Emma Grace Droog

Emma Droog

Donated By The
Mount Vernon
Rotary Club

P9-DMZ-022

MACMILLAN

Dictionary

FOR CHILDREN

Simon & Schuster Books for Young Readers
An imprint of Simon & Schuster Children's Publishing Division
1230 Avenue of the Americas, New York, New York 10020

Conceived and produced by Weldon Owen Pty Ltd
61 Victoria Street, McMahons Point
Sydney, NSW 2060, Australia

Copyright © 2007 Weldon Owen Pty Ltd

BONNIER BOOKS
Group Publisher John Owen

WELDON OWEN PTY LTD
Chief Executive Officer Sheena Coupe
Creative Director Sue Burk
Senior Vice President, International Sales Stuart Laurence
Vice President, Sales: United States and Canada Amy Kaneko
Vice President, Sales: Asia and Latin America Dawn Low
Administration Manager, International Sales Kristine Ravn
Production Manager Todd Rechner
Production Coordinators Lisa Conway, Mike Crowton
Editorial Director Helen Bateman
Manuscript Editors Derek Barton; Anne Bateman; Annette Carter; Robert Coupe;
Barbara Gassmann; Sue Grose-Hodge; Susan Lack; Klay Lamprell; Mark Lamprell;
Kate McAllan; Margaret McPhee; John Mapps; Bronwyn Sweeney; Russell Thomson

Project Editor Carol Natsis
Editor Jasmine Parker
Editor, Features and Captions Carol Natsis
Editor, Reference Section Jennifer Bruce

Senior Art Director Colin Wheatland
Art Director Tom Marotta
Designers Michelle Cutler; Dizign Pty Ltd; Ana Heraud
Designer, Reference Section Andrew Davies
Cover Designer Gaye Allen
Image Coordinator Terence McCann
Photo Researcher Joanna Collard
Image Retoucher Juliana Titin

Database Developer Vincent Robinson

All rights reserved. No part of this publication may be reproduced, stored
in a retrieval system or transmitted in any form or by any means, electronic,
mechanical, photocopying, recording, or otherwise, without the permission
of the copyright holder and publisher.

Color reproduction by SC (Sang Choy) International Pte Ltd
Printed by Craft Print International Ltd
Manufactured in Singapore

A WELDON OWEN PRODUCTION

Simon & Schuster Books for Young Readers is a trademark of Simon & Schuster, Inc.
The text for this book is set in Warnock Pro and Frutiger.
10 9 8 7 6
Cataloging-in-publication data for this book is available from the Library of Congress.

ISBN-13: 978-1-4169-3959-7
ISBN-10: 1-4169-3959-8

0410CPL

MACMILLAN

Dictionary

FOR CHILDREN

GENERAL EDITOR
Christopher G. Morris

SIMON & SCHUSTER BOOKS FOR YOUNG READERS
New York London Toronto Sydney

an·i·mal ▲ [an-uh-mul]
see page 38

ca·the·dral ◀ [kuh-thee-drul]
see page 118

fes·ti·val ▲ [fes-tuh-vul]
see page 264

di·no·saur ▲ [dye-nuh-sore]
see page 205

D·LZ127

RAF ZEPPEL

Contents

au·to·mo·bile ▼ [<u>awt</u>-uh-muh-beel]
see page 57

totem pole [<u>toh</u>-tum-pole] ▶
see page 729

air·ship ◀ [<u>ayr</u>-*ship*]
see page 26

How to use your dictionary

How can I find the word I want?
The word you are looking up is called the **headword** or main entry. It's in **blue letters** to make it stand out more. All the headwords in the dictionary are arranged in alphabetical order. If you're not sure how a word is spelled, use the guide word at the top of each page to get as close to it as you can, then check the words around that section until you find it.

If you still can't find it, it may be a word that starts with a silent letter, which is one that you don't sound when you say the word. The Spelling Guide below may help you find these words. Sometimes two or more headwords are spelled the same way, but they have different meanings. These are called **homographs.** These headwords are listed separately and have small numbers after them to show you they are different.

Headwords that have more than one syllable have been divided into syllables using bullets (•). These bullets show you where you can use a hyphen to break up the word when you are writing it, if it won't all fit on one line.

> **bat·ter**[1] . . . to strike again and again . . .
> **bat·ter**[2] . . . a mixture of flour, milk, or water . . .
> **bat·ter**[3] . . . the player whose turn it is to . . .

How do I say the word?
Sometimes it's difficult to work out how to say a word, so most headwords are followed by their **pronunciation**. Sound out the letters in brackets just the way they look. Put most stress on the letters that are underlined and some stress on the letters that are in italics. Look up the Pronunciation Guide on page 7 for help with the harder words.

What is a part of speech?
The **part of speech** tells you how the headword is used in a sentence. The part of speech might be a noun, such as *cat*; a verb, such as *eat*; an adjective, such as *ugly*; an adverb, such as *quickly*; a preposition, such as *from*; a pronoun, such as *you*; a conjunction, such as *and*; or an interjection, such as *hello*.

What are the other forms of the word?
Words often change their form depending on how you use them. For example, nouns often add an "s" to show that you're talking about more than one (plural); verbs often add "ed" or "ing" to show a change in their timing (tense). These are called **inflections**.

> **eat** [eet] *verb*, **ate, eaten, eating. 1.** to chew and . . .

What does the word mean?
The **definition** of the headword tells you what that word means. If the word has more than one meaning, these are listed separately, and the meaning that is the most common or most important is listed first. Most definitions are followed by an example sentence or phrase to show you how the word is used.

Sometimes words are used in a phrase that means something different from the separate words. These phrases are called **idioms** and they and their meaning are introduced with a small bullet.

> **o·ver·board** [oh-vur-*bord*] *adverb*. from a boat or ship into the water: *A big wave washed three people overboard from the ferry.*
> • **to go overboard.** to be too enthusiastic; go too far: *Rosie went overboard with the Christmas decorations and covered every inch of the tree.*

Anything else?
Sometimes words can be spelled in two different ways. The headword shows the most common spelling, but the other spelling is also included in the entry.

> **for·ward** [for-wurd] *adverb*. moving toward . . . This word is also spelled **forwards**.

Some words belong to quite a large family. Some members of this family are shown at the end of the entry, along with their part of speech.

> **a·lert** [uh-lert] *adjective*. **1.** ready to move or act . . .
> **—alertly,** *adverb*; **—alertness,** *noun*.

Sometimes words sound the same, but they have different meanings. These are called **homophones**, and they are shown with a special symbol of their own.

> **aisle** [ile] *noun, plural* **aisles.** a clear passageway . . .
> 🔊 Different words with the same sound are **I'll** and **isle.**

SPELLING GUIDE
Some words don't look like they sound. Sometimes they start with a letter you don't expect them to start with, and sometimes they start with a letter you don't say at all. Here is a guide to some of those more difficult spellings

If the word sounds like it begins with	then it could begin with	Example
f	ph	photo
h	wh	whoop
j	g	germ
k	ch	chemist
kw	qu	quack
n	gn	gnaw
	kn	kneel
	pn	pneumatic
r	wr	wring
s	c	century
	ps	psalm
sh	ch	chalet
sk	sch	scholar
z	x	xylophone

PRONUNCIATION GUIDE

The pronunciation of a word shows how it sounds when it is spoken out loud. The pronunciation is shown in brackets [ ] after the headword: for example, fan•ta•sy [fan-tuh-see].

The pronunciations use only regular letters of the alphabet, so that they will be easy for you to read and understand. There are no special symbols like ö or ô, such as you would see in a dictionary for adults.

Some words have more than one pronunciation: for example, pa•ja•mas [puh-jahm-uhz or puh-jam-uz]. The one that comes first is used more often, but either one is correct to use.

Not all entries in the dictionary have a pronunciation. An entry that has two separate words, such as *credit card* or *high jump*, does not have one. You can look up the pronunciation of the two words at their own entries.

The following chart shows the way words are pronounced in the dictionary.

CONSONANTS	
Symbol	Examples
b	boy, hobby
ch	chew; watch; nature;
d	dog, ladder
f	fly, off; cough; phone
g	go, buggy
h	hat; who
j	jump; gem; edge
k	king; cat; chorus; back
ks	box
kw	quit
l	low, wall
m	mat, hammer
n	new, bunny; know
p	pig, happy
r	run, carry; write
s	sit, boss; city
sh	shoe; machine
t	ten, butter
th	thin, both
TH	these, mother
v	van
w	way; whale
y	you, toy
z	zone, freeze; has
zh	treasure

VOWELS	
A sounds	Examples
a	at, can
ah	father
ar	park
are	care; fair
aw	law; ball; caught; bought
ay	day; baby; paint
a + consonant + e	make, wave
E sounds	Examples
e	end, bed
ee	ego, we, here; eat; feet; candy; money
I sounds	Examples
i	it, bit; enjoy
eye	eye; idea
i + consonant + e	mine, time
consonant + ie	lie
consonant + y or ye	my; dye
O sounds	Examples
o	hot, honest; watch
oh	over, local
o + consonant + e	hope; bone
oo	cool; do; suit; crew
yoo	you; cute; fuel; few
or	born; order
or + consonant + e	more; store
ow	cow, powder
ou	out
oy	boy; coin
oi	oil
U sounds	Examples
u	cut; ugly
uh	above, operate, terrible; commit
ur	turn; work; perhaps

Stress

When you say a word with more than one **syllable** (part), you say one part with more **stress** (or more loudly) than another.

The dictionary shows a syllable with stress by underlining it. For example, the word *package* has the pronunciation [pak-ij]. This shows that the stress is on the first part. The word *invent* has the pronunciation [in-vent]. This shows that the stress is on the second part.

Some words have more than one kind of stress. In these words, underlining shows the part with a strong stress, and *italic type* shows a lighter stress. For example, in the word *dandelion* the first part has a strong stress, and the third part has a lighter stress: [dan-duh-*lye*-un].

Sample pages

Guide words
These help you find your way around the dictionary by repeating the **first headword** on the left-hand page, and the **last headword** on the right-hand page.

Feature panels
These colored **feature panels** provide more information about interesting headwords.

Illustrations and photos
There are thousands of **illustrations** and **photos** throughout the pages.

Alphabet tabs
Alphabet tabs are color coded to help you find the **letter** you're looking for. The tabs on the left-hand pages show capital letters and those on the right-hand pages show small letters.

DOLPHINS
Closely related to whales and porpoises, dolphins live in groups and are found all over the world. They like to leap in and out of the water, and some even perform spins and flips. Dolphins have excellent sight and hearing, and communicate using sound waves. They can learn to do tricks and even to understand some human language.

Indo-Pacific hump-backed dolphins

Pacific white-sided dolphins

Bottlenose dolphin

doe [doh] *noun, plural* **does**. the female of animals such as the deer, rabbit, antelope, or goat.
◀)) A different word with the same sound is **dough**.

does [duz] *verb.* a present tense of DO used with he, she, or it: *My sister does all her homework on Sunday night.*

does·n't [duz-unt] the shortened form or "does not."

dog [dawg *or* dog] *noun, plural* **dogs**. a four-legged animal that barks and eats meat. Most dogs are kept as pets but some, such as coyotes, wolves, or dingoes, live in the wild.
verb, **dogged, dogging.** to follow someone closely: *I dogged my older sister through the mall to see who she was meeting.*

Traditional wooden Kokeshi dolls from Japan have a large head and cylindrical body, but no arms or legs.

dog·wood [dawg-wud] *noun, plural* **dogwoods.** an ornamental tree or shrub with clusters of greenish flowers and large white or pink leaves that look like petals.

doll ◀ [dol] *noun, plural* **dolls.** a child's toy that is made to look like a person or baby.

dol·lar [dol-ur] *noun, plural* **dollars.** a standard unit of money that is equal to one hundred cents. It is used in many countries such as the United States, Canada, and Australia.

dol·phin ▲ [dol-fin] *noun, plural* **dolphins.** an intelligent sea mammal with flippers and a long, pointed nose.

do·main [doh-mane] *noun, plural* **domains. 1.** an area of land owned or controlled by a person or government: *The king's domain was the land between the sea and the mountain range.* **2.** an area of interest, activity, or knowledge: *Chemistry is not my domain.*

dome ▼ [dome] *noun, plural* **domes.** a rounded roof of a building or room that is shaped like the top half of a ball.

do·mes·tic [duh-mes-tik] *adjective.* **1.** having to do with the home, house, or family: *Washing dishes is a domestic chore.* **2.** living with or under the care of humans: *Our dog is a domestic animal.* **3.** having to do with one's own country: *We took a domestic flight from LA to New York.* —**domestically,** *adverb.*

Lantern and cross

The dome of St. Peter's Basilica in the Vatican City, Italy, is 140 feet across and rises more than 300 feet above the floor.

Dome

do·mes·ti·cate [duh-mes-tuh-kate] *verb,* **domesticated, domesticating.** *Biology.* to tame or train an animal so that it can live with or be used by people: *Dogs and sheep were some of the first animals to be domesticated.* —**domestication,** *noun.*

dom·i·nant [dom-uh-hunt] *adjective.* having the greatest effect; most important or influential: *The dominant issue in this year's election is the high cost of gasoline.* —**dominantly,** *adverb.*

dom·i·nate [dom-uh-nate] *verb,* **dominated, dominating.** to rule or control someone or something: *He dominated the meeting and did not allow anyone else to speak.* —**domination,** *noun.*

do·min·ion [du-min-yuhn] *noun, plural* **dominions. 1.** land controlled by a ruler or government: *The province of Ontario, Canada, was once a dominion of Great Britain.* **2.** the power to rule or control: *The king held dominion over his lands for many years.*

Dominion Day another term for CANADA DAY.

do·mi·no [dom-uh-noh] *noun, plural* **dominoes. 1.** a small, flat piece of wood or plastic marked with different numbers of spots, used for playing a game. **2.** **dominoes.** the game played using these pieces.

do·nate [doh-nate] *verb,* **donated, donating.** to give as a gift; contribute: *I donated some money for cancer research.* —**donation,** *noun.*

done [dun] *verb.* the past participle of DO.
adjective. **1.** finished: *The job is done.* **2.** cooked: *Dinner is almost done.*

don·key ▼ [dong-kee] *noun, plural* **donkeys.** a domestic animal that is related to the horse but is smaller and has longer ears.

do·nor [dohn-ur] *noun, plural* **donors. 1.** someone who gives or contributes something: *The donor of a painting to a museum.* **2.** *Medicine.* someone who allows a part to be taken from their body to be used by another person.

don't [dohnt] the shortened form of "do not."

In everyday talk you may hear a person say something like, "He *don't* want to go with us," or "It *don't* matter what happens." This is wrong. The correct word to use with singular words like *he, she,* or *it* is doesn't: "He doesn't want to go with us."

doom [doom] *noun, plural* **dooms.** a terrible outcome, fate, or death: *The passengers met their doom when the ship sank.*

Donkeys are hardy animals, and can carry heavy loads over rough paths.

verb, **doomed, dooming.** to force a bad outcome or terrible situation: *The prisoner's plan to escape was doomed from the start.* When something is certain to fail or be destroyed it is **doomed.**

door [dor] *noun, plural* **doors.**
1. a swinging or sliding part that is used to open or close an entrance to something. A bell or buzzer located outside the door which is rung to let people know you are there is a **doorbell.** A **doorknob** is a handle that you turn to open the door. **2.** a thing that opens the way to something; an opportunity: *a door to success.*

door·step [dor-step] *noun, plural* **doorsteps.** a step in front of an outside door to a house or building.

door·way [dor-way] *noun, plural* **doorways.** the space in a wall where a door opens into a room or building.

dope [dope] *noun, plural* **dopes. 1.** a slang word for a stupid or silly person. **2.** an illegal drug, especially marijuana. **3.** a varnish-like product used to make a fabric stronger or waterproof.

Mount Rainier is a huge, snow-covered, dormant volcano in Washington State.

dor·mant ◀ [dor-munt] *adjective.* something that is not active or growing at present, but has the ability to become active later on: *The villagers were afraid of living near the dormant volcano.*

The French word **dormir** means "to sleep." When something is dormant (not active), it seems to be asleep.

dorm·i·to·ry [dor-muh-tor-ee] *noun, plural* **dormitories.** a large building with many bedrooms as well as some common facilities. Many colleges or universities have student dormitories.

dormouse [dor-mows] *noun, plural* **dormice.** a small, furry-tailed, squirrel-like rodent, found in Europe and Africa, that hibernates during the cold months of the year.

DOS [dos] *Computers.* an abbreviation for Disk Operating System, which is a type of operating system for computers.

dose [dose] *noun, plural* **doses.**
1. a measured amount of medicine taken at one time. **2.** an amount of radiation absorbed in a person's body at one time. **3.** something hard or unpleasant that is thought to help someone: *a dose of criticism.*

Arrows
A red **arrow** points to an illustration or photo related to the headword.

Captions and labels
The **captions** and **labels** for illustrated headwords provide extra information.

Language notes
A **language note** will help you use a headword correctly. It appears in a yellow box right after the entry for the headword

Word histories
Many headwords have interesting **histories**. These are presented in blue feature boxes close to the entry for that word.

The main entry, or **headword**, is in blue. Headwords of more than one syllable are divided by bullets.

This is the **pronunciation**. It shows you how to say the headword.

This is the **definition**, or meaning, of the headword. Some headwords have more than one definition.

back·ward [back-wurd] *adverb.* **1.** toward the rear; behind: *Looking backward down the trail, I could see everyone following me.* **2.** moving with the back going first; in reverse: *to count backward from fifty to zero.* *adjective.* toward the back: *He climbed aboard without a backward glance.* This word is also spelled **backwards**.

Some headwords can be spelled a different way.

This is the **subject area** in which the headword is used.

bac·te·ri·a [bak-teer-ee-uh] *plural noun, singular* **bacterium.** *Biology.* a group of microscopic single-celled living organisms. Each of the cells is called a **bacterium.** Some bacteria are harmful to humans, as by causing disease. Others are useful, as by helping in digesting food in the body or making certain food products. —**bacterial,** *adjective.*

This is the **part of speech** of the headword. Some headwords have more than one part of speech.

Some entries contain words that are related to the headword, together with their meanings.

base¹ [base] *noun, plural,* **bases. 1.** the part that something rests on; the lowest part: *the base of a lamp.* **2.** the most important part of something: *The sauce has a tomato base.* **3.** a starting place: *The tourists used the hotel as their base.* **4.** one of the four positions on a baseball diamond. **5.** a chemical that combines with an acid to form a salt, and that will turn red litmus paper blue.
verb, **based, basing.** to use something as a base for another thing: *The movie was based on a true story.*
◄)) A different word with the same sound is **bass.**

This is another member of the headword's family.

Some headwords sound the same but have different meanings. These are called **homophones**.

These are the other forms of the headword. They are called **inflections**.

base² [base] *adjective,* **baser, basest. 1.** lacking morals; mean, selfish, or bad: *Cheating in games is a base thing to do.* **2.** being of low value compared with something else: *Brass is a base metal, but gold is a precious one.*
◄)) A different word with the same sound is **bass.**

Some headwords are spelled the same, but have different meanings. These are called **homographs**.

been [bin] *verb.* the past participle of BE.

This is a **cross-reference**. It tells you which word to look up for more information.

bind [bined] *verb,* **bound, binding. 1.** to tie together firmly with string or rope: *Bind those newspapers into bundles.* **2.** to tie a bandage around: *to bind a sprained ankle.* **3.** to fasten the pages of a book together in a cover: *This special edition is bound with a leather cover.* **4.** to force by a promise or an obligation: *This oath binds you to tell the truth.*
• **in a bind.** in a difficult situation: *His injury the day before the game put the coach in a bind about who to use as the pitcher.*

This is a common phrase that uses the headword. It is called an **idiom**.

This is an **example sentence** to show you how the headword is used.

*The **aardvark** uses its long nose to pick up the scent of termites at night.*

A, a *noun, plural* **A's, a's.** the first letter of the English alphabet.

a [uh *or* ay] a word used before a noun or adjective to show there is one of something: *a girl; a lion; a long river; a good book; a hundred dollars.* "A" is called an *indefinite article* and it is used before words that have a CONSONANT sound.

aard·vark ▲ [ard-vark] *noun, plural* **aardvarks.** an African animal with sharp claws for burrowing, long ears, and a long, sticky tongue that it uses to catch ants and termites.

ab·a·cus [ab-uh-kus] *noun, plural* **abacuses** *or* **abaci.** *Mathematics.* a frame with sliding beads on rows of wires or rods. It is used for counting.

a·ban·don [uh-ban-dun] *verb,* **abandoned, abandoning.**
1. to leave and not come back: *to abandon a sinking ship.*
2. to give up; stop: *The search was abandoned after five days.* Something that is left behind or no longer used is **abandoned.**

ab·bey ▶ [ab-ee] *noun, plural* **abbeys.** *Religion.* a large building where monks or nuns live. It is sometimes attached to a church.

ab·bre·vi·ate [uh-bree-vee-ate] *verb,* **abbreviated, abbreviating.** to make shorter: *to abbreviate Street to St.*

ab·bre·vi·a·tion [uh-bree-vee-ay-shun] *noun, plural* **abbreviations.** *Language.* a letter or a group of letters that stand for a longer word or a group of words. *U.S.A.* is an abbreviation for *United States of America.*

The usual way to write an **abbreviation** is with a period at the end, to show it is a shorter word. However, many abbreviations can be correctly written with or without periods, and with or without capital letters.

*Passengers and crew can be seen **aboard** this luxurious seaplane, which flew long-distance routes in the 1930s.*

Pilots

ab·do·men ▼ [ab-duh-mun] *noun, plural* **abdomens.**
1. the part of the body below the chest. It contains the stomach and intestines. Something that has to do with the abdomen is **abdominal.**
2. the rear part of the body of an insect.

ab·duct [ab-dukt] *verb,* **abducted, abducting.** to take away a person by force; kidnap: *Police think the missing man has been abducted by a criminal gang.* **—abduction,** *noun.*

Stinger

a·bide [uh-bide] *verb,* **abided, abiding.**
1. to put up with; tolerate: *I can't abide people who tell lies.* 2. to live in a particular place: *She abides in the country with her aunt.*
• **abide by.** 1. to accept and obey: *to abide by the school rules.*
2. to carry out; be faithful to: *We promised to abide by Grandma's wishes.*

*The **abdomen** of a bulldog ant contains a stinger.*

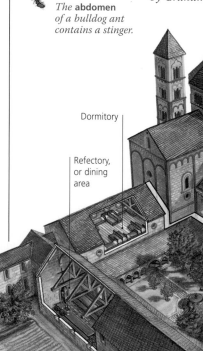

Church

Dormitory

Refectory, or dining area

Cellar and storerooms

*This **abbey** in Germany was built in the twelfth century.*

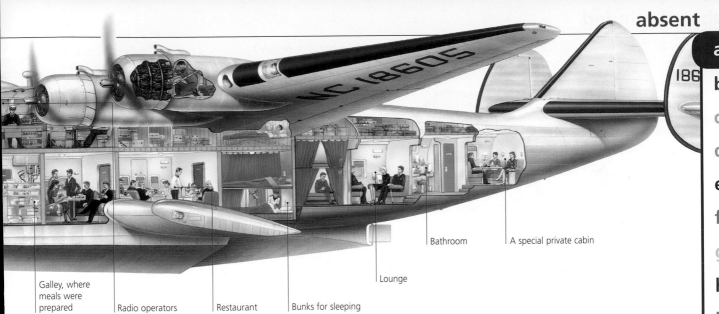

Galley, where meals were prepared

Radio operators

Restaurant

Bunks for sleeping

Lounge

Bathroom

A special private cabin

a·bil·i·ty [uh-<u>bil</u>-i-tee] *noun, plural* **abilities. 1.** the fact of being able to do something: *Both apes and humans have the ability to walk upright on two legs.* **2.** a skill or talent: *She shows great ability as a swimmer.*

a·ble [<u>ay</u>-bul] *adjective,* **abler, ablest. 1.** having the skill, power, or knowledge to do something: *Were you able to answer all the quiz questions?* **2.** having talent or ability that is above average: *Juan is an able dancer.*

-able a suffix that means: **1.** able to be: *washable* means able to be washed; *breakable* means able to be broken. **2.** likely to: *changeable* means likely to change. **3.** deserving of: *lovable* means deserving of being loved.

ab·nor·mal [ab-<u>nor</u>-mul] *adjective.* different to what is usual or expected; not normal. *The scientists were puzzled by the abnormal results of their experiment.* Something unusual or unexpected is an **abnormality.** —**abnormally,** *adverb.*

a·board ▲ [uh-<u>bord</u>] *adverb; preposition.* on a ship, train, bus, or airplane: *The boat will not leave until everyone is aboard; How many passengers were aboard the plane?*

a·bol·ish [uh-<u>bol</u>-ish] *verb,* **abolished, abolishing.** to put an end to: *a law to abolish cruelty to animals.*

ab·o·li·tion [ab-uh-<u>lish</u>-un] *noun.* the act of abolishing: *the abolition of slavery.* A person who wanted slavery abolished in the United States before the Civil War was called an **Abolitionist.**

ab·o·rig·ine [<u>ab</u>-uh-<u>rij</u>-uh-nee] *noun, plural* **aborigines. 1.** one of the first people to live in a country: *Native Americans and Inuit are aborigines of North America.* **2. Aborigine.** one of the dark-skinned people who lived in Australia before the arrival of Europeans. —**aboriginal,** *adjective.*

> **Aborigine** comes from two words meaning "from the first." Aborigines have lived in a place from the first or earliest time.

a·bout [uh-<u>bout</u>] *preposition.* having to do with: *She wrote a story about her pet cat.*

adverb. close to; nearly: *It's about a mile from our house to school; I'm about done with my homework.*

a·bove [uh-<u>bove</u>] *adverb.* in a higher place: *the Moon above; the hills above.*
preposition. **1.** higher than: *The plane flew above the clouds.* **2.** higher in importance or rank: *My cousin thinks she's above me, just because she's older.* **3.** more than: *It feels hot today, is the temperature above normal?*
adjective. mentioned on an earlier page or higher on the same page: *See the illustration, above.*

Ab·ra·ham [<u>abe</u>-ruh-ham] *noun. Religion.* a figure in the Bible. In the Jewish religion Abraham is believed to be the founder of the Hebrew people. He is also important in the religion of Islam.

a·bridge [uh-<u>brij</u>] *verb,* **abridged, abridging.** to shorten a piece of writing, such as a novel or play: *Our homework is to abridge the story from ten pages to two.* A piece of writing that has been made shorter is **abridged.**

a·broad [uh-<u>brawd</u>] *adverb.* in a country other than your own: *My grandmother was born abroad, in Poland.*

a·brupt [uh-<u>brupt</u>] *adjective.* **1.** sudden and not expected: *The rainstorm brought the picnic to an abrupt end.* **2.** not polite or friendly; short and rude in manner: *She seems abrupt at first, but she's really very kind.* —**abruptly,** *adverb.*

ab·scess [<u>ab</u>-ses] *noun, plural* **abscesses.** a painful swelling on the skin or in some part of the body. It contains pus and is usually caused by an infection.

ab·sence [<u>ab</u>-suhns] *noun, plural* **absences. 1.** the fact of being away: *In the absence of the captain, her assistant led the team.* **2.** a period of being away: *an absence of three months.* **3.** the state of being without: *Plants cannot grow in the absence of light.*

ab·sent [<u>ab</u>-sunt] *adjective.* **1.** not present; away: *We all worked harder to make up for the absent team members.* Someone who is absent is an **absentee. 2.** missing: *Accents are usually absent in words from French that have become part of the English language.* —**absently,** *adverb.*

Leaves absorb sunlight.

Roots absorb mineral salts and water from the soil.

To make their food, plants **absorb** *sunlight, water, and mineral salts.*

ab·sent-mind·ed [*ab*-sunt-<u>mine</u>-did] *adjective.* **1.** not paying proper attention: *She kept glancing at the door while turning the pages of the magazine in an absent-minded way.* **2.** not remembering things well; forgetful: *My absent-minded neighbor went to the store but then forgot what he needed to buy.* **—absent-mindedly,** *adverb.*

ab·so·lute [ab-suh-<u>loot</u>] *adjective.* **1.** whole; complete; perfect: *There was absolute silence as the audience waited for her to begin.* **2.** not limited: *The king has absolute power.* **3.** definite; certain: *an absolute fact; absolute proof.* **—absolutely,** *adverb.*

absolute zero *Science.* the lowest temperature possible. This temperature would be so cold that nothing would be able to move.

ab·sorb ▲ [ab-<u>zorb</u>] *verb,* **absorbed, absorbing. 1.** to draw in and soak up: *The sponge absorbed water.* Something that soaks up moisture is **absorbent. 2.** totally holding the attention of: *The class was so absorbed they didn't hear the bell.* **3.** to take in and hold energy such as heat, light, or sound without reflecting it back: *Rocks absorb heat, dark colors absorb light, and a carpet absorbs sound.*

ab·sorp·tion [ab-<u>zorp</u>-shun] *noun.* the act of absorbing: *The absorption of so much water turned the dry soil to mud.*

ab·stract [<u>ab</u>-strakt] *adjective.* **1.** having to do with things that cannot be seen or touched, such as a feeling or an idea, rather than objects, people, or animals. **2.** having to do with general ideas, rather than facts: *The discussion of how to solve crime was too abstract to solve any real cases.* **—abstraction,** *noun.*

abstract noun *Language.* a term that refers to a feeling, idea, or quality: *Hunger, beauty, anger, and height are all abstract nouns.*

An **abstract noun** tells about an idea that cannot really be seen with the eyes, such as *beauty, truth, sorrow,* or *happiness.* Because of this, your writing will be better if you do not depend too much on these words, because the reader cannot picture them. Instead of "There was a lot of *happiness* when we won the game," try "People were laughing, jumping up and down, and hugging each other."

ab·surd [ab-<u>surd</u> *or* ab-<u>zurd</u>] *adjective.* foolish or silly; not sensible: *It was absurd to think he could eat all the cake without anyone noticing.* Something that is silly or foolish is an **absurdity. —absurdly,** *adverb.*

a·bun·dant ▼ [uh-<u>bun</u>-dunt] *adjective.* plentiful or more than enough: *We had such an abundant crop of apples this year that we have been giving them away to friends.* A very large amount of something is an **abundance. —abundantly,** *adverb.*

a·buse [uh-<u>byooz</u> *for verb*; uh-<u>byoos</u> *for noun*] *verb,* **abused, abusing. 1.** to use in a way that is wrong or bad: *She abused my trust by telling everyone my secret.* **2.** to treat in a rough, cruel, or unkind way: *I can't understand why anyone would abuse a harmless animal.* **3.** to insult with harsh words. Someone who abuses someone or something is **abusive.**
noun. **1.** bad or wrong use: *the abuse of drugs.* **2.** rough or cruel treatment: *The man who left his dogs without food was fined for abuse.* **3.** harsh or insulting words: *The crowd shouted abuse at the murderer.*

AC an abbreviation for ALTERNATING CURRENT.

ac·a·dem·ic [ak-uh-<u>dem</u>-ik] *adjective.* having to do with school or college. **—academically,** *adverb.*

An **abundant** *harvest has many kinds of fruits and vegetables.*

a·cad·e·my [uh-<u>kad</u>-uh-me] *noun, plural* **academies.**
1. a private high school.
2. a school where a special subject can be studied: *a music academy; a military academy.*

> **Academy** comes from the name of a famous school thousands of years ago in Greece. The school was led by Plato, one of the great thinkers of that time.

ac·cel·er·ate [ak-<u>sel</u>-uh-*rate*] *verb,* **accelerated, accelerating.** to move faster or speed up: *The police car accelerated in order to catch up with the speeding automobile.*

ac·cel·er·a·tion [ak-*sel*-uh-<u>ray</u>-shun] *noun, plural* **accelerations.** the act of increasing in speed: *The acceleration of the train made me lose my balance.*

ac·cel·er·a·tor [ak-<u>sel</u>-uh-*ray*-tur] *noun, plural* **accelerators.** a pedal in a car that the driver presses with the foot to make the car go faster.

ac·cent [<u>ak</u>-sent] *noun, plural* **accents.** 1. the stronger stress or emphasis given to a word or part of a word. In *fever*, the accent is on the first part of the word. 2. a mark used on a word in some dictionaries to show which letters are spoken with a stronger stress. 3. the way people from another country, or from a particular part of this country speak English: *a French accent; a Southern accent.*
verb, **accented, accenting.** to put stronger stress on or to emphasize a group of letters in a word. In the word *persuade*, the accent is on the second half of the word.

accent mark *Language.* a mark written or printed above or below a letter in some languages to show how the letter is pronounced.

ac·cen·tu·ate [ak-<u>sen</u>-shoo-*ate*] *verb,* **accentuated, accentuating.** to emphasize or draw attention to: *Dark makeup accentuated the shape of her eyes.*

ac·cept [ak-<u>sept</u>] *verb,* **accepted, accepting. 1.** to take something that is offered: *to accept a gift; I am happy to accept your apology.* 2. to receive in a favorable way: *The new puppy was quickly accepted by the other dogs.* 3. to agree to; to say yes to: *He offered her a part in the play and she accepted.* 4. to think of as true or right: *It is generally accepted that smoking can cause lung cancer.*

ac·cept·a·ble [ak-<u>sep</u>-tuh-bul] *adjective.* as is wanted; being good enough; satisfactory: *The arrangements for the trip were acceptable to everyone.* —**acceptably,** *adverb.*

ac·cept·ance [ak-<u>sep</u>-tuns] *noun, plural* **acceptances.**
1. the act of taking something given or offered: *His acceptance of the gift made us happy.* 2. the act of receiving in a favorable way; approval: *If she is admitted to the college, she will receive a letter of acceptance.*

ac·cess ▼ [<u>ak</u>-ses] *noun, plural* **accesses. 1.** the right or opportunity of coming to someone or something: *Only senior students have access to the gym at lunchtime.* 2. a way of getting to or entering a place: *Access to the cave is by a ladder.*
verb, **accessed, accessing.** to get at something: *It's easy to access information from my computer.*

ac·ces·si·ble [ak-<u>ses</u>-i-bul] *adjective.* 1. easy to reach, enter, or get: *The stadium is accessible by bus; Fire drill information should be accessible to all people in the building.* 2. having to do with a place that can be reached or entered by a handicapped person.

ac·ces·so·ry [ak-<u>ses</u>-uh-ree] *noun, plural* **accessories.**
1. an extra item added to the main thing: *The best accessory on the bicycle was the rack at the back for carrying things.* 2. someone who helps carry out a crime: *Although he was not the actual thief, he was charged as an accessory because he hid the stolen watch.* 3. extra items that go with clothes, such as shoes, belts, scarves, and handbags: *Mom chose accessories to match her new dress.*

ac·ci·dent [<u>ak</u>-si-dunt] *noun, plural* **accidents. 1.** something that is not planned or expected: *Kicking the ball into the lake was an accident.* 2. a sad event that is not expected, especially one where people may be injured: *an automobile accident; She broke her leg in a skiing accident.*
• **by accident.** not on purpose: *It was just by accident that we happened to meet at the mall yesterday.*

ac·ci·den·tal [ak-si-<u>dent</u>-ul] *adjective.* having to do with something that is not planned or expected; happening by chance: *The company said the spilling of oil into the river was accidental.* —**accidentally,** *adverb.*

*In ancient China, canals were built to provide easy **access** to inland cities.*

a
b
c
d
e
f
g
h
i
j
k
l
m
n
o
p
q
r
s
t
u
v
w
x
y
z

ac·com·mo·date [uh-<u>kom</u>-uh-*date*] *verb*, **accommodated, accommodating. 1.** to have enough space for; hold: *Is the closet big enough to accommodate all your clothes?* **2.** to provide with a place to live: *The house has three bedrooms and can accommodate up to six people.* **3.** to give as a favor; help out: *I needed to borrow a textbook, and he was kind enough to accommodate me.* Someone who is **accommodating** is willing to make changes as a favor to help someone else.

ac·com·mo·da·tion [uh-*kom*-uh-<u>day</u>-shun] *noun*, *plural* **accommodations.** a place to stay and sleep, often also serving food. A place that offers food and lodgings is often called **accommodations.**

ac·com·pa·ny ▶ [uh-<u>komp</u>-uh-nee] *verb*, **accompanied, accompanying. 1.** to go together with: *I accompany my little sister on the bus to school.* **2.** to happen or appear at the same time as: *Lightning is usually accompanied by thunder.* **3.** to play a musical instrument for a singer, or as a background for another musical instrument: *Ryan will play the violin and Emma will accompany him on the piano.* Music played for a singer or at the same time as another musical instrument is an **accompaniment.**

The music played by Mexican mariachis provides a lively **accompaniment.**

ac·com·plice [uh-<u>komp</u>-lis] *noun*, *plural* **accomplices.** a person who helps another person do something wrong.

ac·com·plish [uh-<u>komp</u>-lish] *verb*, **accomplished, accomplishing.** to complete successfully; achieve: *It was an amazing effort to accomplish so much in such a short time.* Someone who is very good at something, such as cooking or playing the piano, is **accomplished** in that activity. **—accomplishment,** *noun.*

ac·cord [uh-<u>kord</u>] *noun*, *plural* **accords. 1.** being in agreement: *We can't allow that—it is not in accord with the rules.* **2.** a formal agreement or contract; treaty: *a peace accord; an accord between nations.* **Accordance** is the fact of being in agreement. *verb*, **accorded, according.** to agree: *His memory of what happened does not accord with the facts.* • **of/on one's own accord.** without being asked to: *Joe set the table of his own accord.*

according to 1. following a plan or system; as expected or planned: *The actors spoke their lines according to the script.* **2.** in a way that agrees with something: *The children were placed in groups according to their age.* Something treated in a suitable way has been treated **accordingly. 3.** as shown or reported by: *According to the timetable, the next train is in five minutes.*

Each pack of cards has four **aces.**

ac·cor·di·on ◀ [uh-<u>kor</u>-dee-un] *noun*, *plural* **accordions.** *Music.* a musical instrument that is squeezed to force air through metal reeds to make sounds. It is played by pressing keys.

Some **accordions** *have piano-like keys.*

ac·count [uh-<u>kount</u>] *noun*, *plural* **accounts. 1.** a written or spoken description; report: *There was a full account in the newspaper.* **2.** a record of money put in and taken out: *The company's accounts showed business was improving.* **3.** a sum of money kept in a bank until it is needed: *a savings account.* *verb.* **account for. 1.** to explain: *The coach couldn't account for her team's poor record.* **2.** to be the cause of: *I think staying up too late last night accounts for your bad mood today.* **3.** to tell what happened to or what has been done with: *The zookeeper must account for the health of all these animals.*

ac·count·ing [uh-<u>koun</u>-ting] *noun. Business.* the job of keeping the accounts of a person or business. An **accountant** examines and records all of the money earned and spent by a person or business.

ac·cu·mul·ate [uh-<u>kyoom</u>-yuh-*late*] *verb*, **accumulated, accumulating.** to gradually grow into a pile; collect: *Leaves had accumulated under the tree.* **—accumulation,** *noun.*

ac·cu·rate [<u>ak</u>-yuh-rut] *adjective.* exactly correct; precise: *Sarah's drawing of the house is like a photograph—it's so accurate.* **Accuracy** is the state of being exactly correct. **—accurately,** *adverb.*

ac·cu·sa·tion [*ak*-yoo-<u>zay</u>-shun] *noun*, *plural* **accusations.** a statement that someone has done wrong or broken the law; charge: *an accusation of cheating; I have evidence for my accusation.*

ac·cuse [uh-<u>kyooz</u>] *verb*, **accused, accusing.** to say someone has done wrong or broken the law: *The prisoner is accused of murder.* **—accusingly,** *adverb.*

ac·cus·tom [uh-<u>kus</u>-tum] *verb*, **accustomed, accustoming.** to get used to something; become familiar with through use or habit: *Wait for your eyes to become accustomed to the dark.* If you are used to doing something, you are **accustomed** to it.

ace ◀ [ays] *noun*, *plural* **aces. 1.** a playing card with a single mark in the center. It usually has either the highest or the lowest value. **2.** a person who is expert at something: *James is an ace at video games.*

a·cet·y·lene [uh-<u>set</u>-uh-*leen*] *noun. Chemistry.* a gas that burns with a bright, hot flame. It is used in some types of lamps and for welding metals.

ache [ayk] *noun*, *plural* **aches.** a dull, continuing pain: *I had an ache in my legs from riding my bike all day.* *verb*, **ached, aching. 1.** to hurt with a dull, steady pain: *My arms ache from all the rowing I did yesterday.* **2.** to want very much; have a strong desire: *The prisoner ached to see his family again.*

a·chieve [uh-<u>cheev</u>] *verb*, **achieved, achieving. 1.** to do something; accomplish; succeed: *We achieved all our goals.* **2.** to get through hard work or effort: *to achieve first* place in a contest; *His aim is to achieve a score of ten out of ten.* An **achiever** gets good results through hard work.

a·chieve·ment [uh-<u>cheev</u>-munt] *noun, plural* **achievements.** the act of successfully completing or accomplishing something: *Landing men on the Moon was a great achievement.* **An achievement test** measures how much a student has learned or achieved at a particular stage in a particular subject.

A·chil·les tendon [uh-<u>kil</u>-eez] *Medicine.* a part of the back of the leg, just above the heel. It joins the muscles of the calf to the heel bone.

> In the stories of the ancient Greeks, Achilles was a mighty hero whose entire body could not be hurt in any way, except for one small place. That was the part above the heel that we now call the **Achilles tendon.**

ac·id [<u>as</u>-id] *adjective.* **1.** having a sharp, sour, or bitter taste: *Vinegar has an acid taste.* **2.** having to do with actions or speech that are unpleasant or biting: *She was known for her acid comments, and made few friends at school.* *noun, plural* **acids.** *Chemistry.* a chemical substance that dissolves in water and can eat away metal. Acid turns a blue litmus paper red. **—acidic,** *adjective;* **—acidity,** *noun.*

acid rain ▼ *Environment.* rain, snow, or sleet that contains harmful chemicals that have been let into the air by the burning of fuels, such as factories burning coal. Another term for this is **acid precipitation.**

ac·know·ledge [ak-<u>nol</u>-ij] *verb,* **acknowledged, acknowledging.** **1.** to admit or agree that something is true: *I acknowledge that it was my fault.* **2.** to recognize the ability or claims of: *We all acknowledge Ashley as the best tennis player in the school.* Someone whose achievements and abilities are widely known and accepted is **acknowledged** in their field. **3.** to let someone know that something has been received: *The principal acknowledged the letter with an e-mail.* **—acknowledgment** or **acknowledgement,** *noun.*

ac·ne [<u>ak</u>-nee] *noun. Health.* a skin condition that causes pimples on the face and back.

a·corn ◀ [<u>ay</u>-korn] *noun, plural* **acorns.** the nut of an oak tree. It grows in a cup-shaped base.

a·cous·tic [uh-<u>koos</u>-tik] *adjective.* having to do with sound or hearing. An **acoustic guitar** is one that makes its natural sound, and is not helped by an electrical machine to make it louder. This word is also spelled **acoustical.**

a·cous·tics [uh-<u>koos</u>-tiks] *noun. Science.* the quality of a place that makes it good or bad for hearing sound. *The acoustics in the concert hall were so bad they made it hard to hear the orchestra.*

ac·quaint [uh-<u>kwaynt</u>] *verb,* **acquainted, acquainting.** to make familiar with; get to know: *At Back-to-School Night parents can become acquainted with their child's teacher.*

ACID RAIN

Acid rain is a serious environmental problem in parts of North America, Europe, and Asia. Gases released by cars and some industries combine with water drops in the air to form acids. The resulting acid rain can pollute water and soil, harm crops and trees, and even damage the surface of buildings and structures, especially those made out of marble.

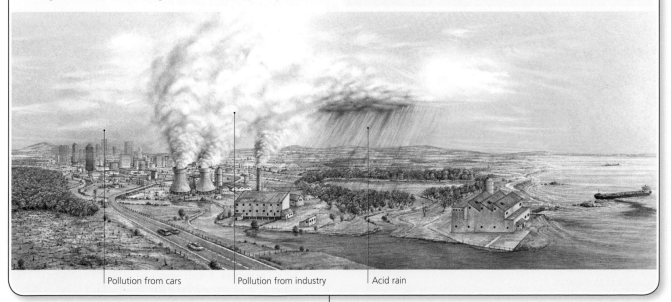

Pollution from cars | Pollution from industry | Acid rain

ac·quaint·ance [uh-<u>kwaynt</u>-tuns] *noun,*
plural **acquaintances. 1.** a person one knows, but not
as a close friend: *a business acquaintance of my mother's.*
2. the fact of knowing; being acquainted: *I have some
acquaintance with caring for pet rabbits.*

ac·quire [uh-<u>kwire</u>] *verb,* **acquired, acquiring.** to get or
obtain something: *She acquired an Australian accent
from her time living in Sydney.* An **acquired** characteristic
is one that is learned or is a result of the environment,
rather than being something that a person is born with.

ac·qui·si·tion [ak-wi-<u>zish</u>-un] *noun, plural* **acquisitions.**
something that is gained: *The painting by Picasso is the
art gallery's latest acquisition.*

ac·quit [uh-<u>kwit</u>] *verb,* **acquitted, acquitting.** *Law.*
to declare not guilty: *The judge told the jury to acquit the
accused person because of a lack of evidence.* An **acquittal**
is the official announcement by a court of law that a
person is innocent.

ac·re [<u>ayk</u>-ur] *noun, plural* **acres.** a unit for measuring land,
equal to 43,560 square feet. An acre is about the size of a
football field. An **acreage** is an area of land that can be
measured in acres.

An **acrobat** *needs balance, flexibility, muscle control,
and body strength.*

ac·ro·bat ▲ [<u>ak</u>-ruh-*bat*] *noun, plural* **acrobats.** a person
who performs daring gymnastic acts, such as walking on
a tightrope or swinging on a trapeze. **Acrobatics** is the
performance of an acrobat.

ac·ro·bat·ic [*ak*-ruh-<u>bat</u>-ik] *adjective.* having to do with
acrobats: *The circus team put on an acrobatic display.*
—**acrobatically,** *adverb.*

ac·ro·nym [<u>ak</u>-ruh-nim] *noun,* **acronyms.** *Language.*
a word formed by using the first letters of other words.
NASA is an acronym for *National Aeronautics and Space
Administration.*

An **acronym** is a lot like an abbreviation in that both are
shorter forms of words. The difference is that an acronym is
formed from the first letter or letters of two or more words
rather than just one. Also, an acronym is written without a
period at the end.

a·cross [uh-<u>kros</u>] *preposition.* **1.** from one side of something
to the other; over: *He jumped across the stream.* **2.** on the
other side of something: *My school is across the park.*
adverb. from one side to another: *You get across at the
bridge.*

a·cryl·ic [uh-<u>kril</u>-ik] *noun.* a type of plastic material used to
make clothes, paint, and many other things.
adjective. made from acrylic material: *Acrylic shirts dry
more quickly than shirts made of cotton.*

act [akt] *noun, plural* **acts. 1.** something a person has done;
an action: *Her gift to the library was an act of generosity.*
2. the process of doing something: *We caught the dog in
the act of eating John's sandwich.* **3.** a law: *an act of
Congress.* **4.** one of the main sections of a stage play,
ballet, or opera. **5.** a brief performance by an entertainer:
The first act of the evening was a magician. **6.** a false
display of feelings: *He was crying, just putting on an act to
get the teacher's attention.*
verb, **acted, acting. 1.** to do something: *After the engine
caught fire, the pilot acted quickly to land the plane.*
2. to be an actor or actress: *Did you act in the school play?*
3. to behave in a particular way: *They acted as if they were
hiding something.* **4.** to produce an effect: *Does the bleach
act quickly?*

act·ing [<u>akt</u>-ing] *adjective.* having to do with replacing
someone for a short period: *While the school principal
is ill her assistant is acting principal.*
noun. the profession of playing parts in plays or films:
Acting is a popular career.

ac·tion [<u>ak</u>-shun] *noun, plural* **actions. 1.** the fact of doing
something: *Throwing a stone and running around a track
are both actions.* **2.** something that is done: *The girl's
quick action saved her brother from drowning.* **3. actions.**
the way people behave. **4.** the act of fighting in battles:
The soldiers were wounded in action.

action verb *Language.* a verb that has to do with
movement or activity. *Run, cut, move, shape, push,* and
raise are all action verbs.

ac·ti·vate [<u>ak</u>-ti-*vat*] *verb,* **activated, activating.** to make
something start working: *If you break the window it will
activate the alarm.* —**activation,** *noun.*

ac·tive ▶ [<u>ak</u>-tiv] *adjective.* **1.** always doing things; busy:
Although Grandad is 90, he is still active. **2.** working;
in action: *The volcano erupts occasionally, so it is
still active.* —**actively,** *adverb.*

active verb *Language.* the type of verb that has
the subject of the sentence doing the action.
In the sentence *Josie kissed Paul,* "kissed" is
an active verb.

ac·tiv·ist [<u>ak</u>-ti-vust] *noun, plural* **activists.**
a person who works hard for something
he or she believes in: *Raquel was an
activist in the peace campaign.*

ac·tiv·i·ty [<u>ak</u>-tiv-uh-tee] *noun,*
plural **activities. 1.** movement or
action: *There was a lot of activity*

in the store on the day of the sales.
2. something that is done for pleasure:
*Swimming is an activity many people
do in the summer.*

ac·tor [ak-tur] *noun, plural* **actors.**
a person who plays a character in a
play, movie, or on TV.

ac·tress [ak-tris] *noun,
plural* **actresses.** a female actor.

ac·tu·al [ak-choo-ul *or* ak-shoo-ul]
adjective. being something
that exists; real: *Johnny
Appleseed was an actual
person who lived almost
200 years ago.*

ac·tu·al·ly [ak-choo-u-lee *or* ak-shoo-u-lee] *adverb.* really;
truthfully: *Actually, I don't like him because he's rude.*

Actually is a word that people often use without thinking
about what it adds to the sentence. "How old is your brother?"
"*Actually*, he's four." That *actually* is not needed. If the
question were, "How old is your brother? He looks like a first
grader," then "*Actually*, he's four" would be a good answer.

ac·u·punc·ture ▲ [ak-yoo-punk-chur] *noun. Medicine.*
the use of needles inserted under the skin to help pain or
treat illness. It has been used in China for hundreds of
years.

ac·ute [uh-kyoot] *adjective.* **1.** very accurate and clear:
*The dog's hearing was so acute it picked up the sound
of the faraway car.* **2.** severe or intense: *Shutting my fingers
in the door caused me acute
pain; There was an acute need
for emergency aid after the
earthquake.*

acute angle *Mathematics.* an angle of less than
90 degrees.

ad [ad] *noun, plural* **ads.** a shortened form of
ADVERTISEMENT.
🔊 A different word with the same
sound is ADD.

AD an abbreviation for *anno
domini*, the Latin for *in the year
of our Lord*: *Paper was
invented in China in about
AD 100.* This is also spelled
A.D.

Ad·am [ad-um] *noun. Religion.*
a figure in the Bible, believed
by Christians to be the first
man created by God.

a·dapt [uh-dapt] *verb,* **adapted, adapting. 1.** to change to
make suitable for a different situation: *The book was
difficult to adapt for television because it was so long.*
Something changed in this way is an **adaptation.**
2. to alter or change to suit circumstances: *We may
need to adapt to different rules at the new school.*
—adaptive, *adjective.*

a·dap·ter [uh-dap-tur] *noun, plural* **adapters.** a device that
joins together two pieces of machinery of different types
or different sizes.

add [ad] *verb,* **added, adding. 1.** to combine two or more
numbers together: *When you add 5 and 6 you get a total
of 11.* **2.** to put on, in, or with something as an extra part:
I added some ice to my drink to make it cooler. **3.** to say or
write something extra to what one has previously written:
*Her teacher added a few words of encouragement to Jane's
school report.*

In 1973 a new volcano became
active *in Iceland and buried a
seaport town in ash.*

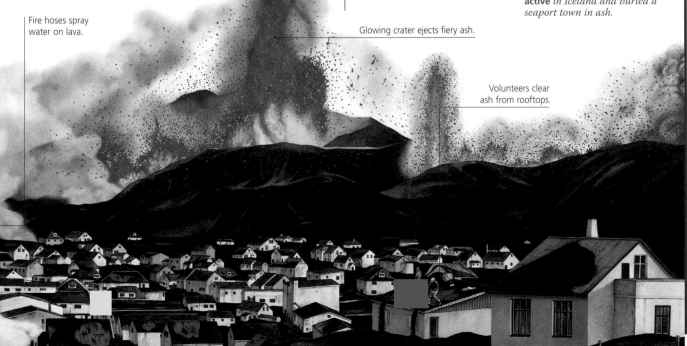

Fire hoses spray
water on lava.

Glowing crater ejects fiery ash.

Volunteers clear
ash from rooftops.

*The **adder** is well camouflaged and likes to lie in wait for its prey.*

ADD *Medicine.* an abbreviation for Attention Deficit Disorder, a medical condition found mainly in children that makes them restless and unable to concentrate, and sometimes causes bad behavior.

add·end [ad-end] *noun, plural* **addends.** *Mathematics.* any of a set of numbers that make up the total: *In the sum 6 + 4 = 10, the addends are 6 and 4.*

ad·der ▶ [ad-ur] *noun, plural* **adders.** a small poisonous snake. It is also called a viper.

ad·dict [ad-ikt] *noun, plural* **addicts. 1.** a person who cannot stop a harmful habit such as smoking cigarettes or taking drugs. **2.** a person who enjoys something with a passion and spends as much time as possible doing it: *Ben is a TV addict.* Someone who cannot stop a harmful habit is described as being **addicted. —addiction,** *noun.*

ad·di·tion [uh-dish-un] *noun, plural* **additions. 1.** the act of adding numbers together: *Addition of 6 and 2 gives 8.* **2.** the act of adding an extra thing or ingredient: *The addition of raisins to the batter made the cake more tasty.* **3.** the act of adding, or the thing that is added: *The Pearsons had an addition to the family when Jake was born.*
• **in addition (to).** as well as: *In addition to selling computers the store also sold books and games.*

ad·di·tion·al [uh-dish-un-ul] *adjective.* beyond what is usual. **—additionally,** *adverb.*

ad·di·tive [ad-i-tiv] *noun, plural* **additives.** something that is added to another to improve it: *Some automobile oils contain an additive that helps the engine last longer.*

ad·dress [ad-res *for noun*; uh-dress *for verb*] *noun, plural* **addresses. 1.** the details of the place where a person lives: *Her address was 1064 Oakleaf Boulevard, Nextville.* **2.** a speech or comment to a person or a crowd: *The school principal gave an address to the students.* *verb,* **addressed, addressing. 1.** to put delivery details on an item that is being delivered. **2.** to make a speech or comment to someone or a crowd.

ad·e·quate [ad-i-kwit] *adjective.* **1.** as it should be; suitable; enough: *All students need adequate supervision.* **2.** only just good enough: *His school grades were adequate but he*

could have done better. **Adequacy** is the state of being great enough in amount.
—adequately, *adverb.*

ADHD *Medicine.* an abbreviation for Attention Deficit Hyperactivity Disorder, which is a medical condition in which children's ability to concentrate is poor, and restlessness is common.

ad·here [ah-heer] *verb,* **adhered, adhering. 1.** to stick firmly to: *The label must adhere to the can.* **2.** to hold a strong belief in a movement or faith: *Religions require followers to adhere to a set of principles.* The act of adhering is **adherence.**

ad·he·sive [ad-hee-siv] *noun, plural* **adhesives.** something that is used to hold two surfaces together: *Glue and cement are both adhesives.*

ad·i·os [ahd-i-ose *or* ahd-yose] *interjection.* the Spanish expression for *goodbye.*

ad·ja·cent ▼ [uh-jay-sunt] *adjective.* next to or near: *Our house is adjacent to the golf course.*
—adjacently, *adverb.*

> **Adios** comes from two words meaning "to" and "God." It was a way of asking God to keep a person safe when they went away.

ad·jec·tive [aj-i-tiv *or* aj-ik-tiv] *noun, plural* **adjectives.** *Language.* a word that describes or adds meaning to a noun or pronoun. In the sentence *It was a sunny day,* "sunny" is an adjective. **Adjectival** is having to do with words that describe a noun.

It is sometimes hard to tell the difference between an **adjective** and a noun when both are being used in front of another noun. For example, in the phrase "an old glove," *old* is an adjective. But in the phrase "a baseball glove," *baseball* is not; it is a noun. To tell the difference, change the phrase to "The (noun) is—" and see if it still makes sense. "The glove is old" makes sense, but "The glove is baseball" does not.

ad·join [uh-join] *verb,* **adjoined, adjoining.** to connect or be joined to: *The coffee shop adjoins the supermarket.*

ad·journ [uh-jurn] *verb,* **adjourned, adjourning. 1.** to cancel or suspend a meeting or court hearing until a later time or date: *The teacher decided to adjourn the meeting until 2.00 o'clock.* **2.** to conclude work for a set period: *Congress was due to adjourn for the Thanksgiving holiday.* **—adjournment,** *noun.*

*These houses along the Rhine River in Germany are built **adjacent** to one another.*

ad·just [uh-<u>just</u>] *verb*, **adjusted, adjusting. 1.** to change the shape or settings of something: *She adjusted the air conditioning to a comfortable temperature.* **2.** to adapt to different circumstances: *They found it hard to adjust to life in the city after living in the country for so long.* —**adjustment,** *noun.*

ad·just·able [uh-<u>just</u>-uh-bul] *adjective.* that can be adjusted; able to be altered by using different settings, such as a tool or the position of a car seat.

ad-lib [*ad*-<u>lib</u>] *verb,* **ad-libbed, ad-libbing.** to speak or perform freely, without preparation: *John forgot to take his notes with him to the school meeting, so he had to ad-lib.* *noun, plural* **ad-libs.** something said on the spot without preparation.

> **Ad-lib** comes from two words meaning "as one pleases." When you ad-lib something, you say what you please at that time, not what was written down before for you to say.

ad·min·is·ter [ad-<u>min</u>-i-stur] *verb,* **administered, administering. 1.** to manage or govern something such as a business or a department: *It took skill and patience to administer the school.* If you **administrate** something, you manage it. **2.** to apply or give something to someone: *The nurse administered the cough medicine.*

ad·min·is·tra·tion [ad-min-i-<u>stray</u>-shun] *noun, plural* **administrations. 1.** the management of the affairs of a business or other organization: *The administration of the company was in good hands.* **2.** the group of people who manage and control an organization: *The school administration included the principal and the school board members.* **3. the Administration.** the President of the United States, the Cabinet, and other federal government officials. **4.** the period of service of a specific government: *the Clinton administration.* —**administrative,** *adjective.*

ad·min·is·tra·tor [ad-<u>min</u>-i-stray-tur] *noun, plural* **administrators.** a person who manages or directs an organization.

ad·mi·ra·ble [<u>ad</u>-mur-uh-bul] *adjective.* worthy of respect: *The teacher's record of persuading pupils to work hard was admirable.* —**admirably,** *adverb.*

ad·mi·ral ▶ [<u>ad</u>-muh-rul] *noun, plural* **admirals.** the highest ranking naval officer.

ad·mi·ra·tion [ad-muh-<u>ray</u>-shun] *noun.* a feeling of pleasure, approval, or respect: *The basketball captain has the admiration of the whole school.*

ad·mire [ad-<u>mire</u>] *verb,* **admired, admiring. 1.** to regard someone or something with respect: *He had admired her courage in speaking out against the bully.* **2.** to look with pleasure or surprise: *She admired her aunt's fancy new car.* A look or comment that is approving or respectful is described as **admiring.**

ad·mir·er [ad-<u>mire</u>-ur] *noun, plural* **admirers.** a person who is attracted to someone else, sometimes in secret: *She had many admirers because of her good sense of humor.*

ad·mis·sion [ad-<u>mish</u>-un] *noun.* **1.** the act of allowing someone to enter: *Universities have strict rules about the* admission of students. **2.** the price charged for entry: *Admission to the football game was $25.* **3.** the act of admitting something is true: *The burglar's full admission of guilt helped him receive a shorter jail sentence.*

ad·mit [ad-<u>mit</u>] *verb,* **admitted, admitting. 1.** to allow to enter, let in: *Will they admit us to the movie theater?* **2.** to agree that something is true: *The thief admitted he had stolen the camera.*

ad·mit·tance [ad-<u>mit</u>-uns] *noun.* the act of allowing entry or access: *The sign said, "No admittance to the park without a permit."*

ad·obe ▶ [uh-<u>doh</u>-bee] *noun, plural* **adobes. 1.** a brick made out of earth, mud, or clay, sometimes with straw to make the material stronger, then dried in the sun. **2.** a building made of such bricks, often- found in the southwestern United States and Mexico.

*In Mexico people have built **adobe** homes for centuries.*

ad·o·les·cent [ad-uh-<u>les</u>-unt] *adjective.* a young person who is between childhood and adulthood. A person who is experiencing changes associated with this age is said to be going through **adolescence.**

ad·opt [uh-<u>dopt</u>] *verb,* **adopted, adopting. 1.** to take a child in as a member of another family through a legal process: *He was adopted by his aunt after his parents died.* A child who has been adopted is an **adopted** child. Someone who adopts a child becomes the child's **adoptive** parent. **2.** to make something one's own: *He was happy to adopt the local football team as his favorite team.* **3.** To accept a decision by taking a vote at a meeting: *The town council adopted the idea of saving water.*

ad·op·tion [uh-<u>dop</u>-shun] *noun, plural* **adoptions.** the legal process by which a child is taken into a new family.

a·dor·a·ble [uh-<u>dor</u>-uh-bul] *adjective.* to be adored; attractive; lovable: *Newborn puppies are adorable.* —**adorably,** *adverb.*

a·dore [uh-<u>dor</u>] *verb,* **adored, adoring. 1.** to love deeply or strongly: *Lucy adores her grandma.* A deeply loving attitude toward someone is described as being **adoring. 2.** to worship or honor as a god. **3.** to like something very much: *She adores eating chocolates.* —**adoration,** *noun.*

*Ancient Egyptians **adorned** mummy cases with pictures and hieroglyphs.*

a·dorn ▶ [uh-<u>dorn</u>] *verb,* **adorned, adorning.** to decorate or make attractive: *Her dress was adorned with jewels.* —**adornment,** *noun.*

ad·re·nal gland [uh-<u>dree</u>-nul] *Medicine.* a gland found near the kidneys. The adrenal gland supplies the body with **adrenalin,** a chemical needed by the heart and blood. This word is also spelled **adrenaline.**

ad·sorb [ad-<u>zorb</u>] *verb,* **adsorbed, adsorbing.** to gather a substance as a thin layer on the surface of a solid: *to adsorb gas on charcoal.* This process is called **adsorption.**

a·dult ▼ [uh-<u>dult</u> *or* ad-ult] *noun, plural* **adults. 1.** a fully grown person. **2.** any fully grown animal or plant. **Adulthood** is the state of being an adult. *adjective:* fully grown: *The adult whale is an awesome sight.*

*A young elephant stays close to its mother or another **adult** elephant.*

ad·vance [ad-<u>vans</u>] *verb,* **advanced, advancing. 1.** to move or bring forward: *The army advanced toward the enemy fort.* **2.** to allow progress to be made: *Science advances the growth of human knowledge.* **3.** to achieve a better position in school or work: *She advanced to a higher-level job with her company.* **4.** to lend money or pay money before it is due: *Mom advanced me the cash to buy a skateboard.*

ad·vanced [ad-<u>vanst</u>] *adjective.* **1.** having made greater progress in life or thought than others: *The society of ancient Greece was very advanced for its time.* **2.** not at an introductory level: *She was studying advanced physics.* **3.** having reached a late stage: *a woman of advanced age.*

ad·vance·ment [ad-<u>vans</u>-munt] *noun, plural* **advancements. 1.** the act of moving forward: *The army's advancement was slowed by bad weather.* **2.** a promotion from one rank or position to a higher one: *His advancement from sales assistant to sales manager was very fast.*

ad·vantage [ad-<u>van</u>-tij] *noun, plural* **advantages.** a thing that is favorable, especially for success or profit: *A good education gives you a big advantage in life.*

ad·van·ta·geous [ad-vun-<u>taje</u>-us] *adjective.* something that is useful or gives a benefit: *Fran found that speaking three languages was advantageous when looking for a job.* —**advantageously,** *adverb.*

ad·vent [ad-<u>vent</u>] *noun.* the coming or arrival of someone or something: *With the advent of fall we needed warmer clothes.* The season that takes in the four Sundays before Christmas is called **Advent.**

ad·ven·ture [ad-<u>ven</u>-chur] *noun, plural* **adventures. 1.** a risky action with an unknown outcome: *For some early explorers, sailing the world's oceans was an adventure.* **2.** an exciting or dangerous event: *Shooting the rapids in a canoe is an adventure.* Taking on bold tasks is being **adventuresome.** —**adventurer,** *noun.*

ad·ven·tu·rous [ad-<u>ven</u>-chur-us] *adjective.* being an adventure; involving danger or excitement: *The first settlers in the New World were adventurous.* —**adventurously,** *adverb;* —**adventurousness,** *noun.*

ad·verb [ad-<u>verb</u>] *noun, plural* **adverbs.** *Language.* a word that adds to the meaning of a verb, adjective, or another adverb by describing how, where, or why something happens. In the sentence *The horse jumped quickly over the fence,* "quickly" is an adverb.

A lot of words have one form that is an adjective and another that is an **adverb** formed from it with *-ly* at the end. You should use this -ly form when you talk about how something happened or was done. For example, "They ate *quickly*" (not *quick*) or "The dog barked *loudly* all night" (not *loud*).

ad·verb·i·al [ad-<u>verb</u>-ee-ul] *adjective.* having to do with an adverb. An **adverbial phrase** is a group of words that does the work of an adverb.

ad·ver·sar·y ▼ [<u>ad</u>-vur-sare-ee] *noun, plural* **adversaries.** an enemy or someone you compete with in life or in sport: *France and England were adversaries in the Hundred Years War.*

ad·verse [<u>ad</u>-vers *or* ad-<u>vers</u>] *adjective.* **1.** not favorable; harmful: *The adverse weather conditions made it hard to play baseball.* **2.** unfriendly; opposing: *The court had an adverse reaction to the prisoner's plea of innocence.* —**adversely,** *adverb.*

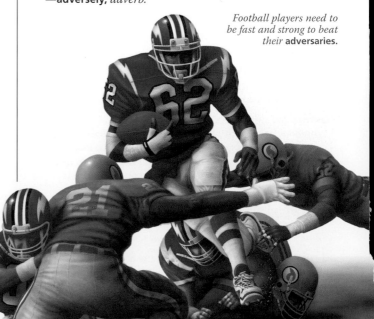

*Football players need to be fast and strong to beat their **adversaries.***

ad·ver·si·ty [ad-<u>vers</u>-i-tee] *noun, plural* **adversities.** bad luck or misfortune: *In the Great Depression of the 1930s many people had to overcome adversity.*

ad·ver·tise [ad-vur-*tize*] *verb,* **advertised, advertising.** **1.** to promote products for sale: *Car makers advertise their new models on TV.* **2.** to place a notice offering or seeking service or goods: *He put a notice in the local paper advertising guitar lessons.* **3.** to make information available to the public: *The movie star didn't advertise the fact that she was married in case it affected her career.*

ad·ver·tise·ment [*ad*-vur-<u>tize</u>-munt *or* ad-<u>vurt</u>-iz-munt] *noun, plural* **advertisements.** *Business.* a public announcement in a newspaper, on television, or the Internet that gives information, or offers goods or a service for sale. **Advertising** has to do with telling people about products in a way that makes them want to buy or use them.

AEROSPACE

Scientists divide aerospace—the air and space above the Earth—into five layers according to their altitude above sea level. The aerospace industry produces all kinds of air and space technology, from gliders to commercial and military airplanes, rockets, missiles, satellites, and spacecraft. The U.S. National Aeronautics and Space Administration (NASA) specializes in aerospace research and development.

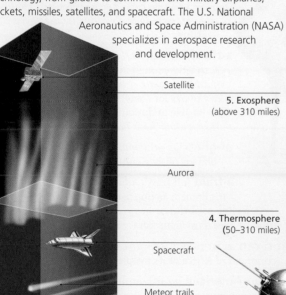

Satellite

5. Exosphere
(above 310 miles)

Aurora

4. Thermosphere
(50–310 miles)

Spacecraft

Meteor trails

Vostok
The first manned spacecraft, 1961

3. Mesosphere
(30–50 miles)

2. Stratosphere
(6–30 miles)

High-altitude balloon

1. Troposphere
(0–6 miles)

Jet airplane

Mount Everest

---

ad·vice [ad-<u>vise</u>] *noun.* an opinion that helps someone make up their mind or offers guidance: *Teachers try to give good advice to their pupils.*

ad·vis·able [ad-<u>vize</u>-uh-bul] *adjective.* something sensible, safe, or worth doing: *It is advisable to wear warm clothing in cold weather.*

ad·vise [ad-<u>vize</u>] *verb,* **advised, advising. 1.** to recommend or offer advice: *The doctor advised him to try to lose weight.* **2.** to inform officially: *The police officer advised the driver of his legal rights after the accident.*

advisor [ad-<u>viz</u>-ur] *noun, plural* **advisors.** a person who helps another with information or advice: *The President of the U.S. has many advisors.* This word is also spelled **adviser.**

ad·vo·cate [<u>ad</u>-vuh-*kate for verb*; <u>ad</u>-vuh-kit *for noun*] *verb,* **advocated, advocating.** to argue the case for something: *She advocates the lowering of the gasoline tax.* *noun, plural,* **advocates.** a person who argues for or supports something: *an advocate for the use of computers in teaching.*

aer·ial [<u>air</u>-ee-ul] *adjective.* **1.** happening in the air: *The eagles gave a display of aerial acrobatics.* **2.** having to do with aircraft: *Aerial photographs of the Earth can be taken from balloons, aircraft, and satellites.* *noun, plural* **aerials.** a device for receiving radio or TV signals; an antenna.

aer·o·bic [uh-<u>robe</u>-ik] *adjective. Science.* able to live only if oxygen is available. An organism that needs oxygen or air to live is called an **aerobe.**

aer·o·bics ▶ [uh-<u>robe</u>-iks] *plural noun. Health.* a form of exercise to work the heart and lungs, often performed to music in a group.

Aerobics helps us to keep fit and healthy.

aer·o·dy·nam·ic [*air*-oh-dye-<u>nam</u>-ik] *adjective. Science.* having to do with an airplane's body shape or wings that allows it to fly more efficiently. The science of bodies, including aircraft, passing through air or gas is called **aerodynamics.** —**aerodynamically,** *adverb.*

aer·o·nau·tics [*air*-oh-<u>nawt</u>-iks] *plural noun. Science.* the study of flight that deals with how airplanes perform in the air. The building of aircraft is called **aeronautical** engineering.

aer·o·sol [*air*-uh-<u>sol</u>] *noun, plural* **aerosols.** *Environment.* a mixture of liquid and gas in which fine particles of solids such as paint or deodorant are stored under pressure, usually in a can, so that the contents are able to be sprayed.

aer·o·space ◀ [*air*-oh-<u>spas</u>] *noun. Science.* **1.** the Earth's atmosphere and the space outside of it. The area that aircraft and spacecraft fly in is called aerospace. **2.** the branch of science that deals with this area.

Affluent *people can afford to buy expensive sports cars.*

aes·thet·ic [es-<u>thet</u>-ik] *adjective. Art.* having to do with the idea of what is beautiful, especially in art: *The new painting was put up in the library because of its aesthetic qualities, but also to cover the mark on the wall.* **Aesthetics** is the study of beauty in art or nature. —**aesthetically,** *adverb.*

a·far [uh-<u>far</u>] *adverb.* at a distance; far away: *Our grandparents traveled from afar to spend Thanksgiving with us.*

af·fair [uh-<u>fare</u>] *noun, plural* **affairs. 1.** something that is done or has to be done: *Cleaning out the garage was a frustrating affair.* **2.** an event: *The Graduation Dinner is going to be a formal affair.* **3. affairs.** business matters: *Dad's accountant handles all of his financial affairs.*

af·fect[1] [uh-<u>fekt</u>] *verb,* **affected, affecting. 1.** to cause something to happen; have an effect on: *The wild winds might affect the electric power lines.* **2.** to bring about a change in feeling or emotion: *The sad music at the end of the film affected us.*
🔊 A different word that sounds like this is **effect.**

af·fect[2] [uh-<u>fekt</u>] *verb,* **affected, affecting.** to pretend to have or feel something. A person who pretends to have something or be something that they are not is **affected.** The fact of pretending to have something or feel something is **affectation.**
🔊 A different word that sounds like this is **effect.**

af·fec·tion [uh-<u>fek</u>-shun] *noun.* a feeling of love, warmth, or fondness: *She has a special affection for her grandson.*

af·fec·tion·ate [uh-<u>fek</u>-shun-it] *adjective.* having or showing affection; warm or loving: *Nan is such an affectionate child, she's always hugging her mom.* —**affectionately,** *adverb.*

af·fil·i·ate [uh-<u>fil</u>-ee-*ate for verb*; uh-<u>fil</u>-ee-it *for noun*] *verb,* **affiliated, affiliating.** to connect or join: *Our local radio station is affiliated with the United Broadcasting Network.*
noun, plural **affiliates.** a person or group associated with another similar person or group. The fact of being associated with another person or group is **affiliation.**

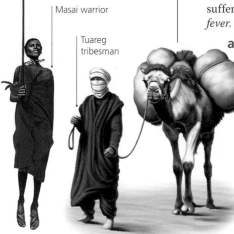

Masai warrior

Tuareg tribesman

African *people belong to many different nations and cultural groups.*

af·firm [uh-<u>firm</u>] *verb,* **affirmed, affirming.** to declare or state something in a positive way: *The witness affirmed that he had seen two men running out of the bank.* A statement asserting something in a positive way is called an **affirmation.**

af·firm·a·tive [uh-<u>firm</u>-i-tiv] *adjective. Language.* agreeing to something or saying it is true: *The school council gave an affirmative answer to my proposal by cheering and clapping their hands.*
noun. a word or phrase, such as "yes," that signifies that you have agreed to something. —**affirmatively,** *adverb.*

affirmative action a policy or program that aims to provide minority groups and women more opportunities for employment and education.

a·fflict [uh-<u>flikt</u>] *verb,* **afflicted, afflicting.** to cause pain or suffering: *She was afflicted with headaches and a high fever.* —**affliction,** *noun.*

af·flu·ent ▲ [<u>af</u>-loo-unt] *adjective.* having a lot of money; wealthy; rich: *The new designer clothing store attracted mostly affluent customers.* —**affluence,** *noun.*

a·fford [uh-<u>ford</u>] *verb,* **afforded, affording. 1.** to have enough money for something: *I can afford a new pair of skis.* When there is enough money to pay for something, it is **affordable. 2.** to be able to do something: *Can you afford to take a whole hour for lunch today?*

af·ghan [<u>af</u>-gan] *noun, plural* **afghans.** a wool blanket, either knitted or crocheted.

a·fraid [uh-<u>frayd</u>] *adjective.* **1.** feeling frightened; having fear: *I'm afraid of spiders.* **2.** feeling regretful or sorry: *I'd like to help you, but I'm afraid I have to go home now.*

Af·ri·can ▲ [<u>af</u>-ri-kun] *adjective.* having to do with the continent of Africa or its people.

African-American [<u>af</u>-ri-kun-uh-<u>mer</u>-i-kun] *noun, plural* **African-Americans.** a black American. *adjective.* having to do with African-American: *We studied influential African-American leaders in history class.* Another word for this is **Afro-American.**

A·fro [<u>af</u>-roh] *noun, plural* **Afros.** a hairstyle in which hair is cut and molded into a full and rounded shape.

Melanorosaurus

Eoraptor

TRIASSIC

248 million years ago

Stegosaurus

Ceratosaurus

JURASSIC

208 million years ago

MESOZOIC ERA

*A flag flies **aft** on this steamship, which made long voyages across the world's oceans in the 1900s.*

aft ▶ [aft] *adverb.* at or toward the rear of a ship.

af·ter [af-tur] *preposition.*
1. later in time: *June comes after May.* 2. behind or following: *Put a period after the last word in a sentence.*
adverb. following in time or place: *The older boys were in front, and the little ones came trailing after.*
conjunction. following the time of: *Please clean up after you finish eating.*

after all despite what was expected or indicated: *Even though it was raining hard, the game was played after all.*

af·ter·life [af-tur-*life*] *noun. Religion.* life after death.

af·ter·math ▶ [af-tur-*math*] *noun.* the conditions that are a result of something happening, like a disaster: *There was a great deal of flooding in the aftermath of the hurricane.*

af·ter·noon [af-tur-noon] *noun, plural* **afternoons.** the time from noon till evening.

af·ter·shock [af-tur-*shok*] *noun, plural* **aftershocks.** *Science.* a smaller tremor or series of tremors that happens after a main earthquake in the same area.

af·ter·ward [af-tur-wurd] *adverb.* at a later time: *I finished all my homework and then afterward I went to my friend's house.* This word is also spelled **afterwards.**

a·gain [uh-gen] *adverb.* one more time; once more: *She didn't hear me, so I called to her again; My little brother likes to hear the same bedtime story again and again.*

a·gainst [uh-genst] *preposition.* 1. in opposition to: *The boss is against changing the name of the company, so it will stay the same.* 2. to go in the opposite direction: *She was riding her bike against the wind.* 3. touching: *I leaned my head against Dad's shoulder and went to sleep.*

age ▼ [aj] *noun, plural* **ages.** 1. the amount of time that someone or something has been alive or existed: *My sister is nine years of age.* 2. a particular stage or time of life: *Mom says she wants to retire in her old age.* 3. a particular period of historical time: *The time when Victoria was called the Queen of England was called the Victorian Age.*

*The **age** of dinosaurs occurred during the Triassic, Jurassic and Cretaceous periods of the Mesozoic era.*

verb, **aged, aging** *or* **ageing.** 1. to grow or look older: *Grandpa has really aged since his operation.* 2. to mature or become ready to be used: *Some wines are aged in oak barrels before they are put in bottles to drink.*

a·ged [aj-id *or* ayjd] *adjective.* 1. elderly; very old: *Our aged grandparents had to move into a retirement home.* 2. having the age of: *He had a hamster aged two.*

age·ism [aj-iz-um] *noun.* unfair treatment or prejudice against a particular age, especially older people.

a·gen·cy [aj-in-see] *noun, plural* **agencies.** 1. an organization that provides a service for other people or organizations: *The employment agency helped me find a job.* 2. a special department or division of the government: *Environmental Protection Agency.*

*In the **aftermath** of a hurricane, houses can be left in ruins.*

a·gen·da [uh-gen-duh] *noun. plural* **agendas.** a list of things to be talked about or done, as at a meeting.

a·gent [aj-int] *noun, plural* **agents.** 1. someone who acts or does things for you: *The travel agent organized our trip to Europe.* 2. something used for a particular purpose: *A special cleaning agent was used to get the stains out of the carpet.*

ag·gra·vate [ag-ruh-vate] *verb,* **aggravated, aggravating.** 1. to make worse: *His headache aggravated his bad temper.* 2. to annoy: *Shouting out in class aggravates the teacher.* —**aggravating,** *adjective;* —**aggravation,** *noun.*

Triceratops
144 million years ago

Velociraptor

Euoplocephalus
65 million years ago

CRETACEOUS

MESOZOIC ERA

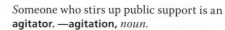
*Juggling on a bicycle requires **agility** and balance.*

ag·gre·gate [ag-ruh-git *for adjective and noun*; ag-ruh-*gate for verb*] *adjective.* having to do with the sum or collection of single things. *noun, plural* **aggregates.** the sum or collection of single things. *verb,* **aggregated, aggregating.** to collect single things into one group: *She aggregated her earnings for the year in one bank account.* —**aggregation,** *noun.*

ag·gres·sion [uh-gres-shun] *noun, plural* **aggressions. 1.** a warlike action or unprovoked attack: *Sending troops to invade another country and take it over by force is an act of aggression.* **2.** hostile behavior, such as starting a fight.

ag·gres·sive ▼ [uh-gres-siv] *adjective.* **1.** ready and likely to attack or fight: *Our neighbors have an aggressive guard dog.* **2.** very forceful: *They got talked into buying a new car by the aggressive salesperson.* —**aggressively,** *adverb;* —**aggressiveness,** *noun.*

ag·ile [aj-ile] *adjective.* **1.** able to move quickly and easily; nimble: *The gymnast had to be agile to perform her routines.*

a·gil·i·ty ▶ [uh-jil-i-tee] *noun.* the ability to move quickly and easily: *Mountain goats demonstrate great agility as they climb up and down steep hillsides.*

ag·ing [aj-ing] *noun.* the process of getting older: *The crumbling walls were a sign that the building was aging.*

ag·i·tate [aj-i-tate] *verb,* **agitated, agitating. 1.** to stir or shake about: *A washing machine works by agitating the clothes and water.* **2.** to disturb or upset: *The bad news agitated my mother.* **3.** to stir up public support: *The students agitated against the increase in fees.*

Someone who stirs up public support is an **agitator.** —**agitation,** *noun.*

ag·nos·tic [ag-nos-tik] *noun, plural* **agnostics.** *Religion.* someone who believes that it is impossible to know whether or not God exists.

> **Agnostic** goes back to two words meaning "not knowing" or "not having knowledge."

a·go [uh-goh] *adjective; adverb.* in the past: *Class started five minutes ago; My grandparents were married many years ago.*

ag·o·nize [ag-uh-nize] *verb,* **agonized, agonizing. 1.** to suffer great pain: *My headache was agonizing.* **2.** to struggle or put in a hard effort: *We agonized over our decision.* Very strong pain is described as **agonizing** pain.

ag·o·ny [ag-uh-nee] *noun, plural* **agonies.** intense physical or mental pain or suffering: *She screamed out in agony after she cut her hand.*

a·gree [uh-gree] *verb,* **agreed, agreeing. 1.** to have the same opinion: *We agreed that it was a good party.* **2.** to say yes; consent: *I agreed to do my sister's chores in exchange for borrowing her shoes.* **3.** to be alike; be consistent: *The two statements did not agree in a few important details.*
• **agree with.** to be pleasing or suitable for: *This blue shirt agrees with my complexion.*

a·gree·a·ble [uh-gree-uh-bul] *adjective.* **1.** pleasing; likeable: *We are lucky to have such agreeable weather.* **2.** willing to agree or accept something: *We will go home early if the teacher is agreeable.* —**agreeably,** *adverb.*

a·gree·ment [uh-gree-munt] *noun, plural* **agreements. 1.** an understanding or arrangement between people or groups: *The lawyers argued for hours before coming to an agreement.* **2.** the act of agreeing: *The team was in agreement about buying new equipment.*

When words are in **agreement** with each other, they talk about the same number of people or things. For example, you should not say "He don't live here." *He* means just one, and *don't* is for more than one, so the two words do not agree. (Either "They don't live here" or "He doesn't live here" would be in agreement.)

ag·ri·cul·ture ▶ [ag-ri-*kul*-chur] *noun.* the science and practice of growing crops and raising farm animals; farming. Having to do with the science and practice of farming is **agricultural.**

Agriculture involves plowing and preparing the soil for crops.

a·gro·no·my [uh-gron-uh-mee] *noun. Science.* the branch of agriculture that deals with soil management and crop production.

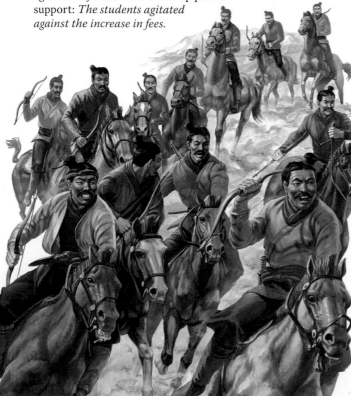

*The conquests of **aggressive** warriors established the rule of the Zhou kings in ancient China.*

GASES IN THE AIR
WE BREATHE

Other 0.1%

Argon 0.9%

Oxygen 21%

Nitrogen 78%

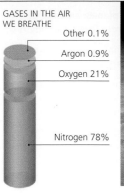

a·head [uh-<u>hed</u>] *adverb.* in the front or in advance; before: *The blue car moved ahead of the others and won the race; If you think ahead, you will be able to plan out your science project.*

AI an abbreviation for ARTIFICIAL INTELLIGENCE.

aid [ayd] *verb,* **aided, aiding.** to give help or assistance: *The community aided our family after the fire.* *noun, plural* **aids. 1.** help or support: *I ran to his aid when I saw him fall.* **2.** a helpful person or device: *Grandma wears a hearing aid.*
🔊 A different word with the same sound is **aide.**

aide [ayd] *noun, plural* **aides.** someone who acts as an assistant or helper: *I'm studying to become a teacher's aide.*
🔊 A different word with the same sound is **aid.**

AIDS [aydz] *noun. Medicine.* a shorter word for Acquired Immune Deficiency Syndrome, a very serious disease caused by a virus that stops the body from defending itself against infections.

ail [ayl] *verb,* **ailed, ailing. 1.** to cause pain or suffering to: *My toothache ails me.* **2.** to be unwell or feel pain: *My grandfather has been ailing for many years.*
🔊 A different word with the same sound is **ale.**

ail·ment [<u>ayl</u>-munt] *noun, plural* **ailments.** something wrong with the body; an illness: *Many minor ailments can be treated by taking vitamins and resting.*

aim [aym] *verb,* **aimed, aiming. 1.** to direct or point something: *I aimed the camera carefully before taking the picture.* **2.** to intend for; direct toward: *The campaign was aimed at raising awareness about human rights.*

noun, plural **aims. 1.** the act of directing or pointing something: *The hunter's aim was accurate.* **2.** goal; purpose: *My aim is to save enough money to buy a car.*

air ◀ [ayr] *noun, plural* **airs. 1.** the invisible mixture of oxygen, nitrogen, and other gases that surrounds the Earth: *I walked outside to breathe in some fresh air.* **2.** the open space above the ground: *They cheered and threw confetti up into the air.* **3.** manner or outward appearance: *There was an air of confidence about him when he spoke.* **4. airs.** showy manners: *When she put on airs, her friends told her not to be conceited.* **5.** a melody or tune: *He was humming an air from last night's show.* *verb,* **aired, airing. 1.** to let air into: *We opened up the windows to air out the room.* **2.** to make your opinion known to others: *He aired his views on the new environmental policy.*
• **off the air.** not broadcasting on the radio or television.
• **on the air.** to be broadcasting on the radio or television: *The news will be on the air every half hour.*

air·bag [<u>ayr</u>-bag] *noun, plural* **airbags.** a bag in a vehicle that automatically inflates to protect passengers in the event of a collision.

air·borne [<u>ayr</u>-born] *adjective.* carried or supported by the air: *Airborne pollen can cause hay fever.*

air con·di·tion·er a machine that cools the temperature and humidity of an enclosed area. **Air conditioning** systems can be set up in homes, buildings, and cars.

air·craft [<u>ayr</u>-kraft] *noun, plural* **aircraft.** any machine that can fly in the air. This includes planes, helicopters, airships, gliders, and balloons.

aircraft carrier ▼ a large naval ship that carries aircraft, with a long, flat deck for taking off and landing out at sea.

air force 1. the part of a country's military forces that uses aircraft for attack and defense. **2. Air Force.** This branch of service in the U.S. armed forces. Someone who is a member of a country's air force is an **airman.**

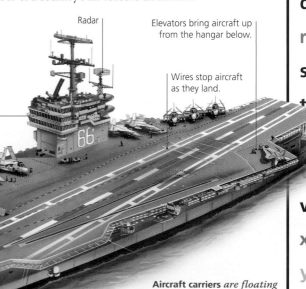

Radar

Elevators bring aircraft up from the hangar below.

Control tower

Wires stop aircraft as they land.

Launching catapult track

66

Aircraft carriers are floating airdromes that allow aircraft to be launched near where they are needed.

*At some large **airports,** more than 2,000 planes can be unloaded, cleaned, and refueled in a day.*

air·line [ayr-*line*] *noun, plural* **airlines.** a company that operates regular plane services for passengers or freight.

air·li·ner [ayr-*line*-ur] *noun, plural* **airliners.** a large passenger airplane.

air·mail [ayr-*mayl*] *noun.* **1.** the system of sending mail by aircraft. **2.** letters and parcels carried by aircraft. *verb,* **airmailed, airmailing.** to send mail by aircraft. *adjective.* the fact of mail being sent by aircraft: *He received an airmail letter from Ireland. adverb.* describing mail sent by aircraft: *I asked the lady to send the letter airmail.* This word is also spelled **air-mail** or **air mail.**

air·plane [ayr-*plane*] *noun, plural* **airplanes.** an aircraft with fixed wings that is driven by propellers or jet engines.

air pollution *Environment.* contamination of the air by smoke, harmful gases, and other materials.

air·port ◀ [ayr-*port*] *noun, plural* **airports.** a place where aircraft take off and land, usually with buildings to accommodate both the aircraft and the passengers.

air pressure *Science.* the force that air exerts on things. Air pressure in the atmosphere is caused by the weight of the air above the Earth pushing down on the air below.

air quality *Health.* the degree to which the pure condition of air is affected by pollutants: *The smog and fumes from the city traffic have a negative impact on air quality.*

air·ship ▼ [ayr-*ship*] *noun, plural* **airships.** a large aircraft with no wings that is filled with gas to make it float. It is powered by engines and can be steered.

air·space [ayr-*spays*] *noun.* the part of the atmosphere above a country that is considered to belong to that country: *The plane entered enemy airspace in order to complete its mission.*

air·speed [ayr-*speed*] *noun.* the speed at which an aircraft travels, relative to the surrounding air.

air·strip [ayr-*strip*] *noun, plural* **airstrips.** a strip of land cleared so that aircraft can take off and land.

The Graf Zeppelin, *the world's most successful* **airship,** *carried twenty passengers and flew at 79 miles per hour.*

Frame made of hooplike rings | Fabric cover

Bags containing gas

Rudders for turning the airship

GRAF ZEPPELIN

D-LZ127

air·tight [ayr-*tite* or ayr-<u>tite</u>] *adjective.* **1.** sealed so that no air can get in or out: *The cookies stayed fresh in the airtight container.* **2.** having planned or done something so carefully that there are no weak points or chance of mistake: *The robbery suspect couldn't be charged because he had an airtight alibi.*

air·y [ayr-ee] *adjective* **1.** having air move through something: *a bright and airy room.* **2.** light and delicate in appearance: *The bride's veil was made out of airy lace.* —**airiness,** *noun.*

aisle [ile] *noun, plural* **aisles.** a clear passageway between two rows or sections of something: *The bride walked down the aisle of the church.*
🔊 Different words with the same sound are **I'll** and **isle.**

a la carte [ah-lah-<u>kart</u>] *adjective.* offering a selection of individual dishes on a menu, each with a separate price. *adverb.* according to a menu that gives a price for each separate dish: *She wasn't hungry enough for a full dinner, so she ordered a hamburger a la carte.*

Al·a·mo ▶ [al-uh-moh] *noun. History.* a famous mission building in San Antonio, where in 1836 Mexican forces and U.S. rebels fought a bloody battle for the control of Texas.

a·larm [uh-<u>larm</u>] *noun, plural* **alarms. 1.** a device that uses a sound or signal to call attention, wake people up, or warn of danger: *Mom set the burglar alarm before we left on vacation.* **2.** a feeling of fear or danger: *The sight of flames filled him with alarm.*
verb, **alarmed, alarming.** to frighten: *The documentary on sharks alarmed the class.* Something that frightens you is **alarming.**

alarm clock a clock that can be set to make a noise at a particular time in order to wake you up.

a·las [uh-<u>las</u>] *interjection.* an exclamation of sorrow, regret, pity, or disappointment. This word is usually used in stories rather than in everyday talk.

al·ba·tross ▶ [al-bu-tros] *noun, plural* **albatrosses.** a large, white sea bird with long, strong wings and webbed feet. The albatross is known for its ability to fly great distances.

al·bi·no [al-<u>bye</u>-noh] *noun, plural* **albinos.** *Biology.* a person or animal that is born with a condition that makes their skin and hair very white and their eyes pink. The fact of having this condition is **albinism.**

Cabin for passengers

ALAMO

Alamo mission building

The battle of the Alamo took place at the beginning of the Texan war of independence from Mexico. Occupying the mission building, a small force of 184 Texan defenders heroically held out against the much larger Mexican army for thirteen days, but were finally overcome and slaughtered. Regarded as a symbol of brave resistance, the Alamo has been preserved as a historic site.

al·bum [<u>al</u>-bum] *noun, plural* **albums. 1.** a book with blank pages used for collecting and keeping things like photographs or stamps: *Mom often looks through her wedding photo album.* **2.** a CD, tape, or record that has several pieces of music recorded on it: *My favorite band has just released their new album.*

al·chem·y [al-kuh-mee] *noun. History.* a type of chemistry studied in the Middle Ages that had three main goals: to change ordinary metals into gold; to discover a medicine to cure all diseases; and to discover how to live forever. A person who practiced this science was known as an **alchemist.**

With its very large wingspan, the **albatross** *can glide for hours.*

al·co·hol [al-kuh-*hol*] *noun, plural* **alcohols.** *Chemistry.* a colorless liquid that can be used in making medicine or chemicals, or burned as fuel. Alcohol can be found in drinks like beer, wine, and whiskey, and can make you drunk if you have too much.

al·co·hol·ic [al-kuh-<u>hol</u>-ik] *adjective.* **1.** having to do with or containing alcohol: *I'm allowed to have an alcoholic drink on special occasions.* **2.** having to do with suffering from alcoholism.
noun, plural **alcoholics.** a person who regularly drinks alcohol to excess and is unable to break the habit. The disease is known as **alcoholism.**

al·cove [al-<u>kov</u>] *noun, plural* **alcoves.** a small section of a room that is built back from the main part.

al·der [<u>awl</u>-dur] *noun, plural* **alders.** a small tree or shrub that grows in moist regions and is related to the birch tree. It has toothed leaves and its rough bark is used for tanning and dyeing.

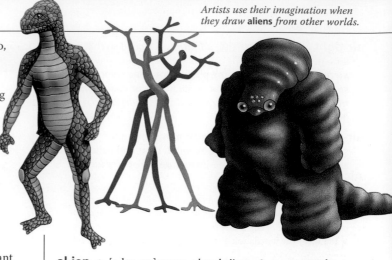

B
C
D
E
F
G
H
K
L
M
N
O
P
Q
R
S
T
U
V
W
X
Y
Z

ale [ayl] *noun, plural* **ales.** an alcoholic drink, similar to, but heavier, than beer, made from malt and flavored with hops.

a·lert [uh-<u>lert</u>] *adjective,* **1.** ready to move or act; paying careful attention: *The deer was suddenly alert to the sound of human voices.* **2.** quick to act or understand.
noun, plural **alerts. 1.** a warning to be ready for possible danger: *We had to evacuate the building after a bomb alert.* **2.** the period that such a warning lasts.
verb, **alerted, alerting.** to warn: *The siren alerted us to the rising floodwaters.* —**alertly,** *adverb;* —**alertness,** *noun.*

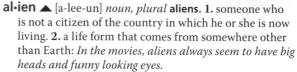

Alfalfa can be planted to improve the soil.

al·fal·fa ◀ [al-<u>fal</u>-fuh] *noun.* a plant with bluish-purple flowers that is grown as food, especially for cattle and other livestock.

al·gae [<u>al</u>-jee] *plural noun, singular* **alga.** *Biology.* simple living organisms that are composed of one or more cells. Most algae are plants without stems or leaves that grow in or near water. Seaweed is a well-known large algae.

al·ge·bra [<u>al</u>-juh-bruh] *noun. Mathematics.* a branch of mathematics that uses letters to represent numbers and values in order to carry out general mathematical processes. Having to do with this type of mathematics that uses letters to represent numbers is **algebraic:**
5x − y = 12 is an algebraic expression.

> **Algebra** is one of many words having to do with mathematics that were invented by the Arabs in the historic time known as the Middle Ages. The Arabs were the world leaders in mathematics at that time.

al·gor·i·thm [*al*-guh-<u>rith</u>-um] *noun, plural* **algorithms.** *Computers.* a set of mathematical instructions that, followed step by step, will help calculate an answer to a mathematical problem. Computers rely on algorithms to help process information.

a·li·as [<u>ay</u>-lee-us] *noun, plural* **aliases.** a false name: *The spy operated under an alias in order to hide his true identity.*
adverb. also known as: *Elvis Presley, alias the King of Rock and Roll.*

al·i·bi [<u>al</u>-i-bye] *noun, plural* **alibis. 1.** a defense by someone to show that they could not have committed a crime because they were not there at the time: *She was already in jail at the time of the robbery, so she had the perfect alibi.* **2.** an excuse used to avoid blame: *Every day he had a new alibi for not doing his homework.*
verb, **alibied, alibiing.** to make an excuse for someone.

> **Alibi** is from a phrase meaning "at another place." If you can prove that when a crime happened you were at another place, then you have an alibi to show that you did not commit the crime.

al·ien ▲ [a-lee-un] *noun, plural* **aliens. 1.** someone who is not a citizen of the country in which he or she is now living. **2.** a life form that comes from somewhere other than Earth: *In the movies, aliens always seem to have big heads and funny looking eyes.*
adjective. **1.** of or from somewhere else: *alien workers in a foreign country.* **2.** strange and unfamiliar: *After living so long in a big city, the slow-paced country life was totally alien to him.*

a·light[1] [uh-<u>lite</u>] *verb,* **alighted** or **alit, alighting. 1.** to get down from something or out of something: *They alighted from the train.* **2.** to land or settle on something: *The bird alighted on a branch.*

a·light[2] [uh-<u>lite</u>] *adjective* **1.** glowing with light or color: *Her eyes were alight with excitement.* **2.** on fire.

a·lign [uh-<u>line</u>] *verb,* **aligned, aligning.** to arrange into a straight line: *She aligned all her pens and pencils on her desk.* —**alignment,** *noun.*

a·like [uh-<u>like</u>] *adverb.* in a similar manner: *People always think my sister and I look alike.*
adjective. being the same; similar: *It's said that no two snowflakes are exactly alike.*

al·i·mo·ny [<u>al</u>-i-*moh*-nee] *noun. Law.* a regular allowance of money that a court orders someone to pay to their former wife or husband after they are divorced or legally separated.

a·live [uh-<u>live</u>] *adjective.* **1.** not dead; living: *I asked my uncle if his old horse was still alive.* **2.** in an active state: *Photographs help to keep our memories alive.* **3.** full of life; lively: *The crowd was alive with excitement.*

al·ka·li [<u>al</u>-kuh-lye] *noun, plural* **alkalis.** *Chemistry.* **1.** a substance that combines with acids to form salts. Alkalis have a bitter taste and turn red litmus paper blue: *Our chemistry teacher asked us to determine whether the test tube contained an acid or an alkali.* **2.** referring to soil containing a large amount of mineral salts. Such soil is described as being **alkaline.**

all [awl] *adjective.* **1.** being everything that there is; the whole of: *Our team won all their games and finished first in the league.* **2.** being every one of: *All fish live in water.*
pronoun. every person or thing: *All of us were too tired to keep playing.*

noun. everything one has: *He'll have to give his all to finish such a long race.*

• **at all.** in any way: *He hasn't any money at all; I thought she'd be mad, but she said, "No, not at all."*

Al·lah [ahl-uh *or* al-uh *or* ah-*lah*] *noun. Religion.* the name of God in the Muslim religion.

all-A·mer·i·can [awl-uh-*mer*-i-kun] *adjective.*
1. representing or typical of America or the United States.
2. selected as one of the outstanding college athletes in the U.S.: *He is an all-American football player.*

all-around [awl-uh-*round*] *adjective.* 1. skilled in many fields: *Most of our team members can only play in one position, but our captain is an all-around player.* 2. not specialized; general: *an automobile that provides an all-around good performance.* This word is also spelled **all-round.**

al·lege [uh-*lej*] *verb,* **alleged, alleging.** to say something is true without proof: *The farmer alleged that his neighbor started the fire.* A statement that something is true without proof is an **allegation.**

al·leged [uh-*lejd*] *adjective. Law.* said to be true without proof; supposed: *The alleged thief is in custody awaiting trial.* —**allegedly,** *adverb.*

al·le·giance [uh-*lee*-juns] *noun, plural* **allegiances.** loyalty to a country, government, ruler, or cause. The **Pledge of Allegiance** is a statement of loyalty to the American nation usually made in the presence of the American flag.

al·ler·gy [al-ur-jee] *noun, plural* **allergies.** *Health.* being unusually sensitive to a substance that is harmless to most people, such as pollen, certain foods, or dust. Hay fever, sneezing, and hives are some of the reactions that allergies can cause. —**allergic,** *adjective.*

Alleys are often found between buildings in old European cities.

al·ley ◀ [al-ee] *noun, plural* **alleys. 1.** a narrow back street or a narrow passageway between buildings. **2.** a place to play the game of bowling; more often called a bowling alley.

al·li·ance [uh-*lye*-uns] *noun, plural* **alliances.** a union between people, groups, or nations formed to achieve a purpose: *The American colonies formed an alliance to fight for their independence from Britain.*

al·lied [al-ide *or* uh-*lide*] *adjective.* **1.** united by an alliance; combined: *The armies of the allied nations were too strong for the enemy forces.* **2.** connected or related: *Building and carpentry are allied trades.*

al·lies [al-ize] *plural noun, singular* **ally. 1.** two or more nations united by a formal agreement. Britain and the United States were among the group of nations known as the **Allies** that defeated Nazi Germany in World War II. **2.** people or groups who unite or cooperate for a purpose: *When the mayor promised to clean up the city, he found many allies among the local business people.*

al·li·ga·tor ▼ [al-uh-*gay*-tur] *noun, plural* **alligators.** a large reptile closely related to crocodiles that lives in swamps and rivers. Like crocodiles, alligators have short legs, a long, flat head, a long tail, and a thick, rough skin. Alligators are native to the southeastern United States and China.

> **Alligator** comes from the Spanish name for this animal, *el legarto,* or "the lizard." When Spanish explorers first saw this animal in the New World, they thought it was a large type of lizard.

al·lit·er·a·tion [uh-*lit*-uh-*ray*-shun] *noun, plural* **alliterations.** *Literature.* the deliberate use of words that start with or include the same sound or letter to produce a special effect, such as *cool, calm, and collected.*

al·lo·cate [al-uh-*kate*] *verb,* **allocated, allocating.** to set aside for; to assign or devote to: *That classroom has been allocated to art classes.* —**allocation,** *noun.*

The female alligator uses her huge jaws to carry her hatchlings gently to safety.

a b c d e f g h i j k l m n o p q r s t

al·lo·sau·rus ▼ [*al*-uh-<u>sore</u>-us]
noun. Biology. a very large, meat-eating dinosaur that lived in North America in prehistoric times. It is related to the tyrannosaur. This animal is also called an **allosaur.**

al·lot [uh-<u>lot</u>] *verb,* **allotted, allotting. 1.** to give out as a share or task: *On the field trip, each child was allotted a sandwich, a piece of fruit, and a drink.* **2.** to set aside for a particular use: *The government allotted funds for a new hospital.* —**allotment,** *noun.*

al·low [uh-<u>low</u>] *verb,* **allowed, allowing. 1.** to let happen; permit: *Our teacher allowed us to leave early.* **2.** to provide for or with: *We allowed ourselves five days to complete the science project.*

al·low·ance [uh-<u>low</u>-uns] *noun, plural* **allowances. 1.** an amount of something or a sum of money given or set aside for a purpose: *My weekly allowance includes the money for my bus fares.* **2.** a discount or deduction: *We traded in our old car and got an allowance on the new one.* • **make allowances for.** to take into consideration; make excuses for: *You have to make allowances for her age.*

al·loy [al-oi] *noun, plural* **alloys.** a substance made by uniting two or more metals or a metal and a nonmetal, usually by melting. Bronze is an alloy of copper and tin. —**alloyed,** *adjective.*

all right *adjective.* **1.** satisfactory; good enough: *The hamburgers aren't as good as the cheeseburgers, but they're still all right.* **2.** safe; well: *He's been really sick, but he's all right now.* *adverb.* yes; very well: *All right, I'm ready. Let's go.*

The **allosaurus** weighed more than a ton and its skull was up to three feet long.

all-star [<u>all</u>-*star*] *adjective.* made up of the best or most famous players or entertainers: *Each year the top players in pro basketball play each other in an all-star game.* *noun, plural* **all-stars.** an outstanding entertainer or player.

al·ly [al-eye] *verb,* **allied, allying.** to unite or form a connection with someone or something to achieve a purpose: *We allied ourselves with the group in favor of longer lunch breaks.* *noun, plural* **allies.** a nation, group, or person united with one or more others to achieve a purpose: *Britain and the United States were allies during World War II.*

To send a hot air balloon **aloft,** the air inside it is heated with a gas burner.

al·ma·nac [awl-muh-*nak*] *noun, plural* **almanacs.** *Literature.* **1.** a book that gives facts and figures on subjects of general interest, usually published once a year: *An American almanac will include a description of state flags.* **2.** a book that contains a calendar giving details of such events as tide changes and the rising and setting of the Sun and the Moon for each day of the year.

al·might·y [awl-<u>mye</u>-tee] *adjective.* having complete or great power. In Christian religions, God is often described as **Almighty,** and referred to as **the Almighty.**

al·mond [ah-mund *or* ahl-mund *or* al-mund] *noun, plural* **almonds.** an oval-shaped nut. The tree it grows on is also called an almond.

al·most [awl-most *or* awl-<u>most</u>] *adverb.* nearly; not quite: *It's almost time to go home now, so you'd better finish your lunch.*

al·oe [al-oh] *noun, plural* **aloes.** *Biology.* **1.** a member of a large group of plants related to lilies, chiefly from southern Africa. **2.** a plant known as the **American aloe,** a type of agave native to Central America. The drink tequila is made from its sap.

a·loft ▲ [uh-<u>loft</u>] *adverb; adjective.* up in the air: *It took him quite a while to get the kite aloft.*

a·lo·ha [uh-<u>loh</u>-hah] *noun, plural* **alohas.** a Hawaiian word meaning both *hello* and *good-bye.*

a·lone [uh-<u>lone</u>] *adjective.* **1.** apart or separated from others: *The rest of the family was out and she was alone in the house.* **2.** exclusively, only: *Enthusiasm alone is not enough—you also have to work hard.* *adverb.* without other people or things: *Jordan likes to work alone.* • **leave/let alone.** to not interfere with or disturb: *I asked you to leave my books alone; Just let me alone for five minutes!* • **let alone.** not to mention: *I'm not sure he can even finish the race, let alone win.*

a·long [uh-<u>long</u>] *preposition.* **1.** on or following the length of: *We rode our horses along the track.* **2.** at one or more points on: *Look out for deer along the way.* *adverb.* **1.** onward; forward: *Can you help me push this cart along.* **2.** with oneself; as a companion: *I brought my little cousin along with us to the movies.* • **get along. 1.** to make progress: *How are you getting along with your studies?* **2.** to be on friendly terms; agree: *My sister and I get along very well.*

a·long·side [uh-*long*-<u>side</u>] *adverb.* beside; next to. *We saw Tenille running, with her dog alongside.* *preposition.* at or by the side of; beside: *I love to walk alongside the canal and look at the boats.*

a lot *adverb.* **1.** a large amount or number of: *That's a lot of money to give to a young child.* **2.** to a considerable degree; much: *That looks a lot better now.*

Please note that this is written as two words, as in "I liked that movie **a lot**." People sometimes write it as one word, "alot," but that is not correct.

a·loud [uh-<u>loud</u>] *adverb.* in a tone of voice that can be heard; not silent or whispering: *My grandfather likes me to read aloud to him.*

al·pac·a ▶ [al-<u>pak</u>-uh] *noun, plural* **alpacas.** an animal with long, silky hair that is native to the mountains of South America. It is related to the llama.

Alpacas are bred mainly for their light, soft wool.

al·pha [al-fuh] *noun. Language.* **1.** the first letter of the Greek alphabet. **2.** the first one in a series. *adjective.* being the first: *The male leader of a group of animals can be called the alpha male.*

ΑΒΓΔΕΖΗΘΙΚΛΜΝΞΟΠΡΣΤΥΦΧΨΩ

al·pha·bet ▲ [*al*-fuh-bet] *noun, plural* **alphabets.** *Language.* the letters or characters used to write a language, usually arranged in a set order.

The ancient Greek alphabet had 24 letters.

The first two letters of the Greek **alphabet** are *alpha* and *beta*, which are like English *a* and *b*. In old times people thought of Greek as being the first or most important language, so they named the English alphabet for these two Greek letters.

al·pha·bet·i·cal [*al*-fuh-<u>bet</u>-i-kul] *adjective.* following the order of the letters of the alphabet: *The entries in an encyclopedia are arranged in alphabetical order.* —**alphabetically,** *adverb.*

al·pha·bet·ize [<u>al</u>-fuh-buh-*tize*] *verb,* **alphabetized, alphabetizing.** to put in alphabetical order: *The first task is to alphabetize this list of names.* —**alphabetization,** *noun.*

al·read·y [*awl*-<u>red</u>-ee] *adverb.* by now; before the time in question: *We arrived to find they had already left.*

al·so [<u>awl</u>-so] *adverb.* in addition; besides; too: *Tigers live in the wild, and also in zoos.*

al·tar [<u>awl</u>-tur] *noun, plural* **altars.** a table or platform used for religious ceremonies.
🔊 A different word with the same sound is **alter.**

al·ter [<u>awl</u>-tur] *verb,* **altered, altering.** to make or become different; change: *The store altered the jacket he bought so that it would fit better.* The thing that is or has changed is an **alteration.**
🔊 A different word with the same sound is **altar.**

al·ter·nate [<u>awl</u>-tur-*nate for verb;* <u>awl</u>-tur-nit *for adjective and noun*] *verb,* **alternated, alternating. 1.** to do in turns: *My sister and I alternate feeding our cat.* **2.** to go back and forth between one thing and another: *The singers alternated between happy and sad songs.* *adjective.* **1.** arranged or appearing one after the other: *My dad and I built the fence using alternate layers of rocks and clay.* **2.** every second; every other: *Justin helps out in the store once every two weeks, on alternate Fridays.* **3.** replacing someone or something else; substitute: *We need to take an alternate route because the main road is closed.* *noun, plural* **alternates.** a person or thing that takes another's place; a substitute: *Ask her to suggest an alternate if she can't play.* —**alternately,** *adverb.*

alternating current *Science.* an electrical current that reverses its direction in regular cycles.

al·ter·na·tive [awl-<u>turn</u>-i-tiv] *noun, plural* **alternatives. 1.** one of two or more choices: *We had the alternative of driving or traveling by train.* **2.** one of two or more possibilities: *We decided on the faster alternative, and went by train.* *adjective.* something available instead of something else: *We had to decide between two alternative designs, one modern and one traditional.*

alternative energy ▼ *Environment.* energy from sources other than coal, oil, and gas, which are the ones most commonly used. Corn and other plants can be used to make an **alternative fuel** called ethanol.

al·ter·nat·or [<u>awl</u>-tur-*nay*-tur] *noun, plural* **alternators.** *Science.* a dynamo that generates an ALTERNATING CURRENT.

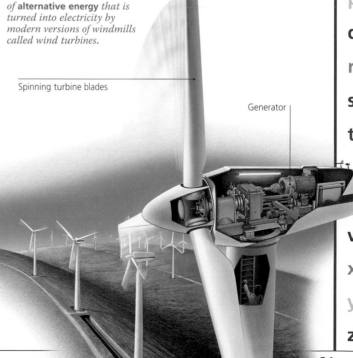

Wind is a natural source of **alternative energy** *that is turned into electricity by modern versions of windmills called wind turbines.*

Spinning turbine blades

Generator

al·though [awl-THO] *conjunction.* **1.** despite the fact that; though: *Although I slept well last night, I feel tired today.* **2.** but; however: *My friends thought the movie was too long, although I enjoyed it.* **3.** even if: *Ask them, although they may refuse.*

al·tim·e·ter [al-*tim*-i-tur] *noun, plural* **altimeters.** *Science.* an instrument that records height above sea or ground level. It is mainly used in airplanes to show the pilot how high the airplane is flying.

al·ti·tude ▲ [al-ti-*tood*] *noun, plural* **altitudes.** the height of an object above ground level or sea level: *The pilot announced that we were flying at an altitude of 12,000 feet; Mount Everest has an altitude of more than 29,000 feet.*

al·to [al-*toe*] *noun, plural* **altos.** *Music.* **1.** the lowest female singing voice and the highest male singing voice. **2.** a singer with such a voice. **3.** a musical instrument with a sound that falls within the range of an alto voice.

al·to·geth·er [awl-tuh-geTH-ur] *adverb.* **1.** in every way; completely; entirely: *You have missed my point altogether.* **2.** in total; including everyone or everything: *There were ten of us altogether on the hike.* **3.** taking everything into account; overall: *Altogether, we can be pleased with our efforts.*

a·lu·mi·num ◀ [uh-*loom*-i-num] *noun.* *Chemistry.* a silver-white metal that is easy to shape and resists tarnishing. It is strong but lightweight, and a good conductor of heat and electricity. Aluminum is used in making a wide range of products, from airplanes, ships, and automobiles to household items. Aluminum is the most abundant metal in the Earth's crust. *adjective.* made of this metal.

al·ways [awl-*waze*] *adverb.* **1.** at all times; continuously: *There is always traffic on the freeway.* **2.** on every occasion; without exception: *Jane always has an excuse for being late.*

Alz·heim·er's disease [awlts-hye-murz] *Medicine.* a serious disorder in which the brain tissue breaks down, leading to the loss of a person's memory over time. The affected person also starts to behave differently from usual, and often has difficulty in performing normal daily activities.

am [am] *verb.* the verb used with the word I: *I am finished with the book.* Am is a form of the word BE.

A.M. *or* **a.m.** an abbreviation used after times of the day to show that they refer to the hours between midnight and noon.

> **A.M.** is an abbreviation of two Latin words, *ante* and *meridiem*. *Meridiem* is the middle of something and *ante* means "before," so time that is **A.M.** is before the middle of the day (noon).

AM an abbreviation for amplitude modulation, a method of radio broadcasting.

a·mass [uh-*mas*] *verb,* **amassed, amassing.** to collect into a heap; to accumulate: *When we cleaned out the attic, we amassed a big pile of rubbish.*

am·at·eur [*am*-uh-chur] *noun, plural* **amateurs.** **1.** someone who does something as a hobby, not as a job or for money: *My mother is happy being an amateur artist and doesn't want to sell her paintings.* **2.** someone who displays a lack of skill or experience: *Only an amateur would make a mistake like that.* —**amateurish,** *adjective.*

> **Amateur** goes back to a Latin word meaning "love." The idea is that **amateurs** do something because they love to do it, not because they get paid to do it.

a·maze [uh-*maze*] *verb,* **amazed, amazing.** to surprise greatly; fill with wonder; astound: *The dancers' speed and coordination amazed us.* —**amazement,** *noun.*

a·ma·zing [uh-*maze*-ing] *adjective.* causing great surprise; wonderful: *My young brother has an amazing singing voice.* —**amazingly,** *adverb.*

Ancient insects are often perfectly preserved in **amber.**

am·bas·sa·dor [am-*bas*-uh-dur] *noun, plural* **ambassadors.** **1.** *Government.* someone sent to represent his or her government in another country. **2.** someone who represents or promotes a specific thing: *Pelé is said to be a wonderful ambassador for the sport of soccer.* —**ambassadorship,** *noun.*

am·ber ▲ [*am*-bur] *noun.* a hardened resin from long-dead trees used to make jewelry and other ornaments. Amber can be highly polished, and is prized for its color, which varies from yellowish to reddish-brown. Most amber is many millions of years old. *adjective.* having a yellow to reddish-brown color.

am·bi·dex·trous [*am*-bi-*deks*-trus] *adjective.* able to use the right and left hands equally well. —**ambidextrously,** *adverb;* —**ambidextrousness,** *noun.*

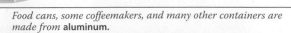

am·bi·ent [am-bee-unt] *adjective.* of the area around something; surrounding: *I find the ambient air temperature in this room very comfortable.* The atmosphere or mood of a place is called its **ambience.**

am·big·u·ous [am-big-yoo-us] *adjective.* open to more than one way of thinking; having an unclear meaning. The sentence, *Evan told his brother he needed a haircut* is ambiguous, as it is not clear which of the two boys needed a haircut. A word or expression with an unclear meaning is an **ambiguity.** —**ambiguously,** *adverb.*

am·bi·tion [am-bish-un] *noun, plural* **ambitions.** a strong desire to reach a certain goal in life: *My ambition is to own a sailboat one day.*

am·bi·tious [am-bish-us] *adjective.* **1.** full of ambition; having a strong urge make a success of oneself: *Sarah is too ambitious to stay in that low-level job for long.* **2.** aiming high: *Building your own house is an ambitious project.* —**ambitiously,** *adverb.*

am·biv·a·lent [am-biv-uh-lunt] *adjective.* having conflicting feelings about someone or something: *I feel ambivalent toward them, as I enjoy their company but don't entirely trust them.* —**ambivalence,** *noun.*

am·bu·lance [am-byuh-luns] *noun, plural* **ambulances.** a specially equipped motor vehicle used to carry sick or injured people to and from a hospital.

am·bush [am-bush] *noun, plural* **ambushes. 1.** a surprise attack by people lying in wait: *This narrow pass is an ideal spot for an ambush.* **2.** a concealed place where people are lying in wait: *The soldiers waited in ambush, listening for sounds of the enemy approaching.* *verb,* **ambushed, ambushing.** to lie in wait for and take by surprise.

a·me·ba [uh-mee-buh] another spelling of AMOEBA.

a·men [ah-men *or* ay-men] *interjection.* **1.** a word people of the Christian and Jewish faiths say at the end of a prayer or hymn meaning *it is so,* or *so be it,* or *truly.* **2.** a word said in response to a statement to show that the speaker strongly approves or agrees.

a·mend [uh-mend] *verb,* **amended, amending. 1.** to make a change, especially to a legal document, according to a formal procedure: *Any proposal to amend the club's rules must be voted on by the members.*
• **make amends.** to compensate for or repay: *Dad bought Mom flowers to make amends for forgetting their wedding anniversary.*

a·mend·ment [uh-mend-munt] *noun, plural* **amendments.** a change, especially to a legal document, made according to a formal procedure. The 5th **Amendment** of the U.S. Constitution gives citizens the right to refuse to testify against themselves in a court of law.

A·mer·i·ca [uh-mer-i-kuh] *noun.* **1.** the United States of America. **2.** North America or South America. **3.** another word for the WESTERN HEMISPHERE.

A·mer·i·can [uh-mer-i-kun] *adjective.* **1.** relating to the United States or its inhabitants: *The American flag is the Stars and Stripes.* **2.** relating to North, Central, or South America. *noun, plural* **Americans. 1.** someone born in or living in the United States, especially a citizen of that country. **2.** someone born in or living in a country in North, Central, or South America, especially a citizen of one of those countries.

American English *Language.* English as spoken by most people living in the United States, as opposed to the way it is spoken in Britain, Canada, Australia, India, and so on.

American Indian ▼ **1.** a member of any of the native peoples of North, Central, or South America. These were the people living in America at the time Europeans first arrived. **2.** a descendant of any of these peoples. American Indians are also called Native Americans or First Peoples.

American Revolution *History.* the war fought between the thirteen American colonies and Great Britain from 1775 to 1781. The colonies formally gained the right to independence in 1783, and set up a free, democratic country known as the United States of America. This war is also called the Revolutionary War.

a·mi·a·ble [ay-mee-uh-bul] *adjective.* having a pleasant and friendly manner; easy to get along with: *Our next-door neighbor is an amiable woman who lets us play in her yard.* —**amiably,** *adverb.*

In the early 1500s the first widely known map of what is now North America used the name **"America"** for this area. It is thought that the map maker named the area for Italian explorer Americo (Americus) Vespucci, though the name may also have come from an earlier Spanish or Indian word.

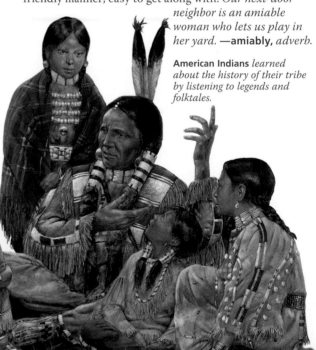

American Indians learned about the history of their tribe by listening to legends and folktales.

a
b
c
d
e
f
g
h
i
j
k
l
m
n
o
p
q
r
s
t
u
v
w
x
y
z

Amish *people often use a horse and buggy for transport instead of a car.*

a·mid [uh-<u>mid</u>] *preposition.* in or into the middle of: *The owner stood amid the ruins of his burnt-out store.* This word is also spelled **amidst**.

a·mi·go [ah-<u>mee</u>-goh *or* uh-<u>mee</u>-goh] *noun, plural* **amigos.** a word for *friend* in Spanish. A female friend is called an amiga.

A·mish ▶ [<u>ahm</u>-ish] *noun. Religion.* a religious group of Swiss-German origin who live in settlements in a number of American states and in Canada. The Amish try to live a simple life without many modern things, and apart from the outside world.
adjective. relating to this group.

am·met·er [<u>am</u>-ee-tur] *noun, plural* **ammeters.** *Science.* an instrument for measuring electric currents.

am·mon·i·a [uh-<u>mone</u>-yuh] *noun. Chemistry.* a colorless gas with a strong, sharp smell, often used in cleaning products.

am·mu·ni·tion [am-yoo-<u>nish</u>-un] *noun.* **1.** objects fired from guns, such as bullets and shells, and explosive objects used in war, such as hand grenades and bombs. **2.** points used to attack or defend an argument: *That new book gave me lots of ammunition to use in the debate.*

am·ne·sia [am-<u>neez</u>-yuh] *noun. Medicine.* being able to remember; loss of memory. It may be partial or complete, and usually results from brain injury or shock.

am·nes·ty [<u>am</u>-nis-tee] *noun, plural* **amnesties.** *Law.* a pardon granted by a government, usually to a group of people and often for political offenses.

a·moe·ba [uh-<u>mee</u>-buh] *noun, plural* **amoebas** *or* **amoebae.** *Biology.* a microscopic animal consisting of one cell that constantly changes its shape as it moves and gathers up food.

a·mong [uh-<u>mong</u>] *preposition.* **1.** in the midst of; surrounded by: *I lost sight of him among the crowd.* **2.** in the company of: *Sonia enjoyed being back among students in college.* **3.** in the class or group of: *Among the many things I must do today is book my flight.* **4.** in shares to each of: *Divide these chocolates among the children.* This word is also spelled **amongst**.

To be very correct in writing, you should use the word *between* only for a connection of two people or things, and **among** for more than two: "Stacy, Emily, and I counted our money and we had $3.50 *among* the three of us." (Not "*between* the three of us.")

a·mount [uh-<u>mount</u>] *noun, plural* **amounts.** **1.** the total sum or number: *Two inches of rain in one day is a large amount.* **2.** any quantity, extent, or size: *I have a huge amount of work to get through today.*
verb, **amounted, amounting. 1.** to add up; to be

in total: *Our hotel bill amounts to a hundred dollars for the two nights.* **2.** to mean the same as; to have the same effect as: *What they did amounts to stealing.*

amp [amp] an abbreviation for AMPERE.

am·pere [<u>am</u>-peer] *noun, plural* **amperes.** *Science.* the unit of measurement used to record the size of an electric current.

am·per·sand [<u>amp</u>-ur-sand] *noun, plural* **ampersands.** *Language.* the symbol (&), which means *and*. It is often used in place of *and* in the name of a company or business.

am·phib·i·an ▶ [am-<u>fib</u>-ee-un] *noun, plural* **amphibians. 1.** *Biology.* an animal able to live both on land and in water, especially one belonging to the group that includes frogs, toads, and newts. The animals in this group are cold-blooded and have backbones. **2.** a vehicle designed to be used on both land and water.

am·phib·i·ous [am-<u>fib</u>-ee-us] *adjective.* **1.** referring to an animal or plant that is able to live both on land and in water. **2.** designed to be used on both land and water. Certain kinds of vehicles such as airplanes and tanks can be amphibious.

am·phi·the·a·ter ▼ [am-fuh-*thee*-uh-tur] *noun, plural* **amphitheaters.** a round or oval building with rows of seats arranged around an open space, used for sporting games and theatrical performances. This word is also spelled **amphitheatre**.

am·ple [<u>am</u>-pul] *adjective,* **ampler, amplest. 1.** plenty of; enough: *We always have an ample supply of light bulbs in our house.* **2.** generous in size or extent; with room to spare: *Their yard has ample room to build a swimming pool.* —**amply,** *adverb.*

am·pli·fi·er [<u>amp</u>-luh-*fye*-ur] *noun, plural* **amplifiers.** an electronic device that increases the strength of electrical signals, especially sound.

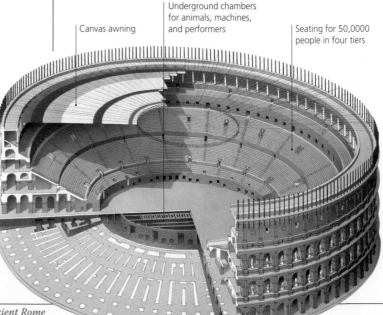

Canvas awning | Underground chambers for animals, machines, and performers | Seating for 50,0000 people in four tiers

The Colosseum was an **amphitheater** *in ancient Rome where special entertainments and contests took place.*

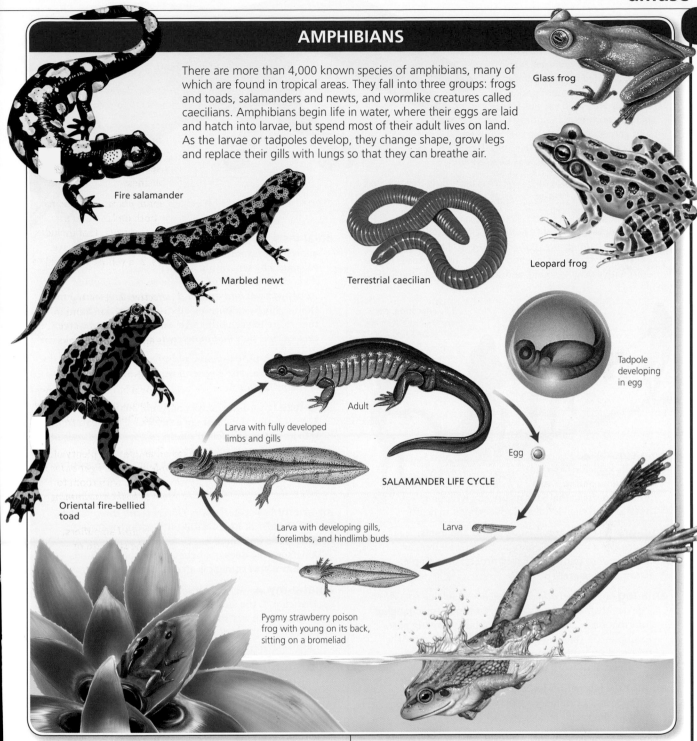

AMPHIBIANS

There are more than 4,000 known species of amphibians, many of which are found in tropical areas. They fall into three groups: frogs and toads, salamanders and newts, and wormlike creatures called caecilians. Amphibians begin life in water, where their eggs are laid and hatch into larvae, but spend most of their adult lives on land. As the larvae or tadpoles develop, they change shape, grow legs and replace their gills with lungs so that they can breathe air.

Glass frog

Fire salamander

Marbled newt

Terrestrial caecilian

Leopard frog

Tadpole developing in egg

Adult

Larva with fully developed limbs and gills

Egg

SALAMANDER LIFE CYCLE

Larva

Larva with developing gills, forelimbs, and hindlimb buds

Oriental fire-bellied toad

Pygmy strawberry poison frog with young on its back, sitting on a bromeliad

am·pli·fy [<u>amp</u>-luh-*fye*] *verb,* **amplified, amplifying.**
1. to add to; to explain in more detail: *If there is time, I am happy to amplify my comments with some examples.* A more detailed explanation is an **amplification.**
2. to increase the strength or extent of: *A loudspeaker can be used to amplify sound.*

am·pu·tate [<u>amp</u>-yoo-*tate*] *verb,* **amputated, amputating.** *Medicine.* to cut off an arm, leg, or other limb by a surgical operation: *One of the climber's fingers was so badly*

frostbitten that it had to be amputated. A person who has had a limb amputated is called an **amputee.** —**amputation,** *noun.*

am·use [uh-<u>myooz</u>] *verb,* **amused, amusing. 1.** to appeal to a person's sense of humor; to make someone laugh or smile: *Sam amused us with his stories about working in a zoo in the summer vacation.* **2.** to occupy someone's time and interest in an agreeable way; entertain: *We amused the baby by playing peekaboo.*

a·muse·ment [uh-<u>myooz</u>-munt]
noun, plural **amusements.**
1. the state of being amused:
*She smiled with amusement
when we tried to guess her dog's
name.* An **amusement park** is an
outdoor area with various forms
of entertainment, including rides
and games. **2.** something that amuses;
a pleasant pastime: *Playing computer
games is my favorite form of amusement.*

a·mus·ing [uh-<u>myooz</u>-ing] *adjective.* appealing to a person's
sense of humor: *I found her jokes to be very amusing.*
—amusingly, *adverb.*

an [an] a word used before a noun or adjective to show there is
one of something: *an egg; an hour; an open door.* "An" is
called an *indefinite article* and it is used before words that
start with a VOWEL sound, and sometimes before the letter *h.*

*The **anaconda**, the
world's longest snake,
can grow to 36 feet.*

an·a·con·da ▲
[*an*-uh-<u>kon</u>-duh] *noun,
plural* **anacondas.** a very large South
American snake that kills its prey by wrapping
itself around the victim and squeezing it to death.

an·a·gram [<u>an</u>-uh-*gram*] *noun, plural* **anagrams.**
Language. a word that contains the same letters as
another word but in a different order. For example,
listen is an anagram of *silent.*

an·a·log [<u>an</u>-uh-*log*] *adjective. Science.* referring to
a device that represents variable, continuously changing
information or signals by a continuously moving part.
Examples are the hands of a clock moving to show the
time and a needle moving to show the output of an
amplifier. This word is also spelled **analogue.**

an·al·o·gy [uh-<u>nal</u>-uh-jee] *noun, plural* **analogies.**
a similarity or resemblance between two otherwise
unlike things: *Our biology teacher pointed out the
analogy between the human heart and a pump.*
When two things have this kind of resemblance,
they are said to be **analogous.**

Using **analogies** can help your writing by bringing in unusual
ideas that would not usually go with what you are writing
about. "My sister had a sad face until she saw my present.
Then she gave a big smile." That is all right, but instead you
might use an analogy: "My sister had a sad face until she saw
my present. Then her smile looked like the sun coming out
from behind a dark rain cloud."

an·al·y·sis [uh-<u>nal</u>-uh-sis] *noun, plural*
analyses. 1. examining the nature of a
substance by separating it into its parts:
*A chemical analysis of water shows that it is made
up of hydrogen and oxygen.* **2.** investigating something
thoroughly by examining all its elements and how
they relate to each other: *An analysis of the two crimes
showed that they had many features in common.*

an·a·lyst [<u>an</u>-uh-list] *noun, plural* **analysts.** someone
skilled in analysis: *A general needs to be a good analyst
of enemy tactics.*

an·a·lyze [<u>an</u>-uh-*lize*] *verb,* **analyzed, analyzing.**
1. to examine the nature of a substance by separating it
into its parts: *The doctor analyzed the blood sample to see
what was causing the infection.* **2.** to investigate
something thoroughly by examining all its elements and
how they relate to each other: *If you analyze the situation,
you will see that there are three important issues.*

an·ar·chy [<u>an</u>-ar-*kee*] *noun. Government.* the complete
lack of order or organization in a nation or society:
During the war, there was anarchy in our country.
A person who does not believe in having any kind
of central government is an **anarchist.**

a·nat·o·my ▲ [uh-<u>nat</u>-uh-mee] *noun, plural* **anatomies.**
Medicine. **1.** the study of human, animal, and plant
bodies. **2.** the way living bodies are structured: *The
anatomy of our bodies is very complicated.* **Anatomical**
means having to do with the study of the body.

an·ces·tor [<u>an</u>-ses-tur] *noun, plural* **ancestors.** a person
who is related to you but who lived in former times:
*My parents can trace their ancestors back to the early
settlers of this country.* All of a person's ancestors make
up that person's **ancestry. Ancestral** means having to do
with ancestors.

an·chor [<u>ang</u>-kur] *noun, plural* **anchors.** a heavy piece
of metal, attached to a chain, that lies on the seabed or
riverbed and keeps a boat or ship from moving. A person
who controls a radio or television news program is called
an **anchorman** or **anchorwoman.**
verb, **anchored, anchoring. 1.** to keep a ship in place:
Their boat is anchored in the harbor. **2.** to prevent
something from moving or blowing away: *She anchored
the table to the floor with a bolt.*

Scientists can reconstruct a dinosaur's **anatomy** *by studying its fossilized bones.*

an·cient ▶ [ayn-shunt] *adjective.*
1. dating from a very long time ago: *The ancient Egyptians grew crops along the Nile River.* **2.** extremely old: *Athens, the capital of Greece, is an ancient city.*
noun, plural **ancients.** a person who lived many centuries ago.

and [and] *conjunction.* a very common word that is used to join words and phrases: *Dogs and cats are pets; For lunch I had soup, bread, and a salad; He left the front door open, and a bird flew in.*

and/or *conjunction.* as well as or instead of: *Pack some apples and/or oranges to eat during the trip.*

an·ec·dote [an-ik-dote] *noun, plural* **anecdotes.** *Literature.* a description of, or story about, something that happened: *This book contains many interesting anecdotes about famous people.* **Anecdotal** means having to do with an anecdote or story.

a·ne·mi·a [uh-nee-mee-uh] *noun. Health.* an illness a person suffers when their blood does not have enough red cells, or when they have lost blood because of an injury. A person who suffers from anemia is **anemic.**

a·nem·o·ne [uh-nem-uh-nee] *noun, plural* **anemones.** a small plant that has mainly red or blue flowers.

an·es·the·sia [an-is-theez-yuh] *noun. Medicine.* a condition in which a person or an animal has no feeling in part or all of their body. An **anesthetist** injects a drug to prevent a person feeling pain during an operation. An **anesthesiologist** is a scientist who is an expert in anesthesia.

an·es·the·tic ▶ [an-is-thet-ik] *noun, plural* **anesthetics.** *Medicine.* a substance that causes a loss of feeling and prevents people feeling pain during surgery: *I was given an anesthetic before my appendix operation.*

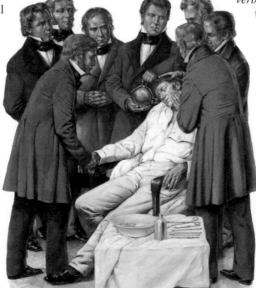

an·gel [ayn-jul] *noun, plural* **angels.** *Religion.*
1. a creature who, according to the beliefs of some religions, serves God in heaven and can also watch over and help people on earth. **2.** a person who is very gentle and lovable. —**angelic,** *adjective.*

an·ger [ang-gur] *noun.* a feeling of being very annoyed or unhappy about something that another person has done or about a particular situation: *People can feel anger when they think they are being treated unfairly.*
verb, **angered, angering.** to make a person annoyed about something: *It angers me when you make fun of me.*

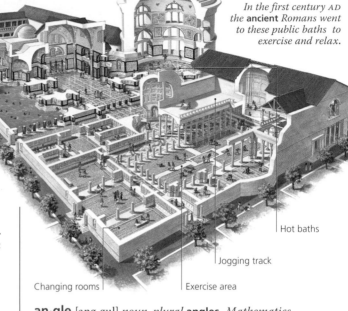

In the first century AD the **ancient** *Romans went to these public baths to exercise and relax.*

Hot baths

Jogging track

Changing rooms

Exercise area

an·gle [ang-gul] *noun, plural* **angles.** *Mathematics.*
1. the space between two straight lines that meet at a point, or between two flat surfaces that come together along a line. **2.** the size of the space between two straight lines that meet at a point. This size is measured in degrees. **3.** a point of view or a way of thinking about an idea or a problem: *Maria and Pablo argue because they often look at the same issue from different angles.*
verb, **angled, angling.** to move something so that it forms a different angle with something else.

An·glo [ang-gloh] *noun, plural* **Anglos.** a word for a white-skinned person whose native language is English. Many people in the United States, Britain, Canada, and Australia can be called Anglos. *adjective.* describing such a person.

Anglo-Saxon [ang-gloh-saks-un] *noun, plural* **Anglo-Saxons.** *History.*
1. one of the people from the area that is now called Germany who invaded England more than 1,600 years ago. **2.** the language of these people, which later developed into the English language.
3. a British person or a person whose ancestors were British.

Ether was an early **anesthetic** *that was first used successfully in 1846 by William Norton to remove a tumor from a man's neck.*

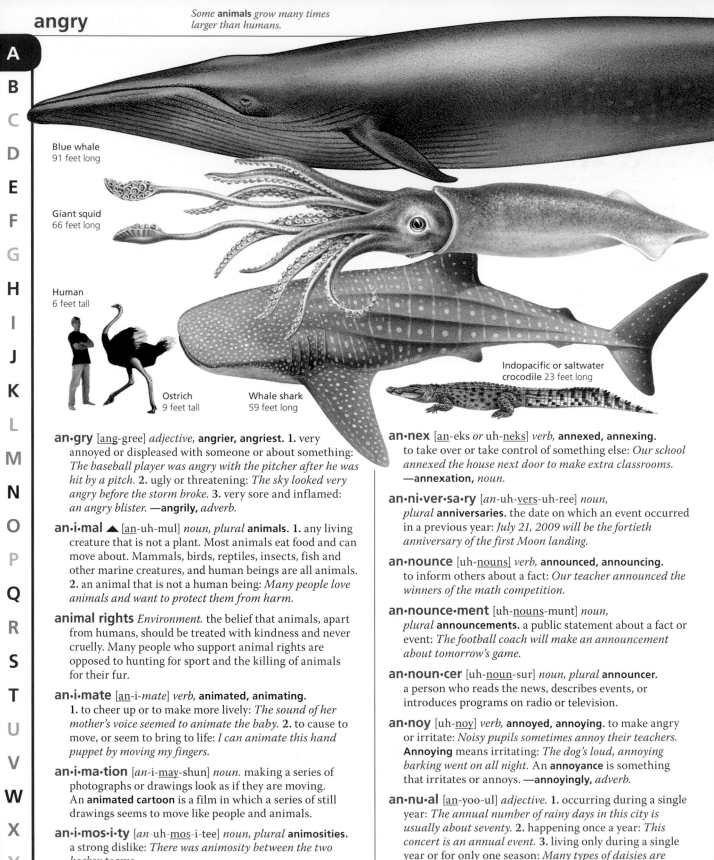

*Some **animals** grow many times larger than humans.*

Blue whale
91 feet long

Giant squid
66 feet long

Human
6 feet tall

Ostrich
9 feet tall

Whale shark
59 feet long

Indopacific or saltwater
crocodile 23 feet long

an·gry [ang-gree] *adjective,* **angrier, angriest. 1.** very annoyed or displeased with someone or about something: *The baseball player was angry with the pitcher after he was hit by a pitch.* **2.** ugly or threatening: *The sky looked very angry before the storm broke.* **3.** very sore and inflamed: *an angry blister.* —**angrily,** *adverb.*

an·i·mal ▲ [an-uh-mul] *noun, plural* **animals. 1.** any living creature that is not a plant. Most animals eat food and can move about. Mammals, birds, reptiles, insects, fish and other marine creatures, and human beings are all animals. **2.** an animal that is not a human being: *Many people love animals and want to protect them from harm.*

animal rights *Environment.* the belief that animals, apart from humans, should be treated with kindness and never cruelly. Many people who support animal rights are opposed to hunting for sport and the killing of animals for their fur.

an·i·mate [an-i-*mate*] *verb,* **animated, animating. 1.** to cheer up or to make more lively: *The sound of her mother's voice seemed to animate the baby.* **2.** to cause to move, or seem to bring to life: *I can animate this hand puppet by moving my fingers.*

an·i·ma·tion [*an*-i-*may*-shun] *noun.* making a series of photographs or drawings look as if they are moving. An **animated cartoon** is a film in which a series of still drawings seems to move like people and animals.

an·i·mos·i·ty [*an*-uh-*mos*-i-tee] *noun, plural* **animosities.** a strong dislike: *There was animosity between the two hockey teams.*

an·kle [ang-kul] *noun, plural* **ankles.** the joint between the leg and the foot.

an·nex [an-eks *or* uh-neks] *verb,* **annexed, annexing.** to take over or take control of something else: *Our school annexed the house next door to make extra classrooms.* —**annexation,** *noun.*

an·ni·ver·sa·ry [*an*-uh-vers-uh-ree] *noun, plural* **anniversaries.** the date on which an event occurred in a previous year: *July 21, 2009 will be the fortieth anniversary of the first Moon landing.*

an·nounce [uh-nouns] *verb,* **announced, announcing.** to inform others about a fact: *Our teacher announced the winners of the math competition.*

an·nounce·ment [uh-nouns-munt] *noun, plural* **announcements.** a public statement about a fact or event: *The football coach will make an announcement about tomorrow's game.*

an·noun·cer [uh-noun-sur] *noun, plural* **announcer.** a person who reads the news, describes events, or introduces programs on radio or television.

an·noy [uh-noy] *verb,* **annoyed, annoying.** to make angry or irritate: *Noisy pupils sometimes annoy their teachers.* **Annoying** means irritating: *The dog's loud, annoying barking went on all night.* An **annoyance** is something that irritates or annoys. —**annoyingly,** *adverb.*

an·nu·al [an-yoo-ul] *adjective.* **1.** occurring during a single year: *The annual number of rainy days in this city is usually about seventy.* **2.** happening once a year: *This concert is an annual event.* **3.** living only during a single year or for only one season: *Many types of daisies are annual plants.*
noun, plural **annuals.** a plant that grows and dies within a single year or season. —**annually,** *adverb.*

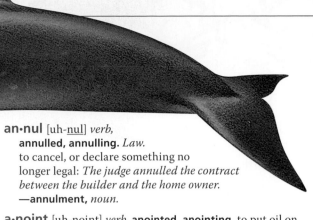

an·nul [uh-<u>nul</u>] *verb,*
annulled, annulling. *Law.*
to cancel, or declare something no
longer legal: *The judge annulled the contract
between the builder and the home owner.*
—**annulment,** *noun.*

a·noint [uh-<u>noint</u>] *verb,* **anointed, anointing.** to put oil on,
usually during a religious ceremony: *The priest anointed
the sick woman.*

a·non·y·mous [uh-<u>non</u>-uh-mus] *adjective.* **1.** written, sent,
or made by an unknown person: *Someone sent my father
an anonymous letter last week.* **2.** unnamed: *The person
who wrote this old folk song remains anonymous.*
—**anonymously,** *adverb.*

a·no·rex·i·a [*an*-uh-<u>reks</u>-ee-uh] *noun. Health.* an illness
that causes people to stop wanting to eat, usually when
they are trying to lose weight very quickly or stay very
thin. **Anorexic** means having to do with this illness, and
an **anorexic** is someone who suffers from it.

an·oth·er [uh-<u>nuth</u>-ur] *adjective.* **1.** one more; an extra:
I would like another biscuit, please. **2.** a different: *Jennie
did not like that book, so she decided to read another one.*
pronoun. **1.** an extra one: *Stephen sang one song, and then
another.* **2.** a different one: *This movie is boring, so I'll
watch another.*

an·swer [<u>an</u>-sur] *noun, plural* **answers. 1.** something
said to respond to something else; a reply: *Please give
me an answer to my question.* **2.** a way of reacting or
dealing with something: *There is an easy answer to
a problem of high gas prices.*
verb, **answered, answering. 1.** to speak or write in
reply to: *We answered all the
questions correctly.* **2.** to act in
response to: *I answered the
phone as soon as it rang.*

Female giant **anteaters**
*grow to six feet long and
carry their young on
their backs.*

ANTS

Ants live in organized groups known as colonies. Each colony
has one large female, or "queen," who stays in the nest to lay
eggs. Many smaller female "workers" collect food and care for
the queen and her eggs. Soldier ants protect the colony, but
the few winged males die after they have mated with a
queen. Ants eat both animal and plant
matter, and communicate using
chemicals called pheromones,
which have a particular smell.

Males, or drones, fly
from the nest to mate
with a new queen.

Touching antennae to check
smells tells these red ants they
are from the same nest.

A worker ant removes
an egg from the queen.

ant ▲ [ant] *noun, plural* **ants.** a common insect that lives
in a large community with many others of the same kind.
Ants are related to bees.

ant·ac·id [ant-<u>ass</u>-id] *noun, plural* **antacids.** a substance
that acts against the effects of acids. People take antacid
medicines when they feel sick in the stomach.

an·tag·o·nism [an-<u>tag</u>-uh-niz-um] *noun, plural*
antagonisms. a feeling of strong dislike or opposition:
There is antagonism between those two countries.
An **antagonist** is a person who shows antagonism.

Ant·arc·tic [ant-<u>ark</u>-tik] *noun.* the part of the world,
around the South Pole, often called the continent of
Antarctica. The word **antarctic** means having to do
with the Antarctic.

ant·eat·er ◀ [<u>ant</u>-eet-ur] *noun, plural* **anteaters.** an animal,
from South America, Central America, or Australia, that
has a long snout and that uses its sticky tongue to get ants
out from their nests and eat them.

an·te·ced·ent [*an*-tuh-<u>seed</u>-unt] *noun, plural* **antecedents.**
Language. something that is mentioned earlier and then
referred to again. In the sentence *I read the letter once and
then read it again,* "letter" is the antecedent of "it."

an·te·lope [<u>an</u>-tuh-lope] *noun, plural* **antelopes.** a tall,
slender, fast-moving animal with long horns. Antelopes
live in parts of Africa and Asia.

*Most male deer lose their **antlers** in winter and grow new ones in the spring.*

Spring: antler buds are covered with soft skin.

Summer: antlers are fully grown.

Fall: skin cover wears away.

Winter: brittle antlers break off easily.

an·ten·na [an-<u>ten</u>-uh] *noun,* plural **antennas** or **antennae.**
1. an object made of metal that sends or receives signals from radio or television transmissions.
2. one of the feelers on the head of an insect, lobster, or crayfish.

an·them [<u>an</u>-thum] *noun,* plural **anthems.** *Music.* a special song that represents and praises a country: *"A Soldier's Song" is the national anthem of Ireland.*

an·thol·o·gy [an-<u>thol</u>-i-jee] *noun,* plural **anthologies.** *Literature.* a collection in a single book of a number of poems, stories, essays, or other kinds of writing: *an anthology of English poetry.*

an·thra·cite [<u>an</u>-thruh-site] *noun. Science.* a kind of hard coal that produces very little smoke or flame when it burns.

an·thrax [<u>an</u>-thraks] *noun. Health.* a disease, caused by bacteria, that people can catch from sheep and cattle.

an·thro·pol·o·gy [an-thruh-<u>pol</u>-i-jee] *noun. Science.* the science that deals with how human societies, beliefs, and cultures have developed through the ages. An **anthropologist** studies how people live all over the world.

anti- a prefix that means *against* or *opposed* to the word it is attached to.

an·ti·bi·ot·ic [an-tye-bye-<u>ot</u>-ik] *noun,* plural **antibiotics.** *Medicine.* a medical drug, such as penicillin, that can help cure illnesses caused by germs.
adjective. acting as a drug in this way.

an·ti·bod·y [<u>an</u>-ti-*bod*-ee] *noun,* plural **antibodies.** *Medicine.* a substance that the blood makes that helps the body fight against germs.

an·tic·i·pate [an-<u>tiss</u>-i-pate] *verb,* **anticipated, anticipating. 1.** to look forward to: *Monica keenly anticipated her cousin's visit.* **2.** to expect and plan for: *A good chess player can often anticipate her opponent's next move.* **—anticipation,** *noun.*

an·ti·dote [<u>an</u>-ti-*dote*] *noun,* plural **antidotes.** a drug or medicine that opposes the effects of a poison or an illness: *Scientists have found antidotes to many kinds of snakebites.*

an·ti·freeze [<u>an</u>-tee-*freez*] *noun.* a liquid that is mixed with another liquid to prevent it from turning to ice in very cold conditions. Antifreeze stops the water in car radiators from freezing in winter.

an·ti·his·ta·mine [an-tee-<u>hiss</u>-tuh-min *or* an-tee-<u>hiss</u>-tuh-meen] *noun,* plural **antihistamines.** *Medicine.* a drug or medicine that can help relieve the effects of some illnesses, such as colds and allergic reactions.

an·tique ▶ [an-<u>teek</u>] *adjective.* very old; from earlier times: *In our house there are some pieces of antique furniture that were made in the 1800s.*
noun, plural **antiques.** something made a long time ago: *This grandfather clock is a real antique.*

an·ti·sep·tic [<u>an</u>-ti-sep-tik] *noun,* plural **antiseptics.** *Medicine.* a substance, such as iodine, that acts against harmful germs and prevents them from growing. *adjective.* describing a substance that acts this way.

ant·ler ▲ [<u>ant</u>-lur] *noun,* plural **antlers.** one of the two large horns that grow on the heads of some animals, such as male elk or deer. Antlers usually have branches.

an·to·nym [<u>an</u>-tuh-*nim*] *noun,* plural **antonyms.** *Language.* a word that means the opposite of another word. *Big* is an antonym of *small; in* is the antonym of *out.*

An **antonym** is not just a word that is very different in meaning from another, but one that is the exact opposite. *Hot* is an antonym for *cold,* but *warm* is not because it is not the direct opposite.

anx·i·e·ty [ang-<u>zye</u>-uh-tee] *noun,* plural **anxieties.** a feeling of worry about something that has happened or that might happen: *Some people feel anxiety when they travel in an aircraft.*

anx·ious [<u>angk</u>-shus] *adjective.* **1.** feeling worried or nervous about something: *The players were anxious before the big game.* **2.** having a strong interest; keen; eager: *Hannah is anxious to know who won the race.* **—anxiously,** *adverb.*

an·y [<u>en</u>-ee] *adjective.* **1.** one, but not a certain one: *Take any seat you want; Are there any gas stations on this road?* **2.** every: *Any day at the beach is fun for me.*
adverb. at all; in some way: *He just doesn't have any good things to say about her.*
pronoun. anybody or anything: *We hoped some famous stars would be there, but we didn't see any.*

an·y·bod·y [<u>en</u>-ee-*bud*-ee *or* <u>en</u>-ee-*bod*-ee] *pronoun.* any person, no matter who: *This job is so easy that anybody could do it.*

an·y·how [<u>en</u>-ee-*how*] *adverb.* no matter what; in spite of something: *Mario is staying home, but we are going out anyhow.*

an·y·more [<u>en</u>-ee-*more*] *adverb.* any longer; these days: *My grandfather does not drive a car anymore.* This word is also spelled **any more.**

an·y·one [<u>en</u>-ee-*wun*] *pronoun.* anybody; no matter who: *Anyone who lives in our town can use this park.*

*This **antique** sewing machine was made in the 1800s.*

APES

Apes can be distinguished from monkeys because they have no tail. They are also more intelligent—for example, they can be taught to communicate using a kind of language and can make simple tools. Orangutans are found in Sumatra and Borneo, and like to live alone. Chimpanzees and gorillas are found in Africa and live in family groups. Gorillas eat only plants. Orangutans feed on fruit, leaves, and small animals. A chimpanzee's diet includes fruits, leaves, birds' eggs, insects, and animals such as antelopes and monkeys.

Orangutan

Western lowland gorilla

Chimpanzee

an·y·place [en-ee-*plas*] *adverb.* anywhere; no matter where: *You can put those books down anyplace you wish.* This word is also spelled **any place.**

an·y·thing [en-ee-*thing*] *pronoun.* any particular thing; no matter what thing: *Because today is a holiday, we can do anything we want.*

an·y·time [en-ee-*time*] *adverb.* whenever; no matter when: *Mom said we could leave anytime we liked.* This word is also spelled **any time.**

an·y·way [en-ee-*way*] *adverb.* **1.** in any manner; no matter how: *Marissa always dresses anyway she likes.* **2.** in any case; anyhow: *It may rain, but we'll come to see you anyway.* This word is also spelled **anyways.**

an·y·where [en-ee-*ware*] *adverb.* no matter where; wherever: *We can play on the grass anywhere we like in this park.*

a·or·ta [an-or-tuh] *noun, plural* **aortas** *or* **aortae.** *Medicine.* the channel, or artery, through which the heart pumps blood to the rest of the body, but not to the lungs.

A·pach·e [uh-patch-ee] *noun, plural,* **Apaches** *or* **Apache.** a person who belongs to a Native American group that lives mainly in the southwest of the United States.

a·part [uh-part] *adverb.* **1.** distant from each other; away: *The two boys were standing together, and then they moved ten feet apart.* **2.** into separate bits or pieces: *To repair the faucet, the plumber had to take it apart.*

a·part·heid [uh-par-tite *or* uh-par-thide] *noun. Government.* a system in a society where people from different racial or religious groups are kept apart from one another by law. Until recently, racial apartheid was practiced in South Africa.

a·part·ment [uh-part-munt] *noun, plural* **apartments.** a dwelling or living space that is part of a larger building. An **apartment house** is a building that contains a number of separate apartments.

ap·a·thy [ap-uh-thee] *noun.* a state of not caring or not being interested: *Apathy was the only reason Rebecca would not join the tennis team.* A person who shows apathy is **apathetic.**

a·pat·o·saur·us [uh-pat-uh-sore-us] *noun, plural* **apatosauruses** *or* **apatosauri.** a huge dinosaur that lived in parts of Central and North America about 150 million years ago. This animal is also called an **apatosaur.**

ape ▲ [ayp] *noun, plural* **apes.** one of a group of large monkeys that have no tails. This group includes chimpanzees, gorillas, gibbons, and orangutans. *verb,* **aped, aping.** to imitate; act exactly like: *Dad makes us laugh when he apes the television announcers.*

ap·er·ture [ap-ur-chur] *noun, plural* **apertures.** a small hole or gap: *The aperture in a camera lens allows a certain amount of light to reach the film inside.*

a·pex [ay-peks] *noun, plural* **apexes** *or* **apices.** the top or highest point: *The apex of a mountain is its peak.*

a·phid ◀ [ay-fid] *noun, plural* **aphids.** a tiny insect that feeds on the juice of plant leaves.

a·pol·o·get·ic [uh-pol-i-jet-ik] *adjective.* expressing regret for doing something, being sorry: *Juan was apologetic about arriving late for the party.* **—apologetically,** *adverb.*

Slow-moving aphids are easy prey for ladybugs.

a·pol·o·gize [uh-pol-uh-*jize*] *verb,* **apologized, apologizing.** to express regret or say sorry for doing something: *I apologized to Rachel for spilling orange juice on her floor.*

a·pol·o·gy [uh-pol-uh-jee] *noun, plural* **apologies.** the act of saying sorry for doing something wrong or offending someone: *You should give an apology to your neighbors for making so much noise.*

A·pos·tle [uh-<u>pos</u>-ul] *noun, plural* **Apostles.** *Religion.*
1. one of the twelve men specially chosen by Jesus to spread his message to others. **2. apostle.** any person who admires and learns from another person and agrees strongly with what that person believes and does.

a·pos·tro·phe [uh-<u>pos</u>-truh-*fee*] *noun, plural* **apostrophes.** *Language.* a mark (') that: **1.** is placed between letters to show that a letter has been left out or two words have been joined together into one. *Can't* is a short form of *cannot*; *don't* is a short form of *do not*. **2.** indicates that someone or something owns something or that something belongs to something else: *Giovanna's hat; the houses' roofs.* **3.** indicates more than one of a single letter or number: *There are two f's in "effort"; My phone number has three 4's in it.* **4.** shows that a date has been shortened: *Both of my parents were born in '73* (meaning 1973).

We use an **apostrophe** to show who owns something, but it is not correct to use it to show the plural of something (more than one). "This is the Johnsons' house" is correct because it shows who owns the house, the Johnson family. "The Johnsons' live here" is not correct because no apostrophe is needed just to say the plural.

ap·pall [uh-<u>pawl</u>] *verb,* **appalled, appalling.** to shock or scare: *The way you behaved yesterday appalled me.* Something that is horrifying or scary is **appalling.**

ap·pa·rat·us [*ap*-uh-<u>rat</u>-us] *noun, plural* **apparatus** *or* **apparatuses.** any equipment or machinery needed for a particular job or purpose, such as a machine used to train in a gym, or a chemistry set used in a laboratory.

ap·par·el ▼ [uh-<u>pare</u>-ul] *noun.* things to wear; clothing; clothes: *The women were dressed in their finest apparel for the celebration.*

ap·par·ent [uh-<u>pare</u>-unt] *adjective.* **1.** easy to understand; obvious: *When Julie's dog died, her sadness was apparent.* **2.** something that appears to be true, but might not be: *Bill might be innocent despite his apparent guilt.*
—**apparently,** *adverb.*

On special occasions, families in ancient China wore their best **apparel.**

ap·peal [uh-<u>peel</u>] *noun, plural* **appeals. 1.** a serious request for help: *In the wake of the hurricane an appeal went out for warm clothes and food.* **2.** the quality of being able to attract or please: *That little puppy has great appeal.* **3.** *Law.* a request to have a case judged again in the hope that the original decision will be reversed: *The accused was found guilty as charged, but his attorney immediately lodged an appeal.* **4.** a request to have a decision reversed in sports.
verb, **appealed, appealing. 1.** to earnestly ask someone to do something for a particular reason: *Harry appealed to the police officer to help him.* **2.** to attract or please: *I love traveling, but sitting on a crowded bus for twenty hours does not appeal to me.* Something that is attractive or pleasing is **appealing. 3.** *Law.* to request a case be heard again by a higher court. **4.** *Sport.* to challenge an umpire or referee's decision.

ap·pear [uh-<u>peer</u>] *verb,* **appeared, appearing. 1.** to become visible; be seen: *The car suddenly appeared out of the thick fog.* **2.** to seem to be or look a certain way: *He appeared to be sad when he heard the news.* **3.** to take part in: *He has appeared in lots of action movies.*

ap·pear·ance [uh-<u>peer</u>-uns] *noun, plural* **appearances. 1.** the act of appearing or becoming visible: *With the sudden appearance of dark clouds on the horizon, it looked like rain.* **2.** how something or someone looks. **Appearances** is how you look to others. **3.** the act of appearing in front of an audience or a group of people: *Everyone at the meeting was waiting for the appearance of the guest speaker.*
• **keep up appearances.** to act in the way that people have come to expect of you: *I've lost my job, so I can no longer afford to keep up appearances.*

ap·pen·di·ci·tis [uh-<u>pen</u>-di-<u>sye</u>-tus] *noun, Medicine.* a painful condition in which a person's appendix becomes inflamed and is usually removed in an operation.

ap·pen·dix [uh-<u>pen</u>-diks] *noun, plural,* **appendixes** *or* **appendices. 1.** *Medicine.* a small, narrow tube attached to the intestines. **2.** material which is added at the end to the main part of a book or document. It supplies the reader with additional information.

ap·pe·tite [<u>ap</u>-uh-tite] *noun, plural* **appetites. 1.** the fact of wanting to have something, especially food: *Bill's appetite is enormous—he ate a whole chicken all by himself.* **2.** enthusiasm for something: *Since the car accident, she has lost her appetite for speed.*

ap·pe·tiz·er [<u>ap</u>-uh-*tize*-ur] *noun, plural* **appetizers.** light food or drink served before the main meal. If you find something tasty, you find it **appetizing.**
—**appetizingly,** *adverb.*

ap·plaud [uh-<u>plawd</u>] *verb,* **applauding, applauding. 1.** to show pleasure or approval by clapping your hands: *After the final act of the play, the audience stood up and applauded for ten minutes.*

2. to support someone and to approve of what they are doing: *I applaud your decision to speak out against drugs.*

ap·plause [uh-<u>plaws</u>] *noun.* **1.** approval and pleasure shown by clapping your hands: *After the concert, the audience's applause was deafening.* **2.** an expression of approval and support: *He received universal applause for his contribution to science.*

ap·ple [<u>ap</u>-ul] *noun, plural* **apples.** a firm, round fruit with red, yellow, or green skin.

ap·pli·ance ▶ [uh-<u>ply</u>-uns] *noun, plural* **appliances.** a machine used for a particular purpose, such as a washing machine, dishwasher, or refrigerator.

ap·pli·ca·ble [<u>ap</u>-li-kuh-bul] *adjective.* having to do with something that is able to be used, or is relevant to a particular situation: *This is a "No Parking" zone, but the rule is not applicable on Sundays.* **—apply,** *verb.*

ap·pli·cant [<u>ap</u>-lu-kunt] *noun, plural* **applicants.** someone who formally applies for a certain position, usually a paying job: *The store owner was amazed when forty applicants replied to his advertisement.*

ap·pli·ca·tion [ap-li-<u>kay</u>-shun] *noun, plural* **applications.** **1.** the act of wanting to get a position, such as a job, or a place at a university or college. **2.** the act of putting something to a specific use: *the application of a formula to solve a math problem; I gave the wall three applications of paint.* **3.** the quality of being relevant or usable: *Carlo said his ladder invention has great practical application for the building trade.* **4.** a computer program specially designed for a particular activity: *a word-processing application.*

ap·ply [uh-<u>ply</u>] *verb,* **applied, applying. 1.** to make use of; employ: *The math problem isn't hard—simply apply the rule.* Something that is used or employed is **applied**: *Applied mathematics means using mathematics to deal with practical problems in everyday life.* **2.** to make a strong effort to do something: *Susan applied herself to her homework.* **3.** to make a formal request for something, such as a university place, a job, or a permit. **4.** to be relevant: *Because of Rory's age, the under-age drinking law applies to him.*

ap·point [uh-<u>point</u>] *verb,* **appointed, appointing. 1.** to choose someone to do a particular job or for a special post: *The President appointed her to the position of Secretary of State.* **2.** to decide on; fix: *It was left to me to appoint the time and place for our next meeting.* If you decide on a certain time or place for something to happen, then that becomes the **appointed** time or place.

ap·point·ment [uh-<u>point</u>-munt] *noun, plural* **appointments. 1.** an arrangement to meet someone at a certain time for a particular reason, such as a patient

The food processor is a small kitchen **appliance** *with many parts.*

meeting a doctor. **2.** the act of choosing someone for a special post, or a particular job: *His recent appointment to the job of chief accountant was a very popular choice.* **3.** a job or position.

ap·praise [uh-<u>prayz</u>] *verb,* **appraising, appraising. 1.** to judge or evaluate the qualities of someone or something: *During the tryout, Tom knew he was being carefully appraised by the team coaches.* **2.** to assess the value of something: *We asked an art expert to come to the house to appraise our paintings.* The act of being judged is **appraisal.** The person who does the judging is the **appraiser.**

ap·pre·ci·ate [uh-<u>pree</u>-shee-*ate*] *verb,* **appreciated, appreciating. 1.** to see the quality or value in someone or something: *Hilary really appreciates beautiful things.* **2.** to be pleased about something and to be grateful for it: *Thanks for lending me the money—I really appreciate it.* **3.** to recognize and understand a situation that exists: *I spent hours repainting his room, but I don't think he appreciated how much time it took.* **4.** to rise in value: *The U.S. dollar has appreciated lately against the euro.*

ap·pre·ci·a·tion [uh-<u>pree</u>-shee-*ay*-shun] *noun.* **1.** the act of seeing quality or value in someone or something, and the pleasure you get from it: *George just loves his Porsche because he has always had a great appreciation of fine things.* **2.** the act of being grateful: *Take this little memento as an indication of my appreciation of your support.* **3.** an increase in value.

ap·pre·hend [ap-ree-<u>hend</u>] *verb,* **apprehended, apprehending. 1.** to catch and arrest someone: *The police apprehended the villain at 4.30 this afternoon.* **2.** to understand or comprehend something: *The problem is complex—have you apprehended it fully?*

ap·pre·hen·sion [ap-ree-<u>hen</u>-shun] *noun, plural* **apprehensions. 1.** a feeling of worry and fear about something, or that something bad might happen: *He was filled with apprehension at the thought of receiving his exam results.* If you have a fear about something happening, you are **apprehensive** about it. **2.** the act of catching and arresting someone.

ap·pren·tice [uh-<u>pren</u>-tis] *noun, plural* **apprentices.** a young person who is employed, usually for a set period of time, by an established company to learn a particular skill, such as mechanics, plumbing, or hairdressing: *Many people think that the best way to learn a trade is to be an apprentice.* The act of taking on an apprentice is an **apprenticeship.**
verb, **apprenticed, apprenticing.** to employ or be employed as an apprentice.

a b c d e f g h i j k l m n o p q r s t u v w x y z

43

*This bridge is part of an ancient **aqueduct** built by the Romans to carry spring water to a town in southern France.*

ap·proach [uh-<u>prohch</u>] *verb,* **approached, approaching.**
1. to come closer or nearer to something: *We are approaching the city center now.* **2.** to talk to someone about a particular subject or plan: *I am going to approach Julia about a babysitting job.* Someone who you feel you can talk to about a subject is **approachable. 3.** to start work on: *We asked many people for their advice about the best way to approach this problem.*
noun, plural **approaches. 1.** the act of coming nearer: *Spring must be approaching because all the flowers are starting to bloom.* **2.** the act of starting work or starting to deal with a subject: *The committee feels this plan represents the best approach.*

ap·pro·pri·ate [uh-<u>pro</u>-pree-ut *for adjective;* uh-<u>pro</u>-pree-ate *for verb*] *adjective.* all right for the purpose or situation; acceptable, suitable: *His rude remark was not an appropriate way to speak to his mother.*
verb, **appropriated, appropriating. 1.** to take for your own use, sometimes illegally: *She was accused of appropriating the money raised at the school fair.* **2.** to set aside for a particular use: *The Town Council appropriated some former army land for a new park.* —**appropriately,** *adverb.*

ap·pro·val [uh-<u>proo</u>-vul] *noun, plural* **approvals.**
1. a feeling of liking; acceptance: *Tracey's new boyfriend met with her parents' approval.* **2.** the act of being allowed to do something; consent.

ap·prove [uh-<u>proov</u>] *verb,* **approved, approving. 1.** to like and admire: *That's a great shirt—I must say I approve of your choice.* **2.** to formally agree to: *The city council approved the developer's plans for a new supermarket.*

ap·prox·i·mate [uh-<u>proks</u>-uh-mut] *adjective.* very near, nearly: *Her approximate height is five feet.*
—**approximately,** *adverb.*

a·pri·cot [<u>ayp</u>-ri-kot *or* <u>ap</u>-ri-kot] *noun, plural* **apricots.**
a small, round, yellowish-orange fruit with furry skin.

A·pril [<u>ay</u>-pril] *noun.*
the fourth month of the year; April has thirty days.

a·pron [<u>ayp</u>-run] *noun, plural* **aprons.** a piece of clothing worn over regular clothes to keep them from getting dirty.

apt [apt] *adjective.* **1.** likely to: *She's apt to forget the time—that's why she's nearly always late.* **2.** clever, quick: *Joe does well at school and his teachers say he is a very apt student.* **3.** fitting or appropriate: *That joke was not an apt remark for such a serious occasion.*
—**aptly,** *adverb.*

> The English words for months go back to Latin, the language of ancient Rome. **April** is said to be from a goddess whose name was Aphrodite, or it may be from a word for "two," since April was the second month in the Roman calendar of ten months.

ap·ti·tude [<u>ap</u>-ti-*tude*] *noun, plural* **aptitudes.** an ability to learn or do something quickly; talent: *She is terrific at English but shows no aptitude for mathematics.*

aq·ua·cul·ture [<u>ak</u>-wi-*kul*-chur] *noun. Environment.* the fact of growing plants and animals in water; farming in water.

aq·uar·i·um [uh-<u>kware</u>-ee-um] *noun, plural* **aquariums.**
1. a pond or tank, usually made of glass, where live fish and other small animals are kept. **2.** a building, usually in a zoo, containing fish and other underwater animals and plants.

a·quat·ic [uh-<u>kwaht</u>-ik] *adjective.* **1.** living or growing in water. Seaweed is an aquatic plant. **2.** related or occurring in water. Sports that are performed in or on water are called **aquatics**.

aq·ue·duct ▲ [<u>ak</u>-wi-*dukt*] *noun, plural* **aqueducts.**
1. a large pipe or channel that carries water over a long distance, often over a valley or river. **2.** a long, high structure that looks like a bridge, usually with arches, that supports such a pipe or channel.

aq·ui·fer [<u>ak</u>-wi-*fur*] *noun, plural* **aquifers.** *Environment.* a layer of rock or sand which holds water, but allows it to seep slowly through to supply springs and wells.

Ar·ab [<u>air</u>-ub] *noun, plural* **Arabs.** a member of a certain group of people living in the Middle East or North Africa, or whose ancestors come from there.
adjective. of, or having to do with the Arabs or Arabia.

A·ra·bi·an ▼ [uh-<u>ray</u>-bee-un] *adjective.* of or having to do with Arabia, a desert region in southwest Asia, its culture, or its people.
noun, plural **Arabians. 1.** a person who was born a member of the Arab race. **2.** a horse of a famous breed originally from Arabia.

Ar·a·bic [<u>air</u>-i-bik] *adjective. Language.* belonging to or relating to the language or culture of the Arabs.
noun. the language of the Arabs.

*Al Hajrah in Yemen is an **Arabian** city.*

Arabic numerals

Mathematics. the number symbols 0, 1, 2, 3, 4, 5, 6, 7, 8, and 9.

These are called **Arabic numerals** because people in Europe first learned of them from the Arabs. Before that, people in Europe used the system of ROMAN NUMERALS, which are not as good for mathematics as Arabic numerals.

ar·bi·trar·y [ar-bi-*trer*-ee] *adjective.* based on emotion, rather than reason, logic, or law: *Nick made an arbitrary decision to go out and buy an expensive car.* —**arbitrarily,** *adverb.*

ar·bi·trate [ar-bi-*trate*] *verb,* **arbitrated, arbitrating. 1.** to settle an argument by making a decision as to who is right: *Mothers and fathers are often called on to arbitrate between their quarreling children.* **2.** to submit to arbitration to be settled: *The United Nations was called upon to arbitrate between the warring factions.* The person who makes the decision is called the **arbitrator** or the **arbiter.** —**arbitration,** *noun.*

ar·bor [ar-bur] *noun, plural* **arbors.** a shelter in a garden that is shaded by trees or vines growing on a frame. **Arbor Day** is a day set aside once a year for the planting of trees and to make people aware of their value.

arc [ark] *noun, plural* **arcs. 1.** *Mathematics.* a section of the line that forms a circle. **2.** a curved shape or line of movement.
🔊 A different word with the same sound is **ark.**

ar·cade [ar-*kade*] *noun, plural* **arcades. 1.** a covered passageway, usually with shops or stalls on both sides. **2.** a place with different video games that people pay to play.

arch [arch] *noun, plural* **arches. 1.** a curved structure over a doorway or open space that usually supports the weight of the material above it. **2.** anything that is curved like an arch, such as the part at the bottom of the foot, between the toes and the heels.
verb, **arched, arching.** to form into an arch; curve: *The horse arched its back, and then took off at a gallop.*

ar·chae·ol·o·gy [ar-kee-*ol*-i-jee] *noun.* *Science.* the scientific study of the way humans lived many years ago. People who do this sort of work are called **archaeologists.** They dig up the remains of ancient civilizations and study the things they find, such as old buildings, tombs, tools, and pottery. This word is also spelled **archeology.**

ar·cha·ic [ar-*kay*-ik] *adjective.* out of date and old fashioned; not in common use today: *I couldn't understand that book—it was full of archaic words like "portmanteau."*

An **archaic** word or phrase is one that was once used commonly in the language, but now is not used very often. An example would be the word *aeroplane* for what we now call an *airplane,* or *aerodrome* for what we now call an *airport.* You can still see these words in books written many years ago. If a word is never used at all any more, it is said to be *obsolete,* not archaic.

arch·bish·op [arch-*bish*-up] *noun, plural* **archbishops.** *Religion.* a bishop of the highest rank, in the Catholic, Protestant, and Orthodox branches of the Christian church.

arch·er·y [arch-uh-ree] *noun.* a sport in which people shoot at a target with a bow and arrow. A person who practices archery is an **archer.**

ar·chi·pel·a·go [ark-i-*pel*-i-go] *noun, plural* **archipelagoes** or **archipelagos. 1.** a large group of small islands. **2.** an area of the ocean containing many small islands.

ar·chi·tect [ark-i-*tekt*] *noun, plural* **architects.** a person who designs new buildings. An architect will also supervise the construction of these.

ar·chi·tec·ture ▼ [ark-i-*tek*-chur] *noun, plural* **architectures. 1.** the act and science of designing and constructing buildings. **2.** a particular style in which buildings were designed: *Notre Dame Cathedral in Paris is a great example of Gothic architecture.* **Architectural** is having to do with architecture.

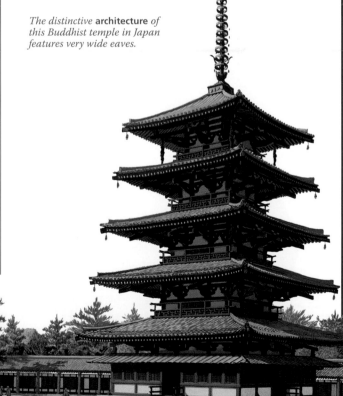

*The distinctive **architecture** of this Buddhist temple in Japan features very wide eaves.*

ARCTIC

The Arctic is the northernmost part of the world that falls inside an imaginary circle around the North Pole, known as the Arctic Circle. At its center is the vast, mostly ice-covered Arctic Ocean. This is surrounded by frozen, treeless land with low-growing plants. The Arctic includes parts of the United States (Alaska), Canada, Greenland, Iceland, Norway, Sweden, Finland, and the Russian Federation.

Alaska

Canada

ARCTIC OCEAN

Russian Federation

Greenland

Norway

Iceland

Finland

Sweden

Snowy owl

CLIMATE
The Arctic is very cold, dry, windy, and often snowy. Arctic winters are long and dark, while summers are short, but with long hours of daylight.

Arctic tern

Arctic fox

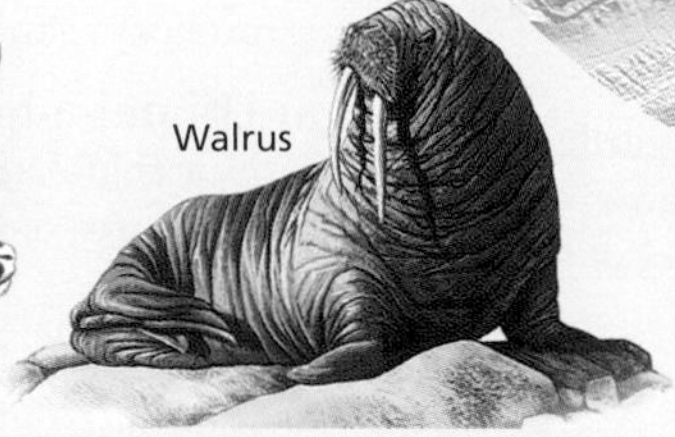

Walrus

Harp seal

Caribou

ANIMALS
Animals that live in the Arctic or migrate there in summer are adapted to the extreme conditions. They include beluga whales, narwhals, seals, sea lions, various seabirds, polar bears, Arctic foxes, walruses, and caribou.

Inuit houses in Greenland

Polar bear and cubs

PEOPLE
The Inuit, or Eskimo, people of the region were once nomadic, hunting and fishing for food. Today they are more likely to live in towns and use snowmobiles instead of dogsleds for transport.

Snow tractor

RESEARCH
To help our understanding of global warming, scientists are investigating the effects of climate change on the unique ecology of the Arctic.

Research ship

Inuit hunters

Researcher

Arc·tic ◀ [ark-tik] *noun.* the area of the world around the North Pole. The word **arctic** means having to do with the North Pole.

ar·dent [ar-dunt] *adjective.* having strong feeling about something; enthusiastic. **—ardently,** *adverb.*

are [ar] *verb.* a present tense of BE, used with *you, we,* or *they.*

ar·e·a [ayr-ee-uh] *noun, plural* **areas. 1.** the total extent of surface, within a set boundary, given in square measurement, such as feet, inches, or miles: *His farm measures close to forty square miles in area.* **2.** a particular part or region: *the suburban area around Washington.* **3.** a field of knowledge, interest, or activity: *His area of expertise is nuclear physics.*

a·re·na [uh-ree-nuh] *noun, plural* **arenas. 1.** a space used for sporting contests or entertainment. In ancient Rome, gladiators fought each other in arenas. **2.** a building with such a space. **3.** any field or area of competitive activity, or conflict: *the arena of politics.*

aren't [arnt] the shortened form of "are not."

ar·gon [ar-gun] *noun. Chemistry.* a chemically inactive gaseous element that has no color or smell.

ar·gue [arg-yoo] *verb,* **argued, arguing. 1.** to express a different opinion, sometimes in an angry fashion; disagree: *Let's stop quarreling—I'm too tired to argue with you anymore.* **2.** to state your reasons for or against something: *James is a great attorney—he is just the man to argue the case for the defense.*

ar·gu·ment [arg-yuh-munt] *noun, plural* **arguments. 1.** a discussion about something between people who do not agree with each other: *The girls were having a heated argument about whose turn it was to drive the family car.* **2.** a reason or reasons given to support or disprove something: *His logical argument about climate warming made me change my mind.*

ar·id ▼ [air-id] *adjective.* dry and hot; without rain: *the arid area of the Sahara Desert.* The state of being dry and without rain is **aridity.**

a·rise [uh-rize] *verb,* **arose, arisen, arising. 1.** to appear or come into being: *I fear that serious problems will arise if we do not take action soon.* **2.** to come up or rise: *As we drove toward the town, a large bear seemed to arise from nowhere and approach us.* **3.** to get up from a lying, sitting, or kneeling position.

ar·is·toc·ra·cy [ar-is-tok-ruh-see] *noun, plural* **aristocracies.** a class of people in some countries, usually old ones such as England, whose family has always had a high social standing, power, and money.

a·ris·to·crat [uh-ris-tuh-krat] *noun, plural* **aristocrats.** a person who belongs to the aristocracy. **—aristocratic,** *adjective.*

a·rith·me·tic [uh-rith-muh-tik] *noun.* **1.** *Mathematics.* a branch of mathematics concerned with the addition, subtraction, multiplication, and division of numbers. **2.** the act of working out the answers to a sum by doing addition, subtraction, multiplication, or division. *adjective.* having to do with arithmetic: *simple arithmetic problems.*

ark [ark] *noun.* **1.** in the Bible, a large, covered boat built by Noah to escape the Flood. He took his family and two of every kind of animal with him. **2.** a sacred chest carried by the ancient Hebrews on their journey to the Promised Land. It contained the two stone tablets on which the Ten Commandments were written.
🔊 A different word with the same sound is **arc.**

arm[1] [arm] *noun, plural* **arms. 1.** the upper limb of the body between the shoulder and the wrist. **2.** anything that is shaped or used like an arm.

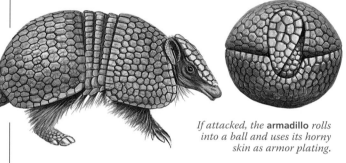

If attacked, the armadillo rolls into a ball and uses its horny skin as armor plating.

arm[2] [arm] *noun, plural* **arms.** any weapon: *Guns, explosives, and missiles are arms.* *verb,* **armed, arming. 1.** to supply with, or have, a weapon: *Police said that the escaped convict was armed with a shotgun.* **2.** to provide something that gives strength or protection: *He easily won the argument, armed as he was, with all the facts and figures.*

ar·ma·da [ar-mah-duh] *noun, plural* **armadas.** a large fleet of warships: *The Spanish Armada was a powerful force in the 1500s.*

ar·ma·dil·lo ▲ [arm-muh-dil-oh] *noun, plural* **armadillos.** a small animal that has a hard, bony shell, a long snout and tail, and sharp claws. The armadillo is a mammal.

Armadillo comes from Spanish, where it means "little armored creature." Many words for animals of North America come from Spanish, because explorers from Spain were the first Europeans to see these animals.

*The Acacus Desert in Libya, northern Africa, is an **arid** region that receives very little rain.*

a
b
c
d
e
f
g
h
i
j
k
l
m
n
o
p
q
r
s
t
u
v
w
x
y
z

ar·ma·ment [ar-muh-munt] *noun,*
plural **armaments.** military
equipment; arms.

arm·chair [arm-*chair*] *noun,*
plural **armchairs.** a comfortable
chair with supports on both sides for
your elbows and arms to rest on.

armed [armd] *adjective.* having a weapon,
especially a gun: *Two armed men tried to
rob the bank.*

armed forces the military forces of a country.
The Army, Navy, Marine Corps, Air Force,
and Coast Guard are the armed forces of the
United States.

ar·mi·stice [arm-i-stis] *noun, plural* **armistices.**
Government. an agreement between two or
more countries to stop fighting to see if a
peaceful settlement can be worked out;
truce. **Armistice Day** is a day specifically
dedicated to members of the armed forces
who were killed during World War I.

*A medieval knight wore a full suit
of* **armor** *when riding into battle.*

ar·mor ▶ [arm-ur] *noun.* **1.** special clothing made of metal
that soldiers and their horses used to wear for protection
during battle. **2.** a thick, hard, outer covering that
protects, such as the metal plates on a military vehicle or
the shell of some animals. —**armored,** *adjective.*

ar·mor·y [arm-uh-ree] *noun, plural* **armories.** a place where
military equipment is kept.

arm·pit [arm-*pit*] *noun, plural* **armpits.** the part of your
body under your arm, where your arm
joins your shoulder.

arms [armz] *plural noun.*
weapons, such as guns,
explosives, and
missiles.

ar·my [arm-ee] *noun,*
plural **armies.** a large
group of people who
are armed and trained
to fight on land in a war.
The United States' **Army** is
organized and trained by
its government.

a·ro·ma [uh-row-muh]
noun, plural **aromas.**
a pleasant smell,
especially of food.

*Sioux boys were taught how to
shoot using small bows and* **arrows.**

a·round [uh-round] *preposition.* **1.** in a circle about: *They
ran around the track.* **2.** here and there in: *The tourists
walked around the town for several hours.* **3.** somewhat
near; about: *We should get there around 5:30.*
adverb. **1.** in a circle: *The wheel spun around.* **2.** in the
opposite direction: *He turned around to see who was calling.*

a·rouse [uh-rouz] *verb,* **aroused, arousing. 1.** to notice or
become interested in something. **2.** to stir up, wake up, or
make angry: *That news story aroused a lot of anger.*

ar·range [uh-raynj] *verb,* **arranged,
arranging. 1.** to position or put in
order: *I am going to arrange my
books on the shelf in alphabetical
order by author.* **2.** to make
plans or make something
happen: *I arranged for the taxi
to come to collect us at 2 P.M.*
3. *Music.* to change a piece of music
from the way it was first written.
—**arrangement,** *noun.*

ar·ray [uh-ray] *noun, plural* **arrays.**
an organized display or collection:
*The teacher set out an array of
colored pencils.*

ar·rest [uh-rest] *verb,* **arrested, arresting. 1.** the action of
police or other authority in taking away a person's
freedom. *The bank robber was arrested by the police.*
noun, plural **arrests.** the act of taking away a person's
freedom, usually with permission or authority.

ar·riv·al [uh-rye-vul] *noun, plural* **arrivals.** the act of
coming to a place: *My parents looked forward to my
arrival home from camp.* **2.** someone who reaches a place:
a new arrival in the neighborhood.

ar·rive [uh-rive] *verb,* **arrived, arriving. 1.** to reach a place:
We arrived too late for the movie. **2.** to reach a state of
being, position, or condition: *After a long discussion we
arrived at an understanding.*

ar·ro·gant [air-uh-gunt] *adjective.* a person who appears to
have too great a sense of their own importance or ability
over others: *The new boy was arrogant in his belief that he
was smarter than the rest of the class.* The fact of being
arrogant is **arrogance.** —**arrogantly,** *adverb.*

ar·row ◀ [air-oh] *noun, plural* **arrows. 1.** a straight, thin
shaft with one sharp, pointed end and one feathered end:
I shot the arrow from my bow. **2.** any image shaped like an
arrow: *Outside the hall were arrows showing where to
enter.* The pointed end of an arrow is an **arrowhead.**

ar·roy·o [uh-roy-oh] *noun, plural* **arroyos.** a deep-sided
ditch or hollow in the earth, originally carved by water
but dry most of the time.

ar·se·nal [ars-uh-nul] *noun, plural* **arsenals.** a place where
weapons are manufactured and kept.

ar·se·nic [ars-uh-nik] *noun. Chemistry.* a metallic, tasteless,
extremely poisonous substance that can be used to kill
weeds and pests.

ar·son [ar-sun] *noun. Law.* the criminal act of intentionally
burning property. A person who intentionally sets fire to
property is an **arsonist.**

art [art] *noun, plural* **arts.** **1.** the creation of something that is beautiful, significant, or meaningful. The arts include painting, dancing, acting, playing music, and writing. **2.** a particular work made or done in a creative way. A statue, an opera, and a novel are works of art. **3.** an ability or craft you learn or have a talent for: *the art of cooking; the art of conversation.*

ar·te·ry [art-uh-ree] *noun, plural* **arteries.** **1.** *Medicine.* a blood vessel that carries blood away from the heart to the body. **2.** something that carries things from place to place in a similar manner to this: *A major highway can be called a traffic artery.* —**arterial,** *adjective.*

ar·thri·tis [ar-thrye-tis] *noun. Health.* a medical condition in which a person has pain, swelling, and stiffness in body joints.

ar·thro·pod ▶ [arth-ruh-*pod*] *noun, plural* **arthropods.** *Biology.* a group of animals with jointed legs, a body divided into parts and no backbone, such as spiders, crabs, and insects.

ar·ti·choke [art-i-*choke*] *noun, plural* **artichokes.** a plant cultivated for its large flower bud, which is eaten as a vegetable. The edible portion of the cooked bud is the fleshy underside of the tough leaves and the soft center, or heart.

ar·ti·cle [art-i-cul] *noun, plural* **articles.** **1.** a complete piece of writing in a newspaper, magazine, or book: *The magazine published an article on child actors.* **2.** an object or item belonging to a group: *an article of clothing.* **3.** a particular section in an official document. **4.** In grammar, a word (*a, an,* or *the*) used before a noun.

ar·ti·cu·late [ar-tik-yuh-lit *for adjective;* ar-tik-yuh-late *for verb*] *adjective.* able to express thoughts easily and clearly: *Her speech is very articulate for such a young girl.* *verb,* **articulated, articulating.** to verbalize thoughts easily and clearly: *She articulated her sense of outrage.* —**articulation,** *noun.*

Artifacts such as this Pueblo vase help us understand how earlier people lived.

ar·ti·fact ▲ [art-i-*fakt*] *noun, plural* **artifacts.** an object made or used by humans in earlier times: *In the cave, they found artifacts such as stone tools and arrowheads.*

ar·ti·fi·cial [art-i-fish-ul] *adjective.* **1.** created by humans rather than nature: *Saccharine is artificial sugar.* **2.** not true or genuine: *She acts so concerned but she is completely artificial.* —**artificially,** *adverb.*

artificial intelligence *Computers.* the use of computers to imitate the learning ability and thinking power of humans.

artificial respiration *Medicine.* the delivering of air into the lungs of a person who is not breathing on their own.

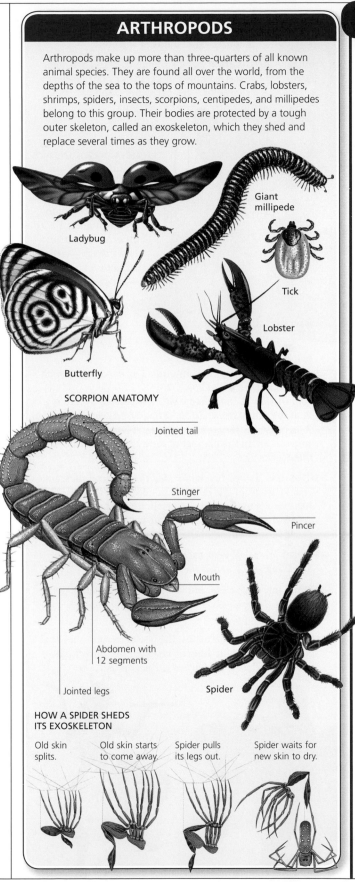

ARTHROPODS

Arthropods make up more than three-quarters of all known animal species. They are found all over the world, from the depths of the sea to the tops of mountains. Crabs, lobsters, shrimps, spiders, insects, scorpions, centipedes, and millipedes belong to this group. Their bodies are protected by a tough outer skeleton, called an exoskeleton, which they shed and replace several times as they grow.

Ladybug

Giant millipede

Tick

Lobster

Butterfly

SCORPION ANATOMY

Jointed tail

Stinger

Pincer

Mouth

Abdomen with 12 segments

Jointed legs

Spider

HOW A SPIDER SHEDS ITS EXOSKELETON

Old skin splits.

Old skin starts to come away.

Spider pulls its legs out.

Spider waits for new skin to dry.

A B C D E F G H I J K L M N O P Q R S T U V W X Y Z

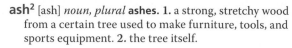

ar·til·ler·y [ar-**til**-uh-ree] *noun.* **1.** heavy weapons used in war, such as cannons. **2.** the army unit that uses these kinds of weapons.

ar·ti·san ▼ [**art**-i-sun] *noun, plural* **artisans.** a worker skilled in a trade or craft. Jewelers, cheese-makers, carpenters, and bakers are artisans.

ar·tist [**art**-ist] *noun, plural* **artists. 1.** someone who creates works of art, such as a painter, musician, or writer. **2.** someone whose work shows creativity or a high level of ability: *She is an artist at putting on makeup.* —**artistic,** *adjective;* —**artistically,** *adverb.*

In ancient Greece, **artisans** *painted scenes from the lives of gods and heroes on pots and vases.*

as [az] *adverb.* to the same amount: *The movie was not as good as I expected it to be.*
conjunction. **1.** in the same way that: *Please do as I say.* **2.** at the same time that: *He called just as we were leaving.* **3.** because: *As she isn't here yet, we'll have to wait.*
preposition. in the manner of or in the role of: *He works as a teacher.*

as·bes·tos [as-**bes**-tus] *noun. Health.* a natural substance that is fireproof and does not conduct electricity, which has made it useful in the construction of buildings. Asbestos is no longer used because it is now known to cause serious illness of the lungs.

as·cend [uh-**send**] *verb,* **ascended, ascending.** to go up: *The climbers ascended the mountain.*

as·cent [uh-**sent**] *noun, plural* **ascents. 1.** the act of going upward: *The onlookers cheered the rocket's ascent.* **2.** a rising slope.

ash¹ [ash] *noun, plural* **ashes.** the powdery substance that remains when something is burned: *Fine, gray flakes of ash were left after we burned the newspaper.*

ash² [ash] *noun, plural* **ashes. 1.** a strong, stretchy wood from a certain tree used to make furniture, tools, and sports equipment. **2.** the tree itself.

a·shamed [uh-**shaymd**] *adjective.* **1.** feeling shame, embarrassment, or regret: *She was ashamed about stealing from the shop.* **2.** choosing not to do something because of guilt: *I was too ashamed to tell my friend the truth.*

a·shore [uh-**shor**] *adverb; adjective.* toward or on land after being on water: *We left the boat to go ashore; The boat's crew enjoyed their time ashore.*

A·sian ▼ [**ay**-zhun] *adjective.* relating to the people, cultures, or languages of the continent of Asia. *noun, plural.* **Asians.** someone who comes from or lives in Asia.

Asian-American [ay-zhun-uh-**mere**-i-kun] *noun, plural* **Asian-Americans.** someone with an Asian family background who was born in, or has come to live in, the U.S. —**Asian-American,** *adjective.*

A·si·at·ic [ay-zhee-**at**-ik] *adjective.* relating to the geography, plants, or animals of Asia.

a·side [uh-**side**] *adverb.* **1.** on or to one side; out of the way: *She stood aside to let him pass.* **2.** not taken into account or considered: *All kidding aside, this is a serious issue.* **3.** kept apart: *I put some of my pocket money aside for the holidays.*
noun, plural **asides.** a comment or speech from an actor directly to the audience that the other characters cannot hear.

a·sleep [uh-**sleep**] *adjective.* **1.** in a state of sleep; not awake. **2.** without sensation; numb: *My hand was asleep.*
adverb. to or into sleep: *The dog fell asleep in front of the fire.*

as·par·a·gus [uh-**spare**-uh-gus] *noun.* a plant with long, green stalks, called spears, that can be eaten as a vegetable.

ask [ask] *verb,* **asked, asking. 1.** to say a question; try to find out something: *I asked the new girl what her name was.* **2.** to make a request; call for: *He didn't understand the problem, so he asked his mom for help.* **3.** to invite: *She asked all the other girls in the class to her party.* **4.** to set as a price: *They are asking $2,000 for that car.*

Indian dancer

Bhutan folk dancer

Korean drum dancer

Thai performers

People who live in **Asian** *countries belong to many different cultures.*

as·pect [as-pekt] *noun, plural* **aspects. 1.** a distinct feature, element, or characteristic: *I studied every aspect of the problem.* **2.** the way a thing appears; a view: *From the windows of my bedroom there is a pretty aspect.*

as·pen ▶ [as-pun] *noun, plural* **aspens.** trees with leaves that flutter in the lightest wind. Aspens are part of a species of trees called poplars.

as·phalt [as-fault] *noun.* a sticky, dark brown or black substance found in the earth or created as a result of refining petroleum. It is mixed with crushed gravel or sand and used for paving.

as·pire [uh-spire] *verb,* **aspired, aspiring.** to have an ambition or want to achieve a goal: *I aspire to being an actor.* The act of wanting to achieve something is **aspiration.**

as·pi·rin [as-puh-run *or* as-prin] *noun, plural,* **aspirins.** *Health.* a drug that is often used to reduce pain, fever, and blood clotting.

ass ▶ [ass] *noun, plural* **asses. 1.** an animal like a horse, though smaller and with longer ears. **2.** someone who is foolish or stupid.

as·sas·si·nate [uh-sas-i-nate] *verb,* **assassinated, assassinating.** to murder an important person: *John Wilkes Booth assassinated the President with a pistol.* Someone who murders an important person is an **assassin. —assassination,** *noun.*

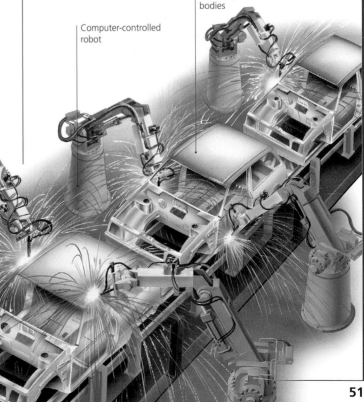

The **ass** *is also known as a donkey, burro, or jackass.*

as·sault [uh-sault] *noun, plural,* **assaults. 1.** a violent physical attack: *The soldiers began their assault on the enemy tanks.* **2.** *Law.* an unlawful attack on a person: *The man who hit him was charged with assault.* *verb,* **assaulted, assaulting.** to attack violently: *The gang assaulted the boy with a metal bar.*

assault rifle any automatic rifle designed for military use.

assault vehicle a tank or armored vehicle, often used to lead an attack.

as·sem·ble [uh-sem-bul] *verb,* **assembled, assembling. 1.** to gather or come together: *We assembled in the hall for the meeting.* **2.** to put together: *He used secondhand parts to assemble a new radio.*

as·sem·bly [uh-sem-blee] *noun, plural* **assemblies. 1.** a group of people gathered for the same purpose: *The assembly of citizens met to discuss plans for a new town hall.* **2.** a group of people who make laws. In some states of the United

In modern **assembly lines,** *car parts are welded together by computer-controlled robots instead of people.*

States, one of the houses of the legislature is called the **Assembly. 3.** the act of putting together: *He carefully followed the instructions for assembly of the model plane.* **4.** a group of parts that belong together: *He could not fly the model plane because a part of the wing assembly was missing.*

assembly line ▼ a line of workers and machines in a factory. A product is put together on an assembly line by adding part after part until the whole product is assembled.

as·sent [uh-sent] *verb,* **assented, assenting.** to agree or approve: *Our principal assented to the changes in the school rules.* *noun.* agreement or approval: *The school board had to give its assent before work on the new library began.*

as·sert [uh-surt] *verb,* **asserted, asserting. 1.** to state confidently: *The police officer asserted that his version of the story was correct.* **2.** to claim or insist: *The students asserted their right to protest.* **—assertion,** *noun.*

as·sess [uh-ses] *verb,* **assessed, assessing. 1.** to set the value of something: *The fake diamonds were assessed as being worthless.* **2.** to set the amount of a tax or fine: *The sheriff assessed a fine of $100.* **—assessment,** *noun.*

Computer-controlled robot

Assembly line of car bodies

Main asteroid belt

Trojan asteroids

Mars

Jupiter

Trojan asteroids

*Most **asteroids** orbit between Mars and Jupiter, but the Trojan asteroids are in Jupiter's orbit.*

as·set [ass-et] *noun, plural* **assets. 1.** a useful thing; an advantage: *Having a strong build is an asset for football players.* **2.** something of value that is owned, such as money, property, or land.

as·sign [uh-sine] *verb,* **assigned, assigning. 1.** to give work; set a task: *The teacher will assign homework before her students leave.* If you are set a job to do, it is an **assigned** task. **2.** to appoint or designate: *The coach assigned her best defender to cover the other team's top scorer.*

as·sign·ment [uh-sine-munt] *noun, plural* **assignments. 1.** a task or job that is assigned: *Your assignment is to write a story about what you did on vacation.* **2.** the act of assigning: *The teacher is responsible for the assignment of homework to her students.*

as·sist [uh-sist] *verb,* **assisted, assisting.** to give help; aid: *The children tried to assist the old lady who had fallen over.* Someone who assists is an **assistant.** —**assistant,** *adjective;* —**assistance,** *noun.*

as·so·ci·ate [uh-soh-see-ate *for verb;* uh-soh-shut *for noun and adjective*] *verb,* **associated, associating. 1.** to join or connect in one's mind: *I always associate the smell of freshly cut grass with summer.* **2.** to join as a partner or friend: *Her mother wants her to associate with people her own age.*
noun, plural **associates.** a partner or friend: *My father asked a work associate to start up a new business with him.*
adjective. **1.** closely connected with another or others in status or responsibility: *Both the associate professors teach at the same college.* **2.** having some, but not all, rights and privileges: *The associate members of the club are allowed to use the pool but not the gym.*

as·so·ci·a·tion [uh-soh-see-ay-shun] *noun, plural* **associations. 1.** a group joined by a common purpose: *My parents joined an association that protects the rights of wild animals.* **2.** the act of associating or the state of being associated: *Our family has a long association with the local church.* **3.** ideas or feelings connected with a person, place, or thing: *Since her grandfather died, she feels a sad association with his old house.*

as·so·ci·a·tive property *Mathematics.* a property of multiplication and addition that allows three or more numbers to be multiplied or added in any order and still give the same answer. For example: $7 \times (3 \times 5)$ gives the same answer as $3 \times (5 \times 7)$; they both equal 105.

as·sort·ed [uh-sort-id] *adjective.* different things mixed together: *After the party we were given an assorted bag of candy to take home.* A collection of different things is called an **assortment.**

as·sume [uh-soom] *verb,* **assumed, assuming. 1.** to take as being true; suppose: *It's a long way to walk so I assume he will catch the bus.* **2.** to take on; undertake: *She feels ready to assume the responsibility of bringing her little sister to school.* **3.** to take for oneself; take over: *Let's hope someone assumes control before things get out of hand.* A person pretending to be someone else might take on an **assumed name.**

as·sump·tion [uh-sump-shun] *noun, plural* **assumptions. 1.** the act of taking something to be true: *She offered us nothing to eat because she made the assumption that we ate lunch earlier.* **2.** something that is taken to be true: *Her assumption that we had eaten turned out to be incorrect.*

as·sur·ance [uh-shur-uns] *noun, plural* **assurances. 1.** a statement given to make a person certain or sure: *Mom asked for an assurance that I would come straight home from school.* **2.** a lack of doubt; certainty: *She played golf with the assurance that comes from being a champion.*

as·sure [uh-shur] *verb,* **assured, assuring. 1.** to state firmly: *I assure you I will be back by dinnertime.* **2.** to make certain or sure: *All those hours of study assured she would pass the exam.* **3.** to make confident: *We assured the terrified girl that the bridge was safe.*

as·ter [ass-tur] *noun, plural* **asters.** a flower like a daisy that blooms in the fall. Asters have white, yellow, pink, or purple petals around a yellow center.

as·ter·isk [ass-tuh-risk] *noun, plural* **asterisks.** *Language.* a star-shaped mark (*) used to tell a reader to look for more information somewhere else on the page.

as·ter·oid ▲ [ass-tuh-roid] *noun, plural* **asteroids.** *Science.* any one of the thousands of small planets that revolve around the Sun.

asth·ma [az-muh] *noun.* *Health.* a medical condition that causes a person to cough and wheeze and find it very hard to breathe. Asthma is often caused by an allergy. Someone suffering from asthma is called an **asthmatic.**

as·ton·ish [uh-ston-ish] *verb,* **astonished, astonishing.** to surprise greatly; amaze: *She was astonished when the magician disappeared in front of her.* If something greatly surprises you, it is **astonishing.** —**astonishment,** *noun.*

as·tride [uh-stride] *preposition.* having one leg on each side of something.

as·trol·o·gy [uh-strol-i-jee] *noun.* the study of the way that stars and planets supposedly affect our lives. A person who makes predictions using astrology is called an **astrologer.** —**astrological,** *adjective.*

as·tro·naut ▶ [as-truh-*nawt*] *noun, plural* **astronauts.** a person who travels in a spacecraft: *The astronaut could look back at the Earth from outer space.*

The word **astronaut** comes from two Greek words that mean "star sailor." Astronauts were thought of as traveling among the stars, though of course they didn't actually travel as far as the stars.

as·tron·o·mer [uh-*stron*-uh-mur] *noun, plural* **astronomers.** a person who studies the stars and planets.

as·tro·nom·i·cal [as-truh-*nom*-i-kul] *adjective.* **1.** of, or having to do with, astronomy: *The scientists used the telescope to make astronomical observations.* **2.** huge or very large: *We were amazed by the astronomical cost of building the new school.* —**astronomically,** *adverb.*

as·tron·o·my [uh-*stron*-i-mee] *noun. Science.* the science that studies the stars, planets, Sun, Moon, and everything in outer space.

a·sy·lum [uh-*sye*-lum] *noun, plural* **asylums. 1.** a place where people receive care when they cannot care for themselves: *The mentally ill man now lives in an asylum.* **2.** a safe place; refuge: *The town hall became an asylum where the whole neighborhood sheltered from the tornado.* **3.** protection given to a refugee: *During a war in their own country, some people seek asylum in another country.*

at [at] *preposition.* **1.** in or near the place of: *I'll be at home all day.* **2.** in or near the time of: *The game starts at noon.* **3.** in the condition of: *The two nations are at war with each other.*

ate [ayt] *verb.* the past tense of EAT.
🔊 A different word with the same sound is **eight.**

a·the·ist [*ayth*-ee-ist] *noun, plural* **atheists.** *Religion.* someone who does not believe in the existence of God. —**atheism,** *noun;* —**atheistic,** *adjective.*

*An **atoll** is created from coral reefs around a volcano that has sunk.*

*An **astronaut** wears a special spacesuit and carries oxygen in a backpack for breathing.*

ath·lete [*ath*-leet] *noun, plural* **athletes.** someone who plays a sport or performs an exercise that takes strength and skill. Runners, swimmers, football players, and hockey players are athletes.

ath·let·ic [ath-*let*-ik] *adjective.* **1.** having to do with athletics or an athlete: *Ice skates and baseball gloves are athletic equipment.* **2.** strong and active: *My sister plays many different sports—she is very athletic.* —**athletically,** *adverb.*

ath·let·ics [ath-*let*-iks] *plural noun.* physical sports or games of any kind: *Athletics are a good way to keep fit.*

at·las [*at*-lus] *noun, plural* **atlases.** *Literature.* a book of maps: *We looked in the atlas to see where the Danube River was in Europe.*

In ancient Greek stories, the giant **Atlas** was forced to hold up the weight of the heavens. Early map books showed him carrying the world on his shoulders and became known as atlases.

ATM *noun, plural* **ATMs.** *Computers.* a machine that lets people withdraw cash, deposit money, and do other banking tasks. ATM is an abbreviation for **automatic teller machine** or **automated teller machine.**

at·mos·phere [*at*-mus-feer] *noun, plural* **atmospheres. 1.** *Environment.* the layer of air surrounding the Earth; it is made up of gases such as oxygen, carbon dioxide, and nitrogen. Beyond the atmosphere lies outer space. **2.** the layer of gases surrounding any heavenly body: *There is no oxygen to breathe in the atmosphere of the Moon.* **3.** mood or feeling: *Grandma's house has a cosy atmosphere.* **4.** the surroundings or environment: *She changed neighborhoods because she wanted to live in a safer atmosphere.* —**atmospheric,** *adjective.*

a·toll ▼ [*a*-tole] *noun, plural* **atolls.** a coral island or group of islands surrounding a lagoon.

a·tom [*at*-um] *noun, plural* **atoms. 1.** *Science.* the smallest particle of a chemical element. An atom is made up of a nucleus of protons and neutrons surrounded by electrons. Atoms make up all matter in the universe. **2.** a tiny piece; a very small bit: *She is so kind—there is not one atom of meanness in her.*

The term **atom** goes back to a Greek word meaning "that cannot be cut." This word was chosen because it was thought that an atom was the smallest piece of matter and could never be divided into something smaller. Modern scientists now know that there are other particles within an atom that are even smaller.

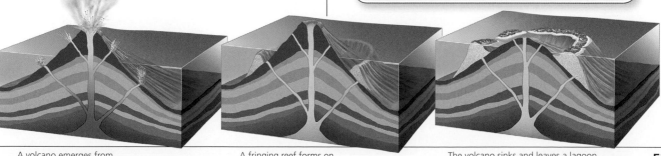

A volcano emerges from the sea to create an island.

A fringing reef forms on the sides of the volcano.

The volcano sinks and leaves a lagoon surrounded by coral islands.

a
b
c
d
e
f
g
h
i
j
k
l
m
n
o
p
q
r
s
t
u
v
w
x
y
z

A B C D E F G H I J K L M N O P Q R S T U V W X Y Z

a·tom·ic [uh-tom-ik] *adjective.* **1.** having to do with atoms: *Our science teacher told us about atomic energy.* **2.** driven by atomic energy: *an atomic submarine.*

atomic bomb a powerful bomb that can wipe out a whole city. The energy released from splitting atoms causes a huge explosion and radiation. Sometimes this bomb is called an atom bomb.

atomic energy *Science.* another term for NUCLEAR ENERGY.

atomic number *Science.* a number given to each element that tells how many protons there are in the nucleus of an atom. Each element has a different atomic number.

a·tro·cious [uh-troh-shus] *adjective.* **1.** very bad or poor taste: *My sister says I have atrocious taste in clothes.* **2.** wicked, cruel, or very unkind: *Bombing the city was an atrocious act.* —**atrocity,** *noun;* —**atrociously,** *adverb.*

at·tach [uh-tach] *verb,* **attached, attaching. 1.** to fasten to something: *I used tacks to attach my poster to the wall.* **2.** to feel strongly connected: *She is very attached to her little dog.* **3.** to assign or attribute: *He attaches great importance to the marks he gets for his homework.* **4.** to add to a document on a computer: *I attached my report to the e-mail.*

at·tached [uh-tacht] *adjective.* joined to something else: *I hope you enjoy my letter—the attached photo will show you how tall I am now.*

at·tach·ment [uh-tach-munt] *noun, plural* **attachments. 1.** the act of joining things: *The attachment of the boat to the trailer takes two people.* **2.** a strong feeling of connection or affection: *My grandmother feels a great attachment to all her grandchildren.* **3.** a device that connects to something: *The computer has an attachment for scanning photos.* **4.** something added to a document of a computer: *If you open the attachment you'll see the homework we have to do.*

at·tack ▼ [uh-takt] *verb,* **attacked, attacking. 1.** to start to fight: *They decided to attack the enemy at dawn.* **2.** to act or speak against: *We attacked the school's harsh new rules in the student paper.* **3.** to start doing

something with lots of energy: *She attacked her dinner as if she hadn't eaten for days.*
noun, plural **attacks. 1.** the act of attacking: *They made the attack under cover of darkness.* **2.** the sudden start of an illness: *After dinner my father had an attack of indigestion.* —**attacker,** *noun.*

at·tain [uh-tane] *verb,* **attained, attaining. 1.** to work hard for something; achieve: *He attained his goal of playing professional baseball.* **2.** to reach; arrive at: *The principal congratulated our teacher for attaining her tenth year at our school.* —**attainment,** *noun.*

at·tempt [uh-tempt] *verb,* **attempted, attempting.** to make an effort; try: *I attempted to jump over the puddle.*
noun, plural **attempts. 1.** an effort; the act of trying: *Each jumper gets three attempts to get over the bar.* **2.** an attack: *The killer made an attempt on her life.*

at·tend [uh-tend] *verb,* **attended, attending. 1.** to be present at: *You have to attend school.* **2.** to be a helper or keep company: *Two bridesmaids attended the bride.* **3.** to take care of: *A kind nurse attended my mother after the operation.*

at·ten·dance [uh-ten-duns] *noun.* **1.** the act of being present: *Attendance at the school dance is not required.* **2.** the number of people at an event.

at·ten·dant [uh-ten-dunt] *noun, plural* **attendants.** someone who helps or takes care of another person: *The attendant at the ball game showed us to our seats.*

at·ten·tion [uh-ten-shun] *noun, plural* **attentions. 1.** the act of watching and listening; focusing on something: *The teacher said she would not go on without our full attention.* **2.** the act of thinking about a situation with the intention of changing it: *The unsafe conditions on our roads require urgent attention.* **3.** a position in which you stand straight

*At the battle of Salamis in 480 BC, the Greeks **attacked** the fleet of the invading Persians and forced them to retreat.*

and still: *The soldiers stood to attention on the parade ground.* **4.** affection and kindness: *She showered lots of attention on her favorite cousin.*

at·ten·tive [uh-<u>ten</u>-tiv] *adjective.* paying attention: *The principal asked the whole school to be attentive during the assembly.* —**attentively,** *adverb.*

at·test [uh-<u>test</u>] *verb,* **attested, attesting.** to show clearly; provide proof: *To use the library's computer you have to attest that you agree with the rules.*

at·tic [<u>at</u>-ik] *noun, plural* **attics.** the area inside the roof of a house.

at·tire ▶ [uh-<u>tire</u>] *noun.* things to wear; clothing: *Everyone at the ball wore formal attire.*
verb, **attired, attiring.** to clothe or dress: *The doormen were attired in fancy uniforms.*

at·ti·tude [<u>at</u>-i-tood] *noun, plural* **attitudes.** how one feels, thinks, or behaves: *Eva's brother had a positive attitude to learning to play the guitar, and he practiced every day.*

at·tor·ney [uh-<u>turn</u>-ee] *noun, plural* **attorneys.** *Law.* a person who acts for another in matters of law; a lawyer: *She hired her own attorney to present her case in court.* An **attorney at law** is a person who has an official license to represent someone in matters of law.

at·tract [uh-<u>trakt</u>] *verb,* **attracted, attracting. 1.** to make come closer; pull closer: *Magnets attract steel pins.* **2.** to gain someone's interest or admiration: *The singer's wonderful voice attracted everyone's attention.* —**attraction,** *noun.*

at·trac·tive [uh-<u>trak</u>-tiv] *adjective.* having a quality that attracts admiration or is pleasing: *Lisa is such an attractive girl when she smiles.* —**attractively,** *adverb.*

at·tri·bute [uh-<u>trib</u>-yoot *for verb;* <u>at</u>-tri-byoot *for noun*] *verb,* **attributed, attributing.** to think of as due to or belonging to: *He attributes doing well on the test to studying hard.*
noun, plural **attributes.** a trait that belongs to someone or something: *Warmer temperatures are an attribute of summer.* —**attribution,** *noun.*

ATV is an abbreviation for **all-terrain vehicle,** which is a small, open, four-wheeled vehicle for off-road use. Another name for this type of vehicle is an **ATC,** which is an abbreviation for **all-terrain cycle.**

au·burn [<u>aw</u>-burn] *noun.* a reddish-brown color. *adjective.* having a reddish-brown color.

auc·tion [<u>awk</u>-shun] *noun, plural* **auctions.** *Business.* a public sale where things are sold to the person who says he will pay the most money: *I couldn't buy the stamp I liked at the auction because the price went too high.* A person who runs an auction is called an **auctioneer.** *verb,* **auctioned, auctioning.** to sell something at an auction.

> **Auction** goes back to a word meaning "to get bigger" or "to increase." In an auction, the amount of money to be paid for something gets larger with each new bid.

au·di·ble [<u>aw</u>-duh-bul] *adjective.* able to be heard: *The explosion was so loud it was audible ten miles away.* —**audibly,** *adverb.*

au·di·ence [<u>aw</u>-dee-uns] *noun, plural* **audiences. 1.** a gathering of people watching or listening to something: *The audience cheered wildly after the President's speech.* **2.** all the people who are reached by a piece of written, recorded, or broadcast information: *The football game was watched by a television audience of two million.* **3.** a formal meeting with an important or high-ranking person: *The queen granted an audience to the mayor.*

Greek guards, called evzons, are **attired** *in a traditional uniform.*

au·di·o [<u>aw</u>-dee-oh] *adjective.* related to sound, especially recording, sending, or receiving it: *The recording of our choir was clear because we used new audio equipment.* An **audiotape** is a tape recording of sound.

au·di·o·vis·u·al [aw-dee-oh-<u>viz</u>-yoo-ul] *adjective.* informing through sound and pictures: *I learned a lot about Antarctica from the museum's audiovisual display.*

au·di·tion [aw-<u>dish</u>-un] *noun, plural* **auditions.** a short performance by an actor, dancer, singer, or musician as a test to show their skills: *The girl had to dance and sing in her audition for the lead part in the musical.* *verb,* **auditioned, auditioning.** to perform in an audition: *I forgot my lines when I was auditioning for the play, so I didn't get the part.*

au·di·to·ri·um [aw-di-<u>tore</u>-ee-um] *noun, plural* **auditoriums.** a building or large room where people gather for meetings or concerts or other performances: *The high school graduation ceremony was held in the auditorium.*

au·di·to·ry [<u>aw</u>-di-tore-ee] *adjective.* having to do with hearing, or with the organs that one hears with: *She has an auditory problem because her ears are blocked.*

aug·ment [awg-<u>ment</u> *or* <u>awg</u>-ment] *verb,* **augmented, augmenting.** to make larger or increase: *At the end of the year he was paid a bonus to augment his regular pay.*

a b c d e f g h i j k l m n o p q r s t u v w x y z

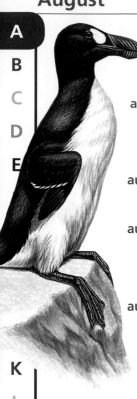

Au·gust [aw-gust] *noun.* the eighth month of the year; August has 31 days.

> The month of **August** is named for *Augustus*, a powerful ruler who was the first emperor of ancient Rome.

auk ◀ [awk] *noun, plural* **auks.** any of certain diving birds that live on northern coastlines. They have black and white feathers and swim using their short paddle-like wings and webbed feet.

aunt [ant *or* ahnt] *noun, plural* **aunts.** 1. your mother or father's sister. 2. your uncle's wife.

au·ri·cle [or-i-kul] *noun, plural* **auricles.** *Medicine.* either of the heart's two upper chambers. Both auricles receive blood from the veins and send it to the heart's two ventricles, or lower chambers.

au·ro·ra [uh-rore-uh] *noun, plural* **auroras** *or* **aurorae.** bands and streams of colored light sometimes seen in the night sky in regions close to the Earth's poles. These lights occur when particles from the Sun enter the Earth's atmosphere.

The great auk, the largest of the **auks,** *was hunted to extinction in the nineteenth century.*

> The people of ancient Rome believed in the goddess Aurora, who was thought of as the spirit of the dawn. From this came the word **aurora**, meaning the light of the Sun coming up at dawn or another bright light in the sky.

aurora borealis ▶ [uh-rore-uh bore-ee-al-is] *Science.* the aurora seen in the area near the North Pole.

aus·tere [aw-steer] *adjective.* 1. serious or stern in appearance or behavior: *The austere teacher never smiled at his students.* 2. extremely simple or plain: *The austere room had no decorations at all.* —**austerely,** *adverb.*

Aus·tra·lian [aw-strale-yun] *noun, plural* **Australians.** someone who was born in, or is a citizen of, Australia. *adjective.* being in, or having to do with, Australia or Australians.

Aus·tri·an [aw-stree-un] *noun, plural* **Austrians.** someone who was born in, or is a citizen of, Austria. *adjective.* being in, or having to do with, Austria or Austrians.

au·then·tic [aw-then-tik] *adjective.* 1. worthy of being believed to be real, true, or correct: *This story gives an authentic account of life in the Middle Ages.* 2. proven to be what it claims to be; genuine: *A jeweler examined the necklace and said it was not made of colored glass, but of authentic rubies.* Something that is proven to be real or true has **authenticity.** —**authentically,** *adverb.*

au·thor [aw-thur] *noun, plural* **authors.** *Literature.* a person who has written a work of literature such as a book, play, article, essay, or story. The act of creating such a work is called **authorship.**

au·thor·i·ta·tive [uh-thor-i-tay-tiv] *adjective.* 1. worthy of being believed in or relied on: *Authoritative sources in the police department said nobody was hurt in the bomb blast.* 2. demonstrating authority: *The captain gave orders to the soldiers in an authoritative manner.* —**authoritatively,** *adverb.*

au·thor·i·ty [uh-thor-i-tee] *noun, plural* **authorities.** 1. the right to command, take control, act, or make decisions: *The judge had the authority to decide for how long the criminal would go to jail.* 2. a person or group of people who has this right. Officials who have this power are known as the **authorities:** *The authorities decided to close the harbor until the oil spill was cleaned up.* 3. a reliable or expert source of information: *The professor of marine biology is an authority on the behavior of dolphins.*

au·thor·ize [awth-uh-rize] *verb,* **authorized, authorizing.** 1. to give authority or power to: *I authorize the bank to pay my bills automatically.* Someone who has this power is **authorized** to act this way. 2. to give official approval: *The mayor authorized the sale of the public land.* —**authorization,** *noun.*

au·tis·im [awt-iz-um] *noun.* a condition where a person has difficulty understanding or communicating with other people. A person who has this condition is said to be **autistic.**

au·to [awt-oh] *noun, plural* **autos.** car; a shortened form of the word AUTOMOBILE.

AURORA BOREALIS

Also known as the northern lights, aurora borealis is a dramatic natural light display. It can be seen mainly in winter from far northern places such as northern Norway, Alaska, and northern Scotland. The aurora occurs when particles thrown out by the Sun collide with gases in the Earth's atmosphere. The energy released appears as a series of colored lights that seem to move across the sky in waves.

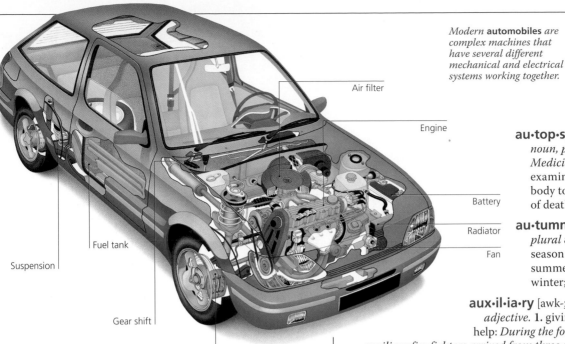

*Modern **automobiles** are complex machines that have several different mechanical and electrical systems working together.*

Air filter

Engine

Battery

Radiator

Fan

Suspension

Fuel tank

Gear shift

Disk brakes

au·top·sy ▼ [aw-top-see] *noun, plural* **autopsies.** *Medicine.* a medical examination of a dead body to learn the cause of death.

au·tumn [awt-um] *noun, plural* **autumns.** the season of the year after summer and before winter; fall.

aux·il·ia·ry [awk-zil-yuh-ree] *adjective.* **1.** giving support or help: *During the forest fire crisis, auxiliary fire fighters arrived from three other states to help battle the blaze.* **2.** extra; additional: *After the hurricane, the hospital was able to stay open because its auxiliary generator supplied electricity.* *noun, plural* **auxiliaries.** a person, group, or thing that gives support or aid: *The volunteers of the hospital auxiliary raised money to build a new ward.*

auxiliary verb *Language.* a verb that is placed before another verb to help express an action or condition. The verbs *be, have, do, must, may,* and *can* are all able to be used as auxiliary verbs. In the sentence *You must clean your bedroom,* the word "must" is an auxiliary verb.

AV an abbreviation for AUDIOVISUAL.

a·vail·a·ble [uh-vale-uh-bul] *adjective.* **1.** possible to get or have: *Only one day after tickets for the concert went on sale, there were no more available.* The **availability** of something is how available it is. **2.** ready to be used: *Once the car had been cleaned, it was available to be rented.*

au·to·bi·og·ra·phy [awt-oh-bye-og-ruh-fee] *noun, plural* **autobiographies.** *Literature.* the story of a person's life written by that person. Such a story is said to be **autobiographical.**

au·to·graph [awt-uh-graf] *noun, plural* **autographs.** a person's name written in their own handwriting. *verb,* **autographed, autographing.** to handwrite one's own name on something: *My favorite basketball player autographed my basketball.*

au·to·ma·tic [awt-uh-mat-ik] *adjective.* **1.** working by itself: *We don't have to wash the dishes because we have an automatic dishwasher.* **2.** taking place without a person's control or without the person thinking about it: *Breathing faster when you are scared is your body's automatic response to danger.* —**automatically,** *adverb.*

automatic pilot **1.** *Science.* a device that flies an airplane automatically: *After the airplane had taken off, the pilot switched to automatic pilot.* **2.** the act of doing something without having to think about it: *She walked home from school the same way every day, so she could do it on automatic pilot.*

au·to·ma·tion [awt-uh-may-shun] *noun.* the creation and use of machines to do the jobs of people: *The rug we bought was not handwoven but made using automation.*

au·to·mo·bile ▲ [awt-uh-muh-beel] *noun, plural* **automobiles.** a motor car; a vehicle that usually carries passengers, has four wheels, and is powered by an engine that uses gasoline.

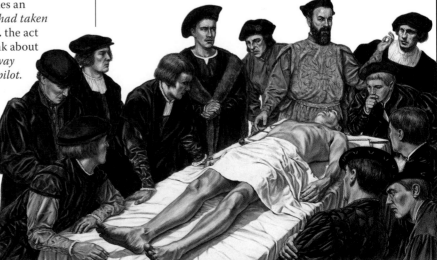

*In the Renaissance, **autopsies** helped medical students understand the anatomy of the human body.* **57**

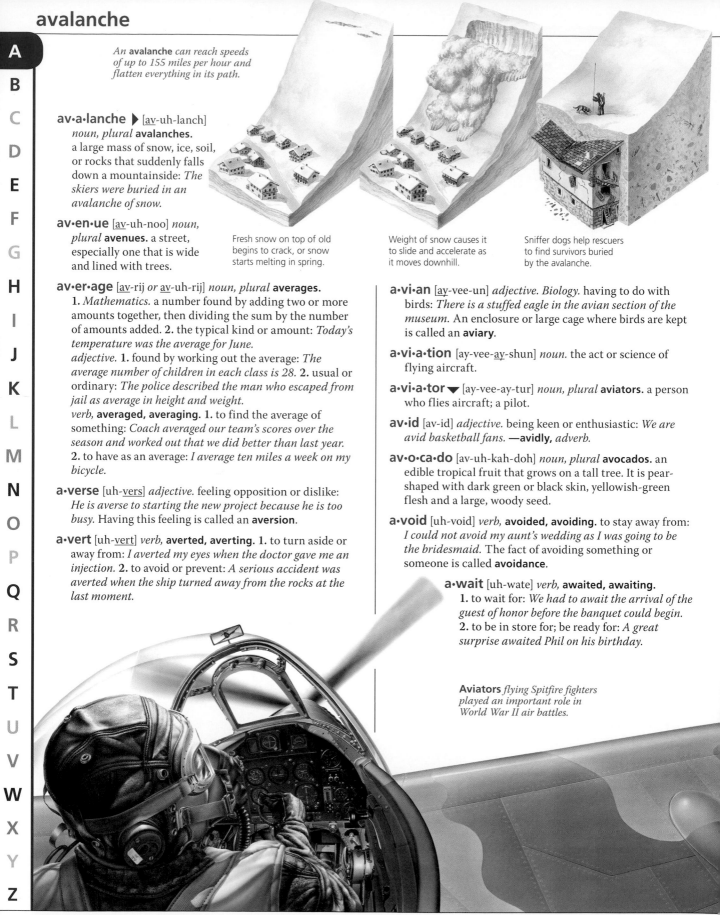

*An **avalanche** can reach speeds of up to 155 miles per hour and flatten everything in its path.*

av·a·lanche ▶ [av-uh-lanch] *noun, plural* **avalanches.** a large mass of snow, ice, soil, or rocks that suddenly falls down a mountainside: *The skiers were buried in an avalanche of snow.*

av·en·ue [av-uh-noo] *noun, plural* **avenues.** a street, especially one that is wide and lined with trees.

Fresh snow on top of old begins to crack, or snow starts melting in spring.

Weight of snow causes it to slide and accelerate as it moves downhill.

Sniffer dogs help rescuers to find survivors buried by the avalanche.

av·er·age [av-rij *or* av-uh-rij] *noun, plural* **averages.**
1. *Mathematics.* a number found by adding two or more amounts together, then dividing the sum by the number of amounts added. 2. the typical kind or amount: *Today's temperature was the average for June.*
adjective. 1. found by working out the average: *The average number of children in each class is 28.* 2. usual or ordinary: *The police described the man who escaped from jail as average in height and weight.*
verb, **averaged, averaging.** 1. to find the average of something: *Coach averaged our team's scores over the season and worked out that we did better than last year.* 2. to have as an average: *I average ten miles a week on my bicycle.*

a·verse [uh-vers] *adjective.* feeling opposition or dislike: *He is averse to starting the new project because he is too busy.* Having this feeling is called an **aversion.**

a·vert [uh-vert] *verb,* **averted, averting.** 1. to turn aside or away from: *I averted my eyes when the doctor gave me an injection.* 2. to avoid or prevent: *A serious accident was averted when the ship turned away from the rocks at the last moment.*

a·vi·an [ay-vee-un] *adjective. Biology.* having to do with birds: *There is a stuffed eagle in the avian section of the museum.* An enclosure or large cage where birds are kept is called an **aviary.**

a·vi·a·tion [ay-vee-ay-shun] *noun.* the act or science of flying aircraft.

a·vi·a·tor ▼ [ay-vee-ay-tur] *noun, plural* **aviators.** a person who flies aircraft; a pilot.

av·id [av-id] *adjective.* being keen or enthusiastic: *We are avid basketball fans.* —**avidly,** *adverb.*

av·o·ca·do [av-uh-kah-doh] *noun, plural* **avocados.** an edible tropical fruit that grows on a tall tree. It is pear-shaped with dark green or black skin, yellowish-green flesh and a large, woody seed.

a·void [uh-void] *verb,* **avoided, avoiding.** to stay away from: *I could not avoid my aunt's wedding as I was going to be the bridesmaid.* The fact of avoiding something or someone is called **avoidance.**

a·wait [uh-wate] *verb,* **awaited, awaiting.** 1. to wait for: *We had to await the arrival of the guest of honor before the banquet could begin.* 2. to be in store for; be ready for: *A great surprise awaited Phil on his birthday.*

Aviators *flying Spitfire fighters played an important role in World War II air battles.*

a·wake [uh-wake] *verb*, **awoke** *or* **awaked**, **awaking**.
to wake up: *When the rooster crowed, she awoke at once.*
adjective. not asleep: *We stayed awake last night to watch the Olympic Games on television.*

a·wak·en [uh-wake-un] *verb*, **awakened**, **awakening**.
to wake up: *The man was awakened by the phone ringing.*

a·ward [uh-ward] *verb*, **awarded**, **awarding**. **1.** to give when judged worthy of merit: *My painting was awarded first prize in the art competition.* **2.** to give because of a decision made in a legal court: *The man injured in the car accident was awarded money by the judge.*
noun, plural **awards**. something given as a result of being judged worthy of merit: *The two sailors who rescued the passengers were given bravery awards.*

a·ware [uh-ware] *adjective*.
being conscious of; knowing: *We were aware that someone was following us.*
—**awareness**, *noun*.

a·way [uh-way] *adverb*.
1. from a place: *He turned and walked away.* **2.** not in the usual place: *She went away on vacation.* **3.** in another direction or to another condition: *He threw away some old papers; We have not had any rain and the grass is just wasting away.*
adjective. **1.** being at a distance: *The airport is ten miles away from here.* **2.** being absent or gone: *He's away for the summer.*
3. in sports, not on one's home field: *an away game.*

Axis

The Earth's **axis** *is an imaginary line from the North Pole to the South Pole.*

awe [aw] *noun*. a feeling of amazement and respect or fear: *They were filled with awe as their plane flew low over the Grand Canyon.*
verb, **awed**, **awing**. to cause such a feeling: *The grizzly bear awed us with its size.*

awe·some [aw-sum] *adjective*. fills with amazement and respect or fear: *The television footage of the tsunami striking the shore was awesome.*

When this word was first used, something that was said to be **awesome** had to be very important, or very unusual, surprising, shocking, frightening, and so on. Now people will use it just to mean "very good," as in "Your brother lets you play his video game? *Awesome.*" This is an example of how a strong word can change over time to have a less powerful meaning.

aw·ful [aw-ful] *adjective*. **1.** causing fear, awe, or dread; terrible: *The awful train smash killed seven people.*
2. very bad or ugly: *Don't buy those awful purple and brown pajamas.* **3.** very large; great: *We will have to save an awful lot of money for our airline ticket.*

aw·ful·ly [aw-flee *or* aw-ful-ee] *adverb*. very much.

a·while [uh-wile] *adverb*. for a short time: *We talked awhile before we sat down to eat.*

awk·ward [awk-wurd] *adjective*. **1.** lacking graceful movement or behavior; clumsy: *The girl was awkward on the ice because she had never skated before.* **2.** in an embarrassing or uncomfortable situation: *I broke my left arm and found it awkward to write with my right hand; The principal felt awkward when he could not remember our names.*
—**awkwardly**, *adverb*.

aw·ning [awn-ing] *noun, plural* **awnings**.
a rooflike shelter from the sun or rain made of metal, canvas, wood, or other material that hangs over a window or door.

Cafes and restaurants often have colorful **awnings**.

a·woke [uh-woke] *verb*. the past tense of AWAKE.

axe [aks] *noun, plural* **axes**. a tool with a metal blade set at the end of a handle. It is used to cut down trees and chop wood. This word is also spelled **ax**.

ax·is ◀ [aks-is] *noun, plural* **axes**. a real or imaginary line that an object rotates around: *The Earth rotates on its own axis as well as orbiting the Sun.*

ax·le [aks-ul] *noun, plural* **axles**. the rod or shaft that goes through the center of a wheel and around which the wheel turns: *When the axle on the cart broke, the wheels would not turn.*

aye [eye] *adverb*. another word for "yes".
noun, plural **ayes**. a yes vote or a person who votes yes.
🔊 Different words with the same sound are **I** and **eye**.

az·a·le·a ▼ [uh-zale-ye] *noun, plural* **azaleas**. a shrub with dark green leaves and brilliant pink, orange, or white flowers that appear in spring.

Az·tec [az-tek] *noun, plural* **Aztec** *or* **Aztecs**. *History*. a member of a Native American people from central Mexico. The Aztec had an advanced and complex empire during the fifteenth and sixteenth centuries AD.

az·ure [az-yur] *noun, plural* **azures**. a blue color like the sky on a clear day.
adjective. having a clear blue color.

Azaleas are covered in a mass of blooms for a month or two in spring.

a
b
c
d
e
f
g
h
i
j
k
l
m
n
o
p
q
r
s
t
w
x
y
z

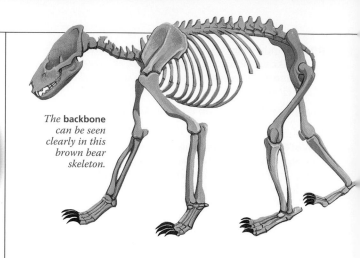

*The **backbone** can be seen clearly in this brown bear skeleton.*

Baboons are the largest members of the monkey family.

Bb

B, b *noun, plural* **B's, b's.** the second letter of the English alphabet.

bab·ble [bab-ul] *verb,* **babbled, babbling. 1.** to make sounds that have no meaning: *The baby could say "Da" but the rest of the time she just babbled.* **2.** to speak in a silly, excitable way; chatter. **3.** to make a murmuring sound: *The stream babbled as it trickled down the rocky hillside.*

ba·boon ▲ [ba-boon] *noun, plural* **baboons.** any one of a number of kinds of large monkeys with doglike faces and short tails. Baboons live in large troops and can travel long distances in search of food.

ba·by [bay-bee] *noun, plural* **babies. 1.** an infant or very young child. **2.** a person who behaves in a childish way: *Stop being a baby and sit down to eat your breakfast.* *adjective.* **1.** belonging to or being for a baby: *A baby bath is much smaller than a bathtub.* **2.** very young or small: *Baby carrots are sweeter than fully-grown ones.* *verb,* **babied, babying.** to treat someone as if they are very young: *My mother babied us and wouldn't let us walk to school by ourselves.*

baby boom *History.* a time when there is a sudden increase in the number of babies being born in a country. Especially in the United States, this was the time after World War II from 1946 to 1960. People born during this time are known as **baby boomers**.

baby-sit [bay-bee-sit] *verb,* **baby-sat, baby-sitting.** to care for babies or young children for a short time while their parents are away. —**baby-sitter,** *noun.*

baby tooth one of a baby's or young animal's first set of teeth.

bach·el·or [bach-lur *or* bach-uh-lur] *noun,* *plural* **bachelors.** a man who is not married, especially one who has never married.

back [bak] *noun, plural* **backs. 1.** the rear part of the human body from the base of the neck to the bottom of the spine. **2.** the similar part of an animal's body. **3.** the part of any object on the opposite side to the front. *verb,* **backed, backing. 1.** to go or move backward: *to back a car out of the driveway.* **2.** to give someone aid or support: *Mom backed my plan to enter the singing competition.* *adjective.* **1.** being at the back, positioned opposite to the front. **2.** having to do with an earlier time; old: *a back issue of a newspaper.* *adverb.* **1.** toward the back; backward. **2.** in a past time or place: *Back in the 1900s, children sometimes rode horses to school.* **3.** in return or in reply: *Give my hat back to me.* ♦ **back up. 1.** to support someone: *Tracy stayed behind Pablo to back up his run.* **2.** to make a copy of computer files or programs in case they are lost or damaged.

back·board [back-bord] *noun, plural* **backboards.** in basketball, the board behind the basket, to which it is attached.

back·bone ▲ [back-bone] *noun, plural* **backbones. 1.** the small bones down the center of the back when joined together; the spine. **2.** someone's strength of character or ability to stand firm: *The boy showed backbone and told the bully to leave him alone.*

back·fire [back-fire] *noun, plural* **backfires.** a small, loud explosion that takes place in a gasoline engine. *verb,* **backfired, backfiring. 1.** to make such an explosion: *The engine must need fixing because it keeps backfiring.* **2.** to go wrong; to have an effect other than that intended: *Our plan to give Dan a surprise party backfired when he didn't show up.*

back·gam·mon ◀ [back-gam-un] *noun.* a board game in which two people take turns throwing dice to determine how to move their checkers.

Backgammon is played on a special board with two different-colored sets of checkers and two pairs of dice.

back·ground [back-*ground*] *noun,*
plural **backgrounds. 1.** the distant part of
a scene. **2.** in design, the plain surface on
which other parts are placed: *Mom chose*
wallpaper with red airplanes on a blue
background for my room. **3.** someone's earlier
education or experience: *She is right for the job*
as she has a background in working with people.

back·hand [back-*hand*] *noun, plural* **backhands.**
a stroke made in a game like tennis where the
back of the hand faces outward. When a stroke
is made in this way, it is said to be **backhanded.**

back·pack [back-*pak*] *noun, plural* **backpacks.** a bag
with shoulder straps that is carried on the back,
as to carry books to school.
verb, **backpacked, backpacking.** to hike or go camping
with one's equipment and supplies carried in a backpack:
When we went backpacking last weekend, we walked
along a canyon.

back·stop [back-*stop*] *noun, plural* **backstops. 1.** a person
or thing that acts as a support or replacement if all else
fails: *I had my speech written down as a backstop in case*
I forgot what to say. **2.** in sport, a screen or fence that
stops the ball going off the playing field. **3.** in baseball,
the catcher or the position of catcher.
verb, **backstopped, backstopping.** to act as a backstop.

back·stroke ▼ [back-*stroke*] *noun.* a swimming stroke
performed by lying on one's back while kicking and
rotating each arm in turn.

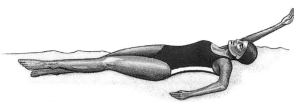

In **backstroke** *swimmers cannot*
see where they are going and must
use their judgment.

back·up [back-*up*] *noun, plural* **backups. 1.** a person or
thing kept as a replacement if needed. **2.** a copy of a
computer file or program kept in case the original is
damaged.
adjective. kept in reserve in case needed: *I have a backup*
inner tube in my bag in case my bicycle gets a puncture.

back·ward [back-*wurd*] *adverb.* **1.** toward the rear; behind:
Looking backward down the trail, I could see everyone
following me. **2.** moving with the back going first; in
reverse: *to count backward from fifty to zero.*
adjective. toward the back: *He climbed aboard without*
a backward glance. This word is also spelled **backwards.**

back·woods [back-*wudz*] *noun.* **1.** an area that is mostly
trees and other wild plant growth where not many people
live: *He lives in the backwoods and his nearest neighbor is*
fifteen miles away. **2.** somewhere thought of as not highly
developed; uncivilized: *Out here in the backwoods there*
are no shopping centers.

back·yard [back-*yard*] *noun,*
plural **backyards.** an area behind a
building that is often fenced off. This
word is also spelled **back yard.**

ba·con [bake-un] *noun.* meat from
the back or sides of a hog, often
salted or smoked; commonly
eaten as a breakfast food.

Spherical

Rod-shaped

With tails

bac·te·ri·a ◄
[bak-*teer*-ee-uh]
plural noun,
singular **bacterium.**
Biology. a group of
microscopic single-
celled living organisms.
Each of the cells is called a
bacterium. Some bacteria
are harmful to humans, as by
causing disease. Other bacteria
are useful, as by helping in
digesting food in the body or
making certain food products.
—bacterial, *adjective.*

Spiral

When seen under the
microscope, different
bacteria *have a variety*
of shapes.

bad [bad] *adjective,* **worse, worst.** not good; of low quality;
poor: *Two right out of ten is a bad score on a test; It was*
a bad meal and I only ate two bites.
✚ **Bad** is used in many other ways to show that something
is wrong, evil, not wanted, not as it should be, and so on:
Killing people is bad; Eating too much is bad for your
health; I felt bad after telling a lie.
• **not bad/not half bad/not so bad.** all right; acceptable,
okay: *My mom's cooking is not bad.*

badge [baj] *noun, plural* **badges.** a small piece of material
or metal worn on clothes to show membership of a group,
achievement, or authority. Police officers wear a badge on
their uniform.

badg·er ▼ [baj-ur] *noun, plural* **badgers.** a small, bearlike
mammal with short, strong legs and claws.
verb, **badgered, badgering.**
to annoy with demands
or questions:
The little boy
badgered his
father for
more candy.

The Eurasian
badger *lives in*
Europe, Asia,
and Japan.

a b c d e f g h i j k l m n o p q r s t u v w x y z

BAGPIPES

Dating back to ancient times, the bagpipe became popular in the British Isles and other parts of Europe around the twelfth century. There are many different kinds of bagpipe, from the well-known Scottish Highland bagpipe, which is now played worldwide, to various folk instruments played across Europe and the Middle East.

A Scottish highland band of bagpipes and drummers

A French bagpipe, called a cabrette

bad·ly [bad-lee] *adverb.* **1.** carried out poorly: *The job was badly done.* **2.** very much: *I'm so dirty I badly need a bath.*

Bad is an adjective and **badly** is an adverb, so *badly* is the word that usually goes with a verb. "We played *badly* and lost the game" is more correct than "We played *bad*…" However, there is an exception to this for the word *feel.* This word is not really an action verb, but one that tells what something is like. So if you were sick or if you were sorry about something, the correct thing to say would be "I feel *bad*," not "I feel *badly*."

bad·min·ton ▼ [bad-min-tun] *noun.* a game for two or four people, who use rackets to hit a small feathered ball, called a shuttlecock, over a net.

baf·fle [baf-ul] *verb,* **baffled, baffling.** to make hard to understand; puzzle or confuse: *Chinese is baffling to an English speaker.*

Badminton *rackets are very light, and shuttlecocks are cone-shaped.*

One of the first places where people played the game of **badminton** was at a grand home in England owned by the Duke of Beaufort. The Duke's estate was known as *Badminton,* and the game took on this name.

bag [bag] *noun, plural* **bags. 1.** a disposable container made of cheap material such as paper or plastic. **2.** a handbag or purse made of cloth or leather for everyday use such as shopping or carrying money. **3.** a large bag made of strong material used for traveling; a suitcase.

ba·gel [bay-gul] *noun, plural* **bagels.** a small, doughnut-shaped roll made of soft dough with a hard crust.

bag·gage [bag-ij] *noun.* any or all of the bags, containers, and suitcases used for carrying items when traveling.

bag·gy [bag-ee] *adjective,* **baggier, baggiest.** loosely fitting; roomy: *Baggy clothes hide a slim figure.*

bag·pipe ▲ [bag-pipe] *noun, plural* **bagpipes.** a musical wind instrument often played in Scotland and Ireland, made from pipes and a leather pouch. It makes a continuous droning sound when played. —**bagpiper,** *noun.*

bail¹ [bale] *noun, plural* **bails.** *Law.* money paid by someone charged with a crime to allow them to stay out of jail until trial, and also to act as a guarantee that they will appear in court and not run away. If the person fails to come to court, they lose the bail money.
verb. **bail out. 1.** to release someone from custody. **2.** to provide help, usually financial assistance: *I bailed Joe out of trouble when he lost his wallet.*
🔊 A different word with the same sound is **bale.**

bail² [bale] *verb,* **bailed, bailing.** to remove water from a boat with a scoop to prevent it from sinking.
• **bail out.** to leave a dangerous or difficult situation: *The pilot bailed out of the aircraft before it crashed.*
🔊 A different word with the same sound is **bale.**

bai·liff [bay-lif] *noun, plural* **bailiffs.** *Law.* **1.** a minor official who serves as a security guard or messenger in some courts. **2.** in Great Britain, an officer who serves and processes legal orders, collects payments, makes arrests, and has the power to confiscate goods.

bait [bate] *noun, plural* **baits. 1.** food put on a hook or in a trap to catch fish or animals. **2.** anything that can be used to attract or persuade: *Using the promise of a holiday as bait, my parents got me to work hard for my exams.*
verb, **baited, baiting. 1.** to put bait on: *We baited the mousetrap with cheese.* **2.** to tease or annoy: *The bully tried to bait the other boy into fighting with him.*

bake [bake] *verb,* **baked, baking. 1.** to cook in an oven. **2.** to harden by heat: *Clay pots are made by baking them in a type of oven called a kiln.* A **baker** is a person who cooks bread in an oven. A **bakery** is a shop that makes and sells bread and cakes.

baking powder a powder used in making cakes or bread to help the dough or batter to rise.

baking soda a powder used to help dough to rise and to help to settle an upset stomach. Another term for this is SODIUM BICARBONATE.

bal·ance [bal-ens] *noun, plural,* **balances. 1.** the condition that exists when two parts or ends of an object are weighted evenly: *Sit on the other end of the seesaw so we can keep it in balance.* **2.** a scale that measures weight with two dishes hanging from a post. The object to be weighed goes in one dish, and an equivalent weight in the other dish balances the scale to show the weight. **3.** the remainder: *The bank teller gave me the balance of my account.* **4.** a feeling of being steady or secure: *The bad news knocked her off balance.*
verb, **balanced, balancing. 1.** to keep in a steady, even position: *The model balanced a book on her head.* **2.** to make equal in number, amount, or force: *I balance my life between work and play.*

balanced diet ▶ *Health.* a diet with food that includes all the important nutrients and vitamins for good health, with not too much or too little of any one food.

bal·co·ny ▼ [bal-kuh-nee] *noun, plural* **balconies.**
1. a projecting platform from the upper window or outside door of a building, with a railing around it.
2. a small floor jutting out over a room in some public buildings, such as movie theaters.

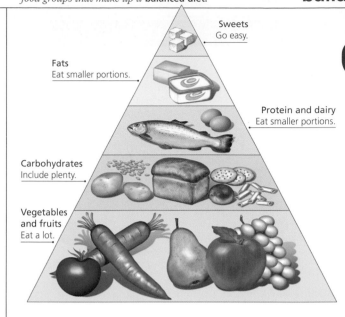

*This healthful-eating pyramid shows the food groups that make up a **balanced diet.***

Sweets
Go easy.

Fats
Eat smaller portions.

Protein and dairy
Eat smaller portions.

Carbohydrates
Include plenty.

Vegetables and fruits
Eat a lot.

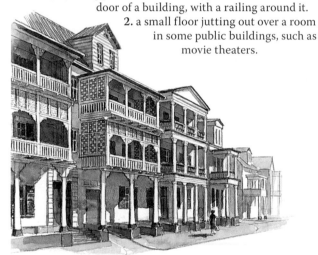

*Dutch colonial buildings in Paramaribo, Suriname, have interesting **balconies.***

ball¹ [bawl] *noun, plural* **balls. 1.** a round object: *a ball of string.* **2.** a round or oval object used in sports: *a tennis ball.* **3.** a game played with a ball: *The girls played ball after school.* **4.** in baseball, a pitch the batter does not swing at and that fails to pass through the strike zone.
🔊 A different word with the same sound is **bawl.**

ball² [bawl] *noun, plural* **balls.** a large, formal, social gathering at which there is dancing.
🔊 A different word with the same sound is **bawl.**

bal·lad [bal-id] *noun, plural* **ballads.** *Music.* a long poem or song, often telling a romantic or historical story, with a strong rhythm.

bald [bald] *adjective* **balder, baldest. 1.** having no hair on the head. **2.** without a natural covering: *a bald mountain with no trees at the top.* **—baldness,** *noun.*

bald eagle ▶ a large brown eagle that lives in North America and is the national symbol of the United States. The white feathers on its head make it look as if it is bald.

bale [bale] *noun, plural* **bales.** a large bundle of materials tied together for convenient storage or removal: *a bale of straw.*
🔊 A different word with the same sound is **bail.**

balk [balk] *verb,* **balked, balking. 1.** to refuse to go on: *The horse balked at the highest fence.* **2.** in baseball, to start to pitch the ball to the batter, then stop or hesitate. This is a play that is against the rules.
noun, plural **balks.** in baseball, the act of breaking the rules in this way.

*The **bald eagle** hunts mainly fish.*

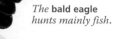

A
B
C
D
E
F
G
H
I
J
K
L
M
N
O
P
Q
R
S
T
U
V
W
X
Y
Z

BALLET

Classical ballet began in seventeenth-century France. By the nineteenth century it had developed into a major art form in which dancers enacted stories set to specially composed music. Tchaikovsky's *Swan Lake* and *The Nutcracker* are two famous classical ballets. To be able to perform the special ballet steps correctly, ballet dancers must train hard and keep fit.

The lead dancers in *Swan Lake*

Ballet shoes

bal·le·ri·na [*bal*-uh-<u>ree</u>-nuh] *noun, plural* **ballerinas.** a female dancer who performs ballet.

bal·let ▲ [ba-<u>lay</u> *or* <u>ba</u>-lay] *noun, plural* **ballets. 1.** a classical form of dance using set formal movements, often telling a story. **2.** a performance by dancers using ballet steps.

bal·lot [<u>bal</u>-it] *noun, plural* **ballots. 1.** a piece of printed paper used in elections with spaces for voters to mark their choices. The ballots are put into a secure **ballot box**, which is later opened to count the votes. **2.** the right to vote: *The United States granted women the ballot in 1920.* *verb,* **balloted, balloting.** to use a ballot for voting.

ball·point pen [<u>bawl</u>-point] a pen that gives smooth delivery of ink through a ball connected to the ink cartridge.

ball·room [<u>bawl</u>-room] *noun, plural* **ballrooms.** a room large enough to hold many people for formal dances and parties.

balm·y [<u>balm</u>-ee] *adjective,* **balmier, balmiest. 1.** not too cold and not really hot; mild and pleasant: *The weather is balmy in Hawaii.* **2.** slightly crazy; eccentric; foolish: *Only a balmy person would wear a swimsuit in winter.*

bal·sa [<u>bawl</u>-suh] *noun.* a light, strong wood from tropical America often used in making model airplanes and boats.

bal·sam [<u>bawl</u>-sum] *noun.* a fragrant aromatic oil used in medicines, perfumes, and ointments that comes from the resin of certain plants. The American **balsam fir** is one of these plants, and is also used as a Christmas tree.

bam·boo ▶ [bam-<u>boo</u>] *noun, plural* **bamboos.** a tall, fast-growing plant with hollow, vertical stems. It is light, strong, and cheap and is used to make furniture, fishing poles, garden canes, and even building scaffolds.

ban [ban] *noun, plural* **bans.** an official order that bars or forbids something: *There is a ban on large trucks on this road.* *verb,* **banned, banning.** to forbid or bar; not allow: *At school, smoking and drinking are banned.*

ba·na·na [buh-<u>nan</u>-uh] *noun, plural* **bananas.** a soft, yellow tropical fruit, about six inches long and curved, that grows in bunches on a tree.

band[1] [band] *noun, plural* **bands. 1.** a number of people or animals gathered together for social or political reasons. Soldiers who fight together have been called "a band of brothers." **2.** a group of musicians. *verb,* **banded, banding.** to form a group: *The townspeople banded together to oppose the new highway.*

band[2] [band] *noun, plural* **bands. 1.** a thin strip of material: *a band of gold* . **2.** a stripe of color: *A bumblebee has yellow and black bands.* **3.** a range of radio frequencies, such as FM, in broadcasting. *verb,* **banded, banding.** to put a band on an animal or bird for identification purposes: *The birds' legs were banded to find out which birds survived long flights.*

ban·dage [<u>ban</u>-dij] *noun, plural* **bandages.** a cloth band used as a dressing over wounds or to support broken or injured limbs. *verb,* **bandaged, bandaging.** to cover or bind up with a bandage: *Mom bandaged my sprained wrist.*

ban·da·na [ban-<u>dan</u>-uh] *noun, plural* **bandanas.** a square of brightly colored or patterned cloth worn around the neck, across the face, or around the head. This word is also spelled **bandanna.**

ban·dit [<u>ban</u>-dit] *noun, plural* **bandits.** a robber who may be violent; often a member of a gang. **Banditry** is the state of being in such a gang; or the crimes committed by such people.

bang [bang] *noun, plural* **bangs.** a short, sudden, loud noise or explosion: *the bang of a firecracker.* *verb,* **banged, banging. 1.** to make a sudden, loud sound. **2.** to hit something loudly or very hard: *He banged on the door until someone opened it.*

ban·gle [<u>bang</u>-gul] *noun, plural* **bangles.** a band worn as a decoration around the wrist or ankle.

bangs [bangz] *plural noun.* a short fringe of hair over the forehead.

ba·nish [<u>ban</u>-ish] *verb,* **banished, banishing. 1.** to send someone far away from their home, often to an isolated place, as a punishment: *The government banished the rebels to a desert island.* **2.** to drive away: *to banish all worries.* —**banishment,** *noun.*

Different kinds of **bamboo** *grow in many parts of the world.*

ban·is·ter [ban-i-stur] *noun, plural* **banisters.**
1. the handrail along a staircase. 2. the posts on the side of the stairs that prevent people from falling.

ban·jo ▶ [ban-*joh*] *noun, plural* **banjos** or **banjoes.** *Music.* a stringed musical instrument with a long neck like a guitar, and a round body.

bank¹ ▼ [bank] *noun, plural* **banks.** the sloping ground beside a lake, stream, or river: *Water rats live in holes along river banks.*
verb, **banked, banking.** to make into a heap: *Dad banked the leaves up by the side of the road.*

bank² [bank] *noun, plural* **banks.**
1. a financial company with local offices where people can keep money safely, or borrow it.
2. a place for keeping reserve supplies: *That writer keeps a notebook with a bank of new ideas for books.*
verb, **banked, banking.** to carry out business at a bank: *I banked my first paycheck today.*
—banker, *noun.*

*Deciduous trees, lush grass, flowers, and reeds line river **banks** in temperate climates in summer.*

bank·rupt [bank-*rupt*] *adjective.* *Business.* having no money left to pay what you owe: *She couldn't pay her bills because she was bankrupt.*
—bankrupted, bankrupting, *verb;*
—bankruptcy, *noun.*

Bankrupt is taken from an Italian phrase meaning "a broken bench." It comes from a time when people who dealt in money would use a bench to do business. If someone was bankrupt (lost all his money), his bench would be broken, to show that he could not do business any more.

ban·ner [ban-ur] *noun, plural* **banners.** a long ribbon of cloth or paper used as a decoration or to show a message; a flag: *the Star-Spangled Banner.*
adjective. special; important: *The swim team made banner headlines when they won the state competition.*

ban·quet ▶ [bank-*wit*] *noun, plural* **banquets.** a large formal dinner, usually with many courses of food, to celebrate a special occasion.

ban·ter [bant-ur] *noun.* lighthearted teasing between friends or by people who feel relaxed with each other: *There was a lot of banter between the boys and the girls at the school dance.*
verb, **bantered, bantering.** to tease or make fun of someone: *My sister is always bantering about how late I get up.*

Bap·tist [bap-tist] *noun, plural* **Baptists.** *Religion.* a person who belongs to the Baptist faith, a Christian religion that believes in the ceremony of baptism. In the Bible, **John the Baptist** baptized Jesus.

bap·tize [bap-tize] *verb,* **baptized, baptizing.** *Religion.* to use water as part of the ceremony of joining a Christian church, as a symbolic way of washing away sins. Traditionally, babies and children are given their names during the ceremony of **baptism.**

bar [bar] *noun, plural,* **bars. 1.** a place where food or drinks are served: *He bought a hot dog at the snack bar.* **2.** the counter over which the food or drinks are served. **3.** a narrow block of something: *a bar of soap; a metal bar.* **4.** something that stops the way: *Being underage is a bar to driving.* **5.** a band of color: *The flag had bars of red and blue.* **6.** *Law.* the profession of attorneys as a group. **7.** *Music.* a short vertical line written across a staff to divide two equal measures of time.
verb, **barred, barring. 1.** to prevent entry: *The road was barred to automobiles.* **2.** to fasten or secure something: *Barring the door will make the house safe.*

*At ancient Chinese **banquets,** guests enjoyed special food and entertainment.*

a b c d e f g h i j k l m n o p q r s t u v w x y z

barb [barb] *noun, plural,* **barbs.** a sharp point facing backward from the main point, as in the hook on a fishing line. A **barbed** remark is sharp or sarcastic.

bar·bar·i·an [bar-<u>bare</u>-ee-un] *noun, plural* **barbarians.** a person who is considered to be cruel, uncivilized, or lacking in culture or education. It is **barbaric** to torture people. Forcing someone into slavery is **barbarous**.

bar·be·cue [bar-bi-kyoo] *noun, plural,* **barbecues. 1.** a meal cooked out of doors over an open fire. **2.** a grill used outside to cook food.
verb, **barbecued, barbecuing.** to cook food outside using a grill or a fire.

barbed wire wire used for fences. It is twisted, with sharp points sticking out that act as a barrier.

bar·ber [<u>bar</u>-bur] *noun, plural* **barbers.** a hairdresser who cuts the hair of boys and men.

bar·code [<u>bar</u>-kode] *noun, plural* **barcodes.** *Computers.* a white label with vertical black lines of different widths that contains a code with information about items for sale. The label, when scanned by a computer in a store, tells the cashier how much the customer should pay.

bare [bare] *adjective.* **1.** having no clothes or covering; naked. **2.** having nothing in it; empty: *The cupboard was bare of food.*
verb, **bared, baring.** to make bare; uncover or show: *My friend bared her feelings to me.*
🔊 A different word with the same sound is **bear.**

bare·back [<u>bare</u>-bak] *adjective; adverb.* riding on a horse without using a saddle.

bare·ly [<u>bare</u>-lee] *adverb.* only just: *He was barely able to speak after the race, he was so out of breath.*

bar·gain [<u>bar</u>-gun] *noun, plural* **bargains. 1.** something of value that is bought or sold more cheaply than usual: *At half price, this coat was a bargain.* **2.** an agreement: *Paul made a bargain to clean the car in return for extra pocket money.*
verb, **bargained, bargaining.** to make a bargain; negotiate: *I bargained hard over how late I could stay up.*

barge ▼ [barj] *noun, plural* **barges.** a type of boat used for carrying cargo such as coal or lumber on inland waterways.
verb, **barged, barging.** to move or go in rudely, as if moving in a barge: *to barge into a room without knocking.*

bar graph *Mathematics.* a graph with vertical or horizontal bars that show information in different amounts so that they can be compared.

Barges are flat-bottomed boats that transport heavy goods along canals and rivers.

bar·i·tone [<u>bare</u>-i-*tone*] *noun, plural* **baritones.** *Music.* **1.** in opera or a choir, an adult male singing voice that is lower than a tenor but not as low as a bass. **2.** someone who sings in this way.

Baritone is one of many words having to do with music that come from Italian, because Italy has always been a leader in music. It goes back to a word meaning "deep," with the idea that a baritone voice has a deep sound.

bark¹ [bark] *noun, plural* **barks. 1.** the noise made by a dog. **2.** a similar noise made by a person who is excited, upset, or being aggressive.
verb, **barked, barking.** to make such a noise: *The general barked orders at his soldiers.*

bark² [bark] *noun, plural* **barks.** the woody covering of tree trunks and branches.
verb, **barked, barking.** to have skin scraped off by accident: *Tom fell over and barked his knees on the rocks.*

bar·ley [<u>bar</u>-lee] *noun.* a type of cereal crop whose grains are used in food and to make beer.

bar mitz·vah [bar <u>mits</u>-vuh] *Religion.* in the Jewish faith, a coming-of-age ceremony for boys when they reach thirteen years and one day old.

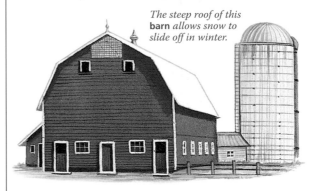

*The steep roof of this **barn** allows snow to slide off in winter.*

barn ▲ [barn] *noun, plural* **barns.** a large building to keep animals or store crops or equipment on a farm. A **barnyard** is the area outside the barn, and is often the place where chickens are kept.

bar·na·cle [<u>barn</u>-i-kul] *noun, plural* **barnacles.** a type of small sea mollusk that attaches itself very firmly to rocks, piers, and the bottoms of ships.

bar·om·e·ter [buh-<u>rom</u>-i-tur] *noun, plural* **barometers.** *Science.* an instrument that measures air pressure, in order to predict the weather.

bar·on [<u>bare</u>-un] *noun, plural* **barons.** in Europe, a man from a noble family. It is the lowest rank in the aristocracy. A woman of this rank is called a **baroness.**
🔊 A different word with the same sound is **barren.**

bar·racks [<u>bare</u>-iks] *plural noun.* a building in which soldiers live when they are serving in the army.

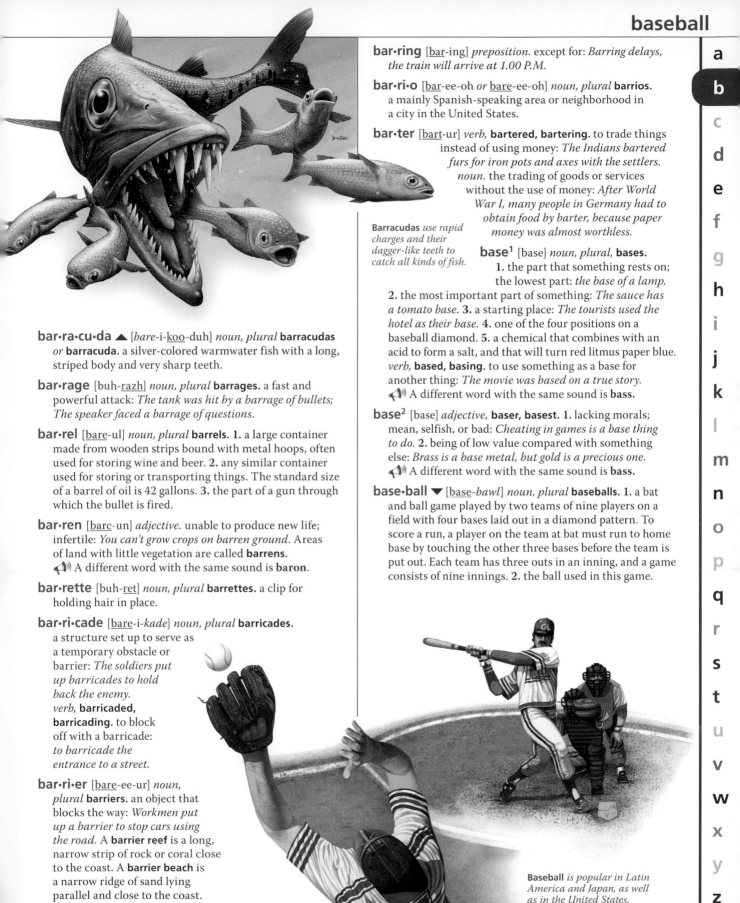

bar·ra·cu·da ▲ [bare-i-<u>koo</u>-duh] *noun, plural* **barracudas** *or* **barracuda.** a silver-colored warmwater fish with a long, striped body and very sharp teeth.

bar·rage [buh-<u>razh</u>] *noun, plural* **barrages.** a fast and powerful attack: *The tank was hit by a barrage of bullets; The speaker faced a barrage of questions.*

bar·rel [<u>bare</u>-ul] *noun, plural* **barrels. 1.** a large container made from wooden strips bound with metal hoops, often used for storing wine and beer. **2.** any similar container used for storing or transporting things. The standard size of a barrel of oil is 42 gallons. **3.** the part of a gun through which the bullet is fired.

bar·ren [<u>barc</u>-un] *adjective.* unable to produce new life; infertile: *You can't grow crops on barren ground.* Areas of land with little vegetation are called **barrens.**
🔊 A different word with the same sound is **baron.**

bar·rette [buh-<u>ret</u>] *noun, plural* **barrettes.** a clip for holding hair in place.

bar·ri·cade [<u>bare</u>-i-*kade*] *noun, plural* **barricades.** a structure set up to serve as a temporary obstacle or barrier: *The soldiers put up barricades to hold back the enemy.* *verb,* **barricaded, barricading.** to block off with a barricade: *to barricade the entrance to a street.*

bar·ri·er [<u>bare</u>-ee-ur] *noun, plural* **barriers.** an object that blocks the way: *Workmen put up a barrier to stop cars using the road.* A **barrier reef** is a long, narrow strip of rock or coral close to the coast. A **barrier beach** is a narrow ridge of sand lying parallel and close to the coast.

bar·ring [<u>bar</u>-ing] *preposition.* except for: *Barring delays, the train will arrive at 1.00 P.M.*

bar·ri·o [<u>bar</u>-ee-oh *or* <u>bare</u>-ee-oh] *noun, plural* **barrios.** a mainly Spanish-speaking area or neighborhood in a city in the United States.

bar·ter [<u>bart</u>-ur] *verb,* **bartered, bartering.** to trade things instead of using money: *The Indians bartered furs for iron pots and axes with the settlers. noun.* the trading of goods or services without the use of money: *After World War I, many people in Germany had to obtain food by barter, because paper money was almost worthless.*

Barracudas use rapid charges and their dagger-like teeth to catch all kinds of fish.

base¹ [base] *noun, plural,* **bases. 1.** the part that something rests on; the lowest part: *the base of a lamp.* **2.** the most important part of something: *The sauce has a tomato base.* **3.** a starting place: *The tourists used the hotel as their base.* **4.** one of the four positions on a baseball diamond. **5.** a chemical that combines with an acid to form a salt, and that will turn red litmus paper blue. *verb,* **based, basing.** to use something as a base for another thing: *The movie was based on a true story.*
🔊 A different word with the same sound is **bass.**

base² [base] *adjective,* **baser, basest. 1.** lacking morals; mean, selfish, or bad: *Cheating in games is a base thing to do.* **2.** being of low value compared with something else: *Brass is a base metal, but gold is a precious one.*
🔊 A different word with the same sound is **bass.**

base·ball ▼ [<u>base</u>-*bawl*] *noun, plural* **baseballs. 1.** a bat and ball game played by two teams of nine players on a field with four bases laid out in a diamond pattern. To score a run, a player on the team at bat must run to home base by touching the other three bases before the team is put out. Each team has three outs in an inning, and a game consists of nine innings. **2.** the ball used in this game.

Baseball is popular in Latin America and Japan, as well as in the United States.

base·ment [base-munt] *noun, plural* **basements.** the floor of a building that is below or partly below the ground.

bash·ful [bash-ful] *adjective.* not liking to meet people; shy: *The boy was too bashful to speak to strangers.* —**bashfully,** *adverb;* —**bashfulness,** *noun.*

ba·sic [bay-sik] *adjective.* being at the base; relating to the main part; fundamental: *The idea that if you drop something it falls to the ground is a basic law of science; Every soldier has basic training when first joining the army. noun.* **basics.** the most important parts: *Running and kicking are the basics of soccer.* —**basically,** *adverb.*

BA·SIC [bay-sik] *noun. Computers.* a simple computer programming language for beginners.

ba·si·cal·ly [bay-sik-lee] *adverb.* **1.** in the most fundamental way; at a basic level: *The car is old, but basically sound.* **2.** in reality; in fact: *She is basically in charge of the entire school.*

bas·il [bay-sil *or* baz-ul] *noun.* a herb with leaves that are used to add flavor in cooking.

ba·sin [bay-sun] *noun, plural* **basins.** **1.** a bowl that holds liquids: *a basin of water.* **2.** a sheltered or partially enclosed area of water: *The yacht sheltered in the basin during the storm.* **3.** the land drained by a river and the streams flowing into it: *The basin of the Nile River is the most fertile part of Egypt.*

ba·sis [bay-sis] *noun, plural* **bases.** the part on which a thing stands or depends; foundation: *The life of Abraham Lincoln has been the basis for many books and movies.*

bask [bask] *verb,* **basked, basking.** to lie in pleasant sunlight or warmth: *They basked in the sun during their vacation at the beach.*

bas·ket [bas-kit] *noun, plural* **baskets. 1.** a container made of grasses, twigs, straw, or other material. **2.** in basketball, a metal ring with a net hanging from it, used as the goal.

bas·ket·ball ▼ [bas-kit-*bawl*] *noun, plural* **basketballs. 1.** a ball game played on a court by two teams of five players each. Players score points by throwing the ball through a basket at the top of a goal post at the opponents' end of the court. **2.** the ball used in this game.

The game of **basketball** was invented and named in 1891 by Dr. James Naismith in Springfield, Massachusetts. At first, the game did not have a metal ring as a goal as it does today. The goal actually was a basket, an empty wooden basket that had been used to hold peaches.

bass¹ [base] *noun plural,* **basses.** *Music.* **1.** the lowest male singing voice. **2.** a singer with such a voice. **3.** a musical instrument with this range.
🔊 A different word with the same sound is **base.**

bass² [bass] *noun, plural* **bass** *or* **basses.** any of several food fish found in North American streams and lakes, and in the sea.

Bass is an example of what is called a *homograph*: a word that has the same spelling as another word, but is not the same because it came into English in a different way. In this dictionary such words are listed separately and identified by a small number after the word. In this case, *bass¹* is the word used in music and is spoken to sound like "face." *Bass²* is the name of the fish and sounds like "mass."

Basset hounds *have an excellent sense of smell and are good trackers.*

bass drum [base] *Music.* a large drum that makes a deep, low sound when it is struck.

bass fiddle another term for BASS VIOL.

basset hound ◀ [bass-it] a short-legged dog with long, drooping ears and a long body.

bas·soon [buh-soon] *noun, plural* **bassoons.** *Music.* a musical instrument that produces low notes when it is played, having a long, straight, wooden body and a smaller, curved, metal tube. It is played by blowing into the metal tube and pressing keys and holes on the body.

bass vi·ol [base] *noun. Music.* the largest musical instrument of the violin family. When played, it makes a rich, low sound. A musician holds the bass viol upright and plays it with a bow or by plucking with the fingers.

baste¹ [bayst] *verb,* **basted, basting.** to moisten meat during cooking with melted butter or another liquid: *Open the oven to baste the turkey.*

baste² [bayst] *verb,* **basted, basting.** to sew with long, loose stitches: *To check the fit of the dress, she first had to baste the seams.*

bat¹ [bat] *noun, plural* **bats.** a strong stick or club, used to hit the ball in baseball, softball, and similar games. *verb,* **batted, batting.** to use a bat.

Spectacular plays like the dunk, where the ball is pushed through the hoop from above, make **basketball** *exciting to watch.*

BATS

Bats are the only mammals that can fly like birds. Their wings are made of two thin layers of skin stretched over arms and long fingers. While many bats eat fruits, some eat insects, fish, frogs, and small animals. Hunting mainly at night, bats find their food by making high-pitched sounds that bounce back off the objects around them.

Long finger on forelimb

Wings formed by two layers of skin and blood vessels

Clawed thumb

Elbow

Large ear

No eyesocket

Hind foot

Tail

Backward-facing knee

A bat's high-pitched sounds bounce off the moth back to the bat.

bat² ▲ [bat] *noun, plural* **bats.** a small flying animal. It has a furry body like a mouse and wings of thin skin.

batch [bach] *noun, plural* **batches.** a set of things made or brought together: *Mom made a batch of cookies for our party.*

bath [bath] *noun, plural* **baths.** 1. the act of washing something in water: *He likes to have a very hot bath.* 2. the water used for bathing: *The bath is too cold.* 3. a room in a house for bathing; bathroom: *The house has only one bath.*

bathe [bayTH] *verb,* **bathed, bathing.** 1. to wash clean: *The doctor had to bathe the girl's sore eye.* 2. to swim: *to bathe in the sea.* 3. to cover or surround as if with water: *The setting sun bathed the field in shades of red and gold.*

bathing suit an article of clothing worn for swimming.

bath·robe [bath-robe] *noun, plural* **bathrobes.** a long, loose article of clothing, worn to and from a bath, or when relaxing.

bath·room [bath-*room*] *noun, plural* **bathrooms.** a room containing a toilet and a sink, and often a shower or bathtub.

bat mitz·vah [baht <u>mits</u>-vuh] *noun, plural* **bat mitzvahs.** *Religion.* a religious ceremony and celebration that takes place for a Jewish girl around the age of thirteen, recognizing her as an adult Jew.

ba·ton [buh-<u>tahn</u>] *noun, plural* **batons.** a rod or stick: *The conductor of the orchestra uses a black baton.*

bat·tal·ion [buh-<u>tal</u>-yun] *noun, plural* **battalions.** a large military unit, made up of several companies of soldiers.

bat·ter¹ [<u>bat</u>-ur] *verb,* **battered, battering.** to strike again and again with hard blows: *The firefighter used an axe to batter down the door.*

bat·ter² [<u>bat</u>-ur] *noun, plural* **batters.** a mixture of flour, milk or water, and other things beaten together and fried or baked to make cakes, muffins, or pancakes.

bat·ter³ [<u>bat</u>-ur] *noun, plural* **batters.** the player who is batting in a game of baseball or softball.

battering ram ▼ *History.* a large beam used in war to break down the walls or gates of a fort or city.

bat·tery [<u>bat</u>-uh-ree] *noun, plural* **batteries.** 1. a device containing materials that produce electricity by chemical changes: *My watch needs a new battery.* 2. a set of things that are similar or that work together: *The President faced a battery of television cameras.*

bat·tle [<u>bat</u>-ul] *noun, plural* **battles.** 1. a violent fight or conflict between two groups of armed persons or forces. Wars are made up of a series of battles. 2. a long, hard struggle; contest: *It was a battle to bring the ship to port in the storm.*
verb, **battled, battling.** to fight or struggle: *The two boxers battled to win the match.*

bat·tle·field [<u>bat</u>-ul-feeld] *noun, plural* **battlefields.** a place where a battle is fought or has been fought. A different word with the same meaning is **battleground.**

bat·tle·ment ▼ [<u>bat</u>-ul-munt] *noun, plural* **battlements.** *History.* a low wall at the top of a tower or fort. A battlement has openings for soldiers to fire weapons through.

At Masada in AD *73, Jewish defenders on the* **battlements** *could not stop the Romans from breaking through the walls with a* **battering ram.**

a
b
c
d
e
f
g
h
i
j
k
l
m
n
o
p
q
r
s
t

A B C D E F G H I J K L M N O

bat·tle·ship [bat-ul-ship] *noun, plural* **battleships.** a large warship having heavy armor and big guns.

bawl [bawl] *verb,* **bawled, bawling.** to shout or cry loudly. *noun.* a loud shout or cry.
🔊 A different word with the same sound is **ball.**

bay¹ [bay] *noun, plural* **bays.** an area of a sea or lake partly enclosed by land.

bay² [bay] *noun, plural* **bays.** the long, deep barking of a dog.
verb, **bayed, baying.** to bark in long, deep tones.
• **at bay.** forced to turn and face pursuers or difficulties; cornered: *Police held the angry protesters at bay.*

bay³ [bay] *noun, plural* **bays.** a small tree whose leaves are used to add flavor in cooking.

bay·ou [bye-ooh] *noun, plural* **bayous.** a slow-moving stream in a marsh or swamp in the southern United States.

ba·zaar ▼ [buh-zahr] *noun, plural* **bazaars.**
1. a market made up of stalls or small shops.
2. a sale of different goods for charity or some other purpose: *They donated some indoor plants for the church bazaar.*

BC an abbreviation for *before Christ.* It is used in giving dates before the birth of Jesus. This abbreviation is also spelled **B.C.**

be [bee] *verb,* **was** or **were, been, being.** a special verb used more often than any other verb in English. Rather than showing action, it tells the condition or state of something: *Be nice and help me finish this; I'll be happy if we win the game. Be* joins with other verbs to form verb phrases: *I have been studying hard for my test.* Forms of *be* are used to join the subject of a sentence to a word or words that tell about it: *The soup is hot; My middle name is David.*

> The verb **be** has a number of different forms that are used according to the subject of the sentence (the subject is the person or thing that is doing or feeling something). For the present tense (something that is going on or that exists now), the correct use is: I *am*, you *are*, he/she/it *is*; we/you/they *are*. For the past tense (something that happened before), the correct use is: I *was*, you *were*, he/she/it *was*; we/you/they *were*.

beach [beech] *noun, plural* **beaches.** an area of sand or pebbles along the edge of a sea or lake.
verb, **beached, beaching.** to run or haul a boat ashore: *He beached the rowboat on the edge of the lake.*
🔊 A different word with the same sound is **beech.**

bea·con [bee-kun] *noun, plural* **beacons.** a signal, such as a light or fire, that warns or guides aircraft or ships.

bead [beed] *noun, plural* **beads. 1.** a small ball of glass, plastic, or wood with a hole through the middle. A number of beads may be strung together on string or wire. **2.** any small, round object; droplet: *beads of sweat.*
verb, **beaded, beading.** to decorate with beads.

bea·gle ◀ [bee-gul] *noun, plural* **beagles.** a small, short-legged dog with drooping ears and a short coat. Beagles were bred as hunting dogs, but are now mainly kept as pets.

beak [beek] *noun, plural* **beaks.** the hard, pointed part of the mouth of a bird or a turtle: *Hummingbirds have very long, thin beaks.*

beak·er [bee-kur] *noun, plural* **beakers.** a flat-bottomed glass container with a pouring lip, used in laboratories to hold liquids or chemicals.

The beagle is a good-tempered dog that likes being with people.

beam [beem] *noun, plural* **beams. 1.** a long, strong piece of wood, concrete, or metal, used as a support in buildings. **2.** a ray of light: *The beam from the flashlight shone in the dark.*
verb, **beamed, beaming. 1.** to shine brightly. **2.** to smile broadly: *He beamed when he saw his birthday present.*

bean [been] *noun, plural* **beans. 1.** an edible seed or pod. Kinds of beans include the kidney bean, navy bean, and broad bean. **2.** any seed shaped like a bean: *coffee beans.*
verb, **beaned, beaning.** to hit on the head with a thrown object, such as a ball: *The pitcher has beaned two batters.*

bear¹ ▶ [bare] *noun, plural* **bears.** a large, strong animal with a thick, furry coat, a very short tail, and sharp claws. The grizzly bear, the polar bear, the black bear, and the brown bear are four kinds of bear.
🔊 A different word with the same sound is **bare.**

Many different goods were sold in the **bazaar** *of old Baghdad, including spices and carpets.*

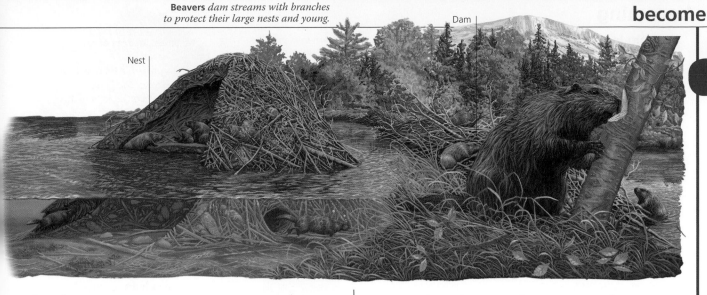

Beavers dam streams with branches to protect their large nests and young.

Nest

Dam

bear² [bare] *verb,* **bore, borne** *or* **born, bearing.**
1. to support or carry something: *The beam will bear the weight of the roof.* 2. to produce offspring: *Trees bear fruits after flowering.* 3. to accept, endure, or tolerate: *I cannot bear this cold weather.* Something that can be accepted or endured is **bearable.** 4. to show physical signs of something: *She bears a strong likeness to her aunt.*
🔊 A different word with the same sound is **bare.**

beard [beeurd] *noun, plural* **beards.**
1. the hair growing on a man's face.
2. a growth of hair that looks like a beard: *The male goat has a beard on its chin.* Something that has a beard or beard-like growth is **bearded.**

bear·ing [bare-ing] *noun, plural* **bearings.** 1. the way that a person walks, sits, stands, or behaves. 2. connection in thought; relevance: *That's an interesting idea, but it has no bearing on the problem at hand.* If someone is working out their position, finding out exactly where they are, they are getting their **bearings.** 3. a part of a machine that contains a moving part and allows it to move easily.

beast [beest] *noun, plural* **beasts.** 1. any four-footed animal: *The lion is the king of the beasts.* 2. a brutal person. —**beastly,** *adjective.*

Brown **bears** *live in northern countries.*

beat [beet] *verb,* **beat, beaten** *or* **beat, beating.** 1. to strike again and again; hit over and over: *It is very cruel to beat a dog.* 2. to defeat or do better than: *We beat their team in the final game.* 3. to flap or move back and forth rapidly: *The butterfly beat its wings; His heart beat fast after the race.* 4. to stir or mix forcefully: *He beat the cream until it was thick.*
noun, plural **beats.** 1. a blow made again and again: *the steady beat of a drum.* 2. a pounding sound, sensation, or rhythm: *The rain beat loudly on the metal roof.*

3. a usual round or route: *The mayor promised to put more police on the beat.* 4. in music, the basic unit of time: *The music was played at two beats to a measure.*
🔊 A different word with the same sound is **beet.**

Beau·fort scale ▼ [boh-furt] *Science.* a scale for measuring wind speeds, ranging from 0 for calm to 12 for a hurricane.

beau·ti·ful [byoo-tuh-ful] *adjective.* pleasing to see, hear, or think about: *That movie star is a beautiful woman; This music is beautiful; He did a beautiful job of cleaning the car.* —**beautifully,** *adverb.*

Force 2

Force 8

Force 12

beau·ti·fy [byoo-tuh-fye] *verb,* **beautified, beautifying.** to make beautiful: *Picking up litter helped to beautify the town.* —**beautification,** *noun.*

The **Beaufort scale** *uses numbers to measure the strength of the wind at sea and the height of the waves.*

beau·ty [byoo-tee] *noun, plural* **beauties.** 1. a quality that makes someone or something pleasing to see, hear, or think about: *The national park is a place of beauty.* 2. someone or something that is beautiful: *Her new car is a beauty.*

bea·ver ▲ [bee-vur] *noun, plural* **beavers.** a furry animal with a broad, flat tail and webbed hind feet for swimming. The beaver is a rodent and lives in or near water.

be·came [bi-kame] *verb.* the past tense of BECOME.

be·cause [bi-kuz] *conjunction.* for the reason that: *I couldn't go to the party because I had a cold.*

beck·on [bek-un] *verb,* **beckoned, beckoning.** to make a signaling gesture by moving the head or hand: *He beckoned to her to come over.*

be·come [bi-kum] *verb,* **became, become, becoming.**
1. to start to be; grow to be: *My uncle has just become a father.* 2. to look good on; suit; flatter: *The color red really becomes you.*

A
B
C
D
E
F
G
H
I
J
K
L
M
N
O
P
Q
R
S
T
U
V
W
X
Y
Z

be·com·ing [bi-<u>kum</u>-ing] *adjective.* looking good on; flattering: *That's a becoming dress.* —**becomingly,** *adverb.*

bed [bed] *noun, plural* **beds. 1.** anything to sleep or rest on. **Bedtime** is the time at which someone usually goes to bed in order to sleep. **2.** a piece of ground to grow plants in: *a bed of roses.* **3.** the bottom of a lake, river, or other body of water: *The bed of the river was very muddy.* **4.** a support or foundation: *The bricks were laid on a bed of concrete.* *verb,* **bedded, bedding.** to provide with a place to sleep. • **bed down.** to lie down, not usually in a bed, in order to sleep: *I'll get my sleeping bag and bed down on the floor.*

bed·ding [<u>bed</u>-ing] *noun.* sheets, blankets, and other coverings for a bed: *They washed the bedding after their guests departed.*

be·drag·gled [bi-<u>drag</u>-uld] *adjective.* wet, limp, and messy: *She changed her bedraggled clothes after coming in out of the rain.*

bed·rid·den [<u>bed</u>-*rid*-un] *adjective.* having to stay in bed, usually because of sickness: *He was bedridden with a bad cold.*

bed·side [<u>bed</u>-*side*] *noun, plural* **bedsides.** the space alongside a bed. The way in which doctors deal with patients is called their **bedside manner.**

bed·spread [<u>bed</u>-*spred*] *noun, plural* **bedspreads.** an outer covering for a bed.

bee ▼ [bee] *noun, plural* **bees. 1.** a common insect with four wings and a stout, hairy body. Some bees produce honey and beeswax. A bee feeds on pollen and nectar. **2.** a gathering of people to have a competition or to work on something as a group: *a sewing bee.*
🔊 A different word with the same sound is **be.**

Beech trees produce triangular nuts and lose their leaves in winter.

beech ▲ [beech] a tree with smooth, gray bark and small, sweet nuts. 🔊 A different word with the same sound is **beach.**

beef [beef] *noun.* meat from a cow, steer, or bull. A **beefsteak** is a slice of beef for frying or broiling.

bee·hive [<u>bee</u>-*hive*] *noun, plural* **beehives. 1.** a nest or house for bees. **2.** a place in which people are very busy: *Her office was a beehive of activity.*

been [bin] *verb.* the past participle of BE.

beep·er [<u>bee</u>-pur] *noun, plural* **beepers.** a small electronic device that makes a sound or vibrates to let the owner know that somebody is trying to make contact.

BEES

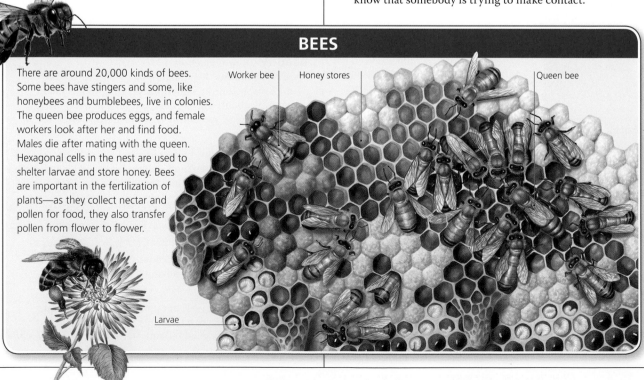

There are around 20,000 kinds of bees. Some bees have stingers and some, like honeybees and bumblebees, live in colonies. The queen bee produces eggs, and female workers look after her and find food. Males die after mating with the queen. Hexagonal cells in the nest are used to shelter larvae and store honey. Bees are important in the fertilization of plants—as they collect nectar and pollen for food, they also transfer pollen from flower to flower.

Worker bee | Honey stores | Queen bee

Larvae

beer [beeur] *noun, plural* **beers.** an alcoholic drink made from water, specially treated grains called malt, and the bud of the hop plant.

beet [beet] *noun, plural* **beets.** a plant with a swollen, fleshy root and leaves that grow on long stalks. The roots and leaves are cooked and eaten as vegetables.
🔊 A different word with the same sound is **beat.**

bee·tle ▶ [bee-tul] *noun, plural* **beetles.** an insect with chewing mouth parts and a pair of hard front wings that fold over and protect a pair of thin hind wings.

be·fall [bee-fawl] *verb,* **befell, befallen, befalling.** to happen, or happen to someone: *We hoped that bad luck would not befall us.*

be·fore [bi-fore] *preposition.* **1.** ahead of; in front of: *Thanksgiving comes before Christmas.* **2.** in the presence of: *The actors performed before an audience.* *adverb.* **1.** at an earlier time; previously: *I'd played on his team once before.* **2.** in advance; in front: *Two of the hikers went on before to put up the tents.* *conjunction.* **1.** in advance of the time when: *We should eat before we leave.* **2.** sooner than; rather than: *I would quit this company before working for him.*

be·fore·hand [bi-fore-hand] *adverb.* in advance: *If we pay beforehand we won't have to bring any money.*

be·friend [bi-frend] *verb,* **befriended, befriending.** to be a friend to: *The new boy at school was befriended by his classmates.*

beg [beg] *verb,* **begged, begging. 1.** to ask humbly: *He begged for forgiveness after smashing the window.* **2.** to ask in an insisting or eager way; plead: *The girl begged to stay up late to see the movie.* **3.** to ask for food or money as charity.

be·gan [bi-gan] *verb.* the past tense of BEGIN.

beg·gar [beg-ur] *noun, plural* **beggars.** a person who lives by asking others for food, money, or clothes.

be·gin [bi-gin] *verb,* **began, begun, beginning. 1.** to take the first step; make a start: *You will begin work on Monday.* **2.** to come into activity or existence: *The new school year begins next week.* A **beginner** is a person who has just started to do or learn something. The point at which something begins is the **beginning.**

be·gon·ia ▶ [bi-goh-nyuh] *noun, plural* **begonias.** a tropical plant with large, fleshy leaves and colorful flowers.

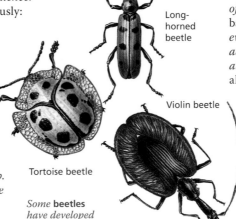

Long-horned beetle

Violin beetle

Tortoise beetle

*Some **beetles** have developed different shapes to suit their way of life.*

*Brightly colored **begonias** are popular garden plants.*

be·half [bi-haf] *noun.* one's interest or benefit.
• **in behalf of.** for the good or benefit of; for: *The telethon raised money in behalf of the flood victims.*
• **on behalf of.** acting for; in the interests of: *The lawyer addressed the court on behalf of his client.*

be·have [bi-hayv] *verb,* **behaved, behaving. 1.** to act in a certain way: *The little boy was tired and upset and he behaved badly.* **2.** to act properly: *Why can't you behave yourself?* —**behavioral,** *adjective.*

be·hav·ior [bi-hayv-yur] *noun.* a way of acting; manner of behaving; conduct: *His behavior in class is terrible.*

be·head [bee-hed] *verb,* **beheaded, beheading.** to cut off a person's head: *The king gave the order to behead the rebels.*

be·hind [bi-hind] *preposition.* **1.** at the back of: *Look behind you!* **2.** not as advanced as; not as high or as far: *She was behind the rest of the class in French.* **3.** supporting or backing someone: *The candidate needs everyone to get behind his plans.* *adverb.* **1.** at the back: *The police officer was attacked from behind.* **2.** in a place or stage already passed: *I left my glasses behind.*

be·hold [bi-hold] *verb,* **beheld, beholding.** to look at; see: *The rocket launch was an incredible sight to behold.*

beige [bayzh] *noun, plural* **beiges.** a pale brown color. *adjective.* having to do with this color.

be·ing [bee-ing] *verb.* the present participle of BE. *noun, plural* **beings. 1.** the fact of having life or being real; existence: *When did that saying come into being?* **2.** a person or animal; creature: *human beings; beings from outer space.*

be·la·ted [bi-lay-tid] *adjective.* coming late; coming after it should: *My aunt called to give the team belated congratulations for their victory in last week's game.* —**belatedly,** *adverb.*

bel·fry [bel-free] *noun, plural* **belfries.** a tower or steeple where a bell or bells hang. Many churches have a belfry.

Bel·gian [bel-jin] *noun.* a person who was born in or lives in Belgium. Belgium is a country in northwestern Europe.

be·lief [bi-leef] *noun, plural* **beliefs.** a feeling that something exists or is true: *The belief in a life after death was an important part of the religion of the ancient Egyptians.*

be·lieve [bi-leev] *verb,* **believed, believing. 1.** to feel sure that something is true or real: *I believe he broke the window, even though I can't prove it.* **2.** to have the opinion that; think: *Pandas live in the wild in China, I believe.* —**believer,** *noun.*

a
b
c
d
e
f
g
h
i
j
k
l
m
n
o
p
q
r
s
t
u
v
w
x
y
z

bell ▲ [bel] *noun, plural* **bells.**
1. a hollow metal object shaped like a cup with a small metal piece hanging inside. It makes a ringing sound when it is hit or shaken. 2. anything that makes a ringing sound like a bell: *a doorbell; a bicycle bell.*

These special monastery **bells** *call Greek orthodox monks to prayer.*

bel·lig·er·ent [buh-lij-uh-runt] *adjective.* 1. angry and wanting to fight: *He pushed the other boy in a belligerent way.* 2. at war; fighting: *The years of war caused great suffering for the people of the belligerent countries.* —**belligerently,** *adverb.*

bel·low [bel-oh] *noun, plural* **bellows.** a loud, deep noise; roar; shout: *A mighty bellow from the injured elephant echoed through the trees.*
verb, **bellowed, bellowing.** to make a sound like this: *to bellow with rage.*

bel·lows [bel-ohz] *plural noun.* a soft leather bag fixed between two wooden boards that press the bag open and shut to push out a current of air: *Some musical instruments, such as the accordion, use a bellows to make sounds.*

bel·ly [bel-ee] *noun, plural* **bellies.** 1. the front part of a person's body between the chest and the legs. 2. the stomach. 3. the lower or under part of the body of an animal. 4. the round or curved under part of something: *the belly of an airplane.*

be·long [bi-long] *verb,* **belonged, belonging.**
1. to have a right or proper place: *Put the history books back on the second shelf where they belong.* 2. to be owned by someone; be the property of: *That pen belongs to me, but you can borrow it for today.* **Belongings** are things that a person owns that are small enough to be carried. 3. to be a member of: *to belong to a club.*

be·lov·ed [bi-luv-id] *adjective.* loved very much: *Megan spent as much time as she could with her beloved pony.*

be·low [bi-loh] *adverb.* in or to a lower place; beneath: *We dropped a stone down the well into the water below.*
preposition. 1. lower than: *We watched as the sun sank below the horizon.* 2. less than: *The temperature is below the freezing point today.*

belt [belt] *noun, plural* **belts.** 1. a strip of leather, cloth, or other material worn around the waist to support clothing or as decoration. 2. a large strip of land with a particular characteristic: *A belt of fir trees sheltered the cabin from the wind.* 3. a loop of strong material used in a machine to drive moving parts or to move objects along: *a conveyor belt.*

bench [bench] *noun, plural* **benches.** 1. a long seat for two or more people: *We sat on a bench beside the river.* 2. a long, heavy table for doing work on: *a carpenter's bench.* 3. the position of a judge in a court of law: *The jury gave their verdict to the bench.* 4. a place where players sit who are not playing in a game.
verb, **benched, benching.** to keep a player out of a game: *The coach benched Alex because he had not been to practice all week.*

bench·mark [bench-mark] *noun, plural* **benchmarks.**
1. a mark made on a post or rock with a known height that can be used as a guide for other measurements. 2. something that other things are measured against or compared with; a standard: *Lauren's good result on the test set a benchmark for the rest of the class.*

bend ▼ [bend] *verb,* **bent, bending.** 1. to turn or force something into a curving direction or shape: *Dad used pliers to bend the wire.* 2. to move the top part of the body downward and forward: *I bent down to tie up my shoelaces.*
noun, plural **bends.** something that is curved or crooked: *He ran around the bend of the river.*

be·neath [bi-neeth] *preposition.* 1. lower than; below; underneath: *Some ants make nests beneath rocks.* 2. not worthy of: *Such rude behavior is beneath you.*
adverb. below; underneath: *From the bridge we watched the water flow beneath.*

ben·e·fi·cial [ben-uh-fish-ul] *adjective.* having to do with helping or with doing good: *Exercise is beneficial to your health.* —**beneficially,** *adverb.*

ben·e·fit [ben-uh-fit] *noun, plural* **benefits.** something that helps or is good for a person or thing: *the benefits of exercise.*
verb, **benefited, benefiting.** to be of use; help: *It would benefit you to study some more for the test.*

When you **bend** *forward, it stretches and relaxes your back, as well as helping to slim your waist.*

ben·ev·ol·ent [buh-<u>nev</u>-uh-lunt] *adjective.* wishing to do good and help others; kind: *I was given money by a benevolent aunt.* **Benevolence** is the fact of being helpful and kind. —**benevolently,** *adverb.*

be·nign [bi-<u>nine</u>] *adjective.* 1. describing something gentle; kind: *Grandma gave us a benign smile.* 2. *Medicine.* not dangerous: *He was very relieved when tests showed that the tumor was benign.*

bent [bent] *verb.* the past tense and past participle of BEND.
adjective. 1. out of its true shape; crooked. 2. set on doing; determined: *He is bent on becoming a pro baseball player.*

ben·zene [bent] *noun. Chemistry.* a colorless liquid that burns easily, obtained mainly from petroleum. It is used to make other chemicals, and in the making of plastic, some adhesives, and synthetic materials such as nylon.

be·queath [bee-<u>kweeth</u>] *verb,* **bequeathed, bequeathing.** to give others after death: *She bequeathed the house to her son.* A **bequest** is a gift of money or property made in a will.

be·reaved [bi-<u>reevd</u>] *adjective.* having to do with someone whose relative or close friend has just died: *The club sent flowers to the bereaved family.* —**bereavement** *noun.*

be·ret ▲ [buh-<u>ray</u>] *noun, plural* **berets.** a round, flat cap, usually woolen.

Ber·mu·da Triangle ▼ [bur-<u>myoo</u>-duh] *Geography.* a triangular area of the Atlantic Ocean between Bermuda and Florida where many ships and airplanes are supposed to have disappeared.

Bowls players in France often wear **berets.**

ber·ry ▶ [<u>ber</u>-ee] *noun, plural* **berries.** a small, round, soft fruit with seeds. Some berries, such as blackberries and strawberries, can be eaten. 🔊 A different word with the same sound is **bury.**

Blueberries are **berries** *that are eaten fresh or cooked.*

ber·serk [buh-<u>zerk</u> *or* bur-<u>serk</u>] *adjective.* not able to be controlled; wild; crazy: *The crowd nearly went berserk when he hit the winning home run.*

berth [burth] *noun, plural* **berths.** 1. a sleeping place on a ship or train. 2. a place at a dock where a ship can stay for a short period. 🔊 A different word with the same sound is **birth.**

be·seech [bee-<u>seech</u>] *verb,* **besought** *or* **beseeched, beseeching.** to ask in an urgent, anxious way; plead; beg: *Have mercy, I beseech you.*

be·set [bee-<u>set</u>] *verb,* **beset, besetting.** to attack from all directions: *Angry bees beset him as he tried to take honey from the hive.*

be·side [bi-<u>side</u>] *preposition.* 1. at or close to the side of; next to: *She stood beside her friend; We stayed in a house beside the beach.* 2. compared with: *My drawing looks terrible beside yours.*
• **beside the point.** having nothing to do with: *We just want a reliable car—its color is beside the point.*

be·sides [bi-<u>sidez</u>] *adverb.* in addition; anyway; also: *It's too far to walk and besides, it's raining now.*
preposition. as well as, in addition to: *We'll need another car besides yours.*

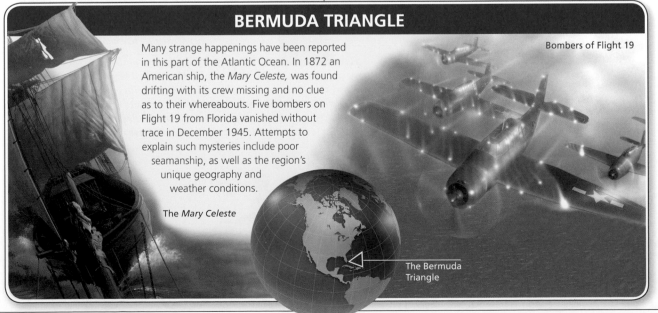

BERMUDA TRIANGLE

Many strange happenings have been reported in this part of the Atlantic Ocean. In 1872 an American ship, the *Mary Celeste,* was found drifting with its crew missing and no clue as to their whereabouts. Five bombers on Flight 19 from Florida vanished without trace in December 1945. Attempts to explain such mysteries include poor seamanship, as well as the region's unique geography and weather conditions.

The *Mary Celeste*

Bombers of Flight 19

The Bermuda Triangle

be·siege [bee-<u>seej</u>] *verb,* **besieged, besieging.**
1. to surround a place with an army in order to capture it: *The troops besieged the enemy town for five weeks.*
2. to crowd around asking for attention: *Reporters besieged the newly married movie stars.*

best [best] *adjective.* 1. of the highest standard or quality; better than the others: *We use the best meat we can buy in our hamburgers.* 2. most suitable; most satisfactory; most preferred: *What is the best way to get to the airport from here?*
adverb. 1. in the best way: *These flowers grow best if you plant the seeds in spring.* 2. most: *Saturday suits me best.*
noun. someone or something of the highest quality: *Our parents want the best for us.*
verb, **bested, besting.** to defeat: *Although we played our hardest, we were bested by the opposing team.*

Best is the word to use with three or more things, and *better* is the word to use with just two. Because of this you should write, "Both books are funny, but I liked this one *better* (not "liked this one *best*").

bet [bet] *noun, plural* **bets.** an agreement to pay money to another person if that person is right and you are wrong about the result of a future event or an uncertain fact: *She made a bet with her father about who would win the race.*
verb, **bet** or **betted, betting.** 1. to make such an agreement. 2. to believe to be true; feel certain about: *Something has chewed up this plant—I bet it was a rabbit.*

be·tray [bi-<u>tray</u>] *verb,* **betrayed, betraying.** 1. to help or give secrets to the enemy: *Spies working for a foreign government betray their own country.* 2. to be disloyal to: *She betrayed our friendship by telling stories about me behind my back.* A **betrayal** is an act or fact of being disloyal or unfaithful to someone.

bet·ter [<u>bet</u>-ur] *adjective.* 1. higher in quality or skill: *I almost failed the first test, but I studied hard and got a better mark this time.* 2. more suitable: *This is a better book for a six-year-old.* 3. improved in health: *She's better now and is back in class.* 4. describing something larger: *I spent the better part of the day at school.*
adverb. 1. in an improved or more effective way: *The team plays better now than they used to.* 2. to a greater degree: *She is better known for singing than for acting.*

noun, plural **betters.** someone or something of higher quality: *Which is the better of these two?*
verb, **bettered, bettering.** 1. to improve: *She bettered her time by 15 seconds.* 2. to do better than: *His swimming record has never been bettered.*

bet·ting [<u>bet</u>-ing] *noun.* the act of making bets; gambling: *Betting takes place at horse races.*

be·tween [bi-<u>tween</u>] *preposition.* 1. in the space or period of time separating two or more things: *In the photo she is standing between her parents; It happened between Monday night and Tuesday afternoon.* 2. concerning or involving: *an argument between Alice and Emily; Can you tell the difference between a star and a planet?*
adverb. in the space or period of time separating two things: *There's a train at noon and one at six, but nothing between.*

People are worried about using the word *me* when *I* would be correct, as in "Maddie and me went to a movie," so they may make what is called an *overcorrection* when they use other words. This means correcting something that does not really need it, such as saying or writing "**Between** you and *I*" when actually "Between you and *me*" is correct. See AMONG for another language note.

bev·er·age [<u>bev</u>-rij or <u>bev</u>-uh-rij] *noun, plural* **beverages.** a drink, such as juice or coffee.

be·ware [bi-<u>ware</u>] *verb.* to be on one's guard against; be very careful: *Beware of sharks when you swim there.*

be·wil·der [bi-<u>wil</u>-dur] *verb,* **bewildered, bewildering.** to puzzle or confuse: *I was bewildered by the complicated instructions.* —**bewildered,** *adjective;* —**bewilderment,** *noun.*

be·witch [bi-<u>wich</u>] *verb,* **bewitched, bewitching.** 1. to cast a magic spell over someone: *The Wicked Queen bewitched Sleeping Beauty into a deep sleep.* 2. to charm, as if by magic: *We were bewitched by her beautiful singing.*

When you bend your arm, the **biceps** *muscle bulges.*

be·yond [bi-<u>yond</u>] *preposition.* 1. on or to the far side of: *He traveled beyond the mountains.* 2. later than: *Cinderella was not to stay at the ball beyond midnight.* 3. outside the limits or range of: *The apples on the top branch are beyond my reach.*
adverb. on or to the far side: *He went across the field and into the forest beyond.*

Dandy horse, 1818

Penny-farthing, 1870

Safety bike, 1879

Aerodynamic bike, early 1980s

Over two centuries, the **bicycle** *developed from a walking machine with wheels to the modern racing bike.*

bi- a prefix that means two: a *bifuel* vehicle can run on two different kinds of fuel.

bi·as [bye-us] *noun, plural* **biases.** a strong feeling for or against a person or thing that stops someone from judging fairly; prejudice; favoritism: *A newspaper should not show bias in its news stories on politics.* A **biased** judgment favors one side and does not judge fairly. *verb,* **biased, biasing.** to show favoritism or be biased.

Bi·ble [bye-bul] *noun, plural* **Bibles.** *Religion.* 1. the holy book of the Christian religion, consisting of the Old Testament and the New Testament. 2. the Old Testament on its own, which is the holy book of the Jewish religion. Any reference book that is seen as the best authority for a particular subject is the **bible** for that subject.

Bib·li·cal [bib-luh-kul] *adjective. Religion.* contained in or having to do with the Bible: *the Biblical story of David and Goliath.* This word is also spelled **biblical.**

bib·li·og·ra·phy [bib-lee-og-ruh-fee] *noun, plural* **bibliographies.** *Literature.* 1. a list of books and other references about a particular subject: *We need to hand in a bibliography of all the books and Internet sources we used in our research.* 2. a list of the books that an author reads or refers to in writing a book or article.

In very early times the making of books was not common, and one reason for this was that so few people knew how to make paper. One place that was famous for making paper was *Byblos,* a town on the coast of the Mediterranean Sea. Several words that have to do with books and writing come from the name of this place, such as **bibliography** and *Bible.*

bi·ceps ◀ [bye-seps] *noun, plural* **biceps** *or* **bicepses.** the large muscle in the front of the upper arm. It runs from the shoulder to the elbow.

bick·er [bick-ur] *verb,* **bickered, bickering.** to argue about small, unimportant things.

bi·cy·cle ◀ [bye-si-kul] *noun, plural* **bicycles.** a two-wheeled vehicle for one rider. It is moved along by turning pedals with the feet, and is steered with handlebars. *verb,* **bicycled, bicycling.** to ride a bicycle: *We bicycled into town along the track beside the river.*

bid [bid] *verb,* **bid** *or* **bidden, bidding.** 1. to give an order; command: *I bid you to kneel before the King.* An order or command is a **bidding.** 2. to say: *She bid farewell and left. noun, plural* **bids.** an offer to pay a certain price: *Dad made a bid of fifty dollars for the old chair.* Someone who makes a bid is a **bidder.**

bide [bide] *verb.* **bide one's time.** to wait until the right moment or for the best opportunity: *Just bide your time, your turn will come.*

bi·en·ni·al [bye-en-ee-ul] *adjective.* 1. lasting or living for two years: *Parsnips and pansies are biennial plants.* 2. happening every two years: *a biennial festival.* Something that happens two times a year is **biannual.** *noun, plural* **biennials.** 1. an event that takes place every two years. 2. a plant that takes two years to complete its life cycle. It produces seed in the second year, then dies. —**biennially,** *adverb.*

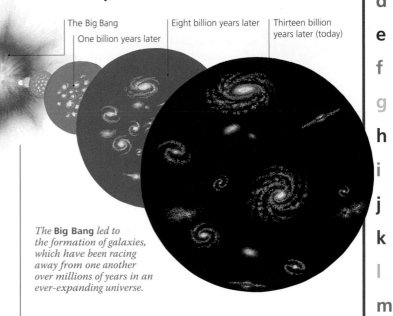

The Big Bang | One billion years later | Eight billion years later | Thirteen billion years later (today)

*The **Big Bang** led to the formation of galaxies, which have been racing away from one another over millions of years in an ever-expanding universe.*

big [big] *adjective,* **bigger biggest.** 1. great in size; large: *That shirt is too big for me—I need a smaller size.* 2. important: *a big mistake; big business; a big event.*

Big Bang ▲ *Science.* the gigantic explosion of a single mass of material that is thought to have caused the beginning of our universe. According to the **Big Bang Theory,** pieces are still flying apart.

Big Dip·per ▼ a group of seven bright stars seen in the northern part of the sky. Its outline looks like a dipper (a bowl with a long handle).

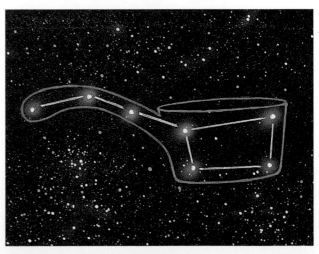

*The **Big Dipper** is part of the constellation of Ursa Major, or the Great Bear.*

big·horn ▼ [big-horn] *noun, plural* **bighorn** *or* **bighorns.** a wild sheep with thick, curved horns that lives in the Rocky Mountains of North America.

bike [byke] *noun, plural* **bikes.** a shortened form of BICYCLE.
verb, **biked, biking.** to ride a bicycle.

bi·ki·ni [buh-kee-nee] *noun, plural* **bikinis.** a bathing suit in two pieces worn by women.

bi·lin·gual [bye-ling-gwul] *adjective. Language.* **1.** able to speak or write in two languages. **2.** spoken or written in two languages.
—**bilingualism,** *noun.*

bill¹ [bil] *noun, plural* **bills. 1.** a written account showing how much money is owed for something bought or for work done: *Jane asked the waiter for her bill.* **2.** a piece of paper money: *a ten dollar bill.* **3.** a poster advertising an event: *Bills pasted in the bus station gave details of the charity concert.* **4.** a suggested law: *Congress votes on the environment bill next week.*
verb, **billed, billing.** to send a written account showing how much money is owed to someone: *The plumber billed us for fixing the broken faucet.*

The horns of the male **bighorn** *can weigh thirty pounds.*

bill² ▶ [bil] *noun, plural,* **bills.** the hard, curved, or pointed part of the mouth of a bird or turtle; beak.

bill·board [bil-bord] *noun, plural* **billboards.** a very large board for displaying advertisements. Billboards are placed outdoors, often along the side of a highway.

BILLS

Birds' bills vary according to how they feed. The African spoonbill traps food with spoonlike tips. The bald eagle's hook-shaped bill is ideal for tearing apart its prey. The palm cockatoo crushes fruits, seeds, and berries with its stout bill, while the Far Eastern curlew has a long, curved bill to probe for food in mud flats. A strong, straight bill allows the pileated woodpecker to dislodge insects from tree bark, and the yellow-billed hornbill's huge, sturdy bill is used to forage for seeds, insects, and scorpions on the ground.

Bald eagle

African spoonbill

Palm cockatoo

Far Eastern curlew

Yellow-billed hornbill

Pileated woodpecker

---

bill·fold [bil-fold] *noun, plural* **billfolds.** a small, flat folding case for holding paper money; a wallet.

bil·liards [bil-yurdz] *plural noun.* a game played using a long stick called a cue to hit hard balls against one another. Billiards is played on a large, felt-covered rectangular table with raised sides.

bil·lion [bil-yun] *noun, plural* **billions.** *Mathematics.* one thousand times one million; 1,000,000,000. A **billionaire** has one billion dollars or more worth of money and property. —**billionth,** *adjective.*

Bill of Rights *Government.* the first ten amendments to the United States Constitution, protecting the basic rights and freedom of people.

bil·low ◀ [bil-oh] *noun, plural* **billows.** a great moving, swelling mass of something: *Billows of steam rose into the air.*
verb, **billowed, billowing.** to move upward or along in billows: *Smoke billowed from the chimney.*

bin [bin] *noun, plural* **bins.** a container, usually with a lid, for storing something. *a coal bin; a grain bin.*
🔊 A different word with the same sound is **been.**

bi·na·ry [bye-nuh-ree *or* bye-nare-ee] *adjective.* **1.** having two parts. **2.** using only the numbers 0 and 1. The **binary system** is a way of counting using only these two numbers. Many computers use the binary system of numbering.

A galleon's many sails **billowed** *as the wind carried it along.*

bind [bined] *verb,* **bound, binding. 1.** to tie together firmly with string or rope: *Bind those newspapers into bundles.* **2.** to tie a bandage around: *to bind a sprained ankle.* **3.** to fasten the pages of a book together in a cover: *This special edition is bound with a leather cover.* **4.** to force by a promise or an obligation: *This oath binds you to tell the truth.*
• **in a bind.** in a difficult situation: *His injury the day before the game put the coach in a bind about who to use as the pitcher.*

bind·er [bine-dur] *noun, plural* **binders. 1.** someone or something that ties or holds things together: *a book binder.* **2.** a cover for holding loose sheets of paper together.

binge [binj] *noun, plural* **binges.** a period when something, such as eating or drinking, is done intensely or more than is sensible or good: *a shopping binge; a chocolate binge.*

bin·go [bing-goh] *noun.* a game in which players cover numbers on a card with numbers chosen by chance and called out. The winner is the first player to cover a row of numbers or the whole card.
interjection. a shout of pleasure at a sudden successful result.

bin·oc·u·lars ▼ [bi-nok-yuh-lurz] *plural noun.* a device with magnifying glasses for both eyes, used for making distant things seem larger and closer.

bio·chem·is·try [bye-oh-kem-i-stree] *Science.* the study of the chemistry of living things. A **biochemist** studies the chemical substances found in living things.
—**biochemical,** *adjective.*

bi·o·de·grad·a·ble [bye-oh-di-grade-uh-bul] *adjective. Environment.* having to do with a substance that can be broken down by the sun or by bacteria into products which can be absorbed by the environment.

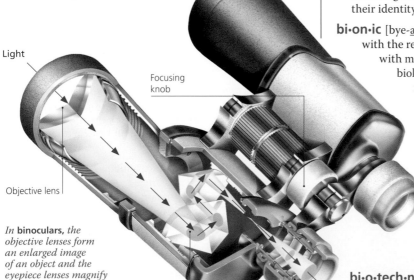

Light

Focusing knob

Objective lens

In **binoculars,** *the objective lenses form an enlarged image of an object and the eyepiece lenses magnify it a little more.*

Two prisms, or glass wedges

Eyepiece with magnifying lenses

bi·o·di·ver·sity [bye-oh-di-vers-uh-tee] *noun. Environment.* the variety of plants, animals, and other living things in a particular area or region.

bio·fuel ▶ [bye-oh-fyool] *noun, plural* **biofuels.** *Science.* a gas or liquid fuel made from plant material or animal waste.

bi·og·ra·phy [bye-ahg-ruh-fee] *noun, plural* **biographies.** the story of a person's life written by someone other than that person. A **biographer** is someone who writes a biography.
—**biographical,** *adjective.*

bi·o·log·i·cal [bye-uh-loj-uh-kul] *adjective.* having to do with plants, animals, and other living things. —**biologically,** *adverb.*

Biofuel *can be made from flax and corn, among other plants.*

bi·ol·o·gy [bye-ol-uh-jee] *noun.* the scientific study of all living things. A **biologist** studies how and where plants, animals, and other forms of life live and grow.

bi·o·lu·mi·nes·cence [bye-oh-loom-i-nes-uns] *Biology.* **1.** the giving off of light by certain living creatures such as fireflies and some fish. **2.** the light given off. —**bioluminescent,** *noun.*

bi·o·mass [bye-oh-mass] *noun.* the total amount of all living things present at a particular time in a specified area of the environment, usually described in terms of the weight or volume of these things.

bi·o·met·rics [bye-oh-met-triks] *plural noun. Science.* a method of using a person's unique body information, including fingerprints, eyes, and voice pattern, to check their identity for security purposes.

bi·on·ic [bye-ahn-ik] *adjective. Science.* having to do with the replacement of natural human body parts with mechanical or electrical ones. **Bionics** uses biological information or devices to deal with mechanical problems.

bi·o·rhyth·m [bye-oh-riTH-um] *noun, plural* **biorhythms.** *Biology.* the natural rhythms of the body, believed to affect people and animals and to control some activities.

bi·o·sphere [bye-uh-sfeer] *noun, plural* **biospheres.** *Biology.* the part of the world in which life can exist; that is, the surface of the Earth and the crust below this, and the atmosphere above the Earth.

bi·o·tech·nol·o·gy [bye-oh-tek-nol-uh-jee] *noun. Science.* the process or business of using living organisms to produce new things to eat or make for industry.

a b c d e f i j k l m n o p q r s t u v w x y z

*This **biplane**, designed and built by Orville and Wilbur Wright, made the first powered flight in 1903.*

A
B
C
D
E
F
G
H
I
O
P
Q
R
S
T
U
V
W
X
Y
Z

bi·plane ▲ [bye-plane] *noun, plural* **biplanes.** an older form of airplane with two sets of wings, one placed above the other.

birch ▼ [birch] *noun, plural* **birches.** any of a group of trees that have hard wood and thin, peeling bark.

*The silver **birch** has a white bark and loses its leaves in winter.*

bird ▶ [burd] *noun, plural* **birds.** an animal with wings and feathers. Birds are warm-blooded and have a body supported by bones. They lay eggs, and most are able to fly.

birth [burth] *noun, plural* **births. 1.** the time when a baby or young animal first comes out of the body of its mother. **2.** an event when something happens for the first time: *A volcano erupting under the sea resulted in the birth of a small island.*
🔊 A different word with the same sound is **berth.**

birth·day [burth-day] *noun, plural* **birthdays. 1.** the day on which someone is born. **2.** the anniversary each year of the same day.

birth·mark [burth-mark] *noun, plural* **birthmarks.** a mark, usually red or brown, found on the skin at birth.

birth·place [burth-plays] *noun, plural* **birthplaces.** the country, region, or town where a person was born.

bis·cuit [bis-kit] *noun, plural* **biscuits. 1.** a small, flat cake baked of dough. **2.** a thin, dry cracker.

bi·sect [bye-sekt] *verb,* **bisected, bisecting.** *Mathematics.* to cut into two parts of equal size. The line that divides the two parts is called the **bisector.**

bish·op [bish-up] *noun, plural* **bishops. 1.** *Religion.* a high-ranking Christian priest. **2.** a chess piece that can move only along diagonal lines.

bi·son ▶ [bye-sun] *noun, plural* **bison.** a large animal with high shoulders and shaggy hair found in North America; also called a buffalo.

bit[1] [bit] *noun, plural* **bits. 1.** a small piece or pieces: *I dropped the cup and it smashed to bits.* **2.** a short time: *The bus will be along in a bit.*

bit[2] [bit] *noun, plural* **bits. 1.** a piece of metal held in a horse's mouth by a bridle. **2.** the sharp metal tip of a drill, separate from the drill itself.

bit[3] [bit] *verb.* the past tense of BITE.

bit[4] [bit] *noun, plural* **bits.** a single unit of information stored in a computer's memory.

> The word **bit** is formed from letters of the phrase "binary digit." A bit is a single digit (number) in a binary (two-digit) numbering system.

bite [byte] *verb,* **bit** or **bitten, biting. 1.** to use teeth to cut into food: *to bite into an apple.* **2.** to wound with the teeth: *The dog bit me.* **3.** to be hurt by cold or ice: *The icy wind bit the tops of our ears.* **4.** to take a bait: *When Dylan went fishing, the fish didn't bite.*
noun, plural **bites. 1.** a small piece of food taken with the teeth: *He took a bite of the melon.* **2.** an injury caused by biting. **3.** a sharp, cutting feeling.
🔊 A different word with the same sound is **byte.**

bit·ten [bit-un] *verb.* the past participle of BITE.

bit·ter [bit-ur] *adjective.* **1.** having a sour taste; sharp: *The vinegar tasted bitter.* **2.** very cold: *The wind was bitter.* **3.** full of anger and hate: *a bitter feud.* —**bitterly,** *adverb;* —**bitterness,** *noun.*

bit·tern [bit-urn] *noun, plural* **bitterns.** a long-legged bird that wades in water to find food.

bi·tu·mi·nous coal [bi-toom-i-nus] *Science.* a coal that easily turns into a gas when heated. It burns with a yellow flame.

bi·zarre [bi-zahr] *adjective.* very strange; odd: *The movie I saw last weekend was about a bizarre monster with two heads.*

black [blak] *noun, plural* **blacks.** the color of night or coal; no light.
adjective, **blacker, blackest. 1.** having the color of coal, darkest. **2.** completely dark, without light: *With no Moon or stars, the night was black.*

Black [blak] *noun, plural* **Blacks.** a member of the dark-skinned races. These include African-Americans, Australian Aborigines, and other generally dark-skinned people around the world.
adjective. having to do with or relating to one of these groups of people.

black·ber·ry [blak-ber-ee] *noun, plural* **blackberries.** a sweet black or purple fruit that grows on bramble bushes.

*Wood **bison** are North America's largest land mammals.*

BIRDS

Barn swallow

There are more than 9,000 different kinds of birds. They range in size from the tiny bee hummingbird to the ostrich, which is taller than a basketball player. Birds are commonly found in marshes, woodland, and forests, but they also live in hot deserts and the cold polar regions. Feathers help birds to fly, protect them from heat, cold, and water, and give them color to attract a mate or hide from an enemy.

BIRD ANATOMY

Wing bone

Large wing muscles give power for flight.

Skeleton is lightweight but strong.

New feather grows at the base of old feather.

Old feather

Feather opens up from the shaft.

New feather pushes out old feather.

New feather

HOW FEATHERS GROW

Keel-billed toucan

Budgerigar

Gouldian finch

Hummingbird

Colorful kingfisher

Splendid fairywren

Emperor penguin

Barn owl

Gray heron

Ostrich

Brown pelican

a
b
c
f
g
h
i
j
k
l
m
n
o
p
q
r
s
t
v
w
x
y
z

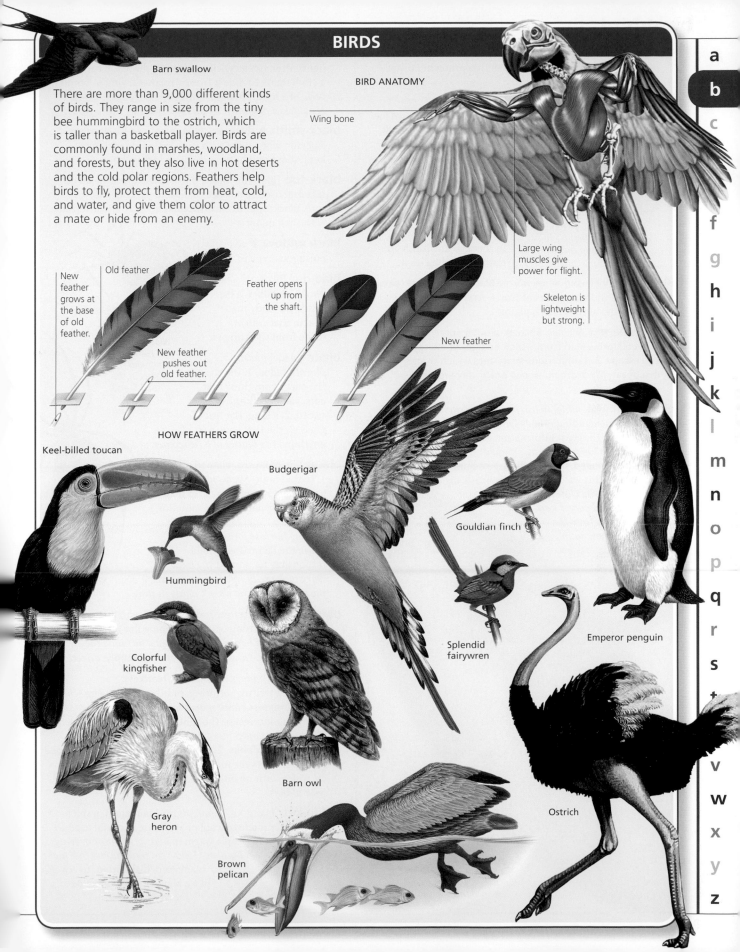

black·bird ▼ [blak-burd] *noun, plural* **blackbirds.** a type of bird, including crows and ravens, common in Europe and North America.

black·board [blak-bord] *noun, plural* **blackboards.** a smooth board for writing or drawing on with chalk, used in classrooms; so called because originally these boards were always black, though now they are often green or another color.

The male tricolored **blackbird** *is found in California, Oregon, and Baja.*

black body *Science.* an imaginary body that, in theory, can absorb all radiation falling on it.

Black·foot [blak-fut] *noun, plural* **Blackfoot** or **Blackfeet.** one of the Indian peoples of North America who once lived on the northwestern plains.

black hole ▼ **1.** *Science.* an area of outer space formed by a collapsing star, from which no light or energy can escape. **2.** a mysterious space into which things disappear: *My bedroom was so untidy my mom called it a black hole.*

black·mail [blak-male] *noun, plural* **blackmails.** *Law.* the act of demanding money from a person by threatening to reveal information about him that would harm his reputation. *verb,* **blackmailed, blackmailing.** to demand money from a person in this way: *Mayor Jones was being blackmailed by someone who claimed to have proof that the mayor had stolen money from the city.* —**blackmailer,** *noun.*

The matter swallowed by a **black hole** *gives off radiation, while excess gas shoots away at high speed.*

black·out [blak-out] *noun, plural* **blackouts. 1.** the loss of lights after an electricity failure. **2.** the act of turning off a city's lights to hide it from airplanes trying to bomb it. *verb.* **black out.** to have a brief loss of consciousness: *He blacked out when he was tackled during the game.*

black·smith ▶ [blak-smith] *noun, plural* **blacksmiths.** a person who works with iron, including making horseshoes and putting them on horses' hooves.

black·top [blak-top] *noun, plural* **blacktops.** the black material used to surface roads and parking lots. *verb,* **blacktopped, blacktopping.** to pave a road surface with such material.

black widow ▶ a very poisonous type of spider.

blad·der [blad-ur] *noun, plural* **bladders.** a bag inside the body made of skin that collects urine from the kidneys.

Northern black widow

Female **black widow** *spiders are the most venomous spiders in the United States, but are not usually deadly.*

blade [blade] *noun, plural* **blades. 1.** the sharp, flat part of anything that cuts, such as a knife or sword. **2.** a long, flat leaf of grass. **3.** the flat, wide part of anything: *the blades of a helicopter.*

blame [blame] *verb,* **blamed, blaming. 1.** to find fault: *She won't blame us if we try really hard.* **2.** to hold someone responsible for something that goes wrong: *I blame you for making me late for school.* *noun.* the fact of being held responsible for something bad: *Gary took the blame for our missing the bus because he wasn't ready in time.*

Southern black widow

bland [bland] *adjective.* **1.** having no flavor; tasteless. **2.** having no strong opinions, hoping not to offend anyone: *Asked how he liked the play, he made the bland remark, "It was OK, I guess."* —**blandly,** *adverb.*

blank [blangk] *adjective,* **blanker, blankest. 1.** without writing, printing, or other marks: *The school report form has blank spaces for teachers' comments.* **2.** with no interest or thought: *He didn't hear my question and just gave me a blank look.* *noun, plural* **blanks. 1.** a space for something to be added: *I've left a blank for you to write your name.* **2.** a gun cartridge with no bullet: *In movies, the guns are loaded with blanks.*

blan·ket [blang-kit] *noun, plural* **blankets. 1.** a thick cover made of wool or synthetic material used to keep people warm in bed. **2.** a thick covering: *A blanket of snow covered the city last night.* *verb,* **blanketed, blanketing.** to cover like a blanket: *Fog blanketed the town.*

*A **blacksmith** heats iron until is is red hot before shaping it into metal objects with hand tools.*

blare [blare] *verb*, **blared, blaring.** to produce a loud, unpleasant sound: *The fire engine's siren blared to make people get out of the way.*
noun, plural **blares.** a loud, grating sound: *The blare from the truck's horn made me jump.*

blas·phe·my [blas-fu-mee] *noun, plural* **blasphemies.**
Religion. the use of bad language about God; swear.
To **blaspheme** is to speak about God without respect.
—**blasphemous,** *adjective.*

blast [blast] *noun, plural* **blasts. 1.** a powerful explosion: *The bomb blast made a huge hole in the road.* **2.** a loud sound, of, or like, that of a brass instrument: *They heard the blast of a horn or bugle.* **3.** a strong, sudden rush of air: *She felt an icy blast when the door swung open.*
verb, **blasted, blasting. 1.** to blow up; destroy: *The explosives team blasted a new entrance to the mine.* **2.** to ruin: *The captain's injury blasted our chances of winning the game.*

blast-off ▶ [blast-*awf*] *noun, plural* **blast-offs.** the act of launching a rocket into the air or a spacecraft into space.
verb. **blast off.** to launch a rocket or spacecraft into space.

bla·tant [blay-tunt] *adjective.* easy to see or notice; obvious; conspicuous: *His cheating at games is quite blatant.*
—**blatantly,** *adverb.*

blaze¹ [blaze] *noun, plural* **blazes. 1.** a strong fire or flame: *We saw the blaze of the forest fire from miles away.* **2.** a dazzling light: *The blaze of the searchlight blinded us.* **3.** a bright show of light or colors: *The flower garden was a blaze of color.*
verb, **blazed, blazing. 1.** to burn strongly: *Once it was going, the fire blazed for hours.* **2.** to shine: *The stars blazed brightly that night.*

blaze² [blaze] *verb,* **blazed, blazing.** to set out marks that show the course of a trail through woods or other wild land, as by cutting marks in the bark of trees or painting marks on rocks.
noun, plural **blazes.** a mark made in this way to show a trail.

blaz·er [blay-zur] *noun, plural* **blazers.** a sport coat in navy blue or another solid color.

bleach [bleech] *verb,* **bleached, bleaching.** to cause something to become white or pale by using a chemical: *I will bleach my blouse before the next school concert.*
noun, plural **bleaches.** a chemical or other substance used for bleaching.

bleach·ers [bleech-urz] *plural noun.* the rows of seats at a sports stadium that are open to the sun, not covered by a roof.

bleak [bleek] *adjective,* **bleaker, bleakest. 1.** open to wind and weather: *The bleak hillside gave us no protection.* **2.** chilly, dark, and unpleasant: *It was a bleak winter afternoon.* —**bleakness,** *noun.*

bled [bled] *verb.* the past tense and past participle of BLEED.

bleed [bleed] *verb,* **bled, bleeding. 1.** to lose blood. **2.** to leak liquid or sap: *Pine trees bleed sap when their bark is cut.*

blend [blend] *verb,* **blended, blending. 1.** to completely mix two or more ingredients together: *To make the cake, blend eggs, flour, butter, and milk.* **2.** to join together; merge: *Julia's friends blended in well at the party.*
noun, plural **blends.** something made up of different parts mixed together: *A mixture of coffee beans from different countries of the world is called a blend.*

In language, a **blend** is a word made by joining together parts of other words. This is a common way of forming new words in today's English. Common examples are *smog* (smoke and fog), *motel* (motor hotel), *brunch* (breakfast/lunch), and *guesstimate* (guess by estimating).

blend·er [blen-dur] *noun, plural* **blenders.** an electrical machine used to mix different foods together or to make solid foods softer or more liquid.

*At **blast-off,** booster rockets generate tremendous heat and power to lift the spacecraft off the launch pad.*

Blimps are often used for advertising, as well as to cover sports events for television.

bless [bless] *verb,* **blessed, blest, blessing. 1.** to ask for God's favor and protection: *The minister blessed the members of the congregation.* **2.** to make something holy by a religious ceremony: *The priest blessed the bread and the wine.* **3.** to bring happiness or good luck to: *The picnic day was blessed with good weather.* Something that brings happiness or good fortune is a **blessing.**

bless·ed [blest *or* bless-id] *adjective.* **1.** having to do with being favored by God; sacred, holy: *"Blessed are the peacemakers" is a famous saying in the Bible.* **2.** having to do with bringing joy or happiness: *When the noise stopped, there was blessed silence.*
noun. the people who have been blessed in a religious ritual.

blew [bloo] *verb.* the past tense of BLOW.
🔊 A different word with the same sound is **blue.**

blimp ▲ [blimp] *noun, plural* **blimps.** a type of aircraft that is a very large balloon filled with a gas that is lighter than air.

blind [blyeind] *adjective.* **1.** not being able to see; not having the power of sight. **2.** difficult to see; hidden or concealed: *It's a blind corner so she didn't see the boy on the bicycle.* **3.** flying without sight of the route, using only instruments: *The pilot had to make a blind landing because of the thick fog.* **4.** with no exit: *We found ourselves in a blind alley.* **5.** without thought or good sense: *When fire broke out there was blind panic.* **Blindness** is the fact of not being able to see.
verb, **blinded, blinding.** to make unable to see: *I was blinded by the strong light.*
noun, plural **blinds.** a cover or shade: *The window is covered by a blind.* —**blindly,** *adverb.*

blind·fold ▶ [blyned-fohld] *verb,* **blindfolded, blindfolding.** to place a piece of cloth over someone's eyes to stop them from seeing: *The prisoner was blindfolded.*
noun, plural **blindfolds.** a cover placed over someone's eyes.

blink [blingk] *verb,* **blinked, blinking. 1.** to close the eyelids and quickly open them again. **2.** to switch on and off again: *The neon signs on the billboard blinked at us.*

blink·er [blingk-ur] *noun, plural* **blinkers.** a flap used to cover a horse's eyes to stop it seeing to the side so that it looks straight ahead.

bliss [bliss] *noun.* complete happiness: *Swimming in the summer sunshine was bliss.* —**blissful,** *adjective;* —**blissfully,** *adverb.*

blis·ter [bliss-tur] *noun, plural* **blisters. 1.** *Health.* a painful bubble or swelling on the skin caused by a burn or rubbing: *I had a blister on my heel after the long walk.* **2.** any swelling or bubble: *The strong sun caused blisters on the paint.*
verb, **blistered, blistering.** to cause blisters to form.

bliz·zard [bliz-urd] *noun, plural* **blizzards.** a heavy snowstorm with high winds that lasts a long time.

bloat [blote] *verb,* **bloated, bloating.** to become too full with solids, liquids, or gas. If someone becomes too full, they are **bloated.**

blob [blob] *noun, plural* **blobs.** a small spot or drop of a thick liquid.

block [blok] *noun, plural* **blocks. 1.** a piece of a hard, solid material: *The bowl was carved from a block of wood.* **2.** an area within a city or town that has a boundary of four streets: *Our block has grocery stores and a pharmacy.* **3.** the distance from one road to another along the side of a city block: *We live four blocks from the shopping center.* **4.** a number of things that are treated as a single unit: *My dad bought a block of tickets for the softball game so our family could all go.* **5.** something that stops a movement or activity: *When a person tries to write but cannot think of what to say, that is called writer's block.* **6.** a mechanism with a pulley in a frame to lift things.
A **blocker** is a person or thing that stops a movement or activity. In football, a blocker tries to stop defensive players from tackling the player with the ball. Drugs called blockers are used in medicine to treat high blood pressure.
verb, **blocked, blocking.** to prevent movement or progress: *The huge truck blocked the street.*

block·ade [blah-kade] *noun, plural* **blockades.** the sealing off of an area or a country by police or soldiers to stop people or goods moving in or out.
verb, **blockaded, blockading.** to seal off, or prevent access to a place: *The navy blockaded the mouth of the river.*

In this game, a **blindfolded** *person has to guess what objects are on the tray.*

bloom

block·house ▶ [blok-*hous*] *noun,
plural* **blockhouses. 1.** a small,
strong building made of logs with
small windows from which to shoot
guns or arrows. **2.** a strong building
near a rocket launch site used to
shelter staff during blast-off.

blog [blog] *noun, plural* **blogs.**
Computers. a diary or story posted
on an Internet Website for others
to read. A **blogger** is someone who
writes a blog. Bloggers often write
comments on politics and news
stories of the day.

*Blockhouses were built as
defensive structures during
the American Civil War.*

Blog is a new word made by putting together parts of
the words "web" and "log." *Web* is another name for the
Internet, and a *log* is a daily written record of events, such
as the things that happen during a ship's voyage or an
airplane flight.

blonde [blond] *adjective,* **blonder, blondest. 1.** pale-
colored yellow hair. **2.** having fair hair and a pale skin:
noun, plural **blondes.** a person with pale-colored
yellow hair.

Blonde has two spellings, with or
without an "e" at the end. According
to strict rules of English, the spelling
blonde should be used for girls or
women having this hair color, and
blond for boys or men. However,
records of how people actually use
the word show that the *blonde*
spelling is used for boys and men
just about as often as *blond*.

Bloodhounds
*are often used
to track escaped
prisoners or to
find earthquake
victims.*

blood [blud] *noun.* **1.** the red
liquid that flows through the
body. **2.** a person's descent or
family origins: *His mother is
of Italian blood.*

blood bank *Medicine.* a store of human blood that is
used when someone has been injured or for an operation.
A person who gives blood to a blood bank is called a
blood donor.

blood·hound ▲ [blud-*hound*] *noun, plural* **bloodhounds.**
a large dog with long ears and a wrinkled face that has a
very good sense of smell and is used to track people who
are lost or missing.

blood pressure *Medicine.* the force with which
the heart pumps blood around the body. It can be
measured precisely. Blood pressure readings give
doctors important information about a patient.

blood·shed [blud-*shed*] *noun.* the fact of
blood flowing, or of people dying in war:
*The war was won, but there was much
bloodshed.*

blood·shot [blud-*shot*] *adjective.* having the white of the
eye colored by small red veins; the result of being tired,
stressed, or injured.

blood·stream [blud-*streem*] *noun, plural* **bloodstreams.**
the blood that flows through the veins and arteries of a
human or animal body.

blood·thirst·y [blud-*thur*-stee] *adjective.* enjoying hurting
people, killing, or causing bloodshed: *The gangsters were
a bloodthirsty crew.*

blood vessel ▼ *Medicine.* any of
the large or small tubes of the body
through which blood flows.

blood·y [blud-ee] *adjective,*
bloodier, bloodiest. 1. bleeding or
covered with blood. **2.** with a lot
of killing or injury: *The battle
was the bloodiest of the war.*

bloom [bloom] *noun,
plural* **blooms.
1.** a flower
or blossom:
*Rhododendrons have blooms shaped
like bells.* **2.** the fact of or time
of growing flowers: *The roses
are in bloom now.*
verb, **bloomed, blooming.**
to produce flowers.

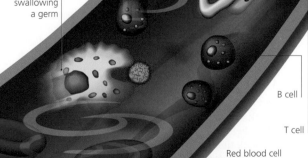

Neutrophil

Macrophage
swallowing
a germ

B cell

T cell

Red blood cell

Blood vessels *carry red blood cells and various white blood cells—macrophages,
neutrophils, and T and B cells—that fight germs.*

blossom

blos·som ◀ [blos-um] *noun, plural* **blossoms.** the flower of a tree, shrub, or plant: *The cherry blossoms are beautiful.* *verb,* **blossomed, blossoming.** 1. to produce flowers. 2. to grow and develop well: *He wasn't a very good pitcher, but when he switched to shortstop he really blossomed.*

blot [blot] *noun, plural* **blots. 1.** a mark or spot, especially one made with ink: *The word was hidden by an ink blot.* **2.** a thing that spoils something else: *The ugly building is a blot on the landscape.* A pad made of thick absorbent paper to soak up wet ink is called a **blotter.** *verb,* **blotted, blotting. 1.** to make a mark or spot on something: *He blotted his paper and had to start again with a new sheet.* **2.** to harm or spoil: *Being arrested blotted his reputation for years afterward.*

blotch [bloch] *noun, plural* **blotches.** a large, uneven stain or mark, especially on the skin.

Bryde's whale

Sei whale

Sperm whale

Humpback whale

Gray whale

Blue whale

Right whale

Fin whale

Bowhead whale

Different kinds of whales shoot air and water out of their blowholes in distinctive patterns.

blouse [blouss] *noun, plural* **blouses.** a piece of girls' or women's clothing similar to a shirt, worn on the upper body. It may be long or short sleeved.

blow¹ [bloh] *verb,* **blew, blown, blowing. 1.** to move the force of wind or air: *The storm blew the ship off course.* **2.** to send out a strong current of air: *I blew on my drink to cool it down.* **3.** to sound by blowing: *He blew the bugle every morning.* **4.** to destroy something with explosives: *The miners blew away some rock to reveal the iron ore.* **5.** to burst because of being old or worn out: *A car tire blew when we were on vacation.*

blow² [bloh] *noun, plural* **blows. 1.** a hit or knock with a fist, hammer, or tool: *He was hurt in the fight by a blow to the head.* **2.** a surprise or shock that has a bad effect: *The news of the accident was a terrible blow to her.*

blow·hole ▼ [bloh-hole] *noun, plural* **blowholes. 1.** a nostril at the top of the head of a whale or dolphin through which it breathes. **2.** a hole in the surface of the ice to which aquatic mammals such as seals come to breathe.

blow·out [bloh-owt] *noun, plural* **blowouts. 1.** the bursting of a tire on a motor vehicle. **2.** the burning out or melting of an electrical fuse. **3.** the sudden bursting of air, oil, or gas from a well. **4.** a large meal or social occasion: *We had a real blowout for my birthday this year.*

blow·torch [bloh-torch] *noun, plural* **blowtorches.** a portable tool that produces a very hot flame. It is used for melting metal and removing old paint.

blow·up [bloh-up] *noun, plural* **blowups. 1.** an explosion. **2.** an enlargement of a photograph: *Mom got a blowup of my school photo as a gift for my grandparents.* **3.** a sudden, big argument or outburst of bad temper: *There was a blowup when Dad saw that I had damaged his car.* *verb.* **blow up. 1.** to destroy by exploding: *The soldiers blew up the bridge.* **2.** to fill up with air: *blow up a balloon.*

blub·ber [blub-ur] *noun, plural* **blubbers.** the thick layer of fat under the skin of whales, seals, and other sea mammals. It is essential for storing energy and helps to keep the animal warm. *verb,* **blubbered, blubbering.** to cry noisily in a childish manner.

blue [bloo] *noun, plural* **blues.** the color of the clear daytime sky. *adjective,* **bluer, bluest. 1.** having this color. **2.** low-spirited; sad: *I felt blue when I broke up with my girlfriend.* A different word with the same sound is **blew.**

blue·ber·ry [bloo-ber-ee] *noun, plural* **blueberries.** a small, dark blue, edible fruit. Blueberries taste sweet and grow on a shrub.

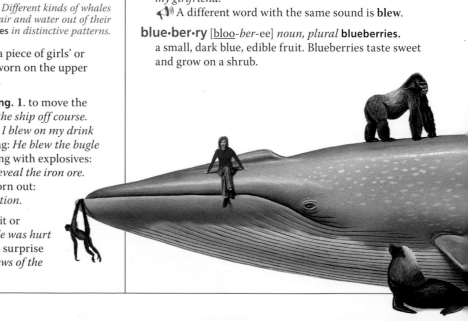

blue·bird [bloo-burd] *noun, plural* **bluebirds.** a small, mostly blue-colored songbird found in North America.

blue·col·lar [bloo-kol-ur] *adjective. Business.* of or relating to the class of people who do physical work rather than working in offices.

> The word **blue-collar** for people who do certain kinds of jobs, such as factory work, comes from the idea that these workers would usually wear blue shirts on the job. People working in an office are said to be *white-collar* workers for a similar reason.

blue·fish [bloo-fish] *noun, plural* **bluefish** *or* **bluefishes.** a bluish saltwater fish that is caught for sport or food.

blue·grass [bloo-grass] *noun, plural* **bluegrasses.** a type of grass with bluish green stems.

blue jay ▶ a North American bird that has a crested head with bright blue feathering and some black and white markings. This term is also spelled **bluejay.**

blue jeans trousers made of a blue material called denim. This term is also spelled **bluejeans.**

blue·print [bloo-print] *noun, plural* **blueprints. 1.** a photographic print of a plan for a building or machine, on a special blue background with white lines: *The builder looked at the blueprints of the building before he started his work.* **2.** a detailed plan of action: *The mayor's plan provided the blueprint for rebuilding the area.*

blues [blooz] *plural noun.* **1.** feelings of sadness or low spiritedness. **2.** *Music.* an American style of popular music that often sounds sad because of its slow melody.

blue whale ▼ a blue-gray whale. It is considered to be the largest animal to have ever lived. It can grow up to 100 feet long and may weigh 150 tons or more.

bluff¹ [bluf] *noun, plural* **bluffs.** a steep headland or cliff.

bluff² [bluf] *verb,* **bluffed, bluffing.** to try to fool others by pretending to have strength, confidence, or knowledge: *She bluffed her dad into letting her drive the car by herself.*

noun, plural **bluffs.** an effort or attempt to fool people in this way, especially a strategy in card games of pretending to have a good hand when really one does not.

blun·der [blun-dur] *noun, plural* **blunders.** a careless or embarrassing mistake: *Kicking the ball into his own goal was a blunder.*
verb, **blundered, blundering. 1.** to make a careless or embarrassing mistake: *The general blundered in attacking the fort with such a small number of troops.* **2.** to move clumsily or unsteadily: *I blundered around in the kitchen while trying to find the light switch.*

blunt [blunt] *adjective,* **blunter, bluntest. 1.** not sharp: *The blunt knife wouldn't cut properly.* **2.** outspoken and insensitive to others' feelings: *His blunt words upset her.*
verb, **blunted, blunting.** to make less sharp.
—**bluntly,** *adverb;* —**bluntness,** *noun.*

blur [blur] *verb,* **blurred, blurring.** to make hard to see; make less clear: *The eyedrops blurred my vision.*
noun, plural **blurs.** something that is unclear or hard to see: *The racing car went by us so fast that it was just a blur.*

blurb [blurb] *noun, plural* **blurbs.** a short description of a book, film, or product, intended to make people want to buy or see it: *I read the blurb on the back cover of the book before deciding to purchase it.*

blurt [blurt] *verb,* **blurted, blurting.** to say something suddenly or without thought: *I was so excited, I blurted out the news even though it was supposed to be a secret.*

blush [blush] *verb,* **blushed, blushing.** to become red in the face when feeling embarrassed, ashamed, or shy: *Mike blushed when Mom asked who ate the cookies, so she knew he had done it.*
noun, plural **blushes.** a reddening of the face from embarrassment, shame, or shyness.

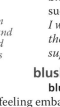

The **blue jay** *lives in southern Canada and the northern United States, but migrates south in winter.*

The **blue whale** *dwarfs all other mammals, and is twenty-six times as heavy as an African elephant.*

87

blus·ter [blus-tur] *verb*, **blustered, blustering. 1.** to blow violently or noisily: *The terrifying storm blustered for hours.* Something that blows in this way is **blustery**: *a blustery wind; a blustery spring day.* **2.** to speak loudly or in a threatening manner: *Our coach blustered from the sidelines when he saw we were losing.*
noun, plural **blusters. 1.** a violent and noisy blowing. **2.** loud or threatening talk.

bo·a constrictor ▼ [boh-uh] a large, non-poisonous snake found in South and Central America that kills its prey by wrapping around it and crushing it to death.

The **boa constrictor** *can grow to nearly twenty feet in length.*

boar [bore] *noun, plural* **boars.** a large, hairy wild pig found in woodlands in North and South America, Europe, and other parts of the world. 🔊) A different word with the same sound is **bore.**

board [bord] *noun, plural* **boards. 1.** a long, flat piece of lumber used for building houses, fences, and the like. **2.** a flat piece of wood or other material designed for a specific purpose: *She prepared the vegetables on the chopping board.* **3.** a group of people who are responsible for being in charge of something: *The members of the Environmental Board voted on the policy.* **4.** regular meals that are provided to guests for a payment. *She got a good price for room and board in the college dormitory.*
verb, **boarded, boarding. 1.** to cover or close with boards: *He boarded up the hole in the wall.* **2.** to pay for a room and regular meals: *The students boarded in a house near college for the first semester.* Someone who pays for a room and regular meals is a **boarder. 3.** to get on a train, bus, ship, or plane: *We boarded the bus for New York.*

boast [bohst] *verb,* **boasted, boasting. 1.** to speak with too much pride about yourself: *She boasted that she would get perfect marks on the test.* **2.** to be proud to be in possession of something: *The school boasts an astounding new technology building.*
noun, plural **boasts.** something that is spoken of with excessive pride: *a pitcher's boast that he could strike out every batter on the other team.* —**boastful,** *adjective.*

boat [bote] *noun, plural* **boats.** a small vehicle that can travel across water, used for carrying people or goods. **2.** a ship, such as a passenger liner. A building where boats are kept or stored is a **boathouse.**
verb, **boated, boating.** to ride or travel by boat: *We spent most of our summer vacation boating on the lake.* The act of riding in a boat is **boating.**

bob [bob] *verb,* **bobbed, bobbing. 1.** to move up and down quickly: *His backpack bobbed on his back as he ran for the bus.* **2.** to cut hair short so that it is neck-length all the way around the head.
noun, plural **bobs. 1.** a short, quick movement up and down: *She said hello to me with a bob of her head.* **2.** a short haircut for women where hair is cut to neck length all the way around the head. **3.** a small float for a fishing line, usually made of cork.

bob·bin [bob-in] *noun, plural* **bobbins.** a small, round, or tube-shaped object on which yarn or thread is wound to use for weaving or in a sewing machine.

bob·cat ▼ [bob-kat] *noun, plural* **bobcats.** a small, wild cat with a brownish coat, dark spots or stripes, and a short "bobbed" tail. It is found in North America.

The **bobcat** *may have been named for its short, stubby tail.*

bob·o·link [bob-uh-lingk] *noun, plural* **bobolinks.** a small American songbird that nests on the ground in open fields. It has a call that sounds something like its name.

bob·sled ▼ [bob-sled] *noun, plural* **bobsleds.** a long racing sled for two or more people. It has long metal blades and a steering mechanism and is built for racing down ice-covered tracks. The sport of riding or racing in such a sled is **bobsledding.**

bob·white [bob-wite] *noun, plural* **bobwhites.** a small North American quail that is hunted for sport. It has reddish-brown plumage and white markings.

bode [bode] *verb,* **boded, boding.** to be a sign of something for the future, especially something bad or unfavorable: *The rough winds bode disaster for our boat trip.*

bod·y [bod-ee] *noun, plural* **bodies. 1.** the entire physical structure of a person or animal. **2.** the main part of a person or animal without the head or limbs: *He had a muscled body, but thin arms and legs.* **3.** the main part or structure of something: *The body of the car needs repainting.* **4.** a group of people or things that are together for a particular purpose: *a body of troops.* **5.** a separate or distinct mass: *a body of water.* Something relating to the human body is **bodily**: *The car was badly damaged, but there was no bodily harm to the passengers.*

The **bobsled** *competition is one of the events at the Winter Olympic Games.*

bod·y·guard [bod-ee-*gard*] *noun, plural* **bodyguards.** someone whose job is to protect another person from danger or attack.

bog [bog] *noun, plural* **bogs.** an area of wet, muddy ground that sometimes contains bushes or grasses.
verb. **bog down.** to sink in or become stuck: *We couldn't leave the house because the truck was bogged down in the mud; Our plan became bogged down in too many details.*

boil¹ [boyle] *verb,* **boiled, boiling. 1.** to cause something to become so hot that bubbles form and steam is given off: *Mom put the kettle on to boil the water.* **2.** to cook in boiling liquid: *We had boiled vegetables as a side dish.*
noun. the condition or state of boiling: *Bring the sauce to the boil before pouring it over the meat.*

boil² [boyle] *noun, plural* **boils.** a painful, infected, swollen sore under the skin.

boil·er [boy-lur] *noun, plural* **boilers. 1.** a sealed container in which water is boiled and changed into steam, which is then used for heating or power.
2. a container with a lid that is used to heat or boil things.

boil·ing point 1. *Science.* the temperature at which a liquid boils and becomes a gas. The boiling point of water is 212 degrees Fahrenheit or 100 degrees Celsius. **2.** the point at which someone is about to lose their temper: *After waiting for the bus for forty minutes, I had reached boiling point.*

The B-25 Mitchell **bomber** *was used in World War II.*

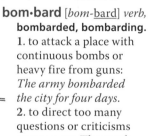

bois·ter·ous [boy-strus *or* boy-stur-us] *adjective.* rough and noisy; rowdy: *The boisterous crowd cheered on their team.* **—boisterously,** *adverb;* **—boisterousness,** *noun.*

bold [bohld] *adjective,* **bolder, boldest. 1.** not afraid of taking risks; brave or daring: *She made a bold leap across the rising floodwaters.* **2.** without respect; rude: *He was a bold and arrogant young man.* **3.** standing out in a noticeable way; clear: *They painted the house in bright, bold colors.*
noun. the shortened form of BOLDFACE. **—boldly,** *adverb;* **—boldness,** *noun.*

bold·face [bohld-*fase*] *noun. Language.* a type of print that is used to make the letters thicker and darker than normal. **This sentence is in boldface.**

boll [bohl] *noun, plural* **bolls.** the capsule-like part of the cotton plant that contains the seeds.
🔊 A different word with the same sound is **bowl.**

boll wee·vil a small, grayish beetle of Mexico and the southern United States that eats and destroys cotton plants.

bo·lo·gna [buh-<u>loh</u>-nee *or* buh-<u>loh</u>-nyuh] *noun, plural* **bolognas.** a smoked sausage made from beef, pork, and veal. This lunchmeat is also called **baloney.**

The word **bologna** comes from Bologna, a very old and important city of northern Italy. Bologna is famous for its food (dishes in the style of Bologna are known as "Bolognese"). One such famous food was *Bologna sausage,* which was the original form of the bologna eaten in the U.S. today.

bol·ster [bowl-stur] *verb,* **bolstered, bolstering.** to support or improve something: *The nice compliment bolstered my confidence level.*
noun, plural **bolsters. 1.** a long, firm pillow shaped like a tube. **2.** something that supports.

bolt ◀ [bohlt] *noun, plural* **bolts. 1.** a thick metal rod that looks like a screw without a pointed end, used with a nut to hold something in place. **2.** a bar that slides across a door or gate to fasten it: *I shut the gate and drew the bolt firmly.* **3.** the part of a lock that moves when a key turns in it. **4.** a flash of lightning. **5.** a roll of cloth or wallpaper.
verb, **bolted, bolting. 1.** to fasten two things together with a bolt. **2.** to move suddenly or rapidly: *She bolted out the door after him.* **3.** to eat food very quickly: *He bolted his lunch and got a stomach ache afterward.*

bomb [hom] *noun, plural* **bombs.** a container filled with an explosive that is used as a weapon to hurt or kill people and damage property.
verb, **bombed, bombing.** to attack with bombs.

bom·bard [bom-<u>bard</u>] *verb,* **bombarded, bombarding. 1.** to attack a place with continuous bombs or heavy fire from guns: *The army bombarded the city for four days.* **2.** to direct too many questions or criticisms at someone: *The coach was bombarded with questions from reporters about why his team lost so badly.* **—bombardment,** *noun.*

bomb·er ▲ [bom-ur] *noun, plural* **bombers.** a military aircraft used to drop bombs.

bon·a fide [boh-nuh-<u>fyde</u> *or* boh-nuh-<u>fye</u>-dee] **1.** made in good faith; sincere: *He made a bona fide offer to buy the house.* **2.** true or real; authentic: *Only bone fide members know the secret handshake.*

bo·nan·za [buh-<u>nan</u>-zuh] *noun, plural* **bonanzas. 1.** a rich mineral deposit. **2.** a lucky or successful situation that brings good fortune or wealth: *The show was a box-office bonanza.*

bond [bond] *noun, plural* **bonds. 1.** something that binds or fastens together: *The glue will act as a bond to hold the two pieces of wood together.* **2.** a close connection or understanding that holds people together: *They had a lifelong bond of friendship.* **3.** *Business.* an official document given by a government or company as a promise that it will pay back money that it has borrowed, with interest paid to the lender.
verb, **bonded, bonding.** to attach firmly; bind.

bond·age [bon-dij] *noun.* the state of being a slave. *The Bible tells of how the Jewish people were held in bondage by the Egyptians.*

bone ▼ [bone] *noun, plural* **bones.** one of the hard parts that makes up the skeleton of a human, animal, or fish. Bones support the body and protect internal organs.
verb, **boned, boning.** to remove the bones from something: *She would eat the fish only once it had been boned.*

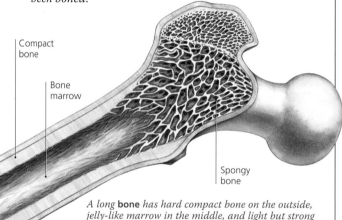

Compact bone

Bone marrow

Spongy bone

A long **bone** *has hard compact bone on the outside, jelly-like marrow in the middle, and light but strong spongy bone at the end.*

bon·fire [bon-fire] *noun, plural* **bonfires.** a large, controlled outdoor fire: *Our camp leader showed us how to build a real bonfire.*

The word **bonfire** once meant "bone fire." It goes back to a time when people made large fires by burning the bones of cattle, sheep, and other farm animals.

bon·go drums [bong-goh] *Music.* a pair of small drums that are held between the knees and played with the fingers.

bon·net [bon-it] *noun, plural* **bonnets. 1.** a close-fitted hat that is tied under the chin with ribbon or string: *I bought a cute pink bonnet for the new baby.* **2.** a headdress made of feathers worn by North American Indians on special occasions.

bon·sai ▶ [bon-sye] *noun, plural* **bonsai. 1.** a very small tree that is kept from getting bigger by continually cutting back the roots and branches. **2.** a tree or shrub that is grown using this method.

bo·nus [boh-nus] *noun, plural* **bonuses.** extra money paid to a worker, in addition to their usual pay, as a reward for good work: *The car salesman is supposed to sell ten cars this month and will get a bonus if he sells fifteen.*

bon·y [boh-nee] *adjective,* **bonier, boniest. 1.** of or relating to bone: *The body has a bony structure.* **2.** full of bones: *a bony piece of fish.* **3.** very thin or scrawny: *She was tall and lean with long, bony fingers*

boo [boo] *interjection.* an expression, usually shouted, used to frighten someone: *I screamed when he appeared out of nowhere and yelled "Boo!".*
verb, **booed, booing.** to express strong disapproval: *The crowd booed when they thought the umpire made a bad call against their team.*

boo·by-trap [boo-bee-*trap*] *noun, plural* **booby-traps.** something dangerous, like a bomb, that is hidden, and triggered by touching something connected with it: *The booby-trap exploded when he accidentally tripped over the wire.*
verb, **booby-trapped, booby-trapping.** to set up something dangerous like a hidden bomb: *He booby-trapped the car.*

book [buk] *noun, plural* **books. 1.** sheets of paper bound together between two covers to be read or written on. **2.** one of the parts making up a larger printed work: *The Bible is divided into many different books.*
verb, **booked, booking.** to arrange to have something at a particular time: *We booked two tickets to the show for Friday night.*
• **by the book.** in the correct way; by the rules: *The police went by the book when they arrested him and made sure to tell him his legal rights.*

book·kee·per [buk-kee-pur] *noun, plural* **bookkeepers.** *Business.* someone who records the sales, payments, and other transactions of a business: *The bookkeeper compiled a detailed report of the store's profits this month.* The practice of recording the transactions of a business is **bookkeeping.**

book·let [buk-lit] *noun, plural* **booklets.** a thin book with a small number of pages and a paper cover.

book·mark [buk-mark] *noun, plural* **bookmarks.** a piece of card, leather, or plastic placed between the pages of a book so that the reader can find their place again.

book·worm [buk-wurm] *noun, plural* **bookworms.** a person who loves reading.

boom¹ [boom] *noun, plural* **booms. 1.** a deep and loud hollow sound: *the boom of a cannon.* **2.** a time of fast growth or prosperity: *There was a boom in umbrella sales after the first day of heavy rain.*
verb, **boomed, booming. 1.** to make a deep and loud hollow sound. **2.** to grow and increase rapidly: *Tourism boomed during summer.*

boom² [boom] *noun, plural* **booms. 1.** a long pole on a boat that is attached to the bottom of a sail, used to change the position of the sail. **2.** a long, movable arm on a crane that is used to load and unload things.

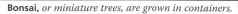

Bonsai, *or miniature trees, are grown in containers.*

boom·er·ang ▶
[boom-uh-*rang*] *noun,*
plural **boomerangs.** a curved stick that when thrown in a particular way, returns to the thrower.

Boomerang is a word that came into English from the native peoples of Australia. It is thought that they had used the boomerang as a weapon for hundreds of years, but there was no English word for it until about 1800, because no English speaker had ever seen one before that.

boon [boon] *noun, plural* **boons.** a great help or advantage: *The new bus service is a boon to me, since I don't own a car.*

boost [boost] *noun, plural* **boosts. 1.** an upward push: *He gave me a boost to climb over the fence.* **2.** the act of giving praise or encouragement: *The coach's talk at halftime gave us a real boost for the second half.* *verb,* **boosted, boosting. 1.** to give an upward push. **2.** to give praise or encouragement. **3.** to increase or improve something: *The new advertisements boosted sales.* Someone who helps something to increase or improve is a **booster**: *The high school football team has a Booster Club that raised money to buy new uniforms.*

boot [boot] *noun, plural* **boots.** a shoe that covers the foot and the lower part of the leg. *verb,* **booted, booting.** to kick: *He booted the ball down the field.*

booth [booth] *noun, plural* **booths. 1.** a small stall where goods are displayed or sold: *The crafts booth was very popular.* **2.** a small, closed-in place usually only big enough for one person: *a polling booth.*

boot·y ▼ [boot-ee] *noun, plural* **booties.** anything taken from people by force, especially in time of war: *The thieves divided their booty of cash and gold.*

bor·der [bore-dur] *noun, plural* **borders. 1.** a line or boundary that separates one country or area from another. **2.** the edge or side of something: *The tablecloth had a lace border.* *verb,* **bordered, bordering. 1.** to lie next to or on the edge of: *Canada borders the United States.* **2.** to form an edging on something: *The farm was bordered by trees.*
♦ **border on.** to resemble or come close to: *That comment is very insulting and borders on racism.*

bore¹ [bore] *verb,* **bored, boring. 1.** to form by digging or drilling into: *The prisoners bored a tunnel through the solid rock.* **2.** to make a hole in: *The drill bored a hole through the piece of wood.* A tool used for drilling is a **borer.**
🔊 A different word with the same sound is **boar.**

bore² [bore] *verb,* **bored, boring.** to act or talk in a way that makes others lose interest: *The new teacher bored us with her long stories.* *noun, plural* **bores.** someone or something that is uninteresting or dull: *I thought the book was a real bore and put it aside after reading one chapter.* The condition of being uninterested is **boredom.**
🔊 A different word with the same sound is **boar.**

bore³ [bore] *verb.* the past tense of BEAR.
🔊 A different word with the same sound is **boar.**

bor·ing [bore-ing] *adjective.* not interesting or exciting: *The party was so boring we left early.* —**boringly,** *adverb.*

born [born] *adjective.* **1.** brought forth into life. **2.** having a strong natural ability: *a born entertainer.* *verb.* a past participle of BEAR.
🔊 A different word with the same sound is **borne.**

born-again [born-uh-gen] *adjective; noun. Religion.* describing someone who has become an evangelical Christian, especially after a spiritual experience. A large number of American Christians refer to themselves as born-again Christians or born-agains. This came from a saying in the Bible that a person must be born again to enter the kingdom of Heaven.

borne [born] *verb.* a past participle of BEAR.
🔊 A different word with the same sound is **born.**

bor·ough [bur-oh] *noun, plural* **boroughs. 1.** a town or part of a town. **2.** one of the five divisions of New York City.
🔊 Different words with the same sound are **burro** and **burrow.**

When ancient Rome was conquered in the fifth century, the barbarians carried off all kinds of valuable **booty** *from buildings and temples.*

bor·row [bor-oh] *verb*, **borrowed, borrowing. 1.** to take something from another with the intention of giving it back: *I borrowed my sister's shoes for the party.* **2.** to take and use a word or idea: *I borrowed the idea for my story from a movie I saw.* —**borrower**, *noun*.

bos·om [buz-um] *noun, plural* **bosoms.** the front part of the chest: *She held the child to her bosom.* *adjective.* describing something beloved; dear: *We are bosom buddies.*

boss [boss] *noun, plural* **bosses.** someone who controls a business and directs others to work. Someone who tells others what to do is described as **bossy.** *verb,* **bossed, bossing.** to direct others to do things: *My older sister always bosses me around.*

bot·a·ny [bot-uh-nee] *noun. Biology.* the scientific study of plants. Someone who studies plants is a **botanist.** Having to do with the study of plants is **botanical.**

both [bowth] *adjective.* referring to two people or things together: *Both girls have brown hair.* *pronoun.* the one and the other: *Both of us were late.* *conjunction.* alike; equally: *Both teachers and students complained about the rule.*

both·er [boTH-ur] *verb,* **bothered, bothering. 1.** to cause trouble for; to annoy or pester: *It bothers me that he always forgets my birthday.* **2.** to make the effort: *I won't bother making my bed today because I'm going to change the sheets later.* *noun, plural* **bothers.** something or someone that annoys or pesters: *Our new neighbor is a bit of a bother.*

bot·tle [bot-ul] *noun, plural* **bottles.** a container with a narrow neck, usually made of glass or plastic, used to hold liquids. *verb,* **bottled, bottling.** to place in a bottle: *to bottle wine.* • **bottle up.** to hold in or to hide: *Jane bottled up her true feelings.*

bot·tle·neck [bot-ul-nek] *noun, plural* **bottlenecks. 1.** a place in a road that narrows, causing the traffic to slow down: *The roadworks caused a major bottleneck this morning.* **2.** anything that slows movement or progress in this way.

bot·tom [bot-um] *noun, plural* **bottoms. 1.** the lowest part or place: *The ball rolled down to the bottom of the stairs.* **2.** the solid surface under a body of water: *the bottom of the ocean.* **3.** the basic cause; fundamental part: *The detective looked everywhere for clues, determined to get to the bottom of the mystery.* *adjective.* in the lowest place or position: *His apartment is on the bottom floor of the building.* If something seems to be without a limit or end, it is said to be **bottomless:** *a bottomless pit that appeared to reach to the center of the Earth.*

*The Devil's Marbles are granite **boulders** in the Australian desert.*

bough [bow] *noun, plural* **boughs.** one of the large branches of a tree. 🔊 Different words with the same sound are **bow**¹ and **bow**³.

bought [bawt] *verb.* the past tense and past participle of BUY.

boul·der ▲ [bowl-dur] *noun, plural* **boulders.** a very large rock that sits on the ground or partly above ground.

boul·e·vard ▼ [bull-uh-*vard*] *noun, plural* **boulevards.** a wide city street lined with trees.

bounce [bouns] *verb,* **bounced, bouncing. 1.** to spring back after impact: *The ball bounced on the sidewalk.* **2.** to throw something and cause it to spring back: *I bounced the ball all the way to school.* *noun, plural* **bounces.** springing movement.

*Norwegians parade down a **boulevard** in Oslo on May 17 to celebrate their national day.*

bound¹ [bound] *adjective.* **1.** not free; tied up: *The hostage had bound hands.* **2.** certain or very likely to happen: *We are bound to get in trouble if we get caught.* **3.** having a duty or obligation: *I felt bound to tell the police the truth.* *verb.* the past tense and past participle of BIND.

bound² [bound] *verb,* **bounded, bounding. 1.** to move quickly up into the air; to leap; jump: *The excited dog came bounding toward its owner.* **2.** to bounce back: *The ball bounded off the tree and landed in the street.* *noun, plural* **bounds.** a leap or jump.

bound³ [bound] *verb,* **bounded, bounding.** to form the border or boundary of: *The town is bounded on the west by the Pacific Ocean.* *noun, plural* **bounds.** the limit or boundary of something.

bound⁴ [bound] *adjective.* headed toward; intending to go: *The plane is bound for San Francisco.*

bound·a·ry [boun-dree *or* boun-duh-ree] *noun, plural* **boundaries.** a real or imagined line that marks the edge of a country, state, or other area: *The Hudson River marks the boundary between the states of New York and New Jersey.*

bounds [boundz] *plural noun.* boundaries or limits: *the bounds of the school yard; Our happiness knew no bounds.* When people are forbidden to enter a particular area it is **out of bounds.** In sport, inside or outside the legal playing area is **in bounds** or **out of bounds.**

boun·ti·ful [boun-tuh-ful] *adjective.* more than enough; plentiful: *The party had a bountiful supply of food.* —**bountifully,** *adverb.*

boun·ty [boun-tee] *noun, plural* **bounties.** **1.** a reward or payment given for killing a predatory or destructive animal. **2.** generosity; kindness: *The success of the fundraiser is dependent on the community's bounty.*

bou·quet [boh-kaye *or* boo-kaye] *noun, plural* **bouquets.** a bunch of flowers.

bout [bowt] *noun, plural* **bouts. 1.** a fight or struggle: *The two boxers fought a title bout to see who would be the world champion.* **2.** a certain period of time, especially a time of struggle: *I have just recovered from a bout of flu.*

bou·tique [boo-teek] *noun, plural* **boutiques.** a small, fashionable shop or business: *My sister bought a dress for her prom at the boutique in the mall.*

bow¹ [bow] *verb,* **bowed, bowing. 1.** to bend forward from the waist to show respect, obedience, or thanks: *When the Queen entered the room the man stood up and bowed to her.* **2.** to give in to; submit: *Even though I didn't agree, I had to bow to my teacher's wishes.*
noun, plural **bows.** a bending forward: *The actors took several bows when the audience clapped and cheered.*
 A different word with the same sound is **bough.**

bow² ▶ [boh] *noun, plural* **bows. 1.** a strip of wood or other material bent by a string attached to each end, used for shooting arrows. **2.** a piece of ribbon, paper, or string with two or more loops: *She wore a red bow in her hair.* **3.** *Music.* a long, thin piece of wood with horsehairs stretched from end to end, used to play musical instruments such as the violin or cello.

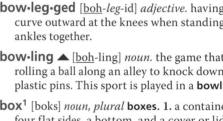

*Buryat archers in Siberia, Russia, once used **bows** made of wood, sheep's horn, and sinew.*

bow³ [bow] *noun, plural* **bows.** the front section of a boat.
 A different word with the same sound is **bough.**

bow·el [bow-ul] *noun, plural* **bowels. 1.** the digestive system below the stomach; the part where food is turned into waste before it is passed out of the body. **2.** the lowest or deepest part of something: *The stowaway hid in the bowels of the ship.*

bowl¹ [bohl] *noun, plural* **bowls. 1.** a wide, round dish that is used to hold or store something, especially food: *a soup bowl; a salad bowl.* **2.** a rounded, hollow part that is shaped like a bowl: *a toilet bowl.* **3.** a large, rounded stadium for football and other events: *Many famous musical shows have been held at the Hollywood Bowl.* **4.** a special football game played after the regular season is over: *The championship of pro football is called the Super Bowl.*
 A different word with the same sound is **boll.**

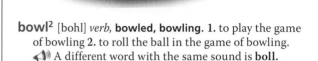

*In **bowling,** the aim is to knock down all the pins with one ball.*

bowl² [bohl] *verb,* **bowled, bowling. 1.** to play the game of bowling **2.** to roll the ball in the game of bowling.
 A different word with the same sound is **boll.**

bow·leg·ged [boh-leg-id] *adjective.* having legs that curve outward at the knees when standing with the ankles together.

bow·ling ▲ [boh-ling] *noun.* the game that is played by rolling a ball along an alley to knock down wooden or plastic pins. This sport is played in a **bowling alley.**

box¹ [boks] *noun, plural* **boxes. 1.** a container, usually with four flat sides, a bottom, and a cover or lid, often made of a stiff material such as cardboard, wood, or plastic. **2.** an area of a theater or court that is separate from where most people sit.
verb, **boxed, boxing.** to put into a box: *After Christmas we boxed up the lights from the Christmas tree.*

box² [boks] *noun, plural* **boxes.** a punch to the head with the closed hand or fist: *When I ignored him, my brother gave me a box on the ear.*
verb, **boxed, boxing. 1.** to hit someone with the closed hand or fist. **2.** to fight with someone as a sport.

box·er [boks-ur] *noun, plural* **boxers. 1.** a person who fights with the closed hand or fist as a sport. **2.** a medium-sized dog with a wide face, flat nose, and short, light brown hair.

box·ing [boks-ing] *noun.* the sport of fighting with closed hands or fists.

Boxing Day the day after Christmas Day. It is a holiday in Great Britain, Canada, Australia, and many other countries.

box office the place in a theater, cinema, or sports stadium where tickets are sold.

The holiday of **Boxing Day** has nothing to do with the sport of boxing, but comes from the custom of giving people gifts in boxes on this day.

A B C D E F G H I J K L M N O P Q R S T U V W X Y Z

boy [boy] *noun, plural* **boys.** a male child from birth to the time he becomes an adult.

boy·cott [boy-kot] *verb,* **boycotted, boycotting.** to refuse to buy or use something, or deal with a person, company, or country as a way of protesting: *We decided to boycott all products made in countries where workers are not paid a proper wage.*
noun, plural **boycotts.** a plan or arrangement in which people join together to refuse to buy or use something, or deal with a person, company, or country.

In 1880 Captain Charles C. *Boycott* was a manager of land in Ireland. The Irish people who farmed the land asked Captain Boycott to lower their rents, but he would not do this. So the people all got together and agreed not to talk to Captain Boycott or to have anything to do with him. Stores would not sell to him, and his mail was not even delivered. It was said that these actions against him were a **boycott.**

boy·friend [boy-frend] *noun, plural* **boyfriends. 1.** a young male friend. **2.** a young man or boy that a girl or woman is having a romantic relationship with.

boy·hood [boy-hood] *noun, plural* **boyhoods.** the time of being a boy.

boy·ish [boy-ish] *adjective.* behaving or looking like a boy: *boyish good looks.* —**boyishly,** *adverb;* —**boyishness,** *noun.*

Boy Scouts ▼ an organization for boys started in England in 1907 to promote physical fitness, spiritual values, outdoor skills, and citizenship. A **boy scout** is a member of the Boy Scouts.

brace [brays] *noun, plural* **braces. 1.** something that strengthens or supports, holds together, or makes stiff: *After she was injured in a car accident, she had to wear a neck brace.* **2.** the handle part of a tool that holds a drill or bit. **3.** two things of the same type: *a brace of pistols.*
verb, **braced, bracing. 1.** to hold something steady by supporting it. **2.** to prepare for something unpleasant that is going to happen: *Brace yourself before I tell you the result of your test.* **3.** to give energy; refresh: *The cold night air was bracing.*

brac·es [brays-iz] *noun.* **1.** a system of metal wires worn on the teeth to make them grow straight. **2.** another name for SUSPENDERS.

brack·et [brak-it] *noun, plural* **brackets 1.** piece of metal, wood, or plastic, fixed to a wall to support something: *The candle sat on a shelf that was held up by two brackets.* **2.** one of the pair of signs, [ ], put around words to show extra information. **3.** a group into which similar things can be placed; category; range: *John's salary puts him in the highest income bracket.*
verb, **bracketed, bracketing. 1.** to put brackets around words or numbers. **2.** to put into groups: *The fastest swimmers were bracketed together for the final race.*

Brackets used in writing look like this: [ ]. The bracket should only be used for special forms of writing (one example is the pronunciation of words in this dictionary). The usual way to enclose words in a sentence is not brackets but parentheses ( ), as in the sentence before this one.

brag [brag] *verb,* **bragged, bragging.** to talk too proudly about what you have done, or how much you own; boast. Someone who brags a lot is called a **braggart.**

Each character in **Braille** *is based on a space and six dots.*

braid [brayd] *noun, plural* **braids.** a narrow band formed by winding or weaving together three or more strands of hair, silk, cotton, or other material: *Mary wears her hair in braids.*
verb, **braided, braiding.** to make a braid: *She braided her hair and tied it up with ribbons.*

Braille ▲ [brayl] *noun. Language.* a way of printing for blind people. They can read by touching raised dots on the paper with their fingers. This word is also spelled **braille.**

The **Braille** alphabet was invented in France in 1821 by Louis *Braille.* He was known as an outstanding teacher of blind people, even though he himself had been blind since he was a very young child.

BOY SCOUTS

The Boy Scouts movement was started by British cavalry officer Robert (later Lord) Baden-Powell and now exists all over the world in more than 200 countries. Scouts learn skills that are needed in camping and other outdoor activities. They also must promise to be loyal to their country, to help others, and to obey simple rules of behavior. The Boy Scouts' motto is "Be prepared."

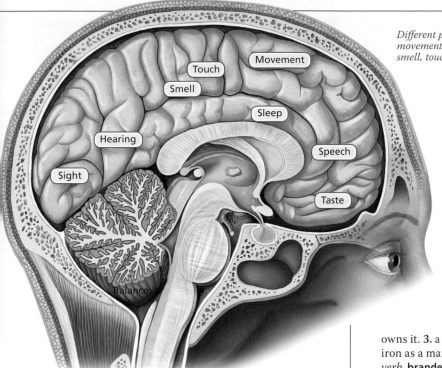

Touch
Movement
Smell
Sleep
Hearing
Speech
Sight
Taste
Balance

Different parts of the **brain** *control our speech, movement, and sleep, as well as our senses of sight, smell, touch, hearing, and taste.*

branch [branch] *noun, plural* **branches.** **1.** a part of a tree that grows out from the main trunk. **2.** a smaller part that leads away from the main body of something: *Pediatrics is the branch of medicine dealing with the health of children.* **3.** a part of a larger organization: *There is a branch of the Bank of America in our suburb.* *verb,* **branched, branching.** to divide from the main part: *A side road branched off from the main highway.*

brand [brand] *noun, plural* **brands.** **1.** a particular name or design of a product: *I'm wearing a new brand of jeans.* **2.** a mark made or burned on an animal's skin to show who owns it. **3.** a mark once put on criminals with a hot iron as a mark of disgrace. *verb,* **branded, branding. 1.** to mark with a brand: *The calves were branded today.* **2.** to describe something as bad or shameful: *It is very unfair to brand all teenagers as lazy.*

brand-new [brand-<u>noo</u>] *adjective.* new and not used: *a brand-new car that has only been driven 120 miles.*

bran·dy [<u>bran</u>-dee] *noun, plural* **brandies.** a strong alcoholic drink made from fermented grapes or other fruits.

brass ▼ [brass] *noun.* **1.** a hard, bright yellow metal that is an alloy of copper and zinc. **2. brasses.** musical instruments made of metal, such as the trumpet, trombone, and French horn.

brat [brat] *noun, plural* **brats.** a badly behaved child.

brave [brave] *adjective* **braver, bravest.** ready to face danger; having no fear; courageous: *The brave firefighter rushed into the burning house to save the family trapped there.* *verb,* **braved, braving.** to deal with a dangerous situation without fear: *Two lifeguards braved the rough waves and rescued a swimmer.* —**bravely,** *adverb.*

brav·er·y [<u>brave</u>-ree *or* <u>brave</u>-uh-ree] *noun.* the ability to be brave; courage: *The soldier was awarded a medal for his bravery during the battle.* A false sense of being brave is **bravado.**

brain ▲ [brane] *noun, plural* **brains. 1.** the large organ inside the head that controls how a person thinks, feels, and moves. It is the main part of the central nervous system in humans and animals. A **brainy** person can think quickly and clearly; a **brainless** person is foolish or stupid. **2. brains.** intelligence: *If you had any brains, you could solve this problem.* *verb,* **brained, braining.** to hit on the head: *He annoyed me so much I wanted to brain him.*

brain·storm [<u>brane</u>-storm] *noun, plural* **brainstorms.** inspiration; a sudden, clever idea.

brain·wash [<u>brane</u>-*wahsh*] *verb,* **brainwashed, brainwashing. 1.** to make someone believe something that is not true, by confusing or torturing the person: *The prisoner was brainwashed into making broadcasts attacking his own country.* **2.** to persuade or convince in an unfair way: *TV ads can brainwash you into wanting to buy something you don't really need.* —**brainwashing,** *noun.*

brake [brake] *noun, plural* **brakes.** equipment that makes a vehicle go more slowly or stop; often friction is used to slow a moving wheel. *verb,* **braked, braking.** to use a brake to make something slow down or stop: *The driver braked as he came to the stop sign.* 🔊 A different word with the same sound is **break.**

bram·ble [<u>bram</u>-bul] *noun, plural* **brambles.** a prickly bush or vine, such as the blackberry.

bran [bran] *noun.* the outer skin of wheat or similar grains. It is separated from the rest of the grain when making white flour and used in breakfast cereals and other foods.

The trumpet has the highest pitch of all the **brass.**

*A windsurfer rides a **breaker** into the shore.*

bra·vo [brah-voh *or* bra-voh] *interjection.* a word used when someone, especially a performer, has done something very well: *The audience clapped loudly and shouted "Bravo!" after the singer finished her performance.*
noun, plural **bravos.** a shout of approval.

braz·en [bray-zun] *adjective.* **1.** made of brass.
2. not embarrassed by one's own bad behavior: *When he got away with telling lies, he became more brazen.*
verb, **brazened, brazening.** to face a situation boldly: *You can admit you lied, or try to brazen it out.* —**brazenly,** *adverb.*

breach [breech] *noun, plural* **breaches.** a break or tear: *The breach in the levee let the water flood the town.*
verb, **breached, breaching.** to break a hole in something; to break through.

bread [bred] *noun, plural* **breads. 1.** food made from flour and water or milk, and baked. **2.** what a person needs for basic living: *I work to earn my daily bread.*
🔊 A different word with the same sound is **bred.**

breadth [bredth] *noun.* the distance from one side of something to the other; width.

break [brayk] *verb,* **broke, broken, breaking. 1.** to separate or smash something into two or more pieces: *That glass will break if you drop it.* **2.** to fracture a bone in the body: *She tripped over the cat and broke her hip.* **3.** to damage something so that it does not work: *He broke the clothes dryer when he left the motor on too long and it overheated.* **4.** to fail to keep or obey: *She broke her word when she promised to help me but didn't.* **5.** to do better than; exceed: *He broke the world record by one second.*
✚ **Break** has many other uses with the idea of a sudden changing or coming apart, such as: *to break some bad news to a person; to break someone's heart with cruel behavior; to break the habit of smoking.*
noun, plural **breaks. 1.** a place where something has come apart or come into pieces: *X-rays showed a break in the bone; Be careful not to fall through that break in the ice.* **2.** a brief stop or rest: *At 10.30 each morning we have a break when people can stop work for fifteen minutes.*
✚ **Break** has other uses with the idea of a sudden change: *He got a lucky break when he struck out, but the catcher missed the third strike; The prisoners attempted a jail break.*
🔊 A different word with the same sound is **brake.**

break·down [brayk-down] *noun, plural* **breakdowns. 1.** a time when something stops working: *We were late because the car had a breakdown on the freeway.* **2.** a loss of physical or mental health: *When she lost her job and her father died, she had a mental breakdown.*
verb. **break down. 1.** to stop working properly: *Dad was in the middle of mowing the lawn when the lawn mower broke down.* **2.** to collapse physically, emotionally, or mentally: *She broke down when she heard the news that her family had been killed.*

break·er ▲ [brayk-ur] *noun, plural* **breakers.** a large wave that curls over and foams as it breaks on the shore.

> The word **breakfast** comes from the phrase "to break the fast." A fast is a time of not eating, and breakfast "breaks the fast" by being the first food eaten after a time of not eating during the night.

break·fast [brek-fust] *noun, plural* **breakfasts.** the first meal that is eaten in the day, usually in the early morning.
verb, **breakfasted, breakfasting.** to have breakfast: *He breakfasted on a bowl of cereal.*

break·through [brake-throo] *noun, plural* **breakthroughs.** something that happens, often suddenly, that removes a block or barrier: *After years of looking for a cure for the disease, scientists had a sudden breakthrough.*

break·up [brake-up] *noun, plural* **breakups.** a time when something falls apart: *The breakup of her marriage made her feel sad; Many independent nations were formed after the breakup of the Soviet Union.*
verb. **break up. 1.** to come apart; disperse: *When he rang from his cell phone, the sound kept breaking up.* **2.** to come to an end; finish: *He was very sad when his marriage broke up.*

break·water [brake-wah-tur] *noun, plural* **breakwaters.** a barrier that is built out into the sea to stop or control the force of the waves.

breast [brest] *noun, plural* **breasts. 1.** the front part of the body between the neck and stomach; chest. **2.** one of the two organs of a female mammal that produce milk after she gives birth.

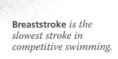

Breaststroke is the slowest stroke in competitive swimming.

breast·bone [brest-bone] *noun, plural* **breastbones.** the long, thin bone in the middle of the chest; the top seven pairs of ribs are connected to it.

breast·stroke ◀ [brest-stroke] *noun.* a swimming stroke made face-down in which both hands are pushed forward and then brought back in a half circle.

breath [breth] *noun, plural* **breaths. 1.** the air that moves in and out of your lungs when you breathe: *It was so cold that we could see our breath in the night air.* **2.** the act of breathing; respiration: *Hold your breath underwater.* **3.** the ability to breathe freely: *He was out of breath after running up the hill.* **4.** a light current of air: *It was so hot, there wasn't a breath of fresh air.*

breathe [breeTH] *verb,* **breathed, breathing. 1.** to move air in and out of your lungs. **2.** to say something quietly: *It's a secret, so don't breathe a word to anyone.*

breath·er [breeTH-ur] *noun, plural* **breathers. 1.** a short rest: *We had to take a breather after all that exercise.* **2.** someone who breathes.

breath·less [breth-lis] *adjective.* **1.** finding it hard to breathe: *After climbing all those stairs, I was breathless.* **2.** breathing lightly because of being excited or afraid: *We were breathless with fear when we watched the horror movie.* —**breathlessly,** *adverb.*

breech·es ▶ [brich-iz *or* breech-iz] *plural noun.* a kind of knee-length trousers, usually worn by men and boys in earlier times. **Britches** is an old-fashioned word for trousers.

breed ▼ [breed] *verb,* **bred, breeding. 1.** to raise plants or animals: *My cousin breeds cattle on his farm.* **2.** to produce young; give birth: *Many wild animals breed in the spring.* **3.** to create a certain condition: *Dirty, crowded living conditions can breed disease; His great wealth may breed jealousy among his friends.* *noun, plural* **breeds.** a distinct kind of thing: *Greyhounds are a breed of racing dog.*

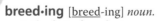

The collie is a Scottish **breed** of dog, while the Siamese cat is from Asia.

breed·ing [breed-ing] *noun.* **1.** the fact of producing young animals or plants. **2.** the way you are brought up: *He is so polite it is obvious he is of good breeding.* A person who raises animals or plants is a **breeder.**

breeze [breez] *noun, plural* **breezes.** a light wind. *verb,* **breezed, breezing.** to do something very easily: *He was so confident, he breezed through the exam.* It is a **breezy** day when the wind is strong.

breth·ren [breTH-run] *plural noun.* members of an organization; usually men; often a religious group: *The Plymouth Brethren were among the early European settlers of New England.*

Breeches *are worn by male musicians in traditional German brass bands.*

brew [broo] *verb,* **brewed, brewing. 1.** to make beer from water, hops, and malt. **2.** to make tea or coffee: *I brewed a fresh pot of coffee.* **3.** to start to form: *A storm is brewing; An argument is brewing over the plans to build a large mall next to the park.* Beer and ale are made in a **brewery.**

briar [brye-ur] *noun, plural* **briars.** a plant or shrub that is covered in prickles or thorns, such as the blackberry or raspberry.

bribe [brybe] *noun, plural* **bribes.** *Law.* money or gifts given to someone to persuade them do something they don't want to do, or to do something illegal. *verb,* **bribed, bribing.** to give someone a bribe: *The dishonest businessman tried to bribe the manager into giving a valuable contract to his company.* **Bribery** is the act of giving someone money illegally in this way.

bric-a-brac [brik-uh-*brak*] *noun.* small ornamental articles that are worth little money but are attractive and interesting.

brick [brik] *noun, plural* **bricks.** a block of baked clay used in building.

bride [bryde] *noun, plural* **brides.** a woman who is about to be married, or has just been married. **Bridal** refers to something having to do with a bride. A **bridesmaid** is a young, usually unmarried woman who helps a bride with her wedding.

bride·groom [bryde-*groom*] *noun, plural* **bridegrooms.** a man who is about to, or has just been, married.

bridge ▼ [brij] *noun, plural* **bridges. 1.** a structure built over a river, road, or railway track to let people or vehicles cross from one side to the other. **2.** the part of the nose between the eyes. **3.** the raised part of a ship from which the officers control it. *verb,* **bridged, bridging. 1.** to build a bridge across: *to bridge a deep canyon.* **2.** to act as a connection between two things: *I need to borrow a little money to bridge the gap until I get my next paycheck.*

The stone Rialto **bridge** *in Venice, Italy, was built across the Grand Canal in 1591.*

bri·dle ▼ [brye-dul] *noun, plural* **bridles.** a device made of leather straps used for controlling a horse. It fits over the horse's head, and includes a bit and a pair of reins. *verb,* **bridled, bridling. 1.** to put a bridle on a horse. **2.** to keep under control; restrain: *He needs to bridle his angry outbursts.*

A horse's **bridle** *holds a bit, which rests on the sensitive places between its teeth.*

brief [breef] *adjective,* **briefer, briefest.** lasting a short time; short in time or length: *We made a brief visit to my aunt on our way to the beach; Just before the game, the coach gave us a few brief instructions. verb,* **briefed, briefing.** to give important information that is needed to do or decide something: *The governor was briefed on the damage done by the hurricane before she visited the area. noun, plural* **briefs.** *Law.* an official statement or summary of the facts to be presented in a court case. —**briefly,** *adverb.*

brief·case [breef-kase] *noun, plural* **briefcases.** a flat case used for carrying books or papers.

bri·er [brye-ur] another spelling of BRIAR.

brig [brig] *noun, plural* **brigs. 1.** a ship with two masts and square sails. **2.** *Law.* a ship's prison.

bri·gade [bri-gayde] *noun, plural* **brigades. 1.** a large body of troops; an army unit of at least two battalions. **2.** a group of people formed for a particular purpose: *a fire brigade.*

bright [brite] *adjective,* **brighter, brightest. 1.** giving off or showing a lot of light; shining: *The full moon is very bright tonight.* **2.** strong in color; vivid: *School buses are painted bright yellow.* **3.** very intelligent: *a bright young woman.* To make something brighter is to **brighten** it: *Putting the fresh flowers on the table really brightened up the room.* —**brightly,** *adverb;* —**brightness,** *noun.*

bril·liant [bril-yunt] *adjective.* **1.** shining brightly; glittering: *brilliant sunshine.* **2.** showing great intelligence; very smart or clever: *Thomas Edison was considered to be a brilliant inventor.* **3.** having great quality; excellent; outstanding: *She wrote a brilliant novel that won many awards from critics.* **Brilliance** is the quality of being brilliant: *the brilliance of a beautifully cut diamond.* —**brilliantly,** *adverb.*

brim [brim] *noun, plural* **brims. 1.** the top edge of a container: *The bathtub was filled to the brim.* **2.** the outer edge of a hat. *verb,* **brimmed, brimming.** to be completely full: *His eyes were brimming with tears.*

bring [bring] *verb,* **brought, bringing. 1.** to take something or someone with you to a different place: *I bring my lunch to school but my sister buys hers there.* **2.** to make something happen: *Winter will bring snowstorms.* **3.** to cause a particular condition: *Bring the car to a stop.* **4.** to sell for: *The painting should bring a good price.*

brink [brink] *noun, plural* **brinks. 1.** the edge of high, steep place: *We stood on the brink of the Grand Canyon in wonder.* **2.** a turning point: *We are on the brink of war.*

brisk [brisk] *adjective,* **brisker, briskest. 1.** full of energy; quick: *a brisk walk.* **2.** cold and refreshing: *The icy wind is brisk.* —**briskly,** *adverb.*

bris·tle ▼ [bris-ul] *noun, plural* **bristles.** short, stiff hair that is rough. *verb,* **bristled, bristling. 1.** to have the hair rise from fear or anger: *The hairs on the back of her neck bristled when she saw the intruder.* **2.** to react with anger: *He bristled when I told him to go away.*

When it is threatened, the crested porcupine raises its **bristles** *to make itself seem larger.*

Brit·ish [brit-ish] *adjective.* having to do with Great Britain or its people. A person who was born in Great Britain is a **Briton,** and can also informally be known as a **Brit.**

British Empire *History.* the group of countries that once were controlled by Great Britain; at its height around 1914–18, it covered a quarter of the world's area. The **British Commonwealth** is a group of countries that used to be part of the British Empire and still recognize the British monarch as their ceremonial head.

British English *Language.* the form of the English language that is used in Great Britain.

British English is the original form of the English language, and it was the only form until British people began to live in other parts of the world such as North America, Australia, and India. The main difference today between British English and American English is in the way words sound.

brit·tle [brit-ul] *adjective.* hard, but easily broken: *The antique glass is very brittle.*

broad [brawd] *adjective,* **broader, broadest. 1.** having great distance from one side to the other; very wide: *a broad river; The famous New York street Broadway got its name because it was originally the widest street in the city.* **2.** having a wide range that includes many things: *The London Times newspaper has broad coverage of world events.* —**broadly,** *adverb.*

broad·band [brawd-band] *noun. Computers.* a system of transferring large amounts of data, such as text, images, and sound, at high speed between computers through the Internet. *adjective.* operating by means of this system: *broadband connection.*

broad·cast [brawd-kast] *verb,* **broadcast** *or* **broadcasted, broadcasting. 1.** to send out programs to the public on radio or television. **2.** to make something known to many people: *Don't broadcast the fact that I failed the exam.* *noun, plural* **broadcasts.** the act of transmitting a radio or television program. **—broadcaster,** *noun.*

> The word **broadcast** comes from the idea of casting (throwing or scattering) seeds over a wide area of the ground, rather than placing them in neat rows. A radio or TV broadcast is thought of as covering a wide area in the same way as these broadcast seeds.

broad·en [brawd-un] *verb,* **broadened, broadening.** to make something wider; expand: *Taking that history course broadened my knowledge of early life in America.*

broad·mind·ed [brawd-mine-did] *adjective.* willing to accept other opinions that are different than your own: *Dad is broadminded about music—he likes opera, but he always lets us put on our rock CDs in the car.* This word is also spelled **broad-minded.**

broc·co·li [broc-uh-lee] *noun, plural* **broccoli.** a plant with thick branching stems and flower buds that are eaten as a vegetable; part of the cabbage family.

bro·chure [broh-shoor] *noun, plural* **brochures.** a thin paper booklet that contains advertising material or other printed information.

broil [broil] *verb,* **broiled, broiling. 1.** to cook food under direct heat: *to broil fish on an outdoor grill.* **2.** to make or become very hot: *We broiled in the scorching sun.*

BRONZE AGE

The Bronze Age began in Greece and China before 3000 BC, but in Britain it started later, around 1900 BC. The use of bronze, a mixture of copper and tin, followed earlier metal-working with copper and gold. Bronze objects produced included spear and arrow heads, shields, chisels, saws, household containers, ornaments, and jewelry.

Bronze disks used to cast verdicts in ancient Greece

Ancient Chinese bronzesmith

Although huge, the **brontosaurus** *was not a threat to other dinosaurs as it ate only plants.*

broil·er [broil-ur] *noun, plural* **broilers. 1.** a pan, grate, or part of a stove used for broiling food. **2.** a chicken that is meant to be cooked by broiling.

broke [broke] *verb.* the past tense of BREAK. *adjective.* having no money.

> "The dishwasher is **broke**; don't use it." People can say this in everyday talk, but the correct word to use here is *broken.* You can say, "I *broke* my watch when I dropped it," but after the words *is/are* or *was/were, broke* is not correct.

bro·ken [broke-un] *verb.* the past participle of BREAK. *adjective.* **1.** no longer in one piece: *a broken plate.* **2.** not kept: *a broken promise.* **3.** not working properly: *The CD player is broken.* **4.** not spoken properly: *broken English.*

bron·chi·tis [brahn-kye-tus] *noun. Medicine.* a disease of the bronchia; one symptom is a bad cough.

bron·co [bronk-oh] *noun, plural* **broncos.** a wild or partly wild horse from Western North America; these are descendants of horses brought over from Spain in the days of Western settlement. This word is also spelled **broncho.**

bron·to·saur·us ▲ [bron-tuh-sore-us] *noun. Biology.* a large dinosaur that had an enormous body, a small head, and long neck. It could grow up to about 80 feet in length. This animal is also called a **brontosaur.**

bronze [bronz] *noun, plural* **bronzes. 1.** a reddish-brown metal that is a mixture of copper and tin; used to make ornaments, medals, and dishes. **2.** a dark red-brown color. *adjective.* **1.** reddish-brown in color. **2.** made of bronze. *verb,* **bronzed, bronzing.** to make the color of bronze: *The surfer's body was bronzed by the sun.*

Bronze Age ◀ *History.* the period in history when bronze was widely used for making tools, weapons, and other implements, about 6,000 to 4,000 years ago.

a
b
c
d
e
f
g
h
i
j
k
l
m
n
o
p
q
r
s
t
u
v
w
x
y
z

brooch [broch *or* brooch] *noun, plural* **brooches.** a piece of jewelry fastened to clothing with a clasp.

brood [brood] *noun, plural* **broods.** a group of young animals, usually birds, that are all born at the same time. *verb,* **brooded, brooding. 1.** to sit on eggs so they will hatch. **2.** to worry about something until you become anxious: *Don't brood over what she said because she didn't really mean it.*

brook [bruk] *noun, plural* **brooks.** a small stream.

broom [broom] *noun, plural* **brooms.** a brush with a long handle, used for sweeping.

broth [brawth] *noun, plural* **broths.** a light soup of meat, fish, or vegetable stock.

broth·er [bruTH-ur] *noun, plural* **brothers.** a male person who has the same parents as you. A **brotherly** person shows the same kind of feelings that you would expect from a brother.

broth·er·hood [bruTH-ur-*hud*] *noun, plural* **brotherhoods. 1.** a feeling of friendship between a group of people, usually males. **2.** a group of people who share common interests, often religious.

bro·ther-in-law *noun, plural* **brothers-in-law.** **1.** the brother of a person's husband or wife. **2.** the husband of someone's sister.

brought [brawt] *verb.* the past tense and past participle of BRING.

brow [brow] *noun, plural* **brows. 1.** the part of the face between the hair and the eyes; forehead. **2.** the small piece of hair just above each eye; eyebrow. **3.** the top edge of a steep place: *the brow of a cliff.*

brown [brown] *noun, plural* **browns.** a color that is darker than yellow but not as dark as black; the color of chocolate, coffee, mud, or wood. *adjective,* **browner, brownest.** being brown in color. *verb,* **browned, browning.** to make something brown, or to turn brown: *You should brown the meat in the pan before putting it in the oven; My skin browns quickly if I stay too long in the sun.*

brown·ie [brow-nee] *noun, plural* **brownies. 1.** a mythical friendly elf that visits and helps people, usually at nighttime. **2.** a kind of thin chocolate cake with nuts in it.

Brown·ie [brow-nee] *noun, plural* **Brownies.** a member of an organization for girls that is the junior division of the Girl Scouts.

brown·out [brown-*owt*] *noun, plural* **brownouts.** a loss of electric power that is less severe than a complete blackout.

browse ▼ [browz] *verb,* **browsed, browsing. 1.** to gaze at or look through without paying a lot of attention: *She browsed through the books in the library but did not find one she wanted to read.* **2.** of an animal, to feed on twigs, leaves, grass, and the like: *Sheep and cattle browse all day on grass and crops.*

brow·ser [browz-ur] *noun, plural* **browsers. 1.** someone or something that browses. **2.** *Computers.* a computer program that provides a way to go on the Internet and view web pages and other material that is found there.

bruise [brooz] *noun, plural* **bruises. 1.** a dark mark caused by a sharp blow or bump, on the surface of a person's skin or on the skin of a fruit, such as a peach or an apple. *verb,* **bruised, bruising. 1.** to create a bruise by hitting or bumping. **2.** to get a bruise or bruises: *Paula has very fair skin and bruises easily if someone bumps against her.*

bru·nette [broo-net] *noun, plural* **brunettes.** a woman or girl who has dark hair and often dark eyes. *adjective.* a way to describe a dark-haired and often dark-eyed woman or girl.

Gerenuks in eastern Africa stand on their hind legs to **browse** *on the leaves of bushes and small trees.*

brush¹ [brush] *noun, plural* **brushes.** an object, usually with a handle, having hair or stiff bristles sticking out of a hard back of wood, plastic, or metal. A brush can be used to clean, paint, dust, or polish surfaces, or to groom hair. *verb,* **brushed, brushing. 1.** to treat or clean with a brush: *He brushed his hair.* **2.** to hit against very lightly: *Amanda's hand brushed the wall as she walked down the alley.* **3.** to sweep away: *I brushed the leaves from the pathway.*

brush² [brush] *noun.* a small area of thick bushes and trees: *We lost our ball when Juan threw it into the brush.*

bru·tal [broot-ul] *adjective.* like a brute; very harsh; cruel: *Soldiers in wars sometimes treat their enemies in a brutal way.* The act of behaving brutally is **brutality.** —**brutally,** *adverb.*

brute [broot] *noun, plural* **brutes. 1.** any animal; a creature that is not human. **2.** a rough, unpleasant person. *Only a brute would be cruel to small children.*
• **brute force.** a rough or violent use of strength: *The police officer overpowered the robber using brute force.*

bub·ble [bub-ul] *noun, plural* **bubbles.** a small ball of air or gas in a liquid or fluid. *verb,* **bubbled, bubbling.** to contain bubbles: *Heat up the sauce until it begins to bubble.* Liquid that has bubbles in it is **bubbly.**
• **on the bubble.** on the edge; in an uncertain or risky position: *Next week the coach will choose twenty players for the final team and ten will be dropped—Jeff is one of three players on the bubble.*

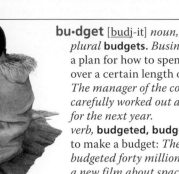

*American Indians wore clothes they made from **buckskin** to keep warm.*

buc·can·eer [*buk*-uh-<u>neer</u>] *noun, plural* **buccaneers.** a person who attacks and robs ships at sea; a pirate.

buck [buk] *noun, plural* **bucks.** the male of some types of animals. Male goats, deer, and antelopes are bucks. **2.** a slang word for a dollar. *verb,* **bucked, bucking. 1.** to jump off the ground with the back pushed upward: *The horse in the rodeo bucked wildly, but the rider did not fall off.* **2.** to struggle against: *If you go into the city today you will have to buck large crowds of people.*

buck·le [<u>buk</u>-ul] *noun, plural* **buckles.** a clasp that holds the ends of a belt or shoe strap together. *verb,* **buckled, buckling. 1.** to close or fasten with a buckle: *As the plane prepared to take off, we were told to buckle our seat belts.* **2.** to bend or curve downward: *Water soaked the floor and caused the floor boards to buckle.*
• **buckle down.** to take on a task or job; get to work: *The attic is really a mess, but we've just got to buckle down and get it cleaned.*

buck·skin ▲ [<u>buk</u>-*skin*] *noun, plural* **buckskins.** a soft leather made from sheepskin or deerskin.

The temple of Borobudur in Indonesia is a shrine of **Buddhism.**

bud [bud] *noun, plural* **buds.** a small growth on the stem of a plant that will develop into a flower, leaf, or shoot. *verb,* **budded, budding.** to grow or produce buds.

Bud·dhism ▲ [<u>bood</u>-iz-um] *noun.* a religion, mainly of central and eastern Asia, that is based on the teachings of Gautama Buddha, a spiritual leader who lived in India about 2,500 years ago.

bud·dy [<u>bud</u>-ee] *noun, plural* **buddies.** a special friend; a pal: *Matt and his buddy Luis often ride their bikes together.*

budge [budj] *verb,* **budged, budging.** to shift slightly or move a very small distance: *Michael was so interested in the book that he did not budge all morning from where he was sitting.*

bu·dget [<u>budj</u>-it] *noun, plural* **budgets.** *Business.* a plan for how to spend money over a certain length of time: *The manager of the company carefully worked out a budget for the next year. verb,* **budgeted, budgeting.** to make a budget: *The company budgeted forty million dollars for a new film about space travel.*

The word **budget** once meant "a little bag or purse." This was used to hold money, and from that came the idea that making a budget is like putting your money into such a bag.

buff [buff] *noun, plural* **buffs. 1.** a kind of leather made from the skin of a wild ox. **2.** a yellowish-brown color. **3.** an object covered with cloth or other soft material that is used for polishing. **4.** a person who knows a lot about a certain subject and has a great interest in it: *Josh is a real sports buff and can name every player on his favorite team. adjective.* being buff-colored. *verb,* **buffed, buffing.** to make shiny; polish: *My father buffed the table with a soft rag.*

buf·fa·lo ▼ [<u>buff</u>-uh-loh] *noun, plural* **buffaloes** or **buffalos** or **buffalo. 1.** a large North American animal with short, curved horns and a shaggy coat; a bison. Large numbers of these animals once lived wild on the Western plains of North America. Today a smaller number live on ranches. **2.** one of several kinds of African or Asian wild oxen.

buf·fet[1] [buh-<u>faye</u> or boo-<u>faye</u>] *noun, plural* **buffets. 1.** a cabinet or sideboard with shelves or drawers for dishes, linen, and other table utensils and a top on which food can be served. **2.** a meal set out in a number of dishes, from which people serve themselves.

buf·fet[2] [<u>buff</u>-it] *verb,* **buffeted, buffeting.** to hit hard against; batter: *The strong winds buffeted our small tent all through the night.*

Plains Indians hunted **buffalo** *on horseback with spears and arrows.*

*This **bug**, called a backswimmer, swims upside down under the water, using its long back legs as oars.*

A B C D E F G H I J K L M N O P Q R S T U V W X Y Z

bug [bug] *noun, plural* **bugs. 1.** one of a group of insects that have four wings and a mouth that can pierce and suck. **2.** any other insect or small animal that is like this type of insect. **3.** a germ that causes a minor illness: *My brother is ill with a stomach bug.* **4.** a fault in a computer or other machine: *The mechanic is trying to get the bugs out of the car engine.* **5.** a microphone or recorder used for listening in to conversations. *verb,* **bugged, bugging. 1.** to put a hidden microphone or recorder in: *In the movie, the soldiers bugged the meeting room to find out what their enemies were planning.* **2.** to bother or annoy in a minor way; irritate: *I tried to study, but my little brother kept bugging me to go out and play with him.*

The word **bug**, as in a problem with a computer, is said to have been made up by one of the most famous computer scientists, Dr. Grace Hopper. She supposedly thought of the word after she found that her computer had stopped working because of a bug trapped inside it. This is an interesting story, but it is also known that the word *bug* was used many years before this to mean a problem with a machine.

bug·gy [bug-ee] *noun, plural* **buggies.** a small carriage with a single seat that is pulled by a horse.

bu·gle ▼ [byoo-gul] *noun, plural* **bugles.** *Music.* a brass musical instrument, similar to a trumpet, that does not have valves. In the past, bugles were used in the army to give signals in battle, and today a bugle is often played at a military funeral or other such ceremony. —**bugler,** *noun.*

build [bild] *verb,* **built, building. 1.** to make something out of materials; construct: *to build a house; to build a bridge; to build a road.* **2.** to increase or develop bit by bit: *Gustav is slowly building a large stamp collection. noun, plural* **builds.** the shape and form of a person's or an animal's body: *Our dog Rufus has a very solid build.* —**builder,** *noun.*

build·ing [bild-ing] *noun, plural* **buildings. 1.** a structure that people live in, work in, store things in, or that they use for many other purposes. **2.** the act of constructing a house, factory, school, or any other building.

built-in [bilt-*in*] *adjective.* **1.** made as a part of a room or building; not able to be moved: *a built-in dresser or bookcase.* **2.** being a basic and permanent feature of something: *The noisy motor is a built-in problem with our lawn mower.*

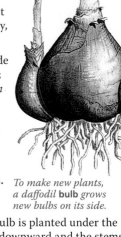

*To make new plants, a daffodil **bulb** grows new bulbs on its side.*

bulb ▶ [bulb] *noun, plural* **bulbs. 1.** a rounded part of certain plants, such as tulips and lilies. When a bulb is planted under the soil, the roots grow downward and the stems, leaves, and flowers grow upward. **2.** anything that has a rounded or swollen part like the bulb of a plant: *a light bulb.*

bulge [bulj] *noun, plural* **bulges.** an upward or outward curve or swelling: *The dampness in the wall caused a bulge in the wallpaper. verb,* **bulged, bulging.** to swell or curve upward or outward.

bulk [bulk] *noun.* **1.** size, especially great size: *Many wrestlers have bodies of great bulk.* **2.** the biggest or most important part: *The bulk of their work has been done—they just have to clean up the job site.* Anything that has great bulk is **bulky.**

Bulldogs are reliable and determined, and are loyal pets.

bull [bull] *noun, plural* **bulls. 1.** the adult male of cattle. **2.** the adult male of certain large mammals, such as the elephant, whale, seal, or moose. **3.** *Business.* a name for a person who thinks that prices in the stock market will go up, or who buys stocks because of this. —**bullish,** *adjective.*

bull·dog ▲ [bull-*dog*] *noun, plural* **bulldogs.** a muscular, small dog with a large head, strong jaws, and short, smooth hair.

bull·doz·er [bull-doh-zur] *noun, plural* **bulldozers.** a large tractor with a curved, metal blade in front that pushes or scoops up earth and rocks and can knock down trees and fences.

bul·let [bull-it] *noun, plural* **bullets.** a piece of metal that can be fired from a pistol or a rifle. Something that a bullet cannot go through is **bulletproof.**

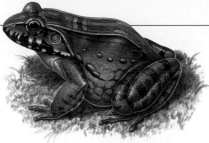

A **bullfrog** eats any moving creature that it can swallow.

bul·le·tin [bull-i-tun] *noun, plural* **bulletins.**
1. a news statement about one or more events: *The hospital issued a bulletin about the people hurt in the accident.* 2. a paper or magazine with news about a particular place or organization: *Every month, our school sends its bulletin to all the pupils' parents.*

bulletin board 1. a board in a public place that displays information, news, or advertisements. 2. *Computers.* a Website that allows people to post announcements, share information, comment on a certain topic, and so on.

bull·fight [bull-*fite*] *noun, plural* **bullfights.** a public performance in which a person called a matador taunts a bull into attacking and then weaves and dodges to escape as the bull charges. After some time, the matador usually kills the bull with a sword. Bullfights are popular entertainments in parts of Spain, Portugal, Mexico, and South America. **—bullfighter,** *noun.*

bull·frog ▲ [bull-*frog*] *noun, plural* **bullfrogs.** a large frog that is native to parts of the United States and Canada and that has a heavy body and a deep, loud croak.

bul·lion [bull-yahn *or* bull-yun] *noun.* 1. a term for gold and silver. 2. gold or silver that has been formed into large bars.

bull's-eye ▶ [bullz-*eye*] *noun, plural* **bull's-eyes.** 1. the circle in the center of a target used for archery, shooting, or darts. 2. a shot, or a throw in darts, that hits the bull's-eye.

A **bull's-eye** is the most difficult part of a target to hit and is worth the most points.

bul·ly [bull-ee] *noun, plural* **bullies.** a person who tries to dominate, threaten, or attack a smaller or weaker person. *verb,* **bullied, bullying.** to stand over, threaten, or attack a smaller or weaker person.

bum·ble·bee [bum-bul-*bee*] *noun, plural* **bumblebees.** a large, hairy bee that buzzes loudly.

bump [bump] *verb,* **bump, bumping.** 1. to hit or knock sharply against: *Nadine bumped her elbow hard against the chair.* 2. to move unevenly: *The bike bumped across the field.*
noun, plural **bumps.** 1. a sharp hit or knock: *The falling branch gave Henry a nasty bump on the shoulder.* 2. something raised or swollen: *a bump in the road; The bump on your face looks painful, but it will disappear soon.* Something that is uneven or has a lot of bumps in it is **bumpy.**

bump·er [bum-pur] *noun, plural* **bumpers.** a bar on the front and back of a vehicle that helps protect it from damage if it bumps into something.
adjective. large in size or amount; big; abundant: *a bumper grain harvest.*

bun [bun] *noun, plural* **buns.** a small roll of baked dough that may be sweetened.

bunch [bunch] *noun, plural* **bunches.** 1. a group of similar things growing, held, or fastened close together: *a bunch of flowers.* 2. a number of people: *Our class is an interesting bunch.* *verb,* **bunched, bunching.** to place or gather together: *Shoppers were bunched up near the door, waiting for the store to open.*

bun·dle [bun-dul] *noun, plural* **bundles.** a group of things wrapped, tied, or placed together: *Please hand me that bundle of papers.* *verb,* **bundled, bundling.** 1. to place things together in a bundle. 2. *Business.* to include some software or other item when selling a computer, without charging extra: *The salesperson bundled some games programs when she sold us the computer.*

bun·gal·ow [bung-guh-loh] *noun, plural* **bungalows.** a small house with only one story. Bungalows are often built near a beach or lake.

The **bungalow** takes its name from a language of India, where this type of building comes from. The word was taken into English when the country of Great Britain ruled over India.

bun·gle [bung-gul] *verb,* **bungled, bungling.** to make a mistake; spoil or ruin something: *He bungled his role in the school play when he forgot his lines.* **—bungler** *noun.*

bunk [bunk] *noun, plural* **bunks.** 1. any small bed. 2. a built-in bed. Built-in bunks are usually placed one above the other. A bunk that is built in is often called a **bunk bed.**

bun·ny [bun-ee] another term for a rabbit.

Bun·sen burner ▶ [bun-sun] *Science.* a small gas jet that produces a hot, blue flame and that is used mainly to heat substances in science experiments.

The **Bunsen burner** is named for a famous German scientist, Robert Wilhelm Bunsen.

bunt [bunt] *verb,* **bunted, bunting.** to purposely bat a baseball very lightly so that it does not travel far. *noun plural,* **bunts.** 1. the act of tapping a baseball very lightly. 2. a baseball that has been hit in this way.

buoy [boo-ee] *noun, plural* **buoys.** 1. one of a number of floats that guide ships or boats away from hidden rocks or other dangers. 2. a vest or inflated ring that prevents a person from sinking in the water. *verb,* **buoyed, buoying.** to support, encourage, or cheer up: *My friends tried to buoy me up when I was upset after losing the tennis final.*

a
b
c
d
e
f
g
h
i
j
k
l
m
n
o
p
q
r
s
t
u
w
x
y
z

buoy·ant ▼ [boy-unt] *adjective.* **1.** able to float; not sinking in water. *A piece of wood is buoyant.* **2.** happy, excited, or confident: *We felt buoyant about our chances of winning the prize.* —**buoyancy,** *noun.*

bur [bur] *noun, plural* **burs.** another spelling of BURR.

bur·den [bur-dun] *noun, plural* **burdens. 1.** something heavy that is carried: *The big bag of groceries was a real burden for the thin old man.* **2.** something difficult to put up with or endure: *Owing a lot of money can be a terrible burden.*
verb, **burdened, burdening.** to place something that is too heavy on: *Her company is short of workers, so she is burdened with a lot of extra jobs.*

bu·reau [byur-oh] *noun, plural* **bureaus. 1.** a piece of bedroom furniture with drawers; a dresser: *Mom keeps her jewelry in her bureau.* **2.** an office or department that provides information or advice: *a weather bureau.*

bu·reau·cra·cy [byur-ok-ruh-see] *noun, plural* **bureaucracies.** *Government.* **1.** a set of rules and regulations that people who work in government departments or large companies have to obey. **2.** the group of people who make decisions in a government department or large business organization. **3.** any system or organization in which progress is difficult because rules and policies are complicated and must be strictly followed. A **bureaucrat** is someone who works in a bureaucracy. —**bureaucratic,** *adjective.*

bur·glar [burg-lur] *noun, plural* **burglars.** *Law.* someone who enters a home or other building in order to steal things. The act of entering a building and stealing from it is **burglary.**

Sea otters are very **buoyant** *and spend a lot of their time floating on their backs.*

bur·i·al [ber-ee-ul] *noun, plural* **burials.** the act of burying a dead body in the earth, lowering it into the sea, or placing it in a tomb.

bur·ly [bur-lee] *adjective,* **burlier, burliest.** having size and strength; large and muscular: *A grizzly bear is a burly animal.*

burn [burn] *verb,* **burned** *or* **burnt, burning. 1.** to set fire to something: *to burn wood in a fireplace; to burn coal to heat a building.* **2.** to be on fire: *That smoke is from dry grass burning along the highway.* **3.** to hurt or damage by heating: *The hot sun burnt my legs.* **4.** to feel or cause to feel heat: *My mouth was burning from the hot pepper sauce.* **5.** to use for heating or lighting: *Keep the light burning outside the front door.*
noun, plural **burns.** an injury or soreness as a result of fire or heat.

bur·ner [burn-ur] *noun, plural* **burners.** the part of a stove, lamp, or furnace where flame appears or heat is produced.

burr [bur] *noun, plural* **burrs. 1.** a rough, prickly case around the seeds or flowers of some plants. **2.** a plant with burrs on it.

bur·ri·to [buh-ree-toh] *noun, plural* **burritos.** a dish from Mexico that consists of a flour tortilla folded around cheese, meat, beans, salad vegetables, or other types of food.

bur·ro [bur-oh] *noun, plural* **burros.** another word for a small donkey.
🔊 Different words with the same sound are **borough** and **burrow.**

bur·row ▼ [bur-oh] *noun, plural* **burrows.** a hole or tunnel that an animal digs in the earth. Rabbits and foxes live in burrows.
verb, **burrowed, burrowing. 1.** of an animal, to dig a hole or tunnel in the earth. **2.** to look hard; search: *She had to burrow around in the dresser drawer to find her keys.*
🔊 Different words with the same sound are **borough** and **burro.**

burst [burst] *verb,* **burst, bursting. 1.** to break open; explode: *A balloon will burst if you poke it with a pin.* **2.** to be very full or too full: *My bag is bursting with schoolbooks.* **3.** to start doing something in a strong and sudden way: *The noisy children burst into the house; The choir burst into song.*
noun, plural **bursts.** a sudden and strong beginning of something: *a burst of laughter; a burst of applause.*

bur·y [ber-ee] *verb,* **buried, burying. 1.** to place a dead body under the ground, in a tomb, or into the sea. **2.** to put something in or as if in the ground: *The dog buried a bone in the yard; When we go to the beach, Jimmy likes to bury himself in the sand.* **3.** to put under or in; hide: *Margaret found five dollars buried at the bottom of her purse; He had his face buried in a book and didn't hear what I said.*
🔊 A different word with the same sound is **berry.**

The colorful jeepney **bus**, originally made from U.S. military jeeps, is a popular form of public transport in the Philippines.

bus ▶ [buss] *noun, plural* **buses** or **busses.** a motor vehicle that can carry a large number of passengers, who pay a fare.
verb, **bused** or **bussed, busing** or **bussing.** to take in a bus or to travel by bus: *to bus students to school.*

bush [bush] *noun, plural* **bushes.**
1. a large plant with branches and leaves that is smaller than a tree. Many bushes have flowers or fruits. 2. an area where many bushes and other wild plants grow close together.

bush·el [bush-ul] *noun, plural* **bushels.** a measure of volume used for dry foods such as grain and vegetables.

bush·y ▼ [bush-ee] *adjective,* **bushier, bushiest.** thick and spreading like the leaves of a bush, or like an area of bush: *a bushy mustache; an animal with a bushy tail.*

busi·ness [biz-nis] *noun, plural* **businesses.** 1. the job a person does to earn money; occupation. Someone who is good at, or serious about, their work is described as **businesslike.** 2. an establishment or activity that involves the buying and selling of goods or the providing of services in return for money. Supermarkets and doctors' practices are examples of businesses. 3. any kind of trade: *Canada and the U.S. do a lot of business with each other.* 4. something that concerns only one person or a number of people: *What I said to Joshua is none of your business.*

busi·ness·man [biz-nis-*man*] *noun, plural* **businessmen.** a man who works in business, especially someone who owns a business or who plays an important part in running it.

busi·ness·wom·an [biz-nis-*wum*-in] *noun, plural* **businesswomen.** a woman who works in business, especially someone who owns a business or who plays an important part in running it.

bus·ing [buss-ing] *noun.* 1. the act of taking people by bus from one place to another, or of traveling by bus. 2. *Education.* the fact of taking students by bus to a school outside their own neighborhood, especially so that schools will have a more balanced student body in terms of race. This word is also spelled **bussing.**

bust [bust] *noun, plural* **busts.** a statue of a person's head, shoulders and upper chest: *There was a bust of George Washington in the art gallery.*

bus·tle [buss-ul] *verb,* **bustled, bustling.** to move about in a hurried way: *She bustled around the house, trying to clean up everything before her guests arrived.*
noun. busy, excited activity: *the afternoon bustle of commuters moving through the station to catch their train for home.* Something that has a lot of activity is **bustling**: *That mine is closed now, but it was really a bustling place during the days of the gold rush.*

The **bushy** tail of the African bat-eared fox can be up to twelve inches long.

bu·sy [biz-ee] *adjective,* **busier, busiest.** 1. active and occupied: *The new baby keeps Mom and Dad busy.* 2. with a lot happening: *We live on a very busy street.* 3. being used; not available: *We tried to buy the tickets by phone, but the line was busy.*
verb, **busied, busying.** to be busy or engaged in: *I busied myself arranging my clothes in the closet.*

but [butt] *conjunction.* a word that is often used to join two parts of a sentence, usually to show that one part has a thought that is the opposite of or different from the other: *I wanted to buy that new CD, but it was sold out; Most birds can fly, but the ostrich cannot.* **But** is also used as a preposition: *We won all our games but one.*

In writing it is better not to use **but** to begin a sentence. "I called her house. *But* she didn't answer." That would read more smoothly as one sentence: "I called her house, *but* she didn't answer." The only time it is good to begin with *but* is when you want the sentence to be short and a bit of a surprise. "When I got up that morning for school, I expected the day to be just like any other day. *But* it wasn't."

butch·er [buch-ur] *noun, plural* **butchers.** 1. a person who cuts up meat and prepares it for sale. 2. any person who sells meat. 3. a cruel and violent person. The act of being cruel and destructive is **butchery.**

but·ler [but-lur] *noun, plural* **butlers.** the chief male servant in a household.

butt[1] [butt] *noun, plural* **butts.** 1. the end of a gun or a rifle that is held in the hand or against the shoulder. 2. the bit that is left after a cigarette or cigar has been smoked.
🔊 A different word with the same sound is **but.**

butt[2] [butt] *noun, plural* **butts.** a person or thing that other people tease or make fun of: *Poor Tim was the butt of many practical jokes.*
🔊 A different word with the same sound is **but.**

butt[3] [butt] *verb,* **butted, butting.** to give a hard blow using the head: *Be careful of that goat because he does butt.*
noun, plural **butts.** a hard blow with the head or horns.
🔊 A different word with the same sound is **but.**

but·ter [butt-ur] *noun, plural* **butters.** 1. a hard, yellow fat made from cream. You can spread it on bread or use it in cooking. **Butterfat** is the yellow fat in milk. **Buttermilk** is the sour liquid that remains when the fat has been removed from cream. 2. a thick, creamy substance like butter, made from a plant or vegetable.
verb, **buttered, buttering.** to spread bread or other food with butter.

a b c d e f g h i j k l m n o p q r s t u v w x y z

buttercup

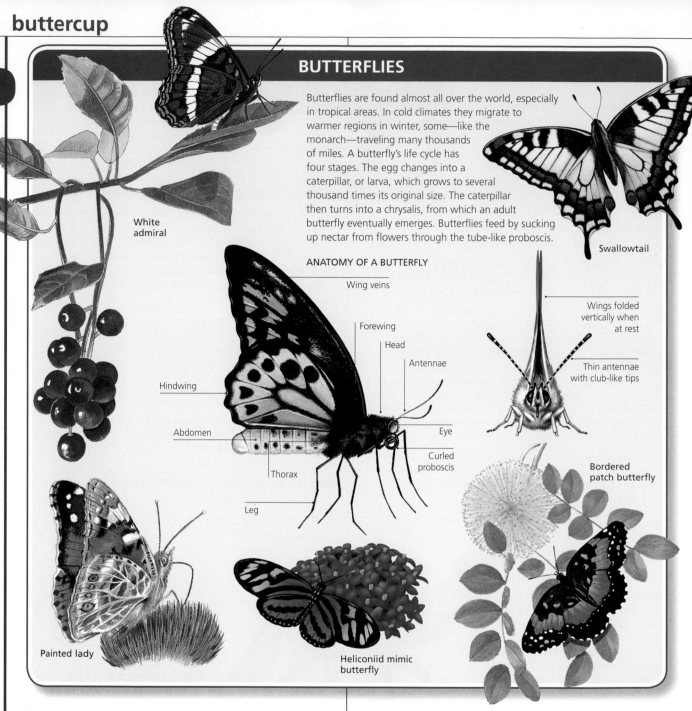

BUTTERFLIES

Butterflies are found almost all over the world, especially in tropical areas. In cold climates they migrate to warmer regions in winter, some—like the monarch—traveling many thousands of miles. A butterfly's life cycle has four stages. The egg changes into a caterpillar, or larva, which grows to several thousand times its original size. The caterpillar then turns into a chrysalis, from which an adult butterfly eventually emerges. Butterflies feed by sucking up nectar from flowers through the tube-like proboscis.

White admiral

Swallowtail

ANATOMY OF A BUTTERFLY

Wing veins
Forewing
Head
Antennae
Hindwing
Abdomen
Thorax
Leg
Eye
Curled proboscis

Wings folded vertically when at rest

Thin antennae with club-like tips

Bordered patch butterfly

Painted lady

Heliconiid mimic butterfly

but·ter·cup [butt-ur-*kup*] *noun, plural* **buttercups.** a small plant with bright yellow flowers.

but·ter·fly ▲ [butt-ur-*flye*] *noun, plural* **butterflies.** an insect with four large, brightly colored wings, and a thin body.
verb, **butterflied, butterflying.** to split and spread something open into the shape of a butterfly: *Mom butterflied the pork chop and it took up most of the plate.*

but·ter·scotch [butt-ur-*skoch*] *noun, plural* **butterscotches.** a candy made from brown sugar and butter.

but·tock [butt-ik] *noun, plural* **buttocks.** the part of your body between your back and your legs, which you sit on.

but·ton [butt-un] *noun, plural* **buttons. 1.** a small, usually round object used to fasten clothing. Buttons can also be used as ornaments. **2.** a small object that you turn, pull, or press in order to make something work, such as a machine, appliance, elevator, or the like: *a dishwasher button.*
verb, **buttoned, buttoning.** to fasten clothing with buttons.

but·ton·hole [butt-un-*hole*] *noun, plural* **buttonholes.** a hole that you push a button through, in order to fasten clothing.
verb, **buttonholed, buttonholing.** to stop someone and make the person listen to you, as if by holding on to the person's coat or buttonhole: *Here comes Jasper. Come on, let's run before he buttonholes us and asks for money.*

106

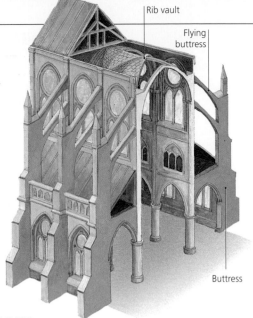

Rib vault

Flying buttress

Buttress

but·tress ▶ [butt-ris] *noun,*
plural **buttresses.** a heavy object
built against a wall to support it.
It is usually made of stone or brick.
verb, **buttressed, buttressing.**
1. to support something with a
buttress. **2.** to give strength and
support in an argument: *As we
had all the facts at our disposal,
we were able to buttress our
position and win the debate.*

buy [bye] *verb,* **bought, buying.**
to get something by paying
money for it.
noun, plural **buys.** something
for sale at a cheap price; bargain:
*The bicycle was offered for half
price, so it was a really good buy.*

buy·er [bye-er] *noun, plural* **buyers.**
1. any person who buys something: *a car
buyer.* **2.** *Business.* a person whose work is buying
things for a company so that they can be offered
for sale to others.

A **buzzard** *can grow
as long as 22 inches
but has a call like a
cat's meow.*

buzz [buzz] *noun, plural* **buzzes.**
1. a continuous, low humming
sound, like the noise that a mosquito
makes when it flies around. **2.** talk,
gossip, or rumor among the public
about a certain thing: *There's a lot
of buzz about the new movie and
it's supposed to be really good.*
verb, **buzzed, buzzing. 1.** to make
a continuous low humming sound.
2. to move around making a
humming sound: *The light aircraft
have been buzzing around all day.*

buz·zard ◀ [buzz-urd] *noun,*
plural **buzzards.** a very large
bird belonging to the hawk family.
It feeds mostly on small animals.

buzz·er [buzz-ur] *noun,*
plural **buzzers.** an electrical device
that makes a buzzing sound.

by [bye] *preposition.* close to in some way; near: *The dog was
sleeping by the fire; Stay by the phone in case Mom calls.*
✚ **By** is used in many other ways to show how something
happens: *to travel by plane; to win by two points; to buy
butter by the pound; to succeed by hard work;
Time went by slowly while we waited.*

by·gone [bye-gone] *adjective.* happening or
existing a very long time ago: *the bygone
era of the American Civil War.* Things that
happened in the past are called **bygones.**

by·pass [bye-pass] *noun, plural* **bypasses.**
1. a road that takes traffic around a town,
rather than through the city center.
2. *Medicine.* an operation to move the

The **buttresses** *of
a Gothic church
support its vaults.*

flow of blood or other fluid around
a blocked or damaged body part.
verb, **bypassed, bypassing.** to travel
around something rather than
through it: *Let's take Route 4 so we
can bypass the bad traffic on the
main highway.*

by-product *noun, plural* **by-products.**
something extra that is obtained
during the making of another
product. Cotton is grown for
clothing but also has several
by-products, such as oil for foods
and seeds for animal feed. This
word is also spelled **byproduct.**

by·stand·er [bye-stan-dur] *noun,*
plural **bystanders.** a person who
is nearby when something happens:
*The blast shattered the window
and several bystanders were
showered with glass.*

byte [byte] *noun, plural* **bytes.**
Computers. a unit of information,
usually eight bits, stored by a computer.
🔊 A different word that sounds like this is **bite.**

Byz·an·tine ▼ [biz-un-teen] *adjective.* **1.** having to do
with **Byzantium,** a powerful city of the ancient world
that is now known as Istanbul. The **Byzantine Empire**
ruled large parts of the Middle East, Europe, and Africa
for about 1,000 years. **2.** *Art.* having to do with a style
of Christian art and architecture that was important
during the time of the Byzantine Empire. **3. byzantine.**
similar to the politics and
government of the Byzantine
Empire, especially in a way that
is tricky, overly complicated,
marked by secret plots,
and so on.

*Gracanica
church in Serbia
was built in the
Byzantine style in
the 1300s.*

a
b
c
d
e
f
g
h
i
j
k
l
m
n
o
p
q
r
s
t
u
v
w
x
y
z

Cc

*American pioneers built log **cabins** as their first homes.*

C, c *noun, plural* **C's, c's. 1.** the third letter of the alphabet. **2.** the Roman numeral for 100.

C an abbreviation for century, cent, centigrade, or Celsius.

cab [kab] *noun, plural* **cabs. 1.** a car that takes people from one place to another one, usually nearby, in return for a certain amount of money; a taxi. **2.** the front part of a truck, bus, train, or other such vehicle where the driver sits to drive it.

cab·bage [kab-ij] *noun, plural* **cabbages.** a large vegetable with green or purple leaves, which grow very tightly together to form a round head.

cab·in ▲ [kab-in] *noun, plural* **cabins. 1.** a small house or hut, often made of wood: *During our summer vacation, we stayed in a cabin in the woods.* **2.** a room on a ship where people live or sleep. **3.** one of the areas of an aircraft where passengers sit, or one reserved for air crew or cargo.

cab·i·net [kab-nit *or* kab-uh-nit] *noun, plural* **cabinets. 1.** a piece of furniture used for storing different things: *He keeps important papers in a filing cabinet.* **2.** a group of senior ministers or advisers who meet regularly to give advice to the leader of a country. **3. Cabinet.** such a group that advises the President of the U.S.

ca·ble [kay-bul] *noun, plural* **cables. 1.** a thick, strong wire or rope, usually made of strands twisted together. **2.** a bundle of insulated wires used to carry an electric current. **3.** a message that is sent along a wire under the ocean, usually to someone a long way away. **—cable,** *verb.*

cable car 1. a small car hanging from overhead moving cables. **2.** a car carried along the ground by underground cables.

cable television a system in which programs are sent along wires to a television set.

ca·ca·o [kuh-kay-oh *or* kuh-kah-oh] *noun, plural* **cacaos.** a small evergreen tropical tree grown for its seeds, which are used to make cocoa and chocolate.

cac·tus ▼ [kak-tus] *noun, plural* **cactuses** *or* **cacti** *or* **cactus.** a thick, fleshy plant that is covered in sharp spikes instead of leaves. It grows in deserts. Most cactuses produce bright flowers and fruits that you can eat.

cad·dy [kad-ee] *noun, plural* **caddies.** someone who carries the golf clubs and other equipment for a person who is playing golf.
verb, **caddied, caddying.** to carry someone else's golf clubs. This word is also spelled **caddie.**

ca·det [kuh-det] *noun, plural* **cadets.** a young man or woman who is being trained in an academy for military or police service.

> The word **cadet** once meant "a younger son." In Europe, the younger son in a family often used to join the army as a way to earn his living, because the family's land always passed on to the eldest son.

caf·e·te·ri·a [kaf-uh-teer-ee-uh] *noun, plural* **cafeterias.** an inexpensive snack bar or restaurant where you choose food from a counter, and then carry it to a table yourself.

caf·feine [kaf-een *or* ka-feen] *noun. Chemistry.* a bitter-tasting chemical substance found in tea, coffee, and many soft drinks. It stimulates your brain and body and if you drink a lot of it, it might make it hard to sleep.

cage [kayj] *noun, plural* **cages. 1.** a box made of wire or metal bars, in which birds or animals are kept, as at a zoo. **2.** a small room where one or more of the walls are made of metal bars, wire, or glass.
verb, **caged, caging.** to put or keep in a cage.

CACTUS

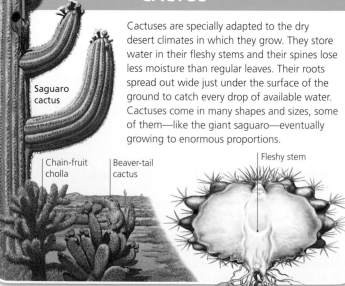

Cactuses are specially adapted to the dry desert climates in which they grow. They store water in their fleshy stems and their spines lose less moisture than regular leaves. Their roots spread out wide just under the surface of the ground to catch every drop of available water. Cactuses come in many shapes and sizes, some of them—like the giant saguaro—eventually growing to enormous proportions.

Saguaro cactus

Chain-fruit cholla

Beaver-tail cactus

Fleshy stem

Ca·jun [kayj-un] *noun, plural* **Cajuns.** a person whose family is descended from French colonists from Canada who settled in Louisiana in the 1700s.
adjective. having to do with the Cajuns, or their language, culture, or cooking.

cake [kayk] *noun, plural* **cakes. 1.** a sweet food made by mixing butter, sugar, flour, milk, eggs, and some sort of flavoring together, and then baking the mixture in the oven: *Every child got a slice of birthday cake.* **2.** a small block or bar of something: *a cake of soap.*
verb, **caked, caking.** to become hard and solid: *The clown's makeup was caked on his face like a mask.*

cal·am·i·ty [kuh-*lam*-i-tee] *noun, plural* **calamities.** a disaster that causes a great deal of sorrow; catastrophe: *First the hurricane, then the flood—it's just one calamity after the other.*

cal·ci·um [*kal*-see-um] *noun. Biology.* a soft white chemical element. It is found in some foods, such as milk and nuts, and helps young people to form healthy bones and teeth.

cal·cu·late [*kalk*-yuh-*late*] *verb,* **calculated, calculating. 1.** to find out the answer to a sum using arithmetic: *to calculate how many people can safely fit in an elevator.* A **calculator** is a small electronic machine for solving mathematical problems. **2.** to be confident that something will happen: *They left Los Angeles at 6 A.M., so I calculate they will arrive here about 3 P.M.* **3.** to plan or mean something to happen: *This movie is calculated to make you laugh.* Someone who plans or means something to happen is **calculating.** —**calculation,** *noun.*

> **Calculate** is taken from a word meaning "a small stone" or "a pebble." In early times, people used to calculate things by using small stones as counters.

cal·cu·lus [*kalk*-yuh-lus] *noun. Mathematics.* a branch of advanced mathematics that is used to deal with quantities that change over time with respect to each other. An example would be predicting the speed of a sailboat whose speed keeps changing because of changes in wind speed and other conditions.

cal·en·dar [*kal*-in-dur] *noun, plural* **calendars. 1.** a chart or table showing the days, weeks, and months in a year. **2.** a list of events that will happen on certain days.

> The **calendar** that we use today developed from one used by the ancient Romans. In Rome, *calends* was the word for the first day of the month.

calf[1] ▼ [kaf] *noun, plural* **calves. 1.** a young cow or bull. **2.** a young seal, elephant, or whale. **3.** leather made from the skin or hide of a calf. This leather is also called **calfskin.**

calf[2] [kaf] *noun, plural* **calves.** the fleshy part of the back of the leg, between the knee and the foot.

cal·i·ber [*kal*-i-bur] *noun.* **1.** the size of the bullets that a gun fires, stated in terms of the width of the barrel of the gun. **2.** a degree of excellence or importance: *a young woman of high caliber.*

cal·i·co [*kal*-i-koh] *noun, plural* **calicoes** or **calicos.** a colorful printed cotton material.
adjective. **1.** made of calico: *a pretty calico dress.* **2.** having large spots of different colors on it.

call [kawl] *verb,* **called, calling. 1.** to speak loudly, shout, or cry out: *She didn't see him, so he called her name.* **2.** to ask to come: *The dog ran over as soon as I called him.* **3.** to get in touch with by telephone: *Don't go out, because I'm going to call you later.* **4.** to visit someone: *Let's call on your grandmother for her birthday.* **5.** to give someone a name: *We called the baby Jessica after her aunt.* **6.** to arrange something, or ask for it to happen: *The principal called for an urgent meeting of the parents.*
noun, plural **calls. 1.** the act of speaking in a loud voice; a shout or cry: *We heard a call for help from the young girl in the water.* **2.** a request to come for a particular purpose: *The TV repairman has to make three service calls this morning.* **3.** the act of contacting someone by phone. **4.** a short visit: *to pay a call on a friend.* **5.** a particular sound, made by a bird or animal: *characteristic call of the magpie.* —**caller,** *noun.*

A female humpback whale is usually very protective her young **calf.**

A
B
C
D
E
F
G
H
I
J
K
L
M
N
O
P
Q
R
S
T
U
V
W
X
Y
Z

Ancient Chinese **calligraphers** *used brushes made from animal hairs.*

cal·lig·ra·phy ▲ [kuh-<u>lig</u>-ruh-fee] *noun. Art.* beautiful handwriting, using a brush or a pen. Someone who does this writing is called a **calligrapher**.

call number a group of numbers or numbers and letters given to a book in a library, so that it can be found easily and quickly.

cal·lous [<u>kal</u>-us] *adjective.* not caring about the feelings of others: *It was very callous of you to say that it was her own fault that she got sick.* —**callously**, *adverb;* —**callousness**, *noun.*
🔊 A different word with the same sound is **callus**.

cal·lus [<u>kal</u>-us] *noun, plural* **calluses.** a hardened area of skin caused by something constantly rubbing against it: *My sneakers are too tight, and I have a nasty callus on my heel.*
🔊 A different word with the same sound is **callous**.

calm [kahm *or* kahlm] *adjective,* **calmer, calmest.**
1. not moving or still; quiet: *the calm waters of a small pond.* **2.** steady and not upset: *Sit down and stay calm.*
noun. a period of peace and quiet.
verb, **calmed, calming.** to become quiet and still.
—**calmly**, *adverb;* —**calmness**, *noun.*

cal·o·rie [<u>kal</u>-uh-ree] *noun, plural* **calories.** *Science.*
1. a way to measure the amount of energy that something has, based on the heat needed to raise the temperature of one gram of water by one degree Celsius. **2.** a unit of measure used to state the energy content of a certain food.

cam·cord·er [<u>kam</u>-kore-dur] *noun, plural* **camcorders.** a television camera and a video cassette together in one unit.

came [kaym] *verb.* the past tense of COME.

cam·el [<u>kam</u>-ul] *noun, plural* **camels.** a large animal with a long, curved neck and long legs, used in desert countries for carrying goods and people. The Arabian camel has one hump, and the camel of central Asia has two.

cam·e·o [<u>kam</u>-ee-oh] *noun, plural* **cameos. 1.** an engraving, often in the shape of a head, that has been carved from a stone or shell so that the design stands out from its background. **2.** a small part in a play or film.

cam·e·ra [<u>kam</u>-ruh *or* <u>kam</u>-uh-ruh] *noun, plural* **cameras.** a device used to take photographs, to make movies, or for television transmission. A man who uses this device is called a **cameraman**.

cam·ou·flage ▼ [<u>kam</u>-uh-*flazh*] *noun, plural* **camouflages.** a false appearance that makes things or people merge into the background so that it is hard to see them. In warfare, leaves and branches can be used as camouflage over something to make it appear to be part of the natural surroundings.
verb, **camouflaged, camouflaging.** to disguise the appearance of something in order to hide it: *to camouflage a truck for desert warfare by painting it the color of the desert sand.*

camp [kamp] *noun, plural* **camps. 1.** an outdoor area with tents or cabins where people live for a short time: *The Boy Scouts spent the weekend at a camp in the woods.* The act or sport of staying in a camp is **camping**. The place where you stay is the **campground**. **2.** huts and other buildings built by an army as a place for soldiers to stay.
verb, **camped, camping.** to stay or live somewhere for a short time in tents or cabins.

cam·paign [kam-<u>pane</u>] *noun, plural* **campaigns. 1.** a series of planned attacks during a war by one country's armed forces against another country: *The famous D-Day landing was part of the European campaign in World War II.* **2.** a set of actions planned and carried out in order to get a particular result: *The company plans a big advertising campaign to promote its new computer.*
verb, **campaigned, campaigning.** to take part in or to plan a series of actions: *Both candidates spent millions of dollars campaigning for the office of President.*
—**campaigner**, *noun.*

Insects are often **camouflaged** *by their color, shape, or patterns.*

cam·phor [kamp-fur] *noun. Chemistry.* a white substance that has a strong odor and a bitter taste used in medicine and in plastics, and in mothballs to keep moths away.

can¹ [kan] *verb, past tense* **could.** a special verb that is often used with other verbs to show these meanings: **1.** to be able or know how to do something: *This car can go about thirty miles on a gallon of gas; Emily can play the piano very well.* **2.** to have the right to: *In our state you can drive a car when you are sixteen.* **3.** to be allowed to: *Mom says I can watch TV after I finish my homework.*

It is often said that the word **can** should not be used in a sentence like, "*Can* I borrow your bike for a while?" The idea is that this should say instead, "*May* I borrow your bike for a while?" because *can* means "be able to" and *may* means "be allowed to." Though it is true that *may* sounds more polite in a sentence like this, people are more likely to use *can*, and it is not really wrong to do this.

can² [kan] *noun, plural* **cans.** a metal container used to store food or liquids: *a can of baked beans; a can of pineapple juice.*
verb, **canned, canning.** to put into or preserve in a can.

Canada Day [kan-uh-duh] July 1, a holiday in Canada. It marks the day when the first four provinces of Canada were joined together, and used to be called **Dominion Day.**

Can·ad·ian [kuh-nay-dee-un] *noun, plural* **Canadians.** a person who was born or lives in Canada.
adjective, belonging to or relating to Canada or its people.

can·al ▼ [kuh-nal] *noun, plural* **canals.** a long, narrow stretch of water made for ships and boats to travel along, or to bring water to and from an area.

ca·nar·y ▶ [kuh-nare-ee] *noun, plural* **canaries.**
1. a small yellow bird, often kept as a pet in a cage, which is known for its beautiful song. **2.** a light, bright yellow color.
adjective. having the same yellow color as a canary.

Canary is the name for a bird, but it comes from a word for "dog." This bird lives on an island in the Atlantic Ocean that was called "the island of dogs," because of the large dogs that once lived there.

can·cel [kan-sul] *verb,* **canceled** *or* **cancelled, canceling** *or* **cancelling. 1.** to call off, give up, or not do something: *All morning flights out of New York were canceled because of fog.* The act of canceling something is the **cancellation** of it. **2.** to cross out, delete, or mark something in a way that shows it can no longer be used: *to cancel a stamp to show that it already has been used to mail a letter.* —**cancellation,** *noun.*

can·cer [kan-sur] *noun, plural* **cancers.** *Medicine.* a serious disease in which cells in a person's body begin to divide and rapidly increase in number, much faster than they usually should. These abnormally growing cells then become **cancerous.** Many different kinds of cancer can affect the body and can cause death.

can·did [kan-did] *adjective.* honest and straightforward in speech and behavior: *Do you like my new dress? Please be candid and tell me if you don't.* —**candidly,** *adverb.*

can·di·date [kan-di-date *or* kan-uh-date] *noun, plural* **candidates. 1.** a person who applies for a job: *I might not get the job because there were ten other candidates.* **2.** a person who puts themselves forward or is proposed by others for an office or honor: *Suzanne was the most popular candidate put forward to be school president.* If you run as a candidate in an election, you announce your **candidacy** for that position.

A pet **canary** *can live for up to fifteen years.*

can·dle [kan-dul] *noun, plural* **candles.** a long, thin object made of wax with a wick through the middle of it that is lit to give light or for decoration. A **candlestick** is a holder for a candle.

can·dy [kan-dee] *noun plural,* **candies.** a sweet made with sugar, syrup, and various other ingredients.
verb, **candied, candying.** to cook something in a syrup so that it becomes coated with it. —**candied,** *adjective.*

cane [kayn] *noun, plural,* **canes. 1.** a stick used to help a person to walk or stand up: *Jane needs a cane to walk now because she broke her leg skiing.* **2.** the long, hollow stems of plants such as bamboo and sugar cane, which can be used to make furniture.

In 1869, the first ships sailed through the new Suez **Canal,** *which linked the Red Sea with the Mediterranean Sea.*

*Over many years, rivers can create **canyons** when they flow over rocks.*

A river flows over a flat rock surface.

The river gradually erodes part of the rock surface.

Slowly, the river gets wider and the canyon deeper.

ca·nine [kay-nine] *adjective.* having to do with dogs, or any member of the dog family.
noun, plural **canines. 1.** a dog or any other animal of the dog family, such as wolves, jackals, hyenas, coyotes, or foxes. **2.** a pointed tooth near the front of the mouth in humans and dogs. Humans have four **canine teeth.**

can·ni·bal [kan-uh-bul] *noun, plural* **cannibals. 1.** a human who eats human flesh. **2.** an animal that feeds on its own species. The act of doing this is called **cannibalism.**

can·non [kan-un] *noun, plural* **cannons** or **cannon.** a large, heavy gun, usually on wheels, used to fire heavy, metal balls at an enemy.

can·not [kan-ot *or* ka-not] can not; not able to.

ca·noe ▼ [kuh-noo] *noun, plural* **canoes.** a small, light boat, often pointed at each end, that is moved and steered through the water with a paddle.
verb, **canoed, canoeing.** to paddle or ride in a canoe.

> When the explorer Christopher Columbus made his famous voyage to the Americas, he saw the native peoples using a type of boat that he had never seen before. They called it *canoa,* and this led to the English word **canoe.**

can·op·y [kan-uh-pee] *noun, plural* **canopies.** a covering hung over the entrance to a building to provide shelter, or used as a decoration over something, such as a bed or throne.

can't [kant] the shortened form of "can not."

can·ta·loupe [kan-tuh-lope] *noun, plural* **cantaloupes.** a small melon with a rough skin, and sweet, yellowish-orange flesh inside.

can·teen [kan-teen] *noun, plural* **canteens. 1.** an inexpensive eating place in a school, office building, or factory where students or workers go to buy their food and drink. **2.** a small metal container used for carrying drinking water.

can·tor [kan-tur] *noun, plural* **cantors.** *Religion.* the chief or solo singer in a synagogue.

can·vas [kan-vis] *noun, plural* **canvases. 1.** a strong, heavy cloth usually made of cotton or linen. It is used to make things such as tents, sails, and awnings. **2.** a piece of strong cloth, on which a painting can be done: *The art exhibition was mainly of oil paintings on canvas.*

can·yon ▲ [kan-yun] *noun, plural* **canyons.** a deep, narrow gorge or valley with very steep sides, often with a river at the bottom.

cap [kap] *noun, plural* **caps. 1.** a type of hat that fits closely on the head, with either no brim or only a visor. **2.** anything that covers or protects like this type of hat, such as a top on a bottle or snow on a mountain. **3.** a tiny package of explosive used in a toy gun to make the sound of a shot.
verb, **capped, capping. 1.** to cover something with a cap or a cap-like object. **2.** to end on a higher point: *They put on a great concert and then capped it off by singing their most popular song.*

ca·pa·ble [kay-puh-bul] *adjective.* having the skill or ability to do something: *A three-year-old really is not capable of riding a bicycle.* The quality of being capable is **capability.**

ca·pac·i·ty [kuh-pas-uh-tee] *noun, plural* **capacities. 1.** the amount that can be contained or managed: *This car has the capacity to carry five people.* **2.** ability, power, or possibility: *The teacher says I have the capacity to do very well in this course.* **3.** a particular role or job: *In his capacity as hall monitor, he checked my pass.*

cape¹ [kape] *noun, plural* **capes.** a sleeveless article of clothing worn over other clothing and across the shoulders.

cape² [kape] *noun, plural* **capes.** a piece of land that extends into a large body of water.

cap·il·lar·y [kap-uh-lare-ee] *noun, plural* **capillaries.** *Biology.* a tiny tube or vessel that carries blood between arteries and veins.

cap·i·tal¹ [kap-uh-tul] *noun, plural* **capitals. 1.** the city or town in which the government of a nation or state has its main offices. **2.** the large form, or upper case, of a letter of alphabet; used as the first letter when writing a sentence or

*Most **canoes** are designed to carry up to two people.*

proper name, such as *Maria, California,* or *Lake Michigan*. **3.** the total wealth, including money and property, of a person or business. **4.** the money or property used to make more money or buy more property. 🔊 A different word with the same sound is **Capitol**.

cap·i·tal² ▶ [kap-uh-tul] *noun, plural* **capitals.** the upper part of a column of a building. 🔊 A different word with the same sound is **Capitol**.

cap·i·tal·ism [kap-uh-tul-*iz*-um] *noun. Business.* a system in which the people of a country have the right to own businesses, factories, and farms, to sell products and services, and to act for the good of themselves. In some countries that do not have capitalism, the government owns the land and stores and has control over the kind of jobs that people have. A person who believes or participates in capitalism is a **capitalist.**

cap·i·tal·ize [kap-uh-tul-*ize*] *verb,* **capitalized, capitalizing.** *Language.* to write or print with capital letters, or start with a capital letter. —**capitalization,** *noun.*

capital punishment *Law.* the fact of legally killing or injuring someone convicted in a court of law of committing murder or another serious crime.

Cap·i·tol [kap-uh-tul] *noun. Government.* the white, domed government building in Washington, D.C. where the U.S. Senate and the House of Representatives meet. A building in which officers of government meet is a **capitol.** 🔊 A different word with the same sound is **capital**.

cap·size [kap-*size*] *verb,* **capsized, capsizing.** to accidentally overturn something, especially a boat: *A large wave caused the sailboat to capsize.*

cap·sule ▶ [kap-sul] *noun, plural,* **capsules. 1.** a very small container that holds a dose of medicine and that can be swallowed whole and digested. **2.** the section of a spacecraft that carries astronauts and instruments. *adjective.* in a small or brief form: *The Website gives a capsule description of each product the company sells.*

cap·tain [kap-tun] *noun, plural* **captains. 1.** an officer in charge of a boat or ship. **2.** an officer in the police or armed forces. **3.** any person who is in charge of a group; a leader. *verb,* **captained, captaining.** to be the captain of.

cap·tion [kap-shun] *noun, plural* **captions.** a short piece of text describing a picture, photo, graph, or other such item in a book, magazine, newspaper, or the like.

cap·tiv·ate [kap-tuh-*vate*] *verb,* **captivated, captivating.** to capture or attract someone's attention: *I was captivated by his good looks.* —**captivation,** *noun.*

cap·tive [kap-tiv] *noun, plural* **captives.** a person or animal held against their will; a prisoner: *The famous book* Kidnapped *tells of a young man taken captive*

Doric capital

Ionic capital

Corinthian capital

Ancient Greek temples had three main types of **capitals**.

to be sold as a slave. The state of being held as a captive is **captivity.** *adjective.* **1.** held as a prisoner; prevented from escaping: *captive animals in a zoo.* **2.** as if held prisoner; kept within bounds: *I had to ride in the car with him, so I was a captive audience for his boring story.*

cap·ture [kap-chur] *verb,* **captured, capturing. 1.** to take control of a person, animal, or thing: *to capture a wild animal; to capture an enemy city in war.* **2.** to attract or draw in: *Her beautiful singing captured my attention.* **3.** to clearly represent or express something: *The film captures the horror of war.* *noun, plural* **captures.** the act of taking control of a person, animal or thing: *the capture of a fort.*

car [kar] *noun, plural* **cars. 1.** a road vehicle, usually with four wheels, powered by an internal engine. **2.** any vehicle that runs on wheels or tracks, such as a cable car or railroad car. **3.** the part of an elevator that carries people and things.

car·at [kare-ut] *noun, plural* **carats. 1.** a measurement of weight for precious stones such as diamonds; a carat is equal to one-fifth of a gram. **2.** a measure of the purity of gold. 🔊 A different word with the same sound is **carrot.**

car·a·van [kare-uh-*van*] *noun, plural* **caravans.** a group of people, vehicles, or pack animals moving forward, often in a line: *In the desert I saw a caravan of camels.*

car·bo·hy·drate [kar-boh-hye-drate] *noun, plural* **carbohydrates.** *Biology.* a combination of the natural chemicals carbon, hydrogen, and oxygen. Carbohydrates are found in certain food sources, such as vegetables, fruits, grains, beans, dairy products, and sugars. A shorter form of this word is **carb.**

car·bon [kar-bun] *noun. Biology.* a chemical found in some amount in all living things. Coal, graphite, and diamonds are almost entirely made up of carbon.

A space **capsule** *orbits the Earth and sends back information about space.*

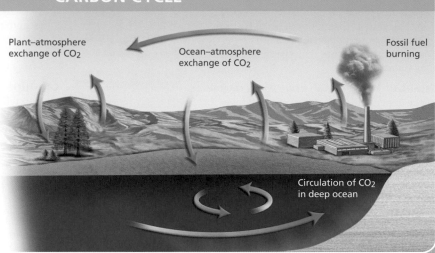

CARBON CYCLE

Carbon in many different forms is cycled between the air, land, and oceans in complex processes. For example, plants absorb carbon dioxide (CO_2) from the atmosphere to help them grow and then return some in a process called respiration. Carbon dioxide is also exchanged between the atmosphere and oceans, where some is used by sea creatures and plants, and some returned to the air. However, when fossil fuels are burned, carbon dioxide moves in one direction only—into the atmosphere, leading to a rise in carbon concentrations in the last 150 years.

Plant–atmosphere exchange of CO_2

Ocean–atmosphere exchange of CO_2

Fossil fuel burning

Circulation of CO_2 in deep ocean

carbon cycle ▲ *Science.* the physical, chemical, and biological processes that move carbon between living organisms and the environment. For example, carbon can be released into the atmosphere when wood or coal is burned. It can be taken from the atmosphere by growing plants.

carbon di·ox·ide [dye-<u>oks</u>-ide] *Biology.* a non-poisonous gas with no color or smell, made of one part carbon and two parts oxygen. Humans make and breathe out carbon dioxide. Plants use carbon dioxide to produce the oxygen we breathe.

carbon mon·ox·ide [muh-<u>noks</u>-ide] *Biology.* a very poisonous gas with no color or smell, made of one part carbon and one part oxygen. It is created when organic materials, such as oil, coal, and wood, are burned with limited access to air. Cars and cigarettes release carbon monoxide into the air.

car·bur·e·tor [<u>kar</u>-buh-*ray*-tur] *noun, plural* **carburetors.** the section of an engine where fuel and air are mixed in the right quantities for the engine to burn fuel properly.

car·cass [<u>kar</u>-kus] *noun, plural* **carcasses.** the dead body of an animal.

card·board [<u>kard</u>-bord] *noun.* a stiff paper often used for making posters, containers, or for packaging.

car·di·ac [<u>kar</u>-dee-ak] *adjective. Medicine.* relating to or affecting the heart: *My uncle developed very serious heart problems, so he had to have cardiac surgery.* The area of medicine that deals with the study or treatment of the heart is **cardiology.** A doctor who specializes in this area is a **cardiologist.**

car·di·nal ▶ [<u>kard</u>-nul *or* <u>kar</u>-duh-nul] *noun, plural* **cardinals. 1.** one of the small group of bishops in the Roman Catholic Church who advise the Pope and elect new Popes. Cardinals wear robes of a bright red color. **2.** a North American songbird with a small, thick bill and a short crest of feathers on its head.

The male is mostly red with a black face; the female is brown with patches of red.
adjective. most important; main: *This book lists five cardinal rules to follow to be a success in business.*

cardinal number *Mathematics.* any number used in counting or to show how many; cardinal numbers do not show the order of things. One, two, and three are cardinal numbers; first, second, and third are not.

care [kare] *noun, plural* **cares. 1.** attention, notice, interest, or concentration: *Carry those glasses with care.* **2.** worry or concern: *Grandpa's main care is Grandma's health.* **3.** safety; protection: *My parents left us in the care of a babysitter.*
verb, **cared, caring. 1.** to feel or show concern or interest: *I care about my school grades.* **2.** to be in favor of or against something; to mind: *Do you care if I eat the leftovers?* **3.** to take responsibility for, look after or protect: *The nurse cared for the patient.*

ca·reer [kuh-<u>reer</u>] *noun, plural* **careers.** someone's job or their different experiences working at a particular type of job: *I am thinking of a career in teaching.*

care·free [<u>kare</u>-*free*] *adjective.* having no worries, concerns, or responsibilities.

care·ful [<u>kare</u>-ful] *adjective.* **1.** showing close attention and concern: *I was careful holding the baby.* **2.** being thorough and showing care: *After careful research, I found the bike I wanted at a price I could afford.* **—carefully,** *adverb.*

care·giv·er [<u>kare</u>-*giv*-ur] *noun, plural* **caregivers.** *Health.* a person who looks after a young child or someone who is sick or disabled.

care·less [<u>kare</u>-lus] *adjective.* not giving attention or concern; not having the proper thought or care: *I was careless while ironing and burned a big hole in my shirt; I made a careless remark to my friend about her new haircut and really upset her.* **—carelessly,** *adverb;* **—carelessness,** *noun.*

A **cardinal** *eats insects, seeds, and fruits.*

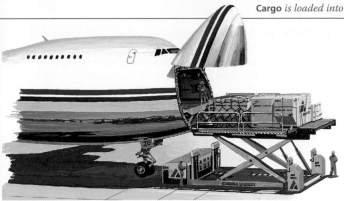

ca·ress [kuh-res] *verb*, **caressed, caressing.** to stroke gently and lovingly: *The grandmother caressed the baby.* —**caress,** *noun*.

care·tak·er [kare-*take*-ur] *noun, plural* **caretakers.** 1. someone who looks after a property or building: *The caretaker of the cemetery trims the grass around the headstones.* 2. someone who looks after other people.

car·go ▲ [kar-goh] *noun, plural* **cargoes** or **cargos.** goods transported by plane, ship, or truck.

car·i·bou [kare-i-*boo*] *noun, plural,* **caribou** or **caribous.** a large animal of the deer family that lives in northern areas of the U.S. and Canada. In Europe and Asia these animals are called reindeer.

car·ies [kare-eez] *noun. Medicine.* decay of the bone or teeth: *If you don't brush your teeth you'll get caries.*

car·na·tion [kar-nay-shun] *noun, plural* **carnations.** a fragrant flower that grows on a long stem and comes in many colors.

car·ni·val [karn-uh-vul] *noun, plural* **carnivals.** a festival or fair that has rides, games, acts, and displays. Some carnivals also have a parade.

car·ni·vor·ous ▶ [kar-niv-ur-us] *adjective. Biology.* describing an animal that lives by eating the flesh of animals: *Tigers, wolves, and jackals are carnivorous animals.* Meat-eating animals are called **carnivores.**

car·ol [kare-ul] *noun, plural* **carols.** *Music.* a happy song or hymn, usually sung at Christmas time. *verb,* **caroled, caroling.** to sing such songs or hymns.

carp [karp] *noun, plural* **carp** or **carps.** a large freshwater fish. Sometimes carp are farmed in dams and used as food.

car·pen·ter [kar-pun-tur] *noun, plural* **carpenters.** someone whose work or skill is building things from wood. Work done by a carpenter is called **carpentry.**

car·pet [kar-put] *noun, plural* **carpets. 1.** a thick, heavy covering for a floor, usually made of wool or synthetic fibers, also called **carpeting**; a rug. **2.** a covering like a carpet: *The field was covered in a colorful carpet of spring flowers.* *verb,* **carpeted, carpeting.** to put a covering on a floor.

car·pet·bag·ger [kar-put-*bag*-ur] *noun, plural* **carpetbaggers. 1. Carpetbagger.** *History.* a Northerner who went to the South after the American Civil War to make money or take advantage of opportunities there. **2.** someone seeking election to political office in a place where he or she has not lived before, and has no local connections.

The Northern **Carpetbaggers** got their name because they were thought to have traveled to the South carrying their belongings in a type of suitcase known as a *carpet bag.*

car·pool [kar-*pool*] *noun, plural* **carpools.** the shared use of a car for traveling to work or school, often by people who each have a car but want to travel together, so as to save costs and cut down on pollution. This word is also spelled **car pool.** *verb,* **car-pooled, car-pooling.** to share the use of a car in this way: *The left lane can only be used by people who car-pool.*

car·riage [kare-ij] *noun, plural* **carriages. 1.** a four-wheeled, horse-drawn, passenger vehicle. **2.** a term for certain other passenger vehicles: *a baby carriage; a train carriage.* **3.** a part of a machine that contains some other part or parts.

car·ri·er [kare-ee-ur] *noun, plural* **carriers.** someone or something that moves or transports things: *Ships, aircraft, and railroad trains are all freight carriers.*

car·rot [kare-ut] *noun, plural* **carrots. 1.** a long, orange-colored vegetable that is pointed at one end. **2.** the plant that produces this vegetable at its root. 🔊 A different word with the same sound is **carat.**

car·ry [kare-ee] *verb,* **carried, carrying. 1.** to move something while holding it: *Let me carry your books.* **2.** to have a supply of something: *The supermarket carries lots of types of candy.* **3.** to continue or keep doing something: *You carry on with the work while I go get us a drink.* **4.** to move from one place to another: *This road carries about 10,000 vehicles per day; To add 15 and 9, put 4 in the first column and carry the 1.*

Weasel

Civet

Hyena

Raccoon

Dingo

Grizzly bear

Carnivorous animals hunt and eat many different creatures.

a
b
c
d
e
f
g
h
i
j
k
l
m
n
o
p
q
r
s
t
u
v
w
x
y
z

A B C D E F G H I J K L M N O P Q R S T U V W X Y Z

cart [kart] *noun, plural* **carts. 1.** a wagon with two wheels, usually pulled by an animal. **2.** a small wagon pushed by a person; often used in supermarkets to carry groceries. *verb,* **carted, carting.** to move in a cart.

car·ti·lage [kart-uh-lij] *noun. Biology.* a tough, flexible tissue found in various parts of the body. It is usually found between bones and helps joints move smoothly. It is also found in the outer ear, larynx, and nose.

car·tog·raph·y ▲ [kar-tog-ruh-fee] *noun.* the science of making maps. Someone who makes maps is a **cartographer.**

car·toon [kar-toon] *noun, plural* **cartoons.** a drawing, often supported with words or a caption. Cartoons are usually supposed to be funny or to tell a story. Sometimes cartoons are animated into movies.

car·tridge [kar-trij] *noun, plural* **cartridges. 1.** a small case containing gunpowder and a bullet, fired from a rifle or handgun. **2.** any small container: *an ink cartridge; a film cartridge.*

cart·wheel [kart-weel] *noun, plural* **cartwheels. 1.** the wheel of a cart. **2.** an acrobatic turn. To do a cartwheel you flip sideways, keeping your arms and legs straight, turning through the air like the spokes of a wheel; finally you end up back on your feet.

carve [karv] *verb,* **carved, carving. 1.** to cut or chisel a shape into material like stone or wood, to create a statue or some other object. **2.** to slice or cut into something hard: *Dad carved the roast beef; I carved my initials into the trunk of the tree.*

The hair of about four goats is needed to make one **cashmere** *sweater.*

cas·cade [kas-kade] *noun, plural* **cascades.** a small waterfall or series of small waterfalls. *verb,* **cascaded, cascading.** to flow like a waterfall: *Water from the broken pipe cascaded down the street.*

case¹ [kase] *noun, plural* **cases. 1.** an example of something: *In a case of mistaken identity, they arrested the wrong man.* **2.** the state of things; the facts: *He said the dog ate his homework, but the teacher certainly does not think that is the case.* **3.** an instance of injury or illness: *There were lots of cases of flu last winter.* **4.** a matter to be dealt with by the police and the court; a matter of law: *The case was closed when the guilty man was sent to prison.*

The **case** of a noun or pronoun is the form of the word that is used, according to what it means in the sentence. Some languages have many different cases for words, but English has only three. The *nominative case* is used when the word is the subject of the sentence: *I called Tyler on the phone.* The *objective case* is used when the word is an object: *Tyler called me back.* The *possessive case* is used when the word shows who has (possesses) something: *Tyler borrowed my book.*

case² ▼ [kase] *noun, plural* **cases.** a container used to protect or store something: *I need to buy a case to hold my laptop computer.*

cash [kash] *noun.* money in the form of bills or coins. *verb,* **cashed, cashing.** to give or receive cash for something: *Mom cashed a check at the bank.*

cash·ew [kash-ooh] *noun, plural* **cashews.** a nut you can eat. Cashews grow on evergreen trees in tropical areas.

cash·mere ◀ [kazh-meer or kash-meer] *noun, plural* **cashmeres.** a soft fabric woven from the hair of certain Asian goats: *My cashmere sweater is especially warm and soft.*

The true **cashmere** wool comes only from a certain type of goat that lives in a region of Asia known as Kashmir. *Cashmere* is an older spelling of *Kashmir.*

cask [kask] *noun, plural* **casks.** a wooden barrel for storing wine or other liquid.

cas·ket [kask-it] *noun, plural* **caskets.** a box to hold a dead body; a coffin.

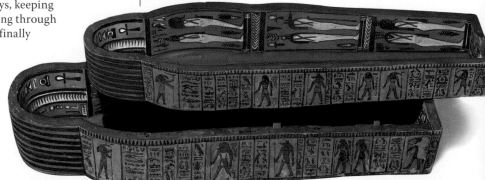

Ancient Egyptian mummy **cases** *were elaborately decorated.*

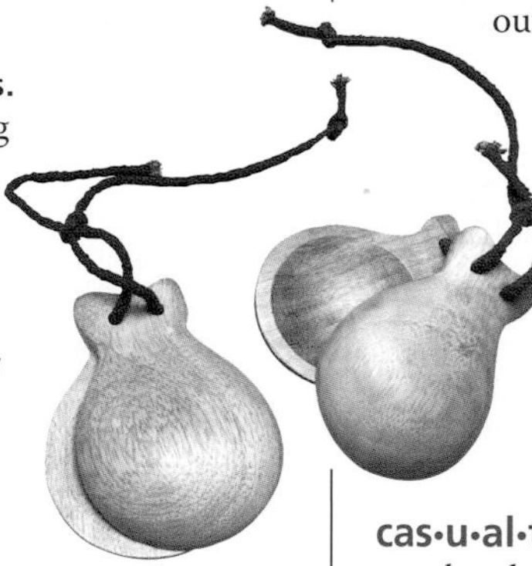

*Spanish dancers use **castanets** to mark the rhythm of the music.*

cas·se·role [kas-uh-*role*] *noun, plural* **casseroles. 1.** a deep dish for cooking and serving food. **2.** food served in such a dish.

cass·ette [kuh-*set*] *noun, plural* **cassettes.** a small case holding a tape for recording or playing music and other sounds.

cast [kast] *verb,* **cast, casting. 1.** to throw something through the air: *He cast his fishing line into the lake.* **2.** to form or put: *As the sun set, we cast long shadows across the sand.* **3.** to choose actors to play a part: *My sister was cast as Snow White in the school play.* **4.** to shape by pouring liquid into a mold and waiting for it to harden: *The art teacher showed us how to cast our statues in plaster.* *noun, plural,* **casts. 1.** the act of throwing something through the air: *Try to practice your cast before you come fishing.* **2.** the actors in a show: *I thought the entire cast of the movie gave a wonderful performance.* **3.** a bandage covered in plaster or other hard material that is put around a broken bone to protect it. **4.** something formed in a mold: *The dentist made a plaster cast of my teeth.*

cas·ta·net ▲ [*kas*-tuh-*net*] *noun, plural* **castanets.** one of two small pieces of wood, each carved in the shape of a half clam shell. They are clicked together in time to the beat of a dance.

cast iron a mixture of iron and other materials melted into a liquid and poured into a mold. When the mixture cools, the iron hardens into a shape.

cas·tle ▼ [*kas*-ul] *noun, plural* **castles. 1.** *History.* a large fort with towers and high, strong walls to keep enemies out. Castles often have moats around them as well. **2.** one of the pieces in a game of chess; also called a rook.

cas·u·al [*kazh*-yoo-ul *or* *kazh*-wul] *adjective.* **1.** doing something without much planning or thought: *As I walked past Tim's house I decided to stop in for a casual visit.* **2.** not formal or serious: *On weekends she wears casual clothing to go to the park or the store.* —**casually,** *adverb;* —**casualness,** *noun.*

cas·u·al·ty [*kazh*-yoo-ul-tee *or* *kazh*-wul-tee] *noun, plural* **casualties. 1.** someone killed or badly injured in war. **2.** someone killed or badly injured in a disaster or large accident, such as a hurricane or plane crash.

Banqueting hall | Lookout towers | Drawbridge

Bedchamber

*Conwy **Castle** was a royal fortress built in Wales in the thirteenth century.*

Hoist | Moat

cat ▶ [kat] *noun, plural* **cats. 1.** a furry animal with pointed ears and a long tail, often kept as a pet. Some cats are used to catch mice and rats. **2.** any animal of the cat family, such as lions, leopards, and tigers.

cat·a·log [kat-uh-*log*] *noun, plural* **catalogs.** a list of things. Stores sometimes have a catalog with pictures and prices of things for sale. Libraries have a catalog with the titles and authors of all their books. *verb,* **cataloged, cataloging.** to make a list of things. This word is also spelled **catalogue.**

*A **catapult** was a powerful and deadly weapon of war.*

cat·a·ma·ran [kat-uh-muh-*ran*] *noun, plural* **catamarans.** a boat with two hulls joined together.

cat·a·pult ▲ [kat-uh-*pult*] *noun, plural* **catapults.** *History.* **1.** a weapon like a huge slingshot, once used to hurl rocks over castle walls. **2.** a machine used to launch planes from an aircraft carrier. —**catapult,** *verb.*

cat·a·ract [kat-uh-*rakt*] *noun, plural* **cataracts. 1.** a large waterfall. **2.** *Medicine.* a clouding in the lens of an eye that can cause blindness. Cataracts are usually cured by surgery.

cat·as·tro·phe [kuh-*tas*-truh-*fee*] *noun, plural* **catastrophes.** a huge, sudden disaster: *When the building collapsed and killed so many people, it was a catastrophe.* If such a disaster happens, the results are often **catastrophic.**

cat·bird [kat-*burd*] *noun, plural* **catbirds.** a long-beaked, gray bird with a song that sounds like a cat meowing.

catch [kach] *verb,* **caught, catching. 1.** to grab hold of a moving thing, especially with the hand: *to catch a baseball; to catch the dog by the collar before he could run away.* **2.** to take and hold; capture: *to catch fish; to catch a wanted criminal.* **3.** to get stuck or hooked on something: *to catch a wool sweater on a nail.* **4.** to surprise or come upon someone doing something: *I caught him trying to copy my homework.* ✚ **Catch** is also used in many other ways with the idea of connecting or coming in contact in some way: *to catch a bus; to catch the measles; to cause a building to catch fire; to catch a movie after work. noun, plural* **catches. 1.** the taking hold of a moving thing: *The outfielder made a great catch.* **2.** something

that fastens or holds: *The catch on the gate is stuck.* **3.** something that has been caught: *Dad came back with a catch of two fish.* **4.** a game where players throw a ball between them. **5.** a hidden condition; a trick: *If they are giving things away for free, there's probably a catch somewhere.*

catch·er [kach-ur] *noun, plural* **catchers. 1.** a player in baseball whose position is behind home plate and who catches balls thrown by the pitcher. **2.** any person or thing that catches.

ca·te·go·ry [kat-uh-*gore*-ee] *noun, plural* **categories.** a type or class of things: *Cats and dogs are just two of the many categories of animals.*

ca·ter [kate-ur] *verb,* **catered, catering.** to provide food or other services for a certain event, such as a wedding: *His mother catered the dinner party.* Someone who does the **catering** for an event is called a **caterer.**

cat·er·pil·lar [kat-ur-*pil*-ur] *noun, plural* **caterpillars.** the larva of a moth or butterfly. Caterpillars look like a short, fat worm; sometimes they are hairy.

> The word **caterpillar** is said to come from a French phrase meaning "a hairy cat." People thought this larva looked like a tiny cat covered with hair.

Lantern

Dome

cat·fish [kat-*fish*] *noun, plural* **catfish** *or* **catfishes.** a type of fish with feelers around its mouth that look like a cat's whiskers.

ca·the·dral ◀ [kuh-*thee*-drul] *noun, plural* **cathedrals.** *Religion.* **1.** a building that is the official church of a bishop. **2.** a large and important church.

*The **cathedral**, or Duomo, in Florence, Italy, was built between 1296 and 1469, and is famous for its huge dome, which contains more than four million bricks.*

Marble mosaic floor

The cat family has 36 members, ranging in size from the South American oncilla, half as big as a domestic cat, to the Siberian tiger, which grows to twelve feet long. All are good hunters, with sharp teeth and claws, strong jaws, and supple bodies. Most cats eat only meat and many are nocturnal. They follow their prey silently, attack suddenly, pull it to the ground and kill it with a bite to the neck or throat. Most cats live alone, but lions live in a family group called a pride.

Wild cat skeleton

Skull
Shoulder blade
Backbone
Tailbone
Jawbone
Ribs
Toe bones

DOMESTIC CATS
For more than 3,000 years some species of small cats have been bred to live with humans.

Domestic cats

CHEETAHS
Cheetahs are the fastest of all land animals and can reach great speeds over short distances. Unlike the great cats, they purr instead of roaring.

Cheetah

Caracal

SMALL CATS
Many small cats purr constantly. They have large eyes and the pupils are usually vertical.

African golden cat

Margay

Eurasian lynx

Kodkod

Puma

GREAT CATS
Like all cats, they are skilled hunters and have keen eyesight. They are the only cats that roar.

Black panther

Tiger

Lion and lioness

Ocelot

Cath·o·lic [kath-lik *or* kath-uh-lik] *adjective. Religion.*
1. having to do with the largest branch of the Christian church, whose leader is the Pope; also called the Roman Catholic Church. This is the earlier branch of the Christian church formed after the life of Christ.
2. **catholic.** very broad in scope or interest; wide-ranging.
noun, plural **Catholics.** a person who is a member of the Catholic Church.

CAT scan another term for CT SCAN.

cat·sup [ketch-up *or* kat-sup] *noun, plural* **catsups.** a thick tomato sauce. This word is usually spelled **ketchup.**

cat·tle ▼ [kat-ul] *plural noun.* animals including cows, steers, bulls, and oxen, often raised for meat, milk, cheese, and other dairy products, and leather.

Cau·ca·sian [kaw-kaye-zhun] *adjective.* **1.** *Geography.* having to do with the Caucasus mountains, a range between the Black Sea and the Caspian Sea in Europe. **2.** having to do with the so-called white race, which was once thought to have come from this mountain area. *noun, plural* **Caucasians.** a member of the so-called white race, generally having lighter skin and originally living in Europe and in nearby areas of Asia and Africa.

caught [kawt] *verb.* the past tense and past participle of CATCH.

caul·dron [kawl-drun] *noun,* *plural* **cauldrons.** a very large pot used for boiling things. This word is also spelled **caldron.**

caulk [kawlk] *verb,* **caulked, caulking.** to make something waterproof or airtight by filling in holes or cracks with tar or some other material. *noun.* a material that is used for this purpose.

cause [kawz] *noun, plural* **causes.**
1. someone or something that makes an event happen: *The cause of the forest fire was lightning striking a dead tree.*
2. something a person believes in: *The cause she supports the most is that ofanimal welfare.*
verb, **caused, causing.** to make an event happen: *Oil on the road caused the car to skid.*

cause·way [kawz-way] *noun,* *plural* **causeways.** a raised roadway crossing swampy ground or shallow water.

cau·tion [kaw-shun] *noun, plural* **cautions. 1.** the fact of taking care; being watchful or careful: *Use caution when you carry boiling water.* **2.** a warning: *After he stopped Mom for speeding, the police officer let her go with a caution.*
verb, **cautioned, cautioning.** to warn or advise to do something with care: *Dad cautioned us to ride our bikes slowly on the wet road.*

cau·tious [kaw-shus] *adjective.* doing something with care or using caution: *He was very cautious about approaching the lion's cage.* —**cautiously,** *adverb.*

cav·al·ry [kav-ul-ree] *noun, plural* **cavalries. 1.** *History.* a group of soldiers who fought on horseback or from tanks. **2.** a modern army unit using tanks and other armored vehicles. A member of the cavalry is called a **cavalryman.**

cave ▲ [kave] *noun, plural* **caves.** an underground hollow with an opening. Caves are often carved out of rocks by wind or water over a long time. *verb,* **caved, caving.** to explore a cave.
♦ **cave in. 1.** to fall in or down; collapse: *The walls of the mine caved in after the explosion, but no miners were hurt.* **2.** to give up; yield: *Dad finally caved in and agreed to let us go.-*

Brahmin

Texas long-horned

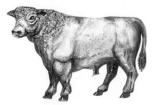

Galloway

Hereford

*There are more than 800 domestic breeds of **cattle** worldwide.*

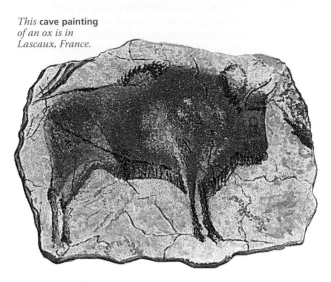
*This **cave painting** of an ox is in Lascaux, France.*

cave dweller someone who lives in a cave. In early human history, many people were cave dwellers. A different term with the same meaning is **cave man.**

cave-in [kave-*in*] *noun, plural* **cave-ins.** a collapse of a tunnel or mine.

cave painting ▲ *Art.* ancient or primitive paintings done on the walls of caves.

cav·ern [kav-urn] *noun, plural* **caverns.** a large or deep cave. **—cavernous,** *adjective.*

cav·i·ty [kav-uh-tee] *noun, plural* **cavities. 1.** a hollow place in something hard; a hole. **2.** a hollow or soft spot in a tooth caused by decay.

CD an abbreviation for COMPACT DISC.

CD-ROM [*see-dee-*rom] *Computers.* an abbreviation for Compact Disc Read-Only Memory, which is a compact disc on which large amounts of digital information are recorded. "Read Only" means that you can read or look at the material, but you cannot change or erase it.

cease [sees] *verb,* **ceased, ceasing.** to put or come to an end; stop: *The company announced that they would cease making that car model at the end of this year.* A **cease-fire** is when two sides in a battle or war agree to stop fighting.

ce·dar ▶ [see-dur] *noun, plural* **cedars.** a type of evergreen tree. Its hard, fragrant wood is used to make furniture.

ceil·ing [see-ling] *noun, plural* **ceilings. 1.** the lining inside the upper part of a room. **2.** the distance between the Earth's surface and the lowest level of clouds: *When the fog came down, the ceiling over the airport was zero.* **3.** the upper limit of something; the highest point or level: *Dad put a ceiling on how much money I could spend on a CD player.*

cel·e·brate [sel-uh-*brate*] *verb,* **celebrated, celebrating. 1.** to mark a special occasion with ceremonies or festivities: *to celebrate a person's birthday.* **2.** to perform with the correct ceremonies: *The priest celebrated Christmas Mass at midnight.*

cel·e·bra·tion [sel-uh-*bray*-shun] *noun, plural* **celebrations. 1.** the ceremonies or festivities held to celebrate a special occasion. **2.** the act of celebrating something.

ce·leb·ri·ty [suh-leb-ruh-tee] *noun, plural* **celebrities.** a famous person whose name often appears in the news, especially a movie star, popular singer, or other entertainer.

cel·er·y [sel-ree *or* sel-uh-ree] *noun.* a plant with white or green stalks that are eaten raw or cooked.

cel·es·ti·al [suh-les-chul] *adjective.* **1.** having to do with heaven; heavenly: *The angels that appeared to the shepherds were celestial beings.* **2.** having to do with the sky: *I used my telescope to look at Jupiter and other celestial objects.*

cell ▶ [sel] *noun, plurals* **cells. 1.** a room in which prisoners are held in a police station or prison. **2.** *Biology.* the basic body unit of all living things. Cells are so small they can only be seen with a microscope. Some things consist of only one cell; the human body is made up of billions of cells. **3.** *Science.* a device that creates electricity by a chemical reaction by energy from the sun; a battery. **—cellular,** *adjective.* 🔊 A different word with the same sound is **sell.**

cel·lar [sel-ur] *noun, plurals* **cellars.** an underground room usually beneath a building and often used for storage.

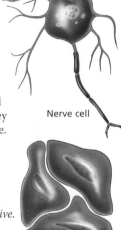
Bone cell

Nerve cell

Skin cell

*Body **cells** have different shapes and structures.*

Cedar trees have narrow, needle-like leaves and hard cones, which contain seeds.

cel·lo ◀ [chel-oh] *noun, plurals* **cellos.** *Music.* an instrument that is similar to a violin but is larger and makes lower sounds. The cello player holds the instrument between the knees and plucks or draws a bow across the strings.

cel·lo·phane [sel-uh-*fane*] *noun.* a thin, see-through, waterproof material made from cellulose; often used for packaging and to make clear sticky tape.

cell phone an abbreviation for **cellular telephone,** a wireless telephone that operates using radio waves. Radio towers receive and send the signals out in overlapping areas called cells, passing them from one area to the next.

cel·lu·loid [sel-yuh-*loyd*] *noun.* **1.** *Chemistry.* a clear plastic material, once used especially to make photographic film. It is strong but burns easily. **2.** another name for motion pictures, from the earlier use of this material for movies.

cel·lu·lose [sel-yuh-*lohs*] *noun. Biology.* the strong material that forms the main part of the cell walls of plants. Cellulose makes up the woody part of plants and gives them their strength.

Cel·si·us [sel-see-us *or* sel-shus] *adjective. Science.* referring to the scale of temperature measurement in which 0 degrees Celsius (0°C) is the freezing point of water and 100 degrees Celsius (100°C) is its boiling point. The **Celsius scale** or centigrade scale is the name of this system of temperature measurement.

> The **Celsius** temperature scale is named for the scientist who developed it, Anders *Celsius* of Sweden.

ce·ment [suh-*ment*] *noun.* **1.** a powdered mixture of burnt clay and limestone. When mixed with water, sand, and rock it makes concrete, which is used in building. **2.** anything soft and sticky that hardens to form a strong bond: *Dad used plastic cement to stick the broken chair back together.*
verb, **cemented, cementing. 1.** to fix something in place with cement: *Use glue to cement the beads onto the box.* **2.** to coat something in cement or concrete. **3.** to join anything together strongly; to unite: *The two leaders met to cement the friendship between their nations.*

cem·e·ter·y [sem-uh-*tare*-ee] *noun, plural* **cemeteries.** a place set aside for the burial of dead bodies; a burial ground.

cen·sor [sen-sur] *noun, plural* **censors.** an official who can ban films, books, plays, radio programs, or news reports, or can remove something from them that is thought to be bad, wrong, or harmful. The act of censoring something is called **censorship.**
verb, **censored, censoring.** to ban something or delete a part of it thought to be harmful.

cen·sus [sen-sus] *noun, plural* **censuses.** *Government.* an official count of the people who live in a country or region. Other details may also be collected, such as each person's age, sex, religion, and the work he or she does.

cent [sent] *noun, plural* **cents.** a unit of money worth one-hundredth part of one dollar. Cents and dollars are used in the United States, Canada, and Australia. ◀)) Different words with the same sound are **sent** and **scent.**

cen·taur ▼ [sen-tore] *noun, plural* **centaurs. 1.** *Literature.* a Greek mythological creature with the body of a man from the waist up and the legs and body of a horse. **2. Centaur.** a group of stars seen in the Southern Hemisphere, thought to look like this creature.

cen·ten·ni·al [sen-ten-ee-ul] *noun, plural* **centennials.** a one-hundredth anniversary of an event or its celebration: *We dressed up in old-fashioned clothes to celebrate the centennial of our school.* This anniversary and its celebration can also be called a **centenary.**

According to legend, **centaurs** *lived in mountain regions.*

cen·ter [sent-ur] *noun, plural* **centers. 1.** the mid-point of a circle or sphere; the point that is the same distance from any point on the circle's circumference or the sphere's surface. **2.** the middle location or part of an area or object: *The fountain stood in the center of the park.* **3.** a place, person, or object that is the main focus of attention or of an activity: *We play basketball at the town's sports center.* **4.** in various sports, the position in the middle of a playing line or area, or the player in this position: *The center on a hockey team lines up in the middle of the ice.*
verb, **centered, centering. 1.** to put something in the center: *The heading of your paper should be centered on the page.* **2.** to bring together around a point; focus: *Today's discussion will center on the cost of health care.* This word is also spelled **centre.**

centi- a prefix that means: **1.** one hundred: *centigrade* means divided into one hundred. **2.** one-hundredth: *centimeter* means one-hundredth of a meter.

cen·ti·grade [sen-tuh-*grade*] *adjective. Science.* using the Celsius temperature scale; an older word for Celsius.

cen·ti·me·ter [sen-tuh-*meet*-ur] *noun, plural* **centimeters.** *Mathematics.* a unit of length in the metric measuring system; one-hundredth of a meter. One centimeter equals approximately four-tenths of an inch.

cen·ti·pede ▶ [sen-tuh-*peed*] *noun,*
plural **centipedes.** a small animal with a long
segmented body, each segment having a pair
of legs. The first pair of legs is modified into
a pair of fangs used to inject poison into
the centipede's prey.

cen·tral [sen-trul] *adjective.* **1.** having to do
with the center of something: *The bank
is in the central part of the city.* **2.** most
important: *The central issue in this year's
election is whether the county should build
a new airport.* —**centrally,** *adverb.*

cen·trif·u·gal [sen-truh-*fyoo*-gul] *adjective.*
Science. moving outward from the center.
Centrifugal force is the tendency of an object that
is spinning to move outward from the point where
it started. When something moves toward the center,
it is described as moving in a **centripetal** way.

cen·tu·ry [sen-shu-ree] *noun, plural* **centuries.** a period
of one hundred years: *In just one century, from 1870
to 1970, the village grew into a city.*

cer·am·ics [suh-*ram*-iks] *noun. Art.* **1.** the art of making
objects such as jars and tiles out of clay; pottery: *When
I studied ceramics I made a vase.* **2.** objects made of baked
clay: *On the archaeological dig we found many ceramics,
including bricks, pots, and beads.*
adjective. **ceramic.** made of baked clay.

ce·re·al ▼ [sere-ee-ul] *noun, plural* **cereals. 1.** any type
of grass plant with seeds that can be eaten, including
grain such as wheat,
rice, or maize. **2.** food
made from these edible
seeds, especially when
eaten for breakfast.
🔊 A different word
with the same sound
is **serial.**

> The ancient Romans believed
> the goddess *Ceres* watched
> over farming and farmers.
> Her name was given to **cereal**
> grains, the most important
> crop of the Romans.

A **centipede**
*feeds at
night on
tiny insects.*

cer·e·mon·y ▼ [ser-uh-*moh*-nee] *noun,*
plural **ceremonies. 1.** a set of serious actions
carried out on a special occasion: *The general led
the ceremony at the opening of the war memorial.*
Something that belongs to or is used for a ceremony
is said to be **ceremonial. 2.** a formal or polite way
of behaving: *He handed me an invitation
with great ceremony.*

cer·tain [surt-un] *adjective.* **1.** known
to be right; absolutely sure: *I am
certain he was at the park today
because his car was parked right
at the entrance.* The state of being
certain of something is a **certainty.**
2. someone or something known
but not named: *I think that certain
people cheated on the test.*

Preparing tea is a traditional **ceremony** *in Japan.*

cer·tain·ly [sur-tun-lee] *adverb.* positively; without a doubt:
He has certainly grown much taller since we last saw him.

cer·tif·i·cate [sur-*tif*-uh-kit] *noun, plural* **certificates.**
a written paper accepted as proof of specific facts:
*I showed my birth certificate to prove who I was when
I opened a bank account.*

chain [chane] *noun, plural* **chains. 1.** a row of rings, usually
made of metal, that are linked to each other. A chain can
be used to fasten something or pull it along, or can be
used for decoration, such as a necklace
or paper chain. **2.** a series of connected
things: *The Rockies are a long chain
of mountains.*
verb, **chained, chaining.** to fasten
with a chain.

chain reaction 1. *Science.* an atomic
reaction in which an atom is split, releasing
neutrons which then split other atoms,
releasing more neutrons, and so on.
2. *Science.* a series of chemical reactions
in which a chemical produced by one
reaction causes further reactions.
3. a series of continuing events caused
by one another.

chair [chare] *noun, plural* **chairs. 1.** a piece
of furniture that a person sits on, with
a seat, legs, back, and sometimes armrests.
2. a shorter word for CHAIRPERSON.
verb, **chaired, chairing.** to lead or run
a meeting or committee.

CEREALS

Cereals make up a substantial part of our diet. Wheat is the most widely produced
cereal, especially in temperate climates, and is used mainly as flour for bread,
cakes, and pastry. Rice is a basic food in all parts of Asia,
where most of the world's rice is grown. The United States is
the largest producer of maize, which is eaten fresh, or can be
canned, frozen, or processed as cornflour and oil.

Planting
rice in Asia

Harvesting wheat
in North America

a
b
c
d
e
f
g
h
i
j
k
l
m
n
o
p
q
r
s
t
u
v
w
x
y
z

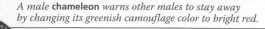
*A male **chameleon** warns other males to stay away by changing its greenish camouflage color to bright red.*

chair·man [chare-mun] *noun, plural* **chairmen.** a person, especially a man, who controls or leads a meeting or committee.

In recent years, people have begun to use the word **chairperson** to refer to either a man or woman. The idea of this is that it is better not to identify the person as being male or female.

chair·per·son [chare-*pur*-sun] *noun, plural* **chairpersons.** a person who controls or leads a meeting or committee.

chair·wo·man [chare-*wum*-un] *noun, plural* **chairwomen.** a woman who controls or leads a meeting or committee.

cha·let [shal-ay *or* shu-lay] *noun, plural* **chalets. 1.** a mountain cottage with a sloping roof and low, wide eaves; originally a traditional house in the Swiss mountains. **2.** a holiday house.

chalk [chawk] *noun.* **1.** a type of soft white pure limestone; used to make lime, cement and added to soil in agriculture. **2.** a stick of this material used for writing or drawing. *verb,* **chalk, chalked.** to mark in some way with chalk.
• **chalk up. 1.** to record or score: *I chalked up a score of seventeen in the spelling bee before I made a mistake.* **2.** to put down to, to say something is the result of: *Coach chalked up our team's victory to hard training.*

chalk·board [chawk-bord] *noun, plural* **chalkboards.** a hard, smooth board on which writing or drawing is done with chalk, especially a large one that a teacher writes on in a classroom. Also called a BLACKBOARD.

chal·lenge [chal-inj] *verb,* **challenged, challenging. 1.** to ask or demand someone take part in a fight or contest: *The champion chess player challenged me to a match.* Someone who challenges another person, or the opponent of a champion, is called a **challenger. 2.** to stop an unknown person and demand they identify themselves: *The airport security guard challenged the woman who forgot to show her passport.* **3.** to make someone stretch or test their abilities: *Going for a ten-mile hike challenged my endurance.* *noun, plural* **challenges. 1.** a call to participate in a fight or contest. **2.** an order for someone to stop and identify themselves. **3.** something that requires a lot of effort: *It is a challenge for babies to learn to walk.*

cham·ber [chame-bur] *noun, plural* **chambers. 1.** an enclosed part of a building; a room, especially a private room: *The king had the grandest chamber in the castle.* **2.** a judge's private office in a courthouse. **3.** the meeting hall of a group of lawmakers. **4.** a lawmaking group: *The Senate is the upper chamber of the United States Congress.* **5.** a cavity inside a plant or an animal's body. **6.** the part of a gun where the cartridge is placed.

cha·me·le·on ◀ [kuh-meel-yun] *noun, plural* **chameleons.** any of a group of lizards that change the color of their skin to blend in with their surroundings so that they cannot be seen.

Many words in English have both a *literal* meaning (the original meaning) and a *figurative* meaning (one that develops in some way from the idea of the first meaning). The literal meaning of **chameleon** is a certain kind of lizard. Because this lizard is known for changing its skin color, chameleon also has the figurative meaning of a person who often changes his or her mind about things.

cham·pagne [sham-pane] *noun, plural* **champagne.** a bubbly white wine often drunk on special occasions.

cham·pi·on [cham-pee-un] *noun, plural* **champions. 1.** the winner of a contest or competition of some kind: *Simon defeated everyone else at the Scrabble tournament and was declared the champion.* **2.** one who fights or speaks out for someone or something: *Mother Teresa was a champion of the poor.*

cham·pi·on·ship [cham-pee-un-*ship*] *noun, plural* **championships. 1.** a contest held to decide who the champion is: *The Super Bowl is the championship game of pro football.* **2.** the title or position belonging to the winner.

chance [chans] *noun, plural* **chances. 1.** a time when one can do something or something can happen; an opportunity: *Everyone went out so I had a chance to study in peace.* **2.** something that may happen; a possibility: *Dad entered the competition for a chance to win a trip to Hawaii.* **3.** the way things happen without being controlled; fate or luck: *I didn't expect to see her, but by chance we met at the mall.* **4.** a possible danger; a risk: *He's going to buy a new furnace rather than taking the chance the old one will break down.* *verb,* **chanced, chancing. 1.** to take place by accident: *She chanced to overhear them talking about the present they were making her.* **2.** to take a risk. *adjective.* not planned; by accident: *a chance meeting.*

chan·de·lier [shan-duh-leer] *noun, plural* **chandeliers.** a branched holder for lights that hangs from the ceiling.

change [chaynj] *verb,* **changed, changing. 1.** to make different; alter: *to change the TV to a different channel; to change the password on a computer.* **2.** to trade one thing for another: *I wanted to change seats because I like to sit by the window.* **3.** to take clothes off and put on different ones. *noun, plural* **changes. 1.** the act or result of something becoming different: *There was a sudden change in the weather from hot to cold.* **2.** the money returned when the amount paid is more than something cost. **3.** money in the form of coins rather than paper bills: *Dad put change in the parking meter.*

chan·nel ▶ [chan-ul] *noun,*
plural **channels. 1.** the deeper part
of a waterway. **2.** a stretch of water that
connects two larger areas of water:
The English Channel joins the Atlantic
Ocean and the North Sea.
3. a frequency band on which
a radio or television station sends
out electronic signals.
verb, **channeled, channeling.**
1. to make a channel in something.
2. to direct in a certain way: *Let's*
channel all our efforts into getting
the yard cleared.

chant [chant] *noun, plural* **chants.**
Music. words shouted, sung, or spoken
repeatedly with a simple, strong
rhythm. —**chant,** *verb.*

Cha·nu·kah [hah-nuh-kuh] another
spelling of HANUKAH.

cha·os [kay-os] *noun.* a total lack of order; complete
confusion; disorder: *There was chaos on the highway*
when the main bridge was closed in both directions.
Something or someone that is completely disorganized
or confused is said to be **chaotic.**

chap[1] [chap] *verb,* **chapped, chapping.** to roughen, crack,
or dry out: *My lips were chapped by the hot desert wind.*
When something, especially skin, is made rough, dry,
and cracked it is **chapped.**

chap[2] [chap] *noun, plural* **chaps.** a fellow; a man or boy.

chap·el ▼ [chap-ul] *noun, plural* **chapels.** *Religion.* a room
or small building used for prayer or religious services,
usually Christian.

chap·er·one [shap-uh-*rone*] *noun, plural* **chaperones.**
an older person who accompanies a younger person
to watch over the person and make sure of proper
behavior: *When Tracy went to lunch with Ewan, her aunt*
went along as a chaperone.
verb, **chaperoned, chaperoning.** to accompany others to
ensure proper behavior. This word is also spelled **chaperon.**

chap·lain [chap-lun] *noun, plural* **chaplains.** *Religion.*
a member of the clergy who conducts religious services
and counsels people in a non-religious organization such
as a school, military unit, or hospital.

chaps [chaps] *plural noun.* sturdy leather trousers with
no seat. Ranch hands wear them over ordinary
trousers to protect their legs when riding horses.

chap·ter [chap-tur] *noun, plural* **chapters.**
1. *Literature.* a main section of a book.
2. a definite period in history or in a person's
life: *Becoming ill marked the beginning*
of a difficult chapter in his life. **3.** a branch
of a society or club.

char [chahr] *verb,* **charred, charring.** to blacken
with fire; to reduce to charcoal: *I left*
the sausages on the barbecue for too long
and charred them on the outside.

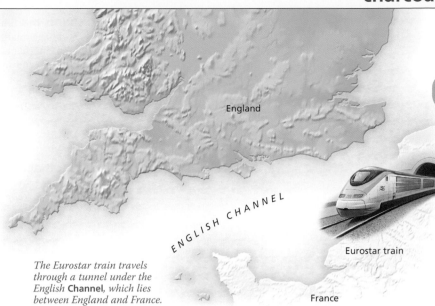

The Eurostar train travels
through a tunnel under the
English **Channel***, which lies*
between England and France.

England

ENGLISH CHANNEL

Eurostar train

France

char·ac·ter [*kare*-ik-tur] *noun, plural* **characters.**
1. the things added together that make a person or object
unique: *The subjects, colors, and brush strokes she uses*
give her paintings a peaceful character. **2.** a person's
inner, true qualities; someone's nature: *Her life wasn't*
easy but her happy character shone through. **3.** someone's
qualities such as honesty and courage; moral worth: *James*
showed strong character when he wouldn't accept the
stolen computer game. **4.** *Literature.* an imaginary person
in a story, play, or film. **5.** someone who is unusual and
interesting: *He was a real character who never behaved*
like everyone else. **6.** a letter, numeral, or other symbol
used in printing or writing.

char·ac·ter·is·tic [*kare*-ik-tuh-*ris*-tik] *noun,*
plural **characteristics.** one of the qualities that
make a person or thing different from others;
a trait: *His most noticeable physical*
characteristic is his red hair.
adjective. in keeping with what is usual; typical:
Even from a distance I knew it was him because
of his characteristic walk.
—**characteristically,** *adverb.*

char·ac·ter·ize [*kare*-ik-tuh-*rize*] *verb,*
characterized, characterizing.
1. to be typical of; show the nature
or character of: *Heavy snowfalls*
characterize winter in the Alps.
2. to describe the qualities
of a person or thing: *That movie*
star is thought to be rude, but
this book characterizes her
as warm and friendly.
—**characterization,** *noun.*

char·coal [char-*kole*] *noun.*
the black carbon that remains
after wood is partly burned.
It is used as fuel or for drawing.

This **chapel** *is in Yosemite National Park, California.*

A
B
C
D
E
F
G
H
I
J
K
L
M
N
O
P
Q
R
S
T
U
V
W
X
Y
Z

Archers rode in **chariots** *in battles fought by the ancient Egyptians.*

charge [charj] *verb,* **charged, charging. 1.** to ask a certain price: *to charge two dollars for a gallon of gas.* **2.** to ask payment for something: *The store charged me for delivery.* **3.** to delay payment for something: *I didn't pay cash for the camera—I charged it to my store account.* **4.** to blame or accuse of a crime: *The man was charged with stealing the car.* **5.** to rush at in a strong and sudden way: *As the ball was kicked, players on the kicking team charged down the field.* **6.** to fill with electrical energy: *I charged my cell phone by plugging it in overnight.* **7.** to assign a responsibility to: *Ben was charged with the job of typing our report.* *noun, plural* **charges. 1.** the payment asked for something. **2.** a responsibility or control: *He'll have charge of the store while the owner is away.* **3.** an accusation or statement of blame: *The charge of murder against the woman was dropped.* **4.** the act of rushing in a sudden attack: *The major led his men in a charge against the enemy.*

char·ger [charj-ur] *noun, plural* **chargers. 1.** *Science.* an item of electrical equipment that allows a battery to be loaded with power. **2.** a fast, strong horse trained to be ridden in battle.

char·i·ot ▲ [chare-ee-ut] *noun, plural* **chariots.** *History.* a horse-drawn vehicle with two wheels, used in battles, processions, and races in ancient times.

This old map **charts** *most of the world's oceans and continents.*

char·is·ma [kuh-riz-muh] *noun.* a quality of great charm that is attractive to others and sometimes leads to a rare ability to influence or impress many people: *The politician had many followers, mostly because of his charisma and not because of his policies.* When someone has charisma, they are said to be **charismatic.**

> The word **charisma** goes back to a term meaning "a gift from God." The idea is that when someone has a powerful ability to attract and inspire, this is a special gift from God.

char·it·able [chare-i-tuh-bul] *adjective.* **1.** generous toward others; giving help or money: *She does charitable work at a shelter for homeless people.* **2.** acting toward others or thinking of them in a kind way, without judging them harshly. **3.** having to do with a charity: *The Red Cross is a charitable organization.* **—charitably,** *adverb.*

char·i·ty [chare-i-tee] *noun, plural* **charities. 1.** the giving of money or other aid to help others. **2.** an organization that provides people with help: *a charity that helps children suffering from cancer.* **3.** kindness toward or tolerance of others: *He had a bad day, so show him some charity if he's cranky tonight.*

charm [charm] *noun, plural* **charms. 1.** the power of pleasing or attracting people: *The movie star Audrey Hepburn was thought to bring a lot of charm to her roles.* **2.** a small, decorative object worn often on a bracelet or necklace. **3.** an act, series of words, or a small object thought to have magical properties. *verb,* **charmed, charming.** to attract or please very much.

charm·ing [charm-ing] *adjective.* pleasing or attractive: *It will be a pleasure to stay in this charming cottage.* **—charmingly,** *adverb.*

chart ◀ [chart] *noun, plural* **charts. 1.** a sheet that gives information in the form of a diagram, graph, or table: *The boss put up a chart showing sales totals for each state in the country.* **2.** a map, especially for sailors. *verb,* **charted, charting.** to make a map or diagram of: *to chart the course of a river.*

char·ter [chart-ur] *noun, plural* **charters. 1.** an official document describing certain rights and obligations granted by a government or ruler to a person, organization, or company. **2.** the hiring of a vehicle. *verb,* **chartered, chartering.** to hire: *They chartered a boat to take them deep-sea fishing.*

charter school *Education.* a school that receives public funds but does not follow the same rules and policies as the public school system. These schools have a charter to operate in a certain way for a given period of time.

chase [chase] *verb*, **chased, chasing.** to follow quickly in order to catch or drive away someone or something: *The lion chased the zebra and soon caught it.* —**chase,** *noun.*

chasm [kaz-um] *noun*, *plural* **chasms.** a deep opening in the ground.

chass·is [chas-ee] *noun*, *plural* **chassis. 1.** the framework, including the wheels and machinery, supporting the body of an airplane or automobile. **2.** the frame holding the electronic parts of a radio, computer, or television.

chat [chat] *verb*, **chatted, chatting.** to have a casual or relaxed conversation; talk in a friendly way. —**chat,** *noun.*

chat·eau [sha-toe] *noun*, *plurals* **chateaus** or **chateaux.** a castle or large country house in France.

chat room *Computers.* an Internet channel or a section of a computer system where people communicate using typed messages as if they were having a conversation.

chat·ter [chat-ur] *verb*, **chattered, chattering. 1.** to talk quickly in a way that is not really serious: *The way he kept chattering on his cell phone bothered the others on the bus.* **2.** to make repeated clicking noises by knocking something together: *We had to get out of the icy-cold stream when our teeth began to chatter.* —**chatter,** *noun.*

chauf·feur [shoh-fur *or* shoh-fur] *noun*, *plural* **chauffeurs.** a person whose job is to drive other people, especially someone who drives people in their own car. —**chauffeur,** *verb.*

cheap [cheep] *adjective.* **1.** priced low: *Dad bought some cheap socks at the sale.* **2.** not charging much money: *a cheap store.* **3.** of poor quality, not worth much: *My shoes were made of cheap leather and soon split.* —**cheaply,** *adverb;* —**cheapness,** *noun.*

Cheap has two different meanings that are close to each other. He bought a **cheap** car might mean that he bought a good car for a bargain price, or that he bought a car that was not very good (and maybe for a high price). Because of this, people usually add more information to show which use of cheap they mean.

cheat [cheet] *verb*, **cheated, cheating. 1.** to act in a dishonest way in order to gain an advantage: *He wrote some words on a hidden piece of paper to cheat on the spelling test.* **2.** to take away from by a trick: *The criminal cheated the old lady out of her savings.* *noun*, *plural* **cheats.** a person who cheats or acts dishonestly. —**cheater,** *noun.*

check [chek] *noun*, *plural* **checks. 1.** a test to make sure something is correct or as it should be: *Before leaving I made a quick check to make sure all the doors were locked.* **2.** a written mark to indicate when something is right. **3.** a slip of paper signed by the owner of a bank account to pay money to someone. **4.** a bill showing what is owed at a restaurant or bar: *The waiter brought us the check.* **5.** a person or thing that delays or holds back something: *A free press can act as a check against the power of the government.* **6.** a pattern of squares: *The coat had a pattern of black and white checks.* **7.** a tag to show ownership of something so it can be claimed later. *verb*, **checked, checking. 1.** to make sure something is correct or as it should be: *Mom checked that we all had our seat belts fastened.* **2.** to make a mark to indicate something is correct. **3.** to leave something for a time to be picked up later: *to check your coat at a restaurant.* **4.** to stop or hold back.

check·ers [chek-urz] *plural noun.* a game for two players using twelve pieces each that move on a squared surface called a **checkerboard.**

check·up [chek-up] *noun*, *plural* **checkups. 1.** *Health.* a regular physical examination to make sure someone is healthy: *I go to the dentist twice a year for a checkup.* **2.** a regular inspection of something to make sure it is in good condition.

cheek [cheek] *noun*, *plural* **cheeks. 1.** the side of the face under the eyes, and the inside of the mouth: *He filled his cheeks with air to blow out the candles.* **2.** a lack of politeness or respect; being rude: *"You've got a cheek talking to your mother like that!" father told me.* A person who acts in a rude or bold way is said to be **cheeky.**

cheer [cheer] *noun*, *plural* **cheers. 1.** a shout of happiness or encouragement, often during a celebration: *Three cheers for the birthday girl!* **2.** good spirits. *A hot drink brought cheer to us all.* *verb*, **cheered, cheering. 1.** to give a shout of happiness or encouragement: *The fans all cheered when their team won the game.* **2.** to make or become happy: *Jack cheered up when I told him the good news.*

cheer·ful [cheer-ful] *adjective.* **1.** full of cheer; very happy: *She has a cheerful way of making visitors feel right at home.* **2.** showing or bringing cheer: *The fresh flowers and the sun streaming through the windows gave the room a cheerful air.* —**cheerfully,** *adverb;* —**cheerfulness,** *noun.*

cheer·leader [cheer-leed-ur] *noun*, *plural* **cheerleaders. 1.** a person who leads others in their cheering for their team at a football game or other sports event. **2.** someone who supports a person or cause in a strong and enthusiastic way.

cheese [cheez] *noun*, *plural* **cheeses.** a food made from the milk of cows, buffaloes, sheep, and goats.

chee·tah ▼ [cheet-uh] *noun*, *plural* **cheetahs.** a large animal of the cat family, having a small head and spotted coat. It lives in the wild in Africa and southern Asia and is the fastest running animal in the world.

The word **cheetah** came into English from a language of India. It originally meant "spotted one."

*A **cheetah** can run as fast as sixty miles per hour, but only for a short time.*

Chefs sometimes wear a special hat and a white uniform.

chef ▶ [shef] *noun, plural* **chefs. 1.** the head cook in a restaurant or hotel. **2.** any person whose job is cooking meals in a restaurant.

chem·i·cal [kem-i-kul] *noun, plural* **chemicals.** a substance found in, on, or above the Earth; any material that can cause a physical change or that results from such a change. *adjective.* **1.** having to do with the science of chemistry: *a chemical experiment.* **2.** made by or involving chemicals: *Wood catching fire is a chemical reaction; Poison gas is a chemical weapon that can be used in war.* —**chemically,** *adverb.*

chem·ist [kem-ist] *noun, plural* **chemists.** a scientist whose work has to do with chemistry.

chem·is·try [kem-i-stree] *noun.* **1.** the area of science in which people examine chemicals to find out what they are made of and how they react with other substances. **2.** the way in which people in a group get along with or react to each other: *a baseball team with good chemistry.*

chem·o·ther·a·py [kee-moh-ther-uh-pee] *noun, plural* **chemotherapies.** *Medicine.* a way of trying to cure certain diseases, such as cancer, by treating them with chemicals. A shorter form of this word is **chemo.**

cher·ish [cher-ish] *verb.* **cherished, cherishing.** to feel or show great affection for: *I cherish the long days of summer.*

Cher·o·kee [cher-uh-kee] *noun, plural* **Cherokee** *or* **Cherokees.** a North American Indian from a tribe who now live in Oklahoma and formerly lived in the area of the Southeastern U.S.

cher·ry [cher-ee] *noun, plural* **cherries. 1.** a sweet-tasting, small, round, red fruit that grows on trees. **2.** a bright red color like the color of this fruit. *adjective.* having a bright red color.

chess ▶ [ches] *noun.* a board game for two people in which each player has sixteen pieces that move in different ways and uses them to try to trap the other person's key piece, the king.

chest [chest] *noun, plural* **chests. 1.** the upper part of the human body. **2.** a large box used for storage.

chest·nut [ches-nut] *noun, plural* **chestnuts. 1.** a shiny brown nut that grows on a tree. It can be eaten by animals and, when cooked, by people. **2.** a rich brown color like this. *adjective.* having a rich brown color.

chew [choo] *verb,* **chewed, chewing.** to grind food using the teeth.

Chey·enne [shy-an] *noun, plural* **Cheyenne** *or* **Cheyennes.** a North American Indian from a tribe now living mainly in Oklahoma and Montana.

Chi·ca·na [chi-kah-nuh] *noun, plurals* **Chicanas.** an American girl or woman having Mexican parents or ancestry.

Chi·ca·no [chi-kah-noh] *noun, plural* **Chicanos.** an American boy or man with Mexican parents or ancestry.

chick [chik] *noun, plural* **chicks.** a young bird, especially a young chicken.

chick·a·dee ▶ [chik-uh-dee] *noun, plural* **chickadees.** a small, North American bird named after the sound of its call.

chick·en [chik-un] *noun, plural* **chickens. 1.** a common bird that is raised for food in many countries of the world. **2.** the meat from this bird eaten as a meal: *We had roast chicken for supper.*

chicken pox [poks] *Medicine.* a common illness, usually appearing in childhood. The symptoms are spots on the skin and a high temperature. This term is also spelled **chickenpox.**

Chickadees are friendly birds that often visit parks and gardens.

During the Middle Ages, crusaders in the Holy Land learned to play **chess** *with Muslim fighters in times of truce.*

chief ▶ [cheef] *noun, plural* **chiefs.** the person who is the leader of a group of people, such as an American Indian tribe or a police or fire department.
adjective. **1.** being in charge; being the leader: *In business the head of a company is often called the Chief Executive Officer.* **2.** most important; main: *The chief thing to remember when climbing is not to look down.*
—**chiefly,** *adverb.*

Chief Justice *Law.* **1.** the head judge of the United States Supreme Court. **2.** the judge who has the most authority in a lower court of law.

chief·tain [cheef-tun] *noun, plural* **chieftains.** the head of some traditional groups or clans: *a Scottish chieftain.*

chi·hua·hua [chi-wah-wah] *noun, plural* **chihuahuas.** a very small dog, originally from Mexico, that is a popular pet.

child [childe] *noun, plural* **children. 1.** the young of human beings; a boy or girl. **2.** a son or daughter of any age.

child·birth [childe-*burth*] *noun, plural* **childbirths.** the act of giving birth to a baby.

child·hood [childe-*hood*] *noun, plural* **childhoods.** the time of life when a person is a child; the time of being young.

child·ish [childe-ish] *adjective.* **1.** of or for a child. **2.** suited only for a child; not adult or mature: *It's childish to believe in fairies.* To be **childlike** is to enjoy oneself like a child.
—**childishly,** *adverb;* —**childishness,** *noun.*

Childish is usually used to mean that someone is acting like a child in a way that is wrong, silly, angry, and so on: *It was childish of him to knock the board over just because he was losing the game. Childlike* is usually used to mean that someone is acting like a child in a good way: *The popular television host Mr. Rogers was known for his childlike qualities of love, honesty, and trust.*

chil·i ◀ [chil-ee] *noun, plural* **chilis. 1.** a very hot spice used in cooking. A **chili pepper** is the seed pod that this spice comes from. **2.** a dish flavored with this spice, made with beef, tomatoes, and usually beans. This is also called **chili con carne.**
🔊 A different word with the same sound is **chilly.**

chill [chil] *noun, plural* **chills. 1.** the fact of being slightly cold, especially in an unpleasant way: *There was a chill in the air this morning, and I could tell fall is coming.* **2.** a cold temperature or feeling: *A chill ran up my spine as I walked down the lonely road.*
verb, **chilled, chilling.** to make cold: *Jane put the lemonade in the refrigerator to chill.*
adjective. slightly cold; chilly: *a chill day in early spring.*

chill·y [chil-ee] *adjective,* **chillier, chilliest. 1.** cold or unpleasant in temperature. **2.** disapproving or unpleasant in feeling: *The librarian gave us a chilly look when we made too much noise.*
🔊 A different word with the same sound is **chili.**

chime [chime] *noun, plural* **chimes.** *Music.* **1.** the sound of bells, or the sound a clock makes when it marks the hour. **2.** a set of bells.
verb, **chimed, chiming.** to make the sound of bells.
• **chime in.** to add one's opinion to a conversation: *Dolores chimed in with her views on the movie we were talking about.*

chim·ney [chim-nee] *noun, plural* **chimneys.** a pipe or hollow structure, usually made of brick or metal, built on the roof of a building to let smoke out from a fireplace.

chim·pan·zee [chim-pan-zee *or* chim-pan-zee] *noun, plural* **chimpanzees.** a type of small ape with brownish-black fur that lives in forests of Africa. Chimpanzees live in social groups and are among the most intelligent animals. A shorter form of this word is **chimp.**

chin [chin] *noun, plural* **chins.** the lower part of the face under the mouth.
verb, **chinned, chinning.** to raise the chin to a bar while pulling up with the arms.

Chili peppers grow abundantly throughout most of Central and South America.

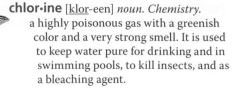

*Antique teapots are often made of fine **china**.*

chi·na ▶ [chye-nuh] *noun.* **1.** a type of fine white material made from clay or porcelain, originally from the country of China. **2.** cups, bowls, and plates made from china.

chin·chil·la ▼ [chin-chil-uh] *noun, plural* **chinchillas.** a small, gray rabbit-like rodent from South America, known for its soft, thick fur. It lives in burrows and hunts at night.

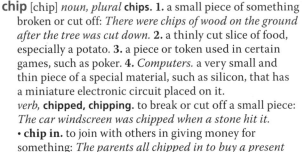

Chinchillas live in mountain areas and feed on fruit, seeds, and grain.

Chi·nese ▼ [chye-neez] *plural noun.* **1.** a person from the country of China. **2.** the language spoken in China. *adjective.* having to do with China or its people.

chink [chingk] *noun, plural* **chinks.** a small crack or opening: *a chink in the wall of an old cabin.*
• **chink in the armor.** a fault or weakness in something that otherwise appears strong.

chip [chip] *noun, plural* **chips. 1.** a small piece of something broken or cut off: *There were chips of wood on the ground after the tree was cut down.* **2.** a thinly cut slice of food, especially a potato. **3.** a piece or token used in certain games, such as poker. **4.** *Computers.* a very small and thin piece of a special material, such as silicon, that has a miniature electronic circuit placed on it. *verb,* **chipped, chipping.** to break or cut off a small piece: *The car windscreen was chipped when a stone hit it.*
• **chip in.** to join with others in giving money for something: *The parents all chipped in to buy a present for the coach of the girls' soccer team.*

chip·munk [chip-munk] *noun, plural* **chipmunks.** a small, lively, striped rodent with large cheek pouches.

chi·ro·prac·tor [kye-ruh-prak-tur] *noun, plural.* **chiropractors.** *Health.* someone who is trained to try to cure pain and disease by moving the spine and limbs in a certain way.

chirp [chirp] *noun, plural* **chirps.** the sound made by birds, especially young birds, and some insects. *verb,* **chirped, chirping.** to make such a sound.

chis·el [chiz-ul] *noun, plural* **chisels.** a tool with a sharp metal edge, used to carve hard materials like wood and stone. *verb,* **chiseled, chiseling.** to shape or cut something with such a tool.

chiv·al·ry [shiv-ul-ree] *noun. History.* a type of behavior that knights of the Middle Ages were expected to show. A **chivalrous** man was brave and honorable, polite and gentle, and kind to the poor and weak.

Chivalry comes from *cheval,* the French word for "horse." The knights who followed the system of chivalry always rode on horseback.

chlor·ine [klor-een] *noun. Chemistry.* a highly poisonous gas with a greenish color and a very strong smell. It is used to keep water pure for drinking and in swimming pools, to kill insects, and as a bleaching agent.

chlo·ro·phyll [klor-uh-fil] *noun. Biology.* the green substance in plants that stores energy from sunlight to change carbon dioxide and water into food and oxygen.

choc·o·late [chok-lit *or* chok-uh-lit] *noun, plural* **chocolates. 1.** a popular type of food made from sweetened cacao seeds. **2.** a candy made of or flavored with chocolate. **3.** a drink made with chocolate: *a cup of hot chocolate.* **4.** a deep brown color. *adjective.* **1.** made with chocolate: *Mom made a batch of chocolate cookies.* **2.** having a deep brown color.

Choc·taw [chok-taw *or* chok-tah] *noun, plural* **Choctaw** *or* **Choctaws. 1.** a member of a Native American tribe from the southern United States. **2.** the language of this tribe.

choice [choys] *noun, plural* **choices. 1.** the act or fact of choosing; picking one from a group: *When you order food in a restaurant, you make a choice from the menu.* **2.** the chance or right to choose: *The microwave is broken, so we have no choice but to get a new one.* **3.** the person or thing chosen; a selection: *I think Shannon was a good choice to be team captain.* *adjective,* **choicer, choicest.** of high quality; worth choosing: *The cabin has a choice location with a beautiful view of the lake.*

choir [kwire] *noun, plural* **choirs.** *Music.* a group of singers.

choke [choke] *verb,* **choked, choking. 1.** to be unable to breathe because the throat is blocked or because of very strong feelings: *He was so angry he choked with rage.* **2.** to stop someone from breathing: *I hugged her so tight she nearly choked.* **3.** to stop the movement or action of; block: *Rush hour traffic was choking the highway.* **4.** to do poorly at something, such as playing in a game or taking a test, because of being nervous.

chol·er·a [kol-uh-ruh] *noun. Medicine.* a disease caused by drinking contaminated water. If not properly treated, a person with cholera can die in a short time.

*According to legend, Laozi was a **Chinese** philosopher who lived about 2,500 years ago.*

cho·les·ter·ol [kuh-les-tuh-rol] *noun. Health.* a fatty substance made by the body which is also present in certain foods. Too much cholesterol can lead to heart disease.

choose [chooz] *verb,* **chose, chosen, choosing.**
1. to pick out one person or thing from two or more; select: *If you order steak, you can choose to have either mashed potatoes, french fries, or rice with it.* **2.** to decide on a certain way of acting; prefer: *The mayor says he will choose not to respond to the attacks on him by the other candidates.* Someone who is **choosy** is very careful and exact in selecting or deciding on something.

chop [chop] *verb,* **chopped, chopping.** to cut into small pieces: *The cook chopped some tomatoes. noun, plural* **chops. 1.** a quick blow with the hand or with a sharp object. **2.** a cut of meat: *a lamb chop.*

chop·py [chop-ee] *adjective,* **choppier, choppiest.** broken up roughly into small parts: *The sea was choppy outside the harbor.* Writing is said to be choppy when it is made up of very short sentences that repeat the same words.

chop·sticks ▼ [chop-stiks] *noun, singular* **chopstick.** two long sticks, held in one hand, used to eat with. Chopsticks were originally from China.

chord[1] [kord] *noun, plural* **chords.** *Music.* more than two musical notes played together to make a pleasant sound.
🔊 A different word with the same sound is **cord.**

chord[2] [kord] *noun, plural* **chords.** *Mathematics.* a straight line linking two points on a curve.
🔊 A different word with the same sound is **cord.**

chore [chore] *noun, plural* **chores.**
1. a task that has to be done regularly: *household chores.*
2. an unpleasant job: *Tidying my room is a real chore.*

cho·re·og·ra·phy [kore-ee-og-ruh-fee] *noun, plural* **choreographies.** *Music.* the composition and arrangement of dance steps. A **choreographer** is a person who arranges dance steps and directs dancers in following them.

cho·rus [kore-us] *noun, plural* **choruses.** *Music.* **1.** a group of people who sing or dance together, often as the supporting act in an opera or ballet. **2.** the last lines of a song when repeated at the end of every verse. *verb,* **chorused, chorusing.** to say or sing together; *Birds chorus loudly in springtime.*

People use **chopsticks** *to eat some kinds of Asian food.*

CHRISTMAS TREES

The tradition of decorating fir trees at Christmas dates back to sixteenth century Germany. In the nineteenth century Queen Victoria's German husband, Prince Albert, encouraged the custom in England. Victorian trees were decorated with candles, candies, small toys and gifts, and little cakes. It was once considered unlucky to bring a Christmas tree indoors before December 24 or to keep it there after twelfth night (January 6).

Decorations

chow·der [chow-dur] *noun, plural* **chowders.** a kind of soup made from seafood or vegetables: *clam chowder; corn chowder.*

Christ [kriste] *noun. Religion.* Jesus, the founder of the Christian religion over two thousand years ago and believed by members of this faith to be the son of God.

chris·ten [kris-un] *verb,* **christened, christening.** *Religion.* **1.** to name a person, usually a baby, during baptism. **2.** to be accepted into the Christian church by baptism. The ceremony of baptism is called a **christening.**

Chris·tian [kris-chun] *noun, plural* **Christians.** *Religion.* someone who believes that Jesus is the son of God and follows his teachings.
adjective. having to do with or believing in the religion of Christianity: *Giving to charity is a Christian thing to do.*

Chris·ti·an·i·ty [kris-chee-an-uh-tee] *noun. Religion.* a worldwide religion based on the teachings of Jesus.

Christ·mas [kris-mus] *noun, plural* **Christmases.** *Religion.* December 25th; the day Christians celebrate Christ's birthday.

Christmas tree ▲ a fir tree cut and brought indoors to be decorated with tinsel and colored balls to celebrate Christmas Day.

a b c d e f g h i j k l m n o p q r s t u v w x y z

Bavaria, Germany

Santorini, Greece

Churches *around the world can be very different in size and architecture.*

Barcelona, Spain

chro·mi·um [krow-mee-um] *noun. Chemistry.* a hard, shiny metal used in making steel because it does not rust. Automobile bumpers are made from chromium. This metal is also called **chrome**.

chro·mo·some [krow-muh-*some*] *noun, plural* **chromosomes.** *Biology.* a microscopic part of each cell in plants and animals that passes on genes, such as eye color, inherited from the parents.

chron·ic [kron-ik] *adjective.* **1.** *Health.* developing slowly or lasting for a long time: *My grandma has chronic arthritis.* **2.** being or having a problem that goes on over time: *He is a chronic gambler; People who live here have chronic complaints about the heavy traffic.* —**chronically,** *adverb.*

There are about a hundred different kinds of **chrysanthemums.**

chron·i·cle [kron-i-kul] *noun, plural* **chronicles.** *Literature.* a document recording events from the past in the order in which they occur. A diary is a kind of chronicle.

chro·nol·o·gy [kruh-nol-uh-jee] *noun, plural* **chronologies.** *Literature.* a way of recording events in the order in which they happen. Someone who keeps a diary would make entries in **chronological** order. —**chronologically,** *adverb.*

chrys·a·lis ▶ [kris-uh-lis] *noun, plural* **chrysalises.** *Biology.* the silk case a caterpillar spins to live in while it develops into a butterfly.

chry·san·the·mum ▲ [kruh-san-thuh-mum] *noun, plural* **chrysanthemums.** a popular garden flower with a round head of many petals.

chub·by [chub-ee] *adjective.* **chubbier, chubbiest.** fat and round in a pleasing way: *The baby waved his chubby arms.* —**chubbiness,** *noun.*

chuck·le [chuk-ul] *verb,* **chuckled, chuckling.** to laugh quietly.
noun, plural **chuckles.** a soft laugh: *We had a good chuckle when the teacher's back was turned.*

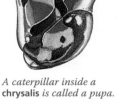

A caterpillar inside a **chrysalis** *is called a pupa.*

chug [chug] *noun, plural* **chugs.** a short, thudding sound made over and over again: *The chug of a steam engine reminds me of my childhood.*
verb, **chugged, chugging.** to move along slowly with such a sound: *His old motorbike chugged along the country road.*

chunk [chungk] *noun, plural* **chunks.** a thick lump or piece: *a chunk of wood; a chunk of ice on a frozen pond.*

chunk·y [chungk-ee] *adjective,* **chunkier, chunkiest.** **1.** containing chunks: *a chunky sauce with small bits of tomato in it.* **2.** thick and short in form or build. —**chunkiness,** *noun.*

church ▲ [church] *noun, plural* **churches.** *Religion.* **1.** a building used for Christian worship. **2.** a Christian organization whose members share the same beliefs: *The Roman Catholic Church is the world's largest religious body.*

churn [churn] *noun, plural* **churns.** a container in which butter is made from cream by beating or shaking. *verb,* **churned, churning. 1.** to beat or shake cream in a special container to make butter. **2.** to stir up something with force: *The tractor churned up the field.*

chute [shoot] *noun, plural* **chutes.** a slide or sloping passage through which objects can travel: *a trash chute.*
◀)) A different word with the same sound is **shoot.**

ci·der [side-ur] *noun, plural* **ciders.** juice from crushed apples, used as a drink and to make vinegar.

ci·gar [si-gar] *noun, plural* **cigars.** a tube of rolled-up tobacco leaves used for smoking.

cig·a·rette [sig-uh-ret or sig-uh-ret] *noun, plural* **cigarettes.** a small roll of shredded tobacco enclosed in a thin sheet of paper and used for smoking. This word is also spelled **cigaret.**

The **circumference** of the Earth is greatest at the equator.

cite

cin·der [sin-dur] *noun, plural* **cinders.** a piece of wood, coal, or other substance that has been burned up or that is still burning without giving off flames.

cin·em·a [sin-uh-muh] *noun, plural* **cinemas.** **1.** a movie theater. **2.** the business or art of making movies.

cin·na·mon [sin-uh-min] *noun.* **1.** a spice made from the dried bark of a southeast Asian tree. **2.** light, reddish brown in color. *adjective.* having a light, reddish brown color.

cir·ca [sirk-uh] *preposition.* as an estimate; about; roughly. Circa is used before dates to show that they are approximate: *Viking explorers came to America before Columbus, circa AD 1,000.* It is abbreviated to **ca.** or **c.**

cir·cle [sirk-ul] *noun, plural* **circles. 1.** *Mathematics.* a round figure with a boundary made up of points that are all the same distance from a point inside called the center. **2.** anything shaped like a circle; a ring: *The pupils gathered in a circle around the teacher.* **3.** a group of people who share the same interests: *a sewing circle.* *verb,* **circled, circling. 1.** to make a circle around: *Circle the number of the answer you choose.* **2.** to move in a circle: *A hawk circled in the sky high above us.*

cir·cuit [sirk-it] *noun, plural* **circuits. 1.** the act of moving around; a path that goes in a circle. **2.** a regular route or course; round: *The singer performed on the nightclub circuit.* **3.** the path of an electric current. In a flashlight, electricity moves in a circuit from the batteries to the light bulb.

cir·cu·lar [sirk-yuh-lur] *adjective.* round like a circle; forming or moving in a circle: *The auto race goes in a circular path around the track.* *noun, plural* **circulars.** an advertisement or a letter sent to a large number of people.

cir·cu·late [sirk-yuh-late] *verb,* **circulated, circulating. 1.** to move around over a wide area: *Blood circulates through the human body.* **2.** to pass from person to person: *That joke has been circulating around the Internet for several weeks now.*

cir·cu·la·tion [sirk-yuh-lay-shun] *noun.* **1.** the act of moving around many different places or from person to person: *The franc is no longer in circulation in France; the new unit of money is the euro.* **2.** the number of copies sold of each issue of a newspaper or magazine. **3.** the movement of blood and other fluids throughout the body.

cir·cu·la·to·ry system ▶ [sirk-yuh-luh-tore-ee] *Medicine.* in the body, the system of the blood, the blood vessels, the heart, and the lymph system.

cir·cum·fer·ence ◀ [sir-kum-fuh-runs] *noun, plural* **circumferences 1.** *Mathematics.* a line that makes up the outside edge of a circle. **2.** the distance around something: *The circumference of the Earth at the equator is about 25,000 miles.*

cir·cum·stance [sirk-um-stans] *noun, plural* **circumstances.** a condition, event, or act that relates to and has an effect on something else: *The painters will start work on Thursday if circumstances permit.*

cir·cum·stan·tial [sirk-kum-stan-shul] *adjective.* **1.** based or depending on circumstances. **2.** *Law.* pointing indirectly to a person's guilt, but not proving it. In a trial, information that by itself does not directly prove a fact is **circumstantial evidence.** For example, if you saw the streets were wet but did not actually see it rain, you would have circumstantial evidence that it had rained.

cir·cus [sirk-us] *noun, plural* **circuses. 1.** a traveling group of trained animals, clowns, acrobats, and other entertainers. **2.** a noisy disturbance or behavior; uproar: *There were so many arguments that the meeting became a circus.*

cite [site] *verb,* **cited, citing. 1.** to repeat the exact words of another person; quote: *She cited Abraham Lincoln in her history paper.* **2.** to mention as support or proof: *He cited the absence of fish to show how badly polluted the river was.* **3.** to praise or honor someone: *The firefighters were cited for bravery.* —**citation,** *noun.*
🔊 Different words with the same sound are **sight** and **site.**

The **circulatory** system pumps blood to and from all parts of the body.

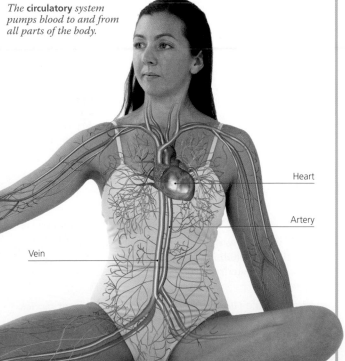

Heart

Artery

Vein

Equator

a
b
c
d
e
f
g
h
i
j
k
l
m
n
o
p
q
r
s
t
u
v
w
x
y
z

cit·i·zen [sit-uh-zun] *noun, plural* **citizens. 1.** *Government.* someone who, by birth or choice, is a member of a certain country. **2.** someone who lives in a city or town: *the citizens of San Francisco.* The fact of being a citizen is **citizenship.**

cit·rus ◀ [sit-rus] *adjective. Biology.* of or relating to a group of trees that produce juicy, acidic fruits, such as an orange, lemon, lime, or grapefruit.

cit·y [sit-ee] *noun, plural* **cities.** a place, larger and more important than a town, where many people live and work.

civ·ic [siv-ik] *adjective. Government.* **1.** of or relating to a city: *The civic leaders met at the town hall.* **2.** of or relating to being a citizen or having citizenship: *It was her civic duty to tell the police what she had seen.* The study of the rights, duties, and privileges of being a citizen is **civics.**

Citrus farmers in Greece sometimes transport lemons by donkey.

civ·il [siv-ul] *adjective.* **1.** of or relating to a citizen or citizens: *The right of all Americans to freedom of speech is called a civil liberty.* **2.** not military or religious in nature: *When order was restored, the civil authorities took over from the military.* **3.** polite but formal: *She was civil to us, but certainly not friendly.*

civ·il·ian [suh-vil-yun] *noun, plural* **civilians.** someone who is not in the armed forces: *Soldiers and civilians worked together to stop the flood waters.*

civ·i·li·za·tion [siv-uh-luh-zay-shun] *noun, plural* **civilizations.** a state of human society in which science, art, government, trade, and farming are well developed. The growth of cities and the use of writing often characterize civilizations.

civ·i·lize [siv-uh-lize] *verb,* **civilized, civilizing.** to bring a people to a more highly developed stage; train in science, culture, and art.

civil rights *Law.* the rights of a country's citizens, including the right to equal protection under the law and the right to vote.

This screw in this **clamp** *prevents the block of wood from moving.*

civil service *Government.* a branch of government service that is not part of the armed forces, the court system, or the legislature. Jobs such as delivering mail, cleaning streets, and taking care of public parks are part of the civil service. A person who works in such a job is called a **civil servant.**

civil war a war between citizens of the same nation.

Civil War *History.* the war fought from 1861 to 1865 between the Northern and Southern states of the United States.

In the Southern states of the U.S., this war has often been called the War Between the States, rather than the **Civil War.** This was thought to be a better description because it indicates two different governments fighting each other (the United States of America and the Confederate States of America), rather than a group of states breaking away from the central government.

claim [klame] *verb,* **claimed, claiming. 1.** to say that one owns or has the right to something: *I went to an attorney to claim my share of the money.* **2.** to say that something is true: *The accused man claimed he had been at home when the crime took place.* **3.** to call for; need; occupy: *My after-school job claims too much of my time right now.* *noun, plural* **claims.** **1.** a statement or demand for something as one's right: *We made a claim with the insurance company for the damage to our roof.* **2.** a statement of something as true: *The jury did not believe the man's claim of innocence.* A person who makes a claim is a **claimant.**

Many kinds of **clams** *can be eaten, but they can be hard to find when they bury themselves in sand or mud.*

clam ▶ [klam] *noun, plural* **clams.** an animal found in the ocean or in fresh water that has a soft body and a shell in two parts joined by a hinge. Something that is unpleasantly moist and sticky is said to be **clammy.** *verb,* **clammed, clamming.** to dig for clams. • **clam up.** to refuse to speak: *The suspect clammed up when the police began to question him.*

clam·or [klam-ur] *noun, plural* **clamors. 1.** a loud noise that goes on and on: *the clamor of the heavy traffic passing over the bridge.* **2.** a noisy demand or protest: *The audience made a clamor for the play to begin.* *verb,* **clamored, clamoring. 1.** to make such a loud noise. **2.** to shout or complain loudly in demand of something.

clamp ▲ [klamp] *noun, plural* **clamps.** a device that holds things together firmly: *The carpenter used a clamp to hold the two frames in position.* *verb,* **clamped, clamping.** to hold together with a clamp.

clan [klan] *noun, plural* **clans.** a group of families related through a common ancestor.

clap [klap] *noun, plural* **claps. 1.** a sudden loud sound like two blocks of wood being hit together: *They heard a clap of thunder.* **2.** a friendly slap: *He gave his friend a clap on the back.*

The **clarinet** *belongs to the woodwind group of instruments.*

verb, **clapped, clapping. 1.** to hit together: *She clapped her hands to keep warm.* **2.** to hit the hands together repeatedly, especially so as to show enjoyment or approval: *The audience began to clap and cheer for the actors at the end of the play.* **3.** to hit in a friendly way.

clar·i·fy [klare-uh-*fye*] *verb,* **clarified, clarifying.** **1.** to make something clear: *Certain chemicals can be put into swimming pool water to clarify it.* **2.** to make something better able to be understood; explain: *The teacher clarified the math problem for me by showing me how to combine the two numbers.* —**clarification,** *noun.*

clar·i·net ▲ [klare-i-*net*] *noun, plural* **clarinets.** *Music.* a musical instrument with a black, tube-shaped wooden body and metal keys. A musician plays the clarinet by blowing into the mouthpiece and pressing keys or covering holes with the fingers.

clar·i·ty [klare-i-tee] *noun.* the fact of being clear; clearness: *The clarity of the lake water made it possible to see the bottom ten feet below; We could understand the legal contract because of the clarity of the writing.*

clash [klash] *noun, plural* **clashes. 1.** a loud, harsh sound like pieces of metal being hit together: *the clash of swords.* **2.** a strong disagreement or struggle; a conflict: *There was a clash at the border between troops from the two nations.* *verb,* **clashed, clashing. 1.** to come together with a clash: *She clashed the cymbals.* **2.** to come into conflict; disagree forcefully: *The two men often clashed over politics.* **3.** to go badly together; not match: *The green baseball cap clashed with his dark blue suit.*

clasp [klasp] *noun, plural* **clasps. 1.** a device that fastens two things or parts together, such as a belt buckle. **2.** a tight grasp: *She held his hand with a firm clasp.* *verb,* **clasped, clasping. 1.** to fasten with a clasp. **2.** to hold tightly.

class [klas] *noun, plural* **classes. 1.** a group of people or things that are alike in some way: *Squares, circles, and triangles belong to the same class of geometric shapes.* **2.** a group of people with the same social rank or status and a similar way of life: *We are part of the middle class.* **3.** a group of students who are taught together. **4.** a period of time in which a group of students are taught. **5.** a grade or quality: *It was a hotel of the first class.* **6.** the fact of having high quality or excellence. *verb,* **classed, classing.** to group in a class; classify.

clas·sic [klas-ik] *adjective.* **1.** *Art.* judged to be excellent over a period of time by many people: *"Huckleberry Finn" is a classic American novel.* **2.** being an outstanding example of its kind that is popular over time: *a classic American car such as the 1957 Chevy.* **3.** typical of its kind: *An apple falling from a tree is the classic example of the law of gravity.* *noun, plural* **classics. 1.** a work of art of the highest quality: *Several paintings by Pablo Picasso are regarded as classics.* **2. the classics.** the writings of ancient Greece and Rome.

clas·si·cal ▼ [klas-i-kul] *adjective.* **1.** relating to the art, writings, and life of ancient Greece or Rome. **2.** not new or experimental; traditional: *She's a classical novelist.* **3.** *Music.* of or having to do with classical music: *Beethoven is my favorite classical composer.* —**classically,** *adverb.*

classical music *Music.* a type of music whose style and form are the result of a long and educated tradition that began in Europe hundreds of years ago. Classical music is different from popular or folk music.

The Parthenon, in Athens, is a **classical** *ancient Greek temple.*

Statue of the goddess Athena

A
B
C
D
E
F
G
H
I
J
K
L
M
N
O
P
Q
R
S
T
U
V
W
X
Y
Z

CLAWS

Animals use their claws—stronger, sharper versions of human nails—to catch food, climb trees, dig up roots, or fight an enemy. Most cats can pull in their claws when they're not needed, to stop them getting blunt. Some animals, such as jaguars, use their long, sharp claws to grab and hold their prey. Clawed forefeet help polar bears grab seals and grizzlies catch salmon. Some birds have long, curved talons and strong toes to snatch fish and small animals.

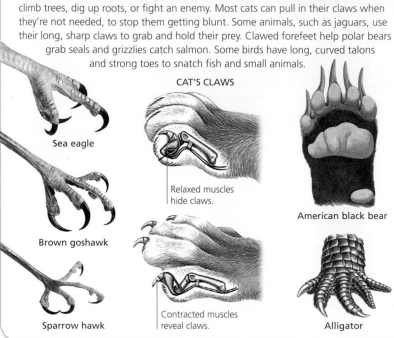

Sea eagle

Brown goshawk

Sparrow hawk

CAT'S CLAWS

Relaxed muscles hide claws.

Contracted muscles reveal claws.

American black bear

Alligator

claw ◀ [klaw] *noun, plural* **claws.**
1. a sharp, curved nail on the foot of an animal or bird. **2.** one of the grasping parts of a crab or lobster. **3.** something that looks similar to a claw. A **claw hammer** has a curved part at the end for pulling out nails. *verb,* **clawed, clawing.** to tear or scratch with claws or fingernails.

clay ▼ [klay] *noun, plural* **clays.** a kind of fine earth that is easily shaped when wet, and hardens when it is dried or baked. Bricks and pottery are made from clay.

clean [kleen] *adjective.* **1.** free from dirt or stains; not dirty. **2.** free from fault or wrong: *She has a clean driving record and has never had a ticket.* **3.** thorough; complete: *The new mayor has made a clean break with the past.*
verb, **cleaned, cleaning.** to remove dirt from. —**cleanly,** *adverb.*

clean energy *Environment.* forms of energy that produce little or no pollution. Examples of clean energy include hydroelectricity, wind power, and solar power.

clas·si·fied [klas-uh-*fyed*] *adjective.* **1.** arranged or put into classes; placed according to class. A **classified ad** is an advertisement in a newspaper placed with others of a similar kind, such as houses for sale. **2.** describing information that is not to be released to the general public: *How the bomb was put together is classified information.*

clas·si·fy [klas-uh-*fye*] *verb,* **classified, classifying.**
1. to arrange in classes: *Books in the library are classified according to their subject matter.* **2.** to assign to a class: *Gold is classified as a precious metal.*
—**classification,** *noun.*

clat·ter [klat-ur] *noun, plural* **clatters.** a rattling sound: *a clatter of horses' hooves.*
verb, **clattered, clattering.** to make a rattling sound.

clause [klawz] *noun, plural* **clauses. 1.** *Language.* a group of words containing a subject and a predicate. **2.** a separate section of a law, treaty, or other formal document: *A clause in the contract set out when the money had to be paid.*

A **clause** may or may not be able to stand on its own as a complete sentence. There are two clauses in the sentence: When we visited the beach, we found some beautiful seashells. "We found some beautiful seashells" is called an *independent clause* because it can be a sentence by itself. "When we visited the beach" is called a *dependent clause* because it does not make sense as a sentence by itself.

claus·tro·pho·bia [klas-truh-*foh*-bee-uh] *noun.* an extreme fear of being in a small, enclosed space, such as a closet or an elevator. Someone who suffers from this fear is described as **claustrophobic.**

clean·er [kleen-ur] *noun, plural* **cleaners. 1.** a person who cleans things for a living, such as a home or a building, or articles of clothing.
2. anything that removes dirt: *a carpet cleaner.*

clean·ly [kleen-lee *for adverb;* klen-lee *for adjective*] *adverb.* in a clean manner: *The axe cut the stick of wood cleanly in two with one blow; The boxing match was conducted cleanly.*
adjective. careful to keep neat and clean. The condition of being clean is **cleanliness.**

Marks carved in **clay** *tablets were an early form of writing.*

cleanse [klenz] *verb,* **cleansed, cleansing.** to make clean. A substance used for cleaning is a **cleanser.**

clear [kleer] *adjective,* **clearer, clearest. 1.** not darkened or obscured; bright: *a sunny day with a clear sky.* **2.** easy to see through: *a clear pane of glass.* **3.** easy to see, hear, or understand: *The actor spoke in a strong, clear voice; We have to finish this today—I hope that's clear to everyone.*
adverb. **1.** in a clear way; distinctly: *He called out his name loud and clear.* **2.** all the way; completely: *I watched the movie clear to the end.*
verb, **cleared, clearing. 1.** to make or become clear;

brighten: *The road finally cleared and we could see what was ahead of us.* **2.** to remove objects or obstructions from: *The bulldozer cleared a path through the rubble.* **3.** to pass or go over without touching: *The plane climbed steeply to clear the power lines.* **4.** to remove guilt, blame, or suspicion: *The accused man wanted to clear his name.*
• **in the clear.** no longer in danger or under suspicion. —**clearly,** *adverb*.

clear·ance [kleer-uns] *noun, plural* **clearances. 1.** the act of clearing: *Clearance of the building was quick after the alarm sounded.* **2.** a clear space that allows one thing to move without touching another thing: *There was only an inch of clearance between the side of the car and the brick wall.*

clear·ing ▼ [kleer-ing] *noun, plural* **clearings.** a piece of open land with no brush or trees, especially in a forest.

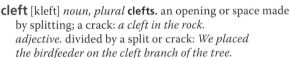

cleav·er ▶ [kleev-ur] *noun, plural* **cleavers.** a tool with a broad blade and a short handle, used by butchers for chopping meat.

Chefs use **cleavers** *to chop up ingredients for meals.*

clef [klef] *noun, plural* **clefs.** *Music.* a sign placed on a staff in music, showing the pitch of the notes written on it.

cleft [kleft] *noun, plural* **clefts.** an opening or space made by splitting; a crack: *a cleft in the rock.*
adjective. divided by a split or crack: *We placed the birdfeeder on the cleft branch of the tree.*

clench [klench] *verb,* **clenched, clenching.** to close or grasp tightly: *to clench your teeth or your wrists.*

cler·gy [klurge-ee] *noun, plural* **clergies.** *Religion.* people appointed to carry on religious work, including priests, ministers, and rabbis. A member of the clergy is a **clergyman** or **clergywoman.**

clerk [klurk] *noun, plural* **clerks. 1.** someone who works in an office keeping records and files. **2.** someone who sells things in a store.
verb, **clerked, clerking.** to be or work as a clerk.

clev·er [klev-ur] *adjective,* **cleverer, cleverest. 1.** having a quick mind; bright; intelligent: *She was a clever student and always topped the class.* **2.** showing intelligence or skill: *My cousin is clever at making things with his hands.* —**cleverly,** *adverb;* —**cleverness,** *noun.*

cli·ché [klee-shay] *noun, plural* **clichés.** *Language.* an idea or saying that has been used too often and has lost much of its original force.

A **cliché** is a phrase or saying that is used very often by a lot of people. The problem is that what one person thinks of as a cliché (*white as snow, raining cats and dogs, eat like a horse*) might be thought of as a new and colorful way to say something by someone else. So for your own writing it is better to avoid using an expression that you hear or read all the time.

click [klik] *noun, plural* **clicks.** a short, sharp noise.
verb, **clicked, clicking.** to make such a noise.

As winter snows melt, a **clearing** *in a coniferous forest attracts animals and birds.*

*A **clipper** had three tall masts and very large sails.*

cli·ent [klye-unt] *noun, plural* **clients.** a person or group using the services of another person or group: *The famous lawyer had many wealthy clients.* The body of clients of a person or group is its **clientele.**

cliff [klif] *noun, plural* **cliffs.** a steep, high rock face rising above the area below, as at the edge of a canyon.

cli·mate [klye-mut] *noun, plural* **climates.** *Environment.* the long-term weather conditions of an area. Aspects of climate include average rainfall, temperature, humidity, and sunlight. A condition having to do with climate is **climatic.**

climate change ▼ *Environment.* long-term changes in the Earth's climate, such as rising temperatures and lower rainfall.

cli·max [klye-maks] *noun, plural* **climaxes. 1.** the most important, intense, or exciting part of something: *The football game reached a climax early.* **2.** *Literature.* in a written work, the peak or turning point of the action, shortly before the end of the story. Relating to or forming a climax is **climactic.**

climb [klime] *verb,* **climbed, climbing. 1.** to go up, over, across, or through something, using the hands and feet. **2.** to grow up or over: *She had roses climbing the fence.* **3.** to move upward; rise: *Fuel prices may climb higher this year.*
noun, plural **climbs. 1.** the act of climbing. **2.** a location to be climbed: *The mountaineers prepared for the long, difficult climb.* **—climber,** *noun.*

clinch [klinch] *verb,* **clinched, clinching. 1.** to make final; settle: *The author clinched a million-dollar deal with a publisher.* **2.** to make winning certain: *A home run clinched the game for our side.*

cling [kling] *verb,* **clung, clinging. 1.** to hold tightly to something: *When the little girl is nervous, she clings tightly to her mother's hand.* **2.** to not give up; keep: *to cling to an old idea or belief.*

clin·ic [klin-ik] *noun, plural* **clinics.** *Health.* a building in which medical care or advice is given.

clin·i·cal [klin-i-kul] *adjective.* **1.** of or relating to medical care that involves the direct examination and treatment of sick people. **2.** showing no feeling or emotion; impersonal: *I thought he'd be upset, but he gave his report in a clinical manner.* **—clinically,** *adverb.*

clip¹ [klip] *verb,* **clipped, clipping.** to cut short; trim: *I clipped the ad from the newspaper.*
noun, plural **clips.** a rate of pace or speed: *We ran at a brisk clip at first, but soon slowed down.*

clip² [klip] *noun, plural* **clip.** a device for holding objects together.
verb, **clipped, clipping.** to fasten or hold with a clip.

clip·board [klip-bord] *noun, plural* **clipboards. 1.** a writing board with a spring clip at the top to hold sheets of paper. **2.** *Computers.* a temporary storage area in a computer program where text or pictures are kept when copied or cut.

clip·per ▲ [klip-ur] *noun, plural* **clipper. 1.** a cutting tool: *a nail clipper for trimming fingernails; a hedge clipper for cutting bushes.* **2.** *History.* a fast sailing ship used for long voyages in the 1800s.

clip·ping [klip-ing] *noun, plural* **clippings.** a piece that is cut out of or from something, especially out of a newspaper or magazine.

clique [klik *or* kleek] *noun, plural* **cliques.** a small group of people who keep to themselves and do not want other people to join the group: *There's a small clique of girls at our school who are not friendly to anyone else.*

The word **clique** comes from the idea is that the people in a clique make a "clicking" sound when they get together and talk about other people.

mya = million years ago   ya = years ago

3,700 mya Climate 18°F warmer than today

PRESENT AVERAGE TEMPERATURE

330 mya Start of long ice age

2,700–1,800 mya Ice sheets widespread

450 mya Brief ice age

245 mya Climate warms; dinosaurs appear.

*This timeline shows how **climate change** has affected the Earth over more than 4,000 million years.*

cloak [kloke] *noun, plural* **cloaks. 1.** a loose outer garment, with or without sleeves. **2.** anything that hides or covers something else: *The burglary took place under a cloak of darkness.*
verb, **cloaked, cloaking.** to cover or hide with or as if with a cloak.

clock ◀ [klok] *noun, plural* **clocks.** an instrument for measuring and showing the time.
verb, **clocked, clocking.** to measure speed by using an instrument like a clock: *He used a stopwatch to clock the runners.*

clock·wise [klok-wize] *adjective.* in the same direction as the moving hands of a clock: *We walked around the lake in a clockwise direction.*

clog ▶ [klog] *verb,* **clogged, clogging.** to fill up; block: *Leaves were clogging the gutter.*
noun, plural **clogs.** a shoe with a thick, wooden sole.

This old cuckoo **clock** *was carved out of wood.*

clois·ter [kloy-stur] *noun, plural* **cloisters. 1.** a covered walk by the side of a building such as a church, monastery, or college building. **2.** *Religion.* a place where members of a religious order live; a monastery or convent. To be secluded or shut in, as if in a monastery or convent, is to be **cloistered.**

clone [klone] *noun, plural* **clones.** *Science.* a plant or animal produced as an exact copy from the cells of another. The fact of producing a clone is called **cloning.**
verb, **cloned, cloning.** to produce a clone of a plant or animal.

close¹ [kloze] *verb,* **closed, closing. 1.** to move something or bring parts together so that a thing is not open; shut: *Close the door when you go out; He stopped reading and closed his book.* **2.** to bring something to an end: *I'm going to close my account and put the money in another bank; She closed the meeting by thanking everyone for coming.* **3.** stop moving, going, or working: *The store closes for the day at 6.00 P.M.*
noun, plural **closes.** the end of something; the finish: *At the close of each day they take down the American flag from its pole.*

People in Holland once wore **clogs** *for some kinds of dances.*

close² [kloze] *adjective,* **closer, closest. 1.** near in position to something else: *My house is close to school and I can walk there in five minutes.* **2.** near in space or time: *a close race between two fast runners; How close are you to finishing your science project?* **3.** near in feeling: *Several close friends came to visit her in hospital.* **4.** not having enough space or fresh air: *a close room.* **5.** with a lot of care or attention: *to keep a close watch on a baby.*
adverb. not far; near: *Mom told us to stay close to shore when we went swimming.* —**closely,** *adverb;* —**closeness,** *noun.*

closed-circuit *adjective.* describing a television system in which cameras send images by cable to connected television sets.

clos·et [kloz-ut] *noun, plural* **closets.** a small room or part of a room in which things are stored, such as clothes.

close-up ▲ [kloze-up] *noun, plural* **close-ups.** a photograph or motion picture scene showing a very close view of the subject.

clot [klot] *noun, plural* **clots.** a thick mass formed when material in a liquid sticks together or thickens: *a blood clot in an artery.*
verb, **clotted, clotting.** to form a clot or clots. —**clotted,** *adjective.*

1.6 mya Cooling continues.

Brief, warm periods occur between ice ages.

AD 900–1100 Warm period

65 mya Gradual cooling begins; dinosaurs vanish.

18,000 ya Peak of last ice age

6,000 ya Warm climate; the birth of farming

1450–1850 Little Ice Age

a b c d e f g h i j k l m n o p q r s t u v w x y z

A
B
C
D
E
F
G
H
I
J
K
L
M
N
O
P
Q
R
S
T
U
V
W
X
Y
Z

CLOUDS

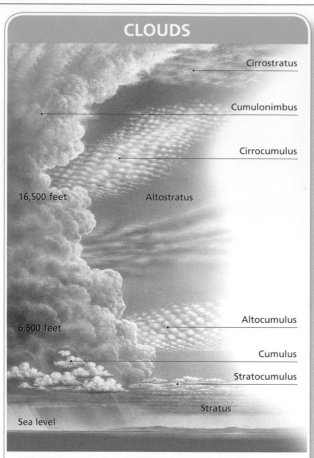

16,500 feet — Altostratus

Cirrostratus

Cumulonimbus

Cirrocumulus

6,500 feet

Altocumulus

Cumulus

Stratocumulus

Stratus

Sea level

Clouds form when warm, moist air comes into contact with cooler air. There are three main kinds: cumulus (puffy clouds), stratus (flat clouds), and cirrus (wispy clouds). The height of clouds is indicated by the prefixes alto- for middle-level clouds and cirro- for high-level clouds. Different kinds of clouds help us to understand the weather. White cumulus clouds are typical of warm, sunny days. High cirrus clouds may mark the beginning of a change in weather, and are often followed by lower altostratus clouds and very low, solid gray stratus rain clouds.

cloth [kloth] *noun, plural* **cloths. 1.** fabric made by knitting or weaving fibers such as cotton, linen, silk, and wool. **2.** a piece of cloth that is used for a particular purpose: *a wash cloth.*

clothe [kloтне] *verb,* **clothed** or **clad, clothing.** to put clothes on; dress: *to clothe a baby.*

clothes [kloтнz] *plural noun.* items worn to cover the body.

cloth·ing [kloтн-ing] *noun.* items worn to cover the body; clothes.

cloud ▲ [klowd] *noun, plural* **clouds. 1.** a white or gray mass of tiny water droplets or ice particles floating in the air. **2.** anything else like this: *a cloud of smoke.* *verb,* **clouded, clouding.** to cover with clouds: *The sky suddenly clouded and it started to rain.* —**cloudiness,** *noun.*

cloud·burst [klowd-burst] *noun, plural* **cloudbursts.** a sudden, heavy rainstorm.

cloud·y [klowd-ee] *adjective* **cloudier, cloudiest. 1.** covered with clouds. **2.** not clear; hard to see or understand: *the reasons she gave for not going on vacation with us are a bit cloudy.* —**cloudiness,** *noun.*

clove[1] [klove] *noun, plural* **cloves.** the dried flower bud of a tropical tree, used as a spice.

clove[2] [klove] *noun, plural* **cloves.** a small segment of a garlic bulb.

clo·ver ▶ [klove-ur] *noun, plural* **clovers.** a low-growing plant with leaves of three leaflets and rounded heads of red, white, or purple flowers.

clown [klown] *noun, plural* **clowns.** someone who makes people laugh by performing tricks or doing foolish things. *verb,* **clowned, clowning.** to act like a clown; be silly.

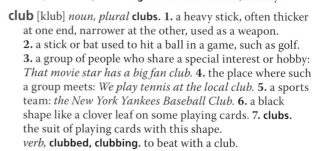

Clover *is used to make hay for animal feed.*

club [klub] *noun, plural* **clubs. 1.** a heavy stick, often thicker at one end, narrower at the other, used as a weapon. **2.** a stick or bat used to hit a ball in a game, such as golf. **3.** a group of people who share a special interest or hobby: *That movie star has a big fan club.* **4.** the place where such a group meets: *We play tennis at the local club.* **5.** a sports team: *the New York Yankees Baseball Club.* **6.** a black shape like a clover leaf on some playing cards. **7. clubs.** the suit of playing cards with this shape. *verb,* **clubbed, clubbing.** to beat with a club.

clue [kloo] *noun, plural* **clues.** something that helps to solve a puzzle or mystery: *The thief left a clue: her fingerprints on the window.* Someone who is helpless is **clueless.**
 • **clue in.** to give someone helpful information: *Can you clue me in on what happened at school today?*

clump [klump] *noun, plural* **clumps. 1.** a group of things close together: *a clump of trees.* **2.** a compact mass or lump: *a clump of dirt.* **3.** a heavy, thudding sound: *The thick book fell to the floor with a clump.* *verb,* **clumped, clumping.** to walk with loud, heavy steps.

clum·sy [klum-zee] *adjective,* **clumsier, clumsiest. 1.** without grace or skill; awkward: *After he hurt his knee, he walked in a clumsy way.* **2.** badly made or done: *The bicycle tire was soon flat again after the clumsy repair job.* —**clumsily,** *adverb;* —**clumsiness,** *noun.*

clung [klung] *verb.* the past tense and past participle of CLING.

clus·ter [klus-tur] *noun, plural* **clusters.** a number of similar things that grow or gather close together: *a cluster of grapes on a vine.* *verb,* **clustered, clustering.** to grow or gather in a cluster.

clutch [kluch] *verb,* **clutched, clutching. 1.** to grasp something tightly; hold tight: *He's a nervous flyer and clutches the arms of the seat when the plane lands.*

2. to try to grab hold of: *I clutched at the branch to stop myself from falling out of the tree.*
noun, plural **clutches. 1.** a firm hold: *The little boy kept a clutch on his teddy bear.* **2.** a part in an automobile engine that connects and disconnects the motor. **3.** a tense situation in a game that will decide who wins or loses.

clut·ter [klut-ur] *noun, plural* **clutters.** a crowded or untidy collection of things: *Rosa couldn't find her jump rope amid all the clutter in her bedroom.*
verb, **cluttered, cluttering.** to fill or cover something with an untidy collection of things.

cm an abbreviation for CENTIMETER. This abbreviation is also spelled **cm.**

co- a prefix that means: **1.** with: *I cowrote the winning project with Dwain.* **2.** together: *The two schools cohosted the dance.*

The British monarch travels in the golden Coronation **Coach** *on ceremonial occasions.*

co. an abbreviation for COMPANY or COUNTY.

CO² an abbreviation for CARBON DIOXIDE.

coach ▲ [kohch] *noun, plural* **coaches. 1.** a closed carriage with four wheels, pulled by horses. **2.** a railroad passenger car. **3.** an area of less expensive seats on a bus, train, or airplane. **4.** someone who teaches or trains athletes or performers.
verb, **coached, coaching.** to train or instruct people.

co·ag·u·late [koh-ag-yuh-late] *verb,* **coagulated, coagulating.** *Medicine.* to change from a liquid to a thick mass: *Blood must coagulate before a wound will stop bleeding.* The state of thickening into something more solid is **coagulation.**

coal [kole] *noun, plural* **coals. 1.** a black or dark brown rock formed over millions of years from decaying plants buried deep underground. It is burned as a fuel for heating or to make electricity. **2.** a piece of glowing or burned wood: *Don't touch those red hot coals!*

coarse [korse] *adjective,* **coarser, coarsest. 1.** made up of large particles; not fine: *Coarse sandpaper has large grains and will rub off a lot of wood.* **2.** thick and rough; harsh: *The stray dog's coat felt coarse and dirty.* **3.** not polite; crude or rude: *My big brother gets in trouble for using coarse language.*
—coarsely, *adverb;* **—coarseness,** *noun.*
🔊 A different word with the same sound is **course.**

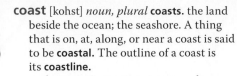

A **coat of arms** *is usually decorated with carved and painted figures.*

coast [kohst] *noun, plural* **coasts.** the land beside the ocean; the seashore. A thing that is on, at, along, or near a coast is said to be **coastal.** The outline of a coast is its **coastline.**
verb, **coasted, coasting.** to move along without any power or effort: *to coast downhill on a bicycle, without pedaling.*

Coast Guard the branch of the United States armed forces that patrols and guards its coast. During wartime, it is part of the United States Navy.

coat [kote] *noun, plural* **coats. 1.** a piece of clothing with sleeves, for wearing over other clothes. **2.** the fur or hair on an animal. **3.** a thin layer over a surface: *Michelle applied a fresh coat of nail polish.*
verb, **coated, coating.** to cover with a layer: *I like to coat my pancakes in maple syrup.* **—coating,** *noun.*

coat of arms ▲ *History.* a special design, often with a motto, on a shield or a drawing of a shield. It can act as the official symbol of a person, family, country, or organization.

coax [koxe] *verb,* **coaxed, coaxing.** to try to get something in a nice way; gently persuade: *I called softly to the frightened cat to coax it down from the roof.*

cob [kob] *noun, plural* **cobs.** the hard central part of an ear of corn, covered in rows of kernels.

co·balt [koh-balt] *noun. Chemistry.* a chemical element. It is a silver-white metal used to make alloys and paint, and to give a blue coloring to pottery.

cob·bler [kob-lur] *noun, plural* **cobblers. 1.** a person who mends or makes shoes. **2.** a fruit dessert with a sweet top crust, baked in a deep dish: *a peach cobbler.*

cob·ble·stone [kob-ul-stone] *noun, plural* **cobblestones.** a round paving stone, used in the past to make roads.

co·bra ▶ [koh-bruh] *noun, plural* **cobras.** a large, very poisonous snake living in Asia and Africa.

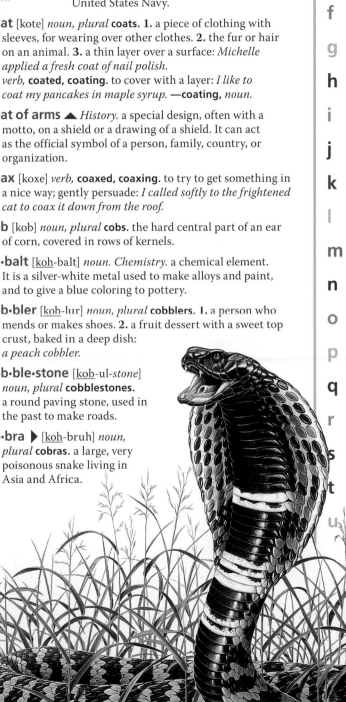

A **coconut's** "milk" is a nutritious drink.

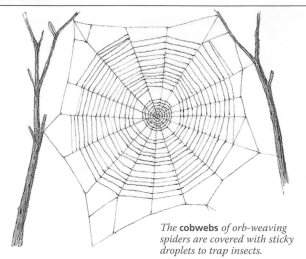

*The **cobwebs** of orb-weaving spiders are covered with sticky droplets to trap insects.*

cob·web ▲ [kob-web] *noun, plural* **cobwebs.** another name for a spider's web.

co·caine [koh-kane] *noun. Health.* a drug used in medicine to reduce pain. It is a powerful and dangerous drug to which people can easily become addicted, and is often used illegally.

cock[1] [kok] *noun, plural* **cocks. 1.** an adult male chicken; a rooster. **2.** any adult male bird. **3.** a device that starts or stops the flow of a gas or liquid through a pipe. *verb,* **cocked, cocking.** to pull back and set the hammer of a gun so that it is ready to fire.

cock[2] [kok] *verb,* **cocked, cocking.** to tilt, turn up, or turn to one side: *He cocked his cap over one eye. noun, plural* **cocks.** an upward tilt.

*A **cockatoo** uses its large beak to crack nuts and pry grubs from trees.*

cock·a·too ◀ [kok-uh-too] *noun, plural* **cockatoos.** a parrot, often white, from Australia and Asia, having a crest of feathers on its head that it can raise or lower.

cock·er spaniel ▼ [kok-ur] a dog with a long, silky coat and short legs.

cock·le [kok-ul] *noun, plural* **cockles.** a sea clam with a ridged, heart-shaped shell. The soft body inside is eaten as food.

cock·pit [kok-pit] *noun, plural* **cockpits.** the place where the pilot operates the controls in an airplane or small boat.

cock·roach [kok-rowch] *noun, plural* **cockroaches.** an insect with a flat, brown or black body and long feelers. It is a common household pest.

cock·tail [kok-tale] *noun, plural* **cocktails. 1.** a drink, usually alcoholic, made from two or more kinds of drink mixed together. **2.** a mixture of fruits or seafood served cold as the first course of a meal: *a shrimp cocktail.*

cock·y [kok-ee] *adjective,* **cockier, cockiest.** thinking too highly of oneself; too self-confident: *They were cocky about doing the puzzle in a short time, until they started it and realized how hard it was.*

co·coa [koh-koh] *noun.* **1.** a brown powder made by roasting and grinding the seeds of the cacao tree and removing the fat. It is used to make chocolate. **2.** a hot drink made from cocoa powder, sugar, and milk or water.

co·co·nut ▲ [koke-uh-nut] *noun, plural* **coconuts.** the very large fruit of the coconut palm tree. It has a hard, hairy shell that is lined with sweet, white meat and full of a milky liquid.

co·coon ▶ [kuh-koon] *noun, plural* **cocoons.** the silky covering that an insect larva such as a caterpillar spins around itself. Inside the cocoon, it changes into adult insect.

Cocoons are often hard to distinguish from twigs and branches.

cod [kod] *noun, plural* **cod** or **cods.** a large fish living in cold, northern oceans, very popular for eating. A different word with the same meaning is **codfish.**

COD an abbreviation for Cash On Delivery, meaning that something must be paid for when it is delivered. This term is also spelled **C.O.D.**

code [kode] *noun, plural* **codes. 1.** a system of signals, letters, numbers, or symbols used to send messages; a special or secret language. **2.** a set of rules or laws that people follow: *Our school dress code says we can't wear hats inside the buildings.* **3.** *Computers.* a system of arranging information so that a computer program can read and process it properly. *verb,* **coded, coding.** to put in the form of a code.

co·ed·u·ca·tion [koh-ed-yuh-kay-shun] *noun. Education.* the education of girls and boys together at the same school. A **coed** is a student (especially a girl) who studies at such a school. —**coeducational,** *adjective.*

co·erce [koh-urs] *verb,* **coerced, coercing.** to make a person do something; force: *He coerced the girl into handing over ten dollars by threatening to hurt her if she didn't.* —**coercion,** *noun.*

*This American **cocker spaniel** has a fine, silky coat that reaches to the ground.*

This **coin** from the Vatican City shows an engraving of St. Peter's Basilica.

cold

cof·fee ▼ [kaw-fee *or* kof-ee] *noun, plural* **coffees. 1.** a dark brown drink that is very popular in the U.S. and other countries, especially as a breakfast drink. It is made from boiling water and the roasted and ground seeds (called coffee beans) of a tropical shrub. **2.** the whole seeds or ground powder used to make this drink.

> The word **coffee** has been traced back to an Arabic word. It is said that a young shepherd noticed that his animals became lively and excited after eating the berries of a certain tree. He then tried some of the berries himself and so discovered coffee.

cof·fin [kof-in] *noun, plural* **coffins.** a box in which the body of a dead person is buried.

cog ▶ [kog] *noun, plural* **cogs.** one of the teeth sticking out from the edge of a wheel on a machine. The cogs fit between the cogs of another wheel and make it turn. A wheel with cogs is called a **cogwheel.**

co·her·ent [koh-here-unt] *adjective.* clear and well thought out; making good sense: *He gave a coherent argument for his idea and the others agreed with him.* If a speech is clear and logical, with well-connected ideas, it has the quality of **coherence. —coherently** *adverb.*

coil [koyl] *noun, plural* **coils. 1.** something wound in a series of loops: *She wound the spare computer cable into a coil and put it in her desk drawer.* **2.** a spiral length of wire through which electricity travels. **—coil,** *verb.*

coin ▶ [koyn] *noun, plural* **coins.** a small piece of metal, usually flat and round, used as money. A coin is stamped with official government markings to show its value.
verb, **coined, coining. 1.** to make money by stamping pieces of metal: *It is illegal for anyone except the government to coin money.* **2.** to invent or make up a new word or saying: *I coined a new nickname for my brother Paul today.*

> In earlier times, it was often possible to identify the first person to **coin** a new word, because only a small number of books and other writings were published. For example, it is known that the word energy was coined by the ancient Greek philosopher Aristotle. Today, with thousands of books published each year and millions of people writing on the Internet, new words are coined all the time, but it is very hard to tell who invented each one.

Cogs

Weight

Pendulum

In a grandfather clock, **cogs** *on interlocking wheels regulate the movement of the hands around the dial.*

co·in·cide [koh-in-side] *verb,* **coincided, coinciding. 1.** to occur at the same time: *The band's world tour coincided with the release of their new album.* **2.** to be exactly the same, be identical: *The suspect's story coincided with what the witness saw, so the police had to let him go.*

co·in·ci·dence [koh-in-suh-duns] *noun, plural* **coincidences.** the fact of two similar things happening at the same time or place, by chance or accident: *What a coincidence that my teacher and I were both on the same plane flight to New York.* **—coincidental,** *adjective;* **—coincidentally,** *adverb.*

coke [koke] *noun.* a grayish-black product that forms when coal is heated in an oven with very little air. It is burned as fuel to make metals.

cold [kohld] *adjective,* **colder, coldest. 1.** having a low temperature: *In the state of Alaska it is very cold in winter.* **2.** not feeling warm; having a chill: *I was cold so I put another blanket on the bed.* **3.** not showing a warm feeling; not kind or nice; unfriendly: *The mayor gave a very cold greeting when he met the writer who had written an article attacking him.*
noun, plural **colds. 1.** a place or condition of low temperature; a lack of heat. **2.** see COMMON COLD.

In the 1700s, farmers in Indonesia grew much of the **coffee** *that was shipped to Europe by Dutch traders.*

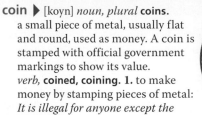

a
b
c
d
e
f
g
h
i
j
k
l
m
n
o
p
q
r
s
t
u
v
w
x
y
z

COLD-BLOODED ANIMALS

Reptiles, amphibians, fish, and insects are all cold-blooded, with the ability to match their body temperature to the air temperature. In hot conditions, their blood can be hotter than that of warm-blooded mammals. To warm themselves, some—like snakes, frogs, and lizards—like to lie in the sun. In cold weather, some insects shiver to keep warm, while others migrate, move underground, or die. Honeybees crowd together and move their wings to produce heat. In areas where winters are cold, fish may move deeper or migrate to warmer waters. Cold-blooded animals are more active when it is warm and slower when it is cold. During the cooler winter months, most reptiles hibernate.

Praying mantis

INSECTS

Butterfly

Fly

Cockroach

Caiman

Vine snake

Painted turtle

Lizards basking in the sun

REPTILES

Carpet python

Two-lined salamander

AMPHIBIANS

Flying frog

Spadefoot toad

Pacific herring

FISH

Seahorse

Ribbon eel

Bulltip shark

People gather and organize **collections** of many objects, including seashells.

collie

cold-blood·ed ◀ [kohld-<u>blud</u>-id] *adjective.* **1.** having a body temperature that changes as the surrounding air or water temperature changes. **2.** without feeling or emotion; cruel: *a cold-blooded criminal.* —**cold-bloodedly,** *adverb.*

col·i·se·um ▼ [kol-uh-<u>see</u>-um] *noun, plural* **coliseums.** 1. a large stadium or building used for sports and other large, public events: *We got tickets to the football game at the Los Angeles Coliseum.* **2. Coliseum** or **Colosseum.** a large amphitheater in Rome, built almost 2,000 years ago for huge public entertainments.

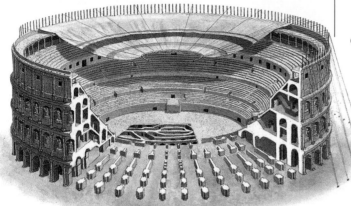

Fifty thousand people could fit into the **Coliseum** *in Rome to watch sporting events.*

col·lab·o·rate [kuh-<u>lab</u>-uh-*rate*] *verb,* **collaborated, collaborating. 1.** to do something with another or others; to work together: *The two writers collaborated on the film script.* **2.** to help the enemy of one's country during a war. Someone who does this is a **collaborator.** —**collaboration,** *noun.*

col·lage [kuh-<u>lahzh</u>] *noun, plural* **collages.** *Art.* a picture made by pasting pieces of paper, photographs, cloth, metal, and other things on a surface.

col·lapse [kuh-<u>laps</u>] *verb,* **collapsed, collapsing. 1.** to fall down or fall apart suddenly: *Our tent collapsed in the wind.* **2.** to fold inward to make smaller in size or flatter in shape: *to collapse an umbrella.* Something that is designed be folded to make it smaller or flatter is **collapsible. 3.** to fall down suddenly because of tiredness, weakness, or poor health: *I was so tired after the soccer game that I just collapsed into bed.* *noun, plural* **collapses.** the act of falling inward, breaking down, or failing.

col·lar [<u>kol</u>-ur] *noun, plural* **collars. 1.** the part of a piece of clothing that goes around the neck. **2.** a band or chain worn around the neck of an animal: *a dog's collar.* *verb,* **collared, collaring. 1.** to put a collar on. **2.** to catch and hold; seize: *The guards collared the escaping prisoner.*

col·lar·bone [<u>kol</u>-ur-*bone*] *noun, plural* **collarbones.** the bone connecting the breastbone and the shoulder blade.

col·lard [<u>kol</u>-urd] *noun, plural* **collards.** a vegetable with large, dark green leaves, related to the cabbage. **Collard greens** are the green leaves of this plant, used as food.

col·league [<u>kol</u>-eeg] *noun, plural* **colleagues.** someone who works at the same workplace or in the same job as another.

col·lect [kuh-<u>lekt</u>] *verb,* **collected, collecting. 1.** to put things together in a group; gather together: *They went around the park collecting empty cans and putting them in the trash.* **2.** to gather things of the same kind together as a hobby: *to collect old coins.* **3.** to get payment for: *The government collects taxes.* Someone who collects a particular thing as a job or a hobby is a **collector.** Someone who is **collected** is calm and in control of himself or herself.

col·lec·tion ▲ [kuh-<u>lek</u>-shun] *noun, plural* **collections. 1.** the act of gathering together: *The next garbage collection is on Tuesday morning.* **2.** a group of things of the same type gathered together: *a stamp collection; a CD collection.* **3.** money collected: *a collection for charity.*

col·lec·tive [kuh-<u>lek</u>-tiv] *adjective.* shared by all in a group; combined: *a collective decision.* *noun, plural* **collectives.** something done as a group. *People on our street formed a collective to buy vegetables together from a farmer.* —**collectively,** *adverb.*

col·lege [<u>kol</u>-ij] *noun, plural* **colleges.** a place for learning that offers more advanced education than high school. —**collegiate,** *adjective.*

College and *university* are both places where a student can go to study after high school. A college offers a four-year course of study leading to a bachelor's degree, or a two-year course leading to an associate degree. A university is larger than a college and can have one or more colleges within it. It also offers courses for college graduates studying to earn higher-level degrees.

col·lide [kuh-<u>lide</u>] *verb,* **collided, colliding. 1.** to crash into another object after one or both have been moving: *The car went through a red light and collided with another car.* **2.** to strongly disagree; clash: *The miners collided head-on with the government over their plans to close the mine.*

col·lie ◀ [<u>kol</u>-ee] *noun, plural* **collies.** a large dog with long thick hair, a long head, and a bushy tail. Collies were originally used by farmers to control sheep.

Collies are fast, intelligent dogs that were bred as sheepdogs.

a b c d e f g h i j k l m n o p q r s t u v w x y z

col·li·sion ▶ [kuh-<u>lizh</u>-un] *noun, plural* **collisions.** the act of crashing into another object, often at high speed.

co·lon[1] [<u>kole</u>-un] *noun, plural* **colons.** *Language.* a punctuation mark (:) that is used to separate the main part of a sentence from a list of examples, a quotation, or an explanation.

co·lon[2] [<u>kole</u>-un] *noun, plural* **colons.** *Medicine.* the part of the body that is made up of most of the large intestine.

A **colon** (:) is used in writing to call attention to what is to follow. It is most often used to introduce a list: The following girls won "Caught Being Good" awards this week: Emily, Hannah, Sarah, and Annie. It is also often used to set off an explanation or a quotation. For instance, the example sentences in this dictionary always follow a colon.

colo·nel [<u>kur</u>-nul] *noun, plural* **colonels.** a high-ranking officer in the United States Army, Marine Corps, or Air Force, ranking above a major but below a general. ◀》 A different word with the same sound is **kernel.**

The word **colonel** is spoken in a way that is not at all like its spelling ("<u>kur</u>-nul" and not "kuh-<u>loh</u>-nul"). At one time there was another word that meant the same thing, spelled *coronel.* Somehow the "r" sound from *coronel* got attached to the word *colonel,* instead of the "l" sound that its spelling suggests.

co·lo·ni·al ▼ [kuh-<u>lone</u>-ee-ul] *adjective.* having to do with a colony: *Spain once had a colonial empire that included Mexico and many parts of South America.* The **Colonial** period has to do with the time before the original thirteen Colonies became the first states of the United States.

co·lo·ni·al·ism [kuh-<u>lone</u>-ee-ul-*iz*-um] *noun. Government.* the control by a powerful country over the government, economy, and culture of a colony that it has claimed ownership of.

col·o·nist [<u>kol</u>-uh-nist] *noun, plural* **colonists.** someone who helps to start a colony or is one of the first to live in a colony; a settler. A **Colonist** was someone who lived in the original thirteen Colonies of North America.

*In the South, large **Colonial** houses were built by wealthy plantation owners.*

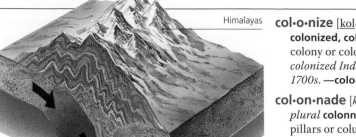

Himalayas

Tectonic plates colliding

*Deep within the Earth, a **collision** of two tectonic plates pushed the land upward to create the Himalayan mountains.*

col·o·nize [<u>kol</u>-uh-*nize*] *verb,* **colonized, colonizing.** to start a colony or colonies in: *The British colonized India in the 1600s and 1700s.* —**colonization,** *noun.*

col·on·nade [kol-uh-<u>nade</u>] *noun, plural* **colonnades.** a row of pillars or columns, often used to hold up a roof or a row of arches.

col·o·ny [<u>kol</u>-uh-nee] *noun, plural* **colonies. 1.** a group of people who leave their own country to settle in a new land. **2.** a territory controlled by a more powerful country. The **Colonies** are the original thirteen colonies of Great Britain that became the first states of the United States. **3.** a group of animals or plants of the same kind living or growing close together: *a colony of bees.*

col·or [<u>kul</u>-ur] *noun, plural* **colors. 1.** the appearance something has because of the way it reflects light: *Red, yellow, and blue are colors.* **2.** the general appearance of the skin: *He felt sick and his face had an unhealthy color.* **3.** an interesting, lively, or notable quality: *Her books about Hawaii have a lot of local color.* Things that have no color at all are **colorless.** *verb,* **colored, coloring.** to add color to.

There are several words in English for **color**, which is the general word and the one used most often. *Shade* means how light or dark a color is: *Navy is a dark shade of blue. Tint* is a slight difference in a color, usually by being lighter and closer to white: *Sky blue is a tint of blue. Hue* is a variety of a certain color that is different from the basic color: *The decorator will use different hues of blue for the room.*

col·or-blind [<u>kul</u>-ur-*blind*] *adjective. Medicine.* not being able to tell the difference between some colors, such as red and green. This condition is called **color-blindness.**

col·or·ful [<u>kul</u>-ur-ful] *adjective.* **1.** having bright colors or many different colors: *colorful parrots.* **2.** interesting or exciting: *a colorful tale about pirates and buried treasure.* —**colorfully,** *adverb.*

col·o·ring [<u>kul</u>-ur-ing] *noun, plural* **colorings. 1.** the particular color or colors of something or somebody: *the bright coloring of butterflies.* **2.** something used to give color to another thing; dye: *hair coloring; food coloring.*

co·los·sal [kuh-<u>los</u>-ul] *adjective.* very great in size: *Based on the size of the bones that were found, this dinosaur was a colossal beast.*

col·our [<u>kul</u>-ur] another spelling of COLOR.

colt [kohlt] *noun, plural* **colts.** a young male horse, or the young male of a similar animal, such as a zebra or donkey.

Columbines *belong to the buttercup family and have distinctive flowers with five petals.*

col·um·bine ◀ [kol-um-*bine*] *noun, plural* **columbines.** a plant with brightly colored, downward hanging flowers.

col·umn ▶ [kol-um] *noun, plural* **columns. 1.** a tall, narrow structure shaped like a post and usually made of stone. It is used as a support or decoration for part of a building or can stand by itself. **2.** anything that has a tall narrow shape like this: *a column of smoke.* **3.** a vertical section of print on a page: *This dictionary has two columns on each page.* **4.** a part of a newspaper or magazine that is always written by the same person: *She writes a weekly column on politics.* A **columnist** is someone who writes a column in a newspaper or magazine. **5.** a long line of things moving one behind the other: *a column of trucks; a column of ants.*

Co·man·che [kuh-man-chee] *noun, plural* **Comanches.** a member of a tribe of Native Americans of the central southern plains of the United States, now living mostly in Oklahoma.

comb [kohm] *noun, plural* **combs. 1.** a narrow piece of plastic, metal, or other material with a row of long thin teeth along one edge. It is used to smooth and tidy the hair, or to hold the hair in place. **2.** the fleshy, red growth on the head of chickens and some other birds. *verb,* **combed, combing. 1.** to make hair smooth and tidy using a comb. **2.** to search everywhere with great care: *We combed the house for the missing keys.*

com·bat ▼ [kom-bat *for noun;* kum-bat *for verb] noun, plural* **combats.** a fight or battle in war. *verb,* **combated, combating.** to fight against; try to defeat: *The job of the police is to combat crime; Jonas Salk developed a medicine to combat polio.*

com·bi·na·tion [kom-buh-nay-shun] *noun, plural* **combinations. 1.** a mixture of different things: *The pop group's success is a combination of talent and hard work.* **2.** a series of letters or numbers needed to open certain locks.

com·bine [kum-bine *for verb;* kom-bine *for noun] verb,* **combined, combining.** to join or mix two or more things together: *Combine the color red with yellow to make orange. noun, plural* **combines.** a farm machine that harvests grain and then separates the seeds from the stems.

This **column** *in Rome depicts the successful military campaigns of the emperor Trajan.*

com·bus·tion [kum-bus-chun] *noun.* the act of catching fire and burning: *the combustion of dry leaves in a forest fire.* Something that can catch fire and burn is **combustible.**

come [kum] *verb,* **came, come, coming. 1.** to move or go nearer to a place: *My dog has learned to come when I call him; Come closer—I want to tell you a secret.* **2.** to get to a certain place; arrive: *Mom comes home from work about four o'clock; Today's mail did not come yet.* **3.** to get to a certain condition: *I didn't like that show at first, but I've come to enjoy it.*

come·back [kum-bak] *noun, plural* **comebacks. 1.** a return to a former position or job: *The ex-lawyer had left politics after being defeated, but then made a successful comeback in this year's election.* **2.** a quick and clever answer; a sharp reply: *Tom was embarrassed by the coach's comeback to his silly remark.*

co·me·di·an [kuh-meed-ee-un] *noun, plural* **comedians.** a performer who tells jokes or acts out funny stories. A female comedian is sometimes called a **comedienne.**

In the past, armies rode into **combat** *on horseback and fought with swords.*

comedy

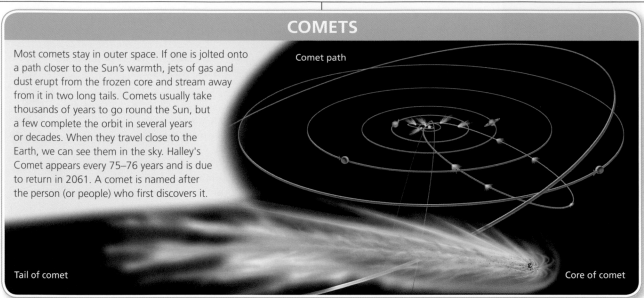

COMETS

Most comets stay in outer space. If one is jolted onto a path closer to the Sun's warmth, jets of gas and dust erupt from the frozen core and stream away from it in two long tails. Comets usually take thousands of years to go round the Sun, but a few complete the orbit in several years or decades. When they travel close to the Earth, we can see them in the sky. Halley's Comet appears every 75–76 years and is due to return in 2061. A comet is named after the person (or people) who first discovers it.

Comet path

Tail of comet

Core of comet

com·e·dy [kom-uh-dee] *noun, plural* **comedies.**
Literature. a movie, television show, play, or other entertainment that is meant to make people laugh and that has a happy ending.

com·et ▲ [kom-ut] *noun, plural* **comets.** a object in space with a bright center and a long trail of light behind it. A comet travels around the Sun. A comet is made of ice, frozen gases, and dust particles.

Comet goes back to a Greek word meaning "long hair." It was thought that the tail of a comet moving across the sky looks like a person's long, flowing hair.

com·fort [kum-furt] *noun, plural* **comforts.**
1. the pleasant state of feeling free from worry, pain, and sadness and having all physical needs met: *She relaxed in the comfort of the warm bed.*
2. something that helps remove worry, pain, or sadness: *After our long trip it was a great comfort to finally see the lights of home.*
verb, **comforted, comforting.** to make someone feel less sad or upset: *She comforted the lost child until his mother arrived.*

com·fort·a·ble [kumft-tur-bul *or* kum-fur-tuh-bul] *adjective.* **1.** giving comfort: *He fell asleep in the comfortable old chair.*
2. at ease; relaxed: *She enjoys acting and is comfortable on stage.* —**comfortably,** *adverb.*

com·ic ▶ [kom-ik] *adjective.* causing laughter; funny or amusing: *a comic actor.*
noun, plural **comics. 1.** a person who tells jokes to make people laugh; a comedian. **2. comics.** a group of comic strips, as in a magazine or newspaper: *the Sunday comics.*

com·i·cal [kom-i-kul] *adjective.* funny or amusing: *He has a comical way of dressing, like wearing odd socks that don't match.* —**comically,** *adverb.*

com·ma [kom-uh] *noun, plural* **commas.** *Language.* a punctuation mark (,) that is used to separate parts of a sentence or items in a list.

In writing, the **comma** (,) shows that there is a slight break in the flow of words. In speech we do this by pausing for a moment between words. The most common uses of the comma are: (1) to separate the two parts of a compound sentence: *I wanted to go to the beach, but it poured with rain all day.* (2) to separate a clause from the main part of the sentence: *When I looked out the window, I could see gray skies everywhere.* (3) to separate different adjectives from one another: *It was a cold, wet, gloomy afternoon.* (4) to separate words or phrases in a list: *So I put on my jacket, got an umbrella, and went for a walk in the rain.*

com·mand [kuh-mand] *verb,* **commanded, commanding.**
1. to tell someone to do something; give an order: *She commanded that they leave her property immediately.* **2.** to have control; be responsible for: *Dwight Eisenhower commanded the U.S. troops in World War II.* A person (especially an officer in the armed forces) who commands is a **commander. 3.** to deserve and be given certain treatment: *to command respect.*
noun, plural **commands. 1.** an order.
2. power or authority to give orders or be in charge: *The police took command of the rescue operation.*
3. the ability to use: *He has a good command of Spanish.*

With their painted mouths and bright clothes, clowns are well-known **comic** *characters.*

com·mand·ment [kuh-mand-munt] *noun, plural* **commandments.** a law or command that should be obeyed. A **Commandment** is one of the ten rules of behavior in the Bible.

com·mem·o·rate ▶ [kuh-mem-uh-rate] *verb,* **commemorated, commemorating.** to honor the memory of someone or something: *The Lincoln Memorial commemorates the life of Abraham Lincoln.* —**commemoration,** *noun.*

com·mence [kuh-mens] *verb*, **commenced, commencing.** to start or begin something: *The company promised that work on the new building would commence in six weeks.*

com·mence·ment [kuh-mens-munt] *noun*, *plural* **commencements. 1.** the beginning; start: *There will be a short talk on safety before the commencement of the flight.* **2.** a ceremony of graduation from a school or college.

com·mend [kuh-mend] *verb*, **commended, commending.** to speak about in a favorable way; praise: *The mayor commended the firefighters for their brave actions.* Something worthy of praise is **commendable.** —**commendation**, *noun.*

com·ment [kom-ent] *noun.* a statement of one's thoughts about something; a remark; opinion: *a rude comment; His comments on my speech were very helpful.* *verb*, **commented, commenting.** to make a remark; give an opinion. *She noticed the broken vase, but did not comment.*

com·men·ta·tor [kom-un-*tay*-tur] *noun*, *plural* **commentators.** a person who gives an opinion about the news or describes an event for a newspaper or radio or television station. Such a person's opinion or description is a **commentary.**

com·merce [kom-urs] *noun.* the buying and selling of goods; trade; business: *The branch of government that promotes business activity and growth is the Department of Commerce.*

com·mer·cial [kuh-mur-shul] *adjective.* **1.** having to do with commerce and business: *The company office is in the commercial part of town.* **2.** producing a profit: *The movie got poor reviews from critics, but it was a commercial success.* *noun*, *plural* **commercials.** an advertisement on radio or television. —**commercially**, *adjective.*

com·mer·cial·ize [kuh-mur-shul-*ize*] *verb*, **commercialized, commercializing.** to make commercial; make a profit from something: *Many people think Christmas has become commercialized and there is too much emphasis on buying gifts.* —**commercialization**, *noun.*

com·mis·sion [kuh-mish-un] *noun*, *plural* **commissions. 1.** a group of people officially appointed to find out about something or control something: *a commission to investigate crime.* **2.** money paid to an employee for a successful effort: *Donna gets a commission on every car she sells.* **3.** the act of committing a crime: *the commission of murder.*

*The Arc de Triomphe in Paris, France, **commemorates** the victories of Emperor Napoleon I.*

4. a certificate giving a rank in the armed forces. A **commissioned officer** is an officer in the armed forces holding by commission the rank of second lieutenant or ensign or above. **5.** the fact of being in working order and ready for use: *We had to bang on the door because the bell was out of commission.* *verb*, **commissioned, commissioning. 1.** to give a person a special job to do: *The king commissioned the artist to paint his portrait.* **2.** to put into active military service: *to commission a warship.*

com·mis·sion·er [kuh-mish-nur *or* kuh-mish-uh-nur] *noun*, *plural* **commissioners. 1.** a member of a commission. **2.** an official in charge of a government department: *the fire commissioner.* **3.** the head of a professional sports league.

com·mit [kuh-mit] *verb*, **committed, committing. 1.** to do something, especially something wrong: *to commit a crime.* **2.** to put someone into the care of an institution, such as a prison or hospital: *The judge committed him to life imprisonment.* **3.** to strongly support something. Someone who is **committed** has a strong belief in or devotion to something such as a religion, a cause, or an opinion. —**commitment**, *noun.*

com·mit·tee [kuh-mit-ee] *noun*, *plural* **committees.** a small group of people chosen from a larger group to discuss and make decisions about certain things: *a committee to investigate new equipment for the park.*

com·mod·i·ty [kuh-mod-uh-tee] *noun*, *plural* **commodities.** *Business.* **1.** anything that can be bought and sold. **2. commodities.** basic products of farming and mining that are traded or sold as raw materials, such as wheat, corn, gold, or crude oil.

com·mon [kom-un] *adjective.* **1.** happening often; usual: *It is common for us to go swimming in summer; Garcia is a common last name around here.* **2.** belonging equally to all; shared: *English is the common language of Australia.* **3.** widely known or found; general: *It's common knowledge that this car model has a lot of problems.* A **commons** is a piece of land, such as a park, that is open to everyone. **4.** not special; ordinary; average: *Crabgrass is a common weed.* —**commonly**, *adverb.*

common cold *Health.* a mild infectious disease that can cause a blocked nose, sore throat, coughing, and sneezing.

common denominator *Mathematics.* a denominator that is shared by two or more fractions. The fractions $1/4$ and $3/4$ have the common denominator 4.

common noun *Language.* a noun that is used to name ordinary places or things. It does not start with a capital letter. The words *grass, star, sister, dog,* and *town* are common nouns.

a b c d e f g h i j k l m n o p q r s t u v w x y z

In an 1880s telephone exchange, women joined hundreds of wires together so that people could **communicate** *by telephone.*

com·mon·place [kom-un-*plase*] *adjective.* happening often; not special; ordinary: *Talk of global warming is now commonplace.*

common sense practical good sense or judgment, gained from experience and logical thinking, not from school or study.

com·mon·wealth [kom-un-*welth*] *noun, plural* **commonwealths.** *Government.* a nation or state governed by the people. The United States is a commonwealth. Certain states, such as Massachusetts, Pennsylvania, Virginia, and Kentucky are officially called commonwealths. **The Commonwealth of Nations** is a group of countries that were once colonies of Britain, such as Australia, Canada, and India.

com·mo·tion [kuh-*moh*-shun] *noun, plural* **commotions.** a noisy or violent disturbance: *There was a commotion in the audience when someone threw a firecracker from the back.*

com·mu·ni·ca·ble [kuh-*myoon*-i-kuh-bul] *adjective.* able to be passed on to others: *Chicken pox is a communicable disease.*

com·mu·ni·cate ▲ [kuh-*myoon*-i-*kate*] *verb,* **communicated, communicating.** to make feelings or information known to others by speech, writing, or electronic means: *My aunt and I communicate by phone and e-mail.*

com·mu·ni·ca·tion [kuh-*myoon*-i-*kay*-shun] *noun, plural* **communications. 1.** the sharing or passing on of information or feelings: *Speaking and writing are both forms of communication.* **2.** a piece of news or information: *The ship's captain received an urgent communication warning of a storm ahead.* **3. communications.** the entire system of electronic connections using telephones, internet, cables, satellites, computers, TV, radio, and cell phones: *Communications to the mountains were cut by heavy snowfall.*

communications satellite ▼ *Science.* a piece of equipment that orbits the Earth to provide electronic links between places on the surface of Earth.

com·mun·ion [kuh-*myoon*-yun] *noun, plural* **communions. 1.** the experience of sharing feelings or thoughts: *Summer camp provided an opportunity for children to have a communion with nature.* **2. Communion.** *Religion.* the religious ceremony in which Christians remember Christ by sharing bread and wine as a symbol of his sacrifice.

com·mu·nism [kom-yuh-*niz*-um] *noun. Government.* a social and political system in which all property and industry is owned by the government on behalf of all people; food and goods are supposed to be shared according to people's needs rather than the wealthy having more. This word is also spelled **Communism.**

com·mu·nist [kom-yuh-nist] *noun, plural* **communists.** someone who believes in communism as a way of life. A **Communist Party** is a political party supporting communism. This word is also spelled **Communist.**

com·mu·ni·ty ▶ [kuh-*myoon*-i-tee] *noun, plural* **communities. 1.** a group of people who live in the same place: *The local community is in favor of building a new hospital.* **2.** a group who have the same interests, language, religion, or ethnic background: *People who teach in universities are known as the academic community.* **3.** *Biology.* a group of different kinds of plants or animals that live together in a certain area and relate to or depend on each other in the same way: *the fish community in a large lake.*

commutative property *Mathematics.* the fact of adding or multiplying two numbers in either order and still getting the same result. For example: 9 + 6 gives the same answer as 6 + 9, and 3 x 8 gives the same answer as 8 x 3.

com·mute [kuh-*myoot*] *verb,* **commuted, commuting.** to travel each morning and evening to and from work by car, bus, or train: *to commute to New York City by railroad. noun, plural* **commutes.** a trip made in this way: *His morning commute takes an hour.* A person who travels to work in this way is a **commuter.**

Like a huge mirror in the sky, a **communications satellite** *receives radio signals and sends them back to the Earth.*

Communications satellite

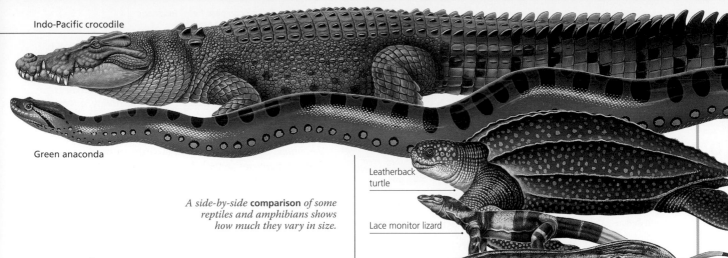

Indo-Pacific crocodile

Green anaconda

*A side-by-side **comparison** of some reptiles and amphibians shows how much they vary in size.*

Leatherback turtle

Lace monitor lizard

Japanese giant salamander

Tuatara

Black-and-white worm-lizard

Banna caecilian

com·pact¹ [<u>kom</u>-*pakt for adjective;* kum-<u>pakt</u> *for verb*]
adjective. **1.** tightly packed together: *The leaves of Brussels sprouts are very compact.* **2.** fitting neatly into a small space: *Our tent folds into a compact carrying bag.*
noun, plural **compacts. 1.** a small flat container with a mirror that holds a woman's face powder.
2. an automobile smaller than a standard sedan.
verb, **compacted, compacting.** to press together firmly: *The weight of the passing cars compacted the snow.*
A **compactor** is a machine that crushes garbage together to make it smaller.

*Living in a **community** helps African meerkats defend the group and look after their young.*

com·pact² [<u>kom</u>-*pakt*] *noun, plural* **compacts.** an agreement between two or more people, groups, or countries.

compact disc a small, round, plastic disc for storing digitally recorded music or information; known as CD for short.

com·pan·ion [kum-<u>pan</u>-yun] *noun, plural* **companions.** a person who spends time with another, either on a journey, as a friend, or by chance: *The two women became good companions on the long voyage.* The bond between companions is **companionship.**

com·pa·ny [<u>kump</u>-uh-nee] *noun, plural* **companies.**
1. the presence of one or more guests: *We had company this weekend—my uncle came to visit us.* **2.** a group of people who join together to do business; a firm. **3.** people or animals with whom one enjoys spending time.
4. a group of people with something in common: *a theater company; The ship's company held a party on the first night of the voyage.* **5.** a unit that is part of an army, usually with about 120 soldiers.

com·par·a·tive [kum-<u>pare</u>-i-tiv] *adjective.* **1.** having to do with a comparison between one thing and another: *a comparative study of the cost of buying a home in Canada and the U.S.* **2.** measured or tested by comparison to something else: *There was comparative silence after the machines stopped.*
noun, plural **comparatives.** *Language.* the form of an adverb or adjective that shows an increase in quantity or degree. *Greater* is the comparative of *great.*
—**comparatively,** *adverb.*

com·pare [kum-<u>pare</u>] *verb,* **compared, comparing.**
1. to judge or note differences between two or more things: *We compared our test results, and hers were better than mine.* **2.** to show similarities or differences between things: *The sound of the crowd was so loud it could be compared to a plane taking off.* When two things are very similar, such as being equally good, they are described as **comparable. 3.** to be worthy of comparison: *She says that nothing compares with the beauty of the Swiss Alps.*

When you write, you can both **compare** and *contrast* two similar things. If you wrote a paper *comparing* your town to Los Angeles, you might mention some things that are the same and others that are different. If you wrote a paper *contrasting* your town with Los Angeles, you would be pointing out just the things that are different.

com·par·i·son ▲ [kum-<u>pare</u>-uh-sun] *noun, plural* **comparisons. 1.** the act of comparing similarities and differences between things or people: *In comparison, the driver's injuries were worse than those of his passenger.*
2. the fact of being similar; a likeness: *To me, there's no comparison between a supermarket tomato and one you grow yourself.* **3.** the changing of the form of an adverb or adjective to show the different degrees of something: *Peter's bike is faster than Duane's, but Mike's is fastest of all.*

h
i
j
k
l
m
n
o
p
q
r
s
t
u
v
w
x
y
z

This early Chinese **compass** *has a magnetic needle floating in a bowl of water.*

com·part·ment [kum-*part*-munt] *noun, plural* **compartments.** any of the parts or divisions of something: *Our refrigerator has compartments for vegetables, meat, and cheese.*

com·pass ▶ [kum-pus] *noun, plural* **compasses. 1.** an instrument used to find direction. It has a needle that always points to magnetic north. **2.** an instrument used to draw circles and mark distances. It has two rods joined at the top, one of which has a sharp point, while the other holds a marker pen or pencil.

com·pas·sion [kum-*pash*-un] *noun.* a strong feeling of sympathy for someone who is suffering and a desire to help them: *When she was ill, the other workers at her job showed great compassion for her.* —**compassionate,** *adjective.*

com·pel [kum-*pel*] *verb,* **compelled, compelling.** to make someone do something they do not want to do; force: *Heavy rain compelled them to postpone the golf tournament.* Something that draws or attracts you to do something is **compelling**: *I only planned to read the first chapter, but the story was so compelling I finished the entire book.*

com·pen·sate [*komp*-in-*sate*] *verb,* **compensated, compensating. 1.** to act as a balance; make up for: *Our teacher's great sense of humor compensates for his making us work so hard.* **2.** to pay money for a loss or damage: *When the store was demolished for road widening the shopkeeper was compensated by city authorities.* **Compensation** is payment to make up for a loss or damage.

com·pete [kum-*peet*] *verb,* **competed, competing.** to take part in a contest: *I will compete in next year's school spelling bee.*

com·pe·tent [*komp*-uh-tunt] *adjective.* having the ability or skill to do something well; enough; capable: *She is not great at playing the guitar, but she's certainly competent.* **Competence** is the ability or skill to do something well enough. —**competently,** *adverb.*

com·pe·ti·tion [*komp*-uh-*tish*-un] *noun, plural* **competitions. 1.** the act of trying to do better than others: *Three schools were in competition for the trophy.* **2.** a test of skill or strength; a game: *The skating competition was popular.*

com·pet·i·tive [kum-*pet*-i-tiv] *adjective.* **1.** based on or determined by competition: *The art prize winner was chosen by a competitive process.* **2.** having to do with liking to compete: *David is a competitive swimmer.* —**competitively,** *adverb;* —**competitiveness,** *noun.*

com·pet·i·tor ▼ [kum-*pet*-i-tur] *noun, plural* **competitors.** a person, team, or product that competes for something: *There were five competitors in the race.*

com·pile [kum-*pile*] *verb,* **compiled, compiling.** to make a report or collect together information from a number of different places: *It takes a lot of research to compile a dictionary.* The result of compiling information is a **compilation.**

com·pla·cent [kum-*play*-sunt] *adjective.* having a good opinion of oneself and not expecting to be challenged, often without a reason to think this: *After six wins the team grew rather complacent.* A feeling of self-satisfaction is called **complacency.** —**complacently,** *adverb.*

com·plain [kum-*playn*] *verb,* **complained, complaining. 1.** to say you are not happy about something: *The neighbor complained when we played loud music.* **2.** to make an official report that something is wrong. —**complainer,** *noun.*

com·plaint [kum-*playnt*] *noun, plural* **complaints. 1.** the act of complaining; saying you are unhappy about something: *His complaint was that the umpire's decision was unfair.* **2.** a cause of annoyance or unhappiness: *The pupils took their complaints about bad food to the head of the school.* **3.** a formal charge: *Leila made a complaint to the police about the burglary.*

Competitors *in a hurdle race need great speed and precision to clear the hurdles while running.*

*Artists in ancient Rome were skilled at creating **complex** mosaic floors.*

com·ple·ment [komp-luh-munt] *noun,*
plural **complements**. the fact of making a thing complete by adding something else: *In a perfect meal, food and drink act as complements to each other.*
verb, **complemented, complementing.** to make something complete: *The fireworks complemented the music to make a great show.* Things that go well together are described as **complementary.**
🔊 A different word with the same sound is **complimentary**.

com·plete [kum-pleet] *adjective.* **1.** having all necessary parts; whole: *If a deck of playing cards is complete, it has 52 cards.* **2.** finished, ended: *Is the new freeway complete yet?* **3.** total, absolute: *His sudden illness came as a complete surprise to us.*
verb, **completed, completing.** **1.** to make a thing whole by adding something missing: *For my birthday I got a new golf club to complete the set.* **2.** to finish or end something: *After Jake completed his schoolwork for the day, he played volleyball.* —**completely,** *adverb.*

com·ple·tion [kum-plee-shun] *noun, plural* **completions.**
1. the act of finishing something: *Completion of this building is due in two years' time.* **2.** the state of being finished: *They worked hard to bring the new science project to completion.*

com·plex ▲ [kum-pleks *or* kom-pleks *for adjective;* kom-pleks *for noun*] *adjective.* **1.** difficult to understand or deal with: *The chemistry experiment was quite complex.* **2.** made from many connecting pieces or elements: *Automobiles are complex machines.* A higher level of **complexity** means things are more difficult to understand. *noun, plural* **complexes. 1.** something made up of many different parts: *They have an apartment in a large housing complex.* **2.** feelings or thoughts that stay in your mind and make you upset or worried: *If you feel you are not as good at things as other people, this is called an inferiority complex.*

com·plex·ion [kum-plek-shun] *noun, plural* **complexions.**
1. the natural color and state of a person's skin, especially the face: *She has a healthy complexion.* **2.** a general character or nature of something: *Mom's injury changed the complexion of the holiday.*

complex sentence *Language.* a sentence consisting of a main part and one or more other parts: *If it rains, we won't be able to play* is a complex sentence.

A **complex sentence** has two or more parts. One part could stand by itself as its own sentence, but the other part or parts could not. "When I saw the smile on her face, I knew right away that her team had won the game." is a complex sentence. One part could be a sentence by itself ("I knew right away that her team had won the game.") but the other part does not make a sentence by itself ("When I saw the smile on her face").

com·pli·cate [komp-luh-kate] *verb,* **complicated, complicating. 1.** to make difficult to do, deal with, or understand: *We have to clean out all the closets today, so it will just complicate matters if we do the garage too.* **2.** to make more serious or more severe: *The injury to his leg was complicated by an infection.* If something is **complicated** it is hard to do or understand: *a complicated jigsaw puzzle that took hours to put together.*

com·pli·ca·tion [komp-luh-kay-shun] *noun,*
plural **complications.** the fact of making a situation more difficult: *Driving in the rain was bad enough, but then there was the added complication of the car running low on gas.*

com·pli·ment [komp-luh-ment] *noun, plural* **compliments.**
1. the act of giving a person praise for something good they have done: *He paid her a compliment on her skating performance.* **2.** **compliments.** good wishes: *Your cousins send their compliments for your birthday.*
verb, **complimented, complimenting.** to say something nice to a person; praise someone: *The music teacher complimented Annette for her flute playing.*
🔊 A different word with the same sound is **complement**.

com·pli·men·ta·ry [komp-luh-men-tree *or* komp-luh-men-tuh-ree] *adjective.* **1.** expressing admiration; giving praise: *The teacher's complimentary comments on my paper were very welcome.* **2.** given as a favor, without cost: *The first 200 customers at the store were given a complimentary box of chocolates.*

Head

*The **components** of a vacuum cleaner include a head, hose, dust bag, fan, and motor.*

com·ply [kum-<u>plye</u>] *verb*, **complied, complying.** to do as one is asked or directed: *The driver told us to get off the bus and everyone complied.* The act or state of doing as directed is **compliance.**

com·po·nent ▶ [kum-<u>poh</u>-nunt] *noun,* *plural* **components.** any of the parts that make up a complete system: *We did not repair our TV as we couldn't buy all the necessary components.*

com·pose [kum-<u>poze</u>] *verb*, **composed, composing.** **1.** to be made up of; consist of: *Water is composed of hydrogen and oxygen.* **2.** to write or create something, such as music or poetry: *He composed a symphony at fourteen years of age.* **3.** to calm or control oneself: *After first being angry I was later able to compose myself.* When you remain **composed** you are able to stay quiet; this is a feeling of **composure.**

Hose

com·pos·er ▼ [kum-<u>poze</u>-ur] *noun,* *plural* **composers.** *Music.* a person who writes music.

*Mozart was one of the greatest **composers** the world has ever known.*

com·pos·ite [kum-<u>poz</u>-it] *adjective.* made up of different parts: *By using everyone's ideas, the class built up a composite story.*

com·po·si·tion [kom-puh-<u>zish</u>-un] *noun,* *plural* **compositions. 1.** the act of bringing two or more parts together to make a whole. **2.** the makeup of something: *The composition of the committee was half Republicans and half Democrats.* **3.** the fact of writing or creating something, such as a piece of music or a piece of writing for school.

com·post ▼ [<u>kom</u>-post] *noun.* a mix of rotting leaves and vegetable matter added to soil to make it better for growing.

com·pound [<u>kom</u>-pownd or kum-<u>pownd</u>] *adjective.* having two or more parts: *Insects have a compound eye with many small parts that can each see.* *noun, plural* **compounds. 1.** a combination of two or more parts. **2.** *Chemistry.* a substance made up of two or more chemical elements:

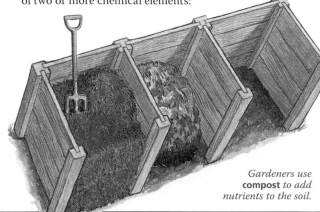

*Gardeners use **compost** to add nutrients to the soil.*

Salt is a compound of sodium and chlorine. **3.** see COMPOUND WORD.
verb, **compounded, compounding.** to make something by combining two or more parts: *The pharmacist compounded ingredients to make up a cough mixture.*

compound sentence *Language.* a sentence that contains at least two simple sentences, often joined by *and, or,* or *but. Julie loves swimming, but I like cycling* is a compound sentence.

compound word *Language.* a compound word is made by joining two or more words together. *Basketball* is a compound word.

> A **compound word** can be written as two separate words (for example, air force, bass drum, credit card); as two words joined by a hyphen (all-star, brand-new, cross-country), or as just one word (airline, background, checkup). Check this dictionary to see which of these forms is correct for a certain compound.

com·pre·hend [kom-pree-<u>hend</u>] *verb*, **comprehended, comprehending.** to understand the meaning of something: *The math problem was too hard for me to comprehend.* The fact of understanding something is **comprehension.**

Fan

com·pre·hen·sive [kom-pree-<u>hen</u>-siv] *adjective.* having to do with including everything possible; broad in scope: *An encyclopedia is a comprehensive book with many different kinds of information.* —**comprehensively,** *adverb;* —**comprehensiveness,** *noun.*

Dust bag   Motor

com·press [kum-<u>pres</u> *for verb;* <u>kom</u>-pres *for noun*] *verb,* **compressed, compressing.** to force into a smaller space: *We compressed our clothes to fit them into the suitcase. noun, plural* **compresses.** a thick pad or cloth used to hold heat or cold against the body after injury.

com·pres·sion [kum-<u>presh</u>-un] *noun,* *plural* **compressions. 1.** the act of compressing or being compressed. **2.** the pressure of an air and gas mixture in the cylinder of an automobile engine before it is burned.

com·prise [kum-<u>prize</u>] *verb,* **comprised, comprising.** to be made up of; consist of; include: *The U.S.A. comprises fifty different states.*

com·pro·mise [<u>komp</u>-ruh-mize] *noun,* *plural* **compromises.** the act of settling an argument in which both sides make a final agreement by giving up some of their demands. *verb,* **compromised, compromising.** to reach agreement by accepting that not all your demands will be met: *After some negotiation Dad and the car salesman compromised on the price.*

com·pul·so·ry [kum-<u>pul</u>-suh-ree] *adjective.* having to do with following a law or instruction: *It is compulsory to attend school meetings.*

com·pute [kum-<u>pyoot</u>] *verb,* **computed, computing.** to make a calculation using mathematics: to compute the cost of building a house. The result of this is a **computation.**

com·put·er [kum-<u>pyoo</u>-tur] *noun, plural* **computers.** an electronic machine that can store and recall large amounts of information in words and pictures. Computers can be used to write, to do calculations with numbers, to use the Internet, and for various other purposes.

computer graphics pictures shown on a computer screen that display information stored in the computer.

com·put·er·ize [kum-<u>pyoo</u>-tur-*ize*] *verb,* **computerized, computerizing.** to install and store information on a computer that was previously held in another form: *The school's academic records used to be on paper, but are all computerized now.* —**computerization,** *noun.*

computer language a system of commands using words and symbols that a computer can read and process.

computer literacy 1. an understanding of what computers can do and how they can be used. **2.** the ability to use a computer to do the basic tasks for which it is intended.

computer science the study of how computers work and what they can do.

com·rade [<u>kom</u>-*rad*] *noun, plural* **comrades.** a friend, companion, or member of the same group: *The soldier risked his life to save his fallen comrade.* **Comradeship** is the friendship that comrades share.

con·cave [kun-<u>kave</u> or kon-<u>kave</u>] *adjective.* curved inward like the inside of a hollow sphere.

con·ceal [kun-<u>seel</u>] *verb,* **conceal, concealing.** to keep something or someone from being seen; hide: *The thief concealed the necklace under his coat.* —**concealment,** *noun.*

con·cede [kun-<u>seed</u>] *verb,* **conceded, conceding. 1.** to admit that something is true, often reluctantly: *He conceded that his exam results were poor.* **2.** to agree an opponent has succeeded in an argument or fight: *A player may concede in a chess match if he sees he has no chance to win.*

con·ceit·ed [kun-<u>seet</u>-id] *adjective.* having an opinion of oneself or one's abilities that is far too high: *She's very conceited about her ability in soccer and thinks she should always be team captain.* The state of having a very high opinion of oneself is **conceit.**

con·ceive [kun-<u>seev</u>] *verb,* **conceived, conceiving.** to think of or imagine something as possible or real: *It is hard to conceive of life existing in outer space.* Something that is able to be imagined is **conceivable.**

con·cen·trate [<u>kon</u>-sun-*trate*] *verb,* **concentrated, concentrating. 1.** to bring together at or around a single point: *Businesses in town are concentrated in the city center.* **2.** to thicken or purify a mixture by boiling it: *We concentrated the chicken stock to make a rich soup.* **3.** to direct one's thoughts to a specific task: *I can't concentrate on my homework while that loud music is playing.* —**concentration,** *noun.*

concentration camp a place where political prisoners or members of ethnic groups are kept, such as Jews in the Nazi camps of World War II.

con·cen·tric ▶ [kun-<u>sen</u>-trik] *adjective.* Mathematics. of two objects, having the same center. —**concentrically,** *adverb.*

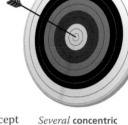

Several **concentric** *circles surround a bull's-eye.*

con·cept [<u>kon</u>-sept] *noun, plural* **concepts.** a thought, idea, or principle: *Everyone needs to understand the concept of right and wrong.* Something made up of a concept or concepts is **conceptual.**

con·cep·tion [kun-<u>sep</u>-shun] *noun, plural* **conceptions.** the act of forming an idea: *The conception of the basic story for the film took only an hour, but actually making it took months.*

con·cern [kun-<u>surn</u>] *verb,* **concerned, concerning. 1.** to be of interest or importance to: *These problems should concern all of us.* **2.** to be about: *The meeting concerned safety at school.* **3.** to cause anxiety or worry: *I am concerned about my sister's health.* Someone who is interested in, or anxious about, something, is **concerned.** You can describe something relating to, or about, something else as **concerning** it.

con·cert ▼ [<u>kon</u>-surt] *noun, plural* **concerts.** *Music.* a public performance by singers or musicians.

A symphony orchestra performs a number of **concerts** *each year.*

Conches *are found among corals and marine plants on the seabed in warm waters.*

con·cer·to [kun-<u>chare</u>-toh] *noun, plural* **concertos.** *Music.* a musical composition for an orchestra and one or more solo instruments.

con·ces·sion [kun-<u>sesh</u>-un] *noun, plural* **concessions. 1.** the act of allowing something to happen that usually or normally would not: *Their soccer team came with only ten players, so as a concession we agreed to use ten also.* **2.** the act of admitting something is true, conceding: *The government made no concession that they had made a mistake.* **3.** a right given by a government or other authority to permit something: *My friend's dad has the concession to sell drinks and hamburgers outside the baseball game.*

conch ▶ [konch] *noun, plural* **conches. 1.** a large tropical sea animal that has a spiral shell. **2.** the shell of this animal.

con·cise [kun-<u>sise</u>] *adjective.* short and clear; expressing a lot of information briefly: *When asked how he would defeat a faster boxer, champion Joe Louis gave a concise answer: "He can run, but he can't hide."* —**concisely,** *adverb.*

con·clude [kun-<u>klood</u>] *verb,* **concluded, concluding. 1.** to bring to an end, finish: *The fireworks showed the performance was concluded.* **2.** to reach a decision after careful consideration: *We concluded it was safe to go back into the house after the earthquake.*

con·clu·sion [kun-<u>kloo</u>-zhun] *noun, plural* **conclusions. 1.** the finish or end: *At the conclusion of the play the hero marries his sweetheart.* **2.** a decision or judgment reached after careful thought: *She came to the conclusion that he was a liar.*

con·coct [kun-<u>kokt</u>] *verb,* **concocted, concocting. 1.** to mix and combine several things: *Mom concocted lunch from what was left over from yesterday's dinner.* Something made by mixing several things together is a **concoction. 2.** to invent or create in order to mislead: *My cousins concocted a story to fool their parents.*

con·crete ▼ [<u>kon</u>-*kreet* or kon-<u>kreet</u>] *noun, plural* **concretes.** a mixture of sand or stones, cement, and water that goes hard when it dries; it is used for buildings, roads, and bridges.
adjective. **1.** made of this substance: *a concrete driveway.* **2.** able to be seen or touched; physically real: *A chair is a concrete object.* **3.** real or definite: *Don't just say we have a problem—please offer a concrete suggestion for solving it.*

concrete noun *Language.* a noun that refers to a real thing.

If something is concrete you can actually see, feel, or touch it. A **concrete noun** is a word of this kind, such as *shirt, tree, table, book,* or *computer.* The opposite kind is an *abstract noun,* which is a word for an idea or thought. For example, *car, truck, bus,* and *train* are concrete nouns but *transportation* is an abstract noun.

con·cur [kun-<u>kur</u>] *verb,* **concurred, concurring.** to share an opinion; agree: *Our views on which movies we should see usually concur.* —**concurrence,** *noun.*

con·cur·rent [kun-<u>kur</u>-unt] *adjective.* at the same time: *The two shows were concurrent, so we could only see one.* —**concurrently,** *adverb.*

The Sydney Opera House in Australia is built mainly of **concrete.**

Concrete ribs

Tiles

Glass

con·cus·sion [kun-<u>kush</u>-un] *noun, plural* **concussions.**
1. a violent shock or shaking: *The concussion of the bomb shook the whole town.* **2.** *Medicine.* a temporary injury to the brain caused by a blow or shock: *The boy suffered a concussion when he fell off the truck.*

con·demn [kun-<u>dem</u>] *verb,* **condemned, condemning.**
1. to express strong disapproval or opposition to something: *She condemned the decision not to allow people to camp at the beach.* **2.** to give a punishment in a court of law: *The judge condemned the murderer to a life sentence.* **3.** to declare that something is unfit for use: *The old building has been condemned because it is no longer safe to work in.* —**condemnation,** *noun.*

con·dense [kun-<u>dens</u>] *verb,* **condensed, condensing.**
1. to reduce something in size or make it thicker by removing some water: *Soup condenses when it is boiled down.* Something that has been changed in this way is **condensed:** *condensed milk; a condensed book.*
2. to change or be changed into a liquid from a gas or vapor: *If steam touches a cold surface it condenses into water.* —**condensation,** *noun;* —**condenser,** *noun.*

con·di·tion [kun-<u>dish</u>-un] *noun, plural* **conditions.**
1. a state of being or existing: *The house is in good condition.* **2.** something necessary for something else to happen: *It is a condition of voting that you must be eighteen years old.* **3.** a general state of illness or of a body part: *My father has a heart condition.* **4. conditions.** the state of things, a set of circumstances: *The weather conditions are poor today.*
verb, **conditioned, conditioning. 1.** to improve something or make healthier: *The shampoo has conditioned my dog's coat.* **2.** to become used or adjusted to something: *Years of working outdoors had conditioned him to cold weather.* —**conditional,** *adjective.*

con·do·lence [kun-<u>doh</u>-luns] *noun, plural* **condolences.**
an expression of sympathy, especially when someone dies: *I sent my condolences to the family of the man who died.*

con·do·min·ium [kon-duh-<u>min</u>-ee-um] *noun, plural* **condominiums. 1.** a group of apartments in which each apartment is owned by the person or people who live in it. **2.** one apartment in such a building. A shorter form of this word is **condo.**

con·dor ▶ [<u>kon</u>-dur] *noun, plural* **condors.**
a type of vulture, a very large bird, found in South America and in California, having wings that can spread out very wide.

con·duct [kun-<u>dukt</u>] *noun.* the way a person acts, behavior: *The students were praised for their good conduct during the school trip.*
verb, **conducted, conducting. 1.** to act in a certain way; behave: *It was the first time he ever gave a speech, but he conducted himself quite well.* **2.** to lead or direct: *The guide conducted a tour of the museum.* **3.** to control or manage: *Conducting a large business is a big responsibility.* **4.** to transmit or carry: *Copper in power cables conducts electricity very well.*

con·duc·tor ◀
[kun-<u>duk</u>-tur] *noun, plural* **conductors.**
1. a person who directs the playing of a group of musicians: *The conductor waved her baton in a vigorous way.* **2.** someone who collects fares on a train, bus, or mass transit system. **3.** a material that carries electricity, sound, or heat: *Metal is a good conductor of heat.*

cone ▼ [kone] *noun, plural* **cones.**
1. *Mathematics.* a solid figure having a round, flat base and narrowing to a point at the top. **2.** any object shaped like this: *an ice-cream cone.* **3.** the fruits of many trees, such as a pine or fir.

Con·fed·er·ac·y [kun-<u>fed</u>-ur-uh-see] *noun. History.* a self-declared independent country that existed between 1860–61 and 1865 in North America. It was made up of eleven southern states that broke away from the Union (The United States of America). The act of independent states joining together for a common purpose is called **confederacy.**

Con·fed·er·ate
[kun-<u>fed</u>-ur-it *or* kun-<u>fed</u>-rit] *noun, plural* **Confederates.** *History.* a person who was a member of or fought for the Confederate States of America. A member of a confederacy is called a **confederate.**

*The **cones** of a pine tree contain the seeds, from which new trees can grow.*

con·fed·er·a·tion
[kun-<u>fed</u>-u-ray-shun] *noun, plural* **confederations.**
1. the act of combining together to form a confederacy. **2.** a group of states or countries with a common interest that agree to act together. The **Articles of Confederation** that established the U.S. Federal government were signed in 1777.

con·fer [kun-<u>fur</u>] *verb,* **conferred, conferring.**
1. to talk together, discuss: *The two leaders conferred on the grades to give their students' papers.* **2.** to give or award: *The university conferred degrees on students at a graduation ceremony.*

con·fer·ence [<u>kon</u>-fruns *or* <u>kon</u>-fur-uns] *noun, plural* **conferences.**
a formal meeting for the exchange of information and ideas: *The conference was held to give delegates a chance to speak on world peace.*

a
b
c
d
e
f
g
h
i
j
k
l
m
n
o
p
q
r
s
t
u
v
w
x
y
z

con·fess [kun-<u>fess</u>] *verb,* **confessed, confessing. 1.** to say or admit something: *Alex confessed that he had stolen the book.* The act of confessing is called a **confession. 2.** to tell a priest about a sin you have committed.

con·fet·ti [kun-<u>fet</u>-ee] *noun.* small pieces of colored paper that people throw in the air to celebrate something. Guests might throw confetti over the bride and groom at a wedding.

con·fide [kun-<u>fide</u>] *verb,* **confided, confiding. 1.** to tell something secret to someone you trust and tell them not to tell anyone else: *He confided the location of the hidden money to his best friend.* **2.** to trust someone with a secret: *I hope I will be able to confide in you.*

con·fi·dence [<u>kon</u>-fuh-duns] *noun,* plural **confidences. 1.** trust or faith in a person or thing: *The coach has confidence in our team.* **2.** trust or faith in your own abilities: *I have more confidence in playing tennis now that I am taking lessons.* **3.** trust or faith that information told to someone will be kept secret: *He spoke to the lawyer in confidence.* **4.** a piece of information that is secret or personal.

con·fi·dent [<u>kon</u>-fuh-dunt] *adjective.* **1.** feeling certain or sure: *I am confident that he will come to the party.* **2.** having faith in your own abilities. —**confidently,** *adverb.*

con·fi·den·tial [<u>kon</u>-fi-<u>den</u>-shul] *adjective.* not meant to be widely known; secret or private: *confidential business records; a confidential phone call.* —**confidentially,** *adverb.*

con·fine [kun-<u>fine</u>] *verb,* **confined, confining.** to hold within certain limits; restrict: *The prisoner is confined to his cell except for one hour of exercise in the yard.* *plural noun.* **confines.** the outer limits or borders: *They were allowed to play within the confines of the schoolyard.* —**confinement,** *noun.*

con·firm [kun-<u>firm</u>] *verb,* **confirmed, confirming. 1.** to show that something is true: *The video tape confirmed the thief's identity.* **2.** to be in favor of; approve; accept: *The Senate confirmed his nomination to the Supreme Court.* **3.** to make certain or definite: *Jane called the restaurant to confirm her reservation for dinner tonight.* Someone who is **confirmed** in their habits or beliefs is not likely to change. **4.** to officially accept a person as a full member of a church in a special ceremony.

con·fir·ma·tion [<u>kon</u>-fur-<u>may</u>-shun] *noun,* plural, **confirmations. 1.** the act of making something definite: *Before lending the money he wanted some confirmation that I could pay him back.* **2.** a statement that an arrangement is definite: *a letter of confirmation.* **3.** a religious ceremony in which someone is admitted as a full member of the church.

con·fis·cate [<u>kon</u>-fis-<u>kate</u>] *verb,* **confiscated, confiscating.** to officially take private property away from someone and keep it: *The illegal goods were confiscated by the police.* —**confiscation,** *noun.*

con·flict [<u>kon</u>-flikt *for noun;* kun-<u>flikt</u> *for verb*] *noun,* plural **conflicts. 1.** a fight, battle, or war: *conflict in the Middle East.* **2.** a difference of ideas or opinions; disagreement or clash: *My sister is often in conflict with our parents.*
verb, **conflicted, conflicting.** to not be in agreement; disagree or clash: *The new evidence conflicted with the suspect's story.*

A good story will usually have some kind of **conflict**. This does not mean that people are actually fighting or arguing in the story, but there should be some kind of a struggle or difference going on. If you begin a story by describing this conflict, that will make the reader interested in knowing what will happen: *I always wanted to learn to ice skate but was afraid to try.*

Confucius, the founder of **Confucianism,** *was known as "The Master" in ancient China.*

con·form [kun-<u>form</u>] *verb,* **conformed, conforming. 1.** to follow a set of rules; obey: *When driving you must conform to road regulations.* To behave within rules is **conformity** with those rules. A person who conforms to certain rules or established ways of acting is a **conformist. 2.** to act or make the same as: *The yacht's design conformed with others in its class.*

con·front [kun-<u>front</u>] *verb,* **confronted, confronting. 1.** to meet or face up to something bravely: *We confronted Julia's illness calmly.* **2.** to come face to face with boldly: *I confronted him and asked him directly if he had taken my watch.* A **confrontation** occurs when two sides clash over an important issue.

Con·fu·cian·ism ◀ [kun-<u>fyoo</u>-shun-<u>iz</u>-um] *noun. Religion.* a way of living that stresses respect for parents and ancestors, kindness, loyalty, intelligence, and proper behavior. It was developed by the teacher and philosopher **Confucius,** who lived in China about 2,000 years ago.

con·fuse [kun-<u>fyooz</u>] *verb,* **confused, confusing. 1.** to cause to be mixed up; puzzle: *I got confused over which street to take to John's house.* **2.** to mistake one thing for another: *Sarah confused the first two questions in the exam paper and put the answer for no. 1 under no. 2.*

con·fus·ing [kun-<u>fyooz</u>-ing] *adjective.* making one feel uncertain or mixed up: *The instructions for setting up the DVD player were very confusing.* —**confusingly,** *adverb.*

con·fu·sion [kun-<u>fyoo</u>-zhun] *noun,* plural **confusions. 1.** a state of not understanding what is happening or what something means: *In his rush and confusion he picked up the wrong suitcase.* **2.** a mistake or mix-up of one person or thing for another.

To reproduce, **conifers** rely on the wind to carry pollen and seeds.

connoisseur

con·geal [kun-<u>jeel</u>] *verb,* **congealed, congealing.** of a liquid, to become thick or solid: *An old can of paint in the garage had dried up and congealed.*

con·gen·i·tal [kun-<u>jen</u>-i-tul] *adjective. Health.* describing a disease or condition that a person has had since birth: *a congenital heart disease.*

con·gest [kun-<u>jest</u>] *verb,* **congested, congesting.** to fill up so as to block the movement or flow of something; overfill or overcrowd: *Traffic is congesting the highway.* Something that has become blocked or overcrowded is **congested.** —**congestion,** *noun.*

con·grat·u·late [kun-<u>grach</u>-yuh-<u>late</u>] *verb,* **congratulated, congratulating.** to praise or express joy for someone's achievement or good fortune: *We congratulated them when they announced their engagement to be married.*

con·grat·u·la·tion [kon-grach-yuh-<u>lay</u>-shun] *noun,* *plural* **congratulations. 1.** the act of giving praise or expressing joy for a person's achievements or good fortune. **2. congratulations.** good wishes or praise given for a person's achievements or good fortune.

con·gre·gate ▼ [<u>kong</u>-gruh-<u>gate</u>] *verb,* **congregated, congregating.** to gather together in a group: *After dinner everyone there congregated around the TV to watch the football game.*

con·gre·ga·tion [<u>kong</u>-gruh-<u>gay</u>-shun] *noun,* *plural* **congregations. 1.** the act of gathering together, or the people or things coming together. **2.** *Religion.* all the people who come together for a certain religious service.

Con·gress [<u>kong</u>-gris] *Government.* **1.** the legislative body of the United States, made up of the Senate and House of Representatives. **2. congress.** any assembly of people who have been elected to make laws in their country.

*At a special time each year, Muslims from around the world **congregate** in Mecca in Saudi Arabia.*

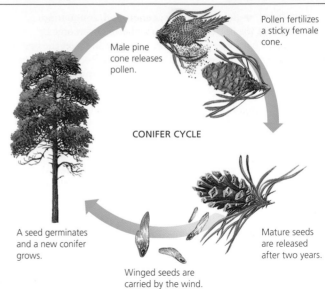

CONIFER CYCLE

Male pine cone releases pollen.

Pollen fertilizes a sticky female cone.

Mature seeds are released after two years.

Winged seeds are carried by the wind.

A seed germinates and a new conifer grows.

con·gress·man [<u>kong</u>-gris-mun] *noun,* *plural* **congressmen.** a man who belongs to a congress.

con·gress·wom·an [<u>kong</u>-gris-wum-un] *noun,* *plural* **congresswomen.** a woman who belongs to a congress.

con·gru·ent [kon-<u>groo</u>-unt] *adjective. Mathematics.* being exactly the same shape and size: *congruent triangles.* —**congruently,** *adverb.*

con·i·fer ▲ [<u>kon</u>-i-fur] *noun,* *plural* **conifers.** *Biology.* a type of evergreen tree, such as a pine or fir, that grows cones. —**coniferous,** *adjective.*

con·junc·tion [kun-<u>junk</u>-shun] *noun,* *plural* **conjunctions.** *Language.* words such as *and, because,* and *but* that connect words, phrases, and clauses in a sentence.

A **conjunction** can join two words: *Dogs <u>and</u> cats are common pets.* It can also join two parts of a sentence: *Before I go out, I have to finish my homework <u>and</u> clean my room.* Or, it can be used to put two sentences together as one: *The sign in the store window said "Closed," <u>but</u> all the lights were still on.*

con·nect [kuh-<u>nekt</u>] *verb,* **connected, connecting. 1.** to join two or more things together: *He connected the printer to the computer.* **2.** to think of together; relate or associate: *He was seen near the bank and may be connected with the robbery.* **3.** to come together with; meet: *This flight connects with a nonstop flight to Los Angeles.*

con·nec·tion [kuh-<u>nek</u>-shun] *noun,* *plural* **connections. 1.** the act of joining two or more things together: *The connection of wires at the back of the TV set took a long time.* **2.** the fact of having something in common; an association or relationship: *Experts continue to study the connection between smoking and lung cancer.* **3.** something that joins: *a telephone connection.*

con·nois·seur [kon-uh-sur *or* <u>kon</u>-uh-soo-ur] *noun,* *plural* **connoisseurs.** someone who has expert knowledge or training on a particular subject such as food, wine, or the fine arts.

a
b
c
d
e
f
g
h
i
j
k
l
m
n
o
p
q
r
s
t
u
v
w
x
y
z

con·quer ▼ [kong-kur] *verb,* **conquered, conquering.**
1. to get the better of in a war or battle; overcome by force: *The troops conquered the enemy.* **2.** to get the better of after a struggle; defeat: *My uncle finally conquered the habit of smoking after many years.* —**conqueror,** *noun.*

con·quest [kong-kwest] *noun, plural* **conquests. 1.** the act or fact of conquering or overcoming something by force: *the conquest of a nation in war; The conquest of that disease took many years.* **2.** something that has been acquired by force: *England was a conquest of the Normans in 1066.*

con·science [kon-shuns] *noun, plural* **consciences.** the awareness of what is right and wrong, and the feeling that you should do what is morally right.

con·sci·en·tious [kon-shee-en-shus] *adjective.* putting a lot of care and effort into something: *She is a conscientious student who always finishes her work on time.* —**conscientiously,** *adverb.*

con·scious [kon-shus] *adjective.* **1.** having knowledge or awareness: *As soon as I walked into the party I was conscious that I was the only girl there.* **2.** mentally alert; awake: *The patient was conscious once the anesthetic from the operation wore off.* **3.** done with intent or purpose; deliberate: *I made a conscious effort to lose weight.* —**consciously,** *adverb.*

con·scious·ness [kon-shus-nis] *noun.* **1.** *Medicine.* the condition of being awake and alert to what is happening around you: *It was three days after the operation before he regained consciousness.* **2.** all of a person's thoughts and feelings.

con·sec·u·tive [kun-sek-yuh-tiv] *adjective.* following one after another without any interruption: *Our team has won four consecutive games.* —**consecutively,** *adverb.*

con·sent [kun-sent] *verb,* **consented, consenting.** to give permission for something; allow: *Mom consented to me buying a car.*
noun, plural **consents.** the fact of allowing something; permission or agreement.

con·se·quence [kon-suh-kwens] *noun, plural* **consequences. 1.** the result of a particular action or situation: *One consequence of letting the dog in the house is that there's fur everywhere.* **2.** importance; value: *The politicians discussed matters of consequence.*

con·se·quent·ly [kon-suh-kwent-lee] *adverb.* as a result: *I stayed up all night finishing my report, and consequently was tired the next day.*

con·ser·va·tion [kon-sur-vay-shun] *noun. Environment.* the act or policy of protecting and preserving animals, plants, and natural areas. Someone who supports the practice of protecting and preserving natural things is a **conservationist.**

con·ser·va·tive [kun-sur-vuh-tiv] *adjective.* **1.** favoring the idea of keeping things as they are; opposing sudden or major change. **2.** wanting to avoid risks; careful: *She was conservative when spending money.* **3.** not fancy or showy: *a conservative dresser who always wears a dark suit and white shirt.*
noun, plural **conservatives.** *Government.* a person who in general thinks that things should continue to be done as they were in the past, especially in politics, and who opposes sudden change or new policies. A member or supporter of the British or Canadian political party that opposes sudden social change or reform is a **Conservative.** —**conservatively,** *adverb.*

The air inside a **conservatory** *is warmer than the air outside.*

con·ser·va·tor·y ▲ [kun-sur-vuh-*tore*-ee] *noun, plural* **conservatories.** a room or building made of glass in which plants are grown and kept.

con·serve [kun-surv] *verb,* **conserved, conserving.** to keep and protect from damage, loss, or change: *We water the garden only twice a week so that we conserve water.*

con·sid·er [kun-sid-ur] *verb,* **considered, considering.** **1.** to think about something carefully: *My parents are considering selling our house.* **2.** to believe someone or something to be: *I consider her to be the best friend I've ever had.* **3.** to show care or respect for others: *I was upset that he was rude and didn't consider my feelings.* **4.** to take into account: *He's quite short if you consider his age.*

con·sid·er·able [kun-sid-ur-uh-bul] *adjective.* large in amount or size; important: *I have saved a considerable amount of money this year.* —**considerably,** *adverb.*

CONSTELLATIONS

Since ancient times, people have imagined that groups of stars, when joined like dot-to-dot drawings, form the outlines of beasts, heroes, and gods. Sometimes different cultures saw different pictures in the same group—for example, the ancient Greeks saw Orion the hunter, but the ancient Egyptians imagined the same constellation as Osiris, the god of light. There are 88 constellations altogether, but which of these you can see depends on the time of night, time of year, and where you live.

Constellation of Orion

Constellation of Leo

con·sid·er·ate [kun-sid-ur-ut] *adjective.* thoughtful of the needs and feelings of others. —**considerately**, *adverb.*

con·sid·er·a·tion [kun-sid-uh-ray-shun] *noun, plural* **considerations. 1.** thoughtfulness and respect for other people: *Cleaning up after using the kitchen shows consideration for others.* **2.** careful thought and deliberation: *The proposed new policy was put forward for consideration by the city council.* **3.** something taken into account: *One important consideration when choosing a college is its reputation.*

con·sign [kun-sine] *verb,* **consigned, consigning. 1.** to send something somewhere to be cared for or sold: *The fitness equipment was consigned to the gym.* **2.** to give over to another's care. —**consignment**, *noun.*

con·sist [kun-sist] *verb,* **consisted, consisting.** to be made up of: *The audience at the concert consisted mainly of teenagers.*

con·sis·tent [kun-sist-unt] *adjective.* **1.** always behaving or acting in a similar way: *Our team has not been consistent this year—we won our first four games, then lost the next four, then won three more.* **2.** in agreement with other facts or previous behavior: *Her story is consistent with the witness's statement.* The quality of always being the same is **consistency. —consistently**, *adverb.*

con·sole¹ [kun-sole] *verb,* **consoled, consoling.** to give someone comfort or sympathy after a bad thing has happened to them: *We tried to console her after she broke up with her boyfriend.* The act of comforting someone is **consolation.**

con·sole² [kon-sole] *noun, plural* **consoles. 1.** a free-standing cabinet for a radio, television, or phonograph. **2.** a control panel for an electronic system such as a computer.

con·sol·i·date [kun-sol-i-date] *verb,* **consolidated, consolidating.** to bring things together; unite: *The three drama classes were consolidated into one big group for the auditions.* —**consolidation**, *noun.*

con·so·nant [kon-suh-nunt] *noun, plural* **consonants.** *Language.* any letter of the alphabet except for the vowels; all the letters but *a, e, i, o,* or *u,* and sometimes *y.* *See* VOWEL *for language note.*

con·spic·u·ous [kun-spik-yoo-us] *adjective.* very noticeable; attracting attention: *I was very conspicuous in my purple spotted raincoat.* —**conspicuously**, *adverb.*

con·spir·a·cy [kun-speer-uh-see] *noun, plural* **conspiracies.** a secret plan made by two or more people to do something illegal: *There was a conspiracy to steal the new computers from school.* Someone who secretly plans with others to do something illegal is a **conspirator.**

con·spire [kun-spire] *verb,* **conspired, conspiring.** to plan secretly with other people to do something illegal.

con·sta·ble ▶ [kon-stuh-bul] *noun, plural* **constables. 1.** a British police officer of the lowest rank. **2.** a peace officer with authority to serve warrants and make arrests.

con·stant [kon-stunt] *adjective.* **1.** staying the same; continuing: *The car traveled at a constant speed of sixty miles per hour.* **2.** faithful or devoted: *He is my constant friend and companion.* —**constantly**, *adverb.*

con·stel·la·tion ▲ [kon-stuh-lay-shun] *noun, plural* **constellations.** a group of stars that people think of as having a certain pattern in the sky and that has a name based on this, such as the Big Dipper or the Serpent.

con·stit·u·ent [kun-stich-yoo-unt] *adjective.* forming a part of a whole: *the constituent parts of a chemical substance.* *noun, plural* **constituents. 1.** one part of a whole; a component: *Sodium is a constituent of salt.* **2.** *Politics.* a person who votes in a particular area.

con·sti·tute [kons-ti-toot] *verb,* **constituted, constituting.** to make up or form: *Women constitute about eighty percent of our church choir.*

con·sti·tu·tion [kons-ti-too-shun] *noun, plural* **constitutions. 1.** a set of basic laws and principles by which a country, state, or organization is governed. **2.** the general state of a person's health: *He has a strong constitution and rarely gets sick.*

British police **constables** *wear dark blue uniforms and distinctive helmets.*

*The **Constitution** of the United States, adopted in 1788, is the country's supreme law.*

Con·sti·tu·tion ▶ [kons-ti-**too**-shun] *noun. Government.* the official document containing the most important laws of the government of the United States.

con·sti·tu·tion·al [kons-ti-**too**-shun-ul] *adjective.* having to do with the basic laws and principles by which a country, state, or organization is governed: *In the U.S. free speech is a constitutional right.* *noun.* walking or other exercise done regularly for the sake of general health.

con·strict [kun-**strict**] *verb,* **constricted, constricting.** to become tighter and narrower: *My bracelet constricted my wrist.*

con·stric·tor [kun-**strict**-ur] *noun, plural* **constrictors.** a type of snake that kills by wrapping itself around its prey and squeezing it to death. The python, boa constrictor, and anaconda are constrictors.

con·struct ▼ [kun-**struct**] *verb,* **constructed, constructing.** to make something by putting parts together; build: *The workers constructed a bridge across the river.* —**construction,** *noun.*

con·struc·tive [kun-**struc**-tiv] *adjective.* serving to be helpful or useful: *The teacher made some constructive suggestions about how I could improve my essay.* —**constructively,** *adverb.*

con·sul [**kown**-sul] *noun, plural* **consuls.** a government official sent to a foreign country to help people from his or her own country who are living or working there.

con·sult [kun-**sult**] *verb,* **consulted, consulting. 1.** to get information or advice from someone: *I consulted my doctor about the headaches I'd been having.* **2.** to discuss together to make a decision: *The senator consulted with his advisors before making an announcement.* A meeting to discuss something or to get advice is a **consultation.**

con·sul·tant [kun-**sult**-unt] *noun, plural* **consultants.** someone who has expert knowledge and advises people on a particular subject, project, or problem.

con·sume [kun-**soom**] *verb,* **consumed, consuming. 1.** to use up or destroy: *Smaller cars consume less fuel per mile than large trucks.* **2.** to eat or drink: *He consumed a large bowl of cereal for breakfast.* **3.** to occupy a person's time, energy, or attention.

con·sum·er [kun-**soom**-ur] *noun, plural* **consumers.** *Business.* any person who buys and uses goods or services.

con·sump·tion [kun-**sump**-shun] *noun, plural* **consumptions.** the eating or using up of something: *Strenuous exercise increases the body's consumption of oxygen.*

con·tact [**kon**-takt] *noun, plural* **contacts. 1.** the fact of two people or things touching each other: *The ice cream began to melt when it came into contact with the hot apple pie.* **2.** the fact of meeting or communicating with another person: *I keep in contact with friends from summer camp.* *verb,* **contacted, contacting.** to communicate with: *She contacted me by e-mail.*

contact lens a small, round piece of transparent plastic that fits closely over the colored part of the eye to improve vision.

*About 2,000 years ago, the Maya people in Mexico **constructed** huge stone temples.*

con·ta·gious [kun-<u>tay</u>-jus] *adjective.* easily spread from one person to another: *Measles is a contagious disease.*

con·tain [kun-<u>tane</u>] *verb,* **contained, containing. 1.** to have within it; hold: *This can contains 46 ounces of juice.* **2.** to include as a part of something: *The candy bar contains nuts.* **3.** to keep under control: *He couldn't contain his anger any longer and started shouting at them.* —**containment,** *noun.*

con·tain·er [kun-<u>tane</u>-ur] *noun, plural* **containers.** a hollow object such as a box or bottle that can be used for holding things: *an ice-cream container.*

con·tam·i·nate [kun-<u>tam</u>-i-*nate*] *verb,* **contaminated, contaminating.** to make dirty or impure: *The water of the lake was contaminated by chemicals from the factory.* A substance that spoils the purity of something is a **contaminant.** —**contamination,** *noun.*

con·tem·plate [<u>kon</u>-tum-*plate*] *verb,* **contemplated, contemplating.** to spend time considering something in a serious and quiet manner: *She's contemplating quitting her job and traveling overseas.* —**contemplation,** *noun.*

con·tem·po·rar·y [kun-<u>temp</u>-uh-*rare*-ee] *adjective.* **1.** belonging to the same time period as something else. **2.** of the current time period; modern: *an exhibition of contemporary photography.*
noun, plural **contemporaries.** a person who lived during the same time period as someone else: *The poet Shakespeare and the famous scientist Galileo were contemporaries—both were born in 1564.*

con·tempt [kun-<u>tempt</u>] *noun.* a strong feeling of dislike and lack of respect for a person or thing: *She had complete contempt for her ex-boyfriend.* Expressing or showing strong dislike and lack of respect is **contemptuous.**

con·tend [kun-<u>tend</u>] *verb,* **contended, contending. 1.** to compete to win something: *In that race she'll be contending against the best athletes in the state.* **2.** to struggle or fight: *He had to contend with a lack of food for almost a week before he was rescued.* **3.** to put forward an argument in favor of something: *The mayor contended that it was too soon to judge the project to be a failure.* —**contender,** *noun.*

con·tent[1] [<u>kon</u>-tent] *noun, plural* **contents. 1.** the things that are inside something: *the contents of a box.* **2.** things that are spoken or written: *the contents of a book.*

con·tent[2] [kun-<u>tent</u>] *adjective.* happy and satisfied: *He isn't wealthy, but he's quite content with what he has.*
verb, **contented, contenting.** to make happy or satisfy.
noun. a feeling of being happy or satisfied. This is also called **contentment.** To be pleased with your situation is to be **contented.** —**contentedly,** *adverb.*

con·test [<u>kon</u>-test for noun; kun-test for verb] *noun, plural* **contests.** an effort to win or get something; a competition: *a dance contest; a contest to see who could eat the most hot dogs.*
verb, **contested, contesting. 1.** to fight for; make an effort to win: *He is contesting a seat on the Board of Directors.* **2.** to argue against the truth or value of something: *The son contested his father's will.*

Contestants *in luge competitions wear special clothing to protect them as they race down a curved track on a sled.*

con·test·ant ▲ [kun-<u>tes</u>-tunt] *noun, plural* **contestants.** someone who takes part in a competition.

con·text [<u>kon</u>-*text*] *noun, plural* **contexts.** *Language.* the text or speech surrounding a particular phrase that helps to explain its meaning: *He said "I hate this!", but within the context of what he was saying, it was obvious that he was not mad, just trying to be funny.* Of or relating to the context is **contextual.**

The **context** of a word is the way in which it is used in a sentence. Context is important in understanding what the word means. For example, suppose you ask someone, "Is it all right to let our dog run on the beach?" and the person answers "Fine." This answer has no context. It probably means, "It's fine (OK) to do that," but it might also mean "You will have to pay a fine if you do that."

con·ti·nent [<u>kon</u>-tuh-nunt] *noun, plural* **continents. 1.** one of the seven large land masses on the Earth; Asia, Africa, North America, South America, Europe, Antarctica, and Australia. **2. the Continent.** a British term for Europe, not including Britain. —**continental,** *adjective.*

Continental Congress *History.* either of two legislative congresses during and after the American Revolutionary War. From these came the Declaration of Independence and the Articles of Confederation.

a b c d e f g h i j k l m n o p q r s t u v w x y z

Seafloor | Continental slope | Continental shelf

continental shelf ▶ *Environment.* the edge of a continent that is under the shallow sea, gradually sloping down steeply to the bottom of the ocean.

The **continental shelf** *becomes the continental slope, which drops steeply to the seafloor.*

con·tin·u·al [kun-<u>tin</u>-yoo-ul] *adjective.* happening again and again; repeating many times: *We've had continual problems with our car.* —**continually,** *adverb.*

con·tin·ue [kun-<u>tin</u>-yoo] *verb,* **continued, continuing. 1.** to keep happening or existing: *The sunny weather continued for the rest of the week.* **2.** to start again after stopping: *The plot of this TV show continues from week to week.* **3.** to stay in the same place or condition; remain: *They met in college and continued to be friends for years afterward.* The act or instance of continuing is **continuance.** —**continuation,** *noun.*

con·tin·u·ous [kun-<u>tin</u>-yoo-us] *adjective.* going on and on; happening or existing without stopping: *the continuous sound of the ocean waves.* —**continuously,** *adverb.*

con·tour [<u>kon</u>-tur] *noun, plural* **contours.** the shape or outline of the surface of something: *the uneven contours of a rocky hillside.*

The large Great Dane **contrasts** *dramatically in size with the tiny chihuahua.*

con·tract [kun-trakt *for verb;* kon-trakt *for noun*] *verb,* **contracted, contracting. 1.** to make shorter or smaller: *Metal contracts when it is cooled.* **2.** to make a legal agreement: *The plumber has contracted to finish the work tomorrow.* **3.** to become affected by something negative: *to contract a cold.*
noun, plural **contracts.** a legal agreement: *a contract of employment.*

con·trac·tion [kun-trak-shun] *noun, plural* **contractions. 1.** the fact of something becoming smaller or shorter: *The contraction of muscle causes movement.* **2.** *Language.* a shortened form of a word or combination of words. *Can't* is the contraction of *cannot.*

Contractions came into use in language because it was easy and natural for people to shorten words as they spoke. An unusual feature of English is that it is possible to say the same thing with two different contractions. For example, "she is not" can be contracted as either "she's not" or "she isn't", and "you have not" can be either "you haven't" or "you've not."

con·trac·tor [*kon*-<u>trak</u>-tur] *noun, plural* **contractors.** a person or company that agrees to do work or provide supplies at a certain price or rate.

con·tra·dict [kon-truh-<u>dikt</u>] *verb,* **contradicted, contradicting. 1.** to say the opposite of something else; deny: *The first witness said the car was blue, but the second contradicted this and said it was red.* **2.** to show the opposite of; be opposed to: *The results of this experiment contradict previous findings.* Two things that are in direct opposition to each other are said to be **contradictory.** —**contradiction,** *noun.*

con·trar·y [<u>kon</u>-trer-ee] *adjective.* **1.** completely different; opposite: *Mom and Dad have contrary opinions as to which candidate would make a better senator.* **2.** liking to argue and disagree: *I ignore my brother when he's being contrary.*
noun. something different or opposite from what was expected: *We thought the meal would be expensive, but quite the contrary, it was cheap.*

con·trast ◀ [kun-<u>trast</u> *for verb;* kon-trast *for noun*] *verb,* **contrasted, contrasting.** to compare things to show the differences between them. *The two pictures contrast the way he looked before and after going on a diet.*
noun, plural **contrasts. 1.** an obvious difference between two or more things. *There are many contrasts in lifestyle between the rich and the poor.* **2.** a person or thing that is specifically compared to another in order to show differences: *Her new hairstyle is quite a contrast to her old one.*

con·tri·bute [kun-<u>trib</u>-yoot] *verb,* **contributed, contributing. 1.** to give money or other things of value for some cause or benefit; donate: *We all contributed toward Grandma's sixtieth birthday present.* **2.** to help to bring about; be a factor in: *News stories about the mayor's income tax problems contributed to his loss in the election.* **3.** to write articles for a newspaper or magazine: *Famous authors sometimes contribute articles to the local newspapers.* —**contributor,** *noun.*

con·tri·bu·tion [*kon*-truh-<u>byoo</u>-shun] *noun, plural* **contributions. 1.** the act of giving or donating something: *The contribution of money will be greatly appreciated.* **2.** something contributed: *We gave contributions of gifts for the underprivileged children.*

con·trive [kun-<u>trive</u>] *verb,* **contrived, contriving.** to invent or plan cleverly: *to contrive an escape route from a prison.* Something false and unnatural is **contrived:** *He told a contrived story about his dog eating his homework.* —**contrivance,** *noun.*

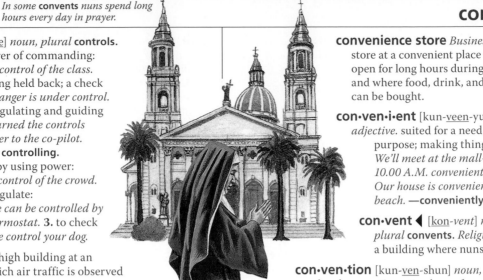

*In some **convents** nuns spend long hours every day in prayer.*

con·trol [kun-<u>trole</u>] *noun, plural* **controls.**
1. the act or power of commanding: *The teacher has control of the class.*
2. the fact of being held back; a check or restraint: *My anger is under control.*
3. a device for regulating and guiding a machine: *He turned the controls of the aircraft over to the co-pilot.*
verb, **controlled, controlling.**
1. to command by using power: *The troops took control of the crowd.*
2. to adjust or regulate: *The temperature can be controlled by changing the thermostat.* **3.** to check or hold in: *Please control your dog.*

control tower a high building at an airport from which air traffic is observed and directed.

con·tro·ver·sial [kon-truh-<u>vur</u>-shul] *adjective.* causing argument or disagreement: *The movie star has become controversial because of his critical remarks about the President.* —**controversially,** *adverb.*

con·tro·ver·sy [kon-truh-<u>vurs</u>-ee] *noun, plural* **controversies.** a dispute or difference of opinion: *The location of the new highway is a matter of controversy.*

con·va·les·cent [kon-vuh-<u>les</u>-unt] *adjective.* for or relating to recovering from illness: *a convalescent hospital. noun, plural* **convalescents.** a person recovering from illness. The period in which a person recovers from illness is **convalescence.**

con·vec·tion ▼ [kun-<u>vek</u>-shun] *noun. Science.* the transfer of heat by the movement of heated air or water.

con·vene [kun-<u>veen</u>] *verb,* **convened, convening.** to assemble or arrange a meeting: *Congress will convene next week for the new session.*

con·ven·i·ence [kun-<u>veen</u>-yuns] *noun, plural* **conveniences 1.** easy to obtain and use: *I like the convenience of buying things with a credit card.*
2. anything that saves or simplifies work: *A microwave oven is a modern convenience.*

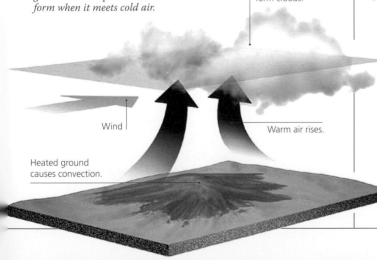

*In **convection**, air warmed by the ground moves upward and clouds form when it meets cold air.*

Water vapor condenses to form clouds.

Wind

Warm air rises.

Heated ground causes convection.

convenience store *Business.* a small store at a convenient place that is open for long hours during the day and where food, drink, and magazines can be bought.

con·ven·i·ent [kun-<u>veen</u>-yunt] *adjective.* suited for a need or purpose; making things easier: *We'll meet at the mall—is 10.00 A.M. convenient for you?; Our house is convenient to the beach.* —**conveniently,** *adverb.*

con·vent ◀ [<u>kon</u>-vent] *noun, plural* **convents.** *Religion.* a building where nuns live.

con·ven·tion [kun-<u>ven</u>-shun] *noun, plural* **conventions. 1.** a large, formal meeting for a particular purpose: *the annual convention of a medical society; a political convention to choose the party's candidates.* **2.** a usual or accepted way of behaving; custom: *In many countries it is the convention to wear all black to a funeral.*

con·ven·tion·al [kun-<u>ven</u>-shun-ul] *adjective.* following the accepted way; traditional or customary: *The conventional fuel for cars is gasoline—some new cars use a plant fuel called ethanol.* —**conventionally,** *adverb.*

con·ver·sa·tion [kon-vur-<u>say</u>-shun] *noun, plural* **conversations.** an informal talk between two or more people: *We had an interesting conversation about diet and exercise.* —**conversational,** *adjective.*

con·verse[1] [kun-<u>vurs</u>] *verb,* **conversed, conversing.** to talk together; have a conversation.

*Large **convertibles** like this one were produced in the 1960s.*

con·verse[2] [<u>kon</u>-vurs] *adjective.* opposite or turned about: *to go in a converse direction.* —**conversely,** *adverb.*

con·vert [kun-<u>vurt</u> *for verb;* kon-vert *for noun*] *verb,* **converted, converting. 1.** to change into something different: *The spare bedroom has been converted into an office.* **2.** to persuade someone to change their beliefs: *Missionaries converted thousands of people to Christianity.* Someone or something changed has been **converted:** *a converted military vehicle now used as an SUV. noun, plural* **converts.** someone who has changed their beliefs: *a convert to a different religion.* —**conversion,** *noun.*

con·ver·ti·ble ▲ [kun-<u>vurt</u>-i-bul] *adjective.* able to be changed and used for a different purpose: *a convertible sofa bed. noun, plural* **convertibles.** an automobile with a roof that can be folded back or repoved.

a b c d e f g h i j k l m o p q r s t u v w x y z

con·vex [kon-_veks_ or kun-_veks_] _adjective. Mathematics._ curved or swelling outward like the outside of a bowl.

con·vey [kun-_vay_] _verb,_ **conveyed, conveying.**
1. to transport; carry from one place to another: _Trains convey people and goods over long distances._ A vehicle for transporting people or things is a **conveyance. 2.** to make known; communicate: _Please convey our congratulations to your parents on their anniversary._

con·vey·or belt [kun-_vay_-ur] a continuously moving belt used for transporting things, especially in a factory.

con·vict ▶ [kun-_vikt_ for verb; _kon_-vikt for noun] _verb,_ **convicted, convicting.** to prove or find a person guilty of a crime, especially in a court of law: _The judge convicted him of robbery._ _noun, plural_ **convicts.** someone convicted of a crime who is serving a prison sentence.

con·vic·tion [kun-_vik_-shun] _noun, plural_ **convictions. 1.** the act of finding someone guilty of a crime. **2.** the fact or state of having been found guilty of a crime. **3.** a strongly held opinion or belief: _It's my conviction that my dog was stolen._

con·vince [kun-_vins_] _verb,_ **convinced, convincing.** to make someone believe that something is true or that a certain thing should be done; persuade: _They convinced me to take the train rather than fly._ Information or evidence that persuades someone to believe or do something is **convincing.**

con·voy [_kon_-voy] _noun, plural_ **convoys.** a group of ships or vehicles traveling together or with an escort.

con·vulse [kun-_vuls_] _verb,_ **convulsed, convulsing.** to cause someone or something to move or shake violently or jerkily: _His impersonations had us convulsed with laughter._

con·vul·sion [kun-_vuls_-un] _noun, plural_ **convulsions. 1.** _Medicine._ a violent movement of the whole body or part of the body as a result of the muscles contracting involuntarily; a fit or seizure: _People who suffer from epilepsy sometimes have convulsions._ **2.** an uncontrollable fit of laughter.

cook [kuk] _verb,_ **cooked, cooking. 1.** to prepare food for eating by heating it. The act of preparing food for eating by heating it is called **cooking.** A **cookout** is an occasion when people cook and eat food outdoors. **2.** to undergo the process of cooking: _Food cooks quickly in our new microwave oven._ _noun, plural_ **cooks.** someone who cooks.

cook·ie [_kuk_-ee] _noun, plural_ **cookies. 1.** a small, sweet cake, either flat or slightly raised. **2.** _Computers._ a small file containing information about the Websites a person has visited from a certain computer. It allows Websites to keep track of visitors to their site. This word is also spelled **cooky.**

cool [kool] _adjective,_ **cooler, coolest. 1.** fairly cold; neither warm nor very cold: _a cool bath._ **2.** not trapping heat; allowing heat to escape: _A straw hat is cool in summer._ **3.** under control; not worried or excited: _To be a major-league relief pitcher you have to stay cool in tight situations._ **4.** not friendly or interested: _They are always cool toward strangers._
noun. a cool place or time: _to go for a walk in the cool of the evening._
verb, **cooled, cooling.** to make or become cool: _When the mixture cools, it will start to set._

British **convicts** sent to Australia were often chained together.

coo·ler [_kool_-ur] _noun, plural_ **coolers.** a container that keeps things cool, especially food and drink.

coop [koop] _noun, plural_ **coops.** a cage or other small enclosure for housing small animals, especially chickens.

co-op [_koh_-op] a shorter form of COOPERATIVE.

co·op·er·ate [koh-_op_-uh-_rate_] _verb,_ **cooperated, cooperating.** to act or work together in a helpful way: _We will do the job faster if we all cooperate._ —**cooperation,** _noun._

co·op·er·a·tive [koh-_op_-uh-ri-tiv] _adjective._ willing to act or work together in a helpful way: _She is one of our most cooperative club members._ _noun, plural_ **cooperatives. 1.** a business, such as a store, or a society owned and run on cooperative principles. Its members share in its benefits, including any profits. **2.** an apartment building that is owned jointly by the people who live in the individual apartments. —**cooperatively,** _adverb._

co·or·di·nate [koh-_or_-duh-_nate_] _verb,_ **coordinated, coordinating.** to organize people or things so that they work smoothly in relation to each other: _Our athletics coach coordinated the program for the meet._ Someone who does this is a **coordinator.**

co·or·di·na·tion [_koh_-or-di-_nay_-shun] _noun._ **1.** the process of organizing people or things so that they work smoothly in relation to each other: _Building a house requires the coordination of many different tradespeople._ **2.** the smooth working together of body parts: _Dancers and sportspeople require a high level of coordination._

cop [kop] _noun, plural_ **cops.** a slang term for a POLICE OFFICER.

cope [kope] _verb,_ **coped, coping.** to deal successfully with a difficult task or situation: _I had to do the whole project in one night, but I coped._

cop·i·er [_kop_-ee-ur] _noun, plural_ **copiers.** a machine or device for copying things, especially documents.

cop·per [_kop_-ur] _noun._ **1.** _Chemistry._ a reddish-brown metal used particularly for electrical wiring because it is a very good conductor of heat and electricity. **2.** a reddish-brown color, like copper. _adjective._ **1.** made of this metal: _copper pipes for a house._ **2.** reddish-brown; of the color of copper.

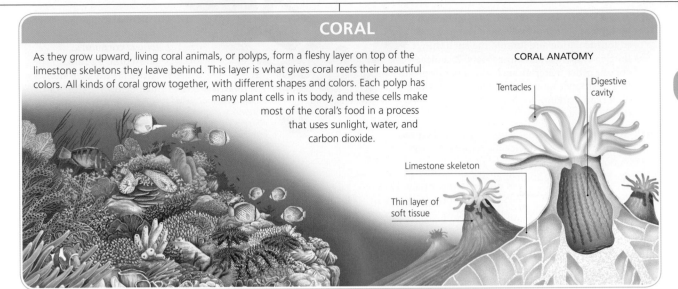

CORAL

As they grow upward, living coral animals, or polyps, form a fleshy layer on top of the limestone skeletons they leave behind. This layer is what gives coral reefs their beautiful colors. All kinds of coral grow together, with different shapes and colors. Each polyp has many plant cells in its body, and these cells make most of the coral's food in a process that uses sunlight, water, and carbon dioxide.

CORAL ANATOMY

Tentacles

Digestive cavity

Limestone skeleton

Thin layer of soft tissue

cop·per·head [kop-ur-*hed*] *noun, plural* **copperheads.** a poisonous snake with a brown body and a copper-colored head that is native to the southeast of the United States. During the American Civil War, a person from the Northern states who sympathized with the South was called a **Copperhead.**

cop·y [kop-ee] *noun, plural* **copies. 1.** a thing made to look exactly like something else; a duplicate. **2.** a single example of a publication; one out of the total number of books, magazines, or newspapers printed at one time: *I was lucky to buy the last copy of the magazine in the store.* *verb,* **copied, copying.** to do or make something that is exactly the same as something else.

cop·y·right [kop-ee-*rite*] *noun. Law.* the exclusive legal right to publish, print, film, record, perform, or sell the contents and form of a literary, artistic, or musical work. *verb,* **copyrighted, copyrighting.** to obtain this right for a creative work: *The author copyrighted his new novel.*

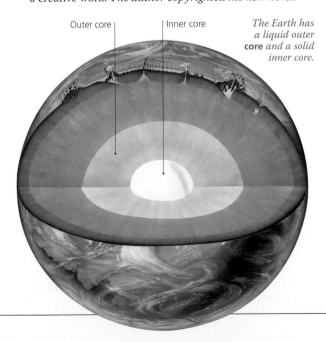

Outer core   Inner core

The Earth has a liquid outer **core** *and a solid inner core.*

cor·al ▲ [kore-ul] *noun, plural* **corals. 1.** a stony or horny substance found in tropical seas, often in the form of reefs, consisting of the skeletons of tiny marine animals massed together. **2.** the tiny marine animal that forms such reefs. **3.** a reddish-pink color, like some types of coral. *adjective.* **1.** made of coral: *a coral necklace.* **2.** reddish-pink; of the color of coral.

coral snake a poisonous snake with brilliant bands of red, black, and yellow or white that is found in the southern United States and tropical South America.

cord [kord] *noun, plural* **cords. 1.** a thin rope or heavy string made from twisted strands, used mainly for tying things. **2.** a length of flexible, insulated wire with a plug at one or both ends; used to connect an electrical appliance to an outlet. **3.** a cord-like structure in the body, such as the spinal cord. **4.** a quantity of firewood equal to a stack of wood 4 feet wide, 4 feet high, and 8 feet long, or 128 cubic feet.

◀)) A different word with the same sound is **chord.**

cor·dial [kore-jul] *adjective.* acting and speaking in a nice way; friendly and welcoming: *My father is known among his friends as a cordial host.* —**cordially,** *adverb.*

cor·du·roy [kord-uh-*roy*] *noun, plural* **corduroys. 1.** a strong cloth with a raised rib pattern like cords, usually made of cotton. **2. corduroys.** trousers that are made from this cloth.

> **Corduroy** comes from the French expression *corde du roi,* meaning "the cord (clothing) of the king." Corduroy was considered to be a very fine fabric that was used for royal clothing.

core ◀ [kore] *noun, plural* **cores. 1.** the hard central part of fleshy fruits such as apples, containing the seeds. **2.** the innermost region of the Earth. **3.** the central or most important part of anything: *Let's get to the core of the problem.* *verb,* **cored, coring.** to remove the core from: *I cored the apples and stuffed them with dried fruits.*

cork [kork] *noun, plural* **corks. 1.** the lightweight outer bark of a certain tree called the **cork oak**, used for insulation and for making such things as bottle stoppers and fishing floats. **2.** a piece of cork or other material, such as rubber or plastic, used as a stopper for a bottle or other container. *verb,* **corked, corking.** to seal with a cork: *to cork a wine bottle.*

cork·screw ▶ [kork-scroo] *noun, plural* **corkscrews.** a usually spiral metal device for removing corks from bottles.

corn [korn] *noun.* a widely grown plant native to the Americas, used as a cereal food and bearing yellow or white seeds on long spikes called ears. The woody core to which the seeds are attached is called a **corncob.**

> **Corn** once meant any kind of seed or food from a grass plant, such as wheat, rye, or barley. The word can still be used this way in British English, with maize used as the word for the one particular plant that Americans call corn.

cor·ne·a [kore-nee-uh] *noun, plural* **corneas.** *Medicine.* the transparent layer over the front of the eye, covering the pupil and iris, that lets light through.

cor·ner [kore-nur] *noun, plural* **corners. 1.** the point where two lines, sides, or edges meet: *the corner of a room.* **2.** the point where two roads or streets meet: *I'll meet you at the corner of Elm Place and Third Street.* **3.** a far-off or private, little-known place: *Volunteers from our organization work in all corners of the globe.* **4.** a difficult or awkward place or position. *verb,* **cornered, cornering.** to force into a corner: *The hunting dogs cornered the bear.*

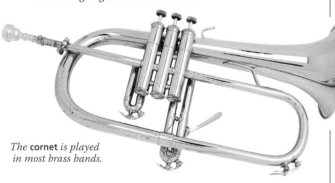

The **cornet** *is played in most brass bands.*

cor·net ▲ [kore-net] *noun, plural* **cornets.** *Music.* a brass instrument similar to a trumpet but shorter and wider, with a softer tone.

corn·meal [korn-meel] *noun.* a food made by grinding corn.

cor·on·ary [kore-uh-nare-ee] *adjective. Medicine.* **1.** relating to the arteries that transport blood to and from the heart. **2.** relating to the heart: *a coronary artery. noun, plural* **coronaries.** a shortened form of **coronary thrombosis,** commonly called a heart attack.

cor·o·na·tion [kore-uh-nay-shun] *noun, plural* **coronations.** the act of crowning a king or queen, or the ceremony at which this takes place.

The **corkscrew** *was based on a tool used to remove unused charges from musket barrels.*

cor·po·ral [korp-rul *or* kore-puh-rul] *noun, plural* **corporals. 1.** an officer's rank in the army, air force, or marines just below the rank of sergeant. **2.** an officer with this rank.

cor·po·ra·tion [kore-puh-ray-shun] *noun, plural* **corporations.** *Business.* a group of people authorized by law to act as an individual person, with the same rights and duties as an individual person.

corps [kore] *noun.* **1.** a special unit of military personnel: *Marine Corps; Signal Corps.* **2.** a group of people engaged in a particular activity: *There is a large corps of doctors among our club members.*

corpse [korps] *noun, plural* **corpses.** a dead body.

cor·pus·cle [kore-pus-ul] *noun, plural* **corpuscles.** *Medicine.* a red or white blood cell.

cor·ral [kuh-ral] *noun, plural* **corrals.** a fenced enclosed space, for keeping or capturing livestock such as horses and cattle. *verb,* **corralled, corralling. 1.** to put in or drive livestock into a corral. **2.** to gain control of by gathering together as if in a corral.

cor·rect [kuh-rekt] *adjective.* **1.** without any mistakes; true; accurate: *You'll get a point for each correct answer.* **2.** done in an appropriate or approved way; proper: *This is the correct way to set a table. verb,* **corrected, correcting. 1.** to adjust or change something to remove mistakes or faults; mark the errors in: *I asked my mother to correct the spelling in my letter.* **2.** to adjust or change something to match an accepted standard: *My father wears shoe inserts to correct his flat feet.* **3.** to draw attention to faults in someone's behavior in order to improve that behavior: *My mother corrected me when I interrupted her conversation.* —**correctly,** *adverb;* —**correction,** *noun.*

cor·re·spond [kore-uh-spond] *verb,* **corresponded, corresponding. 1.** to be equivalent to; be in agreement with; match: *Your version of what happened doesn't correspond with hers.* **2.** to be similar to; be like; have analogies with: *The handlebars of a bicycle correspond to the steering wheel of a car.* **3.** to communicate by writing letters: *My pen pal and I correspond every month.*

cor·re·spon·dence [kore-uh-spond-uns] *noun, plural* **correspondences. 1.** a point or points of similarity or agreement between things. **2.** the process of communicating by writing letters, or the letters exchanged.

cor·re·spon·dent [kore-uh-spond-unt] *noun, plural* **correspondents. 1.** someone who exchanges letters with another person. **2.** someone employed to collect news and send reports to a newspaper or other news outlet, often from a distant place.

cor·ri·dor [kore-uh-*dore*] *noun, plural* **corridors.** a passageway that opens onto rooms or compartments, as in a building or a train.

cor·rode [kuh-<u>rode</u>] *verb,* **corroded, corroding.** to wear or waste away gradually, especially by chemical action: *Metal tools left outdoors for a long time can corrode because of rust.*

cor·ro·sion [kuh-<u>roh</u>-zhun] *noun* **1.** the process of being worn away, especially by chemical action: *Stainless steel resists rust and therefore corrosion.* **2.** the damage resulting from this.

cor·ru·gat·ed [*kore*-uh-<u>gate</u>-id] *adjective.* having alternate ridges and grooves, or having wrinkles, usually to make a material stronger: *Corrugated iron is used as a roofing material.*

The cosmos is made up of groups of galaxies, which gather in clusters.

cor·rupt [kuh-<u>rupt</u>] *adjective.* able to be, or having been, influenced to behave in a wrong or dishonest way: *The corrupt politician secretly took money in return for voting in a certain way.* Improper or dishonest behavior, especially on the part of people in official positions, is **corruption.**
verb, **corrupted, corrupting.** to influence someone to behave improperly or dishonestly: *He tried to corrupt the police officer with a bribe.*

cor·sage [kore-<u>sahzh</u>] *noun, plural* **corsages.** a flower or small bouquet of flowers, usually worn at the shoulder but sometimes at the waist or on the wrist.

cos·met·ic [koz-<u>met</u>-ik] *noun, plural* **cosmetics.** a preparation intended to beautify the skin, the hair, or some other part of a person's appearance, such as lipstick, or hairspray.

cos·mic [<u>koz</u>-mik] *adjective.* **1.** relating to the entire universe. **2.** relating to outer space.

cos·mol·ogy [koz-<u>mol</u>-uh-jee] *noun. Science.* a field of study dealing with the nature of the universe, including how it originated and developed.

cos·mo·naut [<u>koz</u>-muh-*nawt*] *noun, plural* **cosmonauts.** an astronaut who is part of Russia's space program.

The Local Group has around 35 galaxies.

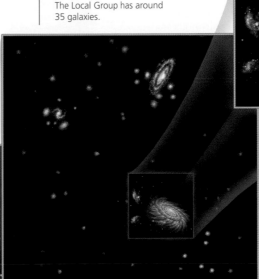

The Milky Way galaxy contains many solar systems.

In the structure of the **cosmos,** *our solar system is one of many in the Milky Way galaxy, which belongs to a group of galaxies known as the Local Group, which in turn is one of many groups in the universe.*

cos·mos ▲ [<u>koz</u>-*mose* or <u>koz</u>-mus] *noun.* the universe as an ordered system.

cost [kost *or* kawst] *noun, plural* **costs. 1.** the sum of money asked or paid for something; price: *The cost of a ticket to the game is ten dollars.* **2.** a loss suffered or a sacrifice made in achieving a goal: *He worked long hours to make his business succeed, but at the cost of his health.*
verb, **cost, costing. 1.** to be priced at; to sell for: *Our hotel room cost a hundred dollars.* **2.** to involve as a loss or sacrifice: *Losing the last two games of the season cost our team the championship.*

cost·ly [<u>kost</u>-lee *or* <u>kawst</u>-lee] *adjective.* **costlier, costliest. 1.** having a high price; expensive: *First-class airplane tickets are very costly.* **2.** causing a loss of sacrifice: *The senator's stand on the issue was costly in terms of his support from conservative votes.*

cos·tume [<u>kos</u>-toom] *noun, plural* **costumes. 1.** special clothes worn to play a role; fancy dress: *I rented a pirate costume for the party.* **2.** a style of dress typical of a certain nation, group, or time: *Wooden shoes are part of the Dutch national costume.*

cot [kot] *noun, plural* **cots.** a light folding bed, usually consisting of canvas stretched over a frame.

cot·tage [kot-ij] *noun, plural* **cottages.** a small, simple house, sometimes for vacation use.

cottage cheese a soft, lumpy cheese made from curds of soured skim milk.

cot·ton ▶ [kot-un] *noun.* **1.** the soft, whitish, downy fibers covering the seeds of certain plants that are spun into yarn. **2.** thread or cloth made from cotton fiber.
adjective. made of cotton: *a cotton shirt.*

cot·ton·mouth [kot-un-*mowth*] *noun, plural* **cottonmouths.** a poisonous snake related to the copperhead that is native to the southern United States. It is also called a water moccasin.

cot·ton·tail [kot-un-*tale*] *noun, plural* **cottontails.** any of several small North American rabbits with brownish-gray fur and a fluffy tail with a white underside.

cot·ton·wood [kot-un-*wud*] *noun, plural* **cottonwoods.** any of several types owf trees native to North America that have seeds covered in cottony hairs.

couch [kowch] *noun, plural* **couches.** a piece of padded furniture big enough for at least two people to sit on or for one person to lie on; a sofa.

couch potato a slang term for a person who likes to lie around at home relaxing, especially by watching television.

cou·gar [koo-gur] *noun, plural* **cougars.** a large, powerful, wild cat with a tawny coat that is native to the mountains of North and South America. It is also called a puma or a mountain lion.

cough [cawf] *verb,* **coughed, coughing. 1.** to force out air from the lungs with a sharp sound or series of sounds: *The smoke at the cookout made me cough.* **2.** to make a sound like this.
noun, plural **coughs.** the act or sound of coughing. **2.** a condition that causes coughing.

could [kud] *verb.* a special verb that is often used with other verbs in these ways: **1.** as the past tense of CAN: *I said I could help.* **2.** to show that something is possible or able to be done: *They could still decide to come; She could run faster if she trained.* **3.** to make a request sound more polite: *Could you put these books away, please?.*

couldn't [kud-unt] *verb.* the shortened form of "could not."

coun·cil [kown-sul] *noun, plural* **councils.** a group of people who are chosen, or elected, to provide advice or make decisions: *a city council.*
🔊 A different word with the same sound is **counsel.**

coun·sel [kown-sul] *noun, plural* **counsels. 1.** advice given by someone about a topic or problem: *My mother gave me good counsel when I was in trouble.* **2.** *Law.* a lawyer who represents someone in a court case: *She served as counsel for the defense.*
verb, **counseled, counseling.** to give advice.
🔊 A different word with the same sound is **council.**

In Uzbekistan, **cotton** *is picked by hand and exported all over the world.*

coun·se·lor [kowns-lur *or* kown-suh-lur] *noun, plural* **counselors. 1.** someone who helps and supports people with problems. *I didn't know what to do, so I spoke to the school counselor.* **2.** a lawyer. This word is also spelled **counsellor.**

count¹ [kownt] *verb,* **counted, counting. 1.** to add up the number of things there are in a group. **2.** to say numbers one at a time in order. **3.** to include something or someone: *You can count me in for the trip to the game.* **4.** to have value; be important: *First impressions really do count.* **5.** to depend upon: *You can always count on Mom to help out.*
noun, plural **counts. 1.** the process of counting: *A count of hands showed that most of the class agreed.* **2.** the total number of things counted.

count² [kownt] *noun, plural* **counts.** a nobleman in some European countries.

count·down [kownt-*down*] *noun, plural* **countdowns.** the process of counting backward to the moment when something happens, such as the launch of a spacecraft, with the final count being zero.

count·er¹ [kownt-ur] *noun, plural* **counters. 1.** a long table where people are served in a shop, bank, or restaurant. **2.** something used for counting, such as a small object that is used to keep score in some board games.

count·er² [kownt-ur] *adverb.* going in the opposite way: *He went counter to the coach's advice and lost the game.* *adjective.* opposite: *My preference is counter to yours.* *verb,* **countered, countering.** to do something in opposition: *"I can't agree with what you want me to do,"* he countered.

counter- a prefix that means the opposite of something: *The enemy forces launched a counterattack.*

count·er·clock·wise [kownt-ur-klok-*wize*] *adverb; adjective.* opposite to the direction that the hands of a clock move: *Turn the lid counterclockwise to open the jar.*

coun·ter·feit [kownt-ur-*fit*] *verb,* **counterfeited, counterfeiting.** to make a copy of something that looks like the original to deceive someone: *It is difficult to counterfeit dollar bills.*
noun, plural **counterfeits.** an imitation that is passed off as the real thing: *That painting is a counterfeit.*
adjective. not real; fake: *The counterfeit money was recognized by the bank teller.*

coun·ter·part [kownt-ur-*part*] *noun, plural* **counterparts.** someone or something that matches another and has the same purpose or effect: *The U.S. President is the counterpart of the British Prime Minister.*

count·ess [kownt-is] *noun, plural* **countesses.** a woman who holds the same rank as a count; usually the wife of a count.

count·less ▶ [kownt-lis] *adjective.* too numerous to be counted; very large in number. *That old joke has been told countless times.* —**countlessly,** *adverb.*

coun·try [kun-tree] *noun, plural* **countries. 1.** a large area of land; a region: *Much of the state of Iowa is farming country.* **2.** a nation or state that is controlled by its own government, such as the United States or Mexico. **3.** the people of a nation or state: *The whole country was shocked by the disaster.* **4.** an area that is away from cities or towns: *It's quiet living in the country.*

coun·try·man [kun-tree-*man*] *noun, plural* **countrymen. 1.** a person from your own country. **2.** someone who lives in the country. A **countrywoman** is a woman who lives in the country.

On a clear night, **countless** *stars can be seen in the sky.*

coun·try·side [kun-tree-*side*] *noun.* the land that is not part of towns or cities.

coun·ty [kownt-ee] *noun, plural* **counties. 1.** a division of a state or country that has its own local government. **2.** the inhabitants of such an area.

coup [koo] *noun, plural* **coups. 1.** a sudden and often violent overthrow of a government. **2.** something very impressive because it was not easy to achieve: *Getting that famous singer to perform at the prom was a real coup for the organizing committee.*

cou·ple [kup-ul] *noun, plural* **couples. 1.** two people or things of the same kind; a pair. **2.** two people who are thought of together in the same way, because they are married, engaged, dating each other, and so on. **3.** a small number: *Your paper is good—there are just a couple of things I would change.* *verb,* **coupled, coupling.** to put two things together; connect: *The rail cars were coupled to each other.*

cou·pon [koo-pon *or* kyoo-pon] *noun, plural* **coupons.** a ticket or piece of paper that shows you are entitled to receive something: *I collected enough coupons to get a free coffee.*

cour·age [kur-ij] *noun.* the ability to face danger or pain and put aside the thought of being afraid; bravery.

cou·ra·geous [kuh-ray-jus] *adjective.* having courage; brave: *The courageous lifeguards rushed into the heavy surf to save the drowning man.* —**courageously,** *adverb.*

cou·ri·er [kur-ee-ur] *noun, plural* **couriers.** a person who is paid to deliver messages or packages.

course [korse] *noun, plural* **courses. 1.** the fact of moving or progressing from one point to another; movement in space or time: *We'll read several stories in the course of the afternoon.* **2.** the planned direction to be taken in order to get somewhere: *We had to change course to avoid the storm.* **3.** the action someone decides to take: *The easiest course would be to say nothing.* **4.** an area where sports or games are played: *a golf course.* **5.** a series of lessons: *I'm taking the history course.* **6.** a part of meal served together: *I had steak and salad for my main course.* *verb,* **coursed, coursing.** to run over or through an area, often quickly: *He could not stop the tears from coursing down his cheeks.*

• **of course. 1.** for certain: *Of course you can come with us.* **2.** as expected: *We heard a strange noise, so of course we locked the door.* 🔊 A different word with the same sound is **coarse.**

court ▼ [kort] *noun, plural* **courts. 1.** *Law.* an official body that has authority to hear legal cases, resolve disputes, and make legal decisions. **2.** *Law.* the place where a trial takes place and judgments are made. **3.** an area open to the sky and surrounded by buildings or walls. **4.** a short street. **5.** an area made for playing games: *a tennis court.* **6.** the place where a royal family lives and works. **7.** the royal family, their followers, and advisers. *verb,* **courted, courting. 1.** to try to win someone's love or affection. **2.** to behave in a way that could be risky: *Skating on melting ice is courting disaster.*

cour·te·ous [kurt-ee-us] *adjective.* showing respect; polite. "Please" and "you're welcome" are courteous remarks. —**courteously,** *adverb;* —**courteousness,** *noun.*

In ancient Chinese **courts,** *a person whose guilt was proven was encouraged to confess.*

COVERED WAGONS

Nineteenth-century pioneers traveled from eastern America to the west in covered wagons pulled by horses, mules, or oxen. For safety and to help one another, they made the long journey in groups, known as wagon trains, usually traveling in single file. At night the wagons were pulled up into a large circle, which provided protection against hostile Indians and other dangers, as well as a pen for the animals.

cour·te·sy [kurt-uh-see] *noun, plural* **courtesies.** polite and respectful behavior; being well-mannered.

court·house [kort-*howse*] *noun, plural* **courthouses.**
1. a building where a court of law is held. **2.** the main building where county government offices are located.

court-mar·tial [kort-*mar*-shul] *noun, plural* **courts-martial.** *Law.* a military court that judges members of the military who may have broken military law. *verb,* **court-martialed, court-martialing.** to put someone on trial in such a court.

court·yard ▼ [kort-*yard*] *noun, plural* **courtyards.** an open space surrounded by walls or buildings.

cous·cous [koos-*koos*] *noun.* a food made from crushed wheat eaten with meat and vegetables; originally from North Africa.

Small trees, shrubs, and bulbs look attractive in a **courtyard.**

cou·sin [kuz-un] *noun, plural* **cousins.** the child of your aunt or uncle. First cousins have the same grandparents; children of first cousins are second cousins to each other and have the same great-grandparents.

cove [kove] *noun, plural* **coves.** a small, sheltered inlet or bay.

cov·er [kuv-ur] *verb,* **covered, covering.**
1. to spread something over a thing: *Cover your head with a scarf; The garden bed was covered with a layer of straw.* **2.** to travel a certain distance: *We should be able to cover two hundred miles in one day.* **3.** to deal with a certain subject: *The lecture covers three hundred years of history. noun, plural* **covers. 1.** something placed over a thing: *I'll put a dust cover on the chairs.* **2.** something that gives protection: *We took cover under the trees.* **3.** the outside of a book, magazine, or the like: *The magazine has a picture of the President on the cover this week.*

covered wagon ▲ *History.* a large wagon with a canvas roof stretched over hoops. Covered wagons were often used by people traveling to the western U.S. in the 1900s.

cov·er·ing [kuv-ur-ing] *noun, plural* **coverings.** something that covers or hides: *She had put up some bright wall coverings.*

cov·et [kuv-it] *verb,* **coveted, coveting.** to want something someone else has; envy: *The Oscars are coveted by many leading actors.* A **covetous** person is someone who is envious of what other people have.

Charros are traditional **cowboys** *who usually work in the north of Mexico.*

cow [kow] *noun, plural* **cows.**
1. an adult female of cattle. **2.** the female of other large animals such as elephants, whales, or seals.

cow·ard [kow-urd] *noun, plural* **cowards.** a person who has no courage or is very easily frightened. A person who is a coward is **cowardly.** The fact of being a coward is **cowardice.**

cow·boy ▲ [kow-*boy*] *noun, plural* **cowboys.** a man who works with cattle on a ranch or at rodeos. A different word with the same meaning is **cowhand.**

cow·girl [kow-*gurl*] *noun, plural* **cowgirls.** a woman who works with cattle on a ranch or at rodeos.

cow·hide [kow-*hide*] *noun, plural* **cowhides. 1.** the skin of a cow, bull, or steer. **2.** leather made from this skin.

coy·o·te [kye-*yoh*-tee *or* kye-*oht*] *noun, plural* **coyotes.** an animal related to the wolf and dog that is often found in western parts of North America. Coyotes are known for their howling call.

co·zy [*koze*-ee] *adjective,* **cozier, coziest.** comfortably warm; snug: *Grandpa likes to sit in his soft, cozy chair by the fire.*

CPR *Medicine.* an abbreviation for **cardiopulmonary resuscitation**, which is a method of treating someone who has suffered a heart attack by blowing air into the lungs and putting pressure on the chest to massage the heart.

crab [krab] *noun, plural* **crabs.** a sea animal that has a flat body, a hard shell, eight legs, and two prominent pincers, or claws. People eat some kinds of crabs.

crab apple a small, wild apple with a sour taste. Crab apples are often used to make jelly or preserves.

crack [krak] *noun, plural* **cracks. 1.** a thin split in something: *There is a long crack in this wall.* **2.** a short, sudden, loud noise: *the crack of a baseball hitting a bat.* **3.** a hard, painful blow: *She got a nasty crack on the shin from an opponent's hockey stick.*
verb, **cracked, cracking. 1.** to split without falling apart. **2.** to break apart noisily: *The branch cracked suddenly in the wind.* **3.** to make a sudden, loud noise; crackle. **4.** to strike with a painful impact.

crack·er [*krak*-ur] *noun, plural* **crackers.** a thin, dry, crispy kind of biscuit.

crack·le [*krak*-ul] *verb,* **crackled, crackling.** to make small, sharp sounds: *Twigs crackle when you snap them.*
noun, plural **crackles.** a small, sharp sound.

cra·dle [*krade*-ul] *noun, plural* **cradles. 1.** a baby's bed, or cot, usually with rockers. **2.** a structure or support that is shaped like a baby's cradle. **3.** a place where something starts or develops: *Ancient Greece was the cradle of democracy.*
verb, **cradled, cradling.** to hold something very gently in a protective way as if in a cradle.

craft [kraft] *noun, plural* **crafts. 1.** the skill used in doing or making something, especially with the hands. **2.** a job or hobby that requires a special kind of skill: *Pottery is a useful and popular craft.* **3.** skill used to deceive or act dishonestly: *The thief used all his craft to convince the police that he was innocent.* **4.** a boat, ship, airplane, or spaceship.

crafts·man [*krafts*-mun] *noun, plural* **craftsmen.** a person who works at a particular craft or who works very skillfully. A different word with the same meaning is **craftsperson.**

craft·y [*kraft*-ee] *adjective,* **craftier, craftiest.** clever at deceiving or acting dishonestly; sly; cunning: *Even though he never went to college he was crafty enough to make them believe he was a doctor.* —**craftily,** *adverb;* —**craftiness,** *noun.*

crag [krag] *noun, plural* **crags.** a high, steep, bare, and uneven cliff or rock. A place that is steep and rocky is **craggy.**

cram [kram] *verb,* **crammed, cramming. 1.** to stuff or force roughly into a small space; jam: *Jeanie crammed the books into her bag.* **2.** to study or learn things in a rush: *The lazy student crammed for her math exam just before the test.*

cramp [kramp] *noun, plural* **cramps. 1.** tightness in a muscle that causes a sudden, severe pain: *The cold water caused a cramp in the swimmer's foot.* **2. cramps.** severe stabbing pains in the stomach.
verb, **cramped, cramping. 1.** to have or cause to have the pain of a cramp: *His leg began to cramp in the last mile of the race.* **2.** to crowd into a tight space; confine or restrict.

cran·ber·ry [*kran*-ber-ee] *noun, plural* **cranberries.** a hard, sour-tasting, dark red berry that grows on shrubs in marshy areas. It is used to make juice, jelly, and a sauce.

crane ▼ [krane] *noun, plural* **cranes. 1.** a tall water bird with long legs and a long neck and bill. **2.** a large machine with a long movable arm that lifts and lowers heavy weights and shifts them from one place to another.
verb, **craned, craning.** to stretch the head upward or forward to get a better view: *The small children had to crane their necks to see past the people in front.*

*A **crane** operator sits in a cab at the top of a tower and moves the load by operating controls.*

a b c d e f g h i j k l m n o p q r s t u v w x y z

crank [krangk] *noun, plural* **cranks. 1.** a handle that is attached at a right angle to a shaft in a machine. When the handle is turned, it sets the machine in motion. The handle of a pencil sharpener is a kind of crank. **2.** a person who believes and states very strange or absurd opinions: *Only a crank would believe that the Earth is flat.* **3.** a person who is usually angry or irritated. *verb*, **cranked, cranking.** to turn a crank in order to start up a machine.

crank·shaft [krangk-*shaft*] *noun, plural* **crankshafts.** the rod or shaft that is attached to a crank handle and that turns to set a machine in motion as in a car or truck.

crank·y [krangk-ee] *adjective,* **crankier, crankiest.** often angry or in a bad mood; irritable; bad-tempered.

crash [krash] *noun, plural* **crashes. 1.** a loud, violent, smashing sound: *There was a loud crash as the tray of dishes fell to the floor and broke.* **2.** a collision in which a vehicle strikes against something at high speed: *a plane crash.* **3.** a sudden fall or failure, as of a business or stock market. **4.** a sudden closing down or loss of information in a computer. *verb*, **crashed, crashing. 1.** to make a loud, violent noise: *The thunder crashed during the big storm.* **2.** to strike very hard: *The car crashed into a tree.* **3.** to enter a place without an invitation or without paying. *Otto crashed the reception at the art gallery.* **4.** of a computer, to stop working suddenly.

crate [krate] *noun, plural* **crates.** a large box, usually made of wooden boards. *verb*, **crated, crating.** to pack in a crate or in crates.

cra·ter ▶ [krate-ur] *noun, plural* **craters.** a large, bowl-shaped hollow in a flat surface, such as can be made in the surface of the Earth by a meteor.

crave [krave] *verb,* **craved craving.** to want very much; feel a strong need for: *I was craving a cold drink after the long, hot walk.*

About three to four billion years ago, asteroids bombarded the Moon and left **craters** *on its surface.*

crawl [krawl] *verb,* **crawled, crawling. 1.** to move along on hands and knees, as a baby does, or to move slowly close to the ground: *The lizard crawled slowly over the rock.* **2.** to move along slowly: *The big truck crawled up the steep, winding mountain road.* **3.** to be covered with or full of moving things: *The rotten log was crawling with ants.* *noun, plural* **crawls. 1.** movement, or something that moves at a slow speed: *On a TV news show, the crawl is the string of words moving across the bottom of the screen.* **2.** a swimming stroke in which a swimmer moves one arm after the other over the head and down through the water while kicking the feet up and down.

cray·fish ◀ [kray-*fish*] *noun, plural* **crayfish, crayfishes.** a freshwater shellfish that is similar to a lobster.

The **crayfish** is not a fish, though it does live in water. English adopted a French word for this animal that sounded like it ended with a "fish" sound. This word has many forms other than *crayfish,* such as *crawfish, crawdad,* and *crawdaddy.*

cray·on [kray-on] *noun, plural* **crayons.** a stick of colored wax for writing, drawing, or coloring. *verb*, **crayoned, crayoning.** to write, draw, or color with a crayon.

cra·zy [kray-zee] *adjective,* **crazier, craziest. 1.** not having a sound and healthy mind; not sane; mentally ill. **2.** not making sense; silly; foolish: *Driving one hundred miles an hour on that narrow road was a crazy thing to do.* **3.** liking very much: *Millie is crazy about horses.* —**crazily,** *adverb;* —**craziness,** *noun.*

creak [kreek] *verb,* **creaked, creaking.** to squeak loudly or make a sharp, high-pitched sound. *noun, plural* **creaks.** a loud squeaking sound. 🔊 A different word with the same sound is **creek.**

cream [kreem] *noun, plural* **creams. 1.** the yellowish, fatty substance that rises and settles on the top of milk. **2.** a food made from cream or that looks or tastes like it: *cream of chicken soup.* **3.** an ointment that is thick like cream: *face cream.* **4.** the very best examples of something: *the speakers at the conference represent the cream of the scientific community.* *verb*, **creamed, creaming.** to beat, rub, or stir until it turns to cream. A substance that is like cream is **creamy.**

crease [krees] *noun, plural* **creases.** a sharp fold or ridge in a soft material: *a crease in a sheet of paper.* *verb*, **creased, creasing.** to form a crease by folding sharply or by ironing.

cre·ate [kree-ate] *verb,* **created, creating.** to make or bring into being; cause to happen or exist: *The sculptor created a wonderful statue; A sudden rainstorm created problems for motorists.* A person who creates something is a **creator.**

cre·a·tion [kree-ay-shun] *noun, plural* **creations.** the act of creating or making something: *the creation of a beautiful painting.* **2.** something created: *I gave him a few ideas, but the story is really his creation.*

Cre·a·tion [kree-ay-shun] *noun. Religion.* the story, told in the Old Testament of the Bible, of how God created the Earth and all living things in a period of six days.

Crayfish are smaller than lobsters and turn red when they are cooked.

cre·a·tion·ism [kree-<u>ay</u>-shun-*iz*-um] *noun. Religion.* the belief that God created the Earth and all living things in a period of six days. People who believe this do not believe that the Earth and the universe developed slowly over many millions of years. The belief that science proves that the Creation really happened is **scientific creationism.** —**creationist,** *noun.*

cre·a·tive [kree-<u>ate</u>-iv] *adjective.* being able to think and do things in an original way: *Thomas Edison was a very creative inventor.* The fact of being creative is **creativity.** —**creatively,** *adverb.*

> **Creative** writing usually refers to writing that requires imagination, such as stories, poems, novels, or screenplays for movies. This contrasts with writing that describes facts about real things, such as a magazine article about sharks. However, in another sense all kinds of writing are creative because the writer always starts with a blank piece of paper and has to decide what to write.

crea·ture [<u>kree</u>-chur] *noun, plural* **creatures.** any living human or animal.

creche [kresh] *noun, plural* **creches.** *Religion.* a scene, made with statues and models, that shows the baby Jesus and the people and animals that were present when he was born. This word is also spelled **crèche.**

cred·en·tial [kruh-<u>den</u>-shul] *noun, plural* **credentials.** something, such as a certificate, that proves that a person has a skill or authority; a qualification: *To prove that she was really an FBI agent, she showed them her credentials.*

cred·it [<u>kred</u>-it] *noun, plural* **credits. 1.** the ability to pay for something over time after buying it: *Dad bought a new shirt on credit.* **2.** an amount of money that can be spent, but need not be paid: *My aunt returned the clock, so she has twenty dollars' credit at the drugstore.* **3.** belief or trust in something: *He's a better writer than people give him credit for.* **4.** approval for doing something or praise: *Jonathon deserves most of the credit over winning the game.* **5.** a unit of study in a college or university. *verb,* **credited, crediting.** to pay back an amount of money: *The bank made an error and credited Monica's account with fifty extra dollars.*

credit card *Business.* a plastic card, issued by a bank or a store, that allows a person to purchase things and not pay for them until later.

cred·i·tor [<u>kred</u>-i-tur] *noun, plural* **creditors.** *Business.* a person or an organization that lends money or provides credit to another person or organization.

creek ▲ [kreek] *noun, plural* **creeks.** a small stream; a body of water smaller than a river. 🔊 A different word with the same sound is **creak.**

creep [kreep] *verb,* **crept, creeping. 1.** to move slowly, silently, and carefully: *The cat was creeping toward the mouse.* **2.** to grow along or on top of: *The thick vine crept over the wall of the house.* **3.** to feel frightened, as if things are crawling over you: *That scary movie made my flesh creep.* *noun, plural* **creeps. 1. the creeps.** a scary or nasty feeling: *I get the creeps whenever I see a snake.* **2.** a person who is annoying or unpleasant.

cre·mate [<u>kree</u>-*mate*] *verb,* **cremated, cremating.** to burn a dead body. The act of burning a dead body is **cremation.**

crepe [krape] *noun, plural* **crepes. 1.** a fabric, such as silk or cotton, with a light, crinkled surface. **2.** a pancake, usually wrapped around a filling. Very light paper that has a crinkly surface is **crepe paper.**

cres·cent [<u>kres</u>-unt] *noun, plural* **crescents. 1.** the moon's shape when it appears small and curved. **2.** a thin, curved shape.

crest ◄ [krest] *noun, plural* **crests. 1.** a group of showy feathers that stands up on the heads of some birds. **2.** the highest part of something: *the crest of an ocean wave.* *verb,* **crested, cresting.** to reach a high point.

cre·vice [<u>krev</u>-is] *noun, plural* **crevices.** a crack or narrow split, as in a rock, cliff, or wall.

crew [kroo] *noun, plural* **crews. 1.** a group or team of people who work together at something: *the crew of a ship or an aircraft.* **2.** any group of people thought of together: *My older brother and his crew are all coming over to watch the football game.*

crib [krib] *noun, plural* **cribs. 1.** a baby's small bed. **2.** a container for feeding farm animals. **3.** a bin or small building where grain is stored.

The male crowned crane displays its elaborate **crest** *to attract a mate.*

a b c d e f g h i j k l m n o p q r s t u v w x y z

crick·et¹ [krik-it] *noun, plural* **crickets.** a jumping insect that is like a grasshopper. A male cricket makes a chirping noise.

crick·et² ▶ [krik-it] *noun.* an English outdoor sport somewhat like baseball, played with bats, hard balls, and wickets between two teams of eleven players each.

cried [kride] *verb.* the past tense and past participle of CRY.

crime [krime] *noun, plural* **crimes. 1.** any deed or action that is against the law: *Murder is a terrible crime.* **2.** the fact of acting in a wrong, wasteful, or unwise way: *It would be a crime to cut down that lovely old tree.*

crim·i·nal [krim-uh-nul] *noun, plural* **criminals.** someone who breaks the law, especially in a serious way: *The jury found the criminals guilty of stealing the gold.* *adjective.* having to do with crime: *a criminal investigations; to face criminal charges.*

crim·son [krim-sun] *noun, plural* **crimsons.** a rich, deep red color. *adjective.* having a rich, deep red color.

crin·kle [kringk-ul] *verb,* **crinkled, crinkling. 1.** to cause ripples or creases, or to become creased: *This silk shirt will crinkle if you wash it.* **2.** to make a gentle, rustling sound: *The dry leaves crinkled when we walked on them.*

crip·ple [krip-ul] *noun, plural* **cripples.** someone who is permanently unable to move or use part of their body. *verb,* **crippled, crippling. 1.** to injure a person so that part of their body becomes damaged or paralyzed: *Polio is a disease that once crippled many young people.* **2.** to disrupt or weaken: *The drought has crippled many farmers' ability to produce their crops.*

cri·sis [krye-sis] *noun, plural* **crises.** a dangerous or difficult situation that may cause conditions to become much worse: *When an engine caught fire, the pilot knew that he was in a crisis.*

crisp [krisp] *adjective,* **crisper, crispest. 1.** firm and easily snapped: *The bread had just been baked and the crust was crisp.* **2.** cool and bracing: *a crisp evening.* **3.** very clear and easily understood: *The general's orders were short and crisp.* **—crisply,** *adverb;* **—crispness,** *noun.*

criss·cross [kris-kros] *adjective.* having lines that cross over each other. *noun, plural* **crisscrosses.** a pattern with crisscross lines. *verb,* **crisscrossed, crisscrossing. 1.** to make lines that cross over. **2.** to travel back and forth across: *The explorers crisscrossed the desert.*

cri·ter·i·on [krye-teer-ee-un] *noun, plural* **criteria.** a reason for choosing , deciding, or judging: *Honesty and intelligence were her main criteria in selecting the best person for the job.*

crit·ic [krit-ik] *noun, plural* **critics. 1.** a person who comments on or writes about the quality of other people's work: *a book critic; a movie critic.* **2.** a person who finds fault with something: *Paul is a very harsh critic of the mayor of our town.*

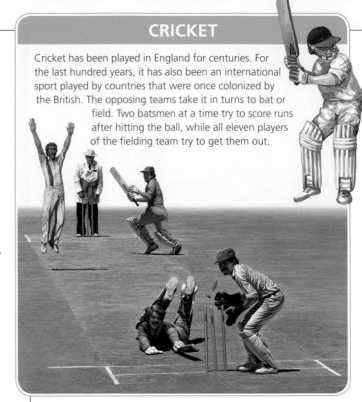

CRICKET

Cricket has been played in England for centuries. For the last hundred years, it has also been an international sport played by countries that were once colonized by the British. The opposing teams take it in turns to bat or field. Two batsmen at a time try to score runs after hitting the ball, while all eleven players of the fielding team try to get them out.

crit·i·cal [krit-i-kul] *adjective.* **1.** likely to find fault; looking for mistakes: *He roots for that team, but is often critical of the way they play.* **2.** given by an expert or critic: *They asked the scientist for his critical opinion of the new theory.* **3.** of great importance for the future; serious: *a critical illness.* **—critically,** *adverb.*

crit·i·cize [krit-i-*size*] *verb,* **criticized, criticizing. 1.** to find fault with; complain about: *Greta's mother criticized her for forgetting to do her chores.* **2.** to act as a critic; judge the value or quality of something.

crit·i·cism [krit-i-*siz*-um] *noun, plural* **criticisms. 1.** the act of finding fault: *He was upset by her criticism of the way he dresses.* **2.** the work of a critic; judging a book, movie, TV show, or the like.

Criticism of writing means making any kind of comment or judgment. The critic could just as easily say the writing is excellent as say it is poor. In fact, for student writing it is always better to use constructive criticism. For example, rather than say, "The end of your story doesn't make sense," it would be better to say, "I was really interested in reading how Mario tried to win the prize. But at the end, I wasn't sure whether he won or not."

croak [kroke] *noun, plural* **croaks.** a harsh, deep noise such as the sound made by a frog or toad. *verb,* **croaked, croaking.** to make a croaking sound.

cro·chet [kroh-shay] *verb,* **crocheted, crocheting.** to make cloth objects by using a hooked needle to link together loops of thread.

croc·o·dile ▶ [krok-uh-*dile*] *noun, plural* **crocodiles.** a reptile with a long body, pointed snout, rough, leathery skin, and four short legs that lives in rivers and swamps in many tropical areas. It is a close relative of the alligator.

cro·cus [kroh-kus] *noun, plural* **crocuses.** a small spring plant with purple, white, or yellow flowers.

crook [kruk] *noun, plural* **crooks. 1.** a curved part of something, such as an umbrella handle. **2.** someone who is not honest; a criminal.
verb, **crooked, crooking.** to bend or curve.

crook·ed [kruk-id] *adjective.* **1.** curving, hooked, bent, or jagged; not straight. **2.** not to be trusted; dishonest; cheating.

crop [krop] *noun, plural* **crops. 1.** a plant that people grow on farms, mainly for food. **2.** the amount of a plant that is produced in a season: *a small grain crop.* **3.** a new group of people or things: *A crop of new movies will be coming out at the end of this year.* **4.** a part of the throat of some birds where food gathers before it is digested. **5.** a small whip with a loop at the end.
verb, **cropped, cropping.** to cut back: *The gardener cropped the hedge.*

cro·quet [krow-kay] *noun.* an outdoor game in which players use mallets with long handles to hit balls through a series of metal hoops.

cross [kros] *noun, plural* **crosses. 1.** the figure formed when one straight line is drawn or placed across another. *+, T,* and *X* are all examples of crosses. **2.** two pieces of wood or other materials that are shaped to form a cross. **3.** also, **the cross.** such a figure used as a symbol of the Christian religion. **4.** a mix of different kinds or species: *Our dog is a cross between a spaniel and a terrier.*
verb, **crossed, crossing. 1.** to go across: *The ship crossed the ocean.* **2.** to put across each other: *The dancers crossed their hands and their feet as they moved around.* **3.** to draw a line across or through: *Mike crossed out what he wrote and started over.* **4.** to argue against; be opposed to: *If John really wants to be team captain we will not cross him.* **5.** to mix different kinds or species.
adjective, **crosser, crossest. 1.** placed or going across. **2.** in a bad mood; angry or unhappy.

cross-coun·try [kros-kun-tree] *adjective.* **1.** moving or stretching over a long distance: *The cross-country race is five miles long.* **2.** moving across all or most of a country: *This cross-country flight goes from California to Florida.* This word is also spelled **cross country.**

cross·bow [kros-boh] *noun, plural* **crossbows.** *History.* a weapon used during the Middle Ages that fired arrows or stones. Its bow was supported by a long, thin, wooden base.

cross·ing [kros-ing] *noun, plural* **crossings.** a place where things go across each other or where something can be crossed: *a river crossing.*

cross-ref·er·ence [kros-ref-uh-runs] *noun, plural* **cross-references.** *Literature.* an indication in a book of where the reader can find other related information about something elsewhere in the book.

cross·road [kros-rode] *noun, plural* **crossroads. 1.** a road that crosses another road or that leads between two main roads. **2. crossroads.** the place where different roads meet and cross each other.

cross-sec·tion ▼ [kros-sek-shun] *noun, plural,* **cross-sections. 1.** a slice or separation made directly through an object so that its internal structure or design can be seen. **2.** an image or drawing showing such a view. **3.** a selection of a small number of people or things from a larger group to try to show what most members of the group think or are like: *The survey represents a cross-section of the population of our city.* This term is also spelled **cross section.**

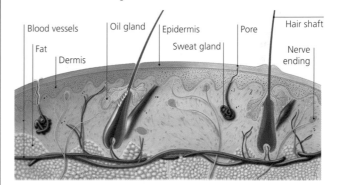

A **cross-section** *of the skin reveals its layers, hair shafts, glands, nerve endings, and blood vessels.*

cross·walk [kros-wawk] *noun, plural* **crosswalks.** a part of a street that has markings to show that pedestrians can cross there.

cross·word puzzle [kros-wurd] a kind of puzzle that has blank squares that must all be filled with letters to spell words, using numbered clues.

crotch [kroch] *noun, plural* **crotches.** the part of the body between the tops of the legs.

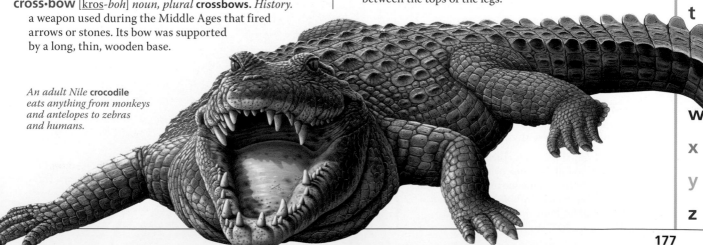

An adult Nile **crocodile** *eats anything from monkeys and antelopes to zebras and humans.*

A
B
C
D
E
F
G
H
I
J
K
L
M
N
O
P
Q
R
S
T
U
V
W
X
Y
Z

crouch [krowch] *verb,* **crouched, crouching.** to bend the knees and lower the rest of the body: *A catcher in baseball crouches down behind home plate.*
noun, plural **crouches.** a crouching position.

crow [kroh] *noun, plural* **crows. 1.** a large bird having shiny black feathers and a loud, grating call; found in large numbers in North America. **2.** the loud call that a rooster makes.
verb, **crowed, crowing. 1.** to make a rooster's loud call. **2.** to call out happily or in a boastful way: *Jeremy crowed about winning the first prize in the competition.*

Crow [kroh] *noun, plural* **Crows.** a member of a North American Indian tribe, now living mainly in Montana.

crow·bar [kroh-*bar*] *noun, plural* **crowbars.** a long metal pole that is wedge-shaped at one end. It is used for lifting or prying things apart.

crowd [krowd] *noun, plural* **crowds.** a lot of people together in one place: *a large crowd at a football game.*
verb, **crowded, crowding.** to fill up a space with many people or things: *The sheep were crowded together in the pen.* A place where there is a large crowd is said to be **crowded.**

crown ▲ [krown] *noun, plural* **crowns. 1.** a decorative kind of hat or head covering worn by kings and queens. **2.** the fact of being king or queen or of governing a country: *The young prince knew that one day he would inherit the crown.* **3.** the top of something: *the crown of a hill.* **4.** an honor, reward, or championship: *to win the heavyweight boxing crown.*
verb, **crowned, crowning. 1.** to make or declare a person officially king or queen. **2.** to be the highest thing on: *The lighthouse crowned the rugged headland.*

crow's-nest ▶ [kroze-*nest*] *noun, plural* **crow's-nests.** a lookout platform high up on the mast of a ship.

The **crow's-nest** is at the very top of a ship. It was so named with the idea that a sailor acting as a lookout there was like a bird looking down from its nest in the treetops.

cru·cial [kroo-shul] *adjective.* very important; having a major effect: *a crucial decision; The Battle of Gettysburg was a crucial event in the Civil War.* —**crucially,** *adverb.*

Cru·ci·fix·ion [kroo-si-fiks-shun] *noun. Religion.* the death of Jesus Christ by nailing him to a cross. A **crucifix** is a cross with the figure of Christ on it.

cru·ci·fy [kroo-si-*fye*] *verb,* **crucified, crucifying. 1.** *History.* to kill someone by nailing them to a cross. **2.** to treat someone in a harsh manner: *The news media have absolutely crucified him for making those insulting remarks.*

Blue war crown

Feathered crown

Double crown

crude [krood] *adjective,* **cruder, crudest. 1.** done in a rough or simple manner; not skilled: *My sketch of the house is pretty crude, but it will give you an idea of what it looks like.* **2.** lacking manners; rude: *a crude joke.* The fact of being rude, simple, or unskilled is **crudity. 3.** in its natural state; raw. —**crudely,** *adverb.*

crude oil *Chemistry.* oil that is in its natural state, as it is when it is pumped from the ground before it has been processed or refined.

cru·el [krool *or* kroo-ul] *adjective,* **crueler, cruelest. 1.** giving pain; deliberately unkind; showing no pity: *Stop kicking that dog—that's cruel.* The act of being deliberately unkind is **cruelty. 2.** causing pain or suffering: *a cruel winter with months of freezing weather.* —**cruelly,** *adverb.*

cruise [krooz] *noun, plural* **cruises.** a holiday on a ship or boat that visits different places: *a cruise in the Caribbean.*
verb, **cruised, cruising. 1.** to sail from one place to another. **2.** to move in a smooth or relaxed way from one place to another: *The car cruised down the highway at a steady seventy miles an hour.*

cruis·er [krooz-ur] *noun, plural* **cruisers. 1.** a large warship, faster than, and with fewer guns than, a battleship. **2.** a motorboat with a cabin where people can live or sleep. **3.** a police car that patrols the streets.

In fifteenth-century sailing ships, crewmen watched for land from the **crow's-nest.**

crum·ble [krumb-ul] *verb,* **crumbled, crumbling.**
1. to break something into many little pieces: *Can you please crumble the bread for the stuffing?* 2. to fall apart; come to pieces; disintegrate: *After the raid, we saw lots of old buildings crumble to the ground.*

crum·ple [krump-ul] *verb,* **crumpled, crumpling.**
1. to cause something to crease or wrinkle: *If you pack your bag carefully, your dress shouldn't crumple.* 2. to fall down; collapse: *The old hut crumpled under the weight of the snow.*

crunch [krunch] *verb,* **crunched, crunching.** to chew or crush something,so that it makes a loud breaking or crushing noise. Hard or crisp food that makes a noise when you bite into it is said to be **crunchy.** *noun, plural,* **crunches.** a breaking or crushing sound: *the crunch of pebbles underfoot.*

cru·sade [kroo-sade] *noun,* *plural* **crusades.** a strong campaign for or against something: *a crusade against reckless driving; a crusade for world peace.* *verb,* **crusaded, crusading.** to fight strongly in a crusade; struggle; fight for a cause.

Cru·sades [kroo-sades] *plural noun. History.* any one of the religious wars fought in the eleventh, twelfth, and thirteenth centuries between the Christians and the Muslims who both wanted control of Palestine. A knight who fought in a Crusade was called a **Crusader.**

crush [krush] *verb,* **crushed, crushing.** 1. to hit, press or squeeze very hard: *A tree fell onto our car in the storm and crushed it.* 2. to put down; defeat: *Tom was crushed by the news that he wasn't picked for the tennis team.* *noun, plural* **crushes.** 1. a large crowd of people: *I tried to make my way through the crush to the other side of the room.* 2. a very strong feeling of love or liking for someone, which usually doesn't last for very long.

crust [krust] *noun, plural* **crusts.** 1. the hard, crispy part on the outside of a loaf of bread. 2. any hard outside layer: *pie crust.* 3. *Science.* the solid outer part of the Earth, extending from the surface to about 25 miles below. Anything that has a hard, crisp, outside layer is **crusty.** A person who is impatient or bad tempered is also described as **crusty.** *verb,* **crusted, crusting.** to cover with a crust: *I'm going to turn the oven up to see if I can crust up the pastry a bit more.*

crus·ta·cean [krus-tay-shun] *noun, plural* **crustaceans.** *Biology.* an animal with a hard shell and many jointed legs, such as a lobster, crab, or shrimp, that usually lives in the sea.

Crystals come in many different shapes, sizes, and colors.

crutch [kruch] *noun, plural* **crutches. 1.** a support or prop for an injured or lame person. It is a pole that usually has a padded part at the top, which you lean on with your arms in order to help you to walk. **2.** something that serves as an extra help or support for a weakness.

cry [krye] *verb,* **cried, crying. 1.** to shed tears; weep. **2.** to utter a call in a loud voice, shout: *Jacky cried out in pain.* *noun, plural* **cries. 1.** a loud call or shout: *a cry for help; a cry of pain; the cry of a bird.* **2.** a period of weeping.

crys·tal ▼ [kris-tul] *noun, plural* **crystals. 1.** *Chemistry.* a mineral that has formed into a regular shape: *crystals of sodium sulfate.* **2.** a rock, like quartz, that is clear and transparent. **3.** very high quality glass

crys·tal·lize [kris-tuh-lize] *verb,* **crystallized, crystallizing.** to form into crystals. —**crystallization,** *noun.*

CT scan *Medicine.* **1.** an image of cross-sections of the body made using X-ray technology and sophisticated computers. **2.** a machine that produces such images. CT scan is a shortened form of **computerized tomography scan.**

cu. an abbreviation for CUBIC.

cub [kub] *noun, plural* **cubs.** a young bear, lion, tiger, or wolf.

Cu·ban [kyoob-un] *noun, plural* **Cubans.** someone who comes from the country of Cuba. *adjective.* belonging to or relating to Cuba and its people.

cube [kyoob] *noun, plural* **cubes. 1.** a solid object with six square surfaces of equal sides. **2.** something shaped like a cube: *cubes of bread; ice cubes.* **3.** *Mathematics.* the product of a number multiplied by itself twice. The cube of 3 is 3 x 3 x 3, which is 27. *verb,* **cubed, cubing. 1.** to cut into cubes. **2.** to multiply a number by itself twice.

cu·bic [kyoob-ik] *adjective.* **1.** shaped like a cube. **2.** *Mathematics.* indicating the volume of something, which is the measurement you get when you multiply together its length, width, and thickness. A **cubic foot** is the volume of a cube whose edges are each one foot long.

Cub Scouts an organization for young boys that teaches them outdoor skills, physical fitness, and how to be a good citizen. A boy who belongs to this group is a **Cub Scout.**

cuck·oo [koo-koo] *noun, plural* **cuckoos.** a gray bird with a long tail that lays its eggs in other birds' nests. It has a very distinctive call of two quick notes, the first one higher than the second.

cu·cum·ber [kyoo-kum-bur] *noun, plural* **cucumbers.** a long, thin vegetable with green skin and white flesh with many seeds inside. It grows on a vine and is often used in salads.

cud [kud] *noun, plural* **cuds.** partly digested food eaten by a cow, sheep, or other animal with more than one stomach. The food is returned from the first stomach to the mouth to be chewed again, before going into the second stomach.

*It takes skill to drive a ball accurately with a **cue.***

A B C D E F G H I J K L M N O P Q R S T U V W X Y Z

cud·dle [kud-ul] *verb,* **cuddles, cuddling.** to hold tightly; hug: *Meg was trying to cuddle all three of her kids at the same time.* **2.** to lie close up next to someone. *noun, plural* **cuddles.** a hug, affectionate embrace.

cue¹ [kyoo] *noun, plural* **cues. 1.** a signal to an actor in a movie or play to do something at a certain time. **2.** any sign that tells someone when to take some action: *When Grandpa shuts his eyes, that's our cue to pack up and go home. verb,* **cued, cuing.** to give a signal to someone to do something.

cue² ▶ [kyoo] *noun, plural* **cues.** a long, thin stick with a leather tip, used to hit the ball in billiards or pool.

cuff¹ [kuf] *noun, plural* **cuffs.** a fold or band at the end of a sleeve or at the bottom of a pair of pants.

cuff² [kuf] *verb,* **cuffed, cuffing.** to hit with an open hand. *noun, plural* **cuffs.** a hit or slap.

cui·sine [kwi-zeen] *noun, plural* **cuisines. 1.** a style of cooking that is characteristic of a certain country: *French cuisine; Spanish cuisine.* **2.** the range and quality of food served, as at a restaurant.

cul-de-sac [kul-di-sak] *noun, plural* **cul-de-sacs.** a street or road that is closed at one end; a dead end.

cul·mi·nate [kul-mi-nate] *verb,* **culminated, culminating.** to end up a certain way because of a gradual series of events that preceded it: *The student demonstration culminated in twenty arrests.* —**culmination,** *noun.*

cul·prit [kul-prit] *noun, plural* **culprits.** someone who has done something wrong; someone who is guilty.

cult [kult] *noun, plural,* **cults. 1.** a small religious group that has beliefs differing in some way from the major religions. **2.** a person or thing who become the object of great devotion: *The worldwide cult of Elvis Presley still has many members.*

cul·ti·vate ▼ [kul-ti-vate] *verb,* **cultivated, cultivating. 1.** to prepare and use land to grow crops. To cultivate land you dig it up, fertilize it, and then plant the crop. **2.** to grow a crop: *to cultivate cotton.* **3.** to develop and make stronger: *The teacher told Sam that he should try to cultivate better manners.* —**cultivation,** *noun.*

cul·ti·va·tor [kul-ti-vay-tur] *noun, plural* **cultivators.** a tool or machine used to break up the soil around growing plants to make it easier to remove the weeds.

cul·tur·al [kulch-uh-rul] *adjective.* having to do with culture: *Our history project is on the cultural changes in the last century.* —**culturally,** *adverb.*

cul·ture [kulch-ur] *noun, plural* **cultures. 1.** the customs, ideas, and art that are shared by a group of people at a particular time: *I love going to foreign countries to see how they live and to discover their culture.* **2.** artistic or intellectual activities: *Tom's family enjoy culture and go to art galleries and museums nearly every weekend.* **3.** the growing and breeding of plants or animals: *the culture of silkworms and bees.* **4.** *Science.* the growing of living cells or microorganisms.

cu·mu·lus ▼ [kyoom-yuh-lus] *noun, plural* **cumuli.** thick, fluffy, white clouds with a sharp outline that form when hot air rises quickly.

cun·ning [kun-ing] *adjective.* good at tricking other people; deceitful; crafty; sly. *noun.* the ability to trick and deceive others, usually in order to achieve what you want. —**cunningly,** *adverb.*

cup [kup] *noun, plural* **cups. 1.** a small, round container, usually with a handle, from which you drink. **2.** the amount that a cup holds: *He had two cups of coffee with breakfast.* **3.** a unit of measure equal to eight ounces. There are four cups in a quart. **4.** a prize or trophy having the shape of a cup. *verb,* **cupped, cupping.** to put your hands around something so that they make the shape of a cup.

Cumulus *clouds dot the sky over west Texas.*

cup·board [kub-urd] *noun, plural* **cupboards.** a piece of furniture with shelves and doors that you can close.

cu·ra·tor [kyur-ay-tur] *noun, plural* **curators.** someone who is in charge of the works on display in an art gallery or museum: *curator of the National Gallery in London.*

curb [kurb] *noun, plural,* **curbs. 1.** a border between the pavement and the road; the paved edge of a road. **2.** anything that holds back or controls: *We are trying to keep a curb on our budget. verb,* **curbed, curbing. 1.** to control something and keep it within fixed limits: *I know I have to try to curb my temper.*

curd [kurd] *noun, plural* **curds.** the thick part of milk that separates from the liquid when the milk turns sour. Curds are used for making cheese.

cur·dle [kurd-ul] *verb,* **curdled, curdling.** to become sour and form into curds: *I'm not drinking this milk—it has curdled.*

Cultivating *rice paddies, such as this one in southern Asia, is hard, wet work.*

cure [kyoor] *verb*, **cured, curing. 1.** to make a person or animal well again, after they have been sick: *This medicine will cure you and make you feel better.* **2.** to make an illness or a problem go away: *The medicine cured his asthma.* **3.** to preserve by salting, drying, or smoking: *to cure ham.*
noun, plural **cures. 1.** something that makes a person or animal healthy again. **2.** a solution to an illness or a problem, which makes it go away: *Mom found the perfect cure to make me stop biting my nails.*

cur·few [kur-*fyoo*] *noun, plural* **curfews. 1.** a rule or law saying that everyone must be off the streets and indoors after a set time at night. 2. any rule that something must end by a certain time of night.

> **Curfew** comes from two words meaning "to cover a fire." In the Middle Ages, fire was used in houses for both heat and light. Each night at a certain time, a bell would ring to tell people to cover or put out their fires for the night.

cu·ri·os·i·ty [kyur-ee-*os*-i-tee] *noun, plural* **curiosities. 1.** a strong desire to find out all there is to know about something: *Curiosity made the explorers want to know what was over the mountains.* **2.** an object that is interesting because it is unusual, strange, or rare.

cu·ri·ous [kyur-ee-us] *adjective.* **1.** having a strong desire to learn or to find out about something: *Sarah is inquisitive and curious about everything.* **2.** unusual, strange, or interesting: *A curious thing happened on our way to the concert.* —**curiously,** *adverb.*

curl [kurl] *noun, plural* **curls. 1.** a piece of hair shaped in a ring or circle. If you have **curls,** you have **curly** hair. **2.** something shaped like a curl: *curls of black smoke.*
verb, **curled, curling.** to form into curls.

cur·rant [kur-unt] *noun, plural* **currants. 1.** a small berry, usually red or black, that grows in bunches on a bush. **2.** small, dried grapes, usually used in cooking.
🔊 A different word with the same sound is **current.**

cur·ren·cy ▶ [kur-un-*see*] *noun, plural* **currencies.**
1. *Business.* the system of money used in a country. Dollars and dimes are part of the currency used in the United States and Canada. **2.** general use and acceptance of ideas and customs at a particular time: *The argument that the world is getting hotter is starting to gain currency.*

cur·rent [kur-unt] *adjective.* **1.** belonging to the present: *a person's current address; the current issue of a magazine.* **2.** generally used or accepted: *Cooking with wood is still the current method in some countries.*
noun, plural **currents. 1.** a strong and continuous flowing movement of water or air: *the current of a river.* **2.** a flow of electricity through a wire or circuit: *The current in the electric fence gave him a shock.* **3.** general tendency of people to do something; trend: *There exists today a strong current of opinion against war.* —**currently,** *adverb.*
🔊 A different word with the same sound is **currant.**

cur·ric·u·lum [kuh-*rik*-yuh-lum] *noun, plural* **curriculums** or **curricula.** *Education.* **1.** all the courses of study offered in a school, college, or university. **2.** the range of study in a particular course.

> The word **curriculum** can be traced back to a word that meant a track or course for running races. The idea is that when a student studies all the courses in a school curriculum, this is like completing a long race around a track.

cur·ry [kur-ee] *noun, plural* **curries.** an Indian dish made with hot spices: *lamb curry.*

curse [kurs] *verb,* **cursed, cursing. 1.** to wish that something unpleasant, evil, or very nasty will happen to another person. **2.** to use bad language; say obscene things; swear. **3.** to complain bitterly about something that is causing you to suffer: *I curse the day I bought that car because it's been nothing but trouble.*
noun, plural **curses. 1.** a wish that something nasty or evil will happen to someone: *The witch doctor placed a curse on the village.* **2.** a swear word, usually said in anger. **3.** something or someone that causes a great deal of trouble or harm.

cur·sor [kurs-ur] *noun, plural* **cursors.** *Computers.* a special symbol on a computer that shows the position where you can enter or change a word or character.

curt [kurt] *adjective,* **curter, curtest.** short, rude, and abrupt: *"Go away!" was his curt reply.* —**curtly,** *adverb.*

cur·tain [kurt-un] *noun, plural* **curtains. 1.** a piece of material that hangs from the top of a window, or at the front of a stage. **2.** something that screens or covers: *a curtain of darkness.* *verb,* **curtained, curtaining.** to put a curtain over; close off with a curtain.

curt·sy ◀ [kurt-see] *noun, plural* **curtsies.** a bow made by girls or woman to show respect, which involves lowering the body slightly and bending the knees. *verb,* **curtsied, curtsying.** to make a curtsy.

*A **curtsy** in a costume with a full skirt can look very graceful.*

*The **currency** of Great Britain is pounds and pence, and comes in notes and coins of various values.*

curve [kurv] *noun, plural* **curves. 1.** a gradually bending line, such as part of the edge of a circle. **2.** something that has the shape of a curve: *a dangerous curve in the road.* **3.** a pitch in baseball that moves to the side as it reaches the batter.
verb, **curved, curving.** to bend or move in a line that has this shape of a curve: *The path curved to the right before heading down to the beach.*

cush·ion [kush-un] *noun, plural* **cushions. 1.** a kind of pillow or pad filled with soft material, as on a chair or sofa. **2.** a soft pad, especially one that protects against a blow.
verb, **cushioned, cushioning.** to soften a blow: *The thick grass cushioned his fall.*

cus·tard [kust-urd] *noun, plural* **custards.** a sweet dessert made from milk, sugar, and eggs.

cus·to·di·an [kuh-stoh-dee-un] *noun, plural* **custodians. 1.** a person who takes care of a public building. **2.** any person responsible for the care of another person or thing: *the custodian of the valuable art collection; the custodian of a wealthy person's estate.*

cus·to·dy [kust-uh-dee] *noun, plural* **custodies. 1.** the fact of holding or arresting a person: *The fire was set on purpose, and the accused man is now in custody.* **2.** the legal right to be in charge of a person, usually a child.

The hilt of a **cutlass** *protected a pirate's hand when he attacked.*

cus·tom [kust-um] *noun, plural* **customs. 1.** a traditional activity of a certain country or group: *Thanksgiving Day is an American custom.* **2.** something that most people do, because it is accepted as the right thing to do or because it has become a habit: *It's my custom to take chocolates when I'm invited out to dinner.* **3. customs.** a tax that a government charges on goods brought into the country. **4.** the place where this tax is collected.
adjective, made especially for a particular buyer: *custom furniture; a custom home.*

cus·tom·ar·y [kust-uh-mer-ee] *adjective.* what usually happens or is usually done: *In many countries it's customary to serve rice with the evening meal.* —**customarily,** *adverb.*

cus·to·mer [kust-uh-mur] *noun, plural* **customers.** a person who buys good or services.

cus·tom·ize [kust-uh-mize] *verb,* **customized, customizing.** to change something to make it look special or unusual: *He had his new car customized by adding a special high-powered engine.* —**customization,** *noun.*

cut [kut] *verb.* **cut, cutting. 1.** to make an opening or break in something with a knife, tool, or other sharp object. **2.** to move or act in a way that is like a knife going into something: *He cut across the neighbor's yard instead of walking on the sidewalk; She started to speak, but he cut her off before she could finish the sentence.* **3.** to make something shorter or smaller, as if by taking a knife to it: *What he wrote was too long and he had to cut about a hundred words from it.*
noun, plural **cuts. 1.** an opening that is made by a sharp object: *The scissors slipped and he got a cut on his finger.* **2.** the way in which something is cut: *Sirloin is my favorite cut of steak; She really likes the cut of that dress.* **3.** the fact of making something shorter or smaller: *The senator promised there would be a cut in taxes.*

cute [kyoot] *verb,* **cuter, cutest.** pretty and appealing; attractive. —**cuteness,** *noun.*

cu·ti·cle [kyoot-i-kul] *noun, plural* **cuticles.** a layer of hardened skin, as at the edge of a fingernail.

cut·lass ◀ [kut-lis] *noun, plural* **cutlasses.** *History.* a sword with one sharp edge once used by sailors and pirates.

cut·lery [kut-luh-ree] *noun,* knives, forks, and spoons.

cut·ter [kut-ur] *noun, plural* **cutters. 1.** a tool that you use to cut things or to cut through them: *wire cutters.* **2.** a person whose job is to cut things: *a diamond cutter.* **3.** a small, fast ship, especially an armed ship used by the Coast Guard.

cut·ting [<u>kut</u>-ing] *noun, plural* **cuttings. 1.** a small piece cut off something. **2.** a small part of an existing plant that you cut off, and replant, in order to start growing another plant. **3.** an article that has been cut from a newspaper or magazine. *adjective.* **1.** able to make a slit; sharp: *a cutting edge.* **2.** hurting a person's feelings; unkind: *We are all scared of that teacher because of his sarcastic and cutting remarks.*

cyber- a prefix that means having to do with computers and the Internet. A cybercafe is a cafe with computers and Internet facilities.

cyb·er·space [<u>sye</u>-bur-*spas*] *noun. Computers.* the world or environment of computer networks and Websites in which online computer communications take place.

cy·cle ▶ [<u>sye</u>-kul] *noun, plural* **cycles. 1.** a series of events that is repeated in the same order, over and over again: *the cycle of the four seasons of the year.* **2.** a bicycle, tricycle, or motorcycle. *verb,* **cycled, cycling.** to ride a bicycle, tricycle, or motorcycle.

cy·clone [<u>sye</u>-klone] *noun, plural* **cyclones.** a violent storm with very powerful winds that move in a clockwise direction.

cyl·in·der ▼ [<u>sil</u>-un-dur] *noun, plural* **cylinders.** *Mathematics.* an object with flat, circular ends and long, straight sides, such as the shape of a soup can. Such an object has a **cylindrical** shape.

cym·bal [<u>sim</u>-bul] *noun, plural* **cymbals.** *Music.* a round brass object, shaped like a plate, which, when you hit two of them together, makes a very loud noise. ◀)) A different word with the same sound is **symbol.**

Batteries are **cylinders** *containing chemicals that provide electrical energy.*

cyn·i·cal [<u>sin</u>-i-kul] *adjective.* describing someone who has a negative view of human nature, thinking that other people always act in a selfish way and expecting them to act in that way. *Tom is so cynical—he just won't believe that I am trying to help him.* A person who thinks like this is a **cynic.** —**cynically,** *adverb.*

cy·press ▶ [<u>sye</u>-pris] *noun.* an evergreen tree with small, dark green, scaly leaves and cones. ◀)) A different word with the same sound is **Cyprus.**

cyst [sist] *noun, plural* **cysts.** a growth on the inside or the outside of the body that contains liquid, and that sometimes needs to be surgically removed.

One of the world's most famous **cycle** *races is the annual Tour de France.*

czar [zahr] *noun, plural* **czars.** *History.* **1.** a Russian king; one of the rulers of Russia before the revolution of 1917 that ended the Russian monarchy. **2.** a person who rules or leads with absolute authority. This word is also spelled **tsar.**

> The word **czar** comes from the ancient Roman word "Caesar." This was the name that was given to the rulers of the Roman Empire, and it then became a word for a king or ruler in various countries of Europe.

cza·ri·na [zah-<u>ree</u>-nuh] *noun, plural* **czarinas.** *History.* the wife of a czar, or a woman who herself ruled as queen of Russia. This word is also spelled **Tsarina.**

Czech [chek] *noun, plural* **Czechs. 1.** a person who comes from the country in central Europe which was formerly known as Czechoslovakia, now divided into the Czech Republic and Slovakia. **2.** *Language.* one of the two main languages spoken in the old Czechoslovakia. The other language is called Slovak. *adjective.* having to do with the Czechs and their language and culture.

The **cypress** *tree is a conifer found mainly in cool, temperate climates.*

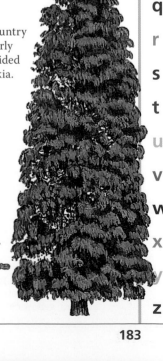

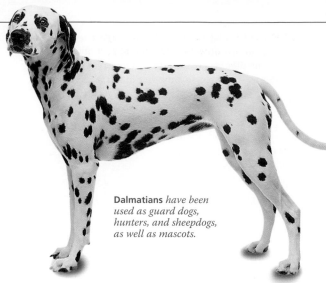

The legs of a **daddy-longlegs** *can be twenty times the length of its body.*

Dalmatians have been used as guard dogs, hunters, and sheepdogs, as well as mascots.

Dal·ma·tian ▲ [dal-<u>may</u>-shun] *noun, plural* **Dalmatians.** a large, short-haired dog with a white coat that has many small, dark brown or black spots.

Dalmatia is a part of Europe along the coast of the Adriatic Sea. This dog is thought to have first come from the area of Dalmatia. It was also once called "the Danish dog" because it was said to have come from Denmark.

D, d *noun, plural* **D's d's.** the fourth letter of the English alphabet.

dab·ble [<u>dab</u>-ul] *verb,* **dabbled, dabbling.** to have some interest in something: *I dabble in photography, but I don't have all the right equipment.*

dachs·hund [<u>doks</u>-und] *noun, plural* **dachshunds.** a small, long dog with very short legs.

dad·dy-long·legs ▲ [*dad*-ee-<u>long</u>-legz] *noun, plural* **daddy-longlegs.** the name used for a spider or spider-like insect with eight long, very thin legs, and a small, round body.

daf·fo·dil ▼ [<u>daf</u>-uh-dil] *noun, plural* **daffodils.** a plant with yellow flowers that look like tiny trumpets and long, thin leaves.

dag·ger [<u>dag</u>-ur] *noun, plural* **daggers.** a short, pointed weapon with a blade that is wider than that of a knife.

dai·ly [<u>day</u>-lee] *adjective.* happening every day: *At camp there is a daily room inspection. adverb.* on each day: *He delivers bread daily. noun, plural* **dailies.** a publication, especially a newspaper, created and printed each day.

dain·ty [<u>dane</u>-tee] *adjective,* **daintier, daintiest.** small, gentle, and delicate. —**daintily,** *adverb.*

dair·y [<u>dare</u>-ee] *noun, plural* **dairies. 1.** a room or building where milk and cream are stored and where butter and cheese are made. **2.** a place where milk cows are fed and cared for.

dai·sy [<u>day</u>-zee] *noun, plural* **daisies.** a common garden plant with white, yellow, or pink petals surrounding a raised, yellow center.

dam ▶ [dam] *noun, plural* **dams.** a barrier built across a river or stream to stop and hold water. *verb,* **dammed, damming.** to stop or block with a dam: *People dam rivers to hold water, such as to form a lake.*

dam·age [<u>dam</u>-ij] *noun, plural* **damages.** harm that causes destruction, injury, or loss: *Mom could not drive her car because of the damage caused by the accident. verb,* **damaged, damaging.** to hurt or cause harm: *My sister damaged my favorite sweater.*

dame [dame] *noun, plural* **dames.** a woman who is highly thought of or in a position of authority.

damp [damp] *adjective,* **damper, dampest.** slightly wet or moist: *The towel was damp from my shower in the morning.*

damp·en [<u>dam</u>-pun] *verb,* **dampened, dampening. 1.** to make slightly wet: *First, sprinkle water to dampen the dough.* **2.** to dull or spoil a good mood: *The argument with my friend dampened our visit.*

dance [dans] *verb,* **danced, dancing. 1.** to move the body to the beat and rhythm of music: *At the concert everyone was dancing.* **2.** to leap about, or bob up and down as if dancing. *noun, plural* **dances. 1.** *Music.* a specific pattern of movement performed to music. The tango, the waltz, and the polka are names of dances. **2.** a gathering where music is played and people dance: *My brother came home late from the dance.* —**dancer,** *noun.*

Daffodils grow from bulbs and bloom for a short time in the spring.

dan·de·li·on [dan-duh-*lye*-un] *noun, plural* **dandelions.** a plant with yellow flowers that become puff-balls full of seeds. The leaves can be eaten.

> The word **dandelion** comes from a French phrase meaning "the tooth of the lion." It was thought that the ragged leaves of a dandelion looked like the sharp teeth of a lion.

dan·druff [dan-druf] *noun.* small, white flakes of dead skin from the scalp.

dan·ger [dane-jur] *noun, plural* **dangers. 1.** the possibility or risk of being hurt: *The danger of climbing a tall tree is that you might fall.* **2.** the cause of possible harm: *Wild bears are a danger to campers.* —**dangerous,** *adjective;* —**dangerously,** *adverb.*

dan·gle [dang-gul] *verb,* **dangled, dangling.** to drop, hang or swing freely: *Charms dangle from my bracelet.*

Dams are built to store water for drinking, irrigation, and flood control, or to provide power for hydroelectricity.

Da·nish [dane-ish] *noun.* the language of Denmark. *adjective.* belonging to the people, culture, history, or geography of Denmark. A person from Denmark is a **Dane.** A **Danish pastry** is a sweet, rich pastry.

dare [dare] *verb,* **dared, daring. 1.** to invite or challenge someone to face adventure, difficulty, or danger as a test of bravery or skill: *I dared my sister to pick up the mouse.* **2.** to be willing to face adventure, difficulty, or danger: *I don't dare go into the park at night.* *noun, plural* **dares.** an invitation or challenge to face adventure or danger: *I took my friend's dare to run barefoot in the snow.*

dar·ing [dare-ing] *noun.* a willingness to face danger or adventure with confidence: *The plan to explore the woods took great daring.* *adjective.* willing to face danger or risk; adventurous; courageous: *She made a daring attempt to beat the world record.* —**daringly,** *adverb.*

dark [dark] *adjective,* **darker, darkest. 1.** having a lack of light: *With the curtains shut the room was dark.* **2.** not light-colored; deeply colored: *a dark green sweater.*

3. sad, wicked, or angry: *He was in a dark mood.* *noun.* **1.** the absence of light: *Without lights we had to cook in the dark.* **2.** the time after the sun sets; night: *We arrived late and had to pitch the tent in the dark.* • **in the dark.** lacking information: *I was kept in the dark about winning the award until prize night.*

dark·en [dar-kun] *verb,* **darkened, darkening.** to become dark or make something darker: *I dimmed the lights to darken the room.*

dar·ling [dar-ling] *noun, plural* **darlings.** a much-loved or adored person or animal: *My puppy is the darling of my life.* *adjective.* **1.** loved very much: *my darling sister.* **2.** adorable and cute: *a darling baby.*

darn [darn] *verb,* **darned, darning.** to sew thread or wool across a worn or torn hole: *My grandmother darned the elbows of my sweater.*

dart ▼ [dart] *noun, plural* **darts. 1.** a small, thin, pointed object that is thrown or shot. **2. darts.** a game in which players take turns throwing such objects at a round, soft board. *verb,* **darted, darting.** a sudden, fast movement: *The fish darted under the rock; Her eyes darted about in fear.*

*Hunters in South America rub **darts** over the backs of some frogs to collect poison for their blow guns.*

Dar·win·ism ▶ [dar-win-iz-um] *noun. Biology.* the ideas of Charles Darwin, who tried to explain why some kinds of plants and animals continue to produce new generations over the years while others die out. Darwin decided that the plants and animals that continue to live have special body features or particular skills that help them to live and reproduce.

dash [dash] *verb,* **dashed, dashing. 1.** to move very quickly; to rush: *I was late and had to dash for the bus.* **2.** to throw or hit something with violence: *Wild winds dashed against the rocks by the coast.* **3.** to destroy or wreck: *A sprained ankle dashed my chances of winning the race.* *noun, plural* **dashes. 1.** a small quantity of something that is added to something else: *My aunt adds a dash of spice to her coffee.* **2.** a quick run or short-distance race run at top speed: *The last race for the day is the 100-yard dash.* **3.** a short horizontal line used as a punctuation mark in writing to show a new thought or idea. Someone who is good-looking, confident, or stylish is described as **dashing.** • **dash off. 1.** to make, write, draw, or finish something in a hurry: *I dashed off a paper the morning it was due.* **2.** to go in a hurry: *She dashed off to school.*

dash·board [dash-bord] *noun, plural* **dashboards.** the section in the front of a vehicle or aircraft that holds dials, controls, and devices to help the driver or pilot.

da·ta [day-tuh *or* dat-uh] *plural noun.* **1.** individual facts and pieces of information: *The data on our town includes measurements, photos, and stories from local people.* A single fact or piece of information is called a **datum.** **2.** a collection of facts and pieces of information: *We researched all the data and decided to buy a poodle instead of a beagle.*

The word **data** is a plural form of the singular word *datum* ("plural" means that it refers to more than one). For this reason, some people use it with other plural words, as in "*These* data *have* been tested and *are* accurate." This is correct from a very strict point of view, and it might be found in scientific writing. However, data is used much more often as a singular form, as in "*This* data *has* been tested and *is* accurate," and it is certainly all right to do this.

Charles Darwin

Insect-eating finch

Seed-eating finch

When English naturalist Charles Darwin visited the remote Galapagos Islands, off the coast of South America, he was amazed at the many new animals and plants he saw. Each island had its own special kind of finch, for example. The reason, Darwin suggested, was that while all the finches probably had a single ancestor, in order to survive they had adapted to the unique conditions of their particular island.

ANIMALS OF THE GALAPAGOS ISLANDS

Penguins

Fur seal

Mockingbird

Marine iguanas

dat·a·base [day-tuh-*base or* dat-uh-*base*] *noun, plural* **databases.** *Computers.* a collection of information stored on a computer and organized so that any part of it can be easily looked at and added to or changed. This word is also spelled **data base.**

data processing *Computers.* the fact of using a computer to store and work with information.

date¹ [date] *noun, plural* **dates. 1.** a particular time when an event occurs: *The date of the final game is July 24.* **2.** the words or numbers that tell the day, month, or year. **3.** a meeting arranged for the future: *My mom has a date with the teacher on Wednesday.* **4.** a person who takes part in a friendly or romantic meeting: *I am meeting my date outside the movies.* *verb,* **dated, dating. 1.** to stamp with a time or date: *The painting is dated 1994.* If something is old-fashioned, it is described as **dated. 2.** to work out or decide on a date: *We are trying to date the old tools we found under our new house.* **3.** to mark the creation or birth of something with a date: *Disneyland dates back to 1955.* **4.** to go out with someone socially or romantically: *My sister dated her best friend's brother.*

date² ◀ [date] *noun, plural* **dates.** the sweet, oval-shaped fruits of date palm trees. These grow in places that are warm.

date·line [date-*line*] *noun, plural* **datelines. 1.** *Geography.* an imaginary line drawn from the North Pole to the South Pole where the date changes by a day. West of the line it is one day later than east of the line.

Dates *grow in bunches beneath the long, feathery leaves of the date palm.*

2. a phrase at the beginning of a newspaper or magazine article that gives the date and place of when and where it was written. This word is also spelled **date line**.

daugh·ter [<u>daw</u>-tur] *noun, plural* **daughters.** the female child of a mother or father.

daughter-in-law [<u>daw</u>-tur-in-*law*] *noun, plural* **daughters-in-law.** the wife of a son.

dawn ▼ [dawn] *noun, plural* **dawns. 1.** the first light in the morning; daybreak. **2.** the start of something: *The dawn of the nuclear age occurred in 1945.*
verb, **dawned, dawning.** to become day.
• **dawn on.** to come to understand: *When he didn't call for so long, it finally dawned on her that he must have lost her phone number.*

day [day] *noun, plural* **days.**
1. the time between sunrise and sunset. The time when the sun rises is called **daybreak. 2.** a twenty-four-hour period. **3.** the part of a day spent doing an activity: *a day at the beach.* **4.** a certain period in history: *the days of the knights of the Middle Ages.*

day care a service that supervises and cares for children who are too young to go to school. This term is also spelled **daycare**.

day·dream [<u>day</u>-*dreem*] *noun, plural* **daydreams.**
a dreamlike thought or fantasy you have while still awake, often about something you especially want: *She had a daydream about being a famous movie star.*
verb, **daydreamed, daydreaming.** to think or fantasize about something: *Sometimes I daydream that I am living on a tropical island.*

day·light ▲ [<u>day</u>-*lite*] *noun.* **1.** the light from the Sun that shines during the day. **2.** daybreak; dawn: *My uncle gets up at daylight to milk the cows.* During summer, when the Sun rises early, some places put their clocks back an hour to take advantage of the extra daylight; they are on **daylight saving time.**

day·time [<u>day</u>-*time*] *noun.* the time when the light from the Sun shines on the Earth; daylight.

daze [daze] *verb,* **dazed, dazing.** to make unable to think or see things clearly; stun or confuse: *The fall from the bike dazed him.* If someone is stunned or confused they are described as **dazed.**
noun, plural **dazes.** the state of being stunned or confused: *After the accident, he wandered around in a daze.*

daz·zle [<u>daz</u>-ul] *verb,* **dazzled, dazzling. 1.** to blind temporarily with bright light: *After leaving the dark room, she was dazzled by the sunlight.* **2.** to surprise or impress greatly: *The teacher said I dazzled her with my brilliance.*

DC *or* **D.C.** an abbreviation for DIRECT CURRENT.

de- a prefix that means: **1.** to undo or do the opposite of: *demote* is the opposite of promote. **2.** to remove: *deregulate* means removing rules and regulations from something.

Sun's rays

Night

Sun

Day

Daylight *begins when your part of the world faces the Sun and is hit by the Sun's rays.*

dea·con [<u>dee</u>-kun] *noun, plural* **deacons.** *Religion.*
1. a church official who assists a minister. **2.** a rank of clergy just below a priest.

dead [ded] *adjective,* **deader, deadest. 1.** no longer alive; not living. **2.** without power or activity: *After the tornado, all the phones went dead; The mall is dead on Sunday afternoons.* **3.** total or exact: *She stood in the dead center of the field.*
adverb. **1.** completely: *After walking all day, they were dead tired.* **2.** straight or directly: *They saw a large ship dead ahead, coming right toward them.*
noun. **1.** the darkest or coldest time: *the dead of night; the dead of winter.* **2. the dead.** people who are no longer alive: *We offered a prayer for the dead.*

dead·en [<u>ded</u>-un] *verb,* **deadened, deadening.** to make dull or weak: *The injection deadened the terrible pain of my broken leg.*

dead end a road or passage that is blocked off at one end. This term is also spelled **dead-end**.

The sky turns golden at **dawn** *in the Southwest desert.*

*When a tornado sweeps through an area, it destroys buildings and trees in its path and leaves a trail of **debris**.*

dead·line [ded-*line*] *noun, plural* **deadlines.** a time limit; the time when something is due: *The deadline for our history project is Monday morning.*

dead·lock [ded-*lok*] *noun, plural* **deadlocks. 1.** a situation where two people or parties cannot come to agreement over something: *The two drama teachers were in a deadlock over who would direct the school play.* **2.** a lock that is opened by a key rather than by turning a latch. *verb,* **deadlocked, deadlocking.** to come to a point where two people or parties cannot agree.

dead·ly ▼ [ded-*lee*] *adjective,* **deadlier, deadliest. 1.** describing the ability of something or someone to cause death: *A loaded gun is a deadly weapon.* **2.** hateful or ill-wishing: *After their fight, the two girls became deadly enemies.*

deaf [def] *adjective,* **deafer, deafest. 1.** unable to hear or hear well: *My deaf cousin wears a hearing aid.* Someone who cannot hear suffers from **deafness. 2.** not wanting to hear something: *Her call for help fell on deaf ears.*

It is sometimes thought that it is more polite to say that someone is "hearing-impaired," rather than "deaf." However, the National Association of the Deaf and the World Federation of the Deaf say that the proper terms to use are either "deaf" or "hard of hearing," and that "hearing-impaired" should not be used.

*The **deadly** Australian funnel-web spider has two sharp fangs on its head.*

deaf·en [def-*un*] *verb,* **deafened, deafening.** to cause someone to lose their hearing: *The sound of the drilling was so loud, it deafened us all for a short time.* Something that causes you to lose your hearing is **deafening.**

deal [deel] *verb,* **dealt, dealing. 1.** to be about a particular topic: *The teacher wants our project to deal with the problem of air pollution.* **2.** to treat or act upon: *Mom said she would deal with us after we cleaned up the mess.* **3.** to trade or do business: *This company deals in toys as well as sports equipment.*

4. to give out: *Deal the cards carefully or they'll think you are cheating.*
noun, plural **deals.** an agreement or bargain: *We did a deal with Dad that if my sister and I do more work around the house, he will take us to the movies more often.*
• **a good/great deal.** a large amount: *She spent a great deal of the day doing homework.*

deal·er [dee-*lur*] *noun, plural* **dealers. 1.** someone who makes a living by buying and selling things: *a car dealer.* **2.** a person who hands out cards in a game.

dear [deer] *adjective,* **dearer, dearest. 1.** liking or loving something or someone: *my dear grandmother.* **2.** showing esteem or respect, usually in a letter: *Dear Carlo, thank you for the lovely gift.* **3.** expensive; costly: *Their clothes were too dear, so we looked in another store.*
noun, plural **dears.** someone you love or like: *What a dear you are for helping clean up.*
interjection. an exclamation of happiness or disappointment: *Oh dear! The cake is burning.* —**dearly,** *adverb.*
🔊 A different word with the same sound is **deer.**

death [deth] *noun, plural* **deaths. 1.** the end of being alive: *The death of a pet is always very sad.* If someone looks like they are close to death, you could describe them as looking **deathly** ill. **2.** the end of something: *If the time comes when everyone drives solar-powered cars, it will be the death of gas stations.*

de·bate [di-*bate*] *noun, plural* **debates.** an argument or discussion between people with different points of view: *a debate between two candidates for President.*
verb, **debated, debating. 1.** to argue or discuss something: *The parents' committee debated whether money should go to the new library.* **2.** to consider or think over: *He debated whether to try out for the school football team.* —**debater,** *noun.*

deb·it [deb-*it*] *noun, plural* **debits.** *Business.* an amount of money owed that is recorded in an account.
verb, **debited, debiting.** to take an amount of money out of something: *The bank debited our account by $100.*

deb·ris ▲ [duh-*bree*] *noun.* the remains of something that has been broken up: *The auto junkyard was filled with car parts, old tires, and other debris.*

debt [det] *noun, plural* **debts. 1.** something, usually money, owed to another person: *She was able to pay off her debt* after she was given money for her birthday. **2.** the state or condition of owing: *My brother has a debt, because he borrowed money from our grandparents.*

• **in debt.** owing money, thanks, or a favor to someone who has helped you: *We are in debt to you for helping our family.*

• **out of debt.** no longer owing money because it has been paid back: *When she made the last payment, she was finally out of debt.*

debt·or [det-ur] *noun.* someone who owes something to someone else.

de·but [day-byoo] *noun, plural* **debuts.** a first public performance or appearance: *Tonight he makes his debut as a professional singer.* A young woman who makes her first appearance in society, usually at a ball, is called a **debutante.** *verb,* **debuted, debuting.** to appear or do something in public for the first time.

*The sound made by a jet engine thirty feet away can reach 150 **decibels.***

dec·a·gon [dek-uh-gon] *noun, plural* **decagons.** *Mathematics.* a shape with ten sides and ten angles.

de·cal [dee-kal] *noun, plural* **decals.** a picture or design transferred to a transparent surface; a decorative sticker: *My sister put a butterfly decal on her bedroom window.*

de·cath·lon [di-kath-lon] *noun, plural* **decathlons.** an athletic event made up of ten different contests, including running, jumping, and throwing weights.

de·cay [di-kay] *noun, plural* **decays. 1.** a slow rotting of matter: *Brush your teeth if you don't want tooth decay.* **2.** a slow breakdown in condition or quality: *The house is in a state of decay because it is too costly to repair.* *verb,* **decayed, decaying.** to suffer from decay; break down slowly in condition or quality: *The fence is decaying and about to fall over.*

de·ceased [di-seest] *adjective.* no longer living; dead: *They named the baby after a deceased uncle.* A dead person or dead people are sometimes called **the deceased.**

de·ceit [di-seet] *noun, plural* **deceits.** the act or fact of lying or cheating: *He never tells the truth because he is full of deceit.* **—deceitful,** *adjective.*

de·ceive [di-seev] *verb,* **deceived, deceiving.** to mislead or lie to someone: *He deceived us by pretending to have no money for the bus fare.*

De·cem·ber [di-sem-bur] *noun.* the twelfth month of the year. December has 31 days.

de·cent [dee-sunt] *adjective.* **1.** thought of as being right or as it should be; respectable or proper: *The teacher said she expects decent behavior from us on the*

school bus trip. If your behavior is respectable or proper, you have acted with **decency. 2.** satisfactory or quite good: *He's not a great ballplayer, but he does a decent job.*

de·cep·tion [di-sep-shun] *noun, plural* **deceptions.** something meant to fool or mislead; a lie or trick: *The teacher said it was an act of deception to pretend I had broken my arm.* If you use a lie or a trick, you are being **deceptive.**

dec·i·bel ◀ [des-uh-bel] *noun, plural* **decibels.** *Science.* a unit that measures the loudness of a sound.

de·cide [di-side] *verb,* **decided, deciding. 1.** to make a choice: *She can't decide whether to wear the pink dress or the blue one.* **2.** to settle an argument or dispute: *The jury decided in favor of the defendant.*

de·ci·ded [di-side-id] *adjective.* without question; certain: *Pedro's enormous strength gave him a decided advantage in the wrestling match.* **—decidedly,** *adverb.*

de·cid·u·ous ▼ [di-sij-oo-us] *adjective. Biology.* describing a plant or tree that drops leaves in the fall and grows them back in spring: *Oaks are deciduous trees.*

The word **deciduous** comes from a Latin word meaning "to fall down" or "to fall off." This shows the main feature of deciduous trees, namely that their leaves fall off each year when colder weather comes at the end of the year.

Summer   Fall

December comes from the Latin word for "ten." The original Roman calendar had ten months, not twelve, and December was the tenth month. (March was the first.)

Spring   Winter

*The **deciduous** plane tree passes through four different stages from spring to winter.* **189**

*This veteran has been **decorated** for his service in war.*

dec·i·mal [des-uh-mul] *adjective.*
Mathematics. describing a system based
on the number 10. In the United States
and many other countries, money is based
on the **decimal system.**
noun, plural **decimals.** a number that is a
multiple of ten (such as 100 or 1,000) or a
number that is divided by 10. You can use
a **decimal point** (.) to describe the fraction
⁷/₁₀ as the decimal fraction 0.7.

de·ci·pher [di-sye-fur] *verb,* **deciphered,
deciphering. 1.** to work out the meaning of a
secret code. **2.** to work out the meaning of
something hard to read or understand: *I gave
my teacher the note but he could not decipher
my mother's handwriting.*

de·cis·ion [di-sizh-un] *noun, plural* **decisions.** the result or
act of making up your mind: *He came to the decision that
he would try for a part in the school play after all.*

de·ci·sive [di-sye-siv] *adjective.* **1.** doing something
that achieves a clear outcome: *They played so well
they won a decisive victory over their opponents.*
2. being determined or firm: *The decisive captain
chose his entire team in less than a minute.*
—**decisively,** *adverb;* —**decisiveness,** *noun.*

deck [dek] *noun, plural* **decks. 1.** the floor of a boat or ship.
2. an outdoor platform attached to a house: *There is a lovely
view from the deck upstairs.* **3.** a pack of playing cards.
verb, **decked, decking.** to decorate or dress up: *We decked
out the house with Christmas lights.*

dec·lar·a·tion [dek-luh-ray-shun] *noun, plural* **declarations.**
the act of announcing something: *a declaration of war;
a declaration of love.*

Declaration of Independence ▼ *History.*
the announcement that thirteen American colonies were
independent of Great Britain; made on July 4, 1776.

declarative sentence *Language.* a sentence
that declares something or makes a
statement. An example of a declarative
sentence is: *School starts tomorrow.*

de·clare [di-klare] *verb,* **declared, declaring.**
1. to announce something: *After years
of fighting, peace was finally declared.*
2. to say something firmly or forcefully:
*She declared she would get revenge if it
was the last thing she did.*

de·cline [di-kline] *verb,* **declined, declining.**
1. to refuse, usually in a polite manner:
to decline an invitation to a party.
2. to weaken or get worse: *Her health
declined after a second dose of the flu.*
noun, plural **declines. 1.** a weakening or
reducing of something: *The power of that country went
into decline after they lost the war.* **2.** a downward slope.

de·code [dee-kode] *verb,* **decoded, decoding.** to work out
the secret meaning of a code; decipher: *The teacher
decoded what our note really meant, and we got into
big trouble.*

de·com·pose [dee-kum-poze] *verb,* **decomposed,
decomposing.** *Environment.* to decay or rot:
*The vegetables and cut grass in the compost heap
decompose into soil.* Something that is decaying or rotting
is in a state of **decompostion.**

de·cor·ate ▲ [dek-uh-rate] *verb,* **decorated, decorating.**
1. to make more attractive by adding beautiful things.
She decorated her room with colorful ornaments. Someone
who decorates is called a **decorator. 2.** to give a medal or
badge to someone: *The captain decorated the private for
bravery above and beyond the call of duty.*

de·cor·a·tion [dek-uh-ray-shun] *noun, plural* **decorations.**
1. the act of decorating: *The decoration of the Christmas
tree took a long time.* **2.** something used to decorate;
an ornament. If an object
is used to decorate, it is
described as **decorative.**
3. a medal or badge:
*Of all his medals, he
was proudest of his
decoration for bravery
in battle.*

de·coy [dee-koy] *noun,*
plural **decoys. 1.** a model
or fake bird used by
hunters to attract real
birds: *The hunter set out
a decoy to lure the ducks
that were flying overhead.*
2. someone who leads
another into a trap
or ambush.
verb, **decoyed, decoying.**
to lead into a trap
or ambush.

DECLARATION OF INDEPENDENCE

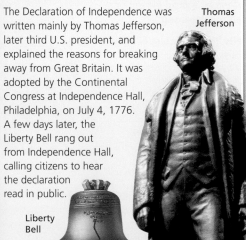

The Declaration of Independence was
written mainly by Thomas Jefferson,
later third U.S. president, and
explained the reasons for breaking
away from Great Britain. It was
adopted by the Continental
Congress at Independence Hall,
Philadelphia, on July 4, 1776.
A few days later, the
Liberty Bell rang out
from Independence Hall,
calling citizens to hear
the declaration
read in public.

Thomas
Jefferson

Liberty
Bell

Independence Hall, Philadelphia

Tube worms

Eelpout

Octopus

Mussels and giant clams

*Although there is no light in the **deepest** part of the ocean, some creatures have adapted to this cold, dark, still environment.*

de·crease [dee-krees *or* di-krees] *verb*, **decreased, decreasing.** to reduce or become less; become smaller: *to decrease the speed of a car; He's trying to decrease the amount of salt he puts on food.*
noun, plural **decreases. 1.** the act of becoming less: *There was a decrease in the number of miles people drove this month because of higher gas prices.*
2. the amount something is reduced by: *A decrease of fifty dollars makes that bike really good value.*

de·cree [di-kree] *noun, plural* **decrees.** an official announcement or order: *By decree of the king, everyone must bow to the princess.*
verb, **decreed, decreeing.** to order or make an official announcement.

ded·i·cate [ded-uh-kate] *verb,* **dedicated, dedicating.** to give or devote entirely to a special person, activity, or purpose: *She decided to dedicate her life to the church.* If you set something aside for a particular purpose, it as been **dedicated:** *a dedicated bus lane on the left side of the highway.*

ded·i·ca·tion [ded-uh-kay-shun] *noun, plural* **dedications. 1.** the act of setting something aside for a special person, activity, or purpose: *the dedication of a new school building.*
2. the act of focusing on an activity: *His dedication to the success of the team inspired all the other players.*

de·duct [di-dukt] *verb,* **deducted, deducting.** to take away from a total; subtract: *If I deduct 4 from 7, I get 3.*

de·duc·tion [di-duk-shun] *noun, plural* **deductions. 1.** the act of figuring something out; a conclusion based on the known facts: *The inspector made a series of deductions that led him to believe that he knew who had committed the crime.*
2. the act of subtracting; taking way from a total: *A deduction of five dollars was made from the price because the scooter had a bent wheel.*

deed [deed] *noun, plural* **deeds. 1.** an act or action: *She did a good deed by helping the old lady with her shopping.*
2. a legal document: *She produced the deed to her land to prove that she owned it.*

deep ▲ [deep] *adjective,* **deeper, deepest. 1.** going far down below the surface: *We dived into the deep part of the river.*
2. from front to back: *The yard is 100 feet wide and 200 feet deep.* **3.** intense or extreme: *to be deep in thought; She studied the swarming ants with deep interest.* **4.** hard to understand: *That book about different religions is too deep for me.* **4.** describing a low-pitched sound: *a deep voice.*
adverb. a long way: *The astronauts flew deep into space.*
—deeply, *adverb.*

deep·en [deep-un] *verb,* **deepened, deepening.** to become or make deeper.

deer ▼ [deer] *noun, plural* **deer.** a large, hoofed animal that runs fast and chews its cud. The males have antlers. Deer are related to moose, elk, and caribou.
🔊 A different word with the same sound is **dear.**

de·face [di-face] *verb,* **defaced, defacing.** to damage by changing the appearance of something: *The students defaced the library with spray paint.*

de·feat [di-feet] *verb,* **defeated, defeating.** to cause someone to lose; win a victory: *In the soccer game the Sharks defeated the Raiders 2–0.*
noun, plural **defeats.** the fact of being beaten or defeated.

de·fect [dee-fekt *or* di-fekt] *noun, plural* **defects.** something that is wrong; a weakness or flaw. *The clock never worked properly because of a defect when it was manufactured.*
verb. **defected, defecting.** to desert or move from one country or organization to another: *The Russian spy defected to America.* Someone who defects is called a **defector.**

*Male fallow **deer** shed their antlers every year and can weigh up to 220 pounds.*

de·fect·ive [di-fek-tiv] *adjective.* having something wrong; flawed, damaged, or not perfect as it should be: *If the washing machine is defective you can return it to the store for a refund.* **—defectively,** *adverb.*

A B C D E F G H I J K L M N O P Q R S T U V W X Y Z

def·end ▼ [di-<u>fend</u>] *verb,* **defended, defending.**
1. to protect or keep from danger: *The knights defended the castle from their enemies.* **2.** to act or argue in support of: *The lawyer defended the man accused of the crime.*
—**defender,** *noun.*

de·fen·dant [di-<u>fen</u>-dunt] *noun, plural* **defendants.**
Law. a person or group brought before a court and accused of a crime.

de·fense [di-<u>fens</u> *or* <u>dee</u>-fens]
noun, plural **defenses. 1.** the act of protecting from or resisting danger: *Their defense of the town crumbled under the army's attack.* To be without protection is to be **defenseless. 2.** a thing or person that protects: *The fort's defenses included a ditch and stockade.* **3.** the argument put forward to defend: *Her defense for taking the food from the store was that she was hungry.* **4.** players on a team that try to prevent the other team from scoring, as in soccer.

The Great Wall of China was built to **defend** *the Chinese kingdom from invaders from the north.*

de·fen·sive [di-<u>fen</u>-siv] *adjective.* **1.** protecting from harm: *Take defensive action against illness by eating fresh fruits and vegetables.* **2.** trying to keep the other team from scoring in a sport. —**defensively,** *adverb.*

de·fer[1] [di-<u>fur</u>] *verb,* **deferred, deferring.** to delay action until a later time: *I deferred going to the dentist until after our vacation.* The act of putting something off is **deferment.**

de·fer[2] [di-<u>fur</u>] *verb,* **deferred, deferring.** to give in to someone else's point of view or wishes out of respect: *Lauren deferred to Jack's decision not to go surfing as he could tell the waves were too rough.* The act of respectfully giving in is **deference.**

de·fi·ant [di-<u>fye</u>-unt] *adjective.* boldly opposing authority: *The defiant child stamped his foot and refused to go to bed.* A bold refusal of authority is called **defiance.**
—**defiantly,** *adverb.*

de·fi·cient [di-<u>fish</u>-unt] *adjective.* lacking something necessary: *She became sick because her diet is deficient in vitamins.* The fact of lacking something is called a **deficiency.**

def·i·cit [<u>def</u>-uh-sit] *noun, plural* **deficits. 1.** *Business.* an amount of money that is lacking: *We took too much money out of our bank account and had a deficit of ten dollars.* **2.** a lack or shortage: *The deficit of rain caused a drought.*

de·fine [di-<u>fine</u>] *verb,* **defined, defining.** to explain the meaning of: *Many thousands of words are defined in this dictionary.*

def·i·nite [<u>def</u>-uh-nit] *adjective.* absolute; clear: *She was definite that she wanted to come along with us.* —**definitely,** *adverb.*

definite article *Language.* the word *the,* which tells us something particular is being talked about.

def·i·ni·tion [def-uh-<u>nish</u>-un] *noun, plural* **definitions.** *Language.* a statement or an explanation of what a word or phrase means.

de·flate [di-<u>flate</u>] *verb,* **deflated, deflating. 1.** to release the air from something: *My bike went over a nail and the tire deflated.* **2.** to reduce in value or size: *His confidence deflated when he got a bad mark on the test.* —**deflation,** *noun.*

de·flect [di-<u>flekt</u>] *verb,* **deflected, deflecting.** to turn something aside from the direction it is traveling in: *The boxer shielded himself with his arms to deflect his opponent's blows.*

de·for·es·ta·tion ▼ [di-<u>for</u>-uh-<u>stay</u>-shun] *noun.* *Environment.* the act or process of removing all or most of the trees from a forest. —**deforest,** *verb.*

de·frost [di-<u>frawst</u>] *verb,* **defrosted, defrosting.** to remove frost or ice; thaw out: *Don't forget to defrost the chicken before you cook it.* —**defroster,** *noun.*

de·fy [di-<u>fye</u>] *verb,* **defied, defying. 1.** to refuse to obey: *The student defied her teacher's directions.* **2.** to dare or challenge someone to do a difficult thing: *He defied me to ride down the steep hill on my skateboard.* **3.** to strongly resist: *The rusty lock defied all attempts to open it.*

Deforestation *has created bare patches in this landscape.*

de·gree [di-<u>gree</u>] *noun, plural* **degrees. 1.** a stage in a process: *There are still fish in the lake, but the number is declining by degrees.* **2.** a level or amount: *That cake contains a high degree of fat.* **3.** a title awarded to a student on completing a university or college course. **4.** a unit of measurement for temperature: *Water freezes at 32 degrees Fahrenheit.* **5.** a unit of measurement for angles or arcs: *There are 360 degrees in a circle.*

degree-day *noun, plural* **degree-days.** *Environment.* a unit of measurement that calculates how much heating or cooling is required to keep a building at a comfortable temperature, usually 65 degrees Fahrenheit. For example, if a day has a high temperature of 67 degrees, a building must be cooled by two degrees to keep it at 65 degrees, which is termed two degree-days. This index allows energy needs to be estimated.

de·hy·drate [dee-<u>hye</u>-drate] *verb,* **dehydrated, dehydrating.** to remove moisture from; dry out: *If you ran for a long time in the hot sun, your body may become dehydrated.* The process of drying something out or the fact of losing too much moisture is called **dehydration.**

de·i·ty ▲ [<u>dee</u>-uh-tee] *noun, plural* **deities.** *Religion.* a god or goddess: *Zeus was the leader of the Greek deities.*

de·jec·ted [di-<u>jek</u>-tid] *adjective.* feeling sad, miserable: *The dejected girl realized nobody had remembered her birthday.* **—dejectedly,** *adverb.*

de·lay [di-*lay*] *verb,* **delayed, delaying. 1.** to put something off until later; postpone: *We will delay our visit until you are feeling better.* **2.** to slow down; cause to be late: *The car broke down and delayed his arrival.* *noun, plural* **delays.** the act of delaying or an instance of being late: *Fog caused the delay of several flights at the airport.*

del·e·gate [<u>del</u>-uh-git *for noun;* <u>del</u>-uh-*gate for verb*] *noun, plural* **delegates.** a person chosen to represent others: *We elected a delegate to speak for us at the meeting.* *verb,* **delegated, delegating.** to give someone the job of doing something: *His boss delegated the job of writing the report to him.*

del·e·ga·tion [del-uh-<u>gay</u>-shun] *noun, plural* **delegations. 1.** a group of people selected to represent others: *The delegation from France voted against the motion.* **2.** the act of delegating: *The delegation of the job was a big decision.*

de·lete [di-<u>leet</u>] *verb,* **deleted, deleting.** to strike out; erase, usually from something written: *He realized he had written "That was the the reason" and he deleted the second "the."* **—deletion,** *noun.*

de·lib·er·ate [duh-<u>lib</u>-rit *or* duh-<u>lib</u>-ur-ut *for adjective;* duh-<u>lib</u>-uh-*rate for verb*] *adjective.* **1.** done with purpose and consideration: *That was a deliberate act of cruelty.* The act of considering an action or decision is called **deliberation.** **2.** carefully and slowly: *She took deliberate steps while learning to roller-skate.* *verb,* **deliberated, deliberating.** to consider or discuss: *My parents deliberated whether or not to buy a new car.* **—deliberately,** *adverb.*

del·i·cate ▼ [<u>del</u>-uh-kut] *adjective.* **1.** finely made or soft; dainty: *She wore a delicate lace gown.* **2.** mild and pleasing: *This delicate perfume is not overpowering at all.* Something that is mild and pleasing to eat is called a **delicacy. 3.** easily weakened; fragile: *The old man has delicate health.* **4.** great care or skill: *Rescuing the men from the mine was a delicate operation.* **—delicately,** *adverb.*

This dragonfly has two pairs of **delicate** *wings.*

del·i·ca·tes·sen [*dcl*-uh-kuh-<u>tcs</u>-un] *noun, plural* **delicatessens.** a store specializing in selling foods that are already prepared, such as cheeses, cold meats, or salads.

> **Delicatessen** comes from the German language; delicatessen foods were very popular in this country. It came into English with the idea of "delicate foods." **Delicate** in this case means "good to eat."

de·li·cious [di-<u>lish</u>-us] *adjective.* tasting or smelling very pleasing: *May I have more of that delicious soup, please?* **—deliciously,** *adverb;* **—deliciousness,** *noun.*

de·light [di-<u>lite</u>] *noun, plural* **delights.** extreme pleasure or enjoyment; happiness: *The little boy shouted with delight when he saw his birthday presents.* *verb,* **delighted, delighting.** to give great pleasure or happiness: *The clown delighted the crowd with her antics.*

de·light·ful [di-<u>lite</u>-ful] *adjective.* causing much pleasure: *The orchestra played delightful music at the concert.* **—delightfully,** *adverb.*

del·ir·i·ous [di-<u>leer</u>-ee-us] *adjective.* **1.** confused and restless because of fever: *The delirious patient didn't know where he was.* **2.** wild with happiness; highly excited: *We were delirious with joy when we won a vacation.* **—deliriously,** *adverb.*

a b c d e f g h i j k l n o p q r s t u v w x y z

A B C **D** E F G H I J K L M N O P Q R S T U V W X Y Z

de·liv·er [di-<u>liv</u>-ur] *verb,* **delivered, delivering. 1.** to take something to a specified person or place: *The florist delivered the flowers to Jane's house.* **2.** to give with words; to pronounce: *The jury delivered a verdict of guilty.* **3.** to send to a target: *The pitcher delivered the ball to the batter.* **4.** to rescue or set free: *Deliver us from evil.*

de·liv·er·y [di-<u>liv</u>-ree *or* di-<u>liv</u>-uh-ree] *noun,* *plural* **deliveries. 1.** the act of taking something to a place or person: *I had to make the delivery to the customer right away.* **2.** the way of doing something: *Abraham Lincoln's delivery of the Gettysburg Address was very dramatic.*

del·ta 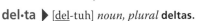 [<u>del</u>-tuh] *noun, plural* **deltas.**
1. the fourth letter of the Greek alphabet.
2. something similar in shape to the Greek capital letter delta (Δ); triangular: *The Concorde airplane had delta wings.* **3.** *Geography.* a lowland area where a river meets the sea and branches out into many channels. This area is often triangular in shape.

de·lu·sion [di-<u>loo</u>-zhun] *noun, plural* **delusions.** a false idea or belief; something imagined: *Her belief that I hated her was a delusion.*

de·mand [di-<u>mand</u>] *verb,* **demanded, demanding.**
1. to command; ask firmly: *Dad demanded that I clean my room.* **2.** to require; need: *Training a puppy demands patience.* Something that has high requirements is said to be **demanding.**
noun, plural **demands. 1.** the act of demanding: *The teacher's demand was that the class work silently.*
2. a great call for something: *Our bookstore can't keep up with the demand for that author's latest novel.*

dem·o·cra·cy 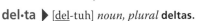 [di-<u>mok</u>-ruh-see] *noun,*
plural **democracies.** *Government* **1.** a type of government controlled by the people. Under this system, the people freely elect representatives who govern for them.
2. a nation governed in this way.

dem·o·crat [<u>dem</u>-uh-krat] *noun, plural* **democrats.**
Government. **1.** a person who agrees with the democratic system. A person who belongs to the Democratic Party in the United States is called a **Democrat.**
2. someone who believes all people are equal and deserve equal rights.

The Greek word for "people" is *demos.* This term was chosen for words like **democracy** and **democratic** because they refer to government by the people, rather than by a king or dictator.

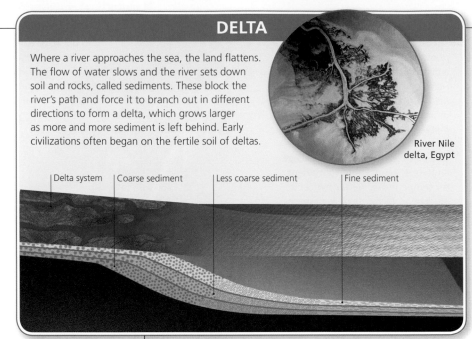

DELTA

Where a river approaches the sea, the land flattens. The flow of water slows and the river sets down soil and rocks, called sediments. These block the river's path and force it to branch out in different directions to form a delta, which grows larger as more and more sediment is left behind. Early civilizations often began on the fertile soil of deltas.

River Nile delta, Egypt

Delta system | Coarse sediment | Less coarse sediment | Fine sediment

dem·o·cra·tic [dem-uh-<u>krat</u>-ik] *adjective.* **1.** having to do with democracy or a democracy: *We have democratic elections in our country.* Something having to do with the U.S. Democratic Party is described as **Democratic.**
2. believing in equal rights: *It would be democratic to ask everyone what they want.* **—democratically,** *adverb.*

Democratic Party one of the two major national political parties in the United States of America, along with the Republican Party.

de·mol·ish [di-<u>mol</u>-ish] *verb,* **demolished, demolishing.** to knock down and break up; destroy: *The earthquake demolished the building.* The act of knocking down or destroying is called **demolition.**

de·mon [<u>deem</u>-un] *noun, plural* **demons. 1.** an evil spirit; devil. Someone or thing which is like a devil is **demonic.**
2. someone who does something with great energy or enthusiasm: *He ran like a demon in the race.*

Public meetings in ancient Athens were the start of modern **democracy.**

dem·on·strate [<u>dem</u>-un-*strate*] *verb,* **demonstrated, demonstrating. 1.** to show, describe, explain, or prove something: *We conducted an experiment to demonstrate the properties of oxygen.* **2.** to show feelings about something by participating in a public meeting or march: *We demonstrated against the closing of our local school.* Someone who does this is a **demonstrator.**

de·mon·stra·tion ▶ [<u>dem</u>-un-<u>stray</u>-shun] *noun, plural* **demonstrations. 1.** something that shows, explains, describes, or proves: *The librarian gave us a demonstration of how to use the on-line catalog.* **2.** a public gathering, such as a march or meeting, to show feelings about an issue: *The demonstration left the mayor in no doubt as to people's feelings.*

demonstrative pronoun *Language.* a word that stands for a noun and also determines which thing, person, or idea is being talked about and how far away it is. The main demonstrative pronouns are *this, that, these,* and *those.*

den [den] *noun, plural* **dens. 1.** an animal's shelter for sleeping or resting in: *Female polar bears make hollows in the ice for their dens.* **2.** a quiet room usually used for studying or reading. **3.** in Cub Scouts, a group of eight to ten members.

de·ni·al [di-<u>nye</u>-ul] *noun, plural* **denials.** the act of saying something is untrue or rejecting something: *Sally was firm in her denial of the crime.*

den·im [<u>den</u>-im] *noun.* a strong cotton cloth, especially used for work and casual clothes such as jeans. Pants or overalls made of this cloth are called **denims.**

> **Denim** comes from the French expression *de Nimes,* which means "of the town of Nimes." Nimes is a city in southern France where the cloth known as *denim* was made.

de·nom·in·a·tion [di-*nom*-uh-<u>nay</u>-shun] *noun, plural* **denominations. 1.** a distinctive religious group where several congregations have the same beliefs and practices. **2.** a class of something in a series: *The one-cent coin is the smallest denomination in United States currency.*

den·om·in·a·tor [di-<u>nom</u>-uh-*nay*-tur] *noun, plural* **denominators.** *Mathematics.* in a fraction, the number below the line. This number is the amount of equal parts by which a whole is divided. For example, in ¾, 4 is the denominator.

de·note [di-<u>note</u>] *verb,* **denoted, denoting. 1.** to show or be a sign of: *Dark shadows under the eyes denote tiredness.* The act or fact of showing something is called **denotation. 2.** to mean: *The prefix "bi" in a word denotes two, such as the two wheels of a bicycle.*

de·nounce [di-<u>nouns</u>] *verb,* **denounced, denouncing. 1.** to speak out against: *We denounced the plan to build an apartment block on the park.* **2.** to accuse or inform against: *The traitor denounced his country to his captors.*

dense [dens] *adjective,* **denser, densest.** closely packed; thick: *The dense smoke made us choke.* The fact of being dense is **density.** —**densely,** *adverb.*

dent [dent] *noun, plural* **dents.** a hollow or impression made in a surface: *The accident made a large dent in the door of our car.*
verb, **dented, denting.** to make an impression or hollow in something: *Don't bang the table or you will dent it.*
• **make a dent in.** to do a significant amount of a task: *I finally made a dent in the paperwork I had to do.*

Crowds gather to make their feelings known in a peace **demonstration***.*

den·tal [<u>den</u>-tul] *adjective.* **1.** having to do with teeth: *Dental cavities can be painful.* **2.** having to do with dentists and their work. A soft, waxed thread used to clean between teeth is called **dental floss.**

den·tin ▼ [<u>den</u>-tin] *noun. Biology.* a hard, bonelike material that teeth are mostly made out of. This material lies under the tooth's enamel and is sensitive to heat, cold, and touch. This word is also spelled **dentine.**

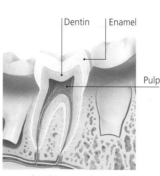
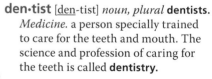

Dentin | Enamel

Pulp

Dentin *lies between the tooth's enamel and the soft pulp.*

den·tist [<u>den</u>-tist] *noun, plural* **dentists.** *Medicine.* a person specially trained to care for the teeth and mouth. The science and profession of caring for the teeth is called **dentistry.**

den·ture [<u>den</u>-chur] *noun, plural* **dentures.** a plate with false teeth attached worn in the mouth. A complete set of false teeth for both upper and lower jaws is called **dentures.**

den·y [di-<u>nye</u>] *verb,* **denied, denying. 1.** to say something is not true: *Tanya denied that she had taken my book.* **2.** to say no to; refuse: *The teacher denied us permissionto leave the room.*

de·o·dor·ant [dee-<u>oh</u>-duh-runt] *noun, plural* **deodorants.** something that blocks or covers unpleasant smells: *Wear underarm deodorant when you play sports.*

de·part [di-<u>part</u>] *verb,* **departed, departing. 1.** to go away; leave: *The train departed at noon.* **2.** to change from a usual pattern; to vary: *I departed from my normal route home from school.*

a b c d e f g h i j k l m n o p q r s t u v w x y z

A
B
C
D
E
F
G
H
I
J
K
L
M
N
O
P
Q
R
S
T
U
V
W
X
Y
Z

de·part·ment [di-<u>part</u>-munt] *noun,* *plural* **departments.** a section of a large organization such as a government, university, hospital, or company: *When Luis broke his leg he went to the hospital's X-ray department.*

department store a large store that sells a variety of goods organized and sold in separate sections.

de·par·ture [di-<u>par</u>-chur] *noun,* *plural* **departures.** a setting out, the act of leaving: *Our star player's departure from the team was disappointing.*

de·pend [di-<u>pend</u>] *verb,* **depended, depending. 1.** to rely on someone or something: *I depended on you to be there on time.* **2.** to rely on for support or care: *The patient depended on the nurses while she got better.* **3.** to be determined by: *Whether we win the league or not depends on today's game.* —**dependence,** *noun.*

de·pen·da·ble [di-<u>pen</u>-duh-bul] *adjective.* that may be depended on; reliable: *Allan was given the job as he is very dependable.* —**dependably,** *adverb.*

de·pict ▲ [di-<u>pikt</u>] *verb,* **depicted, depicting.** to show or describe, either in pictures or words: *The novel depicts life in San Francisco just after the famous earthquake.* —**depiction,** *noun.*

de·port [di-<u>port</u>] *verb,* **deported, deporting.** to make a person leave a country, usually to return to the country they came from: *The immigrant was deported after he was convicted of a crime.* The act of forcibly sending someone from a country is called **deportation.**

Jockeys vie for first place in the Kentucky **Derby.**

de·pos·it [di-<u>poz</u>-it] *verb,* **deposited, depositing. 1.** to put away for safekeeping, usually in a bank: *Maggie deposited the diamond in a safe.* **2.** to put something down: *The waves deposited timber from the shipwreck on the shore.* *noun,* *plural* **deposits. 1.** something put away for safekeeping: *He made a deposit of ninety dollars in his bank account.* **2.** something left as partial payment or promise to pay: *We hired a canoe and left a deposit of ten dollars.* **3.** a layer of material in the ground, especially minerals: *The deposits of gold were too small to be worth mining.*

de·press [di-<u>pres</u>] *verb,* **depressed, depressing. 1.** to lower or press down: *To make the car go faster, you depress the gas pedal.* **2.** to lower the spirits; sadden: *Gray skies depress me.*

de·pres·sion [di-<u>presh</u>-un] *noun,* *plural* **depressions. 1.** *Medicine.* a mental condition involving extreme feelings of despair and hopelessness. **2.** a shallow hole; a hollow: *There was a depression in the bed where the cat had been*

Artists in ancient Egypt **depicted** *their gods on wall paintings in tombs and temples.*

sleeping. **3.** *Business.* a period when business activity slows and stocks lose a lot of their value. The **Great Depression** of the 1920s and 1930s was an extreme case of this and caused much hardship worldwide.

de·prive [di-<u>prive</u>] *verb,* **deprived, depriving.** to take away or keep from having; withhold: *In the United States women were deprived of the right to vote until 1920.* The fact of having something withheld or the act of depriving is called **deprivation.**

depth [depth] *noun,* *plural* **depths. 1.** the distance downward or inward; the fact or amount of being deep. *The ocean here has a depth of about one mile.* The deepest part of something is termed the **depths. 2.** the intensity of something, especially color or feeling: *Parents have a great depth of feeling for their children.*
• **in depth.** in great detail: *He interviewed the celebrity in depth.*

dep·u·ty [<u>dep</u>-yuh-tee] *noun,* *plural* **deputies. 1.** someone appointed to act instead of another: *The mayor was ill, so the deputy mayor led the meeting in his place.* **2.** someone who acts as an assistant to another, especially an officer of the law. To appoint someone as a deputy is to **deputize** them.

der·by ▲ [<u>dur</u>-bee] *noun,* *plural* **derbies. 1.** a stiff, felt hat with a rounded crown and narrow brim. **2.** a horse race: *The Kentucky Derby was first run in 1875.*

The Epsom **Derby** is a famous horse race that has been held in England for hundreds of years. (In British English, the word is said as "<u>dar</u>-bee" and not "<u>dur</u>-bee" as it is in the U.S.) The Kentucky Derby in the United States takes its name from this race. The *derby* hat is so called because men often wore such hats when they went to watch a Derby horse race.

de·rive [di-<u>rive</u>] *verb,* **derived, deriving. 1.** to come from something or somewhere else; originate: *That movie was derived from a book.* **2.** to take from something: *Grandma derives pleasure from knitting.*

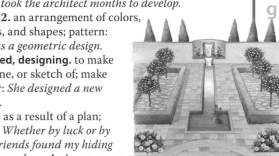

*The **derrick** of an offshore oil well is built on the seafloor and most of the structure is under the sea.*

der·rick ▶ [der-ik] *noun, plural* **derricks.**
1. a machine used to move heavy objects. It consists of a movable arm attached to a fixed post. **2.** the tower-like framework that stands over a drill hole, especially oil wells, to support drilling equipment.

> **Derrick** comes from the name of a man who lived in London about 1600. He was a hangman for the government (someone who executed condemned criminals by hanging them by the neck). The first meaning of the word *derrick* was a place for hanging criminals.

de·scend [di-send] *verb,* **descended, descending. 1.** to go downward: *Descend the ladder slowly.* **2.** to have as your ancestor or origin: *Thanksgiving descends from the traditions of the early settlers in America.*

de·scend·ant [di-send-unt] *noun, plural* **descendants.**
a person or thing that comes from a particular ancestor, group, or source: *His descendants all have the same shaped nose.*

de·scent [di-sent] *noun, plural* **descents. 1.** the act of going downward: *the descent of a plane in order to land.* **2.** a downward slope: *The attic stairs have a steep descent.* **3.** one's ancestral heritage or origins: *I am of Russian and Hungarian descent.*
🔊 A different word with the same sound is **dissent.**

de·scribe [di-skribe] *verb,* **described, describing.** to give a picture of in written or spoken words: *Sam described what happened when he fell off his bike.*

des·crip·tion [di-skrip-shun] *noun, plural* **descriptions. 1.** a picture of something in written or spoken words: *She gave the police an accurate description of the car.* **2.** a kind, type, or sort: *Lisa has flowers of every description in her garden.*

de·scrip·tive [di-skrip-tiv] *adjective.* picturing in words: *His descriptive letter made me feel I had seen Mexico as well.* A **descriptive adjective** describes a noun.

de·seg·re·ga·tion [dee-seg-ruh-gay-shun] *noun. Law.* the doing away with a system in which different races have separate schools and other public facilities. To **desegregate** is to end such a system.

des·ert¹ ▶ [dez-urt] *noun, plural* **deserts.** *Environment.* a very dry region lacking enough rainfall to grow many or any plants.

de·sert² [di-zurt] *verb,* **deserted, deserting.** to leave a person or thing without intending to return: *Because the turtle's mother had deserted it, I took it to be cared for at a wildlife shelter.* The act of leaving a person or thing in this way is **desertion.** —**deserter,** *noun.*
🔊 A different word that sounds like this is **dessert.**

de·ser·ted [di-zurt-id] *adjective.* **1.** describing a feeling of being abandoned; forsaken: *She felt deserted when her teammates voted her out of the competition.* **2.** without inhabitants; *The town has been deserted since the mine closed down.*

de·serve [di-zurv] *verb,* **deserved, deserving.** to be worthy of; have a claim to: *This book deserves to be read and read again.* Something worthy of praise, attention, or assistance is **deserving.**

de·sign ▶ [di-zine] *noun, plural* **designs.**
1. a drawing or plan made to serve as a pattern from which to work: *The design for the house took the architect months to develop.*
2. an arrangement of colors, details, and shapes; pattern: *The quilt has a geometric design.*
verb, **designed, designing.** to make a plan, outline, or sketch of; make a pattern for: *She designed a new family room.*
• **by design.** as a result of a plan; on purpose: *Whether by luck or by design, my friends found my hiding place in the woods.* —**designer,** *noun.*

*This formal garden has a symmetrical **design.***

des·ig·nate [dez-ig-nate] *verb,* **designated, designating. 1.** to point or mark out; indicate; show: *Red paint on the curb designates a no parking zone.* **2.** to give a formal title or name; describe as: *Montana has designated the grizzly bear as its state animal.* **3.** to appoint to a particular position: *He was designated captain of the football team.* —**designation,** *noun.*

DESERTS

Deserts are extremely dry regions found in subtropical areas, on the dry side of mountains, and in the center of continents. Plants and animals have adapted to survive in deserts. Cactuses can store water, and lizards can alter the color of their skin to reflect more or less heat. Not all deserts are hot—the Atacama in northern Chile is quite cool, while the Gobi of central Asia can be freezing.

Leopard gecko

Camel train, Sahara Desert

designated hitter a player in baseball who bats in place of the pitcher.

de·sir·able [di-zire-uh-bul] *adjective.* worth having or seeking; pleasing: *Being a movie star is a highly desirable job.* —**desirably,** *adverb.*

de·sire [di-zire] *verb,* **desired, desiring.** to wish for strongly; want very much: *to desire happiness. noun, plural* **desires.** a strong wish; a longing: *My mother's greatest desire is for peace and quiet at home.*

desk [desk] *noun, plural* **desks.** a piece of furniture with a flat or sloped surface, where a person can read, write, or use a computer.

desk·top [desk-top] *noun, plural* **desktops.** *Computers.* the main area of a computer screen. The desktop contains symbols that represent programs or files. **Desktop publishing** is the production of printed material using a desktop computer and a special program. *adjective.* designed to be used on a desk.

des·o·late ▼ [des-uh-lut] *adjective.* **1.** not lived in; deserted: *The old house was desolate.* **2.** very sad; dismal: *She was desolate after losing her job.* —**desolation,** *noun.*

The surface of the dwarf planet Pluto is cold, barren, and **desolate.**

de·spair [di-spair] *noun.* the loss of all hope. *verb,* **despaired, despairing.** to lose hope; be without hope: *Our team despaired of ever winning a game.*

des·per·ate [des-pur-it] *adjective.* **1.** willing to take any risk because all hope is gone: *Police warned of a desperate criminal on the loose.* **2.** extremely serious or hopeless: *a desperate illness.* The fact of being desperate is **desperation.** —**desperately,** *adverb.*

de·spise [di-spize] *verb,* **despised, despising.** to look down on with scorn; dislike very much: *I despise the way she lied about what happened.* Deserving to be considered in this way is described as **despicable.**

de·spite [di-spite] *preposition.* in spite of: *He ran in the race despite a knee injury.*

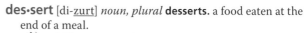

The **destruction** *caused by a major earthquake makes it hard to find survivors.*

des·sert [di-zurt] *noun, plural* **desserts.** a food eaten at the end of a meal.
🔊 A different word that sounds like this is **desert.**

des·ti·na·tion [des-tuh-nay-shun] *noun, plural* **destinations.** the place where someone is going or where something is being sent: *The package took a week to reach its destination.*

des·tine [des-tun] *verb,* **destined, destining.** to choose or intend for a particular use or purpose: *The money is destined for the famine relief fund.* Having to do with being chosen or intended for a particular use or purpose is **destined:** *He seemed destined for the priesthood.*

des·ti·ny [des-tuh-nee] *noun, plural* **destinies.** what happens or will happen to someone, especially when those events seem to be determined beforehand; fate: *She believed it was her destiny to become a teacher like her father.*

de·stroy [di-stroy] *verb,* **destroyed, destroying.** to bring great damage to; wreck completely: *An atomic bomb destroyed Hiroshima.*

de·stroy·er ▶ [di-stroy-ur] *noun, plural* **destroyers.** a small, fast, naval ship.

de·struc·tion ▲ [di-struk-shun] *noun, plural* **destructions.** the act or fact of destroying: *The tornado left a trail of destruction behind it.*

de·struc·tive [di-struk-tiv] *adjective.* causing destruction: *Our town suffered the most destructive storm in over thirty years.* —**destructively,** *adverb.*

A modern **destroyer** *has a crew of around 300 and carries missiles and large guns.*

de·tach [di-<u>tach</u>] *verb,* **detached, detaching.** to unfasten and separate: *The Apollo lunar module was detached from the command module before landing on the Moon.* Having to do with showing no emotional involvement or bias in a situation is **detached:** *a detached observer.* —**detachment,** *noun.*

de·tail [di-<u>tale</u> *or* <u>dee</u>-tale] *noun, plural* **details. 1.** a small individual fact or item: *Please give me all the details of how the accident happened.* **2.** a considering of all matters one by one: *We have not had a chance to discuss her behavior in detail.* Containing a lot of detail is **detailed.** *verb,* **detailed, detailing. 1.** to describe or report fully: *The principal detailed his plans for the year.* **2.** to clean a car inside and out.

de·tect [di-<u>tekt</u>] *verb,* **detected, detecting.** to find evidence of; notice or discover: *This device will detect any motion near the door and cause it to open.* —**detection,** *noun.*

de·tec·tive [di-<u>tek</u>-tiv] *noun, plural* **detectives.** a person whose work is to discover who committed crimes. *adjective.* of or relating to detectives and their work: *detective novels.*

de·tec·tor [di-<u>tek</u>-tur] *noun, plural* **detectors.** a device that detects a particular object or substance, such as smoke or radioactivity.

de·ten·tion [di-<u>ten</u>-shun] *noun.* the punishment of being kept after school or having to come to school early.

de·ter [di-<u>tur</u> *verb,* **deterred, deterring.** to discourage from doing something: *Rain and hail did not deter us from setting out on our vacation.* Something that discourages someone from doing something is a **deterrent.**

de·ter·gent [di-<u>tur</u>-junt] *noun, plural* **detergents.** a powder or liquid used for washing things.

de·te·ri·or·ate [di-<u>teer</u>-ee-uh-<u>rate</u>] *verb,* **deteriorated, deteriorating.** to become gradually worse: *The rubber on my bike's tires has deteriorated over the years.* —**deterioration,** *noun.*

de·ter·min·a·tion [di-<u>tur</u>-muh-<u>nay</u>-shun] *noun, plural* **determinations. 1.** firmness of purpose: *He has a lot of determination to succeed.* **2.** the process of settling or deciding beforehand: *The town council came to a determination about where the new road would go.* **3.** the process of discovering something by checking or observing: *The trial judge will reach a determination after hearing all the evidence.*

de·ter·mine [di-<u>tur</u>-min] *verb,* **determined, determining. 1.** to decide or settle firmly: *My parents determined that I should go to a different school.* **2.** to discover by checking or observing: *Counting tree rings is one way to determine a tree's age.* **3.** to be the cause of: *What determines the sex of a baby?*

de·ter·mined [di-<u>tur</u>-mind] *a djective.* having firmness of purpose; showing determination: *Despite the noisiness of the meeting, she was determined to stand up and state her point of view.*

de·test [di-<u>test</u>] *verb,* **detested, detesting.** to dislike strongly: *I detest spiders.*

det·o·nate [<u>det</u>-uh-<u>nate</u>] *verb,* **detonated, detonating.** to cause to explode: *Sparks from the brush fire threatened to detonate the oil drums.* A device used to set off explosives or a bomb is a **detonator.** —**detonation,** *noun.*

de·tour [<u>dee</u>-toor] *noun, plural* **detours.** a longer way to get somewhere than the usual route: *We followed a detour that took us away from the blocked freeway.* *verb,* **detoured, detouring.** to cause to make a detour: *A burst water main in the road made us detour around the town center.*

dev·as·tate ▼ [<u>dev</u>-uh-<u>state</u>] *verb,* **devastated, devastating. 1.** to cause severe damage; destroy: *San Francisco was devastated by an earthquake in 1906.* **2.** to shock; upset: *He was devastated when his mother died.* Having to do with being severely damaged or upset is **devastated.** —**devastation,** *noun.*

After the eruption of Mount Pinatubo in the Philippines in 1991, a mudflow **devastated** *the area and killed 600 people.*

de·vel·op [di-<u>vel</u>-up] *verb,* **developed, developing. 1.** to come or bring gradually into existence: *Scientists are developing a robot that acts like a human.* **2.** to grow or make grow: *Cycling develops your leg muscles.* **3.** to make available; put to use: *The council wants to develop the vacant lot into a shopping mall.* A **developer** is a person or company that buys land for the purpose of building on it. **4.** to treat photographic film with chemicals to make an image appear.

de·vel·oped [di-<u>vel</u>-upt] *adjective. Government.* having a high standard of living and a high level of industrial production. Canada is an example of a **developed nation.**

de·vel·op·ing [di-<u>vel</u>-up-ing] *adjective. Government.* having a low standard of living and a low level of industrial production; underdeveloped. Haiti is an example of a **developing nation.**

de·vel·op·ment [di-<u>vel</u>-up-munt] *noun, plural* **developments. 1.** the process or act of developing: *We studied the development of the frog, from tadpole to adult.* **2.** an occurrence or event: *What are the latest developments in your grandfather's illness?* **3.** a large area of land with new, similar-looking houses or other buildings on it.

a b c d e f g h i j k l m n o p q r s t u v w x y z

*A stethoscope is a medical **device** used to listen to heartbeats and other sounds in the body.*

de·vice ▶ [di-*vise*] *noun,* *plural* **devices.**
1. a machine or tool designed for a particular purpose. A camera, a battery, and a computer are devices.
2. a scheme or plan; trick: *She often used her limp as a device for getting sympathy.*
• **leave to one's own devices.** to allow someone to do as they wish: *Left to my own devices I wouldn't bother doing homework.*

Dev·il [*dev*-ul] *noun. Religion.* the major spirit of evil; Satan. A **devil** is any evil spirit, or an evil or badly behaved person.

de·vise [di-*vize*] *verb,* **devised, devising.** to plan or invent; think out: *Our teacher has devised a new test for us.*

de·vote [di-*vote*] *verb,* **devoted, devoting.** to give time, attention, or effort to a cause or purpose: *He devoted his evenings to guitar practice.*

de·vot·ed [di-*voh*-tid] *adjective.* very loving or loyal: *a devoted husband.* —**devotedly,** *adverb.*

de·vo·tion [di-*voh*-shun] *noun, plural* **devotions.** a deep love or loyalty: *the devotion of a dog to its master.* Prayers or other religious observances are **devotions.**

de·vour [di-*vowr*] *verb,* **devoured, devouring. 1.** to eat hungrily; consume: *The lions devoured the zebra.*
2. to ruin completely; destroy: *The fire devoured most of the forest.*

dew ◀ [doo] *noun,* *plural* **dews.** drops of water that form on grass, trees, and other outdoor surfaces during the night. Dew comes from moisture in the air.
🔊 Different words with the same sound are **do** and **due.**

Dew forms when air near the ground becomes saturated with water vapor.

di·a·be·tes [*dye*-uh-*beet*-eez *or* *dye*-uh-*bee*-tus] *noun. Health.* a disease in which the body cannot control the level of sugar in the blood. Diabetes results from the body being unable to make or use enough insulin, a substance that maintains proper sugar levels. A **diabetic** is someone who has this disease.

di·a·bol·ic [*dye*-uh-*bol*-ik] *adjective.* very evil or cruel: *The police stopped the terrorists' diabolic plot.* Something that is very bad or shocking is **diabolical.** —**diabolically,** *adverb.*

di·ag·nose [*dye*-ig-*nohs*] *verb,* **diagnosed, diagnosing.** *Medicine.* to form an opinion about what is wrong with a sick person or animal after making an examination: *The doctor diagnosed her as having the flu.*

di·ag·no·sis [*dye*-ig-*noh*-sis] *noun, plural* **diagnoses.** *Medicine.* an opinion about what is wrong with a sick person or animal formed after making an examination. Having to do with diagnosing is described as **diagnostic.**

di·ag·o·nal [*dye*-*ag*-uh-nul] *adjective.* sloping away from a straight line; slanting: *This butterfly has diagonal markings on its wings.* *noun, plural* **diagonals.** *Mathematics.* a straight line that joins the opposite corners of a rectangle or square. —**diagonally,** *adverb.*

di·a·gram [*dye*-uh-*gram*] *noun, plural* **diagrams.** a drawing that shows the parts of something or explains how it works: *a diagram of an automobile engine.* Having the form of such a drawing is **diagrammatic.** *verb,* **diagramed, diagraming.** to make a diagram of; show using a diagram.

di·al ▶ [*dye*-ul] *noun,* *plural* **dials. 1.** the part of an instrument that displays a measurement such as time, pressure, or speed. **2.** a device on some television sets or radios for tuning in to a television or radio station. **3.** the numbered disk on older telephones that is rotated by the finger when a call is made. *verb,* **dialed, dialing.** to control or select by using a television, radio, or telephone dial.

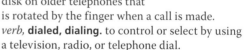

Dials on this medieval clock in Prague, Czech Republic, measure the time in different ways.

di·a·lect [*dye*-uh-lekt] *noun, plural* **dialects.** *Language.* a form of language that is spoken by a certain group of people or in a certain region. —**dialectal,** *adjective.*

A **dialect** is like a language in that both are a way of speaking used by a large number of people. The distinction is that two languages are so different that a person speaking one language cannot understand the other language without special training; for example, English and French. Two dialects are part of the same language and, even though they may be different in certain ways, people who use one dialect can understand the other; for example, American English and British English.

di·a·logue [*dye*-uh-log] *noun, plural* **dialogues.** the act or fact of talking to other people; conversation, especially in a book, play, or movie: *There is almost no dialogue in the first part of the movie.*

dial tone the sound made by a telephone to show that a number may be dialed.

*Colorless and pale **diamonds** are valued as gemstones, and the darker ones are used in industry.*

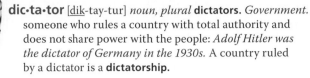

di·a·me·ter [dye-<u>am</u>-uh-tur] *noun, plural* **diameters.** *Mathematics.*
1. a straight line passing from side to side through the center of a circle or sphere. **2.** the length of this line; the width or thickness of a round object or shape: *The diameter of the basketball is about nine inches.*

di·a·mond ▶ [<u>dye</u>-mund *or* <u>dye</u>-uh-mund] *noun, plural* **diamonds. 1.** a clear or pale precious stone, made up of crystals of pure carbon. It is the hardest naturally occurring substance. **2.** a figure with four sides and four angles that is shaped like a diamond. **3.** a playing card marked with a red diamond shape. **4. diamonds.** the suit of cards marked with this shape. **5.** on a baseball field, the area inside the lines that connect the bases.

dia·per [<u>dye</u>-pur *or* <u>dye</u>-uh-pur] *noun, plural* **diapers.** a piece of soft, folded cloth or other material used as underwear for a baby.
verb, **diapered, diapering.** to put a diaper on.

di·a·phragm [<u>dye</u>-uh-*fram*] *noun, plural* **diaphragms.**
1. *Biology.* a curved layer of muscles separating the abdomen from the chest. The diaphragm plays a major role in breathing. **2.** a thin disk, used in microphones and telephones, that changes electrical signals into sound or sound into electrical signals.

di·a·ry [<u>dye</u>-ree *or* <u>dye</u>-uh-ree] *noun, plural* **diaries.** a written record of the daily events and thoughts of a person's life: *My diary is for my own eyes only.*

dice [dise] *plural noun, singular* **die.** small cubes of plastic, wood, or other material with the sides marked with from one to six dots. Dice are used in some games.
verb, **diced, dicing.** to cut into small cubes: *Add the diced carrots.*

dic·tate [<u>dik</u>-tate] *verb,* **dictated, dictating. 1.** to say or read something aloud for someone else to write down: *The teacher dictated a math problem to the class.*
2. to order with authority; impose: *The victors dictated the surrender terms to the defeated army.*
noun, plural **dictates.** an order or rule that is to be carried out: *I follow the dictates of my boss.* —**dictation,** *noun.*

dic·ta·tor [<u>dik</u>-tay-tur] *noun, plural* **dictators.** *Government.* someone who rules a country with total authority and does not share power with the people: *Adolf Hitler was the dictator of Germany in the 1930s.* A country ruled by a dictator is a **dictatorship.**

dic·tion·ar·y [<u>dik</u>-shuh-ner-ee] *noun, plural* **dictionaries.** a book that lists the words of a language in alphabetical order, and gives information about them. A dictionary can be used to find out a word's meaning, spelling, and pronunciation.

People will often say, "Look it up in the dictionary" or "The dictionary defines this word as such and such." This makes it sound like there is just one dictionary, <u>the</u> dictionary, or at least that all dictionaries would agree on the meaning of a certain word. Some words do have an exact meaning that will be given in the same way in all dictionaries, such as the words for months of the year. However, for most of the words in the English language, different dictionaries will have definitions that are not quite the same, and they will not even enter all of the same words.It can be interesting to read them and note the differences.

did [<u>did</u>] the past tense of DO.

didn't [<u>did</u>-unt] the shortened form of "did not."

die¹ [dye] *verb,* **died, dying. 1.** to stop living: *The dog died after being hit by a truck.*
2. to become less strong; stop: *the storm died away.*
3. to want very much: *I was dying to go for a swim.*
◀)) A different word with the same sound is **dye.**

die² [dye] *noun, plural* **dice.** a small cube used in some games. See DICE.
◀)) A different word with the same sound is **dye.**

Heavy trucks and some cars use **diesel** *as their fuel.*

The diesel engine is named for Rudolph **Diesel,** a German engineer who invented in the 1890s. His name is also used in several other ways having to do with this. For example, **diesel fuel** is the kind of fuel used in this engine, and the **diesel cycle** is the way that this engine runs.

die·sel ▲ [<u>dee</u>-zul] *noun, plural* **diesels.** *Science.* **1.** a heavy oil used as a fuel. **Diesel fuel** is a form of petroleum.
2. a vehicle, especially a locomotive, with an engine that burns diesel fuel. In a **diesel engine,** heat produced by the compression of air in the engine is used to set the fuel on fire.

di·et ◀ [<u>dye</u>-ut] *noun, plural* **diets.**
1. the food and drink that a person or animal usually eats: *Koalas live on a diet of eucalyptus leaves.* **2.** a restricted range of food and drink: *a vegetarian diet.*
verb, **dieted, dieting.** to eat a restricted range of foods: *He lost thirty pounds by dieting.*

*Giant pandas are herbivores whose **diet** consists only of certain kinds of bamboo.*

A
B
C
D
E
F
G
H
I
J
K
L
M
N
O
P
Q
R
S
T
U
V
W
X
Y
Z

di·e·ti·tian [dye-uh-<u>tish</u>-un] *noun, plural* **dietitians.** *Health.* a person whose job is to give advice about food and eating. Most dietitians work in hospitals or schools. This word is also spelled **dietician.**

dif·fer [<u>dif</u>-ur] *verb,* **differed, differing. 1.** to be unlike; not be the same or similar: *Both cars are made by Ford, but they differ greatly in price.* **2.** to fail to agree: *My friends and I differed about which movie to see.*

dif·fer·ence [<u>dif</u>-runcs *or* <u>dif</u>-ur-uns] *noun, plural.* **differences. 1.** the condition of being unlike: *There is a big difference between seeing photos of the Grand Canyon and actually being there.* **2.** a way in which someone or something is unlike: *The twins look very much alike, but there are certain differences in the way they act.* **3.** a dispute or disagreement: *The children had a difference over who owned the toy.* **Differences** are instances or causes of a dispute or disagreement. **4.** *Mathematics.* what is left after subtracting one number from another; remainder: *The difference between 23 and 16 is 7.*

dif·fer·ent [<u>dif</u>-runt *or* <u>dif</u>-uh-runt] *adjective.* **1.** not the same; unlike; dissimilar: *We have very different ways of looking at things.* **2.** having to do with being separate: *I visited my brother in the hospital at different times on the same day.* —**differently,** *adverb.*

dif·fi·cult [<u>dif</u>-uh-*kult*] *adjective.* **1.** needing much effort or skill; hard: *Pushing the car up the hill was a difficult task for them.* **2.** not easy to please or get along with: *The new boss is a difficult man.*

dif·fi·cul·ty [<u>dif</u>-uh-*kul*-tee] *noun, plural* **difficulties. 1.** the fact of being hard to do; being difficult: *Some people exaggerate the difficulty of arithmetic.* **2.** something that is hard to do, deal with, or understand: *The firefighters had difficulty rescuing a woman trapped inside the burning building.*

dig ▼ [dig] *verb,* **dug, digging. 1.** to break up and move something, especially earth, with a spade, the hands, or claws: *We have to dig the car out of the snow.* **2.** to obtain or create by digging: *to dig potatoes from a field.*

DIGESTIVE SYSTEM

Our digestive system carries food to various organs for processing and the removal of nutrients. Starting at the mouth food travels down the esophagus to the stomach, then on to the small intestine and the large intestine. Finally, up to 24 hours after the start of this journey, the unwanted "leftovers" pass out of the body through the rectum. Along the way the pancreas, gall bladder, and liver help in the digestion process.

Esophagus
Liver
Stomach
Pancreas
Small intestine
Large intestine
Rectum

3. to search for information: *Police work involves a lot of digging through files.* **4.** to thrust or push: *He dug his feet into the ground.*
noun, plural **digs. 1.** a gentle push or poke: *I give her a dig to get her attention.* **2.** *Science.* a place where scientists, such as archaeologists, look for remains of ancient people or places: *an archaeological dig.* —**digger,** *noun.*

di·gest [dye-<u>jest</u> for verb; <u>dye</u>-jest for noun] *verb,* **digested, digesting.** to change food in the mouth, stomach, and intestine into substances that the body can absorb and use. *noun, plural* **digests.** a summary of material from a document or book: *Reading a digest saves a lot of time.*

di·ges·tion [dye-<u>jes</u>-chun] *noun, plural* **digestions.** the process of changing food into substances that the body can absorb and use. Digestion begins in the mouth and ends in the intestines.

di·ges·tive [dye-<u>jes</u>-tiv] *adjective.* relating to or aiding digestion: *The stomach contains powerful digestive juices.*

digestive system ▲ *Biology.* the system that changes food so that the body can use it. The digestive system in humans includes the mouth, the stomach, the intestines, and particular chemicals that act to break down the food.

dig·it [<u>dij</u>-it] *noun, plural* **digits.** *Mathematics.* **1.** any of the numerals from 1 to 9 and usually the numeral 0. **2.** a finger, toe, or claw: *How many digits does a dog have on each paw?*

dig·i·tal [<u>dij</u>-uh-tul] *adjective. Science.* showing or using information represented by numerical digits: *The alarm of my digital clock wakes me every morning.* A **digital computer** works by processing information represented by the digits 1 and 0. —**digitally,** *adverb.*

dig·i·tize [<u>dij</u>-uh-*tize*] *verb,* **digitized, digitizing.** *Computers.* to convert sound, pictures, or other data into a form that can be processed by a computer. —**digitization,** *noun.*

On a **dig** *in the desert, archaeologists excavate for evidence from the past.*

*A nineteen-mile **dike** was built in the Netherlands to hold back the sea.*

dig·ni·fy [dig-ni-*fye*] *verb,* **dignified, dignifying.**
1. to give dignity to; make worthy of respect: *The war memorial dignified the soldiers who lost their lives.* **2.** to treat someone or something with respect or honor when that is not deserved: *To dignify his rude remark with an answer will only draw more attention to it.* Showing respect for oneself or behaving in a serious, controlled manner is **dignified.**

dig·ni·ty [dig-nuh-tee] *noun, plural* **dignities.** the confident outward show of one's sense of worth: *The teacher kept her dignity even when the children were rude to her.*

dike ▲ [dike] *noun, plural* **dikes.** a bank of earth or a dam built to stop flooding by a river or sea.

di·lap·i·da·ted ▶ [duh-*lap*-uh-*day*-tid] *adjective.* partly ruined or decayed; broken down: *The dilapidated log cabin looked like it was about to collapse.*

> The Latin word for "stone" is *lapis.* The word **dilapidated** comes from this, with the idea that something that is dilapidated looks like it has been knocked to pieces by having stones thrown at it.

di·lem·ma [duh-*lem*-uh] *noun, plural* **dilemmas.** a problem that involves making a difficult choice between two or more things: *The President's dilemma was whether to raise taxes or cut government services.*

dil·i·gent [*dil*-uh-junt] *adjective.* careful and hard-working: *He was a diligent student and deserved his high grades.* **—diligently,** *adverb.*

di·lute [dye-*lute* or duh-*lute*] *verb,* **diluted, diluting.** to make weaker or thinner by adding a liquid: *She diluted the bleach by adding some water.* **—dilution,** *noun.*

dim [dim] *adjective,* **dimmer, dimmest. 1.** not giving or having much light: *The room was too dim for me to be able to read.* **2.** not clearly visible or distinct: *The ship was just a dim outline in the heavy fog.* **3.** not clear to the eyes, ears, or mind: *I had only a dim notion of what was going on in class.* *verb,* **dimmed, dimming.** to make or become dim.

Dinghies *are useful for traveling short distances in calm water.*

dime [dime] *noun, plural* **dimes.** a ten-cent coin in the United States and Canada.

di·men·sion [duh-*men*-shun] *noun, plural* **dimensions.**
1. size as measured in height, length, or width: *Airlines have strict rules about the dimensions of carry-on luggage.* **2.** importance or extent: *The cost of health care is a problem of national dimensions.* Having to do with such measurements is **dimensional.**

di·min·ish [duh-*min*-ish] *verb,* **diminished, diminishing.** to make or become less: *A traffic accident did not diminish my brother's love of driving.*

di·min·u·tive [duh-*min*-yuh-tiv] *adjective.* extremely small: *Their kitchen is diminutive.*

dim·mer [dim-ur] *noun, plural* **dimmers.** a device for varying the brightness of an electric light or automobile headlight: *I used the dimmer to make the room less bright.*

*This **dilapidated** house is gradually falling into ruins.*

dim·ple ▼ [dim-pul] *noun, plural* **dimples.** a small dent or hollow in the surface of something: *The little girl's cheeks formed dimples when she smiled.* *verb,* **dimpled, dimpling.** to produce or show dimples: *The rain dimpled the surface of the lake.*

din [din] *noun, plural* **dins.** a loud, prolonged noise: *The children at the party made a terrible din.*

dine [dine] *verb,* **dined, dining.** to eat dinner: *We usually dine at six o'clock in the evening.*

din·er [dye-nur] *noun, plural* **diners.**
1. a person eating a meal.
2. a small restaurant with a long counter and booths, serving cheap meals: *Mom often has her lunch at the local diner.*

din·ghy ◀ [ding-ee] *noun, plural* **dinghies.** a small rowboat: *He filled the inflatable dinghy with supplies and rowed out to the sailboat.*

din·ing room a room used for serving and eating meals. A small dining area is a **dinette.**

din·ner [din-ur] *noun, plural* **dinners.**
1. the main meal of the day, usually eaten in the evening. **2.** a formal meal that honors a person or special occasion.

*When he smiles, this boy has **dimples** on both sides of his mouth.*

di·no·saur ▶ [dye-nuh-sore] *noun, plural* **dinosaurs.** one of the group of long-tailed reptiles that died out millions of years ago. They lived on land, walking on either two or four feet.

> The word **dinosaur** comes from a Greek phrase meaning "the terrible lizard" or "frightening lizard." This word was first used by the British scientist Richard Owen in 1841. Even though these animals lived millions of years ago, they were not really recognized as dinosaurs until the early 1800s. At first it was thought that they were a type of giant lizard, which is why Owen chose the name "terrible lizard."

di·o·cese [dye-uh-sis *or* dye-uh-sees] *noun, plural* **dioceses.** *Religion.* a church district and the people who live within it, under the authority of a bishop.

dip [dip] *verb,* **dipped, dipping. 1.** to put into a liquid briefly: *He dipped the ice cream in melted chocolate.* **2.** to plunge into water, then get out quickly. **3.** to lower and then quickly raise again: *to dip a flag as a sign of respect.* **4.** to slope downward: *The road dipped suddenly just before the bridge.* *noun, plural* **dips. 1.** the act of dipping: *They went to the lake and jumped in for a quick dip.* **2.** a solution into which something is dipped: *The farmer put the sheep in the dip to kill their parasites.* **3.** a sinking or drop: *a dip in stock prices.* **4.** a thick, savory sauce into which crackers and vegetables are dipped.

diph·the·ria [dif-*theer*-ee-uh *or* dip-*theer*-ee-uh] *noun. Health.* a serious contagious disease with a high fever, in which the throat and nose are coated in a thin membrane, making it hard to breathe.

di·plo·ma ▶ [duh-*ploh*-muh] *noun, plural* **diplomas.** *Education.* an official document that a school or college awards to a graduating student to show that he or she has succeeded in a course of study.

*Students receive a **diploma** when they graduate.*

dip·lo·mat [dip-luh-*mat*] *noun, plural* **diplomats. 1.** *Government.* a person whose work is to manage relations between countries. **2.** a person who can deal tactfully with people or difficult situations, without hurting feelings: *My brother always acts the diplomat to stop my sister and me from fighting.*

dip·lo·mat·ic [dip-luh-*mat*-ik] *adjective.* **1.** relating to diplomats: *The two countries have spent months in diplomatic negotiations.* **2.** good at handling people or difficult situations; tactful: *Dad didn't want to upset Grandma, so he said something diplomatic about her burnt cookies.* —**diplomatically,** *adverb.*

dip·per [dip-ur] *noun, plural* **dippers.** a long-handled cup used for taking up liquids. The **Big Dipper** is the seven bright stars of the constellation Ursa Major, which form a shape like a dipper in the night sky. The **Little Dipper** is the seven bright stars of the constellation Ursa Minor, which also form a dipper shape.

di·rect [di-*rekt*] *verb,* **directed, directing. 1.** to control or manage; guide: *During the fire drill, the teachers directed us in how to leave the building.* **2.** to organize and guide the way a movie, play, or other performance is made: *Mrs. Jackson, the drama teacher, directed the school play.* **3.** to officially order; command: *The judge directed the witness to answer the question.* **4.** to aim in a certain direction or at a certain place: *The firefighters directed the water at the most intense part of the fire.* *adjective.* **1.** going in a straight line or by the shortest possible way: *If I walk the direct way home, I don't stop off at the shops.* **2.** straight to the point; candid and frank: *Please just give us a direct answer: yes or no?* *adverb.* straight; without stopping, turning, or diverting.

direct current *Science.* a steady electric current that flows only in one direction. A battery has a direct current.

di·rec·tion [di-*rek*-shun] *noun, plural* **directions. 1.** the fact of directing; guidance, supervision, or instruction. **2.** the line along which something moves, lies, faces, or points: *We walked in opposite directions.* **3.** an instruction or order on how to do something: *Take the medicine according to the directions on the bottle.*

di·rect·ly [di-*rekt*-lee] *adverb.* **1.** in a direct way, line, or manner; straight: *He looked me directly in the eye and asked if I was lying.* **2.** without delay; immediately: *Turn that music down directly!*

direct object *Language.* the person or thing in a sentence that is directly acted upon by the verb. In the sentence *She ate cake,* the direct object is the noun "cake" because the verb "ate" directly acts upon it.

di·rec·tor [di-*rek*-tur] *noun, plural* **directors. 1.** any person who directs something. **2.** a person who supervises the creation of a performance, such as the making of a movie. **3.** *Business.* a person who controls the running of a company. A person with a position as a director of a company has a **directorship.**

di·rec·tor·y [di-*rek*-tuh-ree] *noun, plural* **directories.** an alphabetical list of names and addresses: *I looked up Juan's address in the telephone directory.*

dir·i·gi·ble [dir-uh-juh-bul] *noun, plural* **dirigibles.** a large aircraft with gas-filled sections to make it float. It is propelled by a motor, and can be steered.

dirt [durt] *noun.* **1.** mud, stains, or any other substance that makes something unclean. **2.** loose earth or soil: *The dog digs holes in the dirt, then buries its bones.*

dirt·y [durt-ee] *adjective,* **dirtier, dirtiest. 1.** not clean: *I packed the dirty dishes in the dishwasher.* **2.** not honest or decent; unfair, low, or mean: *The other team kept tripping us; they were really dirty players.* **3.** hostile or resentful; angry: *Don't be dirty with me just because you don't get your own way.* **4.** obscene or indecent: *a dirty joke.*

DINOSAURS

Dinosaurs walked the Earth for about 150 million years during the Triassic, Jurassic, and Cretaceous periods of an age known as the Mesozoic era. They lived on every continent, some growing as big as jumbo jets, others as small as chickens. Some ate meat, while others ate plants. Many could walk upright on their two hind legs. This allowed them to grow bigger, walk further, and move faster than any other reptiles. Others, like the plant-eating sauropods, moved on all fours. While dinosaurs ruled the land, their distant cousins, marine reptiles and pterosaurs, dominated the sea and skies. It is thought that dinosaurs were wiped out suddenly by a huge volcanic disaster or giant meteorite.

Allosaurus skull

TRIASSIC PERIOD, 248–208 MILLION YEARS AGO

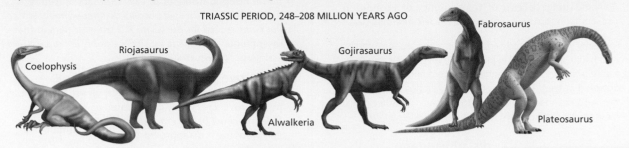

Riojasaurus

Coelophysis

Gojirasaurus

Fabrosaurus

Alwalkeria

Plateosaurus

JURASSIC PERIOD, 208–144 MILLION YEARS AGO

Archaeopteryx

Giraffatitan

Stegosaurus

Scelidosaurus

Diplodocus

Dilophosaurus

CRETACEOUS PERIOD, 1-44–65 MILLION YEARS AGO

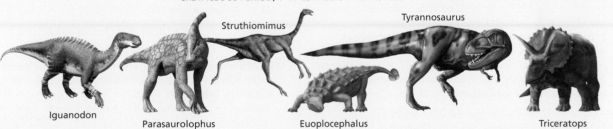

Struthiomimus

Tyrannosaurus

Iguanodon

Parasaurolophus

Euoplocephalus

Triceratops

Sauropod

Pterosaur

The end of dinosaurs

Theropod

dis- a prefix that means: **1.** not or opposite: to *dislike* something means to not like it. **2.** lack of: *disunity* means a lack of unity.

dis·a·bil·i·ty [*dis*-uh-<u>bil</u>-uh-tee] *noun, plural* **disabilities.** a lack of strength, power, or ability in part of the body or brain, which makes it hard for a person to do some things.

dis·a·ble [dis-<u>ay</u>-bul] *verb,* **disabled, disabling.** to remove ability; to cripple or make something stop working.

dis·a·bled ▼ [dis-<u>ay</u>-buld] *adjective.* not being able to do some things because of illness, injury, or a condition present from birth: *A skiing accident left him disabled.*

For many years the word *handicapped* was used for someone who had a serious physical problem. Then people came to feel that this was not quite the right word and began to use **disabled** instead. The idea is that *handicapped* sounds like the person cannot do certain things, while in fact they may do these things, but just have to do them in a different way.

Disabled athletes compete in many sports, including wheelchair racing.

dis·ad·van·tage [*dis*-ud-<u>van</u>-tij] *noun, plural* **disadvantages. 1.** something that makes a situation more difficult; a handicap: *The strained muscle was a serious disadvantage for the runner.* **2.** a loss or damage; harm: *Playing the final game away from home worked to our disadvantage.* **—disadvantageous,** *adjective.*

dis·a·gree [*dis*-uh-<u>gree</u>] *verb,* **disagreed, disagreeing. 1.** to have a different opinion: *She says a mile isn't too far to walk, but I disagree.* **2.** to quarrel; argue: *The boys disagreed angrily about whose turn it was.* **3.** to be different; not be like: *Linda did the math problem three times and so did I, but our answers still disagreed.* **4.** to cause discomfort; have a bad effect on: *Too much fried food disagrees with me.*

dis·a·gree·a·ble [*dis*-uh-<u>gree</u>-uh-bul] *adjective.* **1.** not likable; unpleasant: *Washing the kitchen floor is the most disagreeable household job I have to do.* **2.** likely to quarrel or be bad-tempered; unfriendly: *My sister is always disagreeable when she gets up in the morning.* **—disagreeably,** *adverb.*

dis·a·gree·ment [*dis*-uh-<u>gree</u>-munt] *noun, plural* **disagreements. 1.** a difference of opinion: *The oil company president and the scientist were in total disagreement with each other about global warming.* **2.** a quarrel or argument: *They had a huge disagreement and never spoke to each other again.*

dis·ap·pear [*dis*-uh-<u>peer</u>] *verb,* **disappeared, disappearing. 1.** to go out of sight: *We waved until the train disappeared round the bend.* **2.** to cease to exist; go away or end completely: *My anger disappeared the minute she said she was sorry.*

dis·ap·pear·ance [*dis*-uh-<u>peer</u>-uns] *noun, plural* **disappearances.** the act of disappearing: *After their cat's disappearance, they searched everywhere for him.*

dis·ap·point [*dis*-uh-<u>point</u>] *verb,* **disappointed, disappointing.** to fail to live up to someone's hopes or wishes: *The trip to the beach disappointed us because it rained all day.* When a person or thing doesn't behave as expected, it is **disappointing.**

dis·ap·point·ment [*dis*-uh-<u>point</u>-munt] *noun, plural* **disappointments. 1.** the act or fact of feeling disappointed: *I can't get over my disappointment at not being picked for the team.* **2.** a thing or person that disappoints: *The movie we saw was a big disappointment —it wasn't funny at all.*

dis·ap·prove [*dis*-uh-<u>proov</u>] *verb,* **disapproved, disapproving.** to have a bad opinion of; say to be wrong; not approve: *Everybody disapproved of her decision to leave school before graduating.* The act or state of disapproving is **disapproval.**

dis·arm [dis-<u>arm</u>] *verb,* **disarmed, disarming.** to take weapons away from a person: *They disarmed the soldiers who surrendered.* The act of disarming, especially when a country reduces the number of its weapons or the size of its armed forces, is **disarmament.**

dis·as·ter ▼ [di-<u>zas</u>-tur] *noun, plural* **disasters. 1.** a sudden event that causes great suffering and destruction: *The hurricane left a trail of disaster.* **2.** a complete failure; something very unsuccessful: *The camping trip turned into a disaster after Rob broke his leg.* Something that is very bad or very unsuccessful is **disastrous. —disastrously,** *adverb.*

dis·be·lief [dis-bi-<u>leef</u>] *noun, plural* **disbeliefs.** a refusal to believe; doubt about the truth of something: *Mom looked at my brother in disbelief when he offered to do the laundry for her.*

disc [disk] *noun, plural* **discs. 1.** a phonograph record. **2.** another spelling of DISK.

dis·card [dis-<u>kard</u>] *verb,* **discarded, discarding.** to throw away: *The food and drink containers that people had discarded littered the street.* *noun, plural* **discards.** a thing that has been thrown away or rejected.

*The eruption of Mount Vesuvius in AD 79 was a **disaster** for the people of nearby Herculaneum.*

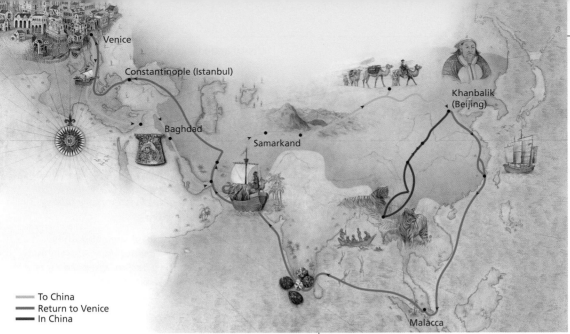

In 1271, Marco Polo left Venice on a journey of **discovery** *that took him across mountains, deserts, and seas to China.*

Venice
Constantinople (Istanbul)
Baghdad
Samarkand
Khanbalik (Beijing)
Malacca

To China
Return to Venice
In China

dis·charge [dis-<u>charj</u>] *verb*, **discharged, discharging.**
1. to let go or release; dismiss: *The hospital discharged Grandma five days after her operation.* **2.** to shoot or fire: *The gun discharged accidentally.* **3.** to give off or let out: *The chimney discharged gases into the atmosphere.*
noun, plural **discharges. 1.** release or dismissal from service or a job: *A soldier who commits a serious offense and must leave the army is given a dishonorable discharge.* **2.** the act of firing a weapon.

dis·ci·ple [di-<u>sye</u>-pul] *noun, plural* **disciples. 1.** a follower of a set of ideas, a person, or a person's teachings: *She is a disciple of the latest dance craze, and is trying to teach all the girls how to do it.* **2.** also, **Disciple.** one of the first twelve followers of Jesus.

dis·ci·pline [<u>dis</u>-uh-plin] *noun, plural* **disciplines.**
1. training that develops good conduct or behavior: *Schools hope their discipline will create good students and good citizens.* **2.** punishment that corrects or trains someone. Having to do with punishment is **disciplinary.**
3. a subject of study: *The scientific disciplines include physics, chemistry, and biology.*
verb, **disciplined, disciplining. 1.** to train in obedience and control: *A professional ice skater must discipline her mind and body.* **2.** to punish: *He was disciplined for stealing.*

dis·close [dis-<u>kloze</u>] *verb,* **disclosed, disclosing.** to make known; reveal: *Don't disclose your address or phone number to strangers on the Internet.* The act of revealing something is a **disclosure.**

dis·col·or [dis-<u>kul</u>-ur] *verb,* **discolored, discoloring.** to change or spoil the color of: *I spilled spaghetti sauce on my white shirt and now it's discolored.*

dis·com·fort [dis-<u>kum</u>-furt] *noun, plural* **discomforts.** the fact of feeling uncomfortable or uneasy; lack of comfort: *Sometimes Grandpa complains about the discomfort from his arthritis.*

dis·con·nect [*dis*-ki-<u>nekt</u>] *verb,* **disconnected, disconnecting.** to break the connection of; undo or separate: *I was disconnected from the Internet and couldn't get on again until this morning.* A person who feels **disconnected** feels detached and alone, not connected to others or the world.

dis·con·tent·ed [*dis*-kun-<u>ten</u>-tid] *adjective.* not contented; restless and dissatisfied: *I feel discontented because I'm bored and I've got nothing to do.*

dis·con·tin·ue [*dis*-kun-<u>tin</u>-yoo] *verb,* **discontinued, discontinuing.** to stop a product or service; put an end to: *They discontinued the newspaper delivery for a month while they were away.* —**discontinuation,** *noun.*

dis·count [<u>dis</u>-kownt] *noun, plural* **discounts.** *Business.* an amount taken off the usual price: *They give you a discount of twenty dollars on each pair of shoes you buy.* A **discount store** sells its products more cheaply than the usual price.

dis·cour·age [dis-<u>kur</u>-ij] *verb,* **discouraged, discouraging.**
1. to make less positive or confident: *He got really discouraged when he failed the test.* **2.** to try to prevent a person from doing something: *Her parents discouraged her from parachuting because it was dangerous.* Results that are **discouraging** make a person feel less confident about his or her abilities.

dis·cour·te·ous [dis-<u>kurt</u>-ee-us] *adjective.* lacking courtesy; rude or impolite: *It is discourteous not to give an elderly person your seat on the train.*

dis·cov·er [dis-<u>kuv</u>-ur] *verb,* **discovered, discovering.**
1. to find or learn about something for the first time: *Gold was first discovered in California in 1848.*
2. to realize or notice; come upon: *I discovered I was good at volleyball.*

dis·cov·er·y ▲ [dis-<u>kuv</u>-ree *or* dis-<u>kuv</u>-uh-ree] *noun, plural* **discoveries. 1.** the act of finding or learning about something for the first time: *The discovery of a cure for cancer would save millions of lives.* **2.** something that is found or found out for the first time: *The mission to Mars has made an important discovery.*

a b c d e f g h i j k l m n o p q r s t u v w x y z

A
B
C
D
E
F
G
H
I
J
K
L
M
N
O
P
Q
R
S
T
U
V
W
X
Y
Z

Throwing a **discus** *was one of the contests in the ancient Olympic Games, which began in Greece more than 2,700 years ago.*

dis·creet [dis-<u>kreet</u>] *adjective.* tactful with other people; avoiding embarrassment: *When our neighbor's son was arrested we were discreet and did not tell other people.* A person who acts in this way is acting with **discretion**. —**discreetly,** *adverb.*

dis·crim·i·nate [dis-<u>krim</u>-uh-*nate*] *verb,* **discriminated, discriminating. 1.** to treat people badly or unfairly because of their religion, sex, or ethnic background: *It is against the law in the U.S. to discriminate against black people in selling or renting a home.* To treat people in this way is called **discriminatory. 2.** to notice the difference between two or more things: *Can you discriminate between butter and margarine?*

dis·crim·i·na·tion [*dis*-krim-i-<u>nay</u>-shun] *noun.* **1.** the act of discriminating on the basis of religion, sex, or ethnic background: *No discrimination is allowed when considering people for employment.* **2.** the act of seeing differences between things, especially good from bad.

dis·cus ▲ [<u>dis</u>-kus] *noun, plural* **discuses.** a flat, heavy, round object that is thrown as far as possible in a track-and-field sports event.

dis·cuss [dis-<u>kus</u>] *verb,* **discussed, discussing.** to consider something from different points of view; talk about: *The committee will discuss plans for the new school library.*

dis·cus·sion [dis-<u>kush</u>-un] *noun, plural* **discussions.** the act of talking about things or exchanging information: *The meeting between the parents and teachers produced a lively discussion.*

dis·ease [duh-<u>zeez</u>] *noun, plural* **diseases. 1.** an unhealthy condition in people, animals, or plants: *Doctors today can treat many diseases with drugs.* **2.** a specific illness: *Her mother has heart disease.* A **diseased** part of the body is one affected by a disease.

dis·fa·vor [dis-<u>fay</u>-vur] *noun.* lack of favor; dislike or disapproval: *The school looked with disfavor on the idea of charging students to use the library.*

dis·grace [dis-<u>grase</u>] *noun, plural* **disgraces. 1.** a loss of respect or honor: *The disgrace of being found guilty was awful.* **2.** the fact of something or someone causing a loss of respect: *The state of our school buildings is a disgrace.* *verb,* **disgraced, disgracing.** to bring about a loss of honor or respect: *Police who take bribes from criminals disgrace the whole police force.*

dis·grace·ful [dis-<u>grase</u>-ful] *adjective.* bringing dishonor or a loss of respect: *His disgraceful behavior at the dance had everyone talking.* —**disgracefully,** *adverb.*

dis·guise ▼ [dis-<u>gize</u>] *verb,* **disguised, disguising. 1.** to change the appearance of someone or something to hide their true identity: *The man disguised his face by wearing a beard and eyeglasses.* **2.** to hide the real situation: *She could not disguise the fact she was angry with me.* *noun, plural* **disguises.** the fact of having changed one's appearance or identity.

dis·gust [dis-<u>gust</u>] *noun.* a strong feeling of dislike caused by a smell or sight of something unpleasant: *The sight of the dead animal filled me with disgust.* *verb,* **disgusted, disgusting.** to cause a strong feeling of dislike or disappointment: *I felt disgusted when we lost the game.*

dish [dish] *noun, plural* **dishes. 1.** a plate or bowl from which food is served: *Please pass the dish of vegetables.* **2.** food cooked or prepared in a special way: *Paella is a Spanish seafood dish.* *verb,* **dished, dishing.** to serve food quickly or in large quantities: *We dished up the food as we were all hungry.*

A mask and costume provide a good **disguise** *at the annual Carnivale in Venice, Italy.*

dis·hon·est [dis-<u>on</u>-ist] *adjective.* not honest; having a tendency to cheat. Someone who is not honest is guilty of **dishonesty.**

dis·hon·or [dis-<u>on</u>-ur] *noun, plural* **dishonors.** the fact of losing honor or good name: *For him, being stripped of the math prize for cheating was a great dishonor.* *verb,* **dishonored, dishonoring.** to bring shame on; disgrace.

dis·hon·or·a·ble [dis-<u>on</u>-ur-uh-bul] *adjective.* not honorable; shameful. —**dishonorably,** *adverb.*

dish·wash·er [<u>dish</u>-wash-ur] *noun, plural* **dishwashers. 1.** a machine that automatically washes pots and pans, plates, knives, forks, and spoons. **2.** a person whose job is washing these things.

dis·il·lu·sion [dis-i-<u>loo</u>-zhun] *verb,* **disillusioned, disillusioning.** to free someone from a belief they hold, causing disappointment: *It was disillusioning to hear later that the story he had told us was all lies.* Someone who experiences this feeling is **disillusioned.**

dis·in·fect [*dis*-in-<u>fekt</u>] *verb*, **disinfected, disinfecting.** to destroy germs in or on something with a chemical.

dis·in·fect·ant [*dis*-in-<u>fek</u>-tunt] *noun, plural* **disinfectants.** *Health.* a chemical used to kill the germs or bacteria that can cause illness.

dis·in·te·grate [dis-<u>in</u>-tuh-*grate*] *verb*, **disintegrated, disintegrating.** to break up into a number of smaller pieces: *The huge explosion caused the building to disintegrate.* The process of breaking up in this way is called **disintegration.**

dis·in·ter·est·ed [dis-<u>in</u>-tuh-*res*-tid] *adjective.* able to act fairly because no personal gain or advantage is involved: *As he does not know any of the people in the contest, he is disinterested.*

English has two similar words formed from the word *interest*, *disinterested* and *uninterested*. To be strictly correct, these should be used in different ways. If you are *uninterested* in something, you don't care about it, you have no interest in what happens. If you are **disinterested,** you are fair, you don't take sides, but you do care about it. In other words, the referee of a soccer game should be *disinterested* (not favoring one team or the other) but should not be *uninterested* (paying no attention to the game).

disk [disk] *noun, plural* **disks. 1.** a flat, round object. **2.** *Computers.* a thin, hard, round piece of plastic used to store computer information. A **diskette** is a disk used in some older computers. This word is also spelled **disc.**

disk drive *Computers.* a piece of electrical equipment built into a computer used for saving information on disks or reading from them.

disk operating system another term for DOS.

dis·like [dis-<u>like</u>] *noun, plural* **dislikes.** a feeling of not liking, finding unpleasant: *I took an instant dislike to him.* *verb*, **disliked, disliking.** to not like someone or something: *We disliked the apartment so we did not rent it.*

dis·mal [<u>diz</u>-mul] *adjective.* expressing or causing unhappiness, sadness, or gloom: *The evening was dismal because we were all in a bad mood.* **—dismally,** *adverb.*

dis·may [dis-<u>may</u>] *verb*, **dismayed, dismaying.** to fill with alarm or anxiety: *The gathering storm dismayed the sailors in the small boat.* *noun.* a feeling of alarm or anxiety: *We were filled with dismay when our automobile broke down in the tunnel.*

dis·miss [dis-<u>mis</u>] *verb*, **dismissed, dismissing. 1.** to send away or allow to go: *The coach dismissed us when the practice session was over.* **2.** to remove someone from a job: *She was dismissed for giving information to a rival company.* When someone is removed from a job in this way it is called a **dismissal.**

dis·mount ▶ [dis-<u>mownt</u>] *verb*, **dismounted, dismounting.** to get down off a horse or bicycle.

dis·o·be·di·ent [*dis*-uh-<u>bee</u>-dee-unt] *adjective.* failing or refusing to obey: *The boys who do not follow orders are being disobedient.* **Disobedience** is the failure to obey. **—disobediently,** *adverb.*

dis·o·bey [*dis*-uh-<u>bay</u>] *verb*, **disobeyed, disobeying.** to fail or refuse to obey: *The troops disobeyed the captain's orders not to shoot.*

A rider **dismounts** *by bringing both legs to one side and jumping down.*

dis·or·der [dis-<u>or</u>-dur] *noun, plural* **disorders. 1.** a lack of normal order or behavior: *A fire in the city center caused massive traffic disorder.* **2.** an illness: *The patient suffered from a stomach disorder.*

dis·or·der·ly [dis-<u>or</u>-dur-lee] *adjective.* **1.** lacking order or organization: *The books in the attic were in a disorderly mess.* **2.** behaving in an unruly, noisy way: *The fire drill at school was disorderly because no one took it seriously.*

dis·or·gan·ized [dis-<u>or</u>-guh-*nized*] *adjective.* confused or lacking good organization: *My bedroom is so disorganized I can never find the things I'm looking for.*

dis·patch [dis-<u>pach</u>] *verb*, **dispatched, dispatching.** to send off swiftly: *The blood bank dispatched plasma to the hospital as quickly as possiblc.* *noun, plural* **dispatches.** a written message sent to a government or newspaper: *The Middle East correspondent sends dispatches back to her newspaper every day.*

dis·pense ▼ [dis-<u>pens</u>] *verb*, **dispensed, dispensing.** to give or offer to people; distribute: *The school's student adviser dispenses a lot of good advice.*
• **dispense with.** to do without or do away with: *Let's dispense with the opening remarks and get right to the business at hand.* **—dispenser,** *noun.*

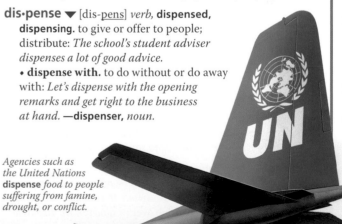

Agencies such as the United Nations **dispense** *food to people suffering from famine, drought, or conflict.*

a b c d e f g h i j k l m n o p q r s t

*An Indian peacock **displays** his colorful feathers to impress a mate.*

dis·perse [dis-<u>purs</u>] *verb,* **dispersed, dispersing.** to scatter in different directions: *After the Easter parade had gone by, the crowd dispersed.* —**dispersal,** *noun.*

dis·place [dis-<u>plase</u>] *verb,* **displaced, displacing.**
1. to replace or take the place of: *The computer has displaced the typewriter for most people.*
2. to force out of its usual place: *Europeans displaced the Native American population of eastern North America.* —**displacement,** *noun.*

dis·play ▶ [dis-<u>play</u>] *verb,* **displayed, displaying.** to lay out for viewing; show: *The store displays clothes beautifully.* *noun, plural* **displays.** the act of displaying something: *The flower show was a great display this year.*

dis·please [dis-<u>pleez</u>] *verb,* **displeased, displeasing.** to not please; annoy or offend: *His refusal to stop smoking displeased his father.*

dis·pos·able [dis-<u>poh</u>-zuh-bul] *adjective. Environment.* made to be thrown away after a single use: *Fast food is served in disposable containers.*

dis·pos·al [dis-<u>poh</u>-zul] *noun, plural* **disposals.**
1. the act of disposing of something; throwing away: *Garbage disposal is a problem in big cities.* **2.** a device for grinding up waste under a kitchen sink into very tiny pieces is called a **garbage disposal.**

dis·pose [dis-<u>poze</u>] *verb,* **disposed, disposing. 1.** to throw away or get rid of: *We disposed of the soda cans by putting them in the recycling bin.* **2.** to complete or settle; conclude: *Once we had disposed of our Saturday morning shopping duties we went to the beach.*

dis·po·si·tion [dis-puh-<u>zish</u>-un] *noun, plural* **dispositions. 1.** a person's usual way of acting: *She still has a pleasant disposition even though she's quite ill.* **2.** an inclination to behave or think in a certain way; tendency: *He has a disposition to support the underdogs in our society.*

dis·prove [dis-<u>proov</u>] *verb,* **disproved, disproving.** to prove that something is false or incorrect: *They will disprove his alibi by calling a witness who saw everything.*

dis·pute [dis-<u>pyoot</u>] *verb,* **disputed, disputing.**
1. to question or argue against: *The newspaper disputed the figures put out by the government as to how much the project will cost.* **2.** to argue over or quarrel: *We disputed their opinion of who would win the game.* *noun, plural* **disputes.** an argument, especially one that goes on for a long time: *The dispute between management and workers lasted for a year.*

dis·qual·i·fy [dis-<u>kwol</u>-uh-*fye*] *verb,* **disqualified, disqualifying.** to make unfit or say to be unable to do something: *The athlete was disqualified from the*

Olympics after testing positive for illegal drugs. **Disqualification** is the act or fact of being disqualified.

dis·re·gard [dis-ri-<u>gard</u>] *verb,* **disregarded, disregarding.** to treat as unimportant; ignore: *Do not disregard safety warnings —they might save your life.* *noun.* a lack of respect or attention: *The captain showed a disregard for his passengers by overloading the boat.*

dis·re·pair ▼ [dis-ri-<u>pare</u>] *noun.* the fact of being in poor condition: *The old house had been allowed to fall into disrepair.*

dis·re·spect [dis-ri-<u>spekt</u>] *noun.* a lack of respect; rudeness: *This school does not permit students to show disrespect to teachers.* To show a lack of respect is to be **disrespectful.**

dis·rupt [dis-<u>rupt</u>] *verb,* **disrupted, disrupting.** to bring about confusion or disorder: *The school timetable has been disrupted by the construction.* The fact of being disrupted is called a **disruption**.

dis·sat·is·fied [dis-<u>sat</u>-us-*fide*] *adjective.* not satisfied; discontented; unhappy: *Raoul is dissatisfied with his position on the team and wants to switch to first base.* **Dissatisfaction** is the experience of being discontented.

dis·sect [di-<u>sekt</u> *or* dye-<u>sekt</u>] *verb,* **dissected, dissecting. 1.** *Science.* to cut up a plant or animal in order to study it: *We dissected a frog in biology and Stephen fainted.* **2.** to study and discuss in detail, sometimes in order to find weaknesses: *Our teacher dissected arguments in favor of the death penalty.* —**dissection,** *noun.*

*This old and rusty scale is in a state of **disrepair.***

dis·sent [di-<u>sent</u>] *verb,* **dissented, dissenting.** to express a different opinion; disagree: *Most of the jurors voted to convict the accused, but one dissented from this view.* *noun.* opposition; a difference of opinion: *The government faced much dissent over its foreign policy.* **Dissension** is the act of disagreeing.
🔊 A different word with the same sound is **descent.**

dis·solve [di-<u>zolv</u>] *verb,* **dissolved, dissolving. 1.** to make into liquid or mix with a liquid: *Sugar dissolves in coffee when you stir it.* **2.** to break up or bring to an end: *The re-election committee was dissolved once the election was over.*

dis·tance [<u>dis</u>-tuns] *noun, plural* **distances. 1.** the amount of space or time between two things or events: *What is the distance from here to the next town?* **2.** a place that is a long way away: *What are those mountains in the distance?*

A B C **D** E F G H I J K L M N O P Q R S T U V W X Y Z

dis·tant [dis-tunt] *adjective.* **1.** far away in time or space: *In the distant past people lived in caves.* **2.** not close to: *Our sports field is so distant from the school we have to take a bus to get there.* **3.** showing a lacking of friendliness: *She has been distant with me ever since I beat her in the tennis match.* —**distantly,** *adverb.*

dis·till [di-stil] *verb,* **distilled, distilling.** *Chemistry.* to make pure by heating, evaporating, and cooling: *Distilled water is free from chemicals or other substances.* Making something pure in this way is called **distillation.**

dis·tinct [dis-tingkt] *adjective.* **1.** having a separate and different identity: *Cats and dogs belong to distinct species.* **2.** clearly seen, heard, smelled, or understood: *There was a distinct smell of perfume in the elevator.* —**distinctly,** *adverb.*

dis·tinc·tion [dis-tingk-shun] *noun, plural* **distinctions.** **1.** the fact of marking a clear difference between two things: *The distinction between the two cars is that one is blue and the other is red.* **2.** something that is particularly good or different: *Roy has the distinction of being president of the school.*

dis·tinc·tive [dis-tingk-tiv] *adjective.* marking someone or something as clearly different from others: *Clara has distinctive red hair.* —**distinctively,** *adverb.*

dis·tin·guish [dis-ting-gwish] *verb,* **distinguished, distinguishing. 1.** to recognize a clear difference between things: *The expert was able to distinguish the real fifty dollar bill from the counterfeit one.* **2.** to make something different; stand out: *The camel's hump distinguishes it from other animals.* **3.** to recognize or make famous by behaving or performing well: *Marie Curie distinguished herself by her research in science.* When someone is recognized in this way we describe them as **distinguished.**

dis·tort [dis-tort] *verb,* **distorted, distorting. 1.** to twist or change the normal shape, sound, or other characteristic of something: *The phone was not working properly and the voice of the caller was distorted.* **2.** to change from the truth: *He sometimes distorts the facts in order to protect his reputation.* When something has changed from the truth or its real identity, it becomes **distorted.** —**distortion,** *noun.*

dis·tract [dis-trakt] *verb,* **distracted, distracting.** to take away someone's attention; divert: *The noise of the fire engine distracted me from what the teacher was saying.* If a person's attention is taken away, they are **distracted.**

dis·trac·tion [dis-trak-shun] *noun, plural* **distractions. 1.** the act or fact of distracting someone; someone or something that interrupts concentration: *The Super Bowl game was a big distraction just before my exams.* **2.** the state of being confused, anxious, or upset: *The noise of the traffic is driving me to distraction.*

dis·tress [dis-tres] *noun.* **1.** great discomfort, pain, or anxiety: *The patient's face showed great distress when she arrived at the hospital.* **2.** a state of acute danger or difficulty: *The ship was in distress after the hurricane hit. verb,* **distressed, distressing.** to cause distress: *We were distressed by the news of his accident.* Things that cause discomfort, pain, or anxiety are **distressing.**

dis·tri·bute [dis-trib-yoot] *verb,* **distributed, distributing. 1.** to divide up and share: *Our teachers distributed the food at the picnic.* **2.** to spread widely over a large area: *The rain was distributed all along the coast.*

dis·tri·bu·tion [dis-truh-byoo-shun] *noun, plural* **distributions.** the act of distributing something: *The distribution of school prizes made the winners happy.*

dis·tri·bu·tor [dis-trib-yuh-tur] *noun, plural* **distributors. 1.** a person or organization that gives out something: *The local distributor of free newspapers has done very well.* **2.** a device in a motor vehicle that distributes electric current to spark plugs so the engine can run.

dis·trict ▼ [dis-trikt] *noun, plural* **districts. 1.** a defined area or region that is part of another; an official division: *U.S. postal districts are called Zip Codes.* **2.** any local area that has a certain identity: *the business district of a city.*

district attorney *Law.* a government legal officer who prosecutes offenders within a defined judicial district.

*The portside **district** of Buenos Aires in Argentina is known for its colorful buildings and its arts and crafts.*

A
B
C
D
E
F
G
H
I
J
K
L
M
N
O
P
Q
R
S
T
U
V
W
X
Y
Z

DIVERS

Exploring a wreck

In ancient times, divers seeking treasure and sea sponges had to hold their breath. Nineteenth-century divers wore heavy suits and helmets, and used breathing devices. Since the invention of portable breathing equipment in the 1940s, divers can move freely, go to greater depths, and stay there longer. Today, scuba diving is a popular recreational activity, while marine biologists, archaeologists, and filmmakers are able to research and record the wonders of the world under the sea.

Modern diver

dis·trust [dis-<u>trust</u>] *verb*, **distrusted, distrusting.** to lack trust or confidence in someone: *I distrusted his judgment after he made several mistakes.*

dis·turb [dis-<u>turb</u>] *verb*, **disturbed, disturbing. 1.** to make uneasy; cause inconvenience, worry, or alarm: *We were disturbed by the news of John's accident.* **2.** to interrupt or break into: *The peace and quiet was disturbed by the sound of gunfire.* The state of being interrupted is called a **disturbance.**

ditch [dich] *noun, plural* **ditches.** a long, narrow hole dug in the earth, as to hold or drain away water.
verb, **ditched, ditching.** to land an airplane in water in an emergency. *When the second engine failed they knew they would have to ditch.*

dive [dive] *verb,* **dived** *or* **dove, dived, diving. 1.** to throw oneself headfirst into water: *When I dive into the pool I close my eyes and hold my breath.* **2.** to fall sharply and at a steep angle: *The airplane dived to within a few hundred feet of the earth before climbing again.* **3.** to move quickly on land or in the air: *The rabbit dived into its burrow when it saw us.*
noun, plural **dives. 1.** an act of diving into water. **2.** a swift, steep movement by someone or something.

Plants grow in a **diversity** *of shapes, sizes, and colors.*

div·er ▲ [<u>dye</u>-vur] *noun, plural* **divers.** a person who dives under water, especially one using breathing equipment and protective clothing.

di·verse [duh-<u>vurs</u> *or* <u>dye</u>-vurs] *adjective.* having a wide variety, not the same: *The citizens had diverse opinions as to which of the many candidates should be elected.* —**diversely,** *adverb.*

di·ver·sion [duh-<u>vur</u>-zhun] *noun, plural* **diversions. 1.** the act of changing the direction of something away from its original course. **2.** the act of diverting attention away from something: *An accomplice created a diversion while the thief stole the watch.* **3.** any form of amusement or entertainment: *Gambling is one of the favorite diversions in Las Vegas.*

di·ver·si·ty ▼ [di-<u>vur</u>-suh-tee] *noun, plural* **diversities.** the fact of having a wide range of difference: *This school has a lot of diversity because its students come from many different countries.*

di·vert [duh-<u>vurt</u> *or* dye-<u>vurt</u>] *verb,* **diverted, diverting. 1.** to cause a change in the use or direction of something: *The water authority diverted a river to flow into the dam because the water level was so low.* **2.** to turn a person's attention or concentration away from something: *The thunderstorm diverted our attention from the TV show for a while.* **3.** to amuse or entertain.

di·vide [duh-<u>vide</u>] *verb,* **divided, dividing. 1.** to separate into two or more parts or groups: *The class divided into two teams to play soccer.* **2.** to separate into several shares and give some to each: *We divided the cake into nine pieces.* **3.** *Mathematics.* to find out how many times one number is contained by another: *When you divide 10 by 5 you get 2 because the number 10 contains the number 5 twice.* **4.** to cause a serious disagreement over an opinion or issue: *People of the town are divided over the question of whether a new airport is needed.*
noun, plural **divides.** a range of mountains separating rivers that flow in opposite directions.

div·i·dend [div-i-*dend*] *noun, plural* **dividends.**
1. *Mathematics.* a number to be divided by another number: *When you divide 9 by 3 the dividend is 9.* **2.** *Business.* money that a company pays to its shareholders: *The oil company paid a good dividend as profits were high this year.*

di·vine [duh-*vine*] *adjective.* having to do with God or with religion; sacred. The belief that a king received his right to rule directly from God was known as the **divine right** of kings.

di·vis·ion [di-*vizh*-un] *noun, plural* **divisions. 1.** the act of separating into parts or divisions: *The division of the former nation of Czechoslovakia into two separate countries took place in 1993.* **2.** one of the sections into which something is divided: *Chapters are the main divisions within most books.* **3.** *Mathematics.* the fact of dividing one number by another; the opposite of multiplication. **4.** a large unit within an army, navy, or air force.

di·vi·sor [di-*vye*-zur] *noun, plural* **divisors.** *Mathematics.* a number by which another number is divided: *When you divide 12 by 4, 4 is the divisor.*

di·vorce [di-*vors*] *noun, plural* **divorces.** *Law.* the official ending of a marriage by a court of law.
verb, **divorced, divorcing.** to officially end a marriage by a court of law.

diz·zy [*diz*-ee] *adjective,* **dizzier, dizziest. 1.** having a feeling of spinning around and being unable to balance: *I was dizzy after I went on the roller coaster three times in a row.* A sensation of spinning and being about to fall is **dizziness. 2.** bewildered, confused, or silly.

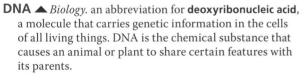

Every cell contains **DNA** *molecules that together make people different from one another.*

DNA ▲ *Biology.* an abbreviation for **deoxyribonucleic acid,** a molecule that carries genetic information in the cells of all living things. DNA is the chemical substance that causes an animal or plant to share certain features with its parents.

do [doo] *verb,* **did, done, doing. 1.** to make a certain action happen; carry out: *to do a job, to do a quick run around the track, to do some business at the bank.* **2.** to act in a certain way: *to do well on a test, to do the right thing.* **3.** to deal with something by acting: *to do the dishes, to do your homework.* **4.** to bring about a certain outcome; result in: *It won't do you any harm to check your paper again.* **5.** to be suitable or acceptable: *The old phone will do for now until we can buy a new one.*
+Do is also often used with other verbs in these ways: **1.** to ask a question: *Do you want to go see that movie?*

2. to show the idea of "not:" *Those boys do not live on our street.* **3.** to say something in a stronger way: *Yes, we really do want to help you.* **4.** to stand for another verb used earlier: *Mom asked if anyone wanted more milk, and I said "I do."*

Do·ber·man pin·scher [*doh*-bur-mun *pin*-chur] a slender, but powerful, dog of German origin with a shiny black or brown coat and a docked tail. They are commonly used as guard dogs, watch dogs, or police dogs.

dock ▼ [dok] *noun, plural* **docks.** a place where a ship ties up to load and unload cargo and passengers.
verb, **docked, docking. 1.** to arrive or sail into such a place. **2.** to join two spacecraft together while in outer space.

Modern **docks** *service ships from all over the world.*

doc·tor [*dok*-tur] *noun, plural* **doctors. 1.** a person who has a license to treat the sick and injured and give them medicine. **2.** a person who has the highest academic degree from a college or university.

doc·trine [*dok*-trin] *noun, plural* **doctrines.** a set of beliefs, usually political or religious, that are taught and accepted by a particular group of people.

doc·u·ment [*dok*-yuh-munt] *noun, plural* **documents.** an official statement that gives proof or information about something, such as a birth certificate or a passport.

doc·u·men·ta·ry [dok-yuh-*men*-tree *or* dok-yuh-*men*-tuh-ree] *noun, plural* **documentaries.** a film or television program about real events or people: *Our class watched a documentary about Martin Luther King, Jr.*

dodge [doj] *verb,* **dodged, dodging.
1.** to move quickly to avoid something: *I dodged the puddle of water just in time.*
2. to deliberately avoid something in a tricky way: *I dodged Dad's questions about my report card by putting on his favorite TV show.*
noun, plural **dodges. 1.** a sudden movement to avoid something.
2. something tricky or dishonest that is done to avoid something: *He says buying a second home is a great tax dodge.*

do·do ▶ [*doh*-doh] *noun, plural* **dodos** or **dodoes.** a large bird that could not fly and is now extinct.

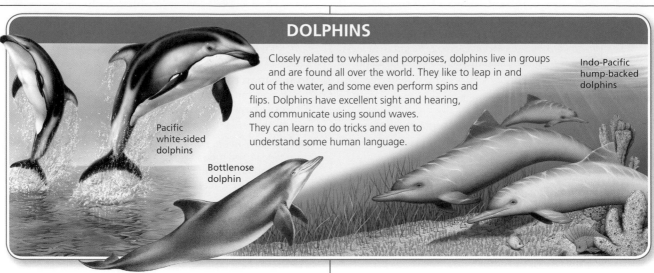

DOLPHINS

Closely related to whales and porpoises, dolphins live in groups and are found all over the world. They like to leap in and out of the water, and some even perform spins and flips. Dolphins have excellent sight and hearing, and communicate using sound waves. They can learn to do tricks and even to understand some human language.

Pacific white-sided dolphins

Bottlenose dolphin

Indo-Pacific hump-backed dolphins

doe [doh] *noun, plural* **does.** the female of animals such as the deer, rabbit, antelope, or goat.
A different word with the same sound is **dough.**

does [duz] *verb.* a present tense of DO used with he, she, or it: *My sister does all her homework on Sunday night.*

does·n't [duz-unt] the shortened form or "does not."

dog [dawg *or* dog] *noun, plural* **dogs.** a four-legged animal that barks and eats meat. Most dogs are kept as pets but some, such as coyotes, wolves, or dingoes, live in the wild.
verb, **dogged, dogging.** to follow someone closely: *I dogged my older sister through the mall to see who she was meeting.*

Traditional wooden Kokeshi **dolls** *from Japan have a large head and cylindrical body, but no arms or legs.*

dog·wood [dawg-wud] *noun, plural* **dogwoods.** an ornamental tree or shrub with clusters of greenish flowers and large white or pink leaves that look like petals.

doll [dol] *noun, plural* **dolls.** a child's toy that is made to look like a person or baby.

dol·lar [dol-ur] *noun, plural* **dollars.** a standard unit of money that is equal to one hundred cents. It is used in many countries such as the United States, Canada, and Australia.

dol·phin ▲ [dol-fin] *noun, plural* **dolphins.** an intelligent sea mammal with flippers and a long, pointed nose.

do·main [doh-mane] *noun, plural* **domains. 1.** an area of land owned or controlled by a person or government: *The king's domain was the land between the sea and the mountain range.* **2.** an area of interest, activity, or knowledge: *Chemistry is not my domain.*

dome ▼ [dome] *noun, plural* **domes.** a rounded roof of a building or room that is shaped like the top half of a ball.

do·mes·tic [duh-mes-tik] *adjective.* **1.** having to do with the home, house, or family: *Washing dishes is a domestic chore.* **2.** living with or under the care of humans: *Our dog is a domestic animal.* **3.** having to do with one's own country: *We took a domestic flight from LA to New York.* —**domestically,** *adverb.*

Lantern and cross

The **dome** *of St. Peter's Basilica in the Vatican City, Italy, is 140 feet across and rises more than 300 feet above the floor.*

Dome

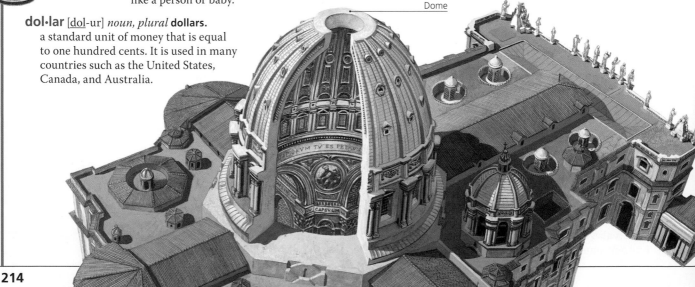

do·mes·ti·cate [duh-<u>mes</u>-tuh-kate] *verb*, **domesticated, domesticating.** *Biology.* to tame or train an animal so that it can live with or be used by people: *Dogs and sheep were some of the first animals to be domesticated.* —**domestication**, *noun.*

dom·i·nant [<u>dom</u>-uh-nunt] *adjective.* having the greatest effect; most important or influential: *The dominant issue in this year's election is the high cost of gasoline.* —**dominantly**, *adverb.*

dom·i·nate [<u>dom</u>-uh-nate] *verb,* **dominated, dominating.** to rule or control someone or something: *He dominated the meeting and did not allow anyone else to speak.* —**domination**, *noun.*

do·min·ion [du-<u>min</u>-yuhn] *noun,* *plural* **dominions. 1.** land controlled by a ruler or government: *The province of Ontario, Canada, was once a dominion of Great Britain.* **2.** the power to rule or control: *The king held dominion over his lands for many years.*

Dominion Day another term for CANADA DAY.

do·min·o [<u>dom</u>-uh-noh] *noun,* *plural* **dominoes. 1.** a small, flat piece of wood or plastic marked with different numbers of spots, used for playing a game. **2. dominoes.** the game played using these pieces.

do·nate [<u>doh</u>-nate] *verb,* **donated, donating.** to give as a gift; contribute: *I donated some money for cancer research.* —**donation**, *noun.*

done [dun] *verb.* the past participle of DO. *adjective.* **1.** finished: *The job is done.* **2.** cooked: *Dinner is almost done.*

don·key ▼ [<u>dong</u>-kee] *noun, plural* **donkeys.** a domestic animal that is related to the horse but is smaller and has longer ears.

do·nor [<u>dohn</u>-ur] *noun, plural* **donors. 1.** someone who gives or contributes something: *the donor of a painting to a museum.* **2.** *Medicine.* someone who allows a part to be taken from their body to be used by another person.

don't [dohnt] the shortened form of "do not."

In everyday talk you may hear a person say something like, "He *don't* want to go with us," or "It *don't* matter what happens." This is wrong. The correct word to use with singular words like *he, she,* or *it* is *doesn't:* "He doesn't want to go with us."

doom [doom] *noun, plural* **dooms.** a terrible outcome, fate, or death: *The passengers met their doom when the ship sank.*

verb, **doomed, dooming.** to force a bad outcome or terrible situation: *The prisoner's plan to escape was doomed from the start.* When something is certain to fail or be destroyed it is **doomed.**

door [dor] *noun, plural* **doors.**
1. a swinging or sliding part that is used to open or close an entrance to something. A bell or buzzer located outside the door which is rung to let people know you are there is a **doorbell.** A **doorknob** is a handle that you turn to open the door. **2.** a thing that opens the way to do something; an opportunity: *a door to success.*

door·step [<u>dor</u>-step] *noun, plural* **doorsteps.** a step in front of an outside door to a house or building.

door·way [<u>dor</u>-way] *noun, plural* **doorways.** the space in a wall where a door opens into a room or building.

dope [dope] *noun, plural* **dopes. 1.** a slang word for a stupid or silly person. **2.** an illegal drug, especially marijuana. **3.** a varnish-like product used to make a fabric stronger or waterproof.

dor·mant ◀ [<u>dor</u>-munt] *adjective.* something that is not active or growing at present, but has the ability to become active later on: *The villagers were afraid of living near the dormant volcano.*

*Mount Rainier is a huge, snow-covered, **dormant** volcano in Washington State.*

> The French word **dormir** means "to sleep." When something is *dormant* (not active), it seems to be asleep.

dor·mi·to·ry [<u>dor</u>-muh-<u>tor</u>-ee] *noun, plural* **dormitories.** a large building with many bedrooms as well as some common facilities. Many colleges or universities have student dormitories.

dor·mouse [<u>dor</u>-mows] *noun, plural* **dormice.** a small, furry-tailed, squirrel-like rodent, found in Europe and Africa, that hibernates during the cold months of the year.

DOS [dos] *Computers.* an abbreviation for Disk Operating System, which is a type of operating system for computers.

Donkeys *are hardy animals, and can carry heavy loads over rough paths.*

dose [dose] *noun, plural* **doses. 1.** a measured amount of medicine taken at one time. **2.** an amount of radiation absorbed in a person's body at one time. **3.** something hard or unpleasant that is thought to help someone: *a dose of criticism.*

dot [dot] *noun, plural* **dots.** a small spot: *Dad's tie is red with white dots.* *verb,* **dotted, dotting. 1.** to put a dot or dots on something: *The teacher said to dot my i's and cross my t's.* **2.** to be spread or scattered across an area: *Trees and shrubs dotted the mountainside.*

dou·ble [duh-bul] *adjective.* **1.** twice as many, as much, or as big: *a double helping of ice cream.* **2.** consisting of two parts: *double doors.* *adverb.* **1.** in two parts or pairs: *Two people can ride double on a horse.* **2.** twice as much: *By mistake he was charged double for the meal.* *noun, plural* **doubles. 1.** something twice another: *Eight is the double of 4.* **2.** something exactly or closely resembling another: *People say I'm the double of my older brother.* **3.** in baseball, a hit that lets the batter reach second base. **4. doubles.** a game between two pairs of players, as in tennis. *verb,* **doubled, doubling. 1.** to make or become twice as many, as much, or as big. **2.** to bend or fold in two: *When the ball hit him, he doubled over in pain.* **3.** to be a substitute: *A stunt man doubled for the actor to do the dangerous fall.* **4.** to serve a secondary use or purpose: *He doubled as a math teacher and football coach.* **5.** in baseball, to hit the ball hard enough to get to second base.

dou·ble-cross [dub-ul-kros] *verb,* **double-crossed, double-crossing.** to deceive or betray someone by doing the opposite to what you had promised to do: *The thief double-crossed his partners by switching their share of the jewels for worthless glass.*

double play in baseball, the action of getting two players out on the same hit, as by throwing the ball quickly from one base to another.

doubt [dout] *verb,* **doubted, doubting. 1.** to not think to be true; distrust: *He doubted my story about where I'd been all day.* **2.** to be uncertain: think of as unlikely: *I doubt I'll get my project finished in time.* *noun, plural* **doubts. 1.** a feeling of distrust: *There is some doubt about her honesty.* **2.** the state of being uncertain: *The coach had doubts about our ability to play well.*

A baker cuts **dough** *into quarters to make buns.*

doubt·ful [dout-ful] *adjective.* being or feeling uncertain: *It was doubtful that we would make it there on time.* —**doubtfully,** *adverb.*

dough ▲ [doh] *noun, plural* **doughs. 1.** a mixture of flour, water, and other ingredients like yeast, fat, and sugar, ready to be baked into bread or pastry. **2.** a slang term for money.

Doves are usually smaller than other pigeons, with whiter feathers and longer tails.

dough·nut [doh-nut] *noun, plural* **doughnuts.** a small ring-shaped cake made of sweet dough which is deep-fried and covered in sugar or icing. This word is also spelled **donut.**

dove¹ ◀ [duv] *noun, plural* **doves.** a small, white bird in the pigeon family, which is often used as a symbol of peace. Something or someone who is harmless or innocent is **dovish.**

dove² [dohve] *verb.* a past tense of DIVE.

down¹ [down] *adverb.* **1.** from higher to lower: *I climbed down from the tree.* **2.** to be in a lower or worse condition: *I am down to my last dollar.* **3.** to or on the ground or floor: *He fell down.* **4.** in or to a calmer state: *The class was excited, but eventually settled down.* *adjective.* **1.** downward: *the down escalator.* **2.** becoming progressively lower: *a down trend in the share market.* **3.** not working, or not in the proper state: *She's down with the flu; We can't get the information now because all the computers are down.* *preposition.* from higher to lower; along; through; toward, and into: *The car raced down the road.* *verb,* **downed, downing. 1.** to put, knock, or throw down: *He downed his opponent with one punch.* **2.** to swallow quickly: *She downed a cup of coffee.* *noun, plural* **downs.** in football, one of the four chances that a team gets to move the ball forward ten yards in order to keep possession of it.

down² [down] *noun.* soft, fine feathers, especially those from a young bird. Something that has soft, fine feathers is described as being **downy.**

Down syndrome *Medicine.* a condition that someone is born with which results in mental retardation, and particular physical characteristics such as a short stature and flattened facial features. This term is also spelled **Down's syndrome.**

> The medical condition known as **Down** or **Down's syndrome** is named for the British doctor James Langdon *Down.* He was the first to identify and report on this condition, in England in the 1860s.

down·load [down-lode] *verb,* **downloaded, downloading.** *Computers.* to transfer information or programs from a computer network or one computer to another: *to download games from the Internet.*

down payment *Business.* an amount of money that you pay when you buy something, such as a house or car, which is only part of the total cost, with the remainder paid over a period of time.

down·pour ▶ [down-por] *noun, plural* **downpours.** a very heavy rain that falls in a short time.

down·right [down-rite] *adjective.* without restriction; complete: *a downright lie.* *adverb.* in an absolute manner; completely: *She is being downright stupid.*

down·stairs [down-stairz] *adverb.*
1. down the stairs: *I wasn't watching where I was going and fell downstairs.*
2. to or on a lower floor: *You can sleep in the bedroom downstairs.*
adjective. on a lower floor: *the downstairs bathroom.*

down·stream [down-streem]
adjective. moving in the direction that a river or other stream of water is flowing.
adverb. **1.** down a stream: *The current carried them downstream.* **2.** further down the stream: *The finishing line was downstream.*

down·time [down-time] *noun. Business.* a time when a machine or computer is not working or not able to be used, such as during repair.

down·town ▲ [down-town] *adverb.* toward or in the central or main part of town: *We went shopping downtown.*
adjective. of or located in the central or main part of town: *The downtown businesses do very well.*
noun. the central or main part of town.

down·ward [down-wurd] *adverb.* toward a lower position: *She glanced downward.*
adjective. moving or pointing towards a lower position: *a downward slope.* This word is also spelled **downwards**.

doze ▼ [doze] *verb,* **dozed, dozing.** to sleep lightly for a short time; take a nap.
noun, plural **dozes.** a short, light sleep.

doz·en [duz-un] *noun, plural* **dozens** *or* **dozen.** a group of twelve: *a dozen eggs.*

Dr. an abbreviation for DOCTOR

draft [draft] *noun, plural* **drafts.**
1. a current of air coming blowing through an enclosed space: *There was a cold draft coming from under the door.*
2. a device for regulating the flow of air in a fireplace, furnace, or stove.
3. a sketch or rough copy of something written: *I asked Mom to edit the first draft of my English essay.* **4.** a system of ordering people by law to join military service.
5. a similar system in professional sports in which new players are each chosen by a certain team.
verb, **drafted, drafting.**
1. to make a sketch or rough copy.
2. to order people by law to join military service: *He was drafted to serve in the war.* **3.** to choose a player for a sports team.
4. to persuade or require someone to do something: *He was drafted as the party's candidate because no one else wanted to run.*
adjective. suited or used for pulling loads: *Oxen are often used as draft animals.*

A hammock is a relaxing place in which to **doze** *on a hot day.*

draf·ty [draft-ee] *adjective.* exposed to a cold current of air: *a drafty room.*

In tropical areas, such as the Amazon rain forest, a heavy **downpour** *can happen suddenly.*

DRAGONS

Dragons, and creatures like them, appear in legends all around the world. In Chinese tradition, dragons are usually seen as kind and represent good luck, but in European tales they are more likely to be evil. A famous legend from the Middle Ages tells how St. George killed a dragon that was terrorizing a region and rescued the young princess who was about to be sacrificed.

Chinese dragon

St. George and the dragon

drag [drag] *verb,* **dragged, dragging. 1.** to pull something along the ground or surface: *She dragged the chair along the kitchen floor.* **2.** to trail along on the ground: *The hem of my skirt dragged on the ground.* **3.** *Computers.* to move words or pictures on a computer screen by using the mouse. **4.** to pull nets and hooks along the bottom of a river or lake to search for something: *The police dragged the lake for more evidence.*

drag·on ▲ [drag-un] *noun, plural* **dragons.** an imaginary monster that is supposed to look like a giant fire-breathing lizard with wings and sharp claws.

drag·on·fly ▼ drag-un-*flye*] *noun, plural* **dragonflies.** a large insect with a long, thin body and two pairs of transparent wings. It lives near water and feeds on flies, gnats, and mosquitoes.

With four large wings, **dragonflies** *can fly very fast.*

drain [drane] *verb,* **drained, draining. 1.** to remove the liquid from something: *We drained the pond.* **2.** to use something up; weaken: *Our European vacation drained our bank account.*
noun, plural **drains. 1.** a pipe or channel that is used to carry liquids away: *Dad got a plumber to fix the blocked drain.* **2.** something that weakens or uses up: *Having to sit through that long and boring speech was a drain on my patience.*

drain·age [drane-ij] *noun, plural* **drainages.** the process or system by which water or waste liquid flows away: *The citizens voted to improve the town's drainage system.*

drain·pipe [drane-*pipe*] *noun, plural* **drainpipes.** a pipe used for carrying waste water or sewage away from buildings.

drake ▼ [drake] *noun, plural* **drakes.** a male duck.

dra·ma [drah-muh] *noun, plural* **dramas. 1.** a story told in the form of a play in theater, on television, or radio. **2.** an exciting event or situation in real life that is like this: *the drama of a championship race or an election for President.* **3.** the quality of being interesting or exciting: *I was sick of seeing comedies, so we chose a movie that was full of drama.*

dra·ma·tic [druh-mat-ik] *adjective.* **1.** having to do with plays or acting: *She is studying dramatic arts at college.* **2.** producing a feeling of excitement; impressive: *We saw some dramatic scenery on our vacation at the Grand Canyon.* —**dramatically,** *adverb.*

dram·a·tist [dram-uh-tist] *noun, plural* **dramatists.** someone who writes plays.

dram·a·tize [dram-uh-*tize*] *verb,* **dramatized, dramatizing. 1.** to take a story and make it into a play: *The best-selling novel was dramatized for television.* **2.** to make a situation seem more exciting, terrible, or emotional than it really is: *He dramatized his tiredness by falling back into his chair with his arms outstretched and a loud sigh.* —**dramatization,** *noun.*

A mallard **drake** *has a distinctive dark green head, a reddish breast, and a gray body.*

drank [drangk] *verb.* the past tense of DRINK.

drape ▶ [drape] *verb,* **draped, draping. 1.** to cover or decorate something with loosely hanging cloth. **2.** to arrange or spread loosely: *I draped my jacket over the back of the chair.*
noun, plural **drapes.** a long, heavy curtain: *We ordered new drapes for the bedroom windows.*

dra·per·y [drape-uh-ree or drape-ree] *noun, plural* **draperies.** cloth hanging or arranged in folds such as window curtains.

dras·tic [dras-tik] *adjective.* extreme or sudden: *Drastic measures were taken to save the drowning child.* —**drastically,** *adverb.*

These people from different countries are wearing their traditional **dress.**

Georgia

The Netherlands

Guatemala

Switzerland

Kenya

Austria

Ukraine

draw [draw] *verb,* **drew, drawn, drawing. 1.** to move by pulling: *a cart drawn by oxen.* **2.** to move in a particular direction: *The ship drew near the shore.* **3.** to pull up or out: *to draw water from a well.* **4.** to produce a picture of something using a pencil or other writing tool. **5.** to bring or cause to come; attract: *The basketball playoffs drew a big crowd of spectators; His performance drew praise from the movie critics.*
noun, plural **draws. 1.** the act of pulling a gun or other weapon: *He was quick on the draw.* **2.** the final result of a game or competition in which there is an even score; a tie: *The hockey game ended in a draw.*

draw·back [draw-bak] *noun, plural* **drawbacks.**
a disadvantage or inconvenience: *The only real drawback to living here is the hot summer weather.*

draw·bridge [draw-brij] *noun, plural* **drawbridges.** a bridge that can be raised or lowered to allow ships to pass under it.

draw·er [drawr] *noun, plural* **drawers.** a box-shaped container that can be pulled out and pushed into a piece of furniture, such as a cupboard or desk.

draw·ing [draw-ing] *noun, plural* **drawings. 1.** a picture or design made using a pencil or other writing tool. **2.** the selection of the winning chance in a raffle or lottery: *The prize drawing for the new car will be held later this evening.*

drawl [drawl] *verb,* **drawled, drawling.** *Language.* to speak slowly, lengthening the vowel sounds.
noun, plural **drawls.** a slow way of speaking with prolonged vowel sounds: *Many people from the Southern U.S. are said to speak with a drawl.*

dread [dred] *verb,* **dreaded, dreading. 1.** to feel extremely frightened or anxious about something that is going to happen: *I always dread the first day of a new school year.* Something that

Ancient Romans **draped** *their tunics and robes around their bodies.*

causes fright or anxiety is described as **dreaded.**
noun. a feeling of fear or anxiety: *The thought of getting on an airplane fills him with dread.*
adjective. causing fear or anxiety: *a dread disease.*

dread·ful [dred-ful] *adjective.* **1.** causing fear or terror: *I heard a dreadful scream from behind the door.* **2.** extremely bad or awful: *She has dreadful table manners.* —**dreadfully,** *adverb.*

dream [dreem] *noun, plural* **dreams. 1.** the thoughts, feelings, and pictures that a person has while they are sleeping: *I had a dream last night that I had magical powers.* **2.** something wished for; a hope or ambition: *My dream is to become a millionaire.* **3.** someone who is very attractive: *My new boyfriend is a real dream.*
verb, **dreamed** *or* **dreamt, dreaming. 1.** to have a dream: *I fell asleep and dreamed I was flying through the air.* **2.** to think or imagine: *I never dreamed the concert tickets would be so expensive.*

drear·y [dreer-ee] *adjective,* **drearier, dreariest.** sad or gloomy; depressing: *a cold and dreary winter's day.*

dredge [drej] *noun, plural* **dredges.** a machine or ship used for scooping up mud, sand, or other material from the bottom of a river or lake.
verb, **dredged, dredging.** to remove unwanted material from the bottom of a river or lake using such a machine: *The canal is dredged on a regular basis.*
• **dredge up.** to talk about something bad that happened in the past.

drench [drench] *verb,* **drenched, drenching.** to make something or someone completely wet: *The unexpected rainstorm left us drenched.*

dress ▲ [dres] *noun, plural* **dresses. 1.** a piece of clothing for women and girls covering the top half of the body and the legs to or below the knees. **2.** a particular style of clothing for an occasion: *I wore formal dress to the wedding.*
verb, **dressed, dressing. 1.** to put clothes on: *She dressed in her nurse's uniform for work.* **2.** to prepare something in a certain way that is like putting on clothes: *to dress the hair; to dress a chicken for cooking; to dress a wound with bandages.*
adjective. describing the type of clothes that are worn to an occasion: *He put on his white dress shirt and bow tie.*
• **dress up.** to wear formal or fancy clothes for a special occasion: *They dressed up for the graduation.*

A B C D E F G H I J K L M N O P Q R S T U V W X Y Z

*Antique **dressers** are now valuable because they were carefully made from fine timber.*

dress·er¹ [dres-ur] *noun, plural* **dressers.** a piece of furniture, often with a mirror attached to it, having shelves and drawers for storing clothes and other things.

dress·er² [dres-ur] *noun, plural* **dressers.** a person who wears a certain type of clothes: *She is a very stylish dresser.*

dress·ing [dres-ing] *noun, plural* **dressings.**
1. the act of putting clothes on yourself or someone else.
2. a mixture of liquids that is put on salad and other foods to add flavor. **3.** a mixture of seasoned ingredients used to put in meat such as turkey.

drew [droo] *verb.* the past tense of DRAW.

drib·ble [drib-ul] *verb,* **dribbled, dribbling. 1.** to flow very slowly in small amounts: *The water dribbled out of the leaky faucet.* **2.** to move a ball along by repeatedly bouncing or kicking it: *He dribbled the soccer ball down the field and scored a goal.* Someone who dribbles a ball is a **dribbler.**
noun, plural **dribbles. 1.** a small amount of liquid.
2. the act of moving a ball along by repeatedly bouncing or kicking it.

dried [dride] *verb.* the past tense and past participle of DRY.

dri·er [drye-ur] *adjective.* the comparative form of DRY.
noun, plural **driers.** another spelling of DRYER.

drift [drift] *verb,* **drifted, drifting. 1.** to move slowly on water or in the air, with no control over direction: *The lifeboat drifted out at sea for days.* **2.** to form a pile of something from the action of the wind: *The snow drifted against the fence.* **3.** to move around without a plan or purpose: *After graduating from college he spent six months drifting around Europe.* A person who does this is a **drifter.**
noun, plural **drifts. 1.** the force of the air or water current that moves something along. **2.** a pile of snow, sand, or something similar, formed by the wind: *a snow drift.*
• **get (the) drift.** to understand the general meaning of what someone is saying: *The science article was hard to read, but I got the drift of the important issues.*

drift·wood ▶ [drift-wud] *noun.* wood floating on the sea or brought in by the water to shore.

drill ▶ [dril] *noun, plural* **drills. 1.** a tool or machine that cuts holes in wood, plastic, and other materials.
2. a method of teaching someone something by making them repeat the same activity many times over: *a multiplication drill.*
verb, **drilled, drilling.**
1. to cut a hole in something using a drill: *They drilled a well in the ground to search for oil.* Someone who is trained in operating such a machine is a **driller.**
2. to train or teach someone by making them repeat the same activity many times over: *The soldiers drilled for hours on the parade ground.*

*A miner uses an electric **drill** to break through rock in a gold mine.*

drink [dringk] *verb,* **drank, drunk, drinking.**
1. to swallow a liquid: *I drink six glasses of water a day.* **2.** to take up a liquid; soak up or absorb.
3. to drink an alcoholic beverage.
noun, plural **drinks. 1.** a liquid that one can drink: *The shop sells fruit drinks and soda.* **2.** an amount of liquid that you swallow: *She took a drink of her coffee.*
3. an alcoholic beverage. Someone who drinks alcohol is a **drinker.**
• **drink in.** to take in through the senses or by paying close attention: *We drank in the gorgeous scenery.*

drive [drive] *verb,* **drove, driven, driving.**
1. to operate and control the movement of a vehicle.
2. to move or travel in a vehicle: *We plan to drive around California for our summer vacation.* **3.** to move or cause to move rapidly or with force: *She drove the ball hard into the corner of the net; The troops drove the enemy back.*
4. to force someone or something into a particular state or condition: *Listening to that singer's squeaky voice is driving me insane.*
noun, plural **drives. 1.** a trip in a vehicle: *It's a short drive from our house to the supermarket.* **2.** a shorter word for DRIVEWAY. **3.** the act of hitting a ball hard: *The batter hit a long drive to left field.* **4.** an effort to achieve a purpose: *Her drive will result in her being very successful.*

drive-by [drive-bye] *adjective.* describing something done from a moving vehicle, usually a crime: *He was the victim of a drive-by shooting.*

drive-in [drive-in] *noun, plural* **drive-ins.** a service you can use or a store you can buy from without getting out of your car, such as a fast-food restaurant, movie theater, or bank.

*Often battered by the sea, **driftwood** comes in many shapes and sizes.*

driv·er [drive-ur] *noun, plural* **drivers. 1.** someone who drives a vehicle, such as a car or train. **2.** a type of golf club used to hit long shots.

drive·way [drive-way] *noun, plural* **driveways.** a short, private road leading from the street to a house, garage, other building, or parking lot.

driz·zle [driz-ul] *verb,* **drizzled, drizzling.** to rain in fine drops.
noun, plural **drizzles.** a fine rain.

drom·e·da·ry ▼ [drom-uh-*der*-ee] *noun, plural* **dromedaries.** a camel with one hump found in western Asia and northern Africa. It is also known as the Arabian camel.

drone¹ [drone] *noun, plural* **drones.** a male bee. Drones have no sting and do not make honey.

drone² [drone] *verb,* **droned, droning. 1.** to make a low, dull, humming or buzzing sound: *The air conditioner droned day and night.* **2.** to talk in a boring, monotonous voice: *The audience dozed as the lecturer droned on.*
noun, plural **drones.** a low, dull, humming or buzzing sound.

*A **dromedary** can drink thirty gallons of water in ten minutes, but can survive for days without drinking.*

drool [drool] *verb,* **drooled, drooling.** to water at the mouth; dribble: *The dog drooled as I put food in his bowl.*

droop [droop] *verb,* **drooped, drooping.** to hang down or sink weakly; sag: *The tree branches drooped under the weight of the snow.*

drop [drop] *verb,* **dropped, dropping. 1.** to fall or let fall; reach a lower point: *I dropped my bag on the ground.* **2.** to pass into a less active state; decline: *Snowboard sales have dropped over the summer.* **3.** to stop doing, saying, or being involved with something; give up: *I dropped the idea as being too expensive.* **4.** to visit casually or unexpectedly: *I dropped by to tell her my news.* **5.** to fail to include; omit: *The coach dropped Shani from the team for missing so many practices.*
noun, plural **drops. 1.** a small quantity of liquid, usually rounded: *a drop of rain.* **2.** the act of falling or reaching a lower point. **3.** the distance something drops or falls: *We were looking at a twenty-foot drop to the ground.*

*On large ranches, farmers control **droves** of cattle with motor vehicles as well as trained cattle dogs.*

*In a **drought**, the soil dries out and crops fail, which creates hardship for farmers in many parts of the world.*

drop·out [drop-out] *noun, plural* **dropouts.** someone who no longer takes part in an activity, especially someone who gives up school, college, or a training program. To stop taking part in an activity or program is to **drop out.**

drought ▲ [drowt] *noun, plural* **droughts.** a long period of dry weather; lack of rain.

drove¹ [drove] *verb.* the past tense of DRIVE.

drove² ▼ drove] *noun, plural* **droves. 1.** a herd or large group of animals being driven or moving together. **2.** a great number of people; crowd: *People arrived in droves for the store's annual sale.*

drown [drown] *verb,* **drowned, drowning. 1.** to die as a result of being under water or some other liquid and unable to breathe. **2.** to overpower a sound with louder noise: *A truck roared past and drowned out his words.*

drow·sy [drow-zee] *adjective* **drowsier, drowsiest.** close to falling asleep; sleepy: *Long car trips always make me feel drowsy.* —**drowsily,** *adverb.*

drug [drug] *noun, plural* **drugs. 1.** *Medicine.* a chemical substance used to treat or cure disease, or to help a person stay healthy: *Aspirin is a drug often used to treat headaches and other body pains.* **2.** *Health.* a type of substance that has a very strong effect on the body, mind, and feelings, and that often can make a person become addicted: *Cocaine and heroin are drugs that it is against the law to use or sell.*
verb, **drugged, drugging.** to give someone a drug, especially a powerful drug.

drug addiction *Health.* the state of having an uncontrollable need for a harmful, habit-forming drug. Someone who has an uncontrollable need for such a drug is a **drug addict.**

a b c d e f g h i j k l m n o p q r s t u v w x y z

drug·gist [drug-ist] *noun, plural* **druggists.** someone licensed to prepare drugs prescribed by a doctor; a pharmacist.

The skin of a **drum** *vibrates when it is hit with a stick, hand, or other object.*

Skin

Vibration

drug·store [drug-stor] *noun, plural* **drugstores.** a store selling medicines and drugs, usually along with a range of other items such as cosmetics and candy.

drum ◀ [drum] *noun, plural* **drums.** **1.** a musical instrument consisting of a hollow cylinder with a material, such as leather, stretched tight over one or both ends, played by striking or beating it with the hand or an object. **2.** a container with a similar shape to this: *an oil drum.* *verb,* **drummed, drumming.** **1.** to play on a drum. **2.** to sound like someone playing on a drum: *The rain drummed on the tin roof.* ♦ **drum into.** to drive a message home by saying it over and over: *His father drummed into him that he must make his own way in life.*

drum major ▶ the leader of a marching band.

drum majorette a member of a female group that marches in front of bands in parades and twirls batons.

drum·mer [drum-ur] *noun, plural* **drummers.** someone who plays a drum or drums.

drum·stick [drum-stik] *noun, plural* **drumsticks.** **1.** a stick for beating a drum. **2.** the lower leg joint of a cooked fowl, such as a chicken or turkey.

drunk [drungk] *verb.* the past participle of DRINK. *adjective,* **drunker, drunkest.** under the influence of alcohol; intoxicated. *noun, plural* **drunks.** someone who regularly drinks too much alcohol, or who has too much to drink at a certain time.

dry [drye] *adjective,* **drier, driest. 1.** having little or no moisture; lacking rain: *Arizona has a dry climate.* **2.** not being in or under water: *It was a relief to step off the boat onto dry land.* **3.** in need of a drink; thirsty. **4.** failing to excite interest; dull: *Some subjects are so dry that no speaker could make them sound interesting.* *verb,* **dried, drying.** to remove the moisture from: *Dry the dishes.*

dry·er [drye-ur] *noun, plural* **dryers.** a device or appliance that dries things with the use of heat or air: *clothes dryer; hair dryer.* This word is also spelled **drier.**

A **drum major** *uses hand gestures, a whistle, or a baton to lead a marching band in a parade.*

Female eider ducks work together to protect their **ducklings** *from danger.*

dry goods goods made of cloth, such as fabrics and lace.

dual [doo-ul] *adjective.* composed of two parts; double: *My father and my uncle have dual ownership of our vacation cottage.* 🔊 A different word with the same sound is **duel.**

du·bi·ous [doo-bee-us] *adjective.* **1.** of doubtful or questionable value or truth: *Being known as the winner of a reality TV show is a dubious claim to fame.* **2.** undecided; hesitating: *I was dubious about going out in the snow.* —**dubiously,** *adverb.*

duch·ess [duch-is] *noun, plural* **duchesses.** a duke's wife or widow.

duck[1] [duk] *noun, plural* **ducks. 1.** a water bird with a broad, flat bill and large, webbed feet. Some types dive under water for food, and some immerse just their head and upper body. Ducks can be wild or domesticated. Domesticated ducks are often raised for food. **2.** a female duck. The male duck is also called a drake.

duck[2] [duk] *verb,* **ducked, ducking. 1.** to go or push momentarily under water: *My father swam up behind me and ducked me.* **2.** to dip the head or body quickly to avoid something: *She ducked to avoid the rock falling from the cliff above.* **3.** to avoid an unpleasant task or duty; dodge: *The mayor thought it best to duck the issue by not answering the question.*

duck·ling ▲ [duk-ling] *noun, plural* **ducklings.** a young duck.

duct ▶ [dukt] *noun, plural* **ducts.** a tube, channel, or pipe for conveying liquid, gas, air, or cables from one point to another. In the human body, tear ducts carry the tears that form in glands behind the eyes to the front of the eyes. In a building, electric cables are fed through ducts to wherever they are needed.

Tear duct   Tear gland

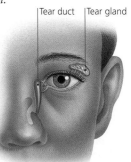

When you cry or sniffle, fluid from your tear glands drains through the tear **ducts** *into your nose.*

due [doo] *adjective.* **1.** owed or owing; needing to be paid: *Club membership fees are due at the end of this month.* **2.** expected or scheduled to happen: *The flight is due at three o'clock.* **3.** as it should be; proper; deserved: *The queen was crowned with due ceremony.* To pay your **dues** is to pay an amount of money you owe, such as a membership fee, or to act in a fitting way toward someone who has a right to your respect or consideration.
• **due to.** caused by; because of: *The damage was due to rust; We canceled the trip due to heavy rain.*

du·el ▼ [doo-ul] *noun, plural* **duels.** **1.** a fight between two people, especially using weapons such as swords or pistols and in the presence of witnesses. In the past, people fought duels to defend their own or someone else's honor or to settle a disagreement. **2.** any struggle or contest like this: *In soccer, a penalty kick is a tense duel between the kicker and the goalkeeper.*
verb, **dueled, dueling.** to fight or take part in a duel.
◀)) A different word with the same sound is **dual.**

du·et [doo-et] *noun, plural* **duets.**
Music. a piece composed for two performers.

dug [dug] *verb.* the past tense and past participle of DIG.

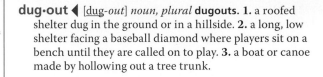

A cedar log was split in two and a stone tool was used to start shaping the dugout.

The sides were slowly chipped away.

The inside was hollowed to the right thickness.

Hot water softened the wood and bands made the dugout wider.

The bow and stern pieces were attached.

dug·out ◀ [dug-out] *noun, plural* **dugouts.** **1.** a roofed shelter dug in the ground or in a hillside. **2.** a long, low shelter facing a baseball diamond where players sit on a bench until they are called on to play. **3.** a boat or canoe made by hollowing out a tree trunk.

In the early days of baseball the **dugout** was an area that was actually *dug out* of the ground, and it was much lower than the rest of the field. Today most baseball fields have a dugout that is on the same level as the playing field, but the name *dugout* is still used.

duke [dook] *noun, plural* **dukes.** a man holding the highest rank of the nobility, especially in Britain. Only a prince is ranked higher. The territory a duke rules is called a **dukedom.**

dull [dul] *adjective,* **duller, dullest. 1.** not sharp; blunt: *My pocketknife was too dull to cut the fishing line.* **2.** not exciting or interesting; boring: *We were disappointed that the concert was so dull.* **3.** not sharp or clear, indistinct: *We heard a dull thud in the next room.* **4.** slow to learn; stupid; slow-witted.
verb, **dulled, dulling.** to make or become dull: *The thick walls dulled the sound of the music.*

dumb [dum] *adjective,* **dumber, dumbest. 1.** lacking the power of speech: *Damage to his vocal cords caused him to become dumb.* **2.** kept silent by surprise or shyness: *Surrounded by so many famous people, she was struck dumb.* **3.** not intelligent; foolish or stupid: *That's a really dumb question to ask.*

The earliest meaning of the word **dumb** was "not able to speak." This was used of people who did not have the ability to talk, and also of animals, since they cannot talk. These uses of the word still exist in expressions like "Be kind to dumb animals" or "She was so surprised by what she saw that she was struck dumb for a moment." The use of dumb to mean "stupid or foolish" is often heard in speech, but it is not a good choice to use in your school writing.

*In the past, some judges ordered people to fight **duels** to settle quarrels, but more often they were private fights.*

*On coastal **dunes**, hardy, salt-resistant plants help to stabilize the shifting sand.*

dumb·bell ▶ [dum-*bel*] *noun, plural* **dumbbells.** a short bar with a weight at each end used for exercise and to build muscle strength.

dumb·founded [dum-*fownd*-id] *adjective.* struck dumb with surprise; astonished; stunned: *They were dumbfounded at the devastation the tornado had caused.* This word is also spelled **dumfounded.**

dum·my [dum-ee] *noun, plural* **dummies. 1.** a model of a person: *We practiced our first aid skills on a dummy.* **2.** something made to look like a real thing and used in place of the real thing: *The impressive rows of books on those shelves are all dummies.* *adjective.* used as a dummy: *They are all dummy books.*

dump [dump] *verb,* **dumped, dumping. 1.** to drop or deposit in a heap: *I dumped my books on the table.* *noun, plural* **dumps. 1.** a place for depositing garbage and other things that are not wanted: *We took our old furniture to the city dump.* **2.** an unattractive, shabby, or dirty place: *The cheap motel turned out to be a dump.*

dune ▲ [doon] *noun, plural* **dunes.** a mound or ridge formed of loose sand deposited by the wind.

dun·ga·rees [dung-guh-*reez*] *plural noun.* pants or work clothes made from blue denim.

dun·geon [dun-jun] *noun, plural* **dungeons.** a dark, usually underground cell or prison. Dungeons were originally built in castles.

dunk [dungk] *verb,* **dunked, dunking. 1.** to dip food, such as bread or a cookie, into a liquid, such as soup or coffee, just before eating it. **2.** to score in a game of basketball by jumping high in the air and shoving the ball down hard into the basket. *noun, plural* **dunks.** a shot in basketball made by jumping high in the air and forcing the ball into the basket. This is also called a **slam-dunk.**

du·pli·cate [doo-pli-*kate*] *adjective.* exactly like something else; identical: *I carry my house key with me and have a duplicate key at home.* *noun, plural* **duplicates.** something that is exactly like something else; an exact copy: *Only an expert would know that this painting is a duplicate and not an original.* *verb,* **duplicated, duplicating. 1.** to make an exact copy of something: *The watchmaker duplicated the old watch in every detail.* **2.** to repeat; match: *I doubt that he will ever be able to duplicate such a great pitching performance.* **—duplication,** *noun.*

du·ra·ble [dur-uh-bul] *adjective.* capable of lasting a long time; sturdy; hard-wearing: *Hiking gear needs to be lightweight but durable.* **—durably,** *adverb.*

dur·ing [dur-ing] *preposition.* **1.** throughout the course of; all through: *He lived in a dormitory during his first year in college.* **2.** at some point in: *A loud noise awoke me during the night.*

Dumbbells *of different weights are used to develop strong muscles.*

dusk [dusk] *noun.* the time of half-light between sunset and nightfall; the darker stage of twilight: *The street lights go on at dusk.*

dust ▶ [dust] *noun.* tiny, powdery particles of earth, dirt, and other solid material: *A layer of dust had settled on the furniture.* *verb,* **dusted, dusting. 1.** to clear of dust by wiping or brushing: *I dust my room every couple of weeks.* **2.** to sprinkle with dust or powder: *She dusted herself with talcum powder.*

dust·y [dust-ee] *adjective,* **dustier, dustiest. 1.** covered or filled with dust: *These old books are very dusty.* **2.** similar to dust; powdery: *The soil was dried out and dusty.*

Dutch [duch] *adjective.* of or relating to the people of the Netherlands, their country, or their language. The people of the Netherlands are called **the Dutch.**

du·ti·ful [doo-ti-ful] *adjective.* doing your duty; conscientious; obedient: *He was a dutiful son, and cared for his parents in their old age.* **—dutifully,** *adverb.*

du·ty [doot-ee] *noun, plural* **duties. 1.** a task or job someone is required or expected to do: *One of the club secretary's duties is to reply to mail.* **2.** *Government.* an official tax on imports and some other goods.

DVD *Computers.* an abbreviation for Digital Video Disk, a plastic disk with a high storage capacity on which information (such as a movie or computer data) is recorded digitally and then read by a laser beam shining on the spinning disk. This can also be called a **Digital Versatile Disk.**

Medieval houses
France

The style and building materials of **dwellings** *vary around the world.*

Shaker house
Kentucky, U.S.A.

Stilt house
Solomon Islands

dwarf [dworf] *noun, plural* **dwarfs** *or* **dwarves. 1.** a person, animal, or plant that is much smaller than normal. **2.** a character in legends and fairy tales that resembles a small man or gnome and has magical powers. *verb,* **dwarfed, dwarfing.** to make something similar seem small or less significant: *The huge amount of money they raised dwarfs the small sum we got.*

dwell [dwel] *verb,* **dwelt** *or* **dwelled, dwelling.** to live somewhere for a time; live in a certain place: *Lions dwell on the African plains.* Someone who lives or resides somewhere for a time is a **dweller** of that place.
• **dwell on.** to keep your attention focused on something; keep thinking or talking about something: *My grandfather says he never dwells on past mistakes.*

dwel·ling ▲ [dwel-ing] *noun, plural* **dwellings.** a house or other place to live in: *Houses and apartments are two common types of dwellings.*

dwin·dle [dwin-dul] *verb,* **dwindled, dwindling.** to become gradually less or smaller; shrink: *As the drought continued, our water supplies dwindled.*

dye [dye] *noun, plural* **dyes.** a liquid substance used to change the color of various kinds of materials, often permanently. *verb,* **dyed, dyeing.** to change the color of something with a dye: *I dyed my white bathrobe blue.*
🔊 A different word with the same sound is **die.**

dy·ing [dye-ing] *verb.* the present participle of DIE.

dy·nam·ic [dye-nam-ik] *adjective.* having a lot of energy; powerful; changing in a productive way: *New York is a dynamic city, full of life and always changing.* **—dynamically,** *adverb.*

dy·na·mite [dye-nuh-mite] *noun.* a powerful explosive that blasts things apart. It is sometimes used to demolish old buildings and blast openings for roads and tunnels.

dy·na·mo [dye-nuh-moh] *noun, plural* **dynamos.** a machine that makes electricity by converting mechanical energy into electrical energy; generator.

dy·nas·ty [dye-nuh-stee] *noun, plural* **dynasties.** a line of rulers who all descend from the same family: *The Zhou dynasty in ancient China ruled for more than eight hundred years.*

dys·lex·ia [dis-lek-see-uh] *noun. Language.* a learning disorder marked by having great difficulty with reading, writing, and spelling. Someone who has this disorder is said to be **dyslexic.**

Strong winds lift dry soil to form a moving cloud of **dust** *that can travel thousands of miles and rise up to 10,000 feet into the air.*

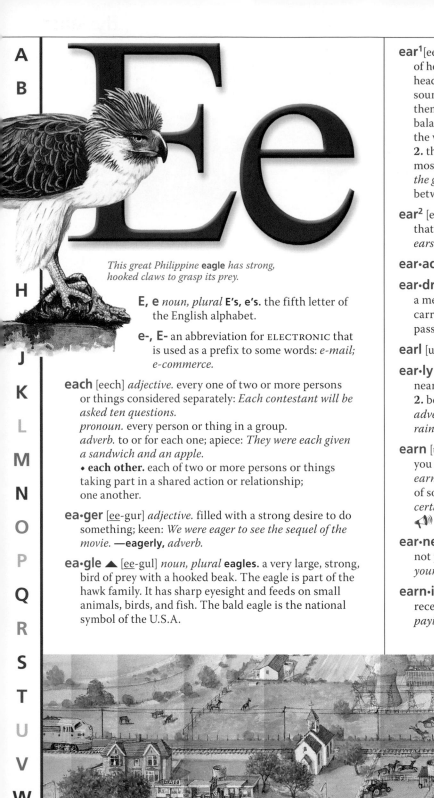

Ee

*This great Philippine **eagle** has strong, hooked claws to grasp its prey.*

E, e *noun, plural* **E's, e's.** the fifth letter of the English alphabet.

e-, E- an abbreviation for ELECTRONIC that is used as a prefix to some words: *e-mail; e-commerce.*

each [eech] *adjective.* every one of two or more persons or things considered separately: *Each contestant will be asked ten questions.*
pronoun. every person or thing in a group.
adverb. to or for each one; apiece: *They were each given a sandwich and an apple.*
• **each other.** each of two or more persons or things taking part in a shared action or relationship; one another.

ea·ger [ee-gur] *adjective.* filled with a strong desire to do something; keen: *We were eager to see the sequel of the movie.* —**eagerly,** *adverb.*

ea·gle ▲ [ee-gul] *noun, plural* **eagles.** a very large, strong, bird of prey with a hooked beak. The eagle is part of the hawk family. It has sharp eyesight and feeds on small animals, birds, and fish. The bald eagle is the national symbol of the U.S.A.

ear¹ [eer] *noun, plural* **ears. 1.** one of the organs of hearing and balance that are on either side of your head. The **outer ear** is the part of the ear that collects sound vibrations. These are amplified in the **middle ear,** then transmitted to the **inner ear,** which helps maintain balance and contains sensory nerve endings that transmit the vibrations to the brain through the auditory nerve. **2.** the external, visible part of this organ in humans and most mammals: *The dog pricked up its ears when it heard the gate open.* **3.** the ability to distinguish accurately between different sounds: *She has a good ear for music.*

ear² [eer] *noun, plural* **ears.** the top part of a cereal plant that contains the seeds, fruit, or grain: *We picked some ears of corn and ate them for lunch.*

ear·ache [eer-*ake*] *noun, plural* **earaches.** a pain in the ear.

ear·drum ▶ [eer-*drum*] *noun, plural* **eardrums.** a membrane between the outer and middle ear that carries the vibrations of sound waves; these are then passed on to the brain via the auditory nerve.

earl [url] *noun, plural* **earls.** a British nobleman.

ear·ly [ur-lee] *adjective,* **earlier, earliest. 1.** in the first part; near the start: *Early morning is the best part of the day.* **2.** before the expected time: *Let's catch the early train today.*
adverb. coming before the usual time: *The game was rained out so we came home early.*

earn [urn] *verb,* **earned, earning. 1.** to get paid for the work you do: *When you graduate from college you'll be able to earn a good living.* **2.** to get a reward or benefit as a result of something well done, or for good behavior: *You've certainly earned a good rest.* —**earner,** *noun.*
🔊 A different word with the same sound is **urn.**

ear·nest [ur-nist] *adjective,* having a serious manner; not playful; sincere. *The new librarian is a very earnest young man.* —**earnestly,** *adverb.*

earn·ings [urn-ingz] *plural noun. Business.* the money received as wages, or profit: *All of his earnings went on paying his debts.*

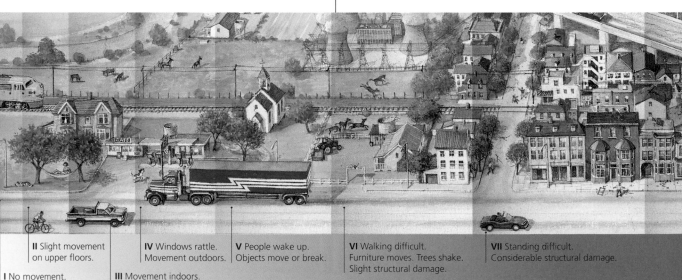

II Slight movement on upper floors.

IV Windows rattle. Movement outdoors.

V People wake up. Objects move or break.

VI Walking difficult. Furniture moves. Trees shake. Slight structural damage.

VII Standing difficult. Considerable structural damage.

I No movement.

III Movement indoors. Objects swing.

ear·phone [eer-fone] *noun, plural* **earphones.** a small electrical device that fits over, or in, your ear so that only you can hear a radio, music player, or telephone.

ear·ring [eer-ing] *noun, plural* **earrings.** jewelry worn on the ear, either clipped to it, or attached by means of a hole pierced in the ear.

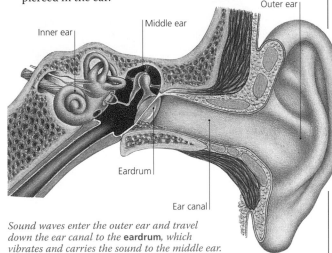

Inner ear · Middle ear · Outer ear · Eardrum · Ear canal

Sound waves enter the outer ear and travel down the ear canal to the **eardrum,** *which vibrates and carries the sound to the middle ear.*

earth [urth] *noun.* **1.** the planet that we live on. It is the third planet in order from the Sun and is 93,000,000 miles from the Sun; it is the only planet in the universe known to support life. This is also spelled **Earth. 2.** the solid, dry land surface of this planet: *When the earthquake hit, we could feel the earth shake under our feet.* **3.** soil and dirt: *He left his footprints in the muddy earth.*

earth·en [urth-un] *adjective.* **1.** made of earth: *The pioneers' huts had earthen floors.* **2.** made of baked clay: *The ancient earthen pot was decorated with figures of animals.* Pottery and utensils made from baked clay are called **earthenware.**

earth·ly [urth-lee] *adjective.* **1.** having to do with the physical world; not spiritual: *Some people believe that our earthly existence is all we can know.* **2.** possible or imaginable: *There is no earthly reason why I shouldn't be allowed to go to the party.*

earth·quake ▼ [urth-kwake] *noun, plural* **earthquakes.** a sudden, violent shaking of the Earth's surface that can cause a lot of damage; movement of rocks and lava deep underground. An earthquake can be the result of volcanic activity.

earth·worm [urth-wurm] *noun, plural* **earthworms.** a common worm with a segmented body that lives in soil and feeds on decaying organic matter. Its burrowing loosens the soil.

ease [eez] *noun.* freedom from pain, worries, or trouble; comfort.
verb, **eased, easing. 1.** to make free from pain or worry: *My increase in salary will ease my money worries.*
2. to move gently and carefully: *He eased his way into the crowded room*
• **at ease. 1.** a military command that gives soldiers permission to relax but not leave their places or talk.
2. having the freedom to act in a way that is comfortable: *I feel at ease with you, now that we have got to know each other well.*

ea·sel [ee-zul] *noun, plural* **easels.** *Art.* a frame, usually made of wood, used for supporting something such as an artist's canvas, a sign, or a blackboard.

eas·ily [ee-zuh-lee] *adverb.* **1.** in an easy way; without trouble or difficulty: *They easily won the game against the team of smaller boys.* **2.** certainly or probably: *If you start smoking you can easily become addicted.*

east [eest] *noun.* one of the four main points of the compass. It lies opposite west and is the direction you face to watch the sun rise in the morning. The part of an area, region, or country in this direction is **East.** The region of the United States along the Atlantic coast is **the East,** which is a term that also refers to Asia and the islands close to it.
adjective. situated toward, near, or facing or coming from the east: *I went into the building by the east entrance.*
adverb. to, toward, or in the east: *Let's drive east to New York City.*

The strength of an **earthquake** *is measured on the Mercalli scale according to the amount of movement and damage.*

a b c d e f g h i j k l m n o p q r s t u v w x y z

VIII Steering cars difficult. Chimneys fall. Branches break. Furniture overturns.

IX Buildings badly damaged. Ground cracks. Pipes break.

X Most buildings destroyed. Landslides. Railroad tracks bend.

XI Most buildings, some bridges, and underground pipes destroyed.

XII Complete destruction. Wave-like ground movements.

ECLIPSE

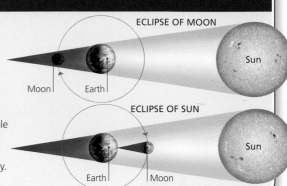

When the Earth is between the Sun and the Moon, the Earth's shadow falls on the Moon, causing an eclipse of the Moon. In an eclipse of the Sun, the Moon passes between the Sun and the Earth, preventing light from reaching a part of the Earth. Eclipses occur at different places, and can be partial, when only part of the Moon or Sun is covered, or total, if the whole is hidden from view. An annular eclipse of the Sun occurs when the Moon is farther from the Earth and does not cover the Sun completely.

ECLIPSE OF MOON

Moon   Earth   Sun

ECLIPSE OF SUN

Earth   Moon   Sun

Annular eclipse of the Sun

Eas·ter [ees-tur] *noun, plural* **Easters.** a holy day when Christians remember the death of Jesus Christ and celebrate his return to life. It falls on the first Sunday following the full moon on or after March 21.

The word **Easter** is thought to come from the name of an ancient goddess whose festival was celebrated in spring. When the Christian holiday of Easter came into being, it was celebrated at the same time as this earlier, non-Christian festival.

east·ern [ees-turn] *adjective.* **1.** in the east: *There is a rain forest on the eastern side of the island.* **2.** coming from the east: *The eastern wind blows hot and dry in summer.* The **Eastern** states of the U.S. are those that lie east of the Mississippi River. Asia, in particular China and Japan, is known as the **Eastern** part of the world.

east·ern·er [ees-tur-nur] *noun, plural* **easterners.** **1.** someone who lives in the east. **2. Easterner.** a person from the eastern United States.

Eastern Hemisphere *Geography.* the half of the Earth to the east of the Atlantic Ocean. This includes Europe, Asia, Australia, and Africa.

east·ward [eest-wurd] *adverb.* moving toward the east: *The ship sailed eastward across the Atlantic Ocean.*
adjective. in an easterly direction. This word is also spelled **eastwards.**

eas·y [ee-zee] *adjective,* **easier, easiest.** **1.** not difficult; not requiring much effort: *That large sign is easy to read.* **2.** relaxed and comfortable, without pain: *Now that we have paid off all our debts we can have an easier life.*

eat [eet] *verb,* **ate, eaten, eating.** **1.** to chew and swallow food: *Eat up all your lunch or you'll be hungry later on.* **2.** to have a meal: *We'll eat now and then go for a walk.* **3.** to destroy; corrode: *The acid in some foods can eat into your tooth enamel.*

eaves ▼ [eevz] *plural noun.* the lower edges of a roof that overhang the wall that supports it.

eaves·drop [eevz-*drop*] *verb,* **eavesdropped, eavesdropping.** to listen in to a private conversation without the speakers being aware of it: *I caught her eavesdropping outside the door.* **—eavesdropper,** *noun.*

In early times, the **eavesdrop** of a house was a space just outside the walls and windows, under the roof. It was thought that someone could stand here to listen in secret to what was being said inside the house; that is, to eavesdrop on the people inside.

ebb [eb] *noun, plural* **ebbs.** the flow of the sea away from the shore as the tide goes out. The **ebb tide** is when the sea is at its lowest point. *verb,* **ebbed, ebbing.** **1.** to flow away: *As the tide ebbed it exposed many shells in the sand.* **2.** to grow less; weaken or fade away: *His life ebbed away as I held his hand.*

eb·o·ny [eb-uh-nee] *noun, plural* **ebonies.** a hard, black wood from trees that grow in southeast Asia, Africa, and southern India, used for making the black keys on pianos.
adjective. made of ebony; a deep, shiny, black color: *Her ebony hair shone in the moonlight.*

ec·cen·tric [ik-sen-trik] *adjective.* behaving or appearing in a way that is odd or strange; unusual; different from normal: *My eccentric aunt has twenty-five cats and wears only yellow clothes.* The state of behaving in an odd way is **eccentricity.**

ech·o [ek-oh] *noun, plural* **echoes.** the repetition of a sound caused when sound waves bounce off a hard surface: *We heard an echo as we walked along the long, empty hallway.*
verb, **echoed, echoing.** **1.** to produce an echo: *Her scream echoed across the canyon.* **2.** to repeat something; imitate: *You are simply echoing what I have already said.*

The roofs and **eaves** *of St. Andrew's church in Borgund, Norway, are made of timber.*

e·clipse ◄ [i-<u>klips</u> *or* ee-<u>klips</u>] *noun, plural* **eclipses.**
Science. an event that occurs when a planet, star, or moon is hidden, or partly hidden, by another. An eclipse of the Moon happens when the Earth moves between it and the Sun.
verb, **eclipsed, eclipsing. 1.** to cause an eclipse: *Last weekend, the Moon eclipsed the Sun.* **2.** to become more powerful or important than; surpass: *The report about the terrorist attack eclipsed all other news.*

eco·log·i·cal [ek-uh-<u>loj</u>-uh-kul] *adjective. Environment.* having to do with how people, plants, and animals interact with each other and the environment.
An **ecological footprint** is a measure of how much land and water a person, a city, or a country needs to provide to support itself and absorb its waste, using the technology that is available at the time.
—**ecologically,** *adverb.*

e·col·o·gy [ee-<u>kol</u>-uh-*jee*] *noun. Environment.* the scientific study of how people, plants, and animals interact with each other and their environment.
An **ecologist** is a scientist who studies ecology.

e-com·merce *noun. Business.* the buying and selling of goods and services and doing other business activities through the Internet. The full name for this activity is **electronic commerce.**

The word **ecology** was made up in the mid-1800s by a German scientist named Ernst Haeckel. He did this by combining two Greek terms, *-logy* meaning "the study or knowledge of" and *eco-* meaning "house" or "place to live." The idea is that ecology studies how plants and animals relate to the place where they live.

ec·o·nom·ic [ek-uh-<u>nom</u>-ik *or* ee-kuh-<u>nom</u>-ik] *adjective.* having to do with the management of money: *In the current economic climate we need to cut our spending.*

ec·o·nom·i·cal [ek-uh-<u>nom</u>-i-kul *or* ee-kuh-<u>nom</u>-i-kul] *adjective.* using resources carefully; without waste: *an economical car that gets good gas mileage.* —**economically,** *adverb.*

ec·o·nom·ics [ek-uh-<u>nom</u>-iks *or* ee-kuh-<u>nom</u>-iks] *noun.* the field of study that deals with the production, distribution, and use of money, goods, and services. An **economist** is a person who studies, or is an expert in, economics.

e·con·o·mize [i-<u>kon</u>-uh-*mize*] *verb,* **economized, economizing.** to reduce spending or the use of something in order to save: *We are trying to economize to save up for our vacation.* —**economization,** *noun.*

e·con·o·my [i-<u>kon</u>-uh-mee] *noun, plural* **economies. 1.** the way a country, state, or other body plans for and organizes its total spending. **2.** the condition of business, sales, employment, and so on at a given time: *The economy of that nation is very strong now.* **3.** the act of saving by spending or using less: *If you waste money now, you will have to make economies in the future.*

e·co·sphere [ek-oh-*sfeer*] *noun, plural* **ecospheres.** *Environment.* the part of the atmosphere around the Earth, or anywhere else in the universe, in which life can exist.

e·co·sys·tem ▼ [ek-koh-*sis*-tum *or* <u>ee</u>-oh-*sis*-tum] *noun, plural* **ecosystems.** *Biology.* all the elements that exist in a particular environment and that interact with each other to maintain or change that environment. Trees, birds, water, and soil are part of a forest's ecosystem.

ec·sta·sy [<u>eks</u>-tuh-see] *noun, plural* **ecstasies.** enormous joy or pleasure: *For some people, listening to great music can be pure ecstasy.*

-ed a suffix that: **1.** indicates the past tense or past participle of most verbs. **2.** describes having the quality of, or having: *barefooted* means having bare feet.

ed·dy [<u>ed</u>-ee] *noun, plural* **eddies.** a place in a stream where the water whirls round in circles.
verb, **eddied, eddying.** to spin or turn around and around swiftly: *The smoke eddied in the wind.*

edge [ej] *noun, plural* **edges. 1.** the part where something begins or ends: *Keep away from the edge of the cliff!* **2.** the thin, sharp, cutting part of something, such as a knife. **3.** a slight advantage or greater skill: *I am good at drawing, but Marissa has the edge on me.*
verb, **edged, edging. 1.** to advance with slow steps: *In the dark, the boys edged carefully down the stairs.* **2.** to create an edge or border: *A row of bushes edged the garden path.*
♦ **on edge.** tense and anxious: *Bella was on edge about the results of her fitness test.*

ed·gy [<u>ej</u>-ee] *adjective,* **edgier, edgiest.** anxious and irritable: *Our teacher gets very edgy if the class is too noisy.*

a
b
c
d
e
f
g
h
i
j
k
l
m
n
o
p
q
r
s
t
u
v
w
x
y
z

These animals, grasses, and small trees are important parts of a savanna **ecosystem.** **229**

ed·i·ble [ed-uh-bul] *adjective*. able to be eaten safely: *Some mushrooms are edible, but some are poisonous.*

ed·it [ed-it] *verb*, **edited, editing.** to correct any mistakes in a text before it is printed or published: *I asked Mom to edit the story I wrote for the class magazine.*

e·di·tion [i-dish-un] *noun, plural* **editions. 1.** the form or style of a book, newspaper, or magazine publication: *There are large-print editions of many books.* **2.** all the copies of something that are published at the same time: *This book had an edition of ten thousand copies.* **3.** the timing of a publication: *The news of the accident was not in the early edition of the newspaper.*

ed·i·tor [ed-uh-tur] *noun, plural* **editors. 1.** a person who corrects or makes changes to text. **2.** a person who controls what is published in a newspaper or magazine: *My uncle is the editor of a popular gardening magazine.* **3.** a person who deals with and helps authors in the publishing of their books.

Spiny eels live in freshwater swamps and feed on insects and other small animals.

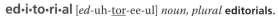

ed·i·to·ri·al [ed-uh-tor-ee-ul] *noun, plural* **editorials. 1.** an article in a newspaper or magazine in which the editor expresses an opinion about something: *Today's editorial criticized the poor condition of the local roads.* **2.** a statement on radio or television that expresses the opinions or policy of the station's owners or managers. *adjective.* having to do with what editors do or decide: *It was an editorial decision to include pictures in that book.* To write an editorial or express an editorial opinion is to **editorialize.**

ed·u·cate [ej-uh-kate] *verb*, **educated, educating.** to develop skills or knowledge in; teach or instruct: *The Smith children were all educated at very good schools.*

ed·u·ca·tion [ej-uh-kay-shun] *noun, plural* **educations. 1.** training or instruction that is given or received: *That school provides its students with a fine education.* **2.** a certain type of skill or knowledge acquired: *To apply for that job, you need a college education.* **3.** the study of teaching and learning and of the proper methods for doing this.

ed·u·ca·tion·al [ej-uh-kay-shun-ul] *adjective.* **1.** having to do with or providing education: *Harvard University is a leading educational establishment.* **2.** designed to educate or instruct: *We went on an educational tour of the local area.* —**educationally,** *adverb.*

ed·u·ca·tor [ej-uh-kay-tur] *noun, plural* **educators.** someone who educates; a teacher or instructor.

eel ▲ [eel] *noun, plural* **eels.** a long, thin, snakelike freshwater or saltwater fish.

ee·rie [eer-ee] *adjective*, **eerier, eeriest.** describing something weird and scary: *At night the old graveyard was an eerie place.*

ef·fect [uh-fekt] *noun, plural* **effects. 1.** a result caused by something else: *One effect of the storm was that the power was off for two hours.* **2.** the ability to change; influence: *The party was indoors, so the weather had no effect on it.* The things that a person owns are that person's **effects.** • **in effect.** as a point of fact; operating; working: *The new school rules are already in effect.* *verb*, **effected, effecting.** to cause to happen: *The oil crisis effected a rise in prices at the gas pump.* 🔊 A different word that sounds like this is **affect.**

Effect and *affect* are two similar words that carry the same meaning of making something happen, but they are used as different parts of speech. *Affect* is a verb: *The development of the jet airliner affected the way people travel around the U.S. Effect* is usually a noun: *The development of the jet airliner had a major effect on the way people travel around the U.S.*

ef·fec·tive [uh-fek-tiv] *adjective.* **1.** working well; efficient: *This cream is effective in preventing sunburn.* **2.** starting from or in operation from: *The price increases are effective tomorrow.* —**effectively,** *adverb.*

ef·fi·cient [uh-fish-unt] *adjective.* able to do things well and on time: *The new employee is an efficient worker and always completes his job assignments on time.* The fact of being able to do things well and on time is **efficiency.** —**efficiently,** *adverb.*

ef·flu·ent [ef-loo-unt] *noun, plural* **effluents.** *Environment.* liquid or other waste material that remains or is spilled out at the end of a process: *That brown stain in the river is effluent from the paint factory.*

ef·fort [ef-urt] *noun, plural* **efforts. 1.** the use of energy and determination to do something, especially a difficult task: *It took a huge effort to read that long book.* **2.** a genuine attempt: *Andrew made a special effort to learn to swim.*

ef·fort·less [ef-urt-lis] *adjective.* not requiring effort; easy: *The gymnast's movements seemed effortless.* —**effortlessly,** *adverb.*

e.g. for example; for instance: *We read about lots of things in history, e.g. the Civil War, the presidents, and the Constitution.* This term is an abbreviation for the Latin words *exempli gratia.*

egg¹ ▼ [eg] *noun, plural* **eggs. 1.** an object that female birds, insects, and many other animals lay and from which newborn birds and animals hatch. Eggs are usually round or oval in shape. **2.** the material inside the shell of eggs that humans eat. **3.** a tiny cell inside the body of a woman or a female animal. When these cells are fertilized, new humans and animals can grow from them.

egg² [eg] *verb*, **egged, egging.** to urge or encourage, especially to do something one should not or does not want to do: *The other boys egged him on to jump from the tree.*

A ladybug lays her tiny, yellow, oval-shaped eggs on a leaf.

egg·plant [eg-*plant*] *noun, plural* **eggplants.**
a large vegetable, shaped a little like an egg, that has purple skin and whitish flesh.

e·go [ee-*goh*] *noun, plural* **egos.** too much pride; love of self: *She has a large ego and has no interest in other people.* A person who shows a lot of excessive pride is **egotistical.**

e·gret ▶ [ee-grit] *noun, plural* **egrets.** one of several kinds of heron. Egrets are tall wading birds and usually have white feathers.

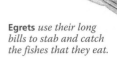

E·gyp·tian ▼ [ee-jip-shun] *noun, plural* **Egyptians.**
1. a person who is a citizen of Egypt, an ancient nation in northeastern Africa. **2.** a person who lived in Egypt in ancient times. **3.** the language that was spoken and written by ancient Egyptian people.
adjective. having to do with Egypt and Egyptian people, in either modern or ancient times.

eight [ate] *noun, plural* **eights.** the number between seven and nine; 8. Something that is number eight in order is the **eighth.**

eight·een [ay-teen] *noun, plural* **eighteens.** the number between seventeen and nineteen; 18. Something that is number eighteen in order is the **eighteenth.**

eight·y [ate-ee] *noun, plural* **eighties.** the number between seventy-nine and eighty-one; 80. Something that is number eighty in order is the **eightieth.**

ei·ther [ee-THur *or* eye-THur] *adjective.* **1.** one of the two: *I will not support either side of this argument.* **2.** each of the two: *The crowd watched the game from either side of the field.*
pronoun. one of the two: *He did not like either of the pictures on display.*
adverb. as well; too: *Helena didn't read that book and I didn't read it either.* A way of indicating a choice between two things is to say **either** before the first and **or** before the second: *Henry said he could come either by bus, or by train.*

e·ject [i-jekt] *verb,* **ejected, ejecting.**
1. to force out; make to leave: *Ian was ejected from the stadium for throwing objects at the players.* **2.** to force oneself out: *The fighter pilot ejected as soon as the missile hit his plane.* **—ejection,** *noun.*

e·lab·o·rate [i-lab-ur-it *for adjective;* ee-lab-uh-*rate for verb*] *adjective.* carefully worked out; complicated: *The architect made elaborate drawings of the house he was designing.*
verb, **elaborated, elaborating.** to explain in great detail; add extra information: *I asked Katrina to elaborate on her description of the movie.* **—elaborately,** *adverb.*

e·land [ee-land] *noun, plural* **elands.** one of two types of ox-like African antelopes that have short, twisted horns.

Egrets use their long bills to stab and catch the fishes that they eat.

e·lapse [i-laps] *verb,* **elapsed, elapsing.** to pass by; slip away: *Ten minutes have elapsed since we started walking.*

e·last·ic [i-las-tik] *adjective.* able to expand and contract and be pushed in and out of shape.
noun, plural **elastics.** a material that can be pulled to expand and will then retract to its original size.

el·bow [el-boh] *noun, plural* **elbows. 1.** the joint in a person's arm. **2.** something that is shaped like an arm bent at the elbow. A sharp bend in a road is called an elbow.
verb, **elbowed, elbowing.** to push or jab with an elbow: *The angry player elbowed his opponent in the ribs.*

*Wealthy ancient **Egyptians** wore colorful clothes and fine jewelry.*

a
b
c
d
e
f
g
h
i
j
k
l
m
n
o
p
q
r
s
t
u

*The **electric eel** is a slow-moving fish that lives in freshwater rivers.*

el·der [el-dur] *adjective.* greater in age; older: *Veronica is Lisa's elder sister.*
noun, plural **elders. 1.** an older person: *My brother is my elder by three years.* **2. elders.** older, influential, or official members of a tribe, community, or religious group. The older of two, such as a father and son with the same name, may be referred to as **the elder.**

Organs that produce electric shocks

eld·er·ly [el-dur-lee] *adjective.* well advanced in age: *The elderly woman needed help to cross the road.*

eld·est [el-dust] *adjective.* oldest of more than two people: *My father is the eldest member of our family.*

e·lect [i-lekt] *verb,* **elected, electing. 1.** to choose for a position by means of a vote: *The team members elected Jules as captain.* **2.** to choose; decide: *Marjorie elected to wear the red dress instead of the white one.*

e·lec·tion [i-lek-shun] *noun, plural* **elections.** *Government.* choice by means of a vote: *People vote in elections for members of Congress, senators, and state governors.*

e·lec·tive [i-lek-tiv] *adjective.* **1.** chosen or decided by an election: *The presidency of the United States is an elective position.* **2.** done by choice: *In this school, history is a required course and music is an elective subject.*

e·lec·tric [i-lek-trik] *adjective.* **1.** having to do with, or powered by, electricity: *Houses today have electric lighting.* **2.** highly emotional; thrilling: *It was an electric moment when the space shuttle landed safely.*

In the year 1600 the English scientist William Gilbert published a book titled *On Magnets.* In this book he was the first to use the word **electric**, which he took from the word for a hard substance called amber. At that time the best-known way to produce electricity was by rubbing a piece of amber.

e·lec·tri·cal [i-lek-truh-kul] *adjective.* having to do with, or powered by, electricity: *There are electrical connections to every part of this building.*

electric eel ◄ a long, eel-like South American fish that can use electric shocks to stun its prey and protect itself against attack.

e·lec·tri·cian [i-lek-trish-un] *noun, plural* **electricians.** a person who works with electricity, does electrical repairs, and installs electrical equipment.

e·lec·tri·ci·ty ▼ [i-lek-tris-uh-tee] *noun.*
1. a form of energy that can generate light and heat and can be used to operate a wide range of engines and appliances. Wind, water, coal, and nuclear energy are some of the things that can be used to create electricity. **2.** an electric current: *In some places underground cables bring electricity to houses and other buildings.* **3.** great emotion or anticipation: *There was electricity in the court as the jury announced its verdict.*

e·lec·tro·cute [i-lek-truh-kyoot] *verb,* **electrocuted, electrocuting.** to kill by giving an electric shock. The **electric chair** is used in some parts of the United States to electrocute convicted criminals. —**electrocution,** *noun.*

e·lec·tro·mag·net [i-lek-troh-mag-nit] *noun, plural,* **electromagnets.** a piece of iron that becomes magnetic when an electric current flows through wire that is coiled around it.

e·lec·tro·mag·net·ism [i-lek-troh-mag-nuh-tiz-um] *noun. Science.* the related properties of electricity and magnetism, or the effects that are produced by these two forces interacting with each other. —**electromagnetic,** *adjective.*

e·lec·tron [i-lek-tron] *noun, plural* **electrons.** *Science.* one of the very small particles that revolves around the nucleus of an atom and carries a negative electrical charge.

e·lec·tron·ic [i-lek-tron-ik] *adjective.* having to do with electrons or electronics.

electronic mail see E-MAIL.

e·lec·tron·ics [i-lek-tron-iks] *noun. Science.* the science that deals with how electrons behave. Radio, television, radar, and computers have all been developed as a result of research in electronics.

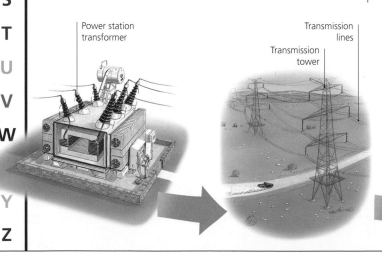

Power station transformer

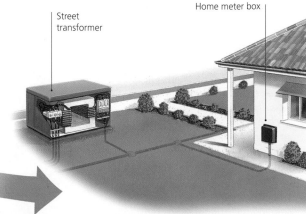

Transmission lines

Transmission tower

Street transformer

Home meter box

Electricity *travels from power stations to homes through transmission lines carried by tall towers and transformers.*

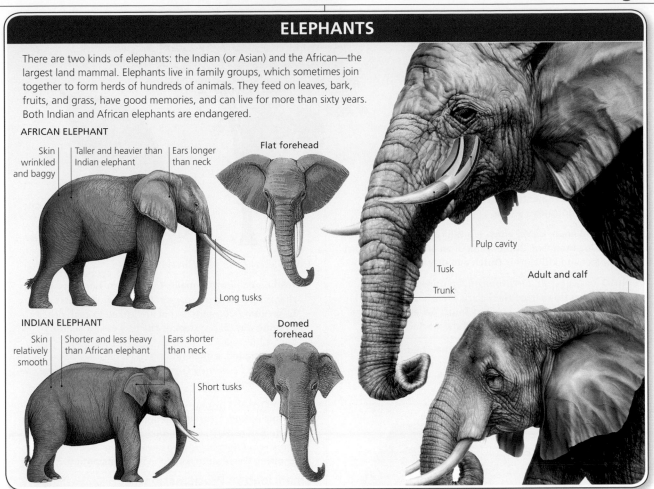

ELEPHANTS

There are two kinds of elephants: the Indian (or Asian) and the African—the largest land mammal. Elephants live in family groups, which sometimes join together to form herds of hundreds of animals. They feed on leaves, bark, fruits, and grass, have good memories, and can live for more than sixty years. Both Indian and African elephants are endangered.

AFRICAN ELEPHANT

Skin wrinkled and baggy

Taller and heavier than Indian elephant

Ears longer than neck

Flat forehead

Long tusks

INDIAN ELEPHANT

Skin relatively smooth

Shorter and less heavy than African elephant

Ears shorter than neck

Short tusks

Domed forehead

Pulp cavity

Tusk

Trunk

Adult and calf

---

el·e·gant [el-uh-gunt] *adjective.* showing good taste; stylish: *The house was full of elegant furniture.* Something that is stylish shows **elegance. —elegantly,** *adverb.*

el·e·ment [el-uh-munt] *noun, plural* **elements.** *Chemistry.* **1.** one of more than a hundred basic substances from which all other substances are formed. Elements cannot be split into simpler substances. Gold, oxygen, tin, and carbon are some of the elements. **2.** something that is a part of something else: *Correct spelling is an important element of good writing.* **3.** a place where something or someone naturally belongs: *An actor is in his element on stage.* Weather and climatic conditions are sometimes referred to as **the elements.**

el·e·ment·ar·y [el-uh-men-tree *or* el-uh-men-tuh-ree] *adjective.* concerned with the early, simple parts; basic: *At her first piano lesson, Greta learned some elementary finger exercises.*

elementary school *Education.* a school that covers the first six or eight grades in a child's education. After elementary school, children go on to junior high school or high school.

el·e·phant ▲ [el-uh-funt] *noun, plural* **elephants.** an Asian or African animal that has a huge body, a long trunk, ivory tusks, and large ears. Elephants are the world's largest animals that live on land.

el·e·vate [el-uh-*vate*] *verb,* **elevated, elevating.** to lift or raise up: *The dentist elevated the patient's chair to get a good look inside his mouth.*

el·e·va·tion [el-uh-vay-shun] *noun, plural* **elevations.** **1.** the act of raising up: *Giovanni was very happy about his elevation to general manager of the firm.* **2.** a high place; a hill: *The house stands on an elevation above the valley.* **3.** the distance above sea level: *We live in the mountains at an elevation of 3,000 feet.*

el·e·va·tor [el-uh-*vay*-tur] *noun, plural* **elevators.** **1.** an enclosed space or a platform that carries people or goods between the stories of a building or up and down into mines. **2.** a tall, hollow building into which grain is elevated and stored.

e·lev·en [i-lev-un] *noun, plural* **elevens.** the number between ten and twelve; 11. Something that is number eleven in order is the **eleventh.**

elf [elf] *noun, plural* **elves.** a small, playful, imaginary being that can perform magic.

el·i·gi·ble [el-uh-juh-bul] *adjective.* entitled to; qualified for: *Because Rhoda has worked here for one year, she is eligible for a pay raise.* The fact of being entitled to or eligible for something is **eligibility.**

e·lim·i·nate [i-<u>lim</u>-uh-*nate*] *verb*, **eliminated, eliminating.** to dispose of; put an end to: *The new police chief aims to eliminate crime in this city.* —**elimination**, *noun.*

elk [elk] *noun, plural* **elk** *or* **elks.** one of a number of large animals of the deer family of North America, Europe, Asia, and parts of Africa, related to and resembling the moose. Male elk have long, branching antlers.

el·lipse [i-<u>lips</u>] *noun, plural* **ellipses.** *Mathematics.* **1.** an oval- or egg-shaped figure that has the same shape at both ends. **2.** *Language.* a punctuation mark (. . .). It shows that letters or words have been left out or indicates a pause.

elm ▶ [elm] *noun, plural* **elms. 1.** a tall tree with spreading or arching branches. **2.** the wood of an elm. A disease that can affect and kill elms is **Dutch elm disease.**

El Niño [el-<u>neen</u>-yoh] *Environment.* an unusually warm current that flows from the Pacific Ocean toward, and then along, the western coast of South America. It alters weather patterns in many parts of the world.

El Niño is a Spanish phrase meaning "the Child." In this case "the Child" means the Christ Child (Jesus Christ). This ocean current generally occurs around Christmas time, the time of the birth of Christ.

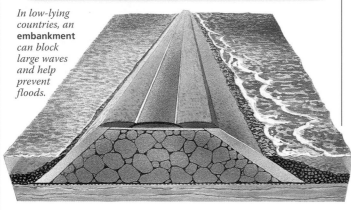

In low-lying countries, an **embankment** *can block large waves and help prevent floods.*

else [elss] *adjective.* **1.** not the same; other or different: *I don't like this food, so can I please have something else?* **2.** in addition; as well: *Stacy and Heather just got here —who else are we waiting for?*
adverb. **1.** differently: *I don't know how else I could have acted.* **2.** in another way or place: *It's too hot here—let's go somewhere else.*
• **or else.** otherwise: *Move into the shade, or else you'll get sunburned.*

else·where [elss-<u>ware</u>] *adverb.* not here; somewhere else: *If we can't get it at this store, we'll have to look elsewhere.*

e·lude [i-<u>lude</u>] *verb,* **eluded, eluding.** to escape from; stay hidden or away from: *He thought hard, but the answer to the question eluded him.*

e·lu·sive [i-<u>loo</u>-siv] *adjective.* difficult to find or catch; hard to understand: *Foxes are sly and elusive animals.*

The deciduous American **elm** *tree has leaves with jagged edges and seeds with two wide "wings."*

elves [elvz] *noun.* the plural of ELF.

e-mail *noun, plural* **e-mails.** *Computers.* **1.** a message that is sent from one person to another or others by means of computers that are linked to each other in some way. **2.** a system or the process for sending such a message.
verb, **e-mailed, e-mailing.** to send a message or messages by e-mail: *I e-mailed Grandpa to tell him what time our flight would arrive.*

e·man·ci·pate [i-<u>man</u>-si-*pate*] *verb,* **emancipated, emancipating.** to grant freedom to; remove restrictions from: *Before they were emancipated, slaves were the property of the people who owned them.* The act of granting freedom to someone is **emancipation.**

Emancipation Proclamation [i-man-si-pay-shun] *History.* an order made by United States President Abraham Lincoln on January 1, 1863, proclaiming the emancipation of slaves in the southern states.

em·bank·ment ◀ [im-<u>bangk</u>-munt] *noun, plural* **embankments.** a raised area of earth, stones, bricks, or other materials designed to support roadways or prevent floods.

em·bark [im-<u>bark</u>] *verb,* **embarked, embarking. 1.** to board a ship, plane, or other form of transport. **2.** to begin a journey or make a new start: *Erica left her job as a nurse and embarked on a career as a teacher.* —**embarkation**, *noun.*

em·bar·rass [im-<u>bare</u>-us] *verb,* **embarrassed, embarrassing.** to cause a person to feel silly, uncomfortable, or ashamed: *My brother embarrassed me by telling my friend about my poor school grades.* The state of feeling silly is **embarrassment.**

em·bas·sy [<u>em</u>-buh-see] *noun, plural* **embassies.** *Government.* the building that contains the offices and residences of an ambassador of a country, and his or her staff, in a foreign country.

em·ber [em-bur] *noun, plural* **embers.** a fragment of wood or coal that continues to glow after a fire has gone out: *We sat up late at night watching the dying embers of our campfire.*

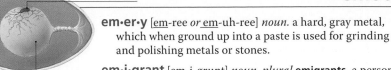

*A bird **embryo** grows inside an egg until the chick is ready to break through the shell and hatch.*

Embryo

Yolk

Embryo

em·bez·zle [im-bez-ul] *verb,* **embezzled, embezzling.** *Law.* to steal money, property, or goods that other people have placed in your care: *The accountant embezzled thousands of dollars from the firm's bank account.* The act of embezzling is **embezzlement.** —**embezzler,** *noun.*

em·blem [em-blum] *noun,* *plural* **emblems.** something that represents something else; a symbol: *The figure of a lion is the emblem of England.* Anything that is an emblem is **emblematic.**

em·brace [im-brays] *verb,* **embraced, embracing. 1.** to put your arms around someone and hold them tightly; hug: *When he returned from his trip, he embraced each member of the family.* **2.** to take up; accept and adopt: *Let's hope he can give up all his bad habits and embrace a new way of life.* *noun,* *plural* **embraces.** a hug: *a warm embrace.*

em·broi·der [im-broy-dur] *verb,* **embroidered, embroidering. 1.** to sew a design onto a piece of cloth or clothing. *I bought a plain, white T-shirt and Mom is going to embroider it for me.* The act of sewing designs on cloth is **embroidery. 2.** to make a story more interesting by adding extra details made up in your imagination.

em·bry·o ▲ [em-bree-oh] *noun,* *plural* **embryos.** *Biology.* an animal or plant in the very early stages of its development, such as a baby inside its mother, a chick inside an egg, or a plant inside a seed. Something that is at a very early stage of its development is **embryonic.**

em·er·ald [em-ruld *or* em-ur-uld] *noun,* *plural* **emeralds. 1.** a precious stone that is clear and bright green in color: *an emerald ring; an emerald necklace.* **2.** a bright green color. *adjective.* having a bright green color.

e·merge [i-murj] *verb,* **emerged, emerging. 1.** to appear or come into view: *A deer emerged from behind the tree.* **2.** to come out, become known: *It emerged that he had been out on the street after curfew.*

e·mer·gen·cy [i-mur-jun-see] *noun,* *plural* **emergencies.** a sudden, unexpected happening, often an accident, that requires swift action: *In case of an emergency such as fire, dial 911.* *adjective.* having to do with or used during an emergency: *emergency supplies such as bandages and medicine.*

emergency services ▶ *Health.* the organizations whose job is to respond quickly to an emergency, such as the fire department, the ambulance service, or the police force.

em·er·y [em-ree *or* em-uh-ree] *noun.* a hard, gray metal, which when ground up into a paste is used for grinding and polishing metals or stones.

em·i·grant [em-i-grunt] *noun,* *plural* **emigrants.** a person who leaves his or her own country to go and live in another country.

Emigrant and the similar word *immigrant* both have to do with people leaving their home country to live in another country. *Emigrant* refers to the country from which the person goes out: *Alexander Graham Bell's famous invention of the telephone was made in the United States, but he was a Scottish emigrant. Immigrant* refers to the country which the person enters: *The radio was invented by Guglielmo Marconi, an immigrant to the United States from Italy.*

em·i·grate [em-uh-*grate*] *verb,* **emigrated, emigrating.** to leave your native country to live in another country: *The actor and political leader Arnold Schwarzenegger emigrated to the United States from Austria.* —**emigration,** *noun.*

em·i·nent [em-uh-nunt] *adjective.* important, highly respected, and well known; being a leader in a field: *an eminent professor of chemistry; an eminent heart surgeon.* —**eminently,** *adverb.*

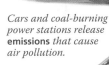

*Cars and coal-burning power stations release **emissions** that cause air pollution.*

e·mis·sions ▶ [i-*mish*-uns] *noun.* *Environment.* the release of some substance into the environment, such as smoke from the burning of coal or exhaust gases from car engines. Monitoring these emissions is known as **emissions control.**

e·mit [i-mit] *verb,* **emitted, emitting.** to send out, give off or produce: *She emitted a loud sob, and ran from the room.* The act of sending something out or giving something off is **emission.**

e·mo·tion [i-moh-shun] *noun,* *plural* **emotions.** a strong feeling such as love, hate, fear, sorrow, or jealousy.

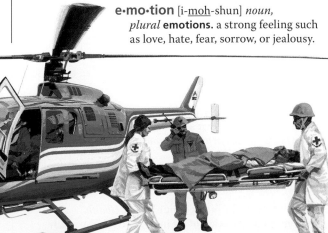
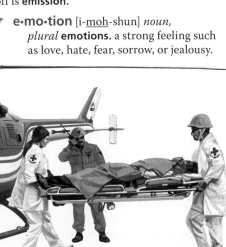

*An **emergency services** helicopter crew rescues an injured person.*

A
B
C
D
E
F
G
H
I
J
K
L
M
N
O
P
Q
R
S
T
U
V
W
X
Y
Z

e·mo·tion·al [i-<u>moh</u>-shun-ul] *adjective.* **1.** having to do with your emotions and the way that you feel: *Joel felt quite emotional when he saw that his sister was safe.* **2.** influenced more by feelings than by fact: *It was an emotional decision to buy the car—he liked the way it looked when he first saw it.* **3.** causing or trying to cause emotion: *The prosecutor's emotional speech was aimed at convincing the jury to convict the accused.* —**emotionally,** *adverb.*

em·per·or ▼ [<u>em</u>-pur-ur] *noun, plural* **emperors.** the male ruler of an empire.

In ancient China, **emperors** *were carried into the palace at the Forbidden City.*

em·pha·sis [<u>em</u>-fuh-sis] *noun, plural* **emphases.** **1.** special or extra importance given to something: *Emphasis should be given to the dangers of drinking and driving.* **2.** extra force placed on a word or syllable; stress: *In the word "giraffe," the emphasis should be on the second syllable.*

There are several different ways to show **emphasis** of a certain word or words in writing. The most common are to write the words in capital letters LIKE THIS; to underline them <u>like this</u>; to write them in bold (black) letters **like this**; or to write them in italics *like this.* It may be that your teacher will ask you to use a certain one of these styles in your school writing, but otherwise it would be correct to choose any of them.

em·pha·size [<u>em</u>-fuh-*size*] *verb,* **emphasized, emphasizing:** to strongly indicate that something is important; stress: *I can't emphasize enough the importance of carefully reading the question.*

em·phat·ic [im-<u>fat</u>-ik] *adjective.* strong and forceful: *Their answer was an emphatic "No!"* —**emphatically,** *adverb.*

em·phy·se·ma [*em*-fuh-<u>see</u>-muh] *noun. Health.* an abnormal collection of air in body tissue, especially the lungs.

em·pire ▶ [<u>em</u>-pire] *noun, plural* **empires.** **1.** a number of separate nations under the control of one government or ruler: *Modern nations such as India, South Africa, and Canada were once part of the empire of Great Britain.* **2.** a country ruled by an emperor or empress.

em·ploy [im-<u>ploy</u>] *verb,* **employed, employing. 1.** to pay someone to work for you; hire: *I will employ the first person who applies for the job.* **2.** to make use of; use: *The hospital always employs the latest medical technology.*
noun. paid work or employment: *That company has twenty workers in its employ.*

em·ploy·ee [im-<u>ploy</u>-ee] *noun, plural* **employees.** *Business.* a person who is paid to work for another person or an organization.

em·ploy·er [im-<u>ploy</u>-ur] *noun, plural* **employers.** *Business.* a person or a company for whom other people work.

em·ploy·ment [im-<u>ploy</u>-munt] *noun, plural* **employments.** *Business.* **1.** the paid work that you do; a job: *He graduates from college next month and hopes to find employment as a salesman.* **2.** the fact or condition of employing: *The workers are calling for the employment of better safety conditions.*

em·press [<u>emp</u>-ris] *noun, plural* **empresses.** the female head of an empire, or an emperor's wife.

emp·ty [<u>emp</u>-tee] *adjective,* **emptier, emptiest. 1.** having nothing in it: *My glass is empty, fill it up, please.* **2.** having no real value or meaning: *empty threats; empty promises.* **3.** having no interest or importance: *After her husband died, her life was sad and empty.*
The fact of having nothing or no real value or meaning is **emptiness.**
verb, **emptied, emptying.**
1. to make or become empty; remove the contents from something: *Please empty the wastebasket.* **2.** to flow into: *The mighty Mississippi River empties into the Gulf of Mexico.*

Emu chicks have stripes that fade as the birds grow.

e·mu ▶ [<u>eem</u>-yoo] *noun, plural* **emus.** a large Australian bird with very long legs, closely related to the ostrich. Emus cannot fly, but they can run along the ground very quickly.

en·a·ble [i-<u>nay</u>-bul] *verb,* **enabled, enabling.** to make able; allow: *The money my grandpa gave me enabled me to go skiing during the holidays.* —**enablement,** *noun.*

en·act [en-<u>akt</u>] *verb,* **enacted, enacting. 1.** to pass a law: *The city enacted a ban on smoking in public places.* **2.** to act out on stage; perform: *to enact a role in a play.* —**enactment,** *noun.*

27 BC The Roman Empire is established under Augustus, the first emperor.

AD 395 The Empire is split into West and East.

AD 476 The Western Empire collapses.

AD 1453 The last city of the Eastern (Byzantine) Roman Empire is captured.

Rome

Mediterranean Sea

e·nam·el [i-<u>nam</u>-ul] *noun, plural* **enamels. 1.** a substance like glass that can be put on metal, pottery, or other material to protect or decorate it. **2.** hard, shiny, paint that is used for painting metal or wood: *Paint the kitchen doors with a glossy enamel.* **3.** *Medicine.* the hard, white substance on the outside of the teeth.
verb, **enameled, enameling.** to cover or decorate with enamel.

en·chant [in-<u>chant</u>] *verb,* **enchanted, enchanting.**
1. to give great delight to; charm: *The little girl enchanted everyone she met.* **2.** to put a magical spell on someone. If someone is delighted or charmed, they are **enchanted.**
—**enchantment,** *noun.*

en·chant·ing [in-<u>chan</u>-ting] *adjective.* having charm; attractive, enjoyable, or delightful: *She had an enchanting smile.*

en·cir·cle [in-<u>sur</u>-kul] *verb,* **encircled, encircling.** to form or move in a circle around: *The police encircled the farmhouse where the escaped criminal was hiding.*
—**encirclement,** *noun.*

en·close [in-<u>kloze</u>] *verb,* **enclosed, enclosing. 1.** to surround on all sides: *The electric wire fence enclosed the back yard.* **2.** to put with; include: *Grandma enclosed a check for my birthday with her card.* The act of enclosing or the thing enclosed is an **enclosure.**

en·core [<u>on</u>-kore] *noun, plural* **encores. 1.** a word that means *again.* It is said by audiences when they want a performance to continue because they want to hear more. **2.** an extra short performance at the end of a show because the audience calls for it: *He sang two more songs as an encore.*

en·coun·ter [in-<u>koun</u>-tur] *verb,* **encountered, encountering. 1.** to meet someone, usually unexpectedly: *As she left, she encountered her teacher at the door.* **2.** to meet with; confront: *I've never encountered any real difficulty in math. noun, plural* **encounters.** an unexpected or unplanned meeting: *The movie star had a brief encounter with some photographers as he left the restaurant.*

en·cour·age [in-<u>kur</u>-ij] *verb,* **encouraged, encouraging. 1.** to support someone by giving them confidence, strength, or courage: *She was encouraged by the news that all signs of her disease were gone.* **2.** to help something happen by supporting it: *The boss encouraged us to meet frequently to discuss any problems in the office.*
—**encouragement,** *noun.*

en·cy·clo·pe·di·a [in-<u>sye</u>-kluh-<u>pee</u>-dee-uh] *noun, plural* **encyclopedias.** *Literature.* a book or set of books containing facts about many different subjects, which are usually set out in alphabetical order. A book that contains a large amount of such reference material is **encyclopedic.**

Encyclopedia comes from a phrase meaning "a circle of education." The idea is that an encyclopedia contains a complete circle, or range, of all the information that a person needs to know.

end [end] *noun, plural* **ends. 1.** the last part: *Put a period the end of a sentence.* **2.** the part where something starts or finishes: *Can you undo this string. I can't find either end.* **3.** the act of stopping something: *I want to put an end to this argument now.* **4.** purpose; goal: *We hope you can put all this study to some good end.*
verb, **ended, ending.** to bring or come to an end; stop: *My holidays end in two days' time.*

ENDANGERED SPECIES

Whales, dolphins, seals, tigers, turtles, elephants, rhinoceroses—these are just some of the animals whose continued existence on the Earth is threatened, mostly by human activity. One very important reason for the endangerment of creatures and plants is the destruction of their natural environment, such as the clearing of tropical forests. Another is the introduction of animals and plants that harm or destroy native species. Diseases, pollution, and uncontrolled practices like twentieth-century whaling also put species at risk.

Ginkgo

Cycad

Venus flytrap

PLANTS AND INSECTS
Plants and insects are threatened when their environment changes.

Monarch butterfly

Killer whale

WATER ANIMALS
Animals that live in the ocean are endangered by pollution.

Crocodiles

Walrus

Pacific hawksbill turtle

Humpback whale

Indian rhinoceros

Andean condor

Red wolf

Aye-aye

LAND ANIMALS
Many land animals have suffered as their habitats have been cleared for farming.

Kiwi

African elephants

Gopher tortoise

Tiger

Rhinoceros

en·dan·ger [in-<u>dane</u>-jur] *verb,* **endangered, endangering.** to put someone or something in danger: *Slow down, you are endangering our lives.* —**endangerment,** *noun.*

en·dan·gered ◀ [in-<u>dane</u>-jurd] *adjective. Biology.* threatened with being destroyed or no longer existing: *In the late 1800s, the American buffalo was endangered because so many were killed.* A kind of animal or plant that is in danger of dying out completely is an **endangered species.**

end·ing [<u>end</u>-ing] *noun, plural* **endings.** the last or final part: *The movie had a surprise ending when the lost dog came back home.*

When you write a story, one of the main things you have to deal with is the **ending.** Probably the most famous ending of a story is, "And they all lived happily ever after." This is thought of as the standard ending for a folk tale or fairy tale. In your own stories, you do not always have to have a happy ending like this. But what this familiar saying does show is that you should not just stop at the end. You should always make clear to the reader what happened to bring the story to a close.

end·less [<u>end</u>-lis] *adjective.* **1.** going on and on; having no limit or end: *the endless movement of the ocean waves.* **2.** without ends. —**endlessly,** *adverb.*

en·do·crine [<u>en</u>-doh-*krin* or <u>en</u>-doh-*krine*] *adjective. Biology.* having to do with a body part that sends chemicals to another part to cause a certain change in the body's action. The thyroid gland is an **endocrine gland.** This area of science is known as **endocrinology.**

en·dorse [in-<u>dors</u>] *verb,* **endorsed, endorsing. 1.** to approve of; support: *The mayor has endorsed Senator Smith in her race for President.* **2.** to write something on a document or sign your name on it: *Don't take the check to the bank until I have endorsed the back of it.* —**endorsement,** *noun.*

en·dow [in-<u>dow</u>] *verb,* **endowed, endowing. 1.** to leave money or property to: *He endowed a large amount of money to his old school.* **2.** to be given a special talent; be blessed with: *Nature endowed her with brains and good looks.* —**endowment,** *noun.*

en·dure [en-<u>dur</u>] *verb,* **endured, enduring. 1.** to continue to exist over time: *Charles Dickens' great books will endure forever.* **2.** to put up with something bad or unpleasant; suffer: *How can you endure that ceaseless chatter?* The act of enduring is **endurance.**

en·e·my [<u>en</u>-uh-mee] *noun, plural* **enemies. 1.** someone who hates another person, and wants to harm him or her. **2.** a country at war with another country: *Our troops were advancing on the enemy.* **3.** someone or something that is against you, or that can cause you harm: *The disease of tuberculosis is an ancient enemy of mankind.*

en·er·get·ic [*en*-ur-*jet*-ik] *adjective.* enthusiastic about doing something; eager to get started: *She is an energetic campaigner for animal rights.* —**energetically,** *adverb.*

Water flows in.

Turbines spin.

Water flows out.

Hydroelectric **energy** *is generated when water makes turbines spin.*

en·er·gy ◀ [<u>en</u>-ur-jee] *noun, plural* **energies. 1.** *Science.* the power to move or heat things or to do other kinds of work, provided by such things as the burning of wood, coal, or oil, the flow of electricity, or the force of wind or moving water. **2.** the strength and power to do something: *I really don't have the energy to play another game.* **3.** enthusiasm and determination: *a woman of great energy and purpose.*

The word **energy** was first used by Aristotle, who lived in Greece more than 2,000 years ago and who was one of the most famous thinkers of the ancient world. He used the word in the sense of "acting toward a goal" or "being at work."

energy crisis *History.* a situation that occurs when oil becomes scarce or hard to get. The price goes up quickly and gasoline and oil supplies become very expensive. This affects private citizens and business interests alike.

en·force [in-<u>fors</u>] *verb,* **enforced, enforcing.** to make sure that a rule or law is obeyed: *Drunken driving is a crime and the police are there to enforce this law.*

en·force·ment [in-<u>fors</u>-munt] *noun,* the act of enforcing a rule, act, or law. **Law enforcement** occurs when the police or some other authority take steps to ensure that this happens.

en·gage [in-<u>gayj</u>] *verb,* **engaged, engaging. 1.** to hire a person to do work; employ. **2.** to be involved; take part in: *I am engaged in fund raising for the school.* **3.** to capture a person's attention or interest: *She was so engaged in her conversation that she didn't hear the phone ring.*

en·gaged [in-<u>gayjd</u>] *adjective.* having agreed to get married: *Alison and Bruce are engaged—she has the most beautiful ring.*

en·gage·ment [in-<u>gaj</u>-munt] *noun, plural* **engagements. 1.** an agreement that two people have made to get married. **2.** an appointment with someone at a certain time: *Sorry, I can't come. I have another engagement for that day.* **3.** an arrangement for someone to do a particular job: *Ruth is so busy singing at the club, she can't take on any more engagements this year.*

a
b
c
d
e
f
g
h
i
j
k
l
m
n
o
p
q
r
s
t
u
v
w
x
y
z

In the past, railroad **engines** like this were powered by steam.

en·gine ▲ [en-jun] *noun, plural* **engines. 1.** a machine that uses energy, such as gasoline, electricity, or coal to produce power in order to make something move. **2.** a machine that pulls a railroad train; a locomotive.

en·gi·neer [en-juh-neer] *noun, plural* **engineers. 1.** a person who is trained to use scientific and mathematical principles to design and build such things as roads, bridges, engines, and machines. **2.** a person who drives a locomotive. **3.** a person who takes care of machinery and electrical equipment.

en·gi·neer·ing [en-juh-neer-ing] *noun. Science.* the work that uses scientific knowledge to solve practical problems, such as the building of roads and bridges, mining of precious metals, drilling for oil, and design and construction of machines and electrical devices.

Eng·lish [ing-glish] *noun.* **1.** a language spoken in Great Britain, Ireland, the United States, Canada, Australia, India, and many other places. **2. the English.** the people of England.
adjective. belonging or relating to England, its people, or its language: *English literature; English weather.*

> The word **English** originally meant "of the Angles," and the English language was "the language of the Angles." England was called "Angle-Land" because a people named the Angles came there from what is now Germany about 1,500 years ago, and ruled over large parts of England for many years after that.

English horn *noun. Music.* a long, thin musical instrument with a deeper tone than the oboe, but resembling it.

Eng·lish·man [ing-glish-mun] *noun, plural* **Englishmen.** a man who was born or lives in England or Great Britain.

Eng·lish·wo·man [ing-glish-wum-in] *noun, plural,* **Englishwomen.** a woman who was born or lives in England or Great Britain.

en·grave [in-grave] *verb,* **engraved, engraving. 1.** to cut or carve a design or words into a surface. *Our team won the match and all our names were engraved onto the cup.* **2.** to cut or carve designs or pictures onto a metal or wooden plate, and then print these designs on paper: *Her name has been engraved at the top of her personal stationery.* **—engraver,** *noun.*

en·grav·ing [in-grave-ing] *noun, plural* **engravings. Art. 1.** the art of cutting or carving designs or words into a surface. **2.** a picture that has been printed from an engraved plate.

en·hance [in-hans] *verb,* **enhanced, enhancing.** to improve the look, value, or quality of something: *Repairing the dents in the car will enhance its resale value.* **—enhancement,** *noun.*

en·joy [in-joy] *verb,* **enjoyed, enjoying. 1.** to get pleasure from; like: *I really enjoy going to the movies.* **2.** to have; possess: *She is lucky enough to enjoy good health.*

en·joy·a·ble [in-joy-uh-bul] *adjective.* giving pleasure and satisfaction; pleasant: *The trip to the zoo was very enjoyable.* **—enjoyably,** *adverb.*

en·joy·ment [in-joy-munt] *noun, plural* **enjoyments.** the fact of enjoying something; pleasure; joy: *The enjoyment we felt from the walk was short lived when it began to pour with rain.*

en·large [in-larj] *verb,* **enlarged, enlarging.** to make or become bigger: *The windows in our house are quite small, so the builder is going to enlarge them.*

en·large·ment ▼ [in-larj-munt] *noun, plural* **enlargements. 1.** the act or process of making something bigger. **2.** something that has been made larger than the original: *This photo is too small, so I arranged for an enlargement.*

en·list [in-list] *verb,* **enlisted, enlisting. 1.** to join the army, navy, or other military service: *Jules enlisted in the Marines.* **2.** to get someone to help and support you: *If I run out of time, may I enlist your help in getting the project finished?* **—enlistment,** *noun.*

e·nor·mous [i-nor-mus] *adjective.* extremely large in size; huge: *Dinosaurs were enormous animals.* **—enormously,** *adverb.*

e·nough [i-nuf] *adjective.* as many or as much as you need; sufficient: *I don't have enough money to go to the movies.*
pronoun. an amount that is as much as or as many as you need.
adverb. to an amount or degree that is needed or necessary: *You have done enough for one day.*

en·rich [in-rich] *verb,* **enriched, enriching. 1.** to improve the quality or value of something by adding something else to it: *The manufacturers say this juice is enriched with extra vitamins.* **2.** to make richer; gain more money or wealth: *I'm entering the competition to try to enrich myself.* **—enrichment,** *noun.*

This **enlargement** *shows the structure of one of the tiny strands of a bird's feather.*

en·roll [in-<u>role</u>] *verb*, **enrolled, enrolling.** to enter your name in a roll or register; join: *She enrolled for an art class.*

en·roll·ment [in-<u>role</u>-munt] *noun, plural* **enrollments.**
1. the act of enrolling or the state of being enrolled.
2. the number of people enrolled.

en·sign [en-sun] *noun, plural* **ensigns. 1.** a flag flown on a ship: *Where's that ship from; can you make out the ensign?* **2.** a junior officer, below lieutenant, in the U.S. Navy.

en·sure [en-<u>shoor</u>] *verb*, **ensured, ensuring. 1.** to make certain; guarantee: *But, can you ensure that it will not rain?* **2.** to protect; make safe: *The police are doing all they can to ensure the safety of the public.*

en·ter [en-tur] *verb*, **entered, entering. 1.** to come or go into: *to enter a room through the door.* **2.** to join in; participate; enroll: *I entered several races but I didn't win any.* An **entrant** is someone who enrolls in a school or university, or participates in a competition. **3.** to write down; record: *Please enter the amount of money you borrowed in this book.* **4.** to type information into a computer.

en·ter·prise [en-tur-<u>prize</u>] *noun, plural,* **enterprises.**
1. a company or business: *large industrial enterprise.*
2. a task that requires a lot of time and effort; an undertaking: *I am really sorry I ever started on that enterprise.* **3.** the ability to think of new and difficult thing to do and the determination to do them: *Young Martha shows such enterprise.* A person who shows this ability is **enterprising.**

en·ter·tain [en-tur-<u>tane</u>] *verb*, **entertained, entertaining.**
1. to do something that other people find interesting or amusing: *Young Harry is such a good singer—he entertains us for hours.* Someone who entertains others is **entertaining. 2.** to give guests food and hospitality: *My mom just loves to entertain.* **3.** to consider an idea: *How can you even entertain the idea of driving Dad's car?* —**entertainer,** *noun.*

en·ter·tain·ment ▼ [en-tur-<u>tane</u>-munt] *noun, plural* **entertainments. 1.** an amusement such as a movie or show that people watch for pleasure: *Tonight's entertainment is a DVD that's just been released.* **2.** the act of entertaining.

*For **entertainment**, the ancient Greeks went to huge outdoor theaters, where as many as five plays would be performed in one day.*

en·thu·si·asm [in-<u>thoo</u>-zee-*az*-um] *noun.* great interest and excitement about something: *The enthusiasm and cheers of the crowd encouraged the swimmers.*

en·thu·si·as·tic [in-<u>thoo</u>-zee-<u>ass</u>-tik] *adjective.* showing excitement, interest, and eagerness: *The class was enthusiastic when the teacher asked if they wanted to visit the history museum.* —**enthusiastically,** *adverb.*

en·tire [in-<u>tire</u>] *adjective.* being the whole of something; nothing left out; the lot: *He was born in Boston and has lived there his entire life.*

en·tire·ly [in-<u>tire</u>-lee] *adverb.* without exception; completely: *I'm not sure that what you are saying is entirely true.*

en·ti·tle [in-<u>tye</u>-tul] *verb*, **entitled, entitling. 1.** to be given the right to: *The coupon entitles you to one free drink with your hamburger.* **2.** to be named, called: *a painting entitled "Sunset."* —**entitlement,** *noun.*

en·trance[1] [en-truns] *noun, plural* **entrances. 1.** a way into a place: *Let's meet outside the library, at the entrance.* **2.** the act of going into a place: *Hank made a dramatic entrance into the room just as everyone else was ready to go home.* **3.** the right to go into a place; permission: *We were denied entrance to the theater because it was already sold out.*

en·trance[2] [in-<u>trans</u>] *verb*, **entranced, entrancing. 1.** to put into a trance; hypnotize. **2.** to fill with great pleasure or wonder: *Jodie was entranced by the magician's tricks.*

en·tre·pre·neur [on-truh-pruh-<u>nur</u>] *noun, plural* **entrepreneurs.** *Business.* someone who starts a new business or who is good thinking of new ideas for business: *Steve Jobs and Steve Wozniak were the entrepreneurs who founded Apple Computer Inc.* The work of starting new businesses and organizations is **entrepreneurship.** —**entrepreneurial,** *adjective.*

en·trust [in-<u>trust</u>] *verb*, **entrusted, entrusting.** to trust someone or give them a position of responsibility: *I entrusted my best friend with my secret.*

A
B
C
D
E
F
G
H
I
J
K
L
M
N
O
P

en·try [en-tree] *noun, plural* **entries. 1.** the action of someone entering: *At the bride's entry into the church, the music began playing and we all stood.* **2.** a door, gate, arch, or other place that lets people through; an entrance way. **3.** information recorded in a book or on a computer. In a catalog or list, there may be a **main entry**, like a heading, under which there are single entries. **4.** someone or something entered into a competition or race: *The entries for the best pet competition included a rabbit, a snake, and a lizard.*

en·vel·op [en-vel-up] *verb,* **enveloped, enveloping.** to surround something completely with a covering: *After the blizzard the parked cars were enveloped in snow.*

en·ve·lope [en-vuh-lope *or* on-vuh-lope] *noun, plural* **envelopes.** a flat covering of paper that can be sealed. Envelopes are used to mail and deliver letters and other papers.

en·vi·ous [en-vee-us] *adjective.* showing envy and jealousy; having a strong feeling of wanting what someone else has: *I am envious of how much allowance she gets.* —**enviously,** *adverb.*

en·vi·ron·ment ▼ [in-vye-ruh-munt *or* in-vye-run-munt] *noun, plural* **environments. 1.** *Science.* all of the surroundings and conditions that affect the growth and health of living things, such as air, water, sun, soil, and plants. **2.** the physical or emotional area surrounding something or someone: *My happy home environment makes me feel safe.*

> **Environment** comes from an older word meaning "what is all around" or "what surrounds something." The idea is that the environment is everything that is around us in the world—the solid earth itself, the air above, the oceans and other bodies of water, the Earth's climate, and the animals and plants living on the Earth.

Insects and other small animals live and feed in the freshwater **environment** *of a pond.*

en·vi·ron·ment·al [in-vye-ruh-ment-ul *or* in-vye-run-ment-ul] *adjective.* having to do with the environment and protection of the environment: *They were not allowed to build a mall on the land because of possible environmental damage.* Concerns and actions to do with protecting the environment from harm are called **environmentalism.** Someone who acts to protect the environment from harm is called an **environmentalist.**

en·vy [en-vee] *noun, plural* **envies. 1.** a strong feeling of wanting something that someone else has; unhappiness that someone has what you want. **2.** a person or thing that makes one feel envy: *Her speed on the track was the envy of all the other runners.*
verb, **envied, envying.** to feel envy about something or of someone: *I envy the way you make friends so easily.* Something that is worthy of being desired or causes envy is **enviable.**

en·zyme [en-zime] *noun, plural* **enzymes.** *Biology.* a substance that speeds up chemical reactions in animals and humans, but is not itself used up. Any changes caused by an enzyme is described as **enzymatic.**

ep·ic [ep-ik] *noun, plural* **epics.** *Literature.* a long poem that tells the story of a hero or heroes in history or legend. *adjective.* **1.** having to do with an epic: *I watched an epic movie about King Arthur and his Knights.* **2.** describing adventures, struggles, and challenges so great they seem like something in an epic: *The sailor set out on his own in an epic voyage across the ocean.*

ep·i·dem·ic [ep-uh-dem-ik] *noun, plural* **epidemics.** *Medicine.* a sudden outbreak of a serious disease that spreads quickly and affects many people.

An **epidemic** is a disease that spreads among many people at the same time, in a given area or in the entire world. It comes from a Greek phrase meaning "among the people," because it affects so many different people at once.

ep·i·dem·iol·ogy [ep-uh-dee-mee-ol-uh-jee] *noun.* *Medicine.* the branch of medicine and science that studies the outbreak and spread of disease. Someone who studies in this field is an **epidemiologist.**

ep·i·lep·sy [ep-uh-lep-see] *noun. Medicine.* a disturbance in the brain that can cause people to lose consciousness or "black out" and suffer violent shaking they cannot control. A person who has this disturbance is an **epileptic.**

E·pis·cop·al·ian [uh-pis-kuh-pale-yun] *noun, plural* **Episcopalians.** *Religion.* someone who follows the teachings and beliefs of the **Episcopal Church,** a part of the Protestant religion. *adjective.* having to do with or belonging to this church.

ep·i·sode [ep-uh-sode] *noun, plural* **episodes.** an event or story that is one part of a series of events or stories: *Last night I watched an episode of my favorite television show.*

*Air movements near the **equator** influence weather in many other parts of the world.*

equator

e·qual [ee-kwul] *adjective.* **1.** having the same quantity, size, or measurement as another: *In cooking, three teaspoons are equal to one tablespoon; The players started the game with an equal number of cards.* **2.** having the same value, opportunities, responsibilities, and status as another: *In America, all citizens over age eighteen have an equal right to vote in elections.* The state or condition of being equal is **equality**. *noun, plural* **equals.** a person who is equal or well-matched to another. *verb,* **equaled, equaling.** to be equal or identical to: *Six times two equals twelve.*

e·qual·ize [ee-kwuh-lize] *verb,* **equalized, equalizing.** to make equal or to match: *Mom equalized the chores amongst us so we wouldn't argue.* —**equalization,** *noun.*

e·qua·tion [i-kway-zhun] *noun, plural* **equations.** *Mathematics.* a mathematical statement that two amounts are equal. $9 - 3 = 6$ is an equation.

e·qua·tor ▲ [i-kway-tur] *noun, plural* **equators.** *Geography.* an imaginary line around the Earth halfway between the North and South poles, dividing the Earth into northern and southern hemispheres. Anything to do with or relating to the equator is called **equatorial**. This word is also spelled **Equator**.

> The word **equator** goes back to a phrase in the Latin language meaning "something that divides equally." The idea is that this imaginary line divides the world exactly into two equal parts, one half north of the equator and one half south of it.

e·qui·lat·er·al [ee-kwuh-lat-ur-ul] *adjective. Mathematics.* describing an object or shape with all sides the same length. A triangle with each side the same length is called an **equilateral triangle.**

e·qui·nox [ee-kwuh-noks] *noun, plural* **equinoxes.** *Geography.* either of the two days of the year when the Sun is directly over the equator so that day and night are of equal length everywhere on the Earth. In the Northern Hemisphere, the **spring equinox** falls in late March and the **fall equinox** occurs in late September. In the Southern Hemisphere the equinoxes are opposite because the seasons are opposite.

e·quip [i-kwip] *verb,* **equipped, equipping.** to provide with what is needed for a particular activity or specific purpose: *The hikers were equipped with the right clothes, plenty of food, water, matches, and a compass.*

e·quip·ment ▶ [i-kwip-munt] *noun.* **1.** the tools, clothing, or other supplies needed for a particular activity or purpose: *My grandfather has rods, hooks, lures, reels, and other fishing equipment.* **2.** the act of providing equipment.

e·quiv·a·lent [i-kwiv-uh-lunt] *adjective.* being the same as, or almost the same as something else, in amount or value: *The hotel costs 100 British pounds per night, which is equivalent to about $200 U.S.* *noun, plural* **equivalents.** a person or thing equal to another: *For deaf people, sign language is the equivalent of speaking.* The state of being equal, equivalent, or equally balanced is **equivalence**.

-er¹ a suffix that indicates: **1.** what something or someone does: a *gardener* is someone who gardens; a *mower* is a machine that mows. **2.** the area in which someone lives: a person living in New York City is a *New Yorker.*

-er² a suffix that means more than; used in comparison to someone or something else: *In the race, I was slow but she was slower, so she came in last.*

e·ra [er-uh *or* eer-uh] *noun, plural* **eras.** a period of time marked by an important event or invention or the significant actions of a person: *The development of the personal computer started a new era in technology.*

e·rase [i-rayss] *verb,* **erased, erasing. 1.** to remove by rubbing or wiping: *I didn't have time to erase the mistake in my test paper.* **2.** to remove material completely, as if by rubbing out: *I erased the part of the videotape that showed the other team scoring the winning goal.*

e·ras·er [i-ray-sur] *noun, plural* **erasers.** an object, often made of rubber, used to erase writing, marks, or stains.

e·rect [i-rekt] *adjective.* in an upright or raised position: *Fresh-cut flowers have erect stalks, but the ones in the shop were drooping.* *verb,* **erected, erecting. 1.** to build or construct: *We erected a tree house.* **2.** to raise up to an upright position: *We erected the goal posts for the football game.*

er·mine [ur-mun] *noun, plural* **ermines** *or* **ermine.** a small animal with a long body and tail, short legs, and brown fur that turns to white in winter.

e·rode [i-rode] *verb,* **eroded, eroding.** to slowly change or destroy by washing away, wearing down, or eating into: *The tides of the river eroded the rocky banks.*

People need special **equipment** *for outdoor activities such as hiking and camping.*

a
b
c
d
e
f
g
h
i
j
k
l
m
n
o
p
q
r
s
t
u
v
w
x
y
z

EROSION

All kinds of landscapes change as a result of erosion. Glaciers, streams, oceans, and wind move rock fragments over exposed rocks, scouring and carving their surfaces and depositing the fragments in rivers, oceans, and lakes. In this way erosion creates jagged mountain peaks, canyons, caves, sea stacks, and unusual rock formations.

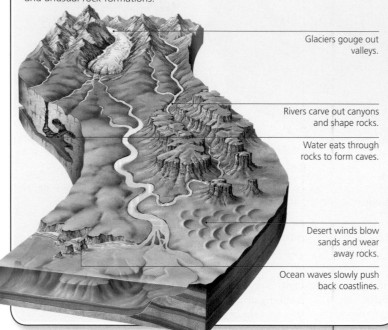

Glaciers gouge out valleys.

Rivers carve out canyons and shape rocks.

Water eats through rocks to form caves.

Desert winds blow sands and wear away rocks.

Ocean waves slowly push back coastlines.

e·ros·ion ▲ [i-<u>roh</u>-zhun] *noun. Environment.* the act of washing away, wearing down, or eating into something over a long time: *The beach community planted grasses in the sand dunes to stop erosion by wind, rain, and waves.*

er·rand [<u>er</u>-und] *noun, plural* **errands. 1.** a quick journey or trip to complete a task: *The teacher sent me on an errand to deliver a message to the principal.* **2.** the task that is the reason for the short trip.

er·rat·ic [i-<u>rat</u>-ik] *adjective.* acting or moving in a way that is not regular or expected: *The teenager's erratic moods meant she might be crying one minute and laughing the next.* —**erratically,** *adverb.*

er·ror [<u>er</u>-ur] *noun, plural,* **errors. 1.** something done wrong accidentally; a mistake: *The store clerk gave me the wrong amount of change in error.* **2.** in baseball, a wrong play by a fielder that allows a batter or base runner to get to a base, when they would have been out if the play had been made properly.

e·rupt [i-<u>rupt</u>] *verb,* **erupted, erupting. 1.** to eject lava out of a volcano. **2.** to break out suddenly, sometimes violently: *The crowd erupted into laughter when he told that joke.*

e·rup·tion [i-<u>rup</u>-shun] *noun, plural* **eruptions.** the act of erupting: *the eruption of a volcano.*

es·ca·la·tor [<u>es</u>-kuh-*lay*-tur] *noun, plural* **escalators.** a moving staircase. The steps move continuously because they are pulled by a circulating belt or chain.

es·cape [es-<u>kape</u>] *verb,* **escaped, escaping. 1.** to get away from: *The prisoner escaped from the jail.* **2.** to be free from something harmful or dangerous; get away from: *The ship sank, but everyone on board escaped safely.* *noun, plural* **escapes. 1.** the act of getting free: *The Great Escape is a famous movie about prisoners sneaking out of a German prison camp.* **2.** a method or way of getting free: *Listening to music is my escape from worry.*

es·cort [<u>es</u>-*kort* for noun; es-<u>kort</u> for verb] *noun, plural* **escorts. 1.** someone who travels with something or someone else: *The President arrived with a police escort.* **2.** airplanes or ships that travel with other airplanes or ships to protect them. *verb,* **escorted, escorting.** to act as an escort: *My father escorted his aunt to the dinner.*

Es·ki·mo [<u>es</u>-kuh-moh] *noun, plural* **Eskimos.** a group of people who live in arctic areas around Canada, Alaska, and Greenland.

The word **Eskimo** is used to describe several groups of people who have lived for many centuries in Alaska, northern Canada, and other Arctic areas. In Canada, the term *Inuit* is now generally preferred to *Eskimo* for these people, because it is thought that *Eskimo* was a name applied to them by other groups. *Inuit* means "the people," and the name that most Native American groups call themselves means "the people" in their own language.

e·soph·a·gus [i-<u>sof</u>-uh-gus] *noun.* the tube that allows food to travel between the throat and the stomach.

ESP the power to sense things that are not obvious to the senses of touch, taste, smell, sight, and hearing: *He believes the fortuneteller uses ESP to communicate with his dead grandmother.* ESP is an abbreviation for **extrasensory perception.**

es·pe·cial·ly [es-<u>pesh</u>-lee *or* es-<u>pesh</u>-uh-lee] *adverb.* **1.** to an unusual extent; in a special way: *It was especially hot this summer.* **2.** for the special purpose of: *Our cousin dropped in especially to see our new car.*

es·pi·o·nage [<u>es</u>-pee-uh-*nahzh*] *noun. Law.* the act of using spies to steal secret information: *Their enemies discovered where the missiles were hidden by use of espionage.*

es·say [<u>es</u>-ay] *noun, plural* **essays.** *Literature.* a written composition about a particular subject: *She wrote an essay about pollution in our rivers.* Someone who writes lots of essays is an **essayist.**

An **essay** is a short piece of writing that deals with a subject in the real world. It usually gives not only facts about that subject but the writer's opinion. Except for poems and made-up stories, most of the writing that students do for school assignments would be called essays. This would include book reports, news stories, biographies, history papers, or science reports.

es·sen·tial [uh-sen-shul] *adjective.* being necessary or important: *The essential ingredient for a good lemonade is fresh lemons.*
noun, plural **essentials.** a necessary or important part: *They brought plenty of candy but forgot essentials like bread and milk.* —**essentially,** *adverb.*

-est a suffix that means the most of something: *hottest* means the most hot; *dearest* means the most dear. This is called the superlative form.

es·tab·lish [uh-stab-lish] *verb,* **established , establishing. 1.** to create or start something: *The school established a drama program.* **2.** to prove that something is true: *The police established the fact that the suspect was carrying a knife.*

es·tab·lish·ment [uh-stab-lish-munt] *noun, plural* **establishments. 1.** the act of setting up something: *the establishment of a new fire station.* **2.** something that has been set up. A school, a business, and a restaurant are all establishments. The group of people who control a society with money and power are sometimes called the **Establishment.**

es·tate [uh-state] *noun, plural* **estates. 1.** a large area of land, usually with a house on it: *My aunt lives on an estate in the country.* **2.** everything that someone owns: *My grandfather's will left his estate to my mother.*

es·teem [uh-steem] *verb,* **esteemed, esteeming.** to think highly of; respect and admire.
noun, plural, **esteems.** respect or admiration: *The teacher was held in high esteem by all her students.* Someone who is well respected can be described as an **esteemed** person.

es·tim·ate [es-tuh-mit] *noun, plural* **estimates.** an opinion or quote about the cost, value, or size of something: *The builder gave an estimate of the cost of building a new library.*
verb, **estimated, estimating.** to think something through and form a general opinion: *The teacher estimated that it would take a week before she finished marking all the exams.* —**estimation,** *noun.*

es·tu·a·ry ▼ [es-choo-er-ee] *noun, plural* **estuaries.** *Environment.* the part of a river that meets the sea where salt water and fresh water mix. Something that lives or grows in an estuary can be described as an **estaurine** plant or animal.

etc. [et set-uh-ruh] and so on: *There are lots of different types of music—rap, blues, rock and roll, classical, etc.* This term is an abbreviation for the Latin words *et cetera.*

etch [ech] *verb,* **etched, etching.** to engrave an image by using acid to eat away parts of a metal or glass surface: *The outline of a tree was etched into the glass panel over my grandparents' front door.*

etch·ing [ech-ing] *noun, plural* **etchings.** *Art.* an image that is stamped or printed from a surface that has been etched.

e·ter·nal [i-tur-nul] *adjective.* **1.** lasting forever: *Some people believe the universe is eternal and others believe it will come to an end.* **2.** seeming to last forever: *Mom complains about my sister and me and our eternal arguing over little things.* —**eternally,** *adverb.*

e·ter·ni·ty [i-tur-nuh-tee] *noun, plural* **eternities. 1.** time without beginning or end; forever. **2.** a period of time that seems to go on forever: *The speech was so boring it felt like an eternity before he finally finished.*

eth·i·cal [eth-i-kul] *adjective.* describing the right way to behave; being in agreement with the accepted rules of right and wrong: *Returning the money when the store accidentally gave him too much change was the ethical thing to do.* —**ethically,** *adverb.*

eth·ics [eth-iks] *noun.* a system of beliefs of what makes something right or wrong: *The scientist couldn't fake the results of his experiment—it would have been acting against proper scientific ethics.*

> The term **etc.** is often used in writing at the end of a list, as in "The farmers' market sells corn, lettuce, tomatoes, beans, peppers, *etc.*" It is short for the Latin phrase *et cetera*, meaning "and the rest" or "and other things."

Estuaries provide food and safety for birds, fishes, crabs, and other kinds of marine life.

In the water cycle, the Sun's heat causes water to **evaporate** *into the air, where it cools to form rain clouds.*

A B C D **E** F G H I J K L M N O P Q R S T U V W X Y Z

eth·nic [eth-nik] *adjective.* having to do with a group of people who share the same language and culture: *Indian, Chinese, and Italian are just three of the many ethnic restaurants in our neighborhood.* People who have the same ethnic background share the same **ethnicity.**
noun, plural **ethnics. 1.** a member of an ethnic group. **2.** a person in the U.S. whose family comes from another country, especially a European country other than Great Britain. —**ethnically,** *adverb.*

et·i·quette [et-uh-ket] *noun, plural* **etiquettes.** the rules of polite behavior: *It is not proper etiquette to eat with your elbows on the table.*

et·y·mol·o·gy [et-uh-mol-uh-jee] *noun, plural* **etymologies.** *Language.* the history of a word from its original use to its current use. An etymology tells you what language a word first came from and whether its spellings and meanings have changed over time.

The word **etymology** comes from a Greek word meaning "true." The idea is that the etymology (history) of a word gives the true story of what the word means and where it comes from, as opposed to what people might guess about this.

Eu·ro·pe·an [yur-uh-pee-un] *adjective.* describing someone or something from the continent of Europe.
noun, plural **Europeans.** someone who was born or lives in Europe.

European Union *Government.* a group formed in 1993, made up of fifteen European countries. The group shares a common market for products and services, as well as the same currency, known as the euro. This group is called the **EU** for short.

e·vac·u·ate [i-vak-yoo-ate] *verb,* **evacuated, evacuating.** to leave or make someone leave; remove or empty: *They evacuated the building because of the bomb threat.* —**evacuation,** *noun.*

e·vade [i-vade] *verb,* **evaded, evading.** to avoid or escape: *We evaded the bullies by taking another route home from school.* The act of evading something is **evasion.** An action done to evade is **evasion.**

e·val·u·ate [i-val-yoo-ate] *verb,* **evaluated, evaluating.** to judge the value of something: *The teacher evaluates our math skills by giving us a regular test.* —**evaluation,** *noun.*

e·vap·or·ate ▲ [i-vap-uh-rate] *verb,* **evaporated, evaporating. 1.** to turn into a gas: *When the sun warms the puddles, the water evaporates into the air.* **2.** to vanish or disappear: *Our interest in the project quickly evaporated when the teacher asked us to do it during summer vacation.*

eve [eev] *noun, plural* **eves.** the evening or day before an important day or holiday: *New Year's Day is January 1st and the night before is New Year's Eve.*

e·ven [ee-vun] *adjective.* **1.** staying the same; regular or unchanging: *The furnace keeps the house at an even temperature of 72 degrees.* **2.** as high or low as something else: *The top of my little brother's head is even with the table.* **3.** at the same level; flat: *We looked for even ground to pitch the tent.* **4.** equal to or the same as: *Mom made sure we all got even amounts of candy.*
adverb. **1.** although it might appear to be unlikely: *The teacher treats everyone equally, even the naughty students.* **2.** yet or still: *Your idea is even better than mine.*
verb, **evened, evening. 1.** to make flat: *We evened the path by filling the holes with pebbles.* **2.** to make equal: *He evened the score by kicking another goal.* —**evenly,** *adverb.*

eve·ning [eev-ning] *noun, plural* **evenings.** the time that is late in the afternoon or early in the night. *adjective.* having to do with the evening: *They ate their evening meal on the porch.*

even number *Mathematics.* a number that can be divided by 2 without having a remainder: *6, 14, and 54 are even numbers.*

e·vent ◀ [i-vent] *noun, plural* **events. 1.** something that happens, often something important: *The teacher asked us to write about the events leading up to the war.* **2.** a contest that is part of a sporting program: *The long jump is his favorite event in track and field.*
• **in the event of.** when something happens: *In the event of an accident, call a doctor.*
• **in any event.** whatever happens: *Rain may fall but in any event the parade will go on anyway.*

Show jumping is a popular sporting **event.**

e·ven·tu·al [i-ven-choo-ul] *adjective.* describing a final outcome: *After the teacher deducted marks for lateness, my eventual grade was B+.* —**eventually,** *adverb.*

e·ver [ev-ur] *adverb.* **1.** at some time: *Have you ever read that book?* **2.** always: *Our dog is ever willing to go for a walk.* **3.** in any way: *How will we ever repay your kindness?*

ev·er·glade [ev-ur-*glade*] *noun, plural* **everglades.** a swampy area with thick grasses and many streams found in warm, rainy climates. The **Everglades** is a large area of this type located in the southern part of the state of Florida.

ev·er·green [ev-ur-*green*] *adjective.* describing a plant or tree that has green leaves or needles all year round. *noun, plural* **evergreens.** plants or trees that have green leaves or needles all year round. Holly, pine, and spruce trees are evergreens.

eve·ry [ev-ree] *adjective.* describing each person or thing that is part of a group: *Every member of the class signed my birthday card; Study every chapter of the book.*

eve·ry·bod·y [ev-ree-*buh*-dee] *pronoun.* every person: *Everybody in the school must attend the assembly.*

eve·ry·day [ev-ree-*day*] *adjective.* **1.** having to do with every day; daily: *Taking the train to his job in the city is an everyday event for him.* **2.** ordinary or not special: *Unless it's a special occasion, we eat dinner from our everyday plates.*

eve·ry·one [ev-ree-*wun*] *pronoun.* everybody; every person: *Everyone in the room heard him scream.*

every other every second; each alternative: *Because she lives so close, my grandmother visits every other day.*

eve·ry·thing [ev-ree-*thing*] *pronoun.* **1.** all the things or every single thing: *I took everything out of the dishwasher after the cycle was finished; The teacher said he didn't expect us to know everything there is to know about the subject.* **2.** an important thing: *Winning the trophy means everything to her.*

eve·ry·where [ev-ree-*ware*] *adverb.* in all areas; in every place: *We searched everywhere for our lost dog.*

e·vict [i-vikt] *verb,* **evicted, evicting.** to make someone move out of the place where they live. The act of evicting someone is called an **eviction.**

ev·i·dence ▶ [ev-uh-duns] *noun.* **1.** *Law.* a statement or fact presented in a court of law to show that something is true or not true. **2.** any proof that something happened: *The teacher demanded to see evidence that the dog ate my homework.*

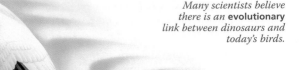

*Many scientists believe there is an **evolutionary** link between dinosaurs and today's birds.*

ev·i·dent [ev-uh-dunt] *adjective* describing something that is clear or easily understood: *It became evident that he was bored when he fell asleep during the lecture.* —**evidently,** *adverb.*

e·vil [ee-vul] *adjective.* very bad or wicked: *The story "Cinderella" tells of a girl who has an evil stepmother who punishes her. noun, plural* **evils. 1.** the fact of being very bad or wicked. **2.** a thing that causes great harm: *Starvation is an evil that no child should suffer.*

ev·o·lu·tion ▲ [ev-uh-loo-shun] *noun, plural* **evolutions.** **1.** a change that happens slowly and step by step: *The book shows the evolution of the airplane from the early propeller models right up to the modern jets.* **2.** *Science.* small changes in the genes of living things that are passed from one generation to the next, so that over a very long time living things will be different from what they were in the past. **3.** *Science.* the theory that all living things developed from much simpler life forms over millions of years; this is called the **theory of evolution.** —**evolutionary,** *adjective.*

e·volve [i-volv] *verb,* **evolved, evolving.** to change gradually; undergo a process of evolution: *Many scientists now believe that birds and dinosaurs evolved from a common ancestor; The idea for the school play evolved out of our drama lessons.*

ewe [yoo] *noun, plural* **ewes.** a female sheep.
🔊 Different words with the same sound are **you** and **yew.**

ex- a prefix that means former: *ex-student* means a former student; *ex-husband* means former husband.

ex·act [ig-zakt] *adjective.* **1.** describing something precise or accurate: *When I called to say I was out, my mother wanted to know my exact location.* **2.** describing something the same: *He walked out of the room at the exact moment that she walked in. verb,* **exacted, exacting.** to demand and receive: *The teacher exacted a promise that I would hand in my essay on time.* A person or task that is particularly demanding can be described as **exacting.**

*Police use fingerprints, handprints, and thumbprints as **evidence** when they investigate crimes.*

A
B
C
D
E
F
G
H
I

ex·act·ly [ig-<u>zakt</u>-lee] *adverb.* **1.** accurately or precisely: *He cut exactly down the middle of the paper.* **2.** in the exact or same way: *She got an A on the test, exactly as I predicted.*

ex·ag·ger·ate [ig-<u>zaj</u>-uh-*rate*] *verb,* **exaggerated, exaggerating.** to make something seem bigger or more important than it is: *My sister exaggerated the pain from her twisted ankle to get more attention.* If you exaggerate something, it is an **exaggeration.**

America has a special type of story called *tall tales,* which are based on the idea of **exaggeration.** One famous hero of tall tales is a giant lumberjack named Paul Bunyan, who was said to weigh 100 pounds when he was born and to be wearing his father's clothes when he was one week old. Exaggeration is a good way to make a story funny and interesting. However, you have to be careful not to exaggerate when you are telling a true story, because this will make the reader doubt what you are saying.

ex·am [ig-<u>zam</u>] *noun, plural* **exams.** a short word for EXAMINATION: *a medical exam.*

ex·am·i·na·tion [ig-<u>zam</u>-uh-<u>nay</u>-shun] *noun, plural* **examinations. 1.** the act of examining something: *The doctor's examination found no sign of a break in her arm.* **2.** a test of how much a person knows about a certain subject: *The college holds examinations during the last week of the semester.*

ex·am·ine ◀ [ig-<u>zam</u>-in] *verb,* **examined, examining. 1.** to look at carefully and in detail: *The police examined the crime scene.* **2.** to test or question carefully: *The prosecutor examined several witnesses to the crime.* —**examiner,** *noun.*

*A doctor **examines** a patient's heart with a stethoscope.*

ex·am·ple [ig-<u>zam</u>-pul] *noun, plural* **examples. 1.** something that shows what similar things are like: *I showed the teacher four photographs as examples of my camera work.* **2.** a problem that shows how similar problems can be solved: *The math teacher gave us an example of how to do the equation.* **3.** someone or something that should be copied: *Dad says I should try to set an example for my younger brother.*
• **for example.** as an example of something: *He loves to eat fast food, for example, hot dogs and hamburgers.*

ex·as·per·ate [ig-<u>zas</u>-puh-*rate*] *verb,* **exasperated, exasperating.** to annoy very much; frustrate: *The teacher was exasperated by Tony's constant interruptions during the lesson.* If someone is annoyed or irritated, they are described as **exasperated.** —**exasperation,** *noun.*

ex·ca·vate ▶ [ek-skuh-*vate*] *verb,* **excavated, excavating. 1.** to dig or scoop out earth. **2.** to uncover or expose by digging: *The archaeologists excavated an ancient tomb.* **3.** to create by digging: *A gigantic hole was excavated for the building's foundations.* —**excavation,** *noun.*

Q
R
S
T
U
V
W
X
Y
Z

ex·ceed [ik-<u>seed</u>] *verb,* **exceeded, exceeding. 1.** to go past or above: *I exceeded my budget by twenty dollars.* **2.** to be better than: *The forest's beauty exceeded my expectations.*

ex·cel [ek-<u>sel</u>] *verb,* **excelled, excelling.** to be better at something than others are; be superior: *Ian excels at math and always tops his class.*

ex·cel·lence [ek-suh-luns] *noun.* the fact of excelling or being outstanding: *The restaurant has a reputation for excellence in the food it serves.*

ex·cel·lent [ek-suh-lunt] *adjective.* extremely good; of very high quality: *He did an excellent job of washing the car and it shone like it was new.* —**excellently,** *adverb.*

ex·cept [ik-<u>sept</u>] *preposition.* not including; apart from all others: *Everyone in the family went to the zoo except me —I was sick and stayed home.*
conjunction. if not for the fact; however: *I'd like to lend you the book, except I haven't finished it yet.* A different word with the same meaning is **excepting.**

ex·cep·tion [ik-<u>sep</u>-shun] *noun, plural* **exceptions. 1.** the act of not including: *Sara gets up early every morning, with the exception of Sundays.* **2.** someone or something not included or different: *All U.S. Presidents have had one or two terms—the exception is Franklin Roosevelt who had four.*

ex·cep·tion·al [ik-<u>sep</u>-shun-ul] *adjective.* standing out from others; rare: *She was admitted into ballet school because of her exceptional dancing talent.* —**exceptionally,** *adverb.*

ex·cerpt [ek-<u>surpt</u>] *noun, plural* **excerpts.** a short part of a written text taken out of a larger whole: *The author read an excerpt from his book on the radio.*
verb, **excerpted, excerpting.** to take a short piece of writing from a longer text: *I excerpted the funniest bit of the story to read out loud in class.*

*Scientists **excavate** fossils of dinosaur bones from rocks.*

ex·cess [<u>ek</u>-ses *or* ek-<u>ses</u>] *noun.* the fact of being more of something than is necessary: *We had an excess of food at the party and a lot was not eaten.* *adjective.* more than is necessary; left over: *Mom made a dress and saved the excess material.*

ex·ces·sive [ek-<u>ses</u>-iv] *adjective.* more than is required or reasonable: *The senator thinks Americans pay an excessive amount of taxes and wants a tax cut.* —**excessively,** *adverb.*

ex·change ▶ [iks-<u>chaynj</u>] *verb,* **exchanged, exchanging. 1.** to give one thing in return for something different: *Ray exchanged the shirt for a larger one.* **2.** to give one thing for another of the same kind; swap: *We exchanged telephone numbers.* *noun, plural* **exchanges. 1.** the act of making an exchange: *We made an exchange of gifts at the party.* **2.** a business place where trading or selling occurs: *Only members can enter the stock exchange.*

ex·cite [ik-<u>site</u>] *verb,* **excited, exciting.** to arouse strong feelings; stir up: *He excited our interest by showing us photos of the beautiful hotel where we would be staying.*

ex·cit·ed [ik-<u>site</u>-id] *adjective.* stirred up, having aroused feelings: *The excited dog ran around barking.* —**excitedly,** *adverb.*

ex·cite·ment [ik-<u>site</u>-munt] *noun.* **1.** the fact of being excited: *On the last day of school, the children's excitement built up all day.* **2.** something that is exciting: *The whole town became caught up in the excitement of the parade.*

ex·cit·ing [ik-<u>site</u>-ing] *adjective.* creating excitement: *We watched the exciting car race on television.* —**excitingly,** *adverb.*

ex·claim [iks-<u>klame</u>] *verb,* **exclaimed, exclaiming.** to speak or cry out suddenly and loudly: *"Watch out!" the girl exclaimed when she saw the car coming toward them.*

ex·clam·a·tion [eks-kluh-<u>may</u>-shun] *noun, plural* **exclamations. 1.** the act of crying out suddenly and loudly. **2.** something suddenly shouted or called out: *The rock went through the window and the exclamation, "Oh no!" came from inside.*

exclamation point *Language.* a mark (!) used after a word or group of words said as an exclamation. Another term for this is **exclamation mark.**

An **exclamation point** shows that a character was shouting out loud, as in: "I thought the pitch was way outside, but the umpire called 'Strike Three!'" You can also use the exclamation point to signal to the reader the idea of "This is surprising" or "This is exciting," as in: "When she got home the house was empty! The dog was gone!" However, too many exclamation points can make it seem you are shouting at your readers, and if your writing is effective, they will get the idea without an exclamation point.

ex·clude [eks-<u>klood</u>] *verb,* **excluded, excluding.** to not let in; not include: *People who don't belong to the club are excluded from playing golf there.* —**exclusion,** *noun.*

ex·clu·sive [iks-<u>kloo</u>-siv] *adjective.* **1.** not shared with others: *That brand of chocolates is exclusive to this store and is not sold anywhere else.* **2.** only allowing a select group to be included: *Harvard is an exclusive college and students must have very high grades to go there.* **3.** complete; absolute: *Jim gave the exam paper his exclusive attention.* —**exclusively,** *adverb.*

ex·crete [eks-<u>kreet</u>] *verb,* **excreted, excreting.** *Biology.* to pass waste material from the body. **Excretory** means having to do with excretion. —**excretion,** *noun.*

ex·cuse [ik-<u>skyoos</u> *for noun;* ik-<u>skyooz</u> *for verb*] *verb,* **excused, excusing. 1.** to forgive someone or something; overlook: *The teacher excused us for being late to class because of the heavy snowstorm.* **2.** to permit not to do something: *Dad excused me from chores because I had a lot of homework.* *noun, plural* **excuses.** a reason given to justify forgiveness: *My excuse for not having my homework was that I left it on the bus.*

ex·e·cute [<u>ek</u>-suh-*kyoot*] *verb,* **executed, executing. 1.** to carry out; complete: *The crew executed the captain's orders; The figure skater executed her routine without a mistake.* **2.** to put to death under order from a higher authority.

*People **exercise** to stay fit and healthy.*

ex·e·cu·tion [ek-suh-<u>kyoo</u>-shun] *noun, plural* **executions.**
1. the act of carrying out: *The execution of our fire drill was perfect.* **2.** the act of putting to someone to death by order. A person who carries out an execution is an **executioner.**

ex·ec·u·tive [ig-<u>zek</u>-yuh-tiv] *noun, plural* **executives.**
1. a person who manages a company or government organization. **2.** the section of a government responsible for running the nation and making sure its laws are enforced. The **Executive Branch** of the U.S. government administers the nation. It includes the President, the presidential staff, the executive agencies, and the Cabinet departments.
adjective. having to do with managing or running a company or government department.

ex·empt [ig-<u>zempt</u>] *verb,* **exempted, exempting.** to release from a duty or rule: *Diane is exempted from entering school via the regular entrance as she uses a wheelchair.*
adjective. released from a duty or rule: *Most property is subject to taxes, but government and church property are exempt.*

ex·emp·tion [ig-<u>zempt</u>-shun] *noun, plural* **exemptions.** the act or fact of exempting; leaving out. A **tax exemption** is something that is not subject to taxes.

ex·er·cise ▲ [<u>ek</u>-sur-*size*] *noun, plural* **exercises. 1.** *Health.* an activity carried out to keep the body fit and healthy, such as running, walking, swimming, lifting weights, or riding a bicycle. **2.** something that you do in order to practice or develop a skill: *There is a set of exercises at the end of each chapter of the textbook.* **3.** the act of putting some skill or ability to use: *Finishing jigsaw puzzles requires the exercise of patience.* **4.** a formal ceremony: *Speeches were given during the college graduation exercises.*
verb, **exercised, exercising. 1.** to carry out exercises: *I exercise by swimming twice a week.* **2.** to make use of; use: *We exercised caution as we approached the large dog.*

ex·ert [ig-<u>zurt</u>] *verb,* **exerted, exerting.** to put to use: *I exerted my powers of thinking and worked out the problem.*

ex·hale [eks-<u>hale</u> *or* <u>eks</u>-hale] *verb,* **exhaled, exhaling.** to breathe out: *Melissa made bubbles by exhaling underwater.* —**exhalation,** *noun.*

ex·haust [ig-<u>zawst</u>] *verb,* **exhausted, exhausting.**
1. to make tired or weaken: *Rick fell asleep as he was exhausted from all the work he did.* **2.** to completely run out of: *Our supply of wood was exhausted, so the fire went out.*
noun, plural **exhausts.** the gases created by a working engine: *The exhaust from cars is a serious cause of pollution.* An **exhaust pipe** is the pipe on an automobile that carries these gases away.

ex·haus·tion [ig-<u>zawst</u>-shun] *noun.* the process of becoming exhausted or the fact of being exhausted: *Exhaustion overcame her as she climbed the mountain.*

ex·hib·it [ig-<u>zib</u>-it] *verb,* **exhibited, exhibiting.**
1. to put out to be seen; display; show: *The paintings were exhibited in the art gallery.* **2.** to give a sign of; indicate: *She exhibited signs of coming down with a cold.*
noun, plural **exhibits.** something put on public show: *The museum has a new exhibit of fossils.*

ex·hi·bi·tion ▼ [ek-suh-<u>bish</u>-un] *noun, plural* **exhibitions.**
1. the act or fact of showing something. **2.** a display for public viewing: *We saw an excellent exhibition of antique automobiles.*

ex·hil·a·rate [ig-<u>zil</u>-uh-*rate*] *verb,* **exhilarated, exhilarating.** to cheer up, excite, or thrill: *Going on the giant slide at the amusement park exhilarated Anthony.* —**exhilaration,** *noun.*

*An **exhibition** of mummy cases helps people understand more about the ancient Egyptians.*

A B C D E F G H I J K L M N O P Q R S T U V W X Y Z

ex·ile [eg-zile *or* ek-sile] *verb*, **exiled, exiling.** to force a person to leave his or her country or home; banish. *noun, plural* **exiles. 1.** the fact of being exiled: *After he surrendered, the French emperor Napoleon lived in exile on a small island.* **2.** someone who is forced to leave his or her country or home.

ex·ist [ig-zist] *verb*, **existed, existing. 1.** to be real: *Few people believe gnomes really exist.* **2.** to continue to live; stay alive: *While the boy was lost in the woods he existed on nuts and berries.* **3.** to be found; occur: *Wild koalas exist only in Australia.*

ex·is·tence [ig-zis-tuns] *noun, plural* **existences. 1.** the state or fact of existing; being real or living: *The existence of an ancient palace was revealed as the archeologists kept digging.* **2.** a way of existing or living: *The herder led a simple existence in the mountains.*

ex·it [ex-it] *noun, plural* **exits. 1.** the way out of a place: *During the fire we left the building through the emergency exit.* **2.** the act of departing: *The actress gave her final speech then made her exit from the stage.* *verb*, **exited, exiting.** to leave; depart: *The flight landed and the passengers exited from the plane.*

ex·ot·ic [ig-zot-ik] *adjective.* **1.** coming from outside an area; *This plant is native to Africa, but exotic to America.* **2.** unusual and fascinating: *She wore a dress made of an exotic printed silk.*

ex·pand [ek-spand] *verb*, **expanded, expanding.** to make larger; increase: *The balloon expanded when I blew into it.*

ex·panse [ek-spans] *noun, plural* **expanses.** a large open area: *We looked up into the expanse of cloudless sky.*

ex·pan·sion [ek-span-shun] *noun, plural* **expansions. 1.** the act of making larger or the fact of being made larger: *The expansion of the computer room will mean forty students can use it at once.* **2.** something resulting from being expanded: *That mansion is the expansion of a smaller home.*

ex·pect [ek-spekt] *verb*, **expected, expecting. 1.** to think of as likely to happen: *John expected to get a good mark in his geography course because he did very well on the final test.* **2.** to firmly believe something should happen: *My grandmother expects all children to be polite.* **3.** to imagine as a possibility; suppose: *If it snows tonight, I expect we can go skiing in the morning.*

ex·pec·tant [ek-spek-tunt] *adjective.* **1.** looking forward to something; anticipating something. *The expectant audience waited for the concert to begin.* **2.** awaiting the birth of a child; pregnant: *an expectant mother.* The state of being expectant or the object of expectations is called **expectancy**. The number of years a person can be predicted to live according to factors such as their place of birth, sex, job, and so on, is called their **life expectancy.** —**expectantly,** *adverb.*

ex·pec·ta·tion [ek-spek-tay-shun] *noun, plural* **expectations. 1.** the act or state of thinking something is likely to happen: *We cleaned the apartment in expectation of our visitors' arrival.* **2.** something expected with good reason: *It had been sunny all week so they had expectations of a good day at the beach.*

Ice often delayed early sea **expeditions** *searching for a northern route to sail from the Atlantic to the Pacific.*

ex·pe·di·tion ▲ [[ek-spuh-dish-un] *noun, plural* **expeditions. 1.** a journey taken for a special purpose: *The marine biologists made an expedition to Antarctic waters to study whales.* **2.** a group of people taking such a journey.

ex·pel [ek-spel] *verb*, **expelled, expelling.** to push out or away; eject: *Four students were expelled from the college for stealing.*

ex·pen·di·ture [ek-spen-duh-chur] *noun, plural* **expenditures.** an amount of something spent; an expense: *Last month their expenditure on food was four hundred dollars.*

ex·pense [ek-spens] *noun, plural* **expenses. 1.** a price paid for something; cost: **2.** something that causes spending: *Household expenses can include food, clothing, rent or a mortgage, and electricity.* **3.** something that causes a loss, penalty, or sacrifice: *The excitement of moving to a new city came at the expense of leaving friends behind.*

ex·pen·sive [ek-spen-siv] *adjective.* costing a lot: *an expensive diamond ring.* —**expensively,** *adverb.*

ex·pe·ri·ence [ek-speer-ee-uns] *noun, plural* **experiences. 1.** something a person did or they saw happen: *Lana found the experience of skydiving very exciting.* **2.** something learned through doing: *We hired her because she is has three years' experience working as a chef.* Someone who has learned through doing is said to be **experienced.** *verb*, **experienced, experiencing.** to have happen to you; go through yourself: *I don't ever want to experience another tornado.*

A
B
C
D
E
F
G
H
I
J
K
L
M
N
O
P
Q
R
S
T

ex·per·i·ment ▶ [ek-<u>sper</u>-uh-ment] *noun, plural* **experiments. 1.** *Science.* a test or procedure carried out carefully under certain conditions to show that some fact is true, or to try to discover a new fact: *Benjamin Franklin ran an experiment with a kite in a storm and learned much about electricity.* **2.** any test or process to find something out or test the truth of something. *verb,* **experimented, experimenting.** to run such a test; try out: *I experimented with several spices to find which ones give my curry the best flavor.*

ex·per·i·ment·al [ek-*sper*-uh-<u>men</u>-tul] *adjective.* relating to an experiment or test: *In experimental theater, actors try out new ways of performing.* —**experimentally,** *adverb.*

ex·pert [<u>ek</u>-spurt] *noun, plural* **experts.** someone who knows a lot about a particular thing or has a particular skill; a specialist: *The fire safety expert gave a talk about preventing fires in the home.* *adjective.* showing a large amount of knowledge or skill: *My uncle is an expert pastry maker.*

ex·pi·ra·tion [ek-spuh-<u>ray</u>-shun] *noun, plural* **expirations.** the act of closing or ending: *The expiration of this coupon is tomorrow so I have to use it today.* The date on processed foods by which they should be used is called the **expiration date.**

ex·pire [ek-<u>spire</u>] *verb,* **expired, expiring.** to go out of use or existence; finish; end: *My subscription to the magazine expired last month.*

ex·plain [ek-<u>splane</u>] *verb,* **explained, explaining. 1.** to make easy to understand or to give the meaning of: *The teacher explained how to do the math problem.* **2.** to give a reason for: *I explained why I don't like playing tennis.* Something used to explain is said to be **explanatory.**

These children are conducting an **experiment** *to see how much weight they can place on inflated balloons before they burst.*

ex·plan·a·tion [*ek*-spluh-<u>nay</u>-shun] *noun, plural* **explanations. 1.** the act of explaining: *The book's explanation of how to set up the computer was very clear.* **2.** a meaning or a reason given to explain: *My flute teacher demanded an explanation for why I hadn't practiced.*

ex·pli·cit [ek-<u>splis</u>-it] *adjective.* shown or stated clearly and fully; leaving nothing to suggestion: *The teacher's explicit note informed my father of what I had done wrong.* —**explicitly,** *adverb.*

ex·plode [ek-<u>splode</u>] *verb,* **exploded, exploding. 1.** to suddenly and forcefully blow apart with a loud bang: *The balloon exploded when she jumped on it.* **2.** to have a sudden, forceful outburst: *to explode with anger.*

ex·ploit [<u>ek</u>-sployte] *noun, plural* **exploits.** a notable, brave, or daring act: *The soldier talked about his war exploits.* *verb,* **exploited, exploiting. 1.** to use selfishly or unjustly: *Some American children were once exploited working in factories for little pay.* **2.** to put to full use: *He exploited every opportunity he got to learn.*

ex·plor·a·tion [*eks*-pluh-<u>ray</u>-shun] *noun, plural* **explorations.** the act of exploring: *an exploration of the surface of the moon.*

ex·plore ▼ [ek-<u>splore</u>] *verb,* **explored, exploring. 1.** to go to a place unknown to others to make discoveries: *The sailors set off in a small boat to explore the coast.* An action such as this is said to be **exploratory. 2.** to search or attempt to work out: *We explored several ideas for our class play.*

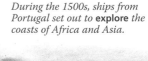

During the 1500s, ships from Portugal set out to **explore** *the coasts of Africa and Asia.*

*Traffic on an **expressway** travels around towns and cities, and not through them.*

ex·plor·er [ek-splore-ur] *noun, plural* **explorers.** one who undertakes a journey of discovery, or who searches.

ex·plo·sion [ek-sploh-zhun] *noun, plural* **explosions.**
1. the act of blowing apart forcefully and loudly: *The explosion of the balloon hurt my ears.* **2.** a sudden, forceful outburst: *The children let out an explosion of laughter when the clowns fell over.*

ex·plo·sive [ek-sploh-siv] *adjective.* **1.** likely to explode or burst out: *Gasoline is an explosive substance.* **2.** likely to suddenly burst out in conflict: *Food shortages created an explosive situation in the city.*
noun, plural **explosives.** a material that can cause an explosion: *The miners broke the rock using dynamite as an explosive.* —**explosively,** *adverb.*

ex·po·nent [ek-spoh-nunt] *noun, plural* **exponents.**
1. *Mathematics.* a number put above and to the right of another number to show how many times it is to be multiplied by itself. For example, in 5^3, 3 is the exponent and means 5 must be multiplied by itself 3 times, giving the answer 125. **2.** a person who puts something forward and explains or argues in favor of it: *Our doctor is an exponent of exercise and healthy eating.*

ex·port [eks-port *or* ek-sport] *verb,* **exported, exporting.**
Business. to send to other nations for sale: *Canada exports minerals such as lead, zinc, and aluminum to other countries.*
noun, plural **exports. 1.** something sold from one country to another: *One of Ecuador's main exports to the United States is bananas.* **2.** the act of selling goods to another country: *The export of oil has made some nations wealthy.*

ex·pose [ek-spoze] *verb,* **exposed, exposing. 1.** to be uncovered and unprotected: *We were exposed to the storm after the roof blew off.* **2.** to uncover or reveal: *His lie was exposed when we discovered the truth.* **3.** to let light fall on a photographic plate or film.

ex·po·sure [ek-spoh-zhur] *noun, plural* **exposures.**
1. the act of exposing or the state of being exposed: *The man who became lost in the desert suffered from heat exposure.* **2.** a position related to weather or sunlight: *This valley is shady and cool because of its northern exposure.* **3.** the act of letting light fall on photographic film.

ex·press [ek-spres] *verb,* **expressed, expressing.** to show through actions or putting into words: *He expressed his anger by kicking the door.* Showing feelings clearly is being **expressive.**
adjective. **1.** particular or definite: *I went to see Grandpa with the express reason of cheering him up.* **2.** traveling directly or fast; without stopping: *The express train doesn't make any stops between the two cities.*
noun, plural **expresses.** a fast transport or delivery service, such as a bus, train, or elevator that travels faster because it makes few stops.

ex·pres·sion [ek-spresh-un] *noun, plural* **expressions.**
1. the act of showing through words or actions: *He wrote her a poem as an expression of his love.*
2. a show of feeling through appearance: *The expression of joy on his face was plain to see.*
3. a manner in which words are expressed: *Dad reads stories to us using lots of expression.* **4.** a group of words often said together; a saying. "Don't judge a book by its cover," is a familiar expression.

ex·press·way ▲ [ek-spres-way] *noun, plural* **expressways.** a major highway made for high-speed automobile travel. An expressway has multiple lanes and few crossroads so traffic rarely has to stop or slow down.

ex·qui·site [ik-skwiz-it *or* ek-skwiz-it] *adjective.* **1.** of rare and flawless beauty; delightful: *Exquisite jewels encrusted the gown.* **2.** made with great skill: *The walls of the palace were covered with exquisite carvings.*
—**exquisitely,** *adverb.*

ex·tend [ik-stend] *verb,* **extended, extending. 1.** to make longer; expand: *I extended my library loan so I could finish reading the book.* **2.** to stretch out to; reach: *The road extends from the town to the river.* **3.** to hold out to; offer or give: *Pauline extended an invitation to my family.*

ex·ten·sion [ik-sten-shun] *noun, plural* **1.** the act or fact of extending: *The extension of shopping hours makes it easier for people to shop after work.* **2.** something that adds to or makes larger: *We have built an extension to our house, including a second bathroom.* **3.** an extra telephone that is added to an existing telephone's line.

ex·ten·sive [ik-sten-siv] *adjective.* large in amount or size; far-reaching or thorough: *An extensive search was carried out for the lost child.* —**extensively,** *adverb.*

ex·tent [ik-stent] *noun, plural* **extents.** the limit, size, area, or degree something extends to: *On October 8, 1871, a great extent of Chicago was destroyed by fire.*

ex·te·ri·or [ek-steer-ee-ur] *noun, plural* **exteriors.** the outside or outward appearance of something: *The exterior of the box is painted gold.*
adjective. having to do with the outside of something: *The exterior walls of the building were made of rough stone.*

ex·ter·min·ate [ik-stur-muh-nate] *verb,* **exterminated, exterminating.** to wipe out; kill all of: *The fish in the stream were exterminated by pollution.* A person who exterminates household pests such as ants is an **exterminator.** —**extermination,** *noun.*

EXTINCT ANIMALS

Many animals that once walked the Earth have died out, either because of changed natural conditions or as a result of human activities. Dinosaurs are thought to have become extinct millions of years ago after some catastrophic natural disaster. Eleven thousand years ago, hunting, climate change, or disease may have caused mammoths to disappear. In the seventeenth century the dodo was lost in Mauritius only eighty years after humans discovered the island, while the passenger pigeon was hunted to extinction in the nineteenth century.

Aphadon

Miss Waldron's red colobus monkey

Passenger pigeon

Ursavus

Dodo

Dinornis

Great auk

Steller's sea cow

ex·ter·nal [ek-stur-nul] *adjective.* having to do with the outside or outer part of something: *They painted the external walls of the house a pale gray color.* —**externally,** *adverb.*

ex·tinct ◀ [ik-stingkt] *adjective.* **1.** having died out; no longer in existence: *Dinosaurs are only known through fossils as they became extinct 65 million years ago.* **2.** no longer active; extinguished: *The extinct volcano has not erupted for two thousand years.*

ex·tinc·tion [ik-stingkt-shun] *noun,* plural **extinctions. 1.** *Biology.* the act or process of becoming extinct or dying out: *Many animal and plant extinctions are occurring because of land clearing by humans.* **2.** the act or process of extinguishing or putting out: *The extinction of the forest fire took many days.*

ex·tin·guish [ik-sting-gwish] *verb,* **extinguished, extinguishing. 1.** to stop something burning; put out: *We extinguished the campfire before we went to our tents.* **2.** to destroy or stop existing: *As the storm worsened, hopes of rescuing people from the sinking ship were extinguished.*

ex·tra [ek-struh] *adjective.* more than usual; additional: *We brought an extra can of gasoline on our drive across the desert. noun,* plural **extras. 1.** something more than usual offered: *The vacation package had many free extras, such as breakfast and a scuba diving lesson.* **2.** a special, additional edition of a newspaper or magazine: *The newspaper ran an extra when Apollo 11 landed on the Moon.* **3.** someone playing a small, non-speaking part in a film. *adverb.* more than the usual amount or degree: *He ran extra fast to get away from the dog.*

ex·tract [ek-strakt] *verb,* **extracted, extracting.** to take from or pull out of something else; *Jill used tweezers to extract the thorn from her foot. noun,* plural **extracts.** something taken out of something else: *Reading the extract of the novel made me want to buy the whole book.* —**extraction,** *noun.*

ex·tra·or·di·nar·y [ek-stror-duh-ner-ee] *adjective.* more than ordinary, remarkable: *That girl is an extraordinary athlete.* —**extraordinarily,** *adverb.*

ex·tra·ter·res·tri·al [ek-struh-tuh-res-tree-ul] *adjective. Science.* not coming from Earth: *The scientists picked up extraterrestrial radio signals with their equipment. noun,* plural **extraterrestrials.** a creature that comes from a planet other than Earth: *Ruby wrote a story about extraterrestrials that lived on Mars.*

A B C D **E** F G H I J K L M N O P Q R S T U V W X Y Z

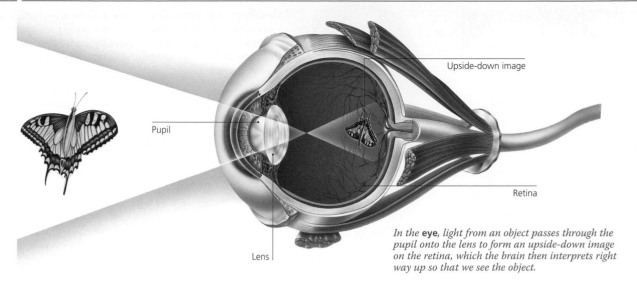

In the **eye,** *light from an object passes through the pupil onto the lens to form an upside-down image on the retina, which the brain then interprets right way up so that we see the object.*

ex·trav·a·gant [ik-<u>strav</u>-uh-gunt] **adjective.** using more of something than necessary, especially money; wasteful: *There is a drought now, so don't be extravagant with water.* The act of being wasteful, especially spending too much money, is called **extravagance. —extravagantly,** *adverb.*

ex·treme [ik-<u>streem</u>] *adjective.* **1.** describing something a long way from the usual; very great or strong: *The tree was blown over by extreme winds.* **2.** farthest from the center; outermost: *The bird sat on the extreme tip of the branch.* *noun, plural* **extremes. 1.** the farthest point of something: *The space probe traveled to the solar system's extreme.* **2.** two things very different to each other; opposites: *Joy and rage are two extremes of emotion.*
• **go to extremes.** to go to great lengths to achieve something; take drastic steps: *He goes to extremes to stay clean, washing his hands twenty or more times a day.*

ex·treme·ly [ik-<u>streem</u>-lee] *adverb.* greatly; very: *I felt extremely sick after I ate a whole pizza.*

ex·trem·ity [ik-<u>strem</u>-i-tee] *noun, plural* **extremities.**
1. the fact of being extreme or something that is extra.
2. extremities. the hands or feet.

eye ▲ [eye] *noun, plural* **eyes. 1.** an organ with which an animal sees or detects light. **2.** the colored section of an eye; the iris: *He has brown eyes.* **3.** the area surrounding an eye: *He got hit with a ball and has a black eye.* **4.** the ability to see or judge: *My mother has a good eye for a bargain.* **5.** the act of watching or looking at: *I kept an eye out for my friend.* **6.** something with a similar shape to a human eye, such as the eye of a needle, which is the small hole through which thread is pushed. **7.** the central part of a hurricane, which is calm and through which clear sky is visible.
verb, **eyed, eyeing.** to look at closely; watch: *Before the race, Huan eyed the other runners.*
• **keep an eye on.** to watch over carefully; mind: *Keep an eye on the saucepan to make sure it doesn't boil over.*
• **see eye to eye.** see in the same way; agree on: *We could not see eye to eye on how to decorate the room.*
◀)) Different words with the same sound are **aye** and **I.**

eye·ball [<u>eye</u>-bawl] *noun, plural* **eyeballs.** the ball-shaped part of the eye without its surroundings parts.

eye·brow [<u>eye</u>-brow] *noun, plural* **eyebrows. 1.** the bony ridge above each eye that protects and shades it. **2.** the arch of short hair growing on this ridge that protects the eye by trapping sweat and dust.

eye·glas·ses [<u>eye</u>-glas-uz] *plural noun.* a pair of lenses worn in front of the eyes to help a person see better. The lenses are held in a frame that rests on the nose and ears.

eye·lash [<u>eye</u>-lash] *noun, plural* **eyelashes.** one of the short, stiff hairs that grow at the edge of each eyelid. Eyelashes help to keep dust out of the eye.
• **within an eyelash.** a narrow margin; very close: *In an exciting finish the Blues came within an eyelash of winning.*

eye·lid [<u>eye</u>-lid] *noun, plural* **eyelids.** a fold of skin that can open and close over the eye. Eyelids protect the eyes and help to keep them moist.

eye·sight [<u>eye</u>-site] *noun.* the power to see; vision. *You have to pass an eyesight test before you can get a driver's license.*

eye·tooth ▼ [<u>eye</u>-tooth] *noun, plural* **eyeteeth.** either of the two pointed teeth toward the front of the upper jaw.

eye·wit·ness [<u>eye</u>-<u>wit</u>-nis] *noun, plural* **eyewitnesses.** *Law.* someone who sees an action or happening and can tell people about it: *an eyewitness to the accident.*

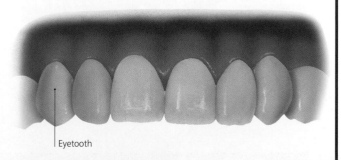
Eyetooth

Eyeteeth *are so called because they are almost directly beneath a person's eyes.*

F, f *noun, plural* **F's, f's.** the sixth letter of the English alphabet.

F or **F.** an abbreviation for FAHRENHEIT.

fa·ble [fay-bul] *noun, plural* **fables.**
1. *Literature.* a short story that teaches a lesson. The main characters in fables are usually animals. **2.** an untrue story: *It was just a fable about her mother having been a Hollywood star.*

Jewelers make gems by cutting and shaping minerals to display their **facets.**

A **fable** is a special kind of story in which animals act like humans. The point is to teach a lesson to the reader from the way the animals act, and especially the mistakes that they make. For example, one famous fable tells of how a fox tricks a crow into giving up its food by saying very nice things to it and appealing to its pride. The lesson is that you should not trust someone who is pretending to be nice just so that they can get something from you.

fab·ric ▼ [fab-rik] *noun, plural* **fabrics.** a material or cloth made by weaving or knitting threads together. Fabric is made from natural fibers such as cotton, wool, or silk and from synthetic fibers such as nylon.

fab·u·lous [fab-yuh-lus] *adjective.* **1.** describing something wonderful; amazing: *Fireworks filled the sky with fabulous patterns of color.* **2.** like something from a story or fable; unbelievable: *Dragons and unicorns are fabulous creatures.* **—fabulously,** *adverb.*

face [fase] *noun, plural* **faces. 1.** the front of the head between the hair and the chin. The eyes, nose, and mouth are part of the face. **2.** a look or expression: *a happy face; a brave face.* **3.** the surface or outward part of something: *the face of a watch; a cliff face; She dealt out the cards face down.* **4.** importance in the opinion of others; reputation: *The student lost face when with his classmates when he was caught cheating.*
verb, **faced, facing. 1.** to look or turn toward: *The house faces north; He turned to face me and waved.* **2.** to accept a difficult or unpleasant situation and deal with it: *Let's face it, the book is lost and we'll need to buy a new one.*

fa·cet ◀ [fas-it] *noun, plural* **facets. 1.** one of the small, flat sides of a cut gem. **2.** any of the many parts of something: *a facet of his personality; Being fit is an important facet of playing a sport.*

fa·cial [fay-shul] *adjective.* having to do with the face: *a facial expression; facial hair; The twins have similar facial features.*
noun, plural **facials.** a beauty treatment for the skin of the face.

fa·cil·i·tate [fuh-sil-uh-tate] *verb,* **facilitated, facilitating.** to make easier; help: *The new freeway will facilitate traffic traveling to the north of the city.* **—facilitation,** *noun.*

fa·cil·i·ty [fuh-sil-uh-tee] *noun, plural* **facilities. 1.** skill and ease in doing something: *a facility for learning languages.* **2.** something that makes an activity or job easier or is provided for a particular purpose: *library facilities; cooking facilities; gym facilities.*

fact [fakt] *noun, plural* **facts.** something that is true or real: *It is a fact that it snows a lot in Alaska.*
• **in fact.** really; actually: *I thought we would be late, but in fact we arrived early.*

In ancient times, Middle Eastern merchants bought silk **fabrics** *from Chinese traders traveling the trade route known as the Silk Road.*

fac·tor [fak-tur] *noun, plural* **factors. 1.** something that helps to bring about a result: *Lack of advertising and bad weather were both factors in the poor attendance at the fair.* **2.** *Mathematics.* any of the numbers that give the product when multiplied together. The factors of 20 are 20 and 1, 10 and 2, and 4 and 5.

fac·to·ry ▶ [fak-tree *or* fak-tuh-ree] *noun, plural* **factories.** a building or group of buildings where goods are made with machines: *an automobile factory; a paint factory.*

fac·tu·al [fak-choo-ul] *adjective.* containing facts; accurate: *a factual report; His talk on the life cycle of frogs was both interesting and factual.* —**factually,** *adverb.*

fac·ul·ty [fak-ul-tee] *noun, plural* **faculties.**
1. the teachers in a school or college. **2.** one of the natural powers of the mind or body, such as hearing or memory. As people get older, they may lose some of their **faculties.**
3. a special ability or skill: *a faculty for doing crosswords; a faculty for making friends.*

Today, most goods are mass-produced in **factories**.

fad [fad] *noun, plural* **fads.** something that is very popular or fashionable for a short time only: *Fad diets come and go.* Something that is very popular or fashionable for a short time is **faddish.**

fade [fade] *verb,* **faded, fading. 1.** to lose or make something lose brightness or color: *My jeans faded after they were washed.* **2.** to become weaker or fainter; disappear gradually: *The sound of the radio faded as the battery went dead; General Douglas MacArthur was famous for saying, "Old soldiers never die, they just fade away."*

Fahr·en·heit [fare-in-*hite*] *adjective. Science.* having to do with the Fahrenheit scale of temperature, in which the freezing point of water is set at 32 degrees and the boiling point of water is set at 212 degrees.

The **Fahrenheit** temperature scale, which has 32° for the freezing point of water and 212° for the boiling point, is named after the man who invented it. Gabriel *Fahrenheit* was a German scientist who developed this scale, probably in about the year 1724.

fail [fale] *verb,* **failed, failing. 1.** to not do what is wanted, expected, or needed; not succeed: *The driver was fined for failing to stop at the red light; The business failed because of bad management.* **2.** to get too low a grade to pass a test or a course of study: *My brother failed the math test.* **3.** to be of no help to; disappoint: *Her friends failed her when she needed them most.* **4.** to lose strength or stop working: *His memory is failing.*
• **without fail.** always happening as expected; completely certain: *The sun will rise tomorrow, without fail.*

fail·ure [fale-yur] *noun, plural* **failures. 1.** a lack of success in doing something: *She was embarrassed by her failure to remember their names.* **2.** a person or thing that does not succeed: *After several failures, the expedition finally reached the North Pole.* **3.** the fact of not working properly or not being good enough: *The lights went off because of an electrical power failure.*

faint [faynt] *adjective,* **fainter, faintest. 1.** not strong or clear: *We could just hear a faint noise of the dog scratching at the door.* **2.** weak and dizzy: *faint with worry; faint from lack of food. noun, plural* **faints.** the act of feeling dizzy and then losing consciousness for a short time: *verb,* **fainted, fainting.** to feel dizzy, then become unconscious for a short time. —**faintly,** *adverb.*
🔊 A different word with the same sound is **feint.**

fair¹ [fare] *adjective.*
1. not showing favor to one more than others; free from bias or prejudice; honest: *A basketball referee must be fair to both teams.* **2.** according to the rules: *a fair tackle in soccer.* **3.** neither very good nor very bad; average in standard: *I'm only a fair swimmer.* **4.** pale or light in color: *He has fair hair and blue eyes.* **5.** fine and clear; not cloudy: *fair skies; fair weather.* **6.** beautiful: *The old story tells of a prince and a fair maiden. adverb.* in an honest manner; according to the rules: *I trust you to play fair.* —**fairness,** *noun.*
🔊 A different word with the same sound is **fare.**

fair² [fare] *noun, plural* **fairs. 1.** a public show for farm goods and products. Fairs take place to display and judge crops and farm animals. Fairs often have music and other entertainment. A **fairground** is an outdoor place where a fair is held. **2.** a large show with products or objects from a particular industry that are for sale: *a book fair; an antiques fair.* **3.** the selling of goods and entertainment for a particular reason or cause: *The school fair raised money to buy new play equipment.*
🔊 A different word with the same sound is **fare.**

fair·ly [fare-lee] *adverb.* **1.** in an honest manner; justly: *We shared the cake fairly, so everyone got the same amount.* **2.** for the most part; in general; rather; quite; somewhat: *He is fairly good at spelling, but his sister is much better.*

fair·y [fare-ee] *noun, plural* **fairies.** a small, imaginary creature that is shaped like a human, has magical powers, and may be able to grant wishes.

faith [fayth] *noun, plural* **faiths. 1.** trust or confidence in someone or something: *I have faith in you to keep our secret.* **2.** a certain system of believing in God; a religion: *the Christian faith; the Islamic faith.*

faith·ful [fayth-ful] *adjective.* **1.** showing faith or trust; loyal and trustworthy: *a faithful dog; a faithful friend.* **2.** holding to truth or fact; accurate or truthful: *The film is faithful to the book it comes from.* —**faithfully**, *adverb;* **faithfulness**, *noun.*

fake [fake] *noun, plural* **fakes.** a person or thing that is not genuine or real; something false: *That beard is a fake.* *verb,* **faked, faking. 1.** to act so as to fool or trick; pretend: *I shut my eyes and faked being asleep.* **2.** to make something false look like it is genuine or real in order to trick or cheat: *He faked his mother's signature on the report card.* Someone who makes something false look like it is genuine, or who pretends to feel something or be someone they are not is a **faker.** *adjective.* not genuine or real: *fake money; a fake yawn.*

In ancient times and the Middle Ages, falcons were trained to catch birds and other animals.

fal·con ◄ [fawl-kun *or* fal-kun] *noun, plural* **falcons.** a hunting bird with a curved beak, powerful wings, and a long tail. Falcons use the claws on their feet to catch other birds and small animals.

fall [fawl] *verb,* **fell, fallen, falling. 1.** to move down from a higher place: *A tile fell from the roof.* **2.** to suddenly drop to the ground or floor from a standing position. **3.** to become less: *I can't afford that jacket unless the price falls.* **4.** to take place; happen: *My birthday falls in May.* **5.** to become: *to fall ill; to fall in love.* *noun, plural* **falls. 1.** the act of moving down from a higher place: *The mountain climber had a bad fall.* **2.** something, or the amount of something, that has come down: *a fall of snow.* **3.** a loss of amount, power, or value;

a decrease or a defeat: *the fall of the Roman Empire.* **4.** also, **Fall.** the season between summer and winter; autumn.
• **fall through.** to fail to finish successfully: *Our plans to go to the lake fell through at the last minute.*

fall·en [fawl-un] *verb.* the past participle of FALL. *adjective.* **1.** having come from a higher place: *Fallen rocks lay at the bottom of the cliff.* **2.** having died in battle or war: *fallen warriors.*

fall·out [fawl-out] *noun.* **1.** *Environment.* dangerous radioactive dust that falls from the air after a nuclear explosion. A **fallout shelter** is a strong building to protect people from radioactive dust. **2.** a difficult or unpleasant situation that results from some other event: *In the fallout from the factory closing, many families moved out of town and a local store also had to close.*

falls ▼ [fawlz] *plural noun.* water from a stream or river moving straight downward from a higher place; a waterfall.

false [fawls] *adjective,* **falser, falsest. 1.** not true or correct: *She is in trouble for making a false statement to the police.* **2.** not genuine or real; artificial: *false teeth.* —**falsely**, *adverb;* **falseness**, *noun.*

false·hood [fawls-hood] *noun, plural* **falsehoods.** a statement that is not true; a lie.

fal·ter [fawl-tur] *verb,* **faltered, faltering. 1.** to walk or move in an unsteady way: *The newborn foal faltered as it took its first steps.* **2.** to hesitate; pause: *The engine faltered, then stopped.*

fame [fame] *noun.* the fact of being very well known: *The movie star's fame spread around the world.*

fa·mil·iar [fuh-mil-yur] *adjective* **1.** well known or often seen; common: *Cactus plants are a familiar sight in the desert.* **2.** known because of being experienced or seen before: *His face looks familiar, but I can't remember his name.* **Familiarity** is the act or fact of knowing or experiencing something before. **3.** knowing or understanding something: *Are you familiar with the word "ecology?"* **4.** friendly: *to be on familiar terms with someone.* —**familiarly**, *adverb.*

fam·i·ly [fam-lee *or* fam-uh-lee] *noun, plural* **families. 1.** a group of people who are related to each other and live together. A family usually consists of parents and their children. A **family room** is a room in a house used by the whole family for activities such as watching television. **2.** the children of a father and mother: *I come from a family of four.* **3.** a larger group of people related to each other, including grandparents, uncles, aunts, and cousins: *All the family got together for my aunt's birthday.* **4.** a group of related things: *Garlic, onions, and leeks belong to the same family of plants.* *adjective.* suitable for a family: *a family car; a family show.*

*The impressive Iguazu **Falls** are on the border between Brazil and Argentina.*

fam·ine [fam-un] *noun, plural* **famines.** a serious lack of food for a large number of people in an area or country. A famine can cause death by starvation.

fa·mous [fay-mus] *adjective.* known to many people; very well known: *The Mona Lisa is a famous painting.*

fan¹ ▶ [fan] *noun, plural* **fans.** a flat object shaped like a half circle. It is held in the hand and waved backward and forward to make air move for cooling. **2.** a machine with blades that are turned by a motor. It is used to make air move for cooling or heating. *verb,* **fanned, fanning. 1.** to move air backward and forward: *to fan your face; to fan a fire.* **2.** to spread gradually in the shape of a fan: *The peacock fanned open its tail; The searchers fanned out across the field.*

fan² [fan] *noun, plural* **fans.** a very enthusiastic follower or supporter: *He is a big fan of the group and buys all their CDs.*

The word **fan** can mean someone who likes a certain sports team and wants that team to win. This word was taken from *fanatic,* a person who is much too interested in or excited about something. The idea was that sports fans may get too excited or upset about how their favorite team is doing. In British sports a fan is more often known as a *supporter,* from the idea that a team gets support (help) from its fans.

fa·na·tic [fuh-nat-ik] *noun, plural* **fanatics.** a person who is too enthusiastic in their support for something. *adjective.* feeling very strongly about something; too enthusiastic: *a computer game fanatic.* **—fanatically,** *adverb.*

fan·cy [fan-see] *adjective,* **fancier, fanciest.** not plain or ordinary; highly decorated: *She wrapped the present in fancy silver paper.* *verb,* **fancied, fancying. 1.** to imagine in a wishful way: *He fancied himself as a baseball star.* **2.** to like; be fond of: *Anyone fancy a game of tennis?* *noun, plural* **fancies. 1.** something made up in the mind; a fantasy. **2.** something wished for that is not likely to happen. **3.** a liking: *Grandma has a fancy for fluffy cats.*

fang ◀ [fang] *noun, plural* **fangs.** a long, pointed tooth of an animal.

*A rattlesnake's **fangs** swing forward to inject poison into its prey.*

fan·tas·tic [fan-tas-tik] *adjective.* **1.** strange or unusual; odd: *Erosion by wind and water has carved the rock into fantastic shapes.* **2.** excellent; pleasing: *Our 7–0 win was a fantastic start to the season.* **—fantastically,** *adverb.*

fan·ta·sy [fan-tuh-see] *noun, plural* **fantasies. 1.** something made up in the imagination; an imaginary wish or thought: *Jacob has never met the President, that is just a fantasy of his.* **2.** *Literature.* a story with strange or magical characters and events: *I enjoy reading fantasies about mysterious worlds and weird creatures.*

FAQ *Computers.* an abbreviation for Frequently Asked Questions, a list of common questions and answers for a particular subject, as on a Website.

far [far] *adverb.* **1.** to, from, or at a great distance: *Can we walk there, or is it too far? They hid in the darkness far from the cave entrance.* **2.** at or to a great distance in time: *She stayed at the office and worked far into the night.* **3.** very much: *The water is far too cold for swimming.* *adjective,* **farther** or **further; farthest** or **furthest.** being a long way away; distant: *It took most of the morning to row to the far side of the lake.* **2.** more distant: *Jupiter is farther from the Sun than Mars.*
• **as far as.** to the distance or degree that: *This bus will take you as far as the river; The test is on Tuesday, as far as I know.*
• **so far.** up to now or to a certain point: *I've really enjoyed that TV show so far.*

far·a·way [far-uh-way] *adjective.* **1.** a long way away; very distant: *faraway stars.* **2.** thinking deeply about other things; dreamy: *She stared out of the window with a faraway look.*

fare [fare] *noun, plural* **fares. 1.** the money paid to travel on a bus, train, taxi, airplane, or ship. **2.** a passenger who has paid to travel: *The taxi took a fare to the station.* *verb,* **fared, faring.** to get on or get along: *How did you fare on the spelling test?*
🔊 A different word with the same sound is **fair.**

Far East *Geography.* a region of Asia east of India and made up of Japan, China, Korea, Vietnam, Cambodia, and other countries.

The part of the world known as the **Far East** (countries such as China, Japan, and Korea) got this name because at one time Western Europe was thought of as the center of the world, and other areas were named in relation to this. Thus certain areas of Asia came to be known as the Near East, the Middle East, and Far East, according to how far they are from Western Europe.

fare·well [fare-wel] *interjection.* goodbye: *Farewell and good luck!* *noun, plural* **farewells.** a saying of goodbye.

farm [farm] *noun, plural* **farms.** an area of land where someone grows crops or keeps animals for food or other use. **2.** an enclosed area of water where fish or shellfish are raised to be sold: *a salmon farm.* *verb,* **farmed, farming.** to prepare and use land to raise crops or animals: *The fertile land beside the river has been farmed for hundreds of years.* **Farming** is the business of growing crops or raising animals on a farm.

a b c d e f g h i j k l m n o p q r s t u v w x y z

farm·er ▼ [farm-ur] *noun, plural* **farmers**. someone who owns or works on a farm.

far·sight·ed [far-*site*-ud] *adjective*. **1.** able to see things more clearly when they are far from the eyes than when they are close up. People who are farsighted may need eyeglasses for reading, but not for driving. **2.** able to understand what is likely to happen in the future and plan for it: *a farsighted policy to deal with global warming.*

Although **farmers** *now use tractors, much of their work is still done by hand in many parts of the world.*

far·ther [far-THur] a comparative of FAR.

See FURTHER for language note.

fas·ci·nate [fas-uh-*nate*] *verb*, **fascinated, fascinating.** to attract and hold the interest of: *The baby was fascinated by the colorful moving shapes.* Something that is extremely interesting is **fascinating. —fascination,** *noun.*

fas·cism [fash-iz-um] *noun, plural* **fascisms.** *Government.* a political system led by a dictator in which all industry is controlled by the government. Fascism encourages extreme nationalism and does not allow people to have opposing political ideas. A **fascist** is someone who believes in fascism as a way of life.

fash·ion ▼ [fash-un] *noun, plural* **fashions. 1.** the way of dressing or behaving that is popular at a particular time or place: *Bonnets were the fashion in the 1800s.* Something that has to do with the current popular way of dressing or behaving is **fashionable. 2.** a way of doing something; manner: *Books were scattered over the table in a disorderly fashion.*
verb, **fashioned, fashioning.** to shape or form: *He fashioned the clay into a small bowl.*

fast¹ [fast] *adjective*. **1.** acting, moving, or done with great speed; quick; rapid: *a fast car; a fast trip on a jet plane.* **2.** ahead of the correct time: *The clock is five minutes fast.* **3.** close; loyal; faithful: *They have been fast friends for years.* **4.** fixed firmly in place; secure; permanent: *The sign was nailed fast to the fence.*
adverb, **faster, fastest. 1.** in a fast way; rapidly; quickly: *Cheetahs run fast.* **2.** firmly; tightly: *I can't open the jar, the lid is stuck fast.*

fast² [fast] *verb,* **fasted, fasting.** to eat little or no food, usually as a choice for religious or health reasons. *noun, plural* **fasts.** a time when someone eats little or no food.

fas·ten [fas-un] *verb,* **fastened, fastening. 1.** to fix firmly in place; attach: *I fastened a name tag to my bag.* **2.** to close firmly: *to fasten a seatbelt.* **3.** to direct; fix: *She ignored us and fastened all her attention on her new friend.* **—fastener,** *noun.*

fast food food such as hamburgers and pizzas that can be cooked quickly and easily and sold to customers to be eaten at once or taken away.

fat [fat] *noun, plural* **fats.** the greasy, white or yellow substance in animal and human bodies that is a store of food and a protection against cold. Fat is also found in the tissues of some plants.
adjective, **fatter, fattest. 1.** having a lot of fat on the body; plump. **2.** having large size or a lot in it; thick or full: *a fat book; a fat suitcase.*

fa·tal [fay-tul] *adjective.* **1.** causing death: *a fatal injury.* A **fatality** is a death caused by an accident or by violence. **2.** causing danger, great harm, or ruin: *Trusting the crook with all their savings was a fatal mistake.* **—fatally,** *adverb.*

fate [fate] *noun, plural* **fates. 1.** a power or force that is believed to control what is going to happen: *Everything is going wrong, fate must be against us.* **2.** the thing that will finally happen to someone or something: *I wonder what my fate will be?* Something that is **fated** is believed to have been planned or fixed by fate and cannot be changed or avoided.

fate·ful [fate-ful] *adjective.* having to do with fate; influencing future events: *a fateful decision that changed the course of history.*

fa·ther [fah-THur] *noun, plural* **fathers. 1.** a male parent. In some religions, **Father** is a respectful title for a priest. **The Father** or **Our Father** is a name for God. **2.** a man who invented or started something: *Washington, Jefferson, and Franklin are among the founding fathers of the United States; The painter Cézanne has been called the father of modern art.*
verb, **fathered, fathering.** to be the father of: *He fathered three children.*

father-in-law *noun, plural* **fathers-in-law.** the father of a person's husband or wife.

Father's Day the third Sunday in June, a day set aside for the honoring of fathers.

fath·om [faTH-um] *noun, plural* **fathoms** or **fathom.** a unit of measurement equal to six feet, used to describe the depth of water in the sea or ocean: *The ship sank thirty fathoms to the seafloor.*
verb, **fathomed, fathoming.** to get to the bottom of something; work out; understand: *Can you fathom how to work the new DVD player?*

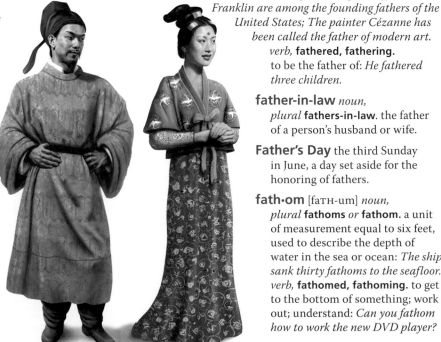

This wealthy Chinese couple of the ninth century wear the latest **fashion** *of the time.*

*The San Andreas **Fault** runs for 650 miles along the coast of California.*

fa·tigue [fuh-<u>teeg</u>] *noun.* **1.** tiredness of mind or body; being tired. **2. fatigues.** work clothes worn by soldiers. *verb,* **fatigued, fatiguing.** to make tired; exhaust: *We were fatigued by hard work in the garden.*

fat·ten [<u>fat</u>-un] *verb,* **fattened, fattening.** to make fatter: *to fatten pigs for market.*

fau·cet [<u>faw</u>-sit] *noun, plural* **faucets.** a device for controlling the flow of water or other liquid from a pipe.

fault ▲ [fawlt] *noun, plural* **faults. 1.** something that spoils someone or something; a mistake, weak point, or defect: *Her main fault is laziness.* Something is **faulty** if it is not working properly or contains a flaw or defect. **2.** a cause for blame; responsibility: *It's my fault the chickens got out.* **3.** *Geology.* a large crack or break in a mass of rock caused by a movement in the Earth's surface. *verb,* **faulted, faulting.** to find something wrong with a person or thing; criticize: *It was hard to fault his argument.* • **at fault.** in the wrong: *The driver of the blue car is at fault for the accident—he went through a red light.*

fau·na ▶ [<u>faw</u>-nuh] *noun, plural* **faunas** or **faunae.** *Biology.* all of the animals living in the wild in a certain area or period of time: *Bison, bald eagles, and alligators are among the native fauna of the U.S.*

fa·vor [<u>fay</u>-vur] *noun, plural* **favors. 1.** a kind or helpful act: *She did me a favor by carrying my bag when I had a sore arm.* **2.** the fact of being thought well of; approval; liking: *The student's hard work soon won favor with the teacher.* **3.** a small gift: *a party favor.* *verb,* **favored, favoring. 1.** to like or support someone or something: *I favor Lucy for class captain.* **2.** to show special treatment or kindness to: *The dog favored its sore foot.* **3.** to look like: *Kayla favors her mother, but her sister is more like their father.*

fa·vor·a·ble [<u>fave</u>-ruh-bul *or* <u>fay</u>-vur-uh-bul] *adjective.* **1.** showing approval: *I was pleased by the favorable report.* **2.** of most benefit; favoring; helpful: *The ship will sail when the weather is favorable.* **—favorably,** *adverb.*

fa·vor·ite [<u>fave</u>-rit *or* <u>fay</u>-vuh-rit] *adjective.* most liked: *Purple is my favorite color.* *noun, plural* **favorites.** someone or something liked better than the rest: *Action movies are my favorites.* **Favoritism** is the act of unfairly treating one individual or group better than all the rest.

fawn [fawn] *noun, plural* **fawns.** a young deer.

fax [faks] *noun, plural* **faxes.** a message consisting of a copy of words or pictures sent over a telephone line by an electronic machine. *verb,* **faxed, faxing.** to send such a message.

fear [feer] *noun, plural* **fears.** a strong feeling that something unpleasant, dangerous, or evil is close or may happen: *Pauline has a terrible fear of the dark.* *verb,* **feared, fearing. 1.** to be frightened; be afraid: *She feared for her life when he pulled out a gun.* **2.** to be worried; anxious: *I fear we will miss the bus if we don't hurry.*

> The word **fax** comes from *facsimile,* which is an exact copy of something. The idea is that a fax machine makes an exact copy of a letter, application form, or other document, and then sends it over a telephone line to another location.

fear·ful [<u>feer</u>-ful] *adjective.* **1.** feeling or showing fear; afraid: *The dog was fearful of the thunder.* **2.** causing fear: *a fearful storm; the fearful threat of war.* **—fearfully,** *adverb.*

fear·less [<u>feer</u>-lis] *adjective.* having or showing no fear; not afraid. **—fearlessly,** *adverb;* **fearlessness,** *noun.*

feast [feest] *noun, plural* **feasts.** a rich meal served on a special occasion for a large group of people. *verb,* **feasted, feasting.** to hold a feast: *We feasted on duck to celebrate the opening of the hunting season.*

feat [feet] *noun, plural* **feats.** an achievement that takes great courage, strength, or skill: *the difficult feat of reaching the South Pole by boat.* 🔊 A different word with the same sound is **feet.**

*Hyraxes, which are as large as rabbits, are among the **fauna** that live on rocky outcrops in Africa and the Middle East.*

A
B
C
D
E
F
G
H
I
J
K
L
M
N
O
P
Q
R
S
T
U
V
W
X
Y
Z

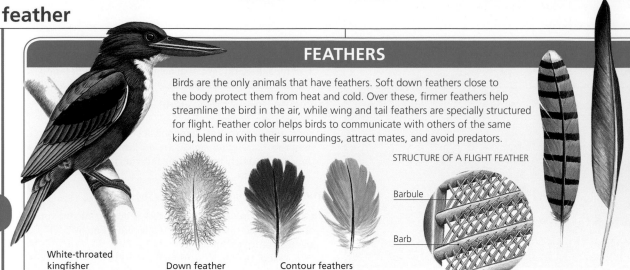

FEATHERS

Birds are the only animals that have feathers. Soft down feathers close to the body protect them from heat and cold. Over these, firmer feathers help streamline the bird in the air, while wing and tail feathers are specially structured for flight. Feather color helps birds to communicate with others of the same kind, blend in with their surroundings, attract mates, and avoid predators.

STRUCTURE OF A FLIGHT FEATHER

Barbule

Barb

White-throated kingfisher

Down feather

Contour feathers

Flight feathers

feath·er ▲ [feTH-ur] *noun, plural* **feathers.** one of the light, fluffy parts that cover a bird's body. Feathers are made up of thin hairs growing from a hard center. They protect the bird's skin, keep the bird warm, and help it to fly. *verb,* **feathered, feathering.** to cover, line, or fill with feathers: *to feather a nest.*

fea·ture [fee-chur] *noun, plural* **features.**
1. a good or noticeable part of something: *Watching dolphins leap out of the water was a feature of our summer vacation.* **2.** a part of the face: *My eyes are my best feature.* **3.** the main film in a movie theater; a full-length movie. **4.** a special story or interview in a newspaper, magazine, or on television.
verb, **featured featuring.** to have as the main attraction: *The circus features a daring trapeze performer.*

Feb·ru·a·ry [feb-yoo-er-ee *or* feb-roo-er-ee] *noun.* the second month of the year. February has 28 days, and 29 days in a leap year.

fed [fed] *verb.* the past tense and past participle of FEED.
• **fed up.** annoyed, bored, tired, or disgusted: *I'm fed up with her constant complaining.*

fed·er·al [fed-rul *or* fed-uh-rul] *adjective. Government.*
1. having to do with one central government, rather than a number of states or territories, each with a separate government: *The United States has a federal government.* This word is also spelled **Federal. 2.** having to do with a central government: *a federal law; federal powers.*
—**federally,** *adverb.*

fed·er·a·tion [fed-uh-ray-shuhn] *noun, plural* **federations.** a union formed by the coming together of states, nations, or other groups.

fee [fee] *noun, plural* **fees.** payment for a service or right: *The museum charges an admission fee.*

The emperor moth has two feather-like **feelers** *on the top of its head.*

fee·ble [fee-bul] *adjective.* lacking strength; weak: *Our dog has gotten old and feeble; He had only a feeble excuse for not doing his work.* —**feebly,** *adverb.*

feed [feed] *verb,* **fed, feeding. 1.** to give food to: *It's my job to feed the dog.* **2.** to take in as food; eat: *Deer feed on twigs, leaves, and other plant parts.* **3.** to supply with something: *We fed the fire with wood.*
noun. food for animals on a farm: *chicken feed.*
—**feeder,** *noun.*

feed·back [feed-bak] *noun.* **1.** the return of some of the sound made by a loudspeaker into a microphone, usually as a high-pitched noise. **2.** opinions or reactions from people about a product or activity: *The car's design was changed as a result of customer feedback.*

feel [feel] *verb,* **felt, feeling. 1.** to examine or know by touching; touch: *My mother felt the bump on my head.* **2.** to be aware of by touch: *It was good to feel the sun's rays again.* **3.** to seem to be: *This cold weather makes it feel like Christmas, even though it's only October.* **4.** to have a sense of in the mind: *to feel sad; I feel I could've done better on the exam.*
noun. **1.** the nature of something, given by touching it: *the feel of a baby's cheek.* **2.** a sense of what something is like: *Reading this book will give you a feel for the subject of biology.*

feel·er ▲ [feel-ur] *noun, plural* **feelers.** a part of an animal's body used to touch things. Feelers are usually located on an animal's head.

feel·ing [feel-ing] *noun, plural* **feelings. 1.** the sense of touch: *The stroke left him with no feeling in one arm.* **2.** the condition of being aware; a sensation: *a feeling of being followed.* **3.** an emotion such as fear, sorrow, joy, or anger. Someone's **feelings** are the sensitive, easily affected part of their nature: *He cares little about the feelings of others.* **4.** a belief; opinion: *Her feeling was that he would go along if we asked him.*

feet [feet] *noun.* the plural of FOOT.
🔊 A different word with the same sound is **feat.**

*A woodsman wears protective clothing as he **fells** a tree with a powerful saw.*

feign [fane] *verb,* **feigned, feigning.** to put on a false appearance of; pretend: *She knew about her surprise birthday party but feigned amazement anyway.*

feint [faynt] *noun, plural* **feints.** a blow, thrust, or other movement meant to distract an opponent's attention from the real objective. *verb,* **feint, feinting.** to make a feint: *The soccer player feinted to the left and then kicked the ball to the right.* 🔊 A different word with the same sound is **faint.**

fell¹ [fel] *verb.* the past tense of FALL.

fell² ▶ [fel] *verb,* **felled, felling.** to knock or cut down; cause to fall: *Power lines were felled by the tornado; I found an ax to fell the tree.*

fel·low [fel-oh] *noun, plural* **fellows. 1.** a man or boy: *a nice fellow.* **2.** a person of similar class or status; associate; comrade: *The doctor had to confer with his fellows about the patient.*
adjective. belonging to the same kind or group: *my fellow Americans; a fellow player.*

FERNS

Ferns are very ancient, leafy plants. Instead of growing from seeds, they reproduce from tiny cells called spores, which form in cases on the underside of the fern's fronds. Most ferns grow in moist, shady, protected areas. Some, like the elkhorn fern, attach themselves to trees. Others, like the rasp fern, grow on the ground from horizontal stems. Tree ferns can grow as tall as palm trees.

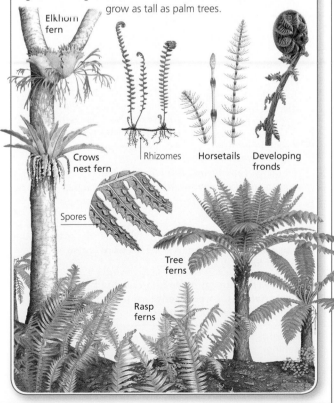

Elkhorn fern

Crows nest fern

Rhizomes

Horsetails

Developing fronds

Spores

Tree ferns

Rasp ferns

fel·on·y [fel-uh-nee] *noun, plural* **felonies.** *Law.* a serious crime that is punished more severely than other crimes. Murder and burglary are examples of felonies. A **felon** is someone who is guilty of such a crime.

felt¹ [felt] *verb.* the past tense and past participle of FEEL.

felt² [felt] *noun, plural* **felts.** a cloth made by rolling and pressing together layers of wool, hair, or fur.

fe·male [fee-male] *adjective.*
1. of or relating to the sex that can bear offspring or produce eggs: *Cows and hens are female animals.* **2.** relating or belonging to women or girls; feminine. *noun, plural* **females.** a female animal or person: *Is the kitten a male or a female?*

fem·i·nine [fem-uh-nun] *adjective.*
1. of or relating to women or girls: *feminine beauty.* **2.** in grammar, a class of nouns and pronouns in certain languages, such as French and Italian.

fem·i·nism [fem-uh-niz-um] *noun.* the belief that women deserve the same power, rights, and opportunities as men. A **feminist** is someone who supports this belief.

fence [fens] *noun, plural* **fences.** a structure used to mark a boundary or to control access to an area: *They put up a wooden fence between their yard and their neighbor's yard* *verb,* **fenced, fencing. 1.** to put up a fence: *Farmers fence their fields to keep the cows in.* **2.** to fight with a sword; take part in the sport of fencing.
• **fence in/off.** to confine or restrict someone: *The farmer used the wire to fence in his chickens; He fenced off a small area to keep them safe.*

fenc·ing ▲ [fen-sing] *noun.* the sport or art of fighting with a sword or foil.

fen·der [fen-dur] *noun, plural* **fenders.** a piece of metal on top of the wheel of an automobile or bicycle that reduces splashing in wet weather. A **fender-bender** is an automobile accident resulting in only minor damage.

fer·ment [fur-ment *or* fur-ment] *verb,* **fermented, fermenting.** *Chemistry.* to cause or undergo a chemical change through the action of substances such as yeast or bacteria: *When apple juice ferments, it turns into cider.* The chemical change brought about by bacteria, yeast, or other similar substances is called **fermentation.**
noun, plural **ferments. 1.** a substance that causes something to ferment. **2.** a state of activity and excitement: *The country was in a ferment leading up to the elections.*

fern ◀ [furn] *noun, plural* **ferns.** a flowerless plant with large leaves called fronds.

Fencing, *which developed from sword fighting, has been an event in the Olympic Games since 1896.*

a
b
c
d
e
f
g

o
p
q
r
s
t
u
v
w
x
y
z

fe·ro·cious [fuh-<u>roh</u>-shus] *adjective.* describing something fierce; violent: *a ferocious dog.* The state of being fierce or violent is **ferocity.** —**ferociously,** *adverb.*

fer·ret [<u>fer</u>-it] *noun, plural* **ferrets.** an animal related to the weasel, with a long, thin body. Ferrets are sometimes used to hunt rabbits and rats.
verb, **ferreted, ferreting.**
1. to hunt with ferrets. **2.** to look for; search: *I had to ferret through my bag to find my pencils.*
♦ **ferret out.** to find something hidden by searching for it again and again: *It took a long time for him to ferret out the cause of problem.*

Ferris wheel [<u>fer</u>-is] an amusement park ride that consists of a large, upright, revolving wheel with seats that hang down from the rim.

The **Ferris wheel** is named after George *Ferris,* an American engineer. He built a huge Ferris wheel (250 feet high, holding 2,000 people or more) for a famous World Fair in Chicago, Illinois, in 1893.

fer·ry ▼ [<u>fer</u>-ee] *noun, plural* **ferries.** a boat used for carrying passengers and goods across a narrow body of water.
verb, **ferried, ferrying.** to travel or carry in a ferry.

fer·tile [<u>fur</u>-tul] *adjective.* **1.** able to produce a lot of vegetation and crops easily: *There is fertile soil by the river.* The **Fertile Crescent** is an area of fertile land in the Middle East, from Israel to the Persian Gulf, where civilizations came into being in ancient times. **2.** able to produce seeds, fruit, eggs, or young: *A chick hatches from a fertile egg.* **3.** able to think up new ideas easily; creative: *a person with a fertile mind.* —**fertility,** *noun.*

fer·til·ize [<u>fur</u>-tuh-*lize*] *verb,* **fertilized, fertilizing.**
1. to make fertile. **2.** to add fertilizer to: *I used chicken manure to fertilize the garden bed.*

fer·ti·liz·er [<u>fur</u>-tuh-*lize*-ur] *noun, plural* **fertilizers.** *Chemistry.* a substance, such as manure or certain chemicals, that is spread on soil to make it more suitable for growing plants.

Large **ferries** *can transport cars, trucks, and even trains across water.*

fes·ti·val ▼ [<u>fes</u>-tuh-vul] *noun, plural* **festivals.**
1. a day or period of celebration; holiday: *a religious festival.* **2.** a program of performances or other events: *a music festival.*

fes·tiv·i·ty [fes-<u>tiv</u>-uh-tee] *noun, plural* **festivities.**
1. fun and joyfulness: *There was great festivity at the wedding.* **2. festivities.** events that are part of a festival: *Fireworks and parties are New Year's Eve festivities.*

fetch [fech] *verb,* **fetched, fetching.** to go and bring back; get: *Teach the dog to fetch the ball.*

fe·tus [<u>fee</u>-tus] *noun, plural* **fetuses.** *Biology.* the young of a person or animal before birth. A fetus is more developed than an embryo.

feud [fyood] *noun, plural* **feuds.** a long and bitter quarrel. *verb,* **feuded, feuding.** to carry on such a quarrel: *The families had been feuding for the last ten years about who owned the strip of land between the two properties.*

The lion dance is a traditional event in the Chinese New Year **festival.**

feu·dal·ism [<u>fyoo</u>-duh-*liz*-um] *noun. History.* an economic and political system of Europe in the Middle Ages. Under feudalism, people known as vassals gave services and a share of their crops to their ruler, the lord. In return, the lord provided land and protection for his vassals. Having to do with this system is **feudal.**

fe·ver [<u>fee</u>-vur] *noun, plural* **fevers.** *Medicine.* a body temperature that is greater than the normal temperature of 98.6 degrees Fahrenheit. A fever is usually caused by an infection. A person affected by a fever is said to be **feverish.**

Fever goes back to a word meaning "a fire" or "to burn." Someone who was suffering from a high fever was thought of as having a fire burning inside their body.

few [fyoo] *adjective,* **fewer, fewest.** not many: *Few cars use this old dirt road.* *noun.* a small number of things or people; some: *All the players were supposed to come to baseball practice, but only a few showed up.*

fi·an·cé [*fee*-ahn-<u>say</u> *or* fee-<u>ahn</u>-say] *noun, plural* **fiancés.** a man engaged to be married. This word is also spelled **fiance.**

fi·an·cée [*fee*-ahn-<u>say</u> *or* fee-<u>ahn</u>-say] *noun, plural* **fiancées.** a woman engaged to be married. This word is also spelled **fiancee.**

The words **fiancée** and **fiancé** come from an older word meaning "promise." The idea is that such a person (someone engaged to be married) has promised to the other person that he/she will marry that person.

A B C D E **F** G H I J K L M N O P Q R S T U V W X Y Z

*A hockey **field** is 100 yards long and 60 yards wide, and often consists of artificial turf.*

fi·ber [fye-bur] *noun, plural* **fibers. 1.** a long, slender piece of material like a thread: *Cotton fibers are woven together to make cloth.* **2.** substances in plant foods, such as fruits and vegetables, that cannot be digested by the body. Fiber helps move food through the digestive system.

fi·ber·glass [fye-bur-*glas*] *noun.* a material made of very fine glass fibers. Fiberglass is strong and does not burn easily. It is used to make many products, including surfboards, boat hulls, and automobile parts.

fic·tion [fik-shun] *noun, plural* **fictions. 1.** *Literature.* a written story, such as a novel, that is made up by the author and that is not about real people or events. **2.** something untrue or imaginary: *Her story about having rich parents was a fiction.* Having to do with something that has to do with fiction is **fictional**: *Sherlock Holmes is a famous fictional detective.*

A well-known teacher of writing once gave a story back to a student and said, "This couldn't happen." The student answered, "But it really did happen." The teacher meant something different. She meant that she did not believe it could have happened, because the characters in it didn't talk and act like real people. When you write a story, you want to make readers think they are reading about something that actually could happen. The question of whether it is **fiction**, or actually based on real life, is not important as long as the writing makes it seem true and real.

fid·dle [fid-ul] *noun, plural* **fiddles.** another word for a violin.
verb, **fiddled, fiddling. 1.** to play a fiddle. Someone who plays the fiddle is a **fiddler. 2.** to move the hands in an aimless way: *He was bored and started to fiddle with his car keys.* **3.** to interfere or tamper with: *My sister keeps fiddling with my computer.*

fidg·et [fij-it] *verb,* **fidgeted, fidgeting.** to move in a restless or nervous manner: *Please don't fidget in class.*
noun, plural **fidgets.** someone who often does this.

field ◀ [feeld] *noun, plural* **fields. 1.** an area of open land. **2.** land that contains or produces a natural resource: *a coal field.* **3.** an area of land used for a sport or game: *a soccer field.* **4.** an area of activity or interest: *She is a leader in the field of medicine.*
verb, **fielded, fielding.** in baseball, to pick, catch, or stop a ball that has been hit: *He fielded the ball well, but his throw was wide.*

field·er feel-dur] *noun, plural* **fielders.** in baseball, a player who is plays out in the field while the other team is at bat and tries to catch the ball.

field goal 1. in football, a score made by kicking the ball over the crossbar. **2.** in basketball, a goal made during normal play.

field hockey a game played on a field by two teams of eleven players each. Players use curved sticks to try to hit a ball into the opposing team's goal.

field trip a trip away from school to study things in person: *The class went on a field trip to the lake to learn about ecology.*

fiend [feend] *noun, plural* **fiends. 1.** an evil being, such as a devil. **2.** a very cruel or evil person. Something very cruel or evil is **fiendish.**

fierce [feers] *adjective,* **fiercer, fiercest. 1.** likely to attack violently; savage: *a fierce guard dog.* **2.** very violent or strong: *a fierce wind.*
—**fiercely,** *adverb;* —**fierceness,** *noun.*

fier·y [fye-ree] *adjective.* **1.** like fire or having to do with fire: *The Sun is a fiery ball.* **2.** full of feeling; very excitable: *a fiery speech.*

fi·es·ta ▶ [fee-es-tuh] *noun, plural* **fiestas.** a celebration or festival.

*A dancer is dressed for the **fiesta** at the annual carnival in Rio de Janeiro, Brazil.*

fife [fife] *noun, plural* **fifes.** *Music.* a high-pitched musical instrument like a flute. The fife is often used with drums in a marching band.

fif·teen [fif-teen] *noun, plural* **fifteens.** the number between fourteen and sixteen; 15. Something that is number fifteen in order is the **fifteenth.**

fifth [fifth] *adjective.* describing something that is number five in a series.
noun, plural **fifths.** one of five equal parts; ⅕.

fif·ty [fif-tee] *noun, plural* **fifties.** ten less than sixty; 50. Something that is number fifty in order is the **fiftieth.**

fig ◀ [fig] *noun, plural* **figs.** a small, sweet fruit that grows in warm regions on a shrub or small tree. Figs can be eaten fresh, but are usually dried.

*There are hundreds of different kinds of **figs,** which grow on bushes or small trees in hot countries.*

fight

fight [fite] *noun, plural* **fights.**
1. a violent struggle between people, animals, or groups. In a fight, each side uses weapons or their own body to hurt the other or to defend itself: *I got a black eye in a fight.*
2. a disagreement; a quarrel or argument: *He had a fight with his parents about doing his homework.*
3. a big effort to reach a goal: *the fight against crime.*
verb, **fought, fighting. 1.** to use violent methods to try to overpower or hurt someone: *Boxers fight in a ring.* **2.** to have an argument or quarrel. **3.** to engage in a struggle, conflict, or contest: *He fought his way through the crowd.*

fight·er [fite-ur] *noun, plural* **fighters.**
1. someone who fights. **2.** someone who boxes; a boxer.

fig·ur·a·tive [fig-yuh-ruh-tiv]
adjective. Language. using words to mean something different than their basic meaning. Figurative language is used to add interest or to make things clearer. To say that a badly beaten football team was massacred is to use figurative language. —**figuratively,** *adverb.*

fig·ure [fig-yur] *noun, plural* **figures. 1.** a symbol that stands for a number: *the figure 9.* **2.** an amount expressed in numbers: *a six-figure salary* **3.** a shape or outline; form: *a woman with a lovely figure.* **4.** a character; person: *Abraham Lincoln is a famous historical figure.*
5. a pattern or design: *wallpaper with geometric figures.*
verb, **figured, figuring. 1.** to use numbers to find a value; calculate. **2.** to think or believe: *He didn't call back, so I figured he wasn't interested.* **3.** to take part; have a part: *The school principal figured in the newspaper report.*
♦ **figure out.** to solve or understand: *I finally figured out the math problem.*

*The **figurehead** of this ancient Greek trading ship is in the shape of a swan's head and neck.*

fig·ure·head ◄ [fig-yur-hed] *noun, plural* **figureheads.** a person who has the title of leader but no real responsibility or authority: *The president of the company was only a figurehead because the owner had the real power.*

In earlier times sailing ships would often have a carved wooden figure on the bow (front) of the boat. This was typically the head and shoulders of a woman. The word **figurehead** as it is used today (a person who does not have real authority) comes from the idea that the figurehead of a ship was just a decoration that was not really needed to sail the ship

figure of speech *Language.*
an expression used to make speaking or writing more forceful and interesting by using words differently from their basic meanings. When President Kennedy said, "The torch has been passed to a new generation of Americans," he was using a figure of speech.

"My feet are *killing* me." "This house is like an *oven*." "That pitcher has a *rocket* for a right arm." All of these are **figures of speech**. Words are being used in a different way from their literal meaning, since obviously your feet are not really killing you, the house is not really an oven, and the pitcher does not have a rocket as an arm. People use a figure of speech because it can be a stronger way to say something than to use the literal and obvious words. You could say, "My feet hurt," "The house is hot," and "That pitcher throws really fast," but in each case that would be a weaker statement than the figure of speech

figure skating ▼ a form of ice skating in which a skater traces patterns on the ice and sometimes performs dance movements and jumps. A **figure skater** is a person who does this kind of skating.

Figure skating *combines artistic and athletic skills.*

fil·a·ment [fil-uh-munt] *noun, plural* **filaments.** a very fine fiber or wire. An electric light bulb contains a wire filament that gives off light when electricity is passed through it.

file[1] [file] *noun, plural* **files. 1.** a cabinet, folder, or other container in which documents or papers are arranged in order. **2.** a set of documents or papers arranged in order: *a file of letters.* **3.** a collection of information stored on a computer with a name that identifies it: *Did you save the file with my letter to the newspaper?* **4.** a row of people, animals, or things one behind the other: *Customers waited outside the shop in a single file.*
verb, **filed, filing. 1.** to place in a file: *Please file these letters.* **2.** to put on a record; make an application: *I want to file a complaint.* **3.** to move in a line or row: *The students filed onto the bus.*
• **on file.** stored in a file: *She said she would keep my job application on file.*

file[2] [file] *noun, plural* **files.** a metal tool that has rough surfaces on it for smoothing, cutting, or grinding down hard surfaces.
verb, **filed, filing.** to smooth, cut, or grind with a file: *File the saw to keep it sharp.*

fi·let [fi-lay] *noun, plural* **filets.** a slice of meat or fish that has no bones or fat.
verb, **fileted, fileting.** to cut up meat or fish into filets. This word is also spelled **fillet.**

fill [fil] *verb,* **filled, filling. 1.** to make or become full: *Fill the glass with milk.* **2.** to occupy all of the space in: *The audience filled the television studio.* **3.** to supply what is asked for or needed: *The pharmacist filled the prescription.* **4.** to put something in so as to close a gap or hole: *All cracks in the wall have to be filled before we start painting.* **5.** to do the job or duties of: *She filled the position of club president.*
noun, plural **fills.** something used to fill: *Earth, rock, and sand were used as fill at the old quarry.*
• **fill in. 1.** to add written information to complete something: *to fill in the blanks on a form.* **2.** to write something needed or missing; insert: *Fill in your date of birth on the second line.* **3.** to replace someone for a short time: *Who wants to fill in for Josh as goalkeeper?*

fill·ing [fil-ing] *noun, plural* **fillings.** a material used to fill something: *The dentist gave me a new filling for my tooth; This sandwich has a cheese filling.*

fil·ly [fil-ee] *noun, plural* **fillies.** a young female horse.

film [film] *noun, plural* **films. 1.** a very thin layer or coating: *There is a film of oil on the water.* Being thin and light like a film or covered with a film is **filmy. 2.** a thin roll or sheet of material with a coating that changes when it is placed in light. It is used in some cameras to produce photographs or movies. **3.** a movie: *Star Wars is a very popular film.*
verb, **filmed, filming. 1.** to cover or become covered with a thin layer or coating. **2.** to take pictures with a movie camera: *My father filmed the school play.*

fil·ter [fil-tur] *noun, plural* **filters.** a material or device with tiny holes in it that is used to remove dirt or other things from a gas or liquid passed through it: *an oil filter.*
verb, **filtered, filtering. 1.** to pass something through a filter; strain: *The water has to be filtered before drinking.* **2.** to separate or take out by a filter: *to filter the dust from air.* **3.** to move gradually through something: *People filtered into the concert hall.*

filth [filth] *noun.* dirt or other matter that is disgusting.

filth·y [filth-ee] *adjective,* **filthier, filthiest.** disgustingly dirty; foul: *Your jeans are filthy!*

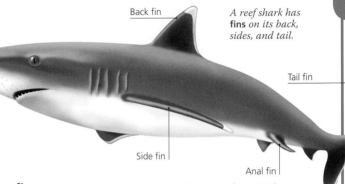

Back fin

A reef shark has **fins** *on its back, sides, and tail.*

Tail fin

Side fin

Anal fin

fin ▲ [fin] *noun, plural* **fins. 1.** a thin upright part that sticks out from the body of a fish and helps in swimming and balance. Other animals, including dolphins and whales, have fins too. **2.** something with the same shape or use as a fin. An airplane's tail has fins that keep the plane stable in flight.

fi·nal [fye-nul] *adjective.* **1.** coming at the end; last: *December is the final month of the year.* **2.** allowing no changes: *I said, "No," and that's final!*
noun, plural **finals. 1.** the examination that occurs at the end of a school or college course of study: *She did well in her math final.* **2.** the last or deciding match or game in a competition. A person who takes part in such a match is said to be a **finalist.** This word is also spelled **finals.**

fi·na·le [fuh-nal-ee] *noun, plural* **finales.** the last part; end: *We turned on the television to watch the series finale.*

fi·nal·ize [fye-nuh-lize] *verb,* **finalized, finalizing.** to put something into final form; complete: *Let's finalize our vacation plans.*

fi·nal·ly [fuh-nal-ee] *adverb.* at last; at the end: *I waited an hour for the bus and then it finally came.*

fi·nance [fuh-nans *or* fye-nans] *noun, plural* **finances. 1.** *Business.* the management of money for governments, businesses, or people: *Accountants have to have a lot of skill in finance.* A person whose work involves managing large amounts of money is a **financier. 2. finances.** the money that a government, business, or person has; funds: *The club's finances are in bad shape.* *verb,* **financed, financing.** to provide money for: *to finance the purchase of a new house.*

fi·nan·cial [fuh-nan-shul] *adjective.* relating to money matters: *Financial institutions include banks and insurance companies.* —**financially,** *adverb.*

a b c d e f g h i j k l m n o p q r s t u v w x y z

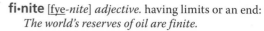

Like other **finches,** *the European goldfinch is a small songbird with a sharp, pointed bill.*

finch ◀ [finch] *noun, plural* **finches.** a small songbird with a strong, cone-shaped bill for cracking seeds.

find [fynde] *verb,* **found, finding.** **1.** to come upon by chance; happen upon: *I found a dollar bill in my old coat.* **2.** to get something back after losing it: *It took me an hour to find my keys.* **3.** to learn or get something that was not known; discover or learn: *Use subtraction to find the difference between these numbers.* **4.** to get by effort: *to find a new job.* **5.** to decide about something and announce the decision: *The jury found the man guilty of murder.*
noun, plural **finds.** something found: *That little restaurant is a great find.*

fine¹ [fine] *adjective,* **finer, finest. 1.** much better than average; very good or excellent: *Nine out of ten is a fine mark on a test.* **2.** very thin or small: *Read the fine print of the contract.* **3.** with no rain or clouds; clear: *a fine day.*
adverb. very well: *I'm feeling fine, thanks.*

fine² [fine] *noun, plural* **fines.** a sum of money that has to be paid as a punishment for a crime or offense.
verb, **fined, fining.** to put a fine on: *He was fined for speeding.*

fin·ger [fing-gur] *noun, plural* **fingers. 1.** each of the long, thin, end parts of the hand. The thumb is often not considered to be a finger. **2.** a part of a glove that fits over a finger.
verb, **fingered, fingering.** to use the fingers to handle, touch, or play: *Please don't finger the fruit.*

fin·ger·nail ▶ [fing-gur-*nale*] *noun, plural* **fingernails.** a thin, hard layer of material at the tip of each finger.

fin·ger·print ▼ [fing-gur-*print*] *noun, plural* **fingerprints.** an impression of the markings of skin on the finger tips. It is believed that no two fingers have exactly the same markings, so fingerprints can be used to identify people.
verb, **fingerprinted, fingerprinting.** to take the fingerprints of: *The police officer's job was to fingerprint suspects.*

fin·ish [fin-ish] *verb,* **finished, finishing.** **1.** to come or bring to an end; complete: *Did you finish the job?; Students go on to first grade after they finish kindergarten.* **2.** to use up completely: *We finished the meal.* **3.** to put a surface or coat on: *She used a wood stain to finish the bookcase.*
noun, plural **finishes.** **1.** the final part of something; end: *the finish of a race.* **2.** the surface of something: *The bowl has a copper finish.*

Fingerprints *taken from a crime scene can be compared with those on file to identify suspects.*

fi·nite [fye-nite] *adjective.* having limits or an end: *The world's reserves of oil are finite.*

Fin·nish [fin-ish] *noun.* the language of Finland, a country in northern Europe.
adjective. of or relating to Finland, its language, or its people. A person who comes from Finland is a **Finn.**
🔊 A different word with the same sound is **finish.**

fiord [fee-ord *or* fyord] *noun, plural* **fiords.** *Geography.* another spelling of FJORD.

fir [fur] *noun, plural* **firs.** an evergreen tree with upright cones and leaves shaped like needles.
🔊 A different word with the same sound is **fur.**

fire [fire] *noun, plural* **fires. 1.** the light, heat, and flames produced by burning. **2.** a collection of burning material: *We lit a fire at the campsite.* **3.** burning that causes damage or destroys: *A fire burned down the church hall.* **4.** a very strong feeling; passion or enthusiasm: *The mayor's speech was full of fire.* **5.** the shooting of guns: *The soldiers opened fire.*
verb, **fired, firing. 1.** to set fire to something; cause to burn. **2.** to remove someone from a job: *His boss had to fire him because he was late for work so often.* **3.** to cause strong emotion in; excite: *Our team was fired up to win the game.* **4.** to shoot: *The submarine fired a torpedo.*

fire·arm [fire-arm] *noun, plural* **firearms.** a gun. Firearms include pistols and rifles.

fire·crack·er [fire-krak-ur] *noun, plural* **firecrackers.** a roll of paper with gunpowder inside and a fuse sticking out. Firecrackers explode with a loud noise.

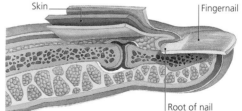

Skin — Fingernail — Root of nail

A **fingernail** *grows from a fold in the skin at the root of the nail.*

fire department a government organization of people trained to prevent and put out fires and to provide other emergency services.

fire drill an event at which people practice what to do in case of fire, such as how to leave a building safely.

fire engine a vehicle that carries equipment for fighting fires and rescuing people.

fire escape a structure, such as an outside stairway on a building, used for escape in the event of a fire.

fire ex·tin·guish·er a container that sprays water, chemicals, or some other substance to put out a fire.

fire·fight·er ▶ [fire *fite* ur] *noun, plural* **firefighters.** someone whose work is to put out fires.

fire·fly [fire-*flye*] *noun, plural* **fireflies.** a small flying beetle whose tail flashes on and off in the dark; also called a lightning bug.

*Spectacular displays of **fireworks** mark special events and occasions.*

fire·house [fire-hous] *noun, plural* **firehouses.** a building for fire engines, fire equipment, and firefighters.

fire·man [fire-mun] *noun, plural* **firemen. 1.** a firefighter. **2.** a person who looks after the fire in a furnace or steam engine.

fire·place [fire-plays] *noun, plural* **fireplaces. 1.** an opening in a room at the base of a chimney, used for building fires. **2.** an outdoor structure of stone, brick, or metal for building fires.

fire·proof [fire-proof] *adjective.* difficult or impossible to burn; not burning easily.

Fireman is an interesting word in that it has two meanings that are the opposite of each other: the familiar one of a person who puts out fires, and another of a person who takes care of a fire and keeps it going, so as to power a train or ship. Today, the first meaning has been largely replaced by the word *firefighter*, and the second meaning is not often used, because coal fires are not used to power trains and ships any more.

fire·wall [fire-wawl] **1.** a wall designed to stop the spread of fire. **2.** *Computers.* software that keeps out computer viruses and stops outside computer users from seeing information they are not meant to see.

fire·wood [fire-wud] *noun.* wood for burning as fuel.

fire·works ◀ [fire-wurks] *plural noun.* devices, such as firecrackers, that burn or explode to make loud noises or bright, colored patterns.

firm¹ [furm] *adjective,* **firmer, firmest. 1.** not soft when pressed; solid: *firm snow.* **2.** solidly in place; secure: *firm shelves on the wall.* **3.** not subject to change; staying the same: *a firm offer to buy the house.*
adverb. so as not to change or move: *He stood firm in his beliefs, despite the criticism.* —**firmly,** *adverb;* —**firmness,** *noun.*

firm² [furm] *noun, plural* **firms.** a business company formed by two or more people together: *a law firm.*

first [furst] *adjective.* before anyone or anything else: *Neil Armstrong was the first person to stand on the Moon; A is the first letter of the alphabet.*
adverb. **1.** before others: *I was here first.* **2.** for the first time: *He first visited Seattle last year.*
noun, plural **firsts. 1.** someone or something that is first: *She was the first to arrive at the party.* **2.** the beginning: *We were friends from the first.*

first aid ▶ basic medical treatment given to a sick or injured person before a doctor comes.

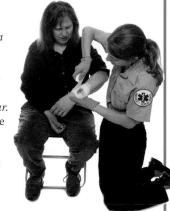

*An injured woman receives **first aid** from a trained paramedic.*

Firefighters *are quick to respond to an emergency such as an earthquake.*

first-class *adjective.* **1.** of the best quality or standard: *a first-class hotel.* **2.** relating to a class of mail that includes personal letters, postcards, and parcels. **3.** relating to the best and most expensive seats or service on an airplane, ship, or train: *a first-class ticket.* *adverb.* by first-class mail or method of transport: *We flew first-class to Europe.* This term is also spelled **first class.**

first·hand [furst-hand] *adjective; adverb.* seen or experienced directly: *The movie was based on a soldier's firsthand account of the Gulf War.*

first-rate *adjective.* of the highest quality or rank; extremely good.

fish ▶ [fish] *noun, plural* **fish** *or* **fishes. 1.** a cold-blooded, scaly animal that lives in water. Fish have a backbone, breathe through their gills, and swim with their fins. **2.** the flesh of fish eaten as food. *verb,* **fished, fishing. 1.** to catch or try to catch fish: *Dad fished for cod from the boat.* The sport or job of catching fish is **fishing. 2.** to feel around, trying to find something: *I fished around in the bag of candy for the one I like best.*

fish·er·man [fish-ur-mun] *noun, plural* **fishermen.** a person who fishes for sport or as a job. A different word with the same meaning is **fisher.**

fish·er·y [fish-uh-ree] *noun, plural* **fisheries. 1.** a place for catching fish. **2.** a place for breeding fish.

fish·ing rod ▼ a long pole usually made of fiberglass, wood, or metal. It supports a line, hook, and reel, and is used to catch fish.

fish·y [fish-ee] *adjective,* **fishier, fishiest. 1.** having a smell or taste like fish: *The whole house smells fishy after Mom cooks tuna casserole.* **2.** not likely to be true; suspicious: *They were whispering and passing notes—something fishy was going on.*

*Fishermen in Sri Lanka perch on wooden poles and use simple **fishing rods** to catch fish.*

*The coastline of Norway features many spectacular **fjords.***

fis·sion [fish-un] *noun. Science.* **1.** the splitting or breaking apart of an atom's nucleus, which releases large amounts of energy. **2.** the dividing of one organism into two or more parts, which grow into new organisms.

fist [fist] *noun, plural* **fists.** a hand with the fingers closed tightly into the palm.

fit¹ [fit] *adjective,* **fitter, fittest. 1.** as it should be or needed; suitable, right, or proper: *The house is not fit to live in with that huge hole in the roof.* **2.** in good physical condition; healthy: *They work out at the gym to keep fit.* *verb,* **fitted, fitting. 1.** to be the right shape or size for: *These shoes fit me well.* **2.** to be or cause to be suitable, right, or proper: *He'll fit the role of class president perfectly; Fit the music to your mood.* **3.** to join, insert, or adjust; put in place properly: *She fitted the light bulb in the socket.* *noun, plural* **fits.** the way that something fits: *Three people applied for the job, but she seems to be the best fit for the position.*

fit² [fit] *adjective,* **fitter, fittest. 1.** a sudden, sharp outburst: *a fit of sneezing; a fit of jealousy.* **2.** a sudden, violent illness, often caused by epilepsy. A person jerks uncontrollably and he or she may lose consciousness.

five [five] *noun, plural* **fives;** *adjective.* the number between four and six; 5.

fix [fiks] *verb,* **fixed, fixing. 1.** to return to the proper condition; mend or repair: *I fixed the broken window.* **2.** to prepare or make ready: *He fixed himself a sandwich.* **3.** to make firm or secure; set in place: *She fixed the poster to her wall with tape; We finally fixed a date for my party.* **4.** to direct or hold steadily: *The man drove with his eyes fixed on the road ahead.* **5.** to try to influence an outcome in a dishonest way: *They fixed the match so that their team won for the third year in a row.* *noun, plural* **fixes.** a difficult or embarrassing situation: *I'm in a fix because I haven't studied for the exam.*
• **fix up. 1.** to mend or repair; improve something: *He fixed up the old house so it looked as good as new.* **2.** to provide or equip with something needed: *The sales assistant promised to fix us up with the latest computer software.*

fix·ture [fiks-chur] *noun, plural* **fixtures. 1.** a permanently attached object in a house or building, such as a toilet or sink. **2.** a person or thing established in a place: *We started feeding the stray cat, and now he's a fixture at our house.*

fjord ▲ [fee-ord *or* fyord] *noun, plural* **fjords.** a long, narrow inlet of the sea with high cliffs on either side. This word is also spelled **fiord.**

flag [flag] *noun, plural* **flags.** a piece of cloth with a particular design and colors, used as a symbol for a country or organization, or for giving signals. A pole used for displaying a flag is a **flagpole.** *verb,* **flagged, flagging.** to stop or signal: *The police officer flagged down our car.*

FISH

There are about 25,000 known kinds of fish, making up the largest group of animals with backbones. They live in fresh and salt water all over the world, and vary in size from the half-inch-long marine dwarf goby found in the Indian Ocean to the whale shark, which can grow to 65 feet. There are three main groups: jawless fish such as lampreys and hagfish; fish with skeletons made of bone—the largest group; and sharks, rays, and dogfish, which have skeletons made of cartilage. The bodies of fish are usually protected by scales, although there are some fish, such as clingfish, that don't have any. Tropical fish that live among coral reefs are brilliantly colored, which helps them to blend in with their surroundings.

JAWLESS FISH
These fish do not have scales or jaws, and many do not have fins.

Pacific hagfish

European brook lamprey

SHARKS, RAYS, AND DOGFISH
There are more than 400 kinds of sharks and dogfish, and more than 500 kinds of rays.

PARTS OF A SHARK

Second dorsal fin

Dorsal fin

Tail fin

Spiracle

Nostril

Keel

Anal fin

Pelvic fin

Pectoral fin

Gill slits

Leopard shark

Sixgill stingray

BONY FISH
Bony fish can be found in all the world's oceans and some live in fresh water.

Moorish idol

FISH RESPIRATION

Water taken into mouth.

Water passes though gill curtain.

Oxygen is absorbed.

Pot-bellied seahorse

PARTS OF A BONY FISH

Dorsal fin

Nostril

Tail fin

Barbels

Pectoral fin

Gill cover

Pelvic fin

Anal fin

Pufferfish

Purplequeen

Anemonefish

Meyer's butterflyfish

Spotted oreo

Sockeye salmon

Slimy loach

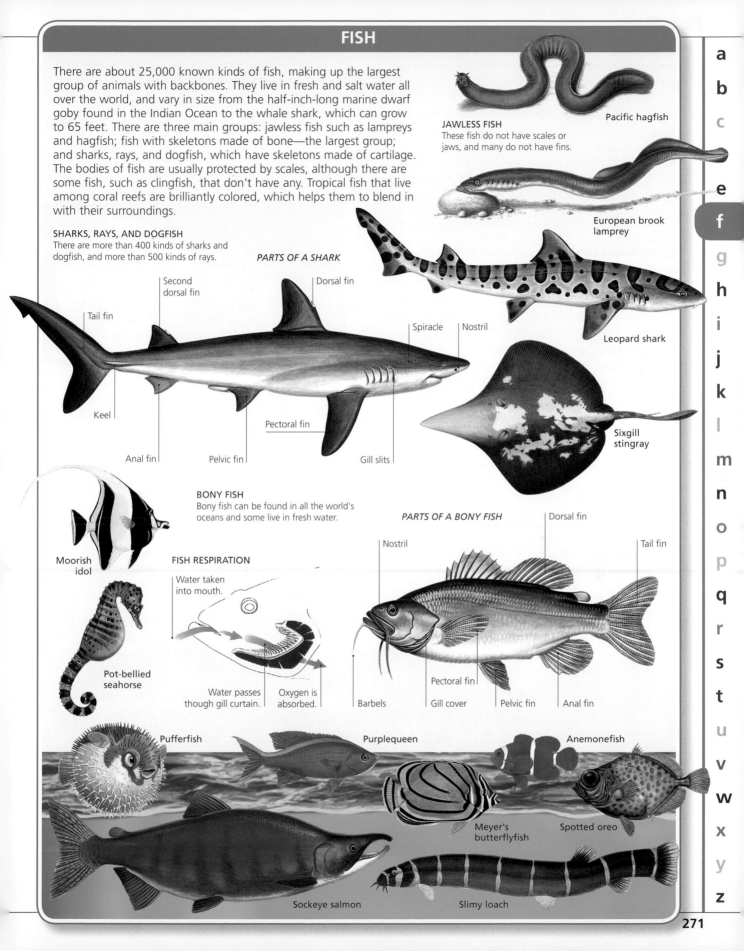

Flag Day June 14, a special day to honor the day in 1777 when the official flag of the United States was adopted.

flair [flare] *noun, plural* **flairs.** a natural talent: *He has a flair for drawing.*
🔊 A different word with the same sound is **flare.**

flake [flake] *noun, plural* **flakes.** a small, flat, thin piece: *flakes of snow.*
verb, **flaked, flaking.** to peel or chip off or separate in flakes: *Paint was flaking off the walls of the old house.*

flame [flame] *noun, plural* **flames. 1.** a glowing stream or band of fire; burning gas or vapor that gives off heat or light. **2.** the state of burning: *The car rolled and burst into flame.*
verb, **flamed, flaming. 1.** to burn brightly; blaze: *The bonfire flamed all night.* **2.** to flash, glow, or color suddenly: *Her cheeks flamed with embarrassment.*

fla·min·go ▼ [fluh-<u>ming</u>-goh] *noun, plural* **flamingos** *or* **flamingoes.** a water bird with a very long, thin neck and legs, webbed feet, and pink or red feathers.

flam·ma·ble [<u>flam</u>-uh-bul] *adjective.* easily set on fire and able to burn quickly. The state of being easy to set alight or of burning quickly is **flammability.**

Flammable is an unusual word in that it means exactly the same thing when used alone as it does when "in-" is added to it: "able to burn; burning easily." Other "in-" words mean the opposite of what the word means when used alone; for example, *incorrect* means not correct, *indirect* means not direct, *insecure* means not secure, and so on.

flank [flangk] *noun, plural* **flanks. 1.** the side of the body, between the ribs and hip. **2.** the side of something, especially the left or right side of a military formation: *Attack the left flank of the enemy.*
verb, **flanked, flanking. 1.** to be at the side of; border: *Two guards flanked the President.* **2.** to attack or threaten the side of: *The commandos flanked the retreating unit.*

flan·nel [<u>flan</u>-ul] *noun, plural* **flannels.** a warm, soft fabric, usually made from wool or cotton. It is often used for shirts, nightgowns, and babies' clothes.

flap [flap] *verb,* **flapped, flapping. 1.** to move up and down: *Birds flap their wings to fly.* **2.** to swing or wave about loosely, usually with a noise: *The flag flapped in the wind.*
noun, plural **flaps. 1.** the movement or sound made when something flaps. **2.** something flat and thin that is attached on one side and hangs loose on the other: *The cat comes in at night through a flap in the back door.*

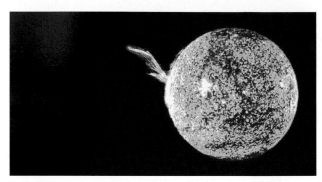

Solar **flares** *are eruptions from the Sun that release massive amounts of energy into space.*

flare ▲ [flare] *verb,* **flared, flaring. 1.** to burst into sudden, bright flame: *The flame above the oil rig flared in the night sky.* **2.** to show a sudden strong feeling: *Tempers flared when the umpire called the runner out.* **3.** to curve outward: *John's jeans flare at the bottom.*
noun, plural **flares. 1.** a sudden bright light that usually lasts only briefly. **2.** a device that sets off a bright light, used as a signal or to give light.
• **flare up.** to break out or intensify: *Her pollen allergies flare up in spring.*
🔊 A different word with the same sound is **flair.**

Flocks of **flamingos** *tramp through shallow water to stir up tiny shellfish, which they strain through their bills.*

flash [flash] *noun, plural* **flashes. 1.** a sudden short burst of light or flame: *a flash of lightning.* **2.** a very brief moment; instant: *He raced out the door and was gone in a flash.* *verb,* **flashed, flashing. 1.** to shine suddenly and brightly: *to flash a light as a signal.* **2.** to shine or appear bright suddenly: *Their eyes flashed with excitement at the thought of the roller coaster ride.* **3.** to move quickly or suddenly: *The cars flashed by at 100 miles per hour.* Clothes that are **flashy** are bright, showy, and even gaudy.

flash·back [flash-*bak*] *noun,* *plural* **flashbacks.** a short section of a movie, play, or story that goes back to events in the past: *The movie about President Nixon had a flashback to his childhood.*

flash·light [flash-*lite*] *noun, plural* **flashlights.** a small light powered by batteries that is held in the hand.

flask ▲ [flask] *noun, plural* **flasks.** a small bottle used for liquids.

flat [flat] *adjective,* **flatter, flattest. 1.** even and smooth; level: *The Great Plains are very flat ground without hills or mountains.* **2.** stretched out; spread out: *He was flat on his back on the floor.* **3.** not likely to change; fixed: *You can rent the skates for a flat rate of ten dollars per hour.* **4.** without much interest or energy: *Life seems a little flat now that the holiday season is over.* **5.** of a tire, having little or no air inside. **6.** *Music.* below the pitch of the correct or intended note. *noun, plural* **flats. 1.** a flat part, side, or surface: *the flat of the hand.* **2.** a tire with little or no air. **3.** *Music.* a note or tone that is one half step, or semitone, below its true pitch. **4.** the symbol ♭ for this note or tone. *adverb.* **1.** in a flat position: *We spread our towels flat on the sand.* **2.** exactly; precisely: *He ran the race in two minutes flat.* **—flatly,** *adverb,* **—flatness,** *noun.*

flat·fish [flat-*fish*] *noun, plural* **flatfish, flatfishes.** any thin, flat sea fish with both eyes on the upper side of its body. Flatfish include halibut, flounder, and sole.

flat·ten [flat-un] *verb,* **flattened, flattening.** to make flat or more flat.

flat·ter [flat-ur] *verb,* **flattered, flattering. 1.** to praise too much or without meaning it: *You're just flattering me because you want to borrow my clothes.* **2.** to make look more attractive than is really true: *That new hairstyle flatters her face.*

flat·ter·y [flat-uh-ree] *noun.* praise that is exaggerated or that is not genuine.

flav·or [flay-vur] *noun, plural* **flavors. 1.** the taste of something: *Maple syrup has a sweet flavor.* Something **flavorful** is full of flavor. **2.** the special quality or nature of something: *This dance music has a Brazilian flavor.* *verb,* **flavored, flavoring.** to add flavor or taste: *to flavor nachos with chili peppers.*

This old glass **flask** *has a decorative metal cover.*

flav·or·ing [flay-vur-ing] *noun, plural* **flavorings.** something added to food or drink to give a particular flavor.

flaw [flaw] *noun, plural* **flaws.** a crack, scratch, fault, or mistake that takes away from the value or quality of something: *A flaw in the model airplane's design meant that it didn't fly.*

flaw·less [flaw-lis] *adjective.* having no faults or weaknesses; perfect. **—flawlessly,** *adverb.*

flax [flaks] *noun.* **1.** a fine, light-colored fiber made from the stem of the flax plant. The fiber is used to make linen fabric, rope, or rugs. **2.** the plant from which this fiber comes. The seeds are used to make linseed oil. Something **flaxen** is made of flax or resembles flax, especially its pale yellow color.

flea ▶ [flee] *noun, plural* **fleas.** a small jumping insect without wings. It sucks blood from humans, cats, dogs, and other mammals, and birds. A flea can sometimes carry disease and pass it to the animal it is living on.
🔊 A different word with the same sound is **flee.**

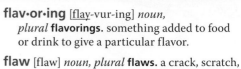

Fleas *can jump up to 200 times the length of their bodies with their strong leg muscles.*

fled [fled] *verb.* the past tense and past participle of FLEE.

flee [flee] *verb,* **fled, fleeing.** to run away or escape: *They had to flee from the hurricane.*
🔊 A different word with the same sound is **flea.**

fleece ▼ [flees] *noun, plural* **fleeces.** the coat of wool covering a sheep or other animal. *verb,* **fleeced, fleecing. 1.** to cut the wool from an animal; shear. **2.** to take someone's money dishonestly, by cheating or fraud: *That hotel tried to fleece us by charging double the standard room price.*

fleet¹ [fleet] *noun, plural* **fleets. 1.** a group of warships under one commander. **2.** a group of boats, airplanes, or vehicles operated as a unit: *the New York City taxi fleet.*

fleet² [fleet] *adjective.* able to move very swiftly and nimbly: *The sprinter was very fleet of foot.*

fleet·ing [fleet-ing] *adjective.* very brief or quick: *This is just a fleeting visit, so we won't stay for lunch.* **—fleetingly,** *adverb.*

flesh [flesh] *noun.* **1.** the soft part of an animal body, made up of layers of muscle and fat between the bones and skin. A person who is **fleshy** has a lot of soft flesh, or is plump. **2.** the soft part of fruits and vegetables used as food: *Peel off the pineapple skin and eat the sweet, yellow flesh inside.* **3.** the meat of an animal.

Today's shearers use electric shears to **fleece** *sheep.*

Flickers spend much of their time flicking ants into their mouths with their pointed bills.

Gilded flicker

Red-shafted flicker

Yellow-shafted flicker

flew [floo] *verb.* the past tense of FLY.
🔊 Different words with the same sound are **flu** and **flue.**

flex [fleks] *verb*, **flexed, flexing.** to move a part of the body; bend: *She flexed her arms and legs as part of her warm-up.*

flex·i·ble [flek-suh-bul] *adjective.* **1.** able to bend or stretch easily; not stiff: *If you can do a split, your body is very flexible.* **2.** able to change or adapt easily: *We can meet whenever you like—I'm flexible.* The act or state of being able to bend or stretch easily is **flexibility. —flexibly,** *adverb.*

flick [flik] *noun, plural* **flicks.** a light, quick touch or movement: *The flick of a cat's tail.*
verb, **flicked, flicking.** to touch or hit with a light, quick movement: *The boys flicked their towels at each other.*

flick·er[1] [flik-ur] *verb*, **flickered, flickering. 1.** to burn unsteadily, with a wavering light: *The match flickered and went out.* **2.** to flutter and quiver; move quickly back and forth: *His shadow flickered on the wall behind him.*
noun, plural **flickers. 1.** an unsteady, wavering light: *the flicker of candlelight.* **2.** a quick, fluttering, back and forth movement.

flick·er[2] ▲ [flik-ur] *noun, plural* **flickers.** a large North American woodpecker. Its feathers are mostly brown and white, with a black curve across its breast.

flied [flide] *verb.* the past tense of FLY, used in baseball: *The batter flied out to right field.*

fli·er [flye-ur] another spelling of FLYER.

flight[1] ▶ [flite] *noun, plural* **flights. 1.** the act of passing through the air using wings; flying.
2. the distance or course traveled by an aircraft or bird: *a flight from Los Angeles to Vancouver.*
3. a group of things flying together: *a flight of geese; a flight of bombers.*
4. an airplane journey.
5. a set of steps or stairs between two floors of a building.

flight[2] [flite] *noun, plural* **flights.** the act of fleeing or escaping: *The movie shows a family's terrifying flight from the war zone.*

flight attendant a person who helps the passengers on an airplane, as by serving food and drink and explaining safety rules.

In the early days of air travel, the people who worked as **flight attendants** were almost always women. The name for this job was not *flight attendant* but *stewardess,* and the very few men who did this job were called *stewards.* Later, as a lot more men took on this job, the name was changed to *flight attendant,* a word that applies to both women and men.

flim·sy [flim-zee] *adjective*, **flimsier, flimsiest.** lacking substance; light; weak; thin: *flimsy sandals; a flimsy argument.*

flinch [flinch] *verb*, **flinched, flinching.** to shrink back from something unpleasant, dangerous, or painful: *He flinched when the nurse took a sample of blood from his finger.*

fling [fling] *verb*, **flung, flinging. 1.** to throw or toss something somewhere, often using a lot of force: *After he lost his temper we saw him fling his tennis racket to the ground.*
noun, plural **flings. 1.** a sudden throw: *a powerful fling of the ball.* **2.** a short period of enjoyment: *Let's go to the lake this weekend because it's our last chance to have a fling before the exams start.*

Flintlocks were invented in France in the 1600s and were used until the mid-1800s.

flint [flint] *noun, plural* **flints.** a very hard, gray-black stone that gives off sparks when you strike it with a piece of steel. Before matches were invented it was used to light fires or to cause a gun to fire.

flint·lock ▲ [flint-lok] *noun, plural* **flintlocks.** *History.* a type of gun that was used many years ago. Sparks struck from a flint in it lit gunpowder, which caused the gun to fire.

flip [flip] *verb*, **flipped, flipping. 1.** to turn something over by making a quick movement with your hand: *Flip through the book and show me the page you are talking about.*
noun, plural **flips. 1.** a light toss: *A flip of a coin decides which team will kick off.* **2.** a somersault.

Spreading wings out

Muscle

Tucking wings in

Pushing forward, wings dropped

End of stroke

Lifting wings

In flight, birds use their muscles, wings, and feathers to launch themselves, keep themselves in the air, and land safely.

A B C D E F G H I J K L M N O P Q R S T U V W X Y Z

flip·per [flip-ur] *noun, plural,* **flippers. 1.** one of the broad, flat limbs of an animal that lives in water, such as a turtle, seal, or penguin, which it uses for swimming, or for moving about on land. **2.** a flat piece of rubber that attaches to your foot to help you to swim faster.

flirt [flurt] *verb,* **flirted, flirting.** to act in a romantic but not very serious fashion: *She flirted with every boy at the party. noun, plural* **flirts.** a person who pretends to like someone, but is not very serious about it.

flit [flit] *verb,* **flitted, flitting.** to fly or move quickly from one place to another: *The birds flit from branch to branch.*

float [flote] *verb,* **floated, floating. 1.** to stay on the surface of a liquid without sinking: *If I throw this empty bottle into the swimming pool I bet it will float.* **2.** to move slowly and gently through water or air; drift: *The current caused the large logs to float down the river. noun, plural* **floats. 1.** something that floats easily on water, such as a raft. **2.** a platform on wheels that carries colorful displays or people in special costumes in a parade.

flock [flok] *noun, plural* **flocks. 1.** a large group of birds, goats, sheep, or other animals: *The road was blocked by a flock of sheep.* **2.** a large group or number: *The fan club of the Atlanta Falcons football team is known as The Flock. verb,* **flocked, flocking.** to go somewhere in large numbers: *We all flocked to see the circus when it was in town.*

floe [floh] *noun, plural* **floes.** a mass or sheet of floating ice. 🔊 A different word with the same sound is **flow.**

flood ▼ [flud] *noun, plural* **floods. 1.** a large flow of water over an area that is usually dry. **2.** a large flow of anything: *a flood of tears; a flood of refugees after a war. verb,* **flooded, flooding. 1.** to cover with water: *The river*

overflowed its banks and flooded the small town below. **2.** to cover with a large amount of something; saturate: *They flooded the market with cheap DVDs.*

floor [flore] *noun, plural* **floors. 1.** the level surface of a room that you walk on or stand on. **2.** the ground at the bottom of something: *the ocean floor; animals that live on the forest floor.* **3.** all the rooms that are at the same level of a building; story: *The doctor's office is on the fifth floor. verb,* **floored, flooring. 1.** to knock someone down: *He floored him with one punch.* **2.** to surprise and confuse: *She was floored by the news that she had won the contest.*

flop [flop] *verb,* **flopped, flopping. 1.** to fall, sit, or lie down heavily: *He was so tired when he came home from work he just flopped down onto the chair.* **2.** to fall somewhere, move around, and hang loosely. *Nadia's long, red hair flopped over her eyes as she was riding her bike.* **3.** to fail completely: *I'm not surprised the play flopped, I thought it was terribly boring. noun, plural* **flops. 1.** the act or sound of falling down heavily. **2.** a complete failure.

The case of this pocket watch is decorated with a floral painting.

flop·py [flop-ee] *adjective.* **floppier, floppiest** limp and bending easily; tending to hang down: *Our dog has floppy ears.*

floppy disk *Computers.* a small, flexible, magnetic disk used to store computer information.

flo·ral ▲ [flore-ul] *adjective.* having to do with flowers: *a floral arrangement; a dress with a floral pattern.*

flo·rist [flore-ist] *noun, plural* **florists.** a person who arranges and sells flowers and indoor plants.

floun·der[1] [floun-dur] *verb,* **floundered, floundering. 1.** to struggle in an awkward way: *We watched them flounder around in the rough surf.* **2.** to stumble on words or struggle to speak: *He floundered, unable to think of an answer to the question.*

floun·der[2] [floun-dur] *noun, plural* **flounders.** a flatfish that lives in salt water.

flour [flou-ur] *noun, plural* **flours.** a white or brown powder made by grinding and sifting grain, such as wheat or rye, and used to make bread, biscuits, and cakes.

flour·ish [flur-ish] *verb,* **flourished, flourishing. 1.** to grow and develop well because of existing conditions: *Our azalea plants flourish in this cool weather, it seems to suit them.* **2.** to be at a strong and successful point: *They reported a fifty percent increase in profits this year—the business has flourished.* **3.** to wave boldly in the air: *Please stop flourishing that knife, it's making me nervous. noun, plural* **flourishes.** a bold, showy movement or gesture: *She finished writing and signed the letter with a flourish.*

*A flash **flood** in northern Italy was caused by the collapse of a dam in torrential rain.*

a
b
c
d
e
f
g
h
j
k
l
m
n
o
p
q
r
s
t
u
v
w
x
y
z

flow [floh] *verb,* **flowed, flowing. 1.** of water or another liquid, to move along in a steady stream: *This river flows into the Pacific Ocean.* **2.** to move along smoothly: *People flowed into the auditorium for the concert.* **3.** to hang or fall freely or loosely: *Lea's blond hair was flowing over her shoulders.*
noun, plural **flows.** the act of flowing; a smooth stream: *the flow of blood in the body; a flow of traffic.*
🔊 A different word with the same sound is **floe.**

flow·er [flou-ur] *noun, plural* **flowers. 1.** the blossom of a plant from which seeds or fruit develop. **2.** a small plant grown especially for its flowers: *Roses are a popular kind of flower.*
verb, **flowered, flowering.** to produce flowers: *The garden looks wonderful in spring because all the plants flower.*

flow·er·y [flou-ur-ee] *adjective.* **1.** having a lot of flowers. **2.** using fancy or ornate language: *a flowery speech.*

flown [flone] *verb.* the past participle of FLY.

flu [floo] *noun, plural* **flus.** an illness like a bad cold but much more serious, which may produce a high temperature and aching joints. It is a virus that spreads easily from one person to another. This word is an abbreviation for INFLUENZA.
🔊 Different words with the same sound are **flew** and **flue.**

flue [floo] *noun, plural* **flues.** a pipe that carries smoke and hot air outside; small chimney: *the flue on the stove; the flue on the clothes dryer.*
🔊 Different words with the same sound are **flew** and **flu.**

fluff [fluf] *noun,* pieces of soft, light material: *When he picked up his coat from the floor it had fluff all over it.* Something that is like this material or covered with it is **fluffy.**
verb, **fluffed, fluffing.** to puff something up by beating or shaking it, in order to make look bigger: *These cushions need fluffing up a bit.*

flu·id [floo-id] *noun, plural* **fluids.** a substance that flows, such as a liquid or gas: *When ice melts it becomes fluid.* Relating to the flow of such a substance is **fluidic.**
adjective. flowing; moving smoothly; not firm: *His pitching motion was easy and fluid.*

The words **fluid** and *liquid* do not mean the same thing. All liquids are fluids, but the opposite is not true. A fluid is any substance that flows; that is, it will move to another place unless it is held where it is in some way, as by being in a container. Thus the word *fluid* includes not only water and other liquids, but also gases such as oxygen and hydrogen.

flung [flung] *verb.* the past tense and past participle of FLING.

fluo·res·cent ▶ [flu-res-unt] *adjective. Science.* giving off light when exposed to radiation or electricity. A **fluorescent lamp** is a glass tube with a special coating inside that provides light when it is exposed to radiation or electricity. The ability to give out such a light is **fluorescence.**

fluor·i·date [flore-uh-*date*] *verb,* **fluoridated, fluoridating.** *Health.* to add fluoride to drinking water to improve dental health. —**fluoridation,** *noun.*

fluo·ride [flore-ide] *noun. Chemistry.* a mixture of chemicals that is sometimes added to a water supply.

fluo·rine [flore-een] *noun. Chemistry.* a pale, yellowish-green gas that combines very easily with other elements. Compounds of fluorine are added to drinking water to help prevent tooth decay.

flur·ry [flur-ee] *noun, plural* **flurries. 1.** a short rush of activity; a sudden outburst: *There was a flurry of activity to clean the house after Mom called to say she'd be home earlier than expected.* **2.** a small amount of something that only appears for a short time, and then disappears: *a flurry of wind; a flurry of snow.*

flush[1] [flush] *verb,* **flushed, flushing. 1.** to turn red; blush: *Nola was so embarrassed and upset she flushed to the roots of her hair.* **2.** to clean or clear something by causing a rush of water: *to flush a toilet; to flush a blocked drain.*
noun, plural **flushes. 1.** a flow of blood to the cheeks. **2.** a rush or flow of water. **3.** a sudden, strong feeling of pleasure: *a flush of excitement.*

flush[2] [flush] *adjective; adverb.* flat and even; level: *That door juts out, it isn't flush with the frame; The tree branch hit him flush in the face.*

flus·ter [flus-tur] *verb,* **flustered, flustering.** to make someone feel nervous and confused: *Stacy was flustered when she arrived late for her job interview.*

flute ▲ [floot] *noun, plural* **flutes.** *Music.* a long, thin, musical instrument with holes in it, made of metal or wood. You hold it sideways to your mouth and play it by blowing into a hole at one end, making different notes by moving your fingers up and down over the holes.

flut·ter [flut-ur] *verb,* **fluttered, fluttering.** to move or fly in a small, quick, or uneven way: *The flag fluttered in the wind.*
noun, plural **flutters. 1.** a quick, light movement: *the flutter of a bird's wings.* **2.** a state of confusion or excitement: *I felt a flutter of nervousness in my stomach as I went up onto the stage to start my speech.*

*These jellyfish glow brightly when they are lit by **fluorescent** light.*

fly¹ [flye] *verb*, **flew, flown, flying. 1.** to move through the air: *The aircraft is flying very low.* **2.** to travel somewhere in an aircraft: *"Learn to fly and pilot your own plane,"* said the advertisement. **3.** to move about freely and loosely: *A flag was flying from the ship's mast.* **4.** to go somewhere fast: *The door burst open and he came flying into the room.* **5.** also, **fly out.** to hit a baseball high in the air that is caught for an out. *noun, plural* **flies. 1.** an opening down the front of a pair of trousers or shorts. **2.** a baseball hit high into the air.

fly² ▼ [flye] *noun, plural* **flies.** one of a group of insects with two wings, such as a housefly or a mosquito.

fly·er [flye-ur] another spelling of FLIER.

flying fish a saltwater fish that lives in warm seas. It has large fins that look like wings, which enable it to leap into the air using its fins to glide above the surface of the water.

flying saucer a spacecraft that some people claim to have seen in the sky, which they believe comes from another planet.

People have reported seeing strange flying objects in the sky for about the past 150 years. However, the number of well-known reports of this increased greatly in the late 1940s, shortly after the end of World War II. A number of people said they had seen objects that could fly at a tremendous speed, and that appeared to have the shape of a disk, saucer, or pie pan. Newspaper stories about these sightings seized upon the idea of **"flying saucers,"** and that became the term for such objects. Today, the preferred term is *UFO* (unidentified flying object).

flying squirrel ▼ a squirrel that has folds of skin that connect its front legs to its back legs, which allow it to make long, gliding leaps.

foal [fole] *noun, plural* **foals.** a young horse, donkey, zebra, or similar animal, not yet one year old. *verb*, **foaled, foaling.** to give birth to a foal.

*A **flying squirrel** uses the skin between its limbs to glide from tree to tree.*

foam [fome] *noun, plural* **foams.** a mass of bubbles on the surface of a liquid; froth. If a liquid has a mass of small bubbles on its surface, it is **foamy.** *verb*, **foamed, foaming.** to form tiny bubbles that are often moving: *He poured the champagne into my glass and it foamed all over the floor.*

foam rubber soft, spongy rubber that is used in upholstery and as filling for mattresses, pillows, and cushions.

fo·cus [foh-kus] *noun, plural* **focuses** or **foci.**
1. a meeting point for rays of light after being bent by a lens. **2.** the distance from the lens to the point where the rays meet. **3.** a point of special interest or attention: *The new plasma TV was the focus of everyone's attention.* **4.** an adjustment to an instrument, such as a camera or telescope, so that the object you are looking at is clear and sharp: *That photo is blurry, it is totally out of focus.* *verb*, **focused, focusing. 1.** to adjust something, so that you can clearly see the thing you are looking at: *to focus a pair of binoculars.* **2.** to take a special interest; concentrate on: *Focus your attention on winning the race.* **3.** to bring to a meeting point.

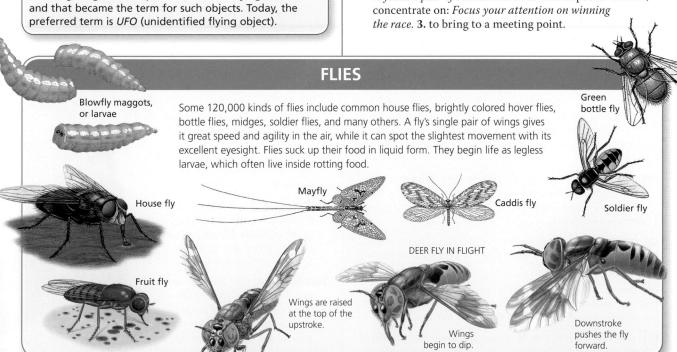

FLIES

Some 120,000 kinds of flies include common house flies, brightly colored hover flies, bottle flies, midges, soldier flies, and many others. A fly's single pair of wings gives it great speed and agility in the air, while it can spot the slightest movement with its excellent eyesight. Flies suck up their food in liquid form. They begin life as legless larvae, which often live inside rotting food.

Blowfly maggots, or larvae

Green bottle fly

House fly

Mayfly

Caddis fly

Soldier fly

Fruit fly

Wings are raised at the top of the upstroke.

DEER FLY IN FLIGHT

Wings begin to dip.

Downstroke pushes the fly forward.

a b c d e f g h i j k l m n o p q r s t u v w x y z

Fog forms at the coast when warm sea air moves over the cold land.

Sometimes fog forms when land cools quickly and the air chills.

Fog clears when the Sun warms the air.

fod·der [fod-ur] *noun, plural* **fodders. 1.** food for farm animals, such as oats, hay, and corn. **2.** something readily available used to supply a strong demand: *The lives of movie stars provide fodder for the gossip columns.*

foe [foh] *noun, plural* **foes.** someone who fights against or opposes; an enemy: *The two clans had been foes for centuries.*

fog ▲ [fog *or* fawg] *noun, plural* **fogs. 1.** tiny drops of water in the air that form a thick cloud; clouds along the ground. **2.** a state of confusion; bewilderment: *I can't think, my brain is in a fog.*
verb, **fogged, fogging.** to cover or become covered with a very fine layer of water: *I can't see because my glasses have fogged up.*

fog·gy [fog-ee *or* fawg-ee] *adjective,* **foggier, foggiest. 1.** having to do with fog; misty: *It was a cold, foggy morning.* **2.** being confused, hazy: *I haven't got the foggiest idea what happened.*

fog·horn [fog-horn *or* fawg-horn] *noun, plural* **foghorns.** a loud horn that is used when there is a fog to warn boats and ships to go carefully.

foil¹ [foyle] *verb,* **foiled, foiling.** to prevent someone from being successful: *His plan to rob the bank was foiled by a security guard who arrived at the last minute.*

foil² [foyle] *noun, plural* **foils.** metal that has been hammered flat into very thin, flexible sheets: *tin foil; aluminum foil.*

foil³ [foyle] *noun, plural* **foils.** a thin, light sword with a button on its tip to prevent injury, used for fencing.

fold¹ [fohld] *verb,* **folded, folding. 1.** to turn or bend something over on itself, so that it becomes smaller: *This bed and chair fold up, so you can put them away in the cupboard.* **2.** to bring together close to the body: *She folded her hands on her lap and sat quietly, listening to the teacher.*
noun, plural **folds. 1.** something bent or turned over on itself. **2.** a mark or bend that you make on something when you fold it: *Make sure you cut along the fold.*

fold² [fohld] *noun, plural* **folds.** a pen, yard, or other such enclosure, especially for sheep.

fold·er [fohl-dur] *noun, plural* **folders.** a holder in which you keep loose papers, usually a piece of cardboard that has been folded into two.

fo·li·age ▼ [foh-lij *or* foh-lee-ij] *noun.* the leaves on trees and plants.

folk [foke] *noun, plural* **folks. 1.** people of a certain type or group: *city folk; middle-class folks.* **2.** people in general; any people: *The neighbors next door are really nice folk.* **3.** a person's close family; parents or other relatives: *I must ring my folks this weekend.*
adjective. being part of a country's traditions; representing the culture of the ordinary people: *German folk songs; folk music.*

In Fall, the **foliage** of deciduous trees turns red, amber, and gold in a colorful display.

The **folk** are people in general, rather than any specific person. A folk tale is so called because it do not have a specific author the way a modern story does. No one knows who was the first person to tell or write down a folk tale, such as the story of Robin Hood. In fact, some folk tales are thought to be so old that they began thousands of years ago, before writing was even invented. Certain of these tales, such as the story of Cinderella, then spread all over the world, having different versions as they were told in different countries.

folk art *Art.* the traditional art of the ordinary people of a particular community or country.

folk dance ▶ **1.** a traditional dance representing the culture and feelings of the ordinary people in a particular region, or country. **2.** *Music.* a piece of music for this kind of dance.

folk·lore [foke-lor] *noun. Literature.* the old customs and traditional beliefs and stories of people in a particular community or country, which have been handed down from one generation to the next.

*The people of Latvia, in eastern Europe, proudly maintain their traditional folk songs and **folk dances.***

folk music *Music.* the traditional music, originating from the ordinary people of a community or country, which has been handed down by them to the next generation. Songs that go with this music are called **folk songs** and the person who sings them is a **folk singer.**

folk tale a story or legend, originating from the people of a region or country and handed down from one generation to the next.

fol·low [fol-oh] *verb,* **followed, following. 1.** to go or come after or behind: *Stay behind me and follow me down the narrow path.* **2.** to go along: *Get on Route 63 and follow it until it meets Highway 9.* **3.** to watch or observe; pay attention to: *Mom doesn't follow golf, but even she has heard of Tiger Woods.* **4.** to understand: *Long division is hard, did you follow my explanation?* **5.** to act in accordance with; obey: *Now, you are in a mess, why didn't you follow my advice?*

fol·low·er [fol-oh-ur] *noun, plural* **followers. 1.** a supporter of a particular person or cause, such as a political party or a religion: *the followers of Jesus Christ.* **2.** someone or something that follows.

fol·low·ing [fol-oh-ing] *adjective.* relating to the next one after the one just mentioned; coming after: *I was really sick on Tuesday, but by the following day I felt better.* *noun, plural* **followings.** a group of people who support a person, cause, or religion: *The singer was very popular and had a big following of fans.*

fol·ly [fol-ee] *noun, plural,* **follies.** silly conduct: foolishness: *Driving fast in this fog would be sheer folly.*

fond [fond] *adjective,* **fonder, fondest.** liking someone or something very much: *Everyone in the class is fond of the teacher.*

font [font] *noun, plural* **fonts. 1.** a basin, often made of stone, which holds water used for baptisms. **2.** a collection of printing type of one style or size.

The type **font** of a word determines the way the word looks in print. Font means the name of the type that is used. For example, the font called Times looks like this, and the font called Helvetica looks like this. Font also means the kind of type used, such as *italics,* **boldface,** SMALL CAPITALS, superscript, or underlining.

In the ocean **food chain,** *fish eat small shellfish, which, in turn, eat microscopic plants.*

Fish   Shellfish   Microscopic plants

food [food] *noun, plural* **foods. 1.** something that people eat, especially something solid rather than a liquid. **2.** anything that promotes growth in people and animals, which they eat or drink to stay alive; nourishment.

food chain ▲ *Biology.* a series of living things that are linked because each thing feeds on the thing below it in the series. A series of related food chains is a **food web.**

food processor a machine used in the kitchen to chop, mix, slice, or blend food.

fool [fool] *noun, plural* **fools. 1.** a silly or stupid person: *He would be a fool to jump in the pool when he knows he can't swim.* **2.** in earlier times, a person who was employed in the court of a king or queen, whose job was to make people laugh. *verb,* **fooled, fooling. 1.** to trick or deceive: *He fooled us all with his pleasant manner, we didn't realize how mean he really is.* **2.** to behave in a childish or silly way: *Stop fooling around and get on with the job.*

fool·ish [fool-ish] *adjective.* lacking common sense; silly: *She is normally a sensible girl, so I was very surprised to see her make such a foolish mistake.* —**foolishly,** *adverb;* —**foolishness,** *noun.*

foot [fut] *noun, plural* **feet. 1.** the part of the body at the end of the leg, which humans and animals stand on. **2.** the bottom, base, or end part of something: *the foot of the stairs; the foot of the bed.* **3.** a unit of measurement, equal to twelve inches.

foot·ball ◄ [fut-bawl] *noun, plural* **footballs. 1.** a game played between two teams, each with eleven players, on a large field with goals at either end. The players attempt to score points by carrying, passing, or kicking the ball over the other team's goal. **2.** the oval-shaped ball used in this game. **3.** another name for the game that is called soccer in the United States.

American **football** *is a tough game that involves blocking, tackling, running, and passing the ball.*

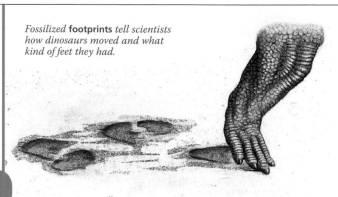

*Fossilized **footprints** tell scientists how dinosaurs moved and what kind of feet they had.*

foot·hill [fut-*hil*] *noun, plural* **foothills.** a hill or a low mountain at the base of a higher mountain or mountain range.

foot·ing [fut-ing] *noun, plural* **footings. 1.** the ability to stand upright with the feet firmly and safely placed without slipping: *He lost his footing and fell down the hill.* **2.** a solid place or foundation. **3.** a relationship: *Unfortunately I've never been on a really good footing with her until now.*

foot·light [fut-*lite*] *noun.* one of the lights that are in a row along the front of the stage in a theater.

foot·note [fut-*note*] *noun, plural* **footnotes.** *Literature.* a note at the bottom of a page in a book that gives more information about something that is already mentioned on the page.

foot·print ▲ [fut-*print*] *noun, plural* **footprints.** a mark made by a foot or shoe.

foot·step [fut-*step*] *noun, plural* **footsteps.** the sound or mark made by someone walking each time their foot touches the ground: *We heard the door opening and then footsteps coming up the stairs.*
• **follow in someone's footsteps.** to do the same thing as someone before you: *Dr. Wilson wanted her daughter to follow in her footsteps and also become a doctor.*

for [for] *preposition.* **1.** to or through a certain time, distance, or amount: *to sleep for eight hours; to run for a mile; to sell a car for $5,000.* **2.** directed to or meant for a certain person, purpose, or cause: *to vote for a candidate; to have a sandwich for lunch; to work for a large company; to campaign for peace in the world.* **3.** in place of or instead of: *to use a sofa for a bed; "Automobile" is another word for "car."*
conjunction. because: *Most fans left the game early, for it was obvious the home team would lose.*

for·age ▶ [for-ij] *verb,* **foraged, foraging.** to search for something, especially food: *We went downstairs for a midnight feast and foraged for cakes and cookies in the pantry.*
noun. crops that are grown as food for cattle and horses.

for·bid [fur-bid] *verb,* **forbade, forbidden, forbidding.** to order not to do something: *It is forbidden to bring a knife or gun on an airplane.* Something that is dangerous or frightening is **forbidding.**

force [fors] *noun, plural* **forces. 1.** strong and violent action: *Wars are usually won by force.* **2.** strength; power: *The force of the earthquake recorded 5.2 on the Richter scale.* **3.** a powerful influence: *China, which has a population of well over one billion people, is becoming a powerful force on the world scene.* **4.** a group of people who work together: *a police force; an air force.* **5.** *Physics.* the pulling or pushing effect that something has on something else: *magnetic force; the force of gravity.*
verb, **forced, forcing. 1.** to make someone do something, against their will: *The thief threatened them with a gun and forced them out of the car.* **2.** to apply a lot of strength to something: *We had to force the window open to get inside.* **3.** to cause someone to do something: *The raging bushfires nearby forced us to leave the house.*
• **in force.** being used or in operation: *I will have to look up exactly which regulations are in force at the moment.*

force·ful [fors-ful] *adjective.* having power and strength; energetic: *He had a strong, forceful personality.*
—forcefully, *adverb.*

ford [ford] *noun, plural* **fords.** a shallow place in a river or stream where it is possible to cross safely, either by foot or in a vehicle.
verb, **forded, fording.** to cross water safely at a shallow place: *We forded the river.*

fore [for] *adjective.* at the front of: *the fore part of a ship.*
🔊 Different words with the same sound are **for** and **four.**

fore·arm [for-*arm*] *noun, plural* **forearms.** the lower part of the arm between the wrist and the elbow.

fore·cast [for-*kast*] *verb,* **forecast** *or* **forecasted, forecasting.** to predict what will happen in the future: *I confidently forecast a 7–0 win for our team in the next football game.*
noun, plural **forecasts.** the act of predicting a future event, especially about weather or business: *The forecast for the wedding on Saturday is sunny and warm.*

fore·fa·ther [for-fah-THur] *noun, plural* **forefathers.** one of a person's ancestors.

fore·fin·ger [for-fing-gur] *noun, plural* **forefingers.** the first finger, next to the thumb; the index finger.

fore·gone [for-*gone*] *adjective.* having something decided or known about beforehand; as predicted: *It was a foregone conclusion that the Senator would win the election.*

*A pig **forages** in the ground for truffles, a fungus that is used in French cooking.*

fore·ground [for-ground] *noun, plural* **foregrounds.** the nearest part of a picture or scene to a person looking at it.

fore·head [for-id *or* for-hed] *noun, plural* **foreheads.** the top part of the face, above the eyes and below the hair.

for·eign [for-un] *adjective.* **1.** of or from a country not your own: *The languages of foreign countries, like France or China, are taught in some schools.* **2.** describing something not belonging where it is found: *A tiny foreign object stuck in her eye.* **3.** having to do with overseas countries or governments: *Foreign policy can involve many problems.*

for·eign·er [for-un-ur] *noun, plural* **foreigners.** a person from another country.

fore·leg [for-leg] *noun, plural* **forelegs.** one of the two front legs of a four-legged animal. The foot on a foreleg is called a **forefoot.**

fore·man [for-mun] *noun, plural* **foremen. 1.** a skilled worker put in charge of a group of other workers. **2.** a male person who speaks on behalf of a jury. If the person is a female she is called the **forewoman.**

fore·most [for-most] *adjective.* being the most important: *Some people say Pablo Picasso was the foremost artist of the twentieth century.*

fore·run·ner [for-un-ur] *noun, plural* **forerunners. 1.** the fact of a thing or person coming before another: *The horse and buggy was the forerunner of the automobile.* **2.** a signal that something is about to happen, a sign: *Big, dark clouds were the forerunner to the snowstorm.*

fore·see [for-see] *verb,* **foresaw, foreseen, foreseeing.** to form an idea of or predict what will happen in the future: *We cannot foresee what changes will take place when the new principal takes over the school.*

fore·sight [for-site] *noun.* the act of seeing into, predicting, or preparing for the future: *Investing money wisely for the future shows foresight.*

for·est ▼ [for-ist] *noun, plural* **forests.** a large area of land covered by trees.

forest ranger a person employed to protect forests and help visitors.

fore·tell [for-tel] *verb,* **foretold, foretelling.** to predict future events; prophesy: *Doctors look for certain signs in a person that may foretell their developing a disease.*

for·ev·er [for-ev-ur] *adverb.* **1.** for all time; to the end of time: *He promised to love her forever.* **2.** without stopping; many times or all the time: *He is forever losing his pens and always has to buy more.*

for·feit [for-fit] *verb,* **forfeited, forfeiting.** to lose the opportunity to do something: *In soccer, a team has to have at least seven players on the field or else they forfeit the game.*

for·gave [for-gave] *verb.* the past tense of FORGIVE.

forge[1] [forj] *noun plural* **forges.** a fireplace or furnace used to heat metal, which is then hammered into shape: *Blacksmiths use a forge to make and shape horseshoes. verb,* **forged, forging. 1.** to heat metal in a forge so it can be turned into metal objects, such as horseshoes. **2.** to draw up an agreement after negotiation: *The two countries forged a trade agreement.* **3.** to copy or change in order to deceive: *He forged a passport to try to get out of the country before the police could find him.*

forge[2] [forj] *verb,* **forged, forging.** to advance steadily and with increasing power: *Joey forged ahead to win the race.*

for·get [fur-get] *verb,* **forgot, forgotten** *or* **forgot, forgetting. 1.** to fail to remember: *He forgot to bring his umbrella and got wet in the rain.* **2.** to stop thinking about: *I tried to forget my problems by going to the movies.*

for·get·ful [fur-get-ful] *adjective.* having the habit of not remembering things: *Grandma is becoming forgetful, so she writes things down.* —**forgetfulness,** *noun.*

A sea stack is a tall coastal rock formation that is caused by erosion.

for·give [fur-_giv_] *verb*, **forgave, forgiven, forgiving.** to stop being angry or laying blame: *David has forgiven me for losing his cell phone now that he has a new one.* **—forgiveness,** *noun.*

for·giv·en [fur-_giv_-un] *verb.* the past participle of FORGIVE.

for·got [fur-_got_] *verb.* the past tense of FORGET.

for·got·ten [fur-_got_-un] *verb.* the past participle of FORGET. *adjective.* describing something or someone not remembered or not noticed: *The old movie starred forgotten actors such as John Derek and Alan Hale.*

fork [fork] *noun, plural* **forks. 1.** a small tool for holding or serving food. Forks have a handle at one end and several sharp points at the other. **2.** a larger tool similar to this, used in gardening and agriculture. **3.** a place where two roads or tracks divide: *Turn left at the fork in the road.* *verb,* **forked, forking. 1.** to lift or toss with a fork. **2.** to loosen earth for planting seed. **3.** to separate into two sections: *The river forks below the town.*

form [form] *noun, plural* **forms. 1.** the shape or outward appearance of something: *We could just make out the form of the building in the darkness.* **2.** one kind; a sort or type: *Democracy is a form of government.* **3.** fitness for or achievement in a sport: *Are you in good form on the tennis court?* **4.** an official piece of paper with questions and blank spaces for answers to be written in. **5.** one of the ways in which a word may occur. *Running is a form of the verb run.* *verb,* **formed, forming. 1.** to make or shape: *The bricklayer formed the arch with the help of a special design.* **2.** to take the shape of something: *The trees formed a semicircle around the bay.*

for·mal [_for_-mu] *adjective.* **1.** describing something official: *As it was a formal document it had to be witnessed and signed.* **2.** being a serious or important occasion, or suited to such an occasion: *a formal dance; formal clothes.* *noun, plural* **formals. 1.** a serious or important occasion. **2.** a dress worn for such an occasion. **—formally,** *adverb.*

for·mat [_for_-mat] *noun, plural* **formats. 1.** the layout, plan, or organization of something: *Part of the format of this book is that the text is divided into two columns.* **2.** the way in which data is stored on a computer disk or program for storage or output. *verb,* **formatted, formatting. 1.** to work out a format for something: *The meeting was formatted so that everyone could speak for two minutes.* **2.** to prepare a computer to store or display information.

A headland is eroded by the sea to form a sea cave.

Sea cave

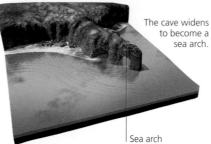

The cave widens to become a sea arch.

Sea arch

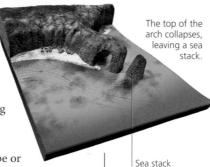

The top of the arch collapses, leaving a sea stack.

Sea stack

for·ma·tion ◀ [for-_may_-shun] *noun, plural* **formations. 1.** the act of making or developing something: *The formation of the mountain range took place thousands of years ago.* **2.** something that is formed: *Geologists study rock formations.* **3.** an arrangement of people, ships, airplanes, or other things: *The fighter jets flew in formation over the parade ground.* **4.** a certain way that a team sets up to play in football or soccer.

for·mer [_for_-mur] *adjective.* **1.** being the first of two things mentioned: *Of the two players named, the former is the better one.* **2.** from an earlier period or previous arrangement: *The former President still spoke on public policy.* **—formerly,** *adverb.*

for·mu·la [_for_-myuh-luh] *noun, plural* **formulas** *or* **formulae. 1.** the proportion of each ingredient in a mixture. **2.** a general rule expressed in numbers or symbols: *The formula for converting imperial to metric units is 1 inch = 2.54 centimeters.* **3.** *Science.* a method of naming a chemical compound that uses a symbol for each molecule: *The formula for salt is NaCl.* **4.** a rule or plan for doing something the best way: *One formula for a happy marriage is to have common interests and a shared sense of humor.*

for·sake [for-_sake_] *verb,* **forsook, forsaken, forsaking.** to abandon or give up: *She decided to forsake eating meat and become a vegetarian.*

for·syth·i·a ▶ [for-_sith_-ee-uh] *noun, plural* **forsythias.** a small bush that has bright yellow, bell-shaped flowers in spring before its leaves grow.

fort [fort] *noun, plural* **forts.** a strong building or enclosure that is easy to defend against attack.

forth [forth] *adverb.* **1.** onward or forward to the future: *Go forth from this school and make your way in the world.* **2.** having come out or into view: *The sun shone forth and ripened the crops.* 🔊 A different word with the same sound is **fourth.**

Forsythia *is a spreading plant whose stems can grow to twenty feet.*

for·ti·fi·ca·tion [_for_-ti-fi-_kay_-shun] *noun, plural* **fortifications. 1.** the act of fortifying a building or wall: *The fortification of the town was ordered by the king.* **2.** something that helps to strengthen defenses, such as a tower or wall.

FOSSILS

Fish fossil

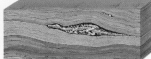
Snakefly fossil

Fossils give us clues about creatures and plants that existed billions of years ago. They are the remains of living things—usually the hard parts such as bones and teeth—that have been preserved in rock. Sometimes fossilized impressions of footprints or traces of body shapes are also found.

The carcass of a dinosaur was washed into a river and its soft parts rotted away or were eaten.

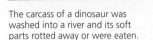

The skeleton, buried under layers of sand or mud, was protected from further decay.

Over time, the river sediments turned to rock and the bones were replaced by hard minerals.

Earth movements eventually lifted the fossil up to the surface, where it was exposed by erosion.

for·ti·fy [for-tuh-*fye*] *verb*, fortified, fortifying.
1. to strengthen against attack: *The castle was fortified by towers and turrets.* **2.** to make stronger or nourish: *They fortified themselves with hot soup before climbing the mountain.*

for·tress ▼ [for-triss] *noun, plural* **fortresses.** a place that can be defended against an enemy.

for·tu·nate [for-chuh-nit] *adjective.* having or bringing good luck; lucky: *She was fortunate to have been born with a calm manner.* **—fortunately,** *adverb.*

for·tune [for-chun] *noun, plural* **fortunes. 1.** the good or bad things that might happen to a person in the future: *I don't want to have my fortune told by a gypsy.* **2.** chance or luck: *It was his good fortune to be healthy.* **3.** a large amount of money: *Her plan is to make a fortune out of real estate.*

for·tune-tell·er someone who claims to be able to tell what will happen during a person's life.

for·ty [for-tee] *noun, plural* **forties.** ten times four; 40. *adjective.* having to do with the number forty. A **fortieth** is one of forty equal parts, or next after the thirty-ninth.

fo·rum [for-um] *noun, plural* **forums. 1.** *History.* an open, public space in ancient Rome where people could talk or do business. The forum was the center of political and religious life. This word is also spelled **Forum.**
2. a meeting or facility for people to say things and give opinions: *A forum will be held next week about the new school timetable.*

for·ward [for-wurd] *adverb.* moving toward the front in place or time; ahead: *We look forward to meeting you; The traffic cop gave the cars a signal to move forward.* This word is also spelled **forwards.**
adjective. **1.** at or toward the front, the end, or the future: *Our seats were in the forward part of the plane.*
2. too friendly or familiar; rude: *She was embarrassed by his forward remarks.*

verb, **forwarded, forwarding.** to send on or to a different address: *We'll forward your mail to you at college.*
noun, plural **forwards.** a member of a sports team who plays close to the other team's goal, in sports such as hockey and soccer.

fos·sil ▲ [fos-ul] *noun, plural* **fossils.** *Science.* a hardened part or print of an animal or plant that died many thousands of years ago: *We found fossils of human footprints in the rock surface.*

fossil fuel *Environment.* a fuel deposit made of trees, plants, or animals from many thousands of years ago. Coal, gas, and petroleum are fossil fuels. New amounts of fossil fuels cannot be produced in modern times and burning them causes pollution.

In the 1300s, Islamic rulers built the Alhambra in Granada, Spain, as a **fortress** *and palace.*

*The large, elaborate **fountain** in Place de la Concorde, Paris, France, is spectacular when lit up at night.*

foun·da·tion [foun-day-shun] *noun, plural* **foundations.**
1. the act of founding something: *The foundation of the new college was good for the town.* **2.** the base upon which something is constructed: *The foundation of a house; The foundations of this church are solid rock.* **3.** the fact or reason behind a belief: *The foundation of his belief was that education is good for children.*

found·ry [foun-dree] *noun, plural* **foundries.** a place where metal is melted down and poured or shaped into tools or other products.

foun·tain ◀ [foun-tun] *noun, plural* **fountains. 1.** a device that sends out a small stream of water for drinking. **2.** a stream of water under pressure that rises into the air from a decorative base, as within a pool or statue. **3.** any strong stream of water rising into the air. **4.** the origin or source of something: *a fountain of wisdom.*

four [for] *noun, plural* **fours.** the number between three and five; 4.
🔊 A different word with the same sound is **for.**

Four-H club a club for young people that promotes the idea that Heads, Hearts, Hands, and Health are all important in maintaining family life and farming.

four·teen [for-teen] *noun, plural* **fourteens.** the number between thirteen and fifteen; 14. A **fourteenth** is one of fourteen equal parts, or next after the thirteenth.

fourth [forth] *adjective.* the place that is number four in a series; the place between third and fifth. *noun, plural* **fourths.** one of four equal parts or quarters.
🔊 A different word with the same sound is **forth.**

Fourth of July the national holiday of the United States; Independence Day. It honors the day when the country was founded—July 4, 1776.

fowl ◀ [foul] *noun, plural* **fowl** or **fowls.** a bird kept for eating or laying eggs. Chickens, ducks, and geese are all fowl.
🔊 A different word with the same sound is **foul.**

fox ▼ [foks] *noun, plural* **foxes. 1.** a small wild animal related to the dog. It has a reddish coat, bushy tail, a slim head, and is known for its cunning. **2.** a fox's fur, worn as a piece of clothing. **3.** a cunning or deceptive person. A sly or cunning person is **foxy.**

fos·ter [faws-tur] *verb,* **fostered, fostering.** to promote the growth of something: *The English teacher fostered an appreciation of literature in her classes. adjective.* having to do with a family that takes care of a child not related to it by birth or adoption: *Jasmine has a strong relationship with her foster family.*

fought [fawt] *verb.* the past tense of FIGHT.
🔊 A different word with the same sound is **fort.**

foul [foul] *adjective.* **fouler, foulest.**
1. dirty or unpleasant: *There's a foul smell coming from the basement.* **2.** describing bad or stormy weather conditions: *It's a foul night outside.* **3.** evil or cruel: *He was the victim of a foul murder.* **4.** against the rules, unfair: *She suspected foul play when she lost her job.* **5.** outside the foul line in a baseball game. *noun, plural* **fouls. 1.** the act of breaking a rule in certain sports such as basketball, football, or soccer: *It is a foul in soccer to trip or kick an opposing player.* **2.** a ball hit outside the foul line in baseball. *verb,* **fouled, fouling. 1.** to make filthy; pollute: *Automobile fumes fouled the city's air.* **2.** to twist or mess up: *The boat's tow rope became fouled in weeds.* **3.** to commit an act against the rules in certain sports. **4.** to hit a ball outside the foul line in baseball.
🔊 A different word with the same sound is **fowl.**

foul line either of the two straight lines in baseball that go from the rear corner of home plate through first and third base to the outer edge of the playing field.

found[1] [found] *verb.* the past tense and past participle of FIND.

found[2] [found] *verb,* **founded, founding.** to establish something: *The company was founded in 1896.* A **founder** is a person who establishes something.

*Various **fowl** have been bred for eating and for their eggs for more than 4,000 years.*

Duck

Turkey

Goose

Rooster

Foxes are mostly meat-eaters and, unlike wild dogs, they usually hunt their prey alone and at night.

Foxhounds *are bred for strength, speed, and their ability to hunt.*

fox·hound ▶
[foks-hound] *noun,*
plural **foxhounds.**
a dog with a good sense
of smell, bred especially
to hunt foxes. These
dogs hunt in a pack and
lead people on horses
to find and chase a fox.

frac·tion [frak-shun]
noun, plural **fractions.**
1. *Mathematics.*
a division or part
of a whole number;
a fraction is shown by one number divided by another:
½ and ⅔ are both fractions. A **fractional** number is
one that is expressed as a fraction. **2.** a small part
of something: *Only a fraction of the class passed the
geography exam; a fraction of a second.*

The word **fraction** originally meant "the breaking off
of a part." A fraction such as ¼ or ⅔ is a part of a whole
number, as if it were a smaller part broken off from
that number.

frac·ture ▶ [frak-chur] *verb,* **fractured, fracturing.**
to crack or break something solid, especially a bone.
noun, plural **fractures.** a break or crack in a bone:
*I got two fractures in my right leg in the
ski accident.*

frag·ile [frag-ul] *adjective.* easily damaged
or broken: *The china teapot is very fragile,
so be careful with it.* **Fragility** is the fact
of being easily damaged.

frag·ment [frag-munt] *noun,*
plural **fragments.** a small piece of
something that has been broken off or
smashed: *There are fragments of glass
where the bottle broke.* Something that
is made up of small pieces broken off
is called **fragmentary.**

fra·grance [fray-gruns] *noun,*
plural **fragrances.** a sweet or pleasant
smell, such as a flower or perfume:
The fragrance of lavender is quite strong.
When a flower smells pleasant, it is **fragrant.**

frail [frale] *adjective,* **frailer, frailest.** having weak or delicate
health or a lack of strength: *The old lady is frail, but her
mind is still sharp.* The state of being weak in strength
or health is **frailty.**

frame [frame] *noun, plural* **frames. 1.** a border or case,
usually in the shape of a square or rectangle, in which
something fits or is enclosed: *a picture frame; a door
frame.* **2.** a set of connected parts giving shape or support
to something: *the metal frame of a bed.* **3.** the shape or
form of a person's body: *a football player with a powerful
frame.* **4.** a single complete picture in a series in a film,
video, or the like.

In a compound
fracture,
*a bone breaks
and pierces
the skin.*

Broken
bone

verb, **framed, framing. 1.** to set within a frame: *to frame
a photograph.* **2.** to put thoughts together in a certain way,
as if organizing them within a frame: *James Madison and
Alexander Hamilton were leaders among those who framed
the U.S. Constitution.* **3.** to make an innocent person seem
to be guilty by means of false evidence. **—framer,** *noun.*

frame·work [frame-wurk] *noun, plural* **frameworks.**
a structure that supports or shapes something:
The framework of houses is often made of wood.

franc [frangk] *noun, plural* **francs. 1.** a unit of money
that was used in France for many years, now replaced
by the euro. **2.** a similar currency used in Switzerland
(Swiss franc) and parts of Africa and Asia.
🔊 A different word with the same sound is **frank.**

frank [frangk] *adjective,* **franker, frankest.** open, honest,
and direct in thought or speech: *To be frank, your exam
results are not as good as they could be.* **—frankly,** *adverb;*
frankness, *noun.*
🔊 A different word with the same sound is **franc.**

frank·furt·er [frangk-fur-tur] *noun, plural* **frankfurters.**
a small, thin, reddish sausage made of spiced, cooked pork
or beef, usually served in a roll with mustard and other
flavorings. Also called a **frank** or a **hot dog.**

The word **frankfurter** comes from *Frankfurt,*
a large and important city in Germany. It is
thought that this food was first served in the
United States by people who came to the
country from the city of Frankfurt.

fran·tic [fran-tik] *adjective.* describing excessive
activity caused by fear, pain, or excitement: *He was
frantic when he realized his dog had got out of the
yard and run away.* **—frantically,** *adverb.*

fra·ter·ni·ty [fruh-turn-i-tee] *noun,*
plural **fraternities. 1.** the fact of feeling a sense
of friendship or community with other people.
2. a group of people who have work, educational,
or other interests in common. **3.** a group of students
at a college or university who form a club and have
shared social events and often live in the same
building, known as a **fraternity house.**

The word **fraternity** comes from the Latin word for
"brother." The idea is that men who are in the same
fraternity, as at a college, are somewhat like a group of
brothers in the way they relate to each other.

fraud [frawd] *noun, plural* **frauds.** *Law.* **1.** the act of
deliberately misleading someone in order to gain an
(illegal) advantage. **2.** a person or thing that is not what
he or it is claimed to be; an impostor. Behavior that is
deliberately misleading is **fraudulent.**

fray[1] [fray] *verb,* **frayed, fraying.** to become worn and
ragged: *The cuffs of this old shirt are frayed.*

fray[2] [fray] *noun, plural* **frays.** a noisy quarrel or
disturbance involving a group of people: *Their friends got
into a big argument at the party, so they joined in the fray.*

a
b
c
d
e
f
g
h
i
j
k
l
m
n
o
p
q
r
s
t
u
v
w
x
y
z

Roads providing access to and exit from two intersecting freeways form a clover-leaf pattern.

freak [freek] *noun, plural* **freaks. 1.** a plant, animal, or person that has developed unusual or abnormal features: *The goat with two sets of horns and two tails was a freak.* **2.** a very unusual thing or event: *The fisherman was hit by a freak wave that was forty feet high.* A very unusual event can be described as **freakish.**

freck·le [frek-ul] *noun, plural* **freckles.** a small brown spot on the skin. Skin that has many such spots is **freckled.**

free [free] *adjective,* **freer, freest. 1.** not costing money; at no cost: *The Independence Day concert in the park was free.* **2.** having the ability to do as one likes; not controlled by others: *The birds are free to fly where they choose.* **3.** not restricted or confined: *After the end of school term we felt free.* **4.** not affected by something; without symptoms: *The patient was free of disease when he left the hospital.* **5.** not blocked; open: *The aisles of the airplane must be free of luggage at all times.* *verb,* **freed, freeing.** to allow to go free: *The prisoner was freed after two years.* —**freely,** *adverb.*

free·dom [free-dum] *noun, plural* **freedoms. 1.** the state of being free; being able to act, speak, write, or move about as one wishes. **2.** the fact of being able to move without restriction: *The loose clothes gave her arms freedom of movement.*

free market *Business.* a system of buying and selling things that is based on having as little control or restriction by the government as possible, so that companies freely compete to offer the best goods and services at the lowest price. The **free enterprise system** allows people and companies to offer labor and goods freely with little state control.

*There may be up to four **French horns** in the brass section of a symphony orchestra.*

free·ware [free-ware] *noun. Computers.* software that is available at no cost for personal use.

free·way ◀ [free-way] *noun, plural* **freeways.** a multi-lane highway with controlled access and no traffic lights, turns, or other restrictions to traffic flow; not all freeways are actually free of tolls.

freeze [freez] *verb,* **froze, frozen, freezing. 1.** to harden because of being very cold: *Water freezes to become ice.* **2.** to become blocked because of extreme cold: *The pipe froze overnight.* **3.** to cause to become very cold: *We were freezing while we watched the outdoor hockey game.* **4.** to stop quickly or be unable to move out of fear: *They all froze at the sight of the gunman.* **5.** to be ruined or damaged by frost or ice: *This year the wine grapes froze before they could be harvested.* *noun.* **1.** a period of very cold weather: *The country was in the grip of a deep freeze.* **2.** a stop or halt: *The stores put a freeze on selling the toy until they could be sure it was safe.*

freez·er [freez-ur] *noun, plural* **freezers.** the part of a refrigerator, or a whole refrigerator, where goods are frozen for storage.

freezing point *Science.* the temperature at which a liquid becomes a solid when cooled; the freezing point of water is 32 degrees Fahrenheit (0 degrees Celsius).

freight [frate] *noun.* **1.** the transportation of goods by land, water, or air. **2.** the goods transported: *A lot of sea and land freight is carried in containers.*

*Modern **freighters** carry cargo in large, sealed containers.*

freight·er ▲ [frate-ur] *noun, plural* **freighters.** a ship or airplane that carries only freight, not passengers.

French [french] *noun.* **1.** the people who live in the country of France. **2.** the language French people speak. *adjective.* having to do with the people, language, or culture of France. A **Frenchman** is a man who was born in France; a **Frenchwoman** is a woman who was born in France.

French fries thin, square-cut strips of deep-fried potatoes.

In 2003 members of the U.S. Congress ordered that **French fries** should be called "freedom fries" when they were served in restaurants run by the House of Representatives. This was part of a movement by certain restaurants to avoid serving food called "French," in protest against the fact that the French nation did not support the U.S. invasion of Iraq. Food experts pointed out that the real name of French fries should be "Belgian fries," because Belgium, not France, was the first nation to have this food.

French horn ◀ *Music.* a brass, wind instrument that is formed by a long, coiled tube that opens into a wide bell. It has a mouthpiece and three valves.

fren·zy [fren-zee] *noun, plural* **frenzies.** a state of extreme excitement or emotion: *The band worked the audience into a frenzy with their music.* Someone who is in a state of extreme excitement is **frenzied.**

fre·quen·cy [free-kwun-see] *noun, plural* **frequencies.**
1. the fact of happening again and again: *The frequency of his sick days made the teachers suspicious.*
2. the number of times something happens within a particular time period: *The doctor measured the frequency of my pulse.* **3.** the number of times per second that a radio wave or other kind of wave or radiation is produced.

fre·quent [free-kwint *for adjective;* free-kwent *for verb*] *adjective.* happening often; common: *My aunt is a frequent visitor to our house.* —**frequently,** *adverb.*

fresh [fresh] *adjective,* **fresher, freshest.**
1. newly made or obtained: *Mom made some fresh coffee.* **2.** different or another: *His shirt got wet so he put on a fresh one.* **3.** pure or refreshing: *fresh mountain air.* **4.** of water, not salty: *Lakes have fresh water.* **5.** improperly forward or rude: *He was scolded by his mother for being fresh.*

fresh·en [fresh-un] *verb,* **freshened, freshening.** to make fresh; renew: *We freshened up before dinner.*

fresh·man [fresh-mun] *noun, plural* **freshmen.** a student in the first year of high school or college.

fresh·wa·ter ▼ [fresh-wawt-ur] *adjective.* of or living in water that is fresh or not salty: *The trout is a freshwater fish.*

fric·tion [frik-shun] *noun.*
1. the rubbing of the surface of one thing against another: *The friction from rubbing my hands together made them hot.*
2. the force that makes it difficult for one surface to move easily over another surface: *Dad put oil on the machine to reduce the friction and get the parts moving smoothly.*
3. a struggle or disagreement: *There was friction between me and my best friend while we were on different Little League teams.*

Fri·day [fry-day *or* fry-dee] *noun, plural* **Fridays.** the sixth day of the week, after Thursday and before Saturday.

The word **Friday** was originally "Frigg's day." Frigg was a goddess of love in the ancient world, and her day, Friday, was considered a lucky day.

When you have a sudden **fright,** *your skin sweats, your eyes open wider, and your hair stands on end.*

fried [fryd] *verb.* the past tense and past participle of FRY.

friend [frend] *noun, plural* **friends. 1.** a person not in your family whom you know and like and who likes you; someone you like to spend time with and do things with. **2.** someone who supports something by giving help or money: *He is a friend of the Arts Society.*

friend·ly [frend-lee] *adjective,* **friendlier, friendliest.**
1. like a friend; showing friendship; warm or kind: *She gave a friendly wave when we arrived.* **2.** not an enemy; not hostile: *A friendly warship is docked in our harbor.* —**friendliness,** *noun.*

friend·ship [frend-ship] *noun, plural* **friendships.** the fact of being friends with someone; the relationship between friends.

fright ◀ [frite] *noun, plural* **frights.**
1. a sudden feeling of fear or terror.
2. a person or thing that looks ugly, shocking, or stupid: *She looked a fright after her terrible haircut.*

fright·en [frite-un] *verb,* **frightened, frightening.**
1. to scare or make afraid: *He jumped out of the closet and frightened me.* **2.** to force or drive away by scaring: *The sound of our voices frightened the deer away.* When something or someone makes you feel afraid or scared, it is **frightening.**

fright·ful [frite-ful] *adjective.* **1.** causing fear or alarm. **2.** revolting or unpleasant: *His bedroom is a frightful mess.* —**frightfully,** *adverb.*

Brolgas, storks, and ducks flock to a **freshwater** *lagoon, where they can find plenty of food and water.*

frigid

A B C D E F G H I J K L M N O P Q R S T U V W X Y Z

frig·id [frij-id] *adjective.* **1.** extremely cold: *Antarctica is a frigid environment.* **2.** not showing warmth; unfriendly: *He gave me a frigid stare.* The fact of being cold or unfriendly is **frigidity.** —**frigidly,** *adverb.*

fringe [frinj] *noun, plural* **fringes. 1.** a decorative edge or border of loose hanging threads or cords: *My red scarf has a white fringe.* **2.** something that resembles this sort of decorative edge or border: *There is a fringe of flowers around the pond.* A **fringe benefit** is a service or advantage received by employees in addition to their wages. Free health insurance, company cars, and paid holidays are examples of fringe benefits.

friv·o·lous [friv-uh-lus] *adjective.* silly or foolish: *I got into trouble for giving frivolous answers to the exam questions.* —**frivolously,** *adverb;* —**frivolousness,** *noun.*

frog ▼ [frog *or* frawg] *noun, plural* **frogs.** a small, tailless animal with long back legs for jumping from place to place. An amphibian, it lives in water or on land and has webbed feet and smooth, moist skin.

from [frum] *preposition.* **1.** showing a certain place, position, or time as the starting point: *to drive from Dallas to Houston; to get a phone call from Grandma; to work from 9:00 until 5:00.* **2.** showing the source or cause of something: *a soup made from tomatoes; She was exhausted from working so hard; I know that boy from school.* **3.** showing a difference between things: *You can tell Indian elephants from African ones by their ears.*

front ▶ [frunt] *noun, plural* **fronts. 1.** the part that faces forward or is seen first: *The mailbox is at the front of the house.* **2.** the land bordering a road or shore: *the lake front.* **3.** in a war, an area where active fighting is going on: *The soldier was wounded at the front.* **4.** in weather, the boundary where two different air masses of different temperatures meet: *Warm fronts often bring light rain and warm, dry air.*
adjective. on or at the front of something: *the front wheel of a bicycle.*
verb, **fronted, fronting.** to have the front toward; face: *The apartment fronts onto the street.*

FROGS

Frogs eggs are usually laid in water, but adult frogs spend much of their lives on land. They can be found in nearly all habitats, from deserts and savannas to mountains and tropical rainforests. Most frogs feed on insects and spiders, but some larger kinds, such as the North American bullfrog, eat small birds, mice, turtles, fish, young snakes, and even smaller frogs of their own species. Frogs communicate by croaking and in some tropical areas their loud chorus can be heard at dusk. Each kind of frog has its own special call. Frogs avoid danger by camouflage or jumping. Some deter attackers with brightly colored poisonous skin or by puffing up their bodies.

Treefrog

Harlequin frog

Orange and black poison frog

FROG LIFE CYCLE

4 About six weeks after hatching the young frog is fully formed and leaves the water.

1 Eggs are laid and fertilized in water.

2 Tadpoles hatch after about two weeks and live in the water, breathing through gills and feeding on algae and weeds.

3 Over the next few weeks, lungs replace gills for breathing, limbs form, and the tail gradually disappears.

*In a cold **front**, cold air pushes into warmer air; in a warm front, warm air moves over cooler air.*

COLD FRONT

Cold air

Warm air

WARM FRONT

Warm air

Cold air

fron·tier [fron-<u>teer</u>] *noun, plural* **frontiers. 1.** *History.* in early America, the border between the area to the west where Indians lived, and the area to the east that was explored and settled by people originally from Europe. The frontier gradually moved westward as time went on. A person who lived on the frontier was known as a **frontiersman** or **frontierswoman. 2.** a border between a part of a country that has been settled and another area where people have not settled. **3.** any border between two countries: *The Niagara River forms part of the frontier between Canada and the United States.* **4.** an underdeveloped field of study or the newest activities in research: *the frontiers of nuclear medicine.*

frost ▼ [frawst] *noun, plural* **frosts. 1.** the white powdery layer of ice that forms when dew freezes. **2.** an extremely cold temperature that causes freezing. Something that is extremely cold is described as **frosty.** *verb,* **frosted, frosting. 1.** to cover with frost: *Our front lawn frosted over.* **2.** to cover with icing or frosting: *Mom frosted the cake.*

frost·bite [<u>frawst</u>-bite] *noun. Health.* damage to some part of the body caused by excessive exposure to the extreme cold. *verb,* **frostbit, frostbitten, frostbiting.** to damage by exposing some part of the body to extreme cold: *The climber's fingers were frostbitten.*

frost·ing [<u>frawst</u>-ing] *noun, plural* **frostings.** a mixture of sugar and butter used to cover, decorate, or fill cakes and cookies; icing.

froth [frawth] *noun, plural* **froths.** a mass of tiny bubbles that rise to the surface of a liquid: *A froth formed as the soup boiled.* A liquid that has lots of small bubbles on top is **frothy.** *verb,* **frothed, frothing.** to produce or give out froth: *The soda frothed up after I shook the can.*

frown [froun] *noun, plural* **frowns.** a wrinkling of the forehead in a look of worry, anger, or deep thought. *verb,* **frowned, frowning. 1.** to wrinkle the forehead in worry, anger, or deep thought. **2.** to disapprove of: *My grandma frowns on some of the clothes I wear.*

froze [froze] *verb.* the past tense of FREEZE.

fro·zen [<u>froh</u>-zun] *verb.* the past participle of FREEZE.

fruit [froot] *noun plural* **fruits. 1.** the part of a plant that contains the seeds such as nuts, berries, or pods. **2.** the part of a plant or tree that contains the seeds and can be eaten such as oranges, apples, or cherries.

frus·trate [<u>frus</u>-trate] *verb,* **frustrated, frustrating.** to stop someone's efforts or prevent something from being achieved: *The strong wind frustrated my attempt to rake the leaves.* When a person feels annoyed or upset that they cannot achieve something, they feel **frustrated.** Something or someone is described as **frustrating** when it makes you feel annoyed or upset because you cannot achieve what you want. **—frustration,** *noun.*

fry [frye] *verb,* **fried, frying.** to cook food in hot oil or fat: *I fried the mushrooms in some butter.* *noun, plural* **fries.** a long, thin piece of potato that is fried and eaten hot: *steak and fries.*

ft., ft an abbreviation for FEET or FOOT.

fudge [fuj] *noun, plural* **fudges.** a soft, creamy candy made from sugar, butter, milk, and flavoring.

fuel [<u>fyoo</u>-ul] *noun, plural* **fuels.** any substance such as coal, wood, or oil that can be burned to provide heat or power. *verb,* **fueled, fueling.** to get or supply with a substance that can be burned to provide heat or power:

Fuel goes back to the Latin word for "fireplace." Though many different things can be used as fuel today, such as oil, coal, or gas, in ancient times there was really only one important fuel, wood, which would be burned in a fireplace.

fuel cell *Science.* a device that combines two different elements of a fuel, such as hydrogen and oxygen, to produce electricity.

*On clear, cold nights, heat from the ground escapes into the air, temperatures fall, and ice crystals form **frost.***

E
F
G
H
I
J
K
L
M
N
O
P
Q
R
S
T
U
V
W
X
Y
Z

fu·gi·tive [fyoo-juh-tiv] *noun,*
plural **fugitives.** a person who
is running away or trying to
escape from the police or a
dangerous situation: *The police
appealed to the public for any
information about the fugitive.*
adjective. trying to or having run
away: *a fugitive slave.*

ful·fill [ful-fil] *verb,* **fulfilled, fulfilling. 1.** to carry out or
achieve something: *Dad fulfilled his promise to buy me a
new bike.* **2.** to provide what is necessary; satisfy: *The layout
of the science lab fulfills safety requirements.*
—**fulfillment,** *noun.*

full [ful] *adjective.* **1.** containing as much or as many as
possible; filled: *My plate was full of food.* **2.** containing
a large number or quantity: *This old jacket is full of holes.*
3. being complete or the maximum amount: *He was driving
the car at full speed.* **4.** being large and rounded: *Her full
figure made her an attractive woman.*
adverb, **fuller, fullest.** completely; entirely: *I filled the jar
full with candy.*

full·back [ful-bak] *noun,*
plural **fullbacks. 1.** a player
in football who plays in
the offensive backfield to
run with the ball or block
for a runner. **2.** a player in
soccer who plays on the
outside as a defender.

full moon ▲ **1.** the moon
when you can see all of it
as a complete illuminated
circle. **2.** the phase of the Moon when this happens:
There's a full moon tonight.

> The **fullback** in football
> or soccer was so called
> because in the earlier
> years of each game, this
> player's position was fully
> (all the way) back from
> the other team's goal.
> The name is still used,
> even though the position
> is not the farthest back.

ful·ly [ful-lee] *adverb.* **1.** in a full way;
totally; completely: *I have fully recovered
from my illness.* **2.** at least: *Fully half the
class forgot their homework.*

fum·ble [fum-bul] *verb,* **fumbled, fumbling.
1.** to feel about clumsily or awkwardly:
*I fumbled in my purse looking for some
spare change.* **2.** to drop a ball:
*The running back fumbled and the other
team got the ball.*
noun, *plural* **fumbles.** the act of fumbling
a ball in sports.

fume [fyoom] *noun, plural* **fumes.** smoke
or gas that can be seen or smelled.
verb, **fumed, fuming.** to be very angry:
I was fuming after the argument with him.

fun [fun] *noun.* **1.** someone or something
that brings enjoyment or pleasure: *Skiing
is a lot of fun.* **2.** playful and energetic
activity: *Young children are full of fun.*
• **make fun of.** to make a joke of someone
or something in an unkind way:
They made fun of his new haircut.

func·tion [fungk-shun] *noun, plural* **functions. 1.** what
something or someone is meant to do; the purpose of
something: *The function of the kettle is to boil water.*
2. a formal occasion or gathering: *Their wedding is
going to be a small and intimate function.*
verb, **functioned, functioning.** to operate properly; work:
The computer isn't functioning very well. Something
that is designed to be useful and work well is said
to be **functional.**

fund [fund] *noun, plural* **funds. 1.** a sum of money saved
or collected for a particular purpose: *I will get my trust
fund when I turn twenty one years old.* **2.** a quantity
of something ready for use: a supply: *He has a fund of
experience in the business world.* **3. funds.** money that
is immediately available: *The church funds were used to
restore the windows.*
verb, **funded, funding.** to provide money to pay for
an event or organization: *My school is funding our team
to go to the championships in New York.*

fun·da·men·tal [fun-duh-men-tul] *adjective.* serving as
a foundation or basis: *Reading music is fundamental to
learning to play a musical instrument.*
noun, plural **fundamentals.** the most important or
essential part: *I am learning the fundamentals of physics.*
—**fundamentally,** *adverb.*

fu·ner·al [fyoon-rul *or* fyoo-nuh-rul] *noun,*
plural **funerals.** a ceremony for burying or cremating
someone who has died.

fun·gi ▼ [fun-jee *or* fun-jye; fung-gee *or* fung-gye] *noun.*
the plural of fungus.

fun·gus [fung-gis] *noun, plural* **fungi** *or* **funguses.** *Biology.*
a simple type of plant that has no leaves or flowers, such
as a mushroom or mold. Something that is characteristic
of or caused by a fungus is **fungal.**

FUNGI

About 70,000 kinds of fungi include mushrooms, molds, mildews,
and rust on plants. Fungi have no roots, stems, or leaves, and often
grow in the dark. They feed on other plants and animals—dead
or alive. Most fungi are made up of threadlike cells called hyphae,
which break down their food. Mushrooms are the fruiting bodies
of fungi and come in different shapes and colors. The gills under
the cap of the fruiting body release spores, from
which new fungi grow. Some mushrooms
are good to eat but others, often called
toadstools, are poisonous.

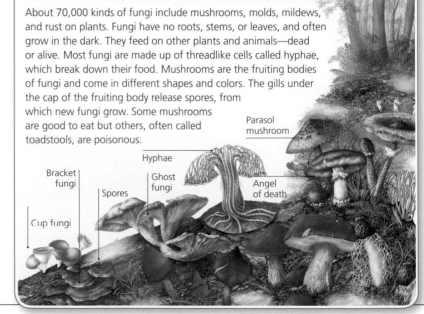

Parasol
mushroom

Hyphae

Bracket
fungi

Ghost
fungi

Angel
of death

Spores

Cup fungi

fun·ny [fun-ee] *adjective,* **funnier, funniest. 1.** causing laughter; amusing: *We saw a really funny movie last night.* **2.** strange or unusual: *I don't know who lives there, but there's something funny about that old house.*

fur [fur] *noun, plural* **furs. 1.** the thick, soft coat of hair that covers some animals: *My dog has shiny, black fur.* **2.** the hair-covered skin of an animal that has been removed from the body. Fur is sometimes treated and used for making clothing or other goods. **3.** a piece of clothing made of fur.

🔊 A different word with the same sound is **fir.**

fu·ri·ous [fyur-ee-us] *adjective.* **1.** being extremely angry: *He was furious when he saw that someone had taken his bike and he had no way to get home.* **2.** describing something violent; strong: *a furious wind.* —**furiously,** *adverb.*

fur·nace ▶ [fur-nis] *noun, plural* **furnaces.** a structure or container in which heat is generated for melting metals or heating buildings.

fur·nish [fur-nish] *verb,* **furnished, furnishing. 1.** to decorate or supply with furniture: *I furnished my bedroom with a bed, dresser, and a recliner chair.* The furniture or other decorations in a room or building are **furnishings. 2.** to provide or supply something needed: *They furnished us with a map to get to the wedding.*

fur·ni·ture [fur-nuh-chur] *noun.* items such as chairs, beds, tables, and other such things put into a house or building to make it comfortable or functional.

fur·row [fur-oh] *noun, plural* **furrows.** a long, narrow groove cut into the surface of something: *There were deep furrows in the plowed field.*

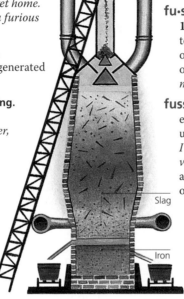

Slag

Iron

In a steel-making **furnace,** *fuel is blasted with hot air to make iron and a waste material called slag.*

fur·ry [fur-ee] *adjective,* **furrier, furriest.** resembling or covered with fur: *A raccoon is a furry animal.*

fur·ther [fur-THur] *adjective.* in addition; more: *She came back for further advice.*
adverb. **1.** to a greater degree or amount; more: *I want to read further on that subject.* **2.** at or to a greater distance; farther: *I ran further than everyone else.*
verb, **furthered, furthering.** to support or advance something: *The movie actor was furthering the cause of cancer research.*

Further and **farther** are similar words. According to an old rule, *farther* should be used for distance that can be measured, and *further* for things that are not measured, such as wanting to go *further* in school. However, people use both words the same way, and this "rule" does not need to be followed.

fur·ther·more [fur-THur-more] *adverb.* in addition; more importantly: *The shoes are stylish and comfortable, and furthermore, they are on sale now.*

fur·thest [fur-THist] *adjective; adverb.* a superlative form of FAR.

fu·ry [fyoo-ree] *noun, plural* **furies. 1.** extreme or violent anger: *She threw the vase at the wall in her fury.* **2.** a violent and dangerous force: *The fury of the storm was frightening.*

fuse[1] [fyooz] *noun, plural* **fuses. 1.** an electrical safety device having a metal or wire strip that interrupts and breaks the circuit if the current is too strong. **2.** a wick connected to an explosive device that, when lit, causes it to explode.

fuse[2] [fyooz] *verb,* **fused, fusing. 1.** to melt by heating: *A blowtorch was used to fuse the lead metal.* **2.** to join or combine: *When a new life is created, the egg and sperm fuse together as one cell.*

fu·sion [fyoo-zhun] *noun, plural* **fusions. 1.** *Science.* the union of two light atomic nuclei to form a single nucleus, resulting in the release of huge amounts of energy. **2.** the act or process of melting or combining: *the fusion of two metals to form an alloy.*

fuss [fuss] *noun, plural* **fusses.** unnecessary excitement or bother over something unimportant: *He made such a fuss when I was late.*
verb, **fussed, fussing.** to give too much attention and unnecessary importance to something or someone. Someone who is **fussy** is often difficult to please and tends to worry too much about unimportant things.

fu·tile [fyoo-tul *or* fyoo-tile] *adjective.* describing something useless and ineffective: *It was futile to try to cheer her up.* —**futilely,** *adverb.*

fu·ture [fyoo-chur] *adjective.* happening or existing in the period of time that is yet to come: *She kept thinking about what her future husband might look like.*
noun. **1.** the period of time that is yet to come: *He's a talented artist with a good future ahead of him.* **2.** another word for FUTURE TENSE.

future tense *Language.* the form of a verb that shows that something is going to happen at a later time.

Many books say that the **future tense** is shown by "will," for example, "We *will* go to the beach tomorrow." However, the normal way to say what you plan to do is *going to* (often said as "gonna"), as in "We're *going to* watch the big game on TV tomorrow." "Will" is used when you want to show that you are determined to do something: "The project is due in just two days, but I *will* get it done on time."

fuzz [fuz] *noun.* fine, soft hair or a substance resembling hair that covers something: *The newborn baby had a fuzz of blond hair on his head.*

fuzz·y [fuz-ee] *adjective,* **fuzzier, fuzziest. 1.** covered with soft hair or a similar substance: *A peach has fuzzy skin.* **2.** as if covered or obscured by fuzz; unclear; blurred: *a fuzzy picture.* —**fuzziness,** *noun.*

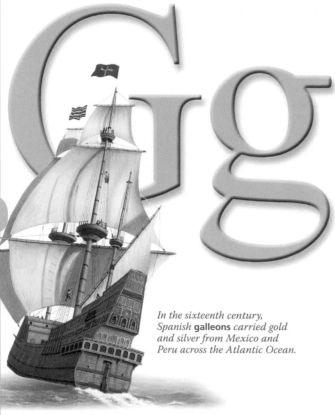

*In the sixteenth century, Spanish **galleons** carried gold and silver from Mexico and Peru across the Atlantic Ocean.*

G, g *noun, plural* **G's, g's.** the seventh letter of the English alphabet.

gad·get [gaj-it] *noun, plural* **gadgets.** a small tool or device that performs a particular purpose: *Dad has a little gadget that shows how much power each appliance in the house is using.*

gag [gag] *noun, plural* **gags. 1.** something that is tied around the mouth or put inside it to stop someone from speaking or making a sound. **2.** something said to be funny; a joke. *verb,* **gagged, gagging. 1.** to prevent someone from speaking or shouting by using a gag. **2.** to be unable to swallow and feel as though you are about to vomit: *The disgusting smell mad me gag.*

gai·ly [gay-lee] *adverb.* in a happy or bright manner: *The dining table was gaily decorated with fresh flowers.*

gain [gane] *verb,* **gained, gaining. 1.** to come to have; obtain or achieve something: *We gained permission to leave class early.* **2.** to get an advantage or benefit: *We all gained from Grandma winning the lottery. noun, plural* **gains.** an increase or advance: *a gain in weight.*

gait [gate] *noun, plural* **gaits.** a way of walking or moving: *He walked with a slow, shuffling gait.*

🔊 A different word with the same sound is **gate.**

gal·axy [gal-ik-see] *noun, plural* **galaxies.** a large group of stars held together by the force of gravitation. The galaxy that contains our Sun and planets is the Milky Way.

gale [gale] *noun, plural* **gales. 1.** a very strong wind. **2.** a noisy outburst: *a gale of laughter.*

> **Galaxy** goes back to a word used by the ancient Greeks for "milk." The one galaxy that ancient people knew about was the Milky Way, because it could be seen without a telescope. This was so called because it looked like a streak of white across the night sky, as if milk had been poured out there.

gal·lant [gal-unt] *adjective.* having to do with being brave and noble: *Sir Lancelot was one of King Arthur's gallant knights of the Round Table.* Courage in battle is known as **gallantry.** —**gallantly,** *adverb.*

gall·blad·der [gawl-blad-ur] *noun. Medicine.* an organ in the body attached to the liver that contains a substance called bile, which helps to digest food. Bile is also known as **gall.**

gal·le·on ◀ [gal-ee-un] *noun, plural* **galleons.** *History.* a large Spanish merchant ship or warship with three or four masts, used from the fifteenth to the seventeenth century.

gal·ler·y [gal-ree *or* gal-uh-ree] *noun, plural* **galleries. 1.** an upper floor or balcony in a theater or other building. **2.** a room, series of rooms, or building where works of art are exhibited or sold.

gal·ley [gal-ee] *noun, plural* **galleys. 1.** *History.* a long, low ship with sails and oars, usually rowed by prisoners or slaves. **2.** the kitchen on a ship or airplane.

gal·lon [gal-un] *noun, plural* **gallons.** a measure of liquid equal to about 3.8 liters. Four quarts make one gallon.

gal·lop ▼ [gal-up] *noun, plural* **gallops.** the fastest movement of a horse. *verb,* **galloped, galloping.** to ride a horse at full speed.

gal·lows [gal-ohz] *noun, plural* **gallows** *or* **gallowses.** a wooden structure used in the past to execute criminals by hanging.

ga·losh·es [guh-losh-iz] *plural noun.* waterproof shoes made of rubber or plastic, worn over ordinary shoes for protection from rain or snow.

*When horses **gallop,** each hoof strikes the ground separately.*

gam·ble [gam-bul] *verb,* **gambled, gambling.**
1. to bet money that something might happen or not happen: *She gambles five dollars each Saturday morning on the state lottery.* The activity or sport of doing this is **gambling,** such as betting on horse races, football games, or games played with cards or dice. A **gambler** is someone who often bets money.
2. to do something risky or take a chance: *I gambled that the shoes would fit and bought them without trying them on.*
noun, plural **gambles.** something that involves a risk: *Having a player who's been hurt all season pitch the big game will be a real gamble.*

game [game] *noun, plural* **games.**
1. something done for fun or amusement: *Jeff and his brother played a game of catch on the way home from school.* **2.** a sport or competition with a set of rules: *a game of football.* **3.** wild animals that are hunted for food or sport.
adjective. having an adventurous or fighting spirit: *Are you game enough to go rock climbing?*

gan·der [gan-dur] *noun, plural* **ganders.** a male goose.

gang [gang] *noun, plural* **gangs. 1.** people who act together to commit crimes. **2.** a group of young people from the same area who are part of a group with a certain name and who act together to fight other gangs and often to commit crimes. **3.** any group of people working or acting together: *Maddie is going to have the whole gang from school over for a party.*
verb. **gang up on.** to combine or unite against: *All the kids ganged up on the new boy.*

gang·plank ▲ [gang-plangk] *noun, plural* **gangplanks.** a movable board used as a bridge to help people get on and off a boat or ship.

gang·ster [gang-stur] *noun, plural* **gangsters.** a member of a gang of criminals.

gang·way [gang-way] *noun, plural* **gangways. 1.** a passageway on a ship. **2.** a gangplank.
interjection. something that is shouted to tell people in a crowd to move aside and let you pass through.

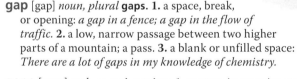

Gardenias are popular with gardeners because of their attractive flowers and strong scent.

gap [gap] *noun, plural* **gaps. 1.** a space, break, or opening: *a gap in a fence; a gap in the flow of traffic.* **2.** a low, narrow passage between two higher parts of a mountain; a pass. **3.** a blank or unfilled space: *There are a lot of gaps in my knowledge of chemistry.*

gape [gape] *verb,* **gaped, gaping. 1.** to stare in surprise or wonder with your mouth wide open: *We stood gaping at her newly dyed hair.* **2.** to be or become wide open: *His pants were gaping at the seams.* Something that is very wide or open is described as **gaping.**

ga·rage [guh-rahzh *or* guh-raj] *noun, plural* **garages.** a building or indoor area where vehicles are parked or repaired.
verb, **garaged, garaging.** to keep or put in a garage. A **garage sale** is a sale of unwanted household and personal goods, usually held in or near someone's garage.

gar·bage [gar-bij] *noun.* waste material that is thrown away, especially waste food from a kitchen.

gar·den [gard-un] *noun, plural* **gardens.** an area where flowers, plants, and vegetables are grown.
verb, **gardened, gardening.** to work in a garden. A person who grows and takes care of plants and flowers is a **gardener.**

gar·de·nia ▲ [gar-deen-yuh] *noun, plural* **gardenias.** a bush that bears large, sweet-smelling white or yellow flowers.

gar·gle [gar-gul] *verb,* **gargled, gargling.** to move a liquid around inside your throat without swallowing, using your breathing to make it bubble.
noun, plural **gargles.** any liquid used for gargling, such as a mouthwash.

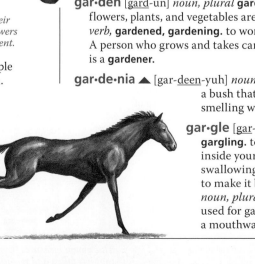

Gargoyles *in the shape of figures were features of medieval architecture.*

gar·goyle ▲ [gar-gole] *noun, plural* **gargolyes.** a spout or pipe that carries rainwater off a roof, carved in the shape of an ugly creature or head.

gar·lic [gar-lik] *noun, plural* **garlics.** a plant of the onion family whose strong-smelling bulb is often used to add flavor in cooking.

gar·ment [gar-munt] *noun, plural* **garments.** a piece of clothing.

gar·net [gar-nit] *noun, plural* **garnets. 1.** a dark red stone used in jewelry. **2.** a deep red color.
adjective. having a deep red color.

gar·nish [gar-nish] *verb,* **garnished, garnishing.** to decorate or add flavor to food with a very small amount of a different food: *The potatoes were garnished with chopped parsley.*
noun, plural **garnishes.** something used to decorate a plate of food or add flavor to it: *a lemon garnish.*

gar·ri·son [gare-uh-sun] *noun, plural* **garrisons. 1.** a group of soldiers who are ready to defend a town or fort. **2.** a post where soldiers are stationed.
verb, **garrisoned, garrisoning.** to occupy a town or fort with soldiers in order to defend it.

gar·ter [gar-tur] *noun, plural* **garters.** a strap or band made of elastic worn around the leg to hold up a sock or stocking.

garter snake a harmless snake found in North America that typically has three longitudinal stripes of color on its back.

gas [gas] *noun, plural* **gases. 1.** *Chemistry.* a substance such as air that is not solid or liquid at normal temperatures and that can move about freely and fill any available space. This is one of the three basic states of matter, along with a solid and a liquid. **2.** a gas or mixture of gases used as a fuel for heating, lighting, and cooking. A substance that is made up of gases or is similar to gas is said to be **gaseous. 3.** an abbreviation for GASOLINE.

gas guzz·ler *Environment.* a vehicle, especially a large automobile, that uses up a lot of gasoline. A gas guzzler gets fewer miles to the gallon than a more economical vehicle.

gas mask a device like a mask that is fitted with a chemical air filter and is worn over the nose and mouth to prevent a person from breathing in poisonous gases and fumes.

gas·o·line [gas-uh-leen *or* gas-uh-leen] *noun, plural* **gasolines.** a liquid made up mainly of refined petroleum that burns easily and is used as a fuel for vehicles such as cars and airplanes.

gasp [gasp] *verb,* **gasped, gasping.** to take a sharp breath through an open mouth when you are surprised, ill, exhausted, and so on: *The hikers gasped for breath as they approached the top of the steep hill.*
noun, plural **gasps.** a sudden, short breath.

gas station a place that sells gasoline from pumps connected to large underground tanks, along with oil and other items motor vehicles and travelers need. Some gas stations are staffed with mechanics who service and repair vehicles.

gas·tric [gas-trik] *adjective. Biology.* relating to the stomach.

gate [gate] *noun, plural* **gates.** a barrier similar to a door, often on hinges, used to close an opening in a wall or fence.
🔊 A different word with the same sound is **gait.**

gate·way [gate-way] *noun, plural* **gateways. 1.** an opening with or for a gate. **2.** a way to or from somewhere or something: *In pioneer days in America, the city of St. Louis was called the Gateway to the West.*

gath·er [gaTH-ur] *verb,* **gathered, gathering. 1.** to bring or come together; collect gradually: *We gathered firewood in the forest.* **2.** to increase in gradual amounts: *The train gathered speed on the open plain.* **3.** to come to understand; conclude; guess: *From what she said, I gathered she hadn't enjoyed the party.*

gath·er·ing [gaTH-ur-ing] *noun, plural* **gatherings.** a coming together of people or things in a group; a meeting or assembly.

gaud·y [gaw-dee] *adjective,* **gaudier, gaudiest.** overly bright and ornamented; showy; flashy: *Her outfit was spoiled by her gaudy bracelets.*

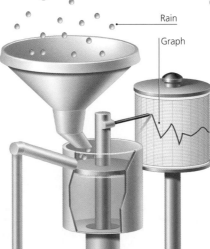

Rain

Graph

gauge ◀ [gayj] *noun, plural* **gauges. 1.** an instrument that measures and records pressure, volume, or dimensions: *a rain gauge; an air pressure gauge.* **2.** a standard measurement for a certain object, such as the capacity of gun barrels or the distance between railroad tracks.
verb, **gauged, gauging. 1.** to measure precisely; calculate: *A depth sounder gauges how deep parts of the ocean are.* **2.** to estimate; judge: *I gauge the distance to camp to be four miles.*

This **gauge** *measures the amount of rain that has fallen and records it in a graph.*

gaunt [gawnt] *adjective,* **gaunter, gauntest.** very thin; haggard; scrawny: *a sick and gaunt old horse.*

gauze [gawz] *noun.* a very thin, loosely woven fabric, like a fine mesh, used for bandages and sometimes as a filter.

gave [gave] *verb.* the past tense of GIVE.

gav·el ▶ [gav-ul] *noun, plural* **gavels.** a small hammer used by someone running a meeting or a judge in a court of law to call those present to order.

gay [gay] *adjective* **gayer, gayest. 1.** in good spirits; light-hearted; merry. **2.** bright; colorful: *A gay scarf brightened her otherwise drab outfit.*

gaze [gaze] *verb,* **gazed, gazing.** to keep your eyes fixed on something for an extended time: *Ben gazed in amazement at the pile of birthday presents on the table. noun, plural* **gazes.** a fixed, intent look.

ga·zelle ▶ [guh-zel] *noun, plural* **gazelles.** a small, swift, graceful antelope with long curved horns, living in Africa and Asia.

gear [geer] *noun, plural* **gears.** wheels designed to engage with each other, so that as one turns the other is made to turn. A **gearshift** is a device that selects or changes gears connected to a motor, especially in a motor vehicle. **2.** equipment for a certain purpose: *fishing gear; scuba-diving gear. verb.* **gear up.** to make ready for something; prepare: *Our school is gearing up for the major athletics meet of the season.*

geese [geese] *noun.* the plural of GOOSE.

Gei·ger counter ▼ *Science.* a device for detecting and measuring radioactivity, which is the amount of nuclear energy given off by a substance.

> The **Geiger counter** is named for Hans *Geiger,* a German scientist who was one of the people who invented it. He and a famous English scientist, Ernest Rutherford, developed this device in 1909 at the University of Manchester.

*In a **Geiger counter,** a tube that conducts electricity measures radioactivity.*

gel [jel] *noun. Chemistry.* a jelly-like substance made up of tiny, solid particles evenly distributed throughout a liquid. *verb,* **gelled, gelling.** to make into or take on the form of a gel.

gel·a·tin [jel-uh-tun] *noun.* a clear, sticky, jelly-like substance obtained by boiling animal bones and skin. It is used as a food (for example, to make jellies and some other desserts), in photography, and for a range of other purposes, such as making glue. This word is also spelled **gelatine.**

gem [jem] *noun, plural* **gems.**
1. a precious or semiprecious stone, especially one that has been cut and polished; a jewel. Such a stone used as a gem is called a **gemstone.**
2. a person or thing of great value or worth: *I told my friend Claudette that she was a real gem for helping me clean up my room.*

gen·der [jen-dur] *noun, plural* **genders.** *Biology.* the set of characteristics associated with being either male or female, including behavior, emotions, and such things as likes, dislikes, and interests.

gene [jeen] *noun, plural* **genes.** *Biology.* a unit of the cells of living things, containing chemical information that helps to determine which characteristics an individual inherits from its parent or parents, such as eye color or hair color.

> The word **gene** goes back to a Greek word meaning "birth." The idea is that when a child is born, the genes of the parents pass on certain characteristics to the child.

ge·ne·al·o·gy [jee-nee-ol-uh-jee] *noun, plural* **genealogies.** *History.* **1.** the line of ancestors from which a person or family has descended, or a statement or chart showing this; a family history or family tree. **2.** the process of investigating a line of ancestors. A person who investigates lines of ancestors, especially as a profession, is called a **genealogist.**

Gazelles are plant-eaters that live in herds and graze on grassy plains.

gen·er·al [jen-rul *or* jen-ur-ul] *adjective.*
1. having to do with everyone or with a group as a whole; common to many; widespread: *This park is for the use of the general public; There was a general feeling of excitement as the first day of the school vacation approached.* **2.** not limited or specific; broad: *Visitors are always surprised at the range of items sold in our town's general store; I could give only a general description of the car, as it was traveling fast. noun, plural* **generals.** a title used for officers of high rank in the armed forces. In the U.S. Army, there are five ranks of general: **brigadier general, major general, lieutenant general, general,** and **general of the army.**
• in general. for the most part; usually: *In general, the people in our neighborhood are very friendly.*

A
B
C
D
E
F
G
H
I
J
K
L
M
N
O
P
Q
R
S
T
U
V
W
X
Y
Z

gen·er·al·ize [jen-ur-uh-*lize*] *verb,* **generalized, generalizing. 1.** to draw a broad conclusion from a number of individual facts or cases: *You need to have experience with many different kinds of dogs before you can generalize about the behavior of all dogs.* **2.** to refer to something in a general or indefinite way: *The mayor told the reporters that he could only generalize about the effects of the storm, as he had not yet had detailed reports.* To speak of something in general terms or to make a sweeping statement is to make a **generalization.**

To **generalize** is to make a broad statement that something is always or almost always true. It is good to generalize in certain ways when you are writing a factual paper. For example: "The state of Florida has warm, sunny weather. The state is very flat, with no mountains, and almost no high hills. Many people from the northeastern U.S. retire to Florida." All these are generalizations, and all are true. What you should be careful about when you write is not to generalize about things that are just your opinion: "All the kids at that school are rich." "Nobody likes that TV show." "Vegetables have a boring taste." Those are the kind of generalizations to avoid.

gen·er·al·ly [jen-ruh-lee *or* jen-ur-uh-lee] *adverb.*
1. as a rule; usually: *My mother generally arrives home from work at four o'clock.* **2.** for the most part; by most people; on the whole: *William Shakespeare is generally thought to be the world's greatest writer.* **3.** without going into detail or taking account of exceptions: *Generally, everyone had a good time at the party.*

gen·er·ate [jen-uh-rate] *verb,* **generated, generating.** to bring into existence; produce: *The advance publicity generated a lot of excitement about the upcoming concert.*

gen·er·a·tion [jen-uh-ray-shun] *noun, plural* **generations.**
1. everyone born and living at a particular time considered as a group: *My grandmother calls herself a "Baby Boomer" because she belongs to the generation born just after World War II.* **2.** a single stage in a family's line of descent: *Our family has lived in this town for four generations, since my great-grandparents settled here.* **3.** the average length of time between the birth of parents and the birth of their offspring, usually taken to be thirty years. **4.** the act or process of generating; production: *the generation of electrical power; the generation of a new idea.*

gen·er·a·tor ▶ [jen-uh-*ray*-tur] *noun, plural* **generators.** a machine that converts mechanical energy into electrical energy.

ge·ner·ic [juh-ner-ik] *adjective.*
1. characteristic of a whole group; general: *When our teacher said cats are hunting animals, she was speaking in generic terms.* **2.** not registered or protected as a trademark; having no brand name: *Generic medicines have the same active ingredients as brand-name medicines, but they are usually cheaper.* **3.** having no distinctive quality; ordinary: *generic wine.*

In stories, **genies** *may take the form of humans or animals.*

gen·er·os·i·ty [jen-u-ros-i-tee] *noun.* the quality of being generous: *We thanked our neighbors for their generosity in inviting us to stay at their vacation cottage.*

gen·er·ous [jen-ur-us] *adjective.*
1. giving or sharing willingly and freely; big-hearted: *My aunt and uncle are very generous and often invite us to spend our vacation on their farm.* **2.** being enough or more than enough; ample or abundant: *We always take a generous supply of food with us when we go camping.* —**generously,** *adverb.*

gene therapy *Medicine.* a method of treating inherited disorders by introducing normal genes into cells to replace missing or defective genes.

ge·net·ic [juh-net-ik] *adjective.*
Biology. having to do with genes or characteristics inherited from parents or other ancestors. The **genetic code** is the chemical code carried in an individual's DNA that ultimately determines which characteristics (such as eye color or hair color) an individual inherits.

ge·net·ics [juh-net-iks] *noun. Biology.* the study of inherited characteristics and how living things with the same line of descent differ from each other. A scientist who specializes in this area of study is called a **geneticist.**

gen·ial [jeen-yul *or* jeen-ee-ul] *adjective.* friendly; good-natured; gracious: *The principal's genial speech at the start of the new school year put all the students in a good mood.*

ge·nie ▲ [jee-nee] *noun, plural* **genies.** *Literature.* a spirit in Arabian tales, often contained in a bottle or lamp, that has the power to grant wishes when it is called forth.

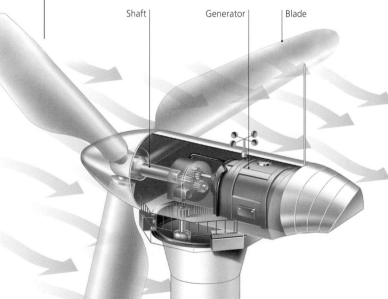

Shaft | Generator | Blade

In this modern windmill, electricity is produced when wind turns blades connected by a shaft to a **generator.**

gen·ius [jeen-yus] *noun, plural* **geniuses. 1.** extraordinary ability to think or act in an original or creative way: *Most people consider the painting known as the Mona Lisa to be a work of genius.* **2.** an exceptionally clever or gifted person: *In the world of science, Einstein was a genius.* **3.** great natural ability or talent in a particular area: *Our coach has a genius for spotting future sports stars.*

ge·nome [jee-*nome*] *noun. Biology.* the complete genetic material of an organism. The study of the genetic material of different organisms is called **genomics.**

Gen·tile [jen-tile] *noun, plural* **Gentiles.** *Religion.* **1.** a person who is not a Jew. **2.** a person who is not a Mormon.
adjective. **1.** not Jewish. **2.** not Mormon.

gen·tle [jen-tul] *adjective,* **gentler, gentlest. 1.** having a mild, peaceful nature. **2.** not harsh; soft; soothing: *a gentle tap on the door; a gentle breeze.* **3.** easy to handle; calm: *a gentle animal.* **4.** not steep; gradual: *a gentle slope.*
—**gently,** *adverb;* **gentleness,** *noun.*

gen·tle·man [jen-tul-mun] *noun, plural* **gentlemen. 1.** a man who has good manners and is honorable. **2.** *History.* an older term for a man whose family had a high position in society. **3.** a polite way of referring to any man: *Her assistant told her that a gentleman was waiting for her in the lobby.*

*A **geologist** closely examines a piece of rock he has found.*

gen·tle·wom·an [jen-tul-*wu*-mun] *noun, plural* **gentlewomen.** *History.* an older term for a woman whose family had a high position in society.

gen·u·ine [jen-yoo-un] *adjective.* **1.** being what it appears or is said to be; real; authentic: *a genuine gold ring.* **2.** not pretended or faked; sincere: *My cousin greeted me with genuine delight.* —**genuinely,** *adverb.*

gen·us [jee-nus] *noun, plural* **genera.** *Biology.* a group of plants or animals that have in common a set of characteristics that is not found in other groups and that distinguishes them from other groups. A genus consists of at least two and usually many different species: *Lions, tigers, and leopards are three species of the same genus, the Panthera or so-called big cats.*

ge·o·chem·is·try [jee-oh-kem-i-stree] *noun. Science.* the study of the chemistry of all the Earth's solid material, including rocks and minerals.

ge·o·des·ic dome ▶ [jee-uh-des-ik] a dome-shaped structure with a framework of short, straight bars that are interlocked in a geometric pattern. The pressure load is shared evenly throughout the structure, making it very strong.

ge·o·graph·ic [jee-uh-graf-ik] *adjective.* having to do with geography. A different word with the same meaning is **geographical.** —**geographically,** *adverb.*

ge·og·ra·phy [jee-og-ruh-fee] *noun, plural* **geographies.** *Science.* **1.** the study of the Earth's physical features, including land forms, climate, and natural resources, as well as human features such as cities, and also of the location of living things on Earth, including people, animals, and plants. **2.** the main physical features of a region: *The geography of the western U.S. varies from deserts to mountains.* A person who specializes in the study of geography is a **geographer.**

ge·ol·o·gist ◀ [jee-ol-uh-jist] *noun, plural* **geologists.** a person who specializes in the study of geology.

ge·ol·o·gy [jee-ol-uh-jee] *noun. Science.* the study of the structure of the Earth, especially its rocks and what these reveal about the changes to the Earth that have taken place in the past and are taking place in the present. —**geological;** —**geologic,** *adjective.*

ge·o·met·ric ▲ [jee-uh-met-rik] *adjective.* **1.** *Mathematics.* having to do with geometry. **2.** made up of or decorated with geometric shapes, such as lines, circles, and triangles. A different word with the same meaning is **geometrical.** **geometrically,** *adverb.*

ge·om·e·try [jee-om-uh-tree] *noun. Mathematics.* the study of points, lines, angles, surfaces, and solids and how they all relate to each other.

ge·o·pol·i·tics [jee-oh-pol-i-tiks] *noun. Government.* the study of the relationship between geography and politics; that is, how a country's physical features affect the way it is governed and its relations with other countries.

*The Biosphere, in Montreal, Canada, is a large **geodesic dome.***

a b c d e f g h i j k l m n o p q r s t u

GEOTHERMAL REGIONS

Chambers deep beneath old volcanoes may still contain hot, liquid material, or magma. In these areas, known as geothermal regions, rising heat warms water that has trickled down from the surface. When pressure is released, the hot water and steam explode upward like a giant fountain, called a geyser, or bubble up gently as hot springs or mud pools. The hot groundwater creates dramatic landscapes with mineral deposits in strange shapes and colors. The world's most famous geothermal regions are in Iceland, New Zealand's North Island, and the U.S.A.'s Yellowstone National Park.

HOW GEYSERS ERUPT

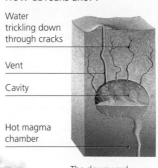

Water trickling down through cracks

Vent

Cavity

Hot magma chamber

The downward pressure of the water in the cracks and vent prevents the water in the cavity from boiling.

As the cavity fills, water overflows at the surface, releasing the pressure in the cavity, and the water boils.

Water and steam rush up to the surface and the geyser erupts. A geyser can spout hundreds of feet.

Geyser

Hot springs

Mud pools

ge·o·ther·mal ▲ [*jee*-oh-<u>thur</u>-mul] *adjective. Science.* relating to or using the Earth's internal heat: *Geysers and hot springs are geothermal features.* A form of energy (such as electricity) that is generated by the use of geothermal heat is called **geothermal energy.**

ge·ra·ni·um [juh-<u>ray</u>-nee-um] *noun, plural* **geraniums.** a garden plant with (usually) red, pink, or white flowers.

gerbil ▲ [<u>jur</u>-bul] *noun, plural* **gerbils.** a small desert animal similar to a mouse but with long hind legs and a long tail. It is kept as a pet. Gerbils are native to Asia, Africa, and southern Russia.

ge·ri·at·ric [*jer*-ee-<u>at</u>-rik] *adjective. Medicine.* relating to the health and care of old people. The medical science concerned with the health and care of old people is called **geriatrics.**

germ [jurm] *noun, plural* **germs.** a microorganism, especially one that can cause disease, such as a virus or a bacterium.

Ger·man [<u>jurm</u>-un] *noun, plural* **Germans. 1.** someone who was born in the country of Germany, is of German descent, or is a citizen of Germany. **2.** the language of Germany. *adjective.* relating to Germany, its people, or its language.

Ger·man·ic [jer-<u>man</u>-ik] *adjective.* **1.** characteristic of German people or people who speak one of the Germanic languages other than English. **2.** referring to a group of related languages that includes English, German, Dutch, Swedish, Danish, and Norwegian.

German measles *Health.* a disease that produces a red rash similar to the rash of mild measles. It is caused by a virus and is very easily spread. It is also called rubella.

German shepherd a large, intelligent breed of dog with black, brown, or gray fur (or a mixture of these colors) often used as a guard or guide dog, and for police work. It was originally bred in Germany.

ger·mi·nate [<u>jur</u>-muh-nate] *verb,* **germinated, germinating.** to sprout or produce shoots: *The packet states that these seeds will take a month to germinate.* —**germination,** *noun.*

ges·ture [<u>jes</u>-chur] *noun, plural* **gestures. 1.** an action or movement that expresses or emphasizes what someone is thinking or feeling: *Juan kept looking at his watch in a gesture of impatience.* **2.** something said or done as a courtesy or for effect: *Her offer of help was an empty gesture, as we had almost finished the work.* *verb,* **gestured, gesturing.** to make or use gestures: *The farmer gestured at me to close the gate.*

A B C D E F G H I J K L M N O P Q R S T U V W X Y Z

get [get] *verb*, **got, got** *or* **gotten, getting. 1.** to come to have: *to get a job; to get a present; to get a new car; to get a cold.* **2.** to come into a certain condition; come to be: *to get excited or angry; to get married; to get home from school.* **3.** to cause to be or to happen: *to get your hair cut; to get packed for a trip.* **4.** to have to or need to: *I've got to leave now; He's got to finish the job today.* **5.** to understand: *to get a joke; to get the point of a story.*

get·a·way [get-uh-*way*] *noun, plural* **getaways.** an escape, especially after committing a crime.

gey·ser [guy-zur] *noun, plural* **geysers.** a naturally occurring hot spring that shoots jets of water and steam into the air from time to time.

ghast·ly [gast-lee] *adjective.* very frightening; dreadful; shocking: *a ghastly accident.*

ghet·to [get-oh] *noun, plural* **ghettos** *or* **ghettoes.** a part of a city where members of a minority group live, often because they are poor or have difficulty finding a place to live elsewhere. Such an area typically has low-quality housing.

The word **ghetto** comes from a name for a certain part of the old city of Venice, Italy. People who were Jewish were required by law to live in this part of the city, and the word then came to mean any area of a city where many people of a certain minority group live.

ghost [gohst] *noun, plural* **ghosts.** the spirit of someone who has died, especially one that is said to appear to living people or to haunt a house or a place. Something that seems unearthly, like a ghost, is said to be **ghostly.**

ghost town ▼ a town that people have deserted, usually because it was established for a particular purpose and it no longer serves that purpose. A mining town, for example, may become a ghost town when the surrounding area is mined out.

When the gold runs out, mining settlements can quickly become **ghost towns.**

gi·ant [jye-unt] *noun, plural* **giants. 1.** a being in legends and fairy tales that is like a person but is of huge size and has extraordinary strength. **2.** someone or something that is much bigger than normal: *A 747 is a giant among airplanes.* **3.** someone or something that is especially powerful or successful: *Elvis Presley was a giant in the world of entertainment.*
adjective. much bigger than normal: *a giant redwood tree; a giant discount store.*

gib·bon ▶ [gib-un] *noun, plural* **gibbons.** a small, tailless ape with very long arms that lives in trees and is native to southeastern Asia.

gid·dy [gid-ee] *adjective,* **giddier, giddiest. 1.** having a feeling of whirling or spinning around and being inclined to stagger or fall over; dizzy: *When I finished the race, I felt giddy and had to sit down.* **2.** not serious; silly; frivolous: *giddy with excitement.*

gift [gift] *noun, plural* **gifts. 1.** something given freely and without requiring payment; a present: *I gave Emily a DVD as a gift for her birthday.* **2.** a special natural ability: *He has a gift for music and can learn a new song in just a few minutes.*

gif·ted [gift-id] *adjective.* possessing a special natural ability: *a gifted teacher.*

giga- *Mathematics.* a prefix that means one billion. A measurement that means 1,073,741,824 bytes of computer memory is a **gigabyte.** An abbreviation for gigabyte is **GB.**

gi·gan·tic [jye-gan-tik] *adjective.* extremely large; huge: *Dinosaurs were gigantic animals.*

gig·gle [gig-ul] *verb,* **giggled, giggling.** to laugh with a light, high-pitched sound.
noun, plural **giggles.** a light, high-pitched kind of laughter.

Gi·la monster ▼ [hee-luh] a lizard with black and orange markings that lives in the southwestern United States. Gila monsters have a poisonous bite.

gild [gild] *verb,* **gilded** *or* **gilt, gilding.** to cover with a coating of gold or gold paint: *The jeweler carefully gilded the small ornament.* Something that has been covered with gold is **gilded.**
◀)) A different word with the same sound is **guild.**

There are nine kinds of plant-eating **gibbons.**

A **Gila monster** *can grow up to twenty inches long.*

gill

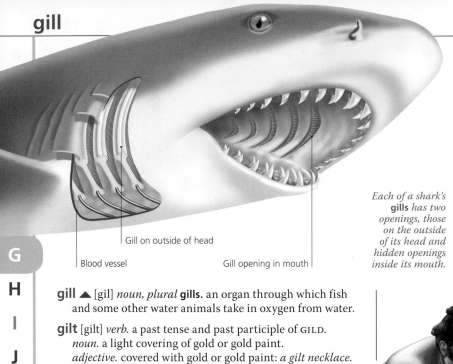

Gill on outside of head
Blood vessel
Gill opening in mouth

Each of a shark's **gills** *has two openings, those on the outside of its head and hidden openings inside its mouth.*

gill ▲ [gil] *noun, plural* **gills.** an organ through which fish and some other water animals take in oxygen from water.

gilt [gilt] *verb.* a past tense and past participle of GILD. *noun.* a light covering of gold or gold paint. *adjective.* covered with gold or gold paint: *a gilt necklace.*

gim·mick [gim-ik] *noun, plural* **gimmicks.** something that is done or said in order to deceive people or to trick them into doing something. Something said or done in order to trick people is described as **gimmicky.**

gin¹ [jin] *noun, plural* **gins.** a strong alcoholic drink made from grain and flavored with juniper berries and other substances.

gin² [jin] *noun, plural* **gins.** one of several kinds of machines or mechanical devices. A machine that separates cotton from the seeds and hulls of the cotton plant is a **cotton gin.**

The long neck of a **giraffe** *helps it to reach the leaves of acacia trees on which it feeds.*

gin·ger [jin-jur] *noun, plural* **gingers.** a kind of tropical plant whose root is used as a spice and sometimes as a medicine. A fizzy drink flavored with ginger is **ginger ale.** A kind of cake flavored with ginger is **gingerbread.**

ging·ham [ging-um] *noun, plural* **ginghams.** a colored cloth, often with a checked pattern.

gi·raffe ◀ [juh-raf] *noun, plural* **giraffes.** the tallest of living animals, a fast-moving, hoofed African mammal that chews its cud and has long legs, a very long neck, a small head, and skin with large, brown spots.

gir·der [gur-dur] *noun, plural* **girders.** a large, sturdy, horizontal beam that supports parts of structures such as buildings and bridges.

girl [gurl] *noun, plural* **girls.** a female who is not yet a woman; a female human baby, child, or adolescent.

girl·friend [gurl-frend] *noun, plural* **girlfriends. 1.** a girl or young woman who is a steady companion of a boy or man, but who is not his wife. **2.** a special female friend of a girl or woman.

girl·hood [gurl-hood] *noun, plural* **girlhoods.** the time or fact of being a girl.

girl·ish [gurl-ish] *adjective.* being or acting like a girl.

Girl Scouts an organization that trains girls between the ages of five and seventeen in a range of skills and that helps them develop positive qualities of behavior and character. A member of the Girl Scouts is a **Girl Scout** or **girl scout.**

girth ◀ gurth] *noun, plural* **girths.** the distance around something: *A thin person is of small girth.*

gist [jist] *noun, plural* **gists.** the main point; most important part: *We didn't see the whole movie, but we understood the gist of the story.*

A sumo wrestler uses his large **girth** *to help overcome his opponent.*

give [giv] *verb,* **gave, given, giving. 1.** to pass a thing from one person to another with the idea that the other can have it: *to give your sister a birthday present; to give some old books to the local library.* **2.** to let have; hand over: *Please give me that pen on the table.* **3.** to provide with something: *Leaving now will give you enough time to catch the bus.* **4.** to cause to have or to happen: *to give a speech; to give someone a hard time.*

give·a·way [giv-uh-way] *noun, plural* **giveaways. 1.** something that is given free, often with something else that is paid for: *This pen was a giveaway with the purchase of the book.* **2.** something that is revealed by mistake: *The robber's mention of the suitcase was a real giveaway.*

gi·ven [giv-in] *verb.* the past participle of GIVE. *noun, plural* **givens.** something that is already known or understood: *It is a given that stealing is wrong.* *adjective.* **1.** having a tendency; likely: *The small child was given to wandering away.* **2.** arranged; understood: *At a given time, we will all meet in the park.*

gla·cial [glay-shul] *adjective.* **1.** having to do with glaciers. **2.** extremely cold; icy: *There was a glacial wind coming off the sea.* **3.** cold and unfriendly: *He gave her a glacial stare as she came in.*

U-shaped valley

Snout, or end, of the glacier

Head of the glacier

Moraine

Glacial lake

As a **glacier** *moves slowly downhill, it carves out a wide U-shaped valley, pushing rock debris, called moraine, to its sides and in front of it.*

gla·cier ▲ [glay-shur]
noun, plural **glaciers.**
a large body of ice that moves extremely slowly down a slope or across flat land.

glad [glad] *adjective,* **gladder, gladdest. 1.** feeling good or happy about something; pleased; content: *Ben was glad to be home after his long trip.* **2.** bringing happiness: *The letter contained the glad tidings that Grandma will be here for a visit next week.* **3.** willing; prepared: *I would be glad to look after your dog while you are on vacation.* **—gladly,** *adverb.*

glad·i·a·tor ▶ [glad-ee-ay-tur] *noun, plural* **gladiators.** *History.* a man in ancient Roman times who entertained large crowds by fighting against and trying to kill other gladiators or ferocious animals.

glad·i·o·lus [glad-ee-oh-luhs] *noun, plural* **gladioli** *or* **gladioluses.** a plant with long, slender, sharply pointed leaves and thick clusters of colorful flowers.

glam·our [glam-ur] *noun.* a power of great beauty and charm; a special appeal or attraction: *The young actor enjoyed the glamour of starring in a big movie.* This word is also spelled **glamor.** Something that has appeal or attraction is **glamorous.**

glance [glans] *noun, plural* **glances.** a brief, rapid look at something: *At first glance, these pictures look very good. verb,* **glanced, glancing. 1.** to look briefly at something: *The speaker glanced down at his notes from time to time as he spoke.* **2.** to brush against without hitting hard: *The door glanced the side of my head as it swung open.*

gland [gland] *noun, plural* **glands.** *Biology.* one of a number of organs in the body that create substances that the body uses or expels. Sweat and saliva are made by glands. Having to do with one of these organs is **glandular.**

glare [glare] *noun, plural* **glares. 1.** a harsh light: *the glare of the searchlight's beam.* **2.** a fixed, angry gaze or stare: *The men gave each other threatening glares as they argued. verb,* **glared, glaring. 1.** to shine with a bright, harsh light. **2.** to stare angrily.

glar·ing [glare-ing] *adjective.* **1.** bright and harsh: *glaring sunlight.* **2.** clearly obvious: *a glaring error.*

glass [glas] *noun, plural* **glasses. 1.** a clear, usually breakable, material made from combining sand, lime, and other substances at very high temperatures. Windows and many types of lenses are made of glass. **2.** a drinking vessel made of glass.

glass·es [glas-iz] *plural noun.* a pair of lenses worn in front of the eyes to improve sight or protect the eyes from glare.

Watching **gladiators** *fight was a popular form of entertainment in Roman times.*

A B C D E F G H I J K L M N O P Q R S T U V W X Y Z

glaze [glaze] *verb,* **glazed, glazing. 1.** to put a shiny coating on: *In the middle of winter, ice glazed the leaves of the trees.* **2.** to fit glass into something, such as a window frame or a door. A person whose work is fitting glass is a **glazier.**
noun, plural **glazes.** a covering that makes something look shiny or polished.

gleam [gleem] *noun, plural* **gleams. 1.** a beam or flash of bright or soft light. **2.** a hint or suggestion: *When we talked to the baby, we thought we saw a gleam of understanding in her eyes.*
verb, **gleamed, gleaming.** to shine brightly or glow softly: *The moonlight gleamed gently through the mist.*

glee [glee] *noun.* joy and excitement: *We jumped with glee when we heard Jessica was coming to stay.* To feel such joy and excitement is to be **gleeful. —gleefully,** *adverb.*

glen [glen] *noun, plural* **glens.** a peaceful, secluded little valley.

glide [glide] *verb,* **glided, gliding. 1.** to slide or move gently and easily: *The boat glided smoothly across the lake.* **2.** to move through the air without using power: *Eagles can glide for long distances without moving their wings.*
noun, plural **glides.** a gliding movement.

glid·er [glye-dur] *noun, plural* **gliders.** a small, light aircraft that has no engine. It flies by riding on air currents.

glim·mer [glim-ur] *noun, plural* **glimmers. 1.** a gentle, flickering light: *a glimmer of firelight.* **2.** a hint or suggestion: *It seemed she would fail, but there was still a glimmer of hope.*
verb, **glimmered, glimmering.** to glow with a gentle, flickering light: *We saw the lights of the town glimmering in the distance.*

glimpse [glimps] *noun, plural* **glimpses.** a very quick view: *I caught just a glimpse of the bird as it flew by.*
verb, **glimpsed, glimpsing.** to see very briefly.

glint [glint] *verb,* **glinted, glinting.** to gleam or flash gently: *The raindrops glinted in the sunlight.*

glis·ten [glis-un] *verb,* **glistened, glistening.** to shine gently; glitter: *Stars glisten in the night sky.*

glitch [glich] *noun, plural* **glitches. 1.** a minor fault or interruption in the operation of a computer or other machine. **2.** a minor problem: *Our plans for the meeting suffered a glitch when one of the speakers didn't turn up.*

glit·ter [glit-ur] *verb,* **glittered, glittering.** to sparkle brightly: *Glowworms glittered in the dark cave.*
noun. **1.** a brightly flickering light: *a glitter of sparks.* **2.** tiny pieces of reflective material: *We put glitter on our Christmas tree to make it sparkle.*

gloat [glote] *verb,* **gloated, gloating.** to take excessive pleasure in someone else's bad luck or in one's own success: *Myra gloated for days after she won the game.*

GLOBAL WARMING

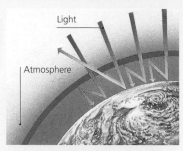

In the last century global temperatures have risen by 1°F. This global warming may be due to an increase in greenhouse gases. These gases occur naturally in the atmosphere and keep the Earth warm by trapping heat reflected from the Earth's surface. However, extra greenhouse gases are being created by burning fossil fuels such as oil and coal, which may be causing the atmosphere to overheat. If this goes on, ice caps could melt, sea levels could rise, and large areas of farmland could become desert.

GREENHOUSE EFFECT
When sunlight enters the atmosphere, some is trapped by cloud. The rest is either absorbed by the Earth's surface or reradiated as heat. Gases called greenhouse gases prevent most of this heat from escaping, leading to an increase in temperature.

ARCTIC ICE CAP
The NASA satellite images below show the diminishing Arctic ice cap.

1979   2005   2006

glo·bal [gloh-bul] *adjective.* **1.** being round like a globe. **2.** referring to, or concerning, the whole of the world: *Air pollution is a global problem.* **—globally,** *adverb.*

glo·bal·i·za·tion [gloh-bul-i-zay-shun] *noun. Government.* the development of rules and practices, in business and other areas, that apply to the whole world and not just to individual countries. The belief in and encouragement of globalization is **globalism.**

global warming ▲ *Environment.* the apparent and continuing gradual increase in the temperature of the Earth's atmosphere, perhaps as a result of the GREENHOUSE EFFECT.

globe [globe] *noun, plural* **globes. 1.** any round object having the shape of a ball or sphere: *an electric light globe.* **2.** the world; the Earth: *People have come to America from all parts of the globe.* **3.** a map of the world in the shape of a sphere.

gloom [gloom] *noun.* **1.** a state of very low light; near darkness: *the gloom of a winter evening.* **2.** great unhappiness; misery: *The prisoner faced the future with a feeling of gloom.*

gloom·y [gloo-mee] *adjective,* **gloomier, gloomiest. 1.** almost dark; dull: *The cellar was a gloomy place.* **2.** unhappy; miserable: *We felt very gloomy after our old dog died.* **—gloomily,** *adverb;* **—gloominess,** *noun.*

glo·ri·fy [glor-uh-fye] *verb,* **glorified, glorifying. 1.** to praise very highly; admire greatly: *People often glorify their favorite sports champions.* **2.** to show as better or more important than it really is: *Nadine glorified her description of the hotel by not saying anything about how small and messy the rooms were.* The act of glorifying is **glorification.**

*Wind and rain make old tree branches **gnarled.***

glo·ri·ous [glor-ee-us] *adjective.* **1.** deserving of great praise: *a glorious act of bravery.* **2.** greatly enjoyable; wonderful: *We had a glorious time exploring the Grand Canyon.* **—gloriously,** *adverb.*

glor·y [glor-ee] *noun, plural* **glories.** **1.** the state of being famous and admired: *The swimmer received much glory for winning the Olympic gold medal.* **2.** something or someone that deserves great fame and admiration: *The Empire State Building is one of New York's great glories.* **3.** wonder or beauty: *I find it hard to describe the glory of that beautiful sunset.* *verb,* **gloried, glorying.** to be proud of; take great pleasure in: *The actor gloried in the applause the audience gave him.*

glos·sa·ry [glos-uh-ree] *noun, plural* **glossaries.** *Language.* a collection of explanations of difficult words in a book or publication. The words are listed in alphabetical order.

glove [gluv] *noun, plural* **gloves.** a covering for the hand and, sometimes, part of the arm. Gloves usually have separate sections for each of the fingers and the thumb.

glow [gloh] *noun, plural* **glows.** **1.** a warm, gentle light: *The lamp shone with a soft, yellow glow.* **2.** a warm, pleasant look: *a glow of happiness.* *verb,* **glowed, glowing.** **1.** to shine with a soft light: *The surface of the lake glowed in the moonlight.* **2.** to have a warm, pleasing appearance: *The bride glowed with pleasure during the wedding ceremony.*

glow·worm [gloh-wurm] *noun, plural* **glowworms.** another word for a FIREFLY.

glu·cose [gloo-kose] *noun. Chemistry.* a form of sugar that exists naturally in many plants and in the blood of animals. Glucose is a source of energy.

glue [gloo] *noun, plural* **glues.** a thick fluid that causes surfaces to stick together. *verb,* **glued, gluing.** **1.** to use glue to stick surfaces together. **2.** to fix or fasten tightly, as if with glue: *His hands were glued to the steering wheel as he drove on the twisting mountain road.*

glum [glum] *adjective.* sad or mildly upset: *Cold, wet weather can make people feel glum.* **—glumly,** *adverb.*

glut [glut] *noun, plural* **gluts.** an excess; too much of something: *There is a glut of tomatoes at the moment, and that's why they are so cheap.*

glut·ton [glut-un] *noun, plural* **gluttons.** **1.** a person who eats too much. **2.** a person who seems able to endure something unpleasant: *Poor Tania is in trouble again—she's a glutton for punishment.* The fact of being a glutton is **gluttony.**

gnarled ◀ [narld] *adjective.* roughly twisted out of shape; disfigured: *After the accident, his fingers were badly gnarled.*

gnat [nat] *noun, plural* **gnats.** one of a number of small flying insects with two wings. Most gnats can give people and animals an itchy bite.

gnaw [naw] *verb,* **gnawed, gnawing.** to chew constantly on something and gradually wear it down: *The goat gnawed on the rope until it snapped.*

gnome ▶ [nome] *noun, plural* **gnomes.** *Literature.* an imaginary small person who in many folk tales lives under the ground and guards buried treasure.

*Plaster **gnomes** are often used as garden decorations.*

The word **gnome** comes from a Greek word meaning "wise" or intelligent." Old stories about gnomes told of them having special knowledge or intelligence that ordinary people did not have.

gnu ▼ [noo] *noun, plural* **gnus** or **gnu.** one of two kinds of large African antelope with two curved horns, a short mane, and a long bushy tail.

🔊 Different words with the same sound are **knew** and **new.**

go [goh] *verb,* **went, gone, going.** **1.** to move from one place to another: *to go to bed; to go the store; to go to Florida by plane.* **2.** to move in a certain direction: *The new highway will go from here to the coast.* **3.** to take part in or do something over time: *to go to medical school; to go fishing in the lake.* **4.** to have a certain result; turn out; happen: *How did it go with your job interview?* **5.** to have a certain place; be suited; fit or match: *Pasta and tomato sauce go well together; These knives go in the top drawer.* **6.** to be in a certain condition; be or become: *to go without sleep; The machine will go off if you push this button.*

goad [gode] *noun, plural* **goads.** a stick with a sharp end that is used to force an animal to move along. *verb,* **goaded, goading.** to force to act in a certain way, as if with a goad: *He goaded me with insults until I finally shouted back at him.*

goal [gole] *noun, plural* **goals.** **1.** something that a person wants to obtain or achieve. **2.** in some games, a net or a space between posts where players have to hit, throw, or kick a ball or some other object to score points. **3.** the score obtained by placing a ball or other object in a goal.

goal·ie [goh-lee] *noun, plural* **goalies.** a person who protects a goal and tries to prevent opponents from scoring in some games, such as hockey, soccer, and lacrosse. This player is also called a **goaltender** or **goalkeeper.**

Gnus live in large herds on the grasslands of the African plains.

a b c d e f g h i j k l m n o p q r s t u v w x y z

A B C D E F G H I J K L M N O P Q R S T U V W X Y Z

GODS AND GODDESSES

Many ancient cultures believed in gods and goddesses. The ancient Egyptians worshipped hundreds of gods, who were often depicted as animals or as humans with the heads of animals or birds. In ancient Greece the gods were thought to look and behave like humans, but to be immortal and live high on Mount Olympus. When the Romans conquered Greece, they adopted the Greek gods, but gave them different names. In German and Scandinavian myths the chief god was Wotan, also known as Odin. Freia, the chief goddess, was linked with love, while Donar, or Thor, was thought to cause thunder and lightning.

EGYPTIAN GODS

Re · Hathor · Anubis · Osiris · Isis

Three times a day, an Egyptian high priest washed and clothed a statue of the sun-god, Amun-Re, and offered it a meal.

ROMAN GODS

Saturn · Neptune · Mercury · Venus

goat [gote] *noun, plural* **goats.** one of a number of types of animal that are related to sheep. Goats have horns that curve backward and short tails. Many have a short growth of hair under the chin.

goat·ee [goh-<u>tee</u>] *noun, plural* **goatees.** a short beard that covers the bottom of the chin and ends in a sharp point. A goatee looks like the hair under a goat's chin.

gob·ble[1] [<u>gob</u>-ul] *verb*, **gobbled, gobbling.** to eat and swallow food greedily and very quickly.

gob·ble[2] [<u>gob</u>-ul] *noun, plural* **gobbles.** the gulping sound that turkeys make. *verb*, **gobbled, gobbling.** to make a gobbling sound.

gob·let ▶ [<u>gob</u>-lit] *noun, plural* **goblets.** a large, tall drinking vessel with a long stem and a wide base.

gob·lin [<u>gob</u>-lun] *noun, plural* **goblins.** *Literature.* an imaginary ugly and mischievous small being in some folk tales.

God [god] *noun. Religion.* the one supreme being believed by Christians, Muslims, and Jews to be the creator of the universe and to have control over everything in it.

god ▲ [god] *noun, plural* **gods.** *Religion.* **1.** a supernatural being that members of some religions believe to have power over parts of people's lives: *In ancient Roman times people believed that Mars was the god of war.* **2.** someone or something that people love greatly or value very highly. A person that many others think to be perfect is sometimes called **godlike.**

god·dess ▲ [<u>god</u>-is] *noun, plural* **goddesses. 1.** a female god that members of some religions believe to have power over parts of people's lives. **2.** a woman who is widely admired for her goodness or her beauty.

god·fa·ther [<u>god</u>-*fahтн*-ur] *noun, plural* **godfathers.** a man who agrees, usually when a child is baptized, to care for that child if its parents are no longer able to do so.

god·moth·er [<u>god</u>-*muтн*-ur] *noun, plural* **godmothers.** a woman who agrees, usually when a child is baptized, to care for that child if its parents are no longer able to do so.

In the past, wealthy people drank from golden **goblets** *at feasts and celebrations.*

*The left-hand side of a **gondola** is wider to accommodate the gondolier.*

god·par·ent [god-*pare*-unt] *noun,* *plural* **godparents.** a godfather or godmother. A child that a godparent agrees to look after is a **godchild.**

goes [goze] *verb.* a present tense of GO.

gog·gles [gog-ulz] *plural noun.* glasses that fit tightly around the eyes to protect them against water, dust, smoke, wind, heat, or very bright light.

go·ing [goh-ing] *verb.* the present participle of GO.
noun, plural **goings.** the way ahead; the state of things: *The poor man can pay his bills now, but he knows that the going will be hard in future.*
adjective. present; current: *Can you tell me what is the going price for potatoes?*

gold [gohld] *noun.* **1.** *Chemistry.* a precious metal that is a chemical element. Gold is a heavy yellow substance, used to make coins and many types of jewelry. **2.** the brilliant yellow color of gold. **3.** something that is thought of as very rare or valuable like gold. *adjective.* **1.** made entirely or partly of gold: *a gold ring.* **2.** having the bright yellow color of gold.

gold·en [gohld-un] *adjective.* **1.** made entirely or mainly of gold: *a golden necklace.* **2.** being gold-colored: *It was a golden sunset.* **3.** valuable like gold; very good; wonderful: *a golden opportunity; The time Joseph spent in Europe was a golden time in his life.*

gold·en·rod [gohld-un-*rod*] *noun, plural* **goldenrods.** one of a number of North American plants that have clusters of small yellow or white flowers that bloom in late summer or early autumn.

gold·finch [gohld-*finch*] *noun, plural* **goldfinches. 1.** one of many types of small, brightly colored European songbirds. **2.** one of three types of small American finches with yellow and black markings.

gold·fish [gohld-*fish*] *noun, plural* **goldfish** or **goldfishes.** a small reddish or orange-colored fish, often kept in home aquariums or ponds.

golf ▼ [golf] *noun.* a game in which players hit a small, hard ball with different types of clubs around a large outdoor course. They must hit the ball into a series of holes, using as few hits, or strokes, as possible.
verb, **golfed, golfing.** to play golf. A person who plays this game is a **golfer.**

gon·do·la ▲ [gon-duh-luh] *noun, plural* **gondolas. 1.** a long, narrow boat, rowed by a person with a long pole, that carries passengers and goods along the canals of Venice in Italy. **2.** a basket or compartment under a balloon for carrying people or goods.

gone [gawn] *verb.* the past participle of GO.
adjective. no longer here; finished: *Gina was giving away some cookies, but they are gone now.*

Golf *dates back to at least the seventeenth century, when Mary, Queen of Scots, is said to have played the game.*

a b c d e f g h i j k l m n o p q r s t u v w x y z

GORILLAS

Gorillas roam through the mountain forests of eastern and central Africa in family groups. They build nests in trees each night, safe from predators and away from the cold ground. Each family is led by a large silverback male. He warns younger males to stay away from his mates and children by standing up, roaring, and slapping his chest. Although gorillas seem fierce, they are actually peaceful vegetarians.

Silverback male

Hand

Foot

gong [gong] *noun, plural* **gongs.** a circular piece of metal that makes a booming, bell-like sound when it is hit with a padded stick or hammer.

good [gud] *adjective,* **better, best. 1.** having what is wanted or needed; of high quality; not bad or poor: *good news; a good mark on a test; a restaurant that serves good food; a good car that does not break down.* **2.** having the right kind of character; honest and kind; not evil: *a good deed; a good person who helps others.* **3.** acting in the right way; well-behaved: *Please be good while you stay with Grandma.* **4.** as it should be; proper, suitable, or correct: *good health; good advice; a good way to lose weight; a good reason to miss school.*
noun. something that is good: *The candidate for mayor promised that he would work for the good of the city.*

Remember that **good** is an adjective and not an adverb. *Well* is the adverb form: "She is a *good* soccer player and she played *well* (not *good*) today." "That's a *good* song and he sang it *well*." The only exception is that *good* can be used with a verb that gives the sense of how something feels, looks, or sounds, because those words take an adjective and not an adverb: "Dad looks *good* (not well) in his new suit."

good-bye [gud-<u>bye</u>] *interjection.* what someone says to another person as a sign of leaving, going somewhere, or finishing a telephone call. *noun, plural* **good-byes.** a farewell: *We dropped Grandma back home and said our good-byes.* This word is also spelled **good-by.**

> **Good-bye** is a shorter form of the words "God be with you." The idea was that when someone said good-bye to a person, they were asking God to watch over that person when the person went away.

Good Friday *Religion.* the Friday before Easter Sunday; Christians have a day of worship on this day to commemorate the death of Jesus Christ on the cross.

good-heart·ed [gud-<u>har</u>-tid] *adjective.* describing a kind, caring, and generous action or personality.

good-na·tured [gud-<u>nay</u>-churd] *adjective.* describing a friendly, cheerful, easygoing action or personality.

good·ness [gud-nis] *noun.* the quality or state of being good: *All the goodness of fresh fruit is in this juice. interjection.* a saying used to show surprise or amazement: *Goodness me, you've done well on this test!*

goods [gudz] *plural noun.* **1.** things for sale: *The store sells kitchen goods such as pots and pans.* **2.** things someone owns; possessions: *In the flood we lost most of our goods.*

good will *noun.* **1.** an act that shows caring or friendliness: *The mayor visited the nursing home as a gesture of good will.* **2.** *Business.* the good opinion customers have of a business. This is taken into account as having a set value when the business is sold: *When my father bought the restaurant, the selling price included the cost of the building, furniture, equipment, and also good will. adjective.* **good-will.** showing care and friendliness: *a good-will gesture.* This term is also spelled **goodwill.**

goose [goos] *noun, plural* **geese. 1.** a bird that is like a duck but larger, with a longer neck and more pointed bill. **2.** the female of this bird. The male is called a gander.

goose bumps raised hairs on the skin caused by cold or stress. These last only a short time.

go·pher [<u>goh</u>-fur] *noun, plural* **gophers.** a small animal from North America that looks somewhat like a squirrel. It has large pouches in its cheeks and it burrows underground.

gorge [gorj] *noun, plural* **gorges.** a deep, narrow space between cliffs of rock, often with a stream. *verb,* **gorged, gorging.** to eat greedily and quickly; eat too much.

gor·geous [gor-jus] *adjective.* having a lovely appearance; very beautiful: *In spring the garden bursts with gorgeous flowers.*

go·ril·la ◀ [guh-<u>ril</u>-uh] *noun, plural* **gorillas.** a large, powerful ape native to rain forests of central Africa. it has a large head, chest, and shoulders, short legs, and long arms.

> The word **gorilla** comes from ancient stories about a wild tribe of hairy people who were called by this name. Adult gorillas look somewhat like human beings when seen from a distance, and at first it was thought that they were a wild race of people rather than animals.

gor·y [gor-ee] *adjective,* **gorier, goriest.** covered with blood; bloody: *The scary movie had many gory scenes.*

Gos·pel [gos-pul] *noun, plural* **Gospels.** *Religion.* **1.** the four accounts in the Bible of the life of Jesus Christ given by his apostles Matthew, Mark, Luke, and John. **2.** the teachings of Jesus Christ and his apostles. **3. gospel.** something believed to be completely true, without question.

gos·sip [gos-ip] *noun, plural* **gossips. 1.** conversation, rumor, or opinion about other people, often with a mean intent and without a real basis in fact: *The school was buzzing with gossip about why the principal left.* **2.** someone who spreads personal or private information about other people: *We never tell our neighbor anything because he is a real gossip.*
verb, **gossiped, gossiping.** to tell personal or private information about other people.

> The word **gossip** once meant "a godparent" or "a very close friend." It was thought that someone like that would be likely to know a person's secret business and talk about this to others.

got [got] *verb.* the past participle and past tense of GET.

Goth·ic ▼ [<u>goth</u>-ik] *adjective. Art.* **1.** describing a style of architecture used from the twelfth century through to the mid-sixteenth century in Europe; noted especially for large, impressive cathedrals built in this style, such as Notre Dame in Paris. **2.** *Literature.* describing a type of story that has a feeling of darkness, gloom, and mystery, and that tells of strange or supernatural events.

got·ten [got-un] *verb.* a past participle of GET.

gouge [gowj] *noun, plural* **gouges. 1.** a type of chisel with a blade shaped like a scoop, used on wood to cut grooves or holes. **2.** a groove, mark, or hole made with or as if with such a tool.
verb, **gouged, gouging.** to scoop out, cut, or carve something in this way.

gourd [gord] *noun, plural* **gourds.** a hard-skinned, rounded fruit related to the squash. Gourds can be dried and used as a decoration, or used to make rounded utensils such as bowls and cups.

gour·met [goor-<u>may</u>] *noun, plural* **gourmets.** someone who has a love for, and a great knowledge of, food and wine.
adjective. having the high standard expected by a gourmet: *a gourmet meal.*

gov·ern [<u>guv</u>-urn] *verb,* **governed, governing. 1.** to have official control of the managing or running of a country, state, city, or other such body. **2.** to act with power over something or someone; control or organize: *He governed the new committee according to rules he made up himself.*

gov·ern·ment [<u>guv</u>-ur-munt *or* <u>guv</u>-urn-munt] *noun, plural* **governments. 1.** the people who have the power to run a country, state, city, or other area. **2.** the type of organization and control used by a government: *Democracy is one type of government–communism is another.*

gov·er·nor [<u>guv</u>-ur-nur] *noun, plural,* **governors. 1.** a person elected to govern a U.S. state. **2.** someone appointed or elected to govern an area for a set amount of time.

It took 150 years to build Notre Dame, a **Gothic** *cathedral in Paris, France.*

a b c d e f g h i j k l m n o p q r s t u v w x y z

Graduates wear traditional academic dress, a gown and cap, when they receive their degree.

gown [gown] *noun, plural* **gowns. 1.** a formal dress worn for special events: *a wedding gown.* **2.** a long, loose-fitting piece of clothing worn over clothes to show a level of importance or authority at official events. A gown may be worn by a college student at a graduation ceremony or by a town mayor at a special occasion.

grab [grab] *verb,* **grabbed, grabbing. 1.** to take hold of something suddenly or forcefully with the hand: *The football player jumped and grabbed the pass out of the air.* **2.** to take or connect with something in a quick or sudden way: *to grab a bite to eat.*
noun, plural **grabs.** the act of taking something suddenly or quickly.

grace [grays] *noun, plural* **graces. 1.** smooth and elegant in appearance or motion: *That ballet dancer is famous for the grace of her performance.* **2.** polite, generous behavior toward others: *My date had the grace not to criticize my dancing.* **3.** also, **Grace.** a short prayer said before a meal. **4.** an extra period of time allowed for something after the usual limit or deadline.
verb, **graced, gracing.** to bring elegance, knowledge, or charm to something: *The author graced our book club with his presence.*
• **good graces.** the fact of being liked or having approval: *I am in Mom's good graces because I have done all my chores.*

grace·ful [grays-ful] *adjective.* describing a smooth, elegant motion or appearance: *The champion figure skater was graceful even off the ice.* —**gracefully,** *adverb;* —**gracefulness,** *noun.*

gra·cious [gray-shus] *adjective.* acting with grace; polite, kind, and considerate: *My sister was gracious enough to let me have the last cookie.* —**graciously,** *adverb;* —**graciousness,** *noun.*

grack·le ▼ [grak-ul] *noun, plural* **grackles.** a noisy type of blackbird with glossy feathers and a long tail.

grade [grade] *noun, plural* **grades. 1.** a class, year, or rank in school. **2.** a mark, letter, or number used to rate the quality of a student's work in comparison to others. **3.** a degree of quality, value, or size on a scale of low to high. **4.** a slope, especially on a road or railroad: *The train chugged up the steep grade in the track.*
verb, **graded, grading. 1.** to arrange, sort, or classify people or things: *The best quality of beef is graded "Prime."* **2.** to assign a rank or rating; mark: *to grade test papers.* **3.** to level out; make even: *They graded the land to build the new house.*

grade school *Education.* a school for the first years of a child's education, usually the first six years; also called an elementary school.

grad·u·al [graj-yoo-ul] *adjective.* proceeding or developing by degrees; bit by bit: *Our wild puppy made a gradual change into a calm dog.* —**gradually,** *adverb.*

grad·u·ate ◄ [graj-oo-ate *for verb;* graj-oo-it *for noun*] *verb,* **graduated, graduating. 1.** *Education.* to be given a degree or diploma after completing studies at a school, college, or university. **2.** to put markings on something in order to show measurements: *The measuring cup is graduated in ounces.*
noun, plural **graduates.** someone who has completed his or her studies and has received a diploma or degree.

grad·u·a·tion [graj-oo-ay-shun] *noun, plural* **graduations.** *Education.* **1.** the act or fact of graduating: *For graduation, we must at least pass all our subjects.* **2.** a ceremony of graduating from school or college. *After graduation, we are having a class photo.*

graf·fi·ti [gruh-fee-tee] *plural noun, singular* **graffito.** words or pictures painted or scratched, usually in places where it is illegal to do this, such as on public buildings, buses, or subways.

> **Graffiti** comes from an Italian word meaning "to scribble" or "to write." The first markings called graffiti were writings found on buildings of ancient Rome, dating back 2,000 years or more.

graft [graft] *verb,* **grafted, grafting. 1.** to attach one part of a plant to another plant so that the two pieces grow as one plant. **2.** to replace damaged skin or bone with pieces of skin or bone from another part of the body.
noun, plural **grafts. 1.** a part of a plant that has been grafted onto another plant. **2.** a piece of bone or skin that is grafted.

grain [grane] *noun, plural* **grains. 1.** the seed of cereal crops such as oats, wheat, and corn. **2.** a tiny piece of something: *grains of sand.* **3.** the pattern of layers in wood or stone.

gram [gram] *noun, plural* **grams.** *Mathematics.* a unit of weight in the metric system. 28 grams approximately equal one ounce; 450 grams approximately equal one pound.

gram·mar [gram-ur] *noun, plural* **grammars.** *Language.* **1.** a system of rules that tells you how words should be arranged in a sentence. These rules help you communicate clearly. You usually learn to use these rules naturally, by listening and talking to other people. Someone who is an expert in grammar is a **grammarian. 2.** a book about the grammar of a particular language: *a French grammar; a Latin grammar.* **3.** the use of words following accepted rules: *My teacher says it's bad grammar to say, "That looks real nice" instead of "really nice."*

grammar school another term for an ELEMENTARY SCHOOL or GRADE SCHOOL.

gram·mat·i·cal [gruh-mat-i-kul] *adjective.* **1.** following or using the rules of grammar. The sentence *The cat sat on the mat* is grammatical while *On the mat cat the sat* is not. **2.** having to do with grammar: *The teacher corrects our grammatical errors.* —**grammatically,** *adverb.*

Sociable **grackles** *live in large flocks, snapping up insects with their bills.*

grand [grand] *adjective*, **grander, grandest. 1.** large and splendid; very impressive: *a grand cathedral.* **2.** being the first or most important: *He won the grand prize in the lottery.* **3.** wonderful or excellent: *She had a grand time at the ball.* **4.** in total; with everything included: *Lunch was a grand total of fifty dollars.*

grand·child [grand-*childe*] *noun, plural* **grandchildren.** the child of a son or daughter. A grandchild is either a grandson or granddaughter.

grand·daugh·ter [grand-*daw*-tur] *noun, plural* **granddaughters.** the daughter of a son or daughter.

grand·fath·er [grand-*fah*-THur] *noun, plural* **grandfathers.** the father of a mother or father.

grandfather clock ▶ a large clock that sits at the top of a tall cabinet with a swinging pendulum below it.

grand jury *Law.* a jury of twelve to twenty-three persons who hear evidence presented by a prosecutor to decide if there is enough evidence to send someone to trial for a crime.

grand·moth·er [grand-*muh*-THur] *noun, plural* **grandmothers.** the mother of a father or mother.

The workings inside a **grandfather clock** *are protected by its case.*

grand·par·ent [grand-*pare*-unt] *noun, plural* **grandparents.** a parent of a father or mother. A grandparent is either a grandfather or grandmother.

grand·son [grand-*sun*] *noun, plural* **grandsons.** the son of a son or daughter.

grand·stand ▼ [grand-*stand*] *noun, plural* **grandstands.** the main stand where people sit to watch a sporting event or parade. Each row of seats gets higher from front to back so that everyone gets a clear view of the action.
verb, **grandstanding.** to show off: *I wish he would stop grandstanding so much after he scores a goal.*

gran·ite [gran-it] *noun.* a very hard rock used in buildings. *adjective.* describing something made of granite: *a granite tile; a granite statue.*

gra·no·la [gruh-<u>noh</u>-luh] *noun.* a food made mainly from oats as well as other things like dried fruits and nuts. It is eaten as a breakfast cereal or snack.

grant [grant] *verb,* **granted, granting. 1.** to let have what is asked for; allow or give: *We were granted permission to use the sports field after school hours.* **2.** to admit that something is right or correct: *She granted that it would be better to arrive late than have an accident trying to get there on time.*
noun, plural **grants.** something that is given; a gift: *The scientist received a grant of fifty thousand dollars to continue his research.*
• **take for granted.** to assume something; suppose something is correct: *She took it for granted that we would give her a ride to school every day.*

A **grapevine** *can provide shade for a sunny patio, as well as producing grapes.*

grape·fruit [grape-*froot*] *noun, plural* **grapefruits.** a large, round, yellow or pink citrus fruit. It tastes something like a cross between an orange and a lemon.

grape·vine ▲ [grape-*vine*] *noun, plural* **grapevines.**
1. a vine that grapes grow on. **2.** an informal network that spreads rumors or news from one person to another: *I heard it on the grapevine that he has a crush on her.*

Grapevine is an unusual word in that it has a lost meaning that was intermediate between the original, literal meaning and the idiom "to hear something through the grapevine." The idiom comes from an old way of sending messages through a series of wires that were thought to spread out like a set of vines.

graph [graf] *noun, plural* **graphs.** *Mathematics.* a picture that uses numbers, lines, figures, and so on to show more clearly how certain facts relate to each other: *The graph showed us how people weigh more today than they did fifty years ago.*

graph·ic [graf-ik] *adjective.* **1.** having to do with a graph; using images or designs to show how certain facts relate to each other. **2.** having to do with handwriting, drawing, printing, photography, and other ways of presenting words and images to be seen. **3.** describing something told in detail: *He gave us a graphic account of the train wreck.*
noun, plural **graphics.** information that is shown by a picture or image.

graphic arts *plural noun. Art.* the different techniques used to display words and pictures in a printed work.

graph·ics [graf-iks] *plural noun. Art.* **1.** pictures in a book, magazine, or other printed work. These can be photos, maps, drawings, or any other such image: *The graphics in this children's book are very colorful.* **2.** pictures made and displayed on a computer.

graph·ite [graf-ite] *noun.* a soft, black substance made of carbon that is used as the writing material in pencils.

The Horseshoe football stadium at Ohio State University has a two-tiered **grandstand.**

A
B
C
D
E
F
G
H
I
J
K
L
M
N
O
P
Q
R
S
T
U
V
W
X
Y
Z

grasp [grasp] *verb*, **grasped, grasping. 1.** to take a firm hold of something, usually with the hand. **2.** to understand or get the meaning of: *I finally grasped what she was trying to tell me.*
noun, plural **grasps. 1.** the act of taking hold of something. **2.** understanding or knowledge: *She has a good grasp of mathematics.*

grass [grass] *noun, plural* **grasses. 1.** any of a large group of green plants with narrow leaves called blades, found all over the world. As well as the grasses that grow in lawns, there are many other types: rice, bamboo, wheat, oats, corn, and sugarcane are all grasses. **2.** one of the certain types of this plant used as the ground cover for lawns, sports fields, pastures, and so on. These grasses include rye, bluegrass, and Bermuda grass. If an area has a lot of grass, it can be described as **grassy.**

grass·hop·per ▼ [grass-*hop*-ur] *noun,*
plural **grasshoppers.** an insect that flies and jumps. Grasshoppers eat many types of grass and crops, and can cause problems for farmers.

grass·land [grass-*land*] *noun, plural* **grasslands.** land covered in grass, often used as pastures for animals.

grate[1] [grate] *noun, plural* **grates. 1.** a grid of metal bars placed over a window, drain, or other opening. **2.** a frame of metal bars used to hold burning wood in a fireplace.
🔊 A different word with the same sound is **great.**

grate[2] [grate] *verb*, **grated, grating. 1.** to shred something by rubbing it against a rough, sharp surface: *Mom likes to grate cheese onto her salad.* **2.** to scrape with a high-pitched noise: *She grated the chalk on the blackboard.* **3.** to irritate or annoy: *She says my silly giggling grates on her.*
🔊 A different word with the same sound is **great.**

grate·ful [grate-*ful*] *adjective.* feeling thankful for something: *I was grateful she found my lost book.* —**gratefully,** *adverb.*

grat·i·fy [grat-*i*-fye] *verb*, **gratified, gratifying.** to please or reward: *The teacher felt gratified that we appreciated all her hard work.* —**gratification,** *noun.*

grat·ing[1] [grate-*ing*] *noun, plural* **gratings.** another word for a GRATE.

grat·ing[2] [grate-*ing*] *adjective.* **1.** describing a high-pitched, grinding noise: *The chalk made a grating sound on the blackboard.* **2.** annoying or irritating: *The way he always interrupts me is very grating.*

grat·i·tude [grat-*uh*-tood] *noun.* the fact of being grateful; a feeling of thankfulness: *She was full of gratitude for our support.*

Grasshoppers *flick their legs backward to launch themselves up into the air.*

grave[1] [grave] *noun, plural* **graves.** a hole in the ground where a dead person is buried. Often a grave has a monument called a **gravestone,** which is marked with a name and other details about the dead person.

grave[2] [grave] *adjective*, **graver, gravest. 1.** very solemn or thoughtful: *The jury foreman had a grave expression on his face as he announced the verdict.* **2.** very serious or important: *a grave illness; The Congress made the grave decision to declare war.* —**gravely,** *adverb.*

grav·el [grav-*ul*] *noun.* crushed rock and pebbles used to make paths and roads.

grave·yard [grave-*yard*] *noun, plural* **graveyards.** an area where dead people are buried; a cemetery.

grav·i·tate [grav-*i*-*tate*] *verb*, **gravitated, gravitating. 1.** to be pulled by the force of gravity or gravitation. **2.** to move toward or be attracted to, as if by a physical force: *Tall athletes seem to gravitate toward basketball.*

grav·i·ta·tion [grav-*i*-tay-shun] *noun. Science.* the force that pulls all bodies in the universe toward each other. Gravitation keeps the Moon revolving around the Earth and the planets revolving around the Sun. This force is described as **gravitational.**

grav·i·ty [grav-*uh*-tee] *noun, plural* **gravities. 1.** *Science.* the force that pulls everything toward the center of a planet. It is the force that makes things fall when they are dropped or thrown into the air. **2.** something that is very serious: *When the boy was expelled, the principal spoke to us about the gravity of the situation.*

To be strictly correct, **gravity** and *gravitation* are not the same thing. Gravity is the force that causes things on Earth to have weight and to move downward toward the ground when they fall or are dropped. Gravitation is the tendency of any two bodies in the universe to tend to move toward each other because of this force; for example, the planets moving in orbit around the Sun.

gra·vy [gray-*vee*] *noun, plural* **gravies.** a sauce made from the juice of cooked meat.

gray [gray] *noun, plural* **grays.** a color made from a mixture of black and white.
adjective, **grayer, grayest. 1.** having the color gray: *a gray sweater.* **2.** dull or gloomy: *It was a cold, gray day.* This word is also spelled **grey.**

graze[1] [graze] *verb*, **grazed, grazing. 1.** to eat growing grass: *The horses grazed in the meadow.* **2.** to put animals out to feed on growing grass: *The rancher grazes his cattle on land near the river.*

graze[2] [graze] *verb*, **grazed, grazing.** to scrape or brush past: *The car grazed the fence before it crashed into the tree.*

grease [grees] *noun.* **1.** melted fat from animals: *There is grease in the pan from frying the bacon.* **2.** any thick, slippery substance like this, such as a substance made from oil used in engines to help different parts move smoothly.
verb, **greased, greasing.** to put grease on something.

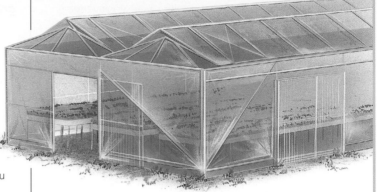

greas·y [grees-ee] *adjective*, **greasier, greasiest.**
1. describing something soiled with grease: *The garage floor was very greasy.* **2.** like grease; oily or fatty: *These French fries are greasy.*

great [grate] *adjective*, **greater, greatest. 1.** having a very large amount or size: *A great, gray cloud appeared in the sky.* **2.** remarkable, excellent, or important: *The development of the electric light bulb was a great invention.* **3.** more or better than usual: *It was a great pleasure to see her.*
🔊 A different word with the same sound is **grate.**

Great is a "great" word to use in your writing as long as you remember that it is a strong word and that not everything should really be called *great*. You can certainly say that Michael Jordan was a *great* basketball player or that you thought "Star Wars" was a *great* movie. But if you said that your friend Michael on your basketball team at school was a great player, or that the five movies you saw last month were all great, you would probably be using the word *great* when it really was not the right choice. It's better to just use *good* for things that are better than the usual, and save *great* for the few things that really stand out above all others.

Great Dane a breed of dog that is very large and strong, and has a short, smooth coat.

great-grand·child [grate-grand-child] *noun*, *plural* **great-grandchildren.** the child of a grandchild.

*The **Greek** site of Olympia is the place where the first Olympic Games were held in ancient times.*

great-grand·par·ent [grate-grand-pare-unt] *noun*, *plural* **great-grandparents.** the parent of a grandparent. A great-grandparent can be either a **great-grandfather** or a **great-grandmother.**

great·ly [grate-lee] *adverb*. highly or very much: *The little dog was greatly loved by the family.*

greed [greed] *noun*, *plural* **greeds.** the fact of wanting more than your fair share of something, especially money or things of value: *to be filled with greed for gold.*

greed·y [gree-dee] *adjective*. wanting more than your fair share: *The greedy boy filled his pockets with candy.*
—greedily, *adverb*.

Greek ▲ [greek] *adjective*. having to do with the country of Greece.
noun, *plural* **Greeks. 1.** someone who was born or is living in Greece. **2.** someone who lived in ancient Greece. **3.** the language of Greece.

green [green] *noun*. **1.** the color of living leaves. You can make this color by mixing yellow and blue. Green vegetables and herbs that you can eat are sometimes called **greens.** **2.** a grass-covered area: *the village green.* **3.** an area on a golf course near a hole where the grass is carefully cut. *adjective*, **greener, greenest. 1.** having the color green. **2.** covered by grasses or plants: *a green valley.* **3.** not ripe: *green tomatoes.* **4.** being someone with little or no experience: *The new player seemed pretty green so we told him it was his job to clean all the other players' cleats.*

green card *Government*. a document given by the U.S. government that allows foreigners to work legally in the country.

green•horn [green-horn] *noun*, *plural* **greenhorns.** an awkward or inexperienced newcomer, especially one who is unfamiliar with rules and procedures.

green·house ▲ [green-hous] *noun*, *plural* **greenhouses.** a glass room where plants can grow all year round.

greenhouse effect ▼ *Environment*. the trapping of the Sun's heat in the Earth's atmosphere. Burning fossil fuels (such as gas or coal) increases the level of carbon dioxide in the layer of air around the Earth. This effect reduces the amount of heat escaping into space, as the glass in a greenhouse stops heat escaping into the air.

greenhouse gas *Environment*. any of the gases that add to the greenhouse effect. These include water vapor, carbon dioxide, methane, fluorocarbons, and ozone.

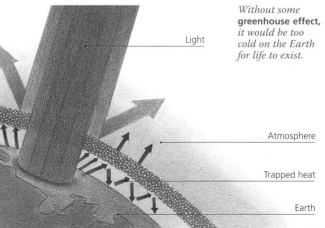

Without some **greenhouse effect,** *it would be too cold on the Earth for life to exist.*

Light

Atmosphere

Trapped heat

Earth

a b c d e f g h i j k l m n o p q r s t u v w x y z

green thumb *noun.* the fact of being good at growing plants: *One look at Grandpa's garden and you can tell he has a green thumb.*

greet [greet] *verb,* **greeted, greeting. 1.** to welcome in a friendly manner: *She greeted each of her guests at the door.* A person whose job is to welcome people in this way is a **greeter. 2.** to meet, receive, or give a response: *News of the victory was greeted with shouts of joy.* **3.** to appear to: *A sunny day greeted us on the first day of spring.*

gree·ting [greet-ing] *noun, plural* **greetings. 1.** the words and actions of someone who greets others: *The teacher gave the new student a friendly greeting.* **2. greetings.** a message of friendship and affection. Such messages can be sent using a **greeting card.**

gren·ade [gruh-nade] *noun, plural* **grenades.** a small bomb, usually thrown by hand. When it lands, it explodes and scatters small pieces of metal (called shrapnel) in all directions.

> In the French language the word **grenade** once meant an apple or other such fruit with seeds. The shape of a grenade is somewhat like a fruit of this kind.

grew [groo] *verb.* the past tense of GROW.

grey [gray] another spelling of GRAY.

grey·hound ▶ [gray-*hownd*] *noun, plural* **greyhounds.** a breed of tall, thin dog, with a smooth coat, narrow head, and long legs that can run very fast. Greyhounds are often used for racing.

Greyhounds have an affectionate and gentle temperament.

grid [grid] *noun, plural* **grids. 1.** a set or series of metal bars that crisscross each other to form a barrier or drain. **2.** a series of intersecting lines that divides a chart or map into squares.

grid·dle [grid-ul] *noun, plural* **griddles.** a thick, flat, metal pan with a handle, used mainly for cooking pancakes.

grid·i·ron [grid-eye-urn] *noun, plural* **gridirons.** another name for the game of football or a football field.

grid·lock [grid-lok] *noun, plural* **gridlocks. 1.** a traffic jam in which cars going in different directions are stopped on the same road. **2.** any situation in which motion or activity is stopped and progress is not possible.

grief [greef] *noun.* **1.** a feeling of great sadness and loss: *She felt terrible grief when her grandmother died.* **2.** a feeling of being criticized or annoyed; an irritation: *She gives him grief every time he forgets his homework.*

grieve [greev] *verb,* **grieved, grieving. 1.** to mourn or feel great sadness: *I grieved the loss of my cat.* **2.** to inflict grief or sorrow: *His rudeness grieves his parents.* Something that causes grief is described as **grievous.**

grill [gril] *noun, plural* **grills. 1.** a framework of metal bars used for cooking food over heat. **2.** a restaurant that serves food cooked on a grill.
verb, **grilled, grilling. 1.** to cook food on a grill. **2.** to ask a person a series of difficult questions: *The principal grilled him until he admitted to cheating.*

grim [grim] *adjective,* **grimmer, grimmest. 1.** describing something stern and joyless: *It was a grim day for the troops when they were forced to surrender.* **2.** refusing to give up or surrender: *grim determination.* **—grimly,** *adverb.*

grim·ace [grim-is] *noun, plural* **grimaces.** the act of twisting your face into an expression. People usually grimace when they are unhappy or displeased.
verb, **grimaced, grimacing.** to make a grimace.

grime [grime] *noun.* dirt that covers or is ingrained in the surface of something. Something that is covered in grime, can be described as **grimy.**

grin [grin] *verb,* **grinned, grinning.** to smile happily; have a big smile.
noun, plural **grins.** a happy smile.

grind [grinde] *verb,* **ground, grinding. 1.** to crush something into a powder or smaller pieces: *The mill grinds the wheat to make flour.* Something that crushes things in this way is called a **grinder. 2.** to sharpen or smooth something by rubbing it against a rough surface: *Dad ground the axe before he chopped the firewood.* **3.** to rub two things together harshly: *My brother grinds his teeth when he is concentrating.*

grind·stone ◀ [grinde-*stone*] *noun, plural* **grindstones.** a round, flat stone used to crush grain or sharpen tools.
• keep one's nose to the grindstone. to keep working hard: *The teacher says that if we keep our nose to the grindstone, we will all do well in the exams.*

grip [grip] *noun, plural* **grips. 1.** a strong grasp; a tight hold: *She kept a grip of her brother's hand crossing the street.* **2.** firm control: *The crowd was held in the grip of the exciting football game.*
verb, **gripped, gripping.** to hold onto tightly: *I gripped the railing so I wouldn't fall down the stairs.* When something holds one's attention firmly, it is said to be **gripping.**

grit [grit] *noun.* **1.** fine particles of stone or sand. **2.** strength of spirit; courage: *Mia fell over during the race, but showed grit by walking to the finish line.*
verb, **gritted, gritting.** to clamp something together hard, especially the teeth.

grits [grits] *plural noun.* ground, boiled grain, such as white corn, served as a cereal.

GRIZZLY BEARS

Grizzly bears, or brown bears, can weigh as much as 850 pounds. They have a large hump of muscle across the shoulders, long, sharp claws, and large, canine teeth. Hairs on their back and shoulders are often white-tipped, giving them a grayish color, which is why they are called "grizzly." They live in a range of places, from dense forest to mountain meadows or the arctic tundra, and eat a varied diet of plants, insects, fish, and smaller animals. The largest grizzly bears are found in coastal areas of Alaska and British Columbia, where salmon are abundant.

Adult grizzly bear

Where grizzly bears live

griz·zly bear ▲ [griz-lee] a large, ferocious bear that lives in western North America. It has long claws, and fur that varies in color from gray to brown.

groan [grone] *noun, plural* **groans.** a low, sad sound made by someone who is unhappy or in pain.
verb, **groaned, groaning.** to make this kind of sound.
🔊 A different word with the same sound is **grown.**

gro·cer [groh-sur] *noun, plural* **grocers.** a person who runs a store selling everyday foods and other household items.

gro·cer·y [grohs-ree *or* groh-suh-ree] *noun, plural* **groceries. 1.** a store where everyday foods and household items are sold. **2. groceries.** the everyday items sold in a grocery.

groom [groom] *noun, plural* **grooms. 1.** a man who is getting married or is just married. **2.** a person with the job of caring for horses.
verb, **groomed, grooming. 1.** to care for horses, especially brushing and washing them. **2.** to make something neat and clean, especially the hair of a person or animal: *Baboons spend much of the day grooming each others' fur.*

groove [groov] *noun, plural* **grooves.** a long, narrow cut or channel: *The chisel cut a groove in the wood.*
verb, **grooved, grooving.** to make such a cut or channel in something.

grope [grope] *verb,* **groped, groping. 1.** to feel around with the hands for something that cannot be seen: *I groped in my bag for a pen.* **2.** to search in a way that is uncertain: *Andy groped for a reason to give for being late.*

gross [gross] *adjective,* **grosser, grossest. 1.** whole and with nothing taken away: *A business's gross profit is the money made before costs are taken out.* **2.** easy to see; obvious; shocking: *The arrest of the innocent man was a gross injustice.* **3.** vulgar or offensive: *He said that he thinks spitting is gross behavior .*
noun, plural **grosses. 1.** a total amount without anything taken out. **2.** twelve dozen of something; 144: *That bakery sells a gross of apple pies every day.*

gro·tesque [groh-tesk] *adjective.* appearing strange or unnatural in shape: *The reflection of his face looked grotesque in the curved mirror.*
—**grotesquely,** *adverb.*

grouch·y [grou-chee] *adjective,* **grouchier, grouchiest.** in a bad mood; grumpy; bad-tempered. Someone who is in a bad mood is called a **grouch.**

ground¹ [ground] *noun, plural* **grounds. 1.** the firm, dry surface of the Earth; land. **2.** land not built on and set aside for a particular use: *a camp ground.*
verb, **grounded, grounding. 1.** to order aircraft down to the ground or to stay there: *All flights to New York were grounded during the snow storm.* **2.** to make a boat or ship strike the earth under water and so bring it to a stop: *The fishing boat became grounded in the shallows.* **3.** to hit a baseball so that it runs along the ground. **4.** to connect an electrical circuit to the ground so that excess electricity passes through it harmlessly.

ground² [ground] *verb.* the past tense and past participle of GRIND.
adjective. having been ground: *Milk and eggs were added to the ground wheat to make dough.*

ground ball in baseball, to strike the ball so that it runs or bounces along the ground. A different word with the same meaning is **grounder.**

ground·hog [ground-hog] *noun, plural* **groundhogs.** a large burrowing rodent that lives in North America. **Groundhog Day** is celebrated on February 2 each year. According to folklore, if a groundhog comes out of its burrow on this day and sees its shadow because the weather is sunny, it will take fright and run back inside and winter will continue. If the weather is cloudy and it does not see its shadow, it stays out, because spring weather will soon arrive. A different name for this animal is WOODCHUCK,

Something that is **grotesque** has a strange or frightening appearance. The word comes from a term meaning "cave." The first things that were called *grotesque* were strange drawings found in caves of ancient Rome.

*These **grubs** chew away the soft parts of a leaf, but leave the veins.*

grounds [groundz] *plural noun.* **1.** the area around a large building that is not built on: *The hospital grounds have pleasant gardens for the patients to look at.* **2.** reasons for doing something: *Leaving your cell phone on in class is grounds for having it confiscated.* **3.** the ground-up material that has settled after being added to a liquid: *coffee grounds.*

ground·wa·ter [ground-waw-tur] *noun. Environment.* water that seeps through the Earth's surface and lies underground. It can come to the surface in springs, or be reached using wells or pumps.

group [groop] *noun, plural* **groups. 1.** a number of things or people gathered together: *A group of his friends went to the beach together.* **2.** a number of people or things that are like each other in some way and go together; category: *Spaghetti and macaroni are part of the group of foods called pasta.*
verb, **grouped, grouping.** to put together in a group: *I grouped the books by subject.*

grouse [grous] *noun, plural* **grouse** or **grouses.** a type of bird related to quail and turkeys. Grouse are plump with mottled gray, brown, or black feathers, often covering their legs. They live in forests and open country mostly in the Northern Hemisphere and are hunted as food.

grove [grove] *noun, plural* **groves.** a group or cluster of trees: *There is an olive grove beside the old house.*

grow ▼ [groh] *verb,* **grew, growing. 1.** to increase in size: *The town's population grew to double its previous size in ten years.* **2.** to come to life and develop: *The seed grew into a tree.* **3.** to plant and cause to grow; cultivate: *Last summer he grew tomatoes in his garden.* **4.** to gradually become: *We grew bored on the rainy afternoon.*

growl [groul] *verb,* **growled, growling.** to make a low, rough sound in the throat, usually as a threat when angry: *The dog growled at me when I went into its yard.*
noun, plural **growls.** a low, rough sound made in the throat.

grown [grohn] *verb.* the past participle of GROW.
🔊 A different word with the same sound is **groan.**

grown-up [grohn-up] *adjective.* **1.** fully grown; adult; mature. **2.** suitable for or like an adult: *The girl was pleased to get a grown-up bike with only two wheels for her birthday.*
noun, plural **grown-ups.** an adult; one who is fully grown: *The grown-ups made lunch while the children played.*

growth [grohth] *noun, plural* **growths. 1.** the act or process of growing: *The growth of many plants slows or stops in winter.* **2.** something that has grown: *The doctor said the growth on my toe was a wart.*

grub ▲ [grub] *noun, plural* **grubs. 1.** a creature that is the first stage of development of many insects that looks like a fat worm; larva. **2.** a slang word for food.
verb, **grubbed, grubbing.** to dig in the dirt; dig up: *Hal grubbed the old tree roots out of the ground.*

grudge [gruj] *noun, plural* **grudges.** a dislike of someone for a particular reason that has been felt for a long while: *She still holds a grudge against me because I didn't invite her to my sleepover party.*

gru·el·ing [groo-ling] *adjective.* very tiring; demanding: *The soldiers went on a grueling march.*

grue·some [groo-sum] *adjective.* causing horror and disgust: *The story was full of gruesome monsters.*

gruff [gruf] *adjective,* **gruffer, gruffest. 1.** low and rough in sound; hoarse: *He answered in a gruff voice.* **2.** bad-tempered and unfriendly: *He often has a gruff manner when he is tired.*
—gruffly, *adverb.*

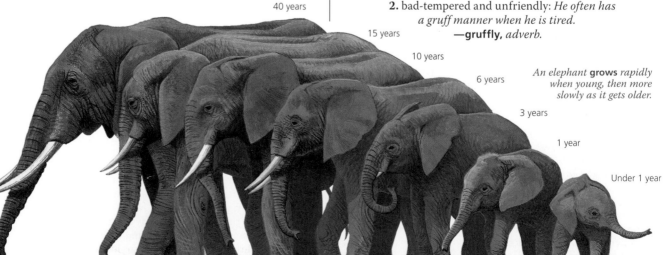

40 years

15 years

10 years

6 years

3 years

1 year

Under 1 year

*An elephant **grows** rapidly when young, then more slowly as it gets older.*

*The path of a **guided missile** can be changed by remote control after it has been launched.*

grum·ble [grum-bul] *verb,* **grumbled, grumbling.**
1. to complain in a bad-tempered way that is not loud: *She grumbled when I forgot to clear the table.* **2.** to make a low, murmuring, rumbling sound: *We could hear thunder grumbling in the distance.*
noun, plural **grumbles. 1.** a bad-tempered complaint. **2.** a deep, murmuring rumble.

grum·py [grum-pee] *adjective,* **grumpier, grumpiest.**
in a bad mood; bad-tempered; cranky.

grunt [grunt] *noun, plural* **grunts.** a short, low sound a bit like the noise a pig makes.
verb, **grunted, grunting. 1.** to make such a sound: *He grunted as he bent over to tie his shoe.* **2.** to speak in a similar, low, short way as this sound: *"Help me up,"* she grunted as she tried to stand.*

guar·an·tee [gare-un-tee] *noun, plural* **guarantees.**
1. a promise made to repair, replace, or return the money for a bought item if it turns out to be faulty. **2.** something that makes a particular result certain: *Studying does not guarantee that you will do well in the test, but it will help.*
verb, **guaranteed, guaranteeing. 1.** to give a guarantee for goods sold. **2.** to make certain; ensure: *Turning off the heater at bedtime guarantees it won't set the house on fire.* **3.** to make a promise: *I guarantee I will be there on time.*

guard ▶ [gard] *verb,* **guarded, guarding. 1.** to protect from harm or danger: *Security men guard the bank at night.* **2.** to watch over and control: *The officers guarding the prison stopped the criminals from escaping.* **3.** in sports, to try to stop a member of the other team moving forward or scoring. **4.** to take an action that can stop something bad from happening: *She used the pedestrian crossing to guard against being hit by a car.*
noun, plural **guards. 1.** a person or group that protects from harm or danger. **2.** the act of guarding: *Keep guard over your bag or someone might take it.* **3.** a device or object that protects: *Put the guard in front of the fireplace to stop sparks falling on the floor.* **4.** in football, one of two offensive linemen positioned on either side of the center. **5.** in basketball, one of two players who generally play farther from their basket when their team has the ball.

guard·i·an [gar-dee-un] *noun, plural* **guardians.**
1. one who protects from harm or danger or watches over: *The guardian at the city gate searched our vehicle before we were allowed to enter.* **2.** a person appointed by a court to care for someone who is unable to look after himself or herself, especially children: *While the children's mother was in the hospital, their aunt was their guardian.*

guer·ril·la [guh-ril-uh] *noun, plural* **guerrillas.**
a member of a small, independent band of soldiers that does not belong to a country's official army. Guerrillas often fight by making surprise attacks or raids. This word is also spelled **guerilla.**
🔊 A different word with the same sound is **gorilla.**

The word **guerrilla** comes from a phrase meaning "a little war." In the way of fighting used by guerrillas, the strategy is to fight a series of small battles, rather than a major war as a large army would.

guess [gess] *verb,* **guessed, guessing.**
1. to reach a conclusion without the knowledge to judge if it is correct: *Tom couldn't see in the dark and had to guess where the door was.* **2.** to give a correct answer without the knowledge to back it up: *She guessed that the capital of Portugal is Lisbon.* **3.** to think or believe something without knowing for sure: *I guess the bus will stop at my street.*
noun, plural **guesses.** a conclusion reached by guessing: *My answer to the question was a guess.*

guest [gest] *noun, plural* **guests. 1.** a person invited to visit another person's home. **2.** a customer at a hotel, club, or restaurant.

guid·ance [gye-duns] *noun.* **1.** the act of guiding or directing; instructing: *Under the teacher's guidance, I soon learned how to use the computer program.* **2.** advice given as to what to do: *The careers adviser gave her guidance about which course to take.*

guide [gide] *verb,* **guided, guiding.** to help by showing the way; instruct or direct: *The store clerk guided Alex to where the CDs were sold.*
noun, plural **guides.** one who shows the way: *A tour guide took us around the town.* A book that provides maps and other information about a place is called a **guidebook.**

guid·ed missile ▲ a missile that is able to be directed to a particular target, either by radio signals sent by people on the ground or by controls on the missile that are set before it is launched.

guide dog a dog that is trained to assist people who are blind or cannot see well. Guide dogs lead the person, making sure it is safe for them to continue walking on. Guide dogs are also called **seeing-eye dogs.**

guide word *Language.* a word printed at the top of a page in a dictionary, telephone book, or other reference book that shows the first or last entry on that page. Guide words help readers search through the book quickly.

guild [gild] *noun, plural* **guilds. 1.** *History.* in the Middle Ages, a group formed by workers who had the same trade or craft. A guild protected its members' interests and made sure they carried out work of a high standard. **2.** an association for people with the same interests, aims, or profession: *The writers' guild holds meetings where writers can read their latest stories.*
🔊 A different word with the same sound is **gild.**

Ceremonial Coldstream **guards** *stand outside London's Buckingham Palace.*

guil·lo·tine [gil-uh-*teen* or *gee*-uh-*teen*] *noun, plural* **guillotines.** *History.* a machine used to execute people by cutting off their head, especially during the French Revolution. It is made up of two grooved posts and a heavy blade that drops between them. *verb,* **guillotined, guillotining.** to execute using this machine: *King Louis XVI of France was guillotined on January 21, 1793.*

The **guillotine** is named for Joseph Ignace *Guillotin,* a doctor who lived at the time of the French Revolution, about 200 years ago. As horrible as it may seem to execute someone by cutting off their head, Guillotin actually was a doctor who argued for this method because the other ways of executing people at the time were even more cruel and horrible. Dr. Guillotin hoped that eventually the death penalty would not be used at all.

Electric **guitars** *are usually made of hardwood and have steel strings.*

guilt [gilt] *noun, plural* **guilts. 1.** the fact of having carried out a crime or done something wrong: *Her guilt for stealing the wallet was proved–we found it in her bag.* **2.** the feeling of something having been your fault: *The guilt of dropping Mom's vase wouldn't leave me.* A different word with the same sound is **gilt.**

guilt·y [gil-tee] *adjective,* **guiltier, guiltiest. 1.** having done something wrong or committed a crime: *He is guilty of murder.* **2.** feeling at fault; ashamed: *I feel guilty for losing your umbrella.*

guin·ea pig [gin-ee] **1.** a small rodent with a stout body and short ears, legs, and tail. They are often kept as pets, are used in scientific experiments. Some are used in scientific experiments and, in some South American countries, for meat. **2.** a person used to test something on, as in a scientific experiment: *Holly used me as a guinea pig for her new recipe for chocolate-flavored omelets.*

Because the **guinea pig** is an animal that has often been used in scientific experiments, it has also come to mean a person or thing used to try out or test something: "When my sister makes a new recipe for cookies, I am her *guinea pig*; she has me taste it first to make sure it is OK."

gui·tar ▲ [guh-*tar*] *noun, plural* **guitars.** *Music.* an instrument with a body shaped like a flat violin, a long neck, and six or more strings that are plucked or strummed. A person who plays the guitar is called a **guitarist.**

gulch ▶ [gulch] *noun, plural* **gulches.** a deep, narrow valley, often with a stream at the bottom; ravine.

gulf [gulf] *noun, plural* **gulfs. 1.** a large area of the ocean partly surrounded by land. **2.** a wide difference between two things; a serious disagreement: *The gulf between the two nations took a long time to overcome.*

gull ▶ [gul] *noun, plural* **gulls.** any of a number of coastal birds with gray and white feathers, long wings, a slightly hooked beak, and webbed feet. This bird is also known as a **seagull.**

gul·li·ble [gul-uh-bul] *adjective.* believing almost anything you are told; easily cheated or tricked: *The gullible boy believed us when we said the Moon is made of cheese.* A person who is gullible is said to have **gullibility.**

Before young **gulls** *grow their adult feathers, they are mottled brown in color.*

gul·ly [gul-ee] *noun, plural* **gullies.** a small ditch or valley formed by flowing water: *During the downpour, water flowed down the gully and carried dirt away.*

gulp [gulp] *verb,* **gulped, gulping. 1.** to swallow something quickly and eagerly in large amounts: *He gulped down his dinner in five minutes.* **2.** to suddenly swallow air: *Sue gulped nervously when the teacher asked to see her. noun, plural* **gulps. 1.** the act of gulping: *The frog swallowed the fly with a gulp.* **2.** a mouthful of something swallowed eagerly or quickly: *She took a gulp of her cold drink.*

gum[1] [gum] *noun, plural* **gums. 1.** a sticky liquid that flows out of some plants when they are cut and that hardens as it dries. Gum is used to make glue, some candy, and in medicines. **2.** a candy for chewing that was originally made from plant gum and other ingredients. *verb,* **gummed, gumming. 1.** to glue together with gum or another sticky material. **2.** to become clogged with something sticky.

• **gum up.** to stop from moving forward or working; interfere with: *The plans for our concert were gummed up by complaints from neighbors about the noise it might make.*

The fast-flowing Yellowstone River carves out **gulches** *through the Rocky Mountains.*

gum² [gum] *noun, plural* **gums.** the pink flesh that covers the part of the jaws in the mouth and the base of the teeth.

gun [gun] *noun, plural* **guns. 1.** a weapon in the form of a long metal tube through which something such as a bullet is shot by an explosive force. Guns include pistols, revolvers, rifles, machineguns, and cannons. The firing of guns is called **gunfire. 2.** something similar in shape to a gun or through which something is forced or shot: *She used a spray gun to paint the car.* *verb,* **gunned, gunning.** to increase the speed of a vehicle rapidly: *The customs officer gunned the engine of his boat to catch up with the other vessel.*

gun·ner [gun-ur] *noun, plural* **gunners.** a soldier responsible for looking after guns and firing them.

gun·pow·der [gun-pow-dur] *noun, plural* **gunpowders.** a dry mixture of chemicals that burn and explode when lit by a spark. Gunpowder is used for fireworks, for guns, and as an explosive in mines and for demolishing buildings.

gup·py [gup-ee] *noun, plural* **guppies.** a small fish native to North and South America. There are many types of guppies and they are often kept in aquariums.

gur·gle [gur-gul] *verb,* **gurgled, gurgling. 1.** to flow with a bubbling noise: *The stream gurgled as it flowed down the hill.* **2.** to make a similar bubbling sound: *My baby brother gurgles when he is happy.* *noun, plural* **gurgles.** such a bubbling sound.

gush [gush] *verb,* **gushed, gushing. 1.** to suddenly flow out in large amounts. **2.** to speak enthusiastically and in a rush: *Everyone gushed over the cute puppy.* *noun, plural* **gushes.** a sudden, large flow: *The gush of water when the dam burst swept the houses away.*

gust [gust] *noun, plural* **gusts. 1.** a sudden, short blast of air or wind. When there are many gusts of air, the weather is said to be **gusty. 2.** a short outburst of feeling: *Simon slammed the door in a gust of temper.* *verb,* **gusted, gusting.** to move in a gust, as wind.

gut [gut] *noun, plural* **guts. 1.** the stomach and the intestines of an animal. The internal organs of an animal are often called its **guts.** Someone with courage is also said to have **guts. 2.** thread made from the intestines of animals. This thread is very strong and is used for such things as the strings of musical instruments and in medicine for sewing up wounds.

gut·ter [gut-ur] *noun, plural* **gutters. 1.** a channel or ditch at the side of a road for carrying away excess water. **2.** a trough attached along the edge of a roof to carry away rain water.

guy¹ [guy] *noun, plural* **guys. 1.** a word for a man or boy used in everyday speech. **2. guys.** in everyday speech, any group of people, male or female.

guy² [guy] *noun, plural* **guys.** a rope or wire used to tie something down and hold it steady: *The guys on our tent will stop it blowing away.*

A famous person in the history of England is Guy Fawkes, a man who was part of a plot in 1605 to blow up the King of England and the buildings where the government met. After this event, people in England celebrated a holiday each year on which they set off fireworks and made statues of Guy Fawkes. Such a figure was known as a **Guy**, and from this came the word *guy* meaning any man or boy.

guz·zle [guz-ul] *verb,* **guzzled, guzzling.** to eat or drink greedily and often: *That dog always guzzles his dinner in minutes and then looks around for more.*

gym [jim] *noun, plural* **gyms. 1.** a gymnasium. **2.** a class in physical education given at school or college.

gym·na·si·um [jim-nay-zee-um] *noun, plural* **gymnasiums.** a large room or building with equipment for physical exercises and sports.

gym·nas·tics ▼ [jim-nas-tiks] *plural noun.* **1.** physical exercises done to increase strength, flexibility, agility, and balance. A person who performs them as a sport or art form is called a **gymnast. 2.** the practice of these exercises.

gy·ne·col·o·gy [guy-nuh-kol-i-jee] *noun. Medicine.* the branch of medicine that deals with illnesses that only women get, especially problems with their reproductive organs. A doctor who works in this area is called a **gynecologist.**

Gyp·sy [jip-see] *noun, plural* **Gypsies.** a person belonging to the group of people thought to have come from India to Europe at least one thousand years ago. They now live as wanderers in many parts of the world.

*Artistic **gymnastics** is a popular spectator sport at the Summer Olympic Games.*

The word **Gypsy** comes from Egyptian, meaning someone from the North African country of Egypt. It was thought that Gypsies originally came from this country. Though it is not known for certain today where they actually came from, it is now thought that Gypsies originated in India, not Egypt.

gypsy moth a type of moth that originally comes from Europe and Asia. It was introduced to North America in the late 1800s, where it has become a pest. Its hairy caterpillars destroy hardwood trees such as oaks by eating their leaves.

gy·ro·scope [jye-ruh-skope] *noun, plural* **gyroscopes.** a wheel mounted on a frame so that its axis can move and point in any direction no matter how the frame moves. Gyroscopes are used in instruments that keep airplanes and ships balanced, and in compasses.

a b c d e f g h i j k l m n o p q r s t u v w x y z

Hh

H, h *noun, plural* **H's, h's.** the eighth letter of the English alphabet.

A rain forest provides an ideal **habitat** *for ferns and many other kinds of plants.*

hab·it [hab-it] *noun, plural* **habits. 1.** something done so often it is done without thinking: *Jamie has a habit of biting his nails when he's nervous.* **2.** a particular type of clothing worn by members of a group, especially a religious order: *The monk's habit was a long, brown shirt tied with a cord.*

hab·i·tat ▲ [hab-uh-tat] *noun, plural* **habitats.** *Environment.* the place where a plant or animal lives naturally: *Clams live in a coastal habitat.*

hab·it·u·al [huh-bich-oo-ul] *adjective.* **1.** done as the result of habit: *He is a habitual fingernail chewer.* **2.** normally used; usual: *Mom drinks a habitual cup of coffee in the morning.* —**habitually,** *adverb.*

ha·ci·en·da ▼ [hah-see-en-duh] *noun, plural* **haciendas.** in Spanish-speaking parts of the Americas, a large country estate, ranch, or farm.

hack [hak] *verb,* **hacked, hacking. 1.** to chop roughly with heavy blows, usually with an axe: *She hacked at the rope to cut the boat free.* **2.** to get access to a computer system illegally: *The criminal hacked into the bank's computer system to steal money.*
noun, plural **hacks. 1.** the act of chopping roughly: *Kyle gave the branch a hack with his hatchet.* **2.** a cut or gash made in something.

Haciendas *date back to the large tracts of land in the New World given to Spanish nobles in the 1500s.*

hack·er [hak-ur] *noun, plural* **hackers.** *Computers.* **1.** someone who is skilled at gaining access to computer systems, especially illegally. **2.** someone who experiments with computers as a hobby.

had [had] *verb.* the past tense of HAVE.

had·dock ▶ [had-ik] *noun, plural* **haddock.** a fish from the North Atlantic Ocean that is similar to the cod and that is used for eating.

Haddock *are found in the northern Atlantic Ocean.*

had·n't [had-unt] the shortened form of "had not."

hai·ku [hye-koo] *noun, plural* **haiku.** *Literature.* a form of poetry originating in Japan that is often about nature. The poem must have three lines, the first line made up of five syllables, the second made up of seven, and the third made up of five.

hail¹ [hale] *noun.* **1.** balls of frozen rain that fall from the sky. **2.** a shower of anything hard: *A hail of nuts fell onto us when we shook the tree.*
verb, **hailed, hailing. 1.** to pour down hail. **2.** to fall in a heavy shower like hail: *Pieces of plaster hailed down from the ceiling.*

hail² [hale] *verb,* **hailed, hailing.** to shout out in greeting or to catch attention: *I called out to hail the bus to stop.*

hair [hare] *noun, plural* **hairs. 1.** a fine strand or thread that grows from the skin of an animal or human. **2.** a mass of these strands that grow together, especially those on a person's head. The way that hair is arranged on the head is called a **hairstyle** or **hairdo. 3.** fine strands that grow on the leaves or stems of some plants.
🔊 A different word with the same sound is **hare.**

hair·cut [hare-kut] *noun, plural* **haircuts.** the act or process of cutting and arranging the hair on a person's head.

hair·dress·er [hare-dres-ur] *noun, plural* **hairdressers.** a person whose job is to wash, cut, and arrange hair.

hair·pin [hare-pin] *noun, plural* **hairpins.** a fine, U-shaped piece of wire used to keep hair in place.
adjective. having a U-shape like a hairpin: *James drove the car carefully around the hairpin turn.*

hair·y [hare-ee] *adjective,* **hairier, hairiest.** having lots of hair or hair-like material: *That sweater prickles my skin because it is too hairy.*

half [haf] *noun, plural* **halves. 1.** one of two equal parts that something can be divided into: *Dozen is another word for twelve, so half a dozen is six.* **2.** in sports, one of two periods into which a game is divided: *I scored a goal in the first half of the match.*
adjective. being one of two equal parts something is divided into: *Add the juice of half a lemon to the mixture.*
adverb. **1.** as much as one half: *He only half filled the cup.* **2.** partly: *The job is half finished.*

half brother a brother who has only one parent the same as someone else: *Alice has the same mother as her half brother, but they have different fathers.*

half·heart·ed [*haf-har-tid*] *adjective.* showing no real effort or interest: *She made a half-hearted attempt to clean up the mess, then gave up.* This word is also spelled **halfhearted. —half-heartedly,** *adverb.*

half-mast ▶ [*haf-mast*] *noun.* a point halfway down a flag pole where a flag flies as a sign of sorrow and respect when someone important dies. A different word with the same meaning is **half-staff.**

half sister a sister who has only one parent the same as someone else.

half·time [*haf-time*] *noun, plural* **halftimes.** the short break between two halves of a game, such as basketball and football.

half·way [*haf-way or haf-way*] *adverb.* to or at half the distance: *Pull the drapes halfway shut; I'm halfway through the book.* *adjective.* in the middle between two points; at the midpoint: *the halfway mark in a race.*

hal·i·but [*hal-uh-but*] *noun, plural* **halibut** *or* **halibuts.** a large flatfish eaten as food. Halibut are found in the northern Atlantic and Pacific oceans.

hall [*hawl*] *noun, plural* **halls. 1.** a passage inside a house with doors or openings that lead to other rooms; corridor. **2.** a room at the entrance to a building; lobby: *We'll wait for you near the information desk in the hall.* **3.** a building or large room that is used for shows, meetings, and other public events: *a music hall; a town hall.*

hal·le·lu·jah [*hal-uh-loo-yuh*] *interjection. Religion.* a word or cry that expresses thanks to God. *noun, plural* **hallelujahs.** a song or exclamation of praise to God.

Hal·low·een [*hal-uh-ween*] *noun, plural* **Halloweens.** October 31, when people dress up in costumes, often as witches or ghosts, and children collect candy and other treats, and sometimes play tricks.

> The holiday of **Halloween** gets its name from the phrase "hallowed evening." The word *hallowed* means "holy," and Halloween was thought of as a holy evening because it came the night before November 1, which is All Saints Day. This is a day on which members of the Catholic Church honor all the saints of the Church, and also honor members of their own family who have died.

hal·lu·ci·na·tion [*huh-loo-suh-nay-shun*] *noun, plural* **hallucinations.** *Medicine.* a seeing or hearing of something that seems real but is not really there. A person may have hallucinations because of an illness or because they have taken a drug.

hall·way [*hawl-way*] *noun, plural* **hallways.** a passageway or hall in a house or other building.

ha·lo ▶ [*hay-loh*] *noun, plural* **haloes.** *Religion.* **1.** a brightness or circle of light drawn around the heads of Jesus, saints, and angels in religious paintings to show that they are holy. **2.** anything that looks like a circle of light around a person or thing: *a halo around the Moon.*

hal·o·gen [*hal-uh-jin*] *noun. Chemistry.* any one of a particular group of five non-metallic elements. These elements are fluorine, chlorine, bromine, iodine, and astatine. A **halogen lamp** uses halogen to produce a very bright white light.

halt [*hawlt*] *noun, plural* **halts.** a stop for a short time: *The car came to a halt at the red light.* *verb,* **halted, halting.** to stop: *The traffic was halted by an accident on the bridge.*

hal·ter [*hawl-tur*] *noun, plural* **halters. 1.** a device made from straps of rope or leather. It is fastened around the head of an animal such as a horse or cow so that it can be led easily. **2.** a woman's blouse with the top part held in place by a narrow band that is fastened or tied behind the neck, leaving the shoulders and back uncovered.

halve [*hav*] *verb,* **halved, halving. 1.** to divide into two equal parts: *James halved the banana so we both had a piece.* **2.** to cut down or reduce something by half: *The new bridge has halved the time it takes me to get to school.*

halves [*havz*] *noun.* the plural of HALF.

ham [*ham*] *noun, plural* **hams.** the salted or smoked meat from the back leg or shoulder of a pig, eaten either hot or cold.

ham·burg·er [*ham-bur-gur*] *noun, plural* **hamburgers. 1.** finely chopped beef. **2.** a flat, round piece of finely chopped beef, cooked and eaten in a bun or round bread roll.

ham·mer [*ham-ur*] *noun, plural* **hammers. 1.** a tool with a heavy metal head, used to drive nails into wood or other material, and for striking metal to force it into a shape. **2.** anything shaped or used like a hammer, such as the padded lever that strikes the strings of a piano. *verb,* **hammered, hammering. 1.** to hit with force again and again; pound: *to hammer in a nail.* **2.** to hit with a hammer to force into a shape: *to hammer gold into jewelry.*

In this old wall painting, Jesus and a follower are shown with **haloes.**

ham·mock [ham-uk] *noun, plural* **hammocks.** a long piece of strong material or netting that is hung between two supports and used as a bed.

ham·per¹ [ham-pur] *verb,* **hampered, hampering.** to slow down or get in the way of action or progress; obstruct: *A heavy rain hampered our efforts to clean up the yard.*

Running on an exercise wheel gives a pet **hamster** *plenty of exercise.*

ham·per² [ham-pur] *noun, plural* **hampers.** a large basket or container with a lid: *a picnic hamper; a laundry hamper.*

ham·ster ▲ [ham-stur] *noun, plural* **hamsters.** a small, furry rodent with a short tail, kept as a pet.

hand [hand] *noun, plural,* **hands. 1.** the part of the body at the end of the arm, below the wrist, having the thumb, four fingers, and palm. **2.** anything that is thought of as being like this part of the body: *the hands of a clock.* **3.** help; aid: *Please give me a hand moving this box.* **4.** a part of something; a role: *He had a hand in planning the attack.* **5. hands.** control or possession: *The thief is now in the hands of the police.* **6.** a worker or crew member: *a hired hand; "All hands on deck," the captain ordered.* **7.** a set of cards held by a player in a card game, or one round of the game.
verb, **handed, handing. 1.** to move or give with the hand: *The waiter handed him the bill.* **2.** to pass on as if with the hand: *That glass bowl was handed down to us from my grandmother.*

hand·bag [hand-bag] *noun, plural* **handbags.** a bag for carrying small articles, such as keys or a wallet.

hand·ball [hand-bawl] *noun, plural* **handballs. 1.** a game in which players use their hands to strike a small rubber ball against a wall. **2.** the ball used in this game. **3.** the deliberate touching of the ball in a soccer game by a player other than the goalkeeper.

hand·book [hand-buk] *noun, plural* **handbooks.** *Literature.* a book that gives useful information about a subject: *a handbook of chemistry; a handbook of car repair.*

> A **handbook** got its name because originally these books were small. A person could hold such a book in one hand to read it.

hand·cuff [hand-kuf] *noun, plural* **handcuffs.** one of a pair of metal rings that are joined by a short chain and fastened with a key. Handcuffs are locked around the wrists of a prisoner to keep the hands close together. *verb,* **handcuffed, handcuffing. 1.** to put handcuffs on a person. **2.** to hold back to progress or action of someone or something: *to be handcuffed by rules and regulations.*

hand·ful [hand-ful] *noun, plural* **handfuls. 1.** the amount that can be held in one hand: *a handful of sand.* **2.** a small number of things or people: *Only a handful of runners finished the marathon in less than three hours.* **3.** someone or something that is difficult to control or manage: *I'm not minding the twins again, they are too much of a handful.*

hand·i·cap [han-dee-kap] *noun, plural* **handicaps. 1.** an injury or medical condition that makes it more difficult to do some things: *Because of her handicap, my sister uses a wheelchair.* **2.** a disadvantage given to a stronger player or team at the start of the game to make the competition more equal.
verb, **handicapped, handicapping.** to make more difficult: *Poor weather and fading light handicapped the search for the missing boat.*

hand·i·capped [han-dee-*kapt*] *adjective.* having a disability: *Some handicapped people use wheelchairs.*

hand·i·craft ▶ [han-dee-*kraft*] *noun, plural* **handicrafts.** *Art.* the art of making things with the hands, such as pottery or quilts.

Making shoes and sandals is a common **handicraft** *in Pakistan.*

hand·ker·chief [hang-kur-chif] *noun, plural* **handkerchiefs.** a small square piece of cloth for wiping the nose or face.

han·dle [han-dul] *noun, plural* **handles.** the part of an object that is grasped by the hand to hold or open it: *the handle of a cup; a door handle.*
verb, **handled, handling. 1.** to feel or touch with the hands: *Eggs can break easily and must be handled with care.* **2.** to control or deal with; manage: *to handle a difficult situation.* A **handler** is someone whose job is to take care of and train an animal, or who works or deals with a particular thing.

han·dle·bars [han-dul-*barz*] *plural noun.* the curved metal bars with a handle at each end that are attached to the front of a bicycle or motorcycle. The rider uses the handlebars to steer.

hand·made [hand-made] *adjective.* made by someone using their hands or tools rather than by a machine: *handmade chocolate; handmade shoes.*

hand·out [hand-out] *noun, plural* **handouts.** something, such as money or food, that is given to someone in need.

hand·rail [hand-rail] *noun, plural* **handrails.** a railing that can be gripped by the hand. Handrails are used for support or protection at the side of stairways, platforms, and balconies.

hand·shake [hand-shake] *noun, plural* **handshakes.** the act of grasping another person's hand and shaking it. A handshake is a sign of greeting, farewell, or agreement.

hand·some [han-sum] *adjective,* **handsomer, handsomest. 1.** attractive or pleasing in appearance: *a handsome man; a handsome street lined with grand buildings.* **2.** large in quantity; generous: *a handsome reward; a handsome contribution.* —**handsomely,** *adverb.*

hand·spring ▶ [hand-*spring*] *noun,*
plural **handsprings.** a kind of somersault in
which the body turns a full circle from a standing
position. The person springs backward or forward
to balance on both hands, while bringing their
heels over their head to land back on their feet.

hand·writ·ing [hand-*rye*-ting] *noun,*
plural **handwritings.** writing done by hand with
a pen or pencil.

hand·y [han-dee] *adjective,* **handier, handiest.**
1. clever with the hands; skillful: *to be handy*
with a paintbrush. **2.** useful and simple to use:
a handy gadget.

hang [hang] *verb,* **hung,** (*for definitions 1, 2, and*
4) *or* **hanged** (*for definition 3*), **hanging. 1.** to attach or
be attached from above only: *an apple hanging on a tree.*
2. to fasten or attach something so it can move back and
forth; suspend: *to hang a door on hinges.* **3.** to kill a person
by tying a rope around their neck then making their body
hang in the air. **4.** to float in the air; hover: *Mist hung over*
the lake.
noun. the way a cloth hangs or falls: *the hang of a skirt.*
• **get the hang of.** to learn the right way to do or use
something: *It took me a few days before I got the hang*
of my new camera.

han·gar [hang-ur] *noun, plural* **hangars.** a building in
which aircraft are kept between flights.
🔊 A different word with the same sound is **hanger.**

hang·er [hang-ur] *noun, plural* **hangers.** a frame of metal,
plastic, or wood with a hook in the center for hanging
it from a rail or peg. A hanger is used for hanging up
clothes.
🔊 A different word that sounds the same is **hangar.**

hang glider ▼ a type of glider like a large kite.
The person riding is suspended in a harness beneath
and launches the hang glider into the air from a cliff
or hilltop. **Hang gliding** is the sport of doing this.

hang·man [hang-mun] *noun, plural* **hangmen.**
a person whose job is to hang those sentenced
to death.

hang·nail [hang-*nale*] *noun,*
plural **hangnails.** a strip of skin that
hangs partly loose at the bottom
or side of a fingernail.

hang·out [hang-*owt*] *noun,*
plural **hangouts.** a place where
someone spends a lot of time:
The beach is Zac's
favorite hangout.

hang·up [hang-up] *noun,*
plural **hangups.** a worry
or difficulty that a person
cannot get out of their
mind: *Nicole won't go*
camping because
she has a hangup
about spiders.

han·ker [hang-kur] *verb,* **hankered,**
hankering. to wish or long for
something: *The exhausted soldiers*
hankered for a hot meal and a dry
bed. —**hankering,** *noun.*

Ha·nuk·kah [hah-nuh-kuh] *noun. Religion.* an eight-day
Jewish holiday in December. It marks the anniversary of
the dedication of the temple in Jerusalem. This word is
also spelled **Chanukah.**

hap·haz·ard [hap-haz-urd] *adjective.* not organized
or arranged according to a plan: *Nothing matched in*
her haphazard collection of plates, cups, and saucers.
—**haphazardly,** *adverb.*

hap·pen [hap-un] *verb,* **happened, happening. 1.** to take
place; occur: *Watch what happens when I push this*
button. **2.** to take place without being planned: *We just*
happened to see her in the park. **3.** to find by chance:
Goldilocks happened upon the house of the three bears.
4. to affect somebody or something in an unpleasant way:
She looks so unhappy, something must have happened.

hap·pen·ing [hap-un-ing] *noun, plural* **happenings.**
anything that happens; an event.

hap·pi·ly [hap-uh-lee] *adverb.* **1.** with pleasure, joy, and
gladness: *to sing happily; They lived happily ever after.*
2. fortunately; luckily: *Happily, the mistake did no harm.*

hap·pi·ness [hap-ee-nis] *noun.* the fact of being pleased,
joyful, or content: *Beaming with happiness, she showed*
us her new baby.

hap·py [hap-ee] *adjective,* **happier, happiest. 1.** feeling
or showing pleasure or joy: *a happy smile.* **2.** pleased or
satisfied: *I'm happy with that result.* **3.** lucky; fortunate:
By a happy coincidence we both caught the same bus.

happy-go-lucky *adjective.* without a care in the world;
trusting luck: *Julie-Ann's happy-go-lucky manner wins*
her lots of friends.

*In **hang gliding** the pilot*
can control the speed and
direction of flight.

har·ass [huh-ras or hare-us] *verb*, **harassed, harassing.** to bother or annoy someone: *The fans were harassing the referee after he made a call against their team.* —**harassment**, *noun*.

har·bor ▼ [har-bur] *noun, plural* **harbors.** an area of water along a coastline where ships can anchor, safe from rough seas.
verb, **harbored, harboring. 1.** to shelter a bad person: *to harbor a criminal.* **2.** to keep bad thoughts in the mind: *I harbored a grudge against him because he took my place in the swimming team.*

hard [hard] *adjective*, **harder, hardest. 1.** firm or solid to touch; not soft: *The cup smashed when it hit the hard floor.* **2.** needing much effort or work: *a hard climb; a hard test.* **3.** full of difficulty, trouble, or worry: *They had little money, and life was hard.* **4.** having or using great force or strength: *a hard kick; I gave the door a hard push.* **5.** not kind or gentle; stern: *The coach is pretty hard on players who miss practice.*
adverb. **1.** with a lot of effort: *Anna couldn't undo the knot, no matter how hard she tried.* **2.** with force or strength: *The wind blew hard.* **3.** in a way that causes pain, sadness, or suffering: *The town was hit hard by the tragedy.*

The words **hard**, *difficult*, and *tough* all mean something that is not easy to do. Usually, *tough* means something that is done with the body, through physical effort: *Cleaning out the garage was a tough job.* *Difficult* is more likely to mean something done with the mind or by means of skill: *Getting around in a foreign county can be difficult if you don't speak or read the language at all.* *Hard* is the most general word and can apply to either physical or mental effort: *the hard work of chopping down a tree; a hard test in mathematics.*

hard-boiled *adjective*. **1.** of an egg, boiled until both the white and the yolk are hard: *Hard-boiled eggs are great for picnics.* **2.** not able to show feelings due to bad experiences; tough: *Some policemen are hard-boiled.*

*Ancient Greek colonies had good **harbors** so that people could keep in touch with their homeland by ship.*

hard copy *Computers*. a copy of a computer file that is printed on paper.

hard·en [hard-un] *verb*, **harden, hardening. 1.** to make or become stiff or firm: *Glue takes hours to harden.* **2.** to make someone tough and less able to feel sympathy for others: *A life of crime can harden someone.*

> A **hard copy** of a computer document is not actually hard, since it is printed on paper. The name came about because it was thought of as hard as compared to the "soft copy" that is displayed by software on the computer screen.

hard·ly [hard-lee] *adverb*. **1.** only just; barely: *The line for tickets was hardly moving.* **2.** not really; almost certainly not: *I didn't ask Naomi to my party, so she's hardly likely to invite me to hers.*

hard·ship [hard-ship] *noun, plural* **hardships.** a state of suffering or need: *The long drought caused farmers great hardship.*

hard·ware [hard-ware] *noun*. **1.** the tools and building supplies used in a home or garden such as hammers and nails, screws, screwdrivers, and locks. **2.** *Computers*. the machinery of a computer such as the disk drive, screen, printer, and keyboard. The programs that run on it are called SOFTWARE.

hard·wood [hard-wud] *noun, plural* **hardwoods.** strong, dense wood from trees that have leaves, such as the oak, beech, and mahogany. Hardwoods are used to make furniture.

har·dy [har-dee] *adjective*, **hardier, hardiest.** able to resist difficult conditions; tough. —**hardiness**, *noun*.

hare [hare] *noun, plural* **hare** or **hares.** an animal related to the rabbit with long ears, a short tail, and strong hind legs that allow it to run very fast.
🔊 A different word with the same sound is **hair**.

harm [harm] *noun, plural* **harms. 1.** the fact of being hurt or damaged: *Much harm was done by the storm.* **2.** a wrong or mistake: *The boys could not see what harm there was in missing school for one day.*
verb, **harmed, harming.** to cause harm or damage: *Smoking cigarettes will harm your health.*
• **in harm's way.** in a dangerous place or condition; at risk; vulnerable: *Allowing the children to walk home at night would put them in harm's way.*

harm·ful [harm-ful] *adjective*. causing harm or injury: *Not sleeping enough is harmful to your health.* —**harmfully**, *adverb*.

harm·less [harm-lis] *adjective*. having no likelihood of causing harm: *The dog may look fierce, but he's quite harmless.* —**harmlessly**, *adverb*.

har·mon·i·ca [har-mon-uh-kuh] *noun, plural* **harmonicas.** *Music*. a small wind instrument with metal reeds that is blown or sucked.

har·mo·ni·ous [har-<u>mone</u>-ee-us] *adjective.* **1.** having to do with pleasing sounds, actions, or ideas: *a harmonious combination of colors.* **2.** friendly and peaceful: *The children played together in a harmonious way.* —**harmoniously,** *adverb.*

har·mo·nize [har-muh-nize] *verb,* **harmonized, harmonizing.** *Music.* to sing or play musical notes that sound right and pleasing together.

har·mo·ny [har-muh-nee] *noun, plural* **harmonies. 1.** *Music.* a pleasing combination of musical notes that are played or sung: *The voices of the choir sang in perfect harmony.* **2.** a pleasing arrangement or combination of parts: *a harmony of colors in the flower garden.* **3.** a state of agreement; being friendly: *Our dog and our cat live in harmony most of the time.*

har·ness [<u>har</u>-nis] *noun, plural* **harnesses.** the straps and buckles used to attach a horse to a cart or buggy to pull it along.
verb, **harnessed, harnessing. 1.** to place a harness on an animal. **2.** to control a natural force to make use of it: *A sailing boat harnesses wind power to move it forward.*

harp [harp] *noun, plural* **harps.** *Music.* a large musical instrument with strings stretched across a triangular frame; the strings are plucked to produce notes.

har·poon ▶ [har-<u>poon</u>] *noun, plural* **harpoons.** a spear attached to a rope line that is thrown or shot by a gun to catch and kill large fish or whales.
verb, **harpooned, harpooning.** to spear or kill large fish or whales with a harpoon.

harp·si·chord [<u>harp</u>-suh-kord] *noun, plural* **harpsichords.** *Music.* a musical instrument like a piano but which is played by strings being plucked, not hit by a hammer.

har·row [<u>hare</u>-oh] *noun, plural* **harrows.** a piece of farm machinery towed by a tractor. It has a heavy metal frame and sharp metal teeth or disks to break up and level soil.
verb, **harrowed, harrowing. 1.** to break up and level soil with a harrow. **2.** to cause suffering or pain to someone. A **harrowing** experience is one that causes great distress.

harsh [harsh] *adjective,* **harsher, harshest. 1.** rough or jarring to the senses: *The icy wind felt harsh on my skin.* **2.** cruel and severe: *The life of crews on early sailing ships was very harsh.* —**harshly,** *adverb;* —**harshness,** *noun.*

har·vest ▶ [<u>har</u>-vist] *noun, plural* **harvests. 1.** the act of gathering in crops when they are ready: *The harvest was early this year.* **2.** the crops gathered in at harvest time: *a potato harvest.*
verb, **harvested, harvesting.** to gather in a crop or crops: *to harvest wheat.*

har·vest·er [<u>har</u>-vi-stur] *noun, plural* **harvesters.** a piece of farm machinery that cuts and gathers in grain crops.

In the nineteenth century whalers used **harpoons** *to hunt whales.*

has [haz] *verb.* a present tense of HAVE.

hash [hash] *noun, plural* **hashes. 1.** a meal of chopped meat mixed with vegetables and browned in a pan. **2.** something disorganized or confused; a mess.
• **hash out.** to talk something over in detail with others: *Jordan's parents were grateful to his teachers for hashing out a plan for his coaching needs with them.*
• **make a hash of.** to make a mess of; ruin: *I tried to connect the DVD player to the TV but made a hash of it.*

has·n't [<u>haz</u>-unt]the shortened form of "has not."

has·sle [<u>has</u>-ul] *verb,* **hassled, hassling.** to annoy someone continuously; bother: *I don't like to get phone calls that hassle you about buying something or giving money.*
noun, plural **hassles. 1.** the act of hassling someone. **2.** an annoying problem: *Getting to school when the bus doesn't run is a real hassle.*

haste [haste] *noun.* speed or quickness in actions; a hurry: *Sophia got ready with great haste as she was late for her job interview.*

has·ten [<u>hase</u>-un] *verb,* **hastened, hastening.** to move or act quickly; hurry: *We'd better hasten so we can get home before the storm hits.*

In India tea is **harvested** *by women, who pick the leaves by hand.*

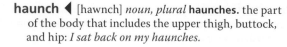

hast·y [hay-stee] *adjective,* **hastier, hastiest. 1.** done in a hurry; swift: *She had a hasty snack before rushing out the door.* **2.** not considered; too quick: *Our decision to buy a puppy was hasty because we could not look after it.* —**hastily,** *adverb.*

hat [hat] *noun, plural* **hats.** a covering for the head, often with a high middle part and a brim around the base.

hatch¹ [hach] *verb,* **hatched, hatching. 1.** to produce young from an egg: *Chickens hatch their chicks.* **2.** to break out from an egg: *The ducklings hatched yesterday.* A **hatchery** is a place for hatching eggs. **3.** to make up a plan or plot, usually in secret: *The king's enemies hatched a plot to capture him.*

hatch² [hach] *noun, plural* **hatches. 1.** an opening in a wall, a floor, or the deck of a ship, which people or goods can pass through. **2.** a cover for such an opening.

hatch·back [hach-*bak*] *noun, plural* **hatchbacks.** a car with a rear door that opens up to load luggage.

hatch·et [hach-it] *noun, plural* **hatchets.** a small axe with a short handle that is used with only one hand.

hate [hate] *verb,* **hated, hating. 1.** to have a very strong dislike of something or someone; detest: *They hated the man who had stolen all their money.* **2.** to dislike and want to avoid: *I hate taking my cough medicine.*

hate·ful [hate-ful] *adjective.* **1.** full of hate: *a hateful person.* **2.** arousing or deserving hatred: *a hateful thing to say.*

ha·tred [hay-trid] *noun, plural* **hatreds.** the fact of hating; a very strong dislike of a person or thing: *The soldiers felt hatred for the enemy they were fighting.*

haugh·ty [haw-tee] *adjective,* **haughtier, haughtiest.** believing oneself to be a lot better than other people; snobbish: *a haughty manner.* —**haughtily,** *adverb.*

haul ◀ [hawl] *verb,* **hauled, hauling. 1.** to pull or drag with effort: *The sailors hauled the boat out of the water.* **2.** to move from one place to another; transport; carry: *The trucks are hauling coal from city to city.*
noun, plural **hauls. 1.** the act of hauling. **2.** the distance over which a thing is hauled: *It's a long haul from here to Kansas City.* **3.** an amount gained or acquired: *The swimming team took in quite a haul of medals.* 🔊 A different word with the same sound is **hall.**

haunch ◀ [hawnch] *noun, plural* **haunches.** the part of the body that includes the upper thigh, buttock, and hip: *I sat back on my haunches.*

haunt [hawnt] *verb,* **haunted, haunting. 1.** to be in or visit a place as a ghost, spirit, or other such strange form: *Some people say the old house is haunted by the ghost of a woman who lived there a hundred years ago.* **2.** to go often to a place: *She haunted the shopping mall.* **3.** to be often present in the mind of: *Memories of the car crash haunted him.* Bringing to the mind a strong emotion that lasts for some time is **haunting:** *a place of haunting beauty.*
noun, plural **haunts.** a place often visited by someone: *The park was one of his favorite haunts.*

have [hav] *verb,* **had, having. 1.** to possess or hold; own: *Giraffes have long necks.* **2.** to be made up of; contain: *Our troop has 31 Scouts.* **3.** to keep in the mind; know: *I have no doubts at all.* **4.** to engage in; carry on: *to have a fight.* **5.** to give birth to: *to have a baby.* **6.** to need or be forced to: *All children have to go to school.* **7.** to cause something to happen; arrange for: *He had the engine working in no time.*
✚**Have** is a special verb often used with other verbs to show that the action of the main verb began in the past: *They have owned that house for twenty years; I have already called the police.*
plural noun, **haves.** people with a lot of money and possessions. People with little money and few possessions are the **have-nots.**
🔊 A different word with the same sound is **halve.**

In American English we use the term **have to** to say that something needs to be done or is required: "In this state you *have to* be 16 years old in order to drive a car." British English usually says have got to in sentences like this: "You *have got to* be 16 years old to drive a car." The word "must" can also be used with the same meaning: "You *must* be 16 years old to drive a car."

ha·ven [hay-vun] *noun, plural* **havens.** a place of shelter or safety: *The park was a peaceful haven for people from the busy city.*

ha·ven't [hav-unt] the shortened form of "have not."

hav·oc [hav-ik] *noun.* great damage or destruction: *A sudden hail storm caused havoc in the orchard.*

Ha·wai·ian [huh-wye-un] *noun, plural* **Hawaiians. 1.** someone from the group of people who were native to the islands of Hawaii. **2.** any person who comes from the state of Hawaii. **3.** the native language of Hawaii. *adjective.* of or relating to Hawaii, its language, or its people.

hawk¹ ▶ [hawk] *noun, plural* **hawks.** a bird with a hooked beak, broad, rounded wings, and sharp eyesight.

hawk² [hawk] *verb,* **hawked, hawking.** to carry around and offer goods for sale by shouting: *Traders hawked their wares on every street corner.*

haw·thorn [haw-*thorn*] *noun, plural* **hawthorns.** a thorny tree or shrub with white or pinkish flowers and small, reddish or dark berries.

hay [hay] *noun, plural* **hays.** grass or other plants that are cut, dried, and used to feed livestock.
🔊 A different word with the same sound is **hey.**

hay fever *Health.* an allergy caused by breathing pollen in the air. A person with hay fever sneezes a lot and has a runny nose and itchy eyes.

hay·loft [hay-*loft*] *noun, plural* **haylofts.** the upper part of a barn or stable, used for the storage of hay.

After harvesting, loose hay is built into **haystacks** *to store it for animal fodder in winter.*

hay·stack ▲ [hay-*stak*] *noun, plural* **haystacks.** a large pile of hay outdoors.

haz·ard [haz-urd] *noun, plural* **hazards.** something that is dangerous or that can cause harm: *Old cans of oil paint can be a fire hazard; Smoking is a hazard to your health.*
verb, **hazarded, hazarding.** to offer an explanation or suggestion without being definite; venture: *Can anyone hazard a guess as to Joe's age?*

haz·ard·ous [haz-ur-dus] *adjective.* involving risk; dangerous: *A coal miner has a hazardous job.*

hazardous waste *Environment.* a substance, such as a nuclear product or a chemical, that is dangerous to living things and can damage the environment. Factories and nuclear power plants are places that can produce hazardous waste.

haze [haze] *noun, plural* **hazes.** dust, smoke, or mist in the air: *A haze covered the city.*

ha·zel [hay-zul] *noun, plural* **hazels. 1.** a shrub or tree with light brown nuts that are good to eat. **2.** a light brown color like the color of a hazelnut.
adjective. having a light brown color: *hazel eyes.*

ha·zy [hay-zee] *adjective,* **hazier, haziest. 1.** covered with a haze: *a hazy sky after a forest fire.* **2.** as if covered with haze; unclear or confused: *I have only a hazy memory of my first day at school.* —**haziness,** *noun.*

H-bomb an abbreviation for HYDROGEN BOMB.

he *pronoun.* **1.** a male person or animal that is being referred to: *My brother said he would meet me outside the theater.* **2.** any person: *Each person sat down in the same seat he had occupied before the break.*
noun, plural **hes.** a male person or animal: *My cat is a he.*

head [hed] *noun, plural* **heads. 1.** the part of the human body above the neck, where the nose, eyes, ears, and mouth are. **2.** the part of an animal that is like the human head. **3.** the top or front part of anything: *the head of a pin.* **4.** a mass of flowers or leaves that is firm and rounded like a head: *a head of cabbage.* **5.** a person in charge; chief: *the head of a company.* **6.** one animal of a group: *Sheep sell for $25 per head.* **7.** mental ability: *She has a good head for business.* **8. heads.** the side of a coin that shows a person's head or other main design.
adjective. chief or main: *the head waiter in a restaurant.*
verb, **headed, heading. 1.** to lead or be at the front of a group: *A marching band headed the parade.* **2.** to be in charge of: *to head a large business.* **3.** to go in a particular direction: *Head for the hills!* **4.** in soccer, to strike the ball with the head: *He headed the ball into the goal.*

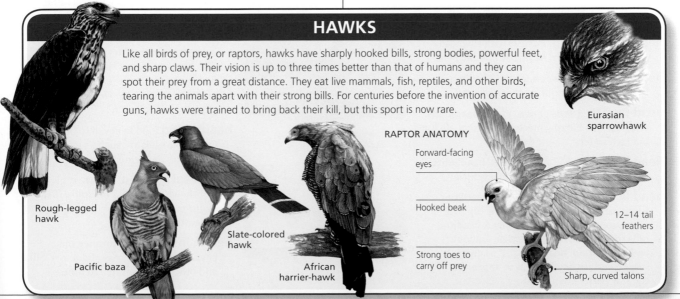

HAWKS

Like all birds of prey, or raptors, hawks have sharply hooked bills, strong bodies, powerful feet, and sharp claws. Their vision is up to three times better than that of humans and they can spot their prey from a great distance. They eat live mammals, fish, reptiles, and other birds, tearing the animals apart with their strong bills. For centuries before the invention of accurate guns, hawks were trained to bring back their kill, but this sport is now rare.

Eurasian sparrowhawk

RAPTOR ANATOMY

Forward-facing eyes

Hooked beak

12–14 tail feathers

Rough-legged hawk

Slate-colored hawk

Strong toes to carry off prey

Sharp, curved talons

Pacific baza

African harrier-hawk

*For special ceremonies, Sioux Indians wore elaborate **headdresses** made of feathers.*

head·ache [hed-*ake*] *noun,* plural **headaches. 1.** a pain in the head. **2.** something that causes worry or difficulty: *Trying to park near the school is a major headache.*

head·band [hed-*band*] *noun, plural* **headbands.** a band worn around the head to keep hair in place or as a decoration.

head·dress ▲ [hed-*dress*] *noun,* plural **headdresses.** a covering or decoration worn on the head: *a tribal headdress.*

head·er [hed-*ur*] *noun, plural* **headers. 1.** in soccer, a shot or pass of the ball made with the head: *She scored a goal with a header.* **2.** a title at the top of each page of a document written on a computer, usually put in place automatically by software.

head·first [hed-*furst*] *adverb.* with the head going first: *He dived headfirst into the pool.*

head·ing [hed-*ing*] *noun, plural* **headings.** a title for a paragraph, page, or chapter.

head·land [hed-*land*] *noun, plural* **headlands.** *Geography.* a narrow piece of land that sticks out into water.

head·light [hed-*lite*] *noun, plural* **headlights.** a powerful light at the front of a vehicle.

head·line [hed-*line*] *noun, plural* **headlines.** a line printed in large type at the top of a newspaper or magazine article. A headline tells the reader what the article is about. *verb,* **headlined, headlining. 1.** to give a story a certain headline. **2.** to appear as the star performer in a show.

head·long [hed-*lawng*] *adverb.* **1.** with the head first: *I fell headlong into bed, exhausted.* **2.** in a great hurry; without thinking: *The child ran headlong across the busy road. adjective.* made with the head first: *a headlong dive.*

head·on [hed-*on*] *adverb.* with the front or head first: *The yacht sailed head-on into a storm. adjective.* taking place head-on: *a head-on collision.*

head·phone [hed-*fohnz*] *noun, plural* **headphones.** a stereo, radio, or telephone receiver that is held over the ear by a headband or placed in the ear.

head·quarters [hed-*kwor*-turz] *noun.* the main office of a company or organization: *NASA has its headquarters in Washington, D.C.*

head·rest [hed-*rest*] *noun, plural* **headrests.** part of a chair or seat that supports the head. Automobile headrests are designed to prevent neck injuries in a crash.

head start an advantage, such as an early start, given to someone in a race or other competition.

head·strong [hed-*strong*] *adjective.* determined to have one's own way; stubborn: *a headstrong teenager.*

heads-up [hedz-*up*] *noun.* a quick message giving notice that something will happen soon; a warning or alert: *The boss sent everyone a heads-up about the next fire drill. adjective.* alert and quick to take advantage of opportunities: *Our team was playing heads-up basketball.*

head·waters [hed-*waw*-turz] *plural noun.* the streams that make up the beginning of a large river.

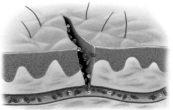
Blood clots to stop bleeding.

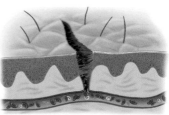
New skin begins to grow under a scab.

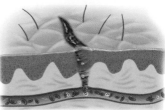
Scab falls off and wound is healed.

*A cut begins to **heal** when blood clots and forms a scab.*

head·way [hed-*way*] *noun.* forward motion or progress: *The bus was unable to make much headway in the heavy snow.*

heal ◀ [heel] *verb,* **healed, healing.** to make or become sound or well again: *This ointment will help to heal the wound.*
🔊 Different words with the same sound are **heel** and **he'll.**

health [helth] *noun.* **1.** the state of being free from injury or disease: *The boy was nursed back to health by his parents.* **2.** the condition of the mind or body: *How is your grandmother's health?*

health food food believed to be good for people's health, such as fruits, vegetables, and cereal grains.

health·ful [helth-*ful*] *adjective.* giving health; wholesome: *a healthful diet; healthful exercise.*
—**healthfully,** *adverb.*

health insurance insurance that covers most of the cost of doctors' bills and other expenses due to illness.

health·y [hel-thee] *adjective,* **healthier, healthiest.**
1. having or showing good health: *I've always had a healthy appetite.* **2.** giving health; healthful.

Strictly speaking, **healthy** and *healthful* are not different words for the same thing. *Healthful* means "giving or bringing good health" and *healthy* means "having good health:" Thus you are more likely to be *healthy* if you eat *healthful* foods.

heap [heep] *noun, plural* **heaps.** a group of things placed untidily one on top of the other; a disorganized pile. *verb,* **heaped, heaping. 1.** to put things into a pile. **2.** to fill or give in large quantities: *She heaped the food onto her plate.* Something that is enough to make a small heap on a spoon or plate is **heaping:** *a heaping teaspoon of sugar.*

hear [heer] *verb,* **heard, hearing. 1.** to take in sound through the ears: *Speak up, I can't hear you!* **2.** to listen to: *Sit down and hear what I have to say.* **3.** to gain information; learn: *I hear our neighbors are moving out.* **4.** to receive a telephone call, letter, or other communication: *We hardly ever hear from our cousins.*
• **hear of.** to consider the idea: *I will not hear of you paying for lunch.*
◀)) A different word with the same sound is **here.**

heard [hurd] *verb.* the past tense and past participle of HEAR.
◀)) A different word with the same sound is **herd.**

hear·ing [heer-ing] *noun, plural* **hearings. 1.** the ability to hear: *The old man's hearing is not very good.* **2.** the act of listening or finding out information: *Hearing my uncle's funny stories is always entertaining.* **3.** an opportunity to be heard: *His ideas should be given a hearing.*

hearing aid *Health.* a small electronic device that allows a person to hear better. It is worn in or behind the ear.

hear·say [heer-say] *noun.* information from other people; rumor: *According to hearsay, Mary is coming home today.*

heart ▲ [hart] *noun, plural* **hearts. 1.** the organ in the chest that pumps blood around the body through the arteries and veins. In humans, the heart is divided into four parts called chambers. **2.** the center of a person's feelings: *The homeless man's story won our hearts.* **3.** strength or courage; spirit: *She took heart from the support of her parents.* **4.** the center of something: *The public library is in the heart of town.* **5.** something shaped like a heart. **6.** a card marked with a red heart shape. The suit of cards marked with this shape is **hearts.**
• **by heart.** memorized word for word: *I know the words to that song by heart.*

heart attack *Health.* a sudden and painful stoppage of the movement of the heart.

heart·beat [hart-beet] *noun, plural* **heartbeats.** one regular movement of the heart.

heart·break [hart-brake] *noun, plural* **heartbreaks.** feelings of great sadness or unhappiness: *The death of the kitten caused heartbreak in our family.* Something that is very sad or causes great unhappiness is **heartbreaking.**

heart·broken [hart-broh-kun] *adjective.* feeling great sadness or unhappiness: *He was heartbroken when his girlfriend left him.*

hearth [harth] *noun, plural* **hearths.** the area of a fireplace or the space in front of it.

heart·less [hart-lis] *adjective.* having no kindness or pity; cruel and unfeeling.

heart·y [har-tee] *adjective,* **heartier, heartiest. 1.** warm-hearted, sincere, and enthusiastic: *hearty laughter.* **2.** large and nourishing: *a hearty lunch.* —**heartily,** *adverb.*

heat [heet] *noun, plural* **heats. 1.** a form of energy that raises the temperature of the place or system it affects. **2.** the condition of being hot; warmth: *I like the heat of a sunny August day.* **3.** a system used to warm a building: *Set the heat at 68 degrees.* **4.** strong feeling: *in the heat of the argument.*
verb, **heated, heating.** to make or become warm or hot: *Turn on the furnace to heat the house.*

heat·er [hee-tur] *noun, plural* **heaters.** a device that gives off heat, such as a radiator or furnace.

heath [heeth] *noun, plural* **heaths.** an area of open land covered with low bushes or heather.

heath·er [heTH-ur] *noun, plural* **heathers.** a low-growing evergreen shrub that grows wild in Europe and Asia. Its flowers are purple, pink, or white.

heave [heev] *verb,* **heaved, heaving. 1.** to pull, throw, lift, or raise with great effort: *The burglar heaved a brick through the window.* **2.** to give voice to loudly or with great effort: *to heave a sigh.* **3.** to rise and fall in turn: *The ship heaved in the heavy seas.*

heav·en [hev-un] *noun, plural* **heavens.** *Religion.* the place regarded in Christianity and other religions as the home of God and the angels. This word is also spelled **Heaven.** The sky or outer space is **the heavens:** *The comet streaked through the heavens.*

heav·en·ly [hev-un-lee] *adjective.* **1.** of or relating to heaven; divine: *a heavenly choir of angels.* **2.** having to do with the sky or outer space. **3.** wonderful, beautiful, or pleasing: *a heavenly birthday cake.*

heav·y [hev-ee] *adjective,* **heavier, heaviest. 1.** weighing a lot; hard to carry, lift, or move: *The men had a hard time moving the heavy refrigerator.* **2.** weighing more than usual for its kind: *Heavy clothing keeps you warm in cold weather.* **3.** large in amount or size: *a heavy crop of apples.* **4.** difficult to manage, do, or carry out: *Flying a jet aircraft is a heavy responsibility.*
—**heavily,** *adverb;* —**heaviness,** *noun.*

Main vein

Main artery, or aorta

Pulmonary artery

Pulmonary vein

Blood flows into the heart from the veins and flows out into the arteries.

a b c d e f g h i j k l m n o p q r s t u v w x y z

He·brew [hee-broo] *noun, plural* **Hebrews. 1.** one of the Jewish people of ancient times. **2.** the language spoken by the ancient Jews. A modern form of Hebrew is the official language of Israel.

heck·le [hek-ul] *verb,* **heckled, heckling.** to interrupt a speaker or performer by making noise and calling out. —**heckler,** *noun.*

hec·tare [hek-tare] *noun, plural* **hectares.** *Mathematics.* a metric unit of area, equal to 10,000 square meters, or about 2½ acres.

hec·tic [hek-tik] *adjective.* full of activity; very busy or confused: *the hectic days leading up to Christmas.*

he'd [heed] **1.** the shortened form of "he had." **2.** the shortened form of "he would."
🔊 A different word with the same sound is **heed.**

hedge [hej] *noun, plural* **hedges.** a fence formed by a row of closely growing bushes or trees. *verb,* **hedged, hedging. 1.** to surround, mark off, or enclose with a hedge. **2.** to avoid giving a direct answer: *Stop hedging and tell the truth!*

hedge·hog [hej-hawg *or* hej-hog] *noun, plural* **hedgehogs. 1.** a small insect-eating animal with a pointed snout and spines on its back and sides. It rolls itself into a ball for protection when attacked or frightened. Hedgehogs are found in Europe. **2.** another word for a PORCUPINE.

heed [heed] *verb,* **heeded, heeding.** to pay attention to; listen or mind: *Heed your doctor's advice and you'll get better.*
noun. careful attention paid to a person or to a piece of advice, a risk, a warning, or a possible problem: *The hikers paid no heed to the warning sign and stood on the cliff edge.*
🔊 A different word with the same sound is **he'd.**

heel [heel] *noun, plural* **heels. 1.** the back part of a person's foot below the ankle. The heel takes much of the body's weight in standing or walking. **2.** something that is like a heel in shape, position, or use, such as the raised back part of a shoe.
verb, **heeled, heeling.** to follow closely: *Tell the dog to heel.*

heif·er [hef-ur] *noun, plural* **heifers.** a young cow that has not had a calf.

height [hite] *noun, plural* **heights. 1.** the distance from bottom to top: *Her height is 5 feet 3 inches.* **2.** a high point or place: *I have always been afraid of heights.* **3.** the highest part or point: *an athlete at the height of her powers; It was the height of rudeness to say something like that.* The highest or most intense level of something is **the heights**: *The pop star's career will one day reach the heights.*

height·en [hite-un] *verb,* **heightened, heightening.** to increase or make something increase: *Our fear heightened as we entered the dark cave.*

Heimlich maneuver
Health. an emergency technique used to force out of a person's mouth an object that is causing him or her to choke. To use the technique, one should stand up, put the arms around the choking victim from behind, and press hard into the upper abdomen.

> The **Heimlich maneuver** is named for the person who is identified as the inventor of this first-aid technique. Henry *Heimlich,* an American doctor, first published a description of this maneuver in 1974.

heir [air] *noun, plural* **heirs. 1.** a person who has the right to receive the property or money of a person after that person has died. **2.** one who receives and continues a particular style, idea, belief, custom, or talent of an earlier person or period: *She is the heir to her mother's cooking skills.*
🔊 Different words with the same sound are **air** and **ere.**

heir·ess [air-us] *noun, plural* **heiresses.** a woman who has the right to receive or has received the property or money of a person after that person has died.

heir·loom [air-loom] *noun, plural* **heirlooms.** an object that has belonged to a family for several generations.

held [held] *verb.* the past tense and past participle of HOLD.

hel·i·cop·ter ◀ [hel-uh-kop-tur] *noun, plural* **helicopters.** a wingless aircraft kept in the air by spinning blades called rotors.

Helicopters *can hover in one place and so are often used to rescue people who are in danger.*

he·li·um [<u>hee</u>-lee-um] *noun. Chemistry.* a gas that has no smell or color, and that is a chemical element. Helium is lighter than air and is used in blimps and balloons.

Hell [hel] *noun, plural* **Hells.** *Religion.* the place regarded in Christianity and other religions as the home of Satan and where wicked people are punished after death. A state or place of great suffering is **hell**: *The wicked stepmother made Cinderella's life a hell on earth.*

he'll [heel] **1.** the shortened form of "he will." **2.** the shortened form of "he shall." 🔊 Different words with the same sound are **heal** and **he'll.**

hel·lo [hel-<u>oh</u> or huh-<u>loh</u>] *noun, plural* **hellos;** *interjection.* a word used to greet someone: *Hello, there!*

helm [helm] *noun, plural* **helms.** the wheel or large lever used to steer a ship: *Who was at the helm when the ship hit the rocks?*

hel·met ▼ [<u>hel</u>-mit] *noun, plural* **helmets.** a covering to protect the head.

help [help] *verb,* **helped, helping. 1.** to give or do something needed, useful, or wanted; assist: *Help me solve this crossword puzzle.* **2.** to make things better; relieve: *The pills helped my hay fever.* **3.** to avoid or stop: *I couldn't help overhearing what she said about me.* *noun, plural* **helps. 1.** the act of helping: *I need some help with my homework.* **2.** someone or something that helps: *A dishwasher is a big help after a party.*
• **help oneself.** to take what is needed or what one wants: *Help yourself to a cookie before you sit down.*

help·ful [<u>help</u>-ful] *adjective.* giving help; useful: *The encyclopedia was helpful to me doing my science report.* —**helpfully,** *adverb;* —**helpfulness,** *noun.*

help·ing [<u>help</u>-ing] *noun, plural* **helpings.** a portion of food served to one person: *small helping of salad.*

helping verb another term for an AUXILIARY VERB.

help·less [<u>help</u>-lis] *adjective.* not able to help oneself: *a helpless baby.* —**helplessly,** *adverb;* —**helplessness,** *noun.*

hem [hem] *noun, plural* **hems.** the edge of a piece of cloth, such as the bottom edge of a dress or curtain. To make a hem, fold back the edge and sew it down. *verb,* **hemmed, hemming.** to fold back the edge of a piece of cloth and sew it down: *I hemmed the curtains.*
• **hem in.** to surround and close in: *The house was hemmed in by skyscrapers.*

The maps show the Earth's Northern and Southern **hemispheres** *as seen from the poles.*

Northern Hemisphere

Southern Hemisphere

hem·i·sphere ◀ [<u>hem</u>-is-*feer*] *noun, plural* **hemispheres.** *Geography.* half of the Earth or another sphere. The Earth is divided into the Northern and Southern hemispheres by the equator. A line through the poles divides the Western Hemisphere and the Eastern Hemisphere. North and South America are in the Western Hemisphere. Australia, Asia, Africa, and Europe are in the Eastern Hemisphere.

hem·lock [<u>hem</u>-*lok*] *noun, plural* **hemlocks.**
1. an evergreen tree of the pine family with small cones and reddish bark. Its wood is used as lumber and as pulp. **2.** a poisonous plant, related to the carrot, that has small white flowers and leaves like a fern.

he·mo·glo·bin [<u>hee</u>-muh-*gloh*-bin] *noun. Biology.* a substance in the blood that carries oxygen around the body.

he·mo·phil·ia [<u>hee</u>-muh-<u>feel</u>-yuh] *noun. Health.* a medical condition in which the blood clots slowly. Someone with hemophilia loses a lot of blood from even a minor cut. A person who suffers from hemophilia is a **hemophiliac.**

hem·or·rhage [<u>hem</u>-ur-ij] *noun, plural* **hemorrhages.** *Medicine.* heavy bleeding from inside the body or from the surface of the body. *verb,* **hemorrhaged, hemorrhaging.** to suffer a hemorrhage.

hemp [hemp] *noun, plural* **hemps.** a tough fiber made from the stem of a tall Asian plant, used to make rope.

hen [hen] *noun, plural* **hens. 1.** a female chicken. **2.** the female of other birds.

hence [hens] *adverb.* **1.** because of this; therefore: *The jury found him innocent— hence he will be set free.* **2.** from this time or place: *What will cars look like thirty years hence?*

hep·a·ti·tis *Health.* a disease in which the liver becomes larger than normal. A person with hepatitis has yellow skin, fever, and pain in the abdomen.

her *pronoun.* a female person or animal that is being spoken about: *I saw her yesterday.* *adjective.* of, belonging to, or having to do with a female person or animal: *Those are her books.*

her·ald [<u>her</u>-uld] *noun, plural* **heralds.**
1. a person who carries and announces important news. **2.** a sign or indication that something is going to happen: *The first automobile was the herald of a new era.* *verb,* **heralded, heralding.** to signal the approach of: *Daffodils herald spring.*

Hockey player

Coal miners
Martial arts fighters

Some sportspeople and workers wear **helmets** *for protection.*

a b c d e f g **h** i j k l m n o p q r s t u v w x y z

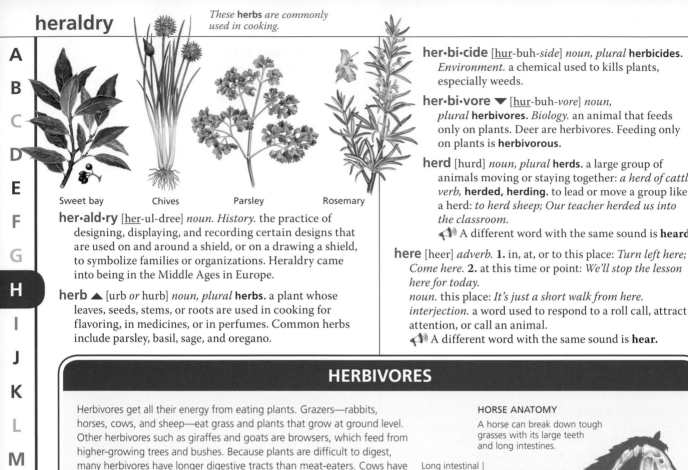

*These **herbs** are commonly used in cooking.*

Sweet bay · Chives · Parsley · Rosemary

her·ald·ry [her-ul-dree] *noun. History.* the practice of designing, displaying, and recording certain designs that are used on and around a shield, or on a drawing a shield, to symbolize families or organizations. Heraldry came into being in the Middle Ages in Europe.

herb ▲ [urb *or* hurb] *noun, plural* **herbs.** a plant whose leaves, seeds, stems, or roots are used in cooking for flavoring, in medicines, or in perfumes. Common herbs include parsley, basil, sage, and oregano.

her·bi·cide [hur-buh-*side*] *noun, plural* **herbicides.** *Environment.* a chemical used to kills plants, especially weeds.

her·bi·vore ▼ [hur-buh-*vore*] *noun, plural* **herbivores.** *Biology.* an animal that feeds only on plants. Deer are herbivores. Feeding only on plants is **herbivorous.**

herd [hurd] *noun, plural* **herds.** a large group of animals moving or staying together: *a herd of cattle.* *verb,* **herded, herding.** to lead or move a group like a herd: *to herd sheep; Our teacher herded us into the classroom.*
🔊 A different word with the same sound is **heard.**

here [heer] *adverb.* **1.** in, at, or to this place: *Turn left here; Come here.* **2.** at this time or point: *We'll stop the lesson here for today.*
noun. this place: *It's just a short walk from here.*
interjection. a word used to respond to a roll call, attract attention, or call an animal.
🔊 A different word with the same sound is **hear.**

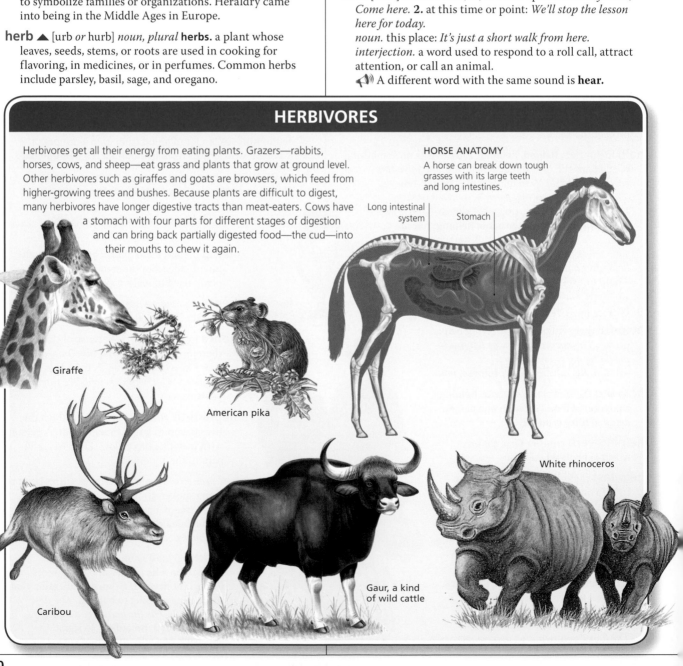

HERBIVORES

Herbivores get all their energy from eating plants. Grazers—rabbits, horses, cows, and sheep—eat grass and plants that grow at ground level. Other herbivores such as giraffes and goats are browsers, which feed from higher-growing trees and bushes. Because plants are difficult to digest, many herbivores have longer digestive tracts than meat-eaters. Cows have a stomach with four parts for different stages of digestion and can bring back partially digested food—the cud—into their mouths to chew it again.

HORSE ANATOMY
A horse can break down tough grasses with its large teeth and long intestines.

Long intestinal system · Stomach

Giraffe

American pika

Caribou

Gaur, a kind of wild cattle

White rhinoceros

Herons use their long bills to catch
frogs, fishes, and other water creatures.

hibernate

here·af·ter [*heer-af-tur*] *adverb.* from now on;
in the future: *The lawyer's letter says that all
payments will stop hereafter.*
noun. life after death: *Most religions believe
in the hereafter.*

here·by [*heer-bye* or *heer-bye*] *adverb.*
by these words; by this act or means:
*The minister said, "I hereby declare you
husband and wife."*

he·red·i·tar·y [*huh-red-uh-ter-ee*] *adjective.*
1. passed down from parents to offspring: *The color
of your hair, skin, and eyes is hereditary.* **2.** passed
down from an ancestor to an heir: *The King or
Queen of England is a hereditary title.*

he·red·i·ty [*huh-red-uh-tee*] *noun, plural* **heredities.**
Biology. **1.** the passing on of characteristics from
parent animals or plants to offspring via genes.
2. the characteristics passed on in this way.

here's [*heerz*] the shortened form of "here is."

her·e·sy [*her-uh-see*] *noun, plural* **heresies. 1.** *Religion.*
a religious opinion that differs from the official
teachings of a church: *In the past, people were burned
to death for heresy.* A **heretic** is a person who commits
heresy. **2.** opinions or beliefs that go against dominant or
generally accepted beliefs: *I think football is boring, which
is a heresy to my football-mad family.*

her·i·tage [*her-uh-tij*] *noun, plural* **heritages.** something
passed on from earlier generations of a country or a
family; tradition: *We're proud of our African heritage.*

her·mit [*hur-mit*] *noun, plural* **hermits.** a person who lives
alone, away from other people, often for religious reasons.

> The word **hermit** is related to an ancient Greek word for
> "desert." In ancient times the desert was thought of as
> the place where hermits would live.

he·ro [*heer-oh*] *noun, plural* **heroes. 1.** a person admired
for his or her great courage, special achievements, or fine
qualities: *Paul Revere was a hero of the Revolutionary War.*
Heroism is the fact of heroic behavior. **2.** the main male
character in a movie, story, or play. **3.** a large sandwich
made of fillings on a long roll: *I ordered a roast beef hero
for lunch.*

he·ro·ic [*hi-roh-ik*] *adjective.* **1.** having a lot of courage; very
brave: *The movie character Superman does heroic deeds.*
2. relating to heroes: *the heroic legends of the Cherokee
Indians.* —**heroically,** *adverb.*

her·o·in [*her-oh-un*] *noun.* a very dangerous illegal drug
that is highly addictive.
◄)) A different word with the same sound is **heroine.**

her·o·ine [*her-oh-un*] *noun, plural* **heroines. 1.** a woman or
girl admired for her great courage, special achievements,
or fine qualities: *Sally Ride was the first American woman
in space—she's my heroine.* **2.** the main female character
in a movie, story, or play.
◄)) A different word with the same sound is **heroin.**

her·on ◄ [*her-un*] *noun, plural* **herons.** a water
bird with long legs, a long, thin neck, and a long,
pointed bill.

her·ring ▼ [*her-ing*] *noun, plural* **herring, herrings.**
a small, silver saltwater fish that is a member of
the sardine family. It is caught in the oceans of
the Northern Hemisphere and eaten smoked,
fresh, or canned.

hers *pronoun.* the thing or things that
belong or relate to her: *That purple
bag is hers.*

her·self *pronoun.* **1.** her own self: *She kept
telling herself that everything would be
okay.* **2.** her normal, proper, healthy self:
*Lisa is herself again now that her case of
the flu is over.*

hertz [*hurts*] *noun. Science.* a unit for
measuring the number of cycles, or
repeated events, that happen every
second, especially in electronics.
One hertz equals one cycle per second.

he's [*heez*] **1.** the shortened form of "he is." **2.** the
shortened form of "he has."

hes·i·tant [*hez-uh-tunt*] *adjective.* tending to hesitate;
unsure or unwilling: *Dad was hesitant about letting me
go to the mall on my own.* —**hesitantly,** *adverb.*

hes·i·tate [*hez-uh-tate*] *verb,* **hesitated, hesitating.**
1. to wait or pause before doing something: *He hesitated
before answering because he wanted to think carefully.*
2. to have doubts or be unwilling: *I hesitate to ask her for
another favor.* **3.** to wait to act because of doubt or fear:
She hesitated before jumping from the high diving tower.

hes·i·ta·tion [*hez-uh-tay-shun*] *noun, plural* **hesitations.**
a pause or delay before doing something, usually because
of fear, forgetting, or being uncertain or indecisive:
*The firefighter ran into the burning building
without hesitation.*

hex·a·gon [*hek-suh-gon*] *noun,
plural* **hexagons.** *Mathematics.* a flat
shape or figure with six straight sides.

hey [*hay*] *interjection.* a word used to get
a person's attention or to show pleasure
or surprise: *Hey! Did you see that!*
◄)) A different word with the same sound is **hay.**

hi [*hye*] *interjection.* a word used as a greeting.
◄)) A different word with the same sound
is **high.**

hi·ber·nate [*hye-bur-nate*] *verb,*
hibernated, hibernating. *Biology.*
to pass through the winter in a state of
being asleep or only partly awake. Some
bears, snakes, turtles, and frogs hibernate.
The act of hibernating is **hibernation.**

Pacific **herring** *swim
in huge schools in the
northern parts of the
Pacific Ocean.*

> **Hibernate** comes from an old term for "winter" or
> "snow." The winter is the time of year when animals
> will hibernate, because food is harder to get and staying
> active takes more energy than in warmer months.

a b c d e f g **h** i j k l m n o p q r s u v w x y z

Egyptian scribes had to learn several hundred hieroglyphics like these.

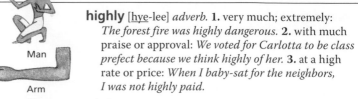

Man

Arm

Reed

Mouth

Flax

Basket

hic·cup [hik-up] *noun, plural* **hiccups.** a quick, uncontrolled catching of the breath that makes a short, sharp sound. It is caused by a spasm of the breathing muscles. The state of having one hiccup after another is **hiccups.**
verb, **hiccupped, hiccupping.** to have hiccups.

hick·or·y [hik-ur-ee] *noun, plural* **hickories.** a tall hardwood tree from North America. It produces sweet nuts that are eaten, and strong, hard timber.

hid [hid] *verb.* the past tense and a past participle of HIDE.

hid·den [hid-un] *verb.* a past participle of HIDE. *adjective.* concealed, obscure: *The spy took photos with a hidden camera.*

hide[1] [hide] *verb,* **hidden** or **hid, hiding. 1.** to put, get, or keep out of sight: *I always hide my diary carefully from my little sister.* **2.** to keep secret: *Will hid his disappointment at not making the team so his friends wouldn't tease him.*

hide[2] [hide] *noun, plural* **hides.** the skin of an animal: *Cow hide is used to make leather jackets.*

hide-and-seek *noun.* a children's game in which a group of children hide, then one child tries to find them.

hid·e·ous [hid-ee-us] *adjective.* horribly ugly; frightening: *a hideous monster.* —**hideously,** *adverb;* —**hideousness,** *noun.*

hide·out [hide-out] *noun, plural* **hideouts.** a safe hiding place, especially a place where criminals hide from the police.

hi·er·o·glyph·ic ▲ [hye-roh-glif-ik] *noun, plural* **hieroglyphics.** *Language.* a symbol or picture that stands for a word, sound, or idea. **Hieroglyphics** is a system of hieroglyphic writing, such as that of ancient Egypt.

high [hye] *adjective,* **higher, highest. 1.** far above the ground; tall: *a high hill; That skyscraper is very high.* **2.** at a point far above the ground: *The sun is high in the sky.* **3.** more important than others: *Mom works long hours because she has a high position in the company.* **4.** above the normal, or ordinary level: *The police were driving at very high speeds in the car chase.* **5.** raised in pitch: *the high notes of a trumpet.* **6.** lofty or noble in character: *Anyone who thinks we can put an end to war has high ideals.*
adverb. at, in, or to a high place: *I bounced high on the trampoline.*
noun, plural **highs. 1.** a high place or level: *The price of gasoline hit a record high.* **2.** the transmission gear of a car, bicycle, or other vehicle that gives the fastest speed.
adverb. to or at a high place: *to fly a kite high in the air.*

high jump an athletics contest in which a person jumps as high as possible over a horizontal bar. A **high jumper** is a person who does the high jump.

high·land [hye-lund] *noun, plural* **highlands.** a high, mountainous area of a country.

highly [hye-lee] *adverb.* **1.** very much; extremely: *The forest fire was highly dangerous.* **2.** with much praise or approval: *We voted for Carlotta to be class prefect because we think highly of her.* **3.** at a high rate or price: *When I baby-sat for the neighbors, I was not highly paid.*

High·ness [hye-nis] *noun, plural* **Highnesses.** a title used when speaking to or about a royal person: *His Highness, Juan Carlos I, King of Spain.*

high-rise [hye-rize] *noun, plural* **high-rises.** a tall, multistory building that has elevators.

high school a school after elementary school or junior high school. It usually goes from ninth or tenth grade up to twelfth grade.

high seas *Law.* the open part of the sea or ocean, beyond the territorial waters controlled by any country.

high-strung [hye-strung] *adjective.* being very nervous or sensitive by nature: *He is too high-strung to cope with the pressure of working with a large class of first-graders.*

high·way [hye-way] *noun, plural* **highways.** a main road, especially one that connects towns or cities: *We escaped the traffic jam once we pulled onto the highway.*

high·way·man [hye-way-mun] *noun, plural* **highwaymen.** *History.* a person who held up and robbed travelers on a road.

hi·jack [hye-jak] *verb,* **hijacked, hijacking.** to seize control of an airplane, truck, or other vehicle by threats or violence. A **hijacker** is a person who hijacks a vehicle, especially an airplane.

hike ▼ [hike] *verb,* **hiked, hiking.** to go on a long walk: *to hike along a nature trail.*
noun, plural **hikes. 1.** a long walk, usually for pleasure or exercise: *We took a hike in the Rockies.* **2.** a sudden sharp increase or rise: *My parents couldn't afford the latest hike in fees for my skating classes, so I had to quit.*

hi·lar·i·ous [huh-lare-ee-us] *adjective.* extremely funny: *The movie was hilarious—I almost fell off my chair laughing.* **Hilarity** is a state of high spirits, when a person laughs a lot at something very funny. —**hilariously,** *adverb.*

*Hiking poles and strong boots are needed for **hikes** in rugged country.*

*Zebras defend themselves against predators by kicking with their strong **hind** legs.*

hill [hil] *noun, plural* **hills. 1.** a raised, rounded area of land, not as high as a mountain. **2.** a small pile or mound: *We slid down the hill of sand that the builders had left.*

hill·side [hil-side] *noun, plural* **hillsides.** the side or slope of a hill.

hill·top [hil-top] *noun, plural* **hilltops.** the top or summit of a hill.

hill·y [hil-ee] *adjective.* having lots of hills: *San Francisco is a hilly city.*

hilt [hilt] *noun, plural* **hilts.** the handle of a sword or dagger. ◆ **to the hilt.** fully; completely: *She played the lead role to the hilt and the audience gave her a standing ovation.*

him *pronoun.* a man, boy, or male animal that is being referred to: *Kick the ball to him.*
🔊 A different word with the same sound is **hymn.**

him·self *pronoun.* **1.** his own self: *He cut himself shaving.* **2.** his normal, proper, healthy self: *Dad hasn't been himself since he's had a bad cold.*

hind ▲ [hinde] *adjective.* behind or rear; at the back: *a dog's hind leg.*

hin·der [hin-dur] *verb,* **hindered, hindering.** to prevent something from happening; interfere with or slow down: *Hank's injured leg will hinder him in the race.*

hin·drance [hin-druns] *noun, plural* **hindrances.** something or someone that hinders you: *The noise coming from the freeway is a hindrance when I try to study.*

Hin·du [hin-doo] *noun, plural* **Hindus.** *Religion.* someone who follows the main religion of India. Hindus have the belief that after death the soul lives on in another body. *adjective.* relating to or having to do with Hindus. This religion is called **Hinduism.**

hinge [hinj] *noun, plural* **hinges.** the movable joint that lets a door, or a lid, open and shut; usually metal, but can also be made of plastic. *verb,* **hinged, hinging. 1.** join together by using a hinge. **2.** to depend on: *The verdict hinged on the jury believing the testimony of the last witness.*

hint [hint] *noun, plural* **hints.** a small amount; just a suggestion: *There was a hint of mint flavor in the ice cream.* *verb,* **hinted, hinting.** to suggest something in a roundabout way: *Instead of asking directly for some lemonade, Jimmy just looked at the pitcher and hinted, "Boy, that sure looks good."*

hip [hip] *noun, plural* **hips.** the area on each side of the body between the waist and the top of the leg; the joint where the leg joins to the body. The **hipbone** is the large bone on either side of the pelvis.

hip·po·pot·a·mus ▼ [hip-uh-pot-uh-mus] *noun, plural* **hippopotamuses.** a very large African animal with a big head, a wide mouth, and thick gray skin; it spends most of its time in water and feeds on plants. This animal is also called a **hippo.**

The word **hippopotamus** literally means "river horse" in the language of ancient Greece. When these people first saw the hippopotamus, they thought it looked like a kind of large horse.

hire [hire] *verb,* **hired, hiring. 1.** to pay someone to do a job; employ: *The school hired the best coach so the team would have a better chance at winning.* **2.** to get the use of something for a short time in exchange for money; rent: *We hired a band to play at our party.* *noun.* the act of hiring: *There are many different types of cars for hire.*

his [hiz] *pronoun.* belonging to a male person or animal: *That shirt is his.* *adjective.* having to do with anything that belongs to a male person or animal: *He pulled his shirt over his head.*

His·pan·ic [hi-span-ik] *adjective.* from or relating to countries where Spanish or Portuguese are spoken, especially in Latin America. *noun, plural* **Hispanics.** a person living in the U.S. whose ancestors were from Spain or Latin America.

The word **Hispanic** is used to refer to people in the Americas who speak Spanish as their native language or who have ancestors coming from Spain. Another word that can mean the same thing is *Latino,* because of the fact that Latin America is the name for the part of the Americas where Spanish-speaking people live. Some people prefer to be called *Hispanic* and others *Latino,* and so both words are often used.

hiss [hiss] *noun, plural* **hisses.** the sound of the letter "s" held for a long time; often used to express disapproval. *verb,* **hissed, hissing.** to make this sound.

*A **hippopotamus** uses its huge, tusk-like lower front teeth to fight other animals that invade its territory.*

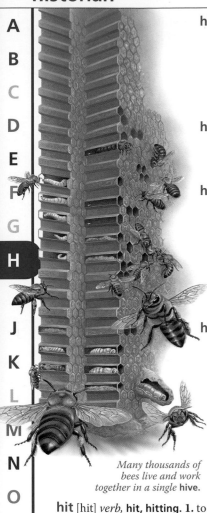

*Many thousands of bees live and work together in a single **hive**.*

his·to·ri·an [hi-<u>store</u>-ee-un] *noun, plural* **historians.** a person who studies history or whose job is to teach or write about history. A historian often writes history books.

his·tor·ic [hi-<u>store</u>-ik] *adjective.* important or well known in history: *a historic battle.*

his·tor·i·cal [hi-<u>store</u>-uh-kul] *adjective.* having to do with history: *We searched the historical records for information on our ancestors.* A **historically** accurate story describes what happened according to historical records.

his·tor·y [<u>his</u>-tree *or* <u>his</u>-tuh-ree] *noun, plural* **histories. 1.** all the things that have happened in past time; all past events: *The Moon landing was a great moment in history.* **2.** a book or record of what happened in the past: *a history of the civil rights movement.* **3.** the teaching of history as a course in school.

hit [hit] *verb,* **hit, hitting. 1.** to strike with force: *He hit me on the arm with his fist.* **2.** to make something move quickly by striking it: *Dave hit the ball right out of the ballpark.* **3.** to move against with force: *The guided missile hit its target.* **4.** to arrive at; realize: *The answer suddenly hit me.* **5.** to affect somebody or something strongly: *The increase in gas price will hit motorists hard.* *noun, plural* **hits. 1.** a blow or impact. **2.** something very popular; a success: *That song will be an instant hit.* **3.** the hitting of a baseball so that the batter can reach base. **4.** *Computers.* the visiting of a Website: *The most popular Websites get thousands of hits a day.*

hit-and-run *adjective. Law.* describing an occasion when a car driver hits someone with a car and keeps driving without stopping to identify themselves, as the law requires.

hitch [hich] *verb,* **hitched, hitching. 1.** to fasten or tie; tether: *Jeb hitched the horse to the rail.* **2.** to raise or move with a jerk: *My pants started to slip down so I hitched them up again.* *noun, plural* **hitches. 1.** a fastening: *I hope the hitch between the tractor and the cart is strong enough.* **2.** an obstacle that causes a problem or delay: *The actors had rehearsed a lot, so the show went off without a hitch.* **3.** a sudden pull; a tug. **4.** a kind of knot.

hitch·hike [<u>hich</u>-hike] *verb,* **hitchhiked, hitchhiking.** to travel by getting free rides from passing vehicles. **—hitchhiker,** *noun.*

HIV *Medicine.* an abbreviation for Human Immunodeficiency Virus; a very serious type of virus that enters the body through blood or intimate contact. HIV reduces the body's ability to fight off infection and can develop into the highly dangerous disease AIDS (Acquired Immune Deficiency Syndrome). Someone who has this virus in their body is **HIV positive.**

hive ◀ [hive] *noun, plural* **hives. 1.** a small box where bees are kept. **2.** the colony of bees that lives in this box.

hives [hivz] *plural noun. Health.* an allergic condition in which the skin, or mucous membrane becomes red, sore, and itchy.

hoard [hord] *verb,* **hoarded, hoarding.** to collect and store large amounts of something, especially much more than one needs at the time: *I hoarded cans of my favorite soft drink.* *noun, plural* **hoards.** the thing or things that someone has stored away. **—hoarder,** *noun.* 🔊 A different word with the same sound is **horde.**

hoarse [horse] *adjective,* **hoarser, hoarsest.** having a low, rough or harsh voice: *When George's throat was sore, he spoke in a hoarse voice.* **—hoarsely,** *adverb;* **—hoarseness,** *noun.* 🔊 A different word with the same sound is **horse.**

hoax [hohks] *noun, plural* **hoaxes.** an attempt to make people believe something is real when it is not: *The author's claim to have found a diary written by Jacqueline Kennedy was a hoax—he actually made it up himself.*

hob·ble [<u>hob</u>-ul] *verb,* **hobbled, hobbling. 1.** to walk unsteadily; limp. **2.** to stop from moving freely: *We hobbled the horse so it couldn't run away.* *noun, plural* **hobbles.** something used to stop an animal from moving freely.

hob·by [<u>hob</u>-ee] *noun, plural* **hobbies.** an activity that you do in your free time for fun, rather than something you have to do for school or work. Collecting stamps or coins, making scrapbooks, and building model railroads are popular hobbies in the U.S. If you have a hobby, you are a **hobbyist.**

A **hobby** was originally a kind of toy horse that a child would ride on as if it were real. The term "riding a hobby" then came to mean doing something over and over for fun, like a child riding such a horse.

hock·ey [<u>hok</u>-ee] *noun.* **1.** a sport between two teams of six players played on ice using long sticks with curved ends to hit a hard rubber disk, called a puck, into the opponents' goal. **2.** a similar game played on a grass field by two teams of eleven players.

hoe [hoh] *noun, plural* **hoes.** a garden tool with a thin, flat blade across the end of a long handle; used for digging up weeds and loosening the soil. *verb,* **hoed hoeing.** to dig with a hoe.

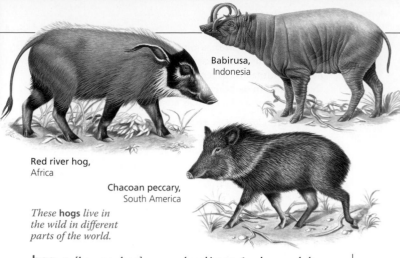

Red river hog,
Africa

Babirusa,
Indonesia

Chacoan peccary,
South America

These **hogs** *live in
the wild in different
parts of the world.*

hog ▲ [hawg *or* hog] *noun, plural* **hogs. 1.** a large, adult pig bred for meat. **2.** any animal of the pig family, either domesticated or wild. **3.** a greedy, selfish, or dirty person. *verb,* **hogged, hogging.** to take or use more than one's share. *She hogs the bathroom every morning so everyone else runs late.*

hogan ▼ [hoh-gun] *noun, plural* **hogans.** a Navajo Indian house made of logs and mud, with a roof covered with earth.

hoist [hoist] *verb,* **hoisted, hoisting.** to raise or lift up: *I hoisted my little brother up on to my shoulder. noun, plural* **hoists.** equipment used for lifting heavy objects: *Joe put the boat on a hoist and lifted it onto the trailer.*

hold¹ [hold] *verb,* **held, holding. 1.** to keep something in your hands or arms: *I'll hold your bag while you take a photo.* **2.** to keep something in the mind: *to hold a grudge; to hold the view that taxes are too high.* **3.** keep or support. *The rafters can hold the weight of the ceiling.* **4.** to maintain or control; keep in a certain place or condition: *to hold a fort; to hold someone captive; The movie held us in suspense for two hours.* **5.** to contain: *a bottle that holds two liters; Our new car holds seven people in comfort.* **6.** to cause to take place: *to hold a meeting; The school will hold a debating competition.* *noun, plural* **holds. 1.** a grasp or grip: *Don't worry! I've got a good hold on the rope.* **2.** something that can be held on to: *The rock climber couldn't find many holds on the steep mountainside.*

hold² [hold] *noun, plural* **holds.** the part of a ship or an aircraft in which cargo is carried.

A **hogan** *has a hole in the roof to let smoke from a fire escape.*

Hollyhocks *are native to central and southwest Asia.*

hollyhock

hold·er [hold-ur] *noun, plural* **holders. 1.** someone who owns or controls something: *Who is the holder of the world record for the highest pole vault?* **2.** a container used to hold something: *How many pens can you fit in that holder?*

hold·up [hold-*up*] *noun, plural* **holdups. 1.** a robbery, often using a weapon such as a gun or knife. **2.** something that stops something else from happening; a delay: *The holdup on the freeway meant that we were late.* This word is also spelled **hold-up.** To **hold up** a store is to commit a robbery in this way.

hole [hole] *noun, plural* **holes. 1.** an empty space in something solid; an opening or gap: *I dug a hole in the garden and planted the tree; The sun shone through the hole in the roof.* **2.** a small, round cavity or cup on a golf course into which the golf ball is hit. *verb,* **holed, holing. 1.** to make a hole in something. **2.** to drive a ball into a hole in golf: *He is a great golfer—he holed the ball in just two strokes.* 🔊 A different word with the same sound is **whole.**

hol·i·day [hol-uh-*day*] *noun, plural* **holidays. 1.** a day free from work, often to celebrate something that happened on that date: *July 4 is a national holiday in the U.S.* **2.** another word for a vacation, as used in British English.

ho·lis·tic [hoh-lis-tik] *adjective.* looking at something as a complete thing, rather than individual parts; being more than the sum of its parts. **Holistic medicine** treats both the mind and the body as a whole, and not just the different symptoms.

hol·low [hol-oh] *adjective.* **1.** having nothing inside; not solid; empty: *a hollow tube.* **2.** curved inward; sunken: *The hollow bowl doesn't hold much liquid.* **3.** having a deep sound: *We heard a hollow sound of footsteps echoing in the long, empty hallway. noun, plural* **hollows. 1.** a hole or cavity: *You could hold the kitten in the hollow of your hand.* **2.** a low-lying area: *When it rains really hard, a pond forms in the hollow of the hills. verb,* **hollowed, hollowing.** to make hollow: *We hollowed out a pumpkin to make a lantern for Halloween.*

hol·ly [hol-ee] *noun, plural* **hollies.** a small evergreen tree that has shiny leaves with sharp-pointed edges, and small red berries. Holly is often used as a Christmas decoration.

hol·ly·hock ▲ [hol-ee-hok] *noun, plural* **hollyhocks.** a tall garden plant with long stems of brightly colored flowers.

Holsters are usually made of leather and may be highly decorated.

Hol·ly·wood [hol-ee-*wud*] *noun.*
1. a section of Los Angeles, California that is the home of the U.S. movie industry. **2.** a name for the U.S. movie business in general
adjective. having to do with the U.S. movie industry.

hol·o·caust [hol-uh-*kost*] *noun, plural* **holocausts.**
1. a great or total destruction and loss of life.
2. the Holocaust. *History.* an event that took place during World War II in Europe, when millions of Jews and other people were killed by the Nazis.

hol·ster ▲ [hole-stur] *noun, plural* **holsters.** a holder for a handgun or pistol. It is often hung on a belt worn around the waist.

ho·ly [hoh-lee] *adjective* **holier, holiest. 1.** having to do with God or religion. **2.** dedicating oneself to or keeping pure for God; religious.
🔊 A different word with the same sound is **wholly.**

Holy Spirit *Religion.* God in the form of a spirit. A different term with the same meaning is **Holy Ghost.**

home [home] *noun, plural* **homes. 1.** the house, apartment, or other place where a person lives: *Our home is a two-bedroom apartment.* **2.** the place where an animal lives or is naturally found: *Australia is the home of the kangaroo.*
3. the place a person or thing comes from or is typically found: *Detroit is the home of the U.S. auto industry.*
4. the safe place or goal in certain sports, such as baseball.
5. a place where some people live to be looked after by others: *The big house on the corner has been made into an old people's home.*
adjective. **1.** in or for the home: *Mom turned our extra bedroom into a home office.* **2.** having to do with a home or central area: *The Boston Red Sox home field is called Fenway Park.*
adverb. to or in a home: *to stay home from school.*
• **at home.** able to relax or be comfortable with something, as if you are in your own home: *When I go to Billy's house his mother always makes me feel at home.*

home economics *Education.* the study of how to manage a household, including budgeting and cooking.

home·land [home-*land*] *noun, plural* **homelands.**
the country where a person was born or has moved to: *Laura's homeland is Australia but she lives in Boston now.*

home·less [home-liss] *adjective.* having no home to live in: *People who are homeless often live on the streets of big cities.* The **homeless** includes all the people in a country who have nowhere to live. **—homelessness,** *noun.*

home·ly [home-lee] *adjective.* **1.** having a plain or ordinary look; not pretty or handsome. **2.** being simple; not stylish.

home·made [home-*made*] *adjective.* made by hand in someone's home, not by a machine or in a factory. Things that are **home-made** often include clothes, rugs, furniture, breads, jams, and preserves.

home·mak·er [home-*may*-kur] *noun.* a person who manages a household, takes care of children, cooks, and cleans.

ho·meo·sta·sis [hoh-mee-oh-*stay*-sis] *noun. Biology.* a natural state of balance in the body; the fact of a human, animal, or other organism being able to maintain the systems in its body in the proper state even when conditions around it change, such as the temperature.

home page *Computers.* the first page that is seen when one opens a browser program to go on the Internet, typically a favorite Website that is often visited.

home plate in baseball, the rubber plate where a batter stands, and which a base runner must touch to score a run.

home·room [home-*room*] *noun, plural* **homerooms.** *Education.* the classroom that all pupils in a class must report to at the start of a school day.

home run a hit in baseball that allows the batter to go around all the bases and score a run. Also known as a **homer,** it is the best hit a batter can make.

home-school *verb. Education.* to teach school subjects to a child or children while they are at home, instead of sending them to school. This type of education is called **home-schooling** and a pupil taught this way is called a **home-schooler.**

home·sick [home-*sik*] *adjective.* having a strong wish to be back at home when one is away from friends and family. **—homesickness,** *noun.*

home·spun [home-*spun*] *noun.* a fabric or clothing that is made by hand at home, not by a machine or in a factory.

home·stead ▼ [home-sted] *noun.* **1.** a farmhouse with its land and buildings. **2.** *History.* a piece of land granted to a settler by the U.S. government on condition that the settler build a house and farm the land. The **Homestead Act** of 1862, signed by President Abraham Lincoln, was in force until 1986.

home·town [home-*town*] *noun, plural* **hometowns.** the town or city where a person was born, or grew up as a child. This word is also spelled **home town.**

home·ward [home-*wurd*] *adverb.* going toward home: *After the long voyage the ship turned homeward.*
adjective, having to do with going home. This word is also spelled **homewards.**

*This **homestead** is on a small farm in Vermont.*

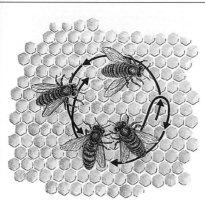

A circular dance indicates that food is close by.

A figure-of-eight dance indicates that food is farther away.

home·work [home-*wurk*] *noun.* schoolwork done while a student is at home, after school hours.

ho·mi·cide [hom-uh-*side or* hoh-muh-*side*] *noun, plural* **homicides.** *Law.* the act of a person killing another person; murder. A person who is likely to commit a murder is **homicidal.**

hom·i·ny [hom-ee-nee] *noun.* kernels of corn that are hulled, ground, and boiled up with water before eating.

ho·mog·e·nize [huh-moj-uh-*nize*] *verb,* **homogenized, homogenizing.** to make a liquid the same consistency throughout. Milk that is treated so that the cream is spread evenly throughout instead of rising to the top is called **homogenized milk. —homogenization,** *noun.*

hom·o·graph [hom-uh-*graf*] *noun, plural* **homographs.** *Language.* a word having the same spelling as another word but a different meaning and a different origin in the language. The words *lead* (to show the way) and *lead* (a heavy metal) are homographs.

Homograph and *homophone* are two similar words based on the form *homo-* meaning "same." The difference can be seen in the other part of each word. The form *-graph* means "writing," so *homograph* means "same writing;" that is, two words that are written (spelled) the same way. The form *-phone* means "sound," so *homophone* means "same sound;" that is, two words that are sounded (spoken) the same way. The older word *homonym* is another word for *homograph,* but it is generally not considered as correct to use.

hom·o·nym [hom-uh-nim] *noun, plural* **homonyms.** *Language.* a word with the same sound and spelling as another word but with a different meaning. The words *bear* (the animal) and *bear* (to carry) are homonyms.

hom·o·phone [hom-uh-*fone*] *noun, plural* **homophones.** *Language.* a word with the same sound as another, but a different spelling and meaning. The words *too* and *two* are homophones.

hon·est [on-ist] *adjective.* **1.** having to do with being truthful, fair, or trustworthy: *President Lincoln was called "Honest Abe" because it was thought that he would never lie or steal.* **2.** earned without cheating or lying: *Seth made an honest living all his life.* **—honestly,** *adverb.*

hon·es·ty [on-is-tee] *noun.* the act or fact of being honest; not lying, cheating, stealing, or doing other such things.

hon·ey [hun-ee] *noun, plural* **honeys. 1.** a sweet, sticky substance made by bees with nectar they collect from flowers. They store it in honeycombs for food. **2.** a person or thing that is very dear or respected.

hon·ey·bee ◀ [hun-ee-*bee*] *noun, plural* **honeybees.** a type of bee that makes and stores honey.

hon·ey·comb [hun-ee-*kohm*] *noun, plural* **honeycombs. 1.** a wax container made by bees with rows of six-sided cells to store honey and pollen in. **2.** a structure that looks like a bee's honeycomb: *The interior of the mountain was a honeycomb of caves and tunnels.* *verb,* **honeycombed, honeycombing.** to carve out a series of linked tunnels and hollow spaces.

honeydew melon a type of melon with pale skin and green or yellow flesh that tastes very sweet.

hon·ey·moon [hun-ee-*moon*] *noun, plural* **honeymoons. 1.** a short vacation taken by two people who have just been married. **2.** an unusually pleasant period often experienced at the beginning of a relationship: *The fans liked the new coach at first, but after six straight losses, the honeymoon is over.* *verb,* **honeymooned, honeymooning.** to go on or take a honeymoon.

hon·ey·suck·le ▶ [hun-ee-*suk*-ul] *noun, plural* **honeysuckles.** a climbing plant or vine that has sweet-smelling yellow flowers.

honk [hongk] *noun, plural* **honks. 1.** the sound made by a wild goose or other bird. **2.** a harsh noise made by an automobile horn as a warning to other road users. *verb,* **honked, honking.** to sound an automobile horn.

There are more than 500 different kinds of **honeysuckles.**

honor [on-ur] *noun, plural* **honors. 1.** a sense of what is right and proper; being fair and honest. **2.** a person's good name: *When I was accused of lying I had to defend my honor.* **3.** something given in recognition to show respect or thanks to someone: *She was given the honor of being seated next to the President at the dinner.* Military decorations or titles given by authorities are called **honors.** The official title **Honor** is used for judges, mayors, and people in other important positions. In court, people call a judge **Your Honor.** A male judge is called **His Honor**; a female judge is called **Her Honor.**

hon·or·a·ble [on-ur-uh-bul] *adjective.* having to do with behavior that is right and proper; respectable: *Josh decided that coming forward and telling the truth was the honorable thing to do.* **—honorably,** *adverb.*

hon·or·ar·y [on-uh-rer-ee] *adjective.* given or received as an honor, without any of the normal requirements or payment: *Rufus's dad was given an honorary degree by the university.*

HOOFED ANIMALS

Plant-eating mammals developed hooves because it was easier for them to escape predators by running on their toes. Their claws gradually turned into hard hooves, and toes that were not needed for support disappeared or became smaller. Some animals, such as elephants and aardvarks, still have most of their toes. Deer, cattle, sheep, goats, antelopes, and giraffes have four toes, but rhinoceroses have three. Pigs, hippopotamuses, and camels have two, while horses and their close relatives have just one.

Camels have two long toes.

Rhinoceroses have three toes.

Elephants have five toes.

Zebras have one toe.

hood [hud] *noun, plural* **hoods. 1.** a loose, soft covering for the head and neck, often attached to a coat. **2.** the metal cover of an automobile's engine compartment.

hood·lum [hood-lum] *noun, plural* **hoodlums.** a violent or destructive person who commits crimes or otherwise causes trouble for others.

hoof ▲ [huf *or* hoof] *noun, plural* **hooves** *or* **hoofs. 1.** the hard covering on the feet of some animals, including horses and cattle. **2.** a foot with this covering: *A blacksmith nails horseshoes to a horse's hooves to protect them.* Animals with hooves are described as **hoofed.**

hook [huk] *noun, plural* **hooks. 1.** a curved piece of metal, wood, plastic, or other material on which to hang something: *Cup hooks are used in many kitchens.* **2.** something that looks or works like a hook. *verb,* **hooked, hooking. 1.** to catch, fasten, or grasp with a hook. **2.** to use a hook to catch something: *The fisherman used good bait and soon hooked a fish.* **3.** to use something as a hook: *We hooked our arms together and danced around the flagpole.*
• **hook up. 1.** to link up to a power source or communications system. **2.** to get together with someone: *Janice asked me to hook up with her after the movie finished so we could go home together.*

hoo·li·gan [hoo-luh-gun] *noun, plural* **hooligans. 1.** a noisy and often violent person who causes trouble by being rude and getting into fights. **2.** specifically, a young male who does this at or near a soccer game.

The origin of the word **hooligan** is not certain, but it was first used to describe gangs of young men who fought and committed crimes. It is thought that "Hooligans" was the name of a notorious gang of that time.

hoop ▼ [hoop] *noun, plural* **hoops.** a circular frame of metal, wood, or other material used in games, sports equipment, or wooden barrels. In basketball, **hoops** are fixed at both ends of the court and players try to shoot the ball into the hoop.
🔊 A different word with the same sound is **whoop.**

hoo·ray [huh-ray *or* hoo-ray] *noun, plural* **hoorays.** a cheer to celebrate excitement or joy. A different word with the same meaning is HURRAH.

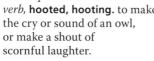

Dolphins can be trained to leap through **hoops.**

hoot [hoot] *noun, plural* **hoots. 1.** the cry or sound of an owl. **2.** a shout of laughter indicating disapproval or scorn: *A hoot went up when they announced everyone had to stay late to clean up the school.* *verb,* **hooted, hooting.** to make the cry or sound of an owl, or make a shout of scornful laughter.

hooves [hoovz] *noun.* the plural of HOOF.

hop [hop] *verb,* **hopped, hopping.** to jump lightly, especially on one leg while the other is raised off the ground or floor: *In some games you must hop from one square to another.* *noun, plural* **hops.** the act of jumping in this way.

hope [hope] *verb,* **hoped, hoping.** to strongly wish that something will happen, and believe that it will: *I hope I pass all my exams.* *noun, plural* **hopes. 1.** the act of strongly wishing that something will happen: *They have hopes of winning the contest.* **2.** someone or something that gives hope: *Kate is our best hope of winning a medal in the race.*

hope·ful [hope-ful] *adjective.* **1.** having a feeling of hope: *Clark is hopeful that he can join the school band.* **2.** offering some cause for hope of success: *The school principal is hopeful that the science lab will be completed by September.*

hope·ful·ly [hope-ful-ee] *adverb.* **1.** in a hopeful manner: *The dog looked hopefully at its owner as she opened the package of treats.* **2.** it is to be hoped: *The flight is supposed to arrive at 9.00, and hopefully it will be on time.*

In the recent past, some critics of writing were very upset by the use of the word **hopefully** to mean "I hope that," as in "*Hopefully*, we will have good weather for the picnic." This use of the word was fairly new then, and the critics hoped that they could drive it out of the English language. One famous writer even said that she would not allow anyone in her house who used this word. Today, however, *hopefully* is used by many people and is an accepted part of the language.

hope·less [hope-lis] *adjective.* having no hope; without hope: *With the team losing 5–0 with two outs in the ninth inning, the situation looked hopeless.*
—**hopelessly,** *adverb;* —**hopelessness,** *noun.*

Hopi [hoh-pee] *noun, plural* **Hopi** or **Hopis.** a Native American people from northwestern Arizona.

hop·per [hop-ur] *noun, plural* **hoppers. 1.** a person or animal that hops: *Kangaroos and rabbits are hoppers.* **2.** a large funnel in which grain, coal, or other bulk products can be stored and loaded into smaller containers for transportation.

hop·scotch [hop-skoch] *noun.* a playground game played by children. A stone is thrown onto a set of numbered squares marked in chalk on the ground. Each child hops and jumps between the squares and has to pick up the stone to score.

horde [hord] *noun, plural* **hordes.** a large group of people, animals, or insects: *A horde of ants swarmed over the dead tree.*
🔊 A different word with the same sound is **hoard.**

hor·i·zon ▼ [huh-rye-zun] *noun, plural* **horizons. 1.** the limit of a person's view over the earth; the point where the sky meets the sea or earth: *As the sun sets, it gradually disappears over the horizon.* **2.** the limit of a person's experience, knowledge, or ideas: *Education can help to broaden a person's horizons.*

hor·i·zon·tal [hor-uh-zon-tul] *adjective.* flat on level ground; level with the horizon. In soccer there is a horizontal bar across the top of the goal.
—**horizontally,** *adverb.*

hor·mone [hor-mone] *noun, plural* **hormones.** *Biology.* any of a number of chemicals produced by organs of the human body that circulate in the bloodstream and help to control growth and development and other activities of the body. A hormone is produced in one part of the body and carried to another part to cause some kind of change. Anything to do with the hormone system is **hormonal.**

horn [horn] *noun, plural* **horns. 1.** a hollow, hard-pointed growth, usually one of a pair, on the head of animals including cattle, sheep, and rhinoceroses. **2.** any growth that looks like the horn of an animal. The **horned owl** has a hornlike growth made of feathers. **3.** one of the brass musical instruments made from a long pipe, bent into shape and played by blowing. **4.** a device in a car, truck, or other vehicle used to make a loud sound as a warning.
• **horn in.** to intrude or meddle in someone else's business.

horned toad ▶ a lizard with scales on its body and spikes on its head that look like animal horns. It lives in the southwestern U.S. These animals are also called **horned lizards.**

The **horned toad** *can squirt blood from its eyes to frighten off another animal.*

hor·net ◀ [hor-nit] *noun, plural* **hornets.** a large wasp with brown markings and a very painful sting.

horn·y [horn-ee] *adjective,* **hornier, horniest. 1.** made of animal horn. **2.** having a hard texture like an animal horn.

Tiny hooks connect the front and back wings of **hornets** *and other wasps.*

hor·o·scope [hor-uh-skope] *noun, plural* **horoscopes.** an analysis of the positions of stars and planets at the time of a person's birth, and predictions of what will happen to him or her as a result of those positions.

hor·ri·ble [hor-uh-bul] *adjective.* **1.** causing shock or horror: *When we drove around the bend, we found ourselves at the scene of a horrible car accident.* **2.** very unpleasant or unkind: *She said some horrible things to me after I beat her in the race.* —**horribly,** *adverb.*

hor·rid [hor-id] *adjective.* very unpleasant, unkind, or frightening: *The science fiction movie was full of horrid, weird-looking creatures.*

hor·ri·fy [hor-uh-fye] *verb,* **horrified, horrifying.** to cause horror or great shock: *We were horrified when we saw the damage caused by the fire.* If something horrifies you, it is **horrifying.**

hor·ror [hor-ur] *noun, plural* **horrors. 1.** a very strong feeling of fear, shock, or disgust: *I have a horror of being in an airplane crash.* **2.** a person or thing that causes such feelings: *The old jail is a real horror.*

A summer sunset lights up the **horizon.**

a b c d e f g h i m n o p q r s t u v w x y z

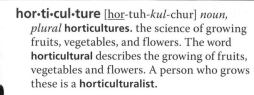

*A **horsefly** has large eyes made up of thousands of tiny eyelets.*

horse [hors] *noun, plural* **horses.**
1. a large, strong animal with four legs, a long neck, pointed ears, and a long mane and tail; used by people to ride on, and to pull carts or wagons. **2.** any animal that belongs to the group of animals that includes zebras, asses, and horses. **3.** a strong wooden frame with legs on which logs are placed while they are being sawed. **4.** a strong padded frame with legs that a person uses to exercise on, or to jump over.
🔊 A different word with the same sound is **hoarse.**

horse·back [hors-*bak*] *noun.* the back of a horse: *The riot police were mounted on horseback.*
adverb. on the back of a horse: *The riding school taught all the skills of riding horseback.*

horse·fly ▲ [hors-*flye*] *noun, plural* **horseflies.** a large, black fly that can sting horses, cattle, and humans.

horse·man [hors-mun] *noun, plural* **horsemen.** a person who rides on a horse, especially someone who is skilled at doing this.

horse·play [hors-*play*] *noun.* any rough or noisy behavior.

horse·pow·er [hors-*pow*-ur] *noun.* a unit that measures the power of an engine. One horsepower is equal to the force needed to pull 550 pounds at a rate of one foot per second. A typical car might have an engine of 150 horsepower.

> The idea of **horsepower** was developed by James Watt, the inventor of the steam engine, because the horse was the main source of energy with which his new engine would be compared.

horse·rad·ish [hors-*rad*-ish] *noun, plural* **horseradishes.** a plant with a strong-tasting white root that is chopped finely and used to make a sauce eaten with meat: *a beef and horseradish sandwich.*

horse·shoe [hors-*shoo*] *noun, plural* **horseshoes.** a strong U-shaped metal plate fitted to a horse's hoof to protect it. The outdoor game of **horseshoes** involves throwing horseshoes so they will land around or near a post fixed in the ground.

horseshoe crab ▼ any of four ancient marine species of arthropod. Horseshoe crabs are common along the east coast of the U.S.

horse·wom·an [hors-*wu*-mun] *noun, plural* **horsewomen.** a woman who rides on a horse, especially one who is skilled at doing this.

Horseshoe crabs *are related to scorpions and are not true crabs.*

hor·ti·cul·ture [hor-tuh-*kul*-chur] *noun, plural* **horticultures.** the science of growing fruits, vegetables, and flowers. The word **horticultural** describes the growing of fruits, vegetables and flowers. A person who grows these is a **horticulturalist.**

hose [hoze] *noun, plural* **hoses. 1.** a flexible rubber or plastic tube used to move liquids from one place to another. **2.** tights, stockings, or socks; hosiery.
verb, **hosed, hosing.** to use a hose on, to spray or wet with water: *When we got home we hosed down the car to wash off the mud.*

ho·sier·y [hoh-zhur-ee] *noun.* knitted garments for the legs: *Tights, pantyhose, stockings, and socks are hosiery.*

hos·pi·ta·ble [hah-*spit*-uh-bul] *adjective.* having a warm and friendly attitude toward guests and strangers; welcoming.

hos·pi·tal [hos-pi-tul] *noun, plural* **hospitals.** a place where people who are ill or have been injured are treated by doctors and nurses.

> The word **hospital** once meant "a guest house" or "a place of shelter and rest for travelers." People who were traveling would be given a bed to sleep in, food to eat, and taken care of in other ways. Later on, buildings to take care of the sick also came to be called hospitals, because they were thought of as giving shelter and care in a similar way.

hos·pi·tal·i·ty [*hos*-pi-*tal*-uh-tee] *noun, plural* **hospitalities.** the act of being hospitable; making guests feel welcome.

hos·pi·tal·ize [*hos*-pit-il-*ize*] *verb,* **hospitalized, hospitalizing.** to put a person into a hospital for treatment. —**hospitalization,** *noun.*

host[1] [host] *noun, plural* **hosts. 1.** a male person who entertains guests: *Stephen is a wonderful host as he remembered everyone's name at his party.* **2.** *Computers.* a central bank of data on a computer that other computers can access, usually via the Internet. *A web host normally offers a range of services to computer users.*
verb, **hosted, hosting.** to act as a host: *Tina hosted the party in her usual efficient, welcoming manner.*

host[2] [host] *noun, plural* **hosts.** a very large number. *The computer I bought has a host of new features.*

hos·tage [hos-tij] *noun, plural* **hostages.** a person who is kept as a prisoner until either money is paid or certain demands are agreed to.

hos·tel [hos-tul] *noun, plural* **hostels.** a building that offers cheap, basic accommodation, mainly to young people who are traveling from place to place.
🔊 A different word with the same sound is **hostile.**

host·ess [hoh-stus] *noun, plural* **hostesses. 1.** a female host who offers hospitality to guests. **2.** a woman who greets customers at a restaurant and shows them to a table.

hos·tile [hos-tul] *adjective.* showing a strong dislike or disapproval; unfriendly: *The home crowd at the football game was quite hostile to the visiting team.*
🔊 A different word with the same sound is **hostel.**

hos·til·i·ty [hos-til-uh-tee] *noun, plural* **hostilities.**
1. the fact of extreme dislike between two people, groups, or countries, often with each preparing to fight the other: *A state of hostility existed between the two nations before war broke out.* **2. hostilities.** acts of war or fighting between two countries: *When hostilities broke out it was the civilians who suffered most.*

hot [hot] *adjective,* **hotter, hottest. 1.** having a high temperature; not cold or cool: *Yesterday was 105°F —the hottest day in ten years.* **2.** having a taste that leaves a burning sensation on the tongue or mouth: *Even after dinner, his mouth was still burning from the hot pepper sauce.* **3.** expressing strong emotions, passionate: *He has a hot temper.* **4.** chasing closely: *The police were hot on the trail of the burglar.* **5.** fresh, new, or exciting: *Daisy is now a hot act with her new band.* **—hotly,** *adverb.*

Grand Prismatic Spring in Yellowstone National Park, Wyoming, is the largest **hot spring** *in the United States.*

hot dog a thin, red sausage, cooked and served in a long roll, often with mustard and other seasonings.

hot spring ▲ a spring whose water flows out naturally from the ground and is at a much higher temperature than the surrounding air.

hound [hound] *noun, plural* **hounds.** a dog bred and trained for hunting game by scent or sight. *verb,* **hounded, hounding.** to keep pestering someone; chase or bother: *Dad keeps hounding me about keeping my room clean.*

hour [our] *noun, plural* **hours. 1.** a period of time equal to sixty minutes. **2.** a fixed time: *I met my friend during my lunch hour.*
🔊 A different word with the same sound is **our.**

hour·glass ▶ [our-glass] *noun, plural* **hourglasses.** an instrument used for measuring time. Two glass bulbs are joined by a narrow passage through which a quantity of sand runs from one bulb down to the next bulb in one hour.

hour·ly [our-lee] *adjective.* happening or done each hour: *There's an hourly train from here into the city.* *adverb.* every hour: *The station broadcasts the news hourly.*

house [hous] *noun, plural* **houses.**
1. a building where people live. **2.** all the people who live in a building or house: *The baby wakes up the whole house when she cries.* **3.** a building used for a particular purpose: *a court house.* **4.** a group of people that make the laws of a country. **5.** an audience: *It was a full house on opening night for the new musical.* **6.** an important or royal family: *the House of Windsor.* *verb,* **housed, housing.** to give a person or animal a place to live or stay: *The hurricane victims were housed in the school hall.*

In the past, **hourglasses** *were used on ships to measure time.*

house·boat ▼ [hous-bote] *noun, plural* **houseboats.** a boat that people use as their home.

house·fly [hous-flye] *noun, plural* **houseflies.** a small, grayish-black fly that commonly lives in and around people's houses.

house·hold [hous-hold] *noun, plural* **households.**
1. a place where people live: *The household was a real mess the day after the party.* **2.** all the people who live together in one house: *The entire household was awakened by the smoke alarm.* *adjective.* belonging or having to do with a house or family: *Heat and electricity are household expenses.*

There are many **houseboats** *on the canals of Amsterdam, Holland.*

*Hummingbirds **hover** by beating and rotating their wings.*

house·keep·er [*hous*-keep-ur] *noun, plural* **housekeepers.** a person whose job is to take care of the cooking, cleaning, and other domestic chores in someone else's home.

House of Commons *Government.* one of the two parts of the British or Canadian Parliament whose members are elected by the people.

House of Lords *Government.* one of the two parts of the British Parliament whose members are not elected but have a high position within society.

House of Representatives *Government.* the larger of the two parts of the United States Congress, made up of 435 members who serve two-year terms..

house·plant [*hous*-plant] *noun, plural* **houseplants.** an indoor plant.

house·wife [*hous*-wife] *noun, plural* **housewives.** a woman, usually married, whose job is inside the home, taking care of the domestic chores and family.

house·work [*houss*-wurk] *noun.* any of the work that keeps a house clean and neat, such as washing, cleaning, cooking, and ironing.

hous·ing [*hou*-zing] *noun, plural* **housings. 1.** buildings that people live in: *There is a lot of new housing on the other side of town.* **2.** a protective covering or support for a machine: *an engine housing.*

hov·el [*huv*-ul] *noun, plural* **hovels.** a small, dirty house or hut where someone lives.

Up and down

Forward and below head

Around shoulder joint

Above and behind head

hov·er ◀ [*huv*-ur] *verb,* **hovered, hovering. 1.** to stay in one place in the air as if by hanging: *The dragonflies hovered over the top of the water.* **2.** to eagerly wait or stand close by: *The waiter hovered around our table while we were looking at the menu.*

how [how] *adverb.* **1.** in what way: *How do I turn on the fan? Dad showed us how to set the table.* **2.** to what amount or extent: *How old is your dog? How far is it to the next exit?* **3.** in what condition: *How is she feeling since her operation?*

how·e·ver *conjunction.* nevertheless: *Our team has several players out with injury, however we will still try our best today.*
adverb. **1.** in whatever way or manner: *You can wear your hair to the prom however you like.* **2.** to whatever degree or extent: *However hard I study, I never seem to get high marks.*

However can be a useful word when you write a report or other factual paper. Often you will need say one thing and then say something else that changes direction or proves an opposite point: "Coyotes once lived only in certain parts of western North America. *However*, they have now spread over other parts of the continent as well. Often when coyotes howl it sounds like a large pack of animals. It may be, *however*, that only one or two animals are making all the noise."

howl ◀ [howl] *verb,* **howled, howling.** to make a long, loud wailing noise: *We heard the wolf howling in the distance.* *noun, plural* **howls.** a long, loud wailing noise: *the howl of the wind blowing fiercely through the trees.*

hr. an abbreviation for HOUR.

ht. an abbreviation for HEIGHT.

HTML *Computers.* a system of producing writing and pictures so that they can be seen on the Internet. It is an abbreviation for Hypertext Markup Language.

hub [hub] *noun, plural* **hubs. 1.** the middle or center part of a wheel to which an axle is joined. **2.** the center of activity or interest: *The mall is a hub of activity on a Saturday.*

hub·cap [*hub*-kap] *noun, plural* **hubcaps.** a round metal cover that goes over the center area of the wheel on a vehicle.

huck·le·ber·ry [*huk*-ul-*ber*-ee] *noun, plural* **huckleberries.** a small, dark blue edible berry found in North America. The berries grow on a small shrub that is also called a huckleberry.

hud·dle [*hud*-ul] *verb,* **huddled, huddling.** to crowd closely together in a group: *We huddled together under the blankets because it was so cold.* *noun, plural* **huddles.** a group gathered closely together: *The football players were standing in a huddle before the start of the play.*

hue [hyoo] *noun, plural* **hues.** a color or shade of color: *We looked in amazement at all the hues of the rainbow.*

*Wolves **howl** in order to communicate with one another.*

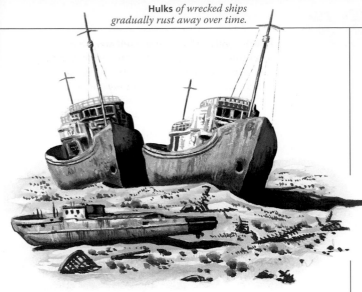

Hulks *of wrecked ships gradually rust away over time.*

huff [huf] *noun, plural* **huffs.** a mood of anger or resentment: *She stormed off in a huff after our argument.* *verb,* **huffed, huffing.** to breathe out in a noisy and heavy way: *I was huffing and puffing after running up the stairs.*

hug [hug] *verb,* **hugged, hugging. 1.** to hold something or someone close to your body with your arms: *I hugged Mom and said goodbye.* **2.** to keep very close to: *The car hugged the curb as it went around the corner.* *noun, plural* **hugs.** a tight hold with the arms.

huge [hyooj] *adjective,* **huger, hugest.** extremely large in size or amount: *An aircraft carrier is a huge ship.* —**hugely,** *adverb.*

hulk ▲ [hulk] *noun, plural* **hulks. 1.** the body of an old ship or vehicle that has been destroyed. **2.** a large, awkward, clumsy or heavy person or thing.

hull [hul] *noun, plural* **hulls. 1.** the shell or outer covering of a seed, grain, or fruit. **2.** the remains of the flower that are attached to strawberries and some other fruits. **3.** the main body or part of a ship that goes underwater. *verb,* **hulled, hulling.** to remove the covering or stem and leaves from a seed or fruit: *We hulled the raspberries.*

hum [hum] *verb,* **hummed, humming. 1.** to make a low continuous sound with your lips closed. **2.** to sing without opening your mouth: *I hummed the tune to myself while I was walking to school.* *noun, plural* **hums.** a low continuous sound: *the hum of the fan in the computer.*

hu·man [hyoo-mun] *adjective.* being or relating to people: *The accident was due to human error, not mechanical error.* *noun, plural* **humans.** a person: *Humans have done a lot of damage to the environment.*

human being a man, woman, or child; a person.

hu·mane [hyoo-mane] *adjective.* showing kindness and sympathy toward others: *Our class watched a documentary on the importance of the humane treatment of animals.* —**humanely,** *adverb.*

hu·man·i·ty [hyoo-man-uh-tee] *noun.* **1.** all humans: *We want a safer world for all humanity.* **2.** deep kindness and concern for others: *He showed great humanity in tending to the patients who couldn't pay for medical care.*

hum·ble [hum-bul] *adjective,* **humbler, humblest. 1.** having a moderate opinion of oneself; modest. **2.** poor and lowly: *She came from a humble background.* *verb,* **humbled, humbling.** to make someone modest: *the world chess champion was humbled when he was beaten by a young competitor.* —**humbly,** *adverb.*

hu·mid [hyoo-mid] *adjective.* moist and damp, particularly when it is warm: *a hot and humid afternoon.*

hu·mid·i·ty [hyoo-mid-i-tee] *noun. Science.* the amount of moisture contained in the air: *I find the humidity in New York in the summer really uncomfortable.*

hu·mil·i·ate [hyoo-mil-ee-ate] *verb,* **humiliated, humiliating.** to make someone feel ashamed or foolish: *I was humiliated when I tripped over and fell in front of the crowd.* —**humiliation,** *noun.*

hum·ming·bird ▼ [hum-ing-burd] *noun, plural* **hummingbirds.** a small, brightly colored bird with a long, narrow bill. The hummingbird beats its wings so fast that it makes a humming noise. It can hover, as well as fly upward, backward, and sideways.

A **hummingbird** *takes nectar from a flower with its long bill.*

a b c d e f g **h** i j k l m n o p q r s t u v w

A
B
C
D
E
F
G
H
I
J
K
L
M
N
O
P
Q
R
S
T
U
V
W
X
Y
Z

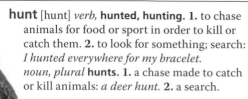

hu·mor [hyoo-mur] *noun,*
plural **humors. 1.** the quality
in something that makes it funny
or amusing. **2.** the ability to make
others laugh: *His outrageous sense
of humor had us falling over
in laughter.* **3.** a mood or frame
of mind: *My brother was in
a bad humor today.*
verb, **humored, humoring.** to do
what someone wants or pretend
to agree with them: *He applied
to college just to humor his parents,
because he really didn't want to go.*

hu·mor·ist [hyoo-mur-ist] *noun,*
plural **humorists.** *Literature.* a person
who is skilled in writing amusing stories.

hu·mor·ous [hyoo-mur-us] *adjective.*
funny or amusing: *Mom told
me some humorous stories
about when she went
to high school.*
—humorously, *adverb.*

hump ▶ [hump] *noun, plural* **humps.** a raised
and rounded lump: *A camel has a hump on its back.*

hu·mus [hyoo-mus] *noun.* the dark material in soil that
is formed from decaying plants and leaves.

hunch [hunch] *verb,* **hunched, hunching.** to raise your
shoulders up and into a rounded shape: *Mom always tells
me to stand straight and stop hunching my shoulders.*
noun, plural **hunches.** an idea based on feeling;
a suspicion: *She had a hunch that he would come over
to ask her out on a date.*

hun·dred [hun-drud] *noun, plural* **hundreds.** ten times
ten; the number 100. One of a hundred equal parts of
something is a **hundredth.**
adjective. amounting to one hundred in number.

hung [hung] *verb.* the past tense and past participle
of HANG.

Hungarian [hung-gare-ee-un] *noun, plural* **Hungarians.**
1. a person from the country of Hungary. **2.** the language
spoken by the people of Hungary.

hun·ger [hung-gur] *noun, plural* **hungers.**
1. an uncomfortable or painful sensation caused by not
eating enough food; the need or desire for food: *Two bowls
of ice cream wasn't enough to satisfy my hunger.* **2.** a strong
desire for something: *a hunger for success.*
verb, **hungered, hungering.** to have a strong desire or need
for something: *I hungered for something sugary to eat.*

hun·gry [hung-gree] *adjective,* **hungrier, hungriest.**
1. having a desire to eat food: *I was hungry all day
because I forgot to bring my lunch.* **2.** having a strong
desire for something: *The puppy was hungry for warmth
and affection.*

hunk [hungk] *noun, plural* **hunks.** a large, thick piece:
a hunk of cheese.

Camels with two **humps** *are not
as common as those with one.*

hunt [hunt] *verb,* **hunted, hunting. 1.** to chase
animals for food or sport in order to kill or
catch them. **2.** to look for something; search:
I hunted everywhere for my bracelet.
noun, plural **hunts. 1.** a chase made to catch
or kill animals: *a deer hunt.* **2.** a search.

hunt·er [hunt-ur] *noun, plural* **hunters.**
1. a person or animal that hunts
other animals for food or sport:
The lion is an excellent hunter.
2. a person who searches for
something: *a treasure hunter.*

hur·dle ▼ [hur-dul] *noun,*
plural **hurdles. 1.** a frame or fence to
be jumped over in a race: *The horse
cleared the final hurdle and sprinted
to the finish.* **2. hurdles.** a race in
which people or horses jump over
hurdles. Someone who competes
in this sort of race is a **hurdler.**
3. a problem to be overcome: *I really
wanted to save money for a car, but
the first hurdle was getting a job.*
verb, **hurdled, hurdling.** to jump over
something while running: *He hurdled
the gate and sprinted for the bus.*

hurl [hurl] *verb,* **hurled, hurling.** to throw something with
a lot of force: *The violent protesters hurled rocks at
the police.*

hur·rah [huh-rah] *noun, plural* **hurrahs.** a shout of
excitement, pleasure, or encouragement: *The crowd
gave a big hurrah when the team walked on the field.*
interjection. a word used to express joy or excitement:
"Hurrah! It's the last day of school!"

Hurdlers *need to run
fast and jump high.*

hur·ri·cane ▼ [hur-uh-*kane*] *noun, plural* **hurricanes.** a violent storm with a very strong wind and heavy rain.

> The word **hurricane** comes from a word used in early times by an American Indian people. When Spanish explorers first came to the Americas, the idea of hurricanes was not well known to them. So they took up the word used by the Indians for this type of storm.

hur·ried [hur-eed] *adjective.* done very quickly: *We arrived just in time for the film after a hurried meal.* —**hurriedly,** *adverb.*

hur·ry [hur-ee] *verb,* **hurried, hurrying.** to move or do things faster than usual: *We had to hurry through the airport in case we missed our connecting flight. noun, plural* **hurries. 1.** the act of moving or doing things faster than usual: *We rushed about in a hurry to get everything cleaned up in time.* **2.** the need to move or do things faster than usual: *I was in a hurry for class to end so I could get home.*

hurt [hurt] *verb,* **hurt, hurting. 1.** to cause pain or damage to: *I hurt my ankle during the soccer game.* **2.** to be painful: *My fingers hurt because I jammed my hand in the car door.* **3.** to cause harm or difficulty: *Her bad attitude hurt her chances of being picked for the team. noun, plural* **hurts.** an injury or pain.

hur·tle [hur-tul] *verb,* **hurtled, hurtling.** to move with great speed, noise, and force: *The truck came hurtling around the corner.*

hus·band [huz-bund] *noun, plural* **husbands.** a man that a woman is married to.

hush [hush] *noun, plural* **hushes.** a silence or stillness after noise stops suddenly. *verb,* **hushed, hushing. 1.** to make or be silent: *The courtroom hushed when the judge walked in.* **2.** to keep secret: *The scandal was hushed up. interjection.* an exclamation used to tell someone to be quiet: *"Hush! I can't hear the TV!"*

HURRICANES

A hurricane begins as a group of smaller thunderstorms over a tropical ocean in summer. The warm water heats the moist air above it, which rises and draws cooler air in beneath the rising current. Huge bands of cloud build up and rotate as the storm moves forward, pulling in more warm, moist air from the ocean and gaining energy. At the center is a small, calm area called the "eye of the storm." When this passes overhead, the rain and wind stop for a short time before resuming.

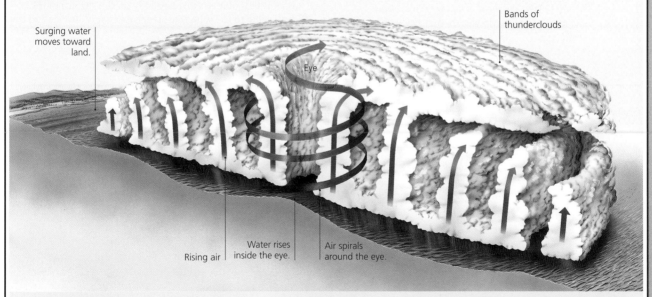

LIFE CYCLE OF A HURRICANE

Day 1: Storm cluster forms.

Day 2: Storms start to spin.

Day 3: Spiral shape becomes more defined.

Day 6: Hurricane has clearly visible eye.

Day 12: Hurricane fades.

husk

husk [husk] *noun, plural* **husks.**
the dry outer covering of seeds,
grain, or fruits: *the husk of
a coconut.*
verb, **husked, husking.** to remove
the husk from: *We husked the corn.*

husk·y¹ [<u>hus</u>-kee] *adjective,* **huskier, huskiest.**
1. big and strong: *a husky man.* **2.** low and rough
in sound: *She has a husky voice because of her sore throat.*

husk·y² ▶ [<u>hus</u>-kee] *noun, plural* **huskies.** a large dog
with thick fur used for pulling sledges over snow.

hus·tle [<u>hus</u>-ul] *verb,* **hustled, hustling. 1.** to move
or go along in a hurry: *The celebrity stopped briefly
for photos and was then hustled up the red carpet.*
2. to get money from someone, often by tricking them.
Someone who tries to trick people into giving them
money is a **hustler.**

hut ▼ [hut] *noun, plural* **huts.** a small shelter or house.

hy·a·cinth [<u>hye</u>-uh-sinth] *noun, plural* **hyacinths.**
a garden plant with sweet-smelling flowers that
grow closely together around one thick stem.

hy·brid [<u>hye</u>-brid] *noun, plural* **hybrids.** *Biology.*
1. the offspring of two animals or plants of
different types, breeds, or species. **2.** something
that comes from the mixture of different sources:
The music was a hybrid of country and blues.
adjective. having to do with being a hybrid:
hybrid corn.

*People living in the Arctic
used to train teams of
huskies to pull sleds.*

hybrid vehicle
an automobile
with more than one
power source, such as
gasoline and electricity.

hy·drant [<u>hye</u>-drunt] *noun,
plural* **hydrants.** a vertical
pipe at the side of a road that
is connected to the main water
supply for access to water in the
case of an emergency.

hy·drau·lic *adjective. Science.*
operated by the pressure of water or other liquid:
a hydraulic pump. The science and system of using
water to produce power is **hydraulics.**

hy·dro·e·lec·tric·i·ty another word for HYDROPOWER.

hy·dro·foil [<u>hye</u>-druh-*foil*] *noun, plural* **hydrofoils.** a large
boat that is able to travel quickly on the surface of the
water due to the winglike structure that is attached to the
hull of the boat.

*In Papua New Guinea, island
people build **huts** from trees,
vines, grass, and leaves.*

hy·dro·gen [hye-druh-jun] *noun. Chemistry.* a colorless, odorless, tasteless, and highly flammable gas. Hydrogen combines chemically with oxygen to form water.

> The word **hydrogen** comes from a phrase meaning "to generate (produce) water." A leading French chemist named Guyton de Morveau named this element in the late 1700s because he noted the way it would produce water when burned.

hydrogen bomb a nuclear bomb, more powerful than an atomic bomb, that explodes when atoms of hydrogen fuse together.

hy·drol·o·gy *Science.* the branch of science dealing with the study of water on the Earth and in the atmosphere.

hy·dro·pow·er ▶ *Science.* the production of electricity by the force of fast-moving water, such as a river or waterfall. This is often referred to as hydroelectric power or **hydroelectricity.**

hy·e·na [hye-ee-nuh] *noun, plural* **hyenas.** a wild, doglike animal found in Africa and Asia. Hyenas hunt in packs, are meat-eaters and make a strange sound similar to a human laugh.

hy·giene [hye-jeen] *noun. Health.* the cleanliness necessary for preserving good health and preventing disease: *A daily shower is important to maintaining good hygiene.*

hy·gien·ist [hye-jee-nist] *noun, plural* **hygienists.** a specialist in hygiene. A dental hygienist is someone who cleans people's teeth and gives them advice on how to keep their mouth and teeth healthy.

hymn [him] *noun, plural* **hymns.** *Religion.* a song praising God. A book of hymns is called a **hymnal.**
🔊 A different word with the same sound is **him.**

hy·per·ac·tive [hye-pur-ak-tiv] *adjective.* being easily excited, restless, and unable to focus the mind for long periods of time: *Hyperactive children can find it difficult to concentrate in class.* The condition of being hyperactive is **hyperactivity.**

hy·per·text *noun. Computers.* a computer-based text retrieval program that uses cross references and links to make it easier to move from one document to the next. The electronic link between one hypertext document and another is called a **hyperlink.**

hy·phen [hye-fun] *noun, plural* **hyphens.** *Language.* the punctuation mark (-) that is used to join two words together, or links two parts of a word when it has to be split at the end of a line.

> The **hyphen** (-) is used in two ways. One is to join together different words into a single word, as in a *half-hearted* attempt, a *high-rise* building, a *happy-go-lucky* attitude, a *hit-and-run* driver. The other way is to divide a word at the end of a line when the whole word is too long to fit. When you write on a computer, you can set the word-processing program so that it puts in these hyphens automatically. If you want to see how to divide a word when you use handwriting, check this dictionary. The symbol (•) shows where the word can be divided.

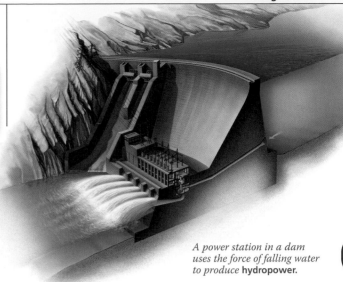

A power station in a dam uses the force of falling water to produce **hydropower.**

hy·phen·ate [hye-fuh-nate] *verb,* **hyphenated, hyphenating.** to join words or syllables with a hyphen. —**hyphenation,** *noun.*

hyp·no·sis [hip-noh-sis] *noun.* a mental state similar to sleep, in which someone's thoughts and actions can be influenced by someone else. When a person is in this state they are said to be in a **hypnotic** trance.

hyp·no·tize [hip-nuh-tize] *verb,* **hypnotized, hypnotizing.** to put someone in a state of hypnosis. The theory or practice of inducing this state is **hypnotism.** A **hypnotist** is a person who uses hypnosis as a form of treatment for entertainment purposes.

hy·po·crite [hip-uh-krit] *noun, plural* **hypocrites.** someone who pretends to have certain beliefs or opinions that he or she does not actually have: *People said the senator was a hypocrite because he made many speeches about saving energy, but he himself traveled in a private jet.* Their false words and actions are described as **hypocritical.** The act or instance of this happening is **hypocrisy.**

hy·po·der·mic [hye-puh-dur-mik] *adjective. Medicine.* used to inject medicine under someone's skin: *a hypodermic needle.*

hy·pot·e·nuse [hye-pot-un-ooze] *noun. Mathematics.* the longest side of any triangle that has one angle of 90 degrees.

hy·po·ther·mi·a [hye-poh-thur-mee-uh] *noun. Health.* a serious medical condition in which the body's temperature is dangerously low as a result of being in the severe cold for a long time.

hy·poth·e·sis [hye-poth-uh-sis] *noun, plural* **hypotheses.** *Science.* an idea that is suggested as an explanation for something, but that has not yet been proved true with facts.

hys·ter·i·cal [hi-ster-uh-kul] *adjective.* **1.** unable to control feelings or behavior because you are really scared, angry, upset, or excited: *He became hysterical and starting throwing things around the room.* **2.** extremely funny: *The movie was hysterical.* —**hysterically,** *adverb.*

a b c d e f g h i j k l m n o p q r s t u v w x y z

Ii

*An **icebreaker** has a specially shaped hull and powerful engines to help it break through thick ice.*

I, i *noun, plural* **I's, i's.** the ninth letter of the English alphabet.

I [eye] *pronoun.* the person speaking: *I have a new jacket.* Different words with the same sound are **aye** and **eye**.

ice [eyess] *noun, plural* **ices. 1.** water that has frozen or become solid: *The car skidded on a patch of ice.* **2.** a frozen dessert made with fruit juice.
verb, **iced, icing. 1.** to chill with ice: *She iced the champagne so it would be ready to drink when the guests arrived.* **2.** to cover or become covered with ice: *This river usually ices over in winter.*

Ice Age *Environment.* a period of time in the past when the temperature was very cold and glaciers covered a large part of the Earth's surface. This term is also spelled **ice age.**

ice·berg ▼ [eyes-berg] *noun, plural* **icebergs.** a very large mass of ice that has broken off from a glacier or polar ice sheet, and is floating in the sea.

ICEBERGS

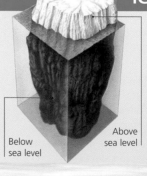

Icebergs separate from polar ice sheets and glaciers mainly in the warmer spring and summer months. They can be as small as a grand piano or as high above sea level as a ten-story building. Only from one-fifth to one-tenth of an iceberg can be seen above water. Icebergs in the Antarctic are both bigger and more plentiful than in the Arctic.

Below sea level — Above sea level

ice·box [ise-boks] *noun, plural* **iceboxes. 1.** a container or chest packed with ice for storing food and drinks. **2.** an older word for a refrigerator.

ice·break·er ◄ [ise-bray-kur] *noun, plural* **icebreakers. 1.** a strong ship designed to break a passage through ice. **2.** a game or joke designed to make people feel more comfortable around each other.

ice·cap [ise-kap] *noun, plural* **icecaps.** *Environment.* a thick sheet of ice that covers an area, sloping in all directions from the center.

ice cream a sweet frozen food made with milk or cream, sugar, and flavorings.

ice hockey ▶ a game played on ice in which two teams of skaters, who each have a curved stick, try to drive a small disk called a puck into the other team's goal.

ice skate a special shoe with a thin metal blade on the bottom that allows fast movement across ice.

ice-skate *verb*, **ice-skated, ice-skating.** to slide on ice wearing ice skates. Someone who participates in the sport of ice skating is an **ice skater.**

i·ci·cle [eye-si-kul] *noun, plural* **icicles.** a long, hanging piece of ice that is formed by the freezing of dripping water.

ic·ing [eye-sing] *noun, plural* **icings.** a sweet mixture of sugar, butter, and flavoring that is used to cover or decorate cakes or cookies.

Icons *are often paintings of saints.*

i·con ▲ [eye-kon] *noun, plural* **icons. 1.** *Art.* a religious picture, often painted on wood. **2.** a small picture or symbol on a computer screen that represents a particular command or operation.

i·cy [eye-see] *adjective*, **icier, iciest. 1.** made of, full of, or covered with ice: *icy roads.* **2.** extremely cold: *The lake was icy cold at this time of the year.* **3.** without warmth; unfriendly: *I got an icy reception from my friend when I arrived late at her party.* **—icily,** *adverb.*

I'd [ide] **1.** the shortened form of "I had" or "I would."

i·de·a [eye-dee-uh] *noun, plural* **ideas. 1.** a picture, thought, or understanding in the mind: *I had a good idea for our science project.* **2.** a belief or opinion about something: *My mother has firm ideas about how children should speak to adults.* **3.** the purpose of something; central meaning: *The idea of the game of soccer is to kick the ball into the goal.*

i·de·al [eye-deel or eye-dee-ul] *noun, plural* **ideals. 1.** a perfect person, thing, or situation: *This restaurant is ideal for Mom's surprise party—it's one of her favorites.* **2.** a principle or high standard: *I believe in the ideal of a democratic society.* *adjective.* describing a perfect example of what something should be like: *I saw my ideal prom dress in the store today.* **—ideally,** *adverb.*

A B C D E F G H I J K L M N O P Q R S T U V W X Y Z

Ice hockey *players wear protective clothing, to prevent injury.*

i·de·a·list [eye-<u>dee</u>-ul-ist] *noun, plural* **idealists.** someone who has high ideals and wants or tries to achieve them. The state of having high ideals and wanting to achieve them is **idealism. —idealistic,** *adjective.*

i·den·ti·cal [eye-<u>den</u>-ti-kul] *adjective.* **1.** the same in every detail: *My brother and I have identical cell phones, so it's easy to mistake his for mine.* **2.** one and the same; the very same: *We saw this identical movie during Christmas season last year.* —**identically,** *adverb.*

i·den·ti·fi·ca·tion [eye-den-tuh-fuh-<u>kay</u>-shun] *noun, plural* **identifications. 1.** the act of stating or recognizing who a person is or what a thing is: *My mother and I went to the dog pound to make an identification of our lost dog.* **2.** something used and accepted as proof of who a person is: *When you travel overseas, you have to carry a passport as a means of identification.* This word is often abbreviated to **ID,** especially when it refers to something used as proof of who a person is: *My father had to show his ID before he could collect the package.*

i·den·ti·fy [eye-<u>den</u>-tuh-*fye*] *verb,* **identified, identifying.** to state or recognize who a person is or what a thing is: *I went to the lost property office to identify the sweater I had left behind in the store.*

• **identify with. 1.** to think of yourself as having the same feelings, problems, or aims as another person or group: *I identified with the girl in the movie who wanted her own horse.* **2.** to link or associate a person, group, or thing very closely with something: *Hollywood is identified with making movies.*

i·den·ti·ty [eye-<u>den</u>-ti-tee] *noun, plural* **identities. 1.** who or what a person or thing is: *He proved his identity by showing his driver's license.* **2.** the state of being exactly alike; sameness: *The identity of the twins' outfits, right down to their shoes, made them even harder to tell apart.*

id·i·om [<u>id</u>-ee-um] *noun, plural* **idioms.** *Language.*
1. a commonly used expression or phrase that means something different from the separate words it is made up of. All languages have idioms. For example, "to pull a fast one" is an idiom that means "to try to trick someone."

When we use an idiom when speaking or writing, we are being **idiomatic. 2.** a special way of using or combining words that is characteristic of a language. For example, we say "show him how to do it," but we don't say "explain him how to do it."

id·i·ot [<u>id</u>-ee-ut] *noun, plural* **idiots.** a stupid or foolish person: *What an idiot to throw a cigarette butt out of the car window on the edge of a forest.* Someone or something that is stupid or foolish can be described as **idiotic.**

i·dle [<u>eye</u>-dul] *adjective,* **idler, idlest. 1.** not in use; out of work: *The strike at the factory left many workers and vehicles idle.* **2.** not active; lazy: *My parents say it's good to be idle sometimes and just to sit and enjoy the beauty of nature.* **3.** having little worth or purpose; trivial; empty: *I don't listen to idle gossip.* *verb,* **idled, idling. 1.** to pass time in a lazy way: *We idled away our vacation fishing and swimming in the river.* **2.** of an engine or motor, to run at minimum speed; to turn over without the gears being engaged: *The mechanic said to let the car idle for a few minutes to allow the engine to warm up.*
🔊 A different word with the same sound is **idol.**

i·dol [<u>eye</u>-dul] *noun, plural* **idols. 1.** an image or statue that represents a god and is worshipped. **2.** someone or something that is greatly admired and loved: *Elvis Presley was the idol of music fans throughout America.*
🔊 A different word with the same sound is **idle.**

i·do·lize [<u>eye</u>-duh-*lize*] *verb,* **idolized, idolizing. 1.** to worship as an idol. **2.** to admire and love someone or something excessively; adore: *My young cousin idolizes his older brother and wants to be just like him.*

if [if] *conjunction.* **1.** in the event that: *Don't come to the party if you are feeling tired.* **2.** on condition that; as long as: *You can have a puppy if you promise to look after it.* **3.** whether: *We wondered if they had heard the good news yet.* **4.** expressing a wish or surprise: *If only they had arrived an hour earlier! If it isn't my old friend Natasha!* See WHETHER *for more information.*

ig·loo ▼ [<u>ig</u>-loo] *noun, plural* **igloos.** a dome-shaped Inuit house, especially one built of blocks of ice or snow.

The word **igloo** simply means "house" in the language of the Inuit, but in English it is used for a particular type of dwelling made from snow. Though it is sometimes thought that all Inuit people lived permanently in igloos, actually they were used more often as temporary shelters, as by hunters traveling away from their usual dwelling.

ig·ne·ous [<u>ig</u>-nee-us] *adjective. Science.* relating to fire; fiery. Igneous rock is formed by the action of a volcano when lava erupts and then hardens.

Blocks of snow insulate an **igloo** *and keep the inside warm.*

a
b
c
d
e
f
g
h
i
j
k
l
m
n
o
p
q
r
s
t
u
v

ig·nite [ig-nite] *verb*, **ignited, igniting. 1.** to set fire to; set on fire; make burn: *I struck a match and ignited the pile of dry twigs.* **2.** to catch fire: *The dry twigs ignited easily.* **3.** to stir up; excite; spark: *Hearing the talk by the famous mountaineer ignited my interest in climbing.*

ig·ni·tion [ig-nish-un] *noun, plural* **ignitions. 1.** the act of igniting: *A responsible person must supervise the ignition of the campfire.* **2.** the act of starting the fuel in an engine burning, or the mechanism (such as an electric spark) for doing this: *The ignition that starts a car's engine is activated when the car's key is turned in a lock.*

ig·no·rance [ig-nur-uns] *noun.* not knowing about or not being aware of some particular thing or many things; lack of education: *We were surprised at the speaker's ignorance of American history.*

ig·no·rant [ig-nur-unt] *adjective.* **1.** not knowing about a particular thing or about many things; not informed or educated: *My grandparents say they are ignorant of computer technology.* **2.** not knowing about or aware of a certain thing: *I was ignorant of the fact that he had been ill.* **3.** showing a lack of knowledge or information: *That was an ignorant remark for someone who has traveled all over the world.* **—ignorantly,** *adverb.*

ig·nore [ig-nore] *verb,* **ignored, ignoring.** take no notice of; pay no attention to: *Everyone in the room was so busy that they completely ignored me when I walked in.*

i·gua·na ▼ [i-gwan-uh] *noun, plural* **iguanas.** a type of large lizard with a spiny ridge along its back and a loose flap of skin under its chin and neck. Iguanas live in tropical parts of America.

ill [il] *adjective,* **worse, worst. 1.** in bad health; not well; sick: *She was so ill that we had to call a doctor.* **2.** bad, evil, or harmful: *Luckily he suffered no ill effects from his fall.* *adverb.* in a harsh or hostile way; unkindly: *We should not speak ill of them when they are not here to defend themselves. noun, plural* **ills.** harm or injury; evil; trouble: *The speaker said that poverty was one of the biggest ills of society.* **◆ ill at ease.** feeling uneasy; uncomfortable; embarrassed: *She felt ill at ease among so many famous people.*

I'll [ile] the shortened form of "I will" or "I shall."
🔊 Different words with the same sound are **aisle** and **isle.**

il·le·gal [i-lee-gul] *adjective. Law.* against the law; unlawful: *It is illegal to park your car in this street during the day.* An act that is against the law is an **illegality.** **—illegally,** *adverb.*

il·leg·i·ble [i-lej-uh-bul] *adjective.* not clear enough to read or very hard to read: *The old letter had faded so badly that the handwriting was now almost illegible.*

il·lit·er·ate [i-lit-ur-it] *adjective. Language.* **1.** unable to read or write at all: *Poor people in many parts of the world are illiterate.* **2.** not able to read and write well enough to get along in the modern world; having a poor education. The state of being unable to read or write is **illiteracy.** *noun.* a person who is unable to read or write.

In the strict sense the word **illiterate** means not being able to read or write at all. In early times many Americans fit this description because not everyone had the chance to go to school to learn these skills. Today, virtually all children do go to school, so the word has added a second meaning that is not as absolute. People say a person is *illiterate* if they do not read and write well enough to do the things needed to get along in modern society, such as reading a newspaper, writing a check, or understanding a supermarket bill.

ill·ness [il-nis] *noun, plural* **illnesses.** the state of being unwell or in bad health; sickness; disease: *Malaria is a serious illness in many parts of the world.*

il·log·i·cal [i-loj-uh-kul] *adjective.* not logical; using faulty reasoning: *It's illogical to say that you love animals but you don't like cats.*

il·lu·mi·nate [i-loo-mi-nate] *verb,* **illuminated, illuminating. 1.** to light up; provide with light: *The Christmas tree was illuminated with flashing lights.* **2.** to help to explain or make clear: *The lecture illuminated the subject for me, and now I'm really interested in it.* The act or process of lighting something up or providing it with light, or of making something clear, is **illumination.**

il·lu·sion [i-loo-zhun] *noun, plural* **illusions.** something unreal or imagined; a false impression; a mistaken idea: *They were surprised to see us, as they were under the illusion that we had moved out of state.*

Marine **iguanas** *of the Galapagos Islands are the only lizards that spend part of their time in the sea.*

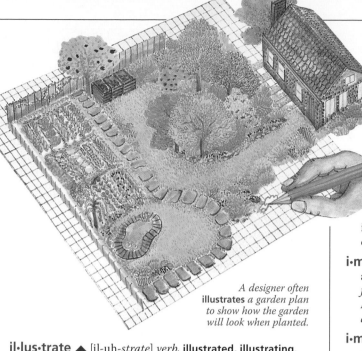

*A designer often **illustrates** a garden plan to show how the garden will look when planted.*

il·lus·trate ▲ [il-uh-*strate*] *verb,* **illustrated, illustrating. 1.** *Art.* to provide a written work with pictures, either to make something clear or for decoration: *The artist illustrated the story with beautiful black-and-white drawings.* **2.** to explain by using examples: *The speaker illustrated her talk with photographs and stories of her personal experiences.*

il·lus·tra·tion [il-uh-*stray*-shun] *noun, plural* **illustrations. 1.** *Art.* a picture or diagram used to explain or decorate a written work: *This book has beautiful black and white illustrations.* **2.** an example that helps to make something clear: *Her success is an illustration of the value of a good education.*

il·lus·tra·tor [il-uh-*strate*-ur] *noun, plural* **illustrators.** *Art.* someone who does illustrations for books, magazines, or other works.

ill will bad or unfriendly feeling: *To show his ill will toward his neighbors, the farmer refused to let them drive across his land.*

I'm [ime] the shortened form of "I am."

im- a prefix that means: **1.** not; without; a lack of: *immature* means not mature. **2.** in or into: *implant* means to plant into or insert. *Im-* has the same meaning as *in-* but is used before words or parts of words starting with *b, m,* or *p.*

im·age [im-ij] *noun, plural* **images. 1.** a picture, statue, or other object made to look like someone or something: *This image of a warrior was made in China thousands of years ago.* **2.** the appearance of someone or something as seen in a mirror or through a lens. **3.** someone who looks very much like someone else: *My cousin is the image of his father.* **4.** a picture of something formed in the mind: *She had an image of exactly how she wanted her garden to look.* **5.** the thoughts or opinions that the public has about a person or thing: *That movie star has the negative image of being rude to fans.* **6.** *Literature.* a word or words used to suggest a certain picture in the mind of the reader.

im·ag·er·y [im-ij-ree] *noun. Literature.* language that creates a vivid picture in the reader's or listener's mind. Describing someone as being "as tense as a coiled spring" or traffic as being "bottlenecked" are examples of imagery.

i·mag·i·nar·y [i-maj-uh-*ner*-ee] *adjective.* existing only in the imagination; not real: *Fairies and gnomes are imaginary beings.*

i·mag·i·na·tion [i-*maj*-uh-*nay*-shun] *noun, plural* **imaginations. 1.** the ability to form mental pictures or ideas of things that are not physically present: *In my imagination I was swimming among dolphins.* **2.** the ability to create or invent new images or ideas: *Unicorns were the product of someone's imagination many hundreds of years ago.*

i·mag·i·na·tive [i-*maj*-uh-nuh-tiv] *adjective.* **1.** having an active imagination: *We need an imaginative illustrator for this book.* **2.** showing an active imagination: *Her imaginative illustrations helped to make the book a success.* —**imaginatively,** *adverb.*

i·mag·ine [i-*maj*-un] *verb,* **imagined, imagining. 1.** to form a picture or an idea of something in your mind: *I imagined sitting in the crescent of the Moon and looking down at the Earth.* **2.** to think something is probably the case; suppose: *I imagine my friend Alicia is having a great time on vacation in Hawaii.* Something that you can form a picture or an idea of in your mind is **imaginable.**

im·i·tate [im-uh-*tate*] *verb,* **imitated, imitating. 1.** to try to behave like someone else; follow someone or something as a model: *I try to imitate my grandmother and always look on the bright side of life.* **2.** to copy or act like another; mimic: *The family all laughed when I imitated the way Dad frowns when he is concentrating.* **3.** to look the same as: *The shelves were covered in plastic that imitated the look of real wood.*

im·i·ta·tion [im-uh-*tay*-shun] *noun, plural* **imitations. 1.** the act of copying the actions or appearance of someone or something: *My friend Marty does very funny imitations of famous movie stars.* **2.** something made as a copy: *This bag is not real leather, but it's a very good imitation.*

im·mac·u·late [i-*mak*-yuh-lit] *adjective.* in perfectly clean and good order; spotless: *The kitchen was immaculate after we all pitched in and helped to clean up.* **2.** with no fault or blemish: *Although her friends were being silly, Carla's behavior was immaculate.* —**immaculately,** *adverb.*

> The source of the word **immaculate** is a word meaning "a spot or stain." The idea is that if something is so completely clean as to be immaculate, it has absolutely no spots or stains.

im·ma·ture [im-uh-*chur* or im-uh-*tur*] *adjective.* **1.** not fully grown or developed; not mature: *A tadpole is the immature stage of a frog.* **2.** showing less good sense, experience, or judgment than might be expected at a certain age; childish: *We all thought it was very immature of Josh to sulk when he didn't get his own way.* The state of being not fully grown or developed is **immaturity.**

A B C D E F G H **I** J K L M N O P Q R S T U V W X Y Z

im·me·di·ate [i-_mee_-dee-it] _adjective._ **1.** happening or done at once; without delay: _My friend Vanessa sent an immediate reply to my e-mail asking her to come on vacation with us._ **2.** near in time or space; not distant: _We haven't decided where we want to live in the long term, but for the immediate future we'll stay in this house._

im·me·di·ate·ly [i-mee-dee-it-lee] _adverb._ at once; right away; without delay: _We need to leave immediately if we are to catch our flight._

im·mense ▼ [i-_mens_] _adjective._ very great in size or amount; enormous: _It's an immense task to have all the costumes ready for the performance on Friday, so everyone will need to help._ The fact of being very great in size or amount is **immensity.** —**immensely,** _adverb._

im·mi·grant [_im_-uh-grunt] _noun, plural_ **immigrants.** someone who comes to live and settle in a country he or she was not born in: _My great-grandparents came to the United States as immigrants from Lithuania._ See EMIGRANT _for more information._

im·mi·grate [_im_-uh-_grate_] _verb,_ **immigrated, immigrating.** to come to live and settle in a country one was not born in: _Her grandparents immigrated to Canada from Greece._

im·mi·gra·tion [_im_-uh-_gray_-shun] _noun._ the act of coming to live and settle in a country one was not born in.

im·mi·nent [_im_-uh-nunt] _adjective._ about to happen; close at hand: _I shouted at him to stop, as he was in imminent danger of being hit by a falling rock._ The state of being about to happen or being close at hand is **imminence.** —**imminently,** _adverb._

im·mor·al [i-_more_-ul] _adjective._ wrong or wicked; not moral; bad: _It's immoral to take things that don't belong to you._ Behavior that is wrong or wicked is **immorality.** —**immorally,** _adverb._

im·mor·tal [i-_more_-tul] _adjective:_ living or lasting forever, or likely to be famous or considered worthy forever: _The works of the composer Mozart are immortal._ The state of living or lasting forever is **immortality.** _noun, plural_ **immortals.** a being that lives forever, or someone whose fame lasts for a very long time: _Shakespeare is an immortal among writers._

The Queen Elizabeth 2 _is an_ **immense** _liner that weighs around 70,000 tons._

im·mune [i-_myoon_] _adjective._ **1.** _Biology._ having a very strong ability to resist catching or developing an infection or disease. This ability can be natural, or acquired as the result of a vaccination: _All the students in our school have had a vaccination that makes them immune from polio._ **2.** free or safe from; not affected by: _It's often helpful to remember that no one is immune from criticism._

> In ancient times a person who was **immune** was someone who was free from having to perform public service. From this came the idea of _immune_ meaning a person who was protected against something harmful or dangerous, then finally the idea of being immune to a disease. (The existence of the body's immune system has only been known for about 100 years.)

immune system _Biology._ the body's system for resisting disease by overpowering and destroying foreign substances and organisms. In humans, the immune system includes antibodies and white blood cells.

im·mu·ni·ty [i-_myoon_-i-tee] _noun._ **1.** _Biology._ the body's ability to resist infections and diseases. This ability can be natural, but it is often the result of a vaccination that protects against a certain infection or disease. **2.** freedom or protection from something negative or harmful: _The thief in custody was granted immunity from prosecution if he revealed the name of the person who had planned the robbery._

im·mu·nize [_im_-yuh-_nize_] _verb,_ **immunized, immunizing.** to make immune to a disease, usually by giving a vaccination: _People who are traveling overseas sometimes have to be immunized against certain infectious diseases._ The fact of being made immune to a disease is **immunization.**

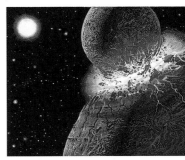
Impacts _in the early solar system created moons and planets._

im·mu·nol·o·gy [_im_-yuh-_nol_-i-jee] _noun. Medicine._ the study of immunity from infections and diseases and how this can be brought about. A person who specializes in this area of study is an **immunologist.**

imp [imp] _noun, plural_ **imps. 1.** _Literature._ a small devil in fairy tales and legends. **2.** a child who gets up to mischief: _When my little brother hid my mother's car keys, she called him an imp._

im·pact ▲ [_im_-pakt] _noun, plural_ **impacts. 1.** the forceful striking of one object against another: _The impact of the truck smashed a hole in the brick wall._ **2.** a strong effect or influence: _The use of computers has had a big impact on the way we live our lives._

im·pair [im-_pare_] _verb,_ **impaired, impairing.** to damage or weaken; make worse: _The skiing accident temporarily impaired his ability to walk._ The state of being damaged or weakened by something is **impairment.**

im·pal·a ▶ [im-<u>pal</u>-uh] *noun,* *plural* **impalas.** a graceful African antelope with a reddish-brown coat and a white underside. The males have large, curving horns. Impalas are very agile, and are able to leap more than ten yards in a single bound.

im·par·tial [im-<u>par</u>-shul] *adjective.* treating all in a fair and equal way; not favoring one more than another: *It is essential that the judge in a court of law be impartial.* Someone who treats everyone in a fair and equal way without favoring one over others is showing **impartiality.** —**impartially,** *adverb.*

im·pa·tient [im-<u>pay</u>-shunt] *adjective.* not putting up with delays or difficulties calmly and without complaining; lacking patience: *The teacher became impatient when the students kept fooling around instead of boarding the bus.* The state of not putting up with delays or difficulties calmly and without complaining is **impatience.** —**impatiently,** *adverb.*

im·peach [im-<u>peech</u>] *verb,* **impeached, impeaching.** *Government.* to formally charge a public official with serious wrongdoing in the course of carrying out his or her duties. The person can be removed from office if the charges are proved. The act of formally charging a public official with wrongdoing is **impeachment.**

im·per·a·tive [im-<u>per</u>-uh-tiv] *adjective.* **1.** extremely important; urgent: *It was imperative that they get the injured climber to the hospital without delay.* **2.** using the form of a verb that expresses a command or request, as in the sentence *Come inside out of the cold!* In grammar, a sentence that uses the form of a verb that expresses a command or request is called an **imperative sentence.** *noun, plural* **imperatives.** the form of a verb that is used to express a command or request, such as *Come here; Stay there; Put that down.*

im·per·fect [im-<u>pur</u>-fikt] *adjective.* having a fault or shortcoming; not perfect: *This shop sells items that are imperfect for much less than the normal price.* The state of having a fault or shortcoming is **imperfection.**

im·pe·ri·al [im-<u>peer</u>-ee-ul] *adjective.* **1.** having to do with an empire or its rulers: *The imperial guard accompanied the emperor and empress when they rode through the streets in their carriage.* **2.** having to do with a country's rule over another country or countries: *During the nineteenth century, Austria was a great imperial power.*

im·pe·ri·al·ism [im-<u>peer</u>-ee-uh-<u>liz</u>-um] *noun. Government.* **1.** the fact of one country ruling over one or more others, often as a result of winning a war or a battle. **2.** the fact of a country's government having a strong desire to gain control of one or more other countries, especially smaller or weaker ones, and taking advantage of any opportunity to do this. A government or country that has control of another or others or is constantly seeking to do this is said to be **imperialist.**

im·per·son·ate [im-<u>pur</u>-suh-*nate*] *verb,* **impersonated, impersonating.** to pretend to be someone or something else in order to amuse or deceive: *My father made my little cousins laugh by impersonating the animals at the zoo.* The act of pretending to be someone or something else is **impersonation.** —**impersonator,** *noun.*

im·per·ti·nent [im-<u>pur</u>-tuh-nunt] *adjective.* rude; not showing proper respect: *My mother said that it was impertinent of our neighbor to ask her how much she earns in her job.* Saying or doing something that is rude or shows a lack of proper respect is **impertinence.**

im·pet·u·ous [im-<u>pech</u>-oo-uhs] *adjective.* acting or done with haste or very suddenly; acting on the spur of the moment: *I made an impetuous decision to accept the puppy I was offered, and hoped my parents would let me keep it.*

im·plant ▼ [im-<u>plant</u>] *verb,* **implanted, implanting.** *Medicine.* to insert an organ or a device into the body by surgery. The process of inserting something into the body by surgery is **implantation.** *noun, plural* **implants.** an organ or a device inserted in the body by surgery, such as an artificial hip or knee.

im·ple·ment [im-pluh-munt *for noun;* <u>im</u>-pluh-ment *for verb*] *noun, plural* **implements.** a device used to carry out a practical task; tool: *Our town's general store sells a range of agricultural implements, such as shovels, hoes, rakes, and wire-cutters.* *verb,* **implemented, implementing.** to make happen; put into action; start doing: *Our club has decided on a program of fundraising events, and next week we will start to implement it.*

im·pli·ca·tion [*im*-pluh-<u>kay</u>-shuhn] *noun,* *plural* **implications.** a meaning that is understood but not stated directly: *When my friend Jess said that she is hopeless at practical jobs, the implication was that she didn't want to help us with painting the clubhouse.*

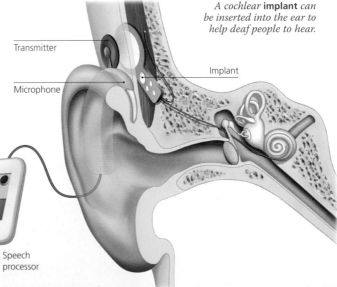

*A cochlear **implant** can be inserted into the ear to help deaf people to hear.*

Transmitter

Microphone

Implant

Speech processor

im·pli·cit [im-<u>plis</u>-it] *adjective.* involved in something said or done as a natural or necessary part of that thing but not said directly; understood but not stated: *How anxious Mom was to hear that Dad had arrived safely at his hotel was implicit in the way she kept looking at the phone as she walked past.* —**implicitly,** *adverb.*

im·ply [im-<u>plye</u>] *verb,* **implied, implying.** to involve or include though this is not stated openly; suggest without said openly: *The way my father kept looking at his watch implied that he was worried we would miss our flight.*

To **imply** something is to give a suggestion or hint, rather than saying it directly: "He said, 'Your cookies look delicious,' *implying* that he would like to have one." To *infer* something is to understand it from such a suggestion or hint: "From what he said, she *inferred* that he wanted a cookie."

im·po·lite [im-puh-<u>lite</u>] *adjective.* not well-mannered; showing rudeness; not polite: *It would be impolite to interrupt while the teacher is talking.*

im·port ▲ [im-<u>port</u> *for verb;* <u>im</u>-port *for noun*] *verb,* **imported, importing.** to bring goods into one country from another: *America imports a lot of food from other countries.*
noun, plural **imports.** a product that is brought into one country from another.

im·por·tance [im-<u>port</u>-uns] *noun.* the fact of being important; the fact of having great value: *People need to understand the importance of eating healthy food.*

im·por·tant [im-<u>port</u>-unt] *adjective.* **1.** very valuable; necessary: *Learning to read is an important part of a child's education.* **2.** having great status or influence; being a leader: *State governors and presidents of large companies are very important people in our society.* —**importantly,** *adverb.*

im·pose [im-<u>poze</u>] *verb,* **imposed, imposing. 1.** to force something onto a person or a group of people: *High food prices can impose hardships on many poor people.* **2.** to trouble or bother; cause inconvenience: *I don't wish to impose on you, but could you please turn down that loud music?* Something or someone that is impressive is **imposing.** Something that is imposed is an **imposition.**

im·pos·si·ble [im-<u>pos</u>-uh-bul] *adjective.* **1.** not possible; unable to be done: *The mystery of the missing treasure was impossible to solve.* **2.** difficult to handle or control: *an impossible situation.* Something that is impossible to do is an **impossibility.** —**impossibly,** *adverb.*

im·pos·tor [im-<u>pos</u>-tur] *noun, plural* **impostors.** a person who disguises himself or herself as someone else or claims to be a different person, usually in order to fool or cheat other people.

im·prac·ti·cal [im-<u>prak</u>-tuh-kul] *adjective.* **1.** not realistic; not possible: *That mountain is so high that it would be impractical to try to climb right to the top.* **2.** not wise; not advisable: *Not buying enough food is an impractical way of trying to save money.* Something that is impractical is an **impracticality.**

im·press [im-<u>pres</u>] *verb,* **impressed, impressing. 1.** to affect strongly and positively: *Fleur's beautiful singing impressed everybody who heard her.* **2.** to make strongly aware of: *The coach impressed on the team the importance of keeping fit.* **3.** *History.* to force people into the army or navy by seizing or kidnapping them.

im·pres·sion [im-<u>presh</u>-un] *noun, plural* **impressions. 1.** the way that something affects someone: *That young actor made a very good impression on the audience.* **2.** thought about something; an opinion; a hunch: *I got the impression that Jack did not enjoy his birthday party.* **3.** an imprint or mark created by stamping, striking, or pressing: *The falling branch made a deep impression in the wet soil.* **4.** a likeness; an imitation of: *Barbara can do good impressions of bird calls.* Someone who does impressions of other people or things is an **impressionist.**

> The style of art known as **Impressionism** got its name from a very famous painting by one of the leading artists of this style of painting. Claude Monet painted *Impression: Sunrise* in 1872. The idea of the word "Impression" is that Monet and his fellow Impressionist artists painted a scene according to the impression that it made on the mind, rather than trying to show exactly what the scene looked like as a photograph would.

Im·pres·sion·ism ▼ [im-<u>presh</u>-un-*iz*-um] *noun. Art.* an artistic movement that began in France in about 1870 in which painters attempted to create impressions of scenes, objects, and people rather than making exact likenesses of them. An artist who practiced Impressionism was an **Impressionist.** Such artists included Claude Monet, Pierre Auguste Renoir, and Paul Cézanne.

im·pres·sive [im-<u>pres</u>-iv] *adjective.* deserving of praise or admiration: *The picture you drew of your brother is a very impressive piece of work.* —**impressively,** *adverb.*

*This painting, by Paul Cézanne, is in the **Impressionist** style.*

im·print [im-*print*] *noun, plural* **imprints. 1.** an image or mark made by pressing, stamping, or striking: *The tight ring left a deep imprint on her finger.* **2.** a lasting effect; a consequence: *The ruined buildings in this city are an imprint of the last war.*
verb, **imprinted, imprinting. 1.** to leave a mark or an impression by pressing, stamping, or striking. **2.** to have an effect on; create consequences: *With many fallen trees, the huge storm imprinted itself on the land.*

im·pris·on [im-*priz*-un] *verb,* **imprisoned, imprisoning.** to send to prison or put in prison; jail. The act of imprisoning is **imprisonment.**

im·prop·er [im-*prop*-ur] *adjective.* **1.** not according to the rules; incorrect: *He is learning to speak English, but he still uses many words in an improper way.* **2.** showing bad manners; rude; impolite: *To lose your temper over such a small thing would be very improper.* An improper act is an **impropriety. —improperly,** *adverb.*

improper fraction *Mathematics.* a fraction that is more than or equal to 1. $^7/_6$, $^5/_4$, and $^4/_4$ are all improper fractions.

im·prove [im-*proov*] *verb,* **improved, improving.** to cause to get better; become better: *Since he started exercising regularly, Ray's fitness has improved greatly.*

im·prove·ment [im-*proov*-munt] *noun, plural* **improvements. 1.** the fact of being better; an increase in quality: *The coach wanted an improvement in the way the players performed.* **2.** a new feature or element that makes things better. **3.** something better than what existed before: *The new coach is a real improvement on the previous one.*

im·pro·vise [im-pruh-*vize*] *verb,* **improvised, improvising. 1.** to make up without preparation: *I quickly improvised an answer to the unexpected question.* **2.** to use whatever is available: *Carlo improvised a meal out of just some tomatoes, rice, and a few vegetables.* Something that is improvised is an **improvisation.**

im·pu·dent [im-pyuh-dunt] *adjective.* not respectful; impolite: *Magritta was an impudent child who never did what her parents asked her to.* A person who is impudent shows **impudence.**

im·pulse [im-puls] *noun, plural* **impulses. 1.** an urge to do something: *Richard bought the new surfboard on a sudden impulse.* **2.** a sudden force or surge of power: *The impulse of the wind caused the door to fly open.*
adjective. acting or happening without thought or preparation: *Henrietta's buying of that expensive necklace was an impulse purchase.*

im·pul·sive [im-*pul*-siv] *adjective.* **1.** inclined to act without planning or thinking: *He is too impulsive to solve this problem carefully and patiently.* **2.** done or performed without proper thinking or planning: *an impulsive remark.* **—impulsively,** *adverb.*

im·pure [im-*pyoor*] *adjective.* **1.** not clean; contaminated: *It is dangerous to breathe the impure air in that old mine.* **2.** mixed with a small amount of another substance: *Most of the fruit juices you buy in supermarkets are slightly impure.* Something that is impure has an **impurity.**

in [in] *preposition.* **1.** within a place; inside: *Stay in the house until we get back.* **2.** into a place: *He put the milk in the refrigerator.* **3.** at or to a certain place, time, or condition: *to live in the suburbs; to make a trip in two hours; to be in a big hurry.* **4.** by a certain method: *to appear in person, to pay in cash.* *adverb.* to the inside; within: *I shut the door to keep the dog in.*

in- a prefix that means: **1.** not; the opposite of: *A measurement that is not accurate is inaccurate.* **2.** in or inside: *Input is what is put into something.* In baseball, the *infield* is inner part of the field, close to the bases.

in. an abbreviation for INCH.

in·a·bil·i·ty [in-uh-*bil*-uh-tee] *noun, plural* **inabilities.** the fact of being unable; a lack of ability: *A deaf person has an inability to hear.*

in·ac·cu·rate [in-*ak*-yuh-rit] *adjective.* not accurate; incorrect: *These scales are inaccurate, so they do not show your correct weight.* **—inaccurately,** *adverb.*

in·ac·tive ▲ [in-*ak*-tiv] *adjective.* **1.** not active; lazy or idle: *There's a lot of work to do so we can't afford to be inactive.* **2.** not in working order; not serving its usual purpose: *an inactive electric wire.*

in·ad·e·quate [in-*ad*-uh-kwit] *adjective.* not good enough; not suitable: *This little stove is inadequate for heating this large room.* **—inadequately,** *adverb.*

in·ap·pro·pri·ate [in-uh-*proh*-pree-it] *adjective.* not suitable; wrong: *Talking loudly during a movie is an inappropriate way to behave.* **—inappropriately,** *adverb.*

in·au·di·ble [in-*aw*-duh-bul] *adjective.* too quiet to be heard: *Genevieve spoke in an almost inaudible whisper.*

in·au·gu·rate [in-*aw*-gyuh-rate] *verb,* **inaugurated, inaugurating. 1.** to install formally in office: *The new President will be inaugurated next month.* **2.** to declare formally open or ready for use: *Many people came to the ceremony that inaugurated the new school building.*

in·au·gu·ra·tion [in-aw-gyuh-*ray*-shuhn] *noun, plural* **inaugurations. 1.** *Government.* the formal installation of someone in office. **2.** the formal declaration that something is open or ready for use: *A large crowd gathered to watch the inauguration of the new airport.*

A
B
C
D
E
F
G
H
I
J
K
L
M
N
O
P
Q
R
S
T
U
V
W
X
Y
Z

INCAS

By the fifteenth century the Incas controlled a huge empire in the Andes mountains, covering much of what is now Peru, Ecuador, Bolivia, and Chile. Its supreme ruler, known as the Inca, was believed to be a descendant of the sun god. The Incas were skilled engineers and built paved roads, aqueducts, and massive forts from huge stone slabs high in the mountains. One of their languages, Quechua, is still spoken in the region today. The Inca Empire came to an end with the arrival of the Spanish in 1532.

Sun god

Machu Picchu

in·cli·na·tion [in-kluh-<u>nay</u>-shun] *noun, plural* **inclinations.**
1. a strong desire; wish; urge: *I have an inclination to stay at home today and read a book.*
2. a lean or slope: *Is that roof flat, or does it have a slight inclination?*

in·cline [in-<u>kline</u> or in-<u>kline</u>] *verb,* **inclined, inclining. 1.** to be on a slope; lean: *The ball rolled out the door because the floor of the room inclined downward.*
2. to have a tendency; be likely to: *I'm inclined to agree with that idea.*
noun, plural **inclines.** a sloping surface; hill: *The car slowed down as it went up the incline.*

in·born [<u>in</u>-*born*] *adjective.* possessed since birth; not learned: *Angelina has an inborn ability to tell interesting stories.*

In·ca ▲ [<u>ing</u>-kuh] *noun, plural* **Inca** *or* **Incas.** a member of an ancient native people of Peru and other parts of South America. The Inca civilization lasted for many centuries until Spanish conquerors arrived in South America during the 1500s.

in·can·des·cent [in-kun-<u>des</u>-unt] *adjective.* **1.** glowing brightly and warmly: *an incandescent flame.* **2.** full of warmth and good cheer; brilliant: *an incandescent personality.* An electric bulb that shines brightly and gives off heat is an **incandescent lamp. —incandescence,** *noun.*

in·ca·pa·ble [in-<u>kay</u>-puh-bul] *adjective.* not having the ability to do something; not able: *When a baby is first born, it is incapable of walking.*

in·cense[1] [<u>in</u>-sens] *noun, plural* **incenses.** a material that produces a strong, perfumed odor when it is burned: *People burn incense in some religious ceremonies.*

in·cense[2] [in-<u>sens</u>] *verb,* **incensed, incensing.** to make very angry; infuriate; annoy: *The noisy couple incensed the other people at the concert.*

inch [inch] *noun, plural* **inches.** a measurement of length equal to $\frac{1}{12}$ of a foot, $\frac{1}{36}$ of a yard, and 2.54 centimeters.

in·ci·dent [<u>in</u>-suh-dunt] *noun, plural* **incidents.** anything that occurs; a happening: *The fight between the two boys was an unpleasant incident.*

in·ci·den·tal·ly [in-suh-<u>dent</u>-lee] *adverb.* by the way; and also: *I'll meet you at ten o'clock—incidentally, could you bring along your camera.*

in·cin·er·a·tor [in-<u>sin</u>-uh-*ray*-tur] *noun, plural* **incinerators.** a container in which garbage and other waste materials are burned.

in·cite [in-<u>site</u>] *verb,* **incited, inciting.** to stir up; urge on: *The leader of the gang incited the others to rob the store.*

inclined plane ▼ *Science.* a flat surface that slopes upward from the ground and that would form an angle of more than ninety degrees with a vertical surface. Inclined planes allow for the relatively easy movement of heavy weights from one level to another.

in·clude [in-<u>klood</u>] *verb,* **included, including. 1.** to have within; contain: *The price of this vacation includes all meals and accommodation.* **2.** to take in as part of a group or a whole: *I include Jacqueline among my best friends.*

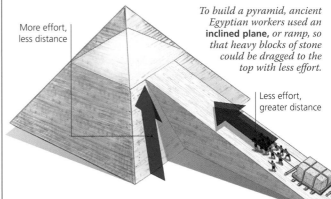

More effort, less distance

Less effort, greater distance

To build a pyramid, ancient Egyptian workers used an **inclined plane,** *or ramp, so that heavy blocks of stone could be dragged to the top with less effort.*

in·clu·sive [in-<u>kloo</u>-siv] *adjective.* including a number of different items; taking in or including: *The sale of the house was inclusive of the washing machine and dishwasher.*

in·come [<u>in</u>-kum] *noun, plural* **incomes.** *Business.* payment that comes to a person for work done, things sold, or return on investments such as bank accounts.

income tax *Government.* a proportion of a person's income that is paid to the government.

in·com·pat·i·ble [in-kum-<u>pat</u>-uh-bul] *adjective.* **1.** not able to live or work together successfully; not able to cooperate with each other: *Arthur quit his job because he and his boss were incompatible.* **2.** not consistent; contradictory: *Gerry's account of the incident is incompatible with Linda's, so one of them is not telling the truth.*

in·com·pe·tent [in-<u>kom</u>-puh-tunt] *adjective.* lacking the ability to do something well or properly: *The carpenter who made this wobbly table was obviously incompetent.* A person who is incompetent shows **incompetence.**

in·com·plete ▶ [*in*-kum-<u>pleet</u>] *adjective.* not finished; having something missing: *The book is incomplete because the writer died before he wrote the last chapter.* —**incompletely,** *adverb.*

in·com·pre·hen·si·ble [*in*-kom-pri-<u>hen</u>-suh-bul] *adjective.* impossible to understand: *Mario was speaking Italian, so what he said was incomprehensible to me.*

in·con·ceiv·a·ble [*in*-kun-<u>see</u>-vuh-bul] *adjective.* not able to be imagined; unbelievable: *It's inconceivable that someone as honest as Amanda would have stolen that money.*

in·con·sid·er·ate [*in*-kun-<u>sid</u>-ur-it] *adjective.* not caring about the needs or wishes of other people: *Playing loud music late at night is very inconsiderate of your neighbors.*

in·con·spic·u·ous [*in*-kun-<u>spik</u>-yoo-us] *adjective.* hard to see or detect; remaining quiet and unnoticed: *Standing in a corner and speaking very quietly, Bert was inconspicuous in the room full of people.*

in·con·ven·ience [*in*-kun-<u>veen</u>-yuns] *noun,* **plural inconveniences.** a situation that is not convenient or comfortable; a difficulty: *Having to travel into the city is a great inconvenience for me.* *verb,* **inconvenienced, inconveniencing.** to cause discomfort or difficulty: *Marika has been badly inconvenienced by her sore ankle.* Anything that is an inconvenience is **inconvenient.**

in·cor·por·ate [*in*-<u>kore</u>-puh-*rate*] *verb,* **incorporated, incorporating. 1.** *Business.* to register a business or organization as a corporation. **2.** to take something into and make it part of something else: *The teacher incorporated the principal's comments into the report she was writing about the year's work.*

in·cor·rect [*in*-kuh-<u>rekt</u>] *adjective.* not right; wrong: *To say that two plus two makes five is incorrect.* —**incorrectly,** *adverb.*

in·crease [in-<u>krees</u> for verb; <u>in</u>-krees for noun] *verb,* **increased, increasing.** to make bigger; add to: *Mom has agreed to increase my allowance to ten dollars a week.* *noun, plural* **increases:** something more; an extra amount: *The workers got a 4 percent pay increase.*

in·cred·i·ble [in-<u>kred</u>-uh-bul] *adjective.* **1.** difficult to believe; unbelievable: *I find it incredible that you could get 100 percent on the test without even studying.* **2.** out of the ordinary; fantastic: *That band wasn't just good—it was incredible!* —**incredibly,** *adverb.*

in·cu·bate [<u>ing</u>-kyuh-*bate*] *verb,* **incubated, incubating.** to protect and keep eggs warm by sitting on them until they are ready to hatch: *Most birds incubate their eggs in nests.*

in·cu·ba·tor [<u>ing</u>-kyuh-*bay*-tur] *noun, plural* **incubators. 1.** a warmed chamber where eggs are kept until they hatch. **2.** a chamber where very tiny babies who are born prematurely are placed for protection.

in·cur·a·ble [in-<u>kyur</u>-uh-bul] *adjective.* not able to be cured: *Modern medicine has found cures for many illnesses that were once thought to be incurable.*

in·debt·ed [in-<u>det</u>-id] *adjective.* **1.** required to pay back something that is borrowed; having a debt or debts. **2.** owing thanks; grateful: *Wendy feels indebted to the lifeguard who rescued her from the rough surf.*

in·deed [in-<u>deed</u>] *adverb.* in fact; absolutely: *Yes, Olga did indeed say she was really angry with you.*

in·def·i·nite [in-<u>def</u>-uh-nit] *adjective.* not known exactly; uncertain: *He may stay with us for quite a while—the length of his visit is indefinite.* —**indefinitely,** *adverb.*

indefinite article *Language.* the words *a* or *an*: *a* book means any book or no particular book; *an* egg means any egg or no particular egg.

in·dent [in-<u>dent</u>] *verb,* **indented, indenting.** to leave a small space at the start of a line of writing or typing: *Our teacher reminded us to indent the first line of each paragraph in our stories.*

in·de·pend·ence [in-di-<u>pen</u>-duns] *noun.* the capacity to control one's own life and destiny; freedom from the authority of others: *During the twentieth century many countries in Africa and Asia gained their independence from European countries that used to govern them.*

Independence Day ▶ *History.* the national holiday in the United States on July 4. It commemorates the Declaration of Independence in 1776, when the United States gained its independence from Britain.

Parades and marching bands are part of **Independence Day** *celebrations.*

in·de·pen·dent [in-di-<u>pen</u>-dunt] *adjective.* able to control one's own life and destiny; free of the authority of others: *When children grow into adults they become independent of their parents.* —**independently,** *adverb.*

in·dex [<u>in</u>-deks] *noun, plural* **indexes.** *Literature.* an alphabetical list of names and topics, usually at the end of a book, that indicates on which pages information about particular topics or people can be found. *verb,* **indexed, indexing.** to compile an index for a book. A person who does this is an **indexer.**

> The word **index** is related to the word *indicate.* It once meant "a person who points out (indicates) things." The idea was that when a person wanted to point out something to others, he or she would use the index finger to show this.

index finger the finger on each hand that is closest to the thumb and that is usually used for pointing.

In·di·an ▼ [<u>in</u>-dee-uhn] *noun, plural* **Indians. 1.** a person who belongs to one of the peoples who have lived in North and South America from long before the time of European settlement there; also called a Native American. **2.** a person who was born in or is a citizen of India. *adjective.* **1.** relating to Indian Americans or Native Americans. **2.** relating to India or the people of India.

The first people to come to the Americas are known as **Indians.** This originally came about because of a mistake; the explorer Christopher Columbus thought he had reached the Asian country of India and not the Americas, which were unknown to Europeans at that time. Because of this, many people recommend that the proper term should be *Native Americans* and not Indians, and this term is often used in schoolbooks. However, polls of the First People themselves generally show that they prefer to be known as Indians or American Indians rather than as Native Americans.

Family groups of American **Indians** *used to follow the buffalo across the Great Plains on horseback.*

Indian summer a period of unnaturally warm weather that sometimes occurs in later autumn or early winter.

in·di·cate [<u>in</u>-duh-*kate*] *verb,* **indicated, indicating. 1.** to provide evidence of; suggest: *Those clouds indicate that it will rain soon.* **2.** to give a sign; point out; show: *The referee blew his whistle to indicate a foul.* Something that indicates or gives a sign or clue is an **indicator.**

in·di·ca·tion [in-di-<u>kay</u>-shuhn] *noun, plural* **indications.** something that indicates or suggests: *The red light will go on as an indication that the car is low on gas.*

in·dict [in-<u>dite</u>] *verb,* **indicted, indicting.** *Law.* to accuse or be accused formally of committing a crime or offense: *The person suspected of robbing the bank was indicted for the crime and will be tried before a court.* The act of indicting someone is an **indictment.**

in·dif·fer·ent [in-<u>dif</u>-runt *or* in-<u>dif</u>-ur-unt] *adjective.* not caring about; not interested in: *I don't follow either of these baseball teams, so I'm indifferent about which one wins this game.* If you are indifferent to something you show **indifference.**

in·di·ges·tion [in-duh-<u>jes</u>-chun] *noun. Health.* a feeling of discomfort experienced while digesting food or drink: *Some people suffer indigestion after eating onions.*

in·di·rect [*in*-duh-<u>rekt</u>] *adjective.* **1.** not direct; taking a longer way: *Going through Pittsburgh would be an indirect way of getting from Boston to New York.* **2.** suggested but not stated directly: *A nod of the head can be an indirect way of saying yes.* **3.** connected, but in a roundabout way: *I got to know Daniel as an indirect result of meeting his brother.* —**indirectly,** *adverb.*

indirect object *Language.* a word, or group of words, that is the object of a verb, but does not receive the action directly; the preposition *to* is understood. In the sentence *She gave them a gift,* "gift" is the direct object and "them" is the indirect object, because she gave the gift *to* them.

in·di·vid·u·al [*in*-duh-<u>vij</u>-oo-ul] *adjective.* **1.** relating or belonging to a single thing, person, or group: *There is an individual gift for every guest at the party.* **2.** different from others; not common; distinct: *This painter has a very individual style.* *noun, plural* **individuals. 1.** a single person; one person: *The Bill of Rights describes freedoms granted to every individual.* **2.** a person or thing thought of in a particular way: *That tall girl in the black dress looks like a very interesting individual.* A person who is individual, or different from others, shows **individuality.** —**individually,** *adverb.*

in·di·vi·sible [*in*-duh-<u>viz</u>-uh-bul] *adjective.* impossible to divide or separate into smaller parts: *Chemical elements are indivisible into smaller kinds of substances.*

In·do·ne·sian ▶ [*in*-doh-<u>neez</u>-yun] *noun, plural* **Indonesians.** a person born in the country of Indonesia. *adjective.* relating to the country of Indonesia, its people, and its language.

in·door [<u>in</u>-*dor*] *adjective.* occurring within a building: *an indoor game; an indoor temperature of 72°F.*

in·doors [<u>in</u>-dorz] *adverb.* inside a building: *It was snowing outside, so we decided to stay indoors.*

in·duce [<u>in</u>-doos] *verb,* **induced, inducing.** to influence or persuade somebody to do something: *The salesperson induced him to buy that new sweater.* Something that encourages a person or group to do something is an **inducement.**

in·dulge [in-<u>dulj</u>] *verb,* **indulged, indulging. 1.** to let yourself or someone else have something enjoyable: *After our workout we indulged in a big breakfast.* **2.** to let someone have what he or she wants: *My parents indulged my little brother's demand for a new bike.* To indulge a person in this way is to be **indulgent.**

in·dus·tri·al [in-<u>dus</u>-tree-ul] *adjective.* **1.** having to do with industry; describing the use of machinery to produce a lot of something: *Before the Industrial Revolution, toys were made by hand in people's homes.* **2.** having many advanced or complex industries: *The factories are in the industrial area of town.*

industrial arts *Education.* an area of school study that deals with methods of using machinery and tools.

in·dus·tri·al·ize [in-<u>dus</u>-tree-uh-*lize*] *verb,* **industrialized, industrializing.** to create an industry or set up many industries in a place: *The Persians industrialized rug production.* The creation of industry on a large scale is **industrialization.**

Industrial Revolution ▶ *History.* the dramatic changes that happened in Britain, the U.S., and Europe in the latter part of the eighteenth century with the move from farming, hunting, and making goods with simple tools at home to producing food and goods using complex machinery in factories. The period of modern history in which industrial methods have been widely used to make and distribute most goods, is said to be the **Industrial Age.**

industrial waste *Environment.* the substances left over from an industrial process, such as dirty water, chemicals, pieces of metal, oil, dirt, chips of wood, and food scraps. This waste material has to be carefully managed so that it does not pollute the environment.

in·dus·tri·ous [in-<u>dus</u>-tree-us] *adjective.* working hard; being constantly busy: *The industrious girls made ten batches of cookies to sell at the fund-raising stall.*

in·dus·try [<u>in</u>-duh-stree] *noun, plural* **industries. 1.** the making and selling of a large number of products or services, especially with the use of machinery: *Our class visited the shoe factory to see industry in action.* **2.** a collection of businesses that make similar goods, or produce similar services: *A lot of my friends want to work in the film industry when they grow up.* **3.** determination and hard work.

in·ef·fi·cient [in-uh-<u>fish</u>-unt] *adjective.* using time, effort, or money in a way that is wasteful or does not produce the required outcome: *You can heat the house with a fire in the fireplace, but it's inefficient compared to using a furnace.* Such a waste of time, effort, or money because of disorganization is called an **inefficiency.** —**inefficiently,** *adverb.*

in·e·qual·i·ty [*in*-i-<u>kwol</u>-uh-tee] *noun, plural* **inequalities.** a situation in which people or things are not equal.

in·er·tia [in-<u>ur</u>-shuh] *noun.* **1.** *Science.* the fact that a still object will stay still until it is moved and a moving object will keep moving in the same way until its movements are stopped or changed. **2.** a reluctance to move: *The more her mother asked her to clean her room, the more she was overcome with inertia.*

in·ev·i·ta·ble [in-<u>ev</u>-uh-tuh-bul] *adjective.* not able to be avoided or stopped: *The changes of the seasons are inevitable.* —**inevitably,** *adverb.*

in·ex·pen·sive [in-ik-<u>spen</u>-siv] *adjective.* not expensive or costly; low in price: *I bought two inexpensive coats at the sale.*

in·ex·pe·ri·enced [*in*-ik-<u>speer</u>-ee-unst] *adjective.* lacking skills, information, or understanding learned from doing something over a period of time.

in·fam·ous [<u>in</u>-fuh-mus] *adjective.* known for extremely bad actions: *Adolf Hitler is infamous for causing the murder of millions of Jewish people.* A state of shame or disgrace caused by very bad behavior is called **infamy.**

in·fant [<u>in</u>-funt] *noun, plural* **infants. 1.** a very young child who is not yet walking or talking. **2.** the first stage of development. The state of being an infant is **infancy**: *Our family business was in its infancy stage when I was born and now we own five restaurants.*

*The invention of the steam engine was an important development in the **Industrial Revolution.***

in·fan·try [in-fun-tree] *noun, plural* **infantries.** an army unit of soldiers who fight on foot: *In ancient battles the infantry would arrive first followed by the cavalry on horseback.*

As you can tell by looking at it, the word **infantry** is related to the word *infant*, meaning "baby." In ancient times, the youngest men in the army were the ones who served in the infantry. Even in modern armies today, members of the infantry will tend to be very young compared to the adult population in general.

in·fect [in-fekt] *verb*, **infected, infecting. 1.** *Health.* to transfer a disease to people or things: *If you don't cover your mouth when you cough, you can infect people around you with your cold.* **2.** to spread rapidly from person to person, as if it were a disease. Something that is able to infect a living thing and spread to others is described as **infectious.**

in·fec·tion [in-fek-shun] *noun, plural* **infections.** *Health.* **1.** the act or fact of infecting. **2.** a sickness resulting from germs getting into the body: *George got an infection in a cut after he rubbed it with dirty hands.*

in·fer [in-fur] *verb*, **inferred, inferring.** to decide something by reasoning; put together information and thought to draw a conclusion: *I inferred my sister was worried about something when she started having nightmares and biting her nails.* A conclusion drawn from reasoning is an **inference.** *See* IMPLY *for more information.*

Hot air was used to **inflate** *this paper-and-cloth balloon.*

in·fe·ri·or [in-feer-ee-ur] *adjective.* **1.** describing something that does not meet a standard; low in quality: *The rooms at that hotel are inferior.* **2.** lower in rank or importance: *The role of assistant coach is inferior to the role of head coach.* The act of being inferior or lesser than is **inferiority.**

in·field [in-feeld] *noun, plural* **infields.** the diamond-shaped area of a baseball field that is inside the bases. A player who plays one of the four positions in this area is an **infielder.**

in·fi·nite [in-fuh-nit] *adjective.* **1.** having no limits or boundaries; not able to be measured: *the infinite size of the universe.* **2.** very great in size, number, or extent: *My mother says she has infinite love for us.* The condition of having no boundaries is **infinity.** —**infinitely,** *adverb.*

in·fin·i·tive [in-fin-uh-tiv] *noun, plural* **infinitives.** *Language.* a basic form of a verb; often used with "to." In the sentence *I like to read*, "to read" is an infinitive.

The **infinitive** of a verb is the root (basic) form used with the word "to" before it. For example: "I'm trying *to learn* Spanish," "She wants *to buy* a new computer," or "I have *to stop* here for a rest." The infinitive is unusual in that it can also be used as a noun, as the subject of a sentence. "*To win* is her goal; coming in second isn't enough" or "*To park* here is against the law."

in·fir·mar·y [in-fur-mur-ee] *noun, plural* **infirmaries.** *Medicine.* a hospital or other place where people go to get medical treatment: *I had a headache so I spent the afternoon in the school infirmary.* Someone who is unwell or is lacking physical strength is said to be **infirm.**

Infirm is an older word meaning "not well; sick." Buildings where sick people were treated then came to be known as *infirmaries,* or places for the sick.

in·flam·ma·ble [in-flam-uh-bul] *adjective.* able to be set on fire quickly and easily: *Dry twigs and paper are inflammable.*

in·flam·ma·tion [in-fluh-may-shun] *noun, plural* **inflammations.** *Health.* a reaction to sickness or injury in an area of the body resulting in redness, pain, swelling, and heat.

in·flate ◀ [in-flate] *verb*, **inflated, inflating.** to fill with air or gas: *The garage attendant inflated our flat tire.* Something that can be inflated is **inflatable.**

in·fla·tion [in-flay-shun] *noun, plural* **inflations. 1.** *Business.* a rise in the cost of things over time. If a quart of milk costs $1.50 and two years later the same brand costs $1.70, that is an example of inflation. **2.** the act of filling something with air or gas: *The inflation of the jumping castle took almost an hour.*

in·flec·tion [in-<u>flek</u>-shun] *noun, plural* **inflections.**
Language. **1.** the changing of a word, usually by adding a different ending, to make the word do a different job in the sentence. For example, the changing of *look* to *looked* makes it past tense. *Looked* is an **inflected form** of *look.* **2.** a change in the pitch or tone of a voice to show a difference in feeling or meaning.

in·flict [in-<u>flikt</u>] *verb,* **inflicted, inflicting.** to impose something unpleasant; cause damage: *The war inflicted terrible losses on the country.*

in·flu·ence [<u>in</u>-floo-uns] *noun, plural* **influences.**
1. a force that produces a change in someone or something else: *Our teacher used her influence to get better food put on the school menu.* **2.** someone or something that can produce a change: *He tries to be a good influence on his little brother.* Someone or something with a lot of influence is **influential.**
verb, **influenced, influencing.** to change something, usually by suggestion or example: *My uncle influenced my father to stop smoking.*

in·flu·en·za [*in*-floo-<u>en</u>-zuh] *noun. Health.* a virus that causes fever, aches, and coughing. A shorter form of this word is **flu.**

> The word **influenza** is related to the word *influence.* In this case, the influence was thought to come from the effect of the stars. Ancient people did not understand how diseases are caused and spread, and many believed that influenza was caused by the stars being in a bad or unfavorable position.

in·form [in-<u>form</u>] *verb,* **informed, informing. 1.** to tell or give information: *Iosie informed the teacher that she would be late.* **2.** to tell damaging or secret information. Someone who does this is an **informer.**

in·for·mal ▶ [in-<u>for</u>-mul] *adjective.* without fuss or ceremony; casual: *It was an informal party so we didn't get very dressed up.* Something that needs to be done but is not official or very important is called an **informality.** —**informally,** *adverb.*

information technology *Computers.* the use of computer hardware and software to provide information to people, especially in business. The abbreviation for this term is **IT.**

in·fre·quent [in-<u>free</u>-kwunt] *adjective.* not happening often: *Rain is infrequent in desert areas.* —**infrequently,** *adverb.*

in·fur·i·ate [in-<u>fyur</u>-ee-*ate*] *verb,* **infuriated, infuriating.** to make someone angry or furious: *The coach is infuriated because Jim never comes to practice.*

-ing a suffix that: **1.** indicates the present participle of most verbs. *Kicking* is the present participle of *kick.* **2.** changes verbs into nouns. In the sentence *Swimming is a popular sport,* "swimming" is a noun formed from the verb "swim."

in·gen·ious [in-<u>jeen</u>-yus] *adjective.* imaginative and clever; like a genius: *She has an ingenious idea for the theme of the school concert.* Some who comes up with ingenious ideas shows **ingenuity.**

in·got ▶ [<u>ing</u>-ut] *noun, plural* **ingots.** a block or bar of metal: *a gold ingot.*

in·gre·di·ent [in-<u>gree</u>-dee-unt] *noun, plural* **ingredients.** one part that goes to make up the whole of something: *Eggs are the main ingredient of an omelet.*

in·hab·it [in-<u>hab</u>-it] *verb,* **inhabited, inhabiting.** to live on or in: *Many different kinds of fish inhabit the sea.*

in·hab·it·ant [in-<u>hab</u>-uh-tunt] *noun, plural* **inhabitants.** a person or animal living in a place.

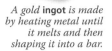

A gold **ingot** *is made by heating metal until it melts and then shaping it into a bar.*

in·hale [in-<u>hale</u>] *verb,* **inhaled, inhaling.** to breathe in: *She inhaled the perfume of the lavender in her garden.*

in·her·it [in-<u>her</u>-it] *verb,* **inherited, inheriting.**
1. to get money or belongings from someone who has died: *My friend inherited a ring from her great aunt.*
2. to receive a feature from a parent or parents: *I inherited my blonde hair from my mother.*

in·her·it·ance [in-<u>her</u>-uh-tuns] *noun, plural* **inheritances.** something inherited: *My mother got money as an inheritance from her uncle.*

in·hu·man [in-<u>hyoo</u>-mun] *adjective.* brutal and cruel; without kindness or mercy: *The prisoners complained about their inhuman treatment by the soldiers.* The fact of being inhuman is called **inhumanity.**

i·ni·tial [i-<u>nish</u>-ul] *adjective.* describing coming first or at the beginning of something: *The initial symptom of a cold is often a headache.*
noun, plural **initials.** the first letter of a word or name: *The initials VIP stand for very important person.*
verb, **initialed, initialing.** to mark or sign with initials: *The teacher asked our parents to initial our homework to show that they had checked it.* —**initially,** *adverb.*

i·ni·ti·ate [i-<u>nish</u>-ee-*ate*] *verb,* **initiated, initiating.**
1. to start or begin something: *The coach initiated a program of two practice games every week.*
2. to introduce someone to the membership of a club or organization: *The new boy was initiated into the Cub Scouts with a ceremony around the campfire.* The act of initiating someone is called an **initiation.**

i·ni·tia·tive [i-<u>nish</u>-uh-tiv] *noun, plural* **initiatives. 1.** the first step toward doing something: *They took the initiative to start a drama group at school.*
2. the drive needed to take the first step toward doing something: *She showed initiative by asking the whole class to help raise money for the new gym.*

in·ject [in-<u>jekt</u>] *verb,* **injected, injecting.**
1. to use a needle to put a liquid into the bloodstream: *The nurse injected everyone with flu vaccine.* **2.** to add or put in: *Our teacher injected some humor by making jokes about past presidents.*

Jeans and T-shirts are popular **informal** *clothes.*

a
b
c
d
e
f
g
h
i
j
k
l
m
n
o
p
q
r
s
t
u
v
w
x
y
z

injection

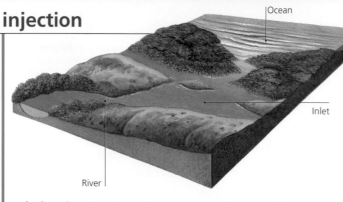

Ocean
Inlet
River

*Fresh water from a river flows into a sheltered **inlet**, where it mixes with salt water from the ocean.*

in·jec·tion [in-jek-shun] *noun, plural* **injections.** *Medicine.* the act of putting a needle into the skin to push a liquid into the blood stream: *The doctor gave my sister an injection to stop her vomiting.*

in·jure [in-jur] *verb,* **injured, injuring.** to cause harm of some kind; hurt or damage: *She injured her ankle when she fell down the stairs.*

in·ju·ry [in-juh-ree] *noun, plural* **injuries.** harm or hurt inflicted on someone or something: *Maria suffered several injuries in the car accident.*

ink [ingk] *noun, plural* **inks.** a colored liquid used for writing, drawing, or printing.
verb, **inked, inking.** to write or draw something with ink.

in·land [in-lund] *adjective.* away from the coast or the center of an area: *an inland lake.*
adverb. away from the coast or toward the center of a country: *We flew inland until we could see the desert below.*

inlet ▲ [in-let] *noun, plural* **inlets.** an opening or passage where water travels from the ocean to a river or lake, or from one lake to another.

inn ▼ [in] *noun, plural* **inns.** a small hotel. Someone who runs an inn is an **innkeeper.**
🔊 A different word with the same sound is **in.**

in·ner [in-ur] *adjective.* **1.** further inside or central: *The store manager's office is in an inner part of the supermarket.* **2.** private or personal: *Although I was furious, I kept my inner feelings to myself.*

in·ning [in-ing] *noun, plural* **innings.** one of the periods of time that divides a game such as baseball, softball, and cricket. In baseball and softball, both teams bat for an inning until three players from each team are out.

in·no·cence [in-uh-suns] *noun.* the state of being not guilty of something: *He protested his innocence when the teacher accused him of cheating.*

in·no·cent [in-uh-sunt] *adjective.* **1.** not having done wrong; not guilty: *An innocent boy was wrongly accused of stealing the watch.* **2.** not hurting anyone; harmless: *I made an innocent remark about my sister's dress but she got upset about it.* —**innocently,** *adverb.*

in·oc·u·late [in-ok-yuh-late] *verb,* **inoculated, inoculating.** *Medicine.* to inject someone with a small amount of disease, which activates their own body to build up a resistance to the disease. This is called an **inoculation.**

in·or·gan·ic [in-ore-gan-ik] *adjective. Chemistry.* describing substances that come from minerals, as opposed to organic substances that come from plants or animals. **Inorganic chemistry** studies substances such as sand, salt, iron, and other minerals.

in·put [in-put] *noun.* **1.** *Computers.* data that is entered into a computer. **2.** feedback or advice: *We asked for the teacher's input before we started on our project.*

in·quire [in-kwire] *verb,* **inquired, inquiring.** to ask about something: *Mom telephoned the theater to inquire about the cost of tickets.*

in·qui·ry [in-kwye-ree] *noun, plural* **inquiries. 1.** an effort to find out something; an investigation: *There will be an inquiry to find out the cause of the bus crash.* **2.** a question or request: *He made inquiries about trading in his old bike for a new one.*

In·quis·i·tion [in-kwuh-zish-un] *noun. History.* a former activity of the Roman Catholic Church created in 1232 to discover and punish people who did not follow the rules of the Church. It operated for almost 600 years.

in·quis·i·tive [in-kwiz-uh-tiv] *adjective.* curious or eager to discover things: *The inquisitive girl kept asking questions.*

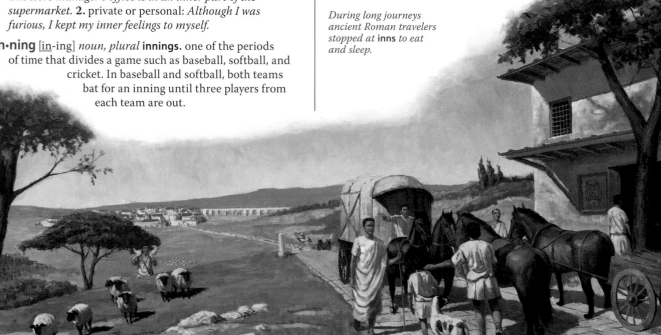

*During long journeys ancient Roman travelers stopped at **inns** to eat and sleep.*

in·sane [in-<u>sane</u>] *adjective.* **1.** not having a sound mind; mentally ill: crazy. The fact or state of being seriously mentally ill is called **insanity**. **2.** very silly or foolish: *You are insane to run around in the snow with no shoes.*

in·scribe ▶ [in-<u>skribe</u>] *verb,* **inscribed, inscribing.** to write or engrave letters or words on something: *He had her name inscribed on the locket.*

in·scrip·tion [in-<u>skrip</u>-shun] *noun, plural* **inscriptions.** words or pictures carved or written on something: *an inscription on a tomb.*

in·sect ▼ [in-<u>sekt</u>] *noun, plural* **insects.** a small animal with a body divided into three parts. Insects have six legs and often a pair of wings, but no backbone. Ants, flies, mosquitoes, and beetles are different types of insects.

> **Insect** goes back to a word meaning "to cut." Insects have a body that is divided into three distinct parts, and people thought it looked like cuts had been made into their bodies to form the three parts.

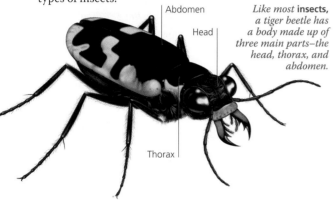

Abdomen
Head
Thorax

Like most **insects,** *a tiger beetle has a body made up of three main parts—the head, thorax, and abdomen.*

in·sect·i·cide [in-<u>sek</u>-tuh-*side*] *noun, plural* **insecticides.** *Environment.* a chemical used to kill insects.

in·se·cure [*in*-si-<u>kyoor</u>] *adjective.* **1.** not properly attached; unstable: *The shelf was so insecure that it fell as soon as I put books on it.* **2.** not safe; in danger: *The prison was insecure because there weren't enough guards.* **3.** not sure or confident; uncertain: *She was very insecure on her first day in the new school.* Someone who suffers fear and self-doubt is suffering from **insecurity.**

in·sen·si·tive [in-<u>sen</u>-suh-tiv] *adjective.* not caring or being careful about other people's feelings: *The insensitive teacher made fun of her when she got the answer wrong.*

in·sert [in-<u>surt</u> *for verb;* <u>in</u>-surt *for noun*] *verb,* **inserted, inserting.** to put inside: *He inserted his ticket into the machine.*
noun, plural **inserts.** something that has been put inside: *The plastic toy came as an insert in our breakfast cereal.* A different word with the same meaning is **insertion.**

in·side [<u>in</u>-side *or* <u>in</u>-side] *noun, plural* **insides. 1.** the interior or inner part of something: *the inside of a box; a coat with a lining on the inside.* **2. insides.** the body's interior. *adjective.* **1.** in or on the inside: *We sat on the inside aisle.* **2.** known by only a few people: *Mom got the inside story about why the neighbors moved away.*

adverb. **1.** into or on the inner part: *He walked inside the house.* **2.** indoors: *We ate inside because the night was cold.* *preposition.* on, in, or into the interior of something: *She looked inside the locker for her book.*

in·sig·ni·a [in-<u>sig</u>-nee-uh] *noun, plural* **insignias.** a badge or emblem that shows someone's official position: *The soldier wore the insignia of his unit, the 101st Airborne Division, which shows the head of an eagle.*

in·sig·ni·fi·cant [in-sig-<u>nif</u>-uh-kunt] *adjective.* of little or no importance: *The teacher said it was an insignificant mistake so she would not deduct marks.* The state or fact of being insignificant is called **insignificance.**

Newspaper Rock in Utah is a sandstone rock **inscribed** *with symbols and pictures from prehistoric times.*

in·sist [in-<u>sist</u>] *verb,* **insisted, insisting.** to demand or say strongly: *She insisted I take the last piece of cake.* The act of insisting something is **insistence.**

in·som·ni·a [in-<u>som</u>-nee-uh] *noun. Health.* a condition of not being able to sleep.

in·spect [in-<u>spekt</u>] *verb,* **inspected, inspecting.** to look at closely; examine: *The nurse inspected our fingernails to make sure they were clean.*

in·spec·tion [in-<u>spek</u>-shun] *noun, plural* **inspections.** the act of looking closely at something: *The new principal completed his inspection of the school.*

in·spec·tor [in-<u>spek</u>-tur] *noun, plural* **inspectors.** **1.** someone who inspects things: *a food inspector.* **2.** a high-ranking police detective.

in·spi·ra·tion [*in*-spuh-<u>ray</u>-shun] *noun, plural* **inspirations.** **1.** the act of having a strong idea or feeling: *She couldn't decide what to paint, so she went to the art gallery for inspiration.* **2.** someone or something that moves you to have such an idea: *The music teacher was the inspiration behind the concert.*

in·spire [in-<u>spire</u>] *verb,* **inspired, inspiring. 1.** to stir the feelings or imagination: *The book inspired me to try writing my own story.* **2.** to move to act: *Her grandmother's visit inspired her to clean her room.*

in·stall [in-<u>stawl</u>] *verb,* **installed, installing. 1.** to put something somewhere to be used: *They installed an air conditioner in the bedroom.* **2.** to place someone in an official position or job: *The president installed a new treasurer.*

in·stal·la·tion [*in*-stuh-<u>lay</u>-shun] *noun, plural* **installations.** the act or fact of putting a thing somewhere to be used: *The installation of the new furnace took two days.*

in·stall·ment [in-<u>stawl</u>-munt] *noun, plural* **installments. 1.** one part of a total amount of money that has to be paid regularly: *I paid the store the fifty dollars I owed in five weekly installments of ten dollars.* **2.** one part or chapter of a story that is published at regular intervals: *The next installment of the outer-space series will be about Venus.*

a b c d h i j k l m n o p q r s t u v w x y z

Electric
guitar

Saxophone

Double
bass

Violin

Taiko drum

*Musical **instruments** come in
many shapes and sizes, and
produce very different sounds.*

in·stance [in-stuns] *noun, plural* **instances.** an example
of something: *There are instances where students have
been expelled from that college for cheating.*
- **for instance.** as an example of something: *Rice is grown
in many Asian countries, for instance, Japan, Vietnam,
and Korea.*

in·stant [in-stunt] *noun, plural* **instances.** a very brief
amount of time: *For an instant, we glimpsed the sun
through the dark clouds.* **2.** a particular moment in time:
I knew I would like her the instant I met her.
adjective. **1.** happening right away; immediate:
*Our teacher says she doesn't always have instant answers
to everything.* **2.** urgent and necessary: *The overflowing
bathtub demanded instant attention.* **3.** something that
can be prepared for drinking or eating right away: *instant
coffee; instant soup.* **—instantly,** *adverb.*

in·stead [in-sted] *adverb.* in place of something or someone
else: *She was going to play tennis for the school this spring,
but decided on softball instead.*
- **instead of.** as a substitute for: *They ate junk food instead
of eating a proper healthy lunch.*

in·stinct [in-stingkt] *noun, plural* **instincts.** something that
comes naturally, without having to be taught: *Many birds
have an instinct to fly south for the winter.*

in·stinct·ive [in-stingkt-tiv] *adjective.* having to do with
something that comes naturally without having to be
taught: *Licking themselves clean is instinctive behavior
for cats.* **—instinctively,** *adverb.*

in·sti·tute [in-stuh-toot] *noun, plural* **institutes.**
an organization that specializes in a particular thing:
She studies French at a language institute.
verb, **institute, instituting.** to introduce an activity:
*My grandparents instituted family picnics so we could
get together every Sunday.*

in·sti·tu·tion [in-stuh-too-shun] *noun, plural* **institutions.**
1. an organization that specializes in a particular thing:
A hospital is a medical institution. **2.** a custom or activity
that has been done for a long time: *Eating turkey at
Thanksgiving is an institution in the U.S.*

in·struct [in-strukt] *verb,* **instructed, instructing. 1.** to teach
or show how to do something: *She instructed him in the
way to make the perfect hamburger.* **2.** to order or give
directions: *We were instructed to use the emergency exit
in case of fire.*

in·struc·tion [in-struk-shun] *noun, plural* **instructions.**
1. the act of showing someone how to do something:
*The coach's instruction on how to kick a ball was
very helpful.* **2.** a direction or explanation: *Read the
instructions before you try to assemble the model plane.*

in·struc·tor [in-struk-tur] *noun, plural* **instructors.**
someone who shows you how to do something; a teacher.

in·stru·ment ▲ [in-struh-munt] *noun, plural* **instruments.**
1. something used for a certain purpose; a tool or
device: *The compass is a mathematical instrument used
to show the direction of true North.* **2.** a device that
shows information: *A jet aircraft has many complicated
instruments in the cockpit.* **3.** something that can be
played to produce musical sounds: *The piano is my
favorite instrument.*

in·suf·fi·cient [in-suh-fish-unt] *adjective.* not enough:
We were given insufficient time to complete the exam.

in·su·late [in-suh-late] *verb,* **insulated, insulating.**
1. to cover or wrap something in a material that stops
sound or heat or electricity from escaping: *Dad insulated
our ceiling to keep the warmth inside during winter.*
2. to protect someone from something bad: *His parents
tried to insulate him from the increasing violence in
the neighborhood.*

in·su·la·tion ▼ [in-suh-lay-shun] *noun,*
plural **insulations. 1.** the act of insulating or fact of
being insulated. **2.** material that stops sound, or heat,
or electricity from escaping: *The insulation around
the toaster cord protects you from getting a shock.*

in·sult [in-sult *for verb;* in-sult *for noun*] *verb,* **insulted,
insulting.** to hurt someone's feelings; say something
bad to a person; offend: *I was insulted by her rude reply.*
noun, plural **insults.** words or actions that hurt
someone's feelings: *She was so upset by the insult
that she burst into tears.*

in·sur·ance [in-shure-uns] *noun. Business.*
financial protection against damage
or loss. If you pay an insurance company
a small amount of money at regular
intervals, they agree to pay you
a certain amount if something bad
happens such as death, accident, theft,
fire, flood, and so on: *Their home
insurance paid for a new house
after the old one burned down.*

*Thick clothing provides **insulation** for
a man fishing in cold conditions.*

in·sure [in-<u>shure</u>] *verb,* **insured, insuring.** to cover something or someone with an insurance policy: *Our house is insured against fire and flood.*

in·te·ger [<u>in</u>-tuh-jur] *noun, plural* **integers.** *Mathematics.* a whole number; a number that does not contain a fraction: *The numbers 1, 0, and -1 are integers, but ½ and 1.5 are not.*

in·te·grate [<u>in</u>-tuh-*grate*] *verb,* **integrated, integrating.**
1. to open an institution to people of all races.
2. to combine parts to form a whole: *The acts from each class were integrated to make a great musical.*

in·te·gra·tion [<u>in</u>-tuh-<u>gray</u>-shun] *noun.* **1.** *Law.* the act of opening an institution or service to all races: *In 1957, President Eisenhower enforced integration at a public high school in Arkansas.* **2.** the act of combining parts into a whole.

in·tel·lec·tu·al [in-tuh-<u>lek</u>-choo-ul] *adjective.* **1.** having to do with the ability to reason, think, and learn. **2.** possessing or showing a great ability to reason, think, and learn. *noun, plural* **intellectuals.** a person who has learned to use their intellectual abilities well.

in·tel·li·gence [in-<u>tel</u>-uh-juns] *noun.* **1.** the ability to think, reason, and understand; using the mind well. **2.** information gathered, especially about an enemy: *The spy had new intelligence about the enemy's plans.*

in·tel·li·gent [in-<u>tel</u>-uh-junt] *adjective.* able to think, learn, and understand well; smart; bright: *an intelligent student with an "A" average; I know Spot is an intelligent dog because he learns commands quickly.* —**intelligently,** *adverb.*

in·tend [in-<u>tend</u>] *verb,* **intended, intending.**
1. to mean to do something; plan: *I intended to return Tina's book but then forgot to bring it.* **2.** to design or mean for a certain person or use: *That small tent is only intended to hold one person.*

in·tense ▶ [in-<u>tens</u>] *adjective.* **1.** extremely strong or great: *The intense sunlight hurt my eyes.* If something has an extreme amount or degree of some quality, it has **intensity.** **2.** strong feelings or focus: *The boy's love of animals is intense.* —**intensely,** *adverb.*

in·tent [in-<u>tent</u>] *noun, plural* **intents.** something one intends to do; an aim or plan: *Ryan's intent is to cycle across Canada to raise money for charity. adjective.* concentrating or focused on something: *He was intent on the television and didn't notice us leave.*

in·ten·tion [in-<u>ten</u>-shun] *noun, plural* **intentions.** something planned, designed, or aimed for: *It is his intention to hand his history assignment in on time.*

in·ten·tion·al [in-<u>ten</u>-shun-ul] *adjective.* done deliberately; aimed for; planned: *I'm sure the fact that she dropped paint on my sweater was intentional.* —**intentionally,** *adverb.*

in·ter·act [in-tur-<u>akt</u>] *verb,* **interacted, interacting.** to act on or influence each other: *The chemicals interacted and caused a large explosion.*

in·ter·ac·tive [in-tur-<u>ak</u>-tiv] *adjective. Computers.* allowing one thing to affect or communicate with another: *That interactive CD-ROM has a story in which you can choose what happens next.*

in·ter·cept [in-tur-<u>sept</u>] *verb,* **intercepted, intercepting.** to stop something moving from one place or person to another: *My friend tried to pass me a note in class but the teacher intercepted it.* Someone or something that intercepts something is called an **interceptor.**

in·ter·cep·tion [in-tur-<u>sep</u>-shun] *noun, plural* **interceptions.** **1.** the act or fact of intercepting: *The interception of the enemy troops stopped them attacking the town.* **2.** something that is intercepted, especially a forward pass in football: *Our team's interception stopped the other team from scoring.*

in·ter·est [<u>in</u>-trist] *noun, plural* **interests.** **1.** a curiosity or wish to know about something: *Mom has a keen interest in finding out what we are doing at school.* **2.** something that is the focus of this: *John's biggest interest is keeping tropical fish.* **3.** the ability to attract curiosity or attention: *There was nothing of interest on television last night.* **4.** a benefit or an advantage: *The nation's interests were improved during the trade talks.* **5.** money paid to someone who lends money or by someone who borrows it: *You can pay a lot of interest on bills you charge to credit cards. verb,* **interested, interesting. 1.** to make curious about, or want to do something: *He is interested in taking scuba diving lessons.* **2.** to attempt to make curious or want to do something: *Caroline could not interest Grandpa in taking a walk with her because he was tired.*

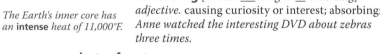
The Earth's inner core has an **intense** *heat of 11,000°F.*

Inner core

in·ter·est·ing [<u>in</u>-tuh-<u>res</u>-ting *or* <u>in</u>-trus-ting] *adjective.* causing curiosity or interest; absorbing: *Anne watched the interesting DVD about zebras three times.*

in·ter·face [<u>in</u>-tur-*fase*] *noun, plural* **interfaces.** *Computers.* a point of contact allowing communication between parts of a computer system: *The interface between the computer and the printer broke down so I couldn't print my letter.*

in·ter·fere [in-tur-<u>feer</u>] *verb,* **interfered, interfering.**
1. to take part in someone else's concerns without being asked: *We can take care of this ourselves, so please don't interfere.* **2.** to disturb or get in the way of: *The baby is tired because the loud music upstairs interfered with her nap.*

in·ter·fer·ence ▶ [<u>in</u>-tur-<u>feer</u>-uns] *noun, plural* **interferences. 1.** unwanted involvement in someone else's concerns: *Interference in their argument will only make them angry with you as well.* **2.** a disturbance of a television or radio signal: *There was too much interference on his cell phone for Mark to hear.* **3.** in sports, illegally stopping an opponent from making a play. For example, in baseball, when a fielder blocks a runner from getting to the base.

Bad weather or other signals can cause **interference** *to television reception.*

a
b
c
d
e
f
g
h
i
j
k
l
m
n
o
p
q
r
s
t
u

The **interior** *of the church of Hagia Sophia, in Istanbul, Turkey, features columns, arches, and high domes.*

A B C D E F G H I J K L M N O P Q R S T U V W X Y Z

in·te·ri·or ▲ [in-<u>teer</u>-ee-ur] *noun, plural* **interiors.**
1. the inner part of something; the inside: *The interior of the car heated up quickly when it was parked in the sun.* **2.** an area within a region such as a country that is a long way from a border or coast: *New Guinea's interior is mountainous.*
adjective. contained within; being inside: *The interior sides of the box are lined with silk.*

in·ter·jec·tion [in-tur-<u>jek</u>-shun] *noun, plural* **interjections.** *Language.* a word or short phrase that shows feelings and can stand alone. Words used in greeting, such as *Hello* and *Good-bye*, are interjections.

Because an **interjection** shows a sudden, strong feeling, you should use an exclamation mark (!) when you write one. You could write, "Hey, watch out for that car" or "Ow. That hurts." However, it would be much better, and would make your meaning much clearer, if your wrote "Hey! Watch out for that car!" or "Ow! That hurts!"

in·ter·me·di·ate [in-tur-<u>mee</u>-dee-it] *adjective.* coming between two things; in the middle: *I am not a beginner or an expert speaker of Spanish, so I took the intermediate class.*

intermediate school *Education.* a school with classes between the elementary and upper secondary levels, usually grades five to eight; also called a middle school or junior high school.

in·ter·mis·sion [in-tur-<u>mish</u>-un] *noun, plural* **intermissions.** a short break taken during an activity; interval: *Gordon went outside for a lemonade during the intermission at the concert.*

in·ter·nal [in-<u>tur</u>-nul] *adjective.* **1.** having to do with or being on the inside of something: *The lungs are the internal organs that we use to breathe.* **2.** having to do with matters within a country as opposed to its foreign relations: *Education is an internal matter that the government must not ignore.*
—**internally,** *adverb.*

in·ter·na·tion·al [in-tur-<u>nash</u>-uh-nul] *adjective.* between or among different nations: *The Olympic Games is an international sporting competition held every four years.*
—**internationally,** *adverb.*

In·ter·net [<u>in</u>-tur-*net*] *noun.* a worldwide communication system created by connecting networks of computers to each other. Computer users can connect to the Internet using a modem and search the system with a browser.

in·ter·pret [in-<u>tur</u>-prit] *verb,* **interpreted, interpreting. 1.** to explain what is said in one language in another language; translate. A person who translates conversations between people who do not speak the same language is an **interpreter. 2.** to explain the meaning of something: *It was difficult to interpret the meaning of the painting.* **3.** to accept or understand as the meaning of: *Most people interpret a dog's snarl as a warning not to touch it.* **4.** to make the meaning of something clear through a performance: *The singer interpreted the sad song so powerfully that it moved the audience to tears.* —**interpretation,** *noun.*

in·ter·ro·ga·tive [in-tuh-<u>rog</u>-uh-tiv] *adjective.* taking the form of a question: *She looked at me in an interrogative way.*
noun, plural **interrogatives.** *Language.* a word that asks something, such as *who, what, how,* or *why.*
An **interrogative sentence** is one that asks a question.

in·ter·rupt [in-tuh-<u>rupt</u>] *verb,* **interrupted, interrupting. 1.** to break in on someone who is talking or doing something: *He kept interrupting so she couldn't finish telling us what happened.* **2.** to stop for a short time: *Our dinner was interrupted when the doorbell rang.*

in·ter·rup·tion [in-tuh-<u>rup</u>-shun] *noun, plural* **interruptions. 1.** the fact of being interrupted: *The interruption in the game was caused by heavy rain.* **2.** something that interrupts: *The teacher disapproved of Julie's constant interruptions during the lesson.*

in·ter·sect [in-tur-<u>sekt</u>] *verb,* **intersected, intersecting.** to come together at the same point and then pass on: *There is a traffic circle where the three main roads intersect.*

in·ter·sec·tion [in-tur-*sek*-shun] *noun, plural* **intersections.** a place where two or more lines meet and cross over each other, especially roads: *There was confusion at the intersection when the traffic lights stopped working.*

in·ter·val [in-tur-vul] *noun, plural* **intervals.** a space or a time that comes between two things; a gap: *There was an interval of a year between the announcement of the new dam and the start of construction.*

in·ter·vene [in-tur-<u>veen</u>] *verb,* **intervened, intervening.** **1.** to lie or occur between two things: *There were two snow-capped mountains but no snow lay in the intervening valley.* **2.** to come between arguing people in order to solve the argument: *When the boys were fighting, their father intervened and sent them to their rooms.* When someone intervenes in a situation or argument, it is called **intervention.**

in·ter·view [in-tur-*vyoo*] *noun, plural* **interviews.** **1.** a meeting, usually held face to face, in which people have a discussion: *At the job interview, Rosie asked the store owner how much she would be paid.* **2.** a meeting where someone is questioned to gather information: *The reporter held an interview with the winning swimmer by the pool right after the race.* *verb,* **interviewed, interviewing.** to conduct an interview with someone: *The student interviewed the elderly man about growing up during the Great Depression.* —**interviewer,** *noun.*

in·tes·tine [in-<u>tes</u>-tin] *noun, plural* **intestines.** *Biology.* a section of the digestive system that is a very long tube; it carries food from the stomach and holds waste products left over from digestion. The intestine is made up of the long, thin **small intestine,** and the shorter, thicker, **large intestine.**

in·ti·mate [in-tuh-mit] *adjective.* **1.** personal and close; familiar: *Intimate friends share their feelings with each other.* The experience of having a close personal relationship is called **intimacy. 2.** having to do with innermost feelings and thoughts; private. —**intimately,** *adverb.*

in·tim·i·date [in-<u>tim</u>-uh-*date*] *verb,* **intimidated, intimidating.** to make timid or fearful; frighten: *The principal intimidated the students by shouting at them.* When someone intimidates another person, it is called **intimidation.**

in·to [in-too] *preposition.* **1.** toward the inside or inner part of: *Put your book into your bag.* **2.** going against; connecting with: *to bump into a chair; I ran into my friend at the park.* **3.** changing the condition of: *The caterpillar turned into a moth.* **4.** *Mathematics.* saying how many times a number is part of another: *6 into 24 is 4.*

in·tri·cate ▶ [in-truh-kit] *adjective.* complicated and detailed: *The intricate carved pattern took days to complete.*

in·trigue [in-<u>treeg</u>] *verb,* **intrigued, intriguing.** to cause interest or curiosity; fascinate: *The detective was intrigued as to how the thief had entered the locked room. noun, plural* **intrigues.** a secret plot or plan: *The general was involved in an intrigue to overthrow the king.*

in·tro·duce [in-truh-<u>duse</u>] *verb,* **introduced, introducing.** **1.** to make known to other people; acquaint: *They met for the first time when they were introduced to each other at a party.* **2.** to bring in something new or make it known: *Tea became popular in the Netherlands soon after it was introduced from China.* **3.** to begin with an explanation of what is to follow: *The biologist introduced his speech by telling us how he came to be interested in parrots.* A statement that prepares one for what is to follow is said to be **introductory.**

in·tro·duc·tion [in-truh-<u>duk</u>-shun] *noun, plural* **introductions. 1.** the act or fact of being introduced: *My introduction to skiing occurred when I was six years old.* **2.** the opening words; a beginning that explains what is to follow: *The book's introduction included information about the author.*

in·trude [in-<u>trood</u>] *verb,* **intruded, intruding.** to go somewhere uninvited or where you are not wanted: *She went into his study and intruded on his privacy.* Entering somewhere uninvited is an **intrusion.** —**intruder,** *noun.*

I·nu·it ▲ [in-oo-it *or* in-yoo-it] *noun, plural* **Inuit** *or* **Inuits.** a native person from Greenland, Alaska, northern Canada, or northeastern Siberia. See ESKIMO for more information. *adjective.* of or relating to the Inuit people or their language: *Inuit clothes are often made of fur for warmth.*

Traditionally, the **Inuit** *fished through holes in the ice or from covered sealskin boats*

in·vade [in-<u>vade</u>] *verb,* **invaded, invading. 1.** to enter into in order to attack and overthrow: *The army invaded the city using tanks.* **2.** to force one's way uninvited somewhere: *Many spectators were arrested when they invaded the football field during the game.*

in·val·id[1] [<u>in</u>-vuh-lid] *noun, plural* **invalids.** someone who is so ill, badly injured, or left weakened by illness that he or she must be looked after by others: *The invalid spent the day resting in bed.*

in·val·id[2] [in-<u>val</u>-id] *adjective.* not valid; without significance, especially according to the law: *Your passport is invalid because the photograph is missing.*

in·val·u·a·ble [in-<u>val</u>-yuh-bul] *adjective.* with a value too large to be measured; very valuable: *The doctor gave Rick invaluable help in curing his illness.*

This embroidery has an **intricate** *pattern.*

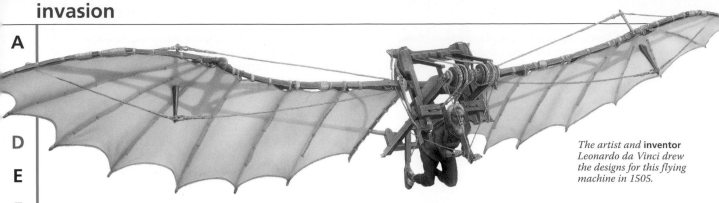

*The artist and **inventor** Leonardo da Vinci drew the designs for this flying machine in 1505.*

in·va·sion [in-<u>vay</u>-zhun] *noun, plural* **invasions. 1.** the act of entering in order to attack and overthrow: *The German invasion of Poland triggered World War II.* **2.** the act of uninvited entry into a place: *He read her diary even though he knew it was an invasion of her privacy.* An act of entry that is unwanted is said to be **invasive.**

in·vent [in-<u>vent</u>] *verb,* **invented, inventing. 1.** to create or think of something for the first time: *Nobody really knows who invented the wheel because it happened thousands of years ago.* Someone who makes or thinks of new things is said to be **inventive.** The new thing that they make or think of is an **invention. 2.** to make up with the imagination: *He invented an excuse about why he was late.*

To **invent** and *discover* both mean to find something new that was not known before. The difference is that if a person *invents* something, he or she makes, puts together, or develops a thing that did not exist before. If a person *discovers* something, that thing already existed but had not been known or found before. For example, Benjamin Franklin is said to have *discovered* electricity when flying a kite in a thunderstorm. Many years later, Thomas Edison *invented* a light bulb to make use of this discovery.

in·vent·or ▲ [in-<u>ven</u>-tur] *noun, plural* **inventors.** a person who thinks of new things, especially a machine, device, or appliance: *Adolphe Sax was the inventor of the saxophone.*

in·ven·to·ry [<u>in</u>-vun-<u>tor</u>-ee] *noun, plural* **inventories.** *Business.* **1.** a detailed list of items held in a store: *The shoe store inventory listed all the shoes in stock along with their prices.* **2.** the items on such a list: *The dealer's inventory of new cars is larger than last year.*

in·vert [in-<u>vurt</u>] *verb,* **inverted, inverting. 1.** to turn something upside down or inside out. **2.** to reverse in direction, order, or position: *Invert the scale and play from the highest note to the lowest.*

in·ver·te·brate ▶ [in-<u>vur</u>-tuh-brit] *adjective. Biology.* having to do with an animal without a backbone. *noun, plural* **invertebrates.** a creature without a backbone, such as a shellfish, insect, or worm.

in·vest [in-<u>vest</u>] *verb,* **invested, investing. 1.** to put money in a business or account in the hope of being paid back extra in return: *Steve invested money in company shares.* One who invests money is called an **investor. 2.** to spend time or effort on something: *He invested all his spare time at the weekend digging a new vegetable garden.*

in·ves·ti·gate [in-<u>ves</u>-tuh-<u>gate</u>] *verb,* **investigated, investigating.** to search, examine carefully, or ask questions about something in order to discover facts: *The detectives investigated the crime scene.*

in·ves·ti·ga·tion [in-<u>ves</u>-tuh-<u>gay</u>-shun] *noun, plural* **investigations.** the act of searching, examining carefully, or asking questions in order to find out facts: *The investigation into the reasons for the airplane crash took many months.*

in·vest·ment [in-<u>vest</u>-munt] *noun, plural* **investments. 1.** the act of investing something: *Jerry's investment of time into his training paid off when he won the high jump.* **2.** the amount of money invested in something: *Her investment in the company is not very large.* **3.** something that is invested in: *Buying that apartment was a good investment.*

in·vis·i·ble [in-<u>viz</u>-uh-bul] *adjective.* existing but not able to be seen: *The road was invisible during the storm.*

in·vi·ta·tion [*in*-vi-<u>tay</u>-shun] *noun, plural* **invitations.** a written or spoken request to go somewhere or do something: *After school, Leah handed out invitations to her party.*

in·vite [in-<u>vite</u>] *noun, plural* **invited, inviting. 1.** to politely ask someone to visit or take part in something: *She invited her neighbor to come swim in our pool.* **2.** to ask for politely: *The school invited donations from parents for the building fund.* **3.** to do something that will probably result in a particular outcome: *Not wearing sunscreen at the beach is inviting sunburn to happen.*

in·vol·un·tar·y [in-<u>vol</u>-un-<u>ter</u>-ee] *adjective.* **1.** done without thought; not deliberate: *She gave an involuntary scream when he jumped out of hiding and shouted at her.* **2.** occurring without control: *The heart works all the time as it is an involuntary muscle.*

in·volve [in-<u>volv</u>] *verb,* **involved, involving. 1.** to be a required part of; include: *Being on the swim team involves hours of training.* **2.** to be drawn into something difficult: *They complained about the bully, but I didn't because I didn't want to get involved.* **3.** to interest greatly or take up one's attention: *The children became so involved in their game that they forgot the time.*

in·ward [<u>in</u>-wurd] *adverb.* going to the inside of something: *The window opens inward. adjective.* toward or on the inside: *The boat sank and there was an inward flow of water.* This word is also spelled **inwards.—inwardly,** *adverb.*

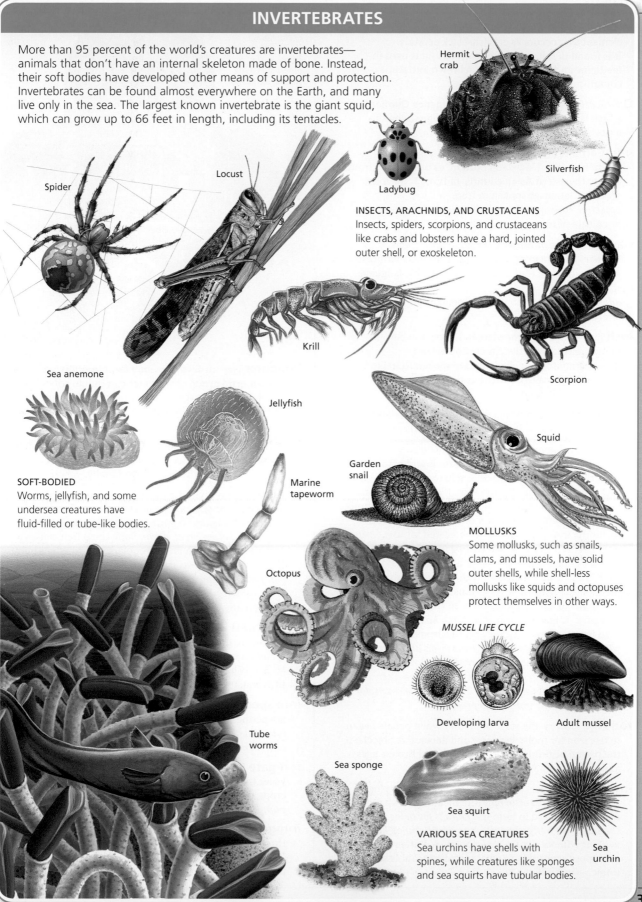

INVERTEBRATES

More than 95 percent of the world's creatures are invertebrates—animals that don't have an internal skeleton made of bone. Instead, their soft bodies have developed other means of support and protection. Invertebrates can be found almost everywhere on the Earth, and many live only in the sea. The largest known invertebrate is the giant squid, which can grow up to 66 feet in length, including its tentacles.

Hermit crab

Ladybug

Silverfish

Spider

Locust

INSECTS, ARACHNIDS, AND CRUSTACEANS
Insects, spiders, scorpions, and crustaceans like crabs and lobsters have a hard, jointed outer shell, or exoskeleton.

Krill

Scorpion

Sea anemone

Jellyfish

Squid

Garden snail

Marine tapeworm

SOFT-BODIED
Worms, jellyfish, and some undersea creatures have fluid-filled or tube-like bodies.

Octopus

MOLLUSKS
Some mollusks, such as snails, clams, and mussels, have solid outer shells, while shell-less mollusks like squids and octopuses protect themselves in other ways.

MUSSEL LIFE CYCLE

Developing larva

Adult mussel

Tube worms

Sea sponge

Sea squirt

Sea urchin

VARIOUS SEA CREATURES
Sea urchins have shells with spines, while creatures like sponges and sea squirts have tubular bodies.

i·o·dine [<u>eye</u>-uh-*dine*] *noun.* **1.** *Chemistry.* a chemical element that occurs as grayish-black crystals. It is found in salt water and seaweed and is used in medicine and photography. **2.** a brown antiseptic containing iodine.

IQ *Education.* an abbreviation of **Intelligence Quotient,** which is a measure of a person's intelligence on the basis of a test.

I·ra·ni·an [ih-<u>rahn</u>-ee-un *or* ih-<u>rane</u>-ee-un] *noun, plural* **Iranians. 1.** a person born in, or originating from, the southwestern Asian country of Iran. **2.** the form of Arabic language spoken in Iran.
adjective. having to do with the people, language, or culture of Iran.

Ir·a·qi [ih-<u>rok</u>-ee *or* ih-<u>rak</u>-ee] *noun, plural* **Iraqis. 1.** a person born in or originating from the southwest Asian country of Iraq. **2.** the form of Arabic language spoken in Iraq.
adjective. having to do with the people, language, or culture of Iraq.

I·rish [<u>eye</u>-rish] *noun, plural* **Irish. 1.** a person born in or originating from the country of Ireland. **2.** the form of the Gaelic language spoken in Ireland.
adjective. having to do with the people, language, or culture of Ireland.

Irish setter a large hunting dog first bred in Ireland, especially noted for its long, red-brown, silky hair.

i·ron [<u>eye</u>-urn] *noun, plural* **irons. 1.** *Chemistry.* a gray-white metallic element used for making tools and many other objects due to its strength. It is able to become magnetic and conducts electricity and heat. Plants and animals need iron, for example to make blood. **2.** any of a number of tools that are made of iron or a mixture of metals including iron and that are often heated for use: *Grandma used to curl her hair with a curling iron.* **3.** an appliance with a flat plate made of iron or a similar metal that is heated and used to smooth cloth. **4.** a golf club with a metal head. **5. irons.** heavy chains attached to a prisoner's legs to make it difficult for them to run.
adjective. **1.** made of iron: *The porch has an iron railing.* **2.** to be strong and hard or gray like iron: *He has an iron will and never wants to change his mind about things.*
verb, **ironed, ironing. 1.** to smooth out cloth with an iron: *Jack ironed his shirt before he went to his job interview.* **2.** to smooth out or get rid of: *The guidance counselor helped the family iron out its problems.*

Iron Age *History.* the stage of history when people began to use iron for tools, weapons, and decorative objects; the period beginning after the Stone and Bronze ages and ending with recorded history.

i·ro·ny [<u>eye</u>-ruh-nee] *noun, plural* **ironies. 1.** a saying or expression that has the opposite meaning of what is really meant; often used in humor: *"Thanks for being so nice,"* she said with irony when the man who bumped her kept walking without saying he was sorry.* A statement that has an opposite meaning to what is really said is said to be **ironic. —ironically,** *adverb.*

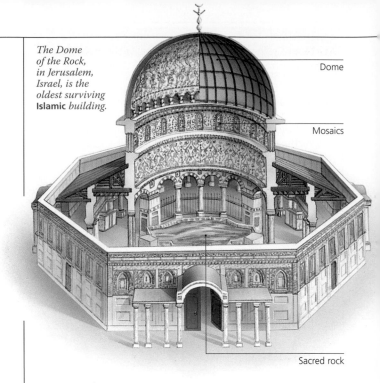

*The Dome of the Rock, in Jerusalem, Israel, is the oldest surviving **Islamic** building.*

Dome

Mosaics

Sacred rock

Ir·o·quois [<u>eer</u>-uh-kwoy] *noun, plural* **Iroquois.** a member of a powerful group of six American Indian tribes based mainly in the area that is now known as New York State.
adjective. having to do with the Iroquois or one of their member tribes.

ir·ra·tion·al [i-<u>rash</u>-uh-nul] *adjective.* not rational or logical; not sensible: *He has an irrational fear of the dark and has to have a light on all night.* **—irrationally,** *adverb.*

ir·reg·u·lar [i-<u>reg</u>-yuh-lur] *adjective.* **1.** not regular in shape, size, length, or spacing; without a pattern: *The ferry service to the island is quite irregular because the ferries are old and often break down.* Something that causes a pattern to be broken is an **irregularity. 2.** rough or bumpy: *The wooden floor was irregular before it was sanded and polished.* **3.** going against the rules or the normal situation: *It is most irregular to shout and run around in a church.* **—irregularly,** *adverb.*

ir·rel·e·vant [i-<u>rel</u>-uh-vunt] *adjective.* not relevant; having nothing to do with something being focused on: *The style of clothes he wears to work is irrelevant to his ability to do his job.* When something is not relevant to a subject or situation, it is an **irrelevance.**

ir·re·spon·si·ble [<u>eer</u>-uh-<u>spon</u>-suh-bul] *adjective.* not acting sensibly; not able to be trusted: *His mother told him he'd been irresponsible leaving his little brother to walk home from school alone.* **—irresponsibly,** *adverb.*

ir·ri·gate [<u>eer</u>-uh-*gate*] *verb,* **irrigated, irrigating.** to supply water through channels or pipes to land planted with crops, especially in an area with little rain: *The farmer pumped water from the river to irrigate his fields.*

ir·ri·ga·tion [<u>eer</u>-uh-<u>gay</u>-shun] *noun.* the supplying of water through channels or pipes to land planted with crops: *The ancient Egyptians were among the first people to use irrigation.*

ir·ri·ta·ble [eer-uh-tuh-buhl] *adjective.* easily annoyed; cranky: *Mom is irritable today because Dad's snoring kept her awake last night.* —**irritably,** *adverb.*

ir·ri·tate [eer-uh-*tate*] *verb,* **irritated, irritating.**
1. to annoy or make cross, especially over something small: *The sound of the dripping water faucet irritated her.*
2. to make sensitive; make itchy or sore: *The dog scratches when fleas bite him and irritate his skin.*

ir·ri·ta·tion [eer-uh-*tay*-shun] *noun, plural* **irritations.**
1. the act of irritating, or the fact of being irritated: *The campfire smoke was a real irritation to my throat.*
2. something that causes one to be irritated: *There were too many irritations for me to enjoy the picnic.*

is [iz] *verb.* a present tense of BE used with *he, she,* or *it,* or words that they stand for: *She is ten years old.*

Is·lam ◀ [iz-lahm *or* is-lahm] *noun. Religion.* a religion that is based on the teachings of the prophet Muhammad, which are written in its holy book, the Koran. Followers of Islam are called Muslims and worship in a mosque. Anything that has to do with Islam, such as art, customs, or beliefs, is **Islamic.**

is·land [eye-lund] *noun, plural* **islands. 1.** a piece of land that is completely surrounded by water: *an island in a lake.* An **islander** is someone who was born on or is living on an island. **2.** something that is like an island: *a traffic island in the middle of a street.*

It seems odd that the first part of the word **island** is spoken to sound like "eye," and not like "is." The original word in English was spelled *iland,* without an **s.** Later the spelling changed to add **s** but the sound of the word stayed the same, without the **s.**

isle [ile] *noun, plural* **isles.** an island, especially a small island. An **islet** is a small isle.
◀)) Different words that have the same sound are **aisle** and **I'll.**

is·n't [iz-unt] the shortened form of "is not."

i·so·late [eye-suh-*late*] *verb,* **isolated, isolating.** to keep separate or apart from other things: *When I had chicken pox I was isolated from my friends so they wouldn't catch it too.* Someone or something that is kept apart or separate is kept in **isolation.**

i·sos·ce·les triangle [eye-*sos*-uh-leez] *Mathematics.* a triangle with two equal sides.

Is·rae·li [iz-*ray*-lee] *noun, plural* **Israelis.** a person born in, or originating from Israel, a country in the Middle East. *adjective.* having to do with the people or culture of Israel.

is·sue [ish-yoo] *noun, plural* **issues. 1.** the act of sending out or producing: *the issue of a new stamp.* **2.** the thing that is sent out or produced: *His photo is in last month's issue of the magazine.* **3.** something important that needs to be talked about: *the issue of wildlife conservation.*
verb, **issued, issuing.** to give or send out: *to issue a parking ticket.*

I·tal·ian [i-*tal*-yun] *noun, plural* **Italians.** a person born in, or originating from Italy, a country in southern Europe. *adjective.* having to do with the people, language, or culture of Italy.

it [it] *pronoun.* **1.** the animal or thing being talked about; this one: *Bring in the newspaper and put in on the table.* **2.** the condition or subject being talked about: *It is a long trip from here to the beach; It was easy to see he was upset.*

i·tal·ic [i-*tal*-ik] *adjective. Language.* having to do with a style of printing that has all the letters sloping to the right. To print something with letters that slope to the right is to **italicize** it.
noun. **italics.** printing that slopes to the right: *This sentence is in italics.*

itch [ich] *noun, plural* **itches. 1.** a prickly or tickling feeling on the skin that causes the desire to scratch. If a part of the body is **itchy,** it feels like it needs to be scratched. **2.** a strong desire; a longing: *the itch to travel to other countries.*
verb, **itched, itching. 1.** to cause or have a prickly or tickling feeling on the skin that makes one want to scratch: *My back itched after I had my hair cut.* **2.** to have a strong desire or longing: *He itched to be home again.*

i·tem [eye-tum] *noun, plural* **items. 1.** a single or separate thing in a list or a collection: *Three items are missing from the set of cups and dishes.* To **itemize** a number of things is to make a list of them. **2.** a piece of the news: *Did you read the item about the earthquake?*

it'll [it-ul] the shortened form of "it will."

its [its] belonging to a particular person, animal, thing, or place: *The puppy has mud on its paws.*

it's [its] the shortened form of: "it is" or "it has."

The words *its* and **it's** look almost the same but are very different in what they mean. *Its* (no apostrophe) means "belonging to it," as in "The dog just had its dinner." *It's* (with the apostrophe) means "it is," as in "The dog looks mean, but it's really friendly." The mistake that people sometimes make is to use *it's* when *its* is the correct word, by writing "The dog had it's dinner."

it·self [it-self] *pronoun.* its own self: *We didn't plant that tree, it just grew by itself.*

-ive a suffix that means doing or likely to: *disruptive* means likely to disrupt.

I've [ive] the shortened form of "I have."

i·vo·ry ▼ [ive-ree] *noun, plural* **ivories. 1.** the hard, smooth, creamy-white material that forms the tusks of elephants. **2.** a creamy-white color.
adjective. **1.** made of ivory or of something like ivory: *ivory beads.* **2.** creamy-white: *ivory gloves; ivory skin.*

i·vy [eye-vee] *noun, plural* **ivies. 1.** a climbing plant with smooth, dark, shiny evergreen leaves. Ivy has roots that can attach to walls; the plant also grows along the ground. **2.** any of a number of similar plants that climb up walls or grow along the ground.

In their spare time, sailors once carved designs onto **ivory** *tusks.*

*The golden **jackal** lives in the dry, open grasslands of eastern Africa.*

A B C D E F I J K L M N O P Q R S T U V W X Y Z

J j

J, j *noun, plural* **J's, j's.** the tenth letter of the English alphabet.

jab [jab] *verb,* **jabbed, jabbing.** to push or poke with something pointed: *He jabbed his fork into the tomato.* *noun, plural* **jabs.** a sudden push or poke with something pointed: *She gave me a jab with her elbow.*

jack [jak] *noun, plural* **jacks. 1.** a tool used for raising and supporting a heavy object, such as a car, a short distance above the ground. **2.** a playing card that has a picture of a prince on it. There are four jacks in a pack of cards. The jack usually has a value just below a queen. **3. jacks.** a game in which each player tries to pick up little metal objects while bouncing and catching a small rubber ball with the same hand. The little metal objects are also called jacks. *verb,* **jacked, jacking.** to lift or move with a jack: *Dad jacked up the front of the car so he could change the flat tire.*

jack·al ▲ [jak-ul] *noun plural* **jackals.** a wild dog of Africa and Asia. Jackals have pointed, upright ears and a bushy tail. They hunt in packs, feeding on small mammals and birds, and also often eat what other animals have killed.

jack·et [jak-it] *noun, plural* **jackets. 1.** a short coat with long sleeves. **2.** an outer covering for a book: *There is a list of other books by the same author on the back of the jacket.*

jack-in-the-box [jak-in-thuh-*boks*] *noun, plural* **jack-in-the-boxes.** a toy with a doll on a spring that pops out of a box when the lid is lifted.

jack·knife [jak-*nife*] *noun, plural* **jackknives. 1.** a large type of knife with a blade that can be folded away into the handle. **2.** a dive in which the body is bent double, so that the hands briefly touch the toes, then straightens out again before the diver enters the water. *verb,* **jackknifed, jackknifing.** to fold up or bend double: *Four of the train cars jackknifed in the crash.*

*The name **jack-o-lantern** comes from an Irish legend about a boy named Jack.*

jack-o-lan·tern ▶ [jak-uh-*lan*-turn] *noun, plural* **jack-o-lanterns.** a lantern made by putting a candle inside a pumpkin that has been hollowed out and had holes cut into it to look like a face. Jack-o-lanterns are used as decorations at Halloween.

jack·pot [jak-*pot*] *noun, plural* **jackpots.** the largest prize in a game, competition, or lottery: *No one won the jackpot this week, so it will increase for next week.*

jack·rab·bit [jak-*rab*-it] *noun, plural* **jackrabbits.** a large hare of western North America that has very long legs and long ears.

jade [jade] *noun, plural* **jades.** a hard stone, usually green in color, that is used for making jewelry and small carved ornaments.

jag·ged [jag-id] *adjective.* sharp and pointed: *a jagged piece of broken glass.*

jag·uar ▼ [jag-wahr] *noun, plural* **jaguars.** a large, fierce, meat-eating member of the cat family found in tropical America. The jaguar has short, golden-colored fur marked with black rings with spots in their centers.

jail [jale] *noun, plural* **jails.** a place where people accused or convicted of a minor crime are locked up. *verb,* **jailed, jailing.** to put or keep in jail: *The shoplifter was jailed for two months.*

*A **jaguar** hunts mainly small animals such as rats, birds, and fish.*

jam¹ [jam] *verb,* **jammed, jamming. 1.** to pack, press, or squeeze into a small space; cram: *We all jammed into the elevator.* **2.** to become stuck so as to not to work: *The drawer jammed.* **3.** to press down hard and suddenly: *to jam on the brakes of the car.* **4.** to catch in and injure or harm: *I jammed my fingers in the door.* *noun, plural* **jams. 1.** a mass of people or things pressed so close together that movement is difficult or impossible: *a traffic jam.* **2.** a difficult situation: *The two boys were in a real jam after getting lost in the woods.*

jam² [jam] *noun, plural* **jams.** a spread for bread and other foods made by cooking fruit with sugar until it is thick.

jan·gle [jang-gul] *verb,* **jangled, jangling. 1.** to make an unpleasant ringing noise: *The chains jangled against the bars.* **2.** to make tense; irritate: *The constant barking of the dog across the street jangled my nerves.* *noun, plural* **jangles.** an unpleasant ringing noise.

jan·i·tor [jan-uh-tur] *noun, plural* **janitors.** a person whose job is to look after and clean a building.

Jan·u·ar·y [jan-yoo-er-ee] *noun.* the first month of the year. January has 31 days.

> The month of **January** gets its name from Janus, a god of the ancient Romans. Janus was the god of doors and entrances, and was thought of as having two heads, one looking forward (as if looking forward to the new year) and the other looking back (as if looking back on the old year).

Jap·a·nese [jap-uh-neez] *noun, plural* **Japanese.** a person born in Japan, an island country in eastern Asia. *adjective.* having to do with Japan, its people, or its culture: *a Japanese garden.*

Japanese beetle a small, shiny, green and brown beetle that came to North America from eastern Asia. It damages crops as a grub by feeding on the roots and as an adult by eating the leaves, flowers, and fruits.

jar¹ [jar] *noun, plural* **jars. 1.** a deep container with a wide opening and a tight lid. A jar is usually made of glass or pottery. **2.** the amount this container holds: *She emptied a jar of pickled onions into the bowl.*

jar² [jar] *verb,* **jarred, jarring. 1.** to shake about; rattle; jolt: *The bumpy ride over the rough track jarred the passengers.* **2.** to have an unpleasant or irritating effect: *The screeching noise of machinery jarred in his ears. noun, plural* **jars.** an unpleasant shaking about; a jolt.

jarg·on [jar-gun] *noun, plural* **jargons.** *Language.* words used by people in a particular job or group, and not often easily understood by other people: *computer jargon; medical jargon.*

jaun·dice [jawn-dis] *noun. Health.* a medical condition in which the skin and the white part of the eyes become yellow. Jaundice is a symptom of disease of the liver.

jaun·diced [jawn-dist] *adjective.* **1.** having an unhealthy yellow color of the skin caused by jaundice. **2.** judging someone or something by bad experiences in the past; negative and unenthusiastic: *The movie star had a jaundiced view of newspaper photographers.*

jaunt [jawnt] *noun, plural* **jaunts.** a short trip, usually made for enjoyment: *a shopping jaunt; a jaunt to the park.*

jaun·ty [jawn-tee] *adjective.* cheerful and confident, carefree: *She gave us a jaunty grin as she collected her prize.*

jave·lin [jav-uh-lun] *noun, plural* **javelins.** a long, light, metal spear used in sporting contests. Competitors try to throw it as far as possible.

jaw ▶ [jaw] *noun, plural* **jaws. 1.** either of the two bones near the mouth that give shape to the mouth and hold the teeth. **2.** a similar mouth part or parts in insects and other animals without backbones. **3.** one of the two parts of a machine or tool that can be opened and closed to grip or crush something.

jay ▶ [jay] *noun, plural* **jays.** a noisy, brightly colored bird belonging to the crow family.

jay·walk [jaw-wawk] *verb,* **jaywalked, jaywalking.** to cross a street at a place other than a regular crossing, or in a careless manner or against a traffic light. —**jaywalker,** *noun.*

jazz ▼ [jaz] *noun.* a style of music with a strong rhythm, in which musicians often make up or vary the music as they play. Jazz was first played by African-Americans in the early 1900s.

Some **jays** *steal the eggs of other birds.*

jeal·ous [jel-us] *adjective.* **1.** fearing the loss of someone's love or friendship to another person or thing: *I think our cat is jealous of the new kitten.* **2.** wanting to have what someone else has; envious: *He was jealous of his friend's success.* —**jealously,** *adverb.*

jeal·ous·y [jel-uh-see] *noun, plural* **jealousies.** a jealous feeling; envy; resentment: *I eventually got over my jealousy about her winning the prize.*

jeans [jeenz] *plural noun.* casual trousers made of denim, corduroy, or other strong cloth, and worn by men, women, and children. Originally dark blue but now made in other colors.

Most bands that play **jazz** *include a trombone player.*

The **jaws** *of a great white shark are huge and wide.*

jeep ▼ [jeep] *noun, plural* **jeeps.** a small, powerful car used for driving over rough ground. Jeeps were originally used by the U.S. army in World War II.

> The history of the **jeep** is well known. This popular vehicle came into use during World War II and millions of vehicles of this type were used by the U.S. and its allies during the war. What is not known is how it came to be called the *Jeep*. One idea is that the name comes from a popular cartoon character of the time, Eugene the Jeep. Another is that it comes from a way to say the letters "G.P.," for <u>G</u>eneral-<u>P</u>urpose vehicle. Or it may just come from a slang word of the time for a truck or other military vehicle.

World War II **jeeps** *could easily ascend very steep slopes.*

jeer [jeer] *verb,* **jeered, jeering.** to shout or laugh at somebody or something in a mean way; insult: *The crowd jeered when the football player dropped the ball for the third time.* *noun, plural* **jeers.** a rude or mocking shout or laugh; an insult: *The appearance of the disgraced politician was met by boos and jeers from the audience.*

Je·ho·vah [juh-<u>hoh</u>-vuh] *noun. Religion.* a name given to God in the Old Testament of the Bible. **Jehovah's Witnesses** is a religious organization. One of its beliefs is that the end of the world is near.

jell [jel] *verb,* **jelled, jelling.** to become firm; set like a jelly.

jel·ly [<u>jel</u>-ee] *noun, plural* **jellies.** a soft, sweet food made from fruit juice boiled with sugar until thick. It is eaten spread on bread, toast, muffins, and other foods.

jel·ly·fish ▼ [<u>jel</u>-ee-*fish*] *noun, plural* **jellyfishes.** a sea animal with a body that looks somewhat like a transparent jelly and that is shaped like an umbrella. A jellyfish has long, thin tentacles, which it uses to sting its prey.

jeop·ar·dy [<u>jep</u>-ur-dee] *noun.* the danger of injury, defeat, or death: *The sailors' lives were in jeopardy as the ship began to sink.* Something that may destroy or damage another thing **jeopardizes** it.

Jellyfish *live in all the world's oceans.*

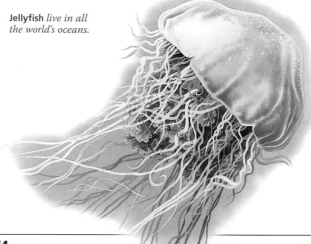

jerk [jurk] *noun, plural* **jerks. 1.** a quick, sharp pull or tug on something: *The deep-sea diver gave the rope two jerks for the boat crew to pull him up.* **2.** a slang term for a stupid or annoying person.
verb, **jerked, jerking.** to move or pull suddenly and roughly: *She jerked the bag from my shoulder.*

jerk·y¹ [<u>jurk</u>-ee] *adjective* **jerkier, jerkiest.** having a sudden, sharp, stopping and starting movement rather than a smooth one: *It was a jerky car trip along the rough road.*

jer·ky² [<u>jurk</u>-ee] *noun.* meat that has been sliced and dried so that it can be stored and eaten at a later time.

jer·sey [<u>jur</u>-zee] *noun, plural* **jerseys. 1.** a fine, soft, machine-knitted cloth, usually woolen, used to make clothing. **2.** a long-sleeved garment made of this cloth, worn as a sweater or shirt. A **Jersey** cow is from a breed of cattle light brown in color and known for their creamy milk.

> **Jersey** is an island near the coast of France that was the original home of the Jersey cow. The article of clothing known as a *jersey* also gets its name from this island, because jerseys were first made with cloth woven on this island. The U.S. state of New Jersey also gets its name from the island of Jersey.

jest [jest] *noun, plural* **jests.** a humorous or playful act; a joke. *verb,* **jested, jesting.** to joke or play the fool.

jest·er ▶ [<u>jes</u>-tur] *noun, plural* **jesters.** *History.* in medieval times, a person who was hired by the king to entertain his friends and guests, as by telling jokes or acting foolish.

Je·sus [<u>jee</u>-zus] *noun. Religion.* the founder of the Christian religion, worshipped by Christians as the son of God. The years of his life are not certain but are typically placed at 4 BC to AD 30. Jesus is also called **Jesus Christ**.

Jesters *wore brightly colored clothes and a special hat with a bell on each point.*

jet [jet] *noun, plural* **jets. 1.** a fast stream of steam, liquid, or gas shooting out from a small opening: *The jet of steam from a kettle is very hot.* **2.** an airplane that has one or more jet engines: *Our family flew to Canada on a jet.*
verb, **jetted, jetting.** to send out a stream of steam, liquid, or gas: *Water jetted into the air from the fountain.*

jet engine an engine that burns fuel in a combustion chamber so that a stream of exhaust gases is pushed out to the rear, producing a strong forward thrust. Such engines use a kerosene-based **jet fuel.**

jet lag *Health.* a feeling of tiredness caused by traveling by airplane through several time zones without allowing the body to have enough time to adjust: *Some people say jet lag is worse when you fly west to east.*

jet plane ▶
an airplane powered by
a jet engine. It can be either
a military plane or passenger plane.
This term is also written as **jet airplane**.

jet propulsion *Science.* the use of one or more
jet engines to drive an aircraft or rocket forward
or upward. A **jet-propelled** aircraft or rocket uses
the power of a jet engine to fly at very fast speeds.

jet stream *Environment.* a current of strong winds
in the upper atmosphere 20,000–30,000 feet
above the Earth that move from west to east.

jet·ti·son [jet-uh-sun] *verb,* **jettisoned,**
jettisoning. to throw away something
that is no longer needed, especially
from a moving vehicle or craft:
*The captain jettisoned some
of the cargo to make
the ship lighter.*

In 1947 this **jet plane**
*was the first to break
the sound barrier.*

jet·ty [jet-ee] *noun, plural* **jetties** a pier or wall built out
into coastal water to control the flow of a river or to
protect the coastline from damage by waves.

Jew [joo] *noun, plural* **Jews.** *Religion.* **1.** a member of
the group descended from the ancient Hebrews.
2. a person whose religion is Judaism.

jew·el [joo-ul] *noun, plural* **jewels. 1.** a small, decorative,
precious stone or gem. Jewels are put in necklaces,
rings, and bracelets, and also used in watches and other
machines because they are very hard. **2.** a decoration
such as a brooch, bracelet, ring, or necklace with precious
stones on it. **3.** a person or thing seen to have beauty
or value: *The Grand Canyon is the jewel of Arizona.*

jew·el·er [jool-ur] *noun, plural* **jewelers.** a person whose
job is to make, sell, or repair jewelry.

jew·el·ry [jool-ree] *noun.* ornaments worn on the body
or clothing. Jewelry includes brooches, rings, bracelets,
necklaces, and earrings.

Jew·ish [joo-ish] *adjective. Religion.* having to do with Jews,
the people whose religion is Judaism.

jif·fy [jif-ee] *noun.* a moment; a very short time: *Don't worry,
I'll have it fixed in a jiffy.*

jig [jig] *noun, plural* **jigs. 1.** a quick, light, and lively dance.
2. the music played for such a dance.

jig·gle [jig-ul] *verb,* **jiggled, jiggling.** to make small, jerky
movements up and down or from side to side: *to jiggle
a key in a lock.*
noun. a jerky movement from side to side.

jig·saw [jig-saw] *noun, plural* **jigsaws.** a saw with a thin,
narrow blade used for cutting curves or shapes in thin
sheets of plywood.

jigsaw puzzle a puzzle consisting of many small
irregular-shaped pieces that when fitted tightly
together make a complete picture.

jin·gle [jing-gul] *noun, plural* **jingles. 1.** a light, tinkling
sound of small bells or metal objects banging together:
*We heard the jingle of the janitor's keys as he unlocked
the door.* **2.** a short, simple tune or song used in TV
or radio advertisements: *I can't get that new jingle out
of my head!*
verb, **jingled, jingling.** to make a light, tinkling sound
of small bells or metal objects: *The coins jingled in
his pocket.*

jinx [jingks] *noun, plural* **jinxes. 1.** a person or thing that
is believed to bring or have bad luck: *This bus has a jinx
on it—this is the third time it's broken down this week.*
2. a run of bad luck. If a person says that someone or
something has **jinxed** them, they believe it has brought
them bad luck.

job [job] *noun, plural* **jobs. 1.** paid work; employment:
My mom has a job at the local supermarket. **2.** any work
or task that needs to be done: *I have to clean my room
and it's a big job.*

jock·ey ▼ [jok-ee] *noun, plural* **jockeys.** a person who rides
racehorses as a job.

Jockeys are usually short and must keep their weight low.

*These models show how hinge **joints**, found in the elbow and the knee, let bones move up and down, while ball-and-socket joints in the hips and shoulders allow all-round movement.*

jog [jog] *verb*, **jogged, jogging.** to run at a slow, steady pace, usually as exercise: *She jogs around the park to keep fit.* A person who runs in this way is called a **jogger.** *noun.* a slow, steady run.

join [joyn] *verb*, **joined, joining. 1.** to fasten or put two things together so that they become one: *A zipper joins the two sides of the jacket.* **2.** to become united with: *This road joins the highway after going through the town.* **3.** to become a member of or take part in an organization: *My dad wants me to join a soccer club.* **4.** to get together with; meet or act with: *Will you join us for a meal after the game?*

joint ▶ [joynt] *noun, plural* **joints. 1.** a point where two or more bones meet. Elbows, knees, and ankles are all joints. **2.** the place where two or more things meet: *The carpenter made neat joints for the kitchen bench.* **3.** a slang word for an inexpensive place to eat or sleep: *We ate at a burger joint down the road.* *adjective.* having to do with a thing owned or done by two or more people: *The brothers are joint owners of a large boat.* —**jointly**, *adverb.*

joke [joke] *noun, plural* **jokes.** something said or done to make people laugh; something to amuse: *I love telling jokes to my mom and dad because they always laugh.* *verb,* **joked, joking.** to make or perform jokes to amuse others: *The magician joked that he might make us all disappear if we did not behave during the show.*

jok·er [joke-ur] *noun, plural* **jokers. 1.** a person who often tells jokes. **2.** a playing card with a picture of a jester on it.

Hinge joint

Ball-and-socket joint

jol·ly [jol-ee] *adjective,* **jollier, jolliest.** very cheerful; full of fun: *Seeing my friends again made me feel very jolly.*

jolt [jolt] *verb,* **jolted, jolting.** to move or cause to move suddenly and violently: *The tractor jolted along the rough farm road.* *noun, plural* **jolts. 1.** a sudden and violent movement: *The earthquake began with a big jolt.* **2.** a big surprise; shock: *It was a jolt not to be picked for the school football team.*

jon·quil [jong-kwil] *noun, plural* **jonquils.** a type of daffodil that has a pleasant-smelling flower with a short center petal shaped like a cup. Jonquils grow from bulbs.

jos·tle [jos-ul] *verb,* **jostled, jostling.** to knock or push roughly: *The students jostled one another when they ran down the staircase after class finished.* *noun, plural* **jostles.** a knock or push.

jot [jot] *verb.* **jot down.** to write briefly or quickly: *Jot down some notes on what the teacher is saying.*

joule [jool] *noun, plural* **joules.** *Science.* a standard unit of energy or work.

The unit of energy known as a **joule** is named for the famous English scientist James Prescott *Joule,* who lived in the 1800s. He was known for his important studies of energy, including the idea that heat is a form of energy—earlier scientists had thought heat was a kind of fluid, like air or water.

jour·nal [jur-nul] *noun, plural* **journals.** *Literature.* **1.** an account or record, such as a diary, kept on a regular basis: *Bob kept a journal during his time in hospital.* **2.** a newspaper or periodical: *a law journal.*

*In **jousts**, the competing knights and their horses wore different colors.*

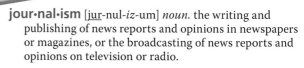

jour·nal·ism [jur-nul-*iz*-um] *noun.* the writing and publishing of news reports and opinions in newspapers or magazines, or the broadcasting of news reports and opinions on television or radio.

jour·nal·ist [jur-nul-ist] *noun, plural* **journalists.** a person who writes news and opinions for newspapers or magazines, or who prepares news and opinions to be broadcast on radio or television.

jour·ney [jur-nee] *noun, plural* **journeys. 1.** a trip from one place to another, especially a long trip: *We made the journey by car from Chicago to Los Angeles.* **2.** the time of distance of such a trip: *From here to the ocean is two days' journey by car.* *verb,* **journeyed, journeying.** to go from one place to another: *He journeyed from the East Coast to the West.*

joust ◀ [jowst] *noun, plural* **jousts.** *History.* a form of combat or contest in the Middle Ages in which two armored knights on horseback fought with a lance. *verb,* **jousted, jousting.** to take part or fight in a joust: *The king allowed only his best knights to joust.*

jo·vi·al [joh-vee-ul] *adjective.* full of fun; cheerful; merry: *My uncle is a jovial host at parties.* —**jovially,** *adverb.*

joy [joy] *noun, plural* **joys. 1.** great happiness: *Linda felt joy when her daughter graduated from college.* **2.** a person or thing that causes great happiness: *Playing the piano is one of my father's greatest joys.*

joy·ful [joy-ful] *adjective.* feeling, causing, or showing great happiness; glad: *I was joyful to see my parents again after being overseas for six months.* —**joyfully,** *adverb.*

joy·ous [joy-us] *adjective.* full of joy or giving joy: *The birthday party was a time for joyous celebrations.* —**joyously,** *adverb.*

ju·bi·lant [joo-buh-lunt] *adjective.* feeling or showing great happiness: *We were jubilant after our team won the final.*

ju·bi·lee [joo-buh-lee] *noun, plural* **jubilees.** a special anniversary, especially a fiftieth anniversary.

Ju·da·ism [joo-dee-iz-um] *noun. Religion.* the religion of the Jews, based mainly on a belief in one God and the teachings of the Torah and Talmud.

judge [juj] *verb,* **judged, judging.**
1. in a court of law, to make a decision or agree on a verdict about a case.
2. to decide or settle a question, dispute, or contest: *Our art teacher has been asked to judge the town's painting competition.* **3.** to form an opinion of: *Don't judge a book by its cover.*
4. to find something wrong with: *We often judge others more harshly than we judge ourselves.*
noun, plural **judges. 1.** in a court of law, a person who decides on legal matters. Some judges are appointed by government officials, others are elected by the people. **2.** someone who decides the winner in a dispute or competition. **3.** a person who has enough knowledge about something to give an opinion about it: *My mother is a good judge of antique clocks.*

judg·ment [juj-munt] *noun, plural* **judgments.**
1. a decision given by a court of law: *The accused man disagreed with the judgment of the court.* **2.** the ability to form sensible opinions or make good decisions: *She shows poor judgment in choosing her friends.*
3. an opinion based on careful thought: *In my judgment, the principal was wrong to punish the girls.* This word is also spelled **judgement.**

ju·di·cial [joo-dish-ul] *adjective. Law.* of or relating to judges or courts of law: *the judicial system.* The branch of government that dispenses justice is the **judiciary.** —**judicially,** *adverb.*

ju·do ▶ [joo-doh] *noun.* a sport in which opponents fight using only their body and no weapons.

This kind of **jukebox** *was popular in the 1950s.*

jug [jug] *noun, plural* **jugs.** a container with a handle, narrow neck, and pouring lip, for holding liquids. A jug may be made of glass, plastic, or pottery.

jug·ger·naut [jug-ur-nawt] *noun, plural* **juggernauts.** a thing so powerful that it can conquer or destroy everything in its path: *The hurricane was a juggernaut—no building could withstand it.*

A **juggernaut** is a huge, powerful force, and the name comes from an important god of the Hindu religion. This god was represented by a large statue that was pulled along the ground during religious ceremonies. It was thought that this statue could run over and destroy anything in its path.

jug·gle ▶ [jug-ul] *verb,* **juggled, juggling.** to continuously toss several objects into the air and catch them in such a way that at least one object stays in the air at any time: *The circus performer can juggle knives.* A person who performs in this way is a **juggler.**

It takes good eye–hand coordination to **juggle** *well.*

juice [joos] *noun, plural* **juices.**
1. the liquid from meats, fruits, or vegetables: *This steak has a lot of juice.*
2. a fluid made in the body: *The digestive juices in your stomach are very strong.*

juic·y [joos-ee] *adjective,* **juicier, juiciest.** containing a lot of juice: *a juicy mango.*

juke·box ◀ [jook-boks] *noun, plural* **jukeboxes.** a machine that plays music when coins are put into it.

Ju·ly [juh-lye] *noun.* the seventh month of the year. July has 31 days.

The month of **July** gets its name from *Julius* Caesar, a great and powerful ruler of the empire of ancient Rome. July became known as "the month of Julius (Caesar)." The following month, August, was named for another ruler of Rome, Caesar *Augustus.*

Since 1964 **judo** *has been an official sport in the Olympic Games.*

jum·ble [jum-bul] *verb,* **jumbled, jumbling.** to mix or confuse: *Her clothes were jumbled up in her suitcase.*
noun, plural **jumbles.** a state of confusion; mess: *A jumble of papers, books, pens, and pencils lay on the student's desk.*

jum·bo [jum-boh] *adjective.* very large: *The largest passenger aircraft are often called jumbo jets.*

a b c d e f g h i **j** k l m n o p q r s t u v w x y z

A B C D E F G H I **J** K L M N O P Q R S T U V W X Y Z

*Many kinds of animals and plants live in thick **jungles**.*

jump [jump] *verb*, **jumped, jumping. 1.** to move into or through the air by pushing with the feet and legs: *I had to jump to catch the basketball in the air.* **2.** to move quickly and suddenly: *She jumped up to answer the phone.* **3.** to pass over through the air: *The athletes jumped over barriers called hurdles.* **4.** to rise or increase suddenly and sharply: *The store's prices for orange juice jumped in a day.* *noun, plural* **jumps. 1.** the act of jumping, or the distance jumped: *The skier won the competition with a jump of 360 feet.* **2.** a sudden movement or increase: *a jump in housing prices.*

jump·er¹ [jum-pur] *noun, plural* **jumpers.** a person who jumps: *Evie is a high jumper on the school team.*

jump·er² [jum-pur] *noun, plural* **jumpers.** a dress with no sleeves that is usually worn over a sweater or blouse.

jump rope 1. the act of jumping over a rope that is held either by the person jumping or by two other people. Jump rope is a game or a form of exercise. **2.** the length of rope used for this activity.

jump·suit [jump-soot] *noun, plural* **jumpsuits.** a garment in one piece that covers the legs and upper body and opens down the front.

jump·y [jum-pee] *adjective,* **jumpier, jumpiest. 1.** very nervous; uneasy: *The scary movie left me feeling jumpy.* **2.** moving by sudden starts and stops.

junc·tion [jungk-shun] *noun, plural* **junctions. 1.** a place where things join or meet, such as two rivers or two railroad systems. **2.** the act of joining or the fact of being joined.

June [joon] *noun.* the sixth month of the year. June has 30 days.

jun·gle ◀ [jung-gul] *noun, plural* **jungles. 1.** an area of tropical forest covered with a thick mass of trees and other plants. **2.** a place or situation that is hard to live in because it is confusing, violent, or competitive: *This city is a jungle.*

jun·ior [joon-yur] *adjective.* **1.** younger, especially if used when referring to a son with the same name as his father: *I am David Williams, Junior; my father is David Williams, Senior.* This word is also spelled **Junior. 2.** of or relating to younger people: *A junior soccer league has been formed.* **3.** having to do with the third year of a four-year course at a high school or college. **4.** having a lower rank or position: *His mother is a junior teacher.* *noun, plural* **juniors. 1.** a person who is younger than another: *My brother is my junior by two years.* **2.** a student who is in the third year of a four-year high school or college course.

junior high school a school between an elementary school and a high school. It generally includes grades seven and eight and sometimes grades six or nine.

ju·ni·per ▼ [joo-nuh-pur] *noun, plural* **junipers.** an evergreen tree or shrub with purple cones that look like berries.

*The small cones, or berries, of **juniper** trees are used to flavor foods and drinks.*

junk¹ [jungk] *noun.* items, such as pieces of metal or wood that are thrown out or considered to be worth nothing; trash: *There was a pile of old junk in the corner of the basement.*
verb, **junked, junking.** to get rid of something because it is no longer useful: *We junked our old computer.*

junk² ▶ [jungk] *noun, plural* **junks.** a flat-bottomed sailing ship, used in Chinese and southeast Asian waters.

In the early 1400s, **junks** *sailed from China to distant parts of the world.*

junk food food that is high in fat or sugar and low in other nutrients.

junk mail mail, especially advertising material, that is sent to people who have not asked for it.

junk·yard [jungk-*yard*] *noun, plural* **junkyards.** a place where junk, especially old cars, is collected and stored before being sold.

Ju·pi·ter ▼ [joo-puh-tur] *noun.* **1.** the fifth planet from the Sun. It is the largest planet in our solar system. **2.** in Roman mythology, the supreme god.

ju·ror [jur-ur] *noun, plural* **jurors.** *Law.* a member of a jury. The number of jurors in a criminal trial is usually twelve.

ju·ry [jur-ee] *noun, plural* **juries.** *Law.* **1.** a group of people chosen to hear all the facts in a matter that has been brought before a court of law. A jury reaches a decision based on those facts and the law. Allowing juries to decide legal matters is the **jury system.** **2.** a group of people chosen to decide the winner of a competition.

just [just] *adjective.* morally correct and fair; honest: *a just decision.*
adverb. **1.** exactly: *That's just what he told me.* **2.** very recently: *I have just seen her in the library.* **3.** by a narrow margin; barely: *The sprinter just managed to get third place in the race.* **4.** no more than; only: *We expected a lot of rain, but got just a few drops.* —**justly,** *adverb.*

jus·tice [jus-tis] *noun, plural* **justices.** *Law.* **1.** correct or fair action or treatment: *She claimed that justice would not be done by sending her son to jail.* **2.** the quality or condition of being morally correct and right: *the justice of our cause.* **3.** the proper carrying out of the law. **4.** a judge of the Supreme Court of the United States.

jus·ti·fy [jus-tuh-*fye*] *verb,* **justified, justifying.** **1.** to show to be reasonable or fair: *Nothing justifies terrorism.* **2.** to prove to be free of blame or guilt: *The court's decision justifies everything I have said.* Something, such as a fact or situation, which explains or justifies is a **justification.**

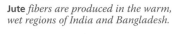

Jute *fibers are produced in the warm, wet regions of India and Bangladesh.*

jut [jut] *verb,* **jutted, jutting.** to extend outward: *The pier juts into the bay.*

jute ▲ [joot] *noun.* a strong fiber taken from the stems of an Asian tropical plant. It is used to make rope and cloth.

ju·ve·nile [joo-vuh-nul *or* joo-vuh-*nile*] *adjective.* **1.** of or relating to children or young people: *The movie was aimed at a juvenile audience.* **2.** immature or childish: *For an adult, he has a juvenile sense of humor.*
noun, plural **juveniles.** a young person: *What are the problems facing today's juveniles?*

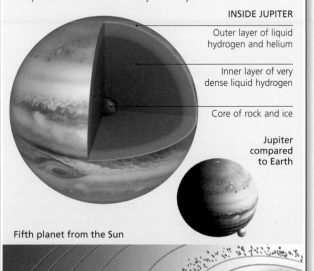

JUPITER

Jupiter is 1,400 times as large as the Earth and 300 times heavier. The planet is mainly made up of the gases hydrogen and helium, topped by bitterly cold, swirling clouds. There is no real surface, but there may be a solid core of rock and ice at the center. Jupiter's fast rotation causes great winds and wild storms, and a day is less than ten Earth hours long. The planet orbits the Sun every twelve years.

INSIDE JUPITER

Outer layer of liquid hydrogen and helium

Inner layer of very dense liquid hydrogen

Core of rock and ice

Jupiter compared to Earth

Fifth planet from the Sun

K k

kay·ak ▼ [kye-ak] *noun, plural* **kayaks. 1.** a traditional boat used by the Inuit. It is made of animal skins stretched over a frame with an opening in the center for a person who paddles. **2.** a light canoe that looks like this is usually made of plastic or fiberglass.

> The word **kayak** comes from the Eskimo (Inuit) word for this kind of boat. The Eskimos were the first to use this kind of boat, and it was not known to the English language until people from Europe came in contact with the Eskimos in the 1600s.

The red kangaroo is the largest **kangaroo** *and can travel as far as 30 feet in one leap.*

K, k *noun, plural* **K's, k's.** the eleventh letter of the English alphabet.

ka·lei·do·scope [kuh-lye-duh-*skope*] *noun, plural* **kaleidoscopes.** a tube that, when looked into and turned, shows colorful, changing patterns. The patterns are produced by mirrors in the tube reflecting the small bits of colored glass or other colored objects inside.

kan·ga·roo ▲ [*kang*-guh-roo] *noun, plural* **kangaroos.** an animal of Australia and New Guinea that has small front legs, a long tail, and powerful back legs on which it moves by hopping. Kangaroos are marsupials, which means that the female has a pouch, in which she carries her young for about six months after birth.

> The **kangaroo** is native to Australia and nearby islands, and it was unknown to people in other parts of the world until the first explorers from Europe came to Australia in the 1700s. It is thought that the English explorer James Cook named this animal *kangaroo* in 1770, taking the name from a word for the animal used by native peoples of Australia.

ka·ra·oke [kare-ee-oh-kee] *noun. Music.* a form of entertainment in which a machine plays only the music of pop songs, allowing a person to sing the words. Karaoke was invented in Japan.

ka·ra·te [kah-rah-tee] *noun.* a Japanese style of fighting in which people use the arms, legs, hands, and feet to kick and punch.

ka·ty·did ▼ [kay-tee-*did*] *noun, plural* **katydids.** a large, green insect like a grasshopper, with two long antennae and wings that look like leaves. By rubbing its wings together, the male katydid makes a shrill noise that sounds like its name.

keel ▲ [keel] *noun, plural* **keels.** a long piece of metal or wood that extends along the center of the bottom of a ship. The keel helps to hold the ship together and keep it stable in water.
verb. **keel over. 1.** to turn over or upside down; capsize: *The cargo ship almost keeled over in the rough seas.* **2.** to fall over suddenly; faint: *Two people in the crowd keeled over in the heat.*

• **on an even keel.** on course; steady: *After we moved to another city, it took time for our lives to get back on an even keel.*

Modern **kayaks** *can be paddled on still water, white water, or over rapids.*

keen [keen] *adjective,* **keener, keenest. 1.** having a sharp point or cutting edge: *Keep the knife's edge keen by sharpening it regularly.* **2.** quick to understand; sharp in hearing or seeing: *I have keen eyesight.* **3.** having or showing enthusiasm or eagerness: *Jenny was keen to go on her first camping trip.*
interjection. used to express approval or agreement: *Keen!—no school today.*

• **keen on.** fond of; enthusiastic about: *We were keen on going to the picnic.* —**keenly,** *adverb.*

keep ▶ [keep] *verb,* **kept, keeping. 1.** to continue to do, hold, or have: *I took back the other shirt I bought, but I'm going to keep this one.* **2.** to continue or cause to continue in a particular state or position; stay or cause to stay: *Keep the door closed.* **3.** to put or store: *Where do you keep your old school photos?* **4.** to hold back or stop: *The police kept the crowd away from the movie stars.* **5.** to be faithful; to fulfill: *Always keep your promises.* **6.** to record, usually by writing down: *The teacher asked us to keep notes of how much money we spend in a week.*
noun, plural **keeps. 1.** food and lodging: *My father says he had to earn his keep when he was only a boy.* **2.** the strongest part of a fort or castle.

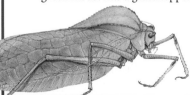

The leaf-like green wings of the **katydid** *help it blend with its surroundings.*

*If a kayak **keels over,** a paddler can return it to an upright position in seconds using a movement called the Eskimo roll.*

Kelp grows in underwater forests in clear, shallow water.

keep·er [keep-ur] *noun, plural* **keepers.** a person who looks after, watches, or guards something or someone.

keep·ing [keep-ing] *noun.* the condition of having control over or being in charge of something: *The stolen bicycle was found and is now in safe keeping with the police.*
• **in keeping with.** suitable or not suitable for a certain situation: *In keeping with tradition, we open our presents under the Christmas tree on Christmas morning.*

keep·sake [keep-sake] *noun, plural* **keepsakes.** a small item kept as a reminder of the person who gave it or originally owned it.

keg [keg] *noun, plural* **kegs.** a small metal or wooden barrel, usually used for storing beer.

kelp ▶ [kelp] *noun.* a large green or brown seaweed that grows in cold waters along ocean coasts. Kelp provides food for people and animals and is used to make many products.

kel·vin [kel-vun] *noun. Science.* a unit of temperature on the **Kelvin temperature scale.** Kelvin (0°K) is the temperature of absolute zero (-459°F), and 273°K is the freezing point of water.

ken·nel [ken-ul] *noun, plural* **kennels. 1.** a shelter for a dog. **2.** a place where dogs are bred or where people leave their dogs while they are away.

kept [kept] *verb.* the past tense and past participle of KEEP.

ker·chief [kur-chif] *noun, plural* **kerchiefs.** a piece of cloth used as a head covering or worn around the neck like a scarf.

ker·nel [kur-nul] *noun, plural* **kernels. 1.** the seed or whole grain of certain plants, such as corn or wheat. **2.** the inner soft part of a nut, seed, or fruit stone. **3.** the central or most important part of something. **4.** *Computers.* the central element of an operating system.

ker·o·sene [ker-uh-seen] *noun.* a thin oil that is made from petroleum. It is used as a fuel for portable heaters, farm machines, and jet engines. Before the electric light bulb was invented, kerosene was used in lamps.

ketch·up [kech-up] *noun.* a red sauce that is added to foods such as steak or hamburgers to give extra flavor. Ketchup is made of tomatoes, onions, salt, vinegar, sugar, and spices. This word is also spelled **catsup.**

*The **kettledrum** belongs to an orchestra's percussion section.*

A hamburger with ketchup on it can be called the most "American" of all foods. However, the sauce known as **ketchup** first became well known in the islands of the western Pacific Ocean and is thought to have originally come from China. Even in its early form, ketchup was a tomato sauce, but it also had ingredients that would be considered strange today, such as mushrooms and walnuts.

Turrets for watching over the castle and countryside

Keep entrance

ket·tle [ket-ul] *noun, plural* **kettles.** a metal container used for boiling liquids or for cooking foods.

ket·tle·drum ▲ [ket-ul-drum] *noun, plural* **kettledrums.** *Music.* a large copper or brass drum, shaped like a bowl, with a thin material called parchment stretched across the top.

*The stone **keep** in Rochester, England, was built in the twelfth century.*

a
b
c
d
e
f
g
h
i
j
k
o
p
q
r
s
t
u
v
w
x
y
z

*An electronic **keyboard** can record music while it is being played.*

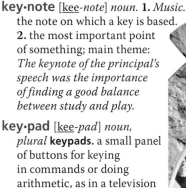

key[1] [kee] *noun, plural* **keys. 1.** a small piece of shaped metal that can open or close a lock: *He used a key to open the desk drawer.* **2.** an item that is used or shaped like such a piece of metal: *You need a key to wind up that old clock.* **3.** a thing that explains or solves: *The key to this mystery will never be found.* **4.** a thing that leads to or is a way of getting something: *The key to his success at baseball is long hours of practice.* **5.** one of the parts of a musical instrument or machine that performs a function when pressed. A piano has black and white keys. The keys of a computer are marked with letters of the alphabet, numbers, and symbols. **6.** *Music.* a group of related musical notes based on a particular note in the group. *adjective.* of great importance; major: *We lost the game because our key player was injured.*

key[2] [kway] *noun, plural* **keys.** a low-lying island or reef: *the Florida Keys.*

key·board ▲ [kee-bord] *noun, plural* **keyboards.** a row or set of keys as in computers and pianos. *verb,* **keyboarded, keyboarding. 1.** to put information into a computer by using a keyboard. **2.** to play a musical instrument that has a keyboard. —**keyboarder,** *noun.*

key·hole [kee-hole] *noun, plural* **keyholes.** the hole in a lock into which a key fits.

key·note [kee-note] *noun.* **1.** *Music.* the note on which a key is based. **2.** the most important point of something; main theme: *The keynote of the principal's speech was the importance of finding a good balance between study and play.*

key·pad [kee-pad] *noun, plural* **keypads.** a small panel of buttons for keying in commands or doing arithmetic, as in a television remote control or a calculator.

key·stone ▶ [kee-stone] *noun, plural* **keystones. 1.** the central stone at the highest point of an arch. The keystone holds the other stones of the arch in place. **2.** the most important part of a system or plan, on which everything else depends: *A new auditorium is the keystone of the plan for remodeling the school.*

kg an abbreviation for KILOGRAM.

khak·i [kak-ee] *noun, plural* **khakis. 1.** a dull, brownish-yellow color. **2.** a cotton cloth of this color, used especially for military uniforms. **3. khakis.** a military uniform or other garment made from khaki.

The word **khaki** comes from the language of Persia, an ancient country of the Middle East located in what is now Iran. Khaki first meant "tan" or "having the color of dust." The first use in English was to describe tan-colored uniforms used by the British Army for troops stationed in warm-weather areas in Asia and Africa.

kick [kik] *verb,* **kicked, kicking. 1.** to strike or hit with the foot: *Don't stand too close to that horse—it kicks.* **2.** to make something move by hitting it with the foot: *The soccer player kicked the ball to his teammate.* **3.** of a gun, to spring back when fired. *noun, plural* **kicks. 1.** a blow or hit with the foot: *He gave the ball a hard kick.* **2.** the springing back of a gun when it is fired: *Be careful, this rifle has a strong kick.* **3.** an exciting feeling; thrill: *Donna gets a kick out of singing in front of an audience.*

kick·er [kik-ur] *noun, plural* **kickers.** a person or animal that kicks: *Steve is the football team's best kicker.*

kick·off [kik-of] *noun, plural* **kickoffs. 1.** in football or soccer, a kick of the ball that begins the action. **2.** the start of something; commencement: *Hundreds of people turned out to see the kickoff of the charity campaign.*

kid [kid] *noun, plural* **kids. 1.** a young goat. **2.** a soft leather that is made from the skin of a young goat: *The gloves were made of kid.* **3.** a child or young person. *verb,* **kidded, kidding.** to tease or make fun of: *We kidded her about her new hairstyle.* A person who often teases someone is a **kidder.**

kid·nap [kid-nap] *verb,* **kidnaped** or **kidnapped, kidnaping** or **kidnapping.** to seize and hold someone by force, usually in order to demand money in return for releasing the person: *The lawyer who was kidnaped was released when his friends paid the money that had been demanded.*

kid·nap·ping [kid-nap-ing] *noun, plural* **kidnappings.** *Law.* the crime of taking away and holding someone by force: *There have been many kidnappings in that country.* Someone who carries out a kidnapping is a **kidnapper.**

*The **keystone** in the center of an arch stops it from collapsing.*

KILLER WHALES

Killer whales, or orcas, actually belong to the dolphin family and are found in all the world's oceans. The largest and most intelligent dolphins, they live, travel, and feed in groups. When playing, they are very active and often leap out of the sea in unison. They also work closely together to catch their prey. For example, one orca may frighten seals by coming right up onto the beach, while the other orcas wait in the sea to catch the seals as they try to escape.

A killer whale can weigh as much as ten tons.

kid·ney ▼ [kid-nee] *noun, plural* **kidneys. 1.** either of two organs in the body that are located in the lower abdomen and look like a very large bean. The kidneys remove waste from the blood and pass it to the bladder as urine. **2.** the kidney of an animal eaten as food.

kill [kil] *verb,* **killed, killing. 1.** to take away life from; cause the death of: *The police had to kill the dangerous dog.* **2.** to put an end to: *A bad teacher can kill a child's enthusiasm for learning.* **3.** to cause great pain to; hurt very much: *I've been walking all day and now my feet are killing me!* **4.** to use up: *We arrived early for our flight, so we killed an hour by watching planes take off.*
noun, plural **kills. 1.** the act of killing: *Lions hunt together to make a kill.* **2.** an animal that has been killed: *The deer hunters carried their kill back to the campsite.*

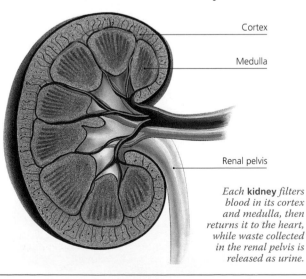

Cortex

Medulla

Renal pelvis

Each **kidney** *filters blood in its cortex and medulla, then returns it to the heart, while waste collected in the renal pelvis is released as urine.*

kill·deer ▶ [kil-deer] *noun, plural* **killdeers** *or* **killdeer.** a bird with a loud song that sounds like its name. The killdeer is a plover with brown and white feathers and two black bands on its breast.

kill·er [kil-ur] *noun, plural* **killers. 1.** someone or something that kills: *Police are searching for the killer of the bank guard.* **2.** something that is very difficult: *That math test was a real killer.*

An adult **killdeer** *will lead predators away from the chicks in its nest by pretending to be injured.*

killer whale ▲ a medium-size dolphin with black-and-white markings and a tall fin on the top of its body. It eats mainly fish, squid, and seals. This animal is also called an **orca.**

The term **killer whale** has been used in English for many years, but in recent times it has become common to call this animal *orca* rather than *killer whale.* It is thought that calling the animal a "killer" gives it a bad reputation that it does not deserve. In nature many kinds of animals kill other animals for food, and they are not specially identified by the word *killer.*

kiln [kiln] *noun, plural* **kilns.** an oven or furnace for baking, burning, or drying. Bricks, pottery, and charcoal are made in a kiln.

ki·lo [kee-loh] *noun, plural* **kilos.** an abbreviation for KILOGRAM.

kilo- a prefix that means 1,000: *kilometer* means 1,000 meters; *kiloliter* means 1,000 liters.

kil·o·byte [<u>kil</u>-uh-*bite*] *noun, plural* **kilobytes.** *Computers.* a unit of computer storage space equal to approximately 1,000 bytes. The abbreviation for kilobyte is **KB.**

kil·o·gram [<u>kil</u>-uh-*gram*] *noun, plural* **kilograms.** in the metric system, a unit of mass and weight. A kilogram is equal to 1,000 grams.

kil·o·hertz [<u>kil</u>-uh-*hurts*] *noun, plural* **kilohertz.** a unit of measurement of radio waves. One kilohertz is equal to 1,000 vibrations per second.

ki·lom·e·ter [kuh-<u>lom</u>-uh-tur *or* <u>kil</u>-uh-*mee*-tur] *noun, plural* **kilometers.** in the metric system, a unit of length. A kilometer is equal to 1,000 meters, or 0.62 of a mile.

kil·o·watt [<u>kil</u>-uh-*waht*] *noun, plural* **kilowatts.** a unit of electrical power equal to 1,000 watts.

kilt [kilt] *noun, plural* **kilts.** a knee-length skirt of pleated, plaid cloth. Kilts are a traditional way of dressing for men in Scotland.

ki·mo·no ▲ [kuh-<u>moh</u>-nuh] *noun, plural* **kimonos.** a long, loose robe that has wide sleeves and is tied with a broad sash called an **obi.** The kimono is a traditional form of clothing in Japan.

kin [kin] *noun.* all of a person's family and relatives: *My father, mother, uncle, and aunt are some of my kin.*

kind[1] [kinde] *adjective,* **kinder, kindest.** having a generous and helpful nature; describing a generous and helpful action: *My uncle seems like a stern man, but he is really very kind.*

kind[2] [kinde] *noun, plural* **kinds. 1.** a group of items or living things that are in some way alike: *Snakes are one kind of reptile; lizards are another.* **2.** one of a group of things or people that are in some way special or different: *That kind of car uses a lot of gasoline.*
  • **kind of.** to some extent; rather: *I'm kind of tired.*

kin·der·gar·ten [<u>kin</u>-dur-*gart*-un *or* <u>kin</u>-dur-*gard*-un] *noun, plural* **kindergartens.** a class in school for children aged from four to six years.

> **Kindergarten** comes from two German words that mean "a children's garden." The name was first used by a German educator of the 1800s, Friedrich Fröbel. He developed the first kindergarten for young children, using building blocks, educational games, songs, dancing, and the like.

kin·dle [<u>kin</u>-dul] *verb,* **kindles, kindling. 1.** to catch fire or set on fire: *The dry brush kindled when it was hit by lightning.* **2.** to cause strong feelings: *The television program on ancient Egypt kindled Sally's interest in learning more about the country.*

kind·ling [<u>kind</u>-ling] *noun.* twigs or other small pieces of material that are used to start a fire: *It was so rainy on our camping trip that it was hard to find dry kindling.*

kind·ly [<u>kinde</u>-lee] *adjective,* **kindlier, kindliest.** showing or having kindness: *Jim was a kindly man who helped his neighbors and took part in charity work.*
  adverb. **1.** in a kind manner; out of kindness: *Rita has kindly offered to drive the children home from the party.* **2.** please: *Kindly keep the car clean.* **3.** sincerely; very much: *Thank you kindly for all your help.*

kind·ness [<u>kinde</u>-nis] *noun, plural* **kindnesses. 1.** the quality or state of being kind: *Thank you for your kindness to me when I was sick.* **2.** a kind act; an act that shows caring: *It would be a kindness to tell him that you really like him.*

ki·net·ic [ki-<u>net</u>-ik] *adjective. Science.* having to do with movement and the forces and energy involved: *The kinetic energy of something moving has to be overcome to make it stop.* **Kinetics** is the science that studies the energy of movement.

king ◀ [king] *noun, plural* **kings. 1.** a male ruler of a country. The position of being a king is usually passed down from generation to generation within a royal family. **2.** someone or something widely believed to be the best or most important: *Elvis Presley is often called the king of rock and roll.* **3.** a playing card with a picture of a king on it. **4.** an important piece in a game of chess or checkers.

king·dom [<u>king</u>-dum] *noun, plural* **kingdoms. 1.** a country that has a king or queen as its ruler. **2.** one of the divisions of the natural world: *the animal, vegetable, and mineral kingdoms.* Some scientists divide all forms of life into five kingdoms.

The English **king** *Henry VIII had six wives.*

king·fish·er [<u>king</u>-*fish*-ur] *noun, plural* **kingfishers.** a small, brightly colored bird with a long bill and a short tail. It usually has a crest and it feeds mainly on fish and insects.

king-size *adjective.* larger, wider, or longer than standard size; extra big: *You need very big sheets for a king-size bed.*

king snake ▼ a large, nonpoisonous snake with bright markings native to North America.

Although not poisonous itself, the **king snake** *hunts and eats poisonous rattlesnakes.*

In ancient Japan, vibrantly colored **kites** *were flown in religious ceremonies and for entertainment.*

kink [kingk] *noun, plural* **kinks. 1.** a tight twist or curl in wire, hair, rope, or something that is usually straight: *The kink in the wire meant I couldn't push it through the hole.* **2.** a spasm in a muscle; cramp: *Gerry got a kink in his neck while watching the movie marathon.* **3.** a small problem that causes a delay: *There are a few kinks to be sorted out before our plans can be successful.*
verb, **kinked, kinking.** to make a kink in something.

kin·ship [kin-ship] *noun.* **1.** a family relationship: *The old church records established his kinship with the Jefferson family.* **2.** a strong connection; an affinity: *Betty felt an immediate kinship with the other members of her team.*

ki·osk [kee-osk] *noun, plural* **kiosks.** a small building, often on a sidewalk, from which goods such as newspapers and candy are sold.

kiss [kis] *verb,* **kissed, kissing.** to touch someone or something with your lips to show them love, or as a greeting: *I always kiss my mother good-bye before I leave for school.*
noun, plural **kisses. 1.** a touch with the lips to show love, or a greeting: *Give me a kiss and say goodnight.* **2.** a small candy: *Peppermint kisses are Gina's favorite candy.*

kit [kit] *noun, plural* **kits. 1.** something that comes in separate parts and is put together to make something: *My favorite hobby is building a model car from a kit.* **2.** a set of articles, tools, or equipment that you use for a particular purpose: *The band bought a new drum kit for the drummer.*

kitch·en [kich-un] *noun, plural* **kitchens.** a room where you prepare and cook food.

kitch·en·ette [kich-uh-net] *noun, plural* **kitchenettes.** a small kitchen.

kite ▲ [kite] *noun, plural* **kites. 1.** a light frame covered in a thin, light material that can be flown in the air on the end of a long string. **2.** a small hawk with long, narrow pointed wings and a forked tail.

kit·ten [kit-un] *noun, plural* **kittens.** a young cat. This animal is sometimes called a **kitty.**

ki·wi ▶ [kee-wee] *noun, plural* **kiwis.** a small brown bird that lives in New Zealand; it has very short wings and cannot fly. A **kiwifruit** is a small, round, furry fruit with green flesh that grows in New Zealand but originally came from China. Someone who comes from New Zealand is often also known as a **Kiwi.**

km an abbreviation for KILOMETER.

knack [nak] *noun.* a natural ability, or a skillful way of doing something: *Ray has a knack for making money.*

knap·sack [nap-sak] *noun, plural* **knapsacks.** a bag with shoulder straps that is carried on the back. It is used to carry personal items.

knead [need] *verb,* **kneaded, kneading.** to fold, press, and stretch with the hands: *You must knead the dough for several minutes when you make bread.*
🔊 A different word with the same sound is **need.**

A **kiwi** *sniffs out food with the sensitive nostrils at the tip of its bill.*

knee ▼ [nee] *noun, plural* **knees.** the joint in the middle of a leg in humans and the back leg in other animals, between the thigh and the lower leg.

knee·cap [nee-kap] *noun, plural* **kneecaps.** the flat, triangular bone in front of your knee; it is movable and protects the knee joint.

kneel [neel] *verb,* **knelt** *or* **kneeled, kneeling.** to move to a position where you are resting on one, or both knees: *I had to kneel down so I could look under the bed.*

The **knee** *joint allows up and down movements and is supported by tendons and ligaments.*

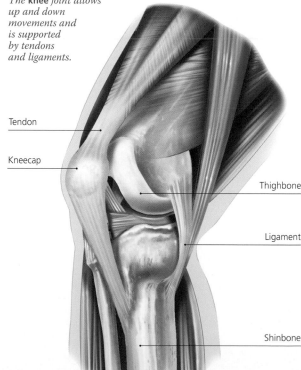
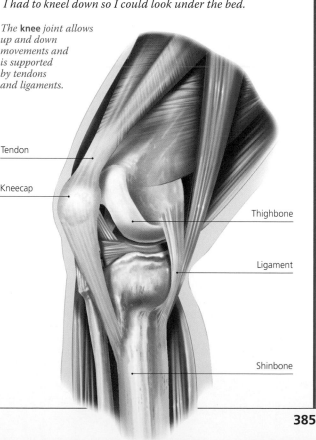

Tendon

Kneecap

Thighbone

Ligament

Shinbone

a b c d e f g h i j **k** l m n o p q r s t u v w x y z

knelt [nelt] *verb.* the past tense and past participle of KNEEL.

knew [noo] *verb.* the past tense of KNOW.
🔊 Different words with the same sound are **gnu** and **new.**

knick·knack [nik-*nak*] *noun, plural* **knickknacks.** a small decorative ornament: *I keep my knickknacks in a special cabinet so I can enjoy looking at them.*

knife [nife] *noun, plural* **knives.**
1. an instrument used for cutting. It has a sharp, metal blade fixed to a handle.
2. a blade in a machine used for cutting.
verb, **knifed, knifing.** to cut or stab with a knife.

Knife is one of a number of English words that have the spelling **kn-** but the sound "n" (that is, the k is not sounded). In earlier times these words could be spoken with a "kn" sound, but since that is not a natural English sound the "n" sound came to be the only one used.

---

knight ▼ [nite] *noun, plural* **knights. 1.** *History.* a noble warrior in the Middle Ages trained to fight for his king or lord, often on horseback. A knight had to serve an apprenticeship as a page or squire. **2.** a man who is given this title by a king or queen to honor him for service to his country. In Great Britain, a knight uses the title "Sir" before his name. **3.** an important chess piece, usually with a horse's head on it.
verb, **knighted, knighting.** to make someone a knight: *The singer Elton John was knighted by Queen Elizabeth II for his charity work.*
🔊 A different word with the same sound is **night.**

knight·hood [nite-*hud*] *noun, plural* **knighthoods.** the rank of a knight: *The doctor received a knighthood after many years of service to medical science.*

knit [nit] *verb,* **knitted, knitting. 1.** to loop wool or other yarn together to make clothing, either with two long needles or a special machine: *I'll knit you a warm scarf for winter.* **2.** to join closely together: *The doctor put my leg in plaster so the broken bones would knit properly.*

knives [nivez] *noun.* the plural of KNIFE.

knob [nob] *noun, plural* **knobs.**
1. a small, rounded handle used for opening a door, or drawer, or adjusting equipment such as a radio or television.
2. a rounded lump; a small piece: *Melt a knob of butter in the pan before cooking the fish.*

knock [nok] *verb,* **knocked, knocking.**
1. to strike with a short, sharp blow; hit: *The oar knocked me on the head as I got out of the boat.* 2. to bump against something so that it falls or moves: *The ball came flying through the window and knocked the vase off the shelf.*
3. to make a repeated, regular sound: *The engine started knocking after I put the wrong gas in the tank.*
4. to find something wrong about something; criticize: *He kept knocking my new purple shirt.*
noun, plural **knocks. 1.** a short, sharp blow; a hit: *a knock on the head.* **2.** a repeated, regular sound: *There was a knock in the engine, so I knew something was wrong.* **3.** a negative or critical comment.

knock·er ▲ [nok-ur] *noun, plural* **knockers.** a hinged knob or ring used to knock on a door, usually made of metal.

knock·out [nok-*owt*] *noun, plural* **knockouts. 1.** the act of making someone unconscious. **2.** in boxing, a punch that makes someone unconscious. If you **knock out** someone in a fight, you make them unconscious. **3.** somebody who is very attractive or successful, or something that is very enjoyable: *That movie star is a real knockout.*

knoll [nole] *noun, plural* **knolls.** a small, round hill.

*When a **knight** rode off to fight, he wore a full suit of armor and his horse wore armor too.*

Knots can be tied in different ways for different purposes.

Overhand knot

Reef knot

knot ▲ [not] *noun, plural* **knots. 1.** the twisting or tying together of a piece of thread, string, rope, or cord: *My father learned to tie some fancy knots when he was in the navy.* **2.** a tangle that is hard to separate: *It hurts when I comb the knots out of my hair.* **3.** a group of people or things close together: *A knot of children stood in the cold waiting for the doors to open.* **4.** a round, dark spot in a piece of wood where a branch once grew out of the tree. **5.** a unit for measuring the speed of boats or airplanes. It equals one nautical mile (6,076 feet) per hour. *verb,* **knotted, knotting.** to tie something in a knot; be tied with a knot; tangle: *It took me a long time to learn how to knot my tie properly.*
🔊 A different word with the same sound is **not.**

knot·ty [not-ee] *adjective,* **knottier, knottiest.**
1. having lots of knots: *Knotty pine is used to make attractive floors.* **2.** hard to understand or solve; complex: *That was a knotty problem—it took me hours to work out the answer.*

know [noh] *verb,* **knew, known, knowing.**
1. to have an understanding or knowledge of; be sure about: *Do you know how many movies Tom Cruise has made?*
2. to be familiar with: *I have known Donald for five years.* **3.** to have a thorough understanding of; be experienced: *Jennifer really knows how to tell a good story.*
• in the know. well informed; having information that only a few people know.
🔊 A different word with the same sound is **no.**

know-how [noh-*how*] *noun.* the knowledge or skill to do something: *Replacing a flat tire takes some know-how.*

knowl·edge [nol-ij] *noun.* **1.** an understanding of facts and information gained through experience; awareness: *Alfredo gained his knowledge of camping from the Boy Scouts.* **2.** the fact of knowing something: *The knowledge that water runs downhill is important for plumbers.*

Knowledge and *information* are both words for facts and ideas that are known or to be known. *Information* is more general and can apply to any collection of things to be known, as through reading, watching, or listening: "The Internet has a lot of *information*; most of it is useful but some is not accurate or not helpful." *Knowledge* usually refers to facts and ideas that have value and that can be put to some good use: "That scientist has a lot of *knowledge* of wolves because she has spent years studying them in the wild."

knowl·edge·a·ble [nol-ij-uh-bul] *adjective.* having or possessing a lot of knowledge about something: *Kurt is very knowledgeable about rap music.*
—**knowledgeably,** *adverb.*

known [nohne] *verb.* the past participle of KNOW. *adjective.* generally recognized: *It is a known fact that football is a popular game.*

knuck·le [nuk-ul] *noun, plural* **knuckles.** a finger joint, especially the ones joining the fingers to the hand.
verb. **knuckle under.** to do what someone else tells you; submit: *The team did not want to go to practice in the rain but they had to knuckle under to the coach's demands.*

ko·a·la ▶ [koh-ah-luh] *noun, plural* **koalas.** an Australian marsupial animal with gray fur, a flat, black nose, big ears, and claws that help it climb around in trees to eat the leaves.

Koalas spend most of their lives in eucalyptus trees and feed on their leaves.

kook [kook] *noun, plural* **kooks.** a strange or eccentric person; someone who is odd or crazy: *People think she is a kook because she wears odd clothing and has rings in her nose.* If someone's behavior or appearance is strange they may be called **kooky.**

kook·a·bur·ra ◀ [kook-uh-*bur*-uh] *noun, plural* **kookaburras.** a large brown bird of Australia and New Guinea with a big beak, blue markings on its wings, and a laughing cry.

Kookaburras eat lizards, snakes, mice, and insects.

Ko·ran [kor-ahn *or* kor-an] *noun. Religion.* the sacred book of the Islamic religion. This word is also spelled **Quran.**

Ko·re·an [kuh-ree-un] *adjective.* having to do with the country, people, or culture of the Asian country of Korea, which is divided into North Korea and South Korea.

ko·sher [koh-shur] *adjective. Religion.* **1.** having been prepared in a way that obeys Jewish food laws. Kosher meat must be killed under the supervision of a rabbi. **2.** any food prepared in this way. **3.** genuine or authentic; not illegal: *The offer seems good, but something makes me think it's just not kosher.*

kung fu [*kung* foo] a Chinese form of self-defense karate using the hands and feet to punch and kick.

Kwan·zaa [kwahn-zuh] *noun.* an African-American harvest festival, celebrated between December 26 and January 1. Kwanzaa is based on traditional African harvest festivals. This word is also spelled **Kwanza.**

The term **Kwanzaa** was developed by the founder of this celebration, Maulana (Ron) Karenga. He has stated that it is based on harvest celebrations of Africa and that the word *Kwanzaa* is taken from the phrase *matunda ya kwanza,* which means "first fruits" in Swahili. (Swahili is the most widely spoken language of Africa.)

a b c h i j k l m n o p q r s t u v w x y z

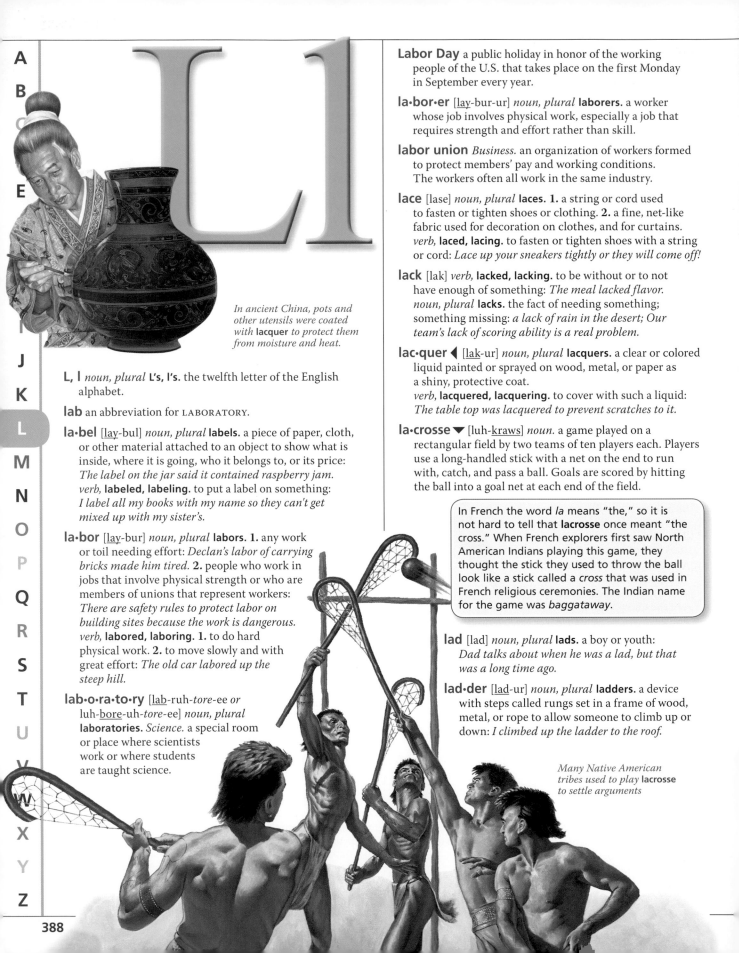

L1

*In ancient China, pots and other utensils were coated with **lacquer** to protect them from moisture and heat.*

L, l *noun, plural* **L's, l's.** the twelfth letter of the English alphabet.

lab an abbreviation for LABORATORY.

la·bel [lay-bul] *noun, plural* **labels.** a piece of paper, cloth, or other material attached to an object to show what is inside, where it is going, who it belongs to, or its price: *The label on the jar said it contained raspberry jam.* *verb,* **labeled, labeling.** to put a label on something: *I label all my books with my name so they can't get mixed up with my sister's.*

la·bor [lay-bur] *noun, plural* **labors. 1.** any work or toil needing effort: *Declan's labor of carrying bricks made him tired.* **2.** people who work in jobs that involve physical strength or who are members of unions that represent workers: *There are safety rules to protect labor on building sites because the work is dangerous.* *verb,* **labored, laboring. 1.** to do hard physical work. **2.** to move slowly and with great effort: *The old car labored up the steep hill.*

lab·o·ra·to·ry [lab-ruh-*tore*-ee *or* luh-*bore*-uh-*tore*-ee] *noun, plural* **laboratories.** *Science.* a special room or place where scientists work or where students are taught science.

Labor Day a public holiday in honor of the working people of the U.S. that takes place on the first Monday in September every year.

la·bor·er [lay-bur-ur] *noun, plural* **laborers.** a worker whose job involves physical work, especially a job that requires strength and effort rather than skill.

labor union *Business.* an organization of workers formed to protect members' pay and working conditions. The workers often all work in the same industry.

lace [lase] *noun, plural* **laces. 1.** a string or cord used to fasten or tighten shoes or clothing. **2.** a fine, net-like fabric used for decoration on clothes, and for curtains. *verb,* **laced, lacing.** to fasten or tighten shoes with a string or cord: *Lace up your sneakers tightly or they will come off!*

lack [lak] *verb,* **lacked, lacking.** to be without or to not have enough of something: *The meal lacked flavor.* *noun, plural* **lacks.** the fact of needing something; something missing: *a lack of rain in the desert; Our team's lack of scoring ability is a real problem.*

lac·quer ◀ [lak-ur] *noun, plural* **lacquers.** a clear or colored liquid painted or sprayed on wood, metal, or paper as a shiny, protective coat. *verb,* **lacquered, lacquering.** to cover with such a liquid: *The table top was lacquered to prevent scratches to it.*

la·crosse ▼ [luh-*kraws*] *noun.* a game played on a rectangular field by two teams of ten players each. Players use a long-handled stick with a net on the end to run with, catch, and pass a ball. Goals are scored by hitting the ball into a goal net at each end of the field.

In French the word *la* means "the," so it is not hard to tell that **lacrosse** once meant "the cross." When French explorers first saw North American Indians playing this game, they thought the stick they used to throw the ball look like a stick called a *cross* that was used in French religious ceremonies. The Indian name for the game was *baggataway.*

lad [lad] *noun, plural* **lads.** a boy or youth: *Dad talks about when he was a lad, but that was a long time ago.*

lad·der [lad-ur] *noun, plural* **ladders.** a device with steps called rungs set in a frame of wood, metal, or rope to allow someone to climb up or down: *I climbed up the ladder to the roof.*

*Many Native American tribes used to play **lacrosse** to settle arguments*

la·dle [lade-ul] *noun, plural* **ladles.** a large spoon with a long handle and a deep bowl on the end. A ladle is used to serve liquids such as milk or soup. *verb,* **ladled, ladling.** to serve something using such a spoon: *The cook ladled the soup into bowls.*

la·dy [lay-dee] *noun, plural* **ladies. 1.** a woman; any adult female: *There was a lady on the TV last night talking about diets.* **2.** a polite, well-bred girl or woman with good manners. **3.** a woman of high social class. In Great Britain, women whose husbands are called Lord are given the title of **Lady.**

la·dy·bug ▶ [lay-dee-*bug*] *noun, plural* **ladybugs.** a type of small beetle, usually red or orange in color and with black spots. Ladybugs eat lice and insects that harm plants. This animal is also called a **ladybird.**

lag [lag] *verb,* **lagged, lagging.** to move more slowly than others: *The younger children were lagging behind the rest of the group on our walk.* *noun, plural* **lags.** the fact of being behind; a delay: *There was a time lag between the planned date for finishing the project and the actual completion.*

la·goon [luh-goon] *noun, plural* **lagoons.** a body of sea water, partly or fully separated from the sea by a sandbar, rocks, or coral reef.

laid [lade] *verb.* the past tense and past participle of LAY.

lain [lane] *verb.* the past participle of LIE.
🔊 A different word with the same sound is **lane.**

lair [lare] *noun, plural* **lairs.** the den or place where a wild animal rests: *The fox ran from its lair when it heard the hounds approaching.*

lake ▶ [lake] *noun, plural* **lakes.** a large area of water surrounded by land.

lamb [lam] *noun, plural* **lambs. 1.** a young sheep. **2.** the meat of such an animal used for food.

lame [lame] *adjective,* **lamer, lamest. 1.** not able to walk properly because of weakness or injury to a leg or foot. **2.** stiff and sore: *My back is lame from lifting all those cartons of books.* **3.** not strong; weak; imperfect: *My older sister said my excuse for handing the assignment in late was pretty lame.* *verb,* **lamed, laming.** to make something lame: *Running on dry, uneven ground lamed the horse.*

lamp [lamp] *noun, plural* **lamps.** any of various lights powered by oil, gas, or electricity. A lamp can usually be easily moved around. Electric lamps have bulbs.

lance [lans] *noun, plural* **lances.** a long spear made of a wooden pole and a sharp metal tip. *verb,* **lanced, lancing.** to puncture or cut flesh open with an instrument to release infected material: *The best way to treat a boil is to lance it.*

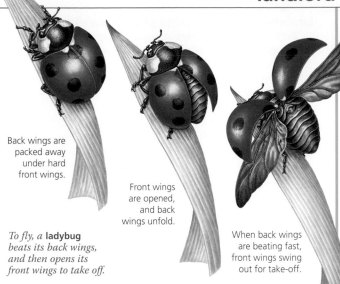

Back wings are packed away under hard front wings.

Front wings are opened, and back wings unfold.

When back wings are beating fast, front wings swing out for take-off.

To fly, a **ladybug** *beats its back wings, and then opens its front wings to take off.*

land [land] *noun, plural* **lands. 1.** any of the Earth's surface that is not water; solid ground: *After sailing for many days we reached dry land.* **2.** a part of the Earth's surface; a country or a region: *The lands to the east of the river are more fertile than those to the west.* *verb,* **landed, landing. 1.** to come or bring down to the land or water from the air: *The airplane landed at Los Angeles Airport.* **2.** to come or bring ashore from a boat: *The Pilgrims landed in America in 1620.* **3.** to bring a fish to land or onto a boat. **4.** to end up; find oneself in: *He landed in a real mess after being caught stealing.*

land·fill [land-*fil*] *noun. Environment.* a method of garbage disposal in which trash is buried in low-lying land or holes in the ground with layers of soil above and below it. If the trash contains harmful materials or chemicals, it can cause serious pollution.

land·ing [land-ing] *noun, plural* **landings. 1.** the act of bringing something to the ground from the air or sea: *The airplane's smooth landing was a credit to the skill of the pilot.* **2.** the place where passengers and goods are loaded or unloaded at a ship's dock. **3.** a level, open area at the top of a flight, or between flights, of stairs.

Lake *Lugano is in a beautiful alpine region in Switzerland.*

land·la·dy [land-*lay*-dee] *noun, plural* **landladies.** a woman who rents out rooms in her own house, or who rents whole houses or land to tenants.

land·locked [land-*lokt*] *adjective.* completely or almost completely surrounded by land: *Liechtenstein is a landlocked country near Germany.*

land·lord [land-*lord*] *noun, plural* **landlords.** a man or organization that rents out rooms in a house, or that rents whole houses or land to tenants.

a
c
d
e
f
g
h
i
j
k
l
m
n
o
p
q
r
s
t
u
v
w
x
y
z

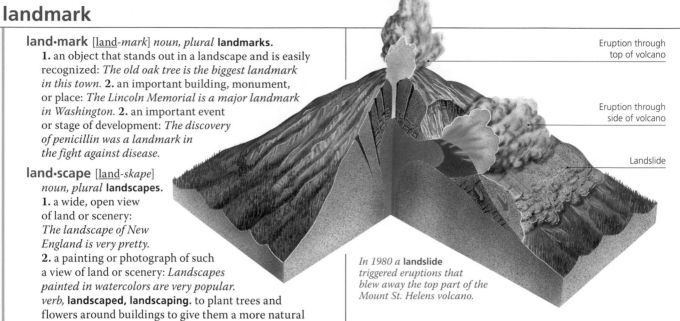

Eruption through top of volcano

Eruption through side of volcano

Landslide

In 1980 a **landslide** *triggered eruptions that blew away the top part of the Mount St. Helens volcano.*

land·mark [land-mark] *noun, plural* **landmarks.**
1. an object that stands out in a landscape and is easily recognized: *The old oak tree is the biggest landmark in this town.* **2.** an important building, monument, or place: *The Lincoln Memorial is a major landmark in Washington.* **2.** an important event or stage of development: *The discovery of penicillin was a landmark in the fight against disease.*

land·scape [land-skape] *noun, plural* **landscapes.**
1. a wide, open view of land or scenery: *The landscape of New England is very pretty.*
2. a painting or photograph of such a view of land or scenery: *Landscapes painted in watercolors are very popular.*
verb, **landscaped, landscaping.** to plant trees and flowers around buildings to give them a more natural appearance: *We are having our garden landscaped.* The **landscaping** of a place refers to the layout and appearance of its gardens. —**landscaper,** *noun.*

land·slide ▲ [land-slide] *noun, plural* **landslides.**
1. the fact of a large quantity of rocks, soil, or mud sliding down a mountain: *The landslide covered everything in its path.* **2.** a big victory in an election: *The local candidate was re-elected in a landslide thanks to our efforts.*

lane [lane] *noun, plural* **lanes. 1.** a narrow, winding track or road in the country: *The lane runs between trees and hedges.* **2.** any of the strips marked with white lines to keep traffic in separate lines on a highway: *Keep in your lane as you approach the bridge.* **3.** a narrow path marked for sporting events so that competitors do not bump into each other: *Swimmers must swim within the lane that has been assigned to them.*
🔊 A different word with the same sound is **lain.**

lan·guage [lang-gwij] *noun, plural* **languages.**
1. the system of spoken or written words by which humans communicate: *Almost all humans are able to use language of one kind or another.* **2.** such a system of words used by a particular group or country: *The French speak one language and the Italians speak another.*
3. a method of communicating without using words: *Sign language is used by people who are unable to speak or cannot hear.* **4.** *Computers.* a system of signs, symbols, and numerals used to tell a computer how to process information.

> The word **language** goes back to Latin word meaning "the tongue." The idea is that a person uses the tongue to speak and produce language.

language arts *Education.* the group of topics that include reading, writing, spelling, and composition, aimed at helping a student's use and understanding of language.

La Niña [neen-yah] *Environment.* a cold current of deep water off the Pacific coast of South America that has the opposite effect to that of El Niño and disrupts weather patterns in the opposite way. It causes cooling and rain periods rather than high temperatures and droughts.

> **La Niña** is a Spanish term meaning "a young girl" or "a female child." This name is used as a companion term to *El Niño,* which is an opposite kind of weather pattern.

lan·tern ▼ [lan-turn] *noun, plural* **lanterns.** a case with a light inside that is shielded from the wind. Many lanterns can be carried.

La·o·tian [lay-oh-shun] *noun, plural* **Laotians.** a person from Laos.
adjective. of or having to do with the southeast Asian country of Laos, its people, or its culture: *The Laotian way of life is similar to many Asian cultures.*

lap¹ [lap] *noun, plural* **laps.** the front part of a person's body from the waist to the knees when they are sitting down, forming a seat: *The girl sat on her father's lap.*

lap² [lap] *verb,* **lapped, lapping.** to lay something partly over something else: *The planks used to make fishing boats lap over each other so the water can't get in.*
noun, plural **laps.** a single trip around a race track or one length of a swimming pool: *The race was six laps long.*

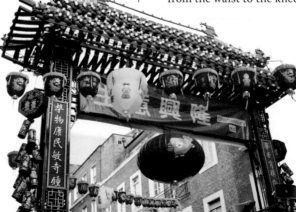

Colorful, paper **lanterns** *often hang at the entrance to the Chinese district of a city.*

lap³ [lap] *verb*, **lapped, lapping. 1.** to drink by using the tongue to take up liquid with quick movements: *The puppy lapped up its milk from the saucer.* **2.** to move or slap gently against something: *The waves lapped against the side of the boat.* *noun, plural* **laps.** the act of drinking by lapping.

la·pel [luh-pel] *noun, plural* **lapels.** the section of the front of a jacket that joins the collar and is folded back toward the arms on each side.

lapse [laps] *noun, plural* **lapses. 1.** a small failure or mistake, especially something easily corrected: *I forgot my cousin's birthday but she forgave me for the lapse of memory.* **2.** the time that passes between events: *After a lapse of two years the museum was opened to the public again.* *verb*, **lapsed, lapsing. 1.** to slip gradually into a different state: *The choir lapsed into silence when the conductor lost his place in the music.* **2.** to come to an end, usually through neglect or non-payment: *Dad's insurance policy lapsed after he forgot to pay to renew it.*

Honeybee **larvae** *mature inside wax cells, where they are fed by worker bees.*

lap·top [lap-top] *noun, plural* **laptops.** *Computers.* a light, portable computer that can be used while placed on the user's lap.

lar·ce·ny [lar-suh-nee] *noun, plural* **larcenies.** *Law.* the act of stealing another person's belongings.

> The word **larceny** comes from an old French word for this crime. Many of the words used in English for matters of the law and crime come from French, because in earlier times the courts of England were run by French-speaking people called Normans who ruled over the country.

lard [lard] *noun.* the fat of a pig, melted down for use in cooking. *verb,* **larded, larding.** to put the fat of a pig into a pan or into or onto food you will cook, such as lean meat: *You may lard a piece of meat to make it tastier.*

large [larj] *adjective,* **larger, largest.** being or having a bigger amount, size, or number than normal: *He had a large collection of baseball cards, more than 1,000.*
• **at large. 1.** not in jail; free: *The murderer is believed to be still at large.* **2.** in general, as a whole: *Can the public at large use this beach or is it private?*

large·ly [larj-lee] *adverb.* for the most part; mainly: *The group largely consists of young children, although there are some adults.*

lar·i·at [lare-ee-ut] *noun, plural* **lariats.** a long rope with a loop at one end, used for roping cattle by the horns; a lasso: *Cowhands are very skilled at throwing a lariat.*

> The word **lariat** comes from the Spanish term *la riata,* meaning 'the rope." The first cowboys of western North America came from Spain, and a number of the words they used for their work with cattle were later passed on to the English language.

Larks nest on the ground, and their dull color helps them blend in with their surroundings.

lark¹ ▲ [lark] *noun, plural* **larks.** a small songbird with brownish feathers that sings beautifully. Larks were originally from Europe, but they now live in many countries.

lark² [lark] *noun, plural* **larks.** an amusing prank or practical joke; something done for fun: *We hid the coach's whistle, just for a lark.*

lar·va ◀ [lar-vuh] *noun, plural* **larvae.** *Biology.* the worm-like form of some young insects that hatch from an egg.

lar·yn·gi·tis [lare-in-jye-tis] *noun. Health.* inflammation of the larynx that makes a person's voice sound hoarse.

lar·ynx [lare-ingks] *noun, plural* **larynxes.** *Biology.* the upper section of the windpipe. In humans, this area contains the vocal cords, also known as the voice box.

la·sa·gna [luh-zahn-yuh] *noun, plural* **lasagnas.** an Italian dish made of layers of wide, flat pieces of pasta noodle with a sauce of cheese, tomato, and spiced meat in between. This word is also spelled **lasagne.**

la·ser [lay-zur] *noun, plural* **lasers.** *Science.* an electronic apparatus for making a thin, very powerful beam of light that can transmit information, perform surgery, and cut through metal. The concentrated light is known as a **laser beam** and has many different uses. Many computers now use **laser printers** in which a laser beam is used to form the images to be printed on paper.

lash¹ [lash] *noun, plural* **lashes. 1.** a hit or blow with a whip: *In former times a sailor in the navy might be given twenty lashes as a punishment.* **2.** a small, curled hair that grows on the end of a person's eyelid; eyelash: *Her lashes were long and curly.* *verb,* **lashed, lashing. 1.** to hit with a whip. **2.** to beat or hit violently: *Rain lashed the windshield of the car during the violent storm.*

lash² [lash] *verb,* **lashed, lashing.** to tie firmly with rope: *The cargo was lashed to the ship's deck ready for the rough voyage.*

lass [las] *noun, plural* **lasses.** a girl or young woman.

las·so ▶ [las-oh *or* la-soo] *noun*, *plural* **lassos** *or* **lassoes.** a long rope with a noose at one end used to rope steers. *verb*, **lassoed, lassoing.** to catch by roping with a lasso: *The cowboy quickly lassoed the steers.*

last[1] [last] *adjective.* **1.** having the final place; being at the end: *December 31 is the last day of the year.* **2.** being the only one left of something: *I ate the last chocolate in the box.* **3.** the most recent; next before the present: *When was the last time you visited your grandma?* **4.** the least likely or expected: *You're the last person I thought I'd see here.* *adverb.* **1.** after anything else: *Clean the bedrooms first and leave the kitchen until last.* **2.** most recently: *I last watched that show three weeks ago.* *noun.* the person or thing that is last: *I was the last to arrive at the party.* • **at last.** after a lot of effort or long period of time: *At last we reached the top of the mountain.*

last[2] [last] *verb*, **lasted, lasting.** **1.** to go on for the set time; continue: *How long will the concert last?* **2.** to remain in good condition: *Your bicycle will last longer if you look after it well.* If something continues to be in good condition, it is said to be **lasting.**

latch [lach] *noun*, *plural* **latches.** a simple bar and U-shaped slot device that fastens a gate or door shut: *Lift the latch to open the gate.* *verb*, **latched, latching.** to fasten a gate or door by closing the latch.

late [late] *adjective*, **later, latest. 1.** after the usual or agreed time: *I arrived at school late because I missed my bus.* **2.** being or occurring toward the end of something: *The storm had passed by late afternoon.* **3.** recent, not long ago: *The Jones family own a late model car.* **4.** having recently died: *Her late husband was a generous man.* *adverb.* **1.** after the usual time: *The teacher was late marking our homework this week.* **2.** toward the end of a period: *We planted the tree late in the year.*

late·ly [late-lee] *adverb.* in the recent past: *Have you seen any good movies lately?*

la·tent [late-unt] *adjective.* present, but not visible or active: *She has latent athletic talent that needs some good coaching to be developed.*

lat·e·ral [lat-ur-ul] *adjective.* having to do with the sides of something: *The gardener advised us to prune the lateral branches of the tree and leave those at the top.* *noun*, *plural* **laterals. 1.** something that goes to the side. **2.** a pass in football thrown from side to side by one offensive player to another. A lateral is not a forward pass. *verb*, **lateraled, lateraling.** to throw a lateral pass in football. —**laterally**, *adverb.*

Cowboys are experts at using **lassos** *to round up cattle.*

la·tex [lay-teks] *noun*, *plural* **latexes.** a thick, milky liquid produced by some trees, particularly the rubber tree. Latex is used to make rubber.

lath·er [laTH-ur] *noun*, *plural* **lathers. 1.** a white foam or froth: *The lather from my soap smells sweet.* **2.** a white foam caused by sweating: *The dog worked up a lather as it ran furiously around the track.* *verb*, **lathered, lathering. 1.** to produce or apply a lather.

Lat·in [lat-un] *noun*, *plural* **Latins. 1.** the language used by the ancient Romans. **2.** a person who speaks a language that comes from Latin. *adjective.* **1.** having to do with Latin: *The Roman Catholic church used the Latin language in its ceremonies for many centuries.* **2.** having to do with countries whose languages are based on Latin. These include Spain, Portugal, Mexico, and the countries of Latin America such as Brazil.

A large number of the words in English were originally used in **Latin,** the language of the ancient city and empire of Rome, Italy. The Roman Empire spread over a great part of western Europe, and various local languages then developed in those areas that were based on Latin. English itself was not one of the languages to come from Latin, but French was. When a group of people called the Normans conquered England in the year 1066, they brought many Latin words from their French language over into English.

La·ti·na [lah-tee-nuh *or* luh-tee-nuh] *noun*, *plural* **Latinas. 1.** a woman or girl born or living in Latin America. **2.** a woman or girl born in Latin America but who lives in the U.S. *adjective.* having to do with such a person.

Latin American a person who was born in or lives in Central or South America and who speaks a language derived from Latin. *adjective.* having to do with Latin America or its people.

La·ti·no [lah-tee-noh *or* luh-tee-noh] *noun*, *plural* **Latinos.** a man or boy born or living in Latin America. **2.** a man or boy born in Latin America but who lives in the U.S. *adjective.* having to do with such a person.

lat·i·tude [lat-uh-tood] *noun*, *plural* **latitudes. 1.** *Geography.* the distance north or south of the equator measured in degrees. Each degree equals about 69 miles. **2.** freedom of choice; room to move: *The teacher gave us quite a bit of latitude as to when we should hand in our work.*

lat·ter [lat-ur] *adjective.* **1.** the second of two things referred to: *If I need to decide between learning Spanish and French, I will choose the latter.* **2.** coming near the end; later: *The credit card bill is due in the latter part of the month.*

laugh [laf] *verb*, **laughed, laughing.** to make the sounds that show that you are happy or think something is funny: *We laughed at the ridiculous joke he told.*
noun, plural **laughs.** the act or sound of laughing: *She gave a nervous laugh.* A situation is **laughable** when it is silly and does not really deserve serious thought or consideration.

laugh·ter [laf-tur] *noun.* the act or sound of laughing: *We heard laughter coming from the other classroom.*

launch¹ ◀ [lawnch] *verb*, **launched, launching.**
1. to send forth: *The troops were ordered to launch a missile.* **2.** to put a boat or ship into water: *He launched the rowboat and settled in for a day's fishing.* **3.** to set going or start: *The advertising campaign was launched last week with huge billboards put up all around the city.*
noun, plural **launches.** the act of launching: *We watched the space shuttle launch on TV.*

launch² [lawnch] *noun, plural* **launches.** a large open motorboat.

launch pad the special platform from which a weapon or spacecraft is sent into the sky. This term is also called a **launching pad.**

Powerful rockets are used to launch a spacecraft.

laun·der [lawn-dur] *verb*, **laundered, laundering.**
1. to wash, dry, and iron clothes and linen: *He laundered his silk shirt by hand.* **2.** to disguise the source of illegal money by transferring it into legal accounts and investments.

laun·dry [lawn-dree] *noun, plural* **laundries. 1.** the clothes and linens that are ready to be washed or have been washed. **2.** a business that washes clothes and linens for paying customers: *Dan collected his shirts from the laundry on the way home from work.*

lau·rel [lor-ul] *noun, plural* **laurels. 1.** a small evergreen tree with dark glossy leaves. **2.** a flowering plant known as the mountain laurel.

la·va ▶ [lah-vuh] *noun.* **1.** the hot liquid rock that comes out of a volcano. **2.** the solid rock formed when this liquid rock cools and hardens.

lav·a·to·ry [lav-uh-tor-ee] *noun, plural* **lavatories. 1.** a room with a toilet and sink in it. **2.** a basin for washing.

lav·en·der ▶ [lav-un-dur] *noun, plural* **lavenders. 1.** a small shrub with fragrant purple flowers and gray-green needle-like leaves. The dried flowers or other parts of the plant are used to perfume linen and clothes. **2.** a pale purple color.
adjective. having a light purple color.

law [law] *noun, plural* **laws. 1.** a rule made by a government for its people to obey: *The police enforce the law against driving faster than the speed limit.* **2.** the system of rules made by a government: *The robber has broken the law and will have to face charges.* **3.** the profession of a lawyer. **4.** a basic rule or custom: *the laws of soccer.* **5.** Science. a statement that an event will always happen in the same way when all conditions are the same: *According to the law of gravity, if you drop a ball, it will fall to the ground.*

law·ful [law-ful] *adjective.* allowed or recognized by the law: *She is his lawful wife.* —**lawfully,** *adverb.*

lawn [lawn] *noun, plural* **lawns.** an open area of grass-covered land that is kept mowed.

lawn mower a machine with rotating blades that is used to cut grass.

When Hawaiian volcanoes erupt, streams of red-hot runny lava can travel for a hundred miles at speeds of up to thirty miles per hour.

Thin, rippled skin forms on lava surface as it cools.

a
b
f
g
h
i
j
k
l
m
n
o
p
q
r
u
v
w
x

law·suit [law-soot] *noun, plural* **lawsuits.** a problem or complaint taken to a court of law for a legal decision.

law·yer [loi-ur *or* law-yur] *noun, plural* **lawyers.** someone who has a license from the state that allows them to advise people on legal matters and represent them in court.

lay¹ [lay] *verb,* **laid, laying. 1.** to put or set down: *She closed the book shut and laid it on the table.* **2.** to spread over a surface: *The new tiles were laid in the bathroom.* **3.** to produce eggs: *Turtles lay their eggs in the sand.*

lay² [lay] *verb.* the past tense of LIE.

lay·er ▼ [lay-ur] *noun, plural* **layers.** a thickness or level of some material laid over another surface: *We stripped two layers of paint off the wall.*

lay·off [lay-of] *noun, plural* **layoffs.** *Business.* the act of ending a worker's employment, often temporarily: *There have been a lot of layoffs recently in the U.S. car industry.* If you end a person's employment you **lay** them **off.**

la·zy [lay-zee] *adjective,* **lazier, laziest.** not willing or making an effort to work: *She drove her car to the store down the street because she was too lazy to walk.* —**lazily,** *adverb;* —**laziness,** *noun.*

> It seems odd that the abbreviation for the word "pound" is **lb**. and not "pd." or "pnd." or the like. This came about because there was an earlier word meaning "pound" that was spelled *libra*, and *lb*. was the abbreviation for that. *Libra* was the Latin word for scales that were used in measuring things.

lb. an abbreviation for POUND¹.

LCD an abbreviation for LIQUID CRYSTAL DISPLAY.

lead¹ [leed] *verb,* **led, leading. 1.** to guide or show the way: *The waitress led us to our table.* **2.** to be at the front of: *The mayor will lead the Thanksgiving Day parade.* **3.** to be a way of getting to: *This winding path leads down to the lake.* **4.** to live or go through: *With all her after-school activities, she really leads a hectic life.*

noun, plural **leads. 1.** the front or first position: *A last-minute goal put us in the lead.* **2.** the amount or distance ahead: *The runner had a lead of three yards.* **3.** a piece of information; clue: *The reporter got a great lead on a new story.* **4.** the main actor in a film or play: *He was cast as the lead in the new Broadway show.*

lead² [led] *noun, plural* **leads. 1.** *Chemistry.* a heavy, soft dark-gray metal that melts easily and is poisonous. It is used to make pipes, bullets, and paint, and for protection against radiation. **2.** the thin stick of black substance in a pencil that makes the marks in writing.
🔊 A different word with the same sound is **led.**

lead·er [leed-ur] *noun, plural* **leaders.** someone who leads or controls: *She was elected as leader of the school dance committee.*

leaf ▶ [leef] *noun, plural* **leaves. 1.** the flat, usually green part of a plant that is joined at one end to the stem or branch. **2.** a thin sheet of paper; page: *He put a bookmark between the leaves of his book.* **3.** a movable or additional part of the top of a table: *We folded the leaf away because there were only the three of us at the dinner table.* *verb,* **leaf, leafed. 1.** to produce leaves. **2.** to quickly turn pages and glance at the content: *She leafed through the magazine while she waited for her friend.*

leaf·let [leef-lit] *noun, plural* **leaflets. 1.** a piece of paper or a pamphlet used to give information or to advertise something: *We handed out leaflets about our garage sale on Saturday.* **2.** a small or young leaf: *The shrub started to sprout leaflets in the spring.* **3.** one of the segments of a larger leaf.

leaf·y [leef-ee] *adjective,* **leafier, leafiest. 1.** having a lot of leaves: *a leafy vegetable.* **2.** having a lot of plants or trees: *a leafy suburb.*

By studying when the different rock **layers** *of the Grand Canyon were formed, geologists can learn a lot about the canyon's history.*

MILLIONS OF YEARS AGO

265
270
275
300
340
375
520
540
560
2000

A B C D E F G H I J K L M N O P Q R S T U V W X Y Z

LEAVES

Leaves have many different sizes and shapes, from flat and wide to thin and spiky. The edges of leaves may be smooth, serrate, lobed, or parted. Some, known as compound leaves, are divided into many separate leaflets. These different leaf characteristics help us to identify plants and trees. Leaves are the part of plants responsible for converting sunlight, water, and carbon dioxide into energy, or food, in a process called photosynthesis. They grow on the stem at different angles in a spiral shape, so that part of each leaf can catch the sunlight.

Serrate Smooth Lobed Parted
LEAF EDGES

LEAF SHAPES

SPIRAL GROWTH

league¹ [leeg] *noun, plural* **leagues.** a group of people or countries joined together for a common interest or purpose: *the National Football League.*

league² [leeg] *noun, plural* **leagues.** *History.* a unit of distance that is no longer used. A league is approximately three miles.

leak [leek] *noun, plural* **leaks. 1.** a hole or crack that lets liquid or gas flow out by accident: *We realized we had a leak in the roof when water started to drip onto the carpet.* **2.** information that was meant to be kept secret, but becomes known.
verb, **leaked, leaking. 1.** to let a substance in or out through a leak: *The gas was leaking through a pipe.* **2.** to allow previously secret information to become well known: *He leaked the news about the President's surprise visit.* Something that escapes by leaking is a **leakage.**
🔊 A different word with the same sound is **leek.**

lean¹ ▶ [leen] *verb,* **leaned, leaning. 1.** to be in or put in a sloping position: *The tree was leaning to one side.* **2.** to rest against something for support: *The sleepy child leaned his head on his mother's shoulder.* **3.** to depend or rely on someone: *She leans on her family when she's feeling down.* **4.** to tend toward: *Either Tim or Mark will be picked to pitch the game, but the coach is leaning toward Tim.*

lean² [leen] *adjective,* **leaner, leanest. 1.** having not much flesh or fat: *lean beef; The athlete was lean and muscular.* **2.** lacking in money or food; poor: *Being a waiter he was on a lean wage and had to rely on tips.*

leap [leep] *verb,* **leaped** *or* **leapt, leaping.** to jump or move quickly: *He leaped up in the air to catch the ball.*
noun, plural **leaps.** a jump or quick movement: *The dog went over the fence in one leap.*

leapt [lept] *verb.* the past tense and past participle of LEAP.

leap year a year of 366 days that happens every fourth year, when February has 29 days instead of 28. The extra day is added so that the calendar and the seasons of the year will match each other, since the actual time it takes the Earth to revolve around the Sun is 365¼ days, not 365.

learn [lurn] *verb,* **learned** *or* **learnt, learning. 1.** to gain knowledge or skill: *I am going to learn how to drive a car this summer.* A **learner** is someone who is gaining knowledge about something. **2.** to know something well; memorize: *The teacher told us to learn the song words by tomorrow.* **3.** to find out; become informed: *We learned that there had been a robbery on our street.*

learn·ed [lur-nid] *adjective.* having or showing much knowledge: *a learned college professor.*

learn·ing [lur-ning] *noun.* knowledge gained through reading and study: *He was known as a man of great intelligence and learning.*

learning disability *Education.* any of numerous conditions, such as dyslexia, that interfere with a person's ability to learn. Someone who has one of these various conditions is described as **learning disabled.**

learnt [lurnt] *verb.* the past tense and past participle of LEARN.

lease [leess] *noun, plural* **leases.** a legal agreement that allows you to rent a house, apartment, or other type of property: *The lease on the apartment expires at the end of the year.* The act of making such an agreement is called **leasing.**
verb, **leased, leasing.** to make a legal agreement to rent: *to lease a car rather than buying it.*

a b c d e f g h i j k l m n o p q r s t u v w x y z

*Today, blood-sucking medicinal **leeches** are used to help control swelling after microsurgery.*

leash [leesh] *noun, plural* **leashes.** a strap fastened to an animal's collar in order to hold or control it: *We need to put the leash on our dog when we take her for a walk.* *verb,* **leashed, leashing.** to fasten such a strap to an animal's collar: *Dogs must be leashed to go on the beach here.*

least [leest] *adjective.* describing the smallest: *She donated the least amount of money to the fund, only one dollar.* *noun.* the smallest in amount, number or importance: *Being late to math class is the least of my worries.* *adverb.* to the smallest degree: *She talks the least out of everyone.*
• **at least. 1.** at the minimum; not less than: *Fixing the car will cost at least two hundred dollars.* **2.** at any rate: *We lost the game, but at least we tried our best.*

leath·er [leTH-ur] *noun, plural* **leathers.** an animal skin that has been cleaned and treated in order to preserve it. Leather is used to make shoes, bags, clothes, and equipment. Something that is **leathery** has the look and feel of leather.

leave[1] [leev] *verb,* **left, leaving. 1.** to go away from a place; depart: *to leave the house in the morning to go to school; The next flight to Dallas leaves at 4 P.M.* **2.** to withdraw from; quit: *Dave is leaving the company to take another job.* **3.** to cause to be or stay in a certain place or condition: *The delivery boy leaves the paper on the porch; Leave the door open when you go out.* **4.** to give to another person to do or have: *I will leave it to you to decide what to do with the old TV; Her will says that she will leave a lot of money to her church when she dies.*

leave[2] [leev] *noun, plural* **leaves. 1.** the fact of being allowed to do something; permission or agreement: *The teacher gave me leave to go to the bathroom during class time.* **2.** time permitted away from work: *The sailor stayed with his parents while he was on leave.*

leaves [leevz] *noun.* the plural of LEAF.

Leb·a·nese [leb-uh-neez] *noun.* an inhabitant of the Middle Eastern nation of Lebanon. *adjective.* of or relating to Lebanon, its people, or its culture.

lec·ture [lek-chur] *noun, plural* **lectures. 1.** a formal talk or speech given to an audience: *We went to a lecture on medieval history.* A person who gives lectures is a **lecturer. 2.** a serious talk given as a scolding or warning about something: *Dad gave me a long lecture about the importance of doing my homework.* *verb,* **lectured, lecturing. 1.** to give a formal speech to an audience: *He lectures at the college three times a week.* **2.** to scold or warn about something: *The coach lectured us about taking our training more seriously.*

led [led] *verb.* the past tense and past participle of LEAD[1].
🔊 A different word with the same sound is **lead.**

ledge [lej] *noun, plural* **ledges. 1.** a narrow, flat shelf: *a window ledge.* **2.** a surface like a shelf that sticks out from something upright: *a rock ledge.*

lee [lee] *noun, plural* **lees.** the side of something such as a ship, hill, tree, and the like, that offers protection from the wind. *adjective.* of or being the side away from the wind: *We set up camp on the lee side of the mountain.*

leech ◀ [leech] *noun, plural* **leeches.** a small worm found in wet places that fixes itself to the skin of humans or animals to suck their blood.

leek ▼ [leek] *noun, plural* **leeks.** a vegetable that tastes like an onion and has a long, white bulb and wide, flat, green leaves.
🔊 A different word with the same sound is **leak.**

left[1] [left] *adjective.* on the side of the body that is to the west when one is facing north: *I wear my watch on my left hand.* *noun.* the left side: *The school yard is on the left of the main building.* *adverb.* toward the left: *Turn left when you reach the end of this road.*

left[2] [left] *verb.* the past tense and past participle of LEAVE.

left-hand [left-hand] *adjective.* **1.** on or to the left: *Their house is about half a mile down the street, on the left-hand side.* **2.** of, for, or with the left hand: *a left-hand glove.*

*The **leek** is a national emblem of Wales and is worn on St. David's Day.*

left-hand·ed [left-hand-id] *adjective.* **1.** using the left hand more often or more effectively than the right: *He is a left-handed pitcher.* **2.** done with the left hand: *a left-handed tennis serve.* **3.** intended or made for the left hand: *a left-handed golf club.* **4.** having two meanings; insincere: *His remark that I was looking better than usual was a left-handed compliment.* *adverb.* with or toward the left hand: *She writes left-handed.*

left·o·ver [left-oh-vur] *noun, plural* **leftovers.** uneaten food at the end of a meal: *I ate the cold leftovers from last night's dinner.* *adjective.* unused or uneaten: *The leftover meatloaf was delicious the next day for lunch.*

leg [leg] *noun, plural* **legs. 1.** one of the long parts of the body that are connected to the feet and used for standing and walking. **2.** something resembling the leg of a human or animal: *the legs of a table.* **3.** a particular section of a journey or race: *The first leg of the trip was from New York to Las Vegas.*

le·gal [lee-gul] *adjective.* **1.** having to do with law: *An attorney is a legal representative; Harvard Law School is famous for providing a good legal education.* **2.** permitted or decided by the law: *She has a legal right to build a house on the land.* The fact of something being allowed by law is **legality. —legally,** *adverb.*

LEGENDS

Legends relate the deeds of ordinary people, but often reality is mixed with fantasy. Ancient Greek legends often tell stories about the amazing exploits of heroes. These ancient "supermen" were mortals but were helped by the gods and goddesses, and sometimes even had a god for a parent. Heracles (called Hercules in Roman legends) had to complete twelve difficult tasks. In one of these he had to kill a serpent with 100 heads and pick three golden apples of eternal youth from the tree the monster guarded.

Heracles and the 100-headed serpent

leg·end ▲ [lej-und] *noun, plural* **legends. 1.** *Literature.* an old, well-known story that is passed down through the years, and that is often considered to be true even though it cannot be proved: *the legend of King Arthur.* **2.** someone who is famous and admired for his or her ability: *Babe Ruth was a baseball legend.*

leg·end·ar·y [lej-un-*der*-ee] *adjective.* **1.** relating to a legend: *The legendary heroes of the Greek myths.* **2.** very famous and admired: *Billie Holliday was a legendary jazz singer.*

leg·gings [leg-ingz] *plural noun.* a pair of leather or canvas trousers worn over other clothes to protect the legs: *The soldiers wore leggings while marching in the snow.*

leg·i·ble [lej-uh-bul] *adjective.* able to be read easily: *The student wrote in big, clear letters so that his writing would be legible.* **—legibly,** *adverb.*

le·gion [lee-jun] *noun, plural* **legions. 1.** *History.* a division of the ancient Roman army consisting of 3,000 to 6,000 foot soldiers. **2.** a large group of soldiers who form part of an army: *the French Foreign Legion.* **3.** a very large number of people or things: *She has a legion of friends.*

leg·is·late [lej-is-*late*] *verb,* **legislated, legislating.** *Government.* to make a law about something: *The government promised to legislate against drugs.*

leg·is·la·tion [lej-is-*lay*-shun] *noun, plural* **legislations.** *Government.* **1.** the action of making laws: *In the U.S. the Senate and House of Representatives are responsible for legislation.* **2.** a law or set of laws: *The legislation on discrimination is very important.*

leg·is·la·tive [lej-is-*lay*-tiv] *adjective. Government.* **1.** of or having to do with making laws: *The City Council has a legislative role.* **2.** having the function or power to make laws: *a legislative body of the government.*

leg·is·la·tor [lej-is-*lay*-tur] *noun, plural* **legislators.** *Government.* **1.** someone who has the power to make laws. **2.** someone who is a member of a group or body that has the power to make laws.

leg·is·la·ture ▼ [lej-is-*lay*-chur] *noun, plural* **legislatures.** *Government.* an organization or body that has the power to make laws: *The state legislature of California.*

le·git·i·mate [luh-*jit*-uh-mit] *adjective.* **1.** according to the law: *She runs a legitimate business.* **2.** reasonable or acceptable: *He did not have a legitimate excuse for not doing his homework.* The fact of being lawful or right is **legitimacy. —legitimately,** *adverb.*

leg·ume [leg-*yoom*] *noun, plural* **legumes.** *Biology.* a plant that has its seeds in a pod, such as peas and beans.

The **legislature** *of the Canadian province of Saskatchewan is in Regina, the capital city.*

lei ◀ [lay] *noun, plural* **leis.** a wreath of flowers for the neck or head, often worn in the Hawaiian Islands. 🔊 A different word with the same sound is **lay.**

lei·sure [lee-zhur] *noun.* time that is free from work or other duties. *adjective.* not occupied by work or other duties: *I spend my leisure time at the beach.* Something done in a relaxed way is said to be **leisurely.**

lem·on [lem-un] *noun, plural* **lemons.** an oval-shaped fruit with a thick, yellow skin and sour taste. *adjective.* made of or with lemon: *I had a lemon tart for morning tea.*

lem·on·ade [lem-uh-nade] *noun, plural* **lemonades.** a drink made from a mixture of lemon juice, sugar, and water.

lend [lend] *verb,* **lent, lending. 1.** to give something to someone for a period of time on condition that will be returned: *I lent my bike to my sister.* **2.** to give an amount of money to someone for a period of time on the condition that it is paid back with interest: *The bank is lending me money for a deposit on an apartment.* **3.** to add quality to something: *Fresh flowers lend a bright and cheerful feeling to the room.* Someone or something that lends money, such as a bank, is known as a **lender.**

length [lengkth] *noun, plural* **lengths. 1.** the distance from one end of something to the other: *The length of the swimming pool is 40 feet and the width is 17 feet.* **2.** amount of time; duration: *Hollywood movies typically have a length of about two hours.* **3.** a piece or portion of something: *a length of string.* **4.** the extent someone goes to in order to achieve something: *She went to great lengths to get to the bottom of the mystery.*

length·en [lengk-thun] *verb,* **lengthened, lengthening.** to make or become longer: *Mom lengthened my skirt because she thought it was too short.*

length·wise [lengkth-wize] *adverb; adjective.* in the direction or position of the longest side. *She cut the paper lengthwise.*

length·y [lengk-thee] *adjective.* continuing for a long time: *The train accident is causing lengthy delays for commuters.*

len·i·ent [leen-yunt or lee-nee-unt] *adjective.* not severe or strict: *I have lenient parents who let me go out a lot on the weekends.* The quality of being lenient is **leniency.** —**leniently,** *adverb.*

lens [lenz] *noun, plural* **lenses. 1.** a piece of curved glass or other clear material that bends rays of light so that objects appear larger, smaller, closer, or farther away. **2.** the part of the eye behind the pupil that focuses rays of light on the retina so that you can see things clearly.

lent [lent] *verb.* the past tense and past participle of LEND.

Lent [lent] *noun. Religion.* in Christianity, the forty weekdays leading up to Easter, during which time many Christians fast, pray, and repent.

> The word **Lent** goes back to a phrase meaning "longer days." The season of Lent is in the spring, when the days begin to get longer after the shorter days of winter.

len·til [len-tul] *noun, plural* **lentils.** a small, round, bean-like seed that is cooked and eaten.

leop·ard ▼ [lep-urd] *noun, plural* **leopards.** a large animal of the cat family that lives in Africa and Southern Asia. Leopards have yellow fur with black spots and are ferocious.

le·o·tard [lee-uh-tard] *noun, plural* **leotards.** a one-piece skintight garment that is worn for dancing or exercising.

> The word **leopard** comes from a combination of two words that were used for other large members of the cat family. The word *leo* was used for the lion, and the word *pard* meant a panther. So the leopard was called a "lion-panther," because it was thought to be like both of these animals.

Leopards are excellent climbers and spend a lot of their time in trees.

lep·re·chaun [lep-ruh-kon] *noun, plural* **leprechauns.** *Literature.* in Irish folklore, a magical creature in the form of a little man.

lep·ro·sy [lep-ruh-see] *noun. Medicine.* an infectious disease that attacks the nerves, skin, and muscles. Leprosy can cause ulcers, deformities, and the loss of sensation in parts of the body. A person who has leprosy can be called a **leper.**

less [less] *adjective.* not as great in size, amount or importance: *I have spent less money this week than I did last week.* *adverb.* to a smaller degree: *She is less happy in her new school than in her old one.* *noun.* a smaller amount: *I eat less now than I used to.* *preposition.* with the deduction of; minus: *The shoes cost $40, less the $10 deposit you have already paid.*

To be strictly correct, **less** should only be used for things that do not express a number, as in *less* money, *less* weight, or *less* time. *Fewer* should be used for things that can be counted, as in "There were *fewer* people there tonight than at last week's meeting." Though it would not sound correct to say, "There were *less* people there," there are many other expressions that do use *less* with numbers, such as "Give your answer in 25 words or *less.*"

-less a suffix that means: **1.** lacking something; without: *tasteless* means lacking or without taste. **2.** unable to be treated or affected in a certain way: *ceaseless* means without stopping.

less·en [less-un] *verb*, **lessened, lessening.** to make or become smaller; reduce: *The medicine will lessen the pain of my headache.*
🔊 A different word with the same sound is **lesson.**

less·er [less-ur] *adjective.* being smaller in size, number, degree, or importance: *The car dealer had asked for a lot of money, but we negotiated him down to a lesser sum.adverb.* to a smaller degree; less: *a lesser-known song of the 1960s.*

les·son [less-un] *noun, plural* **lessons. 1.** something that you learn or from which you learn; something that is taught: *a math lesson in school.* **2.** a period of time in which a person is taught something: *I have a tennis lesson after school today.* **3.** an experience or event that provides some kind of knowledge and awareness: *The near-miss accident taught me a lesson about crossing roads safely.*
🔊 A different word with the same sound is **lessen.**

let [let] *verb*, **let, letting. 1.** to be willing to have happen; allow or permit: *Mom let me stay up late to watch the movie.* **2.** to allow to come, go, or pass: *Please let the dog inside.* **3.** to cause or make: *I let it be known that I wanted a new bike.* **4.** to rent or hire: *We are letting an apartment for a few months while we renovate our house.*

le·thal [lee-thul] *adjective.* causing death: *His death was caused by a lethal dose of drugs.* —**lethally,** *adverb.*

let's [lets] the shortened form of "let us."

let·ter [let-ur] *noun, plural* **letters. 1.** a symbol that represents a sound in language: *the letter K.* **2.** a written or printed message from one person to another: *I wrote a letter to my friend in Germany.* **3.** an emblem in the shape of the initial of a school that is given to a student as an award.
verb, **lettered, lettering. 1.** to write letters or words on something: *She lettered the envelope very neatly.* **2.** to earn a school letter as an award for outstanding performance: *She lettered in high school volleyball for three consecutive years.*

let·ter·ing [let-ur-ing] *noun.* letters that have been written or drawn in a particular color or style: *He gave me a beautiful card with Chinese lettering.*

let·tuce [let-is] *noun, plural* **lettuces.** a round vegetable with large, thin, green leaves that are eaten raw.

leu·ke·mi·a [loo-kee-mee-uh] *noun, plural* **leukemias.** *Medicine.* a type of cancer of the blood in which the body produces too many white blood cells.

lev·ee ▶ [lev-ee] *noun, plural* **levees. 1.** an embankment built along a river to prevent flooding. **2.** a landing place or pier on a river for boats to dock.
🔊 A different word with the same sound is **levy.**

The word **levee** comes from a French word meaning "raise" or "rise up." The idea is that in a levee along a river, the ground is raised up above the usual level, so that water will not overflow onto the nearby land.

lev·el [lev-ul] *adjective.* **1.** having a flat, horizontal surface: *We have a level front lawn.* **2.** having the same height: *The legs of the table need to be level for it to stand firm.*
noun, plural **levels. 1.** the height of something: *The water level in the dam has risen because of the heavy rain.* **2.** a position in a system that has differing ranks of importance: *The book was written to be read at the third-grade level.* **3.** a floor in a building: *Our school library has two levels.* **4.** a tool used by carpenters for checking that a surface is flat. It is a liquid-filled tube containing an air bubble that moves into the middle of the tube when the surface is flat.
verb, **leveled, leveling. 1.** to make flat: *The workers leveled the wet cement before it set.* **2.** to destroy or knock something down to the ground: *The explosion leveled the building.*
• **on the level.** honest and legal: *Is this deal on the level?*

lev·er [lev-ur *or* lee-vur] *noun, plural* **levers. 1.** a stiff rod or bar that can be used to lift heavy objects or pry things open: *The burglar used a crowbar as a lever to pry open the window.* **2.** a bar or handle on a machine or piece of equipment that is moved to operate it: *The worker controlled the crane with two levers.*

lev·er·age [lev-rij *or* lev-ur-ij] *noun.* **1.** the action, power, or use of a lever. **2.** the power to influence others and make them do what you want: *Her high position in the company gives her a lot of leverage.*

lev·y [lev-ee] *verb*, **levied, levying.** to establish, impose, or collect by legal authority: *The government plans to levy more taxes on alcohol.*
noun, plural **levies.** a fee or a tax: *The increased levy on cigarettes surprised many people.*
🔊 A different word with the same sound is **levee.**

lex·i·cog·ra·pher [lex-uh-kog-ruh-fur] *noun, plural* **lexicographers.** *Language.* a person who is an expert on dictionaries or whose job is to write or compile a dictionary. The activity or job of writing dictionaries is **lexicography.**

li·a·bil·i·ty [lye-uh-bil-uh-tee] *noun, plural* **liabilities. 1.** *Law.* the fact of being legally responsible for something: *She accepted liability for the car accident.* **2.** someone or something that is likely to cause trouble: *Our old car is a real liability on long journeys.* **3.** money that a person owes; debts.

li·a·ble [lye-bul *or* lye-uh-bul] *adjective.* **1.** *Law.* having a legal responsibility for something or someone: *The tenant is liable for all the damage he caused to the rented apartment.* **2.** very probable; likely: *I am liable to fail this test if I don't study.*

Levees *have been used to control the Huang River in China for more than 2,200 years.*

*The Statue of Liberty was given to the United States by France as a monument to the love of **liberty** that both nations shared.*

li·ar [lye-ur] *noun, plural* **liars.** someone who tells lies.

lib·er·al [lib-rul *or* lib-ur-ul] *adjective.* **1.** *Government.* favoring progress and reform for more personal freedom and prosperity and the sharing of wealth and power in society: *The liberal candidate was polling well in the elections.* **2.** more than enough; generous: *I receive a liberal allowance from my parents each week.* **3.** not strict; broad: *The movie is a liberal adaptation of a historical novel.* **4.** open-minded and tolerant. *noun, plural* **liberals.** a person with liberal ideas or opinions. —**liberally,** *adverb.*

lib·er·ate [lib-uh-*rate*] *verb,* **liberated, liberating.** to set free: *Troops were sent in to liberate the people from the enemy.* A **liberator** is a person who sets others free. —**liberation,** *noun.*

lib·er·tar·i·an [lib-ur-tare-ee-un] *noun, plural* **libertarians.** a person who believes the government should have as small a role as possible in the way that people speak, act, and conduct their business affairs. **Libertarianism** is the belief that people should be free to think, speak, and act as they please as long as they do not break the law.

lib·er·ty ▲ [lib-ur-tee] *noun, plural* **liberties. 1.** the state of being free to think, speak, and act as one pleases: *The U.S. Constitution guards the liberty of the American people.* **2.** freedom from foreign rule or the rule of another; independence: *The American colonists fought the War of Independence to gain liberty from British rule.* **3.** free time granted to a person away from work or duty: *The sailors looked forward to their liberty in Paris.* The rights of citizens of a country to think, speak, and act as they please as long as they do not break the law are called **civil liberties.**
• **at liberty. 1.** not imprisoned or held captive; free: *The bank robbers are still at liberty, but the police say they are closing in on them.* **2.** being permitted; allowed: *The school principal was not at liberty to reveal the names of the prizewinners before the award ceremony.*

li·brar·i·an [lye-brer-ee-un] *noun, plural* **librarians.** a person who is in charge of or works in a library.

li·brar·y [lye-brer-ee] *noun, plural* **libraries. 1.** a collection of books, magazines, newspapers, and other written records. Many libraries also have collections of records in other forms, such as photographs, recorded music, films, videotape, and DVDs, and information stored on computers. **2.** a place where such a collection is kept for use but not for sale: *the New York Public Library.*

lice [lise] *noun.* the plural of LOUSE.

li·cense [lye-suns] *noun, plural* **licenses.** a card, document, plate, or tag showing that someone has permission from an authority to do, own, or use something: *a driver's license; a marriage license.* *verb,* **licensed, licensing.** to give or have a license to or for someone or something: *My uncle is licensed to work as an electrician.*

li·chen [lye-ken] *noun, plural* **lichens.** a plant made up of an alga and a fungus growing together that is found on surfaces such as rocks, trees, walls, and roofs.

lick [lik] *verb,* **licked, licking. 1.** to pass the tongue over something: *The dog licked his sore paw.* **2.** to pass over or touch lightly, like a tongue: *Flames licked at the roof of the barn; My cat looks cute when she licks her milk from a bowl.* **3.** to do better than; defeat: *Their team beat us at hockey last season, but this season we think we'll lick them.* *noun, plural* **licks. 1.** the act of licking. **2.** a place where salt occurs naturally or has been placed and where animals go to lick it. **3.** a small quantity: *He was so tired that he didn't do a lick of work all day.*

lic·o·rice [lik-ur-ish *or* lik-rish] *noun.* **1.** a plant with a sweet-tasting root that is used in medicines and candy. **2.** a candy, usually black, flavored with licorice.

lid [lid] *noun, plural* **lids. 1.** a cover that can be removed: *If you don't put the lid back on the honey jar, the ants will get in.* **2.** the upper or lower fold of skin that can be closed to cover the eye; eyelid.

lie¹ [lye] *verb,* **lay, lain, lying. 1.** to be in, or to move into, a flat or resting position on a supporting surface: *He suddenly felt dizzy and had to lie on the bed.* **2.** to rest flat on a surface: *I love to lie on the beach and talk with my friends.* **3.** to stay, or be kept in, a certain state or place: *The famous painting was found after lying hidden in an attic for many years.* **4.** to be situated: *Our town lies at the foot of the mountains.* **5.** to be found; occur: *The electrical fault lies in the wiring system itself.* *noun, plural* **lies.** the position or direction in which something lies: *The golfer examined the lie of the ball on the putting green before making his shot.*
🔊 A different word with the same sound is **lye.**

lie² [lye] *noun, plural* **lies.** a statement someone makes knowing that it is not true: *The boy said that he found the wallet in the alley, but it was a lie.* *verb,* **lied, lying.** to make a statement knowing that it is not true; tell a lie: *When asked where she had been all day, the girl lied and said she had been visiting a sick friend.*
🔊 A different word with the same sound is **lye.**

lieu·ten·ant [loo-ten-unt] *noun, plural* **lieutenants. 1.** an officer rank in the armed forces. In the military (the U.S. Army, the Marine Corps, and the Air Force), there are two ranks of lieutenant. A **first lieutenant** ranks just below a captain. A **second lieutenant** has the lowest officer rank. In the U.S. Navy and the Coast Guard, there are also two ranks of lieutenant. A lieutenant ranks just below a lieutenant commander. A lieutenant junior grade has the lowest officer rank. **2.** a rank in the fire or police department just below a captain.

In British English **lieutenant** is spoken with the first sound as "lef" rather than "loo" as in American English. This is because there was an older form of the word that was spelled **lef-** and not **lieu-**. The "lef" pronunciation has lasted even though the word has not been spelled this way for hundreds of years.

life [life] *noun, plural* **lives. 1.** the quality that sets plants and animals apart from non-living objects such as rocks and water and enables them to grow, reproduce, and keep changing until they die. **2.** the state of having this quality: *The man risked his life when he dived in the water to rescue the drowning child.* **3.** a living person: *Many lives were lost in the storm.* **4.** living things: *The forest swarms with insect life.*
5. the period from birth to death, or from birth to the present or the present to death: *My great-aunt's letters show that she had a fascinating life.* **6.** the period during which something lasts or works: *These batteries have a very long life.* **7.** a story of someone's life; biography: *The last book I read was the life of Abraham Lincoln.* **8.** the strength to be active; energy; vigor: *The children were full of life, laughing and shouting.*

life·boat ◀ [life-*bote*] *noun, plural* **lifeboats.** a boat launched from shore to rescue people in danger at sea. It is also often carried on a ship to be used in an emergency.

Lifeboats are often inflatable and carry essential survival needs, such as food and water.

life cycle ▼ *Biology.* the series of stages a living thing passes through from the very earliest form, such as an egg, of one individual to the same stage in its offspring. The life cycle of animals includes birth, development, reproduction, growing old, and death.

life expectancy *Medicine.* the period of time a particular person or a particular group of people can expect to live. This is based on such things as heredity, health, living conditions, and the average period for which people in similar circumstances live.

life·guard [life-*gard*] *noun, plural* **lifeguards.** someone who works at a place where people swim and whose job is to rescue and give first aid to swimmers who get into difficulties.

life jacket a sleeveless jacket made of material that keeps a person afloat in water. It is a type of life preserver.

life·like [life-*like*] *adjective.* looking very like a real, living person or thing: *The painting of a cat was so lifelike that I almost wanted to pet it.*

life·line [life-*line*] *noun, plural* **lifelines. 1.** a line, such as a rope, that people can hang on to for safety or to be rescued. **2.** something that is very important in helping a person to survive or to get through a difficult situation: *When I was ill and had to stay in bed, being able to call my friends on the phone was my lifeline.*

life·long [life-*long*] *adjective.* lasting or continuing throughout life: *My grandmother had a lifelong interest in butterflies.*

life pre·ser·ver a device designed to save a person from drowning by keeping him or her afloat. A life preserver is filled with air or made from material that floats. It can take the form of a ring, a vest, or a belt.

life span *Health.* the average length of life of a person living in a particular society. This average is calculated from official records kept over many years showing how old people were when they died of natural causes.

life·style the particular way in which a person, group, or society lives: *People who live near the beach often have a very relaxed lifestyle.*

life·time [life-*time*] *noun, plural* **lifetimes. 1.** the period of time for which someone or something is alive: *There will be many changes in computer technology in my lifetime.* **2.** the period of time that something works or lasts: *These materials are guaranteed for the lifetime of the house.*

lift [lift] *verb,* **lifted, lifting. 1.** to raise off the ground into the air; pick up: *Please lift that chair so that I can sweep underneath it.* **2.** to rise from the ground into the air; go upward: *The spacecraft lifted off the launch pad.* **3.** to move upward and spread out or disappear: *We'll start off as soon as the fog lifts.*
noun, plural **lifts. 1.** the act of lifting or process of being lifted. **2.** a free ride in someone else's vehicle: *One of Mom's friends gave us a lift to the airport in their car.* **3.** a raising of the spirits: *It gave me a lift when I got such a good mark for my essay.*

lift-off [lift-*of*] *noun, plural* **lift-offs.** the act of a spacecraft or rocket taking off or rising vertically from the ground into the air.

In the **life cycle** *of a dragonfly, young dragonflies live under the water for up to five years before emerging as adults.*

Lightning bugs produce light from special organs in the abdomen.

lig·a·ment [lig-uh-munt] *noun, plural* **ligaments.** *Biology.* a strong, flexible band of tissue that connects bones or holds organs in place in the body.

light¹ [lite] *noun.*
1. *Science.* a form of radiation or energy that stimulates the organs of sight and makes things visible. The Sun gives off light. 2. something that provides light or brightness, such as an electric lamp, a candle, or a flashlight: *Turn on the light before you go downstairs to the basement.* 3. a flame or spark for setting fire to something, or a device that provides a flame or spark: *She struck a light and set fire to the logs in the grate.* 4. knowledge or understanding that comes from certain information: *The research shed new light on the causes of the disease.* 5. the way someone thinks about something: *After I heard her sing so beautifully at the concert, I saw Melissa in a different light.*
verb, **lit** *or* **lighted, lighting. 1.** to begin to burn or to start something burning: *We'll light a fire to keep warm.* **2.** to put lights on; provide with light: *A large lamp is used to light the dining room.* **3.** to make or become bright: *My friend Ryan's face lit up when his mom said he could come on vacation with us.*
adjective, **lighter, lightest. 1.** provided with light; not dark: *It gets light earlier in summer than winter.* **2.** not dark in color; pale: *light green.*

light² [lite] *adjective,* **lighter, lightest.**
1. having little weight; not heavy: *Is that knapsack light enough for you to carry all day?* 2. small in amount or force: *light traffic; a light breeze; Let's walk to the park to get some light exercise.* 3. describing a quick, nimble action; graceful: *She ran down the stairs with a light step.* 4. not serious; entertaining: *light reading, such as popular mystery stories.*
—**lightly,** *adverb;* **lightness,** *noun.*

light·en¹ [lite-un] *verb,* **lightened, lightening.** to make or become lighter or brighter: *I pushed back the curtains to lighten the room.*

light·en² [lite-un] *verb,* **lightened, lightening.**
1. to make or become less heavy, easier, or less of a burden: *The truck driver decided to lighten his load and left some boxes behind for a second trip.* 2. to make or become more cheerful; ease: *The mood among the students lightened when they heard that their classmate was out of danger.*

light·er [lite-ur] *noun, plural* **lighters.** a mechanical device for lighting cigarettes, cigars, and other items.

light-heart·ed [lite-har-tid] *adjective.* free from worry; cheerful; carefree: *The students were light-hearted on the last day of school before vacation.*
—**light-heartedly,** *adverb;* —**light-heartedness,** *noun.*

light·house ▼ [lite-hous] *noun, plural* **lighthouses.** a tower or other structure with a powerful light at the top to warn or guide ships at sea. Lighthouses are built on or near the shore, often in areas that are dangerous to ships.

light·ing [lite-ing] *noun.* the arrangement or method of lights in a room, building, street, or other area: *In earlier times, street lighting was provided by gas lamps.*

light·ning ▶ [lite-ning] *noun.* a flash of bright light or a sudden lighting up of the sky, produced by electricity in the atmosphere moving between clouds or between clouds and the ground.

lightning bug ▲ a small beetle that flies at night and produces flashes of bright light in order to attract a mate; also called a firefly.

lightning rod a metal rod fixed to the roof of a building or the mast of a ship and connected via a wire or cable with the earth or water below to help prevent damage from lightning. The rod provides a path down which the electric charge can travel until it is safely discharged.

*The **lighthouse** on the island of Pharos in Egypt, built in the third century BC, was one of the tallest buildings in the world for many centuries.*

A B C D E F G H I J K L M N O P Q R S T U V W X Y Z

LIGHTNING

Lightning occurs when there is a buildup of opposing electrical charges inside a thundercloud. The charges are strongly attracted to each other. Eventually the attraction becomes so great that the electricity leaps from one area to another. We see this as a bright flash or a jagged white line. There are three common kinds of lightning: cloud to air, cloud to cloud, and cloud to ground.

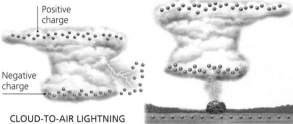

Positive charge

Negative charge

CLOUD-TO-AIR LIGHTNING
Electricity moves from the cloud to the oppositely charged air.

CLOUD-TO-GROUND LIGHTNING
If there is a positive charge on the ground, lightning may strike downward from the negatively charged base of the cloud.

CLOUD-TO-CLOUD LIGHTNING
Lightning may jump within a cloud or between opposite charges in adjacent clouds.

light year *Science.* a unit of length used in astronomy equal to the distance that light travels in one year. Light travels at a speed of about 186,000 miles per second, so it travels about 5,880,000,000,000 (almost 6 million million miles) in one year. Distances to stars are often measured in light years.

like¹ [like] *preposition.* **1.** the same as another in some way; similar to: *My friend Sam has a fishing rod just like mine, except that it's a different color.* **2.** in the same or a similar manner as: *I told my little sister to stop acting like a baby.* **3.** such as: *The store sold a few basic items, like milk and bread.* **4.** in a suitable state or condition for: *Do you feel like playing basketball after school? It looks like a storm is on the way.*
adjective. being the same or nearly the same as: *The twin brothers look the same and also have like personalities.*
• **and the like.** and similar things: *By water sports I mean swimming, surfing, snorkeling, and the like.*

In strictly correct writing, the word **like** should not be used to mean "for example" in giving a list of things. You would write, "The pond is home to many birds such as (not like) ducks, swans, geese, loons, and egrets." Since like also means "similar to," if you wrote "The pond is home to many birds like ducks… " this could give the idea that you are talking about some other kind of bird that is similar to a duck.

like² [like] *verb,* **liked, liking. 1.** to feel good about; be fond of; enjoy: *to like pizza; to like playing soccer; to like spending time with friends.* **2.** to choose to have; want or wish for: *I'd like a pound of hamburger, please; We'd like you to join us for dinner.* **3.** to think of in a certain way; judge: *How do you like that TV show?*
noun, plural **likes.** the things someone enjoys or prefers: *I have strong likes and dislikes in music.*

-like a suffix that means similar to or like: *childlike* means like a child.

like·a·ble easy to like; pleasant; agreeable: *a likeable person with many friends.* This word is also spelled **likable.**

like·li·hood [like-lee-hud] *noun.* the state of being probable or likely; probability: *There is little likelihood of our team winning now that our best pitcher is injured.*

like·ly [like-lee] *adjective,* **likelier, likeliest. 1.** apparently true; believable: *The heavy traffic is the likely reason they have been delayed.* **2.** probably going to happen or be true: *The rope is likely to break at any moment.* **3.** apparently suitable; promising: *This is a likely spot to put up our tent.*
adverb. most probably: *We will likely finish the project by the end of the week.*

like·ness [like-nis] *noun, plural* **likenesses.**
1. the state or quality of being like; similarity; resemblance: *Everyone comments on the likeness between my dad and my brother.*
2. a picture, especially a portrait; representation: *The sketch my sister did of her friend is a very a good likeness.*

like·wise [like-wize] *adverb.* in the same or a similar way; similarly: *Watch how the coach stands to hit the ball and then try to do likewise.*

lik·ing [like-ing] *noun, plural* **likings.**
a fondness or preference or taste for: *All my friends have a liking for computer games.*

li·lac ▲ [lye-luk *or* lye-lak] *noun.*
1. a shrub with large clusters of sweet-smelling pink, purple, or white flowers. **2.** a pinkish-purple color.
adjective. having a pinkish-purple color.

Lilac *is popular with gardeners for its perfume and attractive flowers.*

lily

lil·y [lil-ee] *noun, plural* **lilies. 1.** a type of plant that grows from a bulb and produces a large, trumpet-shaped flower on a long stem. **2.** any plant that looks similar to a lily, such as the WATER LILY.

lily of the valley ▶ a plant that grows from a bulb and produces clusters of tiny, bell-shaped white flowers on a stalk. The flowers hang down as though they are drooping, and have a strong, sweet fragrance.

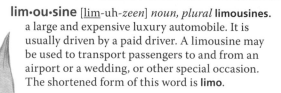

li·ma bean a bean plant native to tropical America with flat, pale green or whitish seeds that are cooked and eaten. The seeds are also called lima beans.

limb [lim] *noun, plural* **limbs. 1.** any of the parts of an animal that grow in pairs (such as an arm, leg, wing, or flipper) and are distinct from the head and trunk. Limbs are used in moving and grasping. **2.** a large branch of a tree: *The lowest limbs of a tree are usually the biggest and strongest.*

lime[1] [lime] *noun, plural* **limes.** a citrus fruit similar to a lemon but smaller and rounder, with a yellowish-green skin.

lime[2] [lime] *noun. Chemistry.* a white, powdery substance made by burning limestone, which is made up of calcium and oxygen. Lime is used in making plaster and cement and as a fertilizer.

lim·er·ick [lim-rik *or* lim-ur-ik] *noun, plural* **limericks.** *Literature.* a funny poem of five lines that follows a set pattern. The first, second, and fifth lines rhyme. The third and fourth lines are shorter and also rhyme. An example is: A minor league pitcher, McDowell/Pitched an egg at a batter named Owl/They cried "Get a hit!"/But it hatched in the mitt/And the umpire called it a fowl.

> **Limerick** is a large city in the western part of Ireland. The humorous poem known as a limerick takes its name from this city. It is said that this comes from a custom of many years ago in which one person in a group would recite a poem of this kind, and then at the end of the poem the rest of the group would say, "Will you all come up to Limerick?"

lime·stone ▶ [lime-*stone*] *noun.* a grayish rock that is made up mainly of calcium carbonate. Limestone is used in building and is burned to produce lime.

lim·it [lim-it] *noun, plural* **limits.** a line, point, or level where something ends or must end; boundary: *Students must stay within the limits of the school grounds during certain hours.* Something that is kept within a certain line, point, or level is **limited.** Something that has no end is **limitless.** *verb,* **limited, limiting.** to keep within certain limits: *I've decided to limit the time I spend playing computer games.*

lim·i·ta·tion [lim-uh-tay-shun] *noun, plural* **limitations.** the act of limiting or the fact of being limited: *Credit cards have a limitation on how much you can charge to them.*

lim·ou·sine [lim-uh-*zeen*] *noun, plural* **limousines.** a large and expensive luxury automobile. It is usually driven by a paid driver. A limousine may be used to transport passengers to and from an airport or a wedding, or other special occasion. The shortened form of this word is **limo.**

> An area of central France known as Limousin gives its name to the car called a limousine. The word **limousine** comes from the shape of a hood or cape often worn by people in this area; the hood of a limousine automobile was thought to look like this type of clothing.

limp[1] [limp] *verb,* **limped, limping.** to walk in a jerky or uneven way because of an injury, or to walk slowly or with difficulty: *I'm limping because I twisted my ankle. noun, plural* **limps.** a limping or lame walk.

limp[2] [limp] *adjective.* not stiff or firm; having no energy: *The flowers in the vase are limp and starting to smell stale.*

Lin·coln's Birthday ▶ *History.* a holiday on February 12 observed in some states to celebrate Abraham Lincoln's birthday. In most states, Abraham Lincoln's birthday is celebrated as part of PRESIDENTS' DAY.

The birth of Abraham Lincoln, on February 12, 1809, is celebrated each year on **Lincoln's Birthday.**

line[1] [line] *noun, plural* **lines. 1.** a straight, thin mark on a piece of paper or other surface: *lines on a paper to write on; a white line down the middle of a road.* **2.** a mark like this on the skin. **3.** a long thin piece of string, paper, or the like: *a telephone line.* **4.** a limit or boundary marked by as if by a line: *the property line between two houses; the finish line*

The Mulu caves in Malaysia are a large underground cave system formed from **limestone.**

of a race. **5.** a row of words or letters going straight across a page. **6.** a group of people or things arranged side by side or one behind the other: *a line of people waiting to buy movie tickets.* **7. lines.** words spoken in a play, movie, TV show, or the like. **8.** a system of public transportation over a regular route: *a city bus line.* **9.** a type of goods for sale: *The store has just put out the new spring line of clothes.* **10.** in football, the group of players who stand at the line of scrimmage at the start of a play, or the place where they stand. The offense must have seven players on the line; the defense can choose how many to have but will typically have four, three, or five.
verb, **lined, lining. 1.** to mark with a line or lines: *Paper is often lined for writing.* **2.** to arrange in a line; form into a line: *The students will line up at the door to go out for recess; A crowd lined the streets as the parade passed by.* **3.** in baseball, to hit the ball hard so that it goes in a straight line: *The batter lined a single to left field.*

line² [line] *verb,* **lined, lining. 1.** to cover the inner surface of: *I lined my drawers with colored paper.* **2.** to form a lining or covering for: *Huge paintings lined the walls of the hotel's dining room.*

lin·e·ar [lin-ee-ur] *adjective. Mathematics.* having to do with lines or length. Inches, feet, yards, miles, meters, and kilometers are examples of linear measurements.

line·back·er [line-bak-ur] *noun, plural* **linebackers.** in football, a player on the defensive team whose position is close behind the linemen, in back of the line of scrimmage.

line·man [line-mun] *noun, plural* **linemen.** in football, a player whose position is on the line of scrimmage at the start of a play.

lin·en [lin-un] *noun, plural* **linens. 1.** a strong cloth woven from flax. **2. linens.** household articles that were often made of linen in earlier times. Sheets, tablecloths, and napkins are called linens, even though today they may be made of cotton or some other fabric.
adjective. made of linen.

line of scrimmage in football, an imaginary line reaching from side to side on the field, marking the spot where the previous play ended. The two teams will set up on either side of the line of scrimmage to start the next play.

lin·er¹ ▲ [line-ur] *noun, plural* **liners.** a ship or airplane that carries passengers and sometimes cargo from one place to another along regular long-distance routes according to a schedule.

lin·er² [line-ur] *noun, plural* **liners.** a layer of material used to cover an inner surface. A liner can usually be removed.

lin·ger [ling-gur] *verb,* **lingered, lingering.** to be slow to leave a place or to stop doing something, usually because you are enjoying it and do not wish to leave or stop. Someone or something that is slow to leave or disappear is described as **lingering**: *There was a lingering smell of paint in the room.*

lin·gui·ne [ling-gwee-nee] *noun.* a kind of pasta that is in long, flat, narrow, thin strips.

lin·guis·tics [ling-gwis-tiks] *noun. Language.* the study of speech and language, and the way in which sounds and words combine and change to create meaning. A person who studies linguistics is a **linguist.**

lin·ing [lye-ning] *noun, plural* **linings.** a material or substance that is attached to or covers the inner surface of something: *The inside of this jewelry box has a soft velvet lining.*

link [lingk] *noun, plural* **links. 1.** a part of a chain that is attached to two other similar parts. Links hold a chain together. **2.** something that provides a connection: *A mutual interest in stamp collecting is a strong link between Eric and Angus.* **3.** something that connects like a link in a chain, such as joined hands in a circle or line of people. **4.** a part of a Website that allows the user to move directly to another Website.
verb, **linked, linking.** to join together; create a connection: *Telephones and e-mails link people who are sometimes long distances apart.*

linking verb *Language.* a verb that connects two other words or parts of a sentence, but that would not make sense on its own. In the sentence *Margot was here,* "was" is a linking verb. In the sentence *Margot seems tired,* "seems" is a linking verb.

A **linking verb** is so called because it links (joins or connects) the subject in the sentence to a word or words after the verb that tell something about the subject, such as "The bus is late" or "She looks angry." The most common linking verb is "be", which has forms such as be, been, is, are, am, was, and were. Other linking verbs also have this same idea of a state of being, such as seem, appear, or become, or they are "sense" words, such as feel, look, taste, sound, or smell.

li·no·le·um [luh-noh-lee-um] *noun, plural* **linoleums.** a hard, thin, often brightly colored floor covering that consists of a canvas or burlap base with a mixture of linseed oil and wood or cork dust on top.

lin·seed oil a yellow-colored oil obtained from flax seeds that is used in the manufacture of paints, printing ink, varnish, linoleum, and other products.

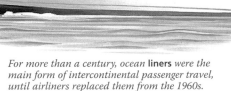

For more than a century, ocean **liners** were the main form of intercontinental passenger travel, until airliners replaced them from the 1960s.

A B C D E F G H I J K **L** M N O P Q R S T U V W X Y Z

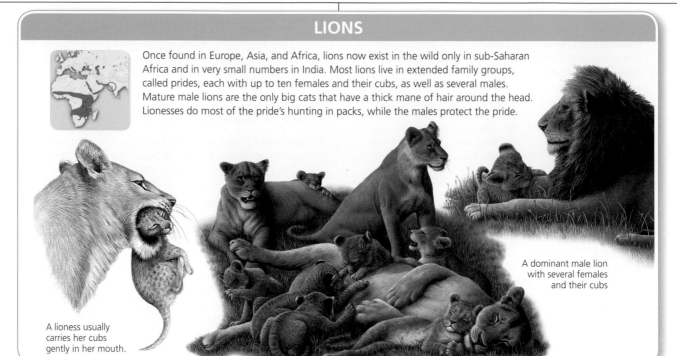

LIONS

Once found in Europe, Asia, and Africa, lions now exist in the wild only in sub-Saharan Africa and in very small numbers in India. Most lions live in extended family groups, called prides, each with up to ten females and their cubs, as well as several males. Mature male lions are the only big cats that have a thick mane of hair around the head. Lionesses do most of the pride's hunting in packs, while the males protect the pride.

A dominant male lion with several females and their cubs

A lioness usually carries her cubs gently in her mouth.

li·on ▲ [lye-un] *noun, plural* **lions.** an animal that is one of the largest members of the cat family and that lives in parts of Africa and Asia. It is strongly built and has short, tawny fur. The male has a prominent brownish mane.

li·on·ess [lye-uh-nis] *noun, plural* **lionesses.** a female lion.

lip [lip] *noun, plural* **lips. 1.** one of the two strips of soft, movable flesh at the front edge of the mouth. **2.** the top edge of a cup, drinking glass, pot, or other container.

lip-read [lip-*reed*] *verb,* **lip-read, lip-reading.** *Language.* to follow what a person is saying by watching the movement of their lips. Many deaf people can lip-read. A person who lip-reads is a **lip-reader.**

lip·stick [lip-*stik*] *noun, plural* **lipsticks.** a waxy substance that is spread on the lips in order to color them.

li·que·fy [lik-wuh-*fye*] *verb,* **liquefied, liquefying. 1.** to change a substance into a liquid. **2.** to become a liquid: *Under extreme heat, some metals will liquefy.*

li·quid [lik-wid] *noun, plural* **liquids.** a substance, such as water, syrup, or oil, that can be poured; a fluid that is not a gas. *adjective.* having the form of a liquid; able to be poured: *Coal is a solid heating fuel—kerosene is a liquid fuel.* The state of being liquid is **liquidity.**

liquid crystal *Science.* a liquid with a molecular structure similar to that of crystals. The use of liquid crystals to show numbers and letters on calculators and some watches and clocks is a **liquid crystal display.**

li·quor [lik-ur] *noun, plural* **liquors.** a kind of alcoholic drink made by heating and then condensing liquid obtained from corn, rye, or other kinds of plant material. Whiskey and brandy are liquors.

lisp [lisp] *noun, plural* **lisps.** a form of speech in which a person uses *th* sounds instead of *s* and *z* sounds. *verb,* **lisped, lisping.** to use *th* sounds instead of *s* and *z* sounds when speaking.

list¹ [list] *noun, plural* **lists.** a set of names, numbers, or other items usually written one under the other: *Dad made a list of all the people we need to buy gifts for at Christmas. verb,* **listed, listing.** to make a list or to include in a list: *Andre listed hiking as one of his favorite pastimes.*

list² ◄ [list] *verb,* **listed, listing.** to lean or tilt sideways: *That pile of books on the table is listing to the left —be careful it doesn't tumble over. noun, plural* **lists.** a sideways lean; tilt.

lis·ten [liss-un] *verb,* **listened, listening.** to hear by paying attention; hear on purpose: *Please listen carefully to the instructions.* Someone who listens is a **listener.**

lit *verb.* the past tense and past participle of LIGHT.

li·ter [lee-tur] *noun, plural* **liters.** a metric unit of volume or capacity. A liter of liquid is just over a quarter of a gallon.

In stormy seas, ancient Phoenician trading ships would **list** *and sometimes capsize.*

lit·er·a·cy [lit-ur-uh-see] *noun. Language.* the capacity to read and write reasonably well: *The level of literacy in the United States is higher than in many other parts of the world.*

lit·er·al·ly [lit-ur-uh-lee] *adverb.* **1.** without changing anything; exactly: *The witness described the events literally as she saw them happen.* **2.** in fact; truly: *Valerie was literally too exhausted to talk after the hockey match.*

Literally means that something really is true according to the exact meaning of what is said. "When he heard that he had won the prize, he *literally* fell out of his chair" would mean that he actually did fall to the floor. However, because this is such a strong word, it is also used for effect to mean the exact opposite of this: "The Senator said, 'Our great Constitution will be *literally* destroyed if this law is in put in effect.'" That would only be *literally* true if the law called for all paper copies of the Constitution to be seized and burned.

lit·er·ate [lit-ur-it] *adjective. Language.* **1.** able to read and write reasonably well. **2.** highly educated; very knowledgeable.

lit·er·a·ture [lit-ur-uh-chur] *noun.* **1.** written works, such as novels, poems, plays, and essays, that are of high quality: *The plays of Shakespeare and the novels of Mark Twain are works of literature.* **2.** any printed matter: *Our teacher gave us some literature about next week's school camp.*

lit·mus test *Chemistry.* **1.** a test that indicates whether a chemical solution is an acid or a base. When a piece of specially treated red paper (**litmus paper**) is placed in a base, it turns blue. When a similar piece of blue paper is placed in an acid, it turns red. **2.** an event that proves or indicates the truth about something: *The marathon race next week will be a real litmus test of the athletes' fitness.*

lit·ter ▶ [lit-ur] *noun, plural* **litters. 1.** items of trash or waste material that are dropped or thrown around: *Careless people sometimes leave litter on the sidewalk.* The act of creating litter is **littering. 2.** a number of young born to an animal at one time: *A lioness usually produces a litter of between two and four cubs.* **3.** a bunk or stretcher used to carry people who are sick, injured, or wounded.
verb, **littered, littering.** to throw or drop trash or waste material onto the ground; make litter.

lit·tle [lit-ul] *adjective,* **less** *or* **lesser** *or* **littler, least** *or* **littlest. 1.** of small size, extent, or amount: *A mouse is a little animal; My uncle is not rich, but he has a little money saved up.* **2.** not long or not far: *Their house is just a little way down this street.*
adverb. not much; slightly: *a little nervous; a little surprised.*
noun. a small or limited amount: *Would you like a little more cake?*

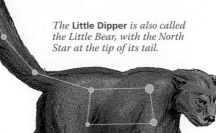

The **Little Dipper** *is also called the Little Bear, with the North Star at the tip of its tail.*

Little Dipper ◀ the seven main stars of the constellation Ursa Minor. These stars appear to be in the shape of a dipper, with the North Star at the end of the handle.

live¹ [liv] *verb,* **lived, living. 1.** to be alive; exist: *We are now living in the twenty-first century.* **2.** to remain alive; survive: *People need food and shelter in order to live.* **3.** to spend one's life or time in a certain way: *to live happily ever after; to live for the moment.* **4.** to have or make one's home: *Our family lives in Dallas.*

live² [live] *adjective.* **1.** not dead; alive: *Andy found a live snake in his house.* **2.** still glowing or burning: *Make sure the fire is out and there are no live coals.* **3.** still able to function; still active: *Years after the war ended, people were still finding live ammunition in the countryside.* **4.** describing something seen as it is occurring; not pre-recorded: *a live interview on radio.*
adverb. in person; not filmed or recorded: *The movie star appeared live at the concert.*

live·li·hood [live-lee-hud] *noun, plural* **livelihoods.** the job or occupation a person has in order to earn money and support themselves: *Medicine is Dr. Jones's livelihood.*

live·ly [live-lee] *adjective,* **livelier, liveliest.** active and energetic; full of life: *We all enjoyed the concert because the music was so lively.*
adverb. in a lively way; energetically: *Step lively!*

liv·er [liv-ur] *noun, plural* **livers. 1.** a large organ in the body of humans and other vertebrate animals that causes changes in the blood and produces bile, which aids the digestion of food. **2.** food made from the liver of certain animals, such as calves.

lives [livez] *noun.* the plural of LIFE.

live·stock [live-stok] *noun.* animals, such as sheep, cattle, horses, and pigs, that are kept on ranches or farms.

The female bandicoot, a marsupial that is native to Australia, produces several **litters** *in a year.*

a b c d e f g h i j k l m n o p q r s t u v w x y z

liv·ing [liv-ing] *adjective.* **1.** not dead; alive: *Many survivors of that shipwreck are still living.* **2.** relating to life: *Living standards in some countries are very harsh.* **3.** still being used; existing now: *The gods of the ancient Greeks and Romans are no longer part of any living religions.*
noun, plural **livings. 1.** the quality or fact of life. **2.** means of support; income: *Samantha's mother makes a very good living as an engineer.* **3.** a manner or form of life: *Some people prefer simple living to having lots of money and possessions.*

liz·ard ▶ [liz-urd] *noun, plural* **lizards.** one of a number of reptiles that have a long, scaly, and often slender body, four short legs, and a tail that tapers off at the end. Iguanas and skinks are lizards.

lla·ma ▼ [lah-muh] *noun, plural* **llamas.** a South American animal that chews its cud. Llamas are related to camels but have no hump. Their shaggy hair is used for making cloth.

load [lode] *noun, plural* **loads. 1.** something large or heavy that is carried or moved: *a load of coal; a load of boxes.* **2.** a quantity or amount that is carried at one time: *We will need two loads of firewood for the rest of the winter.*
verb, **loaded, loading. 1.** to pile up; make a load: *We loaded the shopping bags into the trunk of the car.* **2.** to place something inside a weapon, device, or machine so that it will work: *Joy loaded the batteries into the flashlight.* A person or a machine that loads things is a **loader.**
🔊 A different word with the same sound is **lode.**

loaf¹ [lofe] *noun, plural* **loaves. 1.** a single, fairly large, mass of baked bread. **2.** any food cooked in a single, fairly large piece: *a cheese and spinach loaf.*

loaf² [lofe] *verb,* **loafed, loafing.** to spend time in a lazy way; do little or nothing: *He needs to get a job instead of just loafing around the house all day.*

loaf·er [loh-fur] *noun, plural* **loafers. 1.** an idle, lazy person. **2. loafers.** a type of flat, comfortable shoe without laces, designed for casual wear.

loan [lone] *noun, plural* **loans. 1.** the giving of money for a time with the agreement that it will be paid back: *He got a loan from the bank to buy a new car.* **2.** anything that is lent: *This book does not belong to me—it is a loan from my uncle.*
verb, **loaned, loaning.** to make a loan of: *Jill asked Zoe to loan her ten dollars.*
🔊 A different word with the same sound is **lone.**

loathe [loTHe] *verb,* **loathed, loathing.** to dislike greatly; hate; detest: *I loathe having to do chores after school.* If someone loathes something, they find it **loathesome.**

loaves [lovez] *noun.* the plural of LOAF.

lob [lob] *verb,* **lobbed, lobbing.** to hit or throw something so that it moves in a high arch: *Pat lobbed the ball high over my head.*
noun, plural **lobs.** a hit or throw that causes something to move in a high arch.

lob·by [lob-ee] *noun, plural* **lobbies. 1.** an entrance chamber or reception area at the front of a building: *I met her in the hotel lobby.* **2.** a person or a group of people that attempts to persuade people in government and other positions of authority and power to act in certain ways or to make certain laws.
verb, **lobbied, lobbying.** to attempt to persuade people in authority to act in a certain way: *The airline company lobbied the senator to get a change in laws concerning overseas flights.*

lob·by·ist [lob-ee-ist] *noun, plural* **lobbyists.** *Government.* a person who attempts to persuade people in government and other positions of power and authority to act in certain ways or to pass certain laws. The work that a lobbyist does is called **lobbying.**

A **lobbyist** tries to persuade a lawmaker to act or vote in a certain way. This comes from the idea that such people liked to gather in the lobby outside the room where the lawmakers would meet to vote. They could then stop the lawmakers and talk to them as they either left or went into the meeting room.

lob·ster [lob-stur] *noun, plural* **lobsters.** a saltwater shellfish that has a long tail and five pairs of legs. There is a pair of large claws on each of the two front legs. The flesh of lobsters is used for food. Their shell turns bright red when they are cooked.

lo·cal [loh-kul] *adjective.* **1.** referring to or serving a certain place or a limited area: *Simon and his sister go to the local elementary school.* **2.** making frequent stops along a route: *We catch the local bus to school because it stops near our house.*
noun, plural **locals.** a form of public transportation, such as trains or buses, that stops frequently along the route.
—**locally,** *adverb.*

lo·cal·ity [loh-kal-uh-tee] *noun, plural* **localities.** a place or area and the places close by: *The guide lists all the restaurants in this locality.*

lo·cate [loh-kate] *verb,* **located, locating. 1.** to be in a certain place: *In earlier times, large factories were usually located on or near rivers.* **2.** to place a thing in a certain spot or area: *The new library will be located right next to the high school.* **3.** to find or work out where something is: *The teacher asked the children to locate Peru on the map of South America.*

Llamas were used by the Incas to transport ore from the silver mines in Bolivia.

LIZARDS

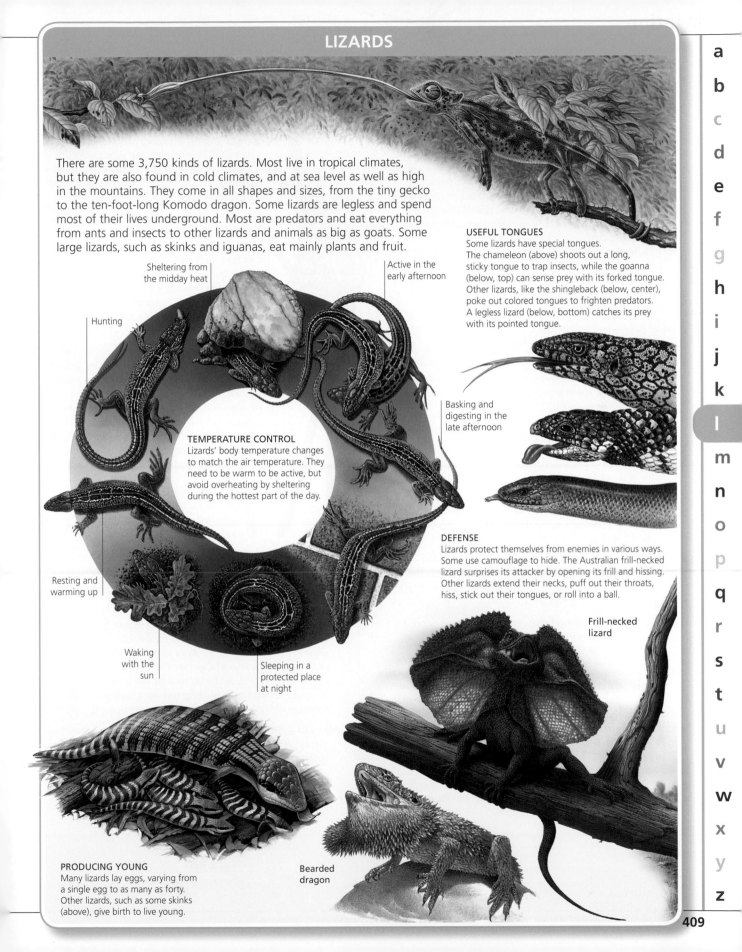

There are some 3,750 kinds of lizards. Most live in tropical climates, but they are also found in cold climates, and at sea level as well as high in the mountains. They come in all shapes and sizes, from the tiny gecko to the ten-foot-long Komodo dragon. Some lizards are legless and spend most of their lives underground. Most are predators and eat everything from ants and insects to other lizards and animals as big as goats. Some large lizards, such as skinks and iguanas, eat mainly plants and fruit.

USEFUL TONGUES

Some lizards have special tongues. The chameleon (above) shoots out a long, sticky tongue to trap insects, while the goanna (below, top) can sense prey with its forked tongue. Other lizards, like the shingleback (below, center), poke out colored tongues to frighten predators. A legless lizard (below, bottom) catches its prey with its pointed tongue.

TEMPERATURE CONTROL

Lizards' body temperature changes to match the air temperature. They need to be warm to be active, but avoid overheating by sheltering during the hottest part of the day.

Sheltering from the midday heat

Active in the early afternoon

Hunting

Basking and digesting in the late afternoon

Resting and warming up

Waking with the sun

Sleeping in a protected place at night

DEFENSE

Lizards protect themselves from enemies in various ways. Some use camouflage to hide. The Australian frill-necked lizard surprises its attacker by opening its frill and hissing. Other lizards extend their necks, puff out their throats, hiss, stick out their tongues, or roll into a ball.

Frill-necked lizard

Bearded dragon

PRODUCING YOUNG

Many lizards lay eggs, varying from a single egg to as many as forty. Other lizards, such as some skinks (above), give birth to live young.

In warm weather locusts form huge swarms and travel widely in search of green plant food.

lo·ca·tion [loh-<u>kay</u>-shun] *noun, plural* **locations. 1.** the fact of where something is; position: *This muddy field is a poor location for a camp site.* **2.** the placing of something in a certain spot or area. **3.** the finding of something: *The police are responsible for the location of the stolen goods.*

lock¹ ▼ [lok] *noun, plural* **locks. 1.** a bolt or mechanism that prevents a door or entrance from being opened without a key, combination code, or other device. **2.** an enclosed stretch of water in a canal or waterway with gates at each end that can be raised or lowered to allow ships and boats to move smoothly from one level to another.
verb, **locked, locking. 1.** to close using a lock: *Don't forget to lock the door when you leave.* **2.** to prevent from leaving or entering: *to lock a prisoner in a cell.* **3.** to join or hold together, as if with a lock: *The two deer locked horns as they fought each other.*

lock² [lok] *noun, plural* **locks. 1.** a small tuft of hair, cotton, or wool. **2. locks.** a person's hair.

lock·er [<u>lok</u>-ur] *noun, plural* **lockers.** a small cupboard or closet where people can lock up and store personal belongings. A room where there are a number of lockers is a **locker room.**

lock·et [<u>lok</u>-it] *noun, plural* **lockets.** a small container that holds a picture or a lock of hair.

lo·co·mo·tion [loh-kuh-<u>moh</u>-shun] *noun.* the power that allows or creates movement; any form of movement: *Wind provides locomotion for sailboats.*

lo·co·mo·tive [loh-kuh-<u>moh</u>-tiv] *noun, plural* **locomotives.** a vehicle that moves using its own power and that pulls railroad cars and vans.

lo·cust ▲ [<u>loh</u>-kust] *noun, plural* **locusts.** a kind of grasshopper that moves in huge numbers across the countryside and that can consume crops and vegetation, causing great harm to farms.

lode [lode] *noun, plural* **lodes.** an underground deposit of rock that contains a valuable metal.
🔊 A different word with the same sound is **load.**

lodge [loj] *noun, plural* **lodges. 1.** a simple dwelling place or shelter: *While they were hiking in the mountains, Jennifer and Robert stayed overnight in small lodges.* **2.** a branch and meeting place of a club or society.
verb, **lodged, lodging. 1.** to live in a place for a time: *While our new house was being built we lodged at our aunt's house.* **2.** to settle or become fixed: *Our ball lodged in the branch of a tree and we couldn't reach it.* **3.** to present to a proper authority; submit: *The prisoner lodged a complaint against his long jail sentence.* A person who lodges somewhere is a **lodger.**

lodg·ing [<u>loj</u>-ing] *noun, plural* **lodgings.** a temporary residence. Rooms that are rented out in such a place are called **lodgings.**

loft [loft] *noun, plural* **lofts. 1.** the room or space immediately below the roof of a building. Lofts are often used as storage areas. **2.** a raised gallery inside a church or hall: *The church organ is in the loft.* **3.** an area without partitions in an upper story of a building: *My uncle's apartment used to be part of a warehouse loft.*

loft·y [<u>lof</u>-tee] *adjective,* **loftier, loftiest. 1.** very tall; high up: *Redwood trees grow to be very lofty.* **2.** describing something grand; impressive: *In her speech the principal expressed some lofty sentiments about the value of education.* **3.** showing contempt; thinking oneself to be superior: *She has a lofty attitude, but she's no better than anyone else.*

log [log] *noun, plural* **logs. 1.** a section of wood cut from the trunk of a tree: *These logs are too thick to burn in our fireplace.* **2.** a detailed written record of what happens during a sea voyage or a flight: *Barbara's parents have a yacht and they keep a log of all the long trips they take.*
verb, **logged, logging. 1.** to fell trees and cut them into logs. **2.** to keep a detailed record of a voyage or a flight.
adjective. built with or made of logs: *a log cabin.* To move out of a computer program is to **log off.** To enter a computer program is to **log on.**

log·book [<u>log</u>-buk] *noun, plural* **logbooks.** a book in which a detailed record of a sea voyage or a flight is kept.

log·ger [<u>log</u>-ur] *noun, plural* **loggers.** a person who fells trees and cuts them into logs.

log·ic [<u>loj</u>-ik] *noun.* **1.** clear and correct reasoning; good sense: *You need to think again because there's no logic in what you are saying.* **2.** a way of thinking, either correct or incorrect: *Gary could not see the logic of going without food to lose weight.* **3.** the science or the study of the rules of good reasoning. According to this, a statement can be tested in certain ways to see if it is true or correct.

log·i·cal [<u>loj</u>-i-kul] *adjective.* **1.** concerned with or showing correct reasoning or good sense: *It is logical to believe that the Earth moves around the Sun.* **2.** able to reason correctly: *Germaine is a very logical person and I agree with most of what she says.* **3.** reasonable to expect; not surprising: *It is only logical that if you go out in the rain you'll get wet.* —**logically,** *adverb.*

*To pass to a higher level of water, a boat enters the **lock** (above) and the gate closes (above right); the water level is raised (opposite left), the gates open and the boat moves forward (opposite right).*

lo·go [loh-*goh*] *noun, plural* **logos.** *Art.* an illustration, picture, or printed symbol that stands for and identifies a group, company, or organization: *The logo of the General Electric Company is a circle with the letters "GE" inside.*

loin [loyn] *noun, plural* **loins. 1.** the section between the hip bone and the ribs on each side of the body of a human or four-legged animal. **2.** meat taken from this part of an animal for use as food.

loi·ter [*loy*-tur] *verb,* **loitered, loitering.** to stand about idly and without purpose: *The owner became annoyed with the boys who were loitering near the front of her store.* Standing around in this way is **loitering.**

lol·li·pop [*lol*-ee-*pop*] *noun, plural* **lollipops.** a lump of hard candy, usually round or spherical in shape, stuck on the end of a small stick.

lone [lone] *adjective.* **1.** not with others; by oneself: *There was just one lone passenger in the bus.* **2.** describing something isolated; deserted: *The big house stood on a lone and windy hilltop.*

A different word with the same sound is **loan.**

lone·ly [*lone*-lee] *adjective,* **lonelier, loneliest. 1.** longing for the company of others; missing other people: *Jason felt lonely when his best friend went on vacation.* **2.** empty and isolated; deserted: *The desert can be a very lonely place.* **3.** describing something alone; by itself: *There was just one lonely ship in the whole harbor.*
—loneliness, *noun.*

lone·some [*lone*-sum] *adjective.* **1.** longing for company; missing other people: *I feel lonesome when I'm all alone in the house.* **2.** having a feeling of being empty or alone; isolated or deserted: *That lonesome old house is very creepy at night.*

long[1] [lawng] *adjective,* **longer, longest. 1.** lengthy in distance or time; having a great extent or amount; not short: *a long movie; a long pass in football; a long drive from New York to Florida; The long train had more than thirty cars.* **2.** indicating an amount of length or time: *A football field is 100 yards long.* **3.** *Language.* slightly slower to say or pronounce; not short: the *a* in *mate* is a long vowel; the *a* in *mat* is a short vowel.
adverb, **longer, longest. 1.** for an extended period: *I need to ask you a few questions, but I won't keep you long; The meeting was meant to end at 3.00, but it went longer.* **2.** during the whole of: *We've been waiting for you to arrive all morning long.* **3.** in the distant past: *George Washington lived long ago.*

long[2] [lawng] *verb,* **longed, longing.** to want very much; have a strong desire for: *I long to travel to the West and see the Grand Canyon.*

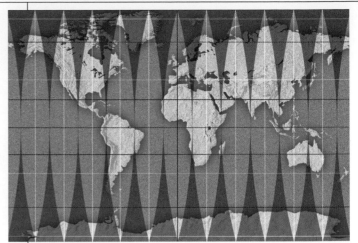

long·horn [*lawng*-horn] *noun, plural* **longhorns.** a breed of cattle of Spanish origin with long, spreading horns. Longhorns were once very common in northern Mexico and the southwestern United States.

long·ing [*lawng*-ing] *noun, plural* **longings.** a very strong wish; a desire for: *My mother has a longing to visit an old friend in England.*
adjective. indicating a strong wish: *Dorothy looked with longing eyes at the puppy in the pet shop window.*

lon·gi·tude ▲ [*lon*-juh-*tood*] *noun,* **longitudes.** *Geography.* the distance east or west on the surface of the Earth, measured in degrees from a meridian that passes through the town of Greenwich in southeast England. On maps and globes, lines of longitude travel from north to south.

long-term *adjective.* **1.** lasting for or taking a long time: *Building a bridge is a long-term project.* **2.** extending far into the future: *long-term plans for a business.*

look [luk] *verb,* **looked, looking. 1.** to see on purpose; see by paying attention: *The teacher asked us to look closely at the map.* **2.** to search for or investigate: *Natasha looked everywhere for her lost earring.* **3.** to give the impression of being; appear; seem: *He looks exhausted after his long journey.* **4.** to face toward; have a view toward: *Their house looks south across the hills.*
noun, plural **looks. 1.** the act of looking: *The doctor took a look at the rash on my arm.* **2.** the way something seems; appearance: *He had an excited look on his face as he opened the present.* The **looks** of something or someone is the way that thing or person appears or seems.

look·out [*luk*-out] *noun, plural* **lookouts. 1.** an alert watch for something that may happen or appear: *When walking on that trail, keep a lookout for snakes.* **2.** a person who watches for something: *The ship's captain placed a lookout on the bridge to see if any small boats were nearby.* **3.** a place to watch from.

a b c d e f g h i j k l m n o p q r s t u v w x y z

loom

loom¹ ▶ [loom] *noun, plural* **looms.**
a machine on which thread or yarn is woven into cloth.

loom² to come suddenly into sight in a frightening or threatening way: *As the campers sat around the fire, a large animal loomed up from the shadows.*

loon ▼ [loon] *noun, plural* **loons.**
one of several large, fish-eating, diving birds with speckled feathers and webbed feet that are placed well back under the body. A loon's wild cry sounds somewhat like a person laughing.

loop [loop] *noun, plural* **loops.**
1. a round shape created when string, ribbon, wire, rope, or a similar material is folded over itself. **2.** anything that has the shape of this: *The Campus Loop is a road that goes in a circle all around the college grounds.*
verb, **looped, looping.** to shape something into a loop or loops: *Mom looped the ribbons to make a bow for my hair.*

loop·hole [loop-hole] *noun, plural* **loopholes. 1.** a small hole or opening in a wall that something can go through or be put through. **2.** a way of escaping the requirements of a rule or law, often because of a small mistake or an unclear meaning: *He didn't have to pay tax on that purchase because of a loophole in the law.*

loose [loos] *adjective,* **looser, loosest. 1.** not fixed in place or firmly fastened: *a loose tooth; The gardener put loose soil around the plant so the roots could grow.* **2.** not held or restrained; free: *The dog got off its leash and is loose in the yard.* **3.** not tightly fitting; baggy: *loose jeans.*
adverb. in a loose way: *A large bull ran loose in the field.*
verb, **loosed, loosing.** make loose; loosen.
—**loosely,** *adverb;* —**looseness,** *noun.*

loose-leaf [loos-leef] *adjective.* describing pages that can be easily removed or rearranged, or a book with rings that hold such pages.

loos·en [loo-sun] *verb,* **loosened, loosening.** to make something less tight or less fixed: *He loosened his belt after eating a big dinner.*

loot [loot] *noun.* money or goods that have been taken by illegal or dishonest means: *The shoplifter hid her loot under her coat.*
verb, **looted, looting.** to steal goods, often those that are valuable, especially during a war or other time of crisis: *During the blackout, people looted the supermarket, taking all the food and other goods.* A person who takes such goods illegally during a war, riot, or other community crisis is a **looter.** The act of stealing in this way is called **looting.**
🔊 A different word with the same sound is **lute.**

lop·sid·ed [lop-sye-did] *adjective.*
having one side that is heavier or bigger than the other; leaning or drooping to one side: *The streetlight was lopsided after a car ran into it.*

Lord [lord] *noun. Religion.* God or Jesus Christ. Different terms for this word are **the Lord** or **Our Lord.**

lord [lord] *noun, plural* **lords.**
1. a person who rules over others, often owning a large amount of land. In earlier times a lord would have authority over the people who lived on his land. **2.** a title given to a man born into a noble class or given noble rank, especially used in Great Britain.
• **lord it over.** to act superior to, higher than, or as the master of: *Now that he is class president, he is lording it over the rest of us.*

> In earlier times a **lord** was an important man who was the head of a large household, where a number of other people worked for him and served him. The word *lord* comes from a phrase meaning "the keeper of the bread." The idea was that a lord kept charge of all the bread (and other food) in the household and gave it out to the other people there.

lose [looz] *verb,* **lost, losing. 1.** to no longer have; to be unable to find something: *I keep losing my sunglasses.* **2.** to be unable to hold on to; fail to keep or have: *If I'm late I will lose my job.* **3.** to fall short of success; not win: *to lose a war; Germany lost in World War II.* **4.** to not take advantage of; waste: *We're losing time arguing over which road to take.* **5.** to have less of: *to lose weight; to lose your hair; to lose money in business.*

lo·ser [looz-ur] *noun, plural* **losers. 1.** someone who loses a competition, contest, or game: *The loser of this game is the one with the most cards left at the end.* **2.** someone who is thought to be unattractive, unsuccessful, or socially unacceptable; a failure.

loss [loss] *noun, plural* **losses. 1.** the act of losing or the state of being lost: *We won our first game, but our second was a 2–0 loss.* **2.** something or someone taken away or not able to be found: *The hurricane caused great property damage but no loss of life.* **3.** the hurt or difficulty suffered because something has been taken away: *I felt a real loss when my pet cat died.*
• **at a loss.** to be confused; uncertain; puzzled: *We are at a loss to understand why she was so mean to us.*

lost [lost] *verb.* the past participle and past tense of LOSE.
adjective. **1.** not where it should be; missing: *I found my lost sweater behind the dresser.* **2.** unable to find the way; not knowing which way to go: *The hikers were lost in the woods.* **3.** not gained or won: *a lost cause; They worked hard to make up for lost opportunities.*

Loons live on northern ponds and lakes in summer, but migrate to the oceans in winter.

lot [lot] *noun, plural* **lots. 1.** a large number or amount of: *There are a lot of kids at our school.* **2.** a bunch, group, or set of things or people: *This puppy is the cutest of the whole lot.* **3.** a piece of land: *We are planting a vegetable garden in the lot next to the school.* **4.** an object, such as a straw, coin, pebble, and the like, chosen at random to help decide something: *We drew lots to decide where to go for our vacation.* **5.** experiences in life; destiny, fate, or luck: *It was my grandmother's lot to be happy and loved.*

lo·tion [loh-shun] *noun, plural* **lotions.** any thick liquid that is gently rubbed into the skin to clean, protect, or heal.

lot·ter·y [lot-ur-ee] *noun, plural* **lotteries. 1.** a game in which numbered tickets are sold or given to players and a winner is chosen by chance. **2.** any situation in which the result is decided by chance and the winner receives a prize, money, or some other benefit: *So many people are interested in the new houses that the buyers will be chosen in a lottery.*

lo·tus ▼ [loh-tus] *noun, plural* **lotuses.** a water plant with large pink or white flowers. The root, which grows under water, can be eaten as a fruit.

loud [loud] *adjective,* **louder, loudest. 1.** having a strong or intense sound; easy to hear: *The trucks made a loud rumble as they passed by.* **2.** surprisingly colorful or overly decorated; not appropriate for a situation: *She wore a loud dress to the funeral.* —**loudly,** *adverb;* —**loudness,** *noun.*

loud·speak·er [loud-*spee*-kur] *noun, plural* **loudspeakers.** a piece of equipment that can turn electrical signals into sounds and can make sounds loud enough to be heard at a distance.

lounge [lounj] *verb,* **lounged, lounging.** to sit in a comfortable position or act in a relaxed way: *He lounged in front of the television. noun, plural* **lounges. 1.** a room where people can relax: *At the airport we waited in the lounge.* **2.** a seat for more than one person; a couch or sofa.

louse [louss] *noun, plural* **lice.** a small wingless insect that lives by biting and sucking the blood of people and animals.

lous·y [louz-ee] *adjective.* **1.** infected with lice. **2.** not good; bad or dreadful: *I had a really lousy day today.*

lov·a·ble [luv-uh-bul] *adjective.* having a nature or characteristics that attract love or affection: *a lovable puppy.* This word is also spelled **loveable.**

love [luv] *noun, plural* **loves. 1.** a powerful feeling of tenderness and warmth toward someone or something: *I have a great love for my sister.* **2.** a great pleasure gained from something; a liking: *They share a love of art.* **3.** a deeply liked person, action, animal, or thing: *Horseback riding is a love of mine. verb,* **loved, loving. 1.** to feel a powerful sense of tenderness and warmth toward someone or something: *I love my parents.* **2.** to gain a deep sense of pleasure from something: *My dog loves to chew on bones.*

Love is a much stronger word than *like,* so your writing will probably be better if you save the word *love* for important things that you care very much about. You can use *like* instead for less important. everyday things. Thus you could say that you *love* your grandmother or your sister or your pet dog or the best movie you ever saw. Then you could use *like* to talk about a nice new friend in your class, or a good meal you had last weekend, or a funny movie you just saw.

love·ly [luv-lee] *adjective,* **lovelier, loveliest. 1.** pleasing to look at; charming and kind: *The famous actress was even more lovely in real life.* **2.** pleasing and enjoyable: *We had a lovely time at the neighbors' Fourth of July party.* —**loveliness,** *noun.*

lov·er [luv-ur] *noun, plural* **lovers. 1.** a person or people in love. **2.** someone's sexual partner. **3.** someone who cares very much about something: *a lover of good wine.*

lov·ing [luv-ing] *adjective.* showing or feeling love: *My grandparents are very loving toward each other.* —**lovingly,** *adverb.*

low [loh] *adjective,* **lower, lowest. 1.** close to the ground or the base of something; not high: *Our dog easily jumps our low fence.* **2.** below the normal height, degree, or amount: *Gas prices are low this month.* **3.** below the common level: *Our team's scores are low compared to the others.* **4.** not having enough; lacking supplies of: *We are low on milk.* **5.** soft in sound; quiet: *Keep your voice low as we go past the baby's room.* **6.** having a depth of sound: *In our band, I sing the low notes.* **7.** not happy; miserable: *When my friend moved away, I felt low for a long time. adverb.* in a low situation or position: *The branches hung low on the tree. noun, plural* **lows. 1.** a low situation or position: *The price of that steak is at an all-time low.* **2.** the first gear in a car, bike, or other vehicle: *I used low on my bike to go up the steep hill.*

The **lotus** *is a common water-garden plant in the warm climates of southern Asia and Australia.*

a
b
c
d
e
f
g
h
i
j
k
l
m
n
o
p
q
r
s
t
u
v
w
x
y
z

*Unlike most modern suitcases, **luggage** did not have wheels in the past.*

low·er [loh-ur] *adjective.* the comparative form of LOW: *The ceiling in our bathroom is lower than the ceilings in the rest of the house.*
verb, **lowered, lowering. 1.** to move something to a level below or underneath: *The crane lowered its cargo of bricks.* **2.** to reduce the value or quality of something; lessen: *The store lowered its price on cat food.* **3.** to bring down the volume of sound: *My mom asked me to lower the CD.*

low·er·case [loh-er-kase] *noun. Language.* letters that are printed or written in the small form, not in capitals.
adjective. describing such letters: *The sign was written in lowercase letters and said, "please keep out."*

loy·al [loy-ul] *adjective.* showing faith, support, and commitment to someone or something: *The girls were being mean about my friend but I was loyal to her and told them to stop.* Someone who is loyal, especially to a government or country, is a **loyalist. —loyally,** *adverb.*

loy·al·ty [loy-ul-tee] *noun, plural* **loyalties.** faith, support, and commitment to someone or something: *The staff felt loyalty to the boss because he had been so good to them.*

lu·bri·cate [loo-bruh-kate] *verb,* **lubricated, lubricating.** to apply a product such as oil or grease to the parts of a machine or other working object so the parts will easily work together: *Dad lubricated the gears on my bike.* **—lubrication,** *noun.*

luck [luk] *noun.* **1.** chance experiences in life; fate or destiny: *His success is the result of hard work, not luck.* **2.** a chance experience that is positive; good fortune: *She had the good luck to win the contest.*

luck·il·y [luk-i-lee] *adverb.* by good luck; with a positive outcome of fate: *Luckily, we got to the station before the train left.*

lug [lug] *verb,* **lugged, lugging.** to carry with difficulty: *We lugged our suitcases from the train station to the hotel.*

lug·gage ▲ [lug-ij] *noun.* a bag or case used to carry clothing and other belongings when traveling.

luke·warm [luke-warm] *adjective.* **1.** somewhat warm; not hot or cold. **2.** showing or feeling little interest or excitement: *The fans showed lukewarm support for the team after they lost three games in a row.*

lull [lul] *verb,* **lulled, lulling.** to cause something or someone to become quiet, calm, or still: *We lulled the children to sleep with a bedtime story.*
noun, plural **lulls.** a quiet period: *a lull in the fighting during a war.*

lul·la·by [lul-uh-bye] *noun, plural* **lullabies.** *Music.* a quiet song to soothe or lull a child into sleep.

lum·ber¹ [lum-bur] *noun.* trees cut and prepared into logs and boards for use as building material.

lum·ber² [lum-bur] *verb,* **lumbered, lumbering.** to move in a slow, heavy, or awkward way: *The bear lumbered through the forest.*

lum·ber·jack [lum-bur-jak] *noun, plural* **lumberjacks.** someone who cuts down trees and organizes the transportation of the logs to the sawmill.

lu·min·es·cence [loom-i-nes-uns] *noun. Science.* **1.** the production of light by means other than heat. **2.** the light created by such a process. This type of light is described as **luminescent.**

lu·min·ous [loo-muh-nus] *adjective.* producing light; shining or glowing: *Luminous fireflies darted through the trees.* The state of producing light or shining is **luminosity.**

lump [lump] *noun, plural* **lumps. 1.** a small, shapeless chunk of something solid: *The children threw lumps of mud at each other.* **2.** a bump or swelling on the body of a person or animal: *A lump has come up where I bumped my knee.*
verb, **lumped, lumping. 1.** to create or form pieces or chunks: *I forgot to stir the sauce and it all lumped together.* When something has lumps it is said to be **lumpy. 2.** to gather together: *We lumped our vacation time into one big overseas trip.*

lu·nar [loo-nur] *adjective.* having to do with the Moon: *From the Earth the lunar surface looks a bit like glowing cheese.*

lu·na·tic [loon-i-tik] *noun, plural* **lunatics.** an insane or wild person. **Lunacy** is the act or fact of being insane, wild, or extremely foolish.

lunch [lunch] *noun, plural* **lunches.** a meal eaten in the middle of the day, between breakfast and dinner.
verb, **lunched, lunching.** to have a meal in the middle of the day: *We lunched from noon to one.*

The word **lunatic** comes from Luna, the Latin name for the Moon. In earlier times it was thought that the way a person acted could be affected by the changes in the appearance of the Moon (full moon, new moon, and so on). A person would be called a lunatic if others thought he was acting crazy because of the influence of the Moon.

lunch·eon [lunch-un] *noun, plural* **luncheons.** a midday meal; often a formal lunch: *The wedding was held in the morning, followed by a luncheon.*

lung [lung] *noun, plural* **lungs.** one of a pair of organs in the chest that allows humans and animals to take in oxygen from the air and remove carbon dioxide from the body.

lunge [lunj] *noun, plural* **lunges.** the act of suddenly thrusting forward: *The boxer made a lunge at his opponent.*
verb, **lunged, lunging.** to suddenly thrust forward: *The cat lunged at the mouse but it ran under the bench.*

lurch [lurch] *verb,* **lurched, lurching.** to move unsteadily: *As the bus lurched to a stop, a couple of passengers fell over.*
noun, plural **lurches.** an unsteady movement.

lure [loor] *noun, plural* **lures. 1.** a powerful attraction: *the lure of fame and fortune.* **2.** a device used as bait in fishing: *He fished with a lure that looked like a real fly.* *verb,* **lured, luring.** to attract. *She was lured to the new job by the promise of higher pay.*

lurk [lurk] *verb,* **lurked, lurking.** to lie in wait; hide or sneak about: *The dog lurked around the picnic blanket, hoping to snatch some food.*

lus·cious [lush-us] *adjective.* describing a delicious smell or taste: *They served luscious chocolate pudding.*

lush [lush] *adjective,* **lusher, lushest.** rich, deeply colored or plentiful: *lush, green hills rolling down to the sea.*

lust [lust] *noun, plural* **lusts.** a very strong desire: *a lust for fame; a lust for money.* *verb,* **lusted, lusting.** to desire something very strongly: *The dictator lusted for power and glory.* —**lustful,** *adjective.*

lute [loot] *noun, plural* **lutes.** *Music.* a stringed instrument that has a body shaped like a pear. A lute looks similar to a guitar.
🔊 A different word with the same sound is **loot.**

Lu·ther·an [looth-uh-run] *noun, plural* **Lutherans.** *Religion.* a member of the Lutheran church. The Lutheran church follows the teachings of Martin Luther, who broke away from the Roman Catholic church 400 years ago in protest against some of its beliefs and practices. A member of the Lutheran church is a follower of **Lutheranism.** *adjective.* having to do with Lutheranism.

The **Lutheran** Church was founded by Martin *Luther,* a German religious leader who lived about 500 years ago. Luther was a priest in the Catholic Church who was known for his writings and speeches on the Bible. He then broke away from the Catholic Church to start a new church because he thought the Catholic Church was no longer being true to the teachings of Jesus.

lux·u·ri·ant [luk-zhur-ee-unt] *adjective.* **1.** describing rich or profuse growth: *a luxuriant garden.* **2.** describing splendor and richness.

lux·u·ri·ous [luk-zhur-ee-us] *adjective.* **1.** providing great comfort and pleasure; splendid: *a luxurious yacht.* **2.** describing liking or depending on luxury: *He has a luxurious taste for dining in fancy restaurants.* —**luxuriously,** *adverb.*

lux·u·ry [luk-shuh ree *or* lug-zhuh-ree] *noun, plural* **luxuries. 1.** something that provides great comfort and pleasure without being essential: *Having a whole hotel suite to himself is a luxury.* **2.** a lifestyle that provides great comfort and pleasure: *My rich uncle loves luxury.*

-ly a suffix that means: **1.** in a particular manner or way: *slowly* means in a slow manner. **2.** to a particular extent or degree: *greatly* means to a great extent.

lye [lye] *noun. Chemistry.* an ingredient used in detergent and soap. Lye is produced by soaking ashes from burnt wood in water.
🔊 A different word with the same sound is **lie.**

ly·ing¹ [lye-ing] *verb.* the present participle of LIE¹. *noun.* the act of not telling the truth: *His parents punished the boy for lying.*

ly·ing² [lye-ing] *verb.* the present participle of LIE².

Lyme disease *Medicine.* a disease caused by bacteria from the bite of a tick. The symptoms are fever, rash, and inflammation of the heart and joints.

lymph [limf] *noun. Biology.* the almost clear fluid made of proteins and water that carries white blood cells around the lymphatic system of the body. This helps fight infections and other diseases.

Lyme disease is named for a small town in the state of Connecticut called *Old Lyme.* It was in this town that people were first identified as having the disease, in 1975.

lymphatic system *Biology.* the system that circulates lymph through the body, and the lymphoid organs such as the **lymph nodes** and **lymph glands** that produce and store infection-fighting cells.

lym·pho·ma [lim-foh-muh] *noun. Medicine.* cancer of the lymph nodes.

lynx [lingks] *noun, plural* **lynxes.** a wild cat that lives in Asia and eastern Europe. Lynxes have mustard-colored fur with black spots and black tufts around the ears. They are a little larger the average domestic cat.

lyre ▶ [lire] *noun, plural* **lyres.** *Music.* a stringed instrument like a harp, that was played in ancient times.

lyr·ic [leer-ik] *adjective.* expressing deep, personal feelings: *a lyric poem.* *noun, plural* **lyrics.** a poem that expresses deep feelings. The words of a song are called **lyrics.**

lyr·i·cal [leer-uh-kul] *adjective.* expressing deep, personal feelings; lyric. —**lyrically,** *adverb.*

*The **lyre** was one of the instruments played to entertain guests at ancient Greek banquets.*

a b c d e f g h i j k l m n o p q r s t u v w x y z

Mm

Mackerels *are an important source of food in many parts of the world.*

M, m *noun, plural* **M's, m's.** the thirteenth letter of the English alphabet.

m. an abbreviation for METER.

ma'am [mam] *noun, plural* **ma'ams.** a shortened form of **madam**: *"Can I carry your package for you, ma'am?" the young man said.*

mac·a·ro·ni [mak-uh-<u>roh</u>-nee] *noun.* a type of pasta. It is made from dried dough in the shape of small hollow tubes, which are then cooked in boiling water.

ma·chine [muh-<u>sheen</u>] *noun, plural* **machines. 1.** a device made of different parts, used to do a particular job. A vacuum cleaner, a blender, and an air conditioner are machines. **2.** a device with a few simple parts that lessens the effort required to move an object. Six devices known as **simple machines** are the screw, lever, pulley, wedge, inclined plane, and wheel and axle.

machine gun a rifle that keeps firing bullets when the trigger is pulled or pressed.

ma·chin·er·y [muh-<u>sheen</u>-ree] *noun.* a group of machines or machine parts: *An automobile factory has many different types of machinery.*

ma·chin·ist [muh-<u>shee</u>-nist] *noun, plural* **machinists.** someone who operates machinery that makes tools or parts.

mack·er·el ▲ [mak-uh-rul] *noun, plural* **mackerels** *or* **mackerel.** a silver fish with dark markings that lives in salt water.

macro- a prefix that means very large in scale. It is used especially in scientific words: *macrocosm* means the greater world or universe (as opposed to *microcosm*); *macroscopic* means something that can been seen without magnifying it (as opposed to *microscopic*).

ma·cron [<u>may</u>-kron] *noun, plural* **macrons.** *Language.* a line (ˉ) above a vowel that shows it has a long sound, such as the **a** in *ate* or the **o** in *open.*

mad [mad] *adjective,* **madder, maddest. 1.** showing or feeling anger or annoyance: *Mom got mad when we didn't clean up our room.* **2.** insane or crazy. **3.** silly or foolish: *Jumping from the roof into the pool is a mad thing to do.* **4.** frantic or wildly excited: *She was in a mad rush to catch the last bus.* **5.** suffering from rabies: *a mad dog.* —**madly,** *adverb;* —**madness,** *noun.*

Mad·am [<u>mad</u>-um] *noun, plural* **Mesdames** *or* **Madams.** a title for a woman: *The store manager greeted her by saying, "Good morning, Madam."* Sometimes this word is spelled **Madame.**

made [made] *verb.* the past participle or past tense of MAKE. 🔊 A different word with the same sound is **maid.**

Mad·e·moi·selle [mad-uh-muh-*zel* or mam-zel] *noun, plural* **Mademoiselles** *or* **Mesdemoiselles.** the French word for an unmarried woman or girl. The shortened form of this word is **Mlle.**

made-up *adjective.* not true; imagined: *The thief gave a made-up address to the police.*

mag·a·zine [<u>mag</u>-uh-zeen] *noun, plural* **magazines. 1.** a collection of articles and pictures, usually published weekly or monthly. **2.** a building or room that stores ammunition. **3.** a container for bullets that is attached to a gun or rifle.

mag·got [<u>mag</u>-ut] *noun, plural* **maggots.** a fly larva; a fly or other insect that has just come out of its egg. Maggots look like short, fat worms and feed on rotting food.

mag·ic [<u>maj</u>-ik] *noun.* **1.** the special use of certain sayings, spells, charms, or potions that are believed to have special powers to control events and make things happen that would not normally be possible: *The book was about a witch who used magic to turn a prince into a frog.* **2.** the performance of tricks that seem impossible to entertain people, such as sawing a woman in half or making a bird fly out of a handkerchief. *adjective.* having to do with or using magic: *a magic trick; a magic show.*

mag·i·cal [<u>maj</u>-i-kul] *adjective.* having to do with or using magic: *The witch used magical powers to fly away on her broomstick.* —**magically,** *adverb.*

ma·gi·cian [muh-<u>jish</u>-un] *noun, plural* **magicians. 1.** someone who does magic tricks. **2.** a witch, wizard, or someone with magical powers.

mag·ma ▶ [<u>mag</u>-muh] *noun. Environment.* very hot, melted rock underneath the Earth's surface. Magma sometimes cools and forms into hard rock. It flows out of volcanoes as lava.

mag·ne·si·um [mag-<u>nee</u>-zee-um] *noun. Chemistry.* a very light metal used in alloys. Because it burns so brightly, magnesium is often used in fireworks.

A B C D E F G H I J K L **M** N O P Q R S T U V W X Y Z

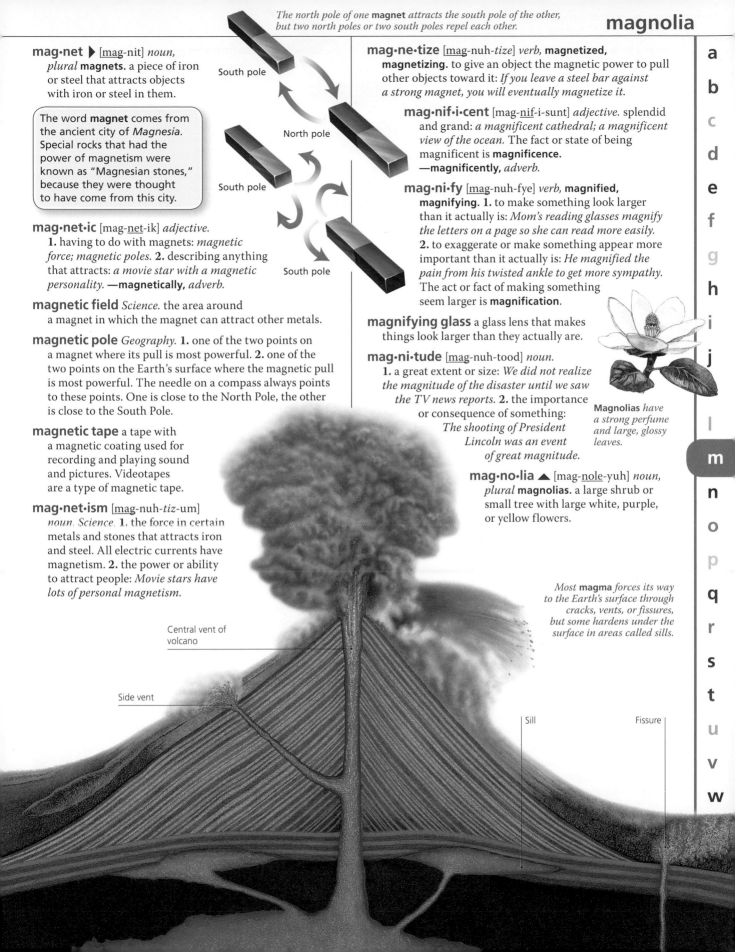

*The north pole of one **magnet** attracts the south pole of the other, but two north poles or two south poles repel each other.*

South pole

North pole

South pole

South pole

mag·net ▶ [mag-nit] *noun, plural* **magnets.** a piece of iron or steel that attracts objects with iron or steel in them.

The word **magnet** comes from the ancient city of *Magnesia.* Special rocks that had the power of magnetism were known as "Magnesian stones," because they were thought to have come from this city.

mag·net·ic [mag-net-ik] *adjective.* **1.** having to do with magnets: *magnetic force; magnetic poles.* **2.** describing anything that attracts: *a movie star with a magnetic personality.* —**magnetically,** *adverb.*

magnetic field *Science.* the area around a magnet in which the magnet can attract other metals.

magnetic pole *Geography.* **1.** one of the two points on a magnet where its pull is most powerful. **2.** one of the two points on the Earth's surface where the magnetic pull is most powerful. The needle on a compass always points to these points. One is close to the North Pole, the other is close to the South Pole.

magnetic tape a tape with a magnetic coating used for recording and playing sound and pictures. Videotapes are a type of magnetic tape.

mag·net·ism [mag-nuh-*tiz*-um] *noun, Science.* **1.** the force in certain metals and stones that attracts iron and steel. All electric currents have magnetism. **2.** the power or ability to attract people: *Movie stars have lots of personal magnetism.*

mag·ne·tize [mag-nuh-*tize*] *verb,* **magnetized, magnetizing.** to give an object the magnetic power to pull other objects toward it: *If you leave a steel bar against a strong magnet, you will eventually magnetize it.*

mag·nif·i·cent [mag-nif-i-sunt] *adjective.* splendid and grand: *a magnificent cathedral; a magnificent view of the ocean.* The fact or state of being magnificent is **magnificence.** —**magnificently,** *adverb.*

mag·ni·fy [mag-nuh-fye] *verb,* **magnified, magnifying. 1.** to make something look larger than it actually is: *Mom's reading glasses magnify the letters on a page so she can read more easily.* **2.** to exaggerate or make something appear more important than it actually is: *He magnified the pain from his twisted ankle to get more sympathy.* The act or fact of making something seem larger is **magnification.**

magnifying glass a glass lens that makes things look larger than they actually are.

mag·ni·tude [mag-nuh-tood] *noun.* **1.** a great extent or size: *We did not realize the magnitude of the disaster until we saw the TV news reports.* **2.** the importance or consequence of something: *The shooting of President Lincoln was an event of great magnitude.*

mag·no·lia ▲ [mag-nole-yuh] *noun, plural* **magnolias.** a large shrub or small tree with large white, purple, or yellow flowers.

Magnolias *have a strong perfume and large, glossy leaves.*

*Most **magma** forces its way to the Earth's surface through cracks, vents, or fissures, but some hardens under the surface in areas called sills.*

Central vent of volcano

Side vent

Sill

Fissure

a b c d e f g h i j l **m** n o p q r s t u v w

*The Australian **magpie** can mimic the calls of other birds.*

mag·pie ▶ [mag-*pye*] *noun, plural* **magpies.** a bird with a long tail, large beak, and a loud, chattering call.

ma·hog·a·ny [muh-*hog*-uh-nee] *noun, plural* **mahoganies. 1.** a large, evergreen tree that grows in tropical America, with hard, reddish-brown wood used for making furniture. **2.** a reddish-brown color. *adjective.* describing a reddish-brown wood or having a reddish-brown color.

maid [made] *noun, plural* **maids. 1.** a woman paid to do housework. **2.** an unmarried woman or girl.

maid·en [*made*-un] *noun, plural* **maidens.** a young, unmarried woman or girl. *adjective.* earliest or first: *The band's maiden tour took them across the Western states.*

maiden name the surname or last name of a woman before she marries and uses her husband's last name.

maid of honor the main, usually unmarried, woman who helps a bride during her wedding.

mail¹ [male] *noun.* **1.** items such as letters and packages that are sent from or to a post office and then delivered to a certain person or place. **2.** the system or organization by which items such as letters and packages are sent, transported, and delivered; the postal system: *My letter to you must have gotten lost in the mail.* *verb,* **mailed, mailing.** to send by mail: *You'll have to mail the present to Kevin today so it reaches him by his birthday.*
🔊 A different word with the same sound is **male.**

mail² [male] *noun. History.* armor made of interlinked metal rings, worn in battle in the Middle Ages.

mail·box [*male*-boks] *noun, plural* **mailboxes. 1.** a public box into which mail is put for a postal worker to pick up. **2.** a private box where mail is put by a postal worker delivering mail.

mail carrier a postal worker whose job is to deliver mail.

mail·man [*male*-man] *noun, plural* **mailmen.** a person whose job is to deliver mail; a mail carrier.

maim [mame] *verb,* **maimed, maiming.** to injure someone badly, or to be injured in this way: *He was maimed in a car accident and will never walk again.*

main [mane] *adjective.* most important or largest: *The town hall is on the town's main street.* *noun, plural* **mains.** a large pipe or electrical cable that runs underground and supplies electricity, water, or gas to buildings.
🔊 A different word with the same sound is **mane.**

main·frame ▶ [*mane*-frame] *noun, plural* **mainframes.** *Computers.* a large and powerful computer that can store great amounts of information. Smaller computers in a system can be connected to it. Mainframe computers are often used by large organizations.

main·land [*mane*-lund] *noun, plural* **mainlands.** *Geography.* the main landmass of a country, not the islands around it: *Tasmania is an island lying about 125 miles off mainland Australia.*

main·ly [*mane*-lee] *adverb.* for the most part; usually: *Sometimes Mom drives me to school but mainly I ride my bike.*

main·stay [*mane*-stay] *noun, plural* **mainstays.** the main support of something: *Mrs. Brown has been a mainstay of the fundraising committee at our school for years.*

main·tain [mane-*tane*] *verb,* **maintained, maintaining. 1.** to continue on with something; keep on: *She put in her best effort to maintain the lead in the race.* **2.** to keep in good condition; look after: *Every three months Kevin takes his car to the auto mechanic to be maintained.* **3.** to keep on saying something is so; hold to be true: *They maintain they weren't the ones who pushed over the trash.*

main·te·nance [*mane*-tuh-nuns] *noun.* **1.** the fact or act of caring for something: *Maintenance of the park is paid for by the town council.* **2.** things that are needed to provide support to live, such as food, shelter, and money.

maize [maze] *noun.* a grain that grows on the large ears of a tall grass plant; corn. It is grown as a cereal crop.
🔊 A different word with the same sound is **maze.**

ma·jes·tic [muh-*jes*-tik] *adjective.* having majesty or grandness: *The Sydney Opera House is a majestic building.* **—majestically,** *adverb.*

ma·jes·ty [*maj*-uh-stee] *adjective.* having a quality of greatness and imposing dignity; splendor or grandeur: *We were awed by the majesty of the giant redwood trees.* Royal rulers are often addressed with the title **Your Majesty, Her Majesty,** and so on.

ma·jor [*may*-jur] *adjective.* larger in size or importance: *The art gallery is holding a major exhibition of Pablo Picasso's work.* *noun, plural* **majors.** an officer in the armed forces who ranks above a captain but below a lieutenant colonel. *verb,* **majored, majoring.** to take courses mainly in a particular subject or area during a course of study: *At college, Tina is majoring in history but is also studying French.*

*A bank of **mainframes** can provide high-speed data processing for industry and business.*

ma·jor·ette [*may-juh-ret*] *noun, plural* **majorettes.**
a woman or girl who leads a marching band, usually
while twirling a baton. Sometimes troupes of majorettes
march together.

ma·jor·i·ty [*muh-jor-uh-tee*] *noun, plural* **majorities.**
1. the greater part or number of something; more than
half: *I dropped the bag of cookies and the majority of
them broke.* **Majority rule** occurs when members of
an organization vote and the whole group follows the
decision of the majority. **2.** the difference between a
larger number and a smaller number: *He won the
election for governor by a majority of about 20,000 votes.*
3. the age at which a person legally becomes an adult.
This age varies from state to state in the U.S.

make [*make*] *verb,* **made, making. 1.** to create, cause
to become, or occur: *to make cookies; to make a noise;
to make a fuss about something.*
2. to force to do; compel: *The teacher
made us finish our homework
at lunchtime.* **3.** to add up to;
the sum of: *Ten plus ten makes
twenty.* **4.** to gain or earn: *Mark
made enough money from his
vacation job to buy a canoe.*
5. to get to; reach: *We didn't make
it to your wedding because we all
came down with flu.* **6.** to gain a
position: *Fran made the school
soccer team.*
noun, plural **makes.** a particular
brand or type of something:
*That make of refrigerator
often breaks down.*
◆ **make up. 1.** to settle an
argument; become friends again: *The men shook hands
and made up.* **2.** to put on cosmetics: *The clown made
up his face before the circus show began.* **3.** to invent
something such as a story; imagine: *My sister likes to
make up silly songs.* **4.** to add up to; form: *A television
is made up of a box, a screen, electronics, and a control.*

There are various words that mean to cause something
to be or come into being. **Make** is the most common and
most general of these. You can make a sandwich, make
a dress, make a movie, make a fire in a fireplace, and so on.
Manufacture means to put parts together for a finished item,
as in manufacturing a car in a factory. To *produce* means to
develop a number of the same kind of thing, as in producing
a large crop of oranges. To *create* is to bring something
new into being that did not exist before, as in creating the
costumes for a movie. To *construct* is to set up something
large according to a plan or design, as in constructing
a new 10-story office building.

make-be·lieve *noun.* something imagined or pretended;
imagination: *In the movie, the children stepped through
a door into a world of make-believe.*
adjective. describing something imaginary or pretended:
*The children's make-believe castle was made of boxes
and blankets.*

make·shift [*make-shift*] *adjective.* used in place of the
usual or correct item for a short time: *Our makeshift tent
made of branches kept the worst of the rain off us.*

make·up [*make-up*] *noun, plural* **makeups. 1.** cosmetics,
especially those worn on the face, such as lipstick.
2. the way something is put together or arranged:
*The makeup of the concert audience was mostly little
children and their parents.* **3.** a person's character or
personality: *It is not in his makeup to stay angry for long.*
adjective. describing something done to replace
something that did not occur when it was supposed to:
The teacher gave me a makeup piano lesson.

ma·lar·i·a [*muh-lare-ee-uh*] *noun. Health.* a deadly tropical
disease that causes high fever and chills. It is caused by
a microscopic organism that destroys red blood cells.
A type of mosquito carries it from person to person.
Something that has to do with malaria, such as an attack
of fever, is said to be **malarial.**

Mal·ay·si·an [*muh-lay-zhun*] *noun, plural* **Malaysians.**
1. a person born in or coming from the southeast Asian
country of Malaysia. **2.** one of the official languages
of Malaysia.
adjective. having to do with
the people, language, or
culture of Malaysia.

male [*male*] *adjective.* **1.** belonging
to or having to do with men
or boys; masculine: *The church
has a male choir.* **2.** of or having
to do with the sex that fertilizes
eggs and does not give birth to young or lay eggs:
Male bald eagles help their mates sit on their eggs.
noun, plural **males.** a person or animal that can fertilize
eggs and does not give birth to young or lay eggs.
◀)) A different word with the same sound is **mail.**

mal·ice [*mal-is*] *noun.* the aim of causing harm or suffering;
ill will; spite: *She knocked over his impressive sandcastle
out of malice.*

mal·i·cious [*muh-lish-us*] *adjective.* showing, feeling,
or acting out of a wish to cause harm or suffering:
The malicious children called the boy bad names.
—maliciously, *adverb.*

mal·ig·nant [*muh-lig-nunt*] *adjective. Medicine.* able to
spread disease through the body: *He had the lump on his
skin tested in case it was malignant.*

mall [*mawl*] *noun, plural* **malls. 1.** a large, enclosed shopping
center. **2.** a street with many stores that is closed off to
automobile traffic. **3.** a large, open, public area where
people can stroll and relax.
◀)) A different word with the same sound is **maul.**

mal·lard ▲ [*mal-urd*] *noun, plural* **mallards** or **mallard.**
a common wild duck in North America, Europe, and Asia.
The male has a green head, white neckband, a brown
front, and a gray back. The female is brown. Both male
and female mallards have blue feathers near the edges
of their wings.

*Mallards are found in
parks, small ponds, rivers,
and other wetlands.*

Manatees have flexible lips that guide plants into their mouth.

mal·let [mal-it] *noun, plural* **mallets.** a hammer with a head made of soft material such as wood or rubber. Short-handled mallets are used to hit another tool such as a chisel. Long-handled mallets are used in sports such as polo to strike a ball.

mal·nu·tri·tion [mal-noo-trish-un] *noun. Health.* an illness caused by eating poor food or not having enough food. When a person or animal becomes ill through not eating properly, they are said to be **malnourished.**

malt [mawlt] *noun.* grain, usually barley, that is sprouted then dried. Malt is used to make beer and whiskey. A powder made from malt, dried milk, and wheat flour is added to milk to make **malted milk.**

ma·ma [mah-muh] *noun, plural* **mamas.** a word for "mother," especially used by children.

mam·mal ▶ [mam-ul] *noun, plural* **mammals.** *Biology.* any of various animals with females that feed their young with milk made by special glands. All mammals are warm-blooded and have backbones, and many have fur. These features are said to be **mammalian.** Examples of mammals are humans, cats, dolphins, bears, and mice.

> The word **mammal** is thought to come from an older word for the gland that female mammals have to give milk to their babies. This way of feeding the young is the most important difference between the mammals and other animals with backbones such as birds or reptiles.

mam·moth ▼ [mam-uth] *noun, plural* **mammoths.** any of various types of elephant with long hair that lived in cold climates in the Northern Hemisphere. The large mammoths became extinct around 10,000 years ago. *adjective.* extremely large; huge; gigantic: *Cleaning out the stadium after the game was a mammoth task.*

man [man] *noun, plural* **men. 1.** an adult male human. **2.** the human race in general; a person: *Man is one of the few animals that walks upright on two legs.* **3.** one of the pieces used in board games like chess or checkers. *verb,* **manned, manning.** to provide people to do a job: *She manned the cake booth at the school picnic.*

Mammoths traveled in herds and were hunted by early humans for their meat, bones, and skin.

man·age [man-ij] *verb,* **managed, managing. 1.** to organize or control; be in charge of: *Mr. Johnson manages a trucking company.* **2.** to be able to do something successfully: *She managed to carry the heavy bags up the steps.*

man·age·ment [man-ij-munt] *noun, plural* **managements. 1.** the organization or control of something: *The management of money is an important skill to learn.* **2.** the person or people who organize, and control something, especially a business: *Yesterday, the factory's management announced that everyone would receive a pay raise.*

man·a·ger [man-uh-jur] *noun, plural* **managers.** a person who organizes and controls something, especially in business: *He has been promoted to the job of bank manager.*

man·a·tee ▲ [man-uh-tee] *noun, plural* **manatees.** a large animal that lives in the coastal waters of the Caribbean Sea, the Gulf of Mexico, the Amazon basin, and West Africa. Manatees are mammals that look a bit like seals.

Man·dar·in [man-dur-in] *noun.* **1.** *Language.* a dialect of Chinese from northern China. Mandarin is the official language used by the Chinese Government. **2. mandarin.** a government official in Imperial China. **3. mandarin.** a small orange-colored citrus fruit with soft skin. This fruit is also known as a **mandarin orange.**

man·date [man-date] *noun, plural* **mandates. 1.** a command or approval to do something granted by voters to their representatives by the act of voting for them in an election: *The new mayor had a mandate to tackle pollution problems.* **2.** an official order to do something; authorization. *verb,* **mandated, mandating.** to tell someone to do something; insist or command: *The U.S. Constitution mandates a minimum age of 35 for the President.*

man·do·lin ▶ [man-duh-lin] *noun, plural* **mandolins.** *Music.* a musical instrument with a small, pear-shaped body, a long neck, and strings made of wire that are played with a plectrum.

The mandolin is related to the lyre.

mane [mane] *noun, plural* **manes.** the long hair that grows on the necks of particular animals. On some, such as horses and male lions, this hair can be a different color from the rest of their fur.
🔊 A different word the same sound is **main.**

MAMMALS

There are nearly 4,000 kinds of mammals. Most of them have hair or fur on their bodies and they all give birth to live young, except for the platypus and echidna. Because they are warm-blooded, mammals can survive in almost any environment. They have adapted to life in jungles, deserts, high mountains, and polar regions. Some, like bats and flying foxes, move mainly in the air; some, like monkeys, lemurs, possums, and koalas, live in the trees. Moles and rabbits burrow under the ground, while whales, dolphins, and seals live in the sea. Like humans, most mammals are social and live in groups. Bears, orangutans, and koalas are among the few mammals that live alone and come together only to mate.

A young koala on its mother's back

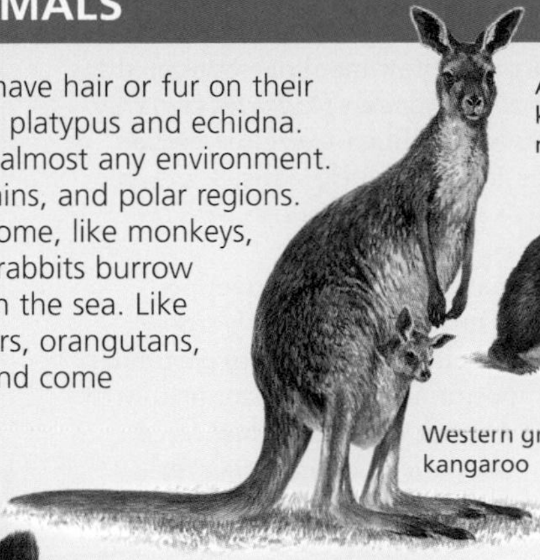

Wombat

Western gray kangaroo

Striped possum

EGG-LAYING MAMMALS
The Australian platypus and the echidnas of Australia and New Guinea are monotremes—mammals that lay eggs from which their young hatch. They have a lower body temperature than other mammals.

Echidna

Platypus

MAMMALS WITH POUCHES
Marsupials are mammals whose newborn young crawl into their mother's pouch and shelter there until they are old enough to be independent. Opossums live in the Americas, and the remaining marsupials live in Australia, New Guinea, and nearby islands.

LAND MAMMALS
Other mammals that live on land are known as placental mammals, and include many different kinds of animals. Before birth, the young of these mammals are nourished by a special organ called a placenta inside their mother's body. They are more developed than marsupials when they are born.

Sun bear

Moonrat

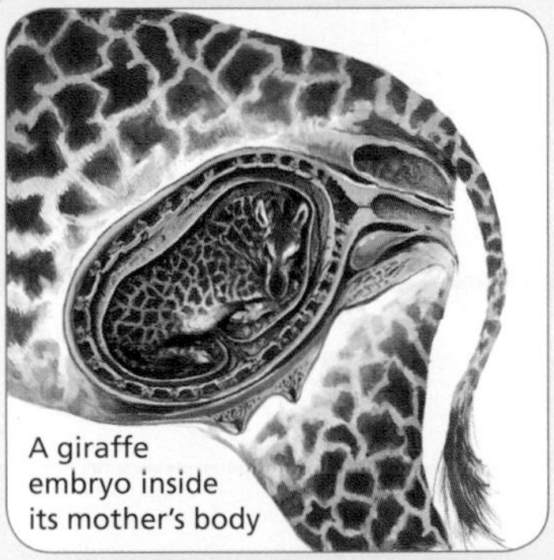

A giraffe embryo inside its mother's body

Philippine tarsier

Red uakari monkey

Spectacled bear

Asiatic golden cat

Greater kudu antelope

Whale

SEA MAMMALS
Some placental mammals live in the sea. Whales and dolphins have sleek, streamlined bodies and a flattened tail that propels them through the water. Sea lions, walruses, and some seals, turn their back flippers around to walk on land. Like all mammals, sea mammals feed their young on milk.

Dolphin

Sea lion

A B C D E F G H I J K L **M** N O P Q R S T U V W X Y Z

ma·neu·ver [muh-<u>noo</u>-ver] *noun, plural* **maneuvers.**
1. a planned and controlled movement of troops or ships: *The maneuver to capture the enemy bridge was carried out at night.* **2. maneuvers.** military exercises carried out by soldiers to practice their battle skills. **3.** a clever move or strategy: *It was the final maneuver with the knight that won the chess match for her.*
verb, **maneuvered, maneuvering.**
1. to move or make move troops or their equipment into particular positions. **2.** to move or plan in a clever way: *Jeff maneuvered the table to a shady spot for our picnic.* Something that can be moved in such a way is **maneuverable.**

Mangoes are a good source of vitamins.

man·ga·nese [mang-guh-neez] *noun. Chemistry.* an easily broken grayish-white metallic element. It is mixed with iron and other metals to make steel.

man·ger [<u>mane</u>-jur] *noun, plural* **mangers.** a box or trough in which food is put for livestock like cattle or horses to eat. The Bible tells of how the baby Jesus was laid in a manger after his birth.

man·gle [<u>mang</u>-gul] *verb,* **mangled, mangling. 1.** to ruin by cutting, crushing, tearing, or beating: *The car was mangled in the accident.* **2.** to spoil or ruin by lack of skill: *She mangled the lullaby by singing in a loud voice.*

man·go ▲ [<u>mang</u>-goh] *noun, plural* **mangoes** *or* **mangos.** an oval, smooth-skinned, yellow-orange fruit with a hard seed. It grows in the tropics on a tree, is sweet and tangy, and is eaten fresh or pickled.

man·grove ▼ [<u>mang</u>-grove] *noun, plural* **mangroves.** a type of tree that grows along the water's edge, particularly the edge of mud flats, swamps, and estuaries. It has many roots that form dense clumps, often above the ground. Mangroves are part of an important ecosystem.

man·hole [<u>man</u>-hole] *noun, plural* **manholes.** a hole with a lid that is large enough for a person to climb through to reach pipes or wires. Manholes can be found in places like roads, sewer pipes, ceilings, or floors.

man·hood [<u>man</u>-hud] *noun.* **1.** the state or time of being an adult male human: *When he reached manhood, he had new responsibilities.* **2.** adult males as a group.

man·i·a [<u>mane</u>-ee-yuh] *noun, plural* **manias. 1.** a state of great excitement or enthusiasm; a craze: *A mania for getting the latest video game swept the country.* **2.** any of various mental illnesses where a person becomes extremely excited and can be violent.

ma·ni·ac [<u>may</u>-nee-ak] *noun, plural* **maniacs. 1.** a person who is insane or acts in a dangerous or violent way. **2.** a person who has great enthusiasm for something: *He is a maniac about vintage automobiles.*

man·i·cure [<u>man</u>-uh-kyoor] *noun, plural* **manicures.** the act of caring for the fingernails by cleaning, shaping, and polishing them. Someone who does this for a job is called a **manicurist.** *verb,* **manicured, manicuring.** to care for the fingernails by cleaning, shaping, or polishing.

This **man-of-war** *was a typical Portuguese battleship in the fifteenth century.*

ma·nip·u·late [man-<u>nip</u>-yuh-late] *verb,* **manipulated, manipulating. 1.** to use or operate something with the hands, especially skillfully: *to manipulate the controls of a video game.* **2.** to control or influence someone, often unfairly: *The politician purposely left out parts of the survey results in order to manipulate the voters into supporting his proposal.* —**manipulation,** *noun.*

man·kind [<u>man</u>-kinde] *noun.* all people; the human race.

man-made *adjective.* not occurring naturally; made by people: *Silk is a natural fiber, but nylon is man-made.*

man·ner [<u>man</u>-ur] *noun, plural* **manners. 1.** the way in which something occurs or is done: *She slammed the door in an angry manner.* **2.** a way of behaving: *The doctor's manner of explaining everything to her was kind and patient.* The accepted ways of acting politely toward others is called **manners.** When a person's manners are good, he or she is said to be **well-mannered.**
🔊 A different word with the same sound is **manor.**

man-of-war ▲ [<u>man</u>-uh-<u>wore</u>] *noun, plural* **men-of-war.** *History.* a ship built for use in battle, especially a sailing ship.

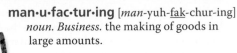

man·or [man-ur] *noun,*
plural **manors.**
1. *History.* in the Middle
Ages, an estate owned
by a lord. His lands were
farmed by peasants who
paid the lord with goods
or by working for him.
2. a grand home;
a mansion.
◄))) A different word
with the same sound
is **manner.**

man·sion [man-shun] *noun, plural* **mansions.**
a large, grand house: *The millionaire lived in
a mansion surrounded by tall fences.*

man·slaugh·ter [man-*slawt*-ur] *noun. Law.* the crime of
killing someone without planning or meaning to do so:
*The driver who hit and killed a pedestrian when speeding
was convicted of manslaughter.*

man·tel [man-tul] *noun, plural* **mantels. 1.** the decorative
structure built on a wall around a fireplace. **2.** the shelf
above the fireplace that is part of this structure.
A different word with the same meaning is **mantelpiece.**
◄))) A different word with the same sound is **mantle.**

man·tis [man-tis] *noun, plural* **mantises.** any of various
predatory insects that hold their front legs up as though
they are praying. The mantis in fact uses its front legs to
catch and hold prey. This insect is also called a **mantid.**

man·tle [man-tul] *noun, plural* **mantles.** a loose cloak
without sleeves; a cape.
◄))) A different word with the same sound is **mantel.**

man·u·al [man-you-ul] *adjective.* using the hands; using
human power, not a machine: *The ancient temple was
built with manual labor.*
noun, plural **manuals.** a book that gives instructions
about how to do something: *The instructions on how to
tune the television are in the manual.* —**manually,**
adverb.

man·u·fac·ture [man-yuh-fak-chur]
verb, **manufactured, manufacturing.**
1. to make goods for sale, especially
many of the same thing: *I work in a factory
where refrigerators are manufactured.*
A person who manufactures goods or
owns a business that does so is called
a **manufacturer. 2.** to make things in a
regular or organized way: *to manufacture
fertilizers.* **3.** to make something up that
is not real: *He manufactured a story
about how the stain got on the carpet.*
noun. the making
of goods, especially
in large amounts:
*Detroit has long
been famous for
the manufacture
of automobiles.*

man·u·fac·tur·ing [man-yuh-fak-chur-ing]
noun. Business. the making of goods in
large amounts.

ma·nure [muh-noor] *noun.* animal
waste matter used as a fertilizer
to make plants grow better.

man·u·script ◄ [man-yuh-skript]
noun, plural **manuscripts.** *Literature.*
a book, poem, article, or other piece
of writing that is written by hand or
typed by the author. If a publisher
accepts a manuscript, many copies
are printed and sold.

man·y [men-ee] *adjective,* **more, most.** made up of a large
number taken together: *Many leaves fell from the tree.*
noun. a large number of something: *Many of the people
who caught flu this winter had to go to the hospital.*
pronoun. a large number of persons or things: *Many
were homeless after the hurricane struck.*

map [map] *noun, plural* **maps.** *Geography.* a plan of an area
showing features such as rivers, towns, streets, railway
lines, and mountain ranges.
verb, **mapped, mapping.** to make a map of an area:
*Captain James Cook mapped the coast of New Zealand
in 1769.*
• **map out.** to plan or arrange: *The teachers mapped out
what the students would do on their trip to the city.*

ma·ple ▼ [may-pul] *noun, plural* **maples.** any of a number
of trees native to the Northern Hemisphere that have
five-pointed leaves that are lost in the fall. They have
small fruits with two wings that spin as they drop. Maple
wood is used in furniture making. The largest type of
American maple is the **sugar maple.** It is the major source
of **maple syrup,** a sweetener made by boiling its sap.

ma·ra·thon [mar-uh-thon] *noun, plural* **marathons.**
1. a running race that is 26 miles and 365 yards long.
2. a contest or task that lasts for a long time and tests
endurance: *I watched a Star Wars movie
marathon all weekend.*
adjective. taking a long time and testing
endurance: *Luke and Gerard played a marathon
Monopoly game that lasted for five hours.*

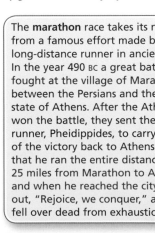

The **marathon** race takes its name
from a famous effort made by a
long-distance runner in ancient times.
In the year 490 BC a great battle was
fought at the village of Marathon
between the Persians and the Greek
state of Athens. After the Athenians
won the battle, they sent their fastest
runner, Pheidippides, to carry the news
of the victory back to Athens. It is said
that he ran the entire distance of
25 miles from Marathon to Athens,
and when he reached the city he cried
out, "Rejoice, we conquer," and then
fell over dead from exhaustion.

*The **sugar maple** may grow as tall as 120 feet
and can live up to several hundred years.*

It takes skill and experience to control the strings of a **marionette.**

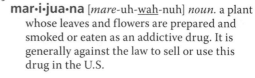

mar·ble [mar-bul] *noun, plural* **marbles. 1.** a type of rock formed when limestone is heated within the Earth. Marble can be white or streaked with colors from different minerals. It is hard and smooth and is used in sculpture and architecture. **2.** a small ball made of glass that is used in games. A game where players try to knock their opponents' marble out of a circle is called **marbles.**

march [march] *verb,* **marched, marching. 1.** to walk in a measured way with steps that are the same in length, often in a group where people walk in step with each other: *Many former service men and women march on Veterans' Day.* A person who marches is called a **marcher. 2.** to go steadily forward: *Time marches on.*
noun, plural **marches. 1.** the act of marching: *The army made its long march in difficult conditions.* **2.** *Music.* a piece of music suitable to be marched to because it is lively and has a strong rhythm: *The army band played a march during the parade.*

March [march] *noun.* the third month of the year. March has 31 days.

The month of **March** gets its name from *Mars,* a god in the religion of the ancient Romans. March was "the month of Mars" and was the first of 10 months in the Roman calendar. The name *March* has nothing to do with the word *march* in the sense of soldiers *marching* to a battle, except that Mars was the Roman god of war.

mare [mare] *noun, plural* **mare.** an adult female horse or other types of animal like the horse, such as the zebra and donkey.

mar·gar·ine [mar-juh-run] *noun, plural* **margarines.** a yellow fat that is used as a spread or in cooking. It is made from animal or vegetable oils, water, salt, and additives such as coloring. It was originally developed as a long-lasting substitute for butter. A different word with the same meaning is **oleomargarine.**

mar·gin [mar-jun] *noun, plural* **margins. 1.** the space around the written or printed area of a page: *The teacher put check marks in the margin beside the parts of my story that she liked.* **2.** a border or edge: *The drapes have red trim on the lower margin.* **3.** an amount that is extra to what is needed: *They won the basketball game by a margin of 20 points.* A **margin of error** is a certain amount used in mathematics to allow for a mistake in calculation, as in a public opinion poll.

mar·gin·al [mar-juh-nul] *adjective.* having to do with a margin, edge, or border of something: *The age of the candidate was only a marginal issue during the election campaign.* —**marginally,** *adverb.*

mar·i·gold ◀ [mare-uh-*gold*] *noun, plural* **marigolds.** a plant with yellow to deep orange flowers. The marigold is a popular garden plant and its flowers have been used in perfume making, medicine, and to keep insects away.

mar·i·jua·na [mare-uh-<u>wah</u>-nuh] *noun.* a plant whose leaves and flowers are prepared and smoked or eaten as an addictive drug. It is generally against the law to sell or use this drug in the U.S.

ma·ri·na [muh-<u>ree</u>-nuh] *noun, plural* **marinas.** a small port within a harbor where yachts and other boats are moored, and where they can be repaired or refueled.

ma·rine [muh-<u>reen</u>] *adjective.* **1.** coming from or having to do with the ocean: *Green turtles are marine creatures that lay their eggs on land.* **2.** having to do with navigation or ships: *The captain used a marine chart to navigate through the islands.*
noun, plural **marines.** a soldier who is part of a unit that stays on board a ship and is trained to fight at sea and on land.

Ma·rine [muh-<u>reen</u>] *noun, plural* **Marines.** a member of the branch of the U.S. armed forces called the **Marine Corps.** Marines are trained to fight at sea and on land.

The United States **Marines** get their name from the Latin word *mare,* which means "the sea." In modern wars the Marines are best known for fighting on land, such as on Pacific Islands in World War II, in Korea and Vietnam, and in Iraq. However, the first troops known as marines served on board ships and were used in naval battles.

marine biology *Biology.* the study of plant and animal life in the ocean. A scientist who studies life in the ocean is a **marine biologist.**

mar·i·o·nette ▲ [mare-ee-uh-<u>net</u>] *noun, plural* **marionettes.** a puppet with arms and legs that can be moved independently, usually made of wood. It is moved by strings or wires.

mar·i·time [mare-uh-*time*] *adjective.* **1.** belonging to or having to do with the ocean, navigation, or shipping; nautical: *There was a display of anchors at the maritime museum.* **2.** being near to or beside the ocean: *Many retired sailors lived in the maritime town.*

mark[1] [mark] *noun, plural* **marks. 1.** a visible trace, such as a spot, stain, line, or scratch, made by one thing on another: *The pen in his shirt pocket leaked and left a blue mark.* **2.** a symbol used in writing: *an exclamation mark.* **3.** a number or letter put on a person's work to show how good it is; a grade: *The teacher gave Sue a mark of 98 out of 100 for her assignment.* **4.** something used to show a position: *The coach said, "On your mark, get set, go!"* **5.** a goal or target that is aimed at: *They lay low so they wouldn't be an easy mark for the enemy.*
verb, **marked, marking. 1.** to make a visible trace on: *She got into trouble for marking the wall with a pencil.* **2.** to show the position of something: *The white lines mark the boundaries of the soccer field.* **3.** to be a feature of or to indicate: *Last month was marked by heavy rainfall.* **4.** to give a piece of work a grade; rank: *The teacher spent all weekend marking all the students' exam papers.*

Marigolds *are often grown among vegetable plants because their strong scent keeps pests away.*

mark² [mark] *noun, plural* **marks.** a unit of money used in Germany until 1999, when it was replaced by the euro.

mark·er [mark-ur] *noun, plural* **markers. 1.** a person who marks or grades something: *The professor is a hard marker who rarely gives an A.* **2.** something that acts as a mark: *The boats in the race sailed around the marker; Ellie started the game by moving her marker three squares.*

mar·ket ▼ [mar-kit] *noun, plural* **markets. 1.** an open place or building where people meet to buy and sell goods: *I bought these flowers from a booth at the market.* **2.** the demand for goods: *There isn't much of a market for wool sweaters in the summer.* **3.** the widespread buying and selling of goods by the general public: *It seems to me that new car model is too expensive, but the market will decide.* The **free market** is where prices are determined by supply and demand and not by government rules.
verb, **marketed, marketing.** to buy or sell goods at a market or store.

mar·ket·ing [mar-kit-ing] *noun. Business.* the process of selling a product, including finding out what would sell well, designing a suitable product, and pricing, advertising, and distributing it for sale.

mar·king [mar-king] *noun, plural* **markings.** a distinctive mark or pattern of marks on an animal: *That horse has unusual brown and white markings on its face.*

mar·lin [mar-lin] *noun, plural* **marlin** *or* **marlins.** a very large, strong sea fish with a long, sharp nose. People often fish for marlin for sport.

English has a number of words for tools and machines that come from the name of an animal, such as a *monkey wrench, bulldozer, Caterpillar tractor,* or *plumber's snake.* The word **marlin** is the opposite of this. The fish is named for a pointed tool used on sailing ships, the *marlinspike,* because the marlin's long, sharp bill is thought to look like this tool.

Hard outer layer of bone

Spongy bone containing marrow

Artery | Vein

In the thighbone, **marrow** *is found in the spaces of the inner bone tissue known as spongy bone.*

mar·ma·lade [mar-muh-*lade*] *noun, plural* **marmalades.** a jam made from citrus fruits, especially oranges, and their peel.

ma·roon¹ [muh-roon] *noun, plural* **maroon.** a brownish-red color.
adjective. having a brownish-red color.

ma·roon² [muh-roon] *verb,* **marooned, marooning.** to be in or be left in a place from which it is difficult or impossible to leave: *The shipwrecked sailors were marooned on a remote island.*

mar·quee [mar-kee] *noun, plural* **marquees.** a permanent canopy jutting out over the entrance to a theater, hotel, or other building.
adjective. well-known or important; leading; prominent: *In pro football, the quarterback is typically the team's marquee player.*

mar·quis [mar-kee] *noun, plural* **marquises** *or* **marquis.** a nobleman who has a rank below a duke and above a count or earl.

mar·quise [mar-kwis] *noun, plural* **marquises.**
1. a noblewoman of the same rank as a marquis.
2. the wife or widow of a marquis.

mar·riage [mare-ij] *noun, plural* **marriages.** the state of being husband and wife. **2.** the legal ceremony to become husband and wife; wedding: *My sister's marriage took place in a church.*

mar·row ▲ [mare-oh] *noun.* the soft substance that fills the hollow spaces within bones. Marrow is important in producing red blood cells.

Chang'an **market,** *in ancient China, was popular with foreign travelers.*

a b c d e f g h i j k l **m** n o p q r s t u v w x y z

marry

*Like other **marsupials**, the female kangaroo protects and feeds her young in her pouch.*

Getting in

Twisting round

Looking out

mar·ry [mare-ee] *verb,* **married, marrying.**
1. to take as a husband or wife: *My cousin asked his girlfriend to marry him.* 2. to join together as husband and wife: *They were married by a priest.*

Mars ▼ [marz] *noun.* 1. the planet in our solar system fourth in order from the Sun. It is between Earth and Jupiter. 2. the ancient Roman god of war.

marsh [marsh] *noun, plural* **marshes.** low, flat land that is very wet and muddy because water cannot drain away properly; a swamp. Land that is very wet and muddy is **marshy.**

mar·shal [mar-shul] *noun, plural* **marshals. 1.** an officer of a federal court whose duties are similar to those of a local sheriff. **2.** a person who organizes certain events and ceremonies.
verb, **marshaled, marshaling.** to organize a group of people or things and get them in the right place or in proper order: *Police helped marshal the crowd through the gates.*
🔊 A different word with the same sound is **martial.**

marsh·mal·low [marsh-*mel*-loh] *noun, plural* **marshmallows.** a soft, round, sweet food that feels like a sponge.

mar·su·pi·al ▲ [mar-soo-pee-ul] *noun, plural* **marsupials.** *Biology.* a type of mammal. The female has a pouch in which young live and feed after birth. A kangaroo is a marsupial.

mar·tial [mar-shul] *adjective.* having to do with war or fighting: *Martial law is the government of a place by the army.*
🔊 A different word with the same sound is **marshal.**

martial arts sports such as judo and karate that have developed from fighting.

Mar·tian [mar-shun] *noun, plural* **Martians.** a fictitious creature imagined to live on the planet Mars. *adjective.* having to do with the planet Mars or its fictitious inhabitants.

mar·tin ▶ [mart-un] *noun, plural* **martins.** a small bird with a forked tail. Martins build nests on cliffs or houses and catch insects while they are flying. They are members of the swallow family.

Martin Luther King Day
the third Monday in January, observed as a holiday to celebrate the birthday of Martin Luther King, Jr., the African-American civil rights leader.

*The tiny sand **martin** spends the summer in Europe and North America, and migrates south for the winter.*

mar·tyr [mar-tur] *noun, plural,* **martyrs.** a person who goes through great suffering or dies rather than give up their political or religious beliefs: *Saint Sebastian was a Christian martyr.* The suffering or death of a martyr is **martyrdom.**
verb, **martyred, martyring.** to kill someone or cause them to suffer very greatly because of their beliefs: *Saint Sebastian was martyred by the Romans.*

mar·vel [mar-vul] *noun, plural* **marvels.** something that causes wonder and admiration: *the marvels of ancient Egypt.*
verb, **marveled, marveling.** to be filled with wonder and surprise: *We marveled at the huge waves churned up by the storm.*

mar·vel·ous [mar-vul-us] *adjective.* **1.** causing great wonder or amazement: *marvelous magic tricks.* **2.** extremely good: *It's marvelous weather today for a picnic.* —**marvelously,** *adverb.*

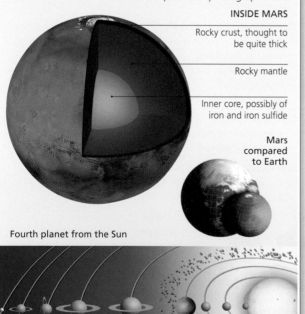

MARS

Mars is the fourth planet from the Sun. Its day lasts just forty minutes longer than a day on the Earth. It has a thin atmosphere of carbon dioxide. On a summer's day temperatures reach only 32°F, and at night they plunge to –110°F. In winter Mars is colder than any place on the Earth—about –190°F. Its dusty surface is covered in ancient volcanoes, canyons, and craters. NASA has sent several probes to photograph Mars.

INSIDE MARS

Rocky crust, thought to be quite thick

Rocky mantle

Inner core, possibly of iron and iron sulfide

Mars compared to Earth

Fourth planet from the Sun

Marx·is·m ▶ [marks-iz-um] *noun. Government.* a political and economic theory based on the writings of the German author and philosopher Karl Marx, who lived from 1818 to 1883. It states that the struggle between people of different social classes has been the main cause of change throughout history, and that it will lead to socialism and eventually a communist society. A **Marxist** is a person who believes in Marxism.

Mar·y [mare-ee] *noun.* the mother of Jesus. Mary is also called **the Virgin Mary.**

mas·car·a [mas-kare-uh] *noun, plural* **mascaras.** a colored substance put on the eyelashes to make them look darker, thicker, and longer.

mas·cot [mas-kot] *noun, plural* **mascots.** something that is thought to bring good luck. A mascot can be an animal, toy, doll, or some other thing. Sports teams often have a mascot, such as the Columbia University lion or the Princeton tiger.

mas·cu·line [mas-kyuh-lin] *adjective.* **1.** having to do with a man; typical of a man: *masculine clothing such as a business suit or a necktie; an actor with a deep masculine voice.* The fact of being a man is **masculinity.** **2.** the form of a word that has to do with males. *Bull, rooster, king, son,* and *wizard* are masculine nouns. *He* is a masculine pronoun.

mash [mash] *noun, plural* **mashes.** **1.** a soft mass or mixture: *The mix of crushed grains and water used to make beer is called a mash.* **2.** a mixture of ground grain that is fed to livestock and poultry. *verb,* **mashed, mashing.** to crush into a soft mass: *Mom mashed the banana so it was easier for my baby sister to eat.*

mask ▼ [mask] *noun, plural* **masks.** **1.** a covering worn over the face to protect it or as a disguise: *a welder's mask; a catcher's mask in baseball; a Halloween mask; The bank robbers wore masks.* **2.** anything that hides, covers up, or disguises something: *He hid his disappointment behind a mask of smiling indifference. verb,* **masked, masking.** **1.** to cover with a mask: *The robber masked his face.* **2.** to hide, cover up, or disguise: *A smile masked her anger; A teaspoon of honey masked the taste of the medicine.*

ma·son [may-sun] *noun, plural* **masons.** a person whose job is to build with stone, brick, or concrete. Something built with stone, brick, or concrete is **masonry.**

mas·quer·ade [mas-kuh-rade] *noun, plural* **masquerades.** **1.** a party or dance at which people wear masks and dress up in costumes: *Brandon went to the masquerade dressed as a Japanese emperor.* **2.** a way of behaving that is intended to hide the truth; a pretense: *Our masquerade of pretending to have forgotten her birthday meant that the party really was a complete surprise. verb,* **masqueraded, masquerading.** to pretend to be someone or something: *The terrorists masqueraded as police officers.*

mass [mas] *noun, plural* **masses.** **1.** a solid lump of matter: *a mass of ice.* **2.** a large number of things grouped together: *a mass of curls; a mass of dark clouds.* **3.** great bulk or size: *We were astonished by the sheer mass of the iceberg.* **4.** the greater part; the majority: *The mass of people at the meeting were opposed to moving the police station.* The amount or level of something that is needed to produce a particular result is the **critical mass.** **5.** *Science.* the total amount of matter that a body contains and that is not affected by the force of gravity. *adjective.* involving or affecting a large number of people or things: *The earthquake caused mass destruction. verb,* **massed, massing.** to gather or form into a large crowd or group: *A crowd massed outside the stadium, waiting for the gates to open.*

In science, the word **mass** refers to the amount of matter that an object has. This can be measured by the extent to which the object will tend to remain in motion if it is already moving, or tend to remain still if it is already stopped. *Mass* and *weight* are similar ideas, but not exactly the same thing. The *weight* of an object depends on the force of gravity. This can be seen by the way an object in a spacecraft far from Earth will float in the air, seeming to have no weight. However, its mass remains the same, even in outer space.

Mass [mas] *noun, plural* **Masses.** *Religion.* a religious ceremony in the Roman Catholic Church and some other churches in which people eat special bread and drink wine to remember the last meal of Jesus Christ.

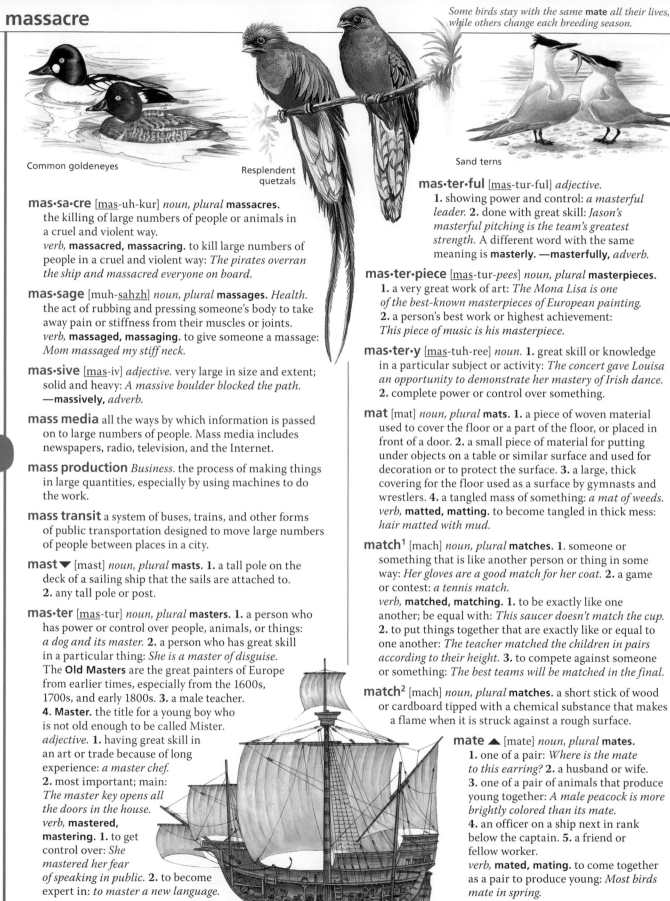

Common goldeneyes

Resplendent
quetzals

Sand terns

mas·sa·cre [mas-uh-kur] *noun, plural* **massacres.**
the killing of large numbers of people or animals in
a cruel and violent way.
verb, **massacred, massacring.** to kill large numbers of
people in a cruel and violent way: *The pirates overran
the ship and massacred everyone on board.*

mas·sage [muh-sahzh] *noun, plural* **massages.** *Health.*
the act of rubbing and pressing someone's body to take
away pain or stiffness from their muscles or joints.
verb, **massaged, massaging.** to give someone a massage:
Mom massaged my stiff neck.

mas·sive [mas-iv] *adjective.* very large in size and extent;
solid and heavy: *A massive boulder blocked the path.*
—**massively,** *adverb.*

mass media all the ways by which information is passed
on to large numbers of people. Mass media includes
newspapers, radio, television, and the Internet.

mass production *Business.* the process of making things
in large quantities, especially by using machines to do
the work.

mass transit a system of buses, trains, and other forms
of public transportation designed to move large numbers
of people between places in a city.

mast ▼ [mast] *noun, plural* **masts. 1.** a tall pole on the
deck of a sailing ship that the sails are attached to.
2. any tall pole or post.

mas·ter [mas-tur] *noun, plural* **masters. 1.** a person who
has power or control over people, animals, or things:
a dog and its master. **2.** a person who has great skill
in a particular thing: *She is a master of disguise.*
The **Old Masters** are the great painters of Europe
from earlier times, especially from the 1600s,
1700s, and early 1800s. **3.** a male teacher.
4. Master. the title for a young boy who
is not old enough to be called Mister.
adjective. **1.** having great skill in
an art or trade because of long
experience: *a master chef.*
2. most important; main:
*The master key opens all
the doors in the house.*
verb, **mastered,
mastering. 1.** to get
control over: *She
mastered her fear
of speaking in public.* **2.** to become
expert in: *to master a new language.*

mas·ter·ful [mas-tur-ful] *adjective.*
1. showing power and control: *a masterful
leader.* **2.** done with great skill: *Jason's
masterful pitching is the team's greatest
strength.* A different word with the same
meaning is **masterly.** —**masterfully,** *adverb.*

mas·ter·piece [mas-tur-*pees*] *noun, plural* **masterpieces.**
1. a very great work of art: *The Mona Lisa is one
of the best-known masterpieces of European painting.*
2. a person's best work or highest achievement:
This piece of music is his masterpiece.

mas·ter·y [mas-tuh-ree] *noun.* **1.** great skill or knowledge
in a particular subject or activity: *The concert gave Louisa
an opportunity to demonstrate her mastery of Irish dance.*
2. complete power or control over something.

mat [mat] *noun, plural* **mats. 1.** a piece of woven material
used to cover the floor or a part of the floor, or placed in
front of a door. **2.** a small piece of material for putting
under objects on a table or similar surface and used for
decoration or to protect the surface. **3.** a large, thick
covering for the floor used as a surface by gymnasts and
wrestlers. **4.** a tangled mass of something: *a mat of weeds.*
verb, **matted, matting.** to become tangled in thick mess:
hair matted with mud.

match[1] [mach] *noun, plural* **matches. 1.** someone or
something that is like another person or thing in some
way: *Her gloves are a good match for her coat.* **2.** a game
or contest: *a tennis match.*
verb, **matched, matching. 1.** to be exactly like one
another; be equal with: *This saucer doesn't match the cup.*
2. to put things together that are exactly like or equal to
one another: *The teacher matched the children in pairs
according to their height.* **3.** to compete against someone
or something: *The best teams will be matched in the final.*

match[2] [mach] *noun, plural* **matches.** a short stick of wood
or cardboard tipped with a chemical substance that makes
a flame when it is struck against a rough surface.

mate ▲ [mate] *noun, plural* **mates.**
1. one of a pair: *Where is the mate
to this earring?* **2.** a husband or wife.
3. one of a pair of animals that produce
young together: *A male peacock is more
brightly colored than its mate.*
4. an officer on a ship next in rank
below the captain. **5.** a friend or
fellow worker.
verb, **mated, mating.** to come together
as a pair to produce young: *Most birds
mate in spring.*

*The Santa Maria, the flagship of Christopher Columbus, had a tall
central **mast** with a lookout platform, or crow's-nest, near the top.*

ma·te·ri·al [muh-<u>teer</u>-ee-ul] *noun, plural* **materials**. the elements or substance of which something is made or can be made: *Wood is a common building material; I went to the library to look up material for my history project.* *adjective*. **1**. made from or having to do with matter rather than ideas and thoughts: *material objects; the material world.* **2**. having to do with money and possessions and the needs of the body: *She longed for the material comforts of a hot meal and a warm bed.* —**materially**, *adverb*.

ma·te·ri·al·is·tic [muh-*teer*-ee-uh-<u>lis</u>-tik] *adjective*. attaching great importance to material things like money and possessions: *The character of Scrooge was a greedy and materialistic man until he realized this was the wrong way to live.*

ma·ter·nal [muh-<u>tur</u>-nul] *adjective*. having to do with or behaving like a mother: *maternal pride.* The state of being a mother is **maternity**. **2**. related through a mother: *My mother's father is my maternal grandfather.* —**maternally**, *adverb*.

math [math] *noun*. an abbreviation for MATHEMATICS.

math·e·mat·i·cal [*math*-<u>mat</u>-i-kul] *adjective*. having to do with or using mathematics: *a mathematical equation; a person who is a mathematical genius.*

math·e·mat·i·cian [*math*-muh-<u>tish</u>-un] *noun, plural* **mathematicians**. a person who studies or works in mathematics.

math·e·mat·ics [math-<u>mat</u>-iks] *noun*. the study of numbers, quantities, measurements, and shapes. Arithmetic, algebra, and geometry are parts of mathematics.

mat·i·nee [mat-uh-<u>nay</u>] *noun, plural* **matinees**. a play or other performance given in the afternoon, or a film shown in the afternoon.

> The word **matinee** goes back to an older word meaning "morning." In early times the "matins" was a special prayer said very early in the morning.

ma·tron [<u>may</u>-trun] *noun, plural* **matrons**. **1**. a middle-aged married woman or widow. A woman who looks like a matron has a **matronly** appearance. **2**. a woman who supervises children in a school or hospital. **3**. a woman who supervises female prisoners in a police station or jail.

mat·ter [<u>mat</u>-ur] *noun, plural* **matters**. **1**. any substance that has weight and takes up space. Matter can be solid, liquid, or gas. All physical things are made of matter. **2**. a subject, situation, or event that needs to be discussed or dealt with: *Building a new hospital is a matter of great importance to the town.* **3**. trouble or difficulty; problem: *What's the matter—have you hurt yourself?* **4**. printed material: *I packed magazines and other reading matter for the long train trip.* **5**. amount or quantity: *The difference between my mother's and father's age is only a matter of months.* *verb*, **mattered, mattering**. to be important: *It won't matter if it rains, because the party is indoors.*

mat·tress [<u>mat</u>-ris] *noun, plural* **mattresses**. a long, flat, thick pad used on or as a bed. A mattress is usually covered with strong cloth and filled with soft material such as foam rubber.

ma·ture [muh-<u>chur</u> *or* muh-<u>tur</u>] *adjective*. **1**. fully grown or developed; ripe: *Fruit is harvested when it is mature.* Something that is fully developed has reached **maturity**. **2**. fully developed in emotional behavior; sensible and reasonable: *He has a very mature attitude for his age.* *verb*, **matured, maturing**. to become fully grown or developed: *A kitten takes about six months to mature into an adult cat.* —**maturely**, *adverb*.

maul [mawl] *verb*, **mauled, mauling**. to injure or damage someone or something by rough handling: *The bear mauled its handler.*

max·i·mum [<u>mak</u>-suh-mum] *noun, plural* **maximums** *or* **maxima**. **1**. the greatest number or amount possible: *The bus holds a maximum of 48 passengers.* **2**. the highest point or degree recorded: *The temperature on the floor of the valley reached a maximum of 110 degrees last summer.* The shortened form of this word is **max**.

may [may] *verb, past tense* **might**. a special verb that is often used with other verbs to show these meanings: **1**. to ask or give permission: *May I come in?* **2**. to say that something is possible: *It may rain tomorrow.* **3**. to express a hope or wish: *May you have a happy birthday.* *See CAN for more information.*

May [may] *noun*. the fifth month of the year. May has 31 days.

Ma·ya ▼ [<u>mye</u>-uh] *noun, plural* **Maya** *or* **Mayas**. a member of the group of Native American peoples of southern Mexico and the Yucatan Peninsula. The **Mayan** people founded a civilization that survived until around AD 1000.

> It is not definitely known how the month of **May** got its name, but it is thought that it was originally known as "the month of *Maia*." Maia was an earth goddess that was associated with this time of year.

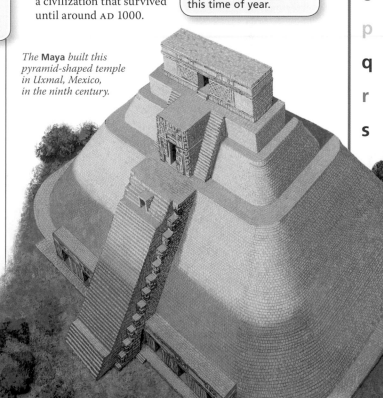

*The **Maya** built this pyramid-shaped temple in Uxmal, Mexico, in the ninth century.*

a
b
c
d
e
f
g
h
i
j
k
l
m
n
o
p
q
r
s

*A river **meanders** through green, fertile farmland.*

maybe [may-be] *adverb.*
it could be; possibly; perhaps: *I didn't hear the phone ring, maybe you imagined it.*

may·on·naise [may-uh-*naze* or may-uh-naze] *noun.*
a thick, creamy, white or yellowish sauce made from egg yolks, oil, and vinegar and used as a dressing on salads, fish, and other food.

may·or [may-ur] *noun, plural* **mayors.** the chief elected official in a town or city; the head of a city government.

maze [maze] *noun, plural* **mazes. 1.** a confusing and complicated network of paths or corridors in which most people lose their way: *We met some people who were just as lost in the maze of hedges as we were.* **2.** something that is very complicated and confusing like this: *To get permission to build on that land, they had to work their way through a maze of regulations.*
🔊 A different word with the same sound is **maize.**

M.D. an abbreviation for **doctor of medicine.**

me [mee] *pronoun.* the person who is speaking or writing; the form of *I* used with an object: *Can you help me open the box? She told me a secret.*

mead·ow [med-oh] *noun, plural* **meadows.** an open area of grassy land used as pasture for animals or for growing hay.

mead·ow·lark ▼ [med-oh-*lark*] *noun, plural* **meadowlarks.** a brown songbird that has a yellow breast with a black bar across it, a short tail and a pointed bill. Meadowlarks live in North and South America.

mea·ger [mee-gur] *adjective.* poor in quality or not enough: *He could not afford to pay for a new car on his meager salary.*

meal[1] [meel] *noun, plural* **meals.** food eaten at one time to stop hunger; breakfast, lunch, or dinner: *Spaghetti and meatballs is my favorite meal.*

meal[2] [meel] *noun, plural* **meals.** grain or nuts that have been crushed or ground into a powder for use in cooking.

mean[1] [meen] *verb,* **meant, meaning.**
1. to stand for; represent: *Do you know what the word "elegant" means?* **2.** to intend to do something: *Did you mean to step on my toe or was it an accident?* **3.** to have a particular purpose: *This book is meant for children.* **4.** to have a certain effect: *She hurt her knee, which means she can't play in today's game.*

mean[2] [meen] *adjective,* **meaner, meanest.**
1. not kind; nasty or cruel: *Don't be mean, let your little sister play the game too.* **2.** causing trouble or difficulty: *Beware of that dog—it has a mean temper.* **3.** poor or low in rank: *In former times coal miners often had to live in mean cottages.*

mean[3] [meen] *noun, plural* **means. 1.** anything that is in the middle between two extremes: *A mean of 70°F is neither too hot nor too cold.* **2. means.** the method or equipment that makes doing something possible: *We have to find some means of getting a message to her.* **3. means.** the money or property a person has; wealth: *He is a man of considerable means.*
adjective. having to do with the average between two extremes: *The mean rainfall for that month was the lowest ever at one inch.*

me·an·der ◀ [mee-an-dur] *verb,* **meandered, meandering.** to flow or wander aimlessly along a winding course: *The river meandered across the plains.*

mea·ning [mee-ning] *noun, plural* **meanings.** the idea or sense intended: *The words "sad" and "unhappy" have the same meaning; The meaning of the poem was not clear to them.*

A dictionary gives the **meaning** of words, but the dictionary itself does not decide what words mean. The job of a dictionary is to study how people actually use words in a correct way, and then record those meanings in the book. If a new meaning comes into the language and it is often used in magazines, books, and other writing, then after a time this new meaning will be included in dictionaries. An example is the word *monitor* to mean "the viewing screen of a computer." The word *monitor* is more than 400 years old, but this computer meaning is new and can only be found in newer dictionaries such as this one.

meant [ment] *verb.* the past tense and past participle of MEAN.

mean·time [meen-time] *noun.* the time between two events: *The next game is on Saturday, but in the meantime make sure you put in some practice.*

mean·while [meen-wile] *adverb.* **1.** during the time in between or since something happened: *I spoke to her yesterday—meanwhile I have been thinking about what she said.* **2.** at the same time: *Dad made a salad and cooked the fish—meanwhile Mom mashed the potatoes.*

mea·sles [mee-zulz] *plural noun. Health.* an infectious disease, usually of childhood, that causes a high temperature and small red spots on the face and body.

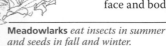

Meadowlarks eat insects in summer and seeds in fall and winter.

meas·ure [mezh-ur] *verb*, **measured, measuring.**
1. to find out the size, length, weight, or amount of something by using a device designed for that purpose: *The shoe shop measured my foot to make sure I bought the right sized shoe.* **2.** to have as its size or amount: *The room measures 10 feet by 12 feet.*
3. to mark a unit of quantity: *Mom measured out two cups of flour to make a cake.*
noun, plural **measures. 1.** the size, length, weight, or amount of something: *The measure of the tree's trunk was over five feet.* **2.** a way of finding the size or amount of something: *Pounds and ounces are measures of weight.* **3.** a device or container for measuring: *Mom used a tape measure to make sure the table was the right size for our kitchen.*
4. an amount, quality, or proportion: *In large measure his success was due to hard work.*
5. an action taken to ensure a particular outcome: *The council took measures to prevent people from parking in the center of town.* **6.** *Music.* a pattern of repeated sounds; a bar.

meas·ure·ment [mezh-ur-munt] *noun,*
plural **measurements. 1.** the act of measuring something: *Thermometers are used for measurements of temperature.*
2. the size, height, or weight of something: *These screws come in measurements of 0.5 inch, 0.75 inch, and 1.0.*
3. a system of measures.

meat [meet] *noun, plural* **meats. 1.** the flesh of animals and birds used for food. The flesh of a cow, pig, or chicken is meat. **2.** the fleshy part of a fruit or nut that can be eaten: *coconut meat.* **3.** the most valuable idea or most important part of something: *The meat of the film is the heroine's story.*
🔊 A different word with the same sound is **meet.**

meat·ball [meet-bawl] *noun, plural* **meatballs.** a small ball of ground meat, seasoned and cooked.

Mec·ca [mek-uh] *noun.* **1.** *Geography.* a city in Saudi Arabia, the birthplace of the prophet Muhammad and a very important place to visit for Muslims. **2. mecca.** any place that is important and that many people want to visit: *The mansion Graceland is a mecca for fans of the late Elvis Presley.*

me·chan·ic [muh-kan-ik] *noun, plural* **mechanics.** a person who is skilled in building, using, or repairing machines: *When the car had engine trouble, we took it to a mechanic.*

me·chan·i·cal [muh-kan-i-kul] *adjective.* **1.** having to do with machines or machinery: *mechanical engineering; Before the invention of the mechanical plow, plows had to be pulled by animals.* **2.** more suitable for a machine than a person: *The actor read his lines in a dull, mechanical voice, without any feeling.* **—mechanically,** *adverb.*

me·chan·ics [muh-kan-iks] *plural noun. Science.*
1. the science of how forces affect objects. **2.** the science of how forces affect the making or working of machines.

me·chan·ism [mek-uh-niz-um] *noun, plural* **mechanisms.** the working parts of a piece of machinery or mechanical device: *The tray-closing mechanism on the CD player broke so we had to replace it.*

med·al ◀ [med-ul] *noun, plural* **medals.** a flat, round metal object with writing on it that looks like a coin. Medals and are given to people for bravery or to honor achievements such as success in sports. A person who wins a medal in sports is a **medalist.**
🔊 A different word with the same sound is **meddle.**

me·dal·li·on [muh-dal-yun] *noun, plural* **medallions.** a large coin-like medal worn around the neck on a chain.

med·dle [med-ul] *verb,* **meddled, meddling.** to take too much interest in the private affairs of other people; interfere: *They were supposed to do the project themselves, but the boss kept meddling in what they were doing.* A person who interferes in the affairs of others is a **meddler.**
🔊 A different word with the same sound is **medal.**

me·di·a [mee-dee-uh] *plural noun, singular* **medium.** the ways by which people receive news and information, such as newspapers, television, radio, and magazines. Another term for this is **the media.**

me·di·an [mee-dee-un] *noun, plural* **medians. 1.** the middle number in a sequence of numbers arranged from smallest to largest. The median is equal to the average of the two middle numbers, if the sequence has an even number of elements. **2.** on highways, the strip of land between the lanes of traffic heading in opposite directions. *adjective.* of or in the middle; middle.

me·di·ate [mee-dee-ate] *verb,* **mediated, mediating.** to try to settle a disagreement between two people or groups: *The United Nations often mediates in disputes between countries.* A person or organization that tries to settle such disagreements is a **mediator.** **—mediation,** *noun.*

med·ic [med-ik] *noun, plural* **medics. 1.** someone who is trained to give medical aid in an emergency or in the military: *Medics treated the wounds of the soldiers on the battlefield.* **2.** an everyday or common word for a physician.

med·i·cal [med-uh-kul] *adjective.* having to do with medicine and doctors: *medical research; a medical school.* **—medically,** *adverb.*

Med·i·care [med-i-kare] *noun. Health.* a United States government program that pays most of the cost of medical care and hospital treatment for people aged 65 and over. The government program that provides medical benefits for poor or needy people not covered by Medicare is **Medicaid.**

med·i·ca·tion [med-i-kay-shun] *noun, plural* **medications. 1.** a chemical substance used to treat an illness; a drug or medicine: *My grandfather is taking medication for high blood pressure.* **2.** treatment using drugs or medicines: *Some diseases need long periods of medication to cure them completely.*

med·i·cine [med-uh-sun] *noun, plural* **medicines. 1.** a drug or other substance used to treat or prevent disease or to relieve pain: *hay fever medicine.* **2.** the practice or science of preventing, treating, or curing disease or injury: *a school of medicine.* Having healing powers or involving medicines is **medicinal**: *Certain herbs have medicinal properties.*

medicine man ▶ among certain North American Indian tribes, a person believed to have magical powers and the ability to cure sickness.

me·di·e·val ▼ [mid-ee-vul *or* med-i-ee-vul] *adjective.* *History.* of or relating to the Middle Ages.

me·di·o·cre [me-dee-oh-kur] *adjective.* of only adequate quality; not very good or very bad; ordinary: *I got mediocre results on my tests.* The quality or condition of being of only adequate quality is **mediocrity**.

In current usage people often think of **mediocre** as a negative word, and they use it to mean "poor" or "below average." To be strictly correct, something that is *mediocre* is neither very good nor very bad, just average, in the middle. For example, if .300 is an excellent batting average in baseball, and .200 is poor, then mediocre would be .240 to .260. Here is a correct example: "Using measures of growth, they determined that two of the bacteria strains were 'high quality' food, two were 'mediocre quality' and one was 'poor quality.'" (*Current Biology Journal*)

med·i·tate [med-i-tate] *verb,* **meditated, meditating.** to think carefully and deeply; reflect: *She tries to set aside some time each day in which to meditate.* The practice of thinking carefully and deeply is **meditation**.

Med·i·ter·ra·ne·an [med-i-tuh-rane-ee-un] *adjective.* *Geography.* of or relating to the Mediterranean Sea or the people, countries, and cultures around it: *a Mediterranean climate; popular Mediterranean foods.*

me·di·um [mee-dee-um] *noun, plural* **media** *or* **mediums.**
1. something in a middle position: *I found a happy medium between studying and relaxing.*
2. a means or substance through which a thing is done or acts: *The Internet is a fairly new medium of communication.*
3. a substance or environment in which a thing can live: *Water is the medium for a fish.*
adjective. having a middle position in quantity, quality, position, size, or degree: *My room is of medium size—not too big, not too small.*

The **medieval** *Chateau de Foix in France was built in the tenth century as a stronghold for a noble family.*

This **medicine man** *is performing the horse dance, a very old Native American religious ceremony.*

med·ley [med-lee] *noun, plural* **medleys. 1.** a mixture, especially of items that do not normally go together: *The actors staged a medley of comedy, drama, and singing at the theater.* **2.** *Music.* a composition that consists of music from a variety of different sources: *The band played a medley of Beatles songs.*

meek [meek] *adjective,* **meeker, meekest.** gentle, quiet, and humble: *Ruth is so meek that I always get my way with her.* —**meekly,** *adverb;* —**meekness,** *noun.*

meet [meet] *verb,* **met, meeting. 1.** to find or come upon by chance: *My mother happened to meet an old school friend at the library yesterday.* **2.** to be introduced to: *I'd like you to meet my brother.* **3.** to come upon by arrangement: *Let's meet for lunch next Sunday.* **4.** to deal with or satisfy: *Where can I get a computer to meet my needs?* **5.** to come together with; join; intersect: *The paths through the woods meet by the lake.* **6.** to assemble for a purpose: *The book club meets at a different person's house each week.* *noun, plural* **meets.** a competition or meeting: *a track meet.*

🔊 A different word with the same sound is **meat.**

meet·ing [mee-ting] *noun, plural* **meetings. 1.** an assembly of people: *The mayor made a speech at the meeting.* **2.** the act of coming together: *The two friends had a chance meeting in the street.* **3.** a place where things meet: *a meeting of two roads.*

meg·a·byte [meg-uh-bite] *noun, plural* **megabytes.** *Computers.* a unit of computer storage space equal to about one million bytes. The abbreviation for megabyte is **MB.**

meg·a·phone ▶ [meg-uh-*fone*] *noun,*
plural **megaphones.** a device shaped like
a cone that makes the voice sound louder.

mel·an·cho·ly [mel-un-*kol*-ee] *adjective.*
1. describing something sad; gloomy:
a melancholy mood. **2.** causing sadness:
*The funeral was a melancholy occasion
for everyone who attended it.*
noun. a feeling of sadness.

mel·a·to·nin [mel-uh-*toh*-nun] *noun. Biology.* a hormone
produced in the pineal gland in the brain of people and
animals. Melatonin helps to regulate the natural cycles
of the body, such as sleep and waking.

mel·low [mel-oh] *adjective,* **mellower, mellowest. 1.** soft
and rich; free from harshness: *The cello has a mellow
sound.* **2.** made wise and gentle by age or experience:
*Her time living overseas made Maria more mellow and
understanding of others.*
verb, **mellowed, mellowing.** to make or become mellow;
soften: *He used to get angry easily, but he's mellowed over
the years.*

mel·o·dra·ma [mel-uh-*drah*-muh] *noun,*
plural **melodramas. 1.** *Literature.* a play, movie, or
television program with exciting events and characters
who show exaggerated emotions: *People always seem
to be crying in melodramas!* **2.** angry or emotional
behavior. Relating to melodrama, or behaving in an overly
emotional way is **melodramatic.**

mel·o·dy [mel-uh-dee] *noun, plural* **melodies.** *Music.*
a sequence of musical notes that make up a tune: *Whistle
the melody and I'll guess the song.* Tuneful or pleasing to
the ear is **melodious.**

mel·on [mel-un] *noun, plural* **melons.** a large, round fruit
with a tough skin and sweet, juicy flesh.

melt [melt] *verb,* **melted, melting. 1.** to change from a solid
to a liquid by applying heat: *The snow melted quickly
when the sun came out.* **2.** to dissolve slowly: *Sugar melts
in coffee.* **3.** to fade away or disappear gradually:
The crowd melted away after the rock concert.
4. to become more tender or loving; soften: *That song
makes my heart melt.*

melt·down [melt-*doun*] *noun, plural* **meltdowns.**
Science. a situation in which the core of a nuclear reactor
overheats, possibly allowing radiation to escape.

melting point *Science.* the temperature at which a
substance changes from a solid to a liquid: *The melting
point of water is 32°F or 0°C.*

mem·ber [mem-bur] *noun, plural* **members. 1.** a person,
animal, or thing that is part of a group: *He is a member
of the Wolves Soccer Club.* **2.** a limb, such as a leg, arm,
or wing, of a person or animal.

mem·ber·ship [mem-bur-*ship*] *noun, plural* **memberships.**
1. the state of belonging to an organization:
Our membership in the health club is due for renewal.
2. all the members of an organization: *Membership
in the club has reached two hundred.*

mem·brane [mem-brane] *noun,*
plural **membranes.** *Biology.* a thin, soft layer
of skin or tissue lining a part of the body.
Relating to, made of, or similar to a membrane
is **membranous.**

me·men·to [muh-*men*-toh] *noun, plural* **mementos**
or **mementoes.** an item kept or given as a reminder
of a person, place, or event: *This old watch is
a memento of my grandfather.*

mem·o [mem-oh] *noun, plural* **memos.**
a memorandum or short message: *The boss is always
sending memos to his employees.* This word is the
shortened form of MEMORANDUM.

mem·oir [mem-*wahr*] *noun, plural* **memoirs.** *Literature.*
1. a written account of historical events, especially
one written from personal experience: *My uncle has
written a memoir of his years in the army.* **2.** the story
of a well-known person's life written by that person;
an autobiography: *The memoirs of the President caused
great excitement when they were published.*

A **memoir** is like an *autobiography* in that the writer tells
about his or her own experiences in life. The difference is that
an autobiography is an account of the person's whole life up
to the point of writing. A memoir is usually shorter than an
autobiography and more focused; that is, it deals with only
one certain part of the person's life. For example, author Frank
McCourt wrote a famous memoir called *Angela's Ashes* about
his childhood in poor conditions in Limerick, Ireland.
The pioneer female pilot Amelia Earhart wrote a memoir
called *Our Flight in the Friendship* about her experience as
the first woman to cross the Atlantic Ocean by air.

mem·o·ra·ble [mem-ruh-bul *or* mem-ur-uh-bul] *adjective.*
worth remembering; easy to remember: *Our family spent
a memorable week on vacation in Mexico.*
—**memorably,** *adverb.*

mem·o·ran·dum [mem-uh-*ran*-dum] *noun,*
plural **memorandums** *or* **memoranda.** a short message
written as a reminder or to inform people at work
about something.

me·mo·ri·al ▶ [muh-*mor*-ee-ul] *noun, plural* **memorials.**
something intended to remind people of an event or
person: *The Lincoln Memorial is a
famous building in Washington D.C.*
adjective. serving as a reminder:
*A memorial service
was held for our
neighbor who
had died.*

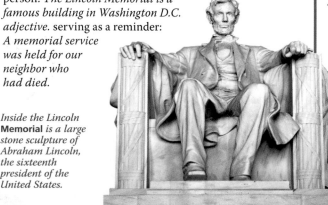

*Inside the Lincoln
Memorial is a large
stone sculpture of
Abraham Lincoln,
the sixteenth
president of the
United States.*

Memorial Day a holiday in the United States that commemorates Americans who fought and died in wars. Memorial Day is observed on the last Monday in May.

mem·o·rize [mem-uh-*rize*] *verb,* **memorized, memorizing.** to fix in the memory; learn by heart: *I memorized my lines for the school play.* The act of learning something by heart is **memorization.**

mem·o·ry [mem-uh-ree *or* mem-ree] *noun,* *plural* **memories. 1.** the ability to remember people, events, and information: *Rose has an excellent memory for phone numbers.* **2.** a thing or person remembered: *One of my happiest memories was the first time I went sailing.* **3.** all that a person can remember: *Play the tune from memory.* **4.** the length of time over which a person's memory extends: *My father told me that the flood was the worst in memory.* **5.** *Computers.* the part of a computer that quickly stores information, either temporarily or permanently. The two basic kinds of memory are ROM and RAM.

men [men] *noun.* the plural of MAN.

men·ace [men-is] *noun, plural* **menaces.** a danger or possible source of danger: *Eating too much junk food could be a menace to a person's health.*
verb, **menaced, menacing.** to put in danger; threaten: *The hurricane menaced the Florida coast.*

men·ac·ing [men-uh-sing] *adjective.* dangerous, threatening, or hostile: *a menacing look.*
—menacingly, *adverb.*

mend [mend] *verb,* **mended, mending. 1.** to make repairs; fix: *The sports store will mend your broken tennis racket.* **2.** to improve in health; heal: *My broken leg is starting to mend.*
noun, plural **mends.** a place that has been mended: *You can tell where the mend is in my jeans.*

me·no·rah ▼ [muh-nor-uh] *noun, plural* **menorahs.** *Religion.* a candlestick used in Jewish worship, with seven or nine candles. A menorah with nine candles is used at Hanukkah.

men·tal [men-tul] *adjective.* **1.** done by or relating to the mind: *Stan was very good at mental arithmetic.* **2.** relating to or affected by a disease of the mind: *mental health; a mental hospital.* **—mentally,** *adverb.*

men·tion [men-shun] *verb,* **mentioned, mentioning.** to write or speak about briefly: *Did I mention that I saw your mother yesterday?*
noun. a brief statement or remark: *Liz made no mention of her illness when I spoke to her.*

men·u [men-yoo] *noun, plural* **menus. 1.** a list of the dishes that can be ordered in a restaurant: *Are French fries on the menu?* **2.** *Computers.* a list on a computer screen from which one can choose a command or other operation.

MERCURY

Mercury is the closest planet to the Sun. It orbits once every 88 days but takes 59 Earth days to turn on its axis. It has daytime temperatures as hot as 800°F, while at night the thermometer plummets to –290°F. Days are long, with sunrises 176 Earth days apart. Only one space probe has been sent to map the surface of Mercury, and little is known about the planet. It is covered with a thick crust of rock that is pitted with craters.

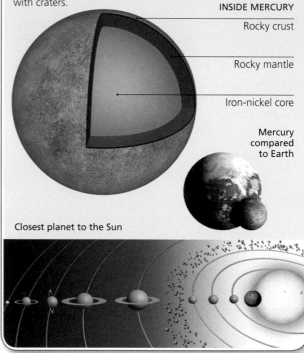

INSIDE MERCURY

Rocky crust

Rocky mantle

Iron-nickel core

Mercury compared to Earth

Closest planet to the Sun

mer·chan·dise [mur-chuhn-dise] *noun. Business.* items for sale; goods: *The warehouse is full of merchandise imported from China.*

mer·chant [mur-chunt] *noun, plural* **merchants. 1.** someone in the business of buying and selling goods for profit: *My father is a wine merchant.* **2.** someone who runs or owns a store: *Many of the merchants in the town made donations to the Christmas charity.*

merchant marine 1. a nation's fleet of cargo and passenger ships. **2.** the officers and crews of such ships.

mer·ci·ful [mur-suh-ful] *adjective.* **1.** having or showing forgiveness or kindness: *The king was merciful to those who had plotted against him.* **2.** providing relief from suffering: *After many hours of discomfort, our flight came to a merciful end.*
—mercifully, *adverb.*

mer·ci·less [mur-see-lis] *adjective.* having or showing no forgiveness or kindness; cruel: *The soldiers launched a merciless attack on the small town.*
—mercilessly, *adverb.*

The seven candles of a **menorah** *represent the seven days in which God is said to have created the Earth.*

*An old-fashioned **merry-go-round** was powered by a steam engine.*

Mer·cu·ry ◀ [mur-kyuh-ree] *noun.* **1.** the closest planet to the Sun. It is the smallest planet in our solar system. **2.** in Roman mythology, the god who served as the messenger for the other gods.

mer·cu·ry [mur-kyuh-ree] *noun. Chemistry.* a heavy, silver-colored metal that is used in dental fillings and thermometers. It is a liquid at ordinary temperatures. Mercury is a chemical element.

In the religion of the ancient Romans, *Mercury* was the messenger of the gods and it was believed that he could move at a tremendous rate of speed. Because of this connection with speed, the chemical element **mercury** was named for him. Mercury is the only metal that is a liquid at ordinary temperatures, and because of this it flows very quickly.

mer·cy [mur-see] *noun, plural* **mercies. 1.** forgiveness or kindness beyond what is deserved or expected: *The guilty man begged the judge for mercy.* **2.** something to be grateful for: *It was a mercy that no one was hurt in the car crash.*
• **at the mercy of.** wholly in the power of; helpless against: *Jill was at the mercy of the school bully.*

mere [meer] *adjective,* **merest.** being nothing more than: *At the doctor's, the mere sight of a needle makes her feel like fainting.*

mere·ly [meer-lee] *adverb.* and nothing more; only; just: *Last week's game was merely practice for next week's final.*

merge [murj] *verb,* **merged, merging.** to combine to form a single thing; come together: *There have been many accidents at the place where the roads merge.*

merg·er [mur-jur] *noun, plural* **mergers.** the joining together of two or more things, especially businesses: *The two small computer stores merged to form one larger firm.*

me·rid·i·an [muh-rid-ee-un] *noun, plural* **meridians.** *Geography.* **1.** an imaginary line on the surface of the Earth passing through the North and South poles. Meridians are drawn on globes and maps to show the exact location of a place. **2.** the highest point that the Sun or any star reaches in the sky. The Sun's meridian is reached at about noon.

mer·it [mer-it] *noun, plural* **merits. 1.** high quality or worth: *This painting shows great merit.* **2. merits.** the features or qualities of a person or thing: *Living in a small town has its merits.*
verb, **merited, meriting.** to be worthy of; deserve: *Your suggestion merits serious consideration.*
• **on merit/on its merits.** with regard to the features or qualities of a person or thing: *On merit, he deserves to be on the all-star team; The principal said he would consider my idea on its merits.*

mer·maid [mur-made] *noun, plural* **mermaids.** *Literature.* an imaginary sea creature. A mermaid is believed to have the head and upper body of a woman and the tail of a fish.

mer·ry [mer-ee] *adjective,* **merrier, merriest.** full of fun; lively and cheerful: *We could hear the merry sound of laughter from the next room.* —**merrily,** *adverb.*

merry-go-round ▲ [mer-ee-goh-*round*] *noun, plural* **merry-go-rounds.** a rotating circular platform that has model animals and seats on which children ride.

me·sa ▼ [may-suh] *noun, plural* **mesas.** *Geography.* a flat-topped hill with steep, rocky sides; a high plateau.

The word **mesa** goes back to the Latin word for "table." This kind of land feature has a flat surface that is raised high above the surrounding land, just as the top of a table is a flat surface above the floor.

mesh [mesh] *noun, plural* **meshes.** a material made of wires or threads woven together with gaps in between, like a net. A fishing net is a type of mesh.
verb, **meshed, meshing.** to fit together: *The mechanic says that the gears of our car are not meshing properly.*

*This **mesa**, in Navajo Nation, Utah, contains rock layers that were formed millions of years ago.*

a
b
c
d
e
f
g
h
i
j
k
l
m
n
o
p
q
r
s
t
u
v
w
x

mesquite

Mating

Laying eggs

Larva, or caterpillar

Pupa

Breaking free

Adult moth

mes·quite [mes-<u>keet</u>] *noun, plural* **mesquite** *or* **mesquites.**
1. a small, spiny tree or shrub with seed pods that can be fed to farm animals. Mesquite grows in Mexico and the southwestern United States. **2.** the wood of the mesquite, used in grilling and barbecuing food.

mess [mes] *noun, plural* **messes. 1.** an untidy group of things; a dirty or untidy condition: *Geoff made a mess in the kitchen when he baked a cake.* **2.** a state of confusion, difficulty, or unpleasantness: *Highway traffic was a mess after the big accident.* **3.** a group of people, such as soldiers, who regularly eat meals together. **4.** the place where such a group eats; also called a **mess hall.**
verb, **messed, messing. 1.** to make dirty or untidy: *I messed my shirt while eating a hamburger.* **2.** to spoil or make a muddle of: *Edie messed up her math exam.*

mes·sage [<u>mes</u>-ij] *noun, plural* **messages. 1.** words or information sent from one person or group to another: *She left a message on the phone saying that she would be late.* **2.** an official communication, such as a speech: *The workers gathered in the cafeteria to hear a message from the head of the company.*

mes·sen·ger [<u>mes</u>-un-jur] *noun, plural* **messengers.** a person who carries messages or runs errands.

Mes·si·ah [muh-<u>sye</u>-uh] *noun. Religion.* the person promised by God to lead the Jews, believed by Christians to be Jesus Christ. Any person who is regarded as a savior or leader is a **messiah.**

mes·sy [<u>mes</u>-ee] *adjective,* **messier, messiest. 1.** dirty or untidy: *a messy bedroom.* **2.** difficult or unpleasant: *Unblocking the kitchen sink was a messy job.*
—messiness, *noun.*

met [met] *verb.* the past tense and past participle of MEET.

me·tab·o·lism [muh-<u>tab</u>-uh-<u>liz</u>-um] *noun, plural* **metabolisms.** *Biology.* all the physical and chemical processes that go on in the body to maintain life and health, especially the changes that make it possible for the body to use food for energy. Having to do with metabolism is **metabolic.**

met·al [<u>met</u>-ul] *noun, plural* **metals.** *Chemistry.* a substance that usually has a shiny surface, is a good conductor of heat and electricity, and can be melted. Metals include steel, iron, brass, aluminum, silver, and copper.

me·tal·lic [muh-<u>tal</u>-ik] *adjective.* typical of metal or containing metal: *There was a metallic sound when the stone hit the car.*

met·al·lur·gy [<u>met</u>-uh-<u>lur</u>-jee] *noun. Science.* the science that is concerned with the properties of metals, and the methods by which a metal is mined, made pure, combined with another metal, and made into objects. A person who works in this field is a **metallurgist.**

met·a·mor·pho·sis ▲ [met-uh-<u>mor</u>-fuh-sis] *noun, plural* **metamorphoses. 1.** *Biology.* in some animals, the changes in function and shape that occur in stages during development from egg to adult. Maggots become flies through the process of metamorphosis. **2.** a complete change in appearance or form. Of or having to do with metamorphosis is **metamorphic:** *A tadpole goes through metamorphic changes to become a frog.*

met·a·phor [<u>met</u>-uh-<u>fore</u>] *noun, plural* **metaphors.** *Literature.* an expression in which a word or phrase is compared to something that is not literally like it in order to suggest a likeness. Metaphors are often used in writing: *In poetry, a rose is used as a metaphor for love.* Having to do with a metaphor is **metaphoric** or **metaphorical:** *Writers often use metaphorical language.* **—metaphorically,** *adverb.*

A **metaphor** is an expression that uses words in a different way from their usual meaning. Metaphors are a good way to bring color to language. Here are some metaphors used by Laura Ingalls Wilder in her book *Little House on the Prairie:* "The wind sang a low, rustling song in the grass." "The big, yellow moon was sailing high overhead." "Even the firelight danced, and all around its edge the shadows were dancing."

me·te·or [<u>mee</u>-tee-ore] *noun, plural* **meteors.** a small body of stone or metal from outer space that enters the Earth's atmosphere. It heats up when it passes at high speed through the atmosphere, and can be seen as a bright streak as it falls to the ground. Something that has to do with meteors, or that is thought to be like a meteor, is **meteoric:** *That singer has had a meteoric rise in popularity.*

me·te·or·ite ◄ [<u>mee</u>-tee-uh-<u>rite</u>] *noun, plural* **meteorites.** a meteor that has fallen to the ground.

Some **meteorites** *are a combination of rocky and metallic material.*

me·te·or·oid [*mee*-tee-uh-*royd*] *noun, plural* **meteoroids.** a small body in outer space that would become a meteor if it entered the Earth's atmosphere.

me·te·or·ol·o·gy [*mee*-tee-uh-*rol*-uh-jee] *noun. Environment.* the science that studies the Earth's atmosphere, especially climate and weather conditions. A person who studies meteorology or who has a good understanding of this science is a **meteorologist.**

me·ter[1] [*mee*-tur] *noun, plural* **meters.** the basic unit of length in the metric system. One meter is equal to 39.37 inches, or just over 3¼ feet.

me·ter[2] [*mee*-tur] *noun, plural* **meters.** a device for measuring or recording something. Meters are used to show such things as the speed of a car or the quantity of water, electricity, or gas used in a building.

me·ter[3] [*mee*-tur] *noun, plural* **meters. 1.** *Literature.* the regular pattern of rhythm in a line of poetry, made by using accented and unaccented syllables. **2.** *Music.* the basic pattern of rhythm in music, made by using strong and weak beats.

meth·ane [*meth*-ane] *noun. Chemistry.* a gas that burns easily and has no odor or color. Natural gas, used for cooking, is made up mostly of methane.

meth·od [*meth*-ud] *noun, plural* **methods. 1.** a way of doing or carrying out something: *What's the best method for making pastry for a pie?* **2.** system or order: *There is no real method to my filing system.*

me·thod·i·cal [muh-*thod*-uh-kul] *adjective.* done, arranged, or acting according to a system or order: *The detective showed a methodical approach to investigating the crime.* —**methodically,** *adverb.*

met·ric [*met*-rik] *adjective.* of or relating to the metric system: *This recipe uses metric measurements, such as 1 kg of flour and 150 ml of milk.* A different word with the same meaning is **metrical.**

met·rics *plural* [*met*-riks] *noun. Mathematics.* measurements expressed in the metric system.

metric system *Mathematics.* a system of measurement based on the number ten. The basic units of the metric system are the meter, which measures length; the gram, which measures weight; and the liter, which measures capacity. The system of measurement based on the foot, pound, and pint is the **English** or **traditional system.**

met·ro·nome ▶ [*met*-ruh-*nome*] *noun, plural* **metronomes.** *Music.* a device that helps musicians keep correct time when they practice. A metronome has a pendulum that can be adjusted to swing at different speeds, with each swing indicated by a ticking noise.

With its high-rise buildings and busy port, Singapore is a busy **metropolis** *and a center of business and trade.*

me·trop·o·lis ▲ [muh-*trop*-uh-lis] *noun, plural* **metropolises.** a large, important city, such as New York, Tokyo, or Paris.

met·ro·pol·i·tan [*met*-ruh-*pol*-uh-tun] *adjective.* relating to or belonging to a metropolis: *The city's subway system is known as the Metropolitan Transportation Authority.*

Mex·i·can [*meks*-i-kun] *noun, plural* **Mexicans.** a person who comes from the country of Mexico. *adjective.* of or relating to Mexico, its people, or its culture.

Mexican War *History.* a war between Mexico and the United States that was fought from 1846 to 1848. It resulted in the United States gaining from Mexico territory that now makes up California and most of the states of the Southwest.

Viruses are **microorganisms** *that cause many infections and diseases, and take on many different forms.*

mice [mise] *noun.* the plural of MOUSE.

micro- a prefix that means very small: *microorganisms* are very small organisms, or living things.

mi·crobe [*mye*-krobe] *noun, plural* **microbes.** *Biology.* a very small living thing; a microorganism. Certain microbes cause disease.

mi·cro·bi·ol·o·gy [*mye*-kroh-kum-*pyoo*-tur] *noun. Science.* the science concerned with living things that are too small to be seen without the aid of a microscope. A person who studies microbiology is a **microbiologist.**

mi·cro·chip [*mye*-kroh-*chip*] *noun, plural* **microchips.** *Computers.* a very small, thin slice of material that usually contains extremely small electronic devices.

mi·cro·com·pu·ter [*mye*-kroh-kum-*pyoo*-tur] *noun, plural* **microcomputers.** *Computers.* a small computer usually meant to be used by one person at a time, now more often called a personal computer or a PC.

mi·cro·or·gan·ism ▲ [*mye*-kroh-*or*-guh-*niz*-um] *noun, plural* **microorganisms.** *Biology.* a living thing that is too small to see without a microscope. Bacteria are microorganisms.

mi·cro·phone [*mye*-kruh-*fone*] *noun, plural* **microphones.** a device that changes sound waves into electrical signals which can then be transmitted, recorded, or made louder.

The **metronome** *was invented by Dietrich Nikolaus Winkel in Amsterdam, Holland, in 1812.*

mi·cro·pro·ces·sor [mye-kroh-*pros*-ses-ur] *noun,* *plural* **microprocessors.** *Computers.* a device that carries out the main operations of a computer. It consists of a small piece of special material containing tiny electrical devices.

mi·cro·scope [mye-kruh-*skope*] *noun, plural* **microscopes.** *Science.* a device with one or more lenses that when looked through will produce a greatly enlarged image of an object. It is used for looking at things that are too small to be seen with the unaided eye: *The scientist used a microscope to see the bacteria in the blood sample.*

mi·cro·scop·ic [mye-kruh-*skop*-ik] *adjective.*
1. so small as to be seen only with a microscope: *Pond water contains microscopic living things.* **2.** using or involving a microscope: *a microscopic investigation of a leaf.* —**microscopically,** *adverb.*

mi·cro·wave [mye-kroh-*wave*] *noun, plural* **microwaves.**
1. *Science.* a type of radio wave that is used to cook food in microwave ovens and to send information over long distances. Microwaves can readily pass through many materials that would block light waves, such as stone and plastic, and weather conditions such as fog.
2. the shortened form of MICROWAVE OVEN.

microwave oven an oven that uses microwaves instead of the heat from electricity or burning gas to cook, warm, or thaw food in a very short time. This is also called a microwave.

mid [mid] *adjective.* in or near the middle: *We are going on vacation in mid August.* This word is also spelled **mid-.**

mid·dle [mid-ul] *adjective.* in a halfway position, point, or part: *I am the middle child in my family—I have an older brother and younger sister.* *noun, plural* **middles.** the halfway position, point, or part: *Jane is the tall one in the middle of the photo.*

middle-aged [mid-ul-*ajd*] *adjective.* in the period of life between early adulthood and old age, from about the years forty to sixty-five. This period of life is **middle age.**

Middle Ages ▼ *History.* the period of European history between about AD 400 and 1450.

middle class the class of people who have more wealth than poor people and less wealth than rich people. Of or having to do with the middle class is **middle-class:** *I grew up in a middle-class neighborhood.*

Middle East *Geography.* a region of northeastern Africa and southwestern Asia. Countries of the Middle East include Syria, Lebanon, Iraq, Iran, Egypt, Israel, and Saudi Arabia. Of or relating to this region is **Middle Eastern:** *Middle Eastern countries produce much of the world's oil.*

Middle English *Language.* the form of the English language spoken and written from about 1100 to 1500.

Today English is the language spoken in the most different countries in the world, and it is also the standard international language for many activities involving people from different countries, as in business dealings, use of the Internet, and airline flights. The development of English as the main international language can be traced back to the Middle Ages, when **Middle English** was used (about the years 1100 to 1500). During this time English grammar and spelling became much simpler, making the language easier to use. English also added thousands of new words from other languages, giving it a larger vocabulary that could be used for more purposes.

Middle West look up MIDWEST.

mid·field [mid-*feeld*] *noun.* **1.** the part of a soccer field that is midway between the two goals. **2.** all of the players whose positions are in the midfield: *We won the game because our midfield played so well.* A member of the midfield is a **midfielder.**

mid·get [mij-it] *noun, plural* **midgets.** a very small person or thing. A person who is a midget is unusually small but has the same body proportions as other people. *adjective.* being much smaller than typical: *a midget racing car.*

mid·land [mid-lund] *noun, plural* **midlands.** the central or inner part of a country or region. *adjective.* of or in a midland: *We visited the midland city of Des Moines.*

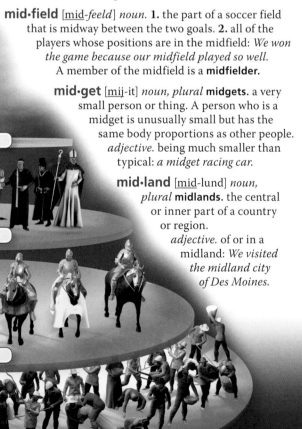

King
Nobles
Knights
Peasants

In the **Middle Ages,** *society was organized in a pyramid system, in which the king had the most power and the peasants had few rights.*

MIGRATION

Animals migrate to avoid winter weather, to find food and water, or to mate and reproduce. Some travel only short distances from water hole to water hole; others go thousands of miles. The gray whale swims some 12,500 miles, while the Arctic tern flies more than 21,000 miles each year. Many birds divide their time between two main locations, leaving Europe, Asia, and North America in the fall for warmer southern climates and returning in the northern spring. Some birds, like the cuckoo, fly alone, but others, like geese, migrate in huge flocks. Insects also migrate—the monarch butterfly leaves Canada for Mexico in the fall on a 2,000 mile journey.

Each year, at the end of the rainy season in the African plains, herds of wildebeest, zebras, and gazelles travel up to 2,000 miles in search of water and grass.

MIGRATION ROUTES

Latham's snipes and far eastern curlews migrate from Asia to their Australian wintering grounds.

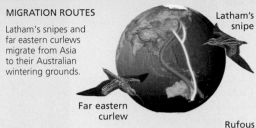

Latham's snipe

Far eastern curlew

Rufous hummingbirds move from Alaska to Mexico. Bobolinks migrate through Central to South America.

Rufous hummingbird

Bobolink

Barn swallows and common cuckoos migrate along heavily used routes between Eurasia and Africa.

Barn swallow

Common cuckoo

mid·night [mid-*nite*] *noun.* twelve o'clock at night; the middle of the night.

midst [midst] *noun.* **1.** the middle; center: *They are in the midst of exams, so they are studying every night.* **2.** a position among a group of people or things: *a stranger in our midst.*

mid·way [mid-*way*] *adjective; adverb.* in the middle; halfway: *We stopped for lunch at the midway point on the hike; She scored the winning goal midway through the second half.*
noun, plural **midways.** the area of a carnival, fair, or circus for sideshows, games, and other amusements.

Mid·west [mid-west] *noun. Geography.* the north-central United States, around the Great Lakes and the Upper Mississippi Valley. This region is also called the Middle West. Something that has to do with this region is **Midwestern.** A **Midwesterner** is a person who lives in this region.

might¹ [mite] *verb.* a special verb that is often used with other verbs to show these meanings: **1.** the past tense of MAY: *Mom packed extra sandwiches because she thought we might get hungry.* **2.** to say that something is possible: *Don't touch the spider—it might be dangerous.* **3.** to ask permission very politely: *Might I leave the table now?* **4.** to make a suggestion: *You might try adding more blue next time, to make a darker purple.*
◄⑴)) A different word with the same sound is **mite.**

might² [mite] *noun.* power, strength, or force: *The lifeguard swam with all his might to reach the drowning boy in time.*
◄⑴)) A different word with the same sound is **mite.**

might·y [mite-ee] *adjective,* **mightier, mightiest.** of great power, strength, size, or amount: *Superman broke down the steel door with one mighty blow.* **—mightily,** *adverb.*

mi·grant [mye-grunt] *noun, plural* **migrants.** a person, animal, or plant that migrates: *The new boy in my class, Vijay, is a migrant from India.* A **migrant worker** is a person who moves from place to place in search of work. *adjective.* having to do with migrating.

mi·grate [mye-grate] *verb,* **migrated, migrating.** to move or travel from one place to another: *As the days get colder, the whales migrate south to warmer waters.*

mi·gra·tion ▲ [mye-gray-shun] *noun, plural* **migrations.** an act or an instance of people or animals migrating in groups: *The fall migration of Canada geese fills the skies with honking birds.* A **migratory** animal is one that migrates to different places, often as the seasons change.

mild [milde] *adjective,* **milder, mildest.** not severe, sharp, or strong; gentle: *mild spring weather; a person with a mild manner; Cindy only had a mild cold, so she could still go to the school camp.* **—mildly,** *adverb;* **mildness,** *noun.*

mil·dew [mil-doo] *noun, plural* **mildews.** a coating of fungus that looks like white powder. It grows on plants and materials such as damp leather, cloth, and paper.

*From above the **Milky Way** has a spiral shape, but from the side it would look like a flying saucer.*

mile [mile] *noun, plural* **miles.** a measure of length equal to 5,280 feet.

mile·age [mile-ij] *noun.* **1.** a total distance in miles: *The car is five years old, with a mileage of about 80,000 miles.* **2.** the distance that a vehicle can travel using a set amount of fuel: *Today's cars get better mileage than those of thirty years ago.* **3.** an amount of use: *The comedian gets a lot of mileage out of his jokes about his mother.*

mile·stone ▼ [mile-stone] *noun, plural* **milestones. 1.** a stone marker at the side of the road that shows the distance to or from a place. **2.** an important event in someone's life or the history of something: *A milestone in the runner's career was when he made the Olympic track team.*

mil·i·tant [mil-uh-tunt] *adjective.* **1.** involved with conflict; warring or fighting. **2.** aggressive and determined, especially for a cause: *The militant conservationists lay down in front of the bulldozer to stop it from destroying more trees.* The fact of fighting aggressively for a cause is **militancy.** *noun, plural* **militants.** a person who is militant.

mil·i·ta·rism [mil-uh-tuh-riz-um] *noun.* **1.** the domination of military values and a military class; glorification of those values. A person who believes in military ideals is **militaristic. 2.** the policy of keeping a large military force and of being ready to use it to attack.

*In the past, the distance to a town or city was carved on a **milestone**.*

mil·i·tar·y [mil-uh-ter-ee] *adjective.* having to do with the armed forces, soldiers, arms, or war: *He volunteered for military service with the Navy.* All the armed forces in a country is **the military.**

mi·li·tia [muh-lish-uh] *noun, plural* **militias.** a group of citizens with military training who can fight or help in emergencies. Each state of the United States has a militia called the National Guard.

milk [milk] *noun.* **1.** a white liquid that female mammals produce to feed their young. The milk of cows, goats, and sheep is used as food by humans. Something that looks like milk or has its color is **milky. 2.** a white liquid, such as plant juice, that looks like milk: *coconut milk.* *verb,* **milked, milking.** to draw milk from a cow or other animal.

milk·shake [milk-shake] *noun, plural* **milkshakes.** a drink made from milk, a flavoring syrup, and sometimes ice cream, shaken or mixed together.

milk·weed [milk-weed] *noun.* any of a group of plants that have a milky juice and dense clusters of flowers.

Milky Way ◀ a galaxy including billions of stars. Our solar system, which contains the Sun, the Earth, and seven other planets, is part of the Milky Way. *See* GALAXY *for more information.*

mill [mil] *noun, plural* **mills. 1.** a building with machines for grinding grain into flour or meal. **2.** a device that crushes grains, beans, or other seeds: *a pepper mill.* **3.** a building with machinery for making goods from raw materials: *a steel mill.* *verb,* **milled, milling. 1.** to grind: *The wheat is still milled into flour locally.* **2.** to move about in a disorderly way: *They milled around the bus stop, waiting for the bus.*

milli- *Mathematics.* a prefix that means one-thousandth (1/1000) of a unit: *A millimeter is 1/1000 of a meter.*

mil·li·gram [mil-i-gram] *noun, plural* **milligrams.** a unit for measuring weight in the metric system. One milligram equals one-thousandth of a gram.

mil·li·liter [mil-i-lee-tur] *noun, plural* **milliliters.** a unit for measuring capacity in the metric system. One milliliter equals one-thousandth of a liter.

mil·li·meter [mil-i-mee-tur] *noun, plural* **millimeters.** a unit for measuring length in the metric system. One millimeter equals one-thousandth of a meter, or about 0.039 of an inch.

mil·lion [mil-yun] *noun, plural* **millions. 1.** one thousand times one thousand; 1,000,000. **2.** an exaggerated number; a lot: *I've told you a million times—Keep out of my room!* —**millionth,** *adjective; noun.*

mil·lion·aire [mil-yuh-nare] *noun, plural* **millionaires.** a person whose wealth is one million dollars or more.

mime [mime] *noun, plural* **mimes.** a performer who tells a story using body and face movements instead of words and sounds.

mim·e·o·graph [mim-ee-oh-graf] *noun, plural* **mimeographs.** a machine that makes copies of written or typed pages using a stencil and ink process. *verb,* **mimeographed, mimeographing.** to make copies on a mimeograph.

*The tall **minarets** of the Blue Mosque in Istanbul, Turkey, make this a distinctive landmark.*

mim·ic [mim-ik] *verb,* **mimicked, mimicking.** to copy or imitate: *My grandma's parrot mimics her—it's always saying, "How y'all?"* An insect that mimics or looks like other, more poisonous insects uses **mimicry** to survive. *noun, plural* **mimics.** a person or thing that copies or imitates.

min. an abbreviation for MINUTE.

min·a·ret ▲ [min-uh-ret] *noun, plural* **minarets.** *Religion.* a tall, slender tower or turret on a mosque. It has a balcony from which a person calls people to prayer.

mince [mins] *verb,* **minced, mincing. 1.** to chop or cut into very small pieces: *The recipe says to mince one pound of chicken finely, then add it to the skillet.* **2.** to avoid speaking plainly; to soften or use milder words: *Don't mince words—say what you mean.*

mince·meat [mins-meet] *noun.* a finely chopped mixture of apples, raisins, currants, sugar, spices, and sometimes meat used as a pie filling.

mind [mined] *noun, plural* **minds. 1.** the part of a person that thinks, feels, wills, remembers, understands, and knows: *I just said the first thing that came into my mind.* **2.** opinion or desire: *Mrs. King changed her mind about who was to blame when we told her exactly what happened.* *verb,* **minded, minding. 1.** to take notice of or be careful about: *Mind the sidewalk—it's slippery with ice.* **2.** to take care of: *Jake minded the neighbors' dog while they were on vacation.* **3.** to not like something; object to: *Do you mind waiting for me after school today?*
• **never mind.** to not worry about: *Never mind about the computer freezing—we'll just reboot it.*
• **make up one's mind.** to decide: *I finally made up my mind to buy the red T-shirt.*

mine¹ [mine] *pronoun.* the one or ones that belong to me: *That skateboard is mine.*

mine² [mine] *noun, plural* **mines. 1.** a large area dug in the ground to remove coal, gold, gems, and other minerals. **2.** a rich source or supply: *The Internet is a mine of information.* **3.** a bomb placed underground or underwater. *verb,* **mined, mining. 1.** to dig a mineral out of the ground: *Mine workers mine gold and copper in Nevada.* **2.** to place or hide mines (bombs) in or under a place: *The soldiers mined the fields around the town.*

min·er [mine-ur] *noun, plural* **miners.** a person who works in a mine: *a coal miner.*

min·er·al [min-ur-ul] *noun, plural* **minerals.** a natural substance that is not a plant or animal. Silver, salt, stone, sand, and petroleum are minerals. *adjective.* having to do with minerals; containing minerals: *a mineral deposit; mineral water.*

min·er·al·o·gy [min-uh-rol-uh-jee] *noun. Science.* the scientific study of minerals. A person who studies minerals is a **mineralogist.**

min·gle [ming-gul] *verb,* **mingled, mingling. 1.** to mix or bring together: *The flavors of mint and chocolate ice cream mingle well together.* **2.** to mix or associate in company: *Boys and girls mingled on the dance floor.*

min·ia·ture ▼ [min-ee-uh-chur *or* min-i-chur] *adjective.* much smaller than the usual size; reduced: *a miniature poodle; miniature golf.* *noun, plural* **miniatures.** a very small model or copy of something: *Roberto builds model airplanes that are perfect miniatures of the real thing.*

min·i·mal [min-i-mul] *adjective.* very small in amount or degree; least: *She does the minimal amount of homework that she needs to do to pass.* **—minimally,** *adverb.*

min·i·mize [min-uh-mize] *verb,* **minimized, minimizing. 1.** to make something as small as possible: *If you wear knee pads when you skate, you'll minimize the chance of injury if you fall over.* **2.** to make something seem less important or smaller than it really is: *The mayor tried to reassure people by minimizing the storm's damage in his speech.* The act of minimizing something is **minimization.**

min·i·mum [min-uh-mum] *noun, plural* **minimums. 1.** the smallest amount or number possible: *The rules of soccer say a team needs a minimum of seven players for a game.* **2.** the lowest number or point reached: *The temperature reached a minimum of minus five degrees last night.* *adjective.* lowest; smallest: *The minimum age in this state to get a driver's license is sixteen.*

minimum wage *Business.* the lowest wage that an employer can legally pay a worker for a particular job: *The minimum wage set by the U.S. Government is now $5.15 per hour.*

*A **miniature** bull terrier is just fourteen inches tall.*

min·ing [mye-ning] *noun.* the act, process, or business of digging minerals out of the ground, such as coal, gold, and gems.

min·is·ter [min-uh-stur] *noun, plural* **ministers. 1.** *Religion.* a person who conducts religious services in certain Christian churches, especially Protestant churches; a member of the clergy. **2.** a person in charge of a government department: *In that country, the Minister of Education heads the department that deals with schools, colleges, and universities.* **3.** a person who represents his or her government and nation in a foreign country. *verb,* **ministered, ministering.** to give help, service, or care: *The doctor ministered to the sick patient.*

mi·ni·van [min-ee-van] *noun, plural* **minivans.** a small passenger van, usually with three rows of seats. The back seat can be removed or laid flat to transport large objects.

a
b
c
d
e
f
g
h
i
j
k
l
m
n
p
q
r
s
t
u
v
w
x
y
z

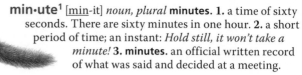
Mink *are raised or trapped for their pelts, which are made into fur coats.*

mink ▶ [mingk] *noun, plural* **mink** or **minks. 1.** a slender, meat-eating animal from the weasel family with soft, thick fur. It lives part of the time in water. **2.** the fur of this animal.

min·now [min-oh] *noun, plural* **minnows.** a very small freshwater fish.

mi·nor [mye-nur] *adjective.* lesser in importance or size: *It's only a minor cut—it doesn't need stitches. noun, plural* **minors.** a person who has not reached the age when he or she legally becomes an adult. A minor cannot vote or be held legally responsible for his or her affairs.

mi·nor·i·ty [muh-nor-uh-tee *or* mye-nor-uh-tee] *noun, plural* **minorities. 1.** the smaller part of something; less than half: *I wanted soup for dinner, but I was in the minority— Mum, Dad, and Tony wanted pasta.* **2.** a group of people who are distinct from other groups in a society because of race, religion, politics, or nationality, and who may be treated differently.

min·strel ▶ [min-strul] *noun, plural* **minstrels.** *Music.* a wandering musician, singer, and poet in past times, especially in the Middle Ages.

mint¹ ▼ [mint] *noun, plural* **mints. 1.** a plant with scented leaves such as spearmint and peppermint; used for its fresh, sharp flavor; also used in medicines. **2.** a small mint-flavored candy.

mint² [mint] *noun, plural,* **mints. 1.** a place where money is made under government control. **2.** a large amount of money: *If your investment is successful, you could make a real mint from it. verb,* **minted, minting.** to make currency: *Next year the government will mint a special dollar coin to commemorate the anniversary.*

min·u·end [min-yoo-end] *noun, plural* **minuends.** *Mathematics.* a number from which another number is subtracted. In 8 - 6 = 2, 8 is the minuend.

mi·nus [mye-nus] *preposition.* **1.** reduced by; less: *Twelve minus eight is four.* **2.** deprived of; without: *Here's the money I owe you, minus three dollars I still need for lunch. adjective.* **1.** less than zero: *The temperature was minus six degrees after the snowstorm.* **2.** less than; below: *I was the only one to get a B minus for the test. noun, plural* **minuses.** a symbol (−) that shows that something is to be subtracted. In the equation 8 − 6 = 2, the symbol between 8 and 6 is a minus.

min·ute¹ [min-it] *noun, plural* **minutes. 1.** a time of sixty seconds. There are sixty minutes in one hour. **2.** a short period of time; an instant: *Hold still, it won't take a minute!* **3. minutes.** an official written record of what was said and decided at a meeting.

mi·nute² [mye-noot] *adjective.* **1.** extremely small: *Even a minute amount of salt will improve the flavor of this dish.* **2.** paying careful attention to the smallest detail: *After a minute examination of the photo, I could see her face in the background.*

min·ute·man [min-it-man] *noun, plural* **minutemen.** *History.* an armed volunteer fighter during the American Revolution, who was not an official soldier but who was said to be ready to fight at a minute's notice.

Minstrels *playing lutes and harps entertained a knight's friends and family at medieval banquets.*

mir·a·cle [meer-uh-kul] *noun, plural* **miracles. 1.** something extraordinary, amazing, or unexpected that cannot be explained: *The Bible tells of a miracle in which Jesus fed thousands of people with just two fish and five loaves of bread.* **2.** something admired as wonderful, or marvelous: *The Empire State Building was seen as a miracle of engineering when it was built. adjective.* describing something that appears to be a miracle: *Penicillin is a miracle drug that has saved countless lives since its discovery.*

mi·rac·u·lous [mi-rak-yuh-lus] *adjective.* **1.** not able to be explained by natural laws: *His survival in the airplane crash was miraculous.* **2.** hard to comprehend; marvelous: *The elephant's disappearance was a miraculous climax to the magician's act.* —**miraculously,** *adverb.*

mi·rage [muh-razh] *noun, plural* **mirages.** something you think you can see when there is actually nothing there; an optical illusion. A mirage can occur in the desert when you think you can see a sheet of water in the distance. This is caused by light waves being distorted by layers of air at different temperatures.

mir·ror [meer-ur] *noun, plural* **mirrors. 1.** a surface that reflects a clear image of anything placed in front of it; usually polished metal, or glass with a silvery, metallic backing. **2.** something that gives an accurate picture of something else: *Do you think popular TV programs are a mirror of today's society? verb,* **mirrored, mirroring.** to reflect an image like in a mirror: *I could see the clouds mirrored in the windows of the building.*

mis- a prefix that means: **1.** bad or wrong: *misconduct* means bad conduct. **2.** the wrong way; badly: *misunderstand* means to understand something incorrectly.

mis·be·have [mis-bee-have] *verb,* **misbehaved, misbehaving.** to behave badly; naughty: *When the little girl misbehaved she was sent to her room.* Being naughty or causing trouble is regarded as **misbehavior.**

The peppermint plant is one of more than 25 kinds of **mint.**

mis·cel·la·ne·ous [mis-uh-lay-nee-us] *adjective.* having to do with a mixture of different things that do not seem to be connected: *He dropped his suitcase and a miscellaneous collection of books, papers, and clothes fell out.* A miscellaneous collection of things is known as a **miscellany.**

mis·chief [mis-chif] *noun.* naughty behavior that is annoying, but does not cause serious harm: *Why do the children always get up to mischief when they are left on their own?*

mis·chie·vous [mis-chuh-vus] *adjective.* **1.** behaving in a naughty but playful way; full of mischief: *The mischievous kitten pulled the cloth off the table and broke the vase.* **2.** deliberately causing trouble: *It's not nice to spread mischievous gossip about someone.* —**mischievously,** *adverb.*

mis·con·duct [mis-kon-dukt] *noun.* behavior that is not right; immoral conduct.

mis·de·mean·or [mis-di-mee-nur] *noun. Law.* a minor crime; one that is not very serious and that does not result in a jail sentence

mis·er [mye-zur] *noun, plural* **misers.** a person who hates spending money and lives as if they were poor; a mean, ungenerous person. Such a person is said to be **miserly.**

mis·er·a·ble [miz-ur-uh-bul *or* miz-ruh-bul] *adjective.* **1.** very unhappy: *Don't look so miserable—it's not the end of the world.* **2.** making a person feel very unhappy, or uncomfortable: *The prisoners were kept in miserable conditions.* **3.** not good enough; poor: *The team gave a miserable performance and lost the game.* —**miserably,** *adverb.*

mis·e·ry [miz-uh-ree] *noun, plural* **miseries.** something that causes great suffering and unhappiness: *The war caused much misery for the whole country.*

mis·fit [mis-fit] *noun, plural* **misfits.** someone or something that does not belong to a group because of being out of place or very different: *I was a complete misfit at school and so was very unhappy.*

mis·for·tune [mis-for-chun] *noun, plural* **misfortunes. 1.** very bad luck: *George's misfortune began when he lost his money gambling.* **2.** an instance of bad luck: *We had the misfortune of being in the elevator when the power went off.*

mis·giv·ing [mis-giv-ing] *noun, plural* **misgivings.** a feeling of doubt or suspicion about what is going to happen: *I had some misgivings about flying in a helicopter, but it was fun.*

mis·guid·ed [mis-gye-did] *adjective.* based on a wrong thought; misled: *He had the misguided idea that he could pass the test without studying.*

mis·hap [mis-hap] *noun, plural* **mishaps.** an unfortunate accident, but not very serious: *The waiter dropped a tray of glasses, but quickly cleaned up the mishap.*

mis·judge [mis-juj] *verb,* **misjudged, misjudging.** to make a mistake when forming an opinion about someone or something: *I misjudged her—she's really very friendly.*

mis·lead [mis-leed] *verb,* **misled, misleading. 1.** to lead someone in the wrong direction: *He misled us and we could not find the complaints department.* **2.** to make someone think or do something that is not right: *We were misled by the local council when we were told the cost of the new development.*

mis·lead·ing [mis-leed-ing] *adjective.* deliberately intended to confuse: *The accountant provided misleading figures to disguise his dishonesty.*

mis·place [mis-plays] *verb,* **misplaced, misplacing. 1.** to forget where you've put something; lose: *I misplaced my watch and it took me all day to find it.* **2.** put in the wrong place: *Our confidence in his ability to tell the truth was misplaced.*

mis·print [mis-print] *noun, plural* **misprints.** *Language.* a mistake in printed material: *Can you find the misprint in the sentence, "I wrote you a lettre yesterday?"*

mis·pro·nounce [mis-proh-nouns] *verb,* **mispronounced, mispronouncing.** *Language.* to pronounce something incorrectly: *Some people mispronounce "nuclear" by saying "nook-yuh-lur" rather than "nook-lee-ur."* A **mispronunciation** is the fact of pronouncing a word incorrectly.

mis·read [mis-reed] *verb,* **misread, misreading.** to read something incorrectly; to misunderstand: *to misread a set of instructions; to misread a person's intentions.*

miss[1] [miss] *verb,* **missed, missing. 1.** to fail to do something intended; fail to hit, catch, reach, or make contact with: *The arrow missed me by a quarter of an inch; We were running late, so we missed the train.* **2.** to be aware that someone or something is not there: *You know I'll miss you when you're gone.* **3.** to avoid something; escape: *If we leave early we'll miss the rush-hour traffic.* **4.** to not have something: *The jigsaw puzzle was missing a piece so we couldn't finish it.* *noun, plural* **misses.** the act or fact of failing to hit, catch, or reach something: *If you have three misses you're out of the game.*

miss[2] [miss] *noun, plural* **misses.** a title for a girl or married woman who is not married. When it is used with a person's name, it is spelled **Miss:** *My teacher's name is Miss Jackson.*

mis·sile ◀ [mis-ul] *noun, plural* **missiles. 1.** something that is thrown or shot through the air; a projectile. **2.** a weapon launched by a rocket and aimed at a target. It usually explodes on contact.

miss·ing [mis-ing] *adjective.* **1.** not in its usual place; lost: *The keys to the front door are missing.* **2.** no longer there; absent: *There's a missing page in this book at the end of Chapter 10.*

A modern **missile** *can hit its target at high speed and with great precision.*

A B C D E F G H I J K L M N O P Q R S T U V W X Y Z

mis·sion ▶ [mish-un] *noun, plural* **missions. 1.** a select group of people given a special task: *That country's trade mission to China has been very successful.* **2.** a special, important task: *A manned mission to Mars will take many more years of planning.* **3.** a place, usually a church, where religious missionaries work.

mis·sion·ar·y [mish-uh-*ner*-ee] *noun, plural* **missionaries.** *Religion.* somebody who is sent to another country by a religious group to teach religion and to carry out social and community work: *Christian missionaries have spread their faith throughout the world.*

mis·spell [mis-spel] *verb,* **misspelled, misspelling.** to spell a word wrongly: *to misspell "running" as "runing."* A spelling mistake is a **misspelling** of the word.

Though there is no way to prove this, it's likely that **misspelled** words were more common before the age of computers. Computer programs have a "spell-check" feature that will identify words that are possible misspellings and point them out to the writer. For example, if you typed "The sky got very dark, and then it started to *rayn*," the spell-checker would tell you that *rayn* should be changed to *rain*. However, you still need to read over your writing even with a spell-checker. If you wrote "The sky got very dark, and *than* it started to rain," the spell-checker would not know that *than* was wrong, because there is such a correct spelling. See also VARIANT.

mist [mist] *noun, plural* **mists.** a cloud of air made up of tiny droplets of water that hangs close to the ground: *The mist made our clothes damp as we walked down the mountain.*

mis·take [muh-stake] *noun, plural* **mistakes.** something done or said incorrectly; an error: *I made two mistakes on the geography test and got the other eight questions right.* *verb,* **mistook, mistaken, mistaking.** to make an error in doing something: *I mistook Ava's tennis racket for my own.* • **by mistake.** in error: *He got on the wrong bus by mistake.*

mis·tak·en [muh-stake-un] *adjective.* describing something wrong; incorrect: *I thought a dolphin was a fish, but I was obviously mistaken.* *verb.* the past participle of MISTAKE. —**mistakenly,** *adverb.*

mis·ter [mis-tur] *noun, plural* **misters.** a title used for a man. When addressing a particular man it is spelled **Mister.** This is often shortened to **Mr.**

mis·tle·toe [mis-ul-*toh*] *noun, plural* **mistletoes.** a climbing plant that lives on trees. It has greenish-yellow leaves and small, white berries It is often used as a Christmas decoration.

mis·took [mis-took] *verb.* the past tense of MISTAKE.

mis·treat [mis-treet] *verb,* **mistreated, mistreating.** to treat something or someone badly or with cruelty: *to mistreat a dog by leaving it chained up without food.* —**mistreatment,** *noun.*

mis·tress [mis-tris] *noun, plural* **mistresses.** a woman who is in control of something, such as a household or a class in school.

*The Cataldo **Mission** in Idaho was built in the nineteenth century by missionaries and Coeur d'Alene Indians.*

mis·trust [mis-trust] *noun, plural* **mistrusts.** the state of lacking trust; suspicion: *Gavin had a deep mistrust of banks and kept all his money hidden in his house.* *verb,* **mistrusted, mistrusting.** to be suspicious of or lack confidence in: *Dorothy mistrusts her neighbor's dog because it once bit her.*

mis·ty [mist-ee] *adjective,* **mistier, mistiest. 1.** consisting of mist or hidden by it: *The boats on the river were lost in the misty morning.* **2.** describing something vague or blurred: *Sam's memories of his grandfather were a little misty.*

mis·un·der·stand [mis-un-dur-stand] *verb,* **misunderstood, misunderstanding.** to understand wrongly; not understand: *I misunderstood Dad's instructions and washed the car with laundry powder.*

mis·un·der·stand·ing [mis-un-dur-stand-ing] *noun, plural* **misunderstandings. 1.** the act or fact of understanding wrongly: *There was a misunderstanding and we went to the wrong church for the wedding.* **2.** a disagreement between two people: *Chad and his teacher had a misunderstanding over whether his paper needed to be rewritten.*

mis·use [mis-yoos *for noun;* mis-yooz *for verb*] *noun, plural* **misuses.** a bad or incorrect use of something: *His misuse of the word "flaw" as something to walk on made us laugh.* *verb,* **misused, misusing.** to use something in the wrong way or for the wrong reason: *The little boy misused his fork at the table by flicking his food with it.*

mite ▼ [mite] *noun, plural* **mites. 1.** a very small spider-like creature that lives on animals. **2.** a small, young, and delicate creature: *The baby was born six weeks early, the poor little mite.* **3.** a very small amount: *He was so ill he couldn't eat a mite of food.* ◀)) A different word with the same sound is **might.**

mitt [mit] *noun, plural* **mitts. 1.** a protective, padded glove used in baseball to catch the ball. **2.** a special glove that covers the hand but leaves the fingers uncovered.

mit·ten [mit-un] *noun, plural* **mittens.** a type of glove that covers the thumb separately but the other fingers all together.

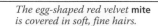

*The egg-shaped red velvet **mite** is covered in soft, fine hairs.*

Moccasins, often made from a single piece of leather, had hard or soft soles depending where they were worn.

mix [miks] *verb*, **mixed, mixing. 1.** to place separate things together: *Teams are mixed in that soccer league, with both boys and girls.* **2.** to blend or combine two or more things: *Ellie mixed the blue and yellow paints together to make green paint.* **3.** to mingle or get together socially: *Parents mixed with children on the school's open day.*
noun, plural **mixes.** the result of combining things: *The cake mix included flour, eggs, and chocolate.*

mixed number *Mathematics.* a number that is the sum of a whole number and a fraction. The number 5⅔ is a mixed number.

mix·er [miks-ur] *noun, plural* **mixers.** a machine or device that mixes things together: *My father uses a paint mixer to make different colors.*

mix·ture [miks-chur] *noun, plural* **mixtures.**
1. a combination of different things put together: *My clothes are a mixture of old and new ones.* **2.** the act of mixing or the process of being mixed: *A mixture of honey and lemon juice makes a refreshing drink.*

mix-up [miks-*up*] *noun, plural* **mix-ups.** a state of confusion: *There was a mix-up over the tickets we ordered and we got only three instead of five.* To confuse something is to **mix** it **up**: *I get the twins mixed up because they look so much alike.*

mm the abbreviation of MILLIMETER.

moan [mone] *noun, plural* **moans.** a soft, low sound with the voice, usually indicating pain or sorrow.
verb, **moaned, moaning.** to make a soft, low sound with the voice: *I moaned because my stomach ached so much.*
🔊 A different word with the same sound is **mown.**

moat ▼ [mote] *noun, plural* **moats.** a long, deep trench dug around a castle or other building and filled with water to protect it from attack. Some large, open zoos have moats to prevent animals escaping.

mob [mob] *noun, plural* **mobs.** any large group of people or animals; an angry, noisy crowd: *The mob ran through the streets breaking windows and setting fire to cars.*
verb, **mobbed, mobbing.** to gather together with others in a noisy, excited way: *The band was mobbed by fans as soon as they left the concert hall.*

mo·bile [moh-bul *for adjective;* moh-*beel for noun*] *adjective.* able to be moved: *The mobile library comes to our area once a week.*
noun, plural **mobiles.** a hanging sculpture consisting of wires or strings, and objects that move freely in a breeze.

mobile home a large trailer big enough for people to live in on a suitable site.

moc·ca·sin ▲ [mok-uh-sun] *noun, plural* **moccasins.** a type of soft leather shoe with no heel, first worn by American Indians.

The type of shoe known as a **moccasin** comes from an American Indian word used by the native peoples of eastern North America. This type of shoe was not known in Europe until early English settlers saw it being worn by the Indians. The first person known to use the word in English was Captain John Smith, the famous leader of an early English colony in Virginia.

mock [mok] *verb,* **mocked, mocking.** to laugh at or make fun of a person in an unkind way: *When Sean broke his leg the other children mocked the way he walked with crutches.* When someone makes a **mockery** of something they ridicule it or make it appear silly.
adjective. not real, but similar; fake: *Leslie wore a mock fur coat because she would never wear a real one.*

The common, or northern, **mockingbird** *can even imitate barking dogs and machines.*

mock·ing·bird ▲ [mok-ing-*burd*] *noun, plural* **mockingbirds.** a songbird that lives in Central and North America and that mimics the sounds made by other birds.

mode [mode] *noun, plural* **modes.**
1. a way in which something is done: *Subways are one mode of transport in big cities.*
2. something that is in fashion, especially clothes: *Who knows how long the mode of wearing faded jeans will last.*

Moats *were built around castles to prevent attackers from climbing the walls or digging underneath them.*

*Lunar **modules** carried astronauts to the Moon from the Apollo spacecraft six times between 1969 and 1972.*

mod·el [mod-ul] *noun, plural* **models.** **1.** a small copy of something: *Ben built a model of the P-51 airplane used in World War II.* **2.** a thing or person that serves as a good example; something to be copied: *Lily-Ann is a model to all students—she always completes her work on time.* **3.** anyone who is paid to pose for an artist or photographer. **4.** a person, especially a young woman, who wears new clothes to display them for other people to buy. **5.** a particular type of product or item of equipment: *What model car does your family drive?* *adjective.* **1.** worthy of being copied: *The Harpers are a model family.* **2.** something that is a small copy: *His birthday present was a set of model cars.* *verb,* **modeled, modeling.** **1.** to make or construct something as a model: *Jack modeled a jumbo jet using a kit.* **2.** to follow or copy someone's behavior: *Karin models herself on her grandmother.* **3.** to be employed as a model: *to model for a clothing store.*

mo·dem [moh-dum] *noun, plural* **modems.** *Computers.* a piece of electronic equipment that allows computers to send and receive data to and from other computers through telephone lines, cable networks, and the Internet.

mod·er·ate [mod-ur-it] *adjective.* not too great or too small: *The family had a moderate income.* *verb,* **moderated, moderating.** to make less in force or degree; calm: *The waves moderated after the storm died down.* **—moderately,** *adverb.*

mod·e·ra·tion [mod-uh-ray-shun] *noun.* the ability to control feelings, appetite, or behavior: *Boris showed moderation in his eating at the barbecue—he only ate two hot dogs.*

mod·er·a·tor [mod-uh-ray-tur] *noun, plural* **moderators.** a person who chairs a town or group meeting, or a discussion panel on TV.

mod·ern [mod-urn] *adjective.* **1.** of the present time or the recent past; not ancient: *Modern inventions include automobiles and airplanes.* **2.** having to do with history from around the year 1500 to the present time: *Anything after the end of the Middle Ages can be called modern history.* **3.** occurring in recent times; not out of date: *The kitchen and bathroom in this house are very modern.*

modern art *Art.* painting, sculpture, and other major art produced between the 1870s and the 1970s, especially works in which artists use unusual shapes and designs rather than showing the way things really look in nature.

mod·ern·ize [mod-ur-nize] *verb,* **modernized, modernizing.** to make or bring something up to date to meet modern needs: *The company modernized the old factory because it wanted to use robots and computers in producing things.* The act of modernizing something is called **modernization.**

mod·est [mod-ist] *adjective.* **1.** not bragging or thinking too much of oneself; not conceited: *I'm glad to say that for someone with so much talent Greg is surprisingly modest.* **2.** not large in size, quantity, or value; moderate: *a modest little house; a modest amount of money.* **3.** proper and decent in dress and action: *That's a modest outfit that is suitable for a young girl to wear.* **—modestly,** *adverb.*

mod·es·ty [mod-ist-ee] *noun, plural* **modesties.** the fact or quality of being modest.

mod·i·fi·ca·tion [mod-i-fuh-kay-shun] *noun, plural* **modifications.** **1.** the act of modifying or changing something: *With just a little modification your school assignment will be fine.* **2.** a change made to something: *The modifications to the school library mean that more students can use computers there.*

mod·i·fi·er [mod-uh-fye-ur] *noun, plural* **modifiers.** *Language.* a word or group of words used with another word to limit its meaning. In the phrase *a shiny, new car,* "shiny" and "new" are modifiers of "car."

mod·i·fy [mod-uh-fye] *verb,* **modified, modifying.** **1.** to change something, usually in a small way: *We modified our travel plan by leaving one day later.* **2.** to limit the meaning of a word by using another word: *In the sentence It was a cold day,* the adjective "cold" modifies the noun "day."

mod·ule ▲ [moj-ool] *noun, plural* **modules.** a section of a spacecraft that can be used separately from the main craft. A special lunar module was used to explore the Moon's surface.

Mo·hawk [moh-hawk] *noun, plural* **Mohawks.** a member of the Native American people from the Mohawk River area of New York. A **mohawk** is a haircut for which the hair is shaved at the side of the head and a strip of hair grown straight up on the crown and down the back of the neck. This is thought to look like the way Mohawk Indians wore their hair.

moist [moyst] *adjective,* **moister, moistest.** damp or slightly wet: *The sea spray in the wind made her hair moist.*

moist·en [moys-un] *verb,* **moistened, moistening.** to make slightly wet: *He moistened his lips with his tongue.*

mois·ture [moys-chur] *noun.* water or other liquid in the air as a mist or on a surface; slight dampness: *Dew is made up of drops of moisture that form on grass at night when the temperature falls.*

mo·lar [moh-lur] *noun, plural* **molars.** any of the large, square teeth at the back of the mouth used for grinding food.

mo·las·ses [muh-las-iz] *noun.* a thick, sticky, brown syrup made from sugarcane.

mold¹ [mold] *noun, plural* **molds.** a specially shaped hollow container into which a liquid is poured, which hardens to form the required shape. *verb,* **molded, molding.** **1.** to model or make something in a special shape: *She molded the clay to form a seashell.* **2.** to influence or shape someone or something: *A person's character can be molded by the way they are raised as a child.*

A **monarch** butterfly can travel more than
1,800 miles in the nine months of its life.

Monday

mold² [mold] *noun, plural* **molds.** a soft, white, or green furry fungus that forms on food and in damp areas. *verb,* **molded, molding.** to grow mold.

mold·ing [mold-ing] *noun, plural* **moldings.** an ornamental band of plaster, stone, or other material around doors and windows or between walls and ceilings.

mold·y [mold-ee] *adjective,* **moldier, moldiest.** covered with or affected by mold.

mole¹ ▼ [mole] *noun, plural* **moles.** a small furry animal that eats insects and burrows under the ground. The mounds of soil it pushes up from the tunnels it makes are called **molehills.**

mole² [mole] *noun, plural* **moles.** a small, dark, slightly raised patch on the skin.

mo·lec·u·lar [muh-lek-yuh-lur] *adjective.* having to do with or involving molecules.

molecular biology *Science.* a study of the large molecules in living cells, such as DNA and proteins. A **molecular biologist** studies the structure and function of large molecules.

mol·e·cule [mol-uh-*kyool*] *noun, plural* **molecules.** *Science.* the smallest unit of a chemical substance that has all the properties of that substance: *a molecule of water.*

> The word **molecule** came into use about 300 years ago, but it was taken from an ancient Latin word meaning "a mass" or "a lump." This word was chosen because of the idea that a molecule is the smallest mass of something that can exist and still have all the important qualities of that thing.

mol·lusk [mol-usk] *noun, plural* **mollusks.** *Biology.* any of a group of soft invertebrate organisms. Most mollusks, such as oysters and clams, have a hard shell to protect them.

molt [molt] *verb,* **molted, molting.** to shed feathers, hair, or fur that is then replaced by new growth. Many animals including snakes and dogs molt.

mol·ten [molt-un] *adjective.* made into a liquid by great heat; melt: *Molten lava from an erupting volcano is liquid rocks.* *verb.* a past participle of MELT.

mom [mom] *noun, plural* **moms.** an everyday word for mother.

mo·ment [moh-munt] *noun, plural* **moments. 1.** a brief period of time: *Hang on a moment—I'll be right with you.* **2.** a particular point of time: *I do have the book, but I can't find it at the moment.*

mo·men·tar·i·ly [moh-mun-ter-uh-lee] *adverb.* **1.** for a moment: *When I was about to jump off the diving board, I momentarily doubted that I could do it.* **2.** at any moment; very soon: *They will be here momentarily.*

mo·men·tar·y [moh-mun-ter-ee] *adjective.* for a short period of time: *After the conductor's signal there was a momentary pause before the orchestra began to play.*

mo·men·tous [moh-men-tus] *adjective.* of great importance, or likely to have serious consequences: *The collapse of the Soviet Union in December 1991 was a momentous event.*

mo·men·tum [moh-men-tum] *noun, plural* **momentums.** the force or speed of an object as it moves forward: *The boulder gathered momentum as it rolled down the hill.*

mon·arch ▲ [mon-urk] *noun, plural* **monarchs. 1.** a king or queen of a country or empire; a ruler. **2.** a large black and orange butterfly found in North America that migrates in large numbers in the spring.

mon·ar·chy [mon-ur-kee] *noun, plural* **monarchies.** *Government.* **1.** a system of government under which a king or queen rules. **2.** a country or empire ruled by a king or queen.

mon·as·ter·y [mon-uh-*ster*-ee] *noun, plural* **monasteries.** *Religion.* **1.** a community where monks live. **2.** the buildings in which a community of monks live.

Mon·day [mun-day *or* mun-dee] *noun, plural* **Mondays.** the second day of the week.

> The word **Monday** goes back to an ancient term meaning "the Moon's day." This particular day was thought of as the Moon's day because it comes after Sunday, "the Sun's day," which was so named because it is the first day of the week.

Tunnel network

Molehill

Mole capturing a grub

Foraging tunnel

Nest

a b c d e f g h i j k l **m** n o p q r s t u v w x y z

mon·e·ta·ry [mon-i-*ter*-ee] *adjective.* having to do with the money or currency in a country: *The monetary system in the U.S. uses dollars and cents.*

mon·ey [*mun*-ee] *noun, plural* **moneys.** currency made up of the coins, paper bills or banknotes, checks, and bank credit, used to pay for the things people buy.

Mongooses hunt snakes like cobras and become immune to their venom.

Mon·go·li·an [mong-*gole*-ee-un] *noun, plural* **Mongolians.** a person born or living in the Asian country of Mongolia. **adjective.** having to do with Mongolia, its people, and its culture.

mon·goose ▲ [mong-*goos*] *noun, plural* **mongooses.** a small, fierce animal with a slim, furry body and a long tail. It lives in Africa and Asia and feeds on smaller animals, including rats, mice, and snakes.

mon·grel [*mong*-grul] *noun, plural* **mongrels.** an animal, especially a dog, that is the offspring of parents of different breeds or species.

mon·i·tor [*mon*-uh-tur] *noun, plural* **monitors.** **1.** a student who is given a responsible task within the school: *Bennie is the library monitor, so hand in your books to him.* **2.** a person who keeps watch or listens for something. **3.** *Computers.* a screen that displays data in text and pictures linked to a computer. **4.** a television set that is similar to such a screen.
verb, **monitored, monitoring.** to listen to or observe something carefully to check progress: *The doctor monitored the patient over several days.*

monk [mungk] *noun, plural* **monks.** *Religion.* a male member of a community who observes rules of that community, such as saying certain prayers each day, wearing certain clothes, or not being married.

mon·key ▶ [*mung*-kee] *noun, plural* **monkeys.** any of a group of small, furry animals with long tails. Monkeys are primates and are closest in evolutionary development to humans apart from the apes. Most monkeys live in tropical forests.
verb, **monkeyed, monkeying.** to play the fool and act up: *Don't monkey with the controls of the machine; Josh is always monkeying around when the teacher is not looking.*

monkey wrench a special tool that can be adjusted to grip and turn nuts and bolts or other objects of different sizes.

mon·o·gram [*mon*-uh-*gram*] *noun, plural* **monograms.** a design combining two or more letters of the alphabet that are the initials of someone's name. Monograms can be printed on stationery or woven into clothes or towels.

mon·o·logue [*mon*-uh-*log*] *noun, plural* **monologues.** **1.** *Literature.* a dramatic or humorous performance by one actor, usually on a stage alone. **2.** a long speech by one member of a group.

mo·nop·o·lize [muh-*nop*-uh-*lize*] *verb,* **monopolized, monopolizing. 1.** to have or get control of something not shared with others: *to monopolize the oil supply in a country.* **2.** to have, get, or use up all of something: *Darren monopolized the conversation with all his questions.*

mo·nop·o·ly [muh-*nop*-uh-lee] *noun, plural* **monopolies.** *Business.* **1.** a power held by a person or a company to control a service or business product: *That company has a monopoly over garden supplies—no one else sells them.* **2.** a person or a company that exercises this control.

MONKEYS

There are two groups of monkeys—Old World monkeys are found in Africa and Asia, and New World monkeys live only in Central and South America. There are about 80 kinds of Old World monkeys, including macaques, langurs, and baboons. They eat insects and other animals, as well as plants. There are about 65 kinds of New World monkeys, including marmosets, spider monkeys, and howlers. Most New World monkeys are plant eaters.

OLD WORLD MONKEYS
Old World monkeys have thin, forward-facing nostrils, walk on all fours, do not have gripping tails, and spend a lot of time on the ground.

NEW WORLD MONKEYS
New World monkeys have widely spaced nostrils, live in the trees, and most have tails that grip.

Old World monkey

New World monkey

Woolly monkey

Proboscis monkey

Vervet monkey

Howler monkey

*When Emperor Shah Jahan's wife died in 1630, he built the Taj Mahal in Agra, India, as a **monument** and tomb for her.*

mon·o·rail [mon-uh-*rale*] *noun, plural* **monorails.**
1. a type of light train with carriages that runs along or is suspended from a single-rail track. **2.** a railroad track with only a single track on which locomotives and carriages run.

mon·o·tone [mon-uh-*tone*] *noun. Language.* a series of vocal sounds in which the voice does not rise or fall but uses the same note.

mo·not·o·nous [muh-not-uh-nus] *adjective.* having a lack of variety or interest; dull and boring: *The job of cleaning windows became monotonous to her after a while.* The lack of change or variety itself is called **monotony.** —**monotonously,** *adverb.*

mon·sieur [muh-shyoor] *noun, plural* **messieurs.** the title French people use when addressing a man.

mon·soon [mon-soon] *noun, plural* **monsoons.** a season of heavy rains in the subcontinent of Asia. In summer, monsoonal southwest winds blow off the ocean onto land and bring heavy rain. In winter, the winds blow off the land to the ocean.

mon·ster [mon-stur] *noun, plural* **monsters. 1.** a strange and frightening imaginary creature. **2.** a plant, animal, or thing that is unusually large or of abnormal structure or appearance. **3.** a wicked, cruel, or horrible person.

mon·strous [mon-strus] *adjective.* **1.** having a frightening or scary quality: *a monstrous creature.* **2.** unusually large; gigantic: *The new multi-story car park is monstrous.* **3.** evil, hideous, or awful: *He committed a monstrous crime.* A thing that is particularly ugly or that someone disapproves of strongly is a **monstrosity.** —**monstrously,** *adverb.*

month [munth] *noun, plural* **months.** any of the twelve parts into which the calendar year is divided.

month·ly [munth-lee] *adjective.* **1.** happening once every month: *the monthly full moon.* **2.** lasting for a month: *a monthly bus ticket.* *adverb.* occurring once a month every month: *The town's parks committee meets monthly.* *noun, plural* **monthlies.** a magazine or other publication that is published once a month.

mon·u·ment ◀ [mon-yuh-munt] *noun, plural* **monuments. 1.** a statue, building, or other structure built in memory of a person or event: *The Taj Mahal was built by the Muslim emperor Shah Jahan as a monument to his late wife.* **2.** an important and lasting achievement: *The publication of* The Origin of Species *is a monument to the scientific work of Charles Darwin.*

mon·u·ment·al [mon-yuh-men-tul] *adjective.* **1.** having to do with monuments. **2.** very large or impressive: *Jasper's contribution to the team's success this year has been monumental.* —**monumentally,** *adverb.*

mood [mood] *noun, plural* **moods.** the state of a person's feelings at a particular time: *Winning the school prize put me in a great mood for a week.*

mood·y [moo-dee] *adjective,* **moodier, moodiest. 1.** having a changeable nature or given to mood swings. **2.** being in a gloomy or depressed state of mind: *She has been moody ever since she broke up with her boyfriend.* —**moodiness,** *noun.*

moon [moon] *noun, plural* **moons. 1.** the round heavenly body that orbits around the Earth and that can be seen shining in the sky at night. This word is also spelled **Moon. 2.** a similar round object that orbits around another planet: *The moons of Jupiter.* *verb,* **mooned, mooning.** to spend time daydreaming or lazing around with no real purpose: *He spent the day mooning about and eating junk food.*

moon·beam [moon-beem] *noun, plural* **moonbeams.** a shining beam or line of light that comes from the Moon.

*The **moors** of Yorkshire and Scotland are popular with walkers.*

moon·light [moon-lite] *noun, plural* **moonlights.** the light of the Moon. *verb,* **moonlighted, moonlighting.** to work at a second job, often at night, in addition to one's full-time job: *He was moonlighting as a cab driver at night because his office job didn't pay him enough.*

moor[1] [moor] *verb,* **moored, mooring.** to secure a boat in place either by ropes or by an anchor: *We moored the boat to the side of the pier with a thick rope.*

moor[2] ▲ [moor] *noun, plural* **moors.** in Britain, an open area of damp wasteland covered with grass or low bushes.

moose ◀ [moos] *noun, plural* **moose.** a large animal of the deer family with a long head and large, flattened antlers. Moose are found in North America, northern Europe, and parts of Asia.

*Male **moose** shed their antlers each winter and grow them again in the spring.*

449

*New **morning glory** flowers bloom each morning and close the same day in the afternoon.*

A B C D E F G H I J K L M N O P Q R S T U V W X Y Z

mop [mop] *noun, plural* **mops. 1.** a long stick with a sponge or a loose bundle of cloth fastened at one end used for washing floors or dishes. **2.** a thick mass of hair.
verb, **mopped, mopping.** to use a mop to wash something: *I had to mop up the floor after I spilled my orange drink.*

mope [mope] *verb*, **moped, moping.** to be depressed and feel sorry for yourself: *He was moping about for days after having a big argument with his girlfriend.*

mo·ped [moh-ped] *noun, plural* **mopeds.** a motorized bicycle.

mor·al [mor-ul] *adjective.* **1.** behaving in a way that others consider to be good, honest, and right: *She is a moral person who always admits to her mistakes.* **2.** having to do with the judgment of what is right and wrong: *Capital punishment is a moral issue for many people.*
noun, plural **morals.** a lesson that you learn from a story or from experience that teaches you about right and wrong: *The moral of the book was that honesty is the best policy.* The beliefs or standards that people have about what is right and wrong are called **morals.** —**morally,** *adverb.*

mo·rale [muh-ral] *noun.* the level of confidence and positive feelings that a person or group of people feels: *It boosted the soldiers' morale when the commanding general made a surprise visit to the battlefield.*

mo·ral·i·ty [muh-ral-i-tee] *noun, plural* **moralities.** a personal or social set of beliefs about right and wrong, and how people should behave: *My father questions the morality of some of the new reality TV shows.*

mor·bid [more-bid] *adjective.* **1.** caused by disease: *a morbid condition.* **2.** having an unhealthy interest in unpleasant or gruesome things: *He has a morbid fascination with funeral parlors.* The state or quality of showing a strong interest in unpleasant things is **morbidity.** —**morbidly,** *adverb.*

more [more] *adjective.* **1.** greater in amount, number, size, or degree: *I spent more money at the mall than I had expected.* **2.** additional: *I need more time to finish my assignment.*
adverb. **1.** to a greater extent or degree: *The movie was more interesting than I thought it would be.* **2.** in addition: *I phoned Mom twice more while I was at camp.*
noun. a greater amount or number: *The more she thought about it, the angrier she became.*

There are two ways to compare things in English, either by using the word **more** or by adding the letters **-er** to the word. Thus you could say "This shirt is *more* expensive than that one" or "That car is *older* than this one." In general, shorter words tend to use **-er** to compare, and longer words tend to use "more." Examples would be *newer* or *more complicated.* The same pattern applies to the use of *most* or **-est.** Shorter words use **-est** (*newest*) and longer words use "most" (*most important*). You should note that **-er** and *more* are not used together. It would be wrong to say "more newer."

more·o·ver [more-oh-vur] *adverb.* in addition to; also: *The shoes fit well and look good and, moreover, they're on sale.*

Mor·mon [more-mun] *noun, plural* **Mormons.** *Religion.* a member of the religious organization officially called the Church of Jesus Christ of Latter-Day Saints.
adjective. having to do with the members of the religious group or their church.

morn [morn] *noun, plural* **morns.** another word for morning.

morn·ing [more-ning] *noun, plural* **mornings.** the time of day from sunrise until noon.
🔊 A different word with the same sound is **mourning.**

morning glory ▲ a vine with funnel-shaped white, pink or blue flowers that open early in the morning and then close in the afternoon.

morph [morf] *verb*, **morphed, morphing. 1.** *Computers.* to change one image into another using a computer program. **2.** to take on a different form or become a different type: *Scientists believe that this type of cell can morph into many other cell types in the body.*

Morse code *Language.* a system used for sending messages in which letters and numbers are represented by signals using dots or dashes or long and short sounds.

mor·sel [more-sul] *noun, plural* **morsels.** a very small piece or amount: *We were so hungry we ate every morsel of food on our plates.*

The **Morse code** is named for Samuel F. B. *Morse,* who lived from 1791 to 1872. He was a man with a wide variety of talents. In addition to inventing the Morse Code, he also developed the first successful electric telegraph in the U.S., was the first president of the American Academy of Design, and was a famous artist known especially for his portrait paintings.

mor·tal [more-thl] *adjective.* **1.** certain to die eventually: *All animals are mortal.* **2.** capable of causing death: *a mortal wound or injury.* **3.** extreme or severe: *The hostages lived in mortal fear of their captors for eight days before they were finally rescued.* **4.** very dangerous or deadly: *a mortal enemy.*
noun, plural **mortals.** a human being.

mor·tar[1] [more-tur] *noun.* a mixture of sand, water, and cement or lime that is used to join bricks or stones together when building.

mor·tar[2] [more-tur] *noun, plural* **mortars.** a heavy bowl in which food or other substances are crushed into a powder by hitting or rubbing them with a tool called a pestle.

mo·sa·ic [moh-zay-ik] *noun, plural* **mosaics.** *Art.* a decoration made by setting small colored stones, glass, or tiles into a pattern or picture.

Mo·ses [moh-zis] *noun. Religion.* a Hebrew prophet and leader of the Jewish people in ancient times who, in the Bible, freed the Israelites from slavery in Egypt.

Mos·lem [moz-lum] another spelling for MUSLIM.

mosque [mosk] *noun, plural* **mosques.** *Religion.* a Muslim temple or place of worship.

mos·qui·to ▼ [muh-skee-toh] *noun, plural* **mosquitoes** *or* **mosquitos.** a small flying insect, the female of which bites the skin and sucks the blood of people or animals. Some mosquitoes carry diseases such as malaria and yellow fever.

moss [mawss *or* moss] *noun, plural* **mosses.** a plant with very small leaves that grows in a thick, soft mat on wet soil, trees, or rocks. Something that is covered with this plant is described as **mossy.**

most [most] *adjective.* **1.** greatest in number, amount, degree, or quantity: *Which team in the league scored the most points this season?* **2.** the majority of; almost all: *Most of the class failed the math test.*
noun. the greatest number, amount, degree, or quantity: *Five dollars is the most that Mom has ever won in the lottery.*
adverb. in or to the highest degree: *Rock climbing was the most terrifying experience of my life.*
See the word MORE for more information.

most·ly [most-lee] *adverb.* for the greatest part; mainly: *My homework is mostly finished by dinnertime.*

Caterpillar

Eggs

Pupa

Adult moth

An Indian moon **moth** *passes through four life stages—eggs hatch into caterpillars, caterpillars become pupas, and pupas turn into adult moths.*

mo·tel [moh-tel] *noun, plural* **motels.** a roadside hotel where travelers can park their cars outside their rooms.

> The word **motel** is what is known as a *blend,* meaning that it was formed by blending (putting together) other words. In this case a motel is a "motor hotel." In the early days of automobiles a car was often called a *motorcar* or simply a *motor.*

moth ◀ [mawth] *noun, plural* **moths.** a flying insect similar to a butterfly, but with a thick body and feathery antennae. Moths usually fly at night and are attracted to lights.

moth·er [muTH-ur] *noun, plural* **mothers.** **1.** a female parent. **2.** the origin or cause of something: *Philosophy is said to be the mother of all the sciences, because it taught people to think carefully and analyze the world.*
verb, **mothered, mothering.** to care or protect someone or something as like a mother: *Our teacher always mothers us when we're on a school trip.*
adjective. **1.** being a mother: *a mother bird.* **2.** relating to a mother: *mother love.* **3.** having an attachment that resembles the relationship between a mother and child: *Britain is often called the mother country of Australia, because that is where Australia's early settlers come from.*

moth·er·board [muTH-ur-bord] *noun, plural* **motherboards.** *Computers.* the main circuit board that holds other boards containing the internal wiring of a computer.

moth·er·in·law *noun, plural* **mothers-in-law.** the mother of a person's husband or wife.

moth·er·ly [muTH-ur-lee] *adjective.* of or like a mother: *She showed motherly concern toward her students.*

Mother Nature the force of nature, represented as a powerful woman that controls the weather: *Mother Nature has hit us with a tough season of hurricanes this year.*

Mother's Day a day, usually the second Sunday in May, on which people honor their mothers.

mo·tion [moh-shun] *noun, plural* **motions. 1.** the act or process of changing place or moving: *The backward and forward motion of the cradle calmed the baby.* **2.** a formal suggestion or proposal made at a meeting: *The head of the School Board put forward a motion to replace the janitor.*
verb, **motioned, motioning.** to make a signal to someone using your hand or head: *Dad motioned to the waiter that we wanted more water.*

mo·tion·less [moh-shun-lis] *adjective.* not moving: *He stood, motionless, as the snake crawled past his feet.*
—motionlessly, *adverb.*

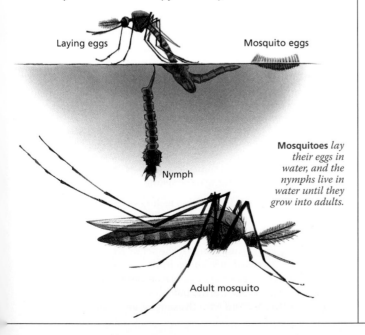

Laying eggs

Mosquito eggs

Nymph

Adult mosquito

Mosquitoes lay their eggs in water, and the nymphs live in water until they grow into adults.

motion picture a movie or moving picture. A series of pictures is projected onto a screen at such high speed that it looks as if the people and objects are actually in motion.

mo·ti·vate [moh-tuh-*vate*] *verb,* **motivated, motivating.** to provide someone a reason for doing something: *I was motivated to study hard for the exam because the student with the highest grade wins a prize.* The reason or enthusiasm for doing something is **motivation.**

mo·tive [moh-tiv] *noun, plural* **motives.** a reason for doing something: *The police were investigating the motive behind the bombing.*

mo·tor [moh-tur] *noun, plural* **motors.** the part of a machine that makes it work by changing electrical or fuel energy into movement: *The motor on the lawn mower runs on gasoline.*
adjective. **1.** having to do with or operated by a motor: *He traded in his bicycle and bought a motor scooter.* **2.** having to do with the nerve impulses that control muscles and movement: *Since the accident, she has poor motor coordination in her hands.*
verb, **motored, motoring.** to travel by car; drive: *We were motoring pretty fast when we were stopped by the police.*

mo·tor·boat [moh-tur-*bote*] *noun, plural* **motorboats.** a boat that is powered by an engine.

mo·tor·cy·cle ▼ [moh-tur-*sye*-kul] *noun, plural* **motorcycles.** a fast, heavy vehicle with two wheels and powered by an engine.

Some modern **motorcycles** *are very powerful machines.*

motor home a large motor vehicle equipped with beds, a kitchen, and bathroom to be used as a traveling home.

mo·tor·ist [moh-tur-ist] *noun, plural* **motorists.** someone who drives a car.

mot·to [mot-oh] *noun, plural* **mottoes** *or* **mottos.** a short saying that sums up the beliefs of a particular group or organization: *The motto for our school is "Strive for Excellence."*

mound [mound] *noun, plural* **mounds. 1.** a large pile or heap of dirt, stones, or other material: *The snow plow left huge mounds of snow along the side of the road; There is a mound of papers on my desk.* **2.** the raised area in the center of a baseball diamond from which the pitcher throws the ball.
verb, **mounded, mounding.** to pile up into a heap or hill: *I mounded an enormous amount of pasta onto my plate at the buffet dinner.*

mount[1] [mount] *verb,* **mounted, mounting. 1.** to go up something: *The workman mounted the ladder and made his way up to fix the roof.* **2.** to get up on something: *to mount a horse or a bicycle.* **3.** to set or fix into position: *They mounted the mirror onto the bathroom wall.* **4.** to gradually increase: *My excitement is mounting as my birthday gets closer and closer.*
noun, plural **mounts. 1.** a horse, other animal, or bicycle for riding: *The pony was a good mount for a beginning rider.* **2.** a backing or setting on which something is fixed: *This colourful painting needs a plain white mount.*

mount[2] [mount] *noun, plural* **mounts.** a mountain.

moun·tain [moun-tun] *noun, plural* **mountains. 1.** a natural raised land mass that is higher than a hill; a very tall feature of the land: *They live near Palamar Mountain, which is about 6,000 feet high.* **2.** a huge amount or pile of something: *I have a mountain of laundry to do.*

moun·tain·eer ▲ [moun-tuh-*neer*] *noun, plural* **mountaineers.** someone who lives in the mountains or someone who climbs mountains for sport.

mountain lion a large and powerful wild cat of North and South America. The mountain lion is also called a **cougar.**

Mountain lions now live only in a few places in the U.S. and Canada, but they were once found all over North America. People in different places called the animal by different names—not only *mountain lion* but also *cougar, puma, panther, catamount,* and many other names. In fact, there is so little agreement on the name of this animal that it has two different scientific names, even though in science each animal is supposed to be called by just one official name. It is known as either *Felis concolor* or *Puma concolor,* and studies show that these two names are equally common.

moun·tain·ous [moun-tuh-nus] *adjective.* **1.** having a lot of mountains: *We live in a mountainous region that is great for hiking in the summer.* **2.** large in amount; huge: *The mountainous waves crashed against the rocks.*

mourn [morn] *verb,* **mourned, mourning.** to feel or show sadness or grief: *She mourned for her husband who died in the war.* A **mourner** is someone who feels or shows sorrow for the loss of something or someone.

mourn·ful [morn-ful] *adjective.* feeling sad or sorrowful: *He had a mournful expression on his face at the funeral.* **—mournfully,** *adverb.*

mourn·ing [morn-ing] *noun,* **1.** the act of grieving or being very sad: *The family was in mourning for their father.* **2.** an outward sign or symbol of grief such as wearing black clothes or black armband.
🔊 A different word with the same sound is **morning.**

moustache another spelling for MUSTACHE.

mouse ▼ [mous] *noun, plural* **mice** *or* **mouses.**
1. a small animal with a long, tail, pointed nose, and sharp teeth; a mouse is a type of rodent. **2.** *Computers.* a device that you hold and move with the hand in order to move and control the cursor on a computer screen or give other commands to the computer.

> The use of the word **mouse** to mean a computer tool is thought to have come into use in the mid-1960s. The first user of the word is thought to have been computer scientist Douglas Engelbart, who received a patent as the inventor of the mouse device. He has said that he called it a "mouse" because the thin wire attaching it to the computer looked to him like the tail of a mouse

mouth [mouth *for noun;* mouTH *for verb*] *noun, plural* **mouths.**
1. the opening through which humans and animals take in food and drink. The human mouth is surrounded on the outside by lips, and contains the tongue and teeth. **2.** an opening of anything: *We rode our horses into the mouth of the canyon.* **3.** the place where a river flows into a larger body of water such as the sea. *verb,* **mouthed, mouthing.** to say things that you do not believe or do not understand: *The losing team's captain mouthed compliments about the winning team.*

mouth·ful [mouth-*ful*] *noun, plural* **mouthfuls.** the amount that can fit into the mouth at one time.

mouth·piece [mouth-*pees*] *noun, plural* **mouthpieces.**
1. the part of a musical instrument, telephone, or other device that is put to, between, or near the lips. **2.** a person who expresses someone else's opinion or beliefs: *That newspaper claims to report the news, but is really just a mouthpiece for the government.*

mouth·wash [mouth-*wahsh or* mouth-*wawsh*] *noun, plural* **mouthwashes.** *Health.* a liquid used to kill germs in the mouth and keep the mouth, teeth, and breath clean and fresh.

mov·a·ble [moov-*uh-bul*] *adjective.* **1.** able to be moved: *Her teddy bear has movable arms and legs.* **2.** changing its date from one year to the next: *Easter is a movable holiday because it depends on the cycle of the Moon.* This word is also spelled **moveable.**

move [moov] *verb,* **moved, moving. 1.** to change the place, position, or direction of something: *She moved the chair from the living room to the dining room; The bird flew away when I moved toward it.* **2.** to change the place where you live or work: *My brother is moving to New York to live with our cousin.* **3.** to make progress; advance: *She'll be moving her way up to a manager's position by the end of the year.* **4.** to cause someone to act or decide something: *The demonstration moved me to change my ideas about animal testing.* **5.** to affect someone's feelings in a strong way: *They were deeply moved by the sad story.* **6.** to make a proposal or suggestion in a meeting: *The Board President moved that they vote on the matter. noun, plural* **moves. 1.** the act of moving; movement: *The prisoner made a sudden move toward the door.* **2.** an action or step taken to achieve something: *Getting to the movie theater early to find good seats was a good move.* **3.** a player's turn in a game: *I've had my turn—it's your move.*

move·ment [moov-munt] *noun, plural* **movements.**
1. the act or process of moving: *The hunter made a sudden movement and frightened the deer away.* **2.** the working or turning parts of a mechanism: *the movement of a watch or clock.* **3.** an organized group of people who share the same beliefs and work for a common purpose: *He was an active leader in the peace movement.* **4.** a gradual change in a situation or in people's opinions: *Over the last twenty years there has been a movement toward equality for women in the workplace.* **5.** *Music.* one section of a long musical piece: *The famous symphony had three movements, each quite different from the other.*

mov·er [moo-vur] *noun, plural* **movers.** someone whose job is to help people pack up their furniture and other possessions and move them to a different home or workplace.

mov·ie [moo-vee] *noun, plural* **movies. 1.** a series of moving pictures that is projected onto a screen; a film or motion picture. **2. movies.** a theater that shows such pictures: *My parents went to the movies on Saturday night.* **3.** the motion picture industry: *I've always dreamed of a career in the movies.*

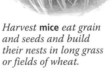

Harvest **mice** *eat grain and seeds and build their nests in long grass or fields of wheat.*

mov·ing [moo-ving] *adjective.*
1. having movement; capable of movement: *I couldn't find my friends in the constantly moving crowd at the concert.* **2.** causing or producing action: *She was the moving force behind setting up the charity.* **3.** causing people to feel strong emotions: *His moving speech had the audience in tears.*

mow [moh] *verb,* **mowed, mowed** *or* **mown, mowing.** to cut plants such as grass or wheat with a machine or a tool.

mow·er [moh-ur] *noun, plural* **mowers.** a machine for cutting grass or grain.

mpg *or* **m.p.g.** an abbreviation for **miles per gallon.**

mph *or* **m.p.h.** an abbreviation for **miles per hour.**

Mr. *plural.* **Messrs.** a title put before a man's name.

Mrs. *plural.* **Mmes.** a title put before a married woman's name.

Ms. *plural.* **Mss.** *or* **Mses.** a title put before a woman's name.

> "*Ms.* Jones and *Mr.* Smith will be in charge of the meeting." The word **Ms.** is believed to have come into the language about the year 1950, and it began to be used widely in the 1970s. The words *Miss* and *Mrs.* were already in common use, but these words indicate either that a woman is married (*Mrs.*) or is not married (*Miss*). The word *Ms.* is equivalent to the word *Mr.* for men; that is, it can be used without referring to whether or not the person is married.

*The ancient Chinese gathered **mulberry** leaves to feed the caterpillars they raised to make silk.*

much [much] *adjective.* **more, most.** in great quantity, amount, or degree: *I can't go out this weekend because I have too much homework.*
adverb, **more, most.**
1. by or to a great amount or degree: *These shoes are much more comfortable than the other pair.* **2.** nearly or approximately: *The food here is much like all the other fast-food outlets.*
noun. a great amount or quantity: *Much that has been written about that celebrity is actually false.*

mu·ci·lage [myoo-suh-lij] *noun, plural* **mucilages.** a sticky substance like glue, produced by certain plants.

mu·cus [myoo-kus] *noun.* a thick, slimy substance produced to moisten and protect the inside of your mouth, nose, throat, and other parts of the body.

mud [mud] *noun.* soil that has become wet, soft, and sticky: *My sneakers were covered in mud after playing baseball in the rain.*

mud·dle [mud-ul] *noun, plural* **muddles.** an untidy or confused mess: *My bedroom is in such a muddle I can't find anything!*
verb, **muddled, muddling. 1.** to mix up or confuse: *The waiter got muddled up with our orders and brought out the wrong food.* **2.** to succeed in doing something, but in a very clumsy or confused way: *I muddled through my exam even though I didn't understand most of the questions.*

mud·dy [mud-ee] *adjective,* **muddier, muddiest.** filled or covered with mud: *a muddy path; muddy shoes.*
verb, **muddied, muddying.** to fill or cover with mud: *We had to take our shoes off so that we wouldn't muddy the new carpet.*

muff [muf] *noun, plural* **muffs.** a roll of fur or woolen material into which you put your hands to keep them warm.

muf·fin [muf-in] *noun, plural* **muffins.** a small, often sweetened, cup-shaped cake.

muf·fle [muf-ul] *verb,* **muffled, muffling.** to deaden or soften the sound of something: *I closed my window to muffle the sound of the party next door.*

muf·fler [muf-lur] *noun, plural* **mufflers. 1.** a scarf worn to protect and keep your neck warm. **2.** a device that fits onto the exhaust pipe of a vehicle to soften the noise of the engine.

mug [mug] *noun, plural* **mugs.** a large, heavy drinking cup with a handle.
verb, **mugged, mugging.** to attack and rob someone, often in a public place.

mug·gy [mug-ee] *adjective,* **muggier, muggiest.** unpleasantly warm, damp, and humid: *Muggy summer weather makes me feel tired and lazy.*

Mu·ham·mad [moo-ham-id *or* moh-ham-id] *noun. Religion.* an Arab prophet who founded the religion of Islam. He lived from about the year 570 to 632.

mul·ber·ry ◀ [muhl-ber-ee] *noun, plural* **mulberries.** a tree with sweet, dark purple, edible berries. The leaves of a mulberry tree are eaten by silkworms.

mulch [mulch] *noun, plural* **mulches.** a covering of leaves, straw, rotting vegetable matter, or grass clippings that is spread over the soil in gardens to protect the plants and soil and to help new growth.
verb, **mulched, mulching.** to cover with mulch.

mule ▼ [myool] *noun, plural* **mules.**
1. the offspring of a female horse and a male donkey. Mules have long ears, a strong muscled horse-like body, and a short mane. **2.** someone who is very stubborn and determined: *He is as stubborn as a mule.*

mul·ti·me·di·a [mul-ti-mee-dee-uh] *adjective.* using or made up of more than one form of communication such as music, television, film, and print: *multimedia software.*

mul·ti·ple [mul-tuh-pul] *adjective.* having or containing many parts: *I had multiple copies of our vacation photos developed.*
noun, plural **multiples.** a number formed by multiplying one number by another: *4, 6 and 8, are multiples of 2.*

Mules *have been used to carry goods for thousands of years.*

mul·ti·pli·cand [mul-tuh-pluh-kand] *noun, plural* **multiplicands.** *Mathematics.* the number that is to be multiplied by another. In 7 x 3 = 21, 7 is the multiplicand.

mul·ti·pli·ca·tion [mul-tuh-pluh-kay-shun] *noun. Mathematics.* a mathematical operation of adding a number to itself a particular number of times. In the multiplication of 6 times 3, you are adding 6 plus 6 plus 6, which equals 18.

mul·ti·pli·er [mul-tuh-plye-ur] *noun, plural* **multipliers.** *Mathematics.* a number by which another is multiplied. In 7 x 3 = 21, 3 is the multiplier.

mul·ti·ply [mul-tuh-plye] *verb,* **multiplied, multiplying.**
1. to add a number to itself a particular number of times: *Multiply 3 times 4 to get 12.* **2.** to increase in number: *Many types of insects multiply rapidly; The amount of homework I have has multiplied now that I'm a senior.*

A B C D E F G H I J K L **M** N O P Q R S T U V W X Y Z

*An Egyptian **mummy** was wrapped in several layers of linen and the face was covered with a painted mask.*

mul·ti·tude [mul-ti-*tood*] *noun, plural* **multitudes.** a very large number of people or things: *I gazed up into the sky at the multitude of stars.*

mum·ble [mum-bul] *verb,* **mumbled, mumbling.** to speak so softly and unclearly that the words are difficult to understand: *The speaker lost points in the debating competition because she was mumbling.*

mum·my ▲ [mum-ee] *noun, plural* **mummies.** a dead body that has been treated with special substances and wrapped in cloth to stop it from decaying. For the ancient Egyptians, this was done to prepare the body for burial.

mumps [mumps] *noun. Health.* an infectious virus that causes painful swelling of the glands at the sides of the face and neck.

munch [munch] *verb,* **munched, munching.** to chew noisily: *The horses munched on the apple cores.*

mun·dane [mun-*dane*] *adjective.* very ordinary and boring: *I hate having to do mundane tasks like washing up and ironing.*

mu·ni·ci·pal [myoo-*nis*-uh-pul] *adjective. Government.* having to do with the government affairs of a town or city: *I study at the municipal library.* The local government of a city or town is called a **municipality.**

mu·ral [*myur*-ul] *noun, plural* **murals.** *Art.* a large picture painted on a wall or ceiling. An artist who paints murals is a **muralist.**

mur·der [*mur*-dur] *noun, plural* **murders.** the crime of deliberately and unlawfully killing someone.
verb, **murdered, murdering.** to deliberately and unlawfully kill someone. A person who is extremely dangerous and likely to commit a murder is **murderous.**

mur·der·er [*mur*-dur-ur] *noun, plural* **murderers.** a person who deliberately and unlawfully kills someone.

mur·ky [*mur*-kee] *adjective,* **murkier, murkiest.** dark, gloomy, and difficult to see through: *The creek water was murky after the big thunderstorm.*

mur·mur [*mur*-mur] *noun, plural* **murmurs.** a low, soft, continuous sound: *I could hear the murmur of the wind in the trees.*
verb, **murmured, murmuring.** to speak softly or quietly: *The students were murmuring in the library even though they were meant to studying.*

mus·cle [*mus*-ul] *noun, plural* **muscles. 1.** one of many tissues in the body that can tighten and relax, making the body move. **2.** a bundle of tissue that moves a particular bone or part of the body: *the heart muscle.* **3.** strength or force: *We need to put a bit of muscle into chopping up this wood.*
verb, **muscled, muscling.** to move with strength or force: *He muscled his way through the crowd.*
🔊 A different word with the same sound is **mussel.**

mus·cu·lar [mus-kyuh-lur] *adjective.* **1.** having well developed muscles: *The athlete had a strong, muscular body as a result of all her training.* **2.** concerning or affecting muscles: *I have a muscular injury in my back.*

muse [myooz] *verb,* **mused, musing.** to think carefully about something for a long period of time: *He mused about all the things he wanted to achieve before he turned 21. noun, plural* **muses.** a source of inspiration: *The artist's muse was his wife, who inspired him to paint beautiful women.*

mu·se·um ▼ [myoo-*zee*-um] *noun, plural* **museums.** a building where important historical, scientific, and artistic objects are kept and displayed: *New York's Metropolitan Museum of Art has many famous paintings.*

In the religion of the ancient Greeks, the *Muses* were nine sister goddesses who each ruled over a different area of the arts, science, and learning. A **museum** was "a home of the Muses," meaning it was a place that would have things relating to these areas of learning and the arts.

mush [mush] *noun.* an unpleasant, soft, thick substance: *I cooked the cabbage for too long and it turned into a green mush.*

mush·room [mush-*room*] *noun, plural* **mushrooms.** a fungus with a stem and a dome-shaped top that grows very fast. Many mushrooms can be eaten, but some are poisonous.
verb, **mushroomed, mushrooming.** to appear or develop suddenly or spread quickly: *Since the new highway was built, housing developments have mushroomed all along the route.*

mu·sic [*myoo*-zik] *noun.* **1.** a pleasing or expressive combination of sounds, especially sounds made by instruments or the voice or both. **2.** the art of making such a pleasing or expressive combination of sounds. **3.** a musical composition: *Many songs are the work of two people—one writes the words, and the other writes the music.* **4.** written or printed instructions for making music in the form of symbols that represent the sounds used: *When I'm learning a new tune, I read the music as I play my guitar.*

*The Guggenheim **Museum,** built between 1956 and 1959 in New York City, has an unusual spiral shape.*

There were some two million **mustangs** in the United States at the beginning of the twentieth century, but since then their numbers have decreased dramatically.

A B C D E F G H I J K L M N O P Q R S T U V W X Y Z

mu·sic·al [myoo-zuh-kul] *adjective.* having to do with or producing music: *A piano keyboard and drums are musical instruments.* *noun, plural* **musicals.** a play or movie with a lot of songs in it. Many musicals have dancing in them as well. —**musically,** *adverb.*

mu·sic·ian [myoo-zish-un] *noun, plural* **musicians.** someone who plays a musical instrument, sings, or composes music, especially as a job.

musk [musk] *noun.* **1.** a substance with a strong smell produced by a male deer called the **musk deer** and used in perfumes. The word **musky** means having a smell like this substance. **2.** the odor of this substance.

mus·ket [mus-kit] *noun, plural* **muskets.** *History.* a gun with a long barrel like a rifle that was loaded with shot through the muzzle. Muskets were used by foot soldiers before rifles were invented. A soldier armed with this type of gun was called a **musketeer.**

musk ox ▼ a wild animal like a small ox, with a dark, thick, shaggy coat and long, curved horns. It is actually more closely related to a goat than to a true ox. The male produces a strong odor similar to musk. The musk ox is native to Canada, Greenland, and Alaska.

musk·rat [musk-rat] *noun, plural* **muskrat** *or* **muskrats.** a North American animal like a large rat that lives in or near water. It has webbed back feet and a long, scaly tail. The name comes from its musky smell.

Mus·lim [muz-lum] *adjective. Religion.* having to do with Islam, the religion founded by the prophet Muhammad. *noun, plural* **Muslims.** someone who follows Islam, the religion founded by the prophet Muhammad.

mus·lin [muz-lun] a cotton cloth with a plain weave, used to make things like sheets and clothing.

mus·sel [mus-ul] *noun, plural* **mussels.** an animal in the group called mollusks. It has a soft body and a hinged double shell. Saltwater mussels have a long, bluish black shell and are eaten. The shells of freshwater mussels have a shiny, pearl-like lining, and are used to make buttons and jewelry.
🔊 A different word with the same sound is **muscle.**

must [must] *verb.* a special verb that is often used with other verbs to show these meanings: **1.** to be obliged to; have to: *We must hand in our biology assignments by Friday.* **2.** to be certain to: *The rain has been pouring down for hours, but it must stop some time.* **3.** to be likely or certain to: *There was no answer when I rang, so they must have gone out.* *noun, plural* **musts. 1.** something that is required or necessary: *Hiking boots are a must if you are going camping in the mountains.* **2.** something that cannot or should not be missed: *If you go to San Francisco, the Golden Gate Bridge is a must.*

mus·tache [mus-tash *or* muh-stash] *noun, plural* **mustaches.** hair left to grow on a man's upper lip, often trimmed to a particular shape. This word is also spelled **moustache.**

mus·tang ◄ [mus-tang] *noun, plural* **mustangs.** a small, wild horse that lives on the western plains of the United States and is a direct descendant of horses brought to America by the Spaniards; bronco.

mus·tard [mus-turd] *noun, plural* **mustards.** a yellow paste or powder with a sharp, hot taste made from the seeds of the mustard plant. It is used to flavor food and in medicines.

mus·ter [mus-tur] *verb,* **mustered, mustering. 1.** to gather together; assemble: *The sergeant mustered the troops for inspection by the visiting general.* **2.** to gather up or summon from within oneself: *I knew how cold the water was and had to muster up my courage to dive in.*

must·n't [mus-unt] the shortened form of "must not."

must·y [mus-tee] *adjective.* having a moldy or stale smell or taste, usually because of dampness or decay.

mu·tant [myoot-unt] *noun, plural* **mutants.** *Biology.* a plant or animal that has one or more genetic characteristics different from its parents and can pass these characteristics on to its own offspring.

mute [myoot] *adjective.* **1.** not able to speak because of a physical disorder, illness, or injury. **2.** not choosing to speak; silent: *My little sister is very shy and stood beside me mute when our new neighbor said hello to her.* **3.** not sounded; not pronounced. The "k" in *knife* is mute. *noun.* **1.** someone who is unable to speak. **2.** a device put on a musical instrument to soften the tone. Mutes are most often used with brass instruments like trumpets. *verb,* **muted, muting. 1.** to soften, muffle, or reduce a sound of. **2.** to tone down; make less harsh: *The coach knew the players had done their best, so he muted his criticism of them.*

mu·ti·late [myoo-tuh-late] *verb,* **mutilated, mutilating.** to damage something severely by cutting or breaking off part of it: *Someone had mutilated the magazine by tearing out pages and cutting out pictures.* —**mutilation,** *noun.*

mu·tin·y [myoot-uh-nee] *noun, plural* **mutinies.** a rebellion or revolt against authority, especially by soldiers or sailors against their officers: *In earlier times, a mutiny on a sailing ship was sometimes caused by sailors being badly treated by their officers.* Someone who takes part in a mutiny is a **mutineer.**

mutt [mut] *noun, plural* **mutts.** a dog, especially one of mixed or unknown breed; a mongrel.

Long hair and thick fur protect a **musk ox** *from the freezing temperatures of its Arctic home.*

Myrtles are native to southern Europe and North Africa.

mut·ter [mut-ur] *verb,* **muttered, muttering.** to speak in a low, unclear voice so that you can hardly be heard: *My dad often mutters to himself when he is making something in his workshop. noun.* words spoken in this way.

mut·ton [mut-un] *noun.* meat from a fully grown sheep.

mu·tu·al [myoo-choo-ul] *adjective.* given and received in equal amount, or felt or experienced in equal amount; shared: *My friend Lisa and I have a mutual interest in horses and often go riding together.* **—mutually,** *adverb.*

mutual fund *Government.* a way of investing money. It is a pool of money collected from a large number of people who want to use some of the money they have to make more money. The people who manage the fund will invest this money in things like stocks and bonds.

muz·zle [muz-ul] *noun, plural* **muzzles. 1.** the part of an animal's face made up of the nose, mouth, and jaws: *A boxer has a short muzzle, and a German shepherd has a long muzzle.* **2.** a guard, usually made of straps or wire, fitted over an animal's nose and mouth to stop it biting or eating. **3.** the open end of a gun from which the bullet or shell is fired.
verb, **muzzled, muzzling. 1.** to put a guard over an animal's muzzle: *The owner had to muzzle his dog to stop it from biting other dogs.* **2.** to stop someone from speaking or expressing an opinion: *The chairman tried to muzzle the protestors by declaring the meeting closed.*

my [mye] *adjective.* of, belonging to, or having to do with me: *I ride my bike to school; After dinner I study in my room.*

my·o·pi·a [mye-oh-pee-uh] *noun. Health.* the state of being short-sighted, or only able to see nearby things clearly. Someone who has this condition is **myopic.**

myrt·le ▲ [murt-ul] *noun, plural* **myrtles. 1.** an evergreen shrub with sweet-smelling white or pink flowers, black berries, and shiny leaves. **2.** an evergreen vine that spreads along the ground and has blue or white flowers and shiny leaves. It is also called a periwinkle.

my·self [mye-self] *pronoun.* **1.** I or me and not someone else: *I hurt myself when I fell out of the tree; My mom said I can decorate my room myself.* **2.** the person I usually, normally, or truly am: *I haven't been myself since my best friend moved to another state.*

mys·te·ri·ous [mis-teer-ee-us] *adjective.* hard or impossible to explain or understand; full of mystery; puzzling: *We heard mysterious noises coming from the basement, and my dad found that a squirrel had been trapped inside.* **—mysteriously,** *adverb.*

mys·ter·y [mis-tur-ee *or* mis-tree] *noun, plural* **mysteries. 1.** something secret or hidden; something that is not known and cannot be explained or understood: *My dog was a stray that just appeared outside our gate one day, and it's a mystery where she came from.* **2.** a book, story, or play about a crime that is puzzling and that keeps the reader or audience guessing.

mys·ti·fy [mis-tuh-fye] *verb,* **mystified, mystifying.** to puzzle or confuse; bewilder: *It mystifies me how my mom hears the baby crying when my dad, my brother, and I hear nothing.* **—mystification,** *noun.*

myth [mith] *noun, plural* **myths. 1.** *Literature.* an old story belonging to a particular group of people that explains how the world began or how the people, animals, and plants in it came to be the way they are. Many of these stories tell about gods or other superhuman beings with magical powers. Some stories explain things in nature, such as storms or how a great river was formed. **2.** a belief or story that many people think is true, or that many people in the past thought was true, but that is not true: *It's a myth that if you rub a wart with a potato and bury the potato, your wart will disappear.*

A **myth** is a story told since very early times, and it is not known who the author of the story is. Many ancient peoples had myths that explained things in the natural world that seemed hard to understand, such as why the seasons change, what causes thunder and lightning, or how a certain river or mountain came to be. The myths of the ancient Greeks and Romans are still famous today. For example, according to Roman mythology the great city of Rome was founded by Romulus and Remus, twins whose mother was human and whose father was the god Mars.

myth·i·cal ▼ [mith-i-kul] *adjective.* found in myths; not real or true: *Dragons and unicorns are mythical animals.*

my·thol·o·gy [mi-thol-uh-je] *noun, plural* **mythologies.** *Literature.* a collection or group of myths, such as the myths belonging to a particular people: *The stories of gods and goddesses like Apollo and Venus are part of Greek mythology.*

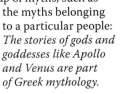
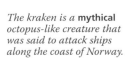

The kraken is a **mythical** *octopus-like creature that was said to attack ships along the coast of Norway.*

N n

Bears prefer the safety of a tree when they take **naps**.

N, n *noun, plural* **N's, n's.** the fourteenth letter of the English alphabet.

nag [nag] *verb,* **nagged, nagging.** to annoy by criticizing, scolding, or asking for something over and over again: *My mother nags me about spending too much time playing video games.*
noun, plural. someone who annoys by criticizing, scolding, or asking for something over and over again.

nail [nale] *noun, plural* **nails. 1.** a thin piece of metal with one end sharp and pointed and the other end flattened so that it can be hammered into something. Nails are used to join pieces of wood or other material together. **2.** the hard, horny layer of material that grows at the end of a finger or toe.
verb, **nailed, nailing.** to join or fasten with a nail or nails: *to nail pieces of wood together.*

na·ked [nay-kid] *adjective.* **1.** without clothes or the natural or usual covering. **2.** with nothing added; plain: *The naked truth is that Shelley's friend lied to her.* **3.** without the help of a device such as a telescope or microscope: *In our biology class we get to examine things like cells that you can't see with the naked eye.* —**nakedness,** *noun.*

name [name] *noun, plural* **names. 1.** the word or words by which a person, animal, place, or thing is known: *The name of the hotel we stayed at is the Parkview Plaza.* **2.** a word or words used to describe or refer to someone or something in an insulting way: *The teacher reported the student to the principal for calling another student names.* **3.** a reputation of a particular kind: *The storekeeper valued her good name in the community.*
verb, **named, naming. 1.** to give a name or names to: *My mom named our cat Chloe.* **2.** to mention by name; state; identify: *The teacher asked us to name the second President of the United States.* **3.** to select for a position; choose: *Winona was named captain of our softball team.*

name·ly [name-lee] *adverb.* that is to say: *My family has lived in two very different cities, namely Pittsburgh and Santa Fe.*

nan·ny [nan-ee] *noun, plural* **nannies.** someone employed by a family to look after their young child or children.

nano- a prefix that means very small.

nan·o·me·ter [nan-uh-*mee*-tur] *noun, plural* **nanometers.** *Science.* a measure of length equal to one billionth of a meter.

nan·o·sci·ence [nan-oh-*sye*-uns] *noun. Science.* the study of objects of the smallest size. The objects studied have to do with different areas of science, such as electrical engineering, biology, physics, and chemistry.

nan·o·sec·ond [nan-oh-*sek*-und] *noun, plural* **nanoseconds. 1.** *Science.* a period of time equal to one billionth of a second. **2.** a tiny amount of time: *When the movie star left the restaurant, it took only a nanosecond for the photographers to start snapping pictures.*

nan·o·tech·nol·o·gy [*nan*-oh-tek-*nol*-uh-jee] *noun, plural* **nanotechnologies.** any technology that comes about through nanoscience. Nanotechnologies use tiny devices or machines, sometimes the size of just a few atoms.

nap[1] ▲ [nap] *noun, plural* **naps.** a short sleep, especially in the daytime: *My grandmother often has a nap in the afternoon.*
verb, **napped, napping.** to sleep for a short while, especially in the daytime.
• **catch napping.** to find someone unprepared or not ready for something: *The troops were caught napping when the enemy attacked and were easily defeated.*

nap[2] [nap] *noun, plural* **naps.** the soft, slightly furry side of woven cloth or leather: *Velvet has a very soft nap.*

nap·kin [nap-kin] *noun, plural* **napkins.** a piece of cloth or paper used during meals to wipe the lips and fingers and to protect clothes from food spills.

nar·cis·sus ▶ [nar-sis-us] *noun, plural* **narcissuses.** a plant that grows from a bulb and produces a single yellow or white flower on a long stem in the spring. The middle part of the flower is shaped like a cup and is surrounded by petals. The daffodil is a kind of narcissus.

In the stories of the ancient Greeks, **Narcissus** was a beautiful young man who was so fascinated with his own good looks that he fell in love with a reflection of himself, after he saw it when he looked into a pool of water. He stared so long at his reflection that he finally wasted away and died, and all that was left where he had been was a single beautiful narcissus flower.

The daffodil, like other **narcissuses,** *stores food in its bulb.*

nar·cot·ic [nar-kot-ik] *noun,*
plural **narcotics.** *Chemistry.*
a drug that dulls the senses,
relieves pain, and makes
a person sleepy. In high
doses, it can make a person
unconscious. People can
become addicted to narcotics.
adjective. having the power
to dull the senses and make
a person sleepy: *Many narcotic*
drugs can be prescribed only
by a doctor.

The word **narcotic** comes from an old
word meaning "to sleep" or "to lack
feeling; be numb." A *narcotic* drug
causes a person to have such feelings
of sleepiness and numbness.

Nasturtium
flowers are
edible and
are sometimes
added to salads.

nar·rate [nare-ate] *verb,* **narrated, narrating.** to tell the
story of or give an account of: *The TV film about the*
Civil War was narrated by a famous actor.

nar·ra·tive [nare-uh-tiv] *noun, plural* **narratives.**
Literature. an account of events told like a story:
The guest speaker gave a narrative of his experiences
working on a fishing boat in Alaska.

nar·ra·tor [nare-ate-ur] *noun, plural* **narrators.** *Literature.*
a person who tells a story in a book, or who provides
a background narrative for a film, play, or radio or
television program.

The **narrator** of a story is the person who tells the story.
If you write a story in which you yourself tell the story, this is
called *first person narrative.* You would use words like *I, me,*
we, or *us*: "*I* heard a noise outside. The dog ran past *me* and
went out the door." If you write a story about another person,
that is *third person narrative*: You would use words like *he,*
she, it, or *they*: "*She* heard a noise outside. The dog ran past
her and went out the door."

nar·row [nare-oh] *adjective,* **narrower, narrowest.**
1. small in width; not broad: *This street is so narrow*
that cars cannot pass each other in it. **2.** small in amount;
restricted; slight: *Julie won the race by a narrow margin.*
verb, **narrowed, narrowing.** to make or get narrow or
narrower: *A bucket is wide at the top, but it narrows*
toward the bottom.
plural noun, **narrows.** a place where a stream or other
stretch of water becomes narrower. **—narrowly,** *adverb.*

nar·row-mind·ed [nare-oh-mined-id] *adjective.*
not prepared or able to accept or consider new ideas or
opinions: *It is very narrow-minded to think that anyone*
who disagrees with you is always wrong. A person who is
narrow-minded shows **narrow-mindedness.**

NASA an organization that controls and coordinates the
United States space exploration programs and activities.
NASA is the abbreviation for **National Aeronautics and**
Space Administration.

na·sal [nay-zul] *adjective.*
relating to the nose or
parts of the nose: *Janine*
is suffering from a nasal
infection and cannot
stop sneezing.

nas·tur·tium ◀
[nuh-stur-shum] *noun,*
plural **nasturtiums.**
one of a number of plants
that are native to Central
and South America and
that have showy red,
orange, or yellow flowers.

nas·ty [nas-tee] *adjective,*
nastier, nastiest.
1. describing something cruel; offensive; spiteful: *Bullies*
are nasty people. **2.** describing something painful or
harmful: *Poor Ned is sick—he has a nasty bout of flu.*
—nastily, *adverb*; **nastiness,** *noun.*

na·tion [nay-shun] *noun, plural* **nations. 1.** a country or
state that has its own government and laws and, usually,
a language which most or all of its people speak: *France,*
Spain, India, and Australia are all nations. **2.** the people
who are citizens of a country or state: *Every four years*
the nation votes to elect its president. The fact of being
a nation is **nationhood.**

na·tion·al [nash-uh-nul] *adjective.* **1.** relating to or
representing a nation or its people: *Each country has its*
own national flag. **2.** applying to a whole nation; existing
throughout a nation: *The Boy Scouts and Girl Scouts are*
both national organizations.
noun, plural **nationals.** a person who is a citizen of
a particular nation: *The tour group consisted mainly*
of British and French nationals. **—nationally,** *adverb.*

national anthem *Music.* a special song that celebrates
and praises a nation and expresses the national pride that
its people feel.

National Guard a national military organization whose
members are volunteers. Its role or purpose is to protect
and defend the public. A member of the National Guard
is a **National Guardsman.**

na·tion·al·ism [nash-nul-iz-um] *noun. Government.*
1. the fact of acting in a way that attempts to give one's
own nation an advantage over other nations. **2.** the feeling
of great love of, and pride in, a nation, and the expression
of that feeling in actions and words.

na·tion·al·ist [nash-nuh-list] *noun, plural* **nationalists.**
a person who feels and expresses a great love of, and pride
in, his or her nation. Some nationalists consider their own
nation to be superior to most or all others. A person who
is a nationalist is **nationalistic.**

na·tion·al·i·ty [nash-nal-uh-tee] *noun, plural* **nationalities.**
1. the fact of being a citizen of or of belonging to a
particular nation. **2.** people who are citizens of or belong
to a nation: *Many nationalities made up the crowd in the*
Olympic stadium.

a
b
c
d
e
f
g
h
i
j
k
l
m
n
o
p
q
r
s
t
u
v
w
x
y
z

*Many artists have painted the **Nativity**, which is also a popular theme for pictures and cards at Christmas.*

national park
Environment. a part of a country's natural environment that has been classified by the government as an area to be preserved and protected for the enjoyment of the public. Most national parks are areas of scenic beauty or of historical or scientific importance.

na·tive [nay-tiv] *noun, plural* **natives.**
1. a person who was born in or belongs to a particular place: *I'm a native of the United States; Boris is a native of Russia.* **2.** one of the people, plants, or animals that originally inhabited a place: *The kangaroo and the platypus are natives of Australia.* *adjective.* **1.** belonging to where a person was born; original: *Heinrich lives in America now, but Germany is his native country.* **2.** originally belonging to or coming from: *Elephants are native animals of Africa and Asia.*

Native American
a person who belongs to one of the peoples, except the Inuit, who have lived in North and South America from long before the time of European settlement there; American Indian.
See INDIAN *for more information.*

Na·tiv·i·ty ▲ [nuh-tiv-uh-tee] *noun, plural* **Nativities.**
the birth of Jesus Christ.

NATO
a military treaty involving the United States, Canada, and a number of European countries, including Great Britain, France, and Germany. Members of NATO have agreed to cooperate with each other and help defend each other. NATO is the abbreviation for **North Atlantic Treaty Organization.**

nat·u·ral [nach-ur-ul] *adjective.*
1. occurring in nature; not artificial: *Caves can provide natural shelters for people and animals.* **2.** not taught or learned; inborn: *Bernie has the lead in our school play—people say he's a natural actor.* **3.** describing something normal; to be expected: *It is natural to want to be happy and successful.* **4.** true to life; like the real thing: *I know those flowers are plastic, but they really look natural.* **5.** describing something genuine; not false: *He was very rude to me yesterday, but his apology today seemed natural and sincere.*
noun, plural **naturals.** a person with an inborn ability: *That singer is great—she's a real natural!*

natural gas
Chemistry. gas that forms naturally under the ground. Natural gas consists largely of methane and is widely used in homes and industry for heating and other forms of useful energy.

natural history
Biology. the study of nature and of the living and non-living things found in nature.

nat·u·ral·ist [nach-ur-uh-list] *noun, plural* **naturalists.**
Biology. a person who studies the natural world and things that exist naturally, especially animals and plants.

nat·u·ral·ize [nach-ur-uh-lize] *verb,* **naturalized, naturalizing.**
to permit someone from another country to become a citizen. People from one country who become citizens of a new country are said to be **naturalized.** —**naturalization,** *noun.*

nat·u·ral·ly [nach-ruh-lee *or* nach-uh-ruh-lee] *adverb.*
1. without effort; easily: *I need to work hard in math, but Sean can do the work naturally.* **2.** in the usual way; normally: *Ilsa tried to talk as naturally as possible during her speech so that people would not know she was nervous.* **3.** by all means; certainly: *"May I borrow your book?" "Naturally!"*

natural resource ▼
Environment. a substance that exists in a natural state and that people use for food, fuel, building materials, energy, or other purposes. Coal, oil, timber, and water are natural resources.

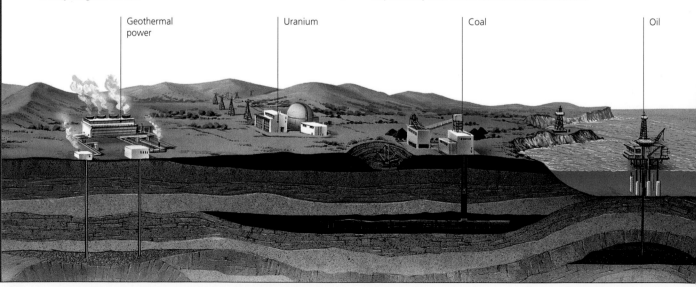

Geothermal power | Uranium | Coal | Oil

*Different kinds of **natural resources** are used to produce energy.*

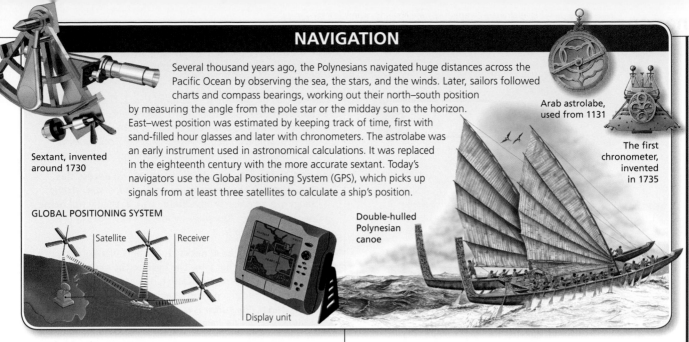

NAVIGATION

Several thousand years ago, the Polynesians navigated huge distances across the Pacific Ocean by observing the sea, the stars, and the winds. Later, sailors followed charts and compass bearings, working out their north–south position by measuring the angle from the pole star or the midday sun to the horizon. East–west position was estimated by keeping track of time, first with sand-filled hour glasses and later with chronometers. The astrolabe was an early instrument used in astronomical calculations. It was replaced in the eighteenth century with the more accurate sextant. Today's navigators use the Global Positioning System (GPS), which picks up signals from at least three satellites to calculate a ship's position.

Sextant, invented around 1730

Arab astrolabe, used from 1131

The first chronometer, invented in 1735

GLOBAL POSITIONING SYSTEM

Satellite | Receiver

Display unit

Double-hulled Polynesian canoe

na·ture [nay-chur] *noun, plural* **natures. 1.** everything that exists in a natural state; the natural world: *We like to go out into the countryside to enjoy the woods, the streams, and other forms of nature.* **2.** the way something naturally is; character: *It is a cat's nature to hunt mice; You will like Trish, she has a very friendly nature.* **3.** a group of things that are alike in some way; type; kind: *A necklace, bracelet, or something of a similar nature would be a good birthday present for Julia.*

naugh·ty [naw-tee] *adjective,* **naughtier, naughtiest.** badly behaved; not obedient: *The naughty child was being rude to his mother.*

nau·sea [naw-zee-uh *or* naw-zhuh] *noun. Health.* a sick feeling; an urge to vomit: *Some people suffer from nausea when they travel on an aircraft.* If you have this feeling, you are **nauseated** or **nauseous.** Anything that causes nausea is **nauseating.**

nau·ti·cal ▼ [naw-tuh-kul] *adjective.* relating to boats, ships, sailors, and other matters having to do with the ocean: *John is taking a course on sailing, navigation, and other nautical subjects.* A **nautical mile** is a measurement of distance, used in the navigation of ships and aircraft, equal to 6,076.115 feet.

Na·va·jo [nahv-uh-hoh] *noun, plural* **Navajo** *or* **Navajos. 1.** a member of a Native American people that lives mainly in northern New Mexico and Arizona. **2.** the language of the Navajo people. *adjective.* relating to the Navajo people or their language. This word is also spelled **Navaho.**

na·val [nay-vul] *adjective.* relating to the navy or to matters concerned with the navy: *Midway was a famous naval battle of World War II.*
🔊 A different word with the same sound is **navel.**

na·vel [nay-vul] *noun, plural* **navels.** a small round scar or hollow in the middle of a person's abdomen. It results from the cutting or breaking of the cord that connects a newborn baby to its mother's body.
🔊 A different word with the same sound is **naval.**

nav·i·gate [nav-uh-gate] *verb,* **navigated, navigating. 1.** to plan or direct the course of a voyage or journey on water or through the air. **2.** to sail or travel across, on, or through: *The kayak navigated the dangerous rapids on the river.*

nav·i·ga·tion ▲ [nav-uh-gay-shun] *noun.* **1.** the act or science of steering or plotting a journey in a ship or aircraft. **2.** the art or skill of navigating: *The navigation of an aircraft requires a great deal of experience and knowledge.*

nav·i·ga·tor [nav-uh-gay-tur] *noun, plural* **navigators. 1.** the person who plots and controls the course of a journey or voyage. **2.** a highly skilled sailor: *Only a very good navigator could sail solo around the world.*

na·vy [nay-vee] *noun, plural* **navies. 1.** the warships that a country possesses, including aircraft carriers, destroyers, submarines, and the like, as well as the people who serve on these ships and also aircraft, weapons, and supplies: *Some people join the navy because they like ships and the sea.* The navy of a particular country is usually spelled **Navy.** **2.** a dark blue color; navy blue. *adjective.* being dark blue in color.

navy blue a dark blue color.

Na·zi [not-see] *noun, plural* **Nazis.** *History.* a member of the National Socialist German Workers' party that was founded in 1919. From 1933 until 1945 the Nazis, led by Adolf Hitler, governed Germany. *adjective.* relating to the ideas and beliefs held by Nazis. The ideas and beliefs held by Nazis, and the practice of these, are called **Nazism** or **Naziism.**

NE an abbreviation for NORTHEAST.

Today, steering wheels and other **nautical** *items are often made of fiberglass instead of wood.*

Nearsightedness occurs when light rays from objects do not reach the retina at the back of the eye, and can be corrected by a curved lens in front of the eye.

A B C D E F G H I J K L M **N** O P Q R S T U V W X Y Z

NEARSIGHTEDNESS

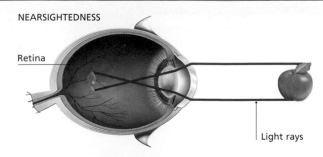

Retina

Light rays

NEARSIGHTEDNESS CORRECTED

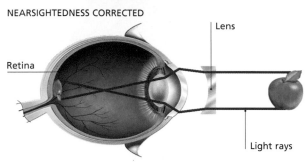

Retina

Lens

Light rays

near [neer] *adverb,* **nearer, nearest.** not far off; close: *The two cars came very near to each other, but they did not collide.* *adjective,* **nearer, nearest. 1.** close by; not far off: *I live here, and my school is quite near.* **2.** having a small margin; narrow. **3.** less distant; closer: *The bridge will be built in the near future.*
preposition. close to; not far from: *Our house is near the river.* *verb,* **neared, nearing.** to come close to; approach: *As we neared home, we felt glad to be back.* —**nearness,** *noun.*

near·by [neer-bye] *adjective.* close by; near to here: *a nearby supermarket.*
adverb. close by; near to here: *One of my grandmothers lives with us and the other lives nearby.*

near·ly [neer-lee] *adverb.* very close to; almost: *It is nearly time to leave; On my way here, I nearly turned into the wrong street.*

near·sight·ed ▲ [neer-sye-tid] *adjective.* unable to see clearly things that are far away; able to see things that are close by more clearly than faraway things. A person who is nearsighted suffers from **nearsightedness,** which is another word for MYOPIA.

neat [neet] *adjective,* **neater, neatest.** **1.** clean and orderly; tidy: *My bedroom is always neat, but my brother's is messy.* **2.** describing something attractive, clever, or impressive: *Jeannie bought herself a neat new outfit to wear to her sister's wedding.* —**neatly,** *adverb;* —**neatness,** *noun.*

neb·u·la ▶ [neb-yuh-luh] *noun, plural* **nebulas** *or* **nebulae.** *Science.* a vast mass of dust particles or gas that appears like a cloud in the night sky.

The Horsehead **Nebula** *can only be seen with a telescope.*

nec·es·sar·i·ly [nes-uh-ser-uh-lee] *adverb.* as a result; definitely: *People with long legs are not necessarily fast runners.*

nec·es·sar·y [nes-uh-ser-ee] *adjective.* **1.** that cannot be done without; essential: *A passport is necessary if you want to travel to other countries.* **2.** naturally following; sure to happen: *The jury ruled that the accident was a necessary result of his reckless driving.*

ne·ces·si·ty [nuh-ses-uh-tee] *noun, plural* **necessities.** **1.** something that is essential or needed: *Good, strong shoes are a necessity on a hiking trip.* **2.** the fact of being necessary: *The champion swimmer was aware of the necessity to keep fit.*

neck [nek] *noun, plural* **necks. 1.** the part of a human or animal body that joins the head to the chest and shoulders. **2.** the part of a shirt, blouse, or other garment that goes around a person's neck. **3.** a narrow section of something: *The guitar is a musical instrument that has a wide body and a long neck.*

neck·er·chief [nek-ur-cheef] *noun, plural* **neckerchiefs.** a scarf or piece of cloth that is worn and tied loosely around the neck.

neck·lace [nek-lis] *noun, plural* **necklaces.** a chain or string worn as jewelry around the neck. Necklaces often contain beads, pearls, and other items of decoration.

neck·tie [nek-tye] *noun, plural* **neckties.** an item of clothing that is often worn by men with a suit for business or another serious occasion. It consists of a colorful length of cloth that is tied in a knot at the front of the neck so that it falls down the front of the chest.

nec·tar [nek-tur] *noun, plural* **nectars.** a sweet liquid produced in the flowers of many plants. Bees collect nectar and turn it into honey.

need [need] *noun, plural* **needs.** **1.** something that is lacking, but wanted: *The club has a need for more members.* **2.** something that is necessary; a requirement or obligation: *Food is a basic human need; Norma feels no need to visit her sister in England this year.* **3.** trouble, distress, or poverty: *The woman was in great need after the fire destroyed her house.* *verb,* **needed, needing. 1.** to lack, but desire: *They badly need a new car, but cannot afford one.* **2.** to be obligated or required to; have to: *We need to leave now to catch the 3.00 P.M. bus.* Things that people need are their **needs.**
🔊 A different word with the same sound is **knead.**

nee·dle [need-ul] *noun, plural* **needles.** **1.** a small, slender piece of metal with a sharp point at one end and a narrow slit, through which thread is passed, at the other. Needles are used for sewing. **2.** a similar piece that acts as a pointer on a compass, meter, or other instrument. **3.** a thin, hollow tube with

*Film **negatives** are developed in long strips and used to print photographs.*

a pointed end that is used to inject liquid beneath the skin or to draw blood from the body. **4.** a long, thin, metal or plastic tool, used in knitting. **5.** the leaves of a pine tree or other such evergreen tree: *Our driveway is covered with long, thin pine needles.* **6.** anything with a sharp end that is shaped like a needle.
verb, **needled, needling.** to bother or annoy someone; tease or mock: *My brother keeps needling me about my poor grades at school.*

need·less [need-lis] *adjective.* not required; that could have been avoided: *The air raid resulted in the needless destruction of many buildings.* **—needlessly,** *adverb.*

need·y [nee-dee] *adjective,* **needier, neediest.** living in poverty; poor: *There are many organizations that provide food and shelter for needy people.*

neg·a·tive ▲ [neg-uh-tiv] *adjective.* **1.** indicating "no": *When I asked if he knew you, he gave a negative answer.* **2.** describing something not positive; unhelpful; hostile: *She was very negative about his plan to buy an expensive car.* **3.** less than zero; minus: *Minus three is a negative number.* **4.** one of two opposite kinds of electrical charge; the kind of electrical charge that electrons have: *A flashlight battery has a negative charge at one end and a positive charge at the other.* **5.** indicating the absence of an illness or medical condition: *The results of Karin's tests for anemia proved negative.*
noun, plural **negatives. 1.** the kind of image that results from developing film. In a negative the dark areas appear light and the light areas appear dark. **2.** any word, phrase, or gesture that indicates "no", or that shows disagreement. A person who has a negative attitude displays **negativity.** **—negatively,** *adverb.*

neg·lect [ni-glekt] *verb,* **neglected, neglecting. 1.** to not care for; ignore: *Good parents never neglect their children.* **2.** not to do; forget to do: *I did not get your message because I neglected to check my e-mails.*
noun. the fact of being neglected: *The ruined church was in a terrible state of neglect.* A person who shows neglect is **neglectful.**

neg·li·gent [neg-luh-junt] *adjective.* showing a lack of care; careless or forgetful: *It would be negligent to let a young child ride in a car without a seatbelt.* A person who is negligent shows **negligence.**

ne·go·ti·ate [ni-goh-shee-ate] *verb,* **negotiated, negotiating.** to discuss to try to reach a decision that all can accept: *The two countries that were at war finally negotiated a peace treaty.* A person who negotiates is a **negotiator.**

ne·go·ti·a·tion [ni-goh-shee-aye-shun] *noun, plural* **negotiations.** a discussion to try to come to a decision that all can accept: *The pay negotiations between the workers and managers broke down because they could not agree.*

Ne·gro [nee-groh] *noun, plural* **Negroes.** a member of a group of humans that have black or very dark skin, black hair, and dark eyes. Such people are usually referred to as Black.

neigh·bor [nay-bur] *noun, plural* **neighbors. 1.** a person who lives next door or very close by. **2.** any person or thing that is near or next to something else: *The Earth and the Moon are neighbors in space.* Something that is close by is **neighboring.**

neigh·bor·hood [nay-bur-hud] *noun, plural* **neighborhoods. 1.** a part of a town, city, or region: *This neighborhood, which is north of the highway, has some interesting old houses.* **2.** the people who live in an area, region, or district: *The whole neighborhood is very interested in the new bridge that is being planned.*
• **in the neighborhood. 1.** in the area of; near. **2.** in the range of; about, approximately: *The final cost is not known yet, but will be in the neighborhood of $1,000.*

neigh·bor·ly [nay-bur-lee] *adjective.* friendly or kind; helpful: *Welcoming newcomers is a neighborly act.* **—neighborliness,** *noun.*

nei·ther [nee-THur *or* nye-THur] *conjunction.* **1.** not one or the other: *A person who is deaf and dumb can neither hear nor speak.* **2.** not either; nor: *I won't be at school tomorrow, and neither will Esther.*
adjective. not one; not either: *Neither choice appeals to me.*
pronoun. not one of the two: *I watched both movies, but neither was interesting.*

neo- a prefix that means new, recent, or revived: *neonatal* means relating to newborn babies.

ne·o·con·ser·vat·ive [nee-oh-kun-surv-i-tiv] *noun, plural* **neoconservatives.** *Government.* in politics, a former liberal who now holds conservative views, especially in matters concerning foreign policy. A person who is neoconservative believes in **neoconservatism.**

ne·on ▲ [nee-on] *noun. Chemistry.* a colorless, odorless gas that is a chemical element and that makes up a small part of the air we breathe. It glows when an electric current passes through it. Tubes with neon in them are used for lighting and as signs.

neph·ew [nef-yoo] *noun, plural* **nephews.** the son of a person's sister, brother, sister-in-law, or brother-in-law.

*Times Square in New York City is famous for its advertisements made from tubes of **neon**.*

The scarlet tanager bird builds a cup-shaped **nest** *to prevent its eggs from rolling out.*

Nep·tune ▼ [nep-toon] *noun.*
1. the fourth largest planet in the solar system and the eighth in terms of distance from the Sun. Neptune cannot be seen from the Earth without the aid of a telescope. **2.** the ancient Roman god of the sea.

nerve [nurv] *noun, plural* **nerves.**
1. a single fiber or cluster of fibers through which messages pass back and forth from the brain to the spinal cord and other parts of the body. **2.** strength of will; courage: *I don't think I have the nerve to climb that cliff.* **3.** the fact of showing rudeness; cheek; boldness: *Kirsty had the nerve to accuse me of cheating on the exam.* **4. nerves.** feelings of fear: *The actor suffered an attack of nerves on opening night.* A person who is **nervy** is bold, especially in a rude way.

ner·vous [nur-vus] *adjective.* **1.** not relaxed or confident; worried about harm or failure: *Gail always feels nervous when she travels on an airplane; The singer was very nervous before the concert.* **2.** having to do with the nerves: *My uncle suffers from a nervous condition that makes his hands shake.* **—nervously,** *adverb;* **nervousness,** *noun.*

NEPTUNE

Neptune is four times bigger than the Earth and is encircled by five thin, dark rings. Its atmosphere is mainly poisonous methane gas, which makes the planet look blue-green. Beneath the gas is a thick, slushy layer of ice and water, and inside this is what astronomers believe to be a hot, rocky core. Among the dozens of satellites orbiting Neptune there are thirteen known moons.

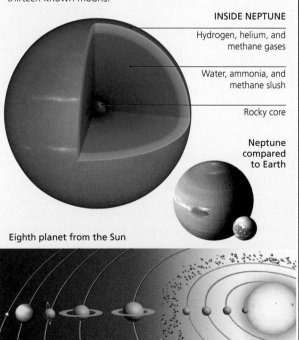

INSIDE NEPTUNE

Hydrogen, helium, and methane gases

Water, ammonia, and methane slush

Rocky core

Neptune compared to Earth

Eighth planet from the Sun

nervous system ▶ *Biology.* the system that controls everything the body does and feels. The nerves, spinal cord, and brain make up a body's nervous system.

-ness a suffix that means the fact of being: *sadness* is the fact of being sad; *softness* is the fact of being soft.

nest ▲ [nest] *noun, plural* **nests. 1.** a structure in which birds lay their eggs and raise very young chicks. Birds build nests using grass, sticks, mud, and other materials. **2.** a structure that some fish, turtles, insects, rabbits, squirrels, and other animals make and in which they lay eggs or raise their young. **3.** a warm, comfortable place that is thought of as being like a bird's nest.
verb, **nested, nesting.** to make a nest, or live in a nest: *Most birds nest in trees, but some nest on the ground.*

nes·tle [nes-ul] *verb,* **nestled, nestling.**
1. to settle or snuggle cozily: *The puppy nestled happily in its basket.* **2.** to be in a protected or sheltered position: *The tiny village was nestled at the foot of the mountain.*

Net an abbreviation for INTERNET.

net¹ ▶ [net] *noun, plural* **nets. 1.** a material made of intersecting strands of cord, rope, or wire with holes through which liquid or air can pass. **2.** a container, cover, or other object made of this material: *Dad used a small net to move our goldfish from one bowl to another.* **3.** such an object used as a goal or dividing line in games such as basketball, hockey, soccer, or volleyball.
verb, **netted, netting.** to catch in a net, or to place or hit into a net: *The tennis player was disappointed when she netted the ball instead of hitting it past her opponent.*

net² [net] *adjective. Business.* remaining as profit or gain after all costs have been deducted.
verb, **netted, netting.** to earn as profit after all costs have been deducted: *Hugo hopes to net about two hundred dollars on the sale of his computer.*

net profit *Business.* the amount of profit made by a business after all expenses of the business have been deducted from the total money received from sales or other sources of income.

net·tle [net-ul] *noun, plural* **nettles.** one of a number of kinds of plants that are covered with stinging hairs.

Brain

Spinal cord

Nerves

Humans have the most complex **nervous system** *in the animal world.*

net·work [net-*wurk*] *noun, plural* **networks.** a structure of lines, roads, tracks, pipes, or other things that intersect or interact to create a working system: *a telephone network; a network of tunnels.* **2.** a number of broadcasting organizations that cooperate closely and often share the same programs. *verb,* **networked, networking. 1.** to connect a number of computers to each other so that their users may interact and share information. **2.** to join with other people or organizations in a group that cooperates for a particular purpose.

> In earlier times a **network** was a kind of system that was thought of as being like the net that is used to catch fish. Some writers used the word *network* to refer to the web of a spider. In modern times radio and television stations that join together came to be called *networks* because they were thought of as spreading out and connecting to each other in this same kind of "web."

net·work·ing [net-*wurk*-ing] *noun.* **1.** the setting up or use of a computer network. **2.** the forming of contacts between people or organizations in order to work toward a common purpose.

neu·rol·o·gy [noo-*rol*-i-jee] *noun. Medicine.* the study of the structure and workings of the nervous system and the treatment of problems and diseases of the nervous system. A person who studies or practices neurology is a **neurologist.**

neu·ro·sci·ence [*noor*-oh-*sye*-uns] *noun. Biology.* the study of nerves and the nervous system and the way they relate to human learning and behavior. A person who studies neuroscience is a **neuroscientist.**

*The northwestern Native American tribes used **nets** to catch salmon in the spring.*

neu·ro·sis [noo-*roh*-sis] *noun, plural* **neuroses.** *Health.* a mental disorder that causes people to become excessively anxious and/or fearful.

neu·rot·ic [nu-*rot*-ik] *adjective.* suffering from a neurosis; being excessively anxious or fearful: *a neurotic fear of animals.*

neu·tral [noo-trul] *adjective.* **1.** not supporting either side in a dispute, argument, war, game, or other contest: *An umpire in a baseball game must always be neutral.* **2.** not striking; not bright: *Neutral colors, such as beige and gray, have a soothing effect.* **3.** neither acid nor base: *In chemical terms, water is a neutral fluid. noun, plural* **neutrals. 1.** anything that is neutral. **2.** a gear position in a vehicle that does not produce movement: *This car won't move if you don't change out of neutral.* The state of being neutral is **neutrality.** —**neutrally,** *adverb.*

neu·tron [noo-tron] *noun, plural* **neutrons.** *Science.* a tiny particle that has no electrical charge, has a mass almost the same as that of a proton, and occurs in the nucleus of every atom except the hydrogen atom.

nev·er [nev-ur] *adverb.* **1.** not even once; on no occasion: *She never eats bananas, because they make her feel sick.* **2.** not possibly; in no way: *I could never climb Mount Everest.*

nev·er·the·less [*nev*-ur-THuh-*less*] *adverb.* despite that; anyhow; regardless: *He had a cold yesterday; nevertheless he still went to school.*

new [noo] *adjective,* **newer, newest. 1.** very recently made, created, or having come into existence: *Amy was born last month—she is my new baby sister.* **2.** not previously known or recognized: *The police found new evidence in their investigation of the robbery.* **3.** not yet used to; unfamiliar: *Jenny is new to this neighborhood—can you show her around?* **4.** recently arrived or acquired: *There are some good new movies to see right now.* —**newness,** *noun.*
🔊 Different words with the same sound are **gnu** and **knew.**

new·born [noo-*born*] *adjective.* describing something or someone just born: *The newborn calf drank milk from its mother.*

new·com·er [noo-*kum*-ur] *noun, plural* **newcomers.** someone who has just arrived or started something: *a newcomer to the school.*

New England a group of states in the northeastern United States including Maine, Vermont, New Hampshire, Massachusetts, Rhode Island, and Connecticut.

new moon the Moon when it disappears from view once a month or the Moon soon afterward when it reappears as a thin crescent.

news [nooz] *noun.* a report of any recent event: *News of the bombing was reported on television and in the newspaper.*

news·cast [nooz-kast] *noun, plural* **newscasts.** a television or radio news presentation: *We watched the newscast for more information about the hurricane.* Someone or some organization that presents the news is a **newscaster.**

a b c d e f g h i j k l m **n** o p q r s t u v w x y z

Newton's laws are said to have been developed after he observed an apple falling from a tree.

news·pa·per [<u>nooz</u>-*pay*-pur] *noun, plural* **newspapers.** a printed publication of news, opinions, and advertisements. Usually newspapers are produced daily or weekly.

news·stand [<u>nooz</u>-*stand*] *noun, plural* **newsstands.** a booth or stall that sells newspapers and magazines.

newt [noot] *noun, plural* **newts.** a small salamander of Europe, North America, or northern Asia. Newts are brightly colored and live in or around water.

New Testament *Religion.* the second part of the Christian Bible that contains stories about Jesus Christ and his followers.

new·ton [<u>noot</u>-un] *noun, plural* **newtons.** *Science.* a measurement of force. One newton is the force needed to give an acceleration of one meter per second per second to a mass of one kilogram.

Newton's laws ▲
Science. three basic laws that describe and explain the movement of objects. These laws were stated more than three hundred years ago by Sir Isaac Newton.

New World the continents of North America and South America.

The area known as the **New World** (North and South America) is of course not really any newer than what is called the *Old World* (Europe and Asia). It was called "new" because it was not known to people in Europe until Columbus made his famous journey to the Americas in 1492.

New Year's Day the first day of the new year. In Western countries, this day falls on January 1 and is usually a public holiday.

next [nekst] *adjective.* **1.** describing something that follows after: *The next time I see you I will bring the money I owe you.* **2.** being or describing the nearest: *The next block is where Dad works.* *adverb.* **1.** immediately following: *My birthday comes first, then my sister's comes next.* **2.** at the first time after this: *I'll return the book when I next visit the library.*

next-door [*nekst*-<u>dore</u>] *adjective.* in the nearest house or building or block: *The Lins are our next-door neighbors.* *adverb.* to or from the nearest house or building or block. *I'm going next door to visit.*

Nez Perce [nez purs] *noun, plural* **Nez Perce** or **Nez Perces.** a member of a Native American tribe from the northwestern United States.

The name **Nez Perce** for this Indian tribe comes from a French term meaning "pierced nose." It was thought by early American explorers that these people would pierce the nose to wear an ornament there, though this was not true. Like many other Native American groups, the name the Nez Perce gave themselves meant simply "the people."

nib·ble ▼ [<u>nib</u>-ul] *verb,* **nibbled, nibbling.** to take small, quick bites: *The squirrel nibbled the nut.* *noun, plural* **nibbles.** a series of small, quick bites.

nice [nise] *adjective,* **nicer, nicest. 1.** describing something enjoyable or pleasant: *We had a nice time on our vacation.* **2.** describing something thoughtful or kind: *It was nice of her to help you.* **3.** being fine or having quality: *a nice piece of furniture.* —**nicely,** *adverb.*

nick [nik] *noun, plural* **nicks.** a cut or chip out of something. *verb,* **nicked, nicking.** to make a small cut or take a chip out of something: *She accidentally nicked her finger with the scissors.*

• **in the nick of time.** just in time: *She grabbed the runaway dog in the nick of time.*

*A parasarolophus dinosaur would have **nibbled** on vegetation with its duck-billed mouth.*

nick·el [<u>nik</u>-ul] *noun, plural* **nickels. 1.** a hard metal used in alloys to give them strength. **2.** a five-cent coin in the United States and Canada.

nick·name [<u>nik</u>-*name*] *noun, plural* **nicknames.** a name used instead of someone's real name. *His nickname is Mac because his family name, or last name, is MacDonald.* *verb,* **nicknamed, nicknaming.** to give someone a nickname: *We nicknamed our tall friend Shorty.*

A B C D E F G H I J K L M **N** O P Q R S T U V W X Y Z

nic·o·tine [nik-uh-*teen*] *noun. Chemistry.* a poison found in tobacco that makes people addicted to cigarettes and can contribute to them getting cancer.

niece [neess] *noun, plural* **nieces.**
1. the daughter of a sister or brother.
2. the daughter of a sister-in-law or brother-in-law.

The drug known as **nicotine,** which is found in tobacco plants, is named for Jacques *Nicot,* who was an official of the French government in the 1500s. He was the person who first brought the tobacco plant to France, after he learned of it while visiting the nearby country of Portugal.

Ni·ger·i·an [nye-*jeer*-ee-un] *noun, plural* **Nigerians.**
someone who was born in or lives in Nigeria, a country in west-central Africa.
adjective. having to do with the country of Nigeria.

night [nite] *noun, plural* **nights. 1.** the time between sunset and sunrise when it is dark: *My sister worked all night to finish her assignment.* The time when night begins is called **nightfall. 2.** a state of darkness because there is no sunlight: *The robbers broke in under the cover of night.*
🔊 A different word with the same sound is **knight.**

night·gown [nite-*goun*] *noun, plural* **nightgowns.** a long, loose dress worn to bed.

night·in·gale [nite-un-*gale*] *noun, plural* **nightingales.** a small bird with brown wings and white chest known for its beautiful song. Nightingales live in Europe and western Asia.

night·ly [nite-lee] *adjective.*
describing something that happens every night: *She takes a nightly dose of medicine.*
adverb. every night: *to take a bath nightly.*

night·mare [nite-*mare*] *noun, plural* **nightmares. 1.** a bad dream: *I had a nightmare that a monster was chasing me.* **2.** a bad experience: *The bus ride home was a nightmare because it was so hot and cramped.* A bad experience can be described as **nightmarish.**

This word comes from an old belief that an evil spirit called a **nightmare** would sneak up on people while they were asleep. This spirit would haunt and frighten people and try to stop their breathing by pressing down on top of them.

nim·ble [nim-bul] *adjective,* **nimbler, nimblest. 1.** quick and light in moving. *My sister made a nimble leap over the laundry basket to answer the phone.* **2.** quick to understand: *a nimble mind.* —**nimbly,** *adverb.*

nine [nine] *noun, plural* **nines.** the number between eight and ten; 9. Something that is number nine in order is the **ninth.**

nine·teen [nine-*teen*] *noun, plural* **nineteens.** the number between eighteen and twenty; 19. Something that is number nineteen in order is the **nineteenth.**

nine·ty [nine-tee] *noun, plural* **nineties.** the number between eighty-nine and ninety-one; 90. Something that is number ninety in order is the **ninetieth.**

nip [nip] *verb,* **nipped, nipping. 1.** to pinch or bite, but not hard: *The dog only nipped her foot.* **2.** to cut by pinching: *Mom nipped the buds off the plant to stop it from growing too tall.* *noun, plural* **nips. 1.** a pinch or bite. **2.** a biting cold: *a nip in the air.* **3.** a small drink of an alcoholic beverage.

nip·ple [nip-ul] *noun, plural* **nipples. 1.** the raised, rounded tip in the middle of a breast or udder. Babies drink milk from their mother's nipple. **2.** the rubber tip of a baby bottle that the baby sucks from.

ni·tro·gen [nye-truh-jun] *noun. Chemistry.* a colorless, odorless tasteless gas that makes up 78 percent of the Earth's air and is a part of all living tissues. Something that has to do with, or contains, nitrogen is **nitrogenous.**

In the Middle Ages, wealthy **nobles** *lived in castles and owned all the land surrounding the castle.*

nitrogen cycle *Environment.* the process in which substances in the soil are soaked up by plants that are eaten by animals that die and, as they decay, put nitrogen back into the soil.

ni·tro·gly·cer·ine [nye-troh-glis-ur-un] *noun. Chemistry.* a heavy, oily, poisonous liquid; used in making explosives and to treat heart conditions by helping the blood to flow more easily. A shorter form of this word is **nitro.**

no [noh] *adverb.* **1.** not right; not so: *No, I don't know her.* **2.** not in any amount or degree; not at all: *Little League is for players no older than twelve.* *adjective.* **1.** not any; none: *I have no reason to doubt her.* **2.** not one; zero: *There were no apples left at the shop.* *interjection.* used to show amazement: *No! Really? He passed the test?* *noun, plural* **nos. 1.** a negative response or refusal: *I said a firm "no."* **2.** an answer or vote against something: *There were twenty noes to one yes.*

no. an abbreviation for NUMBER.

Nobel Prize an award given each year to people who made very important contributions to peace, literature, medicine, economics, chemistry, and physics.

no·ble ▲ [noh-bul] *adjective,* **nobler, noblest. 1.** belonging to a class of people with high rank in society and a title: *She married into a noble family and was given the title of Duchess.* **2.** having or showing goodness or courage: *Helping your friend stand up to the bully was a noble act.* *noun, plural* **nobles.** someone with a title and high rank in society. Such a person is part of the **nobility.**

A
B
C
D
E
F
G
H
I
J
K
L
M
N
O
P
Q
R
S
T
U
V
W
X
Y
Z

NOCTURNAL ANIMALS

Animals that are nocturnal sleep during the day and are active at night. They have highly developed senses and other abilities to help them navigate the dark. Owls, lemurs, and cats have a special kind of eyesight. Other animals, like rabbits, can hear very well. Hedgehogs rely on their noses to sniff out insects and other food, while racoons have an acute sense of touch. Bats use echolocation, a kind of radar, to give them information about their surroundings. Nocturnal birds like the owl, nightjar, and the night parrot have dull or foliage-colored feathers to camouflage them while they sleep during the day.

Gray mouse lemur

Night parrot

Hedgehog

Rabbit

Barn owl

no·ble·man [noh-bul-mun] *noun, plural* **noblemen.** a man with high rank in society and a title.

no·ble·wom·an [noh-bul-*wum*-un] *noun, plural* **noblewomen.** a woman with high rank in society and a title.

no·bod·y [noh-*buh*-dee] *pronoun.* no person; no one: *Nobody is allowed in the classroom at lunchtime.* *noun, plural* **nobodies.** someone who feels, or is, not important: *Those girls make me feel like a nobody.*

noc·tur·nal ▲ [nok-tur-nul] *adjective.* **1.** relating to things that happen at night. **2.** active during the night: *Nocturnal flowers open at night.*

Nocturnal is one of three special words used in science to describe how different kinds of wild animals behave. Animals that are *nocturnal* come out when it gets dark and are active during the night. Animals whose activity and feeding takes place during the day are said to be *diurnal*. A third type of animal is *crepuscular*; these are animals that come out and are active at twilight, the time between light and dark at the end or beginning of the day.

nod [nod] *verb,* **nodded, nodding. 1.** to move the head up and down. **2.** to raise and lower the head repeatedly in order to show agreement: *The music teacher nodded when I hit the right notes.* *noun, plural* **nods.** the action of moving the head up and down.

noise [noyze] *noun, plural* **noises. 1.** a sound that is unwanted, irritating, or loud: *We want to move to a different house because of all the noise here from the traffic.* **2.** any type of sound or combination of sounds: *We heard some strange noises outside our tent.*

noise pollution *Environment.* sounds that upset, disturb, or harm people.

nois·y [noy-zee] *adjective,* **noisier, noisiest.** having or making a lot of noise: *The noisy people were asked to be quiet or leave the library.* —**noisily,** *adverb.*

no·mad ▼ [noh-mad] *noun, plural* **nomads. 1.** someone belonging to a culture or tribe that moves their home from place to place to find food. Nomads often move according to the seasons. **2.** someone who does not settle in one place. Someone who moves from place to place is described as **nomadic.**

In ancient times the name *Nomades* was given to certain tribes that lived on the borders of states such as Greece, Rome, and Carthage. The Nomades lived as **nomads.** The Nomades got their name from a word for "pasture" or "grazing land," because it was thought that they moved from place to place looking for good land to feed their animals.

nom·in·ate [nom-uh-*nate*] *verb,* **nominated, nominating. 1.** to suggest someone to be appointed to or elected into a position: *The Republican Party nominated Gerald Ford to run for President in 1976.* **2.** to appoint someone to a position or give responsibility to someone: *The coach nominated three players to try out for the select team.*

nom·i·na·tion [nom-uh-nay-shun] *noun, plural* **nominations. 1.** the suggestion of someone suitable for a position, or to take part in an election, or to receive an award: *The nominations for mayor have now closed and the election will take place soon.* **2.** the appointment of someone to a position; the announcement of an award or honor.

The **nomads** *of Central Asia sometimes use camels to transport their belongings.*

nom·i·nee [nom-uh-<u>nee</u>] *noun, plural* **nominees.** a person or people who has been nominated: *Tomorrow they will announce the nominees for Best Actress for this year's Academy Awards.*

non- a prefix that means not; without; the opposite of: *nonprofit* means without profit; *nonstop* means without stopping.

non·chal·ant [non-shuh-<u>lahnt</u>] *adjective.* being casual or indifferent: *His nonchalant attitude to homework makes the teacher unhappy.* The fact of being nonchalant is **nonchalance.** —**nonchalantly,** *adverb.*

none [nun] *pronoun.* **1.** not one person: *All the students looked for the lost book but none could find it.* **2.** not any part of something: *None of the cake was left.*
adverb. in no way: *Help for the lost campers arrived none too soon.*
🔊 A different word with the same sound is **nun.**

non·fic·tion [non-<u>fik</u>-shun] *noun. Literature.* writing that deals with real facts and events rather than made-up stories: *Biographies are my favorite nonfiction books.*
adjective. describing writing that deals with real facts and events: *This book about whales is a nonfiction story.*

Writing that is **nonfiction** is about real things and gives facts. This is different from *fiction*, which tells a made-up story. If you wrote a report about wolves or about the Grand Canyon, that would be nonfiction. However, nonfiction and fiction are not completely different. You could use the real Grand Canyon as the place where a made-up story (fiction) takes place, such as a story of a boy exploring the canyon. In the same way, your nonfiction report about wolves could be an interesting story of one certain pack of wolves and how they live.

non·sense [<u>non</u>-sens] *noun.* **1.** ideas or words that are silly or make no sense. Something that makes no sense can be described as **nonsensical. 2.** an action or behavior that is senseless or silly: *The guide said there was to be no nonsense inside the museum.*

non·stop [non-<u>stop</u>] *adjective.* going somewhere directly without stopping along the way: *They took a nonstop flight home.*
adverb. without stopping: *We drove nonstop through the night.*

noo·dle ▶ [<u>noo</u>-dul] *noun, plural* **noodles.** a strip of dough made of eggs, flour, and water. The strips are dried then cooked in boiling water.

It is not known how the word **noodle** came into English. A story is often told that an explorer of the Middle Ages named Marco Polo was the first European to learn about noodles, when he made a famous journey to China. Marco Polo is said to have brought the recipe for noodles from China to Italy, and the word *noodle* then moved to other countries.

noon [noon] *noun.* 12 o'clock in the day; midday. The sun is highest in the sky at **noontime.**

no one nobody or no person: *We came on the wrong night and no one was home.*

noose ◀ [noos] *noun, plural* **nooses.** a loop of rope with a knot that tightens when the rope is pulled.

A **noose** *is made using a simple knot called the hangman's knot.*

nor [nor] *conjunction.* and not. Nor is used together with neither: *Neither my sister nor I like spicy food.* Nor can be used like the word *and*, but only in a negative sense: *Dad did not enjoy skating, nor did Mom.*

nor·mal [<u>nor</u>-mul] *adjective.* **1.** describing something regular or usual: *Today, we went to school at the normal time of 8.00 A.M.* **2.** being healthy; describing average mental or physical development: *My sister's temperature came down and returned to normal, 98.6°.* —**normally,** *adverb.*

north [north] *noun.* one of the four main points of the compass. If you face the rising sun, north is to your left. Any area in that direction can be called **North.** The area in the United States north of Maryland, the Ohio River, and Missouri is called **The North.**
adjective. **1.** having to do with the north: *The field is on the north side of the school.* **2.** being from the north: *a north wind.*
adverb. toward the north: *They traveled north.*

North American 1. someone born or living in Canada, or the United States, or Mexico. **2.** having to do with North America, its people, or its culture.

north·east [north-<u>eest</u>] *noun.* **1.** the point or direction half way between north and east. **2.** an area in this direction. New England, New York, Pennsylvania, states in the northeast of the United States, are called the **Northeast.**
adjective. having to do with or being from the northeast. Also, **northeastern.**
adverb. toward the northeast.

north·ern [<u>nor</u>TH-urn] *adjective.* **1.** having to do with the north: *The lemon tree is in the northern corner of the garden.* **2.** being from the north: *an icy northern wind.* Someone who comes from the north is a **northerner. 3. Northern.** having to do with the northern part of the United States.

Northern Hemisphere *Geography.* the half of the Earth between the North Pole and the equator. North America, Europe, and most of Africa and Asia are in the Northern Hemisphere.

northern lights streams of light that sometimes appear in the northern sky at night. They are also called the **aurora borealis.**

Noodles are part of many Chinese meals.

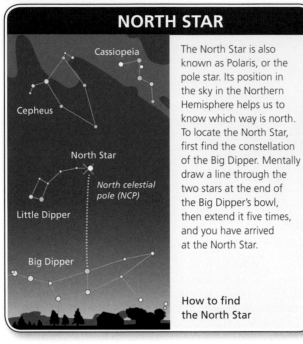

NORTH STAR

The North Star is also known as Polaris, or the pole star. Its position in the sky in the Northern Hemisphere helps us to know which way is north. To locate the North Star, first find the constellation of the Big Dipper. Mentally draw a line through the two stars at the end of the Big Dipper's bowl, then extend it five times, and you have arrived at the North Star.

Cassiopeia

Cepheus

North Star

North celestial pole (NCP)

Little Dipper

Big Dipper

How to find the North Star

North Star ▲ a bright star that shines in the northern sky above the North Pole.

north·west [north-<u>west</u>] *noun.* **1.** the point or direction half way between north and west. **2.** an area in this direction: *The northwest of the town has a lake.* Oregon, Washington State, and other areas in the northwest of the United States are called the **Northwest.**
adjective. having to do with or being from the northwest. Also, **northwestern.**
adverb. toward the northwest: *They flew northwest.*

Nor·we·gian [nore-<u>weej</u>-un] *noun, plural* **Norwegians.**
1. someone born or living in the European country of Norway. **2.** the language of Norway.
adjective. having to do with Norway, its people, or its culture.

nose ▼ [noze] *noun, plural* **noses. 1.** the part of the face used for smelling and breathing. **2.** the sense of smell: *He has a nose for good wine.* **3.** the part of something that sticks out in front: *the nose of an airplane.*
verb, **nosed, nosing.** to use the nose: *They use sniffer dogs at the airport to try to nose out illegal drugs.*
• **under one's nose.** in an obvious place: *The book she thought she lost was right under her nose.*

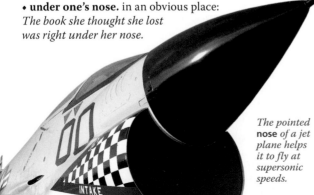

*The pointed **nose** of a jet plane helps it to fly at supersonic speeds.*

nos·tal·gi·a [nuh-<u>stal</u>-juh] *noun.* fond memory or a longing for the past: *Dad feels nostalgia for the town where he grew up.* Someone who feels nostalgia is **nostalgic.**
—nostalgically, *adverb.*

The word **nostalgia** comes from a name used in ancient Greece, *Nestor*. The name Nestor meant "the one who returns." A person who is *nostalgic* about the past is someone who would like to return to that time, or return to a place that he or she knew in the past.

nos·tril [<u>nos</u>-trul] *noun, plural* **nostrils.** one of two openings in the nose through which people and animals breathe and smell.

no·sy [<u>noh</u>-zee] *adjective,* **nosier, nosiest.** describing someone who is overly interested in other people's business: *Our nosy neighbor always knows what everyone on the block is doing.* **—nosily,** *adverb;* **—nosiness,** *noun.*

not [not] *adverb.* in no way; at no time: *She is not in school today—she's sick; Do not cross when the light is red.*
🔊 A different word with the same sound is **knot.**

no·ta·tion ▶ [noh-<u>tay</u>-shun] *noun, plural* **notations.**
1. symbols or signs that represent words, numbers, or other information. The mathematical sign "×" is a notation meaning "multiplied by." **2.** a short note that helps recall or organize information: *We are allowed to write notations in the margin of our workbook.*

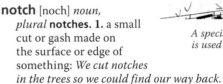

*A special kind of **notation** is used to represent music on paper.*

notch [noch] *noun, plural* **notches. 1.** a small cut or gash made on the surface or edge of something: *We cut notches in the trees so we could find our way back.*
2. a small valley or open place between two mountains.
verb, **notched, notching.** to cut a notch in something.

note [note] *noun, plural* **notes. 1.** words written to help recall and organize information: *She took notes during the lesson.* **2.** a brief explanation in a book: *There are notes at the bottom of each page of our history book.* **3.** a brief letter or message: *She sent a note thanking us for the gift.* **4.** the act of looking at carefully: *Take note of what the doctor says.* **5.** the state or fact of being important: *He is a scientist of some note.* **6.** an indication or suggestion: *The was a note of anger in her voice.* **7.** a single musical sound, or a symbol representing that sound.
verb, **noted, noting. 1.** to write down: *The teacher noted Sue's absence in the attendance book.* **2.** to see or look at: *I note that you included a card with the gift.*

note·book [<u>note</u>-buk] *noun, plural* **notebooks.** a book for keeping notes: *Our teacher wants us to have a separate notebook for each subject.*

notebook computer *Computers.* a portable personal computer about the size of a large book.

not·ed [note-id] *adjective.* well known or famous: *A noted scientist spoke to us about saving the environment.*

noth·ing [nuth-ing] *noun, plural* **nothings.**
1. no thing; not anything: *The dog ate all its dinner and nothing was left in the bowl.* **2.** the fact of being zero: *Five minus nothing equals five.* **3.** someone or something that is not important: *It means nothing to her if I come to the party or not. adverb.* not at all: *That orange drink tastes nothing like real orange juice.*

no·tice [noh-tis] *noun, plural* **notices. 1.** the state of being seen or watched: *It escaped his notice that he had put on two different colored socks.* **2.** the act of seeing or watching: *Her wild hairstyle gained our notice.* **3.** an announcement: *We got a notice that school would close at noon on Friday.* **4.** a printed announcement: *The notice on the board says we all have to attend gym class. verb,* **noticed, noticing.** to see or become aware of: *The teacher noticed that one of her students was missing.*

no·tice·a·ble [noh-tis-uh-bul] *adjective.* able to be noticed easily: *a noticeable improvement.* —**noticeably,** *adverb.*

no·ti·fy [noh-tuh-*fye*] *verb,* **notified, notifying.** to give notice; tell: *The principal notified us about the changes to the class schedule.* The act or fact of notifying is **notification.**

no·tion [noh-shun] *noun, plural* **notions. 1.** an idea or belief: *She had no notion that we were planning a party for her.* Pins, needles, and other small, useful objects are sometimes called **notions. 2.** a wish to do something; a whim or desire: *He gave in to the notion to cut class and left the school grounds.*

no·tor·i·ous ▲ [noh-*tor*-ee-us] *adjective.* famous or widely known for something: *a notorious criminal; That highway is notorious for afternoon traffic jams.* The fact of being notorious is **notoriety.** —**notoriously,** *adverb.*

noun [nown] *noun, plural* **nouns.** *Language.* a word that names someone, something, or some place. In the sentence *The teacher brought her goldfish named Jerry to show the class,* "teacher," "goldfish," "Jerry," and "class" are nouns.

The usual way to describe a **noun** is to say that it is "the name of a person, place, or thing." The largest number of nouns fit into the third group, "things." "Things" has a very general meaning here because it includes not only real objects such as *car, pencil, dish,* or *computer,* but also ideas such as *love, freedom, energy,* and *disease.* In certain sentences another part of speech can even be a noun. The word *swimming* is usually a verb, as in the sentence "Fish were *swimming* in the pond," but it is a noun in the sentence "*Swimming* is good exercise."

*Billy the Kid was a **notorious** outlaw of America's Old West.*

nour·ish [nur-ish] *verb,* **nourished, nourishing. 1.** to provide the things that are needed to live and grow: *Sun and rain nourish the garden.* **2.** to provide things that allow someone or something to do well: *Her musical career was nourished by a wonderful teacher.* Someone or something that nourishes can be described as **nourishing.**

nour·ish·ment [nur-ish-munt] *noun.* things that are needed to live and grow: *There is a lot of nourishment in a good salad.*

nov·el[1] [nov-ul] *noun, plural* **novels.** *Literature.* a long story, usually in the form of a book.

nov·el[2] [nov-ul] *adjective.* new or different from anything seen before: *Taking her students to the zoo to count animals was a novel approach to teaching math.*

nov·el·ist [nov-ul-ist] *noun, plural* **novelists.** *Literature.* someone who writes novels: *Mark Twain was the novelist who wrote Huckleberry Finn.*

nov·el·ty [nov-ul-tee] *noun, plural* **novelties. 1.** the fact of being new: *Once the novelty wore off, she stopped riding her horse every day.* **2.** something new: *It was a real novelty for him to try such spicy food.* **3. novelties.** small, often cheap, toys and ornaments.

No·vem·ber [noh-*vem*-bur] *noun.* the eleventh month of the year. November has 30 days.

nov·ice [nov-is] *noun, plural* **novices. 1.** someone who is new at something; a beginner: *He was a novice at skydiving so he was very nervous.* **2.** someone who enters a religious order for a test period before they take their final vows. Nuns, brothers, and monks all begin their religious life as novices.

The word **November** comes from *novem,* the Latin word for "nine." November is the eleventh month in the modern calendar of twelve months, but the calendar of ancient Rome had only ten months and November was the ninth.

now [now] *adverb.* **1.** at the present time or at that moment. *Say good-bye to Aunt Leah, she's leaving now.* **2.** immediately or at once: *Take your shower now before the hot water runs out.* **3.** under the present conditions: *She slept late, and now she will probably miss her bus. conjunction.* since: *The lesson can start, now that the teacher has arrived. noun.* this moment: *The time to leave is now.*

now·a·days [now-uh-*daze*] *adverb.* at the present time; these days: *There used to be stores on every corner but nowadays they're all in the mall.*

no·where [no-ware] *adverb.* not anywhere: *The lost book was nowhere to be found. noun.* **1.** a remote or unknown place. *Our cousins live on a farm, way out in the middle of nowhere.* **2.** the fact of being unknown: *He came from nowhere to become the most famous actor on television.*

noz·zle [noz-ul] *noun, plural* **nozzles.** a small opening or spout, usually at the end of a hose or pipe: *Dad changed the nozzle on the hose to get a finer spray of water.*

a b c d e f g h i j k l m **n** o p q r s t u v w x y z

nu·cle·ar [noo-klee-ur] *adjective.* **1.** having to do with a nucleus: *Protons and neutrons are nuclear particles.* **2.** having to do with the energy created by splitting or combining the nucleus of an atom: *a nuclear bomb; a nuclear explosion.*

nuclear energy *Science.* energy released by splitting or joining atoms. This energy may be released in an explosion, as in an atomic bomb. This energy may also be released in a controlled way, as to produce electricity. Nuclear energy is used to power some ships and submarines.

At the center of a cell's **nucleus** *is a nucleolus, which is the part of the cell that produces proteins.*

Nucleus

nuclear physics *Science.* the branch of physics that studies the inside of the atom's nucleus, and the interactions of its parts.

nuclear reactor *Science.* a device in which a nuclear chain reaction is started and controlled. The resulting heat is usually used to produce electricity.

nuclear weapon a device, such as a bomb or warhead, that explodes because of a release of nuclear energy. Nuclear weapons are weapons of mass destruction.

nu·cle·i [noo-klee-eye] *noun.* the plural of NUCLEUS.

nu·cle·us ▲ [noo-klee-uss] *noun, plural* **nuclei** *or* **nucleuses.** **1.** *Biology.* the central part found in almost every cell that makes up living things. The nucleus is a rounded mass that contains the genes that control heredity. It also controls the cell's growth and division. **2.** *Physics.* the central part of an atom that is made up of protons and neutrons and carries a positive charge. **3.** the central part or thing around which other parts or things gather: *The conductor is the nucleus of an orchestra.*

> **Nucleus** comes from a word meaning "a nut" or "a kernel," as in a kernel of corn. People thought of the nucleus of something as a small inner part like a nut or kernel.

nug·get ▶ [nug-it] *noun, plural* **nuggets.** **1.** a solid lump of something: *The miner dug up a nugget of gold as big as his hand.* **2.** something of great value, usually surrounded by things of less value: *It was a very long book, but I found a few nuggets of useful information.*

The world's largest gold **nugget,** *called the Welcome Stranger, was found in Australia in 1869.*

nui·sance [noo-suns] *noun, plural* **nuisances.** a person, thing, or action that causes problems or is annoying: *That dog is a nuisance because it always digs up the garden.*

numb [num] *adjective,* **number, numbest. 1.** unable to feel or move properly: *The doctor gave her an injection to make her arm numb before he sewed up the cut.* **2.** without or seeming to be without feelings: *Hearing of our friend's serious illness, we were numb with shock.* *verb,* **numbed, numbing.** to become or to make numb: *The cold wind numbed Jim's fingers so he couldn't untie the rope.* **—numbness,** *adverb.*

num·ber [num-bur] *noun, plural* **numbers. 1.** the total count or amount of something: *The number of students in our class is 28.* **2.** a symbol or word used in counting or to tell which one. Numbers can be written as figures, such as 22, or as words, such as twenty-two. **3.** a certain number assigned for a purpose: *a telephone number; the license number of a car.* **4.** the total or sum; an amount: *A small number of children behaved badly on the school camp.* **4.** a large but not exactly stated amount: *A number of houses were damaged during the storm.* *verb,* **numbered, numbering. 1.** to total in number or amount: *The boats in the race numbered fourteen.* **2.** to give numbers that tell things apart: *The seats in the hall were numbered from one to 400.* **3.** to limit or restrict: *The places available on the cruise are strictly numbered.*

number line *Mathematics.* a line on which marks are made with even spaces in between and each mark is given a number. The numbers on the line are written in order and go up or down.

nu·mer·al [noo-mur-ul] *noun, plural* **numerals.** *Mathematics.* a written sign that stands for the amount or total of something: *In Roman numerals, the number six is written VI.*

In the past, **nuns** *wore special habits and veils, but today many wear ordinary clothes.*

nu·mer·a·tor [noo-muh-ra-tur] *noun, plural* **numerators.** *Mathematics.* in a fraction, the number above the line that is the number of parts of a whole that there are. For instance, in the fraction ½, 1 is the numerator and 2 is the denominator.

nu·mer·i·cal [noo-mer-uh-kul] *adjective.* having to do with numbers: *She arranged the coins in numerical order, from those with the lowest value to those with the highest.* **—numerically,** *adverb.*

nu·mer·ous [noo-mur-us] *adjective.* describing a large number together; many: *Numerous water birds live in and around the pond.*

nun ▲ [nun] *noun, plural* **nuns.** *Religion.* a woman who belongs to a religious order. Nuns devote their life to worship and to good deeds, such as care of the sick. They often live in convents and take special vows. 🔊 A different word with the same sound is **none.**

nurse [nurs] *noun, plural* **nurses. 1.** a person whose job is to take care of sick people or teach people how to look after their health: *In the hospital, the nurse put clean bandages on the girl's wound every day.* **2.** a person whose job is to care for small children.
verb, **nursed, nursing. 1.** to care for a sick person: *It took months to nurse the man back to health after he was hurt in an accident.* **2.** to feed a young animal or baby from a nipple; breast-feed: *The mother cat nursed her kittens.* **3.** to treat carefully: *Michael nursed the seedlings in the greenhouse until they were ready to be planted outside.*

Nuthatches *can store up to forty seeds an hour under tree bark.*

nurse·maid [nurs-made] *noun, plural* **nursemaids.** a girl or woman whose job is to care for small children.

nurs·er·y [nurs-ree *or* nur-sur-ee] *noun, plural* **nurseries. 1.** a baby's bedroom. **2.** a place where babies and young children are brought to be cared for during the daytime. **3.** a place where plants are grown and usually sold.

nursery rhyme *Literature.* a short poem or song for young children.

nursery school *Education.* a school for small children who are not yet old enough to go to kindergarten.

nursing home *Health.* a large residence where people who are disabled, ill, or very old live. People who live there do not need to be in a hospital but cannot be cared for at home.

nut ▼ [nut] *noun, plural* **nuts. 1.** a fruit that is made up of a hard shell with a soft, dry kernel inside. **2.** the soft, edible kernel of a nut. **3.** a metal block with a hole in the middle that is screwed onto a bolt to hold it in place. **4.** a person who acts in a crazy, odd, or wild manner.

nut·crack·er [nut-krak-ur] *noun, plural* **nutcrackers. 1.** a tool used to crack a nut's hard shell to reach the kernel inside. **2.** a type of bird related to jays and crows. It has a strong beak that it uses to dig out kernels from pinecones, spruce cones, and hazelnuts.

Nuts *are a good source of protein, vitamins, and oils, and make a healthy snack food.*

nut·hatch ◀ [nut-hach] *noun, plural* **nuthatches.** a small bird with a large head, short tail, and strong beak that creeps along the branches and trunks of trees gathering seeds, insects, and small nuts.

nut·meg ▼ [nut-meg] *noun, plural* **nutmegs.** the hard, fragrant seed of a tree that grows in tropical Asia. The seed is dried and grated or ground, for use as a spice in cooking.

nu·tri·ent [noo-tree-unt] *noun, plural* **nutrients.** a substance that is taken in by a plant or animal in order to grow or provide energy. Plants absorb nutrients from the soil and water. Animals and people absorb them from food and drink: *Vitamin C is a nutrient that people get from eating oranges.*

nu·tri·tion [noo-trish-un] *noun. Health.* **1.** the fact of taking in food; the diet: *Good nutrition is important for growing children.* **2.** the process by which food is absorbed by living things and used for growth or to provide energy: *Roots absorb water and are an important part of plant nutrition.*

nu·tri·tion·ist [noo-trish-un-ist] *noun, plural* **nutritionist.** *Health.* a person who studies food and nutrition and gives advice to others about good nutrition.

nu·tri·tious [noo-trish-us] *adjective.* providing good nourishment: *Fruits such as apples or peaches can be eaten as a nutritious snack between meals.*

Nutmegs *develop from the yellow, bell-shaped flowers of the nutmeg tree.*

nut·shell [nut-shel] *noun, plural* **nutshells.** the hard shell of a nut.
• **in a nutshell.** in a few words: *The coach told us what she wanted us to do in a nutshell: "get the ball and score."*

nut·ty [nut-ee] *adjective,* **nuttier, nuttiest. 1.** containing nuts or having a flavor or texture like nuts: *Putting walnuts in the cake gave it a nutty flavor.* **2.** not sensible; silly or crazy: *It would be nutty to jump on the trampoline in the pouring rain.*

nuz·zle [nuz-ul] *verb,* **nuzzled, nuzzling.** to rub or push against with the nose: *The pony nuzzled my hand, hoping I had a carrot for him.*

ny·lon [nye-lon] *noun.* a material made from chemicals. It is very strong and elastic and is used to make things such as cloth, tires, and brush bristles.

nymph [nimf] *noun, plural* **nymphs. 1.** *Literature.* in old stories such as Greek and Roman legends, a goddess who lived in the woods, meadows, or ocean and appeared as a beautiful young woman. **2.** a young insect that hatches from its egg looking like a small adult. A nymph changes into an adult in stages, shedding is skin each time. Grasshoppers begin their lives as nymphs.

Oases make it possible for people to survive long journeys across the desert.

Oo

O, o *noun, plural* **O's, o's.** the fifteenth letter of the English alphabet.

oak ▼ [oke] *noun, plural* **oaks.** any of many trees or shrubs that have acorns as fruit. The wood of some oak trees is hard and is used to build furniture, boats, or houses.

oar [or] *noun, plural* **oars.** a pole with a wide blade at one end that is used to row or steer a boat.
🔊 Different words with the same sound are **or** and **ore.**

o·a·sis ▲ [oh-<u>ay</u>-sis] *noun, plural* **oases. 1.** a place in the desert where there is water and trees, and other plants can grow. **2.** a place that offers a break from unpleasant surroundings; a refuge: *Her quiet apartment was her oasis in the noisy city.*

oath [ohth] *noun, plural* **oaths. 1.** a promise a person makes to tell the truth: *In court, the witness gave her evidence under oath.* **2.** a word thought of as rude or offensive that is especially used when angry; a swear word.

oat·meal [<u>ote</u>-meel] *noun, plural* **oatmeals. 1.** a meal or coarse powder made by grinding whole oats. **2.** porridge or cereal made by cooking this meal with milk or water.

oats [ohtz] *plural noun.* a cereal grain that grows well in cool climates. Oats are used to make porridge and in baking. They are also used to feed livestock such as horses.

o·be·di·ent [oh-<u>bee</u>-dee-unt] *adjective.* likely to or willing to do what you are told: *The obedient dog came to its owner when it was called.* The act or practice of being obedient is called **obedience. —obediently,** *adverb.*

o·bese [oh-<u>bees</u>] *adjective. Health.* extremely fat: *The obese man lost weight by going on a diet and doing more exercise.* The condition of being extremely overweight is called **obesity.**

> The word **obese** is taken from a Latin word meaning "to eat." The idea is that a person becomes obese from eating too much.

o·bey [oh-<u>bay</u>] *verb,* **obeyed, obeying. 1.** to carry out orders or instructions that are given to you: *We obeyed the teacher and took out our books.* **2.** to follow the rules: *People who do not obey the law can be sent to jail.*

o·bi [<u>oh</u>-bee] *noun, plural* **obis.** a long, wide sash worn tied around the waist of a kimono.

ob·ject [<u>ob</u>-jikt] *noun, plural* **objects. 1.** something that can be seen or touched but is not alive; a thing: *I saw her put a red object into her bag.* **2.** a person or thing toward which an action or attention is aimed: *an object of hatred.* **3.** a reason for doing something; goal: *The object of my phone call was to make sure you are all right.* **4.** a word or group of words that a verb acts on. For example, in the sentence *The girl kicked the ball,* the "ball" is the object—it is the thing "kicked." **5.** the word or group of words that is the end point of a relationship described by a preposition. For example, in the sentence *He put his shoes on,* "shoes" are the object of the preposition "on." *verb,* **objected, objecting.** to express disagreement with something or someone: *I objected to having to sit next to him because he kept poking and bothering me.*

In some languages the form of a word changes when it is an **object** in a sentence rather than the subject, but not in English. "A soccer *ball* is round" uses *ball* as a subject, and "She kicked the *ball* down the field" uses the same form, *ball,* as an object. The only time there is a difference between subject and object is with pronouns. "Scott and *I* went to a movie" is correct and not "Scott and *me* went," because *I* is the subject. On the other hand, "Mom gave Scott and *I* a ride to the movie" is not correct; it should be "Mom gave Scott and *me* a ride" because *me* is the object.

ob·jec·tion [ub-<u>jek</u>-shun] *noun, plural* **objections. 1.** a reason given for not agreeing with something or someone: *Mom's objection to our game was the loud noise we were making.* **2.** a feeling of dislike or not approving: *Don's objection to going into the cold water was strong.* When a person or thing causes strong disapproval or dislike, it is said to be **objectionable.**

ob·jec·tive [ub-<u>jek</u>-tiv] *adjective.* influenced by facts, not by feelings or opinions; not biased: *My best friend drew that picture but, being objective, I don't like it. noun, plural* **objectives.** an aim or purpose: *The explorer's objective was to reach the North Pole.* **—objectively,** *adverb.*

Oak trees can live for more than two hundred years.

ob·li·gate [<u>ob</u>-li-*gate*] *verb,* **obligated, obligating.** to cause someone do something out of a sense of duty, because of a rule, or to fulfill a promise. When someone feels they must do something, they feel **obligated.**

ob·li·ga·tion [*ob*-luh-<u>gay</u>-shun] *noun, plural* **obligations.** something that is a person's duty to do; a responsibility: *I have an obligation to visit my aunt as I promised I would.* Something done out of a sense of duty is **obligatory.**

The **oboe** has a clear, piercing tone that can be heard above the other instruments in an orchestra.

observatory

o·blige [uh-<u>blyje</u>] *verb*, **obliged, obliging. 1.** to have to do something out a sense of duty, because it is the law, or because of a promise: *All drivers are obliged to stop for red traffic lights.* **2.** to be grateful for someone's assistance: *Our neighbor was obliged to us for looking after her cat.* Someone who is helpful is said to be **obliging.**

ob·lique [oh-<u>bleek</u>] *adjective.* **1.** describing something sloping; slanting: *The wall was no longer straight but oblique, and looked as if it would collapse.* **2.** not direct; misleading or not honest: *The police officer didn't trust her because of her oblique answers to his questions.*

oblique angle *Mathematics.* any angle that is not a right angle.

ob·liv·i·on [uh-<u>bliv</u>-ee-un] *noun.* **1.** the state of being completely forgotten: *His poetry is so bad that it is destined for oblivion.* **2.** the condition of totally forgetting: *After the awful day she'd had, the oblivion of sleep was a relief.*

ob·liv·i·ous [uh-<u>bliv</u>-ee-us] *adjective.* **1.** being forgetful or not remembering: *The oblivious children couldn't remember the rule their teacher had explained a week ago.* **2.** not taking any notice of; unaware of: *The woman in the funny hat was oblivious to people's stares.*

ob·long [<u>ob</u>-lawng] *adjective.* describing something that is longer than it is wide: *Both ovals and rectangles are oblong shapes.*
noun, plural **oblongs.** an object or shape that is longer than it is wide.

ob·nox·ious [ub-<u>nok</u>-shus] *adjective.* very unpleasant or disagreeable: *It's hard for him to make friends because people think he has an obnoxious personality.* **—obnoxiously,** *adverb.*

o·boe ◀ [<u>oh</u>-boh] *noun, plural* **oboes.** *Music.* a long, tube-shaped woodwind instrument. The oboe player blows through a mouthpiece that has two reeds to make high-pitched sounds.

ob·scure [ub-<u>skyoor</u>] *adjective.* **1.** unclear in meaning; not easy to understand: *The writer used lots of difficult words that made her story obscure.* **2.** hard to see, hear, or feel: *The face in the portrait was obscure because of the thick dust covering it.* **3.** not well known: *An obscure singer filled in for the sick pop star.* The state of not being well known is called **obscurity.**

ob·ser·vant [ub-<u>zur</u>-vunt] *adjective.* good at noticing things; watchful: *The observant bank clerk gave the police a good description of the robber.* **—observantly,** *adverb.*

ob·ser·va·tion [ob-zur-<u>vay</u>-shun] *noun, plural* **observations. 1.** the act of noticing or watching: *The zoologist learned about walruses through observation of their behavior.* **2.** the fact of being observed; notice: *They escaped observation by hiding behind the curtains.* **3.** a comment on something or someone; remark.

ob·serv·a·to·ry ▼ [ub-<u>zur</u>-vuh-*tore*-ee] *noun, plural* **observatories.** *Science.* a building or place in which there are telescopes and other scientific equipment for observing the sky, especially the stars and planets.

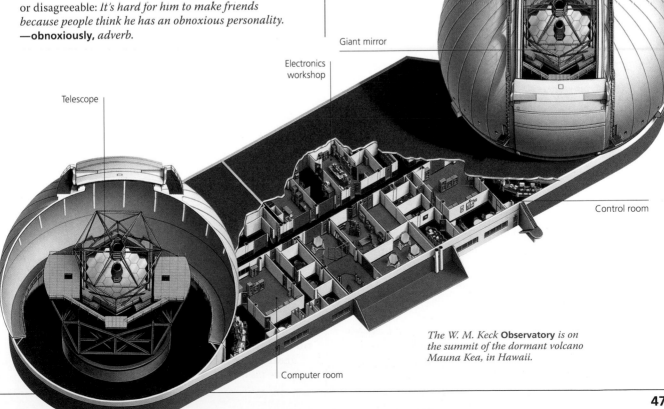

Movable shutter

Dome

Giant mirror

Electronics workshop

Telescope

Control room

Computer room

The W. M. Keck **Observatory** *is on the summit of the dormant volcano Mauna Kea, in Hawaii.*

OCEANS

The Earth's oceans carry up to 97 percent of all the Earth's water. They absorb most of the solar radiation that reaches the Earth. As they carry this heat around the globe, they affect climate. The Gulf Stream, for example, carries warm water from the Caribbean past the United States to northern Europe, where the climate is a lot warmer than northern Canada at the same latitudes.

Southern Ocean

Indian Ocean

Pacific Ocean

Atlantic Ocean

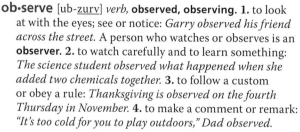

Arctic Ocean

OCEAN LIFE
There is a great diversity of life in the world's oceans. While plants are found only near the surface, marine animals live at all levels.

Sunlight zone
Enough sunlight reaches this top layer for plants to grow. It is here that most of an ocean's life is found, from microscopic plankton to fish of all sizes and sea mammals.

Twilight zone
This layer has insufficient light to support plants. Many of the fish in this zone glow in the dark.

Midnight zone
No light reaches below 3,250 feet. In this cold, slow-moving water, there is total darkness and much less diversity.

Abyssal zone
In the near-freezing, pitch-black bottom layer, there is no food except what falls from above. Creatures found here include the gulper eel, mussels, clams, and giant tubeworms.

ob·serve [ub-<u>zurv</u>] *verb,* **observed, observing. 1.** to look at with the eyes; see or notice: *Garry observed his friend across the street.* A person who watches or observes is an **observer. 2.** to watch carefully and to learn something: *The science student observed what happened when she added two chemicals together.* **3.** to follow a custom or obey a rule: *Thanksgiving is observed on the fourth Thursday in November.* **4.** to make a comment or remark: *"It's too cold for you to play outdoors," Dad observed.*

ob·so·lete [*ob*-suh-<u>leet</u>] *adjective.* no longer practiced or used; outdated: *"Methinks" is an obsolete word that means "I think."* The state of falling out of use is called **obsolescence.**

ob·sta·cle [<u>ob</u>-stuh-kul] *noun, plural* **obstacles.** something that gets in the way; an obstruction: *The fallen rocks formed an obstacle to cars on the road.*

obstacle course a series of obstacles, such as things that must be climbed over or crawled through, that a person attempts to complete, usually while being timed or scored in some way.

ob·struct [ub-<u>strukt</u>] *verb,* **obstructed, obstructing. 1.** to block the way with something; close up: *The avalanche obstructed the railway line.* **2.** to get in the way of: *Our view of the bay is obstructed by the new skyscraper.*

ob·struc·tion [ub-<u>struk</u>-shun] *noun, plural* **obstructions. 1.** something that obstructs; a blockage: *The tree roots formed an obstruction in the pipe and stopped water flowing through.* **2.** the act of obstructing or the state of being obstructed: *The obstruction of the river was caused by a mudslide.*

ob·tain [ub-<u>tane</u>] *verb,* **obtained, obtaining.** to gain by effort or by asking; get: *Cassie obtained her new bag by buying it with her own money.* Something that is possible to be obtained is said to be **obtainable.**

obtuse angle *Mathematics.* an angle that is greater than 90 degrees but less than 180 degrees.

ob·vi·ous [<u>ob</u>-vee-us] *adjective.* extremely easy to understand or see: *He has an obvious lump on his head where the rock hit him.* **—obviously,** *adverb.*

oc·ca·sion [uh-<u>kay</u>-zhun] *noun, plural* **occasions. 1.** a time when an event occurs: *On the occasion Harry and Leanne first met, they got along very well.* **2.** a special event: *The occasion of his graduation was celebrated by the whole family.* **3.** a suitable opportunity: *Dad was driving me to school when he took the occasion to ask me how I was doing in math.*

oc·ca·sion·al [uh-<u>kay</u>-zhuh-nul] *adjective.* occurring now and then; not happening often: *The old school friends still had occasional get-togethers after they grew up and got married.*—**occasionally,** *adverb.*

oc·cu·pant [<u>ok</u>-yuh-punt] *noun, plural* **occupants.** someone who lives in or occupies a place or holds a position: *The new occupant of the house across the street has just moved in.*

oc·cu·pa·tion [ok-yuh-<u>pay</u>-shun] *noun, plural* **occupations. 1.** the job a person does to earn money: *Her occupation is driving a bus.* Something that is related to an occupation is said to be **occupational. 2.** the act of taking over a place: *The army's occupation of the island ended after a month.*

oc·cu·py [<u>ok</u>-yuh-*pye*] *verb,* **occupied, occupying. 1.** to fill a space or time: *The rose bushes occupy the sunniest part of our garden.* **2.** to take over territory by force: *The soldiers occupied the hill.* **3.** to live in a place: *Oscar occupies the apartment upstairs from us.* **4.** to keep someone busy: *It rained all afternoon so we occupied ourselves playing board games.* **5.** to hold or possess: *He occupies the position of treasurer of our school's PTA.*

oc·cur [uh-<u>kur</u>] *verb,* **occurred, occurring. 1.** to take place; happen: *Snowstorms occur only in winter.* **2.** to be found; exist: *Ferns do not occur in desert environments.* **3.** to come into the mind of; be thought of: *It occurred to me that you might like to eat out on your birthday.*

oc·cur·rence [uh-<u>kur</u>-uns] *noun, plural* **occurrences.** the fact of something happening: *For her, forgetting to do homework is a common occurrence.*

o·cean ◀ [<u>oh</u>-shun] *noun, plural* **oceans. 1.** the vast body of salt water that covers around three-quarters of the Earth's surface. **2.** any of the largest areas of salt water on the Earth. These oceans are named the Arctic, the Atlantic, the Indian, the Pacific, and the Southern.

o·cean·og·ra·phy [*oh*-shuh-<u>nog</u>-ruh-fee] *noun. Science.* the scientific study of the ocean, including its movement, chemistry, geology, and the plants and animals that live in it. A scientist who studies the ocean is an **oceanographer.** —**oceanographic,** *adjective.*

o·cel·ot ◀ [<u>os</u>-uh-lut] *noun, plural* **ocelots.** a medium-sized cat with yellowish fur marked with black stripes on the face and neck and spots elsewhere. Ocelots live in the southwestern United States and Central and South America. They mostly eat small animals and hunt at night. They were once hunted for their fur and are now endangered.

The **ocelot** was given its name by a famous scientist of the 1700s, Count de Buffon of France. He developed a huge encyclopedia of 44 volumes, describing everything that was then known about the world of nature. He took the word *ocelot* from a name used by the Indians of Mexico for another related animal, the jaguar.

o'clock [uh-<u>klok</u>] *adverb.* according to the clock: *School finishes at three o'clock.*

oc·ta·gon [<u>ok</u>-tuh-*gon*] *noun, plural* **octagons.** *Mathematics.* a shape that has eight angles and eight straight sides. Something that is eight-sided is said to be **octagonal.**

oc·tave [<u>ok</u>-tiv] *noun, plural* **octaves.** *Music.* **1.** the eight-note distance between a note and the next note of the same name. **2.** the notes or keys of an instrument that are included in this distance, including sharps and flats.

Oc·to·ber [ok-<u>toh</u>-bur] *noun.* the tenth month of the year. October has 31 days.

oc·to·pus ▼ [<u>ok</u>-tuh-pus] *noun, plural* **octopuses** *or* **octopi.** a marine animal with a soft, oval body and eight arms with suckers on their underside. The octopus mainly lives on the sea bottom and catches prey. It is related to the squid.

The **octopus** gets its name from a phrase meaning "having eight feet." The limbs of the octopus are usually called "arms," and are much longer than what one would think of as feet, but for some reason the word "foot" rather than "arm" was used in this name.

odd [od] *adjective,* **odder, oddest. 1.** describing something unusual or peculiar: *It's odd that he didn't call to say he wasn't coming.* **2.** being left over from a pair or set of something: *Throw out this odd sock, as the other one is lost.* **3.** occurring now and then; occasional: *I do odd jobs for my grandmother around her house.* **4.** leaving one behind when a number is divided by two; being the opposite of even: *7 is an odd number but 6 is even.* —**oddly,** *adverb.*

The blue-ringed **octopus** *produces venom that is powerful enough to kill an adult human in minutes.*

a
b
c
d
e
f
g
h
i
j
k
l
m
n
o
p
q
r
s
t
u
v
w
x
y
z

*People light candles, burn incense, and give money as a form of religious **offering**.*

A B C D E F G H I J K L M N O P Q R S T U V W X Y Z

odd·i·ty [od-uh-tee] *noun, plural* **oddities.**
1. a person or thing that is unusual or peculiar: *That rose is an oddity because it is blue instead of white, pink, or red.* **2.** the fact or quality of being unusual or peculiar: *The oddity of his costume made everyone stare at him.*

odds [odz] *plural noun.*
the likelihood of something occurring or being true. This is sometimes expressed as a ratio, such as ten to one. *The odds are that the bus will be late again; The odds against the team winning the championship are a hundred to one.*
• **at odds.** in disagreement or arguing: *They are at odds about whether to repair the old car or buy a new one.*

odds and ends a collection of objects of various kinds; leftovers; scraps: *The children stuck odds and ends together to make funny model animals.*

o·dor [oh-dur] *noun, plural* **odors.** a smell or scent, especially one that is strong and unpleasant: *The odor of rotten eggs makes me feel sick.* Something without a smell is said to be **odorless.**

of [of] *preposition.* **1.** belonging to or having to do with: *a friend of mine; the principal of the school; a lot of money; ten minutes of five.* **2.** made with or containing: *a piece of paper; a fence of iron; a book of poems.* **3.** that is; that is called: *the city of New York.*

off [of *or* awf] *preposition.* not on or connected to; away or down from: *The plate fell off the table.*
adverb. **1.** not on; away or down from: *The dog ran off down the road.* **2.** not happening or working: *Turn off the television.* **3.** away from a job or a duty: *She had to go to the dentist, so she took the day off.*
adjective. **1.** not happening or working: *The engine is off.* **2.** being away from a job or duty: *He is off from work today.* **3.** being away from the truth; incorrect: *They were way off in their estimate of how long the work would take.*

of·fend [uh-fend] *verb,* **offended, offending.** to make upset or angry: *She was offended when they didn't invite her to the party.*

of·fend·er [uh-fen-dur] *noun, plural* **offenders.** a person who does something wrong, especially someone who commits a crime.

off·ense [uh-fens *or* aw-fens] *noun, plural* **offenses.**
1. the act of breaking the law; a crime: *Stealing is an offense.* **2.** something that makes people feel upset or insulted: *The rude joke gave offense to everyone at the dinner table.* **3.** the players on a sports team who attack and attempt to score: *In football, the offense can pass or run with the ball to try to score a touchdown.*

of·fen·sive [uh-fen-siv *or* aw-fens-iv] *adjective.*
1. being rude or upsetting; insulting: *Picking on one person for the team losing the game was unfair and also offensive.* **2.** not pleasant; displeasing: *We complained about the offensive smell.* **3.** used for attack: *In war, bombers and tanks are offensive weapons.*
noun, plural **offensives.** an attacking attitude or position: *The soldiers went on the offensive and pushed far into enemy territory.*
—**offensively,** *adverb.*

of·fer [of-ur] *verb,* **offered, offering. 1.** to be willing to give something if the other person would like to have it: *He offered a slice of cake to each of his sisters.* **2.** to be willing to do something, usually without being asked; volunteer: *Ethan offered to weed the garden.* **3.** to make a show of; put up: *to offer resistance.*
noun, plural **offers. 1.** the act of giving something: *an offer of help.* **2.** something that is offered: *I'll sell the bike to whoever makes the highest offer.*

of·fer·ing ▲ [of-ur-ing] *noun, plural* **offerings.** anything that is offered, especially something that is produced to be sold: *the latest offerings from the world of fashion.* **2.** something that is offered to God.

of·fice [of-is] *noun, plural* **offices. 1.** a place where people work or do business, usually at desks: *a lawyer's office.* **2.** all of the people who work in such a place: *The office bought Daniel a farewell present.* **3.** a position of authority: *to be elected to office; the office of president.*

of·fi·cer [of-uh-sur] *noun, plural* **officers. 1.** a person who commands others in the army, navy, or air force. **2.** a member of the police department. **3.** a person who has a position of trust or authority: *The president of the club is its most important officer.*

of·fi·cial [uh-fish-ul] *noun, plural* **officials.** a person who has the authority to do a particular job: *a government official; a company official.*
adjective. **1.** having to do with a position of authority: *an official uniform; an official letter from the mayor.* **2.** having the authority to do a particular job: *an official photographer for the governor.* **3.** part of a formal event or ceremony: *the official opening of the bridge.*
—**officially,** *adverb.*

off-line [of-line] *adjective; adverb. Computers.* not connected to a computer network: *Use the off-line computers in the library to search their catalog.*

off·set [of-set] *verb,* **offset, offsetting.** to balance a bad thing with a good thing; make up for: *Mom took us to the movies to offset our disappointment at missing the circus.*

off·shoot ▶ [of-shoot] *noun,*
plural **offshoots. 1.** a new stem or
branch. **2.** anything that grows from
something else: *The sports magazine*
was an offshoot of a television network
showing sports programs.

off·shore [of-shore] *adjective.*
1. in the sea and some distance from
the coast: *an offshore reef.* **2.** *Business.*
of a company or investment, being
based in a foreign country, usually
to avoid tax in the country where the
business is owned or the investor lives.
adverb. away from the shore:
The current carried them offshore.

These **offshoots** *have*
grown after a plant
stem was joined, or
grafted to young twigs.

off·side [of-side] *adjective.* being in a position in a game
such as football, hockey, or soccer that is not allowed by
the rules of the game. In football, you are offside if you go
across the line of scrimmage before the play starts. This
word is also spelled **offsides.**

The word **offside** at first was used as "off the side." This
meant to be beyond or away from your own side of the
field; that is, the side where the rest of your team is.
The word was first used in soccer. In the early days of that
game, all the other players on the team had to be behind
the player with the ball, or else they were offside.

off·spring [of-spring] *noun.* the young of an animal,
person, or plant: *The mother duck led her offspring down*
to the pond for their first swim.

of·ten [of-un] *adverb.* many times; frequently: *I see her*
often, but she hardly ever talks to me.

o·gre [oh-gur] *noun, plural* **ogres. 1.** a large, cruel monster
in fairy tales and legends who eats people. **2.** a frightening
person: *My brother thinks our neighbor is an ogre because*
he shouts if we make too much noise.

oh a word used to express surprise, happiness, pain, fear,
or other feelings: *Oh! You frightened me!*
🔊 A different word with the same sound is **owe.**

ohm [ohm] *noun. Science.* a unit in measuring the amount
of resistance that something has to an electric current.

oil ▼ [oil] *noun, plural* **oils.**
1. a greasy substance obtained
from animals, plants, or
minerals. Oils will not mix with
water. Oils are usually liquid,
or will become liquid when
heated. Oils are used for
cooking, heating, and other
purposes: *olive oil; whale oil.*
2. a thick, black liquid that
is found beneath the Earth's
surface and that can be used as a fuel to provide energy to
drive cars, heat homes, fly planes, and so on; petroleum.
verb, **oiled, oiling.** to put oil on: *to oil a squeaky hinge.*

The electrical unit of
measure known as
the **ohm** is named
for a famous scientist
of the 1800s, Georg
Ohm of Germany. He
made important early
studies of electricity
and the way in which
electric current flows.

oil·field [oil-feeld] *noun, plural* **oilfields.** a place where
there are large underground deposits of oil that can be
removed for energy use.

oil spill *Environment.* the accidental release, usually from
a ship, of a large amount of oil into the sea or other large
body of water. Because oil floats on the surface of the
water, oil spills are very damaging to fish, birds, and other
animals that live in the sea and along the coasts.

oil well a deep hole that is dug or drilled into the earth to
get oil for energy use.

oil·y [oil-ee] *adjective,* **oilier, oiliest. 1.** of or like oil: *an oily*
liquid. **2.** containing oil or covered in oil: *oily fried food;*
an oily rag.

oint·ment [oint-munt] *noun, plural* **ointments.** a soft, thick
cream or paste that is rubbed on the skin. Ointments
usually contain medicine.

O·jib·wa [oh-jib-way *or* oh-jib-wah] *noun,*
plural **Ojibwa** *or* **Ojibwas.** a member of a
tribe of Native American people who live
in the area around Lake Superior and the
Northern Great Plains. The Ojibwa are
also known as the **Chippewa.**

An ocean **oil**
platform can provide
for several hundred
workers at a time
and can pump up
millions of barrels of
oil every day.

a
b
c
d
e
f
g
h
i
j
k
l
m
n
o
p
q
r
s
t
u
v
w
x
y
z

OK [oh-<u>kay</u>] *adjective; adverb; interjection.* all right: *He fell, but he's OK—he wasn't hurt; I did OK on the test; OK! I'll go!* This word is also spelled **O.K.** and **okay.**
noun, plural **OKs.** agreement or approval: *Mom gave her OK to our idea.*
verb, **OK'd, OK'ing.** to accept that something is all right; approve: *The coach OK'd my new running shoes.*

> It is still not known for sure where the expression OK comes from. The most likely explanation is that it is an abbreviation of "<u>O</u>ll <u>K</u>orrect," a humorous way of saying "All Correct." Other ideas are that it comes from an abbreviation for Old Kinderhook, a nickname for U.S. President Martin van Buren, or from a political club called the O.K. Club.

old [ohld] *adjective,* **older** *or* **elder, oldest** *or* **eldest.**
1. having lived or existed for a long time: *The Roman Forum is very old, but the Pyramids of Egypt are even older—they were built more than 4,000 years ago.*
2. of a certain age: *Jose is six years old.* **3.** not new or recent: *Our old car was white, but our new car is red; Dad met an old school friend at the game.* **4.** not current; former: *Our old neighbor now lives in Canada.*
noun. a time long ago: *They crossed the seas in a crude sailboat, like Viking warriors of old.*

old·en [<u>ohl</u>-din] *adjective. Literature.* relating to many years ago: *People traveled by wagon in the olden days.*

old-fash·ioned [ohld-<u>fash</u>-und] *adjective.* **1.** preferring old ways, ideas, or customs: *My grandfather always writes an old-fashioned thank-you letter instead of sending an e-mail.* **2.** no longer in fashion; out-of-date: *Jane wore an old-fashioned hat and long skirt as a costume for the play.*

Old Testament *Religion.* a collection of writings about events before the birth of Christ that make up the Jewish Bible and form the earlier part of the Christian Bible.

Old World *Geography.* the part of the world that includes Europe, Asia, and Africa: *Colonists from the Old World settled in the New World of North America.*
See NEW WORLD for more information.

o·le·o·mar·ga·rine see MARGARINE.

ol·ive ◀ [<u>ol</u>-iv] *noun, plural* **olives. 1.** the small, bitter-tasting fruit of a tree that grows in warm parts of the world. Olives have firm flesh and a single seed. They are eaten pickled or are crushed to make olive oil. **2.** a yellowish-green or brownish-green color. *adjective.* having a dull, yellowish-green or brownish-green color.

olive oil a yellow or green oil obtained by crushing olives that is used in cooking and for putting on salads.

O·lym·pics [oh-<u>lim</u>-piks] *plural noun.* **1.** an athletic contest held in ancient Greece every four years. **2.** a modern international sports event held every four years, each time in a different country. The Olympics are also called the **Olympic Games.** An **Olympian** is an athlete who competes in the Olympics.

> The modern athletic event known as the **Olympics** is based on a similar athletic competition that was held in ancient Greece about 2,500 years ago. These earlier Olympic Games were held at a place called *Olympia,* which was thought of as being sacred to Greek gods such as Zeus. The highest mountain in Greece, Mount *Olympus,* was thought of as the home of the gods.

om·e·let [<u>om</u>-lit] *noun, plural* **omelets.** a food made of eggs that are beaten and then fried in a pan. Omelets are usually folded in half, with filling between the two halves. This word is also spelled **omelette.**

o·men [<u>oh</u>-mun] *noun, plural* **omens.** a sign of good or bad luck to come: *Some people believe a ladybug landing on your hand is an omen of good luck.*

om·i·nous [<u>om</u>-uh-nus] *adjective.* giving warning of something bad that is going to happen: *ominous black clouds; An ominous silence came just before the explosion.* —**ominously,** *adverb.*

o·mis·sion [oh-<u>mish</u>-un] *noun, plural* **omissions.** a person or thing that has not been included, either on purpose or by mistake; something left out: *We were surprised by his omission from the starting lineup.*

o·mit [oh-<u>mit</u>] *verb,* **omitted, omitting.** to leave out or not include, either on purpose or by mistake: *He omitted to write his address on the form, so they can't contact him.*

om·ni·vore [<u>om</u>-nuh-vore] *noun, plural* **omnivores.** *Biology.* an animal that eats all kinds of food, including plants and animal flesh. Such an animal is **omnivorous.**

on [on] *preposition.* **1.** above something and held up by it: *Put the book on the desk.* **2.** in a place at or near: *a picture on a wall; a house on a lake.*
✚ **On** is used in many other ways to show that one thing has to do with another: *to be on time; to go to work on Saturday; to ride on an airplane; to talk on the phone; to take the road on the right, to buy a coat on sale; to read a book on whales.*
adverb. **1.** so as to touch or cover: *to put on a sweater.* **2.** so as to be active or in use: *to turn on a radio.* **3.** so as to go forward: *to drive on to the next town.*
adjective. active or in use; not off: *It stopped raining, so the game is on.*

once [wuns] *adverb.* **1.** one time and no more: *We get mail delivered to our house once a day.* **2.** at a time in the past; before: *Frogs were tadpoles once; Our old dog could once run faster than he can now.*
conjunction. from the moment that; as soon as: *The house will feel warmer once we turn on the furnace.*

on·col·o·gy [on-<u>kol</u>-uh-jee] *noun, plural* **oncologies.** *Medicine.* the study and treatment of cancer. An **oncologist** is a special type of doctor who treats people with cancer.

Olives grow on small trees that can produce fruit for hundreds of years.

one [wun] *noun, plural* **ones. 1.** the first and lowest number; **2.** a single person or thing: *The class left the room one at a time.*
adjective. **1.** having to do with a single person or thing: *Take one pill after each meal.* **2.** having to do with a particular person or thing: *She's the one person who always laughs at my jokes.* **3.** some: *We'll go there one day.*
pronoun. **1.** a particular person or thing: *This one is my favorite.* **2.** any person: *One never knows what the future will bring.*
🔊 A different word with the same sound is **won.**

one·self [*wun*-self] *pronoun.* a person's own self: *to cook for oneself; to see oneself in a mirror.*

one-sid·ed [*wun*-sye-did] *adjective.* **1.** showing or for only one side; biased; unfair: *The reporter didn't speak to everyone involved in the argument, so her story ended up being one-sided.* **2.** with one side much stronger than the other: *Without our star pitcher, the game was one-sided and the other team won easily.*

one-way [*wun*-way] *adjective.* allowing movement in one direction only: *a one-way street.*

on·go·ing [*on*-goh-ing] *adjective.* happening for a long time and continuing to happen: *Jake has an ongoing interest in dinosaurs.*

on·ion [*un*-yun] *noun, plural* **onions.** a small, round vegetable with white, brown, or purple skin that grows underground. Onions have a strong smell and sharp taste.

The word **onion** goes back to an old word used by the Romans for this vegetable. It was taken from a word meaning "pearl," the object that can be found in an oyster and that is used in jewelry because of its beautiful shape and color. A round white onion can be thought of as looking something like a pearl.

on·line [*on*-line] *adjective; adverb. Computers.* connected to a computer network: *an online newspaper; You can only send e-mails when you are online.* This word is also spelled **on-line.**

on·look·er ▼ [*on*-luk-ur] *noun, plural* **onlookers.** someone who watches something happen without taking part in it: *The two boys who were fighting were surrounded by a group of onlookers.*

In the Southern Hemisphere, groups of **onlookers** *gather to watch whales and their calves in winter and spring.*

on·ly [*ohn*-lee] *adjective.* **1.** being the single one: *All the others went home so I'm the only person here.* **2.** best of all: *She is the only one for that role.*
adverb. **1.** no more than: *Only two days to go.* **2.** no one else or nothing other than: *Only Lisa spoke.* **3.** no time or place except: *It only snows in winter.*
conjunction. except that; but: *I would love to have a dog, only we don't have a yard.*

on·set [*on*-set] *noun, plural* **onsets. 1.** the beginning or start: *Green plant shoots mark the onset of spring.* **2.** the beginning of something unpleasant: *the onset of war; the onset of a fever.*

on·to [*on*-too] *preposition.* to a place or position on: *Move the plates onto the lower shelf.*

ooze [ooz] *verb,* **oozed, oozing.** to flow out very slowly: *Ketchup oozed out of the bun when I took a bite of my hamburger.*

o·pal ◀ [*oh*-pul] *noun, plural* **opals.** a whitish gem with streaks of different colors.

Nearly all **opals** *come from desert areas in Australia.*

o·pen [*oh*-pun] *adjective.* **1.** not closed or shut; allowing something to pass through: *The door was open and the dog ran out.* **2.** not covered, fastened, enclosed, and so on: *an open can of soda; a picnic out in the open air.* **3.** in operation; active: *a store that is open for business.* **4.** not restricted, limited, controlled, and so on: *a meeting that is open to the public; a person who is honest and open in giving her opinions.*
verb, **opened, opening. 1.** to cause to be not closed or shut; make open: *to open a window; to open an envelope.* **2.** to be or become open: *A wind came up and the door blew open; The store opens at nine.* **3.** to begin; start: *The movie opens with a view of San Francisco; She opened her speech by telling a joke.*
noun. **1. the open.** a place that is not closed in or shut up: *He likes to spend time out in the open viewing the beauties of nature.* **2.** a contest or event that is not limited as to who can compete: *The U.S. Open is a major golf tournament held every year.*

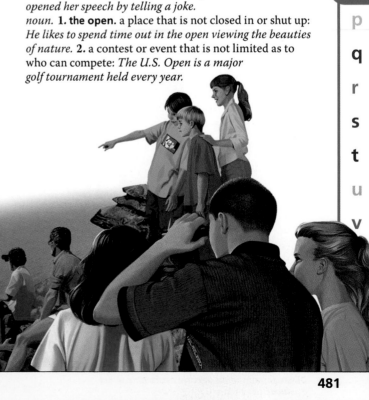

*An **opossum** spends a lot of time climbing in trees and can hang by its tail from branches.*

o·pen·er [oh-puh-nur] *noun, plural* **openers. 1.** a hand tool that is used to open a closed container: *a bottle opener.* **2.** the first thing or part of a series: *This match is the opener of the soccer season.*

o·pen·ing [oh-puh-ning] *noun, plural* **openings. 1.** a hole or empty space; a gap: *The sun shone through an opening in the clouds.* **2.** the first part or stage of something: *At the opening of the movie the star is alone on an island.* **3.** a job position that is not filled: *The company has an opening for an experienced accountant.* **4.** the act of becoming or making open: *the opening of a new wing of a hospital.*

When you write, it is important to have a good **opening** that will get the attention of your audience. If you were writing a paper about the theme park Sea World, you could begin by simply saying "Last summer my family went to visit Sea World." But for a better opening, you might open with something like, "Ever have a ten-foot shark swim right over your head? It happened to me last summer at Sea World."

open·ly [oh-pun-lee] *adverb.* in an open way; without trying to hide any facts or feelings: *She openly admitted her silly mistake.*

o·pen-mind·ed [oh-pun-mind-id] *adjective.* willing to listen to and consider other people's ideas and opinions: *My parents try to be open-minded about the clothes I wear and the music I like.* **—open-mindedness,** *noun.*

op·er·a ▼ [op-ruh *or* op-ur-uh] *noun, plural* **operas.** *Music.* a drama that is sung to music. Operas often have a large number of performers and fancy, colorful costumes. Anything that has to do with opera or the way operas are performed is **operatic.**

> The word **opera** comes from a Latin word meaning "work" and thus it is related to words such as *operate* and *operation.* An opera is a very large stage production that involves the work of many people.

op·er·ate [op-uh-rate] *verb,* **operated, operating. 1.** to be in action or work: *The subway line operates from 5.00 A.M. to midnight.* **2.** to put into action or control the workings of: *to operate the CD player.* **3.** to cut open the body of a sick or hurt person or animal in order to repair or remove a damaged part of it: *The doctors operated on Grandma's right hip.*

operating system *Computers.* an essential program that allows all other programs to work on a computer. A shorter form of this term is **OS.**

op·er·a·tion [op-uh-ray-shun] *noun, plural* **operations. 1.** the activity of making something work or go: *The operation of the farm involved the whole family.* **2.** the fact of being active or being in working order: *The elevator isn't in operation at present.* **3.** a medical treatment for a sick or hurt person or animal in which the doctor cuts into the patient: *The dog needed an operation to fix its leg.*

op·er·a·tor [op-uh-ray-tur] *noun, plural* **operators.** someone who works a machine or other device: *a computer operator.*

op·er·et·ta [op-uh-ret-uh] *noun, plural* **operettas.** *Music.* a short opera that is amusing and light-hearted, and in which many of the words are spoken. An operetta usually includes dancing.

o·pin·ion [uh-pin-yun] *noun, plural* **opinions. 1.** a view held by someone based on personal belief, not known facts: *My dad's opinion is that this TV show is boring, but I like it.* **2.** a formal statement of advice made by an expert or professional: *After he was diagnosed with kidney disease the patient was advised to seek a second doctor's opinion.* When a person holds opinions strongly and without any evidence they are described as **opinionated.**

It is important to know the difference between *fact* and **opinion** in a paper. "The New York Yankees have won the most championships in baseball" is a fact and "The New York Yankees are the best team in baseball" is an opinion. When you write, you can include both fact and opinion, but you should support your opinions with facts: "I think the New York Yankees are the best team in baseball because they have won the most championships."

o·pos·sum ▲ [uh-pos-um] *noun, plural* **opossums.** any member of a group of furry American animals that live in trees. Opossums carry their young in the mother's pouch as kangaroos do. They are active mainly at night.

op·po·nent [uh-poh-nunt] *noun, plural* **opponents.** a person or group that takes the opposite side in a fight, sporting event, or debate: *In the first game, the Lions' opponents will be the Blue Wave.*

*Performers in an **opera** must be able to act as well as sing.*

op·por·tun·ity [op-ur-<u>too</u>-nuh-tee] *noun*, *plural* **opportunities.** a good or favorable time for something; a chance: *The warm weather gave us the opportunity for a swim.*

op·pose [uh-<u>poze</u>] *verb*, **opposed, opposing. 1.** to resist or be against: *The residents opposed the building of a chemicals factory near the town.* **2.** to be in contrast; be the opposite: *Love is opposed to hate.*

op·pos·ite [<u>op</u>-uh-zit] *adjective.* **1.** having to do with something that is directly facing: *Marion sat opposite me at dinner.* **2.** moving the other way: *We waited for the tide to turn in the opposite direction.* **3.** as different as possible: *Good is the opposite of bad.*
noun, *plural* **opposites.** a thing or a person that is opposite: *The North Pole and South Pole are opposites.*

op·po·si·tion [op-uh-<u>zish</u>-un] *noun*, *plural* **oppositions. 1.** the fact of not agreeing with something: *There was much opposition to the increase in the price of hamburgers.* **2.** a political party that is the official opponent of a party in power in a democracy.

opt [opt] *verb*, **opted, opting.** to make a choice; decide: *I opted not to go to Jane's party.*
• **opt out.** to decide not to do something: *If you opt out of the team, we'll need to find a new player.*

op·ti·cal [<u>op</u>-tuh-kul] *adjective.* having to do with the eyes or the sense of sight: *A microscope is an optical instrument.*

optical illusion ▶ something a person believes they can see even though it is not really there: *There appeared to be a lake in the desert, but it was an optical illusion caused by the heat.*

op·ti·cian [op-<u>tish</u>-un] *noun*, *plural* **opticians.** a person whose job is to make and sell eyeglasses and contact lenses.

op·tics [<u>op</u>-tiks] *plural noun, Science.* the study of light and vision.

op·ti·mis·tic [op-tuh-<u>mis</u>-tik] *adjective.* tending to think that things will turn out well: *Despite the dark clouds, we were all optimistic that the weather would improve for the carnival.* —**optimism**, *noun.*

op·tion [<u>op</u>-shun] *noun*, *plural* **options.** the right or ability to choose: *The best option for James was to do as the teacher suggested.*

op·tion·al [<u>op</u>-shuh-nul] *adjective.* having the ability to choose an option: *In some high schools studying a foreign language is optional, but in others students have to do it.*

op·tom·e·trist [op-<u>tom</u>-i-trist] *noun*, *plural* **optometrists.** *Medicine.* a person whose job is to examine people's eyes and sight and to prescribe eyeglasses or contact lenses. The work of such a person is **optometry.**

or [or] *conjunction.* a word that is used to show a choice between things: *Do you want soup or a salad for lunch? The sweater comes in sizes small, medium, or large; The sport is called soccer, or football in Great Britain; Better leave now or you may miss the train.*

OPTICAL ILLUSIONS

Optical illusions occur when something appears to be different from what is really is. These illusions happen when the brain finds incoming visual signals confusing and tries to interpret them in ways that fit with the kinds of patterns it "expects."

Even though you think the red circle on the left is bigger, both red circles are exactly the same size.

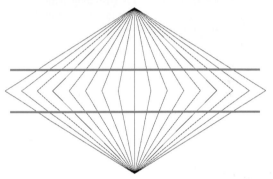

The horizontal green bars in this diagram are actually straight and parallel, but appear to be curving inward.

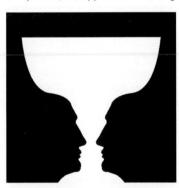

Can you see a goblet or two faces in profile? The brain cannot present both images at once.

o·ral [<u>or</u>-ul] *adjective.* **1.** having to do with spoken, not written words: *All students take a French oral exam in which they have to say certain French words correctly.* **2.** having to do with the mouth: *Oral hygiene is very important.* —**orally**, *adverb.*

or·ange [<u>or</u>-inj] *noun*, *plural* **oranges. 1.** a round citrus fruit with a thick, reddish-gold skin, flesh divided into segments, and with sweet juice. Oranges grow on evergreen trees in hot parts of the world. **2.** a reddish-gold color. *adjective.* having the reddish-gold color of oranges.

o·rang·u·tan ▲ [uh-<u>rang</u>-uh-*tan*] *noun,* *plural* **orangutans.** a large ape with long arms, thick, red-brown hair, and no tail. Orangutans live in the forests of southeast Asia.

or·a·tor [or-uh-tur] *noun, plural* **orators.** *Literature.* a person who speaks in public places and to a large group of people, especially in a skillful or powerful way. A person who speaks in this way is showing the skill of **oratory.** A formal public speech is an **oration.**

Oratory is the art of public speaking and it is considered a form of literature. Famous orators are often people who hold an important position, as in government, and who can move or inspire people with their words. Probably the two most famous orations in American history are Abraham Lincoln's Gettysburg Address (1863) and Martin Luther King's "I Have a Dream" speech (1963).

or·bit ▼ [<u>or</u>-bit] *noun, plural* **orbits.** *Science.* **1.** the roughly circular path that a planet, moon, or other heavenly body follows around another heavenly body: *The Moon makes an orbit of the Earth about every 27 days.* **2.** one entire trip of a spacecraft along such a path: *The space station is in orbit around the Earth.*
verb, **orbited, orbiting.** to move in a roughly circular path around a heavenly body: *Two moons orbit the planet Mars.*

or·chard [or-churd] *noun, plural* **orchards.** an area of land planted with fruit trees.

or·ches·tra [or-kuh-struh] *noun, plural* **orchestras.** *Music.* **1.** a group of musicians who play together on different kinds of instruments. Something having to do with orchestras, or intended for an orchestra, is **orchestral:** *orchestral music.* **2.** the instruments, such as violins, flutes, and cymbals, played by such a group. **3.** the part of a theater where the orchestra plays, usually just in front of the stage. **4.** the main floor of a theater.

or·chid [<u>or</u>-kid] *noun, plural* **orchids.** a tropical plant that bears colorful flowers of various shapes.

or·deal [or-<u>deel</u>] *noun, plural* **ordeals.** a painful or difficult experience or test: *My last visit to the dentist was a real ordeal.*

or·der [<u>or</u>-dur] *noun, plural* **orders.** **1.** an instruction to do something: *I obeyed the coach's orders not to swing at the first pitch.* **2.** the way in which items are arranged or organized; sequence: *The books in the library are arranged in alphabetical order.* **3.** a state in which laws or rules are observed: *It's the job of the police force to maintain law and order.* **4.** a state in which everything is in its correct place: *Jane set to work to bring order to the untidy house.* **5.** a request to supply goods, or the goods that have been supplied or requested: *The store took a long time to deliver our order.* **6.** a group of people who belong to the same organization or live according to the same rules: *a monk of the Franciscan order.* **7.** *Biology.* a related group of plants, animals, or other living things. An order is made up of several families: *Cats and dogs belong to the same order.*
verb, **ordered, ordering. 1.** to command someone to do something: *She ordered the dog to sit.* **2.** to request something: *We ordered French fries and a salad to go with the steaks.* **3.** to arrange things neatly: *The computer files are ordered by date.*
• **in order to.** for the purpose of; so that: *My father cut down the old tree, in order to allow more sunlight to reach the garden.*
• **out of order.** not working properly or at all: *The escalators in the shopping mall were out of order, so we used the stairs.*

or·der·ly [or-dur-lee] *adjective.* **1.** arranged in a neat or proper way; having order: *He placed the clothes in two orderly piles.* **2.** well behaved; peaceful: *an orderly class of students.*

or·di·nal number [ord-un-ul] *Mathematics.* a number that shows the place of something in a series of items. First, second, and third are ordinal numbers.

Orangutans can reach fruit in high places with little effort.

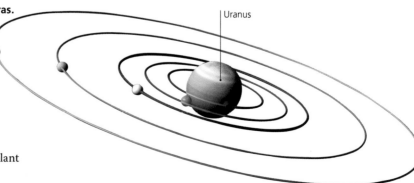

Uranus

Five main satellites, or moons, **orbit** *the planet Uranus.*

These four rock samples contain the following **ores:**
(from left to right) bauxite, galena, uranium, and iron.

Aluminum   Lead   Autunite   Hematite

or·gan·ize [or-guh-*nize*]
verb, **organized, organizing.**
1. to put together in a neat
way; arrange something:
*It took all day for Katie to
organize her collection of
DVDs and CDs.* **2.** to form
workers into a labor union
or other organization.

or·di·nar·i·ly [or-duh-<u>nare</u>-i-lee] *adverb.* most of the time; usually: *Ordinarily, I'm home from school by four o'clock.*

or·di·nar·y [<u>ord</u>-uh-*ner*-ee] *adjective.* **1.** describing something usual; regular: *The ordinary car uses gasoline, but some run on special fuels such as ethanol.* **2.** of no special ability, interest, or quality; average: *This book was supposed to be really good, but I thought it was quite ordinary.*

ore ▲ [or] *noun, plural* **ores.** a mineral or rock that is dug out of the ground and processed to obtain a valuable metal that it contains.

🔊 Different words with the same sound are **oar** and **or.**

or·gan ▶ [or-gun] *noun, plural* **organs.**
1. *Music.* an instrument that consists of a keyboard attached to a bellows that blows air through a number of pipes of different lengths to produce sound. **2.** *Biology.* a part of a plant or animal that performs a particular job and is made up of different kinds of tissues: *The stomach and intestines are organs of the digestive system.*

or·gan·ic [or-<u>gan</u>-ik] *adjective.* **1.** relating to or coming from living things: *Earthworms help to break down organic matter, such as fallen leaves.* **2.** using or raised by farming or gardening methods that avoid the use of manufactured chemicals: *organic fruit.*
—organically, *adverb.*

organic food *Environment.* food produced without the use of manufactured chemicals. Raising crops or animals on a farm in this way is called **organic farming.**

or·gan·ism [or-guh-<u>niz</u>-um] *noun, plural* **organisms.** *Biology.* a living thing. Organisms include humans and other animals, plants, and bacteria.

or·gan·ist [<u>or</u>-guh-nist] *noun, plural* **organists.** *Music.* a person who plays the organ.

or·gan·i·za·tion [or-guh-nuh-<u>zay</u>-shun] *noun, plural* **organizations. 1.** the act of organizing: *The organization of the state basketball tournament took a lot of work.* **2.** the state or method of being organized: *I like the artist's organization of shapes and colors in this painting.* **3.** a body of people who work together for a particular purpose: *My mother does a lot of work for charitable organizations such as the Red Cross.*

The air going into the pipes of an **organ** *is controlled by a keyboard and pedals.*

o·ri·ent [or-ee-ent] *verb,* **oriented, orienting. 1.** to adjust or adapt to new surroundings or a new situation: *It took Jim a while to orient himself at the new school.* **2.** to position a person or thing in a particular direction: *The front part of the house is oriented in a northerly direction.* **3.** to aim or adjust something to particular circumstances: *The pottery course is oriented toward beginners.*

Orient [or-ee-ent] *noun. Geography.* the countries of Asia, especially eastern Asia: *China is in the Orient.*

O·ri·en·tal [or-ee-<u>ent</u>-ul] *adjective.* relating to or belonging to the Orient.
noun, plural **Orientals.** a person from the Orient.

o·ri·en·ta·tion [or-ee-en-<u>tay</u>-shun] *noun.* instruction or preparation for a new situation, such as a course of study: *You should attend the orientation meeting to find out all the information you need for starting college.*

or·i·gin [<u>or</u>-uh-jin] *noun, plural* **origins. 1.** the beginning or cause of something: *The origin of the word "pizza" is the Italian word for "pie."* **2.** a person's ancestors; parents: *My family is of Polish origin.*

o·rig·i·nal [uh-<u>rij</u>-uh-nul] *adjective.* **1.** newly thought of, invented, or carried out: *The architect won an award for the most original design.* **2.** able to do, think of, invent, or carry out something new: *The teacher said that Karin is an original thinker in class discussions.* **3.** earliest or first: *The original church building still stands next to the modern one.*
noun, plural **originals.** the earliest or first form of something: *This copy of the painting is about half the size of the original.*

o·rig·i·nal·i·ty [uh-<u>rij</u>-uh-<u>nal</u>-uh-tee] *noun.* **1.** the quality of being unusual or new: *The originality of that movie was the best thing about it.* **2.** the ability to make, do, or think up something unusual or new: *Charles Dickens was a writer of great originality.*

o·rig·i·nal·ly [uh-<u>rij</u>-uh-nuh-lee] *adverb.* at first or from the beginning: *The potato was originally grown in South America.*

o·rig·i·nate [uh-<u>rij</u>-uh-*nate*] *verb,* **originated, originating. 1.** to give rise to; invent: *The artist Picasso originated a new style of painting.* **2.** to come into being; begin: *Where did the kayak originate?* The act of bringing something into being is **origination.**

The yellow oriole lives in lush vegetation in New Guinea and northern Australia.

o·ri·ole ◀ [*or-ee-ohl*] *noun, plural* **orioles.** any of various colorful songbirds that are found in most parts of the world.

or·na·ment [*or-nuh-munt*] *noun, plural* **ornaments.** an object that is used to decorate something: *Fountains, ponds, and statues are among the ornaments in their garden.* *verb,* **ornamented, ornamenting.** to add ornaments to. Relating to or serving as an ornament is described as **ornamental.**

or·phan [*or-fun*] *noun, plural* **orphans.** a child whose parents are dead. *verb,* **orphaned, orphaning.** to make someone an orphan: *The plane crash orphaned five children.*

or·phan·age [*or-fuh-nij*] *noun, plural* **orphanages.** a place where orphans live.

or·tho·don·tist [*or-thuh-don-tist*] *noun, plural* **orthodontists.** *Health.* a dentist who specializes in correcting the position of the teeth.

or·tho·dox [*or-thuh-doks*] *adjective.* **1.** widely accepted; traditional: *The orthodox way to wear a wedding ring is on the third finger of the left hand.* **2.** following or holding widely accepted or traditional practices or beliefs: *The doctor is very orthodox in his approach to medicine.* The state of being orthodox is **orthodoxy.**

Or·tho·dox [*or-thuh-doks*] *adjective. Religion.* **1.** relating to the Orthodox Church. A different term with the same meaning is **Eastern Orthodox.** **2.** relating to Orthodox Judaism.

os·mo·sis [*oz-moh-sis or os-moh-sis*] *noun. Biology.* the movement of fluid from a solution of low concentration through a membrane into a more concentrated solution until there is an equal concentration on both sides of the membrane. Having to do with osmosis is **osmotic.**

os·trich [*os-trich*] *noun, plural* **ostriches.** a large African bird that cannot fly. It has a small head, a long neck, and fluffy feathers. Its powerful legs allow it to run very quickly. The ostrich is the largest of all living birds.

oth·er [*uhTH-ur*] *adjective.* **1.** different from the one or ones already mentioned: *He turned around and walked the other way; This is the exit—you go in the other door.* **2.** additional, more, or further: *My family owns one other car besides this one.* **3.** of the recent past: *I mailed the card the other day, so it should be there by now.* *pronoun, plural* **others.** **1.** the remaining one or ones of a group: *One cow became separated from the others in the herd.* **2.** an additional or different person or thing: *We'll get someone or other to take Jeff's place on our team.* *adverb.* in another way; otherwise: *How could I feel anything other than angry?*

oth·er·wise [*uhTH-ur-wize*] *adverb.* **1.** in other respects: *The car has a few scratches, but otherwise it's in good condition.* **2.** in different circumstances: *I broke my arm, otherwise I'd be playing baseball today.* **3.** in another way; differently: *You think he's a nice guy—I think otherwise.* *adjective.* being different; other: *The soldier was ordered to fire on the enemy and could not do otherwise.* *conjunction.* or else; because if not: *Write down this phone number, otherwise you'll forget it.*

ot·ter ▼ [*ot-ur*] *noun, plural* **otters** or **otter.** a water animal with thick brown fur, webbed feet, and a long, slightly flattened tail. Otters are good swimmers and eat fish.

ouch [*ouch*] *interjection.* a word expressing sudden pain: *Ouch! The cat scratched me!*

ought [*awt*] *verb.* a special verb that is often used with other verbs to show these meanings: **1.** to indicate a duty or obligation: *I ought to do my homework now.* **2.** to indicate something that is probable: *Harry left an hour ago, so he ought to be home by now.* **3.** to offer advice: *You ought to wear a helmet when you ride your bike.*

ounce [*ouns*] *noun, plural* **ounces.** **1.** a unit of weight of $\frac{1}{16}$ of a pound. There are sixteen ounces in one pound. **2.** a unit of measure for liquids. There are thirty-two ounces in one quart. **3.** a very small amount: *Doing something so silly shows he doesn't have an ounce of common sense.*

our [*our*] *adjective.* of, belonging to, or associated with us: *The President is the head of our country.* ◀)) A different word with the same sound is **hour.**

ours [*ourz or arz*] *pronoun.* the one or ones belonging to or associating with us: *Ours is a big house; Amy's a friend of ours.*

our·selves [*our-selvz*] *pronoun.* our own selves: *We promised ourselves a long vacation this year.*

The webbed feet of a river otter allow it to swim and dig, as well as walk on land.

out [*out*] *adverb.* **1.** in a direction away from the inside or center: *Water rushed out when I turned on the faucet.* **2.** away from one's home or place of work: *I'm just going out for a few minutes.* **3.** at or to an end; so as to be finished: *Let's drive until the gas runs out.* **4.** into the open or to public attention: *When is that film due to come out?* *adjective.* **1.** not in use, operating, or in proper condition: *The power is out because the storm brought down power lines.* **2.** in baseball, not successful in reaching a base. **3.** being outside or away: *He didn't answer the door, so he must be out.* *preposition.* through to the outside: *I walked out the door.*

out- a prefix that means: **1.** away; going out: *outgoing* means going out. **2.** in a way that surpasses or exceeds: *outrun* means to run faster or longer than. **3.** away from; outside: an *outcast* is someone living apart from a group.

out·board motor a motor that is mounted outside the stern of a small boat.

out·break [out-*brake*] *noun, plural* **outbreaks.** a violent or sudden occurrence of something: *an outbreak of war.*

out·burst [out-*burst*] *noun, plural* **outbursts.** a sudden, violent display or release of something: *an outburst of tears.*

out·come [out-*kum*] *noun, plural* **outcomes.** a result of something; an end: *I have to wait a week to know the outcome of my job interview.*

out·dat·ed [out-<u>day</u>-tid] *adjective.* no longer in fashion or use; obsolete: *Blaack and white TV sets became outdated after color TV was introduced.*

out·do [out-<u>doo</u>] *verb,* **outdid, outdone, outdoing.** to do better than: *My friend and I try to outdo each other in spelling bees.*

out·door [out-<u>dore</u>] *adjective.* done, situated, or used in the open air, rather than inside a building: *an outdoor swimming pool.*

out·doors [out-<u>dorz</u>] *adverb.* in the open air; outside: *We set up the table outdoors. noun.* the open air; the world outside buildings: *Lauren had a great love of the outdoors.*

out·er [<u>ou</u>-tur] *adjective.* on the outside; external: *A snail has a shell for an outer covering.*

outer space ▼ the space outside Earth's atmosphere: *The Moon is in outer space.*

out·field [out-<u>feeld</u>] *noun, plural* **outfields.** in baseball, the area beyond the infield and between the foul lines. A player whose position is in the outfield is an **outfielder.**

out·fit [out-*fit*] *noun, plural* **outfits. 1.** a complete set of tools or equipment needed for doing something: *a carpenter's outfit.* **2.** a set of clothes: *She bought herself a new outfit to wear to the wedding.* **3.** a group of people who do a particular activity together: *The outfit John wanted to join was the Marine Corps. verb,* **outfitted, outfitting.** to provide with tools or equipment needed for doing something: *The new fire engines have been outfitted with the most modern equipment.*

out·grow [out-<u>groh</u>] *verb,* **outgrew, outgrown, outgrowing. 1.** to grow too large for: *Young children quickly outgrow their clothes.* **2.** to give up or lose as one matures: *She outgrew her dislike of broccoli.* **3.** to grow bigger or faster than: *In our garden, the lettuce is outgrowing the spinach.*

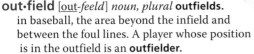

Charles Arthur ("Pretty Boy") Floyd was a gangster who became an **outlaw** *in the 1920s.*

out·ing [out-*ing*] *noun, plural* **outings.** a short trip taken for pleasure or education: *Our class went on an outing to the museum.*

out·law ▲ [out-*law*] *noun, plural* **outlaws.** someone who breaks the law again and again; a criminal. *verb,* **outlawed, outlawing.** to make something illegal; prohibit: *Smoking in restaurants has been outlawed.*

out·let [out-*let*] *noun, plural* **outlets. 1.** an opening through which something comes out: *We called a plumber when the sewer outlet became blocked.* **2.** a means of expressing one's emotions, talents, desires, or energy: *Painting is a good outlet for a person's creative desires.* **3.** a device connected to a power supply into which electrical appliances are plugged.

From **outer space,** *the spiral formation of swirling storm clouds can be clearly seen.*

a
b
c
d
e
f
g
h
i
j
k
l
m
n
o
p
q
r
s
t
u
v
w
x
y
z

*This Sri Lankan canoe has two **outriggers**.*

out·line [out-line] *noun, plural* **outlines. 1.** the shape of an object or figure, without any detail: *I could see the outline of the mountains against the setting sun.* **2.** the main points of a speech, story, or other writing: *Do an outline before writing your final report.*
verb, **outlined, outlining. 1.** to give the main points of: *The principal outlined his plans for the new school library.* **2.** to draw the outline of: *Use a pencil to outline the cookie cutter on paper.*

A good way to plan a piece of writing is to prepare an **outline** of what you want to write. An outline is a list of the things that your paper will cover, in the order that they will be presented. For example, if you were writing a report on polar bears, your outline might be organized as follows: 1) where the polar bear lives; 2) its size and appearance; 3) what it eats and how it behaves; 4) birth and care of young; 5) how its future existence may be threatened. An outline could change as you actually write. For example, in the outline above you might decide that #4 does not have enough information for its own part and should be combined with #3.

out·look [out-luk] *noun, plural* **outlooks. 1.** a view into the future; what seems likely to happen: *The President spoke about the outlook for the economy in the coming year.* **2.** a way of thinking about or looking at something: *Cleaning up the litter in the streets created a positive outlook among people.*

out·ly·ing [out-lye-ing] *adjective.* located far from the central part of a place: *an outlying suburb of the main city.*

out·num·ber [out-num-bur] *verb,* **outnumbered, outnumbering.** to be greater in number than: *In my class, girls outnumber boys by sixteen to eleven.*

out-of-date ◀ *adjective.* out of style or use; old-fashioned: *My uncle has some out-of-date ideas about what jobs women should do.*

out·pa·tient [out-pay-shunt] *noun, plural* **outpatients.** *Medicine.* a person who goes to a hospital for treatment without staying there overnight.

out·put [out-put] *noun.* **1.** the amount of something produced: *The auto factory increased its output of cars this year.* **2.** *Computers.* information produced by a computer and shown on its screen, printed on paper, or sent to another device.

out·rage [out-raje] *noun, plural* **outrages.**
1. a very violent or cruel act: *Some Roman emperors committed outrages against the people.*
2. a great anger: *I feel outrage when I hear about cruelty to animals.*
verb, **outraged, outraging.** to cause anger in: *People were outraged by the bombing attack.*

out·ra·geous [out-ray-jus] *adjective.* describing something shocking: *It was an outrageous act to tear down that beautiful historic building.*
—outrageously, *adverb;*
—outrageousness, *noun.*

out·rig·ger ▲ [out-rig-ur] *noun, plural* **outriggers.** a frame with a float attached that extends outward from the side of a canoe. It keeps the canoe from turning over.

out·right [out-rite] *adjective.* describing something total; complete: *The play was an outright disaster and almost the entire audience walked out before it was over.*
adverb. **1.** without hiding anything; openly: *She told me outright that I was not suitable for the job.*
2. completely and all at once: *The accused man denied the charges outright.*

out·run [out-run] *verb,* **outran, outrun, outrunning.** to run faster or farther than: *The cat outran the dog that was chasing it.*

out·set [out-set] *noun.* the start or beginning: *I knew from the outset that this school would be better than my old one.*

out·side [out-side] *noun, plural* **outsides.** the outer surface, part, or side: *There's a black mark on the outside of this banana, so I won't eat it.*
adjective. **1.** on the outside; external: *You need to fix the outside light.* **2.** very unlikely; slight: *Our team has only an outside chance of winning the final.*
adverb. on or toward the outside; outdoors: *It's raining heavily outside.*
preposition. beyond the boundaries or limits of: *That car is outside their price range.*

out·sid·er [out-side-ur] *noun, plural* **outsiders.** a person who does not belong to a particular group: *He keeps to himself and is regarded as an outsider.*

out·skirts [out-skurts] *plural noun.* the outer parts of a town or city: *He lives on the outskirts of Seattle.*

out·smart [out-smart] *verb,* **outsmarted, outsmarting.** to be more clever than; gain the advantage of: *The outlaw outsmarted the sheriff and got away.*

out·source [out-sorse] *verb,* **outsourced, outsourcing.** *Business.* of a company, to buy some products or services from another company: *Many companies outsource as a way of reducing costs.*

out·spo·ken [out-spoh-kun] *adjective.* being direct and open: *The senator is an outspoken opponent of the President.*

out·stand·ing [out-stand-ing] *adjective.* **1.** much better than others of its kind; extremely good: *an outstanding restaurant; Danny was famous as an outstanding guitar player.* **2.** not paid or decided: *There are many outstanding problems in nuclear physics.* **—outstandingly,** *adverb.*

Out-of-date walkmans have been replaced by CD and MP3 players.

Shutters *open outward to let sunlight into a building.*

out·ward ▶ [out-wurd] *adverb.* away from the inside or a particular point: *This door opens outward.*
adjective. **1.** on or toward the outside: *a fishing boat's outward journey.* **2.** able to be seen from the outside: *There is no outward sign that the sick man is getting better.* This word is also spelled **outwards.**
—outwardly, *adverb.*

out·weigh [out-way] *verb,* **outweighed, outweighing.** to be heavier, more valuable, or more important than: *He gave up cigarettes when he realized that the dangers of smoking outweighed the pleasures.*

out·wit [out-wit] *verb,* **outwitted, outwitting.** to be more clever than; gain the advantage of: *The two chess players tried to outwit each other.*

o·val [oh-vul] *adjective.* shaped like an egg or an ellipse: *an oval mirror.*
noun, plural **ovals.** a thing shaped like an egg or an ellipse.

o·va•ry [oh-vur-ee] *noun, plural* **ovaries.** *Biology.*
1. the part of a female animal in which eggs are produced. **2.** the part of a flowering plant in which seeds form. Of or relating to an ovary is **ovarian.**

ov·en ▶ [uv-un] *noun, plural* **ovens.** an enclosed space that is used to cook or heat food. Most kitchen stoves have an oven.

o·ver [oh-vur] *preposition.* **1.** above in place or position: *A traffic signal has the red light over the green.* **2.** on top of, so as to cover: *Elaine placed a blanket over the sleeping baby.* **3.** above and across from one end or side to the other: *The horse jumped over the fence.* **4.** during; throughout: *I'm planning to learn to ski over the winter vacation.* **5.** more than: *Over fifty people attended the meeting.* **6.** about; concerning: *The workers went on strike over the issue of low pay.*
adverb. **1.** on high; above: *They all looked up when the jet plane flew over.* **2.** above and across the edge or top: *The water in the bathtub ran over.* **3.** across a space or distance; from one end or side to another: *I leaned over and whispered in her ear.* **4.** another time; again: *I got the math problem wrong, so I had to do it over.*
adjective. at an end; finished: *School is over.*

over- a prefix that means: **1.** too much: *overdo* means to do too much. **2.** across; above; beyond: *overseas* means across the seas; *overtime* means time worked beyond regular working hours. **3.** from one point past another point: *overtake* means to catch up with or pass.

o·ver·alls [oh-vur-awlz] *plural noun.* loose trousers worn over clothes to keep them clean. Overalls usually have a part that covers the chest held up by straps over the shoulders.

Traditional **ovens** *for baking bread in Kazakhstan are made of mud.*

o·ver·board [oh-vur-bord] *adverb.* from a boat or ship into the water: *A big wave washed three people overboard from the ferry.*
• **to go overboard.** to be too enthusiastic; go too far: *Rosie went overboard with the Christmas decorations and covered every inch of the tree.*

o·ver·cast [oh-vur-kast] *adjective.* of weather, cloudy with no sun; dull: *The forecast is for overcast skies and a little rain.*

o·ver·charge [oh-vur-charj] *verb,* **overcharged, overcharging.** to charge too much money for something: *The store overcharged me by twenty dollars.*

o·ver·coat [oh-vur-kote] *noun, plural* **overcoats.** a long, thick outer coat worn over other clothing in cold weather.

o·ver·come [oh-vur-kum] *verb,* **overcame, overcome, overcoming. 1.** to get the better of; defeat or conquer: *"We can overcome all our problems," promised the mayor; Peter overcame his fear of flying.* **2.** to make weak or helpless; affect deeply: *After they walked all day, tiredness finally overcame the hikers.*

o·ver·crowd [oh-vur-krowd] *verb,* **overcrowded, overcrowding.** to put too many people or things into a space: *When you have mice as pets, it's important not to overcrowd the cage.* Containing too many people or things is **overcrowded:** *an overcrowded city.*

o·ver·do [oh-vur-doo] *verb,* **overdid, overdone, overdoing. 1.** to use or do too much; carry too far: *After she came out of hospital, my mother had to be careful not to overdo things.* **2.** to cook food for too long: *The fish was overdone and was too dry.*
🔊 A different word with the same sound is **overdue.**

o·ver·dose [oh-vur-dohs] *noun, plural* **overdoses.** too large an amount of a drug or medicine at one time: *an overdose of cough medicine.*
verb, **overdosed, overdosing.** to take or give an overdose of a drug or medicine.

o·ver·due [oh-vur-doo] *adjective.* **1.** not paid at the expected or required time: *an overdue electricity bill.* **2.** past the expected or required time; late: *The librarian said my books were a week overdue.*
🔊 A different word with the same sound is **overdo.**

o·ver·flow [oh-vur-floh] *verb,* **overflowed, overflowing. 1.** to flow beyond normal bounds; be so full that the contents flow over: *Many rivers overflow after the end of winter.* **2.** to spread or cover over; spill out: *The crowd filled the entire stands and overflowed onto the sides of the field.*
noun. something that flows over; an excess: *the overflow of a river.*

a
b
c
d
e
f
g
h
i
j
k
l
m
n
o
p
q
r
s
t
u
v
w
x
y
z

The ancient Chinese believed that colorful kites flying **overhead** carried their prayers to heaven.

o·ver·grow [oh-vur-<u>groh</u>] *verb,* **overgrew, overgrown, overgrowing.** to grow over or beyond: *The ivy had almost overgrown the house.*

o·ver·hand [<u>oh</u>-vur-*hand*] *adjective.* carried out with the hand brought forward and down from above the shoulder: *an overhand throw.*
adverb. in an overhand manner: *In volleyball, I still can't serve overhand very well.* This word is also spelled **overhanded.**

o·ver·head ▲ [oh-vur-<u>hed</u>] *adverb.* above one's head; far above: *The helicopter roared overhead.*
noun. Business. the general cost of running a company, store, or other business: *To increase profits, the business has to reduce its overhead.*
adjective. situated above one's head: *The flight attendant placed my bag in the overhead locker.*

o·ver·hear [oh-vur-<u>heer</u>] *verb,* **overheard, overhearing.** to hear what someone is saying without that person's knowledge: *I could overhear my little sister talking to our new puppy.*

o·ver·joyed [oh-vur-<u>joyd</u>] *adjective.* extremely happy: *She was overjoyed to hear that she had got the job.*

o·ver·night [oh-vur-<u>nite</u>] *adverb.* **1.** during or through the night: *David stayed overnight at my place.* **2.** very quickly; suddenly: *The new hit record was so popular, it reached the top of the charts overnight.*
adjective. **1.** during or through one night: *an overnight flight from Los Angeles to London.* **2.** used for short trips: *an overnight bag.*

o·ver·pass [<u>oh</u>-vur-*pass*] *noun,* plural **overpasses.** a bridge or road that crosses over another road or railroad.

o·ver·pop·u·la·tion [oh-vur-*pop*-yuh-<u>lay</u>-shun] *noun. Environment.* the fact of too large a population living in an area, which can cause overcrowding, loss of natural resources, and damage to the environment.

o·ver·pow·er [oh-vur-<u>pow</u>-ur] *verb,* **overpowered, overpowering.** to defeat by great strength or power: *The army's tanks overpowered the poorly armed rebel forces.*

o·ver·rule [oh-vur-<u>rool</u>] *verb,* **overruled, overruling.**
1. to rule against, reverse, or disallow a decision already made, especially as a higher authority: *The tennis umpire overruled the linesman and said the ball was in.*
2. to decide against: *We wanted to watch a DVD, but Dad overruled us and turned on the news.*

o·ver·run [oh-vur-<u>run</u>] *verb,* **overran, overrun, overrunning.**
1. to spread or swarm over or throughout: *After all the rain, the river overran its banks.* **2.** to run or go beyond the limits of; exceed: *The airplane overran the runway and came to a stop on the grass.*

o·ver·seas [oh-vur-<u>seez</u>] *adverb; adjective.* over, beyond, or across the sea; abroad: *Our cousins live overseas, in Ireland; My dad's job involves travel overseas.*

o·ver·shoe ▶ [oh-vur-*shoo*] *noun,* plural **overshoes.** an item of footwear worn over a shoe to protect against cold, snow, water, or mud. Overshoes are usually made of rubber.

Boot-style **overshoes** provide the best protection in harsh weather.

o·ver·sight [<u>oh</u>-vur-*site*] *noun,* plural **oversights. 1.** a mistake that is not deliberate: *Mom said it must have been an oversight that the hotel billed us for two nights instead of three.* **2.** the fact of watching over and guiding; supervision: *The oversight of all building repairs is the caretaker's responsibility.*

o·ver·sleep [oh-vur-<u>sleep</u>] *verb,* **overslept, oversleeping.** to sleep beyond the time for waking up: *If I oversleep I might miss the school bus.*

o·ver·take [oh-vur-<u>take</u>] *verb,* **overtook, overtaken, overtaking. 1.** to catch up with or pass: *I tried to overtake Laura in the last lap of the swimming race, but she was too fast.* **2.** to come upon suddenly or unexpectedly: *The blizzard overtook the climbers near the top of the mountain.*

o·ver·throw [oh-vur-<u>throh</u>] *verb,* **overthrew, overthrown, overthrowing.** to bring down or defeat by force or a struggle: *The army tried to overthrow the elected government.*
noun. a loss of power; a defeat: *The people celebrated the overthrow of the dictator.*

o·ver·time [oh-vur-*time*] *noun. Business.* extra time in a day before or after the usual working hours: *My mom's job involves a lot of overtime. adverb; adjective.* beyond the set time limit or usual working hours: *They worked overtime to finish the project; Not everyone gets overtime pay.*

o·ver·ture [oh-vur-chur] *noun, plural* **overtures. 1.** *Music.* music played by an orchestra before the start of an opera, ballet, or other large musical show. **2.** an offer or attempt to start something; proposal: *The children made an overture of friendship to the new boy in our class.*

Once an **owl** *has located its prey, it glides silently in for the kill.*

o·ver·turn [oh-vur-<u>turn</u>] *verb,* **overturned, overturning. 1.** to turn over; capsize; upset: *The car hit a pole and overturned.* **2.** to reverse an earlier decision, often by legal means: *The lawyer fought to have the guilty verdict overturned because she was sure her client was not guilty.*

o·ver·weight [oh-vur-*wate*] *adjective.* heavier than the normal, needed, or allowed weight: *He is about ten pounds overweight.*

o·ver·whelm [oh-vur-<u>welm</u>] *verb,* **overwhelmed, overwhelming.** to overpower or make helpless; completely overcome: *Their soccer team overwhelmed the team of younger boys and won by a score of 7–0.*

o·ver·work [oh-vur-<u>wurk</u>] *verb,* **overworked, overworking.** to cause to work too hard or long: *The emergency crews were overworked after the hurricane. noun.* too much work: *He has a bad back from overwork.*

owe [oh] *verb,* **owed, owing. 1.** to have to pay back: *Sharon still owes me the ten dollars I lent her.* **2.** to have to give: *You owe me an explanation for why you took my baseball cards.* **3.** to be indebted or obliged for: *The tennis star owed his success to his family's help and support.* 🔊 A different word with the same sound is **oh.**

owl ▲ [owl] *noun, plural* **owls.** a bird with large, staring eyes and a hooked beak, covered in soft feathers, that makes a hooting sound. It hunts mostly at night for food such as mice, frogs, snakes, and insects.

It is not known for certain how the idea of "a wise old **owl**" came about, possibly because of the way this bird sits silently in a tree observing what goes on below. There are many other similar expressions in which animals are given human qualities based on the way they act. If we say, "He's a fox," the person is thought to be clever and tricky and hard to defeat. In the same way, a rat is someone sneaky, dishonest, or treacherous, a lion is brave and determined, a shark is fierce, hungry, and ruthless, a pigeon can be easily fooled or deceived, and so on.

own [ohn] *adjective.* having to do with or belonging to oneself or itself: *Miss Lewis makes her own clothes. noun.* a thing that belongs to oneself: *I'm tired of borrowing my brother's guitar—I want my own. verb,* **owned, owning. 1.** to have as one's own; possess: *Kenny owns two skateboards.* **2.** to admit to something; confess: *She owned that she'd been stealing money from her mother's purse.*

own·er [ohn-ur] *noun, plural* **owners.** a person who owns something: *They are still looking for the cat's owner.*

ox [oks] *noun, plural* **oxen. 1.** an adult male of domestic cattle, used for pulling loads or for meat. **2.** any of the large, horned animals related to the ox, such as buffaloes, bison, and yaks.

ox·cart [oks-*kart*] *noun, plural* **oxcarts.** a cart pulled by an ox or oxen.

ox·en [oks-in] *noun.* the plural of **ox.**

ox·ide [<u>oks</u>-*ide*] *noun, plural* **oxides.** *Chemistry.* a chemical combination of oxygen and one or more chemical elements.

ox·i·dize [ok-suh-*dize*] *verb,* **oxidized, oxidizing.** *Chemistry.* to combine a chemical substance with oxygen.

ox·y·gen [ok-suh-jun] *noun. Chemistry.* a gas with no color, taste, or smell. It makes up about one-fifth of the air we breathe. Living things cannot live without it, nor can fires burn. It is a chemical element.

> The word **oxygen** was made up by a famous French scientist, Antoine Lavoisier. He discovered and named this gas in the 1770s. Lavoisier is often called "the father of chemistry" because he made so many important contributions to the development of this science.

oy·ster [oy-stur] *noun, plural* **oysters.** a shellfish with a soft body inside a rough, hinged shell, which attaches to rocks or timber in shallow water along coasts. Some kinds of oysters are eaten, while others are grown for their pearls.

oz. an abbreviation for OUNCE or **ounces.**

o·zone [oh-zone] *noun. Chemistry.* a form of oxygen with a strong smell that is formed when lightning passes through the atmosphere. It is used to kill germs and freshen the air.

ozone layer ▼ *Environment.* a layer of ozone high in the Earth's atmosphere. It partly blocks the Sun's harmful ultraviolet rays so they do not reach the Earth. An area of the ozone layer where the ozone has become thinner is an **ozone hole.**

The hole in the **ozone layer** *was first discovered in the 1970s.*

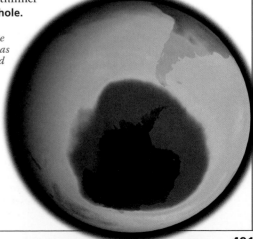

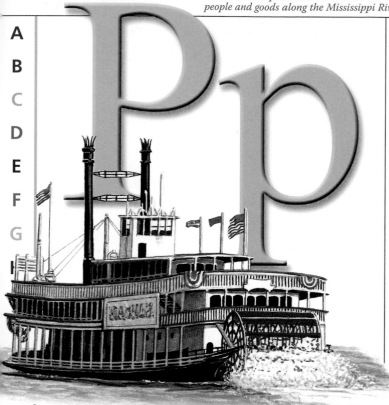

P, p *noun, plural* **P's, p's.**
the sixteenth letter of the English alphabet.

pace [pase] *noun, plural* **paces. 1.** the act of walking a single step, or the distance covered by this: *He reached the door in five paces.* **2.** the speed or rate of movement: *A snail moves at a slow pace.* **3.** a manner or style of stepping; gait: *a lively pace.*
verb, **paced, pacing. 1.** to walk or stride back and forth across: *She paced the room, waiting for the phone to ring.* **2.** to measure a distance by paces: *The referee paced off ten yards to set up the free kick.*

pace·mak·er [pase-*may*-kur] *noun, plural* **pacemakers.** *Medicine.* a small electronic device placed inside a person's body, used to help keep his or her heart beating at the right rate.

It takes skill to **paddle** *in fast-moving water.*

Pa·cif·ic [puh-*sif*-ik] *noun.* the ocean that separates North and South America from Asia and Australia, and extends from the Arctic to Antarctica. It is also called the **Pacific Ocean.**
adjective. of or relating to the Pacific.

pac·i·fi·er [pas-uh-*fye*-ur] *noun, plural* **pacifiers. 1.** a rubber or plastic object for a baby to suck or chew on for comfort. **2.** a person who makes someone or something calm.

pac·i·fist [pas-uh-fist] *noun, plural* **pacifists.** *Government.* a person who is against war and violence as a way to settle disputes. The belief that war is wrong, and that disputes between countries should be settled peacefully, is **pacifism.**

pac·i·fy [pas-uh-*fye*] *verb,* **pacified, pacifying.** to make calm, quiet, or peaceful. Peacekeeping forces aim to carry out **pacification** in areas where fighting and conflict occur.

pack [pak] *noun, plural* **packs. 1.** a collection of things wrapped or tied up for carrying; bundle: *Mom made up a pack of our old clothes to give to the thrift shop.* **2.** a sturdy bag or container that people or animals carry on their back. **3.** a set, group, or collection of similar things: *a pack of cards; an information pack.* **4.** a large number or amount; a lot: *a pack of money.*
verb, **packed, packing. 1.** to place in a container for carrying or storing: *I packed a spare pair of jeans.* **2.** to fill up with items; fill tightly: *A crowd of 50,000 packed into the stadium to watch the final.* **3.** to press together firmly: *To make a snowball, you need to pack a mass of snow tightly together.*

pack·age [pak-ij] *noun, plural* **packages. 1.** a collection of things wrapped, packed, or tied up for carrying; a parcel: *The postman delivered the package.* **2.** a container in which things are packed, wrapped, or sealed: *a package of cookies.* The materials in which goods are sealed before being sold is **packaging.**
verb, **packaged, packaging.** to make into or enclose in a package: *The book was packaged with a free DVD.*

pack·et [pak-it] *noun, plural* **packets.** a small package or parcel.

pact [pakt] *noun, plural* **pacts.** an agreement between countries or people: *The three girls made a pact to be friends forever.*

pad [pad] *noun, plural* **pads. 1.** a thick piece of soft material used for comfort or protection, or as stuffing: *I wear knee and elbow pads for in-line skating.* A thick, soft piece of protective material or stuffing is **padding.**
2. a number of sheets of paper held together along one edge: *José wrote the answers down on his pad.*
3. the soft, cushioned bottom of the feet of dogs, cats, and some other animals. **4.** a block of material soaked in ink and used for inking a rubber stamp.
verb, **padded, padding. 1.** to line or stuff with a pad: *The nurse padded the area around the wound on my arm in case someone bumped it.* **2.** to make longer with useless or trivial material: *The guest speaker padded her talk with jokes so it would last the full ten minutes.*

pad·dle ▲ [pad-ul] *noun, plural* **paddles. 1.** a short oar with a flat blade, used to move and guide a canoe or rowboat. **2.** a small, broad bat with a short handle, used to hit a ball in games such as table tennis. **3.** a flat, wooden tool used for stirring, mixing, or beating.
verb, **paddled, paddling. 1.** to move a canoe or other boat with a paddle or paddles: *We paddled the canoes through the rapids.* **2.** to punish by hitting someone with a paddle or the hand; spank.

paddle wheel ▲ a big wheel with paddles or broad boards around the edge, usually used to move a boat.

pad·dock [pad-ik] *noun, plural* **paddocks. 1.** a small, fenced field or area where animals exercise or graze. **2.** a small, fenced area at a racetrack where racehorses assemble.

pad·dy [pad-ee] *noun, plural* **paddies.** a field that is used to grow rice.

pad·lock [pad-lok] *noun, plural* **padlocks.** a removable lock with a U-shaped bar that is hinged at one end. It can be opened with a key or a dial.
verb, **padlocked, padlocking.** to lock with a padlock.

pa·gan [pay-gun] *noun, plural* **pagans.** *Religion.* a person who does not follow any of the main world religions. A pagan believes in many gods. Pagan beliefs or practices are **paganism.**
adjective. having to do with pagans or pagan beliefs.

page[1] [payj] *noun, plural* **pages.** one side of a sheet of paper in a book, magazine, newspaper, or letter.

page[2] [payj] *noun, plural* **pages. 1.** a young person employed to run errands or deliver messages. **2.** a boy who worked as a servant or a knight's attendant during medieval times.
verb, **paged, paging.** to try to find a person by calling out his or her name on a microphone: *At the mall, they paged the mother of the lost boy.*

pag·eant [paj-unt] *noun, plural* **pageants. 1.** an elaborate show made up of scenes based on history or legend: *a Christmas pageant.* **2.** a colorful parade, procession, or ceremony to mark an important event. A colorful or elaborate display is **pageantry.**

pag·er [pay-jur] *noun, plural* **pagers.** a small, portable electronic device that beeps when the person carrying it is paged; beeper.

pag·i·na·tion [paj-uh-nay-shun] *noun.* the system used to number and arrange pages of written or printed material. To **paginate** a document is to number and arrange its pages.

pa·go·da ▶ [puh-goh-duh] *noun, plural* **pagodas.** a temple or memorial in the form of a multistory tower, found in Asia. The roof of each story usually curves upward.

paid [pade] *verb.* the past tense and past participle of PAY.

pail [pale] *noun, plural* **pails.** a round container with a handle, open at the top; a bucket.
🔊 A different word with the same sound is **pale.**

pain [pane] *noun, plural* **pains. 1.** the feeling of part of your body being hurt or sore: *the pain of a headache or a sprained ankle.* **2.** a bad feeling like this in the mind; sorrow or suffering: *Her illness caused her family a great deal of pain.* **3. pains.** special effort; trouble taken: *I went to great pains to make sure the surprise party was a success.*
verb, **pained, paining.** to cause pain to somebody; to experience pain: *It pains me to hear you say such horrible things about my friend.*
🔊 A different word with the same sound is **pane.**

pain·ful [pane-ful] *adjective.* making you feel pain or hurt: *Listening to her sing was a painful experience.*
—painfully, *adjective.*

pain·kill·er [pane-kil-ur] *noun, plural* **painkillers.** *Medicine.* something that reduces or stops pain: *Shelley had to take some aspirin as a painkiller after the operation to set her broken leg.*

pain·less [pane-lis] *adjective.* **1.** causing no pain: *It was a painless operation that didn't require any anesthetic.* **2.** involving little effort; not difficult: *Paying bills on the Internet is a painless way to take care of your household expenses.* **—painlessly,** *adverb.*

pains·tak·ing [paynz-tay-king] *adjective.* taking great care; very thorough: *A painstaking search of the crash site provided vital evidence.* **—painstakingly,** *adverb.*

paint [paynt] *noun, plural* **paints.** a mixture of coloring material dissolved in a liquid and applied to a surface to color or decorate it.
verb, **painted, painting. 1.** to put paint on something: *to paint a kitchen wall white.* **2.** to create an image of something with paint: *Vincent van Gogh was famous for painting pictures of flowers and other scenes of nature.* Painting is usually done with a **paintbrush.**

paint·er [payn-tur] *noun, plural* **painters. 1.** someone who paints pictures, especially an artist who does this as a work of art. **2.** a person whose job is to paint walls and houses.

paint·ing [payn-ting] *noun, plural* **paintings.**
1. a picture made by painting as a work of art: *The Mona Lisa is a very famous painting by Leonardo da Vinci.*
2. the act or result of applying paint: *I studied painting in my art class.*

Pagodas are a traditional kind of architecture in China.

pair [pare] *noun, plural* **pairs** *or* **pair. 1.** two things of the same kind that are used together: *I gave my mother a pair of earrings for her birthday.* **2.** something made up of two parts joined together: *He bought a new pair of black trousers.* **3.** two people or animals that are connected; a couple: *They are such a well-matched pair—do you think they'll get married?*
verb, **paired, pairing.** to put into groups of two: *The two fastest swimmers were paired in the relay race.*
◀») Different words with the same sound are **pare** and **pear.**

pa·ja·mas [puh-<u>jahm</u>-uhz *or* puh-<u>jam</u>-uz] *plural noun.* loose-fitting clothes that are worn to sleep in.

pal [pal] *noun, plural* **pals.** a close friend: *I like hanging out at the mall with my pals after school.*
verb, **palled, palling.** to spend time with a close friend, or friends: *We could pal around over the weekend.*

> **Pajamas** comes from an ancient word of Persia, the Middle Eastern country now known as Iran. That is where clothes of this type were originally worn. The word was spelled *pyjamas* when it first came into English.

pal·ace ▲ [<u>pal</u>-is] *noun, plural* **palaces. 1.** a large, impressive building that is the official home of a king, queen, ruler, or high-ranking person. **2.** something regarded as grander than it really is: *The tent seemed like a palace to the weary hikers.*

pal·ate [<u>pal</u>-it] *noun, plural* **palates. 1.** the top surface of the mouth. **2.** the sense of taste: *The menu has many dishes to tempt your palate.* The **hard palate** is the bony part at the front of the mouth; the fleshy, muscular part at the back is the **soft palate.**
◀») Different words with the same sound are **palette** and **pallet.**

pale [pale] *adjective,* **paler, palest. 1.** having skin color that is light or whiter than it usually is: *His face went very pale just before he fainted.* **2.** having little color: *The pale yellow shirt set off his dark skin.*
verb, **paled, paling.** to become pale: *Her face paled when she saw that she had failed the test.*
◀») A different word with the same sound is **pail.**

pa·le·on·tol·o·gy [pale-ee-un-<u>tol</u>-uh-jee] *noun. Science.* the study of fossils in order to learn about ancient plant and animal life. A **paleontologist** is a person who studies paleontology.

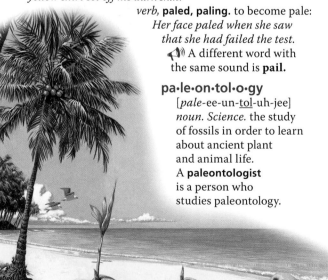

Pa·le·o·zo·ic [pay-lee-uh-<u>zoh</u>-ik] *noun. Science.* the era in Earth's early history, about 570 million to 248 million years ago, during which vertebrates and land plants first appeared. *adjective.* from the time of, or relating to, this era.

Pal·es·tin·i·an [pal-uh-<u>stin</u>-ee-un] *noun, plural* **Palestinians. 1.** a person who comes from, or lives, in Palestine, the area in the Middle East between the Jordan River and the Mediterranean Sea. In ancient times, Palestine was the Jewish homeland, but it is now occupied by Israel and Jordan. It is also known as the Holy Land. **2.** specifically, a person of Arab descent who lives in or comes from this region. *adjective.* having to do with Palestine, its people, or its culture.

pal·ette ▶ [<u>pal</u>-it] *noun, plural* **palettes. 1.** a thin, usually oval-shaped, board used by an artist to mix paints. It has a hole at one end for the thumb. **2.** a range of colors used by an artist or designer, or the choice of shapes and colors available in a computer program.
◀») Different words with the same sound are **palate** and **pallet.**

Palettes allow artists to hold and mix a number of colors while they paint.

pal·i·sades [pal-uh-<u>saydz</u>] *plural noun.* a row of steep, high cliffs alongside a river or lake.

pall·et [<u>pal</u>-it] *noun, plural* **pallets. 1.** a thin mattress filled with straw. **2.** a small, hard, makeshift bed: *We had to sleep on pallets when we stayed at the beach hut.* **3.** a hard frame used for the storage and handling of goods: *The builder had three pallets of bricks delivered to the house so he could start building the new wall.*
◀») Different words with the same sound are **palate** and **palette.**

pall·id [<u>pal</u>-id] *adjective.* pale and unhealthy: *His face looked pallid after his long illness.* An unnatural paleness of the skin is called **pallor.**

palm¹ [pahm *or* pahlm] *noun, plural* **palms.** the inside surface of the hand between the wrist and fingers. *verb,* **palmed, palming. 1.** to hide something in your hand: *The magician palmed the coin and made it reappear out of my ear.* **2.** to fool someone into buying something through deception: *Some fake antiques are palmed off to unsuspecting buyers.*

palm² ◀ [pahm *or* pahlm] *noun, plural* **palms.** any of a group of trees, shrubs, or vines that grow in warm climates.

*When a coconut washes ashore, it may sprout, take root in the sand, and grow into a new coconut **palm.***

A B C D E F G H I J K L M N O P Q R S T U V W X Y Z

PAMPAS

The vast grassy plains of the pampas extend across central Argentina from the Atlantic Ocean to the foothills of the Andes, as well as into Uruguay. They are one of the richest grazing areas in the world and support millions of beef cattle. In the nineteenth century, skilled horsemen called gauchos lived as nomads on the pampas, but today they live and work on large cattle ranches. Some interesting animals are found in these humid, windy, almost treeless grasslands. The maned wolf, for example, has very long legs so it can see above the tall grass, while the coloring and striped legs of the pampas cat help it to hide.

Pampas grass

Pampas cat

Maned wolf

Guanacos

Gaucho with cattle

pal·met·to [pal-<u>met</u>-oh] *noun, plural* **palmettos** *or* **palmettoes.** a low-growing palm plant that has fan-shaped leaves.

Palm Sunday *Religion.* the Sunday before Easter Day; a religious day for Christians to mark Christ's entry into the city of Jerusalem when the people there welcomed him by waving palm branches.

pal·o·mi·no [*pal*-uh-<u>mee</u>-noh] *noun, plural* **palominos.** a light, golden-colored horse with a pale mane and tail.

pam·pas ▲ [<u>pam</u>-puz] *plural noun. Geography.* large, treeless, grassy plains in some parts of South America; similar to prairies.

pam·per [<u>pam</u>-pur] *verb,* **pampered, pampering.** to be very kind to someone; indulge: *She pampered herself with a box of her favorite chocolates.*

pam·phlet [<u>pam</u>-flit] *noun, plural* **pamphlets.** a thin book with a paper cover: *The pamphlet contained a list of all the video games that were on special.*

pan [pan] *noun, plural* **pans. 1.** a shallow metal container used for cooking or baking. It often has a handle but no lid. **2.** a flat, round, metal dish used to wash precious metals, such as gold, from gravel.
verb, **panned, panning. 1.** to wash gravel in a pan to separate metal from the sediment: *We panned for gold in the creek and found a few small nuggets.* **2.** to criticize strongly: *All the critics panned that movie.*

pan·cake [pan-*kake*] *noun, plural* **pancakes.** a thin, round cake made by cooking batter in a flat pan.

pan·cre·as [<u>pan</u>-kree-us] *noun, plural* **pancreases.** *Medicine.* a large gland near the stomach that produces insulin and other liquids that help digest food. Anything to do with the pancreas is described as **pancreatic.**

pan·da ▼ [<u>pan</u>-duh] *noun, plural* **pandas. 1.** a large, bearlike animal with thick black and white fur; native to central China. This animal is also called the **giant panda. 2.** a raccoon-like animal with reddish-brown fur, a long bushy tail, and a white face; native to the Himalayan forests. This animal is also called the **lesser panda.**

pane [pane] *noun, plural* **panes.** a piece of glass used in windows and doors.
◀)) A different word with the same sound is **pain.**

pan·el [<u>pan</u>-ul] *noun, plural* **panels. 1.** a distinct section of something that is different from the surrounding parts. It can have a border, be raised, or sunken. It is often part of a door, wall, furniture, garment, or drapery. **2.** a group of people with special skills or knowledge chosen to advise, judge, or discuss something: *The panel on the TV news program discussed the recent election results.* **3.** a surface that displays dials, measuring instruments, or gauges for operating something: *The control panels of modern cars are easy to see and help make driving safer.* Thin boards, or sheets of other materials used to decorate walls or furniture is called **paneling.**

pang [pang] *noun, plural* **pangs.** a short, sudden feeling: *I felt a pang of jealousy when I saw my boyfriend talking to Jane.*

pan·ic [<u>pan</u>-ik] *noun, plural* **panics.** a sudden, strong feeling of fear or anxiety that stops you from thinking clearly. It can make you lose your self control: *When the plane suddenly lost height, panic spread among the passengers. verb,* **panicked, panicking.** to feel sudden fear or anxiety. Being in a state of panic is sometimes described as being **panicky.**

pan·o·ram·a [pan-uh-<u>rahm</u>-uh] *noun, plural* **panoramas.** an impressive wide view of an area: *From the top of the tower you can see a panorama of the lakes and mountains.* Such a view is described as **panoramic.**

Like the giant panda, the **lesser panda** *feeds only on bamboo shoots.*

Pansies belong to the violet family and come in many different colors.

pan·sy ▶ [pan-zee] *noun, plural* **pansies.**
a small garden plant with flat petals and brightly colored flowers.

pant [pant] *verb,* **panted, panting. 1.** to breathe hard and quickly; take short breaths: *I panted for a few minutes after I had run up the hill.* **2.** to speak while panting or out of breath: *"This dog," Amy panted, "has too much energy!" as it pulled her along by its leash.*

pan·ther [pan-thur] *noun, plural* **panthers.**
a name for a large animal of the cat family, especially a leopard with an almost black coat that lives in Africa or Asia.

pan·to·mime [pan-tuh-*mime*] *noun, plural* **pantomimes.** a play or performance in which actors tell a story using facial gestures, body movements, and music, but do not speak. *verb,* **pantomimed, pantomiming.** to perform with body movements and facial gestures, but without speaking.

pan·try [pan-tree] *noun, plural* **pantries.** a room or cupboard for storing food.

pants [pants] *plural noun.* an article of clothing for the lower part of the body, with both legs covered separately; trousers.

pa·pal [pape-ul] *adjective. Religion.* having to do with the Pope, the worldwide head of the Roman Catholic Church. The position that the Pope holds is known as the **papacy.**

pa·pa·ya [puh-pah-yuh] *noun, plural* **papayas.** a greenish-yellow fruit that grows on a tropical tree. The ripe fruit is sweet, and similar to a melon.

pa·per [pay-pur]
noun, plural **papers.**
1. a substance made from wood pulp, straw, rags, or similar materials that is made into thin sheets. Paper is used to write or print on, to wrap things in, to cover walls, and for many other uses.
2. a sheet of paper. **3.** a printed document: *The scientist has published several papers on global warming.*
4. an assignment or essay written as part of a course of study. **5.** a newspaper: *That story is in today's paper.*
verb, **papered, papering.** to cover with special paper used for walls; put up wallpaper: *We papered Angelina's bedroom last weekend.*

> The word **paper** comes from *papyrus*, the name of a tall plant growing in the Nile River area of Egypt. In ancient times the Egyptians, Greeks, and others used materials from this plant to make paper for writing.

pa·per·back [pay-pur-*bak*] *noun, plural* **paperbacks.** a book with a soft paper or light cardboard cover. Many books are first published in **hardcover** with hard boards and a dust jacket before being published as a paperback.

paper clip a small metal or plastic device to hold several loose sheets of paper together.

pa·per·work [pay-pur-*wurk*] *noun.* any work involving writing reports and letters, keeping records, or administration, usually as part of a normal job.

papier mâché [pay-pur muh-shay] *Art.* a lightweight material made from paper that is soaked in water and made into a mushy pulp. The pulp is mixed with glue and shaped to make simple models or sculptures and objects such as bowls that are painted or lacquered.

When a Native American tribe was on the move, a mother carried her baby in a **papoose.**

pa·poose ▲ [pa-poos] *noun, plural* **papooses.** a baby or small child of Native American parents. It is also the name given to a bag-like device with a frame used for carrying a small child on a person's back.

pap·ri·ka [pa-preek-uh] *noun, plural* **paprikas.** a spicy, reddish-brown powder made from sweet red chili peppers that are dried and ground. It is used to flavor and color food.

pa·py·rus ◀ [puh-pye-rus] *noun, plural* **papyri. 1.** a tall grasslike plant that grows on the banks of rivers. Papyrus was used in ancient times to make paper. **2.** a kind of paper made from this plant.

par [par] *noun, plural* **pars. 1.** an average or normal amount, number, or condition of something: *John's math skills are very good—well above par.* **2.** the fact of being equal in amount or quality: *The two players are on a par with each other.* **3.** the number of strokes a good player should take to complete a particular hole or a golf course: *That hole is a par four but it usually takes Dad five or six strokes.* *verb,* **parred, parring.** to have a score that is the same as par: *Today, Uncle Joe parred the sixth and ninth holes.*

par·a·ble [par-uh-bul] *noun, plural* **parables.** *Literature.* a short, simple story that illustrates a moral or lesson.

par·a·chute ▶ [par-ruh-*shoot*] *noun, plural* **parachutes.** a large, circular piece of cloth with cords attached to a harness that allows people or objects to be dropped safely from an airplane to the ground. Parachutes are folded tightly in a backpack until released by pulling a cord to form a large mushroom-like shape. A person who uses a parachute is known as a **parachutist.**

pa·rade [puh-*rade*] *noun, plural* **parades. 1.** a public procession of people, vehicles, or both, through the streets to celebrate a special occasion: *The Easter parade had a band and a troupe of dancers at the front.* **2.** a ceremonial assembly of military personnel to be inspected by senior officers. *verb,* **paraded, parading. 1.** to march or take part in a parade. **2.** to make a show of or draw attention to something: *Julian's always parading his knowledge of weird music to us.*

par·a·digm [pare-uh-*dime*] *noun, plural* **paradigms.** a pattern or example to be followed.

par·a·dise [pare-uh-*dise*] *noun.* **1.** another word for Heaven. **2.** a place of great beauty and happiness: *The Great Barrier Reef is an paradise for divers.*

par·a·dox [pare-uh-*doks*] *noun, plural* **paradoxes.** a statement or situation that appears to go against common sense, but nonetheless seems to be true: *It is a paradox that the French eat rich food and drink wine but do not become fat or die of heart disease.* To describe this sort of statement or situation is to say it is **paradoxical.**

par·af·fin [pare-uh-fin] *noun.* a white, waxy substance made from petroleum used to make candles and to coat paper, and which is used in some drugs and cosmetics.

par·a·graph [pare-uh-*graf*] *noun, plural* **paragraphs.** *Language.* a group of sentences that are part of a written or spoken work and are written or printed together in one group because they continue the same thought or idea. Paragraphs usually begin on a new line, indented from the other lines, and often there is an extra space between one paragraph and the next.

A long piece of writing is made easier to read by breaking up the writing into **paragraphs.** There is no exact rule about how to do this, but in general a new paragraph should start when a new idea is introduced. In student writing, a paragraph would usually be about four or five sentences. Paragraphs of only two or three sentences will break up writing too much.

par·a·keet ▶ [pare-uh-*keet*] *noun, plural* **parakeets.** a small, often brightly colored parrot found in tropical countries. The Australian budgerigar is a type of parakeet.

par·al·lel [pare-uh-*lel*] *adjective.* having to do with lines running in the same direction and always the same distance apart: *The two streets are parallel to each other.* *noun, plural* **parallels. 1.** a parallel line or surface: *The architect drew a line and then drew a parallel beside it.*

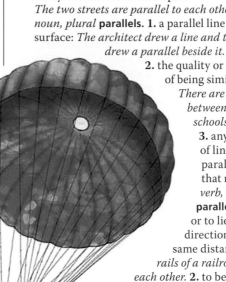

2. the quality or state of being similar: *There are many parallels between the two high schools in this town.* **3.** any of a number of lines on a map parallel to the equator that mark latitude. *verb,* **paralleled, paralleling. 1.** to be or to lie in the same direction and always the same distance apart: *The two rails of a railroad track parallel each other.* **2.** to be very similar to: *The twins' careers in pro football paralleled each other.* *adverb.* always exactly the same distance apart: *The two roads run parallel for almost six miles.*

The first **parachutes** *were canvas, but today they are made from light nylon.*

par·al·lel·o·gram [pare-uh-*lel*-uh-*gram*] *noun, plural* **parallelograms.** *Mathematics.* a four-sided figure in which the two sets of opposite sides are equal in length and parallel to each other, as in a square or a rhombus.

pa·ral·y·sis [puh-*ral*-uh-sis] *noun, plural* **paralyses.** the fact of a loss of movement or feeling in all or part of the body: *After the crash I suffered paralysis in my left leg.*

par·a·lyze [pare-uh-*lize*] *verb,* **paralyzed, paralyzing. 1.** to cause a loss of power or feeling to all or part of the body. **2.** to cause to be unable to move; make something stop working: *The snowstorm paralyzed the city's bus lines.* If someone's body is completely paralyzed, they are described as **paralytic.**

par·a·me·ci·um [pare-uh-*mee*-see-um] *noun, plural* **paramecia.** *Biology.* a tiny animal with hairlike threads to help it move that lives in fresh water and can be seen only through a microscope.

para·med·ic [pare-uh-*med*-ik] *noun, plural* **paramedics.** *Medicine.* a member of a medical team who is not a doctor or a nurse but who helps with auxiliary medical care, such as taking X-rays and giving injections.

par·a·mount [pare-uh-*mount*] *adjective.* having superior importance; above all others: *It is of paramount importance that our school is kept safe from fire.*

par·a·noid [pare-uh-*noyd*] *adjective. Medicine.* having to do with an unjustified fear or belief by someone that they are being persecuted by others who want to harm or threaten them. The state of **paranoia** is a mental disorder in which fear and distrust of others take an extreme form.

par·a·pher·na·li·a [pare-uh-fuh-*nale*-yuh] *plural noun.* a collection of personal belongings, equipment, small articles, or other such items that may be used for a particular purpose: *I keep all my sports paraphernalia in a large canvas bag.*

par·a·phrase [pare-uh-*fraze*] *noun, plural* **paraphrases.** *Language.* a rewritten or reworded piece of writing that is shorter or easier to understand than the original. *verb,* **paraphrased, paraphrasing.** to rewrite or reword a piece of writing to make it shorter or easier to understand: *Please paraphrase your essay to clarify the reasons for the American Civil War.*

par·a·ple·gic [pare-uh-*plee*-jik] *noun, plural* **paraplegics.** *Health.* a person who has lost both arms or both legs or whose arms or legs are paralyzed. The state of having lost the use of both arms or both legs is called **paraplegia.**

par·a·pro·fes·sion·al [pare-uh-pruh-*fesh*-nul] *noun, plural* **paraprofessionals.** a person who has been trained to assist a professional such as a doctor or a teacher.

par·a·site ▶ [pare-uh-*site*] *noun, plural* **parasites.** *Biology.* an animal or plant that obtains its food by living on another animal or plant. The parasite may cause damage or disease to the host animal or plant. Lice and fleas are parasites on animals. The act of an animal or organism living and feeding on another is **parasitism.** —**parasitic,** *adjective.*

par·a·si·tol·o·gy [pare-uh-sye-*tol*-uh-jee] *noun. Medicine.* the study of parasites and the diseases they cause. A person who studies parasites is called a **parasitologist.**

par·a·sol ▼ [pare-uh-sol] *noun, plural* **parasols.** a lightweight, portable sunshade made from cloth or paper that looks like an umbrella.

par·a·troop·er [pare-uh-*troo*-pur] *noun, plural* **paratroopers.** a soldier trained and equipped to parachute from an airplane, especially one dropped to fight behind enemy lines. A large number of paratroopers are called **paratroops.**

par·cel [par-sul] *noun, plural* **parcels. 1.** a bundle or package of articles wrapped up together: *Mom sent her Christmas parcels out early this year.* **2.** a piece or collection of something: *Max bought a parcel of land in the country for his retirement. verb,* **parceled, parceling.** to divide into shares or distribute: *The teacher parceled out the paints and brushes to the children.*

*Buddhist monks in hot countries use **parasols** to shelter from the sun.*

Louse

Flea

*The louse and the flea are tiny **parasites** that cause the skin to itch.*

parch [parch] *verb,* **parched, parching.** to dry out: *The blazing sun parched the crops day after day. adjective.* having to do with a person becoming hot, dried out, and thirsty: *I'm parched after my long walk in the sun.*

parch·ment [parch-munt] *noun, plural* **parchments.** the skin of animals such as sheep or goats that has been dried and prepared for use as a surface for writing on, or a special paper made to look like this.

par·don [pard-un] *verb,* **pardoned, pardoning. 1.** to release someone who has committed a crime from serving a punishment for it: *The king pardoned one hundred prisoners on his birthday.* **2.** to forgive or not blame. *noun, plural* **pardons. 1.** a releasing from punishment: *The prisoners received a pardon from the king.* **2.** the act of not blaming; forgiveness: *I'm so sorry—will you give me your pardon?*
• **pardon me/I beg your pardon.** excuse me: *Pardon me, I didn't quite hear you.*

pare [pare] *verb,* **pared, paring. 1.** to cut or shave off the outer skin of something: *I pared an orange with a small knife.* **2.** to reduce something a little at a time or gradually over time: *They had to pare back their spending on groceries when their father lost his job.*
🔊 Different words with the same sound are **pair** and **pear.**

par·ent [pare-unt] *noun, plural* **parents. 1.** a mother or a father. **2.** a living thing that produces other similar living things. The fact of being or becoming a parent is called **parenthood.**

pa·ren·the·sis [puh-*ren*-thuh-*sis*] *noun, plural* **parentheses.** *Language.* either of two curved lines, ( ), that are used to enclose a word, phrase, mathematical symbol, or other note.

You use parentheses ( ) in writing when you add a thought that is not part of the main point but is needed to explain or give information about it: "He was known as El Jefe (The Chief)." "The plane is able to fly at a speed of Mach 2 (about 1,500 miles per hour)." "With your order, you get bread and a choice of minestrone (a kind of soup) or salad."

par·ent·ing [pare-unt-ing] *noun.* the care of a child by its parents.

par·ish [pare-ish] *noun, plural* **parishes. 1.** an area with its own church and its own priest, minister, or other cleric. **2.** the people who live within this area. A person who lives within the parish and is a regular member of the church congregation is a **parishioner.**

park [park] *noun, plural* **parks. 1.** an area of open space in a town, usually with trees and grass, and often with paths, and playgrounds, set aside for pleasure and recreation. **2.** an area of country recognized for its natural beauty and often with wildlife, preserved by the government for the enjoyment of the people. *verb,* **parked, parking.** to leave an automobile or other motor vehicle in a lot or on the street for a period of time: *We parked on the street and walked half a mile to the game.*

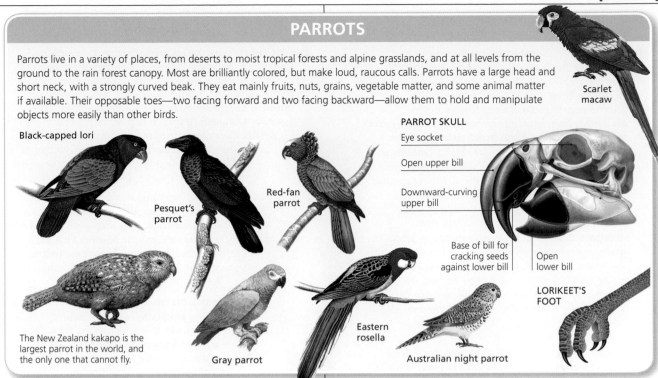

PARROTS

Parrots live in a variety of places, from deserts to moist tropical forests and alpine grasslands, and at all levels from the ground to the rain forest canopy. Most are brilliantly colored, but make loud, raucous calls. Parrots have a large head and short neck, with a strongly curved beak. They eat mainly fruits, nuts, grains, vegetable matter, and some animal matter if available. Their opposable toes—two facing forward and two facing backward—allow them to hold and manipulate objects more easily than other birds.

Scarlet macaw

Black-capped lori

Pesquet's parrot

Red-fan parrot

PARROT SKULL

Eye socket

Open upper bill

Downward-curving upper bill

Base of bill for cracking seeds against lower bill

Open lower bill

LORIKEET'S FOOT

The New Zealand kakapo is the largest parrot in the world, and the only one that cannot fly.

Gray parrot

Eastern rosella

Australian night parrot

---

par·ka [par-kuh] *noun, plural* **parkas.** a warm, waterproof, long-sleeved jacket with a fur-lined hood.

park·ing [par-king] *noun.* the act of leaving an automobile or other motor vehicle in a parking lot, parking garage, or on the street for a period of time.

parking lot an outdoor area for parking automobiles and other motor vehicles.

parking meter an electronic or mechanical device by which people pay to park a vehicle on a street or in a specified area for a limited time.

park·way [park-way] *noun, plural* **parkways.** a landscaped highway with trees and grass in the central strip.

par·lia·ment ▼ [par-luh-munt] *noun, plural* **parliaments.** an assembly of people from all parts of a country who represent the whole population, and who elect the leaders of the government. In most Western democracies including the U.K., Canada, and Australia, the house of national government is called **Parliament.**

par·lor [par-lur] *noun, plural* **parlors. 1.** a room in a house used for entertaining guests. **2.** a room or premises used as a commercial enterprise; a shop: *an ice-cream parlor; a funeral parlor.*

pa·ro·chi·al [puh-roh-kee-ul] *adjective.* **1.** of or relating to a parish: *A priest has a wide range of parochial duties.* **2.** having to do with a narrow or limited view of something: *This town can be very parochial when it comes to politics.* In many parishes, churches run a **parochial school** for the education of parishioners' children.

par·o·dy [pare-uh-dee] *noun, plural* **parodies.** *Literature.* a humorous piece of writing or music in the style of a serious work.
verb, **parodied, parodying.** to make a parody of something.

pa·role [puh-role] *noun, plural* **paroles.** *Law.* the act of releasing a person from prison before they have served their full sentence. People are normally granted parole for good behavior while in prison. A person who has been released on parole is called a **parolee.**
verb, **paroled, paroling.** to release a person from prison before they have served their full sentence.
• **on parole.** the state of a prisoner who has been released before the end of his or her sentence.

parole officer *Law.* a law officer or prison official responsible for supervising a prisoner released on parole.

par·rot ▲ [pare-it] *noun, plural* **parrots.** any of a number of brightly colored birds with a long tail, hooked beak, and fleshy tongue. Some parrots are able to mimic the human voice.
verb, **parroted, parroting.** to mimic exactly or repeat what a person says: *He wants to learn about that issue himself and not just parrot what people say about it in the papers and on radio.*

pars·ley [pars-lee] *noun, plural* **parsleys.** a green garden herb with flat or crinkly leaves that are chopped and used to flavor foods while cooking, or for decoration.

*The **Parliament** in Budapest, Hungary, is one of the largest in the world, with 691 rooms and more than twelve miles of corridors.*

pars·nip ▶ [par-snip] *noun, plural* **parsnips.** a white, cone-shaped root vegetable, often used in soups and stews.

part [part] *noun, plural* **parts. 1.** a piece or unit of something that is not the whole thing; section: *The top part of a tree is called the crown; The book was very long so I skipped over several parts in the middle.* **2.** a component piece of a machine or device: *My car has been in the garage waiting for spare parts to repair the engine.* **3.** a role played by an actor: *Marlon Brando played the part of the Godfather in the movie of that name.* **4.** one side of an argument or disagreement: *Dugald took no part in the debate.* **5.** a line that divides hair brushed or combed in two different directions: *Matt used to wear his part on the left side but now it's on the right.* *verb,* **parted, parting. 1.** to move things or people apart; separate: *The icy waters parted as the huge ship pushed ahead.* **2.** to go in separate ways: *After saying fond farewells to each other the two parted.* **3.** to brush or comb the hair either side of a line on the head: *I part my hair slightly to the left side.* *adverb.* to some extent; partly: *The problem is in part his and in part hers.* *adjective.* having to do with only a proportion of a whole; partial: *A number of different people are part owners of this time-share apartment.*
• **take part.** to join in with an activity: *We took part in the school fair in order to raise money.*

par·tial [par-shul] *adjective.* **1.** not complete: *The movie was only a partial success because it did well in the U.S. but not overseas.* **2.** showing favor mainly to one side; biased: *Naturally, the crowd was partial to the home team.* **3.** fond of: *I'm very partial to a dessert of strawberries and cream.* —**partially,** *adverb.*

par·tic·i·pate [par-tis-uh-pate] *verb,* **participated, participating.** to take part in or join with others: *It is important for parents to participate in the activities of the school.* A person who takes part in something is called a **participant.**

par·tic·i·pa·tion [par-*tis*-uh-*pay*-shun] *noun, plural* **participations.** the act of participating in an activity; taking part: *His participation in the game was cut short when he got hurt.*

par·ti·ci·ple [par-tuh-*sip*-ul] *noun, plural* **participles.** *Language.* a word formed from a verb and used as an adjective or a verb. A phrase or word that is formed from or has to do with a participle is **participial.**

A **participle** is added to the end of a verb to show a certain tense (time). This is usually done by adding the letters **-ed** or **-ing** to the end of a root verb, as in "I was *reading* a book when the door suddenly *opened*." A common error in writing is known as the *dangling participle.* This is a participle that "hangs off" from the rest of the sentence: "*Finding the main highway blocked,* our trip took longer than expected." It is not clear how this participle connects to "our trip," so it would be better as: "Finding the main highway blocked, we had to detour and our trip took longer than expected."

par·ti·cle [par-tuh-kul] *noun, plural* **particles.** a very small piece: *There were particles of dust on her eyeglasses.*

par·tic·u·lar [pur-*tik*-yuh-lur] *adjective.* **1.** describing something single and different from any other; separate: *I want to buy that particular tennis racket; Daphne's particular talent is ballet dancing.* **2.** being special or unusual: *There's no particular reason why I like her— I just do.* **4.** showing a special care for or interest in small details: *Gerry is particular about the food he eats.* *noun, plural* **particulars.** a single point, fact, or part: *The lawyer made sure the document was correct in every particular.* —**particularly,** *adverb.*

part·ing [part-ing] *noun, plural* **partings.** the act of separating or dividing: *The couple's parting was easy as they knew he was only going to be away for a week.* *adjective.* having to do with something said or done on parting: *His parting words were, "Take care of yourself."*

par·ti·tion [par-*tish*-un] *noun, plural* **partitions.** a wall or screen that divides a room or space: *We built a partition in my bedroom to make a separate space for my sister's bed.* *verb,* **partitioned, partitioning. 1.** to separate or divide into parts: *In 1993 the nation of Czechoslovakia was partitioned into the Czech Republic and Slovakia.* **2.** to separate by a wall or screen: *He partitioned off a section of the garage for a workshop.*

part·ly [part-lee] *adverb.* to some degree, in part: *Marilyn's swimming coach was partly responsible for her success in the pool.*

Parsnips look like carrots, but are paler in color and have a stronger flavor.

part·ner ▶ [part-nur] *noun, plural* **partners. 1.** a person who shares a business or other activity with another person or persons: *a partner in a law firm; The two brothers are partners in the town's pizza parlor.* **2.** a person who plays on the same side in a game or sports team: *Frankie and I are great table tennis partners.* **3.** a person who dances with another person: *You need a good partner to dance the waltz well.* *verb,* **partnered, partnering.** to be or act as a partner for an activity: *Jennifer partnered Hans in the mixed doubles tennis competition.*

part·ner·ship [part-nur-*ship*] *noun, plural* **partnerships.** *Law.* the state of having a formal business relationship in which profits and losses are shared equally: *My uncle's law firm has six lawyers who all share in the partnership.*

Dancing **partners** *must practice their steps before entering tango competitions.*

*The gray **partridge** grows up to twelve inches long and feeds on seeds and insects.*

part of speech *Language.* any of the groups into which words are classified according to the function they perform in a sentence. There are eight parts of speech in the English language: noun, pronoun, verb, adjective, adverb, preposition, conjunction, and interjection. Many words can be used as more than one part of speech.

par·tridge ▶ [par-trij] *noun, plural* **partridges. 1.** any of a number of European birds with brown feathers and bright plumage that are shot as game. **2.** another word for QUAIL.

part-time *adjective.* having to do with working or engaging in another activity that takes up less than a full amount of working or other time.

par·ty [par-tee] *noun, plural* **parties. 1.** a group of people who get together for enjoyment; a social gathering: *Are you going to Gordon's birthday party next week?* **2.** a group of people doing the same activity: *A search party set out to look for the lost hikers.* **3.** a group of people who join together in politics to try to win elections and carry on the activities of the government: *the Democratic or Republican Party.* **4.** an individual person: *We found out that the party who wanted to buy our house already lived on our street.*
verb, **partied, partying.** to hold or participate in a party, especially over a long time: *After their team won the Super Bowl they partied all night long.*

pass [pas] *verb,* **passed, passing.**
1. to move beyond; go by: *The bus to school passes my grandmother's house.* **2.** to move, transfer, or go through: *The thought passed my mind that I was lost.* **3.** to give from one person to another: *Please pass me the ketchup.* **4.** to successfully complete a test or examination: *Did your brother pass his test for a driver's license?* **5.** to spend or use time: *Before the movie started, we passed the time telling jokes.* **6.** to get through, approve, or receive approval: *The Senate passed the legislation with a very small majority.*
noun, plural **passes. 1.** a written notice: *You will need a pass to leave school in the middle of the day.* **2.** a free ticket that allows entry to entertainment: *Carlos was given a pass by his brother who works at the theater.* **3.** a route crossing between two mountain peaks: *Great St. Bernard Pass has been used as a route through the Alps for thousands of years.* **4.** the throwing of a ball between two members of the same team in sports such as football, basketball, or soccer.
• **pass out. 1.** to give out; hand out; distribute: *The teacher passed out the exam papers to the whole class.* **2.** to become unconscious; faint: *to pass out at the sight of blood.*

*In the old city of Siena, Italy, there are often narrow **passageways** between buildings.*

pas·sage [pas-ij] *noun, plural* **passages. 1.** the act or fact of passing: *In the film, the passage of time was shown by pages being pulled off a calendar; Passage of the bill in Congress was achieved despite a lot of opposition.* **2.** a means of passing such as a road, lane, route, or corridor: *The soldiers found a secret passage through the mountains.* **3.** a trip or journey. **4.** a short part of a piece of written work or music: *The selected passage was from a short story by Mark Twain.*

pas·sage·way ◀ [pas-ij-way] *noun, plural* **passageways.** a way or route along which a person or goods can pass: *The two offices are connected by a passageway.*

pas·sen·ger [pas-un-jur] *noun, plural* **passengers.** a person who travels in a method of transportation such as a bus, automobile, airplane, or ship.

pas·ser [pas-ur] *noun, plural* **passers. 1.** in football, a player who tries to gain ground by throwing a forward pass. **2.** any player who makes a pass in sports.

pas·sing [pas-ing] *adjective.* **1.** having to do with moving or going: *The children watched the passing horses.* **2.** brief or temporary state: *Bob's interest in baseball cards was a passing fad.*
noun, plural **passings.** the act of going past or going by: *The passing of summer always made us sad.*
• **in passing.** done or said as a secondary thing, incidentally: *In passing, I'd point out that my results were better than you expected!*

pas·sion [pash-un] *noun, plural* **passions. 1.** a really strong emotion or feeling. Love, hate, anger, and grief are all emotions of passion. **2.** a strong liking or enthusiasm: *She developed a passion for ballet at school.*

pas·sion·ate [pash-uh-nit] *adjective.* having to do with showing passion or emotion: *He became a passionate opponent of the death penalty.* —**passionately,** *adverb.*

a b c d e f g h i j k l m n o p q r s t u v w x y z

pas·sive [pas-iv] *adjective.* easily accepting of the will of others; not active: *Louis's dog is a passive creature and wouldn't harm a flea.*
noun. Language. the form of a verb used to show something that happens to the subject. In the sentence *The boy was hit by the tennis ball*, the verb "was hit" is in the passive and it tells what happened to the boy. —**passively**, *adverb.*

In English, verbs are either *active* or **passive**. In a sentence with an active verb, the subject of the sentence causes or carries out the action: "*Sharon kicked* the ball." "*Mom parked* the car." In a sentence with a passive verb, the subject receives or is affected by the action: "To start the game, *the ball is kicked* forward." "*The car was parked* next to a fire hydrant." The choice of active or passive depends on the type of sentence. In the examples above, you will note that an active verb is used when it is known who does the action; the passive is used when this is not clearly known or stated.

Pass·o·ver [pas-oh-vur] *noun. Religion.* an annual Jewish feast and holiday that celebrates the escape of the Jews from slavery in Egypt in ancient times.

pass·port ▶ [pas-port] *noun, plural* **passports. 1.** an official document with a photograph, showing a person's identity and nationality. A passport is issued by the government of one country to a person who wishes to travel to another country. **2.** a means of obtaining something: *A college degree can be seen as a passport to a successful career.*

pass·word [pas-wurd] *noun, plural* **passwords. 1.** a secret word or phrase a person uses to get past a guard or sentry. **2.** *Computers.* a word, or a series of letters or numbers, needed to access a computer system, its data, or programs.

past [past] *adjective.* **1.** having happened in time long since gone by: *In the past, kings led their soldiers into battle.* **2.** having happened before the present time; recently: *I have been in Boston for the past week.* **3.** being former: *The past principal of our school retired two years ago.*
noun, plural **pasts. 1.** a time long since gone by: *Dinosaurs lived in the distant past.* **2.** see PAST TENSE.
preposition. older, beyond, or farther than: *The truck went past my window; That old man is past ninety.*
adverb. passing or going by: *We looked up as a helicopter flew past.*

pas·ta ◀ [pahs-tuh] *noun, plural* **pasta** *or* **pastas.** a mixture of flour and eggs made into a dough and rolled flat or shaped in various ways. Spaghetti, fettucine, and macaroni are all pasta.

paste [payst] *noun, plural* **pastes. 1.** a mixture of flour and water used to glue things together, especially paper. **2.** any thick, soft, smooth mixture: *He added too much tomato paste to the sauce and had to thin it with water.*
verb, **pasted, pasting.** to glue together with paste: *The teacher told us to paste the pictures we drew into our books.*

pas·tel ▶ [pa-stel] *noun.* **1.** a chalk-like crayon used for drawing on paper. **2.** a drawing made by using such crayons. **3.** a soft, delicate color.
adjective. **1.** a picture drawn with pastel crayons. **2.** having a soft, delicate color: *The bathroom curtains are a pastel pink.*

Pastels are usually produced in finger-sized sticks, and come in many colors.

pas·teur·ize [pas-chuh-rize] *verb,* **pasteurized, pasteurizing.** to heat milk or other liquids to reduce the number of microorganisms in it. A liquid that has been treated in this way is described as **pasteurized.** —**pasteurization**, *noun.*

pas·time [pas-time] *noun, plural* **pastimes.** an enjoyable activity that is done to occupy a person's spare time: *Reading detective novels is Mom's favorite pastime.*

pas·tor [pas-tur] *noun, plural* **pastors.** *Religion.* a minister or priest in charge of a church.

past participle *Language.* the form of a verb used with the verb "have" and "be" to show that an action has been completed. In the sentences, *Sarah has already bought her Christmas presents; My bedroom was painted last Saturday; Jim and Mike have both visited New York City*, "bought", "painted," and "visited" are past participles.

pas·try [pay-stree] *noun, plural* **pastries. 1.** sweet baked goods such as cakes and pies. **2.** a mixture of flour, fat, and water that is baked and used for the crust or outer part of foods such as a pie.

past tense *Language.* the form of a verb that shows that something has already happened before the present time. In the sentence *I walked to school this morning*, the verb "walked" is in the past tense.

When you write a story, you will usually use the **past tense**. "Mark Lima *liked* to go fishing with his Dad and older brother. Mark *watched* them put their lines in the water, but they *said* he was too little to do this himself." As you write, you may picture the story in your mind as taking place now, but it is still better to use past tense verbs, as if it you had seen it happen before.

A **passport** *contains a description of the owner and pages for visas and control stamps.*

The word **pasteurize** comes from the name of the man who developed this process, the biologist Louis *Pasteur* of France. Pasteur is considered one of the great figures in the history of science because of his studies of how disease is spread from one person or animal to another.

Pasta is made in a variety of shapes and colors.

pas·ture ▼ [pas-chur] *noun, plural* **pastures. 1.** land covered with grass or other plants that is used for the grazing of livestock. **2.** the grass or other vegetation eaten by such animals: *There is good pasture for the sheep on the other field.*
verb, **pastured, pasturing.** to put livestock on a field to feed on grass or other plants: *The cattle were pastured in the back paddock.*

pat [pat] *verb,* **patted, patting.** to tap or stroke something or someone gently with the hand.
noun, plural **pats. 1.** a light tap or stroke: *I gave the dog a pat good-bye.* **2.** a small, flat piece of butter.

patch [pach] *noun, plural* **patches. 1.** a small piece of material used to cover a hole or weak spot in clothing: *Mom sewed a patch over the hole in my jacket.* **2.** a small piece of material used to cover a wound or injury: *The doctor advised him to wear a patch over his sore eye.* **3.** a small area that is different from the surrounding area: *We had a picnic on the only patch of grass we could find.* **4.** a small area where fruits and vegetables grow: *a cabbage patch.*
verb, **patched, patching.** to cover or mend with a patch: *I patched the hole in my trousers.*
• **patch up.** to deal with something successfully; smooth over: *We patched up our differences and now Rob and I are good friends again.*

patch·work ◀ [pach-wurk] *noun.* a type of sewing in which pieces of cloth of different colors and different shapes are stitched together to make one piece.

pat·ent [pat-unt] *noun, plural* **patents.** *Law.* a special document granted by the government to an inventor, to allow the person to make, use, or sell an invention that no one else is allowed to copy.
verb, **patented, patenting.** to obtain a patent for: *The scientist patented the new drug.*

patent leather a type of leather that has a shiny surface.

pa·ter·nal [puh-tur-nul] *adjective.* **1.** having to do with being or behaving like a father. *The old man who lives next door often takes Tony out fishing and gives him paternal advice.* **2.** related on the father's side of the family: *She vacationed with her paternal grandparents for the summer.*

path [path] *noun, plural* **paths. 1.** a route or track for walking: *We followed the garden path until we reached the pond.* **2.** the route or course along which something or someone moves: *We were scared because our house was directly in the path of the hurricane.* **3.** a course of action that someone takes: *Taking the new job was the first step on his path to success.*

pa·thet·ic [puh-thet-ik] *adjective.* **1.** bringing feelings of sadness; causing pity or sympathy: *The starving child was a pathetic sight.* **2.** very poor; having no value or quality: *It was a pathetic effort by the soccer team and they lost 7–0.* —**pathetically,** *adverb.*

pa·tience [pay-shuns] *noun.* the quality of enduring pain, difficulties, or delay without complaining or getting annoyed: *He showed great patience as he sat in the traffic jam for an hour.*

*Sheep enjoy good **pasture** on this Irish farm.*

*Saint Patrick, who lived in the fifth century, is the **patron saint** of Ireland.*

A B C D E F G H I J K L M N O P Q R S T U V W X Y Z

pa·tient [pay-shunt] *adjective.* having an ability to endure pain, difficulties, or delay without complaining or getting annoyed: *The customer tried to be patient with the new waiter who kept making mistakes with his order.* *noun, plural* **patients.** someone who is under medical care or treatment by a doctor: *a patient in a hospital.* —**patiently,** *adverb.*

pa·ti·o [pat-ee-oh] *noun, plural* **patios.** a paved, outdoor eating and recreation area next to a house: *On Sunday mornings we have breakfast out on the patio.*

pa·tri·ot [pay-tree-ut] *noun, plural* **patriots.** someone who loves his or her country and is willing to support or defend it.

> The word **patriot** comes from the Latin word for "father." People's own country can be thought of as their "fatherland," meaning that they are in effect the children of this nation.

pa·tri·ot·ic [pay-tree-ot-ik] *adjective.* showing love, loyalty, or pride for your country: *The patriotic citizens went to watch the homecoming parade for the troops.* —**patriotically,** *adverb.*

pa·tri·ot·ism [pay-tree-uh-tiz-um] *noun.* devotion, love and support for your country: *The citizens wanted to show their patriotism by raising money for the war effort.*

pa·trol [puh-trole] *verb,* **patrolled, patrolling.** to regularly go around an area or building to check that there is no trouble or danger: *Police cars patrolled the neighborhood streets after the riots.* *noun, plural* **patrols. 1.** the action of regularly going around an area or building to maintain security: *There is an increase in armed patrols when the President visits the city.* **2.** a person or group of people sent out to search a particular area or building: *The guards of the Border Patrol work very long hours.*

pa·tron [pay-trun] *noun, plural* **patrons. 1.** a regular customer of a particular store, service, or business establishment. **2.** a person who supports a cause, activity, or organization: *The senator is a patron of the children's hospital and donates money every year.*

patron saint ▲ *Religion.* a Christian saint who is considered to be the special guardian of a particular place, activity, or person: *Saint George is the patron saint of England.*

pa·tron·ize [pay-truh-nize] *verb,* **patronized, patronizing.** to be a regular customer of a particular shop, service, or business establishment: *My family has been patronizing that restaurant for over three years.* When someone is **patronizing,** it means that they are talking to you as if you are less intelligent or important than they are.

pat·tern [pat-urn] *noun, plural* **patterns. 1.** a regularly repeated arrangement or design of shapes, colors, or lines: *My dress has a black and white striped pattern on the front.* **2.** a guide or model for making something: *The knitting pattern showed her how to knit the jumper.* **3.** a set of characteristics or actions that is regularly repeated: *We are studying the behavior patterns of chimpanzees in biology class.* *verb,* **patterned, patterning.** to make or model something following a pattern: *She is patterning her career as an athlete after her favorite runner.*

pat·ty [pat-ee] *noun, plural* **patties.** a small, flat piece of chopped or ground food made into a disk shape and then cooked.

pau·per [paw-pur] *noun, plural* **paupers.** a very poor person who has little or no money and depends on welfare or charity.

pause [pawz] *verb,* **paused, pausing.** to stop or rest temporarily: *The speaker paused for a moment to gather her thoughts before she started talking again.* *noun, plural* **pauses.** a temporary stop or rest: *There was a pause in the meeting while the boss answered a phone call.*

pave [pave] *verb,* **paved, paving.** to cover a path, road, or area with a hard level surface.
• **pave the way.** to make a later event or development possible or easier: *The work of Dr. Walter Reed paved the way for finding a way to control the disease of yellow fever.*

pave·ment [pave-munt] *noun, plural* **pavements.** a paved footpath, sidewalk, or road.

pa·vil·ion ▼ [puh-vil-yuhn] *noun, plural* **pavilions. 1.** an open building or shelter used for sporting or entertainment events: *The band concert was held in the pavilion overlooking the beach.* **2.** one of a group of buildings that forms a complex.

*The Brighton **Pavilion** was built in the 1820s to look like an Indian palace.*

*Each player in a chess game starts with eight **pawns.***

paw [paw] *noun, plural* **paws.** the foot of an animal that has nails or claws, such as a dog, bear, or lion.
verb, **pawed, pawing.**
1. to strike or scrape with a paw: *The dog was scared of the thunderstorm and began pawing at the back door.* **2.** to touch something or someone in a rough, careless, and rude way: *The customers pawed at the shirts on the sale table.*

pawn¹ [pawn] *verb,* **pawned, pawning.** to leave a valuable possession with a lender when you borrow money, as a guarantee that you will pay it back. The lender, a **pawnbroker,** sells the object if you do not pay the money back. A **pawnshop** is a place where a pawnbroker operates such a business.

pawn² ▲ [pawn] *noun, plural* **pawns.**
1. the piece of lowest value used in the game of chess. **2.** an unimportant person manipulated by someone else to achieve something: *The refugee was used as a pawn in the political battle between the two countries.*

pay [pay] *verb,* **paid, paying. 1.** to give money in return for goods or services: *to pay to see a movie; to pay for a meal in a restaurant; I paid the cab driver and got out of the car.* **2.** to give money to settle a debt: *Don't forget to pay the electricity bill.* **3.** to be worthwhile or be of benefit: *It pays to be honest.* **4.** to suffer or be punished for something: *I paid the penalty for not studying for the test by getting a poor mark.* **5.** to give or offer: *He paid me a compliment about my new haircut.*
noun. wages or salary: *My boss is pleased with my work and is increasing my pay.*

pay·load ▲ [pay-lode] *noun.* the amount of goods or number of passengers that a vehicle can carry.

pay·ment [pay-munt] *noun, plural* **payments. 1.** the act of paying: *The car salesman wanted payment in advance.* **2.** an amount paid: *We repaid the loan in monthly payments to the bank.*

pay-per-view [pay-pur-vyoo] *noun.* a television system that requires viewers to pay for each separate program that they watch. A shortened form of this term is **PPV.**

pay·roll [pay-role] *noun, plural* **payrolls.**
1. a list of the employees in a company and the amount each of them is to be paid: *The company has added 25 new people to the payroll since the beginning of the year.* **2.** the total amount of all the salaries paid to the employees.

PC an abbreviation for PERSONAL COMPUTER.

pea [pee] *noun, plural* **peas.** a small, round, green vegetable that grows in a pod.

*A space shuttle can carry a large **payload,** including a satellite and a fully equipped scientific laboratory.*

peace [pees] *noun.* **1.** a time without war or fighting; freedom from war and violence: *Peace only lasted for five years before war broke out again between the two nations.* **2.** a state of quiet, calm, or stillness: *I need peace and quiet when I'm trying to study.* **3.** public order and security: *The police charged the man with disturbing the peace.*
🔊 A different word with the same sound is **piece.**

peace·ful [pees-ful] *adjective.* **1.** not involving war or fighting; without violence or force: *The nation leaders were hoping for a peaceful solution to the conflict.* **2.** not wanting to fight; not hostile: *The demonstrators were a peaceful group.*
—**peacefully,** *adverb;* —**peacefulness,** *noun.*

peace pipe ▼ a decorated pipe smoked by Native Americans during special ceremonies as a sign of peace.

peach [peech] *noun, plural* **peaches.**
1. a round fruit with sweet, yellow flesh, fuzzy, yellowish-pink skin and a large seed. **2.** a yellowish-pink color.
adjective. having a yellowish-pink color.

Peace pipes were made from hollow wood and had a wooden or clay bowl.

pea·cock ▶ [pee-*kok*] *noun,*
plural **peacocks** *or* **peacock.**
a large bird, the male of which
has bright blue feathers on its
head and neck and colorful,
eye-like patterns on its tail
feathers. The female peacock
is called a **peahen.**

peak [peek] *noun, plural* **peaks.**
1. the pointed top of a hill or
mountain, or the mountain
itself. **2.** the pointed top of
something: *I took a photo
of the peak of the pyramid.*
3. the highest or strongest
point or level: *The athlete was at the peak of her career.*
4. the brim or flat, curved part of a hat that sticks out over
the eyes.
verb, **peaked, peaking.** to reach the highest or strongest
point or level: *Sales peaked during the Christmas period.*
adjective. being at the highest point, maximum frequency,
or most active: *During peak season the beach is really
crowded.*
🔊 A different word with the same sound is **peek.**

peal [peel] *noun, plural* **peals.** a long, loud, drawn-out
sound or series of sounds: *A peal of laughter came from
the audience.*
verb, **pealed, pealing.** to sound loudly: *The bells from
the tower pealed out after the ceremony.*
🔊 A different word with the same sound is **peel.**

pea·nut [pee-nut] *noun, plural* **peanuts.** a pale brown,
edible, oval-shaped nut that grows in a pod underground.
Oil from the peanut is used in cooking.

peanut butter a soft, creamy paste made from crushed
roasted peanuts that is used on a spread or in cooking.

pear [pare] *noun, plural* **pears.** a sweet, juicy, bell-shaped
fruit with a thin pale green or brown skin.
🔊 Different words with the same sound are **pair**
and **pare.**

pearl ▶ [purl] *noun, plural* **pearls. 1.** a small, round,
cream-white jewel that is found in oysters. **2.** something
resembling the shape or color of a pearl: *There were pearls
of sweat on his forehead.*

Pearl Harbor *History.* a harbor on the southern coast of
Oahu, Hawaii. The U.S. naval base located
here was attacked by the Japanese on
December 7, 1941, and the United
States entered World War II the
next day.

peas·ant ◀ [pez-unt] *noun,*
plural **peasants.**
1. someone who lives
and works on a small farm.
2. *History.* in earlier times,
one of a large group of farm
workers, usually poor and
uneducated and working on
farms owned by others.

*In ancient China, **peasants** grew food
for soldiers and city dwellers.*

peat [peet] *noun.* a dark
brown, soil-like substance
found in marshy areas
that is made up of
decaying leaves, roots, and
grasses. **Peat moss** is one
type of moss that decays
to form peat. The area
from which this substance
is taken is called a **peat
bog.** Peat can be used
as a fertilizer or fuel.

peb·ble [peb-ul] *noun,*
plural **pebbles.** a small,
smooth stone, usually
found at the beach or the bottom of a river.

pe·can [pi-kahn *or* pee-kan] *noun, plural* **pecans.** a long,
thin, sweet nut with a smooth, reddish shell.

peck¹ [pek] *verb,* **pecked, pecking.** to strike, bite, or pick up
something with the beak: *The chickens pecked at the corn
scattered on the ground.*
noun, plural **pecks. 1.** a quick striking movement made
with the beak. **2.** a light, quick kiss: *He gave me a peck
goodnight on the cheek.*

peck² [pek] *noun, plural* **pecks. 1.** a unit of measure of
dry goods such as grain, equal to eight quarts. **2.** a large
quantity: *He has a peck of money.*

PEARLS

Pearls are organic gems that form naturally inside the shells of
oysters. When some grit or sand gets into the shell, the animal
inside protects itself by covering the grit with a substance called
nacre. The nacre builds up in layers
and after about seven years forms a
pearl. Cultured pearls are created
by placing a small bead inside a
shellfish, and take three to four
years to produce.

**How natural pearls
are formed**

**How cultured pearls
are formed**

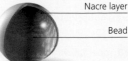

Nacre layer

Sand grain

Nacre layer

Bead

Pearl diver

A natural pearl (left) has more layers than a cultured pearl (right).

A **peddler** in a small Chinese town starts selling his fresh produce early in the morning.

peer

pe·cul·iar [pi-*kyool*-yur] *adjective.* **1.** describing something strange or odd: *There is a peculiar smell coming from the garage.* **2.** having to do with a particular person, place, or thing: *That expression is peculiar to Southerners.* —**peculiarly,** *adverb.*

pe·cu·li·ar·i·ty [pi-*kyool*-*yare*-uh-tee] *noun,* *plural* **peculiarities. 1.** the quality of being strange or odd: *The peculiarity of the house was that the ceilings were so low.* **2.** something that is a feature of only one particular person, place, or thing.

ped·al [*ped*-ul] *noun, plural* **pedals.** a foot-operated lever used to control mechanisms such as a bicycle, sewing machine, or piano.
verb, **pedaled, pedaling.** to push or use the pedals of something: *She pedaled hard on the bicycle to get up the hill.*
🔊 A different word with the same sound is **peddle.**

ped·dle [*ped*-ul] *verb,* **peddled, peddling.** to sell things by traveling about from place to place: *The door-to-door salesman peddled his kitchen products.*
🔊 A different word with the same sound is **pedal.**

ped·dler ▶ [*ped*-lur] *noun, plural* **peddlers.** someone who travels about from place to place to sell goods and wares.

ped·es·tal ▼ [*ped*-i-stul] *noun, plural* **pedestals.**
1. the supporting base on which a column or statue stands. **2.** the supporting base of something upright, such as a vase or lamp.
• **put on a pedestal.** to believe that someone is perfect or has no faults: *When I first met her, I really put her on a pedestal.*

ped·es·tri·an [puh-*des*-tree-un] *noun,*
plural **pedestrians.** someone who travels on foot; a person who walks: *Drivers must be careful of pedestrians crossing the road.*
adjective. not interesting; dull: *His speech was very pedestrian and the audience quickly became bored.*

pe·di·a·tri·cian [*pee*-dee-uh-*trish*-un] *noun,* *plural* **pediatricians.** *Medicine.* a doctor who specializes in treating children and their illnesses. The branch of medicine concerned with the care and treatment of children is **pediatrics.**

ped·i·gree [*ped*-uh-*gree*] *noun,* *plural* **pedigrees.** a list of parents and other past relatives of an animal: *We checked the dog's pedigree with the breeder before we bought it.*

peek [peek] *verb,* **peeked, peeking.** to look quickly while trying to avoid being seen; peep: *I peeked through the curtains to see who was outside.*
noun, plural **peeks.** a quick or secret look.
🔊 A different word with the same sound is **peak.**

peel [peel] *noun, plural* **peels.** the skin or rind of a fruit or vegetable: *a potato peel.*
verb, **peeled, peeling. 1.** to take off the skin or rind of fruits or vegetables: *I helped Mom peel the apples for the apple pie she was baking.* A **peeler** is a utensil used to remove the skin of fruits or vegetables. **2.** to strip or tear off; take or come off in strips: *He peeled off the wallpaper to sand the walls down.* **3.** to lose an outer layer: *The skin on my face is peeling from my day out in the sun.*
🔊 A different word with the same sound is **peal.**

peep[1] [peep] *verb,* **pepped, peeping. 1.** to secretly look at something through a small opening or hiding place: *The little boy peeped through a crack in the door to catch a glimpse of the Christmas presents.* **2.** to appear slowly and only be partially seen: *The sun peeped out over the top of the mountains.*
noun, plural **peeps.** a secret or quick look.

peep[2] [peep] *noun,* *plural* **peeps.** a weak, high noise made by young bird or mouse.
verb, **peeped, peeping.** to make a weak, high noise: *The chicks peeped as they chased after the mother hen.*

peer[1] [peer] *verb,* **peered, peering.** to look closely and carefully in order to see clearly: *She peered into the dark movie theater, trying to figure out where her friends were sitting.*
🔊 A different word with the same sound is **pier.**

peer[2] [peer] *noun, plural* **peers.**
1. someone who is of the same age, social status, or has the same abilities as another: *Teenagers can be easily influenced by their peers.* **2.** a member of one of the five ranks of the British nobility. The rank or title of a peer is called a **peerage.**
🔊 A different word with the same sound is **pier.**

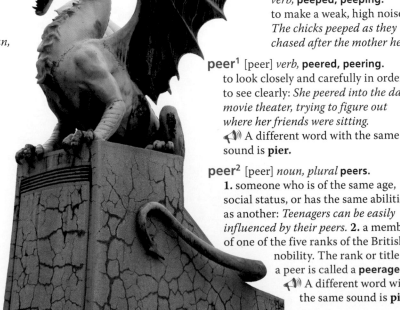

A statue of a dragon stands on a **pedestal** at each corner of the Dragon Bridge in Ljubljana, Slovenia.

507

a b c d e f g h i j k l m n o p q r s t u v w x y z

*The brown **pelican** is found near sandy beaches, lagoons, and other waterfront areas.*

peer pressure pressure from your peers to behave in a similar way to them if you want to be accepted and liked.

peg [peg] *noun, plural* **pegs.** a small wooden, plastic, or metal pin used to pin down, fasten together, mark a place, or hang things on.
verb, **pegged, pegging. 1.** to insert with, fasten, or mark something with pegs. **2.** to restrict something or fix it in place; limit: *to fix the price of gasoline.*

Pe·king·ese [*peek*-uh-*neez*] *noun, plural* **Pekingese.** a Chinese breed of small dog with long, silky hair and a short, flat nose.

pel·i·can ▶ [*pel*-uh-kun] *noun, plural* **pelicans.** a large water bird with a pouch that hangs beneath its bill for holding the fish it catches.

pel·let [*pel*-it] *noun, plural* **pellets.** a small, rounded piece of something: *I cleaned out the rabbit cage and filled the bowl with food pellets.*

pell-mell [*pel-mel*] *adverb.* in a fast and uncontrolled way: *When the fire alarm went off, the crowd ran pell-mell for the nearest exit.*

pelt[1] [pelt] *verb,* **pelted, pelting.** to attack by throwing a large number of things: *The rioters pelted stones and bottles at the police.*

pelt[2] ▼ [pelt] *noun, plural* **pelts.** the skin of a dead animal, usually with the fur or hair still on it, ready to be made into leather.

pen[1] [pen] *noun, plural* **pens.** a long, thin instrument for writing or drawing with ink.

pen[2] [pen] *noun, plural* **pens. 1.** a small fenced area in which farm animals are kept. **2.** a small enclosed area.
verb, **penned, penning.** to shut in pen: *The cows were penned in for the night.*

pe·nal·ize [*pen*-uh-*lize* or *pee*-nuh-*lize*] *verb,* **penalized, penalizing.** to punish or place at a disadvantage: *The football player was penalized for kicking an opponent.*

pen·al·ty [*pen*-ul-tee] *noun, plural* **penalties.**
1. a punishment for breaking a law: *The penalty for drink driving is a fine and a jail sentence.*
2. in sports, an advantage given to one team or player when the opposition has broken the rules: *Our team was awarded a penalty kick.*

pen·cil [*pen*-sul] *noun, plural* **pencils.** a long, thin instrument used for writing or drawing. The wooden or plastic case contains a strip of graphite, which is the marking substance.
verb, **penciled, penciling.** to write, draw, mark, or color with a pencil: *I penciled the name and address onto the envelope.*

pend·ant [*pen*-dunt] *noun, plural* **pendants.** an ornament, such as a jewel or locket, that hangs from a necklace.

pen·du·lum ▶ [*pen*-juh-lum or *pen*-duh-lum] *noun, plural* **pendulums.** a weight suspended from a fixed point that swings backward and forward to control the working of a clock.

pen·e·trate [*pen*-uh-*trate*] *verb,* **penetrated, penetrating.**
1. to pierce or go through something: *The arrow penetrated the target.* **2.** to study something and come to understand it: *The detective tried to penetrate the mystery surrounding the crime.*
—penetration, *noun.*

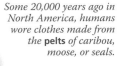

Pendulums were first used in clocks in the seventeenth century.

pen·guin ▶ [*peng*-gwin] *noun, plural* **penguins.** a black and white sea bird that cannot fly. It has webbed feet and flipper-like wings that are used for swimming.

pen·i·cil·lin [*pen*-uh-*sil*-un] *noun. Medicine.* a strong drug used to treat infections caused by bacteria.

*Some 20,000 years ago in North America, humans wore clothes made from the **pelts** of caribou, moose, or seals.*

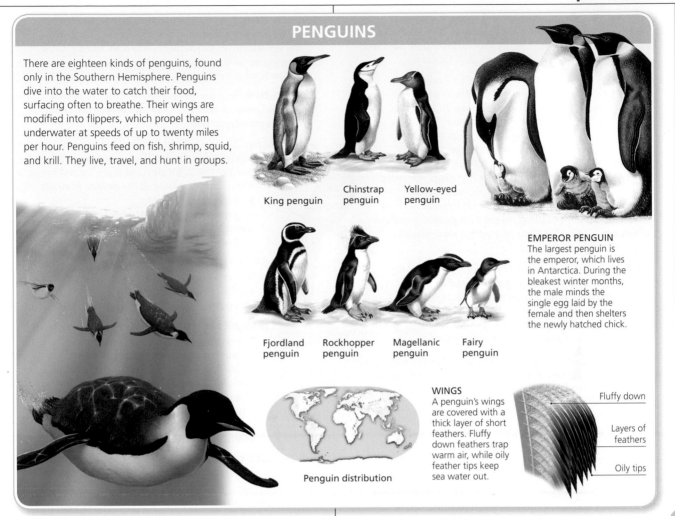

PENGUINS

There are eighteen kinds of penguins, found only in the Southern Hemisphere. Penguins dive into the water to catch their food, surfacing often to breathe. Their wings are modified into flippers, which propel them underwater at speeds of up to twenty miles per hour. Penguins feed on fish, shrimp, squid, and krill. They live, travel, and hunt in groups.

King penguin

Chinstrap penguin

Yellow-eyed penguin

EMPEROR PENGUIN
The largest penguin is the emperor, which lives in Antarctica. During the bleakest winter months, the male minds the single egg laid by the female and then shelters the newly hatched chick.

Fjordland penguin

Rockhopper penguin

Magellanic penguin

Fairy penguin

Penguin distribution

WINGS
A penguin's wings are covered with a thick layer of short feathers. Fluffy down feathers trap warm air, while oily feather tips keep sea water out.

Fluffy down

Layers of feathers

Oily tips

pen·in·su·la [puh-<u>nin</u>-suh-luh] *noun, plural* **peninsulas.** *Geography.* a long piece of land almost completely surrounded by water but still joined to a main area of land. Cape Cod is a peninsula.

> **Peninsula** comes from a phrase meaning "almost an island." The idea is that a peninsula extends far out into water but is still connected to the larger body of land behind it. In other words, it is almost, but not quite, an island.

pen·i·ten·tia·ry [*pen*-uh-<u>ten</u>-chur-ee] *noun, plural* **penitentiaries.** a state or federal prison in which serious offenders are held.

pen·knife [<u>pen</u>-*nife*] *noun, plural* **penknives.** a small pocketknife with a blade that folds into the handle.

pen·man·ship [<u>pen</u>-mun-*ship*] *noun. Language.* the art or practice of handwriting.

pen name *Literature.* a false name used by an author: *The pen name of Charles Lutwidge Dodgson was Lewis Carroll.*

pen·nant ▶ [<u>pen</u>-unt] *noun, plural* **pennants.** a long, narrow pointed flag used as a signal on a ship or as an emblem of victory.

pen·ni·less [<u>pen</u>-ee-lis] *adjective.* having no money whatsoever: *After he lost his job he moved in with his friend because he was almost penniless.*

pen·ny [<u>pen</u>-ee] *noun, plural* **pennies. 1.** a bronze or copper coin worth one cent, used in the United States and Canada. **2.** a British unit of money. One hundred pennies equal one pound.

pen·sion [<u>pen</u>-shun] *noun, plural* **pensions.** an amount of money paid regularly by a company or organization to someone who used to work for the company but is now is retired.

pen·ta·gon [<u>pen</u>-tuh-gon] *noun, plural* **pentagons.** *Mathematics.* a flat shape that has five sides. The **Pentagon** is a five-sided government building that serves as the headquarters of the United States Department of Defense.

pent·house [<u>pent</u>-hous] *noun, plural* **penthouses.** an expensive apartment or dwelling built on the roof or top story of a building.

Different colored **pennants** *have different meanings.*

A B C D E F G H I J K L M N O P Q R S T U V W X Y Z

pe·o·ny ◄ [pee-uh-nee] *noun,*
plural **peonies.** a type of garden
plant with large, round, dark red,
white, or pink flowers.

peo·ple [pee-pul] *noun,*
plural **people** or **peoples**
(for definition 2). **1.** human
beings; persons: *There were*
eighty people at the meeting
today. **2.** the persons who
belong to a particular country, race, or group: *the*
Jewish people. **3.** the public: *The President was voted*
into office by the people. **4.** family or relatives:
My grandfather's people came from Ireland.
verb, **peopled, peopling.** to fill with people; populate;
inhabit: *The early colony of Virginia was peopled*
by settlers from England.

pep [pep] *noun.* lively spirit; energy: *My morning jog*
along the river gives me pep for the rest of the day.
verb, **pepped, pepping.** to make or become lively
or spirited: *We changed the music to try to pep*
up the party. A **pep talk** is an emotional talk to
a person or group to motivate or inspire them.

pep·per [pep-ur] *noun, plural* **peppers. 1.** a hot spice made
from dried berries of a tropical plant used to flavor food.
2. a hollow red, green, or yellow vegetable eaten cooked
or raw. The berry of the black pepper plant is called
a **peppercorn.**
verb, **peppered, peppering. 1.** to flavor or season with
pepper: *I peppered the steak.* **2.** to cover, as if sprinkling
with pepper: *Her face was peppered with freckles after*
her summer vacation.

pep·per·mint [pep-ur-mint] *noun, plural* **peppermints.**
1. a mint herb cultivated for its strong-tasting and
strong-smelling oil. **2.** a candy made with peppermint oil.

per [pur] *preposition.* by or for each: *The buffet meal will*
cost ten dollars per person.

per·ceive [pur-seev] *verb,* **perceived, perceiving.**
1. to become aware of through one of the senses such
as hearing or sight: *She perceived an ambulance siren*
in the distance. **2.** to recognize; understand: *I perceived*
a change in his mood and could tell he was angry.

per·cent [pur-sent] *noun. Mathematics.* one part in
a hundred: *Twenty-five percent of the students failed*
the history test. The symbol used to represent the word
percent is %. For example, "ten percent" is written as
"10%." This word is also spelled **per cent.**

per·cent·age [pur-sen-tij] *noun, plural* **percentages.**
Mathematics. **1.** the rate or proportion in every hundred:
From that class, the percentage of students who went on
to college was high—70 percent. **2.** a part or proportion in
general: *Only a small percentage of students in that school*
will go onto college next year.

per·cent·ile [pur-sen-tile] *noun. Mathematics.*
in statistics, one of one hundred equal-sized parts that
a group of people can be divided into when comparing
things like their scores on a test.

per·cep·tion [pur-sep-shun] *noun, plural* **perceptions.**
1. the act of perceiving or understanding things through
the senses: *My visual perception is poor when I'm not*
wearing my glasses. **2.** the result of having
understood something.

per·cep·tive [pur-sep-tiv] *adjective.* quick to notice
and understand: *She is a clever and perceptive child.*
—**perceptively,** *adverb.*

perch¹ ◄ [purch] *noun, plural* **perches. 1.** a branch, bar, or
any place where a bird roosts: *The pigeon used the head*
of a statue as a perch. **2.** an elevated place for resting or
observing: *He watched the parade from his*
perch in his tree-house.
verb, **perched, perching.** to settle or rest on
a perch: *The child perched on the windowsill,*
waiting for her mother to come home.

Hooked claws
help the greater
racket-tailed
drongo to **perch**
on a branch.

perch² [purch] *noun, plural* **perch** or **perches.**
1. a small freshwater fish with a spiny fin found
in North America and most parts of Europe.
It is used for food. **2.** a similar saltwater fish.

per·co·late [pur-kuh-late] *verb,* **percolated,**
percolating. to flow or make flow gradually
through a substance or small holes; filter:
When you water a container plant, the water
percolates through the soil and seeps out
through the hole in the bottom of the pot.
The act of flowing through a substance or
small holes is called **percolation.** A device used
to make coffee in this way is called a **percolator.**

per·cus·sion [pur-kush-un] *noun.* **1.** the forceful
striking of one thing against another: *The percussion of*
rain water on the sandstone over thousands of years had
worn many holes in the rock. **2.** the sound or vibration
that results from one thing striking forcefully against
another: *The percussion of the waterfall on the rocks*
below drowned out all other sounds.

percussion instrument ▼ *Music.* a musical instrument
that is struck or shaken to produce a sound. Drums,
tambourines, pianos, and xylophones are examples
of percussion instruments.

A drum kit usually includes:
cymbals, a snare drum, and
a bass drum, which are all
percussion instruments.

Yarrow   Violet   Foxglove   Lily   Iris

pe·ren·ni·al ▲ [puh-<u>ren</u>-ee-ul] *adjective.* **1.** lasting or existing through all seasons of the year: *The stream that runs through our farm is perennial and does not dry up in the summer months.* **2.** of plants, living for more than two years: *A perennial plant like the daisy continues to produce flowers year after year.* **3.** lasting for a long time; enduring: *Some singers go on performing for many years and are a perennial favorite with audiences.*
noun, plural **perennials.** a plant that lives and produces flowers for more than two years. —**perennially,** *adverb.*

per·fect [<u>pur</u>-fikt] *adjective.* **1.** having nothing wrong with it; having no fault; so good that it could not be better: *In bowling, if you knock down all the pins with every ball you roll, you have a perfect score of 300.* **2.** as you wish it to be; excellent or ideal: *I think that swimming in the lake is the perfect way to spend a summer afternoon.* **3.** complete; total: *I felt like a perfect fool when I went to introduce our neighbor to my friend and couldn't remember her name.*

per·fec·tion [pur-<u>fek</u>-shun] *noun.* **1.** the state of having no fault or wrong; total excellence: *I took the cake out of the oven and found it was cooked to perfection.* **2.** the act or process of making something perfect or faultless: *The perfection of the plow as a farming tool involved much trial and error.*

per·fect·ly [<u>pur</u>-fikt-lee] *adverb.* **1.** without fault or blemish; in a way that could not be better: *My dad oiled the latch on our gate, and now it closes perfectly.* **2.** completely; totally: *I don't have to tie my little sister's shoelaces, as she is perfectly able to do it on her own.*

perfect tense *Language.* the form of a verb expressing an action or state that has been completed at the time someone is speaking or at the time spoken of. It is made up of "have" or "has" and a past participle. In the sentence *I have finished my work,* the verb "have finished" is in the perfect tense.

per·fo·rate [<u>pur</u>-fuh-*rate*] *verb,* **perforated, perforating.** to make a hole or holes through, especially a row of holes that makes it easy to tear two sheets of paper apart: *Special machines perforate sheets of stamps.* The act of perforating or the state of being perforated, is **perforation.**

per·form [pur-<u>form</u>] *verb,* **performed, performing.** **1.** to carry out; do: *My friend Gerry looked very happy as he performed the ceremony of blowing out the candles on his birthday cake.* **2.** to act in a play, play music, sing, or do something else that requires skill in front of an audience: *When I performed in the school play this year, it was my first time on stage.*

per·form·ance [pur-<u>for</u>-muns] *noun, plural* **performances.** **1.** a public presentation of some kind of entertainment: *Our school concert was so popular that we are giving an extra performance on Friday.* **2.** the act of doing or carrying out something: *The mayor takes the performance of his official duties very seriously.* **3.** the way something runs or functions: *My dad was disappointed with the performance of his car, and wanted to have the engine checked out.*

per·form·er [pur-<u>for</u>-mur] *noun, plural* **performers.** someone who acts, plays music, sings, or does something else that requires skill in front of an audience, especially for entertainment. Movie actors, musicians, and trapeze artists are examples of performers.

per·fume [<u>pur</u>-fyoom] *noun, plural* **perfumes.** **1.** a substance, usually a liquid, used to give people or things a pleasing smell. **2.** a pleasing, usually sweet, smell. *verb,* **perfumed, perfuming.** to fill with a pleasing smell: *A big bunch of roses perfumed the air of the hallway.*

per·haps [pur-<u>haps</u>] *adverb.* maybe; possibly: *Perhaps I'll go to the pool for a swim this afternoon.*

per·il [<u>per</u>-ul] *noun, plural* **perils. 1.** a risk of serious harm or injury; danger: *The father put his own life in peril by diving into the water to save his drowning child.* **2.** something that presents immediate danger: *Frostbite and altitude sickness are two of the perils faced by people who try to climb Mt. Everest.*

per·i·lous [<u>per</u>-uh-lus] *adjective.* full of danger; risky; unsafe: *Rock climbing is a perilous sport.* —**perilously,** *adverb.*

pe·rim·e·ter [puh-<u>rim</u>-uh-tur] *noun, plural* **perimeters.** the outer boundary or edge of an enclosed area: *The fence that surrounds our yard marks the perimeter of property.*

pe·ri·od [<u>peer</u>-ee-ud] *noun, plural* **periods. 1.** a length or portion of time: *A week is a period of seven days.* **2.** a punctuation mark (.) used to mark the end of a sentence other than a question or an exclamation. It is also used at the end of an abbreviation, as in *Dr.* or *etc.*

The **period** is the simplest and most common form of punctuation. Its main use is to show the end of a sentence. (Don't forget to use periods for sentences in your writing.) In British English a period is also called a *full stop.* This is a good name because it means that when you read, a period tells you this is a place to stop for a moment. On the other hand a comma means you should slow down a bit but not make a stop.

pe·ri·od·ic [*peer-ee-od-ik*] *adjective.* happening at regular intervals; occurring every so often: *When we spend the summer in the mountains, we make periodic visits to town to buy supplies.* —**periodically**, *adverb.*

periodic table *Chemistry.* a table listing the chemical elements in a way that groups those with common characteristics. The elements are listed in order of their atomic number and usually arranged in rows, so that elements with a similar atomic structure appear in columns.

pe·ri·od·i·cal [*peer-ee-od-uh-kul*] *noun, plural* **periodicals.** *Literature.* a magazine published every so often at a regular time. Most periodicals come out once every week, every month, or every three months.

per·i·scope ▲ [*per-uh-skope*] *noun, plural* **periscopes.** a device with a tube and mirrors that looks similar to a telescope held upright. When raised up from the top of a submarine, it allows a person to see what is above the surface of the water, such as land and ships.

per·ish [*per-ish*] *verb,* **perished, perishing.** to be destroyed; cease to exist; die: *The mountain climber perished in an avalanche.*

per·ish·a·ble [*per-ish-uh-bul*] *adjective.* likely to spoil or decay within a fairly short time: *Fresh fruits and vegetables are perishable.*

per·ju·ry [*pur-jur-ee*] *noun, plural* **perjuries.** *Law.* the act or crime of lying after swearing to tell the truth, especially in a court of law. Someone who does this is a **perjurer.**

perk [*purk*] *verb,* **perked, perking. 1.** to lift or raise quickly or in a lively way: *My dog perks up her ears whenever she hears the refrigerator door opening.* **2.** to make or become more cheerful; liven up; brighten up: *He was disappointed when his team lost, but he perked up when the coach told him he played a really good game.* Someone or something that is lively and cheerful is **perky.**

per·ma·frost ▶ [*pur-muh-frost*] *noun.* *Environment.* ground that is permanently frozen, as in parts of Alaska and Canada.

per·ma·nent [*pur-muh-nunt*] *adjective.* lasting or meant to last forever or for a very long time; not changing: *Now that the new clubhouse has been built, our club has a permanent home.* The state of lasting forever or for a very long time is **permanence.**
noun, plural **permanents.** a hairdressing technique that uses rollers or rods, chemicals, and heat to produce long-lasting waves. —**permanently**, *adverb.*

per·mis·sion [*pur-mish-un*] *noun.* the fact of being allowed by someone in authority to do something: *I asked my parents for permission to go to the rock concert in the park.* Something that is allowed to be done is **permissible.**

per·mis·sive [*pur-mis-iv*] *adjective.* granting, or being inclined to grant, permission to do things; allowing a lot of freedom to do things. —**permissiveness**, *noun.*

per·mit [*pur-mit for verb;* *pur-mit for noun*] *verb,* **permitted, permitting.** to allow or let: *My parents permit me to spend my pocket money however I like.* **Permitting** is used to indicate that something will happen as long as there is a suitable opportunity to do it: *We'll go for a picnic tomorrow, weather permitting.*
noun, plural **permits.** a document showing you have permission to do something: *My dad has a permit that allows him to park his car on our street.*

per·pen·dic·u·lar [*pur-pin-dik-yuh-lur*] *adjective.* **1.** describing something upright; vertical; very steep: *As we looked up at the perpendicular face of the huge rock, we were amazed to see the tiny figures of two climbers near the top.* **2.** *Mathematics.* at right angles to a given line or surface: *The walls of a house are normally perpendicular to the ground.* —**perpendicularly**, *adverb.*

per·pet·u·al [*pur-pech-oo-ul*] *adjective.* **1.** lasting forever or for a very long time: *The pyramids are a perpetual monument to the pharaohs of ancient Egypt.* **2.** continuing without interruption: *Night follows day in a perpetual cycle.* —**perpetually**, *adverb.*

perpetual motion *Science.* the motion of an object that keeps moving forever without being driven by an outside source of energy. Though various machines to do this were proposed in earlier times, perpetual motion is not possible.

per·pet·u·ate [*pur-pech-oo-ate*] *verb,* **perpetuated, perpetuating.** to make last for a long time or forever; preserve: *Statues perpetuate the memory of important people.* —**perpetuation**, *noun.*

*The Utah Mountains are covered in **permafrost** in winter.*

per·plex [pur-pleks] *verb*, **perplexed, perplexing.** to puzzle or bewilder: *My grandfather says that the way computers work perplexes him.*

per·se·cute [pur-suh-kyoot] *verb*, **persecuted, persecuting.** to continually treat someone badly or in a cruel way, especially because you do not agree with what he or she believes: *The dictator persecuted the citizens who spoke out in favor of democracy.* Someone who acts in this way is a **persecutor.**

per·se·cu·tion [pur-suh-kyoo-shun] *noun*, *plural* **persecutions.** continual bad or cruel treatment of someone, especially because you do not agree with what he or she believes: *The Pilgrims came to America from Europe to escape persecution for their religious beliefs.*

Per·sian ▶ [pur-zhun] *noun*, *plural* **Persians. 1.** someone who lived in the ancient empire of Persia, in southwestern Asia. **2.** the language of ancient Persia or modern Iran. *adjective.* of or having to do with Persia, its people, or its culture.

Handwoven **Persian** *carpets are famous for their individual designs and rich colors.*

Persian Gulf War *History.* a war fought in 1990–1991 in the Middle East between Iraq and the U.S. and a number of other countries as a combined force of the United Nations.

per·sim·mon [pur-sim-un] *noun*, *plural*, **persimmons.** a fruit similar to a plum, but with orange skin. It grows on an evergreen tree. Persimmons are eaten when fully ripe. They are very bitter when unripe.

per·sist [pur-sist] *verb*, **persisted, persisting. 1.** to keep doing something in spite of difficulties or opposition; not give up: *I found it hard to learn to play the guitar, but I persisted, and now I can play lots of songs.* **2.** to last for a long time; continue to exist: *The strong winds persisted all day and finally dropped around nightfall.*

per·sist·ent [pur-sis-tunt] *adjective.* **1.** continuing to do something in spite of difficulties or opposition: *You need to be persistent to achieve your goals in life.* **2.** lasting for a long time; continuing to exist: *My accident left me with a persistent limp for a few months, but my leg is fine now.* The fact of being persistent is **persistence.** —**persistently,** *adverb.*

per·son [pur-suhn] *noun*, *plural* **persons. 1.** an individual human being; a man, woman, or child: *Everyone who knows my doctor says what a kind, gentle person she is.* **2.** the living body of a human being: *The police searched the man to find out if he had any weapons on his person.* **3.** *Language.* one of three groups of personal pronouns and the verb forms they take. The **first person** refers to the person or persons speaking: *I; me; we; us.* The **second person** refers to the person or persons spoken to: *you.* The **third person** refers to the person or persons spoken about: *he; him; she; her; it; they; them.*
• **in person.** physically present; actually there: *The Governor visited our school, and I was thrilled to see him in person.*

per·son·a·ble [pur-suh-nuh-bul *or* purs-nuh-bul] *adjective.* having a pleasing appearance or manner: *Our school principal is very personable, and is popular with the students and parents alike.*

per·son·al [pur-suh-nul *or* purs-nul] *adjective.* **1.** describing something private; not public: *My mom says that love letters are personal and should not be read by outsiders.* **2.** done in person: *The President made a personal appearance at the opening game of the season.* **3.** having to do with a person's body: *personal grooming.*

personal computer *Computers.* a small computer with a microprocessor designed to be used by a single person. Personal computers are used at home, at school, and in offices and other places of business.

per·son·al·i·ty [pur-suh-nal-uh-tee] *noun*, *plural* **personalities. 1.** a person's characteristics, qualities, feelings, and behavior taken as a whole. Personality is an important part of our identity. It is what makes us different from everyone else. *My grandmother has a warm and cheerful personality, and makes everyone feel welcome.* **2.** a famous or well-known person: *Pelé and David Beckham are two of the best-known personalities in the world of soccer.*

per·son·al·ly [pur-sun-uh-lee *or* purs-nuh-lee] *adverb.* **1.** by oneself; in person: *Our neighbor employs many plumbers in his business, but he came around personally to fix our leaking water pipe.* **2.** as far as one oneself is concerned; for oneself: *Personally, I think we should invite all our cousins to the party.* **3.** as a person: *I like the president of our tennis club personally, but I don't think he is very good at getting things done.*

per·son·nel [purs-uh-nel] *noun.* the people employed by a company or other organization.

per·spec·tive ▶ [pur-spek-tiv] *noun*, *plural* **perspectives. 1.** a way of drawing or painting a scene to make it look as though the objects in it have depth and distance. **2.** a point of view: *From the perspective of an old man with a walking stick, the stairs looked impossibly steep.* **3.** a view of the relative size or importance of things or events: *If you get too close to a problem, you can't put it in perspective, and it often seems worse than it is.*

This architect's design for a shopping center is drawn in **perspective.**

per·spi·ra·tion [purs-puh-ray-shun] *noun.* **1.** moisture given off the body through the pores of the skin; sweat. **2.** the process of sweating. Perspiration or sweating is the body's way of cooling down when it gets too hot.

per·spire [pur-spire] *verb*, **perspired, perspiring.** to give off moisture through the pores of the skin; sweat: *It's natural to perspire when you run hard playing sport.*

A B C D E F G H I J K L M N O P Q R S T U V W X Y Z

per·suade [pur-swade] *verb,* **persuaded, persuading.** to cause someone to believe or do something by pleading, giving reasons, or offering something in return; convince: *The doctor persuaded my dad to give up smoking by telling him how harmful it is to his health.*

per·sua·sion [pur-sway-zhun] *noun, plural* **persuasions.** the act or fact of persuading someone to believe or do something by pleading, giving reasons, or offering something in return: *My brother has great powers of persuasion, and we usually end up doing what he wants.* Someone who is able to easily persuade others is **persuasive.**

per·tain [pur-tane] *verb,* **pertained, pertaining.** to refer to or be related to: *I read a lot of magazines pertaining to car racing.*

per·ti·nent [purt-uh-nunt] *adjective.* having to do with what is being discussed or thought about; relevant: *When you write an essay, it's important to keep to pertinent facts and not wander off the point.* —**pertinence,** *noun.*

Pe·ru·vi·an ▶ [puh-roov-ee-un] *noun, plural* **Peruvians.** someone who was born or lives in the country of Peru, in South America. *adjective.* of or having to do with Peru, its people, or its culture.

More than three million **Peruvians** *speak Quecha, the language of the Inca Empire.*

per·vade [pur-vade] *verb,* **pervaded, pervading.** to spread or pass throughout: *The smell of hot doughnuts pervaded the air.* Something that spreads throughout is described as being **pervasive.**

pe·so [pay-soh] *noun, plural* **pesos.** the name of the unit of money used in Mexico and several countries in South America, and also in Cuba, the Dominican Republic, and the Philippines.

pes·si·mist [pes-uh-mist] *noun, plural* **pessimists.** someone who usually expects the worst, or believes that bad things happen more often than good things do: *It's often said that a pessimist sees a glass half empty, while an optimist sees a glass half full.* The way of thinking of someone who expects that bad things will happen more often than good things do, is **pessimism.**

pes·si·mis·tic [pes-uh-mis-tik] *adjective.* expecting the worst; seeing things in a negative way: *When I heard how many students planned to audition for the role in the school play, I was pessimistic about my chances of getting it.* —**pessimistically,** *adverb.*

pest ▶ [pest] *noun, plural* **pests.** someone or something that is annoying or harmful; a nuisance: *My mom calls our dog a pest when he digs up the garden.*

Pest is what is known as a *subjective* word, meaning the idea of the word can change according to the situation and ideas that people have about it. A pest is an animal or plant thought of as damaging, dangerous, annoying, and so on, but this idea can change. An insect, such as a bee, might be useful to humans in one situation but be a pest in another situation.

pes·ter [pes-tur] *verb,* **pestered, pestering.** to keep annoying or bothering someone, especially by asking for something or asking questions: *The child pestered his mother for an ice-cream cone.*

pes·ti·cide [pes-tuh-side] *noun, plural* **pesticides.** a substance that kills harmful or destructive insect or animal pests, such as mosquitoes, mice, and rats.

pes·tle ▶ [pes-ul] *noun, plural* **pestles.** a tool with a heavy, rounded end, like a club, used for pounding or grinding something in a bowl called a mortar.

A **pestle** *can be used to grind spices for cooking.*

pet [pet] *noun, plural* **pets. 1.** a tame animal kept for pleasure and companionship. Cats, dogs, and birds are the most common pets people keep. **2.** a person given special treatment; a favorite: *No student likes to be called the teacher's pet. adjective.* kept or treated as a pet: *a pet donkey.* *verb,* **petted, petting.** to stroke or pat in an affectionate way: *My dog puts her head on my lap when she wants me to pet her.*

pet·al [pet-ul] *noun, plural* **petals.** one of the separate outer parts of a flower. Petals come in many shapes, sizes, and colors. *The petals of a rose start out tightly curled and gradually open to reveal the center of the flower.*

pe·ti·tion [puh-tish-un] *noun, plural* **petitions.** a formal request made to someone in authority, especially a written one signed by many people: *People in our neighborhood signed a petition asking the mayor to turn the city's vacant land into a public park.* *verb,* **petitioned, petitioning.** to make a formal request of this kind: *A group of citizens petitioned the city to widen the bridge into town.*

pet·ri·fy [pet-ruh-fye] *verb,* **petrified, petrifying. 1.** to turn into stone or a stony substance. **Petrified wood** is a fossil formed when fallen trees become buried under soil and other material. **2.** to paralyze or make helpless with fear or amazement: *The sight of a rattlesnake ahead petrified the child, but his father quickly pulled him away to safety.* Something that has been turned to stone, or someone who is paralyzed with fear or amazement, is described as being **petrified.**

pet·ro·chem·i·cal [pet-roh-kem-i-kul] *noun, plural* **petrochemicals.** *Chemistry.* a substance obtained from petroleum or natural gas. Gasoline, kerosene, airplane fuel, and many pesticides are petrochemicals.

Rats are considered to be **pests** *because they spread disease.*

pe·tro·le·um ▲
[puh-<u>troh</u>-lee-um]
noun. Chemistry.
an oily liquid found
beneath the surface
of the earth and
obtained by digging
wells into the ground. It is made into gasoline, kerosene,
fuel for airplanes and heating, and many other products.

> The word **petroleum** is from two Latin words meaning "rock" and "oil." Oil is found under the ground in tiny spaces in rock formations, and early people knew of oil only when it seeped out of the rock and came to the surface.

pet·rol·o·gy [puh-<u>trol</u>-uh-jee] *noun. Science.* the branch
of geology that has to do with the study of rocks.
A **petrologist** studies such things as how rocks form and
what they are made of.

pet·ti·coat [<u>pet</u>-ee-*kote*] *noun, plural* **petticoats.** a skirt
or slip made to be worn under an outer skirt or dress.

pet·ty [<u>pet</u>-ee] *adjective.* **1.** not important; trivial: *Let's
not waste time discussing petty details.* **2.** describing
something mean; not generous: *My mom told me never
to take notice of petty gossip.* —**pettiness,** *noun.*

pe·tu·nia [puh-<u>too</u>-nyuh] *noun, plural* **petunias.** a garden
plant with showy, trumpet-shaped flowers. Petunias are
annuals, and come in many colors.

pew [pyoo] *noun, plural* **pews.** a bench with a back
for people to sit on in church. Pews are arranged
in rows.

pew·ter [<u>pyoo</u>-tur] *noun.* a metallic substance
that is an alloy of tin and one or more other
metals. Originally, pewter was an alloy of tin
and lead, but lead is no longer used. Pewter is used
to make household utensils such as plates, mugs,
and candlesticks.

pg. an abbreviation for PAGE.

pH *noun. Chemistry.* a measure of the amount of acid
or alkali present in something, such as soil, water,
or some other substance.

phan·tom [<u>fan</u>-tum] *noun, plural* **phantoms.**
something that seems to exist, but is not real.
adjective. describing something that seems to exist
but does not.

Phar·aoh ▶ [<u>fare</u>-oh] *noun, plural* **Pharaohs.** the title
for a ruler of ancient Egypt.

phar·ma·cist [<u>far</u>-muh-*sist*] *noun, plural* **pharmacists.**
someone who is trained and legally allowed to
prepare and sell medicine and drugs.

phar·ma·col·o·gy [*far*-muh-<u>kol</u>-i-jee] *noun. Medicine.*
the science or study of drugs and medicines, including
what they are made of, their uses, and their effects.
Someone who practices pharmacology is a **pharmacologist.**

phar·ma·cy [<u>far</u>-muh-see] *noun, plural* **pharmacies.** a place
in which drugs used as medicines are made up and sold;
also called a drugstore.

phase [faze] *noun, plural* **phases. 1.** a particular stage
in a cycle, or a period of time in a sequence of events:
*Measuring ingredients, cooking, and cleaning up are all
phases of food preparation; My little sister went through a
phase of sucking her thumb.* **2.** any of the Moon's changing
shapes of light as the Earth moves around the Sun.
• **phase out.** to discontinue the practice of doing
something: *We're starting to phase out the old school
sports uniforms—by the end of the year, all the teams
will be wearing the new ones.*

phea·sant ▶ [<u>fez</u>-unt] *noun, plural* **pheasants.** a large,
long-tailed bird that lives on the ground and is killed
for its meat. The male usually as bright feathers.

phe·nom·e·non [fuh-<u>nom</u>-uh-nul] *noun,
plural* **phenomena** *or* **phenomenons.**
1. an occurrence, fact, or event that can
be seen: *The phenomenon of salmon
jumping upstream to breed is amazing
to watch.* **2.** an unusual or rare event,
often one that cannot be explained.
3. an extraordinary or amazing person. An amazing
event or action carried out by someone is described
as **phenomenal. —phenomenally,** *adverb.*

Reeves's **pheasant**
*has longer tail
feathers than any
other bird.*

PHARAOHS

The Pharaohs made ancient
Egypt a rich and powerful
nation, and ordered the
building of great temples
for the gods and elaborate
tombs for themselves.
Their subjects believed
that all Pharaohs were
god-kings who controlled
the Nile River, the growth
of crops, and foreign
trade. Everyone had
to kneel and kiss the
ground when they
approached the royal
person. A son inherited
his father's throne.
Pharaohs' wives were
also important, but only
a few women ever ruled
the country.

Foreign visitors at
the Pharaoh's court

*Early **phonographs** had a large funnel to make the sound louder.*

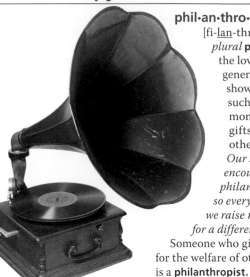

phil·an·thro·py
[fi-*lan*-thruh-*pee*] *noun,* *plural* **philanthropies.** the love of people in general, especially shown by actions such as giving money or other gifts to help other people: *Our school encourages philanthropy, so every month we raise money for a different charity.* Someone who gives money for the welfare of other people is a **philanthropist.**

phil·o·den·dron [fil-uh-*den*-drun] *noun,* *plural* **philodendrons.** any of a variety of tropical American climbing plants, often grown indoors as a houseplant.

phi·los·oph·er [fi-*los*-uh-fur] *noun,* *plural* **philosophers.** someone who studies or is concerned with the nature of life, knowledge, truth, values, and existence.

phi·los·oph·ic·al [fil-uh-*sof*-uh-kul] *adjective.* concerned with understanding the nature of life. —**philosophically,** *adverb.*

phi·los·oph·y
[fi-*los*-uh-fee] *noun,* *plural* **philosophies.**
1. the study of the nature of life, concerned with such matters as knowledge, truth, existence, and values.
2. someone's particular beliefs and values: *My philosophy on war is that no one ever wins.*

> The word **philosophy** comes from two Greek words meaning "the love of knowledge." A philosopher loves to learn and know things and to study questions such as the proper way to think and act and the true nature of life and the universe.

pho·bi·a [*fo*-bee-uh] *noun,* *plural* **phobias.** *Health.* a powerful and ongoing fear or dislike of something: *I cannot go into the woods because of my phobia of snakes.* Someone who has a phobia of something is said to be **phobic.**

phone [fone] *noun,* *plural* **phones.** a telephone.
verb, **phoned, phoning.** to use a telephone to call someone: *She phoned to ask me to go to the movies.*

pho·net·ics [fuh-*net*-iks] *plural noun.* *Language.* the study of speech sounds and how they are made and heard. Things connected with the sounds of speech, and symbols that represent particular sounds of speech, are said to be **phonetic. —phonetically,** *adverb.*

phon·ics [*fon*-iks] *noun.* *Education.* a method of teaching reading by training people to link individual letters or group of letters with their speech sounds.

pho·no·graph ◀ [*foh*-nuh-*graf*] *noun,* *plural* **phonographs.** a machine that plays sound that has been recorded onto a disk called a record.

pho·ny [*foh*-nee] *noun,* *plural* **phonies.** something or someone who is not genuine; a fake: *She's such a phony, she pretended to like me so she could come to my party.*

phos·pho·rus [*fos*-fur-us] *noun.* *Chemistry.* a chemical element that is essential for the growth and development of plants and animals. It is white or yellowish, with an unpleasant smell, and it glows faintly in the dark. Something that continues to glow even after the source of its light is gone is called **phosphorescent.**

pho·to [*foh*-toh] *noun,* *plural* **photos.** the shortened version of PHOTOGRAPH.

pho·to·cop·y [*foh*-toh-*kop*-ee] *noun,* *plural* **photocopies.** a copy made of something written, printed, or drawn by a machine that uses a photographic process. The machine is called a **photocopier.**
verb, **photocopied, photocopying.** to make a copy of something using this process.

pho·to·gen·ic [*foh*-tuh-*jen*-ik] *adjective.* tending to look good in photographs: *Usually my best friend Sarah is photogenic, but she doesn't look as pretty as usual in this photo.*

pho·to·graph [*foh*-tuh-*graf*] *noun,* *plural* **photographs.** a print or slide made from film in a camera, or a digital image captured by a camera.
verb, **photographed, photographing.** to use a camera to capture an image: *The coach photographed us accepting our awards.*

> **Photograph** comes from two Latin words meaning "light" and "writing." The idea is that a photograph captures light and then records it. That is, it "writes" an image on a piece of film or, these days, in a computer file. Other similar words are *phonograph* ("sound writing") and *telegraph* ("distant writing.")

pho·to·graph·er [fuh-*tog*-ruh-fur] *noun,* *plural* **photographers.** someone who takes photos for work or for fun.

pho·to·graph·y [fuh-*tog*-ruh-fee] *noun.* *Art.* the processes involved in making photographs.

pho·to·syn·the·sis [*foh*-toh-*sin*-thuh-sis] *noun.* *Biology.* the process by which plants make food to live on from sunlight, water, and carbon dioxide. This process is described as **photosynthetic.**

pho·to·vol·taic ◀
[*foh*-toh-vol-*tay*-ik] *adjective.* *Science.* able to produce a voltage when exposed to light or other radiant energy. Photovoltaic cells can be used as a source of energy. An abbreviation for this word is **PV.**

Photovoltaic cells power this solar telephone in Saudi Arabia.

phrase [fraze] *noun, plural* **phrases. 1.** *Language.* a group of words that have meaning in themselves, but which do not have the grammatical elements to make up a separate sentence. In the sentence *I jumped over the fence*, "over the fence" is a phrase. **2.** a short saying or expression: *"Go ahead, make my day" is a phrase made famous by Clint Eastwood.*
verb, **phrased, phrasing.** to express using a particular selection of words: *The baseball coach phrased his criticism of our loss gently.*

phys·i·cal [fiz-uh-kul] *adjective.* **1.** having to do with the body; describing something separate from the mind or soul: *His physical appearance is fine, but deep down he is unhappy.* **2.** relating to matter and energy: *The physical law of gravity makes a ball come down after it has been thrown in the air.* **3.** relating to nature or natural objects: *Sand, waves, and salt water are physical features of a beach.* **—physically,** *adverb.*

physical education *Education.* **1.** a school subject that focuses on sports, exercise, and other physical activities. **2.** instruction in the development and healthy maintenance of the human body, often with a focus on sport and exercise. An abbreviation for this term is **PE.**

physical fitness *Health.* the state of the body's health; the condition of health that makes a person suitable for a particular activity: *I go to the gym to increase my physical fitness.*

physical science *Science.* any science that deals with matter and energy, such as chemistry, physics, astronomy, or geology.

physical therapy *Health.* the process of treating illness and injury by physical and mechanical means, such as exercise and massage. Physical therapy differs from treatment that uses drugs and medicines or psychological methods. An abbreviation for this term is **PT.**

phy·si·cian [fuh-zish-un] *noun, plural* **physicians.** someone who is legally qualified to diagnose and treat illness and injury; a doctor.

phys·i·cist [fiz-uh-sist] *noun, plural* **physicists.** *Science.* a scientist whose specialty is physics.

phys·ics [fiz-iks] *noun. Science.* the scientific study of matter and energy and the interaction between them. Physics includes the study of force, motion, light, heat, and sound.

pi [pye] *noun. Mathematics.* the symbol (π) that represents a number that is approximately equal to 3.1416, which is the ratio of the circumference of a circle to its diameter.

pi·an·ist [pee-uh-nist] *noun, plural* **pianists.** *Music.* someone who plays the piano.

pi·an·o [pee-an-oh] *noun, plural* **pianos.** *Music.* a large keyboard instrument. When each key is pressed down, it hits an internal hammer that strikes a tuned metal string and produces sound.

> Like many other English words having to do with music, **piano** is from Italian. It comes from the term *pianoforte*, meaning soft (*piano*) and strong or loud (*forte*). The idea is that this instrument can play both soft and loud tones.

pic·co·lo ▼ [pik-uh-*loh*] *noun, plural* **piccolos.** *Music.* a small flute that plays one octave higher than the standard flute.

pick¹ [pik] *verb,* **picked, picking. 1.** to choose from more than one; select: *I picked out a piece of fruit from the bowl.* **2.** to gather by pulling up, off, or out: *I helped my father pick beans from the vegetable garden.* **3.** *Music.* to play a guitar or other such instrument by pulling at the strings with the fingers. **4.** to act on something in a bad, wrong, or dishonest way: *to pick a lock; to pick a person's pocket; to pick a fight with someone.*
• **pick on.** to blame, tease, or bully someone, verbally or physically.
noun, plural **picks. 1.** the act or fact of choosing something or someone: *The dance teacher gave us the pick of the costumes.* **2.** a small, thin piece of metal, plastic, or ivory used to pluck a stringed instrument.

pick² [pik] *noun, plural* **picks. 1.** a heavy tool with a wooden handle and a metal head with a blade, used for breaking hard surfaces such as rock. **2.** a pointed tool, such as an ice pick, used for cracking or chipping something into smaller pieces.

pick·axe [pik-aks] *noun, plural* **pickaxes.** a pick that has a metal head with a point at one end and a blade at the other end. This word is also spelled **pickax.**

pick·er·el [pik-ur-ul] *noun, plural* **pickerel** *or* **pickerels.** a fish commonly found in fresh water in North America and caught for food. A pickerel is a member of the pike family.

pick·et ▼ [pik-it] *noun, plural* **pickets. 1.** a pointed post hammered into the ground as part of a fence or to hold something in place. A fence made of pointed, upright wooden slats set close together is called a **picket fence. 2.** a group of people demanding attention for their concerns by standing or marching in front of a place such as a building.
verb, **picketed, picketing.** to protest by standing or marching in front of a building: *The workers picketed outside the factory asking for a contract with better pay.*

The **piccolo** *is quite hard to play because it is so small.*

Pickets have traditionally been used for house fences since Colonial times.

*The **picturesque** village of Manarola perched high on cliffs is popular with visitors to northern Italy.*

pick·le [pik-ul] *noun, plural* **pickles.** a food that has been preserved in salt water or vinegar.
verb, **pickled, pickling.** to preserve a food in salt water or vinegar: *We pickle our own cucumbers.*

pick·pock·et [pik-pok-it] *noun, plural* **pickpockets.** someone who steals from pockets or purses, especially in public places.

pick·up [pik-up] *noun, plural* **pickups.** the act of gathering, lifting, picking up, or collecting: *Garbage pickup on this street is on Wednesdays.* A small truck with low sides and a back that drops down for easy loading is called a **pickup truck.**

pick·y [pik-ee] *adjective.* having firm likes and dislikes; fussy: *My mother says I am a picky eater because I won't eat many vegetables.*

pic·nic [pik-nik] *noun, plural* **picnics.** a meal eaten outdoors: *We took a basket of sandwiches and fruits to the park for a picnic.*
verb, **picnicked, picnicking.** to eat outdoors: *We picnicked at the beach.*

pic·tor·i·al [pik-tor-ee-ul] *adjective.* relating to, made of, or containing pictures: *I put photos together for a pictorial history of my family.*
noun, plural **pictorials.** an article in a publication that relies on pictures more than words to tell the story.

pic·ture [pik-chur] *noun, plural* **pictures. 1.** a drawing, painting, or photograph; any visual representation of a person, object, or scene. **2.** images on a television, movie, computer, or other screen: *I get a clear picture on my new cell phone.* **3.** a description in words that gives a strong mental image: *My grandfather's stories gave us a picture of what things were like in the old days.* **4.** a good or useful example: *My puppy is the picture of good health.* **5.** another word for a movie: *In 1997 Titanic won the Academy Award for Best Picture.*
verb, **pictured, picturing. 1.** to draw, paint, photograph, or represent visually in some way. **2.** to give a description in words that creates a strong mental image: *The song "Imagine" pictures a world without war.* **3.** to have a mental image of; imagine: *My sister pictured her wedding in an old church by the sea.*

pic·tur·esque ▲ [pik-chuh-resk] *adjective.* visually pleasing; suitable as the subject of a photo, drawing, or painting: *This valley is a picturesque landscape.*

pie [pye] *noun, plural* **pies.** a filling, such as meat, cheese, or fruits, enclosed in pastry and then baked.

piece [pees] *noun, plural* **pieces. 1.** a section or part separated from the whole: *Grandma cut me the biggest piece of pie.* **2.** an individual item that belongs to a group: *We found pieces of the puzzle under the couch.* **3.** a work by a writer, musician, or artist: *The journalist wrote a long piece on the war.* **4.** an instance of something: *That goal was a great piece of work.* **5.** a coin: *A nickel is a five-cent piece.*
verb, **pieced, piecing.** to join or bring together the parts of something: *We pieced together the broken piggy bank.*

pier [peer] *noun, plural* **piers. 1.** a level area built out from the shore over the water, used as a landing place for ships and boats, a place to fish from, or an area with shops, restaurants, and entertainment. **2.** a support for a bridge or building.

pierce [peers] *verb,* **pierced, piercing. 1.** to make a hole: *The broken glass pierced the bottom of my sneaker.* **2.** to push through something: *The sunlight pierced the tent.* A sound that is loud and sharp is said to be **piercing.**

pig ▶ [pig] *noun, plural* **pigs.**
1. an animal with a flat snout, a round body, short legs with hooves divided into two, and a small, curled tail. Pigs are also called swine or hogs, and the flesh is known as pork.
2. someone who is thought to have negative qualities that are associated with pigs, such as eating too much, being very fat, being dirty, or being greedy and selfish.

Pigs were first domesticated some 9,000 years ago.

pi·geon ▼ [pij-un] *noun, plural* **pigeons.** a medium-sized bird with a small head and plump body, usually with gray feathers. A pigeon is sometimes called a **rock dove.** Pigeons often flock in cities in large numbers.

pig·gy·back [pig-ee-bak] *adjective.* being carried on the back or shoulders: *Dad used to give us piggyback rides around the house.*
adverb. carried on the back.
verb, **piggybacked, piggybacking. 1.** to carry someone in this way. **2.** to join onto or follow something as if riding on its back: *I think someone else has piggybacked onto the wireless network in our house.*

pig·ment [pig-munt] *noun, plural* **pigments.**
1. material used to color things. Pigment is usually a powder that is mixed with a liquid to make paint or dye. **2.** material in living tissue that gives it color: *Pigment gives color to skin, eyes, and hair.*

*The natural habitat of **pigeons** is coastal cliffs, but they are now found throughout the world, especially in cities.*

pig·pen [pig-*pen*] *noun, plural* **pigpens.** an enclosure where pigs are kept.

pig·sty [pig-*stye*] *noun, plural* **pigsties.** another word for PIGPEN. The shortened form of this word is **sty.**

pig·tail [pig-*tale*] *noun, plural* **pigtails.** a braid or bunch of hair that hangs from the back of the head like a tail.

pike[1] [pike] *noun, plural* **pikes** *or* **pike.** a fish with a long, thin body and sharp teeth that lives in fresh water. Pikes belong to the perch family.

pike[2] ▶ [pike] *noun, plural* **pikes. 1.** a long spear formerly used by infantry. **2.** a shorter word for turnpike, a wide road or expressway for high-speed traffic. *verb,* **piked, piking,** to attack or pierce with a pike.

For centuries, soldiers in Europe fought with steel **pikes.**

pile[1] [pile] *noun, plural* **piles. 1.** a stack or mound of things heaped on top of each other: *My sister left a pile of dirty clothes on the floor.* **2.** a large number or amount: *We have a pile of reading to do for History class.* *verb,* **piled, piling. 1.** to heap or put together: *Pile the washing in the laundry.* **2.** to come together as a large number or amount: *Mail piled up in the box while they were away.*

pile[2] [pile] *noun, plural* **pikes.** a thick, upright post that supports a bridge or pier.

pile[3] [pile] *noun.* the fibers that form the surface of a rug or piece of cloth. Loops of yarn are usually used to make pile.

pil·fer [pil-fur] *verb,* **pilfered, pilfering.** to steal bit by bit: *Someone has been pilfering the photocopying paper.* The fact of pilfering is **pilferage.**

pil·grim [pil-grum] *noun, plural* **pilgrims.** someone who makes a journey to a religious or sacred place: *Islamic pilgrims travel to Mecca to honor Muhammad.*

Pil·grim [pil-grum] *noun, plural* **Pilgrims.** *History.* one of a group of English settlers who sailed to North America in 1620 and started the colony of Plymouth in New England.

The first meaning of a **pilgrim** was someone who wandered or traveled around from place to place. It then came to mean someone who travels to a distant place to visit a religious site. The people who came to settle in Massachusetts in 1620 called themselves *Pilgrims* because they felt their religion had brought them to that place.

pil·grim·age [pil-gruh-mij] *noun, plural* **pilgrimages.** a trip or journey taken by a pilgrim.

pill [pil] *noun, plural* **pills. 1.** a small solid tablet containing medicine that is to be swallowed or chewed.

pil·lar [pil-ur] *noun, plural* **pillars. 1.** a column that supports the roof of a building or stands by itself as a monument: *The stone pillars are carved with tiny figures.* **2.** someone who gives support or is an important part of something: *The mayor is a pillar of our community.*

pil·low [pil-oh] *noun, plural* **pillows.** a cloth bag filled with feathers or soft material on which to rest the head. A cover for a pillow is called a **pillowcase.**

pi·lot [pye-lut] *noun, plural* **pilots. 1.** someone who operates an aircraft or spacecraft. **2.** someone who steers ships in and out of harbors and places that are difficult to navigate. *verb,* **piloted, piloting.** to act as a pilot: *The astronaut piloted the shuttle to a safe landing.*

pim·ple [pim-pul] *noun, plural* **pimples.** *Health.* a small bump on the skin where a blocked pore has become infected. Often pimples are filled with pus.

pin [pin] *noun, plural* **pins. 1.** a short, thin piece of metal with a point at one end. Some pins are stiff, straight, and sharp. Safety pins are bent with a sharp end that can be fastened to a metal cover. Bobby pins are bent and blunt, and used for holding hair in place. **2.** an ornament or badge that can be attached to clothing: *My mother wore the diamond pin that she got for graduation.* **3.** a short, thin cylinder, usually of metal or wood, that holds two parts together: *When my brother broke his arm, they put a metal pin in it to hold the bones together.* **4.** one of ten bottle-shaped pieces that you throw the ball at in the game of bowling. *verb,* **pinned, pinning. 1.** to join or attach with a pin or pins: *She pinned the fabric together before she sewed it into a dress.* **2.** to hold or fasten in one place: *The wrestler pinned his opponent to the mat.*
 • **pin down.** to make someone state something clearly and with certainty; locate or find: *It was hard to pin down the teacher about the exact day of the test.*

pi·ña·ta [peen-yah-tuh] *noun, plural* **piñatas.** a container, often in the shape of an animal, that is filled with small toys and candy. Piñatas are hung up as a game for children wearing blindfolds to break open with sticks.

pin·cer ▼ [pin-sur] *noun, plural* **pincers. 1.** a claw that grasps things: *the pincers of a crab.* **2.** a hand tool for holding and grasping things. Pincers are like pliers, but with sharper points.

Crabs wave their **pincers** *to attract mates and use them to dig up food.*

*An American **pinto** has a dark coat with patches of white.*

pinch [pinch] *verb,* **pinched, pinching. 1.** to squeeze between a finger and thumb, or to squeeze between two surfaces: *Be careful not to pinch your hand in the cupboard door as you shut it.* **2.** to crease or wrinkle: *The way she pinched her lips told us she was not pleased.* *noun, plural* **pinches. 1.** the act of pinching; a sharp squeeze. **2.** an amount that can be held between a thumb and finger; a tiny amount: *Add a pinch of salt to the sauce.* **3.** an emergency or time of need: *I can lend you the money in a pinch.*

pinch-hit *verb,* **pinch-hit, pinching-hitting. 1.** to take the place of a player scheduled to bat in a game of baseball, especially when a hit is badly needed. **2.** to take the place of someone else, or help them out, in a time of need: *Her mom is pinch-hitting for the soccer coach who is on vacation.* *noun, plural* **pinch-hits. 1.** the act of batting in place of another player in baseball, or a hit made while doing this. **2.** the act of taking the place of someone else or helping them out. Someone who pinch-hits can be called a **pinch-hitter.**

pine[1] ▶ [pine] *noun, plural* **pines.** an evergreen tree that has cones and needle-shaped leaves. The soft but tough wood of pine is often used to build houses and furniture.

pine[2] [pine] *verb,* **pined, pining. 1.** to long for something desperately: *My brother's dog is pining for him to come home from college.* **2.** to get sick because of grief: *Her grandfather is just pining away since her grandmother died.*

pine·ap·ple [pine-*ap*-ul] *noun, plural* **pineapples.** a large, oval, tropical fruit that is prickly on the outside and has juicy, sweet, yellow meat on the inside.

Ping-Pong [ping-*pong*] *noun.* the trademark for the game of TABLE TENNIS.

pink [pingk] *noun, plural* **pinks. 1.** a light red color made by mixing red and white. **2.** a perfumed plant with pink, or red, or yellow or white flowers. *adjective,* **pinker, pinkest.** having a light red color. • **in the pink.** in good health: *We're glad to hear your aunt is in the pink after her operation.*

pink·eye [pingk-*eye*] *noun. Health.* a disease that causes the eyes to become red and sore.

pin·point [pin-*point*] *verb,* **pinpointed, pinpointing.** to locate or find where something is: *She could not pinpoint exactly where her old house used to be.*

pins and needles a numb, tingling feeling: *My sister got pins and needles in her leg after sitting in one position for so long.* • **on pins and needles.** feeling nervous or anxious: *I was on pins and needles waiting for my exam results.*

The Monterey **pine** *grows quickly and is often planted in forests.*

pin·stripe [pin-*stripe*] *noun, plural* **pinstripes. 1.** a very thin stripe, especially on fabric. **2.** a fabric with very thin stripes that is usually used for suits.

pint [pyent] *noun, plural* **pints.** a measurement of liquid equal to 0.104 gallons.

pin·to ▲ [pin-*toh*] *noun, plural* **pintos.** a pony or horse with patches of two or more colors.

pin·wheel [pin-*weel*] *noun, plural* **pinwheels. 1.** a toy windmill with vanes of colored paper or plastic pinned to a stick that spins when blown. **2.** a whirling firework that throws off light or sparks as it turns.

pi·o·neer ▼ [*pye*-uh-*neer*] *noun, plural* **pioneers. 1.** someone who is one of the first people to settle in a region: *The pioneers traveled from east to west across America.* **2.** someone who develops a field of knowledge: *Madame Curie was a pioneer in the use of X rays.* *verb,* **pioneered, pioneering.** to develop or explore a field of knowledge: *The United States pioneered the use of nuclear power.*

pi·ous [*pye*-us] *adjective.* **1.** describing something very religious. **2.** having to do with religious devotion: *The Lutherans study the pious writings of Martin Luther.* The act of being pious is called **piety. —piously,** *adverb.*

pipe [pipe] *noun, plural* **pipes. 1.** a long tube that carries liquid or gas: *The pipes made clanking noises when we turned the hot water on.* **2.** a tube with a bowl attached, used for smoking tobacco. **3.** a tube with holes in it that is played as a musical instrument. *verb,* **piped, piping. 1.** to carry by means of a pipe: *to pipe oil out of the ground.* **2.** to play a pipe: *My sister piped a song on her recorder.*

*These **pioneers** in astronomy, from ancient Greece to eighteenth-century England, developed new ideas about the universe.*

Claudius Ptolemy Nicolaus Copernicus Galileo Galilei Isaac Newton

pipe·line ▶ [pipe-line] *noun,*
plural **pipelines. 1.** a line
of pipes joined together
to carry liquid or gas over a
long distance. **2.** the fact of
being developed or prepared:
The plans for the new library
are in the pipeline.

Pipelines *carry large amounts of*
oil from wells in the Middle East.

pi·ra·nha [pi-rahn-uh] *noun,*
plural **piranhas** *or* **piranha.**
a tropical American freshwater fish that eats flesh.
Piranhas have sharp teeth and often attack humans.

pir·ate ▶ [pye-rit] *noun, plural* **pirates.**
someone who robs ships at sea.
The act of robbing a ship is called
piracy. The act of copying something
illegally is also called **piracy.**
verb, **pirated, pirating.** to copy
illegally: *Singers try to stop*
people pirating their music
from the Internet. Such a copy
is said to be **pirated:** *We watched*
a pirated DVD of the movie.

pis·ta·chi·o [pi-stash-ee-oh] *noun,*
plural **pistachios.** a small green
nut with a brown shell.

pis·til ▼ [pis-tul] *noun,*
plural **pistils.** *Biology.* the stalk in
the middle of a flower. The pistil is the
female part of the flower where seeds develop.
🔊 A different word with the same sound
is **pistol.**

Pistil

pis·tol [pis-tul] *noun,*
plural **pistols.** a small
gun that can be held
and fired with one hand.
A pistol is also called
a **handgun.**
🔊 A different word
with the same sound
is **pistil.**

Bees deposit
pollen on the
sticky tip of the
pistil, *called*
the stigma.

pis·ton [pis-tun] *noun,*
plural **pistons.** a cylinder that
moves up and down inside another hollow
cylinder. Pistons drive an engine that makes a car move.

pit¹ [pit] *noun, plural* **pits. 1.** a hole in the ground:
The pirates dug a pit to bury their treasure. **2.** a dent on
the surface of something: *The heavy hail left small pits*
all over the roof of the car.
verb, **pitted, pitting. 1.** to make dents in something.
2. to compete against someone or something: *In the*
final round of the spelling bee, the two best spellers
were pitted against each other.

pit² [pit] *noun, plural* **pits.** the seed of fruits like peaches,
plums, and apricots.
verb, **pitted, pitting.** to take the seed out of a fruit:
Mom pitted the peaches before she stewed them.

pitch¹ [pich] *verb,* **pitched, pitching. 1.** to toss or throw:
He pitched the ball to the batter. **2.** to construct or set
up: *Please help me pitch the tent.* **3.** to fall or tilt forward:
The sailing boat pitched and rolled on the stormy seas.
noun, plural **pitches. 1.** a throw by a pitcher to a batter
in a game of baseball. **2.** *Music.* the high or low level of
a musical note: *The judge of the song contest said her pitch*
was perfect. **3.** a slope or incline: *The pitch of their roof*
is so steep that you cannot walk on it.

pitch² [pich] *noun.* a dark, sticky substance used for
constructing paths and for making roofs waterproof.
Pitch is made from tar.

pitch·er¹ [pich-ur] *noun, plural* **pitchers.** a jug or container
with a handle and spout. Pitchers are used for
holding and pouring liquids such as milk
and water.

pitch·er² [pich-ur] *noun, plural* **pitchers.**
the player who throws the ball to the
batter in a game of baseball.

pitch·fork [pich-fork] *noun,*
plural **pitchforks.** a large fork that
is used to lift and throw hay.

pit·fall [pit-fawl] *noun, plural* **pitfalls.**
1. a trap that is a hidden or concealed
hole. **2.** an area of difficulty or danger:
The doctor told the medical students
about several pitfalls that a new doctor
might face.

pit·i·ful [pit-i-ful] *adjective.* **1.** causing
or deserving pity or sympathy:
The stray dog was in such a pitiful state
that we gave him our lunch. **2.** causing
or deserving contempt or scorn: *a pitiful*
excuse; a pitiful attempt to do something.
—**pitifully,** *adverb.*

pi·ty [pit-ee] *noun, plural* **pities. 1.** a kindly
sorrow felt for someone else's suffering:
Everyone felt pity for the victims of the
hurricane. **2.** a cause for regret or sorrow:
What a pity she lost her bike.
verb, **pitied, pitying.** to feel a kindly sorrow for someone
else's suffering: *I pity the poor families who*
can't afford warm clothes this winter.

Edward Teach, known as
Blackbeard, was one of the most
feared **pirates** *of the 1600s.*

piv·ot ▶ [piv-ut] *noun, plural* **pivots.**
a short rod or shaft on which a part
rotates or swings: *The needle*
of a compass turns on a pivot.
verb, **pivoted, pivoting.** to
turn on a pivot, or to turn
on the spot: *The hands of*
the clock slowly pivot from
one number to the next.

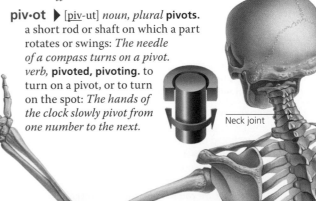

Neck joint

The joint in your neck is like a **pivot**
that allows your head to turn.

a b c d e f g h i j k l m n o **p** q r s t u v w x y z

A
B
C
D
E
F
G
H
I
J
K
L
M
N
O
P
Q
R
S
T
U
V
W
X
Y
Z

pix·el [piks-ul] *noun, plural* **pixels.** one of the small dots that form images and letters on a computer or television screen.

piz·za [peet-suh] *noun, plural* **pizzas.** an Italian pie with a flat yeasted dough base topped with tomato sauce, cheese, and other foods. A restaurant where pizzas are baked and eaten is called a **pizzeria.**

The word **pixel** is thought to come from "pix," a shorter word for *picture* and "el," the first part of the word *element*. The idea is that a pixel is a very small element (part) of a larger picture.

plac·ard [plak-ard] *noun, plural* **placards.** a written or printed notice that is displayed in a public place; a poster or nameplate: *The placard on the wall advertised a concert.*

pla·cate [play-kate] *verb,* **placated, placating.** to make calm or happy; pacify: *The angry customer was placated when the waitress apologized for bringing the wrong order.*

place [plays] *noun, plural* **places. 1.** a certain part of space; a location or position: *Find a place to put your bag.* **2.** a dwelling or home: *Come over to our place for dinner.* **3.** a particular spot or location: *He used a bookmark to mark his place in the novel; Save me a place in the line.* **4.** a position in a series or order; rank: *She won second place in the contest.* **5.** a proper duty or right: *It is not his place to tell me what to do.* *verb,* **placed, placing. 1.** to put or set down in a certain location: *He placed the crown on her head.* **2.** to identify by remembering in a previous location or time: *The witness was able to place the accused man at the scene of the crime.*
• **take place.** to occur or happen: *The meeting will take place on Friday.*

place·ment [plays-munt] *noun, plural* **placements. 1.** the act of placing something or of being placed: *The placement of the window on the south wall makes the room sunny.* **2.** the placing of a person in a suitable position, such as a class, job, or home. A test people do to determine where they will be placed is called a **placement test.**

pla·cid [plas-id] *adjective.* calm and peaceful: *That placid pony never bucks and is good for beginners to ride.* **—placidly,** *adverb.*

pla·gia·rize [play-juh-rize] *verb,* **plagiarized, plagiarizing.** *Literature.* to pass off the ideas or words of another person as your own; copy in a way that is wrong or against the law: *She plagiarized her poem from one she found on the Internet.* The act of doing this is called **plagiarism** and a person who does this is a **plagiarist.**

To **plagiarize** in writing is to take the exact words of another person and pretend you wrote them yourself. This is something that a writer should never do, of course, but it does not mean that you cannot use other people's words when you write. You can do this as long as you show their words as a *quotation*: "When I had made up my mind, I thought of what Davy Crockett said: 'Be sure you're right, then go ahead.'"

plague [playg] *noun, plural* **plagues. 1.** an infectious disease that spreads quickly through a population and causes many deaths. One of the most famous of these diseases is the **bubonic plague,** also known as the **Black Plague** or the **Black Death.** Fleas carry it from rats to humans. During the Middle Ages, outbreaks of plague are estimated to have killed around one-third of Europe's population. **2.** anything that occurs in large numbers and causes widespread calamity: *A plague of locusts destroyed the farmers' wheat crops.*
verb, **plagued, plaguing.** to annoy again and again; trouble or pester: *Autograph seekers plagued the movie star.*

plaid ◀ [plad] *noun, plural* **plaids.** a pattern of stripes of different widths and colors that cross over each other at right angles. This pattern is often used when making cloth.

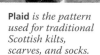

Plaid *is the pattern used for traditional Scottish kilts, scarves, and socks.*

plain [plane] *adjective,* **plainer, plainest. 1.** clear and easy to understand, see, or hear; obvious: *The mark on his leg where the rock had hit him was plain to see.* **2.** describing something direct or straightforward: *Our teacher gave us plain instructions on how to do the experiment.* **3.** describing something not decorated: *I like the plain red shirt, not the fancy, flowery one.* **4.** of food, simply prepared, without extra seasonings or flavorings: *They had a plain meal of soup and bread.* **5.** not extremely attractive or good-looking: *She has a plain face.*
noun, plural **plains.** a wide, flat area of land: *In summer, the plain was covered with long grass.* Vast areas of mostly flat land are often known as **plains. —plainly,** *adverb;* **—plainness,** *noun.*
🔊 A different word with the same sound is **plane.**

plain·tiff [plane-tiv] *noun, plural* **plaintiffs.** *Law.* a person who brings a complaint in court against another person who is known as the defendant.

plan [plan] *noun, plural* **plans. 1.** a strategy for how to do something that is worked out before it is done: *Zac's plan was to save money so he could travel overseas.* **2.** a diagram that shows how the parts of something such as a building or machine are related to each other: *The plan of the building shows the location of the fire exits.*
verb, **planned, planning.** to work out how to do something before it is done: *They carefully planned where they would go on their honeymoon; The landscape designer planned a garden to go around the building.*

plane¹ [plane] *noun, plural* **planes. 1.** a flat surface: *A cube has six planes.* **2.** a level or ranking: *The farm animals were raised on a high plane of nutrition.* **3.** a shorter form of the word AIRPLANE.
adjective. flat or level: *Plane geometry is an area of mathematics dealing with flat surfaces.*
🔊 A different word with the same sound is **plain.**

plane² [plane] *noun, plural* **planes.** a carpenter's tool with a blade that sticks out underneath. It is used to level wood and make it smooth.
verb, **planed, planing.** to make wood smooth or level: *The cabinet maker planed the drawer's edges so it would slide in and out smoothly.*
🔊 A different word with the same sound is **plain.**

plan·et [plan-it] *noun, plural* **planets.** a heavenly body larger than an asteroid or comet that orbits a star. Eight planets orbit the Sun: Mercury, Venus, Earth, Mars, Jupiter, Saturn, Uranus, and Neptune. In 2006 astronomers decided that Pluto was too small to be considered a planet. Something relating to planets is described as **planetary.**

> The word **planet** comes from a term meaning "to wander" or "to move about." In early times people thought that the stars in the heavens were fixed in place and did not change their position, while they could observe that the planets did move about in the sky.

plan·e·tar·i·um [plan-uh-tare-ee-um] *noun, plural* **planetariums** or **planetaria.** a special building where the images of the heavenly bodies, including the stars, the Sun, the planets, and their moons, are projected on the inside of a dome to simulate the night sky.

plank [plangk] *noun, plural* **planks.** a long, narrow, flat piece of wood that is cut thicker than a board.

plank·ton [plangk-tun] *plural noun. Biology.* a general name for various kinds of tiny organisms that live in water. Plankton is eaten in great quantities by fish and baleen whales.

plan·ner [plan-ur] *noun, plural* **planners. 1.** a person who plans. **2.** a notebook or wall calendar where appointments and things to do are written.

plant ▶ [plant] *noun, plural* **plants. 1.** any living thing that makes its own food from non-living substances, has cell walls that contain cellulose, and does not have the power to move from one place to another on its own. Plants include trees, ferns, mosses, and most algae. **2.** a manufacturing complex, including the buildings, machinery, and equipment: *Thousands of vehicles are made each year in that car plant.*
verb, **planted, planting.**
1. to put a plant or seed in the soil to grow: *Morgan planted a window box with pansies.*
2. to put or fix in place: *He planted himself in the back seat and wouldn't budge.*

plan·tain [plan-tin] *noun, plural* **plantains.** a type of banana. Unripe plantains are starchy and are cooked or turned into flour. Ripe plantains are sweeter, and are eaten raw or cooked in sweet dishes.

plan·ta·tion ▼ [plan-tay-shun] *noun, plural* **plantations.** a large farm where crops are grown by laborers who live there: *Cotton plantations in the southern U.S. used slave labor before the Civil War.*

plant·er [plant-ur] *noun, plural* **planters. 1.** a person who plants. **2.** the manager or owner of a plantation: *The planter ordered the workers to pick the tea.* **3.** a decorative holder for a plant; a plant box or pot.

plaque [plak] *noun, plural* **plaques. 1.** a flat piece of metal, wood, or ceramic, often set on a wall. A plaque can be written on, or it can be decorated. It often commemorates something. **2.** a thin layer of food and saliva on the teeth that traps bacteria and helps cause tooth decay.

Tea is grown in **plantations** *in the Malaysian highlands.*

plas·ma [plaz-muh] *noun, plural* **plasmas. 1.** *Biology.* the yellowish liquid part of blood that carries blood cells, salts, hormones, and other material. Plasma makes up a little more than half of blood. **2.** *Science.* a gas that contains an equal number of electrons and positive ions. Plasma is highly conductive and responds strongly to electromagnetic forces. Most of the matter in the universe is thought to exist as plasma.

plas·ter [plas-tur] *noun.* a paste made of lime, sand, water, and sometimes hair that is smoothed over walls and ceilings and becomes hard when dry. Plaster is also used to make molds and statues.
verb, **plastered, plastering. 1.** to coat with plaster: *The walls were plastered before they were painted.* **2.** to cover thickly: *Her bedroom walls were plastered with posters.*

plas·tic [plas-tik] *noun, plural* **plastics.** *Chemistry.* a substance that can be molded when soft but then hardens. There are many strong, light, man-made plastics used to make a wide variety of objects such as toys, cups, furniture, and pens.
adjective. **1.** able to be shaped or molded: *Clay is plastic and can be made into many things.* **2.** made from plastic: *a plastic raincoat.*

plastic surgery *Medicine.* surgery done to repair or reshape parts of the body that have not formed properly or have been damaged. A doctor specializing in plastic surgery is a **plastic surgeon.**

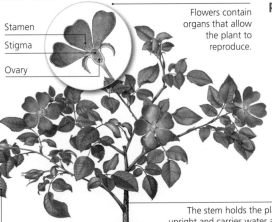

Stamen
Stigma
Ovary

Flowers contain organs that allow the plant to reproduce.

Leaves make food for the plant.

The stem holds the plant upright and carries water and food to the rest of the plant.

Roots anchor the plant and draw water and food from the soil.

Every part of a flowering **plant** *has a role to play in keeping the plant healthy.*

*The Colorado National Monument illustrates the spectacular landscape of **plateaus** and canyons typical of the American West.*

plate [plate] *noun, plural* **plates. 1.** a flat or almost flat dish: *The cake was served on a plate Mom used for special occasions.* **2.** a flat sheet of something hard, such as glass or metal: *The bottom of the wooden ship was covered in copper plates for protection.* **3.** a polished piece of metal on which drawings or writing are engraved. These engraved plates are used in printing. **4.** see HOME PLATE. **5.** one of the vast sheets of rock that join together to form the Earth's crust. These plates move slowly. Earthquakes can take place when these plates become caught against each other and then suddenly tear free.
verb, **plated, plating.** to coat one metal object with a thin coating of another metal: *Those spoons are not made of solid silver, they are just plated with it.*

pla·teau ▲ [pla-<u>toh</u>] *noun, plural* **plateaus.** *Geography.* a wide, flat area of high land.

plate·let [<u>plate</u>-lit] *noun, plural* **platelets.** *Medicine.* disk-shaped blood cells that help the blood clot to stop bleeding. Platelets are made in the bone marrow.

plate tectonics ▼ *Geology.* the study of the movement of the plates that make up the Earth's crust. Many volcanoes and earthquakes occur where these plates meet, and where they separate, vast valley systems are formed.

plat·form [<u>plat</u>-form] *noun, plural* **platforms. 1.** a raised flat area: *We stood on the platform in the school hall to receive our prizes.* **2.** a public declaration of the beliefs or principles of an organization, especially a political party: *The platform of that party includes a promise to reduce crime.*

plat·i·num [<u>plat</u>-uh-num] *noun. Chemistry.* a heavy, silver-colored metallic element. It does not tarnish and is used to make scientific instruments and jewelry.

pla·toon [pluh-<u>toon</u>] *noun, plural* **platoons.** a section of a company of soldiers made up of two squads and usually led by a lieutenant.

Plate tectonics helps scientists understand what causes mountains, volcanoes, eruptions, earthquakes, rift valleys, and underwater formations.

plat·ter [<u>plat</u>-ur] *noun, plural* **platters.** a large plate that food is served on. Each person eating takes a portion of food from a platter.

plat·y·pus ▶ [<u>plat</u>-uh-puss] *noun, plural* **platypuses.** an Australian mammal with webbed feet, brown fur, and a bill that looks like a duck's bill. The platypus is one of only a few monotremes (mammals that lay eggs). It feeds its young milk from pores in its skin.

plau·si·ble [<u>plaw</u>-zuh-bul] *adjective.* appearing to be true; believable or reasonable: *His reason for being late for school sounded plausible.* **—plausibly,** *adverb.*

*A **platypus** uses its bill to search for the small insects on which it feeds.*

play [play] *noun, plural* **plays. 1.** an activity carried out for fun or to pass time in an enjoyable way: *The play of children often involves imaginative games.* **2.** a turn or move in a game: *The chess champion's brilliant play allowed him to capture his opponent's queen.* **3.** a story that can be acted out; a drama: *Our class made up a play and performed it for the whole school.* **4.** the action, operation, or use of something: *Her story was the result of the free play of her imagination.*
verb, **played, playing. 1.** to take part in something for fun or leisure: *The children played in the park.* **2.** to take part in a game: *Their team played in the basketball final.* **3.** to compete against in a game or match: *Mark played Tony in the tennis tournament.* **4.** to use in a careless way: *Don't play with that crystal bowl.* **5.** to act the part of: *A well-known actor played the lawyer in the television program.* **6.** to cause a musical instrument to make sounds: *She plays the trumpet.* **7.** to behave in a particular way: *Games are more fun if you play fair.*

play·er [<u>play</u>-ur] *noun, plural* **players. 1.** a person who plays, as in a game or sport: *The player rolled the dice then moved his marker on the board.* **2.** a person who plays a musical instrument: *He is a flute player.* **3.** a person who performs a part in a drama; an actor: *All the players returned to the stage and the audience applauded.*

play·ful [<u>play</u>-ful] *adjective.* **1.** full of fun; wanting to play: *The playful puppy chased the ball.* **2.** describing something humorous; joking; funny: *Her father made a playful comment about how much she loved chocolate.* **—playfully,** *adverb;* **—playfulness,** *noun.*

Plates collide under the sea, creating trench. | Hot currents | Plates part to form underwater mountain chain. | Magma bursts through crust to make volcanic hotspots appear. | Oceanic and continental plates meet, creating ocean trenches and mountains on land. | Sliding plates cause faults under the sea and sometimes on land. | Parting continental plates form a rift valley. | Continental plates collide and push up mountains.

play·ground [play-ground] *noun, plural* **playgrounds.** an area out of doors set aside for children to play in where there is often equipment to play on, such as slides and swings.

playing card one of a set of cards that is used for playing games. The most common set of cards used in games of chance and skill have 52 cards divided into the four suits of hearts, diamonds, spades, and clubs.

play·mate [play-mate] *noun, plural* **playmates.** someone that you play with, especially a child who plays with another child.

play·pen [play-pen] *noun, plural* **playpens.** a small enclosure where a small child can play safely. Playpens are usually easy to pack up and move from place to place.

play·thing [play-thing] *noun, plural* **playthings.** an object that is played with; a toy.

play·wright ▶ [play-rite] *noun, plural* **playwrights.** someone who writes plays: *Eugene O'Neill was a famous American playwright.*

pla·za [plah-zuh *or* plaz-uh] *noun, plural* **plazas.** an open town or city square: *We had lunch in the open-air cafe in the plaza.*

The **playwright** *William Shakespeare (1564–1616) wrote 36 plays.*

> In ancient times **plaza** meant "a wide street" and then came to mean a large open place in a city, such as a marketplace. The word came into English from Spanish, since plazas were common in cities of Spain.

plea [plee] *noun, plural* **pleas. 1.** a strongly-felt request: *A plea was made for the prisoners to be released.* **2.** an answer given by someone to the charges brought against him or her in a court case: *His plea of guilty to the murders of four people did not surprise anyone.*

plea·bar·gain [plee-bar-gun] *verb,* **plea-bargained, plea-bargaining.** *Law.* to negotiate to reach an agreement where the person accused of a crime will have a reduced sentence if he or she pleads guilty. *noun, plural* **plea-bargains.** the agreement reached by plea-bargaining.

plead [pleed] *verb,* **pleaded** *or* **pled, pleading. 1.** to ask for in an emotional way; make a serious request for: *He pleaded for more time to finish his assignment.* **2.** to use as an excuse: *The hotel clerk pleaded ignorance when we asked him why our room was not cleaned.* **3.** to answer a charge in a court of law: *The man pleaded not guilty to the charges brought against him.*

plea·sant [plez-unt] *adjective.* **1.** describing something pleasing or agreeable: *The weather is pleasant and not too hot or cold.* **2.** acting in a friendly way: *The waiter spoke to us in a pleasant manner.* —**pleasantly,** *adverb;* —**pleasantness,** *noun.*

please [pleez] *verb,* **pleased, pleasing. 1.** to satisfy or give happiness to: *It pleased her to see her friend again.* Something that gives pleasure is said to be **pleasing. 2.** to wish for or prefer: *Choose whatever you please from the menu.* **Please** is also used to ask for something in a polite way: *Pass the milk, please; Please turn the music down.*

pleas·ure [plezh-ur] *noun, plural* **pleasures. 1.** a state of happiness or enjoyment: *Playing in the pool gave them pleasure that hot afternoon.* **2.** a source of happiness or enjoyment: *It is a pleasure to listen to her sing.* *adjective.* giving happiness or enjoyment: *We went on a pleasure cruise on the lake.*

pleat [pleet] *noun, plural* **pleats.** a fold made in cloth by doubling the cloth over on itself and stitching or pressing it in place. Skirts and trousers often have pleats. *verb,* **pleated, pleating.** to make pleats in: *to pleat a skirt.* *adjective.* having pleats: *I wore my pleated trousers last night.*

pled [pled] *verb.* a past tense and past participle of PLEAD.

pledge [plej] *noun, plural* **pledges. 1.** a promise made seriously: *The guard made a pledge to defend the king with his life.* **2.** something of value given to a person to keep until a promise is fulfilled: *He gave his watch as a pledge that he would pay the money back.* *verb,* **pledged, pledging. 1.** to make a serious promise: *They pledged to write to each other every day.* **2.** to give a piece of property as a pledge.

plen·ti·ful [plen-ti-ful] *adjective.* existing in large amounts; abundant: *The salmon are plentiful in the river this year.* —**plentifully,** *adverb.*

plen·ty [plen-tee] *noun.* a large supply of something: *They have plenty of space in the back yard to put in a swimming pool.*

ple·si·o·saur ▼ [plee-see-uh-sore] *noun, plural* **plesiosaurs.** an extinct marine reptile that lived at the time of the dinosaurs. There were many types of plesiosaur, most were large, with a small head, long neck, short tail and four flippers. This animal is also called a **plesiosaurus.**

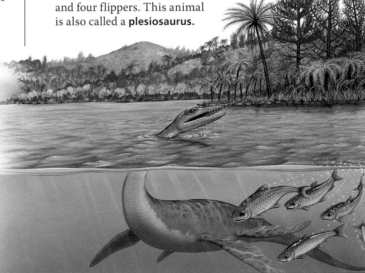

Plesiosaurs *used their flippers to move through the water, flicking their head from side to side in search of fish.*

*This banded pitta has very colorful **plumage**.*

pli·ers [plye-urz] *plural noun.* a pincer tool with long jaws that is used to hold on to fine objects or to bend or cut wire.

plod [plod] *verb,* **plodded, plodding. 1.** to walk slowly and heavily; trudge: *Hank plodded up the steep hill carrying his heavy pack.* **2.** to work slowly and steadily: *She plodded through the pile of paperwork on her desk.*

plop [plop] *verb,* **plopped, plopping. 1.** to make a sound like something landing in water without a splash: *The paint dripped off the brush and plopped onto the floor.* **2.** to fall or let drop heavily: *He was exhausted and plopped down onto the couch.*

plot [plot] *noun, plural* **plots. 1.** a plan made in secret, especially to do something illegal: *The generals carried out a plot to overthrow the king.* A person who plans something secretly is called a **plotter. 2.** the main storyline of a novel, play, poem, or movie: *The plot of that movie is too complicated to follow.* **3.** a small piece of land: *We grow vegetables on our plot.*
verb, **plotted, plotting. 1.** to plan something, especially in secret: *The four prisoners plotted their escape from jail.* **2.** to mark out or map: *We plotted our position on the map.*

plo·ver [ploh-vur] *noun, plural* **plovers.** a type of wading bird with a short, thick bill and long wings. Plovers run and make short flights over wetlands, beaches, or grasslands. They lay their eggs on the ground.

plow [plow] *noun, plural* **plows. 1.** a piece of farm equipment used to break up and turn soil to prepare it to be planted with a crop. A plow can be pulled by a tractor or by animals such as water buffaloes or horses. **2.** a large piece of equipment used to push or clear material away, such as a snowplow.
verb, **plowed, plowing. 1.** to break up and turn soil over with a plow: *The farmer had to plow the field before it could be sown with wheat.* **2.** to move through like a plow in a steady, strong way: *I plowed through my chores so I could go out and play.*

pluck [pluk] *verb,* **plucked, plucking. 1.** to pull or pick off something that is growing: *The bird plucked cherries from the tree.* **2.** *Music.* to quickly pull at the strings of an instrument with the fingers or a pick: *The musician plucked the strings of his violin.* **3.** to give a quick tug: *She plucked at her collar to put it back in place.*
noun, plural **plucks. 1.** a quick or brief pulling movement; a tug. **2.** the act or fact of being brave: *It took pluck for him to cross the rope bridge.* Someone who is courageous is said to be **plucky.**

plug [plug] *noun, plural* **plugs. 1.** a stopper that prevents liquid entering into or draining out of a hole. Plugs can be made from metal, rubber, cork, or other materials: *I put the plug in the basin then filled it with water.* **2.** the connecting end of an electrical cord that has metal prongs that fit into an electrical socket. **3.** an item of good publicity: *The radio station gave the new movie a plug.*
verb, **plugged, plugging. 1.** to stop up a hole: *Julian plugged the hole in the bottom of boat to stop it leaking.* **2.** to provide an electrical appliance with power by inserting its plug into an electricity outlet: *Plug in the television.* **3.** to give something good publicity: *That new book they are plugging sounds exciting.* **4.** to work at steadily: *He plugged away at his assignment and finished it at midnight.*

plum ▶ [plum] *noun, plural* **plums.** a soft, juicy fruit with a pit at its center. Plums can be purple, yellowish, or red. They grow on a tree that is known for its blossom in spring. Dried plums are called prunes.
🔊 A different word with the same sound is **plumb.**

Plums can be eaten fresh or dried, or made into jam or wine.

plum·age ▲ [ploo-mij] *noun.* a bird's entire covering of feathers: *A flamingo's plumage is pink.*

plumb [plum] *noun, plural* **plumbs.** a small, heavy weight on the end of a cord that is used to test how deep something is or whether something is standing straight up and down.
verb, **plumbed, plumbing.** to test something with a plumb.
adverb. **1.** standing straight: *The fence post was no longer plumb, but had a lean to it.* **2.** exactly, directly: *The fly dropped plumb in the middle of my soup.*
🔊 A different word with the same sound is **plum.**

plumb·er [plum-ur] *noun, plural* **plumbers.** a person whose job is to put water and waste pipes into a building or to fix them.

plumb·ing [plum-ing] *noun.* **1.** the system of water and waste pipes in a building. **2.** the work a plumber does.

plume [ploom] *noun, plural* **plumes. 1.** a feather, particularly one that is long, fluffy, or showy: *Turkeys have long plumes that make up their fan-shaped tails.* **2.** a tuft of large, showy feathers worn on a hat, headdress, or helmet. **3.** a long stream or column of something such as smoke or gas.

plum·met [plum-it] *verb,* **plummeted, plummeting.** to rapidly fall straight down; plunge: *The train plummeted off the bridge into the river.*

plump [plump] *adjective,* **plumper, plumpest.** describing something well-rounded and full; chubby: *Babies are often plump, but when they start to walk they usually become thinner.* —**plumpness,** *noun.*

plun·der [plun-dur] *verb,* **plundered, plundering.** to rob with violence, usually during a war or raid; loot: *The soldiers plundered the castle of its riches after they took it over.*
noun. things that are stolen using violence: *The pirates carried their plunder aboard their ship.*

plunge [plunj] *verb,* **plunged, plunging. 1.** to push or thrust suddenly: *He plunged the knife into the attacking wolf.* **2.** to dive or fall suddenly: *The bear plunged into the stream to catch a fish.*
noun, plural **plunges.** the act of thrusting or falling suddenly: *We took a plunge in the ocean.*
• **take the plunge.** to carry out something one has resolved to do: *She took the plunge and asked the boy she liked on a date.*

plu·ral [ploor-ul] *adjective.* of or having to do with a form of word that indicates more than one person or thing: *The words "desks" and "mice" are plural nouns.*
noun, plural **plurals.** the form of a word that indicates it is referring to more than one person or object: *The nouns "children" and "cars" are in the plural.*

In this dictionary the **plural** of a noun is shown in black type after the headword in blue. The plural of most nouns is formed by adding **s**, or **-es** in the case of words ending sounds with certain sounds such as [ch] or [sh]. Certain common words do not use this pattern, such as *foot-feet, mouse-mice,* or *leaf-leaves.* Also, scientific words that are taken from Latin often use the plural forms of that language, such as *fungus-fungi* or *bacterium-bacteria.* Some words that describe ideas do not have a plural form at all, such as *music, health,* or *economics.*

plus [plus] *noun, plural* **pluses.** *Mathematics.* the plus sign (+) that shows something is to be added to something else.
preposition. in addition to: *She has a cold, plus an earache.*
adjective. additional to: *Rex got an A plus for his report.*

plush [plush] *noun.* a cloth with a longer pile (threads above the surface) than that of velvet.
adjective, **plusher, plushest.** describing something luxurious, rich, or costly: *They have had a plush carpet fitted in their living room.*

Plu·to ▶ [ploo-toh] *noun.* a large celestial body made up mainly of ice and rock that orbits the Sun and can only be seen from Earth with a telescope. Pluto was discovered in 1930 and was named as the ninth planet in the solar system. In 2006, astronomers revised this, and called it a dwarf planet.

The dwarf planet **Pluto** was named in 1930 by a young English girl named Venetia Burney. Her grandfather told her that the astronomers who had discovered Pluto did not have a name for it yet. Venetia suggested *Pluto* because it had to do with the religion of the ancient Greeks, a subject that was interesting to her.

plu·to·ni·um [ploo-toh-nee-um] *noun. Chemistry.* a radioactive, silvery-white, metallic element that feels warm to the touch. Plutonium does not occur naturally, but is made from uranium in nuclear reactors. It is used to make nuclear weapons.

ply·wood [plye-wud] *noun.* a wood product made by gluing thin layers of wood together.

P.M. *or* **p.m.** an abbreviation used after times of the day to show that they refer to the hours between noon and midnight.

pneu·mat·ic [noo-mat-ik] *adjective. Science.* worked by air pressure: *He used the pneumatic pump to inflate the tire.* The branch of science that studies the mechanical properties of gases is called **pneumatics.**

pock·et [pok-it] *noun, plural* **pockets. 1.** a cloth fold or pouch that is sewn onto a piece of clothing or bag to hold small items. **2.** a small area of a substance or material that is within a larger area of another type: *The airplane dipped when it flew into a cold pocket of air.*
verb, **pocketed, pocketing.** to put something in your own pocket; take something that is not rightfully yours: *She pocketed the coins lying on the table.*

PLUTO

Pluto lies at the outer edge of the solar system and takes 248 Earth years to orbit the Sun. For most of this time its surface is covered with frozen nitrogen and methane, which turn into gases when it moves closer to the Sun. Beneath the surface, it is made up mainly of ice and rock. Pluto has a moon called Charon, which takes about six days to circle it

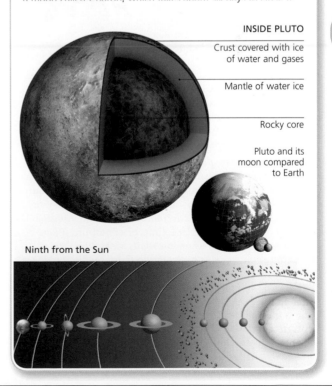

INSIDE PLUTO

Crust covered with ice of water and gases

Mantle of water ice

Rocky core

Pluto and its moon compared to Earth

Ninth from the Sun

pock·et·book [pok-it-*buk*] *noun, plural* **pocketbooks.** a book-like bag used to carry money, papers, and other small items; wallet; also called a purse or handbag.

pock·et·knife [pok-it-*nife*] *noun, plural* **pocketknives.** a small knife with a blade or blades that can be folded back into the handle.

pod ▼ [pod] *noun, plural* **pods. 1.** a seed case with two sides, such as a bean pod, that holds more than one seed. When the seeds are ripe, the two sides of the pod separate. **2.** a small herd of animals, especially whales, dolphins, and seals.

A pod holds several pea seeds.

po·em [poh-um] *noun, plural* **poems.** *Literature.* a piece of writing that expresses feelings and thoughts in language chosen for its beauty. Poetry is often set out in short lines and especially uses words chosen for their rhythm, rhyme, sound, and power.

po·et [poh-ut] *noun, plural* **poets.** *Literature.* a person who writes poetry.

po·et·ic [poh-et-ik] *adjective.* relating to or like poetry: *He used poetic language to describe the beautiful sunset.* —**poetically,** *adverb.*

po·et·ry [poh-i-tree] *noun. Literature.* **1.** a collection of poems: *I bought a book of her poetry.* **2.** the art or work of writing poems.

poin·set·ti·a ▶ [poin-set-uh *or* poin-set-ee-uh] *noun, plural* **poinsettias.** a plant from southern Mexico and Central America that flowers at Christmas time. Poinsettias have small flowers surrounded by large, showy red, white, or pink leaves.

The Aztecs made a red dye from **poinsettia** *plants.*

The **poinsettia** flower is named for Joel *Poinsett*, who was the U.S. ambassador to Mexico in the early 1800s. He was the first to introduce this flower to the United States, after his return from Mexico.

point [point] *noun, plural* **points. 1.** a sharp end of something: *The needle's point pierced the cloth.* **2.** a piece of land that juts out into water and tapers to a fine end: *The ship rounded the point of the headland.* **3.** a dot or mark used in writing: *a decimal point; an exclamation point.* **4.** a particular place, time, or condition: *When you get to the point where the roads meet, turn left; At the point when he began to shout, Jill told him to leave.* **5.** the main thought: *The point of his argument was that he didn't want to pay.* **6.** a characteristic or special quality: *Her best point is that she is always calm.* **7.** a score in a game: *in basketball, a basket counts for two points.* *verb,* **pointed, pointing. 1.** to show where something is, especially by aiming a finger or something else at it: *The sign at the crossroads pointed the way to the town.* **2.** to aim: *He pointed the gun at the target.*

point·er ▼ [point-ur] *noun, plural* **pointers. 1.** something that is used to point with, such as a long stick. **2.** a type of hunting dog that stands still and points at any game animals it detects. **3.** a suggestion or hint: *The teacher gave me some pointers to help me improve my writing.*

point of view a position from which something is seen or thought about: *The artist painted his picture from a bird's point of view; According to his point of view, building the new school would be a waste of money.*

Pointers *are alert and intelligent dogs.*

poise [poiz] *noun.* **1.** calm confidence, especially when dealing with other people: *She dealt with meeting so many new people with poise.* A person who is calm and confident is said to be **poised. 2.** a state of balance: *The gymnast did a somersault on the beam with perfect poise.* *verb,* **poised, poising.** to hold in a balanced position: *She waited, poised to make her entrance onto the stage.*

poi·son [poi-zun] *noun, plural* **poisons.** a substance that harms or kills if it is swallowed or otherwise taken into the body. *verb,* **poisoned, poisoning. 1.** to give a substance that harms or kills: *The exterminator poisoned the cockroaches by spraying them.* **2.** to put a harmful substance in food or drink: *He poisoned the wine meant for the prince.* **3.** to have a harmful effect from: *Her mind was poisoned against us by your lies.*

poison ivy a plant with shiny green leaves that contain a chemical that can cause a severe rash, and if eaten can cause death. Poison ivy grows as a creeping or climbing plant or a shrub and is common in North America. A similar plant that contains the same chemical is **poison oak,** so named because its leaves are similar in shape to oak leaves.

poi·son·ous ▼ [poi-zuh-nus] *adjective.* **1.** containing a poison: *Don't eat those poisonous mushrooms.* **2.** able to harm or kill with a poison; venomous; toxic: *Be careful of poisonous spiders.* **3.** describing something harmful or hateful: *He gave her a poisonous stare.*

poke [poke] *verb,* **poked, poking. 1.** to push with something pointed; jab: *She poked me in the arm with her finger.* **2.** to appear suddenly, especially through, from behind, or from underneath something: *The prairie dog poked its head up out of its hole and looked around.* **3.** to move in a slow, unhurried way: *We poked along behind the rest of the group.*

The strawberry poison frog has a **poisonous** *fluid under its skin.*

*A **polar bear** mother protects and feeds her cubs until they are able to find food for themselves.*

Polish

pok·er¹ [poh-kur] *noun, plural* **pokers.** a metal rod for moving or stirring burning coals or wood in a fireplace.

pok·er² [poh-kur] *noun.* a card game in which the players bet money on the value of the cards they have in their hand.

po·lar [poh-lur] *adjective.* having to do with the North Pole or South Pole: *It is very cold in polar regions; Some scientists are worried that the polar icecaps are melting.* This word is also spelled **Polar.**

polar bear ▲ a large bear that lives in the Arctic. Polar bears have thick, white fur, sharp claws, and are very good swimmers. Their main food is seals.

pole¹ [pole] *noun, plural* **poles.** a long, thin, rounded piece of wood or other material: *a flag pole; ski poles.* *verb,* **poled, poling.** to use a pole or poles to move along: *to pole a boat.*
🔊 Different words with the same sound are **Pole** and **poll.**

pole² [pole] *noun, plural* **poles. 1.** either of the two extreme points of the axis of the Earth, called the North Pole and the South Pole. **2.** either end of a magnet or battery, where the force is strongest.
🔊 Different words with the same sound are **Pole** and **poll.**

Pole [pole] *noun, plural* **Poles.** a person born in Poland, a country in Europe.
🔊 Different words with the same sound are **pole** and **poll.**

pole·cat [pole-kat] *noun, plural* **polecats. 1.** a small, fierce wild animal related to the weasel. It lives in Europe. A polecat gives off an unpleasant smelling spray to mark its territory. **2.** another name for the skunk of North America.

The word **polecat** is used as a name for various wild animals, but this is not connected to the common word *pole.* It comes from the French word *poule,* meaning "chicken." (The English word *poultry* is from this same word *poule.*) A polecat was thought of as an animal that would sneak onto a farm to attack and eat chickens.

pole vault ▼ a sporting contest in which a person uses a long pole to jump over a very high horizontal bar. A person competing in this sport is a **pole vaulter.** *verb,* **pole-vaulted, pole-vaulting.** to use a long pole to jump over a high bar.

po·lice [puh-lees] *noun.* a group of persons employed by the government who have the power to keep order, to make sure people obey the laws, and to protect people and property: *The police caught the bank robbers and arrested them.* *verb,* **policed, policing.** to keep order and make sure people obey the laws: *to police the crowd at a baseball game.*

po·lice·man [puh-lees-mun] *noun, plural* **policemen.** a man who is a member of the police.

police officer a member of the police; a policeman or policewoman.

po·lice·wom·an [puh-lees-*wu*-mun] *noun, plural* **policewomen.** a woman who is a member of the police.

pol·i·cy¹ [pol-uh-see] *noun, plural* **policies.** a set of beliefs or a plan of action worked out and agreed on by a group and used to guide them in making decisions: *Does the town have a policy for saving water?*

pol·i·cy² [pol-uh-see] *noun, plural* **policies.** a signed agreement between an insurance company and the person being insured.

po·li·o [poh-lee-oh] *noun. Medicine.* a serious infectious disease spread by a virus that attacks the spinal cord and can cause paralysis, usually of the legs. There are two vaccines to help prevent polio, and this disease is now rare. This word is the shortened form of **poliomyelitis.**

In the Olympic Games, **pole vaulters** *jump over a bar that is more than sixteen feet high.*

pol·ish [pol-ish] *noun, plural* **polishes. 1.** the fact of being smooth and shiny: *Grace rubbed the silver tray to a bright polish.* **2.** a substance that is put on a surface in order to clean it, protect it, and make it shine: *furniture polish.* *verb,* **polished, polishing.** to make smooth, bright, and shiny by rubbing: *Sam polished the car with a soft cloth.*
• **polish off.** to finish, especially quickly and completely: *He polished off the last piece of pie.*

Po·lish [poh-lish] *noun.* the language of Poland. *adjective.* having to do with Poland, its people, or its culture.

a
b
c
d
e
f
g
h
i
j
k
l
m
n
o
p
q
r
s
t
u
v
w
x
y
z

*Power plants and heavy industry can **pollute** the air with dangerous chemicals and gases.*

po·lite [puh-<u>lite</u>] *adjective,* **politer, politest.** having good manners and behaving in a way that shows consideration for other people: *It is polite to say "thank you" and "please."* —**politely,** *adverb;* —**politeness,** *noun.*

po·lit·i·cal [puh-<u>lit</u>-uh-kul] *adjective.* having to do with politics or government: *The major political parties in the U.S.A. are the Democrats and the Republicans.* —**politically,** *adverb.*

pol·i·ti·cian [pol-uh-<u>tish</u>-un] *noun, plural* **politicians.** **1.** a person whose job has to do with politics, especially someone who has been elected to a government office. **2.** a person who is clever at dealing with people in order to gain something that is to their own advantage.

pol·i·tics [<u>pol</u>-uh-tiks] *plural noun. Government.* **1.** the matters that are connected with controlling the government of a town, state, or country; the management of public affairs: *She began her career in politics by running for the office of mayor.* **2.** the activities of political parties and politicians: *Joe is more interested in sport than politics.* **3.** the beliefs and opinions on how a country should be governed: *Children often have the same politics as their parents.* **4.** the methods people use to gain power in a country or organization: *office politics; to play politics.*

pol·ka [<u>poke</u>-uh] *noun, plural* **polkas.** a quick and lively dance.

polka dot a dot that is part of a pattern of evenly spaced dots printed on a cloth or other material.

poll [pole] *noun, plural* **polls.** a counting of votes or opinions: *The teacher took a class poll on which pets we liked best.* An **opinion poll** is a public survey about important happenings, usually to find out how popular someone or something is. In an election, the place where votes are taken is the **polls.** *verb,* **polled, polling. 1.** to receive votes: *Tom polled well enough to win the election.* **2.** to question a group of people and record their answers: *The radio station polled its listeners on their favorite song.* 🔊 Different words with the same sound are **pole** and **Pole.**

pol·len [<u>pol</u>-un] *noun. Biology.* the fine yellow seed powder produced by the male part, or anther, of a flower and made up of the male cells of the plant.

pol·li·nate ▼ [<u>pol</u>-uh-*nate*] *verb,* **pollinated, pollinating.** *Biology.* to carry pollen from the male part, or anther, of one flower to the female part, or pistil, of another flower of the same species so that the plant can form seeds. Insects such as bees, some birds and animals, and the wind help with **pollination.**

pol·lute ◀ [puh-<u>loot</u>] *verb,* **polluted, polluting.** *Environment.* to make dirty or impure: *Smoke from cars and factories is polluting our atmosphere.* Someone or something that releases harmful substances into air or water is a **polluter.** The harmful substance released into the air or water is a **pollutant.**

pol·lu·tion [puh-<u>loo</u>-shun] *noun, plural* **pollutions.** *Environment.* harmful substances, such as certain gases, chemicals, and wastes, that make the air, water, or soil dirty or impure.

POLLINATION

Pollination is one of several ways that plants reproduce. To make a new plant in this way, the male cells in the pollen must reach and fertilize the female cells in the ovule, inside the ovary. As plants are fixed in one place, this task is carried out by insects, birds, wind, or water. The fertilized female cell develops into a seed, from which the new plant grows.

Bees carry pollen on their back legs from one blossom to another.

HOW A PEACH TREE REPRODUCES

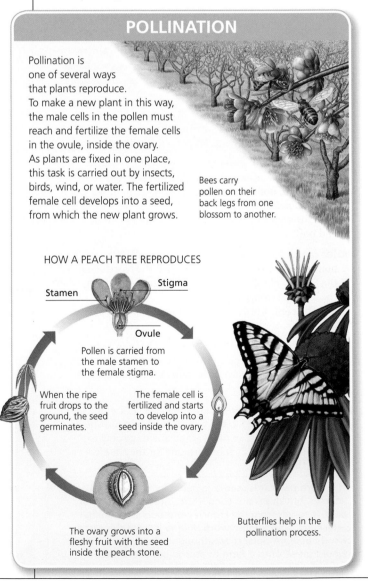

Stamen — Stigma

Ovule

Pollen is carried from the male stamen to the female stigma.

When the ripe fruit drops to the ground, the seed germinates.

The female cell is fertilized and starts to develop into a seed inside the ovary.

The ovary grows into a fleshy fruit with the seed inside the peach stone.

Butterflies help in the pollination process.

po·lo ▶ [poh-loh] *noun.* a ball game played on horseback between two teams using mallets with long handles and a wooden ball.

> The word **polo** comes from an ancient language of Asia. The game was first played in certain parts of Asia, and the word came into English after British people saw it being played in India.

pol·y·gon [pol-ee-gon] *noun, plural* **polygons.** *Mathematics.* a flat shape with three or more straight sides. Triangles, rectangles, and squares are polygons.

pol·yp [pol-ip] *noun, plural* **polyps.** **1.** a small, simple sea animal. A polyp has a tube-shaped body that is closed at one end and at the other end has a mouth that is surrounded by tentacles that catch food. Coral is made of a great many polyps living together in colonies. **2.** *Medicine.* a small, unhealthy growth on a surface inside the body, such as on the inside of the nose or on the lining of the intestines.

pome·gran·ate ▼ [pom-uh-*gran*-it] *noun, plural* **pomegranates.** a round, reddish, thick-skinned fruit with juicy red flesh and many small seeds. Pomegranates grow on trees in warm parts of the world.

pomp [pomp] *noun.* splendid display, as in a ceremony; magnificence: *The king's coronation was conducted with pomp.*

pomp·ous [pom-pus] *adjective.* having too high an opinion of one's importance: *The mayor welcomed the Olympic medalist with a pompous speech about his own sports achievements.*

pon·cho ▶ [pon-choh] *noun, plural* **ponchos.** a cloak with a hole in the center for the head to go through.

pond [pond] *noun, plural* **ponds.** an area of water surrounded by land and smaller than a lake.

pon·der [pon-dur] *verb,* **pondered, pondering.** to think about something deeply or carefully: *Jay stared at the chess board for several minutes, pondering his next move.*

po·ny [poh-nee] *noun, plural* **ponies.** a type of small horse.

Pony Express *History.* a rapid postal service in which relays of riders on fast horses carried mail across the western U.S. The Pony Express operated from 1860 to 1861.

Pomegranate seeds are eaten fresh or dried, and can be made into juice.

po·ny·tail [poh-nee-*tale*] *noun, plural* **ponytails.** a hairdo in which the hair is pulled back and fastened into one bunch so that it hangs down behind the head like a pony's tail.

poo·dle ▼ [poo-dul] *noun, plural* **poodles.** a breed of dog with thick, curly hair that is sometimes trimmed to a special shape.

pool¹ [pool] *noun, plural* **pools.** **1.** an enclosed area of water for swimming in, either indoors or outdoors. **2.** a small area of still water surrounded by land. **3.** a small amount of liquid lying on a surface: *My wet umbrella left a pool of water on the floor.*

pool² [pool] *noun, plural* **pools.** **1.** a game played with hard, colored balls on a large table that has six pockets around the edges. Each player uses a long, thin stick called a cue to strike one ball against another with the aim of hitting the balls into the pockets. **2.** something that is shared by several people or organizations: *The three families formed a car pool and take turns driving the children in the group to school.*
verb, **pooled, pooling.** to put things together so that everyone can share them: *The scientists pooled the results of their research; The children pooled their money to buy a silk scarf for their mother's birthday.*

This black, male miniature **poodle** *has had his coat clipped and styled.*

poor [poor] *adjective,* **poorer, poorest. 1.** having very little money or belongings: *The old man was too poor to afford a new coat.* **2.** of bad quality; below standard: *Jon returned his shirt to the store because the stitching was poor.* **3.** unfortunate or unlucky: *The poor little puppy was whimpering with fright.*
—poorly, *adverb.*

pop [pop] *verb,* **popped, popping. 1.** to make a short, explosive sound: *The balloon popped when I touched it with a pin.* **2.** to come, go, or move quickly or suddenly: *Grandma popped in to say hello on her way to the store.*
noun, plural **pops. 1.** a short, explosive sound: *the pop of a champagne cork.* **2.** a soft drink.

pop·corn [pop-korn] *noun.* a type of corn kernel that bursts open and puffs up when heated. It is then eaten as a snack.

Pope [pope] *noun, plural* **Popes.** *Religion.* the head of the Roman Catholic Church. This word is also spelled **pope.**

Musicians in Bolivia wear colorful **ponchos** *to keep them warm and dry.*

> The word **Pope** comes from an old word for "father." The idea is that the Pope, as head of the Catholic Church, is in the role of a Holy Father to Catholics all over the world.

a b c d e f g h i j k l m n o **p** q r s t u v w x y z

*The Brazilian **porcupine** can grow to a length of forty inches, half of which is its tail.*

pop·lar ▶ [pop-lur] *noun, plural* **poplars.** a type of tall, straight, thin tree. Its wood is used to make paper and cardboard.

pop·py ▼ [pop-ee] *noun, plural* **poppies.** a plant with large, bright red, yellow, or white flowers.

pop·u·lar [pop-yuh-lur] *adjective.* **1.** liked or accepted by many people: *The Grand Canyon is a popular tourist attraction.* **2.** having many friends: *The bus driver's kind nature and good sense of humor made him very popular in the town.* **3.** having to do with the people in general: *The old cinema was reopened by popular demand.* —**popularly,** *adverb.*

pop·u·lar·i·ty [pop-yuh-lare-uh-tee] *noun.* the fact of being liked by many people; the fact of being approved of: *In summer, the popularity of this beach means that it gets very crowded.*

pop·u·la·tion [pop-yuh-lay-shun] *noun, plural* **populations.** **1.** all the people living in a town, country, or other area: *What is the population of Japan?* **2.** the people, animals, or plants living in a place: *a population of rare frogs.*

pop·u·lous [pop-yuh-lus] *adjective.* having a lot of people living in it: *Hong Kong is a populous place.*

por·ce·lain ▶ [por-suh-lin] *noun.* a type of fine, white clay that is used to make very thin, hard pottery. Delicate ornaments and special plates, cups, and other dishes are sometimes made of porcelain.

porch [porch] *noun, plural* **porches.** a covered area at the entrance to a house: *Mom grows pots of herbs on our back porch.*

por·cu·pine ◀ [por-kyuh-pine] *noun, plural* **porcupines.** a short-legged animal with lots of long, thin, sharp spines, called quills, covering its back. The quills stick out to protect the animal when it is attacked.

> **Porcupine** comes from a phrase meaning "spiny pig." A porcupine was thought to look like a pig, although with long, sharp spines or needles rather than a smooth or hairy skin like a pig.

pore¹ [pore] *noun, plural* **pores.** a very small opening in the skin for liquid to be taken in or come out through: *Perspiration comes out through your pores.*
🔊 A different word with the same sound is **pour.**

pore² [pore] *verb,* **pored, poring.** to study or look at something very carefully: *Duncan pored over the map, trying to work out the best way back to the cabin.*
🔊 A different word with the same sound is **pour.**

pork [pork] *noun.* the meat of a pig, eaten as food.

po·rous [pore-us] *adjective.* having a lot of tiny holes or spaces that allow water or air to pass through: *Cotton fabric is porous, but plastic is waterproof.* Materials that have **porosity,** such as loose soil or a towel, are able to absorb water.

por·poise [por-pus] *noun, plural* **porpoises.** a large sea mammal with a short, rounded nose. Porpoises are usually blackish on top and paler underneath, swim about in groups, and often leap out of the water. They are a kind of dolphin.

por·ridge [por-ij] *noun, plural* **porridges.** a soft food made by boiling oatmeal or other ground grains in milk or water.

port [port] *noun, plural* **ports. 1.** a place where boats and ships can load and unload cargo and passengers or can anchor safely; a harbor. **2.** a town or city with such a harbor: *Liverpool is an important port in England.* **3.** the left side of a boat or airplane when you are facing the front.

port·a·ble [por-tuh-bul] *adjective.* able to be easily carried or moved: *We have a portable barbecue that we can put at different places in the yard.*

por·tal [por-tul] *noun, plural* **portals.** a doorway, gate, or entrance, especially one that is large or grand.

por·ter [por-tur] *noun, plural* **porters. 1.** a person whose job is to carry bags or other loads: *a porter at a hotel.* **2.** a person whose job is to look after passengers in the sleeping car or dining car of a train.

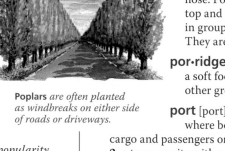

Poplars are often planted as windbreaks on either side of roads or driveways.

*Decorated **porcelain** jugs, bowls, and dishes from China are prized by collectors around the world.*

*The seeds of **poppies** are used in cooking and baking.*

port·hole ▶ [port-*hole*] *noun, plural* **portholes.** a small, round opening like a window in the side of a ship that lets in light and air.

por·ti·co ▼ [por-tuh-koh] *noun, plural* **porticoes** or **porticos.** *Architecture.* a large, covered area at the entrance to a building, with pillars supporting the roof.

por·tion [por-shun] *noun, plural* **portions. 1.** a part of something: *She's going to pay a portion of the bill today and the rest when the work is completed.* **2.** a serving of food: *Alex took two portions of pie.* *verb,* **portioned, portioning.** to divide and share out; distribute: *Donna portioned out the chores so that we all had something to do.*

por·trait [por-trit *or* por-trate] *noun, plural* **portraits. 1.** *Art.* a picture of someone, especially a painting, which often shows only the person's face: *The artist painted a portrait of his mother.* **2.** a description of something in writing: *A Portrait of the Artist as a Young Man is a famous book by James Joyce.*

por·tray [por-tray] *verb,* **portrayed, portraying.** *Art.* **1.** to make a drawing or painting of someone or something: *The artist portrayed his mother standing in her garden.* **2.** to make a picture of someone or something in words; describe: *The book* Huckleberry Finn *portrays the adventures of young boys who live beside the Mississippi River.* **3.** to play the part of: *Gina portrays the mother in the play.* —**portrayal,** *noun.*

Por·tu·guese [por-chuh-geez *or* por-chuh-geez] *noun.* a person born or living in Portugal, a country in Europe. *adjective.* having to do with Portugal, its people, or its culture.

pose [poze] *noun, plural* **poses. 1.** a particular position of the body: *The model took up several different poses for the art class.* **2.** a way of behaving or dressing to give a particular impression or to hide the truth: *Her French accent is just a pose—she has never even visited Europe.* *verb,* **posed, posing. 1.** to stand in a particular way or in a particular place: *The winning team posed with the trophy.* **2.** to pretend to be someone else: *The reporter posed as a waiter to get near the movie star.*

po·si·tion [puh-zish-un] *noun, plural* **positions. 1.** the exact place or location of someone or something: *The cat didn't leave its position beside the fire all night.* **2.** a particular way of being placed: *an upright position; a sitting position.* **3.** an attitude or opinion on a particular subject or situation; point of view: *What is the town's position on changing the route of the highway?* **4.** a job: *He applied for the position of assistant principal.* **5.** a player's assigned place on the field in certain sports: *In football, quarterback is considered to be the most important position.* *verb,* **positioned, positioning.** to put in a particular place: *Zach positioned himself at the back of the room.*

pos·i·tive [poz-uh-tiv] *adjective.* **1.** knowing something without a doubt; certain or sure: *Are you positive that this is the correct address?* **2.** helpful and encouraging; favorable: *The director was pleased with the reviewer's positive comments about the play.* **3.** saying or meaning yes; showing agreement: *Sara nodded a positive reply.* **4.** greater than zero; plus: *Three is a positive number.* **5.** having one of two opposite types of electrical charge: *The positive end of a battery is marked with the "+" symbol.* —**positively,** *adverb.*

pos·se [pos-ee] *noun, plural* **posses.** a group of volunteers who help a sheriff find a criminal or lost person, or keep order.

pos·sess [puh-zes] *verb,* **possessed, possessing. 1.** to own or have: *The city art gallery possesses several paintings by famous artists.* **2.** to be taken over or controlled by something: *I was possessed by the sudden urge to sneeze.* Someone who is **possessed** has been taken over by a strong feeling or madness.

pos·ses·sion [puh-zesh-un] *noun, plural* **possessions. 1.** the act of possessing something; ownership: *When they inherited the farm, the family also came into the possession of two horses and an old tractor.* **2.** the things that someone owns: *She arrived at her new home with all her possessions packed into two large suitcases.* **3.** a place under the control of a foreign power: *Canada was once a possession of Great Britain.*

> The word **posse** comes from a word for "power" and it originally meant "the power of the county." The posse was a group that the sheriff could call upon to help him enforce the law, made up of nearly all the adult men in the county.

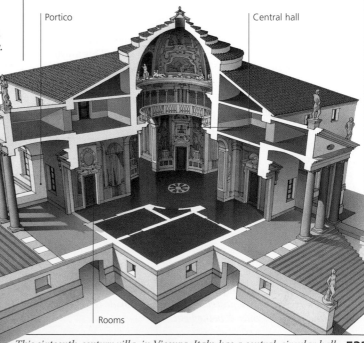

Portico   Central hall

Rooms

This sixteenth-century villa, in Vicenza, Italy, has a central, circular hall surrounded by rectangular rooms with **porticoes** *on all four sides.*

a b c d e f g h i j k l m n o p q r s t u v w x y z

*The Australian striped **possum** hooks grubs out of trees with its long fingers.*

pos·ses·sive [puh-<u>zes</u>-iv] *noun,* *plural* **possessives.** *Language.* the form of a word that shows ownership or connection. In the sentence *He borrowed the teacher's book,* the noun *teacher's* is in the possessive. *adjective.* **1.** having to do with a word that shows ownership or connection. *His* is the possessive form of the pronoun *he.* **2.** not wanting to share the ownership or control of someone or something: *Jason is very possessive about his new bike and won't let anyone else ride it.* —**possessively,** *adverb;* **possessiveness,** *noun.*

To possess something is to own or have it. A **possessive** word shows this sense of ownership, usually by adding **'s** to the end of a word: "That is Susan**'s** book." "The teacher**'s** son visited our class today." Possession can also be shown by certain words, such as *my, mine, our, ours, your, yours, her, hers, his, its, their,* and *theirs*: "That is *her* book." A friend of *mine* visited our class today."

pos·si·bil·i·ty [poss-uh-<u>bil</u>-i-tee] *noun, plural* **possibilities. 1.** the fact of being possible: *Instant communication to most parts of the world is now a possibility, because of the Internet.* **2.** something that might be true or might happen: *There is a possibility that we could finish the project a day early.*

pos·si·ble [poss-uh-bul] *adjective.* **1.** able to be done or happen: *It is possible for a person to stand on one leg, but it is not possible for a person to fly like a bird.* **2.** able to be used or considered; acceptable: *Jack suggested "Tigers" as a possible name for his team.*

pos·si·bly [poss-uh-blee] *adverb.* **1.** in any way at all: *I'll be there if I possibly can.* **2.** it could be; maybe: *I think his coat was black, or possibly very dark blue.*

pos·sum ▲ [poss-um] *noun, plural* **possums.** a small, furry animal. See OPOSSUM for more information. This animal is said to **play possum**—to pretend to be asleep or dead in order to escape danger.

post[1] [post] *noun, plural* **posts.** an upright piece of wood or metal set firmly in the ground to support something, or to mark a place or a boundary: *The large porch was supported by four strong posts.* *verb,* **posted, posting.** to put a public notice in a place where it can be easily seen: *The teacher posted the our new class schedule on the classroom wall.*

post[2] [post] *noun, plural* **posts. 1.** a place where a soldier, sentry, or other guard must stay while on duty: *The sentry post is just outside the main gate.* **2.** a camp or other place where soldiers work or live: *an army post.* **3.** an official position; a job: *My uncle has been offered the post of bank manager.* *verb,* **posted, posting.** to place someone in a certain post: *Guards have been posted to a new job outside the room where the prisoner is being held.*

post[3] [post] *noun, plural* **posts.** a system for collecting and distributing letters and other items; mail: *Please send the book by post.* *verb,* **posted, posting. 1.** to send a letter by the mail system. **2.** to supply current information; inform: *Keep me posted on your exam results.*

post- a prefix that means after: if you *postdate* a letter, you put a date that is after the current date; a *postwar* event happens after the end of the war.

post·age [post-ij] *noun.* the amount of money paid for sending a letter or other item by mail.

postage stamp ▶ a small printed label pasted to an envelope or package that shows the correct amount of postage has been paid.

post·al [post-ul] *adjective.* having to do with the mail: *the U.S. Postal Service.*

post·card [post-*kard*] *noun, plural* **postcards.** a card that can be sent through the mail without an envelope. It usually has a photo, drawing, or design on one side, and the other side has space for the sender to write a short message.

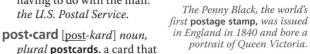

*The Penny Black, the world's first **postage stamp**, was issued in England in 1840 and bore a portrait of Queen Victoria.*

post·er [poh-stur] *noun, plural* **posters.** a large printed picture or notice. Posters advertise goods or services for sale.

post·man [post-mun] *noun, plural* **postmen.** a person employed by the mail service to deliver letters and other postal items.

post·mark [post-*mark*] *noun, plural* **postmarks.** a mark stamped on an envelope or postage stamp showing when and where the letter was posted and canceling the stamp. *verb,* **postmarked, postmarking.** to mark a letter or package in this way: *The card was postmarked New York so I knew that was where my cousin took his vacation.*

post·mas·ter [post-*mas*-tur] *noun, plural* **postmasters.** the official who is in charge of a post office.

post office 1. a government department that is in charge of handling mail. **2.** an office or building where mail is received, sorted, and distributed and where postage stamps are sold.

post·pone [post-<u>pone</u>] *verb* **postponed, postponing.** to cause something to be delayed, or to happen at a later date or time: *I postponed my party because I had a bad cold.* —**postponement,** *noun.*

To **postpone** or *cancel* something, like a game, party, or other event, are similar but not the same. Both mean that the event will not take place, but *postpone* means that it will be held at a later date: "Our baseball game was *postponed* because of rain and will be played next Saturday." *Cancel* means that the event is called off completely: "My flight was *canceled,* so I have to fly on a different airline this afternoon."

post·script [post-skript] *noun, plural* **postscripts.** a short note or sentence added to the end of a letter, after the person's signature, which gives a bit of extra information or late news: *She added in a postscript that the package we sent her had just arrived.* The abbreviation for this word is **P.S.**

*A **potter** shapes a bowl by molding clay on a potter's wheel.*

pos·ture [pos-chur] *noun, plural* **postures.** the way in which someone holds the body when walking, sitting, or standing: *To be sure of good posture while using the computer, sit up straight in a chair that supports your back.* *verb,* **postured, posturing.** to adopt a particular posture; pose: *She's always posturing in front of the mirror.*

pot [pot] *noun, plural* **pots.** a rounded container of metal, baked clay, or glass. Pots are used to store things or for cooking. Something that has been planted or grown in a container such as a pot is described as **potted.**

po·tas·si·um [puh-tas-ee-um] *noun. Chemistry.* a soft, silvery-white metal. Potassium is a chemical element. When combined with other elements, it is used to make glass, fertilizers, soap, and explosives.

Potassium was named by a famous English scientist, Sir Humphrey Davy, who made a number of important discoveries in the field of chemistry. He chose the name *potassium* because he found this chemical in *potash,* a substance obtained from wood ashes.

po·ta·to [puh-tay-toh] *noun, plural* **potatoes.** a roundish vegetable with white flesh. It is the underground stem of a leafy plant.

po·ten·tial [puh-ten-shul] *adjective.* capable of becoming in the future; possible but not yet actual: *The fire inspector told him that the dry grass and dead bushes near the house are a potential problem.* *noun.* something that can become actual or that can develop: *After watching me run, the coach said I have a lot of potential as a sprinter.* —**potentially,** *adverb.*

pot·ter ▲ [pot-ur] *noun, plural* **potters.** a person who makes pottery.

pot·ter·y [pot-ur-ee] *noun.* objects, such as pots and bowls, made from clay.

pouch ▶ [pouch] *noun, plural* **pouches.** **1.** a small sack; a bag: *My grandfather keeps his old silver dollars in a leather pouch.* **2.** in some animals, a fold of skin like a bag: *The female koala carries her young in a pouch.*

poul·try ▼ [pole-tree] *noun.* birds, such as chickens, geese, or turkeys, raised for their meat or eggs.

pounce [pouns] *verb,* **pounced, pouncing.** to leap or swoop down in order to take hold of; attack suddenly: *The eagle pounced on the rabbit.* *noun, plural* **pounces.** the act of pouncing on something.

pound¹ [pound] *noun, plural* **pounds** *or* **pound.** **1.** a unit of weight equal to 16 ounces. There are 2.2 pounds in 1 kilogram. **2.** a unit of currency in the United Kingdom and some other countries.

pound² [pound] *verb,* **pounded, pounding.** **1.** to hit with a lot of force again and again: *The boxer pounded his opponent with many blows.* **2.** to beat or throb heavily: *Running very fast makes my heart pound.*

pound³ [pound] *noun, plural* **pounds.** a place where stray animals, especially dogs, are kept.

pour [pore] *verb,* **poured, pouring. 1.** to flow or cause to flow: *Pour the milk into the bowl.* **2.** to rain heavily: *I got soaked when it suddenly poured.*
🔊 A different word with the same sound is **pore.**

pout [pout] *verb,* **pouted, pouting.** to push out the lips to show annoyance: *Stop pouting and do as I tell you.* *noun, plural* **pouts.** the act of pouting; a sullen mood.

pov·er·ty [pov-ur-tee] *noun.* **1.** a shortage of money; the state of being poor: *Around the world, millions of people live in poverty.* **2.** a shortage of something wanted or needed: *The boring book showed a poverty of imagination on the part of the writer.*

pow·der [pow-dur] *noun, plural* **powders.** **1.** fine, dry particles made by crushing, grinding, or crumbling a solid substance: *The recipe says to grind a cup of almonds into powder.* **2.** any substance in the form of fine, dry particles: *Put the washing powder into the dishwasher.* Something that consists of or looks like powder is described as **powdery.** *verb,* **powdered, powdering. 1.** to turn something into fine, dry particles. **2.** to cover with fine particles: *She finished off the muffins by powdering them with confectioner's sugar.*

Turkey

Goose

Hen

Duck

*Humans have raised **poultry** for more than 4,000 years.*

*Kangaroos and wallabies feed and protect their young in a **pouch.***

pow·er [pow-ur] *noun, plural* **powers. 1.** the ability to do something or act in a certain way; strength: *The bus driver did everything in his power to avoid crashing into the car.* **2.** the official right to do something; authority: *The manager of a company has the power to dismiss his workers.* **3.** a person, organization, or country that has influence or strength: *In ancient times, the Roman Empire was a great power.* **4.** energy that can do work: *Hydroelectric power is electricity generated by rapidly moving water.* **5.** the number that results from multiplying a number by itself a given number of times: *6 to the second power equals 36.*
verb, **powered, powering.** to supply with power: *Many trucks are powered by diesel engines.*

pow·er·ful [pow-ur-ful] *adjective.* having great power or strength: *The United States has the most powerful armed forces in the world.* —**powerfully,** *adverb.*

prac·ti·cal [prak-tuh-kul] *adjective.* **1.** having to do with real life; based on experience: *The mechanic gave me a lot of practical advice about how to fix problems with my car.* **2.** easy to do, use, or put into effect: *One practical way to reduce pollution is to use our cars less often.* **3.** having or showing good judgment; sensible: *To lead hikes in the mountains you have to be a practical person who likes making decisions.* The quality or state of being practical is **practicality:** *The inventor's ideas were praised for their practicality.*

practical joke a trick or prank: *She put peanut butter on the door handle as a practical joke.*

A **praying mantis** *uses its spiny front legs to grip its butterfly prey.*

prac·ti·cal·ly [prak-tik-lee] *adverb.* **1.** almost; nearly: *She is practically finished with her paper and just has to write the conclusion.* **2.** in a manner that is practical, useful, or sensible: *The way to solve the problem is to think practically.*

prac·tice [prak-tis] *noun, plural* **practices. 1.** the process of doing something many times so as to become good at it: *The swimming coach said Susan needs more practice to improve her stroke.* **2.** the usual way of doing something; habit: *It's his practice to get up at six o'clock every morning.* **3.** the process of carrying out something; performance: *The mayor promised to put his plans into practice.* **4.** the business of a doctor, lawyer, or other professional: *a dental practice.*
verb, **practiced, practicing. 1.** to do something many times so as to become good at it: *I need to practice the piano more often.* **2.** to make a habit of; do usually: *"Practice what you preach" means that you should act in the same way you say others should act.* **3.** to work in a profession: *Our doctor has practiced medicine for thirty years.*

prai·rie [prare-ee] *noun, plural* **prairies.** a large area of grassland with few or no trees. A prairie is flat or gently rolling.

prairie dog a small, plump animal, related to the squirrel, that has a short tail and a light brown coat. It lives in groups in underground dens in the prairies of western North America.

praise [praze] *noun, plural* **praises.** words that show admiration and approval: *Dad had nothing but praise for me after he saw my good report card.*
verb, **praised, praising. 1.** to express admiration and approval of: *The police officer praised the girl for handing in the money she had found on the street.* **2.** to pay honor to; worship: *The church choir sang a hymn praising God.*

prance [prans] *verb,* **pranced, prancing. 1.** to move in a lively, happy manner: *David pranced around the room when he heard the good news.* **2.** to spring forward on the hind legs: *The racehorse pranced and leaped about the field.*

prank [prangk] *noun, plural* **pranks.** a mischievous or playful act meant to tease or trick someone: *As a prank, he put salt instead of sugar on his sister's breakfast cereal.*

pray [pray] *verb,* **prayed, praying. 1.** to speak to God to give thanks or to ask for help: *Bill's parents prayed that the boy would recover from his illness.* **2.** to wish or hope for very much: *I pray it doesn't rain on the day of the fair.*
🔊 A different word with the same sound is **prey.**

prayer [pray-ur] *noun, plural* **prayers. 1.** *Religion.* the act of praying to God, or the words used for praying. **2.** something prayed for: *It's my prayer that the world will one day be free of war.* **3.** a chance to succeed; a hope: *The Hawks don't have a prayer of winning that game.*

praying man·tis ◀ an insect with large front legs that it raises up, as if praying. It is related to the grasshopper.

*The conditions inside a cloud, the temperature outside it, and the cloud's height above the ground determine what kind of **precipitation** falls.*

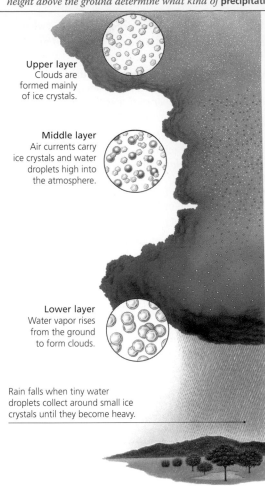

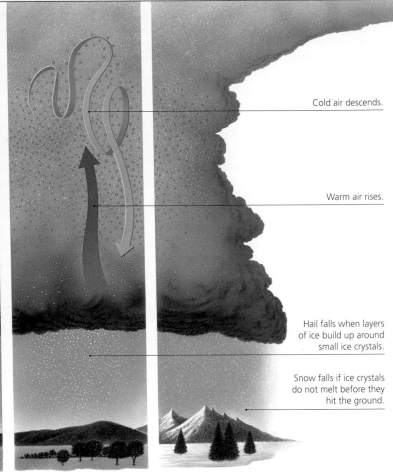

Upper layer
Clouds are formed mainly of ice crystals.

Middle layer
Air currents carry ice crystals and water droplets high into the atmosphere.

Lower layer
Water vapor rises from the ground to form clouds.

Cold air descends.

Warm air rises.

Hail falls when layers of ice build up around small ice crystals.

Rain falls when tiny water droplets collect around small ice crystals until they become heavy.

Snow falls if ice crystals do not melt before they hit the ground.

pre- a prefix that means before or ahead of time: *precede* means to go before; *predict* means to tell ahead of time.

preach [preech] *verb,* **preached, preaching. 1.** *Religion.* to give a religious speech; give a sermon: *The minister devoted his life to preaching the word of God.* **2.** to offer advice; urge: *The principal always preached to us about the need to respect people of different races or cultures.*

preach·er [preech-ur] *noun, plural* **preachers.** *Religion.* a person who preaches, especially a minister of a Protestant church.

pre·cau·tion [pri-kaw-shun] *noun, plural* **precautions.** something done in advance to prevent danger or harm: *Wearing a life jacket is a good precaution to take when you go sailing or canoeing.*

pre·cede [pree-seed] *verb,* **preceded, preceding.** to be, come, or go before: *President John F. Kennedy preceded President Lyndon B. Johnson in the White House.* Being, coming, or going before is **preceding:** *Our baseball team finally won a game after losing the preceding four games.*

prec·e·dent [pres-uh-dunt] *noun, plural* **precedents.** a decision or action that may be used as a guide or example for a future decision or action: *The judge's decision in this case was used as a precedent for other similar cases after that.*

pre·cinct [pree-singkt] *noun, plural* **precincts.** a part of a city or town: *In the election, people vote for candidates in their own precinct.*

pre·cious [presh-us] *adjective.* **1.** of great value: *The queen's crown contains precious jewels.* **2.** greatly loved; dear: *Family vacations have given me many precious memories.* *adverb.* very; extremely: *We have to be at the airport in an hour, so there's precious little time to waste.*

pre·cip·i·tate [pri-sip-i-tate] *verb,* **precipitated, precipitating.** to make something happen suddenly or sooner than expected, especially something bad: *In 1939, the invasion of Poland by Germany precipitated World War II.*

pre·cip·i·ta·tion ▲ [pri-sip-i-tay-shun] *noun.* *Environment.* the falling of water from clouds as rain, sleet, hail, or snow: *The weather forecast for tomorrow is for sunny weather with no precipitation.*

pre·cise [pri-sise] *adjective.* **1.** describing something exact; accurate: *"4 feet 3 inches" is a precise measurement—"about 4 feet" is not.* **2.** careful or strict: *Dad gave us precise orders to be home by eight o'clock.* **—precisely,** *adverb.*

pre·ci·sion [pri-sizh-un] *noun.* the fact of being exact; accuracy: *The missile is designed to hit its target with great precision.*

pre·co·cious [pri-<u>koh</u>-shus] *adjective.* having certain skills, talents, or knowledge at an earlier age than usual: *At age nine the precocious child had the math ability of a child of twelve.* —**precociously,** *adverb;* —**precociousness,** *noun.*

pred·ator ▼ [<u>pred</u>-uh-tur] *noun, plural* **predators.** *Biology.* an animal that hunts, kills, and eats other animals to live. Tigers, sharks, wolves, and eagles are predators. Having to do with being a predator is **predatory:** *Cats have strong predatory instincts.* The act of hunting, killing, and eating other animals is **predation.**

pred·e·ces·sor [<u>pred</u>-uh-*ses*-ur] *noun, plural* **predecessors.** a person who held a job or office before another person: *As the new principal, she hopes to become as well liked by the pupils as her predecessor.*

pre·dic·a·ment [pri-<u>dik</u>-uh-munt] *noun, plural* **predicaments.** an unpleasant, difficult, or embarrassing situation: *The club is in a financial predicament and might have to sell its clubhouse to raise money.*

pred·i·cate [<u>pred</u>-uh-kit] *noun, plural* **predicates.** *Language.* a word or combination of words in a sentence that tells something about the subject and usually comes after it. The predicate explains what the subject does or what is done to the subject, and may also describe the subject. In the sentence *Larry's brother threw the ball across the street,* "threw the ball across the street" is the predicate.
verb, **predicated, predicating.** to use as a basis or proof for a belief, statement, or course of action: *The plan to cut down on pollution is predicated on the belief that most people want cleaner cities.*

An American alligator is a fierce **predator** *that will even leap from the water to catch a young bird.*

pre·dict [pri-<u>dikt</u>] *verb,* **predicted, predicting.** to say what is going to happen ahead of time: *Scientists find it difficult to predict earthquakes.*

pre·dic·tion [pri-<u>dik</u>-shun] *noun, plural* **predictions.** the act of predicting or something predicted: *The prediction of the weather service is that we will have a mild winter this year.*

pref·ace [<u>pref</u>-is] *noun, plural* **prefaces.** *Language.* an introduction to a speech or book: *In the preface to the book, the author explains how she finds her ideas for writing.*
verb, **prefaced, prefacing.** to say or write as an introduction to a speech or book: *The principal prefaced his speech with a joke.*

pre·fer [pri-<u>fur</u>] *verb,* **preferred, preferring.** to like better: *I prefer studying history to studying math.*

pref·er·ence [<u>pref</u>-ur-uns *or* <u>pref</u>-runs] *noun, plural* **preferences.** a person or thing that is liked better; first choice: *My preference is to go to the movies rather than watch TV.*

pre·fix [<u>pree</u>-fiks] *noun, plural* **prefixes.** *Language.* a syllable or combination of syllables that is placed at the beginning of a word or root to change the meaning and make another word. The word *outburst* is made up of the prefix *out-* and the word *burst.*

preg·nant [<u>preg</u>-nunt] *adjective.* *Medicine.* having an unborn child or young developing within the body. The condition or period of being pregnant is **pregnancy.**

pre·his·tor·ic ▶ [<u>pree</u>-hi-<u>stor</u>-ik] *adjective.* relating to the period before history was written down: *Tools, bones, fossils, and other remains tell us much about prehistoric life.* The period before history was written down is **prehistory.**

prej·u·dice [<u>prej</u>-uh-dis] *noun, plural* **prejudices.** **1.** a judgment or opinion that has been formed beforehand or without knowing all the facts; bias: *The judge told the members of the jury that they must reach a decision in the case without prejudice.* **2.** hatred or unfair treatment of a particular group, such as members of a religion or race: *religious prejudice.*
verb, **prejudiced, prejudicing.** to give cause prejudice in: *Being bitten by a dog prejudiced me against all dogs.*

pre·lim·i·nar·y [pri-<u>lim</u>-uh-ner-ee] *adjective.* coming before a more important event or action: *The judge held a preliminary hearing two months before the full court case began.*

pre·ma·ture [*pree*-muh-<u>choor</u> *or* *pree*-muh-<u>toor</u>] *adjective.* happening, arriving, existing, or done before the proper or usual time; too soon or too early: *The premature baby was born after six months of pregnancy instead of the usual nine.* —**prematurely,** *adverb.*

pre·mier [pri-<u>meer</u>] *noun, plural* **premiers.** the name for the head of government in certain countries. *adjective.* first in order, importance, or position; leading: *The Beatles were the premier pop group of the 1960s.*

pre·miere [pri-<u>meer</u>]
noun, plural **premieres.**
the first performance or showing of a play, movie, or other form of entertainment: *Famous actors attended the premiere of the movie.*
verb, **premiered, premiering.** to give the first performance or showing of a play, movie, or other form of entertainment: *The school play premieres on Saturday night.*

prem·ise [<u>prem</u>-is] *noun, plural* **premises. 1.** a statement on which an argument or line of reasoning is based. A premise is accepted as true without the need for proof. **2. premises.** a building with the land belonging to it: *Police came to the factory and searched the premises for stolen goods.*
verb, **premised, premising.** to base an argument or line of reasoning on: *The defense lawyer premised his argument on his belief that his client was innocent.*

prep·a·ra·tion [prep-uh-<u>ray</u>-shun] *noun, plural* **preparations. 1.** the act of preparing something, or the state of being prepared: *Their team lost the game because of a lack of preparation.* **2.** something done beforehand so as to be ready for a future event: *Everyone was busy putting up decorations, making food, and doing other preparations for Mom's birthday party.* **3.** substances, such as food or a medicine, put together for a purpose: *The pharmacist gave me this preparation for my sore throat.*

pre·pare [pri-<u>pare</u>] *verb,* **prepared, preparing.** to get or make ready: *to prepare lunch; We did extra homework to prepare for the exam.*

prep·o·si·tion [prep-uh-<u>zish</u>-un] *noun, plural* **prepositions.** *Language.* a word that shows the relationship of a word to a noun or pronoun. In the sentence *We sat on the park bench and saw a squirrel with a nut*, the words "on" and "with" are prepositions.

> The way the word **preposition** was formed tells you how this part of speech is used. *Preposition* means "in the position before." A preposition is always placed before the word or phrase that is its object, as in "*down* the street."

pre·po·si·tion·al
[prep-uh-<u>zish</u>-uh-nul] *adjective. Education.* having to do with a preposition. A group of words made up of a preposition followed by a noun or nouns is a **prepositional phrase.** *Over the road, across the bridge,* and *before class* are prepositional phrases.

prep school *Education.* a private school that prepares students for college. This term is a shortened form of **preparatory school.**

pre·school [<u>pree</u>-skool] *noun, plural* **preschools.** *Education.* a school for children below the age at which they can enter kindergarten or elementary school.

pre·scribe [pri-<u>skribe</u>]
verb, **prescribed, prescribing. 1.** to order the use of a medicine or other treatment: *The doctor prescribed antibiotics to cure the infection.* **2.** to set down as a rule or course of action to be followed: *In some states, the law prescribes the death penalty for certain crimes.* Setting down a rule or course of action to be followed is **prescriptive.**

pre·scrip·tion [pri-<u>skrip</u>-shun] *noun, plural* **prescriptions. 1.** a written order by a doctor to a pharmacist for medicine: *I gave the pharmacist the prescription for cough medicine.* **2.** medicine ordered in this way. **3.** a recommendation put forward with authority: *The mayor's prescription for fighting crime is to put more police officers on the beat.*

pres·ence [<u>prez</u>-uns] *noun.* **1.** the fact of being in a place at a certain time: *The presence of so many people at my birthday party made me feel happy.* **2.** the area near or around a person: *Please don't be so noisy in my presence.*

pres·ent¹ [pri-<u>zent</u>] *adjective.* **1.** in a place at a certain time: *All students were present to hear the principal's speech.* **2.** being, existing, or happening at this time or now; current: *Who is the present governor of this state?*
noun. **1.** the period of time now occurring: *My grandmother sometimes seems to live in the past, not the present.* **2.** see PRESENT TENSE.
◆ **at present.** at or during this time; now: *At present, China has the highest population of all the world's nations.*

pres·ent² [pri-<u>zent</u>] *verb,* **presented, presenting. 1.** to place or bring before another person or group: *At the airport, I was asked to present my passport.* **2.** to give in a formal manner: *A rich businessman presented the hospital with a check for ten thousand dollars.* **3.** to bring before the public; show: *The children in the Sunday school presented a Christmas play.* **4.** to introduce a person to someone else: *My brother presented his girlfriend to our parents.*
noun, plural **presents.** something given; a gift: *How many presents did you get for your birthday?*

pres·en·ta·tion [prez-un-<u>tay</u>-shun] *noun, plural* **presentations.** the act of presenting something: *Presentation of the awards takes place in the auditorium.*

pres·ent·ly [<u>prez</u>-unt-lee] *adverb.* **1.** in a short while; soon: *Please be patient, the meeting will begin presently.* **2.** at the present time; now: *Out of eight gas stations in our town, only two presently sell diesel fuel.*

present participle *Language.* a form of a verb, ending in *-ing*, which is used with another verb to show that an action is taking place at the time of writing or speaking, is continuing, or will occur in the future. In the sentences *The geese are flying; Dad was washing the car;* and *He's going to Australia next week,* "flying," "washing," and "going" are present participles.

present tense *Language.* the form of a verb that shows that something happens or exists now. In the sentence *He travels to work by car,* the verb "travels" is in the present tense.

The English language actually has not one but two different forms of the **present tense.** Both talk about the time that is now, but only the *present progressive* tense describes action that is going on right now. It uses the verb **BE** with an **-ing** verb to do this: It *is raining* hard outside. Mom *is baking* a pie for dessert. The *simple present* tense uses an **-s** verb to show that something goes on over a long time: It *rains* a lot here in summer. The market *bakes* bread every morning.

pres·er·va·tion [prez-ur-vay-shun] *noun.* the act or fact of preserving; keeping safe from loss, harm, destruction, or decay: *The preservation of historic buildings is an important responsibility.*

pre·serv·a·tive [pri-zur-vuh-tiv] *noun, plural* **preservatives.** a substance that gives something protection from being damaged or spoiled: *I bought some wood preservative from the hardware store to put on the new fence.*

pre·serve ◀ [pri-zurv] *verb,* **preserved, preserving. 1.** to protect from damage, loss, or decay: *The President took an oath to preserve the Constitution of the United States.* **2.** to treat food to protect it from decay. *noun, plural* **preserves.** an area set aside for the protection of animals and plants: *That preserve is one of the last places in the country where this type of wild orchid grows.* Fruits that have been cooked with sugar and sealed in glass jars are **preserves:** *blueberry preserves.*

*People make **preserves** so that they can eat summer fruits all year round.*

pre·side [pri-zide] *verb,* **presided, presiding. 1.** to be officially in charge, as at a meeting: *Jean usually presides at the P.T.A. meetings.* **2.** to exert authority or control: *This government has presided over several years of economic growth.*

pres·i·den·cy [prez-uh-den-see] *noun, plural* **presidencies. 1.** the office of president: *I put my name forward for the presidency of the club.* **2.** the term during which a president holds office: *The atomic bomb was dropped on Japan during the presidency of Harry S. Truman.* This word is also spelled **Presidency.**

pres·i·dent [prez-uh-dent] *noun, plural* **presidents. 1.** the head of the government of a republic, such as the United States: *The President will address the nation on television tonight.* This word is also spelled **President. 2.** the head of an organization such as a company, a club, or a college.

Presidents' Day a holiday observed in most of the United States on the third Monday in February. It commemorates the birthdays of George Washington and Abraham Lincoln.

press [pres] *verb,* **pressed, pressing. 1.** to push something firmly: *I pressed my face to the glass of the window, trying to see inside the house.* **2.** to squeeze firmly: *I pressed my girlfriend's hand under the table.* **3.** to use an iron to remove creases from clothes: *Please press my shirt.* **4.** to make an effort to persuade; urge: *The television interviewer pressed the senator for an answer to the difficult question.*
noun, plural **presses. 1.** an act of pushing. **2.** a piece of equipment that is used for pressing: *The first step in making wine is to remove the juice from the grapes in a wine press.* **3.** a machine for printing things; a printing press. **4.** newspapers and magazines and the people who write them: *The press wants photos of the movie star.* Something that requires quick action is described as **pressing.**

pres·sure [presh-ur] *noun, plural* **pressures. 1.** force exerted by one thing against another thing that it comes into contact with: *When my friend cut her hand, I stopped the bleeding by using my fingers to put pressure on the cut.* **2.** strong persuasion or influence: *The coach put pressure on Nicole to do well at swimming.* **3.** something that is hard to bear; a burden; strain: *The job of an air traffic controller is only for someone who works well under pressure.*
verb, **pressured, pressuring.** to urge strongly: *The man pressured the elderly woman into accepting his offer to buy her house.*

pres·sur·ize [presh-uh-rize] *verb,* **pressurized, pressurizing.** to maintain normal air pressure in an enclosed space: *The cabin of an airplane remains pressurized even when the air pressure outside the airplane is very low.* The state of being pressurized is **pressurization.**

pres·tige [pre-steezh *or* pre-steej] *noun.* respect and admiration from others; high opinion: *The charity organization gained great prestige by caring for victims of war and violence.*

pres·ti·gious [pre-stij-us *or* pre-steej-us] *adjective.* inspiring respect and admiration by others; having prestige: *For his role in the movie, the actor won a prestigious award.*

pres·um·ably [pri-zoo-muh-blee] *adverb.* reasonable to suppose; probably: *He was not at the airport when he said he would be, so presumably he missed the plane.*

pre·sume [pre-zoom] *verb,* **presumed, presuming. 1.** to accept without question as being true; take for granted: *Just because our team has won all our games so far, we should not presume that we'll win the next game.* **2.** to act without authority or permission; dare: *A complete stranger presumed to tell me how I should get my hair cut!*

pre·sump·tion [pri-zump-shun] *noun, plural* **presumptions. 1.** something that is accepted without question as being true: *Under our law, the presumption is that a person accused of a crime is innocent until proven guilty.* **2.** an attitude or behavior that is disrespectful and rude and fails to observe the limits of what is appropriate or permitted: *The new member had the presumption to tell the president how to run the club.*
—presumptive, *adjective.*

pre·sump·tu·ous [pri-<u>zump</u>-choo-us] *adjective.* failing to observe the limits of what is appropriate or permitted; full of presumption: *It was presumptuous of Jim to ask for a raise only a week after taking the job.* —**presumptuously,** *adverb;* **presumptuousness,** *noun.*

pre·tend [pri-<u>tend</u>] *verb,* **pretended, pretending. 1.** to say that something is true; claim: *I can play a few tunes on the piano, but I don't pretend to be a musician.* **2.** to give a false show: *He pretended to be sick so that he could stay home from school.* **3.** to make believe: *They played a game where they pretended to live on a tropical island.*

pre·tend·er [pri-<u>tend</u>-ur] *noun, plural* **pretenders. 1.** a person who gives a false show: *In my opinion Mike is a pretender who will say anything to get his own way.* **2.** a person who lays claim to a title or throne: *Political experts call this candidate the pretender to the presidency.*

pre·tense [<u>pree</u>-tens] *noun, plural* **pretenses.** the act of pretending; a false show: *At the town meeting, the mayor made a pretense of listening to other people's ideas, but she had already made up her mind.*

pret·ty [<u>prit</u>-ee] *adjective,* **prettier, prettiest. 1.** gently pleasing to the eyes; nice to look at: *The flowers in the garden look very pretty.* **2.** pleasing in some other way; nice: *She sang a pretty tune; He made a pretty move to score a basket.*
adverb. quite; fairly: *I'm pretty sure we're lost.*
—**prettily,** *adverb.*

pret·zel [<u>pret</u>-sul] *noun, plural* **pretzels.** a crisp food baked in the shape of a knot or stick and flavored with salt.

> The word **pretzel** comes from the Latin word for "arm." The food was once called "a biscuit of crossed arms," because of the idea that the twisted shape of a pretzel looks like a person with crossed arms.

pre·vail [pri-<u>vale</u>] *verb,* **prevailed, prevailing. 1.** to be greater in influence or strength; triumph: *Our side will prevail against our enemies.* **2.** to be widespread or current: *During the Middle Ages, a belief in witches prevailed in Europe.* Something that is widespread or current is **prevailing.**

prev·a·lent [<u>prev</u>-uh-lunt] *adjective.* occurring, practiced, or accepted widely or commonly: *Poverty and disease are prevalent problems in Africa.* The condition of being prevalent is **prevalence:** *the prevalence of crime in a city.*

pre·vent [pri-<u>vent</u>] *verb,* **prevented, preventing. 1.** to keep something from happening: *Obeying the speed limit while driving helps prevent accidents.* **2.** to keep someone from doing something; hinder: *My broken leg prevented me from swimming for several weeks.*

pre·ven·tion [pri-<u>ven</u>-shun] *noun.* **1.** the act of keeping something from happening: *The police take a leading role in the prevention of crime.* **2.** something that keeps something from happening; a hindrance: *My father takes pills as a prevention against heart problems.*

pre·ven·tive [pri-<u>ven</u>-tiv] *adjective.* designed to keep something from happening: *preventive health care. noun.* something that prevents, especially something that prevents disease or illness: *This pill is a preventive against seasickness.* The branch of medical science that deals with the prevention of disease or illness is **preventive medicine.**

pre·view [<u>pree</u>-vyoo] *noun, plural* **previews.** a show of something ahead of time: *The museum is holding a preview tonight of the dinosaur exhibition that will open next week. verb,* **previewed, previewing.** to show or watch something ahead of time: *to preview a movie.*

pre·vi·ous [<u>pree</u>-vee-us] *adjective.* existing or occurring before; earlier: *We still sometimes get mail addressed to the previous owner of our house.* —**previously,** *adverb.*

prey ▲ [pray] *noun, plural* **preys. 1.** an animal that is hunted by another animal for food: *A tiger may follow its prey for miles before catching and killing it.* **2.** the practice or habit of hunting animals for food: *An eagle is a bird of prey.* **3.** a person who is taken advantage of or harmed: *She was the prey of a dishonest lawyer. verb,* **preyed, preying. 1.** to hunt other animals for food: *Penguins prey on fish.* **2.** to cause distress to: *Worries about not having any money are preying on her mind.*
• **prey on/upon.** to use in an unfair way; take advantage of: *Tourists in that city are preyed upon by thieves.*
🔊 A different word with the same sound is **pray.**

price [prise] *noun, plural* **prices. 1.** the amount of money that is offered or asked for when something is bought or sold: *What's the price of that car?* **2.** something given or lost in order to gain something: *The price of success is hard work. verb,* **priced, pricing. 1.** to put a price on: *The computer is priced at $400.* **2.** to find out what something costs: *I priced three different bicycles before deciding which one to buy.*

a b c d e f g h i j k l m n o **p** q r s t u v w x y z

*The fruit of a **prickly pear** is refreshing to eat but has large seeds.*

price·less [prise-lis] *adjective.* having such a high value that it cannot be measured by price alone: *The museum displays a priceless collection of coins from the ancient Roman Empire.*

prick [prik] *verb,* **pricked, pricking.** to make a small hole with something sharp: *She pricked her arm on a cactus needle.* *noun, plural* **pricks.** a small hole in something: *Use a fork to make pricks in the potatoes before baking them.*

prick·ly [prik-lee] *adjective,* **pricklier, prickliest. 1.** having many sharp points or thorns: *A porcupine's skin is covered with prickly quills.* **2.** irritating to the skin; tingling: *This new sweater gives me a prickly sensation.* **3.** difficult to deal with; easily irritated: *She has a very prickly personality and gets angry quickly.*

prickly pear ▲ a cactus with pear-shaped fruit and large yellow flowers.

pride [pride] *noun.* **1.** a sense of one's own dignity and worth; self-respect: *The elderly woman put aside her pride and asked for her neighbors' help around the house.* **2.** too high an opinion of oneself: *If you cannot ever admit that you are wrong, you are guilty of pride.* **3.** satisfaction or pleasure in something that one does or is connected with: *She takes great pride in her son's success.* *verb,* **prided, priding.** to take pride in.
• **pride oneself.** to feel pride; be proud: *This town prides itself on having streets without litter.*
🔊 A different word with the same sound is **pried.**

pried [pride] *verb.* the past tense and past participle of PRY.
🔊 A different word with the same sound is **pride.**

priest [preest] *noun, plural* **priests.** a member of the clergy in certain religions. Relating to or like a priest is **priestly.**

pri·ma don·na 1. the main female singer in an opera or opera company. **2.** an overly proud person who finds it hard to accept orders or to work as part of a group: *She won't ever do what the coach says and acts like a real prima donna.*

> The phrase **prima donna** literally means "the first lady." The first meaning of *prima donna* was the woman who was the first or most important female singer in an opera.

pri·ma·ry [pry-mer-ee] *adjective.* **1.** more important than anything else; main: *My primary goal in life is to be happy.* **2.** first in time or in order: *You have to attend primary school before going on to secondary school.* *noun, plural* **primaries.** in politics, an election in which members of the same political party vote for different candidates. The winner goes on to represent that party in a general election.

primary color one of the basic colors from which all other colors can be obtained. Red, yellow, and blue are the primary colors in mixing paint.

primary school *Education.* a school that includes the first three or four grades of elementary school and sometimes kindergarten.

pri·mate ▶ [pry-mate] *noun, plural* **primates.** *Biology.* a group of mammals that have a large brain, eyes that can look forward, and fingers and thumbs that can grasp things. Primates include humans, apes, and monkeys.

> The word **primate** comes from a word meaning "the first" or "the most important." The idea was that the primate group of animals is the most important because it includes human beings.

prime [prime] *adjective.* **1.** of the first importance or highest rank; main: *The prime cause of the car accident was excessive speed.* **2.** of the best quality; excellent: *This is a prime location for a restaurant.* **3.** of meat or other food, having the highest grade. *noun, plural* **primes.** the most successful, active, or satisfying stage or period: *He's past his prime as a quarterback after playing for so many years.* *verb,* **primed, priming.** to make ready by putting something on or in: *You have to prime the pump by pouring water into it.*

prime minister ▶
Government. the leader of a group of ministers that form a particular type of government. Canada and Great Britain have prime ministers.

prime number *Mathematics.* a number that can be divided evenly only by itself and the number 1. The numbers 7 and 11 are prime numbers.

*Winston Churchill was **prime minister** of Great Britain during World War II and later in the 1950s.*

prim·i·tive [prim-uh-tiv] *adjective.* **1.** having to do with an early or original stage or state: *A jellyfish is a primitive form of life.* **2.** very simple or basic; crude: *The cabin was very primitive—it had no electricity and no beds.* *noun, plural* **primitives. 1.** a person from a simple, usually tribal society. **2.** an artist, especially a painter, whose work has a simple, direct style. —**primitively,** *adverb.*

prim·rose ▼ [prim-rohz] *noun, plural* **primroses.** a small plant with clusters of showy, colorful flowers. It grows in moist, shady areas.

prince [prins] *noun, plural* **princes. 1.** any male member of a royal family other than a king. **2.** a nobleman of high rank.

prin·cess [prin-sis] *noun, plural* **princesses. 1.** any female member of a royal family other than a queen. **2.** a woman married to a prince. **3.** a noblewoman of high rank.

Primroses grow well in containers.

PRIMATES

Primates are divided into two groups. Lemurs, bushbabies, lorises, and tarsiers belong to the lower primates, while monkeys, apes, and humans are higher primates. Most primates live in trees in tropical regions, but many monkeys in Africa and Asia in drier environments live mainly on the ground. Higher primates have a large brain and are quite intelligent. They have good eyesight using two eyes, nails instead of claws, and sensitive pads on their fingers and toes that give them a highly developed sense of touch.

Ring-tailed lemurs live in groups of up to twenty.

PRIMATE HANDS AND FEET
One of the distinctive characteristics of primates is their special thumb, and sometimes big toe, that allows them to hold and eat food.

Indri foot   Indri hand   Aye-aye foot   Aye-aye hand   Tarsier foot   Tarsier hand

LOWER PRIMATES

Tarsier

Gray mouse lemur

Golden potto

Red ruffed lemur

Indri

HIGHER PRIMATES

Gelada baboon

Cotton-top tamarin

Muriqui

Orangutan

Mandrill

Red howler monkey

Celebes crested macaque

Diana monkey

prin·ci·pal [prin-suh-pul] *adjective.* relating to the most important; describing the main or chief: *The state of Michigan's principal industry is automobile manufacturing.* *noun, plural* **principals. 1.** a person in charge of a school. **2.** a person with a leading or starring role in an activity: *When the ballet finished, the principals received bouquets of flowers.*
🔊 A different word with the same sound is **principle.**

prin·ci·ple [prin-suh-pul] *noun, plural* **principles.**
1. a basic truth, law, doctrine, or belief: *American society runs on democratic principles.* **2.** a rule or code of conduct that a person lives by: *I stuck to my principles and told the truth.* A person who is **principled** lives and behaves according to good principles. **3.** *Business.* an original amount of money that is invested or borrowed, on which interest is then paid or charged.
🔊 A different word with the same sound is **principal.**

The two similar words **principal** and **principle** are often confused with each other. It is not correct to write "The *principle* of Milton School is Mr. Flores" because the head of a school is a *principal*. *Principle* is an important belief or idea, as in "The right to a trial is a basic *principle* of our legal system." One way that people remember the difference is to think, "The *princip**al*** is our **pal** (friend)."

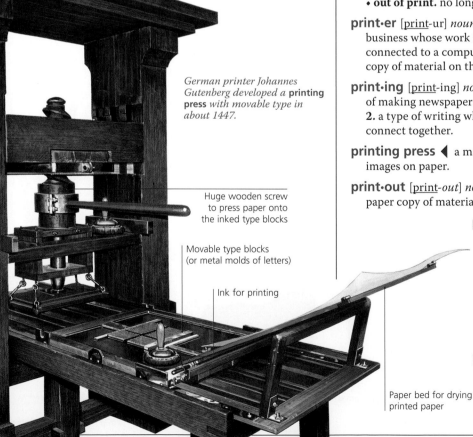

German printer Johannes Gutenberg developed a **printing press** *with movable type in about 1447.*

Huge wooden screw to press paper onto the inked type blocks

Movable type blocks (or metal molds of letters)

Ink for printing

Paper bed for drying printed paper

A **prism** *separates white light into a spectrum of colors ranging from red through to violet.*

Sun

White light

Spectrum

Prism

print [print] *verb* **printed, printing. 1.** to make a copy of writing or pictures on paper using a machine with ink: *He waited for the document to print.* **2.** to publish in a book, magazine, or letter: *The local newspaper printed a photo of us dressed up for Halloween.* **3.** to write in unconnected letters like those in a book: *Please print your name clearly on the label.*
noun, plural **prints. 1.** letters, numbers, or symbols made by printing: *I used bold print for the headings.* **2.** a mark made by pressing into or onto a surface: *The dog tracked muddy prints through the house.* **3.** a picture made by pressing paper onto a raised or engraved surface that is covered with ink. **4.** a photograph developed from a negative. **5.** cloth with a pattern printed on it: *The dress is in a striped cotton print.*
• **in print.** still for sale from a publisher.
• **out of print.** no longer for sale from a publisher.

print·er [print-ur] *noun, plural* **printers. 1.** a person or business whose work is printing. **2.** a machine that is connected to a computer and can print out a paper copy of material on the computer.

print·ing [print-ing] *noun.* **1.** the practice or business of making newspapers, books, or other printed material. **2.** a type of writing where the letters do not connect together.

printing press ◀ a machine that prints writing or images on paper.

print·out [print-out] *noun, plural* **printouts.** a printed paper copy of material on a computer.

prism ▲ [priz-um] *noun, plural* **prisms.** a transparent glass or crystal object that can break up a beam of light into the colors of the rainbow. It has three sides, equal in size and shaped like leaning rectangles, with two triangular ends parallel to one another.

pris·on [priz-un] *noun, plural* **prisons.** a place where people accused or found guilty of crimes are locked up.
See JAIL *for more information.*

pris·on·er [priz-un-ur or priz-nur] noun, plural **prisoners.**
1. a person kept in prison. **2.** any person who is held in a place against their will by someone else: *They planned to hold the hostages prisoner until the government met their demands.* A **prisoner of war** is a person who surrenders to, or is captured by, the enemy during war.

pri·va·cy [pry-vuh-see] noun. the state of being alone or private: *Get out of my room—I want some privacy!*

pri·vate [pry-vit] adjective. **1.** belonging to a particular person or group: *The sign on the old building said: "Private property. Keep out."* **2.** not meant for sharing publicly; personal: *A diary is private.* **3.** not holding an official or public position: *These days, the former governor is a private citizen.*
noun, plural **privates.** a soldier of the lowest enlisted rank, below a corporal.
• **in private.** without other people being present: *Is there somewhere we can talk in private?* —**privately,** adverb.

private school Education. a secondary or elementary school that is run and financed by private individuals or companies, not by a government agency.

priv·i·lege [priv-uh-lij or priv-lij] noun, plural **privileges.** a special right or advantage given to a person or group: *Paul had the privilege of meeting his favorite football star.* A person who is **privileged** has special rights and advantages.

prize [prize] noun, plural **prizes.** something won in a competition or game: *Clara won the prize for best costume at the fancy dress dance.*
adjective. describing someone or something that has won a prize or is worthy of winning a prize: *a prize pig; a prize essay.*
verb, **prized, prizing.** to value highly: *Mom says she prizes the times we all spend together as a family.* A **prized** possession is one that its owner thinks is valuable or important.

pro [pro] noun, plural **pros.** a professional, especially in sports: *The basketball pro earned millions of dollars a year.*

prob·a·bil·i·ty [prob-uh-bil-uh-tee] noun, plural **probabilities. 1.** the chances of a situation or event happening; likelihood: *The probability of winning the lottery is very small.* **2.** a situation or event that is likely to happen: *The temperature dropped overnight, so snow is a strong probability today.*

prob·a·ble [prob-uh-bul] adjective. likely or expected to happen or be true: *The probable causes of the car accident were speed and the icy conditions.*

prob·a·bly [prob-uh-blee] adverb. very likely; almost certainly: *Because of all the snow, the bus will probably be late again today.*

pro·ba·tion [proh-bay-shun] noun, plural **probations. 1.** Law. a set period of time when a person who has committed a crime is not in prison but must act in a proper way to avoid being sent there. Such a person is said to be **on probation. 2.** any other such trial period when a person's fitness for something is tested: *That boy is on probation this term to see if he'll stop disrupting the class.*

probe ▼ [probe] noun, plural **probes. 1.** a thorough investigation: *Congress started its probe into the handling of the disaster.* **2.** a tool or device for examining and exploring: *The space probe to Mars has examined the planet's rocks and soil, and found evidence of water.*
verb, **probed, probing.** to search, examine, or investigate thoroughly: *The doctor probed the wound to make sure she'd removed every bit of glass.*

prob·lem [prob-lum] noun, plural **problems. 1.** a question to be thought about, solved, or answered: *a math problem.* **2.** a situation, person, or thing that causes difficulty or uncertainty: *My little sister is having problems learning to read.* A **problematic** situation is one that is difficult or uncertain.
adjective. difficult to deal with or manage: *a problem child.*

pro·ce·dure [pruh-see-jur] noun, plural **procedures.** a set way of doing something that often involves a series of steps: *We followed the procedure for installing the software.* Something that has to do with such a process is **procedural.**

pro·ceed [pruh-seed] verb, **proceeded, proceeding.** to move on, go on, or continue, especially after stopping: *The man leaned over to pat the dog, then proceeded on his way.*

pro·ceed·ings [pruh-seed-ings] plural noun. a series of events that happen at a particular place or occasion: *The principal started the proceedings by asking everyone to stand for the national anthem.*

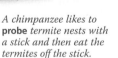
A chimpanzee likes to **probe** *termite nests with a stick and then eat the termites off the stick.*

pro·ceeds [proh-seedz] plural noun. the amount of money raised from an activity, event, or sale: *The sign on the thrift shop says, "All proceeds from sales go to charity."*

pro·cess [pros-es or proh-ses] noun, plural **processes.** a series of actions carried out to achieve a particular result: *Learning to play the saxophone is a slow process.*
verb, **processed, processing.** to treat, prepare, or convert something using a special process or series of steps: *The refinery processes petroleum to make gasoline.*

pro·cessed [proh-sesd] adjective. treated, prepared, or converted using a special process: *Grandma loves processed meats such as salami and bologna.*

*A postage stamp issued in 1963 commemorated the **proclamation** that gave slaves their freedom.*

A B C D E F G H I J K L M N O P Q R S T U V W X Y Z

pro·ces·sion ▼ [pruh-<u>sesh</u>-un] *noun, plural* **processions. 1.** a continuous forward movement of people or things: *The fair will open with a procession led by the Harvest Queen.* **2.** a group or line of people moving along in a particular order: *a funeral procession.*

pro·claim [proh-<u>klame</u>] *verb,* **proclaimed, proclaiming.** to announce publicly or officially: *He was proclaimed king after the death of his father.*

proc·la·ma·tion ▶ [prok-luh-<u>may</u>-shun] *noun, plural* **proclamations.** an official announcement: *The President issued a proclamation for a national day of mourning.*

pro·cras·ti·nate [proh-<u>kras</u>-tuh-*nate*] *verb,* **procrastinated, procrastinating.** to keep putting off doing something: *Dad told me to stop procrastinating and do my book report now.* The act of continually putting off doing a task is **procrastination.**

pro·cure [proh-<u>kyoor</u>] *verb,* **procured, procuring.** to obtain, especially with effort: *She managed to procure two tickets to the Super Bowl.*

prod [prod] *verb,* **prodded, prodding. 1.** to poke or jab; push with a pointed object: *Don't prod me in the arm to get my attention.* **2.** to strongly encourage to do something; urge: *George's teacher liked his stories very much, and prodded him to enter the story writing competition.* *noun, plural* **prods. 1.** a poke, jab, or push: *Give her a prod in the back to wake her up.* **2.** a pointed object used to prod something: *The cowboys used cattle prods to get the steers into the truck.*

pro·duce [pruh-<u>doos</u> *for verb;* proh-<u>doos</u> *for noun*] *verb,* **produced, producing. 1.** to bring into being in some way; make, create, or yield: *The factory produces computer parts.* **2.** to present or bring forth; show: *The magician produced a red silk scarf from her sleeve.* **3.** to supervise and finance the making of a play, film, show, or music: *He produced the singer's new album.* *noun.* things that are made, grown, created, or yielded: *The farmer trucked his fresh produce to market.*

pro·duc·er [pruh-<u>doos</u>-ur] *noun, plural* **producers. 1.** a person, organization, country, or thing that makes, creates, or yields things: *China is the largest producer of cotton in the world.* **2.** a person who supervises and finances the making of a play, film, show, or the like: *The television producer had an idea for a new situation comedy.*

prod·uct [<u>prod</u>-ukt] *noun, plural* **products. 1.** something made, created, or yielded: *The school play was the product of lots of hard work.* **2.** the number arrived at by multiplying two or more numbers together: *The product of 7 times 10 is 70.*

pro·duc·tion [pruh-<u>duk</u>-shun] *noun, plural* **productions. 1.** the act or process of making, creating, or yielding something: *The production of a pearl by an oyster is a long, slow process.* **2.** a thing that is made, created, or yielded: *This year, our school is doing a production of* The Sound of Music.

pro·duc·tive [pruh-<u>duk</u>-tiv] *adjective.* **1.** able to produce large amounts of something: *Grandpa's vegetable patch is so productive that he is able to give away half of what he grows.* The rate at which a company or country produces goods is its **productivity. 2.** having positive results or benefits: *The extra coaching in science was productive because Jenny passed the exam.* —**productively,** *adverb.*

pro·fess [pruh-<u>fes</u>] *verb,* **professed, professing. 1.** to announce or declare openly: *The man professed his Christian faith.* **2.** to claim insincerely; pretend: *She professes to be my friend, then talks about me behind my back.*

pro·fes·sion [pruh-<u>fesh</u>-un] *noun, plural* **professions. 1.** an occupation that needs specialized study and training: *Dr. Garcia's profession is medicine.* **2.** the act of declaring something: *He made a profession of love when he asked his girlfriend to marry him.*

1863-1963 UNITED STATES 5 CENTS
EMANCIPATION PROCLAMATION

*In an Egyptian Pharaoh's funeral **procession,** the mummy was dragged slowly to the tomb on a sled, and was accompanied by servants carrying food and other objects to bury with the dead king.*

pro·fes·sion·al [pruh-<u>fesh</u>-uh-nul *or* pruh-<u>fesh</u>-nul] *adjective.* **1.** having to do with an occupation that needs specialized study and training: *Aunt Carol decided to get a professional opinion from a doctor about her back pains.* **2.** earning money from an activity that others do as a hobby: *She works as a professional photographer.* *noun, plural* **professionals. 1.** a person with an occupation that needs specialized study and training: *Doctors and nurses are health professionals.* **2.** a person who earns money from an activity that others do as a hobby: *The tennis player turned professional after he won the amateur championship.*

pro·fes·sor [pruh-<u>fes</u>-ur] *noun, plural* **professors.** a university or college teacher of high rank.

pro·file ▶ [<u>proh</u>-*file*] *noun, plural* **profiles.** **1.** a side view or outline of an object, especially a person's head: *That photo of me in profile proves that I've got a big nose.* **2.** a short account of a person's life and achievements: *Jamie read the magazine profile about his favorite rap artist.* *verb,* **profiled, profiling.** to draw, write, or produce a profile of: *The school newspaper profiled the new class representatives.*

prof·it [<u>prof</u>-it] *noun, plural* **profits. 1.** *Business.* the amount of money made after all costs or expenses have been subtracted: *The cake stall made a profit of seventy dollars.* **2.** a gain, advantage, or benefit: *There is no profit in arguing all the time.* *verb,* **profited, profiting. 1.** to make a profit; gain money after expenses are paid. **2.** to gain or benefit from something: *We profited from the other team's mistakes and eventually won the game.* 🔊 A different word with the same sound is **prophet.**

> **Profit** goes back to a word meaning "to advance" or "to go ahead." When a business makes a profit, it is as if the business is going forward; that is, going in the right direction.

prof·it·a·ble [<u>prof</u>-i-tuh-bul] *adjective.* resulting in a profit or advantage: *Oil companies such as Exxon are very profitable.* A company that experiences **profitability** is in a state of making a profit. **—profitably,** *adverb.*

This coin bears the **profile** of Vladimir Lenin, the first head of the Soviet Union.

pro·found [pruh-<u>found</u>] *adjective.* **1.** showing a deep understanding or knowledge; not superficial: *a profound thought.* **2.** very deep or intense; complete: *The general expressed his profound regret that the soldiers had died.* **—profoundly,** *adverb.*

pro·fuse [pruh-<u>fyoos</u>] *adjective.* **1.** plentiful or abundant: *The nurse had to stop the profuse bleeding from the deep wound.* A **profusion** of something is a very large amount of it. **2.** given or giving freely or very generously; lavish: *The man was profuse in his apologies for forgetting his father's birthday.* **—profusely,** *adverb.*

pro·gram [<u>proh</u>-gram] *noun, plural* **programs. 1.** a list of the order of events and the performers in a concert, play, or other presentation: *We looked at the actors' names in the program while we waited for the play to start.* **2.** an entertainment, performance, or production: *Maggie watched her favorite television program.* **3.** a plan to be followed; a schedule: *My dad goes to the gym as part of his fitness program.* **4.** *Computers.* a set of coded instructions that makes a computer perform a particular task. *verb,* **programmed, programming. 1.** to schedule or include as part of a program. **2.** to write or prepare a program for a computer. **3.** to train to behave in a particular way: *My body is programmed to wake up every morning at seven o'clock.*

pro·gram·mer [<u>proh</u>-gram-ur] *noun, plural* **programmers.** *Computers.* a person who writes or develops computer programs.

prog·ress *or* **pro·gress** [<u>prog</u>-res *for noun;* pruh-<u>gres</u> *for verb*] *noun.* a forward movement or advance; improvement: *I am making progress with my drawing.* *verb,* **progressed, progressing.** to move forward or advance: *Martin was trying to progress to the next level of the computer game.*
• **in progress.** happening now; under way: *Road work in progress on the highway caused the gridlock.*

pro·gres·sion [pruh-<u>gres</u>-un] *noun.* the process of moving or advancing, especially from one stage to the next: *She's always liked bodyboarding, so it's a natural progression for her to try a surfboard now.*

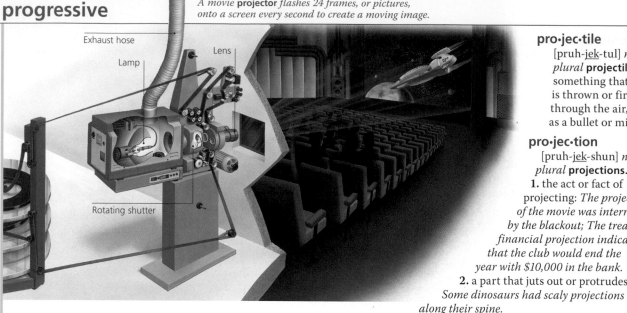

*A movie **projector** flashes 24 frames, or pictures, onto a screen every second to create a moving image.*

Exhaust hose
Lamp
Lens
Rotating shutter

pro·jec·tile [pruh-<u>jek</u>-tul] *noun, plural* **projectiles.** something that is thrown or fired through the air, such as a bullet or missile.

pro·jec·tion [pruh-<u>jek</u>-shun] *noun, plural* **projections.**
1. the act or fact of projecting: *The projection of the movie was interrupted by the blackout; The treasurer's financial projection indicated that the club would end the year with $10,000 in the bank.*
2. a part that juts out or protrudes: *Some dinosaurs had scaly projections along their spine.*

pro·gres·sive [pruh-<u>gres</u>-iv] *adjective.* **1.** describing something developing or advancing: *The snake bite caused progressive paralysis to his hand and then his arm.*
2. in favor of or making change, reform, or improvement: *The progressive politician wanted free health care for all.*
noun, plural **progressives.** a person who believes in change, reform, or improvement in an area of life: *The architect who designs energy-saving houses is a progressive.* —**progressively,** *adverb.*

pro·hib·it [proh-<u>hib</u>-it] *verb,* **prohibited, prohibiting.**
to stop or prevent something; forbid: *People younger than 21 are prohibited from buying alcoholic drinks in the U.S.* If something is forbidden or prevented from happening it is **prohibited.**

pro·hib·i·tion [proh-huh-<u>bish</u>-un] *noun,*
plural **prohibitions.** the act or fact of prohibiting something: *There is a prohibition on smoking in airplanes.* The period between 1919 and 1933, when the production, sale, and transportation of alcoholic drinks was illegal in the U.S., is known as **Prohibition.**

pro·ject [<u>proj</u>-ekt] *noun, plural* **projects. 1.** a planned program to do something, especially a large-scale effort involving many people: *The government began a two-year project to connect all elementary schools to the Internet.*
2. a special assignment in school involving extra work over a period of time: *Her history project is a study of England in the Middle Ages.* **3.** a group of houses or apartment buildings built to a single plan: *The new housing project will provide accommodation for low-income families.*
verb, **projected, projecting. 1.** to throw or make something move forward quickly: *The rocket can project the missile over hundreds of miles.* **2.** to make an image appear on a screen or flat surface: *The lecturer projected his PowerPoint presentation onto the screen.* **3.** to predict or plan what might happen: *This month a 5 percent increase in sales is projected.* **4.** to jut out from; protrude: *The dorsal fin of a shark projects above the surface of the ocean.* Something that is **projected,** is planned or estimated based on the available information.

pro·jec·tor ▲ [proh-<u>jek</u>-tur] *noun, plural* **projectors.** a piece of equipment used to project an image or picture onto a screen or flat surface.

pro·long [pruh-<u>lawng</u>] *verb,* **prolonged, prolonging.** to make something last longer; lengthen: *I ate slowly to prolong my enjoyment of the delicious meal.* An activity that is made to last longer is **prolonged.**

prom [prom] *noun, plural* **proms.** a formal dance for high-school or college students, usually held at the end of the school year.

prom·e·nade [prom-uh-<u>nade</u> or prom-uh-<u>nahd</u>] *noun, plural* **promenades.** a walk or a ride for pleasure, or a place for doing this.
verb, **promenaded, promenading.** to walk or ride for pleasure: *People often get dressed up when they promenade around the town square.*

prom·i·nent [<u>prom</u>-uh-nunt] *adjective.* **1.** describing someone or something important; distinguished: *A group of prominent scientists have confirmed the dangers of global warming.* **2.** having to do with something easily seen; noticeable: *The Empire State Building is a prominent landmark in New York.* The state of being prominent is **prominence.** Land that is higher than the surrounding area is a **prominence.** —**prominently,** *adverb.*

prom·ise [<u>prom</u>-is] *noun, plural* **promises. 1.** an assurance that something will be done, or not done: *My father made a promise to buy me a car when I graduated.*
2. an indication that somebody or something will be successful: *Henry shows great promise as a goalkeeper.*
verb, **promised, promising. 1.** to give an assurance that something will be done, or not done: *I promise I'll give you the money I owe you when I get my allowance.* **2.** to show that something is expected: *The weather pattern promises heavy rain tomorrow.* Something that has been assured of happening is described as **promised.**

prom·is·ing [<u>prom</u>-is-ing] *adjective.* likely to be successful: *He is a promising young gymnast.* —**promisingly,** *adverb.*

prom·on·to·ry ▼ [prom-un-*tore*-ee] *noun,*
plural **promontories.** *Geography.* a high point of land
that sticks out into the ocean or a lake: *When we stood*
on the promontory we could see for miles down the coast.

pro·mote [pruh-*mote*] *verb,* **promoted, promoting.**
1. to move somebody up to a more important, or higher
position: *to be promoted from second grade to third grade;*
After working there for three years, he was promoted to
the head of the mail room. **2.** to help something develop;
encourage growth: *Reading promotes an understanding*
of how other people live.

pro·mot·er [pruh-*mote*-ur] *noun, plural* **promoters.**
somebody who organizes concerts, entertainments,
or sporting events, often providing the financial backing
for them.

pro·mo·tion [pruh-*moh*-shun] *noun, plural* **promotions.**
1. a move up to a more important, or higher position:
After six months she received a promotion to sales
manager. **2.** the act of helping something to develop,
or encouraging growth: *We organized a campaign for*
the promotion of recycling green waste.

prompt [prompt] *adjective.* not late; on time; punctual:
The doctor expects patients to be prompt in arriving for
their appointments. **2.** without delay; quick: *I asked her to*
my party and got a prompt answer saying she would come.
verb, **prompted, prompting. 1.** to encourage somebody
to do something: *Her poor results on the test prompted*
her to study harder. **2.** to help an actor or
speaker remember what they should say:
If you forget your lines, I'll be there to
prompt you. —**promptly,** *adverb;*
—**promptness,** *noun.*

prone [prone] *adjective.* **1.** lying flat with
the face down: *To have your back massaged,*
you need to lie in a prone position. **2.** likely
to do, or be affected by, something: *Both*
infants and the elderly are prone to catching
the flu.

prong [prong] *noun, plural* **prongs.** a thin,
sharp projection at the end of something
that has several points, such as a fork or
a deer's antlers.

prong·horn [prong-horn] *noun, plural* **pronghorns.**
a fast-running animal similar to an antelope that lives
on the plains of western North America. Pronghorns
are now an endangered species.

pro·noun [proh-noun] *noun, plural* **pronouns.** *Language.*
a word that is used in place of a noun or noun phrase.
In the sentence *They saw him kick it with his foot,* "They,"
"him", "it", and "his" are pronouns.

pro·nounce [pruh-*nouns*] *verb,* **pronouncing, pronounced.**
1. to sound out a letter or word in a certain way: *Please*
tell me how to pronounce your name correctly. **2.** to make
a judgment; state: *The judge will pronounce his verdict*
after he reviews the evidence. If something is obvious
or larger than normal it is **pronounced.**

pro·nun·ci·a·tion [pruh-*nuhn*-see-*ay*-shun] *noun,*
plural **pronunciations.** *Language.* a way of sounding
a letter or word: *The words "do," "dew," and "due" all*
have the same pronunciation.

The **pronunciations** in this dictionary show what is considered
to be the most common or most standard way to say a word.
How this actually sounds when someone talks can be slightly
different depending on the person's way of speaking. For
example, many people from the Midwest region of the United
States have a more "flat" sound than people from other parts
of the country when they say the [a] ("short a") sound in
words like *hat* or *back.* People from New England or New York
say the [r] sound less strongly in words like *four* or *more.*

proof [proof] *noun, plural* **proofs.** evidence that something
is true: *He had proof that he was not there when the*
robbery took place.
verb, **proofed, proofing.** to test for mistakes; check against
a correct version: *I had to proof my essay twice to make*
sure there were no spelling mistakes.

-proof a suffix that means not affected by; resistant to:
bulletproof means not affected by bullets; *fireproof*
means resistant to fire.

proof·read [*proof*-reed] *verb,* **proofread, proofreading.**
to read something that is written or printed to find and
correct mistakes: *I will proofread your essay and mark any*
mistakes I find. People who are employed to proofread are
called **proofreaders.** Their job is **proofreading.**

Dunnottar Castle in Scotland was built on a **promontory** *to protect*
it from attack.

prop [prop] *verb,* **propped, propping.** to support something
by putting something under or against it: *We can prop*
the window open with a stick to let in some fresh air.
noun, plural **props.** an object that is used to hold
something in place: *We can use this stick as a prop*
to hold the window open.
• **prop up.** to give support to something, or to help
somebody: *To prop up the failing business, the bank*
reduced the interest on its loan.

prop·a·gan·da [prop-uh-*gan*-duh] *noun.* information
that is often misleading, put out by an organization
or government to influence the way people think:
The government's press release was described as pure
propaganda by their opponents. To spread propaganda
is to **propagandize.**

pro·pane [proh-*pane*] *noun. Chemistry.* a colorless gas used for cooking and heating. It is a by-product of petroleum.

pro·pel [pruh-pel] *verb,* **propelled, propelling.** to make something move forward: *He was so nervous about giving the speech that I had to give him a shove to propel him onto the stage.*

pro·pel·ler [pruh-pel-ur] *noun, plural* **propellers.** a device made of blades attached to a central shaft that revolves to provide the thrust to move an aircraft or ship forward.

prop·er [prop-ur] *adjective.* **1.** describing something correct, appropriate, or suitable: *You must learn the proper way to behave in class.* **2.** strictly defined: *A lot of my friends live in the suburbs, but I prefer to live in the city proper.* —**properly,** *adverb.*

proper noun *Language.* a noun that names a particular person, place, or thing. It is always spelled with a capital letter. In the sentence *Albert Johnson was born in Alabama,* "Albert," "Johnson," and "Alabama" are proper nouns. This is sometimes also called a **proper name.**

prop·er·ty [prop-ur-tee] *noun, plural* **properties.** **1.** anything that is owned: *You need to keep your personal property secure when traveling in foreign countries.* **2.** a piece of land or real estate: *Her father owns several properties in the city.* **3.** a distinctive quality of something: *Many herbs are said to have healing properties.*

proph·e·cy [prof-uh-see] *noun, plural* **prophecies.** **1.** a prediction that something is going to happen: *According to an ancient prophecy the city will some day be overwhelmed by a great flood.* **2.** the act of making a prediction.

proph·et [prof-it] *noun, plural* **prophets. 1.** someone who passes on messages that are believed to come from God. Muhammad, the founder of Islam, is known among Muslims as **the Prophet. 2.** someone who claims to predict future events: *He is known as the Racetrack Prophet because he is thought to be good at picking the winners of horse races.*

🔊 A different word with the same sound is **profit.**

proph·et·ic [pruh-fet-ik] *adjective.* correctly predicting future events: *Emma's prediction about who would win the contest turned out to be prophetic.* —**prophetically,** *adverb.*

pro·por·tion ▼ [pruh-por-shun] *noun, plural* **proportions. 1.** the relationship between two or more things in size, amount, or importance: *The proportion of brown-eyed to blue-eyed students in our class is three to one.* **2. proportions.** the size or dimensions of something.

proportional [pruh-por-shun-ul] *adjective.* having the correct, or most suitable relationship of size, amount, or importance: *The salary paid is proportional to the responsibilities of the job.* —**proportionally,** *adverb.*

pro·pos·al [pruh-poze-ul] *noun, plural* **proposals. 1.** a plan or scheme proposed; suggestion: *The chairman of the company put a proposal to the board of directors to sell the building.* **2.** an offer of marriage.

pro·pose [pruh-poze] *verb,* **proposed, proposing. 1.** to put forward for other people to consider; suggest: *I propose that we end the meeting.* **2.** to intend to do or be something: *What do you propose we should do with all these old books?* **3.** to offer to marry someone: *Geoffrey proposed to Sarah last night and she accepted.*

pro·po·si·tion [prop-uh-zish-un] *noun, plural* **propositions. 1.** a suggestion to be considered: *There is a proposition on this year's ballot to raise the sales tax from 7 percent to 7.25 percent.* **2.** a statement for discussion: *The mayor's proposition is to build a new city art gallery.*

pro·pri·e·tor [pruh-prye-uh-tur] *noun, plural* **proprietors.** *Business.* a person who owns a business: *The proprietor of the store also owns another store in the next town.*

pro·pul·sion [pruh-puhl-shun] *noun.* the act of moving something forward or upward: *The plane was powered by jet propulsion.*

prose [proze] *noun. Literature.* any speech or writing that is similar to normal speech and does not rhyme like poetry.

pros·e·cute [pros-uh-*kyoot*] *verb,* **prosecuted, prosecuting.** *Law.* to take legal action against someone in a court of law. People who are thought to have committed crimes are prosecuted by police or legal authorities.

pros·e·cu·tion [pros-uh-kyoo-shun] *noun, plural* **prosecutions.** *Law.* the act of prosecuting in court someone charged with a crime. The person who leads the case against someone charged with a crime is the **prosecutor.**

pros·pect [pros-pekt] *noun, plural* **prospects. 1.** an event that will take place at some future time: *The prospect of graduating from school the following year filled Graeme with excitement.* **2.** a person who is a good possibility to do something, buy something offered for sale, or take a job offer: *The boss interviewed several prospects for the job.*
verb, **prospected, prospecting.** to search, especially for valuable minerals such as gold.

Ancient Greek architects designed the temple of the Parthenon in Athens, Greece, so that all its measurements were in perfect **proportion.**

*Soldiers provided **protection** for Spanish missionaries in Mexico in the sixteenth century.*

pro·spec·tive [pruh-<u>spek</u>-tiv] *adjective.* expected or likely to happen in the future: *Lydia introduced me to her prospective husband.*

pros·pec·tor [<u>pros</u>-pek-tur] *noun, plural* **prospectors.** a person who explores an area looking for mineral deposits such as gold.

pros·per [<u>pros</u>-pur] *verb,* **prospered, prospering.** to succeed, especially in financial matters; do well: *He has prospered in his career selling stocks and bonds.*

pros·per·i·ty [pros-<u>per</u>-i-tee] *noun.* success or good fortune in financial matters: *The country's prosperity from its oil deposits allowed many people to become rich.*

pros·per·ous [<u>pros</u>-pur-us] *adjective.* describing something rich and successful; wealthy: *The mining company is prosperous after having found a new gold mine.* **—prosperously,** *adverb.*

pro·tect [pruh-<u>tekt</u>] *verb,* **protected, protecting.** to shield from harm or keep safe; defend: *Sunscreens protect our skin against damage from the sun.* When something is **protected** it is defended from harm by a person, substance, or circumstances. **—protector,** *noun.*

pro·tec·tion ▲ [pruh-<u>tek</u>-shun] *noun, plural* **protections.** **1.** the act of protecting something or someone from harm. **2.** the state of being protected from harm: *Warm clothes offer protection from winter cold.*

pro·tec·tive [pruh-<u>tek</u>-tiv] *adjective.* serving to protect from damage or harm. *Scientists wear protective clothing when working with dangerous chemicals.* **—protectively,** *adverb.*

pro·tein [<u>proh</u>-teen] *noun, plural* **proteins.** *Biology.* any of many substances found in the living cells of plants and animals that are needed to keep people healthy. Eggs, meat, and some vegetables contain protein.

pro·test [<u>proh</u>-*test*] *noun, plural* **protests.** the act of expressing opposition, disapproval, or complaint: *The town's residents made strong protests against a nuclear power station being built there.* *verb,* **protested, protesting.** to express opposition; to object: *Allan protested to his next door neighbors about the noise of their dog barking.*

Prot·es·tant [<u>prot</u>-uh-stunt] *noun, plural* **Protestants.** *Religion.* a member of one the Christian churches that are separate from the Roman Catholic and Eastern Orthodox churches. Protestants broke away from the Catholic Church in the sixteenth century. Protestant churches include the Anglicans, Presbyterians, Methodists, Lutherans, and Baptists.

The **Protestant** religion gets its name from the word *protest,* meaning to speak or write saying something is wrong. The people who formed the Protestant religion broke away from the older Catholic Church because they *protested* against certain things that they thought the Catholic Church was doing wrong.

pro·tes·tor [proh-<u>test</u>-ur] *noun, plural* **protestors.** a person who protests about something.

pro·to·col [<u>proh</u>-tuh-kol] *noun.* **1.** a system of rules by which representatives of government and heads of state behave toward each other. **2.** a system of rules governing how data is sent between computers.

pro·ton [<u>proh</u>-ton] *noun, plural* **protons.** *Science.* a very small particle of matter that carries an electrical charge and forms part of an atomic nucleus.

pro·to·plasm [<u>proh</u>-tuh-*plaz*-um] *noun. Biology.* the colorless jelly-like substance that makes up all living cells in plants and animals. It consists of a nucleus and cytoplasm.

pro·to·zo·an [*proh*-tuh-<u>zoh</u>-un] *noun, plural* **protozoans** or **protozoa.** *Biology.* a tiny, living, single-cell organism that can only be seen through a microscope.

pro·trude ▼ [proh-<u>trood</u>] *verb,* **protruded, protruding.** to push through or stick out from a surface: *The tops of trees protruded from the water of the flooded valley.* Something that pushes through or sticks out is a **protrusion.**

proud [proud] *adjective,* **prouder, proudest. 1.** having satisfaction or pride in a person's achievements or possessions: *Keith was proud to win the gold medal.* **2.** having dignity or self-respect: *They were too proud to beg when Dan lost his job.* **—proudly,** *adverb.*

prove [proov] *verb,* **proved** or **proven, proving. 1.** to demonstrate that something is true or genuine by using facts as evidence: *The police used DNA evidence to prove the thief had been at the house.* **2.** to end in a certain way: *Later events proved the decision to build the house on a cliff was a mistake.*

prov·en [<u>proov</u>-un] *verb.* the past participle of PROVE. *adjective.* having to do with facts that have been proved: *The important facts of the case were proven to the jury's satisfaction.*

*The **protruding** nose and ears of a sword-nosed bat help it to find food and avoid danger.*

prov·erb [<u>prov</u>-urb] *noun, plural* **proverbs.** *Literature.* a short phrase or saying containing a useful fact or belief many people regard as true: *A fool and his money are soon parted* is a proverb. Anything seen to be related to a proverb is described as **proverbial.**

pro·vide [pruh-<u>vide</u>] *verb,* **provided, providing. 1.** to supply or make available for use: *Our school provides a good education.* **2.** to state a rule or condition that must be complied with: *The law provides that children must be cared for without violence or neglect.* **3.** to support now or in the future: *Many people provide for the care of their children if anything happens to them by taking out insurance.*

a b c d e f g h i j k l m n o p q r s t u v w x y z

pro·vid·ed *conjunction.* on condition that: *You can bring your little sister to the party, provided that she behaves herself properly.*

prov·ince [prov-uns] *noun, plural* **provinces.** *Government.* **1.** a section or division of a country: *Quebec and Ontario are among the provinces of Canada.* **2.** an area of knowledge or skill: *Designing a house is the province of architects.* **3.** those parts of a country far distant from the capital or major cities: *My aunt prefers to live in the provinces as life is usually simpler and cheaper there.*

pro·vin·cial [pruh-vin-shul] *adjective.* **1.** having to do with a province or the provinces: *Provincial governments in Canada are responsible for health and education.* **2.** having the speech, dress, manners, or thought of a person from the provinces rather than from a major city: *She speaks with a provincial accent that is hard to understand.* *noun, plural* **provincials.** a narrow-minded or simple person from the provinces.

pro·vi·sion [pruh-vizh-un] *noun, plural* **provisions.** **1.** the act of supplying needed goods or services: *The provision of food for the picnic was left to the parents.* **2.** the act of making preparations for the future: *Has any provision been made for late arrivals on the boat trip?* **3.** a condition included in a contract: *A provision of the rental contract for our apartment is that we can't keep a pet.* **Provisions** are food and drink, especially if supplied for a special purpose. *verb,* **provisioned, provisioning.** to supply food, often for a certain purpose like a military campaign or a long sea voyage.

pro·vi·sion·al [proh-vish-uh-nul] *adjective.* provided or arranged for use now, not in the future: *The library gave me a provisional reader's card, to be replaced with a regular one later.* **—provisionally,** *adverb.*

prov·o·ca·tion [prov-uh-kay-shun] *noun, plural* **provocations.** the act of provoking or stirring to action: *The speaker at the peace rally spoke of the government's provocation in calling up more troops.* **Provocative** actions are those that are likely to cause strong reactions or emotions.

pro·voke [pruh-voke] *verb,* **provoked, provoking. 1.** to cause anger: *The man was provoked by the pickpocket who stole his wallet.* **2.** to stimulate to action or emotion: *Our dog was provoked into barking by the arrival of another dog.* **3.** to cause discussion or debate: *The newspaper editorial on crime in the community provoked a lot of letters to the editor.*

prow ▶ [prow] *noun, plural* **prows.** the bow or front part of a ship or boat.

prowl [prowl] *verb,* **prowled, prowling.** to move quietly, staying hidden from view, as if looking for prey: *The burglar prowled around the back of the house.* **• on the prowl.** seeking out something or someone: *Daisy went on the prowl in the local bookshops to find a present for her mother.*

prowl·er [prowl-ur] *noun, plural* **prowlers.** a person who moves quietly and in a secretive way, as if looking for prey.

pru·dent [prood-unt] *adjective.* having or displaying good judgment or caution: *It is prudent to listen to other people's opinions before making up your own mind.* The act of displaying good judgment or caution is called **prudence.** **—prudently,** *adverb.*

prune¹ [proon] *noun, plural* **prunes.** a dried plum.

prune² ▶ [proon] *verb,* **pruned, pruning.** to cut off or shorten the branches of a shrub or tree, or cut back or remove parts of something: *In spring we pruned the apple tree.*

*Gardeners **prune** some plants and small trees to encourage new growth.*

pry¹ [pry] *verb,* **pried, prying.** to look at or inquire excessively: *Don't pry into their private life, as they will not like it.*

pry² [pry] *verb,* **pried, prying.** to prise or lever apart with a tool: *Please pry open this tea chest for me—it's got some of my old books in it.*

P.S. an abbreviation for POSTSCRIPT or PUBLIC SCHOOL.

psalm [sahm] *noun, plural* **psalms.** *Religion.* a sacred song or hymn; a poem praising God, including those forming part of the Bible.

pseu·do·nym [sood-uh-nim] *noun, plural* **pseudonyms.** a name made up to conceal the real identity of a writer. Some female writers used to use male names as pseudonyms, because they thought that their writing would not be taken as seriously if the readers knew they were women.

psy·chi·a·trist [suh-kye-uh-trist] *noun, plural* **psychiatrists.** *Medicine.* a doctor who treats patients with mental or emotional illnesses.

*American Indians decorated the **prows** of ceremonial canoes with carved and painted totems.*

psy·chi·a·try [suh-<u>kye</u>-uh-tree] *noun. Medicine.* a branch of medicine that deals with the diagnosis and treatment of emotional and mental illness. Something that has to do with this area of medicine is said to be **psychiatric:** *a psychiatric hospital; a psychiatric patient.*

psy·cho·log·i·cal [sye-kuh-<u>loj</u>-uh-kul] *adjective.* **1.** having to do with a study of the mind and the ways in which it influences behavior. **2.** having to do with the mind and the way people behave: *Children face both physical and psychological changes as they are growing up.*

psy·chol·o·gist [sye-<u>kol</u>-uh-jist] *noun,* plural **psychologists.** a person trained to work in the field of psychology.

psy·chol·o·gy [sye-<u>kol</u>-uh-jee] *noun.* the branch of science that studies how the brain works and how the mind influences behavior in people and animals.

pter·o·dac·tyl [ter-uh-<u>dak</u>-til] *noun, plural* **pterodactyls.** *Biology.* a large birdlike reptile related to dinosaurs that lived in prehistoric times. Its wings consisted of skin stretched between its body and its toes.

pub [pub] *noun, plural* **pubs.** a place with one or more bars to serve alcoholic drinks and usually also food. This word is a shorter form of **public house**.

pub·lic [<u>pub</u>-lik] *adjective.* **1.** having to do with or concerning all the people in a place or a country: *The public announcement of water restrictions was greeted with dismay.* **2.** employed by the government of a town or city: *The mayor is a public official. noun.* all the people living in a town, city, or country: *The public are invited to comment on the new city plan.* • **in public.** in a place where there are many people; openly: *The first time the band played in public was at a school barbecue.* —**publicly,** *adverb.*

pub·li·ca·tion [pub-luh-<u>kay</u>-shun] *noun, plural* **publications.** a newspaper, magazine, or book published for people to read: *Some publications are published daily, some weekly, and others monthly.*

public health *Health.* the science of maintaining and improving the health of everyone within a community. The provision of clean water, sanitation, and medical and social services are all part of public health.

pub·lic·i·ty [puh-<u>blis</u>-uh-tee] *noun.* **1.** information brought to the notice of the public by means of advertisements, news stories, and word of mouth: *The publicity for Nick and Tom's new rock band has been huge.* **2.** attention or recognition given by the public to prominent people such as politicians or media celebrities: *Publicity can be either good or bad for the person or people involved.*

Words such as **psychiatry** and *psychology* have to do with thoughts and the mind as opposed to the physical body. These terms come from an older word *psyche,* meaning the human soul or spirit. *Psyche* was taken from a word meaning "breath" or "breathing," because of the idea that being able to breathe is absolutely necessary to being alive.

public opinion the thoughts and attitudes of the public, particularly in relation to political policies and issues.

public relations the work and practice of creating and managing favorable impressions of a company, government, or person, within a community.

public school *Education.* any school run by a state or central government that is paid for by taxes and is free to pupils. Public schools are usually open to any child that lives within the local area.

pub·lish [<u>pub</u>-lish] *verb,* **published, publishing.** to organize, print, and make available to the public a newspaper, book, magazine, or other publication.

pub·lish·er [<u>pub</u>-lish-ur] *noun, plural* **publishers.** a person or a company that publishes a newspaper, book, magazine, or newsletter. The industry that prints and sells books and other publications is **publishing.** Some of these products are also published in electronic form on the World Wide Web.

puck [puk] *noun, plural* **pucks.** a thick, flat, hard rubber disk used instead of a ball in the game of ice hockey.

pud·ding [<u>pud</u>-ing] *noun, plural* **puddings.** a sweet dessert usually made from eggs, sugar, and milk, often with fruits added, and eaten with custard or cream.

pud·dle [<u>pud</u>-ul] *noun, plural* **puddles.** a small, shallow area of water or other liquid.

pueb·lo ▼ [<u>pweb</u>-loh] *noun, plural* **pueblo** or **pueblos.** **1.** a Native American village with buildings joined together, made from stone and adobe. Such buildings are found in the Southwestern U.S. in Arizona and New Mexico, built by the **Pueblo** people, one of a number of Native American groups in this area.

To save space in **pueblos,** *buildings were stacked one on top of the other and were reached by ladders.*

a
b
c
d
e
f
g
h
i
j
k
l
m
n
o
p
q
r
s
t
u
v
w
x
y
z

A B C D E F G H I J K L M N O P Q R S T U V W X Y Z

Puerto Rican a person who was born or lives in Puerto Rico, a territory of the United States.
adjective. having to do with Puerto Rico, its people, or its culture.

puf·fin ◀ [puf-un] *noun, plural* **puffins.** a short, black-and-white sea bird with a brightly colored beak. Puffins are found in the North Atlantic Ocean.

Atlantic **puffins** *nest on the top of cliffs in large groups called colonies.*

pull [pul] *verb,* **pulled, pulling.**
1. to bring something forward, toward, or behind oneself by holding on and moving: *I pulled the dog along behind me on its leash because it was walking so slowly.* **2.** to take out or remove: *to pull a badly decayed tooth; The quarterback was pulled from the game because he was playing so poorly.* **3.** to move in a certain direction: *The car pulled away from the sidewalk.*
noun, plural **pulls. 1.** the act or fact of pulling: *the pull of a magnet; The diver gave a pull on the rope for help.* **2.** special influence: *He claims he can get us tickets because he has a lot of pull with the team owner.*

pul·ley ▶ [pul-ee] *noun, plural* **pulleys.** a device for lifting heavy objects. Pulleys have a grooved wheel over which a rope or chain runs and is attached to the object to be lifted.

pulp [pulp] *noun, plural* **pulps. 1.** the soft, fleshy part of a fruit or vegetable. **2.** any soft, moist mixture of vegetable matter: *Paper is made from wood pulp.* **3.** the soft inner section of a tooth.
verb, **pulped, pulping.** to cause to become a pulp by pounding and mixing with water: *Mom pulped the fruit before making jam.*

pul·pit [pul-pit] *noun, plural* **pulpits.** a raised stone or wooden enclosure in a church from which sermons are delivered.

pulse [puls] *noun, plural* **pulses. 1.** a regular, rhythmic beating of blood in the arteries caused by the pumping of the heart: *Doctors and nurses are trained to find a patient's pulse.* **2.** any steady, rhythmic beat: *I could hear the pulse of the music through the wall.*
verb, **pulsed, pulsing.** to display a pulse: *The veins in her neck pulsed after running the race.*

pu·ma ▶ [pyoo-muh *or* poo-muh] *noun, plural* **pumas.** a wild, flesh-eating animal of the cat family, more often called a MOUNTAIN LION.

pump [pump] *noun, plural* **pumps.** a machine for moving liquids or gases through a pipe: *An irrigation pump moves water from a dam to the fields.*
verb, **pumped, pumping. 1.** to move liquids or gases by using a pump: *The tanker pumps gasoline into underground tanks at the gas station.* **2.** to inflate with air or gas: *We pumped up balloons for the party.* **3.** to question repeatedly in order to find out information: *The police officer pumped the boys for information about who had the stolen car.*

pump·kin ▶ [pump-kin] *noun, plural* **pumpkins.** a large, round, pale orange fruit with a thick skin and smooth orange flesh.

pun [pun] *noun, plural* **puns.** a witty play on the meaning of words. Some puns depend on a single word with more than one meaning. Others depend on two words that sound the same but have different meanings: *A bicycle can't stand on its own, because it is two tired.*

A **pun** uses words in a different way in order to be funny or to have another such effect. A typical way to do this is to use the same word or sound in different ways: "The grizzly was cold because he did not have a coat, just his *bear (bare)* skin." "When he got stopped for speeding on the highway, it was a *fine* day." "I don't eat doughnuts any more; I just got tired of the *whole (hole)* thing." Puns are often thought of as silly, but they have been part of the language for hundreds of years and many famous writers have enjoyed using them.

punch¹ [punch] *verb,* **punched, punching. 1.** to hit someone or something hard with the fist: *Milo punched the wall when he heard he had failed the exam.* **2.** to herd or round up: *to punch cattle.*
noun, plural **punches.** a hit made with the fist: *The boxer's last punch knocked out his opponent.*

An old ship's **pulley** *strains to raise its load.*

punch² [punch] *noun, plural* **punches.** a tool for making holes or stamping designs in wood, leather, or metal. *With a leather punch you can make an extra hole in your belt.*
verb, **punched, punching.** to make a hole or stamp a design with a punch: *Jewelers punch beautiful designs onto silver plates and bowls.*

punch³ [punch] *noun, plural* **punches.** a drink made by mixing different fruit juices together, sometimes with spices, wine, or spirits added.

The **puma** *hisses, growls, whistles and purrs, but cannot roar.*

*A **punt** glides under the Mathematician's Bridge in Cambridge, England.*

punc·tu·al [pungk-choo-ul] *adjective.* having to do with being on time; not delayed: *Gayle is always punctual and has never been late for school.* The fact of being on time is **punctuality.** —**punctually,** *adverb.*

punc·tu·ate [pungk-choo-ate] *verb,* **punctuated, punctuating.** *Language.* **1.** to divide written sentences or paragraphs by inserting punctuation marks such as commas and periods, so that the meaning of the words is clear. **2.** to insert a pause, break, or different material when speaking: *Barbara punctuated her speech to the school with photographs of her trip to Africa.*

punc·tu·a·tion [pungk-choo-ay-shun] *noun. Language.* **1.** the system or act of using commas, periods, and other such marks in written work to make the meaning of the words clearer. **2.** any of the marks used to punctuate written language: *The sentence had no punctuation, so I found it hard to follow.*

Punctuation is used in writing to have the same effect for which we use the voice in speaking. For example, a comma (,) shows a pause between words, an exclamation point (!) shows that something would be said more loudly, (?) shows that one is asking or uncertain about something, and *italics* or underlining shows that a certain word would stand out or be emphasized. One famous actor has said that he pays no attention to the punctuation in a script he is reading, because he wants to decide for himself where to pause between words, which words to speak more loudly, and so on.

punctuation mark *Language.* any of the marks commonly used to punctuate written work such as a comma, hyphen, quotation mark, or period.

punc·ture [pung-chur] *verb,* **punctured, puncturing.** to make a hole using a sharp point: *The dog punctured our garden hose by biting it.* *noun, plural* **punctures.** a hole, usually made with a sharp point: *My bicycle tire had a puncture so I could not ride to school.*

pun·ish [pun-ish] *verb,* **punished, punishing.** to make a person who has done something wrong suffer a fine, penalty, pain, or loss of freedom. Anything that hurts or is physically challenging in some way can be described as **punishing.**

pun·ish·ment [pun-ish-munt] *noun, plural* **punishments.** **1.** the act of punishing a person: *Punishments can be imposed by a teacher, a parent, or the justice system.* **2.** the way in which a person is punished for breaking the law: *His punishment for reckless driving was to pay a fine and lose his license.*

punt ◀ [punt] *noun, plural* **punts. 1.** a narrow, flat-bottomed boat used to carry people on a shallow river or lake. Small punts are moved by using a pole to push on the bottom. **2.** the act of kicking a football with the top of the foot after dropping it from the hands. *verb,* **punted, punting. 1.** to move such a boat along by pushing with a pole on the bottom. **2.** to kick a football with the top of the foot after dropping it from the hands. A person who does this is called a **punter.**

pup [pup] *noun, plural* **pups. 1.** a young dog: *Our dog has had six pups.* **2.** the young of a number of other animals such as seals, otters, and foxes.

pu·pa [pyoo-puh] *noun, plural* **pupas** or **pupae.** *Biology.* an insect in the middle stage of its development, after being a larva and before it is fully grown.

pu·pil[1] [pyoo-pul] *noun, plural* **pupils.** a person, especially a child, who is being taught, usually in school.

pu·pil[2] [pyoo-pul] *noun, plural* **pupils.** the opening in the iris in the eye that allows light to reach the retina. The pupil varies in size, depending on the brightness of the light.

pup·pet ▼ [pup-it] *noun, plural* **puppets. 1.** a hollow doll worn on the hand operated by moving the fingers and thumb; or the figure of a person or animal with moving parts controlled by pulling attached strings, wires or rods. **2.** a person or group controlled from a distance by others: *The arts committee are just puppets—they are just told what to do by the Administration.*

*Indonesian shadow puppet masters tell traditional stories using **puppets** made from buffalo or goat skin.*

a b c d e f g h i j k l m n o p q r s t u v w x y z

pup·py [pup-ee] *noun, plural* **puppies.** a young dog or pup.

pur·chase [pur-chus] *verb,* **purchased, purchasing.** to buy something: *I purchased my music system with money I had earned.*
noun, plural **purchases. 1.** the act of buying something with money: *The purchase of my music system was done in a music store.* **2.** something that is bought: *I am very pleased with my purchase.*

pure [pyoor] *adjective,* **purer, purest. 1.** not mixed with anything or diluted: *We buy pure grapefruit juice.* **2.** free from dirt and pollution: *The air around here is really pure.* **3.** utterly and completely: *You are talking pure nonsense.* **4.** free from evil or wicked thoughts; innocent: *Children have such a pure approach to life at the age of five.* **—purely,** *adverb.*

pure·bred ▲ [pyoor-bred] *adjective.* having a family line that is all the same breed: *The kittens are purebred Siamese.*

pu·ri·fy [pyoor-uh-fye] *verb,* **purified, purifying.** to make pure: *The kidneys help purify the blood.* The act of removing harmful substances from something is **purification.** Something that has been made pure has been **purified**: *purified water.*

The Sun and Moon **pyramids** *are huge temples in the ruined city of Teotihuacán, in central Mexico.*

The Siberian husky has been kept a **purebred** *dog for hundreds of years.*

Pu·ri·tan [pyoor-uh-tun] *noun, plural* **Puritans.** *History.* a member of the Protestant religious group in the sixteenth and seventeenth centuries who wanted more discipline and stricter morals within the Church of England. A person who tries to be very pure and strict and believes that pleasure is unnecessary is a **puritan.** Someone who behaves like a puritan is said to be **puritanical.**

pur·ple [pur-pul] *noun, plural* **purples.** a dark color made by mixing red and blue.
adjective. having a purple color.

pur·pose [pur-pus] *noun, plural* **purposes.** the reason why something is done or exists: *The purpose of my studying is so that I would do well on the test.*
♦ **on purpose.** intentionally or deliberately: *The teacher thinks that I left my book at home on purpose, but it was an accident.*

Push-ups are a good way to strengthen arm muscles.

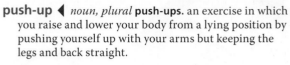

push-up ◀ *noun, plural* **push-ups.** an exercise in which you raise and lower your body from a lying position by pushing yourself up with your arms but keeping the legs and back straight.

pussy willow ▼ [puss-ee] a small tree with silver-colored flowers that are soft and fur-like.

put [put] *verb,* **put, putting. 1.** to place in a certain position: *to put a dish on the table; to put dirty clothes in the washing machine; to put your name on a list.* **2.** to cause to be in a certain condition: *to put on the radio; I hope this won't put you to too much trouble.* **3.** to say in a certain way: *If you put it that way, I guess we have no choice in the matter.*

put·ty [put-ee] *noun.* a soft, oily claylike substance that hardens when it dries. Putty is used for fixing glass into frames or filling holes in wood.

puz·zle [puz-ul] *noun, plural* **puzzles. 1.** something that is difficult to understand: *Mom says that it is a puzzle to her how my room is always so messy.* **2.** a toy or game that is fun because it gives you an interesting problem to solve: *The children spent hours piecing together the jigsaw puzzle.* *verb,* **puzzled, puzzling. 1.** to be difficult to understand; confusing: *My best friend's sudden rudeness and bad attitude really puzzled me.* **2.** to think long and hard about something to try to understand it: *The police officer puzzled over how the accident could have been caused.*

pyr·a·mid ◀ [peer-uh-mid] *noun, plural* **pyramids.** a solid object with a flat square base and four flat triangular sides that meet at a point in the top. **The Pyramids** are huge stone structures built in the shape of a pyramid in Egypt. They were built in ancient times as monuments to hold the bodies and possessions of important people such as Pharaohs.

py·thon ▼ [pye-thon] *noun, plural* **pythons.** a large, non-venomous snake that coils around its prey and crushes it to death.

The buds of a **pussy willow** *are soft and gray.*

By extending its jaws, a **python** *can swallow an animal as large as a wild pig.*

pur·pose·ful [pur-pus-ful] *adjective.* having a clear purpose: *She knew what she wanted to buy, and walked into the shop with a purposeful look on her face.* —**purposefully,** *adverb.*

pur·pose·ly [pur-pus-lee] *adverb.* intentionally or deliberately: *We purposely left early to avoid the rush hour traffic.*

purr [pur] *noun, plural* **purrs.** a low, continuous murmuring sound such as a cat makes when it is happy. *verb,* **purred, purring.** to make a low, continuous murmuring sound: *Our cat purrs when you scratch him behind his ears.*

purse [purs] *noun, plural* **purses. 1.** a small handbag. **2.** a small bag or pouch used to carry money. **3.** a sum of money offered as a prize in a sports competition. *verb,* **pursed, pursing.** to draw tightly together into folds or wrinkles: *The teacher pursed her lips in annoyance.*

pur·sue [pur-soo] *verb,* **pursued, pursuing. 1.** to follow someone or something to catch or capture them: *The leopard pursued its prey.* Someone who follows and chases someone else is a **pursuer. 2.** to continue with an activity or try to accomplish: *I train every day because I am pursuing a career as an professional athlete.*

pur·suit [pur-soot] *noun, plural* **pursuits. 1.** the act of pursuing: *The hunter was in pursuit of the wild pig.* **2.** a pastime or hobby: *My pursuits include sailing and playing soccer.*

pus [puhs] *noun. Medicine.* a thick, yellowish liquid produced in an infected cut or injury. Pus contains white blood cells, germs, and tissue debris.

push [push] *verb,* **pushed, pushing. 1.** to press upon something with force to make it move: *When the car broke down, we pushed it to the side of the road.* **2.** to move forward in a forceful manner: *The rude woman pushed her way through the crowd to the front of the line.* **3.** to insist or persuade someone in order to achieve something: *The mayor pushed hard for more funding for the city's public schools. noun, plural* **pushes. 1.** the act of pushing; a shove: *Someone gave me a push from behind as I got on the bus.* **2.** a strong effort to accomplish something: *The government is making a push for environmental reform.*

*Despite its name, the California **quail** is common and widespread in western North America.*

Q, q *noun, plural* **Q's, q's.** the seventeenth letter of the English alphabet.

quack¹ [kwak] *noun, plural* **quacks.** the harsh cry that a duck makes.
verb, **quacked, quacking.** to make such a sound.

quack² [kwak] *noun, plural* **quacks.** a person who pretends to be a doctor or other expert.
adjective. relating to or characteristic of a quack: *That strange-looking potion is a quack remedy for a cold.*

quad·ran·gle [kwahd-*rang*-gul] *noun, plural* **quadrangles.** a square or rectangular courtyard that is surrounded on all four sides by buildings, as in a school or college. The word quadrangle is often shortened to **quad.**

quad·ri·lat·er·al [kwahd-ruh-*lat*-ur-ul] *noun, plural* **quadrilaterals.** *Mathematics.* a flat shape that has four straight sides such as a square or rectangle.

quad·ru·ped ▶ [kwahd-ruh-*ped*] *noun, plural* **quadrupeds.** *Biology.* any animal that has four feet, such as a lion or cat.

quad·ru·ple [kwah-*droo*-pul] *verb,* **quadrupled, quadrupling.** to become four times as big; multiply by four: *Mom quadrupled the recipe so that we would have enough food for the extra people who arrived.*

quad·ru·plet [kwah-*droo*-plit] *noun, plural* **quadruplets. 1.** any of four children born at the same time to the same mother. **2.** any group of four.

quag·mire [*kwag*-mire] *noun, plural* **quagmires. 1.** an area of wet soggy ground that gives way when you walk on it: *The heavy rain turned the football field into a quagmire.* **2.** a situation that presents serious problems and that is very hard to escape from or avoid.

qua·hog [*kwaw*-hawg *or* *kwaw*-hog] *noun, plural* **quahogs.** an edible clam with a thick, round shell found along the Atlantic coast of North America.

Dogs are agile **quadrupeds** *that enjoy catching and retrieving objects.*

quail ◀ [kwale] *noun, plural* **quail** *or* **quails.** a small, plump brown bird with a short tail that is hunted for sport or food.
verb, **quailed, quailing.** to show fear; lose courage: *The child quailed at the sound of the teacher's angry voice.*

quaint [kwaynt] *adjective,* **quainter, quaintest.** attractive in an old-fashioned and unusual way: *My grandparents live in a quaint little cottage in the country.*
—**quaintly,** *adverb;* —**quaintness,** *noun.*

quake [kwake] *verb,* **quaked, quaking.** to shake or tremble from amusement, fear, cold, shock, or anger: *My legs were quaking with fear when I first boarded the airplane.*
noun, plural **quakes.** a shaking or trembling, especially an earthquake: *Luckily the quake was so small that no one was hurt and there was only minor damage.*

Quak·er [*kway*-kur] *noun, plural* **Quakers.** *Religion.* a member of a Christian group called the **Society of Friends,** that does not have any formal ceremonies or system of beliefs and is strongly opposed to violence.

qual·i·fi·ca·tion [kwahl-uh-fuh-*kay*-shun] *noun, plural* **qualifications. 1.** an ability, skill, or experience that makes a person suitable for a particular job or activity: *She has the academic qualifications for a career in law.* **2.** something that weakens; a restriction or limitation: *The School Board supported the plan without qualification.*

qual·i·fied [*kwahl*-uh-fyed] *adjective.* **1.** having a particular ability, knowledge, or experience to make you suitable to do something: *We hired him because he is a qualified plumber.* **2.** limited or restricted in some way: *Mom gave me only qualified approval to go on spring break with my friends.*

qual·i·fy [*kwahl*-uh-fye] *verb,* **qualified, qualifying. 1.** to make or be suitable to do something: *Her win at the state championships meant she qualified for a spot in the nationals.* **2.** to make less strong; limit or restrict: *The teacher qualified her statement that the test results were poor, by adding that the test had been extra hard this time.* **3.** to change or limit the meaning of: *We use adjectives to qualify nouns so that sentences are more detailed and interesting.*

qual·i·ty [*kwahl*-uh-tee] *noun, plural* **qualities. 1.** a feature of someone or something: *Aluminum is both light in weight and strong—because of these qualities, it is often used to make airplanes; She is very patient, which is one of the qualities of a good teacher.* **2.** a high standard or value: *The fruit at our local store is of very high quality.*

qualm [kwahm *or* kwahlm] *noun, plural* **qualms.** a feeling of uneasiness or slight fear: *I had some qualms about taking on the new job.*

quan·da·ry [*kwahn*-duh-ree] *noun, plural* **quandaries.** a state of confusion or uncertainty: *She was in a quandary about how to stop her two sons from arguing and fighting with each other.*

*In **quarries** heavy-duty construction vehicles are used to crush and collect rock.*

quan·ti·ty [kwahn-tuh-tee] *noun, plural* **quantities.**
1. an amount or measure of something: *Mom bought a small quantity of chocolate for a treat after dinner.*
2. a large amount or measure of something: *The school cafeteria buys macaroni in great quantities.*

quar·an·tine [kwor-un-*teen*] *noun, plural* **quarantines.**
Health. a period of time where a person, animal, or plant is kept away from others to stop the spreading of disease: *The airport officials put the strange plants into quarantine until they could be sure they were safe.*
verb, **quarantined, quarantining.** to put a person, animal, or plant in quarantine.

> The word **quarantine** comes from an Italian phrase meaning "forty days." The practice of quarantine began in Europe in the Middle Ages. When it was thought that a ship coming to port might be carrying a disease, it was the custom to keep it outside the port for a period of forty days to be sure no one on board had the disease.

quark [kwork] *noun, plural* **quarks.** *Science.* in physics, a particle that is smaller than an atom.

quar·rel [kwor-ul] *noun, plural* **quarrels.** an angry argument or disagreement: *I had a quarrel with my sister about who would get to eat the last cookie.* Someone who is **quarrelsome** argues a lot with other people.
verb, **quarreled, quarreling. 1.** to have an angry argument or disagreement: *The two drivers quarreled about which one was at fault for the accident.*
2. to complain or find fault: *The student didn't quarrel with the teacher's negative comments on his report card, because he knew they were true.*

quar·ry¹ ▲ [kwor-ee] *noun, plural* **quarries.** a large, open pit where large amounts of stone are cut or blasted out of the ground.

quar·ry² ▶ [kwor-ee] *noun, plural* **quarries.** an animal or bird that is being hunted: *The foxhounds pursued their quarry into a hole.*

quart [kwort] *noun, plural* **quarts.** a unit for measuring liquids that is equal to two pints or 0.95 liters.

quar·ter [kwor-tur] *noun, plural* **quarters.**
1. one of four equal parts into which something can be divided: *We each had a quarter of an orange during the halftime break of the game.*
2. a coin used in the United States and Canada, worth 25 cents. **3.** the moment that marks the end of each fourth of an hour: *The first morning train to the city leaves at a quarter after six.*
4. one of the four equal periods of playing time into which a game, such as basketball, is divided.
5. an area or district: *The city of Paris, France, has a famous old section called the Latin Quarter.* A place of residence or lodging is referred to as **quarters.**
verb, **quartered, quartering. 1.** to divide into four equal parts. **2.** to provide with a place to stay: *The troops were quartered in the barracks.*

quar·ter·back [kwor-tur-*bak*] *noun, plural* **quarterbacks.** in football, a player who starts the offensive play of the team by taking the ball from the center. He can then pass the ball or hand it to another player.
verb, **quarterbacked, quarterbacking. 1.** to play this position on a football team. **2.** to organize, arrange or direct an event or activity: *He quarterbacked the new advertising campaign.*

> In an earlier time in football the offensive backfield had four players: the **quarterback**, two *halfbacks*, and the *fullback*. These players were named because of where they lined up for a play. The quarterback was the closest to the line of scrimmage, thought of as being one quarter (one-fourth) of the way back. In the modern game of football there is no such position as a halfback, and the fullback sets up next to the line of scrimmage, but the quarterback's position is still the same.

quar·ter·ly [kwor-tur-lee] *adjective.* happening or produced every three months: *My parents receive quarterly school reports on my work performance and behavior.*
adverb. once every three months: *Interest is paid quarterly for this bank account.*

a b c d e f g h i j k l m n o p **q** r s t u v w x y z

*Lizards are among the large **quarries** stalked by the Mexican red-kneed tarantula.*

quar·tet [kwor-<u>tet</u>] *noun, plural* **quartets.** *Music.*
1. a piece of music written for four voices or musicians.
2. an organized group of four people who sing or play musical instruments together. 3. any group or set of four.

quartz [kwortz] *noun.* a hard, colorless mineral substance found in many different types of rocks that is used to make clocks and watches.

qua·sar [<u>kway</u>-zar] *noun, plural* **quasars.** *Science.* an object in space, similar to a star that gives off strong light and powerful radio waves.

quay [kee] *noun, plural* **quays.** a dock or wharf where passengers and cargo are loaded and unloaded from boats and ships.
🔊 A different word with the same sound is **key.**

quea·sy [<u>kwee</u>-zee] *adjective,* **queasier, queasiest. 1.** feeling as if you might vomit. **2.** feeling uneasy or doubtful: *He is feeling queasy about starting a new job tomorrow.*

queen ▼ [kween] *noun, plural* **queens. 1.** the wife or widow of a king. **2.** a woman who rules a kingdom or country. **3.** a woman who is considered the best in a particular area or activity: *She is known in our town as the queen of line dancing.* **4.** the large egg-laying female of a group of insects such as bees or ants. **5.** a playing card with a picture of the queen on it. **6.** the most powerful piece on the board in the game of chess.

queer [kweer] *adjective,* **queerer, queerest.** describing something strange or unusual: *I went to investigate the queer smell coming from the shed in the backyard.*

quench [kwench] *verb,* **quenched, quenching.**
1. to satisfy or make less: *After the game I quenched my thirst with water.* **2.** to put out; extinguish: *They quenched the fire with buckets of water.*

que·ry [<u>kweer</u>-ee] *noun, plural* **queries.** something asked; a question: *The doctor answered my queries about the operation.*
verb, **queried, querying.** to ask questions: *The teacher queried my reasons for not doing my homework.*

quest [kwest] *noun, plural* **quests.** a search for something: *The movie tells about the hero's quest to find a large, very valuable document.*

ques·tion [<u>kwes</u>-chun] *noun, plural* **questions.**
1. something that is said or written to find out information: *The test has ten questions that each have to be answered True or False; The detective had a lot of questions for the suspect.* **2.** a problem or matter for discussion: *The school board met to address the question of government funding.* **3.** doubt or uncertainty: *There is no question about his being the best candidate for the job.* Something that is uncertain or wrong in some way is said to be **questionable.**
verb, **questioned, questioning. 1.** to ask a question: *The police officers questioned the motorist about the accident.* **2.** to express doubts or uncertainty about something or someone: *My parents questioned my story as to why I got home so late.*

The English language has two kinds of **questions.** An information question uses words such as who, what, where, when, why, and how to ask for information in the answer: "When does the movie start?" A yes/no question simply asks for an answer using one of those two words: "Is that your book? No." "Can you give me a ride home? Yes."

question mark *Language.* a punctuation mark (?) put at the end of a written sentence to indicate that a question is being asked.

ques·tion·naire [<u>kwes</u>-chuh-<u>nare</u>] *noun, plural* **questionnaires.** a list of questions that people are asked to gather information about them or their opinions.

quet·zal [ket-<u>sal</u>] *noun, plural* **quetzals.** a brightly colored Central American bird with red and green plumage. The male has long, flowing tail feathers.

queue [kyoo] *noun, plural* **queues.** a line of people or vehicles waiting their turn: *There was a long queue outside the theater of people wanting to buy tickets.*
verb, **queued, queuing.** to form or join a line of people or vehicles waiting in turn: *The passengers had queued up at the gate to get on the plane.*

quib·ble [<u>kwib</u>-ul] *verb,* **quibbled, quibbling.** to argue about small and unimportant things: *He quibbled over the two cents he was owed in change.*

quick [kwik] *adjective,* **quicker, quickest. 1.** taking only a short time; fast: *I had a quick bite to eat and then raced out the door for school.* **2.** able to understand things rapidly; clever: *The student had a quick mind and performed well in class.* —**quickly,** *adverb;* —**quickness,** *noun.*

The sixteenth-century English seaman Sir Francis Drake brought back treasure for **Queen** *Elizabeth I from his raids on Spanish ships.*

quick·sand [kwik-*sand*] *noun.* an area of deep, wet sand into which heavy objects sink and get trapped.

quiet [kwye-ut] *adjective,* **quieter, quietest. 1.** not making much noise: *The audience remained quiet throughout the theater performance.* **2.** not busy; peaceful: *We found a quiet little spot in the park where we could sit and talk. noun.* the condition of being quiet: *I enjoy the peace and quiet of hiking in the woods by myself. verb,* **quieted, quieting.** to make or become quiet: *The teacher quieted down the class so that she could start the exam.* —**quietly,** *adverb;* —**quietness,** *noun.*

quill ▲ [kwil] *noun, plural* **quills. 1.** a large, stiff, bird's feather. **2.** a pen used in the past that was made from the hollow stem of a bird's feather. **3.** any of the long, sharp spines of a porcupine or hedgehog.

quilt ▶ [kwilt] *noun, plural* **quilts.** a bed cover made by sewing two layers of cloth together with feathers or a warm material between them. *verb,* **quilted, quilting. 1.** to make a quilt. **2.** to stitch together cloth and lining in a decorative fashion. Something that resembles a quilt in texture or make is described as being **quilted.** The process of making a quilt is **quilting.**

quin·tu·plet [kwin-tup-lit] *noun, plural* **quintuplets. 1.** any of five children born at the same time to the same mother. **2.** any group of five.

quip [kwip] *noun, plural* **quips.** a witty and clever remark: *My uncle is great fun to visit, because he always makes amusing quips. verb,* **quipped, quipping.** to say something amusing and clever.

quirk [kwerk] *noun, plural* **quirks. 1.** an unusual habit, behavior, or part of someone's personality: *My math teacher has a few quirks, but he's a great teacher all the same.* **2.** a strange or unexpected turn of events: *By a quirk of fate, I bought the same pair of shoes that my sister had bought that morning.* A person who is odd in an interesting sort of way is described as **quirky.**

quirt [kwert] *noun, plural* **quirts.** a riding whip with a short handle and a braided rawhide tip.

quit [kwit] *verb,* **quit** *or* **quitted, quitting. 1.** to stop doing something: *I quit raking the leaves when the rain started.* **2.** to leave or depart from: *The famous actor quit show business to spend more time with his family.* **3.** to give up: *My grandfather quit smoking fifty years ago and hasn't touched a cigarette since.* Someone who gives up easily when things get difficult is called a **quitter.**

quite [kwite] *adverb.* **1.** in all ways; entirely; completely: *I wasn't quite finished my meal so I told the waiter not to take my plate away.* **2.** really or truly: *Wearing sunscreen at the beach is quite the thing to do.* **3.** more than usual; rather or very: *It was quite cold this morning.* • **quite a.** considerable or notable: *He has quite a bit of money.*

quiv·er[1] [kwiv-ur] *verb,* **quivered, quivering.** to tremble or shake slightly: *Her bottom lip quivered and tears started to fall. noun, plural* **quivers.** the act of gently trembling or slightly shaking.

quiv·er[2] [kwiv-ur] *noun, plural* **quivers.** a long, thin case for holding arrows.

quiz [kwiz] *noun, plural* **quizzes.** a short, informal class test: *We had a quiz in math today at school. verb,* **quizzed, quizzing.** to ask questions about something: *Mom quizzed me about who else was going to be at the party.*

> The word **quiz** comes from a Latin word meaning "what." In a quiz it is common to have questions beginning with "What," such as "What is the capital of Michigan?" or "What is another word for 'sad'?"

In this patchwork **quilt,** *pieces of black and white cloth have been carefully stitched together in a pattern.*

quo·rum [kwor-um] *noun.* the smallest number of people that need to be present at a meeting before official decisions can be made: *We need a quorum of ten before we can take a vote.*

quota [kwoh-tuh] *noun, plural* **quotas. 1.** the share or portion of something that you are entitled to: *At the college each student is allowed a quota of 50 MB of space for their e-mail account.* **2.** the amount of a certain type of people or things permitted to enter a place, be hired for a job, be sold, and so on.

quota system a system in which a certain set number of people are admitted or allowed to do something, such as the number of immigrants who are allowed to enter the United States each year.

quo·ta·tion [kwoh-tay-shun] *noun, plural* **quotations. 1.** a piece of writing or speech that is repeated or copied by another person exactly as it was originally said or written: *I began my speech with a quotation from Martin Luther King Jr.* **2.** the act of quoting what someone else has said or written.

quotation mark *Language.* one of a pair of punctuation marks (" ") that are used to indicate the beginning and end of a quotation or direct question.

quote [kwote] *verb,* **quoted, quoting.** to repeat exactly the same words that someone else has said or written: *The minister began the service by quoting from the Bible. noun, plural* **quotes.** a quotation.

quo·tient [kwoh-shunt] *noun, plural* **quotients.** *Mathematics.* the number that is obtained when one number is divided by another. If you divide 18 by 3, the quotient is 6.

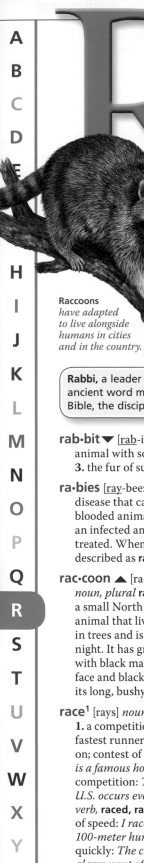

Raccoons
*have adapted
to live alongside
humans in cities
and in the country.*

Rr

R, r *noun, plural* **R's, r's.**
the eighteenth letter of the
English alphabet.

rab·bi [rab-eye]
noun, plural **rabbis.** *Religion.*
a teacher and religious leader
in the Jewish religion.

> **Rabbi,** a leader in the Jewish religion, comes from an
> ancient word meaning "teacher" or "master." In the
> Bible, the disciples of Jesus often address him as "Rabbi."

rab·bit ▼ [rab-it] *noun, plural* **rabbits. 1.** a small burrowing
animal with soft fur, long ears, and a short tail. **2.** a hare.
3. the fur of such an animal.

ra·bies [ray-beez] *noun. Medicine.* an extremely dangerous
disease that can affect humans, dogs, and other warm-
blooded animals. It is spread to humans by the bite of
an infected animal, and can be deadly if the victim is not
treated. When an animal is suffering from rabies, it is
described as **rabid.**

rac·coon ▲ [ra-koon]
noun, plural **raccoons.**
a small North American
animal that lives mostly
in trees and is active at
night. It has grayish fur
with black marks on its
face and black rings on
its long, bushy tail.

race¹ [rays] *noun, plural* **races.**
1. a competition to see who is the
fastest runner, swimmer, diver, and so
on; contest of speed: *The Kentucky Derby
is a famous horse race.* **2.** any contest or
competition: *The race for President of the
U.S. occurs every four years.*
verb, **raced, racing. 1.** to compete in a contest
of speed: *I raced against my best friend in the
100-meter hurdles.* **2.** to move or cause to move very
quickly: *The crowd raced for the nearest exits when the
alarm went off.* **3.** to do something very quickly: *He raced
through his speech because he just wanted to get it over with.*

race² [rays] *noun, plural* **races.** a very large group of people
with the same ancestors. They have similar physical
characteristics, and usually have a culture and language
in common.

rac·er [ray-sur] *noun, plural* **racers. 1.** someone or
something that competes in a race: *That greyhound is
a great little racer.* **2.** a common, fast-moving black or
bluish American snake.

race·track [rays-track] *noun, plural* **racetracks.** a track,
usually oval, on which runners, horses, or cars race.

ra·cial [ray-shul] *adjective.* having to do with a particular
race of human beings: *Racial discrimination should not
be tolerated.* —**racially,** *adverb.*

rac·ist [ray-sist] *adjective.* someone who believes that their
own race is superior to other races. This belief, as well
as unpleasant words or behavior toward other races, is
called **racism.**

rack [rak] *noun, plural* **racks.** a frame or shelf formed by
bars, wires, or pegs on which you can hang, put, or store
things: *I looked through the magazine rack for something
interesting to read in the waiting room.*
verb, **racked, racking.** to cause great physical or mental
pain or suffering: *The high fever racked her entire body.*
• **rack one's brain.** to think very hard about something:
*I've racked my brains about what I was supposed
to tell you, but I just can't remember.*

rack·et¹ [rak-it] *noun, plural* **rackets.**
1. a loud, disturbing noise: *There was such
a racket in the apartment next door that I
couldn't get to sleep.* **2.** a dishonest or illegal
way to get money: *a car-stealing racket.*

rack·et² ▶ [rak-it] *noun, plural* **rackets.** a bat
with a network of strings stretched across a
round or oval frame. It has a long thin handle
and is used for striking a
ball in various sports such
as tennis or badminton.

rac·quet another spelling
of RACKET².

*Modern tennis
rackets are often
made from graphite.*

Rabbits live in warrens, where they build nests for their young.

rac·quet·ball [rak-it-*bawl*] *noun.* **1.** an indoor game played in a four-walled court in which two or four players use rackets to hit a small rubber ball against the walls. **2.** the ball used in the game.

ra·dar ▶ [ray-dar] *noun.* a device that uses radio waves to tell the position and speed of objects such as cars, ships, and planes.

Some **radar** *systems use a special large dish to send out and receive radio signals.*

> The technology known as radar first came into use during World War II. The word radar was made up then to describe this device. It is a combination of the first letters of the words "radio detection and ranging."

ra·di·ant [ray-dee-unt] *adjective.* **1.** shining brightly with light or joy: *She had a radiant smile that showed how happy she really felt.* **2.** heat or energy sent out in the form of waves: *We warmed ourselves by the radiant heater.* Brightness or light is sometimes referred to as **radiance.** —**radiantly,** *adverb.*

ra·di·ate [ray-dee-ate] *verb,* **radiated, radiating. 1.** to send or be sent out in waves or rays: *Heat radiated from the camp fire.* **2.** to spread out from a center point in all directions: *The cat's whiskers radiated from his mouth.* **3.** to show in your manner: *He radiated confidence.*

ra·di·a·tion [ray-dee-ay-shun] *noun. Science.* the process in which energy is given off in the form of waves or particles that cannot be seen.

ra·di·a·tor [ray-dee-ay-tur] *noun, plural* **radiators. 1.** a heating device that is made up of a series of pipes through which steam or hot water passes. **2.** a device that cools automotive engines by cooling the water that is circulated through the engine.

rad·i·cal [rad-i-kul] *adjective.* **1.** having to do with basic or important change: *She has radical ideas about religion.* **2.** expressing the belief that there should be extreme social or political change: *He is a radical politician. noun, plural* **radicals.** someone who supports extreme social or political change. —**radically,** *adverb.*

ra·di·o [ray-dee-oh] *noun, plural* **radios. 1.** a method of sending of electrical signals through the air. **2.** a device that receives or sends these electrical signals. *verb,* **radioed, radioing.** to send a message by radio: *The sailors radioed for help when they realized the ship was sinking.*

ra·di·o·ac·tive [ray-dee-oh-ak-tiv] *adjective.* possessing or producing harmful radiation from the breaking up of atoms: *Uranium is a radioactive mineral used in nuclear weapons.* —**radioactively,** *adverb.*

ra·di·o·ac·tiv·i·ty [ray-dee-oh-ak-tiv-i-tee] *noun. Science.* the energy produced and released by the breaking up of atoms.

ra·di·o·lo·gy [ray-dee-ol-uh-jee] *noun. Medicine.* a branch of science dealing with the use of X-rays and radioactive material in the treatment of disease. Someone who specializes in radiology is a **radiologist.**

rad·ish ▼ [rad-ish] *noun, plural* **radishes.** a small, spicy-tasting vegetable that is usually eaten raw. Radishes have a red or white root and grow underground.

ra·di·um [ray-dee-um] *noun. Chemistry.* a highly radioactive element that is used in the treatment of cancer.

ra·di·us [ray-dee-us] *noun, plural* **radii** or **radiuses.** *Mathematics.* **1.** a straight line going from the center of a circle to the outside edge. **2.** a circular area measured in all directions from a center point: *There are nine churches within a three-mile radius of our house.*

ra·don [ray-don] *noun. Chemistry.* a radioactive gas produced by the decay of radium, used in the treatment of cancer.

raf·fle [raf-ul] *noun, plural* **raffles.** a lottery in which people buy chances to win a prize: *First prize in the school raffle is a plasma screen television. verb,* **raffled, raffling.** to offer something as a prize in a raffle: *The country club raffled off two free lessons with a pro golf player for the charity appeal.*

raft [raft] *noun, plural* **rafts.** a floating platform made of logs or boards fastened together. *verb,* **rafted, rafting.** to travel on a raft: *We rafted down the river for hours until we saw a good spot to set up camp for the night.* The sport of traveling on rivers by raft is known as **rafting.**

The red bulb-like root of the **radish** *is the part that is eaten.*

rag [rag] *noun, plural* **rags. 1.** a small piece of old and torn cloth. Shabby, worn-out, or torn clothes are called **rags.**

rage [rayj] *noun, plural* **rages. 1.** violent, uncontrolled anger: *The man shouted in a rage when he saw the thieves driving off in his car.* **2.** the fact of being a fad or craze; a temporary fashion: *Cowboy boots were the rage in our school last year. verb,* **raged, raging.** to talk or act in a very angry or violent way: *The storm raged all day and caused a huge amount of damage to the town.* Someone who is talking or acting in a very angry or uncontrolled way, or a natural force that is violent, is described as **raging:** *a raging temper; a raging storm.*

rag·ged [rag-id] *adjective.* **1.** worn to rags; torn; frayed: *The young boy was barefoot and wore a ragged shirt.* **2.** wearing torn or worn out clothes; dressed in rags: *The ragged children asked people walking by for money.* **3.** having a rough or uneven outline, or sharp edges that stick out: *The old stone wall was ragged and starting to crumble.* —**raggedly,** *adverb.*

rag·weed [rag-*weed*] *noun, plural* **ragweeds.** a common weed found mainly in North America whose pollen is one of the causes of hay fever. It is related to the daisy.

raid [rade] *noun, plural* **raids.** a sudden attack to take someone or something by surprise: *At dawn, the soldiers made a raid on the enemy camp.* Someone who carries out a sudden surprise attack is a **raider.**
verb, **raided, raiding.** to make a raid on; attack suddenly and take by surprise: *The bandits raided the farmhouse to steal food and horses.*

rail [rale] *noun, plural* **rails. 1.** a level or sloping bar fixed in place that acts as a guard, barrier, or support: *Hold on to the rail as you go down these steep stairs.* The steel bars that trains travel along are called rails. **2.** a shortened form of RAILROAD: *Some people would rather travel by rail than fly.*

rail·ing [*ray*-ling] *noun, plural* **railings.** a barrier or fence made of one or more fixed rails: *The railing around the park is painted dark green to blend in with the trees.*

rail·road ◀ [*rale*-rode] *noun, plural* **railroads. 1.** the track made of parallel steel rails that trains travel on: *The railroad ran alongside the highway for five miles and then turned inland.* **2.** everything that belongs to a system of rail transportation, including tracks, locomotives, cars, stations, and other buildings and equipment: *Until the railroad came to that town, the people who lived there were very isolated.* A different word with the same meaning is **railway.**

rail·way [*rale*-way] *noun, plural* **railways.** another word for a railroad or railroad track.

rain ▼ [rane] *noun, plural* **rains. 1.** drops of water that fall from the clouds: *Is rain expected today?* **2.** the falling of such drops of water; a shower or storm: *Let's get out of the rain under that awning.* **3.** a large amount of anything falling rapidly: *The soldiers came over the hill and were met with a rain of machine gun bullets.*
verb, **rained, raining. 1.** to fall as drops of water from the clouds: *We stayed at home yesterday, as it rained nearly all day.* **2.** to fall like rain: *Confetti rained on the newly married couple.*
🔊 Different words with the same sound are **reign** and **rein.**

rain·bow [*rane*-boh] *noun, plural* **rainbows.** a curve of colored lights that occur in the sky when the sun is shining while it is raining. The sun's rays pass through the raindrops and are reflected as a band of colors.

rain·coat [*rane*-kote] *noun, plural* **raincoats.** a waterproof or water-resistant coat to wear when it rains.

rain·fall [*rane*-fawl] *noun, plural* **rainfalls.** the amount of rain that falls in a certain place or time: *The average yearly rainfall in Seattle is 36 inches.*

Rain falls from clouds.

RAIN

The atmosphere, land, and sea interact to provide us with a continuous supply of fresh water in the form of rain. When the sun heats the ocean, lakes, and rivers, some of the water turns into a gas called water vapor. As this rises and meets cooler air, it condenses to form clouds. The water droplets in clouds merge and eventually fall as rain. Where there are mountains, all the rain falls on the windward side, and the other side, called the rain shadow region, stays dry.

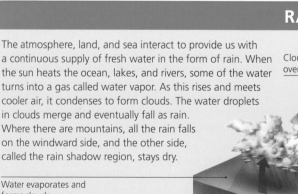

Clouds build up over land.

Water evaporates and forms clouds.

Water flows back to the sea via rivers and underground channels.

Rain shadow region

rain forest ▶ *Environment.* a thick forest with lots of trees and other plants in an area where it rains heavily during the year. In tropical areas, rain forests have very tall trees whose tops touch each other and form a continuous layer, like a roof. This term is also spelled **rainforest**.

rain·y [rane-ee] *adjective,* **rainier, rainiest.** having a lot of rain: *As it was a rainy day, we decided to go to the movies.*

raise [raze] *verb,* **raised, raising. 1.** to move or cause something to move to a higher position, place, or level; lift: *The teacher asked the students to raise their hands if they knew the answer to the question.* **2.** to move to a higher amount or condition: *to raise your voice in anger.* **3.** to bring together; collect: *Our basketball club raised money for a local charity.* **4.** to take care of while growing and developing; bring up: *My uncle raises chickens on his farm.* **5.** to bring to attention or notice: *Our club treasurer raised the issue of members who haven't paid their fees; Our team's win raised our hopes that we would make the final round.*
noun, plural **raises.** an increase in amount: *All the workers at the factory received a raise.*

rai·sin [ray-zin] *noun, plural* **raisins.** a sweet grape that has been dried in the sun or by some other means.

rake [rake] *noun, plural* **rakes.** a gardening tool with a row of prongs or spikes attached to a long handle. It is used to gather up leaves, grass, or hay, or to level or break up the surface of earth.
verb, **raked, raking.** to gather up or level with a rake: *I raked the leaves that had fallen in our yard.*

ral·ly [ral-ee] *verb,* **rallied, rallying. 1.** to bring or come together for a common purpose: *The captain rallied his troops before the assault on the enemy lines; When my mom was ill, our neighbors rallied around to help and often cooked meals for us.* **2.** to recover strength or health; revive: *The man they pulled out of the water rallied when he was given first aid.*
noun, plural **rallies.** a large meeting of people to share a common interest or in support of something: *a rally of sports car fans; a political rally.*

ram ▶ [ram] *noun, plural* **rams. 1.** a male sheep. **2.** a device for pushing hard against or smashing something to force or crush it; also called a battering ram.
verb, **rammed, ramming. 1.** to strike or strike against something with great force; crash or slam into: *The truck skidded and rammed into the stone wall.* **2.** to force down or in with heavy blows: *The farmer used a special machine to ram the fence posts into the ground.*

*The thick horns of a bighorn **ram** are useful weapons in fights with other rams.*

RAM [ram] *noun. Computers.* an abbreviation for Random Access Memory; this allows the user to access all items of information quickly and to change the contents by "overwriting," which means replacing stored information with new information.

Ra·ma·dan [rahm-i-*dahn*] *noun. Religion.* the ninth month of the Muslim year. During this month, Muslims fast between sunrise and sunset.

ram·ble [ram-bul] *verb,* **rambled, rambling. 1.** to walk for pleasure, often with no fixed route in mind; wander about: *We rambled through the woods looking for mushrooms.* **2.** to talk or write without a clear purpose or without keeping to the subject: *When you ask our old neighbor a question, he sometimes rambles on and on and forgets what you said.*
noun, plural **rambles.** a long walk taken for pleasure, often with no fixed route in mind.

A B C D E F G H I J K L M N O P Q R S T U V W X Y Z

ramp ▼ [ramp] *noun, plural* **ramps.** a sloping surface connecting two different levels, such as a passageway or roadway. Ramps are often put in place to enable people in wheelchairs to move about more easily.

ram·rod [ram-rod] *noun, plural* **ramrods.** in older firearms that loaded through the barrel, a straight rod used to push the explosive down the barrel for firing.

ran [ran] *verb.* the past tense of RUN.

ranch [ranch] *noun, plural* **ranches.** a large farm where cattle, sheep, or horses are raised and can graze out in the open. The act or job of raising cattle, sheep, or horses on a large farm where they can graze out in the open is **ranching.**

> The word **ranch** was taken from the Spanish word rancho. Spanish people who settled in the American Southwest in the 1600s were the first to raise cattle and other animals on ranches. Today some towns still carry on the name "Rancho" from those early days, such as Rancho Santa Fe, California or Rio Rancho, New Mexico.

rang [rang] *verb.* the past tense of RING.

range [raynj] *noun, plural* **ranges. 1.** the extent to which, or the limits between which, something can vary: *This vacation resort offers a range of accommodation, from luxury apartments to simple beach huts.* **2.** the distance over which something can extend, travel, or be effective: *The airplane kept out of the range of the enemy's guns.* **3.** a place with targets that is set aside for shooting practice, or a place for testing rockets or military equipment: *You have to be a member of the rifle club to use the rifle range.* **4.** a large area of open grazing land for livestock. **5.** a line or series of

To build Egypt's pyramids, workers pulled huge blocks of stone up giant **ramps.**

mountains: *The Rockies are a range of mountains that extend from Alaska to central New Mexico.* **6.** a large cooking stove with burners and one or more ovens. **7.** *Music.* the upper and lower limits of the tones that someone's singing voice or a musical instrument can produce.

verb, **ranged, ranging. 1.** to vary between two limits; extend: *The prices of computer games in this store range from ten dollars to five hundred dollars.* **2.** to move freely: *Wild horses range over the hills near the ranch.*

ran·ger ▼ [rayn-jur] *noun, plural* **rangers. 1.** someone whose job is to watch over and take care of a forest or other natural area. **2.** one of an organized group of armed people who regularly travel throughout a certain area to enforce the law.

rank¹ [rangk] *noun, plural* **ranks. 1.** a position or grade within a group: *The police officer was promoted to the rank of captain.* **2. ranks.** the large group of men and women in the armed services who are not officers: *The soldier rose from the ranks to become a general.*

verb, **ranked, ranking. 1.** to put in or have a certain position or grade: *Last year I ranked tenth in my class for overall performance.* **2.** to arrange in lines or rows: *The students taking part in the marching display were ranked according to height.*

This **ranger** *helps to take care of Utah's Zion National Park.*

rank² [rangk] *adjective.* **1.** having a strong, offensive smell or taste: *The dead flowers left standing in the vase of water had a rank smell.* **2.** describing something complete; total; outright: *The coach had to explain the basics of the game, as the children were rank beginners.*

ran·som [ran-sum] *noun, plural* **ransoms. 1.** the release of someone held captive, or something stolen, in return for some form of payment, usually money. **2.** the sum of money or other payment demanded in this way: *The kidnappers wanted a ransom of a million dollars.*

verb, **ransomed, ransoming.** to pay money or make the payment demanded to have a captive released or a stolen item returned.

rap [rap] *noun, plural* **raps. 1.** a quick, sharp knock or tap: *I heard a rap on the door and went to see who it was.* **2.** see RAP MUSIC.
🔊 A different word with the same sound is **wrap.**

rap·id [rap-id] *adjective.* describing something quick; fast; speedy: *When the patient was given the new medicine, he made a rapid recovery.* The state of being quick, fast, or speedy is **rapidity.** —**rapidly,** *adverb.*

rap·ids ▼ [rap-idz] *plural noun, singular* **rapid.** a part of a river where the river bed drops to a lower level and the water flows very fast: *You need special training before you attempt to go over those rapids in a boat or canoe.*

rap music *Music.* a kind of music in which words, often in rhyming verses, are spoken to the background of music with a strong beat. Someone who performs this kind of music is a **rapper.**

rap·ture [rap-chur] *noun.* very great delight or joy; ecstasy: *The tourists stared in rapture as the sun set over the Grand Canyon.* Someone who is filled with very great delight or joy is described as being **rapturous.**

rare[1] [rare] *adjectvie,* **rarer, rarest. 1.** not often found, done, or happening; not common: *My uncle has a collection of rare stamps that are worth a lot of money.* **2.** unusually fine; outstanding: *These pearl earrings have a rare beauty.* **3.** less dense than usual; thin: *Mountain climbers have to be prepared for the rare air they encounter at high altitudes.*

rare[2] [rare] *adjective,* **rarer, rarest.** cooked for only a short time so that the inside is still red: *rare steak.*

rare·ly [rare-lee] *adverb.* not often; seldom: *We rarely go skiing, but often go snowboarding.*

rar·it·y [rare-i-tee] *noun, plural* **rarities.** something that is not found or done often, or does not happen often: *The bird called the Californian condor is a rarity, as there are now very few in existence.*

ras·cal [ras-kul] *noun, plural* **rascals.**
1. someone, especially a child, who gets into mischief: *Grandpa called my little sister a rascal when she hid his reading glasses.*
2. someone who is dishonest; a rogue.

rash[1] [rash] *adjective,* **rasher, rashest.** done too hastily and with little or no thought for the consequences: *I made a rash decision to jump ashore from the boat and landed in the water.* —**rashly,** *adverb;* —**rashness,** *noun.*

*Rivers that have powerful **rapids** are good for whitewater rafting.*

rash[2] [rash] *noun, plural* **rashes.** *Health.* an outbreak of red spots or blotches on the skin: *Many plants can cause a rash, especially in people with sensitive skin.*

rasp [rasp] *verb,* **rasped, rasping.** to make a rough, grating sound: *The rusty wheels on the old farm cart rasped as they turned.*
noun, plural **rasps.** a rough, grating sound.

rasp·ber·ry [raz-ber-ee] *noun, plural* **raspberries.** a small, sweet, soft berry that is eaten. Raspberries are usually red but sometimes black. They grow on a prickly plant.

rat ▶ [rat] *noun, plural* **rats.**
1. an animal like a large mouse that belongs to the group called rodents. A rat has a long nose, large front teeth for gnawing things, a long tail, and small, round ears. **2.** a person who is thought to have the negative qualities associated with a rat, as by being dirty, dishonest, sneaky, harmful, and so on.

rate [rate] *noun, plural* **rates. 1.** a way of measuring by relating an amount or number of one thing to an amount or number of something else: *The train was traveling at a high rate of speed, more than a hundred miles per hour.* **2.** the charge for something or the value put on something: *The rates at this motel vary from sixty to a hundred dollars a night.* **3.** rank or class; standard: *We thought the rock band we went to see was second rate.* *verb,* **rated, rating. 1.** to regard as; consider: *My parents rated our school concert this year as one of the best ever.* **2.** to place in or have a certain rank or class: *This meat is rated as prime grade.*

rath·er [ra-THur] *adverb.* **1.** more willingly; preferably: *I would rather go to the movies than to the concert.* **2.** more properly; instead: *I think you should wear the blue jacket rather than the black one.* **3.** more correctly; more exactly: *We'll be leaving at ten o'clock, or rather as soon as the cab arrives.* **4.** somewhat; slightly: *I feel rather tired.*

rat·i·fy [rat-uh-fye] *verb,* **ratified, ratifying.** *Law.* to agree to or confirm officially; accept officially; approve: *Congress ratified the defense treaty.* The act of officially agreeing to or confirming something is **ratification.**

ra·ting [rate-ing] *noun, plural* **ratings.** the act of placing someone or something in a rank or class, or the way someone or something is ranked: *This motel has a three-star rating, so the rooms should be comfortable.* A **credit rating** is an estimate of a person's or an organization's ability to repay the cost of things bought on credit (as when you use a credit card.)

ra·ti·o [ray-shee-oh] *noun, plural* **ratios.** *Mathematics.* the proportional relationship or comparison between the number or amount of one thing and the number or amount of one or more other things. The ratio is the number of times the second thing can be divided into the first thing. For example, if 18 people own cats and 6 people own dogs, the ratio of cat owners to dog owners is 3 to 1. This is often written 3:1.

a b c d e f g h i j k l m n o p q r s t u v w x y z

A
B
C
E
F
G
H
I
J
K
L
M
N
O
P
Q
R
S
T
U

ra·tion [rash-un] *noun,
plural* **rations.** a fixed amount
of something allowed to one
person, especially food: *On the
hike, we each carried our day's
ration of food and water in
our knapsack.*
verb, **rationed, rationing.**
to limit to fixed amounts: *Meat,
gasoline, and other products
were rationed in the U.S. during
World War II.* The act of giving
out something in fixed amounts
or limiting something to fixed
amounts is **rationing.**

*Ravens have
excellent eyesight
and are very
intelligent birds.*

ra·tion·al [ra-shuh-nul] *adjective.* **1.** based
on reasoning or logic; sensible: *We will
solve the problem only if we take a rational
approach and analyze it carefully.* **2.** able
to reason, or think clearly and logically:
*It's foolish to expect babies and very young
children to behave in a rational way.*
The fact of having or taking a reasonable
or logical approach to something is
rationality. —rationally, *adverb.*

rat·tle [rat-ul] *verb,* **rattled, rattling.**
1. to make or cause to make a series
of short, sharp, hard sounds: *The wooden
blind rattled against the window in the
breeze.* **2.** to speak quickly, without
hesitating: *My friend Virginia can rattle
off the names of all the U.S. Presidents in
the correct order.* **3.** to upset or disturb;
confuse: *It was clear that the question
rattled the speaker, as he blushed and
looked uncomfortable.*
noun, plural **rattles. 1.** a series of short,
sharp, hard sounds: *The rattle of the doors
and windows in the wind kept me awake most of the night.*
2. a baby's toy or other object that makes a rattling sound
when shaken.

rat·tle·snake ▼ [rat-ul-*snake*] *noun, plural* **rattlesnakes.**
a poisonous American snake with a series of horny
rings in the end of its tail that make a rattling
sound when shaken. A rattlesnake shakes its tail
to warn people and other animals to keep away.

rave [rave] *verb,* **raved, raving. 1.** to talk wildly, as if crazy
or delirious: *People sometimes rave when they have a high
fever or have been badly injured and are barely conscious.*
2. to talk with great enthusiasm: *My friend Paul raved
about his recent trip to Alaska.*
noun, plural **raves.** enthusiastic praise or approval:
The new movie received raves from all the critics.

ra·ven ◀ [ray-vun] *noun, plural* **ravens.** a large bird with
glossy black feathers that is similar to, but bigger than,
a crow.
adjective. black and shiny: *raven hair.*

rav·e·nous [rav-uh-nus] *adjective.* very hungry.
—ravenously, *adverb.*

ra·vine ▼ [ruh-*veen*] *noun, plural* **ravines.** a deep, narrow
valley or gorge, especially one worn by water.

The Verdon Gorge is a deep **ravine** *in
Provence, France.*

rav·i·o·li [rav-ee-*oh*-lee] *plural noun.*
a food in the form of little square
packets of pasta with a filling, usually
meat, cheese, or spinach. They are
boiled and served with a sauce.

raw [raw] *adjective.* **1.** of food, in its
natural state; not cooked: *raw meat.*
2. being in or close to its natural form;
not treated or processed: *The table
I made for my project will look better
once I have varnished the raw wood.*
3. not trained or experienced: *People
who join the armed forces for the first time
are called raw recruits.* **4.** having the
skin or surface rubbed off: *The wound
was raw and bleeding.* **5.** unpleasantly
cold or damp: *Despite the raw morning
air, we went for a walk.*

raw·hide [raw-*hide*] *noun.* the hide of
cattle that has not been tanned. Ropes
and whips are often made of rawhide.

raw material the material used to make something:
That stack of lumber is the raw material for our new fence.

ray[1] [ray] *noun, plural* **rays. 1.** a narrow beam of light, heat,
or some other form of radiant energy: *The sun's rays are
hottest in the middle of the day.* **2.** one of a set of lines
or parts coming out from a central point: *The petals
of a daisy are like rays.* **3.** a tiny amount of something
cheering: *a ray of hope.*

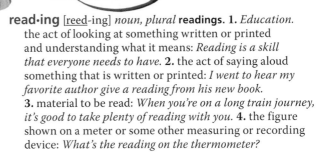

*Mantas, the largest **rays**, have no sting and are completely harmless to humans.*

ray² ▶ [ray] *noun, plural* **rays.** a fish with a broad, flat body and a long tail that lives on or near the bottom of the sea. Rays vary from small to very large. Some types are called **stingrays** because they have a spine at the end of their tail that can cause a severe wound or even death.

ray·on [ray-on] *noun.* a fiber or cloth made from cellulose.

ra·zor [ray-zur] *noun, plural* **razors.** a device with a very sharp blade used for shaving or for cutting hair. Something that is very sharp can be described as **razor-sharp.**

re- a prefix that means: **1.** again: *replay* means to play again. **2.** back: *refund* means to give or pay back.

reach [reech] *verb,* **reached, reaching.**
1. to go as far as; arrive at; come to: *I shouted with joy when I reached the finish line.* **2.** to stretch or extend so as to touch or meet: *The huge doors of the barn reached from the ground to the roof.* **3.** to stretch the arm or hand out to try to touch or grasp something: *I reached up to the top shelf to get the coffee mugs.* **4.** to get in touch with; contact: *You can nearly always reach me on my cell phone. noun, plural* **reaches. 1.** the distance someone or something can reach: *I made sure the knife was out of my little brother's reach.* **2.** the extent of what someone can do or understand: *The tasks given to young children have to be within their reach.* **3.** a stretch of something; an unbroken extent: *We stared at the vast inner reaches of the cave.*

re·act [ree-akt] *verb,* **reacted, reacting.** to act in response to something else: *When I saw the car approaching fast, I reacted by stepping back onto the pavement.*

re·ac·tion [ree-ak-shun] *noun, plural* **reactions.** something done or said in response to something else: *When Luke heard he'd made the all-star team, his reaction was to shout for joy.*

re·ac·tor [ree-ak-tur] *noun, plural* **reactors.** *Science.* short for NUCLEAR REACTOR.

read [reed] *verb,* **read, reading. 1.** to look at something written or printed and understand what it means: *When children go to school, they learn to read and write.* **2.** to say aloud something that is written or printed: *I read a story to my little sister most nights.* **3.** to learn by reading: *I like reading about space travel.* **4.** to know or work out the meaning of; understand: *I knew my friend was upset because I could read the expression on her face.* **5.** to show; indicate; register: *The scale read a hundred and twenty pounds.*
🔊 A different word with the same sound is **reed.**

read·er [reed-ur] *noun, plural* **readers. 1.** someone who reads: *I'm a keen reader of computer magazines.* **2.** *Education.* a book that helps someone to learn to read.

read·i·ly [red-uh-lee] *adverb.* **1.** willingly: *I readily agreed to go to the movie with my friends.* **2.** without difficulty; easily: *When I saw the diagram, I readily understood how the machine works.*

read·ing [reed-ing] *noun, plural* **readings. 1.** *Education.* the act of looking at something written or printed and understanding what it means: *Reading is a skill that everyone needs to have.* **2.** the act of saying aloud something that is written or printed: *I went to hear my favorite author give a reading from his new book.* **3.** material to be read: *When you're on a long train journey, it's good to take plenty of reading with you.* **4.** the figure shown on a meter or some other measuring or recording device: *What's the reading on the thermometer?*

There is an old saying, "To learn to write, **read.**" Obviously reading and writing are two different things, but what this means is that they are closely related. If you study the early life of people who became famous authors, you will almost always find that they loved reading and would read as many books as they could. Often, their first effort to write would be an exact imitation of one of their favorite books, and only later would they develop their own distinct way of writing.

read·y [red-ee] *adjective,* **readier, readiest. 1.** able to do something immediately or able to be used immediately: *Is the picnic basket ready to be loaded into the car?* **2.** willing to do something: *My mom says that you should always be ready to admit your mistakes.* **3.** in a state to or about to do something: *The tree was ready to burst into blossom.* **4.** within reach; easy to get at: *He keeps a ready supply of light bulbs in his house. verb,* **readied, readying.** to make ready; prepare: *We readied the spare bedroom for our cousins' visit.*

real [reel] *adjective.* **1.** actually existing or true; not imagined: *Dragons are not real animals.* **2.** not imitation; genuine: *This purse is made of real leather.*

The words **real** and **really** are very close, but in serious writing *real* should be used only as an adjective: *"Ben and Me* is a made-up story, but it is about Benjamin Franklin, who was a *real* person living in the 1700s." *Really* should be used when the sentence calls for an adverb: "I liked the book *Ben and Me* and thought it was *really* interesting." (not "real interesting.")

*A harvester **reaps** the cotton crop on a U.S. plantation.*

real estate *Business.* property in the form of land together with the trees, plants, water, buildings, and other things on it. A **realtor** is someone whose job is to bring together people who want to sell property and those who want to buy it and to help them to finalize a deal, in return for payment of a fee.

> Land and the buildings and other improvements on it became known as **real estate** because of the idea that land is *real* in the sense that it is permanent, solid, and not able to be moved. Thus it can be thought of as more real than other forms of property that might wear out, waste away, or otherwise lose value over time.

re·al·ism [ree-uh-liz-um] *noun.*
1. an acceptance of life as it really is; the opposite of idealism: *Realism brought Mary back to earth after dreaming of fame and fortune.*
2. in art or literature, a style that tries to show everyday life.

re·al·is·tic [ree-uh-lis-tik] *adjective.* **1.** having the ability to see things as they really are, without distortion or exaggeration: *Bill was realistic about his chance of winning the competition.* **2.** showing something as naturally as possible: *The artist painted a realistic portrait of Dad that showed his bald spot.*
—**realistically,** *adverb.*

re·al·i·ty [ree-al-uh-tee] *noun, plural* **realities. 1.** the fact or state of being real; the truth: *The reality is that they just can't afford a new car right now.* **2.** something that actually happened: *Tom's dream of getting the highest grades in the class became a reality.*

reality show a television program that uses real people rather than actors to compete in stressful or unusual conditions for a prize: *The contestants in the reality show had to survive for a week on a desert island.*

re·al·ize [ree-uh-lize] *verb,* **realized, realizing. 1.** to fully understand something: *She only realized that she had left her wallet at home when she looked for money to pay the bus fare.* A complete understanding of something is a **realization. 2.** to make real: *Mom's dreams were realized when she won the jackpot.*

real·ly [ree-uh-lee *or* ree-lee] *adverb.* **1.** to a great extent; very: *Tom is really tall.* **2.** in actual fact; truly: *She said she was rich, but she was really poor.*

*It takes two dung beetles to roll a dung ball—one from the **rear** and one on top.*

realm [relm] *noun, plural* **realms. 1.** an area ruled over by a monarch; a kingdom. **2.** an area of knowledge: *Chemistry is in the realm of science.*

reap ▲ [reep] *verb,* **reaped, reaping. 1.** to cut down and collect or gather up: *People reap corn at harvest time.* **2.** to get back as a reward: *The athlete reaped praise for her efforts.*

rea·per [reep-ur] *noun, plural,* **reapers.** someone who cuts down and gathers something, usually crops. The **Grim Reaper** is a mythological figure who represents Death. He is portrayed as carrying a harvesting tool called a scythe, with the thought that he uses this to cut off people's lives.

re·ap·pear [ree-uh-peer] *verb,* **reappeared, reappearing.** to come into view again; appear again: *The sun reappeared from behind a cloud.* —**reappearance,** *noun.*

rear[1] ▼ [reer] *noun, plural* **rears.** the back of something; a part or place that is at the back: *The garden was at the rear of the house.*
adjective. having to do with the back: *She had trouble seeing out of the car's rear window.*

rear[2] [reer] *verb,* **reared, rearing. 1.** to bring up a child: *My parents have reared two children—my sister and me.* **2.** of an animal, to stand up on the hind legs. **3.** to lift up or raise, in a threatening way: *The snake slowly reared its head and looked right at its victim.*

re·ar·range [ree-uh-raynj] *verb,* **rearranged, rearranging.** to sort again in a different order: *Fred rearranged his toy cupboard so the biggest games were at the back.* —**rearrangement,** *noun.*

rea·son [ree-zun] *noun, plural* **reasons. 1.** the cause of something: *My reason for missing class was that I had a headache.* **2.** sound judgment; sense: *His plan will never work, so I hope he'll listen to reason and forget about it.*
verb, **reasoned, reasoning. 1.** to think about in order to arrive at a conclusion: *She reasoned out the clues and eventually solved the puzzle.* **2.** to try to change someone's point of view: *He wanted to drive home in the storm so they tried to reason with him and talk him out of it.*

rea·son·a·ble [ree-zun-uh-bul] *adjective.* **1.** showing or using good sense: *a reasonable argument.* **2.** describing something fair: *Jane sold her car for a reasonable price.* —**reasonably,** *adverb.*

rea·son·ing [ree-zun-ing] *noun.* **1.** the process of logical thinking: *The detective solved the crime by using careful reasoning.* **2.** a series of arguments; the reasons for something; a theory.

re·as·sure [ree-uh-shur] *verb,* **reassured, reassuring.** to give comfort or confidence to; put right: *The doctor reassured Mary that her injury was not serious.* To be **reassuring** is to be comforting. —**reassurance,** *noun.*

re·bate [ree-bate] *noun, plural* **rebates.** *Business.* the refund of part of the purchase price: *The company offered a rebate to help sell its less popular products.*

re·bel ▶ [reb-ul] *noun, plural* **rebels.** someone who acts against authority: *The rebels attacked the capital city and took over the government.* A **Rebel** was a soldier who fought against the North in the Civil War of 1861–1865. *verb,* **rebelled, rebelling.** to refuse to obey authority: *The class rebelled against the teacher.*

re·bound [ree-bound] *noun.* **1.** a reaction to something: *He only went out with her on the rebound after breaking up with his girlfriend.* **2.** in basketball, the recovery of the ball after a missed shot on goal. *verb,* **rebounding, rebounded. 1.** to move or bounce back. **2.** to catch a missed shot in basketball.

re·buke [ri-byook] *noun, plural* **rebukes.** a strong scolding; sharp criticism or blame: *My parents gave me a severe rebuke after I crashed their car.* *verb,* **rebuked, rebuking.** to show disapproval; scold.

re·call [ri-kawl] *verb,* **recalled, recalling. 1.** to call back to the mind; remember: *I well recall the day I first met him.* **2.** to bring back: *The casting director recalled the actor for a second audition.* *noun, plural* **recalls.** the act of bringing back: *a company's recall of a faulty product to make necessary repairs; She has a great memory and has almost total recall of the books she has read.*

re·cap·ture [ree-kap-chur] *verb,* **recaptured, recapturing. 1.** to catch again: *The escaped lion was recaptured after a long chase.* **2.** to call back to the mind; remember: *It was so long since they'd seen each other, they couldn't recapture the old, easy feeling of friendship.*

re·cede [ri-seed] *verb,* **receded, receding.** to move back: *Erosion from the ocean causes the shoreline to recede.*

re·ceipt [ri-seet] *noun, plural* **receipts. 1.** a piece of paper that shows that payment or delivery has been received: *The storekeeper gave me a receipt for my purchase.* **2.** the sum of money received: *This week, the company's receipts were the lowest they'd been in years.* **3.** the fact of possessing something: *We are in receipt of your goods.*

re·ceive [ri-seev] *verb,* **received, receiving. 1.** to be given: *Fred received a book for his birthday.* **2.** to allow to enter; welcome: *The bride and groom received guests at their new home.*

re·cei·ver [ri-see-vur] *noun, plural* **receivers. 1.** a person who receives something: *A player who catches a pass in football is called a pass receiver.* **2.** an instrument that accepts radio waves or electrical signals and turns them into sounds or pictures. The earpiece of a telephone is a receiver.

re·cent [ree-sunt] *adjective.* having just occurred or being up to date: *The most recent issue of this magazine went on sale yesterday.* —**recently,** *adverb.*

re·cep·ta·cle [ri-cep-ti-kul] *noun, plural* **receptacles.** something that holds things; a container: *a trash receptacle; The sign at the hotel asked us to place our valuables in the receptacle provided.*

re·cep·tion [ri-sep-shun] *noun, plural* **receptions. 1.** the act of receiving: *The news that the flight would be delayed got a bad reception from the passengers.* **2.** a formal party: *a wedding reception.* **3.** in electronics, the receiving of broadcast signals: *Radio reception is bad in that mountain area.*

re·cep·tion·ist [ri-sep-shuh-nist] *noun, plural* **receptionists.** *Business.* someone who works in the greeting area of an office and whose main job is to arrange appointments, receive clients, and answer the telephone.

re·cess [ree-ses] *noun, plural* **recesses. 1.** a break from activity: *At school we have a snack at recess.* **2.** a niche or hollow in a wall. **3.** an inner, hidden, or secret place: *the deep recesses of the mind.*

*General Jeb Stuart was a famous **Rebel** who fought against the federal army in the American Civil War.*

re·ces·sion [ri-sesh-un] *noun, plural* **recessions.** *Business.* a period of slow financial growth or inactivity: *The coal industry went through a recession last year.*

re·ci·pe [res-i-pee] *noun, plural* **recipes. 1.** a set of instructions for making something: *She has a great recipe for cookies; My recipe for success is to work hard.*

re·cip·i·ent [ri-sip-ee-unt] *noun, plural* **recipients.** a person who receives something: *Jack was the recipient of a gold medal when he won the swimming competition.*

re·ci·tal [ri-sye-tul] *noun, plural* **recitals. 1.** a public performance, as of poetry or music. **2.** the act of repeating something learned by heart. **3.** a detailed statement or account of something; a story: *He gave a long recital of his troubles.*

re·cite [ri-site] *verb,* **recited, reciting. 1.** to repeat something learned by heart: *to recite poetry.* **2.** to give a detailed account: *Alice recited a long list of all her troubles.*

reck·less [rek-lis] *adjective.* acting in a dangerous or thoughtless way: *He raced down the mountain at a reckless speed.* —**recklessly,** *adverb.* —**recklessness,** *noun.*

reck·on [rek-un] *verb,* **reckoned, reckoning. 1.** to take a count of; count up; calculate: *The waiter reckoned up the check.* A **reckoning** is a summing up or the settling of accounts. **2.** to believe: *Grandpa says he reckons I'll be the prettiest girl at the dance.*

re·claim [ri-<u>klame</u>] *verb,* **reclaimed, reclaiming.**
1. to take back something that belongs to you: *I reclaimed my umbrella from the lost property office.* **2.** to change something useless into something useful: *An old industrial part of the city was reclaimed and turned into parkland.* **Reclamation** is the process of making an area of land more useful or more valuable.

re·cline ▼ [ri-<u>kline</u>] *verb,* **reclined, reclining.** to lie down in a relaxed way: *Celia reclined on the sofa, eating chocolates.* A **recliner** is a chair with an adjustable back to lie on.

rec·og·ni·tion [rek-ug-<u>ni</u>-shun] *noun.* **1.** the fact or act of recognizing: *Doctors are trained in the recognition of different kinds of diseases.* **2.** an acceptance of something as legal or valid: *The border between the two countries was given recognition.* **3.** favorable acknowledgment; approval; credit: *She got the recognition she deserved after so much hard work.*

rec·og·nize [rek-ug-<u>nize</u>] *verb,* **recognized, recognizing.**
1. to know a person because of what is remembered from before: *I recognized her voice on the phone as soon as she said hello.* **2.** to accept as being valid: *He recognized that what he had done was wrong.* A **recognized** authority is one that has been accepted as valid by a majority of people.

re·col·lect [rek-uh-<u>lekt</u>] *verb,* **recollected, recollecting.** to call back to the mind; remember: *Grandma enjoys recollecting the things she did for fun in her childhood.*

re·col·lec·tion [rek-uh-<u>lek</u>-shun] *noun,* **recollections.** the act of remembering: *After the car accident, his recollection of exactly what had happened was poor.*

rec·om·mend [rek-uh-<u>mend</u>] *verb,* **recommended, recommending. 1.** to speak in favor of; praise: *The French film was highly recommended by the critics.* **2.** to give support; suggest or advise as a good idea: *Her teacher recommended her for the job; Speaking with your mouth full is not recommended.*

rec·om·men·da·tion [rek-uh-men-<u>day</u>-shun] *noun,* **plural recommendations. 1.** the act or fact of recommending; a suggestion: *The jury's recommendation was that the murderer should go to jail for life.* **2.** a statement of approval: *The teacher had some good recommendations as to how I could improve my paper.*

re·cord [<u>rek</u>-urd] *noun, plural* **records. 1.** a list that stores information about events: *The school attendance record shows how many students were in class each day; He was found guilty of robbery and now has a criminal record.* **2.** the highest score: *She broke the school record in the long jump.* **3.** a plastic disk on which sound has been stored.
verb, **recorded, recording. 1.** to keep an account of events: *He records what happens every day in his diary.* **2.** to show a measurement on an instrument or scale: *A thermometer records temperature.* **3.** to store sound and sometimes images onto an electronic device such as a tape or disk: *We recorded the program on DVD.*

re·cor·der ◀ [ri-<u>kor</u>-dur] *noun, plural* **recorders.**
1. a person who keeps records. **2.** a machine that records sound and sometimes pictures: *a tape recorder; a video recorder.* **3.** *Music.* a wind instrument that looks and sounds like a pipe.

re·cord·ing [ri-<u>kor</u>-ding] *noun, plural* **recordings.** a record of sound, or sound and pictures, on disk or tape: *I made a video recording of my favorite TV program.*

re·cov·er [ri-<u>kuv</u>-ur] *verb,* **recovered, recovering. 1.** to get back to normal: *She was ill last year but has now recovered her health.* **2.** to retrieve something after it has been lost or taken: *The police were able to recover the stolen painting.* **3.** to compensate for: *This hybrid car was more expensive, but we will recover the extra cost by what we save on gas.*

re·cov·er·y [ri-<u>kuv</u>-ree or ri-<u>kuv</u>-uh-ree] *noun, plural* **recoveries. 1.** a return to good health: *The patient made a complete recovery.* **2.** the retrieval of something lost or stolen: *The newspapers reported the recovery of the missing jewelry.*

> **Recreation** comes from the word *recreate*, which means "to make new" or "to make again." The idea is that when someone takes part in a form of recreation, such as running, swimming, or playing a sport, the person feels refreshed and "like new," as if made into a new person.

rec·re·a·tion [rek-ree-<u>ay</u>-shun] *noun, plural* **recreations.** *Health.* an enjoyable or relaxing activity such as playing games or being involved in a hobby. **Recreational** sports include sailing and fishing.

re·cruit [ri-<u>kroot</u>] *noun, plural* **recruits. 1.** a person who has just joined one of the armed forces: *an Army recruit.* **2.** someone who voluntarily joins a group: *I was a new recruit to the fan club.*
verb, **recruited, recruiting.** to enlist in a group: *The teacher recruited volunteers for the class committee.* The act of enlisting of soldiers or sailors in the armed forces is called **recruiting.**

*In ancient Rome, diners at banquets **reclined** on couches and ate mostly with their fingers.*

rec·tang·le [rek-*tang*-gul] *noun, plural* **rectangles.** *Mathematics.* a figure with four sides and four right angles. —**rectangular,** *adjective.*

re·cu·per·ate [ri-*koo*-puh-*rate*] *verb,* **recuperated, recuperating.** *Health.* to get better after an illness: *Tania is recuperating nicely after breaking her ankle playing soccer.* The act or fact of getting better after an illness is **recuperation.**

re·cur [ri-*kur*] *verb,* **recurred, recurring.** to happen again and again: *Hay fever is an allergy that often recurs in people who are affected by it.* Something that happens time after time is described as **recurring** or **recurrent.** —**recurrence,** *noun.*

re·cy·cle [ree-*sye*-kul] *verb,* **recycled, recycling.** *Environment.* to make something able to be used again: *People now recycle many industrial materials, such as newspaper, aluminum cans, glass, and scrap metal.* The act of fact of doing this is called **recycling.**

red [red] *noun, plural* **reds. 1.** a bright color like the color of blood. **2.** something that has this color: *She chose a soft red to paint the dining room walls.* *adjective.* having or relating to the color red.
• **in the red.** in a state of debt: *My bank account was in the red.*

red blood cell *Medicine.* a blood cell that carries oxygen and carbon dioxide to all body tissues.

Red·coat [*red*-kote] *noun, plural* **Redcoats.** *History.* a British soldier of the eighteenth century, especially one who fought in the American Revolution. The name comes from the red jacket worn as part of the uniform.

Red Cross *Health.* an international medical relief organization begun in Switzerland that provides help to victims of war and natural disasters.

re·deem [ri-*deem*] *verb,* **redeemed, redeeming.** **1.** to exchange something for cash or a product: *He redeemed the coupon for a free meal.* **2.** to compensate for: *I redeemed my bad behavior by washing the dishes.* **Redemption** is the act of saving someone from having done bad.
• **to redeem oneself.** to recover one's status after doing something bad.

red-hand·ed *adjective.* in the act of doing something wrong: *The thief was caught red-handed.*

red tape official regulations or paperwork that seem designed to make it unnecessarily complicated and difficult to do something: *The couple went through a lot of red tape to adopt a child.*

> It is said that the phrase **red tape** comes from a historic practice in England. Official papers from a court of law or from the government were wrapped up in a binding of red-colored tape when they were sent from one person to another.

re·duce [ri-*doose*] *verb,* **reduced, reducing. 1.** to make less or smaller; cut down on; decrease: *After his diet he reduced his weight by fifteen pounds; If I can reduce the time I spend watching TV, I'll get more homework done.* **2.** to bring down to a lesser condition: *The bully reduced his victim to tears; The house was reduced to ashes after the wildfire.*

re·duc·tion [ri-*duk*-shun] *noun, plural* **reductions. 1.** the act of reducing: *A reduction in taxes means people have more money.* **2.** the amount by which something is reduced: *There was a reduction of 10 percent in the number of students in our school compared to last year.*

red·wood ▲ [*red*-wood] *noun, plural* **redwoods.** one of the tallest and longest-living trees in the world. It is an evergreen conifer and grows on the western coast of North America.

reed

reed ▼ [reed] *noun, plural* **reeds. 1.** a tall grass that grows in or near water. **2.** *Music.* a thin strip of stiff material in wind instruments that vibrates to make a tone when air passes over it.

🔊 A different word with the same sound is **read.**

reef ▶ [reef] *noun, plural* **reefs.** a ridge of rock, sand, or coral in shallow seas: *The Great Barrier Reef in Australia is the world's largest coral reef.*

reek [reek] *verb,* **reeked, reeking.** to have a very strong or unpleasant smell: *His clothes reeked of smoke after he cooked the barbecue.*

reel[1] [reel] *noun, plural* **reels.** a spool on which something is wound: *a cotton reel; a film reel.*
verb, **reeled, reeling.** to wind in on a reel: *The sailor reeled in the ship's anchor.*
• **to reel off.** to recite something known by heart quickly and with great ease: *He reeled off the names of all the players on his favorite basketball team.*

reel[2] [reel] *verb,* **reeled, reeling. 1.** to be thrown off balance: *He reeled on the slippery ice.* **2.** to seem to spin around: *Her head was reeling with so many facts to learn.*

reel[3] [reel] *noun, plural* **reels.** a country dance in which pairs of dancers face each other along two lines.

re·el·ect [ree-i-lekt] *verb,* **re-elected, re-electing.** to vote someone in to a position for another term: *We re-elected Tom as class president.* **—re-election,** *noun.*

re·ent·ry [ree-en-tree] *noun, plural* **re-entries. 1.** the act or fact of entering again. **2.** in space travel, the process in which a spaceship or missile comes back into the Earth's atmosphere.

ref [ref] *noun, plural* **refs.** the shortened form of REFEREE.

re·fer [ri-fur] *verb,* **referred, referring. 1.** to turn to for help: *David referred to the instruction manual when he was building the model plane.* **2.** to draw attention to: *The judge referred to the man's previous good record in giving him a lighter sentence.* **3.** to pass someone on to a source of help or information: *My grandma was referred to an eye specialist for treatment.*

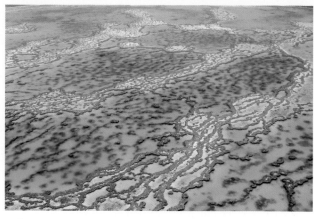

ref·er·ee [ref-uh-ree] *noun, plural* **referees.** an official who makes sure the rules of certain sports and games are followed and makes decisions within the game: *The basketball referee called a foul on the player for tripping an opponent.*
verb, **refereed, refereeing.** to act as a referee: *to referee a football game.*

The word **referee** once meant someone to whom people would *refer* a problem or dispute for a decision. This usually would be two opposing parties in a legal case, who had to agree to accept the decision of the referee. The word then came to mean an official in a sport, such as football or soccer, who makes decisions about plays that are in dispute.

Native Americans made lifelike models of ducks out of **reeds** *to lure real ducks into shallow water.*

ref·er·ence [ref-uh-rens] *noun, plural* **references.**
1. a statement that draws attention to something: *In the letter from the bank, reference was made to their overdue mortgage payment.* 2. a source of information: *Dad was my main reference for the family history I'm writing.* 3. a statement about someone's character or ability: *Her last boss gave her a great reference for the new position.* 4. a connection to something: *In reference to your job application, I am writing to tell you that you have been successful.* 5. see REFERENCE BOOK.

reference book *Literature.* a book that provides well-organized, extensive information on a variety of topics. Dictionaries, encyclopedias, and atlases are reference books.

Some people say there is now no need for **reference books** such as encyclopedias, because the same information is available on the Internet. However, not all information on the Internet has been researched and written by experts, as it would be in a reference book. If you want to know about a certain topic and your Internet search leads you to the Website of a professor who studies this subject, you can feel safe in thinking the information is correct. But if the information appears on a message board and the writer is not known, it may or may not be correct.

re·fill [ree-fil] *verb,* **refilled, refilling.** to fill again: *She refilled her glass with water.*
noun, plural **refills.** a container with material that has to be replaced regularly: *We often have to get a gas refill for our barbecue.*

re·fine [ri-fine] *verb,* **refined, refining.** to make purer or better: *to refine crude oil to make fuel for cars or airplanes.* Something that has all the impurities removed is **refined.**

re·fin·ery [ri-fye-nuh-ree] *noun, plural* **refineries.** *Chemistry.* an industrial building in which raw materials are processed to become useful.

re·flect [ri-flekt] *verb,* **reflected, reflecting.** 1. to give back an image or light from a shiny surface: *The light reflected off the glass.* 2. to think about seriously: *I reflected on my decision to quit school.* 3. to give an impression: *Your style of dressing may reflect the kind of person you are.*

re·flec·tion ▶ [ri-flek-shun] *noun, plural* **reflections.** 1. a mirror image: *I saw a reflection of myself in the window.* 2. a serious thought: *Mary was lost in reflection.* 3. a result of; a sign: *His brave act was a reflection of his courage.*

re·flec·tor [ri-flek-tur] *noun, plural* **reflectors.** something that reflects light, heat, or sound: *A radio transmitter is a reflector of sound waves.*

re·for·est [ree-for-est] *verb,* **reforested, reforesting.** *Environment.* to replant plantations or forests with trees after an earlier period of cutting them down. The act or fact of such replanting is called **reforestation.**

re·form [ri-form] *verb,* **reformed, reforming.** to abandon something bad and make a change for the good: *A criminal can reform his ways and became a model citizen.*
noun, plural **reforms.** the act of making a change for the better: *The government plans reforms to the health care system.*

re·frain [ri-frane] *verb,* **refrained, refraining.** to stop from doing something: *The host asked the guests to refrain from smoking.*
noun, plural **refrains.** the chorus to a poem or song.

re·fresh [re-fresh] *verb,* **refreshed, refreshing.** to make fresh again; stimulate or revive: *A glass of ice water refreshed us after the long hike.* Something that refreshes is described as **refreshing.**

re·fresh·ment [ri-fresh-munt] *noun, plural* **refreshments.**
1. snacks and drinks: *They bought popcorn, soda, and other refreshments before they went in to the movie.*
2. the state of being refreshed: *A week's vacation from work gave her the refreshment she needed.*

re·frig·er·ate [ri-frij-uh-rate] *verb,* **refrigerated, refrigerating.** to make or keep very cold in order to preserve: *Milk is refrigerated in summer to keep it from spoiling.* Something that is being cooled is in a state of **refrigeration.**

At sunset, a **reflection** *of Jacksonville, Florida, can be seen in St. Johns River.*

re·frig·er·a·tor [ri-frij-uh-ray-tur] *noun, plural* **refrigerators.** an appliance, container, or room for storing something at a low temperature.

re·fuel [ree-fyoo-ul] *verb,* **refueled, refueling.** to fill up an aircraft, ship, or car with more fuel: *to refuel an airliner with jet fuel.*

re·fuge [ref-yooj] *noun, plural* **refuges.** a safe or quiet place away from danger or trouble: *When my little brothers get too noisy, my bedroom is my refuge.*

A
B
C
D
E
F
G
H
I
J
K
L
M
N
O
P
Q
R
S
T
U
V
W
X
Y
Z

re·fu·gee [ref-yuh-<u>jee</u>] *noun, plural* **refugees.** a person who has left their own country because of war or persecution, to look for safety somewhere else: *During World War II, many refugees from Europe went to Britain, Australia, and the Americas.*

A *refuge* is a safe place, and a **refugee** is a person who leaves a place that has become dangerous to find safety in another place somewhere else. The word *refugee* was first used in the late 1600s to describe people known as the Huguenots, who left France to go to England because they were afraid of being caught up in a religious war.

re·fund [ri-<u>fund</u>] *verb,* **refunded, refunding.** to return or pay back: *Sally asked the department store to refund her money for the faulty radio.*
noun, plural **refunds.** the giving back of money already paid, or the money that is returned: *Sally got a full refund of thirty dollars.*

re·fuse[1] [ri-<u>fyooz</u>] *verb,* **refused, refusing. 1.** to say no to: *Alex refused Aunty Norma's hugs and kisses.* **2.** to be unwilling to do something or let something happen: *If Mandy refuses to do her homework, then her parents will refuse to let her go to the party.* The fact of saying no to something is a **refusal.**

re·fuse[2] ▲ [<u>ref</u>-yoos] *noun.* anything that is not wanted and thrown away; trash; rubbish: *Please don't leave your refuse in the playground—put it in the trash bin.*

re·gain [ree-<u>gane</u>] *verb,* **regained, regaining.** to get again or recover something that was lost: *After the car accident, it took months for her to regain her memory.*

re·gard [ri-<u>gard</u>] *verb,* **regarded, regarding. 1.** to consider in a certain way: *I regard her as one of the best singers in the country.* **2.** to look at closely; observe; examine: *Jake regarded the praying mantis with interest.*
noun, plural **regards. 1.** proper consideration; care: *Please have some regard for your own safety.* **2.** respect, affection, or love: *This certificate of appreciation is to show our regard for you.* Greetings or best wishes are called **regards:** *Send these flowers to the family, with regards from David.*

re·gard·ing [ri-<u>gar</u>-ding] *preposition.* about or concerning: *We are writing to you regarding your recent job application to this company.*

re·gard·less [ri-<u>gard</u>-lis] *adverb.* even though there are good reasons against it; nevertheless: *We have advised him of the danger, but he is determined to go, regardless.*

reg·gae [<u>reg</u>-ay] *noun. Music.* a style of pop music from the country of Jamaica, with four beats in each bar and an accent on the upbeat.

re·gime [ri-<u>zheem</u>] *noun, plural* **regimes.** the rule or government under a particular leader: *The country celebrated its liberation from the dictator's regime.*

reg·i·ment [<u>rej</u>-uh-munt] *noun, plural* **regiments.** a unit in the military made up of several battalions.

re·gion [<u>ree</u>-jun] *noun, plural* **regions.** an area of land: *the desert region; coastal regions.*

re·gion·al [<u>ree</u>-jun-ul] *adjective.* belonging to a certain: *Our team came first in the regional competition and now we are going to the state level.* —**regionally,** *adverb.*

reg·is·ter [<u>rej</u>-uh-stur] *noun, plural* **registers. 1.** a list or record: *We keep a register of our club members.* **2.** a machine that counts or keeps records: *Please pay for your goods at the cash register.* **3.** *Music.* the range of pitch for a voice or musical instrument: *A soprano has a higher register than an alto.*
verb, **registered, registering. 1.** to write or place on a list or record: *He wants to register as a voter before the next election.* **2.** to show on a measuring device: *The speedometer registered 80 miles per hour.* **3.** to show or express as if on such a device: *Her face registered her surprise at being elected team captain.*

registered nurse *Medicine.* a nurse who has an official qualification and license to practice nursing. An abbreviation for this term is **RN.**

reg·is·tra·tion [<u>rej</u>-uh-*stray*-shun] *noun.* the process of registering something or someone: *When you buy a new car you have to fill out papers for its registration with the state.*

re·gret [ri-<u>gret</u>] *verb,* **regretted, regretting. 1.** to feel sad or sorry for having done something: *Kirsty regrets being so mean to me and she wants to be friends again.*
noun, plural **regrets. 1.** a sad feeling: *My main regret is not joining the team when I had the chance.* **2. regrets.** a polite apology, especially for not accepting an invitation: *Mrs. Jones sends her regrets as she cannot come to the meeting tonight.*

reg·u·lar [<u>reg</u>-yuh-lur] *adjective.* **1.** as is to be expected; normal or usual: *I'll have a regular size drink and he'll have the extra large, please.* **2.** happening repeatedly or at fixed times: *Regular exercise is good for you.* **3.** following a pattern or rule of behavior: *He is one of our regular customers.* **4.** evenly spaced or arranged: *The fence posts must be at regular intervals.* The fact of being regular is **regularity.** —**regularly,** *adverb.*

reg·u·late [<u>reg</u>-yuh-*late*] *verb,* **regulated, regulating.** to put something into a regular pattern or a fixed shape; control: *The government regulates how much wheat can be sold overseas.*

reg·u·la·tion [*reg*-yuh-<u>lay</u>-shun] *noun, plural* **regulations.**
1. a rule that controls (and sometimes punishes) certain behavior; law: *If you choose to break the school regulations, there will be consequences.* **2.** the act of regulating or the state of being regulated: *This gauge controls the regulation of oil pressure in the engine.*

re·hears·al [ri-<u>hurs</u>-ul] *noun, plural* **rehearsals.** a practice session for a performance or other public occasion: *Jamie has had a rehearsal each night for the school musical.*

re·hearse [ri-<u>hurs</u>] *verb,* **rehearsed, rehearsing.** to practice or train for a performance or public occasion: *Please rehearse your parts in the play at home—you must know all your lines by Monday.*

reign [rane] *noun, plural* **reigns. 1.** the time that a king or queen rules as monarch: *England became a powerful nation during the reign of Elizabeth I.* **2.** the power of a ruler or monarch: *They lived in peace under the king's long reign.*
verb, **reigned, reigning. 1.** to hold power as a monarch: *Elizabeth I reigned from 1558 to 1603.* **2.** to be a strong influence or to be widespread: *Thankfully common sense reigned and the problem was solved.*
🔊 Different words with the same sound are **rain** and **rein.**

rein [rane] *noun, plural* **reins. 1.** one of two straps attached to a horse's bridle to guide and control its movement. **2.** anything that acts like a rein to control something: *Keep a tight rein on your tongue—watch what you say!*
verb, **reined, reining.** to keep control of something: *I had to rein him in.*
• **free rein.** complete freedom, without limits.
🔊 Different words with the same sound are **rain** and **reign.**

rein·deer ▶ [<u>rane</u>-deer] *noun, plural* **reindeer.** a large type of deer with branched antlers on its head. Reindeer live in northern or Arctic areas.

re·in·force [*ree*-in-<u>fors</u>] *verb,* **reinforced, reinforcing.** to make stronger, especially by adding something extra: *We need to reinforce the walls and make them thicker.* Something, such as steel, that has been made stronger is **reinforced.**

re·in·force·ment [*ree*-in-<u>fors</u>-munt] *noun, plural* **reinforcements.**
1. the act of reinforcing: *The reinforcement of the bridge will protect it from earthquakes.*
2. something used to reinforce or strengthen: *This building needs concrete reinforcement to stop it collapsing.* **3. reinforcements.** extra people who are sent to help: *The army sent reinforcements to support their troops in the battle.*

When competing for females, male **reindeer** *lock their antlers in a trial of strength.*

re·ject [ri-<u>jekt</u> *for verb;* <u>ree</u>-jekt *for noun*] *verb,* **rejected, rejecting.** to say no to something: *She rejected his invitation to go to the school dance with him.*
noun, plural **rejects.** someone or something that has been rejected, often because they are thought to be unacceptable.

re·joice [ri-<u>jois</u>] *verb,* **rejoiced, rejoicing.** to feel or express great happiness or joy: *She rejoiced at the birth of her granddaughter.*

re·lapse [<u>ree</u>-laps] *noun, plural* **relapses.** a returning or slipping back into an earlier state: *Grandpa is back in the hospital—he's had a relapse of his pneumonia.*

re·late [ri-<u>late</u>] *verb,* **related, relating. 1.** to tell the story of something: *The principal asked us to relate how the fight in the playground started.* **2.** to be connected in some way: *Sean's low score in this test might relate to a problem with reading—could you get his eyes tested?*

re·lat·ed [ri-<u>lay</u>-tid] *adjective.* **1.** part of the same family: *I've just discovered that we're related—our mothers are first cousins.* **2.** connected in some way: *The increase in the number of car accidents on that highway is related to the poor driving conditions.*

re·la·tion [ri-<u>lay</u>-shun] *noun, plural* **relations.**
1. a connection between two or more things: *Do you think there is any relation between violence on TV and bullying at school?* **2.** dealings or connections with other countries, businesses, or people: *international relations; public relations.* **3.** someone in the same family; a relative: *All my friends and relations will be there.*

re·la·tion·ship [ri-<u>lay</u>-shun-ship] *noun, plural* **relationships.** a connection between two or more people or things: *Paul and I are best friends—we have a great relationship.*

rel·a·tive [rel-uh-tiv] *adjective.* having meaning only when it is compared to something else: *The idea of being tall is relative—at six feet five inches, he is not tall for a pro basketball player, but he's very tall among people in general.*
noun, plural **relatives.** a person from the same family; relation: *Katrina invited all her relatives to the wedding.* —**relatively,** *adverb.*

rel·a·tiv·it·y [rel-uh-tiv-uh-tee] *noun.* the state or fact of being relative: *The measurement of what makes a person wealthy is a question of relativity.* Einstein's **theory of relativity** is based on the fact that light has the same speed no matter what it passes through, whether solid, liquid, or gas, but that motion can be relative—that is, position, velocity, and acceleration can be affected by the frame of reference used to measure them.

re·lax [ri-laks] *verb,* **relaxed, relaxing. 1.** to make or become less tense, rigid, or stressed: *The therapist massaged my leg to relax the muscles.* **2.** to make something less firm or strict: *The school relaxed the usual dress rules for the trip and we were allowed to wear casual clothes.* Someone or something that is not suffering from stress is **relaxed.** When something helps people to feel happy or calm it is **relaxing.**

*This **relief** from ancient Persia shows a procession.*

re·lax·a·tion [ree-lak-say-shun] *noun.* **1.** the state or fact of being relaxed: *The family all loves to go to the beach for relaxation and exercise.* **2.** an activity or pastime that helps someone to become relaxed and calm: *She loves to paint as a relaxation.*

re·lay [ree-lay] *noun, plural* **relays.** a set of people or animals that takes turns to move or work: *The rescue teams worked in relays to carry away the rubble.*
verb, **relayed, relaying.** to pass to someone else: *I will relay your message to Katie when I see her tonight.*

relay race ▶ a race between two or more teams, where one person competes over part of the course and is then replaced by another member of their team.

re·lease [ri-lees] *verb,* **released, releasing. 1.** to let something go or set it free: *When the bird's wing had healed, we released it into the wild.* **2.** to announce or publish: *The police have released the names of the people injured in the accident.*
noun, plural **releases.** the fact of being released: *The bird gave a loud cry after its release.*

re·lent [ri-lent] *verb,* **relented, relenting.** to become more forgiving or less strict: *My father relented and said I could go to the party after all, even though he had said no the day before.*

rel·e·vant [rel-uh-vunt] *adjective.* having some connection to the subject being discussed; related; pertinent: *Thank you for your suggestion, which is relevant to our problem.* If something is connected or relevant to the topic it has **relevance.**

When something is **relevant**, it has to do with the subject being written or talked about. In a student paper it is important to stick to your topic and be sure that any details you include are relevant to that. If you are writing a story about a soccer game and you mention that there is a firehouse behind the soccer field, your readers will want to know why that is relevant. (Maybe you will go on to say that there was a fire alarm in the middle of the game, and everyone stopped playing to watch the fire engines roll out.)

re·li·a·ble [ri-lye-uh-bul] *adjective.* able to be depended on; trustworthy; responsible: *The teacher asked for a reliable girl to help the new student learn her way around the school.* The quality of being reliable is **reliability.** —**reliably,** *adverb.*

re·li·ance [ri-lye-uns] *noun.* the act or fact of relying on something; dependence or trust: *His reliance on the crutches will decrease as his broken leg heals and becomes stronger.*

re·lief[1] [ri-leef] *noun.* **1.** the lessening of pain or discomfort: *The cough medicine gave me some relief and helped me sleep.* **2.** aid such as food or housing given to people in need by the government. **3.** a replacement for someone in a job or duty: *He's on duty from 8:00 to 4:00, then his relief takes over.*

re·lief[2] ◀ [ri-leef] *noun, plural* **reliefs.** a design that is raised from its background, such as a carved picture on a stone wall.

relief map *Geography.* a map showing the heights of the different places on the map, such as hills and valleys, usually with contour lines.

relief pitcher in baseball, another pitcher who comes on to replace the pitcher who is in the game. This is often done when the first pitcher gets tired or is not doing well. A different word with the same meaning is **reliever.**

re·lieve [ri-leev] *verb,* **relieved, relieving. 1.** to make lighter or less severe; lessen or ease: *Please give me something to relieve the pain.* **2.** to free someone from pain or discomfort: *The news of his rescue relieved her greatly.* **3.** to replace someone or free them from their work: *The firefighters had to wait until a fresh crew could relieve them.*

*In a track **relay race**, each runner passes a baton to the runner who replaces them.*

The statue of Christ that dominates Rio de Janeiro, Argentina, is considered to be a symbol of the Christian **religion**.

re·li·gion ◀ [ri-<u>lij</u>-un] *noun, plural* **religions.** a system of belief in (and worship of) a particular god or gods. There are many different religions practiced in the world, including Christianity, Buddhism, Judaism, Islam, and Hinduism.

re·li·gious [ri-<u>lij</u>-us] *adjective.* **1.** having a strong faith in a god or a particular religion: *She is very religious and goes to Mass every day.* **2.** relating to religion: *The students at the college come from many different religious backgrounds.* **3.** very careful and strict: *I am religious about walking for exercise every morning.* —**religiously,** *adverb.*

re·lish [<u>rel</u>-ish] *noun, plural* **relishes. 1.** a sauce, usually made with spices and pickles, that adds flavor to a meal. **2.** special interest or enjoyment: *Dad looked at the book catalog with relish.*
verb, **relished, relishing.** to enjoy something very much: *Janet relished the thought of a holiday in Italy.*

re·luc·tant [ri-<u>luk</u>-tunt] *adjective.* unhappy about doing something; unwilling: *Mom was reluctant to lend my brother the car, because he always returns it with the gas on empty.* When someone is unhappy to do something, they feel or show **reluctance** to do it. —**reluctantly,** *adverb.*

re·ly [ri-<u>lye</u>] *verb,* **relied, relying.** to depend on with confidence; trust: *You can't rely on that old car—it will break down, for sure!*

re·main [ri-<u>mane</u>] *verb,* **remained, remaining. 1.** to stay in the same place: *Please remain in your seats until the plane has come to a complete stop.* **2.** to continue in the same way: *I would like to remain in this job for a few more years.* **3.** to be left after others have gone: *Only a few buildings remained standing after the cyclone hit the town.*

re·main·der [ri-<u>mane</u>-dur] *noun, plural* **remainders.
1.** the part left after something has been taken away: *I spent some of my birthday money but I have saved the remainder.* **2.** *Mathematics.* the number found after the process of subtraction: *When you subtract 6 from 10, the remainder is 4.* **3.** *Mathematics.* the number left over after the process of division: *When you divide 25 by 4, the answer is 6 with a remainder of 1.*

re·mains ▼ [ri-<u>maynz</u>] *plural noun.*
1. the section left after other parts have gone or been destroyed: *The tourists visited the remains of the ancient temple.* **2.** the body of someone who has died: *The soldier's remains were transported home for a state funeral.*

Hyssop

re·mark [ri-<u>mark</u>] *noun, plural* **remarks.** something that is said; a comment or statement: *The judge of the skating competition made a few kind remarks about our performance.*
verb, **remarked, remarking.** to make a statement or give a comment: *She remarked that she was very pleased with our progress this year.*

Smooth sow thistle

re·mark·a·ble [ri-<u>mar</u>-kuh-bul] *adjective.* worth noticing; extraordinary; unusual: *She is a remarkable girl because she is both talented and humble.* —**remarkably,** *adverb.*

Motherwort

rem·e·dy ▶ [<u>rem</u>-uh-dee] *noun, plural* **remedies.** a cure or solution for a problem: *Taking aspirin is a common remedy for a headache.*
verb, **remedied, remedying.** to solve a problem or make it better: *You are falling behind with homework—please remedy this situation.* If something is helpful for solving a problem it is **remedial**: *Remedial reading is instruction for students who are having trouble learning to read.*

Eyebright

Physicians in ancient Greece treated many complaints with **remedies** *made from various herbs.*

Paleontologists dig up the **remains** *of dinosaurs and take them away to study.* **579**

Raphael's painting The School of Athens *is one of the masterpieces of* **Renaissance** *art.*

re·mem·ber [ri-mem-bur] *verb,* **remembered, remembering. 1.** to bring something back to mind through use of memory; recall: *I couldn't find my house key and then I remembered I left it on the bookcase.* **2.** to not forget; to keep in mind: *Remember to turn off the light when you leave.* **3.** to give someone a present or reward: *It was kind of you to remember me on my birthday.* **4.** to pass on greetings from: *Please remember me to your parents.* Something that helps people to remember is a **remembrance.**

re·mind [ri-mined] *verb,* **reminded, reminding.** to help someone remember: *I will remind you ten minutes before we have to leave.*

re·min·der [ri-mined-ur] *noun.* something that helps people to remember: *That photo is a good reminder of how happy we were then.*

rem·nant [rem-nunt] *noun, plural* **remnants.** a part or quantity that remains; a fragment: *The family sifted through the remnants of the house after the fire.*

re·mod·el [ree-mod-ul] *verb,* **remodeled, remodeling.** to give something a new structure or design: *We are remodeling our kitchen to make it larger.* *noun, plural* **remodels.** a new structure or design: *Dad's old sports car is getting a remodel.*

re·mote ▼ [ri-mote] *adjective,* **remoter, remotest. 1.** far away; distant: *They explored remote lands across the seas.* **2.** away from cities and towns: *the remote desert.* **3.** very slight or small: *There is only a remote chance of finding your lost ring on this beach.* **—remotely,** *adverb;* **—remoteness,** *noun.*

remote control 1. control of a system by electronic or mechanical means from a distance: *The factory assembles cars by remote control.* **2.** an electronic device that controls appliances such as a television from a distance.

The Nenet people live in the **remote** *northwest of Russia.*

re·mov·al [ri-moov-ul] *noun, plural* **removals.** the act of removing: *Sally has a dentist appointment for the removal of her braces.*

re·move [ri-moov] *verb,* **removed, removing. 1.** to move away from a position or place: *Remove the plastic wrapping before you put the meat in the oven.* **2.** to put an end to: *The safety demonstration removed my doubts.* **3.** to dismiss from a job or position of authority: *The club president was removed from office after he was caught stealing funds.*

ren·ais·sance [ren-uh-sahns] *noun.* a rebirth or renewal; revival: *Ballet has experienced a renaissance in our country, with government support and increased audiences.*

Ren·ais·sance ▲ [ren-uh-sahns] *noun. History.* the period of renewed interest in classical Greek and Roman art, literature, and learning, which lasted from the fourteenth to the sixteenth centuries in Europe. It is often considered to mark the end of medieval times and the beginning of the modern world.

ren·der [ren-dur] *verb,* **rendered, rendering. 1.** to cause to become; make: *The fall from the horse rendered him unconscious.* **2.** to deliver, give, or present: *She was able to render first aid to the accident victim.*

ren·dez·vous [ron-day-voo] *noun, plural* **rendezvous. 1.** an agreement to meet at a certain time and place: *The shuttle has a rendezvous with the space station to transfer equipment.* **2.** the place for such a meeting. *verb,* **rendezvoused, rendezvousing.** to meet at an agreed time and place: *The troops will rendezvous at the river at 1300 hours.*

> The word **rendezvous** goes back to a French phrase meaning "to present yourself," or in simpler terms, "to show up; appear." The idea is that when a rendezvous is planned, this means that the people involved have to appear (meet) at a certain place and certain time.

re·new [ri-noo] *verb,* **renewed, renewing. 1.** to make new or as new; restore: *She felt renewed after her week's vacation at the beach.* **2.** to begin again: *We renewed our conversation outside, where it was quieter.* **3.** to make something continue for a time: *Please renew your magazine subscription by the end of October.* **4.** to make, say, or do again: *He has renewed his demand for a full investigation.*

*Solar panels harness the sun's rays to make **renewable energy.***

re·new·a·ble ▶ [ri-<u>noo</u>-uh-bul] *adjective. Environment.* able to be used and then grown or supplied again. Energy that comes from sources such as the sun, water, or wind (rather than from fossil fuels such as coal or oil) is called **renewable energy.**

re·new·al [ri-<u>noo</u>-ul] *noun, plural* **renewals.** the process of making something new again or restoring it to good condition: *He is going bald, so he went to a clinic for hair renewal.*

ren·o·vate [<u>ren</u>-uh-*vate*] *verb,* **renovated, renovating.** to make something look new again; repair; restore: *We are renovating our house and adding a new bedroom.* A **renovated** building has been restored or repaired.

ren·o·va·tion [*ren*-uh-<u>vay</u>-shun] *noun, plural* **renovations.** **1.** the process of making something new or as new: *The renovation took six months.* **2.** new or redesigned sections, especially of a building.

re·nowned [ri-<u>nownd</u>] *adjective.* known and respected for doing well at something; famous: *She was renowned for her charity work.*

rent [rent] *noun, plural* **rents.** *Business.* payment in return for the use of something: *My sister and her friends share the rent on an apartment.* *verb,* **rented, renting. 1.** to pay money in exchange for the use of something: *We rented a car for our holiday in Europe.* **2.** to allow someone to use something in exchange for money: *The boat company rents out houseboats for the summer.*

re·pair [ri-<u>pare</u>] *verb,* **repaired, repairing.** to get something into good condition again; fix; mend: *We repaired the flat tire on my bike.* *noun, plural* **repairs. 1.** the act of repairing or mending: *The mechanic said it would take two weeks for the car repairs.* **2.** the condition or state that something is in: *The shop buys secondhand furniture if it is in good repair.*

re·pay [ri-<u>pay</u>] *verb,* **repaid, repaying.** to pay or give back: *I'll lend you ten dollars if you promise to repay it tomorrow.* —**repayment,** *noun.*

re·peal [ri-<u>peel</u>] *verb,* **repealed, repealing.** to officially put an end to something: *The lobbying group asked the government to repeal the law.* *noun, plural* **repeals.** the act of repealing something: *The repeal of this law is the first step in reforming the tax system.*

re·peat [ri-<u>peet</u>] *verb,* **repeated, repeating.** to do or say something again: *Please repeat your answer as I could not hear it the first time.* *noun, plural* **repeats.** something that is repeated or done again: *Our dance was so good that the principal has asked for a repeat at the end-of-year concert.* If something happens again it is **repeated.**

re·pel [ri-<u>pel</u>] *verb,* **repelled, repelling. 1.** to drive away by force: *The firemen tried to enter the building but they were repelled by the flames.* **2.** to give someone a feeling of distaste or disgust: *The smell of fish cooking repels me.* **3.** to keep off or away: *This skin lotion repels mosquitoes.*

re·pel·lent [ri-<u>pel</u>-unt] *adjective.* making someone feel distaste or disgust: *She found his odd behavior quite repellent.* *noun, plural* **repellents.** something that repels: *You definitely need mosquito repellent if you're going camping.*

rep·er·toire [<u>rep</u>-ur-*twar*] *noun, plural* **repertoires.** a collection of pieces such as plays, songs, or dances that have been prepared for performance: *Our repertoire includes several comedies by Shakespeare.*

rep·e·ti·tion [rep-uh-<u>tish</u>-un] *noun, plural* **repetitions.** the act of repeating something: *The repetition of the s sound in "sad soft sighs" gives emphasis to the line.*

re·place [ri-<u>plays</u>] *verb,* **replaced, replacing. 1.** to take the place of something: *A new basketball court has replaced the old parking lot.* **2.** to buy or get something similar in the place of: *Felicity lost her school book and needed to replace it.* **3.** to put something back: *Please replace the chairs under the desks when you leave the room.*

re·place·ment [ri-<u>plays</u>-munt] *noun, plural* **replacements.** someone or something that takes the place of another: *Our regular goalkeeper was sick today, so Stacy took over as a replacement.*

re·play [ree-<u>play</u>] *verb,* **replayed, replaying.** to play again: *She replayed the song over and over because she loved listening to it.* *noun, plural* **replays.** a repeated competition, such as when the first game is cancelled or ends in a draw: *The soccer game was rained out, so we had a replay the next day.*

rep·li·ca ◀ [<u>rep</u>-luh-kuh] *noun, plural* **replicas.** a smaller scale copy or model of something: *I built a replica of a P-51 Mustang from World War II.*

re·ply [ri-<u>plye</u>] *verb,* **replied, replying. 1.** to give an answer in speech or writing; respond: *All of my friends have replied to my party invitations.* **2.** to act in some way in response: *The enemy troops replied with fierce gunfire.* *noun, plural* **replies.** anything that is said, written, or given as an answer; a response: *Have you had a reply to your letter?*

*While plaster **replicas** are light to hold, real gold nuggets would be much too heavy.*

re·port [ri-port] *noun, plural* **replies.** a statement or account, often designed for the public: *The newspaper had a front page report about the fire; Lee wrote a report on the field trip for the school magazine.*
verb, **reported, reporting. 1.** to give a formal account or write a report about something: *The government reported that the economy was improving.* **2.** to make a formal complaint about: *I'm going to report you to the principal.* **3.** to come to meet someone in authority: *You will report to the principal, who will give you some extra work to do.*

report card 1. *Education.* an official statement, given to the parents, giving details of how their child is performing at school. **2.** any similar statement giving an evaluation of performance: *After the football season, the newspaper publishes a report card rating each player on the team.*

re·port·er [ri-por-tur] *noun, plural* **reporters.** someone who investigates a story and writes a news report for a newspaper, magazine, or television or radio program.

rep·re·sent [rep-ri-zent] *verb,* **represented, representing. 1.** to stand for something as a symbol: *"Uncle Sam" represents the United States* **2.** to be chosen to speak or act for a group: *to represent the school.*

rep·re·sent·a·tive [rep-ri-zen-tuh-tiv] *noun, plural* **representatives. 1.** someone who is chosen to speak or act for a group: *Tim is our class representative who will welcome our guest speaker today.* **2.** something that shows qualities or characteristics of the whole group: *This cathedral is a good representative of the Gothic style in France in the twelfth century.* *adjective.* **1.** able to represent a whole group: *This song is representative of rock music, with its strong drum beat and guitar solo.* **2.** made up of official representatives: *The leadership committee is a representative group in our school.*

re·pro·duce [ree-pruh-doos] *verb,* **reproduced, reproducing. 1.** *Biology.* to produce young; breed: *Mice can reproduce after 21 days and one female can give birth to ten litters in a year.* **2.** to produce again or make a copy of: *The tape recorder reproduced Gavin's singing, but he hated the sound of his voice.*

re·pro·duc·tion [ree-pruh-duk-shun] *noun, plural* **reproductions. 1.** *Biology.* the process of producing offspring or young: *Reproduction in frogs involves several phases from the laying of eggs to the development of tadpoles and then frogs.* **2.** a copy, usually of something valuable: *That statue is a reproduction of a famous work by Michelangelo.* When something is involved in a process of reproduction it is **reproductive.**

rep·tile ▶ [rep-tile] *noun, plural* **reptiles.** *Biology.* one of a cold-blooded class of animals with backbones, which includes lizards, snakes, turtles, and alligators. Most reptiles lay eggs to reproduce. If something is concerned with or related to reptiles, it is **reptilian.**

re·pub·lic [ri-pub-lik] *noun, plural* **republics.** a system of elected government where the citizens vote for people from a particular political party to represent them and manage the country. A republic usually has a president at its head rather than a king or queen.

re·pub·li·can [ri-pub-li-kun] *adjective.* belonging to or relating to a republic: *The civil war resulted in the overthrow of the monarchy and the setting up of a republican government.*
noun, plural **republicans.** a person who believes that a republic is the best system of government. Someone who is a member of the Republican Party in the U.S.A. is a **Republican.**
See DEMOCRACY *for more information.*

Republican Party *Government.* one of the two major national political parties in the United States of America, along with the Democratic Party.

rep·u·ta·tion [rep-yuh-tay-shun] *noun, plural* **reputations.** the way that people think of someone or something: *Jo has a reputation for always being helpful and kind.*

re·quest [ri-kwest] *verb,* **requested, requesting.** to ask for something: *Dean's parents have requested an interview with his teacher.*
noun, plural **requests. 1.** the act of asking for something: *We made our request in writing to the city council.* **2.** something asked for: *The radio station played my special request for Mom's birthday.*

re·quire [ri-kwire] *verb,* **required, requiring. 1.** to need something, especially in order to work or function: *A car engine requires fuel to run.* **2.** to ask for officially; demand: *The government requires two photos for your application for a passport.*

re·quire·ment [ri-kwire-munt] *noun, plural* **requirements.** something that is required; a need or demand: *Being eighteen years old is one of the requirements for being able to vote; Please tell the school camp coordinator about any special food requirements for your child.*

re·run [ree-run *for verb;* ree-run *for noun*] *verb,* **reran, rerunning. 1.** to run again: *We need to rerun the race as there was a false start.* **2.** to play again: *If you rerun the video tape, you will see where the dancers made the mistake.*
noun, plural **reruns.** a film or television show that is broadcast again: *There's nothing new on TV tonight— only reruns.*

res·cue ◀ [res-kyoo] *verb,* **rescued, rescuing.** to save from danger or harm: *My aunt rescues wild animals when they've been hurt.*
noun, plural **rescues.** the act of rescuing or saving: *There have been twenty surf rescues by lifeguards at our beaches this summer.* —**rescuer,** *noun.*

Rescuers *lift a baby to safety from the rubble of a collapsed building.*

REPTILES

There are four main groups of reptiles: turtles and tortoises, crocodilians, tuataras, and snakes and lizards. They vary in size and structure, but all have features in common. They are mostly found on land and they have bony skeletons with backbones. They have tough skins covered with hard plates or scales to protect them from predators and rough ground. They all lay eggs with shells, and they are all cold-blooded, depending on the sun and warm surfaces to heat their bodies.

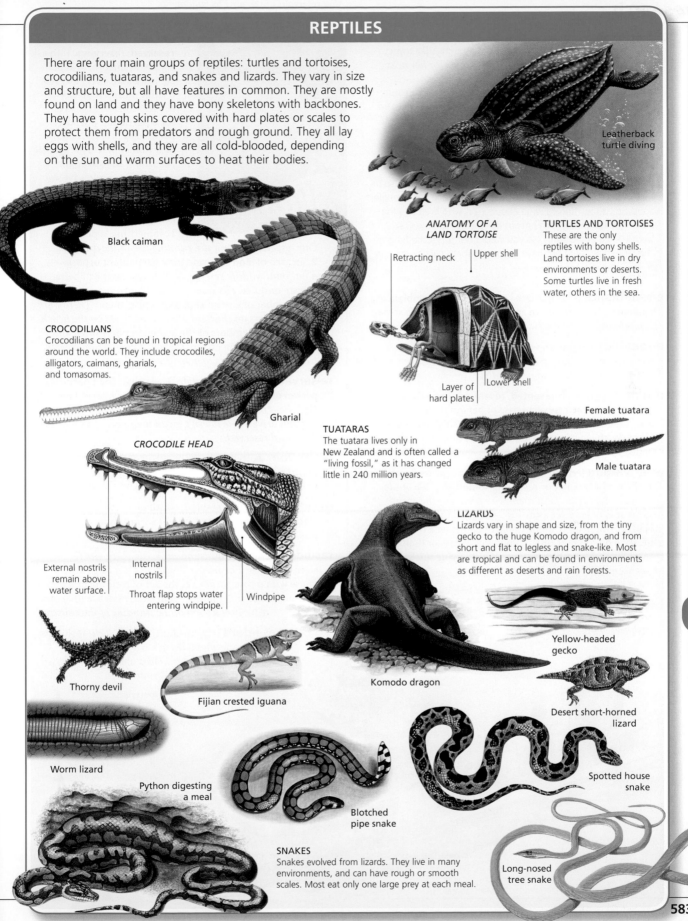

Leatherback turtle diving

Black caiman

ANATOMY OF A LAND TORTOISE

Retracting neck

Upper shell

Layer of hard plates

Lower shell

CROCODILIANS
Crocodilians can be found in tropical regions around the world. They include crocodiles, alligators, caimans, gharials, and tomasomas.

Gharial

CROCODILE HEAD

External nostrils remain above water surface.

Internal nostrils

Throat flap stops water entering windpipe.

Windpipe

TURTLES AND TORTOISES
These are the only reptiles with bony shells. Land tortoises live in dry environments or deserts. Some turtles live in fresh water, others in the sea.

Female tuatara

Male tuatara

TUATARAS
The tuatara lives only in New Zealand and is often called a "living fossil," as it has changed little in 240 million years.

LIZARDS
Lizards vary in shape and size, from the tiny gecko to the huge Komodo dragon, and from short and flat to legless and snake-like. Most are tropical and can be found in environments as different as deserts and rain forests.

Yellow-headed gecko

Thorny devil

Fijian crested iguana

Komodo dragon

Desert short-horned lizard

Worm lizard

Python digesting a meal

Blotched pipe snake

Spotted house snake

SNAKES
Snakes evolved from lizards. They live in many environments, and can have rough or smooth scales. Most eat only one large prey at each meal.

Long-nosed tree snake

re·search ▼ [ree-surch *or* ri-surch] *noun, plural* **researches.**
a study or search to find facts about a particular topic:
*Tammy has to do some research on whales for her next
school project.*
verb, **researched, researching.** to find out about a topic:
*We researched the history of airplanes in the library and
on the Internet.* A person whose work is doing research
is a **researcher.**

As a student writer you probably know how important it is to
do **research** for a paper on a factual subject, such as the life
of Martin Luther King or the behavior of wolves. It can also be
important to do research when you write a story. For example,
suppose you wanted to write about a girl who lived in a log
cabin in pioneer days. You might do research on the way
people lived at that time, so you would not put something in
the story that could not have happened then, such as the girl
riding in an automobile.

re·sem·blance [ri-zemb-luns] *noun, plural* **resemblances.**
a likeness or similarity in appearance: *Jack bears a strong
resemblance to his uncle.*

re·sem·ble [ri-zemb-ul] *verb,* **resembled, resembling.**
to be like or similar to: *Maria resembles her mother,
in both appearance and personality.*

re·sent [ri-zent] *verb,* **resented, resenting.** to feel anger
or bitterness because of a sense of personal hurt:
She resented being treated so unfairly. When someone feels
this way, they feel **resentful.** This hurt or bitter feeling is
called **resentment.**

res·er·va·tion [rez-ur-vay-shun] *noun, plural* **reservations.**
1. the act of keeping or reserving something: *We made
a hotel reservation for a room with a view of the ocean.*
2. an area of land set aside for a particular purpose. Some
Native American tribes are able to continue a traditional
lifestyle on reservations. **3.** concern, worry, or doubt about
something: *I have reservations about buying this sweater
—it seems very expensive.*

Most **reservoirs** *are created by building
a dam across a river valley.*

re·serve [ri-zurv] *verb,*
reserved, reserving. 1. to ask
for something to be kept or
set aside: *We have reserved
a table for seven o'clock at
the restaurant.* **2.** to keep
for a particular purpose:
*Mom likes to reserve the
best dinner plates for special
occasions.* **3.** to keep for
oneself: *Grandma says she
will reserve her opinion until
she gets more information.*
noun, plural **reserves.**
1. something kept aside:
Our reserves of water are running low in the drought.
2. an area of land set aside for a particular purpose:
a national wildlife reserve. **3.** a characteristic of being
private or quiet: *His reserve makes him appear a little shy.*
4. a member of a team kept as a replacement: *There were
eleven players on the field plus two reserves on the bench.*
5. reserves. members of the armed forces trained and
ready for service in an emergency: *The government has
called in the reserves to help after the floods.*

re·served [ri-zurvd] *adjective.* **1.** set apart for a particular
person or purpose: *This parking space is reserved for
the school principal.* **2.** keeping thoughts or feelings to
oneself; private: *He doesn't mean to appear rude—he's just
quiet and reserved.*

res·er·voir ▲ [rez-ur-*vwar or* rez-ur-*vore*] *noun,
plural* **reservoirs.** a storage area for liquids, such as a dam
to collect rainwater.

re·side [ri-zide] *verb,* **resided, residing.** to live in a certain
place, usually for a long time: *Their family has resided in
this town for five generations.*

res·i·dence [rez-uh-duns] *noun.* **1.** the place where
someone lives: *The mayor's residence is a large white
house with a rose garden.* **2.** the act of residing or a period
of time residing: *My father's ten-year residence in Spain
gave him a good understanding of the culture.*

res·i·dent [rez-uh-dunt] *noun, plural* **residents.**
someone who lives in a particular place:
*The local residents held a meeting to discuss
a new children's playground.*

Scientists who **research** *the
ocean live and work on specially
equipped ships.*

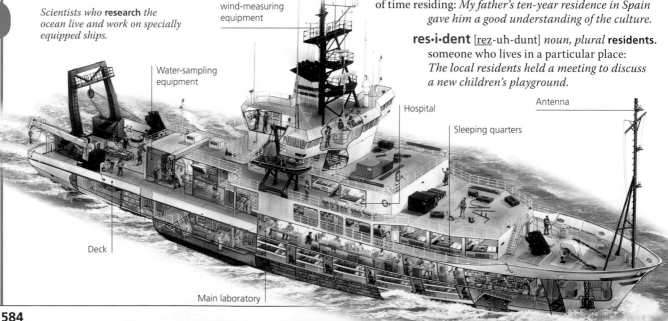

Radar and
wind-measuring
equipment

Water-sampling
equipment

Hospital

Antenna

Sleeping quarters

Deck

Main laboratory

res·i·den·tial [rez-i-den-shul] *adjective.* relating to any area where people live: *The speed limit is lower for residential areas than it is for the main roads.*

res·i·due [rez-uh-doo] *noun, plural* **residues.** the part that remains after something is gone; remainder: *A chemical residue in the building helped police identify the cause of the fire.* When a part has been left behind it is **residual**.

re·sign [ri-zine] *verb,* **resigned, resigning.** to leave a job or position: *One of the teachers has resigned to become the assistant principal at another school.*

re·sig·na·tion [rez-ig-nay-shun] *noun, plural* **resignations.** **1.** the act of resigning: *The manager's resignation was announced yesterday.* **2.** a formal letter or notice that someone intends to resign: *Kieryn handed in her resignation today.* **3.** the acceptance of something with sadness: *When she lost the vote for team captain, resignation was clear on her face.*

re·sin [rez-in] *noun, plural* **resins.** a sticky substance, either obtained from certain trees or manufactured, which is used in making paint, plastics, glue, and rubber.

re·sist [ri-zist] *verb,* **resisted, resisting. 1.** to say no to something tempting: *Susan cannot resist chocolate.* **2.** to fight against; oppose; withstand: *The soldiers resisted the enemy forces.* **3.** to withstand or survive the effect of something destructive: *This paint will resist sun damage for at least five years.*

re·sis·tance [ri-zis-tuns] *noun.* **1.** the act of resisting: *The other team put up a strong resistance, but we won in the end.* **2.** the ability to oppose or withstand: *Eating healthy foods will help your body to build resistance against disease.* **3.** any force that works against movement: *Air resistance slows the car down; Solid earth has good resistance to an electric current.*

res·o·lu·tion [rez-uh-loo-shun] *noun, plural* **resolutions. 1.** a firm or formal decision to do something: *I made a New Year's resolution to do more exercise.* **2.** a mental state of being determined to act in a certain way: *This job will need resolution and hard work.* **3.** the process or act of resolving issues: *We had a workshop on conflict resolution at school; This novel has a surprising resolution—it is not a happy ending!*

Shaft that takes miners down to the mine

Elevator, called a cage, that takes miners to coalface

Coal is loaded onto rail cars for transportation.

Skip taking coal to surface

Coal-cutting machine

Coal is a natural **resource** *that is mined from deep beneath the ground.*

re·solve [ri-zolv] *verb,* **resolved, resolving. 1.** to decide firmly; determine: *David has resolved to train hard to make the team this year.* **2.** to settle an issue or solve a problem: *We have resolved our differences and we can work together now.*
noun. determination or willpower: *His resolve helped him to achieve good results.*

res·o·nant [rez-uh-nunt] *adjective.* **1.** able to make sounds echo or last louder and longer: *A classical guitar has a resonant chamber that amplifies the sound.* **2.** having a full, rich sound; resounding: *Paul's resonant singing filled the concert hall.* The quality of richness or fullness of sound is **resonance**.

re·sort [ri-zort] *verb,* **resorted, resorting.** to use or turn to for help: *When the pain got really bad I had to resort to medication.*
noun, plural **resorts. 1.** a place to go to for rest and relaxation: *a seaside resort for all the family.* **2.** a source of help or protection: *Your best resort is the police—they will know what to do.*

re·sound [ri-zound] *verb,* **resounded, resounding. 1.** to make an echoing, loud, or ringing sound: *The bells resounded through the valley.* **2.** to be filled with sound: *The church resounded with the organ music.* If a sound is loud and full it is **resounding**.

re·source ◀ [ree-sors *or* ri-sors] *noun, plural* **resources. 1.** something useful or helpful for a particular purpose: *This school has excellent resources, including a library, computer rooms, and sports facilities.* **2. resources.** the wealth of a country, or its means of producing wealth: *The nation has many natural resources such as gold, copper, and uranium.* **3.** anything used to help in an emergency: *His only resource was to use his flashlight to send signals and hope that someone would notice.* Someone who is good at overcoming difficulties is **resourceful**.

res·pect [ri-spekt] *noun.* **1.** an attitude of consideration or high regard: *Please show respect for each other by being polite and helpful.* **2.** good opinion, honor, or admiration: *I have a lot of respect for my grandfather, because he did not know English when he came here and now look at what he has achieved.* **Respects** are greetings or signs of regard: *I visited her to pay my respects.* **3.** a particular point or detail: *You are right, in that respect; Terry needs to improve her work, with respect to her spelling.*
verb, **respected, respecting.** to show respect or consideration to: *Sean respects his grandfather; Please respect my wishes.*

a b c d e f g h i j k l m n o p q r s t u v w x y z

re·spect·a·ble [ri-spek-tuh-bul] *adjective.* **1.** having a good reputation; honest; decent: *respectable people; a respectable job.* **2.** above average; good: *This is a respectable report card—well done!* **3.** fit for use in public; appropriate: *You need some respectable clothes for the wedding.* **—respectably,** *adverb.*

RESPIRATORY SYSTEM

In the respiratory system, the air enters through the nose and mouth, goes down the throat, into the windpipe, and then into each lung through the bronchus. The lungs absorb oxygen, which is vital to the function of the human body, and pass it into the blood, which carries it around the body. Carbon dioxide is a waste substance that passes out of the body in the opposite direction, from the blood to the air in the lungs. The diaphragm is the main breathing muscle.

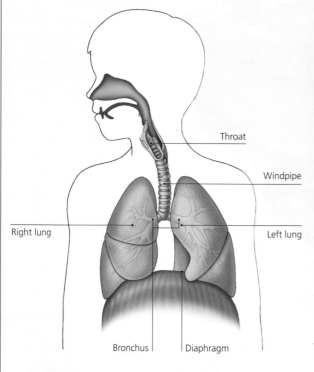

Throat

Windpipe

Right lung

Left lung

Bronchus | Diaphragm

BREATHING IN
Diaphragm flattens; ribs move up and out; lungs expand.

BREATHING OUT
Diaphragm springs up; rib cage sinks; lungs deflate.

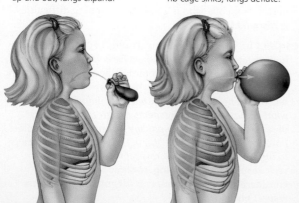

re·spect·ful [ri-spekt-ful] *adjective.* having or showing respect: *There was a respectful minute of silence to remember those who were lost in the war.* **—respectfully,** *adverb.*

re·spect·ive [ri-spek-tiv] *adjective.* relating or belonging to each one: *The aim of the quiz is to match the animals to their respective homes, such as the beaver to the dam.*

re·spect·ive·ly [ri-spek-tiv-lee] *adverb.* in the same order as given: *There are separate cabins for junior and senior campers—Acorn Lodge and Oak Lodge respectively.*

res·pi·ra·tion [res-puh-ray-shun] *noun. Biology* **1.** the natural process in animals of breathing in air to obtain oxygen and breathing out carbon dioxide. **2.** a similar process in plants.

res·pi·ra·to·ry [res-pruh-tore-ee] *adjective. Health.* relating to the process of breathing and the body organs involved: *Asthma is a respiratory illness.*

respiratory system ◀ *Biology.* the parts of the body that are connected and involved in breathing and supplying oxygen to the body. These include the mouth, nose, airways, diaphragm, and lungs.

re·spond [ri-spond] *verb,* **responded, responding.** **1.** to give an answer or reply: *The zoo tries to respond to all the letters that children send.* **2.** to answer a need or call for help: *The fire brigade responded very quickly.* **3.** to act in a certain way in response: *The class has responded well to our new student and has made her feel welcome.*

re·sponse [ri-spons] *noun, plural* **responses.** an answer in word or action: *The government sent army reserves in response to the hurricane disaster.*

re·spon·si·bil·i·ty [ri-spon-suh-bil-uh-tee] *noun, plural* **responsibilities.** **1.** the state or quality of being responsible: *You need to show some responsibility now that you have a younger sister to look after.* **2.** something that one is responsible for; duty: *My responsibility is to feed the dogs each morning.*

re·spon·si·ble [ri-spon-suh-bul] *adjective.* **1.** having a special duty or care of something: *William is responsible for our charity fund-raising.* **2.** able to be trusted; reliable; mature: *We need a responsible person to help run our general store on weekends.* **3.** being the main reason or cause: *The storm was responsible for millions of dollars of damage.* **4.** involving important work: *Being captain is a responsible position.* **—responsibly,** *adverb.*

rest[1] [rest] *noun, plural* **rests.** **1.** a time where one does not work or move: *The doctor ordered her to have two days of bed rest.* **2.** a state of no movement: *The runaway bicycle came to rest in a ditch.* **3.** a support: *Each car seat has a head rest for safety.* **4.** *Music.* a period of silence. *verb,* **rested, resting.** **1.** to stop work or activity in order to refresh oneself: *Please can we rest for a few minutes?* **2.** to be quiet, at peace, or asleep: *The detective said he would not rest until the crime is solved.* **3.** to lie, lean, or be supported: *She rested her head on his shoulder.* **4.** to give rest to: *The coach will rest our best pitcher today and save him for the big game.* **5.** to stay or be fixed: *Her eyes rested on the photograph.*

rest² [rest] *noun.* **1.** the part that is left over; remainder: *I've done most of my homework and I'll finish the rest later.* **2.** other people or things: *Some of my friends are coming, but the rest have a baseball game.*
verb, **rested, resting.** to remain or continue: *Their last chance for victory rests with a final counterattack.*

res·tau·rant [res-tuh-*rahnt* or *res*-tuh-runt] *noun, plural* **restaurants.** a business place that prepares and serves meals for customers.

> The word **restaurant** is fairly new compared to most words in English. The kind of business known as a restaurant began in France about 200 years ago. Before that, people did eat away from home, but only at an inn or tavern while traveling. *Restaurant* comes from "restore," with the idea that when you eat a good meal, you feel *restored* to health and good spirits.

rest·ful [*rest*-ful] *adjective.* giving rest or refreshment: *a restful holiday.*

rest·less [*rest*-lis] *adjective.* **1.** not able to rest or be still: *The animals are very restless because of the storm coming.* **2.** not giving rest or refreshment: *Mom was worried so she had a restless night.* —**restlessly,** *adverb;* —**restlessness,** *noun.*

re·store ▼ [ri-*store*] *verb,* **restored, restoring. 1.** to bring something back to its former condition; repair: *Daniel has bought an old bike and he's going to restore it.* **2.** to bring back: *After the dance we had to restore order in the messy hall.* **3.** to give back (after being taken or lost): *The police restored the lost child to her parents.* The process or the result of restoring something is **restoration.**

re·strain [ri-*strane*] *verb,* **restrained, restraining. 1.** to control or keep back: *The girls could not restrain their giggles.* **2.** to take away someone's freedom or to stop them from doing something: *The suspect was restrained by the police.*

re·straint [ri-*straynt*] *noun, plural* **restraints. 1.** the ability to control one's own behavior; self-control: *Anne showed great restraint in keeping her temper after the way he was so rude to her.* **2.** a device used to control something or hold it back: *The horse broke free from its restraints.*

re·strict [ri-*strikt*] *verb,* **restricted, restricting.** to keep something within a boundary or limit: *The Website has a password to restrict the number of people who can visit it.*

re·stric·tion [ri-*strik*-shun] *noun, plural* **restrictions. 1.** something that restricts or controls: *There is a restriction on the number of books you can borrow from the library at one time.* **2.** the act of restricting or limiting something: *The journalists protested against the restriction of their freedom of speech.*

rest·room [*rest*-room] *noun, plural* **restrooms.** a room with toilets and basins for the public to use.

re·sult [ri-*zult*] *noun, plural* **results. 1.** something that happens because of some other action: *She took up tennis and the result was she became more fit and healthy; We tied the first-place team 1–1, which was a good result for us but not so good for them.* **2.** *Mathematics.* the number that is obtained after a mathematical process: *If you divide 200 by 5, the result is 40.*
verb, **resulted, resulting. 1.** to be produced by some other action: *Success often results from a lot of hard work and a little bit of luck.* **2.** to cause something: *The hailstorm resulted in a lot of damage to cars and houses.*

Scaffolding helped builders **restore** *the golden dome of St. Sophia Cathedral in Moscow, Russia.*

a
b
c
d
e
f
g
h
i
j
k
l
m
n
o
p
q
r
s
t
u
v
w
x
y
z

re·sume [ri-<u>zoom</u>] *verb*, **resumed, resuming. 1.** to continue something after a break: *We resumed studying after lunch.* **2.** to take up a position again or return to: *They resumed their seats after the fire drill.*

res·um·é [<u>rez</u>-uh-*may*] *noun, plural* **resumés.** *Business.* a summary of someone's academic achievements and history of employment: *The supermarket asked for a resumé when I applied for the job.*

re·tail [<u>ree</u>-tale] *noun. Business.* the selling of goods directly to customers, usually in small amounts. Someone who sells goods direct to customers is a **retailer.** *adjective.* related to selling direct to customers: *You pay more at a retail store than at a factory outlet. verb,* **retailed, retailing.** to sell goods directly to customers.

re·tain [ri-<u>tane</u>] *verb*, **retained, retaining.** to keep hold of: *The thermos retained the heat of the soup.* **2.** to keep information or ideas in the mind: *I retained my knowledge of history after the exams.* **3.** to pay someone to do regular work: *We retain a gardener.* The act of retaining something is called **retention.**

re·tard·ed [ri-<u>tard</u>-id] *adjective.* having a mental ability that is slow compared to most people. A retarded person does not learn, act, or think as fast as others.

ret·i·na ▼ [<u>ret</u>-uh-nuh] *noun, plural* **retinas.** *Biology.* a layer of cells at the back of the eye that is sensitive to light. Images picked up by these cells are carried to the brain by the optic nerve.

re·tire [ri-<u>tire</u>] *verb*, **retired, retiring. 1.** to leave a job, business, or career and stop working, usually because of having reached a certain age or a certain number of years on the job: *Our teacher says that when she is 65, she will retire and spend her time traveling and visiting family and friends.* **2.** to go to bed: *Grandma retires around nine o'clock every night.* **3.** to take a break in order to be alone or relax: *Our cousins retire to their beach house in summer and their ski lodge in winter.*

re·tire·ment [ri-<u>tire</u>-munt] *noun, plural* **retirements.** the act of retirement; permanently leaving a certain job or the world of work in general: *Since their retirement, my parents have traveled the world.*

re·treat [ri-<u>treet</u>] *verb*, **retreated, retreating.** to move away from a place or situation, often going back the way you came: *The soldiers retreated when they saw how large the enemy force was; As the floodwaters rose, we retreated to higher ground. noun, plural* **retreats. 1.** the act of moving back from somewhere or something: *The retreat to higher ground saved us from the floodwaters.* **2.** somewhere to be alone or to rest: *a health retreat.* **3.** a signal that tells soldiers to move from a dangerous position: *They used a whistle to call retreat.*

re·trieve [ri-<u>treev</u>] *verb*, **retrieved, retrieving. 1.** to bring back or find again: *My brother retrieved the baseball from the woods.* **2.** in hunting, to find and pick up killed or wounded game: *The dog retrieved the rabbits we shot.* The act of retrieving something is **retrieval.**

re·triev·er [ri-<u>tree</u>-vur] *noun, plural* **retrievers.** any breed of dog trained to find and pick up killed or wounded game.

re·turn [ri-<u>turn</u>] *verb*, **returned, returning. 1.** to go or come back: *We returned to the hotel for a rest before dinner.* **2.** to get or give something back again: *I returned the DVD to the shop.* **3.** to respond to something in a similar way: *to return a phone call; My sister returned my favor by cleaning my room.* **4.** a formal report or statement: *The jury returned its verdict. noun, plural* **returns. 1.** the act of going back: *Mom said she was excited about my return from camp.* **2.** an official report or document: *After working all year my big brother had to file a tax return.* **3.** the money made from a sale: *We made a good return from our lemonade stand.*

re·un·ion [ree-<u>yoon</u>-yun] *noun, plural* **reunions.** the fact of coming together again after time apart: *My cousins are coming from all over the world for a family reunion.*

re·veal [ri-<u>veel</u>] *verb*, **revealed, revealing. 1.** to make something known; tell a secret: *Grandma never reveals her real age.* **2.** to show something that was hidden; make clearly visible: *He took off his mask and revealed his identity.*

rev·e·la·tion [rev-uh-<u>lay</u>-shun] *noun, plural* **revelations. 1.** the act of making something known. **2.** information that has been made known, often something that was a secret: *I was shocked by the revelation that my sister was adopted.*

re·venge [ri-venj] *noun.* actions taken to pay someone back for causing injury, insult, or harm: *They took revenge on the bully by letting the air out of his bike tires. verb,* **revenged.** to take action in order to pay someone back for causing injury, insult, or harm.

Retina

*When we look at a dog, light passes through the eye to form an upside-down image on the **retina,** and then the brain interprets the image the right way up.*

rev·e·nue [<u>rev</u>-uh-*noo*] *noun, plural* **revenues.** *Business.* **1.** money earned through a job, the running of a business, or an investment. **2.** the money a government receives from taxes.

rev·er·ence [<u>rev</u>-ur-uns] *noun.* strong feelings of respect and awe; deep respect and love: *I have reverence for my grandfather.*

re·verse [ri-<u>vurs</u>] *noun plural,* **reverses.** **1.** the direct opposite of what is usual: *I thought our cat was older than our dog but it turns out the reverse is true.* **2.** the gear that makes a machine move backward: *We used reverse to drive back up the hill.* **3.** the other side or back side of something: *On the reverse of the playing cards are pictures of birds.* **4.** a change for the worse; a defeat or setback: *The patient seemed to be getting better, but then suffered a serious reverse.* A change to the opposite condition, position, or direction is a **reversal.** *adjective.* describing the opposite condition, position, or direction: *to count in the reverse order 10 to 1.* *verb,* **reversed, reversing. 1.** to change something so that it is turned around, inside out, or upside down: *She reversed her jacket to reveal a different color.* **2.** to change something so that it is the opposite: *I reversed my opinion of him after his apology.*

re·view [ri-<u>vyoo</u>] *verb,* **reviewed, reviewing. 1.** to examine or study something again: *I reviewed the paper I wrote a few days ago.* **2.** to judge the quality or value of something and give an opinion: *His job was to review new cars for a motor magazine.* **3.** to formally inspect or examine: *The students were suspended until the principal reviewed their case.* *noun, plural* **reviews. 1.** the action of examining or studying something again: *I took time for a review of my speech notes.* **2.** a report giving an opinion on the quality or value of something: *The movie was given a good review.* **3.** inspection by an official or authority.

re·view·er [ri-<u>vyoo</u>-ur] *noun, plural* **reviewers.** someone who examines and gives an opinion on the quality or value of something: *The producers invited reviewers to their first showing of the film.*

re·vise [ri-<u>vize</u>] *verb,* **revised, revising. 1.** to change something in order to improve it: *The chef revised his recipe to make it more simple.* **2.** to make something different: *The journalist revised her article when she received new information.* Something that is improved, made different, or brought up to date is described as being **revised.**

Teachers of writing often say, "Good writing is revising." This means that **revising** (changing) a paper before you hand it in is absolutely necessary, to make it the best that it can be. Even the most famous writers of books do not write something down in final form on the first try and then send it right off to their publisher. They carry out an ongoing process of reading over what they have written and changing it to make it better, before they are finally satisfied it is ready to go.

re·vi·sion [ri-<u>vizh</u>-un] *noun, plural* **revisions. 1.** the act of revising or changing something: *The council asked for a revision of the plans for our house.* **2.** an updated or rewritten version of a text: *The revision of the book included new statistics.*

re·viv·al [ri-<u>vive</u>-ul] *noun, plural* **revivals. 1.** a renewed interest in something that used to be in use or action: *Parent groups are calling for a revival of old-fashioned manners.* **2.** a new production of an old play or showing of a movie that has not been shown for some time: *The local cinema is showing revivals.* **3.** a meeting held to create new interest in religion, often encouraging the open expression of strong religious feeling.

re·vive [ri-<u>vive</u>] *verb,* **revived, reviving. 1.** to bring back to life: *The lifeguards revived the man who had almost drowned.* **2.** to renew interest in something that used to be popular: *Filmmakers are reviving films shot in black and white.* **3.** to bring back to health and vitality; refresh: *A snack and a drink revived the hiker's energy.*

re·voke [ri-<u>voke</u>] *verb,* **revoked, revoking.** to withdraw the power or importance of something; cancel: *My parents revoked my allowance as punishment.* The cancellation of something or the removal of its power is called **revocation.**

re·volt [ri-<u>vohlt</u>] *noun, plural* **revolts.** the overthrow of a government or other officials in authority, often with the use of violence: *The prisoners planned a revolt against the wardens.* *verb,* **revolted, revolting.** to overthrow an authority: *The slaves revolted.*

re·vol·ting [ri-<u>vohlt</u>-ing] *adjective.* to cause feelings of disgust or nausea: *the revolting smell of rotting food.*

rev·o·lu·tion [*rev*-uh-<u>loo</u>-shun] *noun, plural* **revolutions. 1.** the replacement of a government or individual ruler, often with the use of violence. **2.** a large and sudden change: *A revolution in communication has taken place since the introduction of e-mails and cell phones.* **3.** a complete movement in a circle around a fixed object or point: *The Earth makes a revolution around the Sun.*

rev·o·lu·tion·ary ▲ [*rev*-uh-<u>loo</u>-shu-ner-ee] *adjective.* relating to the overthrow of a government or a complete change: *The revolutionary soldiers took over the town.*

Revolutionary War *History.* a war fought by the American colonies against Great Britain from 1775 to 1783, which resulted in the United States becoming a separate nation.

rev·o·lu·tion·ize [*rev*-uh-<u>loo</u>-shuh-*nize*] *verb,* **revolutionized, revolutionizing.** to bring about a change in the most basic nature of something: *Computers have revolutionized almost every aspect of society.*

All the planets of the solar system **revolve** *around the Sun.*

re·volve ▶ [ri-<u>volv</u>] *verb,* **revolved, revolving. 1.** to move in a circle around a fixed object or point: *The Earth revolves around the Sun.* **2.** to spin or turn around: *The front door of the hotel revolves automatically when someone steps up to walk through it.* **3.** to rely on: *The animal's life revolves around the search for food and shelter.*

re·volv·er [ri-<u>vol</u>-vur] *noun, plural* **revolvers.** a handgun that stores bullets in a revolving cylinder so that it can shoot a number of times without reloading.

re·ward [ri-<u>word</u>] *noun, plural* **rewards. 1.** something pleasing given in return for work done or a good deed: *My parents took me out to dinner as a reward for studying hard.* **2.** money that is offered for help finding something lost or for solving a crime: *The police offered a reward for information about the robbery.* *verb,* **rewarded, rewarding. 1.** to give something pleasing in return for work done or a good deed: *The old lady rewarded me with a candy for helping her to cross the road.* **2.** to give a prize in recognition of an ability or talent: *That foundation rewards people who suggest peaceful solutions to conflict.*

re·word [ree-<u>wurd</u>] *verb,* **reworded, rewording.** to give the same message in different words: *The doctor reworded his diagnosis so the patient could understand the problem.*

rheumatic fever *Medicine.* a disease that particularly affects children, causing pain and swelling in the joints, and damage to the heart.

rheu·ma·tism [<u>roo</u>-muh-*tiz*-um] *noun. Medicine.* a painful medical condition involving the joints, muscles, or connective tissues of the body. Someone who is affected by rheumatism is described as **rheumatic.**

rhi·noc·er·os ▼ [rye-<u>nos</u>-ur-us] *noun, plural* **rhinoceroses** or **rhinoceros.** a huge, powerful animals native to southeast Asia and Africa with very thick skin and one or two horns on the snout. The shortened form of this word is **rhino.**

rho·do·den·dron [roh-duh-<u>den</u>-drun] *noun, plural* **rhododendrons.** a shrub that is evergreen with shiny, thick leaves and clusters of bell-shaped flowers.

rhom·bus [<u>rom</u>-bus] *noun, plural* **rhombuses** or **rhombi.** *Mathematics.* a flat shape with four sides of equal length. The opposite sides are parallel.

rhu·barb ▼ [<u>roo</u>-*barb*] *noun, plural* **rhubarbs.** a plant with long green or reddish stalks that can be cooked and eaten. The leaves are poisonous.

rhyme [rime] *noun, plural* **rhymes. 1.** similarity in the sounds of words, used particularly in songs and poetry. For example, in the verse *Twinkle, twinkle, little star, how I wonder what you are,* the word "are" rhymes with the word "star." **2.** a word with a similar sound to another word. For example, the word "pig" rhymes with the word "fig." *verb,* **rhymed, rhyming.** to put words that have a similar sound together: *I rhymed "love" with "dove" in the song I wrote.*

Stewed **rhubarb** *stalks make a delicious filling for pies.*

rhythm [<u>riTH</u>-um] *noun, plural* **rhythms.** repeated, regular movements or sounds: *At the concert the whole crowd moved to the rhythm of the music.*

rhyth·mic [<u>riTH</u>-mik] *adjective.* relating to rhythm; describing repeated, regular movements or sounds: *I feel at peace when I hear the rhythmic chiming of church bells.* A pattern of sounds or movements can also be described as **rhythmical. —rhythmically,** *adverb.*

rib [rib] *noun, plural* **ribs. 1.** one of a group of bones that protect the heart and lungs by curving out from the spine around the chest. **2.** an object similar to a rib in the body. An umbrella has ribs in its metal structure.

rib·bon [<u>rib</u>-un] *noun, plural* **ribbon. 1.** a thin strip of material used in decorating, particularly for hair and gifts: *We tied our hair with ribbons in the team colors.* **2.** a long, thin strip of material with ink on it used in typewriters and some printers.

> **Rhinoceros** goes back to the Greek word for "nose." The thing people noticed when they saw a rhinoceros for the first time was its huge nose (snout) and the large horns attached to this.

Javan rhinoceros

Indian rhinoceros

Sumatran rhinoceros

White rhinoceros

Black rhinoceros

There are only five kinds of **rhinoceroses** *in the world.*

rice [rise] *noun.* the seeds of a grass that is widely grown in warm, wet areas, particularly in India and China, and used for food in many countries throughout the world.

rich [rich] *adjective.* **1.** owning a great amount of material wealth in the form of money, property, and other valuables. **2.** having a large supply of anything: *This fruit is rich in Vitamin C.* **3.** highly fertile or productive: *The farm has rich soil; He is rich in ideas.* **4.** full, deep, and warm: *The opera singer has a rich voice.* **5.** full in flavor or containing a high amount of fatty foods such as cream, eggs, and butter: *a rich dessert.* —**richly,** *adverb;* —**richness,** *noun.*

rich·es [rich-iz] *plural noun.* a large amount of material wealth in the form of money, property, and other valuables.

> The word **ricochet** comes from a type of story told many years ago. The people listening to the story would ask a lot of questions, but the story-teller would dodge the questions and not directly answer them. It was as if the question was sent straight out, but would bounce off in another direction, like a ricochet.

ric·o·chet [rik-uh-*shay*] *verb,* **ricocheted, ricocheting.** to bounce or skip off a surface at an angle; rebound: *The rubber ball ricocheted off the wall.*

rid [rid] *verb,* **rid or ridded, ridding.** to relieve, free from, or clear away something unpleasant or no longer useful: *We got rid of the rubbish.*

rid·dle[1] [rid-ul] *noun, plural* **riddles.** a difficult question or problem. For example: What can you break without touching it? Answer: Your promise.

Riddles are a well-known kind of writing and often appear in humorous books for children. They can even be found in ancient books such as the Bible. This riddle is said to be one of the oldest and most famous in the world: "What kind of creature goes on four legs in the morning, two legs at noon, and three legs in the evening?" The answer is, "A man, because he crawls on four legs as a baby (the 'morning' of life), then walks on two legs as an adult (noon), and finally walks with a cane in old age (evening)."

rid·dle[2] [rid-ul] *verb,* **riddled, riddling.** to make many holes in something: *After the battle, the walls of the fort were riddled with bullets.*

ride [ride] *verb,* **rode, ridden, riding. 1.** to sit on, and control the movement of, a vehicle or animal: *to ride a horse; to ride a motorcycle.* **2.** to be carried in a moving vehicle: *to ride on a train or airplane.* **3.** to float, rise, or be carried along: *The canoe rode the rapids.* *noun, plural* **rides. 1.** a short journey in a vehicle or on an animal: *We took a taxi ride to the airport.* **2.** a mechanical device ridden for entertainment or excitement: *At the amusement park, we went on all the scary rides.*

rid·er [ride-ur] *noun, plural* **riders.** someone who rides: *a horseback rider.* The number of passengers using a particular form of public transport is called a **ridership.**

ridge [rij] *noun, plural* **ridges. 1.** a long, narrow, raised area or edge: *The white goat had a black ridge along its spine.* **2.** any narrow and raised strip: *The ridges of soil in the field held the seeds for the crop.* **3.** a narrow chain of hills or range of mountains.

rid·i·cule [rid-uh-kyool] *verb,* **ridiculed, ridiculing.** to laugh at or make fun of: *The other students ridiculed my silly answer to the question.* *noun.* behavior or language that makes fun of someone or some thing.

ri·dic·u·lous [ri-dik-yuh-lus] *adjective.* not reasonable; silly: *a ridiculous-looking hat with bananas and other fruit on top; He had the ridiculous idea that he could raise the money for his business by winning the lottery.* —**ridiculously,** *adverb;* —**ridiculousness,** *noun.*

ri·fle [rye-ful] *noun, plural* **rifles.** a gun with a long barrel that is fired from the shoulder. *verb,* **rifled, rifling.** to search for something quickly: *She rifled through her papers looking for her homework.*

rig [rig] *verb,* **rigged, rigging. 1.** to put masts, sails, and lines on a boat or ship: *They rigged the yacht and set sail.* **2.** to equip or fit out: *Dad rigged the tree with Christmas lights.* **3.** to put something together in a makeshift way: *He rigged up an aerial using an old coat hanger.* *noun, plural* **rigs. 1.** the arrangement of masts, sails, and lines on a boat or ship. **2.** equipment that is used for a special task: *an oil rig.*

rig·ging ▼ [rig-ing] *noun, plural* **riggings. 1.** ropes, chains, and wires on a boat or ship. **2.** equipment that is used for a special task: *The miner set up the rigging to bore a hole.*

Old ships with many sails had complex **rigging.**

a b c d e f g h i j k l m n o p q r s t u v w x y z

*A bear's claws can **rip** apart almost anything in its path.*

right [rite] *adjective.* **1.** describing something true or correct: *the right answer; the right idea.* **2.** morally correct or good: *Handing in the lost wallet is the right thing to do.* **3.** the opposite of left: *She plays tennis with her right hand.* **4.** as it should be or as is wanted; suitable or appropriate: *He met the right girl and fell in love.* **5.** describing the part that is meant to be showing: *I hope I put the tablecloth right side up.*
noun, plural **rights. 1.** something that is good or morally correct: *Grandpa says that if you do right in the world, you will be rewarded.* **2.** a just or lawful claim: *the right to an attorney.* **3.** the direction that is the opposite of left: *His classroom is on your right.*
adverb. **1.** in the right way: *If you can't spell the word right, ask the teacher; She did right by admitting her mistake.* **2.** to the right: *Look right and you will see the building.*
verb, **righted, righting. 1.** to make something good or act in morally correct way: *He righted the situation by returning the stolen money.* **2.** to return something to its proper position: *They righted the sailing boat after it flipped over.*
A different word with the same sound is **write.**

right angle *Mathematics.* an angle of 90 degrees that forms when two lines are perpendicular to each other.

righ·teous [rye-chus] *adjective.* describing just and moral ideas and behavior: *a righteous person; a righteous judgement.* —**righteously,** *adverb;* —**righteousness,** *noun.*

right-hand *adjective.* **1.** toward or on the right: *The right-hand door leads to the library.* **2.** for the right hand: *her right-hand glove.*

right-hand·ed *adjective.* **1.** describing the use of the right hand more than the left. Someone who does this is called a **right-hander. 2.** done with the right hand: *a right-handed catch.*

right triangle *Mathematics.* a triangle with a right angle inside it.

rig·id [rij-id] *adjective.* **1.** stiff or unbending: *a rigid piece of iron.* The fact of being stiff or unbending is called **rigidity. 2.** difficult to change; strict: *rigid views; a rigid timetable.* —**rigidly,** *adverb.*

rim [rim] *noun, plural* **rims.** the edge or border of something: *The cup is full to the rim.*
verb, **rimmed, rimming.** to form an edge or border around something: *Trees rimmed the park.*

rind [rinde] *noun, plural* **rinds.** a hard skin or outer cover. Some cheeses have wax rinds. Oranges and lemons have rinds.

ring[1] [ring] *noun, plural* **rings. 1.** the fact of being a circle: *They danced in a ring around the singer.* **2.** a circle made of metal or some other substance: *He put the ring on her finger.* **3.** an enclosure or round stage area: *a circus ring.*
verb, **ringed, ringing.** to form a circle around something: *Seats ring the stadium.*
A different word with the same sound is **wring.**

ring[2] [ring] *verb,* **rang, rung, ringing. 1.** to make or cause to make the sound of a bell: *The telephone was ringing.* **2.** to make a loud, echoing sound: *The sound of gunfire rang out.* **3.** to hear an echoing, buzzing sound: *The sound of the explosion rang in her head.* **4.** to announce or call by sounding a bell: *She rang for room service.*
noun, plural **rings. 1.** a sound like a bell: *the ring of a doorbell.* **2.** a telephone call: *Tell your mother to give me a ring.*
A different word with the same sound is **wring.**

rink [ringk] *noun, plural* **rinks.** an area for ice-skating or roller-skating.

rinse [rins] *verb,* **rinsed, rinsing. 1.** to wash soap out with clear water: *The washing machine has a cycle that will rinse the clothes off after the wash cycle.* **2.** to give a light wash to something: *Rinse the plates before you stack them in the dishwasher.*
noun, plural **rinses.** the act of rinsing: *Give the glasses a rinse because they're a little dusty.*

ri·ot [rye-ut] *noun, plural* **riots. 1.** a violent disturbance by a large group of people. Violent behavior by a crowd can be described as **riotous. 2.** something or someone very funny: *That movie is really a riot.*
verb, **rioted, rioting.** to start or take part in a violent disturbance: *The protestors rioted when the police came.*

rip ▲ [rip] *verb,* **ripped, ripping.** to tear apart: *He ripped the paper in two.*
noun, plural **rips.** a tear or cut in something: *She has a rip in her jeans.*

ripe [ripe] *adjective.* **1.** describing something that has finished growing and is ready to be eaten: *ripe fruit.* **2.** in the best condition for use; ready: *After she won the local race, she was ripe for the state finals.* —**ripeness,** *noun.*

rip·en [ripe-un] *verb,* **ripened, ripening.** to become or make ripe: *The grapes ripened on the vine.*

*As the sea goes out, it often leaves **ripples** in the sand.*

rip·ple ▲ [rip-ul] *noun, plural* **ripples. 1.** a tiny wave: *ripples on the water.* **2.** something like a ripple: *Over millions of years, wind and water made ripples in the rock.* **3.** a small wave of sound: *a ripple of applause.*
verb, **rippled, rippling.** to create a series of tiny waves: *Wind rippled the water.*

rise [rize] *verb,* **rose, risen, rising. 1.** to get up: *The people in the courtroom are supposed to rise when the judge enters.* **2.** to get out of bed: *Their family rises at dawn.* **3.** to move or go upward: *Hot air rises; The tower rises above the city.* **4.** to become larger or greater: *The price of gas is expected to rise this summer.* **5.** to revolt or rebel: *The people rose up against the king's harsh rule.*
noun, plural **rises. 1.** the act of moving upward. **2.** a slope leading up: *We drove over the rise and could see the ocean.*

risk [risk] *noun, plural* **risks.** a possibility of harm or loss; danger: *There is a risk we will miss the bus if we don't leave now.*
verb, **risked, risking. 1.** to put in danger: *The policeman risked his life to save the girl.* **2.** to take the risk of: *The teacher risked losing her job when she confronted the parents.*

rit·u·al ▶ [rich-oo-ul] *noun, plural* **ritual. 1.** a formal set of actions done in a certain way; rite or ceremony: *Marriage is a sacred ritual in most churches.* **2.** a regular procedure or event: *Early dinner on Sunday night is a ritual at our house.* An event like this can be described as being ritualistic. —**ritually,** *adverb.*

ri·val [rye-vul] *noun, plural* **rivals.** someone or something that competes against another: *The Yankees and the Red Sox are old rivals in baseball.*
verb, **rivaled, rivaling.** to be as good as: *Nothing rivals playing video games as his favorite activity.*
adjective. describing someone or something competing against another: *rival candidates for the office of mayor.*

ri·val·ry [rye-vul-ree] *noun, plural* **rivalries.** competition between two people or parties: *There was a fierce economic rivalry between the two neighboring countries.*

riv·er [riv-ur] *noun, plural* **rivers. 1.** a large, natural stream of moving water. **2.** a large stream of anything: *A river of oil burst out of the ground.*

riv·et [riv-it] *noun, plural* **rivets.** a metal pin or bolt that holds two or more pieces of metal together.
verb, **riveted, riveting. 1.** to fasten with something with a rivet. A person who does this is called a **riveter. 2.** to hold great interest: *We were riveted by her powerful performance.*

RNA *Biology.* the abbreviation for ribonucleic acid. RNA, DNA, and proteins are the basic molecules of life. RNA provides the "message" and plan by which the information in DNA can be used to build proteins.

roach [roche] *noun, plural* **roaches.** a shortened form of COCKROACH, a brown or black insect that breeds in large numbers.

road [rode] *noun, plural* **roads. 1.** a wide path that cars and other vehicles can travel on. **2.** a way to move forward: *After the cast was taken off his leg, he was on the road to recovery.*
◀)) A different word with the same sound is **rode.**

road map *Geography.* a map or diagram that shows streets and highways.

road·run·ner ▶ [rode-run-ur] *noun, plural* **roadrunners.** a bird that usually runs fast instead of flying. Roadrunners have streaked dark feathers, a long tail, and a crest on the top of the head.

The **roadrunner** gets its name because of the way it can be seen running quickly along the side of a road, at a speed of up to 15 miles per hour. Roadrunners are able to fly, but they are more often seen sitting on a bush, low tree, or fence as they wait to run after their prey of insects and small reptiles.

The **roadrunner** *is the state bird of New Mexico.*

roam [rome] *verb,* **roamed, roaming.** to move about without a particular purpose; wander: *He roamed through the park, looking at the trees and wildflowers.*

roar [rore] *verb,* **roared, roaring. 1.** to make a loud, deep sound: *Lions roar.* **2.** to make a loud laugh: *The audience roared at the comedian's funny lines.*
noun, plural **roars.** a loud, deep sound: *the roar of the ocean waves crashing against the shore.*

*In an ancient Egyptian **ritual** performed on festival days, a shrine containing a god's statue was carried around the temple.*

*In ancient China the emperor and his wife wore fine silk **robes** when they received visiting ambassadors.*

rock¹ [rok] *noun, plural* **rocks.**
1. a small, hard piece of natural material; a stone: *The boy threw a rock at the window and smashed it.* **2.** a mineral that forms inside the earth. Marble and granite are rocks. **3.** a huge amount of stone that forms a cliff or mountain. **4.** something or someone strong and dependable: *Our neighbor was our rock when dad was sick.*

rock² [rok] *verb,* **rocked, rocking.**
1. to gently move back and forth: *to rock a baby to sleep.* **2.** to shake violently: *The earthquake rocked the town.*
noun. see ROCK MUSIC.

rock·er [rok-ur] *noun, plural* **rockers.**
1. a rocking chair. **2.** a curved piece of wood that allows a rocking chair, cradle, or other device to rock back and forth.

rock·et ▶ [rok-it] *noun, plural* **rockets.**
a flying device pushed from behind by burning gas.
verb, **rocketed, rocketing.** to move, fly, or rise very fast: *The car rocketed down the freeway.*

rocking chair a chair that rocks back and forth, usually on two pieces of curved wood.

rocking horse a toy horse that rocks back and forth, usually on two pieces of curved wood.

rock music *Music.* a type of music that grew out of rock 'n' roll in the 1960s. Rock music can range from gentle ballads to loud, harsh music called heavy metal.

rock 'n' roll *Music.* a type of popular, upbeat music, singing, and dancing that developed in the 1950s.

rock·y [rok-ee] *adjective,* **rockier, rockiest.** covered in rocks: *a rocky road.*

The word **robot** became known through a play written by the Czech author Karel Capek. In his play, the Robots were not machines as modern robots are. They were human-like creatures, made up of living parts put together in a factory like an automobile.

*Ariane **rockets** are launched from the European Space Agency base in French Guiana.*

roast [rohst] *verb,* **roasted, roasting. 1.** to cook in an oven or over a flame: *We roasted chestnuts over the fire.*
2. to heat and dry something out: *to roast coffee beans.*
3. to make or be very hot; overheat: *You must be roasting in that heavy wool jacket.*
noun, plural **roasts.** meat that is for roasting or has been roasted: *Beef, lamb, or turkey can be cooked as a roast.*
adjective. describing something that has been roasted: *roast pork; roast vegetables.*

rob [rob] *verb,* **robbed, robbing. 1.** to take something that is not yours, usually secretly or by force: *The house next door was robbed.* **2.** to take a chance or opportunity way from someone: *I was robbed of the math prize by someone who cheated.*

rob·ber·y [rob-ree *or* rob-uh-ree] *noun, plural* **robbers.**
Law. the act of stealing something; theft: *There was a robbery at the corner store.*

robe ▲ [robe] *noun, plural* **robes. 1.** a long, loose flowing gown worn as an outer covering: *She wore a blue robe over her pajamas.* **2.** a gown that shows office or rank: *The professor wore her academic robes when she spoke at the graduation ceremony.*
verb, **robed, robing.** to put on a robe.

rob·in ▶ [rob-in] *noun, plural* **robins.** a small bird that lives in North America and Europe. North American robins have an orange chest with a black head and tail.

rob·ot [roh-bot] *noun, plural* **robots.**
a machine designed to do some of the work of a human being.

ro·bot·ics [roh-bot-iks] *noun.*
Science. the design and making of robots, or the study of the use of robots.

ro·bust [roh-bust] *adjective.*
hardy or tough; strong and in excellent health: *a robust athlete.* **—robustly** *adverb.*

rod [rod] *noun, plural* **rods. 1.** a straight cylinder of wood, metal, or plastic. **2.** a fishing pole. **3.** a stick used to hit someone as a punishment. **4.** a unit that measures distance. One rod equals 16½ feet.

rode [rode] *verb.* the past tense of RIDE.
◀» A different word with the same sound is **road.**

*The song of American **robins** is often heard before dawn.*

ro·dent ▼ [rode-unt] *noun, plural* **rodents**. *Biology.* a member of the group of mammals that gnaw or nibble using a pair of large front teeth. Rats, mice, guinea pigs, squirrels, and beavers are types of rodents.

ro·de·o [roh-dee-oh *or* roh-day-oh] *noun, plural* **rodeos**. a display of the skills of cowboys, such as horseback riding and roping.

roe¹ [roh] *noun.* fish eggs.
🔊 A different word with the same sound is **row**.

roe² [roh] *noun, plural* **roes** *or* **roe**. a small deer that lives in the forests of Europe and northern Asia. Roe have a reddish-brown coat.

> Like many American words having to do with cowboys and the Old West, **rodeo** came into English from the Spanish language. It goes back to a word meaning "wheel," and is related to words like *rotate* or *rotary*. It comes from the idea of cowboys riding around a rodeo ring in a circle, like the spinning of a wheel.

rogue [rohg] *noun, plural* **rogues**. **1.** a person who is dishonest or deceitful; a scoundrel. **2.** a person who likes to play tricks on others; a mischievous person. **3.** a vicious animal, especially a male that lives alone.

role [role] *noun, plural* **roles**. **1.** a part played by a performer in a drama: *Jenny played the lead role in the school play.* **2.** a part taken by a person in life; a position or function: *A parent's role is to guide and care for his or her child.*
🔊 A different word with the same sound is **roll.**

roll [role] *verb*, **rolled, rolling. 1.** to move along by turning over and over: *to roll up a window shade or a sleeping bag.* **2.** to move or be carried on wheels: *The train rolled along the track.* **3.** to turn something over on itself a number of times: *The horse enjoyed rolling in the sand.* **4.** to move up, down, or from side to side: *to roll your eyes; The ship rolled on the rough ocean.* **5.** to make a deep sound that goes on for a long time; rumble: *The thunder rolled.* **6.** to flatten using a roller: *Roll out the pastry.* **7.** to say with a trill of the tongue: *You have to learn to roll your Rs to speak Spanish well.*
noun, plural **rolls. 1.** something that is rolled up: *We need three rolls of wallpaper.* **2.** a list of names of the people in a particular group: *Our teacher called the class roll.* **3.** a type of bread smaller than a loaf: *She ate two rolls for lunch.* **4.** a swaying motion: *The boat's roll made him seasick.* **5.** a number of sounds played rapidly that form a continuous sound: *a drum roll.*
🔊 A different word with the same sound is **role.**

roll·er [roh-lur] *noun, plural* **rollers. 1.** a cylinder around which something is rolled: *He put the paper towels on the roller in the kitchen.* **2.** a heavy cylinder used to smooth, flatten, spread, impress, or crush: *The tar was spread on the road and flattened by a roller.* **3.** a small wheel used to roll something along: *Jed moved the heavy table easily because it is on rollers.* **4.** a long, swelling wave that comes to shore.

RODENTS

More than a third of all the world's mammals are rodents, living in almost every environment. Some spend most of their lives in trees, while others live underground. Several, like beavers, spend much of their time in water. Rodents' front teeth, or incisors, grow constantly, ready to gnaw into hard-shelled nuts, tree bark, or other plant food. Some rodents eat insects and other small animals as well as plants.

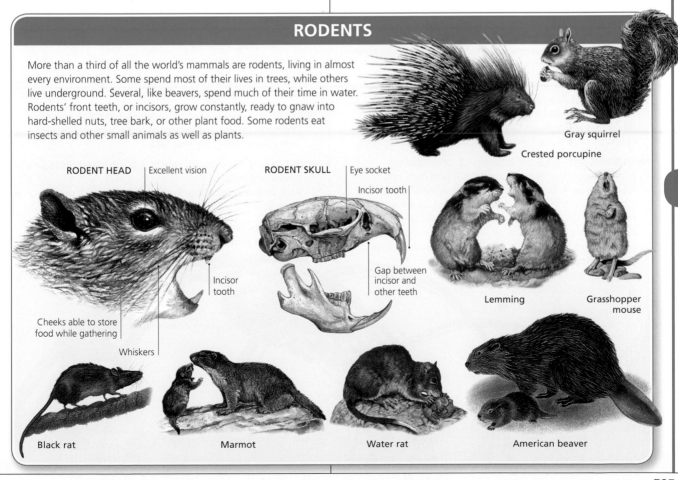

Gray squirrel

Crested porcupine

RODENT HEAD | Excellent vision

Incisor tooth

Cheeks able to store food while gathering

Whiskers

RODENT SKULL | Eye socket

Incisor tooth

Gap between incisor and other teeth

Lemming

Grasshopper mouse

Black rat

Marmot

Water rat

American beaver

roller coaster ▼ an amusement park ride that has small open passenger cars that travel quickly on a track that has many twists, turns, and steep slopes.

roller skate a skate worn over the shoe that has two wheels at the front of the sole and two at the back. People use roller skates to roll quickly on flat, hard surfaces.

roller-skate *verb*, **roller-skated, roller-skating.** to roll across a hard surface wearing roller skates: *We went roller-skating on the sidewalk.*

ROM [rom] *noun. Computers.* an abbreviation of Read-Only-Memory, which is a part of a computer's hardware system that holds information that can be read but not changed.

Ro·man [roh-mun] *adjective.* **1.** of or relating to ancient or modern Rome, including its people and culture. **2. roman.** of or having to do with the upright style of typeface commonly used in modern book printing. *noun, plural* **Romans. 1.** a person born or living in Rome. **2.** a person who lived in Rome in ancient times. **3. roman.** a kind of typeface or lettering.

Roman Catholic Church *Religion.* the Christian church that has the Pope as its leader.

ro·mance [roh-mans *or* roh-mans] *noun, plural* **romances.** **1.** a love affair: *Their romance ended as they were no longer in love.* **2.** an atmosphere or quality of adventure, love, or mystery: *The halls of the old castle have an air of romance about them.* **3.** a tale telling of heroes, their brave deeds, and of love.

Romance language *Language.* one of a group of languages that developed from Latin. Romance languages include Italian, French, Spanish, and Portuguese.

Roman numeral *Mathematics.* a letter that is a symbol in the numbering system used by the ancient Romans. This system is still used on some analog clocks and to number certain things in a series, such as the names of kings, queens, and popes, such as Henry VIII (eighth).

ro·man·tic [roh-man-tik] *adjective.* **1.** of or relating to romance: *That romantic novel is a love story full of adventure.* **2.** having feelings or ideas suitable for a romance; not practical or realistic: *He had a romantic idea about living on a farm until he learned how much hard work was involved.* **3.** showing or expressing feelings of love: *They held hands and went for a romantic stroll.* **—romantically,** *adverb.*

romp [romp] *verb,* **romped, romping.** to play in an active, noisy way: *The puppies romped on the lawn.* *noun, plural* **romps.** play that is active and noisy.

roof [roof *or* ruf] *noun, plural* **roofs. 1.** the outside covering on top of a building. **2.** something like a roof, as it covers or is positioned at the top: *The roof of the car was dented.* *verb,* **roofed, roofing.** to build a roof: *The builders roofed the new house before they worked on the interior.*

rook [ruk] *noun, plural* **rooks.** one of four pieces in a chess set, also known as a castle. Rooks can move parallel to the sides of the board for any number of squares that are unoccupied by other pieces.

rook·ie [ruk-ee] *noun, plural* **rookies. 1.** a person without experience who is new to an organization or job: *The rookie was nervous on his first day on the police force.* **2.** a sports player in his or her first season as a professional.

> The word **rookie** comes from *recruit*; a recruit is a new soldier in the army. A rookie player in professional baseball, football, or other sports is thought of as being like someone who has just joined the army.

room [room] *noun, plural* **rooms. 1.** a space or area that can be filled by someone or something: *There was not enough room between the two cars for her to park her van.* **2.** a part of a building separated by walls: *Their house has six rooms.* **3.** all the people in a room: *When I walked in, the room went quiet.* **4.** a gap that gives an opportunity or chance: *With the lead actor sick, there was room for the understudy to show his ability.* *verb,* **roomed, rooming.** to live in or share a room; lodge: *During college she roomed with her cousin.*

room·mate [room-mate] *noun, plural* **roommates.** a person who shares a rented room with one or more other people.

room·y [roo-mee] *adjective,* **roomier, roomiest.** having generous amounts of room; spacious: *a roomy garage with enough space for four cars.*

roost [roost] *noun, plural* **roosts.** a place where birds perch to rest at night. *verb,* **roosted, roosting.** for a bird, to perch in order to rest at night.

roost·er [roo-stur] *noun, plural* **roosters.** an adult male of certain birds, especially chickens.

ROOTS

There are two basic kinds of roots—tap roots and fibrous roots. All other roots are variations of these. A tap root grows straight down to reach water deep in the soil, and is a single main root with smaller roots branching off it. Fibrous roots have no main root. They spread out to gather water from the top layers of the soil. Aerial roots are adapted fibrous roots. They gather moisture from the air and mineral salts from the surface of the tree upon which they grow.

Aerial root

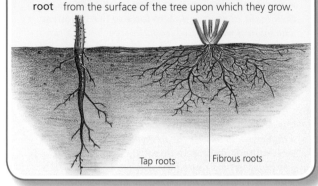

Tap roots

Fibrous roots

root¹ ▲ [root *or* rut] *noun, plural* **roots. 1.** the part of a plant that usually grows downward into the soil. Roots take up fluids and nutrients and hold the plant in place. **2.** a thing that holds something down like a plant's root does: *the root of a tooth.* **3.** the origin or beginning of something: *Money is said to be the root of all evil.* **4.** *Language.* a word to which a prefix or suffix can be added to change its meaning: *watch* is the root of the words *wristwatch* and *watchmen.*
verb, **rooted, rooting. 1.** to send out roots or begin to grow and become established: *He planted the rose bush and it quickly took root.* **2.** to fix in one place: *The acrobats were so amazing that our eyes were rooted to the stage.* **3.** to pull out by the roots; remove completely: *Some weeds must be rooted out or they will grow back.* **4.** to support in a contest: *Natalie rooted for her favorite basketball team.*
🔊)) A different word with the same sound is **route.**

root² [root *or* rut] *verb,* **rooted, rooting. 1.** to turn over soil with the snout: *The pig rooted for food in the dirt.* **2.** to poke about searching for something; to rummage: *Dan rooted around in his bag for a pen.*
🔊)) A different word with the same sound is **route.**

rope [rope] *noun, plural* **ropes. 1.** a strong, thick cord made of twisted fibers or wire. **2.** a number of things strung or twisted together to form a cord: *Ropes of onions hung in the farmers' market.*
verb, **roped, roping. 1.** to tie or fasten with a rope or other cord: *He roped the canoe onto the car roof to take it to the lake.* **2.** to mark off or enclose an area with rope: *The area where the celebrities sat was roped off from the public.* **3.** to capture with a rope: *The calf was roped by the leg.*

rose¹ ▶ [roze] *noun, plural* **roses. 1.** a flower with a sweet smell that comes in many colors and grows on a thorn-covered bush. **2.** a light pinkish-red color.
adjective. having the smell or color of a rose.

rose² [roze] *verb.* the past tense of RISE.

Rosh Ha·sha·nah [rahsh huh-shah-nuh] *Religion.* the holiday held to celebrate the Jewish new year, which falls in September or October. Rosh Hashanah is celebrated with special foods and the blowing of the shofar, a traditional ram's horn trumpet.

ros·y [roh-zee] *adjective,* **rosier, rosiest. 1.** having a pinkish-red color: *a child with rosy cheeks.* **2.** describing something hopeful; cheerful; promising: *The bride and groom looked forward to a rosy future.*

rot [rot] *verb,* **rotted, rotting.** to decay or go bad: *Eating too many sugary foods can rot your teeth.*
noun, plural **rots. 1.** the process of rotting or the fact of being rotten: *Rot destroyed the old wooden boat.* **2.** any of a number of diseases caused by fungi or bacteria that cause decay in animals or plants.

ro·ta·ry [roh-tuh-ree] *adjective.* having a part or parts that turn around: *The rotary hoe has blades that rotate.*

ro·tate [roh-tate] *verb,* **rotated, rotating. 1.** to turn or make turn around a central point: *The wheels on a car rotate around the axles.* **2.** to go through or make go through a series of changes in a set order: *We rotated our jobs in the kitchen so we all got a turn at everything..*

ro·ta·tion [roh-tay-shun] *noun, plural* **rotations.** the act of rotating: *The rotation of the wheels slowed when he put on the brakes.*

ro·tor [roh-tur] *noun, plural* **rotors. 1.** the part of an engine that rotates. **2.** a system of large rotating blades that allows helicopters to fly.

rot·ten [rot-un] *adjective,* **rottener, rottenest. 1.** having gone bad; decayed: *That smelly banana has gone rotten.* **2.** likely to break due to rot: *She almost fell through the rotten wooden stairs.* **3.** bad, evil, or unpleasant: *We are having rotten weather for June.*

rouge [roozh] *noun, plural* **rouges.** a pink or red cosmetic worn on the cheeks.

rough [ruf] *adjective,* **rougher, roughest. 1.** bumpy and uneven; not smooth: *The car bounced along the rough road.* **2.** wild or violent: *We could not go sailing as the sea was too rough.* **3.** rude or bad-mannered; not gentle: *She was offended by his rough manners.* **4.** not in a finished form: *That picture is a rough sketch of the portrait the artist will paint.* **5.** in a natural or crude form: *A rough diamond is one that is yet to be cut and polished.* **6.** describing something unpleasant or difficult: *They have had a rough time lately.*
—**roughness,** *noun.*
verb, **roughed, roughing.** to make a rough plan of: *The illustrator roughed out sketches of what the picture book would look like.*
noun, plural **roughs.** in golf, the part of the course where the grass and other plants are not trimmed.
• **rough it.** to get by without the comforts one is used to living with: *When he goes camping, he roughs it and sleeps out on the bare ground.*
🔊)) A different word with the same sound is **ruff.**

Roses are popular with gardeners because of their strong perfume and beautiful flowers.

a b c d e f g h i j k l m n o p q **r** s t u v w x y z

rough·ly [ruf-lee] *adverb.* **1.** in a violent or harsh way: *He pushed me roughly out the door.* **2.** around about; approximately: *The train comes in roughly half an hour.*

round [round] *adjective,* **rounder, roundest. 1.** shaped like a ball or sphere: *The pearl was perfectly round.* **2.** shaped like a circle; circular: *Rings are round.* **3.** curved like part of a circle: *The top of the human ear is round.*
noun, plural **rounds. 1.** something with the shape of a circle or sphere: *Cut the pastry into rounds.* **2.** movement around a circle or turning about a central point: *The short hand makes two rounds of the clock face each day.* **3.** a set course or circuit that is made regularly; route: *The mailman finished his rounds late.* **4.** a series of events: *a round of golf; The audience gave a round of applause.* **5.** a completed section of a series of bouts, parts, or games in a competition: *At the end of round one, two contestants were eliminated from the singing competition.* **6.** *Music.* a song where singers sing the same words but begin at different times so that they overlap. "Silent Night" is a Christmas carol often sung as a round. **7.** a single gunshot or the ammunition needed for such a shot.
verb, **rounded, rounding. 1.** to make round: *She used a nail file to round the ends of her fingernails.* **2.** to go around something to get to the other side of it: *The truck rounded the corner too fast and turned over.*
adverb; preposition. around: *Turn round to face the front; The ribbon is tied round the present.*
• **round off.** to increase or decrease a number that contains a fraction to the nearest whole number: *On her tax form, she rounded off $45.70 to $46.00 and $138.22 to $138.00.*
• **round up.** to herd or gather together: *The cowhands rounded up the cattle and brought them to the corral.*

Fishermen in northern Italy place their nets using **rowboats.**

round·a·bout [round-uh-*bout*] *adjective.* not direct; the long way: *I was late getting home because I took the roundabout way.*
noun, plural **roundabouts. 1.** a merry-go-round. **2.** a type of road junction in which traffic moves around in a circle.

round number *Mathematics.* a number that has either been increased or decreased to the nearest whole number or to one that ends in a zero: *The nearest round number to 999 is 1,000.*

round trip a journey that begins and ends in the same place; a return trip: *I made the round trip from San Francisco to Los Angeles and back in a day.*

round·up [round-*up*] *noun, plural* **roundups. 1.** the driving together of cattle or other livestock, especially for a particular purpose such as branding or selling. **2.** a bringing together of people, facts, or things: *After the news broadcast there was a roundup of sports results from across the country.*

rouse [rouz] *verb,* **roused, rousing. 1.** to wake someone: *She was roused from her nap by a knock at the door.* **2.** to stir someone up or interest them: *Our interest in the concert was roused when we heard which band would be playing.*

rout [rout] *noun, plural* **routs. 1.** a total defeat in battle, especially when the defeated forces run away in a disorganized manner: *The soldiers were outnumbered so their rout wasn't a surprise.* **2.** any total defeat.
verb, **routed, routing. 1.** to defeat totally: *We routed their team 12 goals to 4.* **2.** to force to flee or retreat: *The soldiers were routed from the trenches and ran away across the field.*

route [root *or* rout] *noun, plural* **routes. 1.** a way or road used to travel from one place to another: *The route to the train station from his house takes him past the corner store.* **2.** a way that is regularly taken, especially by someone making deliveries or sales: *Brian rides a motorbike to deliver the newspapers on his route.*
verb, **routed, routing.** to direct along a particular route: *The police officer routed the cars onto a side street to avoid the accident scene.*
◀)) A different word with the same sound is **root.**

rou·tine [roo-teen] *noun, plural* **routines. 1.** something done in the same way at the same time or place: *I put my lunch in my backpack as part of my routine for getting ready for school.* **2.** a regular or usual way of doing things: *Vacations give you a chance to break away from the old routine.* **3.** an act or part of an act in a performance or show: *the acrobat's routine.*
adjective. done regularly or usually: *The dentist gave the children a routine checkup.* **—routinely,** *adverb.*

row[1] [roh] *noun, plural* **rows. 1.** a line of objects or people arranged side by side: *Joanna planted a row of flowers along the driveway.* **2.** a line of chairs set side by side all facing the same direction: *He sits in the front row in class so he can see the chalkboard.* **3.** a set of things one after the other in a series: *At the start of the season our team won five games in a row.*
◀)) A different word with the same sound is **roe.**

row[2] [roh] *verb,* **rowed, rowing.** to move a boat through water using oars: *My arms soon became sore as I wasn't used to rowing a big boat.*
◀)) A different word with the same sound is **roe.**

row[3] [rou] *noun, plural* **rows.** a loud and angry argument.

row·boat ▲ [roh-*bote*] *noun, plural* **rowboats.** a small boat moved using oars.

row·dy [rou-dee] *adjective,* **rowdier, rowdiest.** wild and making a loud noise: *Mom was cross because we had a rowdy game of hide-and-seek in the house.*
noun, plural **rowdies.** a person who is rough and causes disorder; a hoodlum or ruffian.

> The word **rowdy** is thought to come from *row*, meaning "a fight." The idea is that a person who is a rowdy is very likely to start or get involved in a fight.

*The sap from which **rubber** is made is collected from trees in a process called tapping.*

roy·al [roy-ul] *adjective.* **1.** having to do with a king or queen: *The princess is the youngest member of the royal family.* **2.** given by a king or queen or one of their family: *The execution was carried out by royal command.* **3.** fit for royalty; splendid: *They received royal treatment at the resort hotel.*

roy·al·ty [roy-ul-tee] *noun, plural* **royalties.** **1.** a member of a royal family, such as a king, queen, prince, or princess. **2.** the power and position that belongs to a royal person: *The Chrysanthemum Throne is the symbol of Japanese royalty.*

RSVP a abbreviation of the French phrase *répondez s'il vous plait,* which means "please reply." RSVP is commonly written at the bottom of invitations.

rub [rub] *verb,* **rubbed, rubbing. 1.** to press down while moving back and forth: *The straps of my bag are rubbing on my shoulders.* **2.** to apply something by pressing as you spread it: *He rubbed furniture polish on the table.* **3.** to press against something and move, or to press and move two things together: *The pony rubbed its neck against the fence post.*
noun, plural **rubs.** the act of rubbing: *Give the dirty mark on your shoe a rub with this cloth.*
• **rub it in.** to remind of something unpleasant: *I know I made a lot of spelling mistakes, you don't have to rub it in.*

rub·ber ▲ [rub-ur] *noun, plural* **rubbers. 1.** a stretchy, strong waterproof material used to make things like balls, tires, and rubber bands. Natural rubber is made from the sap of particular tropical trees. **2.** a waterproof overshoe made of rubber.

rubber band a loop made of very stretchy rubber or material like rubber that is used to hold objects together.

rub·bish [rub-ish] *noun.* **1.** useless leftover material; waste; trash: *Please put that rubbish out in the trash can.* **2.** silly or foolish talk; nonsense: *Don't talk rubbish.*

rub·ble [rub-ul] *noun.* rough, broken pieces of stone, brick, or concrete: *The building was demolished and all that was left was a pile of rubble.*

ru·by [roo-bee] *noun, plural* **rubies. 1.** a precious stone that is a deep red color. **2.** a dark red color. *adjective.* having the deep red color of a ruby.

rud·der [rud-ur] *noun, plural* **rudders. 1.** a flat, movable plate attached to the rear of a boat or ship in an upright position. It lies under the water and is moved to steer the vessel. A person or thing that loses direction is said to be **rudderless. 2.** a flat, upright plate at the rear of an airplane that is moved to steer it.

rud·dy [rud-ee] *adjective,* **ruddier, ruddiest.** having a healthy red color: *Being out in the cold wind and rain has given him ruddy cheeks.*

rude [rood] *adjective,* **ruder, rudest. 1.** bad-mannered; not polite: *That rude girl shouted out in class while the teacher was talking.* **2.** made roughly; simple: *The lost hikers made a rude shelter out of branches.*
—**rudely,** *adverb;* —**rudeness,** *noun.*

ruf·fle [ruf-ul] *verb,* **ruffled, ruffling. 1.** to spoil the evenness or calmness of: *The man ruffled his son's hair.* **2.** to annoy or upset: *His rude comment ruffled everyone's feelings.*
noun, plural **ruffles.** a strip of cloth, lace, or ribbon that is gathered on one side to make a frill: *This bedspread has a ruffle around the edge.*

rug [rug] *noun, plural* **rugs.** a piece of heavy material that covers only part of a floor and is not attached to it.

rug·by ▼ [rug-bee] *noun.* a football game in which each team attempts to score goals by touching an oval ball down behind the goal line of the opposing team or kicking it between their goal posts. The game has two forms with slightly different rules, **Rugby Union** and **Rugby League.**

> The game of **rugby** gets its name from *Rugby* School, a famous old school for boys in England. The students of Rugby often used to play football (soccer) on the school grounds. The story is told that one day, a boy named William Webb Ellis picked up the ball and began to run with it. This was the beginning of the game of rugby, since in soccer you cannot carry the ball in your hands, but in rugby you can.

*In **Rugby Union,** each team has fifteen players.*

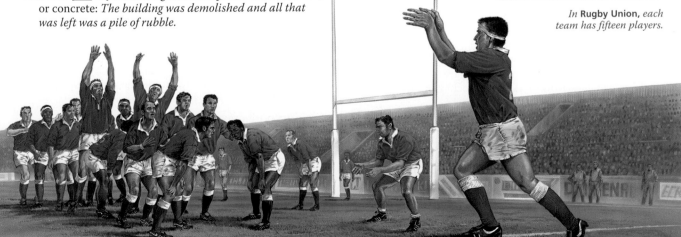

rug·ged [<u>rug</u>-id] *adjective.* **1.** rough, uneven, and difficult to travel over: *The rugged coastline is covered in boulders.* **2.** sturdily built and strong: *The rugged firefighter broke down the door to rescue us.* **3.** harsh and difficult to cope with: *Few people hike in the mountains in winter due to the rugged conditions.* —**ruggedly,** *adverb;* —**ruggedness,** *noun.*

ru·in ▲ [<u>roo</u>-in] *noun, plural* **ruins. 1.** a state of complete destruction or collapse: *The lighthouse's ruin was caused by a storm.* The remains of something that has been destroyed are called **ruins. 2.** something that is a cause of destruction or collapse: *Gambling will be the ruin of him.* *verb,* **ruined, ruining.** to destroy, make collapse, or cause irreversible harm : *Rain ruined the book I left outside.*

rule [rool] *noun, plural* **rules. 1.** an instruction that tells how one should act: *In our school it is against the rules to throw litter on the ground.* **2.** the control of a leader or government; authority: *Many people suffered under the rule of the cruel dictator.* **3.** something that is usual or typical: *As a rule, fish do not leave the water.* **4.** a flat instrument used for measuring; ruler: *The carpenter used her rule to measure the timber.*
verb, **ruled, ruling. 1.** to exercise power over; govern: *The king ruled his country sensibly and with kindness.* **2.** to make a decision: *The umpire ruled that the runner was safe.* **3.** to use a ruler to draw a straight line.
• **rule out.** to decide something is not possible; exclude: *Dad ruled out taking us to the beach as it was too windy.*

rul·er [<u>roo</u>-lur] *noun, plural* **rulers. 1.** a person who rules: *Benito Mussolini was ruler of Italy during World War II.* **2.** a long, flat, narrow tool with straight edges. Rulers are made of wood, plastic, or metal. They are marked along the side in measuring units such as inches and are used for measuring and drawing straight lines.

rum [rum] *noun, plural* **rums.** a strong alcoholic drink that is made from sugar cane or molasses.

rum·ble [<u>rum</u>-bul] *verb,* **rumbled, rumbling. 1.** to make a low, rolling sound: *The thunder rumbled, frightening the dog.* **2.** to move or travel making such a sound: *The freight train rumbled along the tracks.*
noun, plural **rumbles.** a low, rolling sound: *The rumble of my stomach could be heard in the quiet exam room.*

rum·mage [<u>rum</u>-ij] *verb,* **rummaged, rummaging.** to turn things over in an untidy way while searching thoroughly for something: *I rummaged through my drawers looking for two matching socks.* A **rummage sale** is a sale where a variety of goods are put on tables for people to search through.

ru·mor [<u>roo</u>-mur] *noun, plural* **rumors. 1.** information passed from person to person that has not been proved true: *There is a rumor going around school that the principal is leaving for another job.* **2.** general talk; hearsay: *Rumor has it that the dance is going to be cancelled.*
verb, **rumored, rumoring.** to spread or report by rumor: *It is rumored that the movie star has a new boyfriend.*

rump [rump] *noun, plural* **rumps. 1.** the part of an animal above its hind legs where they join onto the back. **2.** a cut of meat from this part of an animal, especially beef.

run [run] *verb,* **ran, run, running. 1.** to move the legs to go quickly over the ground or another surface; go faster than walking: *to run two miles for exercise; A cheetah can run very fast.* **2.** to do something by or as if by running: *to run a race; to run an errand; to run to the store for milk.* **3.** to take part in a contest: *to run for President of the U.S.* **4.** to experience something: *to run a fever; to run into trouble; to run out of money.* **5.** to be in charge of: *to run a large company.* **6.** of a color in clothing, to leak or spread out: *The blue shirt ran when I put it in with the white wash.* **7.** *Computers.* to operate a certain program on a computer.
✚The verb **run** is also used in many other ways to give the sense of something going or moving along in a way that is like a person running: *a bus that runs between downtown and the shopping mall; a play that ran on Broadway for two years; an engine that runs smoothly.*
noun, plural **runs. 1.** the act of moving the legs fast: *They took a run around the field to warm up before the game.* **2.** a place to run: *We like to bring Buster to the dog run at the park.* **3.** the fact of moving or going in a way that is like running: *a movie with a long run in the local theater; a pilot who works on the run between Boston and New York.* **4.** a series of experiences: *a run of bad luck.* **5.** in baseball, a score made by going all the way around the bases without being put out.

run·a·way [<u>run</u>-uh-*way*] *noun, plural* **runaways.** a person or animal that has escaped or run away.
adjective. having run away, escaped or lost control over: *The runaway truck hurtled off the road.*

run-down [<u>run</u>-*down*] *adjective.* **1.** in poor health; tired, weak, and sick: *He became run-down because he keeps staying up late.* **2.** in need of repair or cleaning: *The first thing that run-down barn needs is a new roof.*

rung¹ [rung] *verb.* the past participle of RING.

rung² [rung] *noun, plural* **rungs. 1.** one of the crossbars on a ladder that is used as a step. **2.** a crossbar between the legs or on the back of a chair.

run·ner [run-ur] *noun, plural* **runners. 1.** a person or animal that runs, especially in a race or to carry messages. **2.** a long, thin piece of metal or wood under a skate, sled, or drawer on which it slides. **3.** a long, narrow rug, carpet, or tablecloth. **4.** a thin stem that a plant sends out along the ground from which new roots form: *The strawberry plant sent out runners that soon grew into new plants.*

run·ner-up [run-ur-up] *noun, plural* **runners-up.** a player or team that finishes second in a competition.

running back an offensive player in football who carries the ball.

running mate a candidate from a political party who runs for an office at the same time as another member of the same party runs for a similar office. The running mate of the U.S. presidential candidate runs for the position of Vice President.

run·way ▼ [run-way] *noun, plural* **runways. 1.** a long, narrow strip of land that has been leveled and cleared so that airplanes can use it to take off and land. **2.** a narrow, raised strip that sticks out from a stage into the audience along which fashion models walk to show off clothes.

At large airports, runways often cross one another.

rup·ture [rup-chur] *verb,* **ruptured, rupturing.** to break open, burst, or cut off: *The old sewer pipe ruptured. noun, plural* **ruptures. 1.** the act of breaking or bursting open. **2.** a breaking of good relations or friendship.

ru·ral [rur-ul] *adjective.* having to do with farm areas or other places far away from large cities: *Having access to good health care can be a problem for people in rural communities.*

rush¹ [rush] *verb,* **rushed, rushing. 1.** to move quickly: *Water rushed in through the hole in the boat.* **2.** to do quickly; hurry: *We rushed to catch the ferry on time. noun, plural* **rushes. 1.** the act of rushing; a rapid, fast movement: *He opened the furnace and a rush of hot air hit his face.* **2.** a state of being busy or in a hurry: *I was in a rush to get to school. adjective.* needing to be done in a hurry: *The visitors will arrive soon, so we must do a rush job of cleaning the house.*

rush² ▶ [rush] *noun, plural* **rushes.** a plant with hollow stems with clusters of green or brown flowers along the upper ends.

Rus·sian [rush-un] *noun, plural* **Russians. 1.** a person born in or originating from the country of Russia. **2.** the language of Russia. *adjective.* having to do with Russia, its people, or its culture.

rust [rust] *noun, plural* **rusts. 1.** *Chemistry.* a reddish-brown coating that forms on iron or steel when it corrodes due to being wet and exposed to air. **2.** a plant disease caused by a fungus that causes reddish-brown spots on leaves and stems. **3.** a reddish-brown to orange color. *verb,* **rusted, rusting.** to become coated in rust; corrode: *The iron railing at the cliff top soon rusted in the sea air. adjective.* having the color of rust.

rus·tic [rus-tik] *adjective.* having to do with or like the countryside; rural: *The movie about the farming family had a rustic setting.*

rus·tle¹ [rus-ul] *verb,* **rustled, rustling.** to make or cause a soft, crackling sound: *Her silk skirts rustled as she walked. noun, plural* **rustles.** a soft, crackling sound made by things gently rubbing or bumping together: *The only sound in the forest was the rustle of the wind in the trees.*

rus·tle² [rus-ul] *verb,* **rustled, rustling.** to steal cattle or other livestock. A person who steals livestock is called a **rustler.**

rus·ty [rus-tee] *adjective,* **rustier, rustiest. 1.** coated in rust; corroded: *The rusty lump of metal that the archaeologist dug up had once been a Roman dagger.* **2.** caused or marked by rust: *The pin left rusty marks on the cloth.* **3.** reduced in ability due to lack of use: *She hasn't played tennis for a while, so her game is a bit rusty.*

rut [rut] *noun, plural* **ruts. 1.** a deep groove cut or worn into the ground, especially by wheels: *His motorbike left a deep rut in the muddy track.* **2.** a way of doing something that is so regular it becomes boring. *verb,* **rutted, rutting.** to create ruts in: *The constant passing of carts rutted the dirt track.* • **in a rut.** in a situation of doing something over and over in the same way: *She feels she is in a rut because she has done the same job for ten years.*

ruth·less [rooth-lis] *adjective.* without pity or mercy; cruel: *The ruthless landlord raised the old couple's rent by a thousand dollars a month.* —**ruthlessly,** *adverb;* —**ruthlessness,** *noun.*

rye [rye] *noun, plural* **ryes.** a grass grown as a cereal that is used to make whiskey and bread and as livestock feed. ◀)) A different word with the same sound is **wry.**

Rushes grow along river banks or in marshy areas.

S s

S, s *noun, plural* **S's, s's.** the nineteenth letter of the English alphabet.

Long ago, **saber-toothed tigers** *got stuck in tar pits and their bones were preserved.*

Sab·bath [sab-uth] *noun, plural* **Sabbaths.** *Religion.* the day of the week used for worship by members of various religious groups. Sunday is the Sabbath for most Christians. Saturday is the Sabbath for the Jewish religion.

sab·er [say-bur] *noun, plural* **sabers.** a heavy sword with a long, slightly curved blade that has one cutting edge. This word is also spelled **sabre.**

saber-toothed tiger ▲ a large tiger that lived a very long time ago. It had two long, curved teeth in its upper jaw.

sa·ble [say-bul] *noun, plural* **sables.** a small wild animal that looks like a weasel. It has soft, dark brown fur that is very valuable.

sab·o·tage [sab-uh-*tahzh*] *noun.* damage to machinery, buildings, or other property that is done on purpose in order to weaken an enemy or to interfere with some activity. Sabotage is used during a war or as a form of protest. A person who does this is a **saboteur.** *verb,* **sabotaged, sabotaging.** to carry out acts of sabotage: *To stop supplies reaching the town, enemy spies sabotaged the railway by blowing up the bridge.*

> The word **sabotage** is taken from *sabot,* a French word meaning " a wooden shoe." The first actions to be called sabotage occurred when French factory workers of the 1800s would throw their shoes into a machine to stop it from working.

sac [sak] *noun, plural* **sacs.** a small part of a plant or an animal that is shaped like a little bag. Sacs usually contain liquid.

🔊 A different word with the same sound is **sack.**

sack¹ [sak] *noun, plural* **sacks. 1.** a large bag made of strong woven material for storing and carrying goods: *a sack of potatoes.* **2.** in football, a play in which the quarterback is tackled behind the line of scrimmage as he is trying to pass the ball.
verb, **sacked, sacking. 1.** to dismiss from a job; fire: *The cashier was sacked for stealing from the cash register.* **2.** in football, to tackle the quarterback behind the line of scrimmage.

🔊 A different word with the same sound is **sac.**

sack² [sak] *verb,* **sacked, sacking.** to take away all the valuable things from a town or city captured in a war.
noun, plural **sacks.** the robbing of valuable things from a town or city that has been captured in a war.

🔊 A different word with the same sound is **sac.**

sa·cred [say-krid] *adjective.* **1.** believed to be holy and to have a special connection with God or a god; having to do with religion: *sacred music; a sacred temple.* **2.** worthy of respect; serious and important: *Putting flowers on her grandmother's grave was a sacred duty.*

sac·ri·fice [sak-ruh-fise] *noun, plural* **sacrifices. 1.** the religious ceremony of offering something valuable to God or a god, such as food or lives of animals or people, as an act of worship. **2.** the valuable thing offered: *The goat was killed as a sacrifice to the gods.* Something that has to do with a sacrifice is **sacrificial. 3.** the giving up of something valuable or important for the sake of someone or something else: *The family made many sacrifices to save the money for their daughter's college education.* **4.** in baseball, a bunt that advances a base runner, even though the batter is put out, or a fly ball that is caught for an out but allows a runner to score.
verb, **sacrificed, sacrificing. 1.** to make an offering to God or a god of something or someone: *The ancient Greeks sacrificed sheep to their gods.* **2.** to give up something valuable or important for the sake of someone else or something else: *Todd sacrificed his weekend trip to help his father paint the house.* **3.** in baseball, to advance a runner by making a sacrifice bunt or a sacrifice fly.

sac·ri·lege [sak-ruh-lij] *noun, plural* **sacrileges.** *Religion.* the act of treating a holy place without respect: *It would be a sacrilege to turn the old church into a pizza parlor.* **—sacrilegious,** *adjective.*

sad [sad] *adjective,* **sadder, saddest. 1.** not happy; feeling sorrow: *We were all sad when our team lost the championship game.* **2.** causing sorrow or unhappiness: *the sad news of the accident.* **—sadly,** *adverb;* **—sadness,** *noun.*

sad·den [sad-un] *verb,* **saddened, saddening.** to make sad: *The children were saddened by the death of their grandmother.*

sad·dle [sad-ul] *noun, plural* **saddles. 1.** a padded leather seat on the back of a horse or similar animal for the rider to sit on. **2.** a similar seat on a bicycle.
verb, **saddled, saddling. 1.** to put a saddle on a horse or other animal. **2.** to load or burden someone with difficulties, problems, or responsibilities: *Anne was saddled with feeding her neighbor's cats when he went on vacation.*

On **safaris,** the best time to spot wild animals is at dawn and dusk.

sa·fa·ri ▲ [suh-<u>fah</u>-ree] *noun,* *plural* **safaris.** a trip that involves camping in the wild, usually to look at wildlife and, in the past, to hunt it: *a safari in Africa.*

> The word **safari** comes from Swahili, a language spoken widely in Africa. In Swahili *safari* means "a journey" or "a trip."

safe [safe] *adjective,* **safer, safest. 1.** free from danger, injury, or risk: *We are safe now that the storm has stopped; The mother bear made a den for her cubs in a safe place.* **2.** with little risk of error: *It's safe to say that was one of the worst movies I've ever seen.* **3.** careful in avoiding danger: *a safe driver.* **4.** in baseball, reaching a base without being put out.
noun, *plural,* **safes.** a strong metal box with a special lock. It is used to store money, jewelry, and other valuable things. —**safely,** *adverb.*

safe·guard [safe-*gard*] *noun,* *plural* **safeguards.** something that protects someone or something from possible danger: *At the beach, the children put sunscreen on their skin as a safeguard against sunburn.*
verb, **safeguarded, safeguarding.** to protect or guard: *Painting metal safeguards it against rust.*

safe·ty [safe-tee] *noun.* freedom from danger, harm, or risk: *There was great relief when the little boat finally reached the safety of the harbor.*

safety belt a strong belt for attaching a person to an object to hold them in place or prevent them from falling. People who work in a high place, such as builders roofing houses, wear safety belts.

safety pin a metal pin that is bent back on itself to form a spring. It has a guard at one end to cover the point and is used for fastening things together.

sag [sag] *verb,* **sagged, sagging. 1.** to hang down or sink: *The branch sagged under the weight of the snow.* **2.** to become less firm or strong; weaken: *His spirits sagged when he saw how much work he still had to do.*
noun, *plural* **sags.** a shape that sinks down: *a sag in the middle of the old chair.*

sage¹ [sayj] *noun,* *plural* **sages.** a person who is very wise and knows a lot, usually because of age and experience: *The great patriot, scientist, and author Ben Franklin was known as the Sage of Philadelphia.*
adjective, **sager, sagest.** having or showing good judgment, usually as the result of knowledge and experience gained with age; wise: *The new mother received some sage advice from her grandmother.*

sage² ▶ [sayj] *noun.* a herb used in cooking to add flavor.

sage·brush [sayj-*brush*] *noun.* a bush with silver-green leaves and large clusters of small white or yellow flowers. Sagebrush grows on the dry plains of western North America.

sail [sale] *noun,* *plural* **sails. 1.** a sheet of canvas or other strong fabric, fastened to a mast so that it catches the wind and moves a boat through the water. **2.** something that looks or acts like a sail: *the sails of a windmill.* **3.** a trip in a sailing boat: *We are going for a sail next weekend.*
verb, **sailed, sailing. 1.** to move through water or be carried across the surface of water: *to sail down the Hudson River.* **2.** to manage a sailing boat: *My uncle is teaching me to sail.* **3.** to move quickly and smoothly; glide: *Clouds sailed by overhead.*
◀)) A different word with the same sound is **sale.**

sail·boat ◀ [sale-*boht*] *noun,* *plural* **sailboats.** a boat that is moved along by the wind blowing against its sail or sails. Sailboats are used mainly for racing and pleasure trips.

sail·ing [sale-ing] *noun.* the sport or activity of riding in or directing a sailboat.

sail·or [say-lur] *noun,* *plural* **sailors. 1.** a person whose job is sailing a boat or working on a boat as part of the crew. **2.** a person who is a member of the navy.

saint [saynt] *noun,* *plural* **saints. 1.** *Religion.* a person who is specially honored by certain Christian churches after they have died because their life was very good or holy. **2.** a person who is very kind, patient, and unselfish: *All the parents thought the kindergarten teacher was a saint.*
—**sainthood,** *noun;* —**saintly,** *adverb.*

Saint Bernard a large, powerful dog with thick fur, originally from Switzerland. Saint Bernards are very intelligent and in past times were used as rescue dogs for travelers lost in the mountains.

Sage has been used for thousands of years both in cooking and for medicinal purposes.

Narrow, fast **sailboats,** *called feluccas, are used on the Nile River and off the Mediterranean coast of Egypt.*

> The **Saint Bernard** dog gets its name from an area high in the Alps mountain range, the Great Saint Bernard Pass of Switzerland. Since ancient times this pass was a common route through the Alps, and Saint Bernard dogs were used there to rescue travelers who became lost in the snow.

sake¹ [sake] *noun,* *plural* **sakes. 1.** the advantage of something; a benefit or good: *My aunt joined an exercise program for the sake of her health.* **2.** a particular purpose or reason: *I think he likes arguing just for the sake of hearing his own voice.*

sa·ke² [sah-kee] *noun.* a Japanese wine made from rice.

sal·ad [sal-ud] *noun,* *plural* **salads.** a dish of raw or cooked vegetables, sometimes mixed with rice, pasta, eggs, meat, or fish, and usually served cold with a dressing.

a
b
c
d
e
f
g
h
i
j
k
l
m
n
o
p
q
r
s
t
u
v
w
x
y
z

salamander

Fire salamander

Tiger salamander

Four-toed salamander

Slimy salamander

There are many different kinds of **salamanders**.

sal·a·man·der ▲ [sal-uh-*man*-dur] *noun,* *plural* **salamanders**. a small animal that looks like a lizard. Salamanders are amphibians, which means that they can live on land and in water.

sa·la·mi [suh-*lahm*-ee] *noun, plural* **salamis**. a spicy cooked sausage that is usually sliced and eaten cold.

sal·a·ry [*sal*-ree *or* sal-uh-ree] *noun, plural* **salaries**. *Business*. the fixed amount of money that someone is paid for their job. It is paid at regular times, such as once every two weeks or twice a month.

> The word **salary** comes from the Latin word for "salt." In the time of the ancient Romans, salt was considered to be such a valuable substance that soldiers in the Roman army were paid money for the purpose of buying salt.

sale [sale] *noun, plural* **sales**. **1.** the act of exchanging goods or property for money; selling: *The farmer bought a new tractor after the sale of his crop.* **2.** the selling of something for less than it normally costs: *During the sale, all summer clothing in the store was priced at 20 percent off.* 🔊 A different word with the same sound is **sail**.

sa·lea·ble [*sale*-uh-bul] *adjective.* something that is easy to sell or suitable for being sold: *The tomatoes were old and no longer saleable.* This word is also spelled **salable**.

sales·man [*salez*-mun] *noun, plural* **salesmen**. a man whose job is to sell things.

sales·per·son [*salez*-pur-sun] *noun, plural* **salespersons**. a person whose job is to sell things: *Some department stores hire extra salespersons at Christmas.* A different word with the same meaning is **salespeople**.

sales·wom·an [*salez*-wum-un] *noun plural* **saleswomen**. a woman whose job is to sell things.

sa·line [*say*-leen] *adjective. Environment.* containing or consisting of salt. In some parts of the world, the clearing of land and too much irrigation is making the rivers and soil saline. The salt content of a substance is its **salinity**.

sa·li·va [suh-*lye*-vuh] *noun, plural* **salivas**. the watery liquid that is produced by glands in the mouth. Saliva keeps the mouth moist, helps the chewing and swallowing of food, and starts the process of digestion.

sal·mon ▶ [*sam*-un] *noun, plural* **salmon** *or* **salmons**. **1.** a large, silvery fish with pink flesh that is used for food. Salmon live most of their life in the ocean, but swim up rivers to lay their eggs. **2.** a yellowish-pink color. *adjective.* having a yellowish-pink color.

sal·sa [*sahl*-suh] *noun, plural* **salsas**. a spicy sauce made of tomatoes, onions, chili, and other spices, often used on Mexican food.

salt [sawlt] *noun, plural* **salts**. **1.** white crystals obtained from the earth and sea water. Salt is used in cooking to add flavor and to preserve foods. **2.** a chemical substance formed by combining an acid with a base. *adjective.* containing or preserved with salt: *salt pork.* *verb,* **salted, salting.** to flavor or preserve with salt: *She always salts her potatoes.*
• **salt away.** to save for future use: *to salt away money.*
• **take with a grain of salt.** having some doubt; not believing to be fully true or accurate: *He sometimes makes up stories, so whatever he tells you must be taken with a grain of salt.*

salt·wa·ter [*sawlt*-wawt-ur] *adjective.* having to do with or living in salt water: *a saltwater crocodile.* This word is also spelled **salt-water**.

salt·y [*sawlt*-ee] *adjective,* **saltier, saltiest.** containing or tasting of salt: *salty sea water.* —**saltiness,** *noun.*

sal·u·ta·tion [sal-yoo-*tay*-shun] *noun, plural* **salutations**. a greeting, especially at the start of a speech or letter: *He began his letter with the salutation, "Dear Sir."*

sa·lute [suh-*loot*] *verb,* **saluted, saluting.** to make a sign of respect by raising the right hand to the side of the forehead: *to salute the American flag.* *noun, plural* **salutes**. a military gesture of respect: *a 21-gun salute.*

> **Salute** comes from a Latin word meaning "good health" or "safety." The idea was that in saluting someone, you would be showing that you wished the other person to have good health.

sal·vage [*sal*-vij] *verb,* **salvaged, salvaging.** to save from being lost or destroyed: *When the canoe overturned, I managed to salvage my water bottle, but unfortunately my hat floated away.* *noun, plural* **salvages**. the saving of something from being lost or destroyed: *Many people helped in the salvage of books as rainwater poured in through the damaged roof of the library.*

Atlantic salmon travel more than 2,000 miles to return to their home river to lay eggs.

sal·va·tion [sal-<u>vay</u>-shun] *noun.* **1.** *Religion.* the act of saving someone from sin or delivering them from evil. The **Salvation Army** is a Christian organization that cares for the poor. **2.** anything that saves someone or something from harm or unpleasantness: *The team's salvation was Andrew, who headed in a goal in the last minute of the game.*

salve [sav] *noun, plural* **salves.** an oily substance for putting on a cut, burn, or other wound to soothe it and help the growth of new skin; ointment: *The hiker rubbed salve onto his cracked lips.*

same [same] *adjective.* **1.** just like another in some way: *My friend Jon and I have the same birthday.* **2.** having to do with only one thing, time, or place; not another or other: *This is the same cabin that we stayed in last year.* **3.** not changed or different: *Her smile is the same as ever.* *noun.* someone or something that is identical or very alike: *John climbed over the fence, so I did the same.* Things that are identical or very alike share a **sameness.**

sam·ple [sam-pul] *noun, plural* **samples.** a small part of something that shows what the whole thing is like: *She took home a sample of the fabric to see if it matched her carpet.* *verb,* **sampled, sampling.** to try or test something by taking a small piece: *I sampled several different ice creams before choosing this flavor.* *adjective.* having to do with a small amount that shows what a product is like: *The company gave away sample jars of the new sauce.*

sam·u·rai ▶ [sam-uh-<i>rye</i>] *noun, plural* **samurais.** a Japanese warrior in medieval times.

sanc·tion [sangk-shun] *verb,* **sanctioned, sanctioning.** to agree to something; approve; allow: *The teacher sanctioned the class's choice of music for the school concert.* *noun, plural* **sanctions. 1.** the act or fact of approval or permission: *The mayor gave her sanction to the parade.* **2. sanctions.** actions, such as the stopping of trade, taken by some countries to punish another country for failing to follow international law or for some other unacceptable action.

sanc·tu·ar·y [sangk-choo-er-ee] *noun, plural* **sanctuaries. 1.** protection given to someone running away from danger or cruel treatment: *The escaped slaves were given sanctuary in the church.* **2.** a holy place. **3.** a natural area for birds and animals where they cannot be hunted.

sand [sand] *noun.* tiny, loose grains of rocks that have been worn down by wind and water. Sand is found in deserts and on beaches. *verb,* **sanded, sanding. 1.** to smooth by rubbing with sandpaper or sand: *to sand a wall before painting it.* **2.** to sprinkle with sand: *The city sanded the highway after the oil spill.*

Only **samurai** *were allowed to carry swords, and wealthy landlords hired them to protect their property.*

sand·al [<u>san</u>-dul] *noun, plural,* **sandals.** a light shoe with a sole that is held to the foot by one or more straps.

sand·bag [<u>sand</u>-*bag*] *noun, plural,* **sandbags.** a bag filled with sand or soil and used to form a wall for protection against rising floodwaters or explosions. *verb,* **sandbagged, sandbagging. 1.** to put sandbags around or along: *to sandbag a river bank to stop floodwater entering the town.* **2.** to force someone roughly to do something: *They sandbagged him into doing their share of the cleaning up.*

sand·bar ▲ [<u>sand</u>-*bar*] *noun, plural* **sandbars.** a ridge of sand in a river, a bay, or along the shore, formed by the actions of waves and currents.

sand·box [<u>sand</u>-*box*] *noun, plural* **sandboxes.** a box filled with sand, especially for children to play in.

sand·pa·per [<u>sand</u>-*pay*-pur] *noun.* strong paper coated with a layer of sand on one side and used for smoothing and cleaning wood and similar rough surfaces. *verb,* **sandpapered, sandpapering.** to rub with sandpaper to make smooth and clean: *Dad sandpapered the old varnish off the chair.*

sand·pi·per [<u>sand</u>-*pye*-pur] *noun, plural* **sandpipers.** a small bird with long legs and a long, thin bill that wades in water in search of food.

sand·stone ▼ [<u>sand</u>-*stone*] *noun.* a type of rock made from grains of sand that have been pressed together over a very long time until solid.

Iron-rich water trickled through the porous white **sandstone** *of the Colorado Plateau to create these dramatic colored bands in the cliffs.*

a b c d e f g h i j k l m n o p q r **s** t u v w x y z

A B C D E F G H I J K L M N O P Q R S T U V W X Y Z

sand·wich [sand-wich] *noun, plural* **sandwiches**. two slices of bread with a filling of other food between them: *a cheese sandwich*.
verb, **sandwiched, sandwiching**. to put or squeeze something between two other things: *The ancient church is sandwiched between two huge modern buildings*.

In England in the 1700s, the Earl of *Sandwich* was known for his love of gambling and it was said that he would spend an entire day and night at the card table without once getting up to eat. He is supposed to have invented the **sandwich** so that he could eat right at the table and keep playing.

sand·y [san-dee] *adjective*. **1.** containing or covered with sand: *sandy soil; a sandy beach*. **2.** yellowish-brown in color: *sandy hair*.

sane [sane] *adjective*, **saner, sanest**. **1.** having a normal and healthy mind. **2.** showing or based on good sense and judgment; sensible: *a sane decision; The sane thing would be to wait until it stops raining before walking home*.

sang [sang] *verb*. the past tense of SING.

san·i·ta·ry [san-uh-ter-ee] *adjective. Health*. **1.** having to do with cleanliness or care in preventing disease: *sanitary procedures in a hospital*. **2.** free from dirt and germs: *sanitary areas for preparing food*.

san·i·ta·tion [san-uh-tay-shun] *noun. Health*. the act of keeping a place clean and healthy and free from dirt and germs, especially by the removal of rubbish and waste: *Poor sanitation can cause the spread of disease*.

san·i·ty [san-uh-tee] *noun*. the state of being normal and healthy in the mind.

sank [sangk] *verb*. the past tense of SINK.

San·ta Claus a figure who is associated with the Christmas holiday, thought of as a jolly old man with a long, white beard and a red suit who lives at the North Pole and brings gifts to children on Christmas Eve.

sap[1] [sap] *noun, plural* **saps**. the liquid inside a plant that carries water and food through the plant: *The milky sap of certain tropical trees is collected to make rubber*.

sap[2] [sap] *verb*, **sapped, sapping**. to slowly weaken or destroy over a long period of time: *The explorers returned exhausted, their strength sapped by days of trudging through snow and ice*.

sap·ling ◀ [sap-ling] *noun, plural* **saplings**. a young tree: *Those rows of thin saplings will one day be a leafy avenue*.

sap·phire ▶ [saf-ire] *noun, plural* **sapphires**. a clear blue stone used as a gem. *adjective*. having a clear blue color.

sar·cas·tic [sar-kas-tik] *adjective*. relating to the use of words in a harsh and bitter way so they say the opposite to their meaning in order to mock or insult someone: *"How nice to see you here,"* she sneered in a sarcastic way. The fact or act of saying of harsh and insulting things in this way is **sarcasm**.
—**sarcastically**, *adverb*.

The word **sarcastic** goes back to a term meaning "to bite or tear at something with the teeth." The idea is that when someone makes a bitter, sarcastic remark, this can cut or wound a person's feelings in a way that is like biting the person.

sar·dine ▶ [sar-deen] *noun, plural* **sardines**. a small sea fish that is eaten as food. Sardines are often cooked in oil and packed closely together in flat cans.
• **like sardines**. standing or sitting so close together that it is not possible to move easily: *We were all squeezed onto the bus like sardines*.

Sardines are found in most of the world's oceans.

sa·ri [sah-ree] *noun, plural* **saris**. a piece of clothing that is worn especially by women in India and Pakistan. A sari consists of a long rectangle of thin material that is wrapped around the body to form a skirt, with one end covering one shoulder or the head.

sar·ong ◀ [suh-rong] *noun, plural* **sarongs**. a piece of clothing worn especially by men and women in Southeast Asia. A sarong consists of a rectangle of material that is wrapped around the waist to form a skirt, or around the whole body under the armpits, like a dress.

*Traditional dancers from the Indonesian island of Bali wear colorful **sarongs**.*

sash[1] [sash] *noun, plural* **sashes**. **1.** a broad strip of cloth that is worn around the waist: *Becky's dress had a sash that tied in a bow at the back*. **2.** a strip of cloth that is worn over one shoulder as part of a special uniform.

sash[2] [sash] *noun, plural* **sashes**. the frame that holds the glass in a window or door.

Sa·tan [say-tun] *noun. Religion*. the chief spirit of evil opposed to God; the devil.

*While a tree is a **sapling** it can be dug up and planted in a new place.*

sat·el·lite [sat-uh-*lite*] *noun, plural* **satellites. 1.** any body in space, such as the Moon, that moves in an orbit around another, larger, body, such as a planet. **2.** a spacecraft that moves in an orbit around the Earth, the Moon, or other bodies in space. These satellites are used for gathering information about conditions in space or to help forecast weather, and to connect radio, television, and other communications systems.

satellite dish ▶ a dish-shaped antenna used to receive television signals from a satellite.

sat·in [sat-un] *noun, plural* **satins.** a type of cloth that is smooth and shiny on the front and dull on the back. Satin is made of silk or similar materials such as rayon.

sat·ire [sat-ire] *noun, plural* **satires.** *Literature.* **1.** the use of mocking or exaggerated humor to make fun of foolish or bad people or things. **2.** a novel, poem, play, film, or television show written in this style. Someone who writes or creates a satire is a **satirist.** Something that is done in this style is **satirical.**

Satire is writing that makes fun of a person or group, especially someone who is important, famous, or powerful. The English author George Orwell wrote a very famous satire called *Animal Farm*, in which he made fun of the Soviet Union, a very powerful country at that time. In his satire, the Soviets were talking animals who took over a farm and drove away the farmer and his wife.

sat·is·fac·tion [sat-is-*fak*-shun] *noun, plural* **satisfactions.** a feeling of happiness or pleasure: *Uncle Bill gets great satisfaction from growing vegetables for the family.*

sat·is·fac·to·ry [sat-is-*fak*-tree *or* sat-is-*fak*-tuh-ree] *adjective.* good enough for a particular purpose or to meet a particular standard: *Will a blue shirt be satisfactory to wear to the concert, or do I need to wear white?* —**satisfactorily,** *adverb.*

sat·is·fy [sat-is-fye] *verb,* **satisfied, satisfying. 1.** to be enough of what is wanted or needed to make someone or something pleased or contented: *The kitten lapped at the milk to satisfy its thirst, then curled up and went to sleep.* **2.** to persuade completely; convince: *He satisfied the police that he was telling the truth.*

sat·u·rate [sach-uh-*rate*] *verb,* **saturated, saturating. 1.** to wet all the way through: *Rain water poured in the open window and saturated the drapes.* Something that is wet all the way through is **saturated.** —**saturation,** *noun.*

Sat·ur·day [sat-ur-*day or* sat-ur-dee] *noun, plural* **Saturdays.** the seventh day of the week.

Sat·urn ▶ [sat-urn] *noun.* **1.** the second largest planet in the solar system and the sixth in order of distance away from the Sun. Saturn is surrounded by a number of thin, flat rings of ice and has more than twenty moons. **2.** the Roman god of farming.

sauce [saws] *noun, plural* **sauces. 1.** a tasty liquid served with food: *chocolate sauce; tomato sauce; soy sauce.* **2.** a food made from fruits cooked slowly in a liquid: *cranberry sauce.* A **saucepan** is a pot with a handle used for cooking. *verb,* **sauced, saucing.** to add flavor to by serving with a sauce.

sau·cer [saw-sur] *noun, plural* **saucers.** a small, shallow dish for putting under a cup.

sauc·y [saw-see] *adjective,* **saucier, sauciest.** rude or impudent in an amusing or harmless way: *His grandmother told him to answer politely instead of being saucy.*

Sau·di [sow-dee *or* saw-dee] *noun, plural* **Saudis.** a person who was born in or is a citizen of the southwest Asian country of Saudi Arabia. *adjective.* of or having to do with Saudi Arabia, its people, or its culture.

sau·na [saw-nuh] *noun, plural* **saunas.** a room or bath house for getting clean by taking a steam bath. The steam is made by pouring water over hot stones.

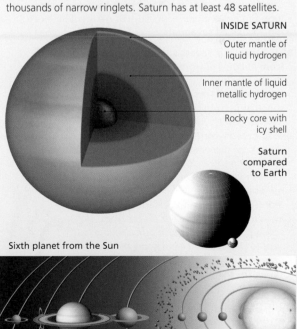

SATURN

More than nine times the size of the Earth, Saturn is made up mainly of the gases hydrogen and helium. It spins very quickly on its axis, is surrounded by bands of clouds, and has a yellowish color. The planet is encircled by seven main rings composed of icy particles and stretching out in a paper-thin disk for thousands of miles. These rings are subdivided into many thousands of narrow ringlets. Saturn has at least 48 satellites.

INSIDE SATURN

Outer mantle of liquid hydrogen

Inner mantle of liquid metallic hydrogen

Rocky core with icy shell

Saturn compared to Earth

Sixth planet from the Sun

A B C D E F G H I J K L M N O P Q R S T U V W X Y Z

saun·ter [sawn-tur] *verb,* **sauntered, sauntering.** to walk along in a slow, leisurely way; stroll: *Donna looked at the window displays as she sauntered past the shops.*

sau·sage [saw-sij] *noun, plural* **sausages.** finely ground meat mixed with spices and usually packed into a thin tube. Frankfurters are a type of sausage.

sav·age [sav-ij] *adjective.* **1.** being wild or untamed: *The sheep were mauled by a savage dog.* **2.** describing something cruel or ferocious: *The man was taken to the hospital after the savage attack.* An act of **savagery** is an act of great cruelty and violence. **3.** describing something thought of as uncivilized; primitive: *a savage tribe living deep in the jungle.*
noun, plural **savages. 1.** a person who is cruel or brutal. **2.** a person who is uncivilized or primitive.
—savagely, *adverb.*

sa·van·na ▲ [suh-van-uh] *noun, plural* **savannas.** *Environment.* a flat grassland with scattered trees, found in hot regions, especially in Africa. This word is also spelled **savannah.**

save [save] *verb,* **saved, saving. 1.** to rescue or guard from harm: *The woman dived in to save the girl from drowning.* **2.** to keep something, especially money, for future use: *We're saving to buy a new car.* **3.** to prevent something from being lost, spent, wasted, or damaged: *Save electricity by remembering to turn off the lights.* **4.** to preserve or copy a computer file onto a hard drive or disk for use or storage: *Don't forget to save your work every ten minutes.* **5.** to make unnecessary; avoid: *Thanks for helping bring in the groceries—it saved me an extra trip.*
noun, plural **saves.** in certain sports, an act that stops another player from scoring: *The goalkeeper made a diving save to stop the ball from going in the net.*
preposition. excluding or leaving out; except: *When the boat sank, all the sailors were lost save one.*

sav·ings [save-ingz] *plural noun.* money that is saved: *Steve used all his savings to buy a fancy new cell phone.* A **savings bank** is a financial organization that keeps people's money, or savings, in accounts.

sav·ior [save-yur] *noun, plural* **saviors.** a person who saves or rescues. In the Christian religion, the **Savior** or **Our Savior** refers to Jesus Christ.

sav·or [save-ur] *verb,* **savored, savoring.** to taste or smell something with pleasure; relish: *Patricia savored every mouthful of the chocolate cake.* Food that is **savory** has a delicious taste or smell, and is very appetizing.

saw¹ [saw] *verb.* the past tense of SEE.

saw² [saw] *noun, plural* **saws.** a hand tool or machine with a blade of sharp metal teeth. It is used to cut hard material such as wood or metal.
verb, **sawed, sawing.** to cut with a saw: *Dad sawed the dead tree into pieces for firewood.*

saw·dust [saw-dust] *noun.* the fine particles of wood that a saw makes when cutting wood.

saw·mill [saw-mil] *noun, plural* **sawmills.** a place where machines saw logs into planks and boards.

sax·o·phone ▼ [sak-suh-fone] *noun, plural* **saxophones.** *Music.* a musical instrument with a curved brass body and finger keys. A person blows through the reed mouthpiece and presses down the keys to produce notes. A shortened form of this word is **sax.**

The **saxophone** is named for the man who invented it. Adolphe *Sax* was a Belgian musician living in Paris, France in the mid 1800s.

say [say] *verb,* **said, saying. 1.** to speak or utter words: *My baby sister says "Mama" and "Dada."* **2.** to express an opinion in words; state or declare: *Mario said that the movie was really boring.* **3.** to judge to be true; suppose or assume: *But say you're right—what will we do then?* **4.** to repeat something from memory; recite: *We say grace before a meal.*
noun. **1.** a turn or chance to speak: *You've already had your say–Let someone else speak now.* **2.** the power or right to decide or to influence a decision: *Everyone in the class has a say in who the class representative will be.*

*The **saxophone** is often played in jazz bands.*

say·ing [say-ing] *noun, plural* **sayings.** a wise or common sense statement that is said often; proverb. *Don't judge a book by its cover* is a saying.

sa·yo·na·ra [*sah*-yuh-*nar*-uh] *interjection.* a Japanese word meaning "good-bye."

scab [skab] *noun, plural* **scabs. 1.** a crust of dried blood and serum that forms over a wound while it heals. **2.** an informal word for a person who works for a company while other workers are on strike or who replaces a striking worker; a strikebreaker.

Scabbards *were usually attached to belts and were often highly decorated.*

scab·bard ▲ [skab-urd] *noun, plural* **scabbards.** a protective holder for the blade of a dagger, sword, or bayonet; a sheath.

scaf·fold [skaf-uld] *noun, plural* **scaffolds.** a temporary or movable platform that workers stand on so they can work on buildings above the ground. A system of scaffolds, and the materials used to make scaffolds, is **scaffolding.**

scale¹ ▼ [skale] *noun, plural* **scales.** a weighing machine. It works by balancing the object being weighed against another weight, or against the force of a spring.

scale² ▶ [skale] *noun, plural* **scales. 1.** one of the thin, flat plates that form the outer covering of fish, snakes, and lizards. **2.** any small, thin, flat piece of something that has flaked or peeled off a surface: *scales of dandruff.* *verb,* **scaled, scaling.** to remove the scales from: *Dad scaled and cleaned the fish we'd caught before he cooked it.*

scale³ [skale] *noun, plural* **scales. 1.** a set of regularly spaced marks along a line, used for measuring things: *The temperature hit 105 degrees on the Fahrenheit scale.* **2.** the size of a picture, plan, map, or model in relation to the size of the thing itself: *Jeff built his model fighter jet on a scale of 1:72.* **3.** size or extent, compared with something else: *Our new two-story house is on a bigger scale than our old one-story house.* **4.** *Music.* a series of notes that go up or down in fixed intervals of pitch: *Every day, Debbie practiced playing scales on her clarinet.* *verb,* **scaled, scaling. 1.** to climb up or over: *The rock climber scaled the cliff.* **2.** to adjust by a set amount or a standard: *The computer company is scaling back its offer of free upgrades.*

sca·lene triangle [skay-leen] *Mathematics.* a triangle with sides that are different lengths.

scal·lion [skal-yun] *noun, plural* **scallions.** a young onion that is pulled from the ground before the white bulb has grown large.

scal·lop [skal-up] *noun, plural* **scallops. 1.** a shellfish that has a soft body inside two fan-shaped shells with wavy edges, which open and close. It is a mollusk, and the soft body is eaten as food. **2.** one of a series of wavy curves like the edge of a scallop shell: *She used a knife to decorate the pie crust with scallops.* *verb,* **scalloped, scalloping.** to edge, shape, or make with a series of wavy curves: *The sleeves and hem of the dress were scalloped.*

scalp [skalp] *noun, plural* **scalps.** the skin on the head that is usually covered with hair. *verb,* **scalped, scalping.** to cut or pull the scalp from a person's head.

scal·pel [skal-pul] *noun, plural* **scalpels.** *Medicine.* a small, straight knife with a very thin, sharp blade, used especially by surgeons in operations.

scal·y [skay-lee] *adjective,* **scalier, scaliest.** covered with or made of scales: *The snakeskin felt scaly.*

scam·per [skam-pur] *verb,* **scampered, scampering.** to run away quickly and playfully: *The kittens scampered off into the garden.*

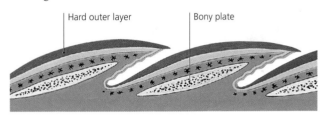

Hard outer layer   Bony plate

The **scales** *of some reptiles have a hard outer layer and a bony inner plate.*

scan [skan] *verb,* **scanned, scanning. 1.** to look at carefully: *He scanned the park for his friends.* **2.** to look or read over quickly: *I scanned the library book to see if it had the information I needed.* *noun, plural* **scans.** a single sweep of a beam of light over something, such as a page in a book, in order to store the information digitally in a computer.

scan·dal [skan-dul] *noun, plural* **scandals. 1.** a disgraceful event; an incident, person, or thing that outrages or offends a society's morality: *The police officers had to resign because of the drug scandal.* A **scandalous** event is one that is disgraceful or shocking. **2.** gossip or talk that harms a person's reputation: *The magazine is full of scandal about famous people.*

Scan·di·na·vi·an [skan-duh-nay-vee-un] *noun, plural* **Scandinavians.** a person who was born in or is a citizen of one of the countries of Scandinavia. These countries are Denmark, Norway, and Sweden; Finland and Iceland are usually also included. *adjective.* of or having to do with Scandinavia, its people, or its languages.

scan·ner [skan-ur] *noun, plural* **scanners.** *Computers.* an electronic device that scans pages of text or images and stores the information digitally on a computer.

This fifteenth-century **scale** *measured moisture in the air by weighing different substances.*

a b c d e f g h i j k l m n o p q r **s** t u v w x y z

*The Andean condor is a South American **scavenger** that feeds on dead llamas and sheep.*

scant [skant] *adjective,* **scanter, scantest. 1.** barely enough; very little: *She paid scant attention in history class because she didn't like the subject.* **2.** a little less than a specific measure; not quite full: *Add a scant cup of milk and mix with the other ingredients.*

scant·y [skan-tee] *adjective,* **scantier, scantiest.** barely enough; meager or not adequate: *Patty's bikini is very scanty.* —**scantily,** *adverb.*

scape·goat [skape-gote] *noun, plural* **scapegoats.** a person or thing that is blamed for something that someone else has done: *Donnie didn't start the fight, but the teachers made him the scapegoat for it and suspended him from school.*

> In ancient times it was believed that when God or the gods became angry with people, certain actions could ease or take away this anger. A **scapegoat** was a goat that was specially chosen to be sent away into the wilderness, with the thought that the peoples' sins would go along with it. From this came the idea that a scapegoat takes the blame for wrongs done by others.

scar [skar] *noun, plural* **scars. 1.** a mark left on the skin after a wound has healed: *I got this scar on my chin when I fell off my bike and cut my chin open.* **2.** a mark or sign of damage or injury: *The bombed-out roads and buildings showed the scars of war.* *verb,* **scarred, scarring.** to mark with or form a scar: *The burns scarred her right arm.*

scarce [skares] *adjective,* **scarcer, scarcest.** difficult to find or obtain; rare: *Feed for the cattle was scarce during the drought.* A **scarcity** of water is the fact of water being difficult to find or obtain.

scarce·ly [skares-lee] *adverb.* **1.** only just or barely; almost not or hardly: *We could scarcely believe it when we won tickets to Disneyland.* **2.** certainly not: *I'd scarcely call him a liar to his face.*

scare [skare] *verb,* **scared, scaring.** to frighten or become frightened: *The horror movie really scared Barbara.* *noun, plural* **scares. 1.** a sudden fright: *My brother gave me a scare when he ran out in front of the car.* **2.** a general state of fear and alarm; panic: *The police closed the subway because of a bomb scare.*

scare·crow ▶ [skare-kroh] *noun, plural* **scarecrows.** a figure that is dressed in old clothes to look like a person. It is put up in fields to scare crows and other birds away from crops that are growing there.

scarf [scarf] *noun, plural* **scarves** or **scarfs.** a piece of fabric worn around the neck, shoulders, or head for warmth or decoration.

scar·let [skar-lit] *noun, plural* **scarlets.** a bright red color. *adjective.* having a bright red color: *Ripe tomatoes are scarlet.*

scarlet fever *Medicine.* a very infectious disease that causes a red rash and a high fever. It occurs mostly in children.

scar·y [skare-ee] *adjective,* **scarier, scariest.** causing fear or alarm; frightening: *It's somewhat scary to have to make a speech in front of the whole school.*

scat·ter [skat-ur] *verb,* **scattered, scattering. 1.** to throw or spread about loosely: *We scattered bits of bread for the birds to eat.* **2.** to separate or drive away in different directions: *As soon as the treasure hunt started, the children scattered throughout the park.* If **scattered** showers are forecast, showers will be spread out and not occur close together.

scav·enge [skav-inj] *verb,* **scavenged, scavenging.** to search through discarded material for useful things: *The man scavenged through the trash cans for bottles and cans to recycle.*

scav·en·ger ▲ [skav-inj-ur] *noun, plural* **scavengers. 1.** *Biology.* an animal that feeds on decaying animal carcasses or plants, or on trash. Hyenas and vultures are scavengers. **2.** a person who searches through discarded material for useful things. A **scavenger hunt** is a game where teams of players are given a list of unusual objects and must try to obtain them within a time limit.

sce·nar·i·o [suh-nare-ee-oh or suh-nah-ree-oh] *noun, plural* **scenarios.** *Literature.* a plot outline of a play, screenplay, or book: *The director went through the scenario with the lead actors.*

scene [seen] *noun, plural* **scenes. 1.** the place where an event or action happens: *The police roped off the crime scene.* **2.** a section of an act in a play or movie. **3.** a view or sight: *The lake at sunset made a peaceful scene.* **4.** an outburst of anger or strong feeling in front of other people: *My little sister made a scene at the supermarket because Dad wouldn't buy her some candy.*

scen·er·y [seen-ree or see-nur-ee] *noun, plural* **sceneries. 1.** the look of a place; the landscape and natural features of an area: *The mountain scenery in the Rockies is spectacular.* **2.** the painted scenes, backdrops, and hangings on a theater stage that show where a scene takes place: *We all helped paint the scenery for the school play.*

scen·ic [see-nik] *adjective.* having to do with beautiful natural scenery: *Aunt Tina always takes the scenic ocean route, by way of Big Sur, to get to San Francisco.*

*For hundreds of years, **scarecrows** have been a traditional feature of the rural landscape.*

scent [sent] *noun, plural* **scents. 1.** a smell, usually pleasant: *The scent of honeysuckle filled the air.* **2.** the distinctive smell left by a passing animal or person, which another animal can follow: *The dogs lost the scent of the escaped prisoner around the river.* **3.** the sense of smell: *My dog used her keen scent and soon found the treat I'd hidden.* **4.** a perfume: *We gave Grandma a bottle of scent for her birthday.*
verb, **scented, scenting.** to detect or notice by or as if by the sense of smell.
🔊 Different words with the same sound are **sent** and **cent.**

sched·ule [skej-ool *or* skej-ul] *noun, plural* **schedules. 1.** a list of times, events, or appointments: *Check the schedule to see what time the train leaves.* **2.** a plan for carrying out a project, which sets out the order and time of each element: *The new highway was finished ahead of schedule.* A **scheduler** is a person who prepares schedules.
verb, **scheduled, scheduling.** to include in a schedule; plan or organize for a certain time or date: *The coach scheduled an extra practice session for Friday afternoon.*

scheme [skeem] *noun, plural* **schemes. 1.** a plan of action; an idea: *Jess has a scheme to raise enough money to buy a digital camera.* A **schemer** is a person who plans and plots. **2.** a secret plan to do something wrong: *a scheme to rob a bank.* **3.** a system of related things or parts; design: *The new transport scheme will include buses, trains, and trams.*
verb, **schemed, scheming.** to make a secret plan or plot: *They schemed to get their revenge.*

schol·ar [skol-ur] *noun, plural* **scholars. 1.** a person who goes to school; a student or pupil. **2.** a person with a great deal of knowledge. A **scholarly** book is a book that contains a great deal of learning and knowledge.

schol·ar·ship [skol-ur-ship] *noun, plural* **scholarships.** *Education.* **1.** money that is awarded to a student to help pay for his or her education: *She won a scholarship to go to Harvard University.* **2.** knowledge, learning, or detailed study: *The scientist's area of scholarship was the feeding habits of polar bears.*

scho·las·tic [skuh-las-tik] *adjective.* having to do with schools and scholars; academic.

school¹ [skool] *noun, plural* **schools. 1.** a place for teaching and learning: *I go to elementary school.* A **schoolbook** is a textbook or other book used at school. A **schoolteacher** is a person who teaches at a school. **2.** the students, teachers, and other people who work at a school: *Mr. Jackson, the music teacher, is popular with the whole school.* **3.** a session or period of school: *She had to stay late after school today.* **4.** a division of a college or university that teaches a particular subject: *a school of medicine.*
verb, **schooled, schooling.** to train or teach: *Our dog has been schooled in obedience.*

school² ▲ [skool] *noun, plural* **schools.** a large number of fish or other water animals swimming together in a group.

school·house [skool-*hous*] *noun, plural* **schoolhouses.** a school building; often a rural elementary school.

school·work [skool-*wurk*] *noun.* work done by a student, either in class, or for homework.

schoon·er [skoo-nur] *noun, plural* **schooners.** a fast sailing ship with two or more masts and sails that are set lengthwise.

sci·ence ▼ [sye-uns] *noun, plural* **sciences. 1.** knowledge about the physical world that has been examined, tested, and proven to be factual. **2.** any branch of such knowledge; biology, chemistry, physics, and astronomy are some examples. **3.** something that is treated like a science, as if it were a topic for serious study: *the science of cooking; the science of clothing design.*

In **science** there is a common saying, "Publish or perish" (be ruined). This means that for scientists to do well and advance in their career, they must often publish their writing in various ways. There are three common forms of science writing. Scientists write for journals in which they publish the results of their research. They also write books themselves, or edit books in which the writings of other scientists are collected. Finally, they write or edit textbooks for science students.

*The modern **science** of oceanography began in 1872, when an expedition left England to study ocean features on board the* Challenger, *the first ship to have its own fully equipped laboratories.*

a b c d e f g h i j k l m n o p q r s t u v w x y z

A B C D E F G H I J K L M N O P Q R **S** T U V W X Y Z

science fiction *Literature.* a type of story based on imagined developments in science. It is usually set in the future and often involves contact with other worlds: *The "Star Wars" movies introduced science fiction to many young people.*

sci·en·tif·ic [sye-un-<u>tif</u>-ik] *adjective.* having to do with science, or using the methods or rules of science: *Scientific research has produced many life-saving medicines.* —**scientifically,** *adverb.*

scientific method the process of finding out information using the methods and rules of science, such as collecting information through observation and experiment, and then testing the result.

sci·en·tist [<u>sye</u>-un-tist] *noun, plural* **scientists.** someone who is trained to work in a branch of science. Biologists, chemists, physicists, and astronomers are scientists.

scis·sors [<u>siz</u>-urz] *plural noun.* an instrument for cutting that is made of two sharp blades connected in the middle. The blades slide past each other and form a double cutting edge.

scold [skold] *verb,* **scolded, scolding.** to criticize angrily or speak harshly to someone: *Margaret's mother scolded her when she arrived home covered in mud. noun, plural* **scolds.** a person who is always scolding.

scoop [skoop] *noun, plural* **scoops. 1.** a tool shaped like a shallow bowl with a handle, used to pick up substances such as flour, sugar, ice cream, or sand. **2.** an exclusive news story that is reported by a media organization before their rivals know about it: *The magazine featured a scoop about the two famous movie stars getting married. verb,* **scooped, scooping. 1.** to pick something up with a scoop, or a scoop-like action: *John scooped up the sugar he had spilled on the floor.* **2.** to be the first media organization to report an exclusive news story.

scoot·er ▲ [<u>skoo</u>-tur] *noun, plural* **scooters. 1.** a child's vehicle that has handlebars on a long rod that is attached to a flat board on which the rider stands. It is propelled by pushing against the ground with one foot. **2.** a light motorcycle with small wheels and a flat plate to support the rider's feet.

scope [skope] *noun.* **1.** the range or extent of an idea, activity, or subject: *What the suspect was doing last year is beyond the scope of this investigation.* **2.** the shortened form of words such as *microscope, telescope,* or *periscope.*

scorch [skorch] *verb,* **scorched, scorching. 1.** to lightly burn the surface of something: *The iron was too hot and I scorched the collar of my shirt.* **2.** to dry up with heat: *The delicate leaves of the ferns will scorch in direct sunlight. noun, plural* **scorches.** a burn mark or slight burn.

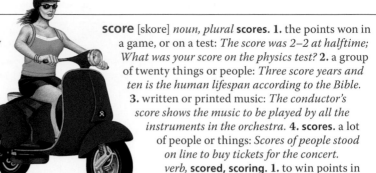

Scooters became a popular form of transport after World War II, when they were used by the U.S. military.

score [skore] *noun, plural* **scores. 1.** the points won in a game, or on a test: *The score was 2–2 at halftime; What was your score on the physics test?* **2.** a group of twenty things or people: *Three score years and ten is the human lifespan according to the Bible.* **3.** written or printed music: *The conductor's score shows the music to be played by all the instruments in the orchestra.* **4. scores.** a lot of people or things: *Scores of people stood on line to buy tickets for the concert. verb,* **scored, scoring. 1.** to win points in a game, or on a test: *Our team scored fifty points in the first half.* Someone who keeps a record of scores in a game is a **scorer. 2.** to cut lines or make small marks along a surface.

scorn [skorn] *noun.* a feeling or show of contempt or dislike; a lack of respect. *verb,* **scorned, scorning.** to treat with scorn: *Many people scorn the idea of cosmetic surgery.*

scorn·ful [<u>skorn</u>-ful] *adjective.* feeling or showing scorn: *My friend was scornful of my attempts at drawing.* —**scornfully,** *adverb.*

scor·pi·on ▼ [<u>skore</u>-pee-un] *noun, plural* **scorpions.** a small insect-like animal related to the spider. It has a long body and a tail divided into sections with a venomous sting in its tip.

SCORPIONS

Scorpions live in places as varied as rain forests, deserts, plains, and high mountains. They belong to a group of insects called arthropods. Their bodies are divided into two segments. The cephalothorax consists of the head, pincers, and four pairs of legs, while the abdomen contains various organs and has a jointed tail with a stinger at the end. Scorpions use their venom to paralyze or kill their prey.

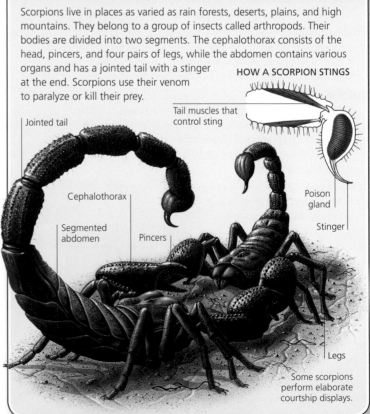

HOW A SCORPION STINGS

Jointed tail

Tail muscles that control sting

Cephalothorax

Poison gland

Segmented abdomen

Pincers

Stinger

Legs

Some scorpions perform elaborate courtship displays.

*Traditional **Scottish** highland bands play bagpipes and wear kilts.*

Scot [skot] *noun, plural* **Scots.** someone from the country of Scotland or whose ancestors come from Scotland.

Scotch [skoch] *adjective.* having to do with the country of Scotland: *Scotch broth warms you up on a cold day. noun, plural* **Scotches.** a kind of whiskey that was first produced in Scotland.

The words **Scotch** and *Scottish* both refer to people or things coming from the country of Scotland. *Scottish* is considered to be the more correct and more polite term, as in "Robert Burns was a famous *Scottish* writer" or "Glasgow is the largest *Scottish* city." The word *Scotch* is preferred only in the names of certain products, such as *Scotch* whisky (whiskey).

Scot·tish ▲ [skot-ish] *noun.* **1. the Scottish.** the people of the country of Scotland. **2.** the version of English as spoken in Scotland.
adjective. relating to Scotland, its people, or its culture.

scoun·drel [skown-drul] *noun, plural* **scoundrels.** a dishonest person or cheat; a villain: *I could tell from his lies and deceit that he was a scoundrel.*

scour[1] [skour] *verb,* **scoured, scouring.** to clean or brighten something by rubbing it with an abrasive cleaning material: *George scoured the pans until you could see your face in them.*

scour[2] [skour] *verb,* **scoured, scouring.** to search carefully and thoroughly: *He scoured the secondhand bookshops for a copy of the textbook.*

scourge [skurj] *noun, plural* **scourges.** someone or something that causes harm, suffering, or destruction: *Terrorism is a scourge on modern society.*

scout [skout] *noun, plural* **scouts. 1.** a person, ship, or plane that is sent out to get information: *The general sent a scout ahead to determine the strength of the enemy.* **2.** someone who is a Boy Scout or a Girl Scout. **3.** a person who looks for talented sports players or performers to offer them professional employment.
verb, **scouted, scouting. 1.** to search for, and bring back, information: *We scouted around for hours before we found a place to camp.* **2.** to look for talented new sports players or performers: *The major league teams in baseball are always scouting for new players.*

scout·mas·ter [skout-mas-tur] *noun, plural* **scoutmasters.** a person who is the leader of a group of Boy Scouts.

scowl [skowl] *noun, plural* **scowls.** an angry facial expression; a frown: *I didn't say anything when I saw the scowl on his face.*
verb, **scowled, scowling.** to make an angry facial expression; frown: *My grandfather scowled at me after I shouted at him.*

scram·ble [skram-bul] *verb,* **scrambled, scrambling. 1.** to mix together; jumble: *He scrambled the letters according to a secret code.* **2.** to move quickly by crawling or climbing: *He scrambled up the tree when he was chased by a bear.* **3.** to compete frantically for something: *Thousands of people scrambled for the best seats in the arena. noun, plural* **scrambles. 1.** the act of scrambling. **2.** a frantic struggle: *There is a scramble for the bathroom in our house every morning.* If you make **scrambled eggs,** you cook eggs, butter and milk together in a pan.

scrap [skrap] *noun, plural* **scraps. 1.** a small piece of something; a fragment: *Give a me a scrap of paper and I'll write down the address.* **2. scraps.** pieces of leftover food: *She was so poor she had to eat whatever scraps she could find.* **3.** worn and discarded material that can be used again in a different way: *After the plane was taken out of service, its metal was used for scrap.* **4.** an informal word for a fight or argument.
verb, **scrapped, scrapping. 1.** to convert into scrap: *Old, unsafe cars should be scrapped.* **2.** to throw away or get rid of as useless: *Some people want to scrap road taxes.*

scrap·book [skrap-buk] *noun, plural* **scrapbooks.** a book with empty pages on which you can place pictures, clippings, photos, and other material you want to keep. The practice of this as a hobby is **scrapbooking.**

scrape [skrape] *verb,* **scraped, scraping. 1.** to rub against a rough surface and cause a slight injury or damage: *If you bump the car against the curb, you may scrape the fender.* **2.** to move something so as to make a harsh rubbing sound: *Please don't scrape your chair on the floor when you stand up.* **3.** to remove something from a surface by rubbing: *If you scrape the old paint away you can see the ancient symbols underneath.* **4.** to barely manage to do something: *Only a few people showed up but we managed to scrape together a team.*
noun, plural **scrapes. 1.** a mark or slight injury caused by rubbing against a rough surface: *I got a scrape on my knee when I fell down the stairs.* **2.** a sharp sound. **3.** an unpleasant situation; predicament: *He was always getting into scrapes when he was younger.* An instrument used for scraping is called a **scraper.**

scratch [skrach] *verb,* **scratched, scratching. 1.** to cut or scrape with something sharp, such as nails or claws: *She accidentally scratched his arm with her nails.* **2.** to rub your skin with your nails or something sharp to relieve itching. **3.** to make a harsh, rough sound: *I heard the birds scratching on the roof.* **4.** to put an end to; cancel or abandon: *We'll scratch that plan because it won't work.*
noun, plural **scratches.** a thin cut, tear, or mark made by scraping or cutting: *John had a scratch across his left cheek.*
• **from scratch.** to start something from nothing: *We lost everything in the hurricane and had to start from scratch.*

a b c d e f g h i j k l m n o p q r s t u v w x y z

scraw·ny [skraw-nee] *adjective.* very thin; weak: *There were a few scrawny hens scratching in the dirt.*

scream [skreem] *verb,* **screamed, screaming.** to cry out and make a loud, high-pitched, piercing sound: *She screamed when the attacker grabbed her.*
noun, plural **screams.** a loud, high-pitched, piercing sound: *Jennifer let out a scream of delight when she heard she had won first prize.*

screech [skreech] *verb,* **screeched, screeching.** to make a high-pitched, unpleasant sound: *We heard the owl screech as it flew out of the barn.*
noun, plural **screeches.** a high-pitched, unpleasant sound: *There was a screech of brakes as the train pulled into the station.*

screen [skreen] *noun, plural* **screens. 1.** a frame that holds a fine mesh or net: *There are so many insects at night we'll need to put screens on all the windows.* **2.** a covered frame used to hide or separate. It can be fixed or movable: *The nurse placed a screen around his bed to give him some privacy.* **3.** something that provides shelter or protection: *A row of trees was planted as a screen against the sun.* **4.** the white or silver surface on which movies or slides are projected: *The new movie theater has the largest screens in the U.S.* **5.** the surface on which the image appears on a television or computer.
verb, **screened, screening. 1.** to keep from view; hide or protect: *The celebrity's house had a high wall to screen it from public view.* **2.** to show a movie or television program: *The movie will be screened at eight o'clock tonight on television.*

screen-sav·er [skreen-*save*-ur] *noun, plural* **screen-savers.** *Computers.* a computer program that displays images when the computer is turned on but is not being used. It protects the screen from damage.

screw [skroo] *noun, plural* **screws.** a type of nail with spiral grooves above its point and a slot in its head: *You will need long screws to fasten the hinge to the door.*
verb, **screwed, screwing. 1.** to attach or join with a screw or screws: *The carpenter screwed the hinge onto the door frame.* **2.** to fasten by turning or twisting: *Don't forget to screw the top back on the toothpaste tube.*

screw·driv·er [skroo-*drye*-vur] *noun, plural* **screwdrivers.** a tool with a metal shaft and a flat or shaped end, used to fit into the head of a screw to tighten or loosen it.

scrib·ble [skrib-ul] *verb,* **scribbled, scribbling.** to write or draw quickly or carelessly: *I scribbled the last page of my English exam as I was running out of time.*
noun, plural **scribbles.** writing or drawing that is done quickly or carelessly.

scribe [skribe] *noun, plural* **scribes.** *History.* a person who copied letters, manuscripts, or books before printing was available, or for people who did not know how to write.

In Europe in the Middle Ages only a few people knew how to read and write, mostly wealthy people or people with religious training. The **scribe** was a person whose work was to write things down; they were hired to keep written records for their community, or to write for people who could not write themselves.

scrim·mage [skrim-ij] *noun, plural* **scrimmages.**
1. a practice game between two teams, or two parts of the same team. **2.** see LINE OF SCRIMMAGE.
3. a disorganized fight or struggle between two or more people to gain an advantage.
verb, **scrimmaged, scrimmaging.** to play a game in the form of a scrimmage: *Our team is going to scrimmage the Lions the week before the actual season starts.*

script [skript] *noun, plural* **scripts. 1.** handwriting in which the letters are joined together: *Eleanor writes a very clear script.* **2.** the text of a play, TV or radio program, or movie, in written or printed form. When someone describes a situation as **scripted** they mean there is a known outcome. If something is unscripted then anything may happen.

A **script** is a special form of writing to be read by actors giving a performance, as in a movie, play, or TV program. A script can tell a story as a book does, but it differs in that the whole message of the story has to be in the *dialogue* (what the actors say) and in the directions for what they do.

Scrip·ture [skrip-chur] *noun, plural* **Scriptures.** *Religion.*
1. the writings in the Bible, usually including both the Old and the New Testament. **2.** a passage from the Bible read out in church. **3.** the sacred writings that form a religion's basic authority or text.

scroll ◀ [skrole] *noun, plural* **scrolls.** *History.* a roll of paper or parchment with writing on it: *The Dead Sea Scrolls were written in Hebrew before the time of Jesus—there are more than eight hundred separate documents.*
verb, **scrolled, scrolling.** to move the text on a computer screen up or down in order to read it: *He scrolled through the school's Website to find the calendar.*

In ancient Greece, teachers used papyrus **scrolls** *for "textbooks," and pupils wrote on wax tablets.*

A B C D E F G H I J K L M N O P Q R S T U V W X Y Z

scrub [skrub] *verb,* **scrubbed, scrubbing.** to make clean by washing and rubbing in a hard or rough way: *to scrub a floor.*
noun, plural **scrubs.** the act of scrubbing something.

scruff [skruf-ee] *noun, plural* **scruffs.** the soft, fleshy back part of the neck: *She grabbed the naughty puppy by the scruff of the neck.*

scrum ▼ [skrum] *noun, plural* **scrums. 1.** in the game of rugby, a play in which the forwards of both teams form a pack pushing against each other and the ball is thrown at their feet. Each team then tries to push the ball backward out of the scrum. **2.** a disorderly struggle.

scru·ple [skroo-pul] *noun, plural* **scruples.** a hesitation or unwillingness to do something wrong because of a moral principle: *She has no scruples, she'll do anything to get her own way.*

scru·pu·lous [skroo-pyuh-lus] *adjective.* **1.** having scruples or moral principles; having a conscience: *Mac was scrupulous about paying back all the money he owed.* **2.** precise attention to detail: *The teacher made sure the marking of papers was scrupulous and fair.*
—scrupulously, *adverb.*

*In a rugby **scrum**, the opposing sets of forwards in each team work to push each other out of position as they battle for the ball.*

scru·ti·nize [skroot-uh-*nize*] *verb,* **scrutinized, scrutinizing.** to look at or examine very carefully: *At the airport immigration desk, they scrutinized my passport for several minutes.*

scru·ti·ny [skroot-uh-nee] *noun, plural* **scrutinies.** the act of studying or examining something very closely: *The police officers gave his driver's license and insurance certificate careful scrutiny.*

The device known as a **scuba** gets its name from the words that describe it. It is a **s**elf-**c**ontained **u**nderwater **b**reathing **a**pparatus.

scu·ba ▲ [skoo-buh] *noun.* a device that allows a diver to breathe while under water. It consists of a breathing tube connected to an oxygen bottle carried on a diver's back. The sport of exploring areas under water is called **scuba diving.**

Scuba equipment allows divers to spend time under water studying ocean life.

scuff [skuf] *verb,* **scuffed, scuffing.** to mark or scratch a shiny surface: *Nate scuffed his new skateboard the day he got it by crashing off the sidewalk.*
noun, plural **scuffs.** a mark or scratch made by scraping something on a shiny polished surface.

scuf·fle [skuf-ul] *noun, plural* **scuffles.** a rough, disorganized struggle or fight: *The police arrested the thieves after a short scuffle.*
verb, **scuffled, scuffling.** to struggle or fight in a rough, disorganized way: *When the two boys saw a $20 note on the street they scuffled with each other to pick it up first.*

sculpt [skulpt] *verb,* **sculpted, sculpting.** to carve, shape, or give form to something: *The Frenchman Auguste Rodin sculpted large statues of famous people in Paris.*

sculp·tor [skulp-tur] *noun, plural* **sculptors.** *Art.* a person who carves, models, or makes figures from clay, metal, wood or other material for exhibition or sale.

sculp·ture ▲ [skulp-chur] *noun, plural* **sculptures.** *Art.* **1.** the art of making, carving, or modeling three-dimensional objects. Sculpture usually involves shaping clay or carving wood, marble, or stone, or casting objects in metal. **2.** a figure or other object created in this way.
verb, **sculptured, sculpturing.** to make, carve, or model three-dimensional objects.

scum [skum] *noun, plural* **scums.** *Environment.* a layer of dirt, chemicals, or pollution that floats on top of water or other liquid, making it unsafe to drink or use.

scur·ry [skur-ee] *verb,* **scurried, scurrying.** to move quickly; hurry: *The people in the street scurried indoors when it started to rain heavily.*

scur·vy [skur-vee] *noun. Health.* a disease caused by not having sufficient vitamin C in the diet. Swollen gums, tiredness, and anemia are all symptoms of scurvy. It can be cured by eating fresh fruits, particularly citrus fruits.

Scythes were first used in medieval Europe, mainly for mowing grass.

scut·tle [skut-ul] *verb,* **scuttled, scuttling. 1.** to move quickly with small, hurried steps to escape: *The cockroach scuttled across the kitchen floor when I put the light on.* **2.** to sink one's own ship deliberately to prevent it from being captured by an enemy.

scythe ▶ [syeTH] *noun, plural* **scythes.** a farm tool with a sharp, curved blade and a long wooden or metal handle, used in the past to cut crops such as wheat.
verb, **scythed, scything. 1.** to cut with a scythe to harvest wheat, other crops, or grass. **2.** to cut down or cut through vigorously: *The cavalrymen scythed through the enemy infantrymen with their swords.*

a b c d e f g h i j k l m n o p q r s t u v w x y z

Seagulls *are common seabirds found all over the world, from the polar ice caps to the equator.*

The colorful tentacles of **sea anemones** *can sting and paralyze fish and other sea creatures.*

sea [see] *noun, plural* **seas.**
1. the body of salt water that covers large areas of the Earth's surface; the ocean. **2.** an area of such water partly enclosed by land, often given its own name such as the *North Sea* or the *Bering Sea.*
3. the movement and action of the waves of such a body of water: *The ship made slow progress in heavy seas.* **4.** a vast number or large area: *The band at the rock concert looked out over a sea of faces.*

♦ **at sea. 1.** on the water of the sea or ocean: *They spent six days at sea before reaching land.* **2.** confused or puzzled: *Matilda confessed she was all at sea trying to work with the new computer.*
A different word with the same sound is **see.**

sea a·nem·o·ne ▲ [uh-nem-uh-nee] a marine creature with a tubelike circular body, and tentacles that are used to trap food.

sea·board [see-bord] *noun, plural* **seaboards.** the coastal area of a landmass nearest to the sea: *The Eastern seaboard of the U.S. has many people living along it.*

sea·coast [see-kohst] *noun, plural* **seacoasts.** an area of land that lies close to the sea.

sea·far·ing [see-fare-ing] *adjective.* having to do with traveling by sea or working on the sea. A person who makes a living in this way is called a **seafarer.**

sea·food [see-food] *noun, plural* **seafoods.** saltwater fish and other sea creatures such as shellfish and octopus eaten as food.

sea·gull ▲ [see-gul] *noun, plural* **seagulls.** a large, white bird with gray wings and a hooked beak that lives in coastal areas. This word is also spelled **sea gull.**

sea·horse ▶ [see-horse] *noun, plural* **seahorses.** a small fish that rides upright in the water. It has a head that looks like that of a horse and a long tail. This word is also spelled **sea horse.**

seal¹ ▼ [seel] *noun, plural* **seals.** a fish-eating marine mammal with a sleek, furry body and flippers instead of feet.

A **seahorse** *moves fins on its back to push itself forward through the water.*

SEALS AND SEA LIONS

There are two kinds of seals. Sea lions and fur seals are known as eared seals. They have small ears and can turn their hind flippers around to walk on land. "True" or earless seals, such as leopard, harp, and Weddell seals, are more streamlined, cannot turn their flippers, and wriggle to move on land. Seals eat crabs, fish, and squid. The Antarctic leopard seal also hunts penguins. The male elephant seal is the largest seal, growing up to twenty feet long and weighing nearly four tons.

A colony of Australian sea lions

Fur seal

Leopard seal

Weddell seals

Harp seals

*Metal stamps with different designs can be used to create special **seals**.*

seal² ▶ [seel] *noun, plural* **seals.**
1. a stamp design made in hard wax or printed with ink on paper to show who something belongs to, or to show that a document is genuine.
2. a thing or substance that closes something tightly, or the fact of being closed in this way: *The seal on my medicine bottle has become loose.*
verb, **sealed, sealing. 1.** to close something tightly so that no liquid or air can enter or escape: *The machine seals soft drink bottles with a metal cap.* **2.** to put an official seal on a document: *The king sealed the royal assent to the new tax.*

sea level *Environment.* the natural level of the sea, especially the level halfway between high and low tide.

sea lion one of several types of large seals that live in the Pacific Ocean.

seam [seem] *noun, plural* **seams. 1.** a line made by sewing two pieces of material together. Seams are made using cloth, leather, or any other soft material: *My old jacket is coming apart at the seams.* **2.** any line or mark, especially one that joins two edges together. **3.** a layer of minerals in the earth, such as coal or iron ore.
verb, **seamed, seaming.** to join two edges together: *The dressmaker seamed the blue and black linen to make a pretty skirt.*

sea·man [see-mun] *noun, plural* **seamen.** a person who makes a living by working on boats or ships at sea. The skills needed to sail ships, such as setting sails and navigating, are called **seamanship.**

seam·stress [seem-strus] *noun, plural* **seamstresses.** a woman who makes a living sewing, usually making women's clothing.

sea·plane ▼ [see-plane] *noun, plural* **seaplanes.** an airplane that takes off from and lands on water by using floats attached below the cabin and wings instead of wheels.

sea·port [see-port] *noun, plural* **seaports.** a town on or near the coast where large ships can berth in a port or harbor.

search [surch] *verb,* **searched, searching. 1.** to look carefully or in great detail for something: *I searched high and low for my keys before I realized I had left them in the car.* **2.** *Computers.* to examine various items of data in order to find a desired type of information.
noun, plural **searches.** the act of looking carefully or in great detail for something: *The police started a search for the thief as soon as they found out the jewels were stolen.*
—**searcher,** *noun.*

search engine *Computers.* a program that lists the location of relevant information available on the Internet or another computer system, when key words are typed into the program.

search·light [surch-*lite*] *noun, plural* **searchlights.** a very bright electric light that can be turned to point upward in any direction. A searchlight is used to search the night sky.

sea·shell [see-*shel*] *noun, plural* **seashells.** any shell of a small sea creature such as a clam, abalone, or oyster. Seashells are often found on ocean beaches.

sea·shore [see-*shore*] *noun, plural* **seashores.** the land closest to the sea, especially the sands uncovered at low tide and under water at high tide.

sea·sick [see-*sik*] *adjective. Health.* having a feeling of nausea or sickness while on a boat due to the rolling movement of the waves.

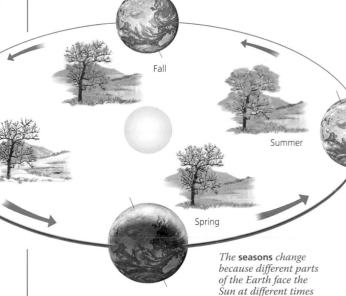

Fall

Summer

Winter

Spring

*The **seasons** change because different parts of the Earth face the Sun at different times of the year.*

sea·son ▲ [see-zun] *noun, plural* **seasons. 1.** any of the four natural divisions of the climate each year: spring, summer, fall, or winter. **2.** any special period during the year: *the wet season in tropical areas; the monsoon season in India.* Anything that occurs during the same season each year, or that lasts only for a certain season, is described as **seasonal.**
verb, **seasoned, seasoning. 1.** to add a seasoning of spices, herbs, or other flavoring to food: *I seasoned the chicken before putting it into the oven.* **2.** to dry wood out slowly to make it ready for use in carpentry.

sea·son·ing [see-zun-ing] *noun, plural* **seasonings.** any mix of herbs and spices used to add flavor to food, usually including salt: *There's too much seasoning on this meat.*

*Small **seaplanes** like this are used to access remote areas.*

*A **sea urchin** uses its sharp spines to protect itself and to move over the seabed.*

A B C D E F G H I J K L M N O P Q R **S** T U V W X Y Z

seat [seet] *noun, plural* **seats.**
1. a piece of furniture used to sit on, such as a chair, bench, or stool. **2.** a place to sit: *There were no seats left at the church service, so we stood in the back.* **3.** any part of something that one can sit on: *The bicycle seat is quite comfortable.* **4.** the part of the body one sits on, or the clothing that covers it: *The seat of my jeans has worn through.* **5.** an official position or membership: *His dad has a seat on the XYZ Company's board of directors.*
verb, **seated, seating. 1.** to place in or on a seat: *The waiter seated everyone around the table.* **2.** to have seats for; accommodate: *The new baseball stadium seats 50,000 people.*

seat·belt [seet-*belt*] *noun, plural* **seatbelts.** a canvas belt or harness in a car, bus, truck, or airplane that holds the passenger safely in place in case of an accident, sudden stop, or other such problem. This word is also spelled **seat belt.**

sea urchin ▲ [ur-chin] any of a group of sea creatures having a round shell with hard spines to protect it.

sea·weed [see-*weed*] *noun, plural* **seaweeds.** any plant that grows under sea water. Most seaweeds are dark green or brown in color.

se·cede [si-seed] *verb,* **seceded, seceding.** to withdraw officially from a country, union, federation, or other political organization: *Norway seceded from Sweden in 1905, creating a new country.* The act of seceding is called **secession.**

se·clud·ed [si-kloo-did] *adjective.* living apart from or away from others: *My uncle lives a secluded life up in the nearby woods.* The act of living apart or away from others is called **seclusion.**

sec·ond¹ [sek-und] *adjective.* **1.** being the next after the first of a series: *February is the second month of the year.* **2.** next best or most important after the first: *Guadalajara has often been called the second city of Mexico, after Mexico City.* **3.** another or other: *Can I have a second helping of cake, please? We have to have a second goalkeeper in case Tim gets hurt.*
adverb. in second place: *Giles came in second in the race, after his friend Todd.*
noun, plural **seconds. 1.** a person who is next after the first: *John was the first to arrive and Sue the second.*
2. an item offered for sale as damaged or inferior goods: *When I buy clothes I sometimes buy seconds with some damage because they are cheaper.*
verb, **seconded, seconding.** to support a nomination or to help with something: *Who will second the motion that we buy some new desks?*

sec·ond² [sek-und] *noun, plural* **seconds. 1.** one of the sixty equal parts into which a minute is divided. **2.** a very short time: *Jean shouted over to us: "Don't worry, I'll be with you in a second."*

sec·ond·ar·y [sek-un-der-ee] *adjective.* coming second in time, place, or importance: *The exercises made his injured leg stronger, and a secondary benefit was that he lost weight.*

secondary school *Education.* another name for HIGH SCHOOL.

sec·ond·hand [sek-und-*hand*] *adjective.* originally owned by someone else; not new: *a secondhand car; I often buy secondhand books.*
adverb. not from the original source; indirectly: *I learned secondhand that I had passed the test, because the teacher didn't tell me.*

secondhand smoke *Health.* the act of inhaling smoke from other people's cigarettes. Sometimes called passive smoking, or environmental tobacco smoke, it poses risks to those who are exposed to it, including children.

se·cre·cy [seek-ruh-see] *noun, plural* **secrecies.** the act of keeping secret, or the fact of being a secret: *The prisoners' escape plan was drawn up in great secrecy.*

se·cret [see-krit] *adjective.* **1.** having to do with keeping knowledge from others; hidden: *The boys told no one about their secret plan to visit the so-called haunted house.* **2.** behaving in a hidden way: *The secret agent posed as a businessman.*
noun, plural **secrets. 1.** knowledge or information that is not known to most other people: *Don't let Sharon know about the party we're having for her—it's a secret.* **2.** a hidden reason or cause: *The secret of her success is her mother's constant encouragement.* —**secretly,** *adverb.*

sec·re·tar·y [sek-ruh-ter-ee] *noun, plural* **secretaries.** *Business.* **1.** a person who writes letters, sends e-mails, answers the phone, and keeps records for another person or a business or other organization. The duties that are carried out by a secretary are described as **secretarial** duties. **2.** a person whose job is to head a government department: *The Secretary of State has important responsibilities in dealing with foreign governments.* **3.** a piece of office furniture having a top to write on, drawers, and some bookshelves.

The original meaning of the word **secretary** was "a person who keeps secrets." The current use of the word in business comes from the idea that a secretary works very closely with her or his boss, and may know secrets about that person or about the business. Today, many businesses do not use the word *secretary,* but prefer to refer to this job as an *assistant* or *executive assistant.*

*This Mercedes Benz **sedan** was a classic of the 1960s.*

se·crete [si-<u>kreet</u>] *verb,* **secreted, secreting.** *Biology.* to produce and release a liquid into the body or onto parts of a plant. Animals and plants produce substances that help with their growth and health. The chemical substances they produce are called **secretions.**

se·cre·tive [<u>see</u>-kri-tiv] *adjective.* tending to have secrets or to keep things hidden: *He's been very secretive about his plans for the new business.* **—secretively,** *adverb.*

sect [sekt] *noun, plural* **sects.** *Religion.* a small group of people who share the same religious beliefs: *Often when a group of people break away from a large religion, they form their own small sect.*

sec·tion ▼ [<u>sek</u>-shun] *noun, plural* **sections.**
1. a separate part taken from a whole; a division: *First-class passengers sit in the front section of the airplane.* **2.** a part of a written work such as a book or newspaper: *My dad often reads the business section of the newspaper first.* **3.** a certain part of a larger region or area: *The section of the forest near the river was the only part not affected by fire.* *verb,* **sectioned, sectioning.** to cut across in order to divide into two or more parts: *We sectioned the orange and ate half each.*

sec·tio·nal [<u>sek</u>-shun-ul] *noun.* a unit of furniture made in sections so that additional units can be added. *adjective.* having to do with a certain part or segment rather than the whole: *In the years before the Civil War there was great sectional rivalry between the Northern and Southern states.*

sec·tor [<u>sek</u>-tur] *noun, plural* **sectors.** one distinct part of an area, group, or field of activity: *The agricultural sector of the economy includes fruit growers and farmers.*

sec·u·lar [<u>sek</u>-yuh-lur] *adjective. Religion.* having to do with a worldly view of existence rather than a religious one: *Most education in the twenty-first century is secular, not religious.*

se·cure [si-<u>kyoor</u>] *adjective,* **securer, securest. 1.** safe from danger or loss: *The cave offered us a secure place to wait during the thunderstorm.* **2.** describing something solid, sturdy, or well fastened: *The painter did not climb the ladder until it was secure.* *verb,* **secured, securing.** **1.** to make secure: *The sailor secured the ropes to the mast; The troops secured the village against enemy attack.* **2.** to get possession of; obtain: *We secured tickets to the new ballet.*

*A **section** of this pitcher plant has been cut away to show how it traps and digests insects.*

se·cu·ri·ty [si-<u>kyoor</u>-uh-tee] *noun, plural* **securities. 1.** the fact of being safe from harm: *An insurance policy gives you security against theft or damage.* **2.** anything that offers protection against harm or loss: *The soldiers ran to the security of the fort.* **3.** something given to make sure that a promise is carried out: *I left my watch as security for the loan.* Certificates of ownership for some investments such as shares are called **securities.** *adjective.* having to do with offering protection: *a strong metal security door; a security guard.*

se·dan ▲ [si-<u>dan</u>] *noun, plural* **sedans.** an automobile with a metal roof, two or four passenger doors, and usually with seats in both front and back.

The word **sedan** is short for *sedan chair.* This was a fancy chair used by wealthy people in earlier times. Two servants would walk in front and back of the chair, holding long poles that supported it as one person sat inside to be carried along.

sed·i·ment ▼ [<u>sed</u>-uh-munt] *noun, plural* **sediments. 1.** any solid material that settles at the bottom of a liquid: *A layer of sediment settled in the bottom of the old wine bottle.* **2.** *Environment.* soil, sand, or rocks left by a glacier, or deposited by wind or water: *The floodwaters let in by broken levees left inches of sediment in many houses.*

sed·i·men·ta·ry [sed-uh-<u>men</u>-tuh-ree] *adjective. Environment.* having to do with layers of rock formed over thousands of years from the compressed sediments of shells, sands, and animal and plant matter. Limestone and sandstone are both sedimentary rocks.

see [see] *verb,* **saw, seen, seeing. 1.** to look at with the eyes; view: *I can see mountains through the living room window.* **2.** to get the meaning of; understand: *Since our teacher explained it to us, I see what a huge problem global warming is.* **3.** to find out; discover: *See who is on the phone, will you?* **4.** to make sure: *Please see that the lights are off when you leave the room.* **5.** to go with; escort: *I'll see you to your car.* **6.** to greet for a visit: *The manager will see you now.* **7.** to meet with; experience: *The troops saw heavy action for several weeks.*
🔊 A different word with the same sound is **sea.**

Sediment in this jar has separated into three layers: gravel (bottom), coarse sand (middle), and fine sand (top).

*The **seeds** of the maple tree spin like tiny helicopters as they fall gently to the ground.*

Spinning maple seed

Seed wing

seed ▲ [seed] *noun, plural* **seeds. 1.** the small, hard part of a plant from which a new plant of the same type will grow: *Spring is the time to plant seeds in the ground.* **2.** the source or origin of something: *The seeds for Simon's book on Hawaii were planted in his mind when he took a holiday there.*
verb, **seeded, seeding. 1.** to plant seeds in the soil: *We seeded the ground to grow pumpkin and beans.* **2.** to remove seeds from a fruit or vegetable: *to seed a red chili pepper.*

seed·ling ▼ [seed-ling] *noun, plural* **seedlings.** a young plant that is grown from a seed.

seek [seek] *verb,* **sought, seeking. 1.** to try to find or search for something: *The fruit pickers moved from town to town seeking work.* **2.** to make an effort; try: *The team will seek to win the next game.* **3.** to try to obtain: *The mayor will seek the newspaper's support in his race for governor.*
—**seeker,** *noun.*

seem [seem] *verb,* **seemed, seeming. 1.** to give the appearance of: *That new store seems to have cheap prices.* **2.** to appear to oneself: *I seem to have upset Sam by telling him a rude joke.*
🔊 A different word with the same sound is **seam.**

seem·ing·ly [seem-ing-lee] *adverb.* **1.** judging by the facts available: *Seemingly it's going to rain, if those big black clouds are anything to go by.* **2.** to have the appearance of: *She has a seemingly endless list of excuses not to attend school.*

seen [seen] *verb.* the past participle of SEE.

A mistake that people can make in speech is to use **seen** instead of *saw,* as in "I don't want to go to that movie; I already *seen* it." The correct way to say this would be either "I already *saw* it" or "I have (I've) already *seen* it." *Saw* is the simple past tense of *see* and does not need another verb with it, but *seen* needs to be used with a form of *have* or *be.*

seep [seep] *verb,* **seeped, seeping.** of a gas or liquid, to pass slowly though a porous substance or material such as earth, rock, or brick: *The water seeped into the house from the broken pipe outside.*

see·saw [see-saw] *noun, plural* **seesaws.** a piece of children's play equipment consisting of a board with seats at both ends, supported in the middle so that each end in turn rises and falls.
verb, **seesawed, seesawing.** to rise and fall over time: *The price of oil seesaws depending on demand and how much is available for sale.*
adjective. having to do with a rising and falling action: *Stock prices have been in a seesaw pattern recently.*

seethe [seeTH] *verb,* **seethed, seething. 1.** to bubble and swirl as if boiling: *The waves below the cliffs seethed and crashed on the rocks.* **2.** to be angry or agitated: *She was seething after she crashed the car.*

seg·ment ◀ [seg-munt] *noun, plural* **segments.** a part of something into which it can be cut, or which separates easily or naturally; a division: *I had grapefruit segments for breakfast.*
verb, **segmented, segmenting.** to cut or separate into parts: *The gardener segmented the flower beds into annual and perennial flowers.*

An orange is easy to eat when it is divided into **segments.**

seg·re·gate [seg-ruh-*gate*] *verb,* **segregated, segregating.** to separate people into two or more groups, by race, religion, or on some other basis: *In the past, public schools in the southern U.S. were segregated—black and white children were required by law to attend different schools.* Communities that are divided according to racial groupings are described as being **segregated.**

seg·re·ga·tion [seg-ruh-gay-shun] *noun. Government.* the act or process of segregating communities into different racial or religious groups. A **segregationist** is a person who believes in the policy of keeping people of different racial or religious groups apart by law.

Broad beans germinate to produce **seedlings** *that eventually grow into new plants.*

seine ▶ [sane] *noun, plural* **seines.** a large fishing net with weights used by fishermen to catch fish at sea. 🔊 A different word with the same sound is **sane.**

seis·mo·graph ▼ [size-muh-*graf*] *noun, plural* **seismographs.** *Science.* a device for measuring and recording the size of earthquakes. The severity of an earthquake is measured on a scale from 1 to 10.

seis·mol·o·gy [size-<u>mol</u>-uh-jee] *noun. Science.* the science of measuring earthquakes on the Earth's crust. A scientist who studies seismology is called a **seismologist.**

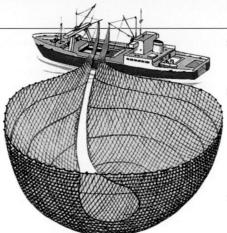

When a school of fish swims into a **seine,** *the net is pulled shut quickly, like a purse.*

seize [seez] *verb,* **seized, seizing. 1.** to take hold of; grab or grasp: *She seized the child's arm to stop him walking onto the road.* **2.** to capture something or take possession of it: *The army seized the bridge to stop the enemy at the river.*

sei·zure [<u>see</u>-zhur] *noun, plural* **seizures. 1.** a sudden, violent shaking of the body; convulsion: *The manager suffered a seizure and his staff called an ambulance.* **2.** the act of seizing someone or something.

sel·dom [<u>sel</u>-dum] *adverb.* not often; hardly ever: *I seldom see my aunt now, as she's moved to L.A.*

se·lect [si-<u>lekt</u>] *verb,* **selected, selecting.** to choose carefully: *Select your apple carefully as some are rotten.* *adjective.* carefully chosen: *Only a select group of students were invited the meet the Governor.*

se·lec·tion [si-<u>lek</u>-shun] *noun, plural* **selections. 1.** the act of selecting from a range of choices: *Robert's selection of music for the show was very thoughtful.* **2.** someone or something that has been selected or may be selected from: *The selection of cheeses on the plate offered a wide variety.*

se·lec·tive [si-<u>lek</u>-tiv] *adjective.* having to do with carefully choosing from a number of options: *That college is very selective and students must have very high grades to be admitted.* **—selectively,** *adverb.*

self [self] *noun, plural* **selves. 1.** your own person apart from all other people: *She knows her own self, and knows that she'd never be patient enough to be a teacher.* **2.** a person's character, nature, or typical behavior: *Dad was back to his usual happy self once he'd had a few days off to rest.*

self- a prefix meaning of or by oneself or itself: a *self-propelled* vehicle is one that powers itself.

self-con·fi·dent [self-<u>kon</u>-fuh-dunt] *adjective.* believing in your own ability or knowledge: *All the girls at school like him because he's funny, smart, and self-confident.* Having **self-confidence** means that you have a belief in yourself or your worth.

self-con·trol [self-kun-<u>trole</u>] *noun.* the ability to stop yourself from doing something, or from letting your emotions or impulses get the better of you: *I don't have much self-control when it comes to chocolate.* When you make yourself do something that you know you ought to, even though you may not want to do it, you show **self-discipline.**

self-de·fense [self-di-<u>fens</u>] *noun. Law.* the act or fact of protecting yourself when attacked: *She shot her attacker in self-defense.*

self-em·ployed [self-im-<u>ployd</u>] *adjective. Business.* working for yourself rather than for someone else; having your own business: *As a self-employed computer technician, he can work whenever he wants.*

self-es·teem [self-uh-<u>steem</u>] *noun.* satisfaction and pride in yourself and your abilities: *Her great score on the test boosted her self-esteem.*

self-gov·ern·ment [self-<u>guv</u>-ur-munt] *noun. Government.* the control of an organization, area, or country by the members or people living there: *The survey showed that the majority of the rural community would support self-government.*

self-help [self-<u>help</u>] *noun. Health.* the use of efforts to overcome your problems without depending on others. *adjective.* of or relating to something, such as a book or course, that encourages individuals to deal with their own problems.

self·ish [<u>sel</u>-fish] *adjective.* thinking only of your own interests and welfare: *The selfish boy didn't share any of his lunch with his friend who had accidentally left his at home.* **—selfishly,** *adverb;* **—selfishness,** *noun.*

self-re·spect [self-ri-<u>spekt</u>] *noun.* a feeling of being happy with your value as a person; respect for yourself: *He kept his self-respect by not cheating on the test even when he had the chance to do it.*

self-ser·vice [self-<u>sur</u>-vis] *adjective.* describing a shop, restaurant, or gas-station set up so that the customers serve themselves and then pay at the cashier: *The self-service salad bar had an excellent range of food.*

self-suf·fi·cient [self-suh-<u>fish</u>-unt] *adjective.* able to provide everything needed without depending on others. **—self-sufficiency,** *noun.*

Until fairly recently **seismographs** *recorded the intensity of earthquakes on long rolls of paper.*

a b c d e f g h i j k l m n o p q r **s** t u v w x y z

A B C D E F G H I J K L M N O P Q R **S** T U V W X Y Z

sell [sel] *verb,* **sold, selling. 1.** to give something to someone in return for money: *I sold my skateboard for eighty dollars.* **2.** to have for sale: *She looked everywhere for a shop that sells red umbrellas.* **3.** to be offered for sale at a particular price: *For today only, these sunglasses are selling for ten dollars.*

🔊 A different word with the same sound is **cell.**

sell·er [sel-ur] *noun, plural* **sellers. 1.** someone who sells something: *a flower seller.* **2.** a product that is popular and a lot of people buy: *The band's latest album has been one of the biggest sellers over the last twelve months.*

sell·out [sel-*out*] *noun.* an event or performance for which all the seats are sold: *The rock concert was a sellout within the first thirty minutes of tickets going on sale.*

selves [selvz] *noun.* the plural of SELF.

se·mes·ter [suh-mes-tur] *noun, plural* **semesters.** *Education.* one of two divisions in the academic year for school or college: *Monica has chosen her subjects for the fall semester.*

semi- a prefix that means: **1.** half: a *semicircle* is half a circle. **2.** partially: *semi-darkness* means partial darkness.

sem·i·cir·cle [sem-ee-*sur*-kul] *noun, plural* **semicircles. 1.** *Mathematics.* a half circle. **2.** an arrangement in the form of a half circle: *We placed the chairs in a semicircle so that we could all see the television screen.*

sem·i·co·lon [sem-ee-*koh*-lun] *noun, plural* **semicolons.** *Language.* a punctuation mark (;) used show more of a break between two parts of a sentence than a comma does. Semicolons can also be used to separate lists of different sets of things.

A **semicolon** (**;**) is a kind of punctuation that is not a strong a break as a period, but stronger than a comma. It is most often used to separate two closely related parts of a short sentence: "She isn't just pretty**;** she's beautiful." "I thought it would be sunny**;** instead it rained." The part that follows the semicolon should be a complete thought, or else a colon (**:**) would be used: "There's only one way to do this**:** the right way.'

sem·i·con·duc·tor [sem-ee-kun-*duk*-tur] *noun, plural* **semiconductors.** *Science.* a material, such as silicon, that has an ability to conduct electricity and is used in electronic equipment.

sem·i·fi·nal [sem-ee-*fye*-nul] *noun, plural* **semifinals.** one of two games or matches that is played to decide who will take part in the final game of a competition. *adjective.* coming before the final round in a competition: *She advanced to the semifinal match.*

sem·i·nar [sem-uh-nahr] *noun, plural* **seminars.** *Education.* **1.** a class at a college or university where a teacher and a small group of students meet to study and discuss a topic: *a medieval art seminar.* **2.** a class or conference on a particular subject where people come to listen and discuss ideas with an expert.

sem·i·nary [sem-uh-*ner*-ee] *noun, plural* **seminaries.** *Religion.* a special college to prepare students to become priests, ministers, or rabbis.

Sem·i·nole [sem-uh-nole] *noun, plural* **Seminole** or **Seminoles.** a member of a tribe of North American Indians who moved to northern Florida in the eighteenth and nineteenth centuries. Many of the Seminole now live in Oklahoma and southern Florida.

Sen·ate [sen-it] *noun.* the upper house of the United States Congress. The Senate has the power to make laws. The legislative assembly of a state or nation is called a **senate.**

> The first group of lawmakers to be known as a **senate** was in ancient Rome. *Senate* comes from a word meaning "old." In ancient Rome the Senate was made up mostly of older men.

Sen·a·tor ▼ [sen-uh-tur] *noun, plural* **senators.** a member of the U.S. Senate. A **senator** is a member of any senate.

In this painting by Cesare Maccari, the famous Roman orator Cicero addresses other **senators.**

send [send] *verb,* **sent, sending. 1.** to cause to go somewhere: *to send a message by e-mail; Mom sent my sister to the store to buy some milk.* **2.** to cause to become: *The news sent her into a panic.*

se·nile [see-*nile*] *adjective. Health.* showing a decline in physical strength or in the ability to think clearly and make decisions as a result of old age: *She had to hire a nurse to help take care of her senile mother.* The state of being senile is **senility.**

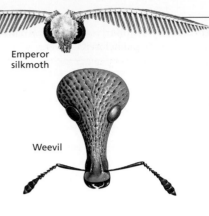

Emperor
silkmoth

Weevil

Cockroach

Butterfly

*Insects use antennae
of varying shapes
and sizes to* **sense**
their surroundings.

sen·ior [seen-yur] *adjective.* **1.** the older of two persons having the same name, such as a father and son: *Edward Jenkins Senior arrived with his son Edward Jenkins Junior.* **2.** higher in rank, level or importance: *She is the senior executive at the office and makes most of the decisions.* **3.** having to do with the final year of high school or college: *I'm looking forward to my senior year next year.* *noun, plural* **seniors.** **1.** someone who is higher in rank, level, or importance. **2.** someone who is older: *My cousin is my senior by two years.* **3.** a student who is in their final year of high school or college. **4.** a shorter form of SENIOR CITIZEN.

senior citizen an elderly or aged person, especially one who has retired: *Senior citizens are entitled to discounts on trains and buses.*

sen·ior·i·ty [seen-yore-i-tee] *noun.* **1.** the state of being higher in rank than someone else. **2.** the status or advantage a person gets for working in the same organization for a long time: *He was given two extra weeks of vacation because of his seniority within the company.*

se·ñor [sen-yore] *noun, plural* **señores.** the Spanish term for a man that is equivalent to "Mr."

se·ño·ra [sen-yore-uh] *noun, plural* **señoras.** the Spanish term for a married woman or an older woman that is equivalent to "Mrs."

se·ño·ri·ta [sen-yore-ee-tuh] *noun, plural* **señoritas.** the Spanish term for a girl or unmarried woman that is equivalent to "Miss."

sen·sa·tion [sen-say-shun] *noun, plural* **sensations.** **1.** the ability of feeling something through one of your five senses; touching, hearing, seeing, smelling, or tasting. **2.** a general feeling or awareness: *I had the strange sensation that I was being watched.* **3.** an extreme feeling of excitement or interest: *The news that the famous actor was visiting our school caused a sensation.*

sen·sa·tion·al [sen-say-shun-ul] *adjective.* causing a strong reaction of great excitement, interest, shock, or surprise: *The newspaper reported a sensational story about a man surviving a bear attack in his backyard.* **—sensationally,** *adverb.*

sense ▲ [sens] *noun, plural* **senses.** **1.** the awareness of your surroundings that comes from using your abilities of sight, hearing, smell, taste, or touch. **2.** a feeling about something: *There was a great sense of relief when we finally found our lost dog.* **3.** the ability to understand something: *She has a good sense of direction and knew exactly where we were going.* **4.** the ability to think and act sensibly; intelligence: *He had the sense to store all his valuables in the safe before he went on vacation.* **5.** the fact of having reason; purpose: *There's no sense in both of us standing in the same ticket line.* **6.** the meaning of something: *The word "fly" has the sense of "to move through the air" or "an insect."*
verb, **sensed, sensing.** to feel or be aware of something: *I sensed the tension between them as soon as I walked in the room.* To become reasonable or to start to think and act clearly and logically is to **come to one's senses.**
• **make sense.** to be easy to understand: *This science report just doesn't make sense.*

sense·less [sens-lis] *adjective.* **1.** being unconscious: *The victim had been beaten senseless and had to be taken to a hospital.* **2.** lacking a use or purpose; pointless: *I had a senseless argument with my friend about the color of her shoes.* **—senselessly,** *adverb;* **senselessness,** *noun.*

sense organ *Biology.* a specialized part of the body such as the eyes, ears, nose, tongue, and skin that take in information and send messages to the brain about your surroundings.

sen·si·ble [sen-suh-bul] *adjective.* having or showing good sense and judgment: *It is sensible to take an umbrella when it looks like it might rain.* **—sensible,** *adverb.*

sen·si·tive [sen-suh-tiv] *adjective.* **1.** easily upset; quick to take offense: *The sensitive girl cried when the coach yelled at her on the field.* **2.** able to feel deeply or understand others: *The school counselor is a very sensitive person.* **3.** easily affected by something: *The baby's skin is very sensitive to the sun.* **—sensitively,** *adverb.*

sen·si·tiv·i·ty [sen-suh-tiv-i-tee] *noun, plural* **sensitivities.** **1.** the ability to be aware and understand other people's problems: *He showed great sensitivity when he comforted the old lady.* **2.** the ability to be easily affected by something: *I have a sensitivity to cow's milk and become ill when I drink it.*

sen·sor ◀ [sen-sur] *noun, plural* **sensors.** a device that is used to detect the presence of something or the change in something such as heat or pressure, and then transmit this information to a control device.

sen·so·ry [sen-suh-ree] *adjective.* having to do with the senses of touch, sight, smell, hearing, and taste: *The eyes are sensory organs.*

A smoke alarm contains a special **sensor** *that sets off a loud warning sound when it detects smoke.*

sen·tence [sen-tuns] *noun, plural* **sentences.** *Language.*
1. a group of words that usually contains a subject and a verb and forms a statement or question. *The cat sat on the mat* is a sentence. **2.** a punishment given by a court after a criminal has been found guilty: *The car thief received a five-year sentence in jail.*
verb, **sentenced, sentencing.** to give a punishment to someone who is guilty of a crime: *The judge sentenced him to prison.*

"I met her when we were in the same swim class. At the town pool." "At the town pool" is not a sentence by itself, and should be part of the sentence before. Your writing should always be made up of complete **sentences**, and you can test for this by seeing if a group of words make sense by themselves. If they do not, this isn't a sentence. This can be a bit tricky because the answer to a question can be a sentence even without a noun and verb. "'Where did you meet her?' 'At the town pool.'" Now "At the town pool" can be a sentence, because it answers a question.

sen·ti·ment [sen-tuh-munt] *noun, plural* **sentiments.** a gentle feeling or emotion: *The teacher appreciated the sentiment behind the students making her a birthday cake.* Opinions or ideas based on feelings are known as **sentiments.**

sen·ti·men·tal [sen-tuh-men-tul] *adjective.* having to do with gentle feelings or emotions: *The necklace my grandmother gave me has great sentimental value to me.* The quality of being sentimental is **sentimentality.** **—sentimentally,** *adverb.*

sen·ti·nel [sen-tuh-nul] *noun, plural* **sentinels.** another term for SENTRY.

sen·try [sen-tree] *noun, plural* **sentries.** a guard, especially a soldier who acts as a lookout: *A sentry stands at the entrance to the army base.*

se·pal ▼ [see-pul] *noun, plural* **sepals.** *Biology.* one of the individual green, leaf-like segments that lie at the base of a flower. The sepals enclose and protect the flower when it is a bud, but then fold back away when it blooms.

sep·a·rate [sep-uh-rate] *verb,* **separated, separating.**
1. to keep apart or divide: *The river separated the two areas of land.* **2.** to move apart: *He separated the two fighting dogs.* **3.** to go in different directions: *We separated when we arrived at the mall and arranged to meet in an hour for lunch.*
adjective. set apart; not connected: *The garage is a separate building behind the house.*
—separately, *adverb.*

sep·a·ra·tion [sep-uh-ray-shun] *noun, plural* **separations. 1.** the process of separating: *the separation of cans and bottles in a recycling bin.* **2.** the condition of being set apart or separated: *The newly married couple had to endure a long period of separation when the husband was sent to war.* **3.** a legal arrangement in which a married couple decide not to live together anymore: *After a year of separation, the couple filed for divorce.*

Sep·tem·ber [sep-tem-bur] *noun.* the ninth month of the year, after August and before October.

The word **September** comes from *septem,* the Latin word for "seven." October is the ninth month in the modern calendar of twelve months, but the calendar of ancient Rome had only ten months and October was the seventh.

se·quel [see-kwul] *noun, plural* **sequels.** *Literature.* a book, film, or play that continues the story of a previous one.

se·quence [see-kwuns] *noun, plural* **sequences. 1.** the following of one thing after another in order: *The school secretary filed all the reports in sequence according to their date.* **2.** a series of related events or actions in a particular order: *There was a sequence of events leading up to Dad finally quitting his job.* When something is **sequential** it is arranged in a sequence or follows a particular order.

se·quoi·a ▶ [suh-kwoy-uh] *noun, plural* **sequoias.** a large, cone-bearing, evergreen Californian tree with reddish bark that can reach a height of over three hundred feet. There are two different types—redwood and **giant sequoia.**

The tree known as the **sequoia** takes its name from a famous American Indian leader. *Sequoyah* was a chief of the Cherokee nation who was especially noted for creating a written alphabet for the Cherokee language. It is not certain how his name came to be connected with the tree, since it grows in a different part of the country from where he lived.

This huge Californian sequoia is called the Stratosphere Giant.

se·rene [suh-reen] *adjective,* **serener, serenest.** describing something calm; peaceful or tranquil: *The serene mountain lake was the perfect spot for a romantic picnic.* The state of being calm or peaceful is **serenity.** **—serenely,** *adverb.*

serf [surf] *noun, plural* **serfs.** *History.* in medieval times, a person who worked on the land and was the property of the person who owned the land. The state of being a serf and the system of using serfs is known as **serfdom.**
🔊 A different word with the same sound is **surf.**

A rosebud sits snugly inside its four **sepals.**

ser·geant [sar-junt] *noun, plural* **sergeants.** any of several ranks of noncommissioned officers or enlisted personnel in the U.S. Army, Air Force, or Marine Corps.

> The word **sergeant** comes from an old word meaning "to serve." The word first meant a household servant, then someone who acted as a servant to a knight, then someone who serves in the army, and then finally a certain rank in the army.

se·ri·al [seer-ee-ul] *noun, plural* **serials.** *Literature.* a story that is broadcast on television or radio or published in a magazine or newspaper in short, regular installments. *adjective.* published in installments or parts.

A different word with the same sound is **cereal.**

serial number a number that is put on an item so that it can be identified and recognized: *Our stolen TV set was tracked down by the police who identified it by its serial number.*

se·ries [seer-eez] *noun, plural* **series.** a number of similar things, events, or actions following one after another: *There is a series of foreign films being played at the local movie theater over the next six weeks.*

In writing, the **series** comma is used at the end of a list (series) of things. "At the farmers market we bought peaches, apples, strawberries, tomatoes, and lettuce. The *series comma* is the one before the "and" at the end of the list. Some people do not use the series comma, but most books on writing recommend it because it makes it clear how the list is arranged.

se·ri·ous [seer-ee-us] *adjective.* **1.** thoughtful, quiet, and solemn in manner: *The school principal had a serious look on his face when he called the student into his office.* **2.** not joking: *Are you being serious about your family moving to Canada?* **3.** requiring much thought; important: *Mom says that marriage is a serious matter.* **4.** having severe or dangerous effects: *He has a serious injury from the car accident.*
—**seriously,** *adverb;*
—**seriousness,** *noun.*

ser·mon [sur-mun] *noun, plural* **sermons.** *Religion.* **1.** a talk given in a Christian church service by the minister, usually about a religious or moral issue. **2.** any long, serious talk about morals, behavior, or conduct: *Dad gave me a sermon about leaving the dinner table without asking.*

ser·pent [sur-punt] *noun, plural* **serpents.** an older word for a SNAKE.

se·rum [seer-um] *noun, plural* **serums.** *Medicine.* **1.** the clear, pale yellow liquid that separates from the blood when a clot forms. **2.** this same liquid taken from an animal that is immune to a particular disease. It can then be put into a sick person's blood to help them fight the infection because it contains antibodies.

ser·vant [sur-vunt] *noun, plural* **servants.** a person who is employed by someone else to serve and perform duties for them such as cooking and cleaning. A **civil servant** is someone who works in the **civil service,** a **public servant** is someone who works for the government.

serve ▼ [surv] *verb,* **served, serving. 1.** to provide food or drink to someone: *Mom served the guests wine and cheese when they arrived.* **2.** to be enough for: *There is enough tea in the teapot to serve four people.* **3.** to be employed as a servant. **4.** to fulfill a term of service; do one's duty for: *My grandfather served in the army for ten years.* **5.** to be used; be of use: *My newspaper served as an umbrella when I was caught in a sudden rainstorm.* **6.** in games such as tennis or volleyball, to put a ball into play. *noun, plural* **serves.** in games such as tennis, the act of putting a ball into play.

ser·ver [surv-ur] *noun, plural* **servers.** *Computers.* a central computer that is used to provide services such as data, file, and program access to other computers on the network.

ser·vice [sur-vis] *noun, plural* **services. 1.** the fact of being a help; a helpful act: *My brother was of great service when I was trying to fill out my college application.* **2.** employment or performance of duties as a servant. **3.** the supplying of something needed or required by people: *The bus service in this town is very efficient.* **4.** a branch of the armed forces: *He spent his first two years in the service doing training.* **5.** a formal religious ceremony or rite: *a burial service.* **6.** the act of repairing; making fit for use: *Dad took the car in for service in the morning and caught the bus to work.* *verb,* **serviced, servicing.** to repair or make fit for use: *Our old car needs to be serviced.*

serv·ice·man [sur-vis-man] *noun, plural* **servicemen.** a man who is a member of the armed forces.

service station a place at the side of the road where services and supplies for your vehicle are provided such as gas, oil, and repairs.

serv·ice·wo·man [sur-vis-wum-un] *noun, plural* **servicewomen.** a woman who is a member of the armed forces.

serv·ing [surv-ing] *noun, plural* **servings.** a portion of food that is enough for one person: *I was so hungry I had two servings of pie.*

ses·sion [sesh-un] *noun, plural* **sessions. 1.** a formal meeting of an organization such as a court or council. **2.** a series of these formal meetings: *Today is the final session of legislature.* **3.** a fixed period of time for any type of meeting: *the fall session of a law school.*

A strong and accurate **serve** *is essential for competitive tennis players like Rafael Nadal.*

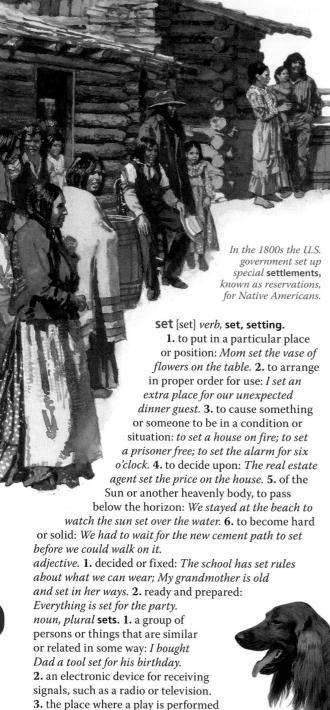

In the 1800s the U.S. government set up special **settlements**, known as reservations, for Native Americans.

set [set] *verb*, **set, setting.**
1. to put in a particular place or position: *Mom set the vase of flowers on the table.* **2.** to arrange in proper order for use: *I set an extra place for our unexpected dinner guest.* **3.** to cause something or someone to be in a condition or situation: *to set a house on fire; to set a prisoner free; to set the alarm for six o'clock.* **4.** to decide upon: *The real estate agent set the price on the house.* **5.** of the Sun or another heavenly body, to pass below the horizon: *We stayed at the beach to watch the sun set over the water.* **6.** to become hard or solid: *We had to wait for the new cement path to set before we could walk on it.*
adjective. **1.** decided or fixed: *The school has set rules about what we can wear; My grandmother is old and set in her ways.* **2.** ready and prepared: *Everything is set for the party.*
noun, plural **sets. 1.** a group of persons or things that are similar or related in some way: *I bought Dad a tool set for his birthday.* **2.** an electronic device for receiving signals, such as a radio or television. **3.** the place where a play is performed or where a television program or movie is filmed. **4.** one of a group of games in tennis.

set·back [set-bak] *noun, plural* **setbacks.** something that delays or slows down your progress: *There was a setback in her singing career when she contracted a terrible case of laryngitis.*

set·ter ▶ [set-ur] *noun, plural* **setters.** a long-haired hunting dog that is trained to help hunters find an animal or bird by standing stiffly and pointing its nose toward the prey.

set·ting [set-ing] *noun.* **1.** the general surroundings or environment: *The cottage is in a beautiful setting nestled in a valley.* **2.** the place and time in which the action of a book, play, or film takes place: *The film has its setting in an Italian fishing village.*

The **setting** of a story is the place where it happens. For most writers, especially student writers, it is easier to write about a place that you know well, such as your home town or a place you often visit. It is also possible to write about a place where you have never been, but it is a lot harder to do this and make it seem real.

set·tle [set-ul] *verb,* **settled, settling. 1.** to reach a decision or agree on something: *Mom says that we should always settle our differences by talking to each other.* **2.** to come to rest: *The fly settled on the kitchen table.* **3.** to live somewhere; set up a home: *My sister got married and settled in Connecticut.* **4.** to sink gradually: *Dust had settled on all the furniture by the time we came home from summer vacation.* **5.** to make quiet or calm: *He settled the baby's nerves by singing softly to her.*

set·tle·ment ◀ [set-ul-munt] *noun, plural* **settlements.**
1. the act or process of settling: *the settlement of parts of New England by the Europeans in the 1600s.* **2.** a small community: *Many new settlements were established in the western U.S. as a result of the coming of the railroad.*

set·tler [set-lur] *noun, plural* **settlers.** someone who comes to a new country or land to live on it and farm it: *Early American settlers lived in log cabins.*

sev·en [sev-un] *noun, plural* **sevens.** the number between six and eight; 7.
adjective. amounting to seven in number.
—**seventh,** *adjective; noun.*

sev·en·teen [sev-un-teen] *noun, plural* **seventeens.** the number between sixteen and eighteen; 17.
adjective. amounting to seventeen in number.
—**seventeenth,** *adjective; noun.*

sev·en·ty [sev-un-tee] *noun, plural* **seventies.** the number between sixty-nine and seventy-one; 70.
adjective. amounting to seventy in number.
—**seventieth,** *adjective; noun.*

sev·er [sev-ur] *verb,* **severed, severing. 1.** to cut through or separate: *The power cables were severed by the ice storm.* **2.** to break off a connection with someone or something: *The two countries could not agree on policy and severed all diplomatic relations with each other.*

Irish **setters** *are also called red setters because of their reddish-brown color.*

sev·er·al [sev-rul *or* sev-ur-ul] *noun.*
a number of people or things that
is more than two, but not many:
*Several of my friends are also applying
for college.*
adjective. **1.** describing more than two but
not many: *Several players on the team are
out with injuries.* **2.** describing something
separate; individual: *They all said good-bye
and went their several ways.*

se·vere [suh-veer] *adjective,* **severer, severest.**
1. describing something harsh; extreme:
*The criminal was given a severe punishment
for his crime.* **2.** causing great pain or difficulty:
*He had severe injuries from the car accident;
The wild storm caused severe damage to the entire city.*
The fact or act of being harsh or the quality of being
severe is **severity. —severely,** *adverb.*

sew ▲ [soh] *verb,* **sewed, sewed** *or* **sewn, sewing.** to join
or attach by using a needle and thread: *My mother taught
me how to sew my clothes both by hand and with a sewing
machine.* The activity or hobby of making or repairing
clothes or decorating with a needle and thread is **sewing.**
• **sew up. 1.** to close or repair a hole or tear: *to sew up a
hole in a pair of trousers.* **2.** to make certain: *We already
had a 2–0 lead and the third goal sewed up the victory.*
🔊 Different words with the same sound are **so** and **sow.**

sew·age [soo-ij] *noun. Environment.* waste matter and
used water that is carried away from houses and other
buildings by sewers and drains under the ground.

sew·er [soo-ur] *noun, plural* **sewers.** a large underground
pipe that is used for carrying waste water and human
waste away from houses and other buildings.

sewn [sohn] *verb.* a past participle of SEW.

sex [seks] *noun, plural* **sexes.** *Biology.* **1.** one of the two
groups, male and female, that humans and animals are
divided into. **2.** the state of being male or female.

sex·ist [seks-ist] *adjective.* having to do with the belief that
members of one sex are less intelligent or skillful than the
other: *He made a sexist remark about women being bad
drivers.* Discrimination based on a person's sex is **sexism.**

sex·u·al [seks-yoo-ul] *adjective.* having to do with being
male or female: *The company released a new policy
on how to deal with sexual discrimination.*
—sexually, *adverb.*

shab·by [shab-ee] *adjective,* **shabbier, shabbiest.**
1. describing something old and very worn:
*The apartment was dirty and smelly with shabby
furniture.* **2.** having to do with being unfair or unkind:
The mean boy played a shabby trick on the new student.
—shabbily, *adverb;* **—shabbiness,** *noun.*

shack [shak] *noun, plural* **shacks.** a roughly-built cabin
or hut: *a rundown old shack by the side of the river.*

shack·le [shak-ul] *noun.* one of a pair of metal rings for
holding the wrist or ankle of a person to stop them
moving easily or escaping.

*Early sewing machines, operated
by a large pedal, made* **sewing**
easier and faster.

shad [shad] *noun, plural* **shads.**
a herring-like fish of Europe and
North America that is usually caught
when it swims up river to lay or
fertilize eggs.

shade [shade] *noun, plural* **shades.**
1. slight darkness in an area caused by
something blocking the direct sunlight:
*We sat in the shade of the beach umbrella
so we wouldn't get too sunburned.*
2. something used to block off or reduce
light: *a lamp shade.* **3.** the darkness or
lightness in a color: *The skirt was two
different shades of blue.* **4.** a slight variation or difference:
*There are many shades of opinion about the issue of
abortion.* **5. shades.** an informal word for SUNGLASSES.
verb, **shaded, shading. 1.** to protect from light or heat:
The tree shaded us from the hot midday sun. **2.** to mark
with changes of darkness or color: *The art student shaded
his drawing so that the lines and wrinkles on the people's
faces really stood out.*

shad·ow [shad-oh] *noun, plural* **shadows. 1.** the figure
or dark area of shade made when light is blocked by
a someone or something: *The huge oak tree cast a long
shadow across our backyard.* **2.** a very little bit; small
amount: *Beyond a shadow of a doubt, our football team
this season is the best that the school has ever produced.*
verb, **shadowed, shadowing.** to follow closely and
secretly: *The undercover police shadowed the suspected
thief for weeks before finally catching him in the act.*

shad·ow·y [shad-oh-ee] *adjective,* **shadowier, shadowiest.**
1. dark and filled with shadows: *The shadowy path
was lined with tall trees.* **2.** like a shadow; hidden, dim,
unclear, and so on: *The book exposes the mayor's shadowy
past, including ties to organized crime.*

shad·y [shay-dee] *adjective,*
shadier, shadiest. 1. sheltered
from the sun or giving
shade: *We found a shady spot
in the park for our picnic.*
2. describing something
dishonest or illegal: *He's a
shady character who is well
known to the police.*

shaft ▶ [shaft] *noun, plural*
shafts. 1. a long, thin pole
that forms the body of a spear
or arrow. **2.** the long, thin
handle of a tool or implement
such as a hammer or a golf
club. **3.** a long, thin, rotating
rod in an engine or machine
used for transmitting power
and motion. **4.** a ray or narrow
beam of light: *A shaft of
sunlight peeped through the
crack in the curtains.* **5.** a long
opening or passage that goes
through a building or into
the ground: *There was a big
explosion in the mine shaft.*

*These trees are so close together that only a very
narrow* **shaft** *of sunlight reaches the forest floor.*

shag·gy [shag-ee] *adjective*, **shaggier, shaggiest.** covered or made up of long, rough, tangled hair or fur: *Our dog's coat is long and shaggy, which makes it hard to keep clean.*

shake [shake] *verb*, **shook, shaken, shaking. 1.** to move backward and forward or up and down with quick, short movements: *He shook the can of soda so that it spurted everywhere when he opened it.* **2.** to tremble with cold or with emotion: *The teacher was so angry he was shaking.* **3.** to make less certain; weaken: *Our team's confidence was shaken after our third straight loss.* **4.** to cause to feel upset: *The news of her serious illness really shook the rest of the family.*
noun, plural **shakes.** the act of shaking: *The boy gave the gift box a shake before unwrapping it.*

shake·up [shake-up] *noun, plural* **shakeups.** a major change or reorganization in the way things are done: *There's been a real shakeup in the company since the new boss arrived.*

shak·y [shake-ee] *adjective*, **shakier, shakiest. 1.** shaking or likely to shake: *His legs were quite shaky since he was still recovering from his operation.* **2.** likely to break down; unsteady: *The old chair was shaky when I sat on it and felt like it would give way at any moment.*

shale [shale] *noun. Environment.* a rock that is formed from hardened clay that breaks easily into thin flat layers.

shall [shal] *verb.* a special verb that is often used with other verbs in these ways: **1.** to express future intentions: *Sir Winston Churchill is famous for saying "We shall never surrender" at the start of World War II.* **2.** to say that something must be done: *The sign said, "All visitors shall report to the school office."* **3.** to ask a question: *Shall we go to the beach today?*

In American English today people do not often use the word **shall**. If you said to someone in your family, "I *shall* go to the store now and I *shall* return in about 15 minutes," they would probably think that sounded strange. People did speak this way in the past, though, so you will find the word in books. In World War II, the famous American general Douglas MacArthur said "I shall return" to make a promise to come back to a place that he had been forced to leave.

shal·low [shal-oh] *adjective*, **shallower, shallowest. 1.** not going or being far from top to bottom; not deep: *The small children waded in the shallow end of the pool.* The shallow part of an area of water is sometimes called the **shallows. 2.** not deep in thought, feeling, or character: *It is a shallow outlook to judge people only by their personal appearance.* —**shallowness**, *noun.*

sham [sham] *noun, plural* **shams.** something that is not what it seems to be; a fraud: *The business scheme turned out to be a sham and the investors lost their money.*
verb, **shammed, shamming.** to give a false show; pretend: *He shammed illness so that he didn't have to go to school.*
adjective. describing something false: *It was a sham diamond ring that was actually worthless.*

shame [shame] *noun.* **1.** an uncomfortable feeling of guilt or foolishness as a result of something said or done: *She felt shame for having spread a nasty rumor about her classmate.* **2.** the fact of dishonor: *His disgraceful behavior brought shame on his family.* **3.** a pity or disappointment: *What a shame you're too sick to come to the party.*
verb, **shamed, shaming. 1.** to cause to feel shame: *He felt shamed and embarrassed that he had been caught cheating.* **2.** to force someone into doing something by making them feel ashamed: *His friends shamed him into telling the truth.*

shame·ful [shame-ful] *adjective.* causing shame; disgraceful: *It is shameful the way some people mistreat animals.* —**shamefully**, *adverb*; —**shamefulness**, *noun.*

shame·less [shame-lis] *adjective.* having or showing no shame: *She was quite shameless about all the terrible lies she had told.* —**shamelessly**, *adverb*; —**shamelessness**, *noun.*

sham·poo [sham-poo] *verb*, **shampooed, shampooing.** to wash the hair with a liquid soap.
noun, plural **shampoos.** a liquid soap for washing the hair.

sham·rock ◀ [sham-rok] *noun, plural* **shamrocks.** a green plant that has three round leaves on each stem. The shamrock is the national emblem of Ireland.

Several different kinds of clover are called **shamrocks.**

shape [shape] *noun, plural* **shapes. 1.** the outline of something; a form or figure: *Mom made my little brother a birthday cake in the shape of a train.* **2.** the state of something; condition: *Despite the uphill climb, the hikers arrived in good shape and set up their camp.* **3.** regular, proper, or good condition: *I need to get my ideas in shape before I start writing my essay.*
verb, **shaped, shaping.** to give form or a particular form to: *In pottery class, I shaped my clay into a bowl.*
• **shape up.** to improve to a good condition: *If the new player doesn't shape up, he'll soon find himself on the bench.*

share [share] *noun, plural* **shares. 1.** a part of something to be divided that is given to or belongs to one person: *Mom gave each of us an equal share of the pie.* **2.** *Business.* one of the equal parts or interests into which the property of a company or business is divided: *My parents own some shares of stock in a mining company.*
verb, **shared, sharing. 1.** to have, use, or experience something with one or more others: *My two sisters and I shared a room in the motel.* **2.** to divide and give out in portions, taking a portion for oneself: *I shared my ice cream with my two friends.* **3.** to have a share; take part: *The whole class shared in the preparations for the concert.*

share·ware *Computers.* software that is available for trial use for little or no cost but that can be upgraded for a fee.

shark ▶ [shark] *noun, plural* **sharks. 1.** a large to very large ocean fish with a rough, often grayish skin, a skeleton made of cartilage, and a prominent fin on its back. **2.** a dishonest person who cheats other people.

SHARKS

There are about 340 kinds of sharks. Some have flattened heads and gaping mouths, while others have snouts like saw blades. They can be as big as a school bus or as small as your hand. All have at least five pairs of gills and gill openings so that they can breathe under water. Sharks also have excellent sensory systems that zero in on prey, as well as powerful muscles to help them accelerate quickly. Some sharks hunt other sea creatures, while others filter their food from the water.

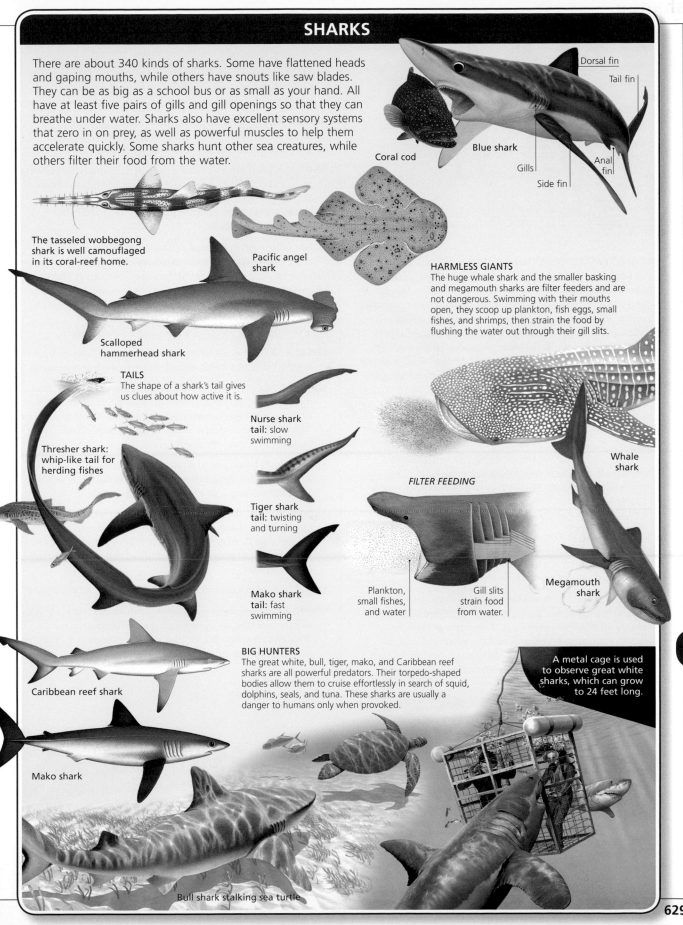

Dorsal fin

Tail fin

Blue shark

Coral cod

Gills

Anal fin

Side fin

The tasseled wobbegong shark is well camouflaged in its coral-reef home.

Pacific angel shark

HARMLESS GIANTS
The huge whale shark and the smaller basking and megamouth sharks are filter feeders and are not dangerous. Swimming with their mouths open, they scoop up plankton, fish eggs, small fishes, and shrimps, then strain the food by flushing the water out through their gill slits.

Scalloped hammerhead shark

TAILS
The shape of a shark's tail gives us clues about how active it is.

Nurse shark tail: slow swimming

Whale shark

Thresher shark: whip-like tail for herding fishes

FILTER FEEDING

Tiger shark tail: twisting and turning

Mako shark tail: fast swimming

Plankton, small fishes, and water

Gill slits strain food from water.

Megamouth shark

BIG HUNTERS
The great white, bull, tiger, mako, and Caribbean reef sharks are all powerful predators. Their torpedo-shaped bodies allow them to cruise effortlessly in search of squid, dolphins, seals, and tuna. These sharks are usually a danger to humans only when provoked.

A metal cage is used to observe great white sharks, which can grow to 24 feet long.

Caribbean reef shark

Mako shark

Bull shark stalking sea turtle

A B C D E F G H I J K L M N O P Q R S T U V W X Y Z

Native women in Bolivia wear bowler hats, ponchos, and colorful **shawls.**

sharp [sharp] *adjective,* **sharper, sharpest. 1.** having an edge or point that cuts or pierces easily; not dull or blunt: *You need a sharp knife to cut steak.* **2.** having a pointed end or edge: *In the distance we saw a mountain range with sharp, jagged peaks.* **3.** having a strong or intense quality: *Mustard has a sharp taste; When I was stung by a wasp, I felt a sharp pain.* **4.** involving a sudden change; abrupt; steep: *As we drove higher up the mountain, we felt a sharp drop in the temperature.* **5.** quick to understand things; clever; alert: *Our neighbor is eighty years old, but he still has a very sharp mind.* **6.** an everyday word describing something fashionable or stylish: *You look very sharp in your new outfit.*
adverb. **1.** exactly: *The meeting starts at nine o'clock sharp.* **2.** in a sharp manner: *As the canoe approached the rapids, the guide told the passengers to look sharp.*
noun, plural **sharps.** *Music.* **1.** a tone or note that is half a note higher than the natural or true note. **2.** a symbol (#) that indicates this tone or note. —**sharply,** *adverb;* **sharpness,** *noun.*

shar·pen [sharp-un] *verb,* **sharpened, sharpening.** to make or become sharp or sharper: *Dad sharpened the carving knife before he cut the turkey.*

shat·ter [shat-ur] *verb,* **shattered, shattering. 1.** to break violently and at once into pieces: *The car windshield shattered when the rock hit it.* **2.** to damage badly or destroy completely; ruin: *When the mast on the yacht broke, it shattered the crew's chances of winning the race.* **3.** to be very upset: *We were shattered to hear the news that our old friend had died.*

shave [shave] *verb,* **shaved, shaving. 1.** to cut off hair close to the skin, usually with a razor: *Most men shave their face every day.* **2.** to remove a thin layer from or cut off in thin layers: *I shaved off a thin slice from the block of cheese.*
noun, plural **shaves.** the act or process of cutting off hair close to the skin, usually with a razor.
♦ **close shave.** a narrow escape; a near miss: *That car almost hit us—that was a close shave!*

shav·er [shave-ur] *noun, plural* **shavers.** a device or tool for shaving, especially an electric razor.

shav·ing [shave-ing] *noun, plural* **shavings.** a thin strip or slice shaved off something: *I decorated the top of the cake with chocolate shavings.*

shawl ◀ [shawl] *noun, plural* **shawls.** a large piece of material, usually cloth, that is worn as a covering for the head or shoulders.

she [shee] *pronoun.* the female person or animal that is being talked about: *I asked my sister if she would like to come shopping with me.*
noun, plural **shes.** a female person or animal: *Is your new kitten a she or a he?*

shear [sheer] *verb,* **sheared** *or* **shorn, shearing. 1.** to cut, trim, or clip with a sharp instrument: *He sheared the hedge with an electric trimmer.* **Shears** are a cutting or clipping instrument with two blades, similar to scissors. **2.** to clip or cut off; remove by cutting or as if by cutting: *to shear the wool from sheep.*
🔊 A different word with the same sound is **sheer.**

sheath [sheeth] *noun, plural* **sheaths.** a close-fitting cover for the blade of a knife, sword, dagger, or similar weapon.

sheathe [sheeTH] *verb,* **sheathed, sheathing. 1.** to put into a sheath: *The knight sheathed his sword.* **2.** to put a close-fitting covering on or over something, usually to protect it: *The workman sheathed the sheets of glass in plastic before loading them onto the truck.*

shed[1] [shed] *noun, plural* **sheds.** a small structure used for storing or sheltering things. A shed may have one or more sides not enclosed, or all sides may be enclosed.

shed[2] ▼ [shed] *verb,* **shed, shedding. 1.** to let fall or flow: *I shed tears of happiness when I heard I had won the scholarship.* **2.** to give off or drop: *Our angora cat sheds a lot of hair.* **3.** to give or send out: *The lamp shed a soft light in the hallway.*

she'd [sheed] the shortened form of "she had" or "she would."

sheep [sheep] *noun, plural* **sheep. 1.** an animal with a thick, woolly coat that eats grass and is raised on farms for its wool and its meat. **2.** a similar but less common animal that lives wild in mountain regions.

New skin | Old skin

Most snakes **shed** *their skin between four and eight times a year.*

sheer [sheer] *adjective,* **sheerer, sheerest.**
1. very fine and thin; so thin that you can see through it; transparent: *a dress made from sheer silk.* **2.** describing something complete; utter: *It was sheer stupidity to jump off that rock into the water like they did.* **3.** describing something very steep; almost vertical: *The sheer cliffs rising from the shoreline were a stunning sight.*

sheet [sheet] *noun, plural* **sheets. 1.** a large piece of cotton, linen, or other fabric used as bedding. **2.** a broad, thin, flat surface or piece of something: *a sheet of paper; a sheet of glass.*

sheik [sheek *or* shake] *noun, plural* **sheiks.** the chief of an Arab tribe, clan, or village.

shelf [shelf] *noun, plural* **shelves. 1.** a flat, thin piece of wood or other material fixed horizontally to a wall or inside a piece of furniture, such as a cupboard, so that things can be placed on it. **2.** something that is like a shelf: *This part of the coastline is dangerous for ships because there is an underwater rock shelf.*
• **on the shelf.** not currently active or of use.

shell [shel] *noun, plural* **shells. 1.** the hard, protective outer covering of eggs, some animals, nuts, and some fruits and seeds. Turtles, snails, and sea animals such as oysters and mussels have shells. **2.** something that is like a shell: *After the huge fire, only the shell of the house remained.* **3.** a case filled with explosive material to be shot from a cannon, or the metal or paper case containing the explosive to be shot from a gun or rifle.
verb, **shelled, shelling. 1.** to remove the shell from: *to shell peas; to shell eggs.* **2.** to fire shells at: *The rebel soldiers shelled the fort with their cannons.*

she'll [sheel] the shortened form of "she will" or "she shall."

shel·lac [shuh-lak] *noun, plural* **shellacs.** a liquid used a wood filler and also as a varnish on floors and furniture to give them a protective coating and make them shine.
verb, **shellacked, shellacking. 1.** to treat or varnish something with shellac. **2.** to defeat thoroughly; thrash: *Our team shellacked the opposition last week.*

shell·fish ▶ [shel-fish] *noun, plural* **shellfish** *or* **shellfishes.** an animal that lives in water and has a shell. Lobsters, crabs, oysters, and mussels are shellfish. Shellfish are not true fish. They belong to one of the two groups of animals called mollusks and crustaceans.

shel·ter [shel-tur] *noun, plural* **shelters. 1.** something that covers or protects: *These trees will make a good shelter for our tent.* **2.** the state of being covered or protected; protection: *The beach umbrella provided us with shelter from the sun.* Someone or something that is protected from something is described as being **sheltered. 3.** a place where people or animals that are lost or have no home can stay and are given food.
verb, **sheltered, sheltering.** to give shelter to: *The awning in front of the store sheltered us from the heavy rain.*

shelve [shelv] *verb,* **shelved, shelving. 1.** to put on a shelf or shelves: *I helped our school librarian to shelve the new books.* **2.** to fit something with shelves. A system of shelves and their supports is called **shelving. 3.** to put something off or aside: *Because he has so many other bills to pay, he has shelved his plans to buy a new car.*

shep·herd ▲ [shep-urd] *noun, plural* **shepherds.** someone whose job is to take care of sheep.
verb, **shepherded, shepherding.** to guide or look after something like a shepherd: *The tour guide shepherded the tourists through the outdoor market.*

sher·bet [shur-but] *noun, plural* **sherbets.** a frozen dessert made of fruit juice with milk, egg white, or gelatin added before freezing. This word is also spelled **sherbert.**

sher·iff [sher-if] *noun, plural* **sheriffs.** the officer who is responsible for enforcing the law in a county and for carrying out the orders of courts and judges.

she's [sheez] the shortened form of "she is" or "she has."

Shetland pony a small, strong pony with short legs that originally came from the Shetland Islands, off the coast of Scotland. It has a thick, rough coat and a long mane and tail.

The *Shetland* Islands are a group of northern islands that are part of the country of Scotland. The **Shetland pony** comes from these islands. They are known as the strongest breed of pony, a strength they developed from living in the cold, harsh conditions of the Shetland Islands.

A crab is a **shellfish** *that has long pincers to catch its prey.*

a b c d e f g h i j k l m n o p q r **s** t u v w x y z

shield ◀ [sheeld] *noun,* *plural* **shields. 1.** *History.* a piece of armor that was carried on the arm or in the hand in earlier times to protect a person's head or body. **2.** someone or something that acts as a defense or protection: *Sunglasses provide a shield against the sun.* **3.** something shaped like a shield. For example, a police officer's badge is called a shield.

shift [shift] *verb,* **shifted, shifting.** to move from one place to another, change position: *I shifted the chair closer to the window; The driver shifted from third gear down to second gear to go up the steep hill.* *noun, plural* **shifts. 1.** a movement or change: *There was a sudden shift in the wind and I nearly lost hold of my kite.* **2.** a group of workers who work together for a set period, or the time that they work: *My mom is a nurse and sometimes works the night shift on weekends.* **3.** a mechanism that connects and disconnects a set of gears to a motor; a gearshift.

shif·ty [shif-tee] *adjective,* **shiftier, shiftiest.** not trustworthy; tricky; evasive: *The customer was behaving in a shifty way, so the sales clerk alerted the store detectives.*

shil·ling [shil-ing] *noun, plural* **shillings.** a coin formerly used in Great Britain. Twenty shillings were equal to one pound. Some early American coins were also called shillings.

shim·mer [shim-ur] *verb,* **shimmered, shimmering.** to shine with a faint, quivering light; glimmer: *The ocean shimmered in the moonlight.*

shin [shin] *noun, plural* **shins.** the front part of the leg between the knee and the ankle. *verb,* **shinned, shinning.** to climb up or down something by using the arms and legs to jerk oneself up or down.

shine [shine] *verb,* **shone** *or* **shined, shining. 1.** to give out or reflect light: *The sun actually shines every day, even when the sky looks dull and cloudy.* **2.** to be or make bright: *Sometimes I shine my dad's shoes for him.* **3.** to be excellent; show talent: *My friend Matt loves performing and really shines when he's up on stage.* *noun, plural* **shines. 1.** light or brightness: *We saw the shine of a flashlight in the distance.* **2.** the act of polishing: *My silver ring is looking dull and needs a shine.*

shin·gle [shing-gul] *noun, plural* **shingles.** a small, thin piece of wood or other material used in overlapping rows to cover the roof and sometimes the sides of a building. *verb,* **shingled, shingling.** to cover with shingles: *The workmen shingled the roof of the house in two days.*

Shin·to [shin-toh] *noun. Religion.* a religion that originated in Japan and is still the main religion in Japan.

shin·y [shy-nee] *adjective,* **shinier, shiniest.** describing something shining; bright or glossy: *I got a shiny new bike for my birthday.*

ship [ship] *noun, plural* **ships. 1.** a large boat that goes to sea. **2.** an airplane, airship, or spacecraft. *verb,* **shipped, shipping. 1.** to send something by ship or transport it by train, truck, or airplane: *We shipped our furniture to our new home by truck.* **2.** to join a ship as a member of the crew: *My uncle shipped out as an engineer on a cruise ship.*

-ship a suffix that means: **1.** the state, condition, or quality of being something: *apprenticeship* means the state of being an apprentice. **2.** the art or skill of: *horsemanship* means the art or skill of a horseman or horsewoman.

ship·ment [ship-munt] *noun, plural* **shipments. 1.** the act or process of shipping: *The tomatoes were loaded onto the truck for shipment to the market.* **2.** the goods shipped or an amount of something shipped: *The store is out of fans, but the clerk told us he expects a shipment next week.*

ship·ping [ship-ing] *noun.* **1.** the act or business of transporting goods by ship, train, truck, or airplane. **2.** ships in general: *That port has a port authority to control the shipping that passes through or docks there each day.*

ship·wreck [ship-rek] *noun, plural* **shipwrecks. 1.** the destruction or loss of a ship: *The shipwreck occurred near a dangerous strip of rocky coastline.* **2.** the remains of a wrecked ship. *verb,* **shipwrecked, shipwrecking.** to cause a ship or boat to be destroyed or lost: *Huge waves shipwrecked the fishing boat.*

ship·yard ▼ [ship-yard] *noun, plural* **shipyards.** a place where ships are built or repaired.

shirk [shurk] *verb,* **shirked, shirking.** to avoid or get out of doing something one should do: *to shirk responsibility.*

shirt [shurt] *noun, plural* **shirts.** a piece of clothing made of cotton or a similar fabric worn on the upper part of the body. The most common type of shirt has a collar, sleeves, and buttons down the front, and is long enough to be tucked inside pants or a skirt.

shiv·er [shiv-ur] *verb,* **shivered, shivering.** to shake involuntarily; tremble, especially with cold or fear: *It was so cold outside that I shivered despite my coat.* *noun, plural* **shivers.** a brief shivering movement: *One of the scenes in the movie sent shivers down my spine.*

shoal [shole] *noun plural* **shoals. 1.** a place where the ocean, a river, or a lake is shallow. **2.** an underwater sandbank or sandbar.

Shipyards are usually located in large ports like this one at Gdansk, Poland.

shock¹ [shok] *noun, plural* **shocks.**
   1. a sudden, very disturbing effect on the mind or feelings: *The news that my cousin had been badly injured in a car accident came as a great shock to us.* **2.** a sudden, violent shake or knock: *The shock of the earthquake was felt hundreds of miles away.* **3.** the effect of an electric charge passing through the body: *You should not use an appliance with a damaged cord, as it may give you a shock.* **4.** *Health.* a great weakness of the body resulting from severe injury, bleeding, or pain or a severe emotional upset. A person goes into shock when not enough blood is flowing through the body.
   verb, **shocked, shocking. 1.** to severely disturb someone's mind or feelings: *The TV images of people caught in the tsunami shocked me.* **2.** to give an electric shock.

shock² [shok] *noun, plural* **shocks. 1.** a bundle of grain or corn stalks stood on end and left in a field to dry. **2.** a bushy, untidy mass of hair: *The baby was born with a shock of red hair.*

shock absorber a device on a vehicle, piece of machinery, or building for absorbing or deadening shocks and vibrations.

shock·ing [shok-ing] *adjective.* causing horror, surprise, or disgust: *We heard the shocking news that two trains had collided and many people were injured.*
   —**shockingly,** *adverb.*

shock wave 1. *Science.* an area of sudden change of pressure moving in a gas (such as air) or a liquid faster than the speed of sound. For example, a shock wave is caused when air is suddenly compressed by an explosion, such as an earthquake. **2.** a violent disturbance or reaction: *The news of President Kennedy's assassination sent shock waves around the world.* This term is also spelled **shockwave.**

shod·dy [shod-ee] *adjective,* **shoddier, shoddiest.** poorly made or done: *This table has uneven legs and is a shoddy piece of workmanship.* —**shoddiness,** *noun.*

shoe [shoo] *noun, plural* **shoes. 1.** an outer covering for the human foot that does not reach beyond the ankle. It is usually made of leather or plastic. **2.** something like a shoe, such as a horseshoe.
   verb, **shod, shoeing.** to put a shoe or shoes on, or to provide with a shoe or shoes: *My uncle owns horses and shoes them himself.*

shoe·lace [shoo-lays] *noun, plural* **shoelaces.** a string or cord used to fasten a shoe.

shone [shohn] *verb.* the past tense and past participle of SHINE.

shook [shuk] *verb.* the past tense of SHAKE.

shoot [shoot] *verb,* **shot, shooting.**
   1. to hit with a bullet fired from a gun or an arrow: *The farmer shot and killed the wolf that had attacked his sheep.*
   2. to let fly or send forth from a weapon: *The king's soldiers shot flaming arrows over the wall of the enemy's castle.*
   3. to cause a weapon to send forth a bullet, arrow, or other missile. **4.** to move or go forward quickly: *My friend shot past me on his skateboard. The lizard shot out its tongue.* **5.** to photograph or film something: *The television series was shot on location in Malibu.*
   noun, plural **shoots.** the new growth of a plant, or a young plant.

shooting star ▲ a small mass of metal or stone traveling very fast that burns up as it enters the Earth's atmosphere; also called a METEOR.

shop [shop] *noun, plural* **shops. 1.** a place where goods or services are sold to the public; a store: *My mom works as a sales clerk in a gift shop.* **2.** a place where a particular kind of work is done, especially work that involves machinery: *I went to see the engineering shop where my cousin works.*
   verb, **shopped, shopping.** to go to shops or stores to look at and buy things: *I shopped for a new pair of boots.*

shop·lift [shop-lift] *verb,* **shoplifted, shoplifting.** to steal goods on display in a store while appearing to shop there. Someone who steals goods in this way is a **shoplifter.**

shop·per [shop-ur] *noun, plural* **shoppers.** someone who goes to shops or stores to look at or buy things.

shopping center a group of stores and other businesses that sell or provide services to the public. Shopping centers are usually located in suburbs, and most have large parking lots.

shore ▼ [shore] *noun, plural* **shores. 1.** the land along the edge of a large body of water, such as the ocean or a lake. **2.** dry land; land: *After spending a day on the fishing boat, we were glad to be back on shore.*

The scenery along an ocean **shore** *may vary from rocky coves and headlands to sandy beaches, large sand dunes, and coastal lagoons.*

short [short] *adjective,* **shorter, shortest. 1.** of little length or height; not long or tall: *I had my hair cut short for the summer.* **2.** not great in distance or amount: *We took a short break from driving to stretch our legs.* **3.** not having or being enough, or not being of the normal or required standard: *I'm short of cash, as I spent my pocket money early in the week.* **4.** *Language.* referring to one of the vowel sounds that takes little time to pronounce. For example, the "a" in *cat* is a short vowel. *adverb.* **1.** suddenly and without warning; abruptly: *The driver pulled up short and managed to avoid hitting a dog that ran out onto the road.* **2.** so as not to reach as far as: *The arrow fell short of the target.* *noun, plural* **shorts.** a SHORT CIRCUIT.
• **for short.** a shorter way of referring to something: *A refrigerator is called a fridge for short.*
• **short for.** a shorter form or abbreviation of: *"Rick" is short for "Richard."*

short·age [shor-tij] *noun, plural* **shortages.** an amount or supply that is not enough; lack; scarcity: *There is a shortage of rooms at the hotel, so some of you will have to share a room.*

short circuit a connection between two points in an electric circuit between which current does not normally flow. Such a connection may be made deliberately or may happen by accident. To **short-circuit** means to make or have such a connection in an electric circuit.

short·com·ing [short-kum-ing] *noun, plural* **shortcomings.** failure to come up to a certain standard; a fault or defect: *Selfishness is a serious shortcoming in a person's character.*

short·cut [short-kut] *noun, plural* **shortcuts. 1.** a shorter or faster route to a place: *I took a shortcut to the park through the alley.* **2.** a quick way of doing or achieving something: *Good carpenters don't take shortcuts when they are building something, as they know that could result in a poor-quality job.* This word is also spelled **short cut.**

short·en [short-un] *verb,* **shortened, shortening.** to make or become shorter or short: *Mom shortened the new curtains to fit the window.*

short·en·ing [short-un-ing] *noun.* a fat such as butter, oil, or lard used in baking or cooking.

short·hand [short-hand] *noun. Language.* **1.** a special method of writing words down as quickly as people say them by using certain symbols and abbreviations instead of writing the words in full. **2.** a short or fast way of communicating or representing something.

short·hand·ed [short-han-did] *adjective.* not having enough or the usual number of people to do a job: *The customers were kept waiting for their meals, as the restaurant was shorthanded.* *adverb.* in certain sports, such as ice hockey, playing with fewer than the full number of players. This word is also spelled **short-handed.**

short·ly [short-lee] *adverb.* in a little while; soon: *The plane will be landing shortly.*

short·ness [short-nis] *noun.* **1.** the fact of being short. **2.** the state of being lacking in something: *Mountaineers may suffer from shortness of breath at high altitudes.*

short-range [short-ranj] *adjective.* **1.** limited to short distances: *a short-range missile.* **2.** related to a short period of time: *short-range plans.*

shorts [shortz] *plural noun.* trousers that end at or above the knee.

short·sight·ed [short-sye-tid] *adjective.* **1.** not able to see distant objects clearly. **2.** not planning for the future: *It was shortsighted of us not to bring umbrellas when the weather forecast predicted rain.* —**shortsightedness,** *noun.*

short·stop [short-stop] *noun, plural* **shortstops.** in baseball or softball, a player whose position is between second and third base.

short story *Literature.* a type of fiction that is shorter than a novel.

The **short story** is a common form of writing for students. It would be very difficult for a student to write a full-length novel, and there aren't many examples of this. However, a short story need only be a page or two long. The British author Somerset Maugham is one of the most famous writers of short stories. One of his best-known stories, called "The Appointment in Samarra," is only 200 words long and takes up less than one printed page.

short·wave [short-wave] *noun, plural* **shortwaves.** in radio communication, a wave length of less than one hundred meters. **Short-wave** broadcasts can be transmitted over long distances to reach foreign audiences.

shot [shot] *noun, plural* **shot** *or* **shots. 1.** the firing of a bullet, arrow, or other such missile: *Shots were fired at the police.* **2.** a person who fires a gun: *To kill deer you have to be a good shot.* **3.** the fact of trying; an attempt: *Marcia gave the test her best shot.* **4.** an injection by hypodermic needle: *The doctor gave him a flu shot.* **5.** the stroke someone makes with a tennis racket or golf club. **6.** an effort to score a goal in games such as basketball, soccer, or ice hockey. **7.** the lead pellets used in guns and cannons.

shot·gun [shot-gun] *noun, plural* **shotguns.** a long-handled, long-barrelled gun that shoots many small pellets, called shot, at once.

shot put ◀ an event in track and field in which athletes try to throw a heavy metal ball as far as possible. An athlete who does this is called a **shot putter.**

A **shot putter** *holds the ball tightly against his neck and shoulder before hurling it.*

should [shud] *verb.* a special verb that is often used with other verbs in these ways: **1.** to express a feeling of obligation: *We should save these newspapers for recycling.* **2.** to give advice: *"You should turn left here,'" I told the cab driver.* **3.** to say that something is likely to happen: *The Democrats should win the next election.* **4.** to say what is to be done if something happens: *If anyone should call while I'm out, please take a message.*

Collarbone

shoul·der [shohl-dur] *noun, plural* **shoulders. 1.** the part of the body between the neck and the upper arm. **2.** in clothing, the piece of material that covers the body between the neck and the upper arms. **3.** the edge of a road: *The car pulled over onto the shoulder.* *verb,* **shouldered, shouldering.** to push aside with the shoulders: *I shouldered my way onto the crowded bus.*

Shoulder blade

shoulder blade ▲ one of the flat, triangular bones that form the back part of the shoulder.

shouldn't [shud-unt] the shortened form of "should not."

shout [shout] *verb,* **shouted, shouting.** to speak loudly: *I had to shout to make myself heard in the crowd.* *noun, plural* **shouts.** a loud call or cry: *Shouts from outside let us know our visitors were here.*

shove [shuv] *verb,* **shoved, shoving.** to push hard, especially in a rough way: *I shoved all my dirty clothes into the laundry basket.* *noun, plural* **shoves.** a strong or rough push: *to give someone a shove to get them to move out of the way.*

shov·el [shuv-ul] *noun, plural* **shovels. 1.** a tool or machine with a broad scoop used for digging and moving loose material: *The snow shovel cleared the road in front of our house .* **2.** the amount of material a shovel can hold: *He dug out five shovels of soil from under the dog's kennel.* *verb,* **shoveled, shoveling. 1.** to move loose material by using a shovel. **2.** to cram in a large amount of material: *The greedy boy shoveled as many potato chips into his mouth as he could fit.*

show [shoh] *verb,* **showed** or **shown, showing. 1.** to come into sight; appear: *The sun showed through the clouds.* **2.** to make evident; reveal: *Jane's smile showed how pleased she was.* **3.** to demonstrate or explain: *The coach showed us how to do head the ball toward the goal.* **4.** to display or exhibit: *My favorite movie is showing at our local theater for a week.* *noun, plural* **shows. 1.** the act or fact of displaying something: *a dog show.* **2.** a movie, play, television, or radio program, or other such public entertainment. **3.** the act or fact of pretending: *She made a show of being grateful for her present, but really she was disappointed.*

show business the entertainment industry: *So many actors want to get into show business, but only a few will make it.*

show·er [shou-er] *noun, plural* **showers. 1.** a brief fall of water in the form of rain, hail, sleet, or snow. **2.** a fall of anything in large numbers: *Showers of leaves drop to the ground in fall.* **3.** a type of bath in which an overhead fixture sprays a stream of water through small holes. **4.** the fixture itself, or an enclosed space where it is contained. **5.** a party where the guests bring gifts for an engaged or pregnant woman: *At a baby shower people bring gifts for the new baby.* *verb,* **showered, showering. 1.** to bathe under a shower. **2.** to fall as a light rain, hail, sleet, or snow: *It often showers in springtime.* **3.** to overwhelm with a great quantity: *He showered her with kisses.*

shown [shone] *verb.* a past participle of SHOW.

show-off [shoh-*of or* shoh-*awf*] *noun, plural* **show-offs.** someone who draws attention to himself or herself: *She's very pretty, but she's such a show-off that people don't like her.*

show·y [shoh-ee] *adjective.* **showier, showiest. 1.** describing something that attracts attention: *a bunch of showy flowers.* **2.** in bad taste; gaudy: *The showiest house on the block was painted pink.*

shrap·nel [shrap-nul] *noun.* **1.** a shell or bomb filled with lead pellets that explodes in flight. **2.** the fragments from such a device after it has exploded.

The artillery shell known as **shrapnel** was invented by a British officer, Henry *Shrapnel.* He developed this type of weapon for a war that Britain fought against France in the early 1800s.

shred [shred] *noun, plural* **shreds. 1.** a small, rough strip of material: *A shred of his clothing was caught on the fence.* **2.** a very small amount: *The lawyer said that the police didn't have a shred of evidence against his client.* *verb,* **shredded** or **shred, shredding.** to tear apart into small pieces: *to shred a piece of paper.*

shred·der [shred-ur] *noun, plural* **shredders.** a machine that tears material into very small pieces: *a document shredder; a leaf shredder.*

shrew ▼ [shroo] *noun, plural* **shrews.** a very small mammal with a long, pointed nose that looks like a mouse.

Rock elephant **shrews** *nest in the gaps between rocks and feed on insects.*

*Banded coral **shrimp** live in tropical waters.*

shrewd [shrood] *adjective,* **shrewder, shrewdest.** showing good judgment; clever: *John made a shrewd decision in selling his stock just before the market crash.*
—**shrewdly,** *adverb;*
—**shrewdness,** *noun.*

shriek [shreek] *noun, plural* **shrieks.** a loud scream of pleasure or fear: *The joke had us in shrieks of laughter.* *verb,* **shrieked, shrieking.** to scream loudly.

shrill [shril] *adjective,* **shriller, shrillest.** having a sharp, high-pitched sound: *The little girl's shrill voice could be heard above the crowd.*

shrimp ▲ [shrimp] *noun, plural* **shrimp** *or* **shrimps.** **1.** a small freshwater or saltwater shellfish that can be eaten. **2.** someone or something very small.

shrine ▼ [shrine] *noun, plural* **shrines.** *Religion.* **1.** a place where people worship. It may contain the tomb of a saint or holy objects belonging to them. **2.** a place people visit where something holy has happened.

shrink [shringk] *verb,* **shrank** *or* **shrunk, shrunk** *or* **shrunken, shrinking. 1.** to become smaller because of heat, cold, or wetness: *My clothes shrank in the laundry.* **2.** to move away in fear or disgust: *He shrank from touching the jellyfish.*

shriv·el [shriv-ul] *verb,* **shriveled, shriveling.** to become smaller by drying up: *With no water, the flowers shriveled in the vase.*

shroud [shroud] *noun, plural* **shrouds.** the cloth in which a corpse is buried: *The Shroud of Turin is believed by many people to have once contained the body of Jesus.* *verb,* **shrouded, shrouding.** to put or keep out of sight; conceal: *a mountain shrouded by clouds; an event shrouded in mystery.*

shrub [shrub] *noun, plural* **shrubs.** any small bushy plant.

shrubb·ery [shrub-ree *or* shrub-uh-ree] *noun, plural* **shrubberies.** a group of shrubs, or the area of the garden in which many shrubs are planted.

shrug [shrug] *verb,* **shrugged, shrugging.** to lift the shoulders to show doubt or lack of interest: *He shrugged when I asked him if he liked playing sports.* *noun, plural* **shrugs.** the act of shrugging.

shudd·er [shud-ur] *verb,* **shuddered, shuddering.** to shake or tremble from fear: *I shudder to think what might have happened if the pilot had not been able to get the plane under control.* *noun, plural* **shudders.** a sudden shiver: *The boy gave a shudder as he thought about diving into the icy water.*

shuf·fle [shuf-ul] *verb,* **shuffled, shuffling. 1.** to drag the feet along the ground, as from being tired or lazy: *The old man shuffled along the sidewalk.* **2.** to change the order in a pack of cards. **3.** to move to a different place: *At the end of the season the veteran player was shuffled off to a different team.* *noun, plural* **shuffles.** the act of shuffling: *She walked with a shuffle.*

shun [shun] *verb,* **shunned, shunning.** to avoid by choice: *The movie star shunned contact with the public because she preferred to be alone.*

shut [shut] *verb,* **shut, shutting. 1.** to close something: *to shut a book; to shut a drawer.* **2.** to become closed: *The door shut after me.* **3.** to bring together parts of: *to shut a book; to shut your eyes.* **4.** to stop the action or operation of: *to shut off the TV set.*
• **shut out. 1.** to block or stop from entering: *The fence shut out trespassers.* **2.** to prevent an opponent from scoring any points in a game.
• **shut up.** to stop talking or prevent from speaking: *She suddenly shut up when she saw everyone else had stopped talking.*

shut·down [shut-down] *noun, plural* **shutdowns.** the temporary or permanent ending of the operation of a machine, system, business, and so on: *the shutdown of a computer; the shutdown of a nuclear reactor.* *verb.* **shut down.** to close down or stop operating.

shut·out [shut-out] *noun, plural* **shutouts.** a game in which one team does not score.

shut·ter [shut-ur] *noun, plural* **shutters. 1.** a window covering, usually made of wooden slats. **2.** in photography, the part of the camera that covers the light-sensitive area at the back that records the image: *I took the photo in very bright light using a fast speed for the shutter.* *verb,* **shuttered, shuttering.** to fit or cover a window with shutters: *The house was shuttered against the light in summer.*

shut·tle [shut-ul] *noun, plural* **shuttles. 1.** a vehicle used for regular or short journeys: *We traveled by bus shuttle from the station to the hotel.* **2.** a regular traffic route: *the Washington–New York air shuttle.* **3.** see SPACE SHUTTLE. **4.** a tool used in weaving cloth that carries the thread back and forth across the material. *verb,* **shuttled, shuttling.** to go back and forth: *We shuttled between classes.*

shy [shye] *adjective,* **shyer** *or* **shier, shyest** *or* **shiest. 1.** easily frightened; timid: *The puppy was shy with strangers.* **2.** unsure or embarrassed in social situations: *Jack was too shy to give a speech at his graduation.* **3.** short of a certain quantity: *She was a week shy of turning eighteen.* *verb,* **shied, shying.** to suddenly jump back from; avoid: *The horse shied at the last fence.*

sib·ling [sib-ling] *noun, plural* **siblings.** a brother or sister: *I have two siblings—one brother and one sister.*

*Bodhnath Stupa is a huge Buddhist **shrine** in Nepal that was built in the fourteenth century.*

A B C D E F G H I J K L M N O P Q R **S** T U V W X Y Z

sick [sik] *adjective*, **sicker, sickest. 1.** having a disease or ailment; not well; ill: *My sister was sick with measles.* **2.** having an upset stomach; feeling nausea: *A rough sea often makes even experienced sailors sick.* **3.** feeling bored or tired: *Jane was sick of doing the household chores.* **4.** feeling unhappy or disgusted: *I was sick to hear the thief had taken our belongings.*

sic·kle ◀ [sik-ul] *noun*, *plural* **sickles.** a tool with a short handle and sharp, curved blade used for harvesting grass or wheat by hand.

sickle cell anemia *Medicine.* a genetic disease in which red blood cells change to become sickle-shaped, causing a certain type of anemia. It mainly affects people from Africa or of African descent.

In Ukraine, people still use **sickles** *to harvest wheat and other crops by hand.*

sick·ly [sik-lee] *adjective*, **sicklier, sickliest. 1.** often or always ill: *My father was sickly as a child but his health improved after good food and exercise.* **2.** having the appearance of being ill: *Her complexion was sickly from spending so much time indoors.*

sick·ness [sik-nis] *noun*, *plural* **sicknesses. 1.** a general state of poor health; the fact of being ill: *There was a lot of sickness in the family.* **2.** a particular disease or illness.

side [side] *noun*, *plural* **sides. 1.** an outer part of something that is not the front, top, bottom, or back: *We planted the roses on the south side of the house.* **2.** any surface of a solid figure: *All four sides of the box were painted white.* **3.** one of the two surfaces of a flat object: *An image of the queen's head was on one side of the coin.* **4.** a line enclosing a drawn figure: *A triangle has three sides.* **5.** a position to the left or right part of the body: *I get a stitch in my side after running.* **5.** the left or right of an imaginary central line: *the west side of a city; Their house is on the other side of the street.* **6.** the place next to someone: *The little boy stood close by his friend's side.* **7.** one of two opposing groups or points of view: *South Africa fought on the Allied side in World War II; I told my side of the story.* **8.** a certain quality of a person in contrast with another: *She likes to joke, but has a serious side, too; Be sure you stay on the coach's good side if you want to be in the starting lineup.*
adjective. **1.** at, to, or near one side: *a side road; a side door.* **2.** less important: *steak with a side dish of fried onions; That's a side issue that we don't need to discuss now.*
• **side by side.** beside each other: *The two red cars were parked side by side.*
• **side with.** in an argument, to support one of the sides: *She always sides with him when we argue—it's not fair.*

Sideburn

Sideburns *can be short and neat, as in this photo, or very long and bushy, as worn by many men in the nineteenth century.*

side·burns ▲ [side-burnz] *plural noun.* the strips of hair on either side of a man's face that grow in front of the ears: *In the 1970s sideburns were very fashionable.*

side effect *Health.* an unwanted additional reaction from using a medicine or treatment: *The doctor warned her that the hay fever tablets she was taking might have the side effect of making her sleepy.*

side·line [side-line] *noun*, *plural* **sidelines. 1.** in sports, a line along the sides of the playing area: *We cheered on our team from the sidelines.* **2.** a second job or hobby: *He works in a factory, and delivers newspapers as a sideline.*
verb, **sidelined, sidelining.** to be kept from taking part in a game or activity: *to be sidelined with a foot injury.*

side·show [side-shoh] *noun*, *plural* **sideshows. 1.** a small show that is part of a larger entertainment: *A circus has many sideshows as well as the main act in the big ring.* **2.** something minor that takes attention away from a more important issue.

side·step [side-step] *verb*, **sidestepped, sidestepping. 1.** to step aside to avoid: *We had to sidestep the rain puddles on the road.* **2.** to dodge an issue: *He sidestepped all responsibility for the disaster.*

side·track [side-trak] *verb*, **sidetracked, sidetracking.** to be distracted from a main course: *It's easy to get sidetracked from studying when it's warm and sunny outside.*

side·walk [side-wawk] *noun*, *plural* **sidewalks.** a path for people to walk on the side of a road.

side·ways [side-waze] *adverb.* **1.** to or from one side: *Fred turned sideways to let the other people pass by on the street.* **2.** with one side forward or to the front.
adjective. moving to one side: *a sideways glance.*

si·ding ◀ [sye-ding] *noun*, *plural* **sidings. 1.** the boards that form the outside walls of a frame house. **2.** a short railway track off the main line used to let other trains pass or to store trains that are not in use.

A train is moved into a **siding** *to clear the main tracks for other trains to pass.*

siege [seej] *noun, plural* **sieges.** in war, the surrounding and isolating of a fortress or town in order to force an enemy to surrender: *After a siege of three months, the villagers had to surrender or starve to death.*

sieve [siv] *noun, plural* **sieves.** a kitchen utensil made of mesh, which is used to separate coarse from fine material: *A sieve is useful for getting rid of lumps in flour.*

sift [sift] *verb,* **sifted, sifting. 1.** to separate lumps or impurities from fine powder such as sugar or flour by passing it through a mesh or sieve. **2.** to pass in between small gaps as if through a sieve: *The sunlight sifted through the branches.* **3.** to examine carefully in order to check or sort: *He sifted through all the applications to make a short list of the good candidates.*

sigh [sye] *verb,* **sighed, sighing. 1.** to let out a long, slow breath as from being disappointed, bored, or tired, and so on, or happy, relieved, and so on. **2.** to make a sound like this: *a pine tree sighing softly in the evening breeze.* *noun, plural* **sighs.** *She gave a sigh of relief when the last guests left the party.*

sight [site] *noun, plural* **sights. 1.** the ability to see; the sense of vision: *He lost his sight after a car accident.* **2.** the act or fact of seeing: *At first sight the room looked a mess.* **3.** the range of vision: *The children hid in the closet, out of sight from their parents.* **4.** the appearance of something visible: *After they were at sea for so long, the view of the harbor was a welcome sight to the sailors.* **5.** something that is worth looking at: *The tour includes all the famous sights of the city.* **6.** something odd or ugly: *She looked a sight in that awful dress.* **7.** an instrument used to help in seeing or aiming, such as on a gun: *to line up the sight with the target.* *verb,* **sighted, sighting. 1.** to see with the eyes; observe: *The lookout sighted an approaching plane.* **2.** to aim at a target with a sight.
🔊 Different words with the same sound are **cite** and **site.**

sight·see·ing [site-see-ing] *noun.* the act of traveling for pleasure to see interesting sights. A **sightseer** is someone who travels to see places of interest.
adjective. describing the act of sightseeing: *She joined a sightseeing group when she arrived in the city.*

sign [sine] *noun, plural* **signs. 1.** a public notice with instructions or information: *The sign shows that this is a one-way street.* **2.** a mark or symbol that stands for something else: *"x" is a multiplication sign.* **3.** a thing that suggests or indicates some fact or quality: *There was no sign that anyone was home; Laughter is a sign of happiness.* **4.** the fact of predicting something: *Some people believe a black cat is a sign of bad luck.* **5.** one of the twelve parts of the zodiac: *My star sign is Leo.* **6.** see SIGN LANGUAGE.
verb, **signed, signing. 1.** to write one's signature: *I signed on the dotted line.* **2.** to use sign language. —**signer,** *noun.*

sig·nal [sig-nul] *noun, plural* **signals. 1.** a symbol, object, sound, and so on that gives some message or warning: *A red traffic light is a signal that cars should stop; The flying of the Union Jack flag at Buckingham Palace is a signal that the Queen is there.* **2.** an electrical current sending out sound or pictures to a radio, television, or other such electronic device.
verb, **signaled, signaling. 1.** to make a sign: *She signaled to the waiter to bring the check.* **2.** to make known: *The bull signaled his anger by pawing the ground.*

sig·na·ture [sig-nuh-chur] *noun, plural* **signatures. 1.** the signing of one's name in handwriting: *I put my signature at the end of the letter.* **2.** *Music.* a sign or signs at the beginning of each written score to indicate the pitch, key, and time of the piece.

sig·nif·i·cance [sig-nif-uh-kuns] *noun.* the fact of being especially important: *Thanksgiving is a celebration of great significance to many people.*

sig·nif·i·cant [sig-nif-uh-kunt] *adjective.* **1.** being especially important: *Teachers can be a significant influence on their students.* **2.** having a special or hidden meaning: *The police think it is significant that the thieves seemed to know exactly where the money was hidden.* —**significantly,** *adverb.*

sig·ni·fy [sig-nuh-fye] *verb,* **signified, signifying. 1.** to express meaning by using a sign: *The umpire raised his hand to signify that the pitch was a strike.* **2.** to be meaningful or of importance: *Your words signify nothing to me if you speak in Chinese.*

sign language ▼ *Language.* a way of communicating by using hand gestures instead of spoken words. People who are deaf are the main users of sign language.

Sikh [seek] *noun, plural* **Sikhs.** *Religion.* a person who follows the Sikh religion, the fifth largest religion in the world. **Sikhism** was begun in India in the fifteenth century and combines elements of Hinduism and Islam.

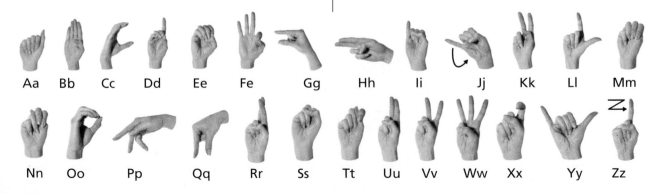

Aa Bb Cc Dd Ee Fe Gg Hh Ii Jj Kk Ll Mm

Nn Oo Pp Qq Rr Ss Tt Uu Vv Ww Xx Yy Zz

In **sign language,** *there is a different hand sign for each letter of the alphabet.*

The **silhouettes** of the boy and the tree against a lake make a striking photograph.

si·lence [sye-luns] *noun, plural* **silences.** **1.** the absence of sound: *There was silence in the woods and then we heard a coyote howling far away.* **2.** the state of being quiet: *His silence showed that he was very upset.*
verb, **silenced, silencing.** to force to become quiet: *The teacher had to raise her voice to silence the class.*

si·lent [sye-lunt] *adjective.* **1.** describing something completely quiet: *It was silent in the house after everyone left.* **2.** not speaking: *It's better to be silent than to say something silly.* **3.** not spoken out loud; not expressed: *My silent wish was to go home, but I had to stay.* **4.** *Language.* describing a letter that appears in the spelling of a word but is not spoken: *The "k" is silent in words like "know," "knife," or "knee."* —**silently,** *adverb.*

sil·hou·ette ▲ [sil-uh-*wet*] *noun, plural* **silhouettes.** **1.** the outline or side view of a figure or object. **2.** a dark form seen against a lighter background: *We could see the silhouette of a man in the lighted window.*
verb, **silhoutted, silhouetting.** to show as a dark form against a lighter background.

sil·i·con [sil-uh-*kon*] *noun. Chemistry.* a common chemical element found in the Earth's crust. It is used to make glass, computer chips, and electronic devices.

sil·i·cone [sil-uh-*kone*] *noun. Chemistry.* a chemical compound containing silicon. It is used in glues, lubricants, and artificial body parts.

silk [silk] *noun, plural* **silks.** **1.** a very fine, shiny material made from the threads spun from silkworm cocoons. It is expensive to make and buy: *Her wedding dress was made of silk.* **2.** the tuft at the tip of an ear of corn.
adjective. made of or like silk: *a silk necktie.*

silk·worm ▶ [silk-*wurm*] *noun, plural* **silkworms.** a white caterpillar originally from China that makes strong silk thread to spin its cocoon. This is used by people to make silk cloth.

sil·ky [sil-kee] *adjective,* **silkier, silkiest.** soft and shiny to look at or touch. A different word with the same meaning is **silken.**

sill [sil] *noun, plural* **sills.** the lower horizontal piece of a window that juts out from the wall.

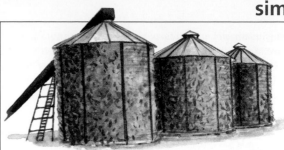

Long slides are used to unload grain from the top of **silos.**

sil·ly [sil-ee] *adjective,* **sillier, silliest.** **1.** lacking in sense; foolish: *You're silly if you think you can pass the exams without studying.* **2.** not serious; meant to be funny: *a silly joke; The boy made silly faces behind the teacher's back.* —**silliness,** *noun.*

si·lo ▲ [sye-loh] *noun, plural* **silos.** **1.** a high tower used for storing grain to feed farm animals. **2.** an underground storage area for keeping missiles.

silt [silt] *noun. Environment.* mud or very fine clay particles carried by flowing water that eventually sink to the bottom to form a layer at the bottom of rivers and streams.

sil·ver ▼ [sil-vur] *noun. Chemistry.* **1.** a chemical element that is a shiny, pale gray precious metal. **2.** objects made of or containing this metal, such as jewelry, coins, or knives, forks, and spoons: *I polished my silver this morning.* **3.** coins, as opposed to paper money. **4.** a shiny, pale gray color.
adjective. **1.** made of silver: *a silver bracelet.* **2.** having the color of silver. As people get older, their hair often turns a **silvery** color.
verb, **silvered, silvering.** to coat with silver or cover with a silvery metal.

sil·ver·smith [sil-vur-*smith*] *noun, plural* **silversmiths.** someone who is skilled in repairing or making objects from silver.

sil·ver·ware [sil-vur-*ware*] *noun.* **1.** anything used to eat with or to hold food that is made of or coated with silver: *Sugar bowls, salt pots, and serving dishes can all be silverware.* **2.** table utensils such as knives, forks, and spoons.

It takes great skill to make highly decorated **silver** objects.

sim·i·lar [sim-uh-lur] *adjective.* being alike but not identical: *My friend and I have similar taste in food, except that she doesn't like eggs.* —**similarly,** *adverb.*

sim·i·lar·i·ty [sim-uh-lare-i-tee] *noun, plural* **similarities.** **1.** the fact of resembling something or someone: *All very young babies share a certain similarity to each other.* **2.** a way in which things are the same: *There are several similarities between different species of ants.*

Cocoon

Silkworm

Mulberry leaf

After hatching, **silkworms** eat mulberry leaves for four to five weeks until they spin their cocoons.

sim·i·le [sim-uh-lee] *noun, plural* **similies.** *Literature.* a figure of speech that expresses a similarity between two different things. A simile usually uses "like" or "as" to make a comparison: *He was as white as a ghost; She sings like a bird.*

Simile is related to the word *similar*, meaning to be like something else. Similes are often used in writing to compare two things that are usually not thought of as being alike. This can make writing stronger and more colorful. Here are some similes used by Patricia MacLachlan in her prize-winning book *Sarah, Plain and Tall*: "Caleb stood up and ran *like the wind.*" "I sank *like a bucket filled with water.*" "At dawn there was the sudden sound of hail, *like stones tossed against the barn.*" "The wild roses were scattered on the ground, *as if a wedding had come and gone there.*"

sim·mer [sim-ur] *verb,* **simmered, simmering.** to cook gently and steadily near the boiling point: *The recipe said to simmer the stew for at least an hour.*

sim·ple [sim-pul] *adjective,* **simpler, simplest. 1.** easily done or understood; not difficult: *a simple math problem such as 12 x 3; Reading textbooks for young children are written in simple language.* **2.** not decorated or fancy; basic and plain: *After eating at expensive restaurants on our vacation, we were glad to have a simple, home-cooked meal.* **3.** without additions; pure: *He gave a simple speech of thanks.* **4.** lacking intelligence; foolish.

simple machine ▶ *History.* any of the six devices once thought to be the basic requirements of all machines. These are the lever, pulley, wedge, inclined plane, screw, wheel, and axle.

sim·plic·i·ty [sim-plis-i-tee] *noun, plural* **simplicities. 1.** the quality of being simple or easy; lacking complexity: *I was surprised by the simplicity of the dressmaking pattern.* **2.** the quality of being natural or truthful: *The witness spoke with the simplicity of a child.*

sim·pli·fy [sim-pluh-fye] *verb,* **simplified, simplifying.** to make something easier or less complicated: *The doctor simplified his explanation of my illness so I could understand it.* The act of making something less complicated is **simplification.**

sim·ply [sim-plee] *adverb.* **1.** in a simple way: *The teacher spoke simply in explaining the lesson; We trimmed the tree simply, with just a few strings of lights.* **2.** only; merely: *To enter the contest, you simply have to fill out this short form.* **3.** to the fullest extent; absolutely; very: *That painting is simply beautiful.*

This pump, used by the ancient Greeks to force water uphill, is an example of a **simple machine** *that uses a screw.*

sim·u·late [sim-yuh-*late*] *verb,* **simulated, simulating. 1.** to copy or reproduce the qualities or appearance of something: *Astronauts train in an environment that simulates conditions in outer space.* **2.** to pretend to experience something: *My sister simulated being sick so she could get out of going to school.* —**simulation,** *noun.*

si·mul·ta·ne·ous [sye-mul-tay-nee-us] *adjective.* happening at exactly the same time: *On New Year's Eve, there were simultaneous celebrations at different places around the city.* —**simultaneously,** *adverb.*

sin [sin] *noun, plural* **sins.** *Religion.* **1.** a thought or behavior that goes against the rules of a particular religion: *Many religions teach that it is a sin to steal.* **2.** any act that is considered wrong.
verb, **sinned, sinning.** to act against the teachings of a particular religion.

since [sins] *adverb.* **1.** from a point of time in the past to now: *My dog has been at the vet since we went on vacation last week.* **2.** happening between a point of time in the past and now: *The pool was closed for repair, but has since reopened.*
preposition. after a general or specific time in the past: *It's been raining hard since Tuesday.*
conjunction. **1.** in the time after a time in the past: *We've lived in this house since I was three years old.* **2.** for the reason that; because: *Since I can't go to the concert, I'm selling my ticket.*

sin·cere [sin-seer] *adjective,* **sincerer, sincerest.** describing something truthful and honest; not false: *a sincere apology for doing something wrong; I have a sincere relationship with my best friend.* The quality of being open and truthful is **sincerity.** —**sincerely,** *adverb.*

sin·ew [sin-oo *or* sin-yoo] *noun, plural* **sinews.** a tough cord or band of tissue connecting a muscle with a bone; a tendon.

sin·ful [sin-ful] *adjective.* acting in a way that goes against the teachings of a particular religion; doing something that is morally or ethically wrong: *Lying and stealing are sinful.* —**sinfully,** *adverb.*

sing [sing] *verb,* **sang** *or* **sung, singing. 1.** to use the voice to create musical sounds or to produce words in a musical way: *When the cake is brought in, we'll all sing "Happy Birthday."* **2.** to make a whistling or humming sound that is like this: *Our kettle sings when the water comes to a boil.*

singe [sinj] *verb,* **singed, singeing.** to burn something lightly on its surface, edge, or end: *I singed my hair when I got too close to the campfire.*

sing·er [sing-ur] *noun, plural* **singers.** a person or bird that sings.

sin·gle [sing-gul] *adjective.* **1.** describing only one person or one of something: *There was a single cookie left in the jar, so Tim and I each had half.* **2.** suitable or useful for only one person: *I asked for a single ticket to the movies.* **3.** describing someone not married: *My oldest brother is still single.*
noun, plural **singles.** a hit in baseball or softball that lets the batter get to first base.
verb, **singled, singling. 1.** to select from a group: *I couldn't have a big party, so I singled out the people I liked most to invite.* **2.** in baseball or softball, to hit a single.

sin·gle-hand·ed *adjective.* describing something done alone and without help: *He made a single-handed trip across the ocean in a small sailboat.*
   —**single-handedly,** *adverb.*

sin·gle-mind·ed *adjective.* having one focus; having one goal in mind: *She's single-minded in her plan to go to medical school and become a doctor.*

sin·gu·lar [sing-gyuh-lur] *adjective.* **1.** *Language.* describing the form of a word that refers to one person or thing. *Dog* and *cat* are singular nouns. *Dogs* and *cats* are plural nouns. **2.** being unusual or unique: *He has a singular fashion sense and uses it to design beautiful clothes.*
noun, plural **singulars.** *Language.* the form of a word that is used when naming or referring to one person or thing. The fact or state of being singular, or having a unique quality is **singularity. —singularly,** *adverb.*

sin·is·ter [sin-uh-stur] *adjective.* threatening or seeming to be evil; menacing: *The ocean seemed sinister to me after I saw the scary shark movie.*

> In the Latin language of ancient Rome, the word **sinister** meant "the left hand." The connection of this with the idea of *sinister* to mean evil, threatening, or frightening came about because in early times the right hand was thought to be connected with good luck and the left hand with bad luck.

sink [singk] *verb,* **sank** or **sunk, sunk** or **sunken. 1.** to go partly or completely below the water or another such surface: *I dropped a stone in the lake and it sank to the bottom.* **2.** to become smaller or weaker; lessen: *My energy sank as the day went on.* **3.** to move or fall from one state of being to another that is thought of as being lower in some way: *Our hopes of winning sank when we gave up an easy goal; I sank into a depression when my friend moved away.* **4.** to make a hole in something such as soil; drill or dig: *They sank a shaft for the mine.*
noun, plural **sinks. 1.** a basin made of metal or porcelain, usually attached to a water supply and a drain for emptying. **2.** a low area of land where water collects.

sin·ner [sin-ur] *noun, plural* **sinners.** someone who sins; a person who breaks the rules of a religion or generally does the wrong thing.

si·nus ▶ [sye-nus] *noun, plural* **sinuses.** *Medicine.* air-filled spaces in the bones of the skull. They are positioned above the eyes and on each side of the nose. Pain in, or infection of the sinuses is called **sinusitis.**

Sioux [soo] *noun, plural* **Sioux.** a member of the North American Indian tribes who once lived across the Great Plains from Lake Michigan to the Rocky Mountains and now live mainly in North and South Dakota.

sip [sip] *verb,* **sipped, sipping.** to take small amounts of a liquid into the mouth: *I sipped my drink to make it last longer.*
noun, plural **sips.** a small amount of liquid taken into the mouth: *My mother gave me a sip of her soup to try.*

si·phon [sye-fun] *noun, plural* **siphons.** a device used to move fluids from one container to another. A siphon is made of a pipe or tube running from a container of liquid to a lower level outside the container, so that air pressure forces the liquid through the pipe or tube.
verb, **siphoned, siphoning.** to move fluids using a siphon: *They siphoned the gas from the spare can to the car's empty gas tank.*

sir [sur] *noun, plural* **sirs.** a formal way of addressing a man in speech and in writing; used instead of a name: *The waiter said, "Excuse me sir, you left your jacket at the table."* In the past, another formal way of addressing a man was **Sire.** The correct way to address a knight is to use **Sir** before the name, as in *Sir Walter Raleigh.*

si·ren [sye-run] *noun, plural* **sirens.** a device that produces a long, loud, piercing sound as a signal or warning: *The ambulance raced past with its siren blaring.*

> Stories of the ancient Greeks told of the *Sirens,* a group of strange creatures who were part woman and part bird. The Sirens had a magical way of singing that could cast a spell over sailors and lead them to wreck their ships on the rocks. The first use of **siren** in the modern sense of the word was a loud horn used to give warnings on a ship.

sis·ter [sis-tur] *noun, plural* **sisters. 1.** a female with the same parents as another person. **2.** the title for a nun, a woman who is a member of a religious community. **3.** a girl or woman with the same interests as another, such as female members of an organization.

sis·ter·hood [sis-tur-hud] *noun, plural* **sisterhoods. 1.** a feeling of friendship, closeness, and loyalty between females. **2.** a group of women who share common interests, often religious.

sister-in-law [sis-tur-in-law] *noun, plural* **sisters-in-law. 1.** the sister of someone's husband or wife. **2.** the wife of someone's brother.

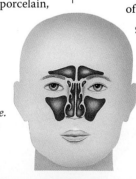

sit [sit] *verb,* **sat, sitting. 1.** to take a position in which the body's weight rests on the buttocks: *I was tired from standing for so long and wanted to sit.* **2.** to place yourself or someone else in this position; seat: *The teacher sat us in a circle.* **3.** to look after a baby or child in place of the parents; baby-sit. **4.** to be located or held in a certain place, as if sitting: *The eagle sat high in the tree; Our photos sit in a box in the attic.* **5.** to be part of a group that has authority: *She sits on the county board of supervisors.*

The amount of air inside the **sinuses** *affects the sound of a person's voice.*

*In 1961 the **site** of a very ancient city, Çatal Hüyük, was discovered in Turkey.*

A B C D E F G H I J K L M N O P Q R **S** T U V W X Y Z

size [size] *noun, plural* **sizes. 1.** the physical space something takes up; the length, height, and width of something: *Your dog is about the same size as mine.* **2.** the number or amount of something: *I would like some new stamps to increase the size of my collection.* **3.** the set of measurements given to articles that are sold in stores, such as clothing or shoes: *I want to buy my mother a blouse but I don't know what size she wears.* *verb,* **sized, sizing.** to have or make a certain size: *The dressmaker sized the dress to a regular 10.*
  • **size up.** to examine something in order to come to a conclusion: *I sized up the new girl and decided she was a nice person.*

site ▲ [site] *noun, plural* **sites.** an area where something is, was, or could be located: *This is the site where the house will be built; Pennsylvania was the site of a famous Civil War battle.*

sit·u·ate [sich-oo-ate] *verb,* **situated, situating.** to position something in a certain place: *They situated the pool in the sunny area of the yard.*

sit·u·a·tion [sich-oo-ay-shun] *noun, plural* **situations.** the circumstances or state someone or something is in: *When our car broke down in the middle of a snowstorm, we found ourselves in a dangerous situation.*

situation comedy a funny television program often with a regular cast of characters and based on situations that might arise in everyday life. The shortened form of this term is **sitcom.**

sit-up [sit-up] *noun, plural* **sit-ups.** a form of exercise in which you lie flat on your back with your legs bent and raise yourself to a sitting position without lifting your feet from the floor. It mainly exercises the stomach muscles.

six [siks] *noun, plural* **sixes.** the number between five and seven; 6. *adjective.* amounting to six in number. The position between fifth and seventh is **sixth.**

six·teen [siks-teen] *noun, plural* **sixteens.** the number between fifteen and seventeen; 16. *adjective.* amounting to sixteen in number. The position between fifteenth and seventeenth is **sixteenth.**

six·ty [siks-tee] *noun, plural* **sixties.** the number between fifty-nine and sixty-one; 60. *adjective.* amounting to sixty in number. The position between fifty-ninth and sixty-first is **sixtieth.**

size·a·ble [size-uh-bul] *adjective.* describing something fairly large: *He inherited a sizeable amount of money—more than $50,000.* This word is also spelled **sizable.**

siz·zle [siz-ul] *verb,* **sizzled, sizzling.** to make the hissing, crackling sound of frying fat or oils: *The steak sizzled on the barbecue.* *noun, plural* **sizzles.** the act or fact of making such a sound.

skate[1] [skate] *noun, plural* **skates. 1.** a shoe with a metal blade attached to the bottom for use when moving over ice; an ice skate. **2.** a shoe with a set of small wheels attached to the bottom for use when moving over a flat surface; a roller skate. *verb,* **skated, skating.** to glide over a surface wearing ice skates, roller skates, or roller blades.

skate[2] ▼ [skate] *noun, plural* **skates** *or* **skate.** a fish with a wide, flat body, side fins that extend out like wings, a short snout, and a long tail.

skate·board [skate-bord] *noun, plural* **skateboards.** a short, flat board with rollers attached to the bottom. It is ridden in a standing or crouching position and pushed along by foot. *verb,* **skateboarded, skateboarding.** to ride a board in this way. The sport of riding a skateboard is called **skateboarding.**

Skates live on the sea bottom in both warm and cold waters.

SKELETON

Your skeleton is a clever structure. It lets you bend, twist, and twirl. It also protects your internal organs and is a sturdy framework that supports the body's muscles and flesh. The skeleton has 206 separate bones, varying in size and shape from the tiny ear bones to the massive thighbones. Some are irregularly shaped, like the vertebrae. Others are flat, like the breastbone. The bones of the ribs and skull are curved, while those of the wrists and ankles are short and stubby.

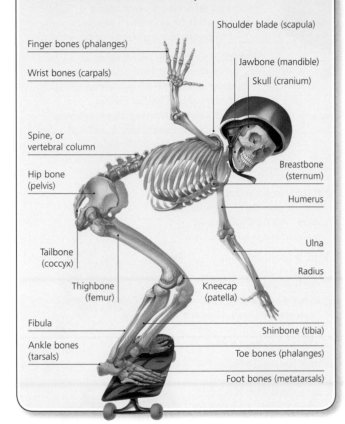

Finger bones (phalanges)
Wrist bones (carpals)
Shoulder blade (scapula)
Jawbone (mandible)
Skull (cranium)
Spine, or vertebral column
Hip bone (pelvis)
Breastbone (sternum)
Humerus
Tailbone (coccyx)
Ulna
Radius
Thighbone (femur)
Kneecap (patella)
Fibula
Ankle bones (tarsals)
Shinbone (tibia)
Toe bones (phalanges)
Foot bones (metatarsals)

skel·e·ton ▲ [skel-uh-tun] *noun, plural* **skeletons.**
1. *Biology.* the inner framework of bones and cartilage that supports and protects the organs of fish, birds, animals, and humans. **2.** any supporting framework or structure: *They put up the wood skeleton of the barn first and then built the rest around it.*

skep·ti·cal [skep-tuh-kul] *adjective.* not believing things easily; doubting: *I was skeptical that my friend really knew the rock star as he claimed.* Someone who tends to doubt things is a **skeptic.** A doubting attitude is **skepticism.**
—**skeptically,** *adverb.*

sketch [skech] *noun, plural* **sketches. 1.** *Art.* a rough drawing done quickly and often without detail: *I found it helpful to make a sketch before starting my painting.* **2.** a short written work, often describing something rather than telling a story.
verb, **sketched, sketching.** to make a quick, rough drawing of something or someone: *I am sketching all kinds of subjects in my art class.*

sketch·y [skech-ee] *adjective.* not complete; lacking detail: *The police could not identify the man from the sketchy description given by the witness.*

skew·er [skyoo-ur] *noun, plural* **skewers.** a smooth, thin, wooden or metal stick with a sharpened end that is used for holding food in position while it is being cooked.

ski [skee] *noun, plural* **skis. 1.** one of a pair of long, thin strips of wood, metal, or other material designed to slide across snow. Skis curve up at the front and are attached to boots. **2.** a similar piece of equipment that attaches to bare feet and is designed for gliding over water; a water-ski.
verb, **skied, skiing.** to glide over the surface of snow or water on skis. A sport that uses skis as the main form of equipment is called **skiing.**

skid [skid] *verb,* **skidded, skidding.** to slide without control: *The bike skidded on the wet road.*
noun, plural **skids.** the act of skidding: *We could see the marks on the road where the car had gone into a skid.*

ski·er [skee-ur] *noun, plural* **skiers.** a person who skis.

skiff ▶ [skif] *noun, plural* **skiffs.** a small, light boat that is moved along by sails or oars.

Skiffs *are small open boats with flat bottoms and flat sterns.*

ski jump ▼ a snow-covered ramp from which skiers can make jumps. Someone who makes these jumps is a **ski jumper.**

skill [skil] *noun, plural* **skills.** an ability to do something well. Skill is learned through practice, training, and experience: *My grandmother has a skill for baking.*

skilled [skild] *adjective.* having or showing a certain skill: *The new restaurant is looking for a skilled chef.*

skil·let [skil-it] *noun, plural* **skillets.** a shallow frying pan.

skill·ful [skil-ful] *adjective.* describing someone or something that shows skill: *She gave a highly skillful performance on the violin.*
—**skillfully,** *adverb.*

skim [skim] *verb,* **skimmed, skimming. 1.** to remove matter floating on the surface of a liquid: *to skim the cream from milk.* **2.** to move or travel across, quickly and lightly: *We skimmed flat stones across the surface of the pond.* **3.** to read quickly or briefly: *Dad skimmed the paper for news of the explosion.*

skim milk milk with the cream removed from it. This is also called **skimmed milk.**

skin

Hair shaft
Epidermis
Dermis
Hair follicle
Fat
Vein
Artery
Pore
Sweat gland
Muscle
Oil gland
Nerve

skin ▲ [skin] *noun, plural* **skins. 1.** the surface covering of an animal body. The skin is the largest organ of the body. **2.** the covering stripped from the body of a dead animal; a pelt. Animal skins are used to make leather for coats, shoes, and bags. **3.** the outer covering of something: a *potato skin.*
verb, **skinned, skinning. 1.** to remove the skin from an animal. **2.** to injure by scraping off an area of skin: *She skinned her arm when she fell.*

skin diving swimming underwater using a mask, snorkel, and flippers. Someone who does this is a **skin diver.**

skin·ny [skin-ee] *adjective,* **skinnier, skinniest.** describing someone who is very thin, especially in an unhealthy way.

skip [skip] *verb,* **skipped, skipping. 1.** to move along by making a small hop on one foot and then the other. **2.** to jump up and down over a rotating rope: *My sisters turned the rope while I skipped.* **3.** to leave out: *The teacher told us to skip the questions that we found too hard.* **4.** to bounce across the surface of something:

We skipped stones across the pond.
5. to not go to or do something: *He had so much work to do that he skipped lunch.* In the past, a bright student might skip a grade in school, as by going from third grade to fifth.
noun, plural **skips.** a movement in which one foot takes a small hop, then the other foot takes a small hop: *You play the game by taking a skip, then a jump.*

skip·per [skip-ur] *noun, plural* **skippers.** a name for the captain of a boat or sports team.
verb, **skippered, skippering.** to act as captain of something: *He skippered the boat.*

skir·mish [skur-mish] *noun, plural* **skirmishes.** a small fight that does not last long: *There was news of a skirmish at the border checkpoint. verb,* **skirmished, skirmishing.** to fight a small fight or in small groups: *The troops skirmished along the border.*

skirt [skurt] *noun, plural* **skirts. 1.** a type of clothing that hangs down from the waist, usually worn by women and girls. **2.** the bottom half of a dress.
verb, **skirted, skirting.** to move along the edge of something: *A pathway skirts along the far side of the field; The mayor did not answer the question directly, but preferred to skirt the issue.*

skit [skit] *noun, plural* **skits.** a short play that is usually comic: *Mom and Dad performed a skit at the family reunion.*

skull ▶ [skul] *noun, plural* **skulls.** the framework of bone in the head that protects the brain. Humans and all other animals with a backbone have a skull.

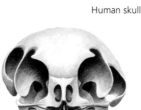

Human skull

skunk [skungk] *noun, plural* **skunks.** an animal with black fur, white stripes, and a bushy tail. Skunks release a foul-smelling liquid when threatened. They belong to the weasel family and are found only in North and South America.

Barn owl skull

sky [skye] *noun, plural* **skies.** the space between the Earth and outer space: *The blue, sunny sky turned gray and rainy.*

sky·div·ing ◀ [skye-div-ing] *noun.* the act of leaping from an airplane, falling through the air, then opening a parachute and floating to earth. A person who does this is a **skydiver.**

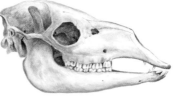

Llama skull

The **skulls** *of a human, a barn owl, and a llama are very different.*

Experienced **skydivers** *may freefall for up to eighty seconds before opening the parachute that will help them to land safely.*

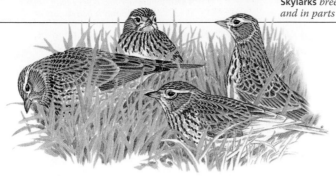

sky·lark ▲ [skye-*lark*] *noun, plural* **skylarks.** a small brown bird that is known for its sweet song while in flight high above the ground.

sky·light [skye-*lite*] *noun, plural* **skylights.** a window in a ceiling or roof to let in outside light.

sky·line [skye-*line*] *noun, plural* **skylines.** the outline of buildings or landscapes where they meet the sky.

sky·rock·et [skye-*rok*-it] *noun, plural* **skyrockets.** a type of firework that flies into the air and explodes, showering colored sparks**.**
verb, **skyrocketed, skyrocketing.** to rise suddenly and dramatically: *House prices in our neighborhood have skyrocketed in the past year.*

sky·scrap·er ▼ [skye-*skray*-pur] *noun, plural* **skyscrapers.** a very tall building: *New York City is filled with skyscrapers.*

slab [slab] *noun, plural* **slabs.** a thick, flat piece of concrete or other material: *Our mom uses a slab of marble for a chopping board.*

slack [slak] *adjective,* **slacker, slackest. 1.** not firm; loose: *This slack rope needs to be tightened.* **2.** not hurried; slow: *We spent a slack day lying around doing nothing.*
noun, plural **slacks.** a part of something that is hanging loose: *If you want to anchor the boat properly, take up the slack on the chain.*

slack·en [slak-un] *verb,* **slackened , slackening.** to make or become slack: *The joggers slackened their pace as they went up the steep hill.*

slacks [slaks] *plural noun.* long trousers worn by men or women.

sla·lom [slah-lum] *noun, plural* **slaloms.** a downhill skiing race that takes a winding course.
verb, **slalomed, slaloming.** to ski in such a race.

slam [slam] *verb,* **slammed, slamming.**
1. to shut with great force: *She slammed the door because she was angry.* **2.** to throw or move something down with great force: *He slammed down his books and stormed off.* **3.** to criticize in a forceful way: *The director was slammed by the critics for having so much violence in his movie.*
noun, plural **slams.** a forceful hit or closing: *The door swung shut with a slam.*

sland·er [slan-dur] *noun, plural* **slanders.** *Law.* an untrue statement that damages someone's reputation.
verb, **slandered, slandering.** to damage someone's reputation by saying something that is not true about them: *The paper slandered the honest policeman by saying he was taking bribes.*

slang [slang] *noun. Language.* casual or informal language that is used in everyday conversation. Using slang involves giving new meanings to old words or creating new words. Sometimes slang words are used so often that they become part of formal language. For example, "skyscraper" used to be a slang word.

Slang is language that is freer, less polite, and more relaxed than the standard language. Slang words are more likely to be used by friends or family talking to each other in a casual way than by someone doing serious writing such as a newspaper story, encyclopedia article, or school textbook. Slang involves the use of words that are new to the language or that are thought of as funny, silly, exaggerated, insulting, and so on.

slant [slant] *verb,* **slanted, slanting. 1.** to be on a slope, or put something on a slope: *That painting was not hung straight, so it slants to the left.* **2.** to report something from a particular angle or point of view: *He slanted the news story to support gun owners because he collects guns himself.*
noun, plural **slants. 1.** a sloping away from a horizontal position: *The roof of the house is on a slant.* **2.** a particular angle or point of view: *The report on pollution had a slant against using oil for fuel.*

slap [slap] *noun, plural* **slaps.** a smack or hit, usually with the hand: *Mom gave him a slap on the wrist to stop him from taking all the candy.*
verb, **slapped, slapping.** to smack or hit, usually with a hand: *She slapped his face in anger.*

slash [slash] *verb,* **slashed, slashing. 1.** to cut violently with a sweeping motion: *The robbers slashed the pillows and mattresses, looking for hidden money.* **2.** to lower or reduce sharply: *The store slashed the price of pineapples and bananas.*
noun, plural **slashes. 1.** a violent cut made with a sweeping motion. **2.** a dramatic lowering: *a slash in house prices.*

slat [slat] *noun, plural* **slats.** a long, thin, narrow piece of metal, wood, plastic, or other material: *The slats in the wooden blind were opened to let in the bright sunlight.*

slate [slate] *noun, plural* **slates. 1.** a type of rock that can easily be split into layers. Slate is usually gray but can also be brown or green. **2.** a piece or tile of this rock that is being used for a particular purpose: *Some floor tiles and roof tiles are made of slate.* **3.** a dark gray color.

From 1931 to 1972 the Empire State Building in New York was the world's tallest **skyscraper.**

*A **sledgehammer** has a very long timber handle and a heavy, flat head.*

slaugh·ter [slaw-tur] *noun, plural* **slaughters. 1.** the killing of animals for food or to use their skins. **2.** a massacre or vicious murder of many people.
verb, **slaughtered, slaughtering. 1.** to kill animals for food or to use their skins. **2.** to massacre or viciously murder people.

slave [slave] *noun, plural* **slaves.
1.** a human being who is the legal property of another person.
2. someone who is controlled by someone or something else: *He's become a slave to his cigarette habit.* **3.** someone who works very long and hard on something, especially for very little money.
verb, **slaved, slaving.** to work very hard: *I slaved over my history assignment.*

> The word **slave** comes from *Slav,* a person from one of the Slavic groups of people. Some of these are Russians, Ukrainians, Czechs, Poles, Slovaks, Bulgarians, Serbs, and Croats. The connection with slavery came about because in early times many of these Slavic peoples lived in very poor conditions after having been captured in war by other European groups.

sla·ver·y ▼ [slave-ree *or* slave-uh-ree] *noun.* **1.** the practice of owning another person as a slave. **2.** the fact of being a slave.

Sla·vic [slah-vik] *noun.* a group of central and eastern European languages that includes Russian, Polish, Bulgarian, Croatian, Czech, Serbian, Slovak, and Slovenian.
adjective. having to do with these languages, the people who speak them, or their cultures. A person from one of these cultures is a **Slav.**

slay [slay] *verb,* **slew, slain, slaying.** to kill with violence: *During the battle, many foot soldiers were brutally slain.*
🔊 A different word with the same sound is **sleigh.**

sled [sled] *noun, plural* **sleds.** a platform mounted on runners that travels across snow and ice.
verb, **sledded, sledding.** to travel on a sled: *We sledded across the snow.*

sledge·ham·mer ▶ [slej-ham-ur] *noun, plural* **sledgehammers.** a large, heavy hammer.

sleek [sleek] *adjective,* **sleeker, sleekest.
1.** describing something shiny and smooth: *sleek hair.* **2.** having a neat, stylish, or elegant appearance: *the sleek design of an expensive yacht.*

sleep [sleep] *noun, plural* **sleeps.
1.** the state of not being awake; a natural condition that occurs regularly from day to day and usually involves lying fairly still with the eyes closed. A person's mind and body rest during sleep. **2.** a state of being inactive or unaware, as if asleep. **3.** another condition thought of as being like sleep, such as a person being in a coma or an animal hibernating.
verb, **slept, sleeping.** to be in a condition of sleep or that is like sleep: *"Why England Slept" is a famous book about how England was not prepared for World War II; to sleep for eight hours a night.*

sleeping bag a large padded bag that someone can sleep in when camping.

sleep·less [sleep-lis] *adjective.* being unable to sleep.
—**sleeplessness,** *noun.*

sleep·walk [sleep-wawk] *verb,* **sleepwalked, sleepwalking.** to walk around while sleeping or not fully awake. Someone who does this is a **sleepwalker.**

sleep·y [slee-pee] *adjective,* **sleepier, sleepiest. 1.** feeling tired or drowsy: *She was so sleepy that she went to bed early.* The fact of being sleepy is **sleepiness. 2.** describing something quiet, inactive, or uneventful: *My uncle lives in a sleepy little village far from the big city.*

sleet [sleet] *noun.* rain and hail or snow falling together.
verb, **sleeted, sleeting.** to fall sleet: *Mom waited for it to stop sleeting before she drove home.*

sleeve [sleev] *noun, plural* **sleeves.** the part of clothing that covers the arm.

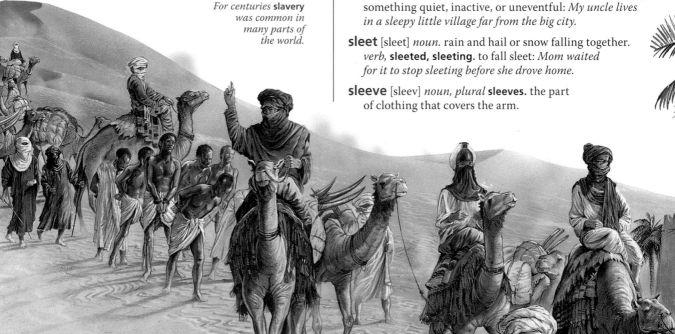

*For centuries **slavery** was common in many parts of the world.*

*In the past, horse-drawn **sleighs** were often used to transport goods long distances across snow and ice.*

sleigh ▶ [slay] *noun, plural* **sleighs.** a carriage on runners for traveling over snow and ice. Sleighs are pulled by dogs or horses.

🔊 A different word with the same sound is **slay.**

slen·der [slen-dur] *adjective,* **slenderer, slenderest.**
1. describing something slim or thin: *The tall, slender tree snapped in the strong wind.* **2.** small in amount or size: *She won the class presidency by a slender margin of six votes.*

Slender is one of several similar words. *Slender* and *slim* usually mean someone whose build looks healthy and attractive. *Lean* is a similar word but is more likely to be used of males than females. *Skinny* suggests someone who has too little weight and looks weak and unhealthy. *Thin* could be used in either a positive way (She's a *thin*, elegant woman known for her stylish way of dressing) or a negative way (He looks very *thin* and tired since his illness).

sleuth [slooth] *noun, plural* **sleuths.** a detective who follows a trail of clues in order to solve a crime or mystery.

slice [slis] *noun, plural* **slices.** a piece cut from something: *a slice of beef; a slice of cake.*
verb, **sliced, slicing. 1.** to cut something: *He sliced the cheese.* **2.** to move through easily: *The boat sliced through the water.*

slick [slik] *adjective,* **slicker, slickest. 1.** describing something smooth and slippery: *She slipped on the slick marble floor.* **2.** clever and efficient: *The salesman had a very slick explanation as to why the car cost so much.*
noun, plural **slicks.** a thin, slippery amount of something, usually spilled on top of something else: *An oil slick polluted the sea.*

slide ▼ [slide] *verb,* **slid, sliding. 1.** to move along a smooth or slippery surface: *The children slid down the snowy hill.* **2.** to lose control of movement on a smooth or slippery surface: *The car slid on the wet road and crashed into a nearby fence.*
noun, plural **slides. 1.** the act of moving along a smooth or slippery surface: *She took a slide across the frozen pond.* **2.** a piece of playground equipment with a smooth or slippery surface for sliding: *Let's play on the slide.* **3.** a small, flat piece of glass or plastic. Glass slides hold tiny objects that can be studied under a microscope. Plastic slides have transparent photos on them that can be projected onto a screen. **4.** a fall of snow or rock: *The mountain road was closed because of heavy snow slides.*

slight [slite] *adjective,* **slighter, slightest. 1.** not large in amount or importance; not significant; small: *The weather report says it will be a clear day, with only a slight chance of rain.* **2.** describing something slim or thin: *My little brother is too slight to play rugby.*
verb, **slighted, slighting.** to ignore or not treat as important: *She felt slighted when the speaker mentioned everyone by name except her.*
noun, plural **slights.** the fact of treating someone or something as if it is not important: *It was a slight that he was not asked to sing at the concert.* —**slightly,** *adverb.*

slim [slim] *adjective,* **slimmer, slimmest. 1.** describing something thin or slender: *My aunt is much slimmer after her diet.* **2.** relating to being small or slight: *There is a slim chance I failed the exam but I am fairly sure I passed.*
verb, **slimmed, slimming.** to lose weight: *She slimmed down with exercise and diet.*

slime [slime] *noun.* a soft, slippery substance such as mud: *Snails leave a trail of slime as they move along.*

slim·y [slye-mee] *adjective,* **slimier, slimiest.** covered in or having to do with slime: *a slimy rock; a slimy toad.*

sling [sling] *noun, plural* **slings. 1.** a device for hurling stones, usually made of a piece of leather with string attached to each end. **2.** a piece of cloth looped around the neck, used for supporting an injured arm or hand.
verb, **slung, slinging. 1.** to hurl a small stone. **2.** to hang or throw loosely: *Sling the hammock between these trees.*

sling·shot ▶ [sling-shot] *noun, plural* **slingshots.** a simple device for shooting small objects such as stones. A slingshot is made from a piece of elastic tied between the two prongs of a Y-shaped stick. A stone is placed in the center of the elastic, which is then drawn back and released.

slink [slingk] *verb,* **slunk, slinking.** to move in a sneaky way; creep: *When the cat heard George come home, she slunk off the bed.*

slip¹ [slip] *verb,* **slipped, slipping. 1.** to slide without meaning to; lose one's footing: *She slipped and fell on the wet floor.* **2.** to leave quietly: *Rob slipped out of the room to make a phone call.* **3.** to move or make move easily, quietly, and smoothly: *He slipped the envelope under the door.* **4.** to escape notice or be forgotten: *My appointment with the dentist slipped my mind.* **5.** to quickly and easily put clothes on or take them off: *Slip off your shoes before you come inside.* **6.** to make a small error: *She slipped and pronounced his name incorrectly.* **7.** to become lower in amount or quality; decline: *The quality of service at the restaurant has slipped since I was there last year.*
noun, plural **slips. 1.** the act of slipping: *That patch of spilled oil could cause a slip.* **2.** a woman's lightweight, sleeveless garment that is worn under a dress or skirt. **3.** an error: *His slip was understandable as he was tired.*
• **slip up.** to make a mistake: *You slipped up when you forgot to telephone him.*

*Simple **slingshots** are sometimes used to hunt small birds and animals.*

*Large water **slides** are a popular attraction in water parks.*

A
B
C
D
E
F
G
H
I
J
K
L
M
N
O
P
Q
R
S
T
U
V
W
X
Y
Z

slip² [slip] *noun, plural* **slips. 1.** a small piece of something, especially paper or cloth: *Mia wrote her shopping list on a slip of paper.* **2.** a small shoot or twig cut from a plant used to grow another plant.

slip·per [slip-ur] *noun, plural* **slippers.** a soft, comfortable, flat shoe that slips on easily and is worn indoors.

slip·pery [slip-ree *or* slip-ur-ee] *adjective.* **1.** likely to cause slipping: *Don't run on that floor—it's very slippery because it's just been polished.* **2.** slipping easily from the hands: *She dropped the slippery bottle.* **3.** not to be trusted or depended on: *I wouldn't trust that slippery man to look after my money.*

slit [slit] *noun, plural* **slits.** a long, narrow cut or opening: *He watched the street through a slit in the curtain.* *verb,* **slit, slitting.** to make a long, narrow cut in something: *The thief slit her bag open with a knife and took her purse.*

slith·er [slɪTH-ur] *verb,* **slithered, slithering.** to slide along a surface: *A snake slithered across the path in front of us.*

sliv·er [sliv-ur] *noun, plural* **slivers.** a small, thin fragment broken or cut off something; a splinter: *When he climbed the fence he got a sliver of wood in his knee.*

slo·gan [sloh-gun] *noun, plural* **slogans.** *Language.* a catch phrase; a motto: *"Make love not war" was a slogan of the 1960s.*

> The first kind of **slogan** was a shout or cry used by the warriors of the Highlands of Scotland as they rushed into battle. Later the word came to mean the special saying or motto of any particular group.

sloop ▼ [sloop] *noun, plural* **sloops.** a sailboat that has a single mast and two sails, one before the mast and one after it.

slop [slop] *verb,* **slopped, slopping.** to spill and splash a liquid: *Soup slopped over the side of the bowl when I was carrying it to the table.*

slope [slope] *verb,* **sloped, sloping.** to go gradually upward or downward; lie on a slant: *The roof isn't flat but slopes toward the back of the house.* *noun, plural* **slopes.** a surface that slopes, especially a piece of ground: *There has been a good snowfall on the ski slopes; You can't build a house on that steep slope.*

slop·py [slop-ee] *adjective,* **sloppier, sloppiest. 1.** describing something that is not tidy: *It is an important occasion, so please do not dress in your usual sloppy manner.* **2.** not properly or neatly done; careless: *Her assignment had many sloppy spelling mistakes in it.* **3.** wet and slushy; muddy: *Heavy rain made the racetrack sloppy.* —**sloppily,** *adverb;* —**sloppiness,** *noun.*

slot [slot] *noun, plural* **slots. 1.** a small, narrow opening or groove, especially one into which something is fitted: *Put the coins in the slot to pay for your drink.* **2.** a certain place or position: *the time slot for a television program.*

sloth ▶ [slawth *or* sloth] *noun, plural* **sloths.** any of a number of tree-dwelling Central and South American animals. Sloths move very slowly and hang upside down using their long claws and arms. They mostly eat leaves but sometimes eat insects and dead animals.

> In early times people identified Seven Deadly Sins, which were thought to be the most serious faults or bad actions that could occur in human life. One of these seven was **sloth,** which meant being too lazy to engage in any physical or mental activity. The animal known as the sloth was given this name because its slow-moving habits made people think it was very lazy.

A **sloth** *feeds at night and sleeps for most of the day.*

slouch [slouch] *verb,* **slouched, slouching.** to move, stand, or sit without holding oneself straight, especially with the head and shoulders bent forward: *Stop slouching and stand up straight.* *noun,* **slouches. 1.** a bending forward of the head and shoulders: *He developed a slouch from sitting at his desk too much.* **2.** a person who is lazy or unable to do something well: *She is no slouch as a volleyball player.*

slow [sloh] *adjective,* **slower, slowest. 1.** moving at a low speed; not quick or fast: *We took a slow walk through the park.* **2.** taking a long time; taking longer than usual: *a person who is slow to anger; a country that has been slow to develop modern industries.* **3.** of a watch or other timepiece, showing a time earlier than the right one. **4.** not fast to learn or understand: *He is a slow learner.* **5.** not busy or active: *Business at the store is usually slow after Christmas.* *adverb.* in a slow way: *Walk slow or you will trip.* *verb,* **slowed, slowing.** to become or make slower: *The driver slowed the bus because of the icy road.*

sludge [sluj] *noun.* mud or any soft, mud-like material, such as the solid material that settles out during sewage treatment.

Sloops *are designed to sail well in strong winds and are popular racing boats.*

*Most **slugs** live in moist surroundings and feed on fungi and leaves.*

slug¹ ▶ [slug] *noun, plural* **slugs.**
1. a small, slimy land animal like a snail, but with only a small shell or sometimes no shell. Slugs have a coating of mucus under their foot to help them cling to things and to protect them. **2.** a piece of lead or other metal fired from a gun. **3.** a metal disk used illegally in a vending or gambling machine instead of a coin.

slug² [slug] *verb,* **slugged, slugging.** to hit hard: *Adam slugged the ball over the neighbour's fence. noun, plural* **slugs.** a heavy or hard hit.

slug·gish [slug-ish] *adjective.* slow-moving and lacking energy: *The sluggish river wound over the plains; The hot weather made us feel sluggish.* —**sluggishly,** *adverb.* —**sluggishness,** *noun.*

sluice [sloos] *noun, plural* **sluices. 1.** an artificial channel that has a gate or valve to control the flow of water or another liquid through it. **2.** a gate or valve in such a channel that controls the flow of liquid.

slum [slum] *noun, plural* **slums.** a crowded part of a city with old, rundown housing where many poor people live.

slum·ber [slum-bur] *verb,* **slumbered, slumbering. 1.** to sleep: *The guard slumbered at his post and the group of enemy soldiers crept past.* **2.** to be calm or not active, as if sleeping: *The town slumbered in the hot midday sun and even the cafes were closed. noun.* a state of being asleep: *Nothing disturbed our slumber that night.*

slump [slump] *verb,* **slumped, slumping.** to fall or drop suddenly and heavily: *The ball hit his head and he slumped to the ground. noun, plural* **slumps.** a sudden marked fall or decline: *The tennis player was in a slump and hadn't won a game for several weeks; There was a slump in the stock market during the Great Depression.*

slur [slur] *verb,* **slurred, slurring. 1.** to run sounds together; to say words in an unclear way: *He slurred so I didn't hear what he said.* **2.** to talk about a person in an insulting or highly critical way. *noun, plural* **slurs. 1.** sounds or words run together or said unclearly. **2.** a hurtful or insulting statement: *To say he is a liar is a slur.*

slush [slush] *noun.* ice or snow that is partly melted: *As the day warmed, the snow on the roads turned to slush.*

sly [slye] *adjective,* **slyer** or **slier, slyest** or **sliest. 1.** being clever and sneaky; cunning: *The sly dog crept out the gate and out of the garden when nobody was looking.* **2.** being playful and mischievous: *Walter pretended to take the last doughnut, then passed it to me with a sly laugh.*
• **on the sly.** in a cunning way; secretly: *They were selling stolen goods on the sly.* —**slyly,** *adverb;* **slyness,** *noun.*

smack [smak] *verb,* **smacked, smacking. 1.** to noisily press together or part quickly: *She smacked her lips together as she ate the pie.* **2.** to hit sharply, especially with a loud noise: *He smacked the ball into the outfield. noun, plural* **smacks. 1.** a loud blow made with an open hand: *I gave the dog a smack for nipping me.* **2.** a loud kiss: *Mom hugged me and smacked me on the cheek. adverb.* straight on; directly: *The snowball hit her smack on the nose.*

small [smawl] *adjective,* **smaller, smallest. 1.** not large in size or amount; little: *A minnow is a small fish; Twenty cents is a small sum of money.* **2.** not of great importance: *Losing my key was only a small problem as I climbed in the open window.* **3.** weak or gentle: *She gave the toy car a small push and it rolled down the slope.* **4.** doing something in a limited way: *Their herb farm is a small business.*

small intestine a section of the digestive system that is a long, coiled tube. Food broken down in the stomach passes into the small intestine, where most of the nutrients are absorbed into the bloodstream as it moves through. The leftover material passes into the large intestine.

small letter *Language.* a lower-case letter; a letter that is not a capital. The letter "b" is a small letter.

small·pox [smawl-poks] *noun. Medicine.* a highly contagious virus carried only by humans. After widespread vaccination campaigns, the United Nations declared the disease to be under control in 1980. Smallpox caused blisters and high temperatures. It killed many people or left them severely scarred or with damaged eyesight.

smart [smart] *adjective,* **smarter, smartest. 1.** able to use the mind well; quick to understand; intelligent; bright: *a smart girl who gets A's in all her courses; The smart dog learned the trick quickly.* **2.** making good decisions; clever: *He's a smart soccer player who always knows what to do when he has the ball.* **3.** clever in a way that shows disrespect: *He got in trouble for giving the teacher a smart answer.* **4.** describing something neat, trim, stylish, or fashionable: *Dad looked smart in his new jacket. verb,* **smarted, smarting. 1.** to cause a stinging pain, or to feel such pain: *My arm still smarts from when she slapped it.* **2.** to have or cause to have hurt feelings: *Their mean comments about my haircut really smarted.*

smash [smash] *verb,* **smashed, smashing. 1.** to break into pieces as it is struck or strikes something; to shatter, especially loudly: *The crystal vase smashed as it fell to the hard floor.* **2.** to hit hard; crash: *The truck skidded and smashed into the wall. noun, plural* **smashes.** the act of breaking to pieces or shattering loudly.

a b c d e f g h i j k l m n o p q r **s** t u v w x y z

smear [smeer] *verb,* **smeared, smearing. 1.** to spread or rub something wet, sticky, or greasy over a surface: *The clown smeared face paint on his chin.* **2.** to become or make blurred: *The ink on the picture I printed is smeared.* **3.** to harm someone or something's good name: *The mayor was smeared by a news story that falsely claimed he had dishonest business dealings.*
noun, plural **smears. 1.** a dirty stain or mark: *There was a smear of lipstick on the cup.* **2.** a false or exaggerated criticism: *a politician's smear of the opposing candidate.*

smell ▼ [smel] *verb,* **smelled** or **smelt, smelling. 1.** to sense using the nose: *They smelled smoke from the forest fire; Smell the flowers to find out which one has the loveliest perfume.* **2.** to give off an odor, especially an unpleasant odor: *Those old shoes smell.*
noun, plural **smells. 1.** the sense used to detect an odor: *A dog's most powerful sense is smell.* **2.** a certain odor or scent: *The smell of baking cookies makes me hungry.*

smelt[1] [smelt] *noun, plural* **smelt** or **smelts.** a small, silvery fish of the Northern Hemisphere. Smelt live in schools in the ocean and migrate up freshwater rivers to spawn. People commonly catch smelt for food.

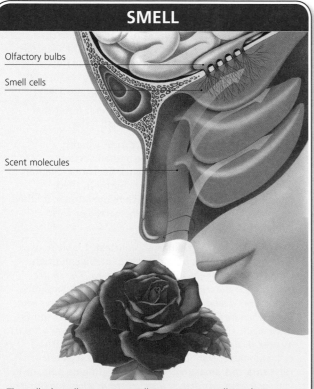

SMELL

Olfactory bulbs

Smell cells

Scent molecules

The cells that allow you to smell occupy two small patches high in your nose and can detect about 1,000 different odors. Scent molecules from different things travel through the air into your nose and reach the smell cells. These send messages to the olfactory bulbs, which then relay the messages to the brain. Your brain combines thousands of messages into a single smell, and then compares this with those it has already stored. That is when you become aware of a particular smell, such as the sweet scent of a rose.

People who work in **smelters** *wear protective gear to shield themselves from the extreme heat.*

smelt[2] ▲ [smelt] *verb,* **smelted, smelting.** the process of heating and melting ore to extract a useful metal from it: *Iron ore is smelted to extract pure iron.* The process of extracting a metal from its ore is **smelting.** A person who does this or a place where it is done is called a **smelter.**

smelt[3] [smelt] *verb.* the past tense and past participle of SMELL.

smile [smile] *noun, plural* **smiles.** a facial expression in which the mouth becomes wider and the corners turn upward. This expression usually shows a person is feeling happy, pleased, amused, or friendly.
verb, **smiled, smiling.** to make or have a smile: *Pat smiled when she saw her friend.*

smock [smok] *noun, plural* **smocks.** a long-sleeved, loose shirt worn over other clothing to protect it: *The artist wore a smock while he painted.*

smog [smog] *noun. Environment.* a fog that has become mixed with smoke. Smog can cause breathing problems. It is a pollution problem in cities, where there are many factories and cars. Air polluted with smog is said to be **smoggy.**

> The word **smog** is a combination of s̲mog̲ke and f̲og̲. This is a fairly new word; it has only been in English for about a hundred years. People began to use the word then to describe the way ordinary fog was made thicker and darker by heavy smoke from large industrial coal fires, as at factories.

smoke [smoke] *noun, plural* **smokes. 1.** the visible gas and other particles given off as something burns. **2.** the act of breathing in the gas given off by burning tobacco and blowing it out again.
verb, **smoked, smoking. 1.** to give off or make smoke: *The tree stump smoked for hours after the forest fire was put out.* **2.** to breathe in the gas given off by tobacco and blow it out again. **3.** to preserve meat or fish by exposing it to the smoke of burning wood.

smoke detector *Health.* an automatic device that gives a loud warning signal when smoke is present; a fire or smoke alarm.

smok·er [smoke-ur] *noun, plural* **smokers. 1.** a person who smokes tobacco, such as in a cigarette or pipe. **2.** something that produces smoke, such as a barbecue used to add a smoky flavor to food.

smoke·stack ▼ [smoke-stak] *noun, plural* **smokestacks.** a large, upright pipe on a ship, steam train engine, or factory that discharges smoke.

In some factories, **smokestacks** *discharge a large amount of smoke that may pollute the atmosphere.*

smok·y [smoh-kee] *adjective,* **smokier, smokiest. 1.** giving off or having a lot of smoke: *The room was smoky because the wood that we used in the fireplace was wet.* **2.** having the color, taste, or smell of smoke: *This cheese you bought has a smoky flavor.*

smol·der [smole-dur] *verb,* **smoldered, smoldering. 1.** to burn giving off smoke but without any or many flames: *Nothing was left of the house but smoldering ruins.* **2.** to exist or linger in a hidden state: *Her jealousy of her friend smoldered until one day she told her what she thought in an angry outburst.*

smooth [smooth] *adjective,* **smoother, smoothest. 1.** not rough to touch; even and without bumps: *Stir the flour, eggs, and milk until you have a smooth batter.* **2.** moving evenly and calmly: *They had a smooth voyage over the calm sea.* **3.** without problems or difficulties: *The play's performance was smooth as we knew our parts.* **4.** skillful or polished: *The smooth piano player gave an enjoyable concert.*
verb, **smoothed, smoothing. 1.** to make something rough or uneven to become level and even: *She smoothed the bedspread and made it tidy.* **2.** to make easier by getting rid of problems or difficulties: *The teacher asked me to smooth the way for the new boy by showing him around.* **—smoothly,** *adverb;* **—smoothness,** *noun.*

smoth·er [smuтн-ur] *verb,* **smothered, smothering. 1.** to cause to die by preventing from breathing air. **2.** to be prevented from breathing: *Don't sleep with the blanket over your head or you might smother.* **3.** to cover a fire to make it burn less or go out: *The firefighter smothered the flames with a fire blanket.* **4.** to cover thickly all over: *She smothered her face with makeup.* **5.** to keep back or hide: *The real facts about the case were quickly smothered to protect the famous movie star's reputation.*

smudge [smuj] *verb,* **smudged, smudging.** to mark with smears and make dirty: *Connor smudged the wet paint on his picture and ruined it.*
noun, plural **smudges.** dirty streaks or marks: *There are smudges on my glasses so I can't see through them.*

smug [smug] *adjective,* **smugger, smuggest.** annoying to others by being pleased with oneself: *I thought the geography exam was hard, but my friend looked smug and said it was really easy.* **—smugly,** *adverb;* **—smugness,** *noun.*

smug·gle [smug-ul] *verb,* **smuggled, smuggling. 1.** *Law.* to secretly move something illegally across a border: *The rare parrot was caught and smuggled out of the country.* The act of carrying something in this way is called **smuggling. 2.** to carry or move something in secret: *He smuggled chewing gum into class inside his pencil case.*

smug·gler [smug-lur] *noun, plural* **smugglers. 1.** a person who smuggles. **2.** a ship used by smugglers to carry goods.

snack [snak] *noun, plural* **snacks.** a small amount of food eaten between meals; a quick, light meal.
verb, **snacked, snacking.** to eat a small amount between meals: *After school, he snacked on crackers and cheese.*

snag [snag] *noun, plural* **snags. 1.** something that sticks out and that other things are likely to catch on, especially the stump of a tree, or a branch: *We had to steer our boat carefully as there were many hidden snags under the water.* **2.** a problem or obstacle that causes delay: *The snag that stopped the dance going ahead was that we couldn't rent a place to hold it.*
verb, **snagged, snagging. 1.** to catch against something that sticks out: *Mary snagged her new sweater on the nail that stuck out of the fence.* **2.** to catch a fish with a hook, but not in its mouth: *He snagged the large trout through its tail.*

snail ◀ [snale] *noun, plural* **snails. 1.** a kind of soft-bodied animal that is protected by a coiled shell. Snails are mollusks. They are slow moving and can live on land or in water. **2.** a slow or lazy person.

If it is threatened, a **snail** *can pull its body back under its shell.*

snake ▶ [snake] *noun, plural* **snakes. 1.** a type of animal that is a reptile with a long body and no limbs. Snakes move by tightening and relaxing muscles along their body. They are cold-blooded and have a scaly skin. They eat meat and some kill their prey with a poisonous bite. **2.** a person who secretly does harm and cannot be trusted.
verb, **snaked, snaking.** to move like a snake in a winding path rather than a straight line: *They snaked their way through the crowd.*

snap [snap] *verb,* **snapped, snapping. 1.** to make or cause a sudden, sharp, cracking sound: *The man snapped his fingers loudly to get the waiter's attention.* **2.** to break suddenly with a cracking sound: *He stepped on the stick and it snapped in two.* **3.** to move or speak sharply and suddenly: *The teacher snapped at the class for making too much noise.* **4.** to open, shut, or move into place with a sharp, cracking sound: *Christopher snapped the lock shut.* **5.** to grab or bite suddenly: *The little dog snapped angrily at the boy's ankle.* **6.** to take an informal photograph: *We snapped lots of photos at Barbara's birthday party.*
noun, plural **snaps. 1.** a sudden, sharp sound, or an action that causes this sound: *She shut the lid of the small box with a snap.* **2.** a catch or fastener that makes a sharp sound: *You better do up the snap on your bag or everything will fall out.* **3.** a quick grab or bite. **4.** a short period of cold weather that arrives suddenly. **5.** a thin, brittle cookie: *Butter snaps are my grandmother's favorite cookies.* **6.** something that was quick and easy to do: *Passing my driving test was a snap.*
adjective. done suddenly without much thought: *They made a snap decision and changed their vacation plans the day before they left.*

snap·shot [snap-shot] *noun, plural* **snapshots.** an informal photograph taken with a handheld camera.

snare [snare] *noun, plural* **snares.** a trap that uses a noose to catch small animals.
verb, **snared, snaring.** to trap or catch with a snare, or in a tricky manner that is thought to be like this: *That advertisement snared our attention because it was really funny.*

snare drum *Music.* a drum with wires stretched underneath that vibrate when the skin of the top of the drum is hit.

snarl¹ [snarl] *verb,* **snarled, snarling. 1.** to growl angrily with the teeth showing: *The guard dog snarled at the intruder.* **2.** to speak angrily in a growling, threatening manner: *"It's to early to get up," the man snarled at his ringing alarm clock.*
noun, plural **snarls.** a fierce growl.

snarl² [snarl] *noun, plural* **snarls. 1.** a knot or tangle in something: *Richard could not untangle the nasty snarl in his fishing line.* **2.** a confused or complicated situation.
verb, **snarled, snarling. 1.** to become or cause to become tangled or knotted: *Susan's hair is snarled because she forgot to brush it this morning.* **2.** to become or cause to become confused or complicated: *The thick fog snarled the traffic at the airport.*

snatch [snach] *verb,* **snatched, snatching.** to grab or take hold of suddenly and quickly: *The bird snatched the moth in its beak.*
noun, plural **snatches. 1.** the act of grabbing or taking hold of something suddenly and quickly. **2.** a bit or small part of something: *I only remember snatches of that song.*

sneak [sneek] *verb,* **sneaked** or **snuck, sneaking.** to act in way that means you will not be noticed: *She sneaked into his room when he was in the kitchen having lunch.*
noun, plural **sneaks.** a person who acts in a secretive, sly way and is not to be trusted: *He is a sneak, so watch what you say when he is around.*
adjective. done in a secretive or sly way: *Let's have a sneak peek at the presents under the Christmas tree.*

snea·ker [sneek-ur] *noun, plural* **sneakers.** a lace-up canvas or nylon shoe with a rubber sole, often worn to play sports.

sneak·y [sneek-ee] *adjective,* **sneakier, sneakiest.** behaving like a sneak; acting in a secretive, sly, or dishonest way.

sneer [sneer] *noun, plural* **sneers.** something said or a facial expression that shows hatred or a lack of respect: *He spoke of his opponent with a sneer in his voice.*
verb, **sneered, sneering.** to show hatred or contempt by something said or by a nasty expression on the face: *The rich lord sneered at his servant.*

sneeze ▼ [sneez] *verb,* **sneezed, sneezing.** to make an explosive rush of air out of the nose and mouth: *Cora sneezed when she smelled the flowers.*
noun, plural **sneezes.** a sudden explosive rush of air out of the nose and mouth: *His loud sneeze could be heard across the playground.*

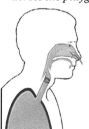 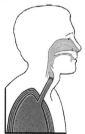 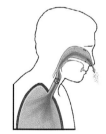

Dust is caught in the nose.

The throat and windpipe close.

They open and air rushes out.

A person **sneezes** *when dust, fur, or pollen irritates the lining of the nose.*

snick·er [snik-ur] *verb,* **snickered, snickering.** to give a rude, disrespectful, or scornful laugh or giggle: *Rude people in the audience snickered when the actor forgot his lines.*
noun, plural **snickers.** a mocking laugh or giggle.

sniff [snif] *verb,* **sniffed, sniffing. 1.** to draw a short, quick breath into the nose. **2.** to smell using a short breath through the nose: *We sniffed the air and smelled smoke.*
noun, plural **sniffs.** the act of sniffing or the sound of this.

snif·fle [snif-ul] *verb,* **sniffled, sniffling.** to sniff over and over again, usually because of having a runny nose from a cold or from crying.
noun, plural **sniffles.** the act or sound of sniffling. When someone has a cold that makes them sniffle, they are said to have **the sniffles.**

SNAKES

There are nearly 2,400 kinds of snakes. They vary in size from the 8-inch thread snake to the 33-foot anaconda, and have many different colors, patterns, and ways of killing their prey. Snakes eat everything from ants, eggs, snails, and slugs to animals as big as caimans and goats. More than half of all snakes kill their prey with venom. Others, like pythons and boa constrictors, squeeze their prey to death.

SIZE COMPARISON

Yellow-bellied sea snake
3 feet

Eastern diamondback rattlesnake
7 feet

Boa constrictor
15 feet

Anaconda
33 feet

ANATOMY OF A RATTLESNAKE

Rattle

Scales

Long, single, narrow lung

Liver

Muscles attached to ribs

Venom duct

Hollow, swinging fang

Forked tongue

Stomach

Small intestine

VENOMOUS SNAKES
Venom is produced by special mouth glands and injected into prey through hollow or grooved fangs, which may be at the back of the mouth, or fixed or swinging in the front of the mouth.

Venom duct

Grooved rear fang

Venom duct

Hollow fixed front fang of cobras

Venom duct

Hollow swinging fang of vipers and rattlesnakes

SNAKES' JAWS
Snakes swallow their prey whole. The upper and lower jaws are attached with elastic connections so that they can open wide and swallow food that may be much larger than the snake's head.

Extended jaw

Resting jaw

YOUNG SNAKES
Most snakes lay eggs and then leave them to develop on their own. Pythons and cobras, however, guard their eggs until they have hatched. Some snakes, like vipers and some water snakes, give birth to live young.

Python guarding eggs

HOW SNAKES MOVE
Snakes move by levering themselves along on the edge of their belly scales, which are connected by tiny muscles to their ribs. Many heavy-bodied snakes, like pythons, crawl in a straight line. The sidewinder, a North American desert rattlesnake, moves sideways so that only small parts of its body touch the hot sand at any one time.

Sidewinder

Red-bellied black snake

South American coral pipe snake

Blood python

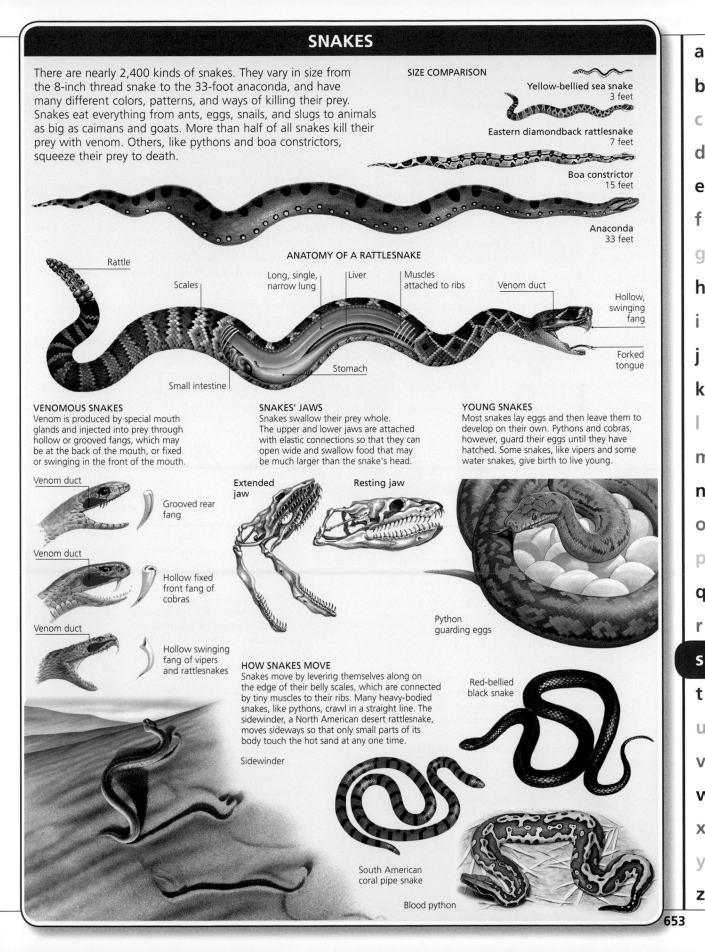

snip [snip] *verb*, **snipped, snipping.** to cut something with short, quick strokes using shears or scissors: *The gardener snipped the shrubs into unusual shapes.* *noun*, *plural* **snips.** the act of snipping, or a piece of something that has been snipped off.

snipe [snipe] *noun, plural* **snipes.** any of several wading birds. Snipes search for small prey in the mud with their long, slender bills.
verb, **sniped, sniping. 1.** to shoot at a person from a hidden place. **2.** to make critical or nasty comments about a person, especially in a sneaky or sly way: *Some players on the team have been sniping about the coach to reporters, without being quoted by name.*

snip·er [snipe-ur] *noun, plural* **snipers.** someone hidden who shoots at people. Some soldiers are trained as snipers.

snob [snob] *noun, plural* **snobs. 1.** someone who thinks great wealth, high social standing, or being stylish and clever are very important. **2.** someone who looks down on people he or she thinks are inferior.

snob·bish [snob-ish] *adjective.* like a snob; stuck-up: *He has a snobbish attitude and judges people by how much money they have.* Someone who acts in this way is also said to be **snobby.**

snoop [snoop] *verb*, **snooped, snooping.** to pry into other people's business in a sneaky, sly way: *I caught him snooping around in my room.* *noun, plural* **snoops.** a person who does this.

snooze [snooz] *verb*, **snoozed, snoozing.** to sleep lightly or for a short time; nap; doze: *The children snoozed in the back seat on the car trip.* *noun, plural* **snoozes.** a light or short sleep; a nap: *Dad had a snooze on the couch after lunch.*

snore [snore] *verb*, **snored, snoring.** to breathe with harsh, snorting sounds while asleep: *He snored all night and kept me awake.* *noun, plural* **snores.** a breathing sound made while asleep that is harsh and snorting.

snor·kel ▼ [snore-kul] *noun, plural* **snorkels.** a tube with a mouthpiece that a person can use to breathe through while swimming face-down in the water: *Tim breathed through his snorkel as he swam over the coral reef looking at the marine life.* Swimming using a snorkel to breathe is called **snorkeling.**

The word **snorkel** comes from the German name for this device. It was invented by the Dutch and then first used by the Germans for their submarines in World War II. It is related to other words that have to do with breathing, such as *snore* and *snort.*

snout ▶ [snout] *noun*, *plural* **snouts.** the part of an animal's head that juts forward and includes the nose, mouth, and jaws.

Gharial

Black caiman

American crocodile

snow [snoh] *noun*. **1.** frozen water that falls to the ground as soft, white crystals. **2.** a layer of these crystals on the ground: *The snow was three feet deep in places.* *verb*, **snowed, snowing.** to fall as snow: *It was snowing so heavily we couldn't see across the street.*

snow·ball [snoh-bawl] *noun, plural* **snowballs.** a pile of snow packed together to form a ball. *verb*, **snowballed, snowballing.** to grow or pile up ever more quickly: *The problems with the project snowballed and soon we had a huge event on our hands.*

snow·flake [snoh-flake] *noun, plural* **snowflakes.** a tiny frozen crystal of water that falls from the sky.

snow·man [snoh-man] *noun, plural* **snowmen.** a figure made out of packed snow that looks like a person.

snow·mo·bile ◀ [snoh-moh-beel] *noun, plural* **snowmobiles.** a small motorized vehicle used for traveling over snow. Snowmobiles are driven by a rubber tread at the rear and are steered by two skis or runners at the front.

snow·plow [snoh-plow] *noun, plural* **snowplows.** a wide, curving blade used to clear snow, or a vehicle with this device attached to the front. Snowplows are often used to remove snow from roads.

Snowmobiles *are used mainly for recreational activities in parts of North America that have good snow cover all through the winter.*

snow·shoe ▶ [snoh-shoo] *noun*, *plural* **snowshoes.** a flat, wide frame with webbing wrapped around it in an open pattern. This footwear is attached to boots to allow you to walk over deep snow without sinking.

snow·storm [snow-storm] *noun*, *plural* **snowstorms.** a storm that has heavy snow instead of rain.

snow·y [snow-ee] *adjective*, **snowier, snowiest. 1.** having much snow or covered in snow: *The weather has been snowy this winter. Our driveway is snowy and needs clearing.* **2.** having the color, texture, or appearance of snow.

Some Native Americans wore **snowshoes** *in dances that celebrated the first winter snowfalls.*

snub [snub] *verb*, **snubbed, snubbing.** to deliberately ignore or treat another person coldly: *She saw him but kept walking without saying hello, snubbing him completely.* *noun, plural* **snubs.** behavior that is deliberately cold or distant; an act of snubbing.

With a mask and **snorkel** *you can take your time exploring the underwater environment.*

The wide wings of eagles help them **soar** high above the ground in search of prey.

social

snug [snug] *adjective,* **snugger, snuggest. 1.** cozy, warm, sheltered, and comfortable: *A storm raged but we were snug and warm in the cabin.* **2.** close fitting; not a loose fit, especially of clothes: *These shoes are snug but not too tight.*

snug·gle [snug-uhl] *verb,* **snuggled, snuggling.** to hold or press close to someone or something for warmth, protection, or to show affection; cuddle: *The baby snuggled up to her mother and fell asleep.*

so [soh] *adverb.* **1.** to the amount or degree described: *I was so tired I fell asleep right after dinner.* **2.** extremely; very: *He is so happy now that he has a puppy.* **3.** for a given reason; therefore: *They forgot their map, so they got lost.* **4.** as well as; too; also: *Mom wants to take a vacation next month, and so does Dad.* **5.** in the way described or shown; thus: *To open the lock, you have to put in the key just so.*
adjective. describing something factual; true: *What the book describes was so.*
conjunction. for the reason that: *Take a water bottle with you, so you can have a drink if you get thirsty.*
pronoun. **1.** around about: *Write a story of two pages or so.* **2.** the same as stated before: *His desk is messy and always will be so.*
interjection. a word used at the beginning of a statement to express surprise or understanding: *So, you have found your pen at last.*
🔊 Different words with the same sound are **sew** and **sow.**

soak [soke] *verb,* **soaked, soaking. 1.** to make people or things very wet: *The hikers were soaked by the sudden storm.* **2.** to let someone or something stay covered with liquid: *Joe let his dirty shirts soak overnight before washing them.* **3.** to take in or absorb liquid: *We used old towels to soak up the spilled water.*
noun, plural **soaks.** the act or fact of letting someone or something stay covered in liquid: *to have a soak in the bathtub.*

soap [sope] *noun, plural* **soaps.** a substance used for washing or cleaning. Soap is made from oil or fat and lye. It can be made into hard pieces, as a powder, or as a liquid.
verb, **soaped, soaping.** to rub or cover something with soap.

soap·y [sope-ee] *adjective.* covered with or containing soap: *Hannah washed the porch with soapy water.*

soar ▲ [sore] *verb,* **soared, soaring. 1.** to rise or fly upward: *The rocket soared into the sky.* **2.** to rise steeply; go very high: *We stayed in the cool of the house as the outdoor temperature soared.*
🔊 Different words with the same sound are **saw** and **sore.**

sob [sob] *verb,* **sobbed, sobbing.** to cry while taking loud, short breaths, because of sadness or fear: *The lost child sobbed for her parents.*
noun, plural **sobs.** the act or sound of crying with short breaths.

so·ber [soh-bur] *adjective.* **1.** not affected by drinking alcohol; not drunk. **2.** thoughtful and serious; solemn: *the sober mood of mourners at a funeral.* The fact of being sober is **sobriety.**
verb, **sobered, sobering.** to make or become serious and thoughtful: *News of their captain's injury sobered the team's victory celebration.*

soc·cer ▼ [sok-ur] *noun.* a game played by two teams of eleven players using a round ball that they try to move into a goal by kicking, striking it with the head, or contacting it with any other part of the body except the hands and arms.

so·ci·able [soh-shuh-bul] *adjective.* enjoying being with others; friendly: *Victoria is very sociable and goes to a lot of parties.*

so·cial [soh-shul] *adjective.* **1.** having to do with the way people as a group are organized or operate: *Governments make laws on social issues such as justice, education, and employment.* **2.** organized for friendly purposes rather than for work or business: *a social gathering; a social club.* **3.** enjoying being with others; sociable: *He's always going out—he's very social.* **4.** having to do with rich or famous people and the things they do. **5.** of animals, living in an organized group rather than alone: *Ants are social insects.*
noun, plural **socials.** a friendly gathering of a group of people. —**socially,** *adverb.*

In **soccer,** *the goalkeeper's job is to stop the other team from scoring goals.*

so·cial·ism [soh-shuh-*liz*-um] *noun. Government.* an economic and political system in which all the important industries are owned and run by the government rather than by private companies or individual people. This is also spelled **Socialism.**

so·cial·ist [soh-shul-ist] *noun, plural* **socialists.** *Government.* a person who believes in socialism. This word is also spelled **Socialist.**

social science the study of people in society. History, anthropology, politics, and economics are all social sciences. A **social scientist** studies human society, both in the past and the present.

Social Security *Government.* **1.** a U.S. government program to provide regular payments to people who have reached retirement age or who are unable to work. The funds for this come from active workers and their employers. **2. social security.** any similar program to provide financial support for those who have low income because they do not work or are unable to work. **3.** money paid to someone through such a program.

social studies *Education.* a course of study taught at an elementary school or a secondary school that includes geography, history, and civics.

social work work done by a government or private organizations to improve the conditions of and provide help to those in need. The job of a **social worker** is to provide these services to those in need.

so·ci·e·ty [suh-sye-uh-tee] *noun, plural* **societies. 1.** people as a whole: *Climate change is one of many problems facing society in the twenty-first century.* **2.** a group of people with a common interest, such as a club: *The Society for the Prevention of Cruelty to Animals.* **3.** the rich, famous, or fashionable people in a particular place. **4.** company; companionship: *Amy enjoyed the society of her grandparents and their friends and loved listening to the stories they told.*

soc·io·eco·nom·ic [soh-see-oh-*ek*-uh-nom-ik *or* soh-shee-oh-*ek*-uh-nom-ik] *adjective.* having to do with both social and economic factors, or the way in which these factors relate to and affect each other: *the socioeconomic effect on the town of closing the factory.*

soci·ol·o·gy [soh-see-ol-uh-jee *or* soh-shee-ol-uh-jee] *noun.* the study of human societies and the behavior of groups in society. A person whose work is doing such studies is a **sociologist.**

sock[1] [sok] *noun, plural* **socks.** a piece of clothing worn under a shoe, covering the foot and ankle and sometimes the lower leg.

sock[2] [sok] *noun, plural* **socks.** a very hard hit, usually with the fist; a punch: *a sock on the jaw.* *verb,* **socked, socking.** to hit very hard: *The boxer socked his opponent on the jaw.*

soc·ket [sok-it] *noun, plural* **sockets.** a hollow area or opening into which something fits: *an eye socket; Dad put the plug of the drill into the electric socket.*

sod [sod] *noun, plural* **sods. 1.** the top layer of the ground, together with the grass and roots growing in it; turf. **2.** such a layer of grass used to make a new lawn. *verb,* **sodded, sodding.** to plant a lawn using sod.

so·da [soh-duh] *noun, plural* **sodas. 1.** a soft drink made with carbonated water and flavoring. Cola drinks are a type of soda. **2.** the shortened form of SODA WATER. **3.** a sweet drink containing soda water, flavoring, and usually ice cream. **4.** a white powder made with sodium that is used in cooking and in medicine, and in making soaps and other cleaners.

soda water a drink made by filling water with bubbles of carbon dioxide gas.

so·di·um [soh-dee-um] *noun. Chemistry.* a soft, silver-white metal found in salt. Sodium is a metallic element.

so·fa [soh-fuh] *noun, plural* **sofas.** a long padded seat for two or more people with a back and arms at each end; also called a couch.

soft [sawft] *adjective* **softer, softest. 1.** easily cut or pressed out of shape; not hard: *soft cheese; a soft cushion.* **2.** smooth and pleasant to touch; not rough: *She rubbed the soft silk against her cheek.* **3.** not harsh or bright; gentle: *Her soft singing helped the baby go to sleep.* **4.** caring about other people's feelings; kind: *a person with a soft heart.* **5.** not in good condition; weak: *Her muscles have gone soft since she stopped exercising.* —**softly,** *adverb;* —**softness,** *noun.*

soft·ball ▶ [sawft-*bawl*] *noun, plural* **softballs. 1.** a type of baseball, played on a smaller field using a softer and larger ball that is pitched underhand. In **fast-pitch softball,** the pitcher throws the ball at full speed, making it difficult for the batter to hit. In **slow-pitch softball,** the ball is delivered at a slower speed and is easier to hit. **2.** the ball used in this game.

Softball *players catch the ball in large mitts that protect their hands.*

soft drink a refreshing cool drink that does not contain alcohol, such as lemonade.

soft·en [sawf-un] *verb,* **softened, softening.** to make or become less hard, stiff, or firm: *Put the ice cream back in the freezer before it softens and melts.* A **softener** is a substance added to water to make washed fabrics feel softer.

soft·ware [sawft-ware] *noun. Computers.* programs that are used to control the functions of a computer. The computer machinery is HARDWARE.

The word **software** came about because of the idea that the physical, solid parts of a computer are called *hardware,* such as the CPU (central processing unit). This comes from the familiar sense of *hardware* as nails, screws, and such other items made of metal. In contrast the programs that run a computer do not have a solid physical identity, and so are called *software.*

soft·wood [sawft-wud] *noun, plural* **softwoods.** wood that is easily cut. Softwood comes from evergreen trees that grow quickly, such as pines and firs.

sog·gy [sog-ee] *adjective.* thoroughly wet; soaked: *I left my magazine out in the rain and now the pages are soggy.*

soil ▶ [soyle] *noun, plural* **soils.**
1. the top layer of the ground that plants grow in; earth or dirt: *The farmer dug the soil before planting the carrots.* **2.** a country, land, or territory: *The homesick sailors longed to set foot again on American soil.*
verb, **soiled, soiling.** to make or become dirty: *The spilled gravy soiled the tablecloth.*

sol·ace [sol-is] *noun.* a feeling of comfort that makes you feel less sad; relief: *He found solace from his troubles listening to his favorite music.*

so·lar [soh-lur] *adjective. Science.* **1.** having to do with or coming from the Sun: *a solar eclipse; solar energy.* **2.** using or powered by the energy from the Sun's rays: *A solar hot water system uses sunshine for energy.*
noun. the shortened form of SOLAR ENERGY.

solar energy ▼ *Environment.* energy from the sun that is used for heating and to make electricity. A **solar cell** is a device that turns sunlight into electricity.

solar system the Sun together with the Earth and all the other planets, comets, asteroids, and other bodies that orbit around it.

Soil — *Between the soil in which plants grow and the solid rock deeper down there are various layers of minerals and other materials.*

Solid rock

sold [sohld] *verb.* the past tense and past participle of SELL.

sol·der [sod-ur] *noun, plural* **solders.** a soft metal that can be melted easily and used to join other metals together.
verb, **soldered, soldering.** to join two metals together in this way.

sol·dier [sole-jur] *noun, plural* **soldiers.** a person who is a member of an army.

> The word **soldier** is related to *solidus*, which was a gold coin used in the Roman Empire. The connection between the two is said to come from a practice of paying soldiers for their services with these solidus coins.

sole¹ [sole] *noun, plural* **soles.** the bottom or underneath part of the foot or of a shoe or boot: *Some sports shoes have special soles to make running easier.*
verb, **soled, soling.** to put a sole on a shoe or boot: *The bootmaker soled my hiking boots.*
🔊 A different word with the same sound is **soul.**

sole² [sole] *adjective.* being the only one; only: *A woman raising children without a husband can be called a sole parent; Apart from a sole phone call, we have not heard from her at all.* **2.** belonging to or allowed to one person or group only: *This bus is for the sole use of school students.* —**solely,** *adverb.*
🔊 A different word with the same sound is **soul.**

sole³ [sole] *noun, plural* **soles** *or* **sole.** a flatfish that is often used as food.
🔊 A different word with the same sound is **soul.**

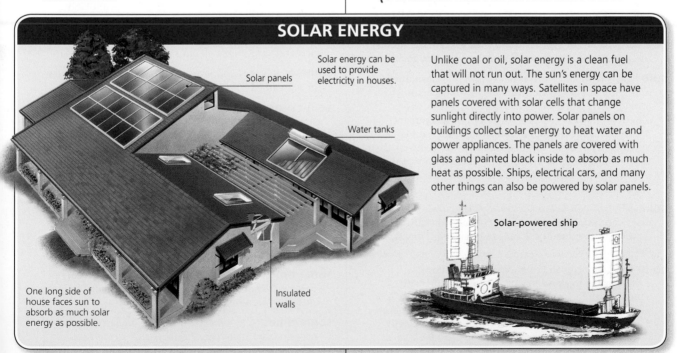

SOLAR ENERGY

Solar energy can be used to provide electricity in houses.

Solar panels

Water tanks

One long side of house faces sun to absorb as much solar energy as possible.

Insulated walls

Unlike coal or oil, solar energy is a clean fuel that will not run out. The sun's energy can be captured in many ways. Satellites in space have panels covered with solar cells that change sunlight directly into power. Solar panels on buildings collect solar energy to heat water and power appliances. The panels are covered with glass and painted black inside to absorb as much heat as possible. Ships, electrical cars, and many other things can also be powered by solar panels.

Solar-powered ship

sol·emn [sol-um] *adjective.* **1.** very serious and formal; not cheerful: *a solemn ceremony in memory of soldiers who died in the war.* An event or ceremony that is serious and formal has **solemnity. 2.** very sincere: *He made a solemn promise that he would return.* —**solemnly,** *adverb.*

sol·id [sol-id] *adjective.* **1.** being hard or firm and with a fixed shape; not liquid or gaseous: *The pond has frozen solid; When I pushed the shovel into the dirt, it banged against something solid.* Something that is strong and firm has **solidity. 2.** made or consisting entirely of the same material, color, or kind; not hollow or mixed: *a solid gold ring; a candy that is solid chocolate.* **3.** without a pause or interruption: *I worked for three solid hours before taking a break.* **4.** very strong; not easily damaged: *These solid castle walls have stood for hundreds of years.* **5.** having good character; dependable: *a solid citizen; a solid friend he could turn to in a time of trouble.* **6.** having length, width, and thickness: *A pyramid is a solid figure.* *noun, plural* **solids. 1.** a substance that is not a liquid or gas and that has a fixed shape. **2.** a figure in geometry that has length, width, and thickness, such as a cube, pyramid, or sphere. —**solidly,** *adverb.*

sol·id·i·fy [suh-<u>lid</u>-uh-*fye*] *verb,* **solidifies, solidifying.** *Chemistry.* to change from a liquid into a solid: *Molten lava solidifies into rock when it cools.* The act of changing from a liquid to a solid is **solidification.**

solid-state [sol-id-<u>state</u>] *adjective.* of an electrical device, working by means of the flow of electricity through solid parts, such as transistors.

sol·i·taire [sol-i-*tare*] *noun, plural* **solitaires. 1.** a single jewel: *a diamond solitaire ring.* **2.** a card game for one player.

sol·i·tar·y [sol-uh-*ter*-ee] *adjective.* **1.** without others nearby; alone: *During the rainstorm, the beach was empty except for a solitary walker.* **2.** relating to one; single: *It's been so busy, I haven't had a solitary minute to myself.* **3.** made, done, or spent without companions: *the solitary life of a hermit.* The fact of being alone is **solitude.**

solo [soh-loh] *noun, plural* **solos.** *Music.* a performance of singing or playing an instrument by one person: *Mark played a solo on the clarinet.* *adjective.* **1.** *Music.* for one singer or one instrument. **2.** made or done without a companion; alone: *a solo airplane flight; a solo voyage around the world in a sailboat.* *verb,* **soloing, soloed. 1.** *Music.* to perform a musical solo. **2.** of a pilot, to fly alone, without an instructor or passengers.

sol·u·ble [sol-yuh-bul] *adjective.* **1.** *Chemistry.* able to be dissolved: *Salt is soluble in water.* A substance that can be dissolved has **solubility. 2.** able to be solved: *This puzzle must be soluble.*

so·lu·tion [suh-<u>loo</u>-shun] *noun, plural* **solutions. 1.** the answer to a problem or a way of dealing with a difficult situation: *the solution to a crossword puzzle; The town is working on a solution to its traffic problems.* **2.** a substance that is made up of a solid spread evenly through a liquid: *Salt can be dissolved in water to form a solution.*

solve [solv] *verb,* **solved, solving.** to find the answer to a problem or question: *to solve a riddle; to solve a murder mystery.*

sol·vent [sol-vunt] *noun, plural* **solvents.** *Chemistry.* a liquid that can dissolve other substances. Solvents that dissolve grease are used to remove certain stains; other types of solvents are used in dry cleaning and to thin paint.

som·ber [som-bur] *adjective.* dark and gloomy; not bright or colorful: *The walls were painted a somber brown.*

som·bre·ro ▼ [som-<u>brer</u>-oh] *noun, plural* **sombreros.** a hat with a very broad brim, originally worn in Mexico and some other Spanish-speaking countries.

some [sum] *adjective.* **1.** having to do with one or ones not named or known: *Some types of dogs are used to herd cattle.* **2.** having to do with a number or quantity not stated exactly: *I picked some flowers; Some children were late.* *pronoun.* a number or amount not stated exactly: *Donna had a box of chocolates and gave me some.*

Mexican **sombreros** *are often elaborately decorated.*

adverb. approximately; about: *The river is some ten minutes walk from our place.*

🔊 A different word with the same sound is **sum.**

some·bod·y [sum-*bud*-ee or sum-*bod*-ee] *pronoun.* a person who is not known or not named: *Can somebody answer the phone please?* *noun, plural* **somebodies.** a person who is important or well known: *She has so much talent as a singer and dancer that I think she'll grow up to be somebody.*

some·day [sum-*day*] *adverb.* at an unknown time in the future: *I hope you'll be able to visit us someday.*

some·how [sum-*hou*] *adverb.* in a way that is not known or stated: *The secret got out somehow.*

some·one [sum-*wun*] *pronoun.* a person who is not known or not named: *Someone forgot to shut the gate.*

som·er·sault [sum-ur-*sawlt*] *verb,* **somersaulted, somersaulting.** to make a complete circular roll of the body, either forward or backward, by bringing the feet over the head. *noun, plural* **somersaults.** a complete circular roll of the body either forward or backward.

some·thing [sum-*thing*] *pronoun.* a thing that is not known or not stated: *I've got something in my eye; Did Mom leave us something for lunch?* *adverb.* to some extent or degree: *A mandarin tastes something like an orange.*

some·time [sum-*time*] *adverb.* at a time in the future or past that is not known or has not been stated: *The baby should be born sometime in the next week.*

some·times [sum-*timez*] *adverb.* on some occasions; occasionally: *Sometimes I walk to school, but I usually take the bus.*

*Scientists use side-scan **sonar** to map the seafloor and search for sunken objects.*

some·what [sum-*what*] *adverb.* to some extent or degree; a little: *The breeze cooled us somewhat. noun.* some part or amount: *Dave's cookie recipe was somewhat of an experiment.*

some·where [sum-*ware*] *adverb.* **1.** in, at, or to a place not known or not stated: *I lost my hat somewhere in the park.* **2.** some number or amount: *The cost should be somewhere between twenty and thirty dollars. noun.* a place not known or stated: *I'm looking for somewhere to put this chair.* Another word with the same meaning is **someplace.**

son [sun] *noun, plural* **sons.** a male child of a mother or father.
🔊 A different word with the same sound is **sun.**

so·nar ▲ [soh-nar] *noun, plural* **sonars.** a device that sends out sound waves under water and measures the time it takes for the echo of the sound waves to return. Sonar is used to find depth or to locate underwater objects such as submarines, mines, or schools of fish.

> The word **sonar** comes from the first letters of <u>so</u>und <u>n</u>avigation <u>a</u>nd <u>r</u>anging. It is one of many new words that entered the language during the days of World War II. This was a time when many new devices and technologies such as sonar first came into use.

so·na·ta [suh-<u>nah</u>-tuh] *noun, plural* **sonatas.** *Music.* a piece of music for one or two instruments with three or more short parts in different styles.

song [sawng *or* song] *noun, plural* **songs.** **1.** a short piece of music with words. **2.** the musical sounds made by some birds, whales, and certain insects.

song·bird ▶ [<u>sawng</u>-*burd or* <u>song</u>-*burd*] *noun, plural* **songbirds.** a bird with a musical call: *Larks and nightingales are well-known songbirds.*

son·ic [<u>son</u>-ik] *adjective. Science.* **1.** having to do with sound or sound waves. **2.** having to do with traveling at the speed of sound. A **sonic boom** is the explosive noise produced by an aircraft traveling faster than the speed of sound.

son-in-law [<u>sun</u>-in-*law*] *noun, plural* **sons-in-law.** the husband of a person's daughter.

son·net [<u>son</u>-it] *noun, plural* **sonnets.** *Literature.* a poem of fourteen lines in which the lines have to rhyme in a certain way.

soon [soon] *adverb.* **1.** within a short time: *Lunch will be ready soon.* **2.** before the expected time; early: *I picked the apples too soon, and they are not properly ripe.* **3.** without delay; quickly: *I'll be home as soon as I can.* **4.** readily; willingly: *I'd just as soon go swimming as go to the movies.*

soot [sut] *noun.* the black, powdery substance that sticks to the inside of a chimney when fuels such as wood, coal, and oil are burned.

soothe [sooTH] *verb,* **soothed, soothing.** to calm, comfort, or ease pain: *Jess sang softly to soothe the crying baby.* Something that calms, comforts, or eases pain, is **soothing. —soothingly,** *adverb.*

so·phis·ti·cat·ed [suh-<u>fis</u>-tuh-*kay*-tid] *adjective.* wise and experienced about the world, especially about things such as culture and fashion, and having a good understanding of the way people behave. The fact of experiencing many different things and knowing a lot about the world is **sophistication.**

soph·o·more [<u>sof</u>-*more or* <u>sof</u>-uh-*more*] *Education.* a student in the second year of college or a four-year high school.

> **Sophomore** goes back to an old phrase that combines two opposite words, one meaning "wise" and the other meaning "foolish." The idea is that a sophomore, having been through the difficult freshman year, may now think of himself as wise, especially in comparison to the new freshman class. However, others who are older and more experienced may think of him as foolish.

Red-capped robin

Golden-fronted leafbird

Orange chat

so·pra·no [suh-<u>prahn</u>-oh *or* suh-<u>pran</u>-oh] *noun, plural* **sopranos.** *Music.* **1.** the highest singing voice in women or boys. **2.** a woman or boy who sings with such a voice.

sor·cer·y [<u>sore</u>-suh-ree] *noun.* magic, especially when used for evil purposes. A **sorcerer** is a person who performs magic by using the power of evil spirits.

sor·did [<u>sore</u>-did] *adjective.* **1.** morally mean or nasty; dishonest: *a sordid story about stealing and blackmail.* **2.** dirty, unpleasant, and neglected: *Half-starved stray cats lived in the sordid back alleys of the city.*

sore [sore] *adjective,* **sorer, sorest. 1.** hurting or painful; aching: *I have a sore knee from falling off my bike.* **2.** angry and upset: *He's sore because we forgot to tell him about the party.* **3.** likely to cause distress, misery, or embarrassment: *Don't ask her how she did on the test, it's a bit of a sore subject. noun, plural* **sores.** a painful or injured spot on the body. **—soreness,** *noun.*

a b c d e f g h i j k l m n o p q r **s** t u v w x y z

Sorrel plants have clusters of reddish-green flowers that bloom in summer.

sore·ly [sore-lee] *adverb.* very much, greatly: *The exhausted hikers were sorely in need of a hot meal and a long sleep.*

so·ror·i·ty [suh-rore-i-tee] *noun.* a social club for women students at a college or university.

sor·rel ▶ [sor-ul] *noun.* a plant with sharp-tasting leaves that are used in salads and sauces.

sor·row [sor-oh] *noun, plural* **sorrows.** **1.** a feeling of deep sadness and loss; grief. People are **sorrowful** when someone they love dies. **2.** a cause of sadness or grief: *Having to leave behind her old friends when she moved was a great sorrow for her.* —**sorrowfully,** *adverb.*

sor·ry [sor-ee] *adjective,* **sorrier, sorriest. 1.** feeling sadness or sympathy: *We felt sorry for the lost child.* **2.** feeling regret or shame: *I am sorry for the unkind things I said about him.* **3.** in poor condition; pitiful: *My lunch was in a sorry state after being squashed at the bottom of my backpack all morning.*

sort [sort] *noun, plural* **sorts.** a group of people or things that are similar in some way; a type or kind: *Frances has the sort of bag that you wear on your back; What sort of movies do you like?*
verb, **sorted, sorting.** to arrange or place according to type or kind: *Dan sorted the books by subject.*
• **sort of.** to some extent; in some way: *Louis can sort of play the guitar, but he needs a lot more practice.*
• **sort out.** to deal with a situation or problem: *They have sorted out their argument and are best friends again.*

SOS *noun.* an urgent call or signal for help.

sought [sawt] *verb.* the past tense and past participle of SEEK.

soul [sole] *noun, plural* **souls. 1.** the invisible part of a person that is thought to control feelings and emotions; the spirit. Many people believe the soul stays alive after the body dies. **2.** a human being; anyone: *a happy soul; I didn't see a single soul I knew.* **3.** the quality of a person or work of art that shows or produces honest and true deep feelings: *a painting with soul.* **4.** a person who inspires or leads: *Many think of Nelson Mandela as the soul of South Africa.* 🔊 A different word with the same sound is **sole.**

soul food food traditionally eaten by African-Americans in the Southern U.S.

soul music a type of modern African-American music with songs about strong emotions.

sound[1] [sound] *noun, plural* **sounds. 1.** something that you can hear. Sounds are vibrations that travel through the air that you hear when they hit your eardrum. **2.** one of the noises that make up speech: *The word "sure" starts with a "sh" sound.* **3.** the distance a noise can be heard: *The cabin is within the sound of the ocean waves.*
verb, **sounded, sounding. 1.** to make or cause something to make a noise: *The church bells sounded.* **2.** to pronounce or say: *Some pairs of words, like "read" and "reed," sound the same, but are spelled differently.* **3.** to seem or appear to be: *That sounds like a good idea.*

sound[2] [sound] *adjective,* **sounder, soundest. 1.** strong and healthy; sturdy: *Exercise and good food helps to keep your body sound.* **2.** in good condition; free from damage or flaws: *Check that all the rungs are sound before you use that ladder.* **3.** showing good judgment; sensible: *sound advice; a sound investment.*

sound[3] [sound] *verb,* **sounded, sounding. 1.** to measure the depth of a body of water by dropping a weighted line or by sending down sonar signals. **2.** of whales, to dive down deeply and suddenly.
• **sound out.** to ask someone questions to find out what they think: *Brandon sounded out the new boy about what sort of music he liked.*

sound[4] ▶ [sound] *noun, plural* **sounds. 1.** a long, narrow stretch of water joining two larger bodies of water, or between an island and the mainland. **2.** a deep inlet or arm of the sea.

sound barrier ▼ *Science.* a point near the speed of sound at which an airplane or other moving body experiences a sudden, large increase in the force of the air it is passing through. The speed of sound is about 740 miles per hour at sea level.

Doubtful Sound is one of the spectacular inlets on the southwest coast of New Zealand's South Island.

Airplanes break the sound barrier when they pass from traveling slower than the speed of sound (subsonic) to traveling faster than the speed of sound (supersonic).

At subsonic speeds, the airplane creates pressure waves in front and behind it.

The airplane catches up with its own pressure waves, which merge to form a shock wave at the speed of sound.

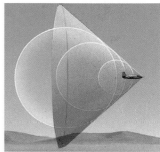

At supersonic speeds, the cone-shaped shock wave hits the ground, causing a loud explosion, or sonic boom.

The Zulu people make up the largest group of native **South Africans.**

sound bite a brief comment that has been taken from an interview or speech recorded on tape and then broadcast in a news report or political advertisement.

sound effects sounds that are made artificially so as to resemble sounds such as traffic, thunder, guns firing, and doors slamming. Sound effects are used in movies, television programs, radio shows, and plays.

sound·proof [sound-*proof*] *adjective.* not allowing sound to enter or escape: *a soundproof room.* *verb,* **soundproofed, soundproofing.** to build a room or building in such a way that no sound can enter or escape: *to soundproof a recording studio.*

sound·track [sound-*trak*] *noun, plural* **soundtracks.** **1.** the sound portion of a movie or television program. **2.** a recording of the music that has been used in a movie or musical play.

sound wave *Science.* vibrations in the form of a wave that move through the air and can be heard by the ear.

soup [soop] *noun, plural* **soups.** a usually hot, liquid food made by boiling vegetables, meat, or fish in water.

sour [sour] *adjective,* **sourer, sourest. 1.** having a sharp taste: *Unripe apples are sour.* **2.** unpleasant or unfriendly: *a sour remark; Our friendship turned sour.* *verb,* **soured, souring.** to get or cause to get a sharp taste: *Milk can quickly sour if it is left out of the refrigerator in hot weather.* **—sourly,** *adverb;* **— sourness,** *noun.*

source [sors] *noun, plural* **sources.** the place, thing, or person from which something comes or begins: *Explorers searched for the source of the Nile River; The newspaper reporter got the facts for his story from a source in the government.*

sour cream a thick cream that is made sour by adding special bacteria. It is used in cooking and baking and as an accompaniment.

sour·dough [sour-*doh*] *noun, plural* **sourdoughs.** **1.** a mixture of flour and water that is left to ferment and later used instead of yeast to make bread. **2.** a bread made with sourdough.

south [south] *noun.* the direction to your right as you watch the sun rise in the morning. South is one of the four main points of the compass and lies opposite north. The part of an area, region, or country in this direction is **South. The South** is the region of the United States south of Missouri, the Ohio River, and Pennsylvania, especially those states that formed the Confederacy in the Civil War. *adjective.* **1.** situated toward, near, or facing the south: *I went into the building by the south entrance.* **2.** coming from the south: *a south wind.* *adverb.* to, toward, or in the south: *Let's drive south to Mexico.*

South African ◀ a person who comes from the country of South Africa.

South American a person who comes from one of the countries of the continent of South America.

south·east [south-*eest*] *noun.* **1.** the direction or point of the compass midway between south and east. **2.** the part of an area, region, or country in this direction. The region in the south and east of the United States is **the Southeast.** *adjective.* **1.** situated toward, near, or facing the southeast. **2.** coming from the southeast: *a southeast wind. adverb.* to, toward, or in the southeast. **—southeastern,** *adjective.*

south·ern [suTH-urn] *adjective.* **1.** situated toward, near, or facing the south: *The southern part of that country gets very hot in summer.* **2.** coming from the south. Having to do with the United States in the South is **Southern.**

south·ern·er [suTH-ur-nur] *noun, plural* **southerners.** a person who comes from the southern part of a region or country. A person who comes from the southern part of the United States is a **Southerner.**

Southern Hemisphere *Geography.* the half of the Earth that is south of the equator. Antarctica, Australia, most of South America, and part of Africa and Asia are situated in the Southern Hemisphere.

South Pole ▼ *Geography.* the southern end of the Earth's axis. The South Pole is the point on the Earth that is farthest south.

south·ward [south-*wurd*] *adverb.* toward the south: *The river flows slowly southward.* *adjective.* toward or in the south. This word is also spelled **southwards.**

south·west [south-*west*] *noun.* **1.** the direction or point of the compass midway between south and west. **2.** the part of an area, region, or country in this direction. The region in the south and west of the United States is **the Southwest.** *adjective.* **1.** situated toward, near, or facing the southwest. **2.** coming from the southeast: *a southwest breeze. adverb.* to, toward, or in the southwest: *The passenger train traveled southwest.*

sou·ve·nir [soo-vuh-neer] *noun, plural* **souvenirs.** something kept as a reminder of a person, place, or event: *Liz bought a toy version of the Statue of Liberty as a souvenir of her visit to New York.*

This research station near the **South Pole** *has provided shelter for scientists since 1975.*

a b c d e f g h i j k l m n o p q r **s** t u v w x y z

sov·er·eign [sov-run] *noun, plural* **sovereigns.**
a king or queen.
adjective. **1.** having the highest rank or greatest authority or power: *the sovereign authority of a queen in the Middle Ages.* **2.** free from the control of others; independent: *A sovereign nation has the right to make its own decisions.*

So·vi·et [soh-vee-et] *adjective.*
having to do with the former Soviet Union, its people, or political system.
The Soviet Union was a large country in eastern Europe and northern Asia. Its largest region was Russia.

sow¹ [soh] *verb,* **sowed, sown** *or* **sowed, sowing. 1.** to plant seeds by scattering them on an area of land: *Farmers use machines to sow seeds over a large area.* **2.** to scatter or spread: *The man's strange behavior sowed suspicion in the minds of others.*
🔊 Different words with the same sound are **sew** and **so.**

sow² [sow] *noun, plural* **sows.**
an adult female pig.

soy·bean [soi-been] *noun, plural* **soybeans.** the seed of the soybean plant. Soybeans are rich in oil and protein and are used as food for people and animals.

space [spays] *noun.*
1. the area in which the whole universe exists. The planet Earth, the Moon, the Sun, and the stars are in space. **2.** the region outside the Earth's atmosphere; outer space: *Astronauts explore space.* **3.** an empty area that is available to be used: *There's no more space on the shelf for your CD collection.* **4.** a period of time: *He washed the car and mowed the lawn within the space of just an hour.*
verb, **spaced, spacing.**
to arrange with spaces between: *I spaced the three paintings evenly along the wall.*

space capsule a small spacecraft or part of a larger one that contains astronauts or equipment and is designed to return to the Earth.

space·craft ◀ [spays-kraft] *noun, plural* **spacecraft.** a vehicle used for traveling in outer space.

space·ship [spays-ship] *noun, plural* **spaceships.** a vehicle used for traveling in outer space; spacecraft.

space shuttle ▼ a spacecraft that is launched into space like a rocket and lands on the Earth like an airplane; it can then be used again, which a rocket cannot. A space shuttle carries astronauts and equipment. It is also called a shuttle.

space station a large spaceship on which astronauts can live for a long time and that is designed to orbit the Earth like a satellite.

In 1976 two **spacecraft** *like this one landed on the planet Mars.*

SPACE SHUTTLE

In the early days of space travel, rockets and spacecraft could be used only once. Now satellites, research crews, space probes, and crews for the International Space Station are carried into space by reusable shuttles. Each shuttle consists of an orbiter space plane, two booster rockets, and an external fuel tank. The first space shuttle in 1981 carried only two astronauts but today's shuttles can take a crew of up to eight people.

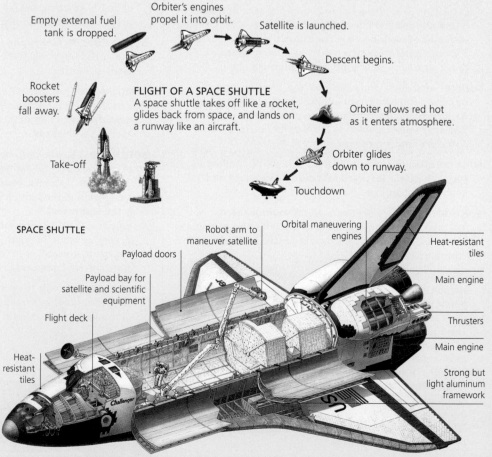

Empty external fuel tank is dropped.

Orbiter's engines propel it into orbit.

Satellite is launched.

Descent begins.

Rocket boosters fall away.

FLIGHT OF A SPACE SHUTTLE
A space shuttle takes off like a rocket, glides back from space, and lands on a runway like an aircraft.

Orbiter glows red hot as it enters atmosphere.

Take-off

Orbiter glides down to runway.

Touchdown

SPACE SHUTTLE

Robot arm to maneuver satellite

Orbital maneuvering engines

Heat-resistant tiles

Payload doors

Main engine

Payload bay for satellite and scientific equipment

Thrusters

Flight deck

Main engine

Heat-resistant tiles

Strong but light aluminum framework

Spacesuits provide astronauts with oxygen to breathe and protect them from the extremes of heat and cold in space.

Life-support backpack

Visor

Headlamp

Spacesuit made of several layers

Control module

Gloves with heaters

Cord attaching astronaut to spacecraft

Tools

Space boots

space·suit ▶ [spays-*soot*] *noun, plural* **spacesuits.** a piece of clothing worn by an astronaut. A spacesuit covers all of an astronaut's body and is designed to protect the astronaut in space. This word is also spelled **space suit.**

space·walk [spays-*wawk*] *noun, plural* **spacewalks.** a period of activity by an astronaut outside a spacecraft in space.

spa·cious [spay-shus] *adjective.* having plenty of room or space; roomy. —**spaciously,** *adverb;* —**spaciousness,** *noun.*

spade¹ [spade] *noun, plural* **spades.** a tool with a flat blade for pressing into the ground and a long handle, used for digging: *a garden spade.* *verb,* **spaded, spading.** to dig with a spade: *I spaded the soil before planting the strawberries.*

spade² [spade] *noun, plural* **spades. 1.** a playing card marked with a black symbol shaped like a spade. **2. spades.** the suit of cards marked with this symbol.

spa·ghet·ti [spuh-get-ee] *noun.* a kind of pasta in the form of long, thin strings. It is served with meat, tomato sauce, or other sauces.

The word **spaghetti** comes from an Italian word meaning "little strings." The word came into English in the late nineteenth century. It was long thought that the famous Italian explorer Marco Polo learned about spaghetti in his travels to China, but now it is believed that it actually originated somewhere in Italy.

spam [spam] *noun. Computers.* e-mail that is not wanted by the person or persons it is addressed to. Spam is sent to large numbers of people at the same time and usually contains advertisements. *verb,* **spammed, spamming.** to send e-mail that is not wanted by the person or persons it is addressed to. The act of sending spam is **spamming.**

span [span] *noun, plural* **spans. 1.** the distance or extent between the two farthest edges of something: *The jet airplane's wings have a span of about 200 feet.* **2.** the full extent, stretch, or length of something: *She has a short attention span.* *verb,* **spanned, spanning.** to stretch over or across.

span·iel ▶ [span-yul] *noun, plural* **spaniels.** any of several breeds of dogs that are small to medium in size, with short legs, a long, silky coat, and long, drooping ears.

Span·ish [span-ish] *noun.* **1.** the people of Spain. **2.** the language of Spain and of most countries in Central and South America. It is also spoken in parts of the United States. *adjective.* of or having to do with Spain, its people, or the Spanish language.

spank [spangk] *verb,* **spanked, spanking.** to hit with the open hand or a flat object, as a punishment.

spare [spare] *verb,* **spared, sparing. 1.** to stop from hurting or treating harshly; show mercy: *The soldier spared the prisoner's life.* **2.** to give up or do without: *Can you spare the time to watch my game on Saturday?* **3.** to have left over, extra, or not used: *Miguel bought the bread and milk and still had money to spare for an ice cream.* *adjective,* **sparer, sparest. 1.** more than is needed; extra: *I used the spare key to let myself in.* A **spare tire** is an extra tire kept in a vehicle to replace one that goes flat. **2.** not lavish or abundant; meager: *When he is fasting, he eats a spare diet.* *noun, plural* **spares. 1.** an extra thing or things: *The batteries on my flashlight have run out and I haven't any spares.* **2.** in bowling, the knocking down of all ten pins with two rolls of the ball.

spark [spark] *noun, plural* **sparks. 1.** a small piece of burning or glowing material: *Sparks from the bonfire blew up into the sky.* **2.** a flash of light, especially from a short electrical discharge. **3.** a very small amount; trace: *That idea shows a real spark of genius.* *verb,* **sparked, sparking. 1.** to give off sparks. **2.** to set off or rouse to action: *The ban on wearing sports caps to school sparked a protest.*

spar·kle [spar-kul] *verb,* **sparkled, sparkling. 1.** to shine with little flashes of light; glitter: *The sequined dress sparkled.* **2.** to release gas bubbles: *The lemonade soda sparkles.* **3.** to be lively or brilliant: *The actress sparkled in her latest comedy role.* *noun, plural* **sparkles.** a bright, glittering quality: *the sparkle of sunlight on a river.*

spark·plug [spark-*plug*] **1.** a part in an engine that produces an electric spark, which sets fire to the fuel and makes the engine start. **2.** a person who provides energy or inspiration for a sports team or other such group. This word is also spelled **spark plug.**

spar·row ▶ [spar-oh] *noun, plural* **sparrows.** a small, brownish or grayish bird with a striped pattern on its feathers, commonly found in North America. It is very hardy, and eats seeds and sometimes insects.

Sparrows are very common birds in most cities and towns.

sparse [spars] *adjective* **sparser, sparsest.** thinly spread or scattered; not dense: *Alaska has a sparse population.* The state of a very small quantity of things living or growing far apart is **sparsity.** —**sparsely,** *adverb.*

The chestnut and white coloring of these King Charles **spaniels** *is known as Blenheim.*

a b c d e f g h i j k l m n o p q r **s** t u v w x y z

Tadpoles will hatch from the jelly-like **spawn** *released into the water when frogs mate.*

spasm [spaz-um] *noun, plural* **spasms.** *Health.* a sudden, uncontrolled tightening and twitching or jerking of a muscle or muscles.

spat¹ [spat] *verb.* the past tense and past participle of SPIT.

spat² [spat] *noun, plural* **spats.** a brief, petty quarrel or disagreement: *Lisa and I had a spat about who should have the last piece of pie.*

spat·u·la [spach-uh-luh] *noun, plural* **spatulas.** a small implement with a flat, thin, sometimes flexible blade, used to lift, turn over, or spread foods.

spawn ▲ [spawn] *noun.* a mass of eggs laid by fish, frogs, and other water creatures. *verb,* **spawned, spawning. 1.** to lay eggs. **2.** to produce or give rise to something: *The hurricane spawned huge waves; The scientist's discovery spawned a new area of medical technology.*

speak [speek] *verb,* **spoke, spoken, speaking. 1.** to use the voice to say words; talk: *I have to speak loudly so Grandpa can hear me.* **2.** to express an idea, fact, or feeling with words: *He spoke about his sadness after his father died.* **3.** to give a speech or talk: *The guest lecturer will speak about climbing Mt. Everest.* **4.** to talk in or be able to talk in a language: *Jasmine speaks Arabic.*

speak·er [spee-kur] *noun, plural* **speakers. 1.** a person who speaks, especially one who gives a public speech. **2. Speaker.** the person who controls a meeting of a law-making assembly: *the Speaker of the House of Representatives.* **3.** a device in a sound system that converts electrical signals into sounds; a loudspeaker.

spear [speer] *noun, plural* **spears. 1.** a weapon that consists of a long pole with a sharply pointed end. **2.** a long, slender stalk, shoot, or sprout of a plant: *an asparagus spear.* *verb,* **speared, spearing.** to pierce with or as if with a spear.

spear·mint ▶ [speer-mint] *noun, plural* **spearmints.** a type of mint. The oil and leaves from this aromatic plant are used to flavor food.

spe·cial [spesh-ul] *adjective.* **1.** different from others; not normal or ordinary; distinctive or unusual: *a special sale in which all goods in a store are sold for half price; Dad took us on a special trip to the zoo.* **2.** meant for one particular purpose or situation: *The field goal kicker wears a special shoe on his kicking foot.* *noun, plural* **specials.** something that is special: *The restaurant has two specials for lunch besides the regular menu; There is a TV news special tonight on the recent flood.* —**specially,** *adverb.*

spe·cial·ist [spesh-uh-list] *noun, plural* **specialists. 1.** a person who is devoted to a particular area of work or study: *Kevin saw the eye specialist about his blurry vision.* **2.** any person who focuses on one specific area of a larger activity: *Their company is a specialist in tours of Alaska.*

spe·cial·ize [spesh-uh-lize] *verb,* **specialized, specializing.** to concentrate on a special activity or an area of work or study: *This radio station specializes in classical music.* —**specialization,** *noun.*

spe·cial·ty [spesh-ul-tee] *noun, plural* **specialties. 1.** a special area of work, study, or skill for a person: *Our dance teacher's specialties are jazz and tap.* **2.** a special product or service: *Gumbo is the specialty of the local Cajun restaurant.*

spe·cies [spee-sheez] *noun, plural* **species.** *Biology.* a group of animals or plants that share many common characteristics. Members of the same species can mate and have offspring. A German Shepherd and a Chihuahua are both dogs and are thus from the same species, but a German shepherd and a coyote belong to two different species.

spe·cif·ic [spi-sif-ik] *adjective.* **1.** having to do with one thing; particular: *He's saving the money for the specific purpose of buying a car.* **2.** stated clearly or in detail; precise; explicit: *Please give me specific instructions on how to get to the ice rink.* *noun, plural* **specifics.** the detailed facts about something: *Tell us the specifics of what happened.* —**specifically,** *adverb.*

spec·i·men [spes-uh-mun] *noun, plural* **specimens.** *Science.* a single thing or part of a thing that is typical of the group or the whole; an example or sample: *The space probe brought back rock specimens from Mars.*

speck [spek] *noun, plural* **specks.** a very small spot, bit, or mark: *I got a speck of grit in my eye.* A **speckled** bird is a bird whose feathers have lots of specks of color.

spec·ta·cle [spek-tuh-kul] *noun, plural* **spectacles. 1.** an unusual or remarkable sight or show: *The Fourth of July fireworks display was an amazing spectacle.* **2. spectacles.** an older term for eyeglasses.

spec·tac·u·lar [spek-tak-yuh-lur] *adjective.* very unusual, exciting, or remarkable: *The eagles soaring high overhead were a spectacular sight.* —**spectacularly,** *adverb.*

spec·ta·tor [spek-tay-tur] *noun, plural* **spectators.** a person who watches but does not take part; an observer: *The spectators crowded into the stadium for the game.* A **spectator sport** is a sport that lots of people like to watch, such as football or baseball.

Spearmint *is one of the most common varieties of mint used in cooking and for medicinal purposes.*

spec·trum ▼ [spek-trum] *noun, plural* **spectra** *or* **spectrums. 1.** *Science.* a band of colors produced when white light passes through a prism or is split up by other means. The colors of the spectrum are red, orange, yellow, green, blue, indigo, and violet, as seen in a rainbow. **2.** a range of related ideas, qualities, or activities: *The student council includes students from across the whole school spectrum—from grades 9 to 12.*

spec·u·late [spek-yuh-*late*] *verb,* **speculated, speculating. 1.** to think about something without having all the facts or evidence; guess: *The reporters speculated about what the President will say in his speech tonight.* The act of reflecting on something, especially of reaching a conclusion without enough evidence to be certain, is **speculation. 2.** to risk losing money while attempting to make a profit: *The businessman speculated in shares on the New York Stock Exchange.*

speech [speech] *noun, plural* **speeches.** *Language.* **1.** the act of expressing thoughts, feelings, and ideas using spoken words. **2.** something spoken, especially a talk in front of an audience: *Jamie has to make a speech at the next school assembly.* **3.** the way a person or group speaks: *Now that she's got braces on her teeth, her speech isn't as clear.*

The two forms of language are **speech** (words that are said out loud) and *writing* (words put down on paper, in a computer, and so on). Almost all humans can learn to use speech on their own by the time they are about two years old. This has been true of all peoples everywhere throughout human history. In fact, the ability to use speech is often said to be the one thing that most distinguishes humans from animals. On the other hand, people don't learn to write on their own and have to be taught to do this. Even today, there are many people in the world who do not know how to write.

speech·less [speech-lis] *adjective.* not being able to speak, especially for a time; silent: *When my brother announced that he was leaving home, my parents were speechless with surprise.*

speed [speed] *noun, plural* **speeds. 1.** quick or fast movement or action: *With a sudden burst of speed, the runner passed all the others.* **2.** the rate of motion: *This airplane can reach speeds of 550 miles per hour.* *verb,* **sped, speeded, speeding.** to go or happen quickly, or to cause to go or happen quickly: *The ambulance sped to the scene of the crash.*

speed·ing [speed-ing] *noun. Law.* the act of driving a vehicle faster than is allowed by law: *She was fined for speeding on the highway.* A **speeder** is a driver who goes faster than the legal or safe speed. A **speed limit** is the highest speed that a vehicle can travel at on a particular stretch of road.

speed·om·e·ter [spi-<u>dom</u>-uh-tur] *noun, plural* **speedometers.** an instrument on a vehicle that measures how fast the vehicle is traveling.

As they pass through raindrops, rays of white sunlight separate into the colors of the **spectrum,** *creating a rainbow.*

speed·y [speed-ee] *adjective,* **speedier, speediest.** describing something very fast; rapid; swift: *The team has a speedy centerfielder; Service at the drive-through restaurant is speedy.*

spell¹ [spel] *verb,* **spelled, spelling. 1.** to say or write the letters of a word in the correct order: *How do you spell "potatoes?"* **2.** to be the letters that form a word: *The letters p-o-t-a-t-o-e-s spell "potatoes."* **3.** to have a sense or indication of; mean: *Getting a flat tire in rush hour spelled trouble.*

• **to spell out.** to make very clear: *Mr. Thomas spelled out how he expected the class to behave at the summer camp.*

spell² [spel] *noun, plural* **spells. 1.** a word or group of words meant to have magic power: *In the story, the wizard cast a spell that made the three children invisible.* **2.** an irresistible power to attract or influence: *The audience sat and watched, transfixed by the spell of the trapeze artists above.*

spell³ [spel] *noun, plural* **spells. 1.** a period of time: *Michael, it's your turn to mind the baby for a spell; We were glad to finally get some rain after a hot, dry spell.* **2.** an attack or fit of something: *a dizzy spell.* *verb,* **spelled, spelt, spelling.** to take a person's place for a time; relieve: *Betty spelled me during the third quarter of the game so I could rest for the last quarter.*

spell·bound [spel-*bound*] *adjective.* held by or as if by a spell; fascinated: *The children listened intently to the story and were spellbound by it.*

spell·er [spel-ur] *noun, plural* **spellers. 1.** a person who spells words: *Christopher is not a very good speller and he always makes mistakes.* **2.** a book with exercises that teach spelling.

spell·ing [spel-ing] *noun, plural* **spellings. 1.** the way words are spelled: *Will you check the spelling in my assignment, please?* **2.** the saying or writing of the letters of a word in the correct order: *The American spelling of "color" is different from the English spelling of "colour."*

spelling bee *Education.* a spelling contest in which competitors are eliminated when they misspell a word. The person who is left has spelled all words correctly and wins the contest.

spend [spend] *verb,* **spent, spending. 1.** to pay money: *She spent seven dollars on a movie ticket.* A person who spends money, especially a lot of money, to buy things is a **spender. 2.** to pass time: *Bradley is spending the week at his friend's house, while his parents visit his uncle.* **3.** to use up: *I've spent all this time trying to get the computer to work.*

sperm [spurm] *noun, plural* **sperm** *or* **sperms.** *Biology.* a reproductive cell produced by a male person or animal. If it joins with a female egg, it can develop into a new person or animal.

a b c d e f g h i j k l m n o p q r s t u v w x y z

sperm whale ▶ a large toothed whale with a huge, squarish head. It lives in tropical and temperate waters, and dives very deep to feed on giant squid. A cavity inside its head contains a valuable oil called sperm oil.

*A **sperm whale** uses its large, powerful tail to propel it into the ocean's depths in search of food.*

sphere [sfeer] *noun, plural* **spheres.** *Mathematics.*
1. a completely round body, such as a ball. All the points on its surface are the same distance from its center.
2. an area of activity, knowledge, or interest; domain: *The President dominates the political sphere in the U.S.*

sphinx [sfingks] *noun, plural* **sphinxes.** a mythical creature with a lion's body and a human head. A huge stone statue of this creature, located in Egypt, is the **Sphinx.**

spice ▶ [spise] *noun, plural* **spices.**
1. any substance from a plant used to flavor food or drinks. Pepper, nutmeg, and ginger are spices. Food that is **spicy** has strong flavors from the use of spices.
2. something that adds interest: *A famous old saying is "Variety is the spice of life."*
verb, **spiced, spicing. 1.** to flavor with spices: *He spiced the pasta sauce with oregano and chili.*
2. to add interest: *To spice things up a bit, the coach had us play the last few minutes with four forwards instead of two.* —**spiciness,** *noun.*

*A merchant sells a range of **spices** in a market in Morocco.*

spi·der ▶ [spye-dur] *noun, plural* **spiders.** a small animal with a body divided into two parts. It has eight legs and two poison fangs. It produces silk for making nests or spinning webs to catch insects for food.

> **Spider** comes from an ancient word meaning "to spin." The thing that most makes a spider different from other creatures is that it is able to spin a web to catch its prey.

spike [spike] *noun, plural* **spikes. 1.** a very large, heavy nail used to hold rails to railroad ties. **2.** a sharp, pointed object, part, or piece that sticks out: *The spikes along the top of the fence keep vandals out.* **3.** a sudden, sharp rise in prices or rates: *a spike in the price of oil.*
verb, **spiked, spiking. 1.** in volleyball, to drive the ball down at a sharp angle into the opponent's court, using a hard blow. **2.** in football, to throw the ball straight down to the ground.

spill [spil] *verb,* **spilled, spilt, spilling.**
1. to make or allow something to fall, flow, or run out: *The little girl spilled her ice cream down her dress; Water spilled over the top of the dam.* **2.** to cause to fall: *The horse spilled the rider at the final jump.*
noun, plural **spills. 1.** an act of spilling or an amount spilled: *The waitress mopped up the spill.*
2. the act of falling; a tumble: *Paulo had a spill coming down the hill on his skateboard.*

spin [spin] *verb,* **spun, spinning. 1.** to turn or make turn around and around quickly; twirl: *The car spun out of control.* **2.** to make thread such as wool by twisting thin fibers. **3.** to form a web or cocoon by producing a sticky substance that quickly hardens into thread: *The silkworm spins a cocoon.* **4.** to feel dizzy: *My head was spinning after I did five cartwheels in a row.*
noun, plural **spins. 1.** a swift turning or whirling motion: *The television host gave the barrel a spin, then reached in for the winning ticket.* **2.** a short ride or drive: *My cousin took me for a spin in her sports car.* —**spinner,** *noun.*

spin·ach [spin-ich] *noun.* a widely grown plant with dark green leaves, which are eaten as a vegetable.

spinal cord *Biology.* a thick cord of nerve tissue that runs from the brain down through the spine, linking the brain to all the nerves in the body.

spin·dle [spin-dul] *noun, plural* **spindles.** a rod used for spinning thread or yarn. Fibers are twisted into thread around the spindle, then wound onto it.

spine [spine] *noun, plural* **spines.** *Biology.* **1.** the column of bones called vertebrae that runs from the skull down the center of the back. This is also called the backbone or **spinal column.** It supports the body and encloses and protects the spinal cord. **2.** a stiff, sharp point growing out of an animal or plant: *Don't touch the cactus—it's covered with spines.* Something that is **spiny** has spines, prickles, or thorns.

spinning wheel ▼ *History.* a small device for spinning thread or yarn used before spinning machines were invented, having a hand-driven or foot-driven wheel to turn a spindle.

spir·al [spye-rul] *noun, plural* **spirals.** a curve that winds around a central point while getting either closer to it or farther away from it. Some springs can be spirals.
verb, **spiraled, spiraling.** to move in the shape of a spiral: *The plane spiraled out of control.*
adjective. having the shape of a spiral: *a spiral staircase.*

*This old **spinning wheel** was driven by a large foot pedal.*

SPIDERS

Spiders live in many different habitats, including forests, grasslands, caves, fresh water, and our homes. Like an insect, a spider has jointed legs and a hard body case, but unlike an insect it has a two-part body and eight legs instead of six. Spiders don't have antennae or wings, but do have many eyes and powerful jaws. A spider uses its poisonous bite to paralyze its prey and then injects digestive juices to dissolve the prey's tissue, which the spider then sucks up. Only thirty of the 35,000 different kinds of spiders have venom that is harmful to humans. Most spiders feed on insects that they trap in their webs, but some, like the huntsman and the tarantula, hunt frogs, lizards, or even small birds and mice.

TWO KINDS OF FANGS

Downward-hinging fangs

Sideways-hinging fangs

SPIDER ANATOMY

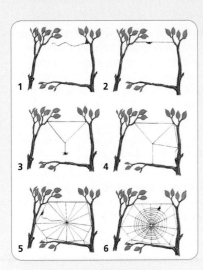

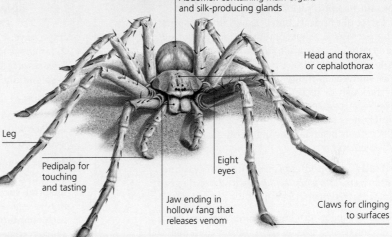

Abdomen containing main organs and silk-producing glands

Head and thorax, or cephalothorax

Leg

Pedipalp for touching and tasting

Eight eyes

Jaw ending in hollow fang that releases venom

Claws for clinging to surfaces

HOW A SPIDER WEAVES ITS WEB

An orb-weaving spider waits for the breeze to blow a silken thread from one stem to another (1), then strengthens it with more thread (2). It attaches more lines in V and Y shapes (3 and 4), and then fills in other lines like the spokes of a wheel (5). Finally it spins a spiral onto the spokes (6).

SPIDERS' WEBS

Scaffold web

Hammock web

Lace-sheet web

Triangle web

SPIDERS' EYES

The arrangement and size of spiders' multiple eyes indicates how they catch their food.

Woodlouse-eating spider Six small eyes and keen sense of touch for night hunting

Ogre-faced spider Huge eyes for seeing prey in total darkness

Crab spider Vibration sensors and sharp vision to detect passing prey

Huntsman Spread-out eyes for all-round vision for active hunting

Nursery-web spider

Trapdoor spider

Huntsman spider

Redback spider

*The **spire** of St. Olaf's church towers above the rooftops of the medieval town of Tallinn, capital of Estonia.*

spire ▶ [spire] *noun, plural* **spires.** a tall, pointed structure built on the top of a tower. Many church buildings have spires.

spir·it [speer-it] *noun, plural* **spirits.**
1. the life force within a person that makes them unique. It is thought to control what they think, feel, and do; the soul. **2.** a supernatural being that has no physical existence; a ghost. **3.** passion, energy, and determination: *The team has a fighting spirit and never gives up, no matter what the score.* **4.** a state of mind; attitude: *He was in good spirits after her visit.* **5.** what something really means: *If you listen carefully you will understand the spirit of what I am saying.*
verb, **spirited, spiriting.** to remove someone or something mysteriously or secretly: *The police spirited the defendant away before the reporters could interview him.* A person's **spirits** refers to the way they feel or think, and that often affects their behavior. Strong alcoholic liquors are also called **spirits.**

spir·it·ed [speer-it-id] *adjective.* full of energy and enthusiasm: *Our class had a spirited debate about capital punishment.*

spir·it·u·al [speer-uh-choo-ul] *adjective. Religion.*
1. having to do with the spirit, rather than material things. **2.** relating to religion: *Most religions place more importance on spiritual values than material ones.*
noun, plural **spirituals.** a folk hymn of the kind originally sung by African-Americans of the southern U.S. The quality of being spiritual is **spirituality.**
—**spiritually,** *adverb.*

spit¹ [spit] *verb,* **spit** *or* **spat, spitting.** to expel saliva or something else out of the mouth: *The food tasted so bad I had to spit it out.*
noun. the watery liquid that is produced in the mouth. See SALIVA.

spit² [spit] *noun, plural* **spits. 1.** a long, thin rod that is put through meat so it can be roasted over an open fire. **2.** a long, narrow piece of land that projects into the ocean, or a river or lake.

spite [spite] *noun.* a feeling of wanting to cause harm or pain to someone, often for a minor or petty reason: *You're only saying those nasty things about her out of spite.*
verb, **spited, spiting.** to deliberately cause harm or pain to someone: *George told Mary's parents what she said, just to spite her.* Deliberately causing harm or pain to someone is **spiteful.**
• **in spite of.** not prevented from doing something; disregarding; despite: *They climbed to the top of the volcano in spite of the warning signs.*

splash [splash] *verb,* **splashed, splashing. 1.** to make a liquid fly up into the air by hitting it or moving around in it: *You'll splash me if you run through the puddles.* **2.** to throw liquid around: *He splashed paint all over the floor when he painted the wall.*
noun, plural **splashes. 1.** the act or sound of liquid being thrown around: *I heard a splash as she fell into the water.* **2.** a small patch where a liquid has hit something; *I had to remove a splash of paint from my new coat.* **3.** something that creates interest or excitement: *The rookie pitcher has made quite a splash in the league this season.*

splen·did [splen-did] *adjective.* **1.** describing something very grand, beautiful, or impressive: *The cathedral has many splendid statues.* **2.** far above the ordinary; excellent: *This race is a splendid opportunity for you to prove what a good swimmer you are.*
—**splendidly,** *adverb.*

splint [splint] *noun, plural* **splints.** *Medicine.* a strip of wood or other rigid material that is used to keep a broken bone in place while it mends. It is often used before a plaster cast is put on.

splin·ter [splint-ur] *noun, plural* **splinters.** a small, sharp piece that has broken off from some kind of hard, brittle material, such as glass or wood: *I got a splinter of glass in my finger as I picked up the pieces of the broken vase.*
verb, **splintered, splintering.** to break into small, thin, sharp fragments: *The window splintered when John threw a rock at it.*

*The **spokes** of old wagon wheels were made of strong timber.*

split [split] *verb,* **split, splitting.** to divide or break into different parts or groups: *The tree split in two when it was struck by lightning; The teacher split up the large class into four smaller groups.*
noun, plural **splits. 1.** a tear or crack in something: *My old leather boot has a split in the sole.* **2.** a division or break in a group: *The decision to ordain women has caused a split in many churches.*

spoil [spoyle] *verb,* **spoiled** *or* **spoilt, spoiling. 1.** to damage or have a bad effect on something: *I didn't tell you the test result because I didn't want to spoil your day.* **2.** to become unfit for use; rot: *Please put the milk back in the refrigerator so it doesn't spoil.* **2.** to allow children such easy treatment that they behave badly: *Some parents spoil their children by letting them do whatever they want without being punished.* Property taken by force in war or obtained through great effort is called **spoils.**
—**spoiler,** *noun.*

spoke¹ [spoke] *verb.* the past tense of SPEAK.

spoke² ▲ [spoke] *noun, plural* **spokes.** a bar or rod that connects the outer ring of a wheel to the center point.

spok·en [spoh-kun] *adjective.* describing the form of language that people speak, rather than write down: *His spoken Japanese was excellent but he couldn't write it very well.*
verb. the past participle of SPEAK.

spokes·man [spokes-mun] *noun, plural* **spokesmen.** a man who is chosen to speak on behalf of another person, or group, or organization: *A White House spokesman said the President would address the nation later in the afternoon.*

spokes·per·son [spokes-*pur*-sun] *noun, plural* **spokespersons.** a person who is chosen to speak on behalf of another person, or group, or organization. It can be either a man or a woman.

spokes·wom·an [spokes-*wum*-un] *noun, plural* **spokeswomen.** a woman who is chosen to speak on behalf of another person, or group, or organization.

sponge ▶ [spunj] *noun, plural* **sponges. 1.** a simple, invertebrate animal that has a porous, fibrous body that can absorb water freely. Sponges live in large colonies, attached to solid objects underwater. They are dried and used for bathing and cleaning. **2.** a cleaning pad that looks like a natural sponge, but is made from a synthetic material.
verb, **sponged, sponging.** to wash or clean with a wet sponge: *When I had a fever, my mother sponged my forehead to cool me down.* —**spongy,** *adjective.*

spon·sor [spon-sur] *noun, plural* **sponsors. 1.** *Business.* a company or organization that pays for all or part of the cost of a television or radio program in return for having its commercials appear on the program. **2.** a person or organization that provides financial support for an event or activity: *All Little League clubs need a sponsor to be able to buy uniforms.* Financial or other support for a person or event is **sponsorship. 3.** a person who is responsible for someone or something: *If you want to apply for permanent residence in the country, you will have to find a sponsor.*
verb, **sponsored, sponsoring.** to act as a sponsor: *The Ford Motor Company sponsors that golf tournament.*

spon·ta·ne·ous [spon-*tay*-nee-us] *adjective.*
1. not planned or organized: *When Margaret won the race, my spontaneous reaction was to stand and cheer.* **2.** taking place with no apparent external force or cause: *The mysterious fire seemed to be caused by spontaneous combustion.* The state of being spontaneous is **spontaneity. —spontaneously,** *adverb.*

spool ▶ [spool] *noun, plural.* **spools.** a cylinder around which thread, tape, wire, or film is wound. It has a rim at each end and a hole through the center.

spoon [spoon] *noun, plural* **spoons.** a utensil used for eating, serving, or preparing food. It has a small, shallow bowl at one end of a long handle. The amount held by a spoon is a **spoonful.**
verb, **spooned, spooning.** to use a spoon: *Once the fruit has been mixed properly, spoon it carefully into the bowls.*

sport [sport] *noun, plural* **sports. 1.** a game or activity in which people use the body in an active way, play according to a certain set of rules, and try to win: *Baseball, basketball, and football are popular sports in the U.S.* **2.** any similar physical activity that people do for recreation or enjoyment, such as hiking or fishing. **3.** amusement or fun: *I like teasing my younger sister for sport.* **4.** a person judged as to how he or she plays a sport or game: *He was a bad sport about losing the game and refused to shake hands afterward.* **5.** a cheerful, easy-going person who has a good attitude: *Be a sport and let me have a ride on your bike.*
verb, **sported, sporting.** to play happily: *We saw a school of dolphins sporting in the sea.*

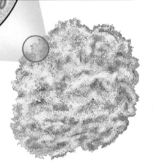

A **sponge** *filters its food from water drawn through its complex inner network of channels.*

Pore

Water current

sporting goods equipment and clothing used in sports: *The local store has a wide range of sporting goods, but it specializes in baseball equipment.*

sports car a low, small car designed for fast acceleration and high-speed driving. It often has a roof that can be removed.

sports·man·ship [sports-mun-*ship*] *noun.* the manner in which players conduct themselves when playing sports; it can be either good or bad: *Even though the team lost the game, they were praised for their good sportsmanship.* Fair, honest, and polite behavior when competing in sports is **sportsmanlike.**

spot [spot] *noun, plural* **spots. 1.** a small mark or stain left on a surface by dirt, blood, paint, or another such substance: *I cleaned a few spots of dirt off the wall.* **2.** a mark on a surface that is different in color or texture from the surrounding area: *The clown had a red spot on each cheek.* **3.** a place or area: *We found a quiet spot on the beach away from the noisy crowds.*
verb, **spotted, spotting. 1.** to make a mark or stain: *The rain spotted the windshield.* **2.** to notice someone or something: *The teacher spotted several mistakes in my history assignment.* Something covered in spots is **spotted.**
• **on the spot. 1.** where or when something is happening: *The reporter was right on the spot when the robbery happened.* **2.** in a difficult or embarrassing situation: *The policeman put him on the spot when he asked for proof he had car insurance.*

The cylindrical shape of a **spool** *of thread makes it easy to use on a sewing machine.*

spot·less [spot-lis] *adjective.* perfectly clean or pure: *My mother keeps the bathroom spotless; The judge has a spotless reputation.*

spot·light [spot-lite] *noun, plural* **spotlights.** a bright light that can be focused on someone or something: *I couldn't see a thing when the spotlight shone in my eyes.* *verb,* **spotlighted** or **spotlit, spotlighting. 1.** to direct a beam of light on to someone or something. **2.** to focus attention on someone or something: *We really need to spotlight the problem of poverty.*

spouse [spous] *noun, plural* **spouses.** a person's husband or wife.

spout ▶ [spout] *verb,* **spouted, spouting. 1.** to discharge a liquid with force: *Whales spout water high into the air through their blowhole.* **2.** to flow out with force: *Blood spouted from the cut on his leg.* *noun, plural* **spouts. 1.** the part on the side of a container through which liquid is poured: *A good teapot has a spout that doesn't drip when the tea is poured.* **2.** a strong stream of liquid pouring out of something.

sprain [sprane] *verb,* **sprained, spraining.** *Health.* to damage a joint or muscle in the body by suddenly twisting it or stretching it too far: *I jumped off the wall and sprained my ankle.* *noun, plural* **sprains.** a painful injury to a joint or muscle caused by twisting or overstretching it: *A sprain made playing tennis impossible.*

sprang [sprang] *verb.* the past tense of SPRING.

sprawl [sprawl] *verb,* **sprawled, sprawling. 1.** to lie or sit with arms and legs spread out awkwardly: *He sprawled on the couch to watch TV and then fell asleep.* **2.** to spread out in an untidy or unplanned manner: *Graffiti sprawled over every surface of the tunnel.* *noun, plural* **sprawls.** buildings on the edge of a city that spread out in an unplanned and ugly way: *The urban sprawl of many big cities makes providing public transport difficult.*

spray [spray] *noun, plural* **sprays. 1.** very fine drops of a liquid: *Farmers use a chemical spray to control insect pests.* **2.** a container that releases liquid in a stream of fine drops: *A light water spray is useful for watering delicate indoor plants.* *verb,* **sprayed, spraying. 1.** to send out a liquid as very fine drops: *to spray water from a hose; The vandals sprayed paint all over the school bus.* **2.** to apply a spray to a surface: *to spray your skin with a sunblock lotion.* A device used for spraying is a **sprayer.**

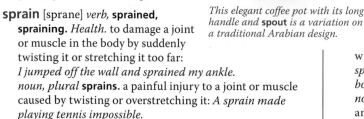

This elegant coffee pot with its long handle and **spout** *is a variation on a traditional Arabian design.*

spread [spred] *verb,* **spread, spreading. 1.** to open out or stretch something to its fullest extent: *Books were spread out across the desk.* **2.** to cover a surface with a soft substance: *Spread the butter on the bread, please.* **3.** to put out or extend over a wide area: *The workers spread sand over the oil spill.* **4.** to become or make widely known: *News of the celebrity's arrival spread and a large crowd gathered.* *noun, plural* **spreads. 1.** the act of spreading: *Recent events have increased the spread of nuclear weapons throughout the world.* **2.** the distance between two points that are extended as far as possible. **3.** a covering for a bed or piece of furniture. **4.** soft food that can be spread: *I like a cheese spread on my toast for breakfast.*

spree [spree] *noun, plural* **sprees.** a period of fun and pleasure, often involving spending a lot of money: *After receiving a bonus for working hard, I went on a shopping spree to buy some new clothes.*

spring [spring] *verb,* **sprang** or **sprung, springing. 1.** to rise or move quickly and lightly; jump: *to spring out of bed in the morning.* **2.** to open or close quickly: *The elevator doors sprang open as soon as he pressed the button.* **3.** to come or appear quickly: *Thoughts of panic sprang into her mind when she saw the flames.* **4.** to say, do, or produce something without warning: *They sprang the idea on the boss at the last minute.* *noun, plural* **springs. 1.** the season of the year after winter and before summer, when plants start to grow again. **2.** the act of springing up; jumping: *Fit gymnasts perform hand springs.* **3.** a metal or plastic device shaped like a spiral that can return to its original shape or position after pressure is applied. **4.** a natural flow of water from the earth: *Mountain springs usually supply clean water.*

> The new season of the year known as **spring** got its name from the idea of something springing (jumping) up or out. This time of year was once known as "the spring of the leaf," because it is the season when new leaves spring out on the trees.

spring·board [spring-bord] *noun, plural* **springboards. 1.** a flexible board attached to the side of a swimming pool, used by divers to give added spring to a jump or dive into the pool. **2.** a point for moving up or off to another job, level, or situation: *David used his job at the corner store as a springboard to get a better job with the supermarket.*

sprin·kle [spring-kul] *verb,* **sprinkled, sprinkling. 1.** to scatter in small bits, particles, or drops of liquid: *She sprinkled water on the plants.* **2.** to rain lightly: *It sprinkled with rain but no one got really wet.*

sprin·kler [springk-lur] *noun, plural* **sprinklers.** a device attached to a hose or pipe for watering lawns and flowerbeds. Some sprinklers rotate or move from side to side with the pressure of water from the hose.

sprint ◀ [sprint] *verb,* **sprinted, sprinting.** to run very fast over a short distance: *They sprinted to catch the bus.* *noun, plural* **sprints.** a short, fast run or race. —**sprinter,** *noun.*

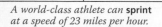

A world-class athlete can **sprint** *at a speed of 23 miles per hour.*

sprout [sprout] *verb,* **sprouted, sprouting.** to start to appear, grow, or develop: *In spring, trees start to sprout new leaves.*
noun, plural. **sprouts.** a new shoot from a seed, vegetable, or tree: *These old potatoes have green sprouts growing from them.*

spruce ▲ [sproos] *noun, plural* **spruce** *or* **spruces.** an evergreen fir tree with long cones and short, needle-like leaves. Spruce grows in the Northern Hemisphere and its wood is used to make paper.

sprung [sprung] *verb.* the past participle of SPRING.

spur ▶ [spur] *noun, plural* **spurs. 1.** a sharp metal device strapped to the heel of a horse rider's boot. Spurs are used to poke the flanks of a horse to urge it to move more quickly. **2.** a short branch line or siding off a main line railroad track.
verb, **spurred, spurring. 1.** to jab or poke a horse with spurs. **2.** to urge on; encourage: *The chance to win a prize spurred Bill to swim his best time.*

spurn [spurn] *verb,* **spurned, spurning.** to angrily reject or refuse with scorn: *Gail spurned all our attempts to help her when she fell off her horse.*

spurt [spurt] *verb,* **spurted, spurting.** a sudden gushing or pouring: *Water spurted from the broken pipe.*
noun, plural **spurts.** a sudden outflow or pouring: *Whales blow water vapor from their lungs out through their blowhole in short, sharp spurts.*

sput·ter [sput-ur] *verb,* **sputtered, sputtering. 1.** to spit or pop noisily and repeatedly: *The popcorn sputtered in the microwave oven.* **2.** to speak in a confused, hurried, or stammering way: *Leonie sputtered angrily that no one had told her of the change of plans.*
noun, plural **sputters.** a popping or spitting noise.

spy [spye] *noun, plural* **spies.** a person who is hired to collect information in secret about someone, such as other people, or something, such as organizations or the governments of enemy countries.
verb, **spied, spying. 1.** to act as a spy; collect information secretly by watching, listening, or by other means: *Orbiting satellites can spy on people on the Earth.* **2.** to see or glimpse; catch sight of: *He spied enemy troops moving in the nearby woods.*

squab·ble [skwab-ul] *noun, plural* **squabbles.** a petty, noisy argument over a trivial matter: *The twins had a squabble about which one was supposed to put away their toys.*
verb, **squabbled, squabbling.** to have a petty, noisy argument: *I told them to stop squabbling.*

squad [skwahd] *noun, plural* **squads. 1.** a small group of soldiers organized in a unit for training, drill, or fighting. **2.** any small group of people acting together or working on the same task: *The varsity football team has a squad of 43 players this year.*

squad·ron [skwad-run] *noun, plural* **squadrons.** a medium-sized group of tanks, ships, or airplanes that are part of a military force.

squall [skwawl] *noun, plural* **squalls.** a sudden, strong gust of wind that may carry with it rain, sleet, or snow.

squan·der [skwan-dur] *verb,* **squandered, squandering.** to spend foolishly or wastefully: *The man squandered the money he inherited on gambling.*

square [skware] *noun, plural* **squares. 1.** *Mathematics.* a four-sided figure with sides of equal length and corners at right angles. **2.** a figure that has this shape, such as a chessboard or checkerboard. **3.** an instrument used to draw right angles: *Some architects use squares that are shaped like a T.* **4.** an open, public area in a town or city bounded by streets: *Many squares have statues, fountains, and grass or trees.* **5.** *Mathematics.* the number obtained by multiplying a number by itself, $5 \times 5 = 25$: *The square of 5 is 25.*
adjective, **squarer, squarest. 1.** having four sides of equal length and four right angles. **2.** having or being a right angle: *A football field has square corners.* **3.** *Mathematics.* a measurement calculated by multiplying one dimension by another: *An area 10 meters by 10 meters is equal to 100 square meters.* **4.** fair or honest value: *When Wayne paid $250 for the guitar he thought it was a square deal.*
verb, **squared, squaring. 1.** to make or mark off something into a square or squares. **2.** to multiply a number by itself: *Three squared equals nine.* **3.** to match or agree with: *His account of who stole the bag does not square with hers.*
adverb. firmly; precisely: *He was hit square on the jaw.*

These working **spurs** *are essential equipment for a cowboy.*

square dance *Music.* a type of folk dance in which four or more pairs of dancers face each other to form a square. The couples then follow instructions called out to them in time to the music to make dance patterns.

square root *Mathematics.* the number that when multiplied by itself equals the given number: *If 3 is the square root of 9, then $3 \times 3 = 9$.*

squash[1] [skwahsh] *verb,* **squashed, squashing.** to press or push into a soft, flat mass; crush: *My sandwich was squashed when I sat on it.*
noun. a sport played in a special four-sided court with racquets and a small, hard rubber ball; players try to hit the ball in such a way that an opponent cannot return it.

*Summer **squash** can be cylindrical or round, and when it is very fresh its blossom may still be attached.*

A B C D E F G H I J K L M N O P Q R S T U V W X Y Z

squash² ▶ [skwahsh] *noun, plural* **squash** *or* **squashes.** any of a number of edible vegetables that grow in different shapes from vines on the ground. Squash are usually a green or orangish-yellow color.

squat [skwaht] *verb,* **squatted, squatting. 1.** to sit on one's heels with knees bent; crouch: *We squatted around the campfire to keep warm.* **2.** to live on land that one does not own or have a legal right to be on. *noun, plural* **squats.** a type of exercise in which you put a weight on your shoulders or chest, squat down, then stand again. *adjective.* describing something short, thick, and low: *a football lineman with a squat build.*

squat·ter [skwaht-ur] *noun, plural* **squatters.** a person who takes up residence in a vacant building or on vacant land, without paying rent or having a right to be there.

squawk [skwawk] *verb,* **squawked, squawking. 1.** to make a harsh, bird-like scream, especially out of fear: *She squawked when the spider dropped onto her head.* **2.** to complain loudly: *Gerry was squawking all day about how hot he was.* *noun, plural* **squawks.** the act of squawking: *Allie let out a squawk when she sat in a puddle on the bench.*

squeak [skweek] *noun, plural* **squeaks.** a short, high-pitched sound or cry: *They heard the squeak of the door opening and closing.* *verb,* **squeaked, squeaking.** to emit a short, high-pitched sound or cry: *The guinea pig squeaked all afternoon in its cage.* When something squeaks, it is described as **squeaky.**

squeal [skweel] *verb,* **squealed, squealing. 1.** to make a shrill, high sound or cry: *The children squealed with joy as the clowns put on the show.* **2.** to inform on someone for a crime; tell the police about a crime: *He squealed about the robbery when the detectives questioned him.* *noun, plural* **squeals.** the act of making a shrill, high sound or cry: *He let out a squeal of delight when he opened his present.* **—squealer,** *noun.*

squeeze [skweez] *verb,* **squeezed, squeezing. 1.** to press firmly together from two sides: *He squeezed the toothpaste tube between his finger and thumb; She squeezed the lemon to get the juice out.* **2.** to embrace or hug someone with affection. **3.** to force by using pressure: *She tried to squeeze her foot into the shoe, but it was too small.* *noun, plural* **squeezes.** the act of pressing firmly: *She gave his arm a squeeze before kissing him on the cheek.*

squid ▶ [skwid] *noun, plural* **squid** *or* **squids.** a sea animal similar to the octopus. Squid are part of a group called cephalopods. They have eight arms and two long tentacles, and are of various sizes, ranging from very small types to the **giant squid**, which can be more than fifty feet long.

squint [skwint] *verb,* **squinted, squinting.** to look with partly closed eyes: *I squinted in the bright headlights.* *noun, plural* **squints.** the act of looking with partly closed eyes.

squire [skwire] *noun, plural* **squires.** *History.* a young man of noble birth who acted as a servant to a knight while he was in training to receive his own knighthood. *verb,* **squired, squiring.** to accompany a person to a social event: *Jason squired Lydia to the formal dance.*

squirm [skwurm] *verb,* **squirmed, squirming. 1.** to wriggle or twist the body around: *My brother squirms around a lot when he rides in the car.* **2.** to act or feel nervous, shy, or embarrassed: *When the spotlight shone on Judith she squirmed with shyness.*

squir·rel ▶ [skwurl] *noun, plural* **squirrels.** a small animal commonly found in North America having reddish-brown or gray fur and a bushy tail, that lives in trees and eats mainly nuts.

The **squirrel** got its name from two words meaning "shade tail." The idea is that the tail of this animal is so long and thick that it can be used to hang over and shade its body.

Squirrels collect nuts and store them in hollow trees for their winter food supply.

squirt [skwurt] *verb,* **squirted, squirting.** to push out liquid in a narrow stream under pressure: *to squirt water on a car with a hose; Oil squirted from the hole in the pipeline.* *noun, plural* **squirts.** the act of pushing out liquid or the amount of liquid pushed out.

St. an abbreviation of STREET.

stab [stab] *verb,* **stabbed, stabbing. 1.** to cut or wound with a sharp, pointed weapon, such as a knife: *The guard stabbed the enemy soldier with his bayonet.* **2.** to pierce something with a sharp object: *Myles stabbed at the sausage with his fork.* *noun, plural* **stabs. 1.** the act or appearance of stabbing with a pointed weapon, or a wound made by doing this. **2** a short, sharp feeling of discomfort: *Arthur felt a stab of pain in his arm when he threw the ball.* **3.** an attempt to do something: *He made a stab at learning Spanish when he was in Mexico last summer.*

sta·ble¹ [stay-bul] *noun, plural* **stables.** a building at a farm or racetrack where horses are housed and fed. *verb,* **stabled, stabling.** to put or keep one or more animals in a stable.

*Deep under the ocean, a **giant squid** may release a large ink cloud to confuse predators like the frill shark.*

*American football is played in large **stadiums** that can seat many spectators.*

sta·ble² [stay-bul] *adjective.* **stabler, stablest.** not likely to collapse or be moved or changed easily; steady: *The ladder needs to be stable before you climb up it; France did not have a stable government after World War II—there were sixteen leaders in just twelve years.* Something that is not likely to fall or collapse has **stability.**

stack [stak] *noun, plural* **stacks. 1.** a large pile of straw, hay, or the like, usually arranged in layers. **2.** a pile of things arranged one on top of the other: *a stack of pancakes; a stack of books.*
verb, **stacked, stacking.** to place in a stack: *He stacked the old magazines to be recycled.*

sta·di·um ▲
[stay-dee-um] *noun, plural* **stadiums.**
a sports arena with rows of spectator seats placed around a flat, open area.

> The word **stadium** comes from a measure of length that was used in ancient Greece and Rome, usually about 200 meters long. The word then came to be used for a race of this length, and then for the large structure in which such a race was held.

staff [staf] *noun, plural* **staffs** *or* **staves.
1.** a rod or pole used as an aid to walking or as a weapon: *Many hikers carry a staff to help them on rough trails.* **2.** a large rod or stick used as a flagpole. **3.** a group of people working under a manager in a business or other organization: *The computer company has just added thirty new employees to their staff.* **4.** *Music.* the pattern of lines and spaces on which music is written.
verb, **staffed, staffing.** to employ people at a place of work: *The factory is fully staffed at present.*

stag ▼ [stag] *noun, plural* **stags.** an adult male deer.

stage [stayj] *noun, plural* **stages. 1.** a raised or open area on which actors or other entertainers perform, especially in a theater. **The stage** is the art or work of actors and the theater. **2.** a location where something important happens: *In Europe the stage was set for World War II when Hitler invaded Poland.* **3.** a single step in a process of development: *The next stage is to test our idea in the lab.* **4.** the shortened form of STAGECOACH.
verb, **staged, staging.** to produce and present an entertainment: *The school staged "Oklahoma" last year.*

stage·coach [stayj-kohch] *noun, plural* **stagecoaches.** *History.* a large, closed-in carriage drawn by a team of horses. Stagecoaches were once used to carry passengers and mail on set routes. At each "stage" the horses were exchanged for fresh ones.

stag·ger [stag-ur] *verb,* **staggered, staggering. 1.** to move or walk unsteadily: *The boxer staggered to his corner of the ring after receiving a hard blow to the head.* **2.** to shock or astonish: *John Lennon's fans were staggered by the news of his death.* **3.** to schedule in alternating or non-overlapping periods: *Classes using the swimming pool were staggered so that it would not become too crowded.*
noun, plural **staggers.** the act of moving or walking unsteadily: *He walked with a stagger.*

stag·nant [stag-nunt] *adjective.* not flowing or moving and as a result, often foul-smelling: *The pond was stagnant during the drought.* The state of something being stagnant is called **stagnation.**

stain [stane] *noun, plural* **stains. 1.** a mark or discolored area left by ink, paint, or another such substance: *The ink from my pen left a stain on my shirt.* **2.** a chemical dye used to color something: *We put a pale brown stain on the picnic table.* **3.** a bad mark or blot on a person's reputation or character: *Failing three subjects put a stain on his school record.*
verb, **stained, staining. 1.** to put a stain on or discolor something: *The paint stained my best jeans.* **2.** to change color by using a dye: *We stained the back fence to help it blend in with the garden.* **3.** to put a bad mark or blot on a person's reputation.

stainless steel a type of metal made from iron and chromium that does not rust, and which is used to make sinks, tools, and knives and forks.

stair [stare] *noun, plural* **stairs. 1.** a series of steps used to walk from one level of a building to another. **2.** a step or series of such steps. A whole series or flight of steps is called a **set of stairs.**
🔊 A different word with the same sound is **stare.**

stair·case [stare-kase] *noun, plural* **staircases.** a set of stairs in a framework leading from one level of a building to another. A different word with the same meaning is **stairway.**

stake [stake] *noun, plural* **stakes. 1.** a post or wooden pole sharpened at one end so that it can be driven into the ground: *Dad put stakes in the garden to help support the tomato plants.* **2.** an amount of money or any other thing promised as payment for a bet. If the risks and returns on a gambling venture are considerable we say the **stakes** are high. **3.** an interest or share in something, such as a business: *My uncle has a stake in a chicken farm.*
verb, **staked, staking.
1.** to tie up to a small wooden stake: *She staked the vine to support it.* **2.** to mark out the boundary of a plot of land or mining claim.
• **at stake.** at risk; involved: *There is much at stake in the launching of this satellite.*
🔊 A different word with the same sound is **steak.**

The wapiti **stag,** *found in northwestern North America, is one of the largest living deer.*

a b c d e f g h i j k l m n o p q r **s** t u v w x y z

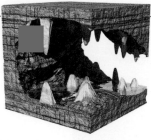

Stalactites *and* stalagmites *take many years to grow.*

Groundwater dissolves limestone to form a cave.

As water containing calcium carbonate slowly drips, it forms downward-growing columns, or stalactites. Where each water drop hits the ground, stalagmites grow upward.

Eventually, a stalactite and a stalagmite may meet to form a single pillar.

sta·lac·tite ▲ [stuh-<u>lak</u>-*tite*] *noun, plural* **stalactites.** a piece of calcium carbonate stone that tapers to look like an icicle hanging from the roof of a limestone cave. It is formed by water containing minerals dripping down the formation.

The words **stalactite** and *stalagmite* are very similar in that both words refer to formations that are found in caves. However, they have different meanings. One way that people tell the difference is to say "Stala<u>c</u>tites, **c**, come down from the <u>c</u>eiling (top) of a cave and stalagmites, **g**, go up from the <u>g</u>round (bottom) of the cave."

sta·lag·mite ▲ [stuh-<u>lag</u>-*mite*] *noun, plural* **stalagmites.** a cone-like formation of calcium carbonate stone on the floor of a limestone cave made by water dripping from a stalactite.

stale [stale] *adjective,* **staler, stalest. 1.** no longer fresh; old: *a stale piece of bread from a loaf baked last week.* **2.** not new, fresh, or interesting: *The politician told some stale jokes at our graduation.*

stale·mate [<u>stale</u>-mate] *noun, plural* **stalemates.** **1.** in chess, when a player whose move it is cannot do so without putting his or her king into check, thus ending the game in a draw. **2.** any situation where two opposing sides cannot act and there cannot be a winner.

stalk[1] [stawk] *noun, plural* **stalks. 1.** the long, thin part of a plant that supports the head of a flower, leaf, or fruit; the stem: *The stalks on sunflowers are very tall.* **2.** something that is like a plant's stalk in shape.

At a famous riding school in Vienna, Austria, Lippizaner **stallions** *are specially trained to perform graceful steps and leaps..*

stalk[2] [stawk] *verb,* **stalked, stalking. 1.** to watch and follow an animal carefully to catch it: *The leopard stalks its prey in silence.* **2.** to follow a person in secret, as if hunting: *The movie star told the police that an unknown man had been stalking her.* **3.** to walk stiffly and proudly with long strides: *Lori was insulted by the manager's pay offer and she stalked out of his office.*

stalk·er [stawk-ur] *noun, plural* **stalkers.** a person who follows another persistently in an unhealthy way, watching and gathering information about their life. Many celebrities attract stalkers.

stall [stawl] *noun, plural* **stalls. 1.** a compartment in a barn that holds one animal, such as a horse or cow. **2.** a table or counter on which goods are offered for sale; a stand. *verb,* **stalled, stalling. 1.** to bring or come to a stop: *The car's engine stalled on the steep hill.* **2.** to act so as to delay something; slow down: *The author is supposed to send his book to the publisher this week, but he's stalling because he hasn't written the last chapter.*

stal·lion ▼ [<u>stal</u>-yun] *noun, plural* **stallions.** an adult male horse, especially one used for breeding.

sta·men [<u>stay</u>-muhn] *noun, plural* **stamens.** *Biology.* the part of a flower that produces pollen. It is made up of a thin stalk called a filament and a pollen-containing tip called the anther.

stam·mer [<u>stam</u>-ur] *verb,* **stammered, stammering.** to speak hesitantly, repeating words, or with a stutter: *I stammered with nervousness at the beginning of my speech.* *noun, plural* **stammers.** the act of speaking with a stammer: *She controlled her stammer as she spoke to the class.*

stamp [stamp] *noun, plural* **stamps. 1.** a small piece of paper used to pay for mailing something; a postage stamp: *I put an airmail stamp on the card.* **2.** a device for shaping or making a mark or design on paper, wax, or other material. *verb,* **stamped, stamping. 1.** to place a postage stamp on a letter, card, or package: **2.** to make a mark with a device or tool on paper, wax, or other material: *At Jon's office they stamp the date of arrival on every letter they receive; The club stamped his hand to show that he'd paid the admission fee.* **3.** to bring one's foot down hard on the ground: *He stamped his foot and refused to go to the dentist.*

♦ **stamp out.** to put a stop to; halt: *The bus company is trying to stamp out the illegal practice of riding without paying the fare.*

stam·pede [stam-<u>peed</u>] *noun, plural* **stampedes. 1.** a sudden, wild rush of frightened cattle, horses, or other animals: *Animals can be easily frightened into a stampede by gunfire or thunder.* **2.** a sudden, wild rush of frightened people: *There was a stampede for the gates when the crowd realized a fire had broken out.* *verb,* **stampeded, stampeding.** to join in a sudden, wild rush: *The mob of cattle stampeded when they saw the wildfire coming.*

stand [stand] *verb*, **stood, standing. 1.** to be on or get to one's feet: *The teacher asked us to stand when the principal came into the room.* **2.** to be or put in an upright position: *The football trophy stood on the prize table.* **3.** to be or remain in a certain condition, situation, or position: *The plane stands ready for the President to use; The City Hall building stands at the center of town.* **4.** to carry out or deal with a certain action or duty: *to stand trial; to stand watch at a fort.* **5.** to remain the same: *My offer to buy the car for $10,000 still stands.* **6.** to put up with; endure; tolerate: *I can't stand the way he talks so rudely to his parents.* **7.** to hold an opinion or position on an issue: *Where does the new candidate stand on the question of gun control?*
noun, plural **stands. 1.** the act of standing or a place where something stands: *The hunters waited for the deer to come within range of their stand.* **2.** a position, opinion, or point of view held by someone: *The governor's stand on greenhouse gas emissions is very controversial.* **3.** the act of stopping to defend a position in battle: *General Custer's Last Stand is one of the most famous events in U.S. history.* **4.** a rack or shelves for storage or display: *a cake stand; a hat stand.* **5.** a counter or table on which to display goods for sale: *a hot dog stand; a news stand.* **6.** a raised platform for a speaker, a performance, or other such purpose: *The last witness to take the stand made a big impression on the jury.* Large raised areas of seats in sports stadiums are called **stands.**
♦ **stand for. 1.** to express the meaning of; represent: *What does the abbreviation "etc." stand for?* **2.** to put up with; tolerate; allow: *I won't stand for so much noise in here!*

It may seem odd that when you go to watch a baseball game you go into the **stands** to sit down. In earlier times the stands were so called because this was a place where people would stand to watch the game, but in modern stadiums the stands will always have seats.

stand·ard [stan-durd] *noun, plural* **standards. 1.** a level or quality or degree of achievement used as a model for others: *There are high standards for people who want to become doctors; The safety standards for toys have improved recently.* **2.** a symbol or emblem, such as a flag: *The soldier bearing the standard led the march down main street.*
adjective. **1.** used as the accepted or established measure of something: *Twelve ounces is the standard size for cans of soda; The U.S. dollar is a standard currency in some foreign countries.* **2.** being the usual, accepted, or typical method: *Saying "hello" is the standard way to answer the telephone.* **3.** used as a guide or authority: *Gray's Anatomy is a standard textbook for training doctors.*

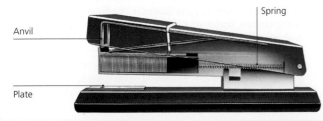

Spring
Anvil
Plate

standard·ize [stan-dur-dize] *verb*, **standardized, standardizing.** to make standard in size, weight, shape, or other characteristic: *Different models of car often use the same standardized parts when they are built.* The act of making things the same is **standardization.**

standard time the time established and adopted for a country or region, usually by law.

stand·by [stand-bye] *noun, plural* **standbys.** a person or thing kept for use if a need arises: *For a quick meal, pasta is a good standby.*
adjective. having to do with being ready at short notice, or when needed: *Many hospitals have a standby generator in case the power fails.*

stand·in [stand-in] *noun, plural* **stand-ins. 1.** a person who takes the place of an important actor who is unable to perform: *The lead actor was sick so we got to see the stand-in.* **2.** a person who takes the place of an actor during the filming of unimportant or dangerous scenes in a movie. **3.** any person who substitutes for another.

stand·ing [stan-ding] *noun, plural* **standings. 1.** rank or reputation, especially in the eyes of others: *Mrs. Brown is a woman of good standing in the community.* **2.** the time during which something has existed: *Bob had an arrangement of long standing with the restaurant to hold his birthday party there each year.* **3. standings.** a listing of individuals or teams in a league or sports competition according to their record of success or performance.
adjective. **1.** done in an upright position: *a standing start.* **2.** continuing or ongoing: *a standing order for a magazine; a standing agreement.* **3.** of water, not flowing; stagnant.

Cassava is a root vegetable that is a dietary **staple** *in western Africa.*

stand·point [stand-point] *noun, plural* **standpoints.** a position from which things are seen and opinions formed; a point of view: *From that standpoint, it seems to be a very good offer.*

stand·still [stand-stil] *noun.* the fact of no movement being made; a halt: *The traffic on the freeway came to a standstill after the crash.*

stan·za [stan-zuh] *noun, plural* **stanzas.** one of a series of groups of lines or patterns that occur in poetry or song.

sta·ple¹ [stay-pul] *noun, plural* **staples.** a piece of thin wire or metal, bent to a U-shape, and used to fasten papers together.
verb, **stapled, stapling.** to fasten papers together using a thin piece of wire or metal: *I stapled the pages of my report together.*

sta·ple² ▲ [stay-pul] *noun, plural* **staples. 1.** an important food product widely used by many people, such as bread or milk. **2.** an important crop produced by a region or a country, such as potatoes and rice

sta·pler ◄ [stape-lur] *noun, plural* **staplers.** a device used to insert staples into pieces of paper, cloth, or other materials in order to fasten them together.

When a **stapler** *is pressed, the anvil pushes a staple down, and a metal plate in the base turns the ends of the staple inward to secure it in the paper.*

a b c d e f g h i j k l m n o p q r s t u v w x y z

A
B
C
D
E
F
G
H
I
J
K
L
M
N
O
P
Q
R
S
T
U
V
W
X
Y
Z

star [star] *noun, plural* **stars. 1.** a huge mass of brightly burning gases in space. A distant star looks like a small point of white light in the sky: *The Earth's nearest star is the Sun.* **2.** a figure, shape, or design that has five points around it, like the shape a star appears to have in the sky. **3.** a very famous or talented person: *a movie star; a major league baseball star.* **4.** a lead actor in a movie, TV series, or play: *an emerging star.*
verb, **starred, starring. 1.** to mark with or as if with a star: *I starred my name on the class list.* **2.** to play the lead role in a play, movie or show: *Carmen starred in the school play.*
adjective. being a star; outstanding or best: *Louis is our star pitcher.*

star·board [star-burd] *noun.* the right-hand side of a boat, ship, or airplane when looking forward from the deck or flight deck.
adjective. on the right-hand side of a boat, ship, or airplane: *The co-pilot's seat is on the starboard side of the aircraft.*

starch [starch] *noun, plural* **starches. 1.** *Biology.* a white substance with no taste that occurs in many plants and foods such as beans, rice, and potatoes. Starch is a common carbohydrate. **2.** a form of this substance used to stiffen linen and clothing such as shirts, collars, or uniforms.
verb, **starched, starching.** to stiffen linen or clothes by spraying starch on before ironing.

stare [stare] *verb,* **stared, staring.** to look hard or for a long time at something: *She stared at the TV when her favorite actor was on.*
noun, plural **stares.** the act of looking hard or for a long time at something.
🔊 A different word with the same sound is **stair.**

star·fish ▶ [star-*fish*] *noun, plural* **starfishes** *or* **starfish.** a marine animal whose body is flat and shaped like a star with five points.

stark [stark] *adjective,* **starker, starkest. 1.** without decoration; hard, severe; bare: *The jagged rocks were stark against the sky.* **2.** being complete and utter: *I think your plan to run away is stark raving madness.*
—**starkly,** *adverb.*

Water enters here.

Tubes pump water.

Tube feet

Tubes inside the body of a **starfish** *pump water in and out of its many tube feet, and this enables the starfish to move along.*

star·ling ◀ [star-ling] *noun, plural* **starlings.** a black bird with greenish-brown sheen, commonly found in Europe. Starlings can mimic the calls of other birds.

The natural habitat of **starlings** *is open country, but they are also found in inhabited areas.*

Star of David ▶ *Religion.* a star-shaped figure that is used as the symbol of the Jewish religion.

star·ry [star-ee] *adjective,* **starrier, starriest. 1.** having to do with stars, or lit up and looking like many of them. **2.** filled with stars: *a starry night sky.*

Stars and Stripes a name given to the flag of the United States.

Star-Spangled Banner *Music.* the national anthem of the United States, chosen by Congress in 1931. The words are taken from a poem by Francis Scott Key written in 1814.

start [start] *verb,* **started, starting. 1.** to bring into being, or begin movement or activity: *The curtain opened and the play started.* **2.** to cause something to happen: *He started the elevator by pressing the button.* **3.** to make a sudden movement out of fright or surprise; jump. **4.** in sports, to be one of the players who is in the lineup to begin a game: *A left-handed pitcher will start for our team in today's game.*
noun, plural **starts. 1.** the act of starting: *I got an early start to the day after my Mom woke me at six o'clock.* **2.** a sudden movement: *I gave a start when the doorbell rang.*

start·er [start-ur] *noun, plural* **starters. 1.** a person who is one of those to start a race. **2.** a person who gives the signal to start a race. **3.** a device that is used to start something, such as the engine of an automobile.

star·tle [star-tul] *verb,* **startled, startling.** to be or cause to be surprised, alarmed, or frightened suddenly: *I was startled when a snake crawled across the road in front of me.* Events or results that cause surprise or alarm are **startling.**

starv·a·tion [star-vay-shun] *noun, plural* s**tarvations.** the fact of suffering from a lack of food.

starve [starv] *verb,* **starved, starving.** to suffer or die from a lack of food.

state [state] *noun, plural* **states. 1.** *Government.* also, **State.** one of the fifty distinct units of the government of the United States: *Alaska is the largest U.S. state, and California has the most people.* **2.** a similar unit of government in other countries. **3.** a number of people living under the same government; a country: *The organization of American States brings together the nations of North and South America.* **4.** the power or actions of the government: *In the U.S. there is a policy of separation of church (religion) and state.* **5.** the land area of a state: *Florida is a very flat state.* **6.** the condition of a person or thing: *Solids, liquids, and gases are the three states of matter; Maggie was in a terrible state after her home was robbed.* The term **the States** is the shortened form of the **United States of America.**
verb, **stated, stating.** to set out clearly in words: *The lawyer stated her client's case.*
adjective. **1.** having to do with a particular state: *a state legislature; a state tax.* **2.** having to do with official government ceremonies or events: *The former President was honored with a state funeral.*

State Department *Government.* the cabinet-level federal department of the United States government that sets and maintains foreign policy.

state·ly [state-lee] *adjective,* **statelier, stateliest.** having to do with a grand style; having a dignified or majestic appearance: *The stately procession went slowly through the capital.*

state·ment [state-munt] *noun, plural* **statements. 1.** something stated, either said or written: *The accused thief read out his statement to the jury.* **2.** a financial record showing the amount of money paid, received, or owed.

state-of-the-art [state-uv-thee-art] *adjective. Business.* describing the most modern and up-to-date methods of technology: *The consultant had a new, state-of-the-art laptop computer.*

states·man [states-mun] *noun, plural* **statesmen.** a politician or government leader, especially one who is respected as being wise and experienced: *The well-known statesman was asked to be a guest speaker at the official dinner.* Having wisdom or ability in the management of government affairs is called **statesmanship.**

stat·ic [stat-ik] *adjective.* showing little or no movement, change, or development: *Experts predict that oil prices will remain static for the next six months.* *noun.* **1.** noise caused by electrical charges in the air. Static interferes with television and radio broadcasts. **2.** criticism or complaints: *Her surprise promotion caused a lot of static in the office.*

static electricity *Science.* electricity that is not flowing in a current, but collects on the surface of objects that can produce an electrical charge when rubbed.

sta·tion [stay-shun] *noun, plural* **stations. 1.** a place where trains and buses regularly stop in order to take on or unload passengers or goods. **2.** a building or establishment used for a particular kind of work or service: *a police station.* **3.** a place where television and radio broadcasts are recorded and transmitted. *verb,* **stationed, stationing.** to place or assign in a position: *The police officers were stationed at the front of the courthouse.*

sta·tion·ar·y [stay-shuh-ner-ee] *adjective.* **1.** not moving; remaining still: *The bus was stationary while the passengers got on.* **2.** not able to be moved; not portable: *In that stadium the seats by the field can be moved, but the upper stands are stationary.*
🔊 A different word with the same sound is **stationery.**

sta·tion·er·y [stay-shuh-ner-ee] *noun.* writing paper and envelopes, as well as writing materials such as pens and pencils: *office stationery.*
🔊 A different word with the same sound is **stationary.**

Statue to tip of flame, 151 feet high

The internal skeleton of the **Statue of Liberty** *is made of iron.*

Seven rays of crown representing the seven continents and seven seas

Tablet inscribed with date of American Independence

Viewing area

Pedestal, 154 feet high

sta·tis·tics [stuh-tis-tiks] *plural noun, singular* **statistic.** *Mathematics.* **1.** numerical data that represent facts or measurements: *Statistics show that women tend to live longer than men.* **2.** a branch of mathematics that deals with the collection and analysis of numerical data. A **statistic** is a single item of information that is collected.

stat·ue [stach-oo] *noun, plural* **statues.** *Art.* an image of a person or animal that is made out of stone, wood, or bronze.

Statue of Liberty ◀ *Art.* a large copper statue of a woman holding a burning torch in her right hand. The statue, which represents freedom, was dedicated to the United States by France in 1886 and stands on Liberty Island in New York Harbor.

stat·ure [stach-ur] *noun.* **1.** a person's height: *She was short in stature with long, curly brown hair.* **2.** the level of achievement or degree which someone has reached: *He is a man of great stature in the political world.*

sta·tus [stat-tus *or* state-us] *noun.* **1.** someone's social or professional rank or position as compared with others: *She enjoys a high status at work because her father owns the company.* **2.** the situation or condition of something: *He asked her about her marital status, to see if she was available for a date.* Something that you own or want to own so that others will admire you is known as a **status symbol,** such as an expensive watch or sports car.

stat·ute [stach-oot] *noun, plural* **statutes.** *Law.* a law that has been officially approved and written down in a formal document. A **statute of limitations** is a law that establishes a specific period of time during which legal action can be taken.

staunch [stawnch] *adjective.* strongly loyal and supportive: *My father is a staunch supporter of the President.* *verb,* **staunched, staunching.** to stop the flow of a liquid such as blood or tears: *to staunch the flow of blood from a cut.* —**staunchly,** *adverb.*

stave [stave] *noun, plural* **staves. 1.** one of a set of narrow pieces of curved wood fitted close together to form part of the side of a barrel. **2.** another word for STAFF.

stay[1] [stay] *verb,* **stayed, staying. 1.** to remain in one place; not leave: *We stayed indoors until the rain cleared.* **2.** to continue doing something or being in a particular state: *He stayed as the school principal for over twenty years.* **3.** to live or be in a place for a short time: *I stayed with my grandparents for my summer vacation.* *noun, plural* **stays.** a period of time spent somewhere: *My parents had a short stay in a luxury hotel for their ten-year wedding anniversary.*

stay[2] [stay] *noun, plural* **stays. 1.** a strong rope or wire used to steady the mast of a ship. **2.** anything that can be used as a support to keep something steady.

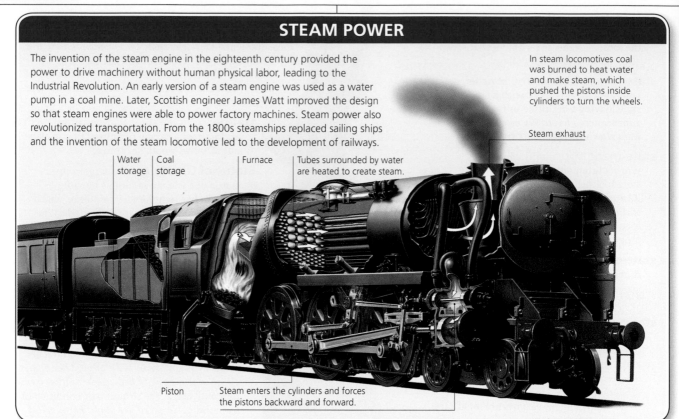

STEAM POWER

The invention of the steam engine in the eighteenth century provided the power to drive machinery without human physical labor, leading to the Industrial Revolution. An early version of a steam engine was used as a water pump in a coal mine. Later, Scottish engineer James Watt improved the design so that steam engines were able to power factory machines. Steam power also revolutionized transportation. From the 1800s steamships replaced sailing ships and the invention of the steam locomotive led to the development of railways.

In steam locomotives coal was burned to heat water and make steam, which pushed the pistons inside cylinders to turn the wheels.

Steam exhaust

Water storage

Coal storage

Furnace

Tubes surrounded by water are heated to create steam.

Piston

Steam enters the cylinders and forces the pistons backward and forward.

stead·fast [sted-fast] *adjective.* being fixed, constant, or unchanging: *She has been a steadfast friend to us for over ten years.* —**steadfastly,** *adverb.*

stead·y [sted-ee] *adjective,* **steadier, steadiest. 1.** describing something fixed; stable: *It's important to hold the camera steady while you take a picture.* **2.** continuing at an even and regular rate: *The student is making steady progress in his math class.* **3.** describing something constant; regular: *He's had a steady job for three years now.* **4.** not easily excited, agitated, or upset: *The student showed steady nerves when he gave his speech in front of the entire school.* *verb,* **steadied, steadying.** to make or become steady: *The bicycle slid in a puddle of water but the rider managed to steady himself.* —**steadily,** *adverb;* —**steadiness,** *noun.*

steak [stake] *noun, plural* **steaks.** a thick, flat piece of meat or fish for grilling or frying. ◀ A different word with the same sound is **stake.**

> The word **steak** goes back to a word used hundreds of years ago in England. This word meant "stick." In those times the usual way to cook a steak was to put it on a stick and hold it over an open fire.

steal [steel] *verb,* **stole, stolen, stealing. 1.** to take something that belongs to someone else: *to steal a car; to steal money; to steal a dress from a store.* **2.** to take or do something secretly: *He stole a look at the answer sheet when the teacher wasn't looking.* **3.** to win over by charm or surprise: *The young actor stole the show with his great performance.* **4.** to move secretly or quietly: *He stole out of the house to meet his friends after his*

parents fell asleep. **5.** in baseball, to advance a base during the throwing of a pitch without the help of a hit or an error: *The baserunner stole third base.* *noun, plural* **steals. 1.** the act of advancing a base in baseball without the ball being hit. **2.** an item that is a bargain or has a very low price. ◀ A different word with the same sound is **steel.**

steam [steem] *noun. Chemistry.* **1.** a colorless gas or vapor that is produced when water is heated to its boiling point (212°F or 100°C). Steam is used for generating power in machines and for heating. **2.** a driving force; energy: *By the time we hiked back to camp, I had completely run out of steam.* *verb,* **steamed, steaming. 1.** to treat with steam for cooking, heating, or softening: *Mom usually steams the vegetables for dinner.* **2.** to give off or be covered with steam: *The hot oven and boiling pans steamed up the kitchen windows.* **3.** to move by steam power: *The passenger train steamed out of the station to its next destination.*

steam·boat [steem-bote] *noun, plural* **steamboats.** a steam-powered boat.

steam engine an engine powered by the force of steam.

steam power ▲ *Science.* the use of steam energy to drive engines, furnaces, and other mechanical devices.

steam·roll·er [steem-roh-lur] *noun, plural* **steamrollers.** a heavy vehicle with very wide rollers for pressing down and smoothing roads. Steamrollers used to be powered by steam in past times.

Stencils make it easy to apply letters and numbers to a surface.

steam·ship [steem-*ship*] *noun,* *plural* **steamships.** a ship powered by the force of steam.

steel [steel] *noun.* a strong, hard, metal formed from a mixture of iron and carbon that is used to make machines, vehicles, and buildings.
adjective. made from steel: *a steel bridge.*
verb, **steeled, steeling.** to make hard or determined: *She steeled herself to jump into the freezing cold water.*
🔊 A different word with the same sound is **steal.**

steel wool a tangled mass of fine steel threads twisted together, used to rub a surface smooth.

steep¹ [steep] *adjective,* **steeper, steepest. 1.** having a sharp slope or high angle: *It was a steep climb to the top of the mountain.* **2.** more than is reasonable; excessive: *Dinner at the restaurant was nice, but the bill was a bit steep.*

steep² [steep] *verb,* **steeped, steeping. 1.** to soak in water or other liquid: *Mom made a fantastic dessert of fruit steeped in red wine.* **2.** to be filled with something: *The college was founded in the 1600s and is steeped in tradition.*

stee·ple [stee-*pul*] *noun,* *plural* **steeples.** a tall, pointed tower with a spire built on the roof of a building or church.

stee·ple·chase [stee-*pul*-*chase*] *noun.* an obstacle race for either people or horses that has ditches, hurdles, water, and hedges to jump.

steer¹ [steer] *verb,* **steered, steering. 1.** to control the direction of a vehicle by using a wheel or rudder: *He steered the car around the fallen tree.* **2.** to be guided in a particular direction: *This bicycle steers easily now that the handlebars have been fixed.* **3.** to follow or pursue a particular course: *The tourist guide steered us to the main shopping district.*

steer² [steer] *noun,* *plural* **steers.** a young sterilized bull that is raised for its meat rather than for breeding.

steg·o·sau·rus ▶
[steg-uh-sore-us] *noun,* *plural* **stegosauri.** a four-footed plant-eating dinosaur with a row of bony plates along its back and a spiky tail.

The type of dinosaur known as a **stegosaurus** gets its name from a phrase meaning "the roof lizard." This animal had a row of bony plates on its back, and people once thought that it could protect itself by causing these plates to lie flat on its back, like the roof of a house.

stem¹ [stem] *noun,* *plural* **stems. 1.** the long, thin stalk of a plant that grows upward from the roots and supports leaves, flowers, or fruits. **2.** anything that resembles the stalk of a plant: *the long stem of a champagne glass.*
verb, **stemmed, stemming.** to remove the stem of: *He stemmed the apples before putting them in the juicer.*
• **stem from.** to originate or develop from: *Their long feud stemmed from a misunderstanding many years ago.*

stem² [stem] *verb,* **stemmed, stemming.** to stop the flow of: *He used a tight bandage to stem the blood flow.*

sten·cil ◀ [sten-*sul*] *noun,* *plural* **stencils.** *Art.* **1.** a thin sheet of paper, cardboard, or metal with a pattern or letters cut out of it so that when ink or paint is applied to the sheet, the pattern comes out on the surface below it. **2.** the design or letters produced on a surface by using a stencil.
verb, **stenciled, stenciling.** to make a design or letters with a stencil.

step [step] *noun,* *plural* **steps. 1.** a movement made by raising the foot and putting it down in a new position: *She took two steps in her new high heels and then tripped over.* **2.** the distance measured by such a movement: *The child was just a few steps away from falling into the pool when I stopped her.* **3.** a support for the foot in going up or coming down: *the bottom step of a ladder.* **4. steps.** a flight of stairs: *The elevator was broken so she climbed the steps to her apartment.* **5.** a stage in a process: *Setting up a bank account was his first step for saving to buy a car.* **6.** a sound or mark made by the foot in walking. **7.** a certain movement that is made with the feet when dancing: *This week we learned the steps for the tango.*
verb, **stepped, stepping. 1.** to move by raising the foot and putting it down in a new position: *She stepped outside into the garden for some fresh air.* **2.** to press the foot onto something: *He stepped on a nail and had to be taken to the hospital.*
• **step up.** to increase or advance: *The airports are stepping up their security measures.*

step·par·ent [step-*pare*-unt] *noun,* *plural* **step-parents.** someone who is a stepmother or stepfather.

step·fa·ther [step-*fath*-ur] *noun,* *plural* **stepfathers.** a man who is married to someone's mother but is not the person's natural father.

step·lad·der [step-*lad*-ur] *noun,* *plural* **stepladders.** a folding portable ladder that has flat steps instead of rungs.

step·moth·er [step-muth-ur] *noun,* *plural* **stepmothers.** a woman who is married to someone's father but is not the person's natural mother.

*The **stegosaurus** used its spiky tail to defend itself against attackers.*

*In spring, the **steppes** of Russia and Asia are carpeted with poppies, daisies, and yellow rapeseed flowers.*

steppe ▲ [step] *noun.*
Geography. a large, grass-covered area of land with no trees.

> The word **steppe** comes from the Russian language and has no connection to the more common word *step*. In fact, the sense is exactly the opposite, since *steps* go up or down as a series of levels. *Steppes* on the other hand are very flat and do not really go up and down at all.

ster·e·o [ster-ee-oh] *noun, plural* **stereos.** a piece of electrical equipment used for producing sound and music through two speakers.

ster·e·o·type [ster-ee-oh-tipe] *noun, plural* **stereotypes.** a fixed belief or idea about someone or something, especially one that is wrong or oversimplified: *She fitted the stereotype of a Californian—she was blonde, fit, and tanned.*
verb, **stereotyped, stereotyping.** to have a fixed belief or idea about someone or something: *Women with blonde hair are sometimes stereotyped as being silly or stupid.*

ster·ile [ster-ul] *adjective. Biology.* **1.** free from germs and bacteria: *Surgeons must use sterile instruments when operating on patients.* **2.** not being able to have children. **3.** unable to produce fruits or crops: *The desert soil was dry and sterile.*

ster·i·lize [ster-uh-lize] *verb,* **sterilized, sterilizing.** *Medicine.* **1.** to make something clean by killing any germs or bacteria: *The dentist sterilized his equipment in a special solution so that it was safe to use.* **2.** to perform a medical procedure in order to make a person or animal unable to produce children or offspring: *The vet sterilized our cat so that she wouldn't have any more kittens.* —**sterilization,** *noun.*

ster·ling [stur-ling] *noun.* **1.** silver that is at least 92 percent pure. This is also called **sterling silver. 2.** the standard unit of money in Britain.
adjective. **1.** made of sterling silver: *He put out the sterling candlestick holders for the special dinner.* **2.** of a very high standard; excellent: *She had sterling manners.*

stern[1] [stern] *adjective,* **sterner, sternest. 1.** describing something strict or severe: *The school principal warned us that there would now be sterner penalties for talking back to teachers.* **2.** being firm and uncompromising: *She showed stern determination in finishing the race with her sprained ankle.* —**sternly,** *adverb.*

stern[2] [stern] *noun, plural* **sterns.** the back part of a boat or ship: *a high stern.*

ster·oid [ster-oid] *noun, plural* **steroids.** *Chemistry.* a chemical that the body produces naturally such as the hormone testosterone. Steroids can also be made artificially to use for treating medical conditions. Sometimes steroids are taken illegally by people in order to increase their strength and fitness and improve their athletic performance.

steth·o·scope [steth-uh-skope] *noun, plural* **stethoscopes.** *Medicine.* a medical instrument that doctors use to listen to the sounds of the heart and lungs.

stew [stoo] *noun, plural* **stews.** a hot meal made by slowly cooking meat and vegetables together in a liquid.
verb, **stewed, stewing. 1.** to cook food slowly in a liquid: *Mom stewed the apples for us to have for dessert.* **2.** to worry or become angry: *He stewed all afternoon about the argument he had with his friend.*

stew·ard [stoo-urd] *noun, plural* **stewards.** a man who serves food and drink to passengers on a ship or plane.

stew·ard·ess [stoo-ur-dis] *noun, plural* **stewardesses.** a woman who serves food and drink to passengers on a ship or plane.
See FLIGHT ATTENDANT for more information.

stick[1] [stik] *noun, plural* **sticks. 1.** a thin piece of wood or a broken twig from a tree. **2.** something shaped like a stick: *We had carrot and celery sticks with dip as a light snack.*

stick[2] [stik] *verb,* **stuck, sticking. 1.** to push a pointed instrument into something else: *to stick a fork into a piece of meat; The nurse stuck the needle into my arm.* **2.** to fasten or attach onto: *The snowflakes stuck on my eyelashes.* **3.** to become fixed in place: *He tried to zip up his jacket but the zipper got stuck halfway.* **4.** to put into a place or position: *The naughty little child stuck her fingers in her ears and stamped her feet.* **5.** to prevent or stop from moving: *The vehicle was stuck in the mud.* **6.** to continue or keep on with a task: *I'm going to stick with this job for at least another six months before I quit.*

stick·er [stik-ur] *noun, plural* **stickers.** an adhesive label with a message or pattern on it.

stick·y [stik-ee] *adjective,* **stickier, stickiest. 1.** made with a substance that stays fixed to surfaces; adhesive: *He used sticky tape to wrap up the birthday presents.* **2.** covered with a sticky substance: *The kitchen table was sticky with maple syrup.* **3.** describing something awkward or difficult: *It was a sticky situation for her to be at a party with her ex-boyfriend.*

stiff [stif] *adjective,* **stiffer, stiffest. 1.** difficult to bend; firm: *He put a stiff piece of cardboard behind the painting when he framed it.* **2.** not able to move easily: *Sarah had stiff leg muscles after her game of tennis.* **3.** not relaxed; formal: *His dance movements were quite stiff because he was so was nervous.* **4.** describing something difficult or severe: *The judge gave him a stiff punishment for his crimes; It was a stiff entrance fee to get into the new amusement park.*
adverb. to a great degree; extremely: *Michael was scared stiff of spiders.* —**stiffly,** *adverb;* —**stiffness,** *noun.*

Stilts were originally used for crossing rivers, but today they are mostly worn for fun.

stiff·en [stif-un] *verb*, **stiffened, stiffening.** to make or become stiff: *She stiffened when she recognized the man who had tried to rob her.*

sti·fle [stye-ful] *verb*, **stifled, stifling: 1.** to smother or stop from breathing: *He was stifled by the smoke and fumes.* **2.** to hold back; suppress: *She stifled a laugh when the guest speaker tripped over on the stage.*

stig·ma [stig-muh] *noun*, *plural* **stigmas.** a symbol of disgrace or shame on a person's reputation: *There used to be a stigma attached to people who got divorced.*

still [stil] *adjective*, **stiller, stillest. 1.** without motion; not moving: *He jumped into the still water of the lake.* **2.** free from sound or noise: *The night was so still the only noise was my own breathing.*
verb, **stilled, stilling.** to make or become silent or calm: *She stilled the baby by rocking it gently in the cradle.*
noun. the state of silence or calm: *He enjoyed sitting out on the porch in the still of the evening.*
adverb. **1.** without movement: *The soldier stood very still.* **2.** up to or at this time: *Let's get to the beach while it's still hot.* **3.** all the same: *I had already eaten breakfast but I was still hungry.*
conjunction. and yet; but yet: *There was no way they could win the match—still they played their hardest until the final whistle.* —**stillness,** *noun.*

still life *Art.* a type of painting or drawing of arrangements of non-moving objects such as fruits, bowls, or flowers.

stilt ▲ [stilt] *noun*, *plural* **stilts. 1.** one of a pair of poles with supports for the feet to allow someone to walk above the ground. **2.** one of the stakes or poles that supports a house or building above the ground or water.

stim·u·lant [stim-yuh-lunt] *noun*, *plural* **stimulants.** *Chemistry.* a substance that makes you feel more awake and active, or makes parts of your body work faster: *Caffeine is a well-known stimulant and is found in tea and coffee.*

stim·u·late [stim-yuh-late] *verb*, **stimulated, stimulating.** to spur on or make more active: *The documentary on the environment stimulated worldwide interest in global warming.* —**stimulation,** *noun.*

stim·u·lus [stim-yuh-lus] *noun*, *plural* **stimuli.** *Biology.* something that causes a part in the body to react, such as a cell, tissue, or organ: *The retina in the eye is sensitive to the visual stimulus of light.*

sting [sting] *verb*, **stung, stinging. 1.** to prick or wound with a sharp-pointed, often poisonous structure or organ: *A wasp stung Dad while he was gardening yesterday.* **2.** to cause pain or hurt: *Mom put antiseptic on my cut knee, which made it sting.*
noun, *plural* **stings. 1.** the sharp, pointed, often poisonous part of an insect or animal that causes a wound. **2.** the wound or pain caused by stinging. **3.** a burning pain in the eyes or on the skin: *She could hardly see because of the powerful sting of smoke in her eyes.*

sting·er ▼ [sting-ur] *noun*, *plural* **stingers.** a sharp, pointed, often poisonous part of an insect or animal that is used to pierce or wound.

sting·ray [sting-ray] *noun*, *plural* **stingrays.** a large, flat fish that has one or more stinging spines near the base of its long, thin, whip-like tail.

stin·gy [stin-jee] *adjective*, **stingier, stingiest. 1.** not generous; reluctant to give or spend: *The rich man was too stingy to give any money to charity.* **2.** too small an amount; meager: *She was hungry after dinner because she had been given such a stingy meal.* —**stinginess,** *noun.*

stink [stingk] *noun*, *plural* **stinks.** a strong and offensive smell:
verb, **stank** or **stunk, stunk, stinking.** to have or give off a strong and offensive smell: *The sour milk in the refrigerator really stank.*

stir [stur] *verb*, **stirred, stirring. 1.** to mix a liquid or other substance by moving a spoon or stick around in it: *He stirred his coffee so that the sugar would dissolve.* **2.** to cause to move: *The wind stirred up all the dust on the road.* **3.** to affect the feelings or reactions of: *When his favorite old song came on the radio, it stirred up happy memories for him.*
noun, *plural* **stirs. 1.** the act of stirring or moving: *She gave the stew a stir and added some herbs.* **2.** an excited reaction; a commotion: *The news that the two movie stars were getting married caused quite a stir among their fans.*

Poison sac

Stinger

The honeybee's **stinger** *is at the end of its abdomen and is connected to a poison sac.*

stir·rup [stur-up] *noun*, *plural* **stirrups.** a metal or leather loop that hangs on both sides of a saddle of a horse to hold the rider's feet.

stitch [stich] *noun*, *plural* **stitches. 1.** one movement of a needle and thread in and out of a cloth or other material. **2.** one complete movement and loop of yarn in knitting or crocheting.
verb, **stitched, stitching.** to join together or mend with stitches: *The doctor stitched up the cut and placed a bandage over the wound.*

a
b
c
d
e
f
g
h
i
j
k
l
m
n
o
p
q
r
s
t
u
v
w
x
y
z

stock [stok] *noun, plural* **stocks. 1.** a supply of goods that a shop keeps to sell to customers: *The market has a large stock of fresh fruits and vegetables.* **2.** farm animals such as cattle; livestock. **3.** the family or race from which a person or animal descends. **4.** *Business.* a share in the ownership of a company: *She sold her stock in the Acme Company and made a profit of thousands of dollars.* **5.** a liquid used to add flavor to food, made by boiling meat, fish, and vegetables in water. **6.** the support or handle of a tool or a gun.
verb, **stocked, stocking. 1.** to fill with a supply of goods: *My parents stocked the fridge with food in preparation for their dinner guests.* **2.** to keep a supply of something: *That department store stocks a large range of children's shoes.*

stock·ade [stah-kade] *noun, plural* **stockades. 1.** a strong wooden fence built as a defense against an attack. **2.** a jail for political or military prisoners.

stock car an ordinary car that has been modified so that it can be raced. **Stock car racing** is a popular form of automobile racing.

stock·ing [stok-ing] *noun, plural* **stockings.** one of a pair of thin, close-fitting coverings for the foot and part of the leg. Stockings are usually worn by women and made of knitted wool, nylon, or similar material.

stock market *Business.* a market where stocks and shares are bought and sold. This is also known as a **stock exchange.**

stock·pile [stok-pile] *verb,* **stockpiled, stockpiling.** to keep adding to a supply of goods, food, or weapons for future use: *The criminals had been stockpiling guns and ammunition for months.*
noun, plural **stockpiles.** a large supply of food or something else kept for future use: *Mom has a stockpile of cough medicine in our bathroom cabinet.*

stocks ▼ [stoks] *plural noun. History.* in past times, a wooden frame used for punishing people who had committed minor crimes, with holes to contain the person's hands and feet.

stock·y [stok-ee] *adjective,* **stockier, stockiest.** having a short, thickset, and sturdy build: *The wrestler was stocky and strong-looking.*

stock·yard [stok-yard] *noun, plural* **stockyards.** a set of pens or enclosures where livestock are kept before being sold or slaughtered.

stoke [stoke] *verb,* **stoked, stoking.** to tend to a fire or furnace by stirring it up or adding fuel: *After Dad had stoked the fire, the sitting room became nice and warm.* —**stoker,** *noun.*

stom·ach [stum-uk] *noun, plural* **stomachs.**
1. the muscular bag-like organ in humans and certain animals that receives food after it has been swallowed and starts to digest it. **2.** the soft part of the body beneath the chest; the belly.
verb, **stomached, stomaching.** to tolerate something, especially if it is unpleasant: *My mother says that she can't stomach watching violence on television.*

stomp [stomp] *verb,* **stomped, stomping.** to walk with heavy steps or bring down the foot heavily: *He was so angry that he stomped out of the room and slammed the heavy door behind him.*

stone [stone] *noun, plural* **stones. 1.** the hard, solid substance that rocks are made of; it is often used in building. **2.** a piece of rock: *The peaceful protest turned violent when some of the demonstrators started to throw stones and other objects at the police.* **3.** a hard, valuable substance or gem: *Charlotte's bracelet and necklace were made of diamonds and other precious stones.* **4.** the hard seed inside fruits such as cherries, peaches, and olives.
adjective. made of stone: *A flight of stone steps led up to the house.*
verb, **stoned, stoning.** to throw stones at someone or something.

Stone Age *History.* the earliest period in which people are known to have existed, when stone rather than metals was used for making tools and weapons.

stool [stool] *noun, plural* **stools.** a low seat with no back or arms: *a milking stool.*

stoop[1] [stoop] *verb,* **stooped, stooping. 1.** to bend the body forward and downward: *I stooped over to tie my shoelaces.* **2.** to stand or walk with the head and upper back bent forward: *The elderly woman stooped as she shuffled along the road with her cane.* **3.** to lower one's moral standards or degrade oneself: *He said that he would never stoop to stealing money from his parents.*
noun, plural **stoops.** a bending forward of the head and upper back.

stoop[2] [stoop] *noun, plural* **stoops.** a raised area for sitting, such as a porch or platform at the door of a house.

stop [stop] *verb,* **stopped, stopping. 1.** to prevent from moving or doing something: *The two security guards stopped us at the door to check our identification.* **2.** to put an end to something: *The referee stopped the game by blowing her whistle.* **3.** to come to an end: *I waited until the rain had stopped before I went outside.* **4.** to block or close up: *The plumber stopped the leak by filling the hole with putty.*
noun, plural **stops. 1.** the act of stopping: *He brought the car to a sudden stop when the neighbor's dog ran across the road.* **2.** a place where vehicles stop in order for passengers to get on or off: *We waited patiently for ten minutes at the bus stop.*

In the eighteenth century, these **stocks** *were used to punish criminals in the city of Williamsburg, Virginia.*

STORMS

The conditions that make a storm are warm, rising air currents, plenty of water vapor, and low air temperatures at the middle and upper levels of the atmosphere. A storm usually progresses through three main stages, which may last from fifteen minutes to several hours.

BUILDING UP
Rising air currents carry water vapor upward into cooler air. The moisture condenses and a cumulus cloud forms.

AT ITS PEAK
The cumulonimbus, or thundercloud, grows and spreads out to form a wide, flat top. A combination of updrafts and downdrafts creates rain, hail, and lightning.

WEAKENING
As the downdrafts outnumber the updrafts, the supply of warm rising air is cut off. The cloud disintegrates, leaving a smaller cumulus cloud and some wispy cirrus clouds.

stop·per [stop-ur] *noun, plural* **stoppers.** something that fits in the top of a bottle or other container in order to close it.

stop·watch [stop-wahch] *noun, plural* **stopwatches.** a watch that can be instantly started and stopped by pushing a button so that an exact time can be measured, such as the time it takes to run a race.

stor·age [store-ij] *noun.* **1.** the keeping of things in a special area for future use: *Her parents put her furniture and belongings in storage when she left for college.* **2.** an area in which things are kept until they are needed: *The attic is a great storage space for all our junk.* **3.** the part in a computer, or a piece of computer equipment such as a disk, that holds and retrieves information.

store [store] *noun, plural* **stores. 1.** an establishment or shop where goods are sold: *Mom sent me to the corner store to buy some milk.* **2.** a supply or stock of goods kept for future use: *We keep a store of candles in the house in case of a power failure.*
verb, **stored, storing.** to put away to be used at a later time: *The squirrel stored a supply of acorns for the winter.*
• **in store.** coming soon; waiting: *The teacher announced that there would be a surprise in store for us in our next lesson.*

stork ▶ [stork] *noun, plural* **storks** *or* **stork.** a large, white wading bird with long legs, a long neck, and a long, straight bill.

> The bird known as a **stork** is said to get its name from a word meaning "stiff." The stork keeps its long legs very stiff as it stands or walks.

storm ▲ [storm] *noun, plural* **storms. 1.** a violent weather condition with heavy rain, wind, thunder, and lightning. **2.** a violent or sudden outburst: *There was a storm of applause and cheering when the celebrity stepped out of the limousine.* **3.** a violent and sudden attack: *The troops took the enemy city by storm.*
verb, **stormed, storming. 1.** to blow forcefully with wind, rain, thunder, or snow: *It stormed all morning, but cleared up in the afternoon.* **2.** to move or rush violently and angrily: *The angry customer stormed out of the shop, shouting and waving his arms about.* **3.** to attack suddenly and violently: *The soldiers stormed the fortress.*

storm·y [storm-ee] *adjective,* **stormier, stormiest. 1.** having strong winds, rain, thunder, lightning, or snow: *The night was dark and stormy.* **2.** having fierce emotions and behavior: *The couple had a stormy argument that could be heard halfway down the street.*

stor·y¹ [stor-ee] *noun, plural* **stories. 1.** the telling of something that has happened: *There was a front-page story in the newspaper about the Super Bowl game.* **2.** a tale made up to entertain: *The little girl's favorite story was Cinderella.* **3.** a piece of writing that is fiction rather than fact: *See* SHORT STORY. **4.** a lie: *He told a story about why he hadn't finished his homework.*

stor·y² [stor-ee] *noun, plural* **stories.** a floor or level in a building: *The office building has twenty stories.*

stout [stout] *adjective,* **stouter, stoutest. 1.** quite fat and heavy-looking: *a short, stout person.* **2.** bold or brave: *The story tells of a boy whose stout heart carries him through many difficulties.* **3.** physically strong and sturdy: *I bought a pair of stout riding boots.*

stove [stove] *noun, plural* **stoves.** a piece of equipment that uses gas, electricity, or wood for cooking or heating.

stow [stoh] *verb,* **stowed, stowing.** to pack something or store it away: *The passenger stowed his luggage in the overhead locker above his seat.*

Storks live near freshwater environments such as marshlands, rivers, lakes, and ponds.

a b c d e f g h i j k l m n o p q r **s** t u v w x y z

A
B
C
D
E
F
G
H
I
J
K
L
M
N
O
P
Q
R
S
T
U
V
W
X
Y
Z

stow·a·way [stoh-uh-*way*] *noun, plural* **stowaways.** someone who hides on a ship, aircraft, or other vehicle to travel secretly or without paying.

strad·dle [strad-ul] *verb,* **straddled, straddling.** to sit or stand with one leg on each side of something: *She straddled the horse.*

strag·gle [strag-ul] *verb,* **straggled, straggling.** to stray or lag behind: *The last of the runners straggled over the finish line.* Someone who strays or falls behind is a **straggler.**

straight [strate] *adjective,* **straighter, straightest. 1.** in one direction; not bending or curving: *The student used a ruler to draw a straight red line across the top of the page.* **2.** in proper order or condition: *It took us all day to get the house straight after the party.* **3.** describing something honest or reliable: *The detective asked the suspect to give him a straight answer. adverb.* **1.** without bending or curving: *The sergeant told the new recruits to stand up straight.* **2.** immediately: *I had some dinner and then went straight to bed; I'll get straight onto it.*
🔊 A different word with the same sound is **strait.**

straight·en [strate-un] *verb,* **straightened, straightening. 1.** to make or become straight: *He straightened his tie and smoothed down his hair before he got up to speak.* **2.** to arrange in neat or proper order: *Mom asked me to straighten up the living room before the guests arrived.*

strain [strane] *verb,* **strained, straining. 1.** to make a great effort to do something: *The students had to strain their ears to hear what the quietly spoken teacher was saying.* **2.** to injure or damage by overuse or the wrong use: *He strained his leg muscle in the race because he didn't warm up properly.* **3.** to stretch to the full; pull tight: *Mom strained the sheets over the mattress.* **4.** to pour or press through a strainer or sieve: *Dad strained the pasta once it had finished cooking. noun, plural* **strains. 1.** a force that stretches, pulls, or puts pressure on something: **2.** an injury caused by too much effort or tension: *Our star player couldn't play in the final because of his knee strain.* **3.** worry that is caused by problems or tension: *He has been under a lot of strain since his marriage broke up.*

strain·er [strane-ur] *noun, plural* **strainers.** a kitchen utensil with many holes in it that is used for separating liquids from solids.

strait [strate] *noun, plural* **straits. 1.** a narrow passage of water that connects two larger bodies of water. **2. straits.** a situation of trouble or difficulty.
🔊 A different word with the same sound is **straight.**

strand¹ ▲ [strand] *verb,* **stranded, stranding.** to leave in a difficult or helpless position: *He was robbed and left stranded in the middle of the city with no money.*

strand² [strand] *noun, plural* **strands. 1.** one of a series of threads, fibers, or wires twisted round each other to make a cord, rope, or cable. **2.** a single thread or a length of fiber: *The girl brushed a strand of hair from her face.*

strange [straynj] *adjective,* **stranger, strangest. 1.** out of the ordinary; unusual; odd: *I was puzzled by my friend's strange behavior— it was so unlike her.* **2.** not known, seen, heard, or experienced before; unfamiliar: *A strange car was parked outside our house for several days.* **3.** out of place; uneasy; uncomfortable: *The girl felt strange on her first day at her new school.* —**strangely,** *adverb;* —**strangeness,** *noun.*

strang·er [strayn-jur] *noun, plural* **strangers. 1.** a person you do not know: *When I tripped and dropped my bag of shopping, a stranger stopped to help me.* **2.** someone who is not known in a place; an outsider or newcomer: *We arrived only yesterday, so we are still strangers in town.*

stran·gle [strang-gul] *verb,* **strangled, strangling. 1.** to kill by squeezing the throat to stop breathing. **2.** to be or feel unable to breathe; choke or suffocate.

strap [strap] *noun, plural* **straps.** a usually flat strip of material such as leather or cloth used to tie or hold things together or in place: *The lock on my suitcase broke, so I put a strap around it to hold it together. verb,* **strapped, strapping.** to tie or fasten with a strap: *Dad strapped our bags to the luggage rack of the car.*

strat·e·gic [struh-tee-jik] *adjective.* **1.** having to do with strategy: *General Eisenhower made the strategic decision that the Allied invasion of France should take place on June 6, 1944.* **2.** giving an advantage in a situation, or helping to achieve a purpose; key: *Hot dog stands were set up at strategic points around the amusement park.* —**strategically,** *adverb.*

strat·e·gy [strat-uh-jee] *noun, plural* **strategies. 1.** the process of planning and directing how military forces and equipment will be used during a war or battle to give the best chance of a favorable outcome. **2.** a plan of action or policy for achieving a goal: *My strategy for winning my tennis match was to mix up my shots and keep my opponent guessing.*

Strategy and *tactics* are both plans for doing things, as in warfare, sports, business, and so on. To make a distinction between these words, *strategy* can be used for planning that takes place beforehand, such as a general in war deciding to attack a certain city. *Tactics* on the other hand would be an immediate decision that takes place on the spot in the middle of the action, such as a sergeant dividing his troops into two groups during the battle.

strat·o·sphere [strat-uh-sfeer] *noun. Environment.* a layer of the Earth's atmosphere between about six miles and thirty miles above the Earth. In this layer, the temperature does not vary very much from one part to another, and clouds are rare.

straw [straw] *noun, plural* **straws. 1.** a thin tube for sucking up a drink. **2.** dry stalks of grain, such as wheat, oats, rye, and barley, after they have been cut and threshed.

straw·ber·ry ▶ [straw-ber-ee] *noun, plural* **strawberries.** the sweet, juicy, red fruit of a low-growing plant that has white flowers and produces long, trailing runners.

*New **strawberry** plants grow from shoots, or runners, that are sent out by the "mother" plant.*

stray [stray] *verb,* **strayed, straying.** to lose one's way; wander: *Our dog strayed when we left the gate open and was found miles away.* *adjective.* **1.** found wandering or lost: *stray cattle.* **2.** occurring here and there; scattered: *The sky was clear except for a few stray clouds.* *noun, plural* **strays.** an animal found wandering, or one that is lost or homeless.

streak [streek] *noun, plural* **streaks. 1.** a long, thin line or mark that has a different color or texture from its background: *At the end of the football game, my uniform was covered in streaks of mud.* **2.** a small amount; trace: *Mom kids me that I have a stubborn streak like my dad.* 3. a brief period of time or a brief series: *The racing driver had a winning streak going and had won five races in a row.* *verb,* **streaked, streaking. 1.** to mark something with streaks. **2.** to move very fast: *The horse streaked to the finish line and won by two lengths.*

stream [streem] *noun, plural* **streams. 1.** a body of water flowing over the earth; a creek. **2.** a steady flow of people or things: *A stream of traffic traveled along the freeway.* *verb,* **streamed, streaming. 1.** to flow steadily; pour: *People streamed out of the stadium at the end of the game.* **2.** to trail out or wave in the air: *My kite streamed in the strong wind.*

stream·lined [streem-lined] *adjective.* **1.** shaped so as to move easily through air or water: *The motor boat had a long, low, streamlined shape.* **2.** made simpler so as to be more efficient: *The club's streamlined procedures make it easier for people who want to join.*

street [street] *noun, plural* **streets.** a public way or road in a town or city, often with sidewalks.

street·car ▶ [street-kar] *noun, plural* **streetcars.** a vehicle for carrying passengers that runs on rails laid in a public road. Streetcars usually operate on city streets.

strength [strengkth] *noun, plural* **strengths. 1.** the state or quality of being strong; power; force: *An elephant has huge strength and can uproot a small tree with its trunk.* **2.** the power to stand up to force or strain: *Our tent is made of a new, lightweight material that has great strength.* **3.** the degree to which something is strong or has power or is effective; intensity: *The strength of this liquid cleaner means that you need to use only a small amount.*

strength·en [strengk-thun] *verb,* **strengthened, strengthening.** to make or become stronger: *Horseback riding strengthens your leg muscles.*

stren·u·ous [stren-yoo-us] *adjective.* **1.** very active; energetic: *Despite our strenuous efforts, we couldn't finish painting the room in one day.* **2.** needing or using great energy or effort: *My dad likes to keep fit with strenuous sports like skiing and rowing.*

stress [stres] *noun, plural* **stresses. 1.** a force that acts on something, such as by pushing against it, pulling or pressing on it, or twisting or squeezing it: *The stress of heavy trucks traveling up and down the road eventually caused cracks in the surface.* **2.** special importance; emphasis: *My parents put great stress on being kind to others.* **3.** the extra force with which you pronounce certain syllables or words: *When you say the word "stretcher," the stress is on the first syllable.* **4.** Health. the state of feeling tense, disturbed, or under pressure because of worries or too much work. This kind of stress can be harmful to health. *verb,* **stressed, stressing. 1.** to place special importance on; emphasize: *Mom stressed that I must be home by five o'clock.* **2.** to pronounce a syllable or word with extra force: *When you say the word "begin," you stress the second syllable.*

stretch [strech] *verb,* **stretched, stretching. 1.** to push out the arms or legs or the whole body to full length: *After sitting at my computer for an hour, I had to stand up and stretch.* **2.** to reach; extend: *The area of the park stretches all the way from here to the river.* **3.** to spread out by pulling, or to become spread out in this way when pulled: *The fabric that my jeans are made of has elastic in it so that it stretches.* *noun, plural* **stretches. 1.** an unbroken area of land or water or period of time: *This stretch of coastline is famous for its beaches.* **2.** the act of stretching.

stretch·er ◀ [strech-ur] *noun, plural* **stretchers.** a device similar to a cot used to carry a sick or injured person. The simplest stretcher is a piece of canvas stretched between two poles.

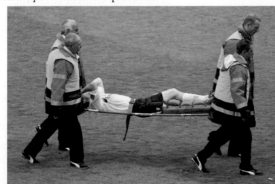

*When players are badly injured during a game, they are carried from the field on a **stretcher**.*

strick·en [strik-un] *verb.* the past participle of STRIKE. *adjective.* showing the effects of being overcome by illness, bad luck, or sorrow: *When she heard that her cat had been run over, her face had a stricken look.*

strict [strikt] *adjective,* **stricter, strictest. 1.** obeying rules or following instructions carefully and exactly, or demanding that this be done: *My parents are strict about good table manners.* **2.** needing to be followed or enforced carefully and exactly: *This restaurant has a strict policy of no smoking.* **3.** describing something complete; absolute: *We made plans for mom's surprise birthday party in strict secrecy.* —**strictly,** *adverb;* —**strictness,** *noun.*

stride [stride] *verb,* **strode, stridden, striding.** to walk with long, firm steps: *The customer was annoyed at being kept waiting and turned on her heel to stride out of the store.* *noun, plural* **strides. 1.** a long step, or the distance covered in a long step. **2.** a step forward; progress; improvement: *Our town has made great strides in attracting tourists over the last few years.*

strife [strife] *noun.* **1.** very serious disagreement between people, sometimes leading to violence; conflict: *The country has a history of strife caused by different groups trying to seize power.* **2.** a struggle or fight: *There was strife outside the bar and the police were called.*

strike [strike] *verb,* **struck, struck** or **stricken.** **1.** to deliver a blow to; hit: *The falling rock struck the climber on the arm.* **2.** to impress in a certain way; make a strong impression on: *My friend's behavior struck me as odd.* Something that makes a strong impression or attracts attention is **striking. 3.** to come upon; discover: *to strike gold; to strike oil.* **4.** to produce fire by scratching or rubbing: *Dad struck a match and lit the campfire.* **5.** of a clock or watch, to indicate the time by sounding: *The grandfather clock struck seven.* **6.** *Business.* to stop work in order to force an employer to meet demands for such things as better pay or working conditions. *noun, plural* **strikes. 1.** *Business.* the stopping of work to gain certain demands: *The factory workers went on strike for better pay.* **2.** a sudden discovery: *The huge gold strike was reported on the front page of the newspaper.* **3.** a pitch in baseball that passes through the strike zone without being hit, or that the batter swings at and either misses or hits foul.

strike·out [strike-out] *noun.* an out called in baseball when a batter has made three strikes.
• **strike out. 1.** to make or cause to make an out in baseball by a strikeout: *The pitcher struck the batter out with a curve.* **2.** to fail to do something, as if striking out in baseball. **3.** to set out on a course of action: *My aunt left her firm and struck out on her own as an architect.*

Some kinds of **string beans** *grow on climbing plants that are trained on frameworks of poles.*

string [string] *noun, plural* **strings. 1.** a thin cord mainly used to fasten or tie something: *I tied up the package with string.* **2.** one of the tightly stretched pieces of gut, wire, or cord on a musical instrument that produce a sound when plucked, struck, or played with a bow. The stringed instruments of an orchestra, as a group, are called the **strings.** *verb,* **stringed, stringing. 1.** to thread on a string: *I strung beads and feathers on nylon thread to make a necklace.* **2.** to equip with strings: *The man at the sporting goods store strung my tennis racket for me.* **3.** to stretch something from one point to another like a string: *Mom strung a washing line between two trees in our yard.*

string bean ◀ any of various beans with a long, green pod. String beans are cooked and eaten whole while they are still young and their seeds are very small.

strip¹ [strip] *verb,* **stripped, stripping. 1.** to take clothing or a covering off someone or something; undress. **2.** to remove a covering layer: *We stripped the old wallpaper from the wall.*

strip² [strip] *noun, plural* **strips.** a long, narrow piece or area: *a strip of paper; a strip of land.*

stripe [stripe] *noun, plural* **stripes.** a long, narrow band or strip that has a different color, appearance, or texture from the surface on either side of it: *The American flag has red and white stripes.* *verb,* **striped, striping.** to mark with a stripe or stripes.

strive [strive] *verb,* **strove** or **strived, striven** or **strived, striving.** to try hard; do all one can: *I strive to do my best at school.*

stroke¹ [stroke] *noun, plural* **strokes. 1.** the act of striking, especially with a weapon or instrument; a hit or blow: *The carpenter drove the nail home with just two strokes of the hammer.* **2.** a mark made by a single movement of a pen, pencil, or brush: *With a few strokes of his pencil, the artist produced a good likeness of her.* **3.** *Health.* a sudden weakness or loss of consciousness, or a state of being unable to feel or move, caused when the blood supply to the brain is interrupted, such as by a blood clot. **4.** the combination of arm and leg movements used in particular styles of swimming: *Freestyle is the fastest swimming stroke.* **5.** an unexpected action or event: *By a stroke of luck they found her lost ring in the sand.*

stroke² [stroke] *verb.* to rub gently or move the hand gently along something in one direction: *I stroked the kitten.*

stroll [strole] *verb,* **strolled, strolling.** to walk in a relaxed, slow way: *We strolled alongside the lake, looking at the sailing boats.* *noun, plural* **strolls.** a relaxed, leisurely walk.

stroll·er [strole-ur] *noun, plural* **strollers. 1.** someone who strolls. **2.** a small carriage in which a baby or small child can be pushed along.

The Burj Al Arab hotel in Dubai, United Arab Emirates, is an unusual **structure** in the shape of a billowing sail.

stuff

strong [strong] *adjective,* **stronger, strongest.**
1. having great physical power, strength, or energy, as to lift or move things: *Two strong men were needed to move the heavy sofa.*
2. having much more than the usual power or force for its kind: *a storm with strong winds; a cheese with a strong taste.* **3.** able to resist; not easily damaged or overcome: *This hammock is made of strong material; That actor always plays a strong character who does the right thing no matter how difficult it is.* —**strongly,** *adverb.*

struc·ture ▶ [struk-chur] *noun,*
plural **structures. 1.** something that is built or constructed. Houses, bridges, and sports stadiums are examples of structures. **2.** an arrangement of parts, or the way the parts of something are arranged: *In our English class we learned about the basic structure of a sentence.*
verb, **structured, structuring.** to give a structure to or give form to; organize: *I structured my story with a beginning, a middle, and an end.*

strug·gle [strug-ul] *verb,* **struggled, struggling. 1.** to make one's way with difficulty or with a great effort: *The hikers struggled up the hill with their heavy backpacks.* **2.** to make a great effort to overcome someone or something; fight; battle: *The police officer struggled with the bank robber.*
noun, plural **struggles. 1.** a great effort: *I found it a struggle to stay awake during the boring movie.*
2. a fight, battle, or contest.

strum [strum] *verb,* **strummed, strumming.** *Music.* to play a stringed instrument, such as a guitar, by brushing the strings with the fingers, especially in a casual or not very skilled way: *I sometimes try to make up songs as I strum on my guitar.*

strut [strut] *verb,* **strutted, strutting.** to walk in a stiff, proud way so as to draw attention to oneself or impress others, or to parade something such as clothes: *The models strutted up and down the runway.*

stub [stub] *noun, plural* **stubs.** a short piece of something left after the rest has been used up or broken off: *a pencil stub; a cigar stub.*
verb, **stubbed, stubbing.** to strike one's toe or foot against something that is sticking out: *I stubbed my toe on a rock.*

stub·born [stub-urn] *adjective.* **1.** hard to persuade or move; not willing to yield: *She is too stubborn to admit that she doesn't like the color she painted her room.*
2. hard to handle or manage: *I have stubborn hair that always sticks up, so I have it cut short.*
—**stubbornly,** *adverb;* —**stubbornness,** *noun.*

stuck [stuk] *verb.* the past tense and past participle of STICK.

stud[1] [stud] *noun, plural* **studs. 1.** an upright support in the framework of a building to which wall materials are attached. **2.** a small knob or a solid button with a curved surface used as decoration or as a fastener: *My favorite belt is decorated with a row of silver studs.*

stud[2] [stud] *noun, plural* **studs.** a male animal kept for breeding: *My uncle breeds racehorses and has a champion stud that is worth a lot of money.*

stu·dent [stood-unt] *noun, plural* **students.**
1. someone who goes to school or college: *How many students does this school have?*
2. someone who studies something: *My grandpa says that he has been a student of human nature all his life.*

stu·di·o ▼ [stoo-dee-oh] *noun,*
plural **studios. 1.** the working place of an artist or craftsperson: *a painter's studio.* **2.** a place where motion pictures are made. **3.** a place where radio or television programs are recorded or broadcast.

stud·y [stud-ee] *verb,* **studied, studying.**
1. to learn about something by reading, thinking, and gathering information about it or by examining it closely: *In our history class we studied the Revolutionary War.* Someone who likes studying or spends a lot of time studying is described as being **studious. 2.** to give close attention to; examine: *I studied the instructions for using our new DVD recorder.*
noun, plural **studies. 1.** the act or process of studying: *I usually do an hour's study before dinner.* **2.** a close examination or investigation of something: *The committee made a study of the changes proposed to the club's constitution.* **3.** something that is studied; a subject: *My cousin is majoring in computer studies at college.*
4. a room used for studying, reading, or writing: *My dad is an engineer and his study is filled with engineering books.*

stuff [stuf] *noun.* **1.** the material that something is made of, or material that can be used to make or do something: *Mom and I went to the store to buy the fabric and other stuff we need to make a quilt.* **2.** things that are useless or of little worth: *Let's clear the basement of all this old stuff.* **3.** things in general: *You can leave your stuff in my locker for now.*
verb, **stuffed, stuffing.**
1. to fill or pack tightly: *I stuffed the trunk with my old toys and games.*
2. to force in; jam; cram: *I stuffed my socks and scarves into the drawer.*
3. to eat too much: *I stuffed myself at lunch and don't feel like eating any dinner.* **4.** to fill out the skin of a dead animal or bird to restore its original shape and make it look lifelike.
5. to fill something with stuffing, such as a food to be cooked or a cushion.

Painters need plenty of natural light in their **studios.**

stuff·ing [stuf-ing] *noun, plural* **stuffings.** material used to fill or pack something: *Mom uses nuts and herbs in the stuffing she makes for turkey.*

stuf·fy [stuf-ee] *adjective,* **stuffier, stuffiest. 1.** lacking fresh air; close: *The house was stuffy when we got back home from our vacation.* **2.** describing something dull and uninteresting; boring: *The guest speaker's manner was so stuffy that the audience kept coughing and looking at their watches.*

stum·ble [stum-bul] *verb* **stumbled, stumbling. 1.** to trip and almost fall: *I stumbled over the crack in the pavement.* **2.** to speak or act in an uncertain or clumsy way: *We stumbled around in the dark basement looking for the light switch.* **3.** to come upon unexpectedly or by chance: *We stumbled on an old-fashioned ice cream parlor that sells delicious sundaes.*

stump [stump] *noun, plural* **stumps. 1.** the part of a tree trunk left in the ground when the top has broken off or been cut off. **2.** the part of anything else left after the rest has been cut off or has worn down: *By the end of the meal, the candle had burned down to a small stump.* *verb,* **stumped, stumping.** to be too hard for someone; baffle; puzzle: *One of the quiz questions stumped me and I had to take a wild guess at the answer.*

stun [stun] *verb,* **stunned, stunning. 1.** to knock someone or something unconscious, or make someone or something dizzy: *A tennis ball hit me on the head and stunned me.* **2.** to cause astonishment or shock: *The announcement that she had won the singing competition stunned her.* Something that stuns, or someone or something that is extremely attractive or impressive, is described as being **stunning:** *The actress wore a stunning evening gown.*

stunt[1] [stunt] *noun, plural* **stunts.** an unusual or daring act done for entertainment or sometimes to gain attention or publicity.

stunt[2] [stunt] *verb,* **stunted, stunting.** to hold back the development or growth of something: *Being grown in too small a container stunts a plant's growth.*

stu·pid [stoo-pid] *adjective,* **stupider, stupidest.** lacking intelligence or common sense; not smart or clever; foolish: *It was stupid of me to go out in the rain without my raincoat.* The state or an instance of lacking cleverness or common sense, or of being foolish, is **stupidity.** —**stupidly,** *adverb.*

stur·dy [stur-dee] *adjective,* **sturdier, sturdiest.** strongly built or made; hardy: *This is a sturdy table, made to last a lifetime.*

stur·geon ▶ [stur-jun] *noun, plural* **sturgeons.** a large fish with a long body like a shark and a thick skin covered with rows of bony, plate-like scales. It is used for food and is especially valued for its eggs, which are made into a very expensive food called caviar.

stut·ter [stut-ur] *verb,* **stuttered, stuttering.** *Language.* to have difficulty making or controlling some sounds when one speaks. Someone who stutters keeps repeating certain sounds, especially the sounds at the beginning of words.

sty[1] [stye] *noun, plural* **sties.** *Health.* a small, sore, red swelling on the edge of the eyelid, caused by an infection.

sty[2] [stye] *noun,* **sties.** a pen or enclosed area for pigs; a pigpen.

style [stile] *noun, plural* **styles. 1.** a particular way of speaking, writing, or performing: *Impressionism is a style of painting; That dancer has an energetic style that is all his own.* **2.** the current fashion: *Simple shapes in bright colors are the style this summer.* **3.** a beautiful, elegant, or excellent quality or manner: *With her elegant clothes and good grooming, she is a person of style.*

A writer's **style** is the special way this person has of using words that is different from other writers. Some famous writers use a plain style with simple words and short sentences. This has been called the "Hemingway style," after the author Ernest Hemingway who became known for writing this way. Other authors have a more complicated style, using longer sentences and more unusual words to give a lot of detail. There is no rule to say that either one of these is right or wrong. However, for a student writer the plain or Hemingway style is probably a better choice.

sty·lish [stile-ish] *adjective.* showing a popular current style; fashionable: *That's a very stylish outfit you are wearing.* —**stylishly,** *adverb.*

sub [sub] **1.** the shortened form of SUBMARINE. **2.** the shortened form of SUBSTITUTE.

sub- a prefix that means under, beneath, or below: *a subway* is an underground railway; *subfreezing* temperatures are temperatures below the freezing point.

sub·di·vide [sub-duh-vide] *verb,* **subdivided, subdividing. 1.** to divide something already divided into more parts. **2.** to divide an area of land into lots for sale: *The land was subdivided and sold as building lots.* A **subdivision** is an area of land that has been divided into lots for sale.

sub·due [sub-doo] *verb,* **subdued, subduing. 1.** to overcome or bring under control; defeat; conquer: *The government soldiers subdued the rebels.* **2.** to make less intense; tone down; soften: *We subdued our laughter so as not to seem impolite.*

sub·ject [sub-jikt *for noun;* sub-jekt *for verb*] *plural* **subjects. 1.** the person or thing being talked or written about: *The subject of my speech is my favorite movie.* **2.** *Language.* the word or words in a sentence naming the person or thing that the sentence tells about. The subject of a sentence usually comes before the verb. In the sentence *My cat likes milk,* "my cat" is the subject. **3.** a field of study: *The subjects I like best in school are history and biology.* **4.** someone under the control or authority of another, or who owes loyalty to a ruler or government: *The king waved to his subjects from his carriage.* **5.** a person or thing that is studied or

The giant **sturgeon** *grows up to nineteen feet long and can live for 150 years.*

sub·merge ◀ [sub-<u>murj</u>] *verb,* **submerged,
submerging. 1.** to cover or overflow with water,
or to put under water or another liquid:
*When the dam wall broke, the waters of the lake
submerged the surrounding land.* **2.** to go under
water: *The submarine quickly submerged
when the enemy planes approached.*

sub·mit [sub-<u>mit</u>] *verb,* **submitted,
submitting. 1.** to yield to someone's
power or authority; stop resisting:
*The employer submitted to his
workers' demands for more pay.*
2. to hand in; present:
*I submitted my book report
a few days before it was due.*

sub·or·di·nate [suh-<u>bord</u>-un-it]
adjective. of lower rank or
importance: *A police sergeant
is subordinate to a captain.*
A **subordinate clause** is
a clause that qualifies the main
clause in a sentence. In the sentence *We'll go to the movies
if it rains*, the main clause is "We'll go to the movies,"
and "if it rains" is a subordinate clause.
noun. a person or thing of lower rank or importance:
*The company president is a popular manager because
he treats all his subordinates with respect.*
verb, **subordinated, subordinating.** to make lower in rank
or importance.

sub·scribe [sub-<u>skribe</u>] *verb,* **subscribed, subscribing.
1.** to put your name down to receive and pay for
a publication or service, especially a regular publication
like a magazine: *My mom subscribes to a monthly
scrapbooking magazine.* **2.** to make it known that
you agree to or approve of something: *We don't subscribe
to the old idea that children should be seen and not heard.*

sub·scrip·tion [sub-<u>skrip</u>-shun] *noun, plural* **subscriptions.**
an agreement to receive and pay for something for a set
period, especially a regular publication like a magazine:
*My parents have a subscription to a magazine about
national parks.*

used in experiments:
*They each took turns
at being the subject and
the experimenter in the
experiment on sound.*
adjective. **1.** under the control
of, or owing loyalty or obedience
to, another: *Citizens of a country are
subject to its laws.* **2.** liable to be affected by or to
have; inclined to: *He is subject to fits of sulking when he
doesn't get his own way.* **3.** depending upon: *We will arrive
at eleven o'clock, subject to the train not being delayed.*
verb, **subjected, subjecting. 1.** to bring under control
or force to accept authority; rule. **2.** to cause or force
to experience: *The storm subjected the townspeople
to devastating floods.*

In student writing, the **subject** of a paper (what it tells about)
may be assigned by the teacher, or it may be up to you to pick
the subject. For example, for a book report you may choose
which book to read, or for a biography you may choose which
person to write about. It's a good idea to choose a subject that
interests you personally, rather than one you think your teacher
or other readers would like but that doesn't especially interest
you. You should also try to choose a subject that is the right
size for your paper. For example, "Birds" is a very big subject
for a science paper. "Western Screech Owls" on the other
hand is a bit narrow. "Owls" is about right.

sub·jec·tive [sub-<u>jek</u>-tiv] *adjective.* expressing one's
personal feelings and opinions; not objective: *The art
teacher asked us to look at the painting and give our
subjective opinion of it.* —**subjectively,** *adverb.*

sub·mar·ine ▼ [<u>sub</u>-muh-<u>reen</u>] *noun, plural* **submarines.
1.** a type of boat that can travel under water, especially
one designed for use by the navy as a warship. **2.** a type
of sandwich made with a long roll split in half lengthwise.
adjective. living or lying under the sea or some other body
of water: *Submarine plants are
plants that live under water.*

*This B-39 attack **submarine** was part of the Soviet
Pacific fleet from the 1970s to the 1990s and was
one of the largest conventionally powered
submarines ever built.*

sub·se·quent [sub-suh-kwunt] *adjective.* coming after in time, order, or place; later: *At the restaurant a soda costs $1.50, but you can get subsequent refills for free.* —**subsequently,** *adverb.*

sub·side [sub-side] *verb,* **subsided, subsiding. 1.** to go down or fall to a lower level; sink down: *The flood waters subsided after a few days.* **2.** to become less or quiet: *My nervousness subsided once I spoke my first words on the stage.*

sub·sid·i·ar·y [sub-sid-ee-er-ee] *adjective.* of secondary importance; lower in rank.
noun, plural **subsidiaries.** *Business.* a company that is owned by a larger company: *The book publishing company in Canada is a subsidiary of a company in the United States.*

sub·si·dy [sub-suh-dee] *noun, plural* **subsidies. 1.** *Business.* a payment of money from the government to a private business: *In some countries, farmers may be paid a subsidy to grow or not grow certain crops.* **2.** a gift of money from one individual or group to another: *Some wealthy companies provide subsidies to charities.* To support individuals or organizations by providing money is to **subsidize** them.

sub·stance [sub-stuns] *noun, plural* **substances. 1.** the matter or material that makes up something: *Wood is the main substance in pencils.* **2.** a certain kind of matter or material: *There was a liquid substance on my desk.* **3.** the most basic and important part of something: *The substance of the story is the love between a boy and his dog.*

sub·stan·tial [sub-stan-shul] *adjective.* **1.** being a large or significant amount: *There was substantial evidence of a break-in; They inherited a substantial fortune.* **2.** in good condition; solid and strong: *The farm has a substantial barn as well as several sheds.* **3.** factual and real; not imaginary. —**substantially,** *adverb.*

sub·sti·tute [sub-stuh-toot] *noun, plural* **substitutes. 1.** someone or something that takes the place of another: *I used lemon juice as a substitute for vinegar in the salad dressing.* **2.** in sports, a player who goes into a game in place of another.
verb, **substituted, substituting. 1.** to put someone or something in the place of another: *To lose weight I am substituting regular milk with low-fat milk.* **2.** to replace someone or something: *My mom substituted for the teacher who was sick.*

sub·sti·tu·tion [sub-stuh-too-shun] *noun, plural* **substitutions.** the act of replacing one with another: *The coach made a smart substitution when he took out the starting quarterback and put in his backup.*

sub·tle [sut-ul] *adjective,* **subtler, subtlest. 1.** not easy to sense or notice; not obvious: *There is a subtle difference between the words "childish" and "childlike;" The beautiful flowers gave off a subtle perfume.* **2.** not open or direct; sly or cunning: *The young lawyer was subtle in his questioning of the witness.* An action that is subtle shows **subtlety.** —**subtly,** *adverb.*

sub·tract [sub-trakt] *verb,* **subtracted, subtracting. 1.** *Mathematics.* to take away one number from another: *If you subtract 9 from 24, the result is 15.* **2.** to take away from a greater or whole amount: *When you subtract all the time he spent on his lunch break, he worked only a few hours.*

sub·trac·tion [sub-trak-shun] *noun, plural* **subtractions.** *Mathematics.* the process of taking one number from another to find the difference between them. This is expressed as an equation using minus and equal signs. $10 - 5 = 5$ is an example of subtraction.

sub·tra·hend [sub-truh-hend] *noun, plural* **subtrahends.** *Mathematics.* the number that is taken away from another number in subtraction. When you subtract 2 from 5, the number 2 is the subtrahend.

sub·urb [sub-urb] *noun, plural* **suburbs.** an area, community, or district where people live, work, and shop that is separate from but near a larger city: *We live in the suburbs and my parents take the train into town to go to work.* Things relating to the suburbs are described as **suburban.**

sub·way ▼ [sub-way] *noun, plural* **subways.** a train system powered by electricity that runs under the ground or mostly underground. Many large cities in North America have subway systems.

*The **subway** in Berlin, Germany, is the city's main form of public transportation.*

suc·ceed [suk-seed] *verb,* **succeeded, succeeding. 1.** to achieve a goal; do well; have a good outcome: *I succeeded in saving enough money to buy the bike I wanted.* **2.** to follow someone in taking up their position; take over from: *When the principal became sick and left the school, the assistant principal succeeded him.*

suc·cess [suk-ses] *noun, plural* **successes. 1.** the achievement of a goal; a good outcome in something that has been desired or attempted: *After years of trying to breed goldfish, we have finally had success.* **2.** someone who achieves a goal or something that does well: *My uncle's book about fishing is a success and has had large sales.*

suc·cess·ful [suk-ses-ful] *adjective.* reaching a desired goal; having success: *She was successful in her effort to complete a marathon run; The new company has become successful and plans to move to a new office and hire more workers.* —**successfully,** *adverb.*

suc·ces·sion [suk-<u>sesh</u>-un] *noun, plural* **successions.**
1. people or things that come after one another:
A succession of planes took off from the airport runway.
2. the process of coming after something or someone
else: *The wedding cars left the church in succession.*
Following one after the other is described as **successive.**
—**successively,** *adverb.*

suc·ces·sor [suk-<u>ses</u>-ur] *noun, plural* **successors.** someone
or something that follows or replaces another: *The senior
team captain made a farewell speech and welcomed in
her successor.*

such [such] *adjective.* **1.** of a certain kind; of this kind:
*We've never had such cold weather as this winter; They
were looking for Edgar Avenue, but there's no such street
around here.* **2.** of the kind just mentioned; similar to:
*The markets sold pottery, handmade jewelry, and other
such items.* **3.** so much: *It was such a great honor to meet
the President.*
pronoun. someone or something of a particular kind:
We need pieces of paper, paints, and such for the posters.

suck [suk] *verb,* **sucked, sucking. 1.** to draw something into
the mouth using the tongue, lips, and an inward breath:
I sucked the water through the straw. **2.** to hold something
in the mouth and lick it: *I sucked on a candy to clear my
ears as the plane took off.* **3.** to draw something out of
or from: *The vacuum cleaner sucked the dog hair out
of the carpet.*

suc·tion [suk-shun] *noun. Science.* the force that draws
something into an empty space: *Our vacuum cleaner
has lost its suction.*

sud·den [<u>sud</u>-un] *adjective.* happening quickly and
without warning; not expected: *There was a sudden
explosion; He made a sudden decision to turn the car
around and head back home.* —**suddenly,** *adverb;*
—**suddenness,** *noun.*

suds [sudz] *plural noun.* water mixed with soap; the bubbles
that form on top of soapy water.

sue [soo] *verb,* **sued, suing.** *Law.* to take action against
someone by bringing a case or complaint against the
person in a court of law.

suede [swade] *noun, plural* **suedes.** a leather that has been
rubbed to make it soft and velvety, or another material
that is similar to this.

su·et [<u>soo</u>-it] *noun.* hard fat from the body of cattle and
sheep, used in cooking and in making candles and soap.

suf·fer [<u>suf</u>-ur] *verb,* **suffered, suffering. 1.** to feel pain
or sadness: *He was suffering from the flu.* **2.** to have a bad
or unpleasant experience: *She suffered a broken leg in
the accident.* **3.** to become worse; be hurt or damaged:
*Brad's been working much too hard and his health has
suffered.* The experience of physical, mental, or emotional
pain or discomfort is **suffering.**

suf·fi·cient [suh-<u>fish</u>-unt] *adjective.* as much as needed;
enough: *There was sufficient food for everyone.*
The state of being or having enough is **sufficiency.**
—**sufficiently,** *adverb.*

suf·fix [<u>suf</u>-iks] *noun, plural* **suffixes.** *Language.* a syllable or
combination of syllables that is added to the end of a word
to make a new word with a similar but slightly different
meaning. The word *golden* is made up of the word *gold*
and the suffix *-en.*

suf·fo·cate [<u>suf</u>-uh-*kate*] *verb,* **suffocated, suffocating.
1.** to die or cause to die from lack of air. **2.** to be kept from
fresh air or from breathing easily: *I felt I was suffocating in
the hot, crowded hall.* **3.** to have a feeling of being closed
in or held back, as if being unable to breathe.

suf·frage [<u>suf</u>-rij] *noun. Government.* the right to vote,
particularly in public elections.

sug·ar [<u>shug</u>-ur] *noun, plural* **sugars.** a sweet substance that
comes mainly from SUGARCANE and **sugar beets** and that
is generally used to flavor food. Something that contains
a great deal of sugar is described as **sugary.**

sug·ar·cane ▲ [<u>shug</u>-ur-*kane*] *noun.* a tall, tough grass
that grows in tropical and subtropical regions and that
is a major source of sugar.

sug·gest [sug-<u>jest</u>] *verb,* **suggested, suggesting. 1.** to put
forward an idea or plan for someone to think about:
I suggested the name "Rex" for our new puppy. **2.** to bring
to mind by having the same qualities or being similar to:
*The leaf pattern in the material suggests the season
of autumn.* **3.** to indirectly bring to mind; hint: *Staring
into the refrigerator suggests you are hungry.*

sug·ges·tion [sug-<u>jes</u>-chun] *noun, plural* **suggestions.
1.** the act of suggesting something; putting forward an idea
or plan for consideration: *She made the suggestion that
we stop the car for lunch at the next rest area.* **2.** a hint or
trace; a small amount: *The weather's been cold and rainy,
without even a suggestion that spring is on the way.*

a
b
c
d
e
f
g
h
i
j
k
l
m
n
o
p
q
r
s
t
u
v
w
x
y
z

Sultan Beyazit was a ruler of the Ottoman Empire during the Middle Ages.

su·i·cide [soo-uh-*side*] *noun, plural* **suicides. 1.** the act of killing oneself on purpose. **2.** someone who has intentionally killed himself or herself.

suit [soot] *noun, plural* **suits. 1.** a set of clothes designed to be worn together. A suit is usually made up of a jacket with matching trousers or skirt. **2.** *Law.* an action in a court of law: *The suit charges that the company illegally dumped harmful chemicals into a nearby river.* **3.** one of the four sets of playing cards in a pack: *The suits are clubs, heart, spades, and diamonds.* *verb,* **suited, suiting. 1.** to meet the needs of; fit; match: *The climate here is well suited to growing fruits and vegetables.* **2.** to be acceptable or convenient to: *You can have either chicken or fish, whichever suits you.* **3.** to look attractive: *The color blue suits you.*

suit·a·ble [soo-tuh-bul] *adjective.* being the right type or having appropriate qualities to fit a situation or purpose: *I am trying to find a gift that is suitable for my best friend.* **—suitably,** *adverb.*

suit·case [soot-*kase*] *noun, plural* **suitcases.** a flat, often rectangular bag for carrying clothes and other personal items when traveling.

suite ▼ [sweet] *noun, plural* **suites. 1.** a set of rooms that are connected: *Our family stayed in a suite at the hotel.* **2.** several things that match: *In our new house we each got a suite of furniture for our bedroom.*

sul·fur [sul-fur] *noun. Chemistry.* a substance in the form of pale yellow crystals used in making matches, gunpowder, and fertilizer. Sulfur is one of the chemical elements. This word is also spelled **sulphur.** **—sulfuric,** *adjective.*

> **Sulfur** was one of the first chemicals to become known to people in ancient times. Its name at that time was *brimstone*, which meant "a burning stone." It got this name because sulfur burns very easily. The word *brimstone* is not used in modern English, but it is often found in the Bible and other ancient writings.

sulfur dioxide *Chemistry.* a colorless, poisonous gas formed during the burning of fuels containing sulfur, such as coal. Sulfur dioxide is used as a preservative and sterilizing agent.

sulfuric acid *Chemistry.* a colorless, corrosive acid made from sulfur dioxide. Sulfuric acid is used in making fertilizers, dyes, and industrial explosives.

sulk [sulk] *verb,* **sulked, sulking.** to express feelings of anger or resentment by refusing to talk; be in a bad mood: *The teenager sulked when her parents said she couldn't go to the party.* *noun, plural* **sulks.** an angry and silent mood.

sul·len [sul-un] *adjective.* **1.** silently angry or resentful: *She gave the teacher a sullen look.* **2.** describing something dull, dark, or gloomy.

sul·tan ◀ [sult-un] *noun, plural* **sultans.** *History.* a former title for the ruler of a Muslim country: *The Ottoman Empire was ruled by sultans.*

sul·try [sul-tree] *adjective.* uncomfortably hot and damp: *The summer nights were so sultry I couldn't sleep.*

sum [sum] *noun, plural* **sums. 1.** *Mathematics.* the number or amount that comes from adding numbers or amounts together: *The sum of 5 and 10 is 15.* **2.** an amount of money: *We paid the Girl Scouts the sum of $5.00 for washing our car.*
• **sum up.** to give a review or shortened version; summarize: *The teacher asked us to sum up what we had learned in the lesson.*

su·mac [soo-mak] *noun.* a small tree or shrub with feathery leaves and clusters of red or whitish berries. Some kinds are known as **poison sumac** because they contain a substance that is poisonous to humans.

sum·mar·ize [sum-ur-*ize*] *verb,* **summarized, summarizing.** to make a summary of; to give a short overview containing the main points: *In my report on the movie, I summarized the action that took place in it.*

sum·mar·y [sum-ur-ee] *noun, plural* **summaries.** a shortened version, containing only the most important points: *At the end of each chapter there is a one-paragraph summary of what has been discussed in that chapter.*

When you write a paper, you often have to provide a **summary** of what you have written at the end. When you do this, you don't need to repeat the facts or ideas you have given earlier in the paper. You just need a short, simple statement that ties together these facts or ideas in a clear way. For example, you might write a paper about your dog and describe several things that he (or she) does. Then you can summarize by saying something like, "That's why I call him my good friend" or "She doesn't try to be funny, she just is."

The pieces of a lounge **suite** *are designed in the same style and color.*

sum·mer [sum-ur] *noun, plural* **summers.** the season of the year between spring and autumn, when days are the longest and the weather is warmest.
verb, **summered, summering.** to spend the summer somewhere: *We summer with our cousins at the beach.*

sum·mit [sum-it] *noun, plural* **summits.** the highest part; the top of something: *We reached the summit of the mountain just at sunset.*

sum·mon [sum-un] *verb,* **summoned, summoning.**
1. to ask to come: *The teacher summoned the parents of the naughty students.* **2.** to stir up; arouse: *The coach asked us to summon all our strength for the game.*

sum·mons [sum-unz] *noun, plural* **summonses.** *Law.* a written order to appear before a court to answer a complaint.

sun ▶ [sun] *noun.* **1.** the star at the center of our solar system that gives heat and light to the Earth and other planets revolving around it. This meaning is also spelled **Sun. 2.** another such star in a different solar system. **3.** the heat and light that comes from the sun: *I love the sun on my skin.*
verb, **sunned, sunning.** to bask in the heat and light of the sun: *Our cat is sunning himself on the back porch.*

sun·bathe [sun-*bayTH*] *verb,* **sunbathed, sunbathing.** to lie in the sun: *We like to sunbathe at the pool.*
—sunbather, *noun.*

Sun Belt *Geography.* an area of the United States stretching across the South and Southwest, thought of as having more sunny weather than other parts of the country.

sun·burn [sun-*burn*] *noun, plural* **sunburns.** *Health.* redness and soreness of the skin caused by the rays of the sun.
verb, **sunburned or sunburnt, sunburning.** to suffer redness and soreness of the skin from exposure to the sun.

sun·dae [sun-day] *noun, plural* **sundaes.** ice cream topped with syrup, fruits, chopped nuts, and sometimes whipped cream.

The type of dessert known as a **sundae** is connected to the word *Sunday,* a day of the week. It is not known for sure what the connection is, but it is thought that it comes from the idea that a sundae was a special food to be eaten only on this day.

Sun·day [sun-day *or* sun-dee] *noun, plural* **Sundays.** the first day of the week.

sun·di·al ▼ [sun-*dye*-ul] *noun, plural* **sundials.** a device that shows the time of day, used to tell the time in the period before the invention of the modern clock. A central needle sticks out of a clock face and casts a shadow. As the sun moves across the sky, the shadow moves too, showing different times.

THE SUN

The Sun is a star around which the Earth and the other planets orbit. It gives us light and heat to grow food and keep warm. The Sun is not the largest star in our galaxy. It just seems big and bright because it is only 93 million miles away from the Earth. It is made up of gases, mostly hydrogen. Energy is produced in the core of the Sun and transferred to its surface through radiation and convection zones in its body.

INSIDE THE SUN

Convective zone, where energy is carried to the surface

Radiative zone, where energy is radiated outward from the core

Core, where energy is produced

The Sun compared to Jupiter, which is nearly twelve times the size of the Earth

Visible surface where sunspots and solar flares occur

The Sun and the planets that orbit it

sun·flow·er ▼ [sun-*flou*-ur] *noun, plural* **sunflowers.** a large, yellow flower with a brown center.

sung [sung] *verb.* the past tense and past participle of SING.

sun·glass·es [sun-*glas*-iz] *plural noun.* tinted glasses that protect the eyes from the sun's glare.

sunk [sungk] *verb.* the past tense and past participle of SINK.

sunk·en [sung-kun] *verb.* a past participle of SINK.
adjective. **1.** placed at a lower level than the surrounding area: *a sunken bathtub.* **2.** describing something deep under water: *sunken treasure.*

sun·light [sun-lite] *noun.* light from the sun.

sun·ny [sun-ee] *adjective.* **1.** filled with or bathed in sunlight: *a sunny day; a sunny room with large windows facing south.* **2.** happy or cheery: *a sunny smile.*

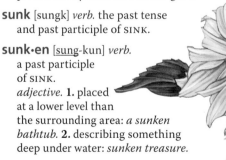

This old brass **sundial** *shows the time to be midday.*

Sunflowers *can grow as tall as ten feet.*

sun·rise ▲ [*sun-rize*] *noun, plural* **sunrises.** the rising of the sun above the horizon. This is also called **sunup.**

sun·screen [*sun-skreen*] *noun. Health.* a lotion that protects the skin from sunburn and the harmful effects of the sun.

sun·set [*sun-set*] *noun, plural* **sunsets.** the setting of the sun below the horizon. This is also called **sundown.**

sun·shine [*sun-shine*] *noun.* light and warmth that comes from the sun.

sun·spot [*sun-spot*] *noun, plural* **sunspots.** *Science.* an area on the surface of the sun that is cooler and darker than the surrounding matter.

sun·stroke [*sun-stroke*] *noun, plural* **sunstrokes.** *Health.* heat stroke caused by too much exposure to the sun. Symptoms include high temperature, convulsions, and coma.

su·per [*soo-pur*] *adjective.* an informal word describing something of superior size, quality, or importance: *The championship of pro football is known as the Super Bowl.*
noun. a shorter word for the superintendent of an office building or apartment.

su·perb [*suh-purb*] *adjective.* describing something excellent; really good: *Thank you for that superb dinner.* —**superbly,** *adverb.*

su·per·fi·cial [*soo-pur-fish-ul*] *adjective.* **1.** being on or near the surface of something: *The cut on her arm was superficial so it didn't need stitches.* **2.** not deep, sensitive, or thoughtful: *The actor played the role of a superficial character who took little interest in other people.* —**superficially,** *adverb.*

su·per·her·o [*soo-pur-heer-oh*] *noun, plural* **superheroes.** *Literature.* a character who has special powers and usually wears a mask or special clothes. Superheroes can do things like fly, lift really heavy things, or see through solid objects. They help ordinary people and fight evil.

su·per·in·ten·dent [*soop-run-ten-dunt or soo-pur-in-ten-dunt*] *noun, plural* **superintendents.**
1. a person who is in charge of something: *The superintendent of schools is in charge of all the schools in our county.* **2.** a person whose work is to clean and maintain a large building, such as a school, office building, or apartment house.

su·per·i·or [*suh-peer-ee-ur*] *adjective.* **1.** of the best quality; better or greater than others of its kind: *Those new homes have a superior grade of kitchen appliances; This airline has a superior record for the number of planes arriving on time.* The fact of being the best quality is **superiority. 2.** having a higher rank or position: *The soldiers had to obey the orders of their superior officer.* **3.** feeling oneself better than others; being snobbish and aloof: *She acts superior because her parents are rich.*
noun, plural **superiors.** someone in a higher position; a leader or boss.

su·per·lat·ive [*suh-pur-luh-tiv*] *adjective.* better than anything else; of the highest quality: *Coming first in every subject was a superlative achievement.*
noun, plural **superlatives.** the form of an adverb or adjective showing the highest degree of comparison. For example, *greatest* is the superlative of *great; fastest* is the superlative of *fast.* —**superlatively,** *adverb.*

su·per·mar·ket [*soo-pur-mar-kit*] *noun, plural* **supermarkets.** a very large food store where customers pick out their own items and then pay for them as they leave. Supermarkets sell many different kinds of food and other types of household goods.

su·per·nat·u·ral [*soo-pur-nach-ur-ul*] *adjective.* not able to be explained by the laws of nature: *Fairies and ghosts are supernatural beings.*
noun. a world apart from the physical world, with forces, effects, and beings that cannot be explained by the laws of nature. This is sometimes called **the supernatural.** —**supernaturally,** *adverb.*

su·per·son·ic ▶ [*soo-pur-son-ik*] *adjective. Science.* moving faster than the speed of sound: *a supersonic rocket.*

su·per·sti·tion [*soo-pur-stish-un*] *noun, plural* **superstitions.** a belief or idea that is not based on reason or knowledge, especially the idea that ordinary circumstances or events can affect the course of the future. Common superstitions include the idea that a person can have bad luck from the number thirteen, from walking under a ladder, or from breaking a mirror, or have good luck from the number seven or finding a four-leaf clover.

> The word **superstition** comes from an old phrase meaning "to stand over." What being superstitious has to do with standing is not clear. One idea is that a superstitious person thinks of something constantly standing over him—a god, luck, Fate, or whatever—and having an effect on what happens to him.

su·per·sti·tious [*soo-pur-stish-us*] *adjective.* describing someone who holds beliefs or ideas that are not based in reason or knowledge: *His superstitious sister thinks black cats bring bad luck.*

su·per·vise [<u>soo</u>-pur-*vize*] *verb*, **supervised, supervising.** to watch over and be in charge of something; direct or manage: *We get to write our own stories for the school paper, but the teacher supervises our work.* The fact of supervising another or others is **supervision.**

su·per·vi·sor [<u>soo</u>-pur-*vye*-zur] *noun, plural* **supervisors.** a person who supervises; someone who directs or manages the work or activity of others: *She wants to take off two days next week for vacation, but first it has to be approved by her supervisor.* Something having to do with the work or position of a supervisor is **supervisory.**

sup·per [<u>sup</u>-ur] *noun, plural* **suppers.** the last meal of the day, especially a lighter meal eaten in the evening when the main meal is eaten earlier in the day.

sup·ple [<u>sup</u>-ul] *adjective*, **suppler, supplest. 1.** bending easily; not stiff, flexible: *Gymnasts are supple athletes.* **2.** describing something adaptable; accepting new ideas: *a person with a supple mind.*

sup·ple·ment [<u>sup</u>-luh-munt] *noun, plural* **supplements.** something added to help, extend, or increase the effect of a thing: *Mom gives us Vitamin C tablets as a supplement to fresh fruits; a newspaper supplement.* Something that supplements is **supplementary.**
verb, **supplemented, supplementing.** to add something to help, extend, or increase the effect of something else: *He supplemented his written report with a folder of photographs and sketches.*

sup·ply [suh-<u>plye</u>] *verb*, **supplied, supplying.** to give or provide something: *The teacher supplied us with new pencils and notebooks.*
noun, plural **supplies.** something needed for use: *There are art supplies in the art room; We bought food and other supplies for our camping trip.* A person or organization that supplies something is a **supplier.**

sup·port [suh-<u>port</u>] *verb*, **supported, supporting. 1.** to bear the weight of; hold up: *Walls support the roof of the school.* **2.** to provide things for: *My aunt supports her family by working two jobs.* **3.** to back or help: *Our class supported my sister when she ran for school president.* **4.** to prove to be true: *Tape from the security camera supported her version of the robbery.*
noun, plural **supports. 1.** the act of supporting someone or something: *The mayor personally thanked Mom for her support.* **2.** someone or something that supports: *If you knock the supports over, the roof will fall down.* —**supporter**, *noun.*

sup·pose [suh-<u>poze</u>] *verb*, **supposed, supposing. 1.** to think or believe to be true without knowing for sure: *When you do suppose you will finish your project?* **2.** to think of as possible: *Let's suppose I want to learn to speak French—how would I start?* **3.** to expect or require: *She was supposed to be here by now; There are supposed to be six rolls in the bag, but I only have five.* The act of supposing something is called **supposition.**

SUPERSONIC FLIGHT

The first supersonic flight was achieved in 1947 in a specially designed Bell X-1 rocket plane. In the 1960s Britain and France joined forces to develop a supersonic passenger plane, Concorde, which began regular transatlantic flights in 1976. Cruising at twice the speed of sound, it could fly from New York to London in three and a half hours. Concorde was not a commercial success, however, and was withdrawn from service in 2003. Many of today's military aircraft are supersonic.

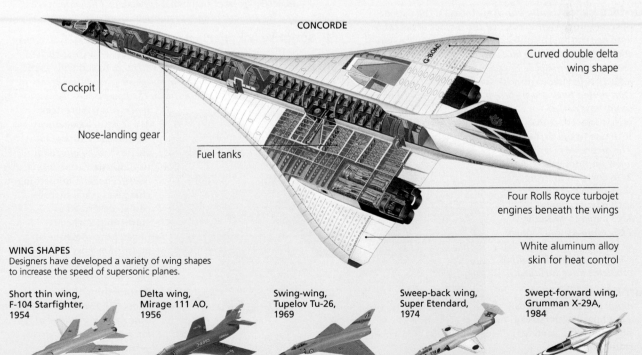

CONCORDE

Cockpit

Nose-landing gear

Fuel tanks

Curved double delta wing shape

Four Rolls Royce turbojet engines beneath the wings

White aluminum alloy skin for heat control

WING SHAPES
Designers have developed a variety of wing shapes to increase the speed of supersonic planes.

Short thin wing, F-104 Starfighter, 1954

Delta wing, Mirage 111 AO, 1956

Swing-wing, Tupelov Tu-26, 1969

Sweep-back wing, Super Etendard, 1974

Swept-forward wing, Grumman X-29A, 1984

sup·pos·ed·ly [suh-poze-id-lee] *adverb.* thought or believed to be the case: *The new teacher supposedly played pro basketball, but he doesn't look tall enough for that.*

sup·press [suh-pres] *verb,* **suppressed, suppressing.** to hold back or keep down: *The principal suppressed the news that she was leaving because of illness.* —**suppression,** *noun.*

su·preme [suh-preem] *adjective.* **1.** highest in authority or power: *God is often called the supreme being; General Eisenhower was the supreme commander of Allied forces in World War II.* The fact of being supreme is **supremacy. 2.** describing the highest or greatest: *She made a supreme effort to be nice to the girl who was mean to her.* —**supremely,** *adverb.*

Supreme Court *Government.* the highest court in the United States. It consists of the Chief Justice and eight other Associate Justices. It is the only court mentioned in the U.S. Constitution.

sure [shoor] *adjective,* **surer, surest. 1.** free from doubt; confident: *She is sure he will be there.* **2.** certain or able to be depended on: *I think he's a sure winner in the election for class president.* **3.** firm and steady: *Take a sure hold of the rope before you jump.*
adverb. certainly; definitely: *Sure, I'll come with you.*

sure·ly [shoor-lee] *adverb.* without doubt; certainly: *Surely you won't need a raincoat on such a sunny day.*

surf [surf] *noun.* the waves where the ocean meets the shore: *a pounding surf.*
verb, **surfed, surfing. 1.** to ride a wave, usually on a surfboard. **2.** to search the Internet, looking for information: *I surfed the Net, looking for sites about bike racing.*
🔊 A different word with the same sound is **serf.**

sur·face [sur-fis] *noun, plural* **surfaces. 1.** the outside of something: *Mom scratched the surface of the table with her ring.* **2.** the outer appearance or impression of something: *On the surface she looked happy, but I knew she was really upset.*
adjective. having to do with the outside of something: *Dad peeled back the surface layers of paint until he got to the bare wood.*
verb, **surfaced, surfacing.
1.** to rise to the surface: *The divers surfaced after a few minutes underwater.*
2. to cover something: *We surfaced the path with paving stones.*
3. to come to be known: *The company was thought to be doing well, but in the past few weeks some major problems have surfaced.*

surf·board [surf-bord] *noun, plural* **surfboards.** a flat board with curved sides and a fin, used for riding waves.

surf·er ▼ [sur-fur] *noun, plural* **surfers.** someone who rides waves on a surfboard. The sport of doing this is called **surfing.**

surge [surj] *verb,* **surged, surging.** to move forward with force: *The audience surged into the hall.*
noun, plural **surges. 1.** a forceful swell: *The surge of a wave crashed the boat onto the rocks.* **2.** a sudden rise: *A surge in oil prices means higher prices for gas.*

sur·geon [sur-jun] *noun, plural* **surgeons.** *Medicine.* a doctor who performs operations.

sur·ger·y [sur-jer-ee] *noun, plural* **surgeries.** *Medicine.*
1. the part of medicine that involves operations on damaged or diseased parts of the body. **2.** an operation to repair or remove a part of the body. Anything having to do with surgery can be described as **surgical.**

> The word **surgery** comes from a phrase meaning "skill with the hands." It is easy to see how the word developed in this way. Of all the things people do with the hands, few if any can be said to require as much skill with the hands as surgery on the brain, heart, or other body parts.

sur·ly [sur-lee] *adjective,* **surlier, surliest.** unfriendly and bad tempered: *Nobody likes to talk to him because of his rude, surly manner.*

sur·name [sur-name] *noun, plural* **surnames.** a person's last name or family name.

sur·pass [sur-pas] *verb,* **surpassed, surpassing.** to excel or be better than: *That guitarist surpasses all the others with her skill and timing.*

sur·plus [sur-plus] *noun.* an amount left over; an amount greater than what is needed: *The surplus of food in rich countries is sometimes sent to poorer countries.*
adjective. greater than what is needed: *The wine maker sold his surplus grapes to another company.*

sur·prise [sur-prize] *verb,* **surprised, surprising. 1.** to amaze or fill with wonder: *It was late fall, so we were surprised to find that the ocean was so warm.* **2.** to suddenly come upon; catch off guard: *The police surprised the three robbers while they were still in the house.*
noun, plural **surprises.
1.** a state of amazement or wonder: *Think of the surprise when our team won, since we were losing 3–0 at the half.* Something that gives you a surprise can be described as **surprising. 2.** the act of catching someone off guard: *The boss was taken by surprise when she said she'd be quitting her job.* **3.** something that is not expected: *Don't tell Mom that Aunt Peg will be at her party—it's a surprise.* —**surprisingly,** *adverb.*

This **surfer** *is wakesurfing—riding the wave generated by a boat.*

sur·ren·der [suh-ren-dur] *verb,* **surrendered, surrendering. 1.** to give up in a fight or struggle: *In 1945 Japan surrendered to the U.S. to end World War II.* **2.** to give up the right to something: *The police officer has been suspended and had to surrender his badge and gun.* **3.** to give in to something; yield: *When he joined the monastery, he agreed to surrender to the will of God. noun, plural* **surrenders.** the act of surrendering: *the surrender of a fort to the enemy.*

sur·round [suh-round] *verb,* **surrounded, surrounding.** to go or be around; enclose on all sides: *At Custer's Last Stand his troops were completely surrounded by Sioux and Cheyenne warriors; A wire fence surrounds the field.*

sur·round·ings [suh-roun-dingz] *plural noun.* the conditions that surround a person, thing, or place: *Rupert sat on the beach, but he was so involved with the book he was reading that he didn't notice his surroundings.*

sur·vey [sur-vay] *verb,* **surveyed, surveying. 1.** to view in detail; study or look over: *The principal surveyed the new menu for the school cafeteria.* **2.** to measure the size, shape, or boundaries of a certain area of land: *They surveyed the land before they built the house.* Someone whose work is to measure land in this way is a **surveyor.** *noun, plural* **surveys. 1.** a study to gain information about a certain issue or topic, often involving answers from a questionnaire: *I answered a survey about which breakfast cereal I preferred.* **2.** the act of measuring land: *They had a survey done before they built the house.*

sur·vi·val [sur-vive-ul] *noun, plural* **survivals. 1.** the act of staying alive: *Pollution in the water threatens the survival of many fish.* **2.** a thing that survives: *Many modern customs are survivals from olden days.*

sur·vive [sur-vive] *verb,* **survived, surviving. 1.** to live through something: *Luckily, the whole family survived the house fire.* Someone who survives something is a **survivor. 2.** to stay alive: *Everyone needs food and water to survive.*

sus·pect [suh-spekt *for verb;* sus-pekt *for noun*] *verb,* **suspected, suspecting. 1.** to think someone is guilty without know for sure: *The police suspect he stole the bike.* **3.** to doubt or not believe: *The teacher suspects that I did not really lose my homework.* **2.** to have an idea about something without knowing for sure: *I suspect I passed my math exam. noun, plural* **suspects.** someone who is thought to be guilty of a crime. *adjective.* that is to be suspected; uncertain: *The company says sales will go up, but based on recent results, that idea is suspect.*

sus·pend ◀ [suh-spend] *verb,* **suspended, suspending. 1.** to hang from: *Baskets of plants are suspended from the roof of the porch.* **2.** to float in something: *The sunlight shows specks of dust suspended in the air.* **3.** to stop for a while: *She suspended her payments to the plumber because the pipes keep leaking.* **4.** to not allow to attend: *The boy was suspended from school for cheating.* —**suspension,** *noun.*

sus·pen·ders [suh-spen-durz] *noun, plural* **suspenders.** a pair of braces or straps that hang each side of the shoulders and hold up trousers.

sus·pense [suh-spens] *noun.* the state of not knowing and being worried about what will happen: *The movie kept us all in suspense until the very end.* Something that keeps you in suspense can be described as **suspenseful.**

sus·pen·sion [suh-spen-shun] *noun, plural* **suspensions. 1.** the act or state of being suspended: *The suspension of the new chandelier from the ceiling was a difficult operation.* **2.** the act of stopping for a while; postponement: *There was a suspension of the court case so that an important witness could be found.* **3.** the state of being banned for a time, especially from school: *The students received a suspension for cheating in the exam.* **4.** a system of springs and shock absorbers that protects the body of a motor vehicle or railroad car from the bumps the wheels travel over.

sus·pi·cion [suh-spish-un] *noun, plural* **suspicions. 1.** the act of suspecting, especially that something is wrong: *I can't find my camera anywhere and I have a suspicion it's been stolen.* **2.** the state of being suspected, especially of doing something wrong: *The men were under suspicion of causing the accident.*

sus·pi·cious [suh-spish-us] *adjective.* **1.** causing to think that something is wrong: *The car parked in front of the bank with the motor running is suspicious.* **2.** feeling something is wrong or showing that feeling: *She was suspicious her brother was being nice because he wanted something.* —**suspiciously,** *adverb.*

sus·tain [suh-stane] *verb,* **sustained, sustaining. 1.** to keep up or keep going; maintain: *He sustained a good speed for the whole of his long race.* **2.** to supply with the necessities of life, especially food: *Our lunch sustained us all afternoon.* **3.** to suffer or experience: *She sustained a broken leg in the accident.* **4.** to accept the value of something; confirm: *The judge sustained the lawyer's objection to what the opposing lawyer had said.*

sus·tain·a·ble [suh-stane-uh-bul] *adjective. Environment.* able to be sustained or kept going: *If you use resources such as energy or plants in a sustainable way, it means you do not use them up and they can continue to be used in the future.* Economic development that aims to meet long-term needs with as little harm to the environment as possible is called **sustainable development.**

SUV an abbreviation of **sports utility vehicle.** This type of motor vehicle is somewhat like a small truck but with room for more passengers; it can be driven on rough roads and is strong enough to tow other vehicles.

Swamps develop over thousands of years from lakes and marshes.

swal·low¹ [swahl-oh] *verb,* **swallowed, swallowing.**
1. to cause something to pass down the throat to the stomach: *He had a sore throat and found it hard to swallow his food.* **2.** to take in and withdraw from view or cover up: *The car drove off and was swallowed by the darkness.* **3.** to hold or take back: *I swallowed my pride and apologized.* **4.** to accept something without questioning it: *The teacher was not willing to swallow the student's story about why she was late.*
noun, plural **swallows. 1.** the act of swallowing. **2.** an amount of something swallowed at one time; a mouthful.

swal·low² [swahl-oh] *noun.* a type of small bird with long wings and a short beak. Swallows are graceful, fast fliers and hunt insects in the air.

swamp ▲ [swahmp] *noun, plural* **swamps.** an area of low ground that is soft and wet and may have bushes and trees growing in it.
verb, **swamped, swamping. 1.** to fill or cover with water: *The dam burst and the town was suddenly swamped.* **2.** to be covered or loaded with a large amount of something: *After the new computer was advertised on TV, the company was swamped with orders.*

swan ▼ [swahn] *noun, plural* **swans.** any of several large water birds with long, slender necks and webbed feet. Swans are related to ducks and geese and can be white or black.

swap [swahp] *verb,* **swapped, swapping.** to exchange one thing for another; trade: *Mom swapped seats with me so I could see out the airplane window.*
noun, plural **swaps.** a trade or exchange: *The two children didn't like their sandwiches so they did a swap with each other.*

The black **swan** *lives in the wetlands of southern Australia.*

swarm ▼ [sworm] *noun, plural* **1.** a large number of bees in a tightly-packed group that leave their hive with a queen to start a new colony. **2.** any such large group of people or animals moving together: *Large swarms of crows flew overhead on the way to their evening roost; A swarm of shoppers rushed into the store for the sale.*
verb, **swarmed, swarming. 1.** of a group of bees, to leave a hive to form a new colony. **2.** to move or gather in a large group in the same direction: *The pond swarmed with fish; Fans wearing their teams' colors swarmed to the stadium to see the football game.*

sway [sway] *verb,* **swayed, swaying. 1.** to swing or move back and forth or cause to do so: *The trees swayed in the breeze.* **2.** to cause to change thoughts or opinions; influence: *Listening to the mayor's latest speech swayed me toward voting for her.*
noun, plural **sways. 1.** the act or condition of swaying: *The sway of the cable car made us feel ill.* **2.** influence or power over others: *The king held sway over his subjects.*

swear [sware] *verb,* **swore, sworn, swearing. 1.** to make a solemn declaration, calling on God or another sacred being to witness its truth: *In court, the witness swore to tell only the truth.* **2.** to make a solemn promise; vow: *She swore she would return the money she borrowed.* **3.** to show anger or hatred by using certain forbidden words; to curse.

sweat [swet] *noun.* **1.** a salty fluid released through pores in the skin, usually when a person is hot or worried; also called perspiration. **2.** droplets of water that form on a surface; condensed moisture. **3.** the act of sweating: *The nervous man broke into a sweat.*
verb, **sweated, sweating. 1.** to give off salty water through pores in the skin; perspire: *The runners sweated during the race.* **2.** to gather moisture from the air on a cold surface; condense: *The jug of cold water sweated in the hot tropical air.*

sweat·er [swet-ur] *noun, plural* **sweaters.** a warm, knitted garment worn on the upper part of the body, usually over other clothes. It can be made of wool, cotton, or an artificial fabric.

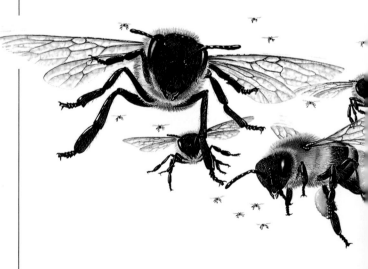

In towns and cities, **swifts** build nests under
roof tiles or in holes in old buildings.

swimmer

sweat·shirt [swet-*shurt*] *noun, plural* **sweatshirts.** a long-sleeved garment with no collar worn on the upper half of the body and usually made of heavy knitted cotton fabric.

Swed·ish [swee̲d-ish] *adjective.* having to do with the country of Sweden or its people or culture.
noun. the language of Sweden. A person born or living in Sweden can be called a **Swede.**

sweep [sweep] *verb,* **swept, sweeping. 1.** to clean by pushing with a broom or brush: *to sweep the kitchen floor.* **2.** to move or clear something with a brushing motion: *to sweep the hair from your eyes with your hand.* **3.** to move quickly and forcefully: *The huge waves swept the boat away.* **4.** to move rapidly across with a single movement: *Their eyes swept the crowd, looking for their friend.* A movement that passes across in a continuous way or something that is wide and continuous is said to be **sweeping.**
noun, plural **sweeps.** the act or motion of sweeping.

sweet [sweet] *adjective,* **sweeter, sweetest. 1.** having a taste of or like sugar. **2.** pleasing to hear, smell, and so on: *The flute makes sweet music.* **3.** pleasing due to being kind, gentle, or innocent; cute: *That little child is very sweet.* **4.** describing something not salted: *Use the sweet butter to bake a cake.*
noun, plural **sweets.** a food made with sugar: *I love sweets like cakes and candy.* —**sweetly,** *adverb;* —**sweetness,** *noun.*
🔊 A different word with the same sound is **suite.**

sweet·en [swee̲t-un] *verb,* **sweetened, sweetening.** to make or cause to become sweeter or more pleasant: *She sweetened her coffee with a sugar cube.* A **sweetener** is something used to make a food or situation sweeter or more pleasant.

sweet·heart [swee̲t-hart] *noun, plural* **sweethearts. 1.** a person who is loved. This word is often used as a term of affection: *She said to her daughter, "Sweetheart, it's time to get ready for school."* **2.** one of two people who are romantically involved: *Paul and Diana have been sweethearts for ages.*

sweet potato a plant originally from the tropical parts of the Americas. It has sweet yellow or orange roots that are eaten baked or boiled and mashed. Sweet potatoes are not related to the white potato or yams.

swell [swel] *verb,* **swelled, swollen** *or* **swelled, swelling. 1.** to grow thicker or larger, especially in a way that is not natural or healthy: *Her face swelled where the bee had stung her.* **2.** to increase above the normal amount or level: *The river was swollen after a week of heavy rain.*
noun, plural **swells.** a wave or number of waves, especially if they have not broken: *The swell was too high to take a boat out.*
adjective. an informal word for something that is good or excellent: *They had a swell time at the party.*

swell·ing [swel-ing] *noun, plural* **swellings.** *Health.* **1.** the act of becoming or the state of being swollen: *the swelling of a sprained ankle.* **2.** a part that has swelled: *Sue has a nasty swelling where the bee stung her.*

swerve [swurv] *verb,* **swerved, swerving.** to suddenly change direction from a set course: *The car swerved to avoid hitting the fallen tree.*
noun, plural **swerves.** the act of swerving.

swift ▲ [swift] *adjective,* **swifter, swiftest. 1.** moving or able to move with great speed: *The swiftest sailboat won the race.* **2.** happening fast or without delay: *We wrote a swift reply to her invitation.*
noun, plural **swifts.** any of various birds with long narrow wings and short legs. Swifts spend much of their lives on the wing catching insects and some even sleep in the air. —**swiftly,** *adverb;* **swiftness,** *noun.*

swim [swim] *verb,* **swam, swum, swimming. 1.** to move in or through water using the arms and legs or fins and a tail. **2.** to move from one point to another through water: *The zebra swam across the river to escape the lion.* **3.** to be covered with or surrounded by a liquid: *My roast beef is swimming in gravy.* **4.** to have a dizzy or light-headed sensation: *Everything swam before him, then he fainted.*
noun, plural **swims.** the act of swimming, or the distance or time taken to swim: *The swim across the lake is a half a mile.*

swim·mer [swim-ur] *noun, plural* **swimmers.** a person who swims. The activity where one swims, especially the sport in which swimmers race each other, is called **swimming.**

Bees travel in **swarms** *when they are looking for a new nest site.*

*Medieval knights sometimes fought with huge two-handed **swords**.*

swin·dle [swin-dul] *verb,* **swindled, swindling.** to fool or deceive a person in order to take their money or other possessions; to cheat: *That man swindled me by selling me a car that didn't even belong to him.* —**swindler,** *noun.*

swine [swine] *noun, plural* **swine.** any of several animals that belong to the pig family; a pig, hog, or boar.

swing [swing] *verb,* **swung, swinging. 1.** to move or cause to move back and forth while held at one end: *The monkey swung through the trees.* **2.** to move or cause to move through a curve or with a sweeping motion: *to swing a basketball bat; He swung the door shut.* *noun, plural* **swings. 1.** a way of moving back and forth or in a curved line: *The swing of the pendulum kept the clock ticking.* **2.** a seat that hangs by ropes or chains that you can swing backward and forward on.

swirl [swurl] *verb,* **swirled, swirling.** to move around and around in a spiraling or spinning motion: *Water swirled around the boat.* *noun, plural* **swirls. 1.** a way of moving in a twisting, spiraling way: *With a swirl of his cloak, the magician appeared to vanish.* **2.** something with a shape as if it has been twisted: *Her hair was arranged in swirls about her head.*

Swiss [swis] *adjective.* having to do with the country of Switzerland or its people or culture. The people of Switzerland are called **the Swiss.**

switch [swich] *noun, plural* **switches. 1.** a slender rod or stick used to whip or beat. **2.** the act of moving in a jerky way as if to whip: *The donkey gave its tail a switch to get rid of the biting flies.* **3.** a shift or change: *For her breakfast she made a switch from eating cereal to toast.* **4.** a device for turning an electrical current on or off: *It was too dark to find the light switch.* **5.** a device that allows a train to go from one track to another. *verb,* **switched, switching. 1.** to beat with a switch. **2.** to move or cause to move in a quick, jerking way: *The lion's tail switched as it crouched, watching its prey.* **3.** to change or make a swap: *Can I switch this pencil for that one?* **4.** to use a switch to turn an electrical current or appliance on or off: *He switched the radio on.* **5.** to move a train from one track to another.

swi·vel [swiv-ul] *noun, plural* **swivels.** a device such as a pivot that holds part of something in place while allowing it to turn: *The swivel on this table allows the top to turn.* *verb,* **swiveled, swiveling.** to turn or move something about a swivel: *He swiveled his chair around.*

swoop [swoop] *verb,* **swooped, swooping.** to suddenly and quickly move downward with a sweeping motion: *The eagle swooped on its prey.*

sword ◀ [sord] *noun, plural* **swords.** a weapon with a long, pointed, metal blade set into a handle.

sword·fish [sord-fish] *noun, plural* **swordfish** or **swordfishes.** a large ocean fish with a long, bony, sword-like bill on its upper jaw. Swordfish are a popular seafood and are now endangered in some areas due to over-fishing.

syc·a·more ▼ [sik-uh-mor] *noun, plural* **sycamores.** a name applied to several types of tree, such as a large tree of North America with large leaves similar to the maple leaf.

syl·la·ble [sil-uh-bul] *noun, plural* **syllables.** *Language.* **1.** a sound that forms part of a word and is made with one flow of air from the lungs. Spoken words are made up of syllables. For example, the word *frog* has one syllable, and the word *tadpole* has two. **2.** in writing, a letter or group of letters that stands for a spoken syllable.

A **syllable** is a part of a word (or a short whole word) that is spoken as a single sound. In this dictionary, syllables are shown in two ways. The syllables in the spoken word (pronunciation) are divided by a hyphen (-), as in [sim-bul]. The syllables in the written word (headword) are divided by a black dot (•), as in **sym•bol.** For most words the two divisions are the same, but not always, because the rules for dividing are not exactly the same for writing and speech. So you should remember that the pronunciation is for saying the word and the headword is for writing it.

Sycamore *trees grow in temperate climates and lose their leaves in winter.*

sym·bol ▶ [sim-bul]
noun, plural **symbols.**
something used to stand for something else: *The symbol for a dollar is $; A figure of the heart is often used as a symbol of love.* Something used to stand for something else is said to be **symbolic.**
🔊 A different word with the same sound is **cymbal.**

sym·me·try ▼ [sim-uh-tree]
noun, plural **symmetries.**
an object or design where one half is the same as, or mirrors, the other. The two sides of the human body are an example of symmetry. Such an object or design is said to be **symmetrical.**

sym·pa·the·tic [sim-puh-thet-ik] *adjective.* **1.** showing or feeling kind understanding for someone else's difficulties: *Mom gave me a sympathetic hug when she heard I failed my geography exam.* **2.** in favor of; agreeable toward: *Our art teacher was sympathetic to our wish to sketch out in the sunshine.* —**sympathetically,** *adverb.*

sym·pa·thize [sim-puh-thize] *verb,* **sympathized, sympathizing.** to have or show kind understanding toward someone who has difficulties: *Jenny's brother sympathized with her after her basketball team lost the final game.* —**sympathizer,** *noun.*

sym·pa·thy [sim-puh-thee]
noun, plural **sympathies.**
1. an ability to understand and share other people's difficulties and sorrows; compassion: *They felt sympathy for their friend when she got into trouble at school.* **2.** the fact or act of agreement: *The sisters were in sympathy about which movie to watch.*

sym·pho·ny [sim-fuh-nee] *noun, plural* **symphonies.** *Music.*
1. a long piece of music written for an orchestra.
2. a large orchestra made up of woodwind, brass, percussion, and stringed instruments.

symp·tom [simp-tum] *noun, plural* **symptoms.**
1. *Medicine.* something that shows a condition exists in the body: *A runny nose, sore throat, aching muscles, and a high temperature are symptoms of the flu.* **2.** a sign or indication of something bad: *The fact that Victoria doesn't say a lot in class is a symptom of her shyness.* Something that is a symptom of something else is said to be **symptomatic.**

syn·a·gogue [sin-uh-gog] *noun, plural* **synagogues.**
Religion. a building in which people of the Jewish religion gather for worship or instruction.

syn·drome [sin-drome] *noun, plural* **syndromes.**
1. *Medicine.* a number of different symptoms that together show evidence of a certain disease. **2.** any group of characteristics that indicate a certain condition.

syn·o·nym [sin-uh-nim] *noun, plural* **synonyms.** *Language.* a word that has the same or nearly the same meaning as another word in the same language. For example, *sad* is a synonym of *unhappy.*

English has taken its words from many other languages, and so the language has many **synonyms**—different words that mean the same thing. You can use synonyms to give variety to your writing. For example, rather than using certain basic words over and over, you can replace them with other words. Instead of writing about *nice* weather, a *nice* girl, or a *nice* day at the beach, instead you could write about *pleasant, mild,* or *balmy* weather, a *friendly, kind,* or *warm-hearted* girl, or a *fine, lovely,* or *enjoyable* day at the beach.

syn·on·y·mous [si-non-uh-mus] *adjective. Language.* meaning the same or nearly the same thing: *The word "stone" is synonymous with the word "rock."*

syn·tax [sin-taks] *noun. Language.* the way words in a language are arranged, using grammatical rules and patterns to create phrases, clauses, and sentences.

syn·the·siz·er [sin-thuh-sye-zur] *noun, plural* **synthesizers.** *Music.* an electronic machine that creates sounds used to make music. Synthesizers are often played using a keyboard. They can imitate the sound of other musical instruments and the human voice.

syn·the·tic [sin-thet-ik] *adjective. Chemistry.* formed by chemical reactions rather than found in nature; artificial; man-made: *Nylon is a synthetic fabric used to make clothes.*

syr·up [sir-up *or* seer-up] *noun, plural* **syrups.** a thick, sticky, sweet liquid often made by boiling sugar with water, juice, or other ingredients.

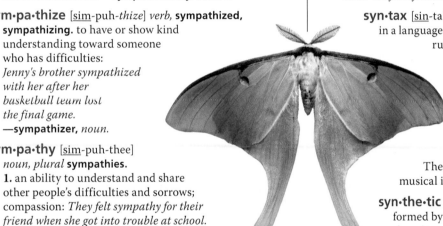

An Indian moon moth is an example of bilateral **symmetry** *commonly seen in nature, where both sides of a living thing look the same.*

sys·tem [sis-tum] *noun, plural* **systems. 1.** a group of things that work or act together in a particular way as a whole: *The Sun, the Earth, and other planets are called the solar system; The railroad system is running on time.* **2.** a group of ideas, facts, or laws that are related and work together: *The legal system controls law and order.* **3.** an organized way of doing something; a procedure: *I have a system for shelving my books so I can find them again easily.* Doing something according to a system is said to be **systematic.** —**systematically,** *adverb.*

a
b
c
d
e
f
g
h
i
j
k
l
m
n
o
p
q
r
s
t
u
v
w
x
y
z

T t

Table tennis *was developed in the late nineteenth century as a miniature indoor version of tennis.*

T, t *noun, plural* **T's, t's.** the twentieth letter of the English alphabet.

tab [tab] *noun, plural* **tabs.** a small flap or loop that sticks out from something and is used to help identify it, open it, or carry it: *Pull the tab on the can of soda to open it.*

ta·ble [tay-bul] *noun, plural* **tables. 1.** a piece of furniture made of a flat top resting on one or more legs: *Please set the table for dinner.* **2.** the food served at a table, or the people who sit there to eat. **3.** a list of facts arranged on a chart, usually in columns and rows: *Make a table of the height of everyone in the class.*

ta·ble·cloth [tay-bul-klawth] *noun, plural* **tablecloths.** a piece of cloth draped over a table to decorate or protect it.

table of contents *Literature.* a list at the beginning of a book or other written work that shows the chapters or other sections of the book and the pages they begin on.

ta·ble·spoon [tay-bul-spoon] *noun, plural* **tablespoons.** a large spoon used to measure ingredients in cooking or to serve food.

tab·let [tab-lit] *noun, plural* **tablets. 1.** several pieces of blank or lined paper joined together along an edge; a pad: *Rajiv brought a tablet of paper to sketch on in art class.* **2.** a small, solid piece of medicine: *I need to take a headache tablet.* **3.** a flat piece of clay, wood, or stone that is written on: *In ancient Babylon, people wrote on wet clay tablets.*

table tennis ▲ a game where two or four players use round paddles to hit a small, light ball back and forth across a low net on a large table.

tab·loid [tab-loid] *noun, plural* **tabloids.** a newspaper with a smaller page size than usual. Tabloids have more pictures and shorter stories than broadsheet newspapers and they often cover news in a more sensational way.

ta·boo [ta-boo] *noun, plural* **taboos.** a social custom or rule that bans a certain food, object, or action. *adjective.* not allowed according to custom or social rule; prohibited; forbidden: *In many societies it is taboo to eat certain foods.*

ta·chom·e·ter [tak-om-uh-tur] *noun, plural* **tachometers.** a device that measures the number of times a shaft rotates. In a motor vehicle, a tachometer measures the number of times a minute the shaft in the engine turns around.

tack [tak] *noun, plural* **tacks. 1.** a short, sharp nail with a wide, flat head. **2.** a course of action; a strategy or approach: *Mom took another tack and promised him an ice cream to get him to clean his room.* *verb,* **tacked, tacking. 1.** to attach something using tacks: *I tacked the poster to the bulletin board.* **2.** to roughly stitch together using large stitches. **3.** to sail a boat in a zigzag course against the wind.

tack·le [tak-ul] *noun, plural* **tackles. 1.** the equipment needed to do a certain activity; gear: *fishing tackle.* **2.** equipment used in a system of ropes and pulleys to lift and lower heavy objects: *They swung the cargo aboard using the tackle.* **3.** the act of stopping by grabbing and pulling to the ground, as in football. **4.** A position in football on the offensive or defensive line. **5.** in sports such as soccer, the act of trying to take the ball from an opponent: A person who carries out a tackle is called a **tackler.** *verb,* **tackled, tackling. 1.** to grab and pull to the ground: *The police officer tackled the thief to stop him escaping.* **2.** in sports such as soccer, to attempt to take the ball from an opposing player: *The defender skillfully tackled the player with the ball and kicked it back up the field.* **3.** to attempt something that is challenging: *I tackled the job of cleaning up after the party.*

ta·co [tah-koh] *noun, plural* **tacos.** a tortilla folded around fillings such as meat, cheese, vegetables, and salsa. The tortilla can be soft, or fried to make it crisp.

tact [takt] *noun.* the skill of saying and doing the right thing in a delicate or difficult situation. Someone who has this skill is said to be **tactful.** —**tactfully,** *adverb.*

tac·tic [tak-tik] *noun, plural* **tactics.** a planned action carried out to achieve a goal; a maneuver: *The soldiers hid until the enemy was upon them—a surprise tactic that won them the battle.* A planned method of attack, especially in warfare or a competition, is called **tactics.** An action that relates to tactics is said to be **tactical.** —**tactically,** *adverb.*

tad·pole ▲ [tad-pole] *noun, plural* **tadpoles.** the young of amphibians, including frogs, toads, newts, and salamanders. Tadpoles live in water and have gills and a tail. As they grow they develop lungs, four legs, and in the case of frogs and toads, lose their tail.

Most **tadpoles** *feed on plants and algae.*

Something that is **taboo** is not allowed, according to a strict rule or custom. The word was first used by native peoples of the western Pacific Ocean. A *taboo* or *tabu* meant that a certain thing or place was set aside for the use of the gods, or only for a select group of people.

taf·fy [taf-ee] *noun, plural* **taffies.** a soft, chewy candy made from boiled sugar or molasses and butter, with other ingredients sometimes added.

tag¹ [tag] *noun, plural* **tags.** a piece of paper, cloth, or other material attached to something, often to mark or identify it: *Look at the tag in the shirt to find out its size.*

tag² [tag] *noun.* a game where one person chases the others until he or she touches another person, who then becomes the chaser.
verb, **tagged, tagging. 1.** to touch, as in a game of tag: *He tagged me, so now I have to chase everyone.* **2.** in baseball, to touch a runner with the ball or the hand holding the ball and so put him out.

tail ▲ [tale] *noun, plural* **tails. 1.** a body part, often long and slender, that sticks out at the back of an animal and can move freely: *The monkey used its tail to swing through the trees.* **2.** anything long and slender that sticks out from the back of something: *The kite has a long tail.* **3.** the back end of something: *the tail section of an airplane.* **4. tails.** the reverse side of a coin; the side that is not the head.
verb, **tailed, tailing.** to follow closely, especially in secret.
🔊 A different word with the same sound is **tale.**

tail·gate [tale-*gate*] *noun, plural* **tailgates.** a hinged board at the back of a pickup truck, station wagon, or similar vehicle that can be lowered to make loading and unloading easier.
verb, **tailgated, tailgating. 1.** of a motor vehicle, to travel too closely behind another vehicle. **2.** to have food and drink in the stadium parking lot before a football game or other sports event; so called because this was originally done using the tailgate of a station wagon.

tail·light [tale-*lite*] *noun, plural* **taillights.** a red light at the back of a motor vehicle, train, or airplane.

*During **takeoff**, the pilot raises the wheels of the airplane into the plane's body.*

tai·lor [tay-lur] *noun, plural* **tailors.** a person who makes, alters, or repairs clothing: *a gentleman's tailor.*
verb, **tailored, tailoring. 1.** to make or alter clothing according to a person's wishes or measurements: *He had his suit tailored after he lost a lot of weight.* **2.** to make or alter something for a specific purpose: *That book about the planets is tailored to children.*

take [take] *verb,* **took, taken, taking. 1.** to get possession of with the hands; hold or grasp: *He took her pen without asking.* **2.** to deal with in some way; to have, obtain, get, or use and so on: *to take a shower; Sara took a photo of us.* **3.** to carry when going; bring along: *Take your towel with you when you go to the beach.* **4.** to use or require: *Teaching takes a lot of patience.* **5.** to remove from: *Take twelve from twenty, and you are left with eight.* **6.** to accept or put up with: *He took the bad news calmly.*
noun, plural **takes. 1.** the act or process of taking. **2.** something that has been taken: *The store's take is hundreds of dollars a day.* **3.** a film or sound recording made without a break: *It took nine takes before the actors got the scene filmed right.*

take·off ▼ [take-*of or* take-*awf*] *noun, plural* **takeoffs. 1.** the act or process of lifting off the ground: *The helicopter's takeoff was delayed due to bad weather.* When something or someone leaves the ground, it is said to **take off. 2.** the act of mimicking or imitating something or someone in an amusing way: *His takeoff of the movie star was funny.*

take·out [take-*out*] *noun.* food bought at a restaurant to be eaten at another location: *We were too tired to cook, so we ate takeout last night.*
adjective. having to do with food bought at a restaurant to be eaten elsewhere: *Go to the takeout counter to pick up your meal.*

take·over [take-*oh*-vur] *noun, plural* **takeovers.** the act of taking something over: *The big company launched a takeover of the small company by buying most of its shares of stock.* When someone or something takes control of someone or something else, this is to **take over.**

a b c d e f g h i j k l m n o p q r s **t** u v w x y z

*The **tambourine** dates back to ancient times and was traditionally played by women to accompany their dancing.*

talc [talk] *noun.* a mineral with a soft, soapy feel that is ground up and used in making face powder, paints, and plastics.

tale [tale] *noun, plural* **tales. 1.** *Literature.* the telling of a story: *"Robin Hood" is a tale set in the Middle Ages.* **2.** an untrue story; a lie: *I know that isn't true, so don't tell tales.*

◀)) A different word with the same sound is **tail.**

tal·ent [tal-unt] *noun, plural* **talents. 1.** a natural ability to do something well; skill: *He has a talent for drawing.* **2.** a person or people with talent: *Plenty of talent turned up for the audition for the musical.* Someone who has an outstanding ability at something is said to be **talented.**

The word **talent** first meant a measure of weight, and someone who had *talent* had gold, silver, or other valuables with a certain weight in *talents.* The word then came to mean someone who had wealth or valuables of a different kind, not in physical possessions but in a special ability to do something, such as singing, dancing, acting, writing, playing a sport, and so on.

talk [tawk] *verb,* **talked, talking. 1.** to communicate using spoken words; speak: *Nadia has a sore throat and can only talk in a whisper.* A person who talks, especially a lot, is called a **talker. 2.** to discuss something: *The group met to talk about their new project.* **3.** to convince by speaking to: *His friend talked him into going to the school dance.* *noun, plural* **talks. 1.** the act of two or more people speaking with each other; a conversation: *We had a talk about where to go on vacation.* **2.** a speech or lecture: *Ross went to a talk at the library on dinosaurs.*

*Huge harpy eagles in the Amazon rain forest use their sharp **talons** to snatch and carry off monkeys.*

talk·a·tive [taw-kuh-tiv] *adjective.* liable to talk a lot: *I'm tired and not feeling very talkative.*

talk show a radio or television program in which a host holds conversations and interviews with noted guests. A radio program in which listeners call in and talk with the host is called **talk radio.**

tall [tawl] *adjective,* **taller, tallest. 1.** higher than is usual; not short or low: *That tree is taller than the other one.* **2.** having a certain height or measurement from bottom to top: *He is six feet tall.* **3.** exaggerated and hard to believe; made-up: *His claim that he stopped a runaway train sounds like a tall story.*

tal·low [tal-oh] *noun.* the hard fat taken from the bodies of cattle, sheep, or horses and used to make soap, candles, and other products.

tal·ly [tal-ee] *noun, plural* **tallies.** a count of something or a record: *Make a tally of the words you spelled correctly.* *verb,* **tallied, tallying. 1.** to count up or keep a record of: *Mary tallied the points and announced that Max had won the game.* **2.** to agree with; match; correspond: *All the witnesses' description of the bank robber tallied.*

Tal·mud [tal-muhd *or* tal-mud] *noun. Religion.* the collection of ancient Jewish writings that cover many subjects, such as geography, history, customs, and religion. Jewish civil and religious laws are based on these writings.

tal·on ◀ [tal-un] *noun, plural* **talons.** the sharp claw of a bird of prey such as an eagle. Talons are used to grab onto prey.

ta·ma·le [tuh-mah-lee] *noun, plural* **tamales.** a traditional South American dish. In Mexico, tamales are made by encasing a mixture of ground meat and peppers in cornmeal dough. They are wrapped in cornhusks and steamed.

tam·bou·rine ▲ [tam-buh-reen] *noun, plural* **tambourines.** *Music.* a small drum made by stretching a skin over a circular frame into which metal disks are set. Tambourines are played by being hit or shaken.

tame [tame] *adjective,* **tamer, tamest. 1.** taken from the wild and trained to be calm around people and do as they say, or brought up to be like this: *Darren has a tame pet parrot.* **2.** describing something gentle, fearless, and without shyness: *The wild dolphins were quite tame and took fish from our hands.* *verb,* **tamed, taming.** to take from the wild and train to be calm and obedient, or to bring up to be like this. A person who tames something or someone is called a **tamer.**

tam·per [tam-pur] *verb,* **tampered, tampering.** to interfere with, especially if this causes damage or harm: *The car's engine had been tampered with so it wouldn't start.*

tan [tan] *verb,* **tanned, tanning. 1.** to soak an animal skin in a chemical solution to turn into leather. **2.** to expose to the sun and make or become brown: *The farmer's hands were tanned from working outside all summer.* *noun.* **1.** a yellowish-brown color. **2.** the brown color that some people's skin turns after being exposed to the sun. *adjective,* **tanner, tannest.** having a yellowish-brown color: *My tan shoes are very comfortable.*

tang [tang] *noun, plural* **tangs.** a distinctive, sharp, strong flavor or smell. When something has such a flavor or smell, it is said to be **tangy.**

tan·ge·rine ▶ [*tan*-juh-<u>reen</u>] *noun, plural* **tangerines.** a small, sweet fruit like an orange that has a loose skin that is easy to remove.

The fruit known as a **tangerine** gets its name from *Tangier*, an ancient port city on the northern coast of Africa. The fruit was first grown in this area.

tan·gi·ble [<u>tanj</u>-uh-bul] *adjective.* describing something real and certain; not imaginary: *The paintings on the cave wall are tangible evidence of the people who lived here thousands of years ago.*

tan·gle [<u>tang</u>-gul] *verb,* **tangled, tangling.** to twist into a confused mass that is hard to undo or smooth out: *My fishing line got tangled in an old branch on the river bed.* *noun, plural* **tangles.** a mass of things such as string, wire, or hair, that are twisted together in an untidy way.

Tangerines are very juicy and contain a lot of vitamin C.

tan·gram ▼ [<u>tang</u>-gram] *noun, plural* **tangrams.** a Chinese puzzle consisting of a square cut into seven pieces, usually five triangles, a square, and a parallelogram, that can be combined in other ways to form many different shapes.

A **tangram** *shape has to use all seven pieces, called tans, without any overlapping.*

tank ▼ [tangk] *noun, plural* **tanks. 1.** a large container for storing liquid or gas: *Many houses have a water heater tank in the basement or garage.* **2.** an enclosed armored military vehicle used in war. It has a cannon and machine guns and moves on two continuous belts of metal plates fastened over the wheels.

tank·er [<u>tang</u>-kur] *noun, plural* **tankers.** a ship, truck, or airplane designed to carry large quantities of oil or other liquids or gas.

tan·trum [<u>tan</u>-trum] *noun, plural* **tantrums.** a childish outburst of bad temper.

tap[1] [tap] *verb,* **tapped, tapping. 1.** to hit or strike gently: *to tap at a computer keyboard; Debbie tapped on the window to get my attention.* **2.** to produce a sound or rhythm by hitting gently again and again: *to tap your feet to music; Matt used his ruler to tap out a tune on the table.* *noun, plural* **taps. 1.** a light or gentle blow: *She gave Tom a tap on the shoulder to let him know she was sitting behind him.* **2.** a small, flat piece of metal attached to the bottom of a shoe for tap dancing.

tap[2] [tap] *noun, plural* **taps.** a device for controlling the flow of a liquid from a pipe, sink, or container; faucet. *verb,* **tapped, tapping. 1.** to take liquid out of a tree by making a hole in its trunk: *to tap a sugar maple tree or rubber tree.* **2.** to use or draw upon something that is needed: *to tap energy from the sun.* **3.** to attach a special device to a telephone to listen secretly to someone's conversations: *The police tapped the criminal's phone.*

tap dance a dance in which the dancer wears special shoes that make a clicking sound on the floor. A person dancing in this way is a **tap dancer** and is **tap-dancing.**

tape [tape] *noun, plural* **tapes. 1.** a long, narrow strip of cloth, paper, plastic, or similar material: *Grandma tied pink tape on the handle of her suitcase so she could recognize it easily at the airport.* **2.** a plastic strip coated with a magnetic substance, used to record sound and pictures and to store information: *audio tape; video tape.* *verb,* **taped, taping. 1.** to fasten or tie with tape: *A notice taped to the door said the meeting had been canceled.* **2.** to record sound or pictures on plastic tape coated with a magnetic substance: *The reporter taped the interview.*

tape measure a long strip of cloth, plastic, or metal marked with standard units of measurement and used for measuring.

ta·per [<u>tay</u>-pur] *verb,* **tapered, tapering. 1.** to make or become gradually narrower at one end: *A pyramid tapers to a point at the top.* **2.** to become less and less; gradually decrease: *Interest in the movie tapered off after a few weeks.* ◀))) A different word with the same sound is **tapir.**

tape recorder a machine that records and plays sound on specially treated tape.

tap·es·try [<u>tap</u>-uh-stree] *noun, plural* **tapestries.** *Art.* a piece of cloth with a design or picture that has been woven or stitched.

A modern United Nations **tank** *has a swiveling gun turret and lookout.*

*The South American **tapir** has young that are brown with yellowish-white streaks and spots.*

tape·worm [tape-wurm] *noun, plural* **tapeworms.** a long, flat worm that lives as a parasite in the intestines of people and animals.

ta·pir ▶ [tay-pir] *noun, plural* **tapirs.** an animal with short legs and a long fleshy nose that looks like a large pig but is related to rhinoceroses. Tapirs live in the forests of South America and Southeast Asia.
🔊 A different word with the same sound is **taper.**

taps [taps] *noun. Music.* a bugle call played in a military camp at the end of the day as a signal to turn out the lights.

tar [tar] *noun.* a black sticky substance obtained from coal or wood. Tar is used to pave roads and to waterproof roofs.
verb, **tarred, tarring.** to cover or spread with tar.

ta·ran·tu·la ▼ [tuh-ran-chuh-luh] *noun, plural* **tarantulas.** a large, hairy spider that lives in warm parts of the world. Tarantulas can give a painful bite.

> The **tarantula** gets its name from *Taranto,* a city of southern Italy where it was commonly found. In early times it was thought that a person bitten by a tarantula would suffer from a strange disease called *tarantism,* which would cause the person to get up and dance wildly for hours at a time. From this idea came a lively Italian dance called the *tarantella,* which is still popular today.

tar·dy [tar-dee] *adjective.* **tardier, tardiest.** coming later than the expected time; slow or late: *The tardy children missed the bus.* —**tardily,** *adverb;* **tardiness,** *noun.*

tar·get [tar-git] *noun, plural* **targets. 1.** something that is aimed at in order to hit or reach it: *The arrow hit the center of the target; Their target for the charity drive is to raise at least $100,000.* **2.** a person or thing that is attacked, criticized, or made fun of: *Dad's battered old hat is the target of family jokes.*
verb, **targeted, targeting.** to aim at something: *As part of its campaign to keep the parks clean, the town introduced fines that target littering.*

tar·iff [tare-if] *noun, plural* **tariffs.** *Business.* the charge or tax paid to the government for importing something into a country.

tar·nish [tar-nish] *verb,* **tarnished, tarnishing. 1.** to make dull and stained: *Air and certain chemicals tarnish silver.* **2.** to lose shine and brightness and become dull and stained: *The brass rail in the bathroom had tarnished from dampness.*
noun, plural **tarnishes.** a dullness or loss of shine on the surface of a metal.

tar·pau·lin [tar-puh-lin] *noun, plural* **tarpaulins.** a large piece of canvas or other waterproof fabric used as a protective cover: *The emergency workers fastened tarpaulins over the damaged part of the roof.* The shortened form of this word is **tarp.**

tar·pon ▼ [tar-pun *or* tar-pahn] *noun, plural* **tarpon** *or* **tarpons.** a large fish with silvery scales and a long body that lives in tropical Atlantic waters near the coast of Central America. It is sometimes caught for sport.

tart[1] [tart] *adjective,* **tarter, tartest.** tasting sharp and sour, like a lemon; not sweet.

tart[2] [tart] *noun, plural* **tarts.** a shallow pie with no top crust, containing custard, fruits, or other filling.

tar·tan [tart-un] *noun, plural* **tartans.** a woolen cloth woven with a plaid pattern, worn originally in Scotland. Each Scottish clan has its own distinctive tartan.

Tarpon grow up to eight feet long.

tar·tar [tar-tur] *noun.* a hard, yellowish substance that forms on the teeth near the gums that can help to cause dental decay if not removed.

task [task] *noun, plural* **tasks.** a piece of work or a duty that has to be done: *One of my tasks is to walk the dog every morning.*

tas·sel [tas-ul] *noun, plural* **tassels. 1.** a bunch of hanging threads tied together into a round ball at one end and used as a decoration. **2.** anything that is like this in shape: *the tassel on an ear of corn.*

*The South American **tarantula** is the largest spider in the world and can easily eat a mouse.*

taste ▶ [tayst] *noun, plural* **tastes.**
1. the sense by which a person or animal experiences flavor when something is taken into the mouth. **2.** a particular flavor of something taken into the mouth. The four basic tastes are sweet, sour, salty, and bitter. **3.** a small amount of a food, taken as a test or sample: *Would you like a taste of my dessert?* **4.** a liking or preference: *The movie was a bit too violent for my taste.* **5.** the ability to choose what is good or attractive: *to have good taste in clothes.*
verb, **tasted, tasting. 1.** to be aware of the flavor of food or drink taken into the mouth. **2.** to have a particular flavor: *This ham tastes very salty.* **3.** to take a small amount of food or drink into the mouth to test its flavor: *Taste this lemonade to see if it needs more sugar.*

taste bud one of the many small structures on the tongue that can tell the difference between foods according to their flavor.

taste·ful [tayst-ful] *adjective.* having or showing a feeling for what is good, attractive, or appropriate: *a tasteful color scheme; a tasteful birthday card.* —**tastefully,** *adverb.*

taste·less [tayst-lis] *adjective.* **1.** having little or no flavor: *The food was cold and tasteless.* **2.** having or showing little feeling for what is good, attractive, or appropriate: *The audience was embarrassed by the speaker's rude and tasteless jokes.*

tast·y [tayst-ee] *adjective* **tastier, tastiest.** having a pleasant taste with lots of flavor: *a tasty cheese; tasty cookies.*

tat·tered [tat-urd] *adjective.* old and torn; ragged: *a tattered coat; The towel was tattered around the edges.*

tat·tle [tat-ul] *verb,* **tattled, tattling.** to tell secrets or gossip about someone. A **tattletale** or **tattler** is a person who gossips about and tells the secrets of others.

tat·too ▶ [ta-too] *noun, plural* **tattoos.** a permanent picture or design on the skin. A tattoo is made by pricking tiny holes in skin with needles and then filling them with colored dyes.
verb, **tattooed, tattooing.** to mark the skin with a tattoo.

taught [tawt] *verb.* the past tense and past participle of TEACH.
🔊 A different word with the same sound is **taut.**

taunt [tawnt] *verb,* **taunted, taunting.** to say or do things to upset someone and make the person angry; tease or insult: *The bully taunted the child by calling him names until he cried.*
noun, plural **taunts.** a teasing remark or action.

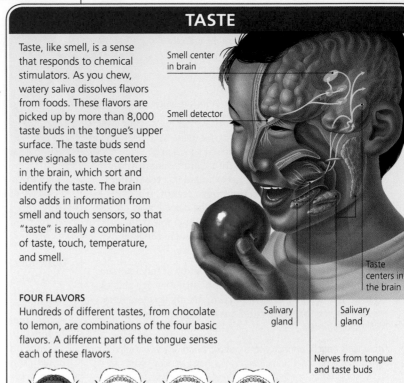

TASTE

Taste, like smell, is a sense that responds to chemical stimulators. As you chew, watery saliva dissolves flavors from foods. These flavors are picked up by more than 8,000 taste buds in the tongue's upper surface. The taste buds send nerve signals to taste centers in the brain, which sort and identify the taste. The brain also adds in information from smell and touch sensors, so that "taste" is really a combination of taste, touch, temperature, and smell.

Smell center in brain
Smell detector
Taste centers in the brain
Salivary gland
Salivary gland
Nerves from tongue and taste buds

FOUR FLAVORS
Hundreds of different tastes, from chocolate to lemon, are combinations of the four basic flavors. A different part of the tongue senses each of these flavors.

Bitter   Sweet   Sour   Salty

---

taut [tawt] *adjective,* **tauter, tautest.** stretched tight; not loose: *Pull the string around the parcel until it is taut, then make a knot.*
🔊 A different word with the same sound is **taught.**

tav·ern [tav-urn] *noun, plural* **taverns.** a place where travelers can stay overnight and where alcoholic drinks also may be sold; an inn.

taw·ny [taw-nee] *adjective,* **tawnier, tawniest.** having a pale brownish-yellow color: *a pile of tawny hay.*

tax [taks] *noun, plural* **taxes. 1.** *Business.* a sum of money that must be paid to a government by citizens and businesses, as when they earn income, buy something, own property, and so on. The government uses the money to provide such things as roads, hospitals, clean water, education, and many other services. **2.** a heavy demand; burden or strain: *The hungry baby birds are a tax on the energy of their parents.*
verb, **taxed, taxing. 1.** *Business.* to put a tax on: *Some governments tax cigarettes and use the money for the health system.* **2.** to make a heavy demand on; strain: *Feeding the extra campers taxed our food supplies.*

tax·at·ion [taks-ay-shun] *noun. Business.* the system that raises money by taxing citizens and businesses so the government can provide services. Something is **taxable** if tax must be paid on it.

a b c d e f g h i j k l m n o p q r s **t** u v w x y z

*In New Zealand, Maori men traditionally **tattooed** their faces, and often their bodies as well, with intricate designs.*

*India grows about thirty percent of the world's **tea** and all the leaves are picked by hand.*

taxi [tak-see] *noun, plural* **taxis.** an automobile with a driver that can be hired to take passengers where they want to go. The payment usually depends on the distance traveled, which is measured by a meter. Another form of this word is **taxicab.**

T cell *Biology.* a type of white blood cell that helps protect the body from infection and cancer.

tea ▶ [tee] *noun, plural* **teas. 1.** a drink made by pouring boiling water onto the dried leaves of a shrub that is grown mainly in China, India, Japan, and Sri Lanka. Water for making tea is boiled in a **teakettle.** The tea is brewed in and served from a **teapot,** which usually has a handle and a spout. **2.** the dried leaves of this shrub. **3.** a hot drink made in the same way from other dried leaves: *mint tea.* **4.** a light meal in the late afternoon when tea is served.

teach [teech] *verb,* **taught, teaching.** to show or tell a person how to do something, and help them until they are able to do it well: *to teach a student to read; My uncle is teaching me how to play the guitar and has taught me three tunes so far this month.*

The words **teach**, *educate, tutor,* and *train* all mean to help a person learn something. *Teach* is the most general word, as in "Schools *teach* students to read and write." *Educate* usually refers to learning at a higher level, such as a college, as in "She was *educated* at Harvard University." *Tutor* means to help someone with a particular subject as in "He earns extra money *tutoring* high school students in math." *Train* means to show someone how to do something practical, as in "The police officers were *trained* in the proper way to question a suspect."

teach·er [teech-ur] *noun, plural* **teachers.** a person who teaches, especially as a job.

*In ancient Greek chariot racing, chariots were drawn by **teams** of two or four horses.*

teal [teel] *noun, plural* **teals.** a small freshwater duck with a short neck. **2.** a bluish-green color. *adjective.* having a bluish-green color.

team ▼ [teem] *noun, plural* **teams. 1.** a group of people who share an activity, such as a sport or work: *a football team; a team of doctors.* The ability of the group to work well together is **teamwork. 2.** a number of animals strapped together to do work: *A team of horses pulled the stagecoach.* *verb,* **teamed, teaming.** to work together for a shared purpose; form a team: *Tim and Joe teamed up to do a joint science project.*
🔊 A different word with the same sound is **teem.**

team·mate [teem-mate] *noun, plural* **teammates.** a person who is a member of the same team: *Haley passed the ball to her teammate who scored a goal.*

tear¹ [tare] *verb,* **tore, torn, tearing. 1.** to pull or force apart: *to tear a piece of paper in two; James tore the poster from the wall.* **2.** to make a hole by pulling sharply or piercing with something sharp; rip: *Sarah tore her skirt climbing over the fence.* **3.** to move quickly; rush: *David tore down the stairs and ran out the door.*
noun, plural **tears.** a hole made by forcing apart or piercing with something sharp: *There's a tear in the sleeve of my favorite shirt.*

tear² [teer] *noun, plural* **tears. 1.** a drop of the salty liquid that falls from the eyes when you cry. Tears keep the eyes clean. They can be caused by sadness, pain, or laughter. **2. tears.** the act of crying: *to burst into tears.*
🔊 A different word with the same sound is **tier.**

tease [teez] *verb,* **teased, teasing.** to mock or make fun of, sometimes in a slightly cruel way: *We teased Dad about his habit of singing opera in the shower.*
noun, plural **teases.** someone or something that puzzles or annoys.

tea·spoon [tee-spoon] *noun, plural* **teaspoons.** a small spoon. Three teaspoons hold the same amount as one tablespoon.

tech·ni·cal [tek-nuh-kul] *adjective.* **1.** having to do with the special knowledge and skills used in industry or practical science: *If doctors talk in technical terms it can be difficult for a patient to follow what they are saying.* **2.** having to do with practical subjects, such as engineering or any of the mechanical industrial arts: *a technical college.* **3.** having to do with a strict or exact meaning of a law or rule: *The final scores were even, but our side was awarded a technical victory because we made fewer fouls.*
—**technically,** *adverb.*

tech·ni·cian [tek-nish-un] *noun, plural* **technicians.** someone with training and special skills for a particular job or science: *He works in the movie business as a sound technician.*

Technology *such as the Hubble Space Telescope, launched in 1990, allows scientists to observe outer space.*

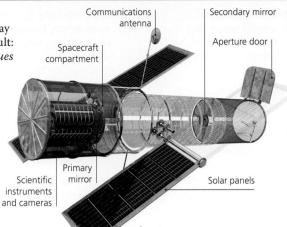

Communications antenna
Secondary mirror
Spacecraft compartment
Aperture door
Scientific instruments and cameras
Primary mirror
Solar panels

tech·nique [tek-<u>neek</u>] *noun, plural* **techniques.** a particular way of bringing about the desired result: *Drivers can learn special techniques to help them drive more safely.*

tech·nol·o·gy ▶ [tek-<u>nol</u>-uh-jee] *noun, plural* **technologies.** *Science.* **1.** the practical use of science, especially in industry, engineering, farming, and medicine; practical science. Something that has to do with the practical use of science is **technological. 2.** the machines, devices, or methods based on practical science that are used in a particular industry or activity: *Agricultural technology has progressed from horse-drawn plows to modern tractors.*

teddy bear a toy bear filled and covered with soft material.

The **teddy bear** is named for U.S. President Theodore ("Teddy") Roosevelt. This is said to come from a political cartoon in which Roosevelt, a famous hunter, is shown sparing the life of a small bear while out hunting. This bear became known as "Teddy's bear" and the term *teddy bear* then came to be used for a stuffed toy bear.

te·di·ous [<u>tee</u>-dee-us] *adjective.* boring and going on for a long time: *The movie was so tedious I nearly fell asleep.* The fact or quality of being tiring and uninteresting is **tedium. —tediously,** *adverb.*

tee [tee] *noun, plural* **tees. 1.** a level area of ground on a golf course that is the starting place for playing each hole. **2.** a wooden or plastic peg on which a golf ball is placed to be hit for the first time for each hole.

teem [teem] *verb,* **teemed, teeming.** to be full of: *The rich compost heap was teeming with earthworms.* 🔊 A different word with the same sound is **team.**

teen·ag·er [<u>teen</u>-*ayj*-ur] *noun, plural* **teenagers.** a person aged between thirteen and nineteen years. Something that has to do with people this age, such as music or fashion, is **teenaged** or **teenage.**

teens [teenz] *plural noun.* the years of being a teenager.

tee·pee ▶ [<u>tee</u>-*pee*] *noun, plural* **teepees.** a tent shaped like a cone made from animal skins, cloth, or canvas on a frame of poles. Teepees were used by Native Americans who lived on the plains. This word is also spelled **tepee.**

teeth [teeth] *noun.* the plural of TOOTH.

teethe [teeTH] *verb,* **teethed, teething.** to grow teeth: *The baby has a red cheek because she is teething.*

tel·e·cast [<u>tel</u>-uh-*kast*] *noun,* **telecasts.** a television broadcast: *Did you watch the telecast of the game? verb,* **telecasted, telecasting.** to broadcast a program on television.

tel·e·com·mu·ni·ca·tions [tel-uh-kuh-myoo-nuh-<u>kay</u>-shunz] *noun. Science.* the science and technology of sending and receiving signals and messages over long distances by computer, telephone, radio, or satellite.

tel·e·com·mute [tel-uh-kuh-<u>myoot</u>] *verb,* **telecommuted, telecommuting.** to work at home by communicating with an office or with other people through the use of a computer or other electronic means.

tel·e·con·fer·ence [*tel*-uh-<u>kon</u>-fruns *or* tel-uh-kon-fur-uns] *noun, plural* **teleconferences.** a meeting in which people from different locations are connected by electronic means, such as telephones and closed-circuit television.

tel·e·gram [tel-uh-*gram*] *noun, plural* **telegrams.** a message sent by telegraph.

tel·e·graph [<u>tel</u>-uh-*graf*] *noun, plural* **telegraphs.** a system for sending a message along electrical wires over a long distance. The message is sent in code and written or printed out at the receiving end. Telegraphs were widely used before the telephone became common.

tel·e·phone [tel-uh-*fone*] *noun, plural* **telephones.**
1. a system for speaking to someone else over a long distance, by sending sound by wire or radio waves.
2. the piece of equipment used to connect to this system. A telephone has a part for speaking into and a part for listening.

Smoke flaps
Family possessions
Entrance
Fireplace

Native Americans of the Great Plains lived in cone-shaped **teepees,** *which were made out of buffalo hides sewn together.*

a b c d e f g h i j k l m n o p q r s **t** u v w x y z

tel·e·scope [tel-uh-*skope*] *noun, plural* **telescopes.**
a tube-shaped instrument with powerful lenses that makes distant things appear nearer and larger. Very powerful telescopes are used to study the stars, planets, and other distant objects in space.

tel·e·vise [tel-uh-*vize*] *verb,* **televised, televising.**
to broadcast a program so it can be seen on television: *Events at the Olympic Games are televised around the world.*

tel·e·vi·sion [tel-uh-*vizh*-un] *noun, plural* **televisions.**
1. a system for sending pictures and sound by electronic signals over long distances. The signals are picked up by the receiving sets of viewers. 2. the receiving set on which these pictures are seen and the sound is heard. This is also called a **television set.**

In the Greek language the form *tele-* means "far away" or "distant." **Television** combines this form with vision, meaning "seeing." Television allows us to see things that are far away. Other similar words are *telephone* ("distant sound") and *telegraph* ("distant writing").

tell [tel] *verb,* **told, telling.** 1. to describe something in words; give information to someone: *Tell us about your vacation.* 2. to give an order; instruct someone to do something: *Mom told us to be back home before dark.* 3. to give away a secret; reveal: *I know where the hiding place is, but I promised not to tell.* 4. to recognize the difference between similar things; identify: *Can you tell whose handwriting this is?*

tell·er [tel-ur] *noun, plural* **tellers.** 1. a person who tells a story or gives an account of something. 2. a person who works in a bank receiving and paying out money.

Deciduous and conifer forests grow in **temperate** *regions.*

tem·per [tem-pur] *noun, plural* **tempers.** 1. a tendency to become angry, impatient, or resentful: *He gets into lots of fights because of his temper.* 2. a usual state of mind; disposition: *The dog's sweet temper makes it a suitable pet for children.* 3. control over the emotions: *He kept his temper and calmly ignored their teasing..*
verb, **tempered, tempering.** to make something less harsh or strong; lessen or soften: *News of the accident was tempered by the fact that no one had been badly injured.*

tem·pe·ra·men·tal [temp-ruh-*men*-tul *or* tem-pur-uh-*men*-tul] *adjective.* having frequent and sudden changes of mood; not calm or quiet: *The rest of the cast had to put up with many outbursts from the temperamental lead actor.*

tem·per·ate ▲ [tem-pur-it *or* temp-rit] *adjective.* not getting either very hot or very cold; moderate. The **Temperate Zone** is the area of the Earth between the tropics and the Arctic and Antarctic circles.

tem·per·a·ture [temp-ruh-chur *or* tem-pur-uh-chur] *noun, plural* **temperatures.** a measure of how hot or cold something or someone is. Temperature is often measured with a thermometer: *The temperature last night was below freezing; She has a fever with a very high temperature.*

tem·plate [tem-plit] *noun, plural* **templates.** 1. a thin plate of cardboard, plastic, or metal used as a pattern for making things with the same shape. 2. *Computers.* a document used to create new documents that follow the same pattern or design: *My dentist uses a template to print out bills for her patients.*

tem·ple¹ ▼ [tem-pul] *noun, plural* **temples.** *Religion.* a building in which people worship a god or gods: *Monks in orange robes climbed the steps to the Buddhist temple.*

tem·ple² [tem-pul] *noun, plural* **temples.** the flat part on either side of the forehead, next to the eyes.

tem·po [tem-poh] *noun, plural* **tempos.** *Music.* the speed at which a piece of music is or should be played: *a solemn march with a slow tempo.*

tem·po·rar·y [tem-puh-*rer*-ee] *adjective.* lasting for a short time only: *Our permanent teacher is away for two weeks, so we have a temporary teacher.* —**temporarily,** *adverb.*

tempt [tempt] *verb,* **tempted, tempting.** 1. to try to persuade someone to do something that seems pleasant, but which may be wrong or foolish: *Advertisements sometimes tempt people to buy things they can't afford.* 2. to appeal strongly to; attract: *It's such a sunny day I'm tempted to stop work now and go for a swim.* Something that is **tempting** is attractive and appealing.

temp·ta·tion [temp-tay-shun] *noun, plural* **temptations.** the feeling of wanting to do or have something that seems pleasant and attractive, but may be wrong or foolish: *I resisted the temptation of eating another chocolate.*

ten [ten] *noun, plural* **tens.** the number between nine and eleven; 10.
adjective. amounting to ten in number.

te·na·cious [tuh-*nay*-shus] *adjective.* not giving up easily; very determined: *Amy is a tenacious fighter for what she believes is right.* —**tenaciously,** *adverb.*

ten·ant [ten-unt] *noun, plural* **tenants.** *Business.* someone who rents a house, apartment, office, or land from the owner.

These Asian **temples** *date back to the Middle Ages.*

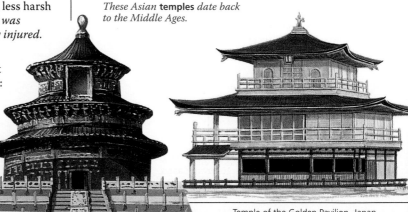

Temple of Heaven, China

Temple of the Golden Pavilion, Japan

An octopus has eight **tentacles** lined with special suction cups
that help it move along or grip its prey.

terminate

tend¹ [tend] *verb,* **tended, tending.** likely to happen: *It tends to snow a lot here in winter.*

tend² [tend] *verb,* **tended, tending.** to look after someone or something; take care of: *to tend a vegetable garden.*

ten·den·cy [ten-dun-see] *noun, plural* **tendencies.** a likelihood that something will keep happening: *That gate has a tendency to jam when it gets wet.*

ten·der¹ [ten-dur] *adjective.* **1.** not hard or tough; soft: *Tender feet are easily hurt on rough ground.* **2.** not strong; delicate: *the tender petals of a rose.* **3.** affectionate or loving: *The mother bathed the baby with tender care.* **4.** sensitive or painful when touched: *The area around the wound is very tender.* —**tenderly,** *adverb;* —**tenderness,** *noun.*

ten·der² [ten-dur] *verb,* **tendered, tendering.** to present or offer something officially: *He went to see the boss to tender his resignation from the company.*

ten·don [ten-dun] *noun, plural* **tendons.** a tough band or cord of tissue that attaches a muscle to a bone or other part of the body.

ten·e·ment [ten-uh-munt] *noun, plural* **tenements.** a large apartment building, usually located in a poor part of a city.

ten·nis ▶ [ten-is] *noun.* a game played by two or four players, who use rackets to hit a small ball over a net. Tennis is played on concrete, grass, clay, or other courts.

The game of **tennis** is thought to have begun in Italy and then moved to France and eventually to England. The name may have come from *tenez,* a French word that a tennis player would shout as he was about to serve the ball. This meant roughly "take this" that is, be ready to receive the serve.

ten·or [ten-ur] *noun, plural* **tenors.** *Music.* **1.** the highest male singing voice. **2.** a singer who has such a voice. **3.** a musical instrument with this range.

tense¹ [tens] *adjective,* **tenser, tensest. 1.** stretched stiff and tight; strained: *A tense rope is easy to climb.* **2.** feeling, showing, or causing anxious feelings or suspense: *The tense scene in the movie made my heart beat faster.* *verb,* **tensed, tensing.** to make or become tense: *She tensed at the sound of footsteps behind her in the dark.*

tense² [tens] *noun, plural* **tenses.** *Language.* a form of a verb that shows the time of the action or state expressed by the verb. In the sentence *I go to school,* the verb "go" is in the present tense. In the sentence *I painted the house,* the verb "painted" is in the past tense.

The **tense** of a verb means its time. This can be the present, as in "She *plays* the piano." It can be the past, as in "I *was eating* dinner when the doorbell *rang.*" You will probably use the past tense when you write stories, because you will be telling about something that happened before. However, you may begin the story with the present tense to set the scene, and then shift to the past to tell what happened: "Dwayne *lives* in a house on a river. One day when he *was walking* by the river, he *saw…*"

ten·sion [ten-shun] *noun.* **1.** the force that acts on objects so as to stretch or pull them: *The string broke because there was too much tension on it.* **2.** a feeling of nervous strain.

tent [tent] *noun, plural* **tents.** a portable shelter made of nylon or canvas and held up by one or more flexible rods or poles. Tents are used for camping.

ten·ta·cle ▲ [ten-tuh-kul] *noun, plural* **tentacles.** one of the long, thin outer parts of certain animals, used to touch, hold, and move: *Many tentacles hang down from the body of a jellyfish.*

tenth [tenth] *adjective; noun.* next after the ninth. *noun, plural* **tenths.** one of ten equal parts of something; ¹/₁₀.

ten·ure [ten-yur] *noun. Education.* a status of guaranteed permanent employment granted to a teacher or professor after they have worked for a certain time and met certain requirements.

te·pee [tee-pee] *noun, plural* **tepees.** another spelling of TEEPEE.

term [turm] *noun, plural* **terms.** **1.** a word or group of words that has a definite meaning: *Terms used in baseball include "diamond," "bat," and "infield."* **2.** a limited or definite period of time: *The judge sentenced the guilty man to a term of five years in jail.* **3.** one of the parts of an agreement or a legal document; a condition: *One of the terms of the building contract states that the roof of the house has to be shingled.* The way in which people get along together is called **terms:** *Bill is now on good terms again with his parents.* *verb,* **termed, terming.** to call or name: *God, in the Muslim religion, is termed "Allah."*

Tennis players competing in the annual Wimbledon Tennis Championships must wear white outfits.

ter·mi·nal [tur-muh-nul] *noun, plural* **terminals.** **1.** a station at the end of a travel route by rail, air, road, or sea. **2.** a monitor and a keyboard that can be linked to a computer. *adjective.* describing a disease that will cause death: *He has terminal cancer.*

ter·mi·nate [tur-muh-*nate*] *verb,* **terminated, terminating.** **1.** to come or bring to an end: *This train terminates at the next station.* **2.** to dismiss from a job; fire: *After ten years in the job, David was terminated by his boss.* —**termination,** *noun.*

ter·mi·nol·o·gy [tur-muh-<u>nol</u>-uh-jee] *noun, plural* **terminologies.** *Language.* words used by people involved in a specific activity or area of work: *The terminology of the science of genetics, such as "allele," "phenotype," or "mutagen," is hard to understand if you have not studied the subject.*

ter·mite ▼ [tur-*mite*] *noun, plural* **termites.** a small, white insect that eats wood, paper, and other similar materials. Termites live in large groups.

ter·race [<u>ter</u>-is] *noun, plural* **terraces. 1.** a paved outdoor area next to a house: *It's nice to have lunch on the terrace in summer.* **2.** a balcony of an apartment house. **3.** a raised area of land with a flat top and sloping sides, built on a hillside and used for growing crops. Of or relating to such areas of land is **terraced.**

ter·rain [tuh-<u>rane</u>] *noun.* ground or a piece of land: *The explorers climbed a hill to see the surrounding terrain.*

ter·ra·pin [ter-uh-*pin*] *noun, plural* **terrapins.** a small turtle that lives in or near fresh water or along the seashore in North America.

ter·rar·i·um [tuh-<u>rer</u>-ee-um] *noun, plural* **terrariums** or **terraria.** a container, usually made of glass, in which small animals or small plants are kept.

ter·res·tri·al [tuh-<u>res</u>-tree-ul] *adjective. Biology.* **1.** of or relating to land, rather than air or water: *A rose is a terrestrial plant–seaweed is not.* **2.** of or relating to the Earth or its inhabitants.

ter·ri·ble [ter-uh-bul] *adjective.* **1.** causing terror or fear; dreadful: *In the movie, a terrible monster destroys the town.* **2.** very bad or serious: *I've got a terrible cold.*

ter·ri·bly [ter-uh-blee] *adverb.* **1.** very badly: *The man was terribly injured in the car accident.* **2.** very; extremely: *I'm terribly tired today.*

ter·ri·er ◀ [ter-ee-ur] *noun, plural* **terriers.** one of a number of small, active dogs that were originally used for hunting.

ter·rif·ic [tuh-<u>rif</u>-ik] *adjective.* **1.** very great or severe; remarkable: *Racing cars move at terrific speeds.* **2.** causing great fear or terror: *a terrific earthquake.* **3.** very good; wonderful: *Greg is a terrific quarterback.* —**terrifically,** *adverb.*

ter·ri·fy [ter-uh-*fye*] *verb,* **terrified, terrifying.** to fill with terror; make greatly afraid: *That big dog terrifies me.*

ter·ri·to·ry [ter-uh-*tore*-ee] *noun, plural* **territories. 1.** a large area of land; region: *It's difficult to hike in mountainous territory during winter.* **2.** all the area of land and water making up a country or state. **3.** a region of a country that does not have the full rights of a state or province: *Alaska was a territory of the United States before it became a state in 1959.* **4.** *Biology.* a certain area occupied by an animal or group of animals, as for breeding, raising young, searching for food, and so on. Animals often will defend their territory against others who try to come there.

ter·ror [ter-ur] *noun, plural* **terrors. 1.** a feeling of great fear: *The sound of thunder filled the little girl with terror.* **2.** a cause of great fear: *The evil king was a terror to his people.*

ter·ror·ism [ter-ur-*iz*-um] *noun.* the use of violence or threats of violence as a way of forcing others to obey or do something, usually for a political goal.

ter·ror·ist [ter-ur-ist] *noun, plural* **terrorists.** a person who uses violence or threats of violence as a way of forcing others to obey or do something, usually for a political goal.

ter·ror·ize [ter-ur-*rize*] *verb,* **terrorized, terrorizing.** to fill with great fear: *A group of hungry lions terrorized an African village.*

test [test] *noun, plural* **tests. 1.** a set of tasks or problems; an examination. A test is used to find out what a person knows or can do: *a math test; a spelling test.* **2.** any method of finding out the quality or nature of something: *An optometrist gives people eye tests to find out how well they can see.* *verb,* **tested, testing.** to give a test to or check: *The doctor tested Susan's blood to find out why she felt sick.*

tes·ta·ment [tes-tuh-munt] *noun, plural* **testaments. 1.** written instructions that state what a person wants done with the things he or she owns after the person dies: *a person's last will and testament.* **2.** something that serves as evidence or proof of a fact, event, or quality: *Myra's recovery from cancer is a testament to the skill of her doctors.* The two main divisions of the Bible are the **Old Testament** and the **New Testament.**

TERMITES

Some termites build huge nests that can be more than twenty feet high. The termites collect plant matter from which fungi grow, providing food for the termites. At the heart of the termite colony is the chamber where the queen termite lives, laying millions of eggs for fifteen years or more. Other chambers are fungus gardens, while others are nurseries where worker termites look after eggs and young termites. A maze of tunnels connects all the chambers and keeps the air circulating.

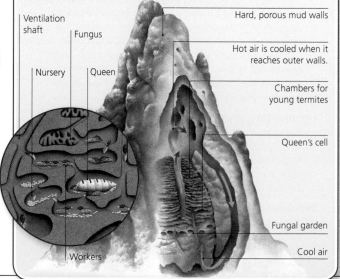

Ventilation shaft
Fungus
Nursery
Queen
Hard, porous mud walls
Hot air is cooled when it reaches outer walls.
Chambers for young termites
Queen's cell
Fungal garden
Workers
Cool air

English thatched cottage

Chinese farmhouse

Nigerian fishing hut

Thatch *is a traditional style of roof covering in many parts of the world.*

tes·ti·fy [tes-tuh-*fye*] *verb,* **testified, testifying. 1.** *Law.* to give evidence under oath as a witness in a court of law: *The police officer was called on to testify in the robbery case.* **2.** to serve as evidence or proof: *The high grades on his report card testify to Mike's intelligence.*

tes·ti·mo·ny [tes-tuh-*moh*-nee] *noun, plural* **testimonies. 1.** *Law.* a statement made under oath by a witness in a court of law: *The testimony of the witness convinced the jury that the accused man was innocent.* **2.** evidence or proof: *Our team's success in soccer is testimony to the skill of our players.*

test tube *Science.* a narrow glass tube that is used in laboratory experiments and tests. A test tube is closed at one end and open at the other.

tet·a·nus [tet-uh-nus *or* tet-nus] *noun. Medicine.* a serious disease that causes great stiffness of muscles, especially those of the jaw. Tetanus is caused by germs that enter the body through a wound. This disease is also called lockjaw.

teth·er [teTH-ur] *noun, plural* **tethers.** a rope or chain used to tie up an animal to keep it in a small area. *verb,* **tethered, tethering.** to tie up with a tether: *The girl tethered her pony to the fence.*

text [tekst] *noun, plural* **texts. 1.** the main body of words in a book: *For homework, we had to read the text of chapter four, then answer the questions at the end of the chapter.* **2.** the original words of a writer or speaker: *The text of Abraham Lincoln's Gettysburg Address is carved into a wall of the Lincoln Memorial.* **3.** a textbook: *My text for science class makes my bag really heavy.*

text·book [tekst-*buk*] *noun, plural* **textbooks.** *Education.* a book containing the information for a course of study in a subject, used by students: *a biology textbook.*

tex·tile ▶ [tek-stile *or* tek-stul] *noun, plural* **textiles.** a woven or knitted fabric.

Tapas cloth is a Samoan **textile** *that is made from the bark of the mulberry tree.*

tex·ture [teks-chur] *noun, plural* **textures.** the appearance and feel of something: *Silk has a smooth, slippery texture.*

than [THan] *conjunction.* **1.** compared with or to: *Sam is a better pitcher than Michael.* **2.** except; but; besides: *I'd rather eat anything else than Brussels sprouts.*

thank [thangk] *verb,* **thanked, thanking. 1.** to show or give thanks; express gratitude: *I thanked Grandma for taking me to the movies.* **2.** to hold responsible; credit; blame: *We have the burst water pipe to thank for the flooding in the basement.*

thank·ful [thangk-ful] *adjective.* feeling or showing thanks; grateful: *The stranded family were thankful to the rescue workers for saving them.* —**thankfully,** *adverb.*

thanks [thangks] *interjection.* thank you: *Thanks for finding my history book.* *plural noun.* a feeling or expression of gratitude: *Our class wrote a letter of thanks to the people who donated the new sports equipment.*

Thanks·giv·ing [thangks-*giv*-ing] *noun, plural* **Thanksgivings. 1.** a holiday in the United States held on the fourth Thursday in November to give thanks for the things one has. It commemorates the Pilgrims' first harvest feast in 1621. **2.** a similar holiday in Canada, held on the second Monday in October.

that [THat] *adjective.* **1.** used to refer to a person or thing being singled out or already mentioned: *I really like that green shirt of yours.* **2.** used to refer to something farther away or less immediate than another thing: *That cake in the back looks nicer than this one in front.* *pronoun, plural* **those. 1.** the person or thing being singled out or already mentioned: *That is my coach standing over there.* **2.** something farther away or less immediate than another thing: *This is a butterfly and that is a moth.* **3.** who, whom, or which: *The cat that we found in the yard had kittens yesterday.* *conjunction.* **1.** used to introduce a clause in a sentence: *She said that she would be home by six.* **2.** used to show a cause or reason: *We were happy that our cousins were coming for a visit; The cut was so deep that he had to go to the hospital for stitches.* *adverb.* to such an extent or degree; so: *I didn't realize it was that important to you.*

Both **that** and *who* are used to begin a clause that tells about someone or something: "Neil Armstrong was the first person *who* walked on the Moon. This completed an effort *that* began nine years earlier." To be correct, you should not use *that* when you are referring to a person. So it would not be proper to write, "Neil Armstrong was the first person *that* walked on the Moon."

thatch ▲ thach] *noun.* a roof covering made from straw, reeds, or other plant stalks or leaves. *verb,* **thatched, thatching.** to cover with thatch: *The villager thatched the roof of the hut with reeds.*

a b c d e f g h i j k l m n o p q r s t u v w x y z

thaw

*Snowmen begin to **thaw** as the weather gets warmer.*

thaw ▶ [thaw] *verb,* **thawed, thawing. 1.** to soften after being frozen; melt: *The frozen pond is thawing in the sun.* **2.** to become less chilled; warm up: *After the snowball fight, we went inside to thaw out in front of the fire.* **3.** to become more friendly: *She was angry with her boyfriend, but she thawed when he apologized and gave her a bunch of roses.* *noun, plural* **thaws.** a period of warm weather when ice and snow melt: *the spring thaw.*

the [THuh *or* THee] a word used in front of a noun that stands for a particular thing, person, or group: *The rocket blasted off into space; Don't forget the CD.* It can also mean a special one or single one: *In our town, that restaurant is the place to eat.* *adverb.* to that extent; by that much: *The farther we walk, the more tired I feel.* "The" is called a *definite article.*

the·ater ▼ [thee-uh-tur] *noun, plural* **theaters. 1.** a building or area where plays, movies, or other entertainments are presented. **2.** the writing and performance of plays; drama: *The movie star started his career in the theater.* This word is also spelled **theatre.**

the·at·ri·cal [thee-at-ruh-kul] *adjective.* **1.** having to do with the theater or with performing plays: *a theatrical costume; theatrical makeup.* **2.** being artificial and exaggerated; not natural: *The way she flutters her eyelashes and waves her hands about is so theatrical.* **—theatrically,** *adverb.*

thee [THee] *pronoun.* an old-fashioned form of YOU.

theft [theft] *noun, plural* **thefts.** *Law.* the act or crime of stealing something that belongs to another person.

their [THare] *pronoun.* of, belonging to, or having to do with them: *The pet hamsters escaped from their cage.* 🔊 Different words with the same sound are **there** and **they're.**

Their, *there,* and *they're* are three words that sound the same, so they are sometimes confused with each other in writing. *Their* is an adjective meaning "belonging to them:" We asked our neighbors to keep *their dog out of our yard. There* is an adverb meaning "in or of a certain place:" The fence has a hole and the dog got through *there. They're* is the shorter form of "they are:" Our neighbors said *they're* sorry this happened.

theirs [THarez] *pronoun.* the thing or things that belong to or have to do with them: *Nancy is a friend of theirs.*

*The Globe **Theatre** in London, England, was built in 1599 by a company of actors to which the famous English playwright Willliam Shakespeare belonged.*

them [THem] *pronoun.* the people or things being discussed: *I called up my friends and asked them to meet me at the park; He picked up the balls and juggled them.*

theme [theem] *noun, plural* **themes. 1.** *Literature.* the main subject or idea of a speech, discussion, book, or other creative work: *The theme of the movie was to follow your dreams.* A **thematic** approach is an approach having to do with or being organized according to a theme. **2.** *Music.* the main melody in a musical composition. **3.** a short written exercise given to a student; essay.

The **theme** of a book or story is the main idea it tells about. This is like the *plot*, but the plot is the action of the story and the theme is the thought that this action expresses. For example, the plot of the famous Western movie *Shane* is a fight between farmers and cattle ranchers about who has the right to the land. The theme of the movie is that the hero, Shane, wants to leave behind his past life as a gunfighter and become peaceful like the farmers, but cannot do this.

theme park an amusement park where all the settings, attractions, and rides have a common theme.

them·selves [THem-selvz] *pronoun.* **1.** their own selves: *They gave themselves plenty of time to get ready.* **2.** their normal, proper, healthy selves.

then [THen] *adverb.* **1.** at that time: *I didn't know her in fourth grade because she was still living in Montana then.* **2.** soon after that; next: *I had a shower, then I got dressed.* **3.** in that case; in those circumstances: *If we miss the bus, then we'll have to walk.*
adjective. being so at that time: *After the bridge was washed away, the then mayor said that the county would rebuild it soon.*
noun. that time: *Let's stay up until then.*

the·ol·o·gy [thee-ol-uh-jee] *noun, plural* **theologies.** *Religion.* the study of religion and religious questions. Something having to do with theology and specialized religious study is **theological.**

the·o·rem [thee-uh-rum *or* theer-um] *noun, plural* **theorems.** *Mathematics.* a formula or proposition that has been or still needs to be proved true using other formulas and propositions.

the·o·ret·i·cal [thee-uh-ret-i-kul] *adjective.* having to do with theory or ideas; not practical: *That's too theoretical —it doesn't tell me how to actually fix the computer.* If something will work **theoretically,** it will work in theory but may not work when put into practice.

the·o·ry [theer-ee] *noun, plural* **theories. 1.** *Science.* a set of ideas or principles that explains a phenomenon, based on observation and reason: *The Big Bang theory is one scientific explanation of how the universe began.* **2.** a belief based on some evidence, but not proved as actual fact: *I have a theory about who stole my skateboard.*

ther·a·py [ther-uh-pee] *noun, plural* **therapies.** *Health.* treatment that helps or heals illness, disability, injury, or psychological problems. A **therapist** is a person trained to give therapy using physical or psychological treatment methods.

there [THare] *adverb.* in, at, to, or into that place: *I'm going to put the poster up there.*
pronoun. used to introduce a sentence that has a linking verb such as "be" before the subject: *There are a lot of rides at the fair.*
noun. that place or position: *Mandy catches the bus from there every day.*
interjection. used to express feelings such as satisfaction, sympathy, or anger: *There! I found it!*
🔊 Different words with the same sound are **their** and **they're.**

"*There's* many good reasons to do that." "*There's* a lot of questions about what really happened." People often use such sentences in speaking. In writing, though, it is better to use *there are* in sentences like this. *There's* is the shorter form of *there is*, which is singular. These are plural sentences, and so it would not be correct to write, "*There is* many good reasons" or "*There is* a lot of questions."

there·af·ter [THare-af-tur] *adverb.* from that time onward; after that: *He graduated from college and moved to Seattle shortly thereafter.*

there·by [THare-bye] *adverb.* by that means; as a result of that: *She untangled the bird from the net, thereby saving its life.*

there·fore [THare-fore] *adverb.* for that reason; because of that: *The school buses can't get through because of the blizzard—therefore, there'll be no school today.*

ther·mal [thur-mul] *adjective.* *Environment.* having to do with or causing heat; warm or hot: *Yellowstone National Park has thermal springs and pools.*
noun, plural **thermals.** a rising current of warm air: *The hang glider soared upward in the thermal.*

ther·mom·e·ter ▲ [thur-mom-uh-tur] *noun, plural* **thermometers.** a device for measuring temperature. The most common thermometer is a glass tube containing a liquid such as mercury or alcohol. The liquid rises or falls against a scale as the temperature rises or falls.

ther·mos ▶ [thur-mus] *noun, plural* **thermoses.** a vacuum bottle used to keep liquids hot or cold. It is also called a **thermos bottle.**

ther·mo·stat [thur-muh-stat] *noun, plural* **thermostats.** a device that controls temperature automatically, as found in cars, air conditioning and heating systems, and refrigerators.

A mercury **thermometer** *(left) is marked with a scale of temperatures, but a digital thermometer displays a person's temperature on a small screen.*

The vacuum between the two walls of a **thermos** *keeps its contents hot or cold.*

the·sau·rus [thi-<u>sore</u>-us] *noun, plural* **thesauri** *or* **thesauruses.** *Language.* a book containing lists of synonyms, and often also antonyms.

A **thesaurus** is a book that gives a list of other words that mean the same thing as a certain word. Writers use a thesaurus when they have an idea they want to express, but are not quite sure which word to use to do this. For example, you might be writing about a fire that happened near where you live. You know that it was a bad fire, but you want to use a stronger and less common word than *bad*. A thesaurus can give you a list of other words to use instead of *bad*.

these [THeez] *adjective; pronoun.* the plural of THIS.

the·sis [<u>thee</u>-sis] *noun, plural* **theses. 1.** an idea, argument, or proposition to be discussed or proved: *His thesis was that if the legal driving age were raised from sixteen to eighteen, there'd be fewer accidents.* **2.** a book-length essay that presents the results of original research, written by a student for an academic degree: *The literature student wrote his thesis on Mark Twain.*

*This house and some beehives are almost hidden by a **thicket**.*

they [THay] *plural pronoun.* **1.** the people or things being talked about; those ones: *Have you seen my skates—they were on the porch a minute ago?* **2.** people in general: *They say there's a pot of gold at the end of the rainbow.*

they're [THare] the shortened form of "they are."

🔊 Different words with the same sound are **there** and **their**.

thick [thik] *adjective,* **thicker, thickest. 1.** having a relatively great depth or extent between one side or surface and the other; not thin: *I wear a thick coat in winter.* **2.** measuring between one side or surface and the other: *The Great Wall of China is up to thirty feet thick.* **3.** closely packed together; dense: *The hikers got lost in the thick forest.* **4.** not flowing easily; not runny: *We spread the thick maple syrup over the pancakes.*
adverb. in a thick manner; thickly: *Snow lay thick on the ground after the blizzard.*
noun. the part or place that is most active or crowded: *Ben threw himself into the thick of the ice hockey game.* **—thickly,** *adverb;* **thickness,** *noun.*

thick·en [<u>thik</u>-un] *verb,* **thickened, thickening.** to make or become thick or thicker: *Use cream to thicken the sauce. The smoke thickened as the fire spread.* **—thickener,** *noun.*

thick·et ▲ [<u>thik</u>-it] *noun, plural* **thickets.** a thick growth of shrubs, bushes, or small trees.

thief [theef] *noun, plural* **thieves.** a person who steals: *The thief snatched the woman's bag and ran off.*

thigh [thye] *noun, plural* **thighs.** the part of the leg from the hip to the knee.

thim·ble ◀ [<u>thim</u>-bul] *noun, plural* **thimbles.** a small plastic or metal cover that is worn on the finger while sewing, to protect the finger when pushing the needle through fabric.

thin [thin] *adjective,* **thinner, thinnest.**
1. having a relatively small depth or extent between one side or surface and the other; not thick: *Mrs. Martinez writes her airmail letters on thin paper.* **2.** slim or lean; not fat: *The fashion model was very thin.* **3.** not dense; sparse: *The balding man's hair was thin on top.* **4.** flowing easily; runny or watery: *The gravy is thin —it needs more flour.* A **thinner** is a liquid that is added to paint or varnish to make it more runny. **5.** having a faint, shrill, or weak sound: *She'd never played the trumpet before, so her notes came out thin.*
adverb. in a thin manner; thinly: *Slice the tomato thin.*
verb, **thinned, thinning.** to make or become thin: *Add more water to thin the soup; The air thinned as the mountain climbers went higher.* **—thinly,** *adverb;* **thinness,** *noun.*

thing [thing] *noun, plural* **things. 1.** a real physical object that is not alive. A pencil, a computer, and a building are all things. **2.** an object, entity, or creature that cannot be named or described precisely: *Pass me the thing with the yellow wire sticking out.* **3.** anything that is spoken of, thought of, or done: *Teasing that girl was a rotten thing to do.* **4.** a person or animal: *That duckling is such a cute little thing.* **5.** a specific state of affairs; situation: *We want to get to the bottom of this thing.* **6. things.** the general state of affairs: *Things are going well for her at work now.* **7. things.** possessions: *We're leaving now, so go and get your things.*

Thing is one of the most common words in English, and one reason is that there is no other word that means exactly what this word does. If you want to get away from using the word *thing* all the time, you can do it by thinking of more exact words that can replace it. "There are a lot of *things* on the bottom of the pool. To pick them up, use this blue *thing* here." This could be, "there are a lot of *leaves and sticks* on the bottom of the pool. To pick them up, use this blue *scoop attached to a long pole.*"

think [thingk] *verb,* **thought, thinking. 1.** to use the mind to form ideas, make decisions, or reason: *I'm trying to think what to do next.* A **thinker** is a person who spends a lot of time considering ideas or subjects. **2.** to consider or believe something; to have an idea or opinion: *Miguel thinks he's the best shooter on the basketball team.* **3.** to bring back to the mind; recall: *Grandma still thinks about when she was a little girl.* **4.** to care about or take account of: *The only person you think about is yourself.*

third [thurd] *adjective.* the position between second and fourth.
noun, plural **thirds. 1.** a person or thing that comes next after the second. **2.** one of three equal parts; ⅓.

thirst [thurst] *noun, plural* **thirsts. 1.** an uncomfortable feeling of dryness in the mouth and throat, caused by the need to drink. **2.** the desire or need to drink: *The marathon runner collapsed from thirst.* **3.** a strong desire or longing: *a thirst for knowledge.*
verb, **thirsted, thirsting. 1.** to feel a need to drink: *I thirsted for a cool drink of water.* **2.** to feel a strong desire or longing: *The politician thirsted for power.*

thirst·y [thur-stee] *adjective,* **thirstier, thirstiest. 1.** having a feeling of thirst; parched: *We're thirsty—can we have some lemonade please?* **2.** having a strong desire: *The football team was thirsty for a new challenge and wanted to play a bigger school.*

thir·teen [thur-teen] *noun, plural* **thirteens.** the number between twelve and fourteen; 13. The position between twelfth and fourteenth is **thirteenth.**

thir·ty [thurt-ee] *noun, plural* **thirties.** the number between twenty-nine and thirty-one; 30. The position between twenty-ninth and thirty-first is **thirtieth.**

this [THis] *adjective.* **1.** referring to a person or thing that is present, close by, or has just been mentioned: *This DVD doesn't work any more.* **2.** referring to something that is nearer than or compared with another thing: *This car goes faster than that one.*
pronoun, plural **these. 1.** the person or thing that is present, close by, or has just been mentioned: *This is Jermaine's baby sister.* **2.** something that is nearer than or compared with another thing: *I didn't ask for this— I asked for that.* **3.** something about to be said: *You're going to laugh when you hear this.*
adverb. to this extent or degree; so: *The fish I caught was this big.*

this·tle ▶ [this-ul] *noun, plural* **thistles.** a plant with prickly leaves and white, yellow, red, or purple flowers.

thong [thong] *noun, plural* **thongs. 1.** a narrow strip of leather used for tying or binding. **2.** a sandal with a V-shaped strap that fits between the big toe and the second toe. It is usually made of rubber or leather.

*The **thistle** is the national flower of Scotland.*

thor·ax ▶ [thore-aks] *noun, plural* **thoraxes.** *Biology.* **1.** the part of the body of mammals and vertebrates between the neck and the abdomen, enclosed by the ribs. It includes the heart and lungs. **2.** the part of an insect's body between its head and its abdomen. It includes the wings and legs.

thorn [thorn] *noun, plural* **thorns. 1.** a sharp, stiff growth on the branch or stem of a plant such as a rose. **2.** a plant that has thorns: *A long hedge of thorns protected the house from the trespassers.* A plant that has thorns is **thorny.**

thor·ough [thur-oh] *adjective.* complete in every detail; extremely careful: *After a thorough examination the doctor said I was fit enough to run in the marathon.*

Thoroughbred horses prized for their elegance and endurance have been raised for more than 2,000 years.

thor·ough·bred ▶ [thur-oh-bred] *noun, plural* **thoroughbreds. 1.** a breed of horse that was developed in England in the seventeenth century by crossing Arabian stallions with European mares. All racehorses are thoroughbreds. **2.** a person who has been well brought up, is well-mannered, and highly educated.
adjective. **1.** relating to a pure-bred horse. **2.** having the qualities of being a well-bred person.

thor·ough·fare [thur-oh-fare] *noun, plural* **thoroughfares.** a street that is open at both ends. It is often a main road.

those [THoze] *pronoun; adjective.* the plural of THAT.

thou [THou] *pronoun.* an old-fashioned form of YOU.

though [THoh] *conjunction.* **1.** despite the fact that; although: *John didn't get an extra serving of popcorn, even though he paid for it.* **2.** and yet; but; however: *I felt it was going to rain, though there were no dark clouds in the sky.*
adverb. nevertheless; however: *The concert was very loud—I really enjoyed it though.*

thought [thawt] *verb.* the past tense and past participle of THINK.
noun, plural **thoughts. 1.** the act or process of thinking: *He stared out the window, deep in thought.* **2.** a person's idea or opinion: *The thought crossed my mind that I should go home early.* **3.** the fact of giving something careful attention or serious consideration: *We all need to give some careful thought to what can be done about climate change.*

thousand [thou-zund] *noun, plural* **thousands.** the number between nine hundred and ninety-nine and one thousand and one; 1,000.
adjective. amounting to one thousand in number. The position between nine hundred and ninety-nine and one thousand and one is the **thousandth.**

Abdomen

Head and thorax

*A spider's legs are attached to its **thorax**.*

a b c d e f g h i j k l m n o p q r s **t** u v w x y z

thrash

thrash [thrash] *verb,* **thrashed, thrashing. 1.** to beat violently as punishment: *It is no longer acceptable to thrash a child for being naughty.* **2.** to toss about violently; to move about in an uncontrolled manner: *He thrashed about in the water because he couldn't swim.* **3.** to defeat decisively, usually in a sports competition: *Our team was thrashed in the final game.*

thread [thred] *noun, plural* **threads. 1.** a thin, fine cord that is used to sew or weave cloth. **2.** a thin strip of something that looks like a thread: *A thread of white smoke rose lazily from the chimney into the still, night air.* **3.** the train of thought that connects the different elements of a story or argument: *When the phone rang, I lost the thread of the movie.* **4.** the continuous ridge of metal that winds around a screw and holds the screw in place. **5.** *Computers.* a series of messages about the same subject in an Internet discussion group. *verb,* **threaded, threading. 1.** to pass something like a thread through a hole: *Alison threaded the rope through the hole and tied it securely.* **2.** to string a number of things together on a thread. **3.** to move carefully around or between things that are blocking the way: *The hikers threaded their way through the narrow mountain pass.*

threat [thret] *noun, plural* **threats. 1.** a declaration of intention to cause hurt or harm: *The kidnappers might carry out their threat to kill their victim.* **2.** someone or something that is likely to cause harm or be dangerous: *That guard dog is a real threat to anyone who goes near it.* **3.** an indication that something very bad will happen: *The threat of a tornado sent everyone running for shelter.*

threat·en [thret-un] *verb,* **threatened, threatening. 1.** to say that hurt or harm will be done; make a threat against someone: *The robbers threatened to shoot us if we didn't hand over our money.* **2.** to be the cause of hurt or harm: *Poor grades in school can threaten your future career.* **3.** to give a sign or warning that something will happen: *The sudden drop in temperature threatened snow.* Someone or something that threatens is **threatening.**

three [three] *noun, plural* **threes.** the number between two and four; 3. *adjective.* amounting to three in number.

thresh ▲ [thresh] *verb,* **threshed, threshing.** to separate grain or seeds from a cereal plant or grass by using some kind of special implement or machine. A person who separates seeds from a plant is called a **thresher.**

thresh·old [thresh-hold] *noun, plural* **thresholds. 1.** the stone, wood, or metal sill of a doorway: *He carried his new bride across the threshold of their new home.* **2.** the starting point of an important event or discovery: *Medical research may be on the threshold of a breakthrough in the treatment of cancer.* **3.** the level that has to be reached before something can be felt or take effect: *People with a low pain threshold need higher doses of painkillers.*

thrift [thrift] *noun.* the wise and careful use of money or valuable resources so as to avoid waste: *You'll have to learn thrift if you want to have enough money for your holiday.* A person who practices such careful use of money is **thrifty.**

thrill [thril] *noun, plural* **thrills. 1.** a sudden, intense feeling of excitement or pleasure: *Many people get a thrill out of skydiving.* **2.** something that gives such a feeling: *It was a real thrill for Jane when her daughter won first prize in the dancing competition. verb,* **thrilled, thrilling.** to give a feeling of great pleasure: *The acrobats thrilled the audience with their death-defying act.* Something that gives this feeling is **thrilling.**

thrill·er [thril-ur] *noun, plural* **thrillers.** a book, play, or movie that tells an exciting story about crime, mystery, or adventure.

thrive [thryve] *verb,* **thrived** or **throve, thrived** or **thriven, thriving. 1.** to be very strong and healthy; grow and develop well: *Some plants are able to thrive in hot, dry climates.* **2.** to be successful; prosper: *She has really thrived as a student since she changed to a different school.* Something that is very successful is said to be **thriving.**

throat [throte] *noun, plural* **throats. 1.** the passage in the body that runs from the back of the mouth to the esophagus. Both food and air pass down the throat. **2.** the front of the neck: *John wore a thick woolen scarf to keep his throat warm.* **3.** something with a narrow opening like a throat: *The throat of the vase was too narrow for the whole bunch of flowers.*

throb [throb] *verb,* **throbbed, throbbing.** to beat rapidly in a forceful manner: *Emma got such a fright she could feel the blood throbbing in her veins. noun, plural* **throbs.** a fast, regular pulsing feeling: *I could feel the throb of the engines as the ocean liner pushed through the waves.*

throne ▶ [throhn] *noun, plural* **thrones. 1.** a special chair used by a monarch on important occasions. **2.** the position and power of a monarch: *The Prince of Wales is next in line to the throne of England.* 🔊 A different word with the same sound is **thrown.**

throng [throng] *noun, plural* **throngs.** a large crowd of people: *I joined the throngs of people watching the parade. verb,* **thronged, thronging.** to move or crowd into a place: *The marketplace thronged with tourists looking for a bargain.*

The last emperor of China, Puyi, was not quite three years old when he ascended the throne in 1908.

thrott·le [throt-ul] *verb,* **throttled, throttling.** to kill or injure a person or animal by holding their throat so tightly that they cannot breathe; strangle.
noun, plural **throttles.** a mechanical device that controls the amount of fuel going into an engine: *You'll have to give the engine full throttle to reach the top of the steep hill.*

through [throo] *preposition.* **1.** passing from one side to the other of something: *That nail is long enough to go right through the board.* **2.** from the beginning to the end of something: *Francis sat through the whole movie even though he didn't really enjoy it.* **3.** traveling from one side of an area or country to the other: *We drove through the Rockies on our way to California.* **4.** as a result of or by means of: *Josh made the swim team through months of hard training; You should receive the book I sent you through the mail.*
adverb. **1.** in one side and out the other: *When I give the signal, walk through the doorway.* **2.** thoroughly; completely: *The soup has to be heated through before being served.*
adjective. **1.** moving or going directly from one place to another: *a through street; The through traffic was moving at a speed of about ten miles an hour.* **2.** reaching the end; finished: *Are you through with the newspaper yet?*
◀ᴵᴵ⁾ A different word with the same sound is **threw.**

through·out [throo-out] *preposition.* **1.** happening or being in all parts of: *The music could be heard throughout the whole building.* **2.** from the beginning to the end: *He was known for his good financial management throughout his two terms as governor.*
adverb. in every part: *The house has beautiful beige carpet throughout.*

throw [throh] *verb,* **threw, thrown, throwing. 1.** to send an object up into or through the air, usually with the arm: *It's dangerous to throw rocks at passing cars.* **2.** to cause someone or something to fall down: *The wrestler threw his opponent to the mat and won the match.* **3.** to put on or place quickly: *She threw a scarf around her head and ran out into the snowstorm.* **4.** to put someone or something in a different state or condition: *The change of plans threw many people into confusion.*
noun, plural **throws.** the act of throwing something: *In soccer you put the ball back into play with a throw with both hands.*

thrush ▶ [thrush] *noun, plural* **thrushes.** a type of small to medium-sized songbird that is usually plain-colored with spots on its breast. These include the robin and the nightingale.

*The scaled plumage of the white **thrush** provides good camouflage when it is on the forest floor.*

thrust [thrust] *verb,* **thrust, thrusting.** to push roughly; shove with force: *Albert thrust the money into my hand and walked out the door.*
noun, plural **thrusts.** a strong shove that happens suddenly: *He was knocked off balance by the thrust of the wave.*

thru·way [throo-way] *noun, plural* **thruways.** a highway that has several lanes in each direction used for fast travel and has limited access. Often drivers have to pay a toll to use it.

thud [thud] *noun, plural* **thuds.** a low sound made when a heavy object hits something else: *I heard a dull thud when the book fell off the shelf.*
verb, **thudded, thudding.** to make a low, heavy sound.

thug [thug] *noun, plural* **thugs.** a brutal and violent person: *A gang of young thugs attacked him in the parking lot.*

The idea of a **thug** as a rough or violent criminal comes from a famous gang in India. The Thugs were a notorious secret band of criminals who were known for robbing and murdering travelers. They are said to have killed thousands of people before they were finally wiped out in the 1830s.

thumb [thum] *noun, plural* **thumbs. 1.** the short, thick finger of the hand. It is next to the forefinger and helps to pick up and grip objects. **2.** the part of a glove or mitten that covers the thumb.
verb, **thumbed, thumbing.** to flip through and glance at pages: *I thumbed through the magazine until I found the article I was looking for.*

thumb·tack [thum-tak] *noun, plural* **thumbtacks.** a short pin with a flat, round head used for attaching notices to bulletin boards or other surfaces.

thump [thump] *noun, plural* **thumps.** a dull sound made by a heavy object hitting a surface: *We heard a squeal of brakes followed by a loud thump.*
verb, **thumped, thumping. 1.** to hit something making a dull, heavy sound: *Henry was so angry he thumped the wall with his fist.* **2.** to pound or beat very fast: *We could hear the drums thumping somewhere in the distance.*

thun·der [thun-dur] *noun.* **1.** the loud noise heard during a storm. It is caused by, and follows lightning. **2.** a noise like thunder: *the thunder of buffalo running across a plain.* A **thunderbolt** is a lightning flash that happens at the same time as a crash of thunder.
verb, **thundered, thundering.** to make a very loud noise: *The trucks thundered past as we waited to cross the road.* Something that is extremely loud and frightening is **thunderous.**

thun·der·cloud ▲ [thun-dur-klowd] *noun, plural* **thunderclouds.** a large, dark cloud that produces thunder and lightning. A **thunderhead** is a large thundercloud that develops before a thunderstorm.

thunderstorm

Thyme is used to flavor many different dishes.

thun·der·storm [thun-dur-*storm*] *noun,*
plural **thunderstorms.** a storm with thunder, lightning, and heavy rain.

Thurs·day [thurz-*day* or thurz-dee] *noun,* plural **Thursdays.** the fifth day of the week.

> The name **Thursday** means "Thor's day." Thor was an important god in the religion of the Norse people, an early people of northern Europe. He was thought of as the god of thunder and lightning, and it was said that he caused thunder by striking things with his giant hammer.

thus [thus] *adverb.*
1. in this way; so: *The math teacher said, "Hold your ruler thus,"* holding one up for the class to see.
2. because of; consequently; therefore: *"Thus, after considering all the evidence, I find the prisoner guilty,"* said the judge. **3.** to this point, so far: *Thus far, we have not had any problems.*

thwart [thwort] *verb,* **thwarted, thwarting.** to prevent something being done; frustrate or hinder: *The builder's plan to develop the whole area was thwarted by one farmer who refused to sell his land.*

thy [thye] *pronoun.* an old-fashioned form of YOUR.

thyme ◀ [time] *noun, plural* **thymes.** a low-growing herb with small, fragrant leaves that are used in cooking. A different word with the same sound is **time.**

thy·roid [thye-*roid*] *noun, plural* **thyroids.** a gland in the neck that has important effects on the development of the brain and body.

tick¹ [tik] *noun, plural* **ticks.** the act of making a light, repeated clicking sound: *The tick of the clock kept her awake.*
verb, **ticked, ticking. 1.** to make a light clicking sound. **2.** of time, to pass by; elapse: *The minutes ticked by until the train was due to leave.* **3.** to make a small mark with a pen or pencil to show that something is correct, has been noted, or a purchase has been made: *I went through my "To do" list, ticking off what I had already done.*

tick² ▶ [tik] *noun, plural* **ticks.** a small blood-sucking creature that looks like a spider and lives on mammals such as cattle, sheep, humans, or dogs.

tick·et [tik-it] *noun, plural* **tickets.**
1. a piece of card or paper that shows the holder is entitled to entry somewhere such as a movie theater or sports event, or to a service such as an airplane flight or a train or bus ride: *You need a ticket to get into a movie.* **2.** a tag or label attached to an item to show its price, or to give other information as on luggage to show its destination: *The ticket showed the price as $10.30.* **3** a notice to pay a fine or summons for a minor offense of the law: *He got a ticket for driving through a red light.*
verb, **ticketed, ticketing. 1.** to attach a label or tag to something. **2.** to give a traffic ticket to: *He was ticketed for parking next to a fire hydrant.*

*Some **ticks** can transmit diseases to the humans they bite.*

TIDES

The gravitational pulls of the Moon and the Sun raise and lower the surfaces of our oceans to produce tides. The Sun has a weaker pull than the Moon. When the Sun, the Moon, and the Earth are in a line, the pulls of the Moon and Sun combine to produce strong, spring tides. Water levels are very high when the tide is in and very low when it is out. When the Sun and the Moon form a triangle with the Earth, their pulls cancel each other to a certain extent and tides, called neap tides, are weaker.

TIDAL PATTERNS
Tidal patterns vary in different parts of the world.

Two tides per day
One tide per day
Two unequal tides per day

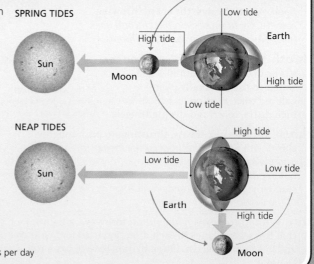

SPRING TIDES

Low tide
High tide
Earth
Sun
Moon
High tide
Low tide

NEAP TIDES

High tide
Low tide
Low tide
Sun
Earth
High tide
Moon

tick·le [tik-ul] *verb,* **tickled, tickling. 1.** to touch the body in a way that causes laughter or a tingling feeling: *The baby giggles when you tickle his feet.* **2.** to have or give a tingling feeling: *This woolen sweater makes my skin tickle.* **3.** to amuse or delight; entertain: *The children were tickled by Dad's funny stories.* *noun, plural* **tickles.** a tingling feeling; an irritation: *a tickle in the throat.*

tick·lish [tik-lish] *adjective.* **1.** sensitive to being tickled: *The soles of my feet are the most ticklish part of my body.* **2.** needing sensitive treatment or special care and attention: *It was a ticklish moment when Tim asked why he hadn't been invited to the party.*

The **tiger** *is the largest member of the cat family and may travel up to twelve miles a day in search of food.*

tic-tac-toe [tik-tak-toh] *noun.* a game in which two players take turns to write "X" or "O" in a pattern of nine squares. The winner is the first player to get three "X"s or three "O"s in a row.

ti·dal [tye-dul] *adjective. Environment.* having to do with or having tides: *tidal movements; a tidal lagoon.* A **tidal wave** is a huge ocean wave produced by an earthquake beneath the ocean. It is not caused by tides.

tid·bit [tid-bit] *noun, plural* **tidbits.** a small, pleasing piece of something, such as food or news: *tasty tidbits left over from the party; tidbits of gossip.*

tide ◀ [tide] *noun, plural* **tides. 1.** the regular rise and fall of the water level of the ocean and seas. Tides are caused by the gravitational pull of the Moon and Sun on the Earth. As the Earth turns, high tide occurs on each body of water twice a day. **2.** a trend or tendency that comes and goes like a tide: *The tide of sympathy from the public soon turned against him.*

tid·ings [tye-dingz] *plural noun.* items of news; information: *My friend sends me e-mails with tidings of her travels.*

ti·dy [tye-dee] *adjective,* **tidier, tidiest.** clean and neat, with everything in its right place: *a tidy room.* *verb,* **tidied, tidying.** to make clean and neat: *I need to tidy my desk—it's a real mess.* **—tidily,** *adverb;* **—tidiness,** *noun.*

tie [tye] *verb,* **tied, tying. 1.** to hold in place with a bow or knot: *to tie shoelaces; Beth tied her hair with a ribbon.* **2.** to be connected in some way: *The amount of money Dan earns is tied to the number of newspapers he delivers.* **3.** to equal the score or total of: *Jose and Nat tied for second place in the spelling contest.* *noun, plural* **ties. 1.** a cord, string, ribbon, or something similar used for fastening something: *Lucy attached the seedlings to stakes with plastic ties.* **2.** a strip of cloth worn around the neck under a collar and knotted at the front; a necktie. **3.** a close connection or relationship; bond: *family ties; cultural ties between France and Quebec.* **4.** an equal score: *The football game was a tie—the score was 7–7.* **5.** a wooden beam laid across a railway track to support the rails.

tier [teer] *noun, plural* **tiers.** a row or level that is one of a series rising one above the other, like the seats in a stadium or the layers of a wedding cake. 🔊 A different word with the same sound is **tear²**.

ti·ger ◀ [tye-gur] *noun, plural* **tigers.** a large wild animal of the cat family. Most tigers have yellow-brown fur with dark brown or black stripes.

tiger lily ▼ a lily with large orange flowers spotted with black. Tiger lilies are originally from Asia.

tight [tite] *adjective,* **tighter, tightest. 1.** not easily moved or loosened; firm: *Make sure the lid is tight before you put the bottle back in the picnic basket.* **2.** fitting the body closely or too closely: *These boots are a bit tight—I need a larger size.* **3.** having little or no space or time to spare: *If you hurry you should catch the train, but it will be tight; It was a tight finish, but Juan won the race by a narrow margin.* **4.** difficult or dangerous: *The ambushed soldiers fought their way out of a tight situation.* **5.** mean with money; not generous: *She's quite wealthy, but is so tight she never gives to charity.* *adverb.* closely; firmly; securely: *Hold on tight!* **—tightly,** *adverb;* **—tightness,** *noun.*

Tiger lilies are impressive garden plants, but in China they are also grown for their edible bulbs.

tighten

A
B
C
D
E
F
G
H
I
J
K
L
M
N
O
P
Q
R
S
T
U
V
W
X
Y
Z

*In some sawmills, **timber** is cut by saws that are specially programmed by computers to minimize waste.*

tight·en [tite-un] *verb,* **tightened, tightening.** to make or become tight or tighter: *to tighten screws; The fishing line tightened as the fish pulled at the bait.*

tight·rope [tite-rope] *noun, plural* **tightropes.** a wire stretched tightly above the ground for acrobats to perform on.

tights [tites] *plural noun.* a close-fitting piece of clothing for the lower body and legs made of thin, stretchy material.

tile [tile] *noun, plural* **tiles.** a thin, flat piece of hard material, often square or rectangular, used to cover roofs, walls, or floors. Most roof tiles are made of baked clay. *verb,* **tiled, tiling.** to cover with tiles: *to tile a floor.*

till[1] [til] *preposition.* up to the time of; until: *The store is open till six; The forecast said the rain would keep falling till tomorrow.*
conjunction. up to the time that or when; until: *Wait here till I come back.*

till[2] ▼ [til] *verb,* **tilled, tilling.** to dig and prepare ground for planting crops.

till[3] [til] *noun, plural* **tills.** a drawer in a store, restaurant, bank, or other business where money is kept: *The store clerk counted the cash before putting it in the till.*

till·er [til-ur] *noun, plural* **tillers.** a handle joined to the rudder of a boat and used for steering.

tilt [tilt] *verb,* **tilted, tilting.** to make something slope or lean by raising one end or side: *Sally tilted the cup to swallow the last of the drink.*
noun, plural **tilts.** a sloping or slanting position or movement: *a sideways tilt of the head.*

tim·ber ▲ [tim-bur] *noun, plural* **timbers. 1.** wood that has been cut and made ready for building; lumber. **2.** a large, heavy piece of wood; a beam. **3.** an area of forest; a group of trees: *hills covered with timber.*

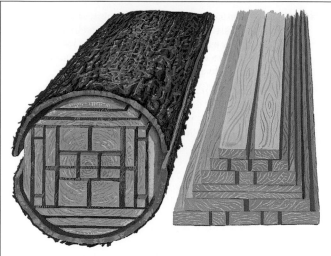

time [time] *noun, plural* **times. 1.** the passing of minutes, hours, days, and years in a continuous progression from the past, through the present, and into the future: *Dinosaurs lived in a past time; The new pool is due to open in three months time.* **2.** an exact or particular moment: *The time now is five minutes past seven o'clock.* **3.** the period needed or taken for an action: *How much time do you spend walking the dog each day?* **4.** a particular period in history: *ancient times; colonial times.* **5.** an experience: *Did you have a good time at the party?* **6.** an occasion when something happens: *How many times have you been camping?* **7.** *Music.* the rhythm or tempo of a piece of music: *The music teacher tapped out the time for the choir to follow.* *verb,* **timed, timing. 1.** to arrange to do something at a particular time: *The fireworks display is timed to start at nine o'clock.* **2.** to measure or record the speed or rate of: *to time runners with a stopwatch.*
◀)) A different word with the same sound is **thyme.**

time·less [time-lis] *adjective.* not affected by the passing of time, changes in fashion, or changes in society: *timeless beauty; the timeless truth of proverbs such as "Honesty is the best policy" or "There's no time like the present."*

time·ly [time-lee] *adjective,* **timelier, timeliest.** happening just at the right time: *The timely rain revived the drooping plants.* —**timeliness,** *noun.*

tim·er [time-ur] *noun, plural* **timers. 1.** a person or thing that measures time: *Grandma uses a timer to make sure her egg is boiled exactly right.* **2.** a device that causes a machine to start or stop working at a particular time: *to set the timer on an oven.*

times [timez] *plural noun.* the fact of being multiplied by: *Seven times two equals 14.* In mathematics, times is often represented by the (x) symbol, as in 7 x 2 = 14.

time·ta·ble [time-tay-bul] *noun, plural* **timetables.** a list that shows the times things are going to happen: *A train timetable shows when trains will arrive and leave.*

*In ancient China, farmers used a simple plow drawn by oxen to **till** the land.*

722

time zone ▼ *Geography.* a region of the Earth in which all the clocks are set to the same time. The Earth is divided into 24 time zones and most time zones are exactly one hour apart. There are seven times zones in the United States and Canada, including Hawaii.

tim·id [tim-id] *adjective.* easily frightened or scared: *Mice are usually thought of as timid animals.* The state of being timid is **timidity.** —**timidly,** *adverb.*

tim·ing [time-ing] *noun.* the skill of doing something at the best possible time: *He's great at telling jokes because he has a good sense of timing.*

tin [tin] *noun, plural* **tins. 1.** a soft, malleable, silver-colored metal used to cover and protect other metals to stop them from rusting. For example, tin is used to coat steel cans. **2.** a container, can, or pan that is made of metal coated with tin: *a tin of beans.*
adjective. made of tin: *The garden shed has a tin roof.*

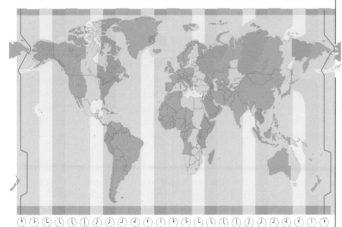

Time zones *make it easier for international businesses to communicate with one another at mutually convenient times.*

tin·der [tin-dur] *noun.* any dry material such as twigs, paper, or grass that catches fire easily: *The hikers collected lots of dry twigs to use as tinder for the campfire.*

tin·foil [tin-*fole*] *noun.* tin or aluminum made into very thin, paper-like sheets used for covering food.

tinge ▶ [tinj] *noun, plural* **tinges.** a very small amount of something: *Her black hair has a tinge of gray in it.*
verb, **tinged, tingeing** or **tinging. 1.** to contain a very small amount of color. **2.** to contain a very small amount of something: *The senator's speech was tinged with sarcasm.*

tin·gle [ting-gul] *verb,* **tingled, tingling.** to have a slight prickly feeling: *My whole arm tingled after I hit my elbow on the table.*
noun, plural **tingles.** a slight prickly feeling: *A tingle went down his spine when he read the first chapter of the crime novel.*

tin·ker [ting-kur] *verb,* **tinkered, tinkering.** to repair something by working in a casual or crude way and experimenting with the parts: *Dad spends most weekends tinkering with the car.*
noun, plural **tinkers.** in the past, someone who traveled from place to place repairing pots and pans or selling trinkets and other things.

tin·kle [ting-kul] *verb,* **tinkled, tinkling.** to ring lightly: *A small bell tinkled when I pushed open the door to the general store.*
noun, plural **tinkles.** a light ringing or jingling sound: *The tinkle of the bell signaled that dinner was about to be served.*

tin·sel [tin-sul] *noun.* long, glittering strips of material used for decoration: *After dinner we decorated the Christmas tree with fairy lights and tinsel.*

tint [tint] *noun, plural* **tints.** a color or a shade of color: *My grandmother's hair has a grayish-blue tint.*
verb, **tinted, tinting.** to slightly change the color: *The windows in their apartment were tinted to stop nosey neighbors from spying.*

ti·ny [tye-nee] *adjective,* **tinier, tiniest.** extremely small: *Dad gets upset when there is even a tiny speck of dirt on his car.*

tip[1] [tip] *noun, plural* **tips.** the pointed end of something: *The tip of the iceberg was high above the water.*

tip[2] [tip] *verb,* **tipped, tipping. 1.** to move or raise so that one side is higher than the other: *The student was scolded for tipping back in his chair.* **2.** to push or knock over: *The child bumped into the table and the vase of flowers tipped onto the floor.* **3.** to touch or raise your hat as a greeting to someone else: *The chauffeur tipped his hat and opened the car door for the Senator.*

tip[3] [tip] *noun, plural* **tips. 1.** an amount of money given to someone to thank them for their good service: *We gave the cab driver a large tip because he was so helpful.* **2.** a useful piece of information: *The Website had some great tips on how to stay fit and healthy over the holiday season.*
verb, **tipped, tipping. 1.** to give an amount of money to someone to thank them for their good service: *She tipped the waiter on the way out of the cafe.* **2.** to give a useful piece of information to someone: *The police were tipped off about the burglary and were ready and waiting when the thief broke in.*

tip·toe [tip-toh] *verb,* **tiptoed, tiptoeing.** to walk quietly and carefully on the tips of your toes: *He tiptoed past his parents' bedroom and sneaked out of the house.*

At sunset, the sky over the Bay Bridge in San Francisco is **tinged** *with pink.*

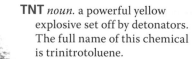

*The leopard **toad** lives in South Africa and has been listed as endangered.*

tire¹ [tire] *verb,* **tired, tiring. 1.** to make or become sleepy or weak: *The five-mile hike up the mountain tired out the campers.* Something that makes you feel sleepy or weak is said to be **tiring. 2.** to wear out the interest of; to bore or be bored: *He's already seen that movie three times, but he never tires of watching it.*

tire² [tire] *noun, plural* **tires.** a thick rubber ring that is filled with air and fitted around the wheel of a car, bicycle, or other vehicle.

tired [tired] *adjective.* feeling exhausted, weary, or bored: *The students were tired of being served the same meals every day at the cafeteria.* **—tiredness,** *noun.*

tire·less [tire-lis] *adjective.* working continuously without becoming weak or tired: *The rescue workers were tireless in their efforts to search for survivors.* **—tirelessly,** *adverb.*

tire·some [tire-sum] *adjective.* causing boredom, annoyance, or fatigue: *At the start of every new school year, the principal gave the same tiresome speech.*

*The fly agaric **toadstool** is easily recognizable by its red and white cap.*

tis·sue [tish-yoo] *noun, plural* **tissues. 1.** *Biology.* a mass of cells that form different organs in plants and animals. In animals, muscle tissue contracts to move a particular bone, part, or substance around the body. **2.** a piece of soft, thin paper used as a disposable handkerchief. **Tissue paper** is a very light, thin paper used for wrapping things.

ti·tle [tye-tul] *noun, plural* **titles. 1.** the name of a book, movie, or piece of music or art. **2.** a name used before a person's last name, such as "Mr.," "Mrs.," "Doctor," or "Professor" to show their occupation or rank in society. Someone who has a high social rank and is called "Sir" or "Lady" is said to be **titled. 3.** the championship: *The Boston Celtics have won the NBA title many times. verb,* **titled, titling.** to give a name to: *I titled my science project "Soil Erosion: The Dirty History".*

Choosing the **title** of a paper is important because a good title can make the paper interesting and appealing to a reader. The title is not necessarily the same as the subject of the paper. Of course you have to know your subject before you start to write, but you can wait until after the paper is finished to choose your title. For example, a paper on the sea creature known as a giant squid could be titled simply as "The Giant Squid," or it could be called "Monster of the Deep Sea."

TNT *noun.* a powerful yellow explosive set off by detonators. The full name of this chemical is trinitrotoluene.

to [too] *preposition.* **1.** in the direction of: *Turn to the right at the end of the street.* **2.** on; against: *Dad applied another coat of paint to the wall.* **3.** in a resulting state or condition: *She tore the letter to pieces.* **4.** for the purpose or intention of: *The paramedics came to the victim's rescue.* **5.** as compared with: *The tennis star was beaten three sets to two.* **6.** in connection with: *What did your mom say to that?* **7.** used to show what or whom an action is connected with: *He is kind to his younger sister.* **8.** used before a verb to form an infinitive: *I'd like to go home.* 🔊 Different words with the same sound are **too** and **two.**

Students, especially those who are learning English, may mix up the three similar words **to**, *too*, and *two*. *To* is a common preposition meaning "in the direction of," and it is also used as part of a verb, such as "to run." *Too* is an adverb meaning "more than enough" or "very much." *Two* is the word for the number that is next after one. So you would write, "I went *to* the park with my *two* friends *to* play ball, but it was *too* cold and windy.

toad ▲ [tode] *noun, plural* **toads.** a small, greenish-brown amphibian that looks similar to a frog. Toads have rough, dry, warty skin and spend more time on land than in water.

toad·stool ◀ [tode-stool] *noun, plural* **toadstools.** a poisonous fungus that has a round, umbrella-shaped top and a narrow stem like a mushroom.

toast¹ [tohst] *noun.* sliced bread that has been made warm and brown by dry heat. *verb,* **toasted, toasting. 1.** to warm and brown bread or other foods with dry heat: *Mom toasted a bagel for breakfast.* **2.** to warm completely: *We toasted our cold, wet feet at the campfire.*

toast² [tohst] *noun, plural* **toasts.** the act of drinking a special drink in honor or out of respect for someone: *The guests were asked to stand for the toast to the President. verb,* **toasted, toasting.** to hold your glass up and drink as a mark of respect for someone: *The guests toasted the bride and groom.*

toast·er [tohs-tur] *noun, plural* **toasters.** an electrical appliance for toasting bread.

to·bac·co ▶ [tuh-bak-oh] *noun, plural* **tobaccos.** a plant cultivated for its leaves that are dried and used for smoking in cigarettes and cigars.

*The **tobacco** plant originally came from the Americas, where its leaves were smoked by Native Americans.*

to·bog·gan ▶ [tuh-<u>bog</u>-un] *noun, plural* **toboggans.** a long, flat-bottomed sled curled upward at the front, used for sliding over ice and snow.
verb, **tobogganed, tobogganing.** to use or travel on a toboggan: *We spent the day tobogganing on the snow-covered hills.*

to·day [tuh-<u>day</u>] *noun.* this present day, time, or age: *Today is my Mom's birthday.adverb.* **1.** on this present day: *Shall we meet up for coffee later today?* **2.** at this present time: *People are more worried about health and fitness today than they were fifty years ago.*

tod·dler[<u>tod</u>-lur] *noun, plural* **toddlers.** a young child who is just learning to walk.

toe [toh] *noun, plural* **toes.** **1.** one of the five separate and movable parts at the end of your foot. **2.** the part of a sock, shoe, or stocking that covers this part: *I scuffed the toe of my shiny black boot.*

🔊 A different word with the same sound is **tow.**

to·fu [<u>toh</u>-foo] *noun.* a soft, pale food made from soybeans. Tofu is high in protein and often used in cooking instead of meat.

to·geth·er [tuh-<u>geth</u>-ur] *adverb.* **1.** with each other: *Mom and Dad went to the movies together.* **2.** forming one whole; combined: *I accidentally sewed the two shirt sleeves together.* **3.** in cooperation: *My sister and I worked together to clean up the yard.* **4.** considered as a whole: *All together, there are seven people in my family.*

toil [toyle] *noun.* hard, unpleasant, and exhausting work: *After three weeks toil picking fruit, I was ready for a break.*
verb, **toiled, toiling.** **1.** to do hard, unpleasant, and exhausting work: *He toiled in the factory for twelve hours straight.* **2.** to move slowly and with great difficulty: *She toiled up eight flights of stairs with heavy bags on each arm because the elevator was broken.*

toi·let [<u>toy</u>-lit] *noun, plural* **toilets.**
1. a bowl-shaped device with a seat on it that uses water to flush body waste down a sewer.
2. a bathroom.

to·ken [<u>toh</u>-kun] *noun, plural* **tokens. 1.** something that represents something else; a symbol: *Wedding rings are a token of love and commitment.*
2. a round metal or plastic disk that is used in place of money: *a bus token.*
adjective. describing an action that is small and has limited effect: *He made a token effort to be her friend by sending her a birthday card once a year.*

told [told] *verb.* the past tense and past participle of TELL.

tol·er·ance [<u>tol</u>-ur-uns] *noun.* **1.** the ability to accept the customs and beliefs of others, regardless of your own beliefs: *Our school prides itself on showing tolerance toward students of all religious backgrounds.*
2. the ability to put up with something that is hard or unpleasant: *The football player had such a high tolerance to pain that he didn't even realize at first that he had broken a rib.*

tol·er·ant [<u>tol</u>-ur-unt] *adjective.* showing respect for the customs and beliefs of others, regardless of your own beliefs.

tol·er·ate [<u>tol</u>-ur-*ate*] *verb,* **tolerated, tolerating.** to accept or put up with: *The teacher stated that she would not tolerate any talking during the exam.*

toll[1] [tole] *noun, plural* **tolls. 1.** a tax or payment for the privilege to use something, such as for crossing a bridge or using an expressway. **2.** the extent of damage done or the number of lives lost: *The death toll from the hurricane has risen to fifty.*

toll[2] [tole] *verb,* **tolled, tolling.** to ring a bell slowly and repeatedly: *The church bells tolled as the family walked sadly out of the funeral service.*
noun, plural **tolls.** the sound of a bell being rung slowly and repeatedly: *The tourists could hear the toll of the cathedral bells marking the middle of the day.*

tom·a·hawk ◀
[<u>tom</u>-uh-*hawk*] *noun, plural* **tomahawks.** a small axe used as a weapon or tool by Native Americans.

to·ma·to [tuh-<u>may</u>-toh *or* tuh-<u>maht</u>-oh] *noun, plural* **tomatoes. 1.** a soft, juicy, round, red fruit that can be eaten raw or cooked. **2.** the plant that produces this fruit.

> The word **tomato** comes from an American Indian name for this plant. The Indians were the first to grow this plant, and people from Europe learned about it from them. Several other common English words beginning with **to-** also describe things that were first developed by the American Indians, such as *tobacco, toboggan,* and *tomahawk.*

After the arrival of Europeans in America, Native Americans traded the stone heads of early **tomahawks** *for iron ones.*

725

a b c d e f g h i j k l m n o p q r s t u v w x y z

tomb ▼ [toom] *noun, plural* **tombs.** a grave or underground room where a person is buried.

tomb·stone [<u>toom</u>-stone] *noun, plural* **tombstones.** a stone that is put on a person's grave, usually with the name and the years of their birth and death carved on it.

to·mor·row [tuh-<u>mor</u>-oh] *noun, plural* **tomorrows.** **1.** the day after today: *Tomorrow is the first day of summer vacation.* **2.** the future in general: *If we solve some of the environmental issues now, the children of tomorrow will have a better future.* *adverb.* on of during the day after today: *It's quite cold today, let's go to the beach tomorrow instead.*

tom-tom [<u>tom</u>-tom] *noun, plural* **tom-toms.** *Music.* a drum played with the hands that originates from Native American or Asian cultures.

ton [tun] *noun, plural* **tons.** a unit for measuring weight equal to 2,000 pounds in the United States and Canada and 2,240 pounds in Britain.

tone [tone] *noun, plural* **tones.** **1.** the quality and character of sound, especially of a musical instrument or a person's voice: *The trumpet has an upbeat and happy tone.* **2.** the difference in pitch between two musical notes on a scale: *D and E are a tone apart on a musical scale.* **3.** the quality of spoken or written language that shows how a person is feeling: *She could tell by the teacher's sharp tone of voice that he was annoyed at the class.* **4.** the quality of style of something: *By starting the meeting with a joke, the President of the Board set a friendly tone for the rest of the afternoon.* **5.** a tint or shade of color: *The bridesmaids' dresses were the same style, but each was a different tone of pink.*

The **tone** of a piece of writing is the feeling or attitude that the writer shows in the paper or story. This might be happy, sad, angry, serious, funny, and so on, depending on how the writer feels about the subject. For example, suppose a man writes about going back to visit a lake where he used to spend summers as a boy. His tone might be happy if he finds that the lake is still as beautiful as he remembers. Or the tone might be sad or angry, if the lake is now dirty and polluted. Either way, his writing should clearly show the reader how he feels, without his having to say directly "I was angry" or whatever.

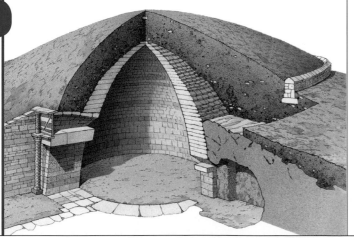

The Treasury of Atreus in Greece dates to around 1300 BC and was once the **tomb** *of a Mycenaean king.*

tongs [tongz *or* tawngz] *plural noun.* a tool with two long movable arms hinged together at one end that is used for picking up objects and holding them.

tongue [tung] *noun, plural* **tongues.** **1.** the large, soft movable piece of flesh in the mouth that is used for eating and speaking. **2.** the tongue of an animal such as an ox or sheep that is cooked and used as food. **3.** a language of a particular country or people: *My grandmother often speaks in her native tongue of Italian when she is having an argument.* **4.** the ability to speak: *The distressed victim eventually found her tongue and gave the police a description of her attacker.* **5.** the loose flap of material shaped like a tongue under the laces of some shoes.

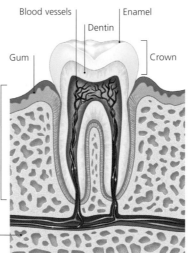

Blood vessels — Enamel — Dentin — Gum — Crown — Root — Bone

Each **tooth** *has three layers and is anchored in its socket by one or more roots.*

ton·ic [ton-ik] *noun, plural* **tonics.** *Health.* something that makes you stronger and healthier: *A weekend in the country is just the tonic I need.*

to·night [tuh-<u>nite</u>] *noun.* the night of this present day: *Tonight we are heading out for a meal at my favorite restaurant.* *adverb.* during the night of this present day: *I'm meeting her at the gym at seven o'clock tonight.*

ton·sil [<u>ton</u>-sul] *noun, plural* **tonsils.** either of the two small round pieces of flesh at the back of the throat. An infection of the tonsils is called **tonsillitis.**

too [too] *adverb.* **1.** in addition; also: *Can I come to the party too?* **2.** more than is needed or wanted: *The T-shirt was too big, so we exchanged it for a different size.* **3.** very; completely: *Mom wasn't too happy with my school report card this year.* 🔊 Different words with the same sound are **to** and **two.**

tool [tool] *noun, plural* **tools.** **1.** an instrument used to help you do work or repair something, such as a knife, hammer, or drill. **2.** something that helps you with a particular task or activity: *The Internet is a useful research tool for school projects.* *verb,* **tooled, tooling.** to work, shape, or decorate with a tool: *The leather craftsman tooled the belt with Celtic designs.*

toot [toot] *noun, plural* **toots.** the short, sharp sound made when a horn is blasted or a whistle is blown. *verb,* **tooted, tooting.** to make or cause to make such a sound: *The driver of the old steam train tooted the whistle as a signal that the train was about to depart.*

tooth ▲ [tooth] *noun, plural* **teeth.** **1.** one of the hard, whitish, bony structures set in the jaws and used for biting and chewing food. **2.** something that looks similar to, or acts like, a tooth or a row of teeth, such as the row of sharp parts on a comb or saw.

*The **topography** of the Mojave Desert, in California, features mountains and flat basins that were once giant salt lakes.*

tooth·ache [tooth-*ake*] *noun, plural* **toothaches.**
a pain in or near a tooth or teeth.

tooth·brush [tooth-*brush*] *noun, plural* **toothbrushes.**
a small brush with a long handle used for cleaning
the teeth.

tooth·paste [tooth-*payst*] *noun, plural* **toothpastes.**
a paste for cleaning the teeth.

tooth·pick [tooth-*pik*] *noun, plural* **toothpicks.** a small,
pointed piece of wood or other material used for
removing pieces of food caught between the teeth.

top[1] [top] *noun, plural* **tops. 1.** the highest point or part
of something: *When we reached the top of the hill, we
sat down to rest.* **2.** the highest or leading place or rank:
That school principal is at the top of her profession.
3. a lid, covering, or stopper: *I put the top back on the pen.*
4. the highest level, pitch, or degree: *The boy was shouting
at the top of his voice.* **5.** a piece of clothing for the upper
part of the body: *I bought a top to match my pants.*
adjective. **1.** at or of the highest place or part: *I reached
up to the top shelf.* **2.** highest in position, degree, or
importance: *The old truck could only do about thirty
miles an hour at top speed.*

top[2] [top] *noun, plural* **tops.** a child's toy with a pointed
end on which it can be made to spin.

top·ic [top-*ik*] *noun, plural* **topics.** what something is about;
the content of a talk, discussion, or piece of writing;
a subject: *The topic of the guest speaker's talk is water
safety.* A **topic sentence** is a sentence that states the main
idea in a paragraph.

The **topic sentence** is a technique that is often used in
student writing, and by famous adult writers as well. This is a
good way to organize a paragraph, by beginning with a topic
sentence that tells what the paragraph is about, and then
following this with several other sentences that give more
detail. For example, the author James Morris begins a book
with this topic sentence: "Queen Victoria of England went
home happy on her Diamond Jubilee day." Following this,
the same paragraph has three other sentences that tell *why*
the Queen was so happy on that day.

top·ic·al [top-uh-kul] *adjective.* **1.** about or relating to
things that are happening at the moment: *This magazine
has topical articles on music and keeps me up to date with
what is happening.* **2.** designed for use on a particular
part of something, such a part of the body: *This antiseptic
solution is for topical use and should be applied to the
wound twice daily.*

to·pog·ra·phy ▲ [tuh-pog-ruh-fee] *noun. Geography.*
1. the shape, height, and depth of the land features in
a particular place. The topography of a place includes such
features as mountains, hills, valleys, plains, rivers, and
lakes. **2.** the practice of showing such features on a map.
A **topographer** is a person who specializes in the study
of topography. —**topographical**, *adverb.*

top·ple [top-ul] *verb,* **toppled, toppling.** to fall or tip
forward from being too heavy at the top, or make fall
or tip over: *I put a book on top of the pile in my room
and the whole pile toppled over.*

top·soil [top-*soil*] *noun. Environment.* the surface or upper
part of the soil. Topsoil usually includes the rich layer of
soil where most plant roots are found.

Tor·ah [tor-uh] *noun. Religion.* **1.** in Judaism, the first five
books of the Old Testament. **2.** a scroll containing the first
five books of the Old Testament used for religious services
in a synagogue.

torch [torch] *noun, plural* **torches. 1.** a light made from a
piece of wood or other material with a burning flame on
the end. It is usually carried in the hand. **2.** a portable
device for producing a hot flame, used for such tasks as
softening metal or burning off old paint.
verb, **torched, torching.** to set fire to; destroy by burning:
*The thieves torched the old barn they had used as
a hideout to destroy any evidence of their activities.*

tor·ment [tor-ment] *verb,* **tormented, tormenting.** to cause
great suffering or distress of the mind or body: *Thoughts
of the opportunities he had wasted tormented him for
many years.*
noun, plural **torments.** great suffering or distress; misery:
*The mosquitoes and other biting insects in the rain forest
caused the hikers great torment.*

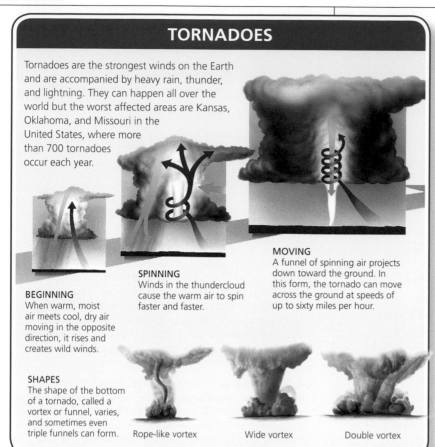

TORNADOES

Tornadoes are the strongest winds on the Earth and are accompanied by heavy rain, thunder, and lightning. They can happen all over the world but the worst affected areas are Kansas, Oklahoma, and Missouri in the United States, where more than 700 tornadoes occur each year.

BEGINNING
When warm, moist air meets cool, dry air moving in the opposite direction, it rises and creates wild winds.

SPINNING
Winds in the thundercloud cause the warm air to spin faster and faster.

MOVING
A funnel of spinning air projects down toward the ground. In this form, the tornado can move across the ground at speeds of up to sixty miles per hour.

SHAPES
The shape of the bottom of a tornado, called a vortex or funnel, varies, and sometimes even triple funnels can form.

Rope-like vortex   Wide vortex   Double vortex

tor·na·do ▲ [tor-<u>nay</u>-doh] *noun, plural* **tornadoes** *or* **tornados.** a violent storm in which a dark, funnel-shaped cloud moves over the land accompanied by extremely strong, whirling winds of 250 miles per hour or more. A tornado can cause great destruction to anything in its path. It is also called a **twister.**

tor·pe·do ▼ [tor-<u>pee</u>-doh] *noun, plural* **torpedoes.** a self-propelled weapon shaped like a tube that is filled with explosives and sent underwater to destroy ships or boats. A torpedo can be launched from a submarine, a ship or other boat, or an aircraft.

torque [tork] *noun. Science.* a force that produces or tends to produce rotation (that is, a revolving movement around a central point). For example, the engine of a car delivers torque to the drive shaft, and this force is what gets a car going.

tor·rent [<u>tor</u>-unt] *noun, plural* **torrents.** a strong, rushing stream of water or other liquid; a great flow or downpour: *When it rains in the tropics, the rain can come down in torrents.*

tor·so [<u>tor</u>-soh] *noun, plural* **torsos.** the human body excluding the head, arms, and legs; also called the trunk.

tor·til·la [tor-<u>tee</u>-yuh] *noun, plural* **tortillas.** a thin round of unleavened, or flat, bread made originally from cornmeal, though wheat flour is now also used. It is cooked on a flat, hot plate. Tortillas come from Mexico. The word is Spanish for "little cake."

tor·toise ▼ [<u>tor</u>-tus] *noun, plural* **tortoises.** a turtle that lives on land and has feet with toes rather than flippers.

tor·ture [<u>tor</u>-chur] *verb,* **tortured, torturing.** to cause great pain or suffering: *After he had sentenced the man to life in prison, the judge was tortured by doubts as to whether he was really guilty.*
noun. **1.** the act of causing great pain, especially as a punishment or to obtain a confession. **2.** something that causes great pain or suffering: *Waiting to hear if anyone had survived the plane crash was sheer torture for the victims' families.*

The giant saddleback **tortoises** *of the Galapagos Islands can stretch their necks to get water and food from tall cactus plants.*

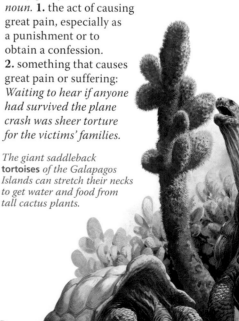

On nuclear-powered attack submarines, **torpedoes** *are launched from a torpedo tube.*

*Native American **totem poles** recorded the history of a family or an important person and featured figures of mythical creatures.*

tourist

toss [taws] *verb,* **tossed, tossing. 1.** to throw quickly and lightly, especially up into or through the air: *Toss me that magazine if you've finished with it.* **2.** to throw or swing unevenly up and down or from side to side: *The storm tossed the boats tied up at anchor.* **3.** to throw a coin into the air to decide something according to which side lands face up: *There was only one piece of pie left, so my brother and I tossed for it.*
noun, plural **tosses.** a quick, light throw or a throw of a coin: *The team that wins the toss will bat last.*

to·tal [toh-tul] *adjective.* **1.** including everything; making up the whole; entire: *The total cost of our vacation was less than we had expected.* **2.** describing something complete; utter; absolute: *Trying to get the old TV to work was a total waste of time.*
noun, plural **totals.** the full amount; sum: *My new outfit came to a total of fifty dollars.*
verb, **totaled, totaling. 1.** to add up: *I totaled my expenses for the field trip.* **2.** to amount to: *The bill for our lunch totaled twenty dollars.*

to·tal·ly [toh-tul-ee] *adverb.* completely; entirely, wholly: *We are totally in agreement with the committee's plans for our club.*

tote [tote] *verb,* **toted, toting.** to carry by hand or on one's person, especially something that is a load or burden: *I toted a stack of books back to the library.* A **tote bag** is a large handbag used to carry shopping or personal items.

to·tem [toh-tum] *noun, plural* **totems. 1.** a natural object, such as an animal or plant, that is the emblem of a family or clan. It may also serve to remind people of where their family or clan came from. **2.** *Religion.* a carved or painted image of such an object. Some Native American peoples carved such images on poles that were placed outside their homes.

totem pole ▲ a pole carved or painted with one or more totems.

tou·can ▶ [too-kan] *noun, plural* **toucans.** a brilliantly colored bird with a very large bill (beak). Toucans are found in tropical America. They eat mainly fruits.

touch [tuch] *verb,* **touched, touching. 1.** to put a finger or some other part of the body lightly on or against something so as to feel it: *I touched the tiny kitten to feel how soft its fur was.* **2.** to be in or bring into contact: *We touched hands as we said good-bye.* **3.** to give rise to tender or painful feelings or emotions; move: *Their concern for my welfare touched me deeply.* Something that gives rise to tender or painful feelings or emotions is **touching.**
noun, plural **touches. 1.** the sense by which someone becomes aware of things by coming into physical contact with them, especially with the fingers: *Our sense of touch tells us, among other things, how hard or soft, or hot or cold, things are.* **2.** the act of touching: *A brief touch was enough to tell me that the leaves were prickly.* **3.** a small amount; trace: *There was a touch of sarcasm in her voice.* **4.** contact or communication between people: *We promised to keep in touch when our friends moved to another state.*

touch·down [tuch-*down*] *noun, plural* **touchdowns. 1.** the act of scoring six points in football by carrying the ball across the opposing team's goal line. **2.** the act of an aircraft or spacecraft making contact with the ground on landing, or the moment when it does this.

touch football a casual form of football in which tackling is replaced by touching.

touch·y [tuch-ee] *adjective.* quick to take offense; easily upset or offended: *He's touchy about his bad haircut, so don't mention it.*

tough [tuf] *adjective,* **tougher, toughest. 1.** hard to cut, tear, break, or chew; strong: *My luggage is made of a very tough fabric.* **2.** able to work hard and endure hardship: *You need to be tough to work as a coal miner.* **3.** having to do with something rough; violent: *a tough neighborhood.* **4.** describing something difficult; challenging: *Our club president was so popular that she'll be a tough act to follow.* **5.** not easily influenced; stubborn; unyielding: *He's a tough man to do business with.* —**toughness,** *noun.*

tou·pee [too-*pay*] *noun.* a small wig or patch of artificial hair worn to cover a bald spot.

tour [toor] *noun, plural* **tours.** a trip or journey that usually starts and finishes at the same place and during which a number of places are visited or a number of things are seen: *When we were in San Francisco, we went on a tour of the city.*
verb, **toured, touring.** to travel around a place: *My parents toured Europe on their vacation.*

tour·ist [toor-ist] *noun, plural* **tourists.** someone who travels for pleasure: *Many tourists visit Hawaii each year.* The practice of traveling for pleasure, and the business of providing services for people traveling for pleasure, is **tourism.**

*The large bill of the toco **toucan** is not heavy because it is hollow.*

*The Petronas twin **towers** in Kuala Lumpur, Malaysia, are 88 stories tall.*

tour·na·ment [tur-nuh-munt] *noun,* *plural* **tournaments.** a contest or series of contests between two or more people or teams to determine the winner of a championship: *a tennis tournament; a baseball tournament.*

tour·ni·quet [tur-nuh-kit] *noun,* *plural* **tourniquets.** *Health.* a strip or piece of cloth that is tied tightly around an injured arm or leg, in order to stop it bleeding.

tow [toh] *verb,* **towed, towing.** to pull a vehicle along behind, using a rope or a chain: *Their car got stuck in the mud and a truck had to tow it out.* *noun.* the act of being pulled along behind: *The car broke down and was given a tow.*

to·ward [tord *or* tuh-word] *preposition.* **1.** in the direction of: *The little girl ran toward her mom.* **2.** in relation to; concerning: *What is the teacher's attitude toward discipline? Nick's parents donated $1,000 toward the cost of the new school bus.* This word is also spelled **towards.**

tow·el [tou-ul] *noun,* *plural* **towels.** a piece of soft cloth or paper that is used to dry wet things: *I can't dry myself on that towel because it's far too wet.* *verb,* **toweled, toweling.** to wipe or dry something with a towel.

tow·er ▲ [tou-ur] *noun,* *plural* **towers.** a tall, narrow building that can stand by itself, or form part of another building, such as a church or a castle. *verb,* **towered, towering.** to stretch upward a long way: *At six feet six, Tom towers over his high school friends even though he's younger than most of them.* A **towering** object or person is taller than everything or everyone else.

town [toun] *noun,* *plural* **towns.** a place with many buildings where people live and work. It is larger than a village but smaller than a city. The people who live in the town are called **townspeople** and a **township** is the town and its surrounding land.

town·house [toun-*hous*] *noun,* *plural* **townhouses.** a tall and narrow house, often two stories, which is built in a town alongside or attached to other similar houses.

tox·ic [tok-sik] *adjective. Environment.* relating to or caused by a poison; poisonous: *The plastics factory was shut down because it was pumping toxic chemicals into the river.* **Toxic waste** is material, often in chemical form, that can pollute the natural environment and contaminate groundwater sometimes causing death or injury.

Words such as **toxic** and *toxin* come from an ancient word referring to a bow and arrow. The first things to be called *toxic* were substances in which an arrow point would be dipped to poison it for shooting an enemy.

tox·i·col·o·gy [tok-si-kol-uh-jee] *noun. Science.* the scientific and medical study of poisons. A **toxicologist** is a person who studies the harmful effects of poisons on humans, animals, plants, and the environment.

tox·in [tok-sin] *noun,* *plural* **toxins.** *Biology.* a poisonous substance produced by an animal or plant, or by bacteria, that is harmful to people, other animals, and the environment.

toy [toy] *noun,* *plural* **toys.** an object that children play with; a plaything. *verb,* **toyed, toying.** to play or fool with something especially while you are really thinking about something else: *She toyed nervously with her pen before she started to answer the questions on her exam paper.*

trace [trays] *noun,* *plural* **traces. 1.** a mark or sign left behind in a particular place that shows that someone or something had been there previously: *No trace was ever found of the missing jewelry.* **2.** a very small amount of something: *Doctors found traces of arsenic in the dead man's body.* *verb,* **traced, tracing. 1.** to look for and find; track down: *The plumber traced the source of the blockage to tree roots inside the pipes.* **2.** to copy a drawing or map by covering it with a piece of transparent paper and following its lines: *After we had traced the map of Africa our teacher asked us to fill in all the countries without looking at our textbook.* **3.** to discover and describe the history of something and how it develops and progresses: *The history students were asked to trace the causes of World War II.*

tra·chea [trake-ee-uh] *noun,* *plural* **tracheae** *or* **tracheas.** the tube that connects the mouth and nose to the lungs; also called the windpipe.

track [trak] *noun,* *plural* **tracks. 1.** a line, path, or marks left by a person, animal, or vehicle. A **tracker** is a person who finds other people or animals by following their track. **2.** an area or course used by athletes, cars, or horses for races: *We watched the girls racing around the track in the 400 yards open running event.* **3.** a rough path or road. **4.** the metal lines on which trains run. *verb,* **tracked, tracking. 1.** to follow the marks, path, or trail left by someone or something: *The police tracked the criminal to his sister's house up in the mountains.* **2.** to leave marks that show where you have been: *The dog tracked mud all over the kitchen floor.*

track and field a group of sports events that include running, jumping, and throwing contests. A **track meet** is a track-and-field competition between two or more teams.

*A **tractor** is a powerful vehicle but can only travel at low speeds.*

tract [trakt] *noun, plural* **tracts. 1.** a large area of land of a certain type: *a housing tract; The hikers had to fight their way through immense tracts of dense forest before they got to the top of the mountain.* **2.** a system of body parts or organs that act together to perform a specific function: *the digestive tract.*

trac·tion [trak-shun] *noun.* the grip that a moving object has on the ground or some other surface: *Branches placed under the tires gave the car traction and stopped it from skidding.*

trac·tor ▲ [trak-tur] *noun, plural* **tractors.** a vehicle with large rear wheels used on a farm for such things as sowing crops, plowing fields, or pulling heavy loads.

trade [trade] *noun, plural* **trades. 1.** the buying, selling, or exchanging of goods or services between people, companies, or countries: *Our country's meat industry is trying to increase its trade with nations in Europe.* **2.** a job, especially one needing special skills; work: *His trade was plumbing and he worked with the same builder for thirty years.*
verb, **traded, trading. 1.** to buy, sell, or exchange goods between people, companies, or countries. **2.** to give one thing for another; exchange: *She wants to trade in her old minivan for a new SUV.* **3.** an exchange of one thing for another: *I made a trade with my friend and got these DVDs for some of his.*

*In the seventeenth century, **trading posts** were set up by the Hudson's Bay Company to provide services for trappers and fur traders in North America.*

trade·mark [trade-mark] *noun, plural* **trademarks.** *Law.* a name, mark, or symbol that a manufacturing company uses on its products. It is registered and protected by law so that no one else can use it.
verb, **trademarked, trademarking.** to put a mark, symbol, or name on a product.

trad·er [trade-ur] *noun, plural* **traders.** a person who buys and sells goods.

trading post ▲ a store in a frontier region where people can get food and supplies in exchange for other things, such as furs and hides.

tra·di·tion [truh-dish-un] *noun, plural* **traditions. 1.** the passing down of practices, beliefs, and customs from one generation to the next. **2.** a belief or custom of a group or society: *They always observed the tradition of a big turkey dinner at Thanksgiving.*

tra·di·tion·al ▼ [truh-dish-un-ul] *adjective.* relating to beliefs and customs that have existed in a place without changing for a long time: *The African wedding was very colorful, as all the guests were wearing traditional costumes and headdress.*
—**traditionally,** *adverb.*

traf·fic [traf-ik] *noun.* **1.** the movement of cars and other vehicles, airplanes, ships, or people between one place and another: *The traffic on the way to the beach was so heavy, the roads were blocked for hours.* **2.** the buying and selling of goods illegally: *The traffic of drugs in the area was of great concern and the police were called in to investigate the problem.*
verb, **trafficked, trafficking.** to buy or sell goods illegally: *to traffic in drugs.*

trag·e·dy [traj-uh-dee] *noun, plural* **tragedies. 1.** a very sad or terrible event: *The headlines described the horrific accident as a tragedy.* **2.** *Literature.* a serious story, play, film, or opera that ends sadly, usually with the death of a main character.

trag·ic [traj-ik] *adjective.* **1.** relating to a very sad or dreadful event: *a tragic death.* **2.** relating to a serious story or play that has a sad ending. —**tragically,** *adverb.*

trail [trale] *noun, plural* **trails. 1.** a path across rough country: *The hiking trail led them over hills and across rivers.* **2.** the footprints, smell, or other signs left by animals or people: *The hunters followed the trail left by the lion.* **3.** something left behind after a person or thing has been somewhere: *They took their shoes off so they wouldn't leave a trail of muddy footprints all over the new carpet.*
verb, **trailed, trailing. 1.** to follow the scent or the tracks of a person or animal: *The police dogs managed to trail the escaped convict to his hideout.* **2.** to drag or be dragged behind: *The bride's veil trailed behind her on the floor of the church.* **3.** to be behind in a contest or competition: *At halftime our team was trailing by twenty points.*

trail·er [trale-ur] *noun, plural* **trailers.** a vehicle that is pulled by a car or a truck. Some trailers are used by people to live in, and others are used to carry goods or equipment: *The car was pulling a trailer with a small boat on it.*

Polish folk costumes

Indian temple dancer

*In some countries people wear **traditional** dress for special occasions or performances.*

a b c d e f g h i j k l m n o p q r s t u v w x y z

*The straddle jump is one of many jumps that can be performed on a **trampoline.***

train ▼ [trane] *noun, plural* **trains. 1.** a line of connected cars, pulled by an engine along a railroad line, that carry passengers or freight from one place to another. **2.** a long line of vehicles, people, or animals moving slowly in the same direction: *The train of refugees stretched as far as the eye could see.* **3.** a chain of connected thoughts or events: *The flood set off a whole train of events that ended in tragedy for the town.* **4.** the long part at the back of a dress or robe that drags or trails on the ground: *She had a long, white train on the back of her wedding dress.*
verb, **trained, training. 1.** to give or be given teaching and practice on how to do something: *She trained as a nurse; They trained their parrot to say "good morning folks."* **2.** to get ready for a sports event by doing lots of exercise and following a special diet. **3.** to make something grow in a certain way: *We trained the climbing rose to grow into an arch over the front door.*

train·er [tray-nur] *noun, plural* **trainers. 1.** a person who trains animals to do things, such as teaching a parrot how to talk. **2.** a person who helps people to get ready to take part in a sport, such as boxing. A trainer may also treat athletes' minor injuries.

train·ing [tray-ning] *noun.* the process of learning the skills that you need for a particular skill or job: *When I applied for a job as a check-out clerk at our local supermarket the manager asked me if I'd already had any training.*

trait [trate] *noun, plural* **traits.** a particular quality of a person or animal; characteristic: *Rose is a wonderful person; loyalty is just one of her traits.*

trai·tor [tray-tur] *noun, plural* **traitors.** someone who betrays his or her country or friends: *When he was found to be selling secret information to the enemy, he was denounced as a traitor and sentenced to twenty years in jail.*

> The word **traitor** goes back to a term meaning "to hand over" or "to give over." The idea is that when a traitor betrays his own country, he is in effect handing his country over to an enemy.

*The French TGV is the fastest **train** on wheels in the world.*

tramp [tramp] *verb,* **tramped, tramping. 1.** to walk or step heavily: *Careful, watch where you are going, you are just about to tramp on the little chicks.* **2.** to walk a long way, usually in a slow and heavy way: *He spent all day tramping the streets looking for a job.*
noun, plural **tramps. 1.** a person who has no home, money, or job, and who moves around from place to place, sometimes doing odd jobs for money. **2.** the sound of heavy steps: *the noisy tramp of soldiers' feet.*

tram·po·line ▲ [tram-puh-leen] *noun, plural* **trampolines.** a piece of equipment that people use to do tumbling exercises, such as acrobatic jumps and somersaults. It consists of a sheet of canvas held to a metal frame by springs.

trance [trans] *noun, plural* **trances.** a state of mind during which a person is conscious but not aware of what is going on around them: *The hypnotist put his subject into such a deep trance that she seemed to be asleep.*

tran·quil [trang-kwul] *adjective.* having to do with something calm and peaceful; serene: *It was so tranquil and peaceful at the lake house that no one wanted to leave.*
Tranquility is the state of being calm and peaceful.

trans- a prefix that means across, beyond, or through: *transatlantic* means across the Atlantic Ocean.

trans·ac·tion [tran-<u>zak</u>-shun] *noun, plural* **transactions.** the act of carrying out a business exchange: *Negotiations for the house had been going on for weeks but the final transaction only took twenty minutes.*

trans·con·ti·nen·tal [trans-kon-tuh-<u>nen</u>-tul] *adjective.* crossing a continent: *a transcontinental railway.*

trans·fer [trans-<u>fur</u> *or* trans-fur] *verb,* **transferred, transferring.** to move from one place or job to another: *Since the plant has grown, I have to transfer it to a larger pot. The company he works for transferred him from its Washington office to its New York office.*
noun, plural **transfers.** a move from one place to another: *All salaries are now paid by direct transfer into an employee's bank account.*

trans·form ▼ [trans-<u>form</u>] *verb,* **transformed, transforming.** to change something completely: *Makeover television shows attempt to transform their stars.* When something changes completely, either in form, appearance, or nature we say that a **transformation** has taken place.

trans·for·mer [trans-<u>for</u>-mur] *noun, plural* **transformers.** a piece of electrical equipment that changes the voltage of a current.

trans·fu·sion [trans-<u>fyoo</u>-zhun] *noun, plural* **transfusions.** *Medicine.* the transfer of one person's blood to another person: *A blood transfusion saved the accident victim's life.*

tran·si·ent [<u>tran</u>-shunt] *adjective.* lasting for only a short time; fleeting; temporary: *Her unhappiness was transient—the next day, everything was fine again.*

tran·sis·tor [tran-<u>sis</u>-tur] *noun, plural* **transistors.** a small electronic device used in televisions, radios, computers, and other electrical equipment.

trans·it [<u>tran</u>-sit *or* <u>tran</u>-zit] *noun, plural* **transits. 1.** the act of carrying goods or people from one place to another: *When I flew from New York to London my luggage got lost in transit.* **2.** the act of passing across or through: *a rocket's transit from the Earth's atmosphere to outer space.* **3.** a system for carrying passengers on subways, buses and other public vehicles: *urban transit.*

tran·si·tion [tran-<u>zish</u>-un] *noun, plural* **transitions.** the process in which something changes from one state or condition to another: *The transition from high school to college is quite a difficult one for some students.*

transitive verb *Language.* a verb that has a direct object. In the sentence *I bought a book about horses,* "bought" is a transitive verb and "book" is its direct object.

trans·late [<u>trans</u>-late] *verb,* **translated, translating.** *Language.* to change speech or writing from one language into another language: *The Spanish word "amigo" can be translated into English as "friend."*

trans·la·tion [trans-<u>lay</u>-shun] *noun, plural* **translations.** *Language.* a piece of writing or speech that has been changed from one language into another one.

trans·lu·cent [trans-<u>loo</u>-sunt] *adjective.* **1.** clear and pure; almost glowing: *Her skin is so beautiful, it's almost translucent.* **2.** clear enough to allow light to pass through. Frosted glass is translucent. The quality of being translucent is **translucence.**

trans·mis·sion [trans-<u>mish</u>-un] *noun, plural* **transmissions. 1.** the act of sending or passing from one person or place to another: *The transmission of infectious diseases in developing countries is a serious problem for the World Health Organization.* **2.** the broadcasting of radio or television waves: *A break in transmission meant the television station was off the air all day.* **3.** the parts of a vehicle that carry power from the engine to its wheels: *The automatic transmission replaced gears in cars.*

trans·mit [trans-<u>mit</u>] *verb,* **transmitted, transmitting. 1.** to send, pass, or carry something from one person, place, or thing to another: *The disease is transmitted by mosquitoes.* **2.** to send out signals by radio or television: *The news was transmitted by satellite throughout the world.*

trans·mit·ter [trans-<u>mit</u>-ur] *noun, plural,* **transmitters.** a device that sends out radio or television signals.

trans·par·ent [trans-<u>pare</u>-unt] *adjective.* **1.** able to be seen through: *She had to line the drapes with a thick material because they were almost transparent.* **2.** easily understood or recognized; obvious: *He wants us to like him—his motives are so transparent.* **Transparency** is the state of being easily understood. **—transparently,** *adverb.*

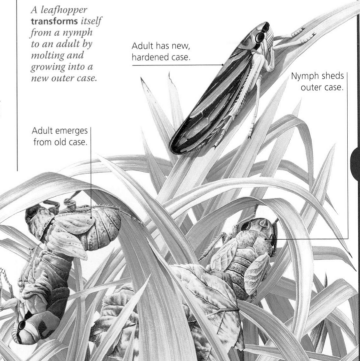

A leafhopper **transforms** *itself from a nymph to an adult by molting and growing into a new outer case.*

Adult has new, hardened case.

Nymph sheds outer case.

Adult emerges from old case.

*When an acrobat performs movements on a **trapeze** without swinging, it is known as static trapeze.*

trans·plant [trans-<u>plant</u> *for verb;* <u>trans</u>-plant *for noun*] *verb,* **transplanted, transplanting. 1.** to move from one place to another: *The best time to transplant the tree is at the end of winter or early spring.* **2.** *Medicine.* to move an organ or part of the body from one person or animal to another. *noun, plural* **transplants.** *Medicine.* the act of transplanting: *The first human heart transplant was done in South Africa in 1967.*

trans·port [trans-<u>port</u> *for verb;* <u>trans</u>-port *for noun*] *verb,* **transported, transporting.** to move or carry goods or people from one place to another by vehicle: *We decided to transport the goods by sea because it was too expensive by air.*
noun. **1.** the moving of goods or people from one place to another by vehicle: *The boxes are all packed up and ready for transport.* **2.** a type of military ship or other vehicle used to move troops and supplies.

trans·por·ta·tion ▶ [trans-pur-<u>tay</u>-shun] *noun.* the act of moving goods or people from one place to another in a vehicle or vehicles: *In Venice, Italy, the main system of transportation is by canal.*

trap [trap] *noun, plural* **traps.**
1. a device that has been placed somewhere in order to catch animals: *The trap was baited with cheese, but it did not attract the mouse.*
2. a plan for tricking someone in order to make them do something that they do not want to do.
verb, **trapped, trapping.** to catch or as if in a trap: *to trap animals for their fur; Coach told him to pass the ball rather than holding it and getting trapped in the corner.*

trap·door [<u>trap</u>-dore] *noun, plural* **trapdoors.** a door in a ceiling or floor. This word is also spelled **trap door.**

tra·peze ▲ [tra-<u>peez</u>] *noun, plural* **trapezes.** a short bar hung from a high place between two ropes, used by acrobats: *She swung on the trapeze above the heads of the circus audience.*

trap·e·zoid [<u>trap</u>-uh-<u>zoid</u>] *noun, plural* **trapezoids.** *Mathematics.* a flat figure with four sides, two of which are parallel.

trap·per [<u>trap</u>-ur] *noun, plural* **trappers.** a person who traps wild animals for their fur.

trash [trash] *noun.* **1.** things to be thrown away; rubbish: *In this town, trash is collected once a week.* **2.** *Computers.* a place on a computer desktop where files can be discarded: *I wanted that file—don't tell me you put into the trash.*

trau·ma [<u>traw</u>-muh *or* <u>trou</u>-muh] *noun, plural* **traumas. 1.** a very unpleasant and upsetting experience: *Final exams can be a cause of trauma and tension.*
2. *Medicine.* damage to the mind or body caused by a sudden emotional shock, accident, or terrible experience: *That psychiatrist sees many patients damaged by the trauma of war.*

trau·mat·ic [truh-<u>mat</u>-ik] *adjective.* being deeply upsetting, shocking: *She never really recovered from the traumatic experience of seeing the terrible car accident.*

trav·el [<u>trav</u>-ul] *verb,* **traveled, traveling. 1.** to make a journey or trip from one place to another: *Christina traveled for four months all over the U.S. by herself.*
2. to move from one place to another: *On the highways in Germany, cars often travel at 150 miles per hour.*
noun, plural **travels.** the act of making a journey from one place to another: *We arrived home tired after two long weeks of travel.* **—traveler,** *noun.*

*A bottom or otter **trawl** is a large net that is towed behind a fishing boat to catch fish that live on the seabed.*

trawl ▲ [trawl] *noun, plural* **trawls.** a strong, wide net that is used by fishermen to drag slowly along the ocean bottom in order to catch fish. A **trawler** is a fishing vessel that uses a trawl.
verb, **trawled, trawling.** to fish with a trawl.

tray [tray] *noun, plural* **trays.** a flat piece of wood, metal, or plastic with raised sides that is used to carry things, especially food and drink.

treach·er·ous [<u>trech</u>-ur-us] *adjective.* **1.** betraying one's country or friends; disloyal: *Don't believe a word he says—he is such a treacherous man.* The act of behaving in this way is called **treachery. 2.** full of hidden dangers; hazardous: *Be careful swimming in the surf—the current can be treacherous and take you into deep water.*

tread [tred] *verb,* **trod, trodden, treading. 1.** to step on something, or place your foot on something: *I don't like dancing with him because he keeps treading on my toes.*
2. to step heavily; trample: *The kids ran into the room treading mud all over Mom's new carpet.*
noun, plural **treads. 1.** the sound made when walking: *I recognized his light tread on the stairs.* **2.** the raised pattern on the outer surface of a tire.

tread·mill ◀ [<u>tred</u>-mil] *noun, plural* **treadmills. 1.** a device moved by persons or animals treading on steps or walking on an endless belt. **2.** a device having an endless belt on which a person can exercise by walking or running.
3. a situation in which one seems to be doing the same thing over and over without making progress.

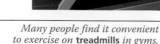

*Many people find it convenient to exercise on **treadmills** in gyms.*

TRANSPORTATION

Transportation allows people to travel on land, in the air, and by sea. While people have moved from place to place for many thousands of years in small groups, new technology has made it possible for large numbers to travel long distances. For example, the ocean liner *Queen Mary 2* is fourteen stories high and can carry more than 3,000 passengers, and the world's largest passenger aircraft, the Airbus A380, can carry 550 people.

LAND TRANSPORTATION
Buses, trains, and trams are forms of mass transport, while cars and motorcycles carry individuals or small groups.

Long-distance passenger coach

Scooters

Electric train

Electric tram

AIR TRANSPORTATION
Air transportation is made up of fixed wing aircraft, such as jet planes and seaplanes, and rotary wing aircraft, such as helicopters.

Bell Jetranger helicopter

Airbus A-320

Flying boat seaplane

Airbus A-320 (from below)

SEA TRANSPORTATION
The first sea transportation was by raft and canoes. Later, ships were powered by sail and, from the nineteenth century, by steam.

The *Mayflower* carried 102 pilgrims to America in 1620.

The *Titanic,* the largest passenger steamboat of its time, struck an iceberg and sank in 1912.

trea·son [tree-zun] *noun. Law.* the crime of betraying one's country by helping an enemy: *If it can be proved that he sold government security secrets to the enemy, he should be tried for treason.*

treas·ure ▶ [trezh-ur] *noun, plural* **treasures.** a collection of money, gold, jewels, or other valuable things: *Buried treasure is the theme of many pirate movies.*
verb, **treasured, treasuring.** to think of something as being very valuable: *I will treasure the watch you gave me for my birthday and keep it safe.*

treas·ur·er [trezh-ur-ur] *noun, plural* **treasurers.** a person responsible for taking care of the money belonging to an organization.

treas·ur·y [trezh-ur-ee] *noun, plural* **treasuries.** the money or other funds of a business, government, or other group. The **Treasury** is the U.S. government department that controls and spends public money.

treat [treet] *verb,* **treated, treating. 1.** to act or behave toward someone, or handle a situation, in a certain way: *His way of handling a difficult situation is to treat it as a joke.* **2.** to give a person medical care: *The doctor is treating him for high blood pressure.* **3.** to buy or give someone something special: *Mary said that as she hadn't bought any clothes lately she was going to treat herself to a new dress.* **4.** to subject to a special process: *The builder said that you should treat the wood with some sort of preservative before it cracks in the sun.*
noun, plural **treats.** something special that gives a lot of pleasure: *We will go to the zoo as a treat for your birthday.*

treat·ment [treet-munt] *noun, plural* **treatments. 1.** the way someone or something is treated: *The mayor is always complaining of unfair treatment by the news media.* **2.** the methods used to help cure a sick or injured person: *He was very ill but recovered after a course of treatment.*

treat·y [tree-tee] *noun, plural* **treaties.** a formal, written agreement between countries: *The Versailles Treaty was signed at the end of World War I.*

tree ▼ [tree] *noun, plural* **trees.** a tall plant with a wooden trunk, branches, and leaves: *The city council planted a beautiful magnolia tree in the middle of the park.*

This old wooden **treasure** *chest is filled with jewels, gold and silver.*

trek [trek] *verb,* **trekked, trekking.** to make a long, hard journey, especially on foot: *They trekked for three days through mud and swamps before reaching their destination.*
noun, plural **treks.** a long, hard journey: *The trek through the mountains was very tiring.*

The word **trek** comes from a term used in South Africa to mean "a long, difficult journey by ox-wagon." The word became known in English because of the Great Trek, a famous movement of the 1800s in which thousands of people called Boers traveled to the interior of South Africa to get away from British rule.

trem·ble [trem-bul] *verb,* **trembled, trembling. 1.** to shake because you are cold, frightened, weak, or angry: *The thunder and lightning made the dogs tremble with fear.* **2.** to move or vibrate: *During the earthquake I could feel our house trembling, but it didn't collapse.*

tre·men·dous [tri-men-dus] *adjective.* **1.** very large or great; enormous: *The new trains can travel at tremendous speeds.* **2.** describing something very good or outstanding: *The school play was a tremendous success.* —**tremendously,** *adverb.*

trem·or [trem-ur] *noun, plural* **tremors.** a shaking or trembling: *I could tell she was very upset because she had a tremor in her voice when she spoke.*

trench [trench] *noun, plural* **trenches. 1.** a long, narrow ditch cut into the ground: *The soldiers dug trenches to protect themselves from enemy fire.* **2.** a deep, narrow valley in the ocean floor.

trend [trend] *noun, plural* **trends.** a direction or course that is being followed; tendency: *The fashion editor said that there seems to be a trend away from dark colors this winter.*

tres·pass [tres-pas] *verb,* **trespassed, trespassing.** *Law.* to go onto someone else's property without permission. The act of going onto someone's property without permission is **trespassing.**
noun, plural **trespasses.** a wrong or bad act; sin.

The word **trespass** goes back to a word meaning "to go beyond" or "pass beyond." The idea is that when you trespass, you are going beyond the place where you should be, onto land where you are not allowed to go.

The baobab **tree** *originally comes from Africa.*

Trestles *support this old railroad bridge in New Mexico.*

tres·tle ▶ [tres-ul] *noun, plural* **trestles.** a framework used to hold up a railroad bridge or to support a table.

tri·al [trye-ul] *noun, plural* **trials.** **1.** *Law.* the legal process in which a judge and jury decide whether or not a person is guilty of a particular crime: *The trial lasted for five weeks, and in the end the verdict was "not guilty."* **2.** a test to find out the quality or performance of something: *There are three hundred patients taking part in the medical trial for the new drug.* **3.** a test of someone's ability to withstand something that causes worry or trouble: *Her illness must be a great trial to her parents.*

tri·an·gle [trye-ang-gul] *noun, plural* **triangles.** **1.** *Mathematics.* a flat shape with three straight sides and three angles. When something is shaped like this it is said to be **triangular** in shape. **2.** *Music.* a small, steel, three-sided instrument that sounds like a bell when it is struck by a steel rod.

tribe [tribe] *noun, plural* **tribes.** a group of people of the same race who share the same culture, language, religious beliefs, and customs. **Tribal** is relating to or belonging to a tribe.

trib·u·tar·y [trib-yuh-ter-ee] *noun, plural* **tributaries.** a river or stream that flows into a larger river: *The Arkansas River is one of the main tributaries of the Mississippi River.*

trib·ute [trib-yoot] *noun, plural* **tributes.** something done, said, or given to show admiration, thanks, or respect: *Everyone stood up and clapped for the soldier as a tribute to his heroic exploits.*

tri·cer·a·tops ▶ [trye-ser-uh-tops] *noun, plural* **triceratopses.** a dinosaur that had a long horn over each eye, a short horn on its snout, and a bony collar over the back of its head.

trick [trik] *noun, plural* **tricks. 1.** something done to cheat or deceive someone: *She didn't seem to care what sort of dirty trick she had to use in order to get her own way.* **Trickery** is the act of using such tricks. **2.** a clever way of doing something or an act needing special skills: *Even though we all watched him do the card trick three times, no one could work out how he did it.*
verb, **tricked, tricking.** to deceive or cheat someone: *It's very hard to trick my mom—she always knows when I'm telling a lie.*

trick·le [trik-ul] *verb,* **trickled, trickling.** to flow in drops or in a thin stream: *She looked so sad and tears started to trickle down her cheeks.*
noun, plural **trickles.** a small flow or thin stream: *The drought slowed the fast-flowing river down to a trickle.*

trick·y [trik-ee] *adjective.* **1.** clever and deceitful: *Some tricky planning by the criminals made it hard for the police to track them down.* **2.** difficult to do or deal with: *Keeping your balance when riding a bike for the first time can be tricky.*

tri·cy·cle [trye-suh-kul] *noun, plural* **tricycles.** a vehicle similar to a bicycle but with three wheels instead of two, two at the back and one at the front. It is often ridden by small children.

tri·fle [trye-ful] *noun, plural* **trifles.** something that is small or of no importance: *After having their luggage stolen, it seemed like a mere trifle when they missed their bus.*
verb, **trifled, trifling.** to be careless of, or not to take seriously: *She's not serious—she's just trifling with you.*

trig·ger [trig-ur] *noun, plural* **triggers.** the small lever on a gun that is pressed or pulled in order to fire it.
verb, **triggered, triggering.** to start something: *It takes only one spark to trigger a forest fire in summer.*

trig·o·nom·e·try [trig-uh-nom-i-tree] *noun. Mathematics.* the branch of mathematics that uses triangle measurement to work out indirect measurements. Trigonometry is used in building, engineering, navigation, and physics.

tril·lion [trig-uh-nom-i-tree] *noun, plural* **trillions.** the number 1,000,000,000,000; one thousand times one billion.

The **triceratops** *was a plant-eating dinosaur that used its horns to defend itself against attackers.*

tri·lo·gy [tril-uh-jee] *noun, plural* **trilogies.** *Literature.* a collection or series of three pieces of writing, connected by subject or theme.

trim [trim] *verb,* **trimmed, trimming. 1.** to cut back something to make it neat: *Fred trimmed the hedge.* **2.** to add decorations to: *Trimming the tree on Christmas Eve was a family tradition.*
noun, plural **trims. 1.** a cut to make something neat: *The barber gave his hair a trim.* **2.** a fringe-like decoration: *My favorite hat has a feather trim.*
adjective. **trimmer, trimmest.** well maintained: *a trim sailboat; a woman with a trim figure.*

trim·ming [trim-ing] *noun, plural* **trimmings. 1.** the act of adding decoration: *the trimming of a Christmas tree.* **2.** something extra; an addition: *At Thanksgiving we have turkey with all the trimmings.* **3.** the act of cutting back: *The trimming of the trees in our street is carried out in late autumn.*

a b c d e f g h i j k l m n o p q r s **t** u v w x y z

tri·o [tree-oh] *noun, plural* **trios. 1.** a group of three. **2.** a piece of music for three singers or instruments.

trip [trip] *noun, plural* **trips.** the act of making a journey: *Every year Joe and Ellen take a trip to Mexico.* *verb,* **tripped, tripping. 1.** to fall over something or cause someone to fall over: *Mary tripped over the dog and fell flat on her face.* **2.** to make a mistake or to cause someone else to make a mistake: *Clever questioning by the detective tripped the guilty person up and forced him into making a confession.*

tripe [tripe] *noun.* **1.** the lining of a cow's intestines, used in cooking. **2.** in everyday speech, something that is of no use or value.

tri·ple [trip-ul] *adjective.* **1.** made up of three parts: *A triple cone has three scoops of ice cream.* **2.** three times as much: *Her promotion meant she was paid triple the amount of her last salary.* *verb,* **tripled, tripling.** to make or become three times the size or amount: *The number of visitors to our state tripled over the last year.* *noun, plural* **triples.** in baseball, a hit that allows the batter to reach third base safely.

trip·let ▼ [trip-lit] *noun, plural* **triplets.** one of three offspring born at the same time to the same mother.

Special three-seater baby carriages make it easy to take **triplets** *out.*

tri·pod ▲ [trye-pod] *noun, plural* **tripods.** a three-legged support, usually for a camera or telescope.

tri·umph [trye-umf] *noun, plural* **triumphs. 1.** a victory over someone or something: *My personal triumph was to overcome my fear of flying.* **2.** the feeling of satisfaction after winning: *After the match the players carried the scorer of the winning goal on their shoulders in triumph.*

tri·umph·ant [trye-um-funt] *adjective.* full of pride after having won a victory or achieved success: *The winner made a triumphant entry on stage.* —**triumphantly,** *adverb.*

triv·i·a [triv-ee-uh] *plural noun.* interesting but unimportant information: *He is the "king" of trivia—he wins all the contests.*

Trivia is information that it is interesting but not really important to know. The word is most often used to describe short factual items dealing with popular subjects such as movies, television shows, music, sports, and famous people. For example, a piece of standard information about Franklin D. Roosevelt is that he was U.S. President during World War II. An item of trivia would be that the name of his dog was Fala. Trivia is different from information that is not useful at all, such as Roosevelt's shoe size or his Social Security number.

Tripods have adjustable legs and tops that swivel to change the viewing direction.

triv·i·al [triv-ee-ul] *adjective.* of little or no importance: *The teacher told them to get on with their work and not to bother him with trivial details.*

troll¹ [trole] *verb,* **trolled, trolling.** to fish by throwing a baited line over the side of a moving boat: *We went trolling for mackerel.*

troll² [trole] *noun, plural* **trolls.** *Literature.* a mischievous dwarf or a giant from folk tales who lives underground, under bridges, or in the hills.

trol·ley [trol-ee] *noun, plural* **trolleys. 1.** an electric-powered streetcar that runs on tracks. **2.** the small wheel that runs along an overhead wire and picks up the electricity that powers streetcars, trains, and buses.

trom·bone [trom-bone *or* trom-bone] *noun, plural* **trombones.** *Music.* a large, brass musical instrument like a trumpet. The pitch is changed by moving the tube up and down a U-shaped slide.

troop [troop] *noun, plural* **troops. 1.** a group of people doing something together: *a Scout troop; a volunteer troop.* **2.** a group of soldiers: *The enemy troops faced each other across the battlefield.* *verb,* **trooped, trooping.** to march or walk together as a group: *The girls trooped up and down the shopping mall looking for dresses for Prom night.* ◀» A different word with the same sound is **troupe.**

troop·er [troo-pur] *noun, plural* **troopers.** a state police officer: *A trooper stopped the car and gave the driver a ticket for speeding.*

tro·phy [troh-fee] *noun, plural* **trophies.** an award such as a plaque, two-handled cup, or statuette given as a prize, especially in sports: *Our team won the championship trophy in swimming.*

trop·i·cal ▶ [trop-uh-kul] *adjective.* *Geography.* found in the region on either side of the equator: *a tropical island; tropical fish.*

trop·ics [trop-iks] *noun.* *Geography.* the region on either side of the equator: *Hawaii lies in the tropics.*

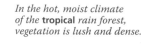

In the hot, moist climate of the **tropical** *rain forest, vegetation is lush and dense.*

Trout *thrive in cool climates and are sought after by those who fish for sport.*

trot [trot] *noun, plural* **trots.** a speed at which an animal or person moves. A trot is faster than a walk but slower than a run: *I went up the stairs at a slow trot.*
verb, **trotted, trotting.** to move or ride at a trot: *The horses trotted around the park.*

trou·ble [truh-bul] *noun, plural* **troubles. 1.** something that causes worry, danger, anger, and so on; a difficult situation: *Mary got into trouble with her parents after she came home very late.* **2.** a problem or inconvenience: *a person suffering from heart trouble; The road sign warned that there was trouble ahead.*
verb, **troubled, troubling. 1.** to make uncomfortable, worried, upset, and so on; disturb or distress: *Freda's decision to join the circus troubled her parents.* **2.** to cause someone an inconvenience: *Can I trouble you to close that window?*

trou·ble·some [truh-bul-sum] *adjective.* having the quality of being difficult or inconvenient: *It's troublesome to be a vegetarian when the rest of the family eats meat.*

trough [trawf] *noun, plural* **troughs.**
1. a long, narrow container for animal feed or water: *The pigs were feeding from the trough.*
2. a long, shallow depression in the earth, the ocean bed, between waves, or in the atmosphere.

troupe [troop] *noun, plural* **troupes.** a group of professional entertainers: *a troupe of actors.* A member of such a group is a **trouper.** A **trouper** is also be someone who is hardworking and uncomplaining: *He was a real trouper, clearing up after the party.* 🔊 A different word with the same sound is **troop.**

trou·sers [trou-zurz] *plural noun.* long pants worn by males and females.

trout ▲ [trout] *noun, plural* **trout** *or* **trouts.** a silver-colored fish that lives in lakes and rivers.

trow·el [trou-ul] *noun, plural* **trowels. 1.** a tool with a flat blade used to spread cement or plaster evenly over surfaces. **2.** a tool with a slightly scooped blade used for digging and planting in the garden.

tru·ant [troo-unt] *noun, plural* **truants.** *Education.* a student who skips class without permission. **Truancy** is the act of being absent from school without permission.

truce [troos] *noun, plural* **truces.** in war, a short stop in fighting, agreed upon by both sides, often so that peace terms can be discussed.

truck [truk] *noun, plural* **trucks.** a large motor vehicle, bigger and heavier than a car, often used to move goods: *A truck delivered the load of firewood to our house.* A **trucker** is the person who drives a truck as a job.
verb, **trucked, trucking.** to move something by truck: *I had all my books trucked to college when I left home.*

trudge [truj] *verb,* **trudged, trudging.** to walk slowly or with some difficulty: *The old man trudged through the snow.*

true [troo] *adjective,* **truer, truest. 1.** not false or made up; according to the facts; factual: *It isn't true to say that the Moon is made of green cheese.* **2.** describing something or someone loyal: *Good friends are true to each other whatever happens.* **3.** relating to being real; genuine: *She wasn't a true vegetarian because she sometimes ate fish.*

tru·ly [troo-lee] *adverb.* **1.** in actual fact; really: *To be truly fit, you have to do a lot of exercise.* **2.** in a true way; sincerely: *Bob said he was truly sorry for the trouble he had caused.*

trum·pet ◀ [trum-pit] *noun, plural* **trumpets.** *Music.* a brass musical instrument with a long tube and a funnel-shaped end.
verb, **trumpeted, trumpeting. 1.** to make a sound like a trumpet: *The elephants trumpeted as they came through the jungle.* **2.** to proclaim loudly and emphatically: *The conservative candidate trumpeted his support for the death penalty.*

trunk ▼ [trungk] *noun, plural* **trunks. 1.** the main growing stem of a tree. **2.** the long nose of an elephant. **3.** a very large box or suitcase: *All their belongings were packed in three trunks.* **4.** in humans, the central part of the body to which the legs, arms, and neck are attached; also called the torso. **5.** the compartment at the rear of an automobile used to store or transport things. **6. trunks.** short pants that end above the knee, worn by males: *swim trunks.*

trust [trust] *verb,* **trusted, trusting. 1.** to have faith in: *to trust in God.* **2.** to have confidence in; hope: *I trust you will approve of my choice.*
noun, plural **trust. 1.** a belief that someone or something is true, honest, or reliable: *My mother has complete trust in her doctor.* **2.** money or property taken care of by one person for another: *The young child's money was held in trust and managed by an attorney.*

trust·wor·thy [trust-wur-thee] *adjective.* able to be trusted; reliable: *He was not a trustworthy witness in court.* A different word with the same meaning is **trusty.**

truth [trooth] *noun, plural* **truths.**
1. something that is not false; a fact: *My parents taught me to always tell the truth.* **2.** the quality of being true: *There's no truth in the belief that the Earth is flat.*

truth·ful [trooth-ful] *adjective.* telling the truth; honest: *Jane was truthful about her age in the job interview.*
—truthfully, *adverb.*

The valves on a trumpet are used to change the pitch of the sound made by blowing.

Elephants eat, drink, and breathe with their trunks.

a b c d e f g h i j k l m n o p q r s **t** u v w x y z

*A **tuber** provides food for the rest of the plant growing above the soil.*

try [trye] *verb,* **tried, trying. 1.** to make an effort; attempt: *John tried to beat the school record in swimming.* **2.** to test something: *She tried the brakes on her bike before riding down the hill.* **3.** to examine a person accused of a crime in a court of law: *The woman was tried for robbery.* **4.** to cause stress: *The teacher said that our constant talking was trying his patience.*
noun, plural **tries.** an attempt: *I had a second try at passing my driving test.*

try·out [trye-out] *noun, plural* **tryouts.** a test for someone applying for a job or a team: *The coach gave John a tryout for the baseball team.* If you **try out** for something, you do a test to demonstrate your skill in that thing.

T-shirt [tee-shirt] *noun, plural* **T-shirts.** a short or long-sleeved under or outer shirt without buttons or a collar. This word is also spelled **tee shirt.**

tsu·na·mi ▼ [soo-nah-mee *or* tsoo-nah-mee] *noun, plural* **tsunamis.** *Environment.* a huge ocean wave caused by a volcanic eruption, an earthquake, or landslide.

tub [tub] *noun, plural* **tubs. 1.** a large container without a lid for holding water: *a wash tub.* **2.** a small container for keeping food: *a tub of butter.*

tub·a [too-buh] *noun, plural* **tubas.** *Music.* a very large brass musical instrument made of a long tube that curves up at the end that produces low notes.

tube [toob] *noun, plural* **tubes. 1.** a long pipe of glass, metal, rubber, or plastic designed to carry liquid or gas. **2.** a soft plastic or metal container which, when squeezed, ejects the contents: *a tube of toothpaste.* **3.** an electric train system that runs under the ground or mostly underground; a subway. Something that is **tubular** is hollow and shaped like a tube.

tub·er ▲ [too-bur] *noun, plural* **tubers.** the swollen underground stem of a plant: *A potato is a tuber.*

tu·ber·cul·o·sis [tu-*bur*-kyuh-loh-sis] *noun. Medicine.* an infection caused by bacteria and usually spread by coughing or sneezing that mainly affects the lungs. It is one of the world's most serious diseases. The shortened form of this word is **TB.**

tuck [tuk] *verb,* **tucked, tucking. 1.** to push or fold the edges of something in place: *Hospital beds have sheets that are neatly tucked in.* **2.** to put something in a secure or hidden place: *She tucked the papers into the folder.*
noun, plural **tucks.** a fold sewed into a piece of clothing: *Mom sewed a tuck in my skirt to make the waist smaller.*

Tues·day [tooz-*day or* tooz-dee] *noun, plural* **Tuesdays.** the third day of the week.

> The word **Tuesday** originally meant "Tiu's day." Tiu was an important deity of ancient times who was believed to be the god of war and the sky.

tuft [tuft] *noun, plural* **tufts.** a bunch of feathers, hair, or grass: *Tufts of grass grew among the sand dunes.*

tug [tug] *verb,* **tugged, tugging.** to pull at something: *I tugged at the handle to make the door open.*
noun, plural **tugs.** a strong pull: *The dog gave a tug on the leash.*

tug·boat ◀ [tug-bote] *noun, plural* **tugboats.** a small, powerful boat used to pull or push ships into or out of a berth or harbor.

Tugboats are used to tow ships through the narrow Corinth Canal in Greece.

tu·i·tion [too-ish-un] *noun. Education.* the money that is paid for studying in a college, university, private school, and so on.

TSUNAMIS

Tsunamis occur mainly in the Pacific area and can cause enormous damage and loss of life. Unlike a surface wave, a tsunami is a whole column of water that reaches from the sea floor up to the surface. It can race across oceans for thousands of miles at speeds of nearly 500 miles per hour. As it approaches shallower water near land, it builds up speed and height, until it hits the shore as an enormous wave.

People enjoy a peaceful harbor moments before a tsunami strikes.

The harbor is suddenly drained of water and people rush to see what is happening.

People and buildings are swept away as the water rushes back.

Tsunamis are often more destructive than the earthquakes or eruptions that cause them.

*Holland produces about three million **tulips** each year.*

tu·lip ▲ [<u>too</u>-lip] *noun, plural* **tulips.** a single, cup-shaped flower with six petals that grows from a bulb. It is the national flower of Holland.

tum·ble [<u>tum</u>-bul] *verb,* **tumbled, tumbling. 1.** to fall by accident: *Fred didn't look where he was going and tumbled downstairs.* **2.** to roll about: *The puppies tumbled together in their basket.* **3.** to do handsprings, somersaults, or rolls. *noun, plural* **tumbles.** the act of falling: *It's easy to take a tumble when the sidewalk is icy.*

tum·bler [<u>tum</u>-blur] *noun, plural* **tumblers. 1.** a cup made of glass or plastic: *a tumbler of water.* **2.** an acrobat or gymnast who performs handsprings, somersaults, and rolls.

tum·ble·weed [<u>tum</u>-bul-*weed*] *noun, plural* **tumbleweeds.** any plant that breaks away from its roots in autumn and is blown around by the wind. Tumbleweeds grow in dry areas of North America.

tu·mor [<u>too</u>-mur] *noun, plural* **tumors.** *Medicine.* a group of cells in the body that grow much faster than usual or do not die out in the normal way. Some tumors spread to other parts of the body and can be fatal. Others grow slowly and are not harmful.

tu·na ▶ [<u>too</u>-nuh] *noun, plural* **tuna** or **tunas.** a large ocean fish that lives in warm waters and is popular for eating.

tun·dra ▼ [<u>tun</u>-druh] *noun, plural* **tundras.** *Environment.* in arctic regions, a huge, mostly flat area where no trees grow.

tune [toon] *noun, plural* **tunes.** *Music.* **1.** a sequence of musical notes, often repeated, that makes a melody easy to remember: *Dad hummed a tune from his favorite opera.* **2.** a song: *She loves to listen to Broadway show tunes.* **3.** the correct pitch or key: *Some people always sing out of tune.* **4.** agreement in opinion or feeling: *We were in tune with each other from the moment we met.* *verb,* **tuned, tuning.** to adjust a musical instrument so that it plays the correct pitch or key: *to tune a piano.*

tung·sten [<u>tung</u>-stun] *noun, plural* **tungsten.** *Chemistry.* a very hard silver-colored metallic element. It is used in making X-ray tubes, electric light globes, television sets, and cutting tools.

tu·nic [<u>too</u>-nik] *noun, plural* **tunics. 1.** a short dress that ends above the knee, sometimes worn as a school uniform. **2.** a short jacket worn by members of the army or police.

tun·nel [<u>tun</u>-ul] *noun, plural* **tunnels.** a passage made under the ground, through rock, or under the water: *The Channel Tunnel, between England and France, is 21 miles long.* *verb,* **tunneled, tunneling.** to make a tunnel: *Rabbits tunnel through soft earth to make their burrows.*

tur·ban ▶ [<u>tur</u>-bun] *noun, plural* **turbans.** a headdress made by winding a long strip of material around the head.

tur·bine [<u>tur</u>-bun or <u>tur</u>-*bine*] *noun, plural* **turbines.** a machine used to make electricity, powered by water, steam, or wind that turns blades on a shaft.

turf [turf] *noun.* the top layer of the soil where grass and roots grow in a mat-like surface.

tur·key [<u>tur</u>-kee] *noun, plural* **turkeys.** a large bird with a red neck and black and brown feathers that is kept for food. The meat of this bird is a traditional meal at Thanksgiving.

*Indian snake charmers usually wear **turbans**.*

The bird known as the **turkey** gets its name from the nation of Turkey, which lies partly in Europe and partly in Asia. Since the bird is found in North America and has never lived wild in Turkey, it is not clear how this name came about. It may be that turkeys were brought from America to sell in Turkey, and so people mistakenly thought they came from there.

Tur·kish [<u>turk</u>-ish] *noun.* the language of Turkey, a country partly in Europe and partly in Asia. *adjective.* of or having to do with Turkey, its language, or its people.

tur·moil [<u>tur</u>-moil] *noun.* the state of being confused; a disturbance: *The country was in turmoil after a civil war.*

*Blue-fin **tuna** can grow to more than fourteen feet in length.*

turn [turn] *verb,* **turned, turning. 1.** to move in a circular direction; revolve: *The Earth turns around the Sun.* **2.** to change direction: *The car turned right.* **3.** to change or become: *Tadpoles turn into frogs.* **4.** to change in feeling: *to turn against something; to turn nasty.* *noun, plural* **turns. 1.** the act of turning: *Go to the end of Cedar Street, then make a right-hand turn into Ridge Road.* **2.** a change in direction: *The patient took a turn for the worse.* **3.** a chance or time to do something: *It was his turn to make dinner.*

*In the Arctic **tundra**, flowering plants and grasses survive cold winters close to the ground where it is warmer.*

a b e f g h i j k l m n o p q r s t u v w x y z

Marine turtles sometimes travel thousands of miles to find a partner and lay eggs.

tur·nip [tur-nup] *noun, plural* **turnips.** a plant with a round yellow or white root. Small varieties are grown for people to eat; larger varieties are grown for animal feed.

turn·out [turn-out] *noun, plural* **turnouts.** a group that gathers for a particular reason: *The Republicans hope for a good turnout of voters on election day.*

turn·o·ver [turn-ove-ur] *noun, plural* **turnovers. 1.** a type of pastry in which the ends are folded over the filling: *an apple turnover.* **2.** in sports such as basketball, the loss of the ball through breaking a rule or because of a player's mistake. **3.** *Business.* the number of workers leaving a job and being replaced: *Stressful jobs often have a high staff turnover.* **4.** *Business.* the amount of money made or activity conducted in a given time: *The travel industry had a good turnover this year.*

turn·pike [turn-pike] *noun, plural* **turnpikes.** a highway that drivers pay to use, with toll gates at its exits and entrances.

turn·stile [turn-stile] *noun, plural* **turnstiles.** a metal barrier that turns to let people in or out of a public area, one at a time: *At the subway station you go through a turnstile to get to the trains.*

turn·ta·ble [turn-tay-bul] *noun, plural* **turntables.** a disk that turns things around: *Old phonograph records are played on a turntable.*

tur·pen·tine [tur-pun-tine] *noun.* a liquid made from the resin of trees, especially pine trees, that is mixed with paints to make them thinner.

tur·quoise [tur-kwoiz or tur-koiz] *noun, plural* **turquoises. 1.** a greenish-blue stone found in arid regions, and often used in jewelry. **2.** the color greenish-blue. *adjective.* having a greenish-blue color.

tur·ret ▼ [tur-it] *noun, plural* **turrets. 1.** a small, usually round tower on a building: *Some castles and churches have turrets.* **2.** a rotating platform on a tank on which guns or cannons are attached so they can be fired in any direction.

*The White Tower of the Tower of London has three square **turrets** and a round turret that once housed a royal observatory.*

tur·tle ▶ [tur-tul] *noun, plural* **turtles.** a reptile with a soft body covered by a wide bony or leather shell that protects its head, limbs, and tail. Some turtles live in water and some live on land.

tur·tle·neck [tur-tul-nek] *noun, plural* **turtlenecks.** a sweater or other garment with a knitted collar that reaches up to the chin and folds over.

tusk ▼ [tusk] *noun, plural* **tusks.** a long, pointed tooth on either side of the mouth of some animals such as elephants, wild boar, and walruses: *The tusks of elephants are made of ivory.*

*Like all teeth, an elephant's **tusks** grow from sockets in its skull.*

tu·tor [too-tur] *noun, plural* **tutors.** *Education.* a teacher who gives private lessons: *Jerry fell so far behind in French he had to have extra lessons from a tutor to help him catch up.* *verb,* **tutored, tutoring.** to teach privately or to give individual lessons: *She tutored me in math.*

tux·e·do [tuk-see-doh] *noun, plural* **tuxedos** or **tuxedoes.** a formal evening jacket for men, usually black, and worn with black trousers.

The type of fancy dress for men known as a **tuxedo** gets its name for a town in New York State, called Tuxedo Park. It is thought that this type of dress jacket was first worn at a club in that town.

TV an abbreviation for TELEVISION.

tweed [tweed] *noun, plural* **tweeds.** a thickly-woven woolen material used for making warm clothing.

The **Tweed** is an important river that flows through southern Scotland and northern England. It is said that the cloth known as tweed got its name because people thought of it as being made along the banks of this river.

twee·zers [twee-zurz] *noun, plural* **tweezers.** a small metal tool with two prongs that is used to pull out hair or pick up tiny objects: *eyebrow tweezers.*

twelve [twelv] *noun, plural* **twelves.** the number between eleven and thirteen; 12. *adjective.* amounting to twelve in number. The position between eleventh and thirteenth is **twelfth.**

twen·ty [twen-tee] *noun, plural* **twenties.** the number between nineteen and twenty-one; 20. *adjective.* amounting to twenty in number. The position between nineteenth and twenty-first is **twentieth.**

twice [twise] *adverb.* two times; double: *The phone rang just twice and then the person hung up.*

twig [twig] *noun, plural* **twigs.** small, thin, woody stick from a tree or other plant: *The wild wind left twigs and branches all over our yard.*

twi·light [twye-*lite*] *noun.* the time of day immediately after sunset or before sunrise when the light is faint.

twin [twin] *noun, plural* **twins.** one of two children born at the same time from the same pregnancy. Twins who develop from the same fertilized egg and look exactly alike are called **identical twins.** Twins who develop from two separate fertilized eggs and may not look alike are called **fraternal twins.**
adjective. **1.** being a twin: *She gave birth to twin girls.* **2.** being a copy, exact match, or very similar: *a small airplane with twin engines; The library has twin statues of lions at the front entrance.*

twine [twine] *noun, plural* **twines.** a string or cord made of strands that have been twisted or spun together.
verb, **twined, twining.** to spin, coil, or twist one thing around another: *We twined the tomato plants around the stake.*

twinge [twinj] *noun, plural* **twinges.** a sudden, short, sharp pain: *I felt a twinge when the needle went in.*

twin·kle [twing-kul] *verb,* **twinkled, twinkling. 1.** to shine with a bright, flickering light: *The stars twinkled in the night sky.* **2.** to appear bright because of happy feelings: *My grandmother's eyes twinkled with delight when I arrived.*
noun, plural **twinkles.** flashes of bright light: *the twinkle of moonlight on the water.*

twirl [twurl] *verb,* **twirled, twirling.** to turn in a circular movement or spin something repeatedly: *My little sister twirled in her new party dress.* —**twirler,** *noun.*

twist [twist] *verb,* **twisted, twisting. 1.** to wind, weave, or coil around something: *The track twisted through the woods.* **2.** to make changes to the natural shape of something: *His face twisted in pain.* **3.** to cause injury to a part of the body by turning it suddenly and forcefully: *I twisted my ankle dancing.* **4.** to misunderstand or distort an intended meaning: *The Senator claimed that the newspaper had twisted his words in the story.*
noun, plural **twists.** a kink or bend: *I can't undo the twist in my necklace.*

twist·er [twis-tur] *noun, plural* **twisters.** a twirling column of wind; tornado.

twitch [twich] *verb,* **twitched, twitching.** to make a sudden, repeated, jerking motion: *After the marathon race my muscles were twitching.*

two [too] *noun, plural* **twos.** the number between one and three; 2.
adjective. amounting to two in number.

ty·coon [tye-koon] *noun, plural* **tycoons.** someone who is very wealthy and powerful, particularly someone in business.

type [tipe] *noun, plural* **types. 1.** a group of people, animals, or things with qualities and characteristics in common: *An eagle is a type of bird.* **2.** a small metal block with raised letters, numbers, and characters that is inked and pressed on paper to produce printed text: *Children's books often use large type.*
verb, **typed, typing.** to write using a keyboard connected to a computer or a typewriter: *I typed my essay so the teacher would be able to read it more easily.*

type·writ·er [tipe-rye-tur] *noun, plural* **typewriters.** a machine with keys that are pressed to print, letters, numbers, and characters onto paper.

ty·phoid fever [tye-foyde] *Medicine.* an infectious disease that is transmitted by contaminated food or water and can kill. Its symptoms are high fever, diarrhea, and intestinal swelling.

The eye of the **typhoon** *is clearly visible in this aerial photograph.*

ty·phoon ▲ [tye-foon] *noun, plural* **typhoons.** a violent tropical storm that occurs in the western Pacific and Indian oceans.

typ·i·cal [tip-u-kul] *adjective.* having or showing the characteristics or qualities shared by a type of person or thing: *Barking is a typical behavior for dogs.* —**typically,** *adverb.*

ty·pist [tye-pist] *noun, plural* **typists.** someone whose job is to type documents using a typewriter or computer keyboard.

ty·ran·no·saur ◀ [ti-ran-uh-sore] *noun, plural* **tyrannosaurs.** a large, powerful, meat-eating dinosaur that lived in North America. It walked upright on its hind legs and had small forelimbs. This animal is also called a **tyrannosaurus rex.**

tyr·an·ny [teer-uh-nee] *noun, plural* **tyrannies.** *Government.* harsh and unjust use of power or a ruler, government, or authority that uses power in this way: *When tyranny took over the nation, people were put in jail without a trial.* Ruling over people by the use of tyranny is described as **tyrannical.**

ty·rant [tye-runt] *noun, plural* **tyrants.** a person in power who uses cruelty and oppression to rule: *The general was a tyrant who ordered the torture of the enemy.*

The gigantic **tyrannosaur** *weighed about seven tons and was taller than a double-decker bus.*

a b c d e f g h i j k l m n o p q r s t u v w x y z

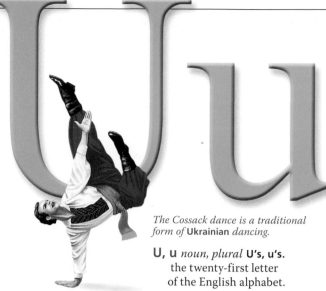

*The Cossack dance is a traditional form of **Ukrainian** dancing.*

U, u *noun, plural* **U's, u's.** the twenty-first letter of the English alphabet.

ud·der [ud-ur] *noun, plural* **udders.** a large sac with nipples that hangs from the underside of animals such as cows, sheep, and goats. The udder contains the glands that produce milk.

UFO an abbreviation for **Unidentified Flying Object,** which is an unknown object that appears to be flying; especially related to objects that are believed to come from outer space.

ug·ly [ug-lee] *adjective,* **uglier, ugliest. 1.** not pleasing to the eyes or other senses; not pretty or attractive: *an ugly house painted purple and green.* **2.** not pleasant; causing offense; dangerous, angry, threatening, and so on: *an ugly tone of voice; an ugly mood.* **3.** extremely unfriendly; threatening: *an ugly crowd that was about to riot.*

u·ke·le·le [*yoo*-kuh-*lay*-lee] *noun, plural* **ukeleles.** *Music.* a small musical instrument similar to a guitar with four strings. The ukelele is traditionally played in Hawaii.

> The musical instrument known as the **ukulele** has been popular in Hawaii since it was introduced there by immigrants from Portugal in 1879. There are several stories of how the instrument got its name. The most generally accepted is that the word meant "jumping flea." People thought that the way the instrument was played, with the musician moving his fingers quickly over the strings, looked like an insect jumping about.

U·krain·i·an ◀ [yoo-*kray*-nee-un] *noun, plural,* **Ukrainians. 1.** someone who was born in the southeastern European country of Ukraine or is a citizen of Ukraine. **2.** the language of Ukraine. *adjective.* relating to the country of Ukraine, its people, or its culture.

ul·cer [ul-sur] *noun, plural* **ulcers.** *Health.* an open sore on the skin or in the stomach or small intestine. The formation of an ulcer is **ulceration.**

ul·ti·mate [ul-tuh-mit] *adjective.* **1.** being the greatest or best; perfect: *Chocolate is my idea of the ultimate treat.* **2.** the highest or most important stage; final: *The ultimate goal of our effort is to make sure the river is kept clean for the future.* **3.** being the essential nature of a thing; basic: *The ultimate theme of the play is love.* —**ultimately,** *adverb.*

ultra- a prefix used to mean more extreme than usual: something that is *ultrasoft* is much softer than normal; to be *ultracareful* means to be especially careful.

ul·tra·sound ▼ [ul-truh-*sound*] *noun, plural* **ultrasounds.** *Science.* a type of sound that is beyond human hearing. This sound can be used to create an image of internal body parts, and is often used to create an image of a baby in the mother's body.

ul·tra·vi·o·let [ul-truh-*vye*-uh-lit] *adjective. Science.* a type of light that is invisible to the human eye and higher in energy than visible light. Ultraviolet light lies just beyond violet in the visible light spectrum. This kind of light is a component of sunlight. **Ultraviolet light** is also known as **UV.**

um·bil·i·cal cord [um-*bil*-uh-kul] *Medicine.* the flexible cord that connects a mother to her baby during pregnancy, carrying blood, oxygen, and nutrients to the baby from the mother's placenta. The umbilical cord is attached at the baby's **umbilicus,** or belly button.

um·brel·la [um-*brel*-uh] *noun, plural* **umbrellas.** a screen of plastic or fabric stretched over a folding frame and used as protection from rain or sun.

> **Umbrella** comes from *umbra,* the Latin word for "shade." The first umbrellas were used in hot climates to give shade from the sun, and only later did people also begin to use them to keep off the rain.

um·pire [um-*pire*] *noun, plural* **umpires.** someone who makes sure that the rules of a game or sport are being followed, such as baseball. An umpire is also responsible for managing arguments between players or teams. *verb,* **umpired, umpiring.** to act as umpire: *Parents umpire our softball games.*

UN an abbreviation for UNITED NATIONS.

un- a prefix used indicate the opposite of something; not: *unloving* is the opposite of loving, and means not loving; *unprepared* is the opposite of prepared, and means not prepared.

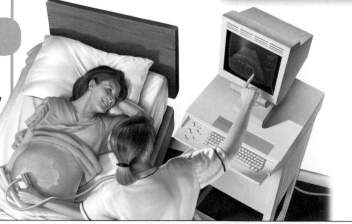

Ultrasound *is used to monitor the development of an unborn baby.*

un·a·ble [un-<u>ay</u>-bul] *adjective.* not able to do something: *I was unable to finish my homework.*

un·ac·cept·a·ble [*un*-uk-<u>sep</u>-tuh-bul] *adjective.* not acceptable; not right: *Interrupting the teacher is unacceptable.*

un·ac·cus·tomed [*un*-uh-<u>kus</u>-tumd] *adjective.* not used to: *I am unaccustomed to giving speeches.*

u·nan·i·mous [yoo-<u>nan</u>-uh-mus] *adjective.* describing a situation in which everyone agrees on something: *She was elected class president by a unanimous vote.* The fact of being unanimous is called **unanimity.** —**unanimously,** *adverb.*

un·armed [un-<u>armd</u>] *adjective.* not carrying guns or weapons: *The police did not shoot because the robber was unarmed.*

un·a·ware [*un*-uh-<u>ware</u>] *adjective.* not realizing or knowing; not aware: *Mom was worried because she was unaware that I was coming home late.*

un·a·wares [*un*-uh-<u>warez</u>] *adverb.* by surprise: *Her friend's sudden arrival caught her unawares.*

un·bear·a·ble [un-<u>bare</u>-uh-bul] *adjective.* not able to be endured; awful or terrible: *When he broke his leg he was in unbearable pain.*

un·be·com·ing [*un*-bi-<u>kum</u>-ing] *adjective.* **1.** not becoming; not flattering: *an unbecoming dress.* **2.** not proper or appropriate: *unbecoming behavior.*

un·be·liev·a·ble [*un*-bi-<u>leev</u>-uh-bul] *adjective.* **1.** hard or impossible to believe: *His list of excuses for being late were completely unbelievable.* **2.** describing something incredible or amazing: *That girl has an unbelievable singing voice.* —**unbelievably,** *adverb.*

un·break·a·ble ▶ [un-<u>bray</u>-kuh-bul] *adjective.* hard or impossible to break: *unbreakable toy building blocks.*

un·can·ny [un-<u>kan</u>-ee] *adjective.* far beyond what is usual or normal; outstanding and remarkable: *He has a uncanny ability to work with computers.* —**uncannily,** *adverb.*

un·cer·tain [un-<u>sur</u>-tun] *adjective.* **1.** not sure or certain: *I am uncertain what day the exams start.* The fact of being uncertain is called **uncertainty. 2.** not dependable or predictable: *They turned the boat back to shore because of the uncertain seas.*

un·chan·ged [un-<u>chaynjd</u>] *adjective.* the same as before; not changed: *I have never liked Sean and my opinion is still unchanged.*

un·cle [<u>ung</u>-kul] *noun, plural* **uncles.** the brother or brother-in-law of a mother or father.

un·clear [un-<u>kleer</u>] *adjective.* not clear; confusing: *We got lost because of the unclear directions.*

Drinking tumblers made out of plastic are **unbreakable.**

Uncle Sam *History.* the U.S. government and its people, represented by a tall, thin man in a top hat, dressed in red, white, and blue.

> "Uncle Sam" is the nickname for the United States of America, but it is not known why this name was chosen. The person most often associated with the name is "Uncle Sam" Wilson, a butcher who supplied meat to American soldiers during the War of 1812. It is said that he would pack the meat in barrels with the label "U.S.," and the soldiers would joke, "This is U.S. meat; it comes from Uncle Sam."

un·com·fort·a·ble [un-<u>kumft</u>-tur-bul *or* un-<u>kum</u>-fur-tuh-bul] *adjective.* not comfortable; feeling or causing discomfort: *a cramped, uncomfortable seat on an airplane; After she started to cry, there was an uncomfortable silence in the room.* —**uncomfortably,** *adverb.*

un·com·mon [un-<u>kom</u>-un] *adjective.* not common; rare or unusual: *Winning the lottery twice is uncommon luck.* —**uncommonly,** *adverb.*

un·con·scious [un-<u>kon</u>-shus] *adjective.* **1.** not conscious: *The football player was knocked unconscious by the hard tackle.* **2.** not knowing; unaware: *She was unconscious of her own beauty.* **3.** not done intentionally: *He made an unconscious error and dialed the wrong number.* —**unconsciously,** *adverb;* —**unconsciousness,** *noun.*

un·con·sti·tu·tion·al [un-<u>kon</u>-stuh-<u>too</u>-shuh-nul] *adjective.* not in keeping with the United States Constitution: *It is unconstitutional for the government to restrict someone's freedom of speech.*

un·con·ven·tion·al [*un*-kun-<u>ven</u>-shun-ul] *adjective.* not conventional; different or unusual: *She has purple hair and wears unconventional clothes.*

un·co·op·er·a·tive [*un*-koh-<u>op</u>-uh-ruh-tiv] *adjective.* not willing to help or go along with something: *The teacher said Tom was uncooperative when he refused to clean the blackboard.*

un·cover [un-<u>kuv</u>-ur] *verb,* **uncovered, uncovering. 1.** to remove the cover or top from: *Cook the stew with the lid on the pot, but then uncover it for the last ten minutes.* **2.** to find out or discover: *Mom uncovered the truth behind the broken window.*

un·de·cid·ed [*un*-di-<u>sye</u>-did] *adjective.* **1.** still thinking about what to do: *She is undecided about which car to buy.* **2.** not settled yet: *The result of the football game was undecided until the last minutes of the game.*

un·der [<u>un</u>-dur] *preposition.* **1.** to or in a lower place; below: *I looked for my shoes under the bed.* **2.** less than: *Children under five are not allowed to go on this side.* **3.** guided or controlled by: *Dad served in the Gulf War under General McCaffrey.* **4.** according to: *It is our right under the Constitution to bear arms.* *adverb.* below or beneath: *This part goes on top and the other part goes under.*

under-

under- a prefix that means. **1.** below or beneath: *underpants* are short pants worn under other clothes; *underage* means below the legal age. **2.** less than enough; not appropriately: *underfed* means fed less than enough food; *underdressed* means not dressed appropriately.

un·der·brush ▶ [un-dur-*brush*] *noun.* small trees and bushes that grow under taller trees in a wood or forest: *A carpet of dense underbrush covered the forest floor.* A different word with the same meaning is **undergrowth**.

un·der·cov·er [un-dur-<u>kuv</u>-ur] *adjective.* working or operating in secret: *an undercover investigation; an undercover agent.*

un·der·de·vel·oped [un-dur-di-<u>vel</u>-upt] *adjective.* **1.** not developed enough: *Poor countries with few industries and not enough food and shelter are called underdeveloped countries.* **2.** not mature or not healthy: *an underdeveloped baby.*

un·der·dog [un-dur-*dawg*] *noun, plural* **underdogs.** a group or a person that is least likely to win: *I love it when the underdogs win because it proves that everyone has a chance to shine.*

> The word **underdog** comes from the idea of two dogs fighting. The underdog would be the one that was losing the fight. In other words, this dog would be underneath the other dog.

un·der·est·i·mate [un-dur-<u>es</u>-tuh-*mate*] *verb,* **estimated, estimating.** to make too low an estimate of the amount, degree, or value of something or someone: *All the team underestimated the batter until he hit a home run.*

un·der·go [un-dur-<u>goh</u>] *verb,* **underwent, undergone, undergoing.** to experience or go though something: *The school will undergo renovations during the vacation.*

un·der·grad·u·ate [un-dur-<u>graj</u>-oo-it] *noun, plural* **undergraduates.** *Education.* a college or university student who has not yet received a degree.

un·der·ground ▶ [un-dur-*ground*] *adjective.* **1.** under the surface of the earth: *an underground tunnel.* **2.** describing something hidden or secret: *During the war, an underground network helped prisoners escape. noun, plural* **undergrounds. 1.** a place under the surface of the earth. **2.** a secret organization. *adverb.* into or in hiding. *The thieves went underground and were never caught.*

Underground Railroad *History.* a secret network that helped slaves escape from the southern states to freedom in the northern states of the United States and Canada.

un·der·hand [<u>un</u>-dur-*hand*] *adjective.* describing something thrown with the hand below the shoulder, as in pitching or bowling a ball: *an underhand pitch. adverb.* from the hand below the shoulder: *The ball was thrown underhand.*

un·der·han·ded [un-dur-*han*-did] *adjective.* **1.** describing something thrown with the hand below the shoulder, as in pitching or bowling a ball. **2.** not open and honest; sneaky: *Letting the air out of the tires on his bike was an underhanded thing to do.*

un·der·line [un-dur-*line*] *verb,* **underlined, underlining. 1.** to draw a line under something: *The teacher asked us to underline all the nouns in the paragraph.* **2.** to emphasize or stress: *She underlined the fact that she wanted the book back by Friday.*

un·der·mine [un-dur-*mine*] *verb,* **undermined, undermining. 1.** to harm or weaken, usually in secret; corrupt: *They undermined her chances of becoming president by spreading rumors about her.* **2.** to make something unstable by digging under it: *When they put in the gas pipes, they undermined the foundations of the house.*

un·der·neath [un-dur-<u>neeth</u>] *preposition.* below or under something: *The children hid underneath the bed. adverb.* positioned below or under: *To stay warm, he wore thick boots with woolen socks on underneath.*

un·der·nour·ish·ed [un-dur-<u>nur</u>-isht] *adjective. Health.* having less nourishment from food than is necessary to stay healthy and grow: *During the drought no grass grew and the cattle became undernourished.*

un·der·pants [un-dur-*pants*] *plural noun.* short pants worn under other clothing.

un·der·pass [un-dur-*pass*] *noun, plural* **underpasses.** a passageway that goes under something, especially a road that goes under another road or a railway line.

un·der·priv·i·leged [un-dur-<u>priv</u>-lijd] *adjective.* not having the benefits of living in a particular society, usually due to being poor or of low social standing: *That charity raises money for underprivileged people in our community.*

un·der·sea [un-dur-<u>see</u>] *adjective.* being, used, or carried out under the sea's surface: *For many years messages were carried between continents using an undersea cable.*

un·der·shirt [<u>un</u>-dur-*shurt*] *noun, plural* **undershirts.** a shirt made from light fabric that is worn beneath a shirt. Undershirts usually have short sleeves, or none at all.

un·der·side [un-dur-*side*] *adjective.* describing the underneath or lower side or surface of something: *A rock lying on the road damaged the car's underside.*

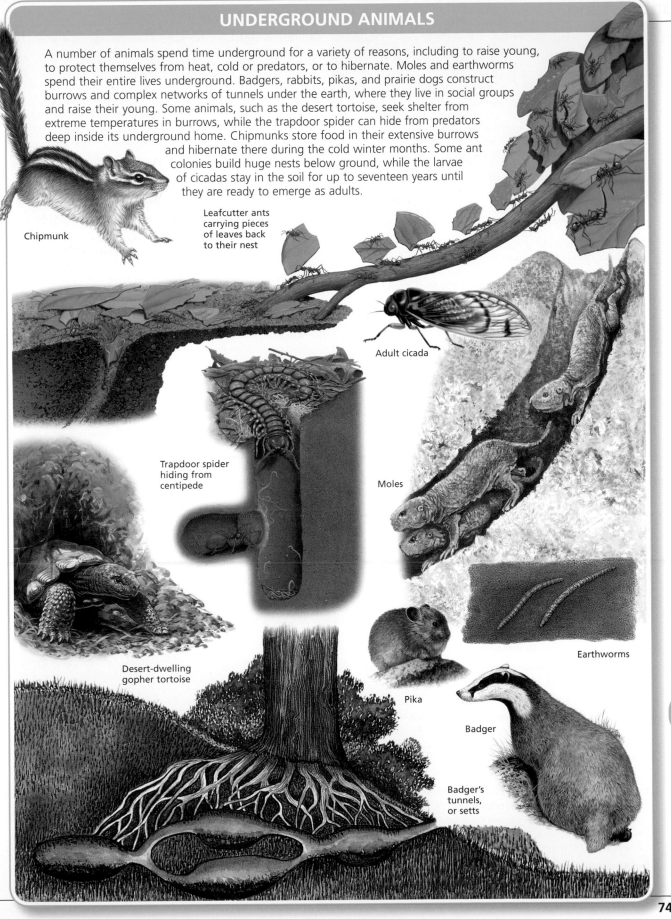

UNDERGROUND ANIMALS

A number of animals spend time underground for a variety of reasons, including to raise young, to protect themselves from heat, cold or predators, or to hibernate. Moles and earthworms spend their entire lives underground. Badgers, rabbits, pikas, and prairie dogs construct burrows and complex networks of tunnels under the earth, where they live in social groups and raise their young. Some animals, such as the desert tortoise, seek shelter from extreme temperatures in burrows, while the trapdoor spider can hide from predators deep inside its underground home. Chipmunks store food in their extensive burrows and hibernate there during the cold winter months. Some ant colonies build huge nests below ground, while the larvae of cicadas stay in the soil for up to seventeen years until they are ready to emerge as adults.

Chipmunk

Leafcutter ants
carrying pieces
of leaves back
to their nest

Adult cicada

Trapdoor spider
hiding from
centipede

Moles

Desert-dwelling
gopher tortoise

Earthworms

Pika

Badger

Badger's
tunnels,
or setts

The ancient Greeks believed that their souls had to travel across the river Styx to reach the **underworld**, so they buried their dead with a coin to pay the ferryman.

un·der·stand [*un*-dur-<u>stand</u>] *verb*, **understood, understanding. 1.** to grasp the meaning of; comprehend: *The students couldn't understand what the poem was about.* **2.** to be familiar with; know well: *He is a good rider because he understands horses.* **3.** to have sympathy and agree with: *She has a sore knee, so we understand why she doesn't want to go dancing.* **4.** to get knowledge of; to learn or find out: *I understand you have never ridden a bicycle before.*

un·der·stand·ing [*un*-dur-<u>stand</u>-ing] *noun*, *plural* **understandings. 1.** the act of grasping the meaning of; knowledge; comprehension: *His understanding of geography isn't good.* **2.** a judgment a person has reached; opinion; conclusion: *My understanding is that the blackout was caused by a lightning strike.* **3.** a settling of differences; an agreement: *They reached an understanding about which DVD to watch.* **4.** an ability to share feelings and sympathize with others: *Mom showed understanding when I said I felt sick.*
adjective. having or showing sympathy with: *Dad gave me an understanding pat on the back after I came in last in the race; an understanding teacher.*

un·der·take [*un*-dur-<u>take</u>] *verb*, **undertook, undertaken, undertaking. 1.** to attempt to carry out; set out to: *He undertook to finish his homework before eight o'clock.* **2.** to promise to carry out; accept a responsibility: *The famous athlete has undertaken to run all the way across the state for charity.* An activity, task, or duty undertaken is called an **undertaking.**

un·der·tak·er [*un*-dur-*tay*-kur] *noun*, *plural* **undertakers.** a person who has the job of preparing dead people for burial or cremation and who organizes funerals.

un·der·tow [*un*-dur-*toh*] *noun*, *plural* **undertows.** a strong underwater current that flows in a different direction to the current of the surface water. Some undertows are formed when the water brought to shore by waves rushes back out to sea. They can be dangerous for swimmers.

un·der·wa·ter ▶ [*un*-dur-*waw*-tur] *adjective*. being, used, or happening under the water's surface: *He wears an underwater watch when he goes scuba diving.*
adverb. beneath the water's surface: *Sperm whales can stay underwater for a long time.*

un·der·wear [<u>un</u>-dur-*ware*] *noun*. clothing worn under outer clothes, usually next to the skin; underclothes.

un·der·weight [*un*-dur-<u>wate</u>] *adjective*. having a weight that is less than is normal, required, or healthy: *The underweight calf didn't get a good price at the livestock sales.*

un·der·world ◀ [<u>un</u>-dur-*wurld*] *noun*. **1.** in Greek and Roman mythology, a place below the earth's surface where the spirits of the dead dwell; also called Hades. **2.** people who take part in organized criminal activities.

un·de·sir·a·ble [*un*-di-<u>zye</u>-ruh-bul] *adjective*.
1. not pleasing or wanted; objectionable: *An undesirable smell was coming from the trash can.*
noun, *plural* **undesirables.** a person who is not pleasing or welcome: *Criminals and other undesirables hang around that part of town.*

un·do [*un*-<u>doo</u>] *verb*, **undid, undone, undoing. 1.** to untie and make loose; unfasten and open: *Undo your shoelaces before you take off your shoes.* **2.** to wipe out; erase: *Dad washed the floor, but the dog undid his work by walking across it with muddy paws.* **3.** to cause the downfall of; destroy: *The election candidate was undone when the scandal hit the papers.* **4.** to make as if something had never been done; reverse: *I wish I could undo what I said to her.*
◀)) A different word with the same sound is **undue.**

un·done¹ [*un*-<u>dun</u>] *adjective*. not done; not completed: *The painter left the last wall of the room undone.*

un·done² [*un*-<u>dun</u>] *adjective*. not tied or fastened: *You might lose your wallet because your bag is undone.*

un·doubt·ed·ly [*un*-<u>dout</u>-id-lee] *adverb*. accepted without doubt; absolutely: *That book is undoubtedly the best I've ever read.*

un·dress [*un*-<u>dres</u>] *verb*, **undressed, undressing.** to remove clothes: *She undressed her doll and gave it a bath.*

un·due [*un*-<u>doo</u>] *adjective*. more than is needed or right; too much; excessive: *There was undue fuss about her staying up an hour past her bedtime.* A different word with the same meaning is **unduly.**
◀)) A different word with the same sound is **undo.**

Mountain ridge

Volcano

Deep valley

*Beneath the sea is an amazing **underwater** landscape of volcanoes, mountain ridges, and deep valleys.*

un·earth [un-<u>urth</u>] *verb,* **unearthed, unearthing. 1.** to dig up from the ground: *The plumber unearthed the old pipes to repair them.* **2.** to find or discover something after a search: *I unearthed my lost sock in the laundry pile.*

un·eas·y [un-<u>ee</u>-zee] *adjective,* **uneasier, uneasiest.** feeling anxious; worried; unsure: *The uneasy campers heard strange noises coming from outside the tent.* —**uneasily,** *adverb;* —**uneasiness,** *noun.*

un·em·ploy·ed [*un*-im-<u>ployd</u>] *adjective.* without paid work, especially without wishing to be: *The unemployed man has a job interview next week.*

un·em·ploy·ment [*un*-im-<u>ploy</u>-munt] *noun. Business.* **1.** the state of being unemployed, especially when you would like to be doing paid work: *Business was not good, and the workers were facing the prospect of unemployment.* **2.** the number of people not doing paid work and actively looking for work: *The economy is booming and unemployment has fallen.*

un·e·qual [un-<u>ee</u>-kwul] *adjective.* not the same in terms such as length, weight, amount, ability, or social status; not equal: *The legs of my pants are unequal in length; The chess match was an unequal contest as one player was experienced, but the other had hardly ever played before.* —**unequally,** *adverb.*

un·e·ven [un-<u>ee</u>-vun] *adjective.* **1.** not smooth or flat; rough: *The uneven road had many bumps and holes.* **2.** not able to be divided into two equal parts. The numbers 3, 15, and 49 are uneven. **3.** not fairly matched; not equal: *It was an uneven race between the old horse and the young colt.* **4.** not always the same; changeable: *The quality of coffee from that cafe is uneven.* —**unevenly,** *adverb.*

un·e·vent·ful [*un*-i-<u>vent</u>-ful] *adjective.* without significant or memorable events: *Our day at school was uneventful and boring.*

un·ex·pect·ed [*un*-ik-<u>spek</u>-tid] *adjective.* happening without warning; surprising: *Grandma's visit was unexpected, so we had not cleaned the house.*

un·fair [un-<u>fare</u>] *adjective.* not reasonable or just: *It is unfair that my sister can stay up late, but I can't.* —**unfairly,** *adverb.*

un·faith·ful [un-<u>fayth</u>-ful] *adjective.* not faithful: *The king's unfaithful servant betrayed him to the enemy.*

un·fa·mil·iar [*un*-fuh-<u>mil</u>-yur] *adjective.* not familiar with; not knowing about or being acquainted with: *Before the trial the jury was unfamiliar with the facts of the case.* The condition of not recognizing or knowing someone or something is called **unfamiliarity.**

un·fa·vor·a·ble [un-<u>fave</u>-ruh-bul *or* un-<u>fave</u>-ur-uh-bul] *adjective.* **1.** likely to cause a problem or disadvantage: *The unfavorable weather meant the parade had to be canceled.* **2.** opposed to; against: *Catherine's suggestion of a party received an unfavorable reaction.*

un·fit [un-<u>fit</u>] *adjective.* **1.** not suited or good enough: *The man was judged unfit to keep his job.* **2.** not physically healthy and strong: *The unfit students found it difficult to run around the playing field.*

un·fold [un-<u>fold</u>] *verb,* **unfolded, unfolding. 1.** to open out something that is folded or closed: *He unfolded the letter to read it; The tree's new leaves unfolded in spring.* **2.** to occur gradually: *The story of how the accident was caused unfolded as the police spoke to witnesses.*

un·fore·seen [*un*-for-<u>seen</u>] *adjective.* not thought of or realized beforehand; unexpected: *We had unforeseen difficulties catching a taxi, so we were late and missed our plane.*

un·for·get·ta·ble [*un*-fur-<u>get</u>-uh-bul] *adjective.* never able to be forgotten due to being so notable: *The Great Chicago Fire was so terrible that it was an unforgettable event to those who lived through it.*

un·for·tu·nate [un-<u>for</u>-chuh-nit] *adjective.* not fortunate; having bad luck; unlucky: *The unfortunate child broke his arm on the first day of the vacation.* —**unfortunately,** *adverb.*

un·friend·ly [un-<u>frend</u>-lee] *adjective,* **unfriendlier, unfriendliest.** not friendly; cold or distant: *She seems unfriendly, but perhaps she's just shy.*

un·grate·ful [un-<u>grate</u>-ful] *adjective.* not expressing thanks for a favor or kind act; not grateful: *How ungrateful of me to forget to thank you for your help.*

un·hap·py [un-<u>hap</u>-ee] *adjective,* **unhappier, unhappiest.** without joy or happiness; sad: *We could tell from Nathan's unhappy face that something was wrong.* —**unhappily,** *adverb;* —**unhappiness,** *noun.*

un·heal·thy [un-<u>hel</u>-thee] *adjective,* **unhealthier, unhealthiest. 1.** not having or showing good health; not fit or well. **2.** not giving good health; not healthy: *an unhealthy diet of fried food and candy bars.*

In the Middle Ages, **unicorns** *were often depicted in paintings, tapestries, and other works of art.*

un·heard-of [un-<u>hurd</u>] *adjective. Literature.* never having happened in the past; very unusual or surprising: *It was unheard-of for Maria to be late for class.*

u·ni·corn ▲ [<u>yoo</u>-nuh-*korn*] *noun,* plural **unicorns.** *Literature.* an imaginary creature similar to a horse with a long, pointed horn growing out from the center of its forehead.

The word **unicorn** comes from *uni-* meaning "one" and *corn*, an older word for horn. It is not known how the legend of the unicorn came about. The only known land animal with one horn is the rhinoceros, which has a much different body shape than the way the unicorn is shown. It may be that the idea comes from people seeing a two-horned animal such as an oryx, but from a sideways view so that the two horns would look like one.

unicycle

*Our solar system is only a minute part of the Milky Way, which in turn is only one of the many galaxies in the **universe**.*

Solar system

Milky Way and its two small satellite galaxies

Close-up of the Milky Way

u·ni·cy·cle [yoo-nuh-*sye*-kul] *noun, plural* **unicycles.** a light vehicle with a seat and a single wheel that is turned by foot pedals to make it go forward: *The clown rode into the circus ring on a unicycle.*

u·ni·form [yoo-nuh-*form*] *adjective.*
1. exactly the same throughout without varying: *Having an air conditioning system means there is a uniform temperature throughout the building.* **2.** looking or being exactly the same; alike: *a field with uniform rows of corn.* To have a **uniformity** of appearance is to have many things looking the same.
noun, plural **uniforms.** the special clothes worn by members of a particular group of people to make them look similar to each other, but different from others: *a police uniform; a nurse's uniform; a soldier's uniform.*
—**uniformly,** *adverb.*

u·ni·fy [yoo-nuh-*fye*] *verb,* **unified, unifying.** to bring separate things together to make one whole thing; unite: *In the nineteenth century a number of states unified to form the modern nation of Italy.*

un·im·por·tant [un-im-*port*-unt] *adjective.* having no special significance, value, or interest; not important: *The color of the umbrella is unimportant to me, as long as it keeps the rain off.*

un·in·formed [un-in-*formd*] *adjective.* not informed; having little information or knowledge about a particular subject: *Like most people who are uninformed about astronomy, I need help to find planets in the night sky.*

un·in·hab·it·ed [un-in-*hab*-uh-tid] *adjective.* having no one living there: *an uninhabited desert island.*

un·in·tel·li·gi·ble [un-in-*tel*-uh-juh-bul] *adjective.* not able to be understood because it cannot be heard or read properly: *The buzzing in the loudspeakers made the announcement unintelligible.*

un·in·ten·tion·al [un-in-*ten*-shuh-nul] *adjective.* not done deliberately; not on purpose: *an unintentional insult.*

un·in·ter·est·ed [un-*in*-truh-stid] *adjective.* having or showing no interest: *The sick child was uninterested in eating.* See DISINTERESTED for more information.

un·ion [*yoon*-yun] *noun, plural* **unions. 1.** the act of joining two or more people or things into one: *the union of two streams into a river.* **2.** a thing formed by joining together. The United States of America is called the **Union;** the states that remained loyal to the federal government during the Civil War are also called the **Union. 3.** an organization formed by the joining together of workers to protect their interests and help with work problems such as pay and working conditions. *adjective.* having to do with a union of workers: *union labor; the union movement.*

u·nique [yoo-*neek*] *adjective.* being the only one of its kind: *Each person has their own unique DNA.*
—**uniquely,** *adverb;*
—**uniqueness,** *noun.*

Something that is **unique** is one of a kind, different from all others: Hawaii is unique among U.S. states, in that it is not part of the mainland of North America. Therefore it is better to avoid using phrases such as "very unique" or "rather unique," as in "Hawaii has a *rather unique* climate" or "In Hawaii we saw some *very unique* sights." Other words such as *different, unusual, distinctive,* or *remarkable* can carry a similar meaning, and *unique* can be saved for something that really is not like any other.

u·ni·son [yoo-nuh-sun] *noun.* **in unison.** the act of speaking or sounding together at the same time: *The class recited the multiplication tables in unison.*

*The **United Nations** flag features a map of the world inside two olive branches, which symbolize peace.*

u·nit [yoo-nit] *noun, plural* **units. 1.** a single person or thing or the whole of a group of people or things: *This month we're studying Unit Four of the math textbook; The family unit for elephants consists of a mature female and her adult daughters and their offspring.* **2.** a fixed quantity or amount used as a standard measurement: *A mile is a unit of measurement.* **3.** a piece of equipment with a special purpose: *a central heating unit.* **4.** the smallest whole number; the number one (1).

u·nite [yoo-*nite*] *verb,* **united, uniting.** to join together as one: *The players' parents were united in the effort to raise money for the volleyball club.*

u·nit·ed [yoo-*nite*-id] *adjective.* with everyone having the same aim and acting together: *There was united opposition to the plan to close the swimming pool.*

United Nations ▲ *Government.* an international organization founded in 1945 that includes nearly all the countries in the world as members. It tries to keep world peace and to help countries work together to deal with international problems.

A B C D E F G H I J K L M N O P Q R S T U V W X Y Z

u·ni·ty [yoo-nuh-tee] *noun, plural* **unities.** the fact or state of being one or a united whole: *A nation has more unity than a group of separate states.*

u·ni·ver·sal [yoo-nuh-vur-sul] *adjective.* **1.** having to do with all people: *a universal desire for world peace.* **2.** present everywhere; affecting everything: *The problem of climate change is universal.* The fact or condition of being or existing everywhere is **universality.** —**universally,** *adverb.*

u·ni·verse ◀ [yoo-nuh-vurs] *noun, plural* **universes.** the whole of space and everything that exists in it, such as stars, planets, and energy. This word is also spelled **Universe.**

university ▼
[yoo-nuh-vur-suh-tee] *noun, plural* **universities.** *Education.* a place for education at the highest level. A university gives training in many professions and may also have facilities for research. *See* COLLEGE *for more information.*

> The word **university** comes from a phrase meaning "the whole thing" or "the entire number" and it is closely related to the word *universe.* It came into use in the Middle Ages to describe the entire group of teachers and students who were gathered at a certain place of learning. The first university in Europe was at Bologna, Italy, and the first one to be called by this name in English was at Oxford, England.

un·just [un-just] *adjective.* not right or fair; not just: *It is unjust that she lost her job because she was away sick too often.*

un·kind [un-kinde] *adjective,* **unkinder, unkindest.** cruel or thoughtless; not kind: *How unkind not to invite him to the party when everyone else is going.* —**unkindly,** *adverb.*

un·known [un-nohne] *adjective.* having to do with a name, date, place, quality, or origin that is not known: *The author of that old folk tale is unknown; The spacecraft will travel to unknown parts of the universe.* *noun, plural* **unknowns.** a person or thing that is not known: *The expedition set off to explore the unknown.*

un·law·ful [un-law-ful] *adjective.* against the law; illegal: *The protesters were asked to move because holding a meeting in the building lobby was unlawful.*

un·lead·ed [un-led-id] *adjective.* having to do with gasoline that does not contain lead additives. Unleaded gasoline is less harmful to the environment.

un·less [un-les] *conjunction.* except on the condition that: *Unless the weather improves, the school will have to cancel the sports carnival.*

un·like [un-like] *preposition.* **1.** not like or alike; different from: *Jason is often late, unlike his sister, who is very punctual.* **2.** not typical of; not usual for: *It's unlike Sadie to get cross, she's usually so good-tempered.* *adjective.* not alike; different: *It's difficult to compare the two movies, because they are so unlike.*

un·like·ly [un-like-lee] *adjective.* **1.** having to do with something that probably will not happen: *It's so late that it is unlikely they will come now.* **2.** having to do with something that is probably not true: *The teacher was not convinced by the student's unlikely explanation for being late.*

un·lim·it·ed [un-lim-uh-tid] *adjective.* having no limit or restrictions: *This special pass gives you unlimited use of the local bus system.*

un·load [un-lode] *verb,* **unloaded, unloading. 1.** to remove from a vehicle: *to unload furniture from a van.* **2.** to remove a load from: *to unload a ship at the dock.* **3.** to remove bullets from a gun. **4.** to dispose of something unwanted; get rid of.

un·lock [un-lok] *verb,* **unlocked, unlocking. 1.** to unfasten the lock of: *Turn the key to unlock the door.* **2.** to explain or make known: *The discoveries made by archaeologists help to unlock the secrets of the past.*

Merton College at the **University of Oxford** *was founded in the thirteenth century.*

a b c d e f g h i j k l m n o p q r s t u v w x y z

*The **unmanned** ROSAT space telescope is controlled remotely from the Earth.*

un·luck·y [un-<u>luk</u>-ee] *adjective,* **unluckier, unluckiest.** having bad luck: *Donna was unlucky to hurt her ankle on the day before the dancing competition.*

un·manned ▶ [un-<u>mand</u>] *adjective.* having no humans on board or in control: *an unmanned space mission.*

un·marr·ied [un-<u>mare</u>-eed] *adjective.* not married; single.

un·moved [un-<u>moved</u>] *adjective.* not affected by excitement or emotion: *Kathleen was unmoved by her daughter's temper tantrum.*

un·nat·u·ral [un-<u>nach</u>-ur-ul] *adjective.* not what is usual or to be expected; not natural: *The actors in the play spoke in an unnatural way because they were nervous; The smoke from the forest fire created an unnatural darkness during the day.* —**unnaturally,** *adverb.*

un·nec·es·sar·y [un-<u>nes</u>-uh-ser-ee] *adjective.* not necessary; needless: *Buying food for six people was unnecessary, because only three people are coming to dinner.* —**unnecessarily,** *adverb.*

un·of·fi·cial [un-uh-<u>fish</u>-ul] *adjective.* not approved by or coming from an authority; not official: *I didn't like my favorite rock star's official Website so I created an unofficial one.*

un·or·tho·dox [un-<u>or</u>-thuh-doks] *adjective.* **1.** different from what most people believe or expect: *Jean teaches her children at home because of her unorthodox ideas about education.* **2.** following or holding practices or beliefs that are not traditional or widely accepted: *That family is very unorthodox in its religious practices.*

un·pack [un-<u>pak</u>] *verb,* **unpacked, unpacking.** to open and remove things from: *I haven't had time to unpack my suitcase.*

un·paid [un-<u>pade</u>] *adjective.* **1.** not paid: *unpaid bills.* **2.** not paying a salary or wage: *an unpaid position.*

un·pleas·ant [un-<u>plez</u>-unt] *adjective.* not pleasing; disagreeable: *This cough medicine has an unpleasant taste.* —**unpleasantness,** *noun.*

un·plug [un-<u>plug</u>] *verb,* **unplugged, unplugging.** **1.** to remove a stopper, cork, or other plug: *Unplug the bathtub.* **2.** to disconnect from the electricity supply by removing a plug.

un·pop·u·lar [un-<u>pop</u>-yuh-lur] *adjective.* not liked or accepted by people in general; not popular: *The governor is unpopular with voters because he has not spent enough money on schools and roads.* The state of being unpopular is **unpopularity.**

un·pre·dict·a·ble [un-pri-<u>dik</u>-tuh-bul] *adjective.* not able to be known beforehand; uncertain or changeable: *The weather has been very unpredictable lately—one day it's cold and raining, the next it's warm and sunny.*

un·pre·pared [un-pri-<u>pared</u>] *adjective.* not ready; not prepared: *The hikers were unprepared for the cold weather in the mountains, having brought only summer clothes.*

un·rav·el ▼ [un-<u>rav</u>-ul] *verb,* **unravel, unraveling. 1.** to separate twisted, woven, or knitted threads: *I had to unravel the knots in the fishing line.* **2.** to remove complications from; solve or make clear: *to unravel a mystery.*

un·real [un-<u>reel</u>] *adjective.* not seeming actual or true; imaginary: *The woods and hills seemed unreal in the early morning mist.*

un·re·al·is·tic [un-ree-uh-<u>lis</u>-tik] *adjective.* **1.** not showing events, things, or people as they appear in everyday life: *an unrealistic movie.* **2.** not tending to see and accept things as they are: *Marion has unrealistic ideas about making lots of money.*

un·rea·son·able [un-<u>ree</u>-zun-uh-bul] *adjective.* not using or showing good sense; not reasonable: *It's unreasonable to expect hot weather in December; He made an unreasonable request to borrow $5,000 from her.*

un·re·li·a·ble [un-ri-<u>lye</u>-uh-bul] *adjective.* not to be depended on; not reliable: *The television is unreliable because it often stops working.* —**unreliably,** *adverb.*

un·rest [un-<u>rest</u>] *noun.* a disturbed or unsettled state: *Bad food caused unrest among the prisoners in the jail.*

un·re·strict·ed [un-ri-<u>strik</u>-tid] *adjective.* having no restrictions or limits: *With unrestricted access to the college, I can go wherever I want to.*

un·ru·ly [un-<u>roo</u>-lee] *adjective,* **unrulier, unruliest.** hard to manage or control: *Rita got detention because of her unruly behavior in class.*

un·safe [un-<u>safe</u>] *adjective.* likely to cause harm; dangerous: *This building may fall down at any time and is unsafe to enter; an unsafe neighborhood.*

un·sa·tis·fac·to·ry [un-sat-is-<u>fak</u>-tree *or* un-sat-is-<u>fak</u>-tuh-ree] *adjective.* not good enough to meet a hope, desire, or need; not satisfactory: *Your results in the spelling test are unsatisfactory.* —**unsatisfactorily,** *adverb.*

un·scru·pu·lous [un-<u>skroo</u>-pyuh-lus] *adjective.* not careful to do what is right or proper; immoral: *The unscrupulous politician lied to the voters.*

un·seen [un-<u>seen</u>] *adjective.* not seen or noticed: *An unseen animal growled in the woods.*

*If you make a mistake when knitting, you can **unravel** the wool and start again.*

un·set·tled [un-<u>set</u>-uld] *adjective.* **1.** not calm, peaceful, or orderly: *She had an unsettled childhood after her parents divorced.* **2.** not determined or decided: *The question of which car we should buy is still unsettled.* **3.** having no settlers or inhabitants: *The unsettled areas of the world are mostly in remote places such as deserts and mountains.*

un·sight·ly ▼ [un-<u>site</u>-lee] *adjective,* **unsightlier, unsightliest.** not pleasant to look at; ugly: *He has an unsightly scar on his forehead from the time someone threw a stone at him.*

Graffiti and garbage combine in an **unsightly** *urban scene.*

un·skilled [un-<u>skild</u>] *adjective.* not having or requiring any special skill or ability: *Unskilled workers get less pay than skilled workers; Digging a hole in the road is an unskilled job.*

un·sound [un-<u>sound</u>] *adjective.* **1.** having a flaw or weakness; damaged: *Many houses were made unsound by the earthquake.* **2.** not based on truth, facts, or good sense: *unsound reasons.*

un·sta·ble [un-<u>stay</u>-bul] *adjective.* **1.** not firm or firmly fixed; unsteady: *The ladder is unstable unless someone holds it.* **2.** likely to change: *The President is concerned about that new country with an unstable government.*

un·stead·y [un-<u>sted</u>-ee] *adjective,* **unsteadier, unsteadiest.** not firm; likely to shake: *This table is unsteady because one leg is shorter than the others.* —**unsteadiness,** *noun.*

un·suc·cess·ful [*un*-suk-<u>ses</u>-ful] *adjective.* failing to achieve something desired; having no success: *He lost all his money in an unsuccessful business deal.*

un·suit·a·ble [un-<u>soo</u>-tuh-bul] *adjective.* not correct or proper: *That movie is unsuitable for children because it contains a lot of violence.* —**unsuitably,** *adverb.*

un·sure [un-<u>shoor</u>] *adjective.* not certain or sure: *The date of the holiday is still unsure; Pete felt nervous and unsure of himself whenever he met new people.*

un·tan·gle [un-<u>tang</u>-gul] *verb,* **untangled, untangling. 1.** to free from tangles or knots: *She tried to untangle her hair, but couldn't get all the knots out.* **2.** to clarify something that is difficult or puzzling; clear up: *The accountant helped us untangle the complications of the tax code.*

un·tie [un-<u>tye</u>] *verb,* **untied, untying.** to undo or loosen; set free: *I untied my scarf after coming in from the cold.*

un·til [un-<u>til</u>] *preposition.* up to the time of: *Franklin D. Roosevelt was President from 1933 until his death in 1945. conjunction.* up to or at the time when; before: *You can't have dessert until you finish your vegetables.*

un·to [<u>un</u>-too] *preposition.* to: *"Do unto others as you would have them do unto you," is a famous saying known as the Golden Rule.*

un·told [un-<u>told</u>] *adjective.* **1.** not told or revealed: *My book is about the untold stories of 9/11.* **2.** too great or too many to be counted or described: *Gold prospectors believe that untold riches lie in those mountains.*

un·touched [un-<u>tucht</u>] *adjective.* not handled, used, or dealt with; not touched: *She left her meal untouched because she was feeling sick; Much of Alaska is untouched by commercial development.*

un·true [un-<u>troo</u>] *adjective.* not true; false: *George's stories about meeting movie stars are all untrue.*

un·used [un-<u>yoozd</u>] *adjective.* **1.** not used or not put to use: *Jane's new bicycle sat unused in the garage.* **2.** not familiar with or accustomed to: *I am unused to driving in such heavy traffic.*

un·u·su·al ▼ [un-<u>yoo</u>-zhoo-ul] *adjective.* not usual or common; out of the ordinary: *The shape of this leaf is unusual.* —**unusually,** *adverb.*

un·veil [un-<u>vale</u>] *verb,* **unveiled, unveiling. 1.** to remove a veil or covering from. **2.** to make public; reveal: *The mayor unveiled plans for a new park.*

un·wel·come [un-<u>wel</u>-kum] *adjective.* not welcome or wanted; not gladly received: *Ants were unwelcome visitors at our picnic.*

un·well [un-<u>wel</u>] *adjective.* feeling sick; ill: *I stayed home from school because I was unwell.*

un·wieldy [un-<u>weel</u>-dee] *adjective.* hard to carry or manage, because of size, shape, or weight: *A sofa is an unwieldy piece of furniture to move from one room to another.*

un·will·ing [un-<u>wil</u>-ing] *adjective.* not willing; reluctant: *Our team was unwilling to accept defeat.*

Volcanic rock at Cappadoccia, Turkey, has eroded to create this **unusual** *landscape of pointed formations.*

un·wind [un-wynde] *verb*, **unwound, unwinding. 1.** to free up; unroll: *The nurse began to unwind the bandage from Nicole's arm.* **2.** to become relaxed: *After work, I took a bath to unwind.*

un·wor·thy [un-wur-thee] *adjective.* not suitable; not worthy: *Such terrible conduct and behavior is unworthy of a school principal.*

up [up] *adverb.* **1.** from a lower to a higher position or place: *The cat climbed up to the top of the fence.* **2.** in, on, or at a higher place: *Looking up, I saw thousands of stars in the night sky.* **3.** to a higher degree or point: *The price of gasoline is going up.* **4.** in or into an erect position: *to stand up straight.* **5.** out of bed: *We got up very early in the morning.* **6.** completely; entirely: *I filled up my glass.* *adjective.* **1.** at or to a higher degree or point: *My grades are up; What time does the sun come up tomorrow? The stock market is up this week.* **2.** out of bed: *I was up by seven o'clock.* **3.** at an end; finished: *Your time is up.* *preposition.* at or toward a point further along or higher on: *There's a gas station up the road from here.*

The simple word **up** is a good example of how the same word can be used as different parts of speech. You can walk *up* a hill (preposition), and when you do this, you go *up* (adverb). At the top of the hill you are *up* (adjective). You can see that the meaning in each case is the same, and the only change is in the way the word is used. Up can even be a noun (Our team has had its *ups* and downs this season) or a verb (That change allowed the business to *up* its profits for the year).

up·beat [up-beet] *adjective.* describing something cheerful; optimistic: *I love seeing upbeat movies and try to avoid sad or violent ones.*

up·bring·ing [up-bring-ing] *noun.* the treatment and training given to a child while growing up: *My upbringing has left me with a very strong religious faith.*

up·date [up-date] *verb*, **updated, updating.** to bring up to date: *I updated our family's Website by adding some new photos.* *noun, plural* **updates.** an act of updating or an updated version: *That movie is an update of a television series from the 1980s.*

up·grade [up-grade *for verb*; up-grade *for noun*] *verb*, **upgraded, upgrading.** to raise to a higher standard or rank; improve: *Jill was upgraded from shipping clerk to junior manager.* *noun, plural* **upgrades. 1.** something that upgrades: *a computer upgrade.* **2.** an upward slope or incline.

up·heav·al ▼ [up-hee-vul] *noun, plural* **upheavals.** a violent or sudden change or disturbance: *That African country has been in upheaval since the army revolted against the government.*

up·hill [up-hil] *adjective.* **1.** leading or sloping upward: *an uphill trail.* **2.** requiring a lot of effort; difficult: *He's had an uphill struggle trying to get the city authorities to listen to him.* *adverb.* upward on a slope or hill: *It's tiring to walk uphill.*

up·hold [up-hold] *verb*, **upheld, upholding.** to support or defend: *A police officer swears to uphold the law.*

up·hol·ster [up-hole-stur] *verb*, **upholstered, upholstering.** to cover furniture with material: *The chairs are upholstered in black leather.*

The **upholstery** *on this old chair is worn and faded.*

up·hol·ster·y ▲ [up-hole-stree *or* up-hole-stur-ee] *noun.* material used to cover furniture: *The old sofa's upholstery is torn and faded.*

At the center of a major earthquake, ground **upheaval** *can cause massive destruction.*

A B C D E F G H I J K L M N O P Q R S T U V W X Y Z

up·keep [up-*keep*] *noun.* the act or process of keeping someone or something in good condition: *The upkeep of a sailing boat includes removing rust, fixing holes, and repairing sails.*

up·load [up-*lode*] *verb,* **uploaded, uploading.** *Computers.* to transfer information from one computer to another: *Alex wants me to upload some software.*

up·on [uh-pon] *preposition.* in a position above and supported by; on top of; on: *He placed the vase upon the table.*

Upon and *on* mean the same thing: "This was an attack *upon* the United States" is the same as "This was an attack *on* the United States." The word *upon* is not used nearly as often as *on*. When it is used, it is usually in older writing, as in the hymn "It Came *Upon* a Midnight Clear" or in some kind of serious or formal expression. Martin Luther King spoke about "a check that will give us *upon* demand the riches of freedom" in his "I Have a Dream" speech.

up·per [up-ur] *adjective.* higher in position or status: *Put the book on the upper shelf of the bookcase.*

up·per·case [up-ur-*kase*] *adjective.* *Language.* describing letters that are capitals. The letters "X," "Y," and "Z" are uppercase letters.

up·per·most [up-ur-*most*] *adjective.* **1.** relating to the highest; topmost: *The apartment is on the uppermost floor of the building.* **2.** having the most importance; foremost: *The uppermost concern of the pilot was the safety of the plane's passengers.* *adverb.* in the highest or most important position, rank, or place: *The problem of terrorism should be uppermost in the minds of our politicians.*

up·right [up-*rite*] *adjective.* **1.** straight up; vertical: *The posts supporting the porch must be in an upright position.* **2.** describing something honorable; honest: *It's good to do business with an upright person.* *adverb.* in or into a vertical position: *She sat upright in her bed.* *noun, plural* **uprights.** something that stands straight up: *Football goal posts are made up of a crossbar and two uprights.*

up·ris·ing [up-*rye*-zing] *noun, plural* **uprisings.** an act of rebellion against an authority; revolt: *Thousands of people took part in the uprising against the government.*

up·roar [up-*rore*] *noun, plural* **uproars.** **1.** a loud and excited noise or disturbance: *The theater was in an uproar after the announcement that the play had been canceled.* **2.** an intense debate or dispute: *The book criticizing the President created an uproar when it was published.*

up·root [up-root] *verb,* **uprooted, uprooting. 1.** to pull up a plant by the roots: *The storm was so intense that it uprooted many trees.* **2.** to move someone from the usual place; displace: *The war uprooted people from their homes.*

up·set [up-set] *verb,* **upset, upsetting. 1.** to knock or tip over: *Heather accidentally upset the vase of flowers.* **2.** to disrupt the usual order or course of things: *The blizzard upset everyone's plans for the weekend.* **3.** to make unhappy, worried, or disappointed; disturb: *Losing her wedding ring upset my mother.* **4.** to make sick: *Spicy foods upset my stomach.* **5.** to defeat unexpectedly: *Our baseball team upset last year's champions.* *adjective.* **1.** unhappy, worried, or disappointed: *Lynne was upset after the car accident.* **2.** relating to being sick: *an upset stomach.* *noun, plural* **upsets.** an unexpected defeat in a game, election, or other contest: *In a stunning upset, the mayor was defeated after twenty years in office.*

up·side-down ▼ [up-side-*down*] *adverb.* **1.** so that the upper part becomes the lower part: *That painting is hanging upside-down.* **2.** in or into total disorder or confusion: *The thief turned the house upside-down looking for valuables.*

Hoffman's two-toed sloth lives in Central and South America and spends most of its time hanging **upside-down** *in trees.*

up·stairs [up-*starez*] *adverb.* **1.** up the stairs: *He went upstairs to the bathroom.* **2.** on or to a higher floor: *I keep my CD collection upstairs.* *adjective.* on a higher floor: *I like the view from the upstairs window.* *noun.* a higher floor.

up·stream [up-*streem*] *adjective; adverb.* moving in the opposite direction to the current of a stream: *It was hard work to paddle the canoe upstream.*

up·tight [up-*tite*] *adjective.* an informal word meaning: **1.** nervous, worried, or tense: *My father gets uptight if I stay out too late at night.* **2.** very formal; conventional: *She's an old-fashioned, uptight sort of person.*

up-to-date [up-tuh-*date*] *adjective.* showing or using the latest ideas, techniques, information, or style; modern: *Use up-to-date software to get the most from your computer.*

up·ward [up-wurd] *adverb; adjective.* toward a higher point, place, or level: *The cost of gasoline has climbed steadily upward; The hikers had a long, upward climb ahead of them.* This word is also spelled **upwards.**

u·ra·ni·um [yu-ray-nee-um] *noun. Chemistry.* a gray, dense metal that is radioactive. It is used as a fuel in nuclear reactors. Uranium is a chemical element.

The chemical known as **uranium** gets its name from the planet *Uranus.* It was discovered in 1789 by a German scientist named Martin Heinrich Klaproth. He chose the name *uranium* because the planet had been discovered shortly before his own discovery.

URANUS

Uranus is nearly four times the size of the Earth and takes 84 Earth years to orbit the Sun. Unlike the other planets, which are tilted only slightly, Uranus moves through the sky completely on its side, so that each pole has constant sunlight for 42 years. Uranus is made up mainly of hydrogen and helium, and may have a slushy interior with an inner core of rock and ice. The planet is also encircled by eleven rings made up of rock and ice, and has a number of moons.

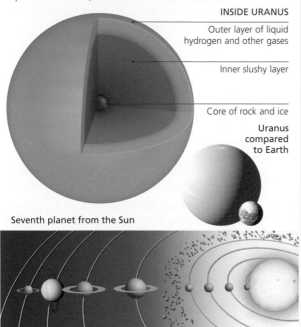

INSIDE URANUS

Outer layer of liquid hydrogen and other gases

Inner slushy layer

Core of rock and ice

Uranus compared to Earth

Seventh planet from the Sun

U·ra·nus ▲ [yur-uh-nus *or* yu-ray-nus] *noun.* **1.** the seventh planet in distance from the Sun. It is the third largest planet in our solar system. Uranus is surrounded by rings. **2.** in Greek mythology, the god who ruled the heavens.

ur·ban ▼ [ur-bun] *adjective.* relating to or belonging to a city: *Most people in the United States live in or near urban areas.*

ur·ban·ize [ur-buh-*nize*] *verb,* **urbanized, urbanizing.** to make an area more like a city in character: *Our little country town was urbanized when developers built more houses, offices, and roads.* **—urbanization,** *noun*

urge [urj] *verb,* **urged, urging. 1.** to try to persuade: *We urged Ray to enter the singing contest because he's got such a great voice.* **2.** to drive, force, or press onward: *The cowboys urged the cattle up the steep slope.* **3.** to speak strongly for something; advocate: *The politician urged immediate reform of the health care system.* *noun, plural* **urges.** a strong desire or impulse: *I had an uncontrollable urge to laugh out loud.*

ur·gent [ur-junt] *adjective.* demanding immediate action or attention; pressing: *The message said, "Come home now. It's urgent."* A matter of **urgency** is a matter that a person should act on right away. **—urgently,** *adverb.*

u·rine [yoor-un] *noun.* Biology. a waste product of the body that is secreted by the kidneys and stored in the bladder. When the bladder empties, urine flows from the body via the **urethra**. It is a clear yellow liquid in mammals. To **urinate** means to release urine.

Some ancient Greek ceramic **urns** *and vases were decorated with figures and scenes in a distinctive red-on-black style.*

URL *Computers.* an Internet address. It is an abbreviation of **Uniform Resource Locator.**

urn ▲ [urn] *noun, plural* **urns. 1.** a vase with a base or pedestal. It is used for decoration or to hold flowers or plants. **2.** a closed container with a spigot, used for heating and serving coffee or tea. 🔊 A different word with the same sound is **earn.**

us [us] *pronoun.* the people who are speaking or writing: *The teacher asked us to be quiet; Will you come with us to the beach?*

U.S. an abbreviation for United States.

U.S.A. an abbreviation for United States of America.

us·a·ble [yooz-uh-bul] *adjective.* fit or ready for use; able to be used: *The computer may be old, but it's still usable.* This word is also spelled **useable.**

High-rise buildings are typical of the **urban** *landscape in New York City.*

us·age [yoo-sij] *noun, plural* **usages. 1.** a way of using or manner of treating something: *This water meter will show our water usage.* **2.** *Language.* the way in which people actually use words when speaking or writing: *"Y'all" is a common usage in the southern United States.*

In language, **usage** means the way a word is actually used in the language. Usage can be what a word means, how it is spelled, or how it is spoken (pronounced). In earlier times, it was thought that correct usage could be determined by a king (this is the idea of "the King's English"), or by a government committee or other official group. Now it is accepted that no single person or small group can dictate what is correct usage. This must be determined by studying how educated people as a whole use the language.

use [yooz *for verb;* yoos *for noun*] *verb,* **used, using.** to put into service for a purpose; employ: *Do you know how to use this computer?*
noun, plural **uses. 1.** the act of using or the state of being used: *They rescued the girl from the water with the use of an inflatable life ring.* **2.** the quality of being suitable; usefulness: *Joe tried to be of use in his father's repair shop.* **3.** the need or purpose for which something is used: *The thrift shop might have a use for those old clothes.* **4.** the ability, permission, or benefit to use something: *He still has the use of his legs after his motor bike accident.*

used [yoozd] *adjective.* having been used already; secondhand: *a used car.*

used to 1. indicating a practice, state, or fact from a time in the past: *We used to live in Denver before we moved to Portland.* **2.** familiar with or accustomed to: *I'm still getting used to my new teacher.*

use·ful [yoos-ful] *adjective.* having a beneficial use; helpful: *A cell phone is very useful when you are traveling.* —**usefully,** *adverb;* —**usefulness,** *noun.*

use·less [yoos-lis] *adjective.* having or being of no use; worthless: *A bicycle with a flat tire is useless.* —**uselessly,** *adverb;* **uselessness,** *noun.*

us·er [yooz-ur] *noun, plural* **users.** a person who uses something: *Mr. Cunningham is a regular user of public transportation.*

user-friend·ly *adjective. Computers.* easy to use or learn to use: *Rosa could install the program quickly because the instructions were user-friendly.*

user group *Computers.* a computer club whose members share information and ideas about a particular type of computer or a software program.

ush·er [ush-ur] *noun, plural* **ushers.** a person who shows people to their seats in a theater, church, or other gathering: *a uniformed usher.*
verb, **ushered, ushering.** to act as an usher; escort or lead: *He took our tickets for the show and promptly ushered us to our seats.*
• **usher in.** to lead in or introduce: *The neighbors ushered in the new year with a block party.*

u·su·al [yoo-zhoo-ul] *adjective.* common, normal, or expected; customary: *There was more snow than usual this winter.*
• **as usual.** as normally happens: *As usual, the mail arrived today at about one o'clock.* —**usually,** *adverb.*

u·ten·sil ▼ [yoo-ten-sul] *noun, plural* **utensils.** an instrument or container that is used to do or make something, especially for cooking or eating: *Spatulas, whisks, and eggbeaters are useful kitchen utensils.*

u·ter·us [yoo-tur-us] *noun, plural* **uteri** *or* **uteruses.** *Biology.* a hollow organ in the pelvic area of female mammals in which a baby develops before birth. It is also called a womb. Having to do with the region of the uterus is **uterine.**

u·til·i·ty [yoo-til-uh-tee] *noun, plural* **utilities.** the quality or state of being useful; usefulness.
adjective. being able to serve or work in various roles or positions as needed: *a utility infielder who can play several positions.*

u·til·ize [yoo-tuh-lize] *verb,* **utilized, utilizing.** to put to use, especially in an effective or practical way: *Solar power utilizes the sun's energy to make electricity.* The **utilization** of the Earth's resources is the act of putting those resources to good use.

ut·most [ut-most] *adjective.* greatest or highest: *They moved the accident victim onto the stretcher with the utmost care.*
noun. the greatest amount or degree possible; maximum: *The swimmer tried her utmost to break the world record.*

Stainless steel cooking **utensils** *are hard-wearing and last a long time.*

u·to·pi·a [yoo-toh-pee-uh] *noun, plural* **utopias.** *Literature.* an ideal or perfect place or society, often described in a novel. A **utopian** society has the characteristics of a utopia.

ut·ter[1] [ut-ur] *verb,* **uttered, uttering.** to express with the voice; speak aloud: *Josie did not utter a single word during class.*

ut·ter[2] [ut-ur] *adjective.* complete or total: *He felt like an utter fool when he asked the girl to dance and she said "no."* —**utterly,** *adverb.*

U-turn *noun, plural* **U-turns. 1.** a turn made by a vehicle so it is facing back the way it has just come. **2.** a complete change from one opinion or action to its opposite.

The word **utopia** comes from the name of a book by Sir Thomas More, a famous English religious leader. *Utopia,* written in 1516, describes an imaginary island on which none of the usual problems of society exist, and people live happily under ideal conditions. More took the name from a Greek term meaning "not a place," since there was no actual place with the conditions he described.

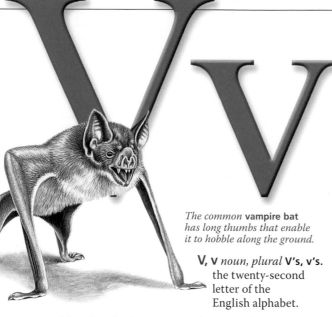

The common **vampire bat** *has long thumbs that enable it to hobble along the ground.*

V, v *noun, plural* **V's, v's.** the twenty-second letter of the English alphabet.

va·cant [<u>vay</u>-kunt] *adjective.* **1.** not being used or occupied; empty: *The family is looking for a vacant apartment to rent.* If a hotel has a **vacancy,** it has a room or rooms not being used. **2.** lacking or seeming to lack intelligence, awareness, or expression: *The girl stared out the window with a vacant look on her face.*

va·cate [<u>vay</u>-kate] *verb,* **vacated, vacating.** to empty or leave empty; to no longer occupy; give up: *Everyone in the school vacated the building when the fire alarm sounded.*

va·ca·tion [vay-<u>kay</u>-shun] *noun, plural* **vacations.** a period of time for rest or freedom from school, work, or other activity; holiday: *Our summer vacation from school starts in June; a beach vacation.*
verb, **vacationed, vacationing.** to take or spend a vacation: *We vacationed in Miami.*

vac·ci·nate [<u>vak</u>-suh-*nate*] *verb,* **vaccinated, vaccinating.** *Medicine.* to give a vaccine to: *The nurse vaccinated the baby against polio.* The act or practice of vaccinating is **vaccination.**

vac·cine [vak-<u>seen</u> *or* vak-seen] *noun, plural* **vaccines.** *Medicine.* a liquid made from the dead or weakened germs that cause a certain disease. The vaccine is swallowed or injected into the body, where it helps protect the person from getting the disease.

vac·u·um [<u>vak</u>-yoom] *noun, plural* **vacuums. 1.** *Science.* a space that is empty of matter. Scientists have not been able to build a perfect vacuum, so a vacuum is usually a space that is empty of most but not all matter. **2.** a VACUUM CLEANER. **3.** a state of being sealed off from outside influences; isolation: *The fight broke out for many reasons—it didn't happen in a vacuum.*
verb, **vacuumed, vacuuming.** to clean with a vacuum cleaner.

vacuum cleaner an electrical appliance that sucks up dirt into its tank or bag. It is used to clean carpets, floors, and other surfaces.

va·grant [<u>vay</u>-grunt] *noun, plural* **vagrants.** *Law.* a person who wanders from place to place, without a permanent home or a regular job or income: *The vagrant waited in the queue at the soup kitchen for a meal.* The state, act, or criminal offense of being a vagrant is **vagrancy.**

vague [vayg] *adjective* **vaguer, vaguest.** not clear or precise; indistinct or hazy: *We could make out the vague outline of the house through the fog; She gave a vague answer of "Maybe so, maybe not; I'm not sure."* —**vaguely,** *adverb;* —**vagueness,** *noun.*

vain [vayn] *adjective,* **vainer, vainest. 1.** overly proud of one's self; conceited: *He is so vain about his clothes—he spends hours trying on outfits.* **2.** not successful; futile: *Linda made a vain attempt to go for help, but the blizzard forced her back inside.* —**vainly,** *adverb.*
🔊 Different words with the same sound are **vane** and **vein.**

val·e·dic·to·ri·an [*val*-uh-dik-<u>tore</u>-ee-un] *noun, plural* **valedictorians.** *Education.* a student who achieves the highest marks of all students in the class at the end of his or her school career. He or she usually gives the farewell speech at the graduation ceremony.

val·en·tine [<u>val</u>-un-*tine*] *noun, plural* **valentines. 1.** a greeting card or gift sent to someone on Valentine's Day to let the person know that the sender loves her or him. **2.** the person who receives such a card or gift.

Valentine's Day February 14, a Christian feast day that celebrates the life of Saint Valentine. It is the day when valentines are sent as tokens of love.

val·i·ant [<u>val</u>-yunt] *adjective.* very brave and courageous: *The firefighters made a valiant effort to rescue the people trapped in the burning building.* —**valiantly,** *adverb.*

Many oceans began life as rift **valleys.**

A rift valley forms when the land drops between splits caused by movement of the Earth's crust.

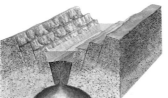

As the land at the sides drops, water floods in.

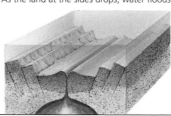

The valley continues to spread and its floor sinks until it becomes part of the ocean.

val·id [<u>val</u>-id] *adjective.* **1.** based on what is true or factual: *You need to have a valid reason for not going to school, such as being sick.* **2.** having standing under the law; legally acceptable: *That rail pass is valid for three months.* The state of being valid is **validity.** —**validly,** *adverb.*

val·ley ◀ [<u>val</u>-ee] *noun, plural* **valleys.** a low-lying area between hills or mountains. Often a stream or river flows through a valley: *The Yosemite Valley in California is a popular tourist destination.*

val·or [<u>val</u>-ur] *noun.* great courage in the face of danger, especially in war: *Since 1862 the Congressional Medal of Honor has been presented to members of the armed forces as an award for valor.* Showing great bravery and courage is **valorous.**

*Water **vapor** rises as steam from the extreme heat of the pool at Grand Prismatic Spring in Yellowstone National Park, Wyoming.*

val·u·a·ble [val-yuh-bul] *adjective.* **1.** worth a lot of money: *The Mona Lisa is one of the most famous and valuable paintings in the world.* **2.** being very useful, or important: *Because George saw the getaway car he was able to give the police valuable information about the robbery.* Things that have great worth are **valuables.**

val·ue [val-yoo] *noun, plural* **values. 1.** the importance, usefulness, or worth of something: *Remember the value of a good education if you want to be successful in life.* **2.** the amount of money something is worth or can be exchanged for: *Houses in this area are likely to go up in value.* **3.** a number or quantity in a mathematical calculation: *If y x 2 equals 16, what is the value of y? verb,* **valued, valuing. 1.** to estimate how much something is worth: *Jewelry valued at $30,000 was stolen from the safe.* **2.** to regard someone or something as important: *Margaret valued John's friendship and support during her long illness.* The principles or standards that guide a person or a group are known as **values.**

valve [valv] *noun, plural* **valves.** a part of a tube or pipe that controls the movement of fluid or gas through it: *There are valves in our veins that stop blood from flowing the wrong way.*

vam·pire [vam-pire] *noun, plural* **vampires.** *Literature.* a fictional person who is dead, but rises from his or her grave at night to suck blood from living people.

vampire bat ◀ a bat that feeds by sucking blood from birds and mammals. It is native to Central and South America.

van [van] *noun, plural* **vans. 1.** an enclosed truck that is used for carrying goods, animals, or large items. It has rear or side doors for loading: *Their furniture was taken to their new home in a moving van.* **2.** a small, boxlike vehicle used for transporting smaller goods. It is often fitted with seats to carry people.

van·dal [van-dul] *noun, plural* **vandals.** someone who deliberately damages or destroys property. Deliberate damage or destruction done to someone else's property is **vandalism.**

van·dal·ize [van-duh-*lize*] *verb,* **vandalized, vandalizing.** to deliberately damage or destroy property: *I couldn't find a public phone that worked, because they had all been vandalized.*

In early times the **Vandals** were a group of warriors from what is now Germany. They invaded and conquered other parts of Europe and also North Africa. The idea of a *vandal* as someone who ruins or destroys things comes from the fact that the Vandals are said to have caused great damage to the city of Rome when they took it over in the year 455 AD.

vane [vane] *noun, plural* **vanes.** a thin, flat, or curved blade that moves by the flow of wind or water. A vane is often used to produce power or to drive a machine.
🔊 Different words with the same sound are **vain** and **vein.**

va·nil·la [vuh-nil-uh] *noun.* a flavoring used in foods and perfumes. It is an extract from the beans of a tropical plant.

van·ish [van-ish] *verb,* **vanished, vanishing.** to disappear or cease to exist suddenly. It often happens in a way that cannot be explained: *The magician made the elephant vanish right before our eyes.*

van·i·ty [van-uh-tee] *noun.* excessive pride in your looks, abilities, or what you have achieved: *Jane's vanity stopped her from getting glasses even though her eyesight was poor.*

va·por ▲ [vay-pur] *noun.* a substance that can be seen suspended in the air, such as steam, smoke, or clouds: *In science class we heated water to see it turn into vapor.*

var·i·a·ble [vare-ee-uh-bul] *adjective.* describing something likely to vary or change: *The level of water in the lake behind the dam is variable. noun, plural* **variables.** a thing, event, or feeling that is likely to vary or change: *The weather is a variable in deciding where to hold the party.* A number of things that are likely to vary or change are called **variables.** —**variably,** *adverb.*

var·i·ant [vare-ee-unt] *noun, plural* **variants.** something that slightly differs from what is expected or considered normal: *My dog's short tail is a variant of the breed. adjective.* differing from what is expected or thought to be usual: *The word "moveable" is a variant spelling of "movable."*

In language a **variant** is a different form of a word. It *varies* (changes) from the usual form. This dictionary lists variants for many words in the way that the word can be spelled or pronounced. For example, the past tense of *cancel* can be spelled either as *canceled* (one **l**) or as the variant *cancelled* (two **l**'s). The word *data* can be pronounced either as [day-tuh] (first syllable sounds like *hay*) or as the variant [dat-uh] (first syllable sounds like *hat*). It is important to note that a variant is not wrong. It is correct, but just not as common or as preferred as the first form.

var·i·a·tion [vare-ee-ay-shun] *noun, plural* **variations.** something that is slightly different from the usual: *The teacher decided we needed a variation in our routine so we had our classes outside yesterday.*

In some countries Muslim women veil their faces and wear modest clothing to show their respect for Islam.

A B C D E F G H I J K L M N O P Q R S T U V W X Y Z

var·ied [vare-eed] *adjective.* relating to different forms or kinds of the one thing: *I like my job because it is varied in terms of what I have to do.*

va·ri·e·ty [vuh-rye-uh-tee] *noun, plural* **varieties.** **1.** the fact of being different or changed; not being the same: *Our coach likes to have variety in our practices so we don't get bored.* **2.** different kinds; things that are different: *The mall has a variety of restaurants.* **3.** one of the different forms of the same thing: *McIntosh and Granny Smith are well-known varieties of apples.*

var·i·ous [vare-ee-us] *adjective.* relating to many different kinds: *Stamp-collecting and photography are two of her various hobbies.* **—variously,** *adverb.*

var·nish [var-nish] *noun, plural* **varnishes.** a liquid used on metal, wood, or other hard surfaces to make a hard, protective coating.
verb, **varnished, varnishing.** to cover or coat with varnish: *My uncle and I varnished the deck of his boat.*

var·si·ty [var-suh-tee] *noun, plural* **varsities.** the main team representing a school or college in a sport or other contest: *the baseball varsity.*
adjective. being part of, or belonging to, a varsity: *a varsity football player.*

var·y [vare-ee] *verb,* **varied, varying. 1.** to change something or make it different: *I vary my route every day when I walk my dog.* **2.** to be different; to show difference: *The colors of the landscape varied as the sun set.*

vase [vays] *noun, plural* **vases.** a container made of glass or pottery that is used to hold cut flowers for decoration.

vas·sal [vas-ul] *noun, plural* **vassals.** *History.* in the Middle Ages, someone who was given the use of land in return for loyalty and services to a feudal lord.

vast [vast] *adjective,* **vaster, vastest.** very large in size or amount: *My summer camp was set in a vast area of woodland.* **—vastly,** *adverb;* **—vastness,** *noun.*

vat [vat] *noun, plural* **vats.** a very large container such as a tank or tub used for holding liquid: *We visited a dairy farm and saw the vats of milk.*

Va·ti·can ▼ [vat-i-kun] *noun. Religion.* the headquarters of the Pope of the Roman Catholic Church. The Pope lives in **Vatican City,** which is an independent state within the city of Rome, Italy. This is also called **the Vatican.**

vault [vawlt] *noun, plural* **vaults. 1.** a roof or ceiling shaped in the form of an arch or many arches: *The vault of the old church in town seems to reach to the heavens.* **2.** a container or room where valuable things can be safely stored: *a bank vault.*
verb, **vaulted, vaulting.** to build as a curve or an arch: *The ceilings were vaulted.*

VCR an abbreviation for **videocassette recorder,** which is a machine into which a videocassette is placed, and which records and plays a videotape.

veal [veel] *noun.* the meat from a calf.

veer [veer] *verb,* **veered, veering.** to turn suddenly; change direction quickly: *She had to veer suddenly when a dog ran in front of her car.*

ve·gan [vee-gun] *noun, plural* **vegans.** someone who only eats foods from plants. A vegan does not eat any foods that come from animals, including not only meat and fish, but also animal products such as butter, cheese, milk, or eggs.

veg·e·ta·ble [vej-tuh-bul *or* vej-uh-tuh-bul] *noun, plural* **vegetables.** a whole plant or part of a plant that is used as food, such as beans, carrots, potatoes, and lettuce.
adjective. made from or relating to vegetables: *a vegetable pie.*

veg·e·tar·i·an [vej-uh-ter-ee-un] *noun, plural* **vegetarians.** someone who does not eat meat, fish, or poultry but lives mainly on a diet of vegetables, fruits, grains, and sometimes dairy products.
adjective. of or having to do with being a vegetarian.

veg·e·ta·tion [vej-uh-tay-shun] *noun.* plant life found in a particular area: *The rain forest has lush green vegetation.*

ve·hi·cle [vee-uh-kul] *noun, plural* **vehicles. 1.** a machine used for transporting people or goods such as a bicycle, car, or ship. Anything relating to vehicles is described as **vehicular. 2.** a way of expressing or achieving something: *The movie was a vehicle for the director's political views.*

veil ▲ [vale] *noun, plural* **veils. 1.** a piece of material worn over the head and face to cover or protect. **2.** something that covers or conceals: *The government finally lifted the veil of secrecy surrounding the senator's death.*
verb, **veiled, veiling.** to cover or conceal with something: *Dirty smog veiled the city.* When something is hidden or unclear it is described as **veiled.**

Vatican Museum

Vatican City wall

St. Peter's Basilica

Sistine Chapel

St. Peter's Piazza

Vatican City is like a small walled town around St. Peter's Basilica and contains many museums and palaces.

vein ▼ [vane] *noun, plural* **veins. 1.** one of the tubes that carries blood from the rest of the body to the heart. **2.** one of the thin, branching tubes that form the framework of a leaf or an insect's wing. **3.** a layer of mineral ore in the middle of a rock: *a vein of silver.* 🔊 Different words with the same sound are **vain** and **vein.**

Vel·cro [vel-*kroh*] *noun.* a registered trademark for a fastening tape that consists of two pieces of material that stick together; one is made up of tiny nylon hooks while the other is made up of tiny nylon loops.

ve·loc·i·ty [vuh-*los*-uh-tee] *noun, plural* **velocities.** *Science.* the speed at which an object is traveling in a particular direction.

vel·vet [vel-vit] *noun.* a thick, soft, furry material usually woven from silk or nylon. *adjective.* made of or resembling velvet: *We bought green velvet cushions for the sofa.*

ven·det·ta [ven-*det*-uh] *noun, plural* **vendettas.** a long and violent feud between two individuals or groups of people, in which each tries to harm the other as revenge for past actions.

vending machine a coin-operated machine that sells items such as candy, soft drinks, and coffee.

ven·dor [ven-dur] *noun, plural* **vendors.** *Business.* a person who sells goods: *Dad buys a cup of coffee from the street vendor each day on his way to work.*

ve·neer [vuh-*neer*] *noun.* a thin layer of wood or other material used to cover another surface: *The bookcase has an oak veneer that makes it look more expensive than it really is.*

ven·er·a·ble [ven-ur-uh-bul] *adjective.* worthy of respect because of age, high position, or importance: *The venerable ex-president was the guest speaker at the formal dinner.*

Venetian blind a window covering made of overlapping horizontal slats that can be opened or closed in order to vary the amount of light coming in. The slats can be drawn together and raised or lowered by pulling a cord.

Ven·e·zue·lan [*ven*-uh-*zway*-lun] *noun.* a person from or an inhabitant of Venezuela, a country in the north of South America. *adjective.* having to do with Venezuela, its people, or its culture.

venge·ance [ven-juns] *noun.* the action of punishing or the desire to punish someone for harm they have done to you: *He swore a vow of vengeance against his attackers.*

Veins *support leaves as well as carrying food and water for the plant.*

The **Venetian blind** gets its name from the famous city of *Venice*, Italy. It is thought that the people of Venice (Venetians) were the first to use such window shades.

ven·i·son [*ven*-uh-sun] *noun.* the meat of a deer.

ven·om [ven-um] *noun, plural* **venoms. 1.** a poisonous liquid that some snakes, spiders, and insects produce when biting or stinging a human or other animal. **2.** a strong feeling of hate, anger, or bitterness: *His Internet posts about politics are often filled with venom.* Something that produces or shows venom is described as **venomous.**

The word **venison** comes from an ancient term meaning "to hunt." At first the word meant the meat of any animal that is hunted, not just deer. However as time passed and people used farm animals for their meat instead of wild game, the word came to apply just to deer because that was the one animal that was still widely hunted.

vent [vent] *noun, plural* **vents. 1.** an opening such as a hole or pipe through which a gas or liquid can escape: *The classroom was hot and stuffy because the air vents were blocked up.* **2.** an outlet or means to release the emotions: *Mom jogs every day as a vent for her stress.* *verb,* **vented, venting.** to release or express emotions: *The naughty child vented her anger by stamping her feet.*

ven·ti·late [ven-tuh-*late*] *verb,* **ventilated, ventilating.** to cause fresh air to circulate around an enclosed space: *A light breeze ventilated the attic when we opened up the window.* The act or process of circulating air is called **ventilation.**

ven·tri·cle [ven-truh-kul] *noun, plural* **ventricles.** *Biology.* either of the two lower chambers on each side of the heart that receive blood from the auricles (upper chambers), and pump it through the arteries to the rest of the body.

ven·tril·o·quism [ven-*tril*-uh-*kwiz*-um] *noun.* the ability of speaking without moving the lips, and projecting the voice so that it appears that something else, such as a wooden doll, is talking. A **ventriloquist** is a person who is skilled in this and does it to entertain others.

ven·ture [ven-chur] *noun, plural* **ventures.** a task or activity that involves some element of uncertainty, risk, or danger: *The company directors argued over how much to invest in a new business venture.* *verb,* **ventured, venturing. 1.** to expose to danger; take a risk: *The man ventured his own life by jumping into the stormy waters to save the child.* **2.** to do something in spite of risk, danger, or objection: *I venture to say we'll have a lot of problems if we do what you want; New campers are supposed to stay with the group rather than venturing off on their own.*

ven·ue [ven-yoo] *noun, plural* **venues.** a place where a meeting, event, or action takes place: *The bride and groom chose a Spanish restaurant as the venue for their wedding reception.*

Ve·nus ▶ [vee-nus] *noun.* **1.** the second nearest planet to the Sun, and the nearest planet to the Earth. **2.** in Roman mythology, the ancient goddess of love and beauty. In Greek mythology she is called Aphrodite.

ve·ran·da [vuh-ran-duh] *noun, plural* **verandas.** a large open porch, usually roofed, that extends along the outside of a house or building. This word is also spelled **verandah.**

verb [vurb] *noun, plural* **verbs.** *Language.* a word that describes an action, condition, or experience. Words such as *run, see, be, bring,* and *keep* are verbs.

The best way to make writing lively and interesting is to use strong, active **verbs** whenever you can. A sentence such as "There was a steak on the fire and I was hungry" may just lie flat on the page. Suppose instead the steak *sizzles,* flames *leap* out from the fire, a delicious smell *floats* on the air, and all this makes your stomach *growl,* as you *pace* back and forth waiting for the steak to be *seared* and ready. The verbs make it easier for the reader to picture this scene.

ver·bal [vur-bul] *adjective. Language.* spoken in words rather than written down: *We had a verbal agreement with our neighbors that they would pay for half of the new fence.* —**verbally,** *adverb.*

ver·dict [vur-dikt] *noun, plural* **verdicts. 1.** *Law.* a finding or judgment of a jury in a trial: *The jury took three days to decide on a verdict of "not guilty."* **2.** any other such judgment or decision: *The film critic's verdict was that the movie was sure to be nominated for an award.*

verge [vurj] *noun, plural* **verges.** a point or condition on the edge or border of something: *She was so upset she was on the verge of tears; The country is in chaos and is said to be on the verge of revolution.*
verb, **verged, verging.** to be on the edge or very close to something.

ver·i·fy [ver-uh-*fye*] *verb,* **verified, verifying.** to prove or check the truth of: *He had to produce his driver's license to verify his identity.* The act of confirming the truth of something is **verification.**

ver·min [vur-min] *plural noun.* animals, birds, or insects that carry diseases or are harmful to people, crops, or other animals. Lice, fleas, locusts, mice, and rats are vermin.

ver·sa·tile [vur-suh-tul] *adjective.* having a wide range of skills; able to do things or be used in different ways: *a versatile actor who can play many different roles; a versatile machine that is able to print, scan, copy, fax, and capture photos.* A person who is versatile shows **versatility.**

verse [vurs] *noun, plural* **verses. 1.** *Music.* a number of lines that form a section of a song or poem; a stanza: *There are four verses in the United States national anthem.* **2.** words that have a rhythmic and/or a rhyming pattern; poetry. **3.** a section of a chapter in the Bible. A person who has a good knowledge of a subject is well **versed** in that subject.

VENUS

In the morning or evening sky, Venus is brighter than any other astronomical body, except the Sun and the Moon. Its surface is covered in a thick layer of clouds, but is four times as hot as boiling water. Even at night the temperatures remain very high. Like the Earth, Venus is heated by the Sun, but its thick cloud cover and atmosphere of carbon dioxide make it impossible for the heat to escape. Venus is similar in size to the Earth, but spins in the opposite direction.

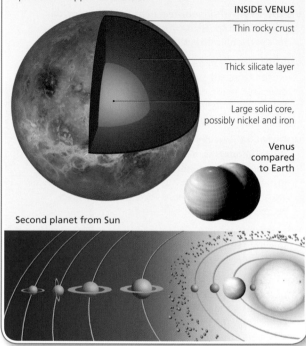

INSIDE VENUS
Thin rocky crust
Thick silicate layer
Large solid core, possibly nickel and iron
Venus compared to Earth
Second planet from Sun

ver·sion [vur-zhun] *noun, plural* **versions.** one way of describing or explaining something: *Martha and Marty gave very different versions of the accident they saw.*

ver·sus [vur-sus] *preposition.* opposed to; against: *It was the Blues versus the Sharks in the final of the soccer tournament.*

ver·te·bra ◀ [vur-tuh-bruh] *noun, plural* **vertebrae** *or* **vertebras.** *Biology.* one of the small bones that together form the backbone or spinal column of a person or animal.

ver·te·brate [vur-tuh-brit *or* vur-tuh-*brate*] *noun, plural* **vertebrates.** *Biology.* any animal that has a backbone, or spinal column. Humans and other mammals, fish, reptiles, amphib ians, and birds are vertebrates.
adjective. being a vertebrate; possessing a backbone, or spinal column: *A bird is a vertebrate animal.*

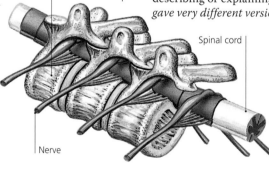

Vertebra

Spinal cord

Nerve

The holes in the **vertebrae** *form a tunnel that protects the spinal cord from knocks and damage.*

ver·tex [vur-teks] *noun, plural* **vertexes** *or* **vertices**. *Mathematics.* **1.** the point of a triangle or a pyramid that is farthest from the base. **2.** the point where two lines or surfaces meet to form an angle.

ver·ti·cal [vur-tuh-kul] *adjective.* describing something that goes straight up and down rather than across; perpendicular to the ground; upright: *The masts of a sailing boat are vertical.* —**vertically**, *adverb.*

ver·y [ver-ee] *adverb.* **1.** to a large extent; extremely: *He was very pleased to win the tennis match.* **2.** really; fully: *This is the very worst movie I have ever seen.* *adjective.* **1.** being the same: *When I met Andrea yesterday, she was the very person I was hoping to see; Please start the story at the very beginning.*

The word **very** can be used with almost any adjective to say that it has the quality of this word to a greater amount than usual; for example, *very* big, *very* old, *very* tired, *very* angry, and so on. However, because *very* is so common and easy to use, it often makes only a weak statement. A better way to do this is to choose a stronger word, so that you will not need to use *very* at all. For example, instead of saying something is *very big*, it can be *huge* or *enormous*. Instead of *very old*, you can say *ancient*, for *very tired* you can say *exhausted*, *very angry* can be *furious*, and so on.

ves·sel [ves-ul] *noun, plural* **vessels**. **1.** a large boat or ship: *The harbor is full of sailing vessels.* **2.** a container that can hold liquids, such as a vase, bowl, or drinking glass. **3.** a vein, duct, or artery through which blood or other bodily fluids flow.

vest [vest] *noun, plural* **vests**. a small garment without sleeves, often worn underneath a jacket or a suit coat. *verb,* **vesting, vested.** to grant a right or power: *The law vests the police with the power to arrest criminals.* A person who is granted the right to do something is **vested** with that right.
• **close to the vest.** not disclosed; secret: *Harvey kept the news about his new job close to the vest.*

ves·tige [ves-tij] *noun, plural* **vestiges**. something remaining or left over; a trace: *A few buildings in ruins were the only vestiges of the ancient city.*

vet·er·an [vet-ur-un *or* vet-run] *noun, plural* **veterans**. **1.** a person who has been doing a job or using a skill for a long time: *When he retired, Arnold Palmer was a veteran of many golf tournaments.* **2.** a former member of the armed forces: *My grandfather is an Air Force veteran.* *adjective.* having long experience in doing a job or using a skill: *Joseph is a veteran doctor who has been practicing medicine for thirty years.*

Veterans Day an annual holiday in the United States, held on November 11, to celebrate the finish of the two world wars in 1918 and 1945 and to honor veterans of the armed forces.

vet·er·i·nar·i·an [vet-ruh-ner-ee-un *or* vet-ur-uh-ner-ee-un] *noun, plural* **veterinarians**. *Medicine.* a person who treats illnesses and injuries in animals; a doctor for animals. This person can be called a **vet** for short. The kind of work a veterinarian does is **veterinary medicine**.

The word **veterinarian** comes from a word meaning "having to do with cattle." The earliest veterinarians were people who were experts in the diseases that affected cattle. Cattle were by far the most useful animals to humans at that time, so their health was very important.

ve·to [vee-toh] *noun, plural* **vetoes**. *Government.* the right or the power to prevent a law being passed or an event from taking place: *The President of the United States has the power of veto over many laws passed by Congress.* *verb,* **vetoed, vetoing.** to use the right or power to prevent something from happening: *The school principal vetoed the students' decision to form an archery club.*

vex [veks] *verb,* **vexed, vexing.** to give trouble to; annoy; irritate: *If you talk during a movie, you may vex the people around you.*

vi·a [vye-uh *or* vee-uh] *preposition.* by way of; by going through: *We traveled from San Francisco to New York via Dallas.*

vi·a·ble [vye-uh-bul] *adjective.* able to be done; possible: *It would not be viable to go sailing in such bad weather.*

vi·a·duct ▼ [vye-uh-dukt] *noun, plural* **viaducts**. a raised road or railroad, supported by piers or arches, often built above a valley, a ravine, or part of a town.

vi·brant [vye-brunt] *adjective.* describing something lively; exciting: *The orchestra played some very vibrant dance music.* —**vibrantly**, *adverb.*

The "Harry Potter" steam train passes over the Glenfinnan **Viaduct** *during its eighty-mile journey through the Scottish Highlands.*

a b c d e f g h i j k l m n o p q r s t u **v** w x y z

A B C D E F G H I J K L M N O P Q R S T U **V** W X Y Z

vi·brate [vye-brate] *verb,* **vibrated, vibrating.** to move or to make move quickly back and forth; to shake or cause to shake: *The earth tremor caused the walls of the hut to vibrate.*

vi·bra·tion [vye-bray-shun] *noun, plural* **vibrations.**
1. a rapid motion back and forth; trembling: *We could feel the vibration of the windows as the wind shook them.*
2. *Science.* the periodic vibrating of a particle, or number of particles, in a body or substance when the equilibrium of that body or substance has been disturbed.

vice [vise] *noun, plural* **vices. 1.** wicked or evil kinds of behavior: *It is the job of the police to combat vice in the community.* **2.** a harmful or annoying habit or type of behavior: *Mom says that chewing my fingernails is my worst vice.*

vice president a person who acts as president when the president is absent or not available; a president's deputy. This term is also spelled **vice-president.** It is spelled **Vice President** when it refers to the Vice President of the United States.

vice versa in reverse order; the other way around: *We'll go to the store first and then to the park, or vice versa if you prefer.*

"We enjoy spending time with her, and *vice versa*" (she enjoys spending time with us). The unusual term **vice versa** comes from two Latin words meaning "place" and "to turn around." The idea is that this expression turns something around on itself; that is, the meaning of the second part of the statement goes back to the first.

vi·cin·i·ty [vuh-sin-uh-tee] *noun, plural* **vicinities.** the district or area that is nearby: *The driver of the car asked us if there was a gas station anywhere in the vicinity.*

vi·cious [vish-us] *adjective.* **1.** describing something nasty; cruel; destructive: *The rebels carried out a vicious attack on the town and its people.* **2.** relating to something threatening; menacing: *The guard dog gave a vicious growl as we approached the house.*
—viciously, *adverb;* **viciousness,** *noun.*

vic·tim [vik-tum] *noun, plural* **victims.**
1. a person or animal that is attacked, injured, killed, or physically harmed in any way: *a victim of a shooting.*
2. a person who is treated badly or unfairly: *Grace often makes fun of people, and today poor Jenny was her victim.*

vic·tim·ize [vik-tuh-mize] *verb,* **victimized, victimizing.**
1. to physically harm or threaten a person or an animal: *The robbers victimized the people in the bank.* **2.** to cheat or treat unfairly or unkindly: *Maria was victimized by the lies that he told about her.* **—victimization,** *noun.*

vic·tor [vik-tur] *noun, plural* **victors.** a person, country, team, or organization that defeats an opponent in any kind of contest; conqueror: *the victor in a war; Amanda was the victor in our class spelling contest.*

vic·to·ri·ous [vik-tor-ee-us] *adjective.* being a winner: *The victorious athlete was presented with a trophy.* **—victoriously,** *adverb.*

vic·to·ry [vik-tuh-ree *or* vik-tree] *noun, plural* **victories.** the winning of a battle, game, or any kind of contest: *At the end of the game, the victory went to the better team.*

vid·e·o [vid-ee-oh] *noun, plural* **videos. 1.** the picture on a television, as apart from the sound: *TV reception is poor in our area so the video on our set is often not clear.*
2. a videotape: *Dad made a video of our school play.*

> The word **video** comes from a Latin word meaning "to see," and is related to the word *vision.* The word *video* was made up to match the earlier word *audio,* which means the part of a film or program you hear, as opposed to *video,* the part you see.

vid·e·o·cas·sette [vid-ee-oh-kuh-set] *noun, plural* **videocassettes.** a plastic case with spools inside, around which videotape is wound.

video game *Computers.* an electronic audiovisual game in which a player, or a number of players, can use controls to move or change images on a television or computer screen.

vid·e·o·tape [vid-ee-oh-tape] *noun, plural* **videotapes.** magnetic tape on which pictures and sound can be recorded and played back.
verb, **videotaped, videotaping.** to make a recording using videotape: *Mom videotaped my basketball game.*

Vi·et·nam·ese ◀ [vee-et-nuh-meez] *noun, plural* **Vietnamese.** a person who was born in or is a citizen of the southeast Asian country of Vietnam. *adjective.* relating to Vietnam, its people, or its culture.

Vietnam War [vee-et-nahm *or* vee-et-nam] *History.* a war fought from 1959 to 1975 in Vietnam between communist forces, supported by the government of North Vietnam, and anti-communist forces, supported by the government of South Vietnam. U.S. forces fought on the side of South Vietnam. In 1975, North Vietnam was victorious and Vietnam became a unified country under a communist government.

view [vyoo] *noun, plural* **views. 1.** the fact of seeing something: *As we reached the top of the hill, the valley below came into view.* **2.** something that can be looked at; scene: *Their house has a nice view of the lake.* **3.** the fact of having an opinion; judgment: *At the debate all the candidates were asked to give their views on immigration.*
verb, **viewed, viewing. 1.** to look at carefully; examine: *Yesterday we went to view the paintings in the art gallery.*
2. to think of as; consider; judge.

Vietnamese *women working in a street market wear traditional conical hats to protect themselves from the sun.*

In ancient times, wealthy Romans owned luxurious **villas** *on large estates in the country.*

view·er [vyoo-ur] *noun, plural* **viewers. 1.** a person who views or watches something, such as television. **2.** a machine or device used for viewing photographs or slides.

view·point [vyoo-point] *noun, plural* **viewpoints.** the fact of having an opinion; a judgment; way of thinking.

vig·il [vij-ul] *noun, plural* **vigils. 1.** the act of staying awake for some purpose at a time a person would normally be asleep: *The soldiers kept vigil all night as they waited for the enemy to attack.* **2.** a time when this is done. **3.** a time spent in prayer, especially on the day or night before an important religious day.

vig·i·lant [vij-uh-lunt] *adjective.* watching for danger; alert: *It is important to be vigilant at all times while riding a bicycle.* Someone who is vigilant shows **vigilance.** —**vigilantly,** *adverb.*

vig·or [vig-ur] *noun.* physical or mental strength or power; healthy energy: *Kylie brought great vigor to the task of running the marathon race.*

vig·or·ous [vig-ur-us] *adjective.* **1.** having lots of vigor; energetic: *Only vigorous people can be good athletes.* **2.** requiring vigor or strength: *Swimming is a vigorous activity.* —**vigorously,** *adverb.*

Vi·king ▶ [vye-king] *noun, plural* **Vikings.** *History.* a member of the warlike seafaring peoples of northwestern Europe who raided and plundered European coastal towns and sailed to North America between the eighth and eleventh centuries.

vile [vile] *adjective,* **viler, vilest. 1.** very bad; extremely unpleasant: *vile weather conditions; a vile taste.* **2.** describing something hateful; evil: *a vile crime.*

vil·la ◀ [vil-uh] *noun, plural* **villas. 1.** a large country property. **2.** a large, comfortable country or suburban house, usually owned by wealthy people.

vil·lage [vil-ij] *noun, plural* **villages. 1.** a community that is larger than a hamlet but smaller than a town: *There were about fifteen houses in the village where we stopped.* **2.** the population of a village: *About half the village came out to meet us when we stopped.* A person who lives in a village is a **villager.**

vil·lain [vil-un] *noun, plural* **villains. 1.** someone who does wrong; an evil person: *Only a villain would steal from poor people.* **2.** *Literature.* an evil character in a book, movie, play, and so on; the opposite of a hero. The evil behavior of a villain is **villainy.** A person who is a villain is **villainous.**

vine [vine] *noun, plural* **vines.** a plant with very long branches that grow along the ground, or on fences, walls, trees, or other types of supports. Some fruits and vegetables, like pumpkin, grapes, and melons, grow on vines.

vin·e·gar [vin-ur-gur] *noun, plural* **vinegars.** a bitter liquid made from the fermented juice of grapes or other fruits: *Mom dressed the salad with her favorite white vinegar.* Vinegar is used to preserve food and add flavor.

The **Vikings** *used wide, flat-bottomed cargo boats, called knorrs, which allowed them to come in close to shore to load goods and livestock.*

a
b
c
d
e
f
g
h
i
j
k
l
m
n
o
p
q
r
s
t
u
v
w
x
y
z

In ancient Greek **vineyards**, *grapes were picked in September and made into wine.*

vi·o·lent [<u>vye</u>-uh-lunt] *adjective.* **1.** describing the use of physical force to cause harm: *a violent attack; Boxing is a violent sport.* **2.** describing a large, destructive force: *a violent hurricane.* —**violently**, *adverb.*

vi·o·let [<u>vye</u>-uh-lit] *noun, plural* **violets.** **1.** a low-growing plant with small, purple, or pink, or white flowers. **2.** a pale purple color. *adjective.* having a pale purple color.

vi·o·lin [vye-uh-<u>lin</u>] *noun, plural* **violins.** *Music.* a four-stringed instrument that is played with a bow. Someone who plays the violin is a **violinist.**

vi·per ▶ [<u>vye</u>-pur] *noun, plural* **vipers.** a poisonous snake.

Wagler's palm **viper** *is a tree-dwelling snake found in Indonesia and Malaysia.*

vir·gin [<u>vur</u>-jin] *adjective.* not used or touched: *There was not a single mark in the virgin snow.*

vir·ol·o·gy [vuh-<u>rol</u>-uh-jee] *noun. Biology.* the study of viruses and viral diseases. Someone who studies viruses is called a **virologist.**

vir·tu·al·ly [<u>vur</u>-choo-uh-lee] *adverb.* almost or in effect: *Her mother virtually did the assignment for her.*

vir·tu·al reality *Computers.* a computer-generated world that allows a user to experience and control it, usually by wearing gloves that monitor hand movements and a helmet that shows images.

vine·yard ▲ [<u>vin</u>-yurd] *noun, plural* **vineyards.** a field where grapes are grown.

vint·age ▼ [<u>vin</u>-tij] *adjective.* describing something old or antique: *a vintage car. noun, plural* **vintages.** a particular age, especially in relation to a crop of grapes: *My uncle said that the year 2000 was a great vintage for that type of wine.*

vi·nyl [<u>vye</u>-nul] *noun, plural* **vinyls.** **1.** *Chemistry.* a plastic material. Vinyl is often used instead of leather to make car upholstery, clothing, and luggage. Thick vinyl can be used to make floor coverings or other objects like phonograph records. **2.** a phonograph record made with this material.

vi·o·la [vee-<u>oh</u>-luh] *noun, plural* **violas.** *Music.* a four-stringed instrument, slightly larger than a violin.

vi·o·late [<u>vye</u>-uh-*late*] *verb,* **violated, violating.** to not obey; break a rule or law: *If you violate the school rules, you may be suspended.*

vi·o·la·tion [*vye*-uh-<u>lay</u>-shun] *noun, plural* **violations.** the act of breaking certain rules: *Speeding is a violation of the traffic laws; She said it was a violation of her rights to stop her from protesting against the war.*

vi·o·lence [<u>vye</u>-uh-luns] *noun.* **1.** the act of using physical force to cause harm: *Punching someone is an act of violence; Mom says there are too many scenes of violence on television.* **2.** a large, destructive force: *the violence of the stormy sea.*

vir·tue [<u>vur</u>-choo] *noun, plural* **virtues.** **1.** goodness of thought and behavior: *Her virtue shines through in everything she says and does.* **2.** a certain type of goodness: *Kindness is a virtue.* **3.** any good quality or characteristic: *Our house has the virtue of being within walking distance to school.*
• **by virtue of.** on the grounds of; by reason of: *By virtue of an academic scholarship, he was able to study overseas.* —**virtuous,** *adjective.*

vir·tu·o·so [*vur*-choo-<u>oh</u>-soh] *noun, plural* **virtuosos.** *Music.* a performer with supreme talent and skill. *adjective.* describing supreme talent and skill: *a virtuoso performance.*

vir·us [<u>vye</u>-rus] *noun, plural* **viruses.** *Biology.* **1.** a tiny organism that reproduces only inside the living cell of a human or animal. Viruses cause many diseases like colds, flu, and measles. **2.** a disease that is caused by a virus. **3.** *Computers.* a program designed to damage computer software, or information stored in a computer.

vi·sa [<u>vee</u>-zuh] *noun, plural* **visas.** *Government.* an official document, attached to a passport, that allows entry into a particular country.

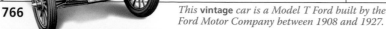

This **vintage** *car is a Model T Ford built by the Ford Motor Company between 1908 and 1927.*

vise [vise] *noun, plural* **vises.** a device used to hold an object firmly in place so that it can be worked on. A vise usually has two jaws that can be closed and opened with a screw or lever.

vis·i·ble [viz-uh-bul] *adjective.* **1.** able to be seen or viewed: *The baseball field is visible from the school library windows.* **2.** easy to see: *The new trees have made a visible improvement to Main Street.* The fact of being visible is called **visibility.** —**visibly,** *adverb.*

vi·sion [vizh-un] *noun, plural* **visions. 1.** the sense of sight; the act of seeing: *Mom wears glasses because she has problems with her vision.* **2.** something that can be seen: *She was a real vision in a red silk dress.* **3.** the fact of being able to think ahead and sense what things will be like in the future: *Dad says our principal is a woman of vision with ground-breaking ideas.* **4.** something dreamed or imagined: *She has a vision of herself living in Paris.*

vis·it [viz-it] *verb,* **visited, visiting. 1.** to stay with or at for a time; go to see: *We visited my friend in the hospital.* **2.** to stay as a guest: *We visited with my aunt for the first week of the vacation.*
noun, plural **visits.** a short stay: *My uncle paid us a visit.*

vis·i·tor [viz-uh-tur] *noun, plural* **visitors.** someone who comes to visit: *Visitors to the school have to check in at the principal's office.*

vi·sor [vye-zur] *noun, plural* **visors.** the brim on the front of a cap that shades the eyes from the sun.

vis·ta [vis-tuh] *noun, plural* **vistas.** a wide, distant view.

vis·u·al [vizh-oo-ul] *adjective.* **1.** having to do with or used in seeing: *Seeing double is a visual problem that can be corrected.* **2.** describing something visible: *If you need help, give a visual signal by waving your hand.* —**visually,** *adverb.*

vi·su·al·ize [vizh-oo-uh-lize] *verb,* **visualized, visualizing.** to imagine or form a mental picture of something: *It might help your game if you visualize yourself scoring a goal.* The act of visualizing something is called **visualization.**

vi·tal [vye-tul] *adjective.* **1.** having to do with life: *The monitor checks the patient's breathing rate, heartbeat, and other vital signs.* **2.** describing something necessary to stay alive: *The heart is a vital organ.* **3.** full of energy and life: *She is such a vital person, we love having her around.* **4.** being necessary or important: *He has vital information about the case that the police need to know.* The fact of being vital is called **vitality.** —**vitally,** *adverb.*

vi·ta·min [vye-tuh-min] *noun, plural* **vitamins.** *Biology.* a substance that is needed by the body for good health. There are many different types of vitamins and they occur naturally in different foods.

> **Vitamin** comes from the word *vita,* meaning "life." The word was made up by Casimir Funk, a Polish-American scientist who was one of the pioneers in working with these substances. He was one of the first to recognize that some diseases can be prevented by having a proper amount of certain vitamins.

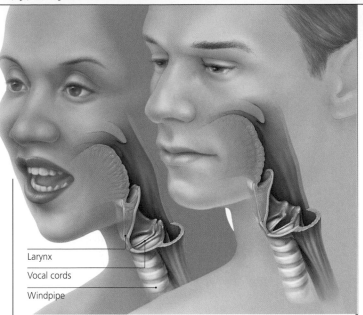

Larynx
Vocal cords
Windpipe

vi·vid [viv-id] *adjective.* **1.** describing something clear and fresh: *His story gave a vivid account of their journey through the mountains.* **2.** describing the brightness and intensity of a color: *a vivid blue sky.* —**vividly,** *adverb;* —**vividness,** *noun.*

vo·cab·u·lary [voh-kab-yuh-ler-ee] *noun, plural* **vocabularies.** *Language.* **1.** all the words that a person knows, understands the meaning of, and can use: *My aunt is a college professor and she has a really big vocabulary.* **2.** all the words of a certain language: *English is said to have the largest vocabulary of any language.* **3.** the words used in a certain activity or by a certain group of people: *the vocabulary of science.* **4.** a lesson in school that has to do with words and their meaning.

A person's **vocabulary** is the complete collection of words that this person knows how to use and understand. It is often thought that an important part of the greatness of famous writers is the fact that they have a very big vocabulary. Actually, studies have shown that most great writers do not use a large number of different words, and they do not use a lot of unusual or uncommon words. What makes them great is that they have complete command of the words they do use and can make these words provide exactly the effect they want.

vo·cal [voh-kul] *adjective.* having to do with the voice: *vocal sounds.* **2.** composed for or performed by the voice: *vocal music.* **3.** using the voice in a strong way; outspoken: *She is a very vocal critic of the mayor's policies.* — **vocally,** *adverb.*

vocal cords ▲ folds of skin in the throat that allow someone to speak or sing. Air passes over the vocal cords, causing them to vibrate and produce sounds. There are two pairs of vocal cords in the part of the throat called the larynx.

vo·cal·ist [voh-kuh-list] *noun, plural* **vocalists.** *Music.* someone who sings.

a b c d e f g h i j k l m n o p q r s t u v w x y z

vo·ca·tion [voh-<u>kay</u>-shun] *noun, plural* **vocations.**
1. a career or occupation. *She will pursue a vocation in medicine.* **2.** a strong desire or calling to take up a certain career, especially religious service. Something having to do with a vocation can be called **vocational:** *vocational advice.*

vocational school [voh-<u>kay</u>-shun-ul] *Education.* a school that offers lessons and practical experience in skilled trades such as carpentry or mechanics.

vod·ka [<u>vod</u>-kuh] *noun, plural* **vodkas.** an alcoholic drink made from wheat, or other cereal grains, or potatoes. Vodka was originally made in Russia.

vogue [vohg] *noun.* the fashion or style of a particular time: *Flared pants have been in vogue in different decades.*

voice [vois] *noun, plural* **voices. 1.** the sound that comes from talking or singing: *I could hear voices outside the door.* **2.** the ability to make sounds with the throat and mouth; speech or singing: *That singer is known for her powerful voice.* **3.** an opinion or point of view: *We should all have a voice in what happens to our school.*
verb, **voiced, voicing.** to say or speak: *He voiced his opinion at the club meeting.*

The **voice** of a writer is the way that this person's thoughts and personality are communicated to the reader by what they write. A great writer will have a voice that is just as easy to recognize, and just as distinctive to that person, as their actual speaking voice would be. When you have finished a piece of writing, you can read it over to yourself to check how it sounds. If the writing sounds like you as you really are, and if someone who knows you well would recognize this, then you have found your voice as a writer.

voice mail a system that records and plays back messages on the telephone.

void [void] *noun, plural* **voids.** a vacant or empty space: *I'm not sure what happens when I delete an e-mail message—I suppose it just goes off into the void somewhere. adjective.* **1.** empty of; lacking any: *It was a good speech except that it was void of any humor.* **2.** with no legal authority; not valid: *The test results were declared void when they discovered he had been cheating.*

vol·ca·no ▼ [vol-<u>kay</u>-noh] *noun, plural* **volcanoes** *or* **volcanos.** a mountain that is pushed up from the earth's surface by lava and gas. Sometimes lava, gas, and ash explode out of the volcano. The set of processes that cause this to happen is called **volcanism.** Volcanoes usually have craters at their peak. **—volcanic,** *adjective.*

> The word **volcano** comes from the name *Vulcan.* He was the god of fire in the religion of the ancient Romans.

vol·can·ol·ogy [*vol*-kuh-<u>nol</u>-uh-jee] *noun. Science.* the study of volcanoes. Someone who studies volcanoes is a **volcanologist.**

vol·ley [<u>vol</u>-ee] *noun, plural* **volleys. 1.** the firing of a number of guns or other weapons together. **2.** a burst or outpouring of many things together: *a volley of words.* **3.** in sports such as tennis and soccer, the act of playing an approaching ball before it bounces on the ground.

vol·ley·ball [<u>vol</u>-ee-*bawl*] *noun, plural* **volleyballs.**
1. a game played by two teams that use their hands to hit a ball to each other over a high net. Each side tries to stop the ball falling to the ground. **2.** the ball that is used in this game.

VOLCANOES

Volcanoes have shaped many of the Earth's islands, mountains, and plains. Vocanoes form either as a result of the movement of two of the Earth's plates or in places where hot molten rock suddenly pierces the Earth's crust. When a volcano erupts, magma rushes up to the surface. Some erupts through the crater or through vents and fissures, but some may stay underground between the rock layers. Steam and gas form clouds of white smoke, small fragments of rock and lava blow out as volcanic ash and cinder, and lava pours down the sides of the volcano and hardens. Large or unexpected eruptions can cause widespread destruction and loss of life.

Measuring crater

Measuring tremors

Sampling gases

Measuring temperature of lava

Because volcanoes are so destructive, scientists try to determine how and when they might erupt by studying crater size, gases, and lava, and measuring tremors.

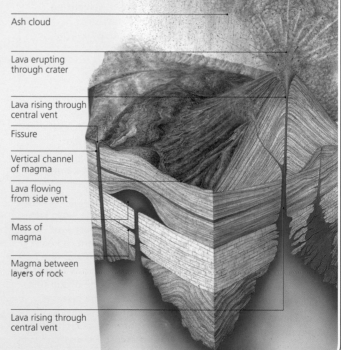

Ash cloud

Lava erupting through crater

Lava rising through central vent

Fissure

Vertical channel of magma

Lava flowing from side vent

Mass of magma

Magma between layers of rock

Lava rising through central vent

volt [vohlt] *noun, plural* **volts.** a unit that measures the force of an electric current.

volt·age [vohl-tij] *noun, plural* **voltages.** the amount of force of an electric current, measured in volts.

vol·ume [vol-yum] *noun, plural* **volumes. 1.** an amount of space that something occupies, determined by multiplying its height by its width by its length: *The volume of that box is ten cubic feet.* **2.** an amount of sound; the loudness of sound: *Turn up the volume on this song so we call hear it better.* **3.** one of a set of books, magazines, or newspapers in the same series: *Our classroom has a five-volume encyclopedia about animals.* **4.** any book: *He took down a large medical volume from the shelf.*

vol·un·tar·y [vol-un-*ter*-ee] *adjective.* **1.** acting or doing with free choice and without being forced: *She made a voluntary decision to leave the club.* **2.** controlled by the mind; done with thought: *The legs move using voluntary muscles, while the heart beats using muscles that are not voluntary.* **—voluntarily,** *adverb.*

vol·un·teer [vol-un-*teer*] *noun, plural* **volunteers. 1.** a person who chooses to enter military service without being drafted or otherwise recruited to do this: *At present the U.S. Army is made up entirely of volunteers.* **2.** someone who chooses to offer to do something, especially for no money: *Parent volunteers created a garden at the school.* *verb,* **volunteered, volunteering. 1.** to offer to do something without being forced to, especially for no money or other reward: *Simon volunteered to clean up the kitchen after the party.* **2.** to give willingly and without being forced: *He quickly volunteered a reply to my question.* *adjective.* having to do with volunteers or being a volunteer: *The volunteer firefighters came when called to help the paid firefighters.*

vo·mit [vom-it] *verb,* **vomited, vomiting.** to bring up the contents of the stomach and eject this through the mouth.

vote [voht] *noun, plural* **votes. 1.** the official expression of a choice carried out by voice, a show of hands, or by marking a ballot. **2.** the right to take part in making such choices: *The Nineteenth Amendment granted the vote to women in the United States.* **3.** the number of votes cast in a ballot: *The club decided to build a new pool, with a vote of 145 for and 23 against.* **4.** a choice or decision: *Each of us in the family will have a vote on where we want to go for vacation; a fair vote.* *verb,* **voted, voting.** to choose by casting a vote: *to vote for a candidate for mayor*

vot·er [voht-ur] *noun, plural* **voters.** a person who votes or has the right to vote.

vouch [vouch] *verb,* **vouched, vouching.** to personally give assurances; guarantee; confirm: *He can vouch for what I'm saying, as he was there and knows it's true.*

The unit of electricity known as the **volt** is named for Alessandro *Volta*, an Italian scientist who was known for important early discoveries in the field of electricity. He was the first to develop a device that could produce an electric current, and this became the basis for all modern batteries.

vouch·er [vouch-ur] *noun, plural* **vouchers. 1.** a written or printed document used to show the proof of something, especially the proof of a purchase or other financial transaction. **2.** a document or certificate used as a substitute for cash.

voucher system *Education.* a system by which the government gives parents a certificate that allows them to pay for their children to attend a school of their choice, rather than having to attend their local public school.

vow [vow] *noun, plural* **vows.** a serious promise or pledge: *The knights took a vow before God to obey King Arthur.* *verb,* **vowed, vowing.** to make a serious promise or pledge.

vow·el [vow-ul] *noun, plural* **vowels.** *Language.* **1.** a sound in speech that is made without blocking air as it travels from the mouth. **2.** a written letter or symbol that stands for a vowel sound. In the English alphabet, these are *a, e, i, o, u* and sometimes *y.*

Every word in English has to have at least one **vowel**, even the shortest words such as *a, be, I, on, up,* or *my.* The pattern of vowels has one unusual feature in that there are six letters that are always vowels (**a, e, i, o,** and **u**), and one other, **y,** that is sometimes a vowel (as in *why* or *happy*) and sometimes a consonant (as in *yet* or *beyond*). In some languages, such as Spanish, the sound of a certain vowel does not change much from one word to another. English is different in that a single vowel letter, such as **o,** can have many different sounds depending on which word it is in. For example, think of the **o** sounds in *bottle, off, open, do, morning, how,* and *melon.*

voy·age [voy-ij] *noun, plural* **voyages.** a journey taken by water or into space, especially one that is long: *the voyage of Christopher Columbus to the Americas.* A person who takes such a journey is called a **voyager.** *verb,* **voyaged, voyaging.** to make a journey by water or into space, especially a long one.

vs. an abbreviation for VERSUS.

vul·gar [vul-gur] *adjective.* **1.** rude in speech or writing; obscene: *I got into trouble for telling a vulgar joke.* **2.** not having good taste or manners; common: *The rich man built a huge, vulgar mansion to show off how much money he had.* The state of being vulgar or a vulgar act is called a **vulgarity.**

vul·ner·a·ble [vul-nur-uh-bul] *adjective.* **1.** not protected against the possibility of being hurt, either physically or emotionally: *Hold the kitten carefully as it is small and vulnerable.* **2.** open to attack; weakly defended: *As the navy was away fighting, the port was vulnerable to attack from the sea.* The state of being vulnerable is called **vulnerability.**

vul·ture ▲ [vul-chur] *noun, plural* **vultures. 1.** any of several large birds with dark feathers and bald heads. Vultures are related to birds of prey such as eagles. They are scavengers and use their excellent eyesight to find dead animals on which to feed.

W w

A B C D E F G H I J K L M N O P Q R S T U V W X Y Z

*Flamingos are **waders** that live in many different parts of the world.*

W, w *noun, plural* **W's, w's.**
the twenty-third letter of the English alphabet.

wad [wahd] *noun, plural* **wads. 1.** a small, tight lump of something soft: *Mike put a wad of cotton in his shoe to stop it rubbing his heel.* **2.** a large roll or bundle of paper, especially paper money.
verb, **wadded, wadding.** to form a small, tight lump out of something soft: *I wadded up sheets of newspaper and put them around the vase I'd packed in the box.*

wad·dle [wad-ul] *verb,* **waddled, waddling.** to walk with short steps while swaying the body from side to side: *The geese waddled along the riverbank.*
noun, plural **waddles.** the act of walking in this way.

wade [wade] *verb,* **waded, wading. 1.** to walk through or in something that makes movement difficult, such as water, snow, mud, or sand: *Judy waded across the creek.*
2. to get through something slowly and with difficulty: *For homework, I waded through a chapter of the textbook.*

wa·der ▲ [way-dur] *noun, plural* **waders. 1.** any of several types of birds with long legs that walk through shallow water searching for food. Storks, cranes, and herons are all waders. **2. waders.** waterproof boots that go up to the thigh. Waders are worn when walking in deeper water, especially by fishermen.

wa·fer [way-fur] *noun, plural* **wafers.** a small, thin, crisp cake, biscuit, candy, or piece of bread.

waf·fle [waf-ul] *noun, plural* **waffles.** a crisp, sweet cake made by cooking batter between two hot metal plates that are usually marked with a deep grid pattern.
verb, **waffled, waffling. 1.** to speak or act in an uncertain, rambling manner, usually to avoid answering a question or making a decision: *Stop waffling and decide which dress to buy.*

wag¹ [wag] *verb,* **wagged, wagging.** to repeatedly move quickly from side to side, up and down, or forward and backward: *The dog wagged its tail; The teacher wagged her finger at the students who were whispering in class.*
noun, plural **wags.** the act or motion of wagging.

wag² [wag] *noun, plural* **wags.** a person who is clever and funny; a joker: *the class wag.*

wage [waje] *noun, plural* **wages.**
the money paid for work, a salary; pay: *My weekly wage has just increased.*
verb, **waged, waging.** to begin and carry on with: *to wage war; The governor is waging a campaign for re-election.*

wag·on ▼ [wag-un] *noun, plural* **wagons. 1.** a vehicle with four wheels used to transport or deliver heavy loads. It is often pulled by horses, oxen, or a tractor. **2.** a small, low, four-wheeled cart pulled by a handle at the front.

wagon train *History.* a group of horse-drawn wagons moving in single file. Settlers in the nineteenth century in the U.S. often traveled west in wagon trains.

waif [wafe] *noun, plural* **waifs.** a person or animal that is homeless, lost, or abandoned, especially a child: *The orphanage cared for waifs who were found wandering the streets.*

wail [wale] *verb,* **wailed, wailing.** to make a long, loud cry, as from pain or sorrow.
noun, plural **wails.** a long, loud cry, or another sound like this: *We heard the wail of the ambulance's siren in the distance.*
🔊 A different word with the same sound is **whale.**

waist [waste] *noun, plural* **waists. 1.** the narrow part of the human body between the hips and the ribs. **2.** the section of a piece of clothing made to cover this part of the body: *The waist of this jacket is too tight.*
🔊 A different word with the same sound is **waste.**

wait [wate] *verb,* **waited, waiting. 1.** to pause and stay somewhere until a certain thing happens or for a certain time: *Isaac waited at the school gate until his dad came to pick him up.* **2.** to put something off; delay; postpone: *You can wait until after dinner to watch television.*
noun, plural **waits.** the act of waiting, or the length of time waited: *We didn't have a long wait until the ferry came; a boring wait.*
• **wait on. 1.** to supply the needs of; serve: *The duke was waited on by his servants.* **2.** to wait for: *She waited on her friend for an hour before she gave up and went home.*
🔊 A different word with the same sound is **weight.**

*Horse-drawn **wagons** have been used to transport crops since ancient times.*

wait·er [way-tur] *noun, plural* **waiters.** a man whose job is to bring customers the food and drink they have asked for in a restaurant, cafe, or the like.

A man who brings people food in a restaurant is a **waiter** and a woman who does this same work is a *waitress.* Both words have been in the language for hundreds of years. In modern times, however, the word *server* has come into use to describe either a man or woman who brings food in a restaurant. This is part of a recent pattern to choose words for jobs that do not tell whether it is a man or woman doing it. Other such words are *flight attendant* instead of *steward/stewardess, firefighter* instead of *fireman/firewoman,* and *chair* or *chairperson* instead of *chairman/chairwoman.*

waiting room a room set aside in which people wait for something or someone, such as in a hospital, doctor's surgery, or railroad station.

wait·ress [way-tris] *noun, plural* **waitresses.** a woman whose job is to bring customers the food and drink they have asked for in a restaurant, cafe, or the like.

waive [wave] *verb,* **waived, waiving.** to willingly put aside or give up: *The man's parking ticket was waived when he explained why he couldn't move his car.*
🔊 A different word with the same sound is **wave.**

waiv·er [wave-ur] *noun, plural* **waivers.** the act of willingly giving up a legal claim or right in an agreement, or a document that proves this right has been given up: *In professional football a club might sign a waiver to release one of their players and allow him to play for another club.*
🔊 A different word with the same sound is **waver.**

wake¹ [wake] *verb,* **waked** *or* **woke, waked** *or* **woken, waking.** to become or cause to become conscious after being asleep: *The little boy was cranky when he woke from his nap; A barking dog woke me during the night.*
• **wake up. 1.** to stop or cause to stop sleeping: *Roy woke up late this morning.* **2.** to become active or aware: *When will people wake up to the fact that this town has a big traffic problem?*

wake² [wake] *noun, plural* **wakes.** a watch kept over a dead body, especially on the night before its burial.

wake³ [wake] *noun, plural* **wakes.** a trail of foam or waves left by something moving through water, especially a boat.

wak·en [wake-un] *verb,* **wakened, wakening.**
1. to stop or cause to stop sleeping: *She wakened early to go for a walk.* **2.** to stir into being active; make alert: *My interest in history was wakened by a documentary on ancient Rome.*

walk [wawk] *verb,* **walked, walking. 1.** to move on foot at a pace that is slower than a run. When walking, people always have one foot on the ground, and four-legged animals always have two or more feet on the ground. **2.** to go through, along, across, or over on foot: *The acrobat walked the tightrope.* **3.** to go with on a walk; accompany: *He walked her home after school.* **4.** to force or help walk; lead or ride at a walk: *The jockey walked his horse around the track after the race.* **5.** in baseball, to go or allow the batter to go to first base after four balls have been pitched.
noun, plural **walks. 1.** the act of walking: *They took a walk in the woods.* **2.** a time taken or distance traveled on foot. **3.** a path or place set aside especially for walking: *Let's sweep the dead leaves off the walk.* **4.** a certain social position or job: *People in his walk of life are usually well off.*

walk·er [wawk-ur] *noun, plural* **walkers. 1.** someone who walks, especially a person who takes other people's dogs on walks for a job. **2.** a piece of equipment used for support by people who have difficulty walking: *The elderly man used a walker to go all the way down the hall.* **3.** a comfortable type of shoe made for walking.

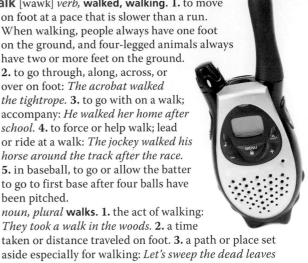

walk·ie-talk·ie ▲ [waw-kee-taw-kee] *noun, plural* **walkie-talkies.** a battery-powered radio receiver and transmitter that is small enough to be carried.

wall [wawl] *noun, plural* **walls.**
1. an upright, solid structure that is built to separate two areas and sometimes supports a roof: *The massive stone wall surrounding the town protected it from attackers.* **2.** something that is like a wall in strength, appearance, or in being difficult to get past; a barrier: *When she asked her class who had drawn on the desk, the teacher was met with a wall of silence.*
verb, **walled, walling.** to build a wall to divide, enclose, separate, or block an area off: *Dad walled in the back yard to keep the dog in.*

When standing still, the forest **wallaby** *of New Guinea bends its tail to touch the ground for support.*

wal·la·by ▲ [wol-uh-*bee*] *noun, plural* **wallabies.** an animal from Australia and New Guinea similar to a kangaroo but usually smaller. Wallabies are marsupials and have pouches.

wal·let [wol-it] *noun, plural* **wallets.** a book-like folding case used to hold banknotes, photographs, documents, or cards.

wal·low [wol-oh] *verb,* **wallowed, wallowing.** to lie down and roll about in something: *The pig wallowed in the muddy pool to cool off.*

a
b
c
d
e
f
g
h
i
j
k
l
m
n
o
p
q
r
s
t
u
v
w
x
y
z

wall·pa·per [wawl-*pay*-pur] *noun, plural* **wallpapers.** paper printed with colorful designs that is pasted on the walls of a room to decorate it.

wal·nut ▶ [wawl-nut] *noun, plural* **walnuts.** an edible nut with a crinkly, hard shell. Walnut trees are large and deciduous. Their timber is used to make furniture and the husks of the nut are used to make a brown dye for cloth.

wal·rus ◀ [wawl-rus] *noun, plural* **walruses** *or* **walrus.** a large marine animal from the Arctic that is related to seals. Walruses have flippers, two long tusks, and thick, tough skin.

The word **walrus** is said to go back to a phrase meaning "the whale horse." When people first saw a walrus, they thought of it as looking like a combination of these two animals.

waltz [wawlts] *noun, plural* **waltzes.** *Music.* **1.** a ballroom dance in which couples step, then slide and step again as they turn around the dance floor. **2.** a piece of music written for this dance. *verb,* **waltzed, waltzing. 1.** to dance the waltz. **2.** to move in a confident, unhesitating way: *He waltzed in and took my book without asking.*

wam·pum [wahm-pum] *noun. History.* strings of polished shell beads made by some Native Americans. Wampum were worn as jewelry and used in ceremonial exchanges between groups. After the arrival of Europeans, they came to be used as money in trade.

wand [wond] *noun, plural* **wands.** a thin stick or rod, especially one used by a magician or fairy, that is said to work magic: *The wizard said the words of the spell, then waved his magic wand.*

wan·der [won-dur] *verb,* **wandered, wandering. 1.** to move about casually with no fixed aim, purpose, or place to go: *The children wandered along the seashore, stopping every now and then to look at shells.* **2.** to leave the right path; stray: *Don't wander off the trail or you could get lost.* **3.** to stop concentrating on something and think about other things: *Although he was supposed to be doing his homework, his mind kept wandering to the baseball game next Saturday.*

wane [wane] *verb,* **waned, waning. 1.** to lose strength; become weaker: *Hope of finding the missing boat waned with each passing day.* **2.** to become or appear to become smaller: *Every month the face of the moon wanes from a full moon to a new moon.*

want [want] *verb,* **wanted, wanting. 1.** to feel a desire to have or do something: *My brother wants a camera for his birthday.* **2.** to need something: *That garden wants weeding. noun, plural* **wants. 1.** something desired: *Her wants have changed from playing with toy ponies to asking for a real pony.* **2.** a lack or need of something: *Months after the devastating earthquake, hundreds of people are still living in want.*

want·ing [want-ing] *adjective.* lacking in something: *He is wanting in modesty, as he is always telling people how clever he is.*

wan·ton [want-un] *adjective.* done or behaving in a way that harms, damages, or wastes something for no good reason: *Some people say that hunting animals for sport is wanton cruelty.*

Persian **walnuts** *have large nuts and thin shells, and are the kind we usually eat.*

war [war] *noun, plural* **wars. 1.** a large-scale, continuous period of fighting between countries or between different groups within a country using armed forces and weapons: *the American Civil War; the Persian Gulf War.* **2.** a campaign or long struggle for a particular purpose: *the war against poverty. verb,* **warred, warring.** to fight with weapons: *The two countries warred over who owned the fishing grounds.* 🔊 A different word with the same sound is **wore.**

war·ble [war-bul] *verb,* **warbler, warbling.** to sing with clear, but slightly vibrating notes: *I woke to the pleasant sound of birds warbling in the trees.*

war·bler ▼ [war-blur] *noun, plural* **warblers.** any of a number of small, usually brightly colored, American songbirds.

ward [ward] *noun, plural,* **wards. 1.** a large room or section of a hospital with many beds for people who need similar kinds of care. **2.** a young person who is officially in the care of an older person or a court of law. **3.** a division of a city or town for the purpose of local government.
    • **ward off.** to drive away; keep at a distance: *A scarecrow wards off birds.*

The garden **warbler** *repeats a loud "chek" sound when it sings.*

ward·en [ward-un] *noun, plural* **wardens. 1.** someone who serves as the official in charge of a prison. **2.** an official who looks after a certain area and makes sure its rules are followed: *Game wardens enforce hunting laws.*

ward·robe [ward-robe] *noun, plural* **wardrobes. 1.** a collection of clothing belonging to one person or group: *The singer is famous for her beautiful wardrobe.* **2.** a large cabinet or closet for hanging and storing clothes.

ware [ware] *noun plural* **wares.** small objects that are made of the same material, such as glass or silver, or are made to be used for cooking or eating: *silverware; kitchen ware.* Someone's **wares** are small objects that they sell in a market or street stall: *The pottery maker sells her wares at the weekly town market.* 🔊 A different word with the same sound is **wear.**

ware·house [ware-hous] *noun, plural* **warehouses.** a large building in which goods to be sold are stored: *The store manager is waiting for a delivery of computers from the warehouse.*

war·fare [war-fare] *noun.* fighting between armies; war.

war·head [war-hed] *noun, plural* **warheads.** the explosive front part of a bomb that is shot or travels through the air: *a nuclear warhead.*

war·like [war-like] *adjective.* ready and eager to attack; aggressive: *The dictator made warlike threats to shoot down all aircraft that flew over his country without permission.*

war·lock [war-lok] *noun, plural* **warlocks.** a male witch; a wizard.

warm [warm] *adjective,* **warmer, warmest. 1.** having heat that can be felt: *Summer is warmer than winter.* **2.** having a pleasant feeling of slight heat; not cold: *The blanket kept me warm.* **3.** giving off heat: *a warm fire.* **4.** able to keep heat in or keep cold out: *You need a warm coat for winter.* **5.** kind and friendly; affectionate: *a warm smile; The new student received a warm welcome.*
verb, **warmed, warming. 1.** to make warm: *Warm your hands by the fire; Warm the baby's milk.* **2.** to become fond of or show friendly feelings toward: *The family quickly warmed to their new neighbors.*
• **warm up. 1.** to make warm: *Warm up the soup on the stove.* **2.** to practice or do exercises a short time before a game or performance.* —**warmly,** *adverb.*

warm-blood·ed ▼ [warm-blud-id] *adjective. Biology.* having a body temperature that remains the same even when the surrounding temperature changes. Mammals and birds are warm-blooded. Reptiles are cold-blooded.

warmer [warm-ur] *noun, plural* **warmers.** a device that heats water or warms an area.

warm·ing [warm-ing] *noun, plural* **warmings.**
1. the fact of becoming warm; a rising in temperature: *With the warming of the weather in spring, the children were able to spend more time playing outdoors.*
2. see GLOBAL WARMING.

warmth [warmth] *noun.* the fact of being warm: *the warmth of the fire; the warmth of Grandma's welcoming smile.*

warm·up [warm-up] *noun, plural* **warmups.** practice or exercises done a short time before a game or performance.

warn [warn] *verb,* **warned, warning. 1.** to tell beforehand of possible dangers or problems: *The flashing sign warned drivers of the flooded road ahead.* **2.** to give advice to in order to avoid possible problems: *Jen warned us that it would be cold in the woods and to bring a coat.*
🔊 A different word with the same sound is **worn.**

warn·ing [warn-ing] *noun, plural* **warnings.** written or spoken advice beforehand of possible dangers or problems: *The radio broadcast grave warnings of a bad storm that was heading our way.*

War of 1812 *History.* a war fought between the United States and Britain between June 1812 and December 1814. The causes included trade restrictions by the British against the United States, the taking by the British of sailors on U.S. trading ships, and U.S. attempts to take Canadian land from the British.

warp [warp] *verb,* **warped, warping.** to twist or bend out of shape: *The top of the wooden table warped after it was left out in the sun and rain.* Someone who is **warped** has a personality or views that are biased or not normal because of a bad influence or experience.

war·rant [war-unt] *noun, plural* **warrants.** *Law.* a written order from a court allowing police to carry out a certain action: *The detectives had a warrant to search the building.* *verb,* **warranted, warranting. 1.** to have proper reasons for an action; justify: *Is it cold enough to warrant putting on the heating?* **2.** to make a promise; guarantee: *The farmer warrants that these vegetables were grown organically, without the use of chemicals.*

war·ran·ty [war-un-tee] *noun, plural* **warranties.** *Business.* a written guarantee of the quality of goods or services sold. A warranty lasts for a set period: *The manufacturer will replace any faulty parts while the bike is under a one-year warranty.*

Bald eagle

Cotton-top tamarins

Samoyed dog

Red kangaroos

Because they are **warm-blooded,** *mammals and birds can survive in almost any environment.* **773**

*Ancient Greek **warriors** defeated the Trojans by hiding inside a huge wooden horse that the Greeks presented as a gift to their enemy.*

A B C D E F G H I J K L M N O P Q R S T U V W X Y Z

war·ri·or ▲ [war-yur *or* war-ee-ur] *noun, plural* **warriors.**
1. a person who fights in a war or who is experienced in fighting: *The Apache chiefs Geronimo and Cochise were famous warriors.* **2.** someone who takes part in a struggle or difficult effort: *That doctor is known as a real warrior in the battle against cancer.*

war·ship [war-*ship*] *noun, plural* **warships.** a ship armed with weapons for use in war.

wart [wart] *noun, plural* **warts.** a small, hard lump that grows on the skin and is caused by a virus.
• **warts and all.** not leaving out any bad parts or faults: *This biography gives an honest description of the President, warts and all* .

wart·hog [wart-*hawg or* wart-*hog*] *noun, plural* **warthogs.** a wild pig of Africa. It has long tusks and growths like warts on either side of its face.

war·y [ware-ee] *adjective,* **warier, wariest.** watchful and careful; cautious: *The deer were wary at first, but eventually came out of the forest to graze on the edge of the meadow.* —**warily,** *adverb;* —**wariness,** *noun.*

was [wuz] *verb.* the past tense of BE.

The normal use of **was** and *were* is that *was* is the singular word and *were* is plural, as in "I *was* sitting in Row 27 on the plane and my brothers *were* in Row 26." There is one special use, thought, that calls for *were* instead of *was.* That is when the verb states something that is not a fact at present or wishes for something to be true: "If I *were* you (not "*was* you"), I would try to get a window seat." "On the plane, I thought about what it might be like if I *were* a pilot." This special type of verb is called the subjunctive.

wash [wahsh *or* wosh] *verb,* **washed, washing. 1.** to clean with water, water and soap, or some other liquid: *Karl washed the sand off his feet with the hose; I washed my dirty socks.* Something that is **washable** can be cleaned with soap and water without damaging it. **2.** to carry away by flowing water: *Rain washed the leaves into the gutter.* *noun, plural* **washes. 1.** the act of washing, or a place where this is done: *a car wash.* **2.** all the clothes, sheets, and other things that are washed together at one time: *Ed loaded a wash into the washing machine.* **3.** a special liquid used to rinse or cleanse something: *The nurse sponged the wound with an antiseptic wash.* **4.** a flow or movement of water, or the sound made by this: *The canoe bobbed about in the wash of the passing motorboat.* **5.** an area of dry land where water sometimes flows.
• **wash up. 1.** to be carried somewhere by water: *We collected driftwood that had washed up on the beach.* **2.** to wash one's face and hands: *Dad needed to wash up after working in the garden.*

wash·er [wahsh-ur *or* wosh-ur] *noun, plural* **washers.**
1. a person or machine that washes. **2.** a flat ring of metal, plastic, rubber, or other material. A washer is placed over a bolt before the nut is screwed on to make a tighter fit: *The plumber fixed the dripping faucet by replacing the worn washer.*

washing machine a machine for washing clothes, sheets, and other things.

Washington's Birthday February 22, the anniversary of the birth of George Washington, formerly a holiday in the U.S. Washington's Birthday is now celebrated on the third Monday in February as Presidents' Day.

wasn't [wuz-unt] the shortened form of "was not."

wasp ▼ [wosp] *noun, plural* **wasps.** a flying insect with a thin, black and yellow striped body and a narrow waist. The female can give a painful sting.

The word **wasp** comes from a term meaning "one who weaves."' The idea is that the nest of wasps, a large and complicated structure, looks as if it is something that has been made by weaving, as a piece of clothing would be.

WASPS

There are many thousand kinds of wasps, but hunting wasps are the kind that might sting you. They use their stings to capture and stun insects for food, or to defend themselves. Some wasps live in groups, but most live alone. The vivid yellow and black coloring of the European wasp warns other animals that it is dangerous. These wasps attack in large swarms when defending their nests and can sting their victims repeatedly.

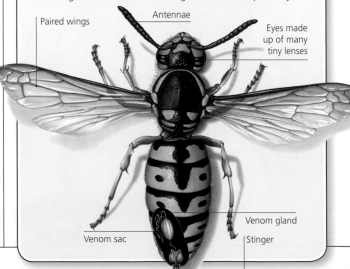

Paired wings
Antennae
Eyes made up of many tiny lenses
Venom gland
Venom sac
Stinger

waste [waste] *verb,* **wasted, wasting. 1.** to spend or use in a careless or useless way: *He wasted half the ketchup by shaking the bottle too hard and spilling it; I wasted five minutes looking for my pen when it was in my bag all the time.* **2.** to lose strength; weaken: *to waste away; The old man's body was wasted by illness.* **3.** to destroy; ruin: *The countryside was wasted by years of war.*
noun, plural **wastes. 1.** the spending or using of something in a careless or useless way: *a waste of money; It's a waste of time trying to fix that old computer.* **2.** something that is left over from a process and is no longer wanted or useful: *industrial waste; nuclear waste.* **3.** material that is eliminated from the body, such as urine. *adjective.* left over or no longer useful: *We collect our waste paper so it can be recycled.*

waste·bas·ket [waste-*bas*-kit] *noun, plural* **wastebaskets.** a small, open container where scraps of unwanted paper and other things are put to be thrown out. Unwanted scraps of paper are **waste paper.**

waste·ful [waste-ful] *adjective.* having to do with wasting something: *It's wasteful to leave all the lights on when no one is in the building.* **—wastefulness,** *noun.*

waste·land [waste-*land*] *noun, plural* **wastelands.** *Environment.* an area of land where little or nothing grows or can survive, such as a desert, or land that has been badly polluted by people.

waste·wa·ter [waste-*waw*-tur] *noun. Environment.* water that has been used for washing, flushing human and animal waste, or in a manufacturing process.

watch [woch] *verb,* **watched, watching. 1.** to look at a person or thing carefully: *Are you going to watch the game on TV today?* **2.** to look after or take care of: *Grandma watched the baby while Mom went to the store.* **3.** to look at or wait for in a careful way: *Watch the milk until it starts to boil, then take it off the stove.*
noun, plural **watches. 1.** the act of watching carefully or guarding: *Can you keep a watch on our picnic things while I get the drinks?* **2.** a person or a group of people whose job is to guard things or the period of time someone is on duty guarding things: *Tim took the first watch while the rest of the crew slept.* **3.** a small object used to keep time, usually worn on the wrist.

watch·ful [woch-ful] *adjective.* careful to notice things; alert: *The children splashed in the pool under the watchful eyes of their parents.* **—watchfully,** *adverb;* **—watchfulness,** *noun.*

watch·man [woch-mun] *noun, plural* **watchmen.** a person whose job is to guard a building or property. A watchman usually works at night, when the building is empty.

wa·ter [waw-tur] *noun, plural* **waters. 1.** the liquid that falls from the sky as rain and in its pure form has no color, taste, or smell. Water forms the oceans, seas, rivers, and lakes. **2.** the liquid of an ocean, sea, river, or spring: *coastal waters; Arctic waters.*
verb, **watered, watering. 1.** to wet something with water: *to water the garden.* **2.** to give water to an animal for drinking: *to water the horses.* **3.** to let out watery liquid: *Cutting up onions makes my eyes water.*
• **water down. 1.** to weaken a liquid by adding water. **2.** to make less forceful or strong; weaken: *The teacher watered down her criticisms because she did not want to sound too discouraging.*

water buffalo a large black buffalo native to tropical Asia that has long horns that curve backward. Water buffalo are often used as working animals and also as a source of milk and cheese.

wa·ter·col·or [waw-tur-*kul*-ur] *noun, plural* **watercolors.** *Art.* **1.** paint made by mixing coloring matter with water. **2.** the art of using such paint, or a painting or design made in this way.

wa·ter·cress [waw-tur-*kres*] *noun, plural* **watercresses.** a plant that grows in water. Its leaves have a peppery taste, and are eaten raw in salads.

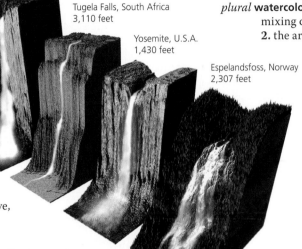

Angel Falls, Venezuela 3,230 feet
Tugela Falls, South Africa 3,110 feet
Yosemite, U.S.A. 1,430 feet
Espelandsfoss, Norway 2,307 feet

Angel Falls, Venezuela, is the world's tallest **waterfall** *with a single drop.*

wa·ter·fall ◀ [waw-tur-*fawl*] *noun, plural* **waterfalls.** the water of a stream or river dropping from a higher to a lower place.

wa·ter·front [waw-tur-*frunt*] *noun, plural* **waterfronts.** the land or the part of a town or city next to an ocean, river, or lake.

Wa·ter·gate [waw-tur-*gate*] *noun. History.* a political scandal in the United States during the early 1970s. Members of the administration of President Richard Nixon organized illegal spying on political opponents. Legal charges were brought, and the President resigned in 1974. A scandal that involves illegal activities and cover-ups may be given a similar name ending in **–gate,** such as Irangate.

The **Watergate** scandal got its name because it began when burglars broke into an office of the Democratic Party at the Watergate building in Washington, D.C. Ever since then, people have made up words ending in *-gate* to describe other scandals that they think are similar in some way to the original Watergate scandal.

a b c d e f g h i j k l m n o p q r s t u v **w** x y z

Water lilies have long, soft stems that carry oxygen from the air down to their roots on the pond bed.

water lily ▲ a plant that grows in freshwater lakes and ponds. It has rounded leaves that float, and showy flowers in various colors.

wa·ter·logged [<u>waw</u>-tur-*logd*] *adjective.* completely soaked or filled with water: *The football game was called off because the field was waterlogged after it rained all week.*

Wa·ter·loo [<u>waw</u>-tur-*loo*] *noun. History.* a battle on June 18, 1815, near the town of Waterloo in Belgium, between the British and French armies. The British won and this was the final defeat of the French Emperor, Napoleon Bonaparte, who was forced into exile. A person has a **waterloo** when he or she suffers a crushing defeat.

wa·ter·mel·on [<u>waw</u>-tur-*mel*-un] *noun, plural* **watermelons.** a large fruit with a thick, green rind and a sweet, juicy flesh of pink, red, or yellow with many seeds. It grows on vines.

water moccasin a type of poisonous snake; also called COTTONMOUTH.

wa·ter·proof [<u>waw</u>-tur-*proof*] *adjective.* not letting water get through: *We wore waterproof jackets when we rode in canoes down the rapids. verb,* **waterproofed, waterproofing.** to make waterproof: *I'm going to waterproof my new boots before I wear them outside in the snow.*

wa·ter·shed [<u>waw</u>-tur-*shed*] *noun, plural* **watersheds. 1.** a ridge of high land that divides two different river basins. **2.** the total area from which water drains into a particular river or lake; a river basin: *The Ohio River's watershed is more than 200,000 square miles.* **3.** a critical point that marks an important change or development; a turning point: *The Revolutionary War was a watershed in American history.*

wa·ter ski one of a pair of broad skis used for water-skiing.

water-ski [<u>waw</u>-tur-*skee*] *verb,* **water-skied, water-skiing.** to glide over water on water skis while being towed by a rope attached to a speedboat. — **water-skier,** *noun.*

wa·ter·tight [<u>waw</u>-tur-*tite*] *adjective.* completely sealed so that water cannot enter or escape: *All the repairs to the roof will make it watertight and stop the rain from coming in.*

wa·ter·way [<u>waw</u>-tur-*way*] *noun, plural* **waterways.** a body of water that a ship can travel through, such as a river, canal, or channel.

wa·ter·wheel ▼ [<u>waw</u>-tur-*weel*] *noun, plural* **waterwheels.** a wheel that is turned by running water falling on it or flowing under it. It is used to power machinery.

wa·ter·works [<u>waw</u>-tur-*wurks*] *plural noun.* **1.** the entire system that supplies water to a city, town, or other area. It includes reservoirs, buildings, machinery, pumps, and pipes. **2.** a building that houses the pumping station that sends water to a city, town, or other area.

wa·ter·y [<u>waw</u>-tur-ee] *adjective,* **waterier, wateriest. 1.** filled with or containing water: *After the rain, the soil was too watery to plant anything.* **2.** having too much water; too weak or diluted: *This fruit drink is watery—I don't like it.*

watt [wot] *noun, plural* **watts.** a unit of measurement for electrical power. An amount of power expressed in watts is **wattage.**

wave ▶ [wave] *verb,* **waved, waving. 1.** to move or cause to move up and down or from side to side: *The stadium was full of fans waving flags and banners.* **2.** to signal by raising and moving the hand or an object held in the hand: *Tony waved good-bye from the car window; The police officer waved to the car to pull over.* **3.** to have or give a wavy form; curve or curl: *Janine's hair has that curl because it waves naturally. noun, plural* **waves. 1.** a ridge, crest, or swell moving on or through the surface of water or another liquid: *The surfers rode the waves into the shore.* **2.** *Science.* a vibration or disturbance that transfers energy through matter or space, and that moves somewhat like a water wave: *a sound wave; a light wave.* **3.** the act of signaling with the hand or an object in the hand: *The movie star gave the cameras a wave before climbing into the limousine.* **4.** a sudden surge, rush, or rise: *He felt a wave of nausea just before he vomited.* **5.** a curve or sequence of curves: *Waves of wheat blew in the wind.*

Waterwheels *were once used to provide power for flour mills.*

wave·length [<u>wave</u>-*length*] *noun, plural* **wavelengths.** *Science.* **1.** the distance of one full wave movement, for example from the top or bottom of one wave to the top or bottom of the next wave. **2.** a way of thinking: *Those two girls get along so well because they're on the same wavelength.*

wa·ver [<u>way</u>-vur] *verb,* **wavered, wavering. 1.** to sway back and forth unsteadily; wobble: *The candle flame wavered in the breeze.* **2.** to swing back and forth when choosing or deciding; be unsure: *He wavered between the apple pie and the lemon meringue pie for dessert.*

wa·vy [<u>wave</u>-ee] *adjective,* **wavier, waviest.** having a wavelike or curvy form or movement; full of waves: *The snake reared back in a wavy motion just before it struck.*

wax[1] [waks] *noun, plural* **waxes. 1.** a fairly hard, greasy or oily substance that comes from plants or animals and that melts with heat. Bees produce **beeswax** for building their honeycombs. **2.** a substance that contains or is like wax. It is used for polishing floors and other surfaces, and for making candles. A **waxy** surface is a surface covered in or made of wax.
verb, **waxed, waxing.** to cover, polish, or treat with wax: *Mom went to the beautician to get her legs waxed.*

wax[2] [waks] *verb,* **waxed, waxing. 1.** to grow or seem to grow larger, greater, or brighter: *The moon waxes as it becomes a full moon.* **2.** to become: *The old lady waxed sentimental as she remembered her childhood.*

way [way] *noun, plural* **ways. 1.** a path or road for traveling from one place to another: *This path is the shortest way to the river.* **2.** a method for doing or getting something: *The way this toy works is by batteries.* **3.** a course of conduct or action: *The clown talked in a funny way to make us laugh.* **4.** a course or route traveled from one place to another; a direction: *Which way is it to town? Dad picks me up from school on his way home from work.* **5.** distance: *Alaska is a long way from Florida.* **6.** something that a person wishes: *If I had my way, I'd never have to clean my room ever again.* **7.** a particular aspect, detail, or feature: *Ben looks like his father in many ways.*
adverb. by or to a great distance or degree; far: *The hermit lives way out in the middle of the woods.*
• **by the way.** an expression used to introduce a new but related subject; incidentally: *By the way, it looks like I'll be able to go on the trip after all.*
• **under way.** already moving or happening; in progress: *The plans for the new library are already underway.*

we [wee] *plural pronoun.* the people who are speaking: *In our house we eat dinner at about six o'clock.*
🔊 A different word with the same sound is **wee.**

weak [week] *adjective,* **weaker, weakest. 1.** lacking strength, energy, force, or power: *Grandpa was very weak after his operation.* **2.** likely to break, fall, or give way: *The wooden fence has stood for forty years, but now it's weak and rotting. —weakly, adverb.*
🔊 A different word with the same sound is **week.**

weak·en [week-un] *verb,* **weakened, weakening.** to make or become weak or weaker: *I was supposed to stay in all weekend, but Mom eventually weakened and let me go skating with my friends.*

weak·ling [week-ling] *noun, plural* **weaklings.** a person who is not strong in body or character: *A weakling wouldn't be able to lift those weights.*

weak·ness [week-nis] *noun, plural* **weaknesses. 1.** the quality or state of being weak: *A weakness in the foundation caused the building to collapse.* **2.** a weak point; defect or flaw: *Our team's weakness is defense—we've got good hitting and pitching, but we make a lot of errors in the field.* **3.** a special fondness: *He has a weakness for fast cars.*

wealth [welth] *noun.* **1.** a large amount of money or possessions; riches: *After finding a huge nugget of gold, the miner was a man of great wealth.* **2.** a large amount of anything: *That tennis star has a wealth of talent.*

wealth·y [wel-thee] *adjective,* **wealthier, wealthiest.** having wealth; rich: *The wealthy woman bought herself a diamond necklace.*

weap·on [wep-un] *noun, plural* **weapons. 1.** an instrument used to attack or defend while fighting. A knife, a gun, and a bomb are all weapons. Weapons in general are **weaponry. 2.** any form of attack or defense: *Maria is our team's secret weapon—she can score a goal from anywhere.*

weapons of mass destruction weapons that can cause great damage and kill many people. They include huge bombs and nuclear, chemical, and biological weapons. The abbreviation for this term is **WMDs.**

wear [ware] *verb,* **wore, worn, wearing. 1.** to have or carry on the body. **2.** to show or display: *We have to wear our hair in a ponytail for dance classes.* **3.** to damage, erode, or reduce by constant use or exposure: *Over millions of years, the Colorado River wore away rock and formed the Grand Canyon.* **4.** to produce by constant use or exposure: *He has worn holes in the knees of his jeans.* **5.** to last or stand up against use or the passing of time: *I've had that coat for three years and it is still wearing well.*
noun. **1.** the act of wearing or the state of being worn: *My favorite sneakers have had a lot of wear.* **2.** articles of clothing: *Lisa needs some beach wear for her vacation in Miami.* **3.** damage from constant use or exposure.
• **wear off.** to become less effective: *My headache is coming back now that the aspirin is wearing off.*
• **wear out. 1.** to make or become useless through too much use: *She wore out her voice cheering for her team in the Super Bowl.* **2.** to make weary; exhaust.
🔊 Different words with the same sound are **ware** and **where.**

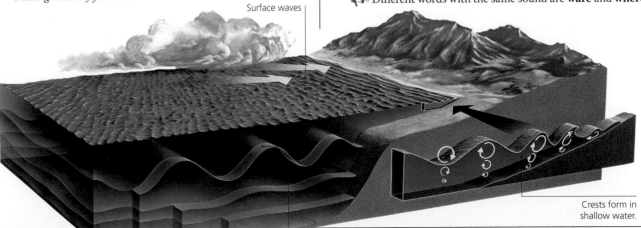

Surface waves

Crests form in shallow water.

Waves under the surface

Surface **waves** *are caused by wind and storms, while those deep under the ocean are generated by tides.*

a b c d e f g h i j k l m n o p q r s t u v **w** x y z

A B C D E F G H I J K L M N O P Q R S T U V W X Y Z

wea·ry [weer-ee]
adjective, **wearier, weariest.** very tired:
I feel weary today because I stayed up late last night.
verb, **wearied, wearying.** to make or become weary:
The long bicycle ride wearied everybody.
—**wearily,** *adverb;*
—**weariness,** *noun.*

wea·sel [wee-zul] *noun,*
plural **weasels** or **weasel.** a small, fierce animal with a long, slender body, a long neck and tail, short legs, and soft, brownish fur. It eats mice, rabbits, and other small animals and birds.

weath·er ▲ [weTH-ur] *noun.* the state of the air or atmosphere at a certain time and place: *Today, the weather will be hot with thunderstorms in the afternoon.*
verb, **weathered, weathering. 1.** to be affected by the weather: *The gate was painted bright blue years ago, but it has weathered to a pale blue-gray.* **2.** to come through safely; survive: *The mayor weathered the crisis and was re-elected.*

It is important to understand the difference between **weather** and *climate.* Global warming applies to *climate,* not *weather. Weather* is the conditions of temperature, sunlight, rain or snow, wind, and so on, in a certain place at a certain limited time. *Climate* is the average of all these weather conditions for a large area over a long period of time, such as several years.

weath·er·man [weTH-ur-*man*] *noun, plural* **weathermen.** a person who studies, forecasts, and reports the weather.

weath·er·vane [weTH-ur-*vane*] *noun,*
plural **weathervanes.** a device that is fixed to a roof or other elevated object. It is moved by the wind and shows the wind's direction.

weave [weev] *verb,* **wove** or **weaved, woven** or **weaved, weaving. 1.** to make by passing lengths of fiber over and under one another: *Native Americans weave baskets from grasses and other plant fibers.* A **weaver** is a person who weaves cloth, baskets, or other objects. **2.** to spin a web or cocoon: *The silkworm has woven a cocoon.* **3.** to move or make by winding in and out or from side to side: *During the movie's car chase, the cars weaved through the streets of Chicago.*
noun, plural **weaves.** a method or pattern of weaving: *The shag pile rug has a loose weave.*

web ▶ [web] *noun, plural* **webs. 1.** a network of fine, sticky threads that a spider spins; cobweb. **2.** a complex crisscrossing structure; network: *We got lost in the web of freeways and interchanges in Los Angeles.* **3.** the skin between the toes of ducks, frogs, and other animals that live in water.

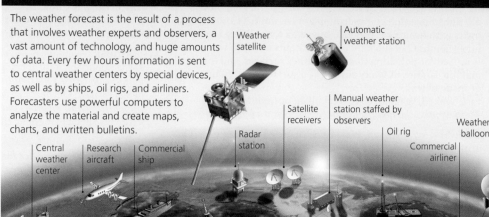

WEATHER

The weather forecast is the result of a process that involves weather experts and observers, a vast amount of technology, and huge amounts of data. Every few hours information is sent to central weather centers by special devices, as well as by ships, oil rigs, and airliners. Forecasters use powerful computers to analyze the material and create maps, charts, and written bulletins.

Weather satellite · Automatic weather station · Satellite receivers · Manual weather station staffed by observers · Oil rig · Weather balloon · Radar station · Commercial airliner · Central weather center · Research aircraft · Commercial ship · Drifting weather buoy

Web [web] *noun. Computers.* the computer network consisting of Internet sites that store information as text and images that people can access easily. Usually called **the Web,** it is the shortened form of WORLD WIDE WEB.

webbed [webd] *adjective.* having or connected by a web: *A beaver has webbed feet.*

Web browser another term for BROWSER.

web-foot·ed [web-fut-id] *adjective.* having feet with toes that are joined by a web: *Alligators swim very well because they are web-footed.*

Web page *Computers.* a page of information that forms part of a Website on the World Wide Web. This term is also spelled **web page, Webpage,** and **webpage.**

Web·site [web-site] *noun, plural* **Websites.** *Computers.* a location on the Internet (World Wide Web) that contains a set of Web pages. This word is also spelled **website** and **Web site.**

Web·zine [web-zeen] *noun, plural* **Webzines.** *Computers.* a magazine that is published on the World Wide Web. People can read it on a computer screen or print it out.

wed [wed] *verb,* **wedded** or **wed, wedding. 1.** to marry someone; get married: *My cousin will wed her fiancé after she graduates from college.* **2.** to join two people in marriage: *A minister will wed three couples on Saturday.* **3.** to be committed or closely attached: *We need some new flowers for the garden, but I'm not wedded to any particular kind.*

Sheet web · Orb web

Spiders' **webs** *vary in size and shape.*

we'd [weed] the shortened form of "we had," "we would," or "we should." A different word with the same sound is **weed**.

wed·ding [wed-ing] *noun, plural* **weddings.** the act of being married; a marriage ceremony or celebration: *We are all invited to George and Emma's wedding on Saturday.*

wedge [wej] *noun, plural* **wedges. 1.** a piece of a substance, such as wood, metal, or plastic, having one thick edge that tapers to a pointed edge. It is used for splitting wood or keeping a door open. **2.** something that is shaped like a wedge: *The restaurant served fish with wedges of lemon.* *verb,* **wedged, wedging. 1.** to force something apart or hold something open with a wedge: *The rescuers used a crowbar to wedge the doors of the elevator apart.* **2.** to force something into or through a narrow place: *The bus was very crowded, and I had to wedge myself into the last seat in the back.*

Wednes·day [wenz-day or wenz-dee] *noun, plural* **Wednesdays.** the fourth day of the week.

The word **Wednesday** originally meant "Woden's day." Woden was the chief god of ancient peoples who lived in northern Europe, in what is now Germany.

wee [wee] *adjective,* **weer, weest.** very small: *We discovered five wee kittens that had just been born.* A different word with the same sound is **we**.

weed ▶ [weed] *noun, plural* **weeds.** a plant that grows where it is not wanted. It can stop other plants from growing properly: *It is a constant battle to stop the weeds from growing in the flower garden.* *verb,* **weeded, weeding. 1.** to remove unwanted plants: *We spent all afternoon weeding the garden.* **2.** to get rid of someone or something that is not wanted: *The coach said he will weed out any players on the team who were not willing to work hard.* A different word with the same sound is **we'd**.

week [week] *noun, plural* **weeks. 1.** a period of seven days, especially one that begins on a Sunday and ends on a Saturday. **2.** the days of the week that a person usually works, goes to school, or does some other regular activity: *My father works a thirty-five hour week with two days off on the weekend.* A different word with the same sound is **weak**.

week·day [week-day] *noun, plural* **weekdays.** any day during the week, except Saturday and Sunday.

week·end [week-end] *noun, plural* **weekends.** the end of the week; Saturday and Sunday. The weekend is regarded as starting at midnight on Friday and ending at midnight on Sunday.

week·ly [week-lee] *adjective.* **1.** done or calculated by the week: *She is paid a weekly salary.* **2.** done or happening once a week: *Jane and Margaret give their dogs a weekly bath.* *noun.* a magazine or other publication that is produced once a week. *adverb.* once a week; by the week: *To save time we shop for groceries weekly.*

weep [weep] *verb,* **wept, weeping.** to show an emotion such as sorrow or happiness by crying: *I wept tears of relief when I heard I had passed the test; Sad stories make Mary weep.*

wee·vil ◀ [wee-vul] *noun, plural,* **weevils.** a small beetle that has a long head and a curved snout. It feeds on grains and other plants and spoils them.

weigh [way] *verb,* **weighed, weighing. 1.** to determine the weight or mass of someone or something: *I weigh myself on the bathroom scales every morning.* **2.** to have a particular weight: *An adult male elephant weighs around 11,000 pounds; Do you know how much that package weighs?* **3.** to consider or think about something carefully: *We'll have to weigh the advantages of the plan against its cost.* **4.** to be a burden; to be difficult or heavy: *George was weighed down by feelings of sadness when his mother died.* A different word with the same sound is **way**.

weight [wate] *noun, plural* **weights. 1.** the mass or heaviness of someone or something: *The weight of snow caused the roof to collapse.* **2.** a measure of the mass of something that is the result of the force of gravity. **3.** an object used because of its heaviness or mass: *The hand-painted stone was useful as a weight to stop the papers on my desk from blowing away.* **4.** an object whose weight is known, such as those used to measure the mass of other objects and in some sports, such as weightlifting: *I usually train with two 100-pound weights on the bar.* **5.** something that weighs you down mentally: *Having to deal with his mother's illness was a weight he could hardly bear.* **6.** something that is important and has the power to influence people: *What that witness said carried a lot of weight with the jury.* A different word with the same sound is **wait**.

weight·less [wate-lis] *adjective.* **1.** having no weight: *A balloon filled with helium appears to be weightless.* **2.** describing the result of being in space where there is little gravity: *Astronauts must undergo special training to be able to deal with being weightless for long periods.* —**weightlessness,** *noun.*

weight·lift·er [wate-lift-ur] *noun, plural* **weightlifters.** someone who lifts heavy, measured weights, either for competition or to keep fit. This sport is called **weight lifting.**

weight·y [wate-ee] *adjective,* **weightier, weightiest.** causing great concern or worry; important or serious: *Being a president of a college is a weighty responsibility.*

weird [weerd] *adjective,* **weirder, weirdest.** very strange and difficult to explain: *Many weird figures and shapes appeared when we rode through the Ghost Tunnel at the amusement park.* —**weirdness,** *noun.*

*Dandelions are common **weeds** that spread very easily.*

*To reconstruct a dinosaur fossil for a museum, metal supports have to be **welded** together.*

wel·come [wel-kum]
verb, **welcomed, welcoming. 1.** to greet someone in a friendly way when they have just arrived: *We welcomed the guests with open arms.* **2.** to be glad to accept something: *The newspaper welcomes letters from readers.*
noun, plural **welcomes.** a friendly greeting: *The rescuers received a warm welcome from the men who had been trapped in the mine.*
adjective. **1.** received in a friendly manner: *My cousin is always a welcome guest at our place.* **2.** free to use or enjoy without obligation: *Everybody is welcome to help themselves to dessert.* **You're welcome** is a polite way of replying to someone who has thanked you for something.

weld ▲ [weld] *verb,* **welded, welding.** to put together two pieces of metal or plastic by heating them until they are soft. The edges are joined by applying pressure: *The split in the gas tank had to be welded so it wouldn't leak.*

weld·er [weld-ur] *noun, plural* **welders.** a person whose job is to weld metal or plastic, as in a factory. The act of fusing materials together in this way is **welding.**

wel·fare [wel-fare] *noun.* **1.** the state of being happy, healthy, and safe: *The teachers hold regular meetings to discuss the welfare of their students.* **2.** help that is given by the government or a private agency to people who are in need, as for people who are very poor or who are not able to look after themselves properly.

well¹ [wel] *adverb,* **better, best. 1.** in a good, successful, or satisfactory manner: *Margaret did very well on the exam and got a mark of 90 out of 100.* **2.** in a complete and thorough way: *To avoid lumps you have to mix the pancake batter very well.* **3.** to a considerable extent; a lot: *Much of the city of Venice, Italy, is well below sea level.* **4.** in a familiar and close way: *I know my next-door neighbors very well.*
adjective. **1.** healthy, both mentally and physically: *I feel really well after my vacation.* **2.** good, satisfactory, or fortunate: *It's just as well we saved that money, now that we have more bills to pay.*
interjection. a word expressing some kind of emotion, such as surprise or disapproval. It is also used to begin or continue a conversation: *Well! Who would have believed that you would ever get married; Well, I guess it's time to go.*
• **as well.** in addition to something: *This fruit is delicious, and it is healthful as well.*
• **as well as.** to the same extent; in addition: *I am studying full-time this year, as well as working on the weekends.*

well² [wel] *noun, plural* **wells. 1.** a deep hole or shaft that is made to get water, oil, or natural gas from the ground: *an oil well.* **2.** a spring or natural source of water. **3.** something that is shaped like a well or is used like a well: *Before you add the milk, you have to make a well in the flour; My grandmother is a well of information about life during the 1950s.*

we'll [weel] the shortened form of "we will" or "we shall."

well- a prefix that means thoroughly or properly: *well-trained* means thoroughly trained; *well-built* means properly built.

well-bal·anced [wel-bal-unst] *adjective.* properly or evenly balanced: *A well-balanced diet is essential for good health.*

well-be·haved [wel-bee-hayvd] *adjective.* behaving in a calm way; having good manners: *Your dog is so well-behaved, you must have trained it well.*

well-be·ing [wel-bee-ing] *noun.* a feeling of being healthy, happy, and doing well: *A hospital's main concern is the well-being of its patients.*

well-known [wel-nohne] *adjective.* known by or to a lot of people; fully understood: *The audience joined in singing the words of many well-known songs.*

well-mean·ing [wel-meen-ing] *adjective.* trying to be helpful or useful but not succeeding: *I know your advice was well-meaning, but it didn't turn out to be very helpful.*

well-off [wel-of *or* wel-awf] *adjective.* having enough money to live comfortably; having as much of something as you need: *Her family is quite well-off, but they are not millionaires.*

well-to-do [wel-tuh-doo] *adjective.* having a good income, or more than enough money to live comfortably.

Welsh [welsh] *noun.* **1.** the people of Wales, which is part of the United Kingdom. **2.** the original language of the Welsh. It is still spoken, but English is now more common in Wales.
adjective. relating to Wales, its people, or their culture.

went [went] *verb.* the past tense of GO.

wept [wept] *verb.* the past tense and past participle of WEEP.

were [wur] *verb.* the past tense of BE.

we're [weer] the shortened form of "we are."

weren't [wurnt *or* wur-unt] the shortened form of "were not."

west [west] *noun.* one of the four main points of the compass. It lies opposite east and is the direction you face to watch the sun set in the evening. The part of an area, region, or country in this direction is **West**. The region of the United States west of the Mississippi River is **the West**.
adjective. situated toward, near, or facing or coming from the west: *Sandra went into the building by the west entrance.*
adverb. to, toward, or in the west: *The road headed west across the Rocky Mountains.*

west·ern [wes-turn] *adjective.* **1.** in, going toward, or facing the west: *The hill's western slope gets the afternoon sun.* **2.** coming from the west: *A western wind was blowing.* Something of or relating to the area of the United States west of the Mississippi River, or to countries in the western part of the world, is said to be **Western.**
noun, plural **westerns.** a story about frontier life in the western United States, especially a book or film.

The **western** is a familiar type of movie that is based in some way on life in the American West in the mid to late 1800s. Westerns tell stories about subjects such as sheriffs battling outlaws, cowboys herding cattle, soldiers fighting Indians, or wagon trains moving West. This was not a very long period in American history, but it is thought of as a very colorful, exciting, and important one. Interestingly, there is no such thing as an "Eastern" movie, although there have been a number of films about wars, Indian fighting, and the like in the Eastern part of America during the early days of the country, such as *The Last of the Mohicans* or *The Patriot.*

west·ern·er [wes-tur-nur] *noun, plural* **westerners.** a person who originates from or lives in the western part of a country or of the world. A person from or living in the western part of the United States is called a **Westerner.**

Western Hemisphere *Geography.* the section of the Earth that includes the Americas and nearby islands such as Greenland and the West Indies.

west·ward [west-wurd] *adverb; adjective.* to or toward the west: *Columbus sailed westward in hope of discovering new lands.*

wet [wet] *adjective,* **wetter, wettest. 1.** damp, covered, or soaked with water or some other liquid: *The grass was wet with dew.* **2.** yet to set firm or dry: *Don't sit on that chair because the paint is still wet.* **3.** having rain; rainy: *It has been a wet month so far.*
verb, **wet** or **wetted, wetting.** to make or cause to become wet: *The rain wet all the clothes on the washing line.*
—**wetness,** *noun.*

Everglades National Park, seen here from above, is a vast area of **wetlands** *in Florida.*

Humpback **whales** *communicate using complex sounds, which they "sing" in a special order for up to fifteen minutes before starting the sequence again.*

wet·land ▼ [wet-*land* or wet-lund] *noun, plural* **wetlands.** *Environment.* a low-lying area of land filled or partly filled with water some or all of the time; also called a marsh or swamp. Such regions have features of both land and aquatic environments and are known as **wetlands.**

we've [weev] the shortened form of "we have."

whack [wak] *noun, plural* **whacks. 1.** a hard, sudden blow: *She gave the tent peg a whack with the hammer.* **2.** in informal usage, an attempt; a try: *He took a whack at fixing his bike himself.*
verb, **whacked, whacking.** to strike with a hard, sudden blow: *The batter whacked the ball.*
• **out of whack.** not working correctly: *The computer monitor is out of whack and has to be repaired.*

whale ▲ [wale] *noun, plural* **whales.** any of various species of water animal that are mammals with a long fishlike body, flippers, a horizontal tail, and one or two blowholes. Whales live in fresh or salt water. **Baleen whales** feed by taking in plankton from the ocean while **toothed whales** catch larger prey such as fish.

The word **whale** comes from a term meaning "great fish" or "large sea fish." A whale is a mammal, but in early times the idea of mammals as a certain type of animal was not known. It was thought that all animals living in the sea could be called fish. Now we know that most of them are fish, but not all.

whal·er [way-lur] *noun, plural* **whalers. 1.** a ship used to hunt whales. **2.** a person whose job is to hunt whales or to process their carcasses.

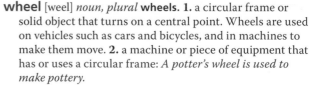
At **wharves,** cranes are often used to unload heavy cargo from ships.

whal·ing [way-ling] *noun.* the act of hunting and killing whales.

wharf ▶ [worf] *noun, plural* **wharves** *or* **wharfs.** a structure built on a shore, projecting out into the water, where ships can dock to load and unload goods or passengers.

what [wut *or* wot] *pronoun.* **1.** used to ask questions about people or things: *What is your name?* **2.** the thing which: *Tell me what you did at school today.* **3.** whatever thing that: *You decide what you want for dinner tonight.*
adjective. **1.** which one or ones of many: *What book are you going to read for your report?* **2.** whatever: *Take what food you need for your trip.* **3.** how surprising, unusual, and so on: *What luck that we should meet like this.*
adverb. how much: *What does it really matter how late for school we are?*
interjection. used to express a strong or sudden feeling such as surprise, anger, or disbelief: *What! When did that happen?*

what·ev·er [wut-ev-ur *or* wot-ev-ur] *pronoun.* **1.** anything that: *The students are allowed to do whatever they like during recess.* **2.** no matter what: *Whatever the cost, I have to buy a new dress for the dance.*
adjective. **1.** in any amount: *Ask whatever questions you need to before the exam starts.* **2.** of any kind: *No food whatever is allowed to be eaten in the classroom.*

what's [wuts *or* wots] the shortened form of "what is" or "what has."

what·so·ev·er [wut-soh-ev-ur *or* wot-soh-ev-ur] *adverb.* used to add emphasis to a negative phrase or statement: *I have no interest whatsoever in seeing that movie.*

wheat ▼ [weet] *noun.* the grain of a cereal grass that is used for making flour. Wheat is used in many foods such as bread, cakes, and pasta.

The word **wheat** comes from a term meaning "white" or "the white plant." This comes from the fact that the plant has white seeds and that it can be made into flour that is pure white in color.

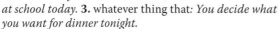

wheat germ the central part of a grain of wheat, often added to foods because it is a good source of vitamins and protein.

Wheat is grown all over the world and is the most important grain food for humans.

wheel [weel] *noun, plural* **wheels.** **1.** a circular frame or solid object that turns on a central point. Wheels are used on vehicles such as cars and bicycles, and in machines to make them move. **2.** a machine or piece of equipment that has or uses a circular frame: *A potter's wheel is used to make pottery.*
verb, **wheeled, wheeling.** **1.** to move or carry on wheels: *The patient was wheeled back to his room after his operation.* **2.** to turn quickly as if on wheels: *The outfielder wheeled around and raced back to the fence to catch a long fly ball.*

wheel·bar·row ▼ [weel-ba-roh] *noun, plural* **wheelbarrows.** an open cart supported at the front end with one or two wheels and with two handles at the back for pushing. Wheelbarrows are used outdoors for moving things.

wheel·chair [weel-chair] *noun, plural* **wheelchairs.** a chair with wheels used to move around by people who cannot walk.

*A **wheelbarrow** is a useful piece of gardening equipment for carrying soil and other items.*

wheeze [weez] *verb,* **wheezed, wheezing.** to breathe with difficulty, making a hoarse, whistling sound: *Dad's chest infection had him wheezing and coughing for weeks.*

whelk ▼ [welk] *noun, plural* **whelks.** a soft and edible sea animal with a hard spiral shell. A whelk looks like a snail.

when [wen] *adverb.* at what time; during which time: *When does the movie start?*
conjunction. **1.** at or during the time that: *I fell over when I was walking home from school today.* **2.** in the event that; whenever: *When I get sick, Mom stays home from work to take care of me.* **3.** after which; and then: *I had just started my homework when the phone rang.* **4.** considering the fact that: *How can you say you don't like boiled cabbage when you've never tried it?*

whence [wens] *adverb; conjunction.* an older word meaning from what source or place; from where: *From whence come all these questions?*

when·ev·er [wen-ev-ur] *conjunction.* any or every time that: *I always think of him whenever I hear that song.*

where [ware] *adverb.* in, at, or to what place: *Where did you buy that shirt?*
conjunction. **1.** in or at the place which: *The gardener planted the tomatoes where they would get the most sun.* **2.** in or at which place: *Stay where you are and I'll come and pick you up.*

where·a·bouts [wair-uh-bouts] *noun.* the location of a person or thing: *The police don't yet know the exact whereabouts of the escaped criminal.*
adverb. in what place; where.

*Mud **whelks** are found in estuaries and among the roots of mangroves in eastern Australia.*

where·as [ware-<u>az</u>] *conjunction.* while on the other hand; but: *Matt is stingy with his money, whereas Tom is always generous with his.*

where·in [ware-<u>in</u>] *adverb; conjunction.* **1.** in what way. **2.** in which.

where·up·on [ware-uh-<u>pon</u>] *conjunction.* at or immediately after which: *I slipped over and broke my wrist, whereupon I was sent to the hospital for treatment.*

wher·ev·er [ware-<u>ev</u>-ur] *adverb.* where: *Wherever did you get that strange hat?*
conjunction. at, in, or to whatever place or situation: *He seems to make friends wherever he goes.*

wheth·er [<u>weth</u>-ur] *conjunction.* **1.** a word used to introduce a choice between two or more possibilities: *I don't know whether to take the dog for a walk or just relax and watch television.* **2.** if: *I wasn't sure whether I would like that book, but it was really good.*

The words **whether** and *if* and can both be used to show a condition or choice that depends on something else. "Scientists do not know yet *whether* these were the bones of a fish or a mammal." This could also be written as, "Scientists do not know yet *if* these were the bones of a fish or a mammal." In serious writing, *whether* is generally preferred to *if* in sentences like this. That is especially true when there is an "or not" kind of choice. "There is not enough evidence yet to know *whether* (not *if*) the vaccine will be effective or not."

whey [way] *noun.* the watery part of milk that is separated from the curd after the milk has soured or thickened during the cheese-making process.

which [wich] *pronoun.* **1.** what one: *You play both soccer and tennis—which do you like better?* **2.** used to refer to something that you have already mentioned: *Unfortunately, that great restaurant, which only opened last year, is closing for good at the end of the month.*
adjective. what particular one or ones: *Which pair of earrings go best with my outfit?*

The words **which** and *that* can both be used to set off a part of a sentence. "This is the road *that* goes to the lake." "This road, *which* was built in the 1930s, is the only way to get to the lake." In the first example, the sentence does not make sense without the "that" part; "this is the road" is not enough by itself. In the second, the sentence could stand on its own without the "which" part: "This road is the only way to get to the lake." In other words, you use *that* when the sentence would not be complete without this part, and *which* when it could be.

which·ev·er [wich-<u>ev</u>-ur] *pronoun.* **1.** any one or ones out of a group: *Choose whichever dress you prefer— I think both of them are very pretty.* **2.** no matter which: *Whichever you decide on is fine with me.*
adjective. **1.** any one or ones out of a group: *You can choose whichever magazine you like—I've finished reading all of them.* **2.** no matter which: *Whichever route you take now, we're still going to be late.*

whiff [wif] *noun, plural* **whiffs.** a slight puff, gust of air, or smell: *There was a whiff of fresh air when she opened up the front door.*

while [wile] *noun.* a particular length of time: *I had to wait a long while for the bus.*
conjunction. **1.** during the time that: *He dropped by unexpectedly while we were having dinner.* **2.** despite the fact that; even though: *While she appreciated the man asking, the old lady did not want any help carrying her shopping bags.* **3.** on the other hand; but: *I wanted to stay longer, while she thought we should leave.*
verb, **whiled, whiling.** to pass time in a relaxing way: *We whiled away the weekend at the beach.*

whim [wim] *noun, plural* **whims.** a sudden idea or desire to do something: *We booked a holiday to Hawaii on a whim.*

whim·per [<u>wim</u>-pur] *verb,* **whimpered, whimpering.** to cry weakly in low, broken sounds: *The dog always whimpers when there's a thunderstorm.*
noun, plural **whimpers.** a weak crying sound.

whim·si·cal [<u>wim</u>-suh-kul] *adjective.* odd or unusual in an amusing way: *My grandfather is always telling us whimsical tales of when he was young.* An odd or fanciful idea is a **whimsy.**

whine [wine] *verb,* **whined, whining.** to complain or express dissatisfaction by making a high-pitched, crying sound: *The little boy whined because he wasn't allowed to have an ice cream.*
noun. a high-pitched, crying sound: *The dog wanted to get in and I could hear his whines outside the door.* Someone who complains by making a constant crying sound is described as **whiny.**

whin·ny [<u>win</u>-ee] *noun, plural* **whinnies.** a low, gentle sound such as a horse makes.
verb, **whinnied, whinnying.** to make this sound.

whip ◀ [wip] *verb,* **whipped, whipping. 1.** to hit a person or animal with a strap or rod: *The rider whipped the horse to make him go faster.* **2.** to beat food such as eggs or cream with light, quick strokes until thick and fluffy: *Mom whipped the cream to put on the strawberries for dessert.* **3.** to move or remove something quickly: *She whipped out the camera just in time to take a photo of the dolphin jumping out of the water.*
noun, plural **whips.** a piece of leather or rope attached to a handle, used to strike people or animals.

The cat-o'-nine tails was a **whip** *with nine thongs that was once used to punish seamen as well as some prisoners in penal settlements.*

whip·lash [<u>wip</u>-lash] *noun. Health.* an injury to the neck caused by sudden movement either forward or backward: *The driver suffered whiplash and some cuts and bruises after his car was hit from behind.*

whipped cream cream that has been beaten until it is thick and fluffy.

whip·poor·will [<u>wip</u>-ur-<u>wil</u>] *noun, plural* **whippoorwills.** a nocturnal North American bird that nests on the ground and has gray, black, and brown plumage. The whippoorwill has a loud repeated call that sounds like its name.

*These dancers **whirl** continuously in a traditional dance originally performed in Turkey by members of a religious group.*

A
B
C
D
E
F
G
H
I
J
K
L
M
N
O
P
Q
R
S
T
U
V
W
X
Y

whir [wur] *verb,* **whirred, whirring.** to move or fly with a low, continuous buzzing sound: *I fell asleep listening to the whirring of the ceiling fans above my head.* *noun, plural* **whirs.** a soft, low, continuous buzzing sound.

whirl ▲ [wurl] *verb,* **whirled, whirling.** to turn or spin around rapidly: *She whirled around to see who had called out her name.* *noun, plural* **whirls.** **1.** a spinning movement: *There was a whirl of dust left behind as the car took off.* **2.** a state of dizziness or confusion: *His head was in a whirl after twenty hours on the plane and no sleep.* • **give it a whirl.** to try something; make an effort or attempt: *She had never done water skiing before, so she decided to give it a whirl with her friends this weekend.*

whirl·pool [wurl-pool] *noun, plural* **whirlpools.** a swift, circular current of water whose spiraling action can draw objects into the center of it.

whirl·wind [wurl-wind] *noun, plural* **whirlwinds.** a swift current of air that blows around in a circle with strong force. *adjective.* something that moves forcefully or quickly like a whirlwind: *It was a whirlwind romance and they were engaged to be married within six weeks after they met.*

whisk [wisk] *verb,* **whisked, whisking.** **1.** to brush or sweep lightly: *He whisked the crumbs off the table.* **2.** to take or move quickly: *The waiter whisked my plate away the second I finished my last bite.*

whisk·er ▶ [wis-kur] *noun, plural* **whiskers.** a long, stiff hair that grows on the face of an animal such as a cat or mouse. A man's beard is often referred to as his **whiskers.** • **by a whisker.** the smallest amount or space: *She lost the race by a whisker.*

whis·key [wis-kee] *noun, plural* **whiskeys.** a strong brown alcoholic drink made from grains such a barley and rye. This word is also spelled **whisky.**

whis·per [wis-pur] *verb,* **whispered, whispering.** to speak very softly with your breath: *They whispered quietly so that they wouldn't wake the baby.* *noun, plural* **whispers.** a way of speaking softly using your breath rather than your voice.

whis·tle [wis-ul] *verb,* **whistled, whistling.** **1.** to make a shrill, sharp noise by forcing your breath out of a small opening formed between your teeth and rounded lips. **2.** to make a similar sound: *The referee whistled for the players to stop for halftime.* *noun, plural* **whistles.** **1.** a device that makes a high, sharp sound when it is held to the lips and air is blown through it: *The police officer used his whistle to help direct traffic.* **2.** any device that makes a similar sound: *a train whistle.* **3.** a shrill, sharp sound.

white [wite] *adjective,* **whiter, whitest.** **1.** having the lightest of colors such as that of milk or snow. **2.** also, **White.** having to do with the group of people having lighter-colored skin. **3.** lighter in color than others of the same type: *white hair; the white meat of a chicken; Riesling is a type of white wine.* *noun, plural* **whites.** **1.** the lightest of all colors, the color of milk and snow. **2.** also, **White.** a person of the group having lighter-colored skin. **3.** something that is lighter in color than another or others of its type: *It was very dark but I could still see the whites of his eyes.* —**whiteness,** *noun.*

white blood cell *Medicine.* a colorless cell in the blood whose function is to help the body fight infections and repair injuries to tissues.

white-collar *adjective. Business.* relating to jobs or occupations that do not involve manual labor or the wearing of special work clothes or protective garments. Professional people, such as lawyers, and most people who work in a business office have white-collar jobs.

> The term **white-collar** comes from the fact that at one time a man who worked in a business office would be expected to wear a dress shirt with a white collar. Today a person in an office might wear a dress shirt that is white, colored, striped, or any of various other designs, or even wear a sport or casual shirt rather than a dress shirt..

White House ▲ *Government.* **1.** the official residence, in Washington D.C., of the President of the United States. **2.** the President and other people who work in the Executive branch: *The White House is expected to make some response to the Senator's remarks.*

whit·en [wite-un] *verb,* **whitened, whitening.** to make or to become white or whiter.

white noise a noise that is created electronically and that covers a wide range of sound frequencies. White noise is sometimes used as a way to block or muffle other noises that are harsh or unpleasant.

white·wash [wite-wahsh *or* wite-wosh] *noun, plural* **whitewashes.** **1.** a thin kind of paint, made of lime and water, that is used to whiten walls and other surfaces. **2.** a report or a description that covers up or ignores faults or errors: *The report on the accident was a complete whitewash that found no one was to blame.* *verb,* **whitewashed, whitewashing.** **1.** to whiten a surface by using whitewash. **2.** to make a report or description that covers up or ignores faults or mistakes.

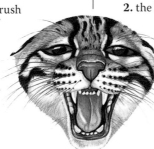

*Like all cats, this margay has very sensitive **whiskers** that help it feel its way around in the dark.*

In November 1800, John Adams was the first President to occupy the **White House.**

whit·tle [wit-ul] *verb,* **whittled, whittling.** to shave or cut a piece of wood or other substance with a knife: *Merry whittled a tiny boat from the fallen branch.* —**whittler,** *noun.*

whiz [wiz] *verb,* **whizzed, whizzing.** to move swiftly with a hissing or buzzing sound: *The windows shook as the jet airplane whizzed by overhead.*
noun, plural **whizzes.** a person who is clever or skilled at doing something: *Maggie is a real whiz at math.*

who [hoo] *pronoun.* **1.** what person or persons: *Do you know who wrote that book?* **2.** that or which, when referring to a person or persons: *Justin, who lives next door, is ten years old.*

whoa [woh] *interjection.* a command, often to an animal, to stop or to slow down: *"Whoa there!" the man called to his excited horse.*

who'd [hood] the shortened form of "who would" or "who had."

who·ev·er [hoo-ev-ur] *pronoun.* any person who; whatever person or persons: *Whoever built this did a great job; Whoever would say such a thing?*

whole [hole] *adjective.* with nothing missing; complete: *Seven days make up a whole week; I've told you the whole story of what happened.*
noun. all parts of; everything: *We spent the whole of our vacation in Florida.*
• **on the whole/as a whole.** all things considered; generally: *On the whole, we enjoyed our vacation; As a whole, our class is good at spelling.*
🔊 A different word with the same sound is **hole.**

whole number *Mathematics.* a number that is not a fraction, or a number and a fraction.

whole·sale [hole-sale] *noun. Business.* the sale of large quantities of goods to stores or other organizations, which then sell them to the public: *This company buys fruit from farmers and then sells it as wholesale to supermarkets.*
adjective. relating to selling in large quantities: *a wholesale fruit merchant.* A person who sells wholesale goods is a **wholesaler.**

whole·some [hole-sum] *adjective.* **1.** promoting health; good for the health: *Fruits and vegetables are wholesome foods.* **2.** describing something good for the mind or character; worthwhile: *She writes wholesome, inspiring books for children.* —**wholesomeness,** *noun.*

whole-wheat [hole-weet] *adjective.* describing bread or flour made using the whole of the ground wheat kernel.

who'll [hool] the shortened form of "who will."

whol·ly [hoh-lee] *adverb.* in every way; completely: *I am wholly convinced that what you say is true.*
🔊 A different word with the same sound is **holy.**

whom [hoom] *pronoun.* **1.** which person or persons: *Whom do you wish to see?* **2.** that or which, when referring to a person or persons: *The girl to whom you lent the book brought it back this morning.*

whom·ev·er [hoom-ev-ur] *pronoun.* any person that; no matter whom: *I'm sure I will like whomever you invite to the party.*

whoop [woop *or* hoop] *noun, plural* **whoops.** an excited cry or yell: *The winner gave a loud whoop as she finished the race; a whoop of delight.*
verb, **whooped, whooping.** to cry out or yell with pleasure or excitement.

whoop·ing cough *Health.* a dangerous contagious illness, often suffered by children and babies, that causes fits of coughing and difficulty in drawing breath.

whooping crane ▼ a large North American water bird that is now almost extinct. It is white with black tips on its wings.

who's [hooz] the shortened form of "who is."

whose [hooz] *adjective; pronoun.* belonging or relating to whom or which: *Whose pen is this? Whose did you say it was?*

Whose and *who's* sound the same, and so they may be confused in writing. *Whose* is a pronoun that is the possessive form of *who:* "*Whose* car is that parked by the mailbox?" "Look at the name tag to see *whose* jacket it is." *Who's* is the shorter form of the words *who is* or *who has:* "*Who's* that on the phone?" "*Who's* been eating all the cookies?"

why [wye] *adverb; conjunction.* for what reason; for what cause: *Why is the dog barking so loudly? I wonder why Mark tried to call me this morning.*
interjection. an expression that indicates surprise, pleasure, curiosity, or some other kind of emotion: *Why, what a lovely surprise!*

Whooping cranes *perform a courtship "dance"by jumping into the air and gracefully floating down.*

a
b
c
d
e
f
g
h
i
j
k
l
m
n
o
p
q
r
s
t
u
v
w
x
y
z

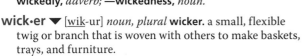

wick [wik] *noun, plural* **wicks.** a piece of cord or twisted thread that, when it is set on fire, draws up fuel to be burned, such as oil in lamps or tallow in candles.

wick·ed [wik-id] *adjective.* **1.** describing someone or something evil; villainous: *Robbery and murder are wicked crimes.* **2.** painful or unpleasant to deal with: *That pitcher has a wicked curve ball.* **3.** mischievous; naughty: *The wicked child refused to drink her milk.* **wickedly,** *adverb;* —**wickedness,** *noun.*

wick·er ▼ [wik-ur] *noun, plural* **wicker.** a small, flexible twig or branch that is woven with others to make baskets, trays, and furniture. *adjective.* made of such material: *a wicker chair.*

wide [wide] *adjective,* **wider, widest. 1.** having a large distance between one side and the other: *The Hudson River is very wide.* **2.** having a particular distance between one side and the other: *The football field is 53 yards wide.* **3.** describing something extensive; broad: *Susan has a wide range of interests and reads all kinds of books.* **4.** far away from an object or target: *His shot was wide of the goal.* *adverb,* **wider, widest.** to a great degree; fully: *The dentist asked me to open my mouth wide; The front door was left wide open.* • **far and wide.** covering a very large area or distance: *We traveled far and wide across America during our vacation.* —**widely,** *adverb;* —**wideness,** *noun.*

wid·en [wide-un] *verb,* **widened widening.** to make wider or become wider: *The workers are widening the road to add two new lanes.*

wide·spread [wide-spred] *adjective.* **1.** spread or happening over a large area: *The drought was very widespread throughout the country.* **2.** happening to or involving many people: *There is a widespread belief in town that the mayor will resign soon.*

Wicker has been used to make baskets since ancient times.

wid·ow [wid-oh] *noun, plural* **widows.** a woman whose husband has died and who has not married again.

wid·ow·er [wid-oh-ur] *noun, plural* **widowers.** a man whose wife has died and who has not married again.

width [width] *noun, plural* **widths.** the extent or distance between the two sides of something; breadth: *The width of this doorway is forty inches.*

wife [wife] *noun, plural* **wives.** a woman who is married.

wig [wig] *noun, plural* **wigs.** something that resembles hair and is worn on the head. Wigs can be made of real or false hair.

wig·gle [wig-ul] *verb,* **wiggled, wiggling.** to twist from side to side in small, jerking movements; wriggle: *The puppy wiggled its way through the small hole in the fence.* *noun, plural* **wiggles.** a small, jerking movement from side to side.

wig·wam ◀ [wig-wahm] *noun, plural* **wigwams.** *History.* a hut used by some Native Americans that consisted of poles covered with skins, bark, or reed mats.

wild [wilde] *adjective,* **wilder, wildest. 1.** of an animal or plant, not under human control; living in nature: *There are tigers, elephants, and other wild animals in Asian forests.* Wild, natural places, such as jungles, are sometimes called **the wild** or **wilds. 2.** out of control; not disciplined: *There was a wild, noisy party last night in our neighbor's house.* **3.** very strong; violent: *A wild wind sprang up during the night.* **4.** not realistic; silly: *Joanna has some wild idea of making a movie about our town.* *adverb.* not controlled; naturally: *Zebra run wild on the African plains.* —**wildly,** *adverb;* —**wildness,** *noun.*

wild·cat ▶ [wilde-kat] *noun, plural* **wildcats. 1.** a small cat, larger than a domestic cat, that lives in the wild. Lynxes and ocelots are both wildcats. **2.** a well that is drilled in a risky or uncertain place in the hope of finding oil or gas. A person who does this is a **wildcatter.**

*The **wildcats** of Europe, Asia, and Africa look very much like larger versions of the domestic tabby cat.*

wil·der·ness [wil-dur-nis] *noun, plural* **wildernesses.** a region, such as a forest, jungle, desert, or coastal area, where humans do not live and where wild animals and plants live and grow naturally.

wild·fire [wilde-fire] *noun, plural* **wildfires. 1.** a fire that burns out of control in a wilderness area. **2.** any fire that is very difficult to control or to extinguish. • **like wildfire.** out of control; with great speed: *The outbreak of flu spread like wildfire through the community.*

wild·flow·er ▼ [wilde-flou-ur] *noun, plural* **wildflowers.** a flower of a plant that grows wild in its natural environment: *a carpet of wildflowers.*

*The French Alps are famous for their beautiful **wildflowers.***

wild·life [wilde-*life*] *noun.* animals and plants that live and grow wild in their natural environment.

will[1] [wil] *verb.* a special verb that is often used with other verbs to: **1.** express future actions: *The shops will be open until nine tonight.* **2.** express intentions: *I have to go out, but I will be back about six o'clock.* **3.** say that something must be done: *ou will finish your chores before you leave.* **4.** show ability: *The printer will not work unless you replace the ink cartridges.*

will[2] [wil] *noun, plural* **wills. 1.** strength of mind; ability to act decisively: *A good leader needs to be a person with a strong will.* **2.** a strong need; determination: *The will to survive helped the lost explorers to find their way.* **3.** *Law.* a document in which a person states what should happen to their property after they die.
verb, **willed, willing. 1.** to use one's strength of mind; to force oneself to act decisively: *The tired climber willed himself to reach the top of the mountain.* **2.** *Law.* to give by means of a will: *The old man willed all his property to his son.*

will·ful [wil-ful] *adjective.* **1.** describing something intended; deliberate. **2.** wanting to get one's way; stubborn: *The willful child refused to eat his dinner.* **—willfully,** *adverb.*

will·ing [wil-ing] *adjective.* agreeing or ready to do something: *He said he's willing to help us; There are plenty of willing players for the chess tournament.* **—willingly,** *adverb;* **—willingness,** *noun.*

wil·low [wil-oh] *noun, plural* **willows.** a tree or bush with tough but flexible branches that are used to make baskets. Willows grow in wet areas such as river banks.

will·pow·er [wil-*pow*-ur] *noun.* the state of having determination and control of mind; a strong will: *It took a lot of willpower for her to stay on her diet.*

wilt [wilt] *verb,* **wilted, wilting.** to droop or loose stiffness: *The flowers wilted in the sun.*

wimp [wimp] *noun, plural* **wimps.** an informal word for a timid or weak person: *They called me a wimp because I wouldn't jump in the icy water.* **—wimpy,** *adjective.*

win [win] *verb,* **won, winning. 1.** to come in first, or beat an opponent in a race or contest: *The fastest runner won the race.* **2.** to receive as a prize: *I won ten dollars in the lottery.* **3.** to gain or achieve: *He won lots of praise for his piano playing.*
noun, plural **wins.** a success or victory: *The club had their first win for the season.*

wince [wins] *verb,* **winced, wincing.** to flinch or pull back suddenly because of pain or a blow: *She winced when she pricked her finger with the needle.*

winch [winch] *noun, plural* **winches.** a machine for pulling or lifting. It is made from a cable wound around a pulley that is turned by a crank or motor. The anchor of a large ship is usually lifted by a winch.

WIND

When the sun heats the land and the air above it, the warm air rises and a low-pressure area, or low, is formed near the ground. Cooler air is drawn in to replace the rising air. When the rising air cools, it begins to sink and an area of high pressure is formed some distance away from the low. Air then moves from the high to the low pressure, and we call this movement wind.

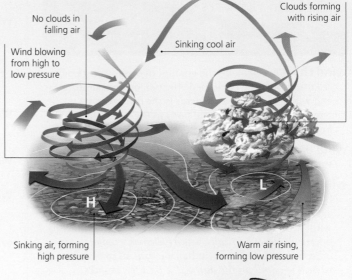

No clouds in falling air

Wind blowing from high to low pressure

Clouds forming with rising air

Sinking cool air

Sinking air, forming high pressure

Warm air rising, forming low pressure

WINDS OF THE WORLD
Air rises at the equator and sinks to the surface at about thirty degrees north and south. From there, some air flows back toward the equator at ground level, completing a circular pattern called a cell. The movement of air at ground level within these cells creates the world's major wind patterns.

Jet stream | Cell

Doldrums, or windless area

Trade winds

Westerlies

Polar easterlies

wind[1] ▲ [wind] *noun, plural* **winds. 1.** air that is moving rapidly over or above the surface of the earth: *The wind blew sand in our faces.* **2.** the fact of having breath: *She can't run because she's short of wind.* **3.** see WIND INSTRUMENT.
verb, **winded, winding.** to cause someone to be unable to breathe: *The kick in the stomach winded him.*

wind[2] [wynde] *verb,* **wound, winding. 1.** to wrap something long, like a rope or cord, around a center or an object: *Wind the rope around the post.* **2.** to move back and forth across something: *The road winds up the side of the mountain.* **3.** to tighten the spring of: *The old clock stopped ticking because we forgot to wind it.*
• **wind up. 1.** to end or finish: *They plan to wind up the meeting before dinner.* **2.** to end up in a certain place or situation: *We wound up having dinner at my grandmother's house.* **3.** in baseball, to move the arms and body before throwing a pitch.

wind·brea·ker [wind-*bray*-kur] *noun, plural* **windbreakers.** a short, light jacket with close fitting, often elastic, cuffs and waistband.

*A **wind farm** near Palm Springs, California, converts wind energy into electricity.*

wind chill *Environment.* the amount of cooling on a body resulting from the combined effect of low temperature and wind. The **wind chill factor** is the difference in temperature between a cold body in the wind and a cold body out of the wind.

wind energy *Science.* energy from machines, such as turbine engines and windmills, that are powered by wind.

wind·fall [wind-*fawl*] *noun, plural* **windfalls. 1.** something blown down by the wind, such as fruit that has fallen from a tree. **2.** money or other good fortune that was received without being expected, and in some cases, without being deserved: *Her inheritance was a welcome windfall. adjective.* received as a windfall: *Several oil companies earned windfall profits during the past few months.*

wind farm ▲ *Science.* a power plant that generates electricity using windmills or wind turbines.

wind·ing [wynde-ing] *adjective.* describing something that turns back and forth: *a winding road.*

wind instrument *Music.* a musical instrument, such as a trumpet, recorder, or clarinet, that you blow air into to play. The sound is produced because the moving air makes the reeds vibrate inside the enclosed column.

wind·mill ▶ [wind-*mil*] *noun, plural* **windmills.** a tower with vanes or sails at the top. The vanes or sails are turned around by the wind. This movement is used to provide energy to do something, such as to pump water or generate electricity, or, in the past, to grind grain.

win·dow [win-doh] *noun, plural* **windows.**
1. an opening in a building that allows light and air to enter. Windows usually have panes of glass in them.
2. *Computers.* a small section of a computer screen that displays a certain file.

> The word **window** comes from an old phrase "eye of the wind." The idea was that a window, an opening in the wall of a house, was like an eye opening to let in the wind from outside.

win·dow·pane [win-doh-*pane*] *noun, plural* **windowpanes.** a piece of glass that fills a window or a section of a window.

window-shop [win-doh-*shop*] *verb,* **window-shopped, window-shopping.** to look at things for sale without intending to buy anything: *My sisters love to go window-shopping in expensive jewelry stores.* Someone who window-shops is called a **window-shopper.**

win·dow·sill [win-doh-*sil*] *noun, plural* **windowsills.** the bottom part of a window frame, made from a horizontal piece of wood, stone, or other material.

wind·pipe [wind-*pipe*] *noun, plural* **windpipes.** the tube that allows air to pass from the throat to the lungs.

wind shear *Environment.* a sudden change in wind direction or speed over a short distance. A sudden down draft is an example of wind shear.

wind·shield [wind-*sheeld*] *noun, plural* **windshields.** the clear screen at the front of a car, truck, or other vehicle that protects the driver and passengers from wind. Windshields are made from glass or plastic. A **windshield wiper** keeps the view clear when it is raining by wiping the water away.

wind·sur·fing [wind-*surf*-ing] *noun.* a sport where someone stands on a sailboard and steers it by moving the sail. —**windsurf**, *verb.*

wind·swept [wind-*swept*] *adjective.* describing somewhere windy: *a rocky, windswept beach.*

wind turbine *Science.* a machine that is turned by the wind and uses the turning movement to generate electricity. Wind turbines power wind farms.

wind·up [wynde-up] *noun* **1.** the act of bringing something to an end: *The chairman's speech will serve as the conference windup.* **2.** in baseball, the act of swinging back the arms and raising the leg before throwing a pitch. *adjective.* describing something operated by a winding mechanism: *a windup toy.*

wind·y [win-dee] *adjective,* **windier, windiest. 1.** describing a place or period of time with strong winds: *It was such a windy day that her umbrella blew away.* **2.** describing a lot of empty talk: *He gave a boring, windy speech and finally sat down.* —**windiness**, *noun.*

wine [wine] *noun, plural* **wines. 1.** the juice of grapes that has been fermented into an alcoholic drink. **2.** a similar drink made from other fruits.

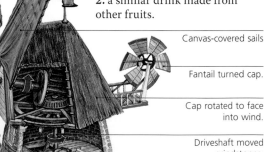

Canvas-covered sails

Fantail turned cap.

Cap rotated to face into wind.

Driveshaft moved grindstones.

Grindstones

*This kind of **windmill** was used many years ago to grind grain.*

The **wingspan** of a gray-headed albatross can be up to ten feet.

wireless

wing ▼ [wing] *noun, plural* **wings. 1.** a part of the body that is used to fly. Birds, bats, and insects have wings. **2.** something that extends out of the side of an airplane, in the manner of a bird's wing. Wings help the airplane lift off the ground and fly. **3.** something that extends out from the main structure: *They built a new wing on the hospital; the chemistry wing.* **4.** either side of a stage that is not seen by the audience: *She made her entrance from the wings.* **5.** a position on the edge of the field in hockey, soccer, and some other sports: *He passed the ball to the wing.* The players who play in such a position are called **wings** or **wingers.**
verb, **winged, winging.** to fly: *The plane winged its way home.*

winged [wingd] *adjective.* having wings: *Airplanes are winged machines.*

wing·span ▶ [wing-span] *noun, plural* **wingspans.** the widest distance between the tip of one wing and the tip of another wing of a bird, bat, insect, or airplane: *The wingspan of the bat was about two feet.* A different word with the same meaning is **wingspread.**

wink [wingk] *verb,* **winked, winking.** to quickly shut and open one eyelid. People signal each other with a wink: *Dad winked at me across the crowded room.*
noun, plural **winks. 1.** the act of winking. **2.** a short period of time. **3.** a short sleep: *It was so noisy outside the hotel that I didn't sleep a wink.*

win·ner [win-ur] *noun, plural* **winners. 1.** someone or something that wins: *The winner of the contest received one hundred dollars.* **2.** someone or something that seems likely to succeed: *Mom said our idea of a garage sale was a real winner.*

win·ning [win ing] *adjective.* **1.** describing someone or something that wins or is successful: *The winning entry had a blue ribbon pinned on it.* **2.** attractive and confident: *Our captain has a winning personality.* Something that is won can be called **winnings.**

win·ter [win-tur] *noun, plural* **winters.** the coldest of the four seasons. Winter comes between autumn and spring.
verb, **wintered, wintering.** to spend the winter: *Many older people winter in Florida or Arizona, where the climate is milder.*

win·ter·green [win-tur-green] *noun, plural* **wintergreens.** an evergreen shrub with red berries and white flowers. Oil from this plant is used for flavoring and in medicines.

win·try [win-tree] *adjective,* **wintrier, wintriest.** having to do with or like winter: *It was an icy, wintry night.*

wipe [wipe] *verb,* **wiped, wiping. 1.** to rub something to clean or dry it: *You wash the dishes and I'll wipe off the table.* **2.** to remove by cleaning or drying:
noun. the act of wiping.
• **wipe out.** to ruin or destroy: *The new vaccine wiped out the disease.* —**wiper,** *noun.*

wire [wire] *noun, plural* **wires. 1.** a metal thread or bunch of metal threads. **2.** a length of such metal threads used to carry electricity. **3.** a message sent by telegraph wire; a telegram.
adjective. describing something made of wire: *a wire cage.*
verb, **wired, wiring. 1.** to install wires or attach using wires: *My brother wired new speakers to his CD player.* **2.** to send a telegram.

wir·ed [wired] *adjective.* describing something attached to wires that carry messages or signals from a source. Cable television is a form of wired communication.

wire·less [wire-lis] *adjective.* describing something that sends or receives messages or signals without using wires. Radios, cell phones, and some computers are forms of wireless communication.
noun, plural **wirelesses.** a radio.

WINGS

Birds' wings vary greatly in size and shape. Birds that fly long distances have long, thin wings, while those that move in thick brush have short, rounded wings. The shape of the wing affects the way a bird flies and determines the amount of lift and drag the wing creates as it moves through the air.

AIRFLOW
Because birds' wings are curved, air flows more quickly across the top. This creates a lower pressure above the wing and provides the lift that keeps the bird in the air.

DIFFERENT KINDS OF WINGS
A bat's wings are made of skin membrane. Birds evolved from a flying reptile called archaeopteryx. Its wings were made of feathers that were arranged in a similar way to those of a living bird, such as a pigeon.

Bat

Archaeopteryx

Pigeon

WING SHAPES
The length and width of a bird's wings affect how fast and how far it can fly.

Albatross
50 mph

Condor
35–40 mph

Swift
37–62 mph

Quail
37–57 mph

Sparrow
17 mph

Hummingbird
50–60 mph

Wisteria is a fast-growing climbing plant that can reach as high as 65 feet.

A B C D E F G H I J K L M N O P Q R S T U V **W** X Y Z

wireless computer
Computers. a computer that uses radio signals rather than cables to carry information. It can be part of a **wireless network** that uses radio signals to send and receive information between different computers.

wireless phone
a phone that uses radio signals rather than wires to send and receive messages.

wire·tap [wire-*tap*] *noun,*
plural **wire-taps.** the fact of tapping or connecting into someone else's phone line in order to listen to what he or she is saying.
verb, **wire-tapped, wire-tapping.** to tap or connect into someone else's phone line in order to listen to what he or she is saying. The act of doing this called **wiretapping.** Someone who does this is a **wiretapper.**

wir·ing [wire-ing] *noun.*
a system of wires carrying electric current: *The wiring in our house is so old that some of our power outlets don't work.*

wir·y [wye-ree] *adjective,* **wirier, wiriest. 1.** thin and stiff like wire: *That dog's hair is not soft—it is wiry.* **2.** thin but tough and strong: *A tall, wiry runner came in first in the Boston Marathon.*

wis·dom [wiz-dum] *noun.*
the quality of being wise and having the intelligence, knowledge, and understanding to judge what is right and true: *It was a sign of the judge's wisdom that she took a lot of time considering the case before pronouncing the sentence.*

wisdom tooth
in humans, the last tooth to erupt at each end of the top and bottom rows of teeth. Wisdom teeth are molars. They usually erupt between the ages of seventeen and twenty-five.

> The name **wisdom tooth** comes from the fact that these teeth move into place later in life, when a person is thought to be wiser (have more wisdom). The other permanent teeth begin to appear when a person is about six years old, but the wisdom teeth typically do not appear until age eighteen or older.

wise [wize] *adjective,* **wiser, wisest.** possessing or showing the ability to judge what is right and true: *It is wise of you not to stay up late the night before your exam.* —**wisely,** *adverb.*

wish [wish] *noun, plural* **wishes. 1.** a desire, wanting, or longing for something: *She has always had a wish to go to Paris.* **2.** the act of expressing a desire or want: *Aladdin made a wish and the genie granted it.* **3.** something wished for: *Reaching the summit of the mountain was my wish come true.*
verb, **wished, wishing. 1.** to desire, want or long for: *They wished the thunder storm would end.* **2.** to express or hold wishes for: *Grandma called and wished me luck in my softball tryout.*

wish·bone [wish-bone] *noun, plural* **wishbones.**
a Y-shaped bone just in front of the breastbone of most birds. According to tradition, after eating a turkey or some other bird, one person holds an end of the wishbone with the little finger, and another person holds the other end with their little finger. While making a wish, both pull until the bone snaps. The wish of the person left holding the longer piece of bone is supposed to come true.

wish·ful [wish-ful] *adjective.* having or showing a feeling of desiring or wanting; longing: *The woman gave the expensive dress in the store window a wishful look.* When someone believes something that is not likely will happen or is so, this is called **wishful thinking.**

wisp [wisp] *noun, plural* **wisps.** a small, thin piece of something: *A wisp of a cloud floated in the valley.* —**wispy,** *adjective.*

wis·te·ri·a ◀ [wi-steer-ee-uh] *noun.* any of several vines with woody stems and hanging clusters of pink, white, blue, or purple flowers. Wisterias are often grown against walls. They are native to Asia and the eastern United States.

wit [wit] *noun, plural* **wits. 1.** the ability to connect unusual ideas in a way that is clever and amusing: *During his speech at the wedding, the best man's wit made everyone laugh.* **2.** a person noted for saying clever, funny things: *He's fun at parties because he is such a wit.* **3. wits.** the ability to think and understand quickly and clearly; intelligence: *They kept their wits about them and found a way out of the burning building.*

witch [wich] *noun, plural* **witches.** a person who is thought to posses magical powers or who practices magic, especially a woman said to use magic for evil purposes.
A different word with the same sound is **which.**

> The word **witch** originally meant someone who had special powers like a god. This could be an actual person or a human-like spirit, and the supernatural power could be used for either good or evil. Later the word came to be used in a narrower way, to refer to a woman who was thought to use supernatural power for evil purposes. Witches were said to be working with the Devil and to do harm in such ways as casting spells on people or causing crops or farm animals to die.

witch·craft [wich-*kraft*] *noun.* the use or practice of magic; sorcery. The use of magic or its influence over something is also called **witchery.**

with [wiTH] *preposition.* **1.** in the company of; associated or connected: *She watched the TV show with her brother; They ate hot dogs with mustard.* **2.** having or showing: *a shirt with blue stripes; Handle the package with care.* **3.** by means of; using: *to cut down a tree with a saw.* **4.** because of; concerning: *He's having trouble with his car.* **5.** on the side of; supporting: *I agree we need a new computer—I'm with you on that.*

with·draw [wiTH-draw *or* with-draw] *verb,* **withdrew, withdrawn, withdrawing. 1.** to remove or take away: *He withdrew fifty dollars from his bank account.* **2.** to take back: *Criminal charges against the man were withdrawn.* **3.** to move away from or leave: *We wanted to talk and withdrew from the living room so the others could watch television in peace.*

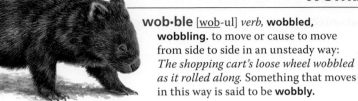

*The common **wombat** has powerful front legs and large paws for digging warrens.*

with·draw·al [WITH-drawl *or* with-drawl] *noun, plural* **withdrawals.** the act of withdrawing: *the withdrawal of money from a bank; The army made a rapid withdrawal from enemy territory.* When a person with an addiction to a drug or alcohol has that substance taken away from them, they may suffer painful and distressing physical symptoms that are called **withdrawal symptoms.**

with·drawn [WITH-drawn *or* with-drawn] *verb.* the past participle of WITHDRAW.
adjective. not sociable; shy and quiet; aloof: *She was very withdrawn and would not talk to anyone.*

with·er [with-ur] *verb,* **withered, withering.** to make or become dry and shriveled: *The tree's leaves withered in the heat.*

with·hold [WITH-hold *or* with-hold] *verb,* **withheld, withholding. 1.** to keep hold of; keep in check: *I withheld my urge to eat the whole cake and left some for you.* **2.** to refuse to give up: *The police withheld the name of the accident victim until his family had been informed.* **3.** *Business.* to keep back an amount of money from a payment, such as wages to a worker, and pay it directly to the government as taxes.

with·in [WITH-in *or* with-in] *preposition.* **1.** in or into the interior of; inside: *Her jewelry is kept within the locked safe.* **2.** inside the limits or boundaries of: *Having a budget plan will help you live within your income.*
adverb. in or into the interior of; inside: *He opened the letter and found a check within.*

with·out [WITH-out *or* with-out] *preposition.* **1.** with none of; not having; lacking: *After the storm, a thousand homes were left without electricity.* **2.** in the absence of; not accompanied by: *She was late, so they left without her.* **3.** done in a way that leaves out or of: *They drove off into the night without their headlights on.*

with·stand [WITH-stand *or* with-stand] *verb,* **withstood, withstanding.** to bear or put up with; hold out against or resist: *The seawall was able to withstand the battering of the waves.*

wit·ness [wit-nis] *noun, plural* **witnesses.** *Law.* someone who personally sees and hears something happen. A witness can give evidence in a court of law about an event: *The witness was questioned in court about the person she had seen running from the scene of the crime.*
verb, **witnessed, witnessing.** to be personally present and see or hear something occur: *We witnessed a terrible accident on the freeway.*

wit·ty [wit-ee] *adjective,* **wittier, wittiest.** amusing in a clever way; possessing or showing wit: *The comedian is well-known for his witty comments.* **—wittily,** *adverb.*

wives [wivz] *noun.* the plural of WIFE.

wiz·ard [wiz-urd] *noun, plural* **wizards. 1.** a person who practices magic or has magical powers; a sorcerer. Wizards are often shown as male. The craft of practicing magic is called **wizardry. 2.** a person who is very skilled at something: *Luis is a wizard at playing the piano.*

wob·ble [wob-ul] *verb,* **wobbled, wobbling.** to move or cause to move from side to side in an unsteady way: *The shopping cart's loose wheel wobbled as it rolled along.* Something that moves in this way is said to be **wobbly.**

woe [woh] *noun, plural* **woes.** great misery, trouble, or suffering: *The refugees faced starvation, illness, and other woes as they fled their war-torn country.*

wok [wok] *noun, plural* **woks.** a wide, round-bottomed, metal pan often used in Chinese cooking.

woke [woke] *verb.* the past tense of WAKE.

wok·en [woke-un] *verb.* a past participle of WAKE.

wolf ▼ [wulf] *noun, plural* **wolves.** any of several types of large wild animal that look like and are related to the domesticated dog. Wolves live in packs and together hunt other animals for food.

wol·ver·ine [wul-vuh-*reen*] *noun, plural* **wolverines.** a thick-set, strong animal with brown fur. They eat meat, hunting large animals such as reindeer. Wolverines belong to the weasel family and are now found only in cold northern regions such as Alaska, Canada, Russia, and Scandinavia.

> The word **wolverine** is said to come from a term meaning "the little wolf." The wolverine is actually a type of weasel, not a wolf, but the two animals were thought to be similar in the ferocious way that they would hunt and kill other animals.

wolves [wulvz] *noun.* the plural of WOLF.

wo·man [wum-un] *noun, plural* **women. 1.** an adult female human. **2.** adult female humans in general.

wo·man·hood [wum-un-*hud*] *noun.* **1.** the state or time of being an adult female human. **2.** adult females as a group.

wom·bat ▲ [wom-bat] *noun, plural* **wombats.** a short-legged, short-tailed, large grazing animal from Australia. Wombats are marsupials and keep their young in pouches that open backward so they do not fill with dirt as they dig their burrows.

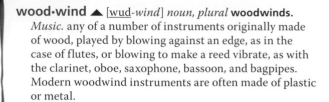

*The Native American cedar flute is a **woodwind** instrument.*

wo·men [wum-in] *noun.* the plural of WOMAN.

won [wun] *verb.* the past tense and past participle of WIN.
🔊 A different word with the same sound is **one.**

won·der [wun-dur] *noun, plural* **wonders. 1.** something unusual or surprising that causes amazement or admiration: *The Great Wall of China is a man-made wonder; It is a wonder she was not completely tired out after running a marathon.* **2.** a feeling of amazement and admiration caused by something unusual or surprising: *In 1969, millions of television viewers watched with wonder as Neil Armstrong walked on the Moon.*
verb, **wondered, wondering. 1.** to be curious or unsure of; to want to know about: *Henry wondered when the next bus would arrive.* **2.** to be amazed or surprised about: *We wondered at the brilliant fireworks display.*

won·der·ful [wun-dur-ful] *adjective.* **1.** causing amazement or wonder; remarkable: *The king had the most wonderful palace built for his queen.* **2.** very good; excellent: *May I have another of those wonderful cookies you baked?* —**wonderfully,** *adverb.*

won't [wohnt] the shortened form of "will not."

wood [wud] *noun, plural* **woods. 1.** the hard material that makes up the trunk and most of the branches of a tree or bush and is covered by bark. People burn wood for fuel and use it as a building material. **2.** an area of land where trees that have not been planted by people grow thickly. Woods are usually thought of as smaller than forests. *adjective.* being of wood or made of wood; wooden.
🔊 A different word with the same sound is **would.**

wood·chuck ▼ [wud-chuk] *noun, plural* **woodchucks.** a small, brownish or gray animal with a stout body, short legs, and a broad, flat tail. It is a type of rodent that lives in a burrow it digs in the ground, where it often hibernates during winter. This animal is also called a GROUNDHOG.

Woodchucks stand up on their hind feet to watch for danger and whistle a warning to other woodchucks.

wood·ed [wud-id] *adjective.* covered with trees or woods: *The hills above the river are heavily wooded.*

wood·en [wud-un] *adjective.* **1.** made out of wood: *Use the wooden spoon to mix the cake batter.* **2.** stiff or awkward: *The actors gave such a wooden performance that they weren't very convincing.*

wood·land [wood-land *or* wud-lund] *noun, plural* **woodlands.** *Environment.* land covered by trees: *Much of the woodland near our town has been cleared for grazing. adjective.* of or relating to woodlands: *Troy saw many woodland creatures as he hiked along the path.*

wood·peck·er ▲ [wud-pek-ur] *noun, plural* **woodpeckers.** any of a number of types of birds with strong claws for clinging to tree trunks and a sharp, strong bill with which they drill holes to reach insects and, in some cases, obtain sap. They also use their bill to chisel out nesting hollows. Woodpeckers are found worldwide.

wood·wind ▲ [wud-wind] *noun, plural* **woodwinds.** *Music.* any of a number of instruments originally made of wood, played by blowing against an edge, as in the case of flutes, or blowing to make a reed vibrate, as with the clarinet, oboe, saxophone, bassoon, and bagpipes. Modern woodwind instruments are often made of plastic or metal.

wood·work [wud-wurk] *noun.* objects or parts of objects made of wood, especially wooden parts of a house: *The woodwork around the porch needs to be repaired.* The craft or skill of working with wood is known as **woodworking.**

wood·y [wud-ee] *adjective,* **woodier, woodiest. 1.** consisting of wood: *When you are pruning the roses, use a saw to cut the thick, woody stems.* **2.** having many trees; wooded: *That bird call came from the woody slope behind the house.*

wool [wul] *noun, plural* **wools. 1.** the soft, curly hair of sheep and some other animals. Wool is spun into yarn, which is made into cloth. **2.** cloth or yarn made of wool. **3.** anything made of a thick mass of fibers: *steel wool. adjective.* made of wool: *a wool coat.* Something made of or like wool is said to be **woolly.**

Woodpeckers are skilled at dislodging insects from the bark of trees.

wool·en [wul-un] *adjective.* made of wool: *My aunt knitted me a woolen scarf for winter.*

word [wurd] *noun, plural* **words.** *Language.* **1.** a sound or a group of sounds standing for an idea, action, or object. A word is the smallest unit of language that can have meaning when spoken or written by itself. **2.** the group of letter used to write down such a sound: *The word "table" has five letters.* **3.** a short talk or speech: *The coach had a word with the team.* **4.** a promise: *I give you my word that I'll never tell your secret.* **5.** a message or piece of news: *Have you had word from the college about your application?*
verb, **worded, wording.** to express in words: *Definitions in a dictionary must be clearly worded so they can be easily understood.*
• **word for word.** using exactly the same words as the original: *Rachel repeated the news report to us word for word.*

word·ing [wur-ding] *noun, plural* **wordings.** the words and phrases used to say something: *Aaron changed the wording of his e-mail message several times before he was happy with it.*

word processing *Computers.* a system for creating, changing, storing, and printing words by means of a computer. The computer program or computer system that does this is a **word processor.**

wor·dy [wur-dee] *adjective,* **wordier, wordiest.** using more words than are needed: *Many in the audience found it hard to follow the mayor's long and wordy speech.* —**wordiness,** *noun.*

Wordy writing uses more words than necessary to make a certain point or get a certain effect. All books on writing will agree on this, and one famous book has a rule saying you should leave out any words you do not need. Unfortunately, this same book also has a rule that you should not make your writing too short, so that it is not clear to the reader. The challenge then for a student writer is to know the difference between extra words and a good detail that is needed.

wore [wore] *verb.* the past tense of WEAR.
🔊 A different word with the same sound is **war.**

work [wurk] *noun, plural* **works. 1.** an effort made by the body or mind to make or do something: *Cutting down that tree was hard work; I still have a lot of work to do on my science project.* **2.** *Science.* the transfer of force to a body, so that it moves some distance in the direction of the force. **3.** what a person does to earn a living; a job: *My uncle has to travel a lot in his work.* **4.** something that has to be done; a task: *I need to finish this work today.* **5.** something made or done by effort: *a musical work; The gallery has many famous works of art.* **6. works.** the moving parts of a machine.
verb, **worked, working. 1.** to use one's effort, energy, or ability to do something: *We worked all morning cleaning the house.* **2.** to have a job: *Alan works as a bus driver.* **3.** to operate or make operate in the proper way: *This hair dryer isn't working; Do you know how to work the DVD player?* **4.** to make happen; cause: *The gardeners worked wonders getting the park ready for the official opening.*
♦ **work out. 1.** to solve: *Can you work out this math problem?* **2.** to have a result; turn out: *The surprise party worked out just as we'd planned.* **3.** to exercise: *to work out at the gym.*

work·bench [wurk-bench] *noun, plural* **workbenches.** a strong table for doing work with tools.

work·book [wurk-buk] *noun, plural* **workbooks.** a school book with questions and exercises to be answered or done by a student.

work·er [wur-kur] *noun, plural* **workers. 1.** a person who works: *My aunt is an office worker.* **2.** *Biology.* a female bee, ant, termite, or other insect that does the work in a hive or colony.

work·man [wurk-mun] *noun, plural* **workmen.** someone who works with his or her hands or with machinery: *A team of workmen prepared the main street for the annual carnival.*

work·man·ship [wurk-mun-ship] *noun.* the skill with which a thing is made: *We admired the workmanship of the beautiful antique furniture.*

work·out [wurk-out] *noun, plural* **workouts.** a session of physical exercises that you do to strengthen your muscles and keep fit.

work·shop [wurk-shop] *noun, plural* **workshops. 1.** a room or building in which work is done with machines or by hand: *The store sent a vacuum cleaner to the workshop to be repaired.* **2.** a group of people who study or work together to develop ideas on a particular subject or activity: *The teacher organized a drama workshop for the class play.*

work·sta·tion [wurk-stay-shun] *noun, plural* **workstations.** a work area in an office equipped with a desk and a computer: *Our school library has several workstations.*

world [wurld] *noun, plural* **worlds. 1.** the planet on which humans live; the Earth: *Mount Everest is the highest mountain in the world.* **2.** a part of the earth: *North and South America are also known as the New World.* **3.** all of the people who live on the earth: *The world was shocked by the huge loss of life from the tidal wave.* **4.** a particular area of interest, activity, or life: *the world of books; the world of sports.* **5.** a large number or amount; a great deal: *There is a world of difference between having a part in the school play and being a Hollywood actor.*

This British tank was captured by German troops during **World War I.**

world·ly [wurld-lee] *adjective,* **worldlier, worldliest. 1.** having to do with life and ordinary activities; not spiritual: *He gave up his worldly possessions to become a monk.* **2.** experienced in the ways of the world; sophisticated: *the worldly manner of the famous author.*

World War I ▲ *History.* the war of 1914 to 1918, which was fought mainly in Europe but involved much of the world. Great Britain, France, Russia, the United States, and their allies were on one side; Germany, Austria-Hungary, and their allies were on the other side.

World War II *History.* the war of 1939 to 1945, which was fought in Europe, Asia, and the Pacific and involved most of the world. Great Britain, France, the United States, Russia, and their allies were on one side; Germany, Italy, and Japan were on the other side.

world·wide [wurld-wide] *adjective.* known or happening all over the world: *The religious leader Mother Teresa was admired worldwide.*

World Wide Web *Computers.* **1.** another name for the INTERNET. **2.** the information and other resources available on the Internet, as opposed to the network itself.

a
b
c
d
e
f
g
h
i
j
k
l
m
n
o
p
q
r
s
t
u
v
w
x
y
z

worm ▼ [wurm] *noun, plural* **worms. 1.** a long, thin animal with no legs and a soft body that moves by sliding along. **2.** *Computers.* a computer program that destroys stored information and can reproduce itself and spread to other computers. A worm is a type of computer virus. **3. worms.** a sickness caused by certain worms that live inside the intestines of another animal as a parasite.
verb, **wormed, worming. 1.** to move gradually by twisting and wriggling like a worm: *Pat wormed his way through the narrow opening.* **2.** to get something by a sly method: *She finally wormed the secret out of her brother by pretending she knew most of the details already.* **3.** to give medicine to an animal in order to kill worms that are living in the intestine.

worn [worn] *verb.* the past tense of WEAR.
adjective. **1.** damaged by a lot of use: *a worn carpet; worn tires.* **2.** tired and weary: *The worn faces of the exhausted soldiers showed how tired they were.*
🔊 A different word with the same sound is **warn.**

worn-out [worn-<u>out</u>] *adjective.* **1.** used until it is so old, thin, or damaged it should not or cannot be used anymore: *worn-out clothes.* **2.** also, **worn out.** tired and weary: *The children were worn out by the long climb.*

wor·ry [wur-ee] *verb,* **worried, worrying. 1.** to have the feeling that something bad may happen; feel uneasy or slightly fearful; be anxious: *The ship's crew were worried about the rough seas.* **2.** to pull, bite, or tear at something: *The dog worried at the bone.*
noun, plural **worries.** something that causes an anxious or troubled feeling: *After our neighbor lost his job, money became a constant worry for the family.*

Worms *are an important source of food and water for birds.*

worse [wurs] *adjective; adverb.* bad to a greater degree; more unpleasant, unfavorable, evil, and so on: *A "D" is a poor mark in school, but an "F" is even worse.*
noun. something that is worse.

wor·ship [wur-ship] *noun, plural* **worships.** *Religion.* the act of showing strong feelings of love and admiration to God with prayer, religious services, and ceremonies: *a song of worship.*
verb, **worshipped** or **worshiped, worshipping** or **worshiping. 1.** to show strong feelings of love and admiration to God. A **worshipper** is a person who believes in and worships God. **2.** to show great love and devotion to a person: *She absolutely worships her father.*

worst [wurst] *adjective.* **1.** bad to the greatest degree; the most unfavorable, harmful, evil, and so on: *It was the worst flood in more than fifty years.*
noun. the most bad person or thing: *None of the pitchers did very well, but he was the worst—he gave up seven runs in one inning.*

worth [wurth] *preposition.* **1.** having the value of: *The jeweler told Mom her ring was worth more than one hundred dollars.* **2.** having possessions or wealth of stated value: *People say that singer is worth millions of dollars.* **3.** good enough for; deserving of: *That book is really worth reading.*
noun. **1.** the value or importance of a person or thing: *The neighbors' kindness to her when she was ill made her really appreciate the worth of their friendship.* **2.** the value of something in money: *The painting's worth is said to be more than a million dollars.* **3.** a quantity or amount: *thirty dollars worth of gasoline.*

worth·less [wurth-lis] *adjective.* of no value or use: *The painting was a worthless forgery.* **—worthlessness,** *noun.*

worth·while [wurth-<u>wile</u>] *adjective.* good or important enough to be worth doing: *Helping to clean up the park was a worthwhile way to spend the afternoon.*

worth·y [wur-thee] *adjective,* **worthier, worthiest. 1.** deserving of support, respect, or admiration: *Caring for lost animals is a worthy job; That boxer should be a worthy opponent for the champion.* **2.** good enough to have something: *Her poem was worthy of first prize.*

would [wud] *verb.* a special verb that is often used with other verbs to: **1.** say what might have happened if something else had happened first: *We would be home by now if we'd caught the earlier train.* **2.** say what is planned or expected: *The weather report said it would rain tomorrow; Jason said he would be home for lunch.* **3.** express something that always used to happen: *When I was younger Mom would walk with me to school.* **4.** make a request: *Would you open the door please?*
🔊 A different word with the same sound is **wood.**

wouldn't [wud-unt] a shortened form of "would not."

wound¹ [woond] *noun, plural* **wounds.** an injury to a part of the body, caused by a cut or blow rather than by disease: *a bullet wound.*
verb, **wounded, wounding. 1.** to injure or damage by cutting, tearing, or piercing the skin: *One police officer was wounded when the criminal fired his gun.* **2.** to hurt a person's feelings: *He was wounded by their insults.*

wound² [wound] *verb.* the past tense of WIND².

wove [wove] *verb.* the past tense of WEAVE.

wo·ven [wove-un] *verb.* the past participle of WEAVE.

wran·gle [rang-gul] *verb,* **wrangled wrangling.**
1. to quarrel or argue over something, especially in a noisy way: *The children wrangled for hours about whose turn it was to wash the dog.* **2.** to herd and care for horses or cattle. A person who does this is a **wrangler.**

wrap [rap] *verb,* **wrapped, wrapping. 1.** to cover by folding paper or some other material around: *to wrap a gift; Chloe wrapped a shawl around her shoulders.* **2.** to hide or conceal by covering: *The valley was wrapped in mist.* **3.** to clasp or coil: *The octopus wrapped its tentacles around the diver's leg.*
🔊 A different word with the same sound is **rap.**

*This rusty old **wreck** sits high and dry on the bank of Lake Baikal, in Siberia.*

wrap·per [rap-ur] *noun, plural* **wrappers.** a piece of paper that forms a covering: *Amy removed the wrapper from the candy.*
🔊 A different word with the same sound is **rapper.**

wrap·ping [rap-ing] *noun, plural* **wrappings.** material used for folding around and covering something.

wrath [rath] *noun.* great and fierce anger: *The king roared in wrath when he discovered his treasure had been stolen.* A **wrathful** person is full of anger and wanting revenge for harm he or she has suffered.

wreak [reek] *verb,* **wreaked, wreaking.** to cause: *The oil spill wreaked terrible damage along the coast.*
🔊 A different word with the same sound is **reek.**

wreath [reeth] *noun, plural* **wreaths.** flowers and leaves woven together to make a ring: *In the ancient Olympic Games, the winners were presented with laurel wreaths.*

wreck ▲ [rek] *verb,* **wrecked, wrecking.** to damage badly or bring an end to; ruin or destroy: *The dogs wrecked our garden with their digging; Rain wrecked the picnic.*
noun, plural **wrecks. 1.** the act of damaging or destroying a car, ship, train, or other vehicle, as by striking another such vehicle or a solid object such as a rock or a tree. **2.** the remains of something that has been ruined or damaged: *At low tide you can sometimes see the wreck of an old ship near the point.*

wreck·age [rek-ij] *noun.* the remains of something that has been ruined or damaged: *The railroad line was closed while the wreckage from the accident was hauled off the tracks.*

wren 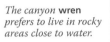 [ren] *noun, plural* **wrens.** a small, brown songbird with a slender bill, short, rounded wings, and a short tail that often points upward.

wrench [rench] *noun, plural* **wrenches.**
1. a tool with an opening that is used to hold and turn a nut or bolt.
2. a sudden, sharp twist, pull, or jerk.
verb, **wrenched, wrenching.** to twist or pull with a sudden, sharp movement: *I wrenched my shoulder when I was playing volleyball.*

*The canyon **wren** prefers to live in rocky areas close to water.*

wrest [rest] *verb,* **wrested, wresting.** to take or obtain by force: *The lords wrested power from the king and had him thrown in the dungeon.*
🔊 A different word with the same sound is **rest.**

wres·tle [res-ul] *verb,* **wrestled, wrestling. 1.** to struggle and fight with an opponent to force or hold him to the ground: *The police officer wrestled the suspect to the ground and handcuffed him.* **2.** to take part in a wrestling match: *Brian wrestles in the 112-pound class for his high school.* **3.** to struggle to master something difficult: *She wrestled with her conscience and finally told the truth.*

wres·tler [res-lur] *noun, plural* **wrestlers.** a person who wrestles as a sport.

wres·tling ▼ [res-ling] *noun.* **1.** an amateur sport in which two competitors struggle with each other, each trying to throw the other to the ground or hold him in a certain position. No punching is allowed. **2.** a form of professional entertainment that developed out of this sport, in which competitors fight with each other in a dramatic and exaggerated way, and typically have special nicknames and wear colorful outfits.

wretch·ed [rech-id] *adjective.* **1.** describing something miserable, unpleasant, poor, or of bad quality: *He had a wretched time at school last year because a bully was always picking on him.* **2.** being or seeming to be mean or cruel: *Hiding that girl's school bag was a wretched trick to play on her.* —**wretchedly,** *adverb;* —**wretchedness,** *noun.*

*In **wrestling,** this move is called a fireman's carry.*

a b c d e f g h i j k l m n o p q r s t u v w x y z

A black rhinoceros has thick skin with folds and **wrinkles,** *which protects it from thorns and sharp grasses.*

wrig·gle [rig-ul] *verb,* **wriggled, wriggling.**
1. to move or twist the body or part of the body with quick, short movements; squirm: *to wriggle your fingers or toes.* **2.** to get into or out of a situation by sly or devious means: *Paul managed to wriggle out of trouble once again.*

wring [ring] *verb,* **wrung, wringing. 1.** to twist or squeeze something, especially to force liquid out: *I will wring out my wet shirt as soon as I change out of it.* **2.** to get or extract something by force: *With her relentless questions, the lawyer wrung the truth from the witness.* **3.** to hold one's hands tightly and twist them when distressed: *The man was wringing his hands in grief.*
🔊 A different word with the same sound is **ring.**

wrin·kle ▲ [ring-kul] *noun, plural* **wrinkles.** a small crease or ridge in a smooth surface: *Dad ironed the wrinkles out of his shirt.*
verb, **wrinkled, wrinkling.** to make or have a small crease or ridge in a smooth surface: *Carole wrinkled her nose at the bad smell.*

wrist [rist] *noun, plural* **wrists.** the joint between the hand and the arm.

wrist·watch [rist-woch] *noun, plural* **wristwatches.** a watch worn on a strap that fastens around the wrist.

write [rite] *verb,* **wrote, written, writing. 1.** to form letters, words, or numbers on a surface such as paper: *Please write your name at the top of your paper.* **2.** to create a book, article, or other such work; be the author of something: *to write a poem or a song; She writes articles for the school newspaper.* **3.** to communicate by letter: *I wrote my pen pal in Kenya about what I've been doing.*
🔊 A different word with the same sound is **right.**

writ·er [rite-ur] *noun, plural* **writers.** a person who writes books, stories, poems, or articles; an author.

writ·ing [rye-ting] *noun, plural* **writings.**
1. letters, words, or numbers written by hand on paper; handwriting: *His writing is neat and tidy.* **2.** the work of a writer: *We are studying the writing of Louisa May Alcott.*

writ·ten [rit-un] *verb.* the past participle of WRITE.
adjective. describing something put down in writing: *Tony handed in his written assignment on time.*

wrong [rawng *or* rong] *adjective.* **1.** not true or correct: *It's wrong to say that New York is the capital of the United States.* **2.** not moral, fair, or just; bad: *It is wrong to tell lies.* **3.** not fitting, suitable, or proper: *Calling the principal by her first name is the wrong thing to do.* **4.** not functioning properly; out of order: *There's something wrong with the computer screen.*
noun, plural **wrongs.** something that is bad, incorrect, unfair, and so on: *There is an old saying that "Two wrongs don't make a right."*
adverb. in a way that is not correct: *Everything is going wrong today.*
verb, **wronged, wronging.** to treat badly, hurtfully, or unjustly: *He felt wronged when the teacher accused him of cheating, since he never cheats.* —**wrongly,** *adverb.*

wrote [rote] *verb.* the past tense of WRITE.

wrought [rawt] *adjective.* put together, shaped, or created, especially by elaborate work or effort: *The gold ring is beautifully wrought with a delicate pattern.*

wrought iron ▼ a type of iron that is tough, relatively soft, and easy to form into decorative shapes. It may be used for garden chairs, gates, and balconies.

wrung [rung] *verb.* the past tense and past participle of WRING.
🔊 A different word with the same sound is **rung.**

wry [rye] *adjective.* **1.** twisted to show displeasure or disgust: *He made a wry face when he tasted the cold, lumpy soup.* **2.** funny in a dry or ironic way: *She is always making wry comments, which everybody laughs at.*

wt. an abbreviation for WEIGHT.

WWW, www abbreviations for WORLD WIDE WEB.

Wrought iron *can be shaped into intricate designs.*

X x

*The word **xylophone** comes from the Greek words for wood and sound.*

X, x *noun, plural* **X's, x's.** the twenty-fourth letter of the English alphabet.

X *noun, plural* **x's.** an unknown or unnamed thing, quantity, or person.

xen·o·phil·i·a [*zee*-nuh-<u>feel</u>-yuh] *noun.* a liking for foreign people, cultures, and things.

xen·o·pho·bi·a [*zee*-nuh-<u>foh</u>-bee-uh] *noun.* a fear of foreign people, cultures, and things. A **xenophobe** is a person with a strong fear or dislike of foreign people.

Xe·rox [<u>zeer</u>-oks] *noun. Business.* a trademark for a machine or process that makes photocopies of written or printed material. A **xerox** is a photocopy of such material.
verb, **xeroxed, xeroxing.** to make a photocopy of written or printed material with a Xerox machine: *The teacher xeroxed the worksheet and handed it out to the class.*

Xho·sa [<u>koh</u>-suh] *noun, plural* **Xhosa, Xhosas.** **1.** a member of a people who live in the country of South Africa. **2.** the language of the Xhosa people.

X·mas [<u>eks</u>-mus] *noun, plural* **Xmases.** an abbreviation for CHRISTMAS.

It is sometimes thought that it is incorrect, and even disrespectful, to use **Xmas** as a substitute for "Christmas." It's said that the word was recently made up by people in the advertising business, who wanted a shorter word that would fit in a space where the longer word Christmas would not. Actually, *Xmas* is a very old word that has been in the language for about 500 years. It comes from the ancient use of the letter X as a symbol for Christ or Christianity, because of its cross shape.

X ray ▼ [<u>eks</u> *ray*] *noun, plural* **X rays.** *Science.* **1.** a type of radiation that can penetrate solid substances that ordinary rays of light cannot. It can pass through the body and take photographs of bones and organs, which are normally hidden from view. This helps doctors to diagnose broken bones and diseases. **2.** a photograph taken with X rays: *After I fell off the roof and hurt my arm, Dad took me to the doctor's for an X ray.*

X rays, which are now a widely used medical technique, were discovered in 1895 by Wilhelm Roentgen, a German scientist. He gave them this name because the nature of these waves was not known at that time, and the letter X was a symbol for the unknown.

X-ray [<u>eks</u> *ray*] *verb,* **X-rayed, X-raying.** *Medicine.* to photograph, examine, or treat with X rays: *The girl had to stay very still while the doctor X-rayed her injured leg.* This word is also spelled **x-ray.**

xy·lo·phone ◀ [<u>zye</u>-luh-*fone*] *noun, plural* **xylophones.** *Music.* a musical instrument consisting of one or two rows of wooden bars of different lengths. It is played by striking the bars with two wooden hammers. A person who plays the xylophone is a **xylophonist.**

*An **X ray** of the boy's arm shows that both bones are broken.*

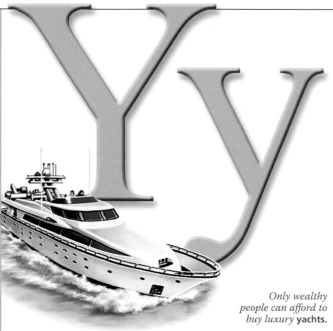

*Only wealthy people can afford to buy luxury **yachts**.*

Y, y *noun, plural* **Y's, y's.** the twenty-fifth letter of the English alphabet.

yacht ▲ [yot] *noun, plural* **yachts.** a small sailing or motor boat used for cruising or racing.

yak ▶ [yak] *noun, plural* **yaks.** a large, long-haired ox that is found in Asia. Some yaks are wild, but most are used as work animals or for meat and milk.

> The word **yacht** comes from a Dutch word meaning "a hunting ship" or "chasing ship." The first type of yacht was a fast sailing ship used to hunt down (chase) pirate ships. *Yacht* is one of various ship names to come into English from the Dutch language, dating back to a time when the Dutch were leaders in the world of ships and sailing.

yam [yam] *noun, plural* **yams. 1.** the potato-like root of a tropical vine. Yams are ground into flour, or baked or broiled and eaten as a vegetable. **2.** a type of SWEET POTATO.

yank [yangk] *verb,* **yanked, yanking.** to pull with a strong, sudden movement; tug or jerk: *As soon as the man yanked the emergency cord, the bus came to a halt. noun, plural* **yanks.** a strong, sudden pull; jerk: *The girl yelled out when her baby brother gave her hair a yank.*

Yank [yangk] *noun, plural* **Yanks.** a nickname for a person who was born in or lives in the United States; an American.

> It is not known for sure why the words **Yank** and **Yankee** became nicknames for a person from the United States. One likely explanation is that it was a name that people in the Dutch colony of New York gave to English colonists in New England. They called them *Janke,* a nickname for *Jan* or *John.* In Dutch, words like *Janke* are spoken with a **y** sound rather than **j.**

Yan·kee [yang-kee] *noun, plural* **Yankees.** a nickname for: **1.** a person who was born in or lives in a state of New England or the northern United States. **2.** a Union soldier during the Civil War. **3.** a person who was born in or lives in the United States; an American.

yard[1] [yard] *noun, plural* **yards. 1.** a unit for measuring length. One yard equals 3 feet or 36 inches, which is a little less than one meter. **2.** a long pole attached to a sailing ship's mast, from which a sail hangs.

yard[2] [yard] *noun, plural* **yards. 1.** an area of ground around or beside a house, school, or other building: *Marco went outside to play in the yard with his dog.* **2.** a fenced area of land used for a particular type of work or business: *The abandoned car was towed to the junk yard.*

yard·stick [yard-stik] *noun, plural* **yardsticks. 1.** a ruler or tape that is one yard long, with units of length along its edge. It is used for measuring. **2.** a test or standard that is used to judge, measure, or compare something: *The yardstick for making the swim team is being able to finish 100 meters of freestyle.*

yar·mul·ke [yah-muh-kuh *or* yar-mul-kuh] *noun, plural* **yarmulkes.** *Religion.* a small, circular covering worn on top of the head by Jewish men and boys, especially for religious ceremonies.

yarn [yarn] *noun, plural* **yarns. 1.** a long strand of twisted fibers or threads such as cotton, wool, or nylon, used for weaving or knitting. **2.** a long, entertaining story; a tale: *My grandpa loves to sit on the porch and tell yarns with his friends.*

yawn [yawn] *verb,* **yawned, yawning. 1.** to open the mouth wide and take in a deep breath, usually as an uncontrolled reaction to being tired or bored. **2.** to open wide; gape: *The mountain climbers stopped and peered into the chasm that yawned below them.* A **yawning** hole is a wide-open or gaping hole. *noun, plural* **yawns.** a deep, usually uncontrolled taking in of breath through a wide-open mouth.

yd. an abbreviation for YARD.

ye [yee] *pronoun.* you. This word was used in English in former times but is rarely used today.

year [yeer] *noun, plural* **years. 1.** a period of twelve months from January 1 to December 31, which is 365 days or 366 in a leap year. This is also called a **calendar year.** **2.** the exact time that the Earth takes to travel around the Sun, calculated as 365 days, 5 hours, 48 minutes and 46 seconds. **3.** any period of this length starting with any date: *Bianca will be twelve years old on June 14.* **4.** a part of a year during which a certain activity is carried out: *After the school year ends, we have a long summer vacation.*

*In Tibet, the dried dung of **yaks** is burned as fuel.*

*The velvet wasp is a **yellowjacket** that nests in the ground and has a painful sting.*

year·book [yeer-buk] *noun, plural* **yearbooks.** a book printed at the end of each year that holds information about the year's activities. Often the graduating class of a high school or college creates a yearbook including photos of the faculty and students, as well as highlights of the year.

year·ling [yeer-ling] *noun, plural* **yearlings. 1.** an animal that is past one year old and is in the second year of life. **2.** a racehorse that is one year old dating from January 1 of the year in which it was born.

year·ly [yeer-lee] *adjective.* **1.** occurring once a year: *Dad went to the doctor for his yearly checkup.* **2.** measured over a year: *The mining company's yearly profit has fallen.*

yearn [yurn] *verb,* **yearned, yearning.** to long for or desire: *By the end of our hike we were yearning for a cool drink.* If you long for something, you have a **yearning** for it.

year-round *adjective.* throughout the year: *That year-round resort has a indoor swimming pool.* *adverb.* throughout the year: *Nowadays you can buy fresh strawberries year-round, not just in summer.*

yeast [yeest] *noun, plural* **yeasts.** *Biology.* a substance made from the minute cells of certain fungi. It is used to make dough rise and to make beer and other alcoholic drinks.

yell [yel] *verb,* **yelled, yelling.** to cry out loudly; shout: *They saw the truck coming and yelled a warning to the people in its path.* *noun, plural* **yells.** a loud cry; shout: *She gave a yell when I stepped on her toe.*

yel·low [yel-oh] *noun, plural* **yellows. 1.** a color like that of gold, butter, or ripe lemons. **2.** something having this color, such as the yolk of an egg. *adjective,* **yellower, yellowest.** having the color yellow. *verb,* **yellowed, yellowing.** to make or become yellow: *The pages of this old book have yellowed with age.*

yellow fever *Medicine.* a disease caused by a virus transmitted mostly by mosquitoes in tropical parts of South and Central America, the Caribbean, and Africa. It causes fever, internal bleeding, and failure of the organs, and it can be fatal. It gets its name from the fact that it can cause a person's skin to turn a yellowish color.

yel·low·jack·et ▲ [yel-oh-jak-it] *noun, plural* **yellowjackets.** any of various wasps with black and yellow markings. They live in colonies and sting to defend their nests.

yelp [yelp] *noun, plural* **yelps.** a short, sharp cry or bark: *The little puppy gave a yelp when the cat scratched its nose; a yelp of surprise.* *verb,* **yelped, yelping.** to give a short, sharp cry or bark.

yen[1] [yen] *noun, plural* **yens.** a desire for something; yearning; longing: *When I was traveling and was homesick I had a yen for hamburgers.*

yen[2] [yen] *noun, plural* **yen.** Japan's basic unit of money.

yes [yes] *adverb.* a word meaning it is so; this is correct; the opposite of "no:" *Yes, I do like the red bag best; Yes, you can come with us.* *noun, plural* **yeses.** a statement, reply, vote, and so on that has this meaning: *Our class voted on whether to hold a party and the result was a definite yes.*

yes·ter·day [yes-tur-day *or* yes-tur-dee] *noun, plural* **yesterdays.** the day coming before this day: *Yesterday was the last day of winter and today is the first day of spring.* *adverb.* on the day coming before this day: *Nicholas arrived home from his trip yesterday.*

yet [yet] *adverb.* **1.** at this time; now: *Did you finish your homework yet?* **2.** up to a certain time; so far: *He has never yet missed a doctor's appointment.* *conjunction.* despite this; however; but: *It was a dark night, yet the cat could still see the mouse.* • **as yet.** up until now; so far: *We have as yet had no news about what caused the accident.*

yew [yoo] *noun, plural* **yews.** any of several evergreen trees and shrubs. Yews are conifers. The slow-growing European yew comes from Europe and Asia and is used in furniture making and to make archery bows. 🔊 Different words with the same sound are **you** and **ewe.**

Yid·dish [yid-ish] *noun. Language.* a language that originated in the Jewish cultures of central and eastern Europe. Yiddish developed from an old form of German, with influences from Hebrew and other languages. It is written with the Hebrew alphabet.

yield [yeeld] *verb,* **yielded, yielding. 1.** to produce or provide: *Our apple trees yielded a good crop this year.* **2.** to hand over control or possession: *The defeated president yielded his power to the new president.* **3.** to give up fighting or arguing and admit defeat: *With only two ships left afloat, the navy yielded to the enemy.* *noun, plural* **yields.** an amount of something produced.

YMCA an abbreviation for the **Young Men's Christian Association,** a service organization that provides community services such as sports activities and health programs. It is also called the **Y** for short.

yo·del [yoh-dul] *verb,* **yodeled** *or* **yodelled, yodeling** *or* **yodelling.** *Music.* to sing switching rapidly between the natural voice and a high voice. **—yodeler,** *noun.*

yo·ga ▼ [yoh-guh] *noun.* a method of exercise and meditation that involves holding unusual body positions and focusing on breathing. Yoga was originally developed as a part of Hindu religious teachings.

yo·gurt [yoh-gurt] *noun, plural* **yogurts.** a custard-like food made by curdling warm milk with certain bacteria. It is often mixed with fruits.

*In **yoga,** a backbend pose is performed to strengthen the arms, legs, and spine.*

a b c d e f g h i j k l m n o p q r s t u v w x y z

yoke

A international **yo-yo** contest
is held every year in Florida.

A B C D E F G H I J K L M N O P Q R S T U V W X Y Z

yoke [yoke] *noun, plural* **yokes. 1.** a device that joins two working animals together, such as oxen. It consists of a wooden cross bar with two pieces underneath to enclose each animal's neck. **2.** a part of a piece of clothing shaped to fit around the shoulders or hips, from which the rest of the garment hangs.
verb, **yoked, yoking.** to join together with a yoke:
The mules were yoked together.
🔊 A different word with the same sound is **yolk.**

yolk [yoke] *noun, plural* **yolks.** the yellow part of an egg that provides the material that forms the embryo and the nutrients to help it grow.
🔊 A different word with the same sound is **yoke.**

Yom Kip·pur [yom kip-ur *or* yom-ki-poor] *noun. Religion.* a Jewish holiday known as the Day of Atonement, when people fast (do not eat) and pray to God for forgiveness of sins. Yom Kippur is held ten days after Rosh Hashanah, the Jewish New Year.

yon·der [yon-dur] *adverb.* in that place indicated; over there: *The knight pointed with his sword and said, "Yonder is the castle of my father."*

Yo·ru·ba [yoh-roo-buh] *noun, plural* **Yoruba** *or* **Yorubas. 1.** a member of a West African people who mostly live in Nigeria. Many people taken to the Americas as slaves were Yoruba. **2.** the language of this group.

you [yoo] *pronoun.* **1.** the person or people being spoken or written to: *You are wearing a nice dress; Will you all please be quiet?* **2.** one; anyone: *You should never cross the street without looking.*
🔊 Different words with the same sound are **ewe** and **yew.**

Using the word **you** when you write means that you are speaking directly to the reader. "Last week I found a little pond with some really big fish. *You* go up Dixon Road all the way to the end. Then *you* walk on the Bobcat Trail. *You'll* see tall bushes on both sides of the trail. After about half a mile, *you* come to an old wooden dock." This use of *you* is a good way to draw people into your story. They will be able to picture the trip to the pond as if they were going along with you, and then when you tell what happened to you there, they will feel part of it.

you'd [yood] the shortened form of "you had" or "you would."

you'll [yool] the shortened form of "you will" or "you shall."

young [yung] *adjective,* **younger, youngest. 1.** in the early stage of life, growth, or existence: *Young swans are called cygnets; In 1790 the United States of America was still a young nation.* **2.** having the appearance, strength, or other qualities of someone young: *Regular exercise and healthy eating keeps my grandfather looking and feeling young.* **3.** of or relating to the early years of life: *In her young days she was a champion swimmer.*
noun. young offspring: *The bear and her young slept in their den.*

young·ster [yung-stur] *noun, plural* **youngsters.** a young person or animal; a child: *The hospital formed a society to support youngsters battling cancer.*

your [yur *or* yor] *adjective.* relating or belonging to you: *You left your bag on the bus—here it is.*
🔊 A different word with the same sound is **you're.**

you're [yur *or* yer] the shortened form of "you are."
🔊 A different word with the same sound is **your.**

yours [yurz *or* yorz] *pronoun.* the possessive form of YOU; used to refer to one or ones belonging to you: *I ate my sandwich and put yours in the refrigerator.*

your·self [yur-self *or* yor-self] *pronoun, plural* **yourselves. 1.** the one that is your own self: *Please fill out the form yourself.* **2.** you in your usual, normal condition: *Once you have a good meal you will feel yourself again.*

youth [yooth] *noun, plural* **youth** *or* **youths. 1.** the condition or quality of being young: *Grandma still has the positive outlook of youth.* **2.** the period of life between childhood and adulthood; adolescence: *He was a good athlete in his youth.* **3.** the early part of something's existence: *Modern physics was in its youth when the Curies discovered uranium.* **4.** a young person, especially a young man, or young people generally: *A youth rescued the family trapped by rising floodwaters; Today's youth are familiar with computer technology.*

youth·ful [yooth-ful] *adjective.* **1.** of or relating to youth or having a quality of youth: *The youthful audience enjoyed the puppet show.* **2.** in the early part of something's existence. **—youthfulness,** *noun.*

yo-yo ▲ [yoh-yoh] *noun, plural* **yo-yos.** a toy made of two disks joined by a central peg. A string is tied to the peg and wound around it. A loop tied in the other end of the string goes around a finger, and the user can make the disk wind up and down the string.

> Different versions of the toy called a **yo-yo** have been known in various lands at different times in history. The current version, and the word *yo-yo* itself, are said to have been brought to America in the 1920s by a man named Pedro Flores. He came from the Philippines, a large island group of the southern Pacific Ocean, and it is likely that he learned the word *yo-yo* there.

Yu·go·sla·vi·an ◄ [yoo-goh-slahv-ee-un] *noun, plural* **Yugoslavian. 1.** a person who was born or lived in the former southeastern European nation of Yugoslavia. **2.** of or relating to the former southeastern European nation of Yugoslavia.

Yule [yool] *noun, plural* **Yules.** another word for Christmas. The Christmas season is known as **Yuletide.**

Yup·pie [yup-ee] *noun, plural* **Yuppies.** a word coming from the first letters of the phrase "Young Urban Professional." A typical Yuppie is thought of as having a well-paying job and as being interested in buying and owning fine things.

*Before the 1990s, the Serbian Parliament building in Belgrade was home to the **Yugoslavian** government.*

Z z

The pattern of stripes of each **zebra** is unique.

Z, z *noun, plural* **Z's, z's.** the twenty-sixth and last letter of the English alphabet.

za·ny [zay-nee] *adjective,* **zanier, zaniest.** amusing in a silly or crazy way: *That cartoon is hilarious because it has zany characters who do strange things.*

zeal [zeel] *noun.* great eagerness; enthusiasm: *They began to clean up the attic with great zeal.*

zeal·ous [zel-us] *adjective.* filled with great enthusiasm or zeal: *The lawyer was zealous in his efforts to win the case.* —**zealously,** *adverb.*

ze·bra ▲ [zee-bruh] *noun, plural* **zebras** or **zebra.** a wild animal that looks like a horse with a black-and-white striped coat. Zebras live in Africa.

ze·nith [zee-nith] *noun, plural* **zeniths. 1.** the point in the sky that is directly above any place or person observing it. **2.** the highest or greatest point of anything: *That ock band is now at the zenith of their career.*

ze·ro [zeer-oh] *noun, plural* **zeros** or **zeroes. 1.** *Mathematics.* the symbol (0), which indicates that something has no value; nothing. **2.** the point from which the numbering or measurement of a scale begins: *The scale has to be adjusted to* zero before you step on, or you won't get a true reading of your weight. *adjective.* **1.** relating to or being zero: *The temperature outside the cabin dropped during the night to zero degrees Fahrenheit.* **2.** having nothing; not any: *Judging by the way they were playing, they had zero chance of winning the game.*
• **zero in on.** to move purposefully in or toward a target: *He had a good look at the situation and immediately zeroed in on the real problem.*

The word **zero** comes from the Arabic term for this mathematical idea. In early times the Arabs were the leaders in mathematics, and our current numbering system of 0, 1, 2, 3, 4, and so on is called *Arabic numerals.* Before the use of the zero was introduced to Europe, probably in the 1200s, Western mathematics was limited by the lack of such a concept.

zest [zest] *noun.* something exciting, interesting, and enjoyable: *a lively energetic person with a zest for life; She brought out a tray of delicious snacks, which added a bit of zest to the otherwise boring party.*

Zeus ▼ [zoos] *noun. Religion.* in mythology, the king of the Greek gods and ruler of the heavens.

zig·zag ▼ [zig-zag] *noun, plural* **zigzags.** a line that has sharp turns from one side to the other: *Her blouse had blue zigzags across the sleeves. verb.* **zigzagged, zigzagging.** to move in a zigzag pattern: *The river zigzagged along through the valley.*

To make it possible to climb a steep mountainside, the road must **zigzag** sharply.

zinc [zingk] *noun. Chemistry.* a bluish-white hard metal that is used to make alloys.

This statue of **Zeus** is in the Fountain of the Four Rivers in Rome, Italy.

a b c d e f g h i j k l m n o p q r s t u v w x y **z**

Zinnias are natives of Mexico and come in many bright colors.

zin·ni·a ◄ [zin-ee-yuh] *noun, plural* **zinnias.** an annual garden plant that has round, colorful flowers.

> The **zinnia** flower took its name from Johann Gottfried *Zinn*, a German botanist of the 1700s. This and many other flowers were officially named by Linnaeus, a famous Swedish scientist of this time. He often chose the names of other scientists such as Zinn for these flowers, as a way to honor their work.

zip [zip] *verb,* **zipped, zipping.** to close something using a fastener called a zipper: *She zipped up her jacket to keep out the cold wind.*

ZIP Code a group of numbers used to identify mail delivery areas in the United States. This term is also spelled **zip code.**

zip·per [zip-ur] *noun, plural* **zippers.** a fastener made of two rows of teeth that can be locked or unlocked by pulling a sliding device up or down.

zith·er [ziTH-ur *or* zith-ur] *noun, plural* **zithers.** a musical instrument consisting of a flat box with more than thirty strings pulled tight across it. It is played by plucking the strings.

zo·di·ac ▲ [zoh-dee-ak] *noun.* an imaginary path in the sky through which the Sun, the Earth, and all the planets travel. The zodiac is divided into twelve parts, called signs, each of which is named after a different constellation (group of stars.)

zone [zone] *noun, plural* **zones. 1.** an area that has been created or set apart for a special purpose: *That area of land has been made a military zone—no one can go there unless they are members of the armed forces.* **2.** any of the five divisions of the Earth's surface. These divisions are based on the climate of the regions. There is a torrid zone, which is also called the **Tropic Zone**, two temperate zones, and one frigid zone.
verb, **zoned, zoning.** to arrange or divide into zones: *The area in my neighborhood is zoned as residential—only private homes can be built there.*

zoning [zone-ing] *noun. Government.* the setting of rules for the use of land and the type of structures that can be built on it.

zoo [zoo] *noun, plural* **zoos.** a park or large area of land where wild animals are kept for people to see.

zo·ol·o·gy [zoh-ol-uh-jee] *noun. Biology.* the science that studies animal life. Someone who studies zoology is a **zoologist.**

A recent book on language has the title *There Is No Zoo in Zoology.* What the author means is that the word *zoo* has an **oo** sound, to rhyme with words like *you, do, few,* and *moose.* **Zoology,** though it is a closely related word, is correctly pronounced with an **oh** sound, as in *go, snow,* or *hoe.* However, many people do say "zoo-ology" rather than "zoh-ology." This shows that people will often pronounce a word in an incorrect way because they think it is supposed to match another more common word.

Capricorn

Sagittarius

Libra

Aries

Virgo

Taurus

Scorpio

Pisces

Gemini

Leo

Aquarius

Cancer

The term **zodiac** *comes from the Greek for "circle of little animals" and many of the signs of the zodiac are represented by creatures.*

zoom [zoom] *verb,* **zoomed, zooming.** to move suddenly and very fast, often in an upward direction: *The airplane zoomed into the clouds and out of sight.*
• **zoom in (on).** to quickly change the focus of a camera so that the object being viewed seems much closer to the observer.

zuc·chi·ni ▼ [zoo-kee-nee] *noun, plural* **zucchini.** a type of squash that is long and narrow and has a dark green skin.

Zu·ni [zoo-nee] *noun, plural* **Zuni** *or* **Zunis.** a member of an Native American people of western New Mexico. *adjective.* of or relating to the Zuni people or their culture.

Zucchini, also known as courgettes, have edible flowers.

North America

Stretching from the Arctic Circle almost to the Equator, North America covers 9.5 million square miles. As well as the mainland, the continent includes Greenland, the islands of the Caribbean, and the Hawaiian Islands. Its 23 nations and 16 dependencies and territories have a combined population of about 518 million. In the north, the large, mainly English-speaking nations of Canada and the United States are industrialized and wealthy. The Spanish-speaking countries and territories in the south are more agricultural and less prosperous.

The moose, the largest of all deer species, is native to Canada and the northern United States.

	U.S.A.	Canada	Mexico
Total area	3,794,080 sq. miles	3,855,100 sq. miles	761,610 sq. miles
Population	298,444,000	33,099,000	107,450,000
Main language	English	English, French	Spanish, regional indigenous dialects
Life expectancy	78 years	80 years	75 years

LARGEST CITIES

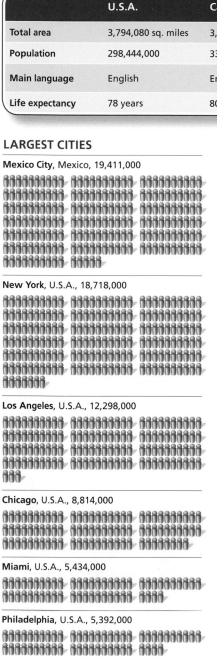

Mexico City, Mexico, 19,411,000

New York, U.S.A., 18,718,000

Los Angeles, U.S.A., 12,298,000

Chicago, U.S.A., 8,814,000

Miami, U.S.A., 5,434,000

Philadelphia, U.S.A., 5,392,000

VEGETATION ZONES

- Tropical forest
- Desert
- Mediterranean forest and scrub
- Grassland
- Temperate forest
- Boreal forest
- Tundra
- Mountain vegetation
- Ice sheet

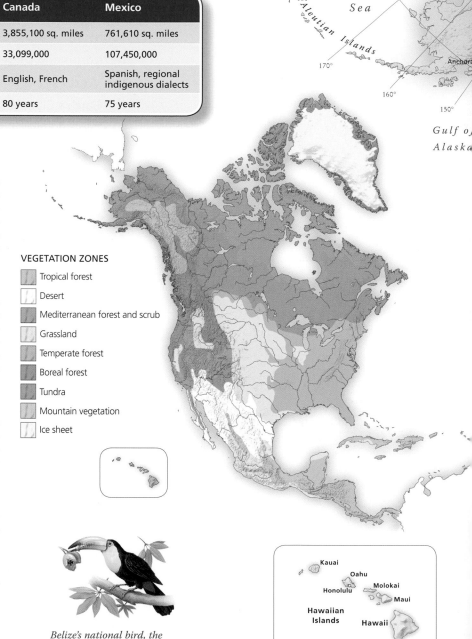

Belize's national bird, the keel-billed toucan, lives in small flocks in rain forests.

Hawaiian Islands — Kauai, Oahu, Honolulu, Molokai, Maui, Hawaii

0   100 miles

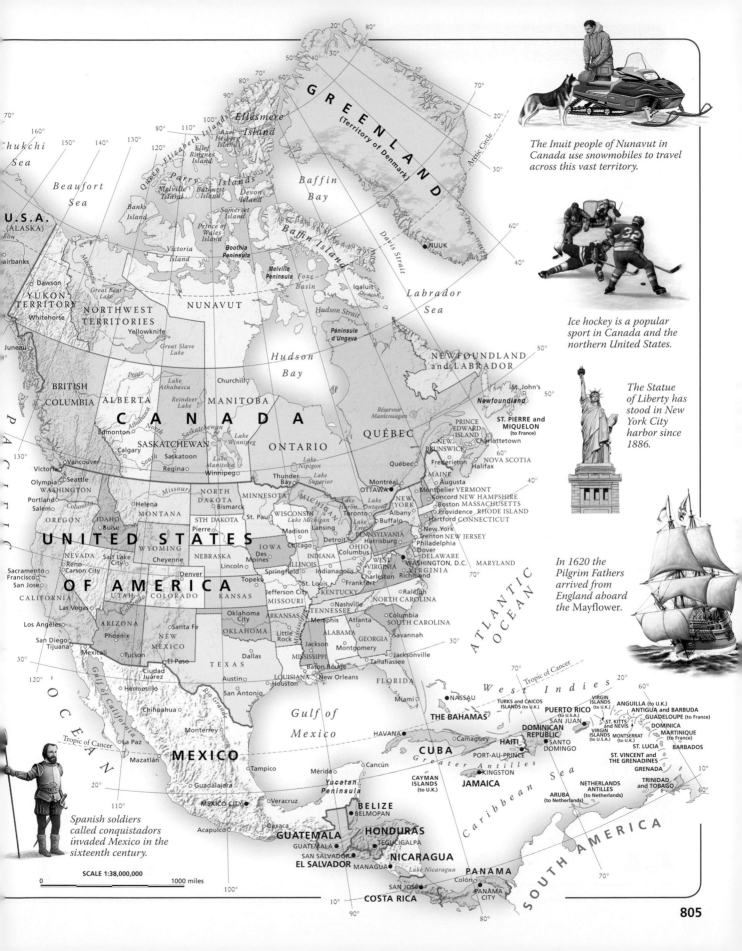

G R E E N L A N D
(Territory of Denmark)

The Inuit people of Nunavut in Canada use snowmobiles to travel across this vast territory.

Ice hockey is a popular sport in Canada and the northern United States.

The Statue of Liberty has stood in New York City harbor since 1886.

In 1620 the Pilgrim Fathers arrived from England aboard the Mayflower.

Spanish soldiers called conquistadors invaded Mexico in the sixteenth century.

Chukchi Sea
Beaufort Sea
Banks Island
Queen Elizabeth Islands
Ellef Ringnes Island
Axel Heiberg Island
Ellesmere Island
Parry Islands
Melville Island
Bathurst Island
Devon Island
Somerset Island
Prince of Wales Island
Boothia Peninsula
Victoria Island
Baffin Bay
Baffin Island
Davis Strait
Foxe Basin
Melville Peninsula
Hudson Strait
Labrador Sea
NUUK

U.S.A. (ALASKA)
Kon
Fairbanks
Dawson
YUKON TERRITORY
Whitehorse
Juneau
Mackenzie
NORTHWEST TERRITORIES
Yellowknife
Great Bear Lake
Great Slave Lake
NUNAVUT
Iqaluit
Péninsule d'Ungava
Hudson Bay
Churchill
NEWFOUNDLAND and LABRADOR

BRITISH COLUMBIA
Peace
ALBERTA
Athabasca
Lake Athabasca
Reindeer Lake
Lake Winnipeg
MANITOBA
CANADA
QUÉBEC
St. John's
Newfoundland
ST. PIERRE and MIQUELON (to France)

Vancouver
Victoria
Seattle
Olympia
WASHINGTON
Portland
Salem
OREGON
Edmonton
Calgary
North Saskatchewan
South Saskatchewan
Saskatoon
Regina
SASKATCHEWAN
Lake Manitoba
Winnipeg
ONTARIO
Lake Nipigon
Thunder Bay
Lake Superior
Québec
Montréal
OTTAWA
PRINCE EDWARD ISLAND
Charlottetown
NEW BRUNSWICK
Fredericton
NOVA SCOTIA
Halifax
MAINE

PACIFIC
Sacramento
San Francisco
San Jose
Reno
Carson City
NEVADA
CALIFORNIA
Las Vegas
Los Angeles
San Diego
Tijuana
Mexicali
ARIZONA
Phoenix
Tucson

Helena
MONTANA
IDAHO
Boise
WYOMING
Cheyenne
Salt Lake City
UTAH
Denver
COLORADO
UNITED STATES
OF AMERICA

NORTH DAKOTA
Bismarck
STH DAKOTA
Pierre
NEBRASKA
Lincoln
KANSAS
Topeka

MINNESOTA
St. Paul
WISCONSIN
Madison
IOWA
Des Moines
MISSOURI
Jefferson City
St. Louis

MICHIGAN
Lansing
Lake Michigan
Chicago
Detroit
ILLINOIS
Springfield
INDIANA
Indianapolis
OHIO
Columbus
Frankfort
KENTUCKY

Lake Huron
Lake Ontario
Toronto
Lake Erie
Buffalo
NEW YORK
Albany
VERMONT
Montpelier
NEW HAMPSHIRE
Concord
Boston MASSACHUSETTS
Providence RHODE ISLAND
Hartford CONNECTICUT
New York
NEW JERSEY
Trenton
PENNSYLVANIA
Harrisburg
Philadelphia
Dover
DELAWARE
WASHINGTON, D.C.
MARYLAND
WEST VIRGINIA
Charleston
Richmond
VIRGINIA

ATLANTIC OCEAN

Santa Fe
NEW MEXICO
El Paso
Ciudad Juárez
Chihuahua
Hermosillo
TEXAS
Dallas
Austin
San Antonio
Houston
Oklahoma City
OKLAHOMA
Little Rock
ARKANSAS
Jackson
MISSISSIPPI
Baton Rouge
LOUISIANA
New Orleans
Nashville
TENNESSEE
Memphis
ALABAMA
Montgomery
Columbia
NORTH CAROLINA
Raleigh
SOUTH CAROLINA
Atlanta
GEORGIA
Savannah
Jacksonville
Tallahassee
FLORIDA
Miami

OCEAN
Gulf of California
Rio Grande
MEXICO
MEXICO CITY
Guadalajara
Veracruz
Mazatlán
La Paz
Tampico
Monterrey
Acapulco
Oaxaca
Mérida
Yucatán Peninsula
Cancún

Gulf of Mexico
Tropic of Cancer
NASSAU
THE BAHAMAS
HAVANA
CUBA
Camagüey
Greater Antilles
JAMAICA
CAYMAN ISLANDS (to U.K.)
TURKS and CAICOS ISLANDS (to U.K.)
West Indies
PUERTO RICO
SAN JUAN
DOMINICAN REPUBLIC
SANTO DOMINGO
HAITI
PORT-AU-PRINCE
Kingston
VIRGIN ISLANDS (to U.K.)
VIRGIN ISLANDS (to U.S.A.)
ANGUILLA (to U.K.)
ANTIGUA and BARBUDA
GUADELOUPE (to France)
ST. KITTS and NEVIS
MONTSERRAT (to U.K.)
DOMINICA
MARTINIQUE (to France)
ST. LUCIA
BARBADOS
ST. VINCENT and THE GRENADINES
GRENADA
Caribbean Sea
NETHERLANDS ANTILLES (to Netherlands)
ARUBA (to Netherlands)
TRINIDAD and TOBAGO

BELIZE
BELMOPAN
GUATEMALA
GUATEMALA
SAN SALVADOR
EL SALVADOR
HONDURAS
TEGUCIGALPA
NICARAGUA
MANAGUA
Lake Nicaragua
COSTA RICA
SAN JOSÉ
PANAMA
Colón
PANAMA CITY

SOUTH AMERICA

SCALE 1:38,000,000
0   1000 miles

States of the United States

	State	Capital	Population	Origin of name	State flower	State bird
	Alabama *AL* The Heart of Dixie / The Yellowhammer State	Montgomery	4,599,000	Means "thicket-clearers" in Choctaw Indian language	Camellia	Yellowhammer
	Alaska *AK* The Last Frontier	Juneau	670,000	Based on an Aleut Indian word *alaxsxaq,* meaning "that which the sea breaks against"	Forget-me-not	Willow ptarmigan
	Arizona *AZ* The Grand Canyon State	Phoenix	6,166,000	From the Papago Indian words for "place of the young spring"	Saguaro cactus blossom	Cactus wren
	Arkansas *AR* The Natural State	Little Rock	2,811,000	French interpretation of an Illinois Indian word *acansa,* meaning "downstream place"	Apple blossom	Mockingbird
	California *CA* The Golden State	Sacramento	36,458,000	Named after a mythical island in a 1510 romance novel by Spanish author Garcia Ordóñez de Montalvo	Golden poppy	California valley quail
	Colorado *CO* The Centennial State	Denver	4,753,000	Taken from the Spanish for "red," which was the color of the Colorado River	Rocky Mountain columbine	Lark bunting
	Connecticut *CT* The Constitution State	Hartford	3,505,000	From the Algonquian Indian name *Quinnehtukqut,* which means "place beside a long river"	Mountain laurel	American robin
	Delaware *DE* The First State	Dover	854,000	Named after an early Virginia governor, Baron de la Warr	Peach blossom	Blue hen chicken
	Florida *FL* The Sunshine State	Tallahassee	18,090,000	Named in honor of Spain's Easter celebration *Pascua Florida,* meaning "feast of flowers"	Orange blossom	Mockingbird
	Georgia *GA* The Peach State / Empire State of the South	Atlanta	9,364,000	Named after King George II of England	Cherokee rose	Brown thrasher
	Hawaii *HI* The Aloha State	Honolulu	1,286,000	May be based on native Hawaiian words for "new homeland"	Native yellow hibiscus	Nene (Hawaiian goose)
	Idaho *ID* The Gem State	Boise	1,467,000	Name made up by mining lobbyist George M. Willing in the early 1860s	Syringa	Mountain bluebird
	Illinois *IL* The Prairie State	Springfield	12,832,000	From the Peoria Indian word *iliniwok,* meaning "warriors"	Native violet	Cardinal
	Indiana *IN* The Hoosier State	Indianapolis	6,314,000	Means "land of the Indians"	Peony	Cardinal
	Iowa *IA* The Hawkeye State	Des Moines	2,982,000	Probably named after a local Indian tribe, whose name was spelled *Ioway* by the English	Wild rose	Eastern goldfinch
	Kansas *KS* The Sunflower State	Topeka	2,764,000	From the Sioux Indian words for "people of the south wind"	Sunflower	Western meadowlark
	Kentucky *KY* The Bluegrass State	Frankfort	4,206,000	Possibly from the Iroquois Indian word for "prairie"	Goldenrod	Cardinal

State	Capital	Population	Origin of name	State flower	State bird
Louisiana *LA* The Pelican State	Baton Rouge	4,288,000	Named in honor of France's King Louis XIV	Magnolia	Eastern brown pelican
Maine *ME* The Pine Tree State	Augusta	1,322,000	Possibly named to distinguish the mainland from nearby islands	White pine cone	Chickadee
Maryland *MD* The Free State / The Old Line State	Annapolis	5,616,000	Named to honor Henrietta Maria, wife of England's King Charles I	Black-eyed Susan	Baltimore oriole
Massachusetts *MA* The Bay State	Boston	6,437,000	Named after the Massachusetts Indian tribe, whose name means "a large hill place"	Mayflower	Chickadee
Michigan *MI* The Wolverine State / The Great Lakes State	Lansing	10,096,000	Based on the Chippewa Indian word *meicigama*, meaning "great water"	Apple blossom	Robin
Minnesota *MN* The North Star State / Land of 10,000 Lakes	St. Paul	5,167,000	From the Dakota Indian name for the Minnesota River, *Mnishota*, which means "sky-tinted water"	Pink and white lady's slipper	Common loon
Mississippi *MS* The Magnolia State	Jackson	2,911,000	Based on the Algonquian Indian words for "great river"	Magnolia	Mockingbird
Missouri *MO* The Show Me State	Jefferson City	5,843,000	Named after the Missouri Indian tribe, whose name means "town of the large canoes"	Hawthorn	Bluebird
Montana *MT* The Treasure State	Helena	945,000	From *montaña*, the Spanish word for "mountain"	Bitterroot	Western meadowlark
Nebraska *NE* The Cornhusker State	Lincoln	1,768,000	Based on an Oto Indian word that means "flat water," referring to the Platte River	Goldenrod	Western meadowlark
Nevada *NV* The Sagebrush State / The Silver State	Carson City	2,496,000	Named after the Sierra Nevada mountains, whose name means "snowy range" in Spanish	Sagebrush	Mountain bluebird
New Hampshire *NH* The Granite State	Concord	1,315,000	Named after the county of Hampshire in England	Purple lilac	Purple finch
New Jersey *NJ* The Garden State	Trenton	8,725,000	Named for the island of Jersey in the English Channel	Purple violet	Eastern goldfinch
New Mexico *NM* Land of Enchantment	Santa Fe	1,955,000	Named after the country of Mexico, which was itself named after the Nahua Aztec tribe, the Mexica	Yucca	Roadrunner
New York *NY* The Empire State	Albany	19,306,000	Named in honor of the Duke of York, who was the brother of England's King Charles II	Rose	Bluebird
North Carolina *NC* The Tar Heel State / The Old North State	Raleigh	8,857,000	Taken from *Carolus*, the Latin word for "Charles," in honor of England's King Charles I	Dogwood	Cardinal
North Dakota *ND* The Peace Garden State / The Sioux State	Bismarck	636,000	Named after a Sioux Indian tribe, the Dakota, whose name means "friends" or "allies"	Wild prairie rose	Western meadowlark

States of the United States

	State	Capital	Population	Origin of name	State flower	State bird
	Ohio *OH* The Buckeye State	Columbus	11,478,000	From the Iroquois Indian word for "great river"	Scarlet carnation	Cardinal
	Oklahoma *OK* The Sooner State	Oklahoma City	3,579,000	Based on two Choctaw Indian words: *okla*, meaning "people," and *humma*, meaning "red"	Mistletoe	Scissor-tailed flycatcher
	Oregon *OR* The Beaver State	Salem	3,701,000	May have come from a misspelled label for the Wisconsin River on a 1715 French map	Oregon grape	Western meadowlark
	Pennsylvania *PA* The Keystone State	Harrisburg	12,441,000	*Penn* honors Admiral William Penn, the father of the state's founder, and *sylvania* is Latin for "woods"	Mountain laurel	Ruffed grouse
	Rhode Island *RI* The Ocean State	Providence	1,068,000	Possibly after the Greek island of Rhodes, or from the Dutch name *Roodt Eylandt,* meaning "red island"	Violet	Rhode Island red
	South Carolina *SC* The Palmetto State	Columbia	4,321,000	Taken from *Carolus,* the Latin word for "Charles," in honor of England's King Charles I	Yellow jessamine	Carolina wren
	South Dakota *SD* The Mount Rushmore State	Pierre	782,000	Named after a Sioux Indian tribe, the Dakota, whose name means "friends" or "allies"	American pasqueflower	Ring-necked pheasant
	Tennessee *TN* The Volunteer State	Nashville	6,039,000	Named after two Cherokee Indian villages called *Tanasi*	Iris	Mockingbird
	Texas *TX* The Lone Star State	Austin	23,508,000	From the Caddo Indian word *teysha,* meaning "hello friend"	Bluebonnet	Mockingbird
	Utah *UT* The Beehive State	Salt Lake City	2,550,000	Named after the Ute Indian tribe, whose name means "people of the mountains"	Sego lily	California gull
	Vermont *VT* The Green Mountain State	Montpelier	624,000	From the French name *Verts Monts,* meaning "green mountains"	Red clover	Hermit thrush
	Virginia *VA* The Old Dominion / Mother of Presidents	Richmond	7,643,000	Named after England's "Virgin Queen," Elizabeth I	Dogwood	Cardinal
	Washington *WA* The Evergreen State	Olympia	6,396,000	Named in honor of George Washington, the first President of the United States	Coast rhododendron	Willow goldfinch
	West Virginia *WV* The Mountain State	Charleston	1,819,000	Named after England's "Virgin Queen," Elizabeth I	Rhododendron	Cardinal
	Wisconsin *WI* The Badger State	Madison	5,557,000	Probably came from a Miami Indian word meaning "river running through a red place"	Wood violet	Robin
	Wyoming *WY* The Equality State	Cheyenne	515,000	Based on a Delaware Indian word meaning "land of vast plains"	Indian paintbrush	Western meadowlark

Presidents of the United States

President, term of office	First Lady	Vice President
1 **George Washington** 1789–97	Martha Washington	John Adams
2 **John Adams** 1797–1801	Abigail Adams	Thomas Jefferson
3 **Thomas Jefferson** 1801–09	Martha Jefferson	Aaron Burr 1801–05 / George Clinton 1805–09
4 **James Madison** 1809–17	Dolley Madison	George Clinton 1809–12 / *vacant 1812–13* / Elbridge Gerry 1813–14 / *vacant 1814–17*
5 **James Monroe** 1817–25	Elizabeth Monroe	Daniel Tompkins
6 **John Quincy Adams** 1825–29	Louisa Adams	John Calhoun
7 **Andrew Jackson** 1829–37	Rachel Jackson (died 1828)	John Calhoun 1829–32 / Martin Van Buren 1833–37
8 **Martin Van Buren** 1837–41	Hannah Van Buren	Richard Johnson
9 **William Henry Harrison** 1841	Anna Harrison	John Tyler
10 **John Tyler** 1841–45	Letitia Tyler (died 1842) / Julia Tyler (from 1844)	*vacant*
11 **James Polk** 1845–49	Sarah Polk	George Dallas
12 **Zachary Taylor** 1849–50	Margaret Taylor	Millard Fillmore
13 **Millard Fillmore** 1850–53	Abigail Fillmore	*vacant*
14 **Franklin Pierce** 1853–57	Jane Pierce	William King 1853 / *vacant 1853–57*
15 **James Buchanan** 1857–61	Harriet Lane (niece)	John Breckinridge
16 **Abraham Lincoln** 1861–65	Mary Lincoln	Hannibal Hamlin 1861–65 / Andrew Johnson 1865
17 **Andrew Johnson** 1865–69	Eliza Johnson	*vacant*
18 **Ulysses S. Grant** 1869–77	Julia Grant	Schuyler Colfax 1869–73 / Henry Wilson 1873–75 / *vacant 1875–77*
19 **Rutherford Hayes** 1877–81	Lucy Hayes	William Wheeler
20 **James Garfield** 1881	Lucretia Garfield	Chester Arthur
21 **Chester Arthur** 1881–85	Ellen Arthur	*vacant*
22 **Grover Cleveland** 1885–89	Frances Cleveland	Thomas Hendricks 1885 / *vacant 1885–89*
23 **Benjamin Harrison** 1889–93	Caroline Harrison	Levi Morton
24 **Grover Cleveland** 1893–97	Frances Cleveland	Adlai Stevenson
25 **William McKinley** 1897–1901	Ida McKinley	Garret Hobart 1897–99 / *vacant 1899–1901* / Theodore Roosevelt 1901
26 **Theodore Roosevelt** 1901–09	Edith Roosevelt	*vacant 1901–05* / Charles Fairbanks 1905–09
27 **William H. Taft** 1909–13	Helen Taft	James S. Sherman 1909–12 / *vacant 1912–13*
28 **Woodrow Wilson** 1913–21	Ellen Wilson (died 1914) / Edith Wilson (from 1915)	Thomas R. Marshall
29 **Warren Harding** 1921–23	Florence Harding	(John) Calvin Coolidge
30 **(John) Calvin Coolidge** 1923–29	Grace Coolidge	*vacant 1923–25* / Charles Dawes 1925–29
31 **Herbert Hoover** 1929–33	Lou Hoover	Charles Curtis
32 **Franklin D. Roosevelt** 1933–45	(Anna) Eleanor Roosevelt	John N. Garner 1933–41 / Henry Wallace 1941–45 / Harry S. Truman 1945
33 **Harry S. Truman** 1945–53	Elizabeth "Bess" Truman	*vacant 1945–49* / Alben Barkley 1949–53
34 **Dwight Eisenhower** 1953–61	Mamie Eisenhower	Richard Nixon
35 **John F. Kennedy** 1961–63	Jacqueline Kennedy	Lyndon B. Johnson
36 **Lyndon B. Johnson** 1963–69	Claudia "Lady Bird" Johnson	*vacant 1963–65* / Hubert Humphrey 1965–69
37 **Richard Nixon** 1969–74	Patricia Nixon	Spiro Agnew 1969–73 / Gerald Ford 1973–74
38 **Gerald Ford** 1974–77	Elizabeth "Betty" Ford	Nelson Rockefeller
39 **Jimmy Carter** 1977–81	Rosalynn Carter	Walter Mondale
40 **Ronald Reagan** 1981–89	Nancy Reagan	George H.W. Bush
41 **George H.W. Bush** 1989–93	Barbara Bush	James Danforth "Dan" Quayle
42 **William "Bill" Clinton** 1993–2001	Hillary Rodham Clinton	Albert "Al" Gore, Jr.
43 **George W. Bush** 2001–	Laura Bush	Richard "Dick" Cheney

The World

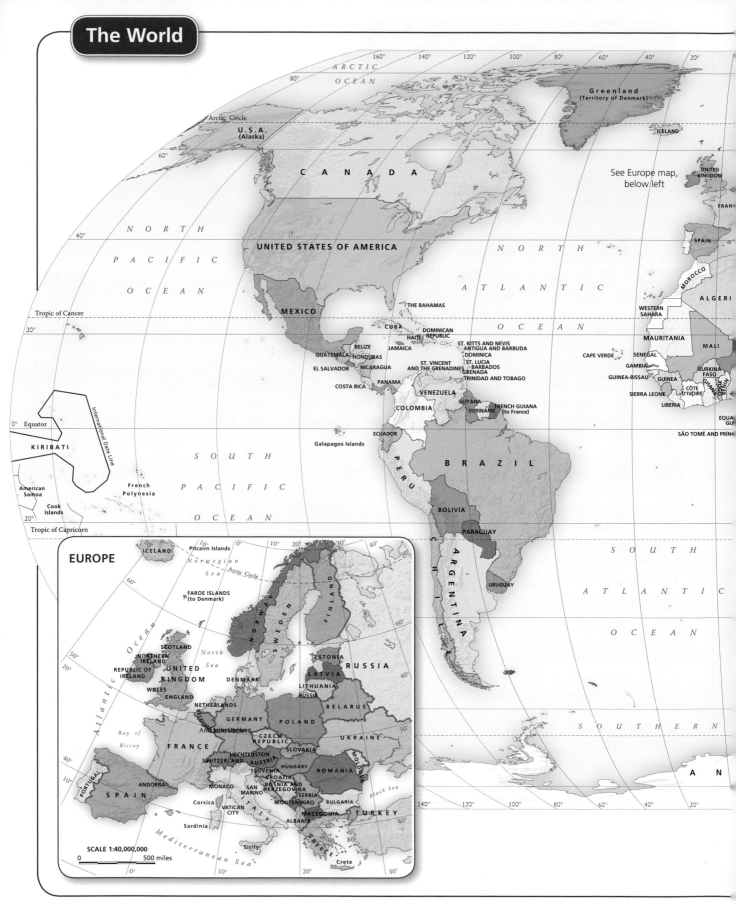

See Europe map, below left

ARCTIC OCEAN

Greenland
(Territory of Denmark)

ICELAND

Arctic Circle

U.S.A.
(Alaska)

C A N A D A

UNITED
KINGDOM

FRAN

N O R T H

SPAIN

P A C I F I C

UNITED STATES OF AMERICA

N O R T H

MOROCCO

O C E A N

A T L A N T I C

ALGERI

Tropic of Cancer

MEXICO

WESTERN
SAHARA

THE BAHAMAS

O C E A N

MAURITANIA

MALI

CUBA

DOMINICAN
REPUBLIC

HAITI

ST. KITTS AND NEVIS
ANTIGUA AND BARBUDA
DOMINICA

CAPE VERDE

SENEGAL

BELIZE

JAMAICA

GUATEMALA

HONDURAS

EL SALVADOR

NICARAGUA

ST. VINCENT
AND THE GRENADINES

ST. LUCIA
BARBADOS
GRENADA

TRINIDAD AND TOBAGO

GAMBIA

GUINEA-BISSAU

GUINEA

BURKINA
FASO

CÔTE
D'IVOIRE

COSTA RICA

PANAMA

VENEZUELA

SIERRA LEONE

LIBERIA

EQUA
GU

COLOMBIA

GUYANA

SURINAME

FRENCH GUIANA
(to France)

SÃO TOMÉ AND PRÍN

ECUADOR

0° Equator

International Date Line

KIRIBATI

Galapagos Islands

P E R U

B R A Z I L

S O U T H

S O U T H

American
Samoa

Cook
Islands

French
Polynesia

P A C I F I C

BOLIVIA

PARAGUAY

O C E A N

A T L A N T I C

A R G E N T I N A

C H I L E

URUGUAY

O C E A N

S O U T H E R N

A N

Tropic of Capricorn

EUROPE

ICELAND

Pitcairn Islands

Norwegian
Sea

Arctic Circle

FAROE ISLANDS
(to Denmark)

Atlantic   Ocean

SCOTLAND

NORTHERN
IRELAND

REPUBLIC OF
IRELAND

UNITED
KINGDOM

WALES

ENGLAND

North
Sea

NORWAY

SWEDEN

FINLAND

RUSSIA

ESTONIA

LATVIA

LITHUANIA

RUSSIA

DENMARK

BELARUS

NETHERLANDS

BELGIUM LUXEMBOURG

GERMANY

POLAND

Bay of
Biscay

FRANCE

CZECH
REPUBLIC

SLOVAKIA

UKRAINE

Andorra

LIECHTENSTEIN

SWITZERLAND

AUSTRIA

HUNGARY

ROMANIA

MOLDOVA

SLOVENIA

CROATIA

PORTUGAL

ANDORRA

MONACO

SAN
MARINO

BOSNIA AND
HERZEGOVINA

SERBIA

Black Sea

SPAIN

VATICAN
CITY

ITALY

MONTENEGRO

MACEDONIA

BULGARIA

Corsica

ALBANIA

TURKEY

Sardinia

GREECE

Sicily

Mediterranean
Sea

Crete

SCALE 1:40,000,000

0   500 miles

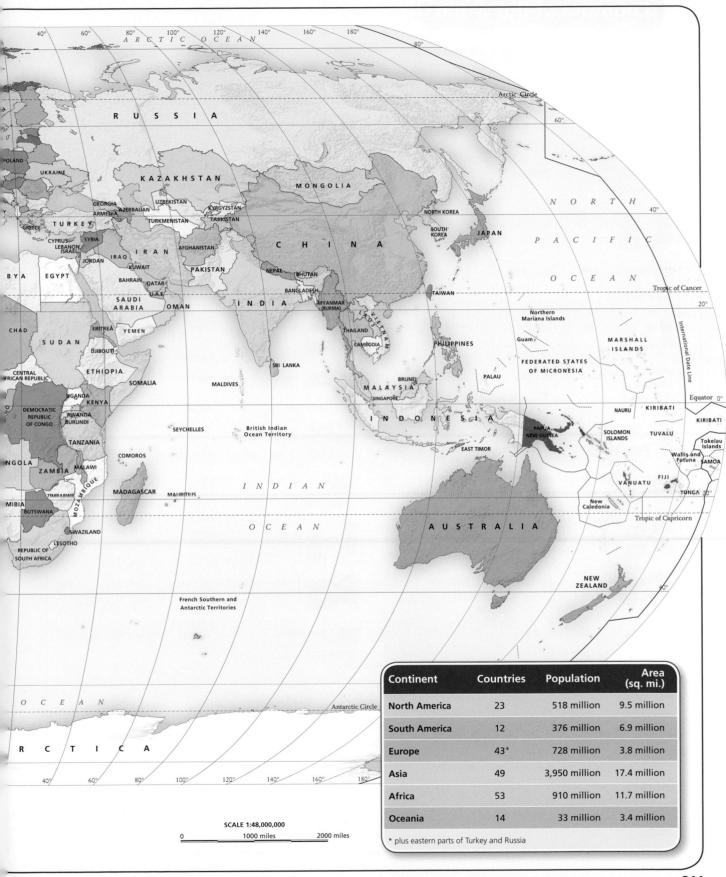

Continent	Countries	Population	Area (sq. mi.)
North America	23	518 million	9.5 million
South America	12	376 million	6.9 million
Europe	43*	728 million	3.8 million
Asia	49	3,950 million	17.4 million
Africa	53	910 million	11.7 million
Oceania	14	33 million	3.4 million

* plus eastern parts of Turkey and Russia

SCALE 1:48,000,000

0   1000 miles   2000 miles

Countries of the World

NORTH AMERICA

Flag	Country	Capital	Population	Area (sq. mi.)	Flag	Country	Capital	Population	Area (sq. mi.)
	Antigua and Barbuda	St. John's	69,000	171		Haiti	Port-au-Prince	8,309,000	10,710
	The Bahamas	Nassau	304,000	5,380		Honduras	Tegucigalpa	7,327,000	43,280
	Barbados	Bridgetown	280,000	166		Jamaica	Kingston	2,758,000	4,240
	Belize	Belmopan	288,000	8,870		Mexico	Mexico City	107,450,000	761,610
	Canada	Ottawa	33,099,000	3,855,100		Nicaragua	Managua	5,570,000	50,000
	Costa Rica	San José	4,075,000	19,730		Panama	Panama City	3,191,000	30,190
	Cuba	Havana	11,383,000	42,800		St. Kitts and Nevis	Basseterre	39,000	101
	Dominica	Roseau	69,000	291		St. Lucia	Castries	169,000	238
	Dominican Republic	Santo Domingo	9,184,000	18,810		St. Vincent and the Grenadines	Kingstown	118,000	150
	El Salvador	San Salvador	6,822,000	8,120		Trinidad and Tobago	Port of Spain	1,066,000	1,980
	Grenada	St. George's	90,000	133		United States of America	Washington, D.C.	298,444,000	3,794,080
	Guatemala	Guatemala	12,294,000	42,040					

SOUTH AMERICA

Flag	Country	Capital	Population	Area (sq. mi.)	Flag	Country	Capital	Population	Area (sq. mi.)
	Argentina	Buenos Aires	39,922,000	1,068,300		Brazil	Brasília	188,078,000	3,286,490
	Bolivia	La Paz / Sucre	8,989,000	424,160		Chile	Santiago	16,134,000	292,260

Flag	Country	Capital	Population	Area (sq. mi.)	Flag	Country	Capital	Population	Area (sq. mi.)
			SOUTH AMERICA						
	Colombia	Bogotá	43,593,000	439,740		Peru	Lima	28,303,000	496,230
	Ecuador	Quito	13,548,000	109,480		Suriname	Paramaribo	439,000	63,040
	Guyana	Georgetown	767,000	83,000		Uruguay	Montevideo	3,432,000	68,040
	Paraguay	Asunción	6,507,000	157,050		Venezuela	Caracas	25,730,000	352,140
			EUROPE						
	Albania	Tirana	3,582,000	11,100		Estonia	Tallinn	1,324,000	17,460
	Andorra	Andorra la Vella	71,000	180		Finland	Helsinki	5,231,000	130,560
	Austria	Vienna	8,193,000	32,380		France	Paris	60,876,000	211,210
	Belarus	Minsk	10,293,000	80,150		Germany	Berlin	82,422,000	137,850
	Belgium	Brussels	10,379,000	11,790		Greece	Athens	10,688,000	50,940
	Bosnia and Herzegovina	Sarajevo	4,499,000	19,740		Hungary	Budapest	9,981,000	35,920
	Bulgaria	Sofia	7,385,000	42,820		Iceland	Reykjavík	299,000	39,770
	Croatia	Zagreb	4,495,000	21,830		Ireland, Republic of	Dublin	4,062,000	27,140
	Czech Republic	Prague	10,236,000	30,450		Italy	Rome	58,134,000	116,310
	Denmark	Copenhagen	5,451,000	16,640		Latvia	Rīga	2,275,000	24,940

Countries of the World

Flag	Country	Capital	Population	Area (sq. mi.)	Flag	Country	Capital	Population	Area (sq. mi.)
EUROPE									
	Liechten-stein	Vaduz	34,000	62		Romania	Bucharest	22,304,000	91,700
	Lithuania	Vilnius	3,586,000	25,170		San Marino	San Marino	29,000	24
	Luxembourg	Luxembourg	474,000	1,000		Serbia	Belgrade	9,396,000	34,120
	Macedonia	Skopje	2,051,000	9,780		Slovakia	Bratislava	5,440,000	18,860
	Malta	Valletta	400,000	122		Slovenia	Ljubljana	2,010,000	7,830
	Moldova	Chişinău	4,467,000	13,070		Spain	Madrid	40,398,000	194,900
	Monaco	Monaco	33,000	0.75		Sweden	Stockholm	9,017,000	173,730
	Monte-negro	Podgorica / Cetinje	631,000	5,420		Switzerland	Bern	7,524,000	15,940
	Netherlands	Amsterdam / The Hague	16,492,000	16,030		Ukraine	Kiev	46,711,000	233,090
	Norway	Oslo	4,611,000	125,020		United Kingdom	London	60,609,000	94,530
	Poland	Warsaw	38,537,000	120,730		Vatican City	Vatican City	930	0.17
	Portugal	Lisbon	10,606,000	35,670					
ASIA									
	Afghanistan	Kabul	31,057,000	250,000		Azerbaijan	Baku	7,962,000	33,440
	Armenia	Yerevan	2,976,000	11,510		Bahrain	Al Manāmah	699,000	257

Flag	Country	Capital	Population	Area (sq. mi.)	Flag	Country	Capital	Population	Area (sq. mi.)
				ASIA					
	Bangladesh	Dacca	147,365,000	55,600		Kazakhstan	Astana	15,233,000	1,049,160
	Bhutan	Thimphu	2,280,000	18,150		Kuwait	Kuwait	2,418,000	6,880
	Brunei	Bandar Seri Begawan	379,000	2,230		Kyrgyzstan	Bishkek	5,214,000	76,640
	Cambodia	Phnom Penh	13,881,000	69,900		Laos	Vientiane	6,369,000	91,430
	China	Beijing	1,313,974,000	3,705,410		Lebanon	Beirut	3,874,000	4,020
	Cyprus	Nicosia	784,000	3,570		Malaysia	Kuala Lumpur	24,386,000	127,320
	East Timor	Dili	1,063,000	5,800		Maldives	Male	359,000	116
	Georgia	T'bilisi	4,662,000	26,910		Mongolia	Ulaanbaatar	2,832,000	603,910
	India	New Delhi	1,095,352,000	1,269,345		Myanmar (Burma)	Rangoon	47,383,000	261,970
	Indonesia	Jakarta	245,453,000	741,100		Nepal	Kathmandu	28,287,000	56,830
	Iran	Tehran	68,688,000	636,300		North Korea	P'yong-yang	23,113,000	46,540
	Iraq	Baghdad	26,783,000	168,750		Oman	Muscat	3,102,000	82,030
	Israel	Jerusalem	6,352,000	8,020		Pakistan	Islamabad	165,804,000	310,400
	Japan	Tokyo	127,464,000	145,880		Philippines	Manila	89,469,000	115,830
	Jordan	Ammān	5,907,000	35,640		Qatar	Doha	885,000	4,420

Countries of the World

Flag	Country	Capital	Population	Area (sq. mi.)	Flag	Country	Capital	Population	Area (sq. mi.)
ASIA									
	Russia	Moscow	142,894,000	6,592,770		Thailand	Bangkok	64,632,000	198,460
	Saudi Arabia	Riyadh	27,020,000	830,000		Turkey	Ankara	70,414,000	301,380
	Singapore	Singapore	4,492,000	268		Turkmen-istan	Ashgabat	5,043,000	188,460
	South Korea	Seoul	48,847,000	38,020		United Arab Emirates	Abu Dhabi	2,603,000	32,280
	Sri Lanka	Colombo / Sri Jayewar-denepura Kotte	20,222,000	25,330		Uzbekistan	Tashkent	27,307,000	172,740
	Syria	Damascus	18,881,000	71,500		Vietnam	Hanoi	84,403,000	127,240
	Taiwan	Taipei	23,036,000	13,980		Yemen	Şan'ā'	21,456,000	203,850
	Tajikistan	Dushanbe	7,321,000	55,250					
AFRICA									
	Algeria	Algiers	32,930,000	919,590		Cameroon	Yaoundé	17,341,000	183,570
	Angola	Luanda	12,127,000	481,350		Cape Verde	Praia	421,000	1,560
	Benin	Porto-Novo	7,863,000	43,480		Central African Republic	Bangui	4,303,000	240,530
	Botswana	Gaborone	1,640,000	231,800		Chad	Ndjamena	9,944,000	495,760
	Burkina Faso	Ouaga-dougou	13,903,000	105,870		Comoros	Moroni	691,000	838
	Burundi	Bujumbura	8,090,000	10,750		Congo	Brazzaville	3,702,000	132,050

Flag	Country	Capital	Population	Area (sq. mi.)	Flag	Country	Capital	Population	Area (sq. mi.)
				AFRICA					
	Côte d'Ivoire	Yamoussoukro	17,655,000	124,500		Liberia	Monrovia	3,042,000	43,000
	Democratic Republic of Congo	Kinshasa	62,661,000	906,570		Libya	Tripoli	5,901,000	679,360
	Djibouti	Djibouti	487,000	8,880		Madagascar	Antananarivo	18,596,000	226,660
	Egypt	Cairo	78,887,000	386,660		Malawi	Lilongwe	13,014,000	45,750
	Equatorial Guinea	Malabo	540,000	10,830		Mali	Bamako	11,717,000	478,770
	Eritrea	Asmara	4,787,000	46,840		Mauritania	Nouakchott	3,177,000	397,960
	Ethiopia	Addis Ababa	74,778,000	435,190		Mauritius	Port Louis	1,241,000	788
	Gabon	Libreville	1,425,000	103,350		Morocco	Rabat	33,241,000	172,410
	Gambia	Banjul	1,642,000	4,360		Mozambique	Maputo	19,687,000	309,500
	Ghana	Accra	22,410,000	92,460		Namibia	Windhoek	2,044,000	318,700
	Guinea	Conakry	9,690,000	94,930		Niger	Niamey	12,525,000	489,190
	Guinea-Bissau	Bissau	1,442,000	13,950		Nigeria	Abuja	131,860,000	356,670
	Kenya	Nairobi	34,708,000	224,960		Rwanda	Kigali	8,648,000	10,170
	Lesotho	Maseru	2,022,000	11,720		São Tomé and Príncipe	São Tomé	193,000	386

Countries of the World

Flag	Country	Capital	Population	Area (sq. mi.)	Flag	Country	Capital	Population	Area (sq. mi.)
	AFRICA								
	Senegal	Dakar	11,987,000	75,750		Tanzania	Dodoma	37,445,000	364,900
	Seychelles	Victoria	82,000	176		Togo	Lomé	5,549,000	21,930
	Sierra Leone	Freetown	6,005,000	27,700		Tunisia	Tunis	10,175,000	63,170
	Somalia	Mogadishu	8,863,000	246,200		Uganda	Kampala	28,196,000	91,140
	South Africa	Pretoria / Bloemfontein / Cape Town	44,188,000	471,010		Zambia	Lusaka	11,502,000	290,580
	Sudan	Khartoum	41,236,000	967,500		Zimbabwe	Harare	12,237,000	150,800
	Swaziland	Mbabane	1,136,000	6,700					
	OCEANIA								
	Australia	Canberra	20,264,000	2,967,910		Palau	Melekeok	21,000	177
	Fiji	Suva	906,000	7,050		Papua New Guinea	Port Moresby	5,671,000	178,700
	Kiribati	South Tarawa	105,000	313		Samoa	Apia	177,000	1,140
	Marshall Islands	Majuro	60,000	70		Solomon Islands	Honiara	552,000	10,980
	Micronesia, Federated States of	Palikir	108,000	271		Tonga	Nuku'alofa	115,000	289
	Nauru	Yaren	13,000	8		Tuvalu	Funafuti	12,000	10
	New Zealand	Wellington	4,076,000	103,740		Vanuatu	Port Vila	209,000	4,710

Territories and Dependencies

Territory/Dependency	Capital	Population	Area (sq. mi.)	Territory/Dependency	Capital	Population	Area (sq. mi.)
UNITED STATES OF AMERICA							
American Samoa	Pago Pago	58,000	77	Navassa Island		–	2.1
Baker Island		–	0.5	Northern Mariana Islands	Saipan	83,000	184
Guam	Hagåtña	171,000	209	Palmyra Atoll		*	5
Howland Island		–	0.6	Puerto Rico	San Juan	3,927,000	3,430
Johnston Atoll		–	1	U.S. Virgin Islands	Charlotte Amalie	109,000	134
Midway Islands		*	2.4	Wake Atoll		*	2.5
DENMARK							
Faroe Islands	Torshavn	47,000	540	Greenland	Nuuk	56,000	836,330
FRANCE							
Clipperton Island		–	2	Mayotte	Mamoutzou	201,000	140
French Guiana	Cayenne	200,000	35,140	New Caledonia	Nouméa	219,000	7,360
French Polynesia	Papeete	275,000	1,610	Réunion	Saint-Denis	788,000	970
French Southern and Antarctic Lands		*	3,020	St. Pierre and Miquelon	Saint-Pierre	7,000	93
Guadeloupe	Basse-Terre	453,000	690	Wallis and Futuna Islands	Matā'Utu	16,000	106
Martinique	Fort-de-France	436,000	420				
NETHERLANDS							
Aruba	Oranjestad	72,000	75	Netherlands Antilles	Willemstad	222,000	371
NORWAY							
Bouvetøya		–	19	Svalbard	Longyearbyen	2,700	23,560
Jan Mayen		*	146				
UNITED KINGDOM							
Anguilla	The Valley	14,000	39	Isle of Man	Douglas	75,000	221
Bermuda	Hamilton	66,000	21	Jersey	St. Helier	91,000	45
British Indian Ocean Territory		*	23	Montserrat	Plymouth	9,400	39
British Virgin Islands	Road Town	23,000	59	Pitcairn Islands	Adamstown	45	18
Cayman Islands	George Town	45,000	101	St. Helena	Jamestown	7,500	158
Falkland Islands	Stanley	3,000	4,700	South Georgia and Sandwich Islands		*	1,510
Gibraltar	Gibraltar	28,000	2.5	Turks and Caicos Islands	Cockburn Town	21,000	166
Guernsey	St. Peter Port	65,000	30				
CHINA							
Paracel Islands		*	4				
AUSTRALIA							
Ashmore Reef and Cartier Islands		*	2	Heard and McDonald Islands		–	159
Christmas Island	The Settlement	1,500	52	Norfolk Island	Kingston	1,800	13
Coral Sea Islands Territory		*	1.1				
NEW ZEALAND							
Cook Islands	Avarua	21,000	93	Tokelau Islands	(a)	1,400	4
Niue	Alofi	2,200	100				

(a) administrative center on each atoll   * no indigenous inhabitants   – uninhabited

The World's People

More than six billion people live on our planet. They are spread very unevenly over its landmasses, with China, India, and Europe being the most crowded areas. People have tended to settle near rivers or the coast, and about half of all people now live in cities. Improved living standards and medical care have allowed people to live longer than ever before, leading to an incredible population explosion. Another one million people are born every five days.

KEY DEVELOPMENTS

130,000 BP* Modern humans (*Homo sapiens*) in Africa

100,000 BP Modern humans in Southwest Asia; first deliberate burials (Israel)

60,000 BP Modern humans in East Asia and Australia; first sea voyages

40,000 BP Modern humans in Europe; early evidence of burials, art, and music

28,000 BP Female statuettes known as "Venus" figurines in Europe

15,000 BP Modern humans spread into America (possibly earlier).

"Venus of Willendorf" 26,000–24,000 BP

13,000 BP Domesticated plants in Southwest Asia

12,500 BP Villages of hunter-gatherers in Southwest Asia

12,000 BP Domesticated dogs in the Levant

10,500 BP Domesticated sheep in Iraq

9000 BP Farming in New Guinea and India; rice cultivation in China

8500 BP Farming in Europe

7000 BP First cities (Southwest Asia); copper work in the Balkans

6300 BP Maize cultivation in Mexico

5500 BP Wheel and plow developed and bronze used in Southwest Asia.

5400 BP Sumerian cuneiform writing

5100 BP Hieroglyphic script in Egypt

Sumerian tablet c. 5000 BP

4500 BP Polynesians use outrigger canoes to migrate throughout South Pacific; Minoans and Mycenaeans build first seagoing cargo ships.

3700 BP The world's first codified laws are recorded in Babylon.

3500 BP Iron smelting in Southwest Asia

AD 1041 Printing with movable clay type invented in China.

1050 Asian astrolabes arrive in Europe and revolutionize navigation.

1183 Magnetic compass invented in China.

1250 Gun invented in China.

1450 First full-rigged ships lead to European Age of Discovery and colonization of much of the globe.

1455 Gutenberg invents printing with movable metal type in Germany.

Columbus's ship Santa Maria

*BP Years before present

WORLD RELIGIONS

- Christianity 33%
- Hinduism 15%
- Buddhism 6%
- Chinese traditional 4%
- Non-religious 14%
- Other 3%
- Primal indigenous 3%
- Islam 22%

NATIVE SPEAKERS

Mandarin Chinese	874,000,000	
Hindi	366,000,000	
English	341,000,000	
Spanish	340,000,000	
Bengali	207,000,000	
Portuguese	176,000,000	
Russian	167,000,000	
Arabic	150,000,000	
Japanese	125,000,000	
German	100,000,000	
Korean	78,000,000	
French	77,000,000	

Ways of worship

The earliest signs of religious belief date back 60,000 years, and virtually every culture since has followed some kind of religion. There are now hundreds of different religious traditions in the world. Of these, Hinduism, Buddhism, Judaism, Christianity, and Islam have had the broadest influence.

Many languages

There are about 6,000 languages, but more than half of all people use one of the twelve shown in this table (left) as their first language. Although English does not have the most native speakers, it is used so much as a second language that it dominates global communication.

Map labels: NORTH AMERICA, Toronto, Chicago, New York, Philadelphia, Los Angeles, Miami, Mexico City, Bogotá, SOUTH AMERICA, Lima, Belo Ho, São Paulo, Rio de, Santiago, Buenos Aires

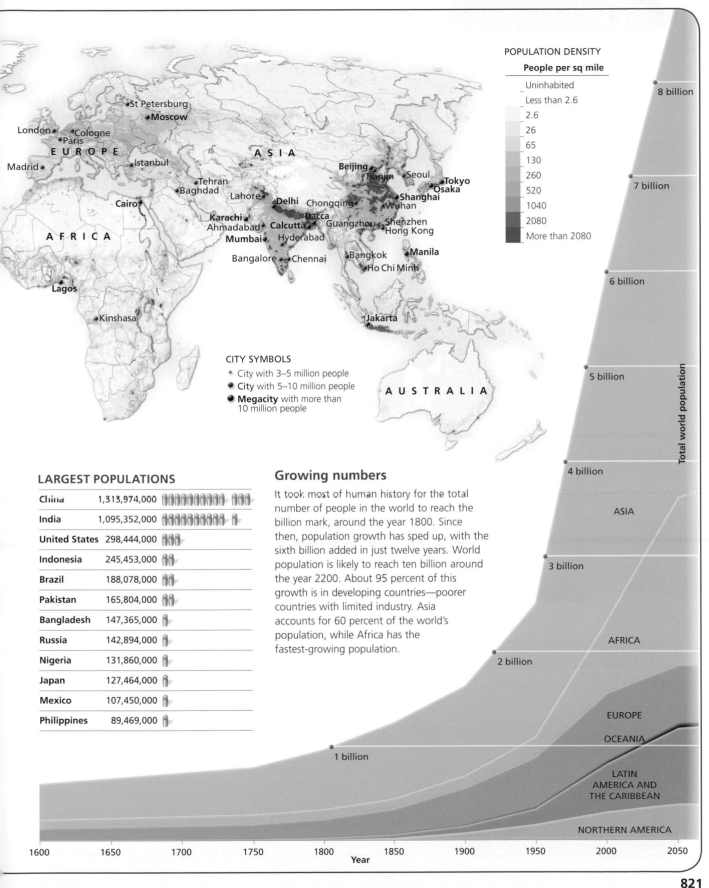

People per sq mile

Uninhabited
Less than 2.6
2.6
26
65
130
260
520
1040
2080
More than 2080

CITY SYMBOLS

• City with 3–5 million people
• City with 5–10 million people
• **Megacity** with more than 10 million people

Total world population

8 billion
7 billion
6 billion
5 billion
4 billion
ASIA
3 billion
AFRICA
2 billion
EUROPE
OCEANIA
1 billion
LATIN AMERICA AND THE CARIBBEAN
NORTHERN AMERICA

LARGEST POPULATIONS

China	1,313,974,000
India	1,095,352,000
United States	298,444,000
Indonesia	245,453,000
Brazil	188,078,000
Pakistan	165,804,000
Bangladesh	147,365,000
Russia	142,894,000
Nigeria	131,860,000
Japan	127,464,000
Mexico	107,450,000
Philippines	89,469,000

Growing numbers

It took most of human history for the total number of people in the world to reach the billion mark, around the year 1800. Since then, population growth has sped up, with the sixth billion added in just twelve years. World population is likely to reach ten billion around the year 2200. About 95 percent of this growth is in developing countries—poorer countries with limited industry. Asia accounts for 60 percent of the world's population, while Africa has the fastest-growing population.

Year

1600 1650 1700 1750 1800 1850 1900 1950 2000 2050

The Earth's Climate

Our planet is home to a vast range of environments, from steamy rain forests to icy polar regions. Distinct weather patterns, known as climates, helped to create this variety. The Earth is unevenly heated by the Sun. Areas around the Equator receive intense sunlight all year long, polar regions receive weak sunlight, and those in between receive varying amounts throughout the year. The circulation of air and ocean waters around the globe determines how much wind and rain an area experiences. The climate influences which plants and animals can survive in each region.

CLIMATE ZONES

Tropical Hot and wet all year round, tropical climates feature dense, lush rain forests with abundant and varied animal life.

Subtropical These climates have hot, wet summers, but winters are drier and cooler. Vegetation is less dense than in the tropics.

Arid Very little rain falls in these desert climates. Days are hot and nights are cold. The life forms have adapted to the harsh conditions.

Semiarid With too little rainfall for forest and too much for desert, semiarid climates feature grassland and herds of grazing animals.

Temperate These climates experience four seasons a year, with warm summers and cold winters. Many trees lose their leaves in fall.

Northern temperate The winters in these zones are long, snowy, and very cold, while the summers are cool.

Polar The Arctic and Antarctic zones are extremely cold and dry all year. They are covered in either low-growing tundra plants or ice.

Mountain These zones are colder, wetter, and windier than low-lying areas. Many animals move down the slopes when winter comes.

Greatest temperature change in a day: 100°F, from 44°F to –56°F, at Browning, Montana, U.S.A., 1916

Most snow in one year: 1,224 inches on Mt. Rainier, Washington, U.S.A., 1971–72

Strongest measured wind gust: 231 miles per hour on Mt. Washington, New Hampshire, U.S.A., 1934

NORTH AMERICA

SOUTH AMERICA

Driest place: 0.02 inches per year in Quillagua, Atacama Desert, Chile, 1964–2001

THE GREENHOUSE EFFECT

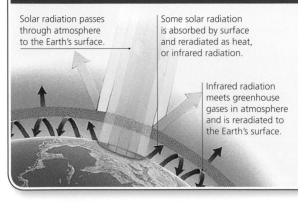

Solar radiation passes through atmosphere to the Earth's surface.

Some solar radiation is absorbed by surface and reradiated as heat, or infrared radiation.

Infrared radiation meets greenhouse gases in atmosphere and is reradiated to the Earth's surface.

The Earth is warm enough for life because the atmosphere contains carbon dioxide, methane, and other "greenhouse gases" that trap the Sun's heat. During the past 150 years, the use of fossil fuels (oil, gas, and coal) and other human activities have dramatically increased the levels of greenhouse gases. Over the same period, the Earth has become warmer, with average temperatures rising about 1°F. If this trend continues, the effects could be devastating. As ice sheets and glaciers melt, sea levels will rise and flood many islands and coastal regions. Rainfall patterns may change, with drought causing serious food shortages in Africa and India. To slow down this climate change, most industrialized countries signed the Kyoto Protocol in 1997 and agreed to reduce greenhouse gas emissions.

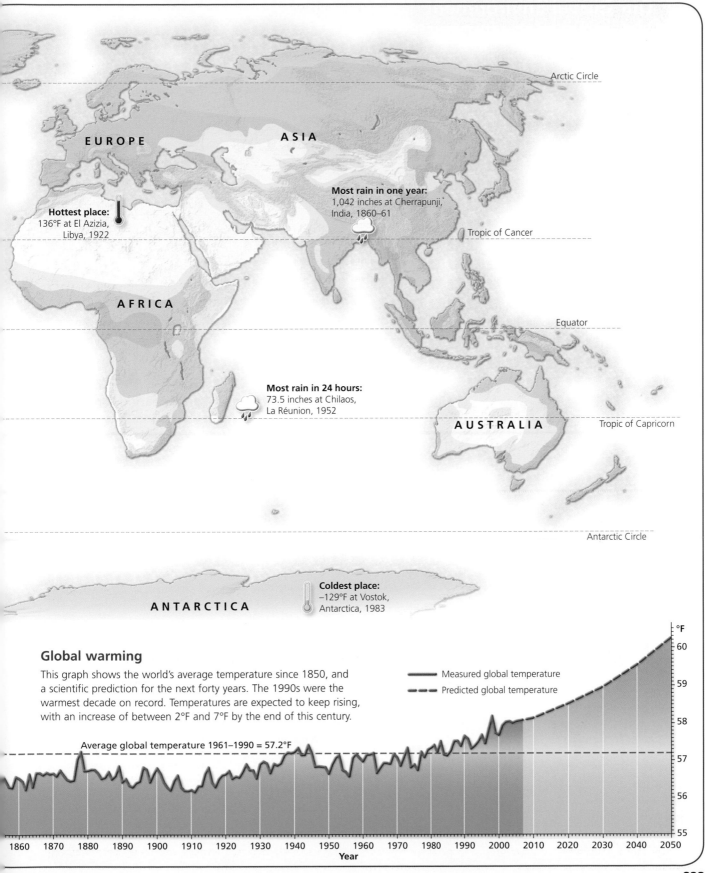

Hottest place:
136°F at El Azizia,
Libya, 1922

Most rain in one year:
1,042 inches at Cherrapunji,
India, 1860–61

EUROPE

ASIA

Arctic Circle

Tropic of Cancer

AFRICA

Equator

Most rain in 24 hours:
73.5 inches at Chilaos,
La Réunion, 1952

AUSTRALIA

Tropic of Capricorn

Antarctic Circle

Coldest place:
−129°F at Vostok,
Antarctica, 1983

ANTARCTICA

Global warming

This graph shows the world's average temperature since 1850, and
a scientific prediction for the next forty years. The 1990s were the
warmest decade on record. Temperatures are expected to keep rising,
with an increase of between 2°F and 7°F by the end of this century.

——— Measured global temperature
- - - Predicted global temperature

Average global temperature 1961–1990 = 57.2°F

°F
60
59
58
57
56
55

1860 1870 1880 1890 1900 1910 1920 1930 1940 1950 1960 1970 1980 1990 2000 2010 2020 2030 2040 2050
Year

Our Global Environment

Humans have shown great ingenuity in using the Earth's rich resources. We have flourished as a species by exploiting wild food supplies, forests, farmland, freshwater, minerals, and fossil fuels. The actions of humans have always affected the environment in some way, but the industrialization and population explosion of the past 150 years have led to an environmental crisis. Supplies of fossil fuels and metals are running out, and there is not enough freshwater to support the population in some regions. In almost every part of the globe, the environment is suffering from serious problems. Vast tracts of forest have been destroyed, soil has become too poor to grow crops, the air in some cities is thick with smog, and many lakes, rivers, and seas are polluted. Animals and plants are showing the strain, with thousands of species becoming extinct every year. Throughout the world, more and more people are supporting campaigns to save threatened wildlife, protect natural habitats, and reduce pollution.

Species under threat

Biologists have checked the status of most mammals, birds, and amphibians, but other groups need more study. For instance, only 0.13 percent of the one million known insects have been assessed. Some experts fear that half of all species could vanish by 2100.

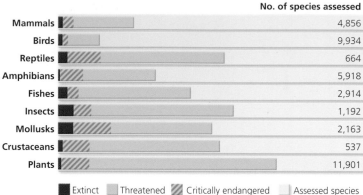

No. of species assessed

Mammals	4,856
Birds	9,934
Reptiles	664
Amphibians	5,918
Fishes	2,914
Insects	1,192
Mollusks	2,163
Crustaceans	537
Plants	11,901

■ Extinct   ■ Threatened   ◨ Critically endangered   ☐ Assessed species

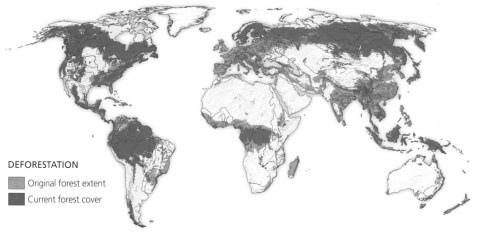

DEFORESTATION

■ Original forest extent
■ Current forest cover

Disappearing forests

At least 40,000 square miles of forest are lost every year, mainly because they are logged for timber or cleared for farming. In Africa and Asia, only about one-third of the original forest cover remains. Once soil has lost its vegetation, it can easily become eroded by water and wind.

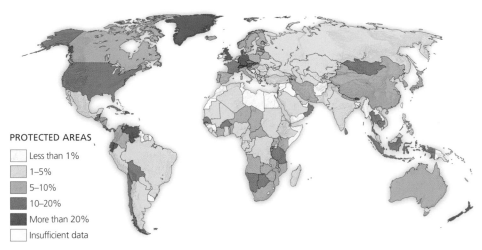

PROTECTED AREAS

☐ Less than 1%
☐ 1–5%
☐ 5–10%
☐ 10–20%
■ More than 20%
☐ Insufficient data

Nature conservation

National parks, nature reserves, wildlife sanctuaries, and other protected areas now make up 6.4 percent of the Earth's land surface. It is vital to conserve areas that are large enough to maintain biodiversity—the variety of living things. Conservation efforts also need to involve and help the local people, especially in poor regions.

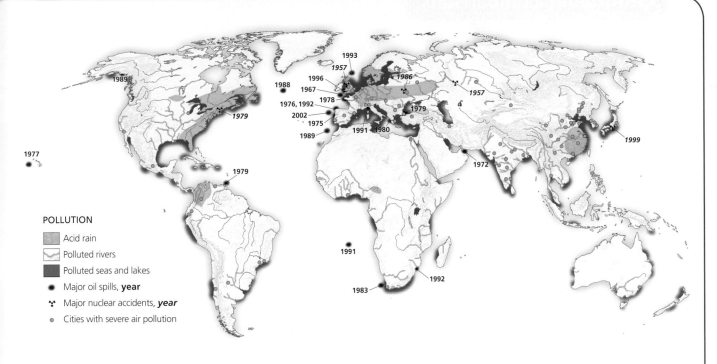

POLLUTION

- Acid rain
- Polluted rivers
- Polluted seas and lakes
- Major oil spills, **year**
- Major nuclear accidents, **year**
- Cities with severe air pollution

A polluted planet

About 93 percent of materials used in modern production end up as waste and pollute the world's ecosystems. Air pollution exceeds safe levels in more than 80 cities. Smogs can deposit acid rain that destroys vegetation and poisons waterways. Fertilizers and sewage end up in lakes, rivers, and oceans. Oil spills and nuclear accidents have widespread effects.

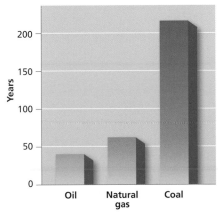

A limited supply

The supply of fossil fuels is finite, and the world may start to run out of oil and natural gas within decades. Many people are looking to cleaner and renewable energy sources, such as water, wind, geothermal, and solar power.

The world's water

Of all the world's resource issues, the scarcity of freshwater may be the most pressing. During the past century, water consumption increased sixfold. At least 35 percent of people are now suffering chronic water shortage, mostly in developing countries such as Ethiopia, Kenya, India, and China.

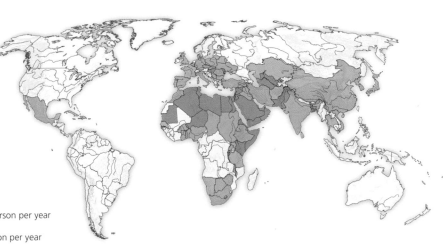

WATER SHORTAGE

- Extreme water shortage: less than 1,300 cubic yards per person per year
- Chronic water shortage: 1,300–2,600 cubic yards per person per year
- Seasonal water shortage: 2,600–6,500 cubic yards per person per year

Geographic Comparisons

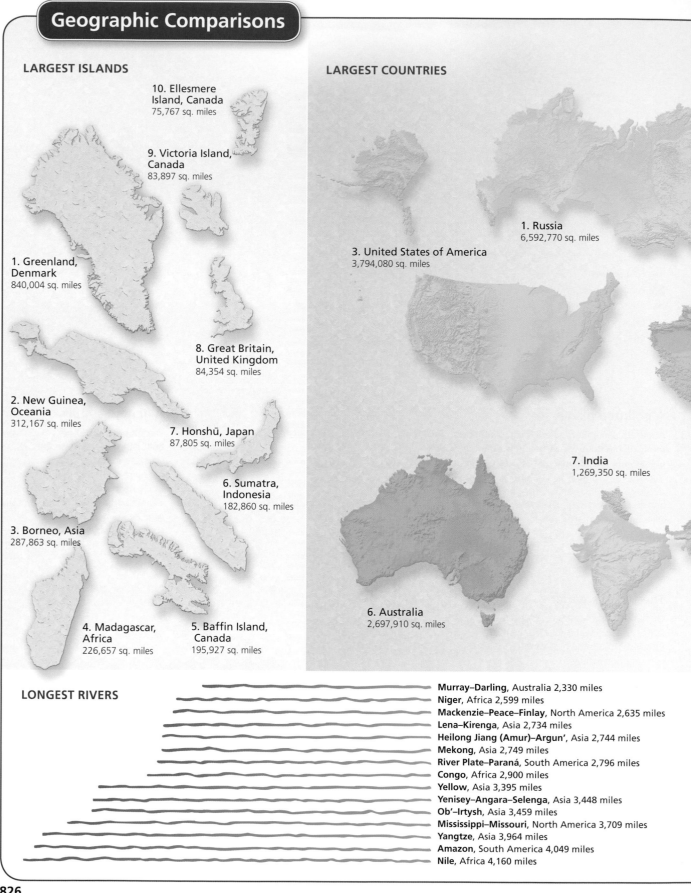

LARGEST ISLANDS

10. Ellesmere Island, Canada
75,767 sq. miles

9. Victoria Island, Canada
83,897 sq. miles

1. Greenland, Denmark
840,004 sq. miles

8. Great Britain, United Kingdom
84,354 sq. miles

2. New Guinea, Oceania
312,167 sq. miles

7. Honshū, Japan
87,805 sq. miles

6. Sumatra, Indonesia
182,860 sq. miles

3. Borneo, Asia
287,863 sq. miles

4. Madagascar, Africa
226,657 sq. miles

5. Baffin Island, Canada
195,927 sq. miles

LARGEST COUNTRIES

1. Russia
6,592,770 sq. miles

3. United States of America
3,794,080 sq. miles

7. India
1,269,350 sq. miles

6. Australia
2,697,910 sq. miles

LONGEST RIVERS

Murray–Darling, Australia 2,330 miles
Niger, Africa 2,599 miles
Mackenzie–Peace–Finlay, North America 2,635 miles
Lena–Kirenga, Asia 2,734 miles
Heilong Jiang (Amur)–Argun', Asia 2,744 miles
Mekong, Asia 2,749 miles
River Plate–Paraná, South America 2,796 miles
Congo, Africa 2,900 miles
Yellow, Asia 3,395 miles
Yenisey–Angara–Selenga, Asia 3,448 miles
Ob'–Irtysh, Asia 3,459 miles
Mississippi–Missouri, North America 3,709 miles
Yangtze, Asia 3,964 miles
Amazon, South America 4,049 miles
Nile, Africa 4,160 miles

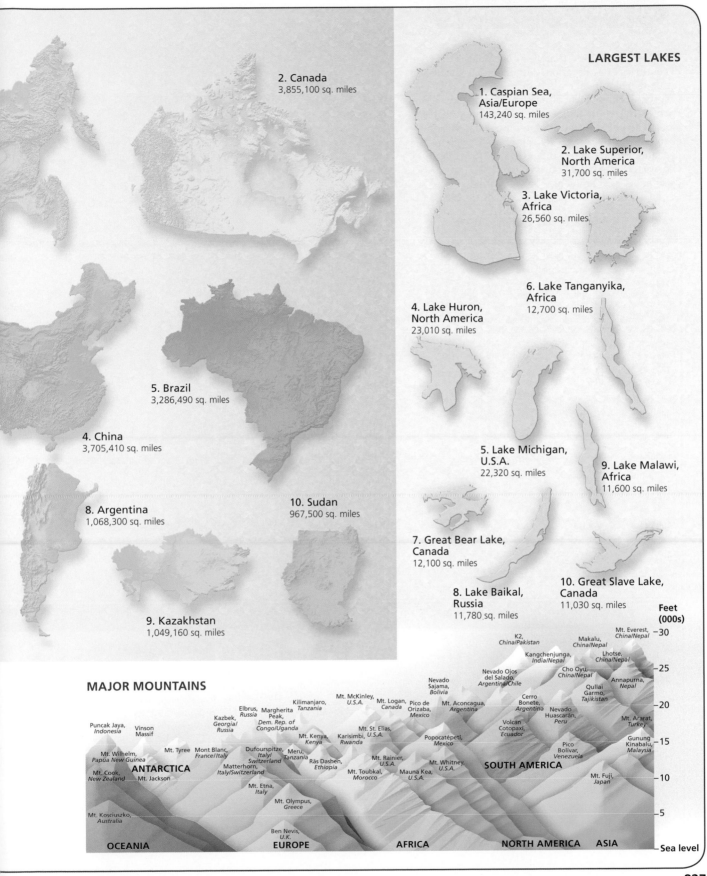

2. Canada
3,855,100 sq. miles

LARGEST LAKES

1. Caspian Sea, Asia/Europe
143,240 sq. miles

2. Lake Superior, North America
31,700 sq. miles

3. Lake Victoria, Africa
26,560 sq. miles

6. Lake Tanganyika, Africa
12,700 sq. miles

4. Lake Huron, North America
23,010 sq. miles

5. Brazil
3,286,490 sq. miles

4. China
3,705,410 sq. miles

5. Lake Michigan, U.S.A.
22,320 sq. miles

9. Lake Malawi, Africa
11,600 sq. miles

8. Argentina
1,068,300 sq. miles

10. Sudan
967,500 sq. miles

7. Great Bear Lake, Canada
12,100 sq. miles

10. Great Slave Lake, Canada
11,030 sq. miles

9. Kazakhstan
1,049,160 sq. miles

8. Lake Baikal, Russia
11,780 sq. miles

Feet (000s)

MAJOR MOUNTAINS

K2, China/Pakistan — 30
Mt. Everest, China/Nepal
Makalu, China/Nepal
Kangchenjunga, India/Nepal
Lhotse, China/Nepal
Nevado Ojos del Salado, Argentina/Chile
Cho Oyu, China/Nepal — 25
Nevado Sajama, Bolivia
Mt. McKinley, U.S.A.
Mt. Logan, Canada
Pico de Orizaba, Mexico
Mt. Aconcagua, Argentina
Cerro Bonete, Argentina
Qullai Garmo, Tajikistan
Annapurna, Nepal
Kilimanjaro, Tanzania
Elbrus, Russia
Margherita Peak, Dem. Rep. of Congo/Uganda
Volcán Cotopaxi, Ecuador
Nevado Huascarán, Peru — 20
Kazbek, Georgia/Russia
Puncak Jaya, Indonesia
Vinson Massif
Mt. St. Elias, U.S.A.
Mt. Ararat, Turkey
Mt. Kenya, Kenya
Karisimbi, Rwanda
Pico Bolívar, Venezuela
Gunung Kinabalu, Malaysia — 15
Mt. Wilhelm, Papua New Guinea
Mt. Tyree
Mont Blanc, France/Italy
Dufourspitze, Italy/Switzerland
Meru, Tanzania
Popocatépetl, Mexico
Mt. Cook, New Zealand
Mt. Jackson
Matterhorn, Italy/Switzerland
Rãs Dashen, Ethiopia
Mt. Rainier, U.S.A.
Mt. Whitney, U.S.A.
SOUTH AMERICA
Mt. Fuji, Japan — 10
ANTARCTICA
Mt. Toubkal, Morocco
Mauna Kea, U.S.A.
Mt. Etna, Italy
Mt. Kosciuszko, Australia — 5
Mt. Olympus, Greece
Ben Nevis, U.K.
OCEANIA   **EUROPE**   **AFRICA**   **NORTH AMERICA**   **ASIA**
— Sea level

827

Journeys of Discovery

The map of the world that we know today is the result of centuries of exploration. Although there had been intrepid explorers in earlier times, no one knew how vast the world was when the Age of Discovery began in the early 1400s. The search for new trade routes, along with advances in shipbuilding and navigation, encouraged the voyages of Columbus, Magellan, da Gama, Drake, Cook, and others. By the time explorers reached the South Pole in 1911, the world map was complete.

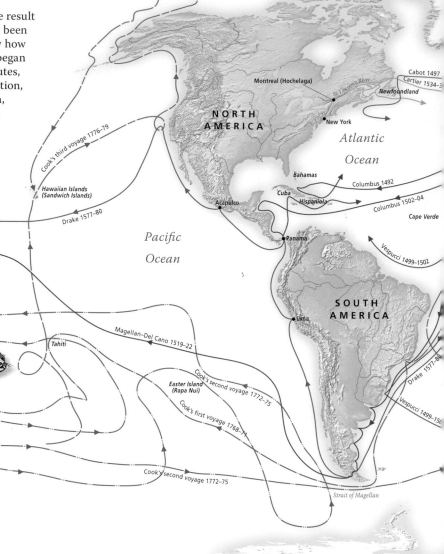

Cabot 1497
Cartier 1534–3
Newfoundland
Montreal (Hochelaga)
St. Lawrence River
NORTH AMERICA
New York
Atlantic Ocean
Cook's third voyage 1776–79
Hawaiian Islands (Sandwich Islands)
Drake 1577–80
Bahamas
Columbus 1492
Cuba
Hispaniola
Columbus 1502–04
Cape Verde
Acapulco
Pacific Ocean
Panama
Vespucci 1499–1502
SOUTH AMERICA
Lima
Magellan–Del Cano 1519–22
Tahiti
Cook's second voyage 1772–75
Easter Island (Rapa Nui)
Drake 1577–8
Cook's first voyage 1768–7
Vespucci 1499–150
Cook's second voyage 1772–75
Strait of Magellan

ANTARCTIC EXPEDITIONS

1773 England's James Cook crosses the Antarctic Circle and circumnavigates Antarctica.

1819–21 Russia's Fabian von Bellingshausen circumnavigates the Antarctic and discovers a number of offshore islands.

1820 First sighting of Antarctica by British naval officers, William Smith and Edward Bransfield.

1821 First landing on continental Antarctica by American sealer Captain John Davis. Disputed.

1823 British whaler James Weddell discovers the sea named for him and finds the most southerly point known at that time.

1840s Separate British, French, and American expeditions establish the status of Antarctica as a continent after sailing along the coastline.

Antarctica's Weddell seals are named after the British explorer James Weddell.

1899 Carsten Borchgrevink leads a British expedition landing at Cape Adare. Believed to be the first confirmed landing.

1909 Australia's Douglas Mawson reaches the South Magnetic Pole.

1911 Norway's Roald Amundsen reaches the South Pole ahead of Britain's Robert Scott.

EXPLORING THE GLOBE

2750 BC First recorded exploring expedition, from Egypt to Arabia

2500 BC Polynesians begin migrating throughout the South Pacific using outrigger canoes.

Polynesian outrigger canoe

7TH C. BC Phoenicians explore the Mediterranean Sea and the Atlantic coasts of Africa and Europe, and circumnavigate Africa on behalf of the Egyptian Pharaoh Necho.

510 BC Greek sailor Scylax explores India and Arabia for Persia.

500 BC Phoenician Hanno sails along northwestern Africa. Himilco, another Phoenician navigator, travels from Carthage to England and establishes tin trade.

4th c. BC Greeks travel to England and India.

138 BC China's Zhang Qian launches the first of several overland expeditions that open up the Silk Road, the main trade route between China and the West.

1st c. AD Chinese invent magnetic compass.

AD 120 Ptolemy of Egypt invents map projections that allow the curved surface of the Earth to be shown on a flat drawing.

AD 860 Vikings discover Iceland.

Viking longship

AD 982 Viking Erik the Red sails from Iceland and discovers Greenland.

1002 Viking Leif Eriksson finds North America.

1050 Asian astrolabes arrive in Europe.

1191 Tea first exported from China.

1271 Venetian Marco Polo travels to China via Silk Road, returning in 1295.

Arab astrolabe from 1131

1325 Arab traveler Ibn Buttuta leaves on a 75,000 mile journey to Asia and Africa, returning almost 30 years later, in 1354.

1405–33 Cheng Ho leads voyages in South Pacific and Indian Ocean on behalf of China's Ming Emperor.

1441 Portuguese sail to West Africa and reestablish the slave trade.

1450 Portugal's Prince Henry the Navigator founds naval observatory for the teaching of navigation, astronomy, and cartography.

1453 Turks overrun Constantinople and shut off the overland trade route between East and West.

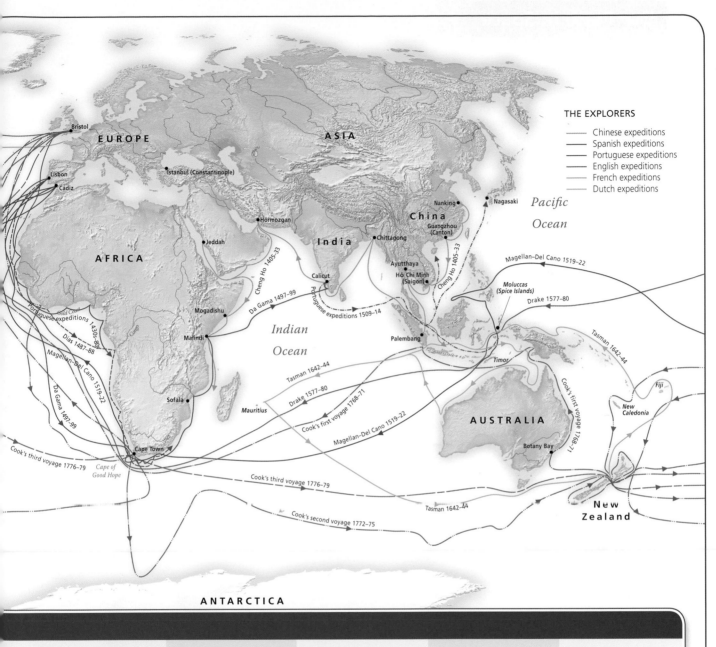

THE EXPLORERS

—— Chinese expeditions
—— Spanish expeditions
—— Portuguese expeditions
—— English expeditions
—— French expeditions
—— Dutch expeditions

EUROPE

Bristol

Lisbon
Cádiz

Istanbul (Constantinople)

AFRICA

Jeddah

Hormozgan

ASIA

India

China

Nanking

Nagasaki

Guangzhou
(Canton)

Chittagong

Calicut

Cheng Ho 1405–33

Da Gama 1497–99

Portuguese expeditions 1509–14

Ayutthaya

Hô Chi Minh
(Saigon)

Cheng Ho 1405–33

Moluccas
(Spice Islands)

Pacific
Ocean

Magellan–Del Cano 1519–22

Drake 1577–80

Mogadishu

Malindi

Gold Coast

Portuguese expeditions 1470s–80s

Dias 1487–88

Magellan–Del Cano 1519–22

Da Gama 1497–99

Cook's third voyage 1776–79

Sofala

Cape Town

Cape of
Good Hope

Indian
Ocean

Mauritius

Tasman 1642–44

Drake 1577–80

Cook's first voyage 1768–71

Magellan–Del Cano 1519–22

Cook's third voyage 1776–79

Cook's second voyage 1772–75

Palembang

Timor

Tasman 1642–44

AUSTRALIA

Botany Bay

Cook's first voyage 1768–71

Tasman 1642–44

Fiji

New
Caledonia

New
Zealand

ANTARCTICA

1470–84 Portuguese find Africa's Gold Coast and the Congo River.

1487 Bartholomeu Dias of Portugal reaches the Cape of Good Hope.

1492 Searching for a sea route to the East, Christopher Columbus sails west from Spain and finds the Bahamas, Cuba, and Hispaniola (today's Haiti and Dominican Republic).

Columbus's ship
Santa Maria

1494 Spain and Portugal sign the Treaty of Tordesillas, dividing the rest of the world between themselves.

1497 John Cabot lands in Newfoundland.

1497 Portugal's Vasco da Gama rounds Cape of Good Hope, reaching India in 1498.

1503 Amerigo Vespucci maps South America for Portugal. Columbus reaches Central America.

1511 Portugal defeats the Arabs and gains control of the Spice Islands, the center of Far East trade.

1519 Ferdinand Magellan begins first circumnavigation of the world for Spain with five ships and 270 men. A single ship with just eighteen crew returns in 1522.

Magellan's
ship Victoria

1534 Jacques Cartier enters Canada's St. Lawrence River and claims land for France.

1577–80 Francis Drake performs second circumnavigation of the world for England.

Cook's ship
Endeavour

1609 Henry Hudson claims New York and Hudson River for the Dutch.

1735 Invention of the chronometer enables precise navigation.

The first
chronometer

1768 James Cook begins the first of his Pacific voyages, reaching New Zealand in 1769 and Australia in 1770.

1778 On his second voyage, Cook crosses the Antarctic Circle.

1778 Cook finds Hawaiian Islands.

1909 American Robert Peary reaches North Pole.

1911 Norwegian Roald Amundsen reaches South Pole.

1969 Americans Neil Armstrong and Buzz Aldrin land on the Moon.

Apollo 11
spacecraft

As vast as our planet may seem to us, it is a mere speck compared to the immensity of the universe. Our local neighborhood is the solar system, where the Earth is the third of eight planets that orbit the Sun. The planets fall into two groups. The inner rocky planets are Mercury, Venus, Earth, and Mars. The outer gas giants are Jupiter, Saturn, Uranus, and Neptune. Other members of the solar system include moons, asteroids, comets, and dwarf planets. The Sun is a star, a giant ball of hydrogen and helium that shines because of nuclear reactions in its core. Beyond the solar system are other stars, some with their own planets. The Sun, billions of other stars, and many clouds of gas and dust make up the Milky Way galaxy. A great spiral galaxy, the Milky Way belongs to a cluster of galaxies known as the Local Group. This cluster belongs to the Local Supercluster, one of the many collections of galaxies that make up the structure of the universe.

The Local Group
With about 40 members, the Local Group is a cluster of galaxies held together by one another's gravity. It features three large spiral galaxies—our own Milky Way, the Andromeda galaxy, and the Pinwheel.

The Milky Way
Our galaxy is made up of the Sun and about 200 billion other stars. The spiral is slowly turning, with the Sun taking 226 million years to complete one revolution.

Uranus
Neptune
Mercury
Venus
Earth
Mars
Jupiter
Saturn

The Earth's neighbors

Shown here to scale, the eight planets range from giant Jupiter, 1,300 times bigger than the Earth, to little Mercury, 18 times smaller than the Earth. All the planets seem small next to the Sun, which could hold almost 1,000 Jupiters or 1,304,000 Earths.

DWARF PLANETS

Considered the ninth planet when it was discovered in 1930, Pluto is now called a dwarf planet. It is just one member of the Kuiper Belt, a vast collection of small, icy worlds at the edge of the solar system. Other dwarf planets include Sedna, Eris, and $2003EL_{61}$.

$2003EL_{61}$
Eris
Sedna
Pluto

THE EIGHT PLANETS

	Mercury	Venus	Earth	Mars	Jupiter	Saturn	Uranus	Neptune
Diameter (miles)	3,032	7,521	7,926	4,222	88,846	74,898	31,763	30,775
Mass (Earth's mass = 1)	0.055	0.82	1.0	0.11	317.8	95.2	14.5	17.1
Distance from Sun (millions of miles)	36	67	93	142	484	891	1,785	2,793
Orbit period	88 days	225 days	365.25 days	687 days	11.9 years	29.5 years	84.0 years	164.8 years
Rotation period	59 days	243 days	23 h 56 m	24 h 37 m	9 h 56 m	10 h 39 m	17 h 14 m	16 h 7 m
Known moons	0	0	1	2	63	56	27	13

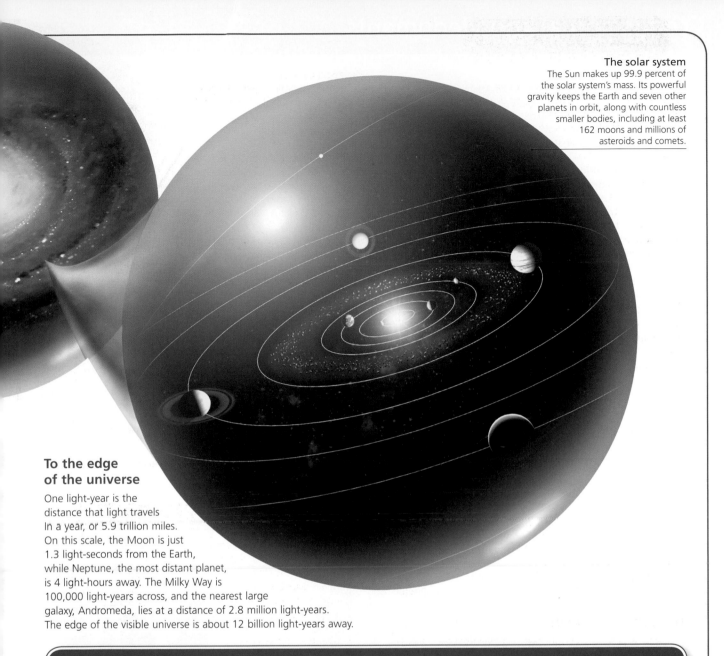

The solar system

The Sun makes up 99.9 percent of the solar system's mass. Its powerful gravity keeps the Earth and seven other planets in orbit, along with countless smaller bodies, including at least 162 moons and millions of asteroids and comets.

To the edge of the universe

One light-year is the distance that light travels in a year, or 5.9 trillion miles. On this scale, the Moon is just 1.3 light-seconds from the Earth, while Neptune, the most distant planet, is 4 light-hours away. The Milky Way is 100,000 light-years across, and the nearest large galaxy, Andromeda, lies at a distance of 2.8 million light-years. The edge of the visible universe is about 12 billion light-years away.

SOLAR SYSTEM BIRTH

Most scientists believe that the solar system formed about 4.6 billion years ago, when a large cloud of dust and gas began to collapse. The densest part of the cloud formed a core that grew hotter and larger, eventually becoming the infant Sun. Meanwhile, some of the cloud formed a broad disk around the hot core. As dust particles in the disk collided, they formed solid bodies, which continued to grow through further collisions. Near the heat of the young Sun, the bodies were rocky and turned into the four small inner planets. Farther out they remained rich in gas and water and ended up as the four gas giant planets.

Spinning disk
A cloud of dust and gas collapses and forms the solar nebula, a broad, thin disk rotating around a dense core.

Colliding bodies
The core becomes the hot infant Sun, as lumps of dust in the disk collide and form solid bodies known as planetesimals.

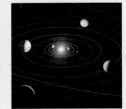

Sun and planets
The Sun becomes a star and, through violent collisions, the planetesimals gradually grow and form the eight planets.

Illustrations Susanna Addario, Mike Atkinson/illustrationweb.com, Paul Bachem, Kenn Backhaus, Cy Baker, Alistair Barnard, Julian Baum, Andrew Beckett, Richard Bonson/The Art Agency, Anne Bowman, Peter Bull Art Studio, Danny Burke, Martin Camm, Dan Cole/The Art Agency, Leslye Cole/The Art Agency, Sam and Amy Collins, Tom Connell, Marcus Cremonese, Marjorie Crosby-Fairall, Barry Croucher/The Art Agency, Claire Davies/The Art Agency, Fiammatte Dogi, Sandra Doyle/The Art Agency, Levent Efe, Simone End, Christer Eriksson, Alan Ewart, Nick Farmer/Brighton Illustration, Rod Ferring, Cecilia Fitzsimons/The Art Agency, Giuliano Fornari, Chris Forsey, Lloyd Foye, John Francis/Bernard Thornton Artists UK, Luigi Gallante/The Art Agency, Lee Gibbons/The Art Agency, Tony Gibbons/Bernard Thornton Artists UK, Jon Gittoes, Mike Gorman, Ray Grinaway, Terry Hadler, Langdon G. Halls, Gino Halser, Lorraine Hannay, David A Hardy/The Art Agency, Tim Hayward, Phil Hood/The Art Agency, Adam Hook/Bernard Thornton Artists UK, Christa Hook/Bernard Thornton Artists UK, Richard Hook/Bernard Thornton Artists UK, Robert Hynes, Mark Iley/The Art Agency, Inklink, Ian Jackson/The Art Agency, Gillian Jenkins, Janet Jones, Steve Kirk/The Art Agency, David Kirshner, Frank Knight, Mike Lamble, Alex Lavroff, Connell Lee, John Mac/Folio, David Mackay, Iain McKellar, James McKinnon, Martin Macrae/Folio, Stuart McVicar/Geocart, Robert Mancini, David Mathews, Peter Mennim, Siri Mills, David Moore/Linden Artists, Colin Newman/Bernard Thornton Artists UK, Kevin O'Donnell, Nicola Oram, Matthew Ottley, Darren Pattenden/illustrationweb.com, Jane Pickering/Linden Artists, Sandra Pond/The Art Agency, Marilyn Pride, Tony Pyrzakowski, Oliver Rennert, Luis Rey/The Art Agency, John Richards, Edwinna Riddell, Steve Roberts/The Art Agency, Trevor Ruth, Claudia Saraceni, Michael Saunders, Peter Schouten, Peter Scott/The Art Agency, Stephen Seymour/Bernard Thornton Artists UK, Christine Shafner/K.E. Sweeny Illustration, Nick Shewring/illustrationweb.com, Chris Shields/The Art Agency, Ray Sim, Marco Sparaciari, R. Spencer Phippen, Kevin Stead, Roger Stewart/Brighton Illustration, Irene Still, Roger Swainston, Kate Sweeney/K.E. Sweeny Illustration, Sharif Tarabay/illustrationweb.com, Steve Trevaskis, Thomas Trojer, Guy Troughton, Chris Turnbull/The Art Agency, Glen Vause, Jane Walkins/The Art Agency, Genevieve Wallace, Ross Watton/illustrationweb.com, Trevor Weekes, Rod Westblade, Steve Weston/Linden Artists, Simon Williams/illustrationweb.com, Ann Winterbotham, David Wood, David Wun

Photographs Stuart Bowey/Adlibitum, iStock International Inc., Shutterstock Inc.

Maps Map Illustrations

Star Maps Wil Tirion

Flags Flag Society of Australia

Reference Section Sources Country statistics (pp. 804, 812–19, 821) are from CIA World Factbook 2007. U.S. state statistics (pp. 806–08) are from the U.S. Census Bureau. City statistics (pp. 804, 820–21) use urban agglomeration data from the United Nations World Urbanization Prospects: The 2005 Revision. Global warming graph (p. 823) is based on data from the Climatic Research Unit, University of East Anglia, and the Intergovernmental Panel on Climate Change Third Assessment Report, Climate Change 2001. Threatened species statistics (p. 824) are from the 2006 IUCN Red List of Threatened Species.

The Publishers would like to thank the following people for their assistance:
Jessica Cox, Mike Crowton, Linda Edwards, Suzanne Keating, Jennifer Losco, Elizabeth Louie, Allister Mackrell, Kathryn Morgan, Danielle Parker, Jacqueline Richards

cog ▲ [kog] *noun, plural* **cogs.**
see page 143